Explore Your World!

Focus on case studies to understand your world.

To learn about the **Eastern Hemisphere**, you will take a close look at specific countries. In each case study, the story of that country will be told through an important world theme—such as the relationship between people and their environment or a nation's quest for independence. After studying each country, you can apply what you've learned to understand other parts of the world.

Interact with exciting online activities.

Journey to different parts of the world by using dynamic online activities on geography, history and culture. Use the web codes listed in the Go Online boxes and in the chart below to tour this region.

Eastern Hemisphere Activities

Web Code	Activity
lep-3700	Composite Volcano Eruption
lep-3701	Water Cycle
lep-3702	The Seasons
lep-3707	Continental Drift
	History Interactive
lap-5803	5 Pillars of Islam
lcp-7004	Explore Two Feudal Societies
ldp-7702	Explore the Magna Carta
ldp-7703	Travel Along a Roman Road
	MapMaster
lap-5801	Geography of Ancient Egypt
lap-5802	Fossil Finds in Africa
lap-5806	West African Empires
lap-5807	Trade Routes of Ghana
lap-5809	Origins of Agriculture
lap-5810	Early River Valley Civilizations
lcp-7001	The Spread of Buddhism
lcp-7002	Geography of Japan
lcp-7003	China under the Tang & Song Dynasties
lcp-7005	The Fertile Crescent
lcp-7006	The Maurya and Gupta Empires
ldp-7701	The Empire of Alexander the Great

For additional activities, please see PHSchool.com, webcode lek-1001

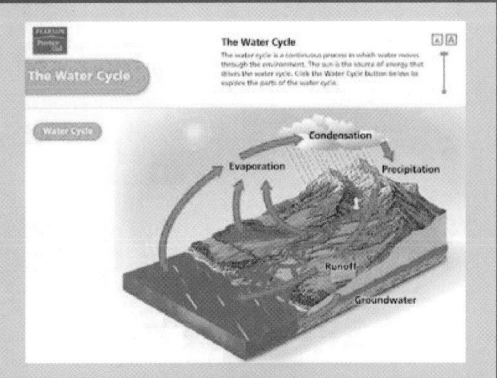

Go Online
PHSchool.com

For: An activity on Central Asia
Visit: PHSchool.com
Web Code: lcd-6203

D1308040

Get hands-on with the Geographer's Apprentice Activity Pack.

Explore the geography, history and culture of the world's regions through hands-on activities. Each activity pack includes maps, data and primary sources to make learning geography fun!

PRENTICE HALL
WORLD STUDIES
EASTERN HEMISPHERE

Geography • History • Culture

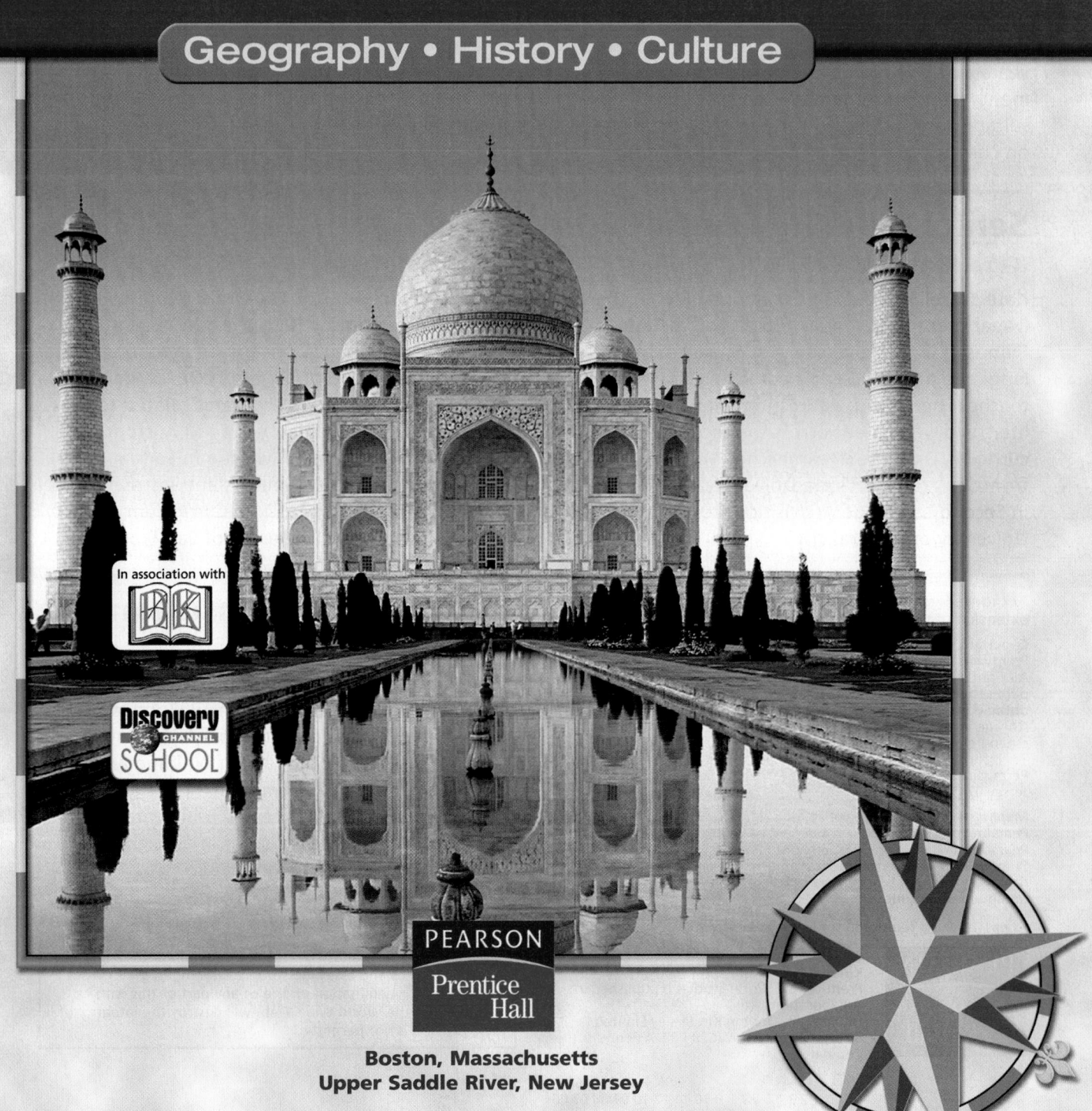

In association with

Discovery CHANNEL SCHOOL

PEARSON

Prentice Hall

Boston, Massachusetts
Upper Saddle River, New Jersey

Program Consultants

Heidi Hayes Jacobs

Heidi Hayes Jacobs has served as an education consultant to more than 1,000 schools across the nation and abroad. Dr. Jacobs serves as an adjunct professor in the Department of Curriculum on Teaching at Teachers College, Columbia University. She has written two best-selling books and numerous articles on curriculum reform. She received an M.A. from the University of Massachusetts, Amherst, and completed her doctoral work at Columbia University's Teachers College in 1981. The core of Dr. Jacobs's experience comes from her years teaching high school, middle school, and elementary school students. As an educational consultant, she works with K–12 schools and districts on curriculum reform and strategic planning.

Michal L. LeVasseur

Michal L. LeVasseur is the Executive Director of the National Council for Geography Education. She is an instructor in the College of Education at Jacksonville State University and works with the Alabama Geographic Alliance. Her undergraduate and graduate work were in the fields of anthropology (B.A.), geography (M.A.), and science education (Ph.D.). Dr. LeVasseur's specialization has moved increasingly into the area of geography education. Since 1996 she has served as the Director of the National Geographic Society's Summer Geography Workshops. As an educational consultant, she has worked with the National Geographic Society as well as with schools and organizations to develop programs and curricula for geography.

Senior Reading Consultants

Kate Kinsella

Kate Kinsella, Ed.D., is a faculty member in the Department of Secondary Education at San Francisco State University. A specialist in second-language acquisition and adolescent literacy, she teaches coursework addressing language and literacy development across the secondary curricula. Dr. Kinsella earned her M.A. in TESOL from San Francisco State University, and her Ed.D. in Second Language Acquisition from the University of San Francisco.

Kevin Feldman

Kevin Feldman, Ed.D., is the Director of Reading and Early Intervention with the Sonoma County Office of Education (SCOE) and an independent educational consultant. At the SCOE, he develops, organizes, and monitors programs related to K–12 literacy. Dr. Feldman has an M.A. from the University of California, Riverside in Special Education, Learning Disabilities and Instructional Design. He earned his Ed.D. in Curriculum and Instruction from the University of San Francisco.

Acknowledgments appear on page 889, which constitutes an extension of this copyright page.

Copyright © 2008 by Pearson Education, Inc., publishing as Pearson Prentice Hall, Boston, Massachusetts 02116.
All rights reserved. Printed in the United States of America. This publication is protected by copyright, and permission should be obtained from the publisher prior to any prohibited reproduction, storage in a retrieval system, or transmission in any form or by any means, electronic, mechanical, photocopying, recording, or likewise. For information regarding permission(s), write to: Rights and Permissions Department, One Lake Street, Upper Saddle River, New Jersey 07458.

MapMaster™ is a trademark of Pearson Education, Inc.
Pearson Prentice Hall™ is a trademark of Pearson Education, Inc.
Pearson® is a registered trademark of Pearson plc.
Prentice Hall® is a registered trademark of Pearson Education, Inc.
Discovery Channel School® is a registered trademark of Discovery Communications, Inc.

ExamView® is a registered trademark of FSCreations, Inc.

is a registered trademark of Dorling Kindersley Limited.
Prentice Hall World Studies is published in collaboration with
DK Designs, Dorling Kindersley Limited, 80 Strand, London WC2R 0RL. A Penguin Company.

Cartography Consultant

 **Andrew Heritage**

Andrew Heritage has been publishing atlases and maps for more than 25 years. In 1991, he joined the leading illustrated nonfiction publisher Dorling Kindersley (DK) with the task of building an international atlas list from scratch. The DK atlas list now includes some 10 titles, which are constantly updated and appear in new editions either annually or every other year.

ISBN 0-13-204160-X
1 2 3 4 5 6 7 8 9 10 11 12 10 09 08 07 06

Academic Reviewers

Africa
Barbara B. Brown, Ph.D.
African Studies Center
Boston University
Boston, Massachusetts

Ancient World
Evelyn DeLong Mangie, Ph.D.
Department of History
University of South Florida
Tampa, Florida

Central Asia and the Middle East
Pamela G. Sayre
History Department,
   Social Sciences Division
Henry Ford Community College
Dearborn, Michigan

East Asia
Huping Ling, Ph.D.
History Department
Truman State University
Kirksville, Missouri

Eastern Europe
Robert M. Jenkins
Center for Slavic, Eurasian and
   East European Studies
University of North Carolina
Chapel Hill, North Carolina

Latin America
Dan La Botz
Professor, History Department
Miami University
Oxford, Ohio

Medieval Times
James M. Murray
History Department
University of Cincinnati
Cincinnati, Ohio

North Africa
Barbara E. Petzen
Center for Middle Eastern Studies
Harvard University
Cambridge, Massachusetts

Religion
Charles H. Lippy, Ph.D.
Department of Philosophy
   and Religion
University of Tennessee
   at Chattanooga
Chattanooga, Tennessee

Russia
Janet Vaillant
Davis Center for Russian
   and Eurasian Studies
Harvard University
Cambridge, Massachusetts

South Asia
Robert J. Young
Professor Emeritus
History Department
West Chester University
West Chester, Pennsylvania

United States and Canada
Victoria Randlett
Geography Department
University of Nevada, Reno
Reno, Nevada

Western Europe
Ruth Mitchell-Pitts
Center for European Studies
University of North Carolina
   at Chapel Hill
Chapel Hill, North Carolina

Reviewers

Sean Brennan
Brecksville-Broadview Heights
   City School District
Broadview Heights, Ohio

Stephen Bullick
Mt. Lebanon School District
Pittsburgh, Pennsylvania

William R. Cranshaw, Ed.D.
Waycross Middle School
Waycross, Georgia

Dr. Louis P. De Angelo
Archdiocese of Philadelphia
Philadelphia, Pennsylvania

Paul Francis Durietz
Social Studies
   Curriculum Coordinator
Woodland District #50
Gurnee, Illinois

Gail Dwyer
Dickerson Middle School,
   Cobb County
Marietta, Georgia

Michal Howden
Social Studies Consultant
Zionsville, Indiana

Rosemary Kalloch
Springfield Public Schools
Springfield, Massachusetts

Deborah J. Miller
Office of Social Studies,
   Detroit Public Schools
Detroit, Michigan

Steven P. Missal
Newark Public Schools
Newark, New Jersey

Catherine Fish Petersen (Retired)
East Islip School District
Islip Terrace, New York

Joe Wieczorek
Social Studies Consultant
Baltimore, Maryland

EASTERN HEMISPHERE

Develop Skills

Use these pages to develop students' reading, writing, and geography skills.

Focus on Geography

Introduce students to the basic tools and concepts of geography.

Build a Regional Background

Introduce students to the geography, history, and culture of Europe and Russia.

Focus on Countries

Create an understanding of the region by focusing on specific countries.

Build a Regional Background

Introduce students to the geography, history, and culture of Africa.

Focus on Countries

Create an understanding of Africa by focusing on specific countries.

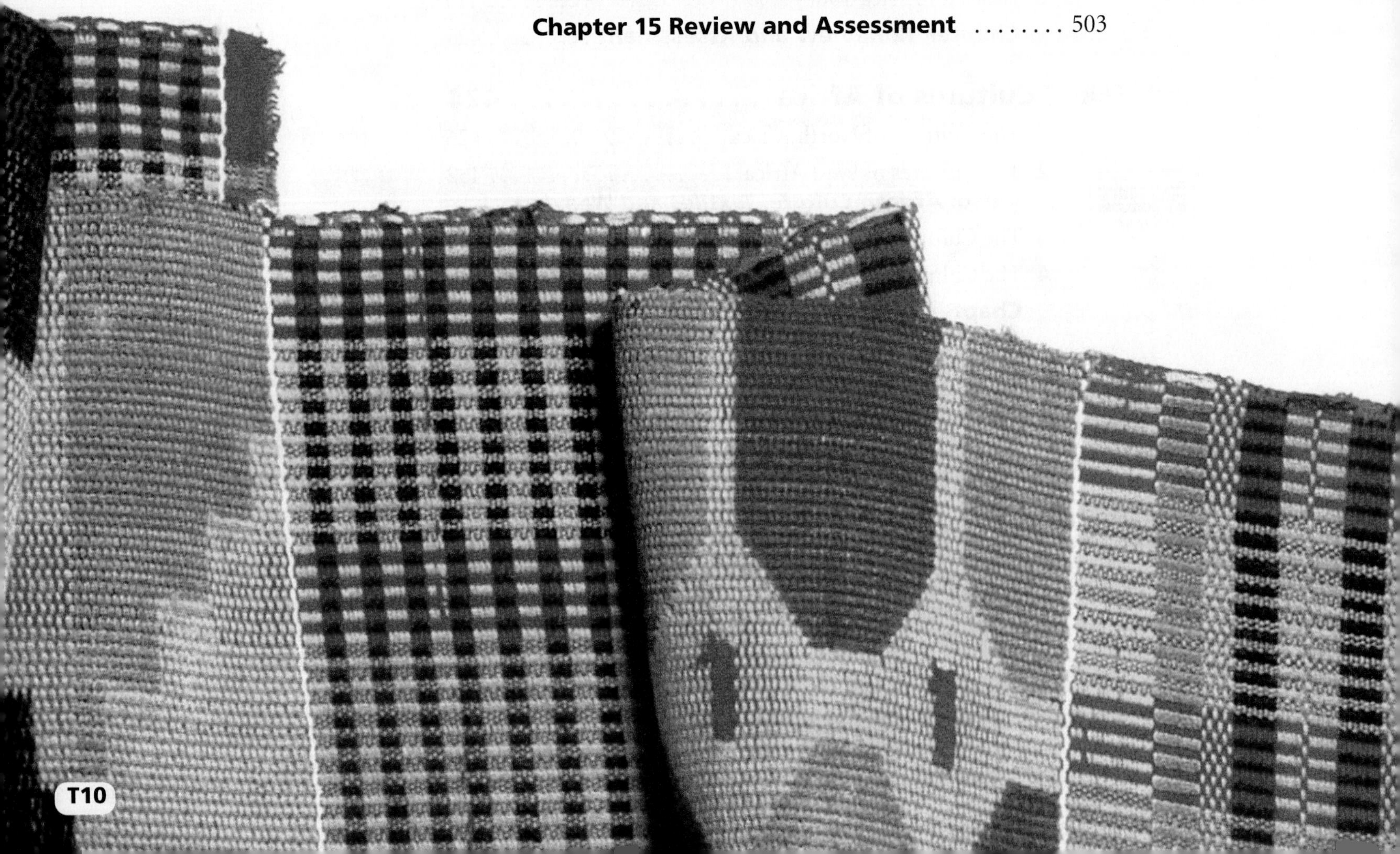

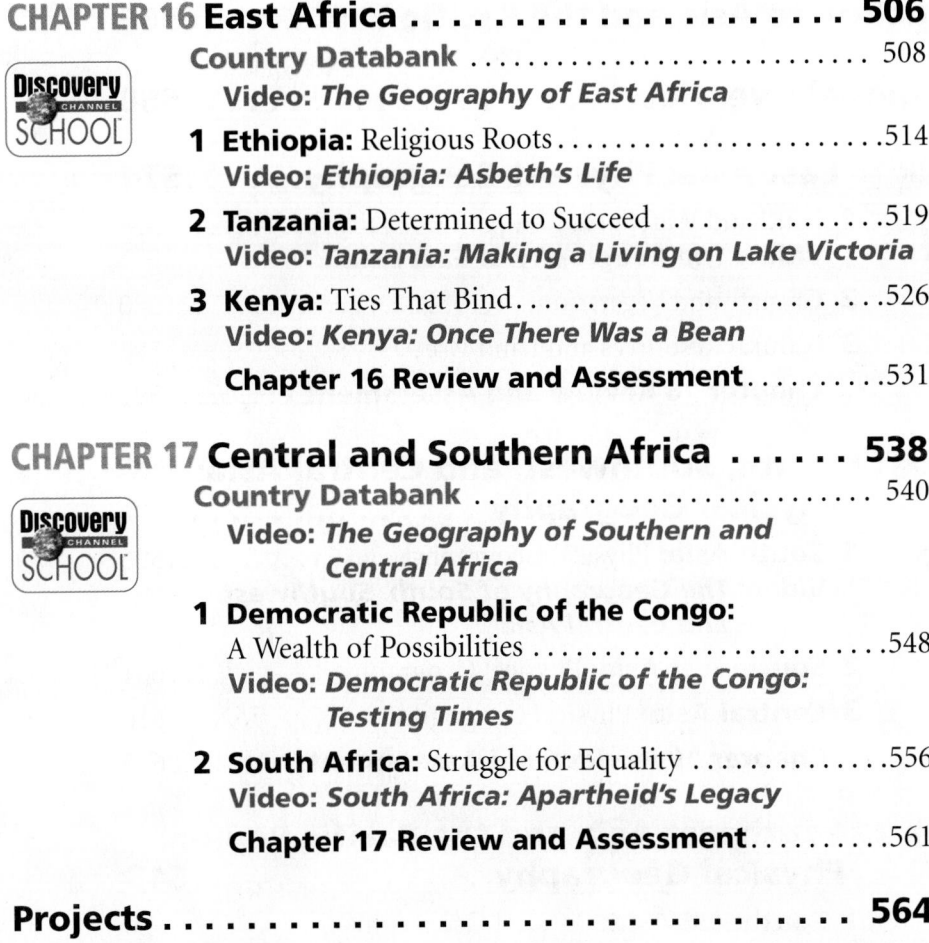

Build a Regional Background

Introduce students to the geography, history, and culture of Asia and the Pacific.

Focus on Countries

Create an understanding of Asia and the Pacific by focusing on specific countries.

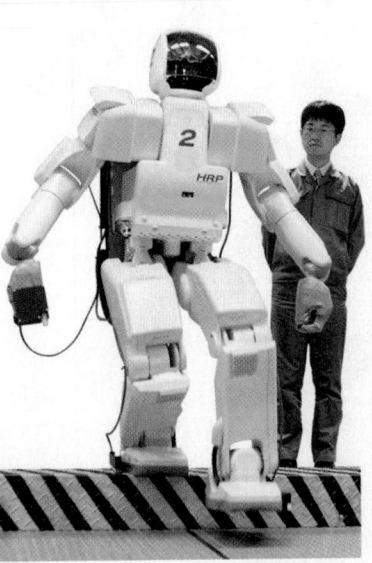

- Learn map skills with the MapMaster Skills Handbook.
- Practice your skills with every map in this book.
- Interact with every map online and on CD-ROM.

Maps and illustrations created by DK help build your understanding of the world. The DK World Desk Reference Online keeps you up to date.

Video/DVD

The World Studies Video Program takes you on field trips to study countries around the world.

The *World Studies* Interactive Textbook online and on CD-ROM uses interactive maps and other activities to help you learn.

COUNTRY DATABANK

Read about Russia and all the countries that make up Europe.

COUNTRY DATABANK

Read about all the countries that make up Africa.

COUNTRY DATABANK

Read about all the countries that make up Asia and the Pacific.

COUNTRY PROFILES

Theme-based maps and charts provide a closer look at countries, regions, and provinces.

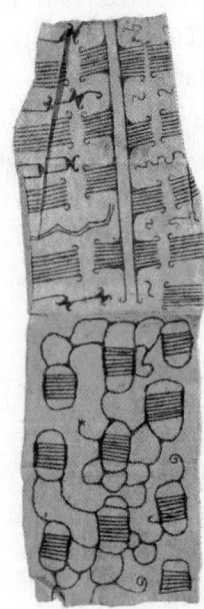

Skills for Life

Teach skills that students will use throughout their lives.

Literature

Selections by noted authors bring social studies to life.

Target Reading Skills

Chapter-by-chapter reading skills help students read and understand social studies concepts.

Citizen Heroes

Introduce people who have made a difference in their country.

Video/DVD

Explore the geography, history, and cultures of the countries of Europe, Africa, Asia, and the Pacific.

Learn how soccer brings Europeans together.

Learn about the different regions of Australia.

Maps and Charts

MAP✦MASTER™

Atlas

MAP MASTER™ Interactive

Go online to find an interactive version of every MapMaster™ map in this book. Use the Web Code provided to gain direct access to these maps.

How to Use Web Codes:

1. Go to www.PHSchool.com.

2. Enter the Web Code.

3. Click Go!

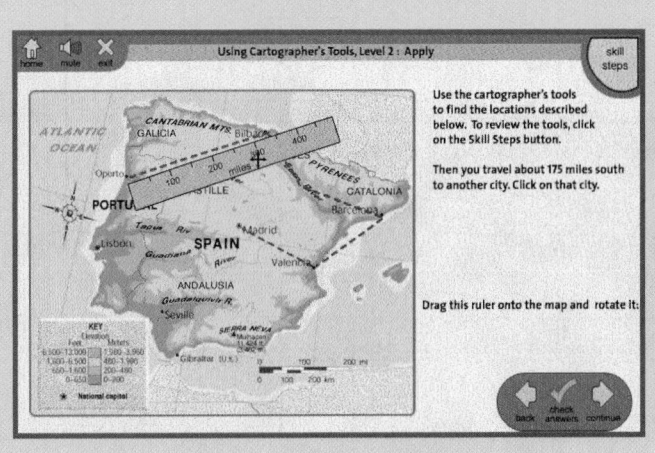

Charts, Graphs, and Tables

NCLB Implications for Social Studies

The No Child Left Behind (NCLB) legislation was a landmark in educational reform designed to improve student achievement and create a fundamental shift in American education. In the essay that follows, we will explore the implications of NCLB on social studies curriculum, instruction, assessment, and instructional programs.

Facts about NCLB

The No Child Left Behind Act of 2001 (NCLB) calls for sweeping educational reform, requiring all students to perform proficiently on standardized tests in reading, mathematics, and (soon to be added) science by the year 2014. Under NCLB, schools will be held accountable for students' academic progress. In exchange for this accountability, the law offers more flexibility to individual states and school districts to decide how best to use federal education funds. NCLB places an emphasis on implementing scientifically proven methods in teaching reading and mathematics, and promotes teacher quality. It also offers parental choice for students in failing schools.

Effects on Curriculum, Instruction, and Assessment

Since the primary focus of NCLB is on raising the achievement of students in reading and mathematics, some educators have wondered how it relates to social studies. Some teachers have expressed concerns that since NCLB does not require yearly testing of social studies, state and school districts may decide to shift resources and class time away from teaching social studies. However, NCLB considers the social studies areas of history, geography, economics, and government and civics to be core academic subjects. Many states are requiring middle grades social studies teachers to be highly qualified in history and geography in order to comply with the principle of improving teacher quality in NCLB.

NCLB sets the goal of having every child meet state-defined education standards. Since social studies educators have been leaders in the development of standards-based education and accountability through student testing over the past decade, many state and local districts have their own standards and assessments for social studies already in place. Assessment, including screening, diagnostic, progress-monitoring—including end-of-year, end-of-schooling, grade level, district, and state testing—and large-scale assessments, will continue to play a significant role in shaping social studies curriculum and instruction in the near future.

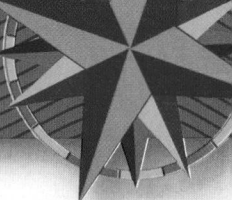

Integrating Reading into Social Studies Instruction

Due to the increased emphasis on reading and mathematics required by NCLB, social studies teachers may be called on to help improve their students' reading and math skills. For example, a teacher might use a graph about exports and imports to reinforce math skills, or a primary source about a historical event to improve reading skills. The connection between reading and social studies is especially important. Since many state and local assessments of reading require students to read and interpret informational texts, social studies passages are often used in the exams. Therefore, social studies teachers may assist in raising reading scores by integrating reading instruction into their teaching of social studies content.

Implications for Instructional Programs

The environment created by the NCLB legislation has implications for instructional programs. In keeping with the spirit of NCLB, social studies programs should clearly tie their content to state and local standards. Programs should also provide support so that all students can master these standards, ensuring that no child is left behind. An ideal instructional program is rooted in research, embeds reading instruction into the instructional design, and provides assessment tools that inform instruction—helping teachers focus on improving student performance.

Prentice Hall Response

We realize that raising the achievement level of all students is the number one challenge facing teachers today. To assist you in meeting this challenge, Prentice Hall enlisted a team of respected consultants who specialize in middle grades issues, reading in the content areas, and geographic education. This team created a middle grades world studies program that breaks new ground and meets the changing needs of you and your students.

With Prentice Hall, you can be confident that your students will not only be motivated, inspired, and excited to learn world studies, but they will also achieve the success needed in today's environment of the No Child Left Behind (NCLB) legislation and testing reform.

In the following pages, you will find the key elements woven throughout this World Studies program that truly set it apart and assure success for you and your students.

Teacher's Edition Contents in Brief

Research on Effective Reading Instruction

Why do many students have difficulty reading textbooks? How can we help students read to learn social studies? In the pages that follow, we examine the research on the challenge of reading textbooks; explain the direct, systematic, and explicit instruction needed to help students; and then show how Prentice Hall has responded to this research.

What is skilled reading?

Recent research (Snow et al., 2002) suggests that skillful and strategic reading is a long-term developmental process in which "readers learn how to simultaneously extract and construct meaning through interaction with written language." In other words, successful readers know how to decode all kinds of words, read with fluency and expression, have well-developed vocabularies, and possess various comprehension strategies such as note-taking and summarizing to employ as the academic reading task demands.

Many students lack reading skills

Sadly, many secondary students do not have solid reading skills. In the early years, students read mainly engaging and accessible narratives, such as stories, poems, and junior biographies. But in the upper elementary years, they shift toward conceptually dense and challenging nonfiction, or expository texts. It is no accident that the infamous "Fourth-Grade Slump" (Chall and Jacobs, 2003; Hirsch 2003)—a well-documented national trend of declining literacy after grade four—occurs during this time. The recent National Assessment of Educational Progress (NAEP, 2002) found that only 33 percent of eighth-grade students scored at or above the proficient level in reading.

Even students quite skilled in reading novels, short stories, and adolescent magazines typically come to middle school ill-equipped for the rigors of informational texts or reading to learn. They tend to dive right into a social studies chapter as if reading a recreational story. They don't first preview the material to create a mental outline and establish a reading purpose. They have not yet learned other basic strategies, including reading a section more than once, taking notes as they read, and reading to answer specific questions.

Dr. Kate Kinsella
Reading Consultant for *World Studies*
Department of Secondary Education
San Francisco State University, CA

Dr. Kevin Feldman
Reading Consultant for *World Studies*
Director of Reading and Early Intervention
Sonoma County, CA

"Even students quite skilled in reading novels, short stories, and adolescent magazines typically come to middle school ill-equipped for the rigors of informational texts or reading to learn."

The unique demands of textbooks

The differences between textbooks and the narratives students are used to reading are dramatic. The most distinctive challenges include dense conceptual content, heavy vocabulary load, unfamiliar paragraph and organizational patterns, and complex sentence structures. Academic texts present such a significant challenge to most students that linguists and language researchers liken them to learning a foreign language (Schleppegrell, 2002). In other words, most secondary students are second language learners: they are learning the academic language of informational texts!

Effective reading instruction

Research illustrates that virtually all students benefit from direct, systematic, and explicit instruction in reading informational texts (Baker & Gersten, 2000). There are three stages to the instructional process for content-area reading:

(1) **before reading:** instructional frontloading;

(2) **during reading:** guided instruction;

(3) **after reading:** reflection and study.

Before reading

Placing a major emphasis on preteaching, or "front-loading" your instruction—building vocabulary, setting a purpose for reading, and explicitly teaching students strategies for actively engaging with the text—helps you structure learning to ensure student success (see Strategies 1 and 2 on pages T32-T33). Frontloading strategies are especially critical in mixed-ability classrooms with English language learners, students with special needs, and other students performing below grade level in terms of literacy.

During reading

In guided instruction, the teacher models approaches for actively engaging with text to gain meaning. The teacher guides students through the first reading of the text using passage reading strategies (see Strategies 3-7 on pages T33-35), and then guides discussion about the content using participation strategies (see Strategies 8-11 on pages T35-T37). Finally, students record key information in a graphic organizer.

After reading

During the reflection and study phase, the teacher formally checks for student understanding, offers remediation if necessary, and provides activities that challenge students to apply content in a new way. To review the chapter, students recall content, analyze the reading as a whole, and study key vocabulary and information likely to be tested.

References

Baker, Scott and Russell Gersten. "What We Know About Effective Instructional Practices for English Language Learners." *Exceptional Children*, 66 (2000):454–470.

Chall, Jeanne S. and Vicki A. Jacobs. "Poor Children's Fourth-Grade Slump." *American Educator* (Spring 2003):14.

Donahue, P.L., et al. *The 1998 NAEP Reading Report Card for the Nation and the States* (NCES 1999-500). Washington, D.C.: U.S. Department of Education, Office of Education Research and Improvement, National Center for Education Statistics, 1999.

Grigg, W.S. et al. *The Nation's Report Card: Reading 2002* (NCES 2003-521). Washington, D.C.: U.S. Department of Education, Institute of Education Sciences, National Center for Education Statistics, 2003.

Hirsch, E.D., Jr. "Reading Comprehension Requires Knowledge—of Words and the World." *American Educator* (Spring 2003):10-29.

Kinsella, Kate, et al. *Teaching Guidebook for Universal Access.* Upper Saddle River, NJ: Prentice Hall, 2002.

Schleppegrell, M. "Linguistic Features of the Language of Schooling." *Linguistics and Education*, 12, no. 4 (2002): 431–459.

Snow, C., et al. *Reading for Understanding: Toward an R&D Program in Reading Comprehension.* Santa Monica, California: The Rand Corporation, 2002.

Putting Research Into Practice

Prentice Hall enlisted the assistance of Dr. Kate Kinsella and Dr. Kevin Feldman to ensure that the new middle grades *World Studies* program would provide the direct, systematic, and explicit instruction needed to foster student success in reading informational texts. To help students rise to the challenge of reading an informational text, *World Studies* embedded reading support right into the student text.

Embedded Reading Support in the Student Text

Before students read

- **Objectives** set the purpose for what students will read.
- **Target Reading Skill** for the section is explained.
- **Key Terms** are defined up front with pronunciation and part of speech.

During the section

- **Target Reading Skill** is applied to help students read and understand the narrative.
- **Key Terms** are defined in context, with terms and definitions called out in blue type.
- **Reading Checks** reinforce students' understanding by slowing them down to review after every concept is discussed.
- **Caption Questions** draw students into the art and photos, helping them to connect the content to the images.

After students read

- **Section Assessment** revisits the **Key Terms**, provides an opportunity to master the **Target Reading Skill**, allows student to rehearse their understanding of the text through the **Writing Activity**.

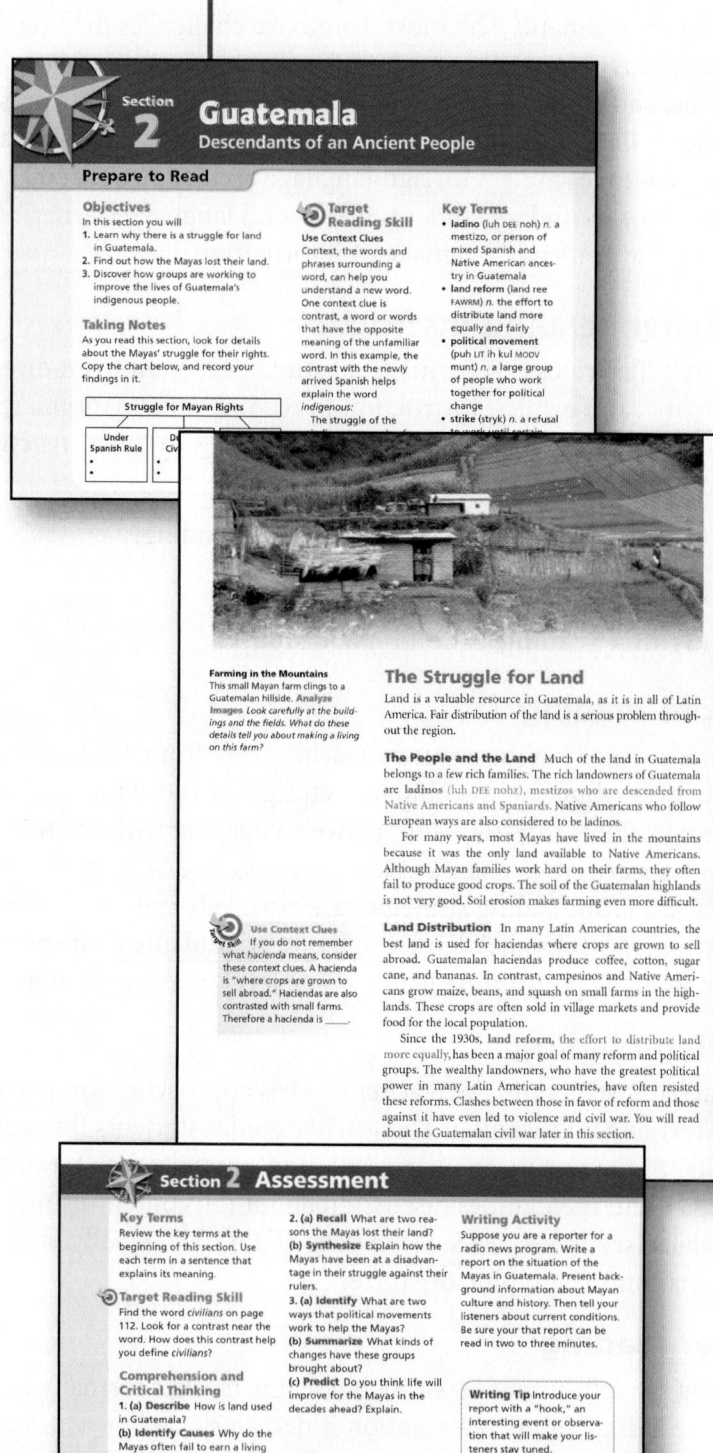

Putting Research Into Practice

World Studies offers teachers guidance in direct, systematic, and explicit reading instruction. The instructional sequence in the Teacher's Edition explicitly guides you in the use of effective strategies at each stage of the instructional process.

Reading Instruction in *World Studies* Teacher's Edition

Before Reading

Every lesson plan begins with suggestions that help you integrate frontloading strategies into your teaching. Build Background Knowledge activates and builds prior knowledge. Set a Purpose for Reading prompts students to predict and anticipate content and motivates students to engage with the text. Preview Key Terms helps students learn Key Terms to understand the text. Target Reading Skill models a reading strategy to help students gain meaning from the text. Vocabulary Builder gives teachers definitions and sample sentences to help teach high-use words.

During Reading

In the Instruct part of the lesson plan, you can use suggestions for getting students actively engaged in the text. Guided Instruction clarifies high-use words, applies a passage-reading strategy to promote text comprehension, and guides discussion to construct meaning. Independent Practice prompts students to reread and take notes in the graphic organizer provided to rehearse understanding.

After Reading

The lesson plan closes with specific strategies for the reflection and study phase after reading is completed. Monitor Progress checks students' note taking, and verifies students' prereading predictions. Assess and Reteach measures students' recall of content and provides additional instruction if needed. Review Chapter Content promotes retention of key concepts and vocabulary.

Integrated Reading Resources

The *World Studies* program provides instructional materials to support the reading instruction in the Teacher's Edition.

The **All-in-One Teaching Resources** provides reading instruction support worksheets, such as a Reading Readiness Guide, Word Knowledge, and Vocabulary Development.

Students can use the **Reading and Vocabulary Study Guide** (English and Spanish) to reinforce reading instruction and vocabulary development, and to review section summaries of every section of the student text.

Instructional Strategies for Improving Student Comprehension

In response to today's environment of the NCLB legislation and testing reform, Prentice Hall asked Dr. Kate Kinsella and Dr. Kevin Feldman to provide specific instructional strategies you can use to improve student comprehension. Their guidance informed the development of the *World Studies* Teacher's Edition. The lesson plans in this Teacher's Edition incorporate the following instructional strategies to enhance students' comprehension.

There is no single magical strategy that will solve all of the difficulties students encounter in reading challenging content area texts. Secondary students in mixed-ability classrooms depend on teachers to use a consistent set of research-informed and classroom-tested strategies in a patient and recursive manner—not the occasional or random use of different strategies. Students will not become skillful readers of content area texts in a week or two of instruction. However, when teachers engage students in the consistent use of a well-chosen set of content reading strategies appropriately matched to the demands of the text and the students' level of knowledge, their ability to comprehend difficult grade level texts will be dramatically enhanced.

Strategy 1: Set a Purpose for Reading

This program has two types of activities designed to help students set a purpose for reading: an Anticipation Guide and a KWL chart. The two types rotate by section.

A. Anticipation Guide

Purpose: To focus students' attention on key concepts, and guide them to interact with ideas in the text

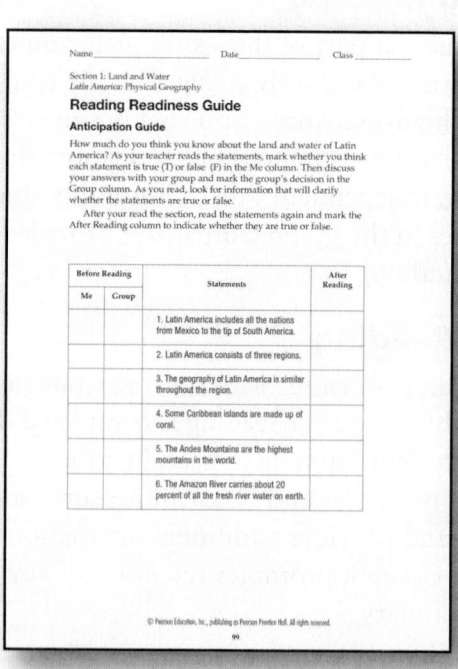

1. Distribute the *Reading Readiness Guide*. Read each statement aloud, and then ask students to react to the statements individually and in groups, marking their responses in the Before Reading column.

2. Use the worksheet as a springboard for discussing the section's key concepts as a unified class. Refrain from revealing the correct responses at this time, to avoid taking away the need for them to read the text.

3. Have students read the section with the purpose of finding evidence that confirms, disproves, or elaborates each statement in the *Reading Readiness Guide*.

4. After students finish reading, have them return to the statements and mark the After Reading column on their worksheets. Have them locate information from the text that supports or disproves each statement.

5. Discuss what the class has learned and probe for any lingering confusion about key concepts.

B. KWL

Purpose: To engage students before, during, and after reading

The KWL worksheet guides students to recall what they **K**now, determine what they **W**ant to learn, and identify what they **L**earn as they read.

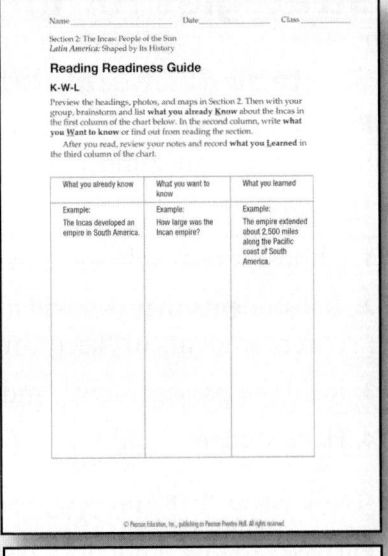

1. Distribute the *Reading Readiness Guide*. Brainstorm with the group about what they already know about the topic. List students' ideas on the board. Encourage students to generate questions at points of ambiguity.

2. Students then list pieces of information they already know and questions they want to answer in the first two columns of their worksheets.

3. As students read the section, ask them to note information that answers their questions or adds to what they know.

4. After reading, facilitate a class discussion about what the students have learned. Clarify any lingering confusion about key concepts.

Strategy 2: Teach High-Use Academic Words

Purpose: To teach students words used often in academic texts, beyond the content-specific Key Terms

How to Do It

1. Have students rate how well they know each word on their *Word Knowledge* worksheets. Tell them there is no penalty for a low rating.

2. Survey students' ratings to decide which words need the most instruction.

3. Provide a brief definition or sample sentence for each word. (See Vocabulary Builder at the beginning of each section for definitions and sample sentences.) Rephrase your explanation, leaving out the word and asking students to substitute it aloud.

4. Work with students as they fill in the "Definition or Example" column of their *Word Knowledge* worksheets.

5. Point out each word in context as you read the chapters. Consider allowing students to earn extra credit if they use a word correctly in class discussion or assignments.

Strategy 3: Oral Cloze

Purpose: To help students read actively while the teacher reads aloud

How to Do It

1. Choose a passage and direct students to "read aloud silently using their inner voices." Be sure students understand reading is an active process, not simply a listening activity, and their job is to follow along—eyes riveted to each word, saying the words to themselves as you read aloud.

2. Tell students to be on their "reading toes," for you will be leaving out an occasional word and their task is to chorally supply the word.

3. The first few times you use the Oral Cloze, demonstrate by telling the students in advance what word you will be leaving out, directing them to read the word at the right time. Practice this a few times until they have the feel for the procedure. Leave out fewer words as students become more familiar with the Oral Cloze and require less direction to remain focused during teacher read alouds.

Strategies for Improving Student Comprehension (continued)

Strategy 4: Choral Reading

Purpose: To have students attend to the text in a non-threatening atmosphere

How to Do It

1. Choose a relatively short passage.

2. Tell students that you will all read the text aloud at once. Direct students to "keep your voice with mine" as they read.

3. Read the passage slowly and clearly.

4. Have students read the text again silently.

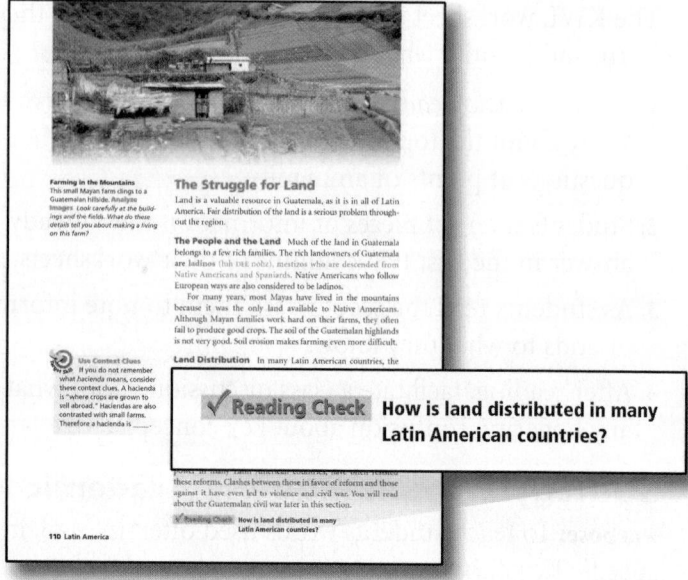

Strategy 5: Structured Silent Reading

Purpose: To give students a task as they read silently to increase their attentiveness and accountability

How to Do It

1. Assign a section to read silently. Pose a question for the whole class to answer from their silent reading, such as the Reading Check question at the end of each subsection. Model how one thinks while reading to find answers to a question.

2. When students get used to reading to answer the Reading Check question, pose more in-depth questions, progressing from factual recall to questions that stimulate interpretive or applied thinking.

3. Teach students to ask and answer their own questions as they read. Model this process by reading a section aloud and asking and answering your own questions as you read.

4. After the students have finished reading, engage the class in a brief discussion to clarify questions, vocabulary, and key concepts.

Strategy 6: Paragraph Shrinking

Purpose: To increase comprehension during reading

How to Do It

1. Partner struggling students with more proficient students and assign a manageable portion of the text.

2. Ask one member of each pair to identify the "who or what" the paragraph is about and tell the other.

3. Have the other member of the pair identify important details about the "who or what" and tell the other.

4. Ask the first member to summarize the paragraph in fifteen to twenty words or less using the most important details. The second member of the pair monitors the number of words and says "Shrink it!" if the summary goes over twenty words.

5. Have the partners reverse roles and continue reading.

6. Discuss the reading as a class to make sure students' paragraphs have correctly hit upon the main ideas of the passage.

Strategy 7: ReQuest (Reciprocal Questioning)

Purpose: To ask and answer questions during reading to establish a purpose for reading and monitor one's own comprehension

How to Do It

1. Prepare students to read by doing the section's Build Background Knowledge, Set a Purpose for Reading, and Preview Key Terms activities.

2. Begin reading a brief portion of the text aloud. Ask and answer your own questions about the text, progressing from recall to critical thinking questions.

3. After modeling this question and response pattern with a brief passage, ask students to read the next section of the text. Tell students that they will be taking turns asking you questions about what they read, and you will answer their questions, just like you modeled for them.

4. Ask students to read the next section. Inform them that you will be asking them questions about the section and they will be answering your questions.

5. Continue to alternate between student-generated questions and teacher-generated questions until the entire designated passage has been read. As students become used to the strategy, they gradually assume more responsibility in the process.

6. When the students have read enough information to make predictions about the remainder of the assignment, stop the exchange of comprehension questions. Instead, ask prediction questions, such as, "What do you think will be discussed in the next section? Why do you think so?"

7. Assign the remaining portion for students to read silently. Then lead a wrap-up discussion of the material.

Strategy 8: Idea Wave

Purpose: To engage students in active class discussions

How to Do It

1. Pose a question or task.

2. Give students quiet time to consider what they know about the topic and record a number of responses.

3. Whip around the class in a fast-paced and structured manner (e.g. down rows, around tables), allowing as many students as possible to share an idea in 15 seconds or less.

4. After several contributions, if there tends to be repetition, ask students to point out similarities in responses rather than simply stating that their idea has already been mentioned.

Strategies for Improving Student Comprehension *(continued)*

Strategy 9: Numbered Heads

Purpose: To engage students in active class discussions

How to Do It

1. Seat students in groups of four and number off one through four (if possible, combine established partners to form groups of four).

2. After giving the discussion prompt, allow students to discuss possible responses for an established amount of time.

3. Remind students to pay close attention to the comments of each group member because you will be randomly selecting one student to represent the best thinking of the entire group.

4. Call a number (one through four), and ask all students with that number to raise their hands, ready to respond to the topic at hand in a teacher-directed, whole-class discussion.

5. Add comments, extend key ideas, ask follow-up questions, and make connections between individual student's comments to create a lively whole-class discussion.

6. Provide any summary comments required to ensure that all students understand critical points.

Strategy 10: Think-Write-Pair–Share

Purpose: To engage students in responding to instruction

How to Do It

1. **Think**—Students listen while the teacher poses a question or a task related to the reading or classroom discussion. The level of questions should vary from lower level literal to higher order inferential or analytical.

2. **Write**—Provide quiet thinking or writing time for students to deal with the question, and go back to the text or review notes. Have students record their ideas in their notebooks.

3. **Pair/Share**—Cue students to find a partner and discuss their responses, noting similarities and differences. Teach students to encourage one another to clarify and justify responses.

4. Randomly call on students to share during a unified class discussion after they have all rehearsed answers with their partners.

5. Invite any volunteers to contribute additional ideas and points of view to the discussion after calling on a reasonable number of students randomly.

6. Direct students to go back to notes and add any important information garnered during the partner and class discussions.

Strategy 11: Give One, Get One

Purpose: To foster independent reflection and peer interaction prior to a unified class discussion

How to Do It

1. Pose a thought-provoking question or a concrete task to the class.

2. Allow three to five minutes of quiet time for students to consider what they may already know about the topic and jot down a number of potential responses.

3. Ask students to place a check mark next to the two or three ideas that they perceive as their strongest and then draw a line after their final idea to separate their ideas from those that they will gather from classmates.

4. Give students a set amount of time (about eight to ten minutes) to get up from their seats and share ideas with classmates. After finding a partner, the two students exchange papers and first quietly read each other's ideas. They discuss the ideas briefly, then select one idea from their partner's list and add it to their own, making sure to accurately copy the idea alongside the partner's name.

5. When one exchange is completed, students move on to interact with a new partner.

6. At the end of the exchange period, facilitate a unified class discussion. Call on a volunteer to share one new idea acquired from a conversation partner. The student whose idea has just been reported then shares the next idea, gleaned from a different conversation partner.

Professional Development

For more information about these strategies, see the end of each chapter's Interleaf.

Research on Differentiated Instruction

It's basic, but it's true—not all our students learn in the same manner and not all our students have the same academic background or abilities. As educators, we need to respond to this challenge through the development and utilization of instructional strategies that address the needs of diverse learners, or the number of children who "fall through the cracks" will continue to rise (Kame'enui & Carnine, 1998).

Providing universal access

Universal access happens when curriculum and instruction are provided in ways that allow all learners to participate and to achieve (Kinsella, et al., 2002). Teachers who teach in heterogeneous, inclusive classrooms can provide universal access by modifying their teaching to respond to the needs of typical learners, gifted learners, less proficient readers, English language learners, and special needs students. Many of these learner populations benefit from extensive reading support (see pages T14-T17).

It is also critical to properly match the difficulty level of tasks with the ability level of students. Giving students tasks that they perceive as too hard lowers their expectations of success. However, giving students assignments that they think are too easy, undermines their feelings of competence (Stipek, 1996). Therefore, it is important for a program to give teachers leveled activities that allow them to match tasks with the abilities of their individual students.

When students connect to and are engaged with the content, comprehension and understanding increase. Technology, such as online activities, can provide an ideal opportunity for such engagement. It also can be used to provide additional opportunities to access content. For example, a less proficient reader may reinforce understanding of a key concept through watching a video. A complete social studies program makes content available in a variety of formats, including text, audio, visuals, and interactivities.

Kame'enui, Edward and Douglas Carnine. *Effective Teaching Strategies that Accommodate Diverse Learners.* Upper Saddle River, NJ: Prentice Hall, 1998.

Kinsella, Kate, et al. *Teaching Guidebook for Universal Access.* Upper Saddle River, NJ: Prentice Hall, 2002.

Stipek, D.J. "Motivation and Instruction," in R.C. Clafee and D.C. Berlinger (Eds.), *Handbook of Educational Psychology.* New York: Macmillan, 1996.

"Universal access happens when curriculum and instruction are provided in ways that allow all learners to participate and to achieve (Kinsella, et al., 2002)."

Putting Research Into Practice

Prentice Hall recognizes that today's classrooms include students with diverse backgrounds and ability levels. Accordingly, the *World Studies* program was designed to provide access to the content for all students. The program provides both the instructional materials to meet the learning needs of all students and the guidance you need to accommodate these needs.

Differentiated Instruction in the Teacher's Edition

The Teacher's Edition was designed to make it easy for teachers to modify instruction for diverse learners. Teaching strategies, provided by Dr. Kate Kinsella and Dr. Kevin Feldman, to help you modify your teaching are incorporated into every lesson plan. Specific activities help you differentiate instruction for individual students in five categories—less proficient readers, advanced readers, special needs students, gifted and talented, and English language learners. Resources are identified as being appropriate for use by each of these categories. All resources are also assigned a level—basic, average, and above average—so you know exactly how to assign tasks of appropriate difficulty level.

All-in-One Teaching Resources

Everything you need to provide differentiated instruction for each lesson, including reading support, activities and projects, enrichment, and assessment—in one convenient location.

World Studies Video Program

Students will benefit from our custom-built video program—the result of an exclusive partnership with Discovery Channel School—making content accessible through dynamic footage and high-impact stories.

Student Edition on Audio CD

The complete narrative is read aloud, section by section, providing extra support for auditory learners, English language learners, and reluctant readers. Also available is the Guided Reading Audio CD (English/Spanish), containing section summaries read aloud.

Interactive Textbook—The Student Edition Online and on CD-ROM

The Interactive Textbook allows students to interact with the content, including reading aids, visual and interactive learning tools, and instant feedback assessments.

Differentiated Instruction

For Less Proficient Readers L1
Have students read the section in the Reading and Vocabulary Study Guide. This version provides basic-level instruction in an interactive format with questions and write-on lines.

Chapter 4, Section 1, **Latin America Reading and Vocabulary Study Guide,** pp. 42–44

For Special Needs Students L1
Have students read the section as they listen to the recorded version on the Student Edition on Audio CD. Check for comprehension by pausing the CD and asking students to share their answers to the Reading Checks.

Chapter 4, Section 1, **Student Edition on Audio CD**

Learn about how natural hazards affect life in Mexico.

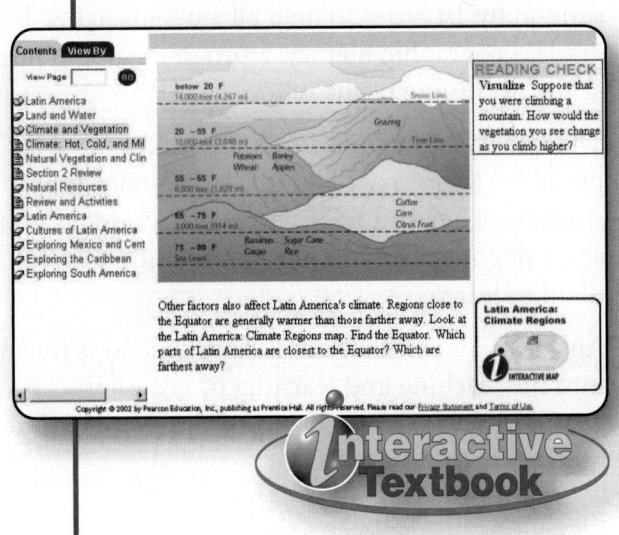

Research on Geographic Literacy

As the *Geography for Life: National Geography Standards* (1994) state, "There is now a widespread acceptance among the people of the United States that being literate in geography is essential if students are to leave school equipped to earn a decent living, enjoy the richness of life, and participate responsibly in local, national, and international affairs." A middle grades social studies program needs to help teachers produce students who are literate in geography.

Geographic literacy defined

Results for the 2001 National Assessment of Educational Progress (NAEP) Geography assessment show that the average scores of fourth- and eighth-grade students have improved since 1994. The average score of twelfth-grade students, however, has not changed significantly. In order to make the critical leap from basic geography skills to the kind of geographic literacy needed by the twelfth grade and beyond, a program must teach both geography content and geography skills, and then help students think critically. Geography content is made up of the essential knowledge that students need to know about the world. Geography skills are the ability to ask geographic questions, acquire and analyze geographic information, and answer these questions. To be truly literate in geography, students must be able to apply their knowledge and skills to understand the world.

Elements for success in middle grades

Students in the elementary grades don't always get enough training in geography. In order to help all students gain a base upon which to build middle grades geographic literacy, a program should introduce basic geography skills at the beginning of the school year.

The quality of maps is also vital to the success of a middle grades world studies program. Maps must be developmentally appropriate for middle grades students. They should be clean, clear, and accurate. Maps should be attractive and present subject matter in appealing ways, so that students *want* to use them to learn.

Another element that can lead to success is the incorporation of technology into the teaching and learning of geography, specifically the Internet. Research has shown that 8th grade students with high Internet usage scored higher in geography (NAEP, 2001).

U.S. Department of Education, Office of Educational Research and Improvement, National Center for Education Statistics, National Assessment of Educational Progress (NAEP), 2001 Geography Assessment.

Andrew Heritage
Head of Cartography
Dorling Kindersley (DK)

"Maps should be attractive and present subject matter in appealing ways, so that students *want* to use them to learn."

Putting Research Into Practice

Prentice Hall partnered with DK—internationally known for their dynamic atlases—to develop the *World Studies* program. DK's Andrew Heritage and his world-renowned cartography team designed all maps, resulting in stunning, high quality maps that are middle grades appropriate.

The MapMaster™ System

World Studies offers the first interactive geography instruction system available with a world studies textbook.

Introduce Basic Map Skills

The MapMaster™ Skills Handbook, a DK-designed introduction to the basics, brings students up to speed with a complete overview at the beginning of every book.

Build Geographic Literacy with Every Map

Scaffolded questions start with questions that require basic geography content and skills, and then ask students to demonstrate geographic literacy by thinking critically about the map.

Activate Learning Online

MapMaster™ Interactive—online and on CD-ROM—allows students to put their knowledge of geography skills and content into practice through interactivities.

Extend Learning with DK

- **DK World Desk Reference Online** is filled with up-to-date data, maps, and visuals that connect students to a wealth of information about the world's countries.

- **DK Compact Atlas of the World** with Map Master™ Teacher's Companion provides activities to introduce, develop, and master geography and map skills.

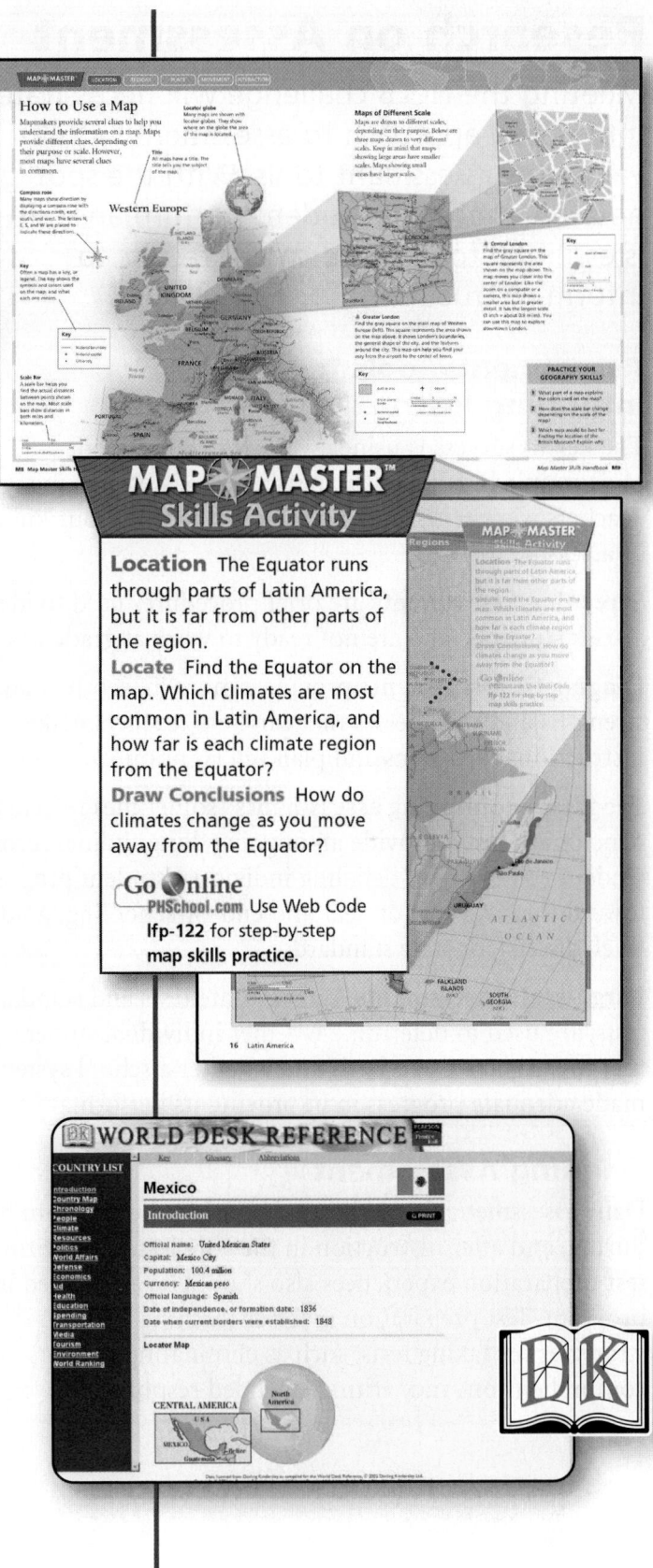

Research on Assessment

Meeting the NCLB challenge will necessitate an integrated approach to assessment with a variety of assessment tools. With the spotlight now on *improving* student performance, it is essential to use assessment results to inform instruction.

Assessments Tools for Informing Instruction

The key to success is using a variety of assessment tools coupled with data analysis and decision making. Teachers work with information coming from four kinds of assessment.

Screening assessments are brief procedures used to identify at-risk students who are not ready to work at grade level.

Diagnostic assessments provide a more in-depth analysis of strengths and weaknesses that can help teachers make instructional decisions and plan intervention strategies.

Progress-monitoring assessments (sometimes referred to as benchmark tests) provide an ongoing, longitudinal record of student achievement detailing individual student progress toward meeting end-of-year and end-of-schooling, grade level, district, or state standards.

Large-scale assessments, such as state tests and standardized tests, are used to determine whether individual students have met the expected standards and whether a school system has made adequate progress in improving its performance.

Ongoing Assessment

Daily assessment should be embedded in the program before, during, and after instruction in the core lessons. Legitimate test preparation experiences also should be embedded in the program. Test preparation involves teaching students strategies for taking tests, such as eliminating answers, reading comprehension, and writing extended response answers.

Eileen Depka
Supervisor of Standards and Assessment
Waukesha, WI

"Meeting the NCLB challenge will necessitate an integrated approach to assessment with a variety of assessment tools."

Putting Research Into Practice

Prentice Hall developed the *World Studies* program with a variety of assessment tools, including ongoing assessment in the student text.

Assessments for Informing Instruction

World Studies was designed to provide you with all four kinds of assessment.

- **Screening test** identifies students who are reading 2-3 years below grade level.

- **Diagnostic tests** focus on skills needed for success in social studies, including subtests in geographic literacy, visual analysis, critical thinking and reading, and communications skills, as well as vocabulary and writing.

- **Benchmark tests**, to be given six times throughout the year, monitor student progress in the course.

- **Outcome test**, to be administered at the end of the year, evaluates student mastery of social studies content standards.

Ongoing Assessment

- **Student Edition** offers section and chapter assessments with questions building from basic comprehension to critical thinking and writing.

- **Test Prep Workbook** and **Test-taking Strategies with Transparencies** develop students' test-taking skills and improve their scores on standardized tests.

- *ExamView® Test Bank CD-ROM* allows you to quickly and easily develop customized tests from a bank of thousands of questions.

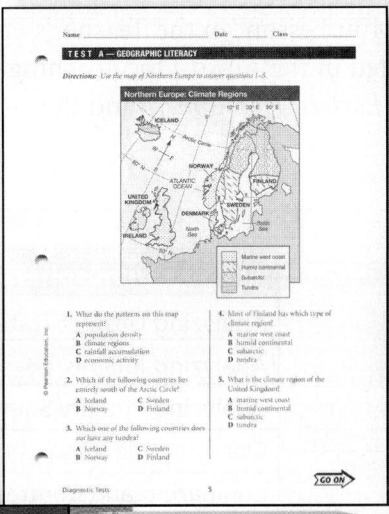
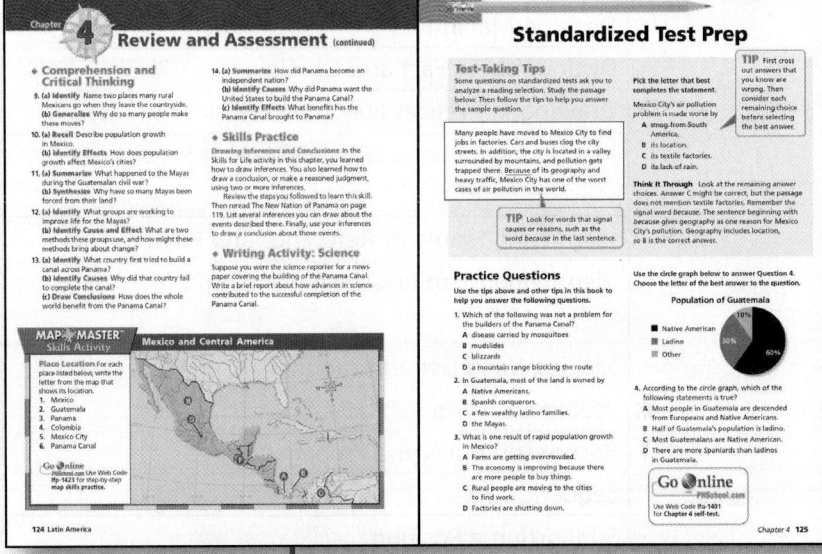
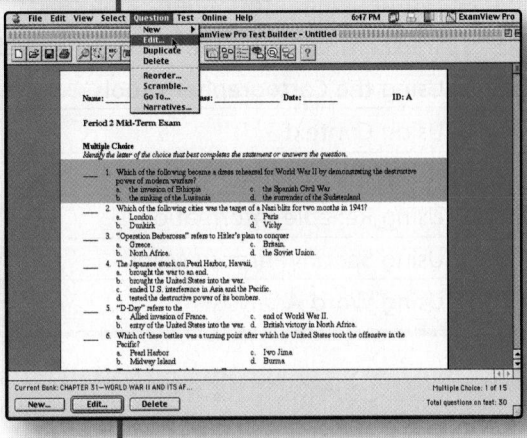

Eastern Hemisphere Skills Scope and Sequence

Prentice Hall *World Studies* contains a comprehensive program of core skills. Each skill is taught in every book of the series. A Target Reading Skill is located at the beginning of each chapter and expanded upon in each section within the chapter. Core skills are also taught either in the "Skills for Life Activity" in the Student Edition, or in a "Skills Mini Lesson" in the Teacher's Edition. In addition, worksheets for the students' use in completing each skill are located in the All-in-One Teaching Resources. The chart below lists the skills covered in *Prentice Hall World Studies: Eastern Hemisphere* and the chapter where each skill is taught.

Eastern Hemisphere Analysis Skills	SE	TE
Analyzing Graphic Data	Chs. 2, 11, 25, 26	Chs. 2, 3, 9, 11, 25, 26
Analyzing Images		Chs. 2, 7, 17, 19
Analyzing Primary Sources	Ch. 17	Chs. 5, 8, 17, 23
Clarifying Meaning	Chs. 1, 7, 11	Chs. 1, 7, 11
Comparing and Contrasting	Chs. 3, 10, 13, 19	Chs. 3, 10, 13, 19
Decision Making	Ch. 15	Chs. 3, 9, 15, 26
Distinguishing Fact and Opinion	Ch. 14	Chs. 4, 8, 14, 24
Drawing Inferences and Conclusions	Ch. 23	Chs. 1, 9, 16, 23
Identifying Cause and Effect/Making Predictions	Chs. 5, 14, 20, 25	Chs. 2, 5, 7, 14, 15, 20, 25
Identifying Frame of Reference and Point of View	Ch. 10	Chs. 3, 10, 13, 21
Identifying Main Ideas/Summarizing	Chs. 5, 8, 15, 16, 19, 20, 26	Chs. 3, 5, 8, 15, 16, 19, 20, 26
Making Valid Generalizations	Ch. 4	Chs. 4, 8, 11, 25
Problem Solving	Ch. 7	Chs. 5, 7, 13, 19
Recognizing Bias and Propaganda	Ch. 22	Chs. 4, 10, 17, 22
Sequencing	Chs. 4, 12, 17, 23	Chs. 1, 4, 7, 12, 17, 23
Supporting a Position	Ch. 8	Chs. 5, 8, 14, 22
Synthesizing Information	Ch. 24	Chs. 4, 10, 12, 24
Transferring Information From One Medium to Another	Ch. 10	Chs. 2, 9, 10, 16, 20
Using the Cartographer's Tools		Chs. 2, 6, 11, 18
Using Context	Chs. 2, 9, 16, 21	Chs. 2, 9, 16, 21
Using the Reading Process	Chs. 6, 12, 18	Chs. 6, 12, 18
Using Reliable Information	Chs. 1, 18	Chs. 1, 7, 15, 18
Using Special-Purpose Maps	Chs. 3, 6, 21	Chs. 3, 6, 12, 21
Using Word Analysis	Ch. 22	Ch. 22

Pacing Options

World Studies offers many aids to help you plan your instruction time, whether regular class periods or block scheduling. Section-by-section lesson plans for each chapter include suggested times, based on the year-long course configuration below. Teacher Express CD-ROM will help you manage your time electronically.

PRENTICE HALL
TeacherEXPRESS™
Plan • Teach • Assess

Pacing Options		Year-long Course
Chapter **1**	Section 1 Section 2	4.5 4
Chapter **2**	Section 1 Section 2 Section 3 Section 4	2 1.5 3 3
Chapter **3**	Section 1 Section 2 Section 3 Section 4	1.5 3 1.5 4.5
Chapter **4**	Section 1 Section 2 Section 3	1.5 3.5 3.5
Chapter **5**	Section 1 Section 2 Section 3	1.5 3 3.5
Chapter **6**	Section 1 Section 2 Section 3	3.5 2 3.5
Chapter **7**	Section 1 Section 2 Section 3 Section 4 Section 5	1.5 1 2 1 4
Chapter **8**	Section 1 Section 2 Section 3	1 2 3

Pacing Options		Year-long Course
Chapter **9**	Section 1 Section 2 Section 3 Section 4 Section 5	2 1.5 1.5 2.5 3.5
Chapter **10**	Section 1 Section 2 Section 3 Section 4	2 1.5 2.5 3.5
Chapter **11**	Section 1 Section 2 Section 3	2.5 2 2.5
Chapter **12**	Section 1 Section 2 Section 3 Section 4 Section 5	1 1 1 2 3
Chapter **13**	Section 1 Section 2 Section 3 Section 4	1 2 1 2.5
Chapter **14**	Section 1 Section 2	2.5 2.5
Chapter **15**	Section 1 Section 2 Section 3	1.5 2 2.5
Chapter **16**	Section 1 Section 2 Section 3	1.5 2 4

Pacing Options		Year-long Course
Chapter **17**	Section 1 Section 2	2.5 2.5
Chapter **18**	Section 1 Section 2 Section 3	3 1.5 2
Chapter **19**	Section 1 Section 2 Section 3	1 1.5 2
Chapter **20**	Section 1 Section 2 Section 3	1 1.5 2
Chapter **21**	Section 1 Section 2	1.5 2
Chapter **22**	Section 1 Section 2 Section 3	1 1.5 2
Chapter **23**	Section 1 Section 2	1.5 2.5
Chapter **24**	Section 1 Section 2 Section 3	1.5 2 2
Chapter **25**	Section 1 Section 2 Section 3 Section 4 Section 5	1.5 1 1.5 2 2
Chapter **26**	Section 1 Section 2	1.5 2.5

Total Number of Days   180

Correlation to *Geography for Life*, the National Geography Standards

On the following pages, *Prentice Hall World Studies: Eastern Hemisphere* is correlated with *Geography for Life*, the National Geography Standards. These standards were prepared in response to the Goals 2000, Educate America Act, by the Geography Education Standards Project. Participating in the project were the American Geographical Society, the Association of American Geographers, the National Council for Geographic Education, and the National Geographic Society. Concepts and skills contained in the Geography Standards are incorporated throughout the program. This correlation displays places where the standards are directly addressed.

Standard	Eastern Hemisphere
The World in Spatial Terms	
Standard 1 Use maps and other geographic representations, tools, and technologies to acquire, process, and report information from a spatial perspective.	MapMaster Skills Handbook, 1:1–2, 2:1–4, 3:1, 3:2, 4:2, 5:1–3, 6:1–3, 7:1, 7:3, 7:4, 8:1, 8:2, 9:1–5, 10:1–4, 11:1–3, 12:1, 12:2, 12:3, 12:4, 13:1, 14:1–2, 15:1–3, 16:1–3, 17:1–2, 18:1–3, 19:1–3, 20:1–3, 21:1–2, 22:1, 22:2, 23:1, 24:1–3, 26:2, Review and Assessment: Chs. 1–26
Standard 2 Use mental maps to organize information about people, places, and environments in a spatial context.	MapMaster Skills Handbook, 2:4, 3:1, 6:2, 7:1, 7:2, 8:1, 8:2, 10:3, 22:3, 23:1, 24:3, 26:2, Review and Assessment: Chs. 1, 6, 8, 9, 10
Standard 3 Analyze the spatial organization of people, places, and environments on Earth's surface.	MapMaster Skills Handbook, 1:1–2, 2:2, 2:3, 2:4, 3:1, 3:2, 3:3, 4:2, 5:2, 6:1–3, 8:1, 8:2, 9:1, 9:4, 10:2, 11:1, 11:2, 14:1–2, 15:1, 15:3, 16:1, 16:3, 17:1–2, 18:1–3, 19:1–3, 20:1–3, 21:1–2, 22:1–3, 23:1, 24:2, 25:1, 25:3, 26:1–2, Review and Assessment: Chs. 1, 2, 4, 6, 7, 8, 11, 14, 18, 19, 20, 21, 22, 25, 26
Places and Regions	
Standard 4 Understand the physical and human characteristics of places.	MapMaster Skills Handbook, 1:1, 2:1–4, 3:1–4, 4:1, 4:2, 5:2, 5:3, 6:1–3, 8:1–3, 9:1–5, 10:1, 10:4, 11:1–3, 12:1, 12:2, 12:5, 13:1–4, 14:1–2, 15:1–3, 16:1–3, 17:1–2, 18:1–3, 19:1–3, 20:1–3, 21:1–2, 22:1–3, 23:1–2, 24:1–3, 25:1–5, 26:1–2, Review and Assessment: Chs. 2–26
Standard 5 Understand that people create regions to interpret Earth's complexity.	MapMaster Skills Handbook, 1:1–2, 2:1, 2:4, 3:1, 3:3, 3:4, 6:1, 8:2, 8:3, 9:1, 9:4, 9:5, 10:1, 10:3, 11:1, 11:2, 13:1–4, 15:1–3, 16:1–3, 17:2, 18:1, 18:2, 19:1–3, 20:1–3, 22:2, 23:1–2, Review and Assessment: Chs. 1, 3, 13, 16, 18, 19, 20
Standard 6 Understand how culture and experience influence people's perception of places and regions.	MapMaster Skills Handbook, 7:5, 8:1–3, 9:1, 9:4, 9:5, 10:1–4, 2:1, 3:1–4, 4:1–3, 5:2, 5:3, 13:1, 13:3, 14:1, 15:1, 15:2, 16:3, 17:1–2, 19:1–3, 20:1, 21:1–2, 22:1–3, 23:1–2, 24:1–3, 25:1–5, 26: 1–2, Review and Assessment: Chs. 3, 4, 5, 8, 9, 10, 21, 22, 23, 24, 25, 26
Physical Systems	
Standard 7 Understand the physical processes that shape the patterns of Earth's surface.	2:1–4, 3:1, 6:1–3, 11:1, 11:2, 15:3, 18:1, 18:2, 19:1, 19:2, 20:1–3, Review and Assessment: Chs. 2, 11, 19, 20
Standard 8 Understand the characteristics and spatial distribution of ecosystems on Earth's surface.	2:2, 2:3, 2:4, 3:1, 5:1–3, 11:1, 11:2, 12:5, 15:3, 17:1, 18:1, 18:2, 20:1–3, 25:5, 26:2, Review and Assessment: Chs. 2, 5, 11, 15, 18, 20

Correlation to *Geography for Life*, the National Geography Standards *(continued)*

Standard	Eastern Hemisphere
Human Systems	
Standard 9 Understand the characteristics, distribution, and migration of human populations on Earth's surface.	MapMaster Skills Handbook, 3:1–4, 4:1–3, 5:1–3, 61–3, 10:4, 11:2, 12:1, 12:2, 12:3, 13:1–4, 14:1–2, 15:1–3, 16:1–3, 17:1–2, 18:1–3, 19:1–3, 20:1, 20:3, 21:1–2, 22:1–3, 23:1–3, 24:1–3, 25:1, 25:2, 25:3, 25:4, 26:1–2, Review and Assessment: Chs. 3, 4, 6, 12, 13, 14, 16, 18, 19, 20, 21, 22, 23
Standard 10 Understand the characteristics, distribution, and complexity of Earth's cultural mosaics.	MapMaster Skills Handbook, 3:1, 3:2, 3:3, 4:1–3, 5:2, 7:1, 7:2, 7:4, 7:5, 8:1–3, 9:2, 9:5, 10:1–4, 12:1, 12:2, 12:3, 12:5, 13:1–4, 14:1–2, 15:1, 15:2, 17:1–2, 19:1–3, 21:1–2, 22:1–3, 23:1–2, 24:1–3, 25:1–5, 26:1–2, Review and Assessment: Chs. 3, 4, 5, 7, 8, 9, 10, 13, 14, 15, 17, 21, 22, 23, 24, 25
Standard 11 Understand the patterns and networks of economic interdependence on Earth's surface.	MapMaster Skills Handbook, 3:1, 3:2, 4:1, 4:2, 5:2, 6:1, 7:1, 7:3, 8:1, 8:2, 9:1, 10:2, 12:1–3, 13:1, 13:2, 13:3, 13:4, 14:1–2, 15:1, 15:3, 16:1, 16:3, 17:2, 18:1–3, 19:1–3, 20:1, 20:3, 21:1–2, 22:1–3, 23:1–2, 24:1–3, 25:1–5, 26:1–2, Review and Assessment: Chs. 3, 5, 6, 7, 12, 13, 15, 19, 20, 24, 25, 26
Standard 12 Understand the processes, patterns, and functions of human settlement.	MapMaster Skills Handbook, 3:1, 3:2, 4:1, 4:2, 5:2, 6:1, 7:1, 7:3, 8:1, 8:2, 9:1, 10:2, 12:1–3, 13:1, 13:2, 13:3, 13:4, 14:1–2, 15:1, 15:3, 16:1, 16:3, 17:2, 18:1–3, 19:1–3, 20:1, 20:3, 21:1–2, 22:1–3, 23:1–2, 24:1–3, 25:1–2, Review and Assessment: Chs. 3, 4, 5, 6, 12, 16, 18, 19, 21, 23, 25
Standard 13 Understand how the forces of cooperation and conflict among people influence division and control of Earth's surface.	3:1, 3:2, 3:3, 4:1–3, 5:1–3, 7:1–5, 8:1–3, 9:1, 9:4, 9:5, 10:1–4, 12:1, 12:2, 12:3, 12:4, 14:2, 15:1, 15:2, 16:1, 17:1–2, 18:1, 18:3, 192, 21:1–2, 22:1–3, 23:1–2, 24:1–3, 25:1, 25:3, 25:5, 26:1–2, Review and Assessment: Chs. 3, 4, 5, 7, 8, 9, 10, 12, 15, 17, 22, 23, 24, 25
Environment and Society	
Standard 14 Understand how human actions modify the physical environment.	3:1, 3:2, 3:3, 4:1, 5:1–3, 6:1, 6:3, 10:1, 10:3, 10:4, 11:1, 11:3, 12:1, 12:5, 13:3, 14:1–2, 15:3, 17:1, 18:3, 19:3, 19:4, 19:5, 20:1, 25:2, 25:3, 25:4, 25:5, Review and Assessment: Chs. 3, 5, 11, 14, 15, 18, 20, 25
Standard 15 Understand how physical systems affect human systems.	2:2, 2:3, 2:4, 3:1, 4:1, 5:1–3, 6:1–3, 10:1, 10:3, 10:4, 11:1, 11:2, 12:2, 12:5, 14:1–2, 15:3, 16:3, 17:1, 18:1–3, 19:3, 19:4, 20:1, 20:3, 23:1–2, 24:2, 24:3, 25:2, 25:3, 26:2, Review and Assessment: Chs. 2, 3, 4, 5, 6, 10, 11, 14, 18
Standard 16 Understand the changes that occur in the meaning, use, distribution, and importance of resources.	2:2, 3:1, 3:2, 3:3, 4:1, 4:3, 5:1–3, 6:1, 6:3, 7:2, 7:3, 9:1, 9:3, 9:4, 10:3, 11:1, 11:3, 12:1, 12:2, 12:3, 12:5, 13:3, 14:1, 15:2, 15:3, 16:2, 16:3, 17:1–2, 18:2, 19:3, 20:1, 20:3, 24:1–3, 25:1–5, 26:1–2, Review and Assessment: Chs. 3, 4, 5, 10, 11, 13, 14, 15, 18, 25, 26
The Uses of Geography	
Standard 17 Understand how to apply geography to interpret the past.	MapMaster Skills Handbook, 1:1, 2:2, 3:1, 3:2, 3:3, 4:1–3, 5:1–3, 7:1, 7:2, 7:3, 7:4, 8:2, 9:1, 9:4, 10:1, 10:3, 10:4, 12:1, 12:2, 12:3, 13:1, 13:3, 14:2, 15:1, 15:3, 16:1, 17:1–2, 18:1–3, 19:1–3, 20:1–3, 23:1–2, Review and Assessment: Chs. 3, 4, , 13, 14, 15, 20
Standard 18 Understand how to apply geography to interpret the present and plan for the future.	3:1, 3:2, 3:3, 4:2, 4:3, 5:1–3, 7:3, 7:5, 8:3, 9:1, 9:3, 9:4, 9:5, 10:1–4, 11:1, 11:3, 12:5, 13:1, 13:3, 14:1–2, 15:1, 15:3, 16:2, 17:1, 18:3, 19:1–3, 20:1, 20:3, Review and Assessment: Chs. 3, 4, 5, 7, 8, 9, 13, 14, 15

Correlation to the NCSS Curriculum Standards

On the following pages *Prentice Hall World Studies: Eastern Hemisphere* is correlated with *Expectations of Excellence*, the Curriculum Standards for Social Studies. These standards were developed by the National Council for the Social Studies to address overall curriculum design and comprehensive student performance expectations.

Standard	Eastern Hemisphere
Performance Expectations 1: Culture	
• compare similarities and differences in the ways groups, societies, and cultures meet human needs and concerns • explain how information and experiences may be interpreted by people from diverse cultural perspectives and frames of reference • explain and give examples of how language, literature, the arts, architecture, other artifacts, traditions, beliefs, values, and behaviors contribute to the development and transmission of culture • explain why individuals and groups respond differently to their physical and social environments and/or changes to them on the basis of shared assumptions, values, and beliefs • articulate the implications of cultural diversity, as well as cohesion, within and across groups	MapMaster Skills Handbook, 4:1–3, 5:2, 6:3, 7:2, 7:5, 8:1–3, 9:1–5, 10:1–4, 13:1–4, 14:1–2, 15:1, 15:2, 16:1–3, 17:1–2, 21:1–2, 22:1–3, 17:1–2, 21:1–2, 22:1–3, 23:1–2, 24:1–3, 25:1–5, 26:1–2, Review and Assessment: Chs. 4, 5, 13, 16, 17, 21, 22, 23, 25, 26
Performance Expectations 2: Time, Continuity, and Change	
• demonstrate an understanding that different scholars may describe the same event or situation in different ways but must provide reasons or evidence for their view • identify and use key concepts such as chronology, causality, change, conflict, and complexity to explain, analyze, and show connections among patterns of historical change and continuity • identify and describe selected historical periods and patterns of change within and across cultures • identify and use processes important to reconstructing and reinterpreting the past • develop critical sensitivities regarding attitudes, values, and behaviors of people in different historical contexts • use knowledge of facts and concepts drawn from history, along with methods of historical inquiry, to inform decision-making about and action-taking on public issues	2:2, 3:1, 3:2, 3:3, 4:1, 4:3, 5:2, 7:1–5, 8:1–3, 9:1, 9:3, 9:4, 9:5, 10:1–4, 12:1–5, 13:3, 13:4, 14:2, 15:1, 15:2, 16:1–3, 17:1–2, 21:1–2, 22:1–3, 23:1–2, 24:1, 24:2, 25:1–5, 26:1–2, Review and Assessment: Chs. 3, 4, 12, 13, 16, 17, 21, 22, 23, 24, 25, 26
Performance Expectations 3: People, Places, and Environment	
• elaborate mental maps of locales, regions, and the world that demonstrate understanding of relative location, direction, size, and shape • create, interpret, use, and distinguish various representations of the earth • use appropriate resources, data sources, and geographic tools to generate, manipulate, and interpret information • estimate distance, calculate scale, and distinguish geographic relationships • locate and describe varying landforms and geographic features and explain their relationship with the ecosystem • describe physical system changes and identify geographic patterns associated with them • describe how people create places that reflect cultural values and ideals • examine, interpret, and analyze physical and cultural patterns and their interactions • describe ways that historical events have been influenced by, and have influenced, physical and human geographic factors in local, regional, national, and global settings • observe and speculate about social and economic effects of environmental changes and crises resulting from natural phenomena • propose, compare, and evaluate alternative uses of land and resources in communities, regions, nations, and the world	MapMaster Skills Handbook, 1:1–2, 2:1–4, 3:1, 3:2, 3:3, 4:1–3, 5:1–3, 6:1–3, 7:1–5, 8:1–3, 9:1–5, 10:4, 11:1–3, 12:1–5, 13:1–4, 14:1–2, 15:1–3, 16:1–3, 17:1–2, 18:1–3, 19:1–3, 20:1–3, 21:1–2, 22:1, 22:2, 23:1–2, 24:1–3, 25:1–5, 26:1–2, Review and Assessment: Chs. 1-26

Correlation to the NCSS Curriculum Standards *(continued)*

Standard	Eastern Hemisphere
Performance Expectations 4: Individual Development and Identity	
• relate personal changes to social, cultural, and historical contexts • describe personal connections to place—as associated with community, nation, and world • describe the ways family, gender, ethnicity, nationality, and institutional affiliations contribute to personal identity • relate such factors as physical endowment and capabilities, learning, motivation, personality, perception, and behavior to individual development • identify and describe ways regional, ethnic, and national cultures influence individuals' daily lives • identify and describe the influence of perception, attitudes, values, and beliefs on personal identity • identify and interpret examples of stereotyping, conformity, and altruism • work independently and cooperatively to accomplish goals	3:1, 3:2, 3:3, 4:1–3, 5:2, 5:3, 8:1–3, 9:1–5, 10:1–4, 12:3, 12:4, 12:5, 13:1–4, 14:1, 15:1–3, 16:1–3, 17:1–2, 21:1–2, 22:1–3, 23:1–2, 24:1–3, 25:1–5, 26:1–2, Review and Assessment: Chs. 3, 4, 5, 12, 13, 16, 21, 22, 23, 24, 25, 26
Performance Expectations 5: Individuals, Groups, & Institutions	
• demonstrate an understanding of concepts such as role, status, and social class in describing interactions of individuals and social groups • analyze group and institutional influences on people, events, and elements of culture • describe the various forms institutions take and the interactions of people with institutions • identify and analyze examples of tensions between expressions of individuality and group or institutional efforts to promote social conformity • identify and describe examples of tensions between belief systems and government policies and laws • describe the role of institutions in furthering both continuity and change • apply knowledge of how groups and institutions work to meet individual needs and promote the common good	3:3, 3:4, 4:1, 4:2, 7:1–5, 8:1–3, 9:1–5, 10:1–4, 12:2, 12:3, 12:4, 12:5, 13:1, 13:2, 13:4, 14:1–2, 15:1, 15:3, 16:1–3, 17:1–2, 21:1–2, 22:1, 22:3, 23:1–2, 24:1–3, 25:1–5, Review and Assessment: Chs. 3, 4, 12, 13, 15, 16, 17, 21, 22, 23, 24, 25
Performance Expectations 6: Power, Authority, and Governance	
• examine persistent issues involving the rights, roles, and status of the individual in relation to general welfare • describe the purpose of government and how its powers are acquired, used, and justified • analyze and explain ideas and governmental mechanisms to meet needs and wants of citizens, regulate territory, manage conflict, and establish order and security • describe the ways nations and organizations respond to forces of unity and diversity affecting order and security • identify and describe the basic features of the political system in the United States, and identify representative leaders from various levels and branches of government • explain conditions, actions, and motivations that contribute to conflict and cooperation within and among nations • describe and analyze the role of technology as it contributes to or helps resolve conflicts • explain how power, role, status, and justice influence the examination of persistent issues and social problems • give examples and explain how governments attempt to achieve their stated ideals at home and abroad	3:3, 3:4, 4:1, 7:1–5, 9:1–5, 10:1–4, 12:3, 12:4, 14:1–2, 15:1, 15:2, 16:2, 16:3, 17:1–2, 21:1–2, 22:1–3, 23:1–2, 24:1–3, 25:1–5, 26:1–2, Review and Assessment: Ch. 3, 12, 15, 16, 17, 21, 22, 23, 24, 25, 26

Correlation to the NCSS Curriculum Standards (continued)

Standard	Eastern Hemisphere
Performance Expectations 7: Production, Distribution, and Consumption	
• give examples of ways that economic systems structure choices about how goods and services are to be produced and distributed • describe the role that supply and demand, prices, incentives, and profits play in determining what is produced and distributed in a competitive market system • explain differences between private and public goods and services • describe a range of examples of the various institutions that make up economic systems • describe the role of specialization and exchange in the economic process • explain and illustrate how values and beliefs influence different economic decisions • differentiate among various forms of exchange and money • compare basic economic systems according to who determines what is produced, distributed, and consumed • use economic concepts to help explain historical and current events in local, national, or global concepts • use economic reasoning to compare different proposals for dealing with contemporary social issues	3:3, 4:3, 5:1–3, 6:2, 6:3, 7:3, 9:1–5, 10:1–4, 11:3, 12:2, 12:3, 13:3, 13:4, 15:1–3, 16:2, 16:3, 17:1–2, 18:3, 19:1–3, 20:1, 20:3, 21:1–2, 24:1–3, 25:1–5, 26:1–2, Review and Assessment: Chs. 3, 5, 12, 13, 15, 21, 24, 25, 26
Performance Expectations 8: Science, Technology, and Society	
• examine and describe the influence of culture on scientific and technological choices and advancement • show through specific examples how science and technology have changed peoples' perceptions of their social and natural world • describe examples in which values, beliefs, and attitudes have been influenced by new scientific and technological knowledge • explain the need for laws and policies to govern scientific and technological applications • seek reasonable and ethical solutions to problems that arise when scientific advancements and social norms or values come into conflict	1:2, 2:1–4, 3:1, 3:3, 4:1, 4:3, 5:1–3, 6:1–3, 7:2, 7:3, 9:1, 9:3, 10:1, 10:3, 10:4, 12:5, 15:1–3, 18:3, 19:2, 19:3, 20:1, 21:1, 24:1–3, Review and Assessment: Chs. 2, 3, 4, 5, 21, 25
Performance Expectations 9: Global Connections	
• describe instances in which language, art, music, and belief systems, and other cultural elements can facilitate global understanding or cause misunderstanding • analyze examples of conflict, cooperation, and interdependence among groups, societies, and nations • describe and analyze the effects of changing technologies on the global community • explore the causes, consequences, and possible solutions to persistent contemporary and emerging global interests • describe and explain the relationships and tensions between national sovereignty and global interests • demonstrate understanding of concerns, standards, issues, and conflicts related to universal human rights • identify and describe the roles of international and multinational organizations	3:1, 3:2, 3:3, 4:1–3, 5:1–3, 7:3, 7:5, 9:1–5, 10:1–4, 12:1–5, 13:1–4, 15:1–3, 16:1–3, 17:1–2, 18:3, 19:2, 19:3, 21:1–2, 22:1–3, 23:1–2, 24:3, 24:4, 25:1–5, 26:1–2, Review and Assessment: Chs. 3, 4, 5, 12, 13, 15, 16, 17, 21, 22, 23, 24, 25

Correlation to the NCSS Curriculum Standards *(continued)*

Standard	Eastern Hemisphere
Performance Expectations 10: Civic Ideals and Practices	
• examine the origins and continuing influence of key ideals of the democratic republican form of government, such as individual human dignity, liberty, justice, equality, and rule of law • identify and interpret sources and examples of the rights and responsibilities of citizens • locate, access, analyze, organize, and apply information about selected public issues—recognizing and explaining multiple points of view • practice forms of civic discussion and participation consistent with the ideals of citizens in a democratic republic • explain and analyze various forms of citizen action that influence public policy decisions • identify and explain the roles of formal and informal political actors in influencing and shaping public policy and decision-making • analyze the influence of diverse forms of public opinion on the development of public policy and decision-making • analyze the effectiveness of selected public policies and citizen behaviors in realizing the stated ideals of a democratic republican form of government • explain the relationship between policy statements and action plans used to address issues of public concern • examine strategies designed to strengthen the "common good," which consider a range of options for citizen action	4:1–3, 5:1, 5:3, 7:1–5, 8:2, 8:3, 9:1, 9:3, 9:5, 10:1–4, 12:2, 12:5, 14:2, 15:2, 16:2, 17:2, 18:3, 24:3, Review and Assessment: Chs. 4, 12, 17, 24

Objective

- Learn how to read nonfiction critically by analyzing an author's purpose, distinguishing between facts and opinions, identifying evidence, and evaluating credibility.

Prepare to Read

Build Background Knowledge **L2**

Write the phrase "Don't believe everything you read" on the board. Ask students to brainstorm examples that illustrate the saying. Provide a few simple examples to get them started (*tall tales, advertisements.*)

Instruct

Reading Informational Texts **L2**

Guided Instruction

- Tell students that they must actively evaluate the information in most of the nonfiction they read.

- Read the sample editorial on this page aloud. Tell students that an editorial usually expresses a person's opinion. Ask students to consider why the author wrote this editorial. (*The author expresses the opinion that the proposal to build the new shopping center should have been approved.*) Ask **How might this purpose affect what the editorial says?** (*The author may present information in the best possible light to prove his or her belief.*)

- Another important step in evaluating nonfiction is distinguishing between facts and opinions. Ask each student to write one fact and one opinion, on any subject, in their notebooks. Use the Idea Wave strategy (TE, p. T35) to get students to share their facts and opinions. If students have incorrectly categorized examples, help them to see why.

Reading Informational Texts

Reading a magazine, an Internet page, or a textbook is not the same as reading a novel. The purpose of reading nonfiction texts is to acquire new information. On page M18 you'll read about some ⊙ **Target Reading Skills** that you'll have a chance to practice as you read this textbook. Here we'll focus on a few skills that will help you read nonfiction with a more critical eye.

Analyze the Author's Purpose

Different types of materials are written with different purposes in mind. For example, a textbook is written to teach students information about a subject. The purpose of a technical manual is to teach someone how to use something, such as a computer. A newspaper editorial might be written to persuade the reader to accept a particular point of view. A writer's purpose influences how the material is presented. Sometimes an author states his or her purpose directly. More often, the purpose is only suggested, and you must use clues to identify the author's purpose.

Distinguish Between Facts and Opinions

It's important when reading informational texts to read actively and to distinguish between fact and opinion. A fact can be proven or disproven. An opinion cannot—it is someone's personal viewpoint or evaluation.

For example, the editorial pages in a newspaper offer opinions on topics that are currently in the news. You need to read newspaper editorials with an eye for bias and faulty logic. For example, the newspaper editorial at the right shows factual statements in blue and opinion statements in red. The underlined words are examples of highly charged words. They reveal bias on the part of the writer.

> More than 5,000 people voted last week in favor of building a new shopping center, but the opposition won out. The margin of victory is irrelevant. Those radical voters who opposed the center are obviously self-serving elitists who do not care about anyone but themselves.
>
> This month's unemployment figure for our area is 10 percent, which represents an increase of about 5 percent over the figure for this time last year. These figures mean unemployment is getting worse. But the people who voted against the mall probably do not care about creating new jobs.

- Tell students that identifying evidence is another way to read nonfiction critically. Ask students to look again at the facts highlighted in the sample editorial. **Does the evidence presented in these facts convince you that building a new shopping center is a good idea?** (*The evidence is incomplete—the author has not shown that the new shopping center would solve the unemployment problem.*)

- Tell students that analyzing an author's purpose, distinguishing between facts and opinions, and identifying evidence are all ways to evaluate the credibility of the author. Tell students to look at the checklist for evaluating Web sites. Ask students to think about Web sites they have visited. Do those Web sites pass the checklist's test? Why or why not?

Identify Evidence

Before you accept an author's conclusion, you need to make sure that the author has based the conclusion on enough evidence and on the right kind of evidence. An author may present a series of facts to support a claim, but the facts may not tell the whole story. For example, what evidence does the author of the newspaper editorial on the previous page provide to support his claim that the new shopping center would create more jobs? Is it possible that the shopping center might have put many small local businesses out of business, thus increasing unemployment rather than decreasing it?

Evaluate Credibility

Whenever you read informational texts, you need to assess the credibility of the author. This is especially true of sites you may visit on the Internet. All Internet sources are not equally reliable. Here are some questions to ask yourself when evaluating the credibility of a Web site.

- ☐ Is the Web site created by a respected organization, a discussion group, or an individual?
- ☐ Does the Web site creator include his or her name as well as credentials and the sources he or she used to write the material?
- ☐ Is the information on the site balanced or biased?
- ☐ Can you verify the information using two other sources?
- ☐ Is there a date telling when the Web site was created or last updated?

Reading and Writing Handbook **RW1**

Independent Practice

Ask students to bring in an editorial from the local newspaper, or distribute copies of an appropriate editorial. Ask students to critically assess their editorial by analyzing the author's purpose; underlining facts and circling opinions in the text of the editorial; summarizing the evidence presented in the editorial; and finally drawing a conclusion about the credibility of the editorial.

Monitor Progress

Pair students and have them share their editorial assessments. Ask them to explain the reasoning behind the conclusions they drew about the editorial's credibility. Circulate and offer assistance as needed.

Assess and Reteach

Assess Progress L2

Collect students' papers and review their assessments.

Reteach L1

If students are struggling, tell them to approach the task by asking themselves the following questions as they read a piece of nonfiction: **Why** did the author write this? **How** has the author made his or her points, using facts or opinions? **What** evidence has the author used to support the main idea? **Who** is the author, and what sources has he or she used?

Extend L3

To extend this lesson, tell students to turn to the Table of Contents in the Student Edition and pick a chapter name that intrigues them. Then, ask them to search the Internet and find two Web sites about the chapter's topic. Finally, ask them to use the checklist on this page to evaluate each Web site and compare the two in terms of credibility.

Differentiated Instruction

For Advanced Readers L3

Draw students' attention to the checklist under the heading "Evaluate Credibility." Ask students to create a similar checklist for analyzing an author's purpose, distinguishing between fact and opinion, and identifying evidence.

For Special Needs Students L1

If special needs students are having trouble making the distinction between facts and opinions, partner them with more proficient students to do the *Distinguishing Fact and Opinion* lesson on the Social Studies Skill Tutor CD-ROM.

⊙ *Distinguishing Fact and Opinion,* **Social Studies Skill Tutor CD-ROM**

Objective

- Use a systematic approach to write narrative, persuasive, expository, and research essays.

Prepare to Read

Build Background Knowledge   L2

As a group, brainstorm all the ways that people use writing to communicate. Start with these examples: labeling a folder or writing an email. Conduct an Idea Wave (TE, p. T35) and write students' responses on the board. Tell them that people often write to express ideas or information. Give them *Four Purposes for Writing* and tell them to keep it in their notebooks for future reference.

All in One Europe and Russia Teaching Resources, *Four Purposes for Writing,* p. 7

Instruct

Narrative Essays   L2

Guided Instruction

- Tell students that narrative essays tell a story about their own experiences. Discuss the steps listed in the Student Edition.

- Choose an event in your own life (or invent one) such as visiting friends in another city. Write your topic on the board and model how to list details. *(what the trip was like, what you did while you were there, what your friends are like)* Cross out the least interesting details.

- Think aloud as you form your topic into a sentence that conveys the main idea of your essay.

- Tell students that you will go on to flesh out the details into a colorful story.

Independent Practice

- Tell students to write a narrative essay about a recent positive experience. Have student pairs brainstorm topics.

Writing for Social Studies

Writing is one of the most powerful communication tools you will ever use. You will use it to share your thoughts and ideas with others. Research shows that writing about what you read actually helps you learn new information and ideas. A systematic approach to writing— including prewriting, drafting, revising, and proofing—can help you write better, whether you're writing an essay or a research report.

Narrative Essays

Writing that tells a story about a personal experience

1 Select and Narrow Your Topic

A narrative is a story. In social studies, it might be a narrative essay about how an event affected you or your family.

2 Gather Details

Brainstorm a list of details you'd like to include in your narrative.

3 Write a First Draft

Start by writing a simple opening sentence that conveys the main idea of your essay. Continue by writing a colorful story that has interesting details. Write a conclusion that sums up the significance of the event or situation described in your essay.

4 Revise and Proofread

Check to make sure you have not begun too many sentences with the word *I*. Replace general words with more colorful ones.

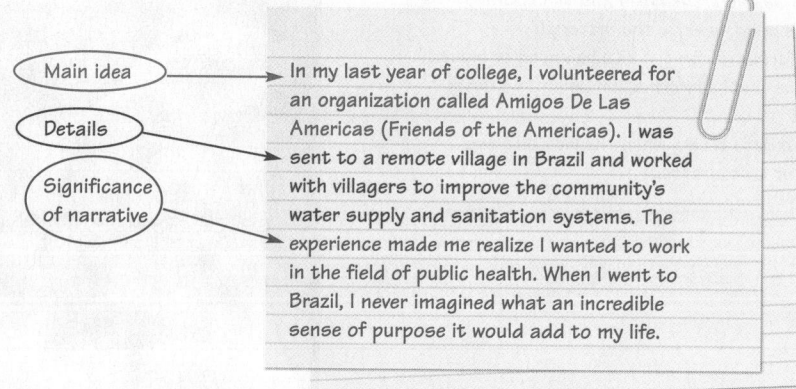

In my last year of college, I volunteered for an organization called Amigos De Las Americas (Friends of the Americas). I was sent to a remote village in Brazil and worked with villagers to improve the community's water supply and sanitation systems. The experience made me realize I wanted to work in the field of public health. When I went to Brazil, I never imagined what an incredible sense of purpose it would add to my life.

Main idea
Details
Significance of narrative

- Give students *Writing to Describe* to help them write their essays. After they have written the body of their essay, give them *Writing the Conclusion* to help them complete it.

All in One Europe and Russia Teaching Resources, *Writing to Describe,* p. 8; *Writing the Conclusion,* p. 9

Monitor Progress

Have students share their drafts with their partners. Give them *Using the Revision Checklist* and ask them to review their partners' papers. Urge them to provide constructive criticism and suggestions for improvement.

All in One Europe and Russia Teaching Resources, *Using the Revision Checklist,* p. 10

Persuasive Essays

Writing that supports an opinion or position

① Select and Narrow Your Topic

Choose a topic that provokes an argument and has at least two sides. Choose a side. Decide which argument will appeal most to your audience and persuade them to understand your point of view.

② Gather Evidence

Create a chart that states your position at the top and then lists the pros and cons for your position below, in two columns. Predict and address the strongest arguments against your stand.

③ Write a First Draft

Write a strong thesis statement that clearly states your position. Continue by presenting the strongest arguments in favor of your position and acknowledging and refuting opposing arguments.

④ Revise and Proofread

Check to make sure you have made a logical argument and that you have not oversimplified the argument.

Main Idea → It is vital to vote in elections. When people

Supporting (pro) argument → vote, they tell public officials how to run the government. Not every proposal is carried

Opposing (con) argument → out; however, politicians do their best to listen to what the majority of people want.

Transition words → Therefore, every vote is important.

Reading and Writing Handbook **RW3**

Guided Instruction

- Tell students that the purpose of writing a persuasive essay is to convince other people to believe your point of view. However, you must use solid, reliable evidence and arguments to make your points.

- Model the thought process by pointing out how the writer presents his or her argument in the paragraph on this page.

Independent Practice

- Tell students to write a persuasive essay about a topic that is important to them. Have students form pairs. One student in each pair should state his or her position. The other student then shares opposing arguments, which the first student should refute in his or her essay. Then the pairs switch roles.

- Give students *Writing to Persuade* to help them write their essays.

  All in One **Europe and Russia Teaching Resources,** *Writing to Persuade,* p. 11

Monitor Progress

If students are having trouble structuring their paragraphs, give them *Structuring Paragraphs* and *Creating Paragraph Outlines* to provide a framework.

  All in One **Europe and Russia Teaching Resources,** *Structuring Paragraphs,* p. 12; *Creating Paragraph Outlines,* p. 13

Differentiated Instruction

For Less Proficient Readers   L1

Tell students to use looping to help them focus on a topic. Have them follow these steps: Write freely on your topic for about five minutes. Read what you have written and circle the most important idea. Write for five minutes on the circled idea. Repeat the process until you isolate a topic narrow enough to cover well in a short essay.

Expository Essays

L2

Guided Instruction

- Read the steps for writing expository essays with students.

- Tell students that the graphic organizer example given on the Student Edition page is for a cause-and-effect expository essay. They might use a Venn diagram for a compare-and-contrast essay and a flow-chart for a problem-and-solution essay.

- Model how to create a topic sentence from the information in the cause-and-effect graphic organizer. (*Sample topic sentence: In Mexico, several factors are causing rural families to move from the countryside to the city.*)

- Create a brief outline showing how you will organize the paragraphs in your essay.

Independent Practice

Tell students to write an expository essay based on a recent current event. Have them brainstorm ideas with a partner, then choose which type of essay best suits their topic (cause and effect, compare and contrast, or problem and solution.) Give them *Writing to Inform and Explain* and *Gathering Details* to help them start drafting their essays.

All in One **Europe and Russia Teaching Resources,** *Writing to Inform and Explain,* p. 14; *Gathering Details,* p. 15

Monitor Progress

If students are struggling with their essays, give them *Writing a Cause-and-Effect Essay* or *Writing a Problem-and-Solution Essay.*

All in One **Europe and Russia Teaching Resources,** *Writing a Cause-and-Effect Essay,* p. 16; *Writing a Problem-and-Solution Essay,* p. 17

Research Papers

L2

Guided Instruction

Go over the steps for writing a research paper carefully. Ask students to share questions about the process, using the Idea Wave strategy (TE, p. T35). Answer any questions they might have.

Reading and Writing Handbook

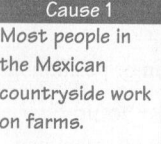

Expository Essays

Writing that explains a process, compares and contrasts, explains causes and effects, or explores solutions to a problem

1 Identify and Narrow Your Topic

Expository writing is writing that explains something in detail. It might explain the similarities and differences between two or more subjects (compare and contrast). It might explain how one event causes another (cause and effect). Or it might explain a problem and describe a solution.

2 Gather Evidence

Create a graphic organizer that identifies details to include in your essay.

Cause 1	Cause 2	Cause 3
Most people in the Mexican countryside work on farms.	The population in Mexico is growing at one of the highest rates in the world.	There is not enough farm work for so many people.

Effect
As a result, many rural families are moving from the countryside to live in Mexico City.

3 Write Your First Draft

Write a topic sentence and then organize the essay around your similarities and differences, causes and effects, or problem and solutions. Be sure to include convincing details, facts, and examples.

4 Revise and Proofread

Research Papers

Writing that presents research about a topic

1 Narrow Your Topic

Choose a topic you're interested in and make sure that it is not too broad. For example, instead of writing a report on Panama, write about the construction of the Panama Canal.

2 Acquire Information

Locate several sources of information about the topic from the library or the Internet. For each resource, create a source index card like the one at the right. Then take notes using an index card for each detail or subtopic. On the card, note which source the information was taken from. Use quotation marks when you copy the exact words from a source.

Source #1
McCullough, David. *The Path Between the Seas: The Creation of the Panama Canal, 1870-1914.* N.Y., Simon and Schuster, 1977.

3 Make an Outline

Use an outline to decide how to organize your report. Sort your index cards into the same order.

Outline
I. Introduction
II. Why the canal was built
III. How the canal was built
 A. Physical challenges
 B. Medical challenges
IV. Conclusion

Differentiated Instruction

For Gifted and Talented
L3

Tell students that a verb is in active voice when the subject performs the action named by the verb. A verb is in passive voice when the subject undergoes the action named by the verb.

Give these examples:

Passive voice: The house is being painted by my sister and me.

Active voice: My sister and I are painting the house.

Tell students that using the active voice whenever possible will make their writing more dynamic and concise.

Introduction

Building the Panama Canal

Ever since Christopher Columbus first explored the Isthmus of Panama, the Spanish had been looking for a water route through it. They wanted to be able to sail west from Spain to Asia without sailing around South America. However, it was not until 1914 that the dream became a reality.

Conclusion

It took eight years and more than 70,000 workers to build the Panama Canal. It remains one of the greatest engineering feats of modern times.

4 Write a First Draft

Write an introduction, a body, and a conclusion. Leave plenty of space between lines so you can go back and add details that you may have left out.

5 Revise and Proofread

Be sure to include transition words between sentences and paragraphs. Here are some examples:

To show a contrast—*however, although, despite.*

To point out a reason—*since, because, if.*

To signal a conclusion—*therefore, consequently, so, then.*

Evaluating Your Writing

Use this table to help you evaluate your writing.

	Excellent	Good	Acceptable	Unacceptable
Purpose	Achieves purpose—to inform, persuade, or provide historical interpretation—very well	Informs, persuades, or provides historical interpretation reasonably well	Reader cannot easily tell if the purpose is to inform, persuade, or provide historical interpretation	Purpose is not clear
Organization	Develops ideas in a very clear and logical way	Presents ideas in a reasonably well-organized way	Reader has difficulty following the organization	Lacks organization
Elaboration	Explains all ideas with facts and details	Explains most ideas with facts and details	Includes some supporting facts and details	Lacks supporting details
Use of Language	Uses excellent vocabulary and sentence structure with no errors in spelling, grammar, or punctuation	Uses good vocabulary and sentence structure with very few errors in spelling, grammar, or punctuation	Includes some errors in grammar, punctuation, and spelling	Includes many errors in grammar, punctuation, and spelling

Reading and Writing Handbook **RW5**

Independent Practice

- Have students consider topics for a research paper. Give them *Choosing a Topic* to help them learn how to evaluate potential topics.

  All in One **Europe and Russia Teaching Resources,** *Choosing a Topic,* p. 18

- Once students have selected a topic, tell them they will need facts to support their ideas. Give them *Using the Library, Summarizing and Taking Notes,* and *Preparing Note Cards* to help them start their research.

  All in One **Europe and Russia Teaching Resources,** *Using the Library,* p. 19; *Summarizing and Taking Notes,* p. 20; *Preparing Note Cards,* p. 21

Monitor Progress

Give students *Writing an Introduction* and *Writing the Body of an Essay* to help them write their essays.

  All in One **Europe and Russia Teaching Resources,** *Writing an Introduction,* p. 22; *Writing the Body of an Essay,* p. 23

Assess and Reteach

Assess Progress L2

Ask students to pick the best essay they have written so far and evaluate it using the rubric on this page.

Reteach L1

Collect students' essays and self-evaluations. Meet with students to go over good points and areas for improvement. Revisit each type of essay as needed with the whole class.

Extend L3

To extend this lesson, tell students there are many other different types of writing. Have them complete *Writing for Assessment* and *Writing a Letter* to learn about two more types of writing.

  All in One **Europe and Russia Teaching Resources,** *Writing for Assessment,* p. 24; *Writing a Letter,* p. 25

Differentiated Instruction

For English Language Learners L2

To help students understand the tasks you have given them, provide them with an example of a well-executed essay from a different class or a previous year. The example essay should be well written and organized but not above grade level. You could look for and save good examples each year you teach.

MapMaster Skills Handbook
Step-by-Step Instruction

Objective
- Identify and define the five themes of geography.

Prepare to Read

Build Background Knowledge L2
Assign students to small groups and give them five minutes to write a definition of geography. Then write the five themes of geography on the board. Remind students that a theme is an important underlying idea. As a class, decide which parts of their definitions go under each of the geography themes. For example, "landforms" would fall under the theme of place.

Instruct

Five Themes of Geography L2

Guided Instruction
- Divide the text using the headings and ask students to read the pages using the Structured Silent Reading technique (TE, p. T34). Clarify the meanings of any unfamiliar words.

- Ask students to give the relative locations of their homes.

- Mention the popularity of different kinds of ethnic foods in the United States. Ask **What theme of geography are these foods a good example of?** *(movement)* Encourage students to name other examples of the movement of cultural traditions from one region to another.

- Discuss the climate in your area. Ask **How does the environment affect how we live?** *(affects dress, travel, sports and other recreational activities, the way homes are built)*

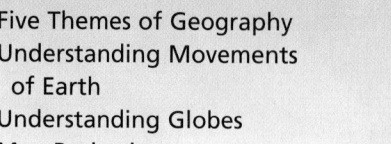

MapMaster™ SKILLS HANDBOOK

CONTENTS

Go Online PHSchool.com — Use Web Code lap-0000 for all of the maps in this handbook.

Five Themes of Geography

Studying the geography of the entire world is a huge task. You can make that task easier by using the five themes of geography: location, regions, place, movement, and human-environment interaction. The themes are tools you can use to organize information and to answer the where, why, and how of geography.

▲ **Location**
This museum in England has a line running through it. The line marks its location at 0° longitude.

LOCATION

1 Location answers the question, "Where is it?" You can think of the location of a continent or a country as its address. You might give an absolute location such as 22 South Lake Street or 40° N and 80° W. You might also use a relative address, telling where one place is by referring to another place. *Between school and the mall* and *eight miles east of Pleasant City* are examples of relative locations.

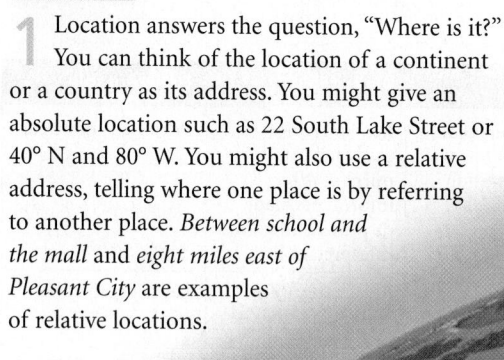

MapMaster Skills Handbook

Differentiated Instruction

For English Language Learners L1
Students may find it difficult to pronounce some of the multisyllable words in this section such as *relative, environment, interaction, government, signature,* and *communicate.* Show students how to break down these words into smaller parts to help them sound out the pronunciation.

For Advanced Readers L3
Have students find articles in newspapers or magazines that illustrate the themes of geography. Have students underline the relevant sections and identify the theme or themes they illustrate. Suggest that students create a bulletin board to share their examples with the class.

REGIONS

2 Regions are areas that share at least one common feature. Geographers divide the world into many types of regions. For example, countries, states, and cities are political regions. The people in any one of these places live under the same government. Other features, such as climate and culture, can be used to define regions. Therefore the same place can be found in more than one region. For example, the state of Hawaii is in the political region of the United States. Because it has a tropical climate, Hawaii is also part of a tropical climate region.

MOVEMENT

4 Movement answers the question, "How do people, goods, and ideas move from place to place?" Remember that what happens in one place often affects what happens in another. Use the theme of movement to help you trace the spread of goods, people, and ideas from one location to another.

PLACE

3 Place identifies the natural and human features that make one place different from every other place. You can identify a specific place by its landforms, climate, plants, animals, people, language, or culture. You might even think of place as a geographic signature. Use the signature to help you understand the natural and human features that make one place different from every other place.

INTERACTION

5 Human-environment interaction focuses on the relationship between people and the environment. As people live in an area, they often begin to make changes to it, usually to make their lives easier. For example, they might build a dam to control flooding during rainy seasons. Also, the environment can affect how people live, work, dress, travel, and communicate.

◄ **Interaction**
These Congolese women interact with their environment by gathering wood for cooking.

PRACTICE YOUR GEOGRAPHY SKILLS

1 Describe your town or city, using each of the five themes of geography.

2 Name at least one thing that comes into your town or city and one that goes out. How is each moved? Where does it come from? Where does it go?

MapMaster Skills Handbook **M1**

Independent Practice
Partner students and have them complete *The Five Themes of Geography*.

All in One Europe and Russia Teaching Resources, *The Five Themes of Geography,* p. 29

Monitor Progress
As students complete the worksheet, circulate to make sure that individuals comprehend the material. Provide assistance as needed.

Assess and Reteach

Assess Progress L2
Have students complete the questions under Practice Your Geography Skills.

Reteach L1
Help students create a concept web that identifies the five themes of geography. Start filling in blank *Transparency B17: Concept Web* to model how to identify information to clarify each theme. For example, under Regions students might write "share common features such as government, climate, and culture." Encourage students to refer to their webs to review the themes.

Europe and Russia Transparencies, *Transparency B17: Concept Web*

Extend L3
To extend the lesson, ask students to find out about any plans for new buildings, highways, or other types of construction in your area. Ask students to predict how these changes will affect the community's environment.

Answers

PRACTICE YOUR GEOGRAPHY SKILLS

1. Answers should include an example of how each of the five themes relates to your community.

2. Students' answers should provide examples of goods, ideas, or things that move into and out of your community.

Objective

- Explain how the movements of Earth cause night and day, as well as the seasons.

Prepare to Read

Build Background Knowledge   L2

Remind students that while Earth revolves around the sun, it also rotates on its own axis. Review the meanings of "revolve" and "rotate" in this context. Ask students to brainstorm ways that Earth's revolving and rotating might affect their lives. Conduct an Idea Wave (TE, p. T35) to generate a list of ideas.

Instruct

Understanding Movements of Earth   L2

Guided Instruction

- Read the text as a class using the Oral Cloze strategy (TE, p. T33). Explain that the illustrations on pp. M2 and M3 show the information in the text visually. Clarify the meanings of any unfamiliar words.

- Ask students **How does Earth rotating on its axis cause day and night?** *(It is daytime on the side of Earth facing the sun, while the side facing away from the sun is dark.)*

- Ask **How does the tilt of Earth affect the seasons?** *(The farther away a part of Earth is from the sun's rays, the colder it is.)*

Independent Practice

Partner students and have them complete *Understanding the Movements of the Earth.*

> **All in One Europe and Russia Teaching Resources,** *Understanding Movements of the Earth,* p. 30

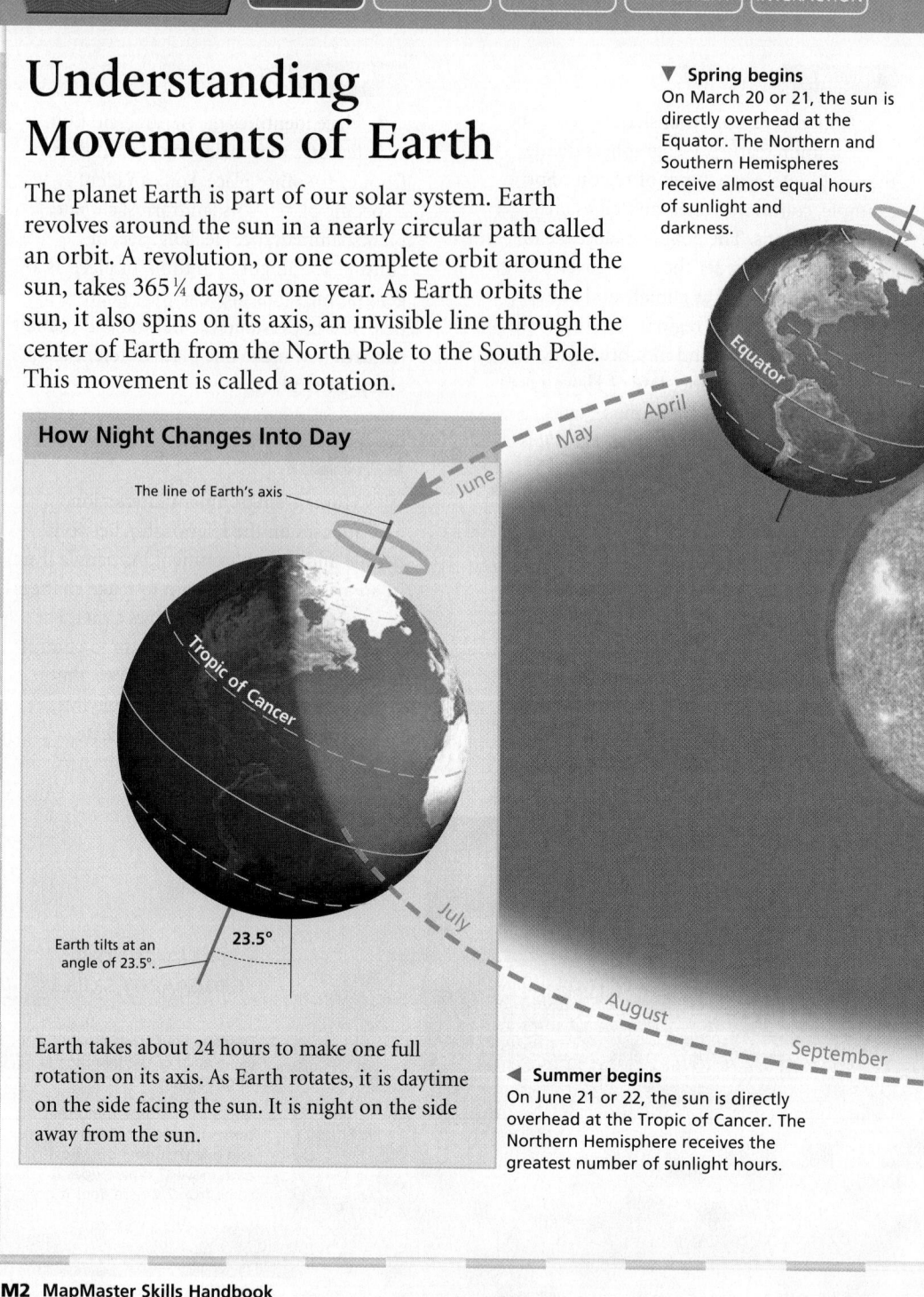

Understanding Movements of Earth

The planet Earth is part of our solar system. Earth revolves around the sun in a nearly circular path called an orbit. A revolution, or one complete orbit around the sun, takes 365 ¼ days, or one year. As Earth orbits the sun, it also spins on its axis, an invisible line through the center of Earth from the North Pole to the South Pole. This movement is called a rotation.

How Night Changes Into Day

The line of Earth's axis

Tropic of Cancer

Earth tilts at an angle of 23.5°.   **23.5°**

Earth takes about 24 hours to make one full rotation on its axis. As Earth rotates, it is daytime on the side facing the sun. It is night on the side away from the sun.

▼ **Spring begins**
On March 20 or 21, the sun is directly overhead at the Equator. The Northern and Southern Hemispheres receive almost equal hours of sunlight and darkness.

Equator

June

May

April

July

August

September

◄ **Summer begins**
On June 21 or 22, the sun is directly overhead at the Tropic of Cancer. The Northern Hemisphere receives the greatest number of sunlight hours.

M2 MapMaster Skills Handbook

Background: Links Across Place

Sunrise and Sunset Most people have heard the saying "The sun rises in the east and sets in the west." However, the sun does not ever actually change position. Every day, Earth rotates on its axis so that as each region faces the sun, it experiences day. The rotation continues so that as a region turns away from the sun, it experiences night. The sun stays in the same place. A person viewing sunrise or sunset is really seeing Earth's slow turn on its axis, not the sun rising or setting.

The Seasons

Earth's axis is tilted at an angle. Because of this tilt, sunlight strikes different parts of Earth at different times in the year, creating seasons. The illustration below shows how the seasons are created in the Northern Hemisphere. In the Southern Hemisphere, the seasons are reversed.

PRACTICE YOUR GEOGRAPHY SKILLS

1 What causes the seasons in the Northern Hemisphere to be the opposite of those in the Southern Hemisphere?

2 During which two days of the year do the Northern Hemisphere and Southern Hemisphere have equal hours of daylight and darkness?

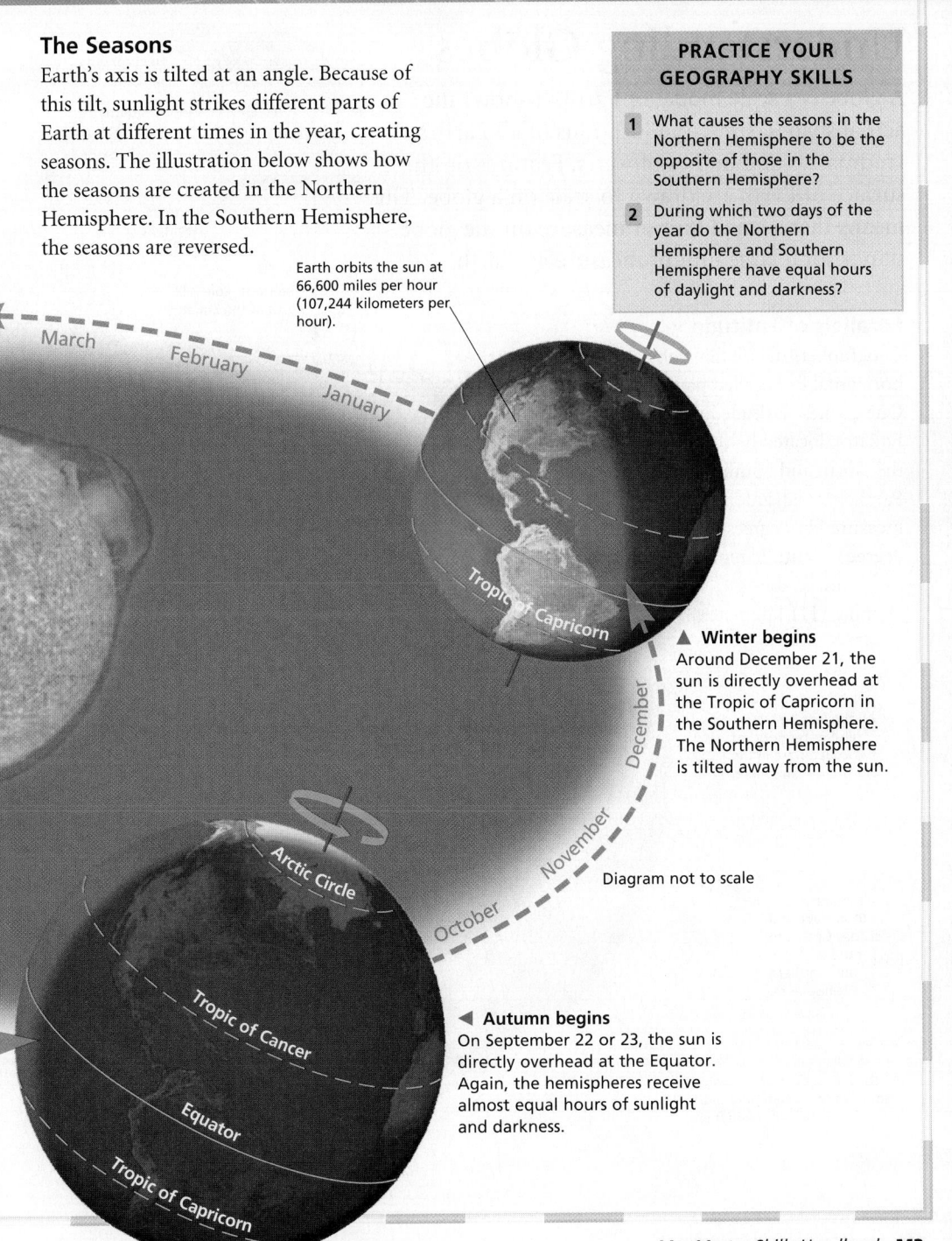

Earth orbits the sun at 66,600 miles per hour (107,244 kilometers per hour).

March
February
January
December
November
October

▲ Winter begins
Around December 21, the sun is directly overhead at the Tropic of Capricorn in the Southern Hemisphere. The Northern Hemisphere is tilted away from the sun.

Diagram not to scale

◀ Autumn begins
On September 22 or 23, the sun is directly overhead at the Equator. Again, the hemispheres receive almost equal hours of sunlight and darkness.

Arctic Circle
Tropic of Cancer
Equator
Tropic of Capricorn

MapMaster Skills Handbook **M3**

Monitor Progress

As students do the worksheet, circulate to make sure individuals comprehend the key concepts. Provide assistance as needed.

Assess and Reteach

Assess Progress   L2

Have students complete the Practice Your Geography Skills questions.

Reteach   L1

If students are having trouble understanding these concepts, create a model to demonstrate Earth's revolution. Use a foam ball to represent Earth. Insert a pencil through the ball to represent Earth's axis, labeling the ends "North Pole" and "South Pole." Draw the Equator perpendicular to the axis. Place a light source in the center of a table to represent the sun. Then tilt the ball at a slight angle and move it around the light to mimic Earth's revolution. Have students notice the point at which each pole is nearest the sun and identify what season it would be in each hemisphere.

Extend   L3

To extend the lesson, ask students to consider Earth's relationship to its satellite, the moon. Ask them to research on the Internet to answer these questions: "Does the moon rotate like Earth? Does the moon revolve around Earth as Earth revolves around the sun?" To help students start their research, give them *Doing Searches on the Internet.*

All in One Europe and Russia Teaching Resources, *Doing Searches on the Internet,* p. 31

Answers

PRACTICE YOUR GEOGRAPHY SKILLS

1. The seasons are reversed in the Northern Hemisphere and Southern Hemisphere because Earth is tilted. When one hemisphere is tilted towards the sun, the other hemisphere is tilted away from the sun.

2. September 22–23 and March 20–21

MapMaster Skills Handbook **M3**

Objectives

- Understand how a globe is marked with a grid to measure features on Earth.

- Learn how to use longitude and latitude to locate a place.

Prepare to Read

Build Background Knowledge   L2

Tell students that in this lesson, they will learn how to use globes. Ask students what it would be like to see Earth from a spacecraft. Discuss the shape that students would see. Then discuss why a globe is a more accurate rendering of Earth than a flat map. Point out that a globe is like a model car in that it is a small version of something larger. If a globe is available, have students examine it.

Instruct

Understanding Globes   L2

Guided Instruction

- Read the text as a class using the Oral Cloze strategy (TE, p. T33). Have students study the illustrations carefully.

- Ask **What line of latitude divides the Northern and Southern Hemispheres?** *(the Equator)* **At what degrees latitude is this line?** *(0°)*

- Ask **Where do the lines of longitude come together?** *(at the North and South Poles)* **What is the name of the meridian at 0 degrees?** *(Prime Meridian)*

- Have students look at the global grid on *Color Transparency ER 3: The Global Grid.* Ask **What is the global grid?** *(a pattern of lines formed where the parallels of latitude and meridians of longitude cross)* **What continent in the Eastern Hemisphere does the 100° E meridian pass through?** *(Asia)*

  Europe and Russia Transparencies, *Color Transparency ER 3: The Global Grid*

Understanding Globes

A globe is a scale model of Earth. It shows the actual shapes, sizes, and locations of all Earth's landmasses and bodies of water. Features on the surface of Earth are drawn to scale on a globe. This means that a small unit of measure on the globe stands for a large unit of measure on Earth.

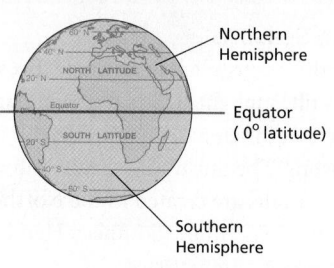

Northern Hemisphere

Equator (0° latitude)

Southern Hemisphere

Parallels of Latitude

Geographers divide the globe along imaginary horizontal lines called parallels of latitude. One of these latitude lines is the Equator, located halfway between the North and South poles. Parallels of latitude are measured in degrees (°). One degree of latitude represents a distance of about 69 miles (111 kilometers).

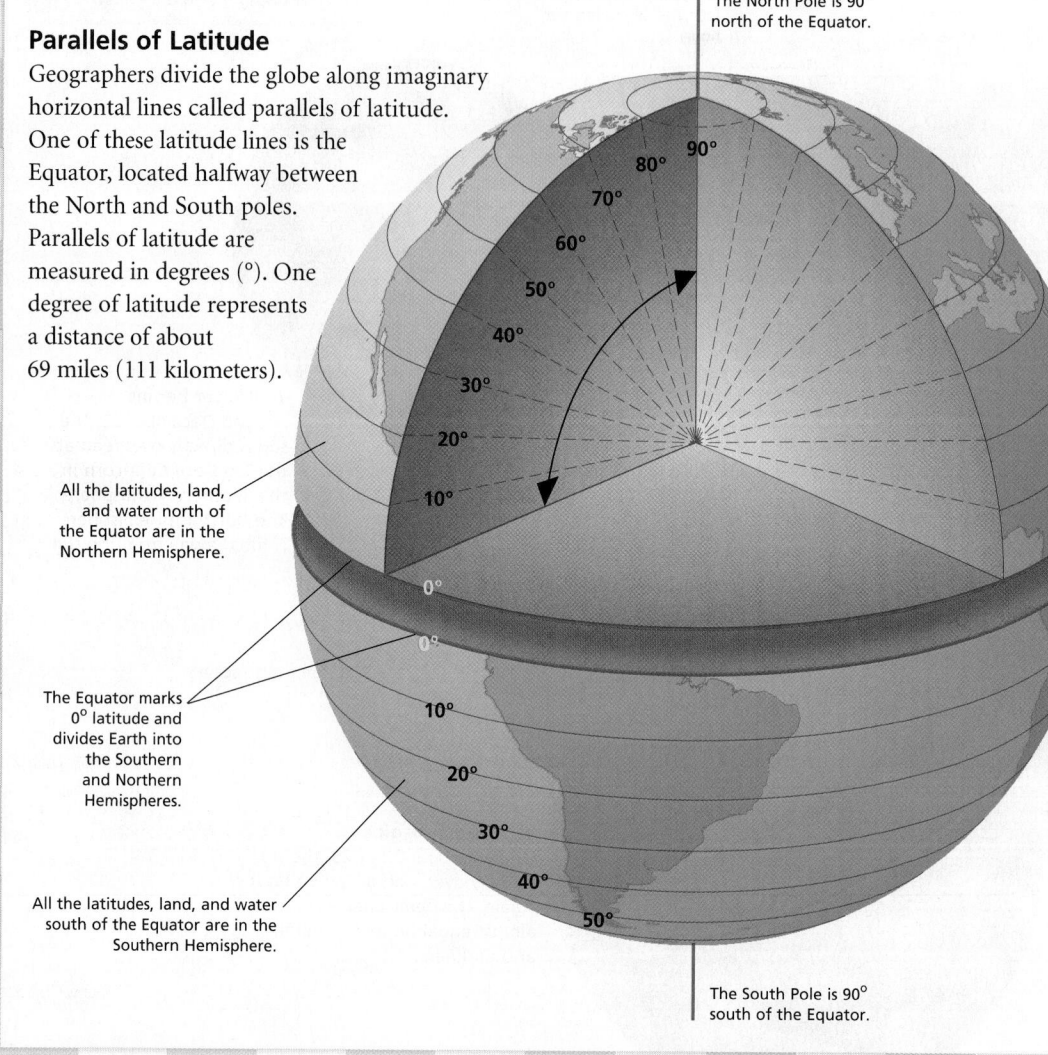

The North Pole is 90° north of the Equator.

All the latitudes, land, and water north of the Equator are in the Northern Hemisphere.

The Equator marks 0° latitude and divides Earth into the Southern and Northern Hemispheres.

All the latitudes, land, and water south of the Equator are in the Southern Hemisphere.

The South Pole is 90° south of the Equator.

M4 MapMaster Skills Handbook

Background: Links Across Time

The First Globes Historians believe that the first globe may have been made in the second century B.C. by a Greek geographer known as Crates of Mallus. The mathematician Ptolemy represented Earth as a globe in his written works in the second century A.D. In late 1492 Martin Behaim made a terrestrial globe that, although inaccurate by today's knowledge, reflected the best geographical knowledge of the time. This globe still exists and is on display in Behaim's hometown of Nuremberg, Germany.

Meridians of Longitude

Geographers also divide the globe along imaginary vertical lines called meridians of longitude, which are measured in degrees (°). The longitude line called the Prime Meridian runs from pole to pole through Greenwich, England. All meridians of longitude come together at the North and South Poles.

All the longitudes, land, and water west of the Prime Meridian are in the Western Hemisphere.

PRACTICE YOUR GEOGRAPHY SKILLS

1 Which continents lie completely in the Northern Hemisphere? In the Western Hemisphere?

2 Is there land or water at 20° S latitude and the Prime Meridian? At the Equator and 60° W longitude?

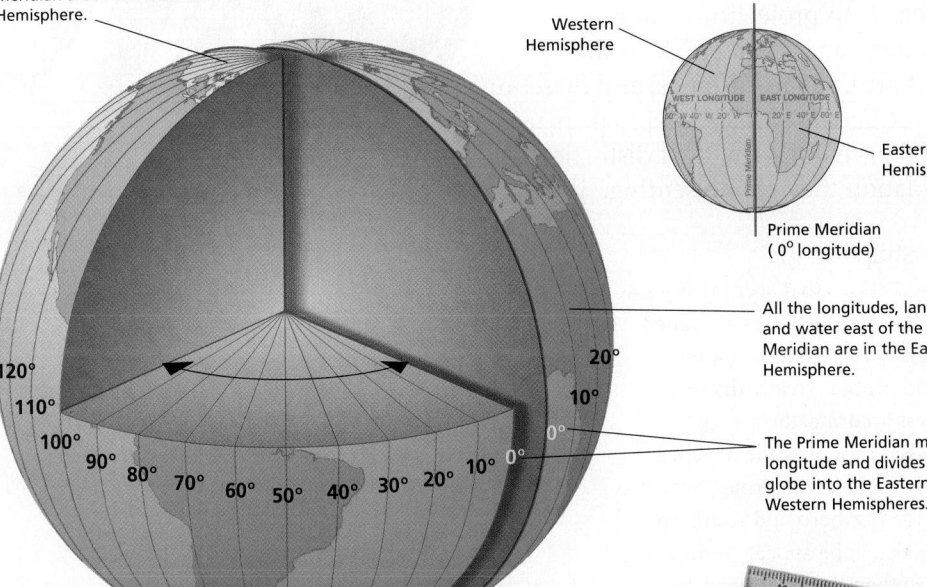

Western Hemisphere

Eastern Hemisphere

Prime Meridian (0° longitude)

All the longitudes, land, and water east of the Prime Meridian are in the Eastern Hemisphere.

The Prime Meridian marks 0° longitude and divides the globe into the Eastern and Western Hemispheres.

The Global Grid

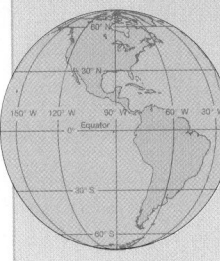

Together, the pattern of parallels of latitude and meridians of longitude is called the global grid. Using the lines of latitude and longitude, you can locate any place on Earth. For example, the location of 30° north latitude and 90° west longitude is usually written as 30° N, 90° W. Only one place on Earth has these coordinates—the city of New Orleans, in the state of Louisiana.

▲ **Compass**
Wherever you are on Earth, a compass can be used to show direction.

Independent Practice

Have students work in pairs to complete *Understanding Hemispheres* and *Understanding Latitude and Longitude*.

All in One Europe and Russia Teaching Resources, *Understanding Hemispheres,* p. 32; *Understanding Latitude and Longitude,* p. 33

Monitor Progress

As students do the worksheets, circulate to make sure pairs understand the key concepts. Show *Color Transparency ER 2: The Hemispheres* to help students.

Europe and Russia Transparencies, *Color Transparency ER 2: The Hemispheres*

Assess and Reteach

Assess Progress   L2

Have students answer the questions under Practice Your Geography Map Skills.

Reteach   L1

Use the DK Atlas activity *Understanding Latitude and Longitude* to review these skills with students. Have students complete the activity in pairs.

All in One Europe and Russia Teaching Resources, *DK Compact Atlas of the World Activity: Understanding Latitude and Longitude,* p. 34

Extend   L3

To extend the lesson, have students complete *Using Latitude and Longitude*. Then have students use the map and with a partner, play a game of Can You Find …? Each partner takes a turn giving the coordinates for a place on the map and the other partner must name the place.

All in One Europe and Russia Teaching Resources, *Using Latitude and Longitude,* p. 35

Differentiated Instruction

For Less Proficient Readers   L1

For students having difficulty understanding the concept of a global grid, give them *Understanding Grids* and help them complete it. Then follow up with *Using a Grid*.

All in One Europe and Russia Teaching Resources, *Understanding Grids,* p. 36; *Using a Grid,* p. 37

For Advanced Readers   L3

Have students complete *Comparing Globes and Maps*. Then ask them to make a chart showing the pros and cons of these two ways of representing Earth.

All in One Europe and Russia Teaching Resources, *Comparing Globes and Maps,* p. 38

Answers

PRACTICE YOUR GEOGRAPHY SKILLS

1. Northern Hemisphere: North America; Europe; Western Hemisphere: North America; South America

2. water; land

Objectives

- Compare maps of different projections.
- Describe distortions in map projections.

Prepare to Read

Build Background Knowledge L1

In this lesson, students will learn how cartographers depict Earth on a two-dimensional map. Remind students that if they were traveling in a spaceship, Earth would look like a globe. Ask if they could ever see the entire Earth at one time from space. Help students recognize that a flat map is the only way to see all of Earth at once.

Instruct

Map Projections L2

Guided Instruction

- Read the text as a class using the Choral Reading strategy (TE, p. T34). Direct students to look at the relevant maps after you read each section together. Follow up by having students do a second silent reading.

- Help students locate Greenland on the Mercator and Robinson maps. Ask **What difference do you notice in the way Greenland is shown?** (*It appears much larger on the Mercator Map.*) **How would you explain this?** (*The Mercator is a same-shape map and the shapes toward the poles are enlarged.*)

- Ask **Where does the distortion usually occur on an equal-area map?** (*at the edges of the map*)

- Have students compare Antarctica on the three projections. (*It is largest and most distorted on the Mercator map; smallest on the equal-area map; covers the entire bottom edge of the Robinson map.*)

Map Projections

Maps are drawings that show regions on flat surfaces. Maps are easier to use and carry than globes, but they cannot show the correct size and shape of every feature on Earth's curved surface. They must shrink some places and stretch others. To make up for this distortion, mapmakers use different map projections. No one projection can accurately show the correct area, shape, distance, and direction for all of Earth's surface. Mapmakers use the projection that has the least distortion for the information they are presenting.

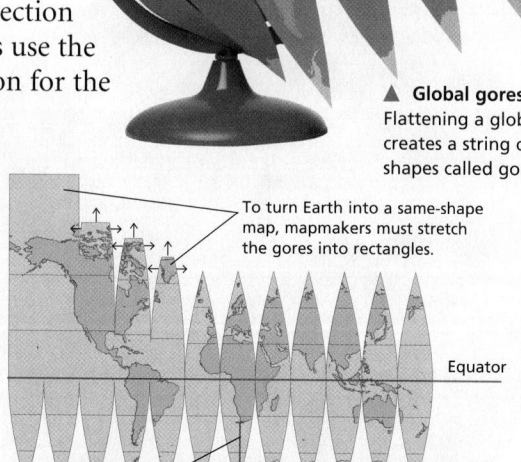

▲ **Global gores**
Flattening a globe creates a string of shapes called gores.

Same-Shape Maps

Map projections that accurately show the shapes of landmasses are called same-shape maps. However, these projections often greatly distort, or make less accurate, the size of landmasses as well as the distance between them. In the projection below, the northern and southern areas of the globe appear more stretched than the areas near the Equator.

To turn Earth into a same-shape map, mapmakers must stretch the gores into rectangles.

Equator

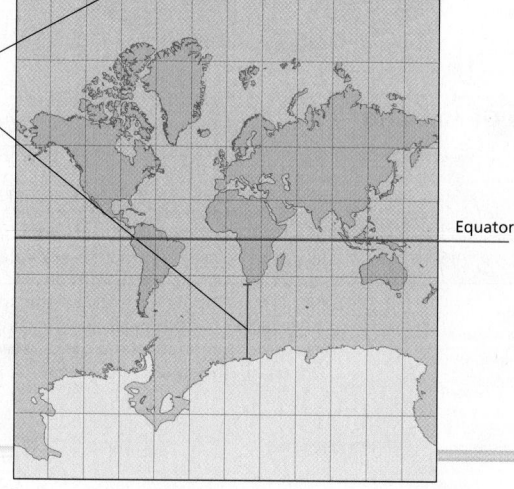

Stretching the gores makes parts of Earth larger. This enlargement becomes greater toward the North and South Poles.

Mercator projection ▶
One of the most common same-shape maps is the Mercator projection, named for the mapmaker who invented it. The Mercator projection accurately shows shape and direction, but it distorts distance and size. Because the projection shows true directions, ships' navigators use it to chart a straight-line course between two ports.

Equator

Differentiated Instruction

For Special Needs Students L1

If students have difficulty understanding why distortion occurs, draw a simple picture on an orange. Then have students try to peel the orange in one piece. Challenge students to place the peel flat on a piece of paper without any tears and spaces. Talk about what happens to the drawing. Explain that mapmakers face this same challenge when drawing Earth on a flat paper.

For Gifted and Talented L3

Have students complete *Great Circles and Straight Lines*. Then ask them to use their completed page and a globe to explain the concept of great circles to the class.

All in One Europe and Russia Teaching Resources, *Great Circles and Straight Lines,* p. 40

Equal-Area Maps

Map projections that show the correct size of landmasses are called equal-area maps. In order to show the correct size of landmasses, these maps usually distort shapes. The distortion is usually greater at the edges of the map and less at the center.

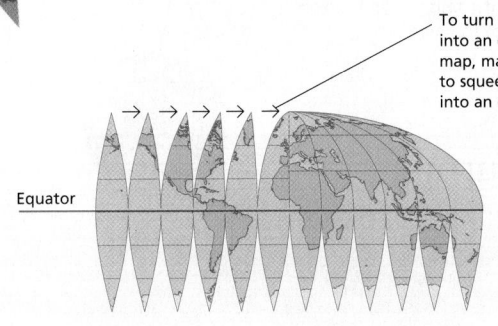

To turn Earth's surface into an equal-area map, mapmakers have to squeeze each gore into an oval.

Equator

PRACTICE YOUR GEOGRAPHY SKILLS

1 What feature is distorted on an equal-area map?

2 Would you use a Mercator projection to find the exact distance between two locations? Tell why or why not.

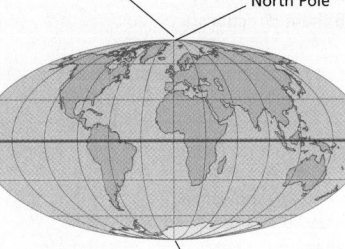

The tips of all the gores are then joined together. The points at which they join form the North and South Poles. The line of the Equator stays the same.

North Pole

Equator

South Pole

Robinson Maps

Many of the maps in this book use the Robinson projection, which is a compromise between the Mercator and equal-area projections. The Robinson projection gives a useful overall picture of the world. It keeps the size and shape relationships of most continents and oceans, but distorts the size of the polar regions.

The entire top edge of the map is the North Pole.

The map is least distorted at the Equator.

Equator

The entire bottom edge of the map is the South Pole.

Independent Practice

Have students work with partners to complete *Understanding Projection*.

All in One Europe and Russia Teaching Resources, *Understanding Projection,* p. 39

Monitor Progress

As students do the worksheet, circulate to make sure individuals comprehend the key concepts. Provide assistance as needed.

Assess and Reteach

Assess Progress   L2

Have students complete the Practice Your Geography Skills questions.

Reteach   L1

Use *Maps with Accurate Shapes: Conformal Maps* and *Maps with Accurate Areas: Equal-Area Maps* to help students go over the information in the lesson. Model thinking for each question and partner students to complete each page together. Circulate to provide explanations and help as students work.

All in One Europe and Russia Teaching Resources, *Maps with Accurate Shapes: Conformal Maps,* p. 41; *Maps with Accurate Areas: Equal-Area Maps,* p. 42

Extend   L3

To extend the lesson, ask students to complete *Maps with Accurate Direction: Azimuthal Maps.* Then have students write a sentence or two describing the different projections they have learned about.

All in One Europe and Russia Teaching Resources, *Maps with Accurate Directions: Azimuthal Maps,* p. 43

Background: Biography

Gerardus Mercator (1512–1594) The Mercator projection takes its name from a Flemish geographer, Gerhard Kremer. Kremer, who used the Latin form of his name, Gerardus Mercator, wrote books on ancient geography and cartography. He made his first world map in 1538. In 1554 he made a map of Europe. In 1568, the first map using the Mercator projection bearing his name appeared. Mercator also began an atlas of his maps which was finished by his son and published in 1594.

Answers

PRACTICE YOUR GEOGRAPHY SKILLS

1. shapes

2. No; the Mercator projection distorts distances.

Objective

- Identify and use the parts of a map.

Prepare to Read

Build Background Knowledge `L1`

In this lesson, students will learn about the practical aspects of maps. Ask students to name reasons that they might use a map: for example, to find directions, boundaries, distances. Conduct an Idea Wave (TE, p. T35) to generate a list of ideas. List the ideas on the board.

Instruct

How to Use a Map `L2`

Guided Instruction

- Divide the text and captions in the lesson using the headings and ask students to read the pages using the Structured Silent Reading strategy (TE, p. T34). Remind students to use the illustrations to acquire additional understanding. Refer to the list on the board, then ask students which map part (key, compass rose, scale, symbol, title) would be helpful in using a map for a specific purpose.

- Ask **What is the purpose of a compass rose?** (to show directions)

- Talk about how the three maps show different amounts of Earth's surface. Ask **Which map shows the largest area?** (Western Europe) **Which map shows the smallest area?** (Central London)

- Ask **What are some symbols that you might find on a map key?** (border, national capital, city, airport, park, point of interest)

Independent Practice

Partner students and have them complete *Using the Map Key* and *Using the Compass Rose*.

> **All in One Europe and Russia Teaching Resources,** *Using the Map Key,* p. 44; *Using the Compass Rose,* p. 45

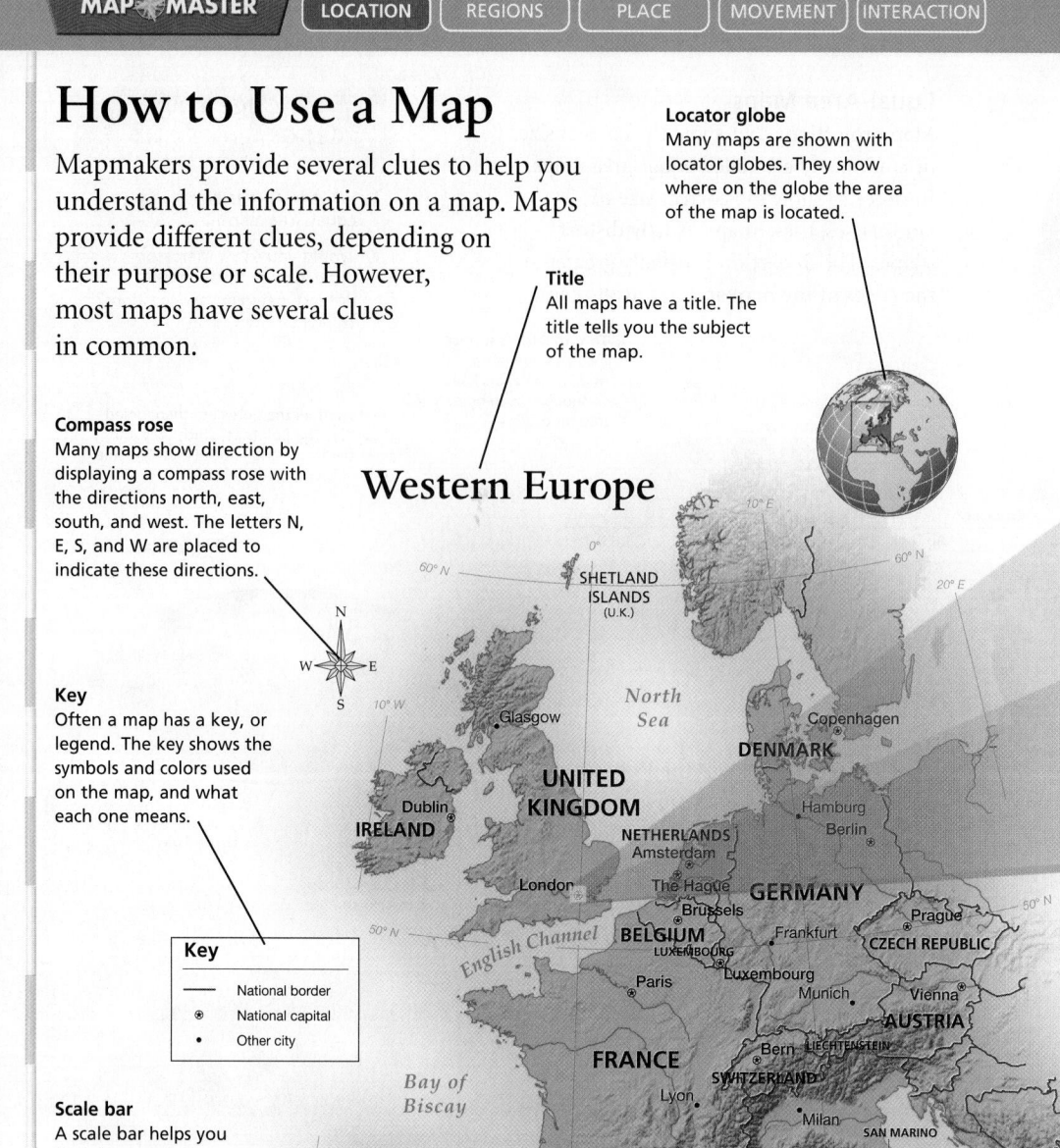

MAP MASTER | LOCATION | REGIONS | PLACE | MOVEMENT | INTERACTION

How to Use a Map

Mapmakers provide several clues to help you understand the information on a map. Maps provide different clues, depending on their purpose or scale. However, most maps have several clues in common.

Locator globe
Many maps are shown with locator globes. They show where on the globe the area of the map is located.

Title
All maps have a title. The title tells you the subject of the map.

Compass rose
Many maps show direction by displaying a compass rose with the directions north, east, south, and west. The letters N, E, S, and W are placed to indicate these directions.

Key
Often a map has a key, or legend. The key shows the symbols and colors used on the map, and what each one means.

Key
— National border
⊛ National capital
• Other city

Scale bar
A scale bar helps you find the actual distances between points shown on the map. Most scale bars show distances in both miles and kilometers.

0 miles 300
0 kilometers 300
Lambert Azimuthal Equal Area

Western Europe

M8 MapMaster Skills Handbook

Differentiated Instruction

For Less Proficient Readers `L1`

If students have difficulty recalling the purposes of different parts of a map, have them make a table using each map part as a heading. Under each heading, help students list the important function or functions of that map part. Students should refer to their table when they are working with maps.

For English Language Learners `L1`

Some of the words in the lesson, such as *symbol* and *scale*, may be unfamiliar to students acquiring English. Have students identify difficult words, look them up in the dictionary, and write sentences explaining what the terms mean.

Maps of Different Scales

Maps are drawn to different scales, depending on their purpose. Here are three maps drawn to very different scales. Keep in mind that maps showing large areas have smaller scales. Maps showing small areas have larger scales.

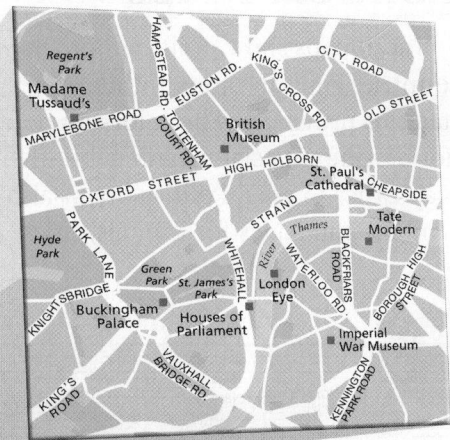

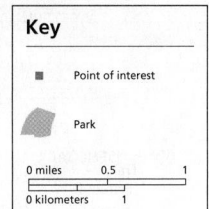

▲ **Greater London**
Find the gray square on the main map of Western Europe (left). This square represents the area shown on the map above. It shows London's boundaries, the general shape of the city, and the features around the city. This map can help you find your way from the airport to the center of town.

▲ **Central London**
Find the gray square on the map of Greater London. This square represents the area shown on the map above. This map moves you closer into the center of London. Like the zoom on a computer or a camera, this map shows a smaller area but in greater detail. It has the largest scale (1 inch represents about 0.9 mile). You can use this map to explore downtown London.

Key

■ Point of interest

▰ Park

0 miles   0.5   1

0 kilometers   1

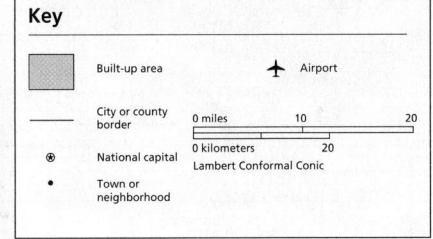

Key

▭ Built-up area

──── City or county border

⊛ National capital

• Town or neighborhood

✈ Airport

0 miles   10   20

0 kilometers   20

Lambert Conformal Conic

PRACTICE YOUR GEOGRAPHY SKILLS

1 What part of a map explains the colors used on the map?

2 How does the scale bar change depending on the scale of the map?

3 Which map would be best for finding the location of the British Museum? Explain why.

Circulate around the room as students complete the worksheets. Make sure that individuals comprehend the material. Provide assistance as needed.

Assess and Reteach

Assess Progress   L2
Have students complete the questions under Practice Your Geography Skills.

Reteach   L1
Some DK Atlas Activities will be helpful in reteaching the lesson. Give students more practice using these concepts by doing the activities for *Using the Map Key, Using the Compass Rose,* and *Using the Map Scale.*

All in One Europe and Russia Teaching Resources, *DK Compact Atlas of the World Activity: Using the Map Key,* p. 46; *DK Compact Atlas of the World Activity: Using the Compass Rose,* p. 47; *DK Compact Atlas of the World Activity: Using the Map Scale,* p. 48

Extend   L3
To extend the lesson, have students complete *Comparing Maps of Different Scale* and *Maps with Accurate Distances: Equidistant Maps.*

All in One Europe and Russia Teaching Resources, *Comparing Maps of Different Scale,* p. 49; *Maps with Accurate Distances: Equidistant Maps,* p. 50

Answers

PRACTICE YOUR GEOGRAPHY SKILLS

1. key
2. The larger the scale of the map, the smaller the distance shown on the scale bar.
3. the map of Central London; it shows the streets in more detail and includes the British Museum as a point of interest

Objectives

- Understand and use political maps.
- Understand and use physical maps.

Prepare to Read

Build Background Knowledge   L1

Tell students that they will learn about political maps and physical maps in this lesson. Explain that a political map is one that shows the boundaries and cities of an area as established by its people. Physical maps show information about the physical features of the area. These physical features would exist whether people lived in a place or not.

Instruct

Political Maps   L2
Physical Maps   L2

Guided Instruction

- Read the text as a class using the Choral Reading strategy (TE, p. T34) and ask students to study the map.

- Ask students to identify what river forms the boundary between Zimbabwe and South Africa. *(Limpopo River)* Then ask them to name at least two capitals on the Mediterranean Sea. *(Tripoli, Algiers, Tunis)*

- Read the text with the class and draw students' attention to the map and its key.

- Explain that sea level is the average height of the ocean's surface; sea level is at zero elevation. Ask students what color represents sea level on the map key. *(dark green)*

- Have students find the Qattara Depression. Ask **What is its elevation?** *(from 0 to 650 feet)*

- Ask **What is the difference between elevation and relief?** *(Elevation is the height of land above sea level while relief shows how quickly the land rises or falls.)*

Answers

PRACTICE YOUR GEOGRAPHY SKILLS

1. solid line, star in a circle, dot
2. Luanda

Political Maps

Political maps show political borders: continents, countries, and divisions within countries, such as states or provinces. The colors on political maps do not have any special meaning, but they make the map easier to read. Political maps also include symbols and labels for capitals, cities, and towns.

PRACTICE YOUR GEOGRAPHY SKILLS

1 What symbols show a national border, a national capital, and a city?

2 What is Angola's capital city?

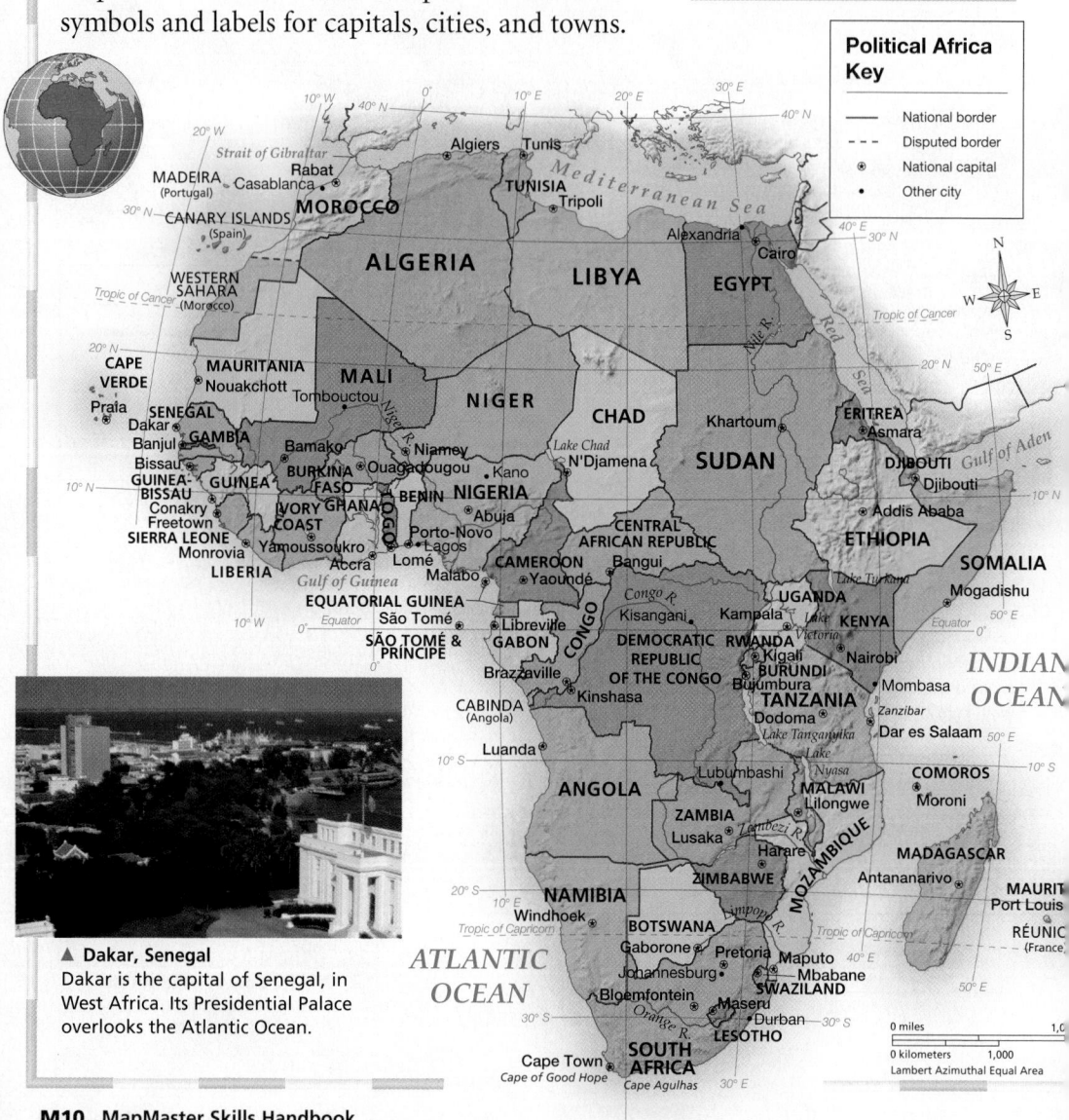

Political Africa Key

——— National border
- - - - Disputed border
⊙ National capital
• Other city

▲ **Dakar, Senegal**
Dakar is the capital of Senegal, in West Africa. Its Presidential Palace overlooks the Atlantic Ocean.

M10 MapMaster Skills Handbook

Background: Global Perspectives

Africa's Highest Peaks Africa's two highest mountains are both extinct volcanoes that rise near the equator on the eastern part of the continent. The tallest mountain, Kilimanjaro in Tanzania, reaches 19,340 feet (5,895 meters) at its highest point. Although snow covers its peaks, farmers raise coffee and plantains on the lower southern slopes of Kilimanjaro. Africa's second highest mountain is Mt. Kenya at 17,058 feet (5,199 meters) located in central Kenya. Like Kilimanjaro, it is snowcapped in its highest regions. Both Kilimanjaro and Mt. Kenya are attractions for mountain climbers from all over the world.

Physical Maps

Physical maps represent what a region looks like by showing its major physical features, such as hills and plains. Physical maps also often show elevation and relief. Elevation, indicated by colors, is the height of the land above sea level. Relief, indicated by shading, shows how sharply the land rises or falls.

PRACTICE YOUR GEOGRAPHY SKILLS

1 Which areas of Africa have the highest elevation?

2 How can you use relief to plan a hiking trip?

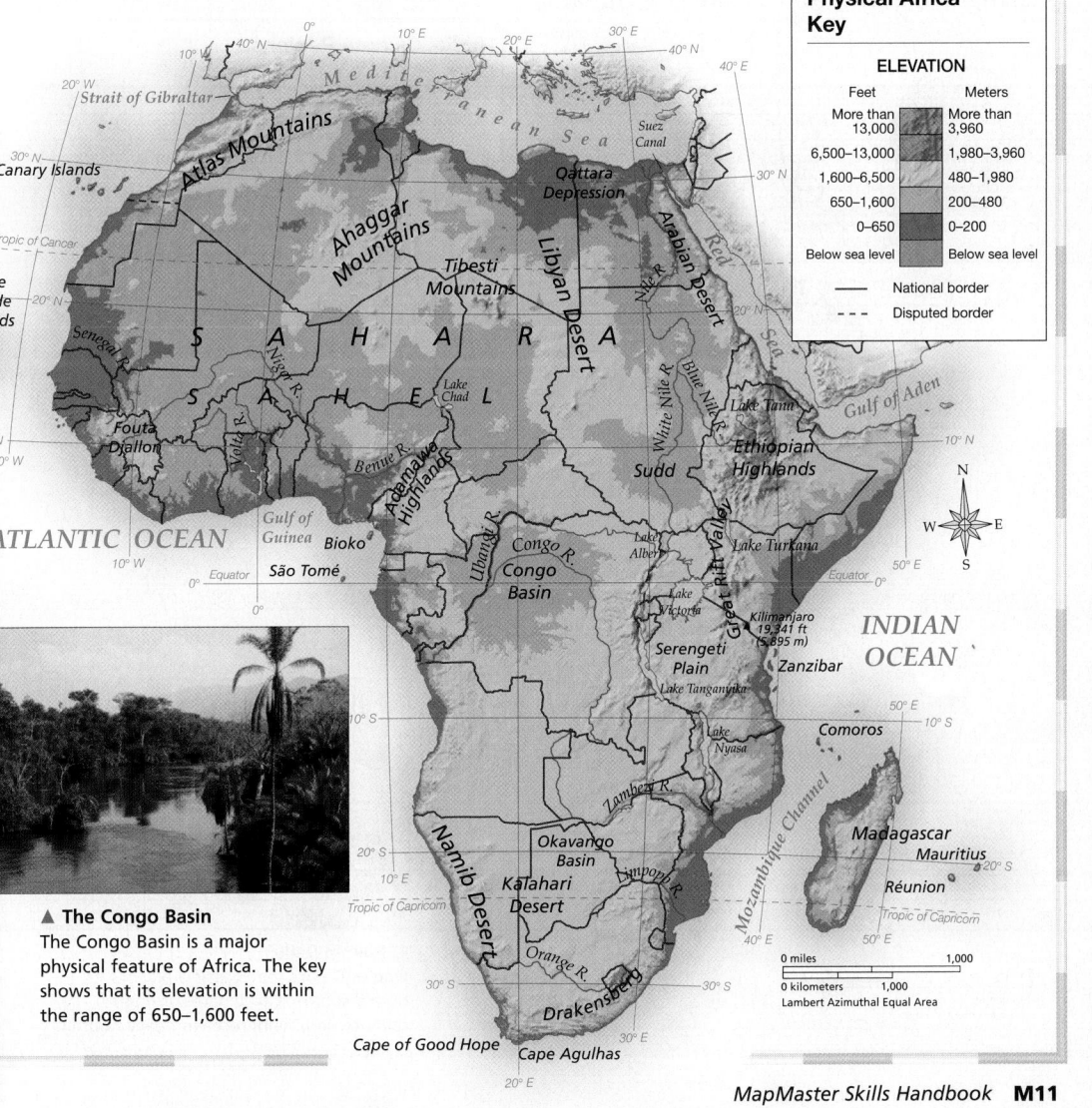

Physical Africa Key

ELEVATION

Feet		Meters
More than 13,000		More than 3,960
6,500–13,000		1,980–3,960
1,600–6,500		480–1,980
650–1,600		200–480
0–650		0–200
Below sea level		Below sea level

—— National border

- - - Disputed border

▲ **The Congo Basin**
The Congo Basin is a major physical feature of Africa. The key shows that its elevation is within the range of 650–1,600 feet.

MapMaster Skills Handbook **M11**

Independent Practice

Have students complete *Reading a Political Map*, *Reading a Physical Map*, and *Elevation on a Map* working with partners.

All in One **Europe and Russia Teaching Resources**, *Reading a Political Map*, p. 51; *Reading a Physical Map*, p. 56; *Elevation on a Map*, p. 57

Monitor Progress

As students complete the worksheets, circulate around the room to make sure individuals understand the key concepts. Provide assistance as needed.

Assess and Reteach

Assess Progress   L2

Have students answer the questions under Practice Your Geography Skills on pp. M10–M11.

Reteach   L1

Use the DK Atlas Activities *Reading a Political Map* and *Reading a Physical Map* to review the concepts in this lesson.

All in One **Europe and Russia Teaching Resources**, *DK Compact Atlas of the World Activity: Reading a Political Map*, p. 52; *DK Compact Atlas of the World Activity: Reading a Physical Map*, p. 58

Extend   L3

To extend the lesson, have students fill in the name of each country and its capital on the outline maps *North Africa*, *West and Central Africa*, and *East and Southern Africa*. Also, ask them to use colors and shading to indicate the Atlas Mountains, the Ethiopian Highlands, the Congo Basin, and the Namib Desert.

All in One **Europe and Russia Teaching Resources**, *Outline Map 22: North Africa*, p. 53; *Outline Map 23: West and Central Africa*, p. 54; *Outline Map 24: East and Southern Africa*, p. 55

Differentiated Instruction

For Special Needs Students   L1
Reuse *Reading a Political Map* to help students understand political maps. Point to the symbol for a national border in the key, then trace the borders of several countries. Invite students to trace others.

All in One **Europe and Russia Teaching Resources**, *Reading a Political Map*, p. 51

For Advanced Readers   L3
Challenge students to explore the concepts of relief and elevation further by completing *Relief on a Map* and *Maps of the Ocean Floor*.

All in One **Europe and Russia Teaching Resources**, *Relief on a Map*, p. 59; *Maps of the Ocean Floor*, p. 60

Answers

PRACTICE YOUR GEOGRAPHY SKILLS

1. Ethiopian Highlands and Great Rift Valley
2. It can help you find out where the land rises and falls.

Objectives

- Understand and use climate maps.
- Understand and use language maps.

Prepare to Read

Build Background Knowledge **L1**

Ask students to think of as many meanings for the word *special* as they can. Tell them that maps can be special too. Ask **What do you think a special-purpose map might show?** List suggestions on the board.

Instruct

Special-Purpose Maps: Climate **L1**

Guided Instruction

- Ask students to read the text using the Structured Silent Reading strategy (TE, p. T34). Point out that the map shows Bangladesh, Bhutan, Nepal, and parts of Myanmar and Pakistan as well as India.

- Point out the map and key. Ask **What areas have a tropical wet climate?** *(area along the southern western coast; eastern part of Bangladesh)*

- Ask **What color represents an arid climate?** *(brown)*

Independent Practice

Partner students and have them complete *Reading a Climate Map.*

All in One **Europe and Russia Teaching Resources,** *Reading a Climate Map,* p. 61

Monitor Progress

As students complete the worksheet, circulate around the room to make sure individuals comprehend the key concepts. Provide assistance as needed.

Answers

PRACTICE YOUR GEOGRAPHY SKILLS

1. the key
2. the northwestern part; No major cities are in the arid region.

Special-Purpose Maps: Climate

Unlike the boundary lines on a political map, the boundary lines on climate maps do not separate the land into exact divisions. For example, in this climate map of India, a tropical wet climate gradually changes to a tropical wet and dry climate.

> ### PRACTICE YOUR GEOGRAPHY SKILLS
>
> **1** What part of a special-purpose map tells you what the colors on the map mean?
>
> **2** Where are arid regions located in India? Are there major cities in those regions?

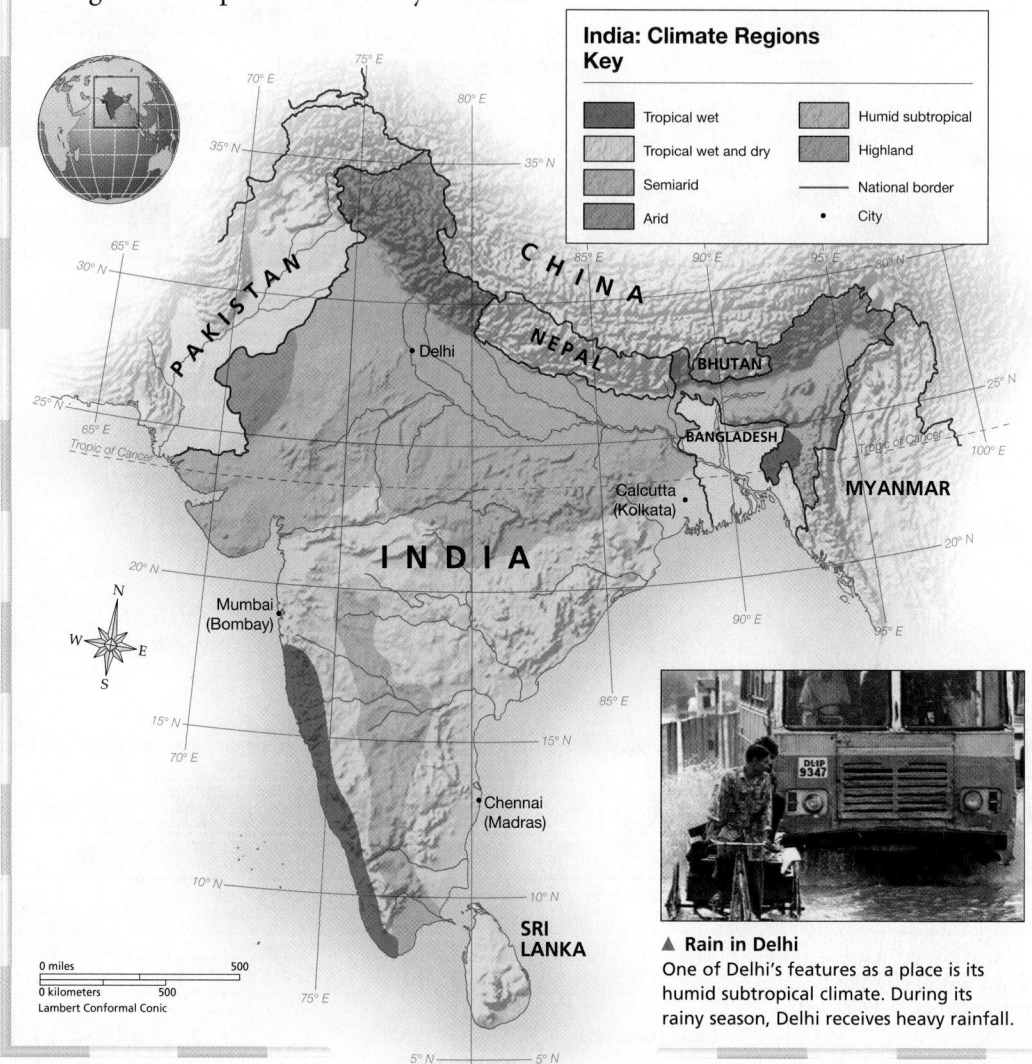

India: Climate Regions Key

- ▓ Tropical wet
- ░ Tropical wet and dry
- ▒ Semiarid
- ▒ Arid
- ░ Humid subtropical
- ▒ Highland
- — National border
- • City

▲ **Rain in Delhi**
One of Delhi's features as a place is its humid subtropical climate. During its rainy season, Delhi receives heavy rainfall.

M12 MapMaster Skills Handbook

Differentiated Instruction

For English Language Learners **L1**

If students are unfamiliar with words in the lesson, help them identify and look up those words in the dictionary. For example: *arid*—adj. having little or no rainfall; dry *humid*—adj. having a lot of water; damp; *semi*—adj. part or partially

Follow up by having students determine the meaning of *semiarid.*

For Gifted and Talented **L3**

Give students *Reading a Climate Graph.* Ask students to compare the information in the graph with the information on the map above. Using the map and the graph, ask them to write a sentence about the climate of Mumbai.

All in One **Europe and Russia Teaching Resources,** *Reading A Climate Graph,* p. 62

Special-Purpose Maps: Language

This map shows the official languages of India. An official language is the language used by the government. Even though a region has an official language, the people there may speak other languages as well. As in other special-purpose maps, the key explains how the different languages appear on the map.

PRACTICE YOUR GEOGRAPHY SKILLS

1 What color represents the Malayalam language on this map?

2 Where in India is Tamil the official language?

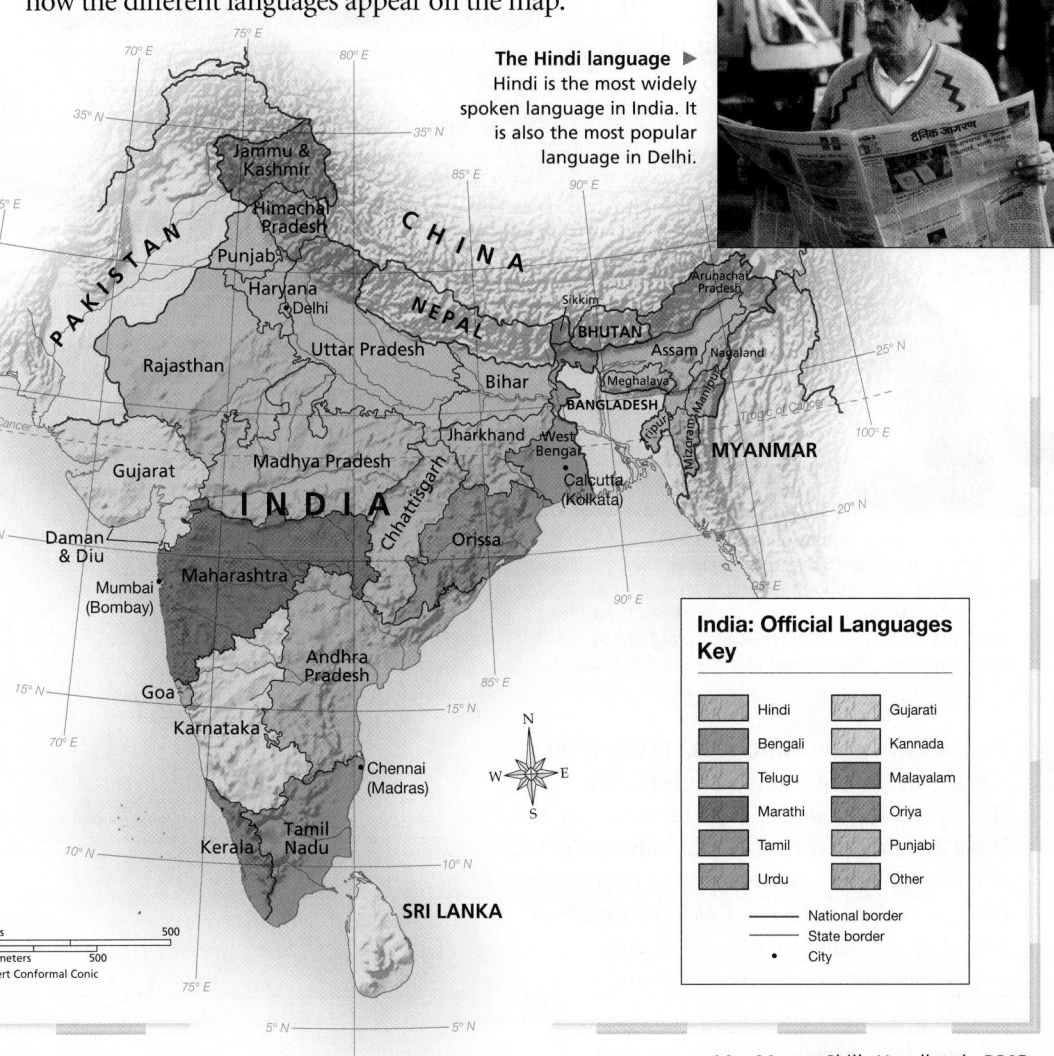

The Hindi language ▶ Hindi is the most widely spoken language in India. It is also the most popular language in Delhi.

India: Official Languages Key

Hindi	Gujarati
Bengali	Kannada
Telugu	Malayalam
Marathi	Oriya
Tamil	Punjabi
Urdu	Other

—— National border
—— State border
• City

MapMaster Skills Handbook **M13**

Background: Daily Life

The Hindi Language Hindi is the official language of India and is the primary language for about 300 million people. English is also spoken by many Indians and is considered the language of politics and commerce. However, the diversity of the country is reflected in the enormous number of languages spoken there, more than 1,500 in all. Ten of India's major states are organized along linguistic lines, and the Indian constitution recognizes 15 regional languages.

Special-Purpose Maps: Language   L2

Guided Instruction

- Read the text as a class. Draw students' attention to the map and its key.

- Have students consider the diversity of official languages. Ask **Why might it be important for a state to have a common language in addition to local ones?** *(Communication is easier with a common language.)*

Independent Practice

Have students work with partners to read another special purpose map, *Reading a Natural Vegetation Map*.

All in One Europe and Russia Teaching Resources, *Reading a Natural Vegetation Map,* p. 63

Monitor Progress

As students complete the worksheet, circulate around the room and make sure individuals understand key concepts. Provide assistance as needed.

Assess and Reteach

Assess Progress   L2

Have students answer the questions under Practice Your Geography Skills on pp. M12–M13.

Reteach   L1

Have students practice using a special purpose map by completing *Analyzing and Interpreting Special Purpose Maps.*

⊙ *Analyzing and Interpreting Special-Purpose Maps,* **Social Studies Skills Tutor CD-ROM**

Extend   L3

Have students learn about another type of special-purpose map by completing *Reading a Time Zone Map.* Then ask students to find out the time zones in India and create their own time zone map, using *Outline Map 26: South Asia: Political.*

All in One Europe and Russia Teaching Resources, *Reading a Time Zone Map.* p. 65; *Outline Map 26: South Asia: Political,* p. 64

Answers

PRACTICE YOUR GEOGRAPHY SKILLS

1. dark purple

2. southeast India

Objectives

- Learn why people migrate.
- Understand how migration affects environments.

Prepare to Read

Build Background Knowledge [L1]

Remind students that they studied the theme of movement earlier in this unit. Brainstorm with students why people move from place to place, particularly those who move from one country to another. Use the Numbered Heads participation strategy (TE, p. T36) to generate ideas.

Instruct

Human Migration [L2]

Guided Instruction

- Divide the text using the headings and ask students to read the pages using the Paragraph Shrinking strategy (TE, p. T34). Clarify the meanings of any unfamiliar words.

- Have students look at the map. Ask **From what European countries did people migrate to the Americas in the years between 1500 and 1800?** (*Portugal, Spain, France, Netherlands, England*)

- Ask **Where did the French settle in the Americas?** (*French Guiana and Haiti*) **Which European country had the most possessions in the Americas?** (*Spain*)

- Ask **Why were some Africans forced to migrate?** (*They were imported as slaves from their homeland. Europeans wanted them to work on the land they claimed in the Americas.*)

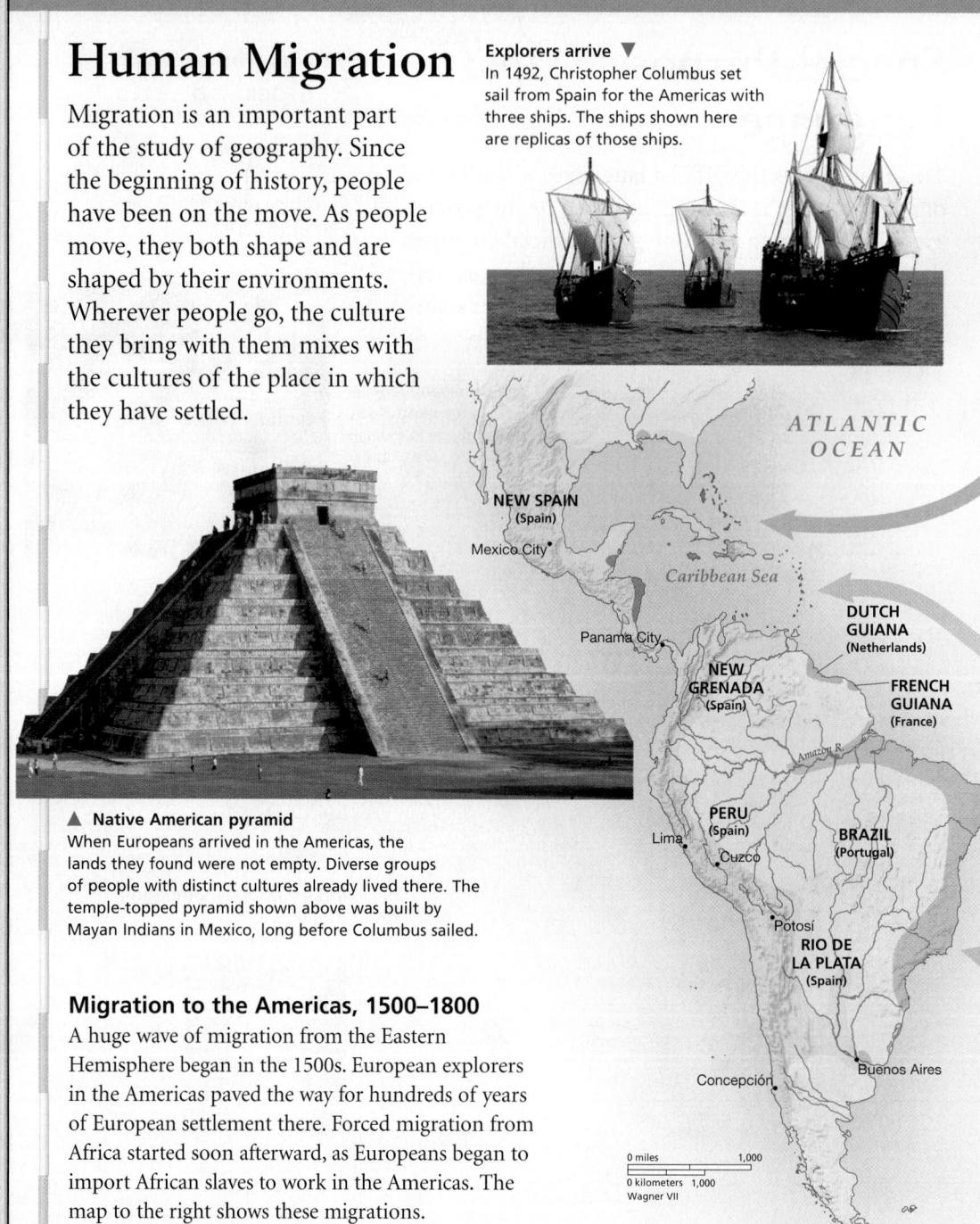

Human Migration

Migration is an important part of the study of geography. Since the beginning of history, people have been on the move. As people move, they both shape and are shaped by their environments. Wherever people go, the culture they bring with them mixes with the cultures of the place in which they have settled.

Explorers arrive ▼
In 1492, Christopher Columbus set sail from Spain for the Americas with three ships. The ships shown here are replicas of those ships.

▲ **Native American pyramid**
When Europeans arrived in the Americas, the lands they found were not empty. Diverse groups of people with distinct cultures already lived there. The temple-topped pyramid shown above was built by Mayan Indians in Mexico, long before Columbus sailed.

Migration to the Americas, 1500–1800

A huge wave of migration from the Eastern Hemisphere began in the 1500s. European explorers in the Americas paved the way for hundreds of years of European settlement there. Forced migration from Africa started soon afterward, as Europeans began to import African slaves to work in the Americas. The map to the right shows these migrations.

ATLANTIC OCEAN

NEW SPAIN (Spain)
Mexico City
Caribbean Sea
Panama City
DUTCH GUIANA (Netherlands)
NEW GRENADA (Spain)
FRENCH GUIANA (France)
Amazon R.
PERU (Spain)
Lima
Cuzco
BRAZIL (Portugal)
Potosí
RIO DE LA PLATA (Spain)
Concepción
Buenos Aires

0 miles   1,000
0 kilometers 1,000
Wagner VII

M14 MapMaster Skills Handbook

Differentiated Instruction

For Less Proficient Readers [L1]
Review with students the meaning of "push" and "pull" factors in terms of human migration. Model for students how to make a table with the headings Push and Pull. Then work with students to list as many factors as they can under each heading.

For Advanced Readers [L3]
Have students complete *Analyzing Statistics*. When they have finished, have them write a paragraph explaining how economic and social statistics are related to "push" and "pull" factors.

All in One Europe and Russia Teaching Resources, *Analyzing Statistics,* p. 67

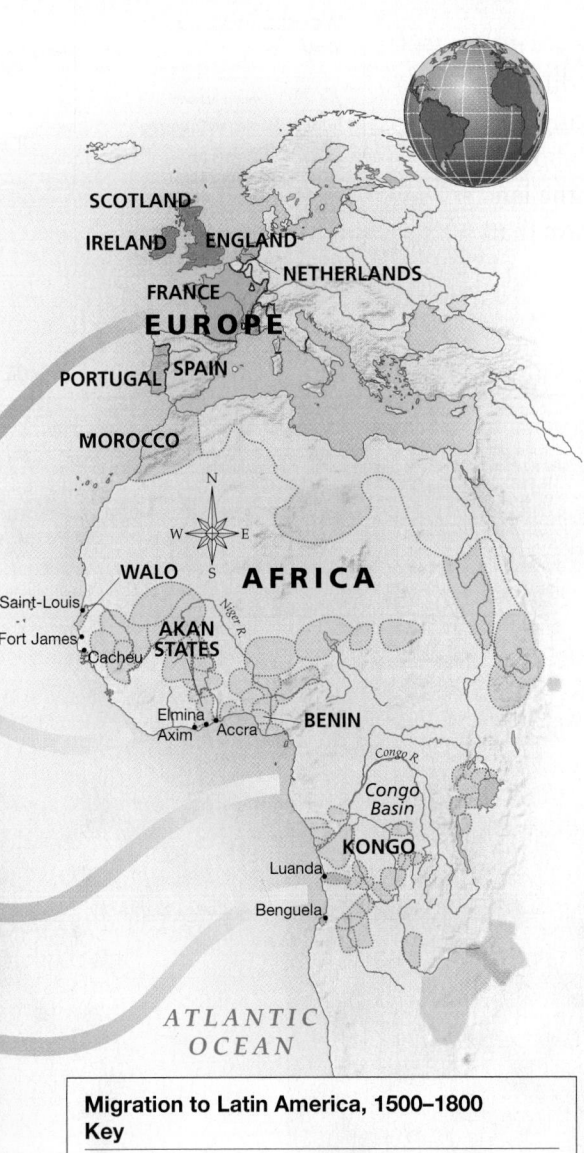

SCOTLAND
IRELAND   ENGLAND
       NETHERLANDS
FRANCE
EUROPE

PORTUGAL SPAIN

MOROCCO

N
W   E
S

WALO   AFRICA

Saint-Louis
Fort James
    Cacheu
        AKAN
        STATES   Niger R.

Elmina   Accra   BENIN
Axim   Congo R.

            Congo
            Basin

        KONGO
Luanda

Benguela

ATLANTIC
OCEAN

Migration to Latin America, 1500–1800
Key

→ European migration
→ African migration
— National or colonial border
⋯ Traditional African border
▨ African State

▨ Spain and possessions
▨ Portugal and possessions
▨ Netherlands and possessions
▨ France and possessions
▨ England and possessions

1 Where did the Portuguese settle in the Americas?

2 Would you describe African migration at this time as a result of both push factors and pull factors? Explain why or why not.

"Push" and "Pull" Factors

Geographers describe a people's choice to migrate in terms of "push" factors and "pull" factors. Push factors are things in people's lives that push them to leave, such as poverty and political unrest. Pull factors are things in another country that pull people to move there, including better living conditions and hopes of better jobs.

▲ **Elmina, Ghana**
Elmina, in Ghana, is one of the many ports from which enslaved Africans were transported from Africa. Because slaves and gold were traded here, stretches of the western African coast were known as the Slave Coast and the Gold Coast.

MapMaster Skills Handbook **M15**

Independent Practice

Have students work with partners to complete *Reading a Historical Map.* Have students be ready to explain how the movement of European groups changed the map of Africa. *(Much of Africa was colonized by Europeans.)*

All in One **Europe and Russia Teaching Resources,** *Reading a Historical Map,* p. 66

Monitor Progress

As students complete the worksheet, circulate around the room to make sure individuals comprehend the key concepts. Provide assistance as needed.

Assess and Reteach

Assess Progress   L2

Have students complete the questions under Practice Your Geography Skills.

Reteach   L1

Help students make an outline of the lesson. Show *Transparency B15: Outline* as a model. Then work with students to identify the main points. Encourage students to refer to their outlines to review the material.

📖 **Europe and Russia Transparencies,** *Transparency B15: Outline*

Extend   L3

To extend the lesson, have students complete *The Global Refugee Crisis.* Then ask them to choose a specific region on the graph and find out more about refugees from one country in that region.

Go Online
PHSchool.com **For:** Environmental and Global Issues: *The Global Refugee Crisis*
Visit: PHSchool.com
Web Code: lfd-1001

Answers

PRACTICE YOUR GEOGRAPHY SKILLS

1. Brazil

2. most likely push factors because people were forced to leave; the need for workers in the Americas was a pull factor although it was the Europeans who responded to it by importing Africans as slaves

MapMaster Skills Handbook **M15**

Objectives

- Understand and use a land use map.
- Learn how land use and economic structures are linked.

Prepare to Read

Build Background Knowledge **L1**

Discuss with the class the ways that people in your community are using land. For example, is all the land used for homes? How much is used for commercial purposes? What kinds? Are there farms or manufacturing facilities? Point out that communities in all parts of the world use land in different ways.

Instruct

World Land Use **L2**

Guided Instruction

- Read the text as a class using the Oral Cloze strategy (TE, p. T33). Follow up by having students do a second silent reading. Encourage students to study the map and photographs.

- Talk about the difference between commercial and subsistence farming. Have them look closely at the photographs on pages M16 and M17. Ask **How do the tools and equipment people use differ in these types of farming?** (*Large power machines are used in commercial farming; hand tools are used in subsistence farming.*) **Why might people use more land in commercial farming?** (*Machines make it possible to cultivate more land. The more land cultivated, the more sales possible.*)

- Ask **What color represents nomadic herding on this map?** (*light purple*) **In what parts of the world is this an economic activity?** (*Africa, Asia, Europe*)

- Ask **Why might some parts of the world have little or no land use activity?** (*Land and/or climate might not be suitable for farming or other activity.*)

World Land Use

People around the world have many different economic structures, or ways of making a living. Land-use maps are one way to learn about these structures. The ways that people use the land in each region tell us about the main ways that people in that region make a living.

World Land Use Key

- Nomadic herding
- Hunting and gathering
- Forestry
- Livestock raising
- Commercial farming
- Subsistence farming
- Manufacturing and trade
- Little or no activity
- ——— National border
- - - - - Disputed border

▲ **Wheat farming in the United States**
Developed countries practice commercial farming rather than subsistence farming. Commercial farming is the production of food mainly for sale, either within the country or for export to other countries. Commercial farmers like these in Oregon often use heavy equipment to farm.

Levels of Development

Notice on the map key the term *subsistence farming*. This term means the production of food mainly for use by the farmer's own family. In less-developed countries, subsistence farming is often one of the main economic activities. In contrast, in developed countries there is little subsistence farming.

▲ **Growing barley in Ecuador**
These farmers in Ecuador use hand tools to harvest barley. They will use most of the crop they grow to feed themselves or their farm animals.

NORTH AMERICA

SOUTH AMERICA

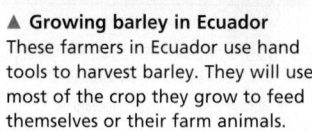

0 miles
0 kilometers   2,000
Robinson

M16 MapMaster Skills Handbook

Background: Global Perspectives

Agriculture Almost 50 percent of the world's population is occupied in agriculture. A much higher proportion of this is in developing countries where dense populations, small land holdings, and traditional techniques predominate. In areas where there is intense cultivation using people and animals but few machines, the yield is low in relation to the output of energy. In leading food producing countries such as the United States, industrial farms make use of new technology and crop specialization to increase output.

▲ **Growing rice in Vietnam**
Women in Vietnam plant rice in wet rice paddies, using the same planting methods their ancestors did.

PRACTICE YOUR GEOGRAPHY SKILLS

1 In what parts of the world is subsistence farming the main land use?

2 Locate where manufacturing and trade are the main land use. Are they found more often near areas of subsistence farming or areas of commercial farming? Why might this be so?

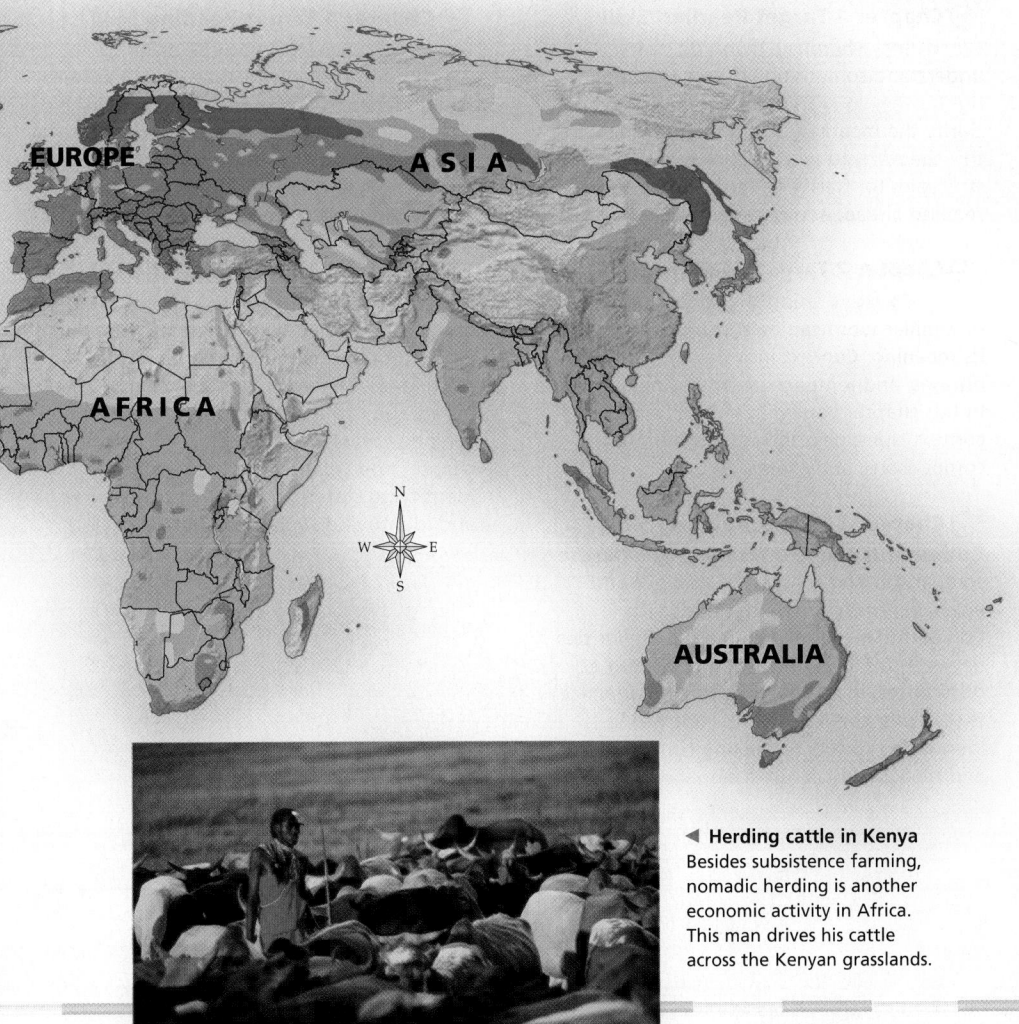

EUROPE

ASIA

AFRICA

AUSTRALIA

◀ **Herding cattle in Kenya**
Besides subsistence farming, nomadic herding is another economic activity in Africa. This man drives his cattle across the Kenyan grasslands.

MapMaster Skills Handbook **M17**

Independent Practice

Partner students and have them complete *Reading an Economic Activity Map*. Have students be ready to offer explanations for how the economic activity in Somalia might affect the lives of people there.

All in One **Europe and Russia Teaching Resources,** *Reading an Economic Activity Map,* p. 68

Monitor Progress

Circulate around the room as students complete the worksheet to make sure individuals comprehend the key concepts. Provide assistance as needed.

Assess and Reteach

Assess Progress   L2
Have students complete the questions under Practice Your Geography Skills.

Reteach   L1
Help students make a table to identify the main kinds of land use. Draw a model on the board for students to follow. Use these headings: Nomadic Herding, Forestry, Livestock Raising, Commercial Farming, Subsistence Farming, Manufacturing and Trade. Under each heading, help students write a short explanation. Then have students find one or two places on the map in their books where that activity takes place.

Extend   L3
To extend the lesson, have students complete *Reading a Natural Resources Map*. Point out that this map shows mineral resources. Then ask students to write a paragraph relating mineral resources to land use.

All in One **Europe and Russia Teaching Resources,** *Reading a Natural Resources Map,* p. 69

Answers

PRACTICE YOUR GEOGRAPHY SKILLS

1. Africa, Asia, South America, North America

2. areas of commercial farming; both manufacturing and trade and commercial farming require technology that subsistence farmers do not have

MapMaster Skills Handbook **M17**

Teaching the Target Reading Skills

The Prentice Hall *World Studies* program has interwoven essential reading skills instruction throughout the Student Edition, Teacher's Edition, and ancillary resources. In the Foundations of Geography section, students will learn five reading skills.

Student Edition The *World Studies* Student Edition provides students with reading skills instruction, practice, and application opportunities in each chapter within the program.

Teacher's Edition The *World Studies* Teacher Edition supports your teaching of each skill by providing full modeling in each chapter's interleaf and modeling of the specific sub-skills in each section lesson.

All in One Teaching Resources The *World Studies* All-in-One Teaching Resources provides a worksheet explaining and supporting the elements of each Target Reading Skill. Use these to help struggling students master skills, or as more practice for every student.

How to Read Social Studies

Target Reading Skills

The Target Reading Skills introduced on this page will help you understand the words and ideas in this section on geography and in other social studies reading you do. Each chapter focuses on one of these reading skills. Good readers develop a bank of reading strategies, or skills. Then they draw on the particular strategies that will help them understand the text they are reading.

Chapter 1 Target Reading Skill

Clarifying Meaning If you do not understand something you are reading right away, you can use several skills to help clarify the meaning of the word or idea. In this chapter you will practice these strategies for clarifying meaning: rereading, reading ahead, and paraphrasing.

Chapter 2 Target Reading Skill

Using Context Using the context of an unfamiliar word can help you understand its meaning. Context includes the words, phrases, and sentences surrounding a word. In this chapter you will practice using these context clues: descriptions, definitions, comparisons, and examples.

Chapter 3 Target Reading Skill

Comparing and Contrasting You can use comparison and contrast to sort out and analyze information you are reading. Comparing means examining the similarities between things. Contrasting is looking at differences. In this chapter you will practice these skills: comparing and contrasting, identifying contrasts, making comparisons, and recognizing contrast signal words.

Chapter 4 Target Reading Skill

Using Sequence Noting the order in which significant events take place can help you understand and remember them. In this chapter you will practice these sequence skills: sequencing, or finding the order of events, sequencing important changes, and recognizing sequence signal words.

Chapter 5 Target Reading Skill

Identifying the Main Idea Since you cannot remember every detail of what you read, it is important that you identify the main ideas. The main idea of a section or paragraph is the most important point and the one you want to remember. In this chapter you will practice these skills: identifying stated and implied main ideas and identifying supporting details.

Assessment Resources

Use the diagnosing readiness tests from **AYP Monitoring Assessments** to help you identify problems before students begin to study geography.

Determine students' reading level and identify challenges:

📄 *Screening Tests,* pp. 1–10

Evaluate students' verbal skills:

📄 *Critical Thinking and Reading Tests,* pp. 25–34

📄 *Vocabulary Tests,* pp. 45–52

📄 *Writing Tests,* pp. 53–60

FOUNDATIONS of GEOGRAPHY

Are you curious about our world? Do you want to know why winters are cold and summers are hot? Have you wondered why some people live and work in cities and others work on farms in the countryside? If you answered yes to any of these questions, you want to know more about geography.

Guiding Questions

The text, photographs, maps, and charts in this book will help you discover answers to these Guiding Questions.

1 **Geography** What are Earth's major physical features?

2 **History** How have people's ways of life changed over time?

3 **Culture** What is a culture?

4 **Government** What types of government exist in the world today?

5 **Economics** How do people use the world's natural resources?

Project Preview

You can also discover answers to the Guiding Questions by working on projects. Project possibilities are listed on page 136 of this book.

Foundations of Geography **1**

Assess students' social studies skills:

- 📄 *Geographic Literacy Tests,* pp. 13–20
- 📄 *Visual Analysis Tests,* pp. 21–24
- 📄 *Communications Tests,* pp. 35–44

The World Studies program provides instruction and practice for all of these skills. Use students' test results to pinpoint the skills your students have mastered and the skills they need to practice. Then use *Correlation to Program Resources* to prescribe skills practice and reinforcement.

📄 *Correlation to Program Resources,* pp. 64–77

Guiding Questions

- This book was developed around five Guiding Questions about the foundations of geography. They appear on the reduced Student Edition page to the left. The Guiding Questions are intended as an organizational focus for the book. The Guiding Questions act as a kind of umbrella under which all of the material falls.

- You may wish to add your own Guiding Questions to the list in order to tailor them to your particular course.

- Draw students' attention to the Guiding Questions. Ask them to write the questions in their notebooks for future reference.

- In the Teacher's Edition, each section's themes are linked to a specific Guiding Question at the beginning of each chapter. Then, an activity at the end of the chapter returns to the Guiding Questions to review key concepts.

Project Preview

- The projects for this book are designed to provide students with hands-on involvement in the content area. Students are introduced to some projects on page 136.

- *Book Projects* give students directions on how to complete these projects, and more.

  All in One **Foundations of Geography Teaching Resources,** *Book Project: Focus on Part of the Whole,* pp. 27–29; *Book Project: The Geography Game,* pp. 30–32; *Book Project: Desktop Countries,* pp. 33–35; *Book Project: World News Today,* pp. 36–38

- Assign projects as small group activities, whole-class projects, or individual projects. Consider assigning a project at the beginning of the course.

Objectives

- Examine country borders that are shaped by geography, politics, and culture.
- Locate and name the seven continents.
- Analyze a physical map of the world to learn about elevation.
- Examine landforms and bodies of water that act as barriers to movement across countries and continents.
- Analyze the population density of the world and investigate the world's urban and rural populations.

Prepare to Read

Build Background Knowledge **L2**

Have students brainstorm similarities and differences among the world's continents. Encourage them to think about physical and cultural similarities and differences. Tell students that they will either confirm or revise these comparisons during their study of Earth's geography.

Instruct

Investigate the Political World **L2**

Guided Instruction

- Read the introductory and Location paragraphs as a class. Direct students' attention to the border between the country of Canada and state of Alaska. Ask **Do you think the border is shaped by politics or geography? Explain.** *(politics, because most of the border is straight)*

- Hand out the *World Overview* worksheet. Direct students to fill in the answers to the questions as they read.

All in One Foundations of Geography Teaching Resources, *World Overview,* pp. 43–45

Answers

LOCATION Rivers and lakes may form the crooked portion of the border in the east. The straight portion of the border was probably shaped by politics.

WORLD OVERVIEW

Investigate the Political World

There are more than 190 independent countries in the world. Some of those countries have dependencies, or areas outside of those countries that belong to them. Every land area where people live belongs to some country. The blue areas on maps in this book show the world's oceans, seas, and lakes. The other colors on this map show the areas of the world's countries and dependencies.

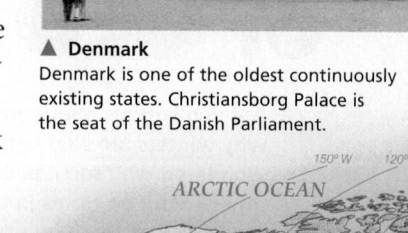
▲ **Denmark**
Denmark is one of the oldest continuously existing states. Christiansborg Palace is the seat of the Danish Parliament.

Go Online
PHSchool.com
Use Web Code **lep-3020** for the **interactive maps** on these pages.

◄ **Niagara Falls**
The border between the United States and Canada runs through the falls. Both countries share its tourist and power-generating benefits.

LOCATION
1 Examine Country Borders

Governments have drawn the borders between countries. Some borders follow mountains or rivers. Others are straight lines. On the map, look at the United States and Canada. These are the large yellow and pink countries in North America. Parts of their borders are straight, but others are crooked. Why might this be? What might explain the location of other borders on this map?

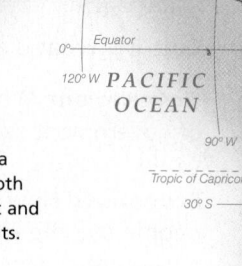

ARCTIC OCEAN
Arctic Circle
60° N
NORTH AMERICA
ATLANTIC OCEAN
30° N
Tropic of Cancer
150° W
0° Equator
120° W PACIFIC OCEAN
SOUTH AMERICA
90° W
Tropic of Capricorn
30° S
ATLANTIC OCEAN
60° S
Antarctic Circle SOUTHERN OC
60° W

The World: Political Key
— National border
--- Disputed border

Mental Mapping

The Shape of the World Have students close their textbooks. Take down or cover any maps of the world that may be hanging in your classroom. Then give each student a blank piece of paper. Ask them to draw a map of the seven continents.

Encourage them to draw the shapes of the continents as accurately as possible. Have them draw in any continent borders that appear on land. Remind them to label the continents.

PLACE
2 Analyze the Continents

Notice the six black labels on the world map. These labels name continents. Which continent's name is also the name of a country? You can see that some continents have more countries than others. Which continent is made up mostly of small countries?

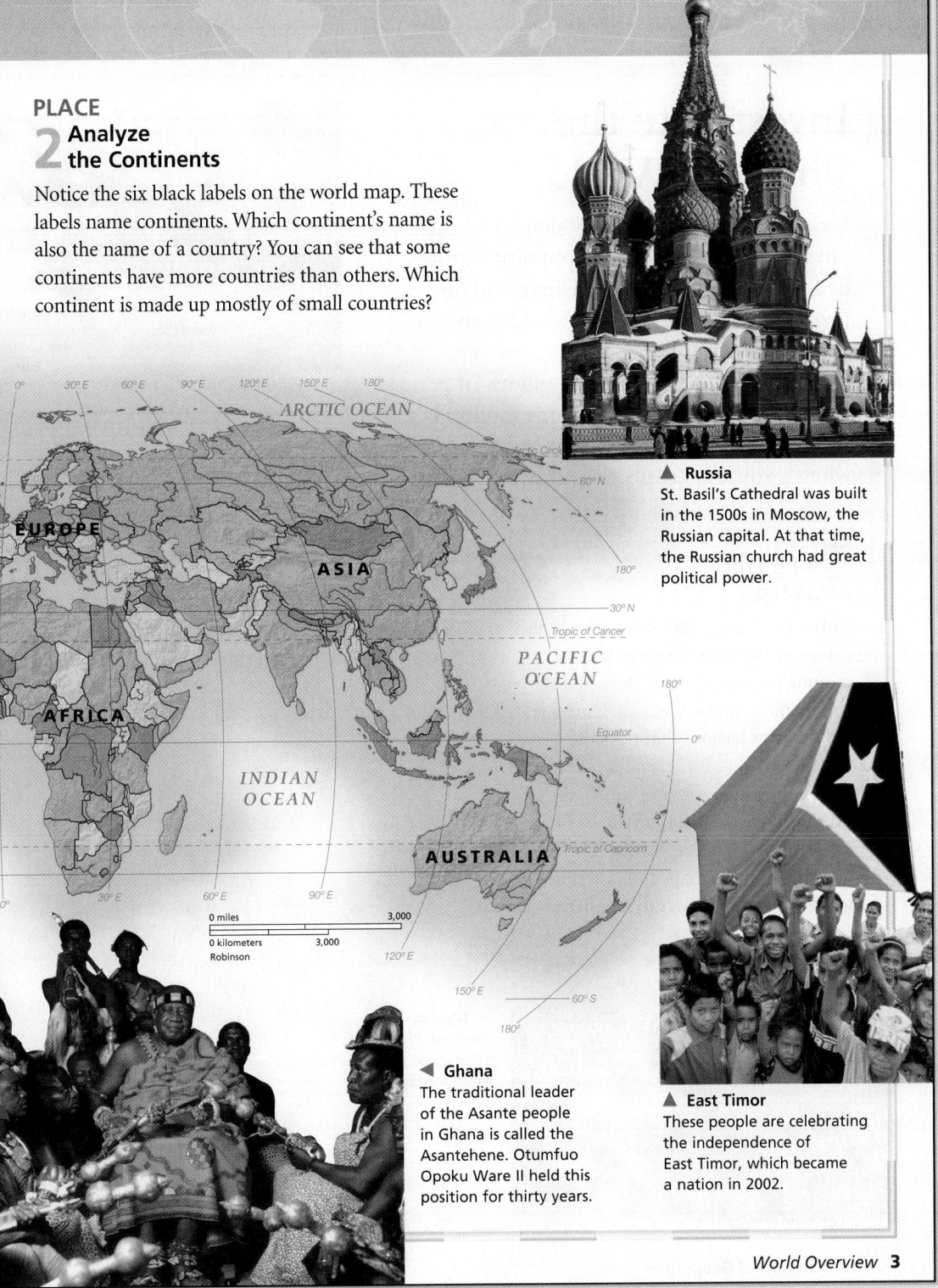

▲ **Russia**
St. Basil's Cathedral was built in the 1500s in Moscow, the Russian capital. At that time, the Russian church had great political power.

◀ **Ghana**
The traditional leader of the Asante people in Ghana is called the Asantehene. Otumfuo Opoku Ware II held this position for thirty years.

▲ **East Timor**
These people are celebrating the independence of East Timor, which became a nation in 2002.

World Overview **3**

Investigate the Physical World

Guided Instruction

- Read the introduction and the Place paragraphs. Have students study the physical map of the world. Ask them to use the map key to determine the highest range of elevations in Asia and Australia. *(Asia—more than 13,000 feet [3,960 meters]; Australia—1,600–6,500 feet [480–1,980 meters])*

- Ask students to identify the elevation range of Scandinavia's northern and western coasts. *(0–650 feet [0–200 meters])*

- Read the Human-Environment Interaction paragraph. Direct students' attention to Europe and Asia. Have them again locate the border between these two continents. Ask **What physical feature serves as a physical barrier between these two continents?** *(Ural Mountains)*

- After students have read the caption about Mount Fuji, ask them to trace their finger over the islands along the rim of the Pacific Ocean. Be sure they locate the islands on both pages of the map. Point out that some of these islands are considered to be part of Asia and others are part of a region that is sometimes called Oceania. The islands off the east coast of Asia from Japan south to Sumatra and Java and east to New Guinea are part of Asia while the islands of Micronesia, Melanesia, and Polynesia are part of Oceania.

- Have students continue to complete the *World Overview* worksheet.

All in One Foundations of Geography Teaching Resources, *World Overview,* pp. 43–45

Answer

PLACE The elevation of the Amazon Basin is 0 to 650 feet or 0 to 200 meters above sea level. The landscape around the Tigre River appears very flat. You would expect to see tall peaks in the Andes.

Investigate the Physical World

People's lives are constantly shaped by their physical environment. The physical features of a place often determine where and how people live. Yet the physical world is always changing, too. Some changes come very slowly. For example, it took millions of years for Earth's crust to lift and form mountains. Other changes are fast and dramatic, such as when a volcano erupts or an earthquake hits.

▲ **Alaska**
Glaciers like this one at Portage, Alaska, have shaped the land for thousands of years.

PLACE
3 Infer From a Map

Notice the bumpy texture and brownish colors on the map. These indicate a mountainous landscape. Now find the continent of South America. Look for the Amazon Basin. What does the key tell you about its elevation? Notice the photograph of the Tigre River as it weaves through the basin. Describe that landscape. Now find the Andes on the map, and describe what you would expect to see there.

◄ **Tigre River**
The Tigre River, a tributary of the Amazon, winds through the Peruvian rain forest.

Differentiated Instruction

For Less Proficient Readers **L1**

For students having trouble reading the physical map of the world, distribute *Reading a Physical Map* and *Elevation on a Map*. Have students complete the activities in pairs.

All in One Foundations of Geography Teaching Resources, *Reading a Physical Map,* p. 47; *Elevation on a Map,* p. 48

For Advanced Readers **L3**

Tell students that another way mapmakers can show elevation on a map is by using isolines. Assign *Understanding Isolines* and *Reading a Contour Map* to help students explore this concept.

All in One Foundations of Geography Teaching Resources, *Understanding Isolines,* p. 49; *Reading a Contour Map,* p. 50

HUMAN-ENVIRONMENT INTERACTION

4 Examine Landforms as Barriers

Physical barriers can make movement between areas difficult. For example, take a look at the continents in the map below. Some of them are separated from one another by vast areas of water. Examine the elevation key. Look closely at the map's labels. What other physical landforms might have acted as barriers to movement?

▲ Mount Fuji, Japan
Volcanoes such as this one have created islands along the rim of the Pacific Ocean.

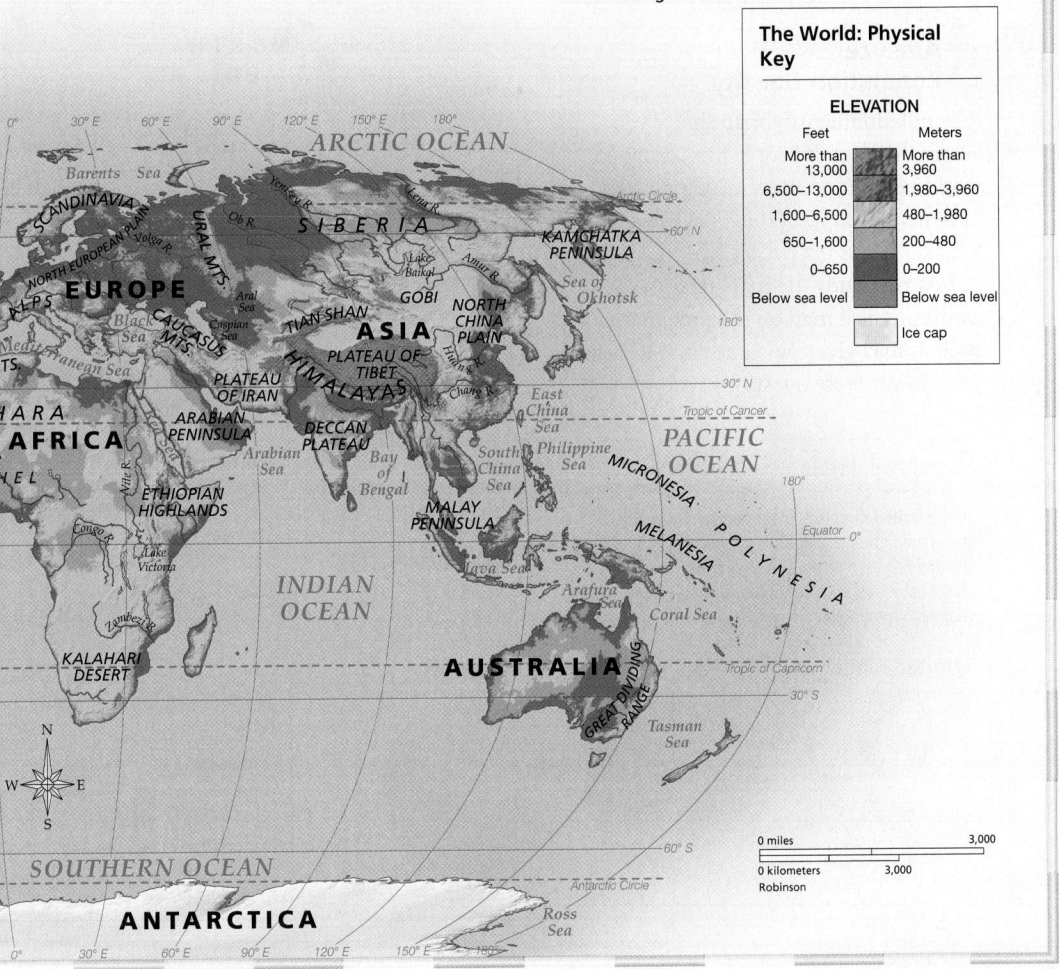

The World: Physical Key

ELEVATION

Feet		Meters
More than 13,000		More than 3,960
6,500–13,000		1,980–3,960
1,600–6,500		480–1,980
650–1,600		200–480
0–650		0–200
Below sea level		Below sea level
	Ice cap	

World Overview **5**

- Have students explore the location of the world's highest peaks by placing them on an outline map.

- Give them the following statistics:

Continent	Highest Point	Elevation
Africa	Kilimanjaro	19,340 feet
Antarctica	Vinson Massif	16,864 feet
Asia	Mount Everest	29,035 feet
Australia	Mount Kosciusko	7,310 feet
North America	Mount McKinley	20,320 feet
South America	Mount Aconcagua	22,834 feet

- Have them research the location of the highest point on each continent. Then distribute *Outline Map 1: The World: Physical.* Ask students to create a symbol to represent the highest point and show it in a map key. Then have them label the points on each continent. Ask them to write in the height of each point near each label.

All in One **Foundations of Geography Teaching Resources,** *Outline Map 1: The World: Physical,* p. 51

Monitor Progress

Make sure students are creating maps correctly. Check student maps for map keys and appropriate labels.

Differentiated Instruction

For Gifted and Talented   L3

Form students into groups or pairs and assign each group one of the continents. Ask them to create a physical map of the continent using information from the map on pp. 4–5 of the Student Edition as well as the Atlas at the back of the book. Tell them to be sure to include labels of geographic features and a key. When students have completed their maps, attach them to form a physical map of the world and display it in your classroom.

Answer

HUMAN-ENVIRONMENT INTERACTION
Possible answer: Mountain ranges and deserts also might have acted as barriers to movement.

Investigate Population

Guided Instruction

- Use the Choral Reading technique (TE, p. 34) to read the text.

- Ask students **Which color on the map represents the most densely populated areas?** *(purple)* **Which color represents the most sparsely populated areas?** *(yellow)*

- Direct students' attention to Africa on the map. Tell them to use what they know about Africa's physical geography to explain why much of North Africa is sparsely populated. *(Much of North Africa is covered by the Sahara.)*

- Have students study the circle graphs at the bottom of p. 6. Ask **In which of these countries does the greatest percentage of people live in urban areas?** *(the United Kingdom)*

Independent Practice

Display *Color Transparency FG 5: The World: Continents and Oceans* and *Color Transparency FG 6: Some Major Cities of the World.* Have students compare them with the population density map on pp. 6–7 in the Student Edition. Ask students to list one densely populated city on each continent. Then have them compare the transparencies with the physical map on pp. 4–5 of the Student Edition. Have them locate the cities they listed on the physical map and their nearby landforms. Finally, ask them to synthesize the information by writing a sentence about each city.

📖 **Foundations of Geography Transparencies,** *Color Transparency FG 5: The World: Continents and Oceans; Color Transparency FG 6: Some Major Cities of the World*

Monitor Progress

Circulate to make sure students are able to locate the most populated cities on the maps. Check students' sentences for appropriate details.

Answer

REGIONS Much of Europe, eastern North America, and southeastern and southern Asia have many people, while Northern North America, Australia, and northern Asia have few people. Possible answer: People choose where to live based on climate and geography.

6 *Foundations of Geography*

Investigate Population

For thousands of years, the world's population grew slowly. In the past 200 years, however, health care, living conditions, and food production have greatly improved. This has led to a huge population burst. In 1800, the world's population numbered less than 1 billion people. Today, it is more than 6 billion, and growing quickly.

▲ **China**
A crowd of people walk through a park in the capital city of Beijing. China has the largest population of any country in the world.

REGIONS

5 Analyze Population Density

A population density map shows you where the world's people live. Study the world population map. Which places have many people? Which have few? Why do you think people live where they do? As you study the map, refer to the world physical map on the previous page. It may give you some clues to help you answer these questions.

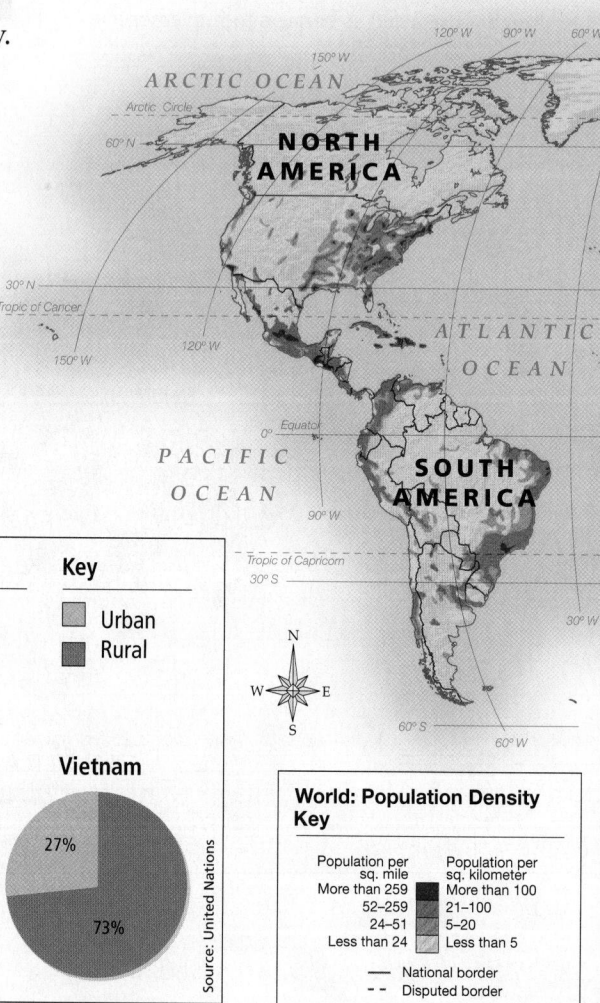

World Population

In the United Kingdom, most people live in cities. In Panama, the population is almost equally divided between urban and rural areas. In some Asian countries, such as Vietnam, people live mainly in rural areas.

Key
- 🟦 Urban
- 🟦 Rural

United Kingdom
- 11%
- 89%

Panama
- 58%
- 42%

Vietnam
- 27%
- 73%

Source: United Nations

World: Population Density Key

Population per sq. mile	Population per sq. kilometer
More than 259	More than 100
52–259	21–100
24–51	5–20
Less than 24	Less than 5

— National border
- - Disputed border

6 Foundations of Geography

Differentiated Instruction

For English Language Learners   L1

Spend extra time reviewing the meaning of important terms that may be difficult for English language learners such as *population density*, *urban*, and *rural*. Point out the map key and review what a square mile is. Have students find at least one area on the map that corresponds to each density range and have them say aloud the number of people it represents as they point to the area on the map.

MOVEMENT

6 Compare Continents

When high population densities cover large areas, those areas have large populations. Look at the continents on the map. Which continent do you think has the largest population, based on the size of its areas of high population density? Which continent do you think has the lowest population? Compare North America and South America on the map. Which continent do you think has the larger population?

▲ New Zealand
The Whanganui River flows through a New Zealand national park. New Zealand has a low population density.

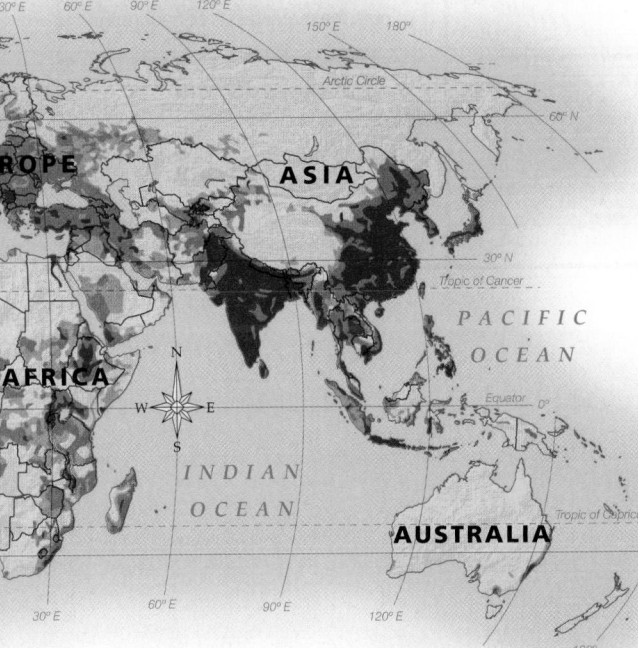

PRACTICE YOUR GEOGRAPHY SKILLS

1 In Asia there is a ring of dense population next to an area with low population. Look at the physical map of the world on pages 4 and 5. What landform may explain this difference?

2 Look at Northern Africa. Find the area of heavy population that forms a curving line on the map. How does the physical map on pages 4 and 5 explain this?

Monaco is the most densely populated European nation. ▶

Differentiated Instruction

For Advanced Readers L3
Have students complete the *Urban Population, Past and Projected* activity individually so they can learn more about the world's urban population.

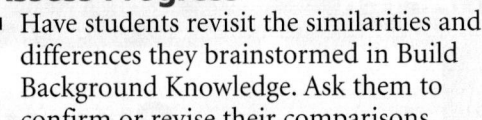

For: Environmental and Global Issues: *Urban Population, Past and Projected*
Visit: PHSchool.com
Web Code: led-3307

Assess and Reteach

Assess Progress L2

■ Have students revisit the similarities and differences they brainstormed in Build Background Knowledge. Ask them to confirm or revise their comparisons.

■ Ask students to complete Practice Your Geography Skills on page 7.

Reteach L1

Have students review key concepts in the World Overview by completing *DK Compact Atlas of the World Activity: Reading a Political Map*, *DK Compact Atlas of the World Activity: Reading a Physical Map*, and *Reading a Population Density Map* in partners or small groups.

 Foundations of Geography Teaching Resources, *DK Compact Atlas of the World Activity: Reading a Political Map,* p. 52; *DK Compact Atlas of the World Activity: Reading a Physical Map,* p. 53; *Reading a Population Density Map,* p. 54

Extend L3

One way of assessing student accomplishments is by having them build a portfolio of their best work. To begin their portfolios for Foundations of Geography, have students choose one of the continents. Then, assign a project on this continent. Students can choose what type of project they would like to do. Options include collages, maps, stories, paragraphs, dioramas, and more.

■ Give students *Writing an Outline for Research* to help them get started.

Foundations of Geography Teaching Resources, *Writing an Outline for Research,* p. 55

Answers

MOVEMENT Possible answer: Asia, because it seems to have the largest areas of high population density. Australia, because most of it has low population density and there is very little area with a high population density. North America, because it has larger areas of high population density.

PRACTICE YOUR GEOGRAPHY SKILLS

1. Possible answer: the Plateau of Tibet, the Gobi desert

2. The Nile River is located along the curving line of dense population.

Overview

Section 1 — The Five Themes of Geography

1. Learn about the study of Earth.
2. Discover five ways to look at Earth.

What Is Geography?

Length: 3 minutes, 25 seconds

Use with Section 1

Explores the many facets of geography.

Section 2 — The Geographer's Tools

1. Find out how maps and globes show information about Earth's surface.
2. See how mapmakers show Earth's round surface on flat maps.
3. Learn how to read maps.

Geography Tools and Map Skills

Length: 4 minutes, 5 seconds

Use with Section 2

Introduces geography as a profession with a focus on maps.

Technology Resources

PHSchool.com

Students use embedded Web codes to access Internet activities, chapter self-tests, and additional map practice. They may also access Dorling Kindersley's Online Desk Reference to learn more about each country they study.

Use the Interactive Textbook to make content and concepts come alive through animations, videos, and activities that accompany the complete basal text—online and on CD-ROM.

PRENTICE HALL

TeacherEXPRESS

Plan • Teach • Assess

Use this complete suite of powerful teaching tools to make planning lessons and administering tests quicker and easier.

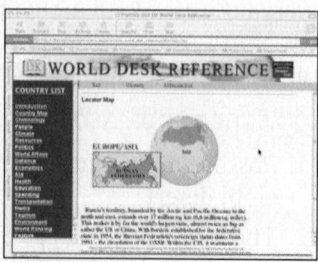

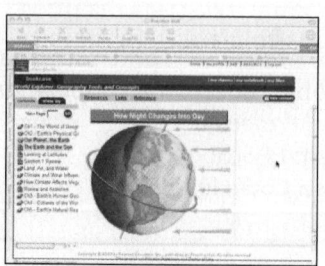

Reading and Assessment

Reading and Vocabulary Instruction

🎯 Model the Target Reading Skill

Clarifying Meaning Explain to students that they can use several strategies to clarify the meaning of unfamiliar words and concepts in the text. They can reread a difficult passage and try to make connections between familiar and unfamiliar words or ideas. They can read ahead to see if the author provides definitions or examples later in the passage. After reading, students can solidify their knowledge of a passage by paraphrasing, or putting what they have read into their own words.

Model clarifying meaning by thinking aloud as you read the paragraph below, from page 17, to the class.

A geographic information system, or GIS, is a computer-based system that links information to locations. Think aloud: What does *link information to locations* mean? I'll keep reading, maybe the author will give me a definition or example. *A GIS is useful not only to geographers but also to governments and businesses. A GIS connects information with places. For example, if a business needs to decide where to open an office, it can use a GIS to choose a location where it will reach the most customers.* Think aloud: This is an example of linking information (number of possible customers) to locations (possible site of new office). To paraphrase, a GIS is used by geographers, governments, and businesses to determine information about specific locations.

Use the following worksheets from All-in-One Foundations of Geography Teaching Resources (pp. 68–69) to support this chapter's Target Reading Skill.

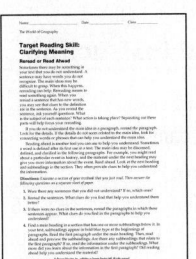 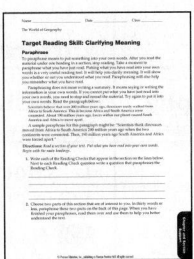

Vocabulary Builder
High-Use Academic Words

Use these steps to teach this chapter's high-use words:

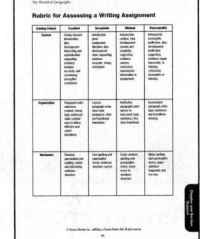

1. Have students rate how well they know each word on their Word Knowledge worksheets (All-in-One Foundations of Geography Teaching Resources, p. 70).
2. Pronounce each word and ask students to repeat it.
3. Provide a brief definition and sample sentence (provided on TE pp. 11 and 17).
4. Work with students as they fill in the "Definition or Example" column of their Word Knowledge worksheets.

Assessment

Formal Assessment

Test students' understanding of core knowledge and skills.

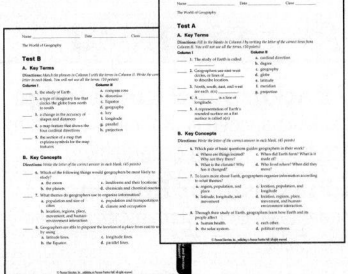

Chapter Tests A and B, All-in-One Foundations of Geography Teaching Resources, pp. 96–101

Customize the Chapter Tests to suit your needs.

ExamView® Test Bank CD-ROM

Skills Assessment

Assess geographic literacy.

MapMaster Skills, Student Edition, pp. 22, 24

Assess reading and comprehension.

Target Reading Skills, Student Edition, pp. 12, 17, and in Section Assessments

Chapter 1 Assessment, Reading and Vocabulary Study Guide, p. 8

Performance Assessment

Assess students' performance on this chapter's Writing Activities using the rubric from All-in-One Foundations of Geography Teaching Resources.

Rubric for Assessing a Writing Assignment, p. 95

Assess students' work through performance tasks.

Small Group Activity: Plotting a Route Around the World, All-in-One Foundations of Geography Teaching Resources pp. 73–76

Online Assessment

Have students check their own understanding.

Chapter Self-Test

Test Preparation

Assess students' skills and diagnose problems as students begin their study of this region.

Screening Tests and Diagnosing Readiness Tests, AYP Monitoring Assessments, pp. 1–11, 13–63

Section 1 The Five Themes of Geography

 3.5 periods, 1.75 blocks (includes Skills for Life)

Social Studies Objectives
1. Learn about the study of Earth.
2. Discover five ways to look at Earth.

Reading/Language Arts Objective
Reread or read ahead to clarify the meaning of unfamiliar words and ideas.

Prepare to Read

Build Background Knowledge
Show students a video, and then ask them to think about the five themes of geography.

Set a Purpose for Reading
Have students evaluate statements on the *Reading Readiness Guide.*

Preview Key Terms
Teach the section's Key Terms using a "See It—Remember It" chart.

Target Reading Skill
Introduce the section's Target Reading Skill of **rereading or reading ahead.**

Instructional Resources

All in One Foundations of Geography Teaching Resources
- L2 Reading Readiness Guide, p. 61
- L2 Reread or Read Ahead, p. 68

World Studies Video Program
- L2 What is Geography?

Differentiated Instruction

Spanish Reading and Vocabulary Study Guide
- L1 Chapter 1, Section 1, pp. 3–4 ELL

Instruct

The Study of Earth
Five Ways to Look at Earth
Discuss the ways people study Earth and its people.

Target Reading Skill
Review **reading ahead.**

Instructional Resources

All in One Foundations of Geography Teaching Resources
- L2 Guided Reading and Review, p. 62
- L2 Reading Readiness Guide, p. 61

Foundations of Geography Transparencies
- L2 Section Reading Support Transparency FG 43

Differentiated Instruction

All in One Foundations of Geography Teaching Resources
- L2 Skills for Life, p. 72 AR, GT, LPR, SN

Spanish Support
- L2 Guided Reading and Review (Spanish), p. 2 ELL

Assess and Reteach

Assess Progress
Evaluate student comprehension with the section assessment and section quiz.

Reteach
Assign the Reading and Vocabulary Study Guide to help struggling students.

Extend
Extend the lesson by having students do a map activity.

Instructional Resources

All in One Foundations of Geography Teaching Resources
- L2 Section Quiz, p. 63
- L3 Understanding Hemispheres, p. 79
- L3 Understanding Grids, p. 80
- L3 Using a Grid, p. 81
- L3 Understanding Latitude and Longitude, p. 82
- L3 Using Latitude and Longitude, p. 83
  Rubric for Assessing a Writing Assignment, p. 95

Reading and Vocabulary Study Guide
- L1 Chapter 1, Section 1, pp. 2–4

Differentiated Instruction

Spanish Support
- L2 Section Quiz (Spanish), p. 3 ELL

Teacher's Edition
- L1 For Less Proficient Readers, TE p. 15
- L1 For Special Needs Students, TE p. 15

Social Studies Skills Tutor CD-ROM
- L1 Using Reliable Information ELL, LPR, SN

Key

L1 Basic to Average	L3 Average to Advanced
L2 For All Students	

LPR Less Proficient Readers
AR Advanced Readers
SN Special Needs Students

GT Gifted and Talented
ELL English Language Learners

Section 2 The Geographer's Tools

 4 periods, 2 blocks (includes Chapter Review and Assessment)

Social Studies Objectives
1. Find out how maps and globes show information about Earth's surface.
2. See how mapmakers show Earth's round surface on flat maps.
3. Learn how to read maps.

Reading/Language Arts Objective
Paraphrase to clarify the meaning of unfamiliar words and ideas.

Prepare to Read	Instructional Resources	Differentiated Instruction
Build Background Knowledge Ask students to preview the section and predict what they will learn about maps and globes. **Set a Purpose for Reading** Have students begin to fill out the *Reading Readiness Guide.* **Preview Key Terms** Teach the section's Key Terms. **Target Reading Skill** Introduce the section's Target Reading Skill of **paraphrasing**.	**All in One Foundations of Geography Teaching Resources** L2 Reading Readiness Guide, p. 65 L2 Paraphrase, p. 69	**Spanish Reading and Vocabulary Study Guide** L1 Chapter 1, Section 2, pp. 5–6 ELL

Instruct	Instructional Resources	Differentiated Instruction
Target Reading Skill Review **paraphrasing**. **Globes and Maps** Ask about the creation and uses of maps and globes. **Getting It All on the Map** Ask about the different kinds of map projections. **Reading Maps** Discuss the parts of a map.	**All in One Foundations of Geography Teaching Resources** L2 Guided Reading and Review, p. 66 L2 Reading Readiness Guide, p. 65 **Foundations of Geography Transparencies** L2 Section Reading Support Transparency FG 44 **World Studies Video Program** L2 Geography Tools and Map Skills	**All in One Foundations of Geography Teaching Resources** L3 Understanding Projection, Maps with Accurate Shapes, Maps with Accurate Areas, Maps with Accurate Directions, pp. 84–87 AR GT L3 Enrichment, p. 71 ELL, LPR, SN L1 Outline Map 1, p. 91 ELL, LPR, SN L3 Captain Scott's Letter to the British Public, pp. 92–93 AR, GT L2 Using the Map Key, Using the Compass Rose, Using the Map Scale, pp. 88–90 ELL L3 Small Group Activity, pp. 73–76 AR, GT **Teacher's Edition** L3 For Gifted and Talented, TE pp. 19, 21 L1 For Special Needs Students, TE p. 20 L3 For Advanced Readers, TE p. 20 L2 For English Language Learners, TE p. 21

Assess and Reteach	Instructional Resources	Differentiated Instruction
Assess Progress Evaluate student comprehension with the section assessment and section quiz. **Reteach** Assign the Reading and Vocabulary Study Guide to help struggling students. **Extend** Extend the lesson by having students create their own maps.	**All in One Foundations of Geography Teaching Resources** L2 Section Quiz, p. 67 Rubric for Assessing a Writing Assignment, p. 95 L2 Vocabulary Development, p. 94 L2 Word Knowledge, p. 70 L2 Chapter Tests A and B, pp. 96–101	**Spanish Support** L2 Section Quiz (Spanish), p. 5 ELL L2 Chapter Summary (Spanish), p. 6 ELL L2 Vocabulary Development (Spanish), p. 7 ELL **Reading and Vocabulary Study Guide** L1 Chapter 1, Section 2, pp. 5–7

Key
L1 Basic to Average   L3 Average to Advanced   LPR Less Proficient Readers   GT Gifted and Talented
L2 For All Students   AR Advanced Readers   ELL English Language Learners
                                               SN Special Needs Students

Reading Background

Previewing and Prereading

Students who do a brief, preliminary reading of complex material are in a strategic position to take control of their learning and comprehension. Previewing also helps students identify the text structure and develop a mental framework for ideas to be encountered in the text. Follow the steps below to teach students how to preview and preread, using Section 1 of this chapter as an example:

1. Tell students that previewing will help them identify the text structure and develop a mental outline of ideas they will encounter in the text.

2. Skim the section, getting clues from such features as titles, bold-faced headings, captions, and discussion questions. Take notes as you go along. (*Notes could include: the study of Earth; five ways to look at Earth; location; latitude and longitude; regions; place; movement; human-environment interaction.*)

3. Use these notes to make predictions about what you will learn from the selection. (*Think aloud: "This section will probably be about how people study Earth. They use five different methods to study it. Some of these might include location, regions, place, movement, and human-environment interaction."*)

4. Reflect on what you've previewed. Write down any questions you may have. (*Questions may include: I am not sure what latitude and longitude are. What kind of movement are they referring to? How do humans interact with their environments and how does this relate to geography?*)

5. Return to the notes and questions after reading part of the selection. Revise your predictions as needed, and answer your questions.

Pre-Teaching Vocabulary

Research literature on academic vocabulary instruction indicates that effective strategies require students to go beyond simply looking up dictionary definitions or examining the context. Vocabulary learning must be based on the learner's dynamic engagement in constructing understanding.

If students are not retaining the meaning of the Key Terms or high-use words, use this extended vocabulary sequence to engage them in learning new words.

World Studies Background

The Longitude Problem

Due to the absence of landmarks at sea, sailors must determine their location by measuring latitude and longitude. In the late 1600s, sailors could measure latitude but had no tool for measuring longitude. After several disasters caused by navigation errors, the British government announced it would give an award to the person who could discover a way to measure longitude at sea.

British carpenter John Harrison solved the problem. He developed a timekeeper that looked like a large pocket watch. This watch kept the time of Greenwich, England. Everywhere the sailors went, they could find the local time by the position of the sun, and compare it to the time in Greenwich, determining longitude.

Fields of Geography

The study of geography is divided into the three professional subcategories of study: physical, human, and regional geography. Although distinct fields, they are interrelated in many ways. Physical geography is the study of the surface of Earth, including the examination of human impact on the environment. Human geography is the analysis of the attributes and populations of different societies. Regional geography is a narrower study of a particular region. It combines elements of physical and human geography because regional geographers look at the physical boundaries, climates, and cultural features of regions.

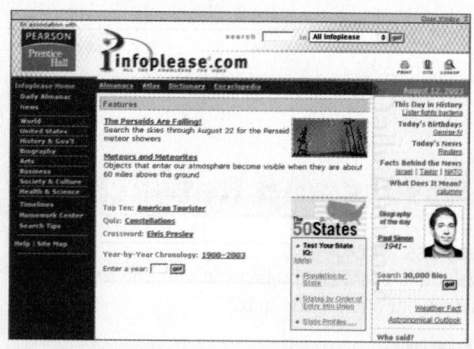

Infoplease® provides a wealth of useful information for the classroom. You can use this resource to strengthen your background on the subjects covered in this chapter. Have students visit this advertising-free site as a starting point for projects requiring research.

Use Web code **led-3100** for **Infoplease.**

1. Present the word in writing and point out the part of speech.
2. Pronounce the word and have students pronounce the word.
3. Provide a range of familiar synonyms (or "it's like" words) before offering definitions.
4. Provide an accessible definition and concrete examples, or "showing sentences."
5. Rephrase the simple definition or example sentence, asking students to complete the statement by substituting the word aloud.
6. Check for understanding by providing an application task/ question requiring critical thinking.

Sample instructional sequence:

1. Our first word is *geography*. It is a noun, a word that names a person, place, or thing.
2. Say the word *geography* after me. (Students repeat.)
3. *Geography* is similar to *geology* because both involve studying something on Earth.
4. The word *geography* means *the study of Earth*. By taking *geography*, we learned a lot more about our world.
5. We learned more about our world by taking _____ . (Students substitute missing word.)
6. Would studying the stars in the sky be part of *geography*? Yes-No-Why? (Students answer the question.)

Scaffolding Tips

Scaffolding is a technique used to help students transition from seeing and hearing the teacher demonstrate and model a particular skill to performing the skill independently. A teacher may begin with a recall question about a topic and lead students toward forming their own interpretive question. Scaffolding is especially effective for less proficient readers, English language learners, and some special needs students. When the teacher uses scaffolding, students should eventually be able to perform the skill completely on their own. To test the effectiveness of scaffolding, ask yourself each time students do an activity how much you had to help them. The answer should decrease with every attempt.

The Trimetrogon Method

Before World War II, many countries lacked detailed maps of their national areas. In fact, by 1940 only about 10 percent of the world was mapped out in any detail. Because airplane pilots needed more comprehensive maps during the war, the United States Air Force developed the trimetrogon method of mapping to create the World Aeronautical Charts.

The trimetrogon mapping technique is a system in which land is photographed, and then plotted for data such as elevation. Remote areas of Earth are now charted in a large enough scale to be significant, using the trimetrogon method. Today, about 62 percent of the world is mapped adequately.

Maps of the Moon

The only celestial body that has been mapped in any detail besides Earth is the moon. Two German astronomers, Wilhelm Beer and Johann Heinrich von Mädler, published the first comprehensive map of the moon in 1836. The map included a detailed study of the moon's surface. A year later, the pair supplemented the map with a book that gave the measurements of 148 of the moon's craters and 830 of its mountains.

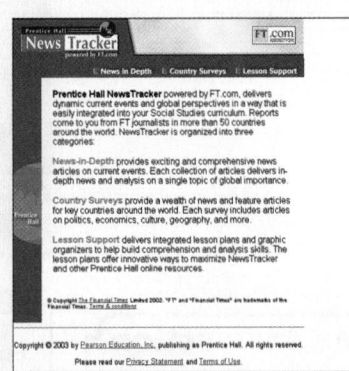

Get in-depth information on topics of global importance with **Prentice Hall Newstracker,** powered by FT.com

 Use Web code **led-3101** for **Prentice Hall Newstracker.**

The World of Geography

Guiding Questions

Remind students about the Guiding Questions introduced at the beginning of the book.

Section 1 relates to **Guiding Question** ❶
What are Earth's major physical features?
(The five central themes of geography are location, regions, place, movement, and human-environment interaction.)

Section 2 relates to **Guiding Question** ❶
What are Earth's major physical features?
(Tools such as globes and maps communicate important information about Earth's physical features.)

⦿ Target Reading Skill

In this chapter, students will learn and apply the reading skill of clarifying meaning. Use the following worksheets to help students practice this skill:

All in One Foundations of Geography Teaching Resources, *Reread or Read Ahead,* p. 68; *Paraphrase,* p. 69

Chapter Preview

This chapter will introduce you to the study of Earth, the planet where we live.

Section 1
The Five Themes of Geography

Section 2
The Geographer's Tools

Target Reading Skill

Clarifying Meaning In this chapter you will focus on clarifying meaning by learning how to read ahead and how to paraphrase.

▶ A satellite launched from the space shuttle *Discovery* orbits Earth.

8 Foundations of Geography

⌐ Bibliography

For the Teacher
Dorling Kindersley. *Geography of the World.* DK Publishing, 2003.
Rhatigan, Joe and Smith, Heather. *Geography Crafts for Kids: 50 Cool Projects and Activities for Exploring the World.* Lark Books, NC, 2002.
Five Themes of Geography. 100 Percent Education, 2002. Videocassette.

For the Student
L1 American Education. *The Complete Book of Maps & Geography.* American Education Publishing, 1998.
L1 Johnson, Sylvia. *Mapping the World.* Atheneum, 1999.
L2 National Geographic Society. *National Geographic Student Atlas of the World.* National Geographic Society, 2001.
L3 Young, Karen Romano. *Maps and Map Making.* Scholastic Paperbacks, 2002.

Reach Into Your Background Draw students' attention to the picture and caption on pages 8–9. Remind them that satellites travel hundreds of miles above Earth's surface.

Discuss the idea that mapmakers can use satellite pictures of Earth to make maps of our planet. There are even detailed satellite maps of cities. Have students discuss ways people might take pictures to make a map of their neighborhood. Have students share their ideas. (*Possible answer: take pictures from a helicopter or airplane*)

Chapter 1 **9**

Chapter Resources

Teaching Resources
Letter Home, p. 59
L2 Vocabulary Development, p. 94
L2 Skills for Life, p. 72
L2 Chapter Tests A and B, pp. 96–101

Spanish Support
Spanish Letter Home, p. 1
Spanish Vocabulary Development, p. 7
Spanish Chapter Summary, p. 6

Media and Technology
L1 Student Edition on Audio CD
L1 Guided Reading Audiotapes, English and Spanish
L2 Social Studies Skills Tutor CD-ROM
ExamView® Test Bank CD-ROM

PRENTICE HALL
Presentation EXPRESS™
(Teach · Connect · Inspire)

Teach this chapter's content using the PresentationExpress™ CD-ROM including:

■ slide shows
■ transparencies
■ interactive maps and media
■ *ExamView®* QuickTake Presenter

Section 1
Step-by-Step Instruction

Objectives

Social Studies
1. Learn about the study of Earth.
2. Discover five ways to look at Earth.

Reading/Language Arts
Reread or read ahead to clarify the meaning of unfamiliar words and ideas.

Prepare to Read

Build Background Knowledge **L2**

Tell students that they will begin their study of geography by learning five important ideas of geography. Show the video *What is Geography?*, then ask students to list the five themes of geography. Ask students what topics they think they will learn about within each theme, and have them use the Think-Write-Pair-Share strategy (TE, p. T36) to share their ideas.

📼 *What Is Geography?*, **World Studies Video Program**

Set a Purpose for Reading **L2**

■ Preview the Objectives.

■ Read each statement in the *Reading Readiness Guide* aloud. Ask students to mark the statements true or false.

All in One Foundations of Geography Teaching Resources, *Reading Readiness Guide*, p. 61

■ Have students discuss the statements in pairs or groups of four, then mark their worksheets again. Use the Numbered Heads participation strategy (TE, p. T36) to call on students to share their group's perspectives.

Vocabulary Builder
Preview Key Terms **L2**

Create a three column "See It—Remember It" chart of the Key Terms on the board. Write a term in the first column, a short definition in the second column, and a sketch in the third column. Guide students as they copy and complete the chart.

Answer

✓ **Reading Check** Where are things located? Why are they there?

Section 1
The Five Themes of Geography

Prepare to Read

Objectives
In this section you will
1. Learn about the study of Earth.
2. Discover five ways to look at Earth.

Taking Notes
As you read the section, look for details about each of the five themes of geography. Copy the web diagram below and write down details related to each theme. Add ovals as needed for additional themes or details.

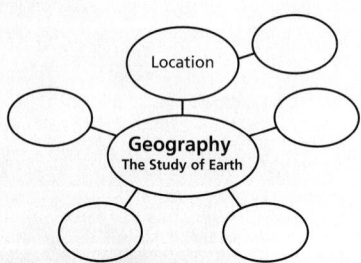

🎯 Target Reading Skill

Reread or Read Ahead If you do not understand a passage, reread it to look for connections among the words and sentences. Reading ahead can also help. Words and ideas may be clarified further on.

Key Terms
• **geography** (jee AHG ru fee) *n.* the study of Earth
• **cardinal directions** (KAHR duh nul duh REK shunz) *n.* the directions north, east, south, and west

• **latitude** (LAT uh tood) *n.* the distance north or south of Earth's Equator, in degrees
• **longitude** (LAHN juh tood) *n.* the distance east or west of the Prime Meridian, in degrees
• **hemisphere** (HEM ih sfeer) *n.* a half of Earth
• **parallel** (PA ruh lel) *n.* a line of latitude
• **meridian** (muh RID ee un) *n.* a line of longitude

Geographers use maps and other tools to understand Earth.

The Study of Earth

Geography is the study of Earth, our home planet. Geographers try to answer two basic questions: Where are things located? and, Why are they there? To find answers to these questions, geographers consider Earth from many points of view.

✓ **Reading Check** What questions do geographers try to answer?

Five Ways to Look at Earth

Five themes can help you organize information about Earth and its people. These themes are location, regions, place, movement, and human-environment interaction. They can help you understand where things are located, and why they are there.

10 Foundations of Geography

🎯 Target Reading Skill **L2**

Reread or Read Ahead Point out the Target Reading Skill. Tell students that rereading a difficult passage or reading ahead in the text can help them clarify meaning.

Model rereading using the first paragraph on this page to find the meaning of the word *geographer*. By rereading, students will see that geographers are people who study Earth. Model reading ahead using this sentence from p. 11: "Longitude is the distance east or west of the Prime Meridian, measured in degrees." Students can read ahead to find an explanation of the Prime Meridian.

Give students *Reread or Read Ahead*. Have them complete the activity in groups.

All in One Foundations of Geography Teaching Resources, *Reread or Read Ahead*, p. 68

Location Geographers begin to study a place by finding where it is, or its location. Geographers use both cardinal and intermediate directions to describe location. The **cardinal directions** are north, east, south, and west. Intermediate directions lie between the cardinal directions. For example, northwest is halfway between north and west.

Geographers also use two special measurements of Earth to describe location. **Latitude** is the distance north or south of the Equator, measured in units called degrees. Degrees are units that measure angles. **Longitude** is the distance east or west of the Prime Meridian, measured in degrees.

Lines of latitude are east-west circles around the globe. All points on the circle have the same latitude. The line of latitude around the middle of the globe, at 0 degrees (0°) of latitude, is the Equator. Lines of longitude run north and south. The Prime Meridian is the line of longitude that marks 0° of longitude.

Learn more about the themes of geography.

Show students *What is Geography*? Ask **Why is geography an important part of everyday life?** (*How people live is often determined by where they live.*)

The Hemispheres

The Equator and the Prime Meridian both divide Earth in two. Each half of Earth is called a **hemisphere.** The Equator divides Earth into Northern and Southern hemispheres. The Prime Meridian divides Earth into Eastern and Western hemispheres.

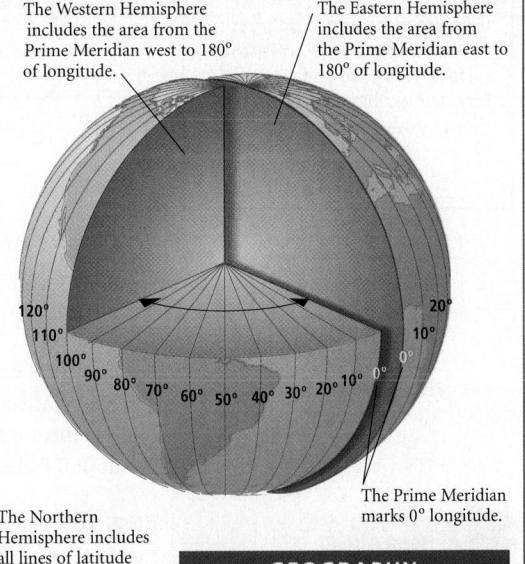

The Western Hemisphere includes the area from the Prime Meridian west to 180° of longitude.

The Eastern Hemisphere includes the area from the Prime Meridian east to 180° of longitude.

The Prime Meridian marks 0° longitude.

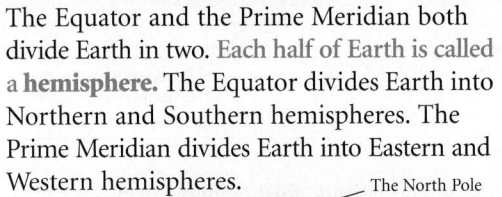
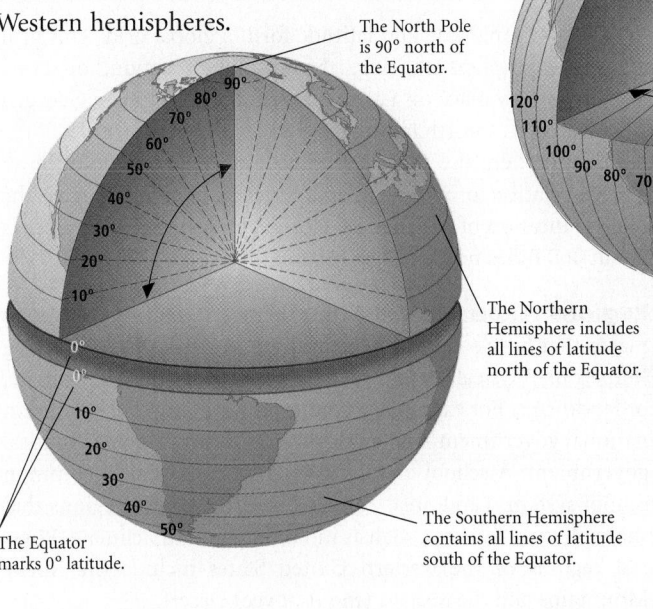

The North Pole is 90° north of the Equator.

The Northern Hemisphere includes all lines of latitude north of the Equator.

The Southern Hemisphere contains all lines of latitude south of the Equator.

The Equator marks 0° latitude.

GEOGRAPHY SKILLS PRACTICE

Location Geographers can pinpoint the location of any place on Earth using lines of latitude and longitude. **Use Latitude and Longitude** What place on Earth is located at 0° longitude and 90° north latitude?

Vocabulary Builder

Use the information below to teach students this section's high-use words.

High-Use Word	Definition and Sample Sentence
theme, p. 10	*n.* the main subject or idea of something The students identified the **theme** of the paragraph.
traditional, p. 13	*adj.* something handed down from generation to generation Her mother taught her to make a **traditional** Italian meal.

Instruct

The Study of Earth L2

Five Ways to Look at Earth L2

Guided Instruction

■ **Vocabulary Builder** Clarify the high-use words **theme** and **traditional** before reading.

■ Read The Study of Earth and Five Ways to Look at Earth, using the Paragraph Shrinking strategy (TE, p. T34). Have students study the diagrams on this page and page 12.

■ Have students name the five themes that geographers use to organize information about Earth and its people, then brainstorm examples of each. (*The five themes and an example of each are: location—the United States is in the Western Hemisphere; regions—a physical region of the United States is the Mojave Desert; place—the climate of the Mojave Desert is hot and dry; movement—radios have helped spread music from the United States to many parts of the world; human-environment interaction— people have cut trails into a mountainside. Other examples will vary, but should illustrate an understanding of each theme.*)

■ Ask students **How are latitude and longitude similar? How are they different?** (*Similar: both are measurements of Earth to describe location; both are measured in degrees. Different: latitude is distance north or south of the Equator; longitude is distance east or west of the Prime Meridian.*)

Answer
Geography Skills Practice Use **Latitude and Longtitude** the North Pole

Guided Instruction (continued)

- Ask students to link their area to the theme of regions. Have them name a region that their location could fall into. Next, ask them to think of an example of the themes of movement and human-environment interaction in their area. *(Responses will vary.)*

Independent Practice

Ask students to create the Taking Notes graphic organizer on a blank piece of paper. Then have them complete the organizer with the information they have just learned. Briefly model how to identify which details to record.

Monitor Progress

- Show *Section Reading Support Transparency FG 43* and ask students to check their graphic organizers individually. Go over key concepts and clarify key vocabulary as needed.

  Foundations of Geography Transparencies, *Section Reading Support Transparency FG 43*

- Tell students to fill in the last column of the *Reading Readiness Guide.* Probe for what they learned that confirms or invalidates each statement.

  All in One Foundations of Geography Teaching Resources, *Reading Readiness Guide,* p. 61

⊙ Target Reading Skill L2

Read Ahead As a follow up, ask students to answer the Target Reading Skill question in the Student Edition. *(Areas that share physical features, such as landforms or a particular climate, are often defined as regions, such as the Rocky Mountains or the Mojave Desert.)*

Answers

Geography Skills Practice Compare and Contrast the Equator; the Prime Meridian

The Global Grid

Lines of longitude and latitude form a global grid. Geographers can identify the absolute location of any point on Earth by finding the latitude and longitude lines that intersect at that point. Lines of latitude are also called **parallels,** because they run east and west and are parallel to one another. This means that they never cross. Lines of longitude are also called **meridians.** Meridians run north and south, from the North Pole to the South Pole.

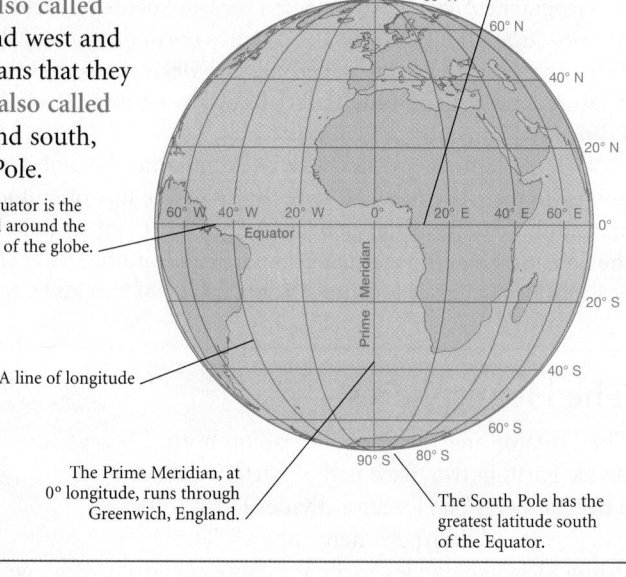

The North Pole has the greatest latitude north of the Equator.

The Equator, at 0° latitude, circles Earth midway between the North and South poles.

The Equator is the parallel around the middle of the globe.

A line of longitude

The Prime Meridian, at 0° longitude, runs through Greenwich, England.

The South Pole has the greatest latitude south of the Equator.

GEOGRAPHY SKILLS PRACTICE

Location Latitude and longitude are measured in degrees from imaginary lines on Earth's surface. **Compare and Contrast** From which line is latitude measured? Where do degrees of longitude start?

Read Ahead Read ahead to see how physical features may define regions.

Lines of longitude and latitude form a global grid. This grid allows geographers to state the absolute location, or exact address, of any place on Earth. For example, Savannah, Georgia, is located at 32° north latitude and 81° west longitude.

Geographers also discuss relative location, or the location of a place relative to another place. A geographer might give the relative location of Tallahassee, Florida, by saying, "Tallahassee is about 400 miles northwest of Miami."

Regions Geographers use the theme of regions to group places that have something in common. A region has a unifying human or physical feature such as population, history, climate, or landforms. For example, a country is a region with a common national government, and a city is a region with a common local government. A school district is a region defined by a common school system. Land areas can also be divided into regions that share physical features, such as mountains or a dry climate. Physical regions of the western United States include the Rocky Mountains and the Mojave (mo HAH vee) Desert.

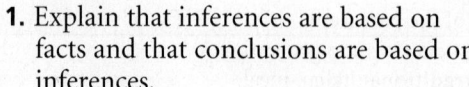 **Skills Mini Lesson**

Drawing Inferences and Conclusions L2

1. Explain that inferences are based on facts and that conclusions are based on inferences.

2. Students can practice the skill using the photograph on p. 10. Have them identify what the photograph shows *(Fact: The geographer is using a map.)*, connect it to the themes of geography *(Inference: She is locating a place on the map.)*, and then draw a conclusion about which theme the geographer is focusing on *(She is focusing on location.)*

3. Have students compare the photographs on pp. 10 and 13, to draw conclusions about where the weather is warmer. *(The farmers' weather is warmer.)*

Place Geographers also study place. Place includes the human and physical features at a specific location. To describe physical features, you might say the climate is hot or cold. Or you might say that the land is hilly. To discuss human features, you might talk about how many people live in a place and the kinds of work they do. You might also describe their religions or the languages they speak.

Movement The theme of movement helps explain how people, goods, and ideas get from one place to another. For example, when people from other countries came to the United States, they brought traditional foods that enriched the American way of life. The theme of movement helps you understand such cultural changes. Movement helps you understand many other facts about the world. For example, radios and computers have helped music from the United States to spread and become popular around the world.

Human-Environment Interaction This theme explores how people affect their environment, or their natural surroundings, and how their environment affects them. Perhaps they have cut trails into the mountainside. Or they may have learned how to survive with little water.

Farmers in India
These women are using the wind to separate grain for flour from chaff, or husks. Farming is an example of human-environment interaction. **Infer** *Do you think that these farmers use much modern machinery?*

✓ Reading Check **What is the purpose of the five themes of geography?**

Section 1 Assessment

Key Terms
Review the key terms at the beginning of this section. Use each term in a sentence that explains its meaning.

🎯 Target Reading Skill
What did you learn about physical features and regions by reading ahead?

Comprehension and Critical Thinking
1. (a) **Recall** What do geographers study?

(b) **Explain** What basic questions guide geographers?
2. (a) **Explain** How can the five themes help geographers?
(b) **Predict** How might a geographer use the theme of movement to describe the area where you live?
3. (a) **Define** What does the theme of location cover?
(b) **Contrast** How would a description of your home town as a place be different from a description of your home town's location?

Writing Activity
Read the passage above on human-environment interaction. Then write a paragraph describing ways that people in your area interact with their natural environment.

For: An activity on the five themes of geography
Visit: PHSchool.com
Web Code: led-3101

Writing Activity
Use the *Rubric for Assessing a Writing Assignment* to evaluate students' paragraphs.
All in One Foundations of Geography Teaching Resources, *Rubric for Assessing a Writing Assignment,* p. 95

Go Online PHSchool.com Typing in the Web code when prompted will bring students directly to detailed instructions for this activity.

Assess and Reteach

Assess Progress L2
Have students complete the Section Assessment. Administer the *Section Quiz.*
All in One Foundations of Geography Teaching Resources, *Section Quiz,* p. 63

Reteach L1
If students need more instruction, have them read this section in the Reading and Vocabulary Study Guide.
📖 Chapter 1, Section 1, **Eastern Hemisphere Reading and Vocabulary Study Guide,** pp. 2–4

Extend L3
Organize students into five groups. Ask each group to complete one of the worksheets listed below to help them fully understand latitude and longitude. Have each group give a brief presentation of its work.
All in One Foundations of Geography Teaching Resources, *Understanding Hemispheres, Understanding Grids, Using a Grid, Understanding Latitude and Longitude, Using Latitude and Longitude,* pp. 79–83

Answers
Infer Probably not, because they are separating grain from straw by hand.

✓ Reading Check They are ways to organize information about Earth and its people

---

Section 1 Assessment

Key Terms
Students' sentences should reflect knowledge of each Key Term.

🎯 **Target Reading Skill**
Physical features refer to climate and landforms, and can be used to form regions.

Comprehension and Critical Thinking
1. (a) Earth (b) Where are things located? Why are they there?

2. (a) They help geographers organize information about Earth and its people. (b) The geographer could explain how people, goods, and ideas came to the area.

3. (a) finding a particular place (b) For place, you might use human and physical features to describe the town; for location, you might use longitude and latitude to describe where the town is.

Objective

Learn to determine the reliability of information.

Prepare to Read

Build Background Knowledge   L2

Ask students to suppose that they are going to a movie. Have them list the information that they will need. *(start time, location of theater, cost of ticket)* Discuss possible sources of information *(newspaper, friend, Web site)* and what may happen if they use unreliable sources. *(may arrive late, may not be able to find the theater, may not have enough money to cover the cost of a ticket)*

Instruct

Using Reliable Information   L2

Guided Instruction

- Read the steps for judging the reliability of information as a class and write them on the board.

- Practice the skill by following the steps on p. 14 as a class. Model each step of the activity by selecting a topic, such as the location of the capital of a country or state, and researching it. Students should identify the source of the information they have found *(examples: an atlas, an encyclopedia, or other source)*, determine whether the information is current *(by checking the publication date)*, consult multiple sources to be sure that they agree *(by comparing information in two or more sources)*, and investigate the author to check for his or her qualifications and possible biases.

Independent Practice

Assign *Skills for Life* and have students complete it individually.

All in One Foundations of Geography Teaching Resources, *Skills for Life,* p. 72

Skills for Life — Using Reliable Information

Would you seek medical advice from a plumber? Would you go to an encyclopedia to keep track of this season's basketball scores? Of course you wouldn't. Information is only as good as its source. To get reliable information, you have to go to an appropriate, trustworthy, and knowledgeable source.

Learn the Skill

Follow these steps to determine whether information is reliable.

1 **Find out the source of the information.** If it comes from a printed source, find out the name of the source, the author, and the date of publication. If it appeared on television, find out the name, date, and type of program (news, drama, or documentary). Do not accept information from Internet sites that do not give a date and an author.

2 **Find out if the information is recent enough for your purpose.** If you need current information, search for recent newspaper articles and up-to-date Web sites. Even if your topic is historic, researchers may have discovered new information about it. Seek the most current information.

3 **Find out if the information is accurate.** On certain topics, nearly all sources agree. For other topics, try to find information on which several respected sources agree. To be clear, you might say, "Several sources agree that" or "According to." If reliable sources disagree, you might note that disagreement in your writing.

4 **Look up the author's qualifications and methods.** When you check out an author's qualifications, always ask yourself whether he or she has a bias, or a one-sided view.

Is it Reliable?

To see if a source is reliable, ask
- What is the source?
- Is it recent enough?
- Is it accurate?
- Is the author qualified or biased?

14 Foundations of Geography

Monitor Progress

Monitor students doing the *Skills for Life* worksheet, checking to make sure they understand the skill steps.

Practice the Skill

Now use steps 1–4 to answer some questions about reliable information.

1. Where might you go to find information on the location of the capital of Japan? On the population of North Carolina? On the major industries of Cuba? On presidential election results in Russia?

2. Would a 20-year-old encyclopedia be a reliable source of information on active volcanoes in Hawaii? On the type of money used in Europe? On the longest river in the world? Explain your answers.

3. If you heard in a television documentary that most of the world's diamonds are mined in southern Africa, how could you check the accuracy of that statement?

4. Suppose you do an Internet search for information on the amount of beef produced in the United States last year. The search leads you to articles by three authors. Who would be the best source of information: an economist for the U.S. Department of Agriculture, the largest cattle rancher in Texas, or a leading university expert on beef production? Explain your answer.

Apply the Skill

If you had to research a report on the health of children in India, what kinds of sources would you search for reliable information? Name at least two sources, and explain why they would be reliable.

These boys are playing ball in front of the famed Taj Mahal, in India.

Differentiated Instruction

For Less Proficient Readers L1

Partner these students with more proficient readers to do Level 1 of the *Using Reliable Information* lesson on the interactive Social Studies Skills Tutor CD-ROM. When they have successfully completed Level 1, they can move on to Level 2 alone.

⊙ *Using Reliable Information,* **Social Studies Skills Tutor CD-ROM**

For Special Needs Students L1

Have students make a two-column chart with the headings *10-Year-Old Encyclopedia* and *This Year's Almanac.* Students should list five questions in each column that could be answered reliably by each source. Then, have students write a sentence explaining how they determined the reliability of each source for their questions.

Assess and Reteach

Assess Progress L2

Ask students to do the Apply the Skill activity.

Reteach L1

If students are having trouble applying the skill steps, have them review the skill using Level 1 of the interactive Social Studies Skills Tutor CD-ROM.

⊙ *Using Reliable Information,* **Social Studies Skills Tutor CD-ROM**

Extend L3

Have students create a bibliography for Chapter 1, Section 1 that contains at least three sources. Students should explain why they consider each source to be reliable.

Answers
Apply the Skill

Possible answers: A Web site containing government data or a recent book by a well-regarded expert would be good sources because the information would be recent, and the authors would be reliable. Student answers will vary, but should reflect that students understand the skill steps for determining if a source is reliable.

Objectives

Social Studies

1. Find out how maps and globes show information about Earth's surface.
2. See how mapmakers show Earth's round surface on flat maps.
3. Learn how to read maps.

Reading/Language Arts

Paraphrase to clarify the meaning of unfamiliar words and ideas.

Prepare to Read

Build Background Knowledge   L2

Tell students that in this section they will learn about maps and globes. Have them glance through the section, paying attention to the visuals and headings. Then write the headings Maps and Globes on the board. Under each heading, make a list of what students already know and what they think they will learn. Use the Idea Wave participation strategy (TE, p. T35) to help generate a list of suggestions. Students can refer to these lists when they are filling in the first two columns of their *Reading Readiness Guides*.

Set a Purpose for Reading   L2

- Preview the Objectives.

- Organize students into pairs or groups of four. Distribute the *Reading Readiness Guide*. Ask the students to fill in the first two columns of the chart. Use the Numbered Heads participation strategy (TE, p. T36) to call on students to share one piece of information they already know and one piece of information they want to know.

All in One Foundations of Geography Teaching Resources, *Reading Readiness Guide,* p. 65

Vocabulary Builder
Preview Key Terms   L2

Pronounce each Key Term, then ask students to say the word with you. Provide a simple explanation such as, "A compass rose is a diagram showing north, south, east, and west on a map."

Prepare to Read

Objectives

In this section you will

1. Find out how maps and globes show information about Earth's surface.
2. See how mapmakers show Earth's round surface on flat maps.
3. Learn how to read maps.

Taking Notes

As you read this section, look for details about each of the following map topics: comparing maps with globes, map projections, and parts of a map. Copy the outline below and write each detail under the correct topic.

> I. Maps and globes
>   A. Globes
>   B.
>   1.
>   2.
> II. Projections
>   A.

A map can help you find directions.

 Target Reading Skill

Paraphrase When you paraphrase, you restate what you have read in your own words. For example, you could paraphrase the first paragraph after the heading Globes and Their Weaknesses this way:

  "Mapmakers found that globes are the best way to show the shapes of continents, but at a different size."

  As you read this section, paraphrase or restate the information after each red or blue heading.

Key Terms

- **scale** (skayl) *n.* relative size
- **distortion** (dih STAWR shun) *n.* loss of accuracy
- **geographic information systems** (jee uh GRAF ik in fur MAY shun SIS tumz) *n.* computer-based systems that provide information about locations
- **projection** (proh JEK shun) *n.* a way to map Earth on a flat surface
- **compass rose** (KUM pus rohz) *n.* a diagram of a compass showing direction
- **key** (kee) *n.* the section of a map that explains the symbols and colors on the map

Globes and Maps

As people explored Earth, they collected information about the shapes and sizes of islands, continents, and bodies of water. Map makers wanted to present this information accurately.

Globes and Their Weaknesses The best way was to put the information on a globe, or a model with the same round shape as Earth itself. By using an accurate shape for Earth, mapmakers could show the continents and oceans of Earth much as they really are. The only difference would be the **scale,** or relative size.

  But there is a problem with globes. Try making a globe large enough to show the streets in your town. The globe might have to be larger than your school building. Imagine putting a globe that big in your pocket every morning! A globe just cannot be complete enough to be useful for finding directions and at the same time small enough to be convenient for everyday use.

Target Reading Skill   L2

Paraphrase Point out the Target Reading Skill. Tell students that saying or writing a difficult passage in their own words can help them clarify meaning.

  Model paraphrasing using the paragraph under the heading Aerial Photographs and Satellite Images on p. 17. (*Aerial photographs and satellite images provide information about* Earth's surface in great detail. However, they cannot show objects that are hidden from the air, and they show a distorted view of Earth's surface.)

  Give students *Paraphrase*. Have them complete the activity in their groups.

All in One Foundations of Geography Teaching Resources, *Paraphrase,* p. 69

Maps and Mapping People, therefore, use flat maps. Flat maps, however, present another problem. Earth is round. A map is flat. Can you flatten an orange peel without stretching or tearing it? There will be sections that are stretched or bent out of shape. The same thing happens when mapmakers create flat maps. It is impossible to show Earth on a flat surface without some **distortion,** or loss of accuracy. Something will look too large, too small, or out of place. Mapmakers have found ways to limit distortion of shape, size, distance, and direction.

Mapmakers rely on ground surveys, or measurements made on the ground, to make maps. They also use aerial photographs and satellite images.

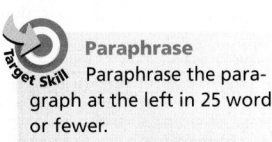
Paraphrase
Paraphrase the paragraph at the left in 25 words or fewer.

Aerial Photographs and Satellite Images
Aerial photographs are photographs of Earth's surface taken from the air. Satellite images are pictures of Earth's surface taken from a satellite in orbit. Both types of image are valuable sources of information for mapmakers because they provide current information about Earth's surface in great detail. But they are not useful for finding objects that are hidden, such as underground transit lines, or features such as streams that may be covered by vegetation. Also, like any map, flat aerial photographs and satellite images give a distorted view of Earth's surface.

Geographic Information Systems A **geographic information system,** or GIS, is a computer-based system that links information to locations. A GIS is useful not only to geographers but also to governments and businesses. A GIS connects information with places. For example, if a business needs to decide where to open an office, it can use a GIS to choose a location where it will reach the most customers. Military planners may use a GIS to improve their knowledge of the places where troops will operate. A GIS also may be used to produce maps.

 **Reading Check** What are the advantages and disadvantages of each way of showing Earth's surface?

Satellite Image of North and South America
This satellite view shows parts of North and South America. A storm system covers part of the southeastern United States. **Analyze Images** How might this image pose problems as a source for making maps?

Paraphrase As a follow up, ask students to complete the Target Reading Skill activity on this page of the Student Edition. *(Answers will vary, but should include an explanation of why flat maps have distortion.)*

Instruct

Globes and Maps L2

Guided Instruction

■ **Vocabulary Builder** Clarify the high-use words **transit** and **vegetation** before reading.

■ Read Globes and Maps using the Oral Cloze reading strategy (TE, p. T33).

■ Have students discuss one use for a globe and one use for a map. *(globe: to see an accurate view of Earth; map: to show roads in your state or streets in your town)*

■ Ask students **How does technology help geographers understand Earth better?** *(Aerial photographs and satellite images provide current information about Earth's surface, while a GIS links geographical information to places.)*

Independent Practice

Ask students to create the Taking Notes graphic organizer on a blank piece of paper. Have them fill in details about maps and globes.

Monitor Progress

As students fill in the graphic organizer, circulate and make sure individuals are choosing the correct details.

Answers

Reading Check globes—show accurate shape, distance, and direction; not convenient for everyday use; maps—easy to use; some distortion of shape, distance, and/or direction; aerial photographs and satellite images—provide current information, but do not show features that are hidden; GIS—links information to location, but is probably not useful for navigating
Analyze Images Clouds and vegetation block the view of parts of Earth's surface.

╓ Vocabulary Builder

Use the information below to teach this section's high-use words.

High-Use Word	Definition and Sample Sentence
transit, p. 17	*adj.* movement from one place to another Many large cities have public **transit** systems.
vegetation, p. 17	*n.* plant life Rainforests have a wide variety of **vegetation**.
available, p. 19	*adj.* that can be gotten, used, or reached She sat in the last **available** seat on the crowded bus.
symbol, p. 21	*n.* a mark or sign that represents another object or an idea A key lists the **symbols** that a map uses.

Show students *Geography Tools and Map Skills.* Ask students to explain why maps are a geographer's most important tool. *(Since geographers study Earth from many points of view, the variety of maps, such as climate maps and relief maps, are essential to a geographer's work.)*

Getting It All on the Map

L2

Guided Instruction

- **Vocabulary Builder** Clarify the high-use word **available.**

- Read Getting It All on the Map with students. As students read, circulate and make sure individuals can answer the Reading Check question.

- Have students describe a Mercator projection. *(Mercator maps expand the area between the longitudes near the poles.)*

- Ask students who these maps were useful to, and why. *(to sailors, because they showed directions accurately)*

- Have students study Making a Mercator Map diagram and discuss the problem with Mercator projections. *(Distances and size become distorted the farther the area is from the Equator.)*

Getting It All on the Map

In 1569, a mapmaker named Gerardus Mercator (juh RAHR dus mur KAY tur) created a flat map to help sailors navigate, or plan journeys, around the globe. To make his map flat and to keep his grid rectangular, Mercator expanded the area between lines of longitude near the poles. Mercator's map was very useful to sailors because it showed directions accurately, even though sizes and distances were distorted. More than 400 years later, nearly all seagoing navigators still use the Mercator **projection,** or method of mapping Earth on a flat surface.

The Mercator Projection Mercator maps make areas near the poles look bigger than they are. This is because on a globe, the lines of longitude meet at the poles. To keep lines of longitude straight up and down, Mercator had to stretch the spaces between them north and south of the Equator. Land near the Equator was about the right size, but land areas near the poles became much larger. For example, on Mercator's map, Greenland looks bigger than South America. Greenland is actually only about one eighth as big as South America. Geographers call a Mercator projection a conformal map. It shows correct shapes but not true distances or sizes. What other areas, besides Greenland, do you think might look larger than they should?

Making a Mercator Map

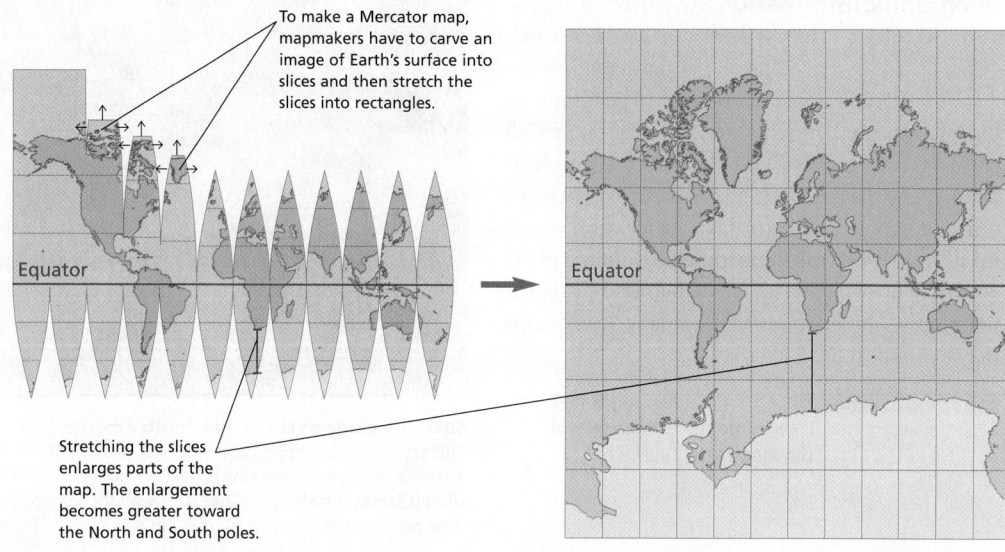

To make a Mercator map, mapmakers have to carve an image of Earth's surface into slices and then stretch the slices into rectangles.

Stretching the slices enlarges parts of the map. The enlargement becomes greater toward the North and South poles.

18 Foundations of Geography

 **Skills Mini Lesson**

Sequencing

L2

1. Teach the skill by explaining that sequencing means putting pieces of information in a logical order, using a diagram if necessary.

2. Help students practice the skill by looking at the visuals on p. 18. As a class, first identify the topic, then the steps in the process, and then the order. Then draw a flowchart of the process on the

board. *(flowchart will have three boxes: get image of Earth's surface, cut image into gores, stretch gores to form rectangle)*

3. Have students apply the skill by creating a similar flowchart about equal-area maps. *(flowchart will have three boxes: get image of Earth's surface, cut image into gores, squeeze gores into oval)*

Equal-Area Projections An equal-area map shows the correct size of landmasses, but their shapes are altered. Lines that would be straight on Earth may be forced into curves to fit on the map's flat surface.

The Robinson Projection This projection is named for its designer, Arthur Robinson. Today, many geographers believe that the Robinson projection is the best world map available. It is used for most of the world maps in this book. This projection shows most distances, sizes, and shapes quite accurately. However, even a Robinson projection has distortions, especially in areas around the edges of the map.

Other Projections There are many other types of projections besides the ones shown here. Some are useful for showing small areas but not for showing the whole world. Others are good for specific purposes, such as planning a plane's flight route.

✓ **Reading Check** What are the strengths and weaknesses of the Mercator, equal-area, and Robinson projections?

Making an Equal-Area Map

To make an equal-area map, the slices are squeezed into an oval.

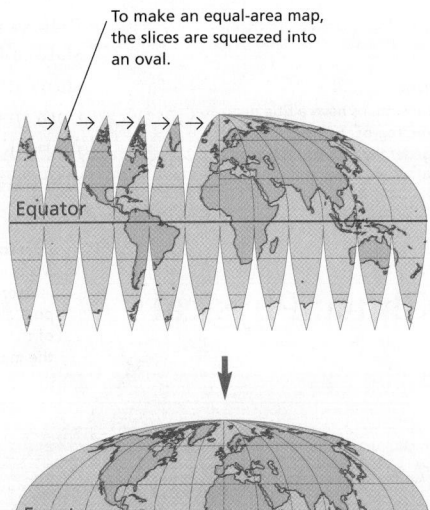

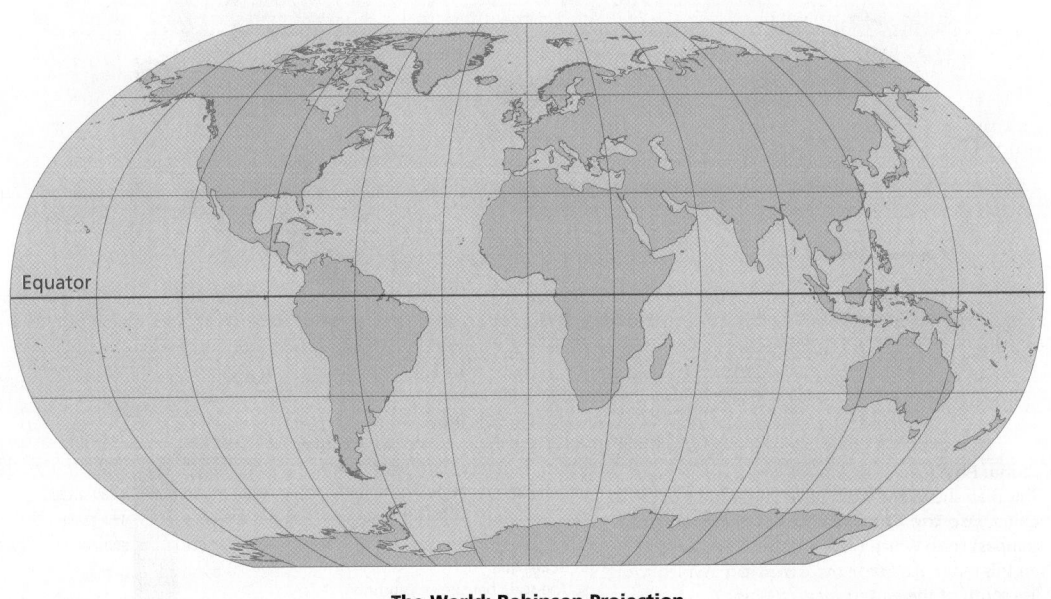

The World: Robinson Projection

Chapter 1 Section 2 **19**

Guided Instruction (continued)

- Have students describe an equal-area projection. (*shows the correct size of landmasses, but alters their shapes*)

- Ask students **Why do geographers believe that the Robinson projection is the best world map available?** (*It shows most distances, sizes, and shapes accurately.*)

- Ask students **If you were planning to travel by ship from Los Angeles to Hong Kong, which map projection would you use? Why?** (*Mercator—its accurate directions are useful for navigation at sea.*)

Independent Practice

Have students continue filling in the graphic organizer with details from the information they have just learned.

Monitor Progress

As students fill in the graphic organizer, circulate and make sure individuals are choosing appropriate details. Provide assistance as needed.

Differentiated Instruction

For Gifted and Talented L3

Challenge students to learn more about map projections. Assign *Understanding Projection, Maps with Accurate Shapes: Conformal Maps, Maps with Accurate Areas: Equal-Area Maps,* and *Maps with Accurate Directions: Azimuthal Maps.*

Then, have students identify one instance in which each type of map would be used.

All in One Foundations of Geography Teaching Resources, *Understanding Projection, Maps with Accurate Shapes: Conformal Maps, Maps with Accurate Areas: Equal-Area Maps,* and *Maps with Accurate Directions: Azimuthal Maps,* pp. 84–87

Answer

✓ **Reading Check** Mercator—shows shapes and directions accurately, but distances and sizes are distorted; equal-area—shows correct size of landmasses, but shapes are distorted; Robinson—most distances, sizes, and shapes are accurate, but some distortions around edges of map

Reading Maps

Guided Instruction

- **Vocabulary Builder** Clarify the high-use word **symbol** before reading.

- Ask students to read Reading Maps and to review the maps on pp. 20–22.

- Have students list the parts of the map shown on the China: Physical and Georgia Highways maps. Then ask students **How does each part help you read a map?** (*title tells you what type of information the map contains and what area it is focusing on; locator globe shows the area's location on a globe; compass rose shows direction; scale bar shows how distances on the map compare to distances on land; a key identifies symbols and coloring*)

- Have students discuss what the colors show on the physical map of China. (*The colors show ranges of elevation.*)

- Ask students **What is the distance between Atlanta and Augusta? Which highway connects the two cities?** (*about 130 miles or 200 kilometers; Interstate 20*)

Reading Maps

Look at the maps shown on these two pages. One is a physical map of the country of China. The other is a highway map of the state of Georgia. These maps cover completely different areas and show different kinds of information. Despite their differences, both maps have all of the basic parts that you will find on most maps. Knowing how to use these parts will help you to read and understand any kind of map.

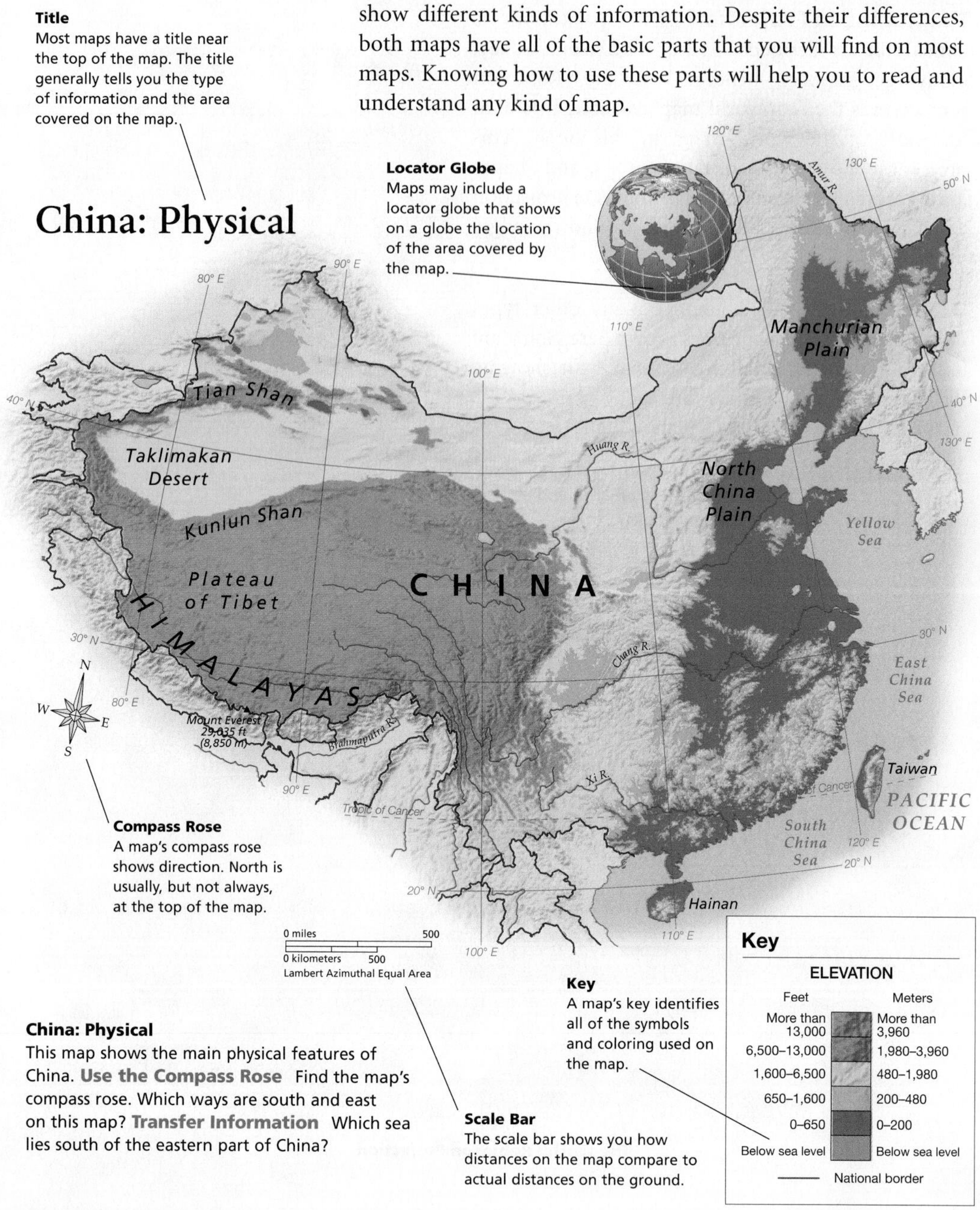

Title
Most maps have a title near the top of the map. The title generally tells you the type of information and the area covered on the map.

Locator Globe
Maps may include a locator globe that shows on a globe the location of the area covered by the map.

China: Physical

Compass Rose
A map's compass rose shows direction. North is usually, but not always, at the top of the map.

0 miles 500
0 kilometers 500
Lambert Azimuthal Equal Area

China: Physical
This map shows the main physical features of China. **Use the Compass Rose** Find the map's compass rose. Which ways are south and east on this map? **Transfer Information** Which sea lies south of the eastern part of China?

Key
A map's key identifies all of the symbols and coloring used on the map.

Scale Bar
The scale bar shows you how distances on the map compare to actual distances on the ground.

Key

ELEVATION

Feet		Meters
More than 13,000		More than 3,960
6,500–13,000		1,980–3,960
1,600–6,500		480–1,980
650–1,600		200–480
0–650		0–200
Below sea level		Below sea level

—— National border

20 Foundations of Geography

Answers

Use the Compass Rose south is down and east is to the right **Transfer Information** South China Sea

---

Differentiated Instruction

For Special Needs Students L1
Have students work with more advanced students to complete *Enrichment*. Then hand out *Outline Map 1* and have them color and label the continents and oceans.

 Foundations of Geography Teaching Resources, *Enrichment,* p. 71; *Outline Map 1: The World: Physical,* p. 91

For Advanced Readers L3
Have students read *Captain Scott's Letter to the British Public* to learn about his expedition to the South Pole. Have students research and chart the journey on a map.

Foundations of Geography Teaching Resources, *Captain Scott's Letter to the British Public,* pp. 92–93

Georgia Highways

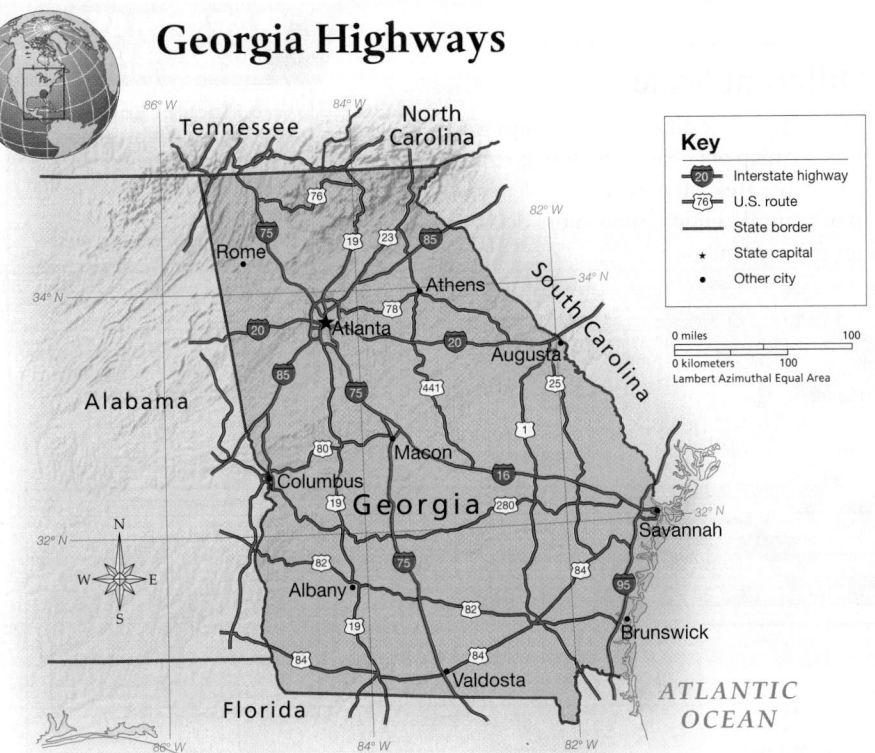

Key

- 20 Interstate highway
- 76 U.S. route
- State border
- ★ State capital
- • Other city

0 miles — 100
0 kilometers — 100
Lambert Azimuthal Equal Area

The Parts of a Map Both maps on these pages have what geographers call a **compass rose,** a diagram of a compass showing direction. If you want to find directions such as north, south, east, or west, just look for the map's compass rose.

Both maps also have a scale bar. The scale bar shows how distances on the map compare to actual distances on the land. Scales vary, depending on the map. If you compare the scale bar on the map of China to the bar on the map of Georgia, you will see that the map of China covers much greater distances on the ground even though the map is not much bigger.

On any map, the **key,** or legend, is the part of the map that explains the symbols and shading on the map. For example, the key on the highway map of Georgia shows the colored lines that stand for different kinds of highways. While some maps use symbols, other maps, like the physical map of China, use coloring to present information. The key shows which colors stand for which elevations.

Georgia Highways
Notice that this map of Georgia has the same basic parts as the physical map of China: a title, a key, a locator globe, a compass rose, and a scale bar.
Use Scale *Using a ruler, measure the distance on the map between Atlanta and Macon. Then hold the ruler against the scale bar. How many miles is Atlanta from Macon?*

✓ **Reading Check** How do the different parts of a map help you to find information?

Guided Instruction (continued)

- Ask students **What are the scales used in the two maps of London on page 22?** (*Greater London: 0 to 10 miles or 0 to 15 km; Central London: 0 to 1 mile or 0 to 1 km*) **Which map provides the most detail?** (*Central London*) **Why would the smaller scale not be used for the map of Greater London?** (*If the map of Greater London showed the same area using a smaller scale, it would make the map quite large and too detailed for its use.*)

Independent Practice

Have students complete their graphic organizers by adding a head labeled "Parts of a Map" and filling in the details they have just learned.

Monitor Progress

- Show *Section Reading Support Transparency FG 44* and ask students to check their graphic organizers individually. Go over key concepts and clarify key vocabulary as needed.

  📖 **Foundations of Geography Transparencies,** *Section Reading Support Transparency FG 44*

- Tell students to fill in the last column of the *Reading Readiness Guide.* Ask them to evaluate if what they learned was what they had expected to learn.

  All in One Foundations of Geography Teaching Resources, *Reading Readiness Guide,* p. 65

Differentiated Instruction

For English Language Learners [L2]
To sharpen students' map skills, have them complete *Using the Map Key, Using the Compass Rose,* and *Comparing Maps of Different Scale.*

All in One Foundations of Geography Teaching Resources, *Using the Map Key, Using the Compass Rose, Using the Map Scale,* pp. 88–90

For Gifted and Talented [L3]
Form students into groups. Have each group plot a trip around the world by completing *Small Group Activity: Plotting a Route Around the World.*

All in One Foundations of Geography Teaching Resources, *Small Group Activity: Plotting a Route Around the World,* pp. 73–76

Answers

Use Scale about 80 miles

✓ **Reading Check** compass rose—shows directions; scale bar—shows how map distances compare to actual distances; key—explains map's symbols and shading; title—tells subject of map; grid—helps find locations

Assess and Reteach

Assess Progress
L2

Have students complete the Section Assessment. Administer the *Section Quiz*.

All in One Foundations of Geography Teaching Resources, *Section Quiz,* p. 67

Reteach
L1

If students need more instruction, have them read this section in the Reading and Vocabulary Study Guide.

📖 Chapter 1, Section 2, **Eastern Hemisphere Reading and Vocabulary Study Guide,** pp. 5–7

Extend
L3

Have students invent their own country and create a map including a title, a key, a scale bar, a grid, and a compass rose. Students should include their country's major cities, physical features, and major sites such as airports or tourist attractions.

Answers

MAP MASTER Skills Activity **Analyze** the map titled Greater London; the map titled Central London

Go Online PHSchool.com Students may practice their map skills using the interactive online version of this map.

Section 2 Assessment

Key Terms

Students' sentences should reflect knowledge of each Key Term.

🔄 **Target Reading Skill**

Answers will vary, but should include the strengths and weaknesses of the Mercator projection.

Comprehension and Critical Thinking

1. (a) ground surveys, aerial photographs, and satellite images **(b)** ground surveys—record details at ground level, but can be out of date; aerial photographs and satellite images—provide current, detailed information, but some features can be hidden from the air and flat photographs and images can distort Earth's curved surface **(c)** ground survey

2. (a) Mercator projection—shows directions and shapes accurately, but distances and sizes are distorted; equal-area projection—shows correct size of landmasses, but shapes are distorted **(b)** Mercator

22 *Foundations of Geography*

Maps of Different Scale

Maps with different scales have different uses. Maps with a large scale, such as the map of Greater London, give a general picture of a large area. Maps with a smaller scale, such as the map of Central London, show more detail and are useful for finding landmarks.

Greater London

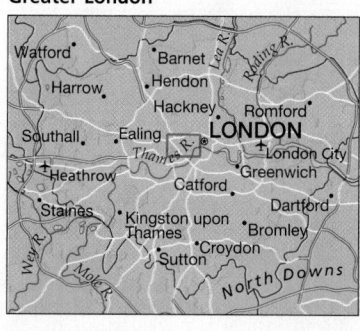

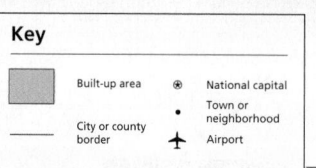

Key

Built-up area · National capital · City or county border · Town or neighborhood · Airport

Central London

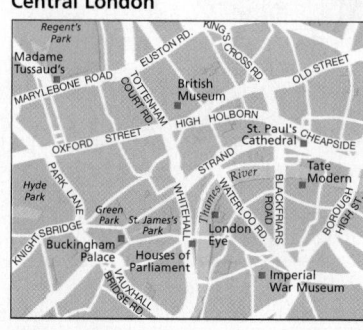

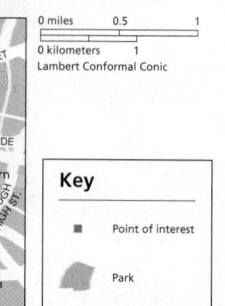

Key

Point of interest · Park

MAP MASTER Skills Activity

Two Maps of London
The map of Central London zooms in on the area inside the red box on the map of Greater London. **Analyze** Which map shows the city's size? Which shows tourist attractions?

Go Online PHSchool.com Use Web Code **lep-3112** for step-by-step **map skills practice.**

Section 2 Assessment

Key Terms

Review the key terms at the beginning of this section. Use each term in a sentence that explains its meaning.

🔄 **Target Reading Skill**

Go back and find the paragraph under the heading The Mercator Projection. Paraphrase this paragraph, or rewrite it in your own words.

Comprehension and Critical Thinking

1. (a) Identify What information sources do mapmakers use?
(b) Evaluate What are the advantages and disadvantages of each information source?

(c) Predict To make a map of small streams in an area of thick vegetation, what source would a mapmaker most likely use?
2. (a) Recall What are the advantages and disadvantages of a Mercator projection and of an equal-area projection?
(b) Apply Information Which projection would you use to plan a voyage by ship in a straight line across an ocean?
3. (a) Define On a map, what are the key, title, compass rose, and scale bar?
(b) Synthesize Information If you made a map of places to shop in your area, what might you put in the map's key?

Writing Activity

Look at the physical map of China. Plan a route for a trip from its east coast to its western border. Using information from the map, describe the landscape that you will see along the way.

Go Online PHSchool.com

For: An activity on maps
Visit: PHSchool.com
Web Code: led-3102

22 Foundations of Geography

---

3. (a) key—explains map's symbols and shading; title—tells subject of map; compass rose—shows directions; scale bar—shows how map distances compare to actual distances **(b)** Answers will vary, but should show an understanding of a key's purpose.

Writing Activity

Use the *Rubric for Assessing a Writing Assignment* to evaluate students' descriptions.

All in One Foundations of Geography Teaching Resources, *Rubric for Assessing a Writing Assignment,* p. 95

Go Online PHSchool.com Typing in the Web code when prompted will bring students directly to detailed instructions for this activity.

Review and Assessment

◆ Chapter Summary

Section 1: The Five Themes of Geography

- Geography is the study of Earth.
- Geographers can pinpoint any location on the surface of Earth using lines of latitude and longitude, which form an imaginary grid.
- There are five themes of geography—location, regions, place, movement, and human-environment interaction. They offer five ways to gather and understand information about places on Earth.

Section 2: The Geographer's Tools

- Maps can show more details of Earth's surface than globes, but showing Earth's round surface on flat maps causes distortion.
- Projections are different ways of showing Earth's round surface on a flat map.
- Parts of the map such as the key, compass rose, and scale bar can help you to find and understand information on any map.

Earth viewed from space

◆ Key Terms

Each of the statements below contains a key term from the chapter. If the statement is true, write *true*. If it is false, rewrite the statement to make it true.

1. The cardinal directions are north, east, south, and west.
2. Latitude is a measure of the distance north or south of Earth's Equator.
3. Longitude is a measure of the distance north or south of the Equator.
4. A hemisphere is a half of Earth.

5. A meridian is a line of latitude.
6. The scale is the part of the map that shows cardinal directions.
7. A projection is a way of mapping the flat surface of Earth onto a round globe.
8. The compass rose is the part of a map that shows symbols and their meanings.
9. The key is the part of the map that shows relative distances.

─ Vocabulary Builder ─

Revisit this chapter's high-use academic words:

available	transit	vegetation
symbol	theme	traditional

Ask students to review the definitions they recorded on their *Word Knowledge* worksheets.

All in One **Foundations of Geography Teaching Resources,** *Word Knowledge,* p. 70

Consider allowing students to earn extra credit if they use the words in their answers to the questions in the Chapter Review and Assessment. The words must be used correctly and in a natural context to earn the extra points.

Review and Assessment

Review Chapter Content

- Tell students that each statement in the Chapter Summary is an answer to one of the chapter's Guiding Questions. Have students determine the number of the Guiding Question that relates to each statement and then pair students to discuss their classifications. Refer to p. 1 of the Student Edition for text of Guiding Questions.

- Assign *Vocabulary Development* for students to review Key Terms.

  All in One **Foundations of Geography Teaching Resources,** *Vocabulary Development,* p. 94

Answers

Key Terms

1. True
2. True
3. False. Longitude is a measure of the distance east or west of the Prime Meridian.
4. True
5. False. A meridian is a line of longitude.
6. False. The scale is the part of the map that shows how distances on the map compare to actual distances on the land.
7. False. A projection is a way of mapping the round surface of Earth onto a flat surface.
8. False. A compass rose shows direction on a map.
9. False. The key is the part of the map that explains the map's symbols and shading.

Review and Assessment

Comprehension and Critical Thinking

10. (a) location, regions, place, movement, human-environment interaction
(b) human-environment interaction

11. (a) by giving its longitude and latitude
(b) Knowing the exact location of a place could enable you to measure its distance from your current location, or find out how to travel there.

12. (a) human or physical features **(b)** Yes; a single place might fit into one political region, but another region based on the physical features of the area.

13. (a) A globe with enough detail for daily use would be enormous. Maps have some degree of distortion of size, distance, shape, and/or direction. **(b)** globe

14. (a) shows directions and shapes accurately, but distances and sizes are distorted **(b)** Navigators are most interested in plotting routes in the correct direction. **(c)** when you were most interested in accurate distances or sizes

15. (a) compass rose, scale bar, key, title, grid **(b)** compass rose—shows directions; scale bar—shows how distances on a map compare to actual distances; key—explains map's symbols and shading; title—tells subject of map; grid—helps find locations

Skills Practice

Students' answers will vary. Some may say that the first three sentences are reliable because the writer makes firsthand observations, while the last sentence is not reliable because the writer is making an assumption.

Writing Activity: Geography

Students' answers will vary, but should show an understanding of each of the five themes of geography.

Use *Rubric for Assessing a Writing Assignment* to evaluate students' descriptions.

All in One Foundations of Geography Teaching Resources, *Rubric for Assessing a Writing Assignment,* p. 95

Review and Assessment (continued)

◆ Comprehension and Critical Thinking

10. (a) List What five themes can help you organize infomation about Earth?
(b) Categorize Under which theme would you discuss building a dam on a river in a desert?

11. (a) Recall How do geographers pinpoint the exact location of any place on Earth?
(b) Infer Why might it be useful to know the exact location of a place?

12. (a) Identify What unifying characteristics might be used to describe a region?
(b) Draw Conclusions Might a single place be part of more than one region? Explain.

13. (a) Recall What are the disadvantages of globes? What are the disadvantages of maps?
(b) Apply Information Which would be more helpful for studying the exact shapes of continents, a globe or a map?

14. (a) Describe What are the main features of the Mercator projection?
(b) Infer Why is the Mercator projection still used by navigators today?
(c) Generalize When might you want to use a projection other than the Mercator projection?

15. (a) List What are the basic parts that most maps have?
(b) Synthesize Information How can you use the parts of a new map to understand it?

◆ Skills Practice

Using Reliable Information In the Skills for Life activity in this chapter, you learned how to use reliable information. Review the steps for this skill. Then apply them to the text below. Suppose you found this text in a teen magazine. Decide whether you think the information is reliable. Write a sentence that explains why or why not.

"Japan is a very clean country. I spent a whole week in Japan. The buses and trains were very clean. I didn't go inside a Japanese home, but I bet they are very clean, too."

◆ Writing Activity: Geography

Write down the name of the place where you live. Below that name, list the five themes of geography. Next to each theme, describe how it applies to your city, town, or state.

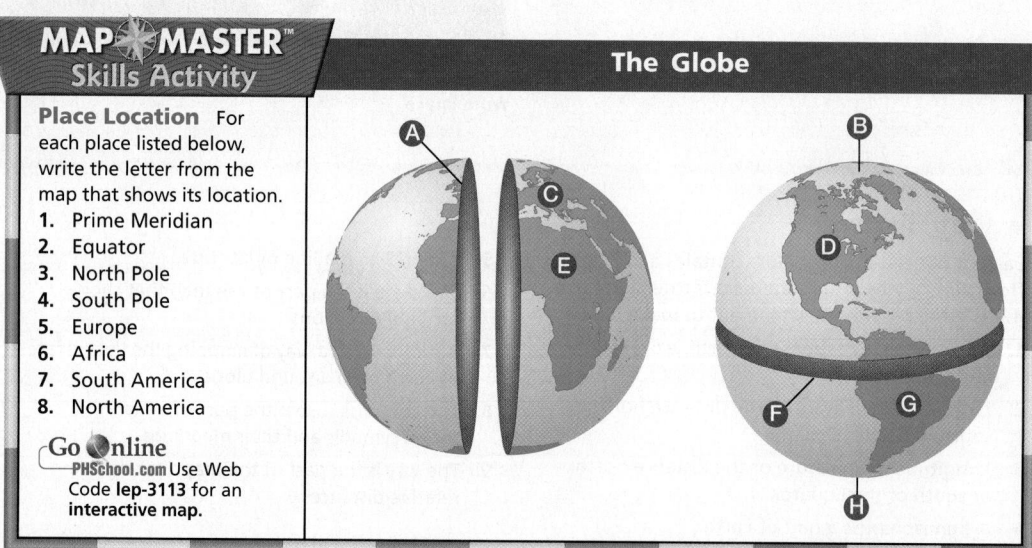

MAP MASTER Skills Activity

Place Location For each place listed below, write the letter from the map that shows its location.
1. Prime Meridian
2. Equator
3. North Pole
4. South Pole
5. Europe
6. Africa
7. South America
8. North America

Go Online PHSchool.com Use Web Code lep-3113 for an interactive map.

The Globe

MAP MASTER Skills Activity

1. A	**2.** F
3. B	**4.** H
5. C	**6.** E
7. G	**8.** D

Go Online PHSchool.com Students may practice their map skills using the interactive online version of this map.

Standardized Test Prep

Test-Taking Tips

Some questions on standardized tests ask you to make mental maps. Do the exercise in the box below. Then follow the tips to answer the sample question.

Draw a simple map of the world based on maps you have seen. Draw a rough shape for each landmass. Draw the Prime Meridian and the Equator across the map.

TIP Find the continents on your map. How is the world divided into hemispheres?

Pick the letter that best answers the question.

Which continent lies completely in both the Northern Hemisphere and the Western Hemisphere?

A Europe
B Greenland
C North America
D Australia

TIP Beware of careless errors. Read the question twice and think carefully about each answer choice.

Think It Through Australia is located completely in both the Southern Hemisphere and the Eastern Hemisphere. Europe is in the Northern Hemisphere but also mostly in the Eastern Hemisphere. Greenland is completely in both the Northern Hemisphere and the Western Hemisphere—as the question asks. But be careful! Greenland is not a continent. The answer is C.

Practice Questions

Use the tips above and other tips in this book to help you answer the following questions.

1. Which of the following is NOT a tool a geographer would use to study absolute location?
   A cardinal directions
   B climate
   C lines of latitude
   D degrees

2. What disadvantage do all flat maps share?
   A They have some sort of distortion.
   B They are hard to carry.
   C There are few sources to create them.
   D They can only show areas at a small scale.

3. A map with cities and colored lines marked with numbers is probably a type of
   A climate map.
   B road map.
   C physical map.
   D vegetation map.

Read the passage below and answer the question that follows.

This area is located in the United States, west of the Mississippi River. It is mainly hot and dry, with little rainfall, so people have built many dams there. Its landforms include rivers, canyons, and deserts.

4. Which of the five themes are used to describe this area?
   A location, movement, regions
   B movement, place, regions, human-environment interaction
   C regions, location, movement
   D location, place, human-environment interaction

Go Online PHSchool.com
Use Web Code lea-3103 for a **Chapter 1 self-test.**

Standardized Test Prep

Answers

1. B
2. A
3. B
4. D

Go Online PHSchool.com Students may use the Chapter 1 self-test on PHSchool.com to prepare for the Chapter Test.

Assessment Resources

Use Chapter Tests A and B to assess students' mastery of chapter content.

All in One Foundations of Geography Teaching Resources, *Chapter Tests A and B,* pp. 96–101

Tests are also available on the *ExamView® Test Bank CD-ROM.*

⊙ *ExamView® Test Bank CD-ROM*

Earth's Physical Geography

Overview

Section 1

Our Planet, Earth
1. Learn about Earth's movement in relation to the sun.
2. Explore seasons and latitude.

Section 2

Forces Shaping Earth
1. Learn about the planet Earth.
2. Explore the forces inside Earth.
3. Explore the forces on Earth's surface.

Section 3

Climate and Weather
1. Learn about weather and climate.
2. Explore latitude, landforms, and precipitation.
3. Discover how oceans affect climate.

Section 4

How Climate Affects Vegetation
1. Investigate the relationship between climate and vegetation.
2. Explore Earth's vegetation regions.
3. Study vertical climate zones.

DISCOVERY CHANNEL SCHOOL Video

The Ever-Changing Earth
Length: 3 minutes, 33 seconds
Use with Section 2
This segment explores how Earth may have looked over 200 million years ago, when all the continents formed a huge single landmass. The segment also examines the theory of plate tectonics. It explains how Earth's surface has changed. Students will learn about the consequences of tectonic plate movements, such as earthquakes and volcanoes.

Technology Resources

Go Online
PHSchool.com

Students use embedded Web codes to access Internet activities, chapter self-tests, and additional map practice. They may also access Dorling Kindersley's Online Desk Reference to learn more about each country they study.

Interactive Textbook

Use the Interactive Textbook to make content and concepts come alive through animations, videos, and activities that accompany the complete basal text—online and on CD-ROM.

PRENTICE HALL
TeacherEXPRESS™
Plan · Teach · Assess

Use this complete suite of powerful teaching tools to make planning lessons and administering tests quicker and easier.

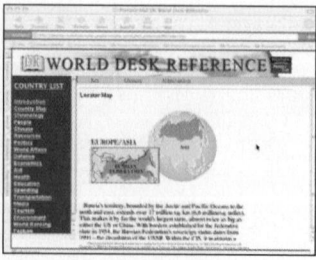

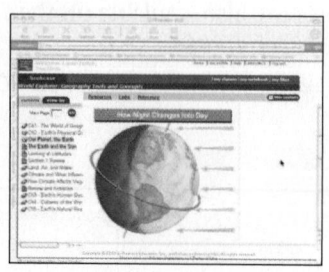

Reading and Assessment

Reading and Vocabulary Instruction

⟲ Model the Target Reading Skill

Using Context Clues Using context clues involves reading the words and sentences that surround an unfamiliar word or idea to clarify its meaning. The context can describe, define, or restate the term, or provide a comparison that allows you to figure out the term's meaning. Model using context clues by writing the following sentences on the board:

1. An archipelago is a series of island chains.
2. A tsunami is like a wall of water 15 to 30 feet above the usual level of the sea.
3. The river carved out an enormous gorge, or deep, narrow valley with steep, rocky walls.

Ask students to circle the unfamiliar word in each sentence, and then underline the context clues that help to define it. Explain that in the first sentence, the context clue is a definition—*is a series of island chains* defines *archipelago*. In the second sentence, *like a wall of water 15 to 30 feet above the usual level of the sea* provides a comparison. In the third sentence, *or deep narrow valley with steep, rocky walls* restates the word *gorge*. Challenge students to find unfamiliar words in the chapter and write down how they used context clues to gain an understanding of these words.

Use the following worksheets from All-in-One Foundations of Geography Teaching Resources (pp. 121–124) to support this chapter's Target Reading Skill.

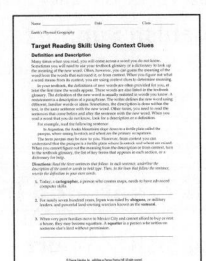
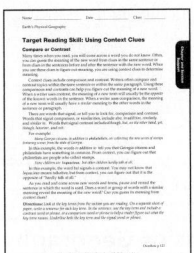

Vocabulary Builder

High-Use Academic Words

Use these steps to teach this chapter's high-use words:

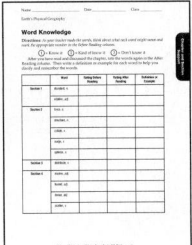

1. Have students rate how well they know each word on their Word Knowledge worksheets (All-in-One Foundations of Geography Teaching Resources, p. 125).
2. Pronounce each word and ask students to repeat it.
3. Give students a brief definition and sample sentence (provided on TE pp. 29, 34, 41, and 51).
4. Work with students as they fill in the "Definition or Example" column of their Word Knowledge worksheets.

Assessment

Formal Assessment

Test students' understanding of core knowledge and skills.

Chapter Tests A and B, All-in-One Foundations of Geography Teaching Resources, pp. 151–156

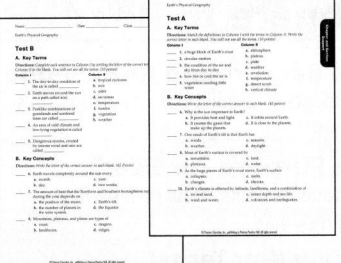

Customize the Chapter Tests to suit your needs.

ExamView Test Bank CD-ROM

Skills Assessment

Assess geographic literacy.

MapMaster Skills, Student Edition, pp. 29, 43, 44, 45, 53, 56

Assess reading and comprehension.

Target Reading Skills, Student Edition, pp. 30, 35, 43, 52, and in Section Assessments

Chapter 2 Assessment, Eastern Hemisphere Reading and Vocabulary Study Guide, p. 21

Performance Assessment

Assess students' performance using the following rubrics from All-in-One Foundations of Geography Teaching Resources.

Rubric for Assessing a Student Poem, p. 146

Rubric for Assessing a Role-Playing Activity, p. 147

Rubric for Assessing a Bar Graph, p. 148

Rubric for Assessing a Line Graph, p. 149

Rubric for Assessing a Poster, p. 150

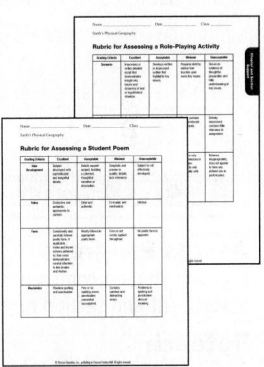

Assess students' work through performance tasks.

Small Group Activity, All-in-One Foundations of Geography Teaching Resources, pp. 128–131

Online Assessment

Have students check their own understanding.

Chapter Self-Test

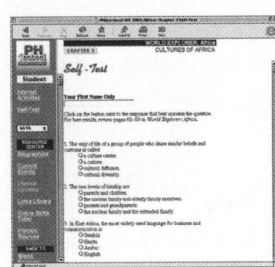

Test Preparation

Foundations of Geography Benchmark Test 1, AYP Monitoring Assessments, pp. 81–84

Section 1 Our Planet, Earth

 2 periods, 1 block

Social Studies Objectives

1. Learn about Earth's movement in relation to the sun.
2. Explore seasons and latitude.

Reading/Language Arts Objective

Use context clues from surrounding phrases to determine the meaning of unfamiliar words.

Prepare to Read

Build Background Knowledge
Ask students to predict the effect of Earth's movements.

Set a Purpose for Reading
Have students begin to fill out the *Reading Readiness Guide*.

Preview Key Terms
Teach the section's Key Terms.

Target Reading Skill
Introduce the section's Target Reading Skill of **using context clues**.

Instructional Resources

All in One Foundations of Geography Teaching Resources
- **L2** Reading Readiness Guide, p. 106
- **L2** Use Context Clues: General Knowledge, p. 121

Differentiated Instruction

Spanish Reading and Vocabulary Study Guide
- **L1** Chapter 2, Section 1, pp. 8–9 ELL

Instruct

Earth and the Sun
Discuss how the Earth's rotation affects the way we keep track of time.

Seasons and Latitude
Ask questions about the Earth's tilt and how it relates to the seasons.

Target Reading Skill
Review **using context clues**.

Instructional Resources

All in One Foundations of Geography Teaching Resources
- **L2** Guided Reading and Review, p. 107
- **L2** Reading Readiness Guide, p. 106

Foundations of Geography Transparencies
- **L2** Section Reading Support Transparency FG 45

Differentiated Instruction

All in One Foundations of Geography Teaching Resources
- **L3** Enrichment, p. 126 AR, GT
- **L1** Understanding Movements of the Earth, p. 134 ELL, LPR, SN

Teacher's Edition
- **L3** For Gifted and Talented, TE p. 31
- **L1** For Less Proficient Readers, TE p. 31

Spanish Support
- **L2** Guided Reading and Review (Spanish), p. 8 ELL

Assess and Reteach

Assess Progress
Evaluate student comprehension with the section assessment and section quiz.

Reteach
Assign the Reading and Vocabulary Study Guide to help struggling students.

Extend
Extend the lesson by assigning an Activity Shop Lab.

Instructional Resources

All in One Foundations of Geography Teaching Resources
- **L2** Section Quiz, p. 108
- **L3** Activity Shop Lab: The Earth's Seasons, pp. 132–133
- Rubric for Assessing a Writing Assignment, p. 145

Reading and Vocabulary Study Guide
- **L1** Chapter 2, Section 1, pp. 9–11

Differentiated Instruction

Spanish Support
- **L2** Section Quiz (Spanish), p. 9 ELL

Key

L1 Basic to Average	**L3** Average to Advanced	
L2 For All Students		

LPR Less Proficient Readers   GT Gifted and Talented
AR Advanced Readers   ELL English Language Learners
SN Special Needs Students

Section 2 Forces Shaping Earth

 1.5 periods, .75 block

Social Studies Objectives
1. Learn about the planet Earth.
2. Explore the forces inside Earth.
3. Explore the forces on Earth's surface.

Reading/Language Arts Objective
Use context clues, such as restatement, to determine the meaning of an unfamiliar word or phrase.

Prepare to Read	Instructional Resources	Differentiated Instruction
Build Background Knowledge Show a video to start a discussion about how forces shape Earth. **Set a Purpose for Reading** Have students begin to fill out the *Reading Readiness Guide.* **Preview Key Terms** Teach the section's Key Terms. **Target Reading Skill** Introduce the section's Target Reading Skill of **using context clues.**	**All in One Foundations of Geography Teaching Resources** L2 Reading Readiness Guide, p. 110 L2 Use Context Clues: Definition/Description, p. 122 **World Studies Video Program** L2 The Ever-Changing Earth	**Spanish Reading and Vocabulary Study Guide** L1 Chapter 2, Section 2, pp. 10–11 ELL

Instruct	Instructional Resources	Differentiated Instruction
Understanding Earth Discuss the properties of Earth, from its core to its atmosphere. **Target Reading Skill** Review **using context clues.** **Forces Inside Earth** Discuss the different forces beneath Earth's surface. **Forces on Earth's Surface** Discuss how the surface of Earth is changing.	**All in One Foundations of Geography Teaching Resources** L2 Guided Reading and Review, p. 111 L2 Reading Readiness Guide, p. 110 **Foundations of Geography Transparencies** L2 Section Reading Support Transparency FG 46	**All in One Foundations of Geography Teaching Resources** L3 A Huge Black Umbrella, pp. 138–140 AR, GT **Teacher's Edition** L1 For English Language Learners, TE p. 36 L3 For Gifted and Talented, TE p. 36 **Spanish Support** L2 Guided Reading and Review (Spanish), p. 10 ELL

Assess and Reteach	Instructional Resources	Differentiated Instruction
Assess Progress Evaluate student comprehension with the section assessment and section quiz. **Reteach** Assign the Reading and Vocabulary Study Guide to help struggling students. **Extend** Extend the lesson by assigning a Small Group Activity.	**All in One Foundations of Geography Teaching Resources** L2 Section Quiz, p. 112 L3 Small Group Activity: Simulation: Making a Poster for the Whitney Classic, pp. 128–131 Rubric for Assessing a Writing Assignment, p. 145 **Reading and Vocabulary Study Guide** L1 Chapter 2, Section 2, pp. 12–14	**Spanish Support** L2 Section Quiz (Spanish), p. 11 ELL

Key
L1 Basic to Average   L3 Average to Advanced   LPR Less Proficient Readers   GT Gifted and Talented

L2 For All Students   AR Advanced Readers   ELL English Language Learners

     SN Special Needs Students

Section 3 Climate and Weather

 3 periods, 1.5 blocks (includes Skills for Life)

Social Studies Objectives
1. Learn about weather and climate.
2. Explore latitude, landforms, and precipitation.
3. Discover how oceans affect climate.

Reading/Language Arts Objective
Use context clues that give a comparison to determine the meaning of a word or phrase.

Prepare to Read

Build Background Knowledge
Have students share ideas about weather and climate.

Set a Purpose for Reading
Have students begin to fill out the *Reading Readiness Guide.*

Preview Key Terms
Teach the section's Key Terms.

Target Reading Skill
Introduce the section's Target Reading Skill of **using context clues.**

Instructional Resources

All in One Foundations of Geography Teaching Resources
- L2 Reading Readiness Guide, p. 114
- L2 Use Context Clues: Compare and Contrast, p. 123

Differentiated Instruction

Spanish Reading and Vocabulary Study Guide
- L1 Chapter 2, Section 3, pp. 12–13 ELL

Instruct

Weather or Climate?
Why Climates Vary
Discuss climate and weather.

Oceans and Climates
Discuss how the ocean affects climate.

Target Reading Skill
Review **using context clues.**

Eyewitness Technology
Have students read about weather forecasting, and then create an outline of the information they learned.

Raging Storms
Ask a question about the characteristics that different storms have in common.

Instructional Resources

All in One Foundations of Geography Teaching Resources
- L2 Guided Reading and Review, p. 115
- L2 Reading Readiness Guide, p. 114

Foundations of Geography Transparencies
- L2 Section Reading Support Transparency FG 47
- L3 Color Transparency FG 41: Climate Graphs

Differentiated Instruction

All in One Foundations of Geography Teaching Resources
- L1 Reading a Climate Map, p. 135 ELL, LPR, SN
  Rubric for Assessing a Student Poem, p. 146 AR, GT
- L3 Writing a Letter, p. 143 AR, GT
- L2 Skills for Life, p. 127 AR, GT, LPR, SN
- L1 Reading a Climate Graph, p. 136 ELL, LPR, SN

Teacher's Edition
- L1 For Special Needs Students, TE p. 42
- L1 For Less Proficient Readers, TE p. 45
- L3 For Gifted and Talented, TE p. 45
- L1 For English Language Learners, TE p. 46
- L3 For Advanced Readers, TE p. 46

Student Edition on Audio CD
- L1 Chapter 2, Section 3 ELL, LPR, SN

Assess and Reteach

Assess Progress
Evaluate student comprehension with the section assessment and section quiz.

Reteach
Assign the Reading and Vocabulary Study Guide to help struggling students.

Extend
Extend the lesson by assigning a role-playing activity.

Instructional Resources

All in One Foundations of Geography Teaching Resources
- L2 Section Quiz, p. 116
  Rubric for Assessing a Role-Playing Activity, p. 147
  Rubric for Assessing a Writing Assignment, p. 145
  Rubric for Assessing a Bar Graph, p. 148
  Rubric for Assessing a Line Graph, p. 149

Reading and Vocabulary Study Guide
- L1 Chapter 2, Section 3, pp. 15–17

Differentiated Instruction

Spanish Support
- L2 Section Quiz (Spanish), p. 13 ELL

Teacher's Edition
- L1 For Special Needs Students, TE p. 49

Social Studies Skills Tutor CD-ROM
- L1 Analyzing Graphic Data ELL, LPR, SN

Key

L1 Basic to Average	L3 Average to Advanced	LPR Less Proficient Readers	GT Gifted and Talented
L2 For All Students		AR Advanced Readers	ELL English Language Learners
		SN Special Needs Students	

Section 4 How Climate Affects Vegetation

 3 periods, 1.5 blocks (includes Chapter Review and Assessment)

Social Studies Objectives

1. Investigate the relationship between climate and vegetation.
2. Explore Earth's vegetation regions.
3. Study vertical climate zones.

Reading/Language Arts Objective

Use context to determine the meaning of a word or phrase when examples are provided.

Prepare to Read

Build Background Knowledge
Have students brainstorm how climate zones affect daily life.

Set a Purpose for Reading
Have students evaluate statements on the *Reading Readiness Guide*.

Preview Key Terms
Teach the section's Key Terms.

Target Reading Skill
Introduce the section's Target Reading Skill of **using context clues**.

Instructional Resources

All in One Foundations of Geography Teaching Resources
- L2 Reading Readiness Guide, p. 118
- L2 Use Context Clues: Examples, p. 124

Differentiated Instruction

Spanish Reading and Vocabulary Study Guide
- L1 Chapter 2, Section 4, pp. 14–15 ELL

Instruct

Climate and Vegetation
Discuss the five broad types of climate.

Earth's Vegetation Regions
Ask a question about the locations of various vegetation regions.

Target Reading Skill
Review **using context clues**.

Vertical Climate Zones
Discuss climates in higher elevations.

Instructional Resources

All in One Foundations of Geography Teaching Resources
- L2 Guided Reading and Review, p. 119
- L2 Reading Readiness Guide, p. 118

Foundations of Geography Transparencies
- L2 Section Reading Support Transparency FG 48
- L2 Color Transparency FG 10: The World: Annual Precipitation (Base)
- L2 Color Transparency FG 12: The World: Desert and Desert Scrub Vegetation Regions (Overlay)

Differentiated Instruction

All in One Foundations of Geography Teaching Resources
- L3 The Endless Steppe, pp. 141–142 AR, GT
- L1 Reading a Natural Vegetation Map, p. 137 ELL, LPR, SN

Teacher's Edition
- L3 For Advanced Readers, TE p. 52
- L1 For Less Proficient Readers, TE p. 52

Spanish Support
- L2 Guided Reading and Review (Spanish), p. 14 ELL

Assess and Reteach

Assess Progress
Evaluate student comprehension with the section assessment and section quiz.

Reteach
Assign the Reading and Vocabulary Study Guide to help struggling students.

Extend
Extend the lesson by having students create posters.

Instructional Resources

All in One Foundations of Geography Teaching Resources
- L2 Section Quiz, p. 120
  - Rubric for Assessing a Poster, p. 150
  - Rubric for Assessing a Writing Assignment, p. 145
- L2 Vocabulary Development, p. 144
- L2 Word Knowledge, p. 125
- L2 Chapter Tests A and B, pp. 151–156

Reading and Vocabulary Study Guide
- L1 Chapter 2, Section 4, pp. 18–20

Differentiated Instruction

Spanish Support
- L2 Section Quiz (Spanish), p. 15 ELL
- L2 Chapter Summary (Spanish), p. 16 ELL
- L2 Vocabulary Development (Spanish), p. 17 ELL

Key

- L1 Basic to Average
- L3 Average to Advanced
- L2 For All Students
- LPR Less Proficient Readers
- AR Advanced Readers
- SN Special Needs Students
- GT Gifted and Talented
- ELL English Language Learners

Professional Development

Reading Background

Paragraph Puzzles

In this activity, students are asked to put a paragraph's sentences in the correct order. Explain to students that this activity will help them understand paragraph structure. The activity teaches students to distinguish a topic sentence that contains the main idea from the supporting details. Doing a paragraph puzzle activity also helps students practice sequencing steps and ideas.

Begin by writing a paragraph on a piece of paper with each sentence on its own line. Cut the sentences into narrow strips, and place the strips in an envelope. Divide students into pairs and distribute one envelope to each pair. Ask students to arrange the sentences into a logical paragraph.

Extend this strategy by challenging students to recall the plot of a short story, the sequence of events necessary to solve a math problem, or the steps involved in a scientific experiment. Ask students to write down the sentences, cut them into individual sentences, and place them in an envelope. Have students exchange envelopes with a partner and put the sentences in the correct order. Students should then explain their rationale.

Power Notes

This strategy can help students clarify the difference between main ideas and details. The Power Notes strategy is similar to creating an outline, but simpler because main ideas and details are assigned different numbers. Main ideas are power 1 ideas. Details are either power 2s or 3s. Students can use this technique to organize information for reading, writing, and studying.

Write the following on the board:

Power 1: Main Idea

Power 2: Detail or support for power 1

Power 3: Detail or support for power 2

Model this approach by using information from the chapter:

Power 1: The effect of Earth's tilt on its axis

Power 2: Toward the sun creates Summer

Power 3: Longer daylight and more direct sunlight

Power 2: Away from the sun creates Winter

Power 3: Shorter daylight and sunlight is less direct

Another way to practice this skill is to write power 1s from the chapter on the board and have students take turns filling in the supporting details.

World Studies Background

Our Solar System

The nine planets of our solar system orbit around the sun in a counterclockwise direction. The innermost planets—Mercury, Venus, Earth, and Mars—are relatively small and have solid surfaces. They have few or no moons and no ring systems. The outermost planets—Jupiter, Saturn, Uranus, and Neptune—are larger and are made up of gases. They have many moons, ranging in number from eight for Neptune to at least 18 for Saturn. Each of the outer planets has a ring system. Pluto is in a category by itself because it resembles the icy moons of the outer planets. It has only one moon and does not have any rings.

Volcanoes

More than 80 percent of Earth's surface—above and below sea level—is of volcanic origin. Most volcanoes are located on the edges of continents, along island chains, or beneath the sea in long mountain ranges. About 500 volcanoes have erupted above sea level throughout history. More than half of them encircle the Pacific Ocean to form the Ring of Fire. After Indonesia and Japan, the United States has the highest number of historically active volcanoes.

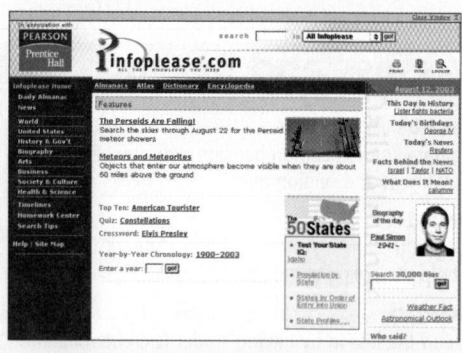

Infoplease® provides a wealth of useful information for the classroom. You can use this resource to strengthen your background on the subjects covered in this chapter. Have students visit this advertising-free site as a starting point for projects requiring research.

Use Web code **led-3200** for **Infoplease.**

Using the Choral Reading Technique Effectively

The Choral Reading strategy encourages participation by all students because it provides a non-threatening reading environment. To maximize success with this strategy, choose shorter passages (fewer than 500 words) and encourage students to stay with your voice, so that everyone reads at the same rate. When students have finished reading in unison, allow time for students to reread the passage silently, focusing on new or unfamiliar words.

Read-Cover-Recite-Check

Read-Cover-Recite-Check is a useful strategy for helping students to retain the information they read. It can be especially effective when students are studying for a test. Model the steps for using Read-Cover-Recite-Check to read the first paragraph on page 28 of the Student Edition.

1. Read the paragraph quickly to grasp the main ideas. (*Think aloud about the main idea: this paragraph is about a galaxy.*)
2. Reread the paragraph, looking for details and key information. (*Think aloud, noting the details: the Milky Way is a galaxy. It is made up of Earth, the sun, other planets, and stars. Our sun is a star in the Milky Way.*)
3. Cover the paragraph with your hand or a piece of paper. Recall and repeat the information from the paragraph, including the topic and important details. (*Think aloud: repeat the main idea and details from steps 1 and 2, using different phrasing.*)
4. Rephrase the paragraph in your own words. (*The Milky Way is a galaxy that includes planets and stars. It looks like a white streak across the sky. The sun is not the center of the Milky Way, but it is the center of Earth's orbit.*)
5. Check to make sure you remembered correctly.

Weather Conditions

Weather takes place in the lowest region of the atmosphere known as the troposphere. Geographic features such as mountains and large bodies of water significantly impact the weather. The temperature of the ocean can be responsible for a drought in one area and heavy rains in another. Because weather has such a great effect on human settlement patterns, food production, and personal comfort, people are often reliant on forecasts. The National Meteorological Center (NMC) collects data from devices such as weather satellites, barometers, and radar. This information is used to create weather maps for geographic regions throughout the world.

The Amazon Rainforest

The Amazon Rainforest in northern South America exists because of the high rainfall, high humidity, and high temperatures of the region. About half of the Amazon's rainfall is evaporated moisture from the Atlantic. The rest is moisture evaporated from the rainforest itself. Blanketing an area of 2,300,000 square miles (6,000,000 sq km), this rainforest is the world's richest and most biologically diverse, with millions of species of animals and plants.

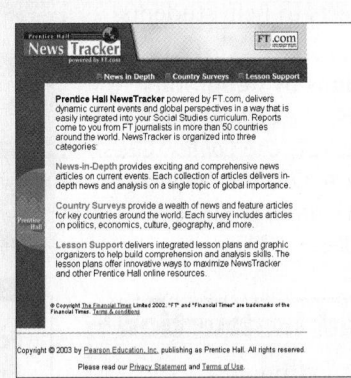

Get in-depth information on topics of global importance with **Prentice Hall Newstracker,** powered by FT.com.

 Use Web code **led-3203** for **Prentice Hall Newstracker.**

Guiding Questions

Remind students about the Guiding Questions introduced at the beginning of the book.

Section 1 relates to **Guiding Question** ❶
What are Earth's major physical features?
(Earth's movement in relation to the sun causes day and night. The tilt of Earth combined with Earth's rotation around the sun causes seasons.)

Section 2 relates to **Guiding Question** ❶
What are Earth's major physical features?
(More than 70 percent of Earth's surface is made up of water. Landforms such as mountains, plains, hills, volcanoes, and plateaus cover the other 30 percent of Earth's surface.)

Section 3 relates to **Guiding Question** ❶
What are Earth's major physical features?
(Earth's oceans and landforms can affect climates. Places located on coasts have more moderate temperatures due to the slow cooling and heating of the ocean. Mountains can also affect climates.)

Section 4 relates to **Guiding Question** ❶
What are Earth's major physical features?
(Vegetation varies widely across Earth according to climate and type of soil.)

⤵ Target Reading Skill

In this chapter, students will learn and apply the reading skill of using context clues. Use the following worksheets to help students practice this skill:

All in One Foundations of Geography Teaching Resources, *Use Context Clues: General Knowledge,* p. 121; *Use Context Clues: Definition/Description,* p. 122; *Use Context Clues: Compare and Contrast,* p. 123; *Use Context Clues: Examples,* p. 124

Differentiated Instruction

The following Teacher's Edition strategies are suitable for students of varying abilities.

Advanced Readers, pp. 46, 52
English Language Learners, pp. 36, 46
Gifted and Talented, pp. 31, 36, 45
Less Proficient Readers, pp. 31, 45, 52
Special Needs Students, pp. 42, 49

Chapter 2 Earth's Physical Geography

Chapter Preview

This chapter will introduce you to the physical geography of Earth, including the planet's structure, climate, and vegetation.

Section 1
Our Planet, Earth

Section 2
Forces Shaping Earth

Section 3
Climate and Weather

Section 4
How Climate Affects Vegetation

Target Reading Skill

Context In this chapter you will focus on using context to help you understand unfamiliar words. Context includes the words, phrases, and sentences surrounding a word.

▶ **Delicate Arch in Arches National Park, Utah**

Bibliography

For the Teacher
Erickson, Jon and Ernest H. Muller. *Plate Tectonics: Unraveling the Mysteries of the Earth.* Checkmark Books, 2001.
Zeilinga De Boer, Jelle and Donald Theodore Sanders. *Volcanoes in Human History: The Far-Reaching Effects of Major Eruptions.* Princeton University Press, 2001.

For the Student
L1 Arthus-Bertrand, Yann. *Earth from Above for Young Readers.* Abrams, 2002.
L2 Berger, Melvin. *Why Do Volcanoes Blow Their Tops?* Scholastic Reference, 2000.
L3 Oldershaw, Cally, *Atlas of Geology and Landforms.* Scholastic Library, 2001.

Chapter 2 **27**

Reach Into Your Background Draw students' attention to the caption accompanying the picture on page 26.

Discuss the visual with your students. What strikes them about the image in this photo? Encourage students to share their ideas about how these rock formations may have formed. Ask students to share any experiences they have had traveling to state and national parks to see unusual landforms.

Chapter Resources

Teaching Resources
L2 Vocabulary Development, p. 144
L2 Skills for Life, p. 127
L2 Chapter Tests A and B, pp. 151–156

Spanish Support
L2 Spanish Chapter Summary, p. 18
L2 Spanish Vocabulary Development, p. 19

Media and Technology
L1 Student Edition on Audio CD
L1 Guided Reading Audiotapes, English and Spanish
L2 Social Studies Skills Tutor CD-ROM
ExamView Test Bank CD-ROM

PRENTICE HALL
Presentation EXPRESS™
Teach · Connect · Inspire

Teach this chapter's content using the PresentationExpress™ CD-ROM including:

- slide shows
- transparencies
- interactive maps and media
- *ExamView*® QuickTake Presenter

Our Planet, Earth

Objectives
Social Studies
1. Learn about Earth's movement in relation to the sun.
2. Explore seasons and latitude.

Reading/Language Arts
Use context clues from surrounding phrases to determine the meaning of unfamiliar words.

Prepare to Read

Build Background Knowledge L2
Tell students that they will learn about Earth's movements and how they affect the seasons and latitude in this section. Ask students to look through the section and predict the effects of Earth's movements. Provide a few simple examples to get students started. Conduct an Idea Wave (TE, p. T35) to generate a list.

Set a Purpose for Reading L2
- Preview the Objectives.

- Form students into pairs or groups of four. Distribute the *Reading Readiness Guide*. Ask students to fill in the first two columns of the chart. Use the Numbered Heads participation strategy (TE, p. T36) to call on students to share one piece of information they already know and one piece of information they want to know.

All in One Foundations of Geography Teaching Resources, *Reading Readiness Guide*, p. 106

Vocabulary Builder
Preview Key Terms L2
Create a three-column "See It—Remember It" chart of the Key Terms on the board. Write a term in the first column, a short definition in the second column, and a sketch in the third column. Guide students as they copy and complete the chart.

Prepare to Read

Objectives
In this section you will
1. Learn about Earth's movement in relation to the sun.
2. Explore seasons and latitude.

Taking Notes
Copy the table below. As you read this section, fill in the table with information about the movements of Earth relative to the sun, days and nights, seasons, and latitude. Add more lines as you need them.

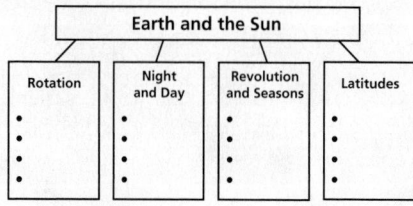

Earth and the Sun

Rotation	Night and Day	Revolution and Seasons	Latitudes
•	•	•	•
•	•	•	•
•	•	•	•
•	•	•	•

Target Reading Skill
Use Context Clues You can sometimes find the meaning of a word by using context—the words and sentences around that word. In some cases the context will describe the word. In this example, the phrase in italics describes a planet:

A planet is a large object that circles a star.

As you read, look at the context for the word *galaxy* in the paragraph below. What do you think *galaxy* means?

Key Terms
- **orbit** (AWR bit) *n.* the path one body makes as it circles around another
- **revolution** (rev uh LOO shun) *n.* circular motion
- **axis** (AK sis) *n.* an imaginary line through Earth between the North and South poles, around which Earth turns
- **rotation** (roh TAY shun) *n.* a complete turn

The Milky Way Galaxy

28 Foundations of Geography

Earth and the Sun

Earth, the sun, the planets, and the stars in the sky are all part of a galaxy, or family of stars. Our galaxy is just one of the billions of galaxies in the universe. We call our galaxy the Milky Way because, in a dark night sky, away from city lights, its billions of stars look like a trail of spilled milk. Our sun is one of those stars. The sun is just a tiny speck compared to the rest of the Milky Way, but it is the center of everything for Earth and the other planets in the solar system. The solar system includes Earth, the other planets, and other objects that orbit the sun.

Even though the sun is about 93 million miles (150 million kilometers) away, it provides Earth with heat and light. Earth travels around the sun in a nearly circular **orbit**, which is the path one body makes as it circles around another. Earth takes $365\frac{1}{4}$ days, or one year, to complete one **revolution**, or circular motion, in its orbit around the sun.

Target Reading Skill L2

Use Context Clues Point out the Target Reading Skill. Tell students that information surrounding an unknown word can provide clues to the word's meaning.

Model context clues to find the meaning of *polar zones* in this sentence from page 32: "The areas above the Arctic Circle and below the Antarctic Circle are the high latitudes, or the polar zones." (*The polar zones are defined in context as the areas of high latitude above the Arctic Circle and below the Antarctic Circle.*)

Give students *Use Context Clues: General Knowledge*. Have them complete the activity in groups.

All in One Foundations of Geography Teaching Resources, *Use Context Clues: General Knowledge*, p. 121

Understanding Days and Nights As Earth circles the sun, it also spins in space. Earth turns around its **axis**—an imaginary line running through Earth between the North and South poles. Each complete turn, or **rotation**, takes about 24 hours. As Earth rotates, it is night on the side away from the sun. As Earth turns toward the sun, the sun appears to rise. When a side of Earth faces the sun, it is daytime. Then, as that side of Earth turns away from the sun, the sun appears to set.

Time Zones Earth rotates toward the east, so the day starts earlier in the east. The time difference is just a few seconds per mile. If every town had its own local time, it would be very confusing. So, governments have divided the world into standard time zones. Times in neighboring zones are one hour apart. There are also a few nonstandard time zones with times less than a full hour away from their neighbors.

✓ **Reading Check** What is the connection between Earth's rotation and the change from day to night?

Links to Math

Time Zones and Longitude
Earth's surface is divided into 360 degrees of longitude: 180 degrees east and west of the Prime Meridian. Since Earth rotates at a steady rate in about 24 hours, its 24 standard time zones are centered the same number of degrees of longitude apart. Can you find this number? (*Hint:* The number is 360° ÷ 24.)

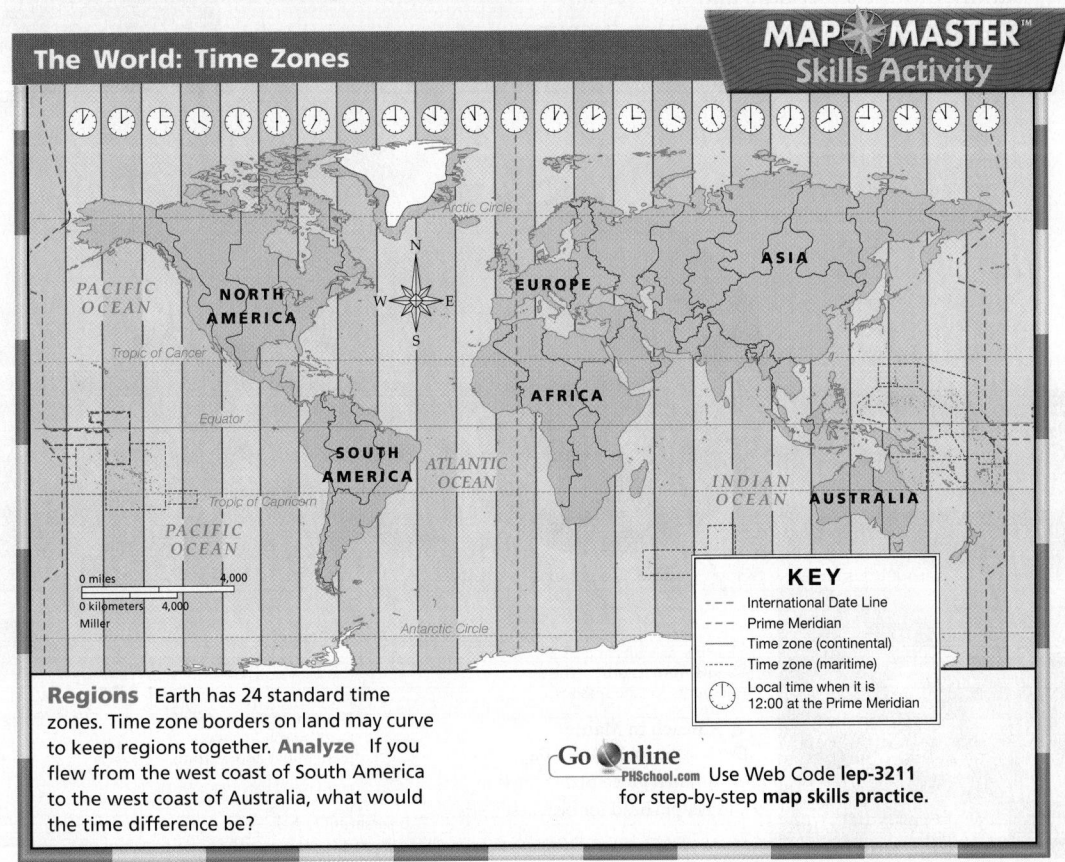

MAP MASTER™ Skills Activity

The World: Time Zones

KEY
- – – International Date Line
- – – Prime Meridian
- —— Time zone (continental)
- ⋯⋯ Time zone (maritime)
- 🕐 Local time when it is 12:00 at the Prime Meridian

Regions Earth has 24 standard time zones. Time zone borders on land may curve to keep regions together. **Analyze** If you flew from the west coast of South America to the west coast of Australia, what would the time difference be?

Go Online PHSchool.com Use Web Code **lep-3211** for step-by-step **map skills practice**.

Chapter 2 Section 1 **29**

Vocabulary Builder

Use the information below to teach students this section's high-use words.

High-Use Word	Definition and Sample Sentence
standard, p. 29	*n.* something set up as a rule or model with which others are compared. Juan's excellent presentation set the **standard** for the rest of the class.
relative, p. 30	*adj.* as compared with someone or something else. My teacher is very short **relative** to the principal.

Guided Instruction

■ **Vocabulary Builder** Clarify the high-use word **standard** before reading.

■ Read Earth and the Sun using the Paragraph Shrinking strategy (TE, p. T34). Ask students to study The World: Time Zones map and the caption on this page.

■ Ask students **What is the relationship between Earth's rotation and time zones?** (*It takes 24 hours for Earth to rotate through each of its 24 time zones.*)

■ Ask students to predict how the cycle of day and night would be affected if Earth's rotation were slower. (*If Earth's rotation were slower, the day would be longer than 24 hours.*)

■ Tell students that every four years is a leap year of 366 days. Have them draw a conclusion as to why. (*If there are 365 1/4 days every year, then every four years there is one extra day, so leap year has 366 days.*)

Independent Practice

Ask students to create the Taking Notes graphic organizer on a blank piece of paper. Then have them fill in the "Rotation" and "Night and Day" boxes with information they have just learned. Briefly model how to identify which details to record.

Monitor Progress

As students fill in the graphic organizer, circulate and make sure individuals are selecting the correct details. Provide assistance as needed.

Links

Read the **Links to Math** box on this page with students. Guide them as they calculate that 360 divided by 24 is 15.

Answers

✓ **Reading Check** As Earth rotates, it is night on the side facing away from the sun. When the side away from the sun faces the sun, it is daytime.

MAP MASTER Skills Activity **Analyze** 11 hours

Seasons and Latitude L2

Guided Instruction

- **Vocabulary Builder** Clarify the high-use word **relative** before reading.

- Read how Earth's movement and latitude affect the seasons in Seasons and Latitude. Ask students to study the diagram titled The Revolution of Earth. As a class, answer the Geography Skills Practice question.

- Ask students **What happens in the Northern Hemisphere during the summer solstice?** *(The Northern Hemisphere is tilted farthest toward the sun.)* **How does this tilt affect the region?** *(The days are longer and the temperature is higher.)*

- Ask students **What is the season in Australia when it is winter in the United States?** *(summer)*

Target Reading Skill L2

Using Context Clues As a follow up, ask students to perform the Target Reading Skill activity in the Student Edition. Then ask **What words in the text describe the summer solstice?** *(the Northern Hemisphere is tilted farthest toward the sun)*

Seasons and Latitude

The axis of Earth is tilted relative to its orbit. At different points in Earth's orbit, the Northern Hemisphere may tilt toward or away from the sun. At other points in the orbit, neither hemisphere tilts toward or away from the sun. The revolution of the tilted planet Earth causes seasons.

At the summer solstice, the Northern Hemisphere is tilted farthest toward the sun. Places in this hemisphere have longer daylight and more direct sunlight at the solstice than at other times of the year. This direct sunlight causes the heat of summer.

Use Context Clues If you do not know what the summer solstice is, look at the words that follow this term in the text. They describe the summer solstice.

The Revolution of Earth

As Earth travels around the sun, the tilt of its axis causes our seasons. Each hemisphere shifts from the long days and direct sun of summer to the short days and indirect sun of winter, and then back again. This diagram shows seasons in the Northern Hemisphere.

Spring ►
At the spring equinox, about March 21, days and nights are nearly equal in length. Earth's axis tilts "sideways." The sun is directly over the Equator.

Summer ►
At the summer solstice, about June 21, the sun is directly over the Tropic of Cancer. North of the Arctic Circle, the sun never sets, and there is continuous daylight.

23.5°

Earth's axis tilts at a 23.5° angle from its orbit. This accounts for the seasons.

◄ A Beach in Maine
During the long, warm days of summer, green plants grow and people head for beaches.

The sun, at the center of Earth's orbit, gives our planet light and warmth.

Diagram not to scale

30 Foundations of Geography

Skills for Life — Skills Mini Lesson

Identifying Cause and Effect

1. Teach identifying cause and effect by pointing out that students can choose a specific event as a starting point and look at earlier events to determine possible causes. They can look at later events to help them identify effects.

2. Help students practice the skill by looking at the diagram on pp. 30–31. Have students determine an effect of Earth's movement.

3. Have students apply the skill by determining the effect of the following cause: the sun is directly over the Tropic of Cancer north of the Arctic Circle at summer solstice.

As Earth moves through its orbit, the Northern Hemisphere is tilted farther from the sun. Sunlight is less direct, and we have the chill of fall. When the Northern Hemisphere is tilted farthest from the sun at the winter solstice, days are short, the sun's rays reach us at a steep angle, and we have cold weather. Finally, Earth's revolution moves the Northern Hemisphere back toward the sun, and we have the warming trend of spring.

When the Northern Hemisphere is tilted toward the sun, the Southern Hemisphere is tilted away, and vice versa, so the seasons are reversed in the Southern Hemisphere.

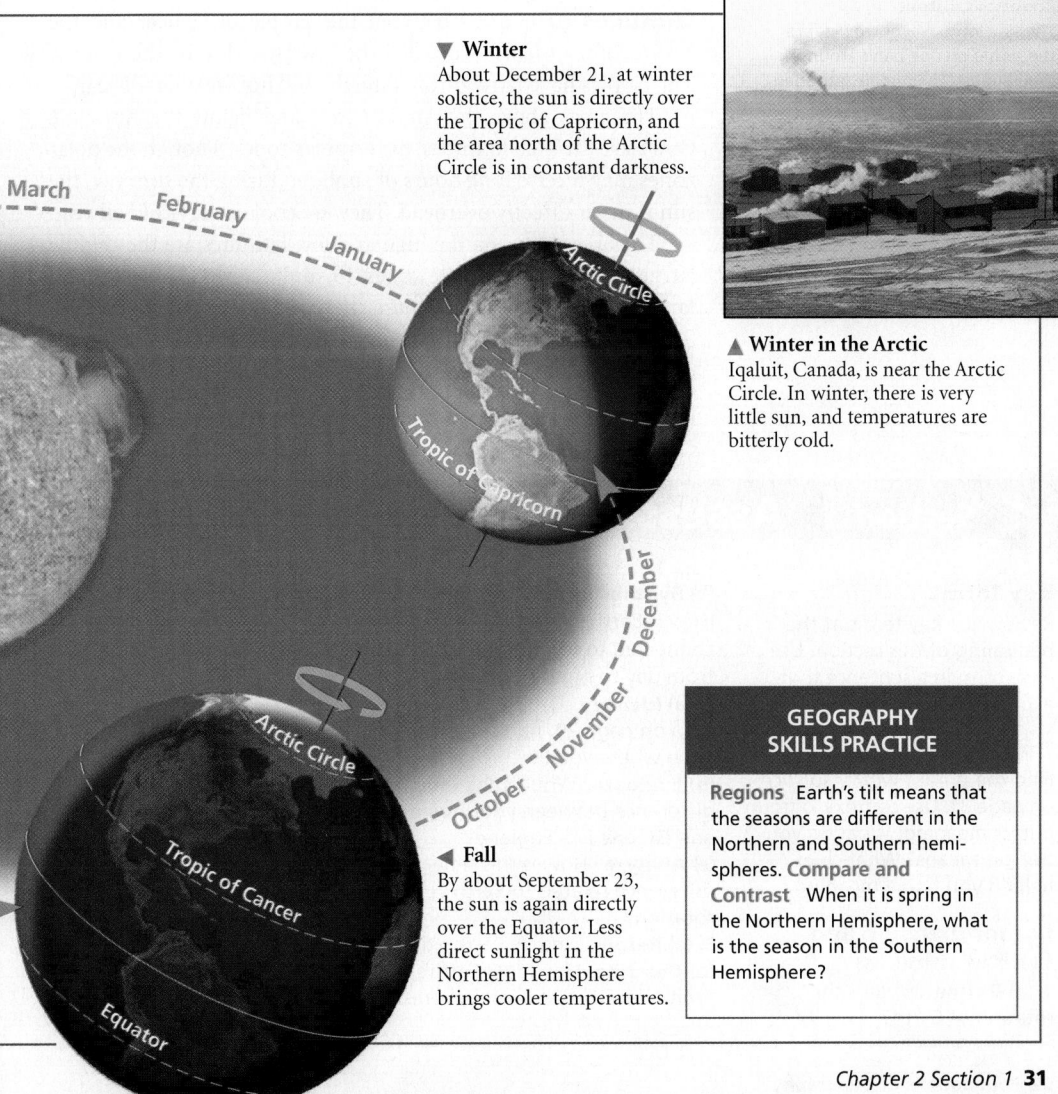

▼ Winter
About December 21, at winter solstice, the sun is directly over the Tropic of Capricorn, and the area north of the Arctic Circle is in constant darkness.

March
February
January
Arctic Circle
Tropic of Capricorn
December
November
October
Arctic Circle
Tropic of Cancer
Equator

▲ Winter in the Arctic
Iqaluit, Canada, is near the Arctic Circle. In winter, there is very little sun, and temperatures are bitterly cold.

◀ Fall
By about September 23, the sun is again directly over the Equator. Less direct sunlight in the Northern Hemisphere brings cooler temperatures.

GEOGRAPHY SKILLS PRACTICE

Regions Earth's tilt means that the seasons are different in the Northern and Southern hemispheres. **Compare and Contrast** When it is spring in the Northern Hemisphere, what is the season in the Southern Hemisphere?

Differentiated Instruction

For Gifted and Talented　　L3
Have students learn more about the Tropics of Cancer and Capricorn by completing the *Enrichment* activity. Then, have them write a brief summary of their research to attach to their map and diagrams.

All in One Foundations of Geography Teaching Resources, *Enrichment,* p. 126

For Less Proficient Readers　　L1
To help students who are having difficulty understanding the concepts described in this section, have students complete *Understanding Movements of the Earth.*

All in One Foundations of Geography Teaching Resources, *Understanding Movements of the Earth,* p. 134

Guided Instruction (continued)

■ Ask students **Where are the high latitudes located?** (*above the Arctic and below the Antarctic circles*) **If this area receives very long hours of sunlight, why do you think it is so cold?** (*The sun is not directly overhead and therefore doesn't cause the temperature to rise.*)

Independent Practice

Have students complete the graphic organizer by filling in the "Revolution and Seasons" and "Latitudes" boxes.

Monitor Progress

■ Show *Section Reading Support Transparency FG 45* and ask students to check their graphic organizers individually. Go over key concepts and clarify key vocabulary as needed.

　📖 **Foundations of Geography Transparencies,** *Section Reading Support Transparency FG 45*

■ Tell students to fill in the last column of their *Reading Readiness Guides.* Ask them to evaluate if what they learned was what they had expected to learn.

　All in One Foundations of Geography Teaching Resources, *Reading Readiness Guide,* p. 110

Answer
Geography Skills Practice Compare and Contrast Fall

Assess and Reteach

Assess Progress L2

Have students complete the Section Assessment. Administer the *Section Quiz.*

All in One **Foundations of Geography Teaching Resources,** Section Quiz, p. 108

Reteach L1

If students need more instruction, have them read this section in the Reading and Vocabulary Study Guide.

Chapter 2, Section 1, **Eastern Hemisphere Reading and Vocabulary Study Guide,** pp. 9–11

Extend L3

To extend the lesson, pair students and distribute the *Activity Shop Lab: The Earth's Seasons.* Have students make a model of Earth's path around the sun. Then, have them describe their observations as they follow the activity's steps as well as answer the questions provided.

All in One **Foundations of Geography Teaching Resources,** *Activity Shop Lab: The Earth's Seasons,* pp. 132–133

Answer

✔ **Reading Check** The higher the latitude the longer the winter, and the lower the latitude the longer the summer. For the middle latitude, the four seasons are more distinct.

Section 1 Assessment

Key Terms
Students' sentences should reflect knowledge of each Key Term.

Target Reading Skill
The winter solstice occurs when the Northern Hemisphere is tilted farthest from the sun. The clue is given in the phrase before the term in the sentence.

Comprehension and Critical Thinking
1. (a) A rotation is one complete turn of Earth around its axis, which takes 24 hours. **(b)** As Earth rotates, it is night on the side facing away from the sun. As that side of Earth turns toward the sun, it becomes day.
2. (a) Answers will vary, but students should be able to identify the correct time zone. **(b)** Answers will vary, but students should correctly calculate the time difference between the Prime Meridian and where they live.

32 *Foundations of Geography*

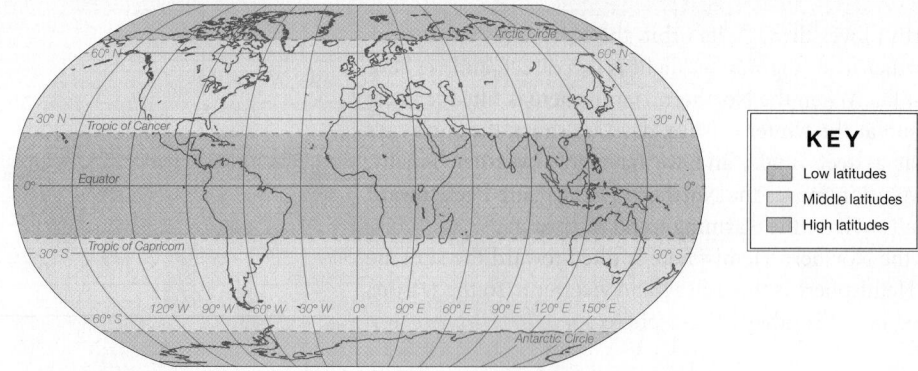

Zones of Latitude
The low latitudes, or tropics, are the single orange band around the Equator. The middle latitudes are the two yellow bands just to the north and south. The two green zones in the far north and south are the high latitudes, or polar zones.

Latitudes The areas between the Tropic of Cancer and the Tropic of Capricorn are called the low latitudes, or the tropics. The tropics have fairly direct sunlight and hot weather all year.

The areas above the Arctic Circle and below the Antarctic Circle are the high latitudes, or the polar zones. Though the polar zones may receive long hours of sunlight during the summer, the sun is never directly overhead. They are cool or very cold all year.

The areas between the high and low latitudes are the middle latitudes, or the temperate zones. In summer, these areas receive fairly direct sunlight. In winter, they get very indirect sunlight. So, the middle latitudes have marked seasons: a hot summer, a cold winter, and a moderate spring and fall.

✔ **Reading Check** What is the relation between seasons and latitude?

Section **1** Assessment

Key Terms
Review the key terms at the beginning of this section. Use each term in a sentence that explains its meaning.

Target Reading Skill
Find the phrase *winter solstice* on page 31. Use context to figure out its meaning. What do you think it means? What clues helped you find a meaning?

Comprehension and Critical Thinking
1. (a) Define What is the rotation of Earth?

(b) Synthesize Information
How is Earth's rotation connected to the change from day to night?
2. (a) Identify On the time zone map on page 29, find the time zone where you live.
(b) Evaluate What is the time difference between your home and Greenwich, England?
(c) Analyze How is this time difference related to Earth's rotation?
3. (a) Recall What is Earth's tilt?
(b) Describe How does Earth's orbit affect its tilted hemispheres?

(c) Identify Cause and Effect
How do Earth's tilt and orbit cause the seasons?

Writing Activity
Write a short passage for a younger child, explaining the movements of Earth.

For: An activity on our planet, Earth
Visit: PHSchool.com
Web Code: led-3201

32 Foundations of Geography

(c) Earth is divided into 24 standard time zones because Earth takes about 24 hours to rotate. The time at a location differs depending on how far from the Prime Meridian its time zone is located.

3. (a) Earth's tilt is the degree to which Earth leans toward or away from the sun. **(b)** At different points in Earth's orbit, the hemispheres tilt at varying degrees toward or away from the sun. **(c)** The shift in Earth's tilt causes the seasons by changing the distance and angle of different parts of the Earth from the sun.

Writing Activity
Use the *Rubric for Assessing a Writing Assignment* to evaluate students' passages.

All in One **Foundations of Geography Teaching Resources,** *Rubric for Assessing a Writing Assignment,* p. 145

Go Online PHSchool.com Typing in the Web code when prompted will bring students directly to detailed instructions for this activity.

32 *Foundations of Geography*

Prepare to Read

Objectives
In this section you will
1. Learn about the planet Earth.
2. Explore the forces inside Earth.
3. Explore the forces on Earth's surface.

Taking Notes
As you read this section, look for details about Earth's structure, Earth's landforms, forces inside Earth, how continents move, and forces on Earth's surface. Copy the web diagram below, add more branches and ovals as needed, and write each detail in the correct oval.

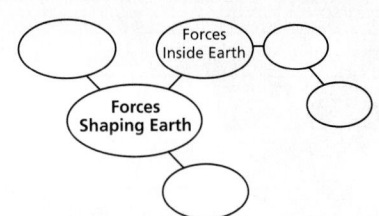

Target Reading Skill
Use Context Clues You can sometimes find the meaning of a word or phrase by using context. Sometimes the context will define or restate the word. In this example, the phrase in italics defines *continent*:

A continent, or *one of Earth's large land areas . . .*

As you read, look at the context for the phrase *Ring of Fire* in the paragraph below. What do you think the phrase *Ring of Fire* means?

Key Terms
- **core** (kawr) *n.* the sphere of very hot metal at the center of Earth
- **mantle** (MAN tul) *n.* the thick layer around Earth's core
- **crust** (krust) *n.* the thin, rocky layer on Earth's surface
- **magma** (MAG muh) *n.* soft, nearly molten rock
- **plate** (playt) *n.* a huge block of Earth's crust
- **weathering** (WETH ur ing) *n.* a process that breaks rocks down into small pieces
- **erosion** (ee ROH zhun) *n.* the removal of small pieces of rock by water, ice, or wind

Understanding Earth

Around the rim of the Pacific Ocean is a string of volcanoes and earthquake belts called the "Ring of Fire." About 80 percent of the world's earthquakes and many of the world's active volcanoes occur in that ring. Earthquakes and volcanoes are two forces that shape and reshape Earth. They are one reason why Earth's surface constantly changes. They also provide clues about Earth's structure.

Hot rock from inside Earth flows into the Pacific Ocean to form new land in Hawaii.

Target Reading Skill

Use Context Clues Point out the Target Reading Skill. Tell students that using context clues, such as definition and restatement, is one way to find the meaning of an unfamiliar word or phrase.

Model using context clues to find the meaning of fresh water in this sentence from page 35: "Very little of Earth's water is fresh water, or water without salt." (*The phrase* fresh water *means* water without salt.)

Give students *Use Context Clues: Definition/Description*. Have them complete the activity in groups.

All in One Foundations of Geography Teaching Resources, *Use Context Clues: Definition/Description,* p. 122

Objectives
Social Studies
1. Learn about the planet Earth.
2. Explore the forces inside Earth.
3. Explore the forces on Earth's surface.

Reading/Language Arts
Use context clues, such as restatement, to determine the meaning of an unfamiliar word or phrase.

Prepare to Read

Build Background Knowledge L2
Tell students that in this section they will learn about the forces that shape Earth, both inside and out. Show students the *The Ever-Changing Earth*. Then ask students how moving plates cause volcanic eruptions. Use the Give One, Get One participation strategy (TE, p. T37) to generate answers.

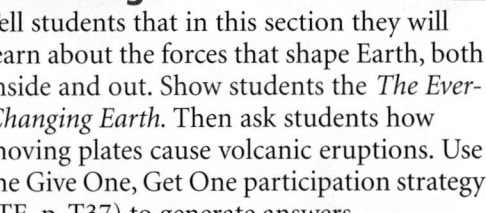

The Ever-Changing Earth, **World Studies Video Program**

Set a Purpose for Reading L2
- Preview the Objectives.
- Read each statement in the *Reading Readiness Guide* aloud. Ask students to mark the statements true or false.
- Have students discuss the statements in pairs or groups of four, then mark their worksheets again. Use the Numbered Heads participation strategy (TE, p. T36) to call on students to share their group's perspectives.

All in One Foundations of Geography Teaching Resources, *Reading Readiness Guide,* p. 110

Vocabulary Builder
Preview Key Terms
Pronounce each Key Term, then ask the students to say the word with you. Provide a simple explanation such as, "The shifting of Earth's plates can sometimes be felt as an earthquake."

Understanding Earth L2

Guided Instruction

- **Vocabulary Builder** Clarify the high-use word **force** before reading.

- Read Understanding Earth using the Oral Cloze strategy (TE, p. T33). Ask students to review the diagram of Earth's Layers on this page. As a class, answer the Analyze Images question. Allow students to discuss their answers with a partner before sharing them with the class.

- Ask students to name the sources of heat that help shape Earth's crust. *(the core: a ball of very hot metal at the center of the earth; the mantle: the hot, rocky layer around the core)*

What Is Earth Made Of? To understand the forces that shape Earth, you must study Earth's structure. A sphere of very hot metal at the center of Earth is called the **core**. The **mantle** is a thick, hot, rocky layer around the core. The thin layer of rocks and minerals that surrounds the mantle is called the **crust**. In effect, the crust floats on top of the mantle. The heat of the core and mantle helps shape Earth's crust. The surface of the crust includes Earth's land areas as well as the ocean floors.

Earth's Layers

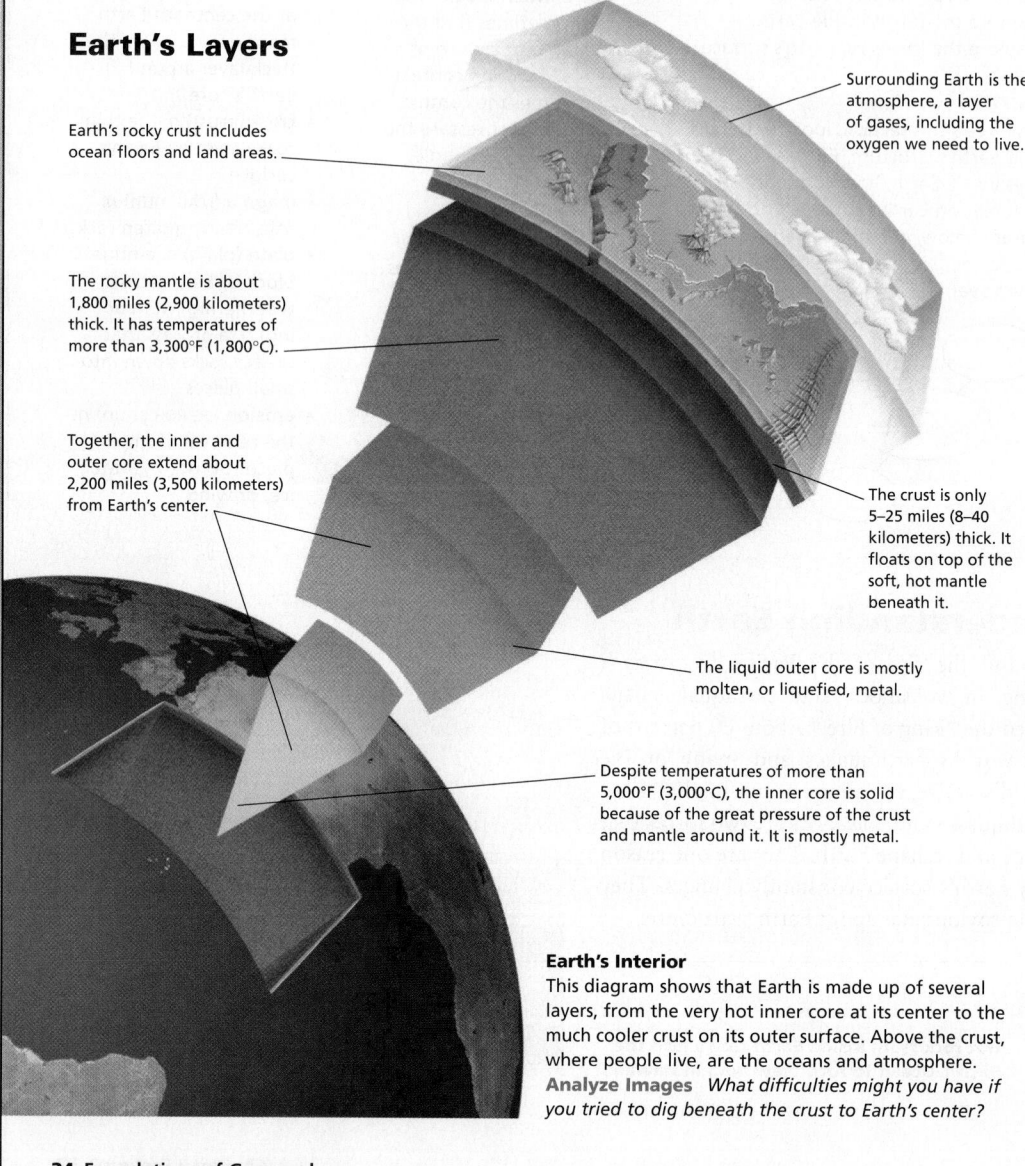

Earth's rocky crust includes ocean floors and land areas.

Surrounding Earth is the atmosphere, a layer of gases, including the oxygen we need to live.

The rocky mantle is about 1,800 miles (2,900 kilometers) thick. It has temperatures of more than 3,300°F (1,800°C).

Together, the inner and outer core extend about 2,200 miles (3,500 kilometers) from Earth's center.

The crust is only 5–25 miles (8–40 kilometers) thick. It floats on top of the soft, hot mantle beneath it.

The liquid outer core is mostly molten, or liquefied, metal.

Despite temperatures of more than 5,000°F (3,000°C), the inner core is solid because of the great pressure of the crust and mantle around it. It is mostly metal.

Earth's Interior
This diagram shows that Earth is made up of several layers, from the very hot inner core at its center to the much cooler crust on its outer surface. Above the crust, where people live, are the oceans and atmosphere. **Analyze Images** *What difficulties might you have if you tried to dig beneath the crust to Earth's center?*

Answers

Analyze Images Possible answers: A person could not withstand the extremely high temperatures; the disturbance might cause a volcano to erupt or an earthquake; the escaping gases might affect the atmosphere that surrounds Earth.

Vocabulary Builder

Use the information below to teach students this section's high-use words.

High-Use Word	Definition and Sample Sentence
force, p. 33	*n.* strength, power, energy The pitcher threw the baseball with great **force**.
collide, p. 37	*v.* to crash against each other The icy road conditions caused the two cars to **collide**.
surge, p. 37	*v.* to swell and move with force She felt her energy **surge** after her third cup of coffee.
splinter, p. 37	*v.* to split into fragments or parts If the wind blows hard enough, the dead tree may **splinter** and fall.

Water and Air Less than 30 percent of Earth's surface is land. Water covers more than 70 percent of Earth's surface in lakes, rivers, seas, and oceans. The oceans hold about 97 percent of Earth's water. This water is salty. Very little of Earth's water is fresh water, or water without salt. Most fresh water is frozen in ice sheets near the North and South poles. People can use only a small part of Earth's fresh water. This fresh water comes from lakes, rivers, and ground water, which are fed by rain.

Above Earth's surface is the atmosphere, a layer of gases a few miles thick. It provides life-giving oxygen to people and animals, and carbon dioxide to plants.

Landforms Many different landforms, or shapes and types of land, cover Earth's land surfaces. Mountains are landforms that rise more than 2,000 feet (610 meters) above sea level or the surrounding flatlands. They are wide at the bottom and rise steeply to a narrow peak or ridge. A volcano is a kind of mountain. Hills are landforms with rounded tops, which rise above the surrounding land but are lower and less steep than mountains. A plateau is a large, mostly flat area that rises above the surrounding land. At least one side of a plateau has a steep slope. Plains are large areas of flat or gently rolling land.

✔ **Reading Check** Which layer of Earth contains all of its landforms?

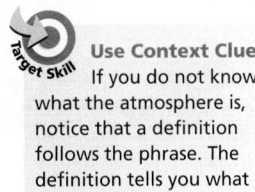

Use Context Clues
If you do not know what the atmosphere is, notice that a definition follows the phrase. The definition tells you what the word means.

Land and Water
Ice floes float near Alexander Island, off the coast of Antarctica. Salt water covers most of Earth's surface. Most fresh water is ice, frozen in polar regions such as Antarctica.
Analyze Images *What landforms can you see in this photograph?*

- Ask students **What is the atmosphere and why is it important to our survival on Earth?** *(The atmosphere is a thick layer of gases, including the air we breathe.)*

- Ask students to draw a conclusion about how much of the world's water is fresh water if 97 percent of the world's water is in oceans. *(about 3 percent)*

- Ask students to name four types of landforms that cover Earth's surface. *(mountains, hills, plateaus, and plains)* Then have students list landforms in your county or state that are one of these four types. *(Answers will vary, but should show an understanding of these landforms.)*

Independent Practice
Ask students to create the Taking Notes graphic organizer on a blank piece of paper. Then have them add more branches and circles in order to fill in the information about Earth's structure and landforms.

Monitor Progress
As students fill in the graphic organizer, circulate and make sure individuals are selecting the correct details. Provide assistance as needed.

Target Reading Skill L2

Using Context Clues As a follow up, ask students to review the Target Reading Skill in the Student Edition. *(a thick layer of gases)*

Skills Mini Lesson

Analyzing Images

1. Teach the skill by pointing out to students that to analyze an image, they can ask these questions: Who or what is the image is showing? When or where does the scene take place? What general feeling do you get from the image? Who created the image and why?

2. Help students practice the skill by looking at the image of the volcano on page 37. Ask students What evidence besides the caption indicates that the molten rock is very hot? *(The color of the liquid pouring out from the top of the volcano shows it is hot.)*

3. Have students apply the skill by answering this question: What might have been the photographer's reason for taking the photo on page 37? *(to show how erupting volcanoes change the surface of Earth)*

Answers
✔ **Reading Check** Earth's crust
Analyze Images mountains

Forces Inside Earth L2

Guided Instruction

- **Vocabulary Builder** Clarify the high-use words **collide, surge,** and **splinter** before reading.

- Read how the movement underneath Earth's surface affects our planet in Forces Inside Earth. As a class, study the diagram and captions under How Continents Move and partner students to answer the Geography Skills Practice question on page 37.

- Ask students **What forces inside Earth cause mountains to form?** (*The pressure exerted where two plates push against each other causes Earth's crust to bend and buckle, forming mountains.*)

- Ask students **Which different forces inside Earth cause volcanoes in Hawaii and earthquakes in California?** (*Volcanoes form when ocean crust plunges beneath continental crust and streams of magma to rise to the surface. Earthquakes occur when blocks of crust rub against each other along faults, releasing huge amounts of energy.*)

Forces Inside Earth

Heat deep inside Earth is constantly reshaping the planet's surface. The intense heat causes rock to rise toward the surface. Where streams of this soft, nearly molten rock called **magma** reach Earth's crust, they push up the crust to form volcanoes. Volcanoes spew molten rock, or lava, from inside Earth. Streams of magma may also push the crust apart along seams. Huge blocks of Earth's crust called **plates** are separated by these seams. Plates may include continents or parts of continents. Each plate also includes part of the ocean floor. Along seams, mainly beneath oceans, streams of magma rise from inside Earth. As the magma cools, it forms new crust and pushes the old crust away from the seams.

How Continents Move

Rising magma forms new crust along seams between Earth's plates. Beneath the surface, some scientists believe, magma moves like a conveyor belt. The belt drags the growing plates and the continents that they carry.

Where two plates push against each other, the pressure makes the crust bend and buckle to form steep mountains.

Plates move only an inch or two (a few centimeters) a year.

Crust

Mantle

Earthquakes occur when blocks of crust slide sideways against each other.

Some scientists think that sheets of mantle act like conveyor belts that move the plates of crust above them.

Sheets of magma rise to the surface from Earth's interior along a seam between plates of crust.

◀ **Two plates rub together along the San Andreas Fault in California.**

Differentiated Instruction

For English Language Learners L1
Students may have difficulty pronouncing some of the longer words in this section, such as *reshaping, continental, boundaries, earthquakes,* and *geographers.* Encourage students to break down these words into smaller parts to help them sound out the pronunciations.

For Gifted and Talented L3
The forces of nature can affect people both directly and indirectly. Ask students to read the selection *A Huge Black Umbrella* to experience how an event altered the lives of several individuals.

All in One Foundations of Geography Teaching Resources, *A Huge Black Umbrella,* pp. 138–140

Volcanoes and Earthquakes Where a plate of ocean crust collides with a plate of continental crust, the ocean crust plunges underneath the continental plate and melts. Molten rock surges upward, exploding onto the surface through a volcano. The Ring of Fire surrounds the plates that make up the Pacific Ocean. Streams of magma also form volcanoes at places other than plate boundaries. Such volcanoes have shaped the Hawaiian Islands, which are far from a plate boundary.

When two plates push together, the crust cracks and splinters from the pressure. The cracks in Earth's crust are called faults. When blocks of crust rub against each other along faults, they release huge amounts of energy in the form of earthquakes.

▲ **Molten rock pours from a volcano in Hawaii.**

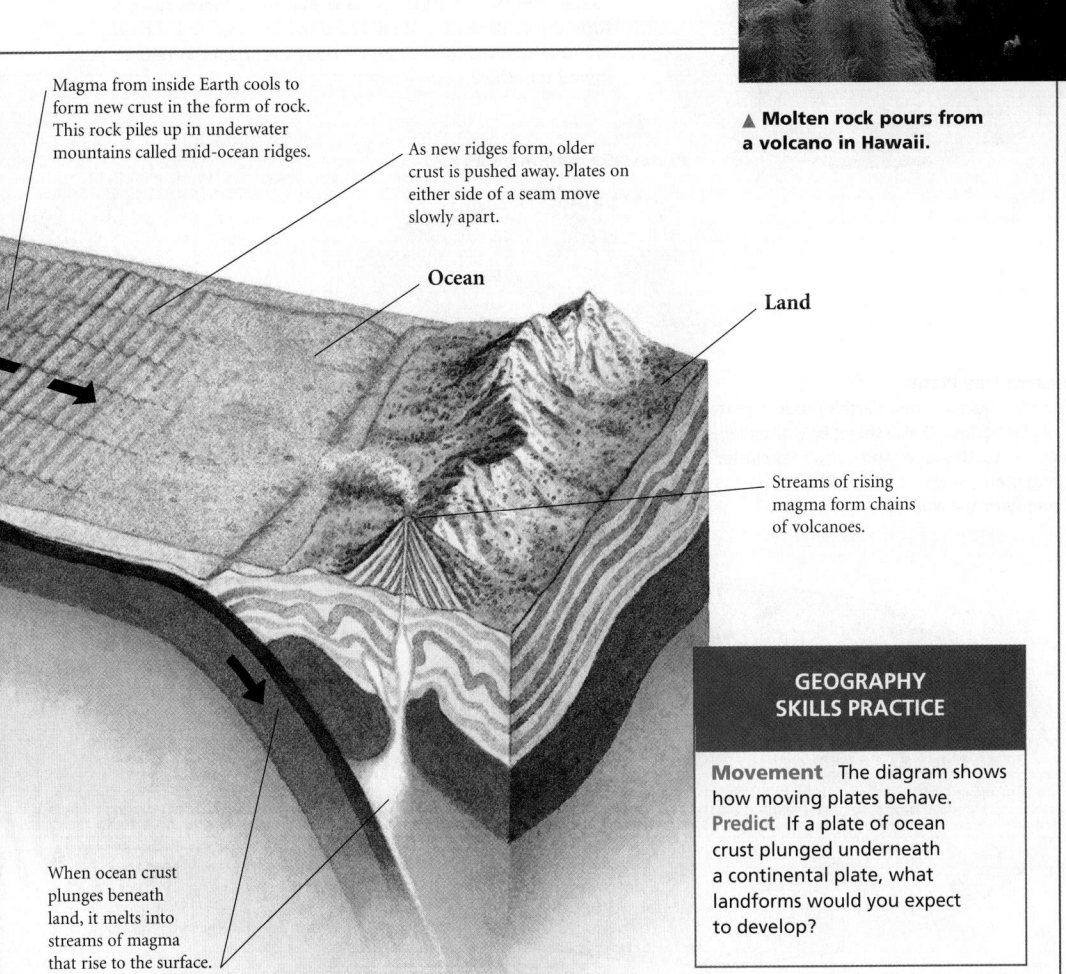

Magma from inside Earth cools to form new crust in the form of rock. This rock piles up in underwater mountains called mid-ocean ridges.

As new ridges form, older crust is pushed away. Plates on either side of a seam move slowly apart.

Ocean

Land

Streams of rising magma form chains of volcanoes.

When ocean crust plunges beneath land, it melts into streams of magma that rise to the surface.

GEOGRAPHY SKILLS PRACTICE

Movement The diagram shows how moving plates behave. **Predict** If a plate of ocean crust plunged underneath a continental plate, what landforms would you expect to develop?

Background: Links Across Time

A New Island For thousands of years, magma from underwater volcanoes built up until it rose above sea level to create the Hawaiian Islands. Today, a new island, named Loihi (low EE hee), is forming just southeast of the big island of Hawaii.

Already more than two miles (about 3.7 kilometers) high, it has 3,180 feet (969 meters) to go before it breaks the ocean's surface. Loihi erupts often, causing earthquakes and tidal waves.

Guided Instruction (continued)

■ Have students review the maps on page 38 and ask **How do some scientists believe that continents move?** *(Magma beneath Earth's crust may act like a slow-moving conveyor belt, dragging the plates that carry the continents a few centimeters a year.)* Then, using The World: Physical map in the Atlas on pp. 140–141, have students discuss ways of how the continents could have once been one land mass.

■ Ask students **How can magma cause the plates that carry the continents to move apart?** *(Sheets of magma rise to the surface along a seam between the plates to form ridges in the crust. As new ridges form, older crust is pushed away, forcing the plates on either side of a seam to move slowly apart.)*

Independent Practice

Have students continue to fill in the graphic organizer web by including details from the information they have just learned. Remind them to add more branches and circles if necessary.

Monitor Progress

Survey the class and determine if individuals are absorbing the content. Provide assistance as needed.

Answer
Geography Skills Practice Predict
volcanoes and islands

Forces on Earth's Surface

Guided Instruction   L2

- Read Forces on Earth's Surface. Circulate to make sure individuals can answer the Reading Check question.

- Ask students **What is weathering?** *(a process that breaks down rocks into tiny pieces)* **How does it differ from erosion?** *(Weathering is the breaking down of rocks into tiny pieces while erosion is the removal of these pieces.)*

- Ask students to predict what the area where they live might look like 10,000 years from now. *(Answers will vary but students should note that forces such as weathering and erosion will change a region over time.)*

Independent Practice

Have students complete their graphic organizers.

Monitor Progress

- Show *Section Reading Support Transparency FG 46* and ask students to check their graphic organizers individually. Go over key concepts and clarify key vocabulary as needed.

  📖 **Foundations of Geography Transparencies,** *Section Reading Support Transparency FG 46*

- Tell students to fill in the last column of their *Reading Readiness Guides.* Probe for what they learned that confirms or invalidates each statement.

  All in One Foundations of Geography Teaching Resources, *Reading Readiness Guide,* p. 110

Answers

✓ **Reading Check** Parts of Earth's crust called plates shift in response to movements of magma beneath the crust.
Analyze According to the first map, all of the present-day continents were once joined together. **Identify** the Cocos Plate

---

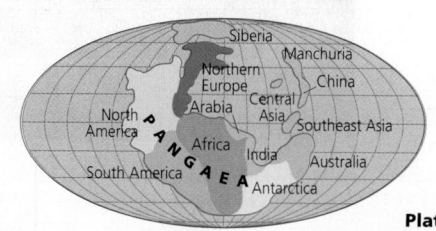

A World of Moving Plates For hundreds of years, geographers wondered how Earth's landmasses took their present shapes and positions. When they looked at the globe, they thought they saw matching shapes in continents that are very far apart. Now that they know how forces inside Earth move continents, they know that those continents were once close together.

✓ **Reading Check** How do continents move apart?

Plate Movements

Plates 250 million years ago

Plates Shifting Through Time
Most geographers believe that long ago Earth had only one huge continent. They call it Pangaea (pan JEE uh). About 200 million years ago, they conclude, plate movement began to split Pangaea apart. They think that these pieces came to form the continents that we know today. **Analyze** According to these maps, which present-day continents were once joined together?

Plates 150 million years ago

Present-Day Plates
The map below shows Earth's modern plates and plate edges. It also shows how the plates are moving. Earthquakes and volcanoes cluster along plate edges. **Identify** Which plate is colliding with the North American Plate?

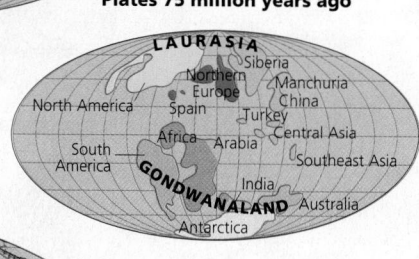

Plates 75 million years ago

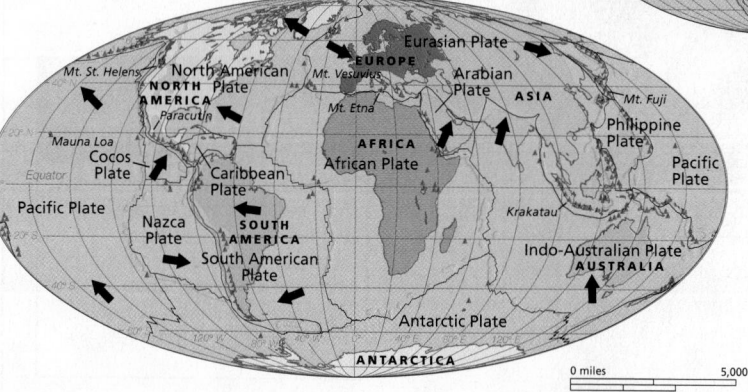

KEY
- Plate boundary
- Plate movement
- Earthquake zone
- Volcano

38 Foundations of Geography

Background: Biography

One Big Landmass Alfred Lothar Wegener (1880–1930) studied astronomy and taught meteorology. Even though his education focused on the sky, Wegener was interested in the shapes of continental landmasses. In 1912, Wegener proposed that a single large landmass broke apart to form the continents we see today. As evidence, he pointed to closely related fossil organisms and similar rock strata that occur on the continents. Geologists rejected his ideas. More than forty years later, precise dating of rocks on the opposite sides of the Atlantic Ocean indicated that Wegener's ideas were not only plausible, but likely.

Forces on Earth's Surface

Forces inside Earth move plates apart, produce volcanoes, and slowly build up Earth's crust. Other forces slowly wear it down and reshape it. The forces that wear Earth down are not as dramatic as volcanoes, but over time they are just as effective.

Weathering is a process that breaks rocks down into tiny pieces. Water, ice, and living things like lichens on rocks all cause weathering. Weathering helps create soil, too. Tiny pieces of rock combine with decayed animal and plant material to form soil.

Once this breaking down has taken place, landforms are reshaped by **erosion,** or the removal of small pieces of rock by water, ice, or wind. Hundreds of millions of years ago, the Appalachian Mountains in the eastern United States were as high as the Rocky Mountains of the western United States now are. Rain, snow, and wind slowly wore them down into much lower peaks.

When water, ice, and wind remove material, they deposit it downstream or downwind to create new landforms. Plains are often made of material carried from upstream by rivers.

Weathering and erosion formed this natural sandstone bridge in Jordan.

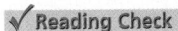 **Reading Check** What landforms are products of weathering and erosion?

Section 2 Assessment

Key Terms
Review the key terms at the beginning of this section. Use each term in a sentence that explains its meaning.

Target Reading Skill
Find the word *landforms* in the last paragraph of page 35. Use the context to find its meaning. What does it mean? What clues did you use to find its meaning?

Comprehension and Critical Thinking
1. (a) List What are Earth's three main layers?

(b) Synthesize Information How do those layers interact?
2. (a) Recall What forces inside Earth shape Earth's surface?
(b) Explain How do these forces explain the movement of the continents?
(c) Predict How might a continent split in two?
3. (a) Identify What forces cause weathering and erosion?
(b) Compare and Contrast How is erosion different from weathering?

Writing Activity
Think about the region where you live. Does it have steep mountains or volcanoes, rounded hills, or plains? Write a paragraph describing some of the natural forces that are slowly reshaping your region.

For: An activity on Pangaea
Visit: PHSchool.com
Web Code: led-3202

Chapter 2 Section 2 **39**

Section 2 Assessment

Key Terms
Students' sentences should reflect knowledge of each Key Term.

Target Reading Skill
Landforms are shapes and types of land. Clue: The meaning of landforms was restated after the word.

Comprehension and Critical Thinking
1. (a) the crust, the mantle, and the core
(b) The crust floats on top of the mantle and the heat of the mantle and the core help shape Earth's crust.

2. (a) magma and moving plates **(b)** Some scientists think that sheets of mantle form conveyor belts that move the plates of crust above them, causing the continents to move. **(c)** A continent that sits on two or more of Earth's plates can split apart when those plates move in opposite directions.

3. (a) water, ice, living things, and wind
(b) Weathering is a process that breaks down rocks into small pieces. Erosion is the removal of small pieces of rock by water, ice, or wind.

Assess and Reteach

Assess Progress `L2`
Have Students complete the Section Assessment. Administer the *Section Quiz.*

> **All in One** **Foundations of Geography Teaching Resources,** *Section Quiz,* p. 112

Reteach `L1`
If students need more instruction, have them read this section in the Reading and Vocabulary Study Guide.

> Chapter 2, Section 2, **Eastern Hemisphere Reading and Vocabulary Study Guide,** pp. 12–14

Extend `L3`
Have students learn more about varying landforms and elevations from Death Valley to Mt. Whitney by completing the *Small Group Activity: Simulation: Making a Poster for the Whitney Classic.*

> **All in One** **Foundations of Geography Teaching Resources,** *Small Group Activity: Simulation: Making a Poster for the Whitney Classic,* p. 128–131

Answer

√ **Reading Check** hills, some mountains, deserts, and plains

Writing Activity
Use the *Rubric for Assessing a Writing Assignment* to evaluate students' paragraphs.

> **All in One** **Foundations of Geography Teaching Resources,** *Rubric for Assessing a Writing Assignment,* p. 145

> **Go Online** PHSchool.com Typing in the Web code when prompted will bring students directly to detailed instructions for this activity.

Section 3
Step-by-Step Instruction

Objectives

Social Studies

1. Learn about weather and climate.
2. Explore latitude, landforms, and precipitation.
3. Discover how oceans affect climate.

Reading/Language Arts

Use context clues that give a comparison to determine the meaning of a word or phrase.

Prepare to Read

Build Background Knowledge L2

Tell students that in this section they will explore climate and weather. Ask students to think about what they know about weather, and then look at the two photographs and related captions on pp. 40 and 41. Then ask what they think the difference between weather and climate is. Conduct an Idea Wave (TE, p. T35) to share ideas as a class.

Set a Purpose for Reading L2

- Preview the Objectives.

- Form students into pairs or groups of four. Distribute the *Reading Readiness Guide*. Ask students to fill in the first two columns of the chart. Use the Numbered Heads participation strategy (TE, p. T36) to call on students to share one piece of information they already know and one piece of information they want to know.

All in One Foundations of Geography Teaching Resources, *Reading Readiness Guide*, p. 114

Vocabulary Builder
Preview Key Terms

Pronounce each Key Term, then ask the students to say the word with you. Provide a simple explanation such as, "The tropical cyclone arrived on shore with such force that roads were flooded, trees and power lines were torn down, and many homes were damaged."

Answer

✓ Reading Check Weather is the condition of the air and sky from day to day. Climate is the average weather of a place over many years.

40 *Foundations of Geography*

Prepare to Read

Objectives

In this section you will

1. Learn about weather and climate.
2. Explore latitude, landforms, and precipitation.
3. Discover how oceans affect climate.

Taking Notes

As you read this section, look for topics related to climate and weather, such as landforms, precipitation, oceans, and storms. Copy the outline below and add headings as needed to show the relationships among these topics.

> I. Weather
> II. Climate
>   A. Latitudes
>   B.
>   1.
>   2.
> III. Storms

🎯 Target Reading Skill

Use Context Clues You can sometimes learn the meaning of a word or phrase when the context gives a comparison. In this example, the word *cyclone* is compared to the phrase in italics.

> A cyclone is like *a huge spiral escalator moving air upward.*

Key Terms

- **weather** (WETH ur) *n.* the condition of the air and sky from day to day
- **precipitation** (pree sip uh TAY shun) *n.* water that falls to the ground as rain, sleet, hail, or snow
- **temperature** (TEM pur uh chur) *n.* how hot or cold the air is
- **climate** (KLY mut) *n.* the average weather over many years
- **tropical cyclone** (TRAHP ih kul SY klohn) *n.* an intense wind and rain storm that forms over oceans in the tropics.

This Inuit woman and child are dressed for their cold climate.

40 Foundations of Geography

Weather or Climate?

Every morning, most people check the weather before they get dressed. But in some parts of India, people have very serious reasons for watching the **weather,** or the condition of the air and sky from day to day. In parts of India, it rains only during one time of year. No one living there wants the rainy days to end too soon. That rain must fill the wells with enough fresh water to last for the entire year.

In India, people are concerned about **precipitation,** or water that falls to the ground as rain, sleet, hail, or snow. When you get dressed in the morning, you may want to know the **temperature,** or how hot or cold the air is. Weather is mainly measured by temperature and precipitation.

The **climate** of a place is the average weather over many years. Climate is not the same as weather. Weather is what people see from day to day. Climate is what usually happens from year to year.

✓ Reading Check What is the difference between weather and climate?

🎯 Target Reading Skill L2

Use Context Clues Point out the Target Reading Skill. Tell students that one way to find the meaning of a word or phrase is to look for comparisons between the unfamiliar word and a familiar word or phrase within the context.

Model using comparison context clues by finding the meaning of *tsunami*. Write the following sentence on the board: "The tsunami approached the southern coast of Japan like an enormous tower of water and crashed upon the shore flooding everything it its path." (enormous tower of water *and* crashed upon the shore *implies a large wave*) Point out to students that words such as *like* and *as* signal that a comparison is being made.

Give students *Use Context Clues: Compare and Contrast.* Have them complete the activity in groups.

All in One Foundations of Geography Teaching Resources, *Use Context Clues: Compare and Contrast*, p. 123

Why Climates Vary

Earth has many climates. Some climates are so hot that people rarely need to wear a sweater. In some cold climates, snow stays on the ground most of the year. And there are places on Earth where more than 30 feet (9 meters) of rain falls in a single year.

Climate depends on location. Places in the low latitudes, or tropics, have hot climates, because they get direct sunlight. Places in the high latitudes, or polar regions, have cold climates, because their sunlight is indirect.

Air and water spread heat around the globe as they move. Without wind and water, places in the tropics would overheat. Oceans gain and lose heat slowly, so they keep temperatures mild near coasts. Mountains can also affect climates.

 **Reading Check** How does latitude affect temperature?

Cherrapunji, India, averages 37 feet (11 meters) of rain a year. The rain then flows into lakes, streams, and waterfalls.

The Water Cycle

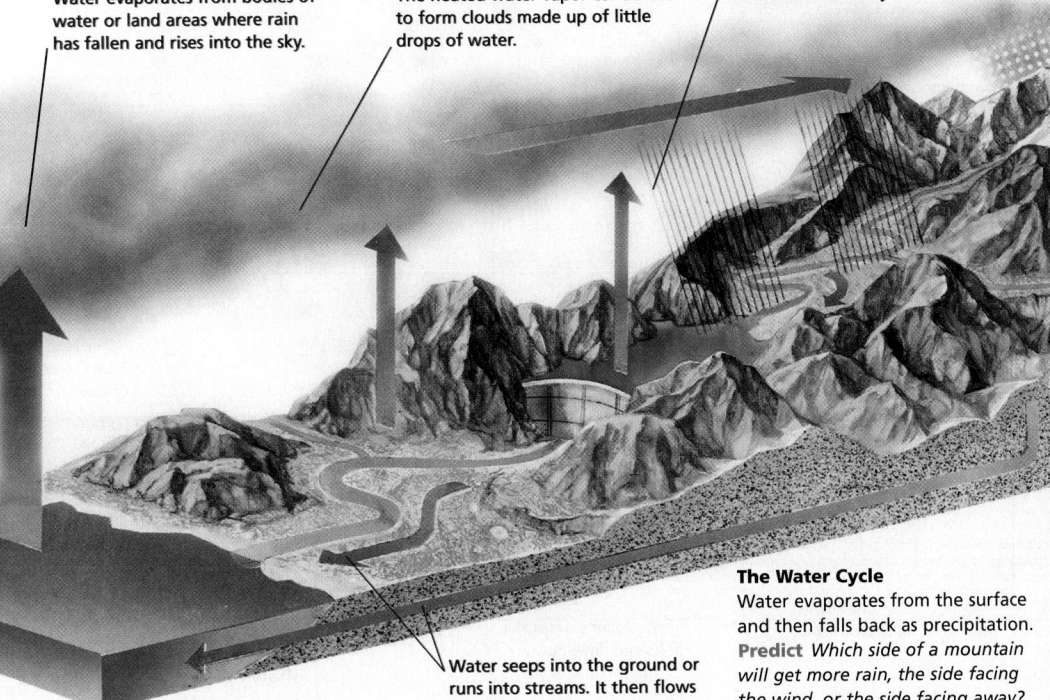

Water evaporates from bodies of water or land areas where rain has fallen and rises into the sky.

The heated water vapor condenses to form clouds made up of little drops of water.

As moist air rises, it cools and drops its moisture. This can happen when air is forced up a mountain slope or when air rises in a storm system.

Water seeps into the ground or runs into streams. It then flows to the sea or evaporates again.

The Water Cycle
Water evaporates from the surface and then falls back as precipitation. **Predict** *Which side of a mountain will get more rain, the side facing the wind, or the side facing away?*

Chapter 2 Section 3 **41**

Guided Instruction

- **Vocabulary Builder** Clarify the high-use word **indirect** before reading.

- Read Weather or Climate? and Why Climates Vary using the Choral Reading strategy (TE, p. T34). Ask students to study the diagram and captions for The Water Cycle. As a class, answer the caption question. Allow students to briefly discuss their responses with a partner before sharing with the class.

- Ask students **What is climate?** (*It is the average weather over many years.*) **Why do climates vary?** (*location, including elevation; wind patterns; mountains*)

- Ask students **How is weather measured?** (*It is mainly measured by temperature and precipitation.*) **What is precipitation and what forms can it take?** (*Precipitation is water that falls to the ground as rain, sleet, hail, or snow.*)

- Ask students **Once rain has fallen, how does water return to the ocean?** (*through rivers, streams, and groundwater runoff*)

Independent Practice

Ask students to create the Taking Notes graphic organizer outline on a blank piece of paper. Have students fill in information related to climate and weather.

Monitor Progress

As students fill in the graphic organizer, circulate and make sure individuals are selecting the correct details. Provide assistance as needed.

Vocabulary Builder

Use the information below to teach students this section's high-use words.

High-Use Word	Definition and Sample Sentence
indirect, p. 41	*adj.* not direct or straight; by a longer way He took an **indirect** route home in order to pass by his friend's house and see if she was home.
distribute, p. 43	*v.* to give or spread out Many people **distribute** candy on Halloween.

Answers

Reading Check Low latitudes receive direct sunlight; therefore, the temperature is hot. High latitudes receive indirect sunlight; therefore, the temperature is cold.
Predict the side facing the wind

Oceans and Climates ⬛L2

Guided Instruction

- **Vocabulary Builder** Clarify the high-use word **distribute** before reading.

- Review the diagram and map on pages 42 and 43 with students. Read how global wind patterns and bodies of water affect the regions of the world in Oceans and Climates.

- Ask students **What do wind and air currents move?** (*heat and moisture between different parts of Earth*) **How are they affected by latitude?** (*The currents flow in regular circular patterns depending on the latitude through which they are moving.*)

- Ask students **What happens when air rises?** (*The moisture it contains condenses and falls as rain or snow.*) **What happens when air sinks?** (*The air becomes drier creating dry climates such as those at the poles or in the desert.*)

Answer

Geography Skills Practice **Compare and Contrast** The regions of heavy precipitation on the map have belts of warm, moist air that rises, causing heavy precipitation.

Air Circulation and Wind

Winds and air currents move heat and moisture between different parts of Earth. These currents follow regular patterns related to latitude. The diagram below shows these circular patterns of air movement, which form a series of belts, or cells, that circle Earth.

A strong onshore wind blows in Miami Beach, Florida.

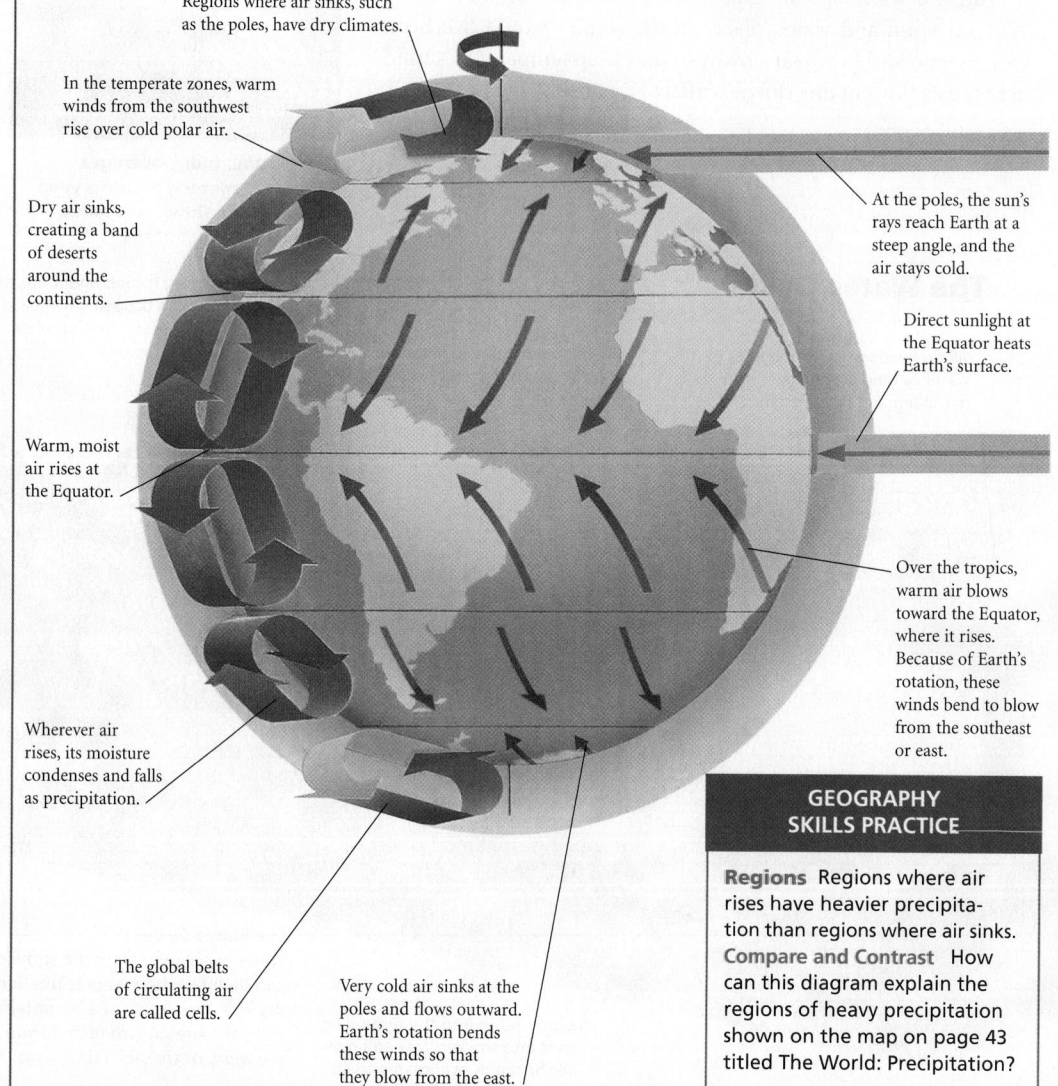

Regions where air sinks, such as the poles, have dry climates.

In the temperate zones, warm winds from the southwest rise over cold polar air.

Dry air sinks, creating a band of deserts around the continents.

Warm, moist air rises at the Equator.

Wherever air rises, its moisture condenses and falls as precipitation.

The global belts of circulating air are called cells.

Very cold air sinks at the poles and flows outward. Earth's rotation bends these winds so that they blow from the east.

At the poles, the sun's rays reach Earth at a steep angle, and the air stays cold.

Direct sunlight at the Equator heats Earth's surface.

Over the tropics, warm air blows toward the Equator, where it rises. Because of Earth's rotation, these winds bend to blow from the southeast or east.

GEOGRAPHY SKILLS PRACTICE

Regions Regions where air rises have heavier precipitation than regions where air sinks. **Compare and Contrast** How can this diagram explain the regions of heavy precipitation shown on the map on page 43 titled The World: Precipitation?

Differentiated Instruction

For Special Needs Students ⬛L1
Have students read the section as they listen to the recorded version on the Student Edition on Audio CD. Check for comprehension by pausing the CD and asking students to share their answers to the Reading Check.

⊙ Chapter 2, Section 3, **Student Edition on Audio CD**

MAP MASTER™ Skills Activity

KEY

Inches	Centimeters
More than 80	More than 200
60–80	150–200
40–60	100–150
20–40	50–100
10–20	25–50
Less than 10	Less than 25

0 miles — 4,000
0 kilometers — 4,000
Robinson

Regions Which areas get the most precipitation? Which get the least? **Analyze** What patterns can you find in precipitation on Earth?

Go Online
PHSchool.com Use Web Code lep-3213 for step-by-step **map skills practice.**

Oceans and Climates

The oceans help distribute Earth's heat and shape climates. Global wind patterns help create ocean currents, which are like vast rivers in the oceans. Ocean currents move across great distances. Generally, warm water flows away from the Equator, while cold water moves toward the Equator.

Oceans and Currents In the Atlantic Ocean, the Gulf Stream, a warm current, travels northeast from the tropics. The Gulf Stream and the North Atlantic Current carry warm water all the way to western Europe. That warm water gives western Europe a milder climate than other regions at the same latitude.

The cold Peru Current moves north from Antarctica along the coast of South America. The city of Antofagasta (ahn toh fah GAHS tah) lies along that coast, in Chile. Even though Antofagasta is closer than Miami, Florida, is to the Equator, the average temperature in Antofagasta during the hottest month of summer is just 68°F (20°C).

Target Skill Use Context Clues
If you do not know what ocean currents are, notice that they are compared to vast rivers in the ocean. How does the comparison help you find the meaning?

Chapter 2 Section 3 **43**

Guided Instruction (continued)

■ Ask students **Why does western Europe have a milder climate than other regions at the same latitude?** (*The Gulf Stream and the North Atlantic Current carry warm water to western Europe.*)

■ Ask students to draw a conclusion about why the temperature in Antofagasta, Chile, is not as warm as Florida, even though it is closer to the Equator. (*The cold-water current from the South Pole called the Peru Current moves north past Chile, giving Antofagasta a cooler climate than Florida.*)

⟳ Target Reading Skill   L2

Use Context Clues As a follow up, ask students to answer the Target Reading Skill question in the Student Edition. (*Possible answer: Since* river *is a familiar concept, it can help one understand a more unfamiliar concept like* ocean current.)

Answers

MAP MASTER Skills Activity **Regions** central region of northern South America; portions of Africa's west coast; parts of Southeast Asia; island countries located in the Pacific Ocean **Analyze** Generally, areas around the Equator get the most precipitation. As you move north or south of the Equator, the amount of precipitation decreases.

Go Online
PHSchool.com Students may practice their map skills using the interactive online version of this map.

Skills Mini Lesson

Using Cartographer's Tools

1. Teach the skill by pointing out that a map key explains symbols and special colors used on a map. Explain that it helps students interpret the information being shown on the map.

2. Help students practice the skill by looking at the map on this page. Read the key with students and have them identify what each color represents on the map.

3. Have students apply the skill by choosing a continent and describing its pattern of precipitation.

Guided Instruction (continued)

- Have students discuss the cooling and warming affects of the ocean and other bodies of water.

- Have students compare and contrast the climates of San Francisco and St. Louis. *(Because San Francisco borders the Pacific Ocean, it is warmer than St. Louis in the winter and cooler than St. Louis in the summer.)* Ask students if there are any bodies of water nearby that may affect the region in which they live.

- As a class, study The World: Climate Regions on these pages. Answer the Map-Master Skills Activity questions as a class. Then, ask the class to compare the climate regions of North America and Europe. *(North America and Europe have similar types of climate regions, but the southern portion of North America has tropical regions while Europe does not.)*

The Ocean's Cooling and Warming Effects Bodies of water affect climate in other ways, too. Water takes longer to heat or cool than land. As the air and land heat up in summer, the water remains cooler. Wind blowing over the water cools the nearby land. So in summer, a region near an ocean or lake will be cooler than an inland area at the same latitude. In the winter, the water remains warmer than the land. So places near lakes or oceans are warmer in winter than inland areas.

The World: Climate Regions

You can see patterns in a map of Earth's climate regions. Notice that tropical wet climate regions hug the Equator on several continents. Farther from the Equator are arid and semiarid climate regions. Elsewhere, regions where the wind blows off the ocean have wetter climates than regions farther inland. Each climate region on this map is described more fully in the next section.

NORTH AMERICA

SOUTH AMERICA

ANTARCTICA

ATLANTIC OCEAN

PACIFIC OCEAN

120° W   90° W   60° W   30° W
150° W
Arctic Circle
60° N
30° N
Tropic of Cancer
120° W
Equator   0°
Tropic of Capricorn
30° S

0 miles   2,000
0 kilometers   2,000
Robinson

60° S
Antarctic Circle
150° W   120° W   90° W   60° W   30° W

▲ **Arid** This view from the air shows the Colorado River winding through the Grand Canyon in Arizona.

 **Skills for Life** — **Skills Mini Lesson**

Comparing and Contrasting

1. Teach the skill by pointing out to students that comparison involves similarities, and contrast involves differences. It is important to first identify the topic and purpose in their comparison and contrast. Similarities and differences will then be easier to determine.

2. Help students practice the skill by looking at The World: Climate Regions map on these pages and comparing and contrasting North and South America.

3. Have students apply the skill by comparing and contrasting the climate regions of Australia and Greenland.

Consider San Francisco, California, and St. Louis, Missouri. Both cities are near 38° north latitude. However, San Francisco borders the Pacific Ocean. In winter, the ocean is warmer than the air. The ocean keeps San Francisco much warmer than St. Louis in winter. In summer, the ocean is cooler than the air, so it keeps San Francisco cool.

✓ **Reading Check** During the summer, are places near the ocean warmer or cooler than places inland?

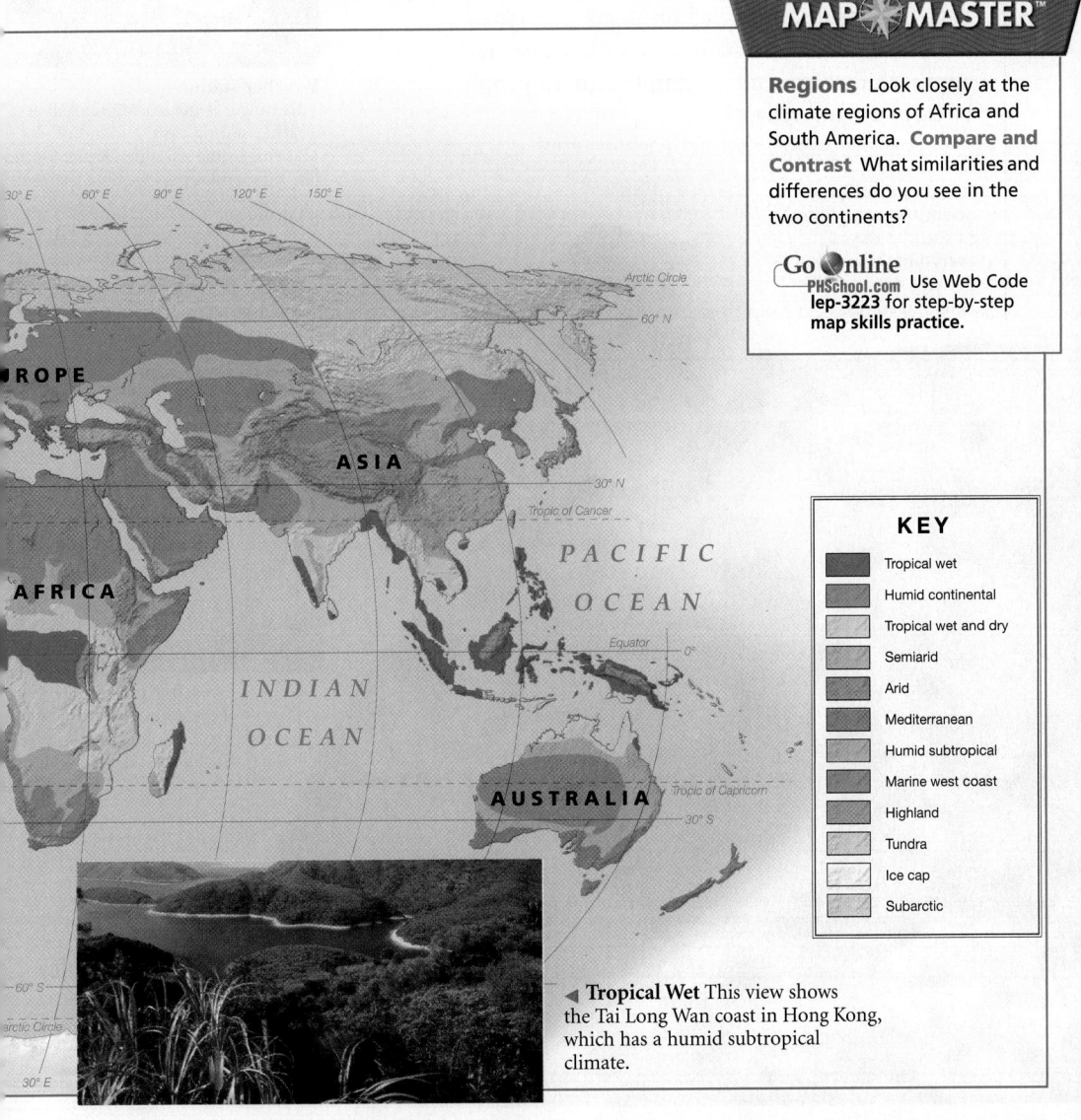

MAP MASTER™

Regions Look closely at the climate regions of Africa and South America. **Compare and Contrast** What similarities and differences do you see in the two continents?

Go Online
PHSchool.com Use Web Code **lep-3223** for step-by-step map skills practice.

KEY

- Tropical wet
- Humid continental
- Tropical wet and dry
- Semiarid
- Arid
- Mediterranean
- Humid subtropical
- Marine west coast
- Highland
- Tundra
- Ice cap
- Subarctic

◄ **Tropical Wet** This view shows the Tai Long Wan coast in Hong Kong, which has a humid subtropical climate.

Differentiated Instruction

For Less Proficient Readers   L1
Some students may have trouble reading the climate map on pages 44 and 45. Pair them with more able students. Ask them to complete *Reading a Climate Map* together.

All in One Foundations of Geography Teaching Resources, *Reading a Climate Map,* p. 135

For Gifted and Talented   L3
Have students choose one of the images on pages 44–45 and write a poem that describes what it must be like to live in this climate region.

All in One Foundations of Geography Teaching Resources, *Rubric for Assessing a Student Poem,* p. 146

Guided Instruction (continued)

■ Partner students to analyze the images on pages 44 and 45. Coach students to think about what each image shows and what general feeling each image inspires. Then ask them **If there were no captions, what climate regions would they assign each image based on its content?** (*The image on page 44 shows a dry, arid landscape; the image on page 45 shows a lush, tropical area with heavy vegetation.*)

Independent Practice
Have students continue to fill in their graphic organizer with details from the information they have just learned.

Monitor Progress
As students fill in the graphic organizer, circulate and make sure individuals are selecting the correct details. Provide assistance as needed.

Answers

✓ **Reading Check** cooler

MAP MASTER Skills Activity **Compare and Contrast**
The two continents share many of the same types of climate regions, but Africa has a much larger arid region.

Go Online
PHSchool.com Students may practice their map skills using the interactive online version of this map.

Weather Forecasting

L2

Guided Instruction

Ask students to read the feature and review the images and captions. Then have students discuss why it might be important to be forewarned about weather conditions. As a class, answer the Analyzing Images question.

Independent Practice

Have students create an outline of the information on this page.

Raging Storms

L2

Guided Instruction

■ Read Raging Storms as a class. Make sure that individuals are able to answer the Reading Check question.

■ Have students list the storms mentioned in the reading. (*tropical cyclones, hurricanes, tornadoes, blizzards, severe rainstorms, and thunderstorms*) Ask **What elements are common to these storms?** (*high winds and heavy precipitation*)

Independent Practice

Tell students to complete their graphic organizers.

Monitor Progress

■ Show *Section Reading Support Transparency FG 47*. Go over key concepts and clarify key vocabulary as needed.

📖 **Foundations of Geography Transparencies,** *Section Reading Support Transparency FG 47*

■ Tell students to fill in the last column of their *Reading Readiness Guides*. Ask them to evaluate if what they learned was what they had expected to learn.

All in One **Foundations of Geography Teaching Resources,** *Reading Readiness Guide,* p. 114

Answer

ANALYZING IMAGES Satellites gather information about locations all over the world. Forecasters might use the weather patterns in other parts of the world to predict what the weather might be like in their area.

Weather Forecasting

Television weather forecasters rely on scientists and equipment from all over the world. Weather stations record local conditions. Satellites orbit overhead to photograph large weather systems. Weather balloons and radar provide still more data. The results, displayed on weather maps or presented in forecasts, can warn citizens of an approaching hurricane or simply remind people to carry an umbrella.

Weather station
This ranger is measuring rainfall at a weather station on the island of Madeira in the Atlantic Ocean. Stations like this send reports to forecasters.

Weather satellites
Scientists use satellites in space to record everything from wind patterns to the height of waves.

Solar cell panels power the spacecraft.

GOES weather satellite
U.S. weather satellites are called GOES (Geostationary Operational Environmental Satellites). They circle Earth in time with Earth's rotation, so they always stay above the same spot.

A hurricane

A gathering storm

Weather map
Forecasters track weather patterns and storm systems, and display data on weather maps.

ANALYZING IMAGES
How might a satellite help forecasters predict the weather?

46 Foundations of Geography

Differentiated Instruction

For English Language Learners   L1

Partner students with English speakers to reread the information on this page. Have them summarize, in their own words, the information they have read. Make sure they clarify words they find difficult to pronounce or understand.

For Advanced Readers   L3

Have students write a letter to a local television weather forecaster asking three questions that would help them learn more about predicting weather. Give them *Writing a Letter* to help them get started.

All in One **Foundations of Geography Teaching Resources,** *Writing a Letter,* p. 143

Raging Storms

Wind and water can make climates milder, but they also can create large and dangerous storms. **Tropical cyclones** are intense wind and rain storms that form over oceans in the tropics. Tropical cyclones that form over the Atlantic Ocean are called hurricanes. The winds near the center of a hurricane can reach speeds of more than 100 miles (160 kilometers) per hour. Hurricanes produce huge swells of water called storm surges, which flood over shorelines and can destroy buildings.

Tornadoes are like funnels of wind that can reach 200 miles (320 kilometers) per hour. The winds and the low air pressure they create in their centers can wreck almost anything in their path. They can be just as dangerous as hurricanes, but they affect much smaller areas.

Other storms are less dangerous. In winter, blizzards dump huge amounts of snow on parts of North America. And severe rainstorms and thunderstorms strike the continent most often in spring and summer.

Hurricane Katrina
In 2005 Hurricane Katrina caused massive destruction along the southeastern coast of the United States.
Synthesizing Information
Is a hurricane more likely on a tropical coast or in a polar region far from the ocean?

✓ **Reading Check** Which storms cover larger areas, hurrricanes or tornadoes?

Section 3 Assessment

Key Terms
Review the key terms at the beginning of this section. Use each term in a sentence that explains its meaning.

🎯 Target Reading Skill
Find the word *tornadoes* in the second paragraph on this page. Using the context, find out its meaning. What clues did you use to find its meaning?

Comprehension and Critical Thinking
1. (a) Identify What is climate?
(b) Explain How is climate different from weather?

(c) Analyze Are hurricanes an example of climate or of weather?
2. (a) Recall What kind of climate occurs in most places near the Equator?
(b) Contrast Why are climates near the poles different from climates near the Equator?
3. (a) Recall How do bodies of water affect temperatures?
(b) Predict A city in the interior of a continent has very cold winters. How would you expect winter temperatures to differ in a coastal city at the same latitude as the interior city?

Writing Activity
Write a paragraph describing your region's climate, or average weather. Are winters usually warm or cold? What can you say about summers? Do oceans affect your climate? How much precipitation does your region get? Is it mostly rain, or snow, or a mix?

Writing Tip Remember that every paragraph needs a main idea. Make a general statement about your climate in a topic sentence. Then add sentences with supporting details about your climate.

Chapter 2 Section 3 **47**

Assess and Reteach

Assess Progress [L2]
Have students complete the Section Assessment. Administer the *Section Quiz*.

📘 **All in One** **Foundations of Geography Teaching Resources,** *Section Quiz*, p. 116

Reteach [L1]
If students need more instruction, have them read this section in the Reading and Vocabulary Study Guide.

📖 Chapter 2, Section 3, **Eastern Hemisphere Reading and Vocabulary Study Guide,** pp. 15–17

Extend [L3]
Form students into groups and have each group choose two cities in the United States, one along the coast and one farther inland. Have them use a newspaper to keep track of the weather in these two cities for a week and chart their findings on two separate bar graphs. Then have students play the role of television forecasters and deliver the weather in these two cities. Ask students to complement their forecasts with their bar graphs and any other maps, charts, or images they think would be helpful.

📘 **All in One** **Foundations of Geography Teaching Resources,** *Rubric for Assessing a Role-Playing Activity*, p. 147

Answers

✓ **Reading Check** hurricanes

Synthesizing Information on a tropical coast

Writing Activity
Use the *Rubric for Assessing a Writing Assignment* to evaluate students' paragraphs.

📘 **All in One** **Foundations of Geography Teaching Resources,** *Rubric for Assessing a Writing Assignment*, p. 145

Section 3 Assessment

Key Terms
Students' sentences should reflect knowledge of each Key Term.

🎯 Target Reading Skill
Tornadoes are funnels of wind that can reach 200 miles per hour, wrecking almost anything in their path. The word *like* signals a phrase that gives a comparison.

Comprehension and Critical Thinking
1. (a) Climate is the average weather over many years. **(b)** Weather is what people experience from day to day. Climate is the average weather over a number of years. **(c)** Hurricanes are examples of weather.

2. (a) a hot climate **(b)** The polar regions receive indirect sunlight, so their climate is cold. Places near the Equator receive direct sunlight, so their climate is hot.

3. (a) In summer, bodies of water heat up more slowly, and wind blowing over the water cools the nearby land. In winter, bodies of water stay warmer than the land. As a result, places near bodies of water are warmer in winter than places inland. **(b)** The temperatures in the interior city would be colder.

Objective
Use and interpret climate graphs.

Prepare to Read

Build Background Knowledge   L2
Invite students to brainstorm a list of all the kinds of graphs they know, such as circle, line, and bar. Then ask them what they usually want or need to know about the weather (*temperature and precipitation*). Tell students that climate graphs answer the questions most people have about weather.

Instruct

Using Climate Graphs   L2

Guided Instruction
■ Read the steps to using climate graphs as a class and write them on the board.

■ Practice the skill by following the steps on page 49 as a class. Model each step in the activity by first reading the labels on the graph (*Fahrenheit degrees; inches; months of the year*); identifying what the bar and line graphs show (*bar: rainfall in inches; line: temperature in Fahrenheit degrees*); describing the shape of the line graph and look of the bar graph (*line: relatively flat indicating little temperature change; bar graph: varying heights indicating higher precipitation during the spring and summer than the fall and winter*). Remind students that seasons in the Southern Hemisphere are the reverse of seasons in the Northern Hemisphere. Then draw conclusions. (*Possible conclusions: São Paulo's temperatures remain in the same small range year round; therefore the city has a moderate climate. São Paulo has a wet and dry season. The wet season runs from October through March and the dry season runs from April through September.*)

Independent Practice
Assign *Skills for Life* and have students complete it individually.

All in One **Foundations of Geography Teaching Resources,** *Skills for Life,* p. 127

Using Climate Graphs

Menghai, China, receives about 40 to 60 inches (100 to 150 centimeters) of rainfall each year.

"**E**verybody talks about the weather, but nobody does anything about it," goes an old joke attributed to the humorist Mark Twain. It's still true, although today we track the weather so that we can predict and prepare for it. One way geographers track weather patterns is by making a climate graph. A climate graph usually presents information about average precipitation and average temperature. Often it shows a whole year of information, so you can see how conditions change with the seasons.

Learn the Skill
To read a climate graph, follow the steps below.

1 **Identify the elements of the graph.** A climate graph is actually two graphs in one: a line graph that shows temperature and a bar graph that shows rainfall. The scale on the left side goes with the line graph, and the scale on the right side goes with the bar graph. The scale along the bottom shows a time period.

2 **Study the line graph.** Notice changes in temperature from month to month and from season to season. Draw a conclusion about the temperature of the place.

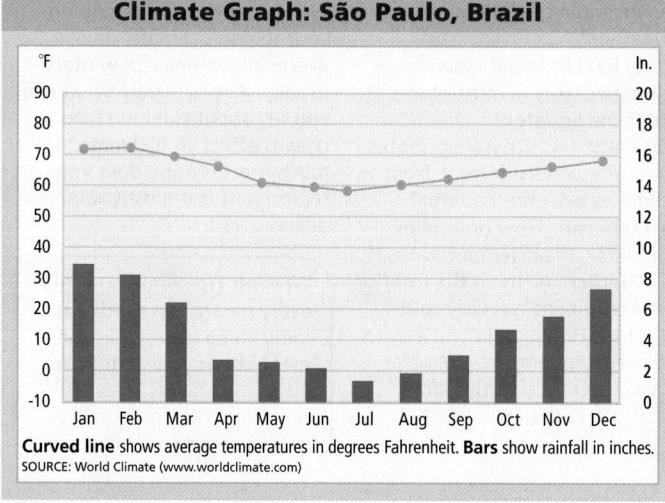

Climate Graph: São Paulo, Brazil

Curved line shows average temperatures in degrees Fahrenheit. **Bars** show rainfall in inches.
SOURCE: World Climate (www.worldclimate.com)

48 Foundations of Geography

3 **Study the bar graph.** Again, notice changes for months and for seasons. Draw a conclusion about rainfall.

4 **Use your conclusions about both graphs to draw an overall conclusion about the climate of the location.** Does the location appear to have hot seasons and cold seasons? Or does it have a rainy season and a dry season? State your conclusion.

Monitor Progress
As students are completing *Skills for Life,* circulate to make sure individuals are applying the skill steps effectively. Provide assistance as needed.

Practice the Skill

Look at the graph of São Paulo, Brazil, on page 48.

1 Read the labels on the sides and bottom of the graph. What do the numbers on the left side measure? What do the numbers on the right side measure? Look at the green bars. Which do they measure, temperature or rainfall? How do you know? Look at the line graph. What does it show? Now, look at the scale along the bottom of the graph. What period of time does it show?

2 Describe the shape of the line graph—is it generally flat, or does it go up and down? What and when is São Paulo's highest average temperature? Its lowest temperature? Do you think São Paulo has a hot season and a cold season? Write a conclusion about temperatures in the city.

3 What do the bars in the bar graph show? Are they generally the same height, or do they differ from month to month? What and when are São Paulo's highest and lowest average rainfall? Do you think São Paulo has a wet season and a dry season? Write a conclusion about rainfall in the city.

4 Using your conclusions about São Paulo's climate, write a summary that includes answers to these questions: What kind of seasons does the city have? Does the weather change much during the year?

Apply the Skill

To make your own climate graph, draw a large square on graph paper. Divide the square into 10 horizontal rows and 12 vertical columns. Title your graph "Climate Graph of Charleston, South Carolina." Then label the left side of your graph using one colored pencil and the right side with a different colored pencil. Write the months of the year along the bottom. Using the temperature and precipitation information in the table above, plot your line graph. Draw the lines with the same colored pencils you used to make the labels for temperature and precipitation.

Charleston, South Carolina

Month	Temperature (°Fahrenheit)	Precipitation (inches)
Jan	48.4	2.9
Feb	50.9	3.0
Mar	57.7	3.6
Apr	65.3	2.4
May	72.7	3.2
Jun	78.8	4.7
Jul	81.7	6.8
Aug	81.0	6.4
Sept	76.6	5.1
Oct	67.8	2.9
Nov	59.5	2.1
Dec	52.2	2.7

Differentiated Instruction

For Special Needs Students **L1**

To provide additional practice in reading graphs, partner special needs students with more proficient students to do Level 1 of the *Analyzing Graphic Data* lesson on the Social Studies Skills Tutor CD-ROM

together. When the students feel more confident, they can move onto Level 2 alone.

⊙ *Analyzing Graphic Data,* **Social Studies Skills Tutor CD-ROM**

Assess and Reteach

Assess Progress   L2

Ask students to do the Apply the Skill activity.

Reteach   L1

If students are having trouble applying the skill steps, pair students and ask them to complete *Reading a Climate Graph.*

All in One **Foundations of Geography,** *Reading a Climate Graph,* p. 136

Extend   L3

To extend the skill, show students *Color Transparency FG 41: Climate Graphs.* Have students follow the steps outlined in the skill feature to draw conclusions on the climates of Karachi, Pakistan, and Chennai, India. Then have students write a brief summary of their findings.

📖 **Foundations of Geography Transparencies,** *Color Transparency FG 41: Climate Graphs*

Answer
Apply the Skill

Student's climate graphs should have the same format as the São Paulo climate graph but reflect the data in the table for Charleston, South Carolina.

All in One **Foundations of Geography Teaching Resources,** *Rubric for Assessing a Bar Graph,* p.148; *Rubric for Assessing a Line Graph,* p.149

Objectives

Social Studies

1. Investigate the relationship between climate and vegetation.
2. Explore Earth's vegetation regions.
3. Study vertical climate zones.

Reading/Language Arts

Use context to determine the meaning of a word or phrase when examples are provided.

Prepare to Read

Build Background Knowledge   L2

Tell students that in this section they will learn about different climates, and the relationship between climate and vegetation. Ask students to think of ways in which their environments would be different if they lived in a different climate zone. Model the thought process by encouraging them to think about how plants and trees would be different, how buildings might be constructed differently, and how their clothing might be different. Use the Numbered Heads participation strategy (TE, p. T36) to have students generate a list.

Set a Purpose for Reading   L2

- Preview the Objectives.

- Read each statement in the *Reading Readiness Guide* aloud. Ask students to mark the statements true or false.

- Have students discuss the statements in pairs or groups of four, then mark their worksheets again. Use the Numbered Heads participation strategy (TE, p. T36) to call on students to share their group's perspectives.

All in One Foundations of Geography Teaching Resources, *Reading Readiness Guide,* p. 118

Vocabulary Builder
Preview Key Terms

Pronounce each Key Term, then ask the students to say the word with you. Provide a simple explanation such as, "The tree canopy was so thick that very little sunlight reached the floor of the rain forest."

Prepare to Read

Objectives

In this section you will
1. Investigate the relationship between climate and vegetation.
2. Explore Earth's vegetation regions.
3. Study vertical climate zones.

Taking Notes

As you read, look for details about Earth's natural vegetation regions. Copy the chart below and list each type of climate in the first row of boxes. Add boxes as needed. In the box underneath each type of climate, list facts about each vegetation region that occurs in that type of climate.

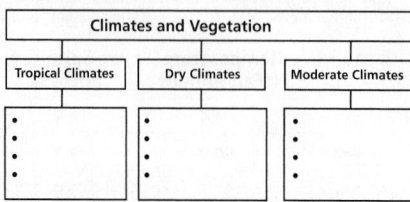

Climates and Vegetation
- Tropical Climates
- Dry Climates
- Moderate Climates

Target Reading Skill

Use Context Clues
You can sometimes learn the meaning of a word or phrase when the context gives examples. In the passage below, the meaning of the word *scrub* is given by the examples in italics.

> Scrub includes *bushes, small trees, and low, woody undergrowth.*

Key Terms

- **vegetation** (vej uh TAY shun) *n.* plants that grow in a region
- **tundra** (TUN druh) *n.* an area of cold climate and low-lying vegetation
- **canopy** (KAN uh pea) *n.* the layer formed by the uppermost branches of a rain forest
- **savanna** (suh VAN uh) *n.* a parklike combination of grasslands and scattered trees
- **desert scrub** (DEZ urt skrub) *n.* desert vegetation that needs little water
- **deciduous trees** (dee SIJ oo us treez) *n.* trees that lose their leaves seasonally
- **coniferous trees** (koh NIF ur us treez) *n.* trees that produce cones to carry seeds

Jackfruit, an Asian fruit, grows huge in the tropical wet climate of Hainan Island, China.

Climate and Vegetation

There are five broad types of climate: tropical, dry, temperate marine, temperate continental, and polar. Each climate has its own types of natural **vegetation,** or plants that grow in a region. This is because different plants require different amounts of water and sunlight and different temperatures to survive. The map titled The World: Natural Vegetation, on page 53, shows the location of Earth's vegetation regions. If you compare this map with the map on pages 44 and 45 titled The World: Climate Regions, you will see that climate regions and vegetation regions often cover similar areas.

Tropical Climates In the tropics, there are two main climates. Both are hot. A tropical wet climate has year-round rainfall. Its typical vegetation is tropical rain forest. A tropical wet and dry climate has two seasons: a rainy season and a dry season. This climate supports grasslands and scattered trees.

Target Reading Skill   L2

Use Context Clues Point out the Target Reading Skill. Tell students that when the context of a sentence provides examples, they can help determine the meaning of an unfamiliar word or phrase.

Model the skill by finding out what vegetation makes up a tropical savanna in this sentence from page 52: "In tropical areas with winter dry seasons or more limited rainfall, there is a parklike landscape of grass- lands with scattered trees known as savanna." *(Tropical savannas are made up of grasslands and scattered trees.)*

Give students *Use Context Clues: Examples.* Have them complete the activity in their groups.

All in One Foundations of Geography Teaching Resources, *Use Context Clues: Examples,* p. 124

Dry Climates Arid and semiarid climates have very hot summers and generally mild winters. They get very little rain. The driest arid climate regions have little or no vegetation. Others have plants that need little water. Semiarid climates get a little more rain. They support shrubs and grasses.

Temperate Marine Climates Temperate marine climates are found in the middle latitudes, usually near coastlines. There are three types: Mediterranean, marine west coast, and humid subtropical. The marine west coast and humid subtropical climates get plenty of rain. In the humid subtropical climate, the rain falls mainly in summer. Mediterranean climates get less rain, and it falls mainly in winter. All of the climates have mild winters. Mediterranean and humid subtropical climates generally have hot summers. With their heavy rainfall, marine west coast and humid subtropical climates support a variety of forests. The drier Mediterranean climates have their own vegetation, known as Mediterranean vegetation.

Temperate Continental Climates In a humid continental climate, summer temperatures are moderate to hot, but winters can be very cold. This climate supports grasslands and forests. Regions with subarctic climates are drier, with cool summers and cold winters. Most subarctic climate regions are forested.

Polar Climates The polar climates are cold all year-round. The **tundra** is an area, near the Arctic Circle, of cold climate and low-lying vegetation. The word *tundra* refers both to the vegetation and the climate, which has short, cool summers and long, very cold winters. Ice cap climates are bitterly cold all year. These areas are covered with ice. No vegetation can grow there.

> ✓ **Reading Check** Why are climate and vegetation related?

Earth's Vegetation Regions

Geographers divide Earth into regions that share similar vegetation. A place's vegetation depends mainly on its climate, but also on other things, such as soil quality.

Polar bears crossing the tundra in Churchill, Manitoba, Canada

Plant Fossils In ancient rocks in Wyoming, scientists have found fossils of palm trees. Millions of years ago, sediments such as sand or ash buried the plants quickly. Over thousands of years, the sediment and plants within turned to rock. Scientists study fossils to learn about ancient climate and vegetation.

Vocabulary Builder

Use the information below to teach students this section's high-use words.

High-Use Word	Definition and Sample Sentence
marine, p. 50	*adj.* of or relating to the sea A **marine** biologist studies ocean plants and animals.
humid, p. 51	*adj.* full of water vapor; moist The weather was hot and **humid**.
dense, p. 52	*adj.* packed in, crowded together We struggled to get through the **dense** bushes.
scatter, p. 52	*v.* to throw loosely about in no specific direction A gust of strong wind made the leaves **scatter**.

Instruct

Climate and Vegetation L2

Guided Instruction

■ **Vocabulary Builder** Clarify the high-use words **marine** and **humid** before reading.

■ Read Climate and Vegetation using the Structured Silent Reading strategy (TE, p. T34). Ask students to study the photos and captions on pp. 50–51.

■ Ask students **What are the five broad types of climate?** *(tropical, dry, temperate marine, temperate continental, and polar)* **What factors are used to distinguish climates?** *(the amount or lack of rainfall and the amount or lack of heat)*

■ Ask students **What kinds of climates have forests?** *(Tropical wet climates, marine west coast, humid subtropical, and temperate continental climates all support forests.)* **Which do not and why?** *(Dry climates, tropical wet and dry climates, and Mediterranean climates do not support forests because there is not enough rainfall. Polar climates do not support forests because the temperatures are too cold.)*

Independent Practice

Ask students to create the Taking Notes graphic organizer on a blank piece of paper. Remind them to add extra boxes to include all of the broad types of climates. Then have them fill in each box with facts about vegetation for each of the five different types of climates.

Monitor Progress

As students fill in the graphic organizer, circulate and make sure individuals are selecting the correct details. Provide assistance as needed.

Links

Read the **Links to Science** box on this page. Ask students **What information do plant fossils give scientists?** *(Plant fossils help scientists learn about ancient climate and vegetation.)*

Answer

✓ **Reading Check** Different plants require different amounts of water and sunlight and different temperatures to survive.

Earth's Vegetation Regions

L2

Guided Instruction

- **Vocabulary Builder** Clarify the high-use words **dense** and **scatter** before reading.

- As a class, show students *The World: Annual Precipitation* and *The World: Desert and Desert Scrub Vegetation Regions* for a more detailed view of desert and desert scrub vegetation regions.

  📖 **Foundations of Geography Transparencies,** *Color Transparency FG 10: The World: Annual Precipitation (Base); Color Transparency FG 12: The World: Desert and Desert Scrub Vegetation Regions (Overlay)*

- Write the different types of vegetation on the board. Ask students to brainstorm locations where they think the types of vegetation would be found. Have students refer to the map on page 53 to get ideas.

Independent Practice

Have students complete their graphic organizers with the information they just learned.

Monitor Progress

- Show *Section Reading Support Transparency FG 48* and ask students to check their graphic organizers individually. Go over key concepts and clarify key vocabulary as needed.

  📖 **Foundations of Geography Transparencies,** *Section Reading Support Transparency FG 48*

🔄 Target Reading Skill

L2

Use Context Clues As a follow up, ask students to answer the Target Reading Skill question in the Student Edition. *(It includes grasses, shrubs, and low trees.)*

This tropical rain forest in Brazil supports dense vegetation.

Use Context Clues If you do not know what Mediterranean vegetation is, consider the examples and other information given by the context. What does the context tell you about this vegetation?

- **Tropical Rain Forest** Because there is so much sunlight, heat, and rain, thousands of kinds of plants grow in a rain forest. Some trees rise 130 feet (40 meters) into the air. The dense, leafy layer formed by the uppermost branches of the rainforest is called the **canopy.** Other plants grow to lower heights in the shade beneath the canopy.

- **Tropical Savanna** In tropical areas with winter dry seasons or more limited rainfall, there is a parklike landscape of grasslands with scattered trees known as **savanna.**

- **Desert** In the driest parts of deserts, there may be no vegetation at all. Elsewhere, plants grow far apart. Their roots absorb scarce water before it evaporates in the heat.

- **Desert Scrub** Semiarid areas and deserts with a little more rain support **desert scrub,** or low desert vegetation that needs little water. Some plants flower only when it rains, so that seeds have a better chance to survive.

- **Mediterranean Vegetation** Mediterranean vegetation includes grasses, shrubs, and low trees. These plants must hold water from the winter rains to survive warm, dry summers.

- **Temperate Grassland** Vast grasslands straddle regions with semiarid and humid continental climates. The wetter grasslands, in humid continental climates, have a mix of tall grasses and other plants that is sometimes called prairie.

- **Deciduous Forest** Marine west coast, humid subtropical, and humid continental climates all support forests of **deciduous trees,** or trees that lose their leaves in the fall.

- **Coniferous and Mixed Forest** These same climates also support areas of coniferous and mixed forest. **Coniferous trees** are trees that produce cones to carry seeds. They generally have needles, not leaves. These features protect trees in drier climates. Mixed forests combine both coniferous and deciduous trees.

- **Tundra** The tundra is an area of cold climate and low-lying vegetation. Tundra vegetation includes mosses, grasses, and low shrubs that bloom during the brief, cool summers.

- **Highland** In highland regions, vegetation depends on elevation, since temperatures drop as elevation rises. Tropical forests may grow at low elevations, with grasslands and coniferous forests farther up. Still higher, tundra vegetation may grow.

- **Ice Cap and Pack Ice** Around the poles, thick ice caps form on land. Masses of ice called pack ice cover the sea. No vegetation can grow there.

✓ **Reading Check** What types of vegetation grow in deserts?

Answer

✓ **Reading Check** desert scrub and vegetation that has roots which can absorb water before it evaporates

---

Differentiated Instruction

For Advanced Readers **L3**

Have students read *The Endless Steppe.* Using its location and description in the selection, have students identify its climate and vegetation regions. Then have students check their conclusions by locating Rubtsovsk in an atlas, encyclopedia, or on the Internet.

All in One Foundations of Geography Teaching Resources, *The Endless Steppe,* pp. 141–142

For Less Proficient Readers **L1**

To ensure students know how to read the natural vegetation map on page 53, have students complete *Reading a Natural Vegetation Map* in pairs.

All in One Foundations of Geography Teaching Resources, *Reading a Natural Vegetation Map,* p. 137

The World: Natural Vegetation

This map shows the natural vegetation regions of the world. The locations of these regions depend mainly on climate. Like the climates that support them, vegetation regions vary according to their distance from the Equator and the amount of precipitation they receive.

The Sahara ▶
The world's largest desert has vast sand dunes with little or no vegetation. This picture also shows an oasis, or a place in the desert where underground water allows trees or crops to grow.

Location In which parts of Earth do you find tropical rain forests? **Compare and Contrast** Find tropical wet climates on the map in the previous section titled The World: Climate Regions. How do those locations compare with the locations of tropical rain forests?

Go Online
PHSchool.com Use Web Code **lep-3214** for step-by-step map skills practice.

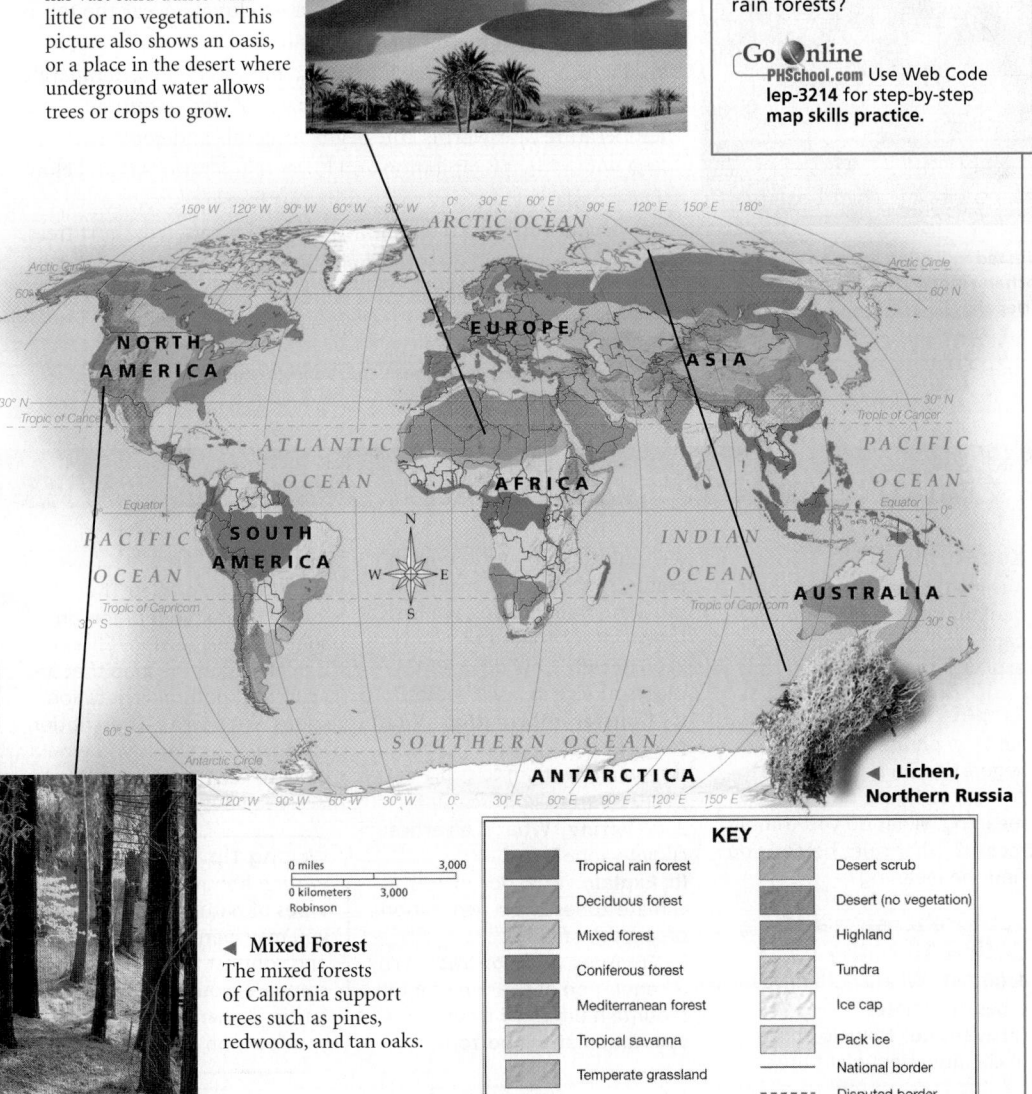

◀ **Lichen, Northern Russia**

◀ **Mixed Forest**
The mixed forests of California support trees such as pines, redwoods, and tan oaks.

KEY

■	Tropical rain forest	▨	Desert scrub
■	Deciduous forest	■	Desert (no vegetation)
■	Mixed forest	■	Highland
■	Coniferous forest	▧	Tundra
■	Mediterranean forest	▫	Ice cap
■	Tropical savanna	▫	Pack ice
■	Temperate grassland	—	National border
		---	Disputed border

0 miles 3,000
0 kilometers 3,000
Robinson

Vertical Climate Zones L2

Guided Instruction

- Read Vertical Climate Zones as a class. As you read, circulate to make sure students are able to answer the Reading Check question.

- Ask students **Why do mountains have a vertical climate?** (*Climate depends on elevation. Elevation changes the farther you go up a mountain causing the climate to change significantly.*)

- Ask students to predict how their clothing might change as they climb a mountain in a temperate climate. (*They might need shorts or light clothing at the base of the mountain; a jacket or coat in the coniferous forest; and polar gear as they climb toward the peak.*)

Independent Practice

Assign *Guided Reading and Review*.

All in One Foundations of Geography Teaching Resources, *Guided Reading and Review,* p. 119

Monitor Progress

Tell students to fill in the last column of their *Reading Readiness Guides*. Probe for what they learned that confirms or invalidates each statement.

All in One Foundations of Geography Teaching Resources, *Reading Readiness Guide,* p. 118

Answers

MAP MASTER Skills Activity **Location** near the Equator **Compare and Contrast** areas with tropical forests are similar to areas of tropical climates

Go Online PHSchool.com Students may practice their map skills using the interactive online version of this map.

Assess and Reteach

Assess Progress   L2
Have students complete the Section Assessment. Administer the *Section Quiz*.

All in One **Foundations of Geography Teaching Resources**, *Section Quiz*, p. 120

Reteach   L1
If students need more instruction, have them read this section in the Reading and Vocabulary Study Guide.

📖 **Eastern Hemisphere Reading and Vocabulary Study Guide**, pp. 18–20

Extend   L3
To extend the lesson, have students create a natural vegetation poster identifying at least five plants that are native to the climate region in which they live. The poster should include information about the climate region, the names of the plants and why they are suited to this particular region, and, if possible, illustrations.

All in One **Foundations of Geography Teaching Resources**, *Rubric for Assessing a Student Poster*, p. 150

Answer

✔ Reading Check   The amount and types of vegetation decrease as the elevation increases until the cold temperature prevents any vegetation.

Section 4 Assessment

Key Terms
Students' sentences should reflect knowledge of each Key Term.

🔄 **Target Reading Skill**
Tundra vegetation includes mosses, grasses, and low shrubs that bloom during brief, cool summers. The examples of mosses and grasses provide clues to the meaning of the phrase.

Comprehension and Critical Thinking
1. (a) tropical, dry, temperate marine, temperate continental, and polar **(b)** Because different plants require different amounts of water, sun, and different temperatures, each climate region has its own types of vegetation. **(c)** Low-lying plants and scrub grow in climates with little precipitation and forests grow in climates with heavier precipitation.

Forested valley at the foot of Machapuchare, a mountain in Nepal

Vertical Climate Zones
The climate at the top of Mount Everest, in southern Asia, is like Antarctica's. But Mount Everest is near the Tropic of Cancer, far from the South Pole. It is so cold at the top of the mountain because the air becomes cooler as elevation increases. Mountains have vertical climate zones, where the climate and vegetation depend on elevation.

In a tropical region, vegetation that needs a tropical climate will grow only near the bottom of a mountain. Farther up is vegetation that can grow in a temperate climate. Near the top is vegetation that can grow in a polar climate.

Picture yourself on a hike up a mountain in a temperate climate. Grassland surrounds the base of the mountain, and temperatures are warm. You begin to climb and soon enter an area with more precipitation and lower temperatures than below. The grassland gives way to a coniferous forest.

As you continue to climb, you find only scattered, short trees. Finally, it is too cold even for them. There are only the low shrubs, short grasses, and mosses of a tundra. At the mountain's peak, you find permanent ice, where no vegetation grows.

✔ Reading Check   How does vegetation change with elevation?

✦ Section 4 Assessment

Key Terms
Review the key terms at the beginning of this section. Use each term in a sentence that explains its meaning.

🔄 **Target Reading Skill**
Find the phrase *tundra vegetation* on page 52. Use context to figure out its meaning. What do you think it means? What clues helped you find the meaning?

Comprehension and Critical Thinking
1. (a) List What are the five main types of climate?
(b) Evaluate How do differences in climate affect plant life?

(c) Analyze Why do low-lying plants, such as scrub or tundra, grow in some climates, while rich forests grow in others?
2. (a) Recall How do desert plants survive in dry climates?
(b) Transfer Information What features of the plants in your region allow them to grow in your region's climate?
3. (a) Define What is a vertical climate zone?
(b) Explain How do vertical climate zones affect vegetation on a mountain?
(c) Compare and Contrast Why is vegetation at the top of a tall mountain different from vegetation at the bottom?

Writing Activity
Look at the map titled The World: Natural Vegetation on page 53 in this section. Choose three places on the map that are in different natural vegetation regions. Then write a description of the types of plants you would expect to see if you visited each place you have chosen.

> **Writing Tip** Since you are writing about three different types of natural vegetation, you may want to compare and contrast them. When you compare, you point out similarities. When you contrast, you focus on differences.

54 Foundations of Geography

2. (a) Desert plants have roots that absorb scarce water before it evaporates; some desert plants flower only when it rains so that as many seeds survive as possible. **(b)** Students' answers will vary by region.

3. (a) A vertical climate zone is one where the climate and vegetation depend on elevation. **(b)** The climate region at the bottom of a mountain can usually support a wide variety of vegetation because it is relatively warm. The climate region at the peak of a mountain is usually much colder and supports less vegetation. **(c)** The climate at the top of a mountain is colder than the climate at the bottom.

Writing Activity
Use the *Rubric for Assessing a Writing Assignment* to evaluate students' essays.

All in One **Foundations of Geography Teaching Resources**, *Rubric for Assessing a Writing Assignment*, p. 145

Review and Assessment

◆ Chapter Summary

Section 1: Our Planet, Earth
- Earth's rotation on its axis changes day to night and night to day.
- The tilt of Earth's axis causes our seasons.

Section 2: Forces Shaping Earth
- Earth's three main layers are the crust, the mantle, and the core.
- Forces inside Earth move plates of crust to form mountains and volcanoes.
- Wind, water, and ice wear down and reshape Earth's surface.

Section 3: Climate and Weather
- Climate is the average weather in a region over a long period of time.
- Climate depends on latitude, landforms, and nearness to an ocean.
- Winds and ocean currents help spread Earth's warmth. They can also cause dangerous storms.

Section 4: How Climate Affects Vegetation
- Vegetation depends mainly on climate.
- Earth can be divided into several natural vegetation regions.
- Climate and vegetation change with elevation.

Delicate Arch, Utah

◆ Key Terms

Each of the statements below contains a key term from the chapter. If the statement is true, write *true*. If it is false, rewrite the statement to make it true.

1. Earth's movement around the sun is called rotation.

2. The mantle is a thick, rocky layer around Earth's core.

3. Earth's crust is at the center of the planet.

4. Magma is hot, flowing rock beneath Earth's surface.

5. The Appalachian Mountains have been worn down over time by erosion.

6. If you want to know how hot it will be tomorrow, you can look at a climate report.

7. Temperature measures how hot or how cold something is.

8. Vegetation is a term for the plants that grow in a region.

9. Deciduous forests grow in polar climates.

┌ Vocabulary Builder ─────

Revisit this chapter's high-use words:

standard	surge	marine
relative	splinter	humid
force	indirect	dense
collide	distribute	scatter

Ask students to review the definitions they recorded on their *Word Knowledge* worksheets.

All in One Foundations of Geography Teaching Resources, *Word Knowledge,* p. 125

Consider allowing students to earn extra credit if they use the words in their answers to the questions in the Chapter Review and Assessment. The words must be used correctly and in a natural context to win the extra points.

Review Chapter Content

- Review and revisit the major themes of this chapter by asking students to classify what Guiding Question each bulleted statement in the Chapter Summary answers. Have students write the Chapter Summary on a separate piece of paper. Then with a partner have them determine which Guiding Question applies to each statement and number the statements accordingly. Refer to page 1 in the Student Edition for the text of the Guiding Questions.

- Assign *Vocabulary Development* for students to review Key Terms.

  All in One Foundations of Geography Teaching Resources, *Vocabulary Development,* p. 144

Answers

Key Terms

1. False. Earth travels around the sun in an oval-shaped orbit.

2. True

3. False. Earth's core is at the center of the planet.

4. True

5. True

6. False. If you want to know how hot it will be tomorrow, you could look at a weather report.

7. True

8. True

9. False. Deciduous forests grow in marine west coast, humid subtropical, and humid continental climates.

Review and Assessment

Comprehension and Critical Thinking

10. (a) 24 **(b)** Earth is divided into 24 time zones because it takes 24 hours for Earth to complete one rotation.

11. (a) the summer solstice, or the longest day of the year **(b)** When a hemisphere tilts toward the sun, it receives direct sunlight, making summers hot. When a hemisphere tilts away from the sun, it receives indirect sunlight, making winters cold. **(c)** The sun is never directly overhead in Antarctica because it is in a high latitude, or polar zone, that is cold year round.

12. (a) three percent **(b)** Possible answer: Lakes, rivers, and ground water might freeze decreasing the fresh water supply.

13. (a) Wind is caused by air currents that follow regular patterns related to latitude. **(b)** Negative—tropical cyclones; hurricanes; tornadoes; Positive—wind and water can make climates milder.

14. (a) Ocean currents help distribute Earth's heat. Warm water flows away from the Equator and cold water moves away from the poles. **(b)** Water remains cooler as the air and land heats up in summer; so wind blowing over the water cools coastal land nearby.

15. (a) Different kinds of vegetation grow in each of the five broad types of climate areas because different plants require different amounts of water and sunlight and different temperatures. **(b)** Tropical climates with year-round rainfall will support a tropical rainforest, because such vegetation requires high rainfall.

Skills Practice

Paragraphs should include information about the average daily temperature changes from month to month and how the amount of precipitation stays about the same.

Writing Activity

Students' plant descriptions will vary but should include information about dry climates and desert vegetation regions.

All in One Foundations of Geography Teaching Resources, *Rubric for Assessing a Writing Assignment,* p. 145

Review and Assessment (continued)

◆ Comprehension and Critical Thinking

10. (a) Recall How many standard time zones is Earth divided into?
(b) Analyze How are time differences related to the rotation of Earth?

11. (a) Identify As Earth moves around the sun, what event happens about June 21?
(b) Explain How does Earth's movement make summers hot and winters cold?
(c) Apply Information Why is Antarctica cold even in summer?

12. (a) Recall How much of Earth's water is fresh?
(b) Predict If Earth's climate became colder, how might the fresh water supply be affected?

13. (a) Recall What causes winds?
(b) Contrast What are some negative and positive effects of wind and water in the tropics?

14. (a) Describe How do oceans shape climate?
(b) Synthesize Information Why do some coastal cities in the tropics stay cool?

15. (a) Describe How does climate affect vegetation?
(b) Evaluate A tropical climate has year-round rainfall. Can forests grow there? Explain why or why not.

◆ Skills Practice

Using Special Geography Graphs Review the steps you learned in the Skills For Life activity in this chapter. Then look at the climate graph for Helsinki, Finland, below. After you have analyzed the graph, write a paragraph that summarizes Helsinki's climate.

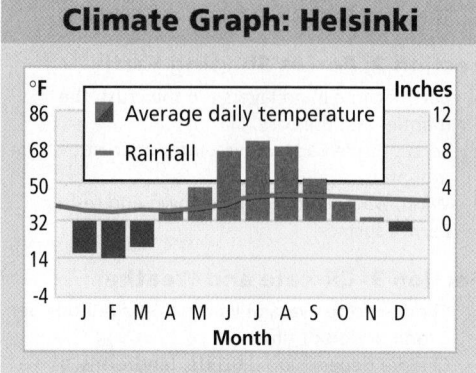

Climate Graph: Helsinki

◆ Writing Activity: Science

Reread the descriptions of dry climates and of desert vegetation regions. Then design a plant that could live in these regions. Describe how it would get light, water, and nutrients.

MAP MASTER Skills Activity

Oceans and Seas

Place Location For each place listed below, write the letter that marks its location on the map.
1. Atlantic Ocean
2. Arctic Ocean
3. Indian Ocean
4. Mediterranean Sea
5. Pacific Ocean
6. Southern Ocean

Go Online
PHSchool.com Use Web Code **lep-3215** for step-by-step map skills practice.

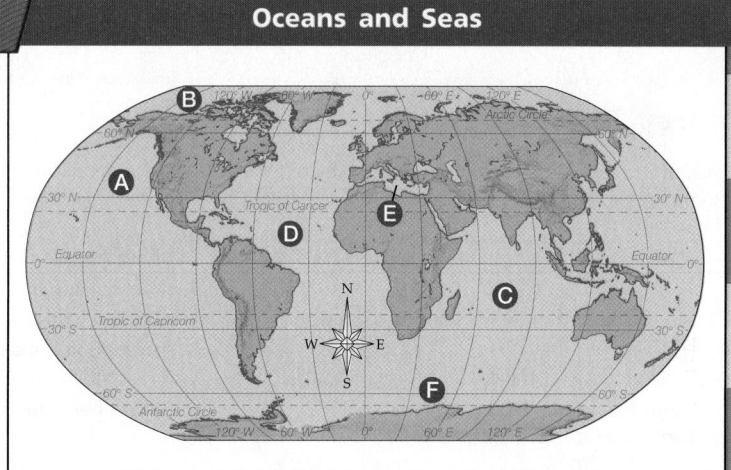

56 Foundations of Geography

MAP MASTER Skills Activity

1. D	**2.** B
3. C	**4.** E
5. A	**6.** F

Go Online PHSchool.com Students may practice their map skills using the interactive online version of this map.

Standardized Test Prep

Test-Taking Tips

Some questions on standardized tests ask you to use map keys. Read the precipitation map key below. Then follow the tips to answer the sample question.

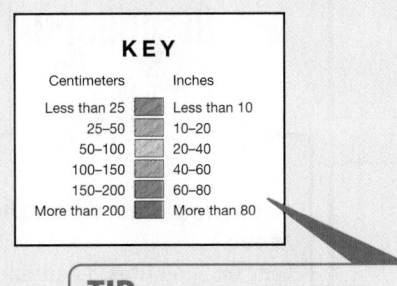

KEY

Centimeters	Inches
Less than 25	Less than 10
25–50	10–20
50–100	20–40
100–150	40–60
150–200	60–80
More than 200	More than 80

TIP On a map key, the colors line up with the data. To find information, read the numbers to the left or right of a given color.

Pick the letter that best answers the question.

On a precipitation map, the southern coastal states are colored dark green. According to the key at the left, how many inches of rain does this region get each year?

A 20–40
B 60–80
C 50–100
D 150–200

TIP To be sure you understand what the question is asking, restate it in your own words: *The color DARK GREEN on the map key stands for how many inches of rain each year?*

Think It Through The question asks about inches of rain, but the answers C and D show numbers from the centimeter column. The numbers 20–40 (answer A) are next to yellow, not dark green. The numbers 60–80 are next to dark green in the inches column. The answer is B.

Practice Questions

Use the tips above and other tips in this book to help you answer the following questions:

1. When the Northern Hemisphere has days and nights of equal length, it is
A summer solstice.
B spring equinox.
C New Year's Day.
D winter solstice.

2. Which of the following is NOT an example of a landform?
A a mountain
B a plateau
C a plain
D an atmosphere

3. In which vegetation region would you find a plant with shallow roots, meant to absorb water before it evaporates?
A desert
B deciduous forest
C coniferous forest
D tropical savanna

Study the following map key and answer the question that follows.

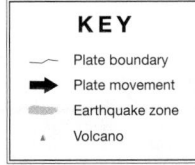

KEY

— Plate boundary
➡ Plate movement
Earthquake zone
▲ Volcano

4. On a map with this key, you would find places where earthquakes happen by looking for
A a brown area.
B a red triangle.
C a black arrow.
D a black line.

Use Web Code **lea-3201** for a **Chapter 2 self-test.**

Assessment Resources

Use *Chapter Tests A and B* to assess students' mastery of the chapter content.

All in One Foundations of Geography Teaching Resources, *Chapter Tests A and B,* pp. 151–156

Tests also available on the *ExamView Test Bank CD-ROM.*

⊙ *ExamView Test Bank CD-ROM*

Use a benchmark test to evaluate students' cumulative understanding of what they have learned in Chapters 1 and 2.

📄 Foundations of Geography Benchmark Test 1, **AYP Monitoring Assessments,** pp. 81–84.

Earth's Human Geography

Chapter Overview

Overview

Section 1 — Population
1. Learn about population distribution.
2. Explore population density.
3. Investigate population growth.

Section 2 — Migration
1. Learn about migration, or people's movement from one region to another.
2. Investigate urbanization, or people's movement to cities.

Section 3 — Economic Systems
1. Examine different kinds of economies.
2. Investigate levels of economic development.
3. Study global trade patterns.

Section 4 — Political Systems
1. Examine different types of states.
2. Investigate types of government.
3. Learn about alliances and international organizations.

Discovery Channel School Video

Migration: People on the Move
Length: 3 minutes, 57 seconds
Use with Section 2
This segment is an overview of human migration and the reasons for it. It discusses human migration in Senegal and the problems that it causes.

Technology Resources

Go Online
PHSchool.com

Students use embedded Web codes to access Internet activities, chapter self-tests, and additional map practice. They may also access Dorling Kindersley's Online Desk Reference to learn more about each country they study.

Interactive Textbook

Use the Interactive Textbook to make content and concepts come alive through animations, videos, and activities that accompany the complete basal text—online and on CD-ROM.

PRENTICE HALL
TeacherEXPRESS
Plan · Teach · Assess

Use this complete suite of powerful teaching tools to make planning lessons and administering tests quicker and easier.

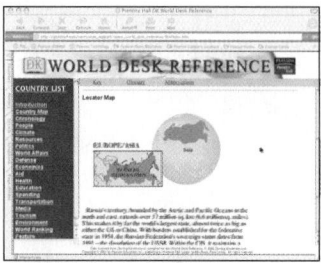

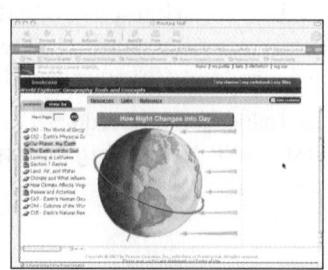

Reading and Assessment

Reading and Vocabulary Instruction

↻ Model the Target Reading Skill

Compare and Contrast Remind students that when they compare and contrast, they analyze two objects or situations to find their similarities and differences. Model comparing and contrasting using information from page 75 of the Student Edition. Draw a Venn diagram on the board. Label the left-hand section "capitalism," the middle section "both," and the right-hand section "communism." Tell students that they make comparisons when they find similarities and contrasts when they find differences.

Ask yourself the following questions aloud, as you fill in the diagram. "What is the same about capitalism and communism? *(they are types of economic systems.)* What are the differences between capitalism and communism? *(capitalism: businesses are privately owned; communism: the government has control of the economy)* How can I summarize these comparisons and contrasts? *(Capitalism and communism are both types of economic systems, but in communism the government controls the entire economy, and capitalism has a free-market economy.)*"

Use the following worksheets from All-in-One Foundations of Geography Teaching Resources (pp. 177–179) to support this chapter's Target Reading Skill.

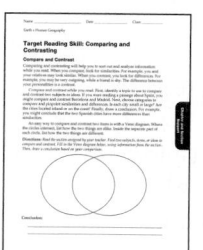 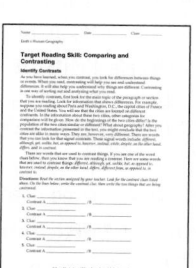 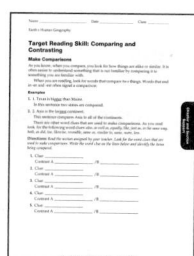

Vocabulary Builder
High-Use Academic Words

Use these steps to teach this chapter's high-use words:

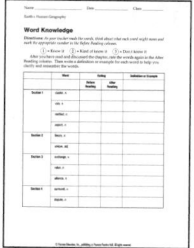

1. Have students rate how well they know each word on their Word Knowledge worksheets (All-in-One Foundations of Geography Teaching Resources, p. 180).
2. Pronounce each word and ask students to repeat it.
3. Give students a brief definition or sample sentence (provided on TE pp. 61, 68, 75, and 81).
4. Work with students as they fill in the "Definition or Example" column of their Word Knowledge worksheets.

Assessment

Formal Assessment

Test students' understanding of core knowledge and skills.

Chapter Tests A and B, Foundations of Geography Teaching Resources, pp. 199–204

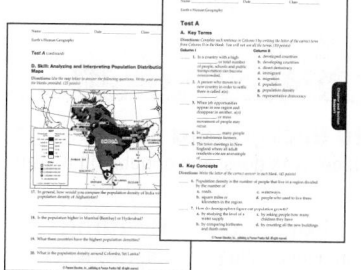

Customize the Chapter Tests to suit your needs.
ExamView Test Bank CD-ROM

Skills Assessment

Assess geographic literacy.

MapMaster Skills, Student Edition pp. 61, 62, 63, 69, 77, 86

Assess reading skills.

Target Reading Skills, Student Edition, pp. 62, 68, 76, 81, and in Section Assessments

Chapter 3 Assessment, Eastern Hemisphere Reading and Vocabulary Study Guide, p. 34

Performance Assessment

Assess students' performance on this chapter's Writing Activities using rubrics from All-in-One Foundations of Geography Teaching Resources.

Rubric for Assessing a Writing Assignment, p. 197

Rubric for Assessing a Bar Graph, p. 198

Assess students' work through performance tasks.

Small Group Activity: Making an Immigration Map, All-in-One Foundations of Geography Teaching Resources, pp. 183–186

Online Assessment

Have students check their own understanding.

Chapter Self-Test

Section 1 Population

 *1.5 periods, .75 block*

Social Studies Objectives

1. Learn about population distribution.
2. Explore population density.
3. Investigate population growth.

Reading/Language Arts Objective

Compare and contrast to analyze information.

Prepare to Read	**Instructional Resources**	**Differentiated Instruction**
Build Background Knowledge Ask students to guess the population densities of local cities. **Set a Purpose for Reading** Have students evaluate statements on the *Reading Readiness Guide*. **Preview Key Terms** Teach the section's Key Terms. **Target Reading Skill** Introduce the section's Target Reading Skill of **comparing and contrasting**.	**All in One Foundations of Geography Teaching Resources** L2 Reading Readiness Guide, p. 162 L2 Compare and Contrast, p. 177	**Spanish Reading and Vocabulary Study Guide** L1 Chapter 3, Section 1, pp. 17–18 ELL

Instruct	**Instructional Resources**	**Differentiated Instruction**
Population Distribution Ask questions about factors that affect population size and distribution. **Target Reading Skill** Review **comparing and contrasting**. **Population Density** Compare and contrast population density and population distribution. **Population Growth** Discuss the relationship between birthrate, death rate, and population.	**All in One Foundations of Geography Teaching Resources** L2 Guided Reading and Review, p. 163 L2 Reading Readiness Guide, p. 162 **Foundations of Geography Transparencies** L2 Section Reading Support Transparency FG 49	**All in One Foundations of Geography Teaching Resources** L3 Analyzing Statistics, p. 187 AR, GT L3 Enrichment, p. 181 AR, GT **Teacher's Edition** L1 For Less Proficient Readers, TE pp. 62, 63 L1 For Special Needs Students, TE p. 62 L3 For Gifted and Talented, TE pp. 63, 64 L3 For Advanced Readers, TE p. 64 **Student Edition on Audio CD** L1 Chapter 3, Section 1 ELL, LPR, SN

Assess and Reteach	**Instructional Resources**	**Differentiated Instruction**
Assess Progress Evaluate student comprehension with the section assessment and section quiz. **Reteach** Assign the Reading and Vocabulary Study Guide to help struggling students. **Extend** Extend the lesson by assigning an Internet activity.	**All in One Foundations of Geography Teaching Resources** L2 Section Quiz, p. 164 Rubric for Assessing a Writing Assignment, p. 197 **Reading and Vocabulary Study Guide** L1 Chapter 3, Section 1, pp. 22–24 **PHSchool.com** L3 **For:** Environmental and Global Issues: Evaluating Solutions **Web Code:** led-3300	**Spanish Support** L2 Section Quiz (Spanish), p. 1923 ELL

Key

L1 Basic to Average   L3 Average to Advanced   LPR Less Proficient Readers   GT Gifted and Talented
L2 For All Students   AR Advanced Readers   ELL English Language Learners
                                        SN Special Needs Students

Section 2 Migration

🕐 *3 periods, 1.5 blocks (includes Skills for Life)*

Social Studies Objectives

1. Learn about migration, or people's movement from one region to another.
2. Investigate urbanization, or people's movement to cities.

Reading/Language Arts Objective

Identify contrasts to understand how situations differ.

Prepare to Read	**Instructional Resources**	**Differentiated Instruction**
Build Background Knowledge Have students brainstorm why people move to different places. **Set a Purpose for Reading** Have students evaluate statements on the *Reading Readiness Guide.* **Preview Key Terms** Teach the section's Key Terms. **Target Reading Skill** Introduce the section's Target Reading Skill of **identifying contrasts.**	**All in One Foundations of Geography Teaching Resources** L2 Reading Readiness Guide, p. 166 L2 Identify Contrasts, p. 178	**Spanish Reading and Vocabulary Study Guide** L1 Chapter 3, Section 2, pp. 19–20 ELL

Instruct	**Instructional Resources**	**Differentiated Instruction**
Why People Migrate Ask questions about migration and discuss the push-pull theory. **Target Reading Skill** Review **identifying contrasts.** **Urbanization** Ask about urbanization and discuss some problems it can cause.	**All in One Foundations of Geography Teaching Resources** L2 Guided Reading and Review, p. 167 L2 Reading Readiness Guide, p. 166 L2 Message from the Rain Forest Amerindians, p. 188 **Foundations of Geography Transparencies** L2 Section Reading Support Transparency FG 50 L2 Transparency B2: Flow Chart **World Studies Video Program** L2 Migration: People on the Move	**All in One Foundations of Geography Teaching Resources** L3 Small Group Activity: Making an Immigration Map, pp. 183–186 AR, GT L2 Skills for Life, p. 182 AR, GT, LPR, SN **Teacher's Edition** L3 For Advanced Readers, TE p. 70 L1 For English Language Learners, TE p. 70 **Spanish Support** L2 Guided Reading and Review (Spanish), p. 20 ELL

Assess and Reteach	**Instructional Resources**	**Differentiated Instruction**
Assess Progress Evaluate student comprehension with the section assessment and section quiz. **Reteach** Assign the Reading and Vocabulary Study Guide to help struggling students. **Extend** Extend the lesson by having students research an American who immigrated to the United States.	**All in One Foundations of Geography Teaching Resources** L2 Section Quiz, p. 168 Rubric for Assessing a Writing Assignment, p. 197 **Reading and Vocabulary Study Guide** L1 Chapter 3, Section 2, pp. 25–27	**Spanish Support** L2 Section Quiz (Spanish), p. 21 ELL **Foundations of Geography Transparencies** L3 Color Transparency FG 5: The World: Continents and Oceans (Base) AR, GT L3 Color Transparency FG 16: The World: Population Density (Overlay) AR, GT **Teacher's Edition** L1 For Special Needs Students, TE p. 73 **Social Studies Skills Tutor CD-ROM** L1 Analyzing and Interpreting Special Purpose Maps ELL, LPR, SN

Key

L1 Basic to Average   L3 Average to Advanced

L2 For All Students

LPR Less Proficient Readers
AR Advanced Readers
SN Special Needs Students

GT Gifted and Talented
ELL English Language Learners

Section 3 Economic Systems

 1.5 periods, .75 block

Social Studies Objectives
1. Examine different kinds of economies.
2. Investigate levels of economic development.
3. Study global trade patterns.

Reading/Language Arts Objective
Make comparisons to understand what things have in common.

Prepare to Read	**Instructional Resources**	**Differentiated Instruction**
Build Background Knowledge Ask students to brainstorm the meaning of *economy*. **Set a Purpose for Reading** Have students evaluate statements on the *Reading Readiness Guide*. **Preview Key Terms** Teach the section's Key Terms. **Target Reading Skill** Introduce the section's Target Reading Skill of **making comparisons.**	**All in One Foundations of Geography Teaching Resources** L2 Reading Readiness Guide, p. 170 L2 Make Comparisons, p. 179	**Spanish Reading and Vocabulary Study Guide** L1 Chapter 3, Section 3, pp. 21–22 ELL

Instruct	**Instructional Resources**	**Differentiated Instruction**
Different Kinds of Economies Discuss various types of economies. **Levels of Economic Development** Discuss the differences between developed and developing countries' economies. **Target Reading Skill** Review **making comparisons.** **World Trade Patterns** Ask questions about and discuss world trade.	**All in One Foundations of Geography Teaching Resources** L2 Guided Reading and Review, p. 171 L2 Reading Readiness Guide, p. 170 **Foundations of Geography Transparencies** L2 Section Reading Support Transparency FG 51	**Teacher's Edition** L1 For Less Proficient Readers, TE p. 77 L3 For Gifted and Talented, TE p. 77 **Spanish Support** L2 Guided Reading and Review (Spanish), p. 22 ELL

Assess and Reteach	**Instructional Resources**	**Differentiated Instruction**
Assess Progress Evaluate student comprehension with the section assessment and section quiz. **Reteach** Assign the Reading and Vocabulary Study Guide to help struggling students. **Extend** Extend the lesson by assigning an Internet activity.	**All in One Foundations of Geography Teaching Resources** L2 Section Quiz, p. 172 Rubric for Assessing a Writing Assignment, p. 197 **Reading and Vocabulary Study Guide** L1 Chapter 3, Section 3, pp. 28–30 **PHSchool.com** L3 For: Environmental and Global Issues: Trade in a Global Economy Web Code: led-3306	**Spanish Support** L2 Section Quiz (Spanish), p. 23 ELL

Key
L1 Basic to Average | L3 Average to Advanced | LPR Less Proficient Readers | GT Gifted and Talented
L2 For All Students | | AR Advanced Readers | ELL English Language Learners
| | SN Special Needs Students |

Section 4 **Political Systems**

 4.5 periods, 2.25 blocks (includes Chapter Review and Assessment, and Literature)

Social Studies Objectives
1. Examine different types of states.
2. Investigate types of government.
3. Learn about alliances and international organizations.

Reading/Language Arts Objective
Recognize contrast signal words to understand how things are different.

Prepare to Read	**Instructional Resources**	**Differentiated Instruction**
Build Background Knowledge Discuss different types of leaders. **Set a Purpose for Reading** Have students evaluate statements on the *Reading Readiness Guide*. **Preview Key Terms** Teach the section's Key Terms. **Target Reading Skill** Introduce the section's Target Reading Skill of **recognizing contrast signal words**.	**All in One Foundations of Geography Teaching Resources** **L2** Reading Readiness Guide, p. 174 **L2** Identify Contrasts, p. 178	**Spanish Reading and Vocabulary Study Guide** **L1** Chapter 3 Section 4, pp. 23–24 ELL

Instruct	**Instructional Resources**	**Differentiated Instruction**
Target Reading Skill Review **using contrast signal words**. **Types of States** Discuss characteristics of different kinds of states. **Types of Government** Compare and contrast different types of government. **International Organizations** Discuss the purpose of alliances and international organizations.	**All in One Foundations of Geography Teaching Resources** **L2** Guided Reading and Review, p. 175 **L2** Reading Readiness Guide, p. 174 **Foundations of Geography Transparencies** **L2** Section Reading Support Transparency FG 52 **L2** Transparency B3: Tree Map/Flow Chart	**All in One Foundations of Geography Teaching Resources** **L3** Your Government Has Returned to You! pp. 189–190 AR, GT **L2** Creating Paragraph Outlines, p. 195 AR, GT, LPR, SN **Teacher's Edition** **L3** For Advanced Readers, TE p. 82 **Spanish Support** **L2** Guided Reading and Review (Spanish), p. 24 ELL

Assess and Reteach	**Instructional Resources**	**Differentiated Instruction**
Assess Progress Evaluate student comprehension with the section assessment and section quiz. **Reteach** Assign the Reading and Vocabulary Study Guide to help struggling students. **Extend** Extend the lesson by having students research alliances or international organizations from the section.	**All in One Foundations of Geography Teaching Resources** **L2** Section Quiz, p. 176 Rubric for Assessing a Writing Assignment, p. 197 **L2** Vocabulary Development, p. 196 **L2** Word Knowledge, p. 180 Rubric for Assessing a Bar Graph, p. 198 **L2** Chapter Tests A and B, pp. 199–204 **Reading and Vocabulary Study Guide** **L3** Chapter 3 Section 4 pp. 31–33	**All in One Foundations of Geography Teaching Resources** **L3** Hatchet, pp. 191–194 AR, GT **Spanish Support** **L2** Section Quiz (Spanish), p. 25 ELL **L2** Chapter Summary (Spanish), p. 26 ELL **L2** Vocabulary Development (Spanish), p. 27 ELL

Key
L1 Basic to Average   **L3** Average to Advanced   LPR Less Proficient Readers   GT Gifted and Talented
L2 For All Students   AR Advanced Readers   ELL English Language Learners
                                          SN Special Needs Students

Reading Background

Structured Silent Reading

In this chapter, students will use the Structured Silent Reading technique. To achieve success, always pose a question for students to answer when they finish reading. If students have trouble reading large sections, break the text into chunks of one to four paragraphs, and give students a question to answer for each one. You may ask students to preview the Reading Check question for a selection and then read to find the answer. Students may also preview the headings to develop their own questions before they read.

Model this approach using the paragraph under the heading *New Population Clusters* on page 61 of the Student Edition. Point out that headings in the text are a good place to start when thinking of a question. Think aloud: *The heading for this paragraph is "New Population Clusters." Population means people, and clusters means groups. It must be about how groups of people came to be. So I am going to read to answer this question: "How did new groups of population form?"*

Have students use this method for other selections. Suggest to students that they write down their questions before reading.

Key Terms

Tell students that the Key Terms in Chapter 3 often appear in the news. Challenge them to find at least three of these Key Terms from the chapter used in their daily lives:

population, immigrants, urbanization, capitalism, developing nations

Encourage students to look at newspapers and magazines, listen to the radio, and watch television to find uses of these words. As "evidence," have them bring in a newspaper clipping with the word or write down the sentence in which the word was used during a radio or television broadcast, and note the time and date of the broadcast.

World Studies Background

People Counting People

Demography can trace its beginnings to the work of an English scholar named John Graunt. In 1662, Graunt published his then unique analysis of over fifty years of death and baptism records. During the next century, nations began conducting basic censuses. In 1790, the United States government conducted the first nationwide census for a political purpose; the Constitution mandates that a census of the United States be taken every ten years because population determines representation in the House of Representatives. The idea caught on, and Britain took its first census in 1801. In 1953, China became the last major area to release its census data. Today, demographers have access to vital statistics such as births, deaths, and marriages, and to census data from virtually the entire world.

Worldwide Urbanization

Urbanization is a worldwide trend, although high levels of urbanization are becoming more common in developing countries. The top ten largest urban centers in 1975 were all in developed countries, including New York, Paris, France, and Beijing, China. In 2000, four of the top ten urban centers were in the developing nations of India and Bangladesh.

Infoplease® provides a wealth of useful information for the classroom. You can use this resource to strengthen your background on the subjects covered in this chapter. Have students visit this advertising-free site as a starting point for projects requiring research.

Use Web code **led-3304** for **Infoplease.**

Discussion Ideas

Discussing what students have read is important for them to absorb information. Empower students by having them provide topics for discussion. Explain that they must begin with a strong idea, or seed, to spark a good discussion. The following questions will motivate students to come up with strong seeds for discussion:

What don't I understand?
What have I learned that I did not know before?
What is interesting or surprising?
What words are confusing?
What reminds me of other things I know?

Write the questions on the board, and have students read *Population Growth* on pages 64–66 of the Student Edition. Ask students to answer one of the questions above on an index card. (*For example: I am surprised that large increases in population could drain Earth of its resources. I wonder what we can do to prevent that from happening?*) When students have finished, put the index cards into a bowl. Have students take turns pulling one out and reading it to the class, and discuss each one for five minutes.

Making Choices

Help students to build their understanding of Key Terms and high-use words from the chapter by asking them to make choices between correct and incorrect examples of the words.

Word: *vary*
Example 1: I eat something different for lunch every day. (*correct*)
Example 2: I always eat chicken for dinner.

Word: *immigrants*
Example 1: People move from the country to the city looking for jobs.
Example 2: Many people move from Mexico to the United States each year. (*correct*)

Word: *consumer*
Example 1: Nancy sells her food at the grocery store.
Example 2: Nancy buys her food at the grocery store. (*correct*)

Word: *dispute*
Example 1: Frank argued with his brother over who would play with the toy. (*correct*)
Example 2: Frank and his brother shared the toy.

UNICEF

One of the best-known organizations in the world is UNICEF, the United Nations Children's Fund. Originally created in 1946 to feed the starving children of postwar Europe and China, it was so successful that it was made a permanent organization in 1953. The organization has grown into a powerful and compassionate group of over 7,000 people working in 158 countries "to overcome the obstacles that poverty, violence, disease and discrimination place in a child's path." UNICEF provides food, vaccinations, and education to children around the world, but focuses its efforts on improving the lives of children in developing nations.

Thomas Malthus

In 1798, English writer Thomas Malthus published a book on population. Malthus expressed concern that the world's population was growing too quickly. He believed that future generations would not be able to raise enough food to keep up with population growth. He predicted widespread misery and starvation unless population growth slowed. Although some of Malthus's ideas have been substantiated, others have proven incorrect.

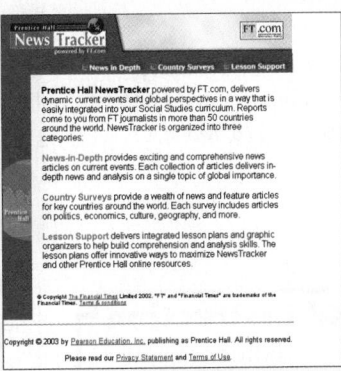

Get in-depth information on topics of global importance with **Prentice Hall Newstracker,** powered by FT.com

Use Web code **led-3305** for **Prentice Hall Newstracker.**

Chapter 3

Guiding Questions

Remind students about the Guiding Questions introduced at the beginning of the book.

Section 1 relates to **Guiding Question** ⑤

How do people use the world's natural resources? *(Many forests are disappearing as the growing world population uses trees for wood and fuel.)*

Section 2 relates to **Guiding Question** ②

How have people's ways of life changed over time? *(Since the 1800s, more people have moved from the countryside to cities.)*

Section 3 relates to **Guiding Question** ⑤

How do people use the world's natural resources? *(Some developing nations sell natural resources, such as oil, to developed nations.)*

Section 4 relates to **Guiding Question** ④

What types of government exist in the world today? *(States are controlled by different types of governments. These include absolute monarchies, dicatorships, oligarchies, constitutional monarchies, and representative democracies.)*

🎯 Target Reading Skill

In this chapter, students will learn and apply the reading skill of comparing and contrasting. Use the following worksheets to help students practice this skill:

All in One Foundations of Geography Teaching Resources, *Compare and Contrast,* p. 177; *Identify Contrasts,* p. 178; *Make Comparisons,* p. 179

Differentiated Instruction

The following Teacher's Edition strategies are suitable for students of varying abilities.
Advanced Readers, pp. 64, 70, 82
English Language Learners, p. 70
Gifted and Talented, pp. 63, 64, 77
Less Proficient Readers, pp. 62, 63, 77
Special Needs Students, pp. 62, 73

Chapter 3
Earth's Human Geography

Chapter Preview

This chapter will introduce you to Earth's human geography, or the patterns of human activity on Earth.

Section 1
Population

Section 2
Migration

Section 3
Economic Systems

Section 4
Political Systems

🎯 Target Reading Skill

Comparison and Contrast In this chapter you will focus on the text structure by learning how to compare and contrast. Comparing and contrasting can help you to sort out and analyze information.

▶ Woman harvesting rice on a terrace built by people in southern China

Bibliography

For the Teacher

Gilbert, Geoffrey. *World Population: A Reference Handbook.* ABC-CLIO, 2001.

Pinder, John. *The European Union: A Very Short Introduction.* Oxford University Press, 2001.

Spellman, William M. *The Global Community: Migration and the Making of the Modern World.* Sutton Publishing, 2002.

For the Student

L1 Giesecke, Ernestine. *Governments Around the World (Kid's Guide).* Heinemean Library, 2000.

L2 Press, Petra. *European Union.* World Almanac, 2003.

L3 Tarsitano, Frank. *United Nations.* World Almanac, 2003.

Using the Visual   L2

Reach Into Your Background Ask students to study the photograph on pp. 58–59. Direct their attention to the caption. Tell students that in this chapter they will learn about the world's urban and rural populations, or populations in cities and the countryside. Ask them if they live in an urban or rural community. Ask students if they think the woman in the picture lives in an urban or rural area. How do they know? (*The woman probably lives in a rural area because she is working on a farm.*)

Chapter Resources

Teaching Resources
- L2 Vocabulary Development, p. 196
- L2 Skills for Life, p. 182
- L2 Chapter Tests A and B, pp. 199–204

Spanish Support
- L2 Spanish Chapter Summary, p. 26
- L2 Spanish Vocabulary Development, p. 27

Media and Technology
- L1 Student Edition on Audio CD
- L1 Guided Reading Audiotapes, English and Spanish
- L2 Social Studies Skills Tutor CD-ROM
- *ExamView Test Bank CD-ROM*

PRENTICE HALL

Presentation EXPRESS™

Teach · Connect · Inspire

Teach this chapter's content using the PresentationExpress™ CD-ROM including:
- slide shows
- transparencies
- interactive maps and media
- *ExamView*® QuickTake Presenter

Section 1
Step-by-Step Instruction

Objectives

Social Studies

1. Learn about population distribution.
2. Explore population density.
3. Investigate population growth.

Reading/Language Arts

Compare and contrast to analyze information.

Prepare to Read

Build Background Knowledge L2

Tell students that in this section they will learn about where on Earth people live, and why they might choose to live there. To introduce the topic, write the names of two locations in your state with which students will be familiar. One should have a high population density and one should have a low population density. Ask students to predict in which location more people live and in which location less people live and why, then conduct an Idea Wave (TE, p.T35) to get students to share their ideas. After they read the section, ask them if their predictions were correct.

Set a Purpose for Reading L2

■ Preview the Objectives.

■ Read each statement in the *Reading Readiness Guide* aloud. Ask students to mark the statements true or false.

All in One Foundations of Geography Teaching Resources, *Reading Readiness Guide,* p. 162

■ Have students discuss the statements in pairs or groups of four, then mark their worksheets again. Use the Numbered Heads participation strategy (TE, p. T36) to call on students to share their group's perspectives.

Vocabulary Builder
Preview Key Terms L2

Pronounce each Key Term, and then ask students to say the word with you. Provide a simple explanation such as, "Demography is the study of where people live and why."

Section 1 Population

Prepare to Read

Objectives

In this section you will

1. Learn about population distribution.
2. Explore population density.
3. Investigate population growth.

Taking Notes

Copy the concept web below. As you read this section, fill in the web with information about the causes and effects of population density and of population growth. Add more ovals as needed.

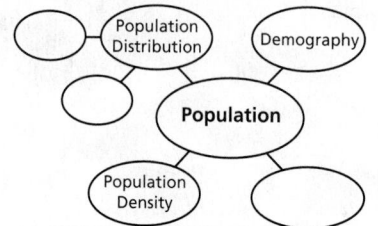

Target Reading Skill

Comparison and Contrast Comparing and contrasting can help you sort out information. When you compare, you examine the similarities between things. When you contrast, you look at the differences. As you read this section, compare and contrast population distribution and population density. Look for the similarities and differences between these two concepts.

Key Terms

- **population** (pahp yuh LAY shun) *n.* total number of people in an area
- **population distribution** (pahp yuh LAY shun dis trih BYOO shun) *n.* the way the population is spread out over an area
- **demography** (dih MAH gruh fee) *n.* the science that studies population distribution and change
- **population density** (pahp yuh LAY shun DEN suh tee) *n.* the average number of people per square mile or square kilometer
- **birthrate** (BURTH rayt) *n.* the number of live births each year per 1,000 people
- **death rate** (deth rayt) *n.* the number of deaths each year per 1,000 people

A crowded village on the Nile River near Aswan, Egypt

60 Foundations of Geography

Population Distribution

The world's **population,** or total number of people, lives in uneven clusters on Earth's surface. Some places have many people. Other places are almost empty. **Population distribution** is the way the population is spread out over an area.

Demography is the science that tries to explain how populations change and why population distribution is uneven. Demographers study rates of birth, marriage, and death. And they ask why people move from one place to another.

Population and Places People usually don't move without a good reason. People may move because they can live better in a new place. Other times, people are forced to move, or they move because they cannot feed their families. However, as long as people can make a living where they are, they usually stay in that area. So, regions with large populations tend to keep them.

Target Reading Skill L2

Compare and Contrast Point out the Target Reading Skill. Tell students that when they compare and contrast information, they identify similarities and differences.

Provide an example of comparing and contrasting by reading the paragraph on p. 63, and then identifying the similarities and differences between Japan and Canada. (*Similarities: Both countries have populations in the millions. Differences: Canada is huge in land area, yet has a population of 32 million people, and a population density of about 9 people per square mile; Japan is small in land area and has a population of 127 million people.*)

Give students *Compare and Contrast.* Have them complete the activity in groups.

All in One Foundations of Geography Teaching Resources, *Compare and Contrast,* p. 177

Population and History In the past, most people lived on farms where they grew their own food. They lived where the climate provided enough water and warm weather to support crops. Regions with a long history of farming, good soil, and plenty of water became crowded. These regions still have large populations. Most places too cold or too dry for farming still have small populations.

New Population Clusters However, after about 1800, improved transportation and new ways of making a living changed things. Railroads and steamships made it easier for people to move long distances, even across oceans. New jobs in factories and offices meant that more people were living in cities, where they could make a living without farming the land. Crowded cities grew in regions that once had few people, such as the United States, Australia, and northern Europe.

Villages in France have grown through centuries of farming.

✓ **Reading Check** Why are some parts of the world more crowded than others?

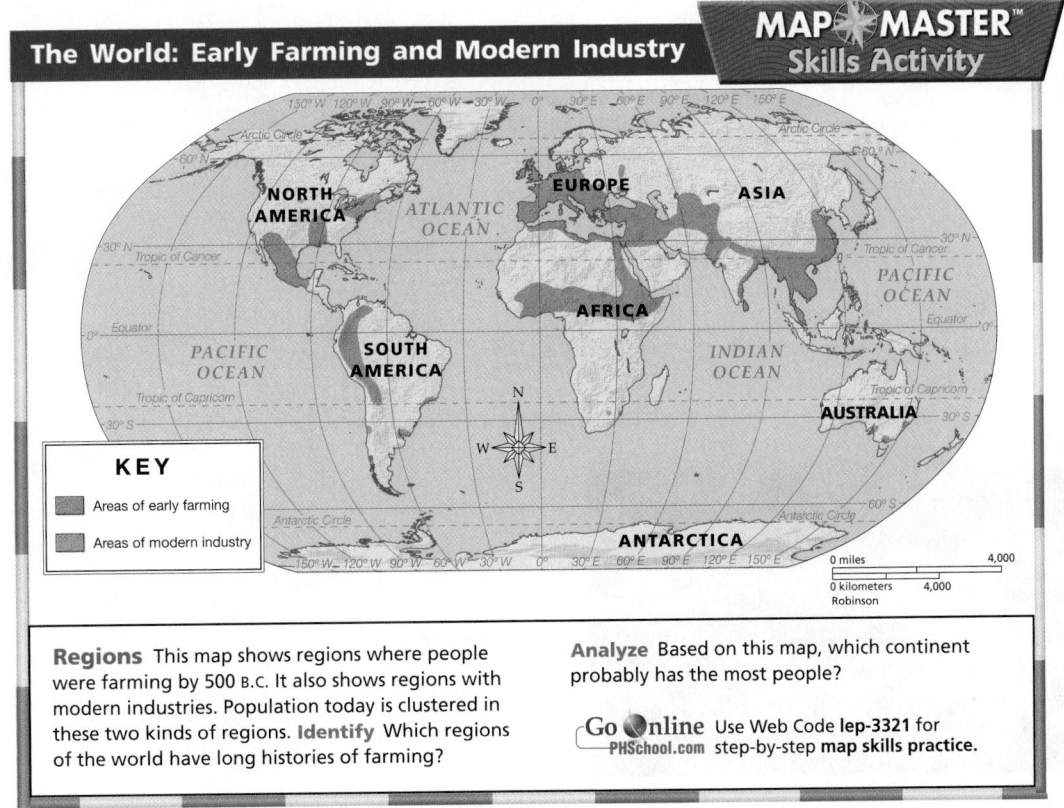

The World: Early Farming and Modern Industry

MAP MASTER™
Skills Activity

KEY
- Areas of early farming
- Areas of modern industry

Regions This map shows regions where people were farming by 500 B.C. It also shows regions with modern industries. Population today is clustered in these two kinds of regions. **Identify** Which regions of the world have long histories of farming?

Analyze Based on this map, which continent probably has the most people?

Go Online
PHSchool.com Use Web Code **lep-3321** for step-by-step **map skills practice.**

Chapter 3 Section 1 **61**

Vocabulary Builder

Use the information below to teach students this section's high-use words.

High-Use Word	Definition and Sample Sentence
cluster, p. 60	*n.* a group of something The clown carried a **cluster** of balloons.
vary, p. 63	*v.* to differ widely The number of students in a class may **vary** from one school to the next.
method, p. 65	*n.* a way of doing something His cleaning **method** helped him finish in half the time.
aspect, p. 66	*n.* appearance or characteristic They considered each **aspect** of the plan before they began building the house.

Target Reading Skill

Compare and Contrast As a follow up, ask students to answer the Target Reading Skill question in the Student Edition. *(Population density is the average number of people who live in a square mile or square kilometer. Population distribution is the number of people who actually live in an area.)*

Population Density

Guided Instruction

- **Vocabulary Builder** Clarify the high-use word **vary** before reading.

- With students, read about the differences between population density and distribution in Population Density.

- Ask **What is population density?** *(the average number of people living in one square mile or square kilometer)* **How does this differ from population distribution?** *(Population distribution gives actual numbers of people for an area.)*

- Have students find the region where their community is located on the map on pages 62 and 63. Discuss whether your area has a high or low population density. Then have students speculate why. *(Answers will vary, but student answers should give the general population density for their community and why.)*

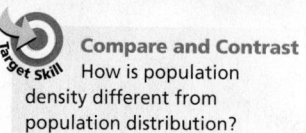

Compare and Contrast How is population density different from population distribution?

Population Density

How many people live in your neighborhood? How big is that neighborhood? If you take the population of an area and divide it by the size of that area in square miles or square kilometers, you can get a sense of how crowded or empty that area is. The average number of people per square mile or square kilometer is called **population density.**

Population distribution and population density both describe where people live. Population density differs from population distribution, however, because it gives an average number of people for an area. Population distribution gives actual numbers of people for an area.

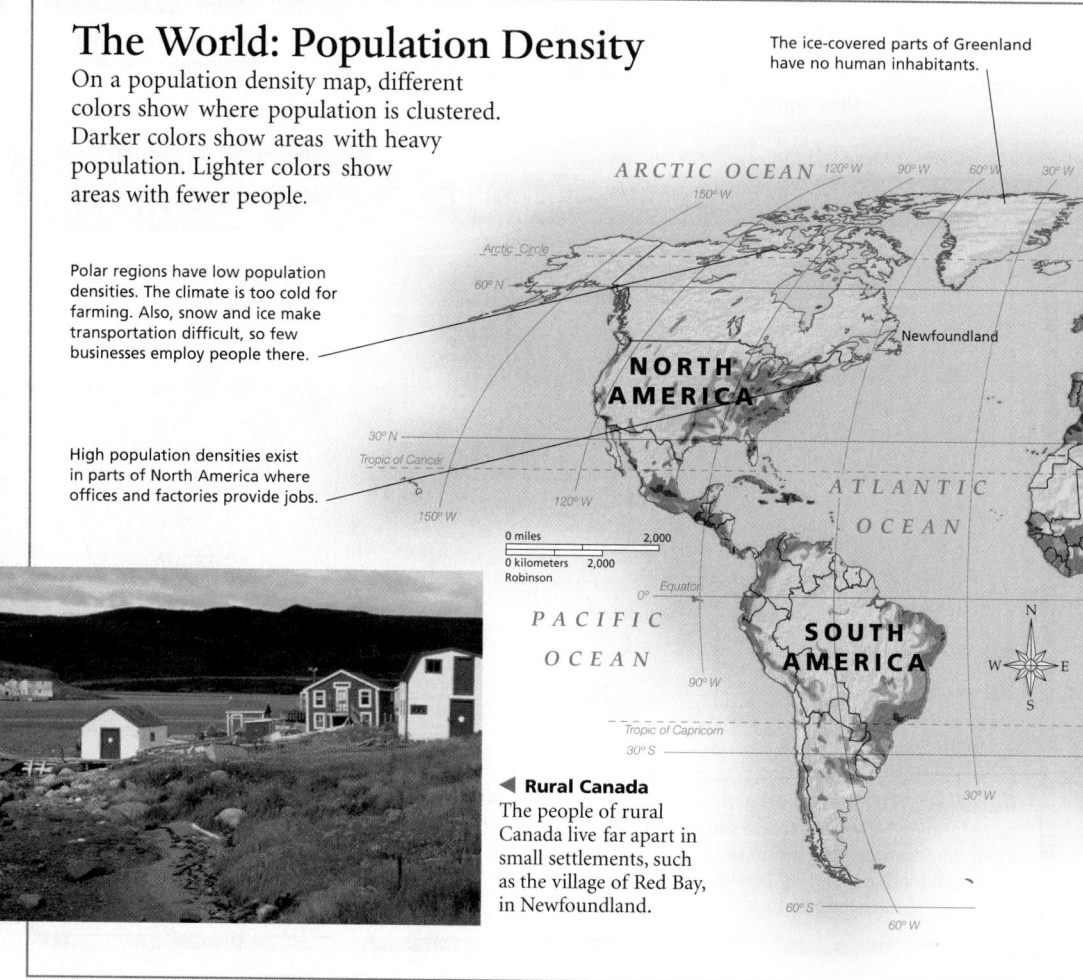

The World: Population Density

On a population density map, different colors show where population is clustered. Darker colors show areas with heavy population. Lighter colors show areas with fewer people.

Polar regions have low population densities. The climate is too cold for farming. Also, snow and ice make transportation difficult, so few businesses employ people there.

High population densities exist in parts of North America where offices and factories provide jobs.

The ice-covered parts of Greenland have no human inhabitants.

◀ **Rural Canada**
The people of rural Canada live far apart in small settlements, such as the village of Red Bay, in Newfoundland.

62 Foundations of Geography

Differentiated Instruction

For Less Proficient Readers

Have students read this section in the Reading and Vocabulary Study Guide. This version provides basic-level instruction in an interactive format with questions and write-on lines.

Chapter 3, Section 1, **Eastern Hemisphere Reading and Vocabulary Study Guide,** pp. 22–24

For Special Needs Students

Have students read the section as they listen to the recording on the Student Edition on Audio CD. Check for comprehension by pausing the CD and asking students to share their answers to the Reading Check questions.

Chapter 3, Section 1, **Student Edition on Audio CD**

Population density varies from one area to another. In a country with a high density, such as Japan, people are crowded together. Almost half of Japan's 127 million people live on only 17 percent of the land, or an area the size of West Virginia. In Tokyo, there is a population density of more than 25,000 people per square mile (9,664 per square kilometer). In contrast, Canada has a low overall population density. It has about 9 people per square mile (3 per square kilometer). Canada is bigger than the United States, but has only about one ninth as many people.

✓ **Reading Check** Which has a higher population density, a city or an area in the countryside?

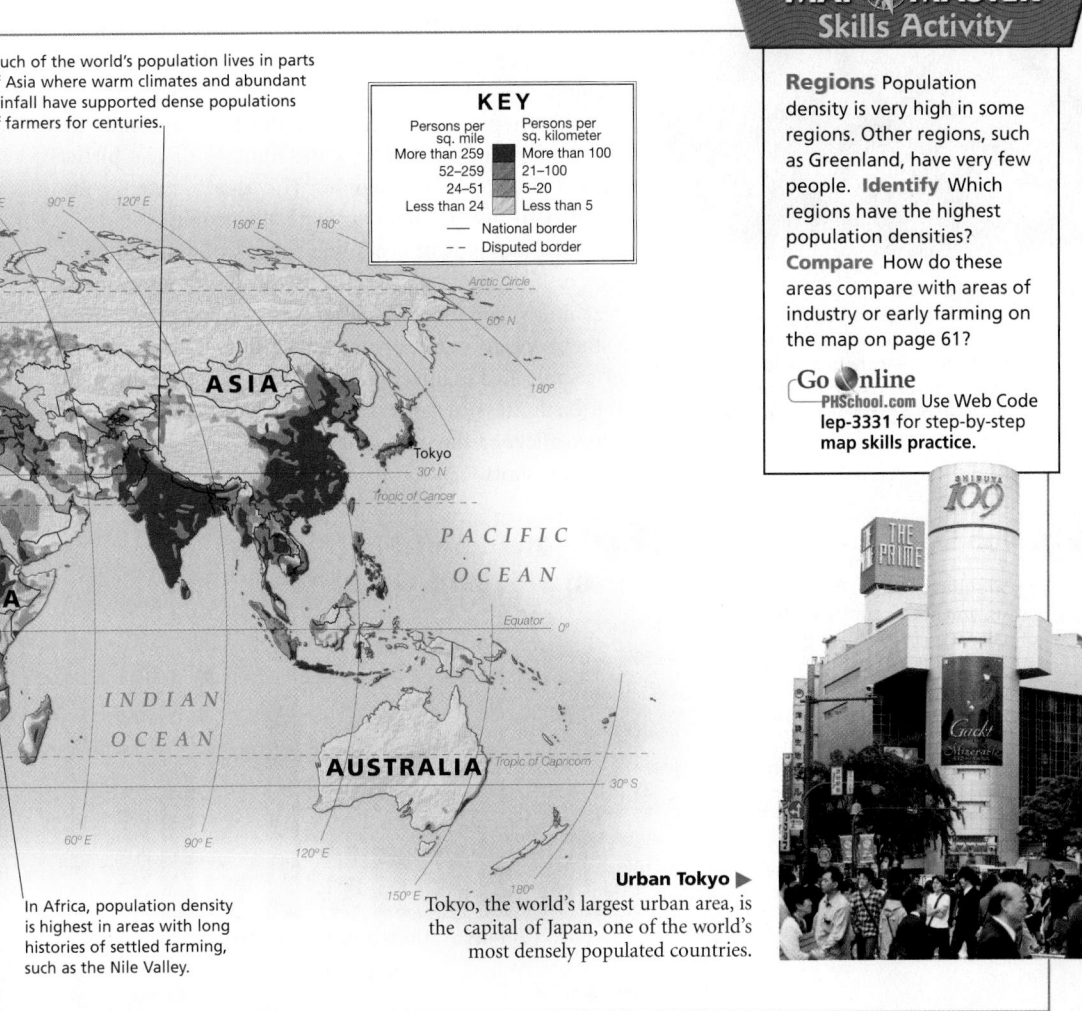

uch of the world's population lives in parts
Asia where warm climates and abundant
infall have supported dense populations
farmers for centuries.

KEY

Persons per sq. mile	Persons per sq. kilometer
More than 259	More than 100
52–259	21–100
24–51	5–20
Less than 24	Less than 5

—— National border
– – Disputed border

In Africa, population density is highest in areas with long histories of settled farming, such as the Nile Valley.

Urban Tokyo ▶
Tokyo, the world's largest urban area, is the capital of Japan, one of the world's most densely populated countries.

MAP ✦ MASTER™
Skills Activity

Regions Population density is very high in some regions. Other regions, such as Greenland, have very few people. **Identify** Which regions have the highest population densities? **Compare** How do these areas compare with areas of industry or early farming on the map on page 61?

Go **Online**
PHSchool.com Use Web Code **lep-3331** for step-by-step **map skills practice.**

Chapter 3 Section 1 **63**

Differentiated Instruction

For Gifted and Talented L3
Have students do research to gather information about population densities for their community, state, and the United States. Then have them create a table showing this information.

For Less Proficient Readers L1
Remind students that it is important to read the captions that appear with pictures or photographs. Direct students' attention to the captions on pages 62 and 63. Have students reread them to find one noun to describe what is shown, and one adjective that describes the climate or vegetation.

When students are finished, ask them to describe one of the photographs without referring to its caption.

Independent Practice
Have students continue to fill in the graphic organizer by recording details about population density.

Monitor Progress
As they fill in details on their webs, make sure students understand the difference between population distribution and population density. Provide assistance as necessary.

Answers

✓ **Reading Check** A city has a higher population density.

MAP ✦ MASTER™ *Skills Activity* **Identify** East, South, and Southwest Asia, Europe, some parts of Africa, northeast North America, Central Europe, and some coastal parts of South America **Compare** Many of the areas of modern industry also have high population densities. Some early farming areas, such as Asia and Europe, have high population densities.

Go **Online**
PHSchool.com Students may practice their map skills using the interactive online version of this map.

Population Growth

Guided Instruction

- **Vocabulary Builder** Clarify the high-use words **method** and **aspect** before reading.

- Read how the world's human population has grown and changed over time in Population Growth.

- Ask **What does population growth depend on?** *(birthrate and death rate)* Then ask **What are birthrate and death rate?** *(Birthrate is the number of live births each year per 1,000 people; death rate is the number of deaths each year per 1,000 people.)*

- Have students study the Birth and Death Rates in Selected Countries, 2006 bar graph on page 64. Then have them predict what kinds of challenges a country like Yemen might face with such a high birthrate and a low death rate. *(Answers will vary, but students should mention that it might become difficult to provide enough food, water, housing, public services, and education for so many people; the environment might also suffer.)*

- Have students look at the line graph of World Population Growth A.D. 1200–2000 on page 65. Ask **About how much has the population increased in the last 100 years?** *(about 4.5 billion)* Ask **How has the development of modern science affected the recent population growth?** *(New farming methods have increased the world's food supply; scientific advances in health and medicine have allowed people to live longer.)*

Modern Medicine
This Rwandan refugee is getting a measles vaccination in Tanzania. Modern medicine has lengthened lifespans worldwide.
Analyze *Does vaccination raise birth rates or lower death rates? Explain why.*

■ Graph Skills

If you subtract deaths from births, you get a country's rate of natural growth. When there are more deaths than births, the native-born population drops. **Identify** Which of the countries shown here has the highest birth rate? **Compare** In which countries is the death rate higher than the birth rate?

Population Growth

Suppose that all the years from A.D. 1 to A.D. 2000 took place in a single day. As the day began at midnight, there would be 300 million people in the world. Twelve hours later, at noon, there would be just 310 million people. By 8:24 P.M., the population would double to 600 million. It would double again by 10:05 P.M. to 1.2 billion. By 11:20, it would double again to 2.4 billion, and then double yet again by 11:48 to 4.8 billion, before reaching 6 billion as the day ended at midnight. As you can see, the world's population has grown very quickly in recent times. There are several reasons for this rapid growth.

Birthrates and Death Rates At different times in history, populations have grown at different rates. Demographers want to understand why. They know that population growth depends on the birthrate and the death rate. The **birthrate** is the number of live births each year per 1,000 people. The **death rate** is the number of deaths each year per 1,000 people.

For thousands of years, the world's population grew slowly. In those years, farmers worked without modern machinery. Food supplies often were scarce. People lived without clean water or waste removal. Many millions of people died of infectious diseases. As a result, although the birthrate was high, so was the death rate. The life expectancy, or the average number of years that people live, was short.

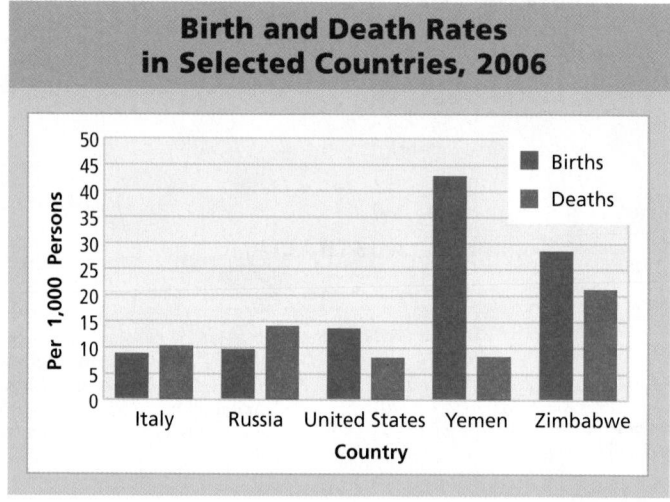

Birth and Death Rates in Selected Countries, 2006

(Bar graph showing Births and Deaths per 1,000 Persons for Italy, Russia, United States, Yemen, and Zimbabwe. Y-axis: Per 1,000 Persons, 0–50. X-axis: Country.)

Differentiated Instruction

For Gifted and Talented   L3

Have students explore the concepts of demographics and statistics further by completing *Analyzing Statistics.*

All in One Foundations of Geography Teaching Resources, *Analyzing Statistics,* p. 187

For Advanced Readers   L3

To gain a better understanding of how population growth can affect the environment, assign students the *Enrichment* activity. Have students complete the activity in pairs.

All in One Foundations of Geography Teaching Resources, *Enrichment,* p. 181

Answers

Analyze Vaccinations lower death rates by improving people's immunity to disease, and therefore their life expectancy.
Graph Skills **Identify** Yemen
Compare Italy and Russia

Reasons for Population Growth Today This all changed after the 1700s. Death rates dropped sharply. In some countries, birthrates increased. As a result, populations have grown very fast. In some countries, the population has doubled in less than 20 years. Meanwhile, people live longer than ever. In the United States, people born in 1900 could expect to live for 47 years. Today, they can expect to live for 77 years.

Scientific progress explains much of this change. First, new farming methods have increased the world's food supply. Scientists have improved important food crops and found new ways to protect crops against insects. Scientists have also found ways to raise crops with less water. These recent scientific improvements in agriculture are called the Green Revolution.

The second set of scientific advances has come in health and medicine. Scientists have convinced local governments to provide clean drinking water and sanitary waste removal. These measures sharply reduce disease. Researchers have also developed vaccines to prevent disease and antibiotics to fight infections. As a result, people live many more years.

Due to a high birthrate and a low death rate, Yemen's population is skyrocketing.

Graph Skills

In recent centuries, population growth has soared. There are now 18 times as many people as there were 600 years ago. **Identify** Around what year did the world's population begin to rise rapidly? **Analyze a Graph** Looking at this graph, how can you tell that the world's population rose more quickly in recent years than in earlier centuries?

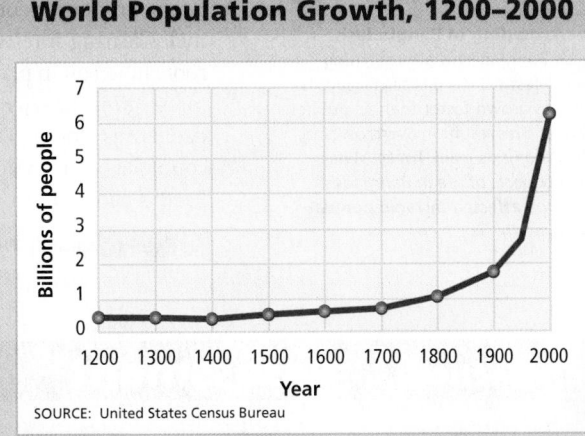

World Population Growth, 1200–2000

SOURCE: United States Census Bureau

Independent Practice
Have students complete their concept webs using the information in this section.

Monitor Progress
- When students are finished with their concept webs, show *Section Reading Support Transparency FG 49* and ask students to check their work individually. Go over key concepts and clarify key vocabulary as needed.

  📖 **Foundations of Geography Transparencies,** *Section Reading Support Transparency FG 49*

- Tell students to fill in the last column of their *Reading Readiness Guides.* Probe for what they learned that confirms or invalidates each statement.

  All in One Foundations of Geography Teaching Resources, *Reading Readiness Guide,* p. 162

Assess and Reteach

Assess Progress   L2
Have students complete the Section Assessment. Then administer the *Section Quiz.*

  All in One Foundations of Geography Teaching Resources, *Section Quiz,* p. 164

Reteach   L1
If students need more instruction, have them read this section in the Reading and Vocabulary Study Guide.

  📖 Chapter 3, Section 1, **Eastern Hemisphere Reading and Vocabulary Study Guide,** pp. 22–24

Chapter 3 Section 1 **65**

Skills Mini Lesson

Analyzing Graphic Data

1. Point out that information is often given in the form of charts and graphs. Tell students that charts and graphs can help them see information quickly, and can also help them draw conclusions.

2. Refer students to the bar graph on page 64. Have them practice the skill by identifying the title of the graph, the labels, and any

similarities or differences they notice in the information being presented in the graph. Then have them draw a conclusion about the populations of the countries shown on the graph.

3. Have students apply the skill by identifying the parts of the graph on this page and drawing conclusions from the information illustrated on the graph.

Answers

Graph Skills Identify 1800 **Analyze a Graph** because of the steep upward movement of the line between 1900 and 2000

Extend

L3

To extend the lesson, have students complete the *Evaluating Solutions* Internet activity to learn about possible solutions to the problem of overpopulation. Then have them answer the questions and partner with another student to create a chart of the options discussed.

Go Online
PHSchool.com **For:** Environmental and Global Issues: *Evaluating Solutions*
Visit: PHSchool.com
Web Code: led-3300

Answers

Infer Jobs, schools, and adequate housing may also be scarce.

✓ **Reading Check** Developments such as better farming methods and advances in health and medicine have led to a population increase.

Section 1 Assessment

Key Terms

Students' sentences should reflect an understanding of each Key Term.

Target Reading Skill

Similar: Both are used to measure and study demographics. Different: Population density is the average number of people who live in a given space; population distribution is the actual number of people who live in an area.

Comprehension and Critical Thinking

1. (a) areas with good soil and plenty of water **(b)** With advances in methods of transportation, people were able to move to other places; as industry developed, people did not need to farm to provide food and could move to work in places with factories. **(c)** Today more people live in cities than in the countryside.

2. (a) the average number of people living in a square mile or square kilometer **(b)** total population and land area.

Overcrowding in Bangladesh
These Bangladeshis are returning from a festival. Bangladesh's population has grown faster than its public services. This results in overcrowding, as seen on this train. **Infer** *What other aspects of life in Bangladesh might be affected by rapid population growth?*

The Challenges of Population Growth Today, food supplies have increased and people live longer. Even so, people in many countries still face serious problems. Some nations, such as those in Southwest Asia, do not have enough fresh water. In parts of Asia and Africa, the population is growing faster than the food supply. Often, these countries do not have enough money to buy food elsewhere.

Population growth puts pressure on all aspects of life. The populations of many countries are increasing so fast that not everyone can find jobs. There are not enough schools to educate the growing number of children. Decent housing is scarce. Public services such as transportation and sanitation are inadequate.

Rapid population growth also affects the environment. For instance, forests in many countries are disappearing. People in poorer countries cut down the trees for wood and fuel. Clearing forests causes other problems. In a forest, tree roots hold soil in place, and forest soils soak up rain. With the forest gone, heavy rainfall may wash away the soil and cause dangerous floods. Demand for wood and fuel in wealthier countries also uses up the world's scarce resources. All of Earth's people must work to meet this challenge.

✓ **Reading Check** Why have populations risen rapidly in recent times?

Section 1 Assessment

Key Terms
Review the key terms at the beginning of this section. Use each term in a sentence that explains its meaning.

Target Reading Skill
How are population density and population distribution similar? How are they different?

Comprehension and Critical Thinking
1. (a) Recall In what parts of the world did most people live before modern times?
(b) Explain How does history help explain population distribution today?

(c) Contrast How is population distribution today different from the days before modern science was developed?
2. (a) Define What is population density?
(b) Transfer Information To figure out the population density of an area, what two pieces of information do you need?
3. (a) Recall How has population growth changed in 100 years?
(b) Explain What accounts for this change?
(c) Identify Cause and Effect What are the effects of this change in population growth?

Writing Activity
Suppose that you are a demographer studying the area where you live. How does population density vary across your area? Where is population growth taking place? Write a short description of your area's demography.

Go Online
PHSchool.com
For: An activity on population
Visit: PHSchool.com
Web Code: led-3301

3. (a) Population growth has been huge in the last 100 years. **(b)** advances in health and medicine and improved farming methods **(c)** Effects can include lack of jobs, schools, and public services and dangers to the environment.

Writing Activity
Use the *Rubric for Assessing a Writing Assignment* to evaluate students' descriptions of local demography.

All in One Foundations of Geography Teaching Resources, *Rubric for Assessing a Writing Assignment,* p. 197

Go Online PHSchool.com Typing in the Web code when prompted will bring students directly to detailed instructions for this activity.

Prepare to Read

Objectives
In this section you will
1. Learn about migration, or people's movement from one region to another.
2. Investigate urbanization, or people's movement to cities.

Taking Notes
Copy the chart below. As you read this section, fill in the chart with information about voluntary and involuntary migration and about urbanization.

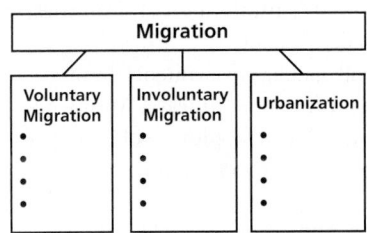

Target Reading Skill

Identify Contrasts
When you contrast two situations, you examine how they differ. Although both voluntary and involuntary migration involve the movement of people, the reasons for that movement differ. As you read, list the differences between voluntary and involuntary migration.

Key Terms
- **migration** (my GRAY shun) *n.* the movement of people from one place or region to another
- **immigrants** (IM uh grunts) *n.* people who move into one country from another
- **urbanization** (ur bun ih ZAY shun) *n.* the movement of people to cities, and the growth of cities
- **rural** (ROOR ul) *adj.* located in the countryside
- **urban** (UR bun) *adj.* located in cities and towns

Why People Migrate

For thousands of years, people have moved to new places. People's movement from one place or region to another is called **migration**. **Immigrants** are people who move into one country from another.

In the years from 1850 to 1930, more than 30 million Europeans moved to live in the United States. Since 1971, more than 4.5 million people have migrated here from Mexico, and more than 2.5 million have migrated from the Caribbean islands. Since 1971, Central America, the Philippines, China, and Vietnam have all lost more than 1 million immigrants to the United States. More than 800,000 immigrants have come from both South Korea and India.

During the late 1800s and early 1900s, millions of immigrants to the United States stopped at Ellis Island in New York Harbor.

Target Reading Skill L2

Identify Contrasts Point out the Target Reading Skill. Tell students that identifying contrasts between two situations will help them understand how they are different.

Read the first paragraph on page 71 to students. Model identifying contrasts by pointing out that in the past most Indonesians lived in rural areas, but today the population is increasingly urban; and, in 1970 about 3.9 million people lived in Jakarta, but in 2000, 11 million people lived there.

Give students *Identify Contrasts*. Have them complete the activity in groups.

All in One Foundations of Geography Teaching Resources, *Identify Contrasts,* p. 178

Objectives
Social Studies
1. Learn about migration, or people's movement from one region to another.
2. Investigate urbanization, or people's movement to cities.

Reading/Language Arts
Identify contrasts to understand how situations differ.

Prepare to Read

Build Background Knowledge L2
Tell students that this section is about the movement of people. Have students brainstorm a list of reasons why people might move from the countryside to the city, from one town to another, or from one country to another. Conduct an Idea Wave (TE p. T35) to elicit student responses, and then record them on the board.

Set a Purpose for Reading L2
- Preview the Objectives.

- Read each statement in the *Reading Readiness Guide* aloud. Ask students to mark the statements true or false.

  All in One Foundations of Geography Teaching Resources, *Reading Readiness Guide,* p. 166

- Have students discuss the statements in pairs or groups of four, then mark their worksheets again. Use the Numbered Heads participation strategy (TE, p. T36) to call on students to share their group's perspectives.

Vocabulary Builder
Preview Key Terms L2
Pronounce each Key Term, and then ask students to say the word with you. Provide a simple explanation such as, "New York City is urban because large numbers of people live close together there."

Instruct

Why People Migrate

Guided Instruction

- **Vocabulary Builder** Clarify the high-use word **theory** before reading.

- Read Why People Migrate using the Oral Cloze strategy (TE, p. T33).

- Discuss with students the push-pull theory. Ask **What is it and how does it work?** *(The theory helps explain why people migrate. It says that bad conditions "push" people to leave their countries, and good conditions in another country "pull" the people to migrate there.)*

- Ask **What kinds of things make people migrate voluntarily?** *(hunger or other difficulties, the search for a better quality of life, better jobs, and political freedom)*
What kinds of things force people to migrate involuntarily? *(punishment, enslavement, war)*

⊙ Target Reading Skill

Identify Contrasts As a follow up, ask students to answer the Target Reading Skill question in the Student Edition *(Involuntary migration is when people are forced to move against their will. Voluntary migration is when people move because they want to.)*

Cubans in Little Havana
These men ordering food at a cafe are part of a large community of Cuban immigrants in Miami, Florida.
Analyze Images *What aspects of their life in Cuba have these immigrants preserved in their new home?*

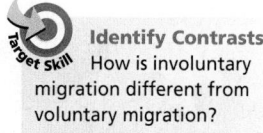
Identify Contrasts How is involuntary migration different from voluntary migration?

Voluntary Migration in the Past Voluntary migration is the movement of people by their own choice. Today, most people move by their own choice. The push-pull theory says that people migrate because difficulties "push" them to leave. At the same time, the hope for a better life "pulls" people to a new country.

The push-pull theory helps to explain the great Irish migration in the 1840s and 1850s. In those years, 1.5 million people left Ireland for the United States. What pushed so many Irish people to come to America? In the 1840s, disease destroyed Ireland's main crop—potatoes. Hunger pushed people to migrate. Job opportunities pulled Irish families to the United States.

Voluntary Migration Today The same theory explains most migration today. The main sources of migration are countries where many people are poor and jobs are few. In some countries, such as Vietnam and Central American countries, wars have made life dangerous and difficult.

In China, Vietnam, and Cuba, governments limit people's freedom. These problems push people to leave. Meanwhile, the possibility of good jobs and political freedom pulls people to the United States and other well-off, democratic countries.

Involuntary Migration Sometimes people are forced to move. Because these people do not choose to move, their movement is known as involuntary migration. During the early 1800s, the British sent prisoners to Australia to serve their sentences. When their sentences were done, many stayed. War also forces people to migrate to escape death or serious danger.

The Transatlantic Slave Trade Perhaps the biggest involuntary migration in history was the transatlantic slave trade. From the 1500s to the 1800s, millions of Africans were enslaved and taken against their will to European colonies in North and South America. These Africans traveled under inhumane conditions across the Atlantic Ocean, chained inside ships for more than a month.

At first, their descendants in the United States lived mainly on the east coast. As cotton farming spread west, many enslaved African Americans were forced to migrate again, this time to new plantations in the Mississippi Valley and Texas.

✓ **Reading Check** Why do people migrate?

Answers

Analyze Images They have preserved their Spanish language and possibly some types of food that might be sold at this cafe.

✓ **Reading Check** Some people migrate for a better quality of life, better jobs, religious or political freedom, or safety from war or violence. Other people are forced to move through enslavement or imprisonment.

⌐ Vocabulary Builder

Use the information below to teach students this section's high-use words.

High-Use Word	Definition and Sample Sentence
theory, p. 68	*n.* an idea or belief about how something is done Laura's **theory** was that she would pass the test if she studied.
unique, p. 71	*adj.* being the only one; having no equal Many rain forest plants are **unique** because they are found nowhere else in the world.

Migration in South Asia

At the end of British colonial rule in 1947, most of South Asia was divided along religious lines into two countries. India had a Hindu majority. Pakistan was mainly Muslim. Fearing religious discrimination or violence, Muslims from India and Hindus from Pakistan fled across the new borders. Many died when violence broke out during these massive migrations.

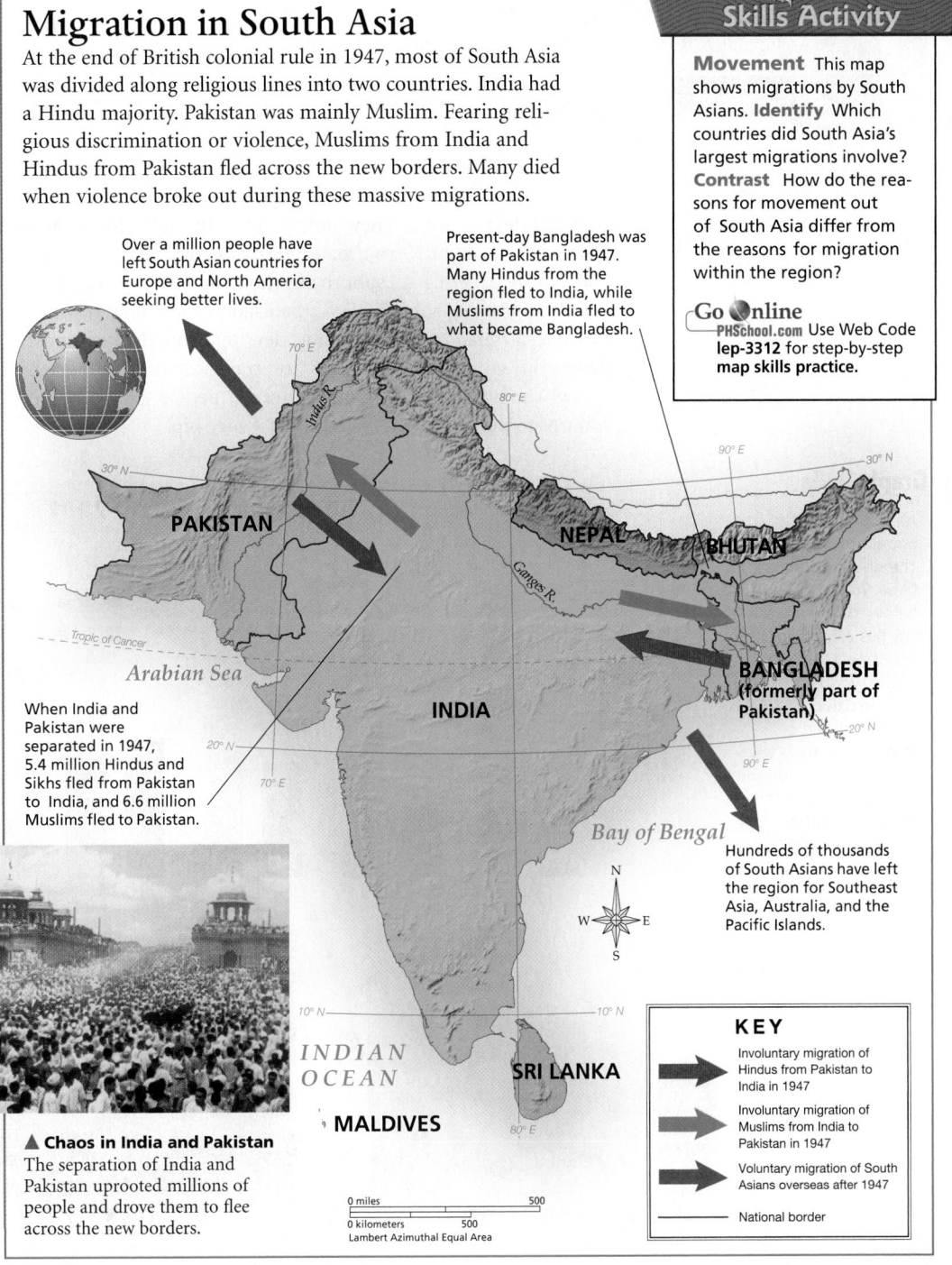

Over a million people have left South Asian countries for Europe and North America, seeking better lives.

Present-day Bangladesh was part of Pakistan in 1947. Many Hindus from the region fled to India, while Muslims from India fled to what became Bangladesh.

When India and Pakistan were separated in 1947, 5.4 million Hindus and Sikhs fled from Pakistan to India, and 6.6 million Muslims fled to Pakistan.

Hundreds of thousands of South Asians have left the region for Southeast Asia, Australia, and the Pacific Islands.

PAKISTAN
NEPAL
BHUTAN
BANGLADESH (formerly part of Pakistan)
INDIA
Arabian Sea
Tropic of Cancer
Indus R.
Ganges R.
Bay of Bengal
INDIAN OCEAN
SRI LANKA
MALDIVES

N W E S

0 miles 500
0 kilometers 500
Lambert Azimuthal Equal Area

KEY

➡	Involuntary migration of Hindus from Pakistan to India in 1947
➡	Involuntary migration of Muslims from India to Pakistan in 1947
➡	Voluntary migration of South Asians overseas after 1947
—	National border

▲ **Chaos in India and Pakistan**
The separation of India and Pakistan uprooted millions of people and drove them to flee across the new borders.

MAP MASTER™ Skills Activity

Movement This map shows migrations by South Asians. **Identify** Which countries did South Asia's largest migrations involve? **Contrast** How do the reasons for movement out of South Asia differ from the reasons for migration within the region?

Go Online
PHSchool.com Use Web Code **lep-3312** for step-by-step map skills practice.

Guided Instruction (continued)

■ Direct students' attention to the map on this page. Ask **What caused the migration of Muslims and Hindus in Southeast Asia in 1947?** *(Following the end of British colonial rule in India, most of South Asia was divided along religious lines into the countries of India and Pakistan; fearing religious discrimination or violence, Hindus and Muslims in the minority fled across the new borders.)* **Do you think this migration was voluntary or involuntary? Why?** *(Possible answer: involuntary, since people migrated to avoid possible religious persecution and violence)*

Independent Practice

Have students create the Taking Notes graphic organizer on a blank piece of paper. Model how to fill in the graphic organizer using the *Flow Chart* transparency. Students should then fill in the chart with information they have just learned.

📖 **Foundations of Geography Transparencies,** *Transparency B2: Flow Chart*

Monitor Progress

As students fill in the graphic organizer, circulate and make sure that individuals are choosing the correct details. Provide assistance as needed.

Skills for Life — Skills Mini Lesson

Identifying Frame of Reference and Point of View

1. Explain that point of view is a person's opinion about an issue. Frame of reference is a person's background and often influences a person's point of view.

2. Have students practice the skill by reviewing the information about the division of India and Pakistan. Discuss how these

people's frame of reference or point of view affected their decision to migrate.

3. Have students apply the skill by identifying Krenak's frame of reference and point of view in the following selection:

All in One Foundations of Geography Teaching Resources, *Message from the Rain Forest Amerindians,* p. 188

Answers

MAP MASTER Skills Activity **Identify** India and Pakistan **Contrast** Within the region, people migrated to avoid violence and religious persecution; they migrated outside the region to seek better lives.

Go Online
PHSchool.com Students may practice their map skills using the interactive online version of this map.

Show students *Migration: People on the Move.* Ask students to name two reasons people are migrating within Senegal. *(People are migrating to Dakar because it has a cooler climate; others are migrating to the north because the desert is encroaching on the land.)*

Urbanization L2

Guided Instruction

- **Vocabulary Builder** Clarify the high-use word **unique** before reading.

- Have students read Urbanization and study the bar graph and photos.

- Ask **What is the general trend in population movement since 1800?** *(More people are moving from rural to urban areas.)* **Why?** *(People are pulled to the city by the promise of better-paying jobs.)*

- Have students discuss some of the problems caused by rapid urbanization. *(Cities often cannot provide enough housing, jobs, schools, hospitals, and other services people need; traffic jams and crowds make it difficult for people to get around.)*

Independent Practice
Have students finish filling in their charts with details about urbanization.

Monitor Progress

- When students are finished with their charts, show *Section Reading Support Transparency FG 50* and ask students to check their work individually.

  📖 **Foundations of Geography Transparencies,** *Section Reading Support Transparency FG 50*

- Tell students to fill in the last column of their *Reading Readiness Guides.* Probe for what they learned that confirms or invalidates each statement.

  All in One Foundations of Geography Teaching Resources, *Reading Readiness Guide,* p. 166

Answers

Graph Skills Identify about 3–4 percent
Predict The urban population will probably be greater than the rural population.

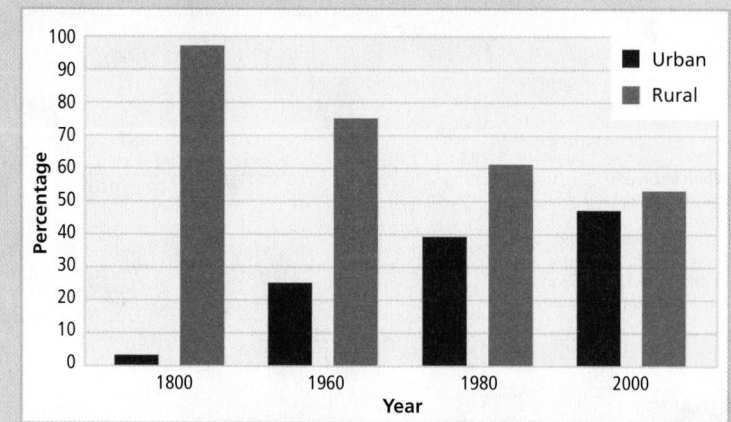

Urbanization

Millions of people in many countries have migrated to cities from farms and small villages. In recent years, the population of some cities has grown tremendously. The movement of people to cities and the growth of cities is called **urbanization.**

Cities and Suburbs In Europe and North America, the growth of industry during the 1800s pulled people from the countryside to cities. They hoped for jobs in factories and offices. Since about 1950, urbanization has given way in Europe and North America to suburbanization, or the movement of people to growing suburbs. Suburbanization sometimes replaces valuable farmland with sprawling development. Because most people in suburbs rely on cars for transportation, suburban sprawl can increase pollution. However, people still move to suburbs to pursue the dream of home ownership.

■ Graph Skills

All over the world, city populations have soared. The photographs of Cape Town, South Africa, below, show how that city has expanded.
Identify What percent of the world's people lived in cities in 1800?
Predict Based on information from the graph, how do you think the world's rural and urban populations will compare in 2050?

World Urban and Rural Populations,1800-2000

Cape Town, 1938

Modern Cape Town

Differentiated Instruction

For Advanced Readers L3

To help students gain better understanding about immigrants and their migrations, divide them into groups to complete the *Small Group Activity: Making an Immigration Map.*

  All in One Foundations of Geography Teaching Resources, *Small Group Activity: Making an Immigration Map,* pp. 183–186

For English Language Learners L1

Students may have difficulty pronouncing some of the longer words in this section, such as *tremendously, urbanization,* and *opportunities.* Encourage students to break down these words into smaller parts to help them sound out the pronunciations.

Urbanization on Other Continents In Asia, Africa, and Latin America, people are still streaming from the countryside to growing cities. Indonesia is an example. In the past, most Indonesians lived in **rural** areas, or areas in the countryside. Recently, more and more Indonesians have moved to **urban** areas, or areas in cities and nearby towns. For example, in 1970, about 3.9 million people lived in Greater Jakarta, Indonesia's capital. By 2000, its population was about 11 million. Jakarta is not unique. Greater São Paulo, Brazil, grew from 8 million residents in 1970 to nearly 18 million residents in 2000.

The problem in cities like Jakarta and São Paulo is that too many people are moving to the city too fast. Cities cannot keep up. They cannot provide the housing, jobs, schools, hospitals, and other services that people need. Traffic jams and crowds often make getting around a struggle.

With so many daily problems, why do people flock to São Paulo and other big cities? As hard as life is in the cities, it can be even harder in the countryside, where there are few jobs and a shortage of land to farm. Most migrants to the city are seeking a better life for their families. They are looking for jobs, modern houses, and good schools. Above all, most want better lives for their children.

São Paulo, Brazil
São Paulo is Brazil's largest city.
Analyze Images *Do you think that this city has a high or a low population density?*

✓ **Reading Check** How is the population of urban areas changing in Africa, Asia, and Latin America?

Section 2 Assessment

Key Terms
Review the key terms at the beginning of this section. Use each term in a sentence that explains its meaning.

Target Reading Skill
Contrast involuntary migration and voluntary migration. How are these two forms of migration different? List at least two differences between the two kinds of migration.

Comprehension and Critical Thinking
1. (a) Identify What are push factors and what are pull factors?
(b) Explain How do push factors and pull factors explain people's decision to migrate?
(c) Compare and Contrast Do push and pull factors account for involuntary migration? Explain why or why not.
2. (a) Recall What is urbanization?
(b) Identify Cause and Effect What are the causes and some of the effects of urbanization?

Writing Activity
Suppose that you are moving to the United States from one of the countries listed in the second paragraph on page 67. Write a paragraph describing your reasons for leaving that country and what attracts you to the United States.

For: An activity on migration
Visit: PHSchool.com
Web Code: led-3302

Chapter 3 Section 2 **71**

Section 2 Assessment

Key Terms
Students' sentences should reflect an understanding of each Key Term.

Target Reading Skill
Involuntary migration is when people are moved against their will. Voluntary migration is when people move because they want to.

Comprehension and Critical Thinking
1. (a) push factors: reasons why people leave a place; pull factors: reasons why people are drawn to a place **(b)** Push factors explain why people leave their own country and pull factors explain why people go to another country. **(c)** Only push factors account for involuntary migration, since people are "pushed," or forced, to move to another place.

2. (a) the movement of people to cities and the growth of cities **(b)** causes: lack of jobs, shortage of land, and population growth in rural areas; effects: lack of housing and jobs, pressure on public services, crowding, traffic problems

---

Assess and Reteach

Assess Progress [L2]
Have students complete the Section Assessment. Then administer the *Section Quiz.*

All in One **Foundations of Geography Teaching Resources,** *Section Quiz,* p. 168

Reteach [L1]
If students need more instruction, have them read this section in the Reading and Vocabulary Study Guide.

📖 Chapter 3, Section 2, **Eastern Hemisphere Reading and Vocabulary Study Guide,** pp. 25–27

Extend [L3]
To extend the lesson, have students do research for a report on either a family member or famous American who immigrated to the United States. Students should identify the immigrant's country of origin and write a brief biography about the person's life and important accomplishments. Students should mention if and how immigration affected their subjects' lives.

Answers

✓ **Reading Check** The populations of urban areas in Africa, Asia, and Latin America are growing rapidly.

Analyze Images high population density

Writing Activity
Use the *Rubric for Assessing a Writing Assignment* to evaluate students' paragraphs.

All in One **Foundations of Geography Teaching Resources,** *Rubric for Assessing a Writing Assignment,* p. 197

Go Online PHSchool.com Typing in the Web code when prompted will bring students directly to detailed instructions for this activity.

Objective

Read and interpret population density maps.

Prepare to Read

Build Background Knowledge **L2**

Briefly review with students the information they learned about population density in Section 1. Ask students why it might be useful to know the population density of a particular area, and who might need to know this information. On the board, begin a concept web with *Population Density* in the center oval and two sub-ovals labeled *Why?* and *Who?* Conduct an Idea Wave (TE p. T35) to elicit student responses.

Instruct

Analyzing and Interpreting Population Density Maps **L2**

Guided Instruction

- Read the steps to read and interpret a population density map as a class and write them on the board.

- Practice the skill by following the steps on p. 73 with the class. Model each step by taking note of the map's topic and features (*South Asia's population density; relief and labels*), studying the map key carefully to note what the colors show (*population density*), using the key to identify the areas of lowest and highest population density (*lowest: parts of Afghanistan and Nepal; highest: parts of Pakistan, India, Bangladesh, and Sri Lanka*), and writing a conclusion about South Asia's population density and possible reasons for its patterns (*Areas with lower population densities are generally mountainous and farther from coasts. This is probably because they are difficult to reach and hard to make a living in. Areas with higher population densities are near the coasts and in non-mountainous areas. This is probably because they are easier to reach and people can make a living there*).

Skills for Life — Analyzing and Interpreting Population Density Maps

Crowds gather in Amsterdam on Queen's Day, a national holiday in the Netherlands.

How dense is the population where you live? If you drew an imaginary five-mile square around your house and counted the number of people who lived within the square, would there be many residents, or few?

Population density is the average number of persons living within a certain area. You can find out how densely populated a place is by reading a population density map.

Learn the Skill

To read and interpret a population density map, follow these steps.

1 **Read the title and look at the map to get a general idea of what it shows.** The title and map key will show you that the topic of the map is population density.

2 **Read the key to understand how the map uses symbols and colors.** Each color represents a different population density range, as explained in the map key.

3 **Use the key to interpret the map.** Identify areas of various densities on the map. Some places average less than one person per square mile. In other places, thousands of people might be crammed into one square mile.

4 **Draw conclusions about what the map shows.** The history, geography, and cultural traditions of a place affect its population density. Draw on this information, plus what you read on the map, to make conclusions about why particular areas have a higher or a lower population density.

Independent Practice

Assign *Skills for Life* and have students complete it individually.

All in One **Foundations of Geography Teaching Resources,** *Skills for Life*, p. 182

Monitor Progress

As students are completing *Skills for Life*, circulate to make sure individuals are applying the skill steps effectively. Provide assistance as needed.

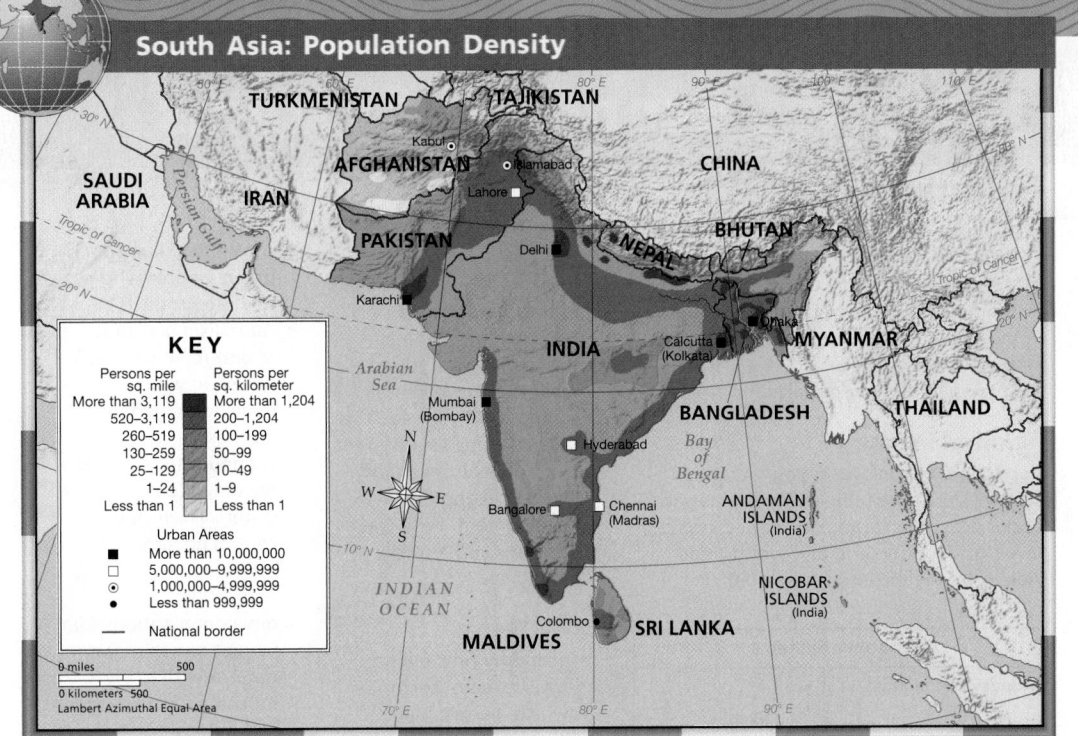

South Asia: Population Density

KEY

Persons per sq. mile | Persons per sq. kilometer
More than 3,119 | More than 1,204
520–3,119 | 200–1,204
260–519 | 100–199
130–259 | 50–99
25–129 | 10–49
1–24 | 1–9
Less than 1 | Less than 1

Urban Areas
■ More than 10,000,000
□ 5,000,000–9,999,999
◉ 1,000,000–4,999,999
• Less than 999,999
— National border

0 miles 500
0 kilometers 500
Lambert Azimuthal Equal Area

Practice the Skill

Use steps 1–4 to read and interpret the population density map above.

① What is the topic of this map? Notice that the map has relief—that is, markings that indicate hills and mountains. It also has labels for cities and nations of South Asia.

② Study the map key carefully. How many different colors are in the key? What color is used for the lowest population density? What color is used for the highest density?

③ Using the key, identify the areas of highest and lowest population densities in South Asia. Write a sentence or two that describes where the most and the fewest people are located.

④ Write a conclusion that makes a general statement about South Asia's population density and suggests possible reasons for the patterns shown on the map.

Apply the Skill

Now take a closer look at the map titled The World: Population Density on pages 62 and 63. Find the areas of greatest density. From what you already know and what you see on the map, what features do you think influence where people choose to live? Think about rivers and mountains as well as nearness to a coast or to the Equator.

Assess Progress `L2`

Ask students to complete the Apply the Skill activity.

Reteach `L1`

If students are having trouble applying the skill steps, have them review the skill using the interactive Social Studies Skills Tutor CD-ROM.

◉ *Analyzing and Interpreting Special Purpose Maps,* **Social Studies Skills Tutor CD-ROM**

Extend `L3`

■ To extend the lesson, ask students to apply the skill steps to the population density map on the transparency *The World: Population Density.*

📖 **Foundations of Geography Transparencies,** *Color Transparency FG 5: The World: Continents and Oceans (Base); Color Transparency FG 16: The World: Population Density (Overlay)*

■ Ask students to identify what the shaded areas indicate. *(population density)* Then have them identify the areas of highest population density in the world. *(parts of North America, Latin America, Asia, Europe, Africa)* Ask **Which continent has the most areas of lowest population density?** *(Antarctica)* Then discuss with students what about certain areas might cause them to have the lowest population densities. *(extremely cold areas, such as the North and South poles, and extremely hot areas, such as deserts, where harsh climates make it difficult for people to live)*

Differentiated Instruction

For Special Needs Students `L1`

Partner special needs students with proficient readers to do Level 1 of the *Analyzing and Interpreting Special Purpose Maps,* lesson on the Social Studies Skills Tutor CD-ROM together. When the students feel more confident, they can move onto Level 2 alone.

◉ *Analyzing and Interpreting Special Purpose Maps,* **Social Studies Skills Tutor CD-ROM**

Answer
Apply the Skill

The areas of the highest population density probably have good farmland, adequate water, and climates that are warm enough to allow many plants to grow.

Section 3
Step-by-Step Instruction

Objectives

Social Studies

1. Examine different kinds of economies.
2. Investigate levels of economic development.
3. Study global trade patterns.

Reading/Language Arts

Make comparisons to understand what things have in common.

Prepare to Read

Build Background Knowledge `L2`

Ask students to quickly preview the headings and visuals in the section. Then, write the word *economy* on the board, and have students use the Think-Write-Pair-Share strategy (TE p. T36) to make a list of five words that they think of when they hear the word *economy (examples: money, goods, services).* Tell students to predict what *economy* might mean, and then read the section to find out if their predictions were correct.

Set a Purpose for Reading `L2`

■ Preview the Objectives.

■ Read each statement in the *Reading Readiness Guide* aloud. Ask students to mark the statements true or false.

   All in One **Foundations of Geography Teaching Resources,** *Reading Readiness Guide,* p. 170

■ Have students discuss the statements in pairs or groups of four, then mark their worksheets again. Use the Numbered Heads participation strategy (TE, p. T36) to call on students to share their group's perspectives.

Vocabulary Builder
Preview Key Terms `L2`

Pronounce each Key Term, and then ask students to say the word with you. Provide a simple explanation such as, "The carpenter who builds a table is a producer. The person who buys the table is a consumer."

Section 3
Economic Systems

Prepare to Read

Key Questions

In this section you will
1. Examine different kinds of economies.
2. Investigate levels of economic development.
3. Study global trade patterns.

Taking Notes

Copy the table below. As you read this section, fill in the table with information about economic terms, kinds of economies, levels of development, and world trade. Add columns and rows as needed.

Economic Systems	
Kinds of Economies	• •
Levels of Development	• •

Target Reading Skill

Make Comparisons Comparing economic systems enables you to see what they have in common. As you read this section, compare different kinds of economies and levels of economic development. Who makes decisions and how do people live?

Key Terms

• **economy** (ih KAHN uh mee) *n.* a system in which people make, exchange, and use things that have value
• **producers** (pruh DOOS urz) *n.* owners and workers

• **consumers** (kun SOOM urz) *n.* people who buy and use products
• **capitalism** (KAP ut ul iz um) *n.* an economic system in which individuals own most businesses
• **communism** (KAHM yoo niz um) *n.* an economic system in which the central government owns factories, farms, and offices
• **developed nations** (dih VEL upt NAY shunz) *n.* nations with many industries and advanced technology
• **developing nations** (dih VEL up ing NAY shunz) *n.* nations with few industries and simple technology

Consumers choose produce at a market in Honolulu, Hawaii.

74 Foundations of Geography

Different Kinds of Economies

An **economy** is a system in which people make, exchange, and use things that have value and that meet their wants or needs. Economies differ from one country to another. In any economy, owners and workers are **producers.** The things they sell are called products **Consumers** are people who buy and use products.

There are three basic economic questions: What will be produced? How will it be produced? And, for whom will it be produced? The answers to these questions depend on the economy.

Modern economies differ in who owns workplaces. The owners generally decide how products are produced. In some countries, most workplaces are privately owned. In others, the government owns most workplaces.

Target Reading Skill `L2`

Make Comparisons Point out the Target Reading Skill. Tell students that making comparisons will help them see what things have in common.

Model the skill by reading the last paragraph on p. 79 and comparing NAFTA and the European Union. (*Both groups are trade* alliances and are made up of several countries in the same region.)

Give students *Make Comparisons.* Have them complete the activity in groups.

All in One **Foundations of Geography Teaching Resources,** *Make Comparisons,* p. 179

Private Ownership Capitalism is an economic system in which private individuals own most businesses. Capitalism is also called a free-market economy because producers compete freely for consumers' business.

In capitalism, people may save money in banks. Banks lend money to people and businesses in return for interest, or a percentage fee for the use of money. Banks also pay interest to savers. Under capitalism, people may directly invest in, or commit money to, a business. Owners of a business are also investors in that business.

Government Ownership Communism is an economic system in which the central government owns farms, factories, and offices. It controls the prices of goods and services, how much is produced, and how much workers are paid. The government decides where to invest resources. Today, only a few of the world's nations practice communism.

Mixed Ownership Hardly any nation has a "pure" economic system. For example, the United States has a capitalist economy. However, governments run schools, build and maintain roads, and provide other services. In communist countries, you may find a few small private businesses.

In some countries, the government may own some industries, while others belong to private owners. This system of mixed ownership is sometimes called a mixed economy.

✓ **Reading Check** What are the differences between capitalism and communism?

New York Stock Exchange
Stocks are bought and sold on the busy trading floor of the New York Stock Exchange. **Draw Conclusions** Would you expect to find a busy stock exchange in a communist economy? Explain why or why not.

Instruct

Different Kinds of Economies

Guided Instruction

- **Vocabulary Builder** Clarify the high-use words **exchange** and **value** before reading.

- Read Different Kinds of Economies using the ReQuest Procedure (TE, p. T35).

- Discuss with students the three different types of economies and the differences among them. (*In capitalism, private individuals own most businesses. In communism, the central government controls the economy. In a mixed economy, the government has partial control of the economy.*)

- Ask **What kind of economy does the United States have?** (*capitalist economy, but the government runs schools, builds and maintains roads, and provides other services*)

Independent Practice

Have students create the Taking Notes graphic organizer on a blank piece of paper. Then have them begin to fill in the organizer with information they have just learned.

Monitor Progress

As students fill in the graphic organizer, circulate and make sure that individuals are choosing the correct details. Provide assistance as needed.

Vocabulary Builder

Use the information below to teach students this section's high-use words.

High-Use Word	Definition and Sample Sentence
exchange, p. 74	*v.* to give and receive Sarah had to **exchange** the large sweater for a smaller one.
value, p. 74	*n.* worth Because it was damaged, the car had little **value**.
alliance, p. 79	*n.* a union The two schools formed an **alliance** to help raise money for their music programs.

Answers

Draw Conclusions No; in a communist country there probably would be no need for a stock market, because the government controls the prices of goods, and goods and shares are not open to free buying and selling.

✓ **Reading Check** Capitalism is an economic system in which producers compete freely for consumers' business. Communism is an economic system in which the government controls the prices of goods and services.

Levels of Economic Development

L2

Guided Instruction

- Read about the differences between developed and developing countries in Levels of Economic Development.

- Have students describe the ways in which people in developed countries and in developing countries produce food. *(In developed countries, most of the food is grown by commercial farmers; in developing countries, most of the people are subsistence farmers.)*

- Ask **What challenges might commercial and subsistence farmers have in common?** *(Bad weather, pollution, and lack of water might be challenges that affect both types of farmers.)*

Target Reading Skill

L2

Make Comparisons As a follow up, ask students to answer the Target Reading Skill question in the Student Edition. *(Both kinds of countries have farms.)*

Make Comparisons What do developed nations have in common with developing nations?

Levels of Economic Development

Three hundred years ago, most people made their own clothes. Then came a great change. People invented machines to make goods. They found new sources of power to run the machines. Power-driven machines were a new technology, or way of putting knowledge to practical use. This change in the way people made goods was called the Industrial Revolution.

The Industrial Revolution created a new economic pattern. Nations with more industries and more advanced technology are considered **developed nations.** Because they are still developing economically, nations with fewer industries and simpler technology are considered **developing nations.** People live differently in developed and developing nations.

Developed Nations Only about one fifth of the world's people live in developed nations. These nations include the United States, Canada, Japan, and most European nations. People in these nations use goods made in factories. Businesses use advanced technologies to produce goods and services.

In developed nations, most people live in towns and cities. They work in offices and factories. Machines do most of the work. Most people have enough food and water. Most citizens can get an education and healthcare.

In developed nations, most food is grown by commercial farmers. These are farmers who grow crops mainly for sale rather than for their own needs. Commercial farms use modern technologies, so they need fewer workers than traditional farms.

Developed nations can have some problems. Unemployment is a challenge. Not everyone can find a job. Industry and cars can cause air, land, and water pollution. Developed nations are working to solve these problems.

Most of Thailand's subsistence farmers grow rice.

76 Foundations of Geography

Skills Mini Lesson

Identifying Main Ideas

1. Tell students that to identify main ideas, they should identify the subject, identify details about the subject, and decide what their overall impression is of the details. Then they should draw a conclusion about what the details tell them.

2. Help students practice the skill by reading the first paragraph on this page with them. Have them note the details and use them to identify the main idea in that paragraph. *(Main idea: The Industrial Revolution changed the way people made goods.)*

3. Have students apply the skill by identifying the details and main idea in the third paragraph on page 77.

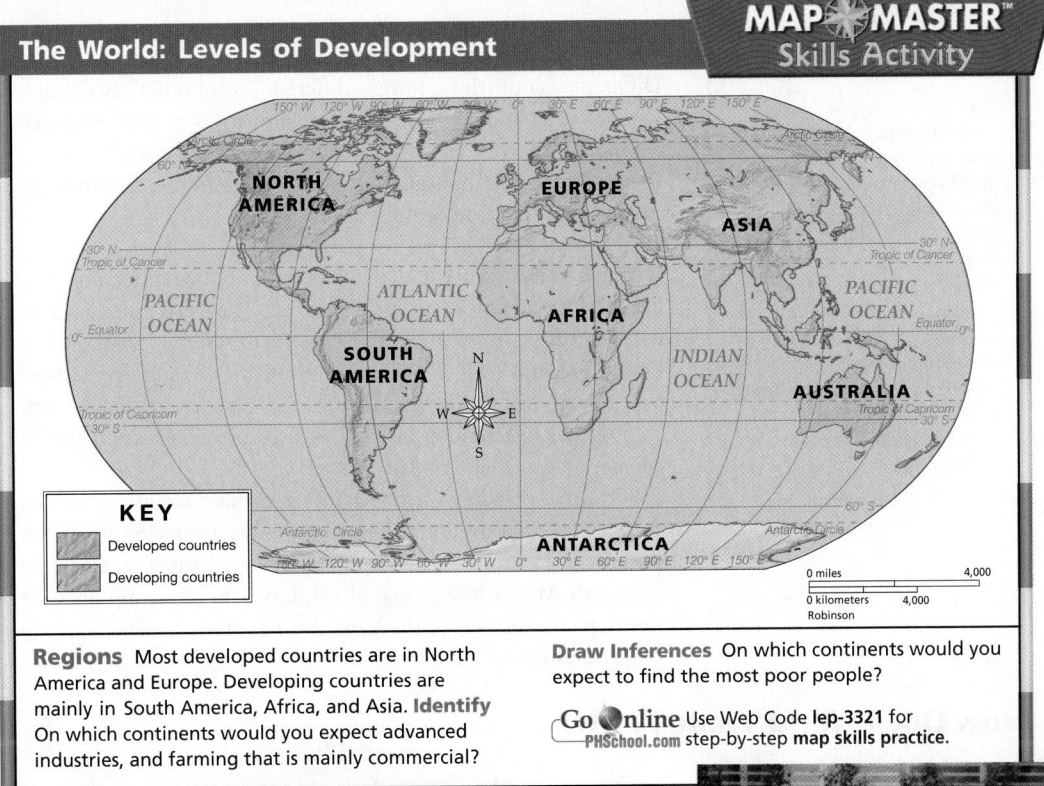

The World: Levels of Development

MAP MASTER™ Skills Activity

KEY

▨ Developed countries

▨ Developing countries

0 miles — 4,000
0 kilometers — 4,000
Robinson

Regions Most developed countries are in North America and Europe. Developing countries are mainly in South America, Africa, and Asia. **Identify** On which continents would you expect advanced industries, and farming that is mainly commercial?

Draw Inferences On which continents would you expect to find the most poor people?

Go Online Use Web Code **lep-3321** for PHSchool.com step-by-step **map skills practice.**

Developing Nations Not every economy is like that of the United States. Most of the people in the world live in developing nations, which are mainly in Africa, Asia, and Latin America.

Developing nations do not have great wealth. Many people are subsistence farmers, or farmers who raise food and animals mainly to feed their own families. Their farms have little or no machinery. People and animals do most of the work.

Many developing nations face great challenges. These include disease, food shortages, unsafe water, poor education and healthcare, and political unrest.

People in developing nations are confronting these challenges. Some nations, such as Saudi Arabia and South Africa, have grown richer by selling natural resources. Others, such as Thailand and China, have built successful industries. The more industrial developing nations are gradually becoming developed countries themselves.

Many people in developed nations work in offices.

✓ **Reading Check** How do developed nations differ from developing nations?

Chapter 3 Section 3 **77**

Independent Practice

Have students add a column entitled "Levels of Development" to their graphic organizers and fill it in with information from this section.

Monitor Progress

As students continue to fill in the graphic organizer, circulate and make sure they are filling in the correct details. Provide assistance as needed.

Answers

MAP MASTER™ Skills Activity **Identify** North America, Europe, the northern half of Asia, Australia **Draw Inferences** Africa, the southern half of Asia, the southern half of North America and South America

✓ **Reading Check** In developed nations food is grown by commercial farmers; in developing nations many people are subsistence farmers. Most people in developed countries live in towns and cities, and can get food, healthcare, good housing, and a good education; in developing countries many face a lack of food, clean water, education, healthcare, and land.

Go Online PHSchool.com Students may practice their map skills using the interactive online version of this map.

Read the **Links Across Time** on this page. Ask students **Why was it important for traders to carry items of value instead of inexpensive items along the Silk Road?** *(To make the trip worthwhile, traders needed to have valuable items to trade along the route.)*

World Trade Patterns ▣

Guided Instruction

■ **Vocabulary Builder** Clarify the high-use word **alliance** before reading.

■ Have students read World Trade Patterns and study the flow chart.

■ Have students summarize the world trade diagram in their own words. *(Country A sells oil to Countries B and C so it can buy wheat and computers; Country B sells wheat to Countries A and C so it can buy computers and oil; Country C sells computers to countries A and B so it can buy wheat and oil.)*

■ **What might be some benefits of belonging to a trade alliance? What might be some drawbacks?** *(Benefits: able to trade goods easily with other member countries. Drawbacks: cannot make decisions about trade alone; member countries might make better, cheaper goods than your country and take business away from your country's producers.)*

Independent Practice

Have students complete the graphic organizer by adding a row entitled "World Trade Patterns" and filling it in with information from this section.

Monitor Progress

■ Show *Section Reading Support Transparency FG 51* and ask students to check their work.

　📖 **Foundations of Geography Transparencies,** *Section Reading Support Transparency FG 51*

■ Tell students to fill in the last column of their *Reading Readiness Guides.*

　All in One Foundations of Geography Teaching Resources, *Reading Readiness Guide,* p. 170

Answer
Predict Country A

The Silk Road
Long-distance trade is nothing new. Hundreds of years ago, merchants brought silks and other luxuries from China to ancient Rome along the Silk Road across Asia. However, those merchants had to load goods on the backs of animals or carry the goods themselves. They could take only light-weight, valuable goods. Today, ships, trains, and trucks can carry heavy and inexpensive goods long distances.

World Trade Patterns

Different countries have different economic strengths. Developed nations have strong industries with advanced technology. Some developing nations have low-cost industries. Other developing nations may grow plantation cash crops, or they may produce oil or minerals.

Different Specialties Countries' economies differ not only because they are more or less developed. They also differ because each country has a different set of economic specialties. For example, Saudi Arabia has vast amounts of oil, and Switzerland has a long history of producing fine watches. Because each country has different specialties, each country has products that consumers in other countries want.

Countries trade with one another to take advantage of one another's special strengths. For example, the United States makes some of the world's best computers. But the United States needs oil. Saudi Arabia has plenty of oil, but it needs computers. So Saudi Arabia sells oil to the United States, and the United States sells computers to Saudi Arabia.

How Does World Trade Work?

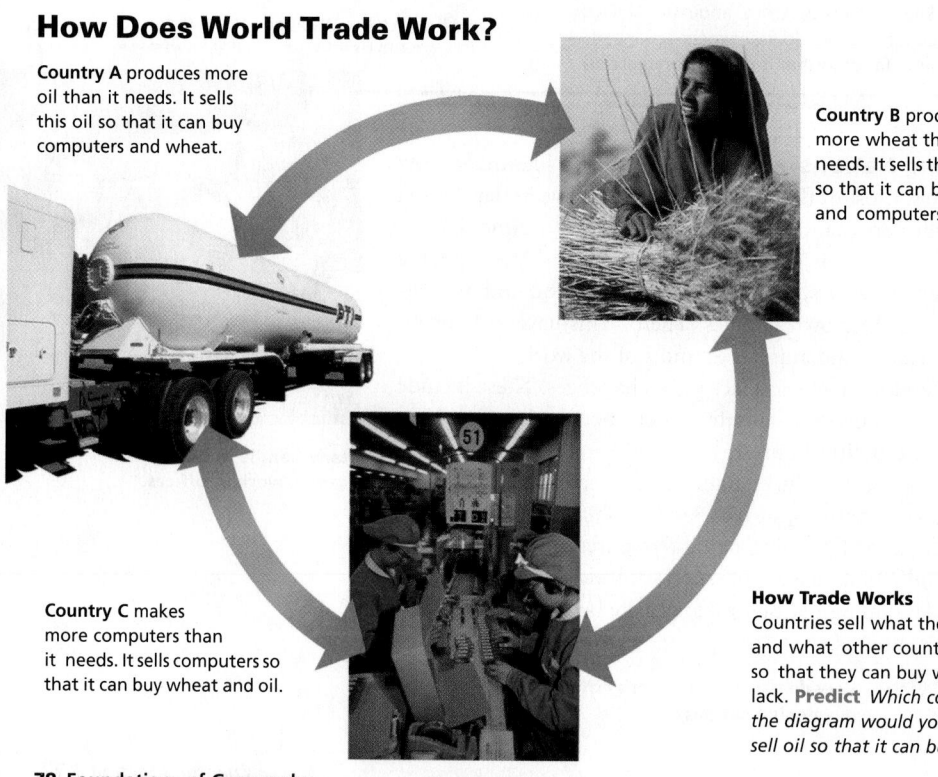

Country A produces more oil than it needs. It sells this oil so that it can buy computers and wheat.

Country B produces more wheat than it needs. It sells this wheat so that it can buy oil and computers.

Country C makes more computers than it needs. It sells computers so that it can buy wheat and oil.

How Trade Works
Countries sell what they have and what other countries want so that they can buy what they lack. **Predict** *Which country from the diagram would you expect to sell oil so that it can buy tea?*

78 Foundations of Geography

Background: Links Across Place

European Union The European Union, or EU, is an organization of European countries that work together on many issues. After the end of World War II, some European leaders believed that a union should be formed between European countries to rebuild Europe and try to prevent future wars. As a result, six countries formed the European Economic Community (EEC) in 1958. More countries eventually joined, and by 1993, the organization changed its name to the European Union. Today goods can be transported freely between countries within the European Union. Representatives from each member country decide on laws that all of the countries will follow. In 2002, 12 EU members replaced their currency with the Euro.

Interdependence As world trade has grown, countries have grown interdependent, or dependent on one another. The United States depends on other countries for oil and inexpensive industrial goods. Meanwhile, other countries depend on the United States for computers and other products.

Developed nations tend to sell products made using advanced technologies. Developing nations tend to sell foods, natural resources such as oil, and simple industrial products. In return, they buy high-technology goods from developed countries.

Some countries have formed trade alliances to reduce the costs of trade. For example, the United States, Canada, and Mexico belong to the North American Free Trade Area, or NAFTA. Most European countries belong to the European Union. Businesses may face increased competition from foreign competitors within these alliances, and workers may lose their jobs. However, businesses may benefit from increased sales in other countries. Consumers benefit from these alliances because they pay less for products from other countries.

Moving Goods
Much of the world's trade travels on container ships, like this one in Dubai, United Arab Emirates. These ships can carry huge loads across oceans. **Draw Conclusions** *How does technology make world trade easier?*

✓ **Reading Check** Why do countries trade with one another?

Section 3 Assessment

Key Terms
Review the key terms at the beginning of this section. Use each term in a sentence that explains its meaning.

Target Reading Skill
What are two ways developed and developing countries are similar?

Comprehension and Critical Thinking
1. (a) Identify Who owns farms, factories, and offices in a communist economy?
(b) Compare and Contrast How is ownership different in a capitalist economy?

2. (a) Identify What is a country's level of development?
(b) Describe What are the main differences in level of development between countries?
(c) Predict What can we predict about a country's economy if we know its level of development?
3. (a) List What are two major trade alliances?
(b) Explain What is the main purpose of these alliances?
(c) Analyze What are some reasons why a country might want to join a trade alliance?

Writing Activity
Suppose you run a company, and you want to expand to another nation. Would you choose a capitalist or communist nation? A developed or developing nation? Would you choose a nation that belongs to a trade alliance? Write a letter to investors explaining your choice.

Go Online
PHSchool.com

For: An activity on economic systems
Visit: PHSchool.com
Web Code: led-3303

Chapter 3 Section 3 **79**

Objectives

Social Studies
1. Examine different types of states.
2. Investigate types of government.
3. Learn about alliances and international organizations.

Reading/Language Arts
Recognize contrast signal words to understand how things are different.

Prepare to Read

Build Background Knowledge L2

Tell students that in this section they will learn about different kinds of rulers and types of governments. To introduce the topic, remind students that the United States is a representative democracy, headed by a President. Ask them to think of other titles they may know for leaders of a country (*prime minister, queen, king*). Conduct an Idea Wave (TE, p. T35) to elicit responses and make a list on the board.

Set a Purpose for Reading L2

- Preview the Objectives.

- Read each statement in *the Reading Readiness Guide* aloud. Ask students to mark the statements true or false.

  All in One Foundations of Geography Teaching Resources, *Reading Readiness Guide,* p. 174

- Have students discuss the statements in pairs or groups of four, then mark their worksheets again. Use the Numbered Heads participation strategy (TE, p. T36) to call on students to share their group's perspectives.

Vocabulary Builder
Preview Key Terms L2

Pronounce each Key Term, and then ask students to say the word with you. Provide a simple explanation such as, "The constitution of the United States set the framework for our government."

Prepare to Read

Objectives
In this section you will
1. Examine different types of states.
2. Investigate types of government.
3. Learn about alliances and international organizations.

Taking Notes

Copy the table below. As you read, fill the table with information about types of states, types of governments, and international organizations.

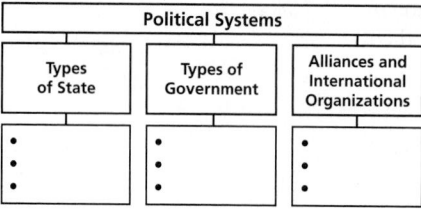

```
              Political Systems

  Types        Types of      Alliances and
 of State     Government      International
                             Organizations

  •             •              •
  •             •              •
  •             •              •
```

Target Reading Skill

Use Contrast Signal Words
Signal words point out relationships among ideas or events. Certain words, such as *like* or *unlike*, can signal a comparison or contrast. As you read this section, notice the comparisons and contrasts among different types of states and governments. What signal words indicate the comparisons and contrasts?

Key Terms
- **government** (GUV urn munt) *n.* a body that makes and enforces laws
- **state** (stayt) *n.* a region that shares a government
- **dependency** (dee PEN dun see) *n.* a region that belongs to another state
- **nation-state** (NAY shun stayt) *n.* a state that is independent of other states
- **city-state** (SIH tee stayt) *n.* a small city-centered state
- **empire** (EM pyr) *n.* a state containing several countries
- **constitution** (kahn stuh TOO shun) *n.* a set of laws that define and often limit a government's power

In 1994, Eritreans celebrated the first anniversary of their country's independence.

80 Foundations of Geography

Types of States

Long ago, most people lived in small, traditional communities. All adults took part in group decisions. Some small communities still make decisions this way, but they are now part of larger units called nations. Nations are too large for everyone to take part in every decision. Still, nations have to protect people and resolve conflicts between individuals and social groups. In modern nations, these needs are met by **governments,** or organizations that set up and enforce laws.

You may remember that a region is an area united by a common feature. A **state** is a region that shares a government. You probably live in a state that is part of the United States. But the political units that we call "states" in the United States are just one kind of state. The entire United States can also be called a state. It is a region that shares a common government—the federal government.

Target Reading Skill L2

Use Contrast Signal Words Point out the Target Reading Skill. Tell students that being able to recognize words that signal a contrast will let them know when a writer is showing how things are different.

Model recognizing contrast signal words using this passage on p. 80: "You probably live in a state that is part of the United States. But the political units that we call 'states' are just one kind of state. The entire country can also be called a state." (*The word* but *signals a contrast. It alerts the reader that the word "state" can have two meanings.*)

Give students *Identify Contrasts.* Have them complete the activity in groups.

All in One Foundations of Geography Teaching Resources, *Identify Contrasts,* p. 178

Dependencies and Nation-States Some regions are **dependencies,** or regions that belong to another state. Others, like the United States, are **nation-states,** or states that are independent of other states. Each has a common body of laws. Nation-states are often simply called nations. Every place in the world where people live is part of a nation-state or dependency.

Most nation-states are large, but some are tiny. The smallest is Vatican City, which is surrounded by the city of Rome in Italy. Vatican City covers only about 109 acres (44 hectares)!

How States Developed The first real states formed in Southwest Asia more than 5,000 years ago when early cities set up governments. Small city-centered states are called **city-states.** Later, military leaders conquered large areas and ruled them as **empires,** or states containing several countries.

After about 1500, European rulers founded the first true nation-states. European nations established dependencies all over the world. When those dependencies became independent, they formed new nation-states.

✓ **Reading Check** What is the difference between a government and a state?

Use Contrast Signal Words

The first sentence in the paragraph at the left begins with the word *some.* The second sentence begins with *others.* These words signal that a contrast will be made. What contrast is being made?

Vatican City
St. Peter's Basilica, shown below, is the seat of the pope. He leads the Roman Catholic Church and rules Vatican City. **Infer** *What must be true about Vatican City for it to be a nation-state?*

Vocabulary Builder

Use the information below to teach students this section's high-use words.

High-Use Word	Definition and Sample Sentence
surround, p. 81	*v.* to shut in on all sides The farmer decided to **surround** the field with a fence to keep his animals from wandering away.
dispute, p. 84	*n.* an argument or disagreement The neighbors settled the **dispute** by agreeing to build a fence between their properties.

⟳ **Target Reading Skill** L2

Use Contrast Signal Words As a follow up, ask students to answer the Target Reading Skill question in the Student Edition. (*Two types of states—dependencies and nation-states—are being contrasted.*)

Instruct

Types of States L2

Guided Instruction

■ **Vocabulary Builder** Clarify the high-use word **surround** before reading.

■ Read Types of States using the Paragraph Shrinking technique (TE, p. T34).

■ Discuss with students the kinds of states that exist today or have in the past, and the characteristics of each type. (*A state is a region that shares the same government. Some regions like the United States are nation-states, which are states that are independent of other states. Some states have dependencies, or regions that belong to them. Empires are states that contain several countries, while many ancient states were small, contained city-states.*)

Independent Practice

Have students create the Taking Notes graphic organizer on a blank piece of paper. Then have them begin to fill in the chart with information they have just learned. Briefly model how to record details by using the *Tree Map/Flow Chart* transparency.

📖 **Foundations of Geography Transparencies,** *Transparency B3: Tree Map/Flow Chart*

Monitor Progress

As students fill in the graphic organizer, circulate and make sure that individuals are choosing the correct details. Provide assistance as needed.

Answers

Infer Vatican City must be independent of any other states.

✓ **Reading Check** Government is a system that sets up and enforces rules; a state is a region that shares a government.

Types of Government

Guided Instruction

- Have students read about the different kinds of governments in Types of Government.

- Have students name the different types of government and who makes the decisions in each. (*direct democracy, all adult residents; tribal rule, the chief or elders; absolute monarchy, the king or queen; dictatorship, the dictator; oligarchy, a small group of people; constitutional monarchy, representatives selected by the people; representative democracy, representatives selected by the people.*)

- Ask **What is the difference between a direct democracy and a representative democracy?** (*In a direct democracy, all adult residents take part in decisions; in a representative democracy, governments are run by representatives that the people choose.*)

Independent Practice

Have students continue to fill in the graphic organizer with details from this section.

Monitor Progress

Circulate to make sure that individuals are choosing relevant details and recording them in the appropriate box on their charts. Provide assistance as needed.

Answer

Analyze Images Kim Jong Il appears before the military, which may be a source of power for him.

Kim Jong Il
Kim Jong Il, the dictator of North Korea, making a rare public appearance.
Analyze Images *What group in North Korea might be a source of power for Kim Jong Il?*

Types of Government

Each state has a government. There are many different kinds of government. Some governments are controlled by a single person or a small group of people. Others are controlled by all of the people.

Direct Democracy The earliest governments were simple. People lived in small groups. They practiced direct democracy, a form of government in which all adults take part in decisions. Many towns in New England today practice direct democracy. Decisions are made at town meetings where all adult residents can speak and vote.

Tribal Rule In time, communities banded together into larger tribal groups. Members of the tribe had a say in group decisions. But chiefs or elders usually made the final decision about what to do. Decisions were based upon the culture's customs and beliefs.

Absolute Monarchy Until about 200 years ago, one of the most common forms of government was absolute monarchy. In that system, a king or queen who inherits the throne by birth has complete control. Few absolute monarchies still exist today. Saudi Arabia is an example of a surviving absolute monarchy.

Dictatorship There are other countries today, however, where just one person rules. A leader who is not a king or queen but who has almost total power over an entire country is called a dictator. Dictatorship is rule by such a leader. Nations ruled by dictators include Cuba, Libya, and North Korea. Dictatorships differ from absolute monarchies because most dictators don't inherit power. Instead, they seize power. Dictators usually remain in power by using violence against their opponents. Dictators deny their people the right to make their own decisions.

Oligarchy Oligarchies are governments controlled by a small group of people. The group may be the leadership of a ruling political party. For example, China is an oligarchy controlled by the leadership of the Communist Party. There are other types of oligarchy. Myanmar, also called Burma, is run by a group of military officers. A group of religious leaders controls Iran. As in a dictatorship, ordinary people have little say in decisions.

Differentiated Instruction

For Advanced Readers

Tell students that sometimes the form of government may change within a country as a result of a revolution or change in leadership. Have students read *Your Government Has Returned to You!* to see an example of this event in the former European country of Czechoslovakia.

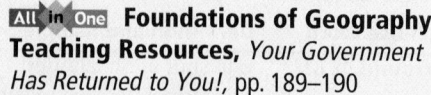 **Foundations of Geography Teaching Resources,** *Your Government Has Returned to You!,* pp. 189–190

Constitutional Monarchy Most monarchies today are constitutional monarchies, or governments in which the power of the king or queen is limited by law. The United Kingdom, the Netherlands, and Kuwait are examples. These nations have **constitutions,** or sets of laws that define and often limit the government's power. In a constitutional monarchy, the king or queen is often only a symbol of the country.

Representative Democracy Representative democracies are governments run by representatives that the people choose. Many constitutional monarchies are also representative democracies. In a representative democracy, the people indirectly hold power to govern and rule. They elect representatives who create laws. If the people do not like what a representative does, they can refuse to reelect that person. Citizens can also work to change laws they do not like. A constitution sets rules for elections, defines the rights of citizens, and limits the powers of the government. This system ensures that power is shared. The United States, Canada, and India are examples of representative democracies.

✓ **Reading Check** What do absolute monarchies, dictatorships, and oligarchies have in common?

Queen Beatrix of the Netherlands heads a constitutional monarchy.

Representative Democracy
Members of the United States House of Representatives, shown below, are elected by the people of their districts. **Contrast** *How does a representative democracy differ from a direct democracy?*

Assess Progress L2

Have students complete the Section Assessment. Then administer the *Section Quiz*.

All in One Foundations of Geography Teaching Resources, *Section Quiz,* p. 176

Reteach L1

If students need more instruction, have them read this section in the Reading and Vocabulary Study Guide.

📖 Chapter 3, Section 4, **Eastern Hemisphere Reading and Vocabulary Study Guide,** pp. 31–33

Extend L3

To extend the lesson, have students do research to learn more about any of the alliances or international organizations mentioned in this section. Students should work in groups to create a display with information about their organization. Then allow students to share their displays with the class.

Answer

✓ **Reading Check** Its purpose is to resolve disputes and promote peace among nations.

Section 4 Assessment

Key Terms

Students' sentences should reflect an understanding of each Key Term.

🔄 **Target Reading Skill**

Governments controlled by a single person are contrasted with governments controlled by all of the people. The words *some* and *others* signal the contrast.

Comprehension and Critical Thinking

1. (a) city-states **(b)** City-states were small and usually controlled only the lands around the city. Modern nation-states are larger.

International Organizations

Nations may make agreements to work together in an alliance. Members of an alliance are called allies. Alliances provide for nations to assist each other with defense. For example, members of the North Atlantic Treaty Organization (NATO) have agreed to defend any fellow member who is attacked.

Military bodies such as NATO are just one type of organization that is international, or involving more than one nation. Some international bodies are mainly economic in purpose. The European Union, for example, promotes economic unity among member nations in Europe.

The United Nations is an international organization meant to resolve disputes and promote peace. Almost all nations of the world belong to the United Nations. Every member has a vote in the General Assembly of the United Nations. But only the United Nations Security Council can make decisions over the use of force. The United States and four other permanent members have the power to prevent action in the Security Council.

The United Nations sponsors other international organizations with special purposes. For example, the Food and Agriculture Organization combats hunger worldwide. The United Nations Children's Fund (UNICEF) promotes the rights and well-being of children.

The United Nations headquarters in New York, New York

✓ **Reading Check** **What is the purpose of the United Nations?**

Section 4 Assessment

Key Terms

Review the key terms at the beginning of this section. Use each term in a sentence that explains its meaning.

🔄 **Target Reading Skill**

Reread the first paragraph on page 82. Which two main types of government are contrasted? Look for contrast signal words.

Comprehension and Critical Thinking

1. (a) Identify What were the earliest types of states?

(b) Compare and Contrast How did those early states differ from modern nation-states?

2. (a) List What are the main types of government?

(b) Categorize In which types of government do ordinary citizens take part in decisions?

3. (a) Define What is an alliance?

(b) Compare and Contrast What are the differences and similarities between alliances and other international organizations?

Writing Activity

Which type of government described in this section appeals most to you? Write a paragraph explaining your preference, and why it appeals to you.

Writing Tip When you write a paragraph, state the main idea in a topic sentence. In this case, the topic sentence will tell the type of government that you prefer. Other sentences should support the main idea with arguments.

84 Foundations of Geography

---

2. (a) direct democracy, absolute monarchy, dictatorship, oligarchy, constitutional monarchy, representative democracy **(b)** direct democracy, constitutional monarchy, representative democracy

3. (a) a group of nations that has agreed to work together **(b)** An alliance is often created to assist members in the event of a military attack, while an international organization may mainly be economic in purpose.

Writing Activity

Use the *Rubric for Assessing a Writing Assignment* to evaluate students' paragraphs.

All in One Foundations of Geography Teaching Resources, *Rubric for Assessing a Writing Assignment,* p. 197

Review and Assessment

Review and Assessment

Review Chapter Content

- Review and revisit the major themes of this chapter by asking students to classify what Guiding Question each bulleted statement in the Chapter Summary answers. Have students write each statement down and work in pairs to determine which statement applies to which Guiding Question. Refer to page 1 in the Student Edition for text of Guiding Questions.

- Assign *Vocabulary Development* for students to review Key Terms.

   All in One **Foundations of Geography Teaching Resources,** *Vocabulary Development,* p. 196

◆ Chapter Summary

Section 1: Population
- Where people live depends on factors such as climate, soil, and history.
- Population density measures the average number of people living in an area.
- Scientific progress has spurred population growth, which is straining Earth's resources.

Section 2: Migration
- People migrate to seek a better life, or, in some cases, because they have no other choice.
- Cities are growing rapidly in some regions.

Section 3: Economic Systems
- Economic systems may have private ownership of businesses, government ownership, or a mixture of both.
- Developed countries have more industry and technology than developing countries.
- Trade connects countries as buyers and sellers.

Section 4: Political Systems
- The world is divided into nation-states.
- States have governments that differ in the amount of power that citizens have.
- Nation-states may join together in alliances and international organizations.

Harvesting rice in China

◆ Key Terms

Each of the statements below contains a key term from the chapter. If the statement is true, write *true*. If it is false, rewrite the statement to make it true.

1. A country's population is the number of people who live there.

2. Population density measures the size of cities.

3. The movement of people from one region to another is migration.

4. Urbanization is the movement of people to cities.

5. An economy is a system of government.

6. Consumers are people who sell products.

7. Developing nations have few industries and simple technologies.

8. A government is a body that makes and enforces laws and resolves conflicts among its people.

9. A state is a system of government.

Chapter 3 **85**

┌ Vocabulary Builder ─────

Revisit this chapter's high-use words:

cluster	theory	rely
vary	unique	alliance
method	exchange	surround
aspect	value	dispute

Ask students to review the definitions they recorded on their *Word Knowledge* worksheets.

All in One **Foundations of Geography Teaching Resources,** *Word Knowledge,* p. 180

Consider allowing students to earn extra credit if they use the words in their answers to the questions in the Chapter Review and Assessment. The words must be used correctly and in a natural context to win the extra points.

Answers

Key Terms

1. True

2. False. Population density measures the average number of people living in an area.

3. True

4. True

5. False. An economy is a system in which people make, exchange, and use things that have value.

6. False. Consumers are people who buy products.

7. True

8. True

9. False. A state is a region that shares a government.

Comprehension and Critical Thinking

10. (a) the way a population is spread out over an area **(b)** climate, natural resources, availability of water, availability of soil for farming **(c)** Because of advancements in food production and transportation, not everyone needs to farm for a living and can therefore live away from rural areas, in cities.

11. (a) It has grown enormously. **(b)** Difficulties include: overcrowding, hunger, unemployment, lack of housing, fresh water, and schools, and inadequate public services

12. (a) when people move by their own choice **(b)** Some people are pulled to a new country by better opportunities, more jobs, or a better climate. Others are pushed to escape hunger, or war, or because they want political freedom.

13. (a) an economic system in which private individuals own most businesses **(b)** Capitalism is an economic system that is controlled by the producers and consumers while communism is an economic system controlled by the government.

14. (a) inadequate healthcare, housing, education, and public services, such as water and electricity **(b)** Developing countries do not have much wealth or industry and have shortages of land and water, which makes it difficult to overcome the challenges.

15. (a) direct democracy and representative democracy **(b)** In democracies a greater number of the citizens get to have a say in government actions than in other forms.

Skills Practice

Purple: more than 260 persons per sq. mile, more than 100 persons per sq. kilometer; pink: 52–259 persons per sq. mile, 21–100 per sq. kilometer; orange: 24–51 persons per sq. mile, 5–20 per sq. kilometer; yellow: less than 24 persons per sq. mile, less than 5 per sq. kilometer; most sparsely populated areas include parts of North and South America, Asia, Africa, and most of Australia; students' conclusions will vary, but may mention that areas that have small populations usually have difficult living conditions, such as climate or terrain, or are not easily accessible.

◆ Comprehension and Critical Thinking

10. (a) Define What is population distribution? **(b) Explain** What factors affect population distribution in a region? **(c) Compare and Contrast** How are those factors different today than they were when most people were farmers?

11. (a) Identify How has the size of world populations changed in recent years? **(b) Identify Cause and Effect** What difficulties have resulted from the change in the size of world populations?

12. (a) Define What is voluntary migration? **(b) Make Generalizations** Why do people choose to migrate?

13. (a) Define What is capitalism? **(b) Contrast** How does capitalism differ from communism?

14. (a) List What are some challenges faced by developing countries? **(b) Infer** Why do developing countries face these challenges?

15. (a) Identify What are two types of democracy? **(b) Contrast** How do democracies differ from other forms of government?

◆ Skills Practice

Using Population Density Maps In the Skills for Life activity in this chapter, you learned how to read a population density map using the map key.

Review the steps you followed to learn this skill. Then review the map on pages 62 and 63, titled The World: Population Density. Using the map key, describe what each color on the map represents and then list the most sparsely populated areas shown. Finally, draw conclusions about why these areas have such small populations.

◆ Writing Activity: Math

Suppose you are a demographer projecting population growth for three countries. Use the following information to create a population bar graph for each country:

	Birthrate	Death Rate
Country A	14.2	8.7
Country B	9.8	9.7
Country C	9.4	13.9

Then, write a brief paragraph explaining your graph. For each country, is the population increasing, decreasing, or stable? Explain why.

MAP ✦ MASTER™
Skills Activity

Place Location For each place listed below, write the letter from the map that shows its location.
1. Asia
2. Antarctica
3. Africa
4. South America
5. North America
6. Europe
7. Australia

Go Online
PHSchool.com Use Web Code **lep-3215** for an **interactive map.**

Continents

Writing Activity: Math

Students' bar graphs should show that Country A has a growing population, Country B's population is staying about the same, and Country C's population is declining. Their paragraphs should explain these findings.

Use *Rubric for Assessing a Bar Graph* to evaluate students' graphs.

All in One Foundations of Geography Teaching Resources, *Rubric for Assessing a Bar Graph,* p. 198

Standardized Test Prep

Test-Taking Tips

Some questions on standardized tests ask you to analyze a reading selection for a main idea. Read the passage in the box below. Then follow the tips to answer the sample question.

This region has one of the highest population densities in the world. As many as 5,000 people per square mile live in parts of the region. There are good reasons for this heavy population density. The land is fertile. Though the desert is not far away, the river contains plenty of water for the people who live there.

TIP As you read each sentence, think about what main idea it supports.

Pick the letter that best answers the question.
Which sentence states this passage's main idea?

A ~~Demographers study human populations.~~

B Egypt's Nile River valley supports a large population.

C ~~People find ways to adapt to their environment.~~

D Many people live near the Mississippi River.

TIP Cross out answer choices that don't make sense. Then pick from the remaining choices the one that BEST answers the question.

Think It Through The passage does not mention demographers. So you can cross out answer A. You can also rule out C, because the passage does not discuss people adapting to their environment. Answers B and D both mention specific regions. Which region does the paragraph describe? The paragraph mentions a desert. There is no desert near the Mississippi River. So the answer is B.

Practice Questions

Use the tips above and other tips in this book to help you answer the following questions.

1. The number of people per square mile is a region's
   A population distribution.
   B population.
   C elevation.
   D population density.

2. People moving to a different region to seek better farming opportunities is an example of
   A trade.
   B voluntary migration.
   C involuntary migration.
   D urbanization.

3. In which of the following does the government own most workplaces?
   A capitalism
   B developing country
   C communism
   D developed country

Read the following passage, and answer the question that follows.

A constitutional monarch has little power. Under some constitutions, elected representatives have the law-making power instead of the monarch. In such cases, the government works much like other representative democracies.

4. What is the main idea of this passage?
   A An absolute monarch has great power.
   B Constitutions are always democratic.
   C A constitutional monarchy may also be a representative democracy.
   D A constitutional monarch cannot interfere with representative democracy.

Go Online
PHSchool.com

Use Web Code lea-3301
for a **Chapter 3 self-test.**

Chapter 3 **87**

MAP MASTER
Skills Activity

1. C   2. G
3. E   4. D
5. A   6. B
7. F

Go Online
PHSchool.com Students may practice their map skills using the interactive online version of this map.

Standardized Test Prep

Answers

1. D
2. B
3. C
4. C

Go Online
PHSchool.com Students may use the Chapter 3 self-test on PHSchool.com to prepare for the Chapter Test.

— Assessment Resources —

Use *Chapter Tests A and B* to assess students' mastery of chapter content.

All in One **Foundations of Geography Teaching Resources,** *Chapter Tests A and B*, pp. 199–204

Tests are also available on the *ExamView Test Bank CD-ROM*

⊙ *ExamView Test Bank CD-ROM*

Objectives

1. Identify the skills Sam needs to survive alone in the wilderness.
2. Discover how Sam came to understand the natural world.
3. Identify devices used by the author to create effects.
4. Analyze the effectiveness of elements of plot, such as setting and character.

Prepare to Read

Build Background Knowledge **L2**

Have students read the Background Information in the Student Edition. Then ask them to brainstorm a list of items they would want to have with them if they were going to live in the woods. Use the Think-Write-Pair-Share strategy (TE, p. T36) to elicit student responses. Then list them on the board.

Instruct

My Side of the Mountain **L2**

Guided Instruction

- Point out that some potentially unfamiliar words are defined in the margin. Clarify the meanings of the words before reading.

- Have students read the selection using the Silent Structured Reading strategy (TE p. T34).

- Tell students that the author of this story uses a literary technique called figurative language to convey Sam's ability to read the weather and animal behavior. One type of figurative language is personification, or describing an object, animal, or idea as if it had human characteristics. Ask students to look through the text to find examples of personification. (*"the moods of storms;" "the air said snow," "trees cry out,"* and *"wind gets caught in a ravine and screams until it dies."*)

- Similes, or phrases that compare things using the words *like* or *as*, are another form of figurative language. Ask students to look through the story and identify similes.

My Side of the Mountain
By Jean Craighead George

Prepare to Read

Background Information

Have you ever camped out overnight? Have you ever built a fire in order to keep warm? Suppose you had no electricity or your home had no heating system. How would you cope with the natural world without modern technology? Do you think that living closer to the natural world would change you in any significant way?

Sam Gribley is the fictional hero of the novel *My Side of the Mountain.* When he decided to live close to nature, he built a tree house in the Catskill Mountains of New York and then moved in with his only companion, Frightful, a falcon. This excerpt describes their first winter in the mountains.

Objectives

As you read this selection, you will

- Identify the skills Sam needed to survive alone in the wilderness.
- Discover how Sam came to understand the natural world.

I lived close to the weather. It is surprising how you watch it when you live in it. Not a cloud passed unnoticed, not a wind blew untested. I knew the moods of the storms, where they came from, their shapes and colors. When the sun shone, I took Frightful to the meadow and we slid down the mountain on my snapping-turtle-shell sled. She really didn't care much for this.

When the winds changed and the air smelled like snow, I would stay in my tree, because I had gotten lost in a blizzard one afternoon and had to hole up in a rock ledge until I could see where I was going. That day the winds were so strong I could not push against them, so I crawled under the ledge; for hours I wondered if I would be able to dig out when the storm blew on. Fortunately I only had to push through a foot of snow. However, that taught me to stay home when the air said "snow." Not that I

Fog-shrouded woodland in the Catskill Mountains, New York

Read Fluently

Form the class into partners. Choose a paragraph from the selection. Have students take turns reading the paragraph aloud. Ask them to underline words that give them trouble as they read. Then, have them decode the problem words with their partner. Provide assistance as needed. Have them reread the paragraph two more times to improve their reading speed. Remind them to stop at the commas and periods and to read with expression. Guide students to see that using figurative language allows the author to make her points about Sam's life among nature more vividly.

was afraid of being caught far from home in a storm, for I could find food and shelter and make a fire anywhere, but I had become as attached to my hemlock house as a brooding bird to her nest. Caught out in the storms and weather, I had an urgent desire to return to my tree, even as The Baron Weasel returned to his den, and the deer to their copse. We all had our little "patch" in the wilderness. We all fought to return there.

I usually came home at night with the nuthatch that roosted in a nearby sapling. I knew I was late if I tapped the tree and he came out. Sometimes when the weather was icy and miserable, I would hear him high in the trees near the edge of the meadow, yanking and yanking and flicking his tail, and then I would see him wing to bed early. I considered him a pretty good barometer, and if he went to his tree early, I went to mine early too. When you don't have a newspaper or radio to give you weather bulletins, watch the birds and animals. They can tell when a storm is coming. I called the nuthatch "Barometer," and when he holed up, I holed up, lit my light, and sat by my fire whittling or learning new tunes on my reed whistle. I was now really into the teeth of winter, and quite fascinated by its activity. There is no such thing as a "still winter night." Not only are many animals running around in the breaking cold, but the trees cry out and limbs snap and fall, and the wind gets caught in a ravine and screams until it dies.

✓ **Reading Check** What did Sam name the nuthatch? Explain why.

hemlock (HEM lahk) *n.* an evergreen tree with drooping branches and short needles
copse (kahps) *n.* a thicket of small trees or shrubs
yank (yangk) *v.* to give the call made by a nuthatch
barometer (buh RAHM uh tur) *n.* an instrument for forecasting changes in the weather; anything that indicates a change
whittle (WHIT ul) *v.* to cut or pare thin shavings from wood with a knife
teeth of winter (teeth uv WIN tur) *n.* the coldest, harshest time of winter

About the Selection

My Side of the Mountain, by Jean Craighead George (New York: E. P. Dutton, 1959), includes sketches of Sam Gribley's adventures.

About the Author

Jean Craighead George (b. 1919) often went camping, climbed trees, and studied living things as she grew up. Ms. George has been writing about nature and its lessons since she was eight years old, and has written more than 80 books for young readers.

Review and Assessment

Comprehension and Critical Thinking

1. (a) **Identify** When the weather is bad, what is Sam's "urgent desire"?
(b) **Compare** To what does Sam compare this desire?
(c) **Interpret** What does Sam tell us about himself when he makes a comparison?
2. (a) **Recall** What are some of the clues Sam has about what the weather will be like?
(b) **Describe** What parts of the natural world does Sam seem to notice most?
(c) **Evaluate** Sometimes Sam talks about the wind and trees as if they were alive. Think about your relationship with nature. How is it like Sam's? How is it different?

Writing Activity

Make a list of sounds you hear only in winter. What are the tastes and smells that make you think of winter? List them. What are the sights of winter? Add them to your list. Then write an essay describing the place you most like to be in winter and explain why.

Literature **89**

Review and Assessment

Comprehension and Critical Thinking

1. (a) to return to his tree (b) to the desire of animals to go to their shelters (c) that he relates to the animals because he thinks of himself as one of them

2. (a) the air smells like snow; the winds change; the nuthatch goes to bed early (b) the behavior of animals (c) Answers

will vary, but students should indicate how their relationship with nature is similar to or different than Sam's.

Writing Activity
Students should create lists of the sights, sounds, tastes, and smells of winter.

All in One **Foundations of Geography Teaching Resources,** *Rubric for Assessing a Writing Assignment,* p. 197

Guided Instruction (continued)

- *Hint:* Have them look at how Sam describes the animals he lives near. *(Examples of similes are: on page 89, "I had become as attached to my hemlock house as a brooding bird to her nest." "...even as The Baron Weasel returned to his den."* Guide students to see that using figurative language allows the author to make her points about Sam's life among nature more vividly.

Independent Practice

Have students write a response to the following statement: "I would/would not want to live like Sam does because…" Make sure that students include at least three reasons why they would or would not like to live like Sam, and that they support each reason with details. Give students *Creating Paragraph Outlines* to help them prepare for writing.

All in One **Foundations of Geography Teaching Resources,** *Creating Paragraph Outlines,* p. 195

Monitor Progress

As students work on their paragraphs, circulate around the room and provide assistance as needed.

Assess and Reteach

Assess Progress　　L2
Have students answer the assessment questions.

Reteach　　L1
If students are having difficulty understanding the story, write the words *Plot, Character,* and *Setting* on the board. Help students identify these elements in the story and list them under the correct heading on the board.

Extend　　L3
To extend the lesson, have students read the selected excerpt from *Hatchet* and answer the questions that follow. Ask students to make a chart in which they compare and contrast the experiences of the boy in each selection.

All in One **Foundations of Geography Teaching Resources,** *Hatchet,* pp. 191–194

Answer

✓ **Reading Check** Barometer; because its actions told Sam when a storm might be coming.

Cultures of the World

Chapter Overview

Overview

Section 1

Understanding Culture
1. Learn about culture.
2. Explore how culture has developed.

Section 2

Culture and Society
1. Learn how people are organized into groups.
2. Investigate language.
3. Explore the role of religion.

Section 3

Cultural Change
1. Explore how cultures change.
2. Learn how ideas spread from one culture to another.

Discovery CHANNEL SCHOOL Video

What is Culture?
Length: 5 minutes, 10 seconds
Use with Section 1
A broad overview of cultures around the world, this segment defines culture and discusses elements of culture. It focuses on the cultures of Sri Lanka as a case study.

Technology Resources

Go Online
PHSchool.com

Students use embedded Web codes to access Internet activities, chapter self-tests, and additional map practice. They may also access Dorling Kindersley's Online Desk Reference to learn more about each country they study.

Interactive Textbook

Use the Interactive Textbook to make content and concepts come alive through animations, videos, and activities that accompany the complete basal text—online and on CD-ROM.

PRENTICE HALL
TeacherEXPRESS™
Plan • Teach • Assess

Use this complete suite of powerful teaching tools to make planning lessons and administering tests quicker and easier.

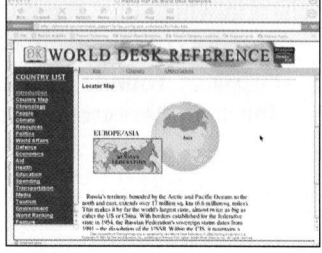

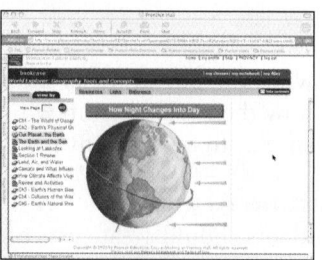

Reading and Assessment

Reading and Vocabulary Instruction

🔄 Model the Target Reading Skill

Sequence Explain to students that recognizing the sequence, or order, of events in written material can help them organize ideas and analyze patterns. Becoming familiar with words that signal sequence is one way for students to strengthen and apply this skill. Have students practice identifying sequence and recognizing sequence signal words by putting the following statements in order:

1. *Then I remembered that there was a shopping list in my pocket.*
2. *Before I left my house, I wrote out a grocery list.*
3. *Later, when I start cooking, I will have all the ingredients I need.*
4. *When I first entered the store, I could not remember what items I needed.*
5. *Soon, my cart was filled up with groceries.*

   Model the approach by thinking out loud: "I am going to look for signal words to put these sentences in order. I see the following signal words: *then, before, later, first, soon.* I think sentence two should be first in the sequence, because it happens *before* the person goes to the store. The first sentence that takes place in the store is four, when she *first entered,* so that comes next. I think sentence one comes after that because she needed the shopping list before she could fill her cart with groceries. She finishes her shopping in sentence five. Finally, she uses the future tense and the word *Later* in sentence three. The correct sequence should be: sentences 2, 4, 1, 5, 3."

   Use the following worksheets from All-in-One Foundations of Geography Teaching Resources (pp. 221–222) to support this chapter's Target Reading Skill.

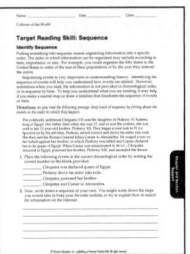 

Vocabulary Builder
High-Use Academic Words
Use these steps to teach this chapter's high-use words:

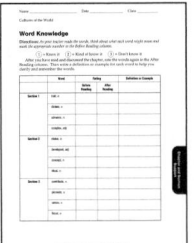

1. Have students rate how well they know each word on their Word Knowledge worksheets (All-in-One Foundations of Geography Teaching Resources, p. 223).
2. Pronounce each word and ask students to repeat it.
3. Give students a brief definition or sample sentence (provided on TE pp. 93, 97, and 105).
4. Work with students as they fill in the "Definition or Example" column of their Word Knowledge worksheets.

Assessment

Formal Assessment
Test students' understanding of core knowledge and skills.

Chapter Tests A and B, All-in-One Foundations of Geography Teaching Resources, pp. 235–240

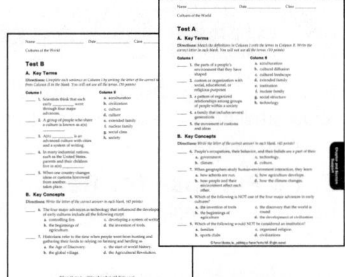

Customize the Chapter Tests to suit your needs.

ExamView Test Bank CD-ROM

Skills Assessment
Assess geographic literacy.

MapMaster Skills, Student Edition, pp. 99, 100, 110

Assess reading and comprehension.

Target Reading Skills, Student Edition, pp. 95, 97, 106, and in Section Assessments

Chapter 4 Assessment, Eastern Hemisphere Reading and Vocabulary Study Guide, p. 44

Performance Assessment
Assess students' performance on this chapter's Writing Activities using the following rubrics from All-in-One Foundations of Geography Teaching Resources.

Rubric for Assessing a Writing Assignment, p. 233

Rubric for Assessing a Journal Entry, p. 234

Assess students' work through performance tasks.

Small Group Activity: Creating a Report on World Music, All-in-One Foundations of Geography Teaching Resources, pp. 226–229

Online Assessment
Have students check their own understanding.

Chapter Self-Test

Section 1 Understanding Culture

 1.5 periods, .75 block

Social Studies Objectives
1. Learn about culture.
2. Explore how culture has developed.

Reading/Language Arts Objective
Identify the sequence of events to help you understand and remember them.

Prepare to Read

Build Background Knowledge
Show students a video and discuss the elements that make up culture.

Set a Purpose for Reading
Have students begin to fill out the *Reading Readiness Guide*.

Preview Key Terms
Teach the section's Key Terms.

Target Reading Skill
Introduce the section's Target Reading Skill of **understanding sequence**.

Instructional Resources

All in One Foundations of Geography Teaching Resources
- **L2** Reading Readiness Guide, p. 210
- **L2** Identify Sequence, p. 221

World Studies Video Program
- **L2** What is Culture?

Differentiated Instruction

Spanish Reading and Vocabulary Study Guide
- **L1** Chapter 4, Section 1, pp. 26–27 ELL

Instruct

What Is Culture?
Discuss how elements of culture differ throughout the world.

The Development of Culture
Ask about the four major advances of early cultures.

Target Reading Skill
Review **understanding sequence**.

Instructional Resources

All in One Foundations of Geography Teaching Resources
- **L2** Guided Reading and Review, p. 211
- **L2** Reading Readiness Guide, p. 210

Foundations of Geography Transparencies
- **L2** Section Reading Support Transparency FG 53

Differentiated Instruction

Spanish Support
- **L2** Guided Reading and Review (Spanish), p. 28 ELL

Assess and Reteach

Assess Progress
Evaluate student comprehension with the section assessment and section quiz.

Reteach
Assign the Reading and Vocabulary Study Guide to help struggling students.

Extend
Extend the lesson by assigning a Book Project.

Instructional Resources

All in One Foundations of Geography Teaching Resources
- **L2** Section Quiz, p. 212
- **L3** Book Project: Desktop Countries, pp. 33–35
  Rubric for Assessing a Writing Assignment, p. 233

Reading and Vocabulary Study Guide
- **L1** Chapter 4, Section 1, pp. 35–37

Differentiated Instruction

Spanish Support
- **L2** Section Quiz (Spanish), p. 29 ELL

Key
- **L1** Basic to Average
- **L3** Average to Advanced
- **L2** For All Students

- **LPR** Less Proficient Readers
- **AR** Advanced Readers
- **SN** Special Needs Students

- **GT** Gifted and Talented
- **ELL** English Language Learners

Section 2 Culture and Society

 3.5 periods, 1.75 blocks (includes Skills for Life)

Social Studies Objectives
1. Learn how people are organized into groups.
2. Investigate language.
3. Explore the role of religion.

Reading/Language Arts Objective
Learning to notice the sequence of important changes can help you understand, remember, and interpret these changes.

Prepare to Read	Instructional Resources	Differentiated Instruction
Build Background Knowledge Discuss three elements of culture: social structure, language, and religion. **Set a Purpose for Reading** Have students evaluate statements on the *Reading Readiness Guide.* **Preview Key Terms** Teach the section's Key Terms. **Target Reading Skill** Introduce the section's Target Reading Skill of **understanding sequence.**	**All in One Foundations of Geography Teaching Resources** L2 Reading Readiness Guide, p. 214 L2 Identify Sequence, p. 221	**Spanish Reading and Vocabulary Study Guide** L1 Chapter 4, Section 2, pp. 28–29 ELL

Instruct	Instructional Resources	Differentiated Instruction
How Society Is Organized Ask about extended and nuclear families. **Target Reading Skill** Review **understanding sequence.** **Language** Discuss language and how it can uphold or reflect particular customs. **Religion** Discuss features of different religions.	**All in One Foundations of Geography Teaching Resources** L2 Guided Reading and Review, p. 215 L2 Reading Readiness Guide, p. 214 **Foundations of Geography Transparencies** L2 Section Reading Support Transparency FG 54 L2 Transparency B15: Outline	**All in One Foundations of Geography Teaching Resources** L3 City Kids in China, pp. 230–231 AR, GT L2 Skills for Life, p. 225 AR, GT, LPR, SN **Teacher's Edition** L3 For Advanced Readers, TE p. 99 L3 For Gifted and Talented, TE p. 99 **Spanish Support** L2 Guided Reading and Review (Spanish), p. 30 ELL

Assess and Reteach	Instructional Resources	Differentiated Instruction
Assess Progress Evaluate student comprehension with the section assessment and section quiz. **Reteach** Assign the Reading and Vocabulary Study Guide to help struggling students. **Extend** Have students work in groups to learn about rituals of world religions.	**All in One Foundations of Geography Teaching Resources** L2 Section Quiz, p. 216 Rubric for Assessing a Journal Entry, p. 234 **Reading and Vocabulary Study Guide** L1 Chapter 4, Section 2, pp. 38–40	**All in One Foundations of Geography Teaching Resources** Rubric for Assessing a Writing Assignment, p. 233 **Teacher's Edition** L1 For Less Proficient Readers, TE p. 103 L1 For Special Needs Students, TE p. 103 **Social Studies Skills Tutor CD-ROM** L1 Making Valid Generalizations ELL, LPR, SN **Spanish Support** L2 Section Quiz (Spanish), p. 31 ELL

Key
L1 Basic to Average   L3 Average to Advanced   LPR Less Proficient Readers   GT Gifted and Talented
L2 For All Students   AR Advanced Readers   ELL English Language Learners
     SN Special Needs Students

Section 3 Cultural Change

 3.5 periods, 1.75 blocks (includes Chapter Review and Assessment)

Social Studies Objectives
1. Explore how cultures change.
2. Learn how ideas spread from one culture to another.

Reading/Language Arts Objective
Identify signal words to help keep the order of events clear.

Prepare to Read

Build Background Knowledge
Ask students to identify elements of their cultures that have been borrowed from others.

Set a Purpose for Reading
Have students evaluate statements on the *Reading Readiness Guide*.

Preview Key Terms
Teach the section's Key Terms.

Target Reading Skill
Introduce the section's Target Reading Skill of **recognizing words that signal sequence.**

Instructional Resources

All in One Foundations of Geography Teaching Resources
- L2 Reading Readiness Guide, p. 218
- L2 Recognize Sequence Signal Words, p. 222

Differentiated Instruction

Spanish Reading and Vocabulary Study Guide
- L1 Chapter 4, Section 3, pp. 30–31 ELL

Instruct

How Cultures Change
Discuss cultural change and have students predict future changes in their own cultures.

How Ideas Spread
Discuss cultural diffusion.

Target Reading Skill
Review **recognizing words that signal sequence.**

Instructional Resources

All in One Foundations of Geography Teaching Resources
- L2 Guided Reading and Review, p. 219
- L2 Reading Readiness Guide, p. 218

Foundations of Geography Transparencies
- L2 Section Reading Support Transparency FG 55
- L2 Transparency B18: Concept Web

Differentiated Instruction

All in One Foundations of Geography Teaching Resources
- L3 Enrichment, p. 224 AR, GT

Teacher's Edition
- L3 For Advanced Readers, TE p. 106
- L1 For English Language Learners, TE p. 106

Spanish Support
- L2 Guided Reading and Review (Spanish), p. 32 ELL

Assess and Reteach

Assess Progress
Evaluate student comprehension with the section assessment and section quiz.

Reteach
Assign the Reading and Vocabulary Study Guide to help struggling students.

Extend
Extend the lesson by assigning a Small Group Activity.

Instructional Resources

All in One Foundations of Geography Teaching Resources
- L2 Section Quiz, p. 220
- L3 Small Group Activity: Creating a Report on World Music, pp. 226–229
  Rubric for Assessing a Writing Assignment, p. 233
- L2 Vocabulary Development, p. 232
- L2 Word Knowledge, p. 223
- L2 Chapter Tests A and B, pp. 235–240

Reading and Vocabulary Study Guide
- L1 Chapter 4, Section 3, pp. 41–43

Differentiated Instruction

Spanish Support
- L2 Section Quiz (Spanish), p. 33 ELL
- L2 Chapter Summary (Spanish), p. 34 ELL
- L2 Vocabulary Development (Spanish), p. 35 ELL

Key
- L1 Basic to Average
- L3 Average to Advanced
- L2 For All Students

- LPR Less Proficient Readers
- AR Advanced Readers
- SN Special Needs Students

- GT Gifted and Talented
- ELL English Language Learners

Reading Background

Oral Cloze Reading

In Section 1 of this chapter, students may use the Oral Cloze Reading strategy to explore the section called Understanding Culture. Help students get the most out of this reading strategy by choosing meaningful words to leave out, such as nouns and verbs, rather than prepositions or conjunctions, and by choosing words that are not particularly long or difficult. For example, in the following paragraph from page 92 of the Student Edition, you might leave out the words indicated in bold.

What Is Culture?

*Culture is the way of life of a **people**, including their beliefs, customs, and practices. The **language** people speak and the way they **dress** are both parts of their **culture**. So are the work people do, what they do after **work** or school, and the **ideas** that influence them.*

Processing Information

Because students will be studying sequence in this chapter's Target Reading Skill, use this opportunity to talk to them about different plans or structures authors may use to organize, or craft, their ideas. Sequence, or chronological order, is one type of author's craft, and others may include comparison and contrast, or cause and effect. Ask students to read the two paragraphs on page 99 of the Student Edition and determine what kind of structure the author is using. Ask: *Is the information in sequence? Is there a clear cause and effect? Is the author highlighting similarities and differences?* Students should see that the author is comparing and contrasting the languages of different groups and countries.

World Studies Background

Folk Art

Folk art can tell us a great deal about a society. Folk artists do not follow the trends of popular art. They develop their own art that reflects the local culture. Folk art includes clothing, toys, and religious figurines that express the typical costumes, forms of entertainment, and beliefs of a society. Because the art is both decorative and functional, it reveals the aesthetic style and everyday routines of a people.

Languages Spread and Shrink

In the 1990s, scholars counted about 6,000 languages spoken across the world. However, scholars predict that within the next 100 years, as societies become more interconnected through improved com-munication, distinct languages will blend together and unique local languages will die out, leaving only 3000 languages in use. This equals a loss of one language every 12 days.

Computers Finding Cures

As technology advances, computer users can help scientists further their research toward curing diseases. In similar pro-grams launched in 2001 and 2003, volun-teers downloaded a screensaver that allowed their computers to perform com-plicated calculations related to disease research. The power of so many comput-ers working on a project is immensely more powerful than the largest supercom-puter and can yield faster results.

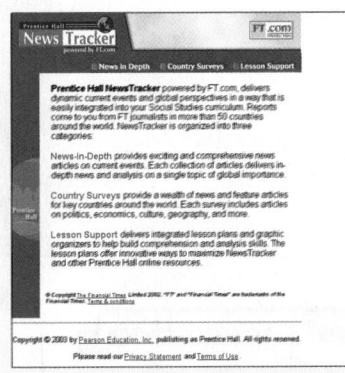

Get in-depth information on topics of global importance with **Prentice Hall NewsTracker,** powered by FT.com.

Use Web Code **led-3400** for **Prentice Hall NewsTracker.**

Chapter 4

Guiding Questions

Remind students about the Guiding Questions introduced at the beginning of the book.

Section 1 relates to **Guiding Question ③**
What is a culture? *(A culture is the way of life of a people, including their beliefs, customs, and practices.)*

Section 2 relates to **Guiding Question ③**
What is a culture? *(Social organization, language, and religion are all parts of a culture.)*

Section 3 relates to **Guiding Question ③**
What is a culture? *(A culture changes through the spread of new technologies and new ideas.)*

◉ Target Reading Skill

In this chapter, students will learn and apply the reading skill of sequence. Use the following worksheets to help students practice this skill:

All in One Foundations of Geography Teaching Resources, *Identify Sequence,* p. 221, *Recognize Sequence Signal Words,* p. 222

Chapter
4 Cultures of the World

Chapter Preview

This chapter will introduce you to the concept of culture, the things that make up culture, and the ways in which cultures change.

Section 1
Understanding Culture

Section 2
Culture and Society

Section 3
Cultural Change

◉ Target Reading Skill

Sequence In this chapter, you will focus on the text structure by identifying the order, or sequence, of events. Noting the sequence of events can help you understand and remember the events.

▶ Young women in traditional dress at a festival in Pushkar, India

---

Bibliography

For the Teacher
Kohl, MaryAnn F., and Jean Potter. *Global Art: Activities, Projects and Inventions from Around the World.* Gryphon House, 1998.
Knight, Margy Burns. *Talking Walls: The Stories Continue.* Tillbury House Publishers, 2003.
Perry, Phyllis Jean. *Keeping the Traditions: A Multicultural Resource.* Fulcrum Publishers, 2000.

For the Student
L1 Wroble, Lisa A. *Kids During the Industrial Revolution* (Kids Throughout History). Rosen Publishing Group, 2003.
L2 Macdonald, Fiona. *Clothing and Jewelry* (Discovering World Cultures). Bt Bound, 2001.
L3 Na, An. *A Step From Heaven.* Front Street Press, 2001.

Reach Into Your Background Have students read the caption and study the photograph on pp. 90–91. Ask them if they have seen or participated in ceremonies where traditional dress is worn. Ask them why wearing traditional dress during special occasions might be important to Indian culture. Have students share their ideas.

Chapter Resources

Teaching Resources
- L2 Vocabulary Development, p. 232
- L2 Skills for Life, p. 225
- L2 Chapter Tests A and B, pp. 235–240

Spanish Support
- L2 Spanish Chapter Summary, p. 34
- L2 Spanish Vocabulary Development, p. 35

Media and Technology
- L1 Student Edition on Audio CD
- L1 Guided Reading Audiotapes, English and Spanish
- L2 Social Studies Skills Tutor CD-ROM
  ExamView Test Bank CD-ROM

PRENTICE HALL

Presentation EXPRESS™
Teach · Connect · Inspire

Teach this chapter's content using the PresentationExpress™ CD-ROM including:
- slide shows
- transparencies
- interactive maps and media
- *ExamView*® QuickTake Presenter

Objectives

Social Studies

1. Learn about culture.
2. Explore how culture has developed.

Reading/Language Arts

Identify the sequence of events to help you understand and remember them.

Prepare to Read

Build Background Knowledge   L2

Tell students that in this chapter they will be learning about the elements that make up culture. Show the video *What is Culture?* and as they watch, ask students to write down a definition of culture and some of its parts. Point out the definition in the text to help students sharpen their answers. Conduct an Idea Wave (TE, p. T35) to generate a list of definitions on the board.

📼 *What Is Culture?,* **World Studies Video Program**

Set a Purpose for Reading   L2

- Preview the objectives.

- Form students into pairs or groups of four. Distribute the *Reading Readiness Guide.* Ask the students to fill in the first two columns of the chart. Use the Numbered Heads participation strategy (TE, p. T36) to call on students to share one piece of information they already know and one piece of information they want to know.

  All in One Foundations of Geography Teaching Resources, *Reading Readiness Guide,* p. 210

Vocabulary Builder
Preview Key Terms   L2

Pronounce each Key Term, then ask the students to say the word with you. Provide a simple explanation such as, "A civilization is a society advanced in art, science, and government."

Section 1 Understanding Culture

Prepare to Read

Objectives

In this section you will
1. Learn about culture.
2. Explore how culture has developed.

Taking Notes

Copy the concept web below. As you read this section, fill in the web with information about culture, its relation to the environment, and how it has developed. Add ovals as needed for concepts in the section.

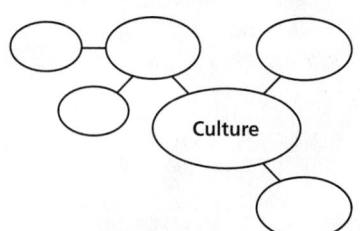

🎯 Target Reading Skill

Understand Sequence
A sequence is the order in which a series of events occurs. Noting the sequence of important events can help you understand and remember the events. You can show the order of events by making a sequence chart. Write the first event, or thing that sets the other events in motion, in the first box. Then write each additional event in a box. Use arrows to show how one event leads to the next.

Key Terms

- **culture** (KUL chur) *n.* the way of life of a people, including their beliefs and practices
- **cultural landscape** (KUL chur ul LAND skayp) *n.* the parts of a people's environment that they have shaped and the technology they have used to shape it
- **civilization** (sih vuh luh ZAY shun) *n.* an advanced culture with cities and a system of writing
- **institution** (in stuh TOO shun) *n.* a custom or organization with social, educational, or religious purposes

A grandfather in Japan teaching his grandson to use chopsticks

What Is Culture?

Culture is the way of life of a people, including their beliefs, customs, and practices. The language people speak and the way they dress are both parts of their culture. So are the work people do, what they do after work or school, and the ideas that influence them.

Elements of Culture Parents pass culture on to their children, generation after generation. Ideas and ways of doing things are called cultural traits. Over time, cultural traits may change.

Some elements of a culture are easy to see. They include material things, such as houses, television sets, food, and clothing. Sports and literature are visible elements of culture as well. Things you cannot see or touch are also part of culture. They include spiritual beliefs, government, and ideas about right and wrong. Finally, language is a very important part of culture.

92 Foundations of Geography

🎯 Target Reading Skill   L2

Understand Sequence Explain that one way to organize ideas is by sequence, or time order. Explain sequence by asking students to consider the order of events in their day. Tell students that events in history also can be organized in a logical sequence.

Model understanding sequence using the first two paragraphs under the head "Technology and Civilization" on p. 94 of the Student Edition. Make a sequence chart on the board using the events leading to the Agricultural Revolution.

Give students *Identify Sequence.* Have them complete the activity in groups.

All in One Foundations of Geography Teaching Resources, *Identify Sequence,* p. 221

People and Their Land Geographers study themes of culture, especially human activities related to the environment. The theme of human-environment interaction deals with these activities. Geographers want to know how the environment affects culture. For example, Japan is a nation of mountainous islands, with limited farmland. So the Japanese have turned to the sea. Fish and seaweed are popular foods in Japan.

However, environment does not dictate culture. Like Japan, Greece is a nation of mountainous islands and peninsulas surrounded by the sea. The Greeks eat some fish, but they have cleared mountainsides as well for use as pasture. Goats and sheep graze on the mountainsides and provide food for the Greeks.

Geographers are also interested in the effect people have on their environment. Often the effect is tied to a culture's technology, even if that technology is simple. For example, the Greeks have cleared their rugged land for pasture. The Japanese harvest seaweed.

A **cultural landscape** is the parts of a people's environment that they have shaped and the technology they have used to shape it. This varies from place to place. On hilly Bali (BAH lee), in Indonesia, farmers have carved terraces into hillsides. On the plains of northern India, farmers have laid out broad, flat fields.

✓ **Reading Check** How are culture and environment related?

Learn more about culture.

Balinese Terraces
A farmer on the island of Bali, in Indonesia, crosses terraced rice fields.
Analyze How has Bali's environment affected its culture? How has Bali's culture affected its environment?

Vocabulary Builder

Use the information below to teach students this section's high-use words.

High-Use Word	Definition and Sample Sentence
trait, p. 92	*n.* distinguishing feature or characteristic One of Adam's **traits** is his unusual sense of humor.
dictate, p. 93	*v.* to control or command Culture often **dictates** the kinds of food people eat.
advance, p. 94	*n.* development Doctors made an important **advance** in fighting the disease.
complex, p. 95	*adj.* complicated, made up of several parts It took him almost an hour to solve the **complex** math problem.

Show students *What is Culture?* Ask students **What elements make up culture?** *(food, festivals, clothing, dance, architecture, spiritual beliefs, language, ideas)*

Instruct

What Is Culture? L2

Guided Instruction
- **Vocabulary Builder** Clarify the high-use words **trait** and **dictate** before reading.

- Read What Is Culture? using the Oral Cloze strategy (TE, p. T33).

- Ask students **What are some elements of culture?** *(houses, television sets, food, clothing, sports, entertainment, literature, spiritual beliefs, government, ideas about right and wrong, and language)*

- Point out to students that people in Japan and Greece share similar physical geography but have chosen to utilize their resources in different ways. Ask students **How do people in Greece interact with their environment differently than people in Japan?** *(The Greeks have cleared their rugged land for pasture; the Japanese fish and harvest seaweed.)*

Independent Practice
Ask students to create the Taking Notes graphic organizer on a blank piece of paper. Have students fill in some of the ovals with information from the passage. Model choosing appropriate details.

Monitor Progress
As students read the passage and expand the Taking Notes concept web, circulate through the classroom to answer questions and provide assistance as needed.

Answers

✓ **Reading Check** Physical environment may influence the types of food, housing, and work that are most common in a culture. The development of technology in a culture can influence environment by allowing people to change the landscape.

Analyze Bali's environment provides a climate suitable for raising rice. The technology of the Balinese culture allows farmers to modify the environment by terracing the land.

The Development of Culture L2

Guided Instruction

- **Vocabulary Builder** Clarify the high-use words **advance** and **complex** before reading.

- Ask students to read The Development of Culture. As students read, circulate to make sure individuals can answer the Reading Check question.

- Ask **What are the four major advances of early cultures? Why do you think each is important?** (*Possible answers: Tools could be used for hunting and building shelters; fire allowed people to live in colder climates and cook food; farming provided a steady food supply; civilizations helped people live better through new technologies.*)

- Ask students why they think the development of cities created a need for institutions such as armies and governments. (*People living together in large groups need more organization, such as laws to ensure safety, as well as means to protect themselves.*)

Independent Practice

Have students complete the Taking Notes graphic organizer by asking them to add more information from the section. Students may add ovals as needed.

Monitor Progress

- Show *Section Reading Support Transparency FG 53* and ask students to check their graphic organizers individually. Go over key concepts and clarify key vocabulary as needed.

  📖 **Foundations of Geography Transparencies,** *Section Reading Support Transparency FG 53*

- Tell students to fill in the last column of the *Reading Readiness Guide.* Ask them to evaluate if what they learned was what they had expected to learn.

  All in One Foundations of Geography Teaching Resources, *Reading Readiness Guide,* p. 210

Answer

Draw Conclusions Farmers were able to harvest more with more powerful tools.

The Development of Culture

Scientists think that early cultures had four major advances in technology. First was the invention of tools millions of years ago. Second and third were the control of fire and the beginning of agriculture. Fourth was the development of **civilizations,** or advanced cultures with cities and the use of writing.

Technology and Civilization For most of human existence, people were hunters and gatherers. While traveling from place to place, they collected wild plants, hunted game, and fished.

Later, people discovered how to grow crops. They tamed wild animals to help them with work or to raise for food. Over time, more and more people relied on farming for most of their food. Historians call this great change the Agricultural Revolution.

Agriculture provided a steady food supply. Agriculture let farmers grow more food than they needed. In parts of Asia and Africa, some people worked full time on crafts such as metalworking. They traded their products for food. People began to develop laws and government. To store information, they developed writing. These advances in culture produced the first true civilizations about 5,000 years ago.

Early civilizations developed new technologies, such as irrigation, that let people grow more crops. Over time, farming and civilization spread throughout the world.

The Development of Agricultural Technology

Sickle
The first farmers used hand-held sickles to harvest grain. The first sickles had stone blades. Later sickles, like the one shown here, had metal blades.

Horse-drawn reaper
By the late 1800s, farmers were using animal-powered machinery, such as this sail reaper, to harvest grain.

Tools for Harvesting When the Agricultural Revolution began, people used simple hand-powered tools. The Industrial Revolution later brought industrial tools to the fields. **Draw Conclusions** *How do you think the development of tools for harvesting affected the amount that each farmer could harvest?*

Combine harvester
Today, farmers harvest grain with large-scale, motorized machinery, such as this combine.

94 Foundations of Geography

Skills for Life Skills Mini Lesson

Recognizing Bias L2

1. Define *bias* as a one-sided view. Explain that to detect bias students should look for false or missing information, words that express emotion, and how the writer's purpose affects the information.

2. Practice the skill using this statement from a school newspaper: *Our team will win the big game because we have better players.* Ask: What words express emotion rather than fact? (*better players*) Why might the paper show a bias? (*The writer wants his or her own team to win.*)

3. Discuss what could make the article less biased.

Then, about 200 years ago, people began to invent new technologies that used power-driven machinery. This change marked the beginning of the Industrial Revolution. It led to the growth of cities, science, and even more advanced technologies, such as computers and space flight.

Development of Institutions Before the Agricultural Revolution, people had simple **institutions,** customs and organizations with social, educational, or religious purposes. These included extended families and simple political institutions, such as councils of elders.

As people gathered in larger groups and formed cities, they needed more complex institutions. People developed organized religions, with priests, ceremonies, and temples. Armies and governments appeared with states. Teachers started schools.

In the modern world, we have many different kinds of institutions, including museums, sports clubs, corporations, political parties, and universities. These institutions are important parts of our culture.

 What allowed civilizations to develop?

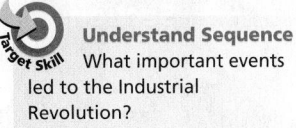 **Understand Sequence**
What important events led to the Industrial Revolution?

Oxford University, in Oxford, England, is more than 800 years old.

Section 1 Assessment

Key Terms
Review the key terms at the beginning of this section. Use each term in a sentence that explains its meaning.

Target Reading Skill
Place the following events in the order in which they occurred: the development of civilization; the invention of tools; the development of industry; and the beginnings of agriculture.

Comprehension and Critical Thinking
1. (a) **Define** What is a cultural landscape?
(b) **Explain** What are the most important cultural traits that shape a people's cultural landscape?
(c) **Identify Cause and Effect** If two cultures occupy similar environments, why might their cultural landscapes still differ?
2. (a) **Identify** What was the Agricultural Revolution?
(b) **Sequence** What cultural advances followed the Agricultural Revolution?

Writing Activity
Think of all the ways that the culture of your region has shaped its landscape. Write a short paragraph describing your cultural landscape and the cultural traits that shaped it.

Go Online
PHSchool.com
For: An activity on culture
Visit: PHSchool.com
Web Code: led-3401

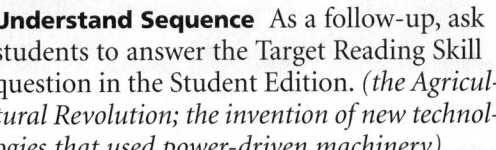

Understand Sequence As a follow-up, ask students to answer the Target Reading Skill question in the Student Edition. (*the Agricultural Revolution; the invention of new technologies that used power-driven machinery*)

Assess and Reteach

Assess Progress L2
Have students complete the Section Assessment. Administer the *Section Quiz.*

All in One Foundations of Geography Teaching Resources, *Section Quiz,* p. 212

Reteach L1
If students need more instruction, have them read this section in the Reading and Vocabulary Study Guide.

Chapter 4, Section 1, **Eastern Hemisphere Reading and Vocabulary Study Guide,** pp. 35–37

Extend L3
Have students complete *Book Project: Desktop Countries.*

All in One Foundations of Geography Teaching Resources, *Book Project: Desktop Countries,* pp. 33–35

Answer

Reading Check advances in culture such as agriculture and writing

Writing Activity
Use the *Rubric for Assessing a Writing Assignment* to evaluate students' paragraphs.

All in One Foundations of Geography Teaching Resources, *Rubric for Assessing a Writing Assignment,* p. 233

Section 1 Assessment

Key Terms
Students' sentences should reflect knowledge of each Key Term.

Target Reading Skill
the invention of tools; the beginnings of agriculture; the development of civilization; the development of industry

Comprehension and Critical Thinking
1. (a) the parts of a people's environment that they have shaped and the technology they have used to shape it (b) a group's customs, ideas, and ways of doing things (c) because of the way they have developed and applied technology, or because of their customs

2. (a) The Agricultural Revolution was a change in which people began growing crops and taming wild animals. They began to depend more on farming for food than hunting and gathering. (b) the rise of birthrates and population, the ability to grow excess crops, the development of crafts, the institution of laws and government, and the development of writing

Section 2
Step-by-Step Instruction

Objectives

Social Studies

1. Learn how people are organized into groups.

2. Investigate language.

3. Explore the role of religion.

Reading/Language Arts

Learning to notice the sequence of important changes can help you understand and remember and interpret these changes.

Prepare to Read

Build Background Knowledge   L2

In this section, students will learn about three elements of culture: social structure, language, and religion. Have students look at the section's headings and photographs with this question in mind: **Why are these ideas important to a society's culture?** Conduct an Idea Wave (TE, p. T35) to generate a list.

Set a Purpose for Reading   L2

■ Preview the Objectives.

■ Read each statement in the *Reading Readiness Guide* aloud. Ask students to mark the statements true or false.

■ Have students discuss the statements in pairs or groups of four, then mark their worksheets again. Use the Numbered Heads participation strategy (TE, p. T36) to call on students to share their group's perspectives.

All in One Foundations of Geography Teaching Resources, *Reading Readiness Guide,* p. 214

Vocabulary Builder
Preview Key Terms   L2

Pronounce each Key Term, then ask the students to say the word with you. Provide a simple explanation such as, "An extended family can include grandparents, aunts, uncles, and cousins."

Section 2   Culture and Society

Prepare to Read

Objectives

In this section you will
1. Learn how people are organized into groups.
2. Investigate language.
3. Explore the role of religion.

Taking Notes

Copy the outline below. As you read this section, fill in the outline with information about how society is organized, about language, and about religion. Add letters and numbers as needed.

```
I. How society is organized
   A. Social classes
   B.
      1.
      2.
II. Language
   A.
```

Target Reading Skill

Understand Sequence Noting the sequence of important changes can help you understand and remember the changes. You can show a sequence of changes by simply listing the changes in the order in which they occurred. As you read this section, list the sequence of the changes in people's ability to improve their status.

Key Terms

• **society** (suh SY uh tee) *n.* a group of people sharing a culture

• **social structure** (SOH shul STRUK chur) *n.* a pattern of organized relationships among groups of people within a society

• **social class** (SOH shul klas) *n.* a grouping of people based on rank or status

• **nuclear family** (NOO klee ur FAM uh lee) *n.* a mother, a father, and their children

• **extended family** (ek STEN did FAM uh lee) *n.* a family that includes several generations

A nuclear family in the United Kingdom

How Society Is Organized

Think about the people you see every day. Do you spend each day meeting random strangers? Or do you see the same family members, classmates, and teachers every day? Chances are, there is a pattern to your interactions.

A group of people sharing a culture is known as a **society.** Every society has a **social structure,** or a pattern of organized relationships among groups of people within the society. A society may be as small as a single community or as large as a nation or even a group of similar nations. Smaller groups within a society work together on particular tasks. Some groups work together to get food. Others protect the community. Still others educate children. Social structure helps people work together to meet one another's basic needs.

The family is the basic, most important social unit of any society. Families teach the customs and traditions of the culture to their children. Through their families, children learn how to dress, to be polite, to eat, and to play.

96 Foundations of Geography

Target Reading Skill   L2

Understand Sequence Explain to students that they can show a sequence of changes by listing the changes in the order in which they occurred.

Model understanding sequence using the text on p. 100 of the Student Edition. Ask **In what order did the religions of Christianity, Islam, and Judaism start?** Then write on the board, *1. Judaism; 2. Christianity; 3. Islam.* Point out the sentence in the passage in which the answer can be found, emphasizing the clue words "first," "then," and "finally."

Give students *Identify Sequence.* Have them complete the activity in groups.

All in One Foundations of Geography Teaching Resources, *Identify Sequence,* p. 221

Social Classes Cultures also have another kind of social organization—**social classes,** or groupings of people based on rank or status. A person's status or position may come from his or her wealth, land, ancestors, or education. In some cultures in the past, it was often hard—or impossible—for people to move from one social class to another. Today, people in many societies can improve their status. They can obtain a good education, make more money, or marry someone of a higher class.

Kinds of Families Not all cultures define family in the same way. In some cultures, the basic unit is a **nuclear family,** or a mother, a father, and their children. This pattern is common in developed nations such as the United States, Australia, and Germany. The nuclear family gets its name from the word *nucleus*, which means "center."

Other cultures have **extended families,** or families that include several generations. In addition to a central nuclear family of parents and their sons or daughters, there are the wives or husbands of those sons or daughters. The family also includes grandchildren, or the children of those sons or daughters. In extended families, older people often help care for the children. They are respected for their knowledge and experience. Older family members pass on traditions. Extended families are less common than they used to be. As rural people move to cities, nuclear families are becoming more common.

√ **Reading Check** What is the basic social unit of societies?

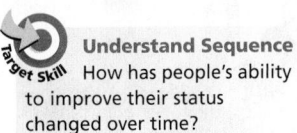

Understand Sequence How has people's ability to improve their status changed over time?

A Salvadoran-American Family This family includes grandparents and more than one set of parents. **Infer** *Is this a nuclear family or an extended family?*

Vocabulary Builder

Use information below to teach students this section's high-use words.

High-Use Word	Definition and Sample Sentence
status, p. 97	*n.* rank or position Going to college is one way to improve your **status** in life.
concept, p. 98	*n.* idea The **concept** behind the invention was very simple.
ritual, p. 101	*n.* ceremony or custom Many religions have a marriage **ritual.**

How Society Is Organized L2

Guided Instruction

- **Vocabulary Builder** Clarify the high-use word **status** before reading.

- Read How Society Is Organized using the Structured Silent Reading technique (TE, p. T34). As students read, circulate to make sure individuals can answer the Reading Check question.

- Have students explain the difference between a nuclear family and an extended family. *(nuclear family: mother, father, and their children; extended family: family that includes several generations)*

- Ask students **Why might movement from rural to urban areas cause nuclear families to become more common?** *(Possible answer: In rural areas, extended families living together might share the work on farms, and there would probably be more room to provide housing for everyone. In urban areas, people generally work outside of the home, and homes are usually smaller and closer together.)*

Independent Practice

Ask students to create the Taking Notes graphic organizer on a blank piece of paper and begin filling in details about how society is organized.

Monitor Progress

As students fill in the graphic organizer, circulate and make sure that individuals are choosing the correct details. Provide assistance as needed.

Target Reading Skill L2

Understand Sequence As a follow-up, ask students to answer the Target Reading Skill question in the Student Edition. *(In the past, it was difficult for people in some cultures to move from one social class to another. Today, people in many societies improve their social status through education, money, or marriage.)*

Answers

√ **Reading Check** The family is the basic social unit of societies.

Infer This is an extended family.

Language

Guided Instruction

■ **Vocabulary Builder** Clarify the high-use word **concept** before reading.

■ Read Language and examine The World: Major Language Groups. Encourage students to ask questions about using the map.

■ Ask students if they can think of examples of a word having different meanings in two different cultures. *(Possible answer: "Football" in the United States is not the same as "football" in England. There, "football" refers to soccer.)*

■ Ask students to examine the photograph at the top of p. 98. Ask **What other forms of cultural communication might depend on senses other than hearing?** *(Answers will vary, but might include a green light that means "go," or a handshake that means "nice to meet you.")*

■ Ask **Why might the customs of a French-speaking Canadian differ from those of an English-speaking Canadian?** *(because people who speak different languages may have different ideas and traditions)*

■ Have students list the language groups found in Australia *(Indo-European, other)*. Ask **Why might Australia share a language group with Europe?** *(Most Australians are descended from British settlers.)*

A teacher using sign language with hearing-impaired students

Language

All cultures have language. In fact, language provides a basis for culture. People learn their cultures mainly through language. Most communication with others depends on language. Think how hard it would be if you had no way to say, "Meet me by the gate after school." How could you learn if you could not ask questions?

A culture's language reflects the things that are important in that culture. For example, English has words for Christian and Jewish concepts, such as *baptism* and *sabbath*. Some languages lack words for these concepts because their speakers are not Jewish or Christian. But those languages have words for concepts in their people's religions that have no English translation.

The World: Major Language Groups

This map shows the locations of the world's major language groups. Languages in each of these groups share a common ancestor, a language spoken long ago that gradually changed to become several related languages. For example, English and German are both Indo-European languages that share a common ancestor. Can you recognize the German words *Land, Mann,* and *Wagen?*

NORTH AMERICA

ATLANTIC OCEAN

PACIFIC OCEAN

SOUTH AMERICA

SOUTHERN OCEAN

ANTARCTICA

Arctic Circle

Tropic of Cancer

Equator

Tropic of Capricorn

Antarctic Circle

0 miles 2,000
0 kilometers 2,000
Robinson

Young boy in China writing Chinese characters

98 Foundations of Geography

Background: Daily Life

Religion Affects Daily Life Many religions require daily activities, such as prayers and rituals, to be performed by believers. In a Jewish group called Hasidim, or "pious ones," religion governs how believers dress, what they eat, and how they wear their hair. Men wear beards and have a long side lock of hair hanging on each side of their faces. Married women cover their hair with wigs or scarves in public. Like other Orthodox Jews, Hasidim observe special laws about food, called *kashrus,* which are outlined in the Jewish Torah. Shellfish and pork are forbidden. Meat and dairy foods may not be eaten at the same meal or cooked in the same pot.

In some countries, people speak more than one language. For example, Canada has two official languages, French and English. In the United States, you may usually hear English, but you can also hear Spanish, Chinese, Haitian Creole, and many other languages. India has 16 official languages, but people there speak more than 800 languages!

People who speak each language are culturally different in some ways from other people in their country who speak other languages. They may celebrate different festivals or have different customs for such things as dating or education. That is because each language preserves shared ideas and traditions.

✓ **Reading Check** What is the relation between language and culture?

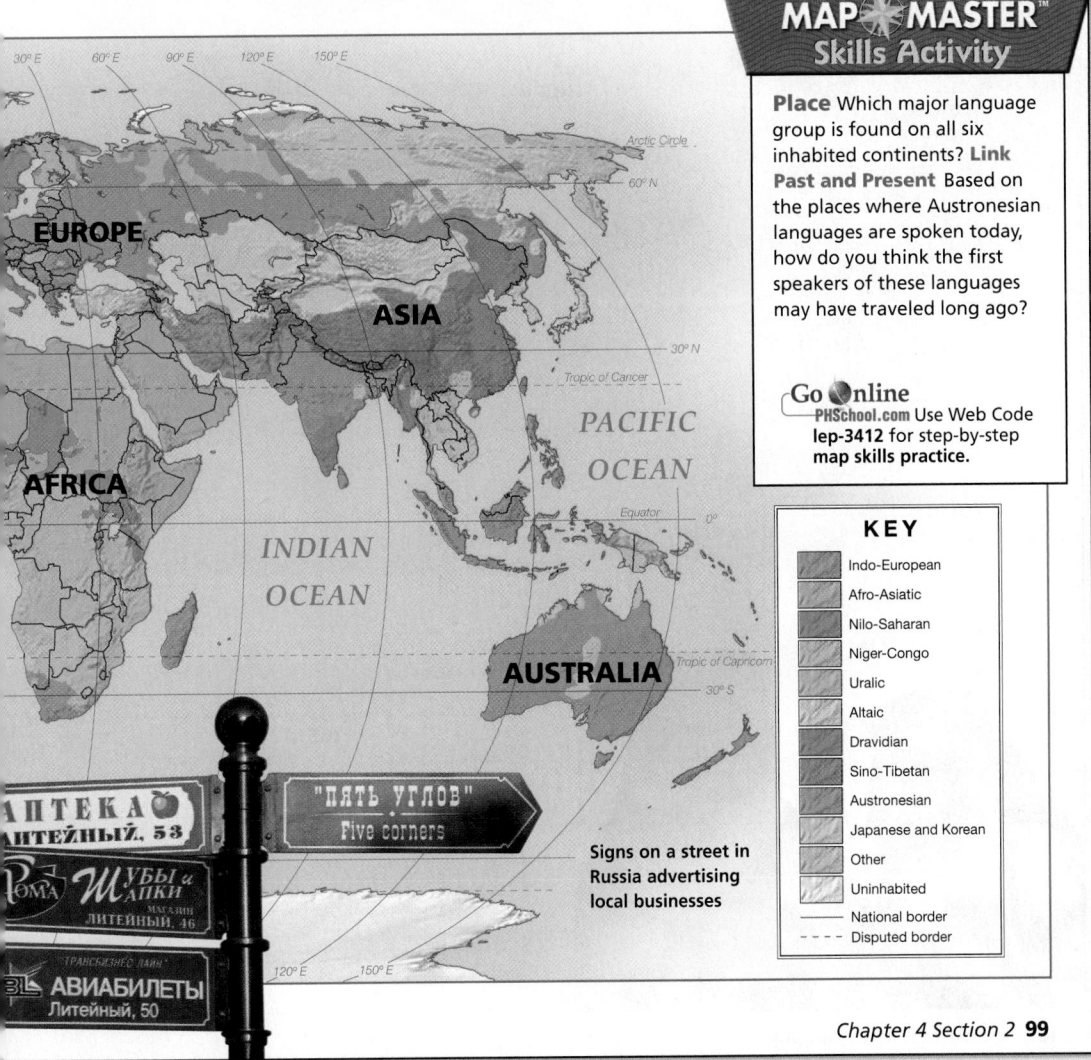

MAP★MASTER™
Skills Activity

Place Which major language group is found on all six inhabited continents? **Link Past and Present** Based on the places where Austronesian languages are spoken today, how do you think the first speakers of these languages may have traveled long ago?

Go Online
PHSchool.com Use Web Code **lep-3412** for step-by-step map skills practice.

KEY

- Indo-European
- Afro-Asiatic
- Nilo-Saharan
- Niger-Congo
- Uralic
- Altaic
- Dravidian
- Sino-Tibetan
- Austronesian
- Japanese and Korean
- Other
- Uninhabited
- —— National border
- - - - Disputed border

Signs on a street in Russia advertising local businesses

Chapter 4 Section 2 **99**

Differentiated Instruction

For Advanced Readers ⬛3
Have students read the primary source *City Kids in China* and look for elements of social structure. Have them compare the Chinese students' experiences to their own and write a paragraph that describes an element of social structure in the United States.

All in One Foundations of Geography Teaching Resources, *City Kids in China,* pp. 230–231

For Gifted and Talented ⬛3
Have students go on a "language hunt." By using the library or Internet and talking to their families, have each student learn ten words in another language. Each student should make a chart with the word, the English translation, and the name of the language. Have students share their new words with the class.

Independent Practice
Have students continue working with the Taking Notes graphic organizer by asking them to expand and complete the section of the outline on Language. If students need assistance, show the blank *Outline Transparency* as a model.

📖 **Foundations of Geography Transparencies,** *Transparency B15: Outline*

Monitor Progress
As students continue to fill in the graphic organizer, make sure individuals are adding appropriate details about language. Provide assistance as needed.

Answers

✓ **Reading Check** Language provides a basis for culture, because people learn their cultures mainly through language.

MAP★MASTER™
Skills Activity **Place** Indo-European **Link Past and Present** Austronesian languages are spoken on many islands in the Pacific and Indian oceans. The first Australians probably traveled by boat to new areas.

Go Online
PHSchool.com Students may practice their map skills using the interactive online version of this map.

Religion

L2

Guided Instruction

- **Vocabulary Builder** Clarify the high-use word **ritual** before reading.

- Have students read Religion and examine The World: Major Religions map and its accompanying text. As students read, circulate to make sure individuals can answer the Reading Check question.

- Direct students' attention to the map and ask **What religions are practiced in South America?** *(Roman Catholic, Protestant, and traditional)*

- Ask students to look at the map key and consider what "Sunni" and "Shi'a" might designate. *(Sunni and Shi'a are branches of Islam, just as Roman Catholic, Protestant, and Eastern Churches are branches of Christianity.)*

- Ask students to list some of the common features among the world's religions. *(All have prayers and rituals, celebrate important places and times, and have standards of proper behavior.)*

Independent Practice

Have students complete the Taking Notes outline by adding a heading on Religion and filling in the appropriate details.

Monitor Progress

- Show *Section Reading Support Transparency FG 54* and ask students to check their graphic organizers individually.

  All in One Foundations of Geography Teaching Resources, *Section Reading Support Transparency FG 54*

- Tell students to fill in the last column of the *Reading Readiness Guide*.

  All in One Foundations of Geography Teaching Resources, *Reading Readiness Guide*, p. 214

Answers

MAP MASTER Skills Activity **Place** Asia **Draw Inferences** It is the largest continent.

Go Online PHSchool.com Students may practice their map skills using the interactive online version of this map.

The World: Major Religions

The major religions of the world all began in Asia. India was the birthplace of Sikhism, Hinduism, and Buddhism, all of which later spread to other countries. The other great world religions had their start in Southwest Asia: first Judaism, then Christianity, and finally Islam. These religions also later spread to other parts of the world.

Young Buddhist monks in Thailand

MAP MASTER Skills Activity

Place Which of the continents has the greatest variety of religions?
Draw Inferences Why do you think this is so?

Go Online PHSchool.com Use Web Code lep-3422 for step-by-step map skills practice.

NORTH AMERICA • EUROPE • ASIA • AFRICA • SOUTH AMERICA • AUSTRALIA
ATLANTIC OCEAN • PACIFIC OCEAN • INDIAN OCEAN • PACIFIC OCEAN • SOUTHERN OCEAN

0 miles 3,000
0 kilometers 3,000
Robinson

Eastern Orthodox Christian priests in Greece

KEY

Islam	Other Major Groups
Sunni	Hinduism
Shi'a	Buddhism
Christianity	Sikhism
Roman Catholic	Judaism
Protestant	Traditional
Eastern Churches	National border
	Disputed border

100 Foundations of Geography

Skills Mini Lesson

Skills for Life

Synthesizing Information

1. Explain that to synthesize information, students should find the main idea of each fact, then find supporting details, and look for connections.

2. State the idea from the text on p. 101, "Most of the people of Saudi Arabia are Muslim." The map and text on p. 100 confirm the fact that Islam started in Southwest Asia. You can conclude: *Many people living near where Islam began are Muslims.*

3. Read the text on p. 101 that says that members of Islam, Judaism, and Christianity believe in one God. The map on p. 100 shows that people of these religions live in the same area. Ask: What conclusion can you draw from this information?

Religion

Religion is an important part of every culture. For example, most of the people of Saudi Arabia are Muslim. In some countries, such as the United States, people follow more than one religion. Beliefs and practices may differ among religions. However, religion remains important to many people.

Religion can help people make sense of the world. Religion can provide comfort and hope for people facing difficult times. And religion can help answer questions about the meaning and purpose of life. Religion also guides people in ethics, or standards of accepted behavior.

Religious beliefs vary. Members of some religions, such as Islam, Judaism, and Christianity, believe in one God. Members of other religions, such as Hinduism and traditional religions, believe in more than one god. But all religions have prayers and rituals. Every religion celebrates important places and times. And all religions expect people to treat one another well and to behave properly.

✓ **Reading Check** Why is religion important to people?

This temple, in Amritsar, India, is a holy place of Sikhism.

Section 2 Assessment

Key Terms
Review the key terms at the beginning of this section. Use each term in a sentence that explains its meaning.

Target Reading Skill
Place the following events in young people's lives in the correct sequence: learning their culture's language and learning their culture's beliefs.

Comprehension and Critical Thinking
1. (a) Identify What is the role of social structure in society?
(b) Explain What is the place of families in a social structure?
(c) Predict Would you expect the members of one family to fall within one social class or more than one?
2. (a) Recall How is language related to culture?
(b) Identify Cause and Effect Why do you think people who speak different languages tend to have different cultures?
3. (a) Identify What values do all religions share?
(b) Draw Conclusions How might those values help people of different religions overcome conflicts?

Writing Activity
In a journal entry, explore the ways in which family and language connect you to other people in your society.

> **Writing Tip** When you write a journal entry, write about experiences from your own life. You may also express your own opinions and perspectives. For this exercise, think about which of your activities and interests involve family or the use of language.

Chapter 4 Section 2 **101**

Section 2 Assessment

Key Terms
Students' sentences should reflect knowledge of each Key Term.

Target Reading Skill
Learning their culture's language; learning their culture's beliefs.

Comprehension and Critical Thinking
1. (a) Social structure organizes a society through a pattern of relationships, and helps people work together to meet the basic needs of individuals, families, and communities. **(b)** Families are the most basic and important unit in a social structure. **(c)** Members of one nuclear family would likely fall within one social class, but the members of an extended family might fall within more than one social class.

2. (a) People learn culture mainly through language. **(b)** Each language preserves shared ideas and traditions.

3. (a) All have prayers and rituals, celebrate important places and times, and have standards of behavior. **(b)** People may be able to focus on their similarities rather than their differences.

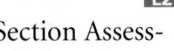

Assess and Reteach

Assess Progress L2
Have students complete the Section Assessment. Administer the *Section Quiz*.

All in One Foundations of Geography Teaching Resources, *Section Quiz*, p. 216

Reteach L1
If students need more instruction, have them read this section in the Reading and Vocabulary Study Guide.

📖 Chapter 4, Section 2, **Eastern Hemisphere Reading and Vocabulary Study Guide,** pp. 38–40

Extend L3
Have students work in small groups to investigate the rituals of world religions. Assign each group a different religion, and ask the groups to use the library or Internet to find out about one major holiday celebrated as part of the religion, including the name of the holiday, what it celebrates, when it is celebrated, and how it is celebrated. Have students create posters using the information they have gathered, and present their posters to the class.

Answer

✓ **Reading Check** Religion is important to people because it helps them make sense of the world, answers questions about the meaning of life, and guides their behavior.

Writing Activity
Use the *Rubric for Assessing a Journal Entry* to evaluate students' journal entries.

All in One Foundations of Geography Teaching Resources, *Rubric for Assessing a Journal Entry*, p. 234

Chapter 4 Section 2 **101**

Objective
Learn how to make valid generalizations.

Prepare to Read

Build Background Knowledge   L2
Ask students to think of words or terms they already know that may help them to determine the meaning of the word *generalization*. Suggest terms such as "generally," "general store," "in general," and "general idea" to get them started. Conduct an Idea Wave (TE, p. T35) to create a list, then point out that the word *general* usually means "for all" or "for the whole." Have students refer to a dictionary to sharpen their definitions.

Instruct

Making Valid Generalizations   L2

Guided Instruction
■ Read the steps to make valid generalizations as a class and write them on the board.

■ Practice the skill by following the steps on p. 103 as a class. Identify the topic of the text and three facts that support it *(corn in the Americas before the 1200s; corn was the principle crop of the Mayas of present-day Mexico and Central America, the Hohokam grew corn in Arizona and the Anasazi grew corn in the northeastern United States.)* Identify what the facts have in common *(all are about Native American groups who grew corn)*. Work with students to create a generalization. *(Possible generalization: Corn was an important and versatile crop in the Americas before the 1200s.)* Ask students to test the generalization using the bulleted questions on p. 102.

Testing for Validity
To find whether a generalization is valid, ask
• Are there enough facts—at least three in a short passage—to support the generalization?
• Do I know any other facts that support the generalization?
• Does the statement overgeneralize or stereotype a group of people? Words such as *all*, *always*, or *every* signal overgeneralization. Words such as *some*, *many*, *most*, and *often* help prevent a statement from being overgeneralized.

102 Foundations of Geography

A generalization is a broad conclusion. Some generalizations are valid—that is, they have value or worth—because they can be drawn reasonably from specific facts. Other generalizations are not valid, because they draw unreasonably broad conclusions and are not based on fact.

Many statements have clues that tell you they should be evaluated for validity. For example, statements with words such as *everybody* or *everyone* are very broad. They should always be evaluated. Is the statement "Everybody needs salt" a valid generalization? It is, because it is based on the scientifically proven fact that humans cannot survive without salt in our diet. However, generalizations such as "Everybody loves chocolate" are not valid. They draw unreasonably broad conclusions and cannot be proved.

You need to know how to evaluate a generalization to see if it is valid. You also have to know how to make a valid generalization yourself.

Learn the Skill
To make a valid generalization, follow these steps:

1 **Identify specific facts contained within a source of information.** Make sure you understand the topic that the facts support.

2 **State what the facts have in common, and look for patterns.** Do any of the facts fit together in a way that makes a point about a broad subject? Do data in a table or graph point toward a general statement?

3 **Make a generalization, or broad conclusion, about the facts.** Write your generalization as a complete sentence or a paragraph.

4 **Test the generalization and revise it if necessary.** You can test the validity of a generalization by using the guidelines in the box at the left.

Practice the Skill

Read the passage at the right describing three cultures, and then make a generalization about these cultures.

1 What is the topic of the text? List at least three specific facts that relate to that topic.

2 What do the facts you listed have in common? Do they suggest a general idea about the topic?

3 Make a generalization about the topic. Write it in a complete sentence. List three facts that support it.

4 Test your generalization to see if it is valid. If it is not valid, try rewriting it so that it is more limited. Be careful of exaggerated wording.

Apply the Skill

Turn to page 97 and read the paragraph under the heading Kinds of Families. Make as many generalizations as you can, and test them for their validity. Explain why each generalization is or is not valid.

The Maya thrived in present-day Mexico and Central America from about A.D. 300 to 900. Corn was their principal crop. They developed a sophisticated civilization, but they had abandoned their great cities by about A.D. 900. At about that time, the Hohokam people were growing corn and beans in what is now Arizona. The Hohokam left their settlements during the 1400s, possibly because of drought. Meanwhile, between about A.D. 900 and 1300, the Anasazi people lived to the northeast. They also grew corn. The Anasazi built multistory dwellings up against high cliff walls. Many families lived in these homes. During a drought in the late 1200s, the Anasazi abandoned some of their villages.

An extended Islamic family, spanning three generations, from the rural east coast of Malaysia

Independent Practice
Assign *Skills for Life* and have students complete it individually.

All in One **Foundations of Geography Teaching Resources,** *Skills for Life*, p. 225

Monitor Progress
As students are completing the *Skills for Life* worksheet, circulate and check to make sure they understand the skill steps.

Assess and Reteach

Assess Progress L2
Ask students to do the Apply the Skill activity.

Reteach L1
If students are having trouble applying the skill steps, have them review the skill using the interactive Social Studies Skills Tutor CD-ROM.

⊙ *Making Valid Generalizations*, **Social Studies Skills Tutor CD-ROM**

Extend L3
Ask students to read the last paragraph on p. 107 of the Student Edition. Point out that the first sentence, "Technology has brought many benefits," is a generalization. Ask them if the paragraph contains enough facts to support this generalization, and have them brainstorm other facts that support it. Students should then write a paragraph explaining whether or not the generalization is valid. Use *Rubric for Assessing a Writing Assignment* to evaluate students' paragraphs.

All in One **Foundations of Geography Teaching Resources,** *Rubric for Assessing a Writing Assignment*, p. 233

Answers
Apply the Skill
Answers will vary, but students should show that they made generalizations and tested them for their validity.

Objectives

Social Studies

1. Explore how cultures change.
2. Learn how ideas spread from one culture to another.

Reading/Language Arts

Identify signal words to help keep the order of events clear.

Prepare to Read

Build Background Knowledge L2

Tell students that in this section they will learn about how cultures change over time. Point out to students that some sports, foods, and words in American culture may have been borrowed or adapted from other cultures. Ask if they are familiar with the sport of karate or have ever eaten shish kebab. Point out that these both originated in different cultures. Have students engage in a Give One, Get One activity (TE, pp. T37) to identify other aspects of American culture that have been borrowed or adapted from different cultures.

Set a Purpose for Reading L2

■ Preview the Objectives.

■ Read each statement in the *Reading Readiness Guide* aloud. Ask students to mark the statements true or false.

■ Have students discuss the statements in pairs or groups of four, then mark their worksheets again. Use the Numbered Heads participation strategy (TE, p. T36) to call on students to share their group's perspectives.

All in One Foundations of Geography Teaching Resources, *Reading Readiness Guide*, p. 218

Vocabulary Builder
Preview Key Terms L2

Pronounce each Key Term, then ask the students to say the word with you. Provide a simple explanation such as "Playing the American sport of baseball in Japan is an example of cultural diffusion."

Prepare to Read

Objectives

In this section you will
1. Explore how cultures change.
2. Learn how ideas spread from one culture to another.

Taking Notes

Copy the concept web below. As you read this section, fill in the web with information about cultural change. Add ovals as needed for the concepts in the section.

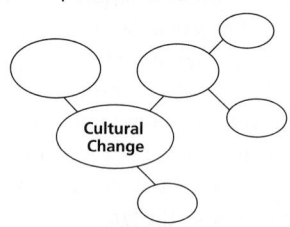

Target Reading Skill

Recognize Words That Signal Sequence
Signal words point out relationships among ideas or events. To help keep the order of events clear, look for words such as *first, later,* or *at that time* that signal the order in which the events took place.

Key Terms

• **cultural diffusion** (KUL chur ul dih FYOO zhun) *n.* the movement of customs and ideas
• **acculturation** (uh kul chur AY shun) *n.* the process of accepting new ideas and fitting them into a culture

Blue jeans and denim shirts have changed with the times.

How Cultures Change

All cultures change over time. The history of blue jeans is an example of cultural change. Some people think that blue jeans are typical American clothes. But many cultures contributed to them. Blue jeans were invented in the United States in the 1800s. They were marketed by Levi Strauss. Strauss was a German-born merchant who moved to California. He made the jeans with a cloth called denim. This may be a shortened form of *serge de Nîmes,* the name of a similar cloth from France.

At first, only Americans wore blue jeans, but they later became popular in other countries. In the 1980s, the Japanese and the French developed stonewashing. It made brand-new denim jeans look worn. Since then, designers from Asia, Europe, and America have promoted new styles, such as ripped and "dirty" denim. Today, jeans are popular all over the world. And the word *jeans* comes from an old French name for Genoa, an Italian city where a cloth similar to denim was first made. What could be more American than jeans?

Target Reading Skill L2

Recognize Words That Signal Sequence
Point out the Target Reading Skill. Explain that by identifying words that signal time order, readers can better understand the sequence of events being presented.

Model recognizing words that signal sequence by reading the second paragraph on p. 104 aloud. Then ask students to make a list of words and terms in the paragraph that signal sequence. On the board, list: "At first," "later," "In the 1980s," "Since then," and "Today." Have students brainstorm other sequence signal words and terms to add to the list *(before, after, then, soon, in the future.)*

Give students *Recognize Sequence Signal Words.* Have them complete the activity in groups.

All in One Foundations of Geography Teaching Resources, *Recognize Sequence Signal Words,* p. 222

Why Cultures Change Just as jeans have changed over time, so, too, has American culture. Cultures change all the time. Because culture is an entire way of life, a change in one part changes other parts. Changes in the natural environment, technology, and ideas all affect culture.

New Technologies New technologies also change a culture. During the 1800s and early 1900s, the growth of industry and the spread of factories drew large numbers of Americans from the countryside to the nation's cities. Factories offered jobs to thousands of men, women, and children. Limited transportation meant that people had to live close to the factories. Cities grew larger as a result.

This all changed after the invention of the car in the late 1800s. Within a few years, advances in technology made cars more affordable. By 1920, many Americans had cars. People could live farther from their jobs and drive to work. Soon after, the idea of owning a house with a yard became more popular. The result has been the growth of sprawling suburbs since the mid-1900s and a new culture based on car travel.

A teenager using a cell phone

A "bullet train" in Japan
Japanese engineers have developed new technologies that allow these trains to travel at speeds of more than 180 miles (300 kilometers) per hour. **Infer** *How might such high speeds affect how far away people can live from their work?*

Vocabulary Builder

Use the information below to teach students this section's high-use words.

High-Use Word	Definition and Sample Sentence
contribute, p. 104	*v.* to give Kim **contributed** cans of food to the food bank.
promote, p. 104	*v.* to help bring about Eating a healthy diet will **promote** a long life.
obtain, p. 106	*v.* to gain possession of You must **obtain** a passport before traveling out of the country.
focus, p. 106	*v.* to concentrate Jenny couldn't **focus** on her book in the noisy airport.

Instruct

How Cultures Change L2

Guided Instruction

- **Vocabulary Builder** Clarify the high-use words **contribute** and **promote** before reading.

- Read How Cultures Change using the Paragraph Shrinking strategy (TE, p. T34). As students read, circulate to make sure they can answer the Reading Check question.

- Ask students to identify three factors that can change a culture. *(changes in the natural environment, technology, and ideas)*

- Discuss the meaning of the sentence "What could be more American than jeans?" Ask students to discuss how, since the passage explains that jeans are a result of the contributions of many different cultures, they could also be called "American." *(America is often recognized as a place where culture is a combination of many different cultures, brought by immigrants from countries around the world. Jeans represent this blending of cultural ideas.)*

- Ask **Since cultures change over time, what kind of changes do you predict may happen to your culture in the future?** *(Answers will vary, but should indicate possible future changes in their culture.)*

Independent Practice

Ask students to create the Taking Notes graphic organizer on a blank piece of paper. Have them fill in some of the blank ovals connected to "Cultural Change." Model one example using the blank *Concept Web* transparency.

All in One **Foundations of Geography Teaching Resources,** *Transparency B18: Concept Web*

Monitor Progress

As students fill in the graphic organizer, circulate through the classroom to make sure individuals select the appropriate details.

Answer

Infer High-speed travel such as bullet trains allows people to commute much greater distances from homes to jobs.

How Ideas Spread

Guided Instruction

- **Vocabulary Builder** Clarify the high-use words **obtain** and **focus** before reading.

- Read How Ideas Spread and direct students' attention to the photographs, Links to Technology, and line graph on these pages.

- Ask students **What is cultural diffusion?** (*the movement of customs and ideas from one culture to another*)

- Ask **How does cultural diffusion occur?** (*As people move they bring customs and ideas with them, and also obtain new customs and ideas.*)

- Discuss with students how the use of computers and the Internet affects their daily lives. (*Libraries, schools, and many homes now have computers and access to the Internet. Students may suggest that this technology helps them with their homework, helps them communicate with their friends or family, or provides entertainment.*)

⟳ Target Reading Skill

L2

Recognize Words That Signal Sequence
As a follow-up, ask students to answer the Target Reading Skill question in the Student Edition. (*The words* before that *signal what comes first in sequence. The events after those words happened before the events in the preceding sentence.*)

Answer

✓ **Reading Check** The invention of cars allowed people to live farther away from their jobs, which led to the growth of suburbs.

Target Skill **Recognize Words That Signal Sequence** What do the words *before that,* in the paragraph at the right, tell you about the sequence of events? Which happened first — the events after those words or the events in the preceding sentence?

A woman practicing yoga, a form of meditation that spread from Asia to Europe and North America

106 Foundations of Geography

How One Change Can Lead to Others Think of other ways technology has changed the culture of the United States. Radio and television brought entertainment and news into homes. Today instant information is part of our culture. Computers change how and where people work. Computers even help people live longer since doctors use computers to diagnose and treat patients. Radio, television, and computers add new words to our language, such as *broadcast, channel surfing,* and *hacker.* What other new words can you think of?

Cultural Change Over Time Cultural change has been going on for a long time. Controlling fire helped early people survive in colder climates. When people started raising animals and growing crops, ways of life also changed. People began to work in the same fields year after year. Before that, they had roamed over a wider area looking for wild plant and animal foods.

✓ **Reading Check** How did the invention of cars change culture?

How Ideas Spread

Advances in transportation technology, such as the airplane, make it easier for people to move all over the world. When they move, people bring new kinds of clothing and tools with them. They also bring ideas about such things as ways to prepare food, teach children, practice their religion, or govern themselves.

Ideas can travel to new places in other ways. People may obtain goods from another culture by trade and then learn to make those goods themselves. People may also learn from other cultures through written material. The movement of customs and ideas is called **cultural diffusion.**

How Cultures Adopt New Ideas One example of cultural diffusion is the game of baseball. Baseball began as an American sport, but today it is played in countries all around the world. That is an example of cultural diffusion. The Japanese love baseball. However, they have changed the game to fit their culture. These changes are an example of **acculturation,** or the process of accepting new ideas and fitting them into a culture. Americans value competition. They focus on winning. A game of baseball does not end until one team wins. But in Japan, a game can end in a tie. The Japanese do not mind a tie game. In Japan, how well you play is more important than winning.

Differentiated Instruction

For Advanced Readers L3
Have students complete the *Enrichment* activity, which centers on the spread of wheat-growing. After they have answered the questions, ask if they can think of other examples of ideas and customs that have spread around the world.

All in One **Foundations of Geography Teaching Resources,** *Enrichment,* p. 224

For English Language Learners L1
As students read, ask them to list unfamiliar words and record any questions they may have about the section on a blank sheet of paper. Label a box "Questions" and tell students that they may place their papers in the box anonymously at a specific time. Go over all of the words and questions with the class.

Communication Technology and the Speed of Change

What's the fastest way to get from your house to Japan? Would you use a jet plane? A phone call? The Internet? A fax? All these answers can be correct. The answer depends on whether you want to transport your body, your voice, a picture, or just words on a sheet of paper.

For thousands of years, cultures changed slowly. People and goods moved by foot or wagon or sailing ship, so ideas and technology also moved slowly. Recently, communication technology has increased the speed of change. Faxes and computers transport information almost instantly. Magazines and television shows can bring ideas and information from all over the world to any home. This rapid exchange of ideas speeds up cultural change.

Technology has brought many benefits. Computers let scientists share information about how to cure diseases. Telephones let us instantly talk to relatives thousands of miles away. In the Australian Outback, students your age use closed-circuit television and two-way radios to take part in class from their own homes.

Links to Technology

Digital Tunes Until recent years, music lovers had to lug around tapes or CDs. The invention of MP3s and MP3 players changed that. Fans can now download and store thousands of songs in MP3 format from the Internet. They no longer need bulky tapes and CDs.

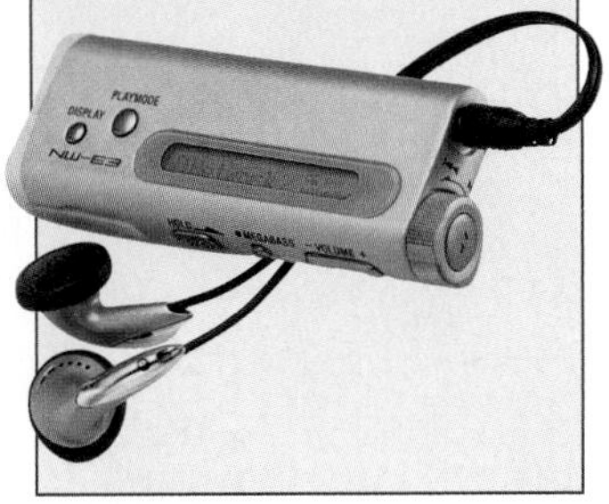

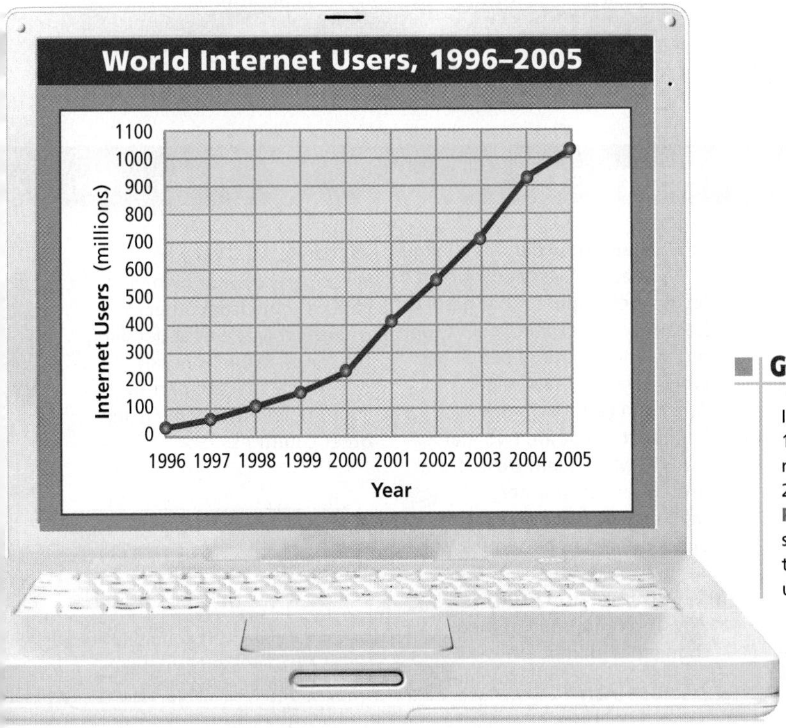

World Internet Users, 1996–2005

Graph Skills

Internet use grew rapidly after 1996. **Identify** What was the number of Internet users in 2005?
Predict Based on the trend shown in the graph, how do you think the number of Internet users has changed since 2005?

Links

Read the **Links to Technology** on this page of the Student Edition. Ask **Why are MP3s more convenient than CDs or tapes?** (*Because MP3s are digital files, they are easier to transport and obtain than CDs or tapes.*)

Guided Instruction (continued)

- Direct students' attention to the graph at the bottom of the page. Ask **According to the graph, which year had the greatest increase of Internet users?** (*2003*)

- Ask students to name one benefit of technology and one challenge of technology. (*Students may say that technology helps people to communicate more quickly or assists people with research, but that the customs of traditional societies may be lost as technology spreads.*)

Independent Practice

Have students complete the Taking Notes graphic organizer by asking them to add more information from the section.

Monitor Progress

- Show *Section Reading Support Transparency FG 55* and ask students to check their graphic organizers individually. Go over key concepts and clarify key vocabulary as needed.

  All in One Foundations of Geography Teaching Resources, *Section Reading Support Transparency FG 55*

- Tell students to fill in the last column of the *Reading Readiness Guide.* Ask them to evaluate if what they learned was what they had expected to learn.

  All in One Foundations of Geography Teaching Resources, *Reading Readiness Guide,* p. 218

Skills Mini Lesson

Distinguishing Fact and Opinion

1. Explain that a fact can be proved to be true or false and an opinion is a personal belief. Tell students that facts answer the question *Who? What? When? Where?* or *Why?* Opinions often use words like *good, bad, think,* or *feel.*

2. Help students practice the skill by writing these statements on the board:

A. *"Dirty" denim jeans are the best jeans.*
B. *Blue jeans were invented in the 1800s.*
Then explain, "I can prove B is true or false using an encyclopedia. I can't prove A. A is an opinion, B is a fact."

3. Have students apply the skill to the following statements: A. *The first telephone was built in 1876.* B. *I think cell phones should be banned.*

Answers

Graph Skills Identify more than one billion
Predict Because the graph shows a steady increase, it is likely that the number of Internet users has grown since 2005.

Assess and Reteach

Assess Progress `L2`

Have students complete the Section Assessment. Then administer the *Section Quiz.*

All in One **Foundations of Geography Teaching Resources,** *Section Quiz,* p. 220

Reteach `L1`

If students need more instruction, have them read this section in the Reading and Vocabulary Study Guide.

📖 Chapter 4, Section 3, **Eastern Hemisphere Reading and Vocabulary Study Guide,** pp. 41–43

Extend `L3`

To learn more about aspects of cultural diffusion, assign the small group activity *Creating a Report on World Music.* Students may work in pairs to complete the activity.

All in One **Foundations of Geography Teaching Resources,** *Small Group Activity: Creating a Report on World Music,* pp. 226–229

Answers

Analyze Images The aborigines in the photo are wearing modern-day clothing.

✓ **Reading Check** New technology allows information to travel more quickly, speeding up cultural change.

Section 3 Assessment

Key Terms
Students' sentences should reflect knowledge of each Key Term.

🎯 Target Reading Skill
the words "For thousands of years" and "Recently"

Comprehension and Critical Thinking
1. (a) the ability of many people to live farther away from their jobs, and the rapid growth of suburbs **(b)** Cars allowed people to travel longer distances between their homes and workplaces, which meant they could live outside cities. **(c)** More Americans might choose to work from their homes, communicating electronically, rather than driving to work. Americans could live even farther away from their workplaces.

---

108 *Foundations of Geography*

Defending Their Heritage
In 1988 Aborigines, descendants of Australia's original inhabitants, protested the 200th anniversary of the arrival of Europeans. **Analyze Images** *What evidence do you see that the Aborigines' culture has changed over the past 200 years?*

Defending Traditions Change can help, but it can also hurt. If things change too fast, people may feel that their culture is threatened. Valuable traditions can disappear. Once traditional knowledge has been lost, it can never be regained. In many parts of the world, people are working to preserve, or save, their own cultures before it is too late. They do not want to lose what is valuable in their culture. They want to save the artistic traditions, the religious beliefs, and the wisdom that enriched the lives of past generations for the sake of future generations.

✓ **Reading Check** How has technology affected the speed of cultural change?

🧭 Section 3 Assessment

Key Terms
Review the key terms at the beginning of this section. Use each term in a sentence that explains its meaning.

🎯 Target Reading Skill
Review the second paragraph on page 107. Find the words that signal a sequence of events related to communication technologies.

Comprehension and Critical Thinking
1. (a) Describe What cultural changes in America followed the invention of cars?

(b) Explain How did cars change where people lived and worked?
(c) Predict Suppose that gasoline became more expensive and computers allowed more people to work at home. How might American culture change?
2. (a) List What are two main ways in which ideas travel from one culture to another?
(b) Describe Give an example of an idea that has passed from one culture to another.
(c) Compare and Contrast How has the spread of ideas changed with modern communication technologies?

Writing Activity
What parts of your own culture come from other countries? Make a list detailing the foods, fashions, music, or customs that are part of your life and that come from other countries.

For: An activity on cultural change
Visit: PHSchool.com
Web Code: led-3403

---

2. (a) trade and written materials **(b)** the people of the culture accepting the idea usually adapt it to fit in with their ideas, customs, and traditions through the process of acculturation. **(c)** The spread of ideas has become much faster due to modern communication technologies.

Writing Activity
Use *Rubric for Assessing a Writing Assignment* to evaluate students' lists.

All in One **Foundations of Geography Teaching Resources,** *Rubric for Assessing a Writing Assignment,* p. 233

Go Online PHSchool.com Typing in the Web code when prompted will bring students directly to detailed instructions for this activity.

Review and Assessment

◆ Chapter Summary

Section 1: Understanding Culture
- Culture is an entire way of life that is shaped by people's environment and that also shapes people's environment.
- Culture developed over time from simple technologies and institutions to more advanced technologies and institutions.

Section 2: Culture and Society
- A society is a group of people sharing a culture and held together by a social structure.
- Language expresses the basic concepts of a culture and transmits those concepts to young people.
- Religions help people make sense of the world. They are an important source of values for cultures and teach people to treat one another fairly.

Section 3: Cultural Change
- Changes in the environment or in technology lead to changes in culture.
- Ideas move among cultures through the movement of people, through trade, and through communication technologies.

Traditional dress in India

◆ Key Terms

Each of the statements below contains a key term from the chapter. If the statement is true, write *true*. If it is false, rewrite the statement to make it true.

1. The culture of a people is their way of life, including their beliefs and customs.

2. A civilization is an organization with social, educational, or religious purposes.

3. An institution is an advanced culture with cities and the use of writing.

4. A society is a group of people sharing a culture.

5. A pattern of organized relationships among groups of people is a social structure.

6. An extended family consists of two parents and their children.

7. A nuclear family includes two grandparents, their children, and their grandchildren.

8. Cultural diffusion is the movement of customs or ideas from one culture to another.

9. Acculturation is an accumulation of several cultures in a single place.

Vocabulary Builder

Revisit this chapter's high-use words:

trait	status	promote
dictate	concept	obtain
advance	ritual	focus
complex	contribute	

Ask students to review the definitions they recorded on their *Word Knowledge* worksheets.

All in One Foundations of Geography Teaching Resources, *Word Knowledge,* p. 223

Consider allowing students to earn extra credit if they use the words in their answers to the questions in the Chapter Review and Assessment. The words must be used correctly and in a natural context to win the extra points.

Review Chapter Content

- Review and revisit the major themes of this chapter by asking students to classify what Guiding Questions each bulleted statement in the Chapter Summary answers. Have students work in groups to match the statements with the appropriate questions. Conduct an Idea Wave (TE, p. T35) with the class to share their answers. Refer to page 1 of the Student Edition for the text of the Guiding Questions.

- Assign *Vocabulary Development* for students to review Key Terms.

  All in One Foundations of Geography Teaching Resources, *Vocabulary Development,* p. 232

Answers

Key Terms

1. True

2. False. A civilization is an advanced culture with cities and the use of writing.

3. False. An institution is an organization with social, educational, or religious purposes.

4. True

5. True

6. False. An extended family includes several generations.

7. False. A nuclear family consists of two parents and their children.

8. True

9. Acculturation is the process of accepting new ideas and fitting them into a culture.

Review and Assessment

Comprehension and Critical Thinking

10. (a) material things, sports, entertainment, literature, spiritual beliefs, ideals, government, morals, language, and technology **(b)** Technology, because through even simple technology, people can change their land.

11. (a) the change from hunting and gathering food to raising crops and animals **(b)** Population increased. **(c)** because people could stay in one area year round, trade extra food for other goods, learn crafts, develop writing systems, and create technologies that gave rise to cities

12. (a) The social class to which a person belongs often comes from his or her wealth, education, or family connections, which affects his or her status in society. **(b)** People's ability to change their status has improved over time, as access to education, the ability to get a high-paying job, or the chance of marrying into a family of high status has increased.

13. (a) Sikhism, Hinduism, and Buddhism in India; and Judaism, Christianity, and Islam in Southwest Asia **(b)** The spread of these religions might be explained by cultural diffusion; as people of various religions traveled to new areas of the world, they brought their beliefs with them and taught them to others, and written materials of different religions could be read by people in other countries.

14. (a) The development of industry and factories led to the advancement of science, the development of even newer technologies, and the growth of cities and institutions, such as governments, schools, and armies. **(b)** Both caused the world to seem smaller by allowing people to work and communicate faster. One difference is that the Internet has changed the way that people find and handle information, while the Industrial Revolution changed the way physical goods were manufactured.

15. (a) forms of communication such as the Internet, scientific advancements in medicine, advances in transportation technology, and other areas **(b)** They have greatly increased the rate of cultural change.

Skills Practice

Students' answers will vary, but should include several facts from the paragraphs and a valid generalization about the information.

Review and Assessment (continued)

◆ Comprehension and Critical Thinking

10. (a) Describe What elements make up a culture?
(b) Apply Information Which of these elements might influence a people's environment, and how?

11. (a) Describe What was the Agricultural Revolution?
(b) Explain How did it affect population?
(c) Draw Conclusions How did it allow the growth of cities?

12. (a) Describe How does social class affect a person's status in society?
(b) Link Past and Present How has people's ability to improve their status changed?

13. (a) Recall Which major religions started in Asia?
(b) Infer What might explain their spread?

14. (a) Describe How did the development of industry and factories change culture?
(b) Compare and Contrast How do those changes compare with the ways technology has changed culture in your lifetime?

15. (a) List What technologies contribute to cultural change today?
(b) Draw Conclusions How have new technologies affected the rate of cultural change?

MAP MASTER™ Skills Activity

Place Location For each religion listed below, write the letter that marks its location on the map.
1. Buddhism
2. Eastern Christianity
3. Hinduism
4. Islam
5. Protestant Christianity
6. Roman Catholic Christianity
7. Traditional religions

Go Online PHSchool.com Use Web Code **lep-3414** for an **interactive map.**

World Religions

◆ Skills Practice

Making Valid Generalizations In the Skills for Life activity in this chapter, you learned to make generalizations. You also learned how to make sure that generalizations are valid, or justified, based on facts. You learned not to overgeneralize, or make claims that go beyond the facts.

Review the steps that you followed to learn this skill. Then reread the paragraphs on pages 94 and 95 under the heading Development of Culture. List several facts about the changes described there. Finally, use these facts to make a valid generalization about those changes.

◆ Writing Activity: Math

Look at the graph titled World Internet Users 1996–2005 on page 107. Find the number of Internet users in 1996 and the number of Internet users nine years later in 2005. How many more users were there in 2005 than in 1996? Based on this information, predict how many Internet users there will be in 2014, nine years after the latest date shown on this graph. Write a short paragraph describing your results and your prediction.

Writing Activity: Math

There were about 990 million more Internet users in 2005 than in 1996. Students' paragraphs should indicate that there is likely to be a similar dramatic increase in Internet users between 2005 and 2014. Students may express that as computer technology becomes more affordable and accessible, the number of Internet users should continue to rise.

Use *Rubric for Assessing a Writing Assignment* to evaluate students' paragraphs.

All in One Foundations of Geography Teaching Resources, *Rubric for Assessing a Writing Assignment,* p. 233

Standardized Test Prep

Test-Taking Tips

Some questions on standardized tests ask you to supply information using prior knowledge. Analyze the web diagram below. Then follow the tips to answer the sample question.

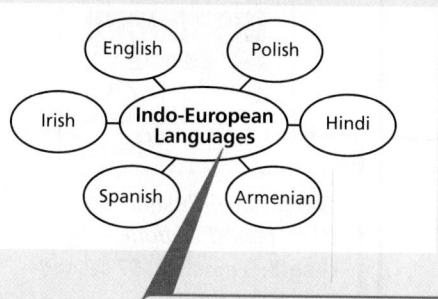

TIP The title in the center circle describes all of the languages. Think about the word *Indo-European* and how it describes languages.

Pick the letter that best answers the question.

Another language that belongs on this web is

A ~~Mandarin Chinese.~~

B Swahili.

C ~~Japanese.~~

D Greek.

TIP Use your prior knowledge—what you know about history, geography, or government—to help you rule out choices.

Think It Through The word *Indo-European* describes languages of India and Europe. Therefore, you can rule out answers A and C because these languages do not come from India or Europe. That leaves Swahili and Greek. You may not be sure about where Swahili is spoken, but you probably know from prior reading that Greece (where people speak Greek) is in Europe. The correct answer is D.

Practice Questions

Use the tips above and other tips in this book to help you answer the following questions:

1. The Agricultural Revolution led
   A to a rebellion by farmers against taxes.
   B to widespread hunger.
   C to an increase in population.
   D people to begin using tools.

2. How does family structure change when countries become more developed?
   A People lose interest in their families.
   B Nuclear families become more common.
   C People move in with their grandparents, aunts, and uncles.
   D Extended families become more common.

3. Which of the following does NOT contribute to cultural change?
   A technological change
   B migration
   C tradition
   D television

Read the following passage, and answer the question that follows.

This country is the birthplace of three major religions. It is located on Earth's largest continent. Its neighbors include Bangladesh and Sri Lanka. The country has more than a billion inhabitants. Its people speak hundreds of different languages. Many people from this country have migrated overseas.

4. What country does the passage describe?
   A Israel
   B Mexico
   C India
   D China

Use Web Code lea-3401
for a **Chapter 4 self-test.**

MAP★MASTER™
Skills Activity

1. F   2. D
3. E   4. C
5. G   6. A
7. B

Go Online PHSchool.com Students may practice their map skills using the interactive online version of this map.

Standardized Test Prep

Answers

1. C
2. B
3. C
4. C

Go Online PHSchool.com Students may use the Chapter 4 self-test on PHSchool.com to prepare for the Chapter Test.

Assessment Resources

Use *Chapter Tests A and B* to assess students' mastery of the chapter content.

All in One Foundations of Geography Teaching Resources, *Chapter Tests A and B,* pp. 235–240

Tests also available on the *ExamView Test Bank CD-ROM.*

◉ *ExamView Test Bank CD-ROM*

5 Interacting With Our Environment

Overview

Section 1

Natural Resources
1. Learn about natural resources.
2. Investigate energy.

Section 2

Land Use
1. Study the relation between land use and culture.
2. Investigate the relation between land use and economic activity.
3. Explore changes in land use.

Section 3

People's Effect on the Environment
1. Investigate how first-level activities affect the environment.
2. Explore how second- and third-level activities affect the environment.

DISCOVERY CHANNEL SCHOOL Video

The Natural Resources of an Island Nation
Length: 3 minutes, 57 seconds
Use with Section 1
This segment explores the relationship between natural resources and a nation's people and economy. We will see how sugarcane, tourism and the people of the island of Mauritius have been used to boost the economy.

Technology Resources

PHSchool.com

Students use embedded Web codes to access Internet activities, chapter self-tests, and additional map practice. They may also access Dorling Kindersley's Online Desk Reference to learn more about each country they study.

Interactive Textbook

Use the Interactive Textbook to make content and concepts come alive through animations, videos, and activities that accompany the complete basal text—online and on CD-ROM.

PRENTICE HALL
TeacherEXPRESS
Plan • Teach • Assess

Use this complete suite of powerful teaching tools to make planning lessons and administering tests quicker and easier.

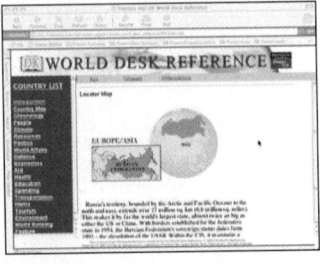

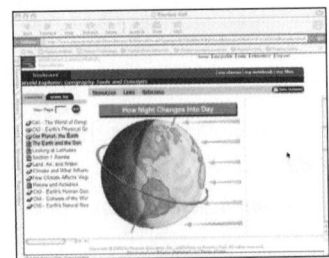

Reading and Assessment

Reading and Vocabulary Instruction

⟳ Model the Target Reading Skill

Main Idea The main idea is the most important point in a written passage. All of the details in a well-written paragraph or section should add up to the main idea. Write the paragraph below, from page 131, on the board. Explain that the main idea is usually stated in the first or last sentence. Model identifying the main idea by thinking aloud: "I will read the first and last sentences to see if either may be the main idea. I think the first sentence is the main idea because it is more general. Let me read the entire paragraph to see if I can find details that support the first sentence."

Point out the supporting details by underlining each one: *Other industrial and service activities have side effects on the environment. For example, <u>shopping malls require large areas to be paved for parking. Industries use large amounts of resources</u> and <u>release industrial wastes</u> into the environment. <u>Service activities require the construction of roads, telephone lines, and power lines.</u>*

Think aloud: "What do these details have in common? They are all examples of how service activities and industries negatively influence the environment. They support the main idea, that *other industrial and service activities have side effects on the environment.*"

Use the following worksheets from All-in-One Foundations of Geography Teaching Resources (pp. 256–258) to support this chapter's Target Reading Skill.

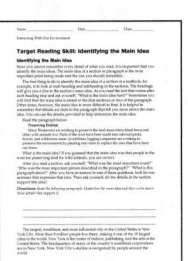 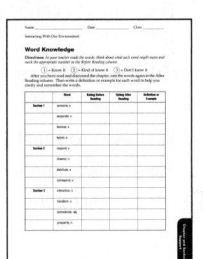 

Vocabulary Builder
High-Use Academic Words

Use these steps to teach this chapter's high-use words:

1. Have students rate how well they know each word on their Word Knowledge worksheets (All-in-One Foundations of Geography Teaching Resources, p. 259).
2. Pronounce each word and ask students to repeat it.
3. Give students a brief definition or sample sentence (provided on TE pp. 115, 121, and 129).
4. Work with students as they fill in the "Definition or Example" column of their Word Knowledge worksheets.

Assessment

Formal Assessment

Test students' understanding of core knowledge and skills.

Chapter Tests A and B, Final Exams A and B, All-in-One Foundations of Geography Teaching Resources, pp. 278–283, 287–292

Customize the Chapter Tests to suit your needs.
ExamView Test Bank CD-ROM

Skills Assessment

Assess geographic literacy.

MapMaster Skills, Student Edition, pp. 115, 124, 134

Assess reading and comprehension.

Target Reading Skills, Student Edition, pp. 115, 122, 131 and in Section Assessments

Chapter 5 Assessment, Eastern Hemisphere Reading and Vocabulary Study Guide, p. 54

Performance Assessment

Assess students' performance on this chapter's Writing Activities using the following rubrics from All-in-One Foundations of Geography Teaching Resources.

Rubric for Assessing a Student Poster, p. 274

Rubric for Assessing a Report, p. 275

Assess students' work through performance tasks.

Small Group Activity, All-in-One Foundations of Geography Teaching Resources, pp. 262–265

Online Assessment

Have students check their own understanding.

Chapter Self-Test

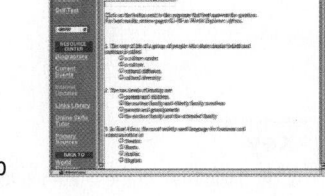

Test Preparation

Foundations of Geography Practice Tests A, B and C, Test Prep Workbook, pp. 49–60

Foundations of Geography Benchmark Test and Outcome Test, AYP Monitoring Assessments, pp. 80–85, 128–131

Section 1 **Natural Resources**

 1.5 periods, .75 block

Social Studies Objectives
1. Learn about natural resources.
2. Investigate energy.

Reading/Language Arts Objective
Learn how to identify the main idea of a paragraph.

Prepare to Read	**Instructional Resources**	**Differentiated Instruction**
Build Background Knowledge Discuss raw materials. **Set a Purpose for Reading** Have students evaluate statements on the *Reading Readiness Guide.* **Preview Key Terms** Teach the section's Key Terms. **Target Reading Skill** Introduce the section's Target Reading Skill of **identifying main ideas.**	**All in One Foundations of Geography Teaching Resources** L2 Reading Readiness Guide, p. 245 L2 Identify Main Ideas, p. 256 **World Studies Video Program** L2 The Natural Resources of an Island Nation	**Spanish Reading and Vocabulary Study Guide** L1 Chapter 5, Section 1, pp. 33–34 ELL

Instruct	**Instructional Resources**	**Differentiated Instruction**
What are Natural Resources? Ask for examples of natural resources and discuss some of them. **Target Reading Skill** Review **identifying main ideas.** **A Special Resource: Energy** Discuss different sources of energy and how they are consumed and protected.	**All in One Foundations of Geography Teaching Resources** L2 Guided Reading and Review, p. 246 L2 Reading Readiness Guide, p. 245 **Foundations of Geography Transparencies** L2 Section Reading Support Transparency FG 56 L2 Transparency B15: Outline	**All in One Foundations of Geography Teaching Resources** Rubric for Assessing a Student Poster, p. 274 GT, AR L1 Reading a Natural Resources Map, p. 267 ELL, LPR, SN L3 Reading an Economic Activity Map, p. 266 AR, GT **Teacher's Edition** L3 For Gifted and Talented, TE p. 116 L1 For Less Proficient Readers, TE p. 116 L3 For English Language Learners, TE p. 117 L3 For Advanced Readers, TE p. 117

Assess and Reteach	**Instructional Resources**	**Differentiated Instruction**
Assess Progress Evaluate student comprehension with the section assessment and section quiz. **Reteach** Assign the Reading and Vocabulary Study Guide to help struggling students. **Extend** Extend the lesson by assigning an online activity.	**All in One Foundations of Geography Teaching Resources** L2 Section Quiz, p. 247 Rubric for Assessing a Journal Entry, p. 276 **Reading and Vocabulary Study Guide** L1 Chapter 5, Section 1, pp. 45–47 **PHSchool.com** L3 For: Environmental and Global Issues: Alternative Sources of Energy **Web Code:** led-3504	**Spanish Support** L2 Section Quiz (Spanish), p. 37 ELL

Key

L1 Basic to Average	L3 Average to Advanced	LPR Less Proficient Readers	GT Gifted and Talented
L2 For All Students		AR Advanced Readers	ELL English Language Learners
		SN Special Needs Students	

Section 2 Land Use

 2 periods, 1 block (includes Skills for Life)

Social Studies Objectives
1. Study the relation between land use and culture.
2. Investigate the relation between land use and economic activity.
3. Explore changes in land use.

Reading/Language Arts Objective
Learn how to identify sentences that include details that support the main idea of a paragraph.

Prepare to Read

Build Background Knowledge
Discuss how land is used to extract raw materials.

Set a Purpose for Reading
Have students begin to fill out the *Reading Readiness Guide.*

Preview Key Terms
Teach the section's Key Terms.

Target Reading Skill
Introduce the section's Target Reading Skill of **identifying supporting details.**

Instructional Resources

All in One Foundations of Geography Teaching Resources
- L2 Reading Readiness Guide, p. 249
- L2 Identify Supporting Details, p. 257

Differentiated Instruction

Spanish Reading and Vocabulary Study Guide
- L1 Chapter 5, Section 2, pp. 35–36 ELL

Instruct

Land Use and Culture
Discuss how different cultures use the materials in their environments.

Land Use and Economic Activity
Discuss first-, second-, and third-level activities related to land use.

Target Reading Skill
Review **identifying supporting details.**

Changes in Land Use
Discuss how human actions can affect land use.

Instructional Resources

All in One Foundations of Geography Teaching Resources
- L2 Guided Reading and Review, p. 250
- L2 Reading Readiness Guide, p. 249

Foundations of Geography Transparencies
- L2 Section Reading Support Transparency FG 57

Differentiated Instruction

All in One Foundations of Geography Teaching Resources
- L2 Celia's Island Journal, pp. 270–271 AR, GT, LPR, SN
- L3 The Road From Coorain, pp. 268–269 AR, GT
- L2 Skills for Life, p. 261 AR, GT, LPR, SN

Teacher's Edition
- L3 For Advanced Readers, TE p. 123
- L1 For English Language Learners, TE p. 123

Reading and Vocabulary Study Guide
- L1 Chapter 5, Section 2, pp. 48–50 ELL, LPR, SN

Assess and Reteach

Assess Progress
Evaluate student comprehension with the section assessment and section quiz.

Reteach
Assign the Reading and Vocabulary Study Guide to help struggling students.

Extend
Extend the lesson by assigning a Book Project.

Instructional Resources

All in One Foundations of Geography Teaching Resources
- L2 Section Quiz, p. 251
- L3 Book Project: World News Today, pp. 36–38 Rubric for Assessing a Report, p. 275

Reading and Vocabulary Study Guide
- L1 Chapter 5, Section 2, pp. 48–50

Differentiated Instruction

Spanish Support
- L2 Section Quiz (Spanish), p. 39 ELL

Teacher's Edition
- L1 For Special Needs Students, TE p. 127

Social Studies Skills Tutor CD-ROM
- L1 Identifying Cause and Effect ELL, LPR, SN

Key
- L1 Basic to Average
- L3 Average to Advanced
- L2 For All Students

- LPR Less Proficient Readers
- AR Advanced Readers
- SN Special Needs Students

- GT Gifted and Talented
- ELL English Language Learners

Section 3 People's Effect on the Environment

🕐 *3.5 periods, 1.75 blocks (includes Chapter Review and Assessment)*

Social Studies Objectives
1. Investigate how first-level activities affect the environment.
2. Explore how second- and third-level activities affect the environment.

Reading/Language Arts Objective
Learn how to identify implied main ideas.

Prepare to Read	**Instructional Resources**	**Differentiated Instruction**
Build Background Knowledge Discuss the natural resources of soil, water and air. **Set a Purpose for Reading** Have students evaluate statements on the *Reading Readiness Guide.* **Preview Key Terms** Teach the section's Key Terms. **Target Reading Skill** Introduce the section's Target Reading Skill of **identifying implied main ideas.**	**All in One Foundations of Geography Teaching Resources** L2 Reading Readiness Guide, p. 253 L2 Identify Implied Main Ideas, p. 258	**Spanish Reading and Vocabulary Study Guide** L1 Chapter 5, Section 3, pp. 37–38 ELL

Instruct	**Instructional Resources**	**Differentiated Instruction**
First-Level Activities Discuss the negative effects of first-level activities on the environment. **Eyewitness Technology** Discuss the hybrid car. **Target Reading Skill** Review **identifying implied main ideas.** **Second- and Third-Level Activities** Discuss the effects of industrial and service activities on the environment.	**All in One Foundations of Geography Teaching Resources** L2 Guided Reading and Review, p. 254 L2 Reading Readiness Guide, p. 253 L2 Small Group Activity: Community Service Project: Protect the Environment, pp. 262–265 **Foundations of Geography Transparencies** L2 Section Reading Support Transparency FG 58	**Spanish Support** L2 Guided Reading and Review (Spanish), p. 40 ELL

Assess and Reteach	**Instructional Resources**	**Differentiated Instruction**
Assess Progress Evaluate student comprehension with the section assessment and section quiz. **Reteach** Assign the Reading and Vocabulary Study Guide to help struggling students. **Extend** Extend the lesson by assigning an Enrichment Activity.	**All in One Foundations of Geography Teaching Resources** L2 Section Quiz, p. 255 L3 Enrichment, p. 260 Rubric for Assessing a Journal Entry, p. 276 L2 Vocabulary Development, p. 273 Rubric for Assessing a Writing Assignment, p. 277 L2 Word Knowledge, p. 259 L2 Chapter Tests A and B, pp. 278–283 L2 Final Exams A and B, pp. 287–292 **Reading and Vocabulary Study Guide** L1 Chapter 5, Section 3, pp. 51–53	**Spanish Support** L2 Section Quiz (Spanish), p. 41 ELL L2 Chapter Summary (Spanish), p. 42 ELL L2 Vocabulary Development (Spanish), p. 43 ELL

Key

L1 Basic to Average	L3 Average to Advanced	LPR Less Proficient Readers	GT Gifted and Talented
L2 For All Students		AR Advanced Readers	ELL English Language Learners
		SN Special Needs Students	

Professional Development

Reading Background

Summarizing

Research has shown that summarizing helps students understand and recall what they have read. Explain to students that good summarizers begin by taking notes while reading. They identify main ideas and list important supporting details. Describe the following steps for writing good summaries:

1. After reading the selection aloud, ask students to recall information from the text. List their responses on the board.
2. Have students reread the selection to verify the accuracy of the recalled information.
3. Have students eliminate any information that is not important enough to include in their summaries.
4. Write the summary together as a class.

Use scaffolding to teach the skill by starting small; ask students to summarize a paragraph from their texts. Then have them extend their summarizing skills by gradually applying the skill to groups of paragraphs, entire sections, and complete chapters.

Using Paragraph Shrinking Effectively

The Paragraph Shrinking strategy can help students extract key ideas from each paragraph they read. To maximize success with this strategy, have students read the paragraph twice. The first time, students should scan the text to understand the general idea of the paragraph. The second time, students should read the paragraph more carefully to identify key ideas.

Demonstrate Paragraph Shrinking by modeling the following steps based on the last paragraph on page 115:

1. Identify the subject of the paragraph. (*types of energy that are renewable resources*)
2. Identify two to three important supporting details. (*The way the sun heats Earth causes wind, which can be used as energy. Solar power and geothermal energy, or the heat within Earth, are types of energy. These resources will never run out.*)
3. Help the student to "shrink" the paragraph by stating the main idea of the paragraph in a complete sentence. The sentence should use approximately ten words or less. (*Wind, solar, and geothermal energy are renewable resources used as energy.*)

World Studies Background

Solar Energy

Solar energy is free, but collecting and converting it to electricity is not. Solar cells can convert only about 10 percent of the sun's energy into electricity. Consequently, several cells must be connected to create power for large areas. This is costly and takes up a great deal of space. Smaller systems used to heat individual homes are more cost-effective.

Raw Materials in the United States

The demand for raw materials in the United States results in substantial internal trade. Forest products from the West are traded particularly to the Northeast and the Midwest. Oil from Texas is essential throughout the United States. Metals from the Midwest are a necessity in the Northeast and the West. These raw materials often travel through manufacturing centers in major cities before the final products are sent to their ultimate destinations.

The Amazon Rainforest and Medicine

Concerns about deforestation in the Amazon rainforest often focus on the threat posed to its unique gene pool. Many organisms found exclusively in the rainforest are essential to the development of pharmaceutical products. About twenty-five percent of the pharmaceuticals used in the Western world are created from rainforest ingredients.

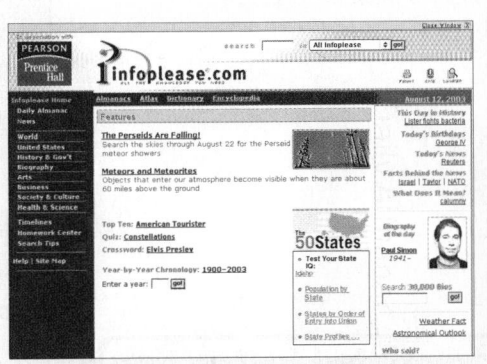

Infoplease® provides a wealth of useful information for the classroom. You can use this resource to strengthen your background on the subjects covered in this chapter. Have students visit this advertising-free site as a starting point for projects requiring research.

Use Web Code **led-3500** for **Infoplease**®.

Chapter 5

Guiding Questions

Remind students about the Guiding Questions introduced at the beginning of the book.

Section 1 refers to **Guiding Question** ③ **How do people use the world's natural resources?** (*Everything that people use or consume is made with natural resources, which can be divided into renewable resources, living resources, and nonrenewable resources.*)

Section 2 refers to **Guiding Question** ③ **How do people use the world's natural resources?** (*People use land in a variety of ways, depending on culture, environment, history, and industrialization.*)

Section 3 refers to **Guiding Question** ③ **How do people use the world's natural resources?** (*People change Earth's landscape through farming and industrialization, and struggle to find a balance between industry and protecting the environment.*)

🔄 Target Reading Skill   L2

In this chapter, students will learn and apply the reading skill of identifying main ideas. Use the following worksheets to help students practice this skill.

All in One Foundations of Geography Teaching Resources, *Identify Main Ideas,* p. 256; *Identify Supporting Details,* p. 257; *Identify Implied Main Ideas,* p. 258

Chapter Preview

This chapter will introduce you to the ways in which people interact with their natural surroundings.

Section 1
Natural Resources

Section 2
Land Use

Section 3
People's Effect on the Environment

🔄 Target Reading Skill

Main Idea In this chapter you will construct meaning by identifying the main idea in a paragraph and the details that support it. Identifying a paragraph's main idea can help you remember what you have read.

▶ Windmills capturing the wind's energy in Tehachapi Pass, California

112 Foundations of Geography

Bibliography

For the Teacher
Nadakavukaren, Anne. *Our Global Environment: A Health Perspective.* Waveland Press, 5th Edition, 2000.
Smith, Dan & Anne Braein. *The Penguin State of the World Atlas.* Penguin USA, 7th Edition, 2003.
The Worldwatch Institute. *State of the World 2003 (annual).* W.W. Norton & Company, 2003.

For the Student
L1 Ditchfield, Christian. *Oil (True Books: Natural Resources).* Children's Book Press, 2003.
L2 Allaby, Michael. *The Environment (How It Works).* Award Publications, 2002.
L3 Morgan, Sally. *Alternative Energy Sources (Science at the Edge).* Heinemann Library, 2002.

Differentiated Instruction

The following Teacher's Edition strategies are suitable for students of varying abilities.
Advanced Readers, pp. 117, 123
English Language Learners, pp. 117, 123
Gifted and Talented, p. 116
Less Proficient Readers, p. 116
Special Needs Students, p. 127

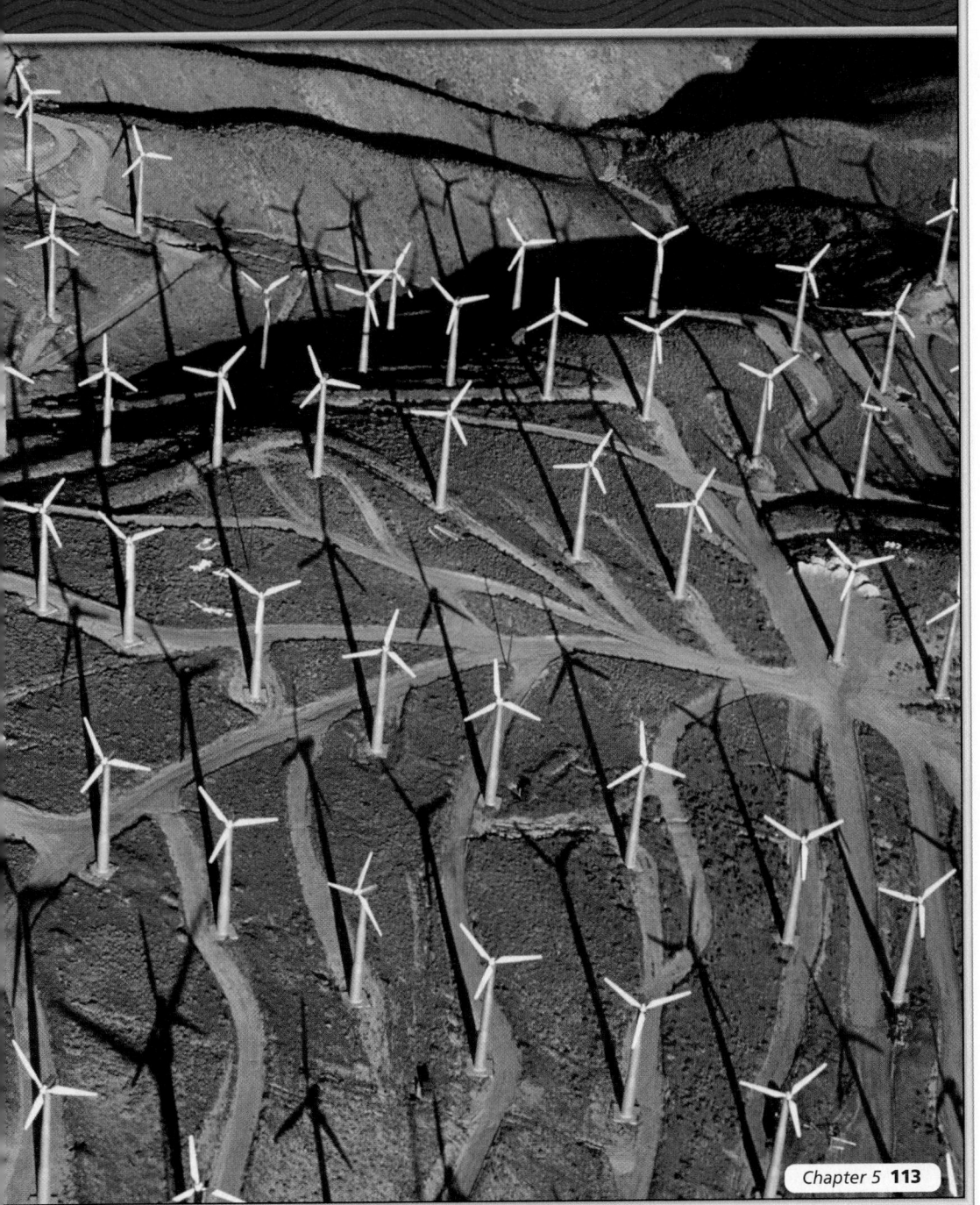

Chapter 5 **113**

Reach Into Your Background Have students study the photo on pp. 112–113 and read the accompanying caption. Draw their attention to the title of the chapter. Ask students to think about how the photograph illustrates interaction between humans and their environment. *(People are using wind to create energy.)* Then ask them to think of some other examples of people interacting with their environment. *(Possible answers: damming rivers to create electricity and regulate water supply; farming; harnessing natural materials to make things used in everyday life, such as clothing)*

Chapter Resources

Teaching Resources
L2 Vocabulary Development, p. 273
L2 Skills for Life, p. 261
L2 Chapter Tests A and B, pp. 278–283

Spanish Support
L2 Spanish Chapter Summary, p. 42
L2 Spanish Vocabulary Development, p. 43

Media and Technology
L1 Student Edition on Audio CD
L1 Guided Reading Audiotapes, English and Spanish
L2 Social Studies Skills Tutor CD-ROM
ExamView Test Bank CD-ROM

PRENTICE HALL
Presentation EXPRESS™
Teach · Connect · Inspire

Teach this chapter's content using the PresentationExpress™ CD-ROM including:
- slide shows
- transparencies
- interactive maps and media
- *ExamView*® QuickTake Presenter

Section 1 — Natural Resources

Objectives

Social Studies

1. Learn about natural resources.
2. Investigate energy.

Reading/Language Arts

Learn how to identify the main idea of a paragraph.

Prepare to Read

Build Background Knowledge   L2

Tell students that in this section they will learn about natural resources and how people use them. Ask students to identify things in the classroom that are in their natural forms, such as a glass of water or a plant. Then have the students name several objects in the room made of raw materials, such as a desk or an item of clothing. Ask them to identify what raw material each was made from and how the raw materials were changed for human use. Conduct an Idea Wave (TE, p. T35) to help students share their ideas.

Set a Purpose for Reading   L2

■ Preview the Objectives.

■ Read each statement in the *Reading Readiness Guide* aloud. Ask students to mark the statements true or false.

> **All in One Foundations of Geography Teaching Resources,** *Reading Readiness Guide,* p. 245

■ Have students discuss the statements in pairs or groups of four, then mark their worksheets again. Use the Numbered Heads participation strategy (TE, p. T36) to call on students to share their group's perspectives.

Vocabulary Builder

Preview Key Terms   L2

Pronounce each Key Term, then ask the students to say the word with you. Provide a simple explanation such as, "Natural resources are things found in nature that people use."

Prepare to Read

Objectives

In this section you will
1. Learn about natural resources.
2. Investigate energy.

Taking Notes

Copy the outline below. Add letters, numbers, and headings as needed. As you read this section, fill in the outline with information about natural resources and energy.

> I. Natural resources
>   A. Renewable resources
>   B.
>   1.
>   2.
> II. Energy
>   A.

🎯 Target Reading Skill

Identify Main Ideas
Good readers identify the main idea in every written paragraph. The main idea is the most important point—the one that includes all of the other points. Sometimes this idea is stated directly. For example, in the first paragraph below, the first sentence states the paragraph's main idea. As you read, note the main idea of each paragraph.

Key Terms

- **natural resources** (NACH ur ul REE sawr siz) *n.* useful materials found in the environment
- **raw materials** (raw muh TIHR ee ulz) *n.* natural resources that must be worked to be useful
- **renewable resources** (rih NOO uh bul REE sawr siz) *n.* natural resources that can be replaced
- **nonrenewable resources** (nahn rih NOO uh bul REE sawr siz) *n.* natural resources that cannot be replaced

Men constructing a wooden hut in Kenya

114 Foundations of Geography

What Are Natural Resources?

Everything that people use or consume is made with **natural resources,** or useful materials found in the environment. When people talk about natural resources, they usually mean such things as water, minerals, and vegetation.

All people need water, food, clothing, and shelter to survive. People drink water. People eat food that the soil produces. So do the animals that provide eggs, cheese, meat, and wool. Homes are made from wood, clay, and steel.

People can use some resources just as they are found in nature. Fresh water is one of these. But most resources must be changed before people can use them. Natural resources that must be worked to be useful are called **raw materials.** For example, people cannot just go out and cut down a tree if they want paper. Trees are the raw materials for paper and wood. To make paper, the wood must be soaked and broken up to create pulp. (Pulp is a kind of soup of wood fibers.) Machines collect the wet fibers on screens to form sheets of paper.

🎯 Target Reading Skill   L2

Identify Main Ideas Direct students' attention to the Target Reading Skill. Tell them that identifying the main idea will help them to focus on the most important points of a paragraph.

Model identifying main ideas by having students read the third paragraph on this page. Students should make a list of the three ideas presented in the paragraph.

Then ask students **Which of these three points is the most important and includes all the other points?** (*Most resources must be changed before people use them.*)

Give students *Identify Main Ideas*. Have them complete the activity in groups.

> **All in One Foundations of Geography Teaching Resources,** *Identify Main Ideas,* p. 256

Renewable Resources The environment is filled with natural resources, but not all resources are alike. Geographers divide them into two main groups.

The first group is **renewable resources,** or resources that can be replaced. Some resources are replaced naturally because of the way Earth works. In the water cycle, water evaporates into the air and falls as rain, snow, hail, or sleet. This happens over and over again. Therefore, Earth has an unchanging amount of water. Other materials that go through natural cycles include nitrogen and carbon.

Some types of energy are also renewable resources. Using wind to make electricity will not use the wind up. Wind results from differences in the way the sun heats Earth. As long as the sun shines, there will always be more wind. Solar energy, or energy from the sun, is a renewable resource. No matter how much people use, there will always be more. Geothermal energy uses differences in heat between Earth's surface and its interior. This heat difference will not disappear in the foreseeable future.

Explore the environment of an island nation.

Target Skill **Identify Main Ideas** Which sentence states the main idea of the paragraph at the left?

The World: Natural Resources

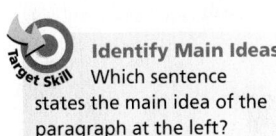
MAP MASTER™ Skills Activity

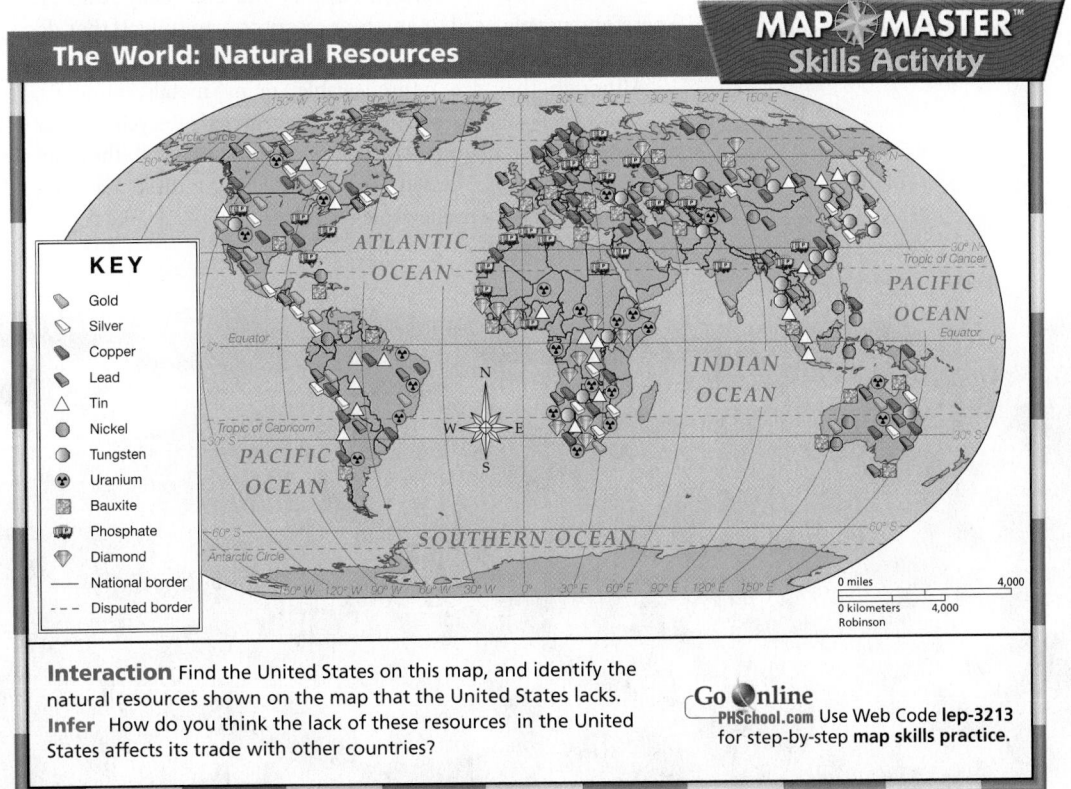

KEY
- Gold
- Silver
- Copper
- Lead
- Tin
- Nickel
- Tungsten
- Uranium
- Bauxite
- Phosphate
- Diamond
- National border
- - - Disputed border

0 miles 4,000
0 kilometers 4,000
Robinson

Interaction Find the United States on this map, and identify the natural resources shown on the map that the United States lacks.
Infer How do you think the lack of these resources in the United States affects its trade with other countries?

Go Online
PHSchool.com Use Web Code lep-3213 for step-by-step **map skills practice.**

Vocabulary Builder

Use the information below to teach students this section's high-use words.

High-Use Word	Definition and Sample Sentence
consume, p. 114	*v.* to use something Larger cars **consume** more gasoline than smaller ones.
evaporate, p. 115	*v.* to change from a liquid into a vapor Puddles **evaporate** quickly on a sunny day.
harness, p. 117	*v.* to bring under control and direct the force of something Windmills **harness** the energy of the wind.
hybrid, p. 119	*n.* something made up of two different elements A **hybrid** car runs on gasoline and electric power.

Show students *The Natural Resources of an Island Nation.* Ask students to name two important parts of Mauritius' economy. *(sugarcane and tourism)* Ask students **How are these related to Mauritius' environment and natural resources?** *(Its climate is suitable for growing sugarcane, and its natural beauty attracts tourists.)*

Instruct

What Are Natural Resources? L2

Guided Instruction

- **Vocabulary Builder** Clarify the high-use words **consume** and **evaporate** before reading.

- Read What Are Natural Resources? using the ReQuest reading strategy (TE, p. T35). Ask students to study the map on p. 115.

- Ask students **What are natural resources?** *(useful materials found in the environment)*

- Ask students **What are renewable resources?** *(natural resources that can be replaced)* **What are some examples of renewable resources?** *(water, wind, solar energy, geothermal energy)*

- Have students examine the map and brainstorm what some of the natural resources shown might be used for. *(Possible answers: gold, silver, diamonds–jewelry; copper—coins, wire; tin—cans; lead— pipes)*

Target Reading Skill L2

Identify Main Ideas As a follow up, ask students to answer the Target Reading Skill question in the Student Edition. *(Some types of energy are also renewable resources.)*

Answers

MAP MASTER Skills Activity **Interaction** nickel and diamonds **Infer** Since the United States does not have these resources, it probably has to purchase them from other countries.

Go Online
PHSchool.com Students may practice their map skills using the interactive online version of this map.

Guided Instruction (continued)

- Ask students **What are living resources?** *(living things that provide natural resources, such as plants and animals)*

- Ask students to define nonrenewable resources and list examples. *(resources that cannot be replaced; metal ores, most minerals, natural gas, petroleum)*

- Ask students **How does recycling help conserve nonrenewable resources?** *(Recycling recovers and processes used materials so they can be used again.)*

- Ask students **What are examples of fossil fuels?** *(coal, natural gas, and petroleum)* Have students discuss how they are created and if they are renewable. *(They were created over millions of years from remains of prehistoric living things. They are renewable, but if used up they would take millions of years to form again. So for the purposes of people living today, fossil fuels are nonrenewable resources.)*

Independent Practice

Show students the *Outline Transparency.* Then ask students to create the Taking Notes graphic organizer on a blank piece of paper. Have them begin to fill in the outline by adding information about natural resources. Briefly model how to create and fill in the outline.

📖 **Foundations of Geography Transparencies,** *Transparency B15: Outline*

Monitor Progress

As students fill in the graphic organizer, circulate and make sure students are choosing appropriate headings and details. Provide assistance as needed.

Solar cells on the roof of a house in Felsberg, Germany

Living Resources Living things that provide natural resources, such as plants and animals, are also renewable resources. Like other resources, they must be properly managed so that people do not overuse them.

For example, a timber company may cut down all the trees in an area for use as wood. But the company may then plant new trees to replace the ones they cut. Even if they do not, seeds left in the ground will probably produce new trees. Every day, the people of the world eat many chickens and ears of corn. But farmers always make sure to grow more corn and chickens to replace what people eat. If people are careful, they can have a steady supply of these renewable living resources.

Nonrenewable Resources The second major group of resources is called **nonrenewable resources,** or resources that cannot be replaced. Most nonliving things, such as metal ores, most minerals, natural gas, and petroleum—or crude oil—are nonrenewable resources. If people keep mining minerals and burning fuels such as coal and oil, they will eventually run out. Therefore, people need to use these resources carefully. If they do run out, people will need to find substitutes for them.

Although they are nonrenewable, many metals, minerals, and materials such as plastics can be recycled. Recycling does not return these materials to their natural state. Still, they can be recovered and processed for reuse. Recycling these materials helps to conserve nonrenewable resources.

Differentiated Instruction

For Gifted and Talented · L3

Have students do library or Internet research to identify their region's resources. Then have them design posters to attract businesses to their region based upon the types of natural resources available.

🔲 **Foundations of Geography Teaching Resources,** *Rubric for Assessing a Student Poster,* p. 274

For Less Proficient Readers · L1

Reinforce students' ability to read and interpret a natural resources map by giving them *Reading a Natural Resource Map* and having them answer the questions.

🔲 **Foundations of Geography Teaching Resources,** *Reading a Natural Resources Map,* p. 267

Fossil Fuels Most scientists think that coal, natural gas, and petroleum are fossil fuels, or fuels created over millions of years from the remains of prehistoric living things. If people continue using coal at today's rate, known supplies may run out in several hundred years. At current rates of use, known supplies of oil and natural gas may run out in less than 100 years.

If oil and natural gas are fossil fuels, they are renewable, since living things today will become fossil fuels in millions of years. But if these fuels take so long to develop, they are nonrenewable for our purposes.

✓ **Reading Check** What is the difference between renewable and nonrenewable resources?

A Special Resource: Energy

Many natural resources are sources of energy. People use energy not only from fossil fuels, but also from the wind and the sun. Dams produce hydroelectric power by harnessing the power of falling water.

Energy is itself a resource that is needed to make use of other natural resources. Consider cotton. It takes energy to harvest cotton from a field, to spin the cotton into thread, and to weave it into fabric. Workers use energy to travel to a garment factory. It takes energy to sew a shirt with a sewing machine. It also takes energy to transport the shirt by ship and truck to a retail store. Finally, the consumer uses energy to bring the shirt home.

Located on the border between Oregon and Washington, the Bonneville Dam produces hydroelectric power.

Strip Mining Coal
The machine below extracts coal from this exposed deposit in Banwen Pyrddin, Wales, United Kingdom. **Apply Information** *Do you think that coal is a recyclable, renewable, or nonrenewable resource?*

Guided Instruction

■ **Vocabulary Builder** Clarify the high-use words **harness** and **hybrid** before reading.

■ Read A Special Resource: Energy with students and have them examine the graph on p. 118. Circulate to make sure individuals can answer the Graph Skills questions.

■ Ask students to name some different sources of energy. *(Possible answers: fossil fuels, wind, water, sun)* Ask students **How is energy needed to make use of other natural resources?** *(It takes energy to convert the natural resource into a usable form, to make it into a product, to transport the product, and to consume the product.)*

Differentiated Instruction

For English Language Learners L3
Tell students that natural resources maps often use symbols to represent different resources. The map key shows what each symbol stands for. Tell students the natural resources of their state. Students can then create a map key to show the symbols and the natural resources they stand for.

For Advanced Readers L1
Pair students and have them complete *Reading an Economic Activity Map.* Ask each pair to use the map on page 115 and the map on the worksheet to compare Somalia's resources and economic activities.

All in One Foundations of Geography Teaching Resources, *Reading an Economic Activity Map,* p. 266

Answers

✓ **Reading Check** Renewable resources are natural resources that can be replaced, whereas nonrenewable resources are natural resources that cannot be replaced.

Apply Information Coal is a renewable resource; over millions of years more coal will be created from the remains of living things. Practically, coal is generally considered to be a nonrenewable resource because its supplies are limited.

Guided Instruction (continued)

- Have students name two countries that can sell oil and two countries that have to buy energy. *(Mexico and Saudi Arabia sell oil; Japan and the United States have to buy energy.)*

- Ask students to list energy alternatives to fossil fuels. *(wind energy, solar energy, tidal energy, geothermal energy, biomass, atomic energy)*

- Direct students' attention to the graph on this page to help them answer the following question: **What are the names of at least three countries that consume more petroleum than they produce?** *(Possible answers: India, China, Germany, Japan, and the United States)*

- Have students list some ways of conserving energy discussed in the text. Then have them brainstorm other ways they could save energy at home or at school. *(In text: hybrid cars, new technologies that conserve energy used for heat and light; other possible answers: turning off lights when not in use at home or in school, turning down heat or air conditioning at night or when not at home)*

Independent Practice

Have students complete the graphic organizer by adding details about energy usage.

Monitor Progress

- Show *Section Reading Support Transparency FG 56* and ask students to check their graphic organizers individually. Go over key concepts and clarify key vocabulary as needed.

  📖 **Foundations of Geography Transparencies,** *Section Reading Support Transparency FG 56*

- Tell students to fill in the last column of their *Reading Readiness Guides*. Probe for what they learned that confirms or invalidates each statement.

  All in One **Foundations of Geography Teaching Resources,** *Reading Readiness Guide, p. 245*

Answers

Graph Skills Identify Germany and Japan **Compare and Contrast** the United States

---

Pipes running across an oil field in Meyal, Pakistan

Energy "Have's" and "Have Not's" People in every country need energy. But energy resources are not evenly spread around the world. Certain areas are rich in energy resources. Others have very few.

Countries with many rivers, such as Canada and Norway, can use water energy to create electricity. Countries like Saudi Arabia and Mexico have huge amounts of oil that they sell to other countries. Countries like Japan and the United States do not produce as much energy as they use. These countries have to buy energy from other countries.

Meeting Energy Needs in the Future Over time, energy use worldwide has grown rapidly. Yet our supplies of fossil fuels may be limited. It seems likely that the world's people will need to find other sources of energy. Many possibilities exist.

Already, some countries, such as Denmark and Germany, are developing renewable energy sources such as wind and solar energy. Other sources of energy that will not run out are tidal energy, from the rise and fall of Earth's oceans, and geothermal energy, or energy from the heat of Earth's interior. Biomass, or plant material, is a renewable source of energy. These energy sources can reduce a country's need for imported oil.

Atomic energy uses radioactive materials, which are non-renewable but plentiful. Some people oppose atomic energy because radioactive materials can be dangerous. Others support it as a plentiful energy source that does not pollute the air.

■ Graph Skills

Some countries produce more oil than they use. These countries can sell their extra oil to other countries. Others consume more oil than they produce and have to buy it from other countries. **Identify** Which of the countries on this graph have to buy almost all of their oil? **Compare and Contrast** Which country buys the most oil?

The World's Top Petroleum Producers and Consumers

Legend:
- Consumption
- Production

(Bar graph: x-axis — Country: Canada, China, Germany, India, Iran, Japan, Mexico, Russia, Saudi Arabia, USA; y-axis — Percentage of World Total, 0 to 30)

SOURCE: *Energy Information Administration*

Skills Mini Lesson

(Skills for Life)

Problem-Solving

1. To solve a problem, students should identify the problem, evaluate its effect, identify possible solutions, choose a solution, and determine its effectiveness.

2. Have students read the second paragraph on this page to identify some problem-solving steps used to meet countries' energy needs.

3. Have students apply the skill by asking them to reread the text under Meeting Energy Needs in the Future on pp. 118–119. Have students suppose they live in a cloudy, windless place with a limited oil supply, no large bodies of water, and no biomass available. Ask them how problem-solving can be used to help them meet their energy needs. *(Possible solutions: geothermal or atomic energy)*

Fossil fuels will last longer if people use less energy. New technologies, such as hybrid cars, can reduce a country's need for imported oil by burning less gas per mile. Other technologies offer energy savings in heating and lighting buildings and in making new products. If people manage to use less energy, they will not need to buy as much from foreign countries. They will also have an easier time meeting their energy needs in the future.

Geothermal power
In addition to producing energy, the geothermal power plant at Svartsengi, Iceland, heats the mineral-rich water of the Blue Lagoon. **Infer** *Are fossil fuels used to heat this pool?*

 Reading Check Why do some countries have to import energy?

Section 1 Assessment

Key Terms
Review the key terms at the beginning of this section. Use each term in a sentence that explains its meaning.

Target Reading Skill
State the main idea of the paragraph on this page.

Comprehension and Critical Thinking
1. (a) **Identify** Why is wood considered a renewable resource?

(b) **Apply Information** What needs to happen after trees are cut in order for wood to remain a renewable resource?
2. (a) **List** Name some sources of energy other than fossil fuels.
(b) **Categorize** What do these energy sources have in common, and how do they differ from fossil fuels?
(c) **Draw Conclusions** Why might we need to use more of these energy sources in the future?

Writing Activity
Think about what you did this morning before you came to school. Write a journal entry describing the natural resources that you used and all of the ways that you used energy at home and on your way to school.

For: An activity on natural resources
Visit: PHSchool.com
Web Code: led-3501

Section 1 Assessment

Key Terms
Students' sentences should reflect knowledge of each Key Term.

Target Reading Skill
Fossil fuels will last longer if people use less energy.

Comprehension and Critical Thinking
1. (a) It can be replaced by the growth of new trees. (b) New trees need to be planted.
2. (a) wind energy, solar energy, geothermal energy, hydroelectric power, tidal energy, biomass, atomic energy (b) All of the types of energy listed above except atomic energy are renewable resources, and fossil fuels are not. (c) Reserves of important fossil fuels will eventually run out.

Assess and Reteach

Assess Progress L2
Have students complete the Section Assessment. Administer the *Section Quiz*.

 Foundations of Geography Teaching Resources, *Section Quiz,* p. 247

Reteach L1
If students need more instruction, have them read this section in the Reading and Vocabulary Study Guide.

Chapter 5, Section 1, **Eastern Hemisphere Reading and Vocabulary Study Guide,** pp. 45-47

Extend L3
Have students explore alternative energy by completing *Alternative Sources of Energy*. Use the activity as a springboard for a discussion about the use of renewable sources of energy.

For: Environmental and Global Issues: *Alternative Sources of Energy*
Visit: PHSchool.com
Web Code: led-3504

Answers

Infer Fossil fuels are not used; geothermal energy is used.

 **Reading Check** Some countries need to import energy because the energy they consume is greater than the energy they produce.

Go Online PHSchool.com Typing in the Web code when prompted will bring students to detailed instructions for this activity.

Writing Activity
Use the *Rubric for Assessing a Journal Entry* to evaluate students' journals.

Foundations of Geography Teaching Resources, *Rubric for Assessing a Journal Entry,* p. 276

Objectives

Social Studies

1. Study the relation between land use and culture.

2. Investigate the relation between land use and economic activity.

3. Explore changes in land use.

Reading/Language Arts

Learn how to identify sentences that include details that support the main idea of a paragraph.

Prepare to Read

Build Background Knowledge **L2**

Tell students they will learn about how people use land resources in this section. Ask students to choose a familiar product *(such as a box of cereal)* that they use in their everyday lives. Then have them think about what raw materials were used to make the product. Finally, ask them to describe how the products are made and relate this process to land use *(For example, farm land is needed to grow the ingredients of cereal.)* Use the Think-Write-Pair-Share participation strategy (TE, p. T36) to structure the activity.

Set a Purpose for Reading **L2**

- Preview the Objectives.

- Form students into pairs or groups of four. Distribute the *Reading Readiness Guide.* Ask students to fill in the first two columns of the chart. Use the Numbered Heads participation strategy (TE, p. T36) to call on students to share one piece of information they already know and one piece of information they want to know.

All in One Foundations of Geography Teaching Resources, *Reading Readiness Guide,* p. 249

Vocabulary Builder
Preview Key Terms **L2**

Pronounce each Key Term, then ask the students to say the words with you. Provide a simple explanation such as, "Manufacturing refers to making many things by hand or using machines."

Prepare to Read

Objectives

In this section you will

1. Study the relation between land use and culture.
2. Investigate the relation between land use and economic activity.
3. Explore changes in land use.

Taking Notes

Copy the concept web below. As you read the section, fill in the ovals with information about land use. Add ovals as needed.

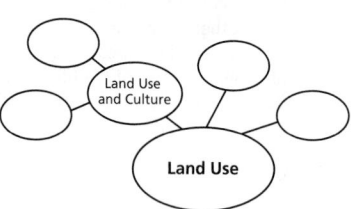

Land Use and Culture

Land Use

Target Reading Skill

Identify Supporting Details Sentences in a paragraph may provide details that support the main idea. These details may give examples or explanations. In the second paragraph on this page, this sentence states the main idea: "Even in similar environments, people may use land differently because they have different cultural traits." Note three details in the paragraph that explain this main idea.

Key Terms

- **environment** (en VY run munt) *n.* natural surroundings
- **manufacturing** (man yoo FAK chur ing) *n.* the large-scale production of goods by hand or by machine
- **colonization** (kayl uh nih ZAY shun) *n.* the movement of settlers and their culture to a new country
- **industrialization** (in dus tree ul ih ZAY shun) *n.* the growth of machine-powered production in an economy

A peanut farmer in Georgia inspecting his crop

Land Use and Culture

How people use the land depends on their culture. People may use their land differently because their cultures have developed in different **environments**, or natural surroundings. For example, the Inuit live in a cold, arctic climate. It is too cold to grow crops, so the Inuit use their land mainly for hunting wild animals, and they rely heavily on fishing. The Japanese live in a warmer, moister climate. Although much of Japan is too steep to farm, the Japanese use much of the remaining land for crops. Their main crop is rice, which grows well in the warm, moist climate of Japan.

Even in similar environments, however, people may use land differently because they have different cultural traits. For example, Georgia has a warm, moist climate like that of southern Japan. But Georgia does not produce much rice. Instead, Georgians raise chickens and grow crops such as peanuts. While the Japanese eat rice at nearly every meal, Americans eat more meat and peanut butter.

Target Reading Skill **L2**

Identify Supporting Details Point out the Target Reading Skill. Tell students that sentences in a paragraph may provide additional details that support the main idea.

Model identifying supporting details by reading the first paragraph on p. 121 aloud. Ask students to identify the main idea. *(People's cultures help shape the landscapes where they live.)* Then ask them to identify one detail that supports the main idea. *(Possible*

supporting details: In some parts of the Philippines, a culture of rice farming and a shortage of level land has led people to carve terraces into hillsides; people cleared forests in Western Europe for farm land.)

Give students *Identify Supporting Details.* Have them complete the activity in groups.

All in One Foundations of Geography Teaching Resources, *Identify Supporting Details,* p. 257

Cultures and Landscapes The examples of the Inuit and the Japanese show how people's environments help to shape their cultures. People's cultures, in turn, help shape the landscapes where they live. For example, in some parts of the Philippines, a culture of rice farming and a shortage of level land has led people to carve terraces into hillsides. Thousands of years ago, Western Europe was covered with forests. As farming cultures spread across that region, people cleared forests to use the land for farming. Today, most of Western Europe is open fields and pastures. Few forests remain.

Land Use and Cultural Differences As the examples of Japan and Georgia show, however, similar environments do not necessarily produce similar cultures. People may respond differently to those environments, depending on their culture. For example, much of the western United States has a dry climate. Many crops need irrigation, or an artificial water supply. The Middle East also has climates too dry for most crops to grow without irrigation. However, the two regions have different cultures and different responses to this challenge. In the western United States, farmers use modern irrigation systems. For example, drip irrigation provides water to each plant through little pipes or tubes. Some Middle Eastern farmers use qanats, or brick irrigation channels, to bring water to their crops. Both cultures face similar environments, but they interact with those environments differently.

✔ Reading Check How is land use related to culture?

Drip irrigation of grape vines in eastern Washington State

Irrigation in Yemen
This man is walking along a qanat, or brick irrigation channel, in Jiblah, Yemen.
Analyze Images What clues do you see in this landscape that suggest a need for irrigation?

Land Use and Economic Activity L2

Guided Instruction

- **Vocabulary Builder** Clarify the high-use words **distribute** and **correspond** before reading.

- Have students read Land Use and Economic Activity. Review the photographs and captions on pp. 122 and 123 with students. Circulate to make sure individuals can answer the Reading Check question.

- Ask students **What are first-level activities?** *(economic activities in which people use land and resources directly to make products)*

- Ask students **How much of the world's land is used for first-level activities?** *(Most of the world's land is used for first-level activities.)* **How much land is used for these activities in developed countries like the United States?** *(In developed countries only a small percentage of the land is used for first-level activities.)*

Target Reading Skill L2

Identify Supporting Details As a follow up, ask students to answer the Target Reading Skill question in the Student Edition. *(Possible answers: hunting, cutting wood, mining, fishing, herding animals, and raising crops)*

Land Use and Economic Activity

In some places, people use the land and its resources to make a living by farming, fishing, or mining. In other places, people work in factories, where they turn natural resources into finished products. In still other places, people sell or distribute products and make a living by providing services. These three ways of making a living correspond to three stages of economic activity. Geographers use stages of economic activity as a way to understand land use.

Identify Supporting Details
Which details in the paragraph at the right give examples of first-level activities?

First-Level Activities In the first stage, people use land and resources directly to make products. They may hunt, cut wood, mine, or fish. They also may herd animals or raise crops. This is the first stage of activities. At this stage, people interact directly with the land or the sea. Most of the world's land is used for first-level activities. However, in developed countries such as the United States, only a small percentage of the people make a living at first-level activities.

Stages of Economic Activity

A series of economic activities connect a flock of sheep in a pasture to a wool sweater in a store. Sheep-raising, a first-level activity, makes it possible to manufacture woolen goods such as sweaters, a second-level activity. Manufacturing makes it possible to deliver sweaters to stores. Stores can then sell the sweaters. Delivery and sales are both third-level activities.

A flock of sheep being driven to a pasture in New Zealand

▲ **Farming, a first-level activity**
This farmer is shearing a sheep, or trimming away its wool. Raising and shearing sheep are first-level activities, or direct uses of natural resources.

122 Foundations of Geography

Skills Mini Lesson

Analyzing Primary Sources

1. Help students define primary and secondary sources. To analyze these sources, students should identify who created the source, when, and why. They should then identify the main idea, separate facts from opinions, look for evidence of bias, and evaluate how reliable the source is.

2. In groups, have students use the steps above to analyze an encyclopedia article, a secondary source, about islands.

3. Have students analyze the primary source *Celia's Island Journal*.

All in One Foundations of Geography Teaching Resources, *Celia's Island Journal,* pp. 270–271

Second-Level Activities At the second stage, people process the products of first-level activities. Most second-level activity is **manufacturing**, or the large-scale production of goods by hand or by machine. Manufacturing may turn a farmer's corn crop into cornflakes for your breakfast. Manufacturing, especially in urban areas, is an important land use in developed countries.

Third-Level Activities At the third stage, a person delivers boxes of cornflakes to your local grocery store. Third-level activities are also known as services. These activities do not produce goods. They may help sell goods. They often involve working directly for customers or for businesses. Many businesses offering services—doctors' offices, banks, automobile repair shops, shopping malls, and fast-food restaurants—are part of everyday living. Services are also clustered in urban areas, especially in developed countries.

✓ **Reading Check** How is most of the world's land used?

▲ **Manufacturing, a second-level activity**
Second-level activities process natural resources to make goods, such as the wool this worker is processing at a New Zealand mill.

Retail sales, a third-level activity ▶
Selling manufactured goods, such as this sweater, in a store is a third-level activity. This woolen-goods store is in New Zealand.

> **GEOGRAPHY SKILLS PRACTICE**
>
> **Human-Environment Interaction** Each activity shown here occurs in a different part of New Zealand.
> **Apply Information** Which activities occur in rural areas, and which activities are likely to occur in urban areas?

Guided Instruction (continued)

■ Ask students **What type of economic activity is performed during second-level activities?** *(For the most part, second-level activities consist of manufacturing.)*

■ Ask students **What are third-level activities?** *(Third-level activities consist of providing services, do not produce goods, and often involve working directly for customers or businesses.)*

■ Ask students to examine the graphic Stages of Economic Activity on pp. 122 and 123. Then have them name and describe other products that use all three levels of economic activity. *(Possible answer: Jewelry is made of raw materials extracted from Earth, such as gold and silver. The raw materials are processed to manufacture things such as necklaces and watches. Finally, the jewelry is sold in stores or online.)*

Independent Practice
Have students continue to fill in their graphic organizers by adding details about land use and economic activity.

Monitor Progress
Circulate among students to provide assistance as needed to individuals as they develop their concept webs.

Differentiated Instruction

For Advanced Readers L3
Ask students to read the primary source *The Road from Coorain*. Have them describe how the natural resources listed in the selection are used for various economic activities.

All in One **Foundations of Geography Teaching Resources,** *The Road from Coorain,* pp. 268–269

For English Language Learners L1
Read the summary of this chapter in the Reading and Vocabulary Study Guide aloud to students. This will provide an oral synopsis of key content before students read the selection on land use and culture.

📖 Chapter 5, Section 2, **Eastern Hemisphere Reading and Vocabulary Study Guide,** pp. 48–50

Answers

✓ **Reading Check** Most of the world's land is used for first-level activities.

Geography Skills Practice Apply Information First-level activities, such as farming, occur in rural areas. Second-level activities, such as manufacturing, and third-level activities, such as retail sales, would probably take place in urban areas.

Changes in Land Use L2

Guided Instruction

- Have students examine the text and visuals on p. 124 and read Changes in Land Use on p. 125.

- Ask students **How has human-environment interaction shaped the city of Boston?** *(Colonists cleared forests and built structures along the waterfront; marshes were drained and filled in to create new land.)*

- Ask **How can colonization affect land use?** *(It may change a landscape to fit colonists' cultural practices.)*

- Ask students **How has industrialization changed land use in developed countries?** *(Since 1900, suburbs have increased around cities in developed countries.)*

Independent Practice

Have students complete the graphic organizer by filling in details about changes in land use.

Monitor Progress

- Show *Section Reading Support Transparency FG 57* and ask students to check their graphic organizers individually. Go over key concepts and clarify key vocabulary as needed.

  📖 **Foundations of Geography Transparencies,** *Section Reading Support Transparency FG 57*

- Tell students to fill in the last column of their *Reading Readiness Guides*. Ask them if what they learned was what they had expected to learn.

  All in One Foundations of Geography Teaching Resources, *Reading Readiness Guide,* p. 249

Answers

MAP MASTER Skills Activity **Identify** Only a small area to the west of South Boston remained forested after colonization. **Compare and Contrast** The city has grown because people created new land.

Go Online PHSchool.com Students may practice their map skills using the interactive online version of this map.

Boston: A Changing Landscape

English colonists founded Boston, Massachusetts, on a narrow peninsula surrounded by water, marshes, and forest. The colonists cleared most of the forest for farmland. The colonists also built dams, piers, and retaining walls along the waterfront. By the 1800s, Boston's growing industries and growing population of workers faced a land shortage. Boston's solution was to drain marshes and to create new land by filling in areas of water. At first, Boston's people filled in around existing piers. Then, they filled in tidal ponds behind dams. Finally, they filled in whole bodies of open water.

Human-Environment Interaction Colonization and industrialization transformed Boston's landscape. **Identify** How much of the forest around Boston remained after colonization? **Compare and Contrast** How did Boston's land area change between colonial times and today?

Go Online PHSchool.com Use Web Code **lep-3312** for step-by-step map skills practice.

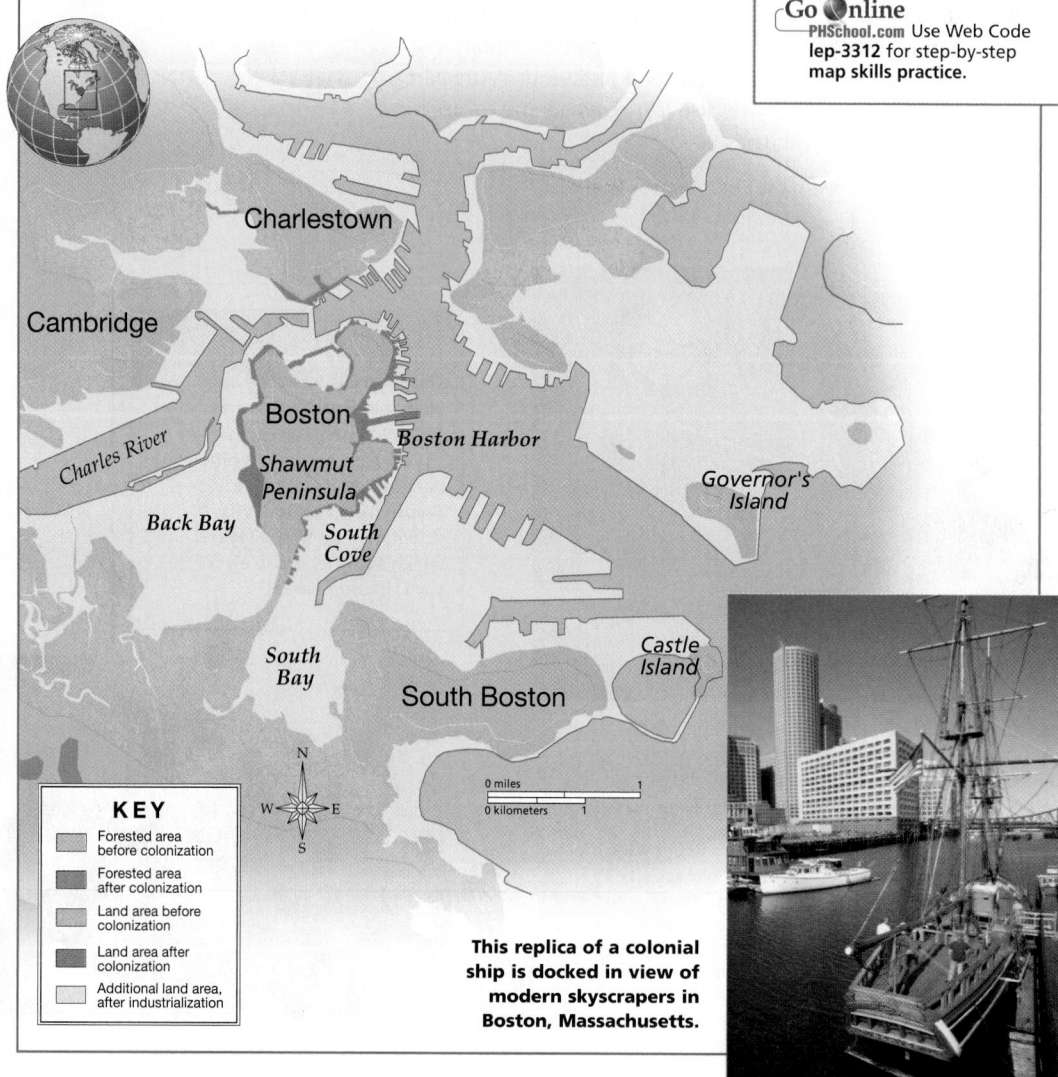

KEY
- Forested area before colonization
- Forested area after colonization
- Land area before colonization
- Land area after colonization
- Additional land area, after industrialization

This replica of a colonial ship is docked in view of modern skyscrapers in Boston, Massachusetts.

124 Foundations of Geography

Background: Links Across Place

The Netherlands Large portions of the Netherlands, a country in northwestern Europe, have been reclaimed from the sea much like the city of Boston. The country is mostly flat, low-lying land. Over one-quarter is located below sea level, and much of the land is naturally lakes or marshes and unusable for farming. However, ingenious civil engineering projects dating as far back as medieval times have managed to make the land more habitable. Lakes and marshes have been drained, and a series of dunes and dikes protect the land from the sea.

Changes in Land Use

When a region undergoes **colonization,** or a movement of new settlers and their culture to a country, the newcomers may change that region's landscape to fit their cultural practices. For example, if farmers move to a region without farms, they will create farms. Similarly, as people find new ways of making a living, they start using the land in new ways, too.

Colonization Before European colonists came to Australia, there was no farming and no livestock raising. In North and South America before colonization, European crops such as wheat and grapes were unknown. So were livestock such as cows and chickens. When Europeans settled these continents, they cleared large areas for use as farmland and livestock pasture.

Industrialization and Sprawl Since the 1800s, the growth of machine-powered production, or **industrialization,** has changed landscapes in many countries. Cities have grown around industrial facilities worldwide. Since 1900, suburbs have spread out from cities in the United States and other developed countries to cover more and more land. The spread of cities and suburbs is known as sprawl.

√ **Reading Check** How did European colonization change landscapes in North and South America?

Vineyards in Australia
Grapes did not grow in Australia before European colonists arrived. Now grapes thrive in Australia's Hunter Valley. **Infer** *What would have been different about this landscape before European colonization?*

Section 2 Assessment

Key Terms
Review the key terms at the beginning of this section. Use each term in a sentence that explains its meaning.

Target Reading Skill
State three details that explain the main idea of the second paragraph on page 120.

Comprehension and Critical Thinking
1. (a) **Describe** How have rice farmers in the Philippines transformed the landscape?

(b) **Infer** Why is the Philippines' farm landscape different from Western Europe's?
2. (a) **Recall** What are second-level activities?
(b) **Categorize** Name some examples of second-level activities.
(c) **Compare and Contrast** How do second-level activities differ from third-level activities?
3. (a) **Recall** What is industrialization?
(b) **Identify Causes** How is industrialization related to sprawl?

Writing Activity
Write a short encyclopedia article on land use around your hometown. Describe how culture has affected land use. Mention the different levels of economic activity around your town. Finally, give an example of a change in land use in or near your hometown.

> **Writing Tip** Encyclopedia articles contain descriptions and statements of facts. Be careful not to express personal thoughts or opinions.

Assess Progress L2
Have students complete the Section Assessment. Administer the *Section Quiz.*

All in One **Foundations of Geography Teaching Resources,** *Section Quiz,* p. 251

Reteach L1
If students need more instruction, have them read this section in the Reading and Vocabulary Study Guide.

Chapter 5, Section 2, **Eastern Hemisphere Reading and Vocabulary Study Guide,** pp. 48–50

Extend L3
Extend students' understanding of the relationship between natural resources and economic activity by having them complete the *Book Project: World News Today.* Have students work in pairs to complete the project.

All in One **Foundations of Geography Teaching Resources,** *Book Project: World News Today,* pp. 36–38

Answers

Infer Possible answer: Before European colonization, grapes were not grown in Australia. The land might have been a forest.

√ **Reading Check** Large areas of land were cleared and transformed for use as farmland and livestock pasture. However, different cultures may respond differently to similar environments.

Writing Activity
Use the *Rubric for Assessing a Report* to evaluate students' encyclopedia articles.

All in One **Foundations of Geography Teaching Resources,** *Rubric for Assessing a Report,* p. 275

Section 2 Assessment

Key Terms
Students' sentences should reflect knowledge of each Key Term.

Target Reading Skill
Possible answers: Georgia and southern Japan both have moist, warm climates; rice is a major crop in Japan; people in Georgia raise chickens and grow crops such as peanuts.

Comprehension and Critical Thinking
1. (a) Due to a shortage of land, Philippine farmers have carved terraces into hillsides in order to grow rice. (b) There is a shortage of level land in the Philippines.

2. (a) Second-level activities are economic activities in which people process the products of first-level activities. (b) Possible answers include: processing food and making sweaters from wool. (c) Second-level activities are based upon the manufacture of goods, whereas third-level activities produce services rather than goods.

3. (a) the growth of machine-powered production in an economy (b) Cities tend to grow around industrial facilities. As cities grow, suburbs grow as well. As cities and suburbs spread out, sprawl is increased.

Objective

Learn how to make predictions.

Prepare to Read

Build Background Knowledge   L2

Tell students that in this skill lesson they will learn how to make an educated prediction. Explain to students that they make predictions every day when they decide whether to take a certain action. For example, students who walk to school may have to choose among several routes they can take. They choose routes based on which they predict is the safest and will get them to school the fastest. Have students brainstorm other common examples of making predictions.

Instruct

Making Predictions   L2

Guided Instruction

■ Read the steps on p. 126 as a class and have student volunteers write them on the board.

■ Practice the skill by following the steps on p. 127 as a class. First, identify the issue in the passage. (*Some countries control water supplies of downstream nations.*) Then have students explain how the issue in the passage is similar to oil issues they already learned about. (*Possible similarity: Both oil and water are important natural resources that are in short supply in some countries.*) Next, have students read aloud the possible effects shown in the graphic organizer. Finally, ask them to predict which effect seems most likely. (*Accept any of the three effects, but be sure students supply a valid reason for their choice.*)

Independent Practice

Assign *Skills for Life* and have students complete it individually.

All in One **Foundations of Geography Teaching Resources,** *Skills for Life,* p. 261

 **Making Predictions**

The Oval Office, where leaders make predictions, is at the center of this photo of the White House.

When you watch an adventure movie, half the fun is in predicting what happens next. Decision makers, such as American presidents, make predictions, too, and their predictions guide their decisions. Good decision makers take actions that they predict will have good results. When you predict, you make an educated guess about the effects of a certain cause. The key word here is *educated*. Without knowledge, you can't predict—you just guess.

Learn the Skill

Follow these steps to make a good prediction.

1 **Identify a situation that has not been resolved.** As you read information, ask yourself questions, such as, "What will happen next? What effects will this situation produce?"

2 **Make a list of probable outcomes, or effects.** If possible, analyze examples of similar causes that have known effects.

3 **Make an educated guess about which outcome is most likely.** In order to make an *educated* guess, use information that you know or that you research.

4 **State your prediction.** In your prediction, explain why you think the cause will produce a particular effect, or outcome.

126 Foundations of Geography

Monitor Progress

As students are completing the *Skills for Life* worksheet, circulate to make sure students are applying the skill steps effectively. Provide assistance as needed.

Practice the Skill

Read the text in the box at the right. Then predict the consequences of global struggles for water.

1 From what you have read about water supplies in Southwest Asia, identify a major issue that has not been resolved. State the problem as a question.

2 This chapter discusses problems in global oil supply. How are oil and water issues similar? What effects have resulted from world oil shortages? Study the graphic organizer below. It shows results that might occur when one country controls other countries' water.

3 Of the possible outcomes in the graphic organizer, which seems the most likely? Make an educated guess, using what you know about the oil issue.

4 Here's how your prediction might begin: "As the world's need for water grows, water-rich countries will probably _____."

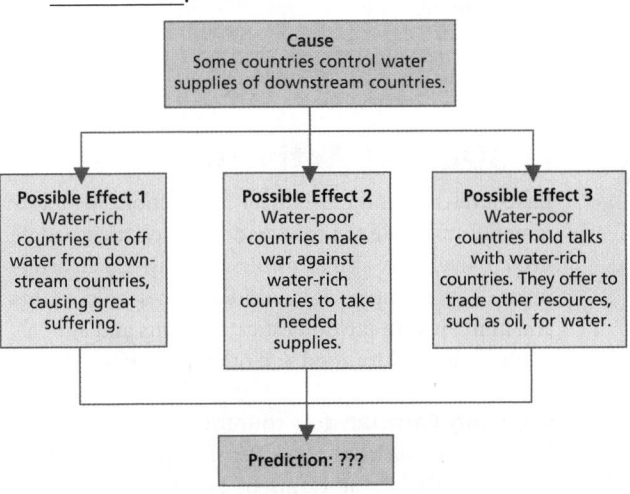

```
                    Cause
          Some countries control water
         supplies of downstream countries.

   ┌──────────────┬──────────────┬──────────────┐
   ▼              ▼              ▼
Possible Effect 1  Possible Effect 2  Possible Effect 3
Water-rich        Water-poor        Water-poor
countries cut off countries make    countries hold talks
water from down-  war against       with water-rich
stream countries, water-rich        countries. They offer to
causing great     countries to take trade other resources,
suffering.        needed            such as oil, for water.
                  supplies.

                  Prediction: ???
```

Apply the Skill

Study the graph on page 118. Note how much oil the United States consumes and produces. What do you learn from these facts? Make a prediction about what America might do when world oil supplies run low. Create a graphic organizer like the one on this page to help you make a prediction.

During the 1900s, oil-rich nations became wealthy and powerful by controlling world oil supplies. In the present century, water supplies may determine who is rich or poor. Much of the world's usable fresh water comes from rivers that flow through many countries. Nearly half the people in the world live in international river basins. Yet many of the countries that share rivers have no water treaties. Countries along these rivers build dams to store water for themselves. Nations downstream worry that they might run out of water. In Southwest Asia, Turkey controls sources of water flowing south into Syria and Iraq. A proposed system of 22 dams could allow Turkey to withhold water from its neighbors. Syria and Iraq have plentiful oil but not enough water.

Assess and Reteach

Assess Progress L2
Ask students to do the Apply the Skill activity.

Reteach L1
Identifying cause and effect is a vital part of making predictions. If students are having trouble with this skill, have them review it using the Social Studies Skills Tutor CD-ROM.

⦿ *Identifying Cause and Effect,* **Social Studies Skills Tutor CD-ROM**

Extend L3
- Have students reread p. 124. Ask them to identify the effect of Boston's growing population and industrialization. (*Boston's people filled in some bodies of water to create more land.*) Explain that this effect can also be a cause.

- Tell students to make a graphic organizer like the one on p. 127. Have them identify two to three possible effects of Boston's people filling in bodies of water to create more land. (*Possible effects: Industries that rely on bodies of water and their resources, such as fishing, may no longer exist; goods may no longer be able to be shipped to and from Boston via waterways.*) Then tell them to predict which effect is most likely. (*Accept any of the effects, but be sure students supply a valid reason for their choice.*)

Answers
Apply the Skill

Students should note from the graph that the United States consumes more oil than any other country in the world.

Students' graphic organizers should look like the graphic organizer on p. 127. Cause: The United States is highly dependent on oil, but world oil supplies are running low. Possible effects: The United States looks for other sources of energy. The United States taps into any oil resources it has not yet used. The United States conserves energy and uses less oil.

Students should choose one of the effects they listed as their prediction and supply a valid reason for their choice.

Section 3
Step-by-Step Instruction

Objectives
Social Studies
1. Investigate how first-level activities affect the environment.
2. Explore how second- and third-level activities affect the environment.

Reading/Language Arts
Learn how to identify implied main ideas.

Prepare to Read

Build Background Knowledge L2

In this section, students will learn about people's effect on the environment. Write the following words on the board: *soil, water, air.* Ask students to list some ways that these natural resources are important. *(Possible answers: soil for growing food, water to irrigate crops and drink, air to breathe)* Then have students describe human activities that could threaten these natural resources. Use the Give One, Get One participation strategy (TE, p. T37) to generate student responses. *(Driving cars can lead to air pollution; cutting down trees can lead to soil erosion and deforestation; dumping trash can cause water pollution.)*

Set a Purpose for Reading L2
- Preview the Objectives.

- Read each statement in the *Reading Readiness Guide* aloud. Ask students to mark the statements true or false.

  All in One Foundations of Geography Teaching Resources, *Reading Readiness Guide,* p. 253

- Have students discuss the statements in pairs or groups of four, then mark their worksheets again. Use the Numbered Heads participation strategy (TE, p. T36) to call on students to share their group's perspectives.

Vocabulary Builder
Preview Key Terms L2
Pronounce each Key Term, then ask the students to say the word with you. Provide a simple explanation such as, "Pollution is waste, such as the exhaust that comes out of cars when we drive, that makes our air, water, or soil less clean."

Section 3
People's Effect on the Environment

Prepare to Read

Objectives
In this section you will
1. Investigate how first-level activities affect the environment.
2. Explore how second- and third-level activities affect the environment.

Taking Notes
Copy the table below. As you read this section, fill in the table with information about people's effect on the environment. Add rows to the table as needed.

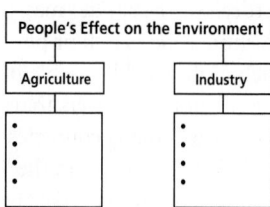

Target Reading Skill
Identify Implied Main Ideas Identifying main ideas can help you remember what you read. The details in a paragraph can add up to the main idea, even if it is not stated directly. For example, the details in the first paragraph below add up to this main idea: "While first-level activities are necessary for human survival, they also reshape the environment."

Key Terms
- **deforestation** (dee fawr uh STAY shun) *n.* a loss of forest cover in a region
- **biodiversity** (by oh duh VUR suh tee) *n.* a richness of different kinds of living things in a region
- **civil engineering** (SIV ul en juh NIHR ing) *n.* technology for building structures that alter the landscape, such as dams, roads, and bridges
- **pollution** (puh LOO shun) *n.* waste, usually man-made, that makes the air, water, or soil less clean

A rancher driving cattle in Manitoba, Canada

128 Foundations of Geography

First-Level Activities

First-level activities, or direct interaction with raw materials, provide the food and resources that people need to live. They also transform the physical environment. For example, agriculture replaces wild plants and animals with the domesticated plants and animals that people need for food and other products.

Creating Farmland As countries have grown, they have met the challenge of feeding their people in different ways. The Great Plains of North America once supported wild grasses and buffalo. Today, farmers in that region grow corn and wheat and raise cattle. In the Netherlands, the people have drained lakes, bays, and marshes to create dry farmland. While creating new farmland destroyed wild grasslands and wetlands, the new land has fed millions.

Target Reading Skill L2

Identify Implied Main Ideas Point out the Target Reading Skill. Tell students that identifying implied main ideas can help them to remember what they read.

Model identifying implied main ideas by reading the first paragraph on p. 132. Think aloud as you read to show how you arrived at the main idea. *(There are many different sources of pollution.)*

Give students *Identify Implied Main Ideas.* Have them complete the activity in groups.

All in One Foundations of Geography Teaching Resources, *Identify Implied Main Ideas,* p. 258

Environmental Challenges Agriculture, forestry, and fishing provide food and resources that people need to live. At the same time, they sometimes have harmful effects on the environment. For example, wood is needed to build houses. But cutting down too many trees can result in **deforestation,** or the loss of forest cover in a region. Cutting forests may result in the loss of more than trees and other plants. Animals that depend on the forest for survival may also suffer. Deforestation can lead to a loss of **biodiversity,** which is a richness of different kinds of living things. So timber companies face the challenge of harvesting needed wood while limiting damage to the environment.

Farmers often use fertilizers and other chemicals to grow more crops. This makes it possible to feed more people. But when rain washes these chemicals into streams, they sometimes harm fish and other water-dwelling creatures. Fish are a tasty and healthy food source. But if fishers catch too many, they may threaten the fishes' survival. Farmers and fishers face the challenge of feeding the world's people without harming important resources.

Finding a Balance The key is to find a balance. Around the world, governments, scientists, and business people are working to find ways of meeting our need for food and resources without harming the environment. One solution is planting tree farms for timber. When the trees are mature, they can be cut and new trees can be replanted without harming ancient forests. Farmers can grow crops using natural methods or use chemicals that will not damage waterways. Fishers can limit their catch of endangered fish and harvest fish that are more plentiful.

✓ **Reading Check** How do people benefit when new farmland is created?

Deforestation
Timber companies and farmers have cut down rain forests in Indonesia.
Apply Information *What are some of the advantages and disadvantages of cutting down forests?*

Links to Math

Acres and Timber Yields
Tree farms, like the one below, in Newbury, England, are one way to fight deforestation. If these oak trees grow to yield 80,000 board feet of timber per acre (466 cubic meters per hectare), and the farm covers 300 acres (121 hectares), how much timber will the farm produce?

Instruct

First-Level Activities L2

Guided Instruction

- **Vocabulary Builder** Clarify the high-use words **interaction, transform,** and **domesticated** before reading.

- Read First-Level Activities using the Paragraph Shrinking technique (TE, p. T34).

- Ask students **What can people do to limit the negative effects of first-level activities?** *(Tree farms can be planted to help preserve ancient forests. Crops can be grown without fertilizers or with chemicals that do not harm the environment. Fishers can avoid catching endangered fish.)*

- Ask students **Why do you think it is important to limit the negative impact of first-level activities on the environment?** *(Possible answer: so that resources such as fish and trees are available to future generations)*

Independent Practice

Ask students to create the Taking Notes graphic organizer on a blank piece of paper. As students read, have them fill in the table with information about people's effect on the environment. Briefly model how to identify which information to record.

Monitor Progress

Circulate throughout the classroom to ensure that individuals are filling in their tables correctly. Provide assistance as needed.

Links

Read the **Links to Math** on this page and have them answer the question. *(Help students calculate that the farm will produce 24 million feet, or 56,386 cubic meters of timber.)*

Answers

Apply Information Advantages: wood can be used to make products; clears land for farming. Disadvantages: threatens the survival of animals and plants; a loss of biodiversity.

✓ **Reading Check** New farmland allows more people to be fed.

The Hybrid Car

Guided Instruction

Ask students to study the Eyewitness Technology feature on this page. Have them silently read the introduction. Then read each caption together with students. Pause after each caption is read aloud to solicit comments and questions from students. Then answer the Analyzing Images question as a class.

Independent Practice

Distribute *Small Group Activity: Community Service Project: Protect the Environment.* Have students work in small groups to propose community education and project proposals that focus on transportation and improving the environment. Possible projects include: an educational campaign about the benefits of using hybrid-car technology; a proposal to establish bike paths for commuters; an education program that encourages carpooling for commuters.

All in One Foundations of Geography Teaching Resources, *Small Group Activity: Community Service Project: Protect the Environment,* pp. 262–265

The Hybrid Car

Cars with gasoline engines are fast and can go long distances, but they pollute. Electric cars don't emit dangerous chemicals, but they can be driven only for a short distance before their batteries need to be recharged. The hybrid car combines the best features of gasoline and electric cars. It is fast and can go long distances, but it uses less gasoline and pollutes less. The hybrid car gets about 46 miles per gallon, while the conventional car of the same size gets about 33.

Traffic Jam
Today, traffic jams are common as drivers commute daily in and out of cities. Waiting in traffic jams wastes a lot of fuel and adds to air pollution.

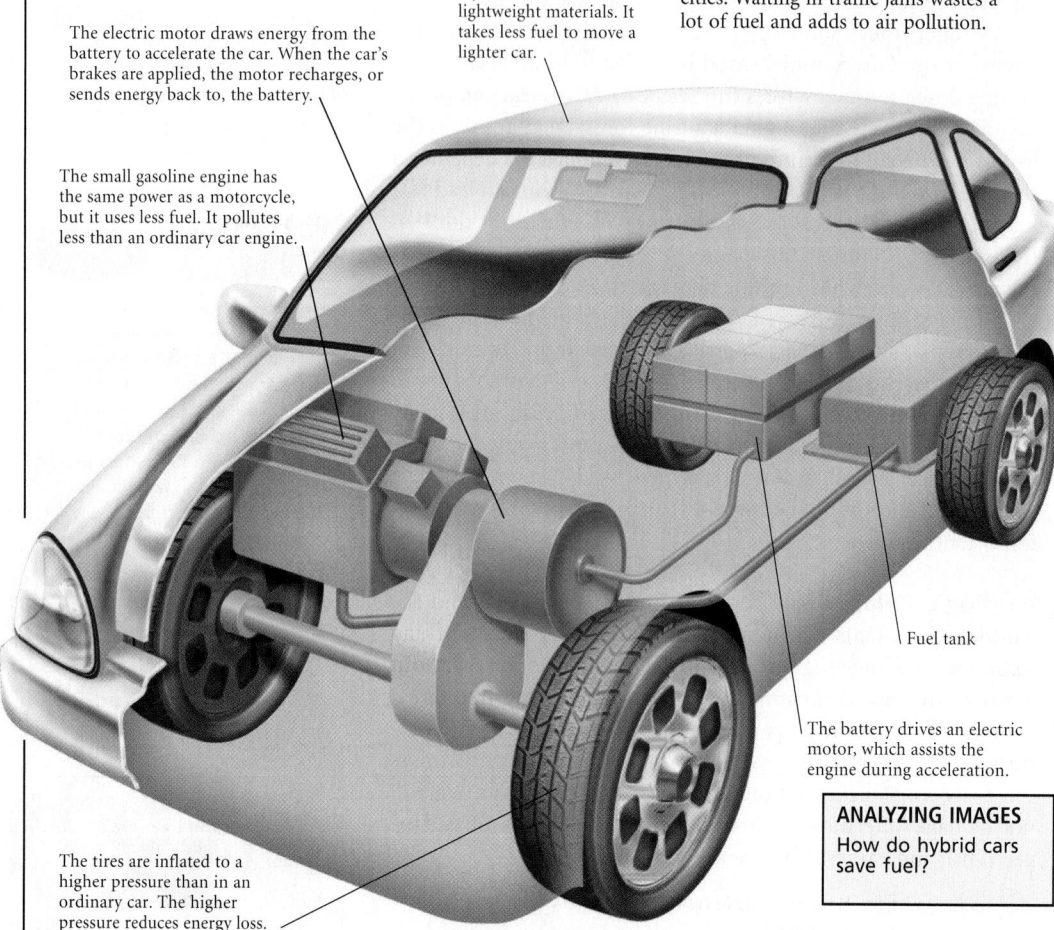

The electric motor draws energy from the battery to accelerate the car. When the car's brakes are applied, the motor recharges, or sends energy back to, the battery.

Hybrid cars are made of lightweight materials. It takes less fuel to move a lighter car.

The small gasoline engine has the same power as a motorcycle, but it uses less fuel. It pollutes less than an ordinary car engine.

Fuel tank

The battery drives an electric motor, which assists the engine during acceleration.

The tires are inflated to a higher pressure than in an ordinary car. The higher pressure reduces energy loss.

ANALYZING IMAGES
How do hybrid cars save fuel?

Background: Global Perspectives

The Kyoto Protocol In 1997, representatives from 160 nations met in Kyoto, Japan, to discuss concerns about increasing global gas emissions. Many scientists believe that these gases cause global warming, a gradual increase in the average temperature on Earth that could lead to melting of polar ice caps and flooding of coastal areas.

At Kyoto, the nations reached an agreement, called the Kyoto Protocol, to reduce the amount of certain gases released into the atmosphere. The agreement called for global emissions to be reduced by approximately 5 percent by 2012. The United States has not ratified the agreement.

Answer

ANALYZING IMAGES by drawing energy from the battery; being lighter in weight reduces the amount of fuel used; higher tire pressure helps reduce energy loss and conserve fuel

Second- and Third-Level Activities

Over the years, industry, or second-level activities, and services, or third-level activities, have transformed deserts, prairies, woodlands, and marshes. They have created our familiar urban landscapes of housing developments, offices, factories, railroads, and highways.

Providing Jobs, Reshaping the Environment Industrial and service activities provide most of the jobs in developed countries such as the United States. Those activities are the basis for the developed countries' prosperity. They are also the main land use in urban areas.

The main purpose of some of these activities is to change the environment. **Civil engineering** is technology for building structures that alter the landscape, such as dams, canals, roads, and bridges. Dams create reservoirs that cover large areas with water. They also provide water for farms and cities and protect areas downstream from flooding.

Other industrial and service activities have side effects on the environment. For example, shopping malls require large areas to be paved for parking. Industries use large amounts of resources and release industrial wastes into the environment. Service activities require the construction of roads, telephone lines, and power lines.

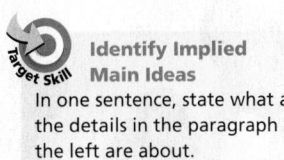

Identify Implied Main Ideas
In one sentence, state what all the details in the paragraph at the left are about.

A Landscape Shaped by Industry
The waterfront in Rotterdam, Netherlands, has been shaped to meet the needs of industry. **Analyze Images** *How might this landscape have been different before it was shaped by industry?*

 **Skills Mini Lesson**

Supporting a Position

1. To support a position, tell students they should state their position clearly in a sentence; identify at least three reasons to support their position; support each reason with accurate evidence; put their reasons and supporting evidence in an effective order; and add a conclusion.

2. Have students practice the skill using information from the section to support this position: All communities should have a recycling program.

3. Have students apply the skill by asking them to follow the steps to state and support their position on reducing car emissions.

Target Reading Skill L2

Identify Implied Main Ideas As a follow up, ask students to answer the Target Reading Skill question in the Student Edition. *(Second- and third-level activities have reshaped the environment we live in.)*

Second- and Third-Level Activities L2

Guided Instruction

- **Vocabulary Builder** Clarify the high-use word **prosperity** before reading.

- Ask students to read Second- and Third-Level Activities. As students read, circulate and make sure individuals can answer the Reading Check question.

- Ask **How is most land used in urban areas?** *(for industrial and service activities)* **Why are these activities important to developed countries?** *(They provide most of the jobs and are the basis of developed countries' prosperity.)*

- Ask students **How are people trying to reduce pollution?** *(by using fuel-efficient vehicles, developing renewable energy resources, and recycling)*

Independent Practice

Have students complete the table by filling in details about people's effect on the environment.

Monitor Progress

- Show *Section Reading Support Transparency FG 58* and ask students to check their graphic organizers individually.

  Foundations of Geography Transparencies, *Section Reading Support Transparency FG 58*

- Tell students to fill in the last column of their *Reading Readiness Guides*. Probe for what they learned that confirms or invalidates each statement.

  All in One Foundations of Geography Teaching Resources, *Reading Readiness Guide,* p. 253

Answer

Analyze Images Possible answer: The land along the water may have been covered by vegetation.

Assess and Reteach

Assess Progress
L2

Have students complete the Section Assessment. Administer the *Section Quiz*.

AllinOne Foundations of Geography Teaching Resources, *Section Quiz,* p. 255

Reteach
L1

If students need more instruction, have them read this section in the Reading and Vocabulary Study Guide.

📖 Chapter 5, Section 3, **Eastern Hemisphere Reading and Vocabulary Study Guide,** pp. 51–53

Extend
L3

Have students complete the *Enrichment* activity so that they may study an instance in which environmental concerns and providing jobs had to be balanced.

AllinOne Foundations of Geography Teaching Resources, *Enrichment,* p. 260

Answers

Apply Information Recycling reduces the amount of waste that local governments must burn or dump and saves natural resources.

✓Reading Check Some industrial activities, such as building dams and bridges, change the environment. Others use large amounts of resources and can harm the environment with the release of industrial wastes.

Section 3 Assessment

Key Terms
Students' sentences should reflect knowledge of each Key Term.

⟳ Target Reading Skill
(1) There are many sources of pollution that affect our air, water, and soil. (2) People are working together to find ways to reduce pollution. (3) Recycling is being used in the United States to reduce waste and save natural resources. (4) By working together, we can find solutions to environmental problems.

Comprehension and Critical Thinking
1. (a) cutting trees to clear land for farms and to use for timber **(b)** Deforestation threatens the survival of animals and plants and can lead to a loss of biodiversity.

2. (a) Industrial and service activities have transformed deserts, prairies, woodlands, and marshes into urban landscapes that include housing developments, offices,

Recycling
These seventh-grade students in Syracuse, New York, are sorting materials for recycling. **Apply Information** *What environmental problems does recycling help to solve?*

Environmental Challenges Industry is not the only source of **pollution,** waste that makes the air, soil, or water less clean. The trash that we throw away may pollute the soil, water, or air. Exhaust from cars and trucks is another source of air pollution. Many scientists believe that air pollution may cause higher temperatures or other changes in our climate.

Finding Solutions Working together, scientists, governments, businesses, and ordinary people can find solutions to these problems. One solution is to use more fuel-efficient vehicles, such as hybrid cars. Vehicles that burn less fuel create less air pollution. Renewable energy sources, such as solar power and wind power, can also reduce the need to burn fuels that pollute the air. In addition, reducing pollution may reduce the risk of harmful climate changes.

Many cities and counties in the United States have introduced waste recycling. Recycling reduces the amount of waste that local governments must burn or dump. It also saves natural resources. For example, when paper is recycled, fewer trees must be cut down to make new paper.

Finding solutions to environmental problems is one of the greatest challenges of our time. If we all work together, we can meet this challenge.

✓Reading Check **How do industrial activities affect the environment?**

Section 3 Assessment

Key Terms
Review the key terms at the beginning of this section. Use each term in a sentence that explains its meaning.

⟳ Target Reading Skill
State the main idea of each paragraph on this page.

Comprehension and Critical Thinking
1. (a) Recall What are the causes of deforestation?

(b) Identify Cause and Effect How does deforestation threaten the environment?
2. (a) List List ways in which industrial and service activities transform landscapes.
(b) Categorize Which of these ways are common to both industrial and service activities?
(c) Analyze How are industrial activities different from service activities in their impact on the environment?

Writing Activity
Write a journal entry in which you discuss how your own activities today may have affected the environment.

For: An activity on the environment
Visit: PHSchool.com
Web Code: led-3503

132 Foundations of Geography

factories, roads, railroads, highways, dams, canals, bridges, reservoirs, shopping malls, and telephone and power lines. **(b)** Service and industrial activities both often require railroads, roads, and telephone and power lines. **(c)** Possible answer: Industrial activities seem to harm the environment more than service activities.

Writing Activity
Use the *Rubric for Assessing a Journal Entry* to evaluate students' entries.

AllinOne Foundations of Geography Teaching Resources, *Rubric for Assessing a Journal Entry,* p. 276

Go Online PHSchool.com Typing in the Web code when prompted will bring students to detailed instructions for this activity.

Review and Assessment

◆ Chapter Summary

Section 1: Natural Resources

- Almost everything that people use or consume is made with natural resources, which are either renewable or nonrenewable.
- Energy is a special resource needed for most economic activities, but some sources of energy are in limited supply, and some nations need to buy energy resources from others.

Section 2: Land Use

- How people use the land depends on their culture.
- Three levels of economic activity account for most land use.
- Land use changes when newcomers settle a region and as cultures change over time.

Section 3: People's Effect on the Environment

- First-level activities provide needed food and resources, but they reduce the land available for wild plants and animals.
- Second- and third-level activities provide jobs, but they can also pollute the environment.

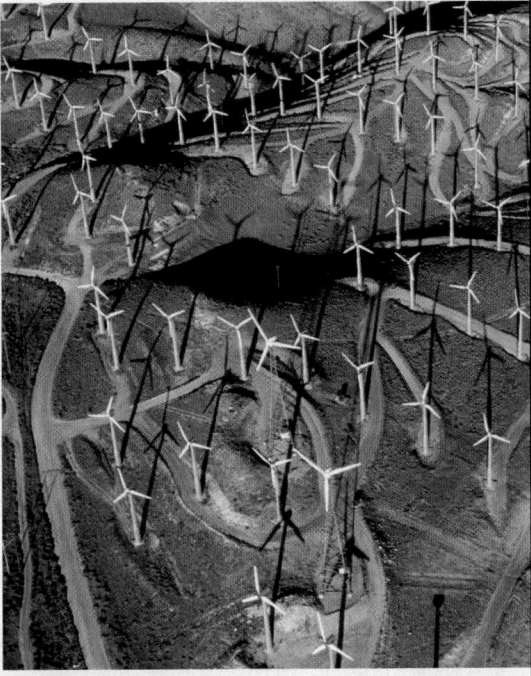

Windmills in California

- Review and revisit the major themes of the chapter by asking students to classify what Guiding Question each bulleted statement in the Chapter Summary answers. Form students into groups and ask them to complete the activity together. Use the Numbered Heads participation strategy (TE, p. T36) to have the groups share their answers in the group discussion. Refer to page 1 of the Student Edition for the text of the Guided Questions.

- Assign *Vocabulary Development* for students to review Key Terms.

  All in One **Foundations of Geography Teaching Resources,** *Vocabulary Development,* p. 273

◆ Key Terms

Each of the statements below contains a key term from the chapter. If the statement is true, write *true*. If it is false, rewrite the statement to make it true.

1. **Raw materials** are natural resources that can be used without reworking.

2. **Renewable resources** are natural resources that can be replaced.

3. Natural resources that cannot be replaced are called **nonrenewable resources**.

4. Our **environment** is our natural surroundings.

5. **Manufacturing** does not produce goods but involves working directly for customers.

6. **Industrialization** is the growth of manufacturing in an economy.

7. **Deforestation** is the planting of trees to replace forests cut down for timber.

8. **Biodiversity** is the loss of plant and animal life due to deforestation.

9. **Pollution** is waste, usually made by people, that makes air, soil, or water less clean.

Chapter 5 **133**

◆ Vocabulary Builder

Revisit this chapter's high-use words:

consume	respond	interaction
evaporate	channel	transform
harness	distribute	domesticated
hybrid	correspond	prosperity

Ask students to review the definitions they recorded on their *Word Knowledge* worksheets.

All in One **Foundations of Geography Teaching Resources,** *Word Knowledge,* p. 259

Consider allowing students to earn extra credit if they use the words in their answers to the questions in the Chapter Review and Assessment. The words must be used correctly and in a natural context to win the extra points.

Answers

Key Terms

1. False. Raw materials are natural resources that must be reworked to be useful.
2. True
3. True
4. True
5. False. Manufacturing is the large-scale production of goods by hand or by machine.
6. False. Industrialization is the growth of machine-powered production in an economy.
7. False. Deforestation is a loss of forest cover in a region.
8. False. Biodiversity is a richness of different kinds of living things in a region.
9. True

Review and Assessment

Comprehension and Critical Thinking

10. (a) Possible answers: water; wind, geo-thermal energy, solar energy; living things **(b)** because they can be replaced **(c)** Renewable resources can be replaced, while non-renewable resources cannot be replaced.

11. (a) no **(b)** solar and wind energy and biomass

12. (a) yes **(b)** Possible answer: The land might be used differently, based on how the colonial culture traditionally uses the type of land available in the region.

13. (a) Possible answers: fishing, hunting, cutting wood, mining, herding, raising crops **(b)** Workers engaging in first-level activities use the land and its resources directly to make products. Second-level activities process the products of first-level activities. Third-level activities do not involve the process of creating goods at all; they may involve working directly for customers or for businesses.

14. (a) Tree farms can be planted and used to produce wood. **(b)** Biodiversity would be preserved.

15. (a) industrial and service activities, trash disposal, and car exhaust **(b)** Possible answers: by using more fuel-efficient vehicles such as hybrids, using renewable energy sources such as solar and wind power, and waste recycling

Skills Practice

Students' answers will vary, but should show an understanding of the skill steps.
Possible facts Worldwide energy usage has grown rapidly; fossil fuel supplies may be limited; some countries are using alternative energy resources; alternative energy resources include wind, solar, tidal, atomic, and geo-thermal energy, as well as biomass; atomic energy uses radioactive materials, which are plentiful; some people oppose atomic energy because radioactive materials can be danger-ous; new technologies that help people to use less energy, such as hybrid cars and those that offer energy savings in heating and lighting, can be used to help fossil fuels last longer.
Possible prediction Advancements in energy technology will help us meet the energy needs of the future.

◆ Comprehension and Critical Thinking

10. (a) List List at least three renewable resources.
 (b) Explain Why is each of these resources renewable?
 (c) Compare and Contrast How do renewable resources differ from nonrenewable resources?

11. (a) Recall Do all countries have adequate energy supplies?
 (b) Analyze What energy sources are available to all countries?

12. (a) Recall Does culture affect land use?
 (b) Predict What might happen to land use in a region if people with a different culture colonized it?

13. (a) List List three first-level activities.
 (b) Compare and Contrast How do those activities differ from second- and third-level activities?

14. (a) Describe How can people obtain wood without cutting down wild forests?
 (b) Predict How would leaving forests in place affect biodiversity?

15. (a) Describe What causes pollution?
 (b) Infer How might companies and individuals reduce pollution?

◆ Skills Practice

Making Predictions In the Skills for Life activity on pages 126 and 127, you learned to make predictions. You also learned how to make sure that a prediction is an educated guess. That is, predictions should be based on information about the situation or about similar situations.

 Review the steps that you followed to learn this skill. Then reread the paragraphs on pages 118 and 119 under the heading Meeting Energy Needs in the Future. List several facts about the issues described there. Finally, use these facts to make a prediction about how those issues might be resolved in the future.

◆ Writing Activity: Language Arts

Identify an environmental problem that interests you. Write a story about people solving the environmental problem. For your story, create characters with different roles in creating or solving the environmental problem. You should also create a plot for your story that describes how people come up with a solution to the problem and carry out that solution.

MAP MASTER™ Skills Activity

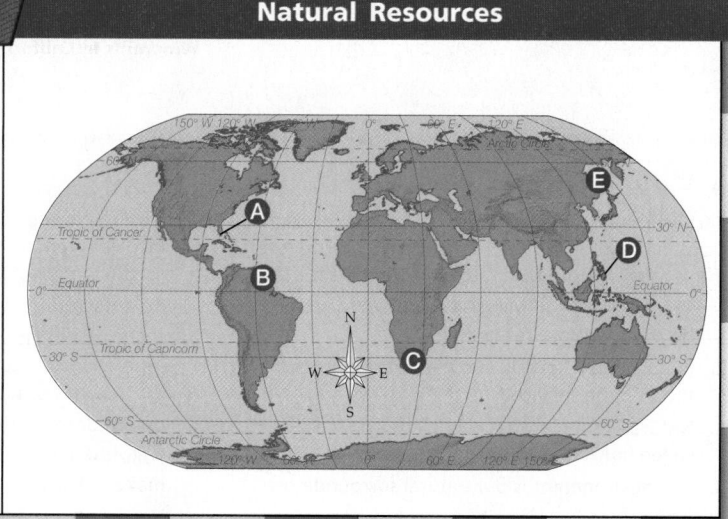

Natural Resources

Place Location Refer to the map titled The World: Natural Resources on page 115. For each natural resource listed below, write the letter from the map at the right that shows its location.
1. Bauxite
2. Diamond
3. Nickel
4. Phosphates
5. Tungsten

Go Online
PHSchool.com Use Web Code lep-3514 for an **interactive map.**

134 Foundations of Geography

Writing Activity: Language Arts

Students' stories will vary, but should include a problem, a solution, characters with various roles, and a plot.
Use *Rubric for Assessing a Writing Assignment* to evaluate students' stories.

All in One Foundations of Geography Teaching Resources, *Rubric for Assessing a Writing Assignment,* p. 277

Standardized Test Prep

Test-Taking Tips

Some questions on standardized tests ask you to find a main idea by analyzing a reading selection. Read the passage below. Then follow the tips to answer the sample question.

Saudi Arabia, Mexico, Iraq, Venezuela, and Russia have large oil reserves. The United States and China are rich in coal and natural gas. Many Northern European countries have rivers with water energy to create electricity. By contrast, Japan has few energy sources.

TIP As you read the paragraph, try to identify its main idea, or most important point. Every sentence in a paragraph supports this main idea.

Pick the letter that best answers the question.
This paragraph describes which kind of resources?

- A capital resources
- B human resources
- C natural resources
- D entrepreneurial resources

TIP Look for key words in the question and in the answer choices that connect to the paragraph. In this case, the key word is *resources*.

Think It Through Start with the main idea of the paragraph: Different countries have different energy sources. What kind of resources are these energy sources: oil, coal, gas, and water? Energy is not a human resource. You may not know the words *entrepreneurial* or *capital*. But you probably recognize *natural resources* as useful materials found in the environment—such as oil, coal, gas, and water. The correct answer is C.

Practice Questions

Use the tips above and other tips in this book to help you answer the following questions:

1. Wind energy is a
   - A fossil fuel.
   - B raw material.
   - C renewable resource.
   - D nonrenewable resource.

2. When colonists settle in a new environment,
   - A they will use land just as they did in their old environment.
   - B the environment will not change.
   - C they will adjust their previous land uses to the new environment.
   - D they will give up all familiar land uses.

3. Which of the following environmental problems does paper recycling help solve?
   - A deforestation
   - B pollution
   - C deforestation and pollution
   - D neither deforestation nor pollution

Read the following passage and answer the question that follows.

Sierra Leone's economy produces raw materials and cash crops. The country's people mine diamonds, iron ore, and aluminum ore. People on the coast catch fish. Its farmers produce coffee, cocoa, rice, and palm oil. They also raise poultry and other livestock.

4. The passage's main idea refers to which type of activities?
   - A first-level activities
   - B second-level activities
   - C third-level activities
   - D financial activities

Use Web Code **lea-3501**
for a **Chapter 5 self-test.**

1. B   **2.** C
3. D   **4.** A
5. E

Go Online
PHSchool.com Students may practice their map skills using the interactive online version of this map.

Standardized Test Prep

Answers

1. C
2. C
3. C
4. A

Go Online
PHSchool.com Students may use the Chapter 5 self-test on PHSchool.com to prepare for the Chapter Test.

Assessment Resources

Teaching Resources
Chapter Tests A and B, pp. 190–195
Final Exams A and B, pp. 196–201

Test Prep Workbook
Foundations of Geography Study Sheet, pp. 113–115
Foundations of Geography Practice Tests A, B, and C, pp. 49–60

AYP Monitoring Assessments
Foundations of Geography Benchmark Test 2 and Report Sheet, pp. 85–88
Foundations of Geography Outcome Test, pp. 170–175

Technology
ExamView Test Bank CD-ROM

- Students can further explore the Guiding Questions by completing hands-on projects.

- Three pages of structured guidance in All-in-One Foundations of Geography Teaching Resources support each of the projects described on this page.

  All in One Foundations of Geography Teaching Resources, *Book Project: Focus on Part of the Whole, pp. 27–29; Book Project: Desktop Countries, pp. 33–35*

- There are also two additional projects introduced, explained, and supported in the All-in-One Foundations of Geography Teaching Resources.

  All in One Foundations of Geography Teaching Resources, *Book Project: The Geography Game, pp. 30–32; Book Project: World News Today, pp. 36–38*

- Go over the four project suggestions with students.

- Ask each student to select one of the projects, or design his or her own. Work with students to create a project description and a schedule.

- Post project schedules and monitor student progress by asking for progress reports.

- Assess student projects using rubrics from the All-in-One Foundations of Geography Teaching Resources.

  All in One Foundations of Geography Teaching Resources, *Rubric for Assessing a Student Performance on a Project, p. 39; Rubric for Assessing Performance of an Entire Group, p. 40; Rubric for Assessing Individual Performance in a Group, p. 41*

 Tell students they can add their completed Book Project as the final item in their portfolios. Assess student portfolios with *Rubric for Assessing a Student Portfolio.*

  All in One Foundations of Geography Teaching Resources, *Rubric for Assessing a Student Portfolio, p. 42*

Projects

Create your own projects to learn more about geography. At the beginning of this book, you were introduced to the Guiding Questions for studying the chapters and the special features. But you can also find answers to these questions by doing projects on your own or with a group. Use the questions to find topics you want to explore further. Then try the projects described on this page or create your own.

1. **Geography** What are Earth's major physical features?

2. **History** How have people's ways of life changed over time?

3. **Culture** What is a culture?

4. **Government** What types of government exist in the world today?

5. **Economics** How do people use the world's natural resources?

Project

CREATE A PHYSICAL MAP

Focus on Part of the Whole
The world and its population are extremely varied. Choose a particular region or country. If you are working with a group, have each person choose a different country on a continent. Learn everything you can about the country's physical geography, the population, and the lifestyles of the people there. Use encyclopedias, almanacs, or other books.

Set up a display based on your research. Prepare a large map that includes important physical features of the land. Add captions that explain how the land's physical geography affects people's lives.

Project

RESEARCH A COUNTRY'S CULTURE

Desktop Countries
What countries did your ancestors come from? Select one country and do some research on it. Interview someone, perhaps a relative from that country, or read about it. Find a recipe you can prepare to share with the class. Then make a desktop display about the country you have chosen. Write the name of the country on a card and put it on your desk. Add a drawing of the country's flag or map, or display a souvenir. On place cards, write several sentences about each object. Take turns visiting everyone's "desktop countries."

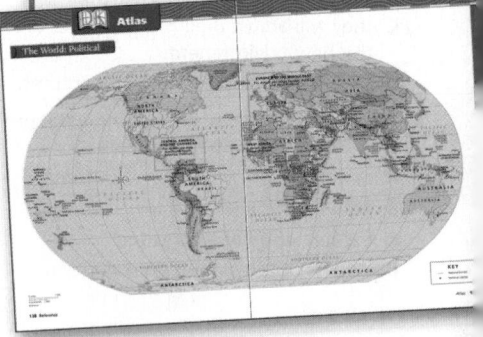

Teaching the Target Reading Skills

The Prentice Hall *World Studies* program has interwoven essential reading skills instruction throughout the Student Edition, Teacher's Edition, and ancillary resources. In Europe and Russia, students will learn five reading skills.

Student Edition The *World Studies* Student Edition provides students with reading skills instruction, practice, and application opportunities in each chapter within the program.

Teacher's Edition The *World Studies* Teacher Edition supports your teaching of each skill by providing full modeling in each chapter's interleaf and modeling of the specific sub-skills in each section lesson.

All in One Teaching Resources The *World Studies* All-in-One Teaching Resources provides a worksheet explaining and supporting the elements of each Target Reading Skill. Use these to help struggling students master skills, or as more practice for every student.

Target Reading Skills

The Target Reading Skills introduced on this page will help you understand the words and ideas in this book and in other social studies reading you do. Each chapter in the Europe and Russia section focuses on one of these reading skills. Good readers develop a bank of reading strategies, or skills. Then they draw on the particular strategies that will help them understand the text they are reading.

Chapter 6 Target Reading Skill

Using the Reading Process Previewing can help you understand and remember what you read. In this chapter you will practice using these previewing skills: setting a purpose for reading, predicting what the text will be about, and asking questions before you read.

Chapter 7 Target Reading Skill

Clarifying Meaning If you do not understand something you are reading right away, you can use several skills to help clarify the meaning of the word or idea. In this chapter you will practice these strategies for clarifying meaning: rereading, reading ahead, and paraphrasing.

Chapter 8 Target Reading Skill

Identifying the Main Idea Since you cannot remember every detail of what you read, it is important that you identify the main ideas. The main idea of a section or paragraph is the most important point and the one you want to remember. In this chapter you will practice these skills: identifying stated and implied main ideas and identifying supporting details.

Chapter 9 Target Reading Skill

Using Context Using the context of an unfamiliar word can help you understand its meaning. Context includes the words, phrases, and sentences surrounding a word. In this chapter you will practice using these context clues: descriptions, definitions, comparisons, and examples.

Chapter 10 Target Reading Skill

Comparing and Contrasting You can use comparison and contrast to sort out and analyze information you are reading. Comparing means examining the similarities between things. Contrasting is looking at differences. In this chapter you will practice these skills: comparing and contrasting, identifying contrasts, making comparisons, and recognizing contrast signal words.

138 Europe and Russia

Assessment Resources

Use the diagnosing readiness tests from **AYP Monitoring Assessments** to help you identify problems before students begin to study Europe and Russia.

Determine students' reading level and identify challenges:

📄 *Screening Tests*, pp. 1–10

Evaluate students' verbal skills:

📄 *Critical Thinking and Reading Tests*, pp. 25–34

📄 *Vocabulary Tests*, pp. 45–52

📄 *Writing Tests*, pp. 53–60

EUROPE and RUSSIA

Europe and Russia lie on a gigantic landmass that stretches from the Atlantic Ocean to the Pacific. The countries of this region are as diverse as their geography, with distinctive cultures and societies. Ancient civilizations that developed in Europe still influence people around the world. Today, the region contains countries with histories that stretch back hundreds of years as well as countries that were formed just a decade or two ago.

Guiding Questions

The text, photographs, maps, and charts in this book will help you discover answers to these Guiding Questions.

1. **Geography** What are the main physical features of Europe and Russia?

2. **History** How have Europe and Russia been affected by their history?

3. **Culture** How have the people of Europe and Russia been shaped by their cultures?

4. **Government** What types of government have existed in Europe and Russia?

5. **Economics** How have Russian and European economies developed into what they are today?

Project Preview

You can also discover answers to the Guiding Questions by working on projects. Several project possibilities are listed on page 346 of this book.

Europe and Russia **139**

Guiding Questions

- This book was developed around five Guiding Questions about Europe and Russia. They appear on the reduced Student Edition page to the left. The Guiding Questions are intended as an organizational focus for the book. The Guiding Questions act as a kind of umbrella under which all of the material falls.

- You may wish to add your own Guiding Questions to the list in order to tailor them to your particular course.

- Draw students' attention to the Guiding Questions. Ask them to write the questions in their notebooks for future reference.

- In the Teacher's Edition, each section's themes are linked to a specific Guiding Question at the beginning of each chapter. Then, an activity at the end of the chapter returns to the Guiding Questions to review key concepts.

Project Preview

- The projects for this book are designed to provide students with hands-on involvement in the content area. Students are introduced to some projects on p. 346.

- *Book Projects* give students directions on how to complete these projects, and more.

   All in One Europe and Russia Teaching Resources, *Book Project: Changing Climates,* pp. 77–79; *Book Project: Tourism in Eastern Europe,* pp. 80–82; *Book Project: Olympic Cities,* pp. 83–85; *Book Project: Folklore Corner,* pp. 86–88

- Assign projects as small-group activities, whole-class projects, or individual projects. Consider assigning a project at the beginning of the course.

Assess students' social studies skills:

- 📄 *Geographic Literacy Tests,* pp. 13–20
- 📄 *Visual Analysis Tests,* pp. 21–24
- 📄 *Communications Tests,* pp. 35–44

The *World Studies* program provides instruction and practice for all of these skills. Use students' test results to pinpoint the skills your students have mastered and the skills they need to practice. Then use *Correlation to Program Resources* to prescribe skills practice and reinforcement.

- 📄 *Diagnosing Readiness Test Correlations,* pp. 64–77

Objectives

- Describe the relative size and location of Europe and Russia.
- Locate the countries that make up Europe.
- Examine the physical features of Europe and Russia.
- Study the population density of Europe and Russia.

Prepare to Read

Build Background Knowledge   L2

Use the Give One, Get One strategy (TE, p. T37) to help students create a list of impressions related to Europe and Russia.

Instruct

Investigate Europe and Russia   L2

Guided Instruction

- Read the introductory, Location, and Regions paragraphs as a class.
- Hand out the *Regional Overview* worksheet. Direct students to fill it in as they study the Regional Overview.

All in One **Europe and Russia Teaching Resources,** *Regional Overview,* pp. 93–95

Independent Practice

Form students into pairs and have them write a statement comparing Europe and Russia's location and size to that of the United States.

Monitor Progress

Circulate and make sure the pairs are measuring correctly.

Answers

LOCATION Atlantic Ocean; west; both regions are about the same distance from the Equator; Alaska and the northern portions of Europe and Russia are located about the same distance from the Arctic Circle; Possible answer: their location.

REGIONS Europe and Russia are bigger than the United States. The United States is larger than Europe alone.

Investigate Europe and Russia

Europe and Russia extend across more than half the world's longitudes, from Iceland in the west at about 25° W to easternmost Siberia at 175° E. Europe is a continent made up of many countries, while Russia is one country that actually lies on two continents—Europe and Asia. Together, Europe and Russia form a rich pattern of different cultures, histories, and languages.

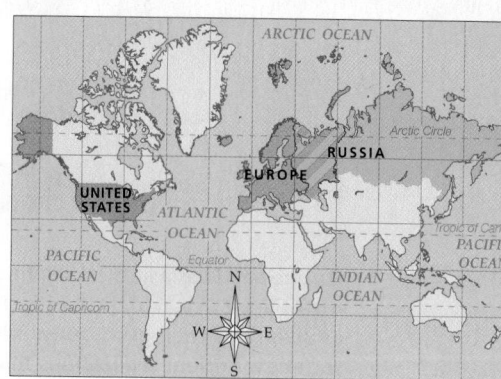

▲ **Amsterdam, the Netherlands**
Skating on one of the city's many frozen canals

REGIONS

2 Estimate the Size of Europe and Russia

How big are Europe and Russia? To find out, compare the size of Europe and Russia together to that of the 48 states of the United States mainland. Now compare Europe alone to those states. Notice that Russia lies in two continents, Asia and Europe. The striped area shows the European part of Russia. The solid green area shows the Asian part of Russia.

LOCATION

1 Investigate Europe and Russia's Location

The location of an unfamiliar place can be described in relation to a familiar place. Use the map above to describe the location of Europe and Russia in relation to the United States. What ocean lies between Europe and the United States? If you were on the west coast of the United States, in what direction would you travel to get to the east coast of Russia most quickly? How close to the Equator are the two regions—Europe and Russia and the United States? How close are they to the Arctic Circle? Many people think the climates of Europe and the United States are similar. Look at the map, and explain why this might be so.

Background: Global Perspectives

Europe-Asia Borders The Ural Mountains are not the only mountains that form a border between Europe and Asia. The Caucasus Mountains separate European Russia and the country of Georgia, which is part of Central Asia. The third land boundary between Europe and Asia is located where the country of Turkey borders the European countries of Greece and Bulgaria. Half of this border is formed by another natural feature—the Maritsa River, which serves as the boundary between Greece and Turkey.

Political Europe and Russia

Key
— National border
⊕ National capital
• Other city

LOCATION

3 Investigate the Countries of Europe

The landmass upon which Europe and Asia are located is known as Eurasia. Russia is the largest country in that landmass and the largest country in the world. Some of the world's smallest countries are in Europe. Name three of them. Name four countries that share a border with Germany. What are the names of the seas and oceans that surround Europe?

▲ **Moscow, Russia**
The historic building called the Kremlin is the headquarters for Russia's government.

Mental Mapping

Everything in Its Place Divide students into four groups. Assign each group one of the following European regions and distribute the appropriate outline map: Northern Europe, Southern Europe, Western Europe, and Eastern Europe and Russia. Write the names of some of the countries from each region on the board. Ask students to locate as many countries on the maps as they can without looking in

their textbooks. They can fill in countries they could not locate as they study the region.

All in One **Europe and Russia Teaching Resources,** *Outline Map 14: Western Europe: Political, p. 97; Outline Map 15: Northern Europe, p. 98; Outline Map 16: Southern Europe, p. 99; Outline Map 18: Eastern Europe and Russia: Political, p. 100*

Guided Instruction

- Read the Location paragraph. Direct students' attention to the political map of Europe and Russia. Ask students to try to locate the three biggest countries in Europe and write their answers on the board. Direct students to the Country Databanks on pp. 112–121 and 166–173 to check their answers. *(Ukraine, France, Spain)*

- Ask students to name the European countries that border Russia. *(Finland, Estonia, Latvia, Belarus, and Ukraine)* Then ask students to locate the small portion of Russia that is separate from the rest of the country. Ask **What countries border this part of Russia?** *(Lithuania and Poland)*

- Ask students to continue completing the *Regional Overview* worksheet.

  All in One **Europe and Russia Teaching Resources,** *Regional Overview, pp. 93–95*

Independent Practice

Distribute *Reading a Political Map*. Have students practice their map skills by answering the questions about the political map of Western Europe.

All in One **Europe and Russia Teaching Resources,** *Reading a Political Map, p. 51*

Monitor Progress

Circulate to make sure that individuals are filling in the correct answers on their worksheets. Provide assistance as needed.

Answers

LOCATION Possible answers: Vatican City, Monaco, San Marino, Andorra, and Liechtenstein; Possible answers: Denmark, Poland, Czech Republic, Austria, Switzerland, France, Luxembourg, Belgium, Netherlands; Arctic and Atlantic oceans, North, Baltic, Mediterranean, Tyrrhenian, Ionian, Adriatic, Aegean, and Black seas

Physical Europe and Russia

L2

Guided Instruction

- Read the Location paragraph. Point out that Europe is a peninsula, or a body of land nearly surrounded by water. Then ask students to name the four smaller peninsulas found on the continent. *(Iberian, Scandinavia, Italian, and Balkan peninsulas)*

- Ask students to continue completing the Regional Overview worksheet.

  All in One Europe and Russia Teaching Resources, *Regional Overview,* pp. 93–95

Independent Practice

Have students do research to find the highest and lowest points in Europe, including European Russia. Ask them to write down the height of each in feet and meters. Then ask students to locate each point on the map on p. 142. Tell students to put their finger on each point and circulate to check their answers. *(Highest point: Elbrus located in the Caucasus Mountains—18,510 feet, or 5,642 meters; lowest point: Caspian Sea shore—92 feet, or 28 meters, below sea level)*

Monitor Progress

Circulate to be sure students have written down the correct heights of each point and that their fingers are on the correct locations.

Answers

LOCATION Pyrenees, Alps, Apennines, Carpathian Mountains, Dinaric Alps, Transylvanian Alps, Balkan Mountains, Pindus Mountains, Caucasus Mountains; Pyrenees

---

Physical Europe and Russia

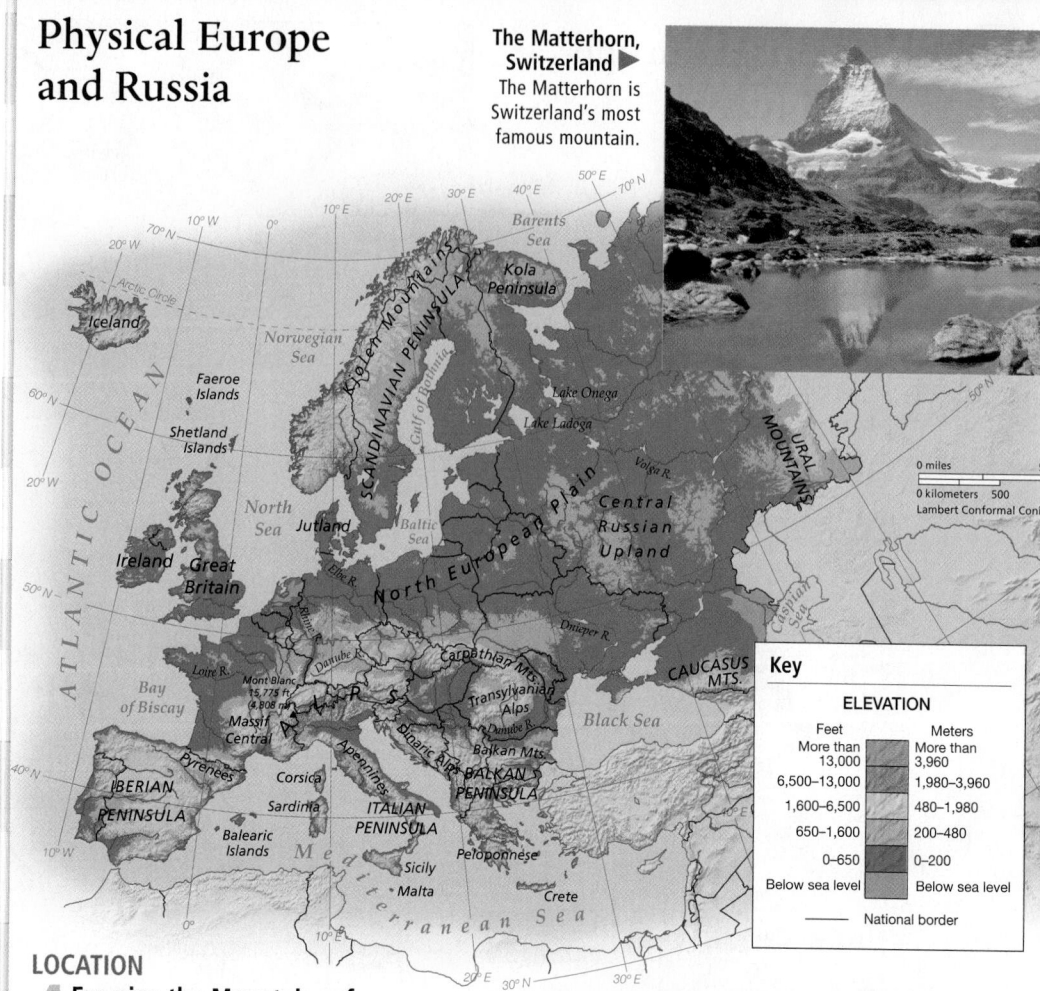

The Matterhorn, Switzerland ▶ The Matterhorn is Switzerland's most famous mountain.

Key

ELEVATION

Feet	Meters
More than 13,000	More than 3,960
6,500–13,000	1,980–3,960
1,600–6,500	480–1,980
650–1,600	200–480
0–650	0–200
Below sea level	Below sea level

—— National border

LOCATION

4 Examine the Mountains of Europe and Russia

Several mountain ranges stretch through Central and Southern Europe, from the Bay of Biscay to the Caspian Sea. Find and name four of these mountain ranges. What mountain range separates France from Spain? Now locate Russia's Ural Mountains. Most of Russia lies in Asia, east of the Ural Mountains. Most Russians, however, live in the European part of Russia, west of the Ural Mountains.

Differentiated Instruction

For Less Proficient Readers   L1

Show students the Europe and Russia fly-over segment on the Passport to the World CD-ROM. Ask students to list several of the region's major landforms on the board after viewing the segment.

 Europe and Russia Flyover, **Passport to the World CD-ROM**

Europe and Russia: Population Density

Population density describes how crowded a particular place is. Use the key below to determine what color on the map represents an area where many people live. What color represents an area where very few people live? Compare the parts of Europe where there are very few people with the parts of Europe where there are very many. How might the locations of these areas explain the differences?

KEY

Persons per sq. mile	Persons per sq. kilometer
More than 3,119	More than 1,204
520–3,119	200–1,204
260–519	100–199
130–259	50–99
25–129	10–49
1–24	1–9
Less than 1	Less than 1

Urban Areas
☐ 5,000,000–9,999,999
⊙ 1,000,000–4,999,999
• Less than 1,000,000
— National border

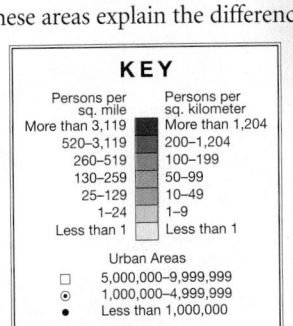

▼ Norway
Sami children on a snowmobile

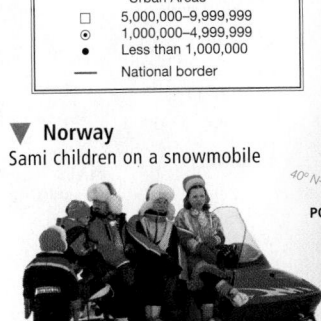

▲ Sergivev Posad, Russia
Trinity Monastery of St. Sergius

PRACTICE YOUR GEOGRAPHY SKILLS

1 You begin to explore Europe from its west coast. From Portugal you fly over the headwaters of the Danube and the Rhine rivers. In what direction are you flying?

2 You board a train in Moscow and travel east. When you get to the farthest point in Siberia, you have gone about one third of the way around the world. What mountain range did you cross?

3 You are going to drive from Warsaw to Moscow. In what direction will you travel?

Regional Overview 143

Europe and Russia: Population Density   L2

Guided Instruction
- Read the Interaction paragraph and have students study the population density map.
- Ask students to list the areas with the highest population densities. (*Portions of the United Kingdom, Germany, the Netherlands, Poland, Ukraine, and coastal areas of Italy.*)
- Ask **Why do you think the population density of the Scandinavian Peninsula is less dense than that of Central and Southern Europe?** (*Possible answer: The climate of the Scandinavian Peninsula is colder because it is located closer to the Arctic Circle, so fewer people want to live there.*)
- Direct students to finish the *Regional Overview* worksheet.
  All in One **Europe and Russia Teaching Resources,** *Regional Overview,* pp. 93–95

Independent Practice
Have students complete *Reading a Population Density Map* to practice the skill.
  All in One **Europe and Russia Teaching Resources,** *Reading a Population Density Map,* p. 101

Monitor Progress
Circulate to make sure that students are able to correctly answer the questions at the end of the activity. Provide assistance as needed.

Answers
Locations that are farther north and in colder climates often have fewer people.

PRACTICE YOUR GEOGRAPHY SKILLS
1. east
2. Ural Mountains
3. east

Focus on Countries in Europe and Russia [L2]

Guided Instruction

- Assign a number from 1–4 to each caption. Have students pick a number (1–4) from a hat and divide the class according to the numbers they selected.

- Have each group read the text on the country relative to their group number and write down important details.

Independent Practice

Have each group use the Country Databanks on pp. 250–259 and 304–311, DK Compact Atlas of the World, and the DK World Desk Reference Online (see student pages for Web code) to research the country they have been assigned. Ask groups to focus on the geography, climate, government, and people of the countries. Then, have each group present the information they gathered to the class.

Monitor Progress

Use *Rubric for Assessing an Oral Presentation* to assess students' presentations.

All in One **Europe and Russia Teaching Resources,** *Rubric for Assessing an Oral Presentation, p. 103*

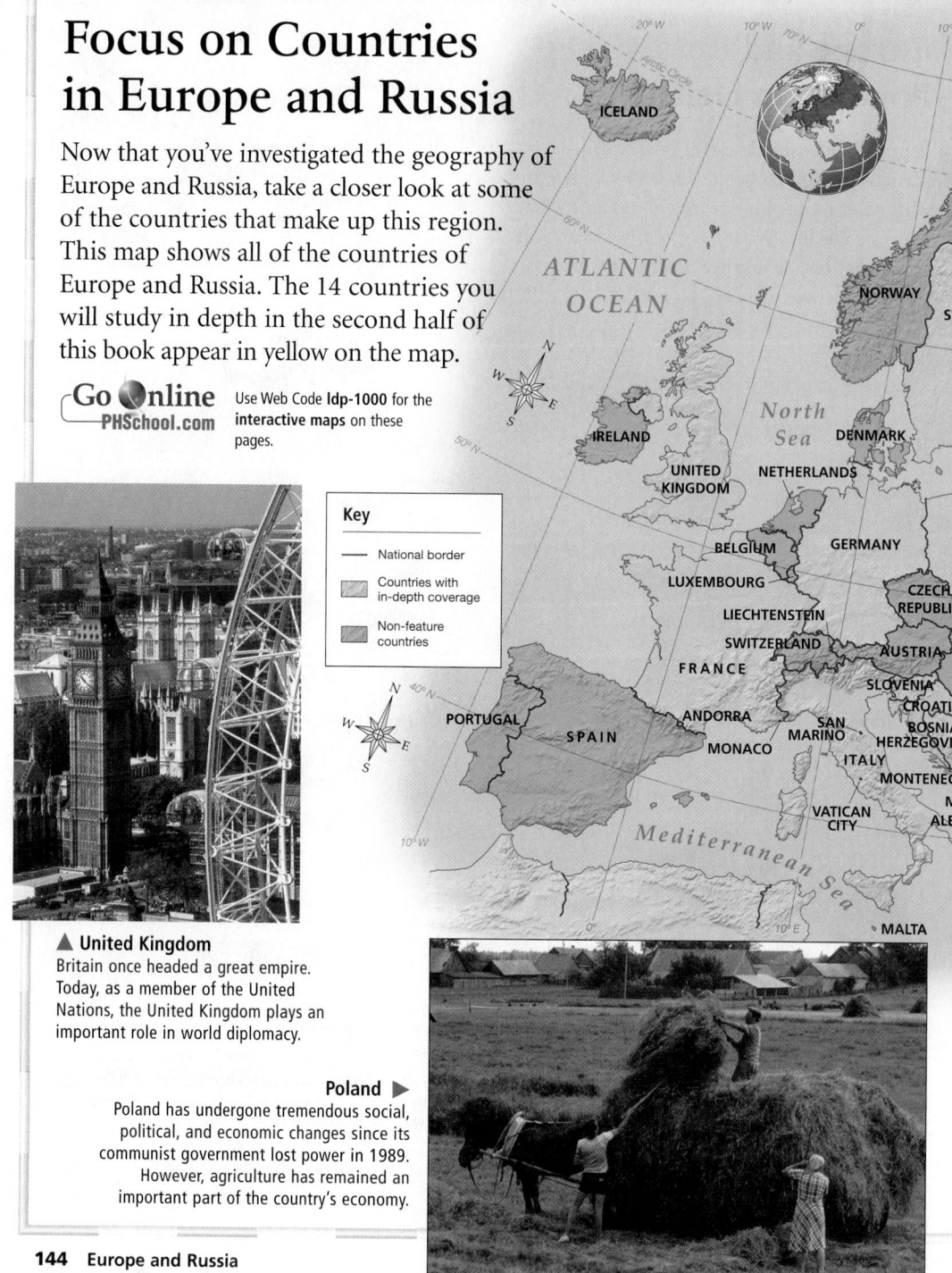

Focus on Countries in Europe and Russia

Now that you've investigated the geography of Europe and Russia, take a closer look at some of the countries that make up this region. This map shows all of the countries of Europe and Russia. The 14 countries you will study in depth in the second half of this book appear in yellow on the map.

Go Online PHSchool.com Use Web Code **Idp-1000** for the **interactive maps** on these pages.

Key

— National border

▨ Countries with in-depth coverage

▨ Non-feature countries

▲ **United Kingdom**
Britain once headed a great empire. Today, as a member of the United Nations, the United Kingdom plays an important role in world diplomacy.

Poland ▶
Poland has undergone tremendous social, political, and economic changes since its communist government lost power in 1989. However, agriculture has remained an important part of the country's economy.

144 Europe and Russia

Background: Links Across Time

Britain's Empire By 1820, Britain controlled so many colonies and territories around the world, that it governed more than 200 million people. This was 26 percent of the world's population at the time. Britain ruled territories on every continent.

RUSSIA

Barents
Sea

Arctic Circle

RUSSIA

US

Aral
Sea

KRAINE

MOLDOVA

Caspian Sea

Black Sea

0 miles 500
0 kilometers 500
Lambert Azimuthal Equal Area

▲ Russia
Russia is the world's largest country. Since its communist government collapsed, it has faced many challenges as it has made the transition to democracy and capitalism.

◀ Germany
Divided after World War II, East and West Germany were reunited in 1990. Today, Germany is Europe's most industrialized nation.

Regional Overview 145

Assess and Reteach

Assess Progress L2

- Have students revisit the impressions they brainstormed in Build Background Knowledge. Using the information they have learned so far, ask them to confirm or revise some of the impressions. If some aspects have yet to be touched on, tell students to write them in their notebooks and look for more information as they begin their study of Europe and Russia.

- Ask students to complete the Practice Your Geography Skills questions on p. 143.

Reteach L1

For more exploration of the region, have students view the Europe and Russia portion of the Passport to the World CD-ROM and complete the Customs Quiz.

⊙ *Europe and Russia,* **Passport to the World CD-ROM**

Extend L3

Portfolio Activity

One way of assessing students' accomplishments is by having them build a portfolio of their best work. To begin their portfolios for Europe and Russia, have students choose a country in the region that they will not be exploring in depth in this textbook. Have students research their country to create a magazine advertisement that encourages people to visit the country. Tell students to use text, illustrations, and maps in their advertisements.

- Give students *Doing Searches on the Internet* to teach them how they can gather information for their advertisements.

All in One **Europe and Russia Teaching Resources,** *Doing Searches on the Internet,* p. 31

CHAPTER **6** Europe and Russia: Physical Geography

Chapter Overview

Overview

Section **1**

Land and Water
1. Learn about the size, location, and population of Europe and Russia.
2. Examine the major landforms of Europe and Russia.
3. Find out about the waterways of Europe and Russia.

Section **2**

Climate and Vegetation
1. Find out about the wide range of climates in Europe and Russia.
2. Learn about the major climate regions of Europe and Russia.
3. Examine the natural vegetation regions of Europe and Russia.

Section **3**

Resources and Land Use
1. Learn about the natural resources of Western Europe.
2. Find out about the natural resources of Eastern Europe.
3. Examine Russia's natural resources.

DISCOVERY CHANNEL SCHOOL

Video

The Geography of Europe and Russia

Length: 7 minutes, 2 seconds

Use with Section 1

This segment provides an overview of the geography of Europe and Russia, with a focus on population density. The climates, geographic features, and natural resources of the two regions are compared and contrasted.

Technology Resources

Go Online
PHSchool.com

Students use embedded Web codes to access Internet activities, chapter self-tests, and additional map practice. They may also access Dorling Kindersley's Online Desk Reference to learn more about each country they study.

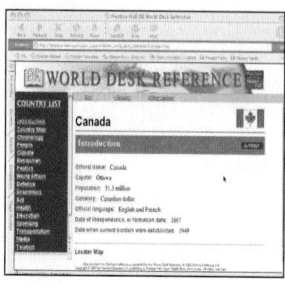

Interactive Textbook

Use the Interactive Textbook to make content and concepts come alive through animations, videos, and activities that accompany the complete basal text—online and on CD-ROM.

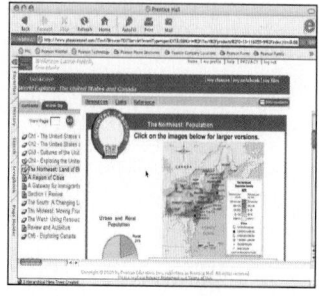

PRENTICE HALL

TeacherEXPRESS
Plan • Teach • Assess

Use this complete suite of powerful teaching tools to make planning lessons and administering tests quicker and easier.

Reading and Vocabulary Instruction

⟲ Model the Target Reading Skill

Reading Process Previewing the text, setting a purpose for reading, predicting what the section will be about, and asking questions before reading all give students a task to complete while reading. This can sharpen students' focus and enhance their understanding of a selection. Model the reading process by thinking about this chapter aloud:

"This chapter's title is *Europe and Russia: Physical Geography*. I will read to learn about the physical features of Europe and Russia. The first section is called *Land and Water*. I predict that this section will explain whether the land in Europe and Russia is made up of deserts, forests, mountains, or something else. It will probably describe the rivers, lakes, oceans, and seas as well. The second section is called *Climate and Vegetation*. I wonder if I will learn about a connection between climate and plant life in Europe and Russia? If a place is rainy and not too cold, then I imagine it would be a good place for plants to grow. The third section is called *Resources and Land Use*. I know that *resources* are things that people use. I wonder if there is a connection between the resources people have and how they use the land. I predict that I will learn about the relationship between humans and the environment."

Use the following worksheets from All-in-One Europe and Russia Teaching Resources (pp. 118–120) to support the chapter's Target Reading Skill.

Vocabulary Builder
High-Use Academic Words

Use these steps to teach this chapter's high-use words:

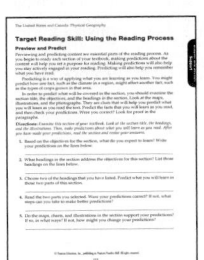

1. Have students rate how well they know each word on their Word Knowledge worksheets (All-in-One Europe and Russia Teaching Resources, p. 121).

2. Pronounce each word and ask students to repeat it.

3. Give students a brief definition or sample sentence (provided on TE pp. 149, 156, and 165).

4. Work with students as they fill in the "Definition or Example" column of their Word Knowledge worksheets.

Assessment

Formal Assessment

Test students' understanding of core knowledge and skills.

Chapter Tests A and B, All-in-One Europe and Russia Teaching Resources, pp. 138–143

Customize the Chapter Tests to suit your needs.

ExamView® Test Bank CD-ROM

Skills Assessment

Assess geographic literacy.

MapMaster Skills, Student Edition, pp. 147, 150, 156, 159, 160, 165, 168, 172

Assess reading and comprehension.

Target Reading Skills, Student Edition, pp. 153, 157, 169, and in Section Assessments

Chapter 6 Assessment, Eastern Hemisphere Reading and Vocabulary Study Guide, p. 65

Performance Assessment

Assess students' performance on this chapter's Writing Activities using the following rubrics from All-in-One Europe and Russia Teaching Resources.

Rubric for Assessing a Journal Entry, p. 136

Rubric for Assessing a Writing Assignment, p. 137

Assess students' work through performance tasks.

Small Group Activity: Europe and Russia Map and Climate Charts, All-in-One Europe and Russia Teaching Resources, pp. 124–127

Online Assessment

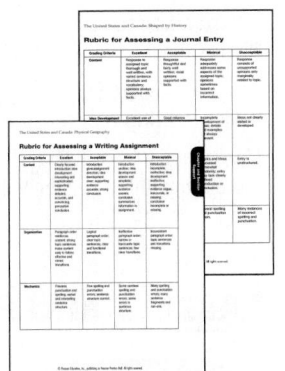

Have students check their own understanding.

Chapter Self-Test

Test Preparation

Assess students' skills and diagnose problems as students begin their study of this region.

Screening Tests and Diagnosing Readiness Tests, AYP Monitoring Assessments, pp. 1–11, 13–63

Section 1 Land and Water

 1.5 periods, .75 block

Social Studies Objectives

1. Learn about the size, location, and population of Europe and Russia.
2. Examine the major landforms of Europe and Russia.
3. Find out about the waterways of Europe and Russia.

Reading/Language Arts Objective

Set a purpose for reading in order to focus on important ideas.

Prepare to Read	**Instructional Resources**	**Differentiated Instruction**
Build Background Knowledge Ask students to preview the section and predict the geographic features they will learn about. **Set a Purpose for Reading** Have students evaluate statements on the *Reading Readiness Guide*. **Preview Key Terms** Teach the section's Key Terms. **Target Reading Skill** Introduce the section's Target Reading Skill of **setting a purpose for reading.**	**All in One Europe and Russia Teaching Resources** L2 Reading Readiness Guide, p. 107 L2 Preview and Set a Purpose, p. 118	**Spanish Reading and Vocabulary Study Guide** L1 Chapter 6, Section 1, pp. 41–42 ELL

Instruct	**Instructional Resources**	**Differentiated Instruction**
Size, Location, and Population Discuss how the size and location of Europe and Russia affect climate and population. **Major Landforms** Discuss the land regions of Europe and Russia. **Target Reading Skill** Review **setting a purpose for reading.** **Waterways of Europe and Russia** Discuss the Rhine and the Volga Rivers.	**All in One Europe and Russia Teaching Resources** L2 Guided Reading and Review, p. 108 L2 Reading Readiness Guide, p. 107 **Europe and Russia Transparencies** L2 Section Reading Support Transparency ER 32 **World Studies Video Program** L2 The Geography of Europe and Russia	**All in One Europe and Russia Teaching Resources** L3 Activity Shop Lab: Tracking the Midnight Sun, pp. 128–129 AR, GT **Teacher's Edition** L3 For Advanced Readers, TE p. 152 L1 For English Language Learners, TE p. 153 **Spanish Support** L2 Guided Reading and Review (Spanish), p. 58 ELL

Assess and Reteach	**Instructional Resources**	**Differentiated Instruction**
Assess Progress Evaluate student comprehension with the section assessment and section quiz. **Reteach** Assign the Reading and Vocabulary Study Guide to help struggling students. **Extend** Extend the lesson by assigning a Small Group Activity.	**All in One Europe and Russia Teaching Resources** L2 Section Quiz, p. 109 L3 Small Group Activity: Europe and Russia Map and Climate Charts, pp. 124–127 Rubric for Assessing a Journal Entry, p. 136 **Reading and Vocabulary Study Guide** L1 Chapter 6, Section 1, pp. 56–58	**Spanish Support** L2 Section Quiz (Spanish), p. 59 ELL

Key

L1 Basic to Average	L3 Average to Advanced	LPR Less Proficient Readers	GT Gifted and Talented
L2 For All Students		AR Advanced Readers	ELL English Language Learners
		SN Special Needs Students	

Section 2 Climate and Vegetation

 2 periods, 1 block (includes Skills for Life)

Social Studies Objectives
1. Find out about the wide range of climates in Europe and Russia.
2. Learn about the major climate regions of Europe and Russia.
3. Examine the natural vegetation regions of Europe and Russia.

Reading/Language Arts Objective
Make predictions about the text to help set a purpose for reading and remember what you read.

Prepare to Read

Build Background Knowledge
Have students compare the climates of Barcelona and Irkutsk to that of their own region.

Set a Purpose for Reading
Have students evaluate statements on the *Reading Readiness Guide*.

Preview Key Terms
Teach the section's Key Terms.

Target Reading Skill
Introduce the section's Target Reading Skill of **predicting**.

Instructional Resources

All in One Europe and Russia Teaching Resources
- **L2** Reading Readiness Guide, p. 111
- **L2** Preview and Predict, p. 119

Differentiated Instruction

Spanish Reading and Vocabulary Study Guide
- **L1** Chapter 6, Section 2, pp. 43–44 ELL

Instruct

A Wide Range of Climates
Discuss how oceans and location affect the climates of Europe and Russia.

Target Reading Skill
Review **predicting**.

Major Climate Regions
Discuss the different climate regions in Europe and Russia.

Natural Vegetation Regions
Discuss different types of vegetation native to Europe and Russia.

Instructional Resources

All in One Europe and Russia Teaching Resources
- **L2** Guided Reading and Review, p. 112
- **L2** Reading Readiness Guide, p. 111

Europe and Russia Transparencies
- **L2** Color Transparency ER 20: Western Europe: Physical-Political
- **L2** Transparency B2: Flow Chart
- **L2** Section Reading Support Transparency ER 33

Differentiated Instruction

All in One Europe and Russia Teaching Resources
- **L3** Doing Searches on the Internet, p. 133 AR, GT
- **L3** Preparing for Presentations, p. 134 AR, GT
- **L3** Book Project: Changing Climates, pp. 77–79 AR, GT
- **L1** Reading a Natural Vegetation Map, p. 130 ELL, LPR, SN
- **L2** Skills for Life, p. 123 AR, GT, LPR, SN

Teacher's Edition
- **L3** For Advanced Readers, TE p. 157
- **L1** For English Language Learners, TE p. 157
- **L3** For Gifted and Talented, TE p. 160
- **L1** For Less Proficient Readers, TE p. 160

Reading and Vocabulary Study Guide
- **L1** Chapter 6, Section 2, pp. 59–61 ELL, LPR, SN

Assess and Reteach

Assess Progress
Evaluate student comprehension with the section assessment and section quiz.

Reteach
Assign the Reading and Vocabulary Study Guide to help struggling students.

Extend
Extend the lesson by assigning an Enrichment activity.

Instructional Resources

All in One Europe and Russia Teaching Resources
- **L2** Section Quiz, p. 113
- **L3** Enrichment, p. 122
  Rubric for Assessing a Writing Assignment, p. 137

Reading and Vocabulary Study Guide
- **L1** Chapter 6, Section 2, pp. 59–61

Differentiated Instruction

Teacher's Edition
- **L1** For Special Needs Students, TE p. 163

Social Studies Skills Tutor CD-ROM
- **L1** Analyzing and Interpreting Special Purpose Maps ELL, LPR, SN

Spanish Support
- **L2** Section Quiz (Spanish), p. 61 ELL

Key
- **L1** Basic to Average
- **L3** Average to Advanced
- **L2** For All Students
- **LPR** Less Proficient Readers
- **AR** Advanced Readers
- **SN** Special Needs Students
- **GT** Gifted and Talented
- **ELL** English Language Learners

Section 3 **Resources and Land Use**

 3.5 periods, 1.75 blocks (includes Chapter Review and Assessment)

Social Studies Objectives
1. Learn about the natural resources of Western Europe.
2. Find out about the natural resources of Eastern Europe.
3. Examine Russia's natural resources.

Reading/Language Arts Objective
Preview and ask questions to help you remember important ideas in the section.

Prepare to Read

Build Background Knowledge
Discuss the importance of soil, water, and fuel.

Set a Purpose for Reading
Have students evaluate statements on the *Reading Readiness Guide.*

Preview Key Terms
Teach the section's Key Terms.

Target Reading Skill
Introduce the section's Target Reading Skill of **previewing and asking questions.**

Instructional Resources

All in One Europe and Russia Teaching Resources
- L2 Reading Readiness Guide, p. 115
- L2 Preview and Ask Questions, p. 120

Differentiated Instruction

Spanish Reading and Vocabulary Study Guide
- L1 Chapter 6, Section 3, pp. 45–46 ELL

Instruct

Resources of Western Europe
Discuss natural resources and where they are found in Western Europe.

Resources of Eastern Europe
Discuss the benefits of having a variety of natural resources, and compare the resources of Eastern and Western Europe.

Resources of Russia
Discuss the challenge of collecting the natural resources of Russia.

Target Reading Skill
Review **previewing and asking questions.**

Instructional Resources

All in One Europe and Russia Teaching Resources
- L2 Guided Reading and Review, p. 116
- L2 Reading Readiness Guide, p. 115
- L3 The Endless Steppe, pp. 131–132

Europe and Russia Transparencies
- L2 Section Reading Support Transparency ER 34

Differentiated Instruction

Teacher's Edition
- L3 For Gifted and Talented, TE p. 167
- L1 For Less Proficient Readers, TE p. 168
- L1 For Special Needs Students, TE p. 168
- L3 For Advanced Readers, TE p. 169

Student Edition on Audio CD
- L1 Chapter 6, Section 3 ELL, LPR, SN

PHSchool.com
- L3 **For:** Environmental and Global Issues: World Oil Reserves
  Web Code: ldd-7104 AR, GT

Assess and Reteach

Assess Progress
Evaluate student comprehension with the section assessment and section quiz.

Reteach
Assign the Reading and Vocabulary Study Guide to help struggling students.

Extend
Extend the lesson by assigning an Internet activity.

Instructional Resources

All in One Europe and Russia Teaching Resources
- L2 Section Quiz, p. 117
- L2 Vocabulary Development, p. 135
- L2 Word Knowledge, p. 121
- L2 Chapter Tests A and B, pp. 138–143

Reading and Vocabulary Study Guide
- L1 Chapter 6, Section 3, pp. 62–64

PHSchool.com
- L3 **For:** Long-Term Integrated Projects: Reporting to an Environmental Conference
  Web Code: ldd-7105

Differentiated Instruction

Spanish Support
- L2 Section Quiz (Spanish), p. 63 ELL
- L2 Chapter Summary (Spanish), p. 64 ELL
- L2 Vocabulary Development (Spanish), p. 65 ELL

Key

L1 Basic to Average	L3 Average to Advanced	
L2 For All Students		

LPR Less Proficient Readers
AR Advanced Readers
SN Special Needs Students

GT Gifted and Talented
ELL English Language Learners

Professional Development

Reading Background

Previewing and Prereading

This chapter's Target Reading Skill asks students to preview each section and set a purpose for reading. Students who do a brief, preliminary reading of complex material are in a strategic position to take control of their learning and comprehension. Previewing helps students consider what they already know about a topic they will be studying and gives some idea of what a text selection is about before they read it. Previewing also helps students identify the text structure and develop a mental framework for ideas to be encountered in the text. This can help them formulate a more realistic reading and study plan. Follow the steps below to teach students how to preview and preread.

1. Tell students that previewing will help them identify the text structure and develop a mental outline of ideas they will encounter in the text.

2. List the various text features you will be previewing in the order in which you would like students to examine them: section title, text headings, introduction, list of Key Terms, questions or tasks in the reading selection, photographs, drawings, maps, charts, and other visuals in the text. Focus students' attention on some of these items, or ask them to look at all of them.

3. Prompt students to reflect after examining various text features. They may ask themselves questions such as: What is this reading selection about? What are some key words I will learn? How should I tackle this reading and divide up the task?

Mapping Word Definitions

Research shows that mapping word definitions can help students develop the ability to investigate word meanings independently and provide elaborated definitions.

Model mapping word definitions using the Key Term *fossil fuel*. Begin by asking students a series of questions: What are some examples of fossil fuels? *(oil, natural gas)* What are these used for? *(providing power for automobiles and other modes of transportation, heating homes)* Where are these found? *(deep inside Earth)*

Finally, develop a graphic organizer with information about the term *fossil fuel*:

the definition (in their own words)	*a source of energy that forms from ancient plant and animal remains*
a synonym	*petroleum*
a sentence using the word	*Fossil fuel is an important natural resource because it is used to provide energy throughout Earth.*

World Studies Background

Urban Development in Europe

Many European cities developed as Roman colonies and still reflect the typical Roman layout. Roman cities were often concentrated around a public gathering place. On the edge of this forum were the main commercial, governmental, and religious buildings. The streets usually emerged from this center in a grid design.

Siberia

The name of this vast region that lies mainly in Russia comes from a Tatar word meaning "sleeping land," in reference to the long, harsh winters during which much of the vegetation lies dormant.

Parts of Siberia have experienced temperatures as low as –90° Fahrenheit (–68° C). Because of its remoteness, Siberia has been used as a place of exile for criminals and political prisoners.

European Cheese

Many regions in Europe make local cheeses from the milk of sheep, goats, and cows. In the caves of Roquefort, France, cheese is left to gather the bacteria that give it a distinctive flavor and coloring. In Italy, provolone cheese is heated and kneaded. In Greece, feta cheese is cured in brine, giving it a salty flavor. In Holland, Gouda and Edam cheeses are preserved by a wax coating. True Gouda and Edam have the word "Holland" stamped on the rind.

Infoplease® provides a wealth of useful information for the classroom. You can use this resource to strengthen your background on the subjects covered in this chapter. Have students visit this advertising-free site as a starting point for projects requiring research.

Use Web code **ldd-7100** for **Infoplease®**.

Guiding Questions

Remind students about the Guiding Questions introduced at the beginning of this section.

Section 1 refers to **Guiding Question** ➊
What are the main physical features of Europe and Russia? *(Europe is a small continent made up of many small countries, while Russia is the largest country in the world. Both have mountains, plains, highlands, plateaus, and major waterways.)*

Section 2 refers to **Guiding Question** ➊
What are the main physical features of Europe and Russia? *(Europe and Russia have a wide range of climate regions; climates are affected by nearness to the ocean, the North Atlantic Current, and mountains. Europe and Russia also have diverse vegetation. Both are heavily forested, but plant life varies by climate.)*

Section 3 refers to **Guiding Question** ➊
What are the main physical features of Europe and Russia? *(Europe's natural resources include fertile soil used for farming, water used for drinking and creating hydroelectric power, and fuels used for producing energy. Russia has large fuel and forest reserves. Fish are an important resource, as is water, used for hydroelectric energy. However, it is difficult for Russia to transport and take advantage of its resources due to its size and climate.)*

🎯 Target Reading Skill

In this chapter, students will learn and apply the reading process. Use the following worksheets to help students practice the skill.

 Europe and Russia Teaching Resources, *Preview and Set a Purpose,* p. 118; *Preview and Predict,* p. 119; *Preview and Ask Questions,* p. 120

Chapter Preview

This chapter will introduce you to the geography of Europe and Russia and show how geography affects the people who live there.

Section 1
Land and Water

Section 2
Climate and Vegetation

Section 3
Resources and Land Use

🎯 **Target Reading Skill**

Reading Process In this chapter you will use previewing to help you understand and remember what you read.

▶ Waves splash against the rocky coast of Cornwall in southern England.

146 Europe and Russia

Bibliography

For the Teacher
Geography of the World. Dorling Kindersley Publishing, 2003.
Milner-Gulland, R.R., et al. *Cultural Atlas of Russia and the Former Soviet Union.* Checkmark Books, 1998.
Recht, Roland. *The Rhine.* Thames & Hudson, 2001.

For the Student
L1 Boraas, Tracey. *England (Countries and Cultures).* Bridgestone Books, 2002.
L2 Bramwell, Martyn. *Europe: The World in Maps.* Lerner Publications Company, 2000.
L3 Murrell, Kathleen Berton. *Eyewitness: Russia.* Dorling Kindersley Publishing, 2000.

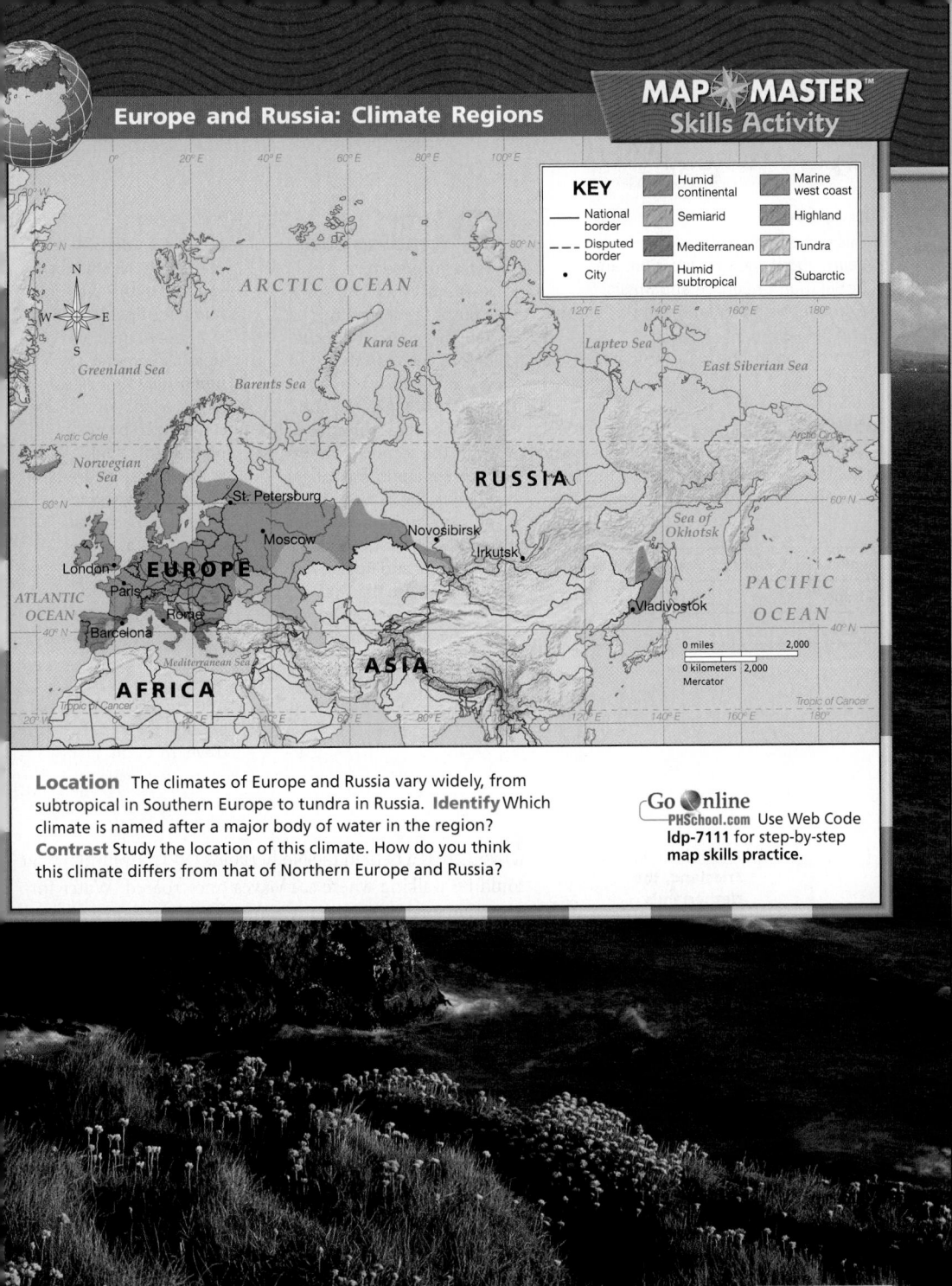

Europe and Russia: Climate Regions

KEY

— National border	Humid continental
- - - Disputed border	Semiarid
• City	Mediterranean
	Humid subtropical
	Marine west coast
	Highland
	Tundra
	Subarctic

ARCTIC OCEAN

Greenland Sea

Norwegian Sea

Kara Sea

Laptev Sea

East Siberian Sea

Barents Sea

Sea of Okhotsk

PACIFIC OCEAN

RUSSIA

St. Petersburg

Moscow

Novosibirsk

Irkutsk

Vladivostok

London

EUROPE

Paris

Rome

Barcelona

Mediterranean Sea

ASIA

AFRICA

ATLANTIC OCEAN

Arctic Circle

Tropic of Cancer

0 miles 2,000
0 kilometers 2,000
Mercator

Location The climates of Europe and Russia vary widely, from subtropical in Southern Europe to tundra in Russia. **Identify** Which climate is named after a major body of water in the region? **Contrast** Study the location of this climate. How do you think this climate differs from that of Northern Europe and Russia?

Go Online PHSchool.com Use Web Code ldp-7111 for step-by-step map skills practice.

Chapter 6 **147**

- Direct students' attention to the map of Europe and Russia. Have students trace the borders of Europe and Russia with their fingers. Point out that Russia is much larger than Europe, and extends much farther north.

- Ask students to create a chart with two columns and label the columns "Climates of Europe" and "Climates of Russia." Have students use the map to list the climates of each region in the appropriate column.

Go Online PHSchool.com Students may practice their map skills using the interactive online version of this map.

Using the Visual   L2

Reach Into Your Background Draw students' attention to the caption accompanying the picture on pp. 146–147. Tell students that Cornwall is a county in southwestern England and is located on a peninsula. Point out that Cornwall's climate is greatly affected by its proximity to the sea; high winds, sea mists, and rainfall are common. Ask students to brainstorm ways that geography affects their own region. Conduct an Idea Wave (TE, p. T35) to elicit responses.

Answers

MAP MASTER Skills Activity **Identify** Mediterranean **Contrast** Because the Mediterranean climate is closer to the Equator, it is probably warmer than the climates of northern Europe and Russia.

Chapter Resources

Teaching Resources
Letter Home, p. 105
L2 Vocabulary Development, p. 135
L2 Skills for Life, p. 123
L2 Chapter Tests A and B, pp. 138–143

Spanish Support
Spanish Letter Home, p. 57
L2 Spanish Chapter Summary, p. 64
L2 Spanish Vocabulary Development, p. 65

Media and Technology
L1 Student Edition on Audio CD
L1 Guided Reading Audiotapes, English and Spanish
L2 Social Studies Skills Tutor CD-ROM
ExamView® Test Bank CD-ROM

PRENTICE HALL
Presentation EXPRESS™
Teach · Connect · Inspire

Teach this chapter's content using the PresentationExpress™ CD-ROM including:
- slide shows
- transparencies
- interactive maps and media
- *ExamView®* QuickTake Presenter

Objectives

Social Studies

1. Learn about the size, location, and population of Europe and Russia.
2. Examine the major landforms of Europe and Russia.
3. Find out about the waterways of Europe and Russia.

Reading/Language Arts

Set a purpose for reading in order to focus on important ideas.

Prepare to Read

Build Background Knowledge **L2**

Tell students that they will be reading about Europe and Russia's size, land, and bodies of water. Ask students to preview the section's headings and visuals. Have them predict the geographic features they expect to learn about, and conduct an Idea Wave (TE, p. T35) to generate a list. Then encourage students to share information they may already know about these features.

Set a Purpose for Reading **L2**

- Preview the Objectives.

- Read each statement in the *Reading Readiness Guide* aloud. Ask students to mark the statements true or false.

    All in One **Europe and Russia Teaching Resources,** *Reading Readiness Guide,* p. 107

- Have students discuss the statements in pairs or groups of four, then mark their worksheets again. Use the Numbered Heads participation strategy (TE, p. T36) to call on students to share their groups' perspectives.

Vocabulary Builder
Preview Key Terms **L2**

Pronounce each Key Term, then ask the students to say the word with you. Provide a simple explanation such as, "A navigable river is wide and deep enough for a ship to pass through."

Section **1**

Land and Water

Prepare to Read

Objectives

In this section you will
1. Learn about the size, location, and population of Europe and Russia.
2. Examine the major landforms of Europe and Russia.
3. Find out about the waterways of Europe and Russia.

Taking Notes

As you read this section, look for the main ideas about land and water. Copy the table below and record your findings in it.

Region	Landforms	Bodies of Water
Europe		
Russia		

🎯 Target Reading Skill

Set a Purpose for Reading When you set a purpose for reading, you give yourself a focus. Before you read this section, look at the headings, the maps, and the photographs to see what the section is about. Then set a purpose for reading the section. Your purpose might be to find out about the geography of Europe and Russia. As you read, use the Taking Notes table to help you achieve your purpose.

Key Terms

- **population density** (pahp yuh LAY shun DEN suh tee) *n.* the average number of people living in a square mile or a square kilometer
- **peninsula** (puh NIN suh luh) *n.* a land area nearly surrounded by water
- **plateau** (pla TOH) *n.* a large raised area of mostly level land bordered on one or more sides by steep slopes or cliffs
- **tributary** (TRIB yoo tehr ee) *n.* a river or stream that flows into a larger river
- **navigable** (NAV ih guh bul) *adj.* wide and deep enough for ships to travel through

A windmill in Friesland, the Netherlands

148 Europe and Russia

If you cross a field in the Netherlands (NETH ur lundz), you could be walking where sea waves once roared. Water formerly covered more than two fifths of the country. Centuries ago, the people of the Netherlands began an effort to create land where there was water. They built long walls called dikes to hold back the water. They pumped the water into canals that empty into the North Sea. In this way, they created polders (POHL durz), or patches of new land.

The polders that lie below sea level are always filling with water. Netherlanders must continually pump them out. Keeping the polders dry is important. Like much of Europe, the country's many people must find living space on a small amount of land. The richest farmlands and some cities in the Netherlands are located on polders.

🎯 Target Reading Skill **L2**

Set a Purpose for Reading Direct students' attention to the Target Reading Skill. Tell them that setting a purpose will give them a focus as they read.

Model setting a purpose for reading by thinking aloud as you preview the headings and photographs on p. 149: "The information on this page tells me that I will learn about land and people in Europe and Russia. My purpose for reading this page is to learn about the size, location, and population of that area."

Give students *Preview and Set a Purpose.* Have them complete the activity in groups.

All in One **Europe and Russia Teaching Resources,** *Preview and Set a Purpose,* p. 118

Size, Location, and Population

Europe and Russia are parts of Eurasia, the world's largest landmass. This landmass is made up of two continents, Europe and Asia. The country of Russia stretches over both continents. About one fourth of Russia is in Europe; the rest is in Asia. The Ural (YOOR ul) Mountains divide Europe from Asia.

Location Trace a latitude line from the United States to Eurasia in the map titled World: Political in the Atlas. You will see that much of Europe and nearly all of Russia are farther north than is the United States. Berlin, the German capital, lies at about the same latitude as the southern tip of Canada's Hudson Bay.

A Small Continent With Many People Europe is a small continent. Only Australia is smaller. While Europe lacks size, it has 44 different countries. Many are the size of an average state in the United States. Russia, though, is the largest country in the world. It is almost twice the size of the United States.

Most of the countries of Europe have a much higher population density than other countries in the world. **Population density** is the average number of people living in a square mile or a square kilometer. The Netherlands has more than 1,236 people per square mile (477 people per sq kilometer). By comparison, the world average is about 106 people per square mile (42 people per sq kilometer). Russia, on the other hand, has a much lower population density—only about 22 people per square mile (9 people per sq kilometer).

✓ **Reading Check** What is the largest landmass in the world?

Rural Regions of Europe and Russia
The Ural Mountains, shown at the bottom, mark the dividing line between Europe and Russia. The inset photo shows a church situated in the highlands of northern Scotland. **Analyze Images** *Use clues from the photographs to estimate which of these places has a greater population density.*

Vocabulary Builder

Use the information below to teach students this section's high-use words.

High-Use Word	Definition and Sample Sentence
landmass, p. 149	*n.* a large area of land Africa is the world's second largest **landmass**.
enable, p. 150	*v.* to allow; to make possible The loan **enabled** Cliff to attend college.
level, p. 151	*adj.* flat; horizontal We looked for a **level** spot to pitch our tent.
link, p. 153	*v.* to join together The two highways **link** and become one in the northern part of the state.

Size, Location, and Population L2

Guided Instruction

■ **Vocabulary Builder** Clarify the high-use word **landmass** before reading.

■ Read Size, Location, and Population using the Choral Reading strategy (TE, p. T34).

■ Have students describe Europe and Russia's size and location. *(Eurasia is made up of the continents of Europe and Asia. Europe is a small continent with many small countries. Russia is the largest country in the world.)*

■ Ask students **Which natural feature divides Europe from Asia?** *(the Ural Mountains)* **Is Russia in Europe, Asia, or both?** *(Both—about one fourth of Russia is in Europe; the rest is in Asia.)*

■ Ask students to predict how the climate of Europe and Russia might compare to that of the United States. *(The climate of Europe and Russia is probably colder than that of the United States because Europe and Russia are mainly located farther north. Some of Europe probably has a similar climate to that of the United States.)* Tell students that they will learn more about the region's climate in the next section.

Independent Practice

Ask students to create the Taking Notes graphic organizer. Have them fill in the Landforms column with information about the Ural Mountains.

Monitor Progress

Circulate among students to make sure they are filling in the correct details. Provide assistance as needed.

Answers

Analyze Images Since the photo of the highlands of northern Scotland shows a church, and the photo of the Ural mountains does not show any buildings, the highlands probably have a higher population density.

✓ **Reading Check** Eurasia

Major Landforms

Guided Instruction

- **Vocabulary Builder** Clarify the high-use words **enable** and **level** before reading.
- Read Major Landforms with students. Circulate and make sure they can answer the Reading Check question.
- Ask students **Why is the continent of Europe described as a peninsula?** (*Europe is a peninsula because it is a body of land nearly surrounded by water.*)
- Ask students **What effect have Western Europe's harbors had on its economy?** (*Western Europe's harbors have helped it to become a world leader in the shipping industry.*)
- Have students look at the map on this page. Point out that although there are no physical barriers between Russia and other European countries, there are some barriers between other countries on the continent. Ask **Why might physical barriers impede travel today less than they may have in the past?** (*Today, people can travel by airplane. Roads have been built through some mountains, allowing cars to travel over them. In the past, people had to travel by foot or on animals, so physical barriers such as mountains were difficult to cross.*)

Major Landforms

Study the shape of Europe on the map below. The continent of Europe forms a **peninsula** (puh NIN suh luh), or a body of land nearly surrounded by water. The European peninsula juts out into the Atlantic Ocean. Europe also has many smaller peninsulas with bays. These bays include harbors, or sheltered bodies of water where ships dock. Good harbors enabled Western European countries to become world leaders in the shipping industry.

Now look at the small physical map of Russia on page 142. Notice how much of Russia lies on the Arctic Ocean. For most of the year, this body of water is frozen and cannot be used for shipping. Between Russia and the other countries of Europe, however, there are no physical barriers. Movement between these two regions has always been easy.

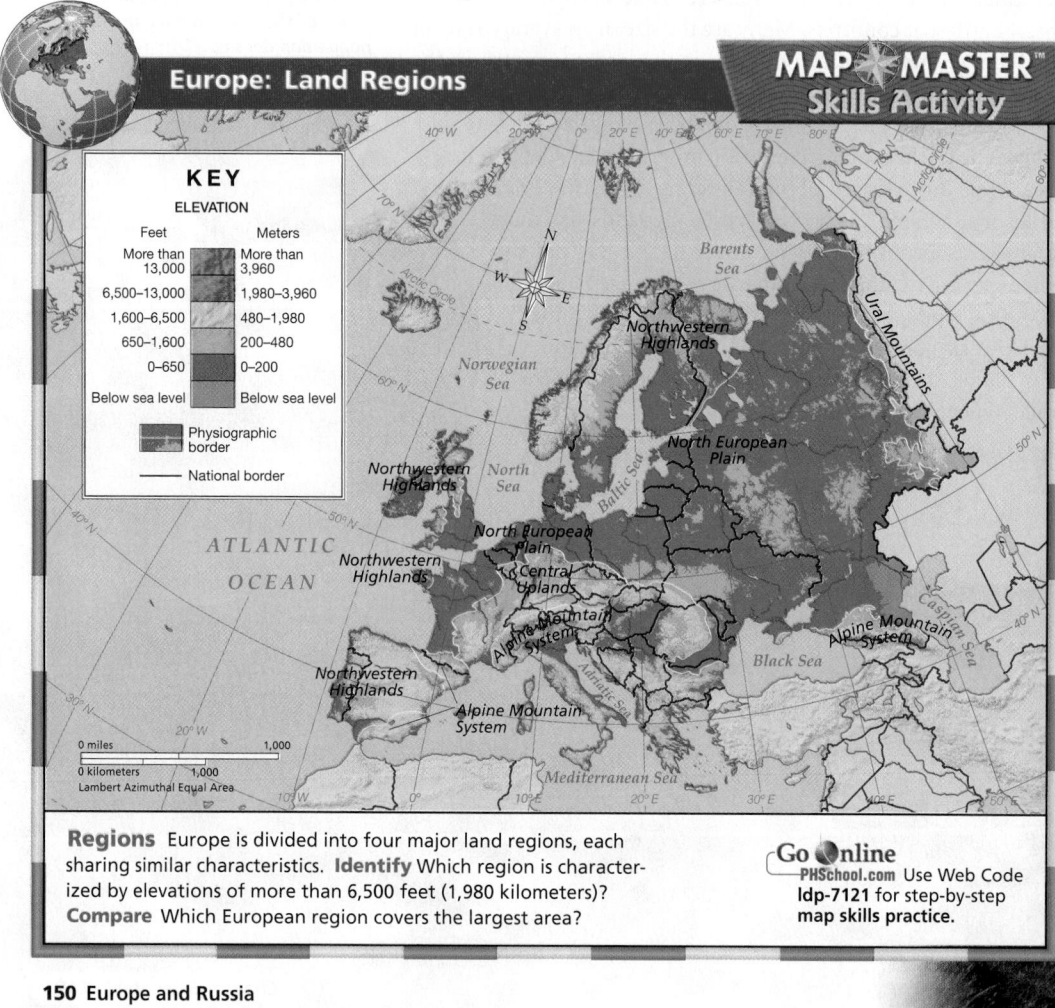

MAP MASTER Skills Activity

Europe: Land Regions

KEY — ELEVATION

Feet	Meters
More than 13,000	More than 3,960
6,500–13,000	1,980–3,960
1,600–6,500	480–1,980
650–1,600	200–480
0–650	0–200
Below sea level	Below sea level

Physiographic border
National border

0 miles 1,000
0 kilometers 1,000
Lambert Azimuthal Equal Area

Regions Europe is divided into four major land regions, each sharing similar characteristics. **Identify** Which region is characterized by elevations of more than 6,500 feet (1,980 kilometers)? **Compare** Which European region covers the largest area?

Go Online PHSchool.com Use Web Code **ldp-7121** for step-by-step map skills practice.

150 Europe and Russia

Answers

MAP MASTER Skills Activity **Identify** an area of the Alpine Mountain System east of the Black Sea **Compare** North European Plain

Go Online PHSchool.com Students may practice their map skills using the interactive online version of this map.

Skills for Life — Skills Mini Lesson

Using the Cartographer's Tools

1. Teach the skill by pointing out that there are certain elements common to most maps, such as a scale and compass rose.
2. Have students practice the skill by using the compass rose to determine where the North European Plain is located in relation to the Alpine Mountain System.

(*It is northeast of the Alpine Mountain System.*)

3. Have students apply the skill by answering this question: Which land region extends the farthest east, the Central Uplands or the North European Plain? (*the North European Plain*)

150 *Europe and Russia*

Plains, Uplands, and Mountains of Europe Within the peninsula of Europe are four major land regions: the Northwestern Highlands, the North European Plain, the Central Uplands, and the Alpine Mountain System. Find these regions on the map on page 150.

The Northwestern Highlands stretch across the far north of Europe. It is a region of old mountains that have been worn down by wind and weather. Because they have steep slopes and thin soil, they are not good for farming, and few people live there. But the forests there support a successful timber industry. And people there raise goats and sheep, especially in Spain and Scotland.

Notice that the North European Plain covers more than half of Europe. These plains includes most of the European part of Russia and reach all the way to France. This region has the most productive farmland and the largest cities in Europe.

In the center of southern Europe are the Central Uplands. The Central Uplands are a region of highlands, made up of mountains and plateaus. **Plateaus** (pla TOHZ) are large raised areas of mostly level land bordered on one or more sides by steep slopes or cliffs. Most of the land there is rocky and not good for farming. But the uplands have other uses, including mining, industry, and tourism.

The mountains of the Alpine Mountain System stretch from France to the Balkan Peninsula. They include the Alps, the highest mountains in the system. Some families do small-scale farming in the mountain valleys and meadows of the Alps.

Learn about the geography of Europe and Russia.

Show students *The Geography of Europe and Russia.*
Ask **What is the main reason for Russia's low population density?** (*Large parts of the country have a harsh, cold climate.*)

Guided Instruction (continued)

- Ask students **What are Europe's four major land regions?** (*the Northwestern Highlands, the North European Plain, the Central Uplands, and the Alpine Mountain System*)

- Ask students **In which part of Europe are the Northwestern Highlands located?** (*They stretch across the far north of Europe.*) Have students discuss why this region is not good for farming. (*The Northwestern Highlands have steep slopes and thin soil.*)

- Ask students **Which land region has the most productive farmland and the largest cities in Europe?** (*the North European Plain*)

- Ask students **How do people use the land in the Alps?** (*Some land in the Alps is used for small-scale farming.*) Have students discuss why they think only small-scale farming takes place in the Alps. (*Students' responses may vary, but should reflect the understanding that large-scale farming is difficult in mountainous terrain.*)

Traveling in the Alps
A train carries people between alpine villages in southern Switzerland. The country has an extensive rail system. **Infer** *What geographical challenges does a nation like Switzerland face when building a rail system?*

Background: Links Across Place

The Alps When most people think of the mountains that form the Alps, they think of Switzerland and perhaps France, Italy, Germany, or Austria. In fact, the Alps stretch across a total of nine European countries, including Slovenia, Croatia, Bosnia and Herzegovina, and Serbia and Montenegro.

Major rivers that originate in the peaks of Alpine mountains include the Rhône, the Rhine, the Po, and a number of tributaries from the Danube River. As these rivers wind their way through Europe, they eventually drain into the Adriatic, Black, North, and Mediterranean seas.

Answer

Infer Possible answer: It is probably difficult to build a railroad over mountainous terrain.

Guided Instruction (continued)

- Ask students to name Russia's two largest cities. *(Moscow and St. Petersburg)*

- Ask students **Why do you think more people live in the North European Plain than in other regions of Russia?** *(Possible answer: The North European Plain has a milder climate than the rest of Russia.)*

Independent Practice

Have students continue filling in the table with details about Europe and Russia's landforms. Briefly model how to identify which details to record.

Monitor Progress

Provide assistance to individuals as needed as they add landforms to their tables.

Making a Living in Siberia
The nomadic Chukchi people make their living by herding reindeer in the uplands of northeastern Siberia. The name *Chukchi* means "rich in reindeer." **Infer** *Why does it make sense for the Chukchi to be nomadic—moving from place to place—rather than to live in fixed settlements?*

Plains, Uplands, and Mountains of Russia Europe and western Russia share the North European Plain. Russia's largest cities, Moscow (MAHS kow) and St. Petersburg, are in this region. Most of Russia's industries are there, too. More people live in this region than in any other part of Russia.

Where the plains end, the uplands begin. On the eastern border of the North European Plain, you will find the Ural Mountains. To the east of the Urals is the Asian part of Russia—a region known as Siberia (sy BIHR ee uh). This region makes up about 75 percent of Russian territory, but the climate is so harsh that only about 20 percent of Russia's people live there.

If you continue east into Siberia from the Ural Mountains, you will cross the largest plain in the world—the West Siberian Plain. This low, marshy plain covers more than one million square miles (2.59 million sq kilometers). More than half of it rises only 328 feet (100 meters) above sea level. Farther east is the Central Siberian Plateau, which slopes upward from the West Siberian Plain. If you travel still farther east, you will find the East Siberian Uplands, which include more than 20 active volcanoes among the rugged mountains and plateaus.

√ **Reading Check** **Where are most of Russia's industries located?**

152 Europe and Russia

Answers

Infer Possible answer: The Chukchi probably have to move often to find food for their reindeer herds.

√ **Reading Check** Most of Russia's industries are located in the North European Plain.

Waterways of Europe and Russia

Rivers and lakes provide the people who live in Europe and Russia with water and transportation.

Major Rivers High in the Alps in Switzerland (SWIT sur lund), melting glaciers create two streams that combine to form the Rhine River. Winding through forests and plains, the Rhine makes a journey of 865 miles (1,392 kilometers), from Switzerland to the Netherlands and the North Sea. The Rhine River is connected to the farthest reaches of Western Europe by canals and **tributaries** (TRIB yoo tehr eez). A tributary is a river or stream that flows into a larger river.

Another major waterway is the Danube (DAN yoob) River. The Danube is Europe's second-longest river. It begins in the Black Forest region of western Germany. It travels 1,770 miles (2,850 kilometers) to the Black Sea of southeastern Europe. Along the way, the Danube passes through nine countries.

The longest river in Europe is Russia's Volga (VOHL guh) River. It flows 2,291 miles (3,687 kilometers) through western Russia and empties into the Caspian (KASP ee un) Sea. Canals link the Volga and its tributaries to the Baltic Sea and other seas. Unfortunately, the Volga freezes along much of its length for three months of each year. During the winter months, it is not **navigable** (NAV ih guh bul), or clear enough for ships to travel through.

Set a Purpose for Reading
If your purpose is to learn about the geography of Europe and Russia, how do these paragraphs help you meet your goal?

A Historical Waterway
The Rhine flows past old castles, mills, and factories along its course through Germany. Just as they did in ancient times, ships today use the river to transport goods. **Analyze Images** What advantages would this location have given the people who settled here?

Differentiated Instruction

For English Language Learners `L1`
Make the meanings of Key Terms and high-use words as concrete as possible by linking each to an object, photo, drawing, or movement. For instance, to demonstrate the word *navigable*, set up several desks and chairs so that there is enough space between them for students to walk through. Then move the desks closer together so that students cannot squeeze through to demonstrate a path that is not navigable.

Target Reading Skill `L2`

Set a Purpose for Reading As a follow up, ask students to answer the Target Reading Skill question in the Student Edition. (*The paragraphs describe Europe and Russia's major rivers, which are an important part of the geography of Europe and Russia.*)

Waterways of Europe and Russia `L2`

Guided Instruction

- **Vocabulary Builder** Clarify the high-use word **link** before reading.

- Read Waterways of Europe and Russia with students.

- Ask students **Where does the Rhine River begin and end?** (*It begins high in the Alps in Switzerland and flows to the Netherlands, where it empties into the North Sea.*)

- Have students compare and contrast the Rhine and Volga rivers. (*Both rivers have canals and tributaries and empty into the sea. Both rivers are long, although the Volga is longer. Both rivers serve as trade routes, although the Volga freezes for three months each year and during that time it is not navigable.*)

Independent Practice

Have students complete the graphic organizer by filling in details about the waterways of Europe and Russia.

Monitor Progress

- Show *Section Reading Support Transparency ER 32* and ask students to check their graphic organizers individually. Go over key concepts and clarify key vocabulary as needed.

  📖 **Europe and Russia Transparencies,** *Section Reading Support Transparency ER 32*

- Tell students to fill in the last column of the *Reading Readiness Guide.* Probe for what they learned that confirms or invalidates each statement.

  All in One **Europe and Russia Teaching Resources,** *Reading Readiness Guide,* p. 107

Answer

Analyze Images They were located on a major trade route, so they would have had access to goods from many places and could have been able to prosper through trade.

Assess and Reteach

Assess Progress L2
Have students complete the Section Assessment. Administer the *Section Quiz*.

All in One Europe and Russia Teaching Resources, *Section Quiz,* p. 109

Reteach L1
If students need more instruction, have them read this section in the Reading and Vocabulary Study Guide.

📖 Chapter 6, Section 1, **Eastern Hemisphere Reading and Vocabulary Study Guide,** pp. 56–58

Extend L3
Have students learn more about the physical geography of Europe and Russia by completing the *Small Group Activity: Europe and Russia Map and Climate Charts.* Have gifted and talented and special needs students work together in small groups to complete the activity.

All in One Europe and Russia Teaching Resources, *Small Group Activity: Europe and Russia Map and Climate Charts,* pp. 124–127

Answers

Analyze Images No, the river appears to be frozen.

✓ Reading Check the Volga River

Section 1 Assessment

Key Terms
Students' sentences should reflect knowledge of each Key Term.

⟳ **Target Reading Skill**
Answers will vary, but should reflect that having a purpose for reading helped students to focus on the main ideas of the section.

Comprehension and Critical Thinking
1. (a) Russia **(b)** Europe is a small continent with many small countries, while Russia is the largest country in the world.

2. (a) the Northwestern Highlands, the North European Plain, the Central Uplands, and the Alpine Mountain System **(b)** the North European Plain, the Ural Mountains, the West Siberian Plain, the Central Siberian Plateau, and the East Siberian Uplands **(c)** Possible responses: Much of the land in the Northwestern Highlands and the Central Uplands is not suitable for farming, so most

A Seasonal Harbor
Ships wait in the harbor of Nizhny Novgorod, Russia, on the Volga River. **Analyze Images** *Is it likely that the river was navigable at the time the photo was taken?*

Lakes Though Europe is criss-crossed by rivers, it contains few lakes compared to other regions. Russia, in contrast, has a huge number of lakes, both large and small. The world's largest fresh-water lake is found in Russia. Called Lake Baikal (by KAHL), it is located in southern Russia. Lake Baikal is nearly 400 miles long and has an average width of 30 miles. It is also the world's deepest lake, with some parts reaching 5,315 feet (1,620 meters). Lake Baikal contains about one fifth of Earth's fresh water and is home to hundreds of animal and plant species. In fact, the Russian word *baikal* means "rich lake."

✓ Reading Check **What is the longest river in Europe?**

★ Section 1 Assessment

Key Terms
Review the key terms at the beginning of this section. Use each term in a sentence that explains its meaning.

⟳ **Target Reading Skill**
How did having a purpose for reading help you understand important ideas in this section?

Comprehension and Critical Thinking
1. (a) Locate Which country is located on both the continents of Europe and Asia?

(b) Compare and Contrast How does the land size of Europe differ from the land size of Russia?
2. (a) Name What are the four major land regions of Europe?
(b) Identify What are the major land regions of Russia?
(c) Draw Conclusions How have physical features affected life in Europe and Russia?
3. (a) Explain Why is the Volga River in Russia not navigable year-round?
(b) Identify Effects How might Russia's industries be affected by ships not being able to travel on the rivers all year long?

Writing Activity
Write an entry in your journal describing what you learned about the landforms and waterways of Europe or Russia.

> **Writing Tip** Remember that writing in a journal is writing you do for yourself. In a journal, you can let your ideas flow without stopping to correct your writing.

154 Europe and Russia

---

farming is done in the North European Plain; frozen land and water in northern Russia limit settlement, industry, and movement; the rocky land in the Central Uplands favors grazing over farming.

3. (a) The Volga River is not navigable for three months of the year when much of it freezes over. **(b)** Possible response: Industries may not be able to make much money during the months in which they are unable to ship goods.

Writing Activity
Use the *Rubric for Assessing a Journal Entry* to evaluate students' journals.

All in One Europe and Russia Teaching Resources, *Rubric for Assessing a Journal Entry,* p. 136

Go Online PHSchool.com Typing in the Web code when prompted will bring students to detailed instructions for this activity.

Climate and Vegetation

Prepare to Read

Objectives
In this section you will
1. Find out about the wide range of climates in Europe and Russia.
2. Learn about the major climate regions of Europe and Russia.
3. Examine the natural vegetation regions of Europe and Russia.

Taking Notes
As you read this section, look for details about factors that affect climate and vegetation. Copy the flowchart below, and write each detail under the correct heading.

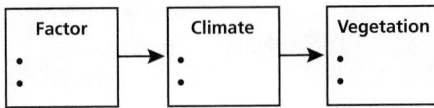

Factor	Climate	Vegetation
• •	• •	• •

Target Reading Skill
Predict Making predictions about the text helps you set a purpose for reading and helps you remember what you read. Before you begin, preview the section by looking at the headings, photographs, charts, and maps. Then predict what the text might discuss about climate and vegetation. As you read this section, connect what you read to your prediction. If what you learn doesn't support your prediction, change your prediction.

Key Terms
- **rain shadow** (rayn SHAD oh) *n.* the area on the dry, sheltered side of a mountain, which receives little rainfall
- **steppes** (steps) *n.* the grasslands of fertile soil suitable for farming in Russia
- **tundra** (TUN druh) *n.* a cold, dry, treeless region covered with snow for most of the year
- **permafrost** (PUR muh frawst) *n.* a permanently frozen layer of ground below the top layer of soil

It is February in Barcelona (bahr suh LOH nuh), Spain. Twelve-year-old Pablo wakes up to the sun streaming through his bedroom window. It's another comfortable day, and the temperature is already 52°F (11°C). Pablo dresses quickly in jeans and a t-shirt and eats a breakfast of thick hot chocolate and *churros*, twisted loops of fried dough. He wants to go out and play soccer with his friends on this sunny Saturday morning.

At the very same moment, it is late afternoon in Irkutsk (ihr KOOTSK), a city in southern Siberia. Anya (AHN yuh) returns home from a day of cross-country skiing. She takes off her fur hat, gloves, boots, ski pants, and coat. The day has been sunny but cold, with an average temperature of −15°F (−26°C). Now Anya warms up with a dinner of *pelmeny* (PEL muh nee), chicken broth with meat-filled dumplings.

Boys in Spain (right) and in Siberia (below)

Objectives

Social Studies
1. Find out about the wide range of climates in Europe and Russia.
2. Learn about the major climate regions of Europe and Russia.
3. Examine the natural vegetation regions of Europe and Russia.

Reading/Language Arts
Make predictions about the text to help set a purpose for reading and remember what you read.

Prepare to Read

Build Background Knowledge   L2
Use the Think-Write-Pair-Share participation strategy (TE, p. T36) to structure the following activity. Ask students to describe the climate where they live. Then have students read the text on this page about the children in Barcelona and Irkutsk. Encourage students to summarize what this passage tells them about the variety of climates found in Europe and Russia. Ask students to compare the climates in Barcelona and Irkutsk in February to their own climate.

Set a Purpose for Reading   L2
- Preview the Objectives.
- Read each statement in the *Reading Readiness Guide* aloud. Ask students to mark the statements true or false.

    All in One Europe and Russia Teaching Resources, *Reading Readiness Guide,* p. 111

- Have students discuss the statements in pairs or groups of four, then mark their worksheets again. Use the Numbered Heads participation strategy (TE, p. T36) to call on students to share their group's perspectives.

Vocabulary Builder
Preview Key Terms   L2
Pronounce each Key Term, then ask the students to say the term with you. Provide a simple explanation such as, "Some places are so cold that there is a layer of ground called permafrost that is frozen all the time."

Target Reading Skill   L2

Predict Point out the Target Reading Skill. Tell students that predicting will help them refine their purpose for reading and remember what they read.

Model predicting by previewing the headings and map on p. 156. Use the previewing process to make a prediction about what students will learn on this page: "I predict we will learn about various climates

and how the ocean affects them." Then tell students that they should connect and compare what they read to their predictions.

Give students *Preview and Predict.* Have them complete the activity in groups.

All in One Europe and Russia Teaching Resources, *Preview and Predict,* p. 119

Instruct

A Wide Range of Climates

L2

Guided Instruction

- **Vocabulary Builder** Clarify the high-use word **dramatic** before reading.

- Have students use the Paragraph Shrinking strategy (TE, p. T34) to read A Wide Range of Climates. Circulate throughout the classroom to ensure that individuals are able to answer the Reading Check question.

- Ask students **How do oceans affect climate?** (*Areas near an ocean or sea have mild weather, while areas farther from the ocean have more extreme weather.*)

- Have students describe the impact of the North Atlantic Current on climate in much of northwestern Europe. (*The North Atlantic Current carries warm water from the Gulf of Mexico to northwestern Europe and warms winds blowing across the Atlantic Ocean. The warm water and wind bring mild weather to much of northwestern Europe.*)

Achill Island, Ireland

A Wide Range of Climates

Barcelona, where Pablo lives, lies on the Mediterranean Sea. There, the summers are hot and dry, and the winters are mild. In Irkutsk, Anya's home, summers are short, and the winters are long and very cold. Temperatures in winter can drop to −50°F (−45°C). Snow covers the ground for about six months of the year.

How Oceans Affect Climate The two cities' distances from an ocean or a sea help explain their climate. Areas that are near an ocean or a sea have milder weather year-round than areas at the same latitude that are far from an ocean or sea. Look at the map below and find the Gulf Stream. Notice that it becomes the North Atlantic Current as it crosses the Atlantic Ocean. This powerful ocean current carries warm water from the tropical waters of the Gulf of Mexico to northwestern Europe. It also warms winds blowing from the west across the Atlantic Ocean. The warm waters and winds bring mild weather to much of northwestern Europe.

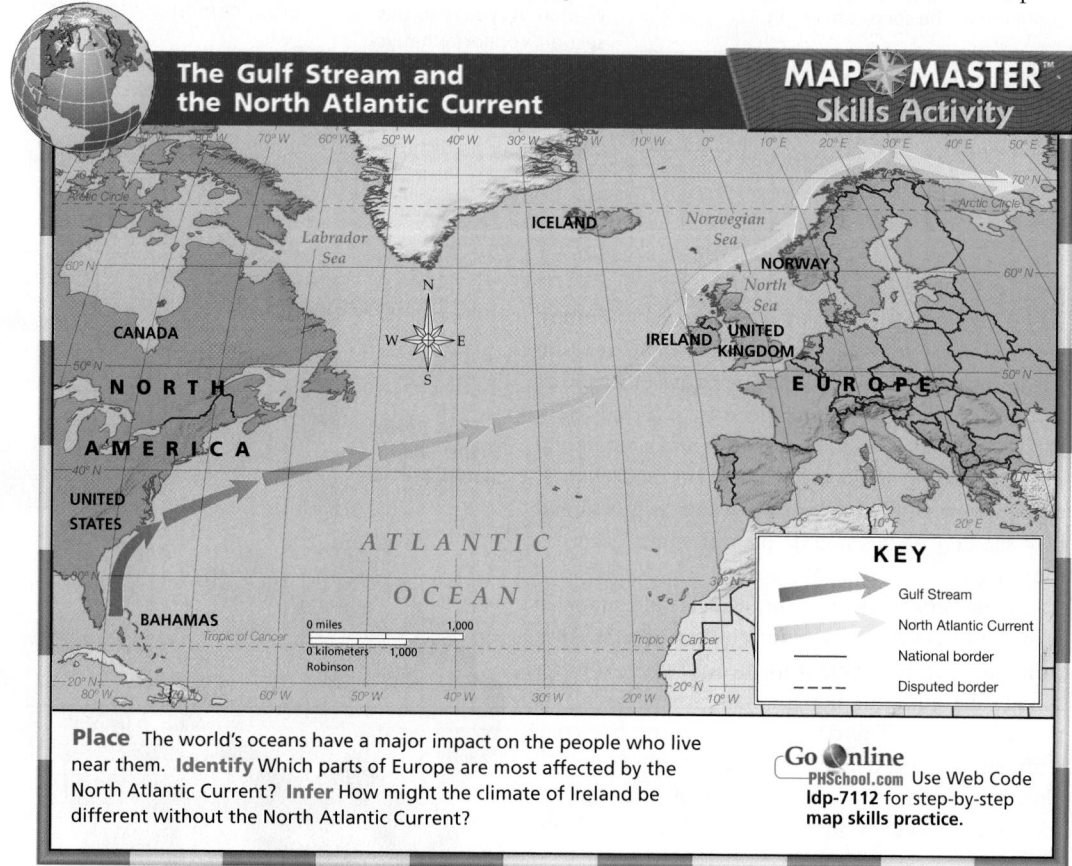

MAP MASTER™ Skills Activity

The Gulf Stream and the North Atlantic Current

KEY

➡	Gulf Stream
➡	North Atlantic Current
—	National border
- - -	Disputed border

Place The world's oceans have a major impact on the people who live near them. **Identify** Which parts of Europe are most affected by the North Atlantic Current? **Infer** How might the climate of Ireland be different without the North Atlantic Current?

Go Online
PHSchool.com Use Web Code ldp-7112 for step-by-step map skills practice.

156 Europe and Russia

Answers

MAP MASTER™ Skills Activity **Identify** Ireland, The United Kingdom, Norway **Infer** The climate of Ireland might be much colder without the North Atlantic Current.

Go Online
PHSchool.com Students may practice their map skills using the interactive online version of this map.

Vocabulary Builder

Use the information below to teach students this section's high-use words.

High-Use Word	Definition and Sample Sentence
dramatic, p. 157	*adj.* striking in effect Marcus barely recognized his friend after her **dramatic** weight loss.
overlap, p. 159	*v.* to occupy the same area in part A Venn diagram is made up of two circles that **overlap.**
brief, p. 161	*adj.* short in time, duration, or length The **brief** quiz took up only five minutes of class time.

Two Cities, Two Climates

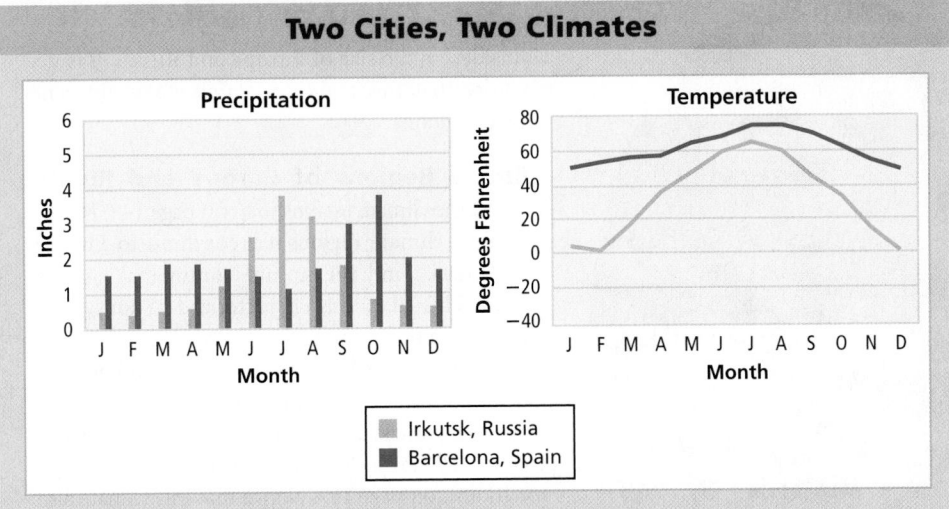

Precipitation

Temperature

■ Irkutsk, Russia
■ Barcelona, Spain

London, England, is farther north than any city in the continental United States, yet it has mild weather. How is this possible? The North Atlantic Current is the reason. But the most dramatic effect of the North Atlantic Current can be seen in northern Norway. Snow and ice cover most of this area in winter. Yet Norway's western coast is free of ice and snow all year. Snow melts almost as soon as it falls. Norway's ice-free ports have helped make its fishing industry one of the largest in Europe.

The ocean affects climate in other ways. Winds blowing across the ocean pick up a great deal of moisture. When these winds blow over land, they drop the moisture in the form of rain. Winds blowing from the west across the Atlantic bring a fairly wet climate to much of Western Europe.

How Mountains Affect Rainfall Mountains also affect the amount of rainfall in an area. In Europe, areas west of mountains receive heavy rainfall. These areas include parts of the United Kingdom, France, Germany, and Norway. Areas east of mountains have much lighter rainfall.

Why is this so? As winds rise up a mountain, they cool and drop their moisture. The air is dry by the time it reaches the other side of the mountain. Areas on the leeward side of a mountain, or the side away from the wind, are in a rain shadow. A **rain shadow** is an area on the dry, sheltered side of a mountain, which receives little rainfall.

✓ Reading Check **How do mountains affect the climates of Western Europe?**

■ Graph Skills

A city's climate is affected by its location and the geographical features that are located near it. **Identify** In which city does the temperature change most from season to season? **Draw Conclusions** What explains this city's greater range in temperature?

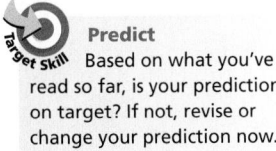 **Predict** Based on what you've read so far, is your prediction on target? If not, revise or change your prediction now.

Guided Instruction (continued)

■ Have students explain why London and Norway have mild climates despite being located far to the north. (*The North Atlantic Current keeps London and Norway mild, despite their distance from the Equator.*)

■ Ask students **Why is the climate in much of Western Europe wet?** (*Winds blowing east across the Atlantic Ocean pick up moisture. When the winds arrive over Western Europe, the moisture falls as rain.*)

■ Review the text of How Mountains Affect Rainfall with students. Then display *Color Transparency ER 20: Western Europe: Physical-Political.* Ask students to point to the areas described in the text as having heavy rainfall. (*the western portions of Great Britain, France, Germany, and Norway*) Then ask them to point to the areas they predict would have less rainfall. (*Students should point to areas east of mountain ranges, such as eastern Italy.*)

📖 **Europe and Russia Transparencies,** *Color Transparency ER 20: Western Europe: Physical-Political*

Independent Practice

Ask students to create the Taking Notes graphic organizer on a blank piece of paper. Then have them begin to fill in the flow chart by listing factors that affect climate. Display the blank *Flow Chart Transparency.* Briefly model how to identify which details to record.

📖 **Europe and Russia Transparencies,** *Transparency B2: Flow Chart*

Monitor Progress

As students begin to fill in the graphic organizer, circulate and help individuals understand which details to include in their charts. Provide assistance as needed.

🔁 Target Reading Skill

Predict As a follow up, ask students to answer the Target Reading Skill question in the Student Edition. (*Students should either explain why their predictions are on target, or revise them if necessary.*)

Answers

Graph Skills Identify Irkutsk **Draw Conclusions** Barcelona is close to an ocean, which provides mild weather year-round, but Irkutsk is not close to an ocean.

✓ Reading Check In Europe, areas west of mountains receive heavy rainfall, while areas east of mountains are drier.

Major Climate Regions L2

Guided Instruction

- Have students read about the variety of climate regions found in Europe and Russia in Major Climate Regions.

- Ask students **What climate regions are found in Europe and Russia?** (*humid continental, subarctic, arctic, semiarid, marine west coast, Mediterranean, humid subtropical*)

- Have students compare the marine west coast climate to the subarctic climate region. (*The marine west coast climate is mild and rainy throughout the year, while the subarctic climate has short summers and long, cold winters.*)

- Ask students **In which climate regions would you expect most people to live?** (*Possible answer: More people probably live in the milder and wetter climates such as humid subcontinental, Mediterranean, and marine west coast.*)

Independent Practice

Have students continue to fill in their graphic organizers by adding details about the major climate regions of Europe and Russia in the climate box.

Monitor Progress

Circulate among students and provide assistance as needed.

Two Very Different Climates
Much of Russia has a tundra climate, as shown in the top photo of Siberia. In contrast, London, England (at bottom), enjoys a mild climate year-round. **Infer** How might the population densities of the places in these photos differ?

Major Climate Regions

Considering the size of Europe and Russia, it is no surprise that this region contains many different climate regions.

Climate Regions of Europe and Russia
Look at the climate regions map on page 147. Notice that four climate regions are common to Europe and Russia. Find the humid continental climate region. This climate is characterized by long, cold winters and hot summers.

Now find Irkutsk, Russia, on the map. It is located in a huge subarctic climate region. There summers are short, and winters are long and cold. You can see how cold it is all year by looking at the temperature graph for Irkutsk on page 157. Notice that this climate also stretches across northern Europe.

Europe and Russia share two other climate regions. The northernmost areas of Europe and Russia have an arctic climate. It is very cold in these areas. On the warmest days of the short summer, temperatures sometimes barely reach 60°F (14°C). In contrast, southeastern Europe and southwestern Russia have a semiarid climate region, with hot temperatures and little rainfall.

Moderate Climate Regions of Europe
As you can see on the climate regions map, Europe has moderate climate regions that Russia does not have. For example, the marine west coast climate affects much of northwestern Europe, stretching from northern Spain to northern Norway. As you have read, winds and currents from the Atlantic Ocean keep this climate mild and rainy all year.

Another climate region surrounds the Mediterranean Sea. It is easy to remember the name of this type of climate—Mediterranean, just like the sea. Remember that Barcelona, Spain, is on the Mediterranean Sea. In the Mediterranean climate, summers are hot and dry. Winters are mild and rainy.

Finally, a band of humid subtropical climate is located in southern Europe. Warm temperatures and year-round rainfall characterize this climate.

✓ Reading Check **What two climate regions are found in Europe but not Russia?**

Answers

Infer Possible answer: London probably has a much higher population density than Siberia.

✓Reading Check marine west coast and Mediterranean

Skills Mini Lesson

Comparing and Contrasting

1. Teach the skill by pointing out to students that to make comparisons and contrasts, they should look for ways things in a group are similar and different. Then, they should draw a conclusion based on their comparisons and contrasts.

2. Have students practice the skill by comparing and contrasting the climate of London with the climate in their own community.

3. Have students apply the skill by drawing a conclusion about the climates of the two cities.

Natural Vegetation Regions

The natural vegetation, or plant life, of Europe and Russia is as varied as the climate. Vegetation regions are related to climate regions. Vegetation in Europe and Russia varies from ice cap to desert. However, the main vegetation regions are forest, grassland, tundra, and Mediterranean. Compare the climate map on page 147 with the natural vegetation map below to see how the climate and vegetation regions overlap.

Forests of Europe and Russia The natural vegetation of much of Europe is forest. However, most of these forests have been cleared to make way for farms, factories, and cities. In northern Europe, you can still find large coniferous (koh NIF ur us) forests, which have evergreen trees with cones that carry and protect the seeds. Deciduous (dih SIJ oo us) forests, which contain trees that lose their leaves in fall, cover most of Western and Central Europe.

Russia is also heavily forested. One forest, called the taiga (TY guh), covers more than 4 million square miles (10 million square kilometers). Located in Siberia, it is the largest forest in the world.

Links Across The World

The Boreal Forest The boreal forest includes one third of all Earth's forests. The name comes from an ancient Greek god named Boreas, the god of the north wind. Russia's taiga makes up half of the boreal forest. The rest is located in the northern parts of Canada, Alaska, China, Mongolia, Scandinavia, and Scotland. Boreal forests play an important role in the environment, by filtering out carbon dioxide and other gases from the atmosphere.

Links

Read the **Links Across the World** on this page. Ask students **What role do boreal forests play in the environment?** *(They filter out carbon dioxide and other gases from the atmosphere.)*

Natural Vegetation Regions

L2

Guided Instruction

- **Vocabulary Builder** Clarify the high-use words **overlap** and **brief** before reading.

- Have students read Natural Vegetation Regions to learn about the many types of plant life found in Europe and Russia.

- Ask students **What natural vegetation covers much of Europe?** *(forests)*

- Have students discuss what has happened to most of the forests in Europe. *(The forests have been cleared to make way for farms, factories, and cities.)*

- Ask students **What is the land that was once covered by grasslands now used for?** *(farming)*

- Have students compare the vegetation map on this page with the climate map of Europe on p. 147. Ask them to draw a conclusion about how climate affects vegetation. *(Possible answer: Warmer, wetter climates such as the marine west coast climate promote the growth of more vegetation, while colder climates such as the subarctic climate region only allow for the growth of sparse vegetation.)*

Europe: Natural Vegetation

KEY

- Deciduous forest
- Mixed forest
- Coniferous forest
- Mediterranean forest
- Temperate grassland
- Tundra
- Ice cap
- National border
- City

MAP MASTER Skills Activity

Regions Europe's vegetation regions, shaped by precipitation and temperature, vary widely. **Use the Map Key** What major kind of vegetation dominates most of Europe? **Analyze Information** You have read that Europe has a high population density. How has the vegetation in the region you identified probably been affected by people?

Go Online
PHSchool.com Use Web Code ldp-7122 for step-by-step map skills practice.

Chapter 6 Section 2 **159**

Background: Daily Life

Country Homes On the weekends, many Russians travel to their *dacha* (DAH cha), or country home. Dachas are located in the countryside and provide Russians in urban areas with a retreat from busy city life. Traditionally, dachas are wooden shacks located on small areas of land, but today some people build dachas with many levels and swimming pools. Dacha owners usually have a small garden where they grow fruits and vegetables. Some people grow an entire year's supply of food for their families in these gardens.

Answers

MAP MASTER Skills Activity **Use The Map Key** deciduous forest **Analyze Information** Possible answer: Much of the forests has probably been cleared to make way for farms, factories, and cities.

Go Online
PHSchool.com Students may practice their map skills using the interactive online version of this map.

Guided Instruction (continued)

- Ask students **What are the three main vegetation regions in Russia?** *(tundra, forest, and grassland)*

- Ask students **What are the grasslands called in Russia?** *(steppes)* **Why are the steppes good for farming?** *(The soil is fertile.)*

- Ask students **What is the tundra?** *(a cold, dry, treeless region that is covered with snow for most of the year)*

- Have students discuss their similarities and differences between the vegetation regions of Europe and Russia. *(Similarities—both have grasslands and forests; differences— much of Russia is covered by tundra and coniferous forest while Europe's vegetation is more varied.)*

Independent Practice

Have students complete their flowcharts by filling in details about the vegetation found in Europe and Russia.

Monitor Progress

- Show *Section Reading Support Transparency ER 33* and ask students to check their graphic organizers individually. Go over key concepts and clarify key vocabulary as needed.

  📖 **Europe and Russia Transparencies,** *Section Reading Support Transparency ER 33*

- Tell students to fill in the last column of the *Reading Readiness Guide*. Probe for what they learned that confirms or invalidates each statement.

  All in One **Europe and Russia Teaching Resources,** *Reading Readiness Guide,* p. 111

Answers

MAP MASTER Skills Activity **Use the Key** it borders the Arctic Ocean, an area of land approximately 4,000 miles long **Apply Information** The region is cold, treeless, and covered with snow most of the year.

Go Online PHSchool.com Students may practice their map skills using the interactive online version of this map.

Russia: Natural Vegetation

MAP MASTER™ Skills Activity

KEY
- Deciduous forest
- Mixed forest
- Coniferous forest
- Temperate grassland
- Desert scrub
- Tundra
- Ice cap
- National border
- • City

0 miles 1,500
0 kilometers 1,500
Lambert Azimuthal Equal Area

Location Russia is located far from the Equator and the warm ocean currents that bring mild climates to most of Europe. **Use the Key** Describe the location of Russia's tundra. **Apply Information** Why are few major cities located in this region?

Go Online PHSchool.com Use Web Code **ldp-7132** for step-by-step map skills practice.

Grasslands of Europe and Russia Grasslands, also called prairies, are a major vegetation region in Europe and Russia. In Europe, grasslands once covered the central and southern parts of the North European Plain. Like the forests, most of the prairies have also disappeared. Today, the land is used for farming.

In Russia, the grasslands are called **steppes.** Steppes are located mainly in the southwestern parts of the country. They contain a mix of grasses and low-growing vegetation such as mosses. Below that vegetation, the soil of the steppes is fertile and black and good for farming. The steppes are similar to the Great Plains of the United States.

Mediterranean Regions of Europe Just as the area of southern Europe near the Mediterranean Sea has its own climate, it also has its own vegetation region. Mediterranean vegetation is a mix of trees, scrub, and smaller plants, usually less than about 8 feet (2.5 meters) tall.

160 Europe and Russia

Differentiated Instruction

For Gifted and Talented L3
Form students into groups and have them begin working on the *Book Project: Changing Climates* to learn more about European climates.

All in One **Europe and Russia Teaching Resources,** *Book Project: Changing Climates,* pp. 77–79

For Less Proficient Readers L1
Some students may have difficulty reading the vegetation map. Have them work in pairs to complete *Reading a Natural Vegetation Map.*

All in One **Europe and Russia Teaching Resources,** *Reading a Natural Vegetation Map,* p. 130

Tundra of Europe and Russia Northern parts of Europe—including northern Scandinavia and Iceland—as well as northern Russia have a tundra vegetation region. **Tundra** is a cold, dry, treeless region that is covered with snow for most of the year. There winters last as long as nine months and the ground contains **permafrost,** a layer of permanently frozen ground below the top layer of soil. During the brief season when the top surface of the permafrost thaws, grasses, mosses, and other plant life grow quickly. Few people live in the tundra region.

✓ **Reading Check** Where is the world's largest forest located?

Flowers bloom during the short Siberian summer.

Section 2 Assessment

Key Terms
Review the key terms at the beginning of this section. Use each term in a sentence that explains its meaning.

Target Reading Skill
What did you predict about this section? How did your prediction guide your reading?

Comprehension and Critical Thinking
1. (a) Describe How do oceans affect climate?
(b) Identify Effects How does the North Atlantic Current affect northern Europe?

2. (a) Recall What are the major climate regions of Europe and Russia?
(b) Draw Conclusions Why are summers in Barcelona, Spain, hot and dry?
3. (a) List What are the natural vegetation regions of Europe and Russia?
(b) Summarize How are vegetation regions and climate regions related?
(c) Generalize What geographic features might lead someone to settle in Europe, rather than in Russia?

Writing Activity
Suppose you are planning a trip to one of the cities mentioned in this section. Decide what time of year you would want to go. Based on the climate of the city, make a list of the clothes that you would pack. Then write a brief paragraph explaining why you would pack the items on your list.

For: An activity about Ireland
Visit: PHSchool.com
Web Code: ldd-7101

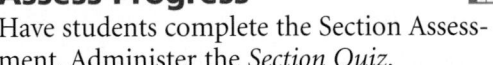

Assess Progress · L2
Have students complete the Section Assessment. Administer the *Section Quiz.*

All in One **Europe and Russia Teaching Resources,** *Section Quiz,* p. 113

Reteach · L1
If students need more instruction, have them read this section in the Reading and Vocabulary Study Guide.

📖 Chapter 6, Section 2, **Eastern Hemisphere Reading and Vocabulary Study Guide,** pp. 59–61

Extend · L3
Extend students' knowledge by having them complete the *Enrichment* activity in which they will learn about a threat to some of Europe's forests.

All in One **Europe and Russia Teaching Resources,** *Enrichment,* p. 122

Answer
✓ **Reading Check** Siberia

Writing Activity
Use the *Rubric for Assessing a Writing Assignment* to evaluate students' paragraphs.

All in One **Europe and Russia Teaching Resources,** *Rubric for Assessing a Writing Assignment,* p. 137

Go Online PHSchool.com Typing in the Web code when prompted will bring students to detailed instructions for this activity.

Section 2 Assessment

Key Terms
Students' sentences should reflect knowledge of each Key Term.

Target Reading Skill
Students should explain how their predictions helped them focus their reading on important ideas in the section.

Comprehension and Critical Thinking
1. (a) Areas near the ocean are fairly mild throughout the year. **(b)** The North Atlantic Current carries warm water from the Gulf of Mexico to northwestern Europe and warms the winds that blow from the west across the Atlantic Ocean. The warm waters and winds cause much of northwestern Europe to have a mild climate.

2. (a) humid continental, subarctic, arctic, semiarid, marine west coast, Mediterranean, and humid subtropical **(b)** Barcelona is located in a Mediterranean climate region, which is characterized by hot and dry summers.
3. (a) forest, grassland, tundra, and Mediterranean **(b)** Climate affects the type of vegetation that can grow in an area. **(c)** possible answer: the warmer climate of some areas

Objective

Learn how to use a precipitation map.

Prepare to Read

Build Background Knowledge   L2

Tell students to look at the special purpose maps in the first two sections of the chapter. Have them identify what each map shows, and then think about why it is useful. Conduct an Idea Wave (TE, p. T35) to help students share their answers.

Instruct

Using a Precipitation Map   L2

Guided Instruction

- Read the steps to using a precipitation map aloud and write them on the board.

- Practice the skill by following the steps on p. 163 as a class. Model each step in the activity by reading the map title and looking over the map to get a general idea of what it shows. *(The World: Precipitation shows how much precipitation different areas of the world receive.)* Students should continue by studying the key *(Different amounts of precipitation are shown using various colors.)*, looking at the precipitation amounts for different regions *(Most of North Africa, Central Asia, Australia, Greenland, and Antarctica receive less than ten inches of precipitation a year. Most of South America, Central Africa, and Southeast Asia receive more than 40 inches of precipitation a year.)*, and using the information to compare precipitation in the United States and Russia. *(Most of the U.S. and Russia receive between ten and 40 inches of precipitation each year, although the eastern and southern coasts of the U.S. receive an average of more than 40 inches a year. The U.S. has more variation in precipitation, and Russia is generally drier.)*

Using a Precipitation Map

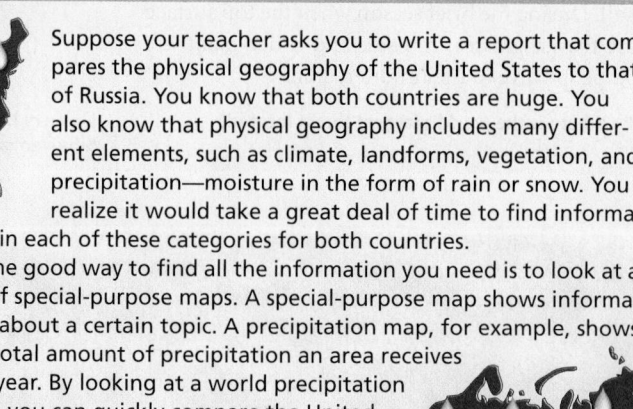

Suppose your teacher asks you to write a report that compares the physical geography of the United States to that of Russia. You know that both countries are huge. You also know that physical geography includes many different elements, such as climate, landforms, vegetation, and precipitation—moisture in the form of rain or snow. You realize it would take a great deal of time to find information in each of these categories for both countries.

One good way to find all the information you need is to look at a set of special-purpose maps. A special-purpose map shows information about a certain topic. A precipitation map, for example, shows the total amount of precipitation an area receives in a year. By looking at a world precipitation map, you can quickly compare the United States' precipitation with that of Russia.

A rainy day in St. Petersburg, Russia

162 Europe and Russia

Learn the Skill

Follow the steps below to learn how to use a precipitation map.

1. **Read the map title and look over the map to get a general idea of what it shows.** Notice that a precipitation map includes common map features, such as a title, key, scale, and labels.

2. **Read the key to understand how the map uses symbols, colors, and patterns.** A precipitation map often shows colors to represent different amounts of precipitation. Notice that the amounts are indicated in both inches and centimeters.

3. **Use the key to interpret the map.** Look on the map for the different colors shown in the key. Notice where areas with different amounts of precipitation are located on the map.

4. **Draw conclusions about what the map shows.** Information you discover when you analyze a precipitation map can help you draw conclusions about how precipitation affects people's lives.

Independent Practice

Assign *Skills for Life* and have students complete it individually.

All in One **Europe and Russia Teaching Resources,** *Skills for Life*, p. 123

Monitor Progress

As students are completing *Skills for Life*, circulate to make sure individuals are applying the skill steps effectively. Provide assistance as needed.

The World: Precipitation

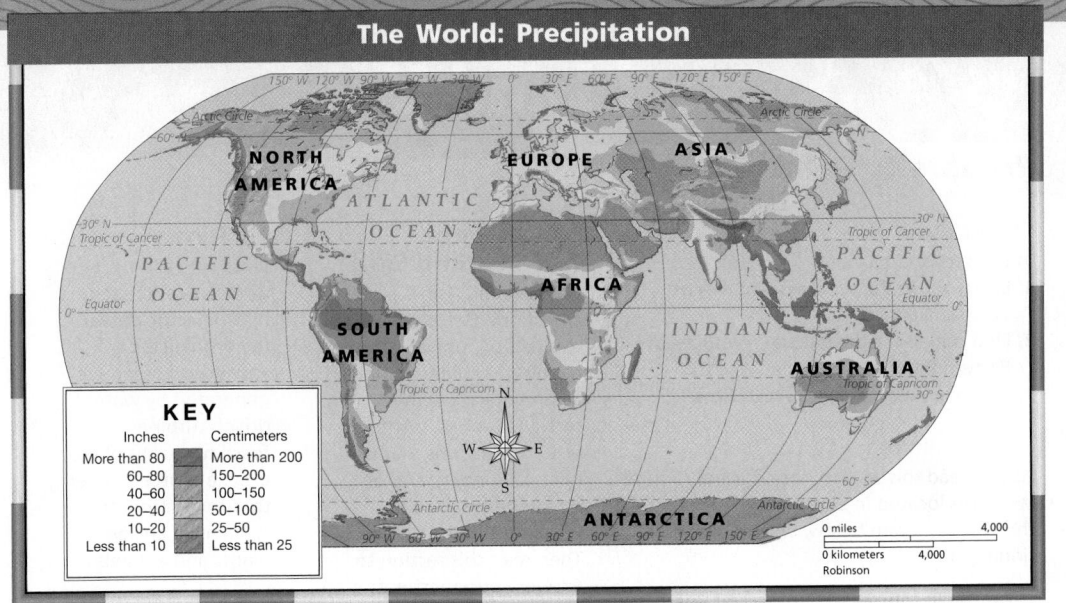

KEY

Inches	Centimeters
More than 80	More than 200
60–80	150–200
40–60	100–150
20–40	50–100
10–20	25–50
Less than 10	Less than 25

Practice the Skill

Use the precipitation map above to complete the following steps.

1 Become familiar with the map. What is the map's title? In general, what does it show?

2 Look at the key to see how different amounts of precipitation are shown. Familiarize yourself with the colors on the key.

3 Look for areas on the map with different amounts of precipitation. Because you want to compare the United States with Russia, find those two regions within the continents of

North America, Asia, and Europe on the map. (If you need help finding the areas of the two countries, compare this map with the World: Political map in the Atlas).

4 Study the map. Use the information on it to compare precipitation in the United States and Russia. Which country has more variation in precipitation? Which country is generally drier? Write a conclusion that summarizes your comparison.

Apply the Skill

Turn to Section 2 of Chapter 6 and look at the Europe: Natural Vegetation map on page 159. Use the steps of this skill to analyze and draw conclusions about this special-purpose map.

Assess and Reteach

Assess Progress   **L2**
Ask students to do the Apply the Skill activity.

Reteach   **L1**
If students are having trouble applying the skill steps, have them review the skill using the interactive Social Studies Skills Tutor CD-ROM.

⊙ *Analyzing and Interpreting Special Purpose Maps,* **Social Studies Skills Tutor CD-ROM**

Extend   **L3**
Have students use the map on this page to create a chart with the amounts of precipitation for different areas of the world. Assign each student different cities, countries, and regions. Have them use an atlas, if necessary, to locate these places on the map in the Student Edition. Then display the finished charts on a class bulletin board.

Answer
Apply the Skill
Students should recognize that the Europe: Natural Vegetation map shows the vegetation regions of Europe. The key should help students identify the countries, major cities, and vegetation regions. Students may conclude that most of Europe is made up of deciduous forest, although it contains large areas of other types of vegetation as well.

Objectives

Social Studies

1. Learn about the natural resources of Western Europe.

2. Find out about the natural resources of Eastern Europe.

3. Examine Russia's natural resources.

Reading/Language Arts

Preview and ask questions to help you remember important ideas in the section.

Prepare to Read

Build Background Knowledge L2

Write the following words on the board: *soil; water; fuel.* Tell students that in this section they will read about the distribution of these resources throughout Europe and Russia. Have students discuss and debate which of these resources they think are most important. Use the Give One, Get One participation strategy (TE, p. T37) to structure the discussion.

Set a Purpose for Reading L2

- Preview the Objectives.

- Read each statement in the *Reading Readiness Guide* aloud. Ask students to mark the statements true or false.

  All in One Europe and Russia Teaching Resources, *Reading Readiness Guide,* p. 115

- Have students discuss the statements in pairs or groups of four, then mark their worksheets again. Use the Numbered Heads participation strategy (TE, p. T36) to call on students to share their group's perspectives.

Vocabulary Builder
Preview Key Terms L2

Pronounce each Key Term, then ask the students to say the word with you. Provide a simple explanation such as, "Hydroelectric power is electricity that is created by moving water."

Prepare to Read

Objectives

In this section you will

1. Learn about the natural resources of Western Europe.

2. Find out about the natural resources of Eastern Europe.

3. Examine Russia's natural resources.

Taking Notes

As you read this section, look for the natural resources located in Europe and Russia. Copy the Venn diagram below, and record your findings in it.

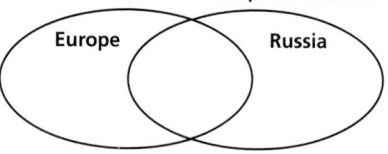

Natural Resources of Europe and Russia

Target Reading Skill

Preview and Ask Questions Before you read this section, preview the headings and illustrations to find out what the section is about. Write one or two questions that will help you understand or remember something important in the section. Then read this section to answer your questions.

Key Terms

- **loess** (LOH es) *n.* a type of rich, dustlike soil

- **hydroelectric power** (hy droh ee LEK trik POW ur) *n.* the power generated by water-driven turbines

- **fossil fuel** (FAHS ul FYOO ul) *n.* a source of energy that forms from the remains of ancient plants and animals

A North Sea oil rig

How would you like to live and work on an ocean? Oil workers on the North Sea do just that. Their job is to pump oil from deep beneath the ocean floor. They work on a tower called an oil rig anchored over an oil field. Oil rig workers live and work as if they were on a ship. But they cannot seek the safety of a harbor when a big storm is stirring.

The North Sea, located between the United Kingdom and mainland northwestern Europe, sometimes has violent weather. Severe storms with winds of as much as 100 miles (160 kilometers) an hour are common. Waves as high as 90 feet (27 meters) batter oil rig platforms. Despite the harsh conditions, crews work around the clock to operate, inspect, and repair the rigs.

Making sure a rig operates properly is a very important job. The United Kingdom and other nations around the North Sea depend on oil and natural gas from the rigs.

Target Reading Skill L2

Preview and Ask Questions Point out the Target Reading Skill. Tell students that previewing and asking questions can help them to focus on and remember important details about what they will read.

Model the skill by previewing the headings and the map on p. 165 and asking the following question: Why is fertile soil an important natural resource in Western Europe? Tell students to read the section and answer the question. *(It is needed to grow food.)*

Give students *Preview and Ask Questions.* Have them complete the activity in groups.

All in One Europe and Russia Teaching Resources, *Preview and Ask Questions,* p. 120

Resources of Western Europe

Western Europe is a wealthy region and a world leader in economic development. Part of this wealth and success comes from Western Europe's rich and varied supply of natural resources. These natural resources include fertile soil, water, and fuels.

Fertile Soil Soil is one of Earth's most important natural resources because it is needed to grow food. Much of Western Europe is covered with rich, fertile soil, especially the region's broad river valleys.

Wind has helped create the fertile soil of the North European Plain. Over thousands of years, winds have deposited **loess** (LOH es), a type of rich, dustlike soil. This soil, combined with plentiful rain and moderate temperatures, provides for a long growing season. These conditions allow European farmers to produce abundant crops.

Tulips brighten the landscape at a flower farm in the Netherlands.

Europe: Natural Resources

KEY

- Copper
- Iron
- Lead
- Uranium
- Bauxite
- Coal
- Phosphates
- Petroleum
- Natural gas
- Hydroelectric power
- National border

0 miles 1,000
0 kilometers 1,000
Lambert Azimuthal Equal Area

MAP MASTER Skills Activity

Human-Environment Interaction A region's natural resources often influence the kinds of activities that take place there. **Locate** Where in Europe is hydroelectric power produced? **Infer** What does the material on the next page suggest about the physical geography of those parts of Europe?

Go Online
PHSchool.com Use Web Code **ldp-7123** for step-by-step map skills practice.

Chapter 6 Section 3 **165**

Vocabulary Builder

Use the information below to teach students this section's high-use words.

High-Use Word	Definition and Sample Sentence
deposit, p. 165	*v.* to set down or drop The storm **deposited** three feet of snow onto our roof.
nourish, p. 166	*v.* to promote growth For a garden to thrive, it must be **nourished** with water and sunlight.
element, p. 168	*n.* an essential part Exercise is an important **element** of a healthy lifestyle.
transport, p. 170	*v.* to carry from one place to another Overnight mail is a good way to **transport** small goods quickly.

Instruct

Resources of Western Europe L2

Guided Instruction

- **Vocabulary Builder** Clarify the high-use words **deposit** and **nourish** before reading.

- Read Resources of Western Europe, using the Paragraph Shrinking strategy (TE, p. T34).

- Have students scan the map of Europe's natural resources before they read the text. Ask students to choose a Western European country and describe its natural resources, using an atlas to locate the countries if necessary. *(Possible answer: Portugal has water for hydroelectric power.)*

- Ask students **What three factors contribute to the abundance of crops in Europe?** *(rich soil in the form of loess, plentiful rain, and moderate temperatures)*

Answers

MAP MASTER Skills Activity **Locate** Most hydroelectric power in Europe is produced in the far north and in the south. **Infer** Possible answer: The regions where hydroelectric power is produced must have rivers. These areas may also have mountains, since many rivers that flow down mountains have been dammed to generate power.

Go Online
PHSchool.com Students may practice their map skills using the interactive online version of this map.

- Ask students **Why is water an important resource for Western Europe?** (*People need water for drinking; water is needed to grow crops; water can be used to generate hydroelectric power.*)

- Ask students **Where must hydroelectric power plants be located?** (*Hydroelectric plants must be located where there are sources of fast-flowing water, such as dammed rivers or waterfalls.*)

- Ask students **What are fossil fuels?** (*Fossil fuels are sources of energy such as natural gas, oil, and coal that are formed from the remains of ancient plants and animals.*)

- Ask students to name three countries in Western Europe that have large supplies of coal. (*the United Kingdom, Germany, and Norway*)

- Have students make generalizations about the natural resources of Western Europe. (*Possible generalizations: Western Europe has a rich variety of important natural resources; Western Europe is a leading world industrial power due to its rich natural resources; Western Europe's major natural resources include fertile soil, water, and fuel deposits.*)

Independent Practice

Have students create the Taking Notes graphic organizer on a blank piece of paper. Ask them to begin by listing the resources of Western Europe in the appropriate circle.

Monitor Progress

Circulate throughout the classroom to ensure that individuals are listing the appropriate resources. Help students as needed.

Answer

✓ Reading Check Hydroelectric power is generated by fast-flowing water from a river that has been dammed or a waterfall that is used to spin turbines. As the turbines spin, they create electric power.

166 *Europe and Russia*

Abundant Water Another important resource in Western Europe is water. People need water for drinking. Water nourishes crops. Water can also be used to produce electricity for industries and homes. To be used as a source of energy, water must flow very quickly. The force of water from a waterfall or a dam can be used to spin machines called turbines (TUR bynz). Spinning turbines generate, or create, electric power. Power generated by water-driven turbines is called **hydroelectric power** (hy droh ee LEK trik POW ur).

Many countries in Western Europe have favorable locations for the development of hydroelectric power. Some rivers that flow down through the mountains have been dammed to generate hydroelectric power. Norway gets almost all of its electric power from water. Hydroelectric power also keeps factories in Sweden, Switzerland, Austria, Spain, Scotland, and Portugal operating.

Fuel Deposits Like flowing water, fuel deposits are another source of energy for many industries. **Fossil fuels** are sources of energy that formed from the remains of ancient plants and animals. Fossil fuels include natural gas, oil, and coal.

Both the United Kingdom and Norway have large deposits of oil and natural gas. The United Kingdom also has large coal fields, as does Germany. The largest coal deposits in Germany are located in the Ruhr (ROOR), a region named for the Ruhr River. Because of its fuel resources, the Ruhr has long been one of Western Europe's most important industrial regions.

An abundance of coal and iron ore gave Western European industries a head start in the 1800s, when industries grew rapidly. Today, countries in Western Europe remain among the world's leading industrial powers.

✓ Reading Check **How is hydroelectric power generated?**

Producing hydroelectric power on the Tay River in Scotland

166 Europe and Russia

Background: Links Across Time

The Industrial Revolution Prior to the Industrial Revolution, the great majority of human labor was devoted to farming. However, technological innovations made farming more efficient and industries such as manufacturing, mining, and communications began to grow.

The Industrial Revolution began around 1760 in Great Britain. Initially, the British banned the export of their technology in an effort to keep their industrial advantages to themselves. However, this policy eventually failed as new inventions spread to nearby European countries, such as Belgium, as well as the United States.

Resources of Eastern Europe

Now, shift your view from Western to Eastern Europe. Turn back to the map on page 165 showing Europe's natural resources. Notice that Eastern Europe has resources similar to those of Western Europe. Place a finger on the area just west of 50°N and 20°E. This is in southern Poland, on the border of the Czech Republic. This area is called Silesia (sy LEE zhuh). Large deposits of coal there have helped to make Silesia a major industrial center.

Ukraine (yoo KRAYN), a large country in Eastern Europe, has coal deposits, too. It also has other fuel resources—especially oil and natural gas. However, the most important resource is probably its soil. The region's black earth is very fertile. Not surprisingly, farming is an extremely important activity in Ukraine.

Eastern Europe has fewer water resources than does Western Europe. However, the nations of the Balkan Peninsula produce a large amount of hydroelectric power.

✓ **Reading Check** What is Silesia, and where is it?

Energy and Land Resources
The photo at the left shows miners on the job in a Silesian coal mine. Above, a Ukrainian woman harvests flowers to use in making perfume.
Compare and Contrast What do mining and farming have in common? How are they different?

Chapter 6 Section 3 **167**

Differentiated Instruction

For Gifted and Talented L3
Have students extend their understanding of the distribution of oil reserves by completing the *World Oil Reserves* Internet activity.

Go Online PHSchool.com

For: Environmental and Global Issues: *World Oil Reserves*
Visit: PHSchool.com
Web Code: ldd-7104

Resources of Eastern Europe L2

Guided Instruction
- Ask students to read Resources of Eastern Europe. As students read, circulate and make sure individuals can answer the Reading Check question.
- Ask students **Why is fertile soil an important resource in Ukraine?** *(Farming is an important activity there.)*
- Ask students **What natural resources do Eastern and Western Europe have in common?** *(They both have fertile soil and fuel resources, such as coal and oil.)*
- Ask students **Why do you think it might be better for a country or region to have a variety of natural resources rather than just one type?** *(Possible answers: Varied resources help countries or regions to have diversified economies; possessing many natural resources provides a country or region with a certain amount of self-sufficiency.)*

Independent Practice
Have students continue to fill in the graphic organizer by listing all of Eastern Europe's natural resources.

Monitor Progress
Circulate among students to make sure individuals are using both the map and the text to compile their resource lists.

Answers

✓ **Reading Check** Silesia is a major industrial area with large coal deposits. It is located where Poland, the Czech Republic, and Germany meet.

Compare and Contrast They both require natural resources; farmers use the fertile soil to grow crops, and miners uncover resources like coal and oil. Mining generally occurs in deep pits of underground shafts; farming activities occur in open fields and barns.

Chapter 6 Section 3 **167**

Resources of Russia ▪②

Guided Instruction

- **Vocabulary Builder** Clarify the high-use words **element** and **transport** before reading.

- Have students read about the variety of Russia's natural resources in Resources of Russia.

- Ask students **What geographic factors make it difficult for Russia to take advantage of its resources?** (*Russia's harsh climate, huge size, and lack of navigable rivers; it also has few places suited for farming*)

- Ask students to name the four major energy resources that are found in Russia. (*oil, natural gas, coal, and hydroelectricity*)

- Ask students **Why do you think steel is useful for many industries in Russia?** (*Possible answer: Steel is a basic material used in industries such as automobile production, manufacturing, and construction.*)

A tugboat pushes a barge loaded with logs along a Russian river.

Resources of Russia

Russia has a much greater supply of natural resources than does the United States. The United States has used its resources to become the richest nation on Earth. You might wonder why Russia has not done the same.

One answer is that Russia's harsh climate, huge size, and few navigable rivers have made it difficult to turn the country's resources into wealth. In addition, Russia has relatively few places that are suited for farming. Much of Russia lacks one or more of the key elements for farming: favorable climate, good soil, and plentiful water.

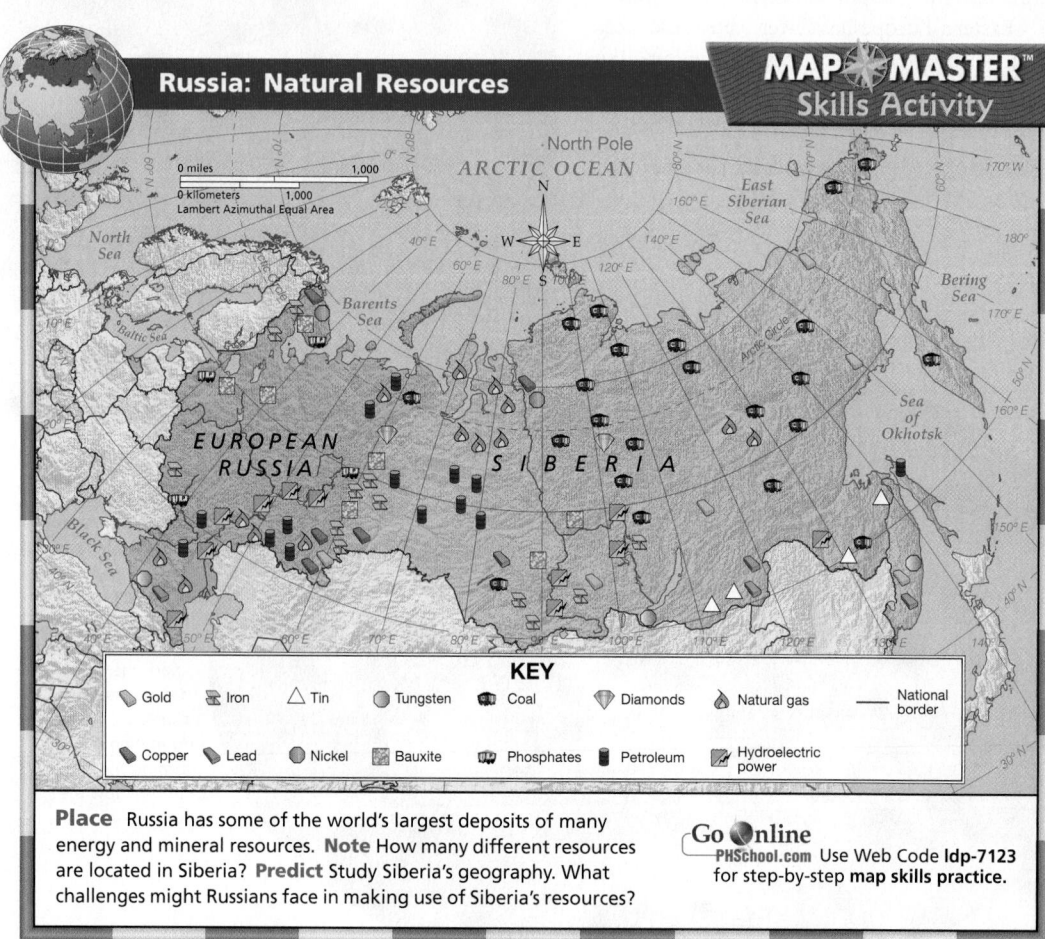

Russia: Natural Resources

MAP ✦ MASTER™
Skills Activity

KEY

Gold	Iron	Tin
Tungsten	Coal	Diamonds
Natural gas	National border	
Copper	Lead	Nickel
Bauxite	Phosphates	Petroleum
Hydroelectric power		

Place Russia has some of the world's largest deposits of many energy and mineral resources. **Note** How many different resources are located in Siberia? **Predict** Study Siberia's geography. What challenges might Russians face in making use of Siberia's resources?

Go Online PHSchool.com Use Web Code ldp-7123 for step-by-step **map skills practice**.

Answers

MAP ✦ MASTER™ **Note** fourteen **Predict**
Possible answer: Siberia is so far north that its cold climate might make it difficult to access and transport its resources. Siberia's large size might restrict the transportation of resources.

Go Online PHSchool.com Students may practice their map skills using the interactive online version of this map.

Differentiated Instruction

For Less Proficient Readers ▪①
Have students read the section as they listen to the recorded version on the Student Edition on Audio CD. Check for comprehension by pausing the CD after each paragraph and asking students to summarize what they have just read.

▸ Chapter 6, Section 3, **Eastern Hemisphere Student Edition on Audio CD**

For Special Needs Students ▪①
Explain to students that they can use word roots to help find the meaning of unfamiliar words. Break down the word *hydroelectric* into its parts—*hydro* and *electric*. Explain that "hydro" is a prefix meaning "water." Ask students to explain what "electric" means. Then help students to understand the full meaning of the word.

From Plants to Fossil Fuel

1. Peat is made of partially decayed plant material. ▶

2. Over millions of years, material ▶ built up over ancient peat deposits. The pressure of this material gradually changed the peat into brown coal.

◀ 3. Continuing pressure gradually turned brown coal into soft coal. Soft coal is the most common coal found on Earth. It is often used in industry.

Fossil Fuels and Minerals Russia has the largest reserves, or available supply, of natural gas in the world. It is also one of the world's five leading oil producers. Scientists estimate that the country has about one third of the world's coal reserves. In addition, Russia has huge deposits of minerals, including cobalt, chromium, copper, and gold.

Russia also has the world's largest reserves of iron ore, which is used to make steel. Many of these iron ore deposits are in the part of Russia that is on the continent of Europe. That is one reason why most of Russia's industry is west of the Ural Mountains. Fueled by its natural resources, Russian factories produce automobiles, cloth, machinery, computers, and chemicals.

Forest, Fishing, and Energy Resources Russia has the world's largest forest reserves. Wood harvested from these forests is used to make paper and pulp, and it also supplies wood for houses and furniture.

Because of Russia's location on the Pacific Ocean, fish provide another abundant resource. Russians also fish the Black and Caspian seas, as well as the country's many inland lakes. The fishing industry is an important part of Russia's economy.

Finally, Russia has ample energy resources. It uses much of its fossil fuel resources to produce electricity. In addition, many Russian rivers are dammed to generate electricity in hydroelectric plants. Russia is one of the world's largest producers of electricity.

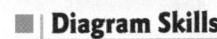

▌ Diagram Skills

A man in Ireland cuts pieces of peat from the ground. **Explain** If this peat stayed in the ground, how long would it take to turn into brown coal? **Apply Information** Explain why coal is a nonrenewable resource, using information from the diagram.

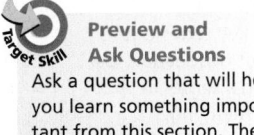

Preview and Ask Questions
Ask a question that will help you learn something important from this section. Then read the section, and answer your question.

Chapter 6 Section 3 **169**

Guided Instruction (continued)

- Ask students **What major natural resources are found in Siberia?** (*oil, natural gas, coal, and forests*)

- Ask students **Why is it difficult for Russians to transport their natural resources from Siberia?** (*Siberia is far from the population and industrial centers of the country. Transport is difficult due to Russia's huge size. Transport via water is difficult because most of Siberia's rivers do not flow toward important cities.*)

- Ask students **What generalization can you make about the natural resources of Russia?** (*Possible answer: Russia has an abundance of natural resources, yet they are often difficult to reach and transport.*)

Independent Practice
Have students complete the graphic organizer by moving the resources common to both Europe and Russia into the overlapping portion of the circles.

Monitor Progress
- Show *Section Reading Support Transparency ER 34* and ask students to check their graphic organizers individually. Go over key concepts and clarify key vocabulary as needed.

  📖 **Europe and Russia Transparencies,** *Section Reading Support Transparency ER 34*

- Tell students to fill in the last column of the *Reading Readiness Guide.* Probe for what they learned that confirms or invalidates each statement.

  All in One Europe and Russia Teaching Resources, *Reading Readiness Guide,* p. 115

⟳ Target Reading Skill L2
Preview and Ask Questions As a follow up, have students answer the Target Reading Skill question in the Student Edition. (*Students' questions and answers should reflect an understanding of the section and the skill.*)

Answers
Diagram Skills **Explain** millions of years **Apply Information** Possible answers: Once all existing coal is used up, it will take millions of years for more to form.

Differentiated Instruction

For Advanced Readers L3
Have students read *The Endless Steppe* to learn more about the harsh lands of Siberia. Then ask them to answer the questions at the end of the selection.

All in One Europe and Russia Teaching Resources, *The Endless Steppe,* pp. 131–132

Assess and Reteach

Assess Progress
Have students complete the Section Assessment. Administer the *Section Quiz*.

 Europe and Russia Teaching Resources, *Section Quiz,* p. 117

Reteach
If students need more instruction, have them read this section in the Reading and Vocabulary Study Guide.

 Chapter 6, Section 3, **Eastern Hemisphere Reading and Vocabulary Study Guide,** pp. 62–64

Extend
Remind students that efforts to get and use resources in Siberia have led to some environmental problems. Have students begin to work on *Reporting to an Environmental Conference,* a long-term project that will help them learn more about environmental problems that affect regions in Europe and Russia and other parts of the world.

Go Online
PHSchool.com

For: Long-Term Integrated Projects: *Reporting to an Environmental Conference*
Visit: PHSchool.com
Web Code: ldd-7105

Answers

Infer possible answer: pollution

✓ Reading Check Most of these resources are located in Siberia.

Section 3 Assessment

Key Terms
Students' sentences should reflect knowledge of each Key Term.

Target Reading Skill
Students' questions will vary. Students should explain how asking questions helped them as they read this section.

Comprehension and Critical Thinking
1. (a) fertile soil, water, and fuel **(b)** Water is used for drinking, growing crops, and producing hydroelectric power.

2. (a) coal, oil, natural gas, and fertile soil **(b)** Many Ukrainians probably farm for a living and to feed their families.

3. (a) minerals, oil, natural gas, coal, iron ore, and forests **(b)** Western Europe has developed its resources to become an important industrial region while Russia has not been able to fully develop its resources. **(c)** The size of the country, the cold climate, and a lack of river transportation routes have hindered Russia's ability to develop its resources fully and bring wealth to its people.

Writing Activity
Use the *Rubric for Assessing a Writing Assignment* to evaluate students' paragraphs.

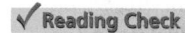 **Europe and Russia Teaching Resources,** *Rubric for Assessing a Writing Assignment,* p. 137

Breaking Up Old Ships
When ships are no longer seaworthy, they are broken apart like this oil tanker in the harbor of Murmansk, Russia. Breaking up ships often causes environmental and health problems. **Infer** *What specific problems might breaking up an oil tanker cause?*

Challenges to Using Russia's Resources Most of Russia's deposits of oil, natural gas, and coal are located in Siberia. Three fourths of Russia's forests are located there, too. These forests contain half of the world's reserves of softwood timber. However, Siberia is far from the population and industrial centers of the country.

Russia's huge size presents a major challenge to transporting Siberian resources to areas where they are needed. Except for the Volga, Russia's rivers are not very useful for transportation. Siberia's rivers do not flow toward Russia's most important cities. Instead, they flow north into the Arctic Ocean. In spite of these problems and the bitter-cold winter weather, Russia has found ways to move resources from Siberia. Pipelines carry oil and natural gas, and railroads transport coal to European Russia.

Extracting Russia's resources has created a new challenge—protecting the environment. Some of the world's worst cases of pollution are found in Russia, especially Siberia. Nuclear waste has been dumped into rivers for 40 years. Air pollution from factories is very severe. Besides finding ways to develop its valuable resources, Russia must also consider how to restore polluted areas.

✓ **Reading Check** Where are most of Russia's oil, natural gas, and coal deposits located?

Section 3 Assessment

Key Terms
Review the key terms at the beginning of this section. Use each term in a sentence that explains its meaning.

Target Reading Skill
Look at the list of questions you asked. Which ones helped you learn and remember something from this section?

Comprehension and Critical Thinking
1. (a) List Name Western Europe's major natural resources.

(b) Summarize How is water used as a natural resource in Western Europe?
2. (a) Recall Which important natural resources are located in Ukraine?
(b) Draw Conclusions Why is farming important to Ukraine?
3. (a) List Name Russia's major natural resources.
(b) Compare and Contrast How do Western Europe and Russia differ in their use of natural resources?
(c) Draw Conclusions Why is Russia not as wealthy as Western Europe?

Writing Activity
What do you think is the most important natural resource in Europe and Russia? What makes that resource so important? Write a paragraph explaining your choice. Be sure to include a main idea statement in your paragraph.

Writing Tip Before you begin writing, list all the natural resources discussed in the section. Then choose which you think is most important.

Review and Assessment

◆ Chapter Summary

Section 1: Land and Water
- Europe and Russia are part of Eurasia, the world's largest landmass.
- Both Europe and Russia have plains, uplands, and mountains.
- Europe's major rivers are the Rhine and the Danube, and Russia's is the Volga.

Section 2: Climate and Vegetation
- Oceans and mountains both affect the climates of Europe and Russia.
- The climate regions of Europe and Russia range from Mediterranean to subarctic.
- The natural vegetation of Europe and Russia is as varied as its climate and includes forest, grassland, and tundra.

London

Ukraine

Section 3: Resources and Land Use
- The resources of Western Europe include fertile soil, water, and fossil fuels.
- Eastern Europe has resources similar to those of Western Europe, including coal, oil, and natural gas.
- Russia has abundant mineral, energy, and other resources, with the majority of these resources located in Siberia.

◆ Key Terms
Use each key term below in a sentence that shows the meaning of the term.

1. population density
2. navigable
3. peninsula
4. plateau
5. tributary
6. rain shadow
7. loess
8. tundra
9. permafrost
10. steppes
11. hydroelectric power
12. fossil fuel

┌ Vocabulary Builder ─

Revisit this chapter's high-use words:

landmass	dramatic	nourish
enable	overlap	element
level	brief	transport
link	deposit	

Ask students to review the definitions they recorded on their *Word Knowledge* worksheets.

All in One Europe and Russia Teaching Resources, *Word Knowledge,* p. 121

Consider allowing students to earn extra credit if they use the words in their answers to the questions in the Chapter Review and Assessment. The words must be used correctly and in a natural context to win the extra points.

- Review and revisit the major themes of this chapter by asking students to classify what Guiding Question each bulleted statement in the Chapter Summary answers. Place students in groups to classify the statements. Use the Numbered Heads participation strategy (TE, p. T36) to have the groups share their answers in a group discussion. Refer to p. 1 in the Student Edition for the text of the Guiding Questions.

- Assign *Vocabulary Development* for students to review Key Terms.

All in One Europe and Russia Teaching Resources, *Vocabulary Development,* p. 135

Answers

Key Terms

1–12. Students' sentences should reflect knowledge of each Key Term.

Comprehension and Critical Thinking

13. (a) The countries of Europe are more densely populated than Russia. More people live in the North European Plain than in any other part of Russia. **(b)** The plains are less mountainous than other areas and have a relatively mild climate. The most productive farmland is found there.

14. (a) The Central Uplands are a region of Europe made up of mountains and plateaus. **(b)** The uplands are used for raising sheep and goats, as well as mineral mining. **(c)** The Central Uplands are characterized by mountains and plateaus, while the North European Plain consists of a broad plain that is more favorable for human settlement.

15. (a) two of the following: oceans, the North Atlantic Current, and mountains **(b)** Warm ocean currents bring warm air and winds to northwestern Europe, making the region's climate mild. The fact that much of Russia is far from oceans is one reason for the climate's harshness.

16. (a) A Mediterranean climate has hot, dry summers and mild, rainy winters. **(b)** A Mediterranean climate is much milder and enjoys longer summers than a subarctic climate.

17. (a) Western and Eastern Europe both share fertile soil, water, fuel deposits, and iron ore; Russia has fuel deposits, iron ore, and forests. **(b)** If a river flows toward major cities and is navigable year-round, ships can easily travel along it to transport goods at any time of the year. **(c)** Western Europe's resources are more fully developed than Russia's because they are accessible, and it is easier to transport them along Europe's many rivers. Russia's resources are often located far from industrial centers, and transportation of resources along rivers is hampered by the fact that many rivers either flow away from industrial centers or freeze during winter.

18. (a) oil, coal, natural gas **(b)** The development of natural resources affects how people in an area make a living. For example, in areas with rich oil deposits, many people might work at oil refineries.

Skills Practice
Students' conclusions should use accurate information from the map and show that they are able to apply the skill steps.

◆ Comprehension and Critical Thinking

13. (a) Identify Which areas of Europe and Russia are the most densely populated?
(b) Summarize What physical features encouraged people to settle in those areas?

14. (a) Define What are the European Central Uplands?
(b) List Name two uses of these uplands.
(c) Contrast How do the Central Uplands differ from the North European Plain?

15. (a) Name List two factors that affect the climates of Europe and Russia.
(b) Summarize What effect do large bodies of water have on climate in Europe and Russia?

16. (a) Describe Explain what a Mediterranean climate is.
(b) Compare and Contrast How is a Mediterranean climate similar to or different from a subarctic climate?

17. (a) Identify What are the major natural resources of Western Europe, of Eastern Europe, and of Russia?
(b) Predict What factors might influence how well a river can be used to transport resources?
(c) Identify Cause and Effect Why are Western Europe's natural resources more fully developed than Russia's natural resources?

18. (a) List Name three kinds of fossil fuels.
(b) Draw Conclusions How does the development of natural resources affect the way that people live?

◆ Skills Practice

Using a Precipitation Map In the Skills for Life activity in this chapter, you learned how to use a precipitation map. The steps you followed to learn this skill can be applied to other kinds of special purpose maps.

Review the steps you used to learn the skill. Then turn to the map titled Europe: Natural Resources on page 165. Use the map title and key to read and interpret the map. Then write a conclusion about the information the map contains.

◆ Writing Activity: Geography

Suppose you are visiting a fourth-grade classroom. You have been asked to report to the students on Europe and Russia's geography. Write a brief report on this subject. To get started, write down the various kinds of landforms and bodies of water that are discussed in the chapter. Do the same for the human and natural resources of Europe and Russia. Then explain in your report how life is similar and different for the people who live in different regions of Europe and Russia.

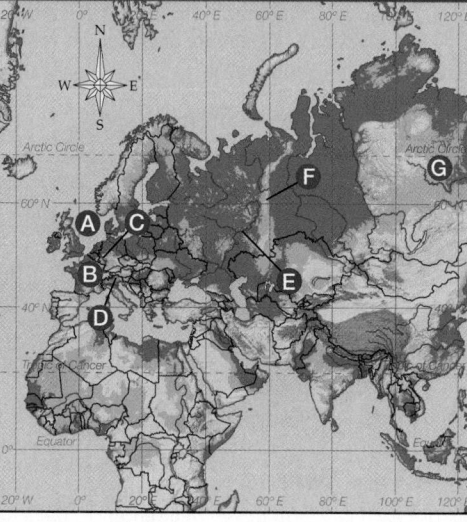

MAP✦MASTER™
Skills Activity
Europe and Russia

Place Location For each place listed below, write the letter from the map that shows its location.
1. France
2. Ural Mountains
3. Alps
4. Siberia
5. Rhine River
6. Volga River
7. North Sea

Go Online
PHSchool.com Use Web Code **ldp-7183** for an **interactive map.**

Writing Activity
Students' reports will vary, but should compare and contrast the ways in which landforms, waterways, climate, vegetation, and natural resources affect the lives of people in Europe and Russia.

Use the *Rubric for Assessing a Writing Assignment* to evaluate students' reports.

All in One Europe and Russia Teaching Resources, *Rubric for Assessing a Writing Assignment,* p. 137

Standardized Test Prep

Test-Taking Tips

Some questions on standardized tests ask you to make mental maps. Read the passage below. Then follow the tips to answer the sample question.

Ben is playing a trivia game. One of the geography questions asks, "Which mountain range divides Russia between two continents, Europe and Asia?" What is the correct answer?

Choose the letter that best answers the question.

A Kjolen Mountains

B Ural Mountains

~~**C** Pyrenees~~

~~**D** Alps~~

TIP Rule out choices that do not make sense. Then choose the best answer from the remaining choices.

Think It Through You can rule out the Alps and Pyrenees because both are inside Europe. Which sounds more familiar to you, the Ural Mountains or the Kjolen Mountains? The correct answer is an important range and is likely to be a name you have heard. As it turns out, the Kjolen Mountains are in Scandinavia—in northern Europe. The correct answer is B.

TIP Try to picture a physical map of Europe and Russia. Then try to place each of these mountain ranges on your mental map.

Practice Questions

Use the tips above and other tips in this book to help you answer the following questions.

1. Which Russian feature covers more than 4 million square miles (10 million square kilometers)?

   A grasslands   **B** taiga

   C polders   **D** tundra

2. Because of its location near the Mediterranean Sea, Barcelona's summers are

   A mild and wet.

   B cold and snowy.

   C hot and dry.

   D short and wet.

3. The climate of the northernmost areas of Europe and Russia is called

   A marine west coast.

   B Mediterranean.

   C humid continental.

   D arctic.

4. What is the location of Siberia relative to that of Spain?

   A northeast

   B southeast

   C northwest

   D west

5. The major vegetation region of Europe and Russia that is now mainly used for farming is

   A grasslands.

   B tundra.

   C taiga.

   D Mediterranean.

Use Web Code lda-7101
for a **Chapter 6 self-test.**

Standardized Test Prep

Answers

1. B

2. C

3. D

4. A

5. A

Assessment Resources

Use *Chapter Tests A and B* to assess students' mastery of the chapter content.

All in One Europe and Russia Teaching Resources, *Chapter Tests A and B,* pp. 138–143

Tests are also available on the *ExamView® Test Bank CD-ROM.*

⊙ *ExamView® Test Bank CD-ROM*

Europe and Russia: Shaped by History

Chapter Overview

Overview

Section 1
From Ancient Greece to the Middle Ages
1. Learn how the heritage of ancient Greece influences life today.
2. Discover the glory of the ancient Roman Empire.
3. Learn about Europe in the Middle Ages.

Section 2
Renaissance and the Age of Revolution
1. Discover what the Renaissance was like at its peak.
2. Examine the effects of increased trade and stronger rulers in the Renaissance.
3. Learn about revolutions in government and science in the 1600s and 1700s.

Section 3
Industrial Revolution and Nationalism
1. Learn how the Industrial Revolution changed people's lives.
2. Examine how nationalism and war can be related.

Section 4
Imperial Russia to the Soviet Union
1. Discover how Russia built its empire.
2. Understand the fall of the Russian tsars.
3. Examine the rise and fall of the Soviet Union.
4. Learn the causes and effects of the Cold War.
5. Learn about the Russian Federation today.

Section 5
The European Union
1. Learn about the history of the European Union.
2. Understand the purpose of the European Union.
3. Examine the structure of the European Union.
4. Find out what the future holds for the European Union.

Discovery CHANNEL SCHOOL Video

St. Petersburg and Peter the Great
Length: 3 minutes, 30 seconds
Use with Section 4
This segment describes how Peter the Great built the city of Saint Petersburg. It concentrates on how the city was important to Russia, and how it brought Eastern and Western Europe together.

Technology Resources

Go Online
PHSchool.com

Students use embedded Web codes to access Internet activities, chapter self-tests, and additional map practice. They may also access Dorling Kindersley's Online Desk Reference to learn more about each country they study.

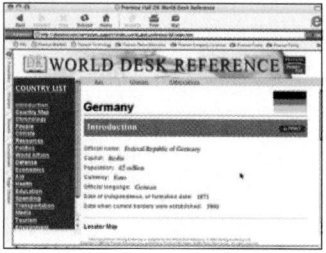

Interactive Textbook

Use the Interactive Textbook to make content and concepts come alive through animations, videos, and activities that accompany the complete basal text—online and on CD-ROM.

PRENTICE HALL
TeacherEXPRESS
Plan • Teach • Assess

Use this complete suite of powerful teaching tools to make planning lessons and administering tests quicker and easier.

Reading and Assessment

Reading and Vocabulary Instruction

🎯 Model the Target Reading Skill

Clarifying Meaning Explain to students that they can use several strategies to clarify the meanings of new words and ideas. They can reread a passage and try to link familiar and unfamiliar words and ideas. They can also read ahead to see if the author provides definitions or examples later in the passage. After reading, students can paraphrase or summarize the information to better understand and remember it.

Write the following selection from page 184 of the Student Edition on the board. Model techniques for clarifying meaning by thinking aloud as you read it to the class.

Michelangelo was an accomplished painter, poet, architect, and sculptor. Think aloud: "I'll reread to make sure I understand. I'm not sure what *accomplished* means. I'll read ahead to find out." *His lifelike statues were remarkably realistic and detailed. In some, you can see veins bulging in the hands. Or the drape of a cloak across the sculpted person looks so real that it appears to be made of cloth rather than of marble.* Think aloud: "I'll paraphrase this segment: Michelangelo was so skilled at carving that he could make marble appear to be flesh or cloth. Therefore, *accomplished* must mean very skillful. To summarize, Michelangelo was remarkably skilled in many art forms."

Use the following worksheets from All-in-One Europe and Russia Teaching Resources (pp. 169–171) to support the chapter's Target Reading Skill.

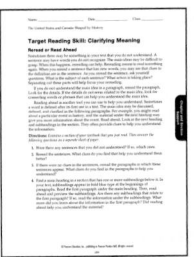 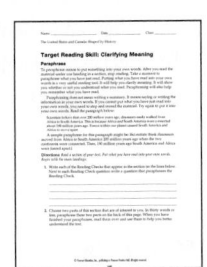 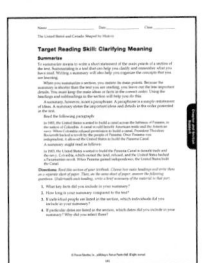

Vocabulary Builder
High-Use Academic Words

Use these steps to teach this chapter's high-use words:

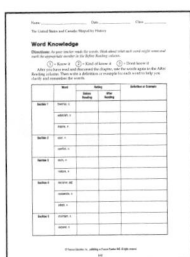

1. Have students rate how well they know each word on their Word Knowledge worksheets (All-in-One Europe and Russia Teaching Resources, p. 172).
2. Pronounce each word and ask students to repeat it.
3. Give students a brief definition or sample sentence (provided on TE pp. 177, 184, 192, 201, and 209).
4. Work with students as they fill in the "Definition or Example" column of their Word Knowledge worksheets.

Assessment

Formal Assessment

Test students' understanding of core knowledge and skills.

Chapter Tests A and B, All-in-One Europe and Russia Teaching Resources, pp. 203–208

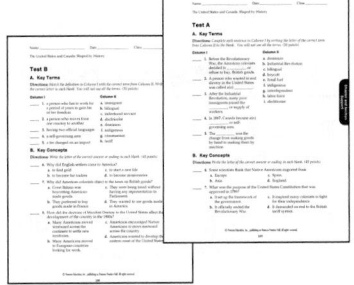

Customize the Chapter Tests to suit your needs.

ExamView Test Bank CD-ROM

Skills Assessment

Assess geographic literacy.

MapMaster Skills, Student Edition, pp. 175, 178, 195, 201, 209, 214

Assess reading and comprehension.

Target Reading Skills, Student Edition, pp. 180, 186, 195, 203, 211, and in Section Assessments

Chapter 7 Assessment, Eastern Hemisphere Reading and Vocabulary Study Guide, p. 81

Performance Assessment

Assess students' performance on this chapter's Writing Activities using the following rubrics from All-in-One Europe and Russia Teaching Resources.

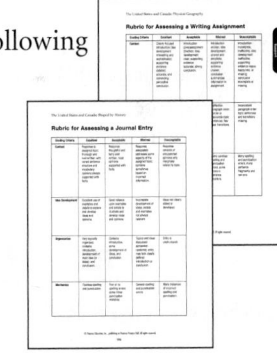

Rubric for Assessing a Journal Entry, p. 200

Rubric for Assessing a Writing Assignment, p. 201

Rubric for Assessing a Letter to the Editor, p. 202

Assess students' work through performance tasks.

Small Group Activity: Castle Mural, All-in-One Europe and Russia Teaching Resources, pp. 175–178

Online Assessment

Have students check their own understanding.

Chapter Self-Test

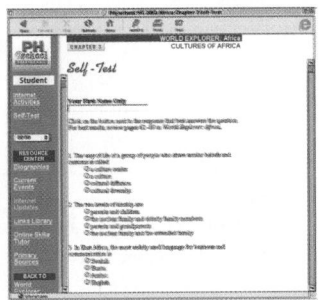

Section 1 From Ancient Greece to the Middle Ages

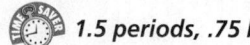 *1.5 periods, .75 block*

Social Studies Objectives
1. Learn how the heritage of ancient Greece influences life today.
2. Discover the glory of the ancient Roman Empire.
3. Learn about Europe in the Middle Ages.

Reading/Language Arts Objective
Reread to look for connections among words and sentences.

Prepare to Read	Instructional Resources	Differentiated Instruction
Build Background Knowledge Discuss how Greek and Roman cultures have influenced modern culture. **Set a Purpose for Reading** Have students evaluate statements on the *Reading Readiness Guide*. **Preview Key Terms** Teach the section's Key Terms. **Target Reading Skill** Introduce the section's Target Reading Skill of **rereading**.	**All in One Europe and Russia Teaching Resources** L2 Reading Readiness Guide, p. 150 L2 Reread or Read Ahead, p. 169	**Spanish Reading and Vocabulary Study Guide** L1 Chapter 7, Section 1, pp. 48–49 ELL

Instruct	Instructional Resources	Differentiated Instruction
The Greek Heritage Discuss ancient Greek influence on modern culture. **The Glory of Ancient Rome** Discuss the Roman Empire and its demise. **Target Reading Skill** Review **rereading**. **Europe in the Middle Ages** Discuss the changes that occurred during the Middle Ages.	**All in One Europe and Russia Teaching Resources** L2 Guided Reading and Review, p. 151 L2 Reading Readiness Guide, p. 150 **Europe and Russia Transparencies** L2 Section Reading Support Transparency ER 35	**All in One Europe and Russia Teaching Resources** L3 A Spartan Reply, p. 182 AR, GT L3 Storm in the State, p. 183 AR, GT **Teacher's Edition** L3 For Advanced Readers, TE p. 178 L3 For Gifted and Talented, TE p. 178 L1 For English Language Learners, TE p. 180 **Spanish Support** L2 Guided Reading and Review (Spanish), p. 66 ELL

Assess and Reteach	Instructional Resources	Differentiated Instruction
Assess Progress Evaluate student comprehension with the section assessment and section quiz. **Reteach** Assign the Reading and Vocabulary Study Guide to help struggling students. **Extend** Extend the lesson by assigning a Small Group Activity.	**All in One Europe and Russia Teaching Resources** L2 Section Quiz, p. 152 L3 Small Group Activity: Castle Mural, pp. 175–178 Rubric for Assessing a Journal Entry, p. 200 **Reading and Vocabulary Study Guide** L1 Chapter 7, Section 1, pp. 66–68	**Spanish Support** L2 Section Quiz (Spanish), p. 67 ELL

Key

L1 Basic to Average   L3 Average to Advanced
L2 For All Students

LPR Less Proficient Readers
AR Advanced Readers
SN Special Needs Students

GT Gifted and Talented
ELL English Language Learners

Section 2 Renaissance and the Age of Revolution

 *1 period, .5 block*

Social Studies Objectives
1. Discover what the Renaissance was like at its peak.
2. Examine the effects of increased trade and stronger rulers in the Renaissance.
3. Learn about revolutions in government and science in the 1600s and 1700s.

Reading/Language Arts Objective
Paraphrase to restate what you have read in your own words.

Prepare to Read	Instructional Resources	Differentiated Instruction
Build Background Knowledge Discuss how the invention of the printing press has influenced people's lives. **Set a Purpose for Reading** Have students begin to fill out the *Reading Readiness Guide.* **Preview Key Terms** Teach the section's Key Terms. **Target Reading Skill** Introduce the section's Target Reading Skill of **paraphrasing.**	**All in One Europe and Russia Teaching Resources** **L2** Reading Readiness Guide, p. 154 **L2** Paraphrase, p. 170	**Spanish Reading and Vocabulary Study Guide** **L1** Chapter 7, Section 2, pp. 50–51 ELL

Instruct	Instructional Resources	Differentiated Instruction
Glories of the Renaissance Discuss cultural and ideological changes that occurred during the Renaissance. **More Trade, Stronger Rulers** Discuss how overseas trade affected Europe. **Target Reading Skill** Review **paraphrasing.** **Revolutions in Government** Discuss the American and French Revolutions. **Revolutions in Science** Discuss the Scientific Revolution.	**All in One Europe and Russia Teaching Resources** **L2** Guided Reading and Review, p. 155 **L2** Reading Readiness Guide, p. 154 **Europe and Russia Transparencies** **L2** Section Reading Support Transparency ER 36	**All in One Europe and Russia Teaching Resources** **L3** Enrichment, p. 173 AR, GT **Teacher's Edition** **L1** For Less Proficient Readers, TE p. 185 **L3** For Gifted and Talented, TE p. 185 **Spanish Support** **L2** Guided Reading and Review (Spanish), p. 68 ELL

Assess and Reteach	Instructional Resources	Differentiated Instruction
Assess Progress Evaluate student comprehension with the section assessment and section quiz. **Reteach** Assign the Reading and Vocabulary Study Guide to help struggling students. **Extend** Extend the lesson by assigning a primary source reading.	**All in One Europe and Russia Teaching Resources** **L2** Section Quiz, p. 156 **L3** Testing a Theory, p. 184 Rubric for Assessing a Writing Assignment, p. 201 **Reading and Vocabulary Study Guide** **L1** Chapter 7, Section 2, pp. 69–71	**Spanish Support** **L2** Section Quiz (Spanish), p. 69 ELL

Key
L1 Basic to Average   **L3** Average to Advanced
L2 For All Students

LPR Less Proficient Readers
AR Advanced Readers
SN Special Needs Students

GT Gifted and Talented
ELL English Language Learners

Section 3 Industrial Revolution and Nationalism

 2 periods, 1 block (includes Skills for Life)

Social Studies Objectives
1. Learn how the Industrial Revolution changed people's lives.
2. Examine how nationalism and war can be related.

Reading/Language Arts Objective
Summarize to better understand the text.

Prepare to Read	Instructional Resources	Differentiated Instruction
Build Background Knowledge Discuss ways that countries show nationalism. **Set a Purpose for Reading** Have students evaluate statements on the *Reading Readiness Guide*. **Preview Key Terms** Teach the section's Key Terms. **Target Reading Skill** Introduce the section's Target Reading Skill of **summarizing.**	**All in One Europe and Russia Teaching Resources** L2 Reading Readiness Guide, p. 158 L2 Summarize, p. 171	**Spanish Reading and Vocabulary Study Guide** L1 Chapter 7, Section 3, pp. 52–53 ELL

Instruct	Instructional Resources	Differentiated Instruction
The Industrial Revolution Discuss changes in Europe during and after the Industrial Revolution. **Eyewitness Technology** Discuss a textile mill. **Target Reading Skill** Review **summarizing.** **A Century of War and Nationalism** Discuss nationalism and World Wars I and II.	**All in One Europe and Russia Teaching Resources** L2 Guided Reading and Review, p. 159 L2 Reading Readiness Guide, p. 158 **Europe and Russia Transparencies** L2 Transparency B6: Flow Chart L2 Section Reading Support Transparency ER 37	**All in One Europe and Russia Teaching Resources** L3 A Child in Prison Camp, pp. 185–187 AR, GT L2 Skills for Life, p. 174 AR, GT, LPR, SN **Teacher's Edition** L1 For English Language Learners, TE p. 193 L3 For Advanced Readers, TE p. 196 L1 For Special Needs Students, TE p. 196 **Student Edition on Audio CD** L1 Chapter 2, Section 3 ELL, LPR, SN

Assess and Reteach	Instructional Resources	Differentiated Instruction
Assess Progress Evaluate student comprehension with the section assessment and section quiz. **Reteach** Assign the Reading and Vocabulary Study Guide to help struggling students. **Extend** Extend the lesson by assigning an online activity.	**All in One Europe and Russia Teaching Resources** L2 Section Quiz, p. 160 Rubric for Assessing a Writing Assignment, p. 201 **Reading and Vocabulary Study Guide** L1 Chapter 7, Section 3, pp. 72–74 **PHSchool.com** L3 For: Long-term Integrated Projects: Making a Book About World Technologies **Web Code:** ldd-7206	**Spanish Support** L2 Section Quiz (Spanish), p. 71 ELL **Teacher's Edition** L1 For Special Needs Students, TE p. 199 **Social Studies Skills Tutor CD-ROM** L1 Problem Solving ELL, LPR, SN

Key

L1 Basic to Average	L3 Average to Advanced	LPR Less Proficient Readers	GT Gifted and Talented
L2 For All Students		AR Advanced Readers	ELL English Language Learners
		SN Special Needs Students	

Section 4 Imperial Russia to the Soviet Union

1 period, .5 block

Social Studies Objectives
1. Discover how Russia built its empire.
2. Understand the fall of the Russian tsars.
3. Examine the rise and fall of the Soviet Union.
4. Learn the causes and effects of the Cold War.
5. Learn about the Russian Federation today.

Reading/Language Arts Objective
Read ahead to help clarify an unfamiliar word or passage.

Prepare to Read	Instructional Resources	Differentiated Instruction
Build Background Knowledge Ask students to generate a list of words that describe Catherine the Great. **Set a Purpose for Reading** Have students evaluate statements on the *Reading Readiness Guide* worksheet. **Preview Key Terms** Teach the section's Key Terms. **Target Reading Skill** Introduce the section's Target Reading Skill of **reading ahead**.	**All in One Europe and Russia Teaching Resources** L2 Reading Readiness Guide, p. 162 L2 Reread or Read Ahead, p. 169	**Spanish Reading and Vocabulary Study Guide** L1 Chapter 7, Section 4, pp. 54–55 ELL

Instruct	Instructional Resources	Differentiated Instruction
Building a Vast Empire Discuss the Russian Empire. **The Fall of the Tsars** Discuss some of the challenges Russia faced in the early 1900s. **Target Reading Skill** Review **reading ahead**. **The Rise of the Soviet Union** Ask about Lenin, Stalin, and World War II. **The Cold War** Discuss the Cold War and the collapse of the Soviet Union. **The Russian Federation** Discuss some of the challenges the Russian Federation has faced.	**All in One Europe and Russia Teaching Resources** L2 Guided Reading and Review, p. 163 L2 Reading Readiness Guide, p. 162 **Europe and Russia Transparencies** L2 Section Reading Support Transparency ER 38 **World Studies Video Program** L2 St. Petersburg and Peter the Great	**All in One Europe and Russia Teaching Resources** L3 A Letter from Napoleon's Army, pp. 188–189 AR, GT L3 Lenin's Deathbed Words, p. 190 AR, GT L3 Kampf, p. 191 AR, GT **Teacher's Edition** L3 For Advanced Readers, TE p. 203 L2 For English Language Learners, TE p. 203 L3 For Gifted and Talented, TE p. 205 L1 For Less Proficient Readers, TE pp. 205, 206 **Reading and Vocabulary Study Guide** L1 Chapter 7, Section 4, pp. 75–77 ELL, LPR, SN

Assess and Reteach	Instructional Resources	Differentiated Instruction
Assess Progress Evaluate student comprehension with the section assessment and section quiz. **Reteach** Assign the Reading and Vocabulary Study Guide to help struggling students. **Extend** Extend the lesson by assigning The Endless Steppe.	**All in One Europe and Russia Teaching Resources** L2 Section Quiz, p. 164 L3 The Endless Steppe, pp. 192–193 Rubric for Assessing a Writing Assignment, p. 201 **Reading and Vocabulary Study Guide** L1 Chapter 7, Section 4, pp. 75–77	**Spanish Support** L2 Section Quiz (Spanish), p. 73 ELL

Key

L1 Basic to Average L3 Average to Advanced	LPR Less Proficient Readers GT Gifted and Talented
L2 For All Students	AR Advanced Readers ELL English Language Learners
	SN Special Needs Students

Section 5 The European Union

 4 periods, 2 blocks (includes Chapter Review and Assessment and Literature)

Social Studies Objectives

1. Learn about the history of the European Union.
2. Understand the purpose of the European Union.
3. Examine the structure of the European Union.
4. Find out what the future holds for the European Union.

Reading/Language Arts Objective

Reread or read ahead to help understand words and ideas in the text.

Prepare to Read

Build Background Knowledge
Discuss the word *union*.

Set a Purpose for Reading
Have students evaluate statements on the *Reading Readiness Guide* worksheet.

Preview Key Terms
Teach the section's Key Terms.

Target Reading Skill
Introduce the section's Target Reading Skill of **rereading or reading ahead.**

Instructional Resources

All in One Europe and Russia Teaching Resources
- **L2** Reading Readiness Guide, p. 166
- **L2** Reread or Read Ahead, p. 169

Differentiated Instruction

Spanish Reading and Vocabulary Study Guide
- **L1** Chapter 7, Section 5, pp. 56–57 ELL

Instruct

History of the European Union
Discuss the history of the European Union.

What does the European Union Do?
Discuss goals and policies of the EU.

Structure of the European Union
Discuss the institutions responsible for making policy.

Future of the European Union
Ask questions about nations joining the European Union in the future.

Target Reading Skill
Review **rereading or reading ahead.**

Instructional Resources

All in One Europe and Russia Teaching Resources
- **L2** Guided Reading and Review, p. 167
- **L2** Reading Readiness Guide, p. 166

Europe and Russia Transparencies
- **L2** Section Reading Support Transparency ER 39

Differentiated Instruction

All in One Europe and Russia Teaching Resources
- **L3** Whose Falkland Islands Are They? pp. 194–196 AR, GT

Teacher's Edition
- **L1** For Special Needs Students, TE p. 210
- **L3** For Advanced Readers, TE p. 210
- **L3** For Gifted and Talented, TE p. 218

Reading and Vocabulary Study Guide
- **L1** Chapter 7, Section 5, pp. 78–80 ELL, LPR, SN

Spanish Support
- **L2** Guided Reading and Review (Spanish), p. 74 ELL

Assess and Reteach

Assess Progress
Evaluate student comprehension with the section assessment and section quiz.

Reteach
Assign the Reading and Vocabulary Study Guide to help struggling students.

Extend
Extend the lesson by assigning a map activity.

Instructional Resources

All in One Europe and Russia Teaching Resources
- **L2** Section Quiz, p. 168
- **L3** Outline Maps 14, 17, and 18, pp. 179–181
  Rubric for Assessing a Letter to the Editor, p. 202
- **L2** Vocabulary Development, p. 199
- **L2** Word Knowledge, p. 172
- **L2** Rubric for Assessing a Writing Assignment, p. 201
- **L2** Chapter Tests A and B, pp. 203–208

Reading and Vocabulary Study Guide
- **L1** Chapter 7, Section 5, pp. 78–80

Differentiated Instruction

All in One Europe and Russia Teaching Resources
- **L3** Lords and Vassals, p. 197 AR, GT
  Rubric for Assessing a Writing Assignment, p. 201

Spanish Support
- **L2** Section Quiz (Spanish), p. 75 ELL
- **L2** Chapter Summary (Spanish), p. 76 ELL
- **L2** Vocabulary Development (Spanish), p. 77 ELL

Key
- **L1** Basic to Average
- **L2** For All Students
- **L3** Average to Advanced
- **LPR** Less Proficient Readers
- **AR** Advanced Readers
- **SN** Special Needs Students
- **GT** Gifted and Talented
- **ELL** English Language Learners

Reading Background

Pre-Teaching Vocabulary

Research literature on academic vocabulary instruction indicates that effective strategies require students to go beyond simply looking up dictionary definitions or examining the context. Vocabulary learning needs to be based on the learner's dynamic engagement in constructing understanding.

If students are not retaining the meaning of the Key Terms or high-use words, use this extended vocabulary sequence to engage them in learning new words.

1. Present the word in writing and point out the part of speech.
2. Pronounce the word and then have students pronounce the word.
3. Provide a range of familiar synonyms (or "it's like" words) before offering definitions.
4. Provide an accessible definition and concrete examples, or "showing sentences."
5. Rephrase the simple definition or example sentence, asking students to complete the statement by substituting the word aloud.
6. Check for understanding by providing an application task/ question requiring critical thinking.

Sample instructional sequence:

1. Our first word is *monarch*. It is a noun, a word that names a person, place, or thing.
2. Say the word *monarch* after me. (Students repeat.)
3. A *monarch* is like a *king* or *queen*.
4. The word *monarch* means *a ruler of a kingdom or empire*; A *monarch* has power over his or her people.
5. A _____ usually inherits his or her title, whereas a president is an elected official. (Students substitute the word.)
6. What are some of the differences between a monarch and a president? (Students answer the question.)

Encourage Active Participation

In this chapter, students may use an Idea Wave to share their ideas. Remind students that if their idea is closely related to another person's idea, they should acknowledge the other person's ideas when they share theirs. Below are some language strategies for active classroom participation:

> *My idea is similar to _____'s idea.*
> *As _____ already pointed out, it seems like….*
> *I don't agree with _____ because….*

World Studies Background

Michelangelo

Like Leonardo da Vinci, Michelangelo Buonarroti (1475–1564) was an important figure during the Renaissance. He worked in his native Italy as a sculptor, painter, architect, and poet. Some of his most famous works include the sculpture *David* and the paintings on the ceiling of the Sistine Chapel at the Vatican in Rome. At the rear of the chapel is *The Last Judgment*, thought by many to be Michelangelo's greatest masterpiece.

Luddites

Bands of handicraft workers known as Luddites led uprisings in the industrial areas of England during the early 1800s. These textile workers took their name from a mythical figure, King Ludd. Their riots, in which they destroyed power looms and other machines, were carried out in anger over low wages and employment issues.

A Great Debate

A famous debate about the differences in Soviet and American lifestyles took place during the Cold War. While touring a U.S. exhibit of a model home in Moscow in 1959, then Vice President Richard Nixon and Russian Premier Nikita Khrushchev began an argument over which nation had the better economic system. This informal debate over capitalism and communism became known as the "kitchen debate."

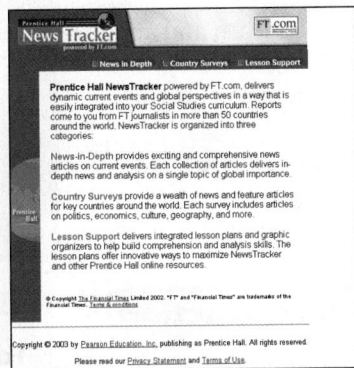

Get in-depth information on topics of global importance with **Prentice Hall Newstracker,** powered by FT.com.

Use Web code **ldd-7200** for **Prentice Hall Newstracker.**

Chapter 7
Europe and Russia: Shaped by History

Guiding Questions

Remind students about the Guiding Questions at the beginning of this section.

Section 1 relates to **Guiding Question ➋** **How have Europe and Russia been affected by their history?** *(Ancient Greek and Roman ideas influenced many European legal systems.)*

Section 2 relates to **Guiding Question ➌** **How have the people of Europe and Russia been shaped by their culture?** *(Europeans were influenced by Renaissance ideas in the 1500s.)*

Section 3 relates to **Guiding Question ➋** **How have Europe and Russia been affected by their history?** *(The Industrial Revolution changed industry and society. During the 1900s, destructive nationalism contributed to two world wars and the deaths of millions.)*

Section 4 relates to **Guiding Question ➍** **What types of government have existed in Europe and Russia?** *(Tsars ruled Russia until 1917. The Communists established the Soviet Union, which broke apart in 1991. Russia became more democratic.)*

Section 5 relates to **Guiding Question ➎** **How have Russian and European economies developed into what they are today?** *(The European Union was formed to promote a strong economy among European nations.)*

➲ Target Reading Skill

In this chapter, students will learn and apply the reading skill of clarifying meaning. Use the following worksheets to help students practice this skill:

All in One Europe and Russia Teaching Resources, *Reread or Read Ahead,* p. 169; *Paraphrase,* p. 170; *Summarize,* p. 171

Chapter Preview

This chapter presents the history of Europe and Russia and shows how that history affects the region to this day.

Section 1
From Ancient Greece to the Middle Ages

Section 2
Renaissance and the Age of Revolution

Section 3
Industrial Revolution and Nationalism

Section 4
Imperial Russia to the Soviet Union

Section 5
The European Union

➲ Target Reading Skill

Clarifying Meaning In this chapter you will focus on clarifying, or better understanding, the meaning of what you read.

▶ A bridge built in the 1100s still spans the Rhone River in Avignon, France.

Differentiated Instruction

The following Teacher's Edition strategies are suitable for students of varying abilities.

Advanced Readers, pp. 178, 196, 203, 210
English Language Learners, pp. 180, 193, 203
Gifted and Talented, pp. 178, 185, 205, 218
Less Proficient Readers, pp. 185, 205, 206
Special Needs Students, pp. 196, 199, 210

Bibliography

For the Teacher
Carlson, Laurie. *Classical Kids: An Activity Guide to Life in Ancient Greece and Rome.* Chicago Review Press, 1998.
Cole, Alison, *The Renaissance.* Dorling Kindersley, 2000.
Fitzpatrick, Sheila. *Everyday Stalinism: Ordinary Life in Extraordinary Times: Soviet Russia in the 1930s.* Oxford University Press, 2000.

For the Student
L1 Collins, Mary. *The Industrial Revolution* (Cornerstones of Freedom Series). Children's Book Press, 2001.
L2 Herbert, Janis. *Marco Polo for Kids.* Chicago Review Press, 2001.
L3 Rogers, Stillman D. *Russia* (Enchantment of the World Series). Children's Book Press, 2002.

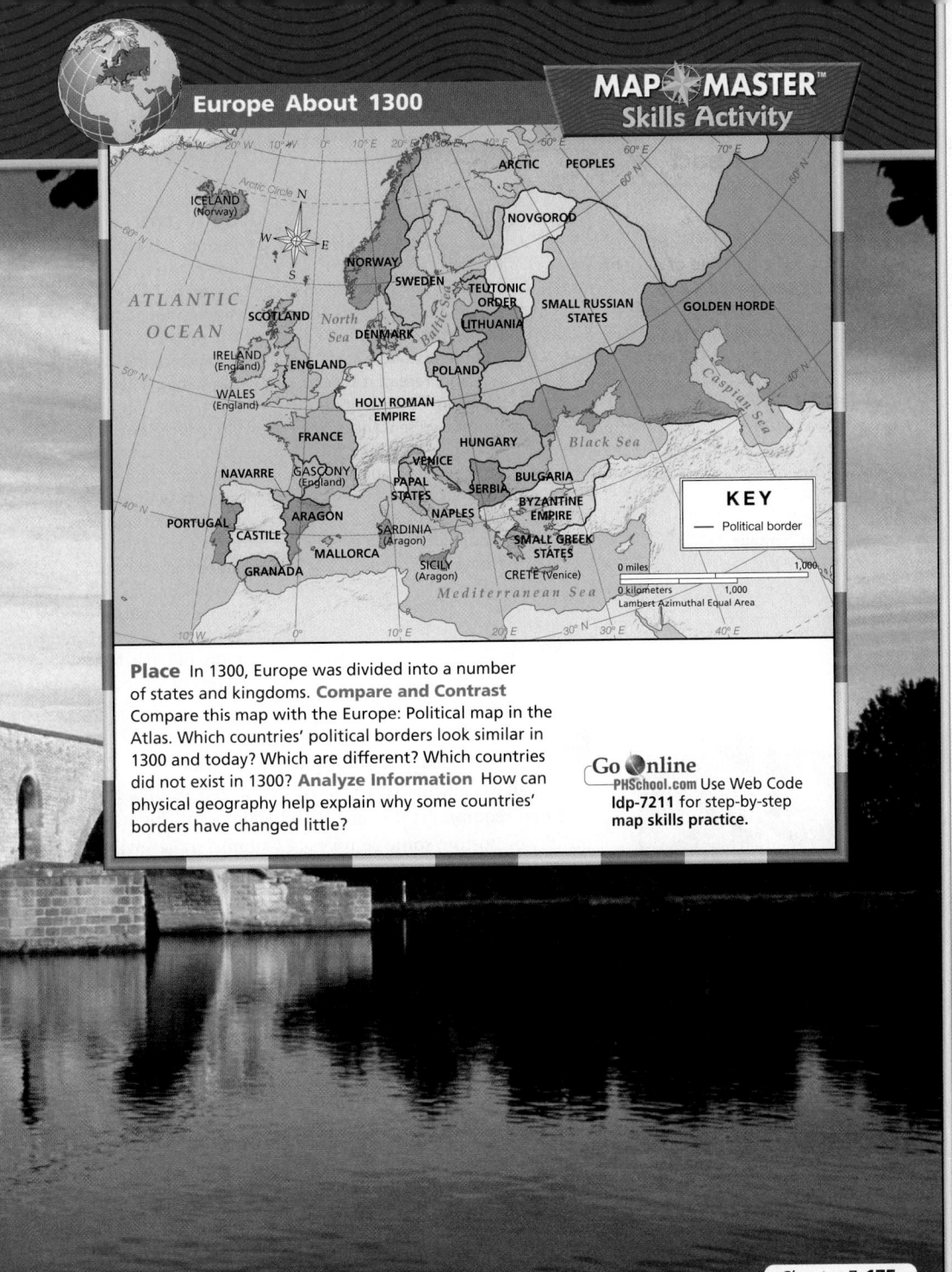

Europe About 1300

MAP MASTER™ Skills Activity

ARCTIC PEOPLES

ICELAND (Norway)

NOVGOROD

NORWAY

SWEDEN

TEUTONIC ORDER

SMALL RUSSIAN STATES

GOLDEN HORDE

ATLANTIC OCEAN

SCOTLAND

North Sea

DENMARK

LITHUANIA

IRELAND (England)

ENGLAND

POLAND

WALES (England)

HOLY ROMAN EMPIRE

FRANCE

HUNGARY

Black Sea

NAVARRE

GASCONY (England)

VENICE

PAPAL STATES

SERBIA

BULGARIA

BYZANTINE EMPIRE

PORTUGAL

ARAGON

NAPLES

SARDINIA (Aragon)

SMALL GREEK STATES

CASTILE

MALLORCA

GRANADA

SICILY (Aragon)

CRETE (Venice)

Mediterranean Sea

Caspian Sea

KEY

— Political border

0 miles 1,000
0 kilometers 1,000
Lambert Azimuthal Equal Area

Place In 1300, Europe was divided into a number of states and kingdoms. **Compare and Contrast** Compare this map with the Europe: Political map in the Atlas. Which countries' political borders look similar in 1300 and today? Which are different? Which countries did not exist in 1300? **Analyze Information** How can physical geography help explain why some countries' borders have changed little?

Go Online PHSchool.com Use Web Code ldp-7211 for step-by-step map skills practice.

Chapter 7 **175**

MAP MASTER™ Skills Activity

Have students carefully study the map on this page. Then have them create a two-column chart on a piece of paper. In the first column, students should make a list of all of the countries on the map. Then, have students study the political map of Europe in the Atlas, and identify which present-day countries correspond to the countries of Europe around 1300. Have them write these countries in the second column of their charts.

Go Online PHSchool.com Students may practice their map skills using the interactive online version of this map.

Using the Visual L2

Reach Into Your Background Point out the photograph on pp. 174–175 and its caption. Ask students to think about how the bridge in the photograph is similar to and different from modern bridges. Use an Idea Wave (TE, p. T35) to create a list of responses.

Answers

MAP MASTER Skills Activity **Compare and Contrast** Similar: Iceland, Norway, Denmark, Ireland, Portugal, Serbia, Bulgaria; Different: Sweden, Hungary, Lithuania, Poland, France; Did not exist: Finland, Belarus, Ukraine, Romania, Moldova, Macedonia, Albania, Bosnia and Herzegovina, Croatia, Slovakia, Austria, Czech Republic, Switzerland, Belgium, the Netherlands, Latvia, Estonia, Russia, United Kingdom, Germany, Turkey, Spain, Italy, Greece **Analyze Information** Physical barriers that form a border may prevent a country from changing in size.

Chapter Resources

Teaching Resources
L2 Vocabulary Development, p. 199
L2 Skills for Life, p. 174
L2 Chapter Tests A and B, pp. 203–208

Spanish Support
L2 Spanish Chapter Summary, p. 76
L2 Spanish Vocabulary Development, p. 77

Media and Technology
L1 Student Edition on Audio CD
L1 Guided Reading Audiotapes, English and Spanish
L2 Social Studies Skills Tutor CD-ROM
ExamView Test Bank CD-ROM

PRENTICE HALL
Presentation EXPRESS™
Teach · Connect · Inspire

Teach this chapter's content using the PresentationExpress™ CD-ROM including:
- slide shows
- transparencies
- interactive maps and media
- *ExamView*® QuickTake Presenter

Objectives

Social Studies

1. Learn how the heritage of ancient Greece influences life today.
2. Discover the glory of the ancient Roman Empire.
3. Learn about Europe in the Middle Ages.

Reading/Language Arts

Reread to look for connections among words and sentences.

Prepare to Read

Build Background Knowledge **L2**

Tell students that in this section they will learn about Europe's history, beginning with ancient Greece. Have students briefly preview the headings and visuals in this section, paying careful attention to the examples of architecture. Explain that aspects of modern architecture can be traced to ancient Greek and Roman cultures. If possible, show students a photo of the White House, and explain that its columns were inspired by Greek and Roman architecture. Ask students to think of other ancient architectural features *(arches, aqueducts)* that are still in use today. Conduct an Idea Wave (TE, p. T35) to generate ideas.

Set a Purpose for Reading **L2**

- Preview the Objectives.

- Read each statement in the *Reading Readiness Guide* aloud. Ask students to mark the statements true or false.

- Have students discuss the statements in pairs or groups of four, then mark their worksheets again. Use the Numbered Heads participation strategy (TE, p. T36) to call on students to share their group's perspectives.

All in One Europe and Russia Teaching Resources, *Reading Readiness Guide,* p. 150

Vocabulary Builder
Preview Key Terms **L2**

Pronounce each Key Term, then ask students to say the word with you. Provide a simple explanation such as, "In a democracy such as the United States, citizens elect officials to represent them in the government."

From Ancient Greece to the Middle Ages

Prepare to Read

Objectives

In this section you will
1. Learn how the heritage of ancient Greece influences life today.
2. Discover the glory of the ancient Roman Empire.
3. Learn about Europe in the Middle Ages.

Taking Notes

As you read this section, look for information about ancient times and the Middle Ages. Copy the outline below and record your findings in it.

> **I. The Greek heritage**
>   **A. Democracy**
>   **B.**
> **II.**

 Target Reading Skill

Reread Rereading is a strategy that can help you to understand words and ideas in the text. If you do not understand a certain passage, reread it to look for connections among the words and sentences. For example, rereading the second paragraph below can make it clear that marathons today are modeled after an event from ancient times.

Key Terms

- **Middle Ages** (MID ul AY juz) *n.* the time between the ancient and modern times, about A.D. 500–1500
- **democracy** (dih MAHK ruh see) *n.* a kind of government in which citizens govern themselves
- **city-state** (SIH tee stayt) *n.* a city with its own government that was both a city and an independent state
- **feudalism** (FYOOD ul iz um) *n.* a system in which land was owned by lords, but held by vassals in return for their loyalty

Runners beginning the Boston Marathon

176 Europe and Russia

Every April thousands of people from around the world gather in a small Massachusetts town. At noon, they begin a marathon race that requires great strength and willpower. The race ends in the city of Boston, some 26 miles (42 kilometers) away.

The Boston Marathon was inspired by an event that is said to have happened 2,500 years ago in the ancient Greek city of Athens. In 490 B.C., the people of Athens were at war with the Persians. The Athenians defeated the Persians at the Battle of Marathon. To announce their victory, an Athenian soldier named Pheidippides (fuh DIP ih deez) ran all the way to Athens, about 25 miles (40 kilometers) away. Pheidippides shouted, "Rejoice, we conquer!" as he entered the city. Then he died of exhaustion.

The Greeks loved the story, and people all over the world still run marathons. When they do, they show how history lives on. This chapter discusses three periods in the history of Europe and Russia—ancient times, modern times, and the **Middle Ages,** or the time between the ancient and modern times. We will see how the past affects the present in Europe and Russia.

Target Reading Skill **L2**

Reread Point out the Target Reading Skill. Tell students that rereading can help them understand words and ideas in the text.

Model the skill by reading and rereading the second paragraph on p. 179. Tell students that rereading can help them better understand the Roman system of roads.

Give students *Reread or Read Ahead.* Have them complete the activity in groups.

All in One Europe and Russia Teaching Resources, *Reread or Read Ahead,* p. 169

The Greek Heritage

The Athenians and other ancient Greeks were Europe's first great philosophers, historians, poets, and writers. They invented new ideas about how the world worked and how people should live.

The Growth of Democracy One such idea was **democracy,** or a kind of government in which citizens, not a king or other ruler, govern themselves. In ancient times, Greece had more than a hundred **city-states,** or cities with their own governments that were both cities and independent states. The Greek city-states had several different kinds of government. Many of them were democracies.

One of the most famous democratic Greek city-states was Athens. Every citizen there had the right to vote on laws and government policies, or the methods and plans a government uses to do its work. Citizens were either elected or chosen at random for government positions.

Democracy was a fresh idea for the Greeks. However, it was not the same as the democracy we practice today. Most Greeks were not citizens. Only freeborn males whose fathers held Athenian citizenship were citizens of Athens. Women, slaves, freed slaves, non-Greeks, and people whose families came from other parts of Greece were not citizens. They could not vote. Still, the Greek idea that citizens should have a voice in their own government had a strong influence on people in later times.

The Golden Age of Athens Democracy reached its highest point in Athens from about 479 to 431 B.C., during Athens' "Golden Age." During that period, the arts, literature, and philosophy also flourished. The Greeks studied the nature of plants, animals, and the human body. In the process, they developed ways of thinking that still influence life today.

Chart Skills

Greek ideas that developed over two thousand years ago still influence societies around the world today. **Note** When were democratic ideals of government formed in Athens? **Apply Information** Which of these ideals can be seen in today's United States government?

The Legacy of the Greeks

Topic	Influence on Modern Society
Drama	Aristotle created the rules for drama in his work *The Poetics*. Today, playwrights and movie scriptwriters still use his ideas.
Architecture	Many modern building designs reflect the common Greek styles known as Ionic, Doric, and Corinthian.
Science	The ancient Greeks introduced many principles of modern medicine, physics, biology, and mathematics.
Politics	The democratic ideals of government by the people, trial by jury, and equality under the law were formed in Athens around 500 B.C.
History	Herodotus collected information from people who remembered the events of the Persian wars. This method of research set the standard for the way history is recorded today.

Guided Instruction

- **Vocabulary Builder** Clarify the high-use word **process** before reading.

- Read The Greek Heritage with students using the Choral Reading strategy (TE, p. T34).

- Ask students **Why are the ancient Greeks considered Europe's first great philosophers, poets, and writers?** *(They did not accept old ways of thinking; they had new ideas about how people should live.)*

- Have students discuss how ancient Greek democracy differed from democracy in the United States today. *(In ancient Greece, only male citizens were allowed to vote. In the United States, all citizens 18 and older have the right to vote.)*

- Draw students' attention to the chart of Greek achievements. Ask **What are the fields in which Greece made important contributions?** *(drama, architecture, science, politics, history)*

Vocabulary Builder

Use the information below to teach students this section's high-use words.

High-Use Word	Definition and Sample Sentence
process, p. 177	*n.* a series of actions We had to be careful to follow the steps for the chemical **process** carefully.
rely, p. 179	*v.* to depend on I **relied** on my brother to give me a ride to school.
collapse, p. 181	*n.* a breakdown The **collapse** of the economy led to the government's defeat.

Answers

Chart Skills Note around 500 B.C.
Apply Information government by the people, trial by jury, and equality under the law

Guided Instruction (continued)

- Ask students **How did Alexander the Great spread Greek ideas?** *(He established Greek cities, the Greek language, and Greek ideas throughout the empire he built.)*

Independent Practice

Ask students to create the Taking Notes outline on a blank piece of paper. Then have students begin to fill it in using information from the text they have read so far. Briefly model how to organize information on an outline.

Monitor Progress

As students work on their outlines, circulate around the room and make sure individuals are choosing the correct information. Provide assistance as needed.

Answers

MAP MASTER Skills Activity **Use a Scale** His original kingdom was about 200 miles (520 kilometers) wide and 200 miles (520 kilometers) long. His empire at its height stretched over about 3,000 miles (7,800 kilometers) from east to west and was almost 1,000 miles (2,600 kilometers) long from north to south in some places. **Infer** It provided a common way of life for all of the people in the empire.

Go Online PHSchool.com Students may practice their map skills using the interactive online version of this map.

✓ Reading Check a collection of lands ruled by a single government

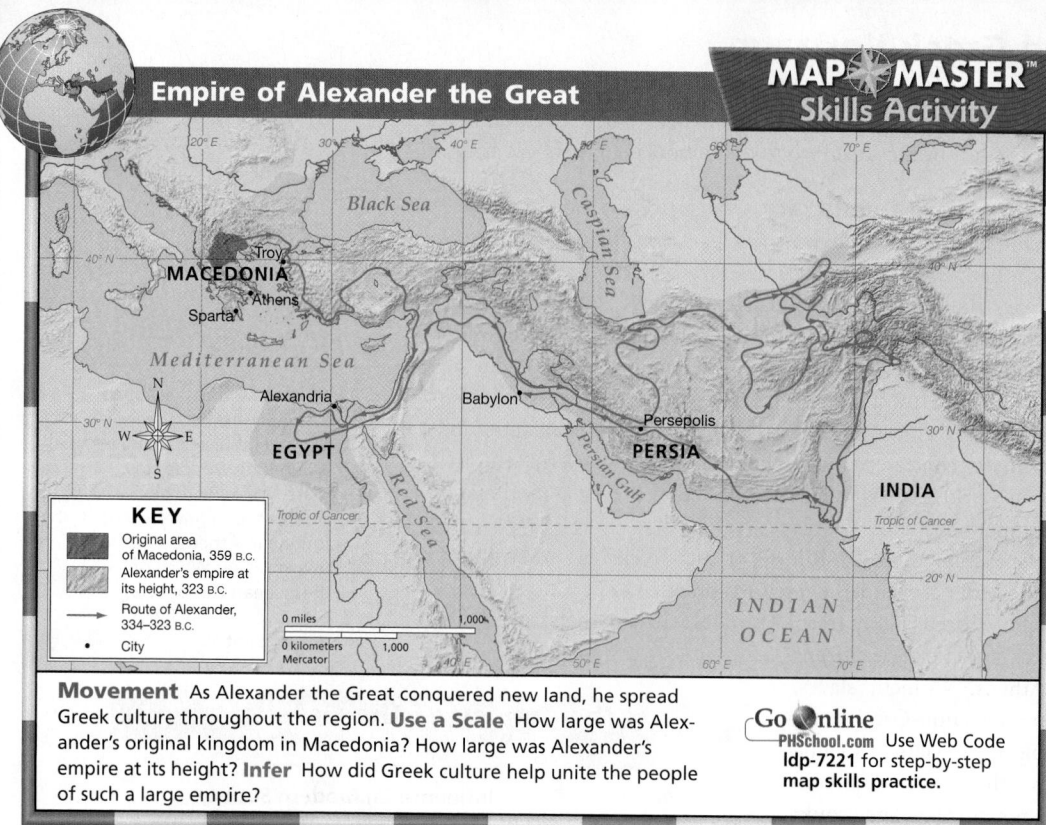

Empire of Alexander the Great

MAP MASTER™ Skills Activity

KEY

- Original area of Macedonia, 359 B.C.
- Alexander's empire at its height, 323 B.C.
- → Route of Alexander, 334–323 B.C.
- • City

0 miles 1,000
0 kilometers 1,000
Mercator

Movement As Alexander the Great conquered new land, he spread Greek culture throughout the region. **Use a Scale** How large was Alexander's original kingdom in Macedonia? How large was Alexander's empire at its height? **Infer** How did Greek culture help unite the people of such a large empire?

Go Online PHSchool.com Use Web Code ldp-7221 for step-by-step map skills practice.

The Spread of Greek Ideas A young man named Alexander, later called Alexander the Great, helped spread the ideas of the Greeks. At age 20, he became king of Macedonia (mas uh DOH nee uh) in northern Greece. But he was not satisfied with his small kingdom. In 334 B.C., Alexander set out to conquer the world. Within only ten years, he had conquered an empire almost as great in size as the United States is today. An empire is a collection of lands ruled by a single government. The map above shows Alexander's travels and the lands he conquered.

In all his new lands, Alexander established Greek cities, the Greek language, and Greek ideas. At the time of his death in 323 B.C., Greek culture linked the entire Mediterranean world. The people who next ruled the region, the Romans, also borrowed much from the Greeks.

✓ Reading Check What is an empire?

This ancient Italian mosaic shows Alexander the Great in battle.

178 Europe and Russia

Differentiated Instruction

For Advanced Readers L3

Have students read about Alexander the Great's father, King Philip, in the primary source *A Spartan Reply*. Have students follow up by writing sentences using the words "laconic" and "Spartan." Ask students to explain the origins of these words to the class.

All in One Europe and Russia Teaching Resources, *A Spartan Reply*, p. 182

For Gifted and Talented L3

Ask students to read the poem *Storm in the State* by Alcaéus of Mytiléne. After reading the poem and answering the questions, suggest that students do research to learn about the kinds of political struggles with which an ancient Greek nobleman might be involved.

All in One Europe and Russia Teaching Resources, *Storm in the State*, p. 183

The Glory of Ancient Rome

Have you ever heard someone say, "All roads lead to Rome" or "Rome was not built in a day"? These expressions refer to the Roman Empire. At its peak, the Roman Empire covered a huge area, and Romans built magnificent cities and structures.

About 50,000 miles (80,500 kilometers) of hard-surfaced roads linked the cities of the Roman Empire. The Roman system of roads was one of the most outstanding transportation networks ever built. Constructed more than 2,000 years ago, many of these roads are still in use today.

The Romans also built aqueducts, or canals that carried water to the cities from distant sources. Like Roman roads, some of these aqueducts are still in use.

The Pax Romana The Romans began building their empire soon after the death of Alexander the Great. The first emperor of Rome, Augustus, took control in 27 B.C. This began the *Pax Romana* (paks roh MAH nah), which means "Roman peace." It lasted for about 200 years. During the Pax Romana, Rome was the most powerful state in Europe and in the Mediterranean. With Rome in control, these regions remained stable.

Roman Law One of Rome's greatest gifts to the world was a system of written laws. Roman lawmakers were careful and organized. They did not rely on word of mouth to pass their laws from one generation to the next. Instead, they wrote the laws down. When a judge made a decision, he based it on written law. His decision was also put in writing to guide other judges. After a while, the law became so complex that it was difficult to learn. Various groups were appointed to gather the laws together into an organized system. Today, the legal system of almost every European country reflects the organization of ancient Roman law.

Roman laws protected all citizens. At first, citizens included only free people who lived in Rome. In time, the term came to include people all over the empire. Roman laws thus protected the rights of all citizens, not just the powerful and wealthy. Modern laws and government are based on this idea.

Roman Art and Architecture
The Colosseum (above) held as many as 50,000 people for public events. The sculpture below is of Rome's first emperor, Augustus. **Conclude** *What does the art a society produces tell you about its culture and wealth?*

Guided Instruction

- **Vocabulary Builder** Clarify the high-use word **rely** before reading.

- Have students read The Glory of Ancient Rome to learn more about the Roman Empire. As students read, circulate and make sure individuals can answer the Reading Check question.

- Ask **Why would a good network of roads be important in building an empire?** *(Possible answer: it would enable people to travel, ideas and information to be communicated, and allow the government in Rome to control a large territory.)*

- Point out the photo of the Colosseum in the Student Edition and tell students that like many ancient Roman roads and aqueducts, the Colosseum is still standing today. Ask **What does this tell you about the Roman Empire?** *(Possible answer: Their civilization was technically advanced enough to create buildings that have lasted thousands of years.)*

- Have students discuss why the Roman system of written laws was so important. *(Roman laws were organized and documented, and almost every modern European country is influenced by them.)*

Answer

Conclude Art can show what is important to a society. For example, the Colosseum reflects the fact that the Romans enjoyed attending public events. Generally, a wealthy society has more elaborate and expensive art than a less wealthy society.

Skills for Life **Skills Mini Lesson**

Analyze Images

1. Tell students that by analyzing an image, they can learn more about a topic. They should look for clues to help them by asking themselves: Who or what is this image? When and where did the scene take place? What feeling does the image suggest? Who created the image and why?

2. Have students analyze the statue of Augustus on this page. Suggest that they make a chart listing the type of details they notice (clothing, posture, etc.) and the conclusions they suggest.

3. Have students apply the skill by analyzing the image of Jesus on p. 180.

Guided Instruction (continued)

- Ask students **How did Emperor Constantine help spread Christianity?** *(He encouraged the spread of Christianity and it became the official religion of the Roman Empire.)*

- Ask students to list some reasons for the fall of the Roman Empire. *(centuries of warfare; higher taxes to pay for warfare weakened the economy; the empire grew too large and was divided, after which the western Roman Empire was attacked and collapsed in A.D. 476)*

Independent Practice

Have students add information about the Roman Empire to their outlines. Suggest that students use the different headings in the text to help them organize information.

Monitor Progress

As students continue to fill in the graphic organizer, circulate and make sure individuals are choosing the correct details. Provide assistance as needed.

⟳ Target Reading Skill   L2

Reread As a follow up, have students perform the Target Reading Skill activity in the Student Edition. *(Students should reread the paragraphs to understand that a spiritual leader is a person who serves as a leader for people who observe a certain religion.)*

Christian Art

This mosaic of Jesus, at the right, decorates the dome of a monastery in Daphni, Greece. Symbols of Christianity—a cross and a fish—are shown below. Early Christians used the symbol of the fish because each letter in the Greek word for fish, *ichthys*, stood for a word describing Jesus. **Analyze Information** *Why might early Christians have depended on symbols to express their faith, rather than doing so openly?*

⟳ **Reread**
Reread the paragraphs under Beginnings of Christianity to understand the phrase "spiritual leader."

Beginnings of Christianity Roman emperors allowed a certain amount of religious freedom within the empire. Jews were allowed to practice their religion as long as they obeyed Roman law. For centuries, the Jewish people had believed that God would send them a messiah, or a savior, who would free them from outside rule. Many Jews were content to cooperate with the Romans, but others began resisting Roman rule. In present-day Israel, the Romans crushed their attempts to revolt.

In about A.D. 30 a spiritual leader, Jesus of Nazareth, traveled and preached throughout the region. His followers believed that God was acting through him. They later called him Jesus Christ. *Christ* means "someone anointed, or a savior sent by God." After the Romans put Jesus to death, his followers began spreading his teachings. They eventually became known as Christians. At first, they were treated poorly by Roman emperors.

After three centuries, Christianity had become so strong that a Roman emperor, Constantine, became a Christian. Within decades, it became the official religion of the Roman Empire. Many people who had suffered under Roman rule turned to the church for comfort at this time.

The Decline of Rome Over time, it grew more difficult to govern the huge Roman Empire. Germanic invaders outside the empire broke through Roman lines of defense. More than once, they terrorized and looted Rome itself.

180 Europe and Russia

Differentiated Instruction

For English Language Learners   L1
Suggest that students use sticky notes to mark words with which they are unfamiliar. Students can go back to these words and use a dictionary to find the meaning. For a concrete noun such as *canal*, have students draw pictures based on their definition.

Answer

Analyze Information They might have wanted to keep their faith secret from groups that might persecute them, and using symbols that only early Christians understood was one way to do this.

To fight the invaders, the empire needed more soldiers. The government raised taxes to pay for the warfare. This hurt the empire's economy. The empire had also grown too large for one person to govern, so it was divided into two empires, one in the eastern Mediterranean and one in the west. The eastern empire remained strong, but the western one continued to weaken. In the A.D. 450s, invaders attacked Rome itself. Finally in A.D. 476, the western Roman Empire collapsed.

√ Reading Check **What was the Pax Romana?**

Europe in the Middle Ages

The collapse of the Roman Empire in western Europe led to a time of uncertainty. The legal system of the Roman Empire no longer protected people. The invading peoples did gradually settle down and establish kingdoms. But no kingdom was able to provide unity and security like the Roman Empire. Europe entered a long period of turmoil and warfare. Government, law, and trade broke down.

Eventually, a new structure of European society arose to provide order and security. It was based on a new political system and the Roman Catholic Church. The Roman Catholic Church was the name for the Christian church in the former western Roman Empire.

Feudalism To bring about order, people in western Europe developed **feudalism,** or a system in which land was owned by kinds of lords, but held by vassals in return for their loyalty. In each country, the king held the highest position. His greatest obligation was to provide security for his kingdom, which meant that he needed soldiers to build an army. Nobles provided the king with knights and foot soldiers. In exchange for knights, soldiers, and the nobles' loyalty, the king—also called a lord—gave land to the nobles—also called vassals.

The noble landholders needed people to work their estates, or manors. They gave peasants the right to farm their land in exchange for a large portion of their crops and any other income from the land. In exchange, they maintained order, enforced laws, and protected the peasants. This economic system is called manorialism. It provided a basis for the feudal political system.

The peasants who worked the land were called serfs. Serfs were not free people. They were bound to the land and could not leave without their lord's permission. But serfs were not slaves. They could not be sold away from the land.

Details from books and calendars dating from the 1400s show farming scenes at medieval manors.

Background: Biography

Julius Caesar Before the days of the Roman Empire, one of Rome's leaders was Julius Caesar. Born in about 100 B.C., Julius Caesar was a natural leader. He was known for his military strategies and led Roman armies to victory over Gaul (parts of today's France, Belgium, and Italy). Many in Rome thought Caesar had too much power. When he refused to give up that power, a civil war began. Caesar's army won, and he became dictator in 49 B.C. He was assassinated five years later, in 44 B.C. The continuing civil strife after his death finally led to new leadership and to the beginnings of the Roman Empire.

Guided Instruction

- **Vocabulary Builder** Clarify the high-use word **collapse** before reading.

- Have students read Europe in the Middle Ages.

- Discuss how the fall of the Roman Empire affected life in western Europe. Ask students **What were some of the problems that the collapse of Rome created?** *(Roman laws no longer protected people, and kingdoms established by invading peoples could not provide unity and security. Government and trade broke down. It was a time of turmoil and warfare.)*

- Have students explain the role of kings, nobles, and peasants in the feudal political system. *(The king held the highest position and kept the kingdom secure. Nobles provided the king with knights and soldiers and in return were provided with land. Noble landholders gave peasants the right to farm their land in exchange for a portion of the crop.)*

- Ask **What role did Christianity play in the Middle Ages?** *(It offered people a sense of community and security in a time of hardship.)*

- Ask **How had Europe changed by the 1400s?** *(Trade increased, and towns grew into cities.)*

Independent Practice

Have students complete their graphic organizers with information about Europe in the Middle Ages.

Monitor Progress

Show *Section Reading Support Transparency ER 35* and ask students to check their graphic organizers individually. Go over key concepts and clarify key vocabulary as needed.

📖 **Europe and Russia Transparencies,** *Section Reading Support Transparency ER 35*

Tell students to fill in the last column of their *Reading Readiness Guides.* Probe for what they learned that confirms or invalidates each statement.

All in One **Europe and Russia Teaching Resources,** *Reading Readiness Guide,* p. 150

Answer

√ Reading Check the Roman peace that lasted for 200 years

Assess and Reteach

Assess Progress L2

Have students complete the Section Assessment. Administer the *Section Quiz.*

All in One **Europe and Russia Teaching Resources,** *Section Quiz,* p. 152

Reteach L1

If students need more instruction, have them read this section in the Reading and Vocabulary Study Guide.

Chapter 7, Section 1, **Eastern Hemisphere Reading and Vocabulary Study Guide,** pp. 66–68

Extend L3

Have students work in pairs to complete the *Small Group Activity: Castle Mural.* Ask students to discuss their research before they begin work on their murals. Follow up with a discussion about the functions of castles during the Middle Ages.

All in One **Europe and Russia Teaching Resources,** *Small Group Activity: Castle Mural,* pp. 175–178

Answers

Analyze Images large, elaborate stained glass windows and carved statues

✔ Reading Check Unlike slaves, serfs could not be sold, although they were bound to the land and could not leave without their lord's permission.

Section 1 Assessment

Key Terms

Students' sentences should reflect knowledge of each Key Term.

Target Reading Skill

Answers will vary, but students should identify a word or idea they were able to clarify by rereading.

Comprehension and Critical Thinking

1. ( ) democracy **(b)** In ancient Athens, only freeborn males whose fathers were citizens could participate in the government. In the United States, all citizens can participate in government.

2. ( ) Many modern legal systems are based on the Romans' system of written laws and their idea that laws should protect the rights of all citizens. **(b)** Invaders grew strong and broke through Roman defenses; the govern-

Cathedral of Notre Dame
The Notre Dame cathedral in Paris, France, dates from the 1100s. It is one of the largest and most spectacular in the world. A carved figure from the roof of the cathedral is shown at the right. **Analyze Images** *What features from the cathedral do you think were meant to inspire awe in the people who worshipped there?*

The Byzantine Empire The eastern Roman Empire, later called the Byzantine Empire, was not divided into feudal kingdoms. The empire survived largely intact in southeastern Europe and southwestern Asia until the 1400s. The Byzantine Empire followed a form of Christianity that became known as the Orthodox Christian Church. Today, this is the main form of Christianity in Russia and much of Eastern Europe.

Christianity Most people's lives centered on the church during the Middle Ages. Religious ceremonies marked major events in the calendar and in the lives of individuals. Wealthy nobles and kings donated money for the construction of grand cathedrals, churches, and monasteries. In a world where most people's lives were marked by hardship and uncertainty, these grand buildings were awe-inspiring. Their brilliant stained-glass windows taught religious stories to peasants who were unable to read.

Europe Begins to Change As the centuries passed, trade increased in Europe. Towns offered opportunities to merchants and other tradespeople. Towns grew into cities. By the A.D. 1400s, a new way of life centered around cities had begun to develop in Europe.

 **✔ Reading Check** How did serfs differ from slaves?

Section 1 Assessment

Key Terms

Review the key terms at the beginning of this section. Use each term in a sentence that explains its meaning.

Target Reading Skill

What word or idea did you clarify by rereading certain passages?

Comprehension and Critical Thinking

1. (a) Recall What kind of government did ancient Athens have?

(b) Contrast How was the government of ancient Athens different from today's United States government?

2. (a) List What were the most important lasting ideas of the ancient Romans?

(b) Sequence Explain how the Roman Empire declined.

3. (a) Name Which institutions brought order and security to people in the Middle Ages?

(b) Summarize How did the feudal system work?

(c) Draw Conclusions Who benefited the most from feudalism? Explain.

Writing Activity

Suppose you are a Roman governor in Britain, far from your home and family in Rome. Write a journal entry describing the things you miss about Rome.

Writing Tip Remember to write your description in the first person, using the pronouns *I* or *we.* Use vivid words to describe Rome. You might write about things such as Rome's weather, art, and architecture.

ment raised taxes to pay for the warfare, which hurt the economy; the empire was divided, and eventually the western Roman empire collapsed and was overrun by invaders.

3. ( ) feudalism and the Roman Catholic Church **(b)** The king held the highest position and provided security for his kingdom. The nobles provided the king with knights and soldiers in exchange for land. The noble landholders allowed peasants to farm land in exchange for some of the crops.

( ) Possible answer: The king and nobles benefited from feudalism more than peasants because they held more power and were free.

Writing Activity

Use the *Rubric for Assessing a Journal Entry* to evaluate students' journal entries.

All in One **Europe and Russia Teaching Resources,** *Rubric for Assessing a Journal Entry,* p. 200

Prepare to Read

Objectives
In this section you will
1. Discover what the Renaissance was like at its peak.
2. Examine the effects of increased trade and stronger rulers in the Renaissance.
3. Learn about revolutions in government and science in the 1600s and 1700s.

Taking Notes
As you read this section, look for details about the Renaissance and the Age of Revolution. Copy the chart below and record your findings in it.

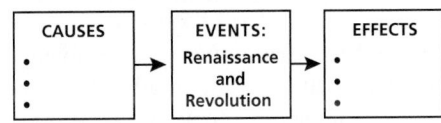

Target Reading Skill

Paraphrase When you pharaphrase, you restate what you have read in your own words. You could paraphrase the first two paragraphs of this section this way: "Marco Polo recorded his world travels in a book that influenced Christopher Columbus." As you read, paraphrase the information following each red or blue heading.

Key Terms
- **Renaissance** (REN uh sahns) *n.* a period of European history that included the rebirth of interest in learning and art
- **monarch** (MAHN urk) *n.* the ruler of a kingdom or empire, such as a king or a queen
- **revolution** (rev uh LOO shun) *n.* a far-reaching change
- **colony** (KAHL uh nee) *n.* a territory ruled by another nation

In about A.D. 1324 an elderly explorer named Marco Polo said before he died, "I have only told the half of what I saw!" Marco Polo indeed had an interesting life. For a time, he was a messenger of the great Mongol (MAHN gul) emperor Kublai Khan (KOO bly kahn), ruler of China. Polo also traveled across burning deserts and sailed south of the Equator. He visited the Spice Islands, which were the sources of the spices cinnamon, nutmeg, and cloves that Europeans valued. He earned great riches, only to be robbed on his way home to Italy.

These stories were published in a book we know today as *The Travels of Marco Polo.* Two hundred years later, Marco Polo's book inspired Christopher Columbus, another explorer. When Columbus sailed west from Europe, he was searching for a new route to the rich lands Marco Polo had described: China, Japan, and India.

Marco Polo and Kublai Khan

Target Reading Skill

Paraphrase Point out the Target Reading Skill. Tell students that paraphrasing, or restating what they have read in their own words, will help them better understand what they have read.

Model paraphrasing by restating the information in the first paragraph under the heading Printing Spreads the Renaissance on p. 185. (*The printing press, invent-ed in Germany around 1450, encouraged the spread of the ideas during the Renaissance. Instead of being copied by hand, books could now be made quickly on a printing press.*)

Give students *Paraphrase*. Have them complete the activity in groups.

All in One Europe and Russia Teaching Resources, *Paraphrase,* p. 170

Objectives
Social Studies
1. Discover what the Renaissance was like at its peak.
2. Examine the effects of increased trade and stronger rulers in the Renaissance.
3. Learn about revolutions in government and science in the 1600s and 1700s.

Reading/Language Arts
Paraphrase to restate what you have read in your own words.

Prepare to Read

Build Background Knowledge
Tell students that in this section they will read about the Renaissance and important inventions of the Renaissance, such as the printing press. Ask students to suppose that the printing press had never been invented, and books were very difficult to obtain. How would this affect their lives? For example, would this affect their knowledge about places far away from where they live? Use the Think-Write-Pair-Share participation strategy (TE, p. T36) to encourage class discussion.

Set a Purpose for Reading
- Preview the Objectives.
- Form students into pairs or groups of four. Distribute the *Reading Readiness Guide.* Ask students to fill in the first two columns of the chart. Use the Numbered Heads participation strategy (TE, p. T36) to call on students to share one piece of information they already know and one piece of information they want to know.

All in One Europe and Russia Teaching Resources, *Reading Readiness Guide,* p. 154

Vocabulary Builder
Preview Key Terms
Pronounce each Key Term, then ask students to say the word with you. Provide a simple explanation such as, "Queen Elizabeth II is the monarch of the United Kingdom today."

Instruct

Glories of the Renaissance L2

Guided Instruction

- **Vocabulary Builder** Clarify the high-use word **focus** before reading.

- Have students read Glories of the Renaissance, using the Paragraph Shrinking strategy (TE, p. T34).

- Ask **How did cultural life change during the Renaissance?** *(There was a renewed interest in learning and the arts, especially poetry, plays, architecture, sculpture, and painting.)*

- Explain to students that humanism is both the revival of the study of Greek and Roman ideas, and a theory that focuses on human dignity and values. Then ask **How did humanism affect the way people thought about life and death?** *(They began thinking about improving the world they lived in rather than hoping for a better life after death.)*

- Ask students **Who was Michelangelo?** *(an Italian painter, poet, architect, and sculptor)* **How did his statues reflect the ideas of humanism?** *(His statues were lifelike and incredibly realistic, rather than being stiff symbols.)*

Answer

Compare and Contrast Alike—both have pointed spires extending upward; Different—Notre Dame has stained glass windows and a pointed roof, whereas St. Peter's has no stained glass and a domed roof.

Works of Michelangelo
Michelangelo used themes from the Bible in many of his art works. Above is his sculpture of Moses. As an architect, Michelangelo worked on the dome of St. Peter's, the church of the Pope, in Rome. **Compare and Contrast** Compare the photo of St. Peter's with that of Notre Dame on page 182. How are they alike? How are they different?

184 Europe and Russia

Glories of the Renaissance

Columbus's search for a new route to the riches of the East was only one example of the movement sweeping Europe. The changes began in Italy in the 1300s and spread over the continent. Traders bought and sold goods across the region. The rich grew even richer. They had the time to enjoy art and learning—and the money to support artists and scholars. This period is called the **Renaissance** (REN uh sahns), or the rebirth of interest in learning and art. The Renaissance reached its peak in the 1500s.

Looking to the Past In trying to understand the world around them, Renaissance thinkers re-examined, or looked at once again, the ideas of Greek and Roman thinkers. People learned again about the ancient world's great poetry, plays, ideas, buildings, and sculpture. What they learned changed them. Writers began writing fresh, powerful poetry. The wealthy built glorious new buildings and filled them with breathtaking paintings.

Humanism: A New View Recall that during the Middle Ages much of Europe was in chaos, and religion was a way to bring order to people's lives. Renaissance thinkers began to focus on improving this world rather than hoping for a better life after death. This new approach to knowledge was called humanism (HYOO muh niz um). Humanistic thinkers emphasized the importance of human nature and the abilities of human beings to change the world.

Humanism affected every part of Renaissance life. For example, in the early Middle Ages, statues had been carved as stiff symbols. In contrast, during the Renaissance period artists carved lifelike statues.

An Important Renaissance Artist The Italian Michelangelo (my kul AN juh loh) was one such artist. Michelangelo was an accomplished painter, poet, architect, and sculptor. His lifelike statues were remarkably realistic and detailed. In some, you can see veins bulging in the hands. Or the drape of a cloak across the sculpted person looks so real that it appears to be made of cloth rather than of marble. Like other Renaissance artists, Michelangelo's work gave art a new importance. During the Renaissance, the role of art changed.

Vocabulary Builder

Use the information below to teach students this section's high-use words.

High-Use Word	Definition and Sample Sentence
focus, p. 184	*v.* to concentrate Nick made sure to **focus** on the teacher during science class.
radical, p. 188	*adj.* extreme or sweeping The new chef made **radical** changes to the restaurant's menu.

Art came to be seen as an important way to understand man, God, and nature. You can read about another important Renaissance figure, Leonardo da Vinci (lee uh NAHR doh duh VIN chee) in the box below.

Printing Spreads the Renaissance An important invention encouraged the spread of the Renaissance. Around 1450, the printing press was invented in Germany. Before printed books, books were made by carefully copying them by hand—a process that took a very long time. With the printing press, books could be made quickly.

Printed books made in large quantities could reach far more people than could books copied by hand. For that reason, the spread of printing had two important effects. First, it increased literacy, or the ability of people to read and write. Second, it allowed ideas of the Renaissance, written in books, to spread to large numbers of people. To understand the difference that the printing press made, consider this example. Before the printing press, there were a few thousand hand-copied books in Europe. Within 50 years after the printing press was invented, there were about 9 million books in Europe.

✓ **Reading Check** What is literacy?

Leonardo da Vinci: Renaissance Man

◀ **Painting**
Leonardo's *Mona Lisa* (1503–1506) is one of the most famous paintings in the world. The lady is believed to have been a merchant's wife. The style of her portrait and the misty background behind her continue to influence artists today.

Inventions ▶
Leonardo built machines of all kinds, but was especially interested in the possibility of human flight. He studied birds and drew imaginary flying machines. This helicopter-like machine, designed in 1487, was inspired by a child's toy.

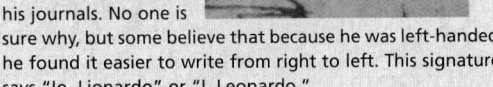

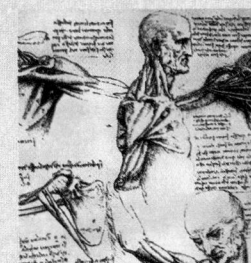

Science ▶
Leonardo studied the anatomy of the living and the dead to learn how the human body works. He often referred to his studies, like this one done in 1510, to make his paintings more realistic.

Mirror Writing ▶
Leonardo used "mirror writing"—writing from right to left—in his journals. No one is sure why, but some believe that because he was left-handed, he found it easier to write from right to left. This signature says "Io, Lionardo" or "I, Leonardo."

Chapter 7 Section 2 **185**

Guided Instruction (continued)
- Ask students **Where and when was the printing press invented?** *(around 1450; Germany)*

- Ask students **What two important effects did the spread of printing have on the people of Europe?** *(It increased literacy and allowed the ideas of the Renaissance to spread to large numbers of people.)*

- Draw students' attention to the graphic Leonardo da Vinci: Renaissance Man. Ask students **What makes da Vinci a Renaissance man?** *(his talents in many different fields, including art and science)*

Independent Practice
Have students create the Taking Notes graphic organizer on a blank piece of paper. Ask them to begin filling in causes and effects of the Renaissance. Briefly model how to choose details.

Monitor Progress
Circulate as students work on their charts and make sure individuals are choosing the correct information. Provide assistance as needed.

Answer

✓ **Reading Check** the ability of people to read and write

More Trade, Stronger Rulers

L2

Guided Instruction

■ Read More Trade, Stronger Rulers with students. As students read, circulate and make sure individuals can answer the Reading Check question.

■ Ask **Why did traders begin to travel outside of Europe?** *(exploration, trade of gold, silver, ivory, slaves, and spices)*

■ Ask **Which European countries were active in overseas trade and settlement?** *(Portugal, Spain, France, England, and the Netherlands)*

■ Ask **How did the wealth from trade affect feudalism?** *(Traders and merchants formed a middle class between the nobles and the peasants. The taxes they paid made monarchs even richer and less dependent on feudal lords. Feudalism declined and kings gained power.)*

 Target Reading Skill   L2

Paraphrase As a follow up, ask students to complete the Target Reading Skill activity in the Student Edition. *(Europeans searched for wealth in the Americas, and brought back precious metals and trade goods to Europe. Most of the wealth went to European monarchs, while some went to traders and merchants who formed a new middle class. Taxes on these goods paid by merchants and traders made monarchs wealthier and ultimately led to the decline of feudalism.)*

Answers

Diagram Skills Identify dishes of various metals **Analyze Information** Possible answer: monarchs, traders, and other merchants probably bought items from merchants such as this one; they had the most wealth to purchase such goods.

■ **Diagram Skills**

By the mid-1400s, European merchants like the one shown here sold a wide variety of goods, some from as far away as China. **Identify** What items in the diagram were made in Germany? **Analyze Information** What kinds of people most likely bought things from merchants such as this one? Why do you think so?

Woolen cloth came from the British Isles, while other kinds of cloth were made in France.

Dishes of various metals were made in present-day Germany.

Leather goods, such as shoes, came from towns in Spain.

More Trade, Stronger Rulers

During the Renaissance, traders began to travel more often outside of Europe. In the 1400s, Portuguese explorers traveled along the western coast of Africa. There they traded in gold, ivory, and slaves. This trade was very profitable. Some Portuguese traders traveled as far east as the Indian Ocean.

Then in 1492, a discovery brought even more possibilities for wealth. While searching for a shortcut to the Indian Ocean spice trade, Christopher Columbus landed in the Americas. He claimed the lands for Spain. Other Spanish explorers soon followed.

While Portugal grew rich from spices, Spain grew wealthy from American gold and silver. Other European countries grew envious. By the 1600s, France, England, and the Netherlands took a growing share of the riches to be gained from overseas trade and settlement.

The Effects of Trade Europeans raced to the Americas in search of wealth. Precious metals, such as gold and silver, and trade goods, such as fur and tobacco, poured into Europe. Much of the wealth went to European **monarchs** (MAHN urks), or rulers such as kings and queens. Some of it went to traders and merchants. These people formed a new social class. They became the middle class, the class between the privileged nobles and the lowly peasants or farmers. The taxes paid by prosperous merchants and traders made monarchs even wealthier. Soon, kings no longer needed the support of feudal lords. Feudalism declined, local lords grew weaker, and kings gained power.

 Paraphrase
Paraphrase the paragraph under the blue heading The Effects of Trade.

Skills for Life **Skills Mini Lesson**

Identifying Cause and Effect

1. Explain that a cause is an event or condition that makes something else, an effect, happen. Students should identify an event or condition as a starting point, look at earlier events for causes, look at later events for effects, and summarize the relationships they find.

2. Have students work in groups to identify cause and effect using The Effects of Trade on p. 186 of the Student Edition.

3. Have students identify causes and effects independently using Revolutions in Government on p. 188 of the Student Edition.

The Age of Monarchs The period in European history from the 1600s to the 1700s can be called the Age of Monarchs. During this time, many European monarchs became absolute monarchs, meaning that they exercised complete power over their subjects.

One such monarch was France's King Louis (LOO ee) XIV, who ruled from 1643 to 1715. One of Europe's most powerful kings, Louis XIV ruled at a time when France was a leading world power. Like other kings of his time, Louis was an absolute monarch. As he said, "I am the state." His wishes were law, and no one dared to disagree with him. Like other European monarchs, Louis believed that his power to rule came from God. To oppose him was the same as opposing God.

Louis used his power to make people pay heavy taxes. These taxes, in part, paid for his very expensive lifestyle. But Louis also wanted to make France strong. Other rulers wanted their countries to be strong as well. Over time, these monarchs made their countries stronger and more unified. As these changes took place, people began thinking again about government. Should the monarchs have such great power? What should the role of the government be?

✓ **Reading Check** What is an absolute monarch?

A Wealthy Monarch
Louis XIV, king of France, rides a horse in this painting from the mid-1600s. He built the palace of Versailles, shown below, to be his personal residence as well as the center of France's government.
Analyze Images How does Versailles reflect Louis XIV's lifestyle? What does it say about his vision of government?

Background: Daily Life

Versailles Louis XIV spent his days at Versailles, the palace where he also had his official court. This magnificent palace includes formal gardens and could accomodate up to 5,000 people. The famous Hall of Mirrors, which stretches across the west façade of the palace, was designed by French architect Jules Hardouin-Mansart. After the French Revolution, Versailles was never again used as a royal residence. However, several important treaties were signed there, including the 1919 Treaty of Versailles at the conclusion of World War I.

- Ask **What period in European history is known as the Age of Monarchs?** (*the period of history from the 1600s to the 1700s during which much of Europe was ruled by absolute monarchs*)

- Have students discuss what King Louis XIV of France meant when he said, "I am the state." (*Possible answer: His wishes were law, and no one dared challenge him.*)

Independent Practice
Instruct students to continue filling in their graphic organizers.

Monitor Progress
Circulate to make sure individuals are choosing appropriate information for their charts.

Answers

Analyze Images Versailles is lavishly decorated with expensive items. It shows that Louis XIV believed that absolute rulers should have power and wealth.

✓ Reading Check a ruler who exercises complete power over his or her subjects

Revolutions in Government

L2

Guided Instruction

- **Vocabulary Builder** Clarify the high-use word **radical** before reading.

- Read Revolutions in Government aloud.

- Ask students **Why are the 1600s and 1700s often called the Age of Revolution?** (*Because many significant revolutions, or far-reaching changes, occurred during this time.*)

- Discuss how revolutions can change governments. Ask **How did revolutionary ideas about government in Great Britain affect the American colonists?** (*The idea that people should have a say in government spread to the colonists, who rebelled against the British king because they felt the laws were unfair. This led to the independence of the United States.*)

- Ask **What was the immediate result of the French Revolution?** (*It created chaos in France.*) **What was a long-term result?** (*Ideas born in the French Revolution influenced Europe long afterwards.*)

Independent Practice

Instruct students to continue filling in their graphic organizers.

Monitor Progress

Circulate to make sure individuals are choosing appropriate information for their charts.

Answer

✓ Reading Check The English removed King Charles from the throne for claiming too much power, causing a revolutionary change in England's government; the American Revolution and the French Revolution brought political change to those nations.

188 *Europe and Russia*

Citizen Heroes

Chemistry and Revolution

Antoine Laurent Lavoisier (1743–1794) is considered one of the founders of modern chemistry. He was the first scientist to recognize oxygen as an element, and he gave it its name. He was also an important public servant. He built workhouses, savings banks, and canals to improve the lives of people in his district.

During the French Revolution, people turned against Lavoisier and other people who were wealthy or had been part of the government. In 1793, Lavoisier was arrested and given an unfair trial. On May 8, 1794, he and 28 others were executed. Lavoisier is shown in this 1788 painting by Jacques-Louis David with his wife Marie-Anne, who helped her husband in his lab.

This painting captures the scene of angry colonists pulling down a statue of British King George III after declaring independence in 1776.

188 Europe and Russia

Revolutions in Government

The 1600s and 1700s are often called the Age of Revolution. A **revolution** is a far-reaching change. European thought, beliefs, and ways of life all changed. This period was the beginning of the modern age of science and democracy that we know today.

The English Revolution One revolutionary change was that people began to believe that kings should not have all the power. For example, in England, King Charles I refused to share power with Parliament (PAHR luh munt), the elected legislature. Parliament then went to war with the King. Charles I was defeated, tried in court, and then put to death. No English ruler could ever again claim absolute power.

The American and French Revolutions The idea that people should have a say in government spread to North America, where Great Britain had several colonies. A **colony** is a territory ruled by another nation. In 1776, 13 of the colonies rebelled against the British king because they felt that the laws applied to them were not fair. The colonists defeated the British and formed the independent nation of the United States.

In 1789, 13 years after the Americans declared their independence, a revolution occurred in France. In order to create a democracy, the French people used extreme violence to overthrow their government. They did this in the name of freedom, equality, and brotherhood. The French Revolution created chaos in France. It also inspired new, radical theories about political and economic change. Ideas born in the French Revolution continued to influence Europeans long after the revolution ended.

✓ Reading Check **What revolutions took place during the 1600s and 1700s?**

Revolutions in Science

For centuries, Europeans had based their view of the world on their religious faith. Scientists had studied nature to explain how the world fit with their religious beliefs. Slowly, scientists began to change their approach. Influenced by humanism and the Renaissance, scientists began to observe nature carefully and record only what they observed. Then they based their theories on facts instead of making the facts fit their religious beliefs. This change in outlook is called the Scientific Revolution.

The Scientific Method It is difficult to pinpoint the exact beginning of the Scientific Revolution. Yet many sources agree that it started at least in part with the work of a scientist named Copernicus (koh PUR nih kus), who lived during the Middle Ages. Before Copernicus, people believed that Earth was the center of the universe. Copernicus shocked the world by suggesting that the sun was the center of the universe, and that Earth moved around the sun. Over time, he was proved to be right. His theories sparked other scientists to look at the world in different ways.

Copernicus and other scientists needed new procedures to test their ideas. These procedures make up what is called the scientific method, in which ideas are tested with experiments and observations. Scientists will accept an idea only if it has been tested repeatedly. The chart on the right shows the steps of the scientific method. Using the scientific method, scientists made dramatic advances.

Other Scientific Developments Some of the greatest advances were in the fields of chemistry and medicine. Before the 1600s, chemistry as we know it today did not exist. Instead, the main idea of chemistry was that any metal could be turned into gold. A scientist named Robert Boyle changed that. Boyle's ideas about temperatures and the behavior of gases set the stage for modern chemistry.

New ideas in medicine came about at that same time. People made efforts to learn about the human body, both inside and out. An English doctor named William Harvey discovered how blood circulates inside the body. The Dutch inventor Antonie van Leeuwenhoek (ahn TOH ne van LAY vun hook) developed techniques for making lenses for microscopes. He used his microscopes to study small lifeforms, such as insects and bacteria.

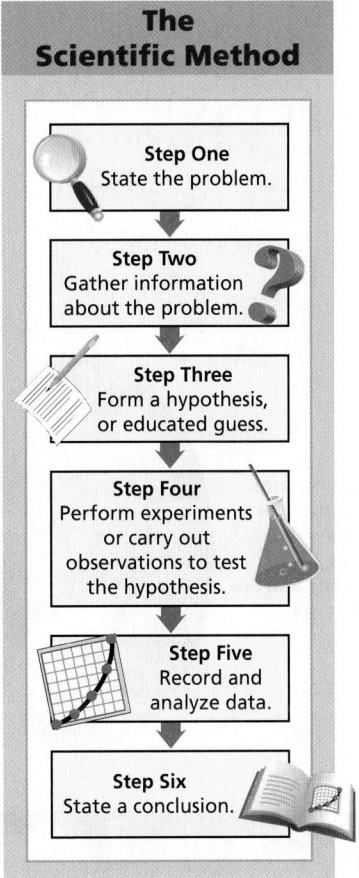

The Scientific Method

Step One
State the problem.

Step Two
Gather information about the problem.

Step Three
Form a hypothesis, or educated guess.

Step Four
Perform experiments or carry out observations to test the hypothesis.

Step Five
Record and analyze data.

Step Six
State a conclusion.

■ Diagram Skills

Though the scientific method is simple, it greatly changed the way science is done. **Explain** What is a hypothesis? How is it tested? **Apply Information** What was Copernicus's hypothesis about the universe?

Chapter 7 Section 2 **189**

Revolutions in Science L2

Guided Instruction

- Ask **What was the Scientific Revolution?** *(It was a change in thinking in which scientists formed theories based on facts observed from nature. Previously, scientists had tried to make facts fit religious beliefs.)*

- Ask students **What is the scientific method?** *(a series of procedures in which ideas are tested with experiments and observations)* **How did the use of the scientific method reflect changes in European attitudes?** *(It showed that Europeans had been influenced by humanism and the Renaissance, since they began basing their theories on facts rather than making them fit with their religious beliefs.)*

Independent Practice

Have students complete their graphic organizers with additional information from their reading.

Monitor Progress

- Show *Section Reading Support Transparency ER 36* and ask students to check their graphic organizers individually. Go over key concepts and clarify key vocabulary as needed.

  Europe and Russia Transparencies, *Section Reading Support Transparency ER 36*

- Tell students to fill in the last column of the *Reading Readiness Guide*. Ask them to evaluate if what they learned was what they had expected to learn.

  All in One **Europe and Russia Teaching Resources,** *Reading Readiness Guide,* p. 154

Answers

Diagram Skills **Explain** an educated guess; by performing experiments or making observations **Apply Information** that the sun was the center of the universe, and that Earth moved around the sun

Assess and Reteach

Assess Progress [L2]

Have students complete the Section Assessment. Administer the *Section Quiz*.

All in One Europe and Russia Teaching Resources, *Section Quiz,* p. 156

Reteach [L1]

If students need more instruction, have them read this section in the Reading and Vocabulary Study Guide.

Chapter 7, Section 2, **Eastern Hemisphere Reading and Vocabulary Study Guide,** pp. 69–71

Extend [L3]

Partner students and have them read the primary source *Testing a Theory* to learn how scientists in the seventeenth century tested their ideas. Have pairs work together to answer the questions.

All in One Europe and Russia Teaching Resources, *Testing a Theory,* p. 184

Answer

✓ **Reading Check** a new branch of mathematics called calculus

Section 2 Assessment

Key Terms
Students' sentences should reflect knowledge of each Key Term.

Target Reading Skill
Isaac Newton was one of the greatest scientists of the Scientific Revolution. He invented calculus to test his ideas, because existing mathematics could not explain them. With calculus and other simple laws, he was able to explain the movement of the moon and planets. His laws are still used today.

Comprehension and Critical Thinking
1. (a) a rebirth of interest in learning and art that reached its peak in the 1500s **(b)** the printing press
2. (a) a shortcut to the Indian Ocean spice trade **(b)** Their desire for wealth led them to travel outside Europe for goods that they could bring back and sell.

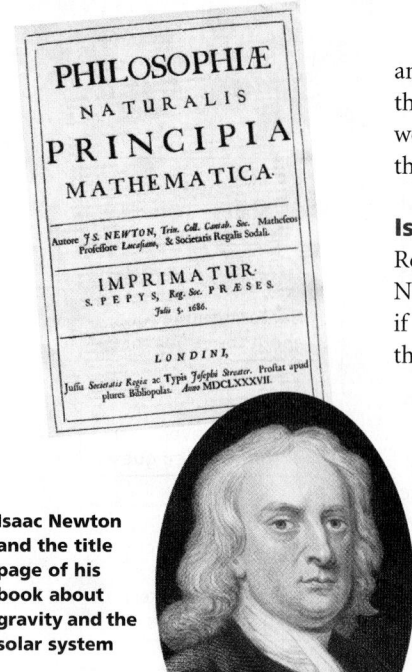

Isaac Newton and the title page of his book about gravity and the solar system

These and other developments led to a new way of thinking among scientists. With each new discovery, scientists began to see the universe as a giant machine. They believed this machine worked in a regular way, with set rules. They also believed that they could eventually learn everything about it.

Isaac Newton One of the greatest scientists of the Scientific Revolution was Isaac Newton. You may have heard a story about Newton, in which he saw an apple fall from a tree. He wondered if the force that pulled the apple to the ground was the same force that kept the moon in orbit around Earth.

To test this idea, Newton invented a new branch of mathematics called calculus (KAL kyoo lus). He had to invent calculus because the mathematics that existed at the time could not be used to explain his ideas. Using calculus and a few simple laws, Newton was able to demonstrate how the moon and planets move. Newton's laws and his mathematics are still used in science today.

By the end of the Age of Revolution, the nations of Europe were bustling with trade and bursting with new scientific ideas. Europe was about to begin a new kind of revolution. This time it would be an economic one.

✓ **Reading Check** What did Isaac Newton invent?

Section 2 Assessment

Key Terms
Review the key terms at the beginning of this section. Use each term in a sentence that explains its meaning.

Target Reading Skill
Paraphrase the text under the blue heading Isaac Newton above.

Comprehension and Critical Thinking
1. (a) Define What was the Renaissance?
(b) Identify Causes What invention helped spread the ideas of the Renaissance?

2. (a) Recall What was Christopher Columbus searching for when he landed in the Americas?
(b) Identify Effects How did Europeans' desire for wealth lead to voyages of exploration?
3. (a) Explain Why are the 1600s and 1700s called the Age of Revolution?
(b) Summarize How did the thinking of European scientists change during this period?
(c) Make Inferences How did humanism and advances in art help bring about changes in science?

Writing Activity
Marco Polo's writings excited readers and made them want to explore the places he had visited. Think about a place that you have visited. What makes it special? Describe in detail the features that you especially liked. Write about the place in a way that would make a reader want to go there.

For: An activity about Leonardo da Vinci
Visit: PHSchool.com
Web Code: ldd-7202

3. (a) European thought, beliefs, and ways of life changed dramatically during this time. **(b)** Scientists began using new methods of experimentation and observation. **(c)** Scientists changed their approaches based on the ideas of humanism and the Renaissance, observing nature carefully and recording what they observed.

Writing Activity
Use the *Rubric for Assessing a Writing Assignment* to evaluate students' work.

All in One Europe and Russia Teaching Resources, *Rubric for Assessing a Writing Assignment,* p. 201

Go Online PHSchool.com Typing in the Web code when prompted will bring students directly to detailed instructions for this activity.

Industrial Revolution and Nationalism

Prepare to Read

Objectives

In this section you will
1. Learn how the Industrial Revolution changed peoples' lives.
2. Examine how nationalism and war can be related.

Taking Notes

As you read this section, look for details about how life changed as a result of the Industrial Revolution. Copy the chart below and record your findings in it.

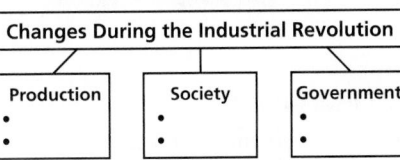

Changes During the Industrial Revolution

Production	Society	Government
•	•	•
•	•	•

Target Reading Skill

Summarize You can better understand a text if you pause to restate the key points briefly in your own words. A good summary includes important events and details, notes the order in which the events occurred, and makes connections between the events or details. Because a summary leaves out less important details, it is shorter than the original text.

Key Terms

- **Industrial Revolution** (in DUS tree ul rev uh LOO shun) *n.* the life-changing period in the 1800s when products began to be made by machines in factories
- **textile** (TEKS tyl) *n.* a cloth product
- **imperialism** (im PIHR ee ul iz um) *n.* the pursuit of economic and political control over foreign territories
- **nationalism** (NASH uh nul iz um) *n.* pride in one's country
- **alliance** (uh LY uns) *n.* an agreement between countries to protect and defend each other

It was dawn. Thick, black smoke rose from the tall smokestack of the factory. The smoke and the roar of machines signaled that the factory workday had begun. Inside, women and children worked at rows of machines that wove cotton thread into cloth. Their work was dirty, noisy, and dangerous. The day before, a worker had severely injured his hand in a machine. Today, another worker stood in his place. Both were only 13 years old. But the machines kept going. Workers fed them thread for 12 hours every day—six days a week. Vacations did not exist, and there were few breaks.

Factories like this one could be found all across Europe in the early 1800s. They were a result of the **Industrial Revolution,** a life-changing period when goods changed from being made by hand to being made by machines in factories. Industrialization caused great suffering at first, but in time brought an easier way of life to people all over the world.

Workers grind razors at a factory in Sheffield, England, in 1866.

Chapter 7 Section 3 **191**

Objectives

Social Studies

1. Learn how the Industrial Revolution changed peoples' lives.
2. Examine how nationalism and war can be related.

Reading/Language Arts

Summarize to better understand the text.

Prepare to Read

Build Background Knowledge　L2

Tell students that in this section they will learn about nationalism, or pride in one's country. Ask them to think of the ways that Americans show pride in their country. Have them discuss how events, such as Memorial Day or Veterans Day, and symbols, such as the American flag or the Statue of Liberty, reflect American nationalism. If you have students from different countries in your classroom, have them explain ways in which their home countries use events or symbols to reflect their citizens' nationalism, and how they are different than or similar to those in the United States. Use the Give One, Get One participation strategy (TE, p. T37) for this activity.

Set a Purpose for Reading　L2

- Preview the Objectives.
- Read each statement in the *Reading Readiness Guide* aloud. Ask students to mark the statements true or false.
- Have students discuss the statements in pairs or groups of four, then mark their worksheets again. Use the Numbered Heads participation strategy (TE, p. T36) to call on students to share their group's perspectives.

All in One **Europe and Russia Teaching Resources,** *Reading Readiness Guide,* p. 158

Vocabulary Builder
Preview Key Terms

Pronounce each Key Term, then ask students to say the word with you. Provide a simple explanation such as, "Cotton is an important material in the textile industry."

Target Reading Skill　L2

Point out the Target Reading Skill. Tell students that when summarizing text, they should include only the key points in the correct order, and omit the less important details.

Model the skill by summarizing the second paragraph on this page aloud. "The Industrial Revolution occurred in Europe during the 1800s. Goods changed from being made by hand to being made by machines. Although it first caused great suffering for many, it eventually made life easier for people worldwide."

Give students *Summarize.* Have them complete the activity in their groups.

All in One **Europe and Russia Teaching Resources,** *Summarize,* p. 171

Instruct

The Industrial Revolution L2

Guided Instruction

- **Vocabulary Builder** Clarify the high-use word **policy** before reading.

- Have students read The Industrial Revolution, using the Structured Silent Reading strategy (TE, p. T34).

- Ask **Where did the Industrial Revolution begin?** *(Great Britain)* **What did the first machines make?** *(textiles)*

- Ask **What do you think were the advantages of making goods by machine rather than by hand?** *(Possible answer: goods could be made more quickly and cheaply and in greater numbers. This enabled business owners to earn greater profits.)*

- Ask **What other improvements did the new factory system bring about?** *(new inventions in machinery, transportation, and communication, and improvements in agriculture)*

Improvements in Making Cloth
For generations, people used spinning wheels like the one above to spin cloth. After the Industrial Revolution, huge machines called "spinning mules" in factories like the one at the right produced cloth cheaper and more quickly. **Evaluate Information** *How do you think the shift from using simple tools to complex machinery affected the average worker?*

The Industrial Revolution

Until the late 1700s, nearly all goods were made by hand. People made what they needed, or bought it from a craftsperson or at a store for a high price. The Industrial Revolution—a revolution in the way goods were made and in the ways people lived and worked—changed all that.

Changes in Production The first machines of the Industrial Revolution were invented in Great Britain to speed up the weaving of **textiles, or cloth products.** Large factories housed the machines. Factory work was very different from work done by hand. For example, a person weaving cloth would first spin the thread, then dye it, and then weave it. He or she might work on every step of the finished product. In contrast, in a factory each worker tended a specific machine, which performed a specific job over and over again. The machine worked much faster than a person could. This meant that goods could be made quickly and much more cheaply than they had been by hand.

This new factory system was improved by new inventions in machinery, transportation, and communication. Other new inventions also brought about improvements in agriculture. Food could be grown in larger quantities by fewer people, and transported quickly to supply factory workers in the cities.

Vocabulary Builder

Use the information below to teach students this section's high-use words.

High-Use Word	Definition and Sample Sentence
policy, p. 195	*n.* a plan adopted by a government, organization, or individual The school's **policy** was to reward students who had perfect attendance.
invade, p. 196	*v.* to enter by force The war started after the country **invaded** its neighboring country.
generation, p. 196	*n.* a group of individuals born and living at the same time My parents belong to a different **generation** than my sister and I.

Answer

Evaluate Information Possible answer: It allowed the average worker to produce more goods in less time.

Changes in Society Because Great Britain's factories were so successful, business people in other countries began to build factories. By 1900, factories produced many of the goods made in the United States and Western Europe.

The Industrial Revolution changed life in almost every way. Inventions created to fuel the Industrial Revolution were soon used in everyday life. Improved transportation meant that people could travel more quickly and often more cheaply. Better communications meant that people separated by long distances could talk to one another almost instantly.

Yet not all of the effects of the Industrial Revolution were positive. For hundreds of years, families had farmed the land. Now they moved to industrial centers to work in factories. Cities grew rapidly. People lived in cramped, dirty housing. Because of unclean and crowded conditions, diseases spread rapidly.

Factory work was also difficult. Factory owners took advantage of workers. Wages were low. Factory conditions were not safe. However, workers slowly began to form labor unions and to demand better working conditions. In the early 1900s, governments began passing laws to protect workers. Over time, conditions improved and wages rose. The Industrial Revolution helped give working people a greater voice in government. Many European nations became more democratic as a result.

Timeline Skills

Important inventions of the late 1700s and early 1800s had a major impact on industry and society. **Note** When was the spinning jenny invented? **Apply Information** Which inventions helped improve transportation?

Guided Instruction (continued)

- Have students discuss how the Industrial Revolution affected the growth of cities. (*Cities grew quickly as people moved from farms to work in new factories in the cities.*)

- Ask **Why did factory workers form unions?** (*Wages were low; factory owners took advantage of workers; working conditions were unsafe. Unions had more influence than individuals in fighting management.*)

- Have students discuss how the Industrial Revolution caused European nations to become more democratic. (*Making and selling goods was a big part of a country's economy, so governments had to listen to workers. As a result, working people got a greater voice in government.*)

- Ask **How did the Industrial Revolution lead to imperialism?** (*Colonies served useful purposes for European nations. They supplied raw material for industry and buyers for European products.*)

Inventions in Industry, 1700s–1800s

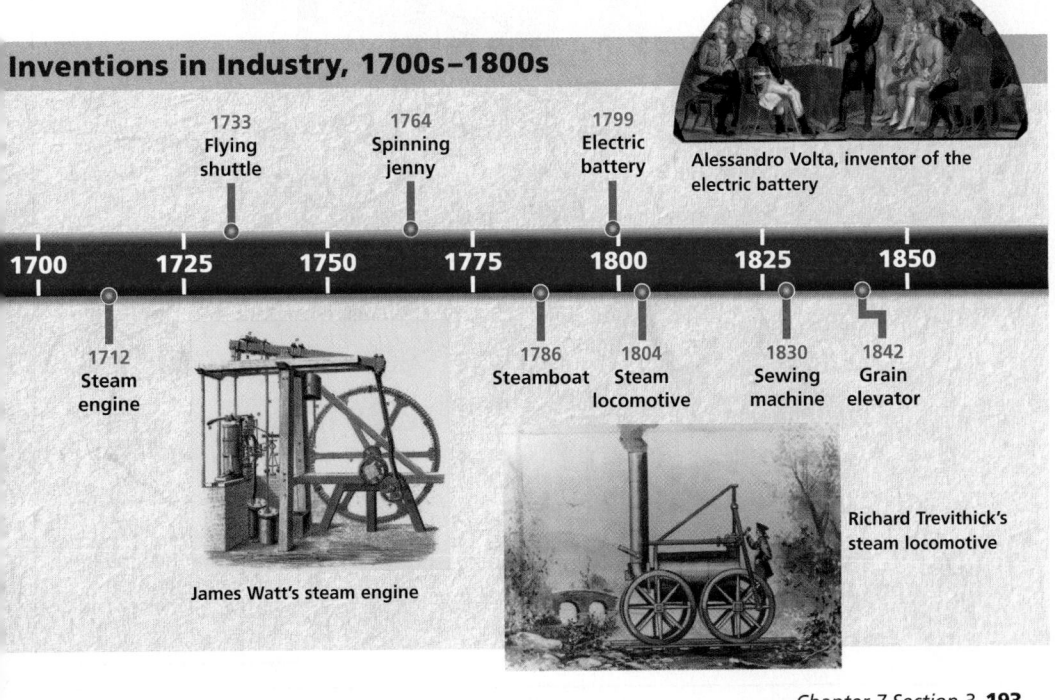

1733 Flying shuttle

1764 Spinning jenny

1799 Electric battery

Alessandro Volta, inventor of the electric battery

1700 1725 1750 1775 1800 1825 1850

1712 Steam engine

1786 Steamboat

1804 Steam locomotive

1830 Sewing machine

1842 Grain elevator

James Watt's steam engine

Richard Trevithick's steam locomotive

Chapter 7 Section 3 **193**

Differentiated Instruction

For English Language Learners L1
Students may find it difficult to pronounce some of the words on these pages, such as *industrial, economy, imperialism*, and *aggressive*. Show students how to break these words down into smaller parts to help them sound out the pronunciations.

Answers

Timeline Skills Note in 1764
Apply Information the steamboat; the steam locomotive

Textile Mill

Guided Instruction

Have students read the main paragraph on this page. As a class, look at the diagram and read the numbered captions. Direct students' attention to the photo and its caption. Then have students discuss their answers to the Analyzing Images question.

Independent Practice

Display *Transparency B6: Flow Chart,* and have students work in pairs to create a flow chart showing the activities in a mill. Using the diagram and numbered captions, have students identify the features of the mill and the jobs each feature performs. Remind students to put the descriptions in the correct order, to show how the features of the mill are linked.

Europe and Russia Transparencies, *Transparency B6: Flow Chart*

Textile Mill

Weaving, or making cloth from threads or yarns, is one of the oldest crafts in the world. It was also the first to take advantage of the inventions that fed the Industrial Revolution. Water, and then steam, powered the first textile factories and their machines. In England, this new form of manufacturing produced goods for trade and export, and wealth and power for the nation.

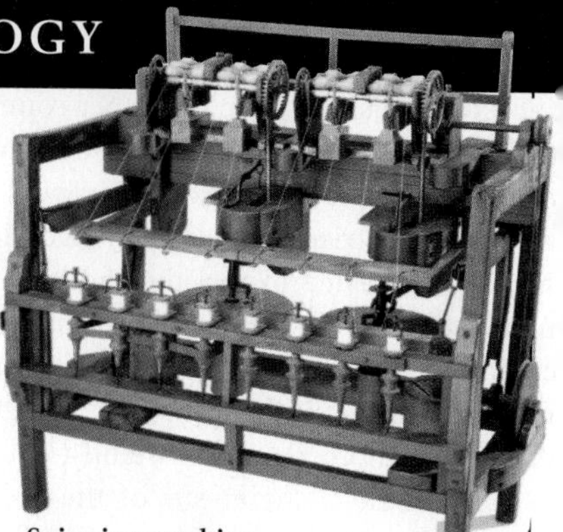

Spinning machine
A water-powered spinning machine (called a water frame) was invented by Sir Richard Arkwright.

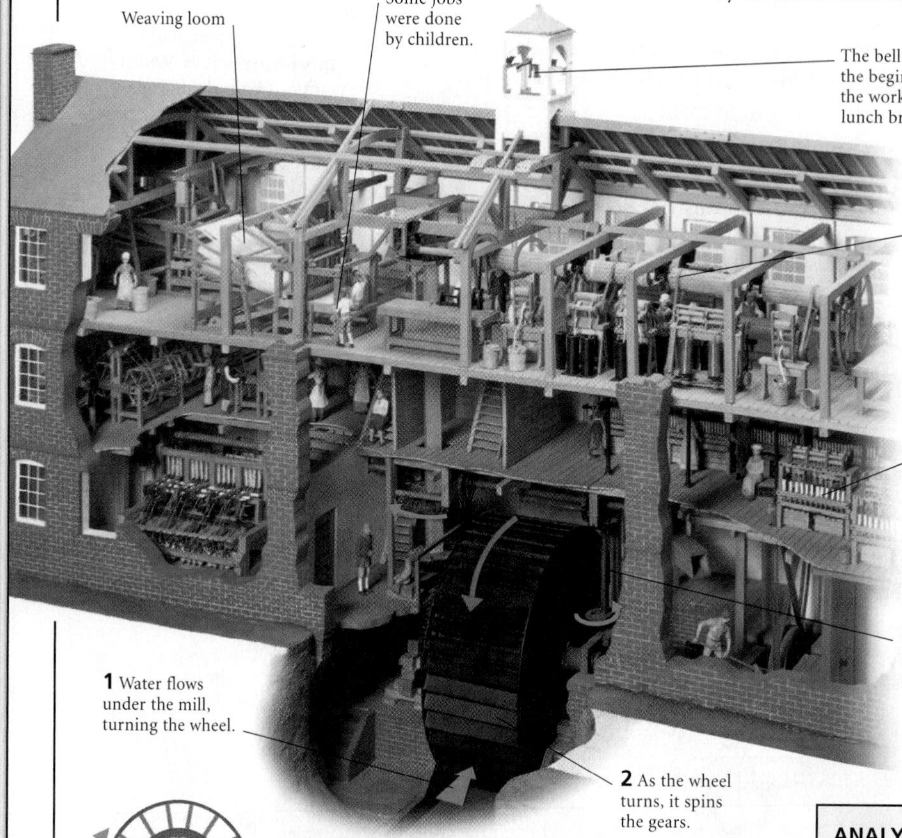

Weaving loom

Some jobs were done by children.

The bell is used to signal the beginning and end of the workday, and the lunch break.

4 Belts, attached to pulleys, power the mill's many machines.

Spindles hold the cotton thread.

3 Gears transfer power to different parts of the mill.

1 Water flows under the mill, turning the wheel.

2 As the wheel turns, it spins the gears.

Water wheel
Flowing water turns the mill wheel, driving gears that cause the overhead shafts to turn. These shafts drive belts that power the machines.

ANALYZING IMAGES
Near what geographical feature must this textile mill have been located?

194 Europe and Russia

Answer
ANALYZING IMAGES flowing water

Changes in Government At the same time, though, European governments were becoming more aggressive abroad. Beginning in the 1600s, many European nations had followed the policy of **imperialism,** or the practice of taking control of foreign territories as colonies in order to form an empire. Colonies provided the raw materials, such as cotton, wood, and metals, that industry needed. Colonies also supplied markets for European goods. Finally, European countries hoped to spread their influence over people in those colonies by converting them to their own religions.

The late 1800s are called the Age of Imperialism. During this time, the nations of Belgium, France, Italy, Spain, Portugal, Germany, and the United Kingdom colonized most of Africa. Some of these countries also took over much of Southeast Asia and many South Pacific islands. In time, struggles among the colonial powers would bring disaster to Europe.

✔ **Reading Check** Why are the late 1800s called the Age of Imperialism?

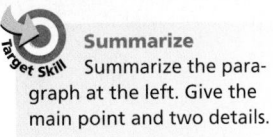

Summarize Summarize the paragraph at the left. Give the main point and two details.

Summarize As a follow up, have students perform the Target Reading Skill activity in the Student Edition. (*Main Idea: European nations used the policy of imperialism to colonize other countries. Students' examples of details will vary, but should be drawn from the paragraph.*)

Independent Practice

Have students create the Taking Notes graphic organizer on a blank piece of paper and begin filling it in with details about the Industrial Revolution.

Monitor Progress

As students work on their graphic organizers, circulate and make sure individuals are choosing appropriate information. Provide assistance as needed.

European Imperialism, 1910

MAP★MASTER™
Skills Activity

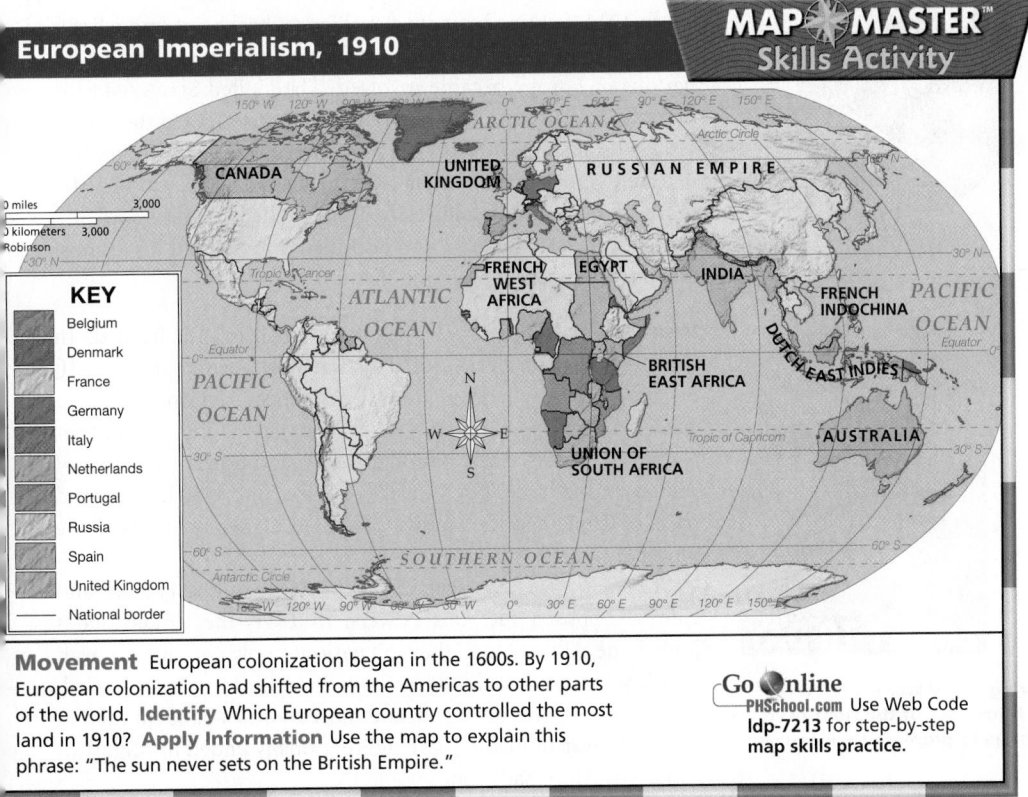

KEY
- Belgium
- Denmark
- France
- Germany
- Italy
- Netherlands
- Portugal
- Russia
- Spain
- United Kingdom
- — National border

Movement European colonization began in the 1600s. By 1910, European colonization had shifted from the Americas to other parts of the world. **Identify** Which European country controlled the most land in 1910? **Apply Information** Use the map to explain this phrase: "The sun never sets on the British Empire."

Go Online
PHSchool.com Use Web Code
ldp-7213 for step-by-step
map skills practice.

 **Skills Mini Lesson**

Sequencing

1. Tell students that sequencing—showing events in chronological order—helps them to keep track of historical events. To make a timeline, students should determine the topic and time span, identify the events, and place them in order.

2. Have students study the timeline on p. 193 of the Student Edition. Ask them to find one or two events to add to the timeline and indicate where on the timeline they would place these events.

3. Have students make a timeline of events leading up to World War II. Students may do library or Internet research to add to their timelines.

Answers

✔ **Reading Check** During these years, many European nations took over much of Africa, parts of Southeast Asia, and many South Pacific Islands and turned them into colonies.

MAP★MASTER *Skills Activity* **Identify** the United Kingdom **Apply Information** Because the United Kingdom colonized countries all over the world, there was always daylight in at least one British colony.

Go Online PHSchool.com Students may practice their map skills using the interactive online version of this map.

A Century of War and Nationalism

Guided Instruction

- **Vocabulary Builder** Clarify the high-use words **invade** and **generation** before reading.

- Read A Century of War and Nationalism with students. As students read, circulate and make sure individuals can answer the Reading Check question.

- Ask **How was nationalism a destructive force in Europe in the early 1900s?** (*European nations feared one another and were afraid of invasion. As a result, they made alliances to protect themselves. Soon, Europe was divided into two major alliances. Eventually, fighting broke out between them.*)

- Ask **Who were the two opposing alliances in World War II?** (*Axis Powers: Germany, Italy, and Japan; Allies: Great Britain, the Soviet Union, France, China, and the United States.*)

- Ask **How did nationalism in Western Europe change after World War II?** (*Nations began to work together as trading partners and in building a common European community.*)

Independent Practice

Have students complete their graphic organizers by filling in details about World War II.

Monitor Progress

- Show *Section Reading Support Transparency ER 37* and have students check their graphic organizers individually. Go over key concepts and clarify key vocabulary as needed.

   Europe and Russia Transparencies, *Section Reading Support Transparency ER 37*

- Ask students to fill in the last column of the *Reading Readiness Guide*. Probe for what they learned that confirms and invalidates each statement.

   All in One Europe and Russia Teaching Resources, *Reading Readiness Guide*, p. 158

A Century of War and Nationalism

At the start of the 1900s, the people of Europe were filled with **nationalism,** or pride in their countries. Nationalism can be either a destructive or a constructive force, depending on what it leads people to do. It can make one nation harm another in an effort to get ahead. It can also prevent nations from working with one another. Then, hatred and warfare can erupt between countries. Between 1900 and 1950, destructive nationalism played a part in causing two world wars and the deaths of millions of people.

World War I During the early 1900s, European nations feared one another. Each nation was afraid another would invade, or try to take over, its territory. To protect themselves, nations made **alliances** (uh LY un sez), or agreements with one another. In such alliances, a nation promises to protect its friends if someone attacks them. Soon, Europe was divided into two major alliances. On one side were Germany, Austria-Hungary, and Turkey. On the other side were Great Britain, France, and Russia.

In 1914, fighting between the alliances broke out into what is now called World War I. Over the course of the war, most of the nations of Europe became involved. The United States—on the side of Great Britain, France, and Russia—also joined the war in 1917. The alliance of Germany, Austria-Hungary, and Turkey was defeated, but at an enormous cost. By the end of the war in 1918, more than 9 million soldiers had been killed. About 13 million civilians, or non-soldiers, had also died. Europe had lost almost an entire generation of young men.

World War II But the flame of nationalism still burned. In 1939, another war broke out. This war was called World War II. As in World War I, there were two alliances. On one side were the Axis Powers—Germany, Italy, and Japan. These countries sought to increase their national wealth and power by means of military conquest. They quickly captured most of Europe and parts of China and the South Pacific. Germany also attacked the Soviet Union.

The Allies—Great Britain, the Soviet Union, France, and China—opposed the Axis Powers. In 1941, the United States joined the Allies. More than 50 nations took part in this war, which was the most destructive ever fought. More people died, more property was damaged, and more money was spent than in any other war in history. The fighting finally ended in August of 1945. The Allies had won.

During World War I, countries on both sides of the fight used posters to promote their causes.

Differentiated Instruction

For Advanced Readers   L3

Ask students to read the primary source *A Child in Prison Camp*. Students should work with a partner to answer and discuss the questions. Ask students to summarize this account for the class.

   All in One Europe and Russia Teaching Resources, *A Child in Prison Camp*, pp. 185–187

For Special Needs Students   L1

Have students reread the section as they listen to the recorded version on the Student Edition on Audio CD. Check for comprehension by pausing the CD and asking students to share their answers to the Reading Check questions.

   Chapter 7, Section 3, **Student Edition on Audio CD**

Two Paths Emerge in Europe After World War II, the Soviet Union and the United States emerged as the world's two superpowers. These nations had very different ideas about government and its role in society. Both nations used their ideas to influence people around the world.

After the war, much of Europe was in ruins. It was time to rebuild. The nations of Western Europe allied themselves with the United States. They also grew together as a region. With the shared values of peace and prosperity, they worked together to restore the economies and standards of living that had been shattered by war.

The nations of Eastern Europe, in contrast, took a different path. Many of the nations of Eastern Europe followed the example of the Soviet Union. Their economies failed to recover after the war, and their governments suspended many of their people's freedoms. You will read more about the Soviet Union and its influence on Eastern Europe in the next section.

Western and Eastern Europe remained divided, with very different governments and standards of living, until the 1990s. You will read about their recent history in Chapters 9 and 10.

The United States led an effort called the Marshall Plan to rebuild the economies of Europe. In this photo, a parade in Greece celebrates the delivery of Marshall Plan food supplies.

✓ **Reading Check** Which countries made up the Axis Powers? Which made up the Allies?

Section 3 Assessment

Key Terms
Review the key terms at the beginning of this section. Use each term in a sentence that explains its meaning.

Target Reading Skill
Summarize the information in the paragraphs on this page.

Comprehension and Critical Thinking
1. (a) Recall Where did the Industrial Revolution begin?

(b) Find the Main Idea How did the Industrial Revolution change the way that goods were made?
(c) Identify Effects How did this change affect the lives of Europeans?
2. (a) Describe Give an example of destructive nationalism.
(b) Identify Cause and Effect How did nationalism help to cause World War I and World War II?
(c) Predict How might nationalism be used in the future as a creative force for peace?

Writing Activity
After World War II, colonies in Africa and Asia demanded their freedom. Suppose you were a citizen of a colony of one of the European nations. Write a paragraph explaining why you would want your country to be independent.

> **Writing Tip** Use the following topic sentence to help you organize your thoughts: It is important for people to control their own destiny.

Chapter 7 Section 3 **197**

Section 3 Assessment

Key Terms
Students' sentences should reflect knowledge of each Key Term.

Target Reading Skill
After World War II, the Soviet Union and the U.S. became superpowers, influencing countries world-wide. Western Europe allied itself with the U.S., and its nations worked together to rebuild their economies. Eastern Europe failed to rebuild its nations' economies, and the two regions became divided.

Comprehension and Critical Thinking
1. (a) Great Britain **(b)** Machines in large factories could produce goods more quickly and cheaply than by hand. **(c)** Factory owners became wealthy; people moved from the country to the city; cities grew rapidly; diseases spread because of unclean and crowded conditions.

Assess and Reteach

Assess Progress **L2**
Have students complete the Section Assessment. Administer the *Section Quiz*.

All in One **Europe and Russia Teaching Resources,** *Section Quiz*, p. 160

Reteach **L1**
If students need more instruction, have them read this section in the Reading and Vocabulary Study Guide.

📖 Chapter 7, Section 3, **Eastern Hemisphere Reading and Vocabulary Study Guide,** pp. 72–74

Extend **L3**
As an extension of this section, have students work in small groups on the long-term project *Making a Book About World Technologies.* You may wish to suggest that students concentrate on technologies that helped propel the Industrial Revolution.

> **Go Online** PHSchool.com
>
> **For:** Long-term Integrated Projects: *Making a Book About World Technologies*
> **Visit:** PHSchool.com
> **Web Code:** ldd-7206

Answer

✓ **Reading Check** Axis Powers: Germany, Italy, and Japan; Allies: Great Britain, the Soviet Union, France, China, and the United States

Writing Activity
Use the *Rubric for Assessing a Writing Assignment* to evaluate students' paragraphs.

All in One **Europe and Russia Teaching Resources,** *Rubric for Assessing a Writing Assignment,* p. 201

2. (a) the creation of alliances between countries in World War I and World War II which led to disagreements and fighting **(b)** The alliances formed in Europe in the early 1900s by nations trying to protect themselves helped to pull these nations into World War I and World War II. **(c)** Answers will vary, but students might suggest that nations should work together to bring peace and stability to their region.

Objective

Learn how to solve problems.

Prepare to Read

Build Background Knowledge **L2**

Tell students that problem solving is a skill that they can use every day to solve small or large problems. Introduce students to the skill by asking them to think of a problem they had recently, either at school or in some other aspect of their lives. If students are uncomfortable talking about their personal experiences, they may make up a fictional problem. Ask students to think about how they solved or did not solve the problem. If they were able to solve it, what strategies did they use? If the problem was not solved, why do they think that was so? Could they have done anything differently? Use the Numbered Heads participation strategy (TE, p. T36) to elicit responses.

Instruct

Problem Solving **L2**

Guided Instruction

- Read the steps to problem solving as a class and write them on the board.

- Practice the skill by following the steps on p. 199 as a class. Model each step in the activity by identifying the problem (*invaders were attacking the Roman empire*), listing possible solutions (*have a better organized army of only trained military officers; invest more time in training peasants and slaves; station all soldiers in one place; repair roads so travel would be easier*), reviewing the possible solutions (*having only trained officers would mean fewer people to fight in the army; spending more time training peasants and slaves would require more work and time and would mean that peasants and slaves would not be performing their other jobs; stationing all soldiers in one place would require soldiers to travel to the location and might make it difficult for them to return home; repairing roads would require money and workers, but traveling from place to place would be easier*), and iden-

Marco Polo dressed in clothes worn by the Tatars, a nomadic tribe of eastern Asia

> In 1275, Marco Polo arrived at the court of Kublai Khan in China. The Mongol leader appointed Marco Polo governor of Yangchow, a busy Chinese city. After three years had passed, Marco Polo wanted to return to Venice. He had enemies within the court. The khan was getting older. Marco Polo worried that when the khan died, those enemies would have him killed. But the khan refused to let him return to Venice.
>
> One year, a Mongol princess was promised as a bride to the Persian khan. Marco Polo proposed that he accompany the princess on the journey, to keep her safe. He knew that at the end of the trip he could escape to Venice. The khan agreed, and Marco Polo set out by sea with the princess and hundreds of men. The trip was dangerous, and most of the men died. But it might have been even more dangerous to go by land, because of robbers.

Solving a problem requires a range of skills. You must first state the problem clearly and identify the possible solutions. Then you must think about the likely outcome of each solution and choose the best option. In the passage above, Marco Polo identified and solved two problems.

Learn the Skill

Follow the steps below to learn how to solve problems.

1 **Identify the problem.** State the problem in a direct, complete, and accurate way. Your statement should contain facts, not opinions. The facts should be directly related to the problem.

2 **List possible solutions.** There may be more than one way to solve the problem. Identify all possible solutions.

3 **Review the possible solutions.** Identify the resources that would be needed to carry out each solution. Also identify consequences of each solution.

4 **Choose the best solution.** Decide which solution is the most effective, or the easiest to carry out. What will the likely outcome be?

198 Europe and Russia

tifying the solution they think is best (*Students' answers will vary, but they should identify the solution they think is the best, why it is best, and what they think its outcome would be*).

Independent Practice

Assign *Skills for Life* and have students complete it individually.

All in One **Europe and Russia Teaching Resources,** *Skills for Life,* p. 174

Monitor Progress

As students are completing *Skills for Life,* circulate to make sure individuals are applying the skill steps effectively. Provide assistance as needed.

Mosaic of Roman gladiators in battle

The Roman Empire was in trouble. Invaders from Germany were attacking the empire's western and northern borders. At the same time, Persians were attacking the empire in the east. The Roman army was poorly organized. It was made up mainly of slaves and peasants instead of trained soldiers. Soldiers were permitted to marry and grow crops. They also held many non-military jobs, such as collecting taxes. As a result, they spent little time training for fighting. In addition, soldiers were stationed in cities throughout the empire. When attacks on the empire occurred, it was difficult to gather the soldiers together in one place for defense. Finally, the government had not kept the roads in repair, so travel was very difficult.

Practice the Skill

Read the passage above. Use the steps from Learn the Skill to identify the Roman Empire's problem and possible solutions.

1 Identify the Roman Empire's problem. State the problem in a clear sentence or two.

2 Identify possible solutions. Does the passage bring to mind any obvious solutions? Does it suggest any solutions that aren't as obvious?

3 Review the possible solutions. What kind of resources would each solution require? Think of what the possible outcome would be for each solution.

4 Identify the solution you think is best. Explain why you think it is the best one, and what its outcome would be.

Apply the Skill

Reread the passage titled Revolutions in Government on page 188. Then use the steps in this skill to identify the problem described in the passage, note its possible effects, and explain the solutions used.

Bronze statue of a
Roman soldier

Chapter 7 **199**

Objectives

Social Studies

1. Discover how Russia built its empire.
2. Understand the fall of the Russian tsars.
3. Examine the rise and fall of the Soviet Union.
4. Learn the causes and effects of the Cold War.
5. Learn about the Russian Federation today.

Reading/Language Arts

Read ahead to help clarify an unfamiliar word or passage.

Prepare to Read

Build Background Knowledge L2

Draw students' attention to the photo of Catherine the Great on this page. Help students get a sense of the Russian court by conducting an Idea Wave (TE, p. T35) to generate a list of words and phrases that might describe Catherine. Provide an example to get students started. (*regal, wealthy, powerful*)

Set a Purpose for Reading L2

- Preview the Objectives.

- Read each statement in the *Reading Readiness Guide* aloud. Ask students to mark the statements true or false.

- Have students discuss the statements in pairs or groups of four, then mark their worksheets again. Use the Numbered Heads participation strategy (TE, p. T36) to call on students to share their group's perspectives.

All in One Europe and Russia Teaching Resources, *Reading Readiness Guide,* p. 162

Vocabulary Builder
Preview Key Terms L2

Pronounce each Key Term, then ask students to say the word with you. Provide a simple explanation such as, "Ivan IV was the first tsar, or emperor, of Russia."

Prepare to Read

Objectives

In this section you will
1. Discover how Russia built its empire.
2. Understand the fall of the Russian tsars.
3. Examine the rise and fall of the Soviet Union.
4. Learn the causes and effects of the Cold War.
5. Learn about the Russian Federation today.

Taking Notes

As you read this section, look for important dates in Russia's development as an empire. Copy the timeline below and record your findings on it.

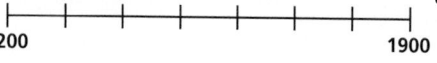

1200   1900

Target Reading Skill

Read Ahead Reading ahead can help you understand something you are not sure of in the text. If you do not understand a certain word or passage, keep reading. The word or idea may be clarified further on. For example, in the last paragraph below you may not be sure what is meant by the word *expansion*. As you read the section, that word will be clarified by the text.

Key Terms

- **westernization** (wes tur nuh ZAY shun) *n.* the adoption of western European culture
- **tsar** (zahr) *n.* a Russian emperor
- **revolutionary** (rev uh LOO shuh neh ree) *adj.* ideas that relate to or cause the overthrow of a government, or other great change
- **communism** (KAHM yoo niz um) *n.* a political system in which the central government owns farms, factories, and offices

---

Catherine the Great

200 Europe and Russia

The Russian court under Catherine the Great was dazzling. Catherine loved the arts, literature, philosophy, and French culture. She dreamed of creating a great nation, as glorious as France had been under Louis XIV.

Early in her rule, she made many efforts to improve the lives of the Russian people. She built schools and hospitals and gave people more religious freedom. She also became interested in ideas about liberty. Catherine did not bring freedom to all of her people, but she did make Russia a great empire. By the time of her death in 1796, she had expanded Russia southward to the Black Sea and westward into parts of Poland.

The history of Russia is a story with four themes: invasion and expansion, harsh treatment of the common people, slow **westernization,** or the process of becoming more like Western Europe, and autocratic (aw toh KRAT ik) government. An autocratic government is one in which one person has absolute power. As you read Russia's story, notice how these four themes appear again and again.

Target Reading Skill L2

Read Ahead Point out the Target Reading Skill. Tell students to keep reading if they come across a word or passage they do not understand, because it may be clarified later on in the text.

Model reading ahead by reading aloud the third sentence in the second paragraph on this page. "She also became interested in ideas about liberty." Tell students to read the next sentence in the paragraph to clarify the meaning of the word "liberty". (*freedom*)

Give students *Reread or Read Ahead.* Have them complete the activity in groups.

All in One Europe and Russia Teaching Resources, *Reread or Read Ahead,* p. 169

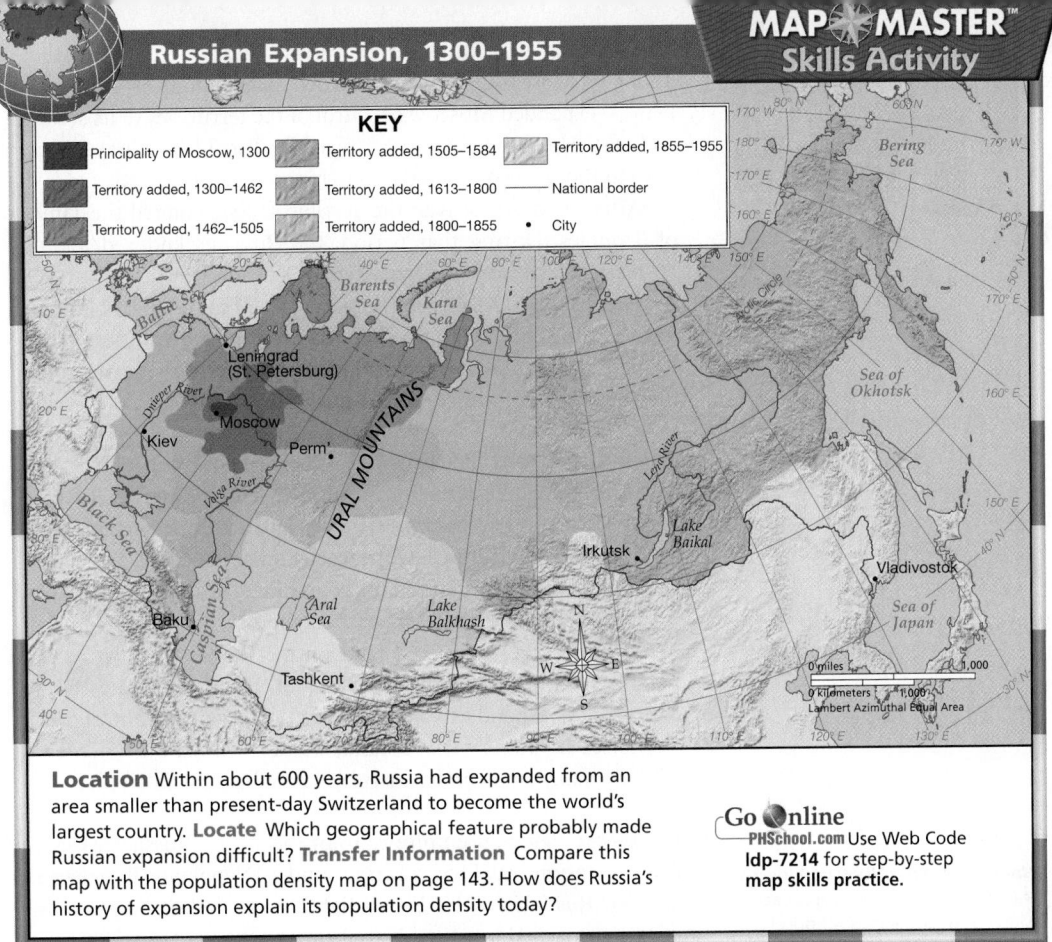

KEY

Principality of Moscow, 1300	Territory added, 1505–1584	Territory added, 1855–1955
Territory added, 1300–1462	Territory added, 1613–1800	—— National border
Territory added, 1462–1505	Territory added, 1800–1855	• City

Location Within about 600 years, Russia had expanded from an area smaller than present-day Switzerland to become the world's largest country. **Locate** Which geographical feature probably made Russian expansion difficult? **Transfer Information** Compare this map with the population density map on page 143. How does Russia's history of expansion explain its population density today?

Go **Online**
PHSchool.com Use Web Code
ldp-7214 for step-by-step
map skills practice.

Building a Vast Empire

Russia's story begins long before Catherine the Great. Many centuries before, various groups of people known as Slavs (slahvz) lived in small settlements. The Slavs lived in the region that eventually became the Russian Empire. In the 1200s, Mongol invaders from Asia swept in and conquered them.

The Rise of Moscow The prince of Moscow made clever agreements with the Mongols that helped him grow rich and powerful. By the 1330s, he had become the strongest ruler in the region. Slowly Moscow conquered surrounding territory. By the end of the 1400s, Moscow had freed itself entirely from Mongol rule. The map above shows how the small principality, or territory ruled by a prince, of Moscow grew into a huge country.

Chapter 7 Section 4 **201**

Vocabulary Builder

Use the information below to teach students this section's high-use words.

High-Use Word	Definition and Sample Sentence
reign, p. 202	*n.* period of time during which a monarch rules During the queen's **reign,** there was peace in the country.
reform, p. 203	*n.* a change for the better The principal made **reforms** to the school schedule, giving us more time to use the computer room.
withdraw, p. 204	*v.* to move back or out We **withdrew** from the room so we would not disturb the sleeping baby.

Instruct

Building a Vast Empire

L2

Guided Instruction

- **Vocabulary Builder** Clarify the high-use word **reign** before reading.

- Have students use the Oral Cloze reading strategy (TE, p. T33) to read Building a Vast Empire. They should also study the map showing Russian expansion.

- Ask **Which groups of people lived in the region that became the Russian Empire?** *(Slavs lived in the region in small settlements; Mongol invaders from Asia conquered the Slavs in the 1200s.)*

- Have students study the map of Russian Expansion. Ask **In what time period was Kiev added to Russian territory?** *(1613–1800)*

Answers

MAP★MASTER **Locate** the Ural Mountains
Skills Activity
Transfer Information Russia has a low population density, partly because it is such a large country.

Go **Online**
PHSchool.com Students may practice their map skills using the interactive online version of this map.

Chapter 7 Section 4 **201**

Show students *St. Petersburg and Peter the Great.* Ask **Who was Peter the Great?** *(He was the tsar of Russia from 1682–1725.)* **How did he make St. Petersburg into a great city?** *(He brought artists and architects from around the world to make a beautiful city; he made it the capital of the Russian Empire.)*

Guided Instruction (continued)

■ Ask **Who was the first tsar of Russia?** *(Ivan IV, known as Ivan the Terrible)* **What happened in Russia after his death?** *(Russia entered the Time of Troubles, during which there were 20 years of civil wars and invasions by the Poles.)*

■ Ask **What changes did Peter the Great bring to Russia?** *(He encouraged the westernization of the country, founded new schools, reorganized the government and army, conquered land on the Baltic and Black Seas, and moved the capital to St. Petersburg.)*

■ Ask **How was Napoleon's army in Russia defeated in 1812?** *(The early Russian winter surprised the troops and about 90,000 soldiers died.)*

Independent Practice

Have students create the Taking Notes graphic organizer on a blank piece of paper and begin to fill in dates and events from Building a Vast Empire.

Monitor Progress

As students begin work on their timelines, circulate and make sure individuals are choosing correct information. Provide assistance as needed.

Answers

Analyze Images the man on the horse; he appears to be leading the army

✓ Reading Check He wanted seaports to help Russia become a world power.

Learn how Peter the Great built St. Petersburg.

The Rise of the Tsars In the 1540s, Ivan IV became the leader of Moscow. He called himself **tsar** (zahr), or emperor. Ivan IV expanded Moscow's control of the territories to its south and east. He earned the name Ivan the Terrible for his cruelty both to those he conquered and to his own people.

After the death of Ivan the Terrible, Russia entered the Time of Troubles. During that period, the Russians endured about 20 years of civil wars and invasions by the Poles.

Finally, in 1613, Michael Romanov (ROH muh nawf) became tsar. During his reign, order was restored to Russia. The Romanovs continued expanding Russian territory throughout the 1600s and continued to rule Russia for more than 300 years.

Peter the Great Peter the Great came to power in 1689. Peter began bringing Western European ideas and culture to Russia. He hired foreign professors, scientists, and advisors, and encouraged Russians to adopt European customs. He also established new schools and reorganized his government and the army.

Peter believed that Russia needed good seaports to become a world power. He conquered land on the Baltic (BAWL tik) and Black seas, and moved the capital to St. Petersburg. Later tsars continued to expand Russian territory. Russia gained control over territories in present-day Poland, Turkey, China, and Sweden. With so many lands under its rule, Russia became an empire.

Invasion Being an empire did not mean that Russia was safe from invasion. A French army under Napoleon Bonaparte invaded Russia in 1812. Fierce fighting erupted as Napoleon's army approached Moscow. Napoleon's invasion plan, which did not take into account Russia's early winter, resulted in disastrous losses for the French. Of the 100,000 soldiers that reached Moscow, only about 10,000 survived.

✓ Reading Check **Why did Peter the Great want to control land on the Baltic Sea?**

Napoleon's First View of Moscow Napoleon and his troops approach Moscow in 1812 in this historical painting. **Analyze Images** *Which figure in the painting is Napoleon? How can you tell?*

202 Europe and Russia

Skills Mini Lesson

Using Reliable Information

1. Tell students that they should answer these questions when checking if a source is reliable: Is the information recent enough for your purposes? Is it accurate? What are the author's qualifications and methods? Does the author have a bias or one-sided view?

2. Ask students if a speech by Peter the Great about the value of his policy of westernization would be a reliable source of information about Russian history during the late 1600s.

3. Ask students to apply the skill using an article about Russia from a current source, such as a newspaper article.

The Last of the Tsars
A photo from the early 1900s shows Tsar Nicholas II with his family. **Compare and Contrast** *Describe the tsar and his family. How do you think their lives were different from those of poor Russians?*

The Fall of the Tsars

Russia had become a powerful empire, but the lives of most of its people had not improved. For hundreds of years, the tsar made all the important decisions. Below the tsar, Russian society was divided into two main groups. The first was a small number of landowners. The second group was a large number of very poor serfs. Tensions between the two groups began to rise.

Freeing of the Serfs In 1855, Alexander II became tsar. He soon freed the serfs and gave them their own land. He also gave towns more control over their own affairs. However, Alexander's son, Alexander III, reversed many of his father's reforms. Once again, the tsar ruled with absolute power.

Rumblings of Revolution In 1894, Nicholas II became tsar. He would be the last Russian tsar. Russia was badly beaten in a war with Japan in 1904 and 1905, and unrest grew among peasants, workers, and a small middle class. In 1905, thousands of workers in St. Petersburg marched to the tsar's Winter Palace. They wanted to appeal directly to the tsar for reforms. Troops stopped them and fired into the crowd, killing hundreds. This mass killing was known as Bloody Sunday.

Tsar Nicholas II was forced to agree to establish the Duma (DOO mah), a kind of congress. The people elected its members. In theory, the Duma shared power with the tsar. In fact, the Duma had very little power. Some progress toward reform was made, but many people wanted more.

Read Ahead
Keep reading to learn why the Russian people were not satisfied with this reform.

✔ **Reading Check** What event is known as Bloody Sunday?

The Fall of the Tsars L2

Guided Instruction

- **Vocabulary Builder** Clarify the high-use word **reform** before reading.

- Read The Fall of the Tsars with the class.

- Have students discuss why there were tensions between serfs and landowners. *(A small number of people owned all the land, but there was a large number of very poor serfs.)*

- Ask students to explain what happened when workers sought reforms in 1905. *(Troops killed hundreds of workers marching to the Winter Palace to ask the tsar for reforms. Tsar Nicholas II was forced to establish the Duma and share power with its elected members.)*

Independent Practice

Have students add information about the freeing of the serfs and the beginnings of revolution in Russia to their graphic organizers.

Monitor Progress

As students work on their graphic organizers, circulate to make sure individuals are choosing the correct events and placing them in order. Provide assistance as needed.

↻ Target Reading Skill L2

Read Ahead As a follow up, ask students to perform the Target Reading Skill activity in the Student Edition. *(Students should read ahead to find out why the Russian people were not satisfied with this reform.)*

Differentiated Instruction

For Advanced Readers L3
Have students read about Napoleon's campaign on the Russian battlefield in *A Letter from Napoleon's Army*. Have students share their responses to the questions in a discussion with a partner.

All in One **Europe and Russia Teaching Resources,** *A Letter from Napoleon's Army,* pp. 188–189

For English Language Learners L2
You may wish to have Spanish-speaking students complete the *Guided Reading and Review (Spanish)* for Section 4 of this chapter.

📄 **Eastern Hemisphere Spanish Support,** *Guided Reading and Review (Spanish),* p. 72

Answers

Compare and Contrast The tsar and his family were wealthy and probably lived much more comfortably than poor Russians.

✔ **Reading Check** the mass killing of protesting workers at the Winter Palace in 1905

The Rise of the Soviet Union

Guided Instruction

- **Vocabulary Builder** Clarify the high-use word **withdraw** before reading.

- Read The Rise of the Soviet Union with students.

- Ask **Why did communism appeal to the Russian people?** (*The nation was made up of mostly poor people who suffered terribly while a few rich people lived in luxury. Communism seemed to offer the poor the hope of making everyone equal and improving life for many Russians.*)

- Ask **What country did Lenin create when the Communists won the Russian civil war?** (*the Soviet Union*) **What did it include?** (*Russia and several smaller republics under Russian control—most of the territory of the old Russian Empire*)

- Ask **How did Stalin achieve his goals for the Soviet Union?** (*He developed industry by forcing peasants to give their crops to the government to feed factory workers and sending millions who opposed this policy to their death in Siberian prison camps.*)

- Have students discuss how the Soviet Union became involved in World War II. (*Despite an agreement between the Soviet Union and Germany, the Germans invaded the Soviet Union in 1941.*)

Independent Practice

Have students continue to work on their timelines, adding new dates and events.

Monitor Progress

Circulate to make sure individuals are choosing appropriate events.

Answer

Synthesize the idea that everyone would be equal and would enjoy a better standard of living

Promoting Communism
At the top, Lenin gives a speech to a crowd in Moscow in 1918. The poster above promotes communism, reading, "You are still not a member of the cooperative? Sign up immediately!" **Synthesize** *What about communism might have appealed to poverty-stricken Russians?*

The Rise of the Soviet Union

On an afternoon in April 1917, a small group of Russians gathered at a German railroad station. Among them was a man named Vladimir Ulyanov, who was also called Lenin. Earlier, the Russian government had imprisoned Lenin for spreading ideas that they believed were **revolutionary,** or ideas that could cause the overthrow of a government. Later, the government gave him permission to leave Russia.

Now the Germans were taking Lenin back to Russia. The Germans made two rules. First, no member of Lenin's group could leave the train, and second, none of them could talk to any Germans during their journey. The Germans, like the Russians, knew that ideas could be more powerful than any army. At the time, Germany was at war with Russia and hoped that Lenin would cause changes in Russia. And he did.

The Russian Revolution To understand why the Germans helped Lenin, you need to go back to 1914. That year, Russia entered World War I against Germany. Millions of Russian soldiers were killed or wounded. At home, people suffered severe food and fuel shortages. By March 1917, the Russian people began rioting. Troops were sent to put down the uprising. They joined the rioters instead. Tsar Nicholas II was forced to give up his throne. The tsar and his family were held as prisoners, and were later killed by Lenin's followers. A weak government took over.

In November 1917, after his return to Russia, Lenin and his supporters pushed the weak government aside. Lenin knew that Russians wanted peace more than anything else. In March 1918, Russia signed an agreement with Germany and withdrew from World War I. Under Lenin's leadership, Russia also agreed to give up the Baltic republics, a large area of its territory that had been occupied by the Germans. This was just what the Germans had hoped for.

As the new leader of Russia, Lenin wanted to establish a communist government. **Communism** (KAHM yoo niz um) is a political system in which the central government owns farms, factories, and offices. No one person can own factories or land. Each person is supposed to work and share equally in the rewards of this work.

The idea of communism appealed greatly to many Russians. For hundreds of years, Russia's poor had suffered terrible hardships while the rich lived in luxury. Lenin promised that everyone would be equal and enjoy a better standard of living, but he broke that promise. Instead, the government took all power and most of the wealth for itself.

Background: Biography

Joseph Stalin Joseph Stalin, the leader of the USSR from 1925–1953, was one of the most brutal dictators of modern times. In 1928, he launched programs that dramatically changed Soviet economic and social structures. Stalin crushed any opposition to his policies. In 1932–33, he created a famine in the Ukraine that killed 3 million farmers who had protested giving their lands to the state. In 1936, he conducted purges that resulted in the execution of many military officers and Communist party members that he believed were plotting against him. Stalin accomplished many of his goals, such as industrialization and involving the Soviet Union in international affairs, but after his death his methods were denounced by the Soviet government.

Building a Communist State The treaty with Germany ended the war, but peace still did not come to Russia. After the Communists came to power, there was a terrible civil war. On one side were Lenin's followers. On the other side were many groups who opposed them.

The Russian civil war lasted three years and cost millions of lives. Eventually, the Communists won. In 1922, Lenin created the Union of Soviet Socialist Republics (USSR), also called the Soviet Union. The Soviet Union was made up of Russia and several smaller republics under Russian control. It included most of the territory of the old Russian Empire. And as in the old empire, most of the people in the smaller republics were not Russian.

Lenin began turning the Soviet Union into a communist country. He jailed and even killed people who opposed him, calling them enemies of the revolution. Lenin died in 1924. Josef Stalin became the next leader. Under Stalin's form of Soviet communism, the government tried to control all aspects of citizens' lives.

Stalin's Dictatorship Josef Stalin was a dictator (DIK tayt ur), a leader who has absolute power. Stalin did not care about the suffering his decisions caused the Russian people. For example, he wanted to develop more industry in the Soviet Union. He knew that the increased number of factory workers would require great amounts of food. Therefore, Stalin forced the peasants to give their farm products to the government. Many peasants opposed the plan. As punishment, Stalin sent millions of peasants to prison camps in Siberia. Most died there. Stalin eventually succeeded in industrializing Russia. But all of the Soviet Union lived in terror of Stalin.

World War II Stalin signed an agreement with the Germans in 1939. It stated that the two countries would not go to war against each other. Despite the agreement, the Germans invaded the Soviet Union two years later. Three million German soldiers, with tanks and airplanes, advanced deep into the Soviet Union.

For a time, a German victory appeared likely. Many Soviet cities were destroyed. Millions of soldiers died or were captured. But the Soviet people fought bravely. By 1943, the Soviets had begun pushing the Germans out of Russia. Two years later, Soviet troops had captured Berlin, the capital of Germany.

✓ **Reading Check** Why was Stalin called a dictator?

Ending World War II
In the photo at the top, a Russian soldier celebrates the Soviet victory in Berlin by raising the Soviet flag. Above, the leaders of the Soviet Union, the United States, and the United Kingdom meet to discuss their countries' roles in the post-war world. **Recognize Causes** *How did the Soviet Union's role in World War II help it become a world power?*

The Cold War
L2

Guided Instruction

- Have students read about growing tension between the United States and the Soviet Union in The Cold War.

- Ask students **What were the world's two superpowers after World War II?** *(the United States and the Soviet Union)* **Why were they called "superpowers"?** *(They were extremely powerful countries.)*

- Ask **What were the main causes of the Cold War?** *(The Soviet Union forced Eastern European nations to become Communist and cut off their contact with the West. The Soviets attempted to expand their power in the world by encouraging rebels in other countries to turn to communism. The United States was determined to stop the spread of communism.)*

- Have students discuss some of the causes of the collapse of the Soviet Union. *(Its economy did not grow fast enough; basic consumer goods were in scarce supply; people did not want to be controlled by the government in every part of their lives.)*

Independent Practice

Have students add events from The Cold War to their graphic organizers.

Monitor Progress

As students continue to work on their timelines, circulate to make sure individuals are choosing the correct events. Provide assistance as needed.

Differentiated Instruction

For Gifted and Talented   L3
Have students read *Lenin's Deathbed Words* and *Kampf*, by Joseph Stalin. Ask students to write a brief paragraph explaining if they think Lenin's concerns about Joseph Stalin were valid.

All in One Europe and Russia Teaching Resources, *Lenin's Deathbed Words,* p. 190; *Kampf,* p. 191

For Less Proficient Readers   L1
Students who are less proficient readers may have difficulty absorbing the information in this section. Pair students with more proficient readers and have them create an outline of the material. Tell students to use the headings in the section as guidelines for their outline.

Answers

Recognize Causes It had a major role in the victory against Germany, which ultimately gave it more power after World War II.

✓ **Reading Check** because he ruled with absolute power

The Russian Federation

Guided Instruction

- Have students read about the Russian Federation. Circulate to make sure individuals can answer the Reading Check question.

- Ask **What is the Russian Federation?** (*the name that Russia took after the breakup of the Soviet Union; it includes Russians and many different ethnic groups.*)

- Ask **What are some of the challenges the Russian Federation has faced?** (*The transition from a Communist system to a western-style economy has caused economic chaos; ethnic conflict has arisen.*)

- Have students discuss the ways in which some groups have decided to break away from Russian rule. (*The republic of Tatarstan negotiated with the Russians to have more rights, while the republic of Chechnya has fought for its independence.*)

Independent Practice

Have students complete their timelines by adding events from The Russian Federation.

Monitor Progress

- Show *Section Reading Support Transparency ER 38* and ask students to check their graphic organizers individually. Go over key concepts and clarify key vocabulary as needed.

   📖 **Europe and Russia Transparencies,** *Section Reading Support Transparency ER 38*

- Tell students to fill in the last column of the *Reading Readiness Guide.* Probe for what they learned that confirms or invalidates each statement.

   All in One **Europe and Russia Teaching Resources,** *Reading Readiness Guide,* p. 162

A Nuclear Threat
By the 1980s, the superpowers had built enough powerful nuclear weapons to destroy the entire world. The top photo shows the explosion of a nuclear bomb. The bottom photo shows the universal yellow and black symbol of fallout shelters—underground rooms meant to protect people from fallout, or dangerous particles, after a nuclear explosion.
Sequence *What events led to the buildup of nuclear weapons by the Soviet Union and the United States?*

The Cold War

As you have read, after World War II the United States and the Soviet Union were so powerful that people called them superpowers. Relations between the superpowers became extremely tense. However, the two sides never fought each other. This time of tension without actual war is called the Cold War. It lasted roughly from 1945 until 1991 and shaped events within the two nations and around the world.

Causes of the Cold War The first cause of the Cold War was the situation in Eastern Europe. During World War II the Soviet army moved westward to Berlin, freeing the Eastern European countries that the Germans had conquered. But after the war, the Soviet troops did not leave. They forced those countries to become communist. Trade and most contact with the West were cut off. British leader Winston Churchill said that it was as if an "iron curtain" had fallen across Eastern Europe, dividing the East from the West.

Second, the Soviets tried to expand their power beyond Eastern Europe. They encouraged rebels in other nations to turn to communism. The United States was determined to stop this. The superpowers often backed opposing sides in conflicts in Latin America, Asia, and Africa. They also built powerful nuclear (NOO klee ur) weapons to use against each other.

Collapse of an Empire The Soviet Union's economy grew weak during the Cold War. The government had invested most of its money in heavy industries and weapons. It did not produce enough basic consumer goods, such as food and clothing. Also, the government's central control of the economy was not working.

Many of the Soviet people had lost faith in the communist system by the early 1980s. They were still poor and no longer believed the government's promises. One Soviet leader responded. Mikhail Gorbachev (mee kah EEL GAWR buh chawf), who took power in 1985, made many changes in the Soviet system. He allowed more personal freedom. He also reduced the government's control of the economy.

When people who have lived under harsh rule are given a taste of freedom, they often want more. This happened across Eastern Europe and the Soviet Union by the late 1980s. Eastern European countries abandoned communism. The Soviet republics demanded their independence. Finally, at the end of 1991, the Soviet Union broke apart.

✓ **Reading Check** What was the "Iron Curtain"?

Answers

Sequence the United States and the Soviet Union became superpowers after World War II; the Soviet Union took over Eastern Europe; the Soviet Union tried to spread communism in other parts of the world; the United States tried to stop the spread of communism; both countries built powerful nuclear weapons to use against each other.

✓ Reading Check a term used to describe the division between Eastern and Western Europe after World War II

Differentiated Instruction

For Less Proficient Readers L1
Have students read the section in the Reading and Vocabulary Study Guide. This version provides basic-level instruction in an interactive format with questions and write-on lines.

📖 Chapter 7, Section 4, **Eastern Hemisphere Reading and Vocabulary Study Guide,** pp. 75–77

The Russian Federation

After the breakup of the Soviet Union, all of its republics became independent nations. By far the largest of these, the republic of Russia, changed its name to the Russian Federation. A federation is a union of states or republics. In a federation, each member agrees to give certain powers to a central government. The Russian Federation includes Russians and peoples of many different ethnic groups. However, the Russian Federation is smaller in size than the old Soviet Union.

The Russian Federation made efforts to build a free-market economy, or an economy in which producers compete freely for consumers' business. It sold its state-owned factories and businesses to private individuals. It also tried to become more democratic. The transition away from a communist system was difficult, however. Russia experienced economic chaos.

Russia also experienced conflicts among its ethnic groups. Many of the non-Russian peoples were tired of being ruled by Russians, who are the majority in Russia. The republic of Tatarstan, for example, negotiated with the Russians to have more rights. The republic of Chechnya (CHECH nee uh), however, has fought bitterly for its independence. Russia today faces many challenges to building a new way of life.

Russian president Vladimir Putin in 2000

✓ **Reading Check** Why did the Russian Federation sell businesses to private individuals?

Section 4 Assessment

Key Terms
Review the key terms at the beginning of this section. Use each term in a sentence that explains its meaning.

Target Reading Skill
What word or idea were you able to clarify by reading ahead?

Comprehension and Critical Thinking
1. (a) Name Who was the first Russian leader to begin westernization?
(b) Draw Conclusions Why did he encourage Russians to adopt western customs?

2. (a) Define What was the Russian Duma?
(b) Identify Causes Why did Tsar Nicholas II create the Duma?
3. (a) Explain Why had Lenin been imprisoned by the Russian government?
(b) Sequence How did Lenin become Russia's leader?
4. (a) Define What is a federation?
(b) Summarize How did the Russian Federation try to westernize its economy?

Writing Activity
Today, some people in Russia want to return to their lives under communist rule. Write a paragraph arguing either for or against returning to communism.

Go Online
PHSchool.com

For: An activity about Leo Tolstoy
Visit: PHSchool.com
Web Code: ldd-7204

Assess and Reteach

Assess Progress　L2
Have students complete the Section Assessment. Administer the *Section Quiz*.

All in One **Europe and Russia Teaching Resources,** *Section Quiz,* p. 164

Reteach　L1
If students need more instruction, have them read this section in the Reading and Vocabulary Study Guide.

📖 Chapter 7, Section 4, **Eastern Hemisphere Reading and Vocabulary Study Guide,** pp. 75–77

Extend　L3
To extend students' understanding of the hardships people who were sent to Siberia suffered, have them read the primary source *The Endless Steppe* by Esther Hautzig. Have students work with partners to answer the questions.

All in One **Europe and Russia Teaching Resources,** *The Endless Steppe,* pp. 192–193

Answer

✓ **Reading Check** to begin building a free-market economy

Writing Activity
Use the *Rubric for Assessing a Writing Assignment* to evaluate students' paragraphs.

All in One **Europe and Russia Teaching Resources,** *Rubric for Assessing a Writing Assignment,* p. 201

Go Online
PHSchool.com Typing in the Web code when prompted will bring students directly to detailed instructions for this activity.

Section 4 Assessment

Key Terms
Students' sentences should reflect knowledge of each Key Term.

⟳ Target Reading Skill
Answers will vary, but students should identify a word or idea in the section that they were able to clarify by reading ahead.

Comprehension and Critical Thinking
1. ( ) Peter the Great **(b)** To make Russia a world power, Peter the Great probably felt that Russians needed to be familiar with western culture and ideas.

2. ( ) a kind of congress with elected members that was set up in Russia **(b)** He needed to meet the people's demand for reforms after the events of Bloody Sunday.

3. ( ) The government felt he had been spreading dangerous revolutionary ideas. **(b)** After the tsar was forced to give up his throne, a weak government was formed. Lenin and his supporters pushed that government aside.

4. ( ) a union of states or republics **(b)** It sold state-owned businesses to individuals and tried to become more democratic.

Section 5 The European Union

Objectives

Social Studies

1. Learn about the history of the European Union.

2. Understand the purpose of the European Union.

3. Examine the structure of the European Union.

4. Find out what the future holds for the European Union.

Reading/Language Arts

Reread or read ahead to help understand words and ideas in the text.

Prepare to Read

Build Background Knowledge L2

Tell students that in this section they will learn about the European Union. Write the word *union* on the board and invite students to suggest how this applies to governments and international affairs. Use an Idea Wave (TE, p. T35) to generate ideas. To get students started, ask them to think about how *union* applies to the United States. *(The word expresses how the individual states are united to make one country.)*

Set a Purpose for Reading L2

■ Preview the Objectives.

■ Read each statement in the *Reading Readiness Guide* aloud. Ask students to mark the statements true or false.

■ Have students discuss the statements in pairs or groups of four, then mark their worksheets again. Use the Numbered Heads participation strategy (TE, p. T36) to call on students to share their group's perspectives.

All in One Europe and Russia Teaching Resources, *Reading Readiness Guide,* p. 166

Vocabulary Builder
Preview Key Terms L2

Pronounce each Key Term, then ask students to say the word with you. Provide a simple explanation such as, "Many countries in Europe use the same currency, the euro."

Prepare to Read

Objectives

In this section you will
1. Learn about the history of the European Union.
2. Understand the purpose of the European Union.
3. Examine the structure of the European Union.
4. Find out what the future holds for the European Union.

Taking Notes

As you read this section, look for details about the European Union. Copy the concept web below and record your findings in it.

Target Reading Skill

Reread or Read Ahead
Both rereading and reading ahead can help you understand words and ideas in the text. If you do not understand a word or passage, use one or both of these techniques. In some cases, you may wish to read ahead first to see if the idea is clarified later on. If it is not, try going back and rereading the original passage.

Key Terms

• **euro** (YUR oh) *n.* the official currency of the European Union

• **single market** (SIN gul MAHR ket) *n.* a system in which goods, services, and capital move freely, with no barriers

• **foreign minister** (FAWR in MIN is tur) *n.* a government official who is in charge of a nation's foreign affairs

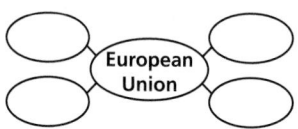

Robert Schuman worked to repair war-torn Europe.

At the end of World War II, Europe lay in ruins. Many of the nations of Europe had been at war with one another for years. Europeans needed to work together to bring about peace, rebuild their nations, and strengthen their shattered economies.

A French government official named Robert Schuman had a plan. He wanted European nations to work together to control their coal and steel industries. He proposed a new organization called the European Coal and Steel Community (ECSC). Six nations—Belgium, France, Italy, Luxembourg, the Netherlands, and West Germany—joined the group in 1951.

Over time, this small group grew into a much larger group, with many more roles and responsibilities. Today, it is called the European Union (EU), and has 25 member states. Many additional countries are waiting to become members.

208 Europe and Russia

Target Reading Skill L2

Reread or Read Ahead Point out the Target Reading Skill. Tell students to reread or read ahead to help them understand unfamiliar words or clarify ideas.

Model rereading and reading ahead using the two paragraphs on this page. Tell students that rereading the first paragraph can help clarify why European nations needed to rebuild and strengthen their economies.

Then tell students that reading ahead to the second paragraph will help them understand one of the ways in which Europeans wanted to rebuild their nations after World War II.

Give students *Reread or Read Ahead.* Have them complete the activity in their groups.

All in One Europe and Russia Teaching Resources, *Reread or Read Ahead,* p. 169

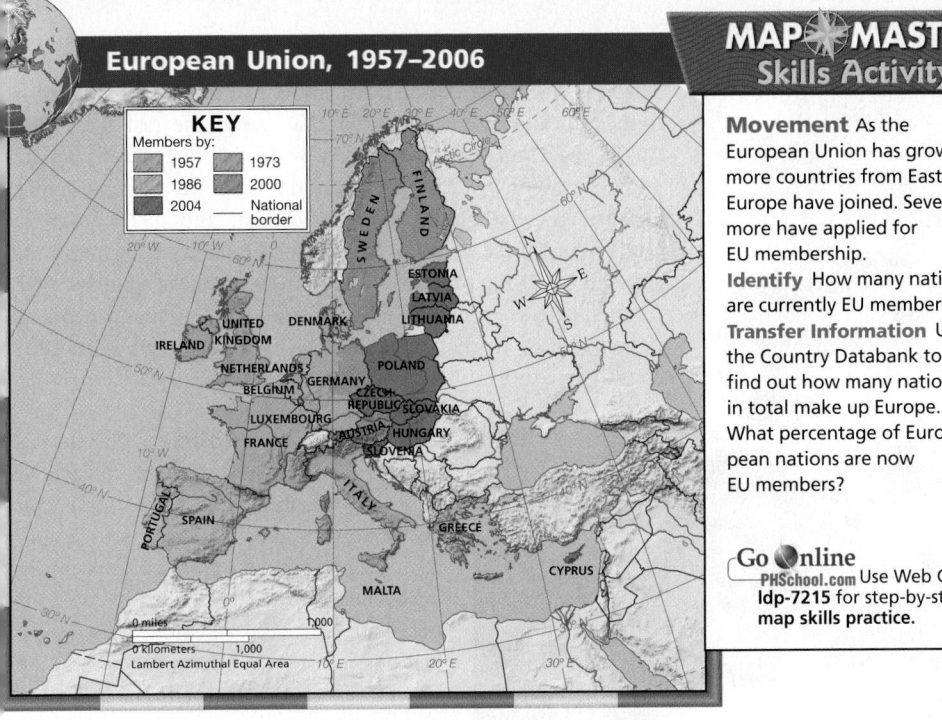

KEY

Members by:
- 1957
- 1986
- 2004
- 1973
- 2000
- National border

0 miles 1,000
0 kilometers 1,000
Lambert Azimuthal Equal Area

Movement As the European Union has grown, more countries from Eastern Europe have joined. Several more have applied for EU membership.
Identify How many nations are currently EU members?
Transfer Information Use the Country Databank to find out how many nations in total make up Europe. What percentage of European nations are now EU members?

Go Online
PHSchool.com Use Web Code ldp-7215 for step-by-step map skills practice.

History of the European Union

The ECSC created the European Economic Community (EEC) in 1957. The EEC expanded the ECSC, giving it greater economic powers. It also added the power to make social policies.

Expanding Membership Throughout the 1970s and 1980s, more and more nations wanted to join the EEC. The United Kingdom, Ireland, and Denmark joined in 1973. Greece followed in 1981. Portugal and Spain joined in 1986. Soon, the member nations began working on a new plan for an even stronger union.

The EEC Becomes the EU In 1992 the member nations of the EEC signed the Maastricht (MAH strikt) Treaty. This treaty, which went into effect the next year, established the European Union. It also laid out the plan for EU nations to adopt a single currency, or money. Europe's common currency is called the **euro,** (YUR oh). By 2001, twelve countries had adopted the euro. Denmark, Sweden, and the United Kingdom chose not to adopt the euro.

At first, only banks and other businesses used the euro. In 2002, nations adopting the euro withdrew their own coins and paper bills from circulation and began using euros instead.

✓ **Reading Check** What is the currency of the European Union?

Chapter 7 Section 5 **209**

Vocabulary Builder

Use the information below to teach students this section's high-use words.

High-Use Word	Definition and Sample Sentence
legal, p. 211	*adj.* relating to the law The presidents signed the bill, making the new law **legal.**
debate, p. 211	*v.* to discuss both sides of an issue We spent a long time **debating** whether to go away or stay at home during the vacation.

Instruct

History of the European Union L2

Guided Instruction

- Have students read History of the European Union using the Paragraph Shrinking reading strategy (TE, p. T34).

- Ask **What was the origin of the EU?** (*Six European nations formed the European Coal and Steel Community, which eventually became the EU.*)

- Ask **Which countries joined the EEC in 1973?** (*the United Kingdom, Ireland, and Denmark*) **Which joined in 1986?** (*Portugal and Spain*)

- Ask **What did the Treaty of Maastricht accomplish?** (*It established the European Union and laid out the plan for its members to adopt a single currency.*)

Independent Practice

Have students create the Taking Notes graphic organizer on a blank piece of paper. Briefly model how to begin filling in the concept web.

Monitor Progress

As students work on their graphic organizers, circulate to make sure individuals are choosing correct information. Provide assistance as needed.

Answers

MAP MASTER™ Skills Activity **Identify** twenty-five
Transfer Information about 60 percent

Go Online PHSchool.com Students may practice their map skills using the interactive online version of this map.

✓ **Reading Check** the euro

What Does the European Union Do? L2

Guided Instruction

- **Vocabulary Builder** Clarify the high-use word **legal** before reading.

- Read What Does the European Union Do? with students. As they read, circulate and make sure individuals can answer the Reading Check question.

- Ask **What was the main goal of the European Union when it first formed as the EEC?** *(to make future wars impossible by binding together the people and governments of Europe)* **How does the EU work to achieve this goal?** *(by promoting economic and social progress)*

- Ask **How is EU membership economically beneficial?** *(In the EU's single market, member nations can trade with one another without having to pay taxes on international trade.)*

- Ask **How do EU member nations still retain control over many of their own policies?** *(Each nation makes its own decisions about health care, national defense, education, and housing policies.)* **Why might this be important?** *(Answers will vary, but students should recognize that each country has its own culture, heritage, language, and sense of pride.)*

Independent Practice

Have students add information about the origins of the European Union to their graphic organizers.

Monitor Progress

As students work on their graphic organizers, circulate to make sure individuals are choosing correct information. Provide assistance as needed.

Answer

Generalize Possible answer: People traveling between countries do not have to carry many different currencies to buy goods.

A Market With Two Currencies
A Spanish market lists prices in both euros (top) and pesetas, the old Spanish currency. Many European markets used both currencies before changing over completely to euros.
Generalize *What are some advantages of having just one currency throughout several countries?*

What Does the European Union Do?

The EEC was created when the memory of a terrible war was fresh in the minds of all Europeans. For that reason, the goal of the EEC was to make future wars impossible by binding together the people and governments of Europe. Today the EU works to achieve that goal by cooperating to promote economic and social progress. Unlike the United States or Russia, the EU is not a federation of states. It is a group of individual countries that have agreed to give certain powers to the EU. Each EU nation remains an independent nation. But by working together, the EU has strength and influence that no individual nation could have alone.

Common Social Policies The citizens of all EU member nations are considered equal. Throughout the EU, people can move around freely without needing special visas or permits. They can even move permanently to another EU nation without receiving official permission. When new nations join the EU, however, it may be several years before their citizens gain all of these rights.

EU member nations also establish common policies in areas such as education, the environment, and fighting crime. For example, EU nations have similar policies for combating poverty. EU nations also follow over 200 environmental guidelines set up by the EU.

Finally, the EU strives to protect European heritage and culture. European students are encouraged to learn foreign languages and study in other EU countries. The EU also sponsors cultural projects—such as theater, dance, and film—that are produced by EU member nations working together.

Common Economic Policies EU member nations can trade freely with one another without having to pay tariffs, or taxes, on international trade. In effect, the EU has a **single market**, or a system in which goods, services, and capital move freely, with no barriers. EU nations also cooperate to create jobs for citizens in all countries throughout the EU.

All EU member nations help plan and contribute to the EU's central budget. A special bank manages this budget, which pays for all of the EU's expenses.

Common Government and Foreign Policies

The EU has many different roles relating to government and foreign policy. It creates laws that govern its member nations. It also signs treaties with non-EU countries and organizations. Most of these treaties have to do with trade or industry. Finally, the EU oversees policies that have to do with crime and the national security of the region.

A court called the Court of Justice ensures that the EU's policies are applied fairly in every EU member nation. It settles any legal disputes between member nations, EU organizations, or EU citizens. The Court is made up of one judge from each EU member state.

Things the EU Does Not Handle Recall that all EU member nations still remain independent countries. Although EU member nations work together, they keep control over many of their countries' own policies. For example, each nation decides how best to handle its own healthcare, national defense, education, and housing policies. Still, member nations try to make policies that agree with the policies made by other member nations.

✓ **Reading Check** What is the court that ensures EU policies are applied fairly?

Structure of the European Union

The EU has three main policy-making institutions. These institutions are the European Parliament, the Council of the European Union, and the European Commission.

European Parliament The European Parliament passes the majority of the EU's laws. It is the only EU institution that meets and debates in public. It is elected by all the citizens of the EU and represents their interests.

The number of representatives to Parliament differs according to the size of each country. When the Parliament meets, the representatives are assembled by political party, not by nation.

Council of the European Union The Council of the European Union is made up of the foreign ministers from individual EU nations. A **foreign minister** is a government official who is in charge of a nation's foreign affairs, or relations with other nations. The Council represents the separate national interests of the member nations.

A Seat of Government
The European Parliament is located in Strasbourg, France. **Infer** What challenges might EU nations have faced in deciding on where to locate its parliament?

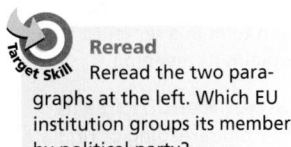

Reread Reread the two paragraphs at the left. Which EU institution groups its members by political party?

Chapter 7 Section 5 **211**

Structure of the European Union [L2]

Future of the European Union [L2]

Guided Instruction

- **Vocabulary Builder** Clarify the high-use word **debate** before reading.

- Have students read Structure of the European Union and Future of the European Union.

- Ask **What are the three main institutions that make policy?** (*the European Commission, the Council of Ministers, and the European Parliament*)

- Ask **Why do you think more nations are becoming interested in joining the European Union?** (*Possible answer: It is becoming more successful and stronger, which means that its member nations benefit more.*)

Independent Practice

Have students complete their graphic organizers.

Monitor Progress

- Show *Section Reading Support Transparency ER 39*, and have students check their graphic organizers individually. Go over key concepts and clarify key vocabulary as needed.

  📖 **Europe and Russia Transparencies,** *Section Reading Support Transparency ER 39*

- Tell students to fill in the last column of the *Reading Readiness Guide*.

  All in One Europe and Russia Teaching Resources, *Reading Readiness Guide,* p. 166

🎯 Target Reading Skill [L2]

Reread As a follow up, have students answer the Target Reading Skill question in the Student Edition. (*the European Parliament*)

Answers

Infer Possible answer: Since the EU has many member nations, it might have been difficult to decide which nation should contain the European Parliament.

✓ **Reading Check** the Court of Justice

Skills Mini Lesson

Identifying the Main Idea

1. Explain that to find the main idea of a passage, students should identify the subject and supporting details, decide what overall impression the details present, and make a general statement about what the details tell them.

2. Have students practice the skill using the first paragraph on this page. Suggest that

they identify the topic sentence (*the first sentence of the paragraph*). Draw attention to the details in the later sentences. Have students make a general statement about the main idea.

3. Have students practice the skill using a paragraph under the heading Structure of the European Union.

Assess and Reteach

Assess Progress `L2`
Have students complete the Section Assessment. Administer the *Section Quiz*.

All in One **Europe and Russia Teaching Resources,** *Section Quiz,* p. 168

Reteach `L1`
If students need more instruction, have them read this section in the Reading and Vocabulary Study Guide.

📖 Chapter 7, Section 5, **Eastern Hemisphere Reading and Vocabulary Study Guide,** pp. 78–80

Extend `L3`
To help students extend their understanding, have them use *Outline Maps 14, 17,* and *18* to label the nations currently in the European Union and those expecting to join in the near future. They may do library or Internet research to help them find countries being considered for membership.

All in One **Europe and Russia Teaching Resources,** *Outline Map 14: Western Europe: Political,* p. 179, *Outline Map 17: Eastern Europe: Physical,* p. 180, *Outline Map 18: Eastern Europe and Russia: Political,* p. 181

Answers

✔ **Reading Check** the Council of the European Union

✔ **Reading Check** It must accept existing EU laws, values, and policies.

Section 5 Assessment

Key Terms
Students' sentences should reflect knowledge of each Key Term.

🎯 **Target Reading Skill**
Answers will vary, but students should identify how rereading or reading ahead helped their understanding of an idea in the text.

Comprehension and Critical Thinking
1. (a) Denmark, Sweden, and the United Kingdom **(b)** Possible answer: They might have taken pride in their own currency as part of their national identity.

2. (a) People can move freely between member countries; common policies have been established for the countries; European heritage and culture are protected. **(b)** It wants

---

Members of the EU discuss energy resources with non-EU members.

Other EU Institutions The European Commission represents the interests of the whole EU community. It is made up of several different offices, each overseeing a certain area of policy. Each EU member nation sends representatives to the Commission. Other EU institutions perform services such as monitoring the EU's income and spending, advising on economic policy, and overseeing long-term investment.

✔ **Reading Check** **Which institution in the European Union represents each nation's national interests?**

Future of the European Union

In just over 50 years, the EU has enjoyed great success. It has brought peace and prosperity to almost 500 million Europeans.

The EU continues to expand. In 2004, ten nations from Eastern and Southern Europe joined. By 2006, several more countries had applied to join and were working to meet EU requirements. To join, new members must accept existing EU laws, values, and policies. The EU will continue to draw its strength from following its own rules and honoring its traditions. Its long-term goal is to bring all the democracies of Europe together. This process will be a careful and gradual one.

✔ **Reading Check** **What must a nation do to join the EU?**

Section 5 Assessment

Key Terms
Review the key terms at the beginning of this section. Use each term in a sentence that explains its meaning.

🎯 **Target Reading Skill**
How did rereading or reading ahead help your understanding?

Comprehension and Critical Thinking
1. (a) Name Which three nations in the EU did not adopt the euro?
(b) Infer Why might these countries not have wanted to adopt a single currency?

2. (a) List What are some examples of the EU's social policies?
(b) Analyze Information What do these policies tell you about how the EU views its citizens?
3. (a) Recall What are the EU's main policy institutions?
(b) Draw Conclusions Why do you think the representatives in Parliament are assembled by political group and not by nation?
4. (a) Recall What must new members of the EU accept before they can join the EU?
(b) Infer Why might some European countries not want to join the EU?

Writing Activity
Suppose that you are a citizen of a nation that is interested in joining the European Union. Write a letter to your local newspaper describing both the benefits and the disadvantages of joining.

> **Writing Tip** A letter should begin with an overview sentence or two. After describing the benefits and disadvantages, end the letter with a closing statement.

---

to improve the quality of life for its citizens and protect their national identities.

3. (a) European Commission, Council of the European Union, European Parliament **(b)** Members of the same political groups probably have more goals in common than representatives of the same country.

4. (a) EU laws, values, and policies **(b)** Possible answer: They do not agree with EU laws and policies; they may feel as though joining

the EU will compromise their sense of nationalism.

Writing Activity
Use the *Rubric for Assessing a Letter to the Editor* to evaluate students' letters.

All in One **Europe and Russia Teaching Resources,** *Rubric for Assessing a Letter to the Editor,* p. 202

7 Review and Assessment

◆ Chapter Summary

Section 1: From Ancient Greece to the Middle Ages

- The first great philosophers, historians, and writers were the ancient Greeks.
- Ancient Romans created a system of written laws that are still in use today.
- In the Middle Ages, many people found order and security in feudalism and Christianity.

Section 2: Renaissance and the Age of Revolution

- The ideas, writing, and art of the ancient world later inspired Renaissance scholars and artists.
- Explorers began to travel beyond Europe in search of wealth.
- Revolutions in government and science changed European ways of life.

Section 3: Industrial Revolution and Nationalism

- The Industrial Revolution changed the way that goods were made and how people lived and worked.
- Workers began to demand better working conditions and a voice in government.
- Europe experienced a century of war and nationalism in the 1900s.

Section 4: Imperial Russia to the Soviet Union

- By the 1900s, Russia was a huge empire.
- Following the Russian Revolution, Vladimir Lenin came to power and a communist state was established.
- The Cold War was a time of great tension between the United States and Russia that lasted for nearly 50 years.
- After the collapse of the Soviet Union, the Russian Federation was formed.

Section 5: The European Union

- The European Union was officially created in 1992.
- The European Union works to achieve common security and economic goals.
- Three main institutions create European Union policy.
- The European Union continues to expand.

Euro bills and coins

◆ Key Terms

Match the vocabulary words with their correct definitions.

1. Industrial Revolution
2. euro
3. foreign minister
4. alliance
5. Renaissance
6. tsar

A   a Russian emperor

B   a government official who is in charge of relations with other nations

C   the currency of the European Union

D   the period of history when products began to be made by machines in factories

E   a period of history that included the rebirth of interest in learning and art

F   an agreement between countries to protect and defend each other

Vocabulary Builder

Revisit this chapter's high-use words:

process	policy	withdraw
rely	invade	legal
collapse	generation	debate
focus	reign	
radical	reform	

Ask students to review the definitions they recorded on their *Word Knowledge* worksheets.

All in One Europe and Russia Teaching Resources, *Word Knowledge,* p. 172

Consider allowing students to earn extra credit if they use the words in their answers to the questions in the Chapter Review and Assessment. The words must be used correctly and in a natural context to win the extra points.

Review and Assessment
Review Chapter Content

- Review and revisit the major themes of this chapter by asking students to classify what Guiding Question each bulleted statement in the Chapter Summary answers. Have students work in groups to classify the statements. Use the Numbered Heads participation strategy (TE, p. T36) to have the groups share their answers in a class discussion. Refer to p. 139 in the Student Edition for the text of the Guiding Questions.

- Assign *Vocabulary Development* for students to review Key Terms.

   All in One Europe and Russia Teaching Resources, *Vocabulary Development,* p. 199

Answers

Key Terms

1. D
2. C
3. B
4. F
5. E
6. A

Review and Assessment

Comprehension and Critical Thinking

7. (a) democracy and the idea of learning through observation **(b)** He acquired a huge empire in which he established Greek cities, the Greek language, and Greek ideas.

8. (a) in the 1500s **(b)** the ancient world of Greek and Roman thinkers **(c)** The art of the Renaissance was more lifelike than the stiff art of the Middle Ages.

9. (a) People worked long hours in unsafe factories for low wages. The rapid growth of cities caused people to live in cramped, dirty housing where diseases spread rapidly. **(b)** to fight for better working conditions **(c)** As governments responded to workers' demands, people gained a greater voice in government and many European nations became more democratic.

10. (a) Millions of soldiers had been killed or wounded in World War I, and people at home were suffering shortages of food and fuel. **(b)** He promised poor Russians that everyone would be equal and enjoy a better standard of living to convince them to support communism.

11. (a) In the 1300s, the prince of Moscow conquered the territory surrounding Moscow. Ivan IV expanded Moscow's control; Peter the Great and Catherine the Great later added to the empire. **(b)** Under the tsars most people were poor and lived lives of hardship. **(c)** Under the tsars, only a few people owned the land and the rest were poor peasants. Under communism, the state owned everything. People were supposed to work and share the rewards equally, but the government took all the power.

12. (a) to promote security and a strong economy **(b)** to preserve national independence and identity

Skills Practice

Possible Answer: Problem—Wages were low and factory conditions were not safe. Solution—Workers formed labor unions and demanded better working conditions.

◆ Comprehension and Critical Thinking

7. (a) List Name two important ideas given to us by the ancient Greeks.
(b) Synthesize How did Alexander the Great spread Greek ideas?

8. (a) Recall When did the Renaissance reach its peak?
(b) Explain To what culture did Renaissance scholars and artists look for inspiration?
(c) Contrast How did the art of the Renaissance differ from the art of the Middle Ages?

9. (a) Name In what ways did people suffer as a result of industrialization?
(b) Draw Conclusions Why did labor unions begin to form during the Industrial Revolution?
(c) Identify Effects How did changes in society during the Industrial Revolution lead to changes in government?

10. (a) Explain Why was there rioting in Russia in 1917?
(b) Identify Effects How did Lenin use the power of ideas to persuade Russians to follow him?

11. (a) Explain How did Russia gain more territory and become an empire?
(b) Summarize Why did the Russian people come to oppose the tsars?
(c) Contrast How was Russia under the tsars different from the Soviet Union under communism?

12. (a) Recall What are the main goals of the European Union?
(b) Analyze Why might EU member nations prefer to handle some issues, such as healthcare, education, and housing policies, on their own?

◆ Skills Practice

Problem Solving In the Skills for Life activity in this chapter, you learned how to solve problems. Review the steps you followed to learn this skill. Then turn to the section titled Changes in Society on page 193 of this chapter. Identify the problem that factory workers faced. Then explain how the problem was solved.

◆ Writing Activity: Math

Rome's emperor Hadrian had a wall built from coast to coast across northern England, in order to defend his empire's land. The wall extends 73 miles (118 kilometers) from Wallsend in the east to Bowness in the west. There are many towers and gates along the wall. About every seven miles there is a fort. Calculate how long it would have taken an army to march the entire length of the wall, if their marching speed was three miles per hour. Write a paragraph explaining your opinion on whether a wall would work as a type of defense.

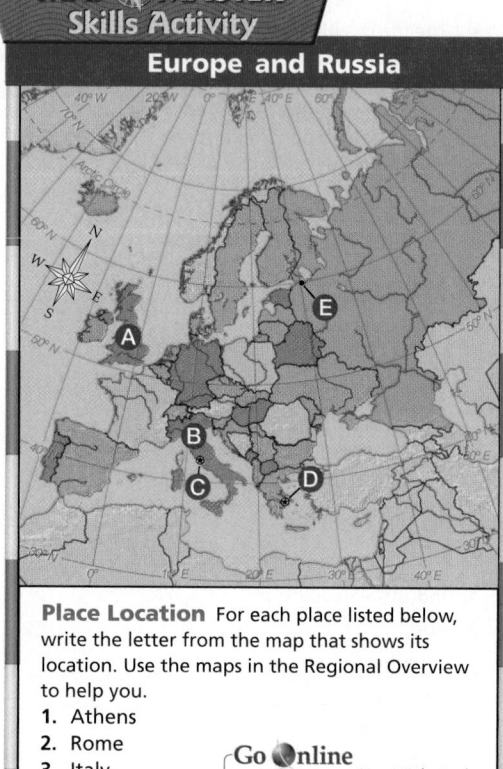

MAP MASTER™ Skills Activity

Europe and Russia

Place Location For each place listed below, write the letter from the map that shows its location. Use the maps in the Regional Overview to help you.
1. Athens
2. Rome
3. Italy
4. Great Britain
5. St. Petersburg

Go Online
PHSchool.com Use Web Code **ldp-7225** for an **interactive map**.

Writing Activity: Math

Students should note that it would take a soldier about 24 hours and 20 minutes to walk the length of the entire wall. Students might point out that this figure does not take into account resting or eating. Most students will conclude that this is not the best defense, although they should note the period in which it was used. They might also mention other walls erected for defense, such as the Great Wall of China. Use the *Rubric for Assessing a Writing Assignment* to evaluate students' paragraphs.

All in One Europe and Russia Teaching Resources, *Rubric for Assessing a Writing Assignment,* p. 201

Standardized Test Prep

Test-Taking Tips

Some questions on standardized tests ask you to find main ideas or topic sentences. Read the paragraph below. Then follow the tips to answer the sample question.

> In 334 B.C., Alexander the Great set out from Greece to conquer the world. Within ten years, his empire extended from Egypt to northern India. He founded many new cities across these lands. Greek culture linked the whole Mediterranean world by the time of his death in 323 B.C.

Pick the letter that best answers the question.

Which topic sentence is missing from this paragraph?

- **A** Alexander the Great was a great soldier, thinker, and artist.
- **B** Alexander the Great was one of the world's greatest military minds.
- **C** The accomplishments of Alexander the Great were enormous.
- **D** Alexander's conquest spread Greek language, culture, and ideas.

TIP Some paragraphs have a topic sentence that states the main idea. All the other sentences in the paragraph support this point.

Think It Through What is the main point of the paragraph? You can eliminate C because it is too general. Answer A may or may not be true, but even if it is true, it doesn't completely describe every sentence in the paragraph. That leaves B and D. Alexander was a great military mind, but the paragraph includes other accomplishments as well. The correct answer is D.

TIP Make sure that you read each answer choice carefully. Carelessness can easily cost points on a multiple-choice test.

Practice Questions

Use the tips above and other tips in this book to help you answer the following questions.

1. In a feudal system, there is a special relationship between
   - **A** knights and foot soldiers.
   - **B** lords and vassals.
   - **C** peasants and knights.
   - **D** peasants and kings.

2. Which of the following would not be discussed under the topic sentence, Renaissance sculptors made powerful lifelike statues?
   - **A** the work of Michelangelo
   - **B** the importance of human beings to Renaissance artists
   - **C** the role of printing in the Renaissance
   - **D** the 1500 sculpture named *David*

3. After World War II, Eastern Europe was under the influence of which country?
   - **A** the Soviet Union
   - **B** France
   - **C** Germany
   - **D** the United States

4. What type of leader was Joseph Stalin?
   - **A** president
   - **B** tsar
   - **C** prime minister
   - **D** dictator

Use Web Code lda-7201 for a **Chapter 7 self-test.**

Chapter 7 **215**

Standardized Test Prep

Answers

1. B
2. C
3. A
4. D

Go Online PHSchool.com Students may use the Chapter 7 self-test on PHSchool.com to prepare for the Chapter Test.

Assessment Resources

Use *Chapter Tests A and B* to assess students' mastery of chapter content.

All in One Europe and Russia Teaching Resources, *Chapter Tests A and B*, pp. 203–208

Tests are also available on the *ExamView Test Bank CD-ROM.*

⊙ *ExamView Test Bank CD-ROM*

Objectives

1. Learn about the everyday life of a young serf in the Middle Ages.

2. Understand the importance of work on a feudal manor.

3. Determine the author's purpose and point of view.

Prepare to Read

Build Background Knowledge L2

Ask students to recall what they have read about feudalism. Discuss what it would have been like to be a serf in the Middle Ages. Use the Think-Write-Pair-Share participation strategy (TE, p. T36) to have students identify what responsibilities someone their own age might have had as a serf.

Instruct

Pearl in the Egg L2

Guided Instruction

- Point out that some potentially unfamiliar words are defined for students in the margin. Clarify the meaning of the words before reading.

- Pair students and have them use the Paragraph Shrinking strategy (TE, p. T34) to read the selection.

- Ask students **What is Pearl's home like?** (*It is a hut made of mud and timber that has a dirt floor, a bed of straw, and is lit by a rushlight.*)

- Ask students **Why is it important for Pearl to work in the fields?** (*It is harvest time and her family needs the food for the coming winter. Her father is ill and cannot help, so her brother has to take their father's place working in the manor fields.*)

From Pearl in the Egg
By Dorothy Van Woerkom

Prepare to Read

Background Information

In Europe in the Middle Ages, a typical day for a person your age was quite different than it is for you. For one thing, a child at that time was considered much closer to being an adult than is a child today. This is because people had shorter life expectancies. More people in those days died of diseases that today can be cured.

Pearl in the Egg was the name of a real girl who lived in the 1200s. Historians know little about her. Dorothy Van Woerkom has written a book of historical fiction about Pearl. Her descriptions of Pearl's life are based on what historians know about life in England in the 1200s. At that time, people in Europe were just beginning to use family names. Usually they gave themselves names that described their work or their families in some way.

In this part of Pearl's story, you will read about a typical day in her life.

Objectives

In this selection you will

1. Learn about the everyday life of a young serf in the Middle Ages.

2. Understand the importance of work on a feudal manor.

---

rushlight (RUSH lyt) *n.* a lamp made with grease and part of a rush, or swamp plant

dripping (DRIP ing) *n.* fat and juices drawn from cooking meat

serfs (surfs) *n.* peasant farmers who worked the land as the slaves of a wealthy landowner

Pearl set the bowl of cabbage soup down on the floor near the rushlight. She knelt beside the box of straw that was her father's bed. She wiped his forehead, listening to his heavy breathing.

"Please, Fa," she coaxed. She broke off a piece from a loaf of black bread and dipped it into the soup. She placed it on his lips, letting the soup trickle into his mouth. She ate the chunk of bread, and dipped another.

"I will be in the fields until the nooning," she said, "so you must try to eat a little now. See, I have put a bit of dripping in the soup."

She forced the warm, mild liquid down his throat until the bowl was half empty. She drank the rest herself, chewing hungrily on the lump of fat that the sick man had not been able to swallow.

Again she wiped his face, and then she blew out the light. She crossed the smooth dirt floor, and pulled a sack from a peg on the wall near the door as she left the hut. Outside, the sky was gray with the dawn. Ground fog swirled around her feet. The air smelled of ripening grain and moist earth.

From other huts of mud and timber, serfs hurried out into the early morning mist. Some, like Pearl, would spend the day in their own small holdings in the fields. It was the time for har-

Read Fluently

Partner students and have them choose a paragraph from the selection. Have students take turns reading the paragraph aloud. Ask them to underline words that give them trouble as they read. Then, have them decode the problem words with their partner. Provide assistance as needed. Have students reread the paragraph two more times to improve their reading speed. Remind them to stop at the commas and periods and to read with expression.

vesting their crops, which would feed their families through the winter. Others, like Pearl's older brother, Gavin, had already left for work in the manor fields to bring in Sir Geoffrey's crops.

Sir Geoffrey was lord of the manor, which included his great stone house and all the land surrounding it. He owned this tiny village. He even owned most of the people in it. A few, like the baker, the miller, and the soapmaker, were freemen and free women. They worked for themselves and paid the lord taxes. For tax, Sir Geoffrey collected a portion of everything they produced. No one in the village had money.

But the serfs were not free. They could never leave the manor, or marry without the lord's permission. They could not fish in the streams or hunt in the forest. They owned only their mud huts and small gardens, called holdings, and an ox or cow, or a few geese or sheep. The serfs also paid taxes. Each year they gave Sir Geoffrey a portion of their crops. He took a share of their eggs; if a flock of sheep or geese increased, he took a share; and if a cow had a calf, he took that also. On certain days of the week each family had to send a man—and an ox if they had one—to help plow the lord's fields, harvest his crops, and do their work. Each woman had to weave one garment a year for the lord and his family.

The sun was up when Pearl reached the long <u>furrows</u> of her field, where the flat green bean pods weighed down their low bushes. She bent to see if the leaves were dry. Wet leaves would wither when she touched them.

The sun had dried them. Pearl began filling her sack, wondering how she could finish the harvest all by herself before the first frost. She had other plots to work as well.

Now that their father was ill, twelve-year-old Gavin was taking his place for three days each week in the manor fields. Sir Geoffrey would get his crops safely in! But if the frost came early, or if the only one left at home to work was an eleven-year-old like Pearl, that was of small matter to Sir Geoffrey.

Pearl stood up to rub her back. A serf's life was a hard life. Her father's was, and his father's before him. She sighed. Who could hope to change it?

Old <u>Clotilde</u> came swaying up the narrow path between her field and Pearl's. She waved her empty sack by way of greeting and squatted down among her plants.

"How be your Fa this morning?" she asked Pearl.

A page from a French book dating from around 1460 shows people planting seeds.

furrows (FUR ohz) *n.* grooves in the earth made by a plow

Clotilde (kluh TILD)

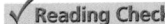
√ **Reading Check**

Why does Pearl work alone in her family's holdings?

Guided Instruction (continued)

- Ask students **What responsibilities do the freemen and free women in the village have to the lord?** (*Though they work for themselves, they are required to pay the lord taxes.*)

- Ask students **How does Sir Geoffrey control the lives of the serfs?** (*They cannot leave the manor or marry without the lord's permission; they cannot fish in the streams or hunt in the forest; they own only their mud huts, their small gardens, and some livestock; Sir Geoffrey takes a portion of any gains in their livestock each year. Each family must send a man to work in the lord's fields on certain days, and each woman must weave one garment per year for the lord and his family.*)

- Ask students **Why do you think the author includes the flashback to Pearl's meeting with Jack in the woods?** (*Possible answer: The author wanted to show how unfairly and cruelly the serfs were treated.*)

- Ask students **What will be the result of the hunters' damage to the crops?** (*Many villagers won't have enough to eat.*)

- Have students discuss what the author's purpose might have been in writing this story. (*Possible answers: to share the story of a real girl's life in the 1200s; to let readers know what feudalism was like*)

- Ask students **Based on the selection, how do you think the author feels about feudalism?** (*Possible answer: It was a hard and unfair life for serfs.*)

Answer

√ **Reading Check** Her mother is dead, her father is ill, and her brother must take the place of their father in the manor fields, so Pearl is the only one left at home to work in her family's holdings.

Literature **217**

Independent Practice

If students are having trouble following the selection, have them reread it with a partner, taking turns reading every few paragraphs aloud to each other. Ask them to write down the answers to the Reading Check questions as they read.

Monitor Progress

Circulate to make sure students are communicating effectively and are able to answer the Reading Check questions. Provide assistance as needed.

A painting of nobles hunting illustrates this manuscript, created in 1515.

bowmen (BOH mun) *n.* men with bows and arrows; archers

defiant (dee FY unt) *adj.* bold or resistant

"He took some soup. But he wanders in his head. He thinks I am my mother, though she's been dead three summers now."

"Ah, and he'll join her soon, Big Rollin will." Clotilde's wrinkled face was nearly the same dirty gray as her cap. "They all do, soon as they take a mite of sickness. For the likes of us to stay alive, we must stay well! Get the priest for him! He won't plow these fields again."

Before Pearl could reply, the shrill blare of a hunting horn sounded across the meadow, followed by the baying of hounds on the trail of a wild boar. Startled to their feet, the serfs watched the terrified boar running in and out among the rows of crops.

"Run, lest you get trampled!" Clotilde screamed, dashing down the path toward the forest. The others followed her. Someone pulled Pearl along as she stumbled forward, blinded by angry tears, her fingers tightly gripping her sack.

The hounds came running in pursuit of the boar. Behind the hounds rode the hunting party of twenty horsemen, led by Sir Geoffrey. At the rear was another man Pearl recognized. Jack, one of Sir Geoffrey's <u>bowmen</u>, had come upon her one day as she scrounged for dead branches near the edge of the forest. He had baited her with cruel words, rudely ruffling her hair with the shaft end of an arrow.

"Jack's my name. What's yours?" he had demanded, taking pleasure in her discomfort. For answer she had spat at him, and he had pressed the arrow's metal tip against her wrist until she'd dropped her bundle. Laughing, he had scattered the branches with his foot and grabbed her hair.

"Spit at me again, girl, and that will be the end of you!" Though his mouth had turned up in a grin, his eyes had been bright with anger. His fingers had tightened on the nape of her neck, bending her head back. She stared up at him, frightened, but <u>defiant</u>.

"Perhaps you need a lesson in manners right now," he'd said, raising his other hand. He probably would have struck her, but for the rattle of a wagon and the tuneless whistle signaling someone's approach. He had let her go with a suddenness that had left her off balance, and had stalked away.

Shaken, Pearl had turned to see Sir Geoffrey's woodcutter driving out of the forest with a wagonload of wood for the manor house.

218 Europe and Russia

Differentiated Instruction

For Gifted and Talented　L3

Ask students to create a schedule for a day in Pearl's life. Remind them that her day depended on the hours of light available. Then have each student make another schedule showing a day in his or her own life. Ask students to write a paragraph comparing their lives with Pearl's. Students should include hours spent at work or other responsibilities, hours spent learning, hours spent at recreation, sleeping, and any other categories they can think of.

Now Pearl shuddered at the memory; but Jack was taking no notice of her. His eyes were on the boar and on his master. If the boar became maddened during the chase and turned on one of the hunters, Jack was ready with his arrows to put an end to the beast.

Over the meadow they galloped, and onto the fields. They churned up the soft earth, trampled down the precious bean plants, crushed the near-ripe ears of the barley and oats, tore up the tender pea vines. They chased the boar across the fields and back again, laughing at the sport.

When they had gone, Pearl ran back to her field. She crawled in the turned-up earth, searching for unbroken bean pods. The other serfs were doing the same.

"What is the matter with us?" she demanded of Clotilde, "Why do we stay silent, with spoiled crops all around us, just so Sir Geoffrey will have his sport?"

"Shish!" Clotilde warned, looking quickly around to see who might have heard. "Do you want a <u>flogging</u> for such bold words? Hold your tongue, as you see your elders do."

For the rest of the morning they worked in silence. At midday, Pearl picked up her half-filled sack. It should have been full by now. She glared fiercely across the meadow at the manor house, but she held her tongue.

Pearl returned home to find that her father had worsened. When she could not rouse him, she went for the priest.

flogging (FLAHG ing) *n.* a beating or whipping

✓ **Reading Check**

What stopped Jack from hitting Pearl?

Review and Assessment

Thinking About the Selection

1. (a) **Recall** What did the serfs use to pay their taxes?
(b) **Explain** Why did the serfs give Sir Geoffrey a portion of their crops every year?
(c) **Infer** The feudal system existed for more than 400 years. Why do you think it lasted for such a long time?
2. (a) **Explain** What did Clotilde mean when she said, "Do you want a flogging for such bold words?"

(b) **Predict** Based on what you know about Pearl, how do you think she might act the next time she sees the lord or one of his men?

Writing Activity

Write a Short Story
Write a preface to Pearl's story telling how she received the name Pearl in the Egg. Or write a short story in which Pearl awakens in 2005. She is still 11 years old, and her father is still ill. Describe her reaction to today's world.

About the Author

Dorothy Van Woerkom (b. 1924) was born in Buffalo, New York. She was an elementary school teacher before becoming a writer. She is most noted for her folktale translations and her religious stories. She often rewrites folktales, sometimes changing the characters' names and the settings, but keeping the plot.

Literature 219

Assess and Reteach

Assess Progress L2

Have students answer the assessment questions.

Reteach L1

To help students understand and analyze the characters, have them make a chart listing each of these characters—Pearl, Clotilde, Jack—as a heading. Under each name, have students write words that describe the character in terms of feelings and actions. (*Pearl: worried about her father and the harvest; hard worker at home and in the fields: angry and defiant toward Jack; angry at the hunters. Clotilde: concerned and resigned about Pearl's father; fearful about the hunters; fearful about speaking out about the ruined crops. Jack: cruel and bold toward Pearl; angry at her resistance; dutiful during the hunt.*)

Extend L3

To broaden students' understanding of how feudalism worked, have them read *Lords and Vassals.* Partner students to discuss this selection and to compare it with *Pearl in the Egg.*

All in One Europe and Russia Teaching Resources, *Lords and Vassals,* p. 197

Review and Assessment

Thinking About the Selection

1. (a) They gave the lord part of their crops, livestock, and labor. (b) He owned the village and the land they farmed. (c) Possible answer: The lords benefited from it, and probably did not want the system to end; many of the serfs were probably too afraid to speak up for their rights.

2. (a) She meant that Pearl could be punished for criticizing Sir Geoffrey and his men. (b) Answers will vary but students might suggest that Pearl will have angry words for the lord and his men.

Writing Activity

Use *Rubric for Assessing a Writing Assignment* to evaluate students' work.

All in One Europe and Russia Teaching Resources, *Rubric for Assessing a Writing Assignment,* p. 201

Answer

✓ **Reading Check** The woodcutter drove his wagon past them.

Overview

Section 1 The Cultures of Western Europe
1. Find out how industry has led to the growth of cities and increased wealth.
2. Learn about the cultural centers of Western Europe.
3. Understand how open borders affect life in Western Europe.

Section 2 The Cultures of Eastern Europe
1. Learn about the different ethnic groups in Eastern Europe.
2. Understand the impact of foreign domination on the region.
3. Find out about ethnic conflict in Eastern Europe.
4. Learn about Eastern Europe's cultural centers.

Section 3 The Cultures of the Russian Federation
1. Learn about Russia's ethnic groups.
2. Find out about the Russian culture and its educational system.

Uniting Europe: Football
Length: 4 minutes, 43 seconds
Use with Section 1
Explores the origins of the game of soccer, or "football," as it is known in Europe. Explains how the game has brought Europeans together.

Technology Resources

Go Online
PHSchool.com

Students use embedded Web codes to access Internet activities, chapter self-tests, and additional map practice. They may also access Dorling Kindersley's Online Desk Reference to learn more about each country they study.

interactive Textbook

Use the Interactive Textbook to make content and concepts come alive through animations, videos, and activities that accompany the complete basal text—online and on CD-ROM.

PRENTICE HALL
TeacherEXPRESS™
Plan • Teach • Assess

Use this complete suite of powerful teaching tools to make planning lessons and administering tests quicker and easier.

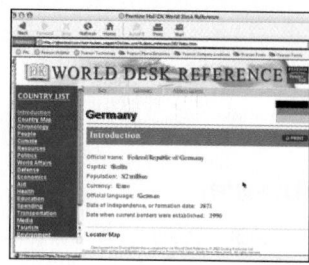

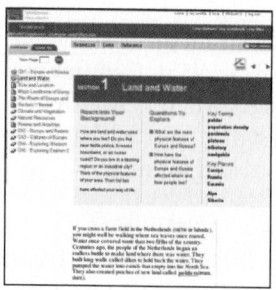

Reading and Assessment

Reading and Vocabulary Instruction

⟳ Model the Target Reading Skill

Main Idea The main idea is the most important point in a written passage. All of the details in a well-written paragraph or section should add up to the main idea. Write the paragraph below, from page 224 of the Student Edition, on the board. Explain that the main idea is often stated in the first or last sentence.

Model identifying the main idea by thinking aloud: "I will read the first and last sentences to see if either may be the main idea. I think the first sentence is the main idea because it is more general. Now I will read the entire paragraph to see if I can find details that support the first sentence."

Point out the supporting details by underlining each one:

Most Western European cities are a mix of the old and the new. Both <u>public buildings and houses from the Middle Ages</u> are a common sight. They stand next <u>to modern apartments and office buildings</u>. Cars and buses drive along <u>cobblestone streets once used by horse-drawn carriages</u>. <u>Monuments honor leaders who lived hundreds of years ago</u>.

Think aloud: "What do these details have in common? They all describe features of Western European cities. They support the main idea, that *Most Western European cities are a mix of the old and the new.*"

Use the following worksheets from All-in-One Europe and Russia Teaching Resources (pp. 227–229) to support the chapter's Target Reading Skill.

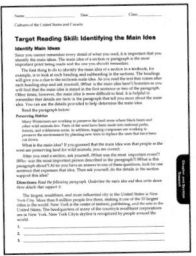 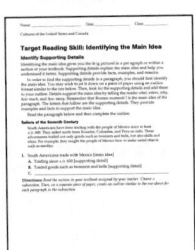 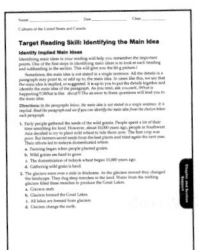

Vocabulary Builder
High-Use Academic Words

Use these steps to teach this chapter's high-use words:

1. Have students rate how well they know each word on their Word Knowledge worksheets (All-in-One Europe and Russia Teaching Resources, p. 230).

2. Pronounce each word and ask students to repeat it.

3. Give students a brief definition or sample sentence (provided on TE pp. 223, 230, and 239).

4. Work with students as they fill in the "Definition or Example" column of their Word Knowledge worksheets.

Assessment

Formal Assessment

Test students' understanding of core knowledge and skills.

Chapter Tests A and B, All-in-One Europe and Russia Teaching Resources, pp. 247–252

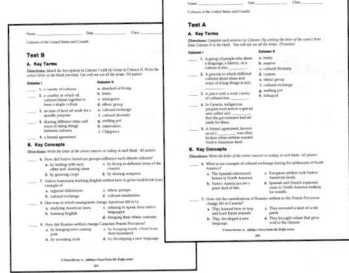

Customize the Chapter Tests to suit your needs.

ExamView Test Bank CD-ROM

Skills Assessment

Assess geographic literacy.

MapMaster Skills, Student Edition, pp. 221, 224, 230, 232, 239, 247

Assess reading and comprehension.

Target Reading Skills, Student Edition, pp. 225, 231, 240 and in Section Assessments

Chapter 8 Assessment, Eastern Hemisphere Reading and Vocabulary Study Guide, p. 91

Performance Assessment

Assess students' performance on this chapter's Writing Activities using the following rubrics from All-in-One Europe and Russia Teaching Resources.

Rubric for Assessing a Writing Assignment, p. 244

Rubric for Assessing a Student Poster, p. 245

Rubric for Assessing an Oral Presentation, p. 246

Assess students' work through performance tasks.

Small Group Activity: European and Russian Music, All-in-One Europe and Russia Teaching Resources, pp. 233–236

Online Assessment

Have students check their own understanding.

Chapter Self-Test

Test Preparation

Europe and Russia Benchmark Test 1, AYP Monitoring Assessments, pp. 105–108

Section 1 The Cultures of Western Europe

1 period, .5 block

Social Studies Objectives
1. Find out how industry has led to the growth of cities and increased wealth.
2. Learn about the cultural centers of Western Europe.
3. Understand how open borders affect life in Western Europe.

Reading/Language Arts Objective
Learn how to identify main ideas.

Prepare to Read	Instructional Resources	Differentiated Instruction
Build Background Knowledge Discuss countries in Western Europe and their capital cities. **Set a Purpose for Reading** Have students begin to fill out the *Reading Readiness Guide.* **Preview Key Terms** Teach the section's Key Terms. **Target Reading Skill** Introduce the section's Target Reading Skill of **identifying main ideas.**	**All in One Europe and Russia Teaching Resources** L2 Reading Readiness Guide, p. 216 L2 Identify Main Ideas, p. 227 **Europe and Russia Transparencies** L2 Color Transparency ER 16: Western Europe: Political	**Spanish Reading and Vocabulary Study Guide** L1 Chapter 8, Section 1, pp. 59–60 ELL

Instruct	Instructional Resources	Differentiated Instruction
Growth of Industry Discuss changes in industry after World War II. **Centers of Culture** Discuss cultural attractions and popular recreational activities. **Target Reading Skill** Review **identifying main ideas.** **Open Borders** Discuss travel in Europe.	**All in One Europe and Russia Teaching Resources** L2 Guided Reading and Review, p. 217 L2 Reading Readiness Guide, p. 216 **Europe and Russia Transparencies** L2 Section Reading Support Transparency ER 40 **World Studies Video Program** L2 Uniting Europe: Football	**All in One Europe and Russia Teaching Resources** L3 Small Group Activity: European and Russian Music, pp. 233–236 AR, GT **Teacher's Edition** L3 For Advanced Readers, TE p. 224 L1 For Special Needs Students, TE p. 224 **Spanish Support** L2 Guided Reading and Review (Spanish), p. 78 ELL

Assess and Reteach	Instructional Resources	Differentiated Instruction
Assess Progress Evaluate student comprehension with the section assessment and section quiz. **Reteach** Assign the Reading and Vocabulary Study Guide to help struggling students. **Extend** Extend the lesson by assigning an Enrichment activity.	**All in One Europe and Russia Teaching Resources** L2 Section Quiz, p. 218 L3 Enrichment, p. 231 Rubric for Assessing a Writing Assignment, p. 244 **Reading and Vocabulary Study Guide** L1 Chapter 8, Section 1, pp. 82–84	**Spanish Support** L2 Section Quiz (Spanish), p. 79 ELL

Key
L1 Basic to Average   L3 Average to Advanced
L2 For All Students

LPR Less Proficient Readers
AR Advanced Readers
SN Special Needs Students

GT Gifted and Talented
ELL English Language Learners

Section 2 The Cultures of Eastern Europe

 2 periods, 1 block (includes Skills for Life)

Social Studies Objectives
1. Learn about the different ethnic groups in Eastern Europe.
2. Understand the impact of foreign domination on the region.
3. Find out about ethnic conflict in Eastern Europe.
4. Learn about Eastern Europe's cultural centers.

Reading/Language Arts Objective
Learn how to identify supporting details in a text to help understand the main idea.

Prepare to Read

Build Background Knowledge
Discuss the origins of different ethnic groups.

Set a Purpose for Reading
Have students evaluate statements on the *Reading Readiness Guide.*

Preview Key Terms
Teach the section's Key Terms.

Target Reading Skill
Introduce the section's Target Reading Skill of **identifying supporting details.**

Instructional Resources

All in One Europe and Russia Teaching Resources
- L2 Reading Readiness Guide, p. 220
- L2 Identify Supporting Details, p. 228

Differentiated Instruction

Spanish Reading and Vocabulary Study Guide
- L1 Chapter 8, Section 2, pp. 61–62 ELL

Instruct

Eastern Europe's Ethnic Groups
Discuss the Slavs.

Target Reading Skill
Review **identifying supporting details.**

Foreign Domination Ethnic Conflict
Discuss conflicts in Czechoslovakia and Yugoslavia.

European Centers of Culture
Discuss the major cities of Prague and Budapest.

Instructional Resources

All in One Europe and Russia Teaching Resources
- L2 Guided Reading and Review, p. 221
- L2 Reading Readiness Guide, p. 220
- L2 Your Government Has Returned to You! pp. 237–238

Europe and Russia Transparencies
- L2 Section Reading Support Transparency ER 41

Differentiated Instruction

All in One Europe and Russia Teaching Resources
- Rubric for Assessing a Student Poster, p. 245 AR, GT
- L2 Skills for Life, p. 232 AR, GT, LPR, SN

Teacher's Edition
- L3 For Gifted and Talented, TE p. 233
- L3 For Advanced Readers, TE p. 234

PHSchool.com
- L3 For: Long Term Integrated Project: Genocide in the Balkans AR, GT
  Web Code: ldd-7304

Assess and Reteach

Assess Progress
Evaluate student comprehension with the section assessment and section quiz.

Reteach
Assign the Reading and Vocabulary Study Guide to help struggling students.

Extend
Extend the lesson by assigning a Book Project.

Instructional Resources

All in One Europe and Russia Teaching Resources
- L2 Section Quiz, p. 222
- L3 Book Project: Tourism in Eastern Europe, pp. 80–82
  Rubric for Assessing a Writing Assignment, p. 244

Reading and Vocabulary Study Guide
- L1 Chapter 8, Section 2, pp. 85–87

Differentiated Instruction

Spanish Support
- L2 Section Quiz (Spanish), p. 81 ELL

Teacher's Edition
- L1 For Special Needs Students, TE p. 237

Social Studies Skills Tutor CD-ROM
- L1 Supporting a Position ELL, LPR, SN

Key
- L1 Basic to Average
- L3 Average to Advanced
- L2 For All Students
- LPR Less Proficient Readers
- AR Advanced Readers
- SN Special Needs Students
- GT Gifted and Talented
- ELL English Language Learners

Section 3 The Cultures of the Russian Federation

 3 periods, 1.5 blocks (includes Chapter Review and Assessment)

Social Studies Objectives
1. Learn about Russia's ethnic groups.
2. Find out about the Russian culture and its educational system.

Reading/Language Arts Objective
Learn how to identify implied main ideas to help remember the most important information.

Prepare to Read

Build Background Knowledge
Ask students to discuss works of art that they like or dislike.

Set a Purpose for Reading
Have students evaluate statements on the *Reading Readiness Guide*.

Preview Key Terms
Teach the section's Key Terms.

Target Reading Skill
Introduce the section's Target Reading Skill of **identifying main ideas.**

Instructional Resources

All in One Europe and Russia Teaching Resources
- L2 Reading Readiness Guide, p. 224
- L2 Identify Implied Main Ideas, p. 229

Differentiated Instruction

Spanish Reading and Vocabulary Study Guide
- L1 Chapter 8, Section 3, pp. 63–64 ELL

Instruct

Russia's Ethnic Groups
Discuss ethnic groups in Russia.

Target Reading Skill
Review **identifying main ideas.**

Eyewitness Technology
Discuss the beginning of the space age.

Russian Culture and Education
Discuss art and education in Russia.

Instructional Resources

All in One Europe and Russia Teaching Resources
- L2 Guided Reading and Review, p. 225
- L2 Reading Readiness Guide, p. 224

Europe and Russia Transparencies
- L2 Section Reading Support Transparency ER 42

Differentiated Instruction

All in One Europe and Russia Teaching Resources
- Rubric for Assessing an Oral Presentation, p. 246 AR, GT
- L3 Writing Plays, p. 242 AR, GT

Teacher's Edition
- L1 For Less Proficient Readers, TE p. 240
- L3 For Gifted and Talented, TE p. 240
- L2 For English Language Learners, TE p. 241
- L3 For Advanced Readers, TE p. 243
- L1 For Special Needs Students, TE p. 243

Student Edition on Audio CD
- L1 Chapter 8, Section 3 ELL, LPR, SN

Passport to the World CD-ROM
- L1 Russia ELL, LPR, SN

Assess and Reteach

Assess Progress
Evaluate student comprehension with the section assessment and section quiz.

Reteach
Assign the Reading and Vocabulary Study Guide to help struggling students.

Extend
Extend the lesson by assigning a literature reading.

Instructional Resources

All in One Europe and Russia Teaching Resources
- L2 Section Quiz, p. 226
- L3 Lenin's Deathbed Words, p. 239
- L2 Vocabulary Development, p. 243
- L2 Word Knowledge, p. 230
- L2 Chapter Tests A and B, pp. 247–252

Reading and Vocabulary Study Guide
- L1 Chapter 8, Section 3, pp. 88–90

Differentiated Instruction

Spanish Support
- L2 Section Quiz (Spanish), p. 83 ELL
- L2 Chapter Summary (Spanish), p. 84 ELL
- L2 Vocabulary Development (Spanish), p. 85 ELL

Key
- L1 Basic to Average
- L2 For All Students
- L3 Average to Advanced
- LPR Less Proficient Readers
- AR Advanced Readers
- SN Special Needs Students
- GT Gifted and Talented
- ELL English Language Learners

Professional Development ★

Reading Background

Applying New Words Outside the Classroom

Expand students' understanding of this chapter's vocabulary by assigning an activity which applies the chapter's Key Terms and high-use words to students' lives. Choose five or six vocabulary words from the chapter, such as *urbanization, immigrant, ethnic group, conflict,* and *campaign,* and ask students to list them in their notebooks.

Next, ask students where they might *see* these words outside of their textbook. List the responses on the board. Suggestions might include signs, newspapers, magazines, history books, fiction books, and biographies. Then ask students where they might *hear* these words. Answers might include television or radio news broadcasts, conversations with parents or other adults, and political speeches. Finally, ask students how they might *use* these words. Students can suggest sample sentences or topics of conversation.

Have students keep a log for one week in which they record where and how they see their selected words printed or spoken. Have students share their logs at the end of the week.

Encourage Active Participation

In this chapter, students may use the Choral Reading strategy to engage them in actively reading the chapter. Remember that the following tips can help improve the effectiveness of the Choral Reading strategy:

1. Make sure that students say the words with you, without lagging behind or racing ahead in their speech.
2. Use only short passages of less than 500 words. Follow the choral reading with a silent reading of the same passage to allow students to review the materials silently now that they have heard the content.

World Studies Background

Languages of Western Europe

The two major language divisions in Western Europe are Romance and Germanic languages. Both divisions stem from the language of the ancient peoples who migrated to Europe from Asia. The Romance languages, such as French, Spanish, and Italian, are prevalent in western and Mediterranean regions. The Germanic languages, such as German, Netherlandic (Dutch or Flemish), and Swedish, are found in central, northern, and northwestern regions of Europe.

Roma of Eastern Europe

One of the least-understood groups in Eastern Europe is the Roma, sometimes mistakenly called Gypsies. They are descended from a group of people who originated in India. The Roma reside throughout the world, although most live in Europe. Many still speak the Romany language and live a nomadic lifestyle, traveling from place to place to find work. Few non-Roma know or understand much about this culture. In some countries of Europe, Roma have often been a persecuted minority.

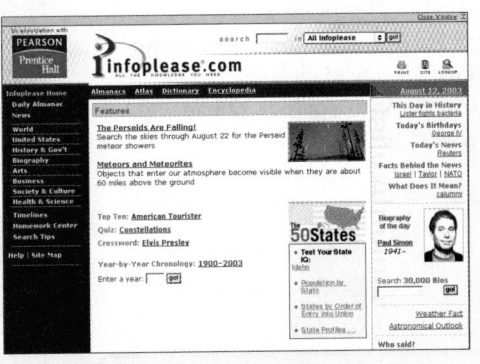

Infoplease® provides a wealth of useful information for the classroom. You can use this resource to strengthen your background on the subjects covered in this chapter. Have students visit this advertising-free site as a starting point for projects requiring research.

Go Online PHSchool.com

Use Web Code **ldd-7300** for **Infoplease®**.

Chapter 8

Guiding Questions

Remind students about the Guiding Questions introduced at the beginning of this section.

Section 1 relates to **Guiding Question ③**
How have the people of Europe and Russia been shaped by their culture? *(Many European cities are centers of culture, and have museums, concert halls, restaurants, nightclubs, theaters, and stores.)*

Section 2 relates to **Guiding Question ②**
How have Europe and Russia been affected by their history? *(Most ethnic groups in Eastern Europe are descended from Slavs. Throughout European history, as the Slavs separated and migrated across Eastern Europe, they developed different languages and dialects, and adopted different religions.)*

Section 3 relates to **Guiding Question ②**
How have Europe and Russia been affected by their history? *(Under communism, artistic creativity nearly ended because the government only approved art that supported its propaganda campaign. The collapse of communism in 1991 led to a revival of artistic traditions in Russia.)*

⟳ Target Reading Skill

In this chapter, students will learn and apply the reading skill of identifying main ideas. Use the following worksheets to help students practice this skill:

All in One Europe and Russia Teaching Resources, *Identify Main Ideas,* p. 227; *Identify Supporting Details,* p. 228; *Identify Implied Main Ideas,* p. 229

Differentiated Instruction

The following Teacher Edition strategies are suitable for students of varying abilities.

Advanced Readers, pp. 224, 234, 243
English Language Learners, p. 241
Gifted and Talented, pp. 233, 240
Less Proficient Readers, p. 240
Special Needs Students, pp. 224, 237, 243

Chapter 8 Cultures of Europe and Russia

Chapter Preview

This chapter will introduce you to the cultures of Europe and Russia.

Section 1
The Cultures of Western Europe

Section 2
The Cultures of Eastern Europe

Section 3
The Cultures of the Russian Federation

⟳ **Target Reading Skill**

Identify Main Ideas In this chapter you will focus on finding and remembering the main idea, or the most important point, of sections and paragraphs.

▶ The golden domes of the Annunciation Cathedral brighten up the sky above Moscow, Russia.

220 Europe and Russia

Bibliography

For the Teacher
Egert-Romanowska, Joanna, and Magorzata Omilanowska. *Eyewitness Travel Guide to Germany.* Dorling-Kindersley Publishing, 2001.
Hancock, Ian. *We Are the Romani People.* University of Hertfordshire Press, 2003.
Richmond, Yale. *From Nyet to Da: Understanding the Russians.* Intercultural Press, 2003.

For the Student
L1 Flux, Paul. *Wassily Kandinsky.* Heinemann Library, 2002.
L2 Lane, Kathryn. *Germany: The Culture.* Bt Bound, 2002.
L3 Marcovitz, Hal. *The Balkans: People in Conflict (People at Odds).* Chelsea House Publications, 2002.

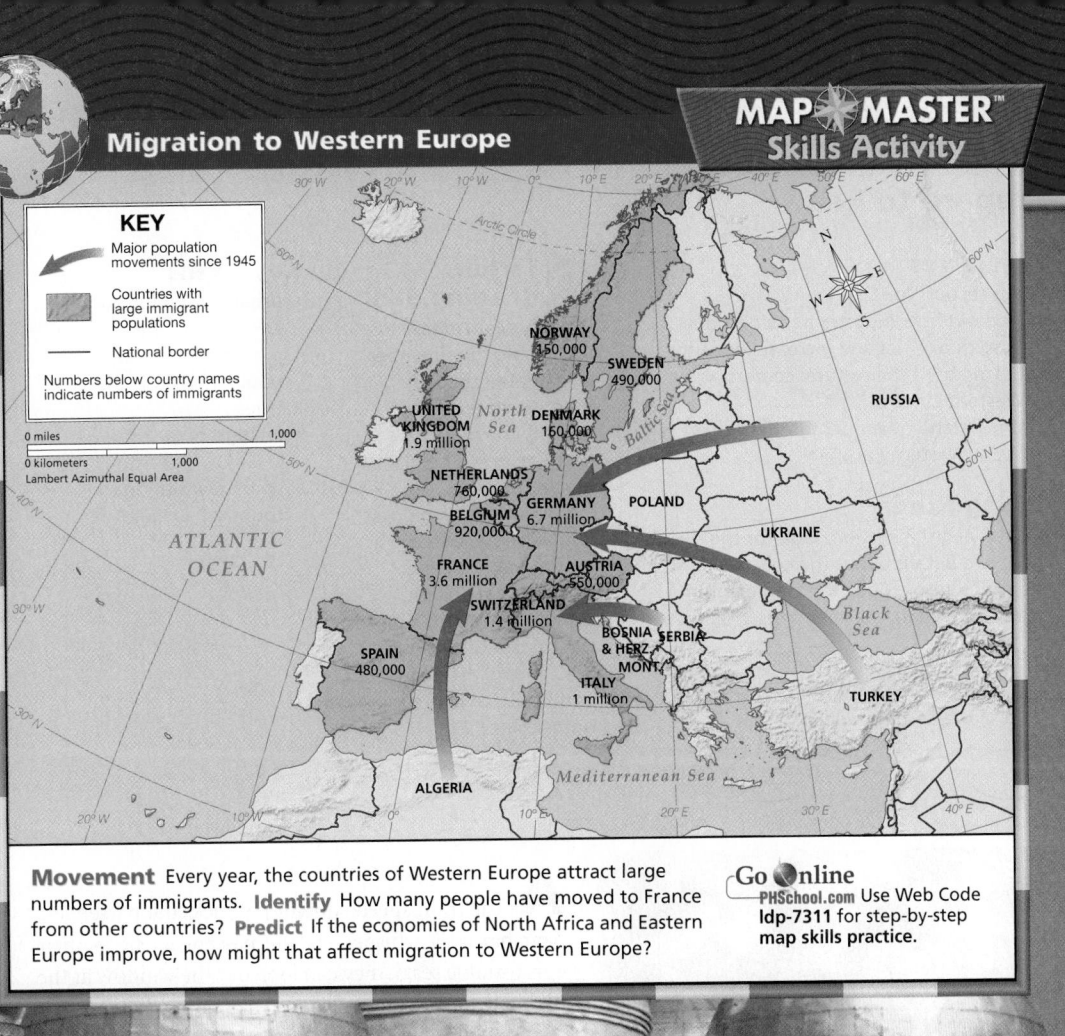

Migration to Western Europe

MAP MASTER™
Skills Activity

KEY

⬅ Major population movements since 1945

▨ Countries with large immigrant populations

— National border

Numbers below country names indicate numbers of immigrants

0 miles 1,000
0 kilometers 1,000
Lambert Azimuthal Equal Area

Arctic Circle

NORWAY 150,000

SWEDEN 490,000

RUSSIA

North Sea

DENMARK 150,000

Baltic Sea

UNITED KINGDOM 1.9 million

NETHERLANDS 760,000

GERMANY 6.7 million

POLAND

BELGIUM 920,000

UKRAINE

ATLANTIC OCEAN

FRANCE 3.6 million

AUSTRIA 550,000

SWITZERLAND 1.4 million

Black Sea

BOSNIA & HERZ. MONT. SERBIA

SPAIN 480,000

ITALY 1 million

TURKEY

ALGERIA

Mediterranean Sea

Movement Every year, the countries of Western Europe attract large numbers of immigrants. **Identify** How many people have moved to France from other countries? **Predict** If the economies of North Africa and Eastern Europe improve, how might that affect migration to Western Europe?

Go Online
PHSchool.com Use Web Code ldp-7311 for step-by-step map skills practice.

Chapter 8 **221**

MAP MASTER™
Skills Activity

Make a chart on the board with three columns labeled "Migration To," "Migration From," and "Number of People." Have student volunteers come to the board and fill in the information based on the map. Then lead a discussion as to why Western Europe might attract so many immigrants.

Go Online
PHSchool.com Students may practice their map skills using the interactive online version of this map.

Using the Visual   L2

Reach Into Your Background Draw students' attention to the caption accompanying the photograph on pp. 220–221. Ask students to compare and contrast the cathedral in the photograph to houses of worship that they have seen in their own community. Conduct an Idea Wave (TE, p. T35) with students to create a list of similarities and differences on the board.

Answers

MAP MASTER™ Skills Activity **Identify** 3.6 million
Predict It might decrease migration to Western Europe because people from those regions won't need to leave their homelands for financial security.

Chapter Resources

Teaching Resources
L2 Vocabulary Development, p. 243
L2 Skills for Life, p. 232
L2 Chapter Tests A and B, pp. 247–252

Spanish Support
L2 Spanish Chapter Summary, p. 84
L2 Spanish Vocabulary Development, p. 85

Media and Technology
L1 Student Edition on Audio CD
L1 Guided Reading Audiotapes, English and Spanish
L2 Social Studies Skill Tutor CD-ROM
ExamView Test Bank CD-ROM

PRENTICE HALL
Presentation EXPRESS™
Teach · Connect · Inspire

Teach this chapter's content using the PresentationExpress™ CD-ROM including:
■ slide shows
■ transparencies
■ interactive maps and media
■ *ExamView®* QuickTake Presenter

Chapter 8 **221**

Section 1
Step-by-Step Instruction

Objectives

Social Studies
1. Find out how industry has led to the growth of cities and increased wealth.
2. Learn about the cultural centers of Western Europe.
3. Understand how open borders affect life in Western Europe.

Reading/Language Arts
Learn how to identify main ideas.

Prepare to Read

Build Background Knowledge   L2
Tell students that they will learn about the cultures of Western Europe in this section. Show students *Color Transparency ER 16: Western Europe: Political*, and identify the locations of several countries' capital cities. Point out to students the close proximity of the countries and their capitals, and have students list the ways they think that this might affect the people living in Western Europe. Use the Think-Write-Pair-Share strategy (TE, p. T36) to elicit student responses, and then list them on the board.

📖 **Europe and Russia Transparencies,** *Color Transparency ER 16: Western Europe: Political*

Set a Purpose for Reading   L2
- Preview the Objectives.
- Form students into pairs or groups. Distribute the *Reading Readiness Guide*. Ask the students to fill in the first two columns of the chart. Use the Numbered Heads participation strategy (TE, p. T36) to call on students to share one piece of information they already know and one piece of information they want to know.

All in One Europe and Russia Teaching Resources, *Reading Readiness Guide, p. 216*

Vocabulary Builder
Preview Key Terms
Pronounce each Key Term, then ask the students to say the word with you. Provide a simple explanation such as, "Urbanization occurs when large numbers of people move from the countryside into cities."

Section 1
The Cultures of Western Europe

Prepare to Read

Objectives
In this section you will
1. Find out how industry has led to the growth of cities and increased wealth.
2. Learn about the cultural centers of Western Europe.
3. Understand how open borders affect life in Western Europe.

Taking Notes
As you read this section, look for the main ideas and details about the cultures of Western Europe. Copy the web diagram below and record your findings in it.

Western European Cultures

🎯 Target Reading Skill
Identify Main Ideas It is impossible to remember every detail that you read. Good readers identify the main idea in every section. The main idea is the most important or the biggest point—the one that includes all the other points in the section. Sometimes this idea is stated directly. As you read, record the main ideas of this section in the Taking Notes chart.

Key Terms
- **urbanization** (ur bun ih ZAY shun) *n.* the movement of populations toward cities
- **immigrant** (IM uh grunt) *n.* a person who moves to one country from another

A high-speed train travels across Europe.

222 Europe and Russia

As the train speeds down the track, the passengers hear hardly a whisper. As the passengers sit in their comfortable seats, they can look out the window at the highway next to the railroad. They know that the cars are traveling at least 60 miles (96 kilometers) per hour, but the cars seem to be moving backward. That's because the train is traveling three times faster than the cars—about 180 miles (289 kilometers) per hour.

Would you like to take a trip like that? You can if you go to France, which has some of the world's fastest trains. Great Britain also has speedy rail travel. Some British trains reach speeds of 140 miles (225 kilometers) per hour. In Western Europe, high-speed trains have made travel between countries easy and fast. Someone in a European country can be in another country in hours. Such easy movement through Western Europe affects the entire culture of the region.

🎯 Target Reading Skill   L2

Identify Main Ideas Point out the Target Reading Skill. Tell students that identifying main ideas will help them remember the most important information in their reading.

Model identifying main ideas by reading the second paragraph on p. 224. Point out that the main idea of the paragraph is that European cities have a mixture of old and new structures. Note that this idea is stated in the first sentence of the paragraph.

Give students *Identify Main Ideas*. Have them complete the activity in their groups.

All in One Europe and Russia Teaching Resources, *Identify Main Ideas, p. 227*

Growth of Industry

Most Western European countries are prosperous, or wealthy. This prosperity is based on strong economies. The economies of Western Europe have grown because of productive industries and high-quality services.

A Farming Revolution

The Industrial Revolution of the late 1700s sped up the development of industry in Western Europe. Before the Industrial Revolution, most people worked on farms. They could grow little beyond their basic food needs. Over time, new and better farm machines were able to do tasks that once required many workers. Farmers also learned ways to improve soil quality and fight insects. With these advances, farms could produce more and better crops with fewer laborers.

This revolution in farming grew out of the Industrial Revolution. Factory-made farm equipment and chemicals helped each farmer to grow more. Thus, as the need for farm workers declined, the need for industrial workers grew. Many people began moving to cities, where factories were located.

The Growth of Cities

Urbanization (ur bun ih ZAY shun), or the movement of populations toward cities, was a trend throughout the 1800s and 1900s. Following World War II, it increased rapidly. The United States provided billions of dollars to help Western Europe recover from the war. With this help, the region's industries came back stronger than ever. And even more people left rural areas to work in cities.

Today, the majority of Western Europeans have a comfortable life. They earn good wages working in factories or in service industries such as banking and food service.

✓ **Reading Check** How was farming transformed?

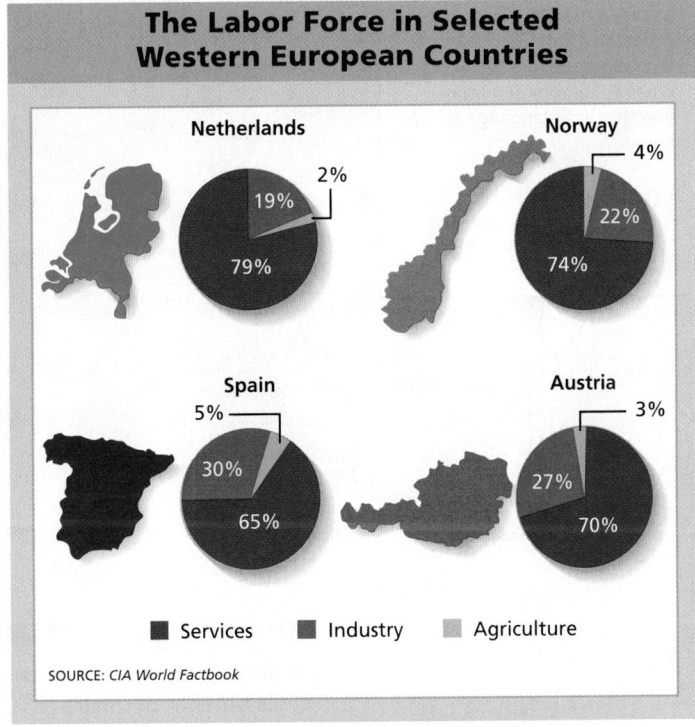

The Labor Force in Selected Western European Countries

Netherlands: Services 79%, Industry 19%, Agriculture 2%
Norway: Services 74%, Industry 22%, Agriculture 4%
Spain: Services 65%, Industry 30%, Agriculture 5%
Austria: Services 70%, Industry 27%, Agriculture 3%

■ Services ■ Industry ■ Agriculture

SOURCE: *CIA World Factbook*

■ Diagram Skills

The economies of most Western European countries today are based on service industries. **Identify** Which country has the highest percentage of its labor force in services? **Compare** In what ways are the labor forces in all four countries similar?

Instruct

Growth of Industry L2

Guided Instruction

- **Vocabulary Builder** Clarify the high-use word **revolution** before reading.

- Read Growth of Industry, using the Choral Reading strategy (TE, p. T34).

- Ask students **What kinds of improvements led to the Agricultural Revolution?** *(New and better farm machines could do tasks that had once required many workers, and farmers learned ways to improve soil quality and fight insects.)*

- Explain the factors that increased urbanization in Europe after World War II. *(Billions of dollars from the United States helped European industries rebuild, causing more people to move to cities in search of jobs.)*

Independent Practice

Ask students to create the Taking Notes graphic organizer on a blank piece of paper. Then have them fill in one of the circles with the information they have just learned. Briefly model how to identify which details to record.

Monitor Progress

As students fill in the graphic organizer, circulate to make sure individuals are recording the correct details.

Answers

Diagram Skills Identify the Netherlands **Compare** The labor forces of all four countries are similiar in that each is mainly dependent on services.

✓ **Reading Check** new and better farm machines improved farm production while reducing the number of laborers needed

Chapter 8 Section 1 **223**

Vocabulary Builder

Use the information below to teach students this section's high-use words.

High-Use Word	Definition and Sample Sentence
revolution, p. 223	*n.* a complete or drastic change Modern sewing machines brought about a **revolution** in the fashion industry.
scholar, p. 225	*n.* a person with great knowledge in a particular area The history professor was a **scholar** in his field.
recreational, p. 225	*adj.* for the purpose of play or amusement Soccer is Sarah's favorite **recreational** activity.
exchange, p. 228	*v.* to give and receive The friends **exchanged** phone numbers and agreed to talk that evening.

Centers of Culture L2

Guided Instruction

- **Vocabulary Builder** Clarify the high-use words **scholar** and **recreational** before reading.

- With students, read Centers of Culture. As students read, circulate and make sure individuals can answer the Reading Check question.

- Ask **What kinds of cultural attractions can be found in European cities?** *(museums, concert halls, restaurants, nightclubs, theaters, and stores)*

- Have students carefully examine the map on this page. List the names of the countries found on the map on the board. Divide students into pairs, and have each pair identify what language group or groups are found in each country.

Answers

MAP MASTER Skills Activity **Locate** Spain, France, Finland **Infer** Ural Mountains

Go Online PHSchool.com Students may practice their map skills using the interactive online version of this map.

Place Though more than 50 languages are spoken in Western Europe, many of these languages are related. **Locate** Where are languages other than Indo-European languages spoken? **Infer** For what geographical feature was the Uralic language group named?

Go Online PHSchool.com Use Web Code **ldp-7321** for step-by-step map skills practice.

KEY

Indo–European Languages
- Celtic
- Germanic
- Romance
- Greek

Other Language Groups
- Uralic
- Basque
- National border
- National capital

Centers of Culture

It is difficult to travel far in Europe without coming across a city. People travel from small towns and villages to cities to find jobs. Some people go to cities to attend school. People also travel to cities to enjoy cultural attractions. These include museums, concerts, restaurants, nightclubs, theaters, and stores.

A modern entrance was added to the over-400-year-old Louvre Museum in Paris, France.

The Old and the New Most Western European cities are a mix of the old and the new. Both public buildings and houses from the Middle Ages are a common sight. They stand next to modern apartments and office buildings. Cars and buses drive along cobblestone streets once used by horse-drawn carriages. Monuments honor leaders who lived hundreds of years ago. Market plazas dating back to medieval times still thrive today.

224 Europe and Russia

Differentiated Instruction

For Advanced Readers L2

To learn more about aspects of different cultures in Europe and Russia, assign students the *Small Group Activity: European and Russian Music*. Students may work in pairs or groups to complete the activity.

All in One **Europe and Russia Teaching Resources,** *Small Group Activity: European and Russian Music,* pp. 233–236

For Special Needs Students L1

Ask students to pick out a paragraph or sentence under Centers of Culture that describes life in a European area or city. Have them draw a picture that illustrates what the text describes. *(To illustrate the description of Madrid in the text, students might draw images of people eating.)*

Vibrant Cities Each city in Western Europe is different from every other city. However, they all share certain characteristics. The majority of Western Europeans live and work in cities. Cities are also the centers of Western European culture.

Let's take a look at some Western European capital cities. Paris, the capital of France, attracts scholars, writers, and artists from all over the world. England's capital, London, is known for its important financial center as well as for its grand historic buildings and lovely parks. The Spanish capital city of Madrid (muh DRID) is known as a place with a vibrant street life, a place where people meet on café terraces to relax outdoors after work. As a cultural and economic center for the Spanish-speaking world, the city is rich in both business and the arts. The German capital, Berlin, is always full of activity and attracts many visitors to its theaters and museums.

Work and Leisure Let's focus on life in Germany for a moment. Most visitors to Germany think that the Germans are efficient. In other words, Germans do their work without waste or extra effort. Visitors get this idea from what they see. German cities, streets, and buses are kept clean. Hotels are well run. German cars are well designed. Travel is swift on an excellent system of highways. Travel is equally fast on high-speed trains.

But life in Germany is not all hard work and fast-paced activity. Many workers enjoy as much as six weeks of vacation each year. Skiing, hiking, and camping are popular recreational activities throughout the country's mountains and highlands. The country's many rivers, as well as the North and Baltic seas, are good for swimming and boating. Those who prefer city life enjoy the museums, concerts, and plays. Life is similar in countries throughout Western Europe.

The European Union and the Arts One of the goals of the European Union is to support Europe's cultural community. Although different from one another geographically and politically, European nations often share a common history and cultural heritage. They all belong to the European community. The EU organizes concerts, cultural events, exhibits, and conferences to bring Europeans together. The EU's goal is to respect individual cultures, while encouraging cooperation among them.

European City Scenes
A trolley passes by historical buildings in Amsterdam, the Netherlands, in the top photo. The photo above shows Germany's Parliament building, called the Reichstag, in Berlin. It was built in 1995 after the country was reunified. **Infer** Why do you think the German government chose a modern style of architecture for its new Parliament building?

Identify Main Ideas
Which sentence states the main idea under the heading The European Union and the Arts?

- Discuss with students the examples of recreational activities that Germans participate in. Ask **How are these similar to or different from the recreational activities where you live?** *(Answers will vary, but students should identify which of their recreational activities are similar and which are different.)*

- Ask students **What kinds of events does the EU organize to bring Europeans together?** *(concerts, cultural events, exhibits, and conferences)*

- Ask students **What is the DEBORA project?** *(a project that gives Internet users access to documents from the Renaissance)* **How did EU support help this project?** *(Access to the collections of books and materials stored in libraries throughout Europe was often limited, but with support from the EU, people are now able to view the collections on the Internet.)*

☉ Target Reading Skill ⬛

Identify Main Ideas As a follow up, ask students to answer the Target Reading Skill question in the Student Edition. *(One of the goals of the European Union is to support Europe's cultural community.)*

Skills Mini Lesson

Making Valid Generalizations

1. Teach the skill by telling students that valid generalizations can be made about a group if the statement is supported by facts that relate to the vast majority of the group.

2. Help students practice the skill by identifying a generalization in the first paragraph on this page.

3. Have students apply the skill by identifying a generalization in the section Growth of Industry on p. 223. Then have them explain what details support the generalization.

Answer

Infer Possible answer: Germany had just reunified, so it may have wanted to break away from the past by using a new style of architecture unlike the style used when the country was divided.

Have students read the **Links Across Time** on this page. Ask **How are the UK's immigration patterns expected to change?** *(As more countries from Eastern and Central Europe join the EU, large numbers of people from those regions are expected to immigrate to the UK.)*

Guided Instruction (continued)

- Ask students **Why did millions of Western Europeans leave Europe in the 1800s and early 1900s?** *(They left in search of more opportunities and better lives.)* **Where did they go?** *(Most went to the United States, Canada, and South America.)*

- Ask students **Where do most of the current immigrants to Western Europe come from?** *(Eastern Europe, North Africa, South Asia, and the Middle East)*

- Ask students **How have many Western European countries become multicultural?** *(Immigrants to these countries have brought their own languages, religious beliefs, values, and customs, causing the cultures of these countries to blend and change.)*

Independent Practice

Have students continue filling in the graphic organizer with details about Western European cultures. Encourage them to add extra circles as necessary.

Monitor Progress

As students continue to fill in the graphic organizer, circulate and make sure individuals are including as many details as possible.

Immigrants in the United Kingdom The United Kingdom's immigrant population today reflects its history as a world power. In 2004, almost half of the immigrants came from countries—including Pakistan, India, and Nigeria—that were once under British rule. In the future, the UK's immigration patterns are expected to change. As more countries from Eastern and Central Europe join the EU, large numbers of people from those regions are expected to immigrate to the UK and other Western European countries.

LIBRAIRIE AFRICAINE المكتبة الإفريقية
كتب عطور ملابس إسلامية

To achieve that goal, the EU finances programs that help cultural development and encourage cultural exchange. One of the programs that the EU funds is the DEBORA (Digital Access to Books of the Renaissance) project. It gives Internet users access to documents from the Renaissance. The books and materials dating from the 1500s are stored in libraries throughout Europe. However, access to these collections is often limited. With the EU's support, Internet technology now makes viewing the collections possible. The EU helps museums, libraries, and other cultural institutions make these collections accessible to more people. By doing so, it helps connect people to their cultural heritage.

Changing Immigration Patterns Although life in Western Europe is good now, it was not always so. In the 1800s and early 1900s, millions of Western Europeans left Europe. Most went to the United States, Canada, and South America. They left in search of more opportunities and better lives.

Since World War II, patterns of human movement have been reversed. Large numbers of people stopped leaving Western Europe. Industry continued to expand in the postwar years and more workers were needed. As a result, people from other countries began moving to Western Europe.

Today's Immigrants Today, about 6 percent of workers in Western Europe are **immigrants** (IM uh grunts), or people who move to one country from another. Most of the immigrants in Western Europe are from Eastern Europe, North Africa, South Asia, and the Middle East. The four largest countries in the European Union—France, Germany, Italy, and the United Kingdom—all have large immigrant populations.

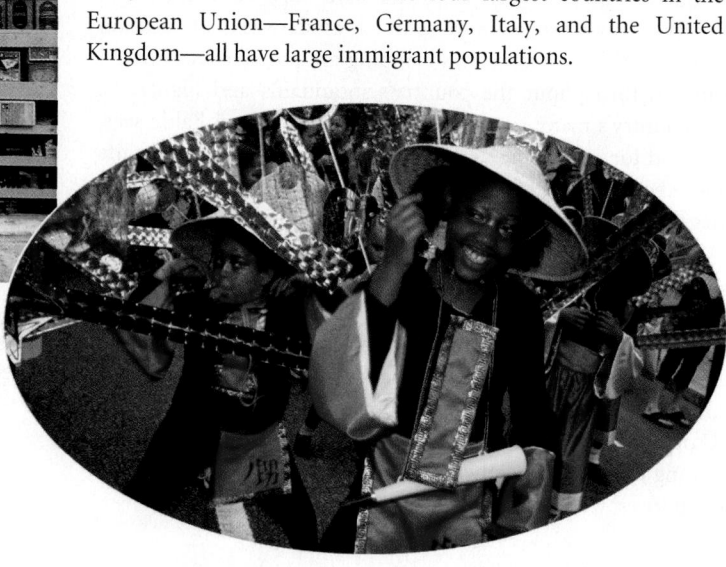

Background: Links Across Place

German Expressionism and Hollywood Germany has a long history of artistic achievements, ranging from opera to great works of literature. One German art form that had a strong influence on popular culture in the United States was early German filmmaking, especially during the period from 1919 to 1933. During this time a group of German artists created a style of filmmak- ing called German Expressionism. Their films, which were mostly thrillers, experimented with uses of light, settings, and make-up to create feelings of fear in audiences. This style greatly influenced most early American horror films. After the Nazi Party came to power in 1933, many German filmmakers moved to the United States and became leaders in the Hollywood movie industry.

More than 6 million immigrants live in France, making up more than 10 percent of the total population. Algerians make up the largest group of immigrants. In 2005, the number of immigrants in Germany accounted for about 12 percent of its total population, or more than 10 million people. Many of Germany's immigrants come from Poland, Turkey, and the former Yugoslavia, with smaller numbers of other Europeans and Asians.

About 4 percent of Italy's population is foreign-born, with Romanians, Moroccans, and Albanians being the largest groups. Most of the United Kingdom's 5 million immigrants come from Ireland, India, Pakistan, and Central and Eastern Europe. They make up about 9 percent of the country's population.

Blending Cultures Immigrants do not leave their cultures behind when they leave their homelands. They bring their languages, religious beliefs, values, and customs to their new homes. But most immigrants make changes in their ways of life. They may change the way they dress. They may try new foods and discover new ways of cooking. Most immigrants learn the language of their new country.

In many ways, immigration has changed the cultures of Western Europe. In countries like the United Kingdom and France, people from many different backgrounds live and work together. They learn about one another's ways of life. In the process, the cultures blend and change. In this way, many Western European countries have become multicultural.

✓ Reading Check **What does the European Union hope to gain by supporting the arts?**

Learn how soccer brings Europeans together.

Faces of Western European Immigration
The photos from left to right show Africans in France, Caribbean Islanders in the UK, a Turkish woman in Germany, and a South American in Italy. All are immigrants.
Analyze Images *What details in the photographs show cultural traditions that these people have brought with them?*

Chapter 8 Section 1 **227**

Show students *Uniting Europe: Football.* Ask **How does European football bring people together?** *(Many Europeans share a common love of the game, which brings them together, regardless of nationality.)*

Open Borders L2

Guided Instruction

- **Vocabulary Builder** Clarify the high-use word **exchange** before reading.

- As students read Open Borders, ask them to think back to the examples they listed in the Build Background Knowledge activity at the beginning of the lesson.

- Ask students **How does geography influence travel in Europe?** *(Since most of the countries are small and close together, travel between them is quick and easy.)*

- Ask students to look at the map on p. 224. Then ask **What language skills would be helpful to a person traveling across Western Europe?** *(Knowledge of several languages would probably be helpful, since there are many different language groups in Western Europe.)*

Independent Practice
Have students complete the graphic organizer with information from the section.

Monitor Progress

- Show *Section Reading Support Transparency ER 40* and ask students to check their graphic organizers individually. Go over key concepts and clarify key vocabulary as needed.

  Europe and Russia Transparencies, *Section Reading Support Transparency ER 40*

- Tell students to fill in the last column of the *Reading Readiness Guide.* Probe for what they learned that confirms or invalidates each statement.

  Europe and Russia Teaching Resources, *Reading Readiness Guide,* p. 216

Answers

Analyze Images Possible answer: their traditional style of dress

✓ Reading Check It hopes to respect individual cultures, while encouraging cooperation among them.

Assess and Reteach

Assess Progress `L2`

Have students complete the Section Assessment. Administer the *Section Quiz*.

All in One **Europe and Russia Teaching Resources,** *Section Quiz,* p. 218

Reteach `L1`

If students need more instruction, have them read this section in the Reading and Vocabulary Study Guide.

Chapter 8, Section 1, **Eastern Hemisphere Reading and Vocabulary Study Guide,** pp. 82–84

Extend `L3`

Remind students that elements of a country's culture also include literature, such as plays. Have them learn more about one of England's most famous playwrights, William Shakespeare, by completing the *Enrichment* activity.

All in One **Europe and Russia Teaching Resources,** *Enrichment,* p. 231

Answer

✓ **Reading Check** the transportation of goods and people flowing freely across borders, and the use of the euro

Section 1 Assessment

Key Terms
Students' sentences should reflect knowledge of each Key Term.

Target Reading Skill
Possible answers: Western European cultures are a combination of old and new. The growth of industry has led to urbanization and prosperity. Western Europeans of different countries easily share goods and ideas.

Comprehension and Critical Thinking
1. (a) industry **(b)** Cities grew, along with the immigrant population.

2. (a) France, Germany, Italy and the United Kingdom **(b)** They bring their languages, religious beliefs, values, and customs to their new homes.

3. (a) The countries are small and close together. **(b)** Possible answer: It would be difficult for people to travel across borders, and there might not be such a large exchange of cultural ideas.

Goods are transferred from a train to a truck in Munich-Reim, Germany.

Open Borders

You read that on a high-speed train, travelers can go from one country to another in a matter of hours. Ideas, goods, and raw materials can travel quickly as well. In addition to the closeness of the countries and the good train service, Western Europe is becoming more prosperous because goods and people can now flow freely across its borders.

Adding to the ease of movement across the borders is the use of a single European currency, the euro, which you read about in Chapter 7. Think about how different it was when a traveler had to stop at every country's border to show a passport and to change money to the local currency. Since 2002, the euro has replaced old currencies such as the French franc, the German mark, and the Italian lira.

Adopting the euro is one step in a series of efforts to move Europe toward both economic and political unity. Even the colorful design of the euro coins and bills reflects this effort. They do not have any famous people on them. Instead, they symbolize European unity by featuring a map of Europe, flags of the EU member nations, and bridges, gateways, and windows. The open exchange of ideas, goods, and money is an outcome of the European Union and has helped Western Europe thrive.

✓ **Reading Check** Which factors have created a prosperous Western Europe?

 ## Section 1 Assessment

Key Terms
Review the key terms at the beginning of this section. Use each term in a sentence that explains its meaning.

Target Reading Skill
State the main ideas in Section 1.

Comprehension and Critical Thinking
1. (a) Recall What is Western Europe's prosperity based on?

(b) Identify Effects How has the growth of industry affected cities in Western Europe?

2. (a) List Which four Western European countries have large immigrant populations?

(b) Summarize How have immigrants changed the cultures of Western Europe?

3. (a) Explain Why is it easy to travel among Western European countries?

(b) Make Generalizations How would life be different for travelers in Western Europe if borders were not open?

Writing Activity
Write down two facts about Western Europe that you were surprised to learn. How has this new information changed the way you think about Western Europe or its people?

For: An activity on the European Union
Visit: PHSchool.com
Web Code: ldd-7301

228 Europe and Russia

Writing Activity
Use the *Rubric for Assessing a Writing Assignment* to evaluate students' answers.

All in One **Europe and Russia Teaching Resources,** *Rubric for Assessing a Writing Assignment,* p. 244

Go Online PHSchool.com Typing in the Web code when prompted will bring students to detailed instructions for this activity.

Section 2
The Cultures of Eastern Europe

Prepare to Read

Objectives

In this section you will
1. Learn about the different ethnic groups in Eastern Europe.
2. Understand the impact of foreign domination on the region.
3. Find out about ethnic conflict in Eastern Europe.
4. Learn about Eastern Europe's cultural centers.

Taking Notes

As you read, create an outline of this section. The outline below has been started for you.

> I. Eastern Europe's ethnic groups
>   A. Slavic heritage
>   1.
>   2.
>   B. Non-Slavic groups
> II.

🎯 Target Reading Skill

Identify Supporting Details The main idea of a section is supported by details that explain or develop the main idea with reasons or examples. The main idea of the section titled Eastern Europe's Ethnic Groups is stated in the first sentence of the first paragraph under the heading Slavic Cultures. As you read, note the details following each of the blue headings that tell more about the cultures of Eastern Europe.

Key Terms

- **migration** (my GRAY shun) *n.* movement from place to place
- **ethnic group** (ETH nik groop) *n.* a group of people who share the same ancestors, culture, language, or religion
- **dialect** (DY uh lekt) *n.* a version of a language found only in a certain region

---

If you look at a map of Europe as it was one hundred years ago, you may notice something odd. Many of today's Eastern European countries are missing. Until 1918, three large empires ruled most of this region.

Eastern Europe formed a crossroads between east and west. To the east lay the Russian and Ottoman empires. To the west lay Germany and Austria. There were few mountains or other natural barriers to keep invaders out of Eastern Europe. For example, Russia, Prussia, and Austria moved into Poland and divided it among themselves in 1795. Poland did not become independent again until the end of World War I in 1918.

Movement throughout much of Eastern Europe has always been easy. For thousands of years, various groups have entered or crossed this region. This movement from place to place, called **migration** (my GRAY shun), is still happening today.

A European map from 1911

Chapter 8 Section 2 **229**

🎯 Target Reading Skill

L2

Identify Supporting Details Point out the Target Reading Skill. Tell students that identifying supporting details in the text will help them remember the most important ideas in their reading.

Model identifying supporting details by reading the first paragraph on p. 231. Note that the main idea is that most of Eastern Europe's ethnic groups are descendants of Slavs. Identify supporting details that can help students remember this idea. *(One main Slavic group existed two thousand years ago. It separated, developing into about ten different Slavic language groups.)*

Give students *Identify Supporting Details.* Have them complete the activity in their groups.

All in One **Europe and Russia Program Resources,** *Identify Supporting Details,* p. 228

Objectives

Social Studies

1. Learn about the different ethnic groups in Eastern Europe.
2. Understand the impact of foreign domination on the region.
3. Find out about ethnic conflict in Eastern Europe.
4. Learn about Eastern Europe's cultural centers.

Reading/Language Arts

Learn how to identify supporting details in a text to help understand the main idea.

Prepare to Read

Build Background Knowledge

L2

Tell students that in this section they will learn about the different ethnic groups in Eastern Europe. Ask students to list some of the different ethnic groups in their community. Then have them identify where these groups originally came from. Are any of them from Eastern Europe? Conduct an Idea Wave (TE, p. T35) to generate a list. Point out that ethnic groups move for different reasons, such as finding better jobs or escaping religious or political persecution.

Set a Purpose for Reading

L2

- Preview the Objectives.

- Read each statement in the *Reading Readiness Guide* aloud. Ask students to mark each statement true or false. Have students discuss the statements in pairs or groups of four, then mark their worksheets again. Use the Numbered Heads participation strategy (TE, p. T36) to call on students to share their group's perspective.

All in One **Europe and Russia Teaching Resources,** *Reading Readiness Guide,* p. 220

Vocabulary Builder
Preview Key Terms

Pronounce each Key Term, then ask the students to say the word with you. Provide a simple explanation such as, "The movement of people from one place to another is called migration."

Instruct

Eastern Europe's Ethnic Groups [L2]

Guided Instruction

- **Vocabulary Builder** Clarify the high-use word **descendant** before reading.

- Read Eastern Europe's Ethnic Groups, using the Paragraph Shrinking strategy (TE, p. T34).

- Ask **What ethnic groups are most Eastern Europeans descended from?** *(Slavs)*

- Ask **How did differences develop among the descendants of the Slavs?** *(As the Slavs separated, they developed different languages and dialects, and adopted different religions.)*

- Ask students **What might have happened if the Slavs had not migrated across Eastern Europe?** *(Possible answer: They probably would not have divided into so many groups, and another ethnic group might have populated Eastern Europe.)*

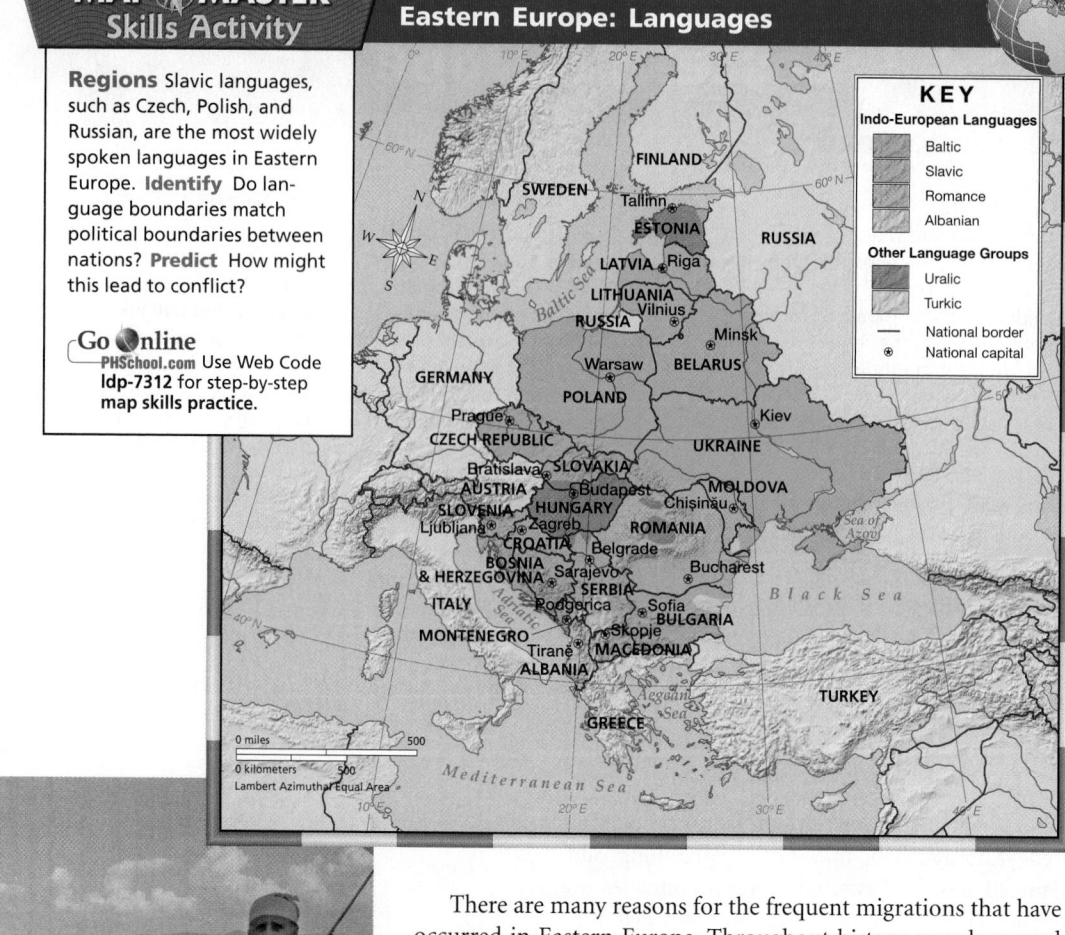

MAP MASTER™ Skills Activity — Eastern Europe: Languages

Regions Slavic languages, such as Czech, Polish, and Russian, are the most widely spoken languages in Eastern Europe. **Identify** Do language boundaries match political boundaries between nations? **Predict** How might this lead to conflict?

Go Online
PHSchool.com Use Web Code **ldp-7312** for step-by-step map skills practice.

KEY

Indo-European Languages
- Baltic
- Slavic
- Romance
- Albanian

Other Language Groups
- Uralic
- Turkic

— National border
⊛ National capital

There are many reasons for the frequent migrations that have occurred in Eastern Europe. Throughout history, people moved in search of good farmland or plentiful natural resources. Sometimes people moved to escape enemies. People have also fled places where their religious or political beliefs put them in danger. And they have often moved in search of a better life.

Eastern Europe's Ethnic Groups

One of the groups that migrated across Eastern Europe long ago was the Slavs (slahvz). These people first lived in present-day Poland, Slovakia (sloh VAH kee uh), and Ukraine. By the 700s, the Slavs had spread south to Greece, west to the Alps, north to the Baltic Sea, and east into Russia.

A Roma family

230 Europe and Russia

Answers

MAP MASTER Skills Activity **Identify** No, languages cross political boundaries.
Predict Language barriers could create a breakdown in communication.

Go Online
PHSchool.com Students may practice their map skills using the interactive online version of this map.

Vocabulary Builder

Use the information below to teach students this section's high-use words.

High-Use Word	Definition and Sample Sentence
descendant, p. 231	*n.* a person related to an earlier ancestor or family Paul is a **descendant** of his grandfather.
conflict, p. 233	*n.* a disagreement My sister and I were in a **conflict** over who would have the bigger bedroom.
thrive, p. 234	*v.* to grow vigorously; flourish Mia's boat rental business **thrives** in the summer.

Slavic Cultures Today, descendants of Slavs make up most of Eastern Europe's ethnic groups. An **ethnic group** is a group of people with a shared culture, language, or religion that sets them apart from their neighbors. Two thousand years ago, there was a single Slavic language. As the Slavs separated and moved to different areas, different Slavic languages developed. Today, about ten Slavic languages are spoken in Eastern Europe. These include Czech, Polish, and Russian.

Some countries in Eastern Europe are almost entirely Slavic-speaking. These countries include Poland, Croatia (kroh AY shuh), Slovenia (sloh VEE nee uh), and the Czech Republic.

However, even two people who speak the same Slavic language may not speak the same dialect. A **dialect** (DY uh lekt) is a version of a language that can be found only in a certain region.

There are also major religious differences among descendants of Slavs. Most follow the Eastern Orthodox faith or Roman Catholicism. Others may be Protestant or Muslim.

Other Ethnic Groups Many other ethnic groups live in Eastern Europe as well. About 90 percent of the people of Hungary belong to an ethnic group called the Magyars (MAG yahrz). In Romania, most people are Romanians. Similarly, in Albania, most people are Albanian. Roma, sometimes called Gypsies, and Germans live in several of the countries of Eastern Europe.

✓ **Reading Check** Name three Slavic languages that are spoken in Eastern Europe.

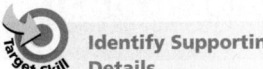

Identify Supporting Details
What details in these paragraphs give examples of Slavic languages?

Worshiping in Different Ways
Below, hundreds of Muslims pray at a mosque in Bosnia. At the left, women participate in a religious ceremony in an Eastern Orthodox church in Macedonia.
Synthesize *Though these Eastern Europeans practice different religions, what other cultural traditions might they share?*

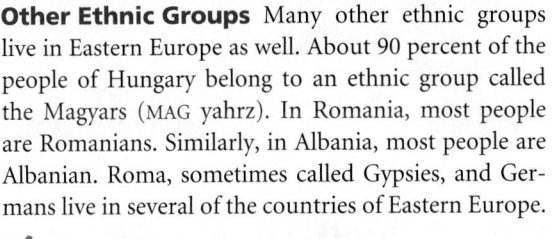

Background: Global Perspective

Slavic Migration Migration has continued to play an important part in the history of Eastern Europe. In the late 1800s, many Slavs began to leave the region. A large number of them immigrated to the United States, greatly increasing the Slavic population there.

Economic and political hardships influenced this migration. It was also aided by changes in global transportation. The expansion of railroads and the use of steamships for ocean travel made what was once a long and very expensive journey possible for many.

Many Jews living in Eastern European countries also migrated, to escape persecution.

L2

🎯 **Target Reading Skill**

Identify Supporting Details As a follow up, ask students to answer the Target Reading Skill question in the Student Edition. (*Two thousand years ago there was one Slavic language; as Slavs separated, different Slavic languages developed; today there are about ten Slavic languages in Eastern Europe.*)

Independent Practice
Ask students to create the Taking Notes graphic organizer on a blank piece of paper. Then have them fill in the outline with headings and details from the section. Briefly model how to identify which details to record.

Monitor Progress
Circulate to make sure students are filling in their outlines correctly. Provide assistance as needed.

Answers

Synthesize They might share similar ways of dressing, similar languages, and other ways of life.

✓ **Reading Check** Czech, Polish, and Russian

Foreign Domination L2

Ethnic Conflict L2

Guided Instruction

- **Vocabulary Builder** Clarify the high-use word **conflict** before reading.

- Read Foreign Domination and Ethnic Conflict as a class. As students read, circulate to make sure individuals can answer the Reading Check questions.

- Ask **How did the Soviets try to control people's lives in Eastern Europe?** *(They took private land, punished people for criticizing the government, and discouraged cultural traditions such as religion.)*

- Discuss the role cultural traditions played in Eastern Europe. *(Cultural traditions brought people together. For example, in Poland, Roman Catholics united in their opposition to the Soviets.)*

- Ask **Who controlled Czechoslovakia after World War II?** *(Communists heavily influenced by the Soviet Union)*

- Discuss how many Czechoslovakians reacted to the Communist government. *(Many were unhappy, and students and writers formed groups protesting communism and calling for a return to democracy.)*

MAP MASTER™ Skills Activity

Eastern Europe: Political

Regions This book uses the term *Eastern Europe* to describe the region including the former Yugoslavia and the nations dominated by the Soviet Union after World War II. **Identify** Which nation is physically in the eastern half of Europe, but is not part of what we call Eastern Europe? **Apply Information** Why is this country not considered part of Eastern Europe?

Go Online
PHSchool.com Use Web Code ldp-7322 for step-by-step map skills practice.

KEY
— National border
⊛ National capital
• Other city

Foreign Domination

As you read at the beginning of this section, Eastern Europe is a region with a history of foreign domination. As you read in Chapter 7, most of Eastern Europe came under Soviet control following World War II. Communist leaders, influenced by the Soviet Union, led the governments of most Eastern European countries.

As in the Soviet Union, the Communists tried to control almost every aspect of people's lives. They took private land, and punished people for criticizing the government. They discouraged traditional expressions of culture such as religion. However, they did not succeed in destroying Eastern European culture. Instead, the cultural traditions you have read about brought people together. In Poland, for example, the Roman Catholic faith unified people in opposition to the Soviets. In Ukraine, people continued to speak Ukrainian even though Russian was the official language.

✓ **Reading Check** What country influences Eastern Europe's leaders?

Answers

 **Identify** Russia **Apply Information** because much of Russia is located in Asia

✓ Reading Check the Soviet Union

Skills for Life **Skills Mini Lesson**

Analyzing Primary Sources

1. Teach the skill by telling students that when they read a primary source, they should identify who wrote or spoke the information, and when and why they did so. They should then identify the main idea, identify facts and opinions, and determine whether the source is reliable.

2. Help students practice the skill by analyzing the primary source on p. 95 using the steps above.

3. Have students apply the skill by analyzing another of Havel's speeches, *Your Government Has Returned to You!*

All in One **Europe and Russia Teaching Resources,** *Your Government Has Returned to You!,* pp. 237–238

Ethnic Conflict

Eastern Europe's long history of migration and foreign domination have made it an ethnically diverse region. At times, that diversity has brought ethnic conflict. Ethnic conflict in the region has been resolved both peacefully and violently.

Czechs and Slovaks: A Peaceful Division
Czechoslovakia (chek uh sloh VAH kee uh) had two main ethnic groups. The Czechs lived mostly in the western regions of Bohemia and Moravia. The Slovaks lived mostly in the eastern region of Slovakia. Hungarians, Ukrainians, Germans, and Poles lived in both areas.

Czechoslovakia was taken over by Communists, heavily influenced by the Soviet Union, after World War II. From the 1960s to the 1980s, students and writers formed groups protesting communism and calling for a return to democracy. Vaclav Havel, a playwright, explained his reasons for staying in Czechoslovakia.

> **"I am Czech. . . . This is my language, this is my home. I don't feel myself to be patriotic, because I don't feel that to be Czech is to be something more than French, English, or European, or anybody else. . . . I try to do something for my country because I live here. "**
>
> —Vaclav Havel

Such protests helped end communism in Czechoslovakia. However, Czechs and the Slovaks disagreed about how to run the newly democratic country. In 1993, they agreed to peacefully separate into two countries—the Czech Republic and Slovakia.

Yugoslavia: A Violent Division
Unlike in Czechoslovakia, ethnic differences in the former country of Yugoslavia (yoo goh SLAH vee uh) led to violence and the breakup of the country. You will read more about this conflict in Chapter 10.

✓ **Reading Check** Who is Vaclav Havel?

The Velvet Revolution
Crowds celebrate Czechoslovakia's transition to a democratic government, which took place in a peaceful movement called the Velvet Revolution. Playwright Vaclav Havel, shown below, became the country's first president. **Infer** Why was Czechoslovakia's change in government called the "Velvet Revolution"?

Chapter 8 Section 2 **233**

Differentiated Instruction

For Gifted and Talented   L3
To learn more about the conflicts that occurred during the breakup of Yugoslavia, have students read *Genocide in the Balkans*, and answer the questions.

Go Online
PHSchool.com

For: Long Term Integrated Project: *Genocide in the Balkans*
Visit: PHSchool.com
Web Code: ldd-7304

Guided Instruction (continued)
- Ask **Why did Czechoslovakia divide in 1993?** (*The Czechs and Slovaks disagreed about the future of the country.*) **What countries emerged as a result of this split?** (*the Czech Republic and Slovakia*)
- Ask **How did the division of Yugoslavia differ from that of Czechoslovakia?** (*Conflicts and violence broke out within Yugoslavia, leading to its breakup.*)

Independent Practice
Have students continue to fill in their outlines as they read the section.

Monitor Progress
As students fill in details from the section, circulate to check students' outlines and provide assistance as needed.

Answers
Infer Possible answer: Velvet is a smooth fabric, and the transition went smoothly and peacefully.

✓ **Reading Check** the playwright who became the first president of Czechoslovakia

European Centers of Culture

Guided Instruction

- **Vocabulary Builder** Clarify the high-use word **thrive** before reading.

- Read European Centers of Culture as a class.

- Discuss the ways in which Prague has been an important center of culture through history. *(In the past, several famous composers lived there. Today, the music of these composers is still performed there. The city is well-known for its theaters, and is an important center for art.)*

- Ask **How did geography play a part in the development of Prague and Budapest into major cities?** *(Possible answer: Both are located on major rivers which may have provided transportation, ports for trade, and water for drinking, making these locations good for the development of cities.)*

- Ask **How was Budapest different from many other European cities during Communist rule?** *(It was able to remain a thriving cultural center because Hungary's ties to Western Europe were stronger than those of other Eastern European countries.)*

Independent Practice

Have students complete their outlines with the information they have just read.

Monitor Progress

- Show *Section Reading Support Transparency ER 41* and ask students to check their graphic organizers individually. Go over key concepts and clarify key vocabulary as needed.

  📖 **Europe and Russia Transparencies,** *Section Reading Support Transparency ER 41*

- Tell students to fill in the last column of their *Reading Readiness Guides*. Probe for what they learned that confirms or invalidates each statement.

  All in One Europe and Russia Teaching Resources, *Reading Readiness Guide,* p. 220

Answer

Apply Information Because of the Czech Republic's architecture and cultural attractions, tourism is probably an important part of the economy.

Prague: A Historic City
Prague's buildings are a rich mix of architectural styles, including Renaissance, Gothic, and modern. Many of Prague's historic buildings house art collections. **Apply Information** *What role do you think tourism plays in the economy of the Czech Republic?*

European Centers of Culture

As in Western Europe, Eastern Europe's cities are important centers of life and culture throughout the region. These cities have thrived particularly since the fall of communist governments in the region in the 1980s.

Prague: A City Rich in Culture Prague (prahg) is the capital of the Czech Republic. Though people settled in the region thousands of years ago, the city first developed in the A.D. 800s. The Vltava (VUL tuh vuh) River winds its way through the city. Prague Castle, built in the late 800s, sits high on a hill overlooking the city. Houses dating back hundreds of years line the narrow streets of the historic city center.

Prague has always been an important center of culture. Antonín Dvořák (AHN toh nin DVAWR zhahk) and several other famous Czech composers lived in Prague. Today, their music is performed every year at a spring music festival in the city. The composer Wolfgang Mozart, an Austrian, also lived and wrote some of his famous pieces in Prague.

Prague is well known for its many theaters. It is also an important center for art, with its many museums and galleries.

234 Europe and Russia

Practice the Skill

Reread the passages about immigration and culture on pages 226–227. Then decide what *your* position is about immigration. Use the steps in Learn the Skill to support your position.

1 Prepare to write a statement summarizing your position by first jotting down your ideas about immigration. Think about these questions as you decide on your position: Why do people emigrate? Why do some countries welcome immigrants? Why do other countries sharply limit immigration? How do immigrants affect the countries they move to? Now choose a position, and write a statement that summarizes it.

2 Add at least three reasons to explain why you hold your position. Clarify your reasons with examples or other details.

3 Research your position using reliable sources. Add additional reasons, details, and examples.

4 Review the information you have gathered and organize it in order to strengthen your argument. Does one reason lead to another?

5 Summarize your position about immigration in a one-sentence conclusion.

I support immigration because....

I do not support immigration because....

Apply the Skill

Reread the passage titled Growth of Industry on page 223. Use the steps you have learned in this lesson to identify and support a position on whether the trend toward urbanization in Europe is a positive or a negative thing.

Assess and Reteach

Assess Progress [L2]
Ask students to do the Apply the Skill activity.

Reteach [L1]
If students are having trouble applying the skill steps, have them review the skill using the interactive Social Studies Skills Tutor CD-ROM.

 Supporting a Position, **Social Studies Skills Tutor CD-ROM**

Extend [L3]
Write the following on the board: "Immigrants should try and blend into their new country's culture as much as possible." Then write, "Immigrants should learn about their new country's culture, but should also retain some of their own customs and traditions." Have students reread the text under the subheading Blending Cultures on p. 227. Working together in pairs, have students write a paragraph that supports one of the positions.

Answer
Apply the Skill
Answers will vary, but students should identify and support a position on whether or not they think urbanization in Europe is a positive or negative trend.

Section 3
Step-by-Step Instruction

Objectives
Social Studies
1. Learn about Russia's ethnic groups.
2. Find out about Russia's culture and its educational system.

Reading/Language Arts
Learn how to identify implied main ideas to help remember the most important information.

Prepare to Read

Build Background Knowledge **L2**
Tell students that in this section they will learn about the cultural achievements of Russia. Ask students to preview the headings, photographs, art, and captions in the section, keeping the following questions in mind: **What artwork did they like? Did they dislike any artwork? Do they think that artists should be able to create whatever they like without outside interference, such as government involvement?** Use the Give One, Get One participation strategy (TE, p. T37) to elicit student responses, and then record them on the board.

Set a Purpose for Reading **L2**
■ Preview the Objectives.

■ Form students into pairs or groups. Distribute the *Reading Readiness Guide*. Ask the students to fill in the first two columns of the chart. Use the Numbered Heads participation strategy (TE, p. T36) to call on students to share one piece of information they already know and one piece of information they want to know.

All in One Europe and Russia Teaching Resources, *Reading Readiness Guide*, p. 224

Vocabulary Builder
Preview Key Terms
Pronounce each Key Term, then ask the students to say the word with you. Provide a simple explanation such as, "A government represses a group of people when it does not allow them to practice their religion freely."

Section 3
The Cultures of the Russian Federation

Prepare to Read

Objectives
In this section you will
1. Learn about Russia's ethnic groups.
2. Find out about Russia's culture and its educational system.

Taking Notes
As you read this section, look for information about how cultural expression differed in the Soviet Union and Russia. Copy the table below and record your findings in it.

Cultural Expression	
Soviet Union	**Russia**
•	•
•	•
•	•

Target Reading Skill
Identify Main Ideas
Identifying main ideas can help you remember what you read. Sometimes the main idea is not stated directly. To find the main idea, add up all the details in the paragraphs and then state the main idea in your own words. Carefully read the details in the two paragraphs below. Then state the main idea of that section.

Key Terms
• **heritage** (HEHR uh tij) *n.* the customs and practices passed from one generation to the next
• **propaganda** (prahp uh GAN duh) *n.* the spread of ideas designed to support a cause or hurt an opposing cause

Moscow's St. Basil's Cathedral was built in the 1500s.

238 Europe and Russia

For many years, Russians passing the Church of Saints Cosmas and Damian in Moscow never heard a choir. They never saw a bride and groom leave the church. They never heard religious services. The only sound they heard was the hum of machines printing government documents. The government of the Soviet Union owned the church and used it as a printing shop. In the Soviet Union, the government tried to prevent people from practicing religion.

In 1991, the Soviet Union collapsed. Two years later, Russians who had never given up their faith took back their church. Now the Church of Saints Cosmas and Damian is filled with people singing songs of worship. In recent years, hundreds of other churches in Moscow have reopened their doors. The same return to religion can be seen in places of worship across all of Russia.

Target Reading Skill **L2**

Identify Main Ideas Point out the Target Reading Skill. Tell students that when the main idea of a text is not stated directly, they must read the text carefully to figure out the implied idea, and then state it in their own words.

Model identifying implied main ideas by reading the second paragraph on p. 244. Note that the first sentence of the passage states important information, but not the main idea. State the main idea in your own words. *(After the fall of the Soviet Union, free education continued, but students had greater freedom to study what they wanted.)*

Give students *Identify Implied Main Ideas*. Have them complete the activity in their groups.

All in One Europe and Russia Teaching Resources, *Identify Implied Main Ideas*, p. 229

238 *Europe and Russia*

Russia's Ethnic Groups

The Russian Orthodox religion is a branch of Christianity closely related to the Eastern Orthodox Church. It has been a powerful bond among many Russians for hundreds of years. It is part of the Russian **heritage** (HEHR uh tij), or the customs and practices that are passed from one generation to the next.

Russia's ethnic culture is another part of the Russian heritage. More than 80 percent of Russian citizens belong to the ethnic group of Russian Slavs. These people generally speak the Russian language. Most of them live in the western parts of the Russian Federation. However, Russia is also home to many non-Russian ethnic groups.

Both of the families at the right live in Siberia.

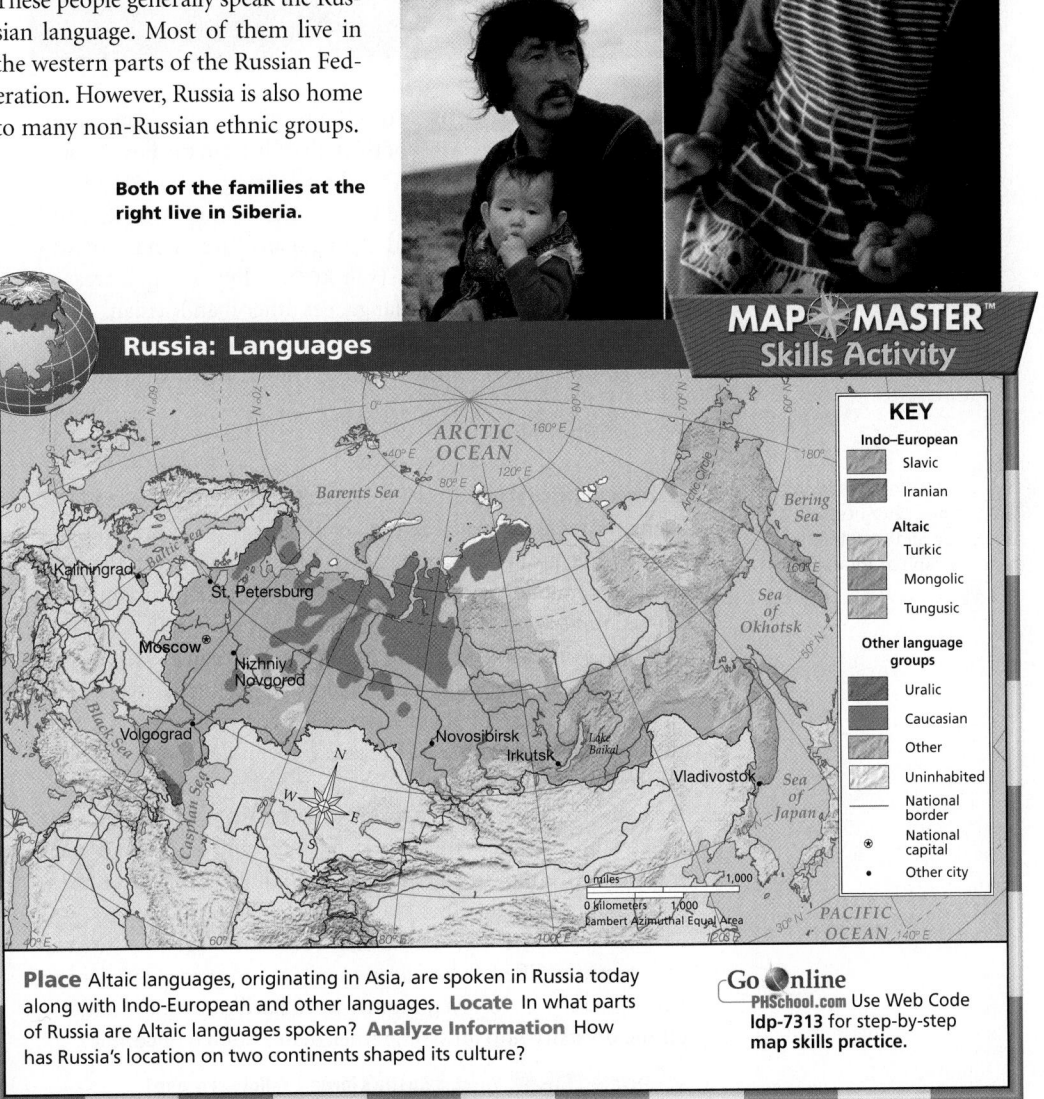

Russia: Languages

KEY

Indo–European
- Slavic
- Iranian

Altaic
- Turkic
- Mongolic
- Tungusic

Other language groups
- Uralic
- Caucasian
- Other
- Uninhabited
- National border
- National capital
- Other city

Place Altaic languages, originating in Asia, are spoken in Russia today along with Indo-European and other languages. **Locate** In what parts of Russia are Altaic languages spoken? **Analyze Information** How has Russia's location on two continents shaped its culture?

Go Online PHSchool.com Use Web Code ldp-7313 for step-by-step map skills practice.

Vocabulary Builder

Use the information below to teach students this section's high-use words.

High-Use Word	Definition and Sample Sentence
unify, p. 240	*v.* to combine into one A common language and culture **unified** the community.
intricate, p. 242	*adj.* full of detail, complex The beading on the fancy dress was very **intricate.**
campaign, p. 242	*n.* series of activities to achieve a goal The goal of the election **campaign** was to get as many votes as possible for the candidate.

Guided Instruction

- **Vocabulary Builder** Clarify the high-use word **unify** before reading.

- Read Russia's Ethnic Groups, using the Oral Cloze reading strategy (TE, p. T33).

- Discuss what ethnic group has had the greatest influence on Russia's heritage. *(Russian Slavs, who make up over 80 percent of the population and speak the Russian language)*

Answers

MAP MASTER Skills Activity **Locate** Altaic languages are spoken mainly in northern and eastern Russia, as well as a few areas in southern and western Russia. **Analyze Information** Russia's culture is influenced by both European and Asian cultures.

Go Online PHSchool.com Students may practice their map skills using the interactive online version of this map.

Guided Instruction (continued)

- Discuss how other ethnic groups have shaped Russia. *(More than 60 other ethnic groups live within Russia, mostly far from the western Russian areas. They speak languages other than Russian and practice Islam, Buddhism, and other religions. Some groups, like the Chechens, have tried to break away from Russia politically.)*

- Ask students **Why do you think some non-Russian ethnic groups have not tried to break away from Russia?** *(Answers will vary, but students might argue that some groups might be afraid of Russia's military power, while others might say that many groups do not feel the need to break away since they are allowed to rule themselves.)*

Independent Practice

Assign *Guided Reading and Review.*

All in One **Europe and Russia Teaching Resources,** *Guided Reading and Review,* p. 225

Monitor Progress

As students complete the worksheet, circulate to answer questions and provide assistance as needed.

🔄 Target Reading Skill   L2

Identify Main Ideas As a follow up, ask students to perform the activity of the Target Reading Skill in the Student Edition. *(The Russian government wants to keep the country united.)*

Buddhism in Russia
A Buddhist monastery in southern Siberia reflects the Tibetan heritage of the people who live there. **Compare and Contrast** *Compare this photo with the ones on page 231. Besides religion, what other cultural differences might there be among the three groups?*

Identify Main Ideas
In one sentence, summarize all the details in the paragraph at the right.

Other Ethnic Groups More than 60 non-Russian ethnic groups live in Russia. Most of them live far from the heavily populated western areas. People speaking languages related to Finnish and Turkish live near the Ural and Caucasus (KAW kuh sus) mountains. Armenians and Mongolians live along Russia's southern edges. The Yakuts (yah KOOTS) live in small areas of Siberia. These groups speak languages other than Russian.

They also follow different religions. Muslims make up Russia's second-largest religious group, after Russian Orthodox. Many followers of Buddhism (BOOD iz um) live near Russia's border with China.

Ethnic Majorities Recall that the Soviet Union was made up of many republics. Each Soviet republic was the homeland of a large ethnic group. When the Soviet Union came apart, the non-Russian republics broke away and formed their own countries. For example, Armenia is a former Soviet republic with a majority of ethnic Armenians. It gained its independence in 1991.

Other ethnic groups remained part of Russia, sometimes unwillingly. Many of them have called for more rights to rule themselves. Some have even called for independence. These efforts have brought much ethnic tension. Yet despite this great tension, fighting has broken out only between Russia and one other ethnic group—the Chechens. You will read about their independence movement, and the Russian government's repression of it, in Chapter 10.

The government of the Russian Federation has tried to keep the country unified. It has given many ethnic groups the right to rule themselves. However, it must work hard to turn the nation's ethnic diversity into an asset, rather than a source of conflict.

✓ **Reading Check** What is Russia's largest religious group?

240 Europe and Russia

Differentiated Instruction

For Less Proficient Readers   L1
To learn more about Russia, have students view the maps, photo tour, and timeline about Russia on the Passport to the World CD-ROM.

⊙ *Russia,* **Passport to the World CD-ROM**

For Gifted and Talented   L3
Have students research and give an oral presentation on one of the non-Russian ethnic groups that live in Russia. Use the *Rubric for Assessing an Oral Presentation* to assess students' work.

All in One **Europe and Russia Teaching Resources,** *Rubric for Assessing an Oral Presentation,* p. 246

Answers

Compare and Contrast The people in the three photographs live in different areas, and are probably from different ethnic groups. They also may of different socio-economic backgrounds.

✓ **Reading Check** Russian Orthodox

The Space Age Begins

When the Soviet Union launched the first artificial satellite on October 4, 1957, it took the world by surprise. Less than four years later, the Soviet Union shocked the world again by sending the first human being into space. On April 12, 1961, twenty-seven-year-old Cosmonaut Yuri Gagarin spent one hour and 48 minutes in space. Gagarin completed a single orbit in the spacecraft *Vostok I*, before returning to Earth.

Yuri Gagarin
Yuri Gagarin completed two years of secret training before the flight.

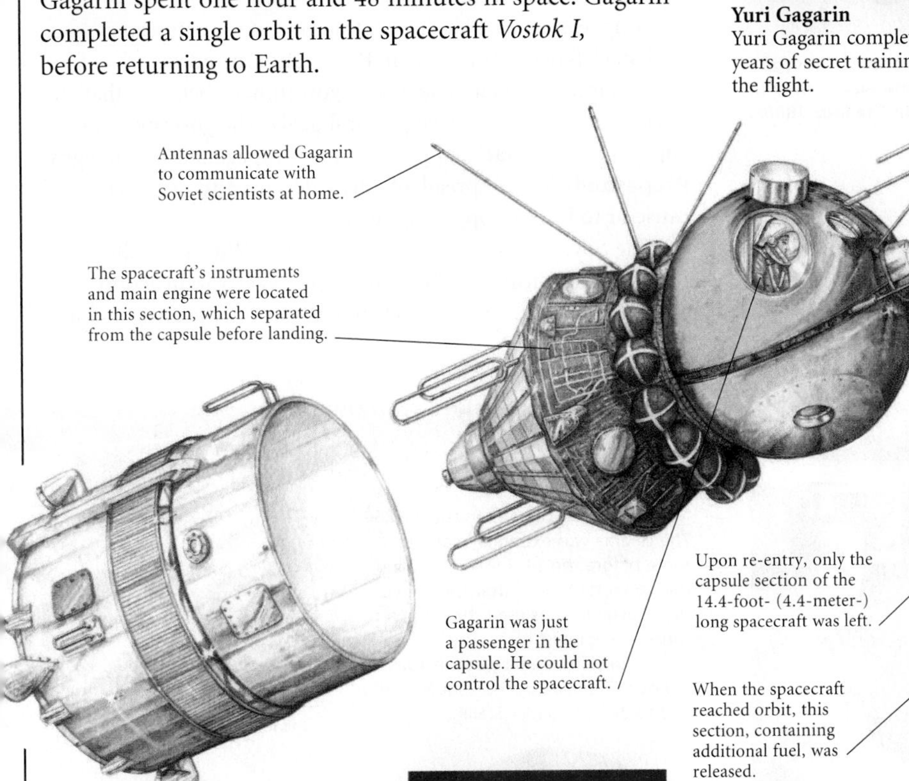

Antennas allowed Gagarin to communicate with Soviet scientists at home.

The spacecraft's instruments and main engine were located in this section, which separated from the capsule before landing.

Gagarin was just a passenger in the capsule. He could not control the spacecraft.

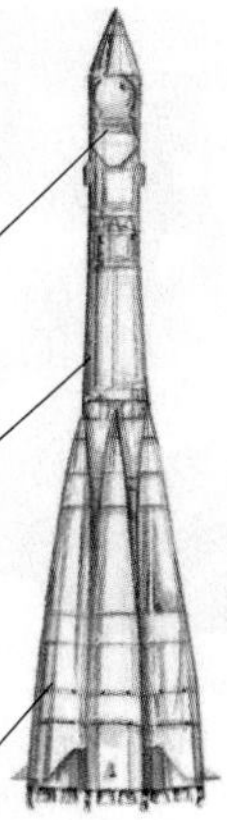

Upon re-entry, only the capsule section of the 14.4-foot- (4.4-meter-) long spacecraft was left.

When the spacecraft reached orbit, this section, containing additional fuel, was released.

This section, containing fuel to lift the heavy spacecraft, was released within two minutes after liftoff.

Four jets at the base of this section helped turn and tilt the spacecraft as it headed for orbit.

Blasting off
Vostok I takes off with Yuri Gagarin on board. After 15 minutes, Gagarin reported, "The flight is proceeding normally. I feel well."

ANALYZING IMAGES
In which section of *Vostok I* did the cosmonaut sit?

Chapter 8 Section 3 **241**

The Space Age Begins L2

Guided Instruction
Have students read the text on this page of the Student Edition. As a class, study the art and photographs and read the captions. Then have students answer the Analyzing Images question.

Independent Practice
Ask students to suppose it is April 1961, and Yuri Gagarin has just become the first person to orbit Earth. Using the information in the captions and text, ask them to write a short paragraph from the point of view of Yuri Gagarin describing what happened as he traveled in the spacecraft.

Differentiated Instruction

For English Language Learners L2
Students may have trouble understanding some of the more difficult words on this page, such as *antennas, capsule, proceeding,* and *tilt*. Have students use a dictionary to find the meaning of the words, their parts of speech, and their pronunciations.

Answer
ANALYZING IMAGES He sat in the capsule.

Russian Culture and Education

Guided Instruction

- **Vocabulary Builder** Clarify the high-use words **intricate** and **campaign** before reading.

- Read about Russian Culture and Education. Draw students attention to the graphic Artistic Traditions in Russia at the bottom of pp. 242–243 and read the captions together.

- Identify some of the kinds of art produced by Russian artists, musicians, and writers. *(Fabergé eggs, works by Leo Tolstoy, music by Peter Tchaikovsky, paintings by Wassily Kandinski)*

- Discuss how communism affected Russian art. *(Artistic creativity nearly ended because the government only approved art that supported its propaganda campaign.)*

- Ask **What event in 1991 led to the return of artistic traditions in Russia?** *(the collapse of Soviet communism)*

Elaborately decorated Fabergé eggs like this one were made in St. Petersburg in the late 1800s.

Russian Culture and Education

Russia has produced many great artists. Russia's artistic heritage includes outstanding architecture, fine paintings, great plays, and intricate art objects like Fabergé (FAB ur zhay) eggs.

Russian Artists The novelist Leo Tolstoy (TOHL stoy) wrote powerful stories of life in Russia in the 1800s. Peter Tchaikovsky (chy KAWF skee) composed moving classical music. Russian painters, such as Wassily Kandinsky (VAS uh lee kan DIN skee), were leaders in the modern art movement in the early 1900s. Creating works of art has been a tradition among Russians.

Under Soviet communism, the creation of new works of art nearly came to a halt. The Soviet government believed that the purpose of art was to serve political goals. The government only approved art that supported its propaganda campaigns. **Propaganda** is the spread of ideas designed to support some cause or to hurt an opposing cause.

The Soviet Union broke apart in 1991. With the collapse of Soviet communism, the Russian people eagerly returned to their artistic traditions. Creating new works was once again possible.

Artistic Traditions in Russia

Painting ▲
Russian painter Wassily Kandinsky (1866–1944), above, was an influential abstract artist. Abstract artists do not try to depict things the way that they appear to the eye. His style ranged from pure bursts of color to exact geometric shapes.

Cinema ▶
Motion pictures came to Russia in 1896. The cinema was extremely popular there before the 1917 revolution and during World War I. After the revolution, Soviet leaders used the cinema to spread communist ideas. The golden age of Russian cinema was the 1920s, although filmmaking techniques continued to develop under Stalin.

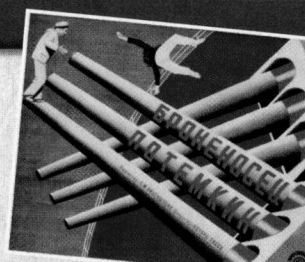

A 1929 Russian movie poster

Tolstoy and Chekhov in 1901

◀ Literature
Russian literature is rich and varied, from the short stories of Nikolay Gogol to the novels of Leo Tolstoy and the plays of Anton Chekhov. Often writing in a harsh political environment, Russian authors have influenced writers all over the world with their wit, expressiveness, and insight into the human mind.

 **Skills Mini Lesson**

Distinguishing Fact and Opinion

1. Teach the skill by explaining that facts are statements that can be proved or disproved, while opinions are statements that cannot be proved or disproved.

2. Help students practice the skill by writing the following sentences on the board, and then having them determine if the statements are fact or opinion and

why. "Leo Tolstoy was born in 1828." *(Fact: it can be proven true or false.)* "I think *War and Peace* is the greatest book ever written. *(Opinion: it cannot be proven true or false.)*

3. Have students apply the skill by finding other examples of facts and opinions in the text as they read.

St. Petersburg: A Cultural Symbol The second-largest city and the largest seaport in Russia, the city of St. Petersburg lies on the Gulf of Finland and is an important center of Russian culture. Visitors to the city can clearly see the mixture of Russian and other European cultures. St. Petersburg was founded by Peter the Great in 1703. His goal was to create a Russian city as beautiful as any Western European city. He employed Western architects to design the city. St. Petersburg was the capital of Russia for more than 200 years before it was renamed Leningrad in 1924. In September 1991, its name was changed back to St. Petersburg.

Because of its grand architecture and many canals, St. Petersburg was once called Venice of the North. The Neva (NEE vuh) River winds gracefully through the city. Along the river's banks are palaces and public buildings hundreds of years old. St. Petersburg's grandest sight, the Winter Palace, is on the Neva. The palace has more than 1,000 rooms and was the winter home of Russia's tsars. Part of the palace is now the Hermitage (HUR muh tij) Museum. Built in 1764, it houses one of the world's finest art collections of Russian, Asian, and European art.

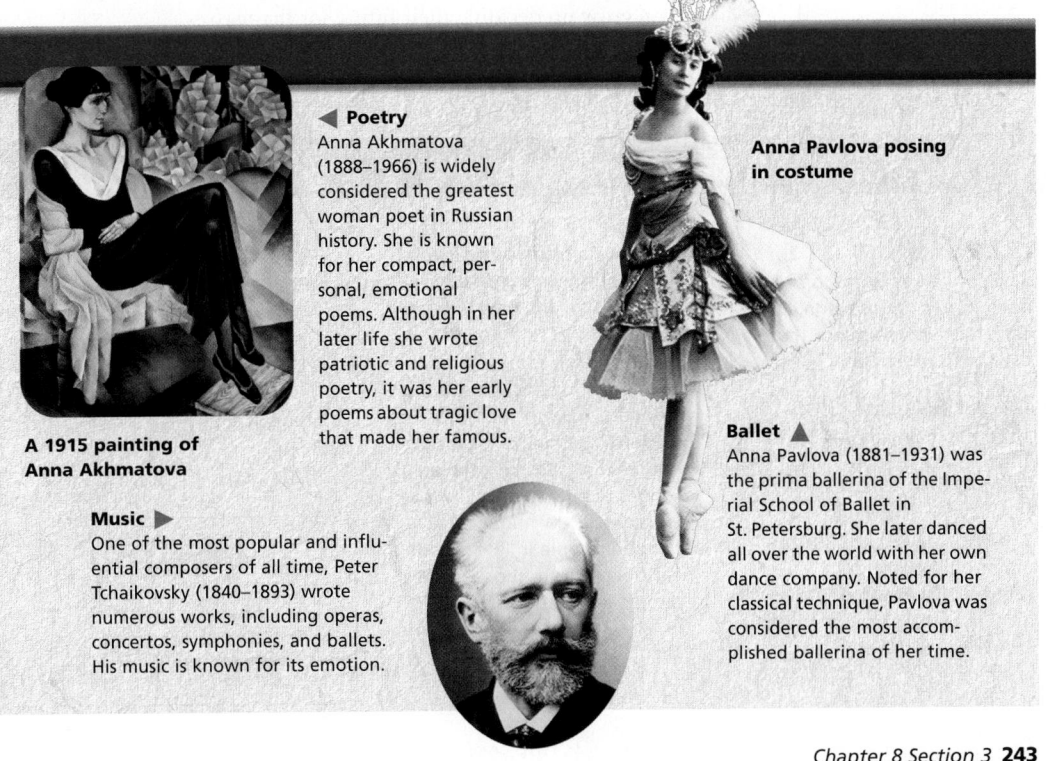

◀ Poetry
Anna Akhmatova (1888–1966) is widely considered the greatest woman poet in Russian history. She is known for her compact, personal, emotional poems. Although in her later life she wrote patriotic and religious poetry, it was her early poems about tragic love that made her famous.

A 1915 painting of Anna Akhmatova

Music ▶
One of the most popular and influential composers of all time, Peter Tchaikovsky (1840–1893) wrote numerous works, including operas, concertos, symphonies, and ballets. His music is known for its emotion.

Anna Pavlova posing in costume

Ballet ▲
Anna Pavlova (1881–1931) was the prima ballerina of the Imperial School of Ballet in St. Petersburg. She later danced all over the world with her own dance company. Noted for her classical technique, Pavlova was considered the most accomplished ballerina of her time.

Guided Instruction (continued)

- Ask students to describe the Winter Palace. (*It is a palace on the Neva River, with more than 1,000 rooms, and was the winter home of Russia's tsars. Part of the palace is now the Hermitage Museum.*)

- Ask students **How did old Soviet Union policies lead to a more educated population?** (*Education was free, increasing the percentage of the population that could read and write from 40 percent to almost 100 percent.*)

- Ask students **What other new courses do you think Russia's young people might be interested in?** (*Possible answers: art, religion, music, politics*)

Independent Practice

Have students create the Taking Notes graphic organizer on a piece of paper. Then have them complete it using the information from this section.

Monitor Progress

- Show *Section Reading Support Transparency ER 42* and ask students to check their graphic organizers individually. Go over key concepts and clarify key vocabulary as needed.

    Europe and Russia Transparencies, *Section Reading Support Transparency ER 42*

- Tell students to fill in the last column of their *Reading Readiness Guides*. Probe for what they learned that confirms or invalidates each statement.

    All in One Europe and Russia Teaching Resources, *Reading Readiness Guide*, p. 224

Assess and Reteach

Assess Progress [L2]

Have students complete the Section Assessment. Administer the *Section Quiz*.

All in One Europe and Russia Teaching Resources, *Section Quiz*, p. 226

Reteach [L1]

If students need more instruction, have them read this section in the Reading and Vocabulary Study Guide.

📖 Chapter 8, Section 3, **Eastern Hemisphere Reading and Vocabulary Study Guide,** pp. 88–90

Extend [L3]

Have students learn more about Russia's political history and how it affected the people of Russia by reading *Lenin's Deathbed Words*, *Kampf*, and *Housekeeping in Russia Soon After the Revolution*.

All in One Europe and Russia Teaching Resources, *Lenin's Deathbed Words*, p. 239; *Kampf*, p. 240; *Housekeeping in Russia Soon After the Revolution*, p. 241

Section 3 Assessment

Key Terms
Students' sentences should reflect knowledge of each Key Term.

🎯 Target Reading Skill
Possible answers: While most Russians share a common ethnic background, many different groups live there. Russia has a rich artistic heritage that includes great artists, thinkers, and writers. St. Petersburg is an important center of Russian culture. Education is also an important part of Russia's culture, and has been since it came under Communist rule.

Comprehension and Critical Thinking
1. (a) Russian Slavs **(b)** Some ethnic groups want to rule themselves. **(c)** Some groups have tried to break ties with the Russians, leading the Russians to use force against them.

2. (a) There has been a return to religion since the fall of the Soviet Union. Artistic traditions that were not allowed under the Soviets are being practiced once more. **(b)** The Soviet Union introduced free education. After the end of Soviet rule, education

Children learning computer skills in a Russian school

Russia's Educational System One of the strengths of the Soviet Union was its free public education system. Under that system, the number of Russians who could read and write rose from about 40 percent to nearly 100 percent. Higher education was also free for Soviet citizens.

The Russian Federation continued free public schooling for children between ages 6 and 17. When students finish ninth grade, they can choose to continue their education in a secondary school or a vocational school. Secondary schools emphasize academic subjects such as mathematics and science, while the vocational schools prepare students for careers in industry and agriculture. Schools are updating their old courses of study, which used to emphasize only one official point of view.

These changes show that Russia is trying to recover the riches of its past even as it prepares for a new future. Religion and art, two important parts of Russia's cultural heritage, can now be freely expressed. And Russia's young people, unlike their parents, can grow up deciding their future for themselves.

✓ **Reading Check** Who founded the city of St. Petersburg?

Section 3 Assessment

Key Terms
Review the key terms at the beginning of this section. Use each term in a sentence that explains its meaning.

🎯 Target Reading Skill
State the main ideas in Section 3.

Comprehension and Critical Thinking
1. (a) Recall What is Russia's major ethnic group?
(b) Identify Point of View Why do some ethnic groups in Russia seek independence?

(c) Draw Conclusions How has Russia's ethnic mix created challenges for the new Russian government?
2. (a) List Give some examples of the ways in which Russians are reconnecting with their past.
(b) Identify Effects How have political changes in Russia led to changes in education?
(c) Predict How might the lives of young people in Russia today be different from those of their parents' generation?

Writing Activity
Suppose that you are visiting St. Petersburg. Write a postcard to your family describing the works of art, architecture, and other expressions of Russian culture that you have seen.

Go Online PHSchool.com
For: An activity on Russian cities
Visit: PHSchool.com
Web Code: ldd-7303

244 Europe and Russia

continued to be free, and schools have updated their courses. **(c)** Answers will vary, but students might say that they probably have more freedom and more choices than their parents did.

Writing Activity
Use the *Rubric for Assessing a Writing Assignment* to evaluate students' postcards.

All in One Europe and Russia Teaching Resources, *Rubric for Assessing a Writing Assignment* p. 244

Typing in the Web code when prompted will bring students to detailed instructions for this activity.

Review and Assessment

Celebrating Carnival in London

◆ Chapter Summary

Section 1: The Cultures of Western Europe

- Industry has made many Western European countries wealthy.
- Western European cities are the cultural centers of their countries.
- Goods, materials, and ideas can travel easily and quickly across Western Europe.

Section 2: The Cultures of Eastern Europe

- Long ago, many ethnic groups migrated across Eastern Europe.
- Under foreign domination, some expressions of Eastern European culture were discouraged.
- Ethnic conflict has influenced the modern history of Eastern Europe.
- Prague and Budapest are important cultural centers of Eastern Europe.

Section 3: The Cultures of the Russian Federation

- Russia has more than 60 different ethnic groups.
- Russia has a rich cultural heritage.

A Fabergé egg from Russia

◆ Key Terms

Each of the statements below contains a key term from the chapter. If the statement is true, write *true*. If it is false, change the term to make it true.

1. A tariff is a different version of a language.
2. Propaganda is the spread of ideas designed to support a cause.
3. Someone who moves to one country from another is an immigrant.
4. People in the same ethnic group share the same ancestors, culture, or religion.
5. Heritage is the customs and practices passed from one generation to the next.
6. Diversification is the movement of populations toward cities and the resulting city growth.
7. Migration is a movement from place to place.

Chapter 8 **245**

─ Vocabulary Builder ─

Revisit this chapter's high-use words:

revolution   descendant   intricate
scholar   conflict   campaign
recreation   thrive
exchange   unify

Ask students to review the definitions they recorded on their *Word Knowledge* worksheets.

Review Chapter Content

- Divide the class into pairs, and have them review the major themes of this chapter by reading each bulleted statement of the Chapter Summary. Then have each group identify which Guiding Question each bulleted statement in the Chapter Summary answers. Discuss the answers as a class using the Idea Wave participation strategy (TE, p. T35). Refer to p. 1 in the Student Edition for the Guiding Questions.

- Assign *Vocabulary Development* for students to review Key Terms.

  All in One Europe and Russia Teaching Resources, *Vocabulary Development*, p. 243

All in One Europe and Russia Teaching Resources, *Word Knowledge*, p. 230

Consider allowing students to earn extra credit if they use the words in their answers to the questions in the Chapter Review and Assessment. The words must be used correctly and in a natural context to win the extra points.

Answers

Key Terms

1. False. A dialect is a different version of a language.
2. True.
3. True.
4. True.
5. True.
6. False. Urbanization is the movement of populations toward cities and the result of city growth.
7. True.

Review and Assessment

Comprehension and Critical Thinking

8. (a) Answers may vary; possible answers include: Paris, London, Madrid, Berlin **(b)** museums, parks, theaters, nightclubs, shops, restaurants, monuments, historical sites

9. (a) People, goods, and ideas can travel easily between countries. **(b)** The Industrial Revolution, urbanization, and continued economic development before and after World War II has made them prosperous.

10. (a) An ethnic group found in many parts of Eastern Europe. **(b)** Today, descendants of Slavs make up most of Eastern Europe's ethnic groups. The different groups of Slavs speak 10 different, but related, languages and practice many different languages.

11. (a) Czechs and Slovaks **(b)** The breakup of Czechoslovakia was peaceful, while the breakup of Yugoslavia led to many conflicts. **(c)** The Czechs and Slovaks already lived in separate parts of the country, which made it easier to divide the land.

12. (a) more than 60 **(b)** Some groups have tried to form their own countries.

13. (a) 1991 **(b)** There is greater political, religious, and cultural freedom. **(c)** Students' answers will vary, but might predict greater artistic, financial, and political achievements.

Skills Practice
Answers will vary, but students should show that they used the skill steps to support their positions.

Writing Activity: Language and Arts
Students' travel guides will vary, but should reflect accurate information about the places they have chosen.

Use the *Rubric for Assessing a Writing Assignment* to evaluate students' answers.

All in One Europe and Russia Teaching Resources, *Rubric for Assessing a Writing Assignment,* p. 244

Review and Assessment (continued)

◆ Comprehension and Critical Thinking

8. (a) List Name three cities in Western Europe.
(b) Summarize What features make cities in Western Europe centers of culture?

9. (a) Explain What does the concept of open borders mean?
(b) Infer Why do Western Europeans generally have a higher standard of living than do Eastern Europeans?

10. (a) Identify Who were the Slavs?
(b) Synthesize How does Slavic culture live on in Eastern Europe today?

11. (a) Recall Name two of Czechoslovakia's ethnic groups.
(b) Compare and Contrast How was the breakup of Czechoslovakia different from the breakup of Yugoslavia?
(c) Draw Conclusions Why was Czechoslovakia able to break up peacefully?

12. (a) Note About how many ethnic groups live in Russia?
(b) Analyze How have non-Russian ethnic groups reacted to recent changes in Russia?

13. (a) Recall When did the Soviet Union break apart?
(b) Find Main Ideas How has life changed for the Russian people since the collapse of the Soviet Union?
(c) Predict What might the future hold for the Russian people?

◆ Skills Practice

Supporting a Position In the Skills for Life activity in this chapter, you learned how to support a position. Review the steps you followed to learn this skill. Then turn to the section titled Ethnic Majorities on page 240. Read about Russia's republics. Decide whether you support or oppose independence for Russia's republics and then support your position.

◆ Writing Activity: Language Arts

Suppose you had friends who were visiting Europe and Russia for the first time. What information would you want to share with them? Create a brief travel guide that your friends could use to plan their trip. Mention interesting places and activities, and provide background information on the cultures of the people they will meet.

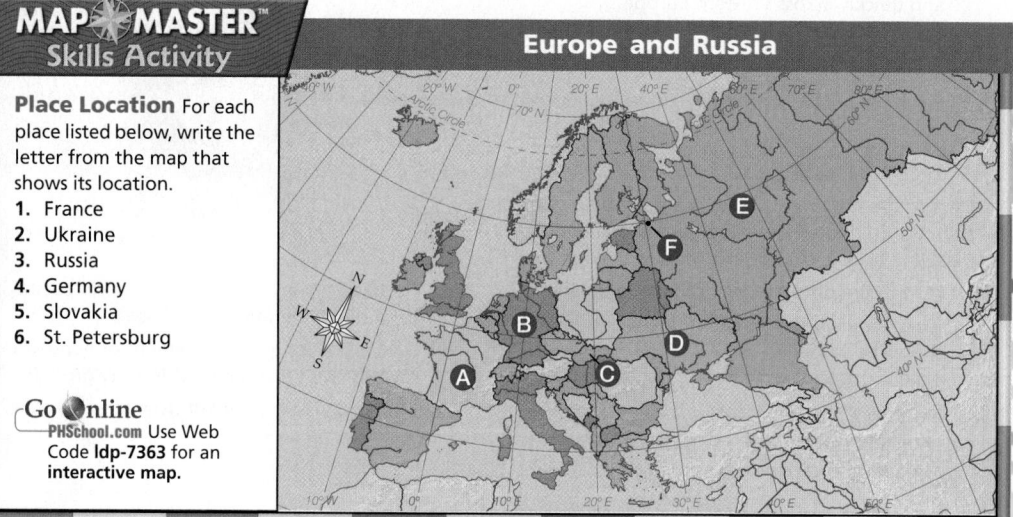

MAP MASTER™ Skills Activity

Europe and Russia

Place Location For each place listed below, write the letter from the map that shows its location.
1. France
2. Ukraine
3. Russia
4. Germany
5. Slovakia
6. St. Petersburg

Go Online
PHSchool.com Use Web Code **ldp-7363** for an **interactive map.**

Standardized Test Prep

Test-Taking Tips

Some questions on standardized tests ask you to analyze graphic organizers. Study the concept web below. Then follow the tips to answer the sample question at the right.

TIP Preview the question. Keep it in mind as you study the information in the web.

Pick the letter that best answers the question.
Another name that belongs on this web is

- **A** Peter the Great.
- **B** Tsar Nicholas II.
- **C** Pablo Picasso.
- **D** Peter Tchaikovsky.

TIP Be sure that you read all four options. If you don't read each one, you can't be certain that you've found the best choice.

Think It Through What other name belongs in the web? The center of the web says Russian Artists—meaning painters, writers, musicians, dancers, and so on. You can rule out A and B, because both are political figures in Russian history. That leaves C and D. You may know that Picasso is Spanish. That leaves Tchaikovsky, answer D.

Practice Questions

Use the tips above and other tips in this book to help you answer the following questions.

1. Advances in farming about 200 years ago led to
   - **A** the Velvet Revolution.
   - **B** increased immigration.
   - **C** the growth of cities.
   - **D** open borders in Western Europe.

2. Which group's descendants make up most of Eastern Europe's ethnic groups?
   - **A** the Romanians
   - **B** the Albanians
   - **C** the Russians
   - **D** the Slavs

3. More than 80 percent of Russian citizens belong to this ethnic group.
   - **A** Russian Slavs
   - **B** Mongolians
   - **C** Yakuts
   - **D** Buddhists

Study the concept web and answer the question that follows.

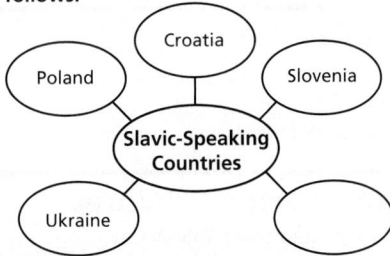

4. What other country belongs on the web?
   - **A** Hungary
   - **B** Romania
   - **C** Austria
   - **D** Czech Republic

Use Web Code lda-7303 for a **Chapter 8 self-test.**

Chapter 8 **247**

MAP MASTER
Skills Activity

1. A	2. D
3. E	4. B
5. C	6. F

Go Online
PHSchool.com Students may practice their map skills using the interactive online version of this map.

Standardized Test Prep

Answers

1. C
2. D
3. A
4. D

Go Online
PHSchool.com Students may use the Chapter 8 self-test on PHSchool.com to prepare for the Chapter Test.

Assessment Resources

Use *Chapter Tests A and B* to assess students' mastery of the chapter content.

All in One **Europe and Russia Teaching Resources,** *Chapter Tests A and B,* pp. 247–252

Tests are also available on the *ExamView Test Bank CD-ROM.*

⊙ *ExamView Test Bank CD-ROM*

Use a benchmark test to evaluate students' cumulative understanding of what they have learned in Chapters 1 through 3.

📄 *Europe and Russia Benchmark Test 1,* **AYP Monitoring Assessments,** pp. 105–108

Discovery CHANNEL SCHOOL Video

Overview

Introducing Western Europe
1. Analyze the data to compare the countries.
2. Identify the characteristics that the countries of Western Europe share.
3. Find out some of the key differences among the countries.

The Geography of Western Europe
Length: 5 minutes, 9 seconds
Gives overview of the different regions and landforms of Western Europe.

 **Section 1**

The United Kingdom: Democracy and Monarchy
1. Examine the regions that make up the United Kingdom.
2. Learn about the United Kingdom's democratic heritage.
3. Find out how the United Kingdom combines democracy and monarchy.
4. Understand why trade is important to the United Kingdom.

Great Britain: London Fog and Suburbia
Length: 4 minutes, 17 seconds
Explains how the suburbs in Britain reflect British history.

 **Section 2**

France: Cultural Heritage and Diversity
1. Find out why the French take pride in their traditional culture.
2. Learn about growing cultural diversity in France.

France: The Rise of Napoleon Bonaparte
Length: 5 minutes, 53 seconds
Explores Napoleon's power.

 Section 3

Sweden: A Welfare State
1. Learn about Sweden's welfare state.
2. Find out how Sweden became a welfare state.
3. Examine possible solutions to Sweden's economic problems.

Sweden: Land of Forests
Length: 4 minutes, 15 seconds
Discusses the importance of forestry in Sweden.

 **Section 4**

Italy: Northern and Southern Divisions
1. Discover that there is another country within Italy called Vatican City.
2. Understand why there are divisions between northern and southern Italy.

Ancient Rome
Length: 4 minutes, 37 seconds
Describes the daily lives and achievements of the Romans.

 **Section 5**

Germany: A Unified Nation
1. Learn about Germany's past.
2. Find out how Germany became reunited.

Germany: The Berlin Wall
Length: 4 minutes, 22 seconds
Discusses the history of the Berlin Wall.

 # Technology Resources

 **PHSchool.com**

Students use embedded Web codes to access Internet activities, chapter self-tests, and additional map practice. They may also access Dorling Kindersley's Online Desk Reference to learn more about each country they study.

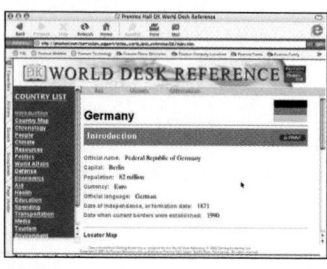

 **Interactive Textbook**

Use the Interactive Textbook to make content and concepts come alive through animations, videos, and activities that accompany the complete basal text—online and on CD-ROM.

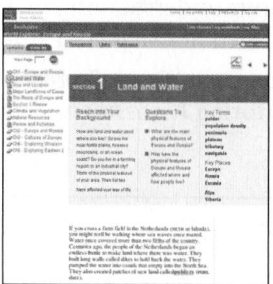

 PRENTICE HALL **TeacherEXPRESS** Plan · Teach · Assess

Use this complete suite of powerful teaching tools to make planning lessons and administering tests quicker and easier.

Reading and Vocabulary Instruction

🔊 Model the Target Reading Skill

Context Understanding how to derive meaning from context clues can help students become more confident and better readers. Learning the importance of context allows students to see patterns between terms and understand larger concepts.

Model using context clues by thinking aloud about the following selection from p. 267. Begin by writing the selection on the board.

The United Kingdom has many strong industries, or businesses. For example, it has good supplies of fossil fuels—especially oil from deposits beneath the North Sea. It also continues to export many manufactured goods, such as clothing and electronic products.

Think aloud: "The first sentence uses the word *industries*. I think this is an important word, but I'm not completely sure of its meaning. The word *or* comes after the word *industries*. This is a clue that a definition might follow. Reading ahead, I see that *industries* means *businesses*. Why are the United Kingdom's industries strong? I will underline the items in the next two sentences that give me clues. (*underline* good supplies of fossil fuels *and* export many manufactured goods) By looking at the context, I was able to determine that the United Kingdom has strong businesses because a great deal of goods are manufactured for export, and a large amount of fossil fuel is found there."

Use the following worksheets from All-in-One Europe and Russia Teaching Resources (pp. 277–279) to support the chapter's Target Reading Skill.

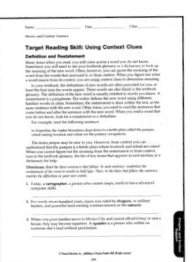 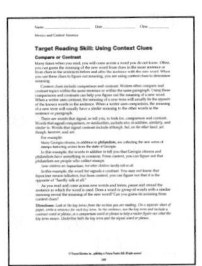 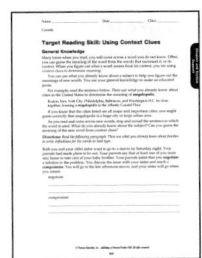

Vocabulary Builder
High-Use Academic Words

Use these steps to teach this chapter's high-use words:

1. Have students rate how well they know each word on their Word Knowledge worksheets (All-in-One Europe and Russia Teaching Resources, p. 280).
2. Pronounce each word and ask students to repeat it.
3. Give students a brief definition or sample sentence (provided on TE pp. 261, 269, 277, 284, and 293).
4. Work with students as they fill in the "Definition or Example" column of their Word Knowledge worksheets.

Assessment

Formal Assessment

Test students' understanding of core knowledge and skills.

Chapter Tests A and B, All-in-One Europe and Russia Teaching Resources, pp. 300–305

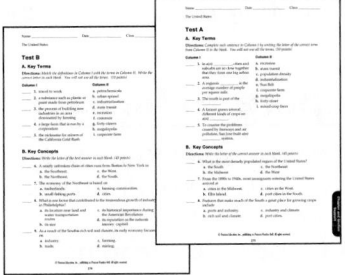

Customize the Chapter Tests to suit your needs.

ExamView Test Bank CD-ROM

Skills Assessment

Assess geographic literacy.

MapMaster Skills, Student Edition, pp. 249, 261, 293, 300

Country Profile Map and Chart Skills, Student Edition, pp. 262, 272, 278, 285, 294

Assess reading and comprehension.

Target Reading Skills, Student Edition, pp. 263, 274, 280, 286, 296 and in Section Assessments

Chapter 9 Assessment, Eastern Hemisphere Reading and Vocabulary Study Guide, p. 107

Performance Assessment

Assess students' performance on this chapter's Writing Activities using the following rubrics from All-in-One Europe and Russia Teaching Resources.

Rubric for Assessing a Writing Assignment, p. 298

Rubric for Assessing a Journal Entry, p. 299

Assess students' work through performance tasks.

Small Group Activity: Comparing Types of Government, All-in-One Europe and Russia Teaching Resources, pp. 283–286

Portfolio Activity, Teacher Edition, p. 121

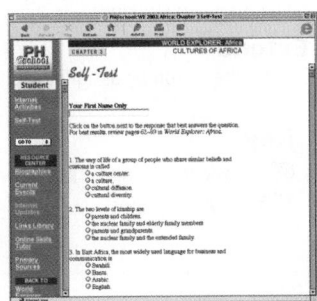

Online Assessment

Have students check their own understanding.

Chapter Self-Test

Section 1 The United Kingdom: Democracy and Monarch

⏱ *2 periods, 1 block (includes Country Databank)*

Social Studies Objectives
1. Examine the regions that make up the United Kingdom.
2. Learn about the United Kingdom's democratic heritage.
3. Find out how the United Kingdom combines democracy and monarchy.
4. Understand why trade is important to the United Kingdom.

Reading/Language Arts Objective
Use context clues to clarify unfamiliar words and ideas.

Prepare to Read

Build Background Knowledge
Ask students to discuss words having to do with the United Kingdom's government.

Set a Purpose for Reading
Have students begin to fill out the *Reading Readiness Guide*.

Preview Key Terms
Teach the section's Key Terms.

Target Reading Skill
Introduce the section's Target Reading Skill of **using context clues**.

Instructional Resources

All in One Europe and Russia Teaching Resources
- **L2** Reading Readiness Guide, p. 258
- **L2** Use Context Clues: Definition and Description, p. 277

Differentiated Instruction

Spanish Reading and Vocabulary Study Guide
- **L1** Chapter 9, Section 1, pp. 66–67 ELL

World Studies Video Program
- **L2** The Geography of Western Europe AR, GT, LPR, SN

Instruct

Regions of the United Kingdom
Discuss the formation of Great Britain.

Country Profile
Ask students to derive information from maps, charts, and graphs.

Target Reading Skill
Review **using context clues**.

A Democratic Heritage
Discuss democracy in the United Kingdom.

A Changing Monarchy
Discuss aspects of the British constitution.

The Importance of Trade
Discuss trade and colonies.

Instructional Resources

All in One Europe and Russia Teaching Resources
- **L2** Guided Reading and Review, p. 259
- **L2** Reading Readiness Guide, p. 258
- **L2** Reading a Circle Graph, p. 287

Europe and Russia Transparencies
- **L2** Section Reading Support Transparency ER 43

World Studies Video Program
- **L2** Great Britain: London Fog and Suburbia

Differentiated Instruction

All in One Europe and Russia Teaching Resources
- Rubric for Assessing a Writing Assignment, p. 298 AR, GT, LPR, SN
- **L3** Enrichment, p. 281 AR, GT

Teacher's Edition
- **L3** Gifted and Talented, p. 256
- **L3** For Advanced Readers, TE pp. 256, 264
- **L1** For Less Proficient Readers, TE p. 264
- **L1** For English Language Learners, TE p. 265

Student Edition on Audio CD
- **L1** Chapter 9, Section 1 ELL, LPR, SN

Spanish Support
- **L2** Guided Reading and Review (Spanish), p. 86 ELL

Assess and Reteach

Assess Progress
Evaluate student comprehension with the section assessment and section quiz.

Reteach
Assign the Reading and Vocabulary Study Guide to help struggling students.

Extend
Extend the lesson by assigning a Small Group Activity.

Instructional Resources

All in One Europe and Russia Teaching Resources
- **L2** Section Quiz, p. 260
- **L3** Small Group Activity: Comparing Types of Government, pp. 283–286

Reading and Vocabulary Study Guide
- **L1** Chapter 9, Section 1, pp. 92–94

Differentiated Instruction

Spanish Support
- **L2** Section Quiz (Spanish), p. 87 ELL

Key
L1 Basic to Average	**L3** Average to Advanced	
L2 For All Students		

LPR Less Proficient Readers   GT Gifted and Talented
AR Advanced Readers   ELL English Language Learners
SN Special Needs Students

Section 2 France: Cultural Heritage and Diversity

 1.5 periods, .75 block

Social Studies Objectives

1. Find out why the French take pride in their traditional culture.
2. Learn about growing cultural diversity in France.

Reading/Language Arts Objective

Use context clues to understand new words.

Prepare to Read	Instructional Resources	Differentiated Instruction
Build Background Knowledge Have students learn about France using the Passport to the World CD-ROM. **Set a Purpose for Reading** Have students begin to fill out the *Reading Readiness Guide*. **Preview Key Terms** Teach the section's Key Terms. **Target Reading Skill** Introduce the section's Target Reading Skill of **using context clues**.	**All in One Europe and Russia Teaching Resources** L2 Reading Readiness Guide, p. 262 L2 Use Context Clues: Compare and Contrast p. 278 **Passport to the World CD-ROM** L2 France	**Spanish Reading and Vocabulary Study Guide** L1 Chapter 9, Section 2, pp. 68–69 ELL

Instruct	Instructional Resources	Differentiated Instruction
Pride in French Culture Discuss various aspects of French culture. **Country Profile** Ask students to derive information from maps, charts, and graphs. **Diversity in France** Discuss how other cultures have influenced that of France. **Target Reading Skill** Review **using context clues**.	**All in One Europe and Russia Teaching Resources** L2 Guided Reading and Review, p. 263 L2 Reading Readiness Guide, p. 262 L2 Reading a Table, p. 288 **Europe and Russia Transparencies** L2 Section Reading Support Transparency ER 44 **World Studies Video Program** L2 France: The Rise of Napoleon Bonaparte	**Teacher's Edition** L3 For Gifted and Talented, TE p. 270 L3 For Advanced Readers, TE p. 274 **Spanish Support** L2 Guided Reading and Review (Spanish), p. 88 ELL

Assess and Reteach	Instructional Resources	Differentiated Instruction
Assess Progress Evaluate student comprehension with the section assessment and section quiz. **Reteach** Assign the Reading and Vocabulary Study Guide to help struggling students. **Extend** Extend the lesson by assigning a research project.	**All in One Europe and Russia Teaching Resources** L2 Section Quiz, p. 264 Rubric for Assessing a Writing Assignment, p. 298 **Europe and Russia Transparencies** L3 Color Transparency 24: The Cathedral at Reims L3 Color Transparency 25: The Cathedral at Reims: Interior **Reading and Vocabulary Study Guide** L1 Chapter 9, Section 2, pp. 95–97	**Spanish Support** L2 Section Quiz (Spanish), p. 89 ELL

Key

L1 Basic to Average	**L3** Average to Advanced	**LPR** Less Proficient Readers	**GT** Gifted and Talented
L2 For All Students		**AR** Advanced Readers	**ELL** English Language Learners
		SN Special Needs Students	

Section 3 Sweden: A Welfare State

 1.5 periods, .75 block

Social Studies Objectives
1. Learn about Sweden's welfare state.
2. Find out how Sweden became a welfare state.
3. Examine possible solutions to Sweden's economic problems.

Reading/Language Arts Objective
Learn to use context clues to determine how familiar words are being used in the text.

Prepare to Read	Instructional Resources	Differentiated Instruction
Build Background Knowledge Ask students to discuss benefits the government provides. **Set a Purpose for Reading** Have students evaluate statements on the *Reading Readiness Guide*. **Preview Key Terms** Teach the section's Key Terms. **Target Reading Skill** Introduce the section's Target Reading Skill of **using context clues**.	**All in One Europe and Russia Teaching Resources** L2 Reading Readiness Guide, p. 266 L2 Use Context Clues: General Knowledge, p. 279	**Spanish Reading and Vocabulary Study Guide** L1 Chapter 9, Section 3, pp. 70–71 ELL

Instruct	Instructional Resources	Differentiated Instruction
A Welfare State Discuss the welfare system in Sweden. **Country Profile** Ask students to derive information from maps, charts, and graphs. **Building a Welfare State** Discuss change in Sweden during the 1800s and 1900s and the way the country became a welfare state. **Target Reading Skill** Review **using context clues**. **Problems and Solutions** Discuss challenges that Sweden's government and businesses faced in the late 1900s.	**All in One Europe and Russia Teaching Resources** L2 Guided Reading and Review, p. 267 L2 Reading Readiness Guide, p. 266 L2 Reading a Line Graph, p. 289 **Europe and Russia Transparencies** L2 Section Reading Support Transparency ER 45 **World Studies Video Program** L2 Sweden: Land of Forests	**Teacher's Edition** L1 For Special Needs Students, TE p. 280 L3 For Gifted and Talented, TE p. 280 **Europe and Russia Transparencies** L3 Transparency B5: Flow Chart AR, GT **Student Edition on Audio CD** L1 Chapter 9, Section 3 ELL, LPR, SN **Spanish Support** L2 Guided Reading and Review (Spanish), p. 90 ELL

Assess and Reteach	Instructional Resources	Differentiated Instruction
Assess Progress Evaluate student comprehension with the section assessment and section quiz. **Reteach** Assign the Reading and Vocabulary Study Guide to help struggling students. **Extend** Extend the lesson by assigning a literature excerpt.	**All in One Europe and Russia Teaching Resources** L2 Section Quiz, p. 268 L3 The Boy, pp. 292–295 Rubric for Assessing a Writing Assignment, p. 298 **Reading and Vocabulary Study Guide** L1 Chapter 9, Section 3, pp. 98–100	**Spanish Support** L2 Section Quiz (Spanish), p. 91 ELL

Key

L1 Basic to Average   L3 Average to Advanced   LPR Less Proficient Readers   GT Gifted and Talented

L2 For All Students   AR Advanced Readers   ELL English Language Learners

SN Special Needs Students

Section 4 Italy: Northern and Southern Divisions

 *2.5 periods, 1.25 blocks (includes Skills for Life)*

Social Studies Objectives
1. Discover that there is another country within Italy called Vatican City.
2. Understand why there are divisions between northern and southern Italy.

Reading/Language Arts Objective
Use what you already know about an unfamiliar word to confirm information given in context clues.

Prepare to Read

Build Background Knowledge
Show a video and discuss the Roman influence in Italy today.

Set a Purpose for Reading
Have students evaluate statements on the *Reading Readiness Guide*.

Preview Key Terms
Teach the section's Key Terms.

Target Reading Skill
Introduce the section's Target Reading Skill of **using context clues.**

Instructional Resources

All in One Europe and Russia Teaching Resources
- L2 Reading Readiness Guide, p. 270
- L2 Use Context Clues: General Knowledge, p. 279

World Studies Video Program
- L2 Ancient Rome

Differentiated Instruction

Spanish Reading and Vocabulary Study Guide
- L1 Chapter 9, Section 4, pp. 72–73 ELL

Instruct

Target Reading Skill
Review **using context clues.**

Vatican City
Discuss Vatican City.

Country Profile
Ask students to derive information from maps, charts, and graphs.

Divisions Between North and South
Discuss the differences between northern and southern Italy and the challenges they face.

Instructional Resources

All in One Europe and Russia Teaching Resources
- L2 Guided Reading and Review, p. 271
- L2 Reading Readiness Guide, p. 270
- L2 Reading a Bar Graph, p. 290

Europe and Russia Transparencies
- L2 Transparency B16: Venn Diagram
- L2 Section Reading Support Transparency ER 46

Differentiated Instruction

All in One Europe and Russia Teaching Resources
- L2 Skills for Life, p. 282 AR, GT, LPR, SN

Teacher's Edition
- L1 For Special Needs Students, TE p. 285
- L3 For Advanced Readers, TE p. 286
- L1 For English Language Learners, TE p. 288

Europe and Russia Transparencies
- L1 Transparency B17: Concept Web ELL

PHSchool.com
- L3 For: Long-Term Integrated Projects: Keeping a Scrapbook of Daily Life Around the World AR, GT
  Web Code: ldd-7406

Assess and Reteach

Assess Progress
Evaluate student comprehension with the section assessment and section quiz.

Reteach
Assign the Reading and Vocabulary Study Guide to help struggling students.

Extend
Extend the lesson by assigning an online activity.

Instructional Resources

All in One Europe and Russia Teaching Resources
- L2 Section Quiz, p. 272
  Rubric for Assessing a Writing Assignment, p. 298

Reading and Vocabulary Study Guide
- L1 Chapter 9, Section 4, pp. 101–103

PHSchool.com
- L3 For: Environmental and Global Issues: Urban Population, Past and Projected
  Web Code: ldd-7407

Differentiated Instruction

Spanish Support
- L2 Section Quiz (Spanish), p. 93 ELL

Teacher's Edition
- L1 For Less Proficient Readers, TE p. 291

Social Studies Skills Tutor CD-ROM
- L1 Transferring Information from One Medium to Another ELL, LPR, SN

Key
- **L1** Basic to Average
- **L3** Average to Advanced
- **L2** For All Students
- **LPR** Less Proficient Readers
- **AR** Advanced Readers
- **SN** Special Needs Students
- **GT** Gifted and Talented
- **ELL** English Language Learners

Section 5 Germany: A Unified Nation

 3.5 periods, 1.75 blocks (includes Chapter Review and Assessment)

Social Studies Objectives
1. Learn about Germany's past.
2. Find out how Germany became reunited.

Reading/Language Arts Objective
Learn to use context clues in several paragraphs to determine the meaning of an unfamiliar word.

Prepare to Read	Instructional Resources	Differentiated Instruction
Build Background Knowledge Discuss the concept of the Berlin Wall with students. **Set a Purpose for Reading** Have students begin to fill out the *Reading Readiness Guide*. **Preview Key Terms** Teach the section's Key Terms. **Target Reading Skill** Introduce the section's Target Reading Skill of **using context clues**.	**All in One Europe and Russia Teaching Resources** **L2** Reading Readiness Guide, p. 274 **L2** Use Context Clues: Definition and Description, p. 277	**Spanish Reading and Vocabulary Study Guide** **L1** Chapter 9, Section 5, pp. 74–75 ELL

Instruct	Instructional Resources	Differentiated Instruction
Germany's Past Discuss World War I, World War II, the Cold War, and the fall of the Berlin Wall in Germany. **Country Profile** Ask students to derive information from maps, charts, and graphs. **Target Reading Skill** Review **using context clues**. **Germany Reunited** Discuss the effects of the fall of the Berlin Wall on Germany.	**All in One Europe and Russia Teaching Resources** **L2** Guided Reading and Review, p. 275 **L2** Reading Readiness Guide, p. 274 **L2** Reading a Timeline, p. 291 **Europe and Russia Transparencies** **L2** Section Reading Support ER Transparency 47 **World Studies Video Program** **L2** Germany: The Berlin Wall	**Teacher's Edition** **L3** For Gifted and Talented, TE p. 294 **L1** For English Language Learners, TE p. 296 **L1** For Less Proficient Readers, TE p. 297 **Europe and Russia Transparencies** **L1** Color Transparency ER Set 1: Europe Today With Eastern Europe Updated ELL, LPR, SN **PHSchool.com** **L3** **For:** Environmental and Global Issues: The Universal Declaration of Human Rights AR, GT **Web Code:** ldd-7408

Assess and Reteach	Instructional Resources	Differentiated Instruction
Assess Progress Evaluate student comprehension with the section assessment and section quiz. **Reteach** Assign the Reading and Vocabulary Study Guide to help struggling students. **Extend** Extend the lesson by assigning a research project.	**All in One Europe and Russia Teaching Resources** **L2** Section Quiz, p. 276 **L3** Writing to Inform and Explain, p. 296 Rubric for Assessing a Journal Entry, p. 299 **L2** Vocabulary Development, p. 297 **L2** Word Knowledge, p. 280 **L2** Chapter Tests A and B, pp. 300–305 **Reading and Vocabulary Study Guide** **L1** Chapter 9, Section 5, pp. 104–106	**Spanish Support** **L2** Section Quiz (Spanish), p. 95 ELL **L2** Chapter Summary (Spanish), p. 96 ELL **L2** Vocabulary Development (Spanish), p. 97 ELL

Key
L1 Basic to Average **L3** Average to Advanced
L2 For All Students

LPR Less Proficient Readers
AR Advanced Readers
SN Special Needs Students

GT Gifted and Talented
ELL English Language Learners

Reading Background

Summarizing

Research shows that summarizing can help students comprehend and recall text. Use the following steps to model how to write a one-sentence summary using the following paragraph from p. 279 of the Student Edition:

1. Write the selection on the board, and read it aloud to students.
2. Underline the important ideas:

   Swedish people believe that welfare benefits are very important. They are willing to pay the highest taxes in Europe in order to have these benefits. Swedes pay as much as 60 percent of their income in taxes. Food is taxed at 12 percent. Clothing and other goods are taxed at 25 percent. _But in exchange for these high taxes, all Swedes have financial security._

3. Show how to combine these ideas into one sentence.

(Swedish people are willing to pay taxes for welfare benefits in exchange for financial security.)

Seed Discussions

Give students the opportunity to lead their own discussions about what they are reading in the chapter. Tell students that in order to lead a discussion with their classmates, they will need a strong "seed" to start with. Have the class list ideas for strong seeds, such as questions or opinions about what they have learned, or things in the chapter that surprised them.

Model a strong seed versus a weak seed. A strong seed might be an opinion, such as: "I believe the fall of the Berlin Wall was good for Germany." A weak seed might be a restatement of fact, such as: "Hitler was the dictator of Germany."

Once students are comfortable with the concept of a strong seed, have each student write a seed on a sheet of paper. Then have students form small groups. In the groups, each person should take a turn leading a discussion from the seed he or she has written. Divide time equally so every person gets an equal opportunity to lead the discussion.

World Studies Background

The Chunnel

Although France and England are separated by the English Channel, they are now connected by the Channel Tunnel (often called "the Chunnel"). This tunnel consists of three passages: two are for trains and their passengers, and one is for maintenance and ventilation. Train service began in 1994. The train ride between Folkestone, England and Calais, France takes about 35 minutes.

Brittany

Before the Chunnel, history connected England and France. The Bretons, a Celtic people who lived in England, were driven out of England by the Anglo-Saxon invasion in the A.D. 400s and 500s. They settled in the northwest part of France, called Brittany. Brittany fought for independence, but was integrated into France in 1532. The Breton language is still spoken in some areas.

Swedish Holidays

Many people in Sweden celebrate St. Lucia day on December 13, in honor of the saint also known as St. Lucy. Traditionally on this day, the oldest daughter in the family wears a white robe and a candle-lit wreath on her head and serves pastries to her family. People also celebrate with parades and bonfires. On Midsummer Day, the longest day of the year, many Swedes celebrate by singing and dancing around a May pole.

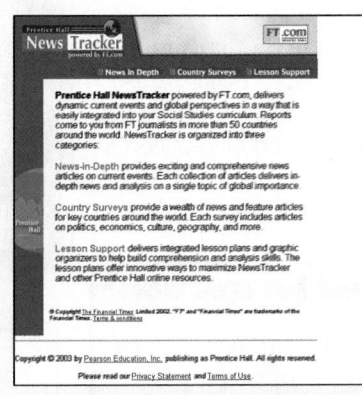

Get in-depth information on topics of global importance with **Prentice Hall Newstracker,** powered by FT.com.

 Use Web code **ldd-7400** for **Prentice Hall Newstracker.**

Chapter 9

Guiding Questions

Remind students about the Guiding Questions at the beginning of this section.

Section 1 relates to **Guiding Question 4** **What types of government have existed in Europe and Russia?** *(The United Kingdom is a constitutional monarchy.)*

Section 2 relates to **Guiding Question 3** **How have the people of Europe and Russia been shaped by their culture?** *(The French have made important contributions to the arts, architecture, food, philosophy, and fashion.)*

Section 3 relates to **Guiding Question 5** **How have Russian and European economies developed into what they are today?** *(Economic problems led to the establishment of Sweden's modern welfare programs.)*

Section 4 relates to **Guiding Question 2** **How have Europe and Russia been affected by their history?** *(Roman Catholicism has been a strong influence on Italy.)*

Section 5 relates to **Guiding Question 2** **How have Europe and Russia been shaped by their history?** *(Germany was divided into two countries after World War II; they were reunited in 1990.)*

Target Reading Skill

In this chapter, students will learn to use context clues. Use the following worksheets to help students practice this skill:

All in One **Europe and Russia Teaching Resources,** *Use Context Clues: Definition and Description,* p. 277; *Use Context Clues: Compare or Contrast,* p. 278; *Use Context Clues: General Knowledge,* p. 279

Differentiated Instruction

The following Teacher Edition strategies are suitable for students of varying abilities.

Advanced Readers, pp. 256, 264, 274, 286
English Language Learners, pp. 265, 288, 296
Gifted and Talented, pp. 256, 270, 280, 294
Less Proficient Readers, pp. 264, 281, 297
Special Needs Students, pp. 280, 285

Chapter 9 Western Europe

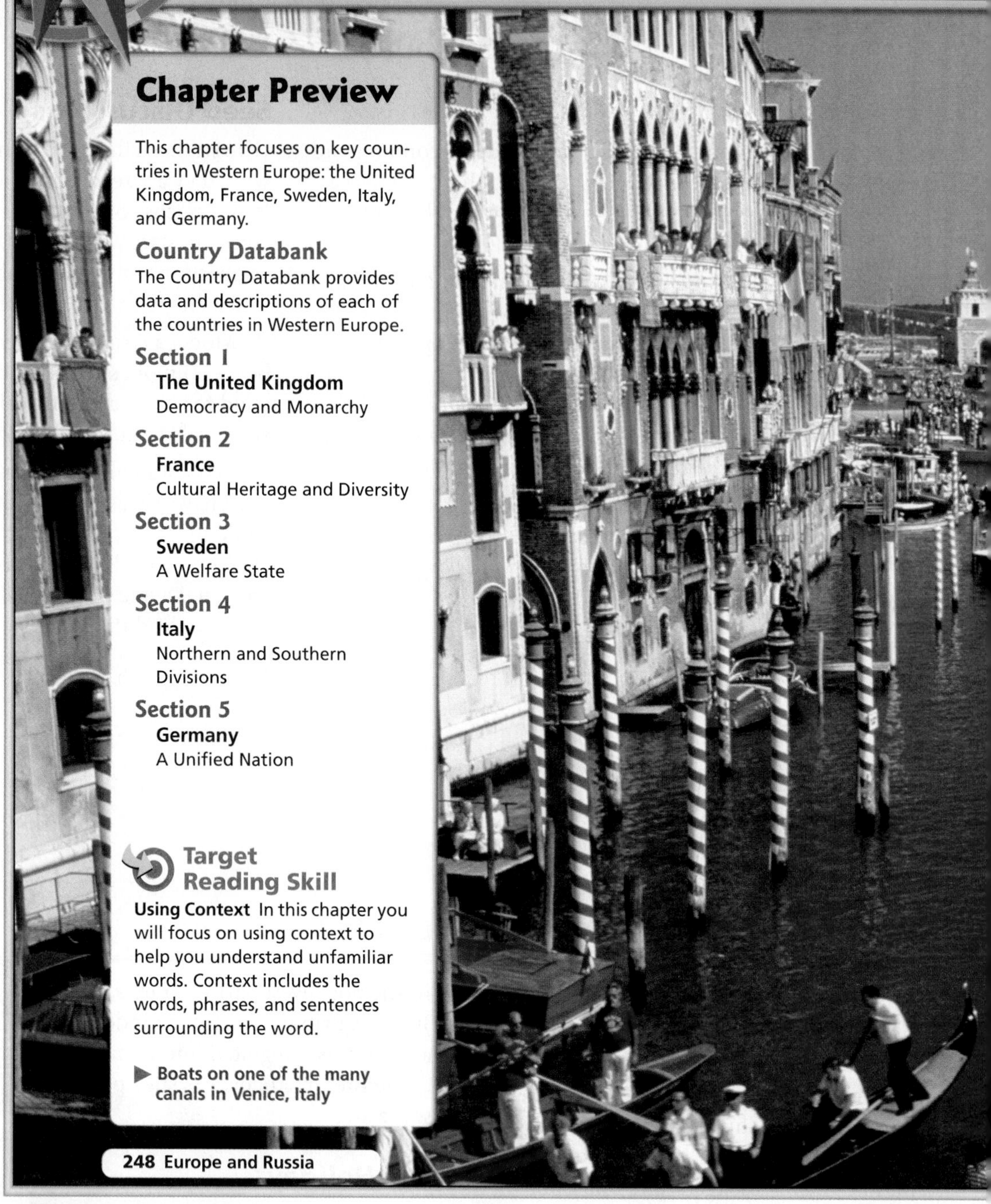

Chapter Preview

This chapter focuses on key countries in Western Europe: the United Kingdom, France, Sweden, Italy, and Germany.

Country Databank

The Country Databank provides data and descriptions of each of the countries in Western Europe.

Section 1
The United Kingdom
Democracy and Monarchy

Section 2
France
Cultural Heritage and Diversity

Section 3
Sweden
A Welfare State

Section 4
Italy
Northern and Southern Divisions

Section 5
Germany
A Unified Nation

Target Reading Skill

Using Context In this chapter you will focus on using context to help you understand unfamiliar words. Context includes the words, phrases, and sentences surrounding the word.

▶ **Boats on one of the many canals in Venice, Italy**

Bibliography

For the Teacher

Cannon, John Ashton, ed. *The Oxford Companion to British History.* Oxford Press, 2003.

Hilton, Christopher. *The Wall: The People's Story.* Sutton Publishing, Limited, 2003.

Subervie, Maurice. *Paris in 500 Photos.* Flammarion, 2003.

For the Student

L1 Thomas, Keltie. *Sweden: The People.* Crabtree, 2003.

L2 Stanley, Diane. *Michelangelo.* HarperTrophy, 2003.

L3 Rochman, Hazel, ed. *Bearing Witness: Stories of the Holocaust.* Orchard Books, 1999.

248 Europe and Russia

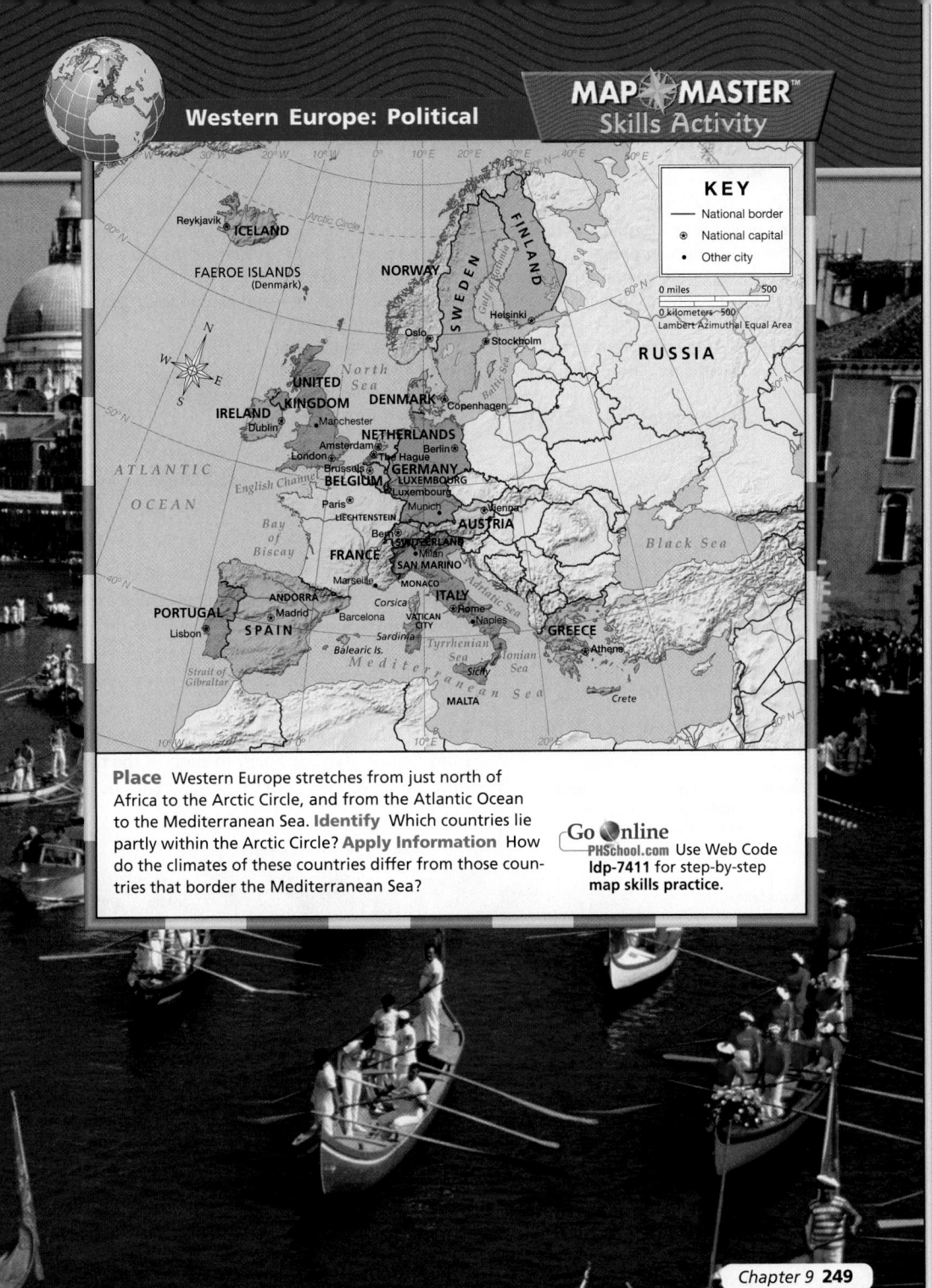

Western Europe: Political

MAP MASTER™
Skills Activity

KEY

— National border
⊙ National capital
• Other city

0 miles 500
0 kilometers 500
Lambert Azimuthal Equal Area

Reykjavik — ICELAND
FAEROE ISLANDS (Denmark)
NORWAY
SWEDEN
FINLAND
Arctic Circle
RUSSIA
Oslo
Stockholm
Helsinki
North Sea
UNITED KINGDOM
DENMARK
Copenhagen
IRELAND
Dublin
Manchester
NETHERLANDS
Amsterdam
The Hague
Berlin
London
Brussels
GERMANY
BELGIUM
LUXEMBOURG
Luxembourg
ATLANTIC OCEAN
English Channel
Paris
LIECHTENSTEIN
Munich
Vienna
AUSTRIA
Bern
SWITZERLAND
FRANCE
Milan
SAN MARINO
Bay of Biscay
Marseille
MONACO
Black Sea
Corsica
ITALY
Rome
PORTUGAL
ANDORRA
Madrid
Barcelona
VATICAN CITY
Naples
Lisbon
SPAIN
Sardinia
Balearic Is.
GREECE
Athens
Strait of Gibraltar
Sicily
Tyrrhenian Sea
Ionian Sea
Mediterranean Sea
MALTA
Crete
Adriatic Sea

Place Western Europe stretches from just north of Africa to the Arctic Circle, and from the Atlantic Ocean to the Mediterranean Sea. **Identify** Which countries lie partly within the Arctic Circle? **Apply Information** How do the climates of these countries differ from those countries that border the Mediterranean Sea?

Go Online
PHSchool.com Use Web Code ldp-7411 for step-by-step map skills practice.

MAP MASTER™
Skills Activity

Tell students to trace the outline of Western Europe with their fingertips. Point out that much of the region is bordered by either seas or oceans. Ask them to brainstorm how this fact may have affected the region. Use the Think-Write-Pair-Share strategy (TE, p. T36) to elicit responses.

Go Online
PHSchool.com Students may practice their maps skills using the interactive online version of this map.

Using the Visual   L2

Reach Into Your Background Direct students' attention to the caption accompanying the photo on pp. 248–249. Tell students that people in Venice use canals and bridges to travel within the city. Then ask **How does Venice differ from where you live? Are there any similarities?**

Answers

MAP MASTER™ Skills Activity **Identify** Russia, Norway, Sweden, and Finland lie partly within the Arctic Circle. Iceland lies very close to the circle's edge. **Apply Information** The climate is much colder within the Arctic Circle.

Chapter Resources

Teaching Resources
L2 Vocabulary Development, p. 297
L2 Skills for Life, p. 282
L2 Chapter Tests A and B, pp. 300–305

Spanish Support
L2 Spanish Chapter Summary, p. 96
L2 Spanish Vocabulary Development, p. 97

Media and Technology
L1 Student Edition on Audio CD
L1 Guided Reading Audiotapes, English and Spanish
L2 Social Studies Skills Tutor CD-ROM
ExamView Test Bank CD-ROM

PRENTICE HALL
Presentation EXPRESS™
Teach · Connect · Inspire

Teach this chapter's content using the PresentationExpress™ CD-ROM including:
■ slide shows
■ transparencies
■ interactive maps and media
■ *ExamView®* QuickTake Presenter

Objectives

- Look at the map on the previous page and then read the paragraphs to learn more about each nation.

- Analyze the data to compare the countries.

- Identify the characteristics that the countries of Western Europe share.

- Find out some of the key differences among the countries.

Show *The Geography of Western Europe.* Then ask **What are the four major geographic regions of Western Europe?** *(Northwestern Highlands, the Alpine Mountain system, the Central Uplands, and the European Plain)* **What are the major bodies of water?** *(Students may mention the Rhine River and the Mediterranean Sea.)*

Prepare to Read

Build Background Knowledge   L2

Write a list of the countries that students will be learning about across the top of the board. Then ask students what they already know about the countries listed. *(For example, students may say that France's capital is Paris, or that the United Kingdom is also sometimes referred to as Britain.)* Conduct an Idea Wave (TE, p. T35) to share students' answers, and add their responses under the name of the country on the board. Tell students that they will be learning more about these countries as they read the Country Databank.

Introducing Western Europe

Guide for Reading

This section provides an introduction to the 24 countries of Western Europe.

- Look at the map on the previous page and then read the paragraphs to learn about each nation.
- Analyze the data to compare the countries.
- What characteristics do most of these countries share?
- What are some key differences among the countries?

Viewing the Video Overview

View the World Studies Video Overview to learn more about each of the countries. As you watch, answer these questions:

- What are the four major geographic regions of Western Europe?
- What are the major bodies of water and why are they important?

Explore the geography of Western Europe.

Andorra

Capital	Andorra la Vella
Land Area	181 sq mi; 468 sq km
Population	68,403
Ethnic Group(s)	Spanish, Andorran, French, Portuguese
Religion(s)	Roman Catholic
Government	parliamentary democracy
Currency	euro
Leading Exports	tobacco products, furniture
Language(s)	Catalan (official), Spanish, French, Portuguese

The small country of Andorra (an DAWR uh) lies high in the eastern Pyrenees mountain range between France and Spain. France and Spain together ruled Andorra from the 1200s until the first full elections were held in 1993. Today, a 28-member legislature governs the country. Andorra's main source of income is its tourist industry. Most tourists come from France, Italy, or Spain to shop in the tax-free stores or to ski. Andorra's wealthiest citizens are its hotel owners.

The town of Andorra la Vella, Andorra

250 Europe and Russia

Austria

Capital	Vienna
Land Area	31,945 sq mi; 82,738 sq km
Population	8.2 million
Ethnic Group(s)	German, Croatian, Slovene, Hungarian, Czech, Slovak, Roma
Religion(s)	Roman Catholic, Protestant, Muslim, Jewish
Government	federal republic
Currency	euro
Leading Exports	machinery and equipment, motor vehicles and parts, paper and paper-board, metal goods, chemicals, iron and steel, textiles, foodstuffs
Language(s)	German (official), Croatian, Slovenian

Austria (AWS tree uh) borders several countries including the Czech Republic, Germany, Hungary, Italy, and Slovenia. In 1273, Austria came under the control of the Hapsburg Empire. Present-day Austria was established in 1918 after the fall of the Austro-Hungarian Empire during World War I. In 1938, Germany took control of Austria. Austria regained full independence 17 years later, in 1955. Having few natural resources, Austria imports large amounts of fossil fuels and energy from Russia.

A poster for the 1924 Commercial Fair in Brussels, Belgium

Belgium

Capital	Brussels
Land Area	11,672 sq mi; 30,230 sq km
Population	10.3 million
Ethnic Group(s)	Fleming, Walloon
Religion(s)	Roman Catholic, Protestant
Government	federal parliamentary democracy under a constitutional monarch
Currency	euro
Leading Exports	machinery and equipment, chemicals, diamonds, metals and metal products
Language(s)	Dutch (official), French (official), German (official)

Belgium (BEL jum) is a small country bordered by Germany, France, Luxembourg, and the Netherlands. It only takes about four hours to cross Belgium by car or by train. Belgium is one of the most densely populated countries in Europe. More than 95 percent of its citizens live in cities. The city of Antwerp is Belgium's main commercial center and Europe's second-largest port. Antwerp is important because Belgium has few natural resources and depends on the export of goods and services from other countries.

Denmark

Capital	Copenhagen
Land Area	16,368 sq mi; 42,394 sq km
Population	5.4 million
Ethnic Group(s)	Scandinavian, Inuit, Faeroe, Southwest Asian, Central Asian
Religion(s)	Protestant, Roman Catholic, Muslim
Government	constitutional monarchy
Currency	Danish krone
Leading Exports	machinery and instruments, meat and meat products, dairy products, fish, chemicals, furniture, ships, windmills
Language(s)	Danish (official)

Denmark (DEN mahrk) is the southernmost country in the region of northern Europe known as Scandinavia (skan duh NAY vee uh). Denmark contains many hundreds of islands, including self-governing Greenland. Greenland, located in the North Atlantic Ocean, is the world's largest island. Denmark itself is one of the flattest countries in the world. More than 65 percent of its land is used to raise crops. The North Atlantic current creates a damp but usually mild climate. These conditions help to make the region's farming profitable.

Chapter 9 **251**

Guided Instruction

- Read each country paragraph in the Databank as a class using the Choral Reading strategy (TE, p. T34). Then ask students to read through the data tables on pp. 250–251.

- Ask students **What are the leading exports of Andorra?** *(tobacco products, furniture)* **What is the country's official language?** *(Catalan)*

- Ask students **What exports are important in both Austria and Belgium?** *(machinery and equipment, metal goods and products, and chemicals)*

- Have students compare and contrast Denmark and Andorra's land area and population. *(At 16,368 square miles, Denmark's land area is much larger than Andorra's, at 181 square miles; Denmark's population is 5.4 million, while Andorra's is only 68,403.)*

- Ask students to discuss how Denmark's geography might influence the way land is used there. *(Denmark's flat land is probably one of the reasons farming is so important there.)*

- Point out the Religions data on pp. 252–253. Ask students **Which religions do almost all the countries on these pages share?** (*Roman Catholicism and Protestantism*)

- Ask students to compare the ethnic groups of France and Germany. Ask **Which ethnic group do they have in common?** (*German*) **Which ethnic groups are unique to France?** (*French, Breton, North African, Basque*) **Which are found only in Germany?** (*Turkish, Southeast Asian*)

- Ask students why they think Swedish is one of the official languages of Finland. (*Sweden borders Finland, so perhaps this is why many people speak Swedish there.*)

COUNTRY DATABANK

Introducing Western Europe

A brown bear in Lappi, Finland

Finland

Capital	Helsinki
Land Area	11,610 sq mi; 305,470 sq km
Population	5.2 million
Ethnic Group(s)	Finnish, Swedish, Sami, Roma, Tartar
Religion(s)	Protestant, Russian Orthodox
Government	republic
Currency	euro
Leading Exports	machinery and equipment, chemicals, metals, timber, paper, pulp
Language(s)	Finnish (official), Swedish (official), Sami

Bordered by Norway, Sweden, and Russia, Finland (FIN lund) is a low-lying country that can be divided into three geographic zones. There is a low-lying coastal strip in the south and west, where most of the cities are located. The interior of Finland is made up of vast forests and woodlands. This area also contains more than 60,000 lakes. Finland's third region is thinly wooded or barren and lies north of the Arctic Circle. The climate is extreme there. Temperatures fall well below zero degrees Fahrenheit during the six-month winter.

France

Capital	Paris
Land Area	210,668 sq mi; 545,630 sq km
Population	59.8 million
Ethnic Group(s)	French, North African, German, Breton, Basque
Religion(s)	Roman Catholic, Protestant, Jewish, Muslim
Government	republic
Currency	euro
Leading Exports	machinery and transportation equipment, aircraft, plastics, chemicals, pharmaceutical products, iron and steel, beverages
Language(s)	French (official), Provençal, German, Breton, Catalan, Basque

Located between the English Channel and the Mediterranean Sea, France (frans) is bordered by Italy, Switzerland, Germany, Belgium, and Spain. France has a long history of wars, invasions, and foreign occupations. Though it suffered great damage during both world wars, France is currently an economic leader among the nations of Europe. France helped to establish the European Union. It is the fourth-largest exporter in the world. Paris, the capital, is considered to be one of the world's great cultural centers.

252 Europe and Russia

Background: Global Perspectives

France and the New World French culture has had a significant influence on North America. The Canadian province of Quebec was originally founded by the French. Although later conquered by the British, Quebec was allowed to retain its French language and institutions. Today, many French-speaking Canadians feel that they might be better represented and their French traditions better preserved if Quebec broke away from Canada and formed its own country.

Germany

Capital	Berlin
Land Area	134,835 sq mi; 349,223 sq km
Population	83 million
Ethnic Group(s)	German, Turkish, Southeast Asian
Religion(s)	Protestant, Roman Catholic, Muslim
Government	federal republic
Currency	euro
Leading Exports	machinery, vehicles, chemicals, metals and manufactured goods, foodstuffs, textiles
Language(s)	German (official), Turkish

Germany (JUR muh nee) is located in Central Europe, with coastlines on the Baltic and North seas. It is bordered by nine countries, including France, Poland, and Austria. Germany was divided into two countries from 1949 to 1990. Today the country faces problems such as unemployment and an aging population. Germans are also still working to rebuild the former East Germany. However, Germany, an EU member, is now an economic leader. It is the second-largest exporter in the world. Germany's economy—based mainly on services and industry—is Europe's largest.

Greece

Capital	Athens
Land Area	50,502 sq mi; 130,800 sq km
Population	10.6 million
Ethnic Group(s)	Greek, Albanian, Turkish
Religion(s)	Eastern Orthodox, Muslim
Government	parliamentary republic
Currency	euro
Leading Exports	food and beverages, manufactured goods, petroleum products, chemicals, textiles
Language(s)	Greek (official), Turkish, Macedonian, Albanian

Greece (grees) is located in southern Europe. It is made up of the southern tip of the Balkan Peninsula and more than 2,000 islands. It is surrounded by the Aegean, Ionian, and Mediterranean seas. Greece's landscape is dominated by mountains and coastlines. Greece is famous for its ancient culture, which influenced the development of the modern world. Today, Greece is a member of the EU. However, it has one of the weakest economies in that organization. Efforts to strengthen the Greek economy have been slowed by government policies and conflicts with Greece's neighbors.

Iceland

Capital	Reykjavík
Land Area	38,707 sq mi; 100,250 sq km
Population	279,384
Ethnic Group(s)	Norse, Celtic
Religion(s)	Protestant, Roman Catholic
Government	constitutional republic
Currency	Icelandic króna
Leading Exports	fish and fish products, animal products, aluminum, diatomite, ferrosilicon
Language(s)	Icelandic (official)

Iceland (EYES lund) is an island in northern Europe, between the Greenland Sea and the North Atlantic Ocean. Located just south of the Arctic Circle, Iceland's climate is generally cold. However, the warm waters of the Gulf Stream keep its ports ice-free in the winter. Iceland's varied landscape includes volcanoes, glaciers, fjords, and hot springs. More than half the population of Iceland lives in or near Reykjavík, the capital city. Fishing is the country's largest industry. The people of Iceland enjoy a high standard of living and a strong economy.

Chapter 9 **253**

Guided Instruction (continued)

■ Ask **What is the capital of Germany?** *(Berlin)* **What is the capital of Greece?** *(Athens)*

■ Have students compare and contrast the geography and economies of Greece and Iceland. *(Geography—Much of both countries border the ocean; Greece is made up of the southern tip of the Balkan Peninsula and over 2,000 islands, while Iceland is a large island off the coast of northern Europe. Greece is closer to the Equator than Iceland. Economies—Greece's economy is relatively weak, while Iceland's is strong.)*

Guided Instruction (continued)

- Tell students that the countries on pp. 254–255 vary greatly in size. Have students read through the data tables to find the land area for each country. Then ask them to list the countries from largest to smallest. *(Italy, Ireland, Luxembourg, Malta, Liechtenstein, Monaco)*

- Ask students **Which country on these two pages has a land area less than one square mile?** *(Monaco)* Then ask **Are any countries in the Country Databank smaller than Monaco?** *(Vatican City is smaller than Monaco.)*

- Have students compare and contrast the religions and governments of Ireland and Italy. *(They are both republics, and both have Roman Catholics, but Ireland also has Protestants.)*

- Ask students to study Italy's leading exports. Then ask **What do these exports tell you about land use in Italy?** *(Possible answer: Much of the land is probably used for agriculture.)*

Introducing Western Europe

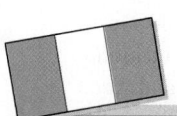

Ireland

Capital	Dublin
Land Area	26,598 sq mi; 68,890 sq km
Population	3.9 million
Ethnic Group(s)	Celtic, English
Religion(s)	Roman Catholic, Protestant
Government	republic
Currency	euro
Leading Exports	machinery and equipment, computers, chemicals, pharmaceuticals live animals, animal products
Language(s)	Irish Gaelic (official), English (official)

Ireland (EYER lund) is located in the North Atlantic Ocean off the west coast of Britain. It is an independent republic that occupies most of the island of Ireland. About one sixth of the island is Northern Ireland, which is part of the United Kingdom. Despite decades of violent conflict with Northern Ireland, Ireland's economy has grown at a remarkable rate in recent years. Its low taxes have brought in businesses from around the world. It is a member of the European Union and helped launch the euro currency. Often called the Emerald Isle, Ireland is known for its rolling green hills and mild, damp climate.

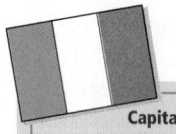

Italy

Capital	Rome
Land Area	113,521 sq mi; 294,020 sq km
Population	57.7 million
Ethnic Group(s)	Italian, Sardinian
Religion(s)	Roman Catholic
Government	republic
Currency	euro
Leading Exports	fruits, vegetables, grapes, potatoes, sugar beets, soybeans, grain, olives, beef, dairy products, fish
Language(s)	Italian (official), German, French, Rhaeto-Romanic, Sardinian

Italy (IT ul ee) is a peninsula in southern Europe. It lies in the Mediterranean Sea northeast of Tunisia. Italy also includes Sicily, Sardinia, and several other islands. Italy has a long and influential history. As the center of the Roman Empire, it was once a world leader. A system of law developed in Rome more than 2,000 years ago still influences law and citizenship in many countries today. Modern Italy became a democratic republic in 1946. Italy, a founding member of the European Union, has a strong economy based largely on manufacturing and industry.

Liechtenstein

Capital	Vaduz
Land Area	62 sq mi; 160 sq km
Population	32,842
Ethnic Group(s)	Alemannic, Italian, Southwest Asian
Religion(s)	Roman Catholic, Protestant
Government	hereditary constitutional monarchy
Currency	Swiss franc
Leading Exports	small specialty machinery, dental products, stamps, hardware, pottery
Language(s)	German (official), Alemannic dialect, Italian

Liechtenstein (LIK tun styn) is a small country in the Alps of central Europe, between Austria and Switzerland. Despite its small size, Liechtenstein has a strong free-enterprise economy and a high standard of living. It has a low tax rate, which attracts businesses from other countries. It also has many banks, with laws that protect international investors. Liechtenstein is closely tied to Switzerland, which provides the smaller country's defense. Liechtenstein uses Switzerland's franc as its national currency. Tourists visit Liechtenstein to ski, climb, and hike in the mountains.

254 Europe and Russia

Background: Links Across Time

The Cradle of Civilization The Mediterranean Sea is located between three continents — Africa, Asia, and Europe. The early civilizations of Egypt, Greece, and Phoenicia developed in the area surrounding the Mediterranean, which is often called the "cradle of civilization." By the first century A.D., the region was controlled by the Romans. The sea has a long history of trade; it was used by many early civilizations to transport goods between Asia and Europe. The Mediterranean declined as a trade route in the late fifteenth century with the establishment of an ocean route around Africa. However, much of the oil transported today from Southwest Asia to Europe crosses the Mediterranean Sea.

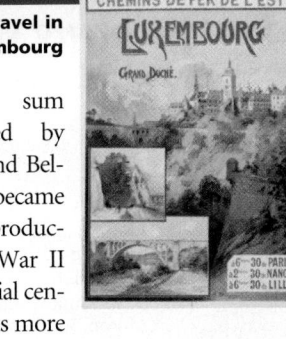
A 1900 poster for railroad travel in Luxembourg

Luxembourg

Capital	Luxembourg-Ville
Land Area	998 sq mi; 2,586 sq km
Population	448,569
Ethnic Group(s)	Celtic, French, German, Portuguese, Italian, Slavic
Religion(s)	Roman Catholic, Protestant, Jewish, Muslim
Government	constitutional monarchy
Currency	euro
Leading Exports	machinery and equipment, steel products, chemicals, rubber products, glass
Language(s)	French (official), German (official), Luxembourgish (official)

Luxembourg (LUK sum burg) is bordered by France, Germany, and Belgium. Luxembourg became wealthy from steel production before World War II and today is a financial center. Its capital city has more banks than any other city in the world. Luxembourg is also the home of important EU organizations. The people of Luxembourg enjoy high income, low unemployment, and few social problems. More than 90 percent of the population lives in cities. Tourists visit Luxembourg to see its forests, mountains, and historic castles.

Malta

Capital	Valletta
Land Area	122 sq mi; 316 sq km
Population	397,499
Ethnic Group(s)	Maltese
Religion(s)	Roman Catholic
Government	republic
Currency	Maltese lira
Leading Exports	machinery and transport equipment, manufactured goods
Language(s)	Maltese (official), English (official)

Malta (MAWL tuh) is a group of islands south of Italy in the Mediterranean Sea. Only three islands of this rocky archipelago are inhabited. Malta fell under British rule in 1814, and the United Kingdom defended Malta through World War I and World War II. In 1964, Malta gained its independence and ten years later became a republic. Since that time, Malta has become an important transportation port, financial center, and tourist destination. Economically, it depends on trade with other countries, manufacturing, and tourism. Malta has recently joined the European Union.

Monaco

Capital	Monaco
Land Area	0.75 sq mi; 1.95 sq km
Population	31,987
Ethnic Group(s)	French, Monégasque, Italian
Religion(s)	Roman Catholic
Government	constitutional monarchy
Currency	euro
Leading Exports	no information available
Language(s)	French (official), Italian, Monégasque, English

Monaco (MAHN uh koh) is located on the southeastern coast of France, bordering the Mediterranean Sea. In the late 1800s, Monaco was linked to France with a railroad. This event brought tourists and money to the small country. Since that time, Monaco has grown into a popular vacation destination for tourists seeking beautiful scenery, a pleasant climate, and shopping. The government is focused on developing other services and industries as well. Monaco has no income tax and low business taxes. However, the cost of living is high.

Chapter 9 **255**

Guided Instruction (continued)

- Ask students **Why is Monaco such a popular tourist spot?** (*It offers beautiful scenery, a pleasant climate, and shopping.*)

- Ask **What do Luxembourg and Liechtenstein have in common?** (*Their ethnic groups both include Italians; the Roman Catholic and Protestant religions are practiced in both; their governments are both constitutional monarchies; they both produce machinery; German is an official language in both.*)

Guided Instruction (continued)

- Have students read the data tables on pp. 256–259.

- Ask **What ethnic groups live in the Netherlands?** *(Dutch, Southwest Asian, North African, Southeast Asian, South American, West Indian)*

- Ask **Which of Norway's exports might be related to its long coastline?** *(ships, fish)*

- Ask students **What religion is practiced in all the countries on pp. 256–257?** *(Roman Catholicism)*

Introducing Western Europe

The Netherlands

Capitals	Amsterdam and The Hague
Land Area	13,082 sq mi; 33,883 sq km
Population	16.1 million
Ethnic Group(s)	Dutch, Southwest Asian, North African, Southeast Asian, South American, West Indian
Religion(s)	Roman Catholic, Protestant, Muslim
Government	constitutional monarchy
Currency	euro
Leading Exports	machinery and equipment, chemicals, fuels, foodstuffs
Language(s)	Dutch (official), Frisian

The Netherlands (NETH ur lundz) is located in northwest Europe between Belgium and Germany, bordering the North Sea. The country is also known by the name *Holland.* The Netherlands suffered through German invasion and occupation during World War II. Very active in international politics, the nation helped to form both NATO and the European Union. Stable relationships with other industrial countries help to keep its economy strong and growing. The Netherlands also serves as an important transportation center in Europe—particularly Rotterdam, on the Mans River.

Norway

Capital	Oslo
Land Area	118,865 sq mi; 307,860 sq km
Population	4.5 million
Ethnic Group(s)	Norwegian, Sami
Religion(s)	Protestant, Roman Catholic
Government	constitutional monarchy
Currency	Norwegian krone
Leading Exports	petroleum and petroleum products, machinery and equipment, metals, chemicals, ships, fish
Language(s)	Norwegian (official), Sami

Norway (NAWR way) is located in northern Europe west of Sweden. In 995, Norway's king converted to Christianity. He also ended two hundred years of Viking raids. In 1397, the nation became part of Denmark, and it remained so for more than four hundred years. The following two hundred years saw Norway gain independence, fall under Swedish rule, gain its independence again, fall under German rule, and regain its independence a third time, in 1945. In the 1960s, the discovery of oil and gas strengthened the Norwegian economy. Like Sweden, Norway has a mix of modern capitalism with many social welfare benefits, and has a very high standard of living. Norway has decided not to join the European Union.

A Sami man trains a reindeer to pull a sleigh.

Differentiated Instruction

For Advanced Readers [L3]

Have students scan the Country Databank for languages or ethnic groups they may not be familiar with, such as the Monégasque of Monaco, or the Sami language, spoken in Norway. Have students choose one of these languages or ethnic groups to research in the library or on the Internet. Ask students to write a one-page summary of their research, to be read aloud for the class.

For Gifted and Talented [L3]

Using a calculator, ask students to find the population density of each country in the Databank by dividing each country's population by its land area. Students should record the population density for each nation, then organize the information in a poster-sized chart, table, or bar graph. Allow students to explain to the class how they chose to organize their information.

Portugal

Capital	Lisbon
Land Area	35,502 sq mi; 91,951 sq km
Population	10.1 million
Ethnic Group(s)	Portuguese, African
Religion(s)	Roman Catholic, Protestant
Government	parliamentary democracy
Currency	euro
Leading Exports	clothing and footwear, machinery, chemicals, cork and paper products, hides
Language(s)	Portuguese (official)

Portugal (PAWR chuh gul) is located in southwestern Europe. It is west of Spain, bordered by the North Atlantic Ocean. Though Portugal is a fairly small country, it has played a major role in world history. From the 1400s to the 1600s, Portugal dominated the world sea trade. Portuguese explorers sailed the world, seeking wealth and colonies. They established colonies throughout the Americas and in Africa, some of which they ruled into the 1900s. Portugal became part of the European Union in 1986. Since then, the Portuguese economy has grown stronger, but a poor educational system is hindering greater growth.

San Marino

Capital	San Marino
Land Area	23.6 sq mi; 61.2 sq km
Population	27,730
Ethnic Group(s)	Sammarinese, Italian
Religion(s)	Roman Catholic
Government	independent republic
Currency	euro
Leading Exports	building stone, lime, wood, chestnuts, wheat, baked goods, hides, ceramics
Language(s)	Italian (official)

San Marino (sahn mah REE noh) is located in southern Europe, in the Italian Apennine Mountains. It is completely surrounded by the nation of Italy. San Marino is the third-smallest country in Europe and claims to be the world's oldest republic. It has remained independent since around A.D. 300. San Marino's political and social trends are similar to those of Italy. The tourist industry is extremely important to San Marino. Other industries include banking, clothing, electronics, ceramics, and cheese-making. San Marino enjoys a standard of living similar to the wealthiest areas of Italy.

Spain

Capital	Madrid
Land Area	192,873 sq mi; 499,542 sq km
Population	40.1 million
Ethnic Group(s)	Castilian Spanish, Catalan, Galician, Basque, Roma
Religion(s)	Roman Catholic
Government	parliamentary monarchy
Currency	euro
Leading Exports	machinery, motor vehicles, foodstuffs, other consumer goods
Language(s)	Spanish (official), Galician (official), Catalan (official), Basque (official)

Spain (spayn) is located in southwestern Europe between Portugal and France. It has coasts on the North Atlantic Ocean, the Mediterranean Sea, and the Bay of Biscay. Spain was a powerful world empire in the 1500s and 1600s. However, Spain's economy did not industrialize as quickly in later centuries as did other Western European countries such as Britain, Germany, and France. Spain was neutral during World War I and World War II but suffered through its own civil war in the 1930s. Spain joined the EU in 1986, and was among the first countries to begin using the euro currency. The country's economy is generally strong, though high unemployment continues to be a problem.

Guided Instruction (continued)

■ Ask students **Why do you think the official language of San Marino is Italian?** (*Possible answer: San Marino is completely surrounded by Italy, so Italy has probably had a strong influence on its culture.*)

■ Have students compare the information given about San Marino and Italy. Ask **What other characteristics do they have in common?** (*Their ethnic groups both include Italian, their religions both include Roman Catholicism, they are both republics, and they both use the euro.*)

■ Have students compare and contrast the populations, languages, and governments of Portugal and Spain. (*Portugal has 10.1 million people, while Spain has roughly four times as many; Portugal's official language is Portuguese, while Spain's four official languages are Spanish, Galician, Catalan, and Basque; Portugal is a parliamentary democracy, while Spain is a parliamentary monarchy.*)

Guided Instruction (continued)

- Have students compare and contrast the governments and political histories of Sweden and Switzerland. *(Sweden is a constitutional monarchy, while Switzerland is a federal republic. Both countries have maintained peace over time by not taking sides in wars.)*

- Ask students **What is the currency of Sweden?** *(the Swedish krona)* **What is the currency of the United Kingdom?** *(the pound sterling)*

- Have students describe how the United Kingdom has changed since the 1800s. *(In the 1800s, the United Kingdom was a growing empire with industrial and military strength. The nation was weakened by World War I and World War II, gradually withdrew from its colonies, and rebuilt itself to become a modern world power.)*

- Ask students **What characteristics make Vatican City different from the rest of the places you have learned about?** *(Vatican City is the smallest independent state in the world; it is an enclave of the city of Rome; its government is ecclesiastical and is headed by the pope; it has no exports; its economy is supported by a yearly tax on Catholics around the world.)*

Independent Practice

Explain to students that the euro is the monetary unit and currency of many of the nations of the European Union, and notes and coins began being used by participating countries in 2002. Have students make a list of the countries in Western Europe that use the euro, and another list of those that do not. Then ask students to write a paragraph explaining what they think the benefits of many countries having the same currency are, and think about why some countries have not adopted the euro. Use the *Rubric for Assessing a Writing Assignment* to review students' paragraphs.

All in One **Europe and Russia Teaching Resources,** *Rubric for Assessing a Writing Assignment,* p. 298

Monitor Progress

Circulate to make sure students are organizing their ideas appropriately.

Introducing Western Europe

Sweden

Capital	Stockholm
Land Area	158,662 sq mi; 410,934 sq km
Population	8.9 million
Ethnic Group(s)	Swedish, Finnish, Sami
Religion(s)	Protestant, Roman Catholic, Muslim, Jewish, Buddhist
Government	constitutional monarchy
Currency	Swedish krona
Leading Exports	machinery, motor vehicles, paper products, pulp and wood, iron and steel products, chemicals
Language(s)	Swedish (official), Finnish, Sami

Sweden (SWEED un) is located in northern Europe between Norway and Finland, bordering the Baltic Sea and the Gulf of Bothnia. Sweden has a high standard of living, with a mixture of modern capitalism and broad social welfare benefits. The nation joined the EU in 1995 but has not accepted the euro as its own currency. Beginning in the 1990s, Sweden faced high unemployment and other economic problems. However, with a population of skilled workers, rich resources, and a modern transportation system, Sweden's economy is still relatively strong. Sweden is one of the world's leaders in equal rights for women.

Swedish soccer player Malin Moestroem in 2003

Switzerland

Capital	Bern
Land Area	15,355 sq mi; 39,770 sq km
Population	7.3 million
Ethnic Group(s)	German, French, Italian, Romansch
Religion(s)	Roman Catholic, Protestant
Government	federal republic
Currency	Swiss franc
Leading Exports	machinery, chemicals, metals, watches, agricultural products
Language(s)	French (official), German (official), Italian (official), Swiss German, Romansch

Switzerland (SWIT sur lund) is located between France and Italy. It is the source of all four of the region's major river systems: the Po, the Rhine, the Rhône, and the Inn-Danube. Politically, Switzerland is famous for its neutrality. Switzerland is also economically neutral and has so far remained outside the European Union. Switzerland does, however, participate in international organizations, including the UN. This small, landlocked Alpine country has one of the strongest market economies in Europe. It is a center of international finance.

258 Europe and Russia

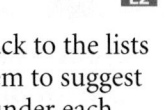

United Kingdom

Capital	London
Land Area	93,278 sq mi; 241,590 sq km
Population	59.8 million
Ethnic Group(s)	English, Scottish, Irish, Welsh, Ulster, West Indian, South Asian
Religion(s)	Protestant, Roman Catholic, Muslim
Government	constitutional monarchy
Currency	pound sterling
Leading Exports	manufactured goods, fuels, chemicals, food, beverages, tobacco
Language(s)	English (official), Welsh (official), Scottish Gaelic, Irish Gaelic

The United Kingdom (yoo NYT id KING dum) is made up of several islands lying northwest of France, between the North Atlantic Ocean and the North Sea. In the 1800s, the United Kingdom was an expanding empire with great industrial and military strength. However, World War I and World War II seriously weakened the nation. In the following decades, the United Kingdom withdrew from its colonies around the world. It then rebuilt itself into a modern world power. The United Kingdom is a founding member of NATO and one of the five permanent members of the UN Security Council. It is also a member of the European Union, although the British have not accepted the euro.

Vatican City

Capital	Vatican City
Land Area	0.17 sq mi; 0.44 sq km
Population	900
Ethnic Group(s)	Italian, Swiss, Polish
Religion(s)	Roman Catholic
Government	ecclesiastical
Currency	euro
Leading Exports	none
Language(s)	Latin (official), Italian (official)

Vatican City (VAT ih kun SIH tee), also known as the Holy See, is an enclave of Rome. This means it is entirely surrounded by Italy's capital city. The Vatican is the world's smallest independent state. It is the home of the pope, who is the leader of the Roman Catholic Church. The pope is also the head of the Vatican City government. The Vatican's unique economy is supported by donations from Roman Catholics around the world. It also earns income from investments and tourism.

SOURCES: DK World Desk Reference Online; CIA World Factbook Online, 2002; *The World Almanac*, 2003

Assessment

Comprehension and Critical Thinking

1. Compare and Contrast Which countries in the region are the largest and the smallest?

2. Make Generalizations What are some characteristics that many of the region's countries share?

3. Infer Which countries do not have any exports? Why might this be so?

4. Categorize What kinds of exports do many of the countries of Western Europe rely on?

5. Make a Circle Graph The total population of Western Europe is about 392 million. Find the Western European country with the largest population. Make a circle graph that shows this country's population as a percent of the population of Western Europe as a whole.

Keeping Current

Access the **DK World Desk Reference Online** at **PHSchool.com** for up-to-date information about the 24 countries in this region.

Go Online
PHSchool.com

Web Code: lde-7400

Assess Progress

- Direct students' attention back to the lists on the board. Encourage them to suggest more information to fill in under each head based on what they learned from the Country Databank.

- Ask students to answer the Assessment questions.

Reteach L1

Ask students to create a bar graph showing the populations of the countries of Western Europe. Have them display the countries in order, from the smallest population to the largest population. Remind them to label their information and give the graph a title.

Extend L3

Have students choose one country in the Country Databank. Ask students to learn more about one or two aspects of the country's culture, using the Internet or other reference sources. Have students create a poster explaining their topic and what they learned through their research to the class.

Answers

Assessment

1. France is the largest; Vatican City is the smallest.

2. Many countries in Western Europe use the euro; many share the Roman Catholic and Protestant religions; many are members of the European Union; many countries export machinery and equipment.

3. Monaco and Vatican City; probably because they are so small

4. machinery and equipment, motor vehicles and parts, paper, metals, chemicals, textiles, foodstuffs, ships, wood products, manufactured goods

5. Germany has the largest population in Western Europe, with 83 million. Students' graphs should show that Germany's population is about 21 percent of the total population of Western Europe.

Objectives

Social Studies
1. Examine the regions that make up the United Kingdom.
2. Learn about the United Kingdom's democratic heritage.
3. Find out how the United Kingdom combines democracy and monarchy.
4. Understand why trade is important to the United Kingdom.

Reading/Language Arts
Use context clues to clarify unfamiliar words and ideas.

Prepare to Read

Build Background Knowledge **L2**
Tell students that in this section, they will learn about the United Kingdom and its democratic heritage. Then write the following words on the board: *King, President, Parliament, Congress, Representative, Constitution,* and *Democracy.* Give students several minutes to write down what they think about when they see or hear these words. Then conduct an Idea Wave (TE, p. T35) to allow students to share their responses.

Set a Purpose for Reading **L2**
■ Preview the Objectives

■ Form students into pairs or groups of four. Distribute the *Reading Readiness Guide.* Ask students to fill in the first two columns of the chart. Use the Numbered Heads participation strategy (TE, p. T36) to call on students to share one piece of information they already know and one piece of information they want to know.

All in One Europe and Russia Teaching Resources, *Reading Readiness Guide,* p. 258

Vocabulary Builder
Preview Key Terms **L2**
Pronounce each Key Term, then ask students to say the word with you. Provide a simple explanation such as, "A country's constitution is its plan of government."

Prepare to Read

Objectives
In this section you will
1. Examine the regions that make up the United Kingdom.
2. Learn about the United Kingdom's democratic heritage.
3. Find out how the United Kingdom combines democracy and monarchy.
4. Understand why trade is important to the United Kingdom.

Taking Notes
As you read this section, look for important events that have taken place in British history. Copy the table below, and write each event in the correct time period.

Events in British History			
1500s	1700s	1800s	1900s

Target Reading Skill
Use Context Clues When reading, you may come across a word that is used in an unfamiliar way. Look for clues in the context—the surrounding words, sentences, and paragraphs—to help you understand the meaning. Sometimes the context will define the word. In the first paragraph below, for example, you know the words *crown* and *jewels,* but may not know what the term *crown jewels* means. The context of the second paragraph helps explain this term.

Key Terms
• **Parliament** (PAHR luh munt) *n.* the lawmaking body of the United Kingdom
• **representative** (rep ruh ZEN tuh tiv) *n.* a person who represents, or speaks for, a group of people
• **constitution** (kahn stuh TOO shun) *n.* a set of laws that describes how a government works
• **constitutional monarchy** (kahn stuh TOO shuh nul MAHN ur kee) *n.* a government in which a monarch is the head of state but has limited powers

A Beefeater in front of the Tower of London

260 Europe and Russia

The line of tourists seems to go on forever. People in the line are speaking English, French, Arabic, and Japanese. In all of these languages, the tourists are talking about the same thing: the British crown jewels.

The jewels are kept under guard in the Tower of London. The priceless collection includes crowns worn by the kings and queens of England. After a long wait, the tourists finally reach the amazing jewels. Their eyes widen at the sight of huge diamonds, bright-red rubies, and cool-blue sapphires.

British history can be felt everywhere in and around the Tower of London. Near the Tower, rebellious nobles met their deaths on the executioner's block. Young King Edward V and his brother were most likely murdered in the Tower of London. The Tower is watched over by guards called Beefeaters. No one knows for sure where this name came from. But Beefeaters in their colorful red uniforms have guarded the Tower for hundreds of years.

Target Reading Skill **L2**

Use Context Clues Point out the Target Reading Skill. Tell students that using context clues will help them determine the meaning of unfamiliar words or ideas in a text.

Model using context clues with the word *specific* from the first paragraph on p. 261. *(Since the paragraphs following the sentence explain that each name for the United King-*
dom has a slightly different meaning, students should be able to determine that specific *means "exact" or "particular.")*

Give students *Use Context Clues: Definition and Description.* Have them complete the activity in groups.

All in One Europe and Russia Teaching Resources, *Use Context Clues: Definition and Description,* p. 277

Regions of the United Kingdom

You may have heard people use different names for the nation located on the British Isles: England, Great Britain, and the United Kingdom. Each name has a specific meaning.

England England is a region within the United Kingdom. Find England on the map below. About two thousand years ago, Romans ruled over present-day England. After the Roman Empire fell, many small kingdoms arose. Over time, one of these kingdoms, Wessex, grew stronger than the others. By conquering other kingdoms, Wessex unified England into a single nation by the 800s.

Great Britain England grew in power and strength. Soon, it began to exert power over its neighbors, including Wales and Scotland. Wales officially became part of the English nation in the 1500s. By the early 1700s, England and Scotland had joined together. Now all of the nations on the island of Great Britain were united. The name of the nation changed to Great Britain.

Hadrian's Wall, built in about A.D.122 by the Roman emperor Hadrian, marked the northern boundary of the Roman Empire. It still stands today in northern England.

Regions of the United Kingdom

KEY
- England
- Great Britain
- United Kingdom
- National border

0 miles 200
0 kilometers 200
Lambert Azimuthal Equal Area

Map labels: Shetland Islands, Orkney Islands, Outer Hebrides, SCOTLAND, NORTHERN IRELAND, UNITED KINGDOM, IRELAND, Isle of Man, GREAT BRITAIN, WALES, ENGLAND, ATLANTIC OCEAN, Irish Sea, Celtic Sea, North Sea, Isle of Wight, English Channel

MAP MASTER™ Skills Activity

Regions The United Kingdom is a single nation made up of several smaller regions. **Identify** Which three regions do the islands called the Outer Hebrides belong to? **Compare and Contrast** How does the political structure of the United Kingdom compare to that of the United States?

Go Online
PHSchool.com Use Web Code ldp-7421 for step-by-step map skills practice.

Vocabulary Builder

Use the information below to teach students this section's high-use words.

High-Use Word	Definition and Sample Sentence
exert, p. 261	*v.* to apply Hiking requires one to **exert** great energy.
symbol, p. 264	*n.* something that represents or suggests another thing An olive branch is a **symbol** of peace.
finance, p. 267	*n.* the management of money matters The treasurer of our book club is in charge of **finance.**

Instruct

Regions of the United Kingdom   L2

Guided Instruction

- **Vocabulary Builder** Clarify the high-use word **exert** before reading.

- Read Regions of the United Kingdom, using the Structured Silent Reading strategy (TE, p. T34).

- Have students discuss the formation of Great Britain. (*England became a united nation by the 800s and began to exert power over its neighbors. Wales became a part of England in the 1500s, and Scotland joined later, in the 1700s, forming Great Britain.*)

- Discuss the Act of Union with students. Ask **Do you think Ireland was in favor of joining with Great Britain? Why or why not?** (*Answers will vary, but students should point out that the southern part of Ireland became an independent nation in the 1920s, and some Northern Irish groups seek to break away from Great Britain and join Ireland, which might indicate that the Irish did not want to join with Great Britain.*)

Independent Practice

Ask students to create the Taking Notes graphic organizer on a blank piece of paper. Then have them enter the details of important events in British history. Briefly model how to identify which details to include.

Monitor Progress

As students fill in the graphic organizer, circulate to make sure individuals are placing the events in the correct boxes. Provide assistance as needed.

Answers

MAP MASTER Skills Activity **Identify** Scotland **Compare and Contrast** Possible answer: Just as the United States is made up of fifty separate states, the United Kingdom is comprised of separate regions.

Go Online
PHSchool.com Students may practice their map skills using the interactive online version of this map.

Guided Instruction L2

Ask students to study the Country Profile on this page. As a class, answer the Map and Chart Skills questions. Allow students to briefly discuss their responses with a partner before sharing answers.

Independent Practice

Distribute *Reading a Circle Graph*. Have students work in pairs to complete the worksheet. Then direct their attention to the two circle graphs on this page. Ask **What is the percentage of mineral fuels exported from the United Kingdom?** *(6%)* **What is the percentage imported?** *(9%)*

All in One Europe and Russia Teaching Resources, *Reading a Circle Graph*, p. 287

COUNTRY PROFILE Focus on Economics

United Kingdom

The United Kingdom has few mineral resources. Yet it has more energy resources—including coal, natural gas, and petroleum—than any other EU member. In the early 2000s, it was among the world's top ten oil producers. From about the mid-1970s on, the United Kingdom has produced enough fuel to export it to other countries. The United Kingdom also uses its energy resources to run the factories that produce manufactured goods, the country's most important export. Study the map and graphs to learn more about the United Kingdom's economy.

United Kingdom: Natural Resources
KEY
- Iron
- Tin
- Coal
- Peat
- Kaolin
- Salt
- Petroleum
- Natural gas
- Hydroelectric power
- — National border
- ⊛ National capital
- • Other city

0 miles 200
0 kilometers 200
Lambert Azimuthal Equal Area

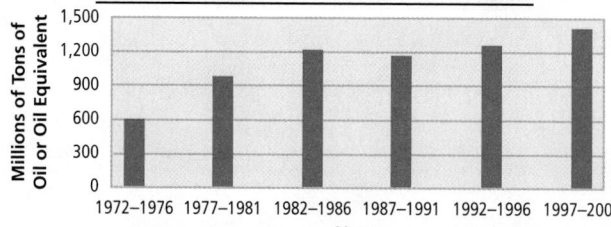

Leading Exports*

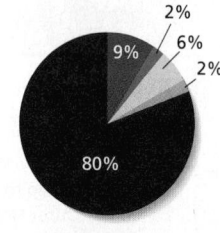

2%
6%
2%
9%
80%

Leading Imports*

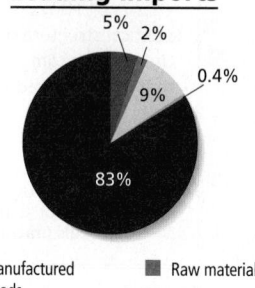

5% 2%
0.4%
9%
83%

- ■ Manufactured goods
- ■ Food, beverages, and tobacco
- ■ Raw materials
- ▨ Mineral fuels
- ▨ Other

*Note: Numbers may not equal 100% due to rounding.
SOURCE: U.K. Office for National Statistics, 2004

Fossil Fuel Production, 1972–2001

Millions of Tons of Oil or Oil Equivalent

1,500
1,200
900
600
300
0

1972–1976 1977–1981 1982–1986 1987–1991 1992–1996 1997–2001
Years

SOURCE: U.K. Office for National Statistics, 2002

Map and Chart Skills

1. **Locate** Where is the United Kingdom's petroleum located?
2. **Identify** What products make up the United Kingdom's largest import and export?
3. **Compare** How did the United Kingdom's fossil fuel production change from 1972 to 2001?

 Use Web Code **ldp-7431** for step-by-step **map skills practice**.
PHSchool.com

Answers

Map and Chart Skills

1. in the North Sea
2. manufactured goods
3. Fossil fuel production in the United Kingdom more than doubled between 1972 and 2001.

Go Online PHSchool.com Students can find more information about this topic on the DK World Desk Reference Online.

Skills for Life Skills Mini Lesson

Transferring Information from One Medium to Another

1. Tell students that to transfer information from one medium to another, they should state the main idea they wish to communicate, identify key information, choose a format to express the information, and transfer the information into the new format.

2. Practice the skill by having students write a paragraph expressing the information on the Leading Imports circle graph on this page in pairs.

3. Apply the skill by having students write a paragraph expressing the information on the bar graph on this page independently.

United Kingdom In 1801, Great Britain officially united with Ireland with a law called the Act of Union. The name of the nation changed to the United Kingdom of Great Britain and Ireland. In the 1920s, the southern part of Ireland became an independent nation. The rest of the island, Northern Ireland, has remained part of the United Kingdom. However, some Northern Irish groups seek to break away from Great Britain and join Ireland.

Today, the full name of this nation is the United Kingdom of Great Britain and Northern Ireland. Most people use the shortened form of the name, United Kingdom, or UK. Within the United Kingdom are four regions: England, Scotland, Wales, and Northern Ireland. Each region continues to have its own culture, traditions, and customs. The British government unifies them all.

✓ **Reading Check** **Which regions make up Great Britain?**

A Democratic Heritage

Today, the United Kingdom is headed by Queen Elizabeth II. As the country's monarch, she is a symbol of Britain's past and its customs. The United Kingdom also has a strong democratic government. The roots of British democracy go back many centuries.

The Magna Carta During the Middle Ages, kings needed large sums of money for major undertakings, such as going to war. If they did not have the money themselves, they asked the nobles to provide the funds. In the 1200s, the nobles used the influence their money gave them to limit the power of the king. In 1215, a group of nobles required King John to sign a document called the Magna Carta, or "Great Charter." The Magna Carta required the king to obey the laws of the land.

Target Skill **Use Context Clues**
How do the sentences in this paragraph explain what an *Act of Union* is?

Links Across
Time

The Magna Carta King John signed the Magna Carta in 1215 in a meadow called Runnymede, beside the River Thames in southeastern England. The Magna Carta holds an important place in history because it was the first written document that limited the power of a monarch. Hundreds of years later, British colonists in the Americas used the Magna Carta to support their fight for more rights. The document itself was written in Latin, which was the language of formal documents at that time. Four copies of the original charter still exist today in England, including the one shown at the right. Two are held in the British Library, while the other two are stored in the archives of the cathedrals at Lincoln and Salisbury.

Chapter 9 Section 1 **263**

Background: Biography

Another Elizabeth Queen Elizabeth I (1533–1603) reigned as queen of England from 1558 to 1603. The period of her reign is called the "Elizabethan Age," and it marked one of England's greatest eras. During her rule, England became a major power in Europe, building a navy formidable enough to defeat the great Spanish Armada. England also experienced a cultural golden age during her reign, as exemplified by writers such as William Shakespeare.

⟳ **Target Reading Skill** L2

As a follow up, have students answer the Target Reading Skill question on this page. *(Surrounding sentences say that Great Britain brought Ireland under its control in 1801, and that the nation's name changed to the United Kingdom of Great Britain and Ireland. So the Act of Union must have unified Britain and Ireland.)*

A Democratic Heritage L2

Guided Instruction

- Have students read how democracy developed in the United Kingdom in A Democratic Heritage.

- Have students discuss how the nobles were able to force King John to sign the Magna Carta, limiting the king's powers. *(The nobles used the influence their money gave them.)*

- Ask students **What groups make up the modern United Kingdom Parliament?** *(the House of Lords and the House of Commons)* **How are they different?** *(Members of the House of Lords are not elected, and their power is limited; members of the House of Commons are elected, and they govern the nation.)*

Independent Practice

Have students continue to fill in their graphic organizers by adding events from this section.

Monitor Progress

As students fill in the graphic organizer, circulate to make sure individuals are adding the appropriate information.

Links

Read the **Links Across Time** on this page. Ask students **Why does the Magna Carta hold an important place in history?** *(It was the first written document that limited the power of a monarch.)*

Answer

✓ **Reading Check** England, Scotland, and Wales

A Changing Monarchy L2

Guided Instruction

- **Vocabulary Builder** Clarify the high-use word **symbol** before reading.

- Have students read about the current basis of British government in A Changing Monarchy. As students read, circulate to make sure individuals can answer the Reading Check question.

- Ask students **What is a constitutional monarchy?** *(a government in which the power of kings and queens is limited)* **What role does Britain's monarchy play today?** *(It is a symbol of Britain's past and helps to unify the British people.)*

- Discuss the components of the British constitution. *(laws passed by Parliament, significant court decisions, and certain legal practices)* Ask **How is this different from the United States Constitution?** *(The Constitution of the United States is a single written document.)*

- Ask students **What do you think are some of the benefits and challenges of devolution?** *(Answers will vary, but may include: benefits—regional assemblies have a better idea of what their citizens need and can adopt specific laws for their citizens; challenges—regional assemblies may pass laws that conflict with one another; the national Parliament might lose some of its power over certain areas)*

Parliament, Past and Present

Below, an illustration shows King Edward I before the Parliament in the late 1200s. At the bottom, Queen Elizabeth II attends a session of Parliament in 1995. **Compare** *Compare the two images. What traditions has Parliament kept throughout its history?*

264 Europe and Russia

Parliament In time, the group of nobles became known as the Parliament. **Parliament** is the legislature, or lawmaking body, of the United Kingdom. This word comes from the French word *parler* (PAHR lay), which means "to talk." Parliament is the place where officials discuss laws and other government business. Parliament changed over time. It later came to include common people as well as nobles. As it became more responsive to the needs of the people, it also gained more power. It helped decide the kinds of taxes paid by citizens. People elected from each region of the country served as representatives in the Parliament. A **representative** represents, or speaks for, a group of people.

The modern Parliament is made up of the House of Lords and the House of Commons. Members of the House of Lords are not elected. They are high-ranking clergy and judges or people who have distinguished themselves in public life. Their power has become limited over the years. In contrast, members of the House of Commons are elected. They govern the nation.

✓ **Reading Check** What was the purpose of the Magna Carta?

A Changing Monarchy

Today, the monarchy serves as an important symbol of Britain's past. It also helps to unify the British people. The British honor the monarchy in many ways. When the queen is in London, a royal flag is flown over her home at Buckingham (BUK ing um) Palace. A ceremony called the changing of the guard takes place there every day. Trumpets blare and guardsmen march back and forth at the palace gate.

A Constitutional Monarchy While Parliament gained power, the power of British monarchs lessened. They no longer make laws or collect taxes. The United Kingdom is now governed by a constitution. A **constitution** is a set of laws that describes how a government works. Some nations have one written document that serves as a constitution, such as the Constitution of the United States. The British constitution is different. It is not one written document. Instead, the British constitution is made up of laws passed by Parliament, important court decisions, and certain legal practices. Parliament can change it as necessary. One of the greatest strengths of the United Kingdom's government is its ability to adopt modern ideas while keeping old ideas that still work.

Answers

Compare Possible answer: The seating arrangements and clothing of the monarch and members of Parliament are very similar in both images.

✓ **Reading Check** Its purpose was to force the king to obey the law of the land.

Differentiated Instruction

For Less Proficient Readers L1
Have students read the section as they listen to the recorded version on the Student Edition on Audio CD. Check for comprehension by pausing the CD after a paragraph or two and asking students to paraphrase what they have read.

⊙ Chapter 9, Section 1, **Student Edition on Audio CD**

For Advanced Readers L3
To learn more about daily life and language in Britain, have students complete the *Enrichment* activity about understanding British English.

All in One **Europe and Russia Teaching Resources,** *Enrichment,* p. 281

The British government is a **constitutional monarchy,** or a government in which the power of kings and queens is limited. In a constitutional monarchy, kings and queens must obey the laws. And in the United Kingdom, the laws are made by Parliament, not by the monarch. This is very different from an absolute monarchy. An absolute monarch makes all the laws and has the power to ignore them as he or she chooses.

Devolution Until the late 1990s, Parliament made the laws for the entire nation. It even made specific laws for each of the country's regions—laws that affected only England, Scotland, Wales, or Northern Ireland. By the end of the 1990s, the national Parliament turned over some of its lawmaking powers to regional assemblies. Now, the Scottish Parliament makes certain laws that apply only to Scotland. The Welsh Assembly makes laws for Wales, and the Northern Ireland Assembly makes laws for Northern Ireland. Only England does not have a regional assembly. Its laws are still made by the national Parliament. The process of moving lawmaking power from the national level to the regional level is called devolution.

✓ **Reading Check** What is devolution?

Links Across
The World

The Brightest Jewel Rare spices, silks, and other riches attracted the British East India Company to India in the 1600s. The company established trading outposts in India, with the goal of making huge profits. Over time, the company's goals changed. It gained great political power, and called for social change such as ending India's system of discrimination against people of lower class. In 1858, the British government took over the company, and officially turned India into a colony. Many people called India the "brightest jewel" in the British "crown" of colonies. The coat of arms shown here was a symbol of the British East India Company.

Regional Seats of Government
At the left, Queen Elizabeth II opens the Scottish Parliament in 1999—Scotland's first parliament in nearly 300 years. Northern Ireland's Assembly building is shown below. **Apply Information** *In what ways does allowing more power to regional lawmakers strengthen the United Kingdom's government?*

The Importance of Trade

Guided Instruction

- **Vocabulary Builder** Clarify the high-use word **finance** before reading.

- Have students read The Importance of Trade.

- Discuss how the United Kingdom acquired the natural resources it needed during the period of the British Empire. *(It traded with other nations and established colonies in other areas of the world.)*

- Ask students **How has the United Kingdom become successful in today's world economy?** *(It has become a leading member of the European Union, with expertise in shipping and finance; its membership also allows easy access to European markets for trade.)*

Independent Practice

Have students complete the graphic organizer with events from this section.

Monitor Progress

- Show *Section Reading Support Transparency ER 43* and ask students to check their graphic organizers individually.

    📖 **Europe and Russia Transparencies,** *Section Reading Support Transparency ER 43*

- Tell students to fill in the last column of the *Reading Readiness Guide.*

    All in One Europe and Russia Teaching Resources, *Reading Readiness Guide,* p. 258

Show students *Great Britain: London Fog and Suburbia.* Ask **What was the main cause of the "London Fog" of the 1800s?** *(The smoke from burning coal mixed with natural fog and created a thick smog.)*

Answer

Analyze Images the feeling of unity among the different regions of the British Empire

A Far-Flung Empire
The postcard below shows several of the British Empire's colonies in 1919. At the right, Lord Curzon, the British monarch's deputy in India, poses with an Indian prince in 1907. **Analyze Images** Read the words and phrases on the postcard. What kind of image of the British Empire is the postcard trying to convey?

Learn about the suburbs of Great Britain.

The Importance of Trade

As an island nation, the United Kingdom has limited natural resources. It must trade with other nations for resources. For that reason, trade has been important throughout the United Kingdom's history.

The British Empire In the 1500s, trade enabled the British to begin building a large empire. The British Empire grew to include colonies in British-ruled areas on six continents. Its empire was so vast that one could say in the 1800s, "The sun never sets on the British Empire." Recall that 13 of today's United States used to be British colonies. The American and other colonies provided British factories with raw materials. They also provided markets to sell the goods made in British factories. Its many colonies helped the United Kingdom become a world economic power.

But that changed in the 1900s. Fighting World War I and World War II weakened the United Kingdom. In the years after World War II, most of the colonies within the British Empire began seeking independence. The British Empire rapidly came to an end. It had turned over most of its colonies by the mid-1960s. The last colony, Hong Kong, was returned to China in 1997. However, the United Kingdom continues to trade with its former colonies.

Background: Links Across Time

The American Colonies Great Britain suffered a major setback when it lost the 13 colonies in North America that became the United States. This setback occurred in the late 1700s, when Britain was nearing the height of its power. Some believe that the British government failed to take the colonists' complaints regarding trade and taxation seriously. Also, not only had the colonists inherited strong democratic values from England, but much of the motivation for migrating to the colonies had been centered on individual freedom and independence. Ultimately, Britain's attempts to control commerce in the colonies for its own benefit led first to widespread protest and then the American Revolution.

A European Union Member The United Kingdom has many strong industries, or businesses. For example, it has good supplies of fossil fuels—especially oil from deposits beneath the North Sea. It also continues to export many manufactured goods, such as clothing and electronic products. However, the United Kingdom is not as strong a world power as it once was.

The United Kingdom no longer relies on its colonies to boost its economy. In 1973, the United Kingdom joined the European Union. As you have read, the EU is a group of nations that promotes trade and other forms of cooperation among its members.

The United Kingdom today is a leading member of the EU. Its experience in such areas as shipping and finance has strengthened the EU in global trade. In turn, easier access to European markets has helped replace the trade the United Kingdom lost when its empire broke apart. With new links to the resources and markets of other European countries, the British look forward to a bright economic future.

A woman paints figures by hand at a British company that exports tableware and gifts.

✓ **Reading Check** In what ways did the United Kingdom rely on its colonies?

Section 1 Assessment

Key Terms
Review the key terms at the beginning of this section. Use each term in a sentence that explains its meaning.

◉ **Target Reading Skill**
Find the phrase *common people* on page 264. How do the other words in the same sentence explain its meaning?

Comprehension and Critical Thinking
1. (a) Explain What is the difference between the terms *Great Britain* and *United Kingdom*?

(b) Sequence List four events, in order, that led to the formation of the United Kingdom.
2. (a) Name What are the two houses of the British Parliament?
(b) Contrast How do the two houses of Parliament differ?
3. (a) Recall What kind of government does the United Kingdom have?
(b) Contrast How does the British constitution differ from that of the United States?
4. (a) Note What factor led the British to build a large empire?
(b) Draw Conclusions How did the United Kingdom remain strong after losing its colonies?

Writing Activity
Suppose that you are a British tour guide operator. You tell an American tourist that you are from three places: England, Great Britain, and the United Kingdom. Write a paragraph that explains to the tourist how this can be so.

Go Online
PHSchool.com
For: An activity on the British Empire
Visit: PHSchool.com
Web Code: ldd-7401

Assess Progress **L2**
Have students complete the Section Assessment. Administer the *Section Quiz*.

All in One **Europe and Russia Teaching Resources,** *Section Quiz,* p. 260

Reteach **L1**
If students need more instruction, have them read this section in the Reading and Vocabulary Study Guide.

📖 Chapter 9, Section 1, **Eastern Hemisphere Reading and Vocabulary Study Guide,** pp. 92–94

Extend **L3**
Have students complete the *Small Group Activity: Comparing Types of Government* to learn more about the governments of Great Britain and the United States.

All in One **Europe and Russia Teaching Resources,** *Small Group Activity: Comparing Types of Government,* pp. 283–286

Answer

✓ **Reading Check** It relied on the colonies for raw materials and as markets for goods made in British factories.

Writing Activity
Use the *Rubric for Assessing a Writing Assignment* to assess students' paragraphs.

All in One **Europe and Russia Teaching Resources,** *Rubric for Assessing a Writing Assignment,* p. 298

Go Online
PHSchool.com Typing in the Web code when prompted will bring students directly to detailed instructions for this activity.

Section 1 Assessment

Key Terms
Students' sentences should reflect knowledge of each Key Term.

◉ **Target Reading Skill**
The phrase *as well as of nobles* tells students that *common people* are people who are not nobles or royalty, but ordinary citizens.

Comprehension and Critical Thinking
1. (a) *Great Britain* refers to England, Scotland, and Wales. *United Kingdom* refers to those three regions plus Northern Ireland.
(b) The Roman Empire fell; the kingdom of Wessex conquered other kingdoms to unify England; England incorporated Scotland and Wales; Great Britain brought Ireland under its control.
2. (a) the House of Lords and the House of Commons **(b)** In the House of Lords, the members are not elected, and they have limited power; in the House of Commons, the members are elected, and they govern the nation.
3. (a) a constitutional monarchy **(b)** The British constitution is not a single written document, but is made up of laws passed by Parliament, significant court decisions, and certain legal practices.
4. (a) trade **(b)** The United Kingdom's participation in the European Union has replaced some of the trade it lost with its colonies.

Section 2
Step-by-Step Instruction

Objectives

Social Studies
1. Find out why the French take pride in their traditional culture.
2. Learn about growing cultural diversity in France.

Reading/Language Arts
Use context clues to understand new words.

Prepare to Read

Build Background Knowledge **L2**

In this section, students will learn about France and French culture. Have students begin their exploration of France by viewing the Passport to the World CD-ROM section about France. As they use the CD-ROM, ask students to note several facts about France to share with the class using the Give One, Get One strategy (TE, p. T37).

> ⊙ *France,* **Passport to the World CD-ROM**

Set a Purpose for Reading **L2**

■ Preview the Objectives

■ Form students into pairs or groups of four. Distribute the *Reading Readiness Guide.* Ask students to fill in the first two columns of the chart. Use the Numbered Heads participation strategy (TE, p. T36) to call on students to share one piece of information they already know and one piece of information they want to know.

> **All in One** **Europe and Russia Teaching Resources,** *Reading Readiness Guide,* p. 262

Preview Key Terms **L2**

Pronounce the Key Term, then ask students to say the word with you. Provide a simple explanation such as, "A person's philosophy often influences his or her lifestyle."

Section 2 France
Cultural Heritage and Diversity

Prepare to Read

Objectives
In this section you will
1. Find out why the French take pride in their traditional culture.
2. Learn about growing cultural diversity in France.

Taking Notes
As you read this section, look for details about French culture, including recent influences on it. Copy the chart below, and record your findings in it.

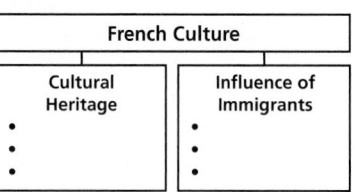

Target Reading Skill
Use Context Clues
Context, the words and phrases surrounding a word, can help you understand a new word. In this example, the phrase in italics helps explain what Impressionism is: French Impressionist artists such as Claude Monet developed *new techniques to paint light and shadow.*

Key Term
• **philosophy** (fil LAHS uh fee) *n.* a system of ideas and beliefs

It's July of 1998 in Paris, France. Hundreds of thousands of people crowd onto the Champs Elysées (shawnz eh lee ZAY), one of the most fashionable streets in the world. The sidewalks are packed. Some people have even climbed to the tops of lampposts or newspaper stands for a better view. They're all here for a huge celebration. The French soccer team has just won the World Cup championship for the first time ever.

Fans are waving French flags. Others have their faces painted in the colors of the French flag—red, white, and blue. But in the crowd, many fans are waving the Algerian flag and chanting, "Zizou! Zizou!" They are calling for Zinedine Zidane, the midfielder who scored two of the goals in the winning game. Like many of the team's players, Zidane, of Algerian descent, is the son of immigrants.

This victory celebration is symbolic of a new France—a France that is fiercely proud of its culture and is increasingly diverse.

In 1998, the words "world champions" were projected onto France's Arc de Triomphe.

268 Europe and Russia

⊙ Target Reading Skill **L2**

Use Context Clues Point out the Target Reading Skill. Tell students that sometimes, the context will contain a contrast word that tells the reader that the next idea will be different than the idea it follows.

Model using contrast in the context using the word *permanent* from the second paragraph on p. 274. (*Students should recognize that the word "instead" signals a contrast between "temporarily" and "permanent." Therefore, "permanent" means the opposite of "temporarily.")*

Have students complete *Use Context Clues: Compare and Contrast* in their groups.

> **All in One** **Europe and Russia Teaching Resources,** *Use Context Clues: Compare and Contrast,* p. 278

Pride in French Culture

French people generally take great pride in their culture—for good reason. Over centuries, the French have made many important contributions to art, religion, music, literature, and philosophy. A **philosophy** is a system of ideas and beliefs. Many French people are committed to preserving their traditional French culture.

The French Language Some people want to prevent the French language from changing too much. An organization called the French Academy determines which words are officially accepted as part of the French language. Since 1635, it has published dictionaries explaining the usage of these words. The Academy is one example of how the French strive to preserve their culture.

Enduring Philosophies Many important philosophies originated in France. Some of these philosophies had to do with government, and they had a great influence on many other nations. For example, the idea that government should be divided into three branches comes from a French philosopher named Baron de Montesquieu (MAHN tus kyoo). A Swiss philosopher living in France named Jean-Jacques Rousseau (zhahn zhahk roo SOH) developed the idea that no laws are binding unless the people have agreed to them. These ideas helped shape the United States Constitution.

Achievements in the Arts French painters are world-famous for their achievements. For example, Eugène Delacroix (ooh ZHEHN deh la KWAH) painted works full of intense emotion and rich color in the early 1800s. Impressionist artists such as Claude Monet (moh NAY) developed new techniques for painting light and shadow.

French composers have written beautiful works of classical music. Claude Debussy (deh boo SEE), for example, composed music in the late 1800s and early 1900s. His work was influenced by artists such as Monet. In turn, Debussy influenced other composers.

French literature is world-famous. For example, Alexandre Dumas (doo MAH) wrote novels in the 1800s. Even today, many of his novels are read by people around the world and have been made into movies.

French Cultural Milestones

1637 René Descartes publishes ▶ *Discourse on Method*, one of the world's most important works in philosophy.

1664 Molière, considered to be France's greatest comic playwright, writes his masterpiece, *Tartuffe*.

1751 Denis Diderot publishes an important encyclopedia of science and philosophy that reflects the ideals of the Scientific Revolution.

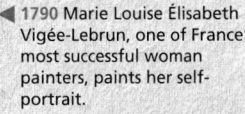

◀ **1790** Marie Louise Élisabeth Vigée-Lebrun, one of France's most successful woman painters, paints her self-portrait.

1830s A French artist and a French inventor together develop the first methods for making photographs.

1899 Claude Monet paints ▶ *The Water-Lily Pond*, an important Impressionist painting.

◀ **1908** Auguste Rodin, considered to be France's finest sculptor, creates *The Cathedral*.

1939 Film director Jean Renoir produces his masterpiece *The Rules of the Game*, which influences cinema around the world.

1957 Writer Albert Camus, who wrote about human emotion in the post–World War II world, wins the Nobel Prize in Literature.

■ Diagram Skills

The French have made major contributions to the world's art, literature, cinema, and philosophy. **Identify** Which event had an influence on cinema around the world? **Identify Causes** What earlier event in this diagram paved the way for this event?

Chapter 9 Section 2 **269**

- Ask students to describe Gothic architecture. *(Gothic architecture developed in and around Paris in the 1100s. It is characterized by high ceilings, thin walls, and the use of columns and arches.)*

- Ask students **How did French style influence other parts of the world in the 1700s and 1800s?** *(In the 1700s, Russian aristocrats followed French fashion, used French manners, and spoke French. In the 1800s, wealthy British and American women had their clothes made in France, and less wealthy women copied French styles.)*

The Eiffel Tower
Paris's Eiffel Tower was built in 1889 to celebrate the French Revolution. The 984-foot- (300-meter-) tall tower was the tallest structure in the world until 1930. **Infer** *What feelings about the French Revolution might this tower bring about in French people?*

270 Europe and Russia

Innovative Architecture French architects have created magnificent buildings. In the 1100s, a style of art and architecture called Gothic developed in and around Paris. Gothic architecture is characterized by high ceilings, thin walls, and the use of columns and arches. French architects built stunning Gothic-style medieval cathedrals, like the Cathedral of Notre Dame (noh truh DAHM). Built in the 1200s in Paris, Notre Dame is one of Europe's most famous cathedrals. It has a number of huge stained-glass windows, one of which is 42 feet (13 meters) in diameter.

In later years, French architects designed other important buildings. For example, work on the Louvre (LOO vruh) Museum was begun during the Renaissance. At first, the Louvre was a royal palace. Over time, many of France's monarchs added to the original building. As they collected great works of art, they housed them in different parts of the Louvre. By the late 1700s, monarchs no longer used the Louvre as a palace, and it became a national museum.

French architects today continue to design great buildings, such as the national library that opened in 1998. This library is made up of four glass skyscrapers surrounding an open square. Though the building is new and modern, the collection it holds is one of the oldest in the world.

Answer

Infer Possible answer: They may view it as symbol of their national pride and as a celebration of their history.

Links to

Economics

The Department Store In 1852, a French merchant named Aristide Boucicaut (BOO sih koh) took over the Bon Marché, a fabric shop in Paris. By 1914, he had transformed it into the world's first single department store. The department store allowed people, mainly women, to choose from a variety of ready-made clothing and household items in one attractive store. Before this, people went to individuals who specialized in making or selling one type of product. The department store also introduced innovations such as advertising, fixed prices on goods, and a system of returns or exchanges. Department stores were also introduced in the late 1800s in the United States and England.

The Bon Marché, in an engraving made around 1880

New Styles in Fashion For centuries, many people looked to France for the latest styles. Russian aristocrats of the 1700s followed French fashion and used French manners. They even spoke French. Wealthy British and American women traveled to Paris in the 1800s to have their clothes made. Less wealthy women admired French fashions in magazines. They often had their local seamstresses make copies of French originals.

French fashion continued to set trends in the 1900s. For example, a French fashion designer named Christian Dior (dee AWR) created a "New Look" in 1947. His designs featured narrow shoulders and long, full skirts. His fashions became popular all over the world.

Paris continues to be one of the most important centers of the fashion industry. Each year, people come from countries around the world to see the latest fashions from French designers.

Fine Food French cooking has long been one of the most respected styles of cooking in the world. In about 1805, a French pastry chef named Marie-Antoine Carême (muh REE ahn TWAHN kuh REM) delighted the rich and powerful people of France with his desserts. Some of his cakes looked like buildings or monuments. His puddings looked like birds or flowers.

In 1833, Carême wrote a book on the art of French cooking. His book was similar to the dictionaries of the French Academy. It set strict standards of excellence for cooking. Today, many of the world's best chefs are trained in France.

✓ **Reading Check** Name two examples of the influence of French culture on the rest of the world.

Learn about Napoleon Bonaparte.

Background: Biography

"Coco" Chanel (1883–1971) Gabrielle "Coco" Chanel created fashion designs that dominated Parisian and international *haute couture* (oht koo TOOR) for much of the 1900s. Orphaned at age six, Chanel was raised by her aunts, who taught her how to sew and gave her the nickname "Coco." Chanel's styles attracted the attention of wealthy women seeking style and comfort. Her classic innovations included jersey dresses, bell-bottom pants, trench coats, turtleneck sweaters, and the "little black dress." She also created a line of perfumes, including the famous Chanel No. 5, which brought her company great financial success.

Guided Instruction L2

Ask students to study the Country Profile on this page. As a class, answer the Map and Chart Skills questions. Allow students to briefly discuss their responses with a partner before sharing answers.

Independent Practice

Distribute *Reading a Table*. Have students work in partners to complete the worksheet. Then have students transform the information in the two circle graphs on this page into tables similar to the Export Partners table.

All in One **Europe and Russia Teaching Resources,** *Reading a Table,* p. 288

Answers

Map and Chart Skills

1. 35 percent; Large areas of arable land are located in southern and northwestern France. Commercial agriculture also takes place near the English Channel, along the Mediterranean coast, and in parts of the interior.

2. Using modern agricultural techniques, a small number of laborers can farm a large amount of land.

3. 50 percent; the EU is very important to the economy of France

Go Online PHSchool.com Students can find more information about this topic on the DK World Desk Reference Online.

France

Like most developed countries, France's economy is increasingly based on services. Agriculture, however, is still very important to the nation's economy. France is the leading agricultural exporter among EU nations. Agricultural products, mainly cereals such as wheat and corn, make up about 16 percent of France's total exports. Use the data on this page to learn more about France's land use and economy.

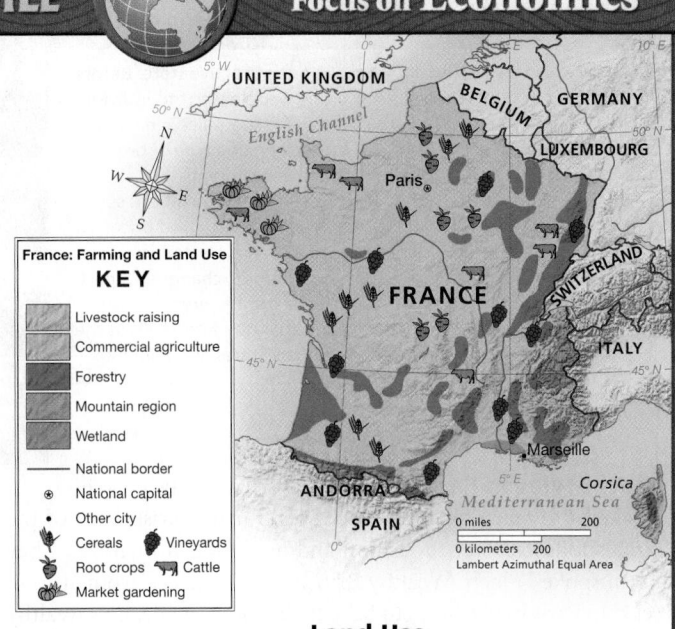

France: Farming and Land Use
KEY
- Livestock raising
- Commercial agriculture
- Forestry
- Mountain region
- Wetland
- — National border
- ⊛ National capital
- • Other city
- 🌾 Cereals 🍇 Vineyards
- 🥕 Root crops 🐄 Cattle
- 🌱 Market gardening

Export Partners

Export Destination	Percent of France's Exports
European Union	
Germany	15
Spain	10
United Kingdom	9
Italy	9
Belgium	7
United States	7
Other	43

SOURCE: *CIA World Factbook*

Land Use

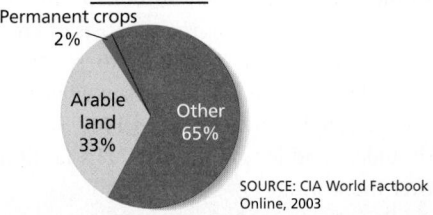

Permanent crops 2%
Arable land 33%
Other 65%

SOURCE: CIA World Factbook Online, 2003

Labor Force by Occupation

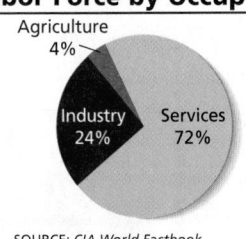

Agriculture 4%
Industry 24%
Services 72%

SOURCE: *CIA World Factbook*

Map and Chart Skills

1. **Note** How much of France's land can be used to grow crops? Where is this land located?

2. **Infer** Compare the percentage of France's arable land and cropland with the percentage of France's labor force in agriculture. From this information, what can you infer about how many laborers are needed to carry out modern agriculture?

3. **Transfer Information** What is the total percentage of France's exports to EU countries? What does this tell you about the importance of the EU to France's economy?

Use Web Code **Ide-7412** for **DK World Desk Reference Online.**

Diversity in France

Many French citizens believe French culture is both unique and valuable. Yet the cultures of other nations are influencing French culture more and more.

The French language, for example, has picked up words from other languages. French has borrowed words from English, such as *weekend, barbecue, laser,* and *cross-country.* French also includes words from languages such as Italian, Malaysian, Turkish, and Hindi. These words are a sign of France's ties with many other nations.

Cultural influences from other nations come from many different sources, such as film, television, and radio. Another source is immigration.

A History of Immigration Between 1850 and about 1940 France welcomed 7 million immigrants from European countries such as Poland, Italy, Spain, and Belgium. Because these immigrants came from cultures similar to that of France, they quickly and easily adopted French culture.

After World War II France had a shortage of workers. The French government began to encourage immigration to France. By the 1950s, the largest group of immigrants came from Algeria, a French colony in North Africa. In the past few decades, many immigrants have also arrived from Southeast Asia.

Influences on French Culture
At the top, Indian immigrants celebrate a Hindu festival. Above, a cable advertisement on a bus uses both French and English words.
Identify Effects *How might increasing immigration continue to affect the French language?*

- Discuss the ways in which North African immigrants have contributed to French culture. *(They have brought their Arab culture with them, including different kinds of food, clothing, and music.)*

- Ask students **Why do you think there are more restaurants and grocery stores in France selling foreign foods?** *(Possible answer: There are more immigrants from other countries, and they wish to preserve their traditional customs, including special foods.)*

Independent Practice

Have students complete their graphic organizers with information from this section.

Monitor Progress

- Show *Section Reading Support Transparency ER 44* and ask students to check their graphic organizers individually. Go over key concepts and clarify key vocabulary as needed.

   📖 **Europe and Russia Transparencies,** *Section Reading Support Transparency ER 44*

- Tell students to fill in the last column of the *Reading Readiness Guide*. Ask them to evaluate if what they learned was what they had expected to learn.

   All in One Europe and Russia Teaching Resources, *Reading Readiness Guide*, p. 262

🎯 Target Reading Skill   L2

Use Context Clues As a follow up, have students answer the Target Reading Skill question on this page. *(The text says that the French government thought that Algerian immigrants would be in France only temporarily. The next sentence says that many stayed permanently instead, so students should conclude that* temporarily *means "not permanently" or "for a short while.")*

A Political Protest
Muslim women protest a French law proposed in 2004 to ban students from wearing headscarves, Jewish caps, or other religious symbols in school. The women are holding a French flag. **Evaluate Information** *What point are the women making by displaying a French flag?*

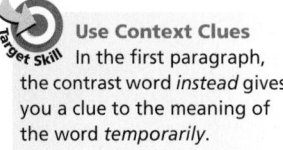

Use Context Clues In the first paragraph, the contrast word *instead* gives you a clue to the meaning of the word *temporarily*.

Rising Tensions After World War II, Algerians and other immigrants helped rebuild France's economy. They took jobs that French employers found hard to fill. The French government assumed that these immigrants would work in France temporarily and then return home. Instead, many North African immigrants decided to make France their permanent home. Large numbers of immigrants along with their families moved to France in the 1970s, a time when the French economy was weak. Tension began to build between native-born French citizens and recent immigrants.

Some native French people had questions about the immigrants. Would they take jobs away from people already in France? Would the immigrants adopt French culture, or would they try to change it? Unlike earlier European immigrants, these recent immigrants often came from very different cultures. As they thought about these questions, some French people felt threatened by the immigrants. In the 1970s, the French government began to limit immigration.

In November 2005, discouraged immigrants in several French cities began to riot. Immigrants faced economic disadvantages and claimed that the French government and people had treated them unfairly. To combat the violence, the French government imposed temporary security measures, such as curfews and police raids, in affected areas. French leaders also promised to fight discrimination and improve opportunities for France's immigrants.

274 Europe and Russia

Differentiated Instruction

For Advanced Readers   L3
Working in pairs, have students do research in the library or on the Internet to find the numbers and origins of immigrants to France for the last five years. Then have them create a table that shows this information.

Answer

Evaluate Information Possible answer: that French citizens should unite and protect each other's freedoms

Immigrants' Influences Today the debate over immigration continues. Immigrants from Algeria, Morocco, and Tunisia bring African and Arab cultures with them. Their food, dress, and music are quite different from those of traditional French culture. The same is true of immigrants from Asia and other regions. The influence of all these groups can be seen especially in the big cities. In Paris and in many other large cities in France, it is common to hear people speaking languages other than French. Every year, there are more and more restaurants and stores that sell foreign food.

France has always been a diverse society. But unlike in the past, recent immigrants have arrived from countries with very different cultures from that of France. France and its people are making adjustments. Many French people were shocked when a politician who promoted an anti-immigrant message won significant popular support in the 2002 presidential election. But most people have come to value the benefits of a diverse population.

An African immigrant selling fresh fish

✓ **Reading Check** How are France's immigrants today different from those of the past?

Section 2 Assessment

Key Terms
Review the key terms at the beginning of this section. Use each term in a sentence that explains its meaning.

Target Reading Skill
Find the word *aristocrat* on page 271. What clues in that paragraph helped you figure out its meaning?

Comprehension and Critical Thinking
1. (a) List Name two French cultural contributions to the arts.

(b) Explain What were Montesquieu's and Rousseau's philosophies about government?
(c) Synthesize How did these philosophies influence the United States?
2. (a) Recall Why did the French government encourage immigration following World War II?
(b) Summarize Why did tensions arise between native-born French citizens and immigrants to France in the 1970s?
(c) Identify Effects When immigrants move to a new country, how do they change a country for better or worse?

Writing Activity
Suppose that you are a television reporter covering a story on French culture. You interview an elderly woman for your report. What questions might you ask her to determine how French culture has changed and how it has stayed the same over the past few decades?

> **Writing Tip** Use the blue headings in this section to help you decide on topics. Reread the text under the headings to get ideas for your questions.

Chapter 9 Section 2 **275**

Assess and Reteach

Assess Progress L2
Have students complete the Section Assessment. Administer the *Section Quiz*.

All in One **Europe and Russia Teaching Resources,** *Section Quiz,* p. 264

Reteach L1
If students need more instruction, have them read this section in Reading and Vocabulary Study Guide.

📖 Chapter 9, Section 2, **Eastern Hemisphere Reading and Vocabulary Study Guide,** pp. 95–97

Extend L3
To learn more about France's historical architecture, show students *Color Transparency 24* and *Color Transparency 25* of the Cathedral at Reims. Then have students research the history of the Cathedral, and write a short paragraph about one historical event that occurred there.

📖 **Europe and Russia Transparencies,** *Color Transparency 24: The Cathedral at Reims; Color Transparency 25: The Cathedral at Reims: Interior*

Answer

✓ **Reading Check** Most of France's immigrants today come from North Africa, and unlike those in the past, bring cultures that are very different from that of France.

Writing Activity
Use the *Rubric for Assessing a Writing Assignment* to assess students' interviews.

All in One **Europe and Russia Teaching Resources,** *Rubric for Assessing a Writing Assignment,* p. 298

Section 2 Assessment

Key Terms
Students' sentences should reflect knowledge of each Key Term.

➔ Target Reading Skill
Because the paragraph states that Russian aristocrats followed French manners, fashion, even spoke French, and that French clothing was very expensive, students can deduce that an aristocrat is a wealthy, educated person.

Comprehension and Critical Thinking
1. (a) Answers should include two of the following: painting, music, architecture, literature. **(b)** The government should be divided into three branches; no law is binding unless agreed to by the people. **(c)** The United States government has three branches and is a republic, which means that laws are voted on by representatives of the people.

2. (a) because there was a shortage of workers in France **(b)** As the French economy became weak, native French people worried that immigrants would take jobs from them and would change French culture and traditions. **(c)** Better—They bring their own culture and traditions to the country, including foods, religions, and languages. Worse—Some might think that immigrants take jobs away from people who already live in the country, or cause the traditional culture of the country to change.

Objectives

Social Studies

1. Learn about Sweden's welfare state.
2. Find out how Sweden became a welfare state.
3. Examine possible solutions to Sweden's economic problems.

Reading/Language Arts

Learn to use context clues to determine how familiar words are being used in the text.

Prepare to Read

Build Background Knowledge L2

Tell students that they will learn about government benefits in Sweden. Ask them if they know of any benefits that their local, state, or federal government provides for citizens in the United States. Model the thought process by encouraging them to think about transportation, education, and protection. Provide simple examples to get students started. Conduct an Idea Wave (TE, p. T35) to generate a class list.

Set a Purpose for Reading L2

- Preview the Objectives.

- Read each statement in the *Reading Readiness Guide* aloud. Ask students to mark the statements true or false.

  All in One **Europe and Russia Teaching Resources,** *Reading Readiness Guide,* p. 266

- Have students discuss the statements in pairs or groups of four, then mark their worksheets again. Use the Numbered Heads participation strategy (TE, p. T36) to call on students to share their group's perspectives.

Vocabulary Builder
Preview Key Terms L2

Pronounce each Key Term, then ask students to say the word with you. Provide a simple explanation such as, "In a welfare state, the government provides services and benefits to citizens."

Prepare to Read

Objectives

In this section you will
1. Learn about Sweden's welfare state.
2. Find out how Sweden became a welfare state.
3. Examine possible solutions to Sweden's economic problems.

Taking Notes

As you read this section, look for details about Sweden's welfare state. Copy the table below and record your findings in it.

Sweden's Welfare State	
Benefits	Economic Challenges
•	•
•	•
•	•

Target Reading Skill

Use Context Clues
Remember that a word that looks familiar to you may have a different meaning in the context of the text you are reading. For example, you have probably heard of the word *welfare*. As you read the text under the red heading A Welfare State, you will learn that the word has a different meaning than the one you have thought of. The last sentence of the first paragraph under A Welfare State makes that difference clear.

Key Terms

- **welfare state** (WEL fayr stayt) *n.* a country in which many services and benefits are paid for by the government
- **national debt** (NASH uh nul det) *n.* the amount of money a government owes

A baby being examined by a doctor in Sweden

A young Swedish couple is expecting a new baby any day now. Excited, they decorate the baby's room and talk about how they will raise her. They even joke about where she will go to college and what career she might choose when she grows up.

Like all new parents, they have many hopes and plans for their baby. They have concerns, too—concerns about her health and well-being. But they feel confident about certain things. For example, both parents will have paid time off from work to care for the baby. The baby will also receive excellent health care, child care, and schooling—all for free or at a very low cost. To understand why the government provides these services, you need to understand the nature of Sweden's society.

276 Europe and Russia

Target Reading Skill L2

Use Context Clues Point out the Target Reading Skill. Tell students that a word that looks familiar to them may have a different meaning in the context of the text they are reading. Students can use their own knowledge and context clues to determine how the word is being used.

Model the skill using the term *cradle-to-grave* on p. 277. (*Students will be familiar with the words "cradle" and "grave," and from* the context should be able to discern that the term *cradle-to-grave* means "lifelong" or "at every stage of life.")

Give students *Use Context Clues: General Knowledge.* Have them complete the activity in their groups.

All in One **Europe and Russia Teaching Resources,** *Use Context Clues: General Knowledge,* p. 279

A Welfare State

Sweden is a welfare state. In a **welfare state,** the government provides many services and benefits either for free or for a very low cost. These services and benefits include medical care, paid time off from work, and child care. A welfare system means something very different in Sweden than it does in the United States. The American welfare system helps people who are in great need—people who cannot afford medical care or food. The Swedish system helps everyone.

A Cradle-to-Grave System Sweden has a "cradle-to-grave" welfare system. That means that the system provides basic services for all people at every stage of life. When a child is born, the government pays for parents to stay home from work for at least 12 months. The state then provides child care at a reduced cost, so that parents can work or continue their education. The government pays the costs of schooling, including books and lunches for all students. College education is also paid for every student, through a combination of grants and loans. And every Swedish citizen has access to free or inexpensive health care.

As part of the government benefits program, all workers receive five weeks paid vacation. Most workers generally take their vacation at the same time during the summer. That is because in the summer, the nights in this far-northern country are very short. It is daylight for most of the day.

Swedish people take more paid sick days than the workers of any other European nation. Some of the money for this leave comes from the government. And when workers retire, they receive a monthly payment from the government. This payment generally equals more than half of the pay they received when they were working.

Daily Life in Sweden
Sweden's government funds this day care center (below) and senior citizen community center (bottom left). Both are located in Stockholm, Sweden's capital. **Summarize** What other benefits do Swedes receive from the government?

Vocabulary Builder

Use the information below to teach students this section's high-use words.

High-Use Word	Definition and Sample Sentence
benefit, p. 277	*n.* money or service provided by a government to its citizens Her **benefits** allowed her to get job training.
fund, p. 280	*v.* to provide money or resources for specific costs Public schools are **funded** largely by property taxes.

A Welfare State · L2

Guided Instruction

- **Vocabulary Builder** Clarify the high-use word **benefit** before reading.

- Read A Welfare State, using the Choral Reading strategy (TE, p. T34).

- Discuss the difference between the meaning of a welfare system in the United States and in Sweden. *(The American welfare system helps people who are in great need. The Swedish system helps everyone.)*

- Ask students **Explain why Sweden is said to have a "cradle-to-grave" welfare system?** *(The government pays for benefits at every stage of life, including day care, education, health care, vacation, sick days, and retirement payments.)*

- Discuss with students how the Swedish government pays for benefits. *(Swedish people pay very high taxes on take-home pay, food, and clothing to pay for the benefits.)*

Independent Practice

Ask students to create the Taking Notes graphic organizer on a blank piece of paper. Have them fill in details in the Benefits column. Briefly model how to identify which details to record.

Monitor Progress

As students fill in the graphic organizer, circulate to make sure individuals are choosing the correct details. Provide assistance as needed.

Answer

Summarize The government pays for the costs of schooling, including higher education, and provides access to inexpensive or free health care. Workers receive five weeks of paid vacation, and Swedish people are allowed more paid sick days than the workers of any other European nation. The government pays for parents to stay home from work with their newborn children. When workers retire, they receive a monthly payment from the government.

Guided Instruction [L2]

Ask students to study the Country Profile on this page. As a class, answer the Map and Chart Skills questions. Allow students to briefly discuss their responses with a partner before sharing answers.

Independent Practice

Distribute *Reading a Line Graph*. Have students work in partners to complete the worksheet. Then draw their attention to the line graph on this page. Ask **How does the rainfall in Sweden fluctuate over a year?** (*Slightly more rain falls in the months of June, July, August, and September, but overall rainfall does not fluctuate very much.*)

AllinOne Europe and Russia Teaching Resources, *Reading a Line Graph*, p. 289

Answers

Map and Chart Skills

1. in the southern half of Sweden

2. The northern interior is cold and receives heavy snowfall, while in the south temperatures are more moderate and coastal waters do not freeze.

3. Sweden's large cities are located there in the south, where temperatures are more moderate and coastal waters do not freeze.

Go Online PHSchool.com Students can find more information about this topic on the DK World Desk Reference Online.

Sweden

Sweden is located far to the north, with about a fifth of its land within the Arctic Circle. Because of its great length from north to south, its climate varies greatly. The northern interior receives heavy snowfall and is cold for months, while in the southern regions temperatures are moderate, and the coastal waters do not freeze. The country is heavily forested, especially in the northern part of the country. Study the map and the charts to learn how Sweden's geography shapes the lives of its people.

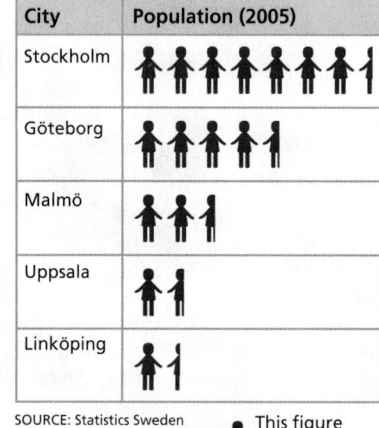

Sweden: Natural Vegetation
KEY

- Deciduous forest
- Mixed forest
- Coniferous forest
- Highland (vegetation varying with elevation)
- Tundra

— National border
⊛ National capital
• Other city

0 miles 300
0 kilometers 300
Lambert Azimuthal Equal Area

Largest Cities

City	Population (2005)
Stockholm	
Göteborg	
Malmö	
Uppsala	
Linköping	

SOURCE: Statistics Sweden

This figure represents 100,000 people.

Sweden's Weather

— Average temperature   ■ Rainfall

°F: 104, 86, 68, 50, 32, 14, −4
in.: 16, 12, 8, 4, 0

J F M A M J J A S O N D

SOURCE: DK World Desk Reference

Map and Chart Skills

1. **Locate** Where are Sweden's five largest cities located?

2. **Contrast** How is the vegetation of that area different from that of the regions with no large cities?

3. **Synthesize Information** What factors might explain the location of the majority of Sweden's population?

Go Online PHSchool.com Use Web Code lde-7413 for DK World Desk Reference Online.

Urban and Rural Population

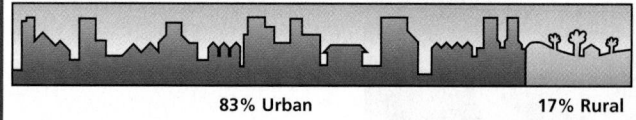

83% Urban   17% Rural

SOURCE: United Nations Population Division

Background: Global Perspectives

Health Insurance National health insurance has been adopted throughout Europe and in parts of Asia. For example, Great Britain has provided comprehensive health coverage since 1948, while Canada has had similar coverage since 1971. The United States, by contrast, is the only Western industrialized nation without a form of national comprehensive health insurance. However, the U.S. government does provide health coverage to older retired persons and low-income citizens. Many people in the United States have no health care coverage. This issue has been an important one in recent elections.

High Taxes Swedish people believe that welfare benefits are very important. They are willing to pay the highest taxes in Europe in order to have these benefits. Swedes pay as much as 60 percent of their income in taxes. Food is taxed at 12 percent. Clothing and other goods are taxed at 25 percent. But in exchange for these high taxes, all Swedes have financial security. Whether they are rich or poor, they know that their children will get a good education. Medical costs are low. Rents are affordable.

√ **Reading Check** What is a "cradle-to-grave" system?

Building a Welfare State

As it has been for hundreds of years, Sweden is a monarchy. Yet the government has changed greatly throughout Sweden's history.

Sweden's History The history of Sweden begins with the Vikings—an early sailing people from Scandinavia who colonized many parts of Europe. Beginning in about the 900s, Sweden was ruled by a series of kingdoms. In the 1600s, Sweden emerged as a great power in northern Europe. From its capital city, Stockholm, Sweden ruled a thriving empire. However, the country's strength declined in the 1700s after Sweden lost a war with Russia. Sweden remained neutral in both world wars.

Like the monarchy in the United Kingdom, Sweden's monarchy changed over time. The monarch slowly gave more and more power to the people, represented in a parliament. And political parties arose to represent the people and bring about change in government. Today Sweden is a constitutional monarchy. The monarch is the ceremonial leader, but parliament makes the laws.

A 2002 photo shows the current Swedish monarch, King Carl Gustaf XVI, with other members of the royal family.

Learn the importance of Swedish forests.

Show students *Sweden: Land of Forests.* Then ask **Why are forests important to Sweden?** *(Forests cover much of Sweden, and the forestry industry pays taxes that help to provide the many benefits Swedes enjoy.)*

Building a Welfare State
L2

Guided Instruction

■ Read about Sweden's past in Building a Welfare State. As students read, circulate and make sure individuals can answer the Reading Check question.

■ Discuss why life in Sweden was not always so secure. *(By the late 1800s, industry had not grown, farming methods had not changed, and many people were poor.)*

■ Ask students **How did the country change in the early 1900s?** *(Sweden became an industrial country and the economy grew stronger.)*

■ Discuss how Sweden became a welfare state. *(A political party called the Social Democrats came to power in the mid-1900s, promised Swedes a better life, and changed Sweden into a welfare state.)*

Independent Practice

Have students continue to fill in the graphic organizer with details about Sweden's welfare state. Ask them to include details under the Economic Challenges column.

Monitor Progress

As students fill in the graphic organizer, make sure individuals are entering the correct details. Provide assistance as necessary.

Background: Biography

Alfred Nobel (1833-1896) Industry came to Sweden slowly, but Swedish inventor and businessman Alfred Nobel became a successful industrialist in the 1800s. Nobel developed a safer form of the explosive nitroglycerin, which he called dynamite. He opened factories throughout Europe to manufacture dynamite and soon became rich. He also opened laboratories to develop new products. He registered more than 350 patents for his inventions, which included artificial leather and silk. In his will, he left money for the establishment of the Nobel Prizes. These prizes honor people who have made advances in science, literature, economics, and peace.

Answer

√ **Reading Check** a system that provides basic services for all people at every stage of life

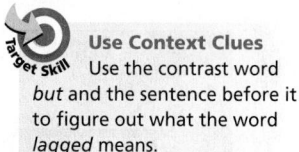

Target Reading Skill L2

As a follow up, have students answer the Target Reading Skill question on this page. (*Using the previous sentence and the contrast word* but, *students should answer that* lagged *means "delayed" or "fail to keep up."*)

Problems and Solutions L2

Guided Instruction

- **Vocabulary Builder** Clarify the high-use word **fund** before reading.

- Read how Sweden is trying to meet its challenges in Problems and Solutions.

- Discuss Sweden's tax problem in the late 1980s. (*Because taxes were high, people bought fewer products, there was less money to boost the economy, and economic growth stalled.*)

- Ask **What measures did the government take to continue to pay for benefits?** (*The government borrowed money, which raised the national debt. It then increased taxes and cut some spending to try to control the debt.*)

Answers

✓ Reading Check the Social Democrats

Chart Skills Compare Sweden's sales tax is about 5–9 percent higher than the other European countries shown, and almost twenty percent higher than those of Florida and California. **Generalize** Possible answer: probably fewer, because they have less money to spend on social services than governments with higher taxes

---

Target Skill **Use Context Clues** Use the contrast word *but* and the sentence before it to figure out what the word *lagged* means.

■ Chart Skills

Sales tax is a tax on goods and services. This chart shows the rate, or percent, of sales tax in various Western European countries and two American states. **Compare** How does Sweden's sales tax compare to those of the other European countries shown? To the states shown? **Generalize** Do you think governments with very low taxes generally provide many or few social services? Why do you think so?

Sales Tax Rates in Western Europe and the United States

Country or State	Standard Rate (%)
France	19.6
Germany	16.0
Sweden	25.0
United Kingdom	17.5
United States: Florida	6.0
United States: California	7.25

SOURCE: The Economist Intelligence Unit Limited; Federation of Tax Administrators (www.taxadmin.org), California State Board of Equalization

280 Europe and Russia

Meeting Economic Challenges Economic problems led to the rise of Sweden's modern welfare state. By the late 1800s, industry had grown in the United States and most of Europe. But Sweden lagged far behind. There were few factories or railroad lines or even good roads. Farming methods had not changed much since the Middle Ages. Many people were very poor. By the end of the 1800s, about 1.5 million Swedes had left the country in search of a better life. Most of them settled in the midwestern states of the United States, such as Minnesota and Wisconsin.

In 1932, a political party called the Social Democrats came to power. The Social Democrats promised a better life for Swedes. Over the next few decades, the party made Sweden into a welfare state. At the same time, Sweden became an industrial country, and its economy grew stronger. Today the Social Democrats are still the country's largest political party.

✓ Reading Check **Which political party created Sweden's welfare state?**

Problems and Solutions

Sweden's welfare state has served as a model for government throughout Europe. Still, the system has its problems. Everyone in Sweden receives benefits, but the government has faced challenges in providing those benefits.

Facing Challenges For decades, Sweden was able to offer its citizens generous benefits. But things changed in the 1980s. People bought fewer items because of the high taxes on groceries, clothing, and other goods. Thus, there was less spending to boost the economy. Sweden's economic growth stalled. The government had to borrow money to continue paying for the benefits provided under the welfare system. Soon, the **national debt**, or the amount of money their government owed, began to grow.

The government increased taxes and cut spending in the 1990s to control the debt. Eventually, the Swedish government no longer had to borrow money to fund welfare benefits. In fact, every year since 1998, the government has had a budget surplus, or more money than is needed to pay for benefits. However, as its population ages, Sweden will need more money to care for its people.

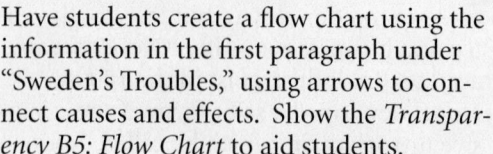

Differentiated Instruction

For Special Needs Students L1
Have students read the section as they listen to the recorded version on the Student Edition on Audio CD. Check for comprehension by pausing the CD after each paragraph and asking students to summarize what they have just read.

⊙ Chapter 9, Section 3, **Student Edition on Audio CD**

For Gifted and Talented L3
Have students create a flow chart using the information in the first paragraph under "Sweden's Troubles," using arrows to connect causes and effects. Show the *Transparency B5: Flow Chart* to aid students.

📖 **Europe and Russia Transparencies,** *Transparency B5: Flow Chart*

A Graying Population Sweden has 1.5 million retired people out of a population of about 9 million. This means that about one out of six people is retired. That is the highest proportion of retired people in the world. Sweden's aging population presents many challenges for the nation. Elderly people often need increased health care and medicines.

Yet an aging population presents an even greater problem. As you have read, Swedes receive many benefits. The money for these benefits comes from the paychecks of Swedish workers, who pay high taxes on their salaries. In an aging population, there are fewer workers, because so many people are retired. As a result, there is less tax money to pay for benefits.

Over time, the money received from taxes may not be enough to pay for the extra care needed by an elderly population. Raising taxes even higher to cover the high costs of benefits has been proposed, but it is not a popular idea. The government is trying to save money now to pay for this care in the future. However, if Sweden does not stick to its budget reforms, money for welfare benefits could run out.

Government Solutions Sweden's government is working to solve these problems. The government reformed its own budget process through new rules, such as balanced budget requirements, surplus goals, and spending limits. In addition, the government tried to reduce benefits in the 1990s. It reduced the payments for sickness benefits and required workers to save more of their own money for retirement. But the reduction in benefits angered Swedish voters, who voted against their leaders in two major elections.

Links to Science

Sun at Midnight It is midnight in northern Sweden, and some friends are playing volleyball outside. How is this so? From about March 20 to September 23 in the most northern arctic regions, the sun can be seen on the horizon 24 hours a day. This is because the northern hemisphere is tilted directly toward the sun at this time. In northern Sweden, the sun never sets for a few days around June 21. The Swedes celebrate this time as Midsummer's Eve, with dancing (below), food, and music.

12:05 AM

Chapter 9 Section 3 **281**

Links

Read the **Links to Science** on this page. Then ask **When do Swedes celebrate Midsummer's Eve?** *(for a few days around June 21, when the sun never sets)*

Guided Instruction (continued)

■ Discuss how Sweden has tried to solve its problems and whether its efforts were successful. *(It tried to reduce benefits and required workers to save more of their own money for retirement, but angry Swedish voters voted against their leaders.)*

■ Ask **Why have Swedish companies had problems competing with firms in other countries?** *(Companies became less productive because they could not make products as quickly and cheaply as other countries.)*

■ Ask **How might businesses help solve Sweden's problems?** *(Sweden's businesses might take advantage of natural resources.)*

Independent Practice

Have students complete the graphic organizer by filling in additional details in the Economic Challenges column.

Monitor Progress

■ Show *Section Reading Support Transparency ER 45* and ask students to check their graphic organizers individually. Go over key concepts and clarify key vocabulary as needed.

📖 **Europe and Russia Transparencies,** *Section Reading Support Transparency ER 45*

■ Tell students to fill in the last column of the *Reading Readiness Guide.* Probe for what they learned that confirms or invalidates each statement.

All in One Europe and Russia Teaching Resources, *Reading Readiness Guide,* p. 266

 **Skills Mini Lesson**

Decision Making

1. Teach the skill by explaining the steps used in decision making: identify a problem, gather information, list and evaluate the options, and choose the best option.

2. Help students practice the skill by identifying the problems Sweden has faced

in continuing to provide benefits to all its citizens.

3. Have students apply the skill by answering these questions: What are some options the government and businesses have to solve this problem? What might be possible negative effects of these options? What would you decide?

Assess and Reteach

Assess Progress `L2`

Have students complete the Section Assessment. Administer the *Section Quiz*.

All in One **Europe and Russia Teaching Resources,** *Section Quiz,* p. 268

Reteach `L1`

If students need more instruction, have them read this section in the Reading and Vocabulary Study Guide.

Chapter 9, Section 3, **Eastern Hemisphere Reading and Vocabulary Study Guide,** pp. 98–100

Extend `L3`

Have students learn more about comparing daily life today to life in the past by reading the literature excerpt *The Boy* by Erik Christian Haugaard in pairs or groups. Discuss the Think It Over questions at the end. Ask students how Dag's government might have been able to help him if it offered benefits like Sweden's today.

All in One **Europe and Russia Teaching Resources,** *The Boy,* pp. 292–295

Answer

√ Reading Check Natural resources such as iron ore, steel, rivers, waterfalls, and timber could help the Swedish economy.

Section 3 Assessment

Key Terms

Students' sentences should reflect knowledge of each Key Term.

Target Reading Skill

Because the forests are large enough to supply Sweden's timber needs as well as those of other countries, *vast* must mean "large" or "extensive."

Comprehension and Critical Thinking

1. (a) Swedish citizens receive medical care, family leave, child care, education, five weeks paid vacation, sick leave, and retirement payments. **(b)** Many Swedes are willing to pay high taxes for the security the benefits give them.

2. (a) There were few factories or railroad lines or good roads, farming methods had changed little, many people were poor. Many left the country in search of a better life. **(b)** With industrialization, Sweden's economy grew stronger.

A woman assembles parts at a car factory in Göteborg, Sweden.

Business Solutions Another solution would be for businesses to earn more, giving more money to the government in the form of taxes. One way for businesses to grow is to take better advantage of Sweden's natural resources. Sweden has high-grade iron ore and produces enough steel for itself and for export. Hydroelectric turbines run by Sweden's fast rivers and many waterfalls produce half of Sweden's electricity. Sweden's vast forests support the timber industry, which supplies Sweden's needs as well as those of other countries.

Even with these ample resources, Swedish companies have had trouble competing with firms in other countries. Most Swedish products are of high quality. But the Swedes have not been able to make them as quickly and cheaply as other countries. Some companies have found a solution to this problem. Swedish automakers, for example, have followed the example of American companies. Using the methods of American auto factories, the Swedes can now make a car in about 40 hours. It used to take them about 100 hours.

Improving the economy means changing the ways that things are done in Sweden. Because the welfare system is very important to Swedes, they are working to find better ways of paying for it. That is one challenge facing Sweden today.

√ Reading Check **What natural resources could help the Swedish economy?**

Section 3 Assessment

Key Terms

Review the key terms at the beginning of this section. Use each term in a sentence that explains its meaning.

Target Reading Skill

Find the word *vast* in the first paragraph on this page. How does its context explain its meaning?

Comprehension and Critical Thinking

1. (a) Describe What benefits do Swedish citizens receive?

(b) Identify Frame of Reference Why are some Swedes willing to pay such high taxes?

2. (a) Explain Why did many Swedes leave their country in the late 1800s?

(b) Identify Effects What effect did industrialization have on Sweden's economy?

3. (a) Explain Why did the Swedish economy stall in the late 1980s?

(b) Apply Information How did the government and businesses work together to solve Sweden's economic problems?

Writing Activity

Consider that in the United States, most people pay 20 to 30 percent of their income in taxes, compared to about 60 percent in Sweden. What lessons do you think the two countries might learn from each other? Write a paragraph summarizing your thoughts.

For: An activity on the Vikings
Visit: PHSchool.com
Web Code: ldd-7403

282 Europe and Russia

3. (a) People were buying fewer items because of high taxes. **(b)** The government reformed its own budget process, and businesses have followed the examples of American companies.

Writing Activity

Use the *Rubric for Assessing a Writing Assignment* to evaluate students' paragraphs.

All in One **Europe and Russia Teaching Resources,** *Rubric for Assessing a Writing Assignment,* p. 298

Go Online PHSchool.com Typing in the Web code when prompted will bring students directly to detailed instructions for this activity.

Prepare to Read

Objectives
In this section you will
1. Discover that there is another country within Italy called Vatican City.
2. Understand why there are divisions between northern and southern Italy.

Taking Notes
As you read this section, look for ways that life is similar and different in northern and southern Italy. Copy the Venn diagram below and record your findings in it.

Life in Italy

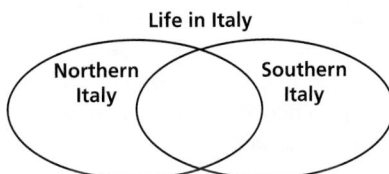

Target Reading Skill
Use Context Clues To make sure you have correctly determined the meaning of an unfamiliar word by looking at its context, look at the word itself for clues. For example, examine the word *guidance* in the first paragraph below. The sentence in which the word appears tells you that it has something to do with the leader. To double check, look at the word itself. What verb sounds like *guidance*?

Key Terms
- **basilica** (buh SIL ih kuh) *n.* a Roman Catholic church that has special, high status because of its age or history
- **manufacturing** (man yoo FAK chur ing) *n.* the process of turning raw materials into finished products
- **land reform** (land ree FAWRM) *n.* the process of dividing large properties into smaller ones

Can you solve this riddle? A magazine photographer spent about a year exploring a certain country, yet the country is so tiny that he was able to walk around it in 40 minutes. Its population is only about 1,000. But about one billion people look to its leader for guidance. What is the country?

The tiny country is called Vatican City (VAT ih kun SIH tee). It is the world headquarters of the Roman Catholic Church. The pope is its leader. Every day, Roman Catholics all over the world look to him for leadership. Politically, Vatican City is not part of Italy. Yet it holds an important place in the culture of all Italians.

St. Peter's Basilica rises above Vatican City.

Target Reading Skill L2
Point out the Target Reading Skill. Tell students that when they use context clues to determine the meaning of a word, they can double check the meaning by studying the word itself for clues.

Model the skill using the word *modernize* in the fourth paragraph on p. 288. (*Students should use what they know about the word "modern" to determine that mod-* ernize *means to "renovate" or "bring up to date."*)

Give students *Use Context Clues: General Knowledge.* Have them complete the activity in groups.

All in One Europe and Russia Teaching Resources, *Use Context Clues: General Knowledge,* p. 279

Objectives
Social Studies
1. Discover that there is another country within Italy called Vatican City.
2. Understand why there are divisions between northern and southern Italy.

Reading/Language Arts
Use what you already know about an unfamiliar word to confirm information given in context clues.

Prepare to Read

Build Background Knowledge L2
Tell students that they will learn about similarities and differences between the northern and southern regions of Italy. Show the video *Ancient Rome.* Ask students how the Roman Empire's legacy is evident in Italy today, and if they think it contributes to the unity or division of the Italian people. Use the Give One, Get One strategy (TE, p.T37) to encourage class discussion.

Ancient Rome, **World Studies Video Program**

Set a Purpose for Reading L2
- Preview the Objectives.
- Read each statement in the *Reading Readiness Guide* aloud. Ask students to mark the statements true or false.

  All in One Europe and Russia Teaching Resources, *Reading Readiness Guide,* p. 270

- Have students discuss the statements in pairs or groups of four, then mark their guides again. Use the Numbered Heads participation strategy (TE, p. T36) to call on students to share their group's perspectives.

Vocabulary Builder
Preview Key Terms L2
Pronounce each Key Term, then ask students to say the word with you. Provide a simple explanation such as, "A basilica is a Roman Catholic church that has special importance."

Use Context Clues As a follow up, have students answer the Target Reading Skill question on this page of the Student Edition. (*Students should conclude that* priceless *means "too valuable to be assigned a price" or "irreplaceable".*)

Instruct

Vatican City   L2

Guided Instruction

■ Read A Unifying Force, using the Oral Cloze reading strategy (TE, p. T33).

■ Ask students **How is the Vatican both a city and a country?** (*The Vatican is located within the city of Rome. It has its own police force, radio station, newspaper, and fire department. Like other countries, it is a member of the United Nations and has its own banks and money.*)

■ Discuss why tourists come to the Vatican. (*Tourists come to see St. Peter's Basilica, the Vatican's palace, the Sistine Chapel, and art museums.*)

Independent Practice

Assign *Guided Reading and Review*.

All in One **Europe and Russia Teaching Resources,** *Guided Reading and Review*, p. 271

Monitor Progress

As students complete *Guided Reading and Review*, circulate and make sure that individuals are completing the worksheet correctly.

Answers

✓ Reading Check   The Vatican is an independent city-state and country within Rome. It symbolizes the Roman Catholic Church and unites most Italians.

Apply Information Many famous Renaissance artists and architects contributed to St. Peter's Basilica.

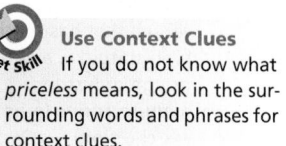

Use Context Clues If you do not know what *priceless* means, look in the surrounding words and phrases for context clues.

A View Inside St. Peter's
Tourists gaze in awe at the art decorating St. Peter's Basilica, including these sculptures by the Italian Renaissance artist Bernini. **Apply Information** *How was the Vatican influenced by the Renaissance?*

Vatican City

Vatican City is also known as the Vatican. It is a country within a country. Located within Rome, the capital of Italy, the Vatican is an independent city-state. The Vatican has its own banks and its own money, although you can also use euros there. It is a member of the United Nations. It also has its own police force, radio station, newspaper, and fire department.

Vatican City symbolizes the Roman Catholic Church that unites most Italians. Every day, Catholics and non-Catholics stream into this little country. Most visitors come to see St. Peter's Basilica. A **basilica** is a Roman Catholic church that has a special, high status because of its age or history. The Vatican's palace and art museums are also popular attractions. These museums have priceless collections of religious art, as well as artwork from ancient Greece and Rome.

The Sistine (SIS teen) Chapel, located inside the Vatican, contains many famous paintings, sculptures, and other works of art. Tourists crowd into this chapel, but there is nearly perfect silence inside. No one is allowed to speak above a whisper. Everyone leans back to see the religious scenes painted on the ceiling. The artist Michelangelo painted the ceiling in the 1500s. It is the most famous ceiling in the world.

✓ **Reading Check** What is the Vatican?

284 Europe and Russia

Vocabulary Builder

Use the information below to teach students this section's high-use words.

High-Use Word	Definition and Sample Sentence
retain, p. 287	*v.* to maintain possession of Banks **retain** detailed records of all transactions.
abundant, p. 288	*adj.* plentiful The **abundant** rain allowed the flowers to bloom.

Italy

Historically, Italy's location on the Mediterranean Sea made it an important agricultural center and a crossroads of world trade. Today, Italy's economy is shifting toward services, and its main trade partners are other EU members. The "two Italies"—northern and southern—continue to have unequal economies. Use the data on this page to learn more about the economy of Italy.

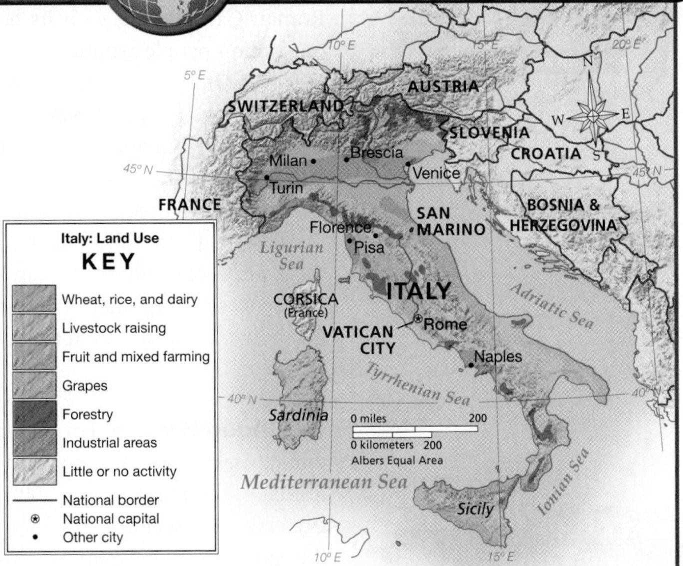

Italy: Land Use
KEY

- Wheat, rice, and dairy
- Livestock raising
- Fruit and mixed farming
- Grapes
- Forestry
- Industrial areas
- Little or no activity
- ─── National border
- ⊛ National capital
- • Other city

0 miles 200
0 kilometers 200
Albers Equal Area

Economic Output per Person, 2001

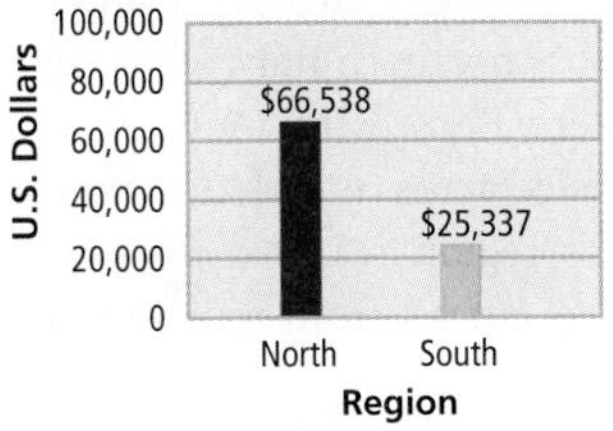

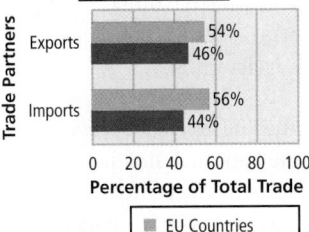

- North: $66,538
- South: $25,337

U.S. Dollars / Region

SOURCES: The European Commission; The World Bank Group

Structure of Italy's Economy

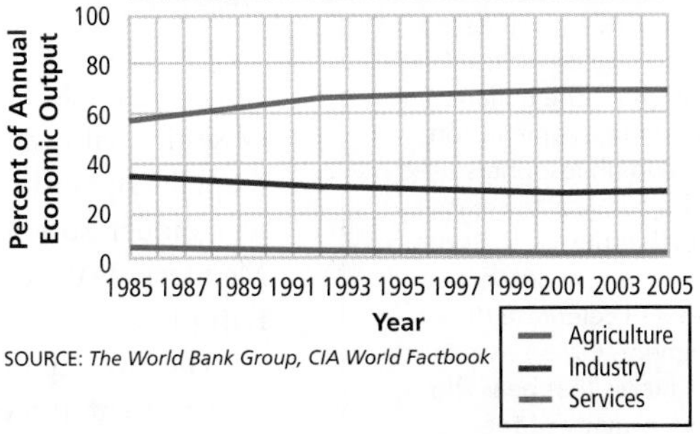

Percent of Annual Economic Output vs. Year (1985–2005)

- Agriculture
- Industry
- Services

SOURCE: The World Bank Group, CIA World Factbook

Trade, 2001

Exports: 54% / 46%
Imports: 56% / 44%

Percentage of Total Trade

- EU Countries
- Non-EU Countries

SOURCE: Italy in Figures

Map and Chart Skills

1. **Identify** Where is most of Italy's industry?
2. **Compare and Contrast** How does northern Italy's economic output per person compare to that of southern Italy?
3. **Predict** What changes might southern Italy need to make to its economy in order to catch up with the economy of northern Italy?

Go Online
PHSchool.com

Use Web Code **lde-7414** for **DK World Desk Reference Online.**

Chapter 9 Section 4 **285**

Guided Instruction [L2]

Ask students to study the Country Profile on this page. As a class, answer the Map and Chart Skills questions. Allow students to briefly discuss their responses with a partner before sharing answers.

Independent Practice

Distribute *Reading a Bar Graph*. Have students work in pairs to complete the worksheet. Then ask them to study the bar graphs on this page. Ask them to describe what information the bar graph Trade, 2001 tells them. *(EU countries traded more than non-EU countries in 2001.)*

All in One **Europe and Russia Teaching Resources,** *Reading a Bar Graph,* p. 290

Answers

Map and Chart Skills

1. in northern Italy, especially near Milan
2. The north's economic output per person is much higher than the south's.
3. Possible answer: building factories to increase manufacturing

Go Online
PHSchool.com Students can find more information about this topic on the DK World Desk Reference Online.

Differentiated Instruction

For Special Needs Students [L2]

Tell students that to paint the ceiling of the Sistine Chapel, Michelangelo had to paint lying on his back on top of a platform raised 60 feet above the ground. Help students appreciate the difficulties the artist faced by having each student first draw a picture sitting at a table. Then have them try to duplicate their efforts by drawing the same picture while lying on their backs. Students might tape their papers to the bottoms of chairs or desks. Have students compare their two drawings.

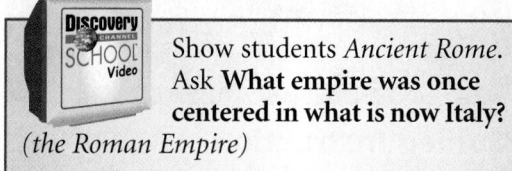

Show students *Ancient Rome.* Ask **What empire was once centered in what is now Italy?** *(the Roman Empire)*

Divisions Between North and South L2

Guided Instruction

■ **Vocabulary Builder** Clarify the high-use words **retain** and **abundant** before reading.

■ Read about Italy's past and present in Divisions between North and South.

■ Ask students **How does the Roman Catholic Church unite the people of Italy?** *(Though not every Italian is Catholic, Italy's history is closely tied to the history of Catholicism.)*

■ Ask students **What are some differences among Italians?** *(Italians in the north live, work, and practice Roman Catholicism differently from those in the south.)*

■ Have students discuss how northern and southern Italy developed differently after the fall of the Roman Empire. *(Italy was divided into many separate city-states, territories, and small kingdoms. Northern Italy was influenced by invaders from Western Europe. Southern Italy was colonized by invaders from the Byzantine Empire. Their different cultures influenced northern and southern Italy—northern Italy is more industrial, while the south is more agricultural.)*

Links

Read the **Links Across Time** on this page. Ask students **How is the Risorgimento remembered in Italy today?** *(Italian schoolchildren learn about and celebrate the movement, and streets and squares are named after its heroes.)*

Learn about life in ancient Rome.

Links Across Time

The Risorgimento: "Rising Again" The Risorgimento was a movement in the 1800s that inspired the Italian people to unite as one nation. Poets and philosophers used words and ideas to create a sense of nationalism. Today, Italian school children learn about and celebrate the movement. Cities have streets and squares that bear the names of many of the Risorgimento's heroes. Giuseppe Garibaldi (right) was one of the Risorgimento's leaders and is today considered an Italian patriot.

Divisions Between North and South

Roman Catholicism, with its base in the Vatican, unites about one billion people around the world. It also unites most Italians. Not every Italian is a Catholic, but Italy's history is closely tied to the history of Catholicism. Other things also bring Italians together. Most people living in Italy are ethnic Italians. There are few ethnic minorities. Strong family ties are common among Italians. Even a love of soccer unites many Italians.

Despite these things that many Italians have in common, there are many differences among Italians. Some of the major differences are regional. Italians in the north and Italians in the south live, work, and even practice Roman Catholicism in different ways.

A Divided History For hundreds of years, there was no single, unified Italy. What we now call Italy was once the center of the Roman Empire. Around 2,000 years ago, the Roman Empire stretched across Europe and into northern Africa. When the Roman Empire broke up, Italy itself was divided into many separate city-states, territories, and small kingdoms. The people in these areas had different governments and spoke different languages.

Over time, a regional pattern emerged. Invaders came by land from the north. They swept across northern Italy, which retained close ties with the rest of Western Europe. In contrast, invaders from the Byzantine Empire traveled across the Mediterranean Sea to conquer southern Italy. This region retained links to other Mediterranean countries but was cut off from much of Western Europe.

The two regions also developed differently in terms of government and economy. In northern Italy, city-states became bustling cities. In modern times, this region became a center of industry. In contrast, in southern Italy, feudal kingdoms dominated, with large numbers of peasants working the land. As a result, southern Italy has always been heavily agricultural.

Italy Unites In the late 1800s, the regions of Italy were united into one nation. A standard form of the Italian language was introduced to help unify the people. After hundreds of years of a divided history, it was not always easy for Italians to identify themselves with this new nation. Even today, there are strong differences between life in the north and in the south.

Differentiated Instruction

For Advanced Readers L3
Have students learn more about daily life in Italy and the rest of the world by working on *Keeping a Scrapbook of Daily Life Around the World.*

Go Online
PHSchool.com
For: Long-Term Integrated Projects: *Keeping a Scrapbook of Daily Life Around the World*
Visit: PHSchool.com
Web Code: ldd-7406

Life in the North Milan (mih LAN) is typical of northern Italy. Abundant minerals, fast rivers, and a well-developed economy have brought wealth to the region. Many international businesses are located there. Northern Italy is much more prosperous than southern Italy.

The cities of Milan, Turin, and Genoa are home to most of Italy's manufacturing industries. **Manufacturing** is the process of turning raw materials into finished products. Milan's factories produce cars, planes, leather goods, and plastics.

Milan has a more stylish side, too. Every season, people interested in fashion crowd into Milan to see the new collections from clothing designers. Milan is now second only to Paris as a fashion capital.

Like many European cities, Milan is a mix of the old and the new. In a 400-year-old palace, you can see one of the oldest public libraries in Europe. Millions of dollars have been spent to keep it in good condition. Less than a mile away, you can drive past modern steel and glass office buildings.

Life in the South Southern Italy is very different from Milan. Southern Italy is mostly agricultural. Fertile areas near the coast receive enough rainfall to grow abundant crops. Olives, tomatoes, fruits, and other crops grow there. Inland, farmers have difficulty making a living because of the thin soil and dry climate.

Locorotondo (loh koh roh TOHN doh) is a small town located in the southernmost part of Italy. It is on the "heel" of the Italian "boot." Most people in Locorotondo make a living by farming. They grow wheat, olives, and fruits there. Fishing is also an important business for people there.

Most people in southern Italy follow a more traditional way of life. Many people in southern Italy talk about northern Italy as if it were another country. There are fewer large cities in southern Italy. The high fashions of Milan and the busy city of Turin seem very far away.

Cars being assembled at the Ferrari factory in Maranello, Italy

Making Cheese
These men use traditional methods to make cheese. **Contrast** *How does this work differ from that performed by the men in the photo at the top of this page?*

Background: Links Across Time

A Papal Division The establishment of the Holy Roman Empire in the early 800s is linked to the division of north and south evidenced in Italy today. The pope was given political power over central Italy, and the Papal States effectively separated northern and southern Italy. The separation was heightened by the influence that France, Spain, and Austria exerted on northern Italy. These associations led northern city-states to create commercial and financial empires. Italy was unified in 1861.

Guided Instruction (continued)
- Ask students to explain how Milan is typical of northern Italy. (*Milan has abundant minerals, fast rivers, a developed economy, international businesses, manufacturing industries, and fashion designers, and is more prosperous than areas of southern Italy.*)
- Have students discuss how Locorotondo is typical of southern Italy. (*Locorotondo is a small town where most people make a living in agriculture and live a more traditional way of life than northern Italians.*)

Answer

Contrast The men in the photo at the top of the page are assembling machinery and seem to be working in an urban environment. The man in the photo at the bottom of the page seems to be using tools that are less modern. He probably works in a more rural area.

Guided Instruction (continued)

- Discuss with students how life is organized in small towns in Italy's countryside. *(Life is organized around the Roman Catholic Church and family.)*

- Ask **How did Italy's government work to improve life in southern Italy after World War II?** *(The government introduced land reform and modernized the region by building new roads and irrigation systems.)*

- Ask **Why do you think that the Northern League want to turn northern Italy into a separate country?** *(Possible answer: because the two regions are so different; perhaps so northern Italy would not have to support the poorer southern part of Italy)*

- Ask **Do you think northern and southern Italy will become separate countries?** *(Possible answer: Probably not, because Italians have a strong identity and are linked by religion and their focus on family.)*

Independent Practice

Ask students to create and complete the Taking Notes graphic organizer on a blank piece of paper. Have them fill in the graphic organizer with details about similarities and differences between the northern and southern regions of Italy. Briefly model how to identify which details to record. As an additional aid, show the blank *Venn Diagram Graphic Organizer Transparency*.

📖 **Europe and Russia Transparencies,** *Transparency B16: Venn Diagram*

Monitor Progress

- Show *Section Reading Support Transparency ER 46* and ask students to check their graphic organizers individually. Go over key concepts and clarify key vocabulary as needed.

📖 **Europe and Russia Transparencies,** *Section Reading Support Transparency ER 46*

- Tell students to fill in the last column of the *Reading Readiness Guide*. Probe for what they learned that confirms or invalidates each statement.

All in One **Europe and Russia Teaching Resources,** *Reading Readiness Guide,* p. 270

Answer

Analyze Images There is a large church in the lower righthand corner of the photgraph.

A Coastal Scene
The town of Positano clings to a steep cliff on the edge of the ocean in southern Italy. **Analyze Images** *What evidence do you see in the photo of the importance of religion to southern Italians?*

Religion in the Two Italies The Roman Catholic Church provides a focus particularly for southern Italians. Today, in the small towns of the south, life is organized around the larger family of the Church and the smaller family in the home. In the north, these ties may not be as strong.

Many religious events are celebrated in the streets of southern towns. Every year, the Feast of Corpus Christi, a Catholic religious festival, takes place several weeks after Easter. In this festival, women hang their wedding clothes over their balconies and place flowers on them. Additional displays are set up on the streets around town. People walk together around the town, from church to church and from display to display.

Economics and the Two Italies After World War II, Italy's economy boomed. Because most of its large cities and industrial centers are located in the north, northern Italy boomed, too. Meanwhile, the agriculture-based economy of southern Italy failed to thrive. Southern Italians moved to the north in large numbers to find jobs.

Italy's government took measures to help the south catch up with the north. First, it introduced land reform. **Land reform** is a process of dividing large properties into smaller ones. Governments sponsor land reform so that more people can own land. Italy's government hoped that land reform would increase agricultural production. The government also modernized the southern region by building roads and new irrigation systems.

Differentiated Instruction

For English Language Learners L1
As a vocabulary-building activity, create a word web using the blank *Concept Web Graphic Organizer Transparency* as an aid. Write "agriculture" in the center circle and invite students to suggest words on p. 150 that are related to that topic. Students may include related words not found in the text.

📖 **Europe and Russia Transparencies,** *Transparency B17: Concept Web*

These measures increased agricultural output in the south. Still, southern Italy today lags behind northern Italy. Unemployment in southern Italy is higher than elsewhere in the country. And many southern Italians still move north, particularly to the cities of Rome and Milan. There, they seek jobs and a better standard of living.

Politics and the Two Italies Northern and southern Italy are so different that some Italians have urged northern Italy to become a separate country. Throughout the 1990s, a party called the Northern League called for northern Italy to secede, or leave the rest of Italy to form its own country. In 1996, the party won 10 percent of the vote in a national election.

However, in recent elections, the Northern League has not done so well. For most Italians, no matter how much they differ, they will never lose their strong Italian identity. Religion and family will probably keep the people of Italy unified for many years to come.

 **Reading Check** Why do some Northern Italians support the Northern League?

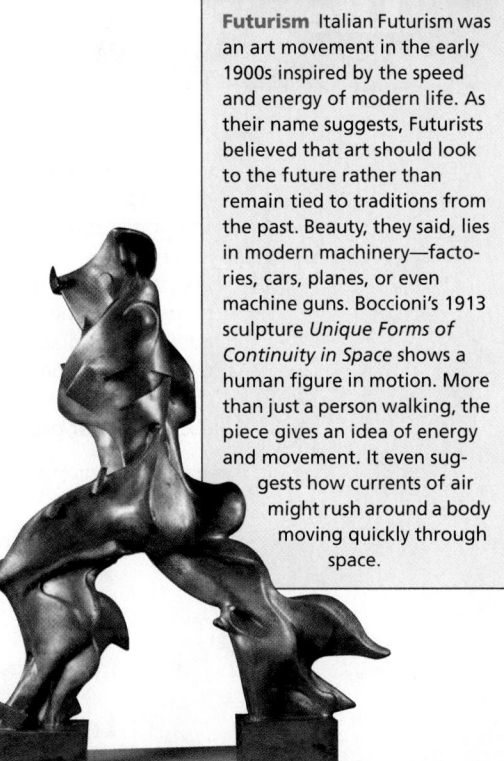

Links to Art

Futurism Italian Futurism was an art movement in the early 1900s inspired by the speed and energy of modern life. As their name suggests, Futurists believed that art should look to the future rather than remain tied to traditions from the past. Beauty, they said, lies in modern machinery—factories, cars, planes, or even machine guns. Boccioni's 1913 sculpture *Unique Forms of Continuity in Space* shows a human figure in motion. More than just a person walking, the piece gives an idea of energy and movement. It even suggests how currents of air might rush around a body moving quickly through space.

Section 4 Assessment

Key Terms
Review the key terms listed at the beginning of this section. Use each term in a sentence that explains its meaning.

Target Reading Skill
Use context clues to explain the meaning of the word *secede* in the second paragraph on this page.

Comprehension and Critical Thinking
1. (a) Locate Where is Vatican City?
(b) Summarize How does the Vatican operate as a city-state?

(c) Synthesize Information How does the Roman Catholic religion unite Italians?
2. (a) List Name three differences between life in northern Italy and life in southern Italy.
(b) Sequence How did regional differences emerge in Italy over time?
(c) Make Generalizations Do you think Italy's government should continue to introduce reforms to make northern Italy and southern Italy equal? Explain why or why not.

Writing Activity
Write a letter as if you are an Italian writing to a relative about life in either northern or southern Italy. Write details about your life, including what you do for fun, what kinds of work your parents do, and so on.

> **Writing Tip** Be sure to include a greeting, a closing, and a signature in your letter. Also decide on the age, gender, and personality of the person writing the letter.

Section 4 Assessment

Key Terms
Students' sentences should reflect knowledge of each Key Term.

Target Reading Skill
The phrase following *secede* explains that it means that a part of the country breaks away to form its own country.

Comprehension and Critical Thinking
1. (a) The Vatican is in Rome, the capital of Italy. **(b)** It has its own money, police force, radio station, newspaper, and fire department, and is located entirely within the city of Rome. **(c)** Though not all Italians are Roman Catholic, Roman Catholicism is an important part of the history of Italy.

2. (a) Northern Italy has international businesses, manufacturing industries, and is more prosperous. Southern Italy is mostly

---

Assess and Reteach

Assess Progress [L2]
Have students complete the Section Assessment. Administer the *Section Quiz*.

All in One Europe and Russia Teaching Resources, *Section Quiz*, p. 272

Reteach [L1]
If students need more instruction, have them read this section in the Reading and Vocabulary Study Guide.

📖 Chapter 9, Section 4, **Eastern Hemisphere Reading and Vocabulary Study Guide,** pp. 101–103

Extend [L3]
Have students complete the *Urban Population, Past and Projected* online activity.

Go Online PHSchool.com

For: Environmental and Global Issues: *Urban Population, Past and Projected*
Visit: PHSchool.com
Web Code: ldd-7407

Answer

✓ **Reading Check** Possible answer: Some northern Italians may feel that northern and southern Italy are too different to remain one country.

Writing Activity
Use the *Rubric for Assessing a Writing Assignment* to evaluate students' letters.

All in One Europe and Russia Teaching Resources, *Rubric for Assessing a Writing Assignment*, p. 298

agricultural and more traditional. **(b)** After the fall of the Roman Empire, different groups settled in northern and southern Italy. Their cultures shaped the people who lived in the regions. **(c)** Answers and explanations will vary, but should be supported with evidence from the text.

Objective

Learn how to transfer information from one medium to another by using visual information to write a paragraph.

Prepare to Read

Build Background Knowledge L2

Tell students that there are many ways to present information, such as photographs, numbers, charts, tables, and text. Ask students to look through the sections they have covered so far in this chapter. Have them choose a visual from the chapter, such as a chart or a photograph, and make a list of the information that the image communicates. Then have each student share what they found with the class.

Instruct

Using Visual Information to Write a Paragraph L2

Guided Instruction

- Read the steps to using visual information to write a paragraph as a class and write them on the board.

- Practice the skill by following the steps on p. 291 as a class. Model each step in the activity by identifying the title and what it reveals about the subject of the table *(The title, "Italy: Population Statistics," tells you that the table will focus on the population of Italy.)*, studying the headings of the table and what they indicate *(The table is comparing and contrasting population, birth rate, death rate, fertility rate, and life expectancy in Italy in 1990 with an estimate of what they would be in 2006.)*, analyzing the meaning of the facts and drawing conclusions, and writing a paragraph with the major pieces of information from the table, including conclusions that can be drawn from the information. *(Possible conclusions: The population of Italy has not changed very much in 16 years. The birth rate has gone down slightly, while the death rate has gone up slightly. This means that the population of Italy is not growing significantly through births.)*

Skills for Life
Using Visual Information to Write a Paragraph

Jerry had to write a report on Rome's Vatican City. He was surprised to discover that Vatican City is a country. He had thought that it was only a religious center in Italy. To write his report, Jerry looked at different charts, graphs, maps, and diagrams. He found that the Vatican has been a country since 1929. From a chart, Jerry learned that the Vatican is about 109 acres (44 hectares) in area. Looking at a diagram, he saw that it is surrounded by a wall with gates that can be locked at night. Its population is fewer than a thousand people. The number of tourists who visit the Vatican each day is far greater than the number of its residents.

St. Peter's Basilica

Information can be presented as pictures, as numbers, or as text. When you translate the meaning of visual information into words, you are transferring information from one medium into another. Jerry transferred visual information from charts, graphs, and diagrams into a written report.

Learn the Skill

Use these steps to transfer visual information into a paragraph.

1. **Identify the topic of the chart, diagram, or graph by reading the title.** Then look at it to get a general idea of its purpose.

2. **Identify the key pieces of information.** Read headings and other key pieces of information carefully. The headings are usually set off in some way. If you are using a chart or a table, look for similarities and differences among the types of information in the columns.

3. **Analyze the meaning of the information.** Write down several conclusions that can be drawn from the information you have put together.

4. **Rewrite the key pieces of information and your conclusions in a clear paragraph.**

Independent Practice

Assign *Skills for Life* and have students complete it individually.

All in One Europe and Russia Teaching Resources, *Skills for Life,* p. 282

Monitor Progress

As students are analyzing the table, circulate and make sure individuals are applying the skill steps effectively.

Practice the Skill

Use the steps in Learn the Skill to translate the information in the table into a paragraph.

1 What is the title of the table? What does it tell you about the subject of the table?

ITALY: POPULATION STATISTICS		
	1990	2006 (Estimated)
Population	57,664,405	58,133,509
Birth Rate	10 births per 1,000 population	9 births per 1,000 population
Death Rate	9 deaths per 1,000 population	10 deaths per 1,000 population
Fertility Rate	1.4 children born per woman	1.3 children born per woman
Life Expectancy	74, male; 81, female	77, male; 83, female

2 What are the important headings in the table? Do they indicate key pieces of information? Note the information that is compared and contrasted in the table. How are all the statistics shown on this table related? In what ways are the two sets of numbers similar and different? Which categories have changed over time? Why do you think they have changed?

3 Analyze the meaning of the facts you have learned. What conclusions can you draw? For example, how might the change in the birth rate have affected Italy's population? How might the change in the death rate have affected Italy's population? Is the population getting older or younger? In what ways might the changes in Italy's population affect life in Italy in the future? Consider jobs, school, family life, health care, and so on.

4 Write a paragraph that contains the major pieces of information you have learned. Include the conclusions you have drawn.

Italian Workforce by Occupation

1990
5%
37% 58%

2003
5%
32% 63%

■ Services   ■ Industry   ■ Agriculture

Apply the Skill

Compare the circle graphs. Then use the steps above to write a short paragraph. Include key facts from the graphs, explaining what has changed from 1990 to 2003. Note that agriculture has remained the same. Why do you think that is so? Look at the two graphs and draw some conclusions about how these changes might have affected the country.

Assess and Reteach

Assess Progress   L2
Ask students to do the Apply the Skill activity.

Reteach   L1
For additional practice, have students complete the *Transferring Information from One Medium to Another* lesson on the Social Studies Skills Tutor CD-ROM.

 Transferring Information from One Medium to Another, **Social Studies Skills Tutor CD-ROM**

Extend   L3
Ask students to use the skill steps to analyze a chart or table from one of the Country Profiles in this chapter. They should follow the skill steps to write a paragraph, then exchange papers with a partner. Pairs should check each other's information and conclusions, revising their papers as necessary.

Answer
Apply the Skill
Students' conclusions will vary, but should be supported with information from the graphs.

Section 5
Step-by-Step Instruction

Objectives

Social Studies
1. Learn about Germany's past.
2. Find out how Germany became reunited.

Reading/Language Arts
Learn to use context clues over several paragraphs to determine the meaning of an unfamiliar word.

Prepare to Read

Build Background Knowledge L2
Ask students to suppose that there is a wall around their city or town. They are not allowed to cross the wall, and people on the other side of the wall are not allowed to cross either. Ask students how they would feel in this situation. Conduct an Idea Wave (TE, p. T35) to generate a list of student responses. Then tell them that until 1989 Germany was divided by a wall into two separate countries—East Germany and West Germany.

Set a Purpose for Reading L2
- Preview the Objectives.

- Form students into pairs or groups of four. Distribute the *Reading Readiness Guide.* Ask students to fill in the first two columns of the chart. Use the Numbered Heads participation strategy (TE, p. T36) to call on students to share one piece of information they already know and one piece of information they want to know.

  All in One Europe and Russia Teaching Resources, *Reading Readiness Guide,* p. 274

Vocabulary Builder
Preview Key Terms L2
Pronounce each Key Term, then ask students to say the word with you. Provide a simple explanation such as, "The reunification of Germany brought people from East and West Germany together for the first time since the end of World War II."

Section 5
Germany
A Unified Nation

Prepare to Read

Objectives
In this section you will
1. Learn about Germany's past.
2. Find out how Germany became reunited.

Taking Notes
As you read this section, look for the events that caused Germany to be divided and later reunited. Copy the flowchart below and record your findings in it.

Target Reading Skill
Use Context Clues When you first encounter an unfamiliar word, jot down some ideas about its meaning. As you read and reread the paragraphs that provide its context, adjust the word's definition until you are certain of it. For example, find the word *desperate* in the first paragraph on the next page. You may need to read several paragraphs before you can be certain of its meaning.

Key Terms
- **Holocaust** (HAHL uh kawst) *n.* the mass murder of six million Jews
- **reunification** (ree yoo nih fih KAY shun) *n.* the process of becoming unified again
- **standard of living** (STAN durd uv LIV ing) *n.* the level of comfort in terms of the goods and services that people have

A guard stands watch while East Berlin workmen add blocks to the Berlin Wall in October, 1961.

292 Europe and Russia

In 1961, Conrad Schumann, a 19-year-old policeman, stood guard at a barbed-wire fence in East Berlin. His job was to shoot anyone who tried to get across the fence. East Berlin was part of communist East Germany. The fence was built to prevent East Berliners from escaping to West Berlin, where they could reach democratic West Germany.

To Schumann, the fence was a terrible thing. He could see the buildings of West Berlin on the other side. They seemed very beautiful. On television, he had seen a program from West Berlin that showed people dancing to Western music and speaking their views freely. In East Germany, the government did not approve of Western music and free speech. The stores had few interesting things to buy.

Schumann thought about all these things. Then he made a decision and jumped over the barbed wire. A moment later, he was on the other side—in the freedom of the West. Just a few days after Schumann jumped to freedom, a concrete wall replaced the barbed-wire fence. The Berlin Wall separated families and friends. On one side of it, communism ruled. On the other side, the people did. What were the effects of a divided Germany?

Target Reading Skill L2
Point out the Target Reading Skill. Tell students that clues to the meaning of an unfamiliar word may appear near the word, or later on in the text.

Model using context clues using the word *communism* from the last paragraph on this page. Point out to students that more information about life under communism can be found throughout the section. *(Students should be able to determine that* communism *is a system under which people have few individual rights, and the government controls most of the economy.)*

Give students *Use Context Clues: Definition and Description.* Have them complete the activity in their groups.

All in One Europe and Russia Teaching Resources, *Use Context Clues: Definition and Description,* p. 277

Germany's Past

To understand the importance of the Berlin Wall, you need to understand part of Germany's past. Germany lost World War I in 1918. The German government had to pay billions of dollars as punishment for attacking other countries. In the early 1920s, the German economy collapsed. Prices soared. Germans became desperate.

Hitler and World War II When World War I began, Adolf Hitler (AD awlf HIT lur) was a 25-year-old Austrian soldier in the German army. When Germany lost the war, he promised himself that Germany would never suffer such a defeat again. Hitler became deeply involved in politics. In speech after speech, he promised to make Germany great again. By 1933, this former soldier had become dictator of Germany.

Hitler blamed Germany's economic problems on Jews. He spread hateful theories about Jews, Roma, and other groups in Germany. He claimed that they were inferior to other Germans. He claimed that Germans were a superior ethnic group—and that they should rule Europe.

Adolf Hitler salutes a crowd of people in 1934.

MAP MASTER™ Skills Activity

Divided Berlin

KEY
- Berlin Wall
- City border
- ✈ Airport

0 miles 10
0 kilometers 10
Transverse Mercator

Berlin
EAST GERMANY
WEST GERMANY

East Berlin
Tegel Airport
Reichstag
Brandenburg Gate
Gatow Airport
Tempelhof Airport
West Berlin
Schönefeld Airport
Havel River
Spree River

Location Though Berlin was divided into eastern and western halves, the entire city itself lay within the country of East Germany. **Locate** Which half of the city contained three airports? **Identify Point of View** How might Germans living in West Berlin have felt being surrounded by a communist nation?

Go Online
PHSchool.com Use Web Code ldp-7415 for step-by-step map skills practice.

Vocabulary Builder

Use the information below to teach students this section's high-use words.

High-Use Word	Definition and Sample Sentence
theory, p. 293	*n.* an idea or a plan about what something is or how it should be done It was Steve's **theory** that if the team practiced harder, they would win more games.
superior, p. 293	*adj.* greater in quality My new bicycle is **superior** to the old one.
elimination, p. 298	*n.* removal The **elimination** of sugar from the recipe made the cake less sweet.
aid, p. 298	*v.* to help Many charities **aid** people in need.

Germany's Past L2

Guided Instruction

- **Vocabulary Builder** Clarify the high-use words **theory** and **superior** before reading.

- Together with students, read Germany's Past, using the Oral Cloze reading strategy (TE, p. T33). As students read, circulate to make sure individuals can answer the Reading Check question.

- Have students discuss the effects of Germany's loss of World War I. (*The German government had to pay billions of dollars as punishment for attacking other countries, and the German economy collapsed while prices soared.*)

- Ask students **Who was Adolf Hitler?** (*an Austrian who became dictator of Germany in 1933*) **How did his actions lead to the start of World War II?** (*Hitler ordered attacks on neighboring countries and forced them under German rule. Great Britain, the Soviet Union, and the United States joined other nations to stop the Germans.*)

Answers

MAP MASTER Skills Activity **Locate** West Berlin
Identify Point of View they might have felt isolated and vulnerable

Go Online
PHSchool.com Students may practice their map skills using the interactive online version of this map.

Guided Instruction
Ask students to study the Country Profile on this page. As a class, answer the Map and Chart Skills questions. Allow students to briefly discuss their responses with a partner before sharing answers.

Independent Practice
Distribute *Reading a Timeline*. Have students work in partners to complete the worksheet. After they have finished, direct their attention to the timeline on this page and ask the following questions: **How many years after Germany was divided was the Berlin Wall built?** *(12 years)* **How many years after that did the Berlin Wall fall?** *(28 years)*

All in One **Europe and Russia Teaching Resources,** *Reading a Timeline,* p. 291

Germany

Germany has a long, complex history. At the time of the Roman Empire, various Germanic tribes lived all across Central Europe and into Scandinavia. Present-day Germany developed in the late 1800s out of a patchwork of kingdoms and small states. Just a few decades later, the country dramatically altered its history by fighting a global war. Use the data on this page to learn about modern Germany's history.

Germany: Population Density

KEY

Persons per sq. mile	Persons per sq. kilometer
More than 519	More than 199
260–519	100–199
130–259	50–99
25–129	10–49

Urban Areas
☐ More than 4,999,999
◉ 1,000,000–4,999,999
● 500,000–999,999
· Less than 500,000
— National border

0 miles 300
0 kilometers 300
Lambert Azimuthal Equal Area

Germany Since 1914

1914–1918 Germany is defeated in World War I; loses land, colonies, and wealth.

1933 Adolf Hitler and Nazi Party take political control.

1939–1945 Germany fights in World War II; is defeated by Allies.

1961 Berlin Wall is built.

1990 East Germany and West Germany reunite.

1910 — 1920 — 1940 — 1960 — 1980 — 2000

1920s Germany faces severe economic challenges.

1935 Nuremberg Laws legalize the persecution of Jews.

1949 Germany divides into communist East Germany and democratic West Germany.

1989 Berlin Wall falls.

2002 Germany adopts euro as its currency.

SOURCE: DK World Desk Reference

A World War I gas mask

German Capital Cities

Years	German Region	Region's Capital
1871–1918	German Empire	Berlin
1919–1949	Germany	Berlin
1949–1990	East Germany	East Berlin
1949–1990	West Germany	Bonn
1990–1999	Germany	Bonn
1999–present	Germany	Berlin

SOURCE: Encyclopedia Britannica Online

Map and Chart Skills

1. **Note** What was the capital of West Germany from 1949 to 1990?
2. **Explain** Why did Germany have two different capitals during the years 1949–1990?
3. **Predict** How might the population density of eastern Germany change as long as Berlin remains the capital?

 **Go Online** PHSchool.com
Use Web Code **Ide-7415** for **DK World Desk Reference Online.**

Answers

Map and Chart Skills

1. Bonn
2. because the country was divided into East Germany and West Germany
3. It might increase as more businesses and people move to Berlin.

Go Online PHSchool.com Students can find more information about this topic on the DK World Desk Reference Online.

Differentiated Instruction

For Gifted and Talented   L3
Tell students that since the end of World War II, countries and organizations around the world have taken steps to try to prevent another Holocaust. Have students read *The Universal Declaration of Human Rights* to see one example of this.

Go Online PHSchool.com
For: Environmental and Global Issues: *The Universal Declaration of Human Rights*
Visit: PHSchool.com
Web Code: Idd-7408

Soviet soldiers free Holocaust survivors from an Austrian concentration camp in 1945. **Synthesize** *How might images like this one have helped Europeans' resolve to avoid another world war?*

Many people did not believe Hitler's ideas. But Hitler was deadly serious. He ordered attacks on neighboring countries and forced them to submit to German rule. His actions led to the start of World War II in 1939. Great Britain, the Soviet Union, and finally the United States joined other nations to stop the Germans.

By the end of the war, Europe was in ruins. People around the world learned that the Germans had forced countless Jews, Roma, Slavs, and others into brutal concentration camps. Millions of people were murdered in these camps. The majority of them were Jews. This horrible mass murder of six million Jews is called the **Holocaust** (HAH luh kawst).

A Divided Capital At the end of the war, the victors divided up Germany. The Americans, British, and French joined their sections together to create the Federal Republic of Germany. This democratic country was also known as West Germany. The Soviet Union created a communist system in the German Democratic Republic, or East Germany.

The city of Berlin was in East Germany. But the western half of the city, called West Berlin, became part of democratic West Germany. The western half of Berlin was turned into an island of democracy in the middle of communism. The Berlin Wall separated the two halves of Berlin. It also stood as a symbol of a divided world.

Berlin had once been the capital of all of Germany. But now Germany was divided. The city of Bonn became the new capital of West Germany. East Berlin was the capital of East Germany.

Citizen Heroes

Raoul Wallenberg

Raoul Wallenberg (rah OOL WAHL un burg) came from a wealthy Swedish family of bankers and diplomats. Wallenberg studied architecture in the United States. But in 1944, with World War II raging, he persuaded the Swedish government to send him to Hungary as a diplomat. In Hungary, Wallenberg used Sweden's status as a neutral nation to create "safe houses" for Hungarian Jews. Wallenberg's safe houses sheltered several thousand Hungarian Jews and ultimately saved their lives. Wallenberg's efforts put his own life at great risk. In 1945, he was mistakenly arrested as a spy by Soviet troops in Hungary. Wallenberg died in a Soviet prison.

Guided Instruction (continued)

■ Ask students **How did Hitler's theories lead to the Holocaust?** (*He blamed Germany's problems on Jews and claimed Jews and other ethnic groups were inferior to other Germans. The Germans forced millions of Jews, Gypsies, Slavs, and others into concentration camps, where millions were murdered.*)

■ Discuss how Germany was divided at the end of World War II. (*The victors of the war divided Germany: the American, British, and French joined their sections to create a democratic country called the Federal Republic of Germany, also known as West Germany. The Soviet Union created a communist system called the German Democratic Republic, also known as East Germany. In addition, Berlin was divided by the Berlin Wall, creating West Berlin and East Berlin. East Berlin became the capital of East Germany and Bonn became the capital of West Germany.*)

Citizen Heroes

Read the **Citizen Heroes** on this page. Ask students **How did Raoul Wallenburg work to help Hungarian Jews during World War II?** (*He created "safe houses" to hide them during the Holocaust.*)

Skills Mini Lesson

Drawing Inferences and Conclusions

1. Tell students that to draw inferences and conclusions, they should identify what they know to be true, make an educated guess based on what they assume to be true, and use inferences to draw a conclusion.

2. Help students practice the skill using this situation: On Friday, students always have a spelling test. Today is Friday, and the teacher tells them to take out a piece of paper. (*Conclusion: The teacher is giving a spelling test.*)

3. Have students draw a conclusion about what life was like in Germany after the end of World War II.

Answer

Synthesize Pictures like these probably strengthened European's resolve to work for peace by reminding them how victims of the Holocaust suffered during World War II.

Use Context Clues As a follow up, have students perform the Target Reading Skill activity on this page. *(By reading ahead, students learn that* installed *means "established" or "set up.")*

Guided Instruction (continued)

- Have students compare the United States and its partners with the Soviet Union and its partners during the Cold War. *(The United States and its Western European partners had democratic governments and opposed communism. The Soviet Union and its Eastern European partners had communist governments.)*

- Ask students **What were some of the effects of the Cold War on European countries?** *(Cold War borders separated families, friends, and relatives.)*

- Ask students **What was life like for people living in East Germany?** *(The government of East Germany required people to obey without asking questions and encouraged people to spy on family members and neighbors. Children were taught to respect only communist ideals. Western ideas and products were banned.)*

- Ask students **What happened on November 9, 1989?** *(Crowds of East Germans were allowed to cross into West Berlin; people climbed on top of the Berlin Wall, dancing and celebrating, and began to take the wall apart.)*

- Ask students **Why do you think Germans wanted to be united again?** *(Possible answer: East Germans wanted more democracy and a better economy, and did not want to be separated from friends and family any longer.)*

Independent Practice

Have students create the Taking Notes graphic organizer on a blank piece of paper. Then have them fill it with dates and events from the section.

Monitor Progress

As students fill in their graphic organizers, check to make sure they are listing events in chronological order. Provide assistance as needed.

⟲ **Target Skill** **Use Context Clues** If you are unsure of the meaning of *installed,* read on. The next sentence clarifies its meaning.

While Eastern German border guards look on, a protestor hammers against the Berlin Wall in November, 1989.

The Cold War During the Cold War, the United States and Western Europe became partners. These countries had democratic governments and were opposed to communism. Eastern European countries had communist governments that had been installed by the Soviet Union. Soviet troops stayed in Eastern Europe to make sure that these countries remained communist.

Think about the effects of the Cold War on European countries. Recall that these countries are small and close together. Cold War borders separated families and friends. Even some who had managed to escape to the West suffered. They could no longer see the relatives they had left behind.

East Germans led far different lives from West Germans. The communist government required people to obey without asking questions. It even encouraged people to spy on family members and neighbors. Children were taught to respect only those things that promoted communism. Western movies, music, and magazines were seen as harmful influences.

The Communists Weaken In time, communist rule started to change. The East German economy fell far behind the West German economy. The average West German had a much more comfortable life than the average East German had. Many East Germans wanted to go to the West, but the East German government did not let them.

In the late 1980s, changes in the Soviet Union weakened the East German government. It became clear that the Soviets would no longer use force to protect communism in Eastern Europe. Fear of the Soviets had helped keep the East German government in power. Now this fear was gone, and the people were ready for change.

Some East Germans began to escape to West Germany by way of Hungary, Czechoslovakia, and Poland. Others began protesting in the streets. To stop the protests, the East German government softened its rules. It announced that under certain conditions, East Germans could visit West Germany.

The East German Government Falls Many people misunderstood the announcement. They thought that the government was opening the Berlin Wall permanently. On November 9, 1989, huge crowds of people demanded to cross into West Berlin. The border guards let them

Differentiated Instruction

For English Language Learners L1
To help students visualize the countries that were formed after the end of the Cold War, show them *Color Transparency ER Set 1: Europe Today With Eastern Europe Updated.* Using the Think-Write-Pair-Share strategy (TE, p. T36), have students examine each map and note the differences and similarities between the maps.

📖 **Europe and Russia Transparencies,** *Color Transparency ER Set 1: Europe Today With Eastern Europe Updated*

Thousands of East Berliners crossed into West Berlin that night. People climbed on top of the wall. They danced and celebrated their new freedom. They also began to destroy the wall, taking it apart piece by piece. The hated wall that had separated them for so long was now gone.

The destruction of the Berlin Wall was the beginning of the end for the East German government. People continued protesting against the government. They wanted more democracy. They wanted Germany to be united again. Less than a year later, the governments of East Germany and West Germany united. Germany had become a single country again.

✓ **Reading Check** How was Germany divided after World War II?

Germany Reunited

Most Germans were thrilled about the fall of the Berlin Wall. Despite having been separate countries for about 50 years, the cultures of East Germany and West Germany had remained similar in many ways. People in both East Germany and West Germany spoke the same language and ate the same foods. They knew the same German composers, writers, and painters. Still, **reunification** (ree yoo nih fih KAY shun), or the process of becoming unified again, would not be easy.

Changing East Germany The East German economy was very weak. Germans in the west had to spend huge amounts of money to improve the economy in the east. The government sold the state-owned factories of East Germany to private companies. They modernized factories and businesses. They cleaned up toxic waste sites. They began producing more consumer goods, such as televisions and cars. This process was very expensive.

East Germans had some concerns about life after communism. For example, in communist East Germany, people had had guaranteed jobs. There were no such guarantees under the democratic system of West Germany. Even today, there are many more people in the east without jobs than there are in the west. Even so, Germans in the east now enjoy a much better standard of living than they did under communism. A **standard of living** is the level of comfort in terms of the goods and services that people have.

Chapter 9 Section 5 **297**

Links to
Science

Albert Einstein German-born scientist Albert Einstein (below) was teaching physics at the University of Berlin when World War I broke out. He was also developing the important scientific theories that would make him world famous. Einstein was strongly opposed to the war. When Hitler rose to power, Einstein gave up his German citizenship and emigrated to the United States. When scientists began to investigate ways to create the atomic bomb in the 1930s, Einstein urged U.S. President Roosevelt to develop the bomb first, before Germany could. Yet Einstein was still opposed to war and spent the last years of his life promoting peace.

Learn about the history of the Berlin Wall.

Links

Read the **Links to Science** on this page. Ask students **Why do you think Einstein urged President Roosevelt to develop the atomic bomb?** *(Possible answer: Einstein believed Hitler was dangerous and had to be defeated.)*

Germany Reunited L2

Guided Instruction

■ **Vocabulary Builder** Clarify the high-use words **elimination** and **aid** before reading.

■ Read Germany Reunited with students.

■ Discuss the steps Germans took to improve the economy in East Germany. *(Germans spent money to improve the economy; the government sold state-owned factories to private companies; factories were modernized and toxic waste sites were cleaned; more consumer goods were produced.)*

Independent Practice

Have students complete their graphic organizers.

Monitor Progress

■ Show *Section Reading Support Transparency ER 47* and ask students to check their graphic organizers individually.

📖 **Europe and Russia Transparencies,** *Section Reading Support Transparency ER 47*

■ Tell students to fill in the last column of the *Reading Readiness Guide.*

All in One **Europe and Russia Teaching Resources,** *Reading Readiness Guide,* p. 274

 Show students *Germany: The Berlin Wall.* Ask **Why was the Berlin Wall built?** *(to prevent East Germans from defecting to West Germany)*

Answer

✓ **Reading Check** It was divided into two parts—East Germany and West Germany.

Assess and Reteach

Assess Progress L2

Have students complete the Section Assessment. Administer the *Section Quiz*.

All in One Europe and Russia Teaching Resources, *Section Quiz*, p. 276

Reteach L1

If students need more instruction, have them read this section in the Reading and Vocabulary Study Guide.

Chapter 9, Section 5, **Eastern Hemisphere Reading and Vocabulary Study Guide,** pp. 104–106

Extend L3

Have students choose one aspect of one topic discussed in this section, such as the Holocaust or the Cold War, for further study. Have them research and then write a short essay about their topic that presents new information not found in the lesson. Give students *Writing to Inform and Explain* to help get them started.

All in One Europe and Russia Teaching Resources, *Writing to Inform and Explain,* p. 296

Answer

✓ Reading Check It was chosen because of its central location and because it had previously been the capital of a united Germany.

Section 5 Assessment

Key Terms
Students' sentences should reflect knowledge of each Key Term.

Target Reading Skill
Using the surrounding text, students should be able to determine that *elimination* means "removal" or "taking something away."

Comprehension and Critical Thinking
1. (a) It had to pay billions of dollars. **(b)** It led to soaring prices and the collapse of the economy. Hitler promised that he would make Germany great again. **(c)** After the defeat of Germany, the victorious countries divided the country among themselves. The Americans, British, and French joined their sections to create the Federal Republic of Germany, also known as West Germany. The Soviet Union created a communist system in the German Democratic Republic, or East Germany.

The German flag flies in front of the Reichstag, Germany's parliament building.

Moving Forward When Germany reunited, the German legislature decided Berlin would be the nation's capital once more. By 1999, most government offices had been moved back to Berlin from Bonn.

The cost of moving the capital was enormous. It led to budget cuts and the elimination of many public-service jobs. Still, Germans believed that the move benefited the "new Germany." Berlin's central location, they said, would aid reunification by linking Germans in the east with Germans in the west.

Reunification has been a huge undertaking. It has been difficult and expensive to merge two countries into one unified nation. Even so, Germany remains strong. Despite the high cost of reunification, Germany still has one of the world's strongest economies. It is also a powerful member of the European Union. As the European Union adds new members from Eastern Europe, Germany's central location will be to its advantage. Finally, because Germany was divided for only about 50 years, its people remember their shared history and culture. They will build on this common heritage as they move forward.

✓ Reading Check Why was Berlin chosen as the reunified nation's capital?

Section 5 Assessment

Key Terms
Review the key terms listed at the beginning of this section. Use each term in a sentence that explains its meaning.

Target Reading Skill
Find the word *elimination* at the top of this page. How do the surrounding phrases help explain it?

Comprehension and Critical Thinking
1. (a) Explain What was Germany's punishment for its role in World War I?

(b) Identify Effects How did that punishment lead to the rise of Adolf Hitler and the beginning of World War II?

(c) Sequence Describe the events that led to the division of Germany.

2. (a) Recall How did most Germans feel about the fall of the Berlin Wall?

(b) Sequence Describe the events that led to the reunification of Germany.

(c) Identify Effects How has the reunification of Germany affected life in the former East Germany?

Writing Activity
Write a journal entry from the point of view of an East Berliner. Describe the night the Berlin Wall was torn down. How did you feel? Whom and what did you want to see?

Writing Tip Before you write, decide what your age will be. If you are a young East Berliner, write as if you have never lived without the wall. If you are older, write as if you have experienced life both with and without the wall.

2. (a) They were happy. **(b)** After the destruction of the Berlin Wall, people continued to protest against the government, demanding democracy. A year later, the country became united again. **(c)** The government privatized state-owned factories, modernized factories and businesses, cleaned up toxic waste sites, and began producing more consumer goods. However, many more people are unemployed because there are no guaranteed jobs.

Writing Activity
Use the *Rubric for Assessing a Journal Entry* to evaluate students' journal entries.

All in One Europe and Russia Teaching Resources, *Rubric for Assessing a Journal Entry,* p. 299

Review and Assessment

Review Chapter Content

- Review and revisit the major themes of this chapter by asking students to classify what Guiding Question each bulleted statement in the Chapter Summary answers. Form students into groups and ask them to complete the activity together. Refer to p. 139 in the Student Edition for text of the Guiding Questions.

- Assign *Vocabulary Development* for students to review Key Terms.

  All in One **Europe and Russia Teaching Resources,** *Vocabulary Development*, p. 297

◆ Chapter Summary

Section 1: The United Kingdom
- There are four regions within the United Kingdom: England, Scotland, Wales, and Northern Ireland.
- The Magna Carta and Parliament played important roles in the development of British democracy.
- The United Kingdom is a constitutional monarchy.
- Trade is important to the United Kingdom because it is an island with limited natural resources.

Section 2: France
- France has made important contributions to art, philosophy, architecture, fashion, and cooking.
- France is becoming more culturally diverse.

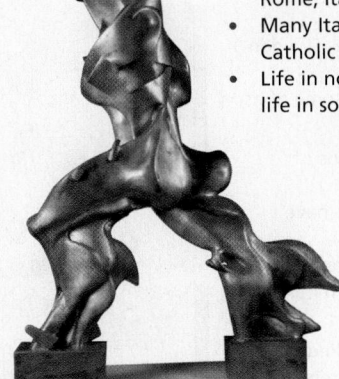

Boccioni's *Unique Forms of Continuity in Space* (1913)

Section 3: Sweden
- Sweden is a welfare state that provides many services to its citizens.
- Sweden became an industrialized country in the early 1900s.
- The Swedish government faces challenges as it tries to continue providing benefits to everyone.

Section 4: Italy
- Vatican City is an important city-state within Rome, Italy.
- Many Italians have close ties to the Roman Catholic Church.
- Life in northern Italy differs in many ways from life in southern Italy.

Section 5: Germany
- The Berlin Wall divided communist East Germany from democratic West Germany.
- After the fall of the Berlin Wall, the governments of East and West Germany reunited.

◆ Key Terms

Complete each sentence with a key term from the list.

Parliament

standard of living

land reform

philosophy

national debt

reunification

welfare state

constitutional monarchy

1. A _____ is a system of ideas or beliefs.
2. _____ is the lawmaking body of the United Kingdom.
3. A _____ is the level of comfort in terms of the goods and services that people have.
4. A _____ is a government in which a monarch is the head of state but has limited powers.
5. The process of dividing large properties into smaller ones is called _____.
6. In a _____, the government provides many services and benefits for free or at a low cost.
7. _____ is the amount of money a government owes.
8. The process of becoming unified again is called _____.

Chapter 9 **299**

Vocabulary Builder

Revisit this chapter's high-use words:

exert	standard	theory
symbol	benefit	superior
fund	elimination	aid
finance	retain	abundant
contribution		

Ask students to review the definitions they recorded on their *Word Knowledge* worksheets.

All in One **Europe and Russia Teaching Resources,** *Word Knowledge*, p. 280

Consider allowing students to earn extra credit if they use the words in their answers to the questions in the Chapter Review and Assessment. The words must be used correctly and in a natural context to win the extra points.

Answers

Key Terms
1. philosophy
2. Parliament
3. standard of living
4. constitutional monarchy
5. land reform
6. welfare state
7. national debt
8. reunification

9. (a) The British monarch is a symbol of Britain's past and customs. (b) to unify the British people (c) Answers will vary, but should show clear reasoning and examples from the text.

10. (a) It is an organization that determines which words are officially accepted as part of the French language. (b) Possible answer: Because of the variety of cultures in Western Europe, different languages probably influence each other regularly.

11. (a) The Swedish government provides child care at a reduced cost, access to free or inexpensive health care, generous vacation and sick days for all workers, and money for retirement. The government also pays for parents to stay at home from work with their newborn children for up to 15 months, and pays for the costs of schooling through college. (b) Sweden does not have enough money to pay for all the benefits to its citizens. (c) The government may provide fewer benefits and businesses may pay more in taxes by taking advantage of Sweden's natural resources.

12. (a) Italians are united by a common ethnicity, the Roman Catholic faith, the legacy of the Roman Empire, and strong family ties. (b) It is both a city and an independent country that is led by the pope. (c) Northern Italy has international businesses and manufacturing industries, and is more prosperous. Southern Italy is mostly agricultural and more traditional, and religion plays a major part in daily life.

13. (a) The victors of World War II divided the country into democratic and communistic nations. (b) After the destruction of the Berlin Wall, East Germans continued to protest against the East German government and demand reunification. (c) West Germans had to spend much money to modernize factories, clean up toxic waste, and to improve the economy of East Germany.

14. (a) The East German government disapproved of Western movies and free speech. (b) East Germans could not travel where they wanted, question the government, or enjoy things produced by a noncommunist country. West Germans enjoyed the movies, music, and magazines they wanted, and freedom of speech.

◆ Comprehension and Critical Thinking

9. (a) **Explain** What is the role of the British monarch?
(b) **Draw Conclusions** Why does Britain remain a monarchy even though the monarch now has little power?
(c) **Predict** Do you think the United Kingdom will continue to have a monarch in the future? Explain why or why not.

10. (a) **Explain** What is the French Academy?
(b) **Infer** Why do foreign words enter the French language even though the French Academy tries to limit them?

11. (a) **Explain** What benefits does Sweden's welfare system provide?
(b) **Summarize** What challenges does Sweden face today?
(c) **Predict** How might Sweden solve some of its economic challenges?

12. (a) **Identify** What is the political status of Vatican City?
(b) **List** Which things do most Italians have in common?
(c) **Compare and Contrast** How is life in northern Italy different from life in southern Italy?

13. (a) **Recall** How was Germany divided?
(b) **Explain** Why was Germany reunified?
(c) **Summarize** What challenges has reunification brought to Germany?

14. (a) **List** Name two things that the East German government did not allow.
(b) **Compare and Contrast** Compare personal freedom in East Germany and West Germany during the Cold War.

◆ Skills Practice

In the Skills for Life activity in this chapter, you learned how to use visual information to write a paragraph. Review the steps you followed to learn this skill. Then turn to the Country Profile on page 294. Use the data on this page to write a paragraph titled A History of Germany Since World War I.

◆ Writing Activity: Government

You read about Germany's division after World War II. Recall that some Italians today are in favor of dividing Italy. Write a paragraph comparing Germany's situation after World War II with Italy's situation today.

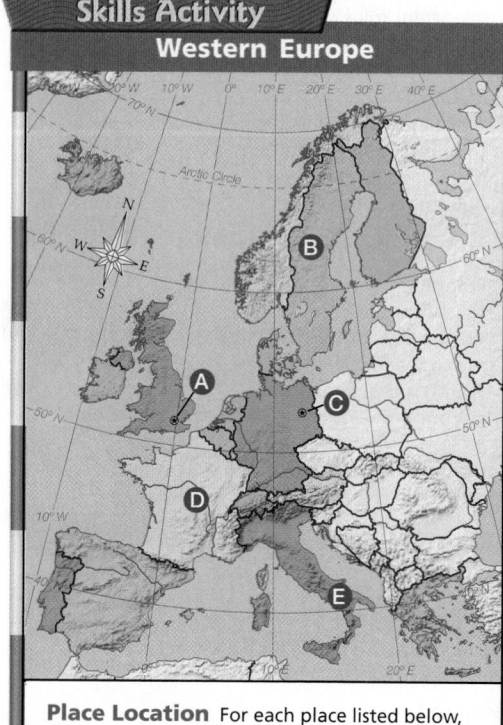

MAP MASTER™ Skills Activity

Western Europe

Place Location For each place listed below, write the letter from the map that shows its location.
1. France
2. London
3. Sweden
4. Italy
5. Berlin

Go Online
PHSchool.com Use Web Code ldp-7455 for an interactive map.

Skills Practice
Students' paragraphs should accurately reflect the information from the Country Profile.

Writing Activity: Government
Students' essays should use at least five key terms to explain the role of government in Western Europe.

Use the *Rubric for Assessing a Writing Assignment* to evaluate students' essays.

All in One Europe and Russia Teaching Resources, *Rubric for Assessing a Writing Assignment,* p. 298

Standardized Test Prep

Test-Taking Tips

Some questions on standardized tests ask you to analyze a point of view. Read the passage below. Then follow the tips to answer the sample question.

> On November 9, 1989, crowds began to tear down the Berlin Wall, block by block. People helped each other over the wall to the other side. Someone watching from a window nearby said, "Today they are happy. But will they still be cheering when they realize that they no longer have the promise of either a job or food to eat?"

Choose the letter that best answers the question.

Who might have made this statement?

- **A** an old East German who wants to have his son visit from West Germany
- **B** a young East German who dreams of finding a job in West Germany
- **C** an East German communist with a job running a state business
- **D** a West German whose parents live in East Germany

Think It Through
The person who made this statement is not happy that the wall is coming down. He or she wonders whether the people tearing it down will still be cheering about it in the future. Who would not be happy about the wall coming down? You can eliminate A and D because both people have families that will be reunited with the wall torn down. You can also rule out B because that person will now be able to go to West Germany to look for work. The correct answer is C.

> **TIP** Use good reasoning to help you choose an answer that makes sense.

> **TIP** Be sure that you understand the question: Who might have said the words that begin, *Today they are happy. But will they still be cheering . . .?*

Practice Questions

Use the tips above and other tips in this book to help you answer the following questions.

1. What historical document first limited the power of the British king?
   - **A** the Magna Carta
   - **B** Parliament
   - **C** the British constitution
   - **D** the Northern League

2. Which style of architecture began in the region of Paris hundreds of years ago?
   - **A** Renaissance
   - **B** French Academic
   - **C** Gothic
   - **D** classical

3. What happened when the Roman Empire broke up?
   - **A** The nation of Italy was formed.
   - **B** It broke into a number of kingdoms, city-states, and territories.
   - **C** Italy became part of the United Kingdom.
   - **D** The Italian language became standardized.

4. When was Germany divided into two countries?
   - **A** at the end of the Cold War
   - **B** at the end of World War I
   - **C** during the Cold War
   - **D** at the end of World War II

Use Web Code lda-7405 for a **Chapter 9 self-test.**

Chapter 9 **301**

Standardized Test Prep

Answers

1. A
2. C
3. B
4. D

Go Online PHSchool.com Students may use the Chapter 9 self-test on PHSchool.com to prepare for the Chapter Test.

Assessment Resources

Use *Chapter Tests A and B* to assess students' mastery of chapter content.

All in One **Europe and Russia Teaching Resources,** *Chapter Tests A and B,* pp. 300–305

Tests are also available on the *ExamView Test Bank CD-ROM.*

⊙ *ExamView Test Bank CD-ROM*

10 Eastern Europe and Russia

CHAPTER

Overview

Introducing Eastern Europe and Russia

1. Look at the map and study the data to learn about Russia and the countries of Eastern Europe.
2. Analyze data to compare the countries.
3. Identify characteristics that most of these countries share.
4. Find some of the key differences among the countries.

The Geography of Eastern Europe and Russia
Length: 5 minutes, 52 seconds
Provides overview of the countries, geography and resources of Eastern Europe and Russia.

Section 1 — Poland: Preserving Tradition Amidst Change

1. Find out about Polish traditions.
2. Learn about economic changes that have taken place in Poland since the collapse of communism.
3. Understand the future challenges that Poland faces.

Jewish Life in Poland
Length: 3 minutes, 32 seconds
Explores the experience of Polish Jews before, during, and after World War II.

Section 2 — Five Balkan Nations: A Region Tries to Rebuild

1. Identify the groups of people who live in the Balkans.
2. Understand how Yugoslavia was created and how it broke up.
3. Identify issues that these Balkan nations face in the future.

Rebuilding Kosovo
Length: 3 minutes, 48 seconds
Describes the rebuilding of Kosovo after years of struggle with the Serbian government.

Section 3 — Ukraine: Independence and Beyond

1. Understand how Ukraine's history has been shaped by foreign rule.
2. Explain the major issues that Ukrainians have faced since independence.
3. Describe life in Ukraine today.

The After-Effects of Chernobyl
Length: 3 minutes, 27 seconds
Explains how Ukrainians have coped with the accident at Chernobyl.

Section 4 — Russia: A Huge Country Takes a New Path

1. Investigate the changes that capitalism has brought to Russia.
2. Understand the cultural traditions that have endured throughout Russia.
3. Identify the issues that create challenges for Russians.

Life in the "New" Russia
Length: 4 minutes, 6 seconds
Discusses how the collapse of the Soviet Union improved the lives of Russians. Shows how old traditions and modern ways mix in the "new" Russia.

Technology Resources

Students use embedded Web codes to access Internet activities, chapter self-tests, and additional map practice. They may also access Dorling Kindersley's Online Desk Reference to learn more about each country they study.

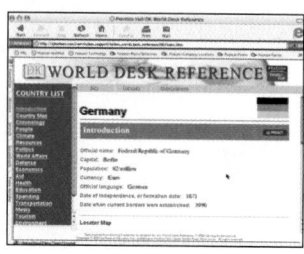

Use the Interactive Textbook to make content and concepts come alive through animations, videos, and activities that accompany the complete basal text—online and on CD-ROM.

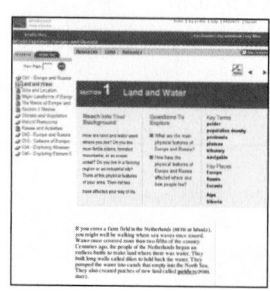

PRENTICE HALL

Use this complete suite of powerful teaching tools to make planning lessons and administering tests quicker and easier.

Reading and Vocabulary Instruction

↻ Model the Target Reading Skill

Comparison and Contrast Tell students that comparing and contrasting can be a helpful tool both for clarifying what they read and for remembering information. Comparing allows students to see patterns of similarities, and contrasting elucidates patterns of difference. Help students learn this skill by comparing and contrasting the Serbs and the Croats after reading the selection Land of Many Peoples from pp. 321–322 of the Student Edition.

Ask students **What are some similarities between the Serbs and the Croats?** *(Both are ethnic groups of the Balkan Peninsula; both groups speak Serbo-Croatian.)* Then ask **What are some differences between the two groups?** *(They use different alphabets; most Serbs belong to the Christian Orthodox Church, while most Croats are Roman Catholic.)* Finally, have students summarize what they learned to help them remember the information. *(Serbs and Croats, two ethnic groups of the Balkan Peninsula, both speak the same language. However, they use different alphabets and have different religions.)*

Use the following worksheets from All-in-One Europe and Russia Teaching Resources (pp. 329–331) to support the chapter's Target Reading Skill.

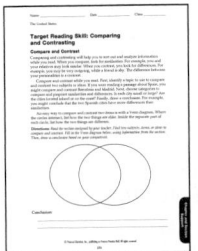 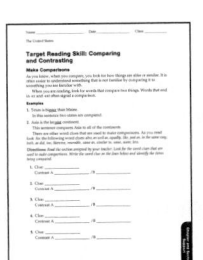

Vocabulary Builder

High-Use Academic Words

Use these steps to teach this chapter's high-use words:

1. Have students rate how well they know each word on their Word Knowledge worksheets (All-in-One Europe and Russia Teaching Resources, p. 332).

2. Pronounce each word and ask students to repeat it.

3. Give students a brief definition or sample sentence (provided on TE pp. 313, 320, 328, and 337).

4. Work with students as they fill in the "Definition or Example" column of their Word Knowledge worksheets.

Assessment

Formal Assessment

Test students' understanding of core knowledge and skills.

Chapter Tests A and B, and **Final Exams A and B**, All-in-One Europe and Russia Teaching Resources, pp. 351–356, pp. 363–368

Customize the Chapter Tests to suit your needs.

ExamView Test Bank CD-ROM

Skills Assessment

Assess geographic literacy.

MapMaster Skills, Student Edition, pp. 303, 322, 325, 344

Country Profile Map and Chart Skills, Student Edition, pp. 314, 320, 328, 339

Assess reading and comprehension.

Target Reading Skills, Student Edition, pp. 316, 322, 330, 340 and in Section Assessments

Chapter 10 Assessment, Eastern Hemisphere Reading and Vocabulary Study Guide, p. 120

Performance Assessment

Assess students' performance on this chapter's Writing Activities using the following rubrics from All-in-One Europe and Russia Teaching Resources.

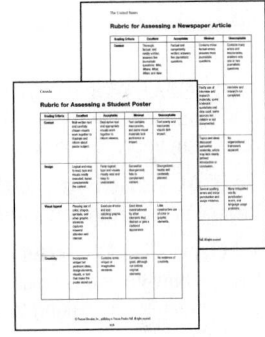

Rubric for Assessing a Bar Graph, p. 347

Rubric for Assessing a Newspaper Article, p. 348

Rubric for Assessing a Timeline, p. 349

Assess students' work through performance tasks.

Small Group Activity, All-in-One Europe and Russia Teaching Resources, pp. 335–338

Portfolio Activity, Teacher Edition, p. 173

Online Assessment

Have students check their own understanding.

Chapter Self-Test

Test Preparation

Europe and Russia Practice Tests A, B and C, Test Prep Workbook, pp. 37–48

Europe and Russia Benchmark Test 2 and Outcome Test, AYP Monitoring Assessments, pp. 109–112, 188–193

Section 1 Poland: Preserving Tradition Amidst Change

 2 periods, 1 block (includes Country Databank)

Social Studies Objectives
1. Find out about Polish traditions.
2. Learn about economic changes that have taken place in Poland since the collapse of communism.
3. Understand the future challenges that Poland faces.

Reading/Language Arts Objective
Compare and contrast to help you sort out and analyze information.

Prepare to Read	**Instructional Resources**	**Differentiated Instruction**
Build Background Knowledge Discuss traditions in students' communities. **Set a Purpose for Reading** Have students evaluate statements on the *Reading Readiness Guide*. **Preview Key Terms** Teach the section's Key Terms. **Target Reading Skill** Introduce the section's Target Reading Skill of **comparing and contrasting**.	**All in One Europe and Russia Teaching Resources** L2 Reading Readiness Guide, p. 314 L2 Compare and Contrast, p. 329	**Spanish Reading and Vocabulary Study Guide** L1 Chapter 10, Section 1, pp. 77–78 ELL **World Studies Video Program** L2 The Geography of Eastern Europe and Russia AR, GT, LPR, SN

Instruct	**Instructional Resources**	**Differentiated Instruction**
Tradition in Poland Discuss the major religions in Poland and how language links the Polish people. **Country Profile** Ask students to derive and use information from maps, charts, and graphs. **Great Economic Changes** Ask about how the transition from communism to capitalism improved Poland's economy. **Target Reading Skill** Review **comparing and contrasting**. **Future Challenges** Discuss how Poland is repairing its damaged environment and working to reduce the level of unemployment.	**All in One Europe and Russia Teaching Resources** L2 Guided Reading and Review, p. 315 L2 Reading Readiness Guide, p. 314 L2 Reading a Table, p. 342 **Europe and Russia Transparencies** L2 Transparency B15: Outline L2 Section Reading Support Transparency ER 48 **World Studies Video Program** L2 Jewish Life in Poland	**All in One Europe and Russia Teaching Resources** L2 Outline Map 18: Eastern Europe and Russia: Political, p. 344 AR, ELL, GT, LPR, SN L2 Using a Map Key, p. 341 AR, GT, LPR, SN Rubric for Assessing a Newspaper Article, p. 348 AR, GT **Teacher's Edition** L1 For Special Needs Students, TE pp. 305, 315 L3 For Gifted and Talented, TE pp. 306, 315 L1 For Less Proficient Readers, TE pp. 307, 314, 317 L3 For Advanced Readers, TE p. 308 **Europe and Russia Transparencies** L1 Transparency B16: Venn Diagram ELL, LPR, SN

Assess and Reteach	**Instructional Resources**	**Differentiated Instruction**
Assess Progress Evaluate student comprehension with the section assessment and section quiz. **Reteach** Assign the Reading and Vocabulary Study Guide to help struggling students. **Extend** Ask students to research the collapse of Poland's communist government and create a timeline based on their findings.	**All in One Europe and Russia Teaching Resources** L2 Section Quiz, p. 316 Rubric for Assessing a Timeline, p. 349 Rubric for Assessing a Writing Assignment, p. 350 **Reading and Vocabulary Study Guide** L1 Chapter 10, Section 1, pp. 108–110	**All in One Europe and Russia Teaching Resources** Rubric for Assessing a Bar Graph, p. 347 AR, GT, LPR, SN **Spanish Support** L2 Section Quiz (Spanish), p. 99 ELL

Key
L1 Basic to Average   L3 Average to Advanced   LPR Less Proficient Readers   GT Gifted and Talented
L2 For All Students   AR Advanced Readers   ELL English Language Learners
SN Special Needs Students

Section 2 New Balkan Nations: A Region Tries to Rebuild

 *1.5 periods, .75 block*

Social Studies Objectives
1. Identify the groups of people who live in the Balkans.
2. Understand how Yugoslavia was created and how it broke up.
3. Identify issues that these Balkan nations face in the future.

Reading/Language Arts Objective
Make comparisons to find out how two or more situations are alike.

Prepare to Read	Instructional Resources	Differentiated Instruction
Build Background Knowledge Show students the video for this section and discuss the lasting effects of land mines. **Set a Purpose for Reading** Have students evaluate statements on the *Reading Readiness Guide*. **Preview Key Terms** Teach the section's Key Terms. **Target Reading Skill** Introduce the section's Target Reading Skill of **making comparisons.**	**All in One Europe and Russia Teaching Resources** **L2** Reading Readiness Guide, p. 318 **L2** Make Comparisons, p. 330 **World Studies Video Program** **L2** Rebuilding Kosovo	**Spanish Reading and Vocabulary Study Guide** **L1** Chapter 10, Section 2, pp. 79–80 ELL

Instruct	Instructional Resources	Differentiated Instruction
Country Profile Ask students to derive and use information from maps, charts, and graphs. **Land of Many Peoples** Discuss the Slavic groups in the Balkans. **Target Reading Skill** Review **making comparisons.** **The Creation of Yugoslavia** Discuss Yugoslavia's government before and after World War II. **Yugoslavia Breaks Up** Discuss war and conflict in Yugoslavia. **The Region's Future** Discuss Slobodan Milosevic and the future of the Balkan nations.	**All in One Europe and Russia Teaching Resources** **L2** Guided Reading and Review, p. 319 **L2** Reading Readiness Guide, p. 318 **L2** Using a Map Key, p. 341 **Europe and Russia Transparencies** **L2** Section Reading Support Transparency ER 49	**All in One Europe and Russia Teaching Resources** **L1** DK Compact Atlas of the World Activity: Reading a Political Map, p. 343 ELL, LPR, SN **Teacher's Edition** **L1** For Special Needs Students, TE p. 322 **L1** For English Language Learners, TE p. 323 **L3** For Gifted and Talented, TE p. 325 **PHschool.com** **L3** For: Environmental and Global Issues: Genocide in the Balkans **Web Code:** ldd-7506 AR, GT **Spanish Support** **L2** Guided Reading and Review (Spanish), p. 100 ELL

Assess and Reteach	Instructional Resources	Differentiated Instruction
Assess Progress Evaluate student comprehension with the section assessment and section quiz. **Reteach** Assign the Reading and Vocabulary Study Guide to help struggling students. **Extend** Extend the lesson by assigning an Enrichment activity.	**All in One Europe and Russia Teaching Resources** **L2** Section Quiz, p. 320 **L3** Enrichment, p. 333 Rubric for Assessing a Writing Assignment, p. 350 **Reading and Vocabulary Study Guide** **L1** Chapter 10, Section 2, pp. 111–113	**Spanish Support** **L2** Section Quiz (Spanish), p. 101 ELL

Key
L1 Basic to Average **L3** Average to Advanced
L2 For All Students

LPR Less Proficient Readers
AR Advanced Readers
SN Special Needs Students

GT Gifted and Talented
ELL English Language Learners

Section 3 Ukraine: Independence and Beyond

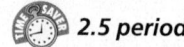 2.5 periods, 1.25 blocks (includes Skills for Life)

Social Studies Objectives

1. Understand how Ukraine's history has been shaped by foreign rule.
2. Explain the major issues that Ukrainians have faced since independence.
3. Describe life in Ukraine today.

Reading/Language Arts Objective

Compare and contrast different points in history to understand how a nation has changed over time.

Prepare to Read

Build Background Knowledge
Discuss how independence affected Ukraine.

Set a Purpose for Reading
Have students evaluate statements on the *Reading Readiness Guide*.

Preview Key Terms
Teach the section's Key Terms.

Target Reading Skill
Introduce the section's Target Reading Skill of **comparing and contrasting**.

Instructional Resources

All in One Europe and Russia Teaching Resources
- L2 Reading Readiness Guide, p. 322
- L2 Compare and Contrast, p. 329

Differentiated Instruction

Spanish Reading and Vocabulary Study Guide
- L1 Chapter 10, Section 3, pp. 81–82 ELL

Instruct

Country Profile
Ask students to derive and use information from maps, charts, and graphs.

A History of Occupation
Discuss Ukraine's relationship with the Soviet Union.

Target Reading Skill
Review **comparing and contrasting**.

Independence Brings Challenges
Ask about changes after independence.

Life in Ukraine
Discuss life in Ukraine before and after independence and ask about the future of the nation.

Instructional Resources

All in One Europe and Russia Teaching Resources
- L2 Guided Reading and Review, p. 323
- L2 Reading Readiness Guide, p. 322

Europe and Russia Transparencies
- L2 Section Reading Support Transparency ER 50

World Studies Video Program
- L2 The After-Effects of Chernobyl

Differentiated Instruction

All in One Europe and Russia Teaching Resources
- L2 Guided Reading and Review, p. 323 ELL
- L3 Small Group Activity: Chernobyl: Report on a Disaster, pp. 335–338 AR, GT
- L2 Skills for Life, p. 334 AR, GT, LPR, SN

Teacher's Edition
- L2 For English Language Learners, TE p. 329
- L1 For Special Needs Students, TE p. 329
- L3 For Gifted and Talented, TE p. 330
- L3 For Advanced Readers, TE p. 331

Student Edition on Audio CD
- L1 Chapter 10, Section 3 ELL, LPR, SN

Assess and Reteach

Assess Progress
Evaluate student comprehension with the section assessment and section quiz.

Reteach
Assign the Reading and Vocabulary Study Guide to help struggling students.

Extend
Extend the lesson by assigning an online activity.

Instructional Resources

All in One Europe and Russia Teaching Resources
- L2 Section Quiz, p. 324
  Rubric for Assessing a Newspaper Article, p. 348

Reading and Vocabulary Study Guide
- L1 Chapter 10, Section 3, pp. 114–116

PHSchool.com
- L3 **For:** Environmental and Global Issues: Using Nuclear Power
  Web Code: ldd-7507

Differentiated Instruction

Spanish Support
- L2 Section Quiz (Spanish), p. 103 ELL

Teacher's Edition
- L1 For Special Needs Students, TE p. 335

Social Studies Skills Tutor CD-ROM
- L1 Identifying Frame of Reference and Point of View ELL, LPR, SN

Key

L1 Basic to Average	L3 Average to Advanced	
L2 For All Students		

LPR Less Proficient Readers
AR Advanced Readers
SN Special Needs Students

GT Gifted and Talented
ELL English Language Learners

Section 4 Russia: A Huge Country Takes a New Path

3.5 periods, 1.75 blocks (includes Chapter Review and Assessment)

Social Studies Objectives
1. Investigate the changes that capitalism has brought to Russia.
2. Understand the cultural traditions that have endured throughout Russia.
3. Identify the issues that create challenges for Russians.

Reading/Language Arts Objective
Identify contrasts to find out how two things are different.

Prepare to Read

Build Background Knowledge
Discuss the effects of capitalism on Moscow.

Set a Purpose for Reading
Have students evaluate statements on the *Reading Readiness Guide*.

Preview Key Terms
Teach the section's Key Terms.

Target Reading Skill
Introduce the section's Target Reading Skill of **identifying contrasts**.

Instructional Resources

All in One Europe and Russia Teaching Resources
- L2 Reading Readiness Guide, p. 326
- L2 Identify Contrasts, p. 331

World Studies Video Program
- L2 Life in the "New" Russia

Differentiated Instruction

Spanish Reading and Vocabulary Study Guide
- L1 Chapter 10, Section 4, pp. 83–84 ELL

Instruct

Emerging Capitalism
Discuss the dissolution of the Soviet Union.

Country Profile
Ask students to analyze maps, charts, and graphs.

Target Reading Skill
Review **identifying contrasts**.

Cultural Traditions Continue
Discuss how old and new cultural traditions are mixing in Russia.

Uniting a Vast Nation
Discuss changes in Russia after the dissolution of the Soviet Union.

Instructional Resources

All in One Europe and Russia Teaching Resources
- L2 Guided Reading and Review, p. 327
- L2 Reading Readiness Guide, p. 326

Europe and Russia Transparencies
- L2 Transparency B2: Flow Chart
- L2 Section Reading Support Transparency ER 51

Differentiated Instruction

All in One Europe and Russia Teaching Resources
- L3 Activity Shop Interdisciplinary: Plan a New Railroad Line, pp. 339–340

Teacher's Edition
- L1 For Less Proficient Readers, TE p. 339
- L3 For Advanced Readers, TE pp. 339, 341

Europe and Russia Transparencies
- L1 Color Transparency ER 13 ELL, LPR, SN
- L1 Color Transparency ER 15 ELL, LPR, SN

PHSchool.com
- L3 For: Environmental and Global Issues: Why Do Wars Begin?
  Web Code: ldd-7508 AR, GT

Assess and Reteach

Assess Progress
Evaluate student comprehension with the section assessment and section quiz.

Reteach
Assign the Reading and Vocabulary Study Guide to help struggling students.

Extend
Extend the lesson by assigning a primary source reading.

Instructional Resources

All in One Europe and Russia
- L2 Section Quiz, p. 328
- L3 Housekeeping in Russia Soon After the Revolution, p. 345
- L2 Vocabulary Development, p. 346
- L2 Word Knowledge, p. 332
- L2 Chapter Tests A and B, pp. 351–356

Reading and Vocabulary Study Guide
- L1 Chapter 10, Section 4, pp. 117–119

Differentiated Instruction

Spanish Support
- L2 Section Quiz (Spanish), p. 105 ELL
- L2 Chapter Summary (Spanish), p. 106 ELL
- L2 Vocabulary Development (Spanish), p. 107 ELL

Key
- L1 Basic to Average
- L3 Average to Advanced
- L2 For All Students

- LPR Less Proficient Readers
- AR Advanced Readers
- SN Special Needs Students

- GT Gifted and Talented
- ELL English Language Learners

Reading Background

Learning Vocabulary by Making Choices

Help students build their understanding of Key Terms and high-use words from the chapter by asking them to make choices between correct and incorrect examples of the words. For each word below, read the two examples and ask students to say which example best shows the true meaning of the word.

Word: *entrepreneur*
Description 1: Seth started a business to buy and sell baseball cards, and opened offices around the world. *(correct)*
Description 2: The employee followed her boss' orders to get the job done.

Word: *secede*
Description 1: The organization withdrew its membership. *(correct)*
Description 2: The student joined the study group.

Word: *inflation*
Description 1: The price of food has increased over the years. *(correct)*
Description 2: The price of food has decreased over the years.

Using the Choral Reading Strategy Effectively

For many less proficient readers, it is often a lack of confidence that is key to their reading difficulties. You can use a combination of reading strategies, such as Choral Reading followed by silent reading, to teach students the skills they need to read confidently.

Keep the following points in mind as you practice the Choral Reading strategy:

1. Encourage students to stay with your voice as you read rather than racing ahead or lagging behind.
2. Use shorter passages of about 300 to 500 words.
3. For students to have a better understanding of the text, follow with a silent reading of the same passage. Then begin to ask questions about the content of the passage.

World Studies Background

Lech Walesa (1943–)

Poland was still under communist control in 1980 when Lech Walesa, a shipyard electrician, led a strike against a government-owned shipyard in Gdansk. Walesa soon became the leader of Solidarity, an independent labor federation that challenged the communist government. The government outlawed Solidarity in 1981. Walesa was arrested and detained by the government for a year. He and other union activists were harassed by the government throughout the 1980s, until a new wave of labor unrest swept Poland in 1988. The government was forced to negotiate with Walesa and restore Solidarity. Walesa won the Nobel Peace Prize in 1983. In 1990, he became the first democratically elected president of a free Poland.

The Original Yugoslavia

The Kingdom of Serbs, Croats, and Slovenes was created in 1918 as a result of World War I. It was formed from regions that had been part of the Ottoman Empire and the Austro-Hungarian Empire and ruled by a Serb dynasty. In 1929, King Alexander, a Serb, attempted to unite the different ethnic groups and officially changed the country's name to Yugoslavia. After World War II, Yugoslavia was controlled by Joseph Broz Tito's Communist Party.

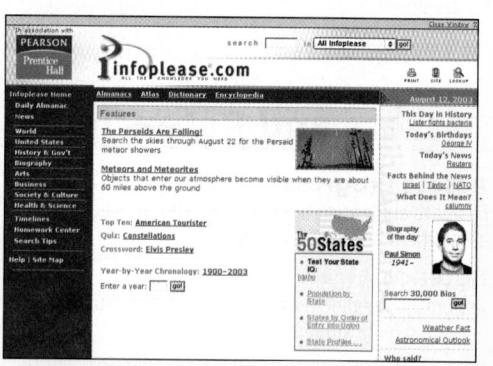

Infoplease® provides a wealth of useful information for the classroom. You can use this resource to strengthen your background on the subjects covered in this chapter. Have students visit this advertising-free site as a starting point for projects requiring research.

Use Web code **Idd-7500** for **Infoplease®**.

Build Vocabulary by Developing Expanded Definitions

Give students a tool to create rich definitions, discover word relationships, and learn vocabulary independently by teaching them to develop expanded definitions. Students can build their understanding of a word by answering the three questions below. Students can then combine the answers into a definition to which they can relate. Model the skill by walking students through the steps with a high-use word from the chapter, such as *consume*.

1. What does it mean?
   to purchase goods and services
2. What is a synonym for *consume*?
   buy
3. Provide a sentence using the word.
   It becomes a problem when a society consumes goods faster than they can be produced.

As a class, create an expanded definition of *consume*: *To consume means to purchase goods or services. People who buy food are consumers.*

Ask students to use this skill to create definitions for other Key Terms and high-use words from the chapter.

Tips for Writing Paragraphs

Knowing the components that make up a paragraph is essential for writing successful paragraphs. Model the following steps using a paragraph from p. 313 of the Student Edition before students write paragraphs related to this chapter:

1. Begin with a topic sentence. (*Poland has experienced great change in its long history.*)
2. Provide examples that support the topic sentence. (*Borders have shifted. Rulers have come and gone. Economic systems have changed.*)
3. End with a summary sentence. (*But throughout all these changes, some parts of Polish life have remained the same.*)

Have students write their own paragraphs that relate to the chapter. Remind students to use transition words and vary the length and structure of their sentences.

Siberian Chronicles

The Siberian Chronicles are a series of stories and historical accounts about Siberia dating from the 1500s through the 1700s. Historians hold conflicting theories about the origins of the chronicles. One widely held hypothesis is that survivors of a Siberian expedition in the 1500s wrote a work which was copied and reinterpreted, then eventually modified into the Siberian Chronicles. The chronicles describe the travels of Yermak Timofeyevich, who led an expedition to explore Siberia and defeat local tribes. The chronicles also include aspects of Russian folklore.

Black Earth

Chernozem, the black soil abundant in Ukraine, occurs in other parts of the world as well. Present in the middle latitudes of both hemispheres, chernozem forms in regions with cold winters and hot summers. In the United States, the Black Belt is a fertile area that spans Alabama and northeastern Mississippi. Beef cattle and soybeans are raised in this region of dark, rich soil. Similar soils are also found in India and in the Pampas region of Argentina.

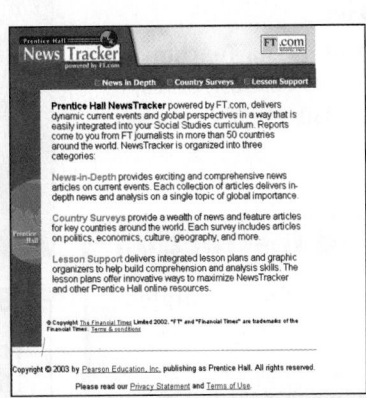

Get in-depth information on topics of global importance with **Prentice Hall Newstracker,** powered by FT.com.

Use Web code **ldd-7501** for **Prentice Hall Newstracker.**

Chapter 10

Guiding Questions

Remind students about the Guiding Questions introduced at the beginning of this section.

Section 1 relates to **Guiding Question** (5)
How have Russian and European economies developed into what they are today? (*Poland transitioned from communism to capitalism, which has strengthened the economy.*)

Section 2 relates to **Guiding Question** (2)
How have Europe and Russia been affected by their history? (*The formation of Yugoslavia brought together many ethnic groups. Tensions between the groups have led many to break away.*)

Section 3 relates to **Guiding Question** (5)
How have Russian and European economies developed into what they are today? (*After Ukraine gained independence from the Soviet Union, Ukrainians had to learn how to build their economy.*)

Section 4 relates to **Guiding Question** (3)
How have the people of Europe and Russia been shaped by their cultures? (*Today, traditional ways exist alongside new ways in Russia.*)

Target Reading Skill

In this chapter, students will learn and apply the reading skill of compare and contrast. Use the following worksheets to help students practice this skill:

All in One Europe and Russia Teaching Resources, *Compare and Contrast,* p. 329; *Make Comparisons,* p. 330; *Identify Contrasts,* p. 331

Differentiated Instruction

The following Teacher's Edition strategies are suitable for students of varying abilities.

Advanced Readers, pp. 308, 331, 339, 341
English Language Learners, pp. 323, 329
Gifted and Talented, pp. 306, 315, 325, 330
Less Proficient Readers, pp. 307, 314, 317, 339
Special Needs Students, pp. 305, 315, 322, 329, 335

Chapter 10 Eastern Europe and Russia

Chapter Preview

This chapter focuses on Poland, new Balkan nations, Ukraine, and Russia.

Country Databank
The Country Databank provides data and descriptions of Russia and each of the countries in Eastern Europe.

Section 1
Poland
Preserving Tradition Amidst Change

Section 2
New Balkan Nations
A Region Tries to Rebuild

Section 3
Ukraine
Independence and Beyond

Section 4
Russia
A Huge Country Takes a New Path

Target Reading Skill
Comparing and Contrasting In this chapter you will focus on comparison and contrast to help you sort out and analyze information.

▶ Harvesting lavender on a hillside in Croatia

302 Europe and Russia

Bibliography

For the Teacher
Hudgins, Sharon. *The Other Side of Russia: A Slice of Life in Siberia and the Russian Far East.* Texas A&M University Press, 2003.
Prazmowska, Anita J. *A History of Poland.* Palgrave, Macmillan, 2004.
Rogel, Carole. *The Breakup of Yugoslavia and Its Aftermath: Revised Edition.* Greenwood Publishing Group, 2004.

For the Student
L1 Steele, Philip. *Moscow.* Gareth Stevens, 2003.
L2 Bryan, Nichol. *Chernobyl: Nuclear Disaster.* Gareth Stevens, 2003.
L3 Taylor, David. *The Wars of Former Yugoslavia (Troubled World).* Raintree/Steck Vaughn, 2003.

302

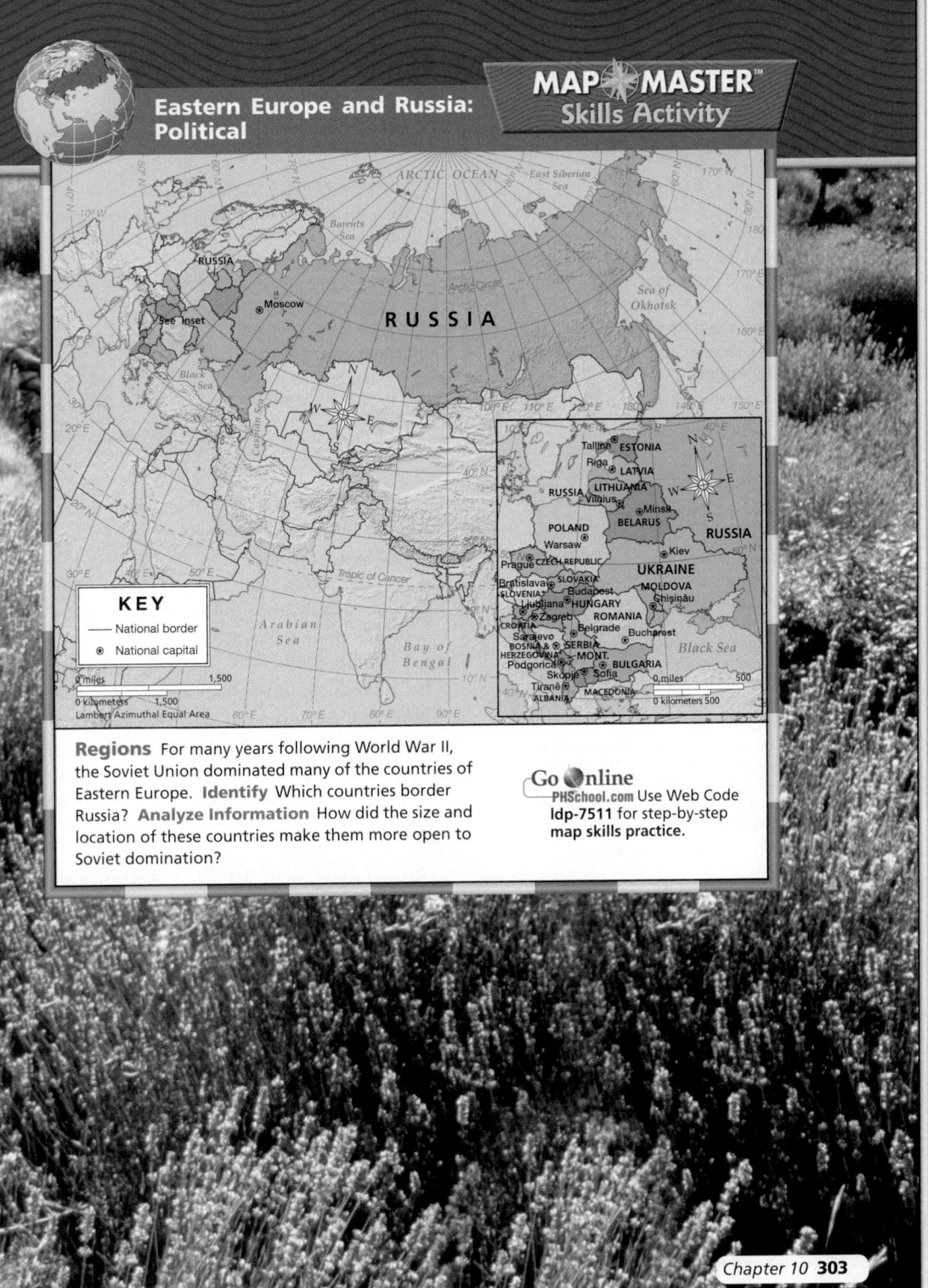

MAP★MASTER™ Skills Activity

Eastern Europe and Russia: Political

KEY
— National border
⊛ National capital

0 miles 1,500
0 kilometers 1,500
Lambert Azimuthal Equal Area

0 miles 500
0 kilometers 500

Regions For many years following World War II, the Soviet Union dominated many of the countries of Eastern Europe. **Identify** Which countries border Russia? **Analyze Information** How did the size and location of these countries make them more open to Soviet domination?

Go Online
PHSchool.com Use Web Code ldp-7511 for step-by-step map skills practice.

MAP★MASTER™ Skills Activity

Create a blank chart with two columns on the board. Label the columns "Countries of Eastern Europe and Russia" and "Capitals." Call on students to list the countries from the map on this page, and write them in the first column of the chart. Then, have students name the capital of each country, and fill them in the second column.

Go Online
PHSchool.com Students may practice their map skills using the intermediate online version of this map.

Using the Visual   L2

Reach Into Your Background Draw students' attention to the photograph on pages 302–303. Discuss the photograph with students. Have them discuss what details stand out to them. Can they relate this scene to something in their own lives? Encourage students to share their ideas with the class.

Answers

MAP★MASTER Skills Activity **Identify** The map shows that Estonia, Latvia, Belarus, and Ukraine border Russia. **Analyze Information** They are relatively small and close to Russia, making it easier for Soviets to enter and gain control over them.

Chapter Resources

Teaching Resources
L2 Vocabulary Development, p. 346
L2 Skills for Life, p. 334
L2 Chapter Tests A and B, pp. 351–356

Spanish Support
L2 Spanish Chapter Summary, p. 106
L2 Spanish Vocabulary Development, p. 107

Media and Technology
L1 Student Edition on Audio CD
L1 Guided Reading Audiotapes, English and Spanish
L2 Social Studies Skills Tutor CD-ROM
ExamView Test Bank CD-ROM

PRENTICE HALL
Presentation EXPRESS™
Teach · Connect · Inspire

Teach this chapter's content using the PresentationExpress™ CD-ROM including:
■ slide shows
■ transparencies
■ interactive maps and media
■ *ExamView®* QuickTake Presenter

Objectives

- Look at the map and study the data to learn about Russia and the countries of Eastern Europe.

- Analyze data to compare the countries.

- Identify characteristics that most of these countries share.

- Find some of the key differences among the countries.

Show *The Geography of Eastern Europe and Russia.* Ask **What are the major land regions in Eastern Europe?** *(East European Plains, Alpine Mountain System, and the plains and plateaus of Siberia)* **How is the terrain both different from and similar to that in Western Europe?** *(Both have plains that contain valuable resources, and the Alpine Mountain System runs through both. Western Europe, however, does not contain a region as large and barren as Siberia.)*

Prepare to Read

Build Background Knowledge L2

Tell students that Russia and the Eastern European countries they saw in the video have many similarities and differences. Have students brainstorm any similarities or differences among these countries that they can recall from the video. Conduct an Idea Wave (TE, p. T35) to elicit student responses and write them on the board in two columns labeled "Similarities" and "Differences."

The Geography of Eastern Europe and Russia, **World Studies Video Program**

Guide for Reading

This section provides an introduction to Russia and the 20 countries of Eastern Europe.

- Look at the map on the previous page and then read the paragraphs to learn about each nation.
- Analyze the data to compare the countries.
- What characteristics do most of these countries share?
- What are some key differences among the countries?

Viewing the Video Overview

View the World Studies Video Overview to learn more about each of the countries. As you watch, answer these questions:

- What are the major land regions in Eastern Europe?
- How is the terrain both different from and similar to that in Western Europe?

Explore the geography of Eastern Europe and Russia.

Albania

Capital	Tirana
Land Area	10,578 sq mi; 27,398 sq km
Population	3.5 million
Ethnic Group(s)	Albanian, Greek
Religion(s)	Muslim, Eastern Orthodox, Roman Catholic
Government	emerging democracy
Currency	lek
Leading Exports	textiles and footwear, asphalt, metals and metallic ores, crude oil, vegetables, fruits, tobacco
Language(s)	Albanian (official), Greek

Albania (al BAY nee uh) is located in southeastern Europe on the Adriatic and Ionian Seas. It is bordered by Serbia, Montenegro, Macedonia, and Greece. Albania became a communist state during World War II. In the early 1990s, the country tried to establish democracy. But government instability, high unemployment rates, and violence have prevented Albania from achieving that goal. Economically, the country is poor and struggling. Today, the country depends on aid from other countries to survive. However, the Albanians are slowly creating an open-market economy.

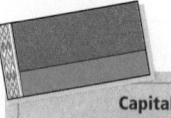

Belarus

Capital	Minsk
Land Area	80,154 sq mi; 207,600 sq km
Population	10.3 million
Ethnic Group(s)	Belarusian, Russian, Polish, Ukrainian
Religion(s)	Eastern Orthodox, Roman Catholic, Protestant, Muslim, Jewish
Government	republic
Currency	Belarusian ruble
Leading Exports	machinery and equipment, mineral products, chemicals, textiles, foodstuffs, metals
Language(s)	Belarusian (official), Russian (official)

Belarus (bay luh ROOS) is located between Poland and Russia. It was a Soviet republic for seven decades until its independence in 1991. Unlike many other former Soviet republics, Belarus has remained politically close to Russia. Russia also supplies Belarus with resources, as the country has few natural resources of its own. Belarus does have the potential, however, to develop its agriculture and forestry industries. Belarus faces major health and environmental problems caused by the 1986 Chernobyl explosion in neighboring Ukraine.

Bosnia and Herzegovina

Capital	Sarajevo
Land Area	19,741 sq mi; 51,129 sq km
Population	4.0 million
Ethnic Group(s)	Serb, Bosniak, Croat
Religion(s)	Muslim, Eastern Orthodox, Roman Catholic, Protestant
Government	emerging federal democratic republic
Currency	marka
Leading Exports	miscellaneous manufactured goods, raw materials
Language(s)	Serbo-Croat (official)

Bosnia and Herzegovina (BAHZ nee uh and hurt suh goh VEE nuh) is located on the Adriatic Sea in southeastern Europe, bordered by Croatia, Serbia, and Montenegro. Bosnia and Herzegovina declared independence from Yugoslavia in 1992. However, conflict among Serbs, Bosniaks, and Croats drew the country immediately into civil war. Peace was reached in 1995 with the help of NATO. Today, Bosnia and Herzegovina is struggling to recover from the years of war. Because of its natural resources, it has the potential to develop a thriving economy.

Bulgaria

Capital	Sofia
Land Area	42,683 sq mi; 110,550 sq km
Population	7.6 million
Ethnic Group(s)	Bulgarian, Southwest Asian, Roma, Macedonian, Armenian, Tartar, Circassian
Religion(s)	Eastern Orthodox, Muslim, Roman Catholic, Jewish
Government	parliamentary democracy
Currency	lev
Leading Exports	clothing, footwear, iron and steel, machinery and equipment, fuels
Language(s)	Bulgarian (official), Turkish, Macedonian, Romany

Bulgaria (bul GEHR ee uh) is located in southeastern Europe between Romania and Greece, bordering the Black Sea. The first Bulgarian state was created in the 600s when a central Asian Turkic tribe merged with the Slavic people of the region. Bulgaria was ruled by the Ottoman Empire for hundreds of years. The country regained its independence in 1878 but fell under communist rule after World War II. In 1990 the first open elections were held. Since then, the country has continued to develop a democratic political system with a free-market economy. Bulgaria is a member of NATO and is on a path to becoming an EU member in 2007.

Croatia

Capital	Zagreb
Land Area	21,781 sq mi; 56,414 sq km
Population	4.4 million
Ethnic Group(s)	Croat, Serb, Bosniak, Hungarian, Slovene, Czech, Albanian, Montenegrin, Roma
Religion(s)	Roman Catholic, Eastern Orthodox, Muslim
Government	presidential-parliamentary democracy
Currency	kuna
Leading Exports	transport equipment, textiles, chemicals, foodstuffs, fuels
Language(s)	Croation (official)

Croatia (kroh AY shuh) is located in southeastern Europe between Slovenia and Bosnia and Herzegovina. It borders the Adriatic Sea. Croatia was formerly part of the nation called Yugoslavia. Croatia declared its independence in 1991, but Serbian armies remained and fought on Croatian land for several years afterward. Economically, the country is struggling to recover from costly war damage and a high unemployment rate. The EU has spent over $1 billion in aid to help Croatia rebuild. The nation has rich fishing resources in the Adriatic Sea.

Instruct

Introducing Eastern Europe and Russia L2

Guided Instruction

- Read each country paragraph as a class using the Choral Reading strategy (TE, p. T34). Then, ask students to read through each data table.

- Ask **What religions are common to all of the countries on pp. 304–305?** *(Muslim, Eastern Orthodox, and Roman Catholic)*

- Have students study the Belarus data. Ask **In what ways are Belarus' ties to Russia visible?** *(Russian is one of Belarus' official languages, and Russian is one of the country's major ethnic groups.)*

- Discuss the changes that have taken place in Bulgaria since 1990. *(The country now holds free elections, it is moving toward democracy and a free-market economy, it is a member of NATO, and it has taken the first steps to joining the EU.)*

Differentiated Instruction

For Special Needs Students L1

Distribute *Outline Map 18: Eastern Europe and Russia: Political*. As you read about each country in the region as a class, have students fill in the name of the country on their outline maps. Refer them to the map on p. 165 if they need guidance.

All in One Europe and Russia Teaching Resources, *Outline Map 18: Eastern Europe and Russia: Political*, p. 344

- Have students study the paragraphs and data for the countries on pp. 306–307. Tell them to think about what the countries have in common and what the major differences are as they read. Encourage them to make a table to keep track of the similarities and differences.

- Ask students to find the similarities between the Czech Republic and Hungary. (*population size; Slovak is a major ethnic group; parliamentary democracy as government; machinery and equipment, manufactured goods, and raw materials are major exports; Hungarian language; once under communist rule; both have strengthening economies*)

Introducing Eastern Europe and Russia

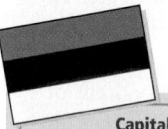

Czech Republic

Capital	Prague
Land Area	29,836 sq mi; 78,276 sq km
Population	10.3 million
Ethnic Group(s)	Czech, Moravian, Slovak, Polish, German, Silesian
Religion(s)	Roman Catholic, Protestant, Eastern Orthodox
Government	parliamentary democracy
Currency	Czech koruna
Leading Exports	machinery and transportation equipment, intermediate manufactured goods, chemicals, raw materials, fuel
Language(s)	Czech (official), Slovak, Hungarian

The Czech Republic (chek rih PUB lik) is a landlocked nation surrounded by Germany, Slovakia, Austria, and Poland. In 1918, the Slovaks joined with the Czechs to form Czechoslovakia. Czechoslovakia fell under Soviet rule after World War II but gained back its freedom in 1989. In 1993, the Czechs and the Slovaks peacefully separated into two nations, the Czech Republic and Slovakia. The Czech Republic has become one of the most stable and successful countries of those dominated by the Soviet Union during the Cold War. It has strong industries, mineral resources, and a thriving tourist industry. The Czech Republic has become a member of NATO and the EU.

Estonia

Capital	Tallinn
Land Area	16,684 sq mi; 43,211 sq km
Population	1.4 million
Ethnic Group(s)	Estonian, Russian, Ukrainian, Belarusian, Finnish
Religion(s)	Protestant, Eastern Orthodox, Jewish
Government	parliamentary republic
Currency	kroon
Leading Exports	machinery and equipment, wood products, textiles, food products, metals, chemical products
Language(s)	Estonian (official), Russian

Estonia (es TOH nee uh) borders the Baltic Sea, Latvia, and Russia. It is actually a small peninsula, and includes more than 1500 small islands. For centuries, foreign powers controlled the region. But in 1918, Estonia gained its independence. Like several other eastern European states, it was taken over by the Soviet Union in 1940 and regained its independence in 1991. Since then, Estonia has adopted political and economic ideas from Western Europe. Its three major trading partners are Finland, Sweden, and Germany. The country has joined the EU and NATO.

A hawk moth in Viidumae Nature Reserve, Estonia

Differentiated Instruction

For Gifted and Talented　　L3

Have students choose two of the five countries found on pp. 306–307. Tell them to use the DK World Desk Reference Online to make information cards similar to the ones in the Country Databank using different statistics, such as the percentage of people living in rural and urban areas and literacy rates. Ask them to use the same types of statistics for both countries. Then have them write a short paragraph explaining the similarities and differences between the countries based on what they found.

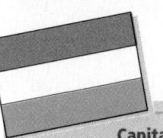

Hungary

Capital	Budapest
Land Area	35,652 sq mi; 92,340 sq km
Population	10.1 million
Ethnic Group(s)	Hungarian, Roma, German, Serb, Slovak, Romanian
Religion(s)	Roman Catholic, Protestant
Government	parliamentary democracy
Currency	forint
Leading Exports	machinery and equipment, other manufactured goods, food products, raw materials, fuels and electricity
Language(s)	Hungarian (official)

Hungary (HUNG guh ree) is landlocked among Austria, Romania, and five other countries in central Europe. For hundreds of years the nation was part of the Austro-Hungarian Empire. After World War II, the country came under communist rule. In the late 1960s, Hungary took some steps away from a government-controlled economy. But real reforms came in 1990 with the first open elections and a free-market economy. Since then, Hungary has had strong economic growth, and has become a member of both NATO and the EU. Hungary's capital, Budapest, has long been a cultural center of the region.

Latvia

Capital	Riga
Land Area	24,552 sq mi; 63,589 sq km
Population	2.4 million
Ethnic Group(s)	Latvian, Russian, Belarusian, Ukrainian, Polish, Lithuanian
Religion(s)	Protestant, Roman Catholic, Eastern Orthodox
Government	parliamentary democracy
Currency	lat
Leading Exports	wood and wood products, machinery and equipment, metals, textiles, foodstuffs
Language(s)	Latvian (official), Russian

Located between Estonia and Lithuania, Latvia (LAT vee uh) sits on the eastern coast of the Baltic Sea. The entire country lies on a flat, low plain. Its climate is temperate, with cool summers and cold winters. Between World War I and World War II, Latvia enjoyed a period of independence, but in 1940 it was taken over by the Soviet Union. Along with many other Soviet republics, it declared its independence in 1991. Since then it has adopted many of the political and economic ideas of Western Europe. After a Russian economic crisis in 1998, Latvia further decreased is dependence on Russia. It has joined the EU and NATO.

Lithuania

Capital	Vilnius
Land Area	25,174 sq mi; 65,200 sq km
Population	3.6 million
Ethnic Group(s)	Lithuanian, Russian, Polish, Belarusian
Religion(s)	Roman Catholic, Protestant, Russian Orthodox, Muslim, Jewish
Government	parliamentary democracy
Currency	litas
Leading Exports	mineral products, textiles and clothing, machinery and equipment, chemicals, wood and wood products, foodstuffs
Language(s)	Lithuanian (official), Russian

Lithuania (lith oo AY nee uh) is located between Latvia and Poland and borders the Baltic Sea. It was an independent state before World War II, but the Soviet Union claimed it in 1940. Lithuania was the first Soviet republic to declare independence in 1990. Since independence, the Lithuanians have taken steps toward establishing a free-market economy and privatizing businesses. Most of Lithuania's income is from services and agriculture. However, it has few natural resources and is one of the poorer nations in the region. Lithuania has joined the EU and NATO.

Chapter 10 **307**

Guided Instruction (continued)

■ Ask **Which countries on pp. 306–307 were once under Soviet rule?** (*Czech Republic, Estonia, Latvia, and Lithuania*) **What types of government do these countries have now?** (*Czech Republic, Latvia, and Lithuania are parliamentary democracies; Estonia is a parliamentary republic.*)

■ Ask students **Do you think migration is common within Eastern Europe? Why or why not?** (*Students should see that many Eastern European countries contain major ethnic groups from other Eastern European countries. For example, Latvia's major ethnic groups include Russian, Belarusian, Ukrainian, Polish, and Lithuanian. Therefore, migration among Eastern European countries is probably fairly common.*)

Differentiated Instruction

For Less Proficient Readers
Have students create a Venn diagram to show the similarities and differences between Estonia and Latvia. Display the *Venn Diagram Transparency* to show

L1 students how to sketch the organizer. Circulate to make sure students are filling in the organizers correctly.

📖 **Europe and Russia Transparencies,** *Transparency B16: Venn Diagram*

Guided Instruction (continued)

- Have students place the countries on pp. 308–309 in order from largest population to smallest population. *(Russian Federation, Poland, Romania, Moldova, Macedonia, Montenegro)* Remind students how to find population density. *(Divide the population by the land area.)* Ask them to find out which country on these pages has the highest population density. *(Moldova)* Ask **Which has the lowest?** *(Russian Federation)* **Why does the Russian Federation have the lowest when it is the largest country in the world and has a large population?** *(Its large population is spread out over a very large land area.)*

- Ask **Why is Moldova's economy based mostly on farming?** *(It has a good climate for farming, and it has few minerals and energy resources to fuel the economy.)* **Why do you think Moldova's economy has not improved as much as Poland's economy?** *(Moldova had few free market reforms and in 2001 elected a communist president who would most likely not implement any more. Poland changed rapidly to an open economy.)*

Introducing Eastern Europe and Russia

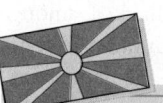

Macedonia

Capital	Skopje
Land Area	9,597 sq mi; 24,856 sq km
Population	2.1 million
Ethnic Group(s)	Macedonian, Albanian, Southwest Asian, Serb, Roma
Religion(s)	Eastern Orthodox, Muslim
Government	emerging democracy
Currency	Macedonian denar
Leading Exports	food, beverages, tobacco, miscellaneous manufactured goods, iron and steel
Language(s)	Macedonian (official), Albanian (official), Serbo-Croat

Macedonia (mas uh DOH nee uh) is located in southeastern Europe north of Greece. It gained its independence from Yugoslavia in 1991. Macedonia is the poorest of the countries that used to make up Yugoslavia. The nation has a weak economy, and one third of its labor force is unemployed. Macedonia faces ethnic conflict and government instability. It has also faced political conflict with its neighbor, Greece. Because Macedonia is the name of a region in northern Greece, Greece opposed the country's choice of name. However, a treaty signed in 1995 settled the dispute.

Moldova

Capital	Chisinau
Land Area	12,885 sq mi; 33,371 sq km
Population	4.4 million
Ethnic Group(s)	Moldovan, Ukrainian, Russian, Bulgarian, Gagauz
Religion(s)	Eastern Orthodox, Jewish
Government	republic
Currency	Moldovan leu
Leading Exports	foodstuffs, textiles and footwear, machinery
Language(s)	Moldovan (official), Romanian, Russian

Moldova (mohl DOH vuh) is located between Romania and Ukraine. Before World War II, Moldova was ruled by Romania. It became part of the Soviet Union after World War II and gained its independence in 1991. With few minerals and energy sources, Moldova's economy is based mostly on farming. One of the poorest nations in Europe, it recently saw an improvement in its economy due to some free-market reforms. However, in 2001 Moldova became the first former Soviet state to elect a communist president. Consequently, fewer free-market reforms are expected in the future.

Montenegro

Capital	Podgorica
Land Area	5,333 sq mi; 13,812 sq km
Population	620,145
Ethnic Group(s)	Montenegrins, Serbs, Albanians
Religion(s)	Eastern Orthodox, Muslim, Roman Catholic
Government	republic
Currency	euro
Leading Exports	foodstuffs
Language(s)	Serbian (official)

Montenegro (mahnt uh NEE groh) is located in southeastern Europe. It borders Bosnia and Herzegovina, Serbia, Croatia, Albania, and the Adriatic Sea. Montenegro was once part of Yugoslavia. It experienced years of ethnic conflict after Yugoslavia broke up in the 1990s. In 2003, it formed a partnership with Serbia, another part of the former Yugoslavia. However, in 2006, Montenegrins voted to become an independent country. After years of war and political instability, the Republic of Montenegro is focused on rebuilding its troubled economy. Promising industries include tourism, metal processing, and textiles.

308 Europe and Russia

Differentiated Instruction

For Advanced Readers   L3

Help students learn the capitals of each of the countries in the Country Databank by dividing the class into pairs, and having each pair create a set of flashcards. One side of the flashcard should have the country name, and the other side should have the country capital. Have students take turns quizzing each other. Once students have learned the country capitals, you may choose to have students repeat the exercise using different information, such as currency or government.

Poland

Capital	Warsaw
Land Area	117,554 sq mi; 304,465 sq km
Population	38.6 million
Ethnic Group(s)	Polish, German, Ukrainian, Belarusian
Religion(s)	Roman Catholic, Eastern Orthodox
Government	republic
Currency	zloty
Leading Exports	machinery and transport equipment, intermediate manufactured goods, miscellaneous manufactured goods, food and live animals
Language(s)	Polish (official)

Polish postage stamps

Poland (POH lund) is located in central Europe between Germany and Ukraine. Poland was taken over by Germany and the Soviet Union during World War II. Following the war, Poland was dominated by the Soviet Union. Since the fall of the Soviet Union, Poland has changed successfully from a government-controlled economy to an open economy, and has entered the EU and NATO. Poland has an almost homogeneous population, and the vast majority of Poles are Roman Catholic.

Romania

Capital	Bucharest
Land Area	88,934 sq mi; 230,340 sq km
Population	22.3 million
Ethnic Group(s)	Romanian, Hungarian, Roma, Ukrainian, German, Russian
Religion(s)	Eastern Orthodox, Protestant, Roman Catholic
Government	republic
Currency	Romanian leu
Leading Exports	textiles and footwear, metals and metal products, machinery and equipment, minerals and fuels
Language(s)	Romanian (official), Hungarian, German, Romany

Romania (roh MAY nee uh) is located in southeastern Europe between Ukraine and Bulgaria, bordering the Black Sea. Following World War II, Romania was occupied by the Soviet Union. It became a communist republic in 1947. A single harsh dictator ruled Romania from 1965 to 1989. In the late 1990s, the country became a limited democracy. Today, the country still struggles with widespread poverty and government instability. Romania is carrying out political and economic reforms required for it to join the European Union. It aims to join the EU in 2007.

Russian Federation

Capital	Moscow
Land Area	6,592,100 sq mi; 16,995,800 sq km
Population	145 million
Ethnic Group(s)	Russian, Tatar, Ukrainian, Chuvash, Bashkir, Belarusian, Moldavian
Religion(s)	Russian Orthodox, Muslim, Jewish
Government	federation
Currency	Russian ruble
Leading Exports	petroleum and petroleum products, natural gas, wood and wood products, metals, chemicals
Language(s)	Russian (official), Tatar, Ukrainian, Chuvash, and others

Russia (RUSH uh), the world's largest country, is located in northern Asia between Ukraine and China, bordering the Arctic and North Pacific Oceans. The region west of the Ural Mountains is considered part of Europe. Throughout most of its history, Russia was ruled by royal families. The last royal dynasty was overthrown in 1917. The world's first communist government, the Soviet Union, was formed after World War I and ruled for decades. In 1991, the USSR split into 15 independent nations. Russia is by far the largest, with most of the former Soviet Union's area and population.

Chapter 10 **309**

Guided Instruction (continued)

■ Ask students to describe Romania's population. (*Romania has a population of about 22.3 million people. It has a diverse population, with seven major ethnic groups including Romanian, Hungarian, and Southwest Asian. Most people are Christian.*) Ask **How does it differ from Po-land's population?** (*Poland has a more homogenous population, and Islam is not a major religion practiced there.*)

■ Ask **What challenges do you think Russia's large land area presents to its people and government?** (*Possible answer: Extensive transportation and communication systems are needed so that people and goods can be transported throughout the country and the government can rule the large territory effectively.*)

■ Ask **How do Russia's leading exports reflect the country's standing as one of the world's leaders in natural resources?** (*Russia's leading exports include natural resources such as petroleum, natural gas, and wood.*)

Background: Links Across Time

St. Petersburg The name of the second largest city in Russia, now called St. Petersburg, has changed several times during the country's history. Peter the Great, who founded the city in the early 1700s, used the German word *burg*, meaning "city," as part of his city's name. In 1914, however, when Russia and Germany went to war, the city's name was changed to the more Russian-sounding Petrograd. After the communists came to power, the city's name was changed again, this time to Leningrad, in honor of one of Russian Communism's founders, Vladimir Lenin. Finally when the Soviet Union collapsed in the early 1990s, the city's name was changed back to its original, St. Petersburg.

Guided Instruction (continued)

- Ask students to compare and contrast Serbia and Slovenia. *(Similarities: Both have Serb and Hungarian ethnic groups, Christians and Muslims, manufactured goods and food as leading exports, and Serbo-Croat as a language; both were once part of Yugoslavia. Differences: Slovenia has a better economy and is more stable. There are also differences in land area, population size, some ethnic groups, government, currency, some exports, and some languages.)*

- Have students create a short timeline showing important events in Slovakia's history. *(1918: Slovaks join with Czechs to form Czechoslovakia; 1989: gains independence from Soviet rule; 1993: Slovaks and Czechs peacefully separate into Slovakia and the Czech Republic)*

- Have students review the map on p. 165, and ask them to draw conclusions about Ukraine's geographic location and its different ethnic groups. *(Ukraine is bordered by several countries, including Russia, Belarus, Poland, Hungary, and Moldova. A number of its ethnic groups come from these places.)*

Independent Practice

Have students complete *Using a Map Key,* and then divide the class into pairs and distribute *Outline Map 18: Eastern Europe and Russia: Political.* Then ask students to use the Country Databank to help them create a map that shows the official language for each country in the region. Tell students to use different colors for each official language, and shade the countries with the color that corresponds to the official language. If a country has more than one official language, have them alternate bands of two or three colors to show that information. They should explain what each color represents in their map keys.

All in One Europe and Russia Teaching Resources, *Using a Map Key,* p. 341; *Outline Map 18: Eastern Europe and Russia: Political,* p. 344

Monitor Progress

Circulate to make sure students are filling in their maps correctly. Provide assistance as needed.

Introducing Eastern Europe and Russia

Serbia

Capital	Belgrade
Land Area	34,116 sq mi; 88,361 sq km
Population	9.4 million
Ethnic Group(s)	Serb, Albanian, Hungarian, Bozniak, Roma
Religion(s)	Eastern Orthodox, Muslim, Roman Catholic
Government	republic
Currency	dinar
Leading Exports	foodstuffs and live animals, manufactured goods, raw materials
Language(s)	Serbian (official)

Serbia (SUR bee uh) is a diverse country in southeastern Europe with about 40 different ethnic groups. It was once part of Yugoslavia and experienced years of civil war after Yugoslavia broke up. Serbia's violence against ethnic Albanians in Kosovo caused NATO troops to invade the region in 1999 to restore peace. In 2003, Serbia formed a partnership with Montenegro, another part of the former Yugoslavia. However, in 2006, Montenegro voted to become independent. The Republic of Serbia is now focused on rebuilding its economy and recovering from years of war.

Slovakia

Capital	Bratislava
Land Area	18,842 sq mi; 48,800 sq km
Population	5.4 million
Ethnic Group(s)	Slovak, Hungarian, Roma, Czech, Moravian, Silesian, Ruthenian, Ukrainian, German, Polish
Religion(s)	Roman Catholic, Protestant, Eastern Orthodox
Government	parliamentary democracy
Currency	Slovak koruna
Leading Exports	machinery and transport equipment, manufactured goods, chemicals
Language(s)	Slovak (official), Hungarian, Czech

Slovakia (sloh VAH kee uh) is located in Central Europe between the Czech Republic and Ukraine. In 1918, the Slovaks joined with the Czechs to form Czechoslovakia. Czechoslovakia fell under Soviet domination after World War II but gained back its freedom in 1989. In 1993, the Slovaks and the Czechs peacefully separated into two democratic nations, Slovakia and the Czech Republic. Slovakia has a stable economy and has joined the EU and NATO.

An Eastern Orthodox Church in Montenegro

Slovenia

Capital	Ljubljana
Land Area	7,780 sq mi; 20,151 sq km
Population	1.9 million
Ethnic Group(s)	Slovene, Croat, Serb, Bosniak, Yugoslav, Hungarian
Religion(s)	Roman Catholic, Protestant, Muslim
Government	parliamentary democratic republic
Currency	tolar
Leading Exports	manufactured goods, machinery and transport equipment, chemicals, food
Language(s)	Slovene (official), Serbo-Croat

Slovenia (sloh VEE nee uh) is located in Central Europe between Austria and Croatia, bordering the Adriatic Sea. The Slovene lands were once part of Austria and the Holy Roman Empire. In the mid-1900s, they became part of Yugoslavia. Since independence in 1991, Slovenia has become a stable democracy with a strong economy and a good relationship with Western Europe. Slovenia has joined the EU and NATO. The country has Eastern Europe's highest standard of living.

Ukraine

Capital	Kiev
Land Area	233,090 sq mi; 603,700 sq km
Population	48.4 million
Ethnic Group(s)	Ukrainian, Russian, Belarusian, Moldovan, Crimea Tartar, Bulgarian, Hungarian, Romanian, Polish
Religion(s)	Eastern Orthodox, Jewish
Government	republic
Currency	hryvnia
Leading Exports	ferrous and nonferrous metals, fuel and petroleum products, machinery and transport equipment, food products
Language(s)	Ukrainian (official), Russian, Tartar

Ukraine (yoo KRAYN) is located between Poland and Russia, bordering the Black Sea. During the 900s and 1000s, Ukraine was the center of the largest and most powerful state in Europe. However, since that time, the region has suffered invasions, occupations, and rebellions. Millions of Ukrainians died under Soviet occupation in the 1920s and 1930s and millions more during World War II. Although Ukraine gained independence from the Soviet Union in 1991, many of its leaders have been slow to encourage political or economic reforms.

SOURCES: CIA World Factbook Online; DK World Desk Reference Online; *The World Almanac*, 2003

Assessment

Comprehension and Critical Thinking

1. Compare and Contrast Compare the physical size and the population of Ukraine to those of Macedonia.

2. Make Generalizations Identify the six countries that were once part of Yugoslavia. What are some characteristics that they share?

3. Categorize Which religions do most people in the region practice?

4. Draw Conclusions The governments of some of these countries are listed as "emerging," or developing democracies. Read about these countries' histories. Why might it be difficult for them to establish democratic governments?

5. Make a Bar Graph Create a bar graph that shows the populations of the countries in the region.

Keeping Current

Access the **DK World Desk Reference Online** at **PHSchool.com** for up-to-date information about the 20 countries in this region.

Go Online
PHSchool.com

Web Code: lde-7500

Assess and Reteach

Assess Progress L1

- Have students create a chart similar to the one you created on the board at the beginning of the lesson. Have them choose any two countries and list their similarities and differences on the chart.

- Ask students to answer the Assessment questions.

Reteach L1

Ask students to create a table on a large piece of poster board that shows the data for all of the countries in the Country Databank. Have them list the categories across the top of the table and the names of the countries along the side. Model filling in the information for one country on the board.

Extend L3

Portfolio Activity

Have students choose one country in the Country Databank. Ask them to research the country, using the DK World Desk Reference Online as a starting point. Then, have them create a paragraph, short story, chart, graph, map, or illustration about the country to add to their portfolios.

Answers

Assessment

1. Ukraine has a much larger area and population size than Macedonia.

2. Bosnia and Herzegovina, Croatia, Macedonia, Serbia, Montenegro, and Slovenia; all have the Serb ethnic group, Muslim and Christian religions, and food as a leading export; all have struggled with instability and are working to improve their economies.

3. Christianity, Islam, and Judaism

4. Most of these countries are struggling to rebuild their government after gaining independence from communist rule.

5. Students' bar graphs should reflect the populations of the countries in the Databank. Use the *Rubric for Assessing a Bar Graph* to evaluate students' work.

All in One **Europe and Russia Teaching Resources,** *Rubric for Assessing a Bar Graph,* p. 347

Section 1
Step-by-Step Instruction

Objectives

Social Studies

1. Find out about Polish traditions.
2. Learn about economic changes that have taken place in Poland since the collapse of communism.
3. Understand the future challenges that Poland faces.

Reading/Language Arts

Compare and contrast to help you sort out and analyze information.

Prepare to Read

Build Background Knowledge **L2**

Tell students that in this section they will learn about the country of Poland. Explain that although many changes have affected Poland throughout its history, many Polish traditions have remained. Ask students if they know of any such cultural traditions in their communities. Then have them discuss why they think these traditions have lasted. Conduct a Think-Write-Pair-Share activity (TE, p. T36) to help students generate ideas.

Set a Purpose for Reading **L2**

- Preview the Objectives.

- Read each statement in the *Reading Readiness Guide* aloud. Ask students to mark the statements true or false.

  All in One Europe and Russia Teaching Resources, *Reading Readiness Guide*, p. 314

- Have students discuss the statements in pairs or groups of four, then mark their guides again. Use the Numbered Heads participation strategy (TE, p. T36) to call on students to share their group's perspectives.

Vocabulary Builder
Preview Key Terms **L2**

Pronounce each Key Term, and then ask the students to say the word with you. Provide a simple explanation such as, "An entrepreneur is a person who starts new businesses."

Section 1
Poland
Preserving Tradition Amidst Change

Prepare to Read

Objectives

In this section you will
1. Find out about Polish traditions.
2. Learn about economic changes that have taken place in Poland since the collapse of communism.
3. Understand the future challenges that Poland faces.

Taking Notes

As you read, create an outline of this section. The outline below has been started for you.

> I. Tradition in Poland
>   A. Catholicism
>   B.
>   1.
>   2.
> II.

Target Reading Skill

Compare and Contrast
When you compare, you look for the similarities between things. When you contrast, you look at the differences. Comparing and contrasting can help you sort out and analyze information. As you read this section, look for similarities and differences in Polish life during and after Soviet domination.

Key Terms

- **shrine** (shryn) *n.* a holy place
- **capitalism** (KAP ut ul iz um) *n.* an economic system in which businesses are privately owned
- **entrepreneur** (ahn truh pruh NOOR) *n.* a person who develops original ideas in order to start new businesses

Dancers at a traditional festival in Mazuka, Poland

In June of 2003, Polish citizens celebrated an event that could not possibly have occurred just two decades earlier. Poland had voted to join the European Union. It was an exciting event for a nation that at one time did not even appear on maps of Europe.

Poland has had a difficult history. In medieval times, it was the largest state in Europe. But by the late 1700s, it had been divided up among its stronger neighbors. For the next two hundred years, Polish territory changed hands many times. Controlled at different times by Russia, Germany, and Austria, Poland became free again at the end of World War I. But after World War II, the Polish government fell under the influence of the Soviet Union. For several decades, Poles lived under a harsh communist government. Poles regained their freedom when that government fell in 1989. Poland then began a long process of reform and rebuilding.

312 Europe and Russia

Target Reading Skill **L2**

Compare and Contrast Point out the Target Reading Skill. Tell students that comparing and contrasting ideas will help them to better understand and organize them.

Model the skill by reading the Capitalism paragraph on p. 315 and comparing and contrasting Poland's economy before and after January 1, 1990. (*After January 1, the government no longer controlled prices, taxes and wages were frozen, and a stock market was set up a year later.*)

Give students *Compare and Contrast.* Have them complete the activity in groups.

All in One Europe and Russia Teaching Resources, *Compare and Contrast*, p. 329

Tradition in Poland

Poland has experienced great change in its long history. Borders have shifted. Rulers have come and gone. Economic systems have changed. But many parts of Polish life have remained the same.

Catholicism in Poland Catholicism has been at the center of Polish tradition for centuries. The communist government tried to discourage Catholicism, but it could not change the devotion many Poles have for the Roman Catholic Church.

Today, about 90 percent of Poles are Catholic. Poles have their own way of observing Catholic holidays and their own way of prayer. Polish Catholics felt tremendous pride in 1978, when a Pole was selected as pope of the Catholic Church. Pope John Paul II quickly became the most widely traveled Catholic leader in history. He also made the world more aware of Poland and its struggle under communism.

In 1979, the pope visited Poland. About one million joyful and enthusiastic Poles gathered to see him. Mothers held babies over their heads for the pope's blessing. The crowd sang hymns and threw flowers toward the stage on which he sat. For most of these people, the pope stood for traditional Poland.

Orthodoxy in Poland However, not all Poles are Catholic. A minority of Poles are Polish Orthodox. An example of Polish Orthodox religious life can be seen in northeastern Poland, near the forest of Bialowieza (byah woh VYEH zhah). Not far from the forest is the holy hill of Grabarka, with an Orthodox church at the top. In mid-August, visitors climb this hill to visit the church. Each visitor plants a cross in the earth. Among the trees on the hillside are hundreds of crosses. Some are as tall as trees, and others as tiny as flowers. You can see such Orthodox **shrines,** or holy places, all over Poland.

Judaism in Poland A small minority of Poles are Jewish. Today, Poland's Jewish population numbers only in the thousands. However, more than 3 million Jews used to live in Poland. During the Holocaust, about 85 percent of Polish Jews were killed by the German government.

Polish Religious Traditions
Roman Catholic Pope John Paul II, at the top, waves to crowds in his hometown of Wadowice (vah duh VEET seh). Above, Eastern Orthodox worshipers take part in a festival in Bialowieza. **Apply Information** *What role does religion play in the lives of most Poles?*

Vocabulary Builder

Use the information below to teach students this section's high-use words.

High-Use Word	Definition and Sample Sentence
unique, p. 315	*adj.* having no like or equal Each painting the artist created was truly **unique.**
transition, p. 315	*n.* a change from one situation to another Some students find the **transition** from high school to college difficult.
invest, p. 316	*v.* to spend money on something in the hope of making a profit Amanda **invested** her money in stocks of growing companies.

Tradition in Poland   L2

Guided Instruction

- **Vocabulary Builder** Clarify the high-use word **unique** before reading.

- Read Tradition in Poland, using the Oral Cloze strategy (TE, p. T33).

- Ask students **What is the major religion of Poland?** *(Catholicism)* **How is Polish Catholicism unique?** *(Polish Catholics have their own way of observing holidays and praying.)*

- Have students discuss why Poles felt such pride in Pope John Paul II. *(He stood for traditional Poland, and became the most widely traveled Catholic leader in history, working to make the world more aware of Poland's struggle under communism.)*

- Ask students **What other religion do many Poles practice?** *(Polish Orthodox)* **What is a shrine?** *(a holy place)* **How do you think shrines reflect Polish traditions?** *(They are important to Polish religions, which are a large part of Polish tradition.)*

- Ask students **How does the Polish language link Poles to each other and to other nations?** *(It ties Poles together by making them feel different and special, and because it is a Slavic language, it links Poland with other Slavic nations in Eastern Europe.)*

Independent Practice

Ask students to create the Taking Notes graphic organizer on a blank sheet of paper. Then have them fill in the outline with information they have just learned. Briefly model how to add details using *Transparency B15: Outline.*

> **Europe and Russia Transparencies,** *Transparency B15: Outline*

Monitor Progress

As students begin to fill in the graphic organizer, circulate and help individuals understand which details to include. Provide assistance as needed.

Answer

Apply Information Religion is very important to many Poles.

Guided Instruction L2

Ask students to study the Country Profile on this page. As a class, answer the Map and Chart Skills questions. Allow students to briefly discuss their responses with a partner before sharing answers.

Independent Practice

- Distribute *Reading a Table*. Have students work in pairs to complete the worksheet.

  All in One **Europe and Russia Teaching Resources,** *Reading a Table*, p. 342

- Turn students' attention to the charts on this page. Ask them to write a few sentences summarizing the information they learned from each chart.

Poland

A few powerful people had run Poland's communist government. In contrast, as a republic, Poland has a three-branch form of government similar to that of the United States. Poland's economy has also changed. Under communism, the government took control of most privately owned businesses and industries. Poland's republic has encouraged the development of small businesses, as well as foreign trade. Study the map and charts to learn more about Poland's government.

Poland: Economic Activity
KEY

- Forestry
- Commercial farming
- Manufacturing and trade

City Population
- ⊙ 1,000,000–4,999,999
- ⊙ 250,000–999,999
- — National border

Employment by Sector and Ownership

1989				2001		
Sector	Privately Owned	Government Owned		Sector	Privately Owned	Government Owned
Agriculture	79%	21%		Agriculture	99%	1%
Industry	15%	85%		Industry	77%	23%
Construction	27%	73%		Construction	94%	6%
Transport	6%	94%		Transport	48%	52%
Trade	8%	92%		Trade	98%	2%

SOURCES: Glowny Urzad Statystyczny (GUS), Rocznik Statystyczny

Poland's Government

Executive Branch	Legislative Branch	Judicial Branch
President Elected by the people for a five-year term	**National Assembly** Made up of two houses, the Sejm and the Senate	**Supreme Court** Judges appointed by the president for life
Prime Minister Appointed by the president, and confirmed by the Sejm	**Sejm** Includes 460 members, who are elected to four-year terms	**Constitutional Tribunal** Judges appointed by the Sejm for nine-year terms
Council of Ministers Appointed by the President, and approved by the Sejm	**Senate** Includes 100 members, who are elected to four-year terms	SOURCE: CIA World Factbook Online, 2003

Map and Chart Skills

1. **Locate** Around which Polish cities are the manufacturing industries and trade centered?
2. **Compare** How did the percentage of people employed in privately owned industries change from 1989 to 2001?
3. **Apply Information** How does Poland's government compare to that of the United States?

 Use Web Code lde-7501 for **DK World Desk Reference Online.**

Answers

Map and Chart Skills

1. Warsaw, Katowice, Kraków
2. It increased.
3. Poland has a three-branch government similar to that of the United States.

Go Online PHSchool.com Students can find more information about this topic on the DK World Desk Reference Online.

Differentiated Instruction

For Less Proficient Readers L1

To help reinforce students' understanding of the shift from government ownership to private ownership of businesses and industries in Poland, have them choose one of the sectors in the chart and create a pie graph showing the portions that are privately-owned and government-owned. They should create one graph for the sector in 1989 and another for the same sector in 2001. Remind students to label the graphs properly and give each an appropriate title.

The Polish Language The language of the Poles has stood the test of time. In the past, some foreign rulers banned the use of Polish in schools and in the government. Although the communists did not ban Polish, they did force Polish schoolchildren to learn Russian, the official language of the Soviet Union.

Today, Polish is spoken by the majority of the population. The Polish language is a cultural tie that unites Poles, giving them pride in their unique heritage. As a Slavic language, it also links the nation to other Slavic nations in Eastern Europe.

✓ **Reading Check** What religion do most Poles belong to?

Great Economic Changes

Communism ended in Poland in 1989. After that, Poland underwent rapid change. The greatest of these changes occurred in Poland's economy.

Capitalism Poland has been very successful in making the change from communism to capitalism. **Capitalism** is an economic system in which businesses are privately owned. Most former communist countries made this change gradually. Poland changed almost overnight. On January 1, 1990, Polish leaders made a number of changes. They ended the government's control over prices. They also froze taxes and wages. A year later, Poland set up a stock market. Although these were dramatic changes, they helped Poland successfully make the difficult transition to capitalism.

Learn about life for Jews in Poland.

Links to
Government

Poland's Solidarity Movement In the 1980s, a radical group formed in Poland. This was a labor union—a group of people seeking workers' rights—called Solidarity. This group was radical because it was the first independent labor union to form in a Soviet-dominated country. Solidarity was formed to protest rising food prices. It organized strikes and demonstrations such as the 1987 march shown in the photo at the left. Solidarity's first leader was an electrician named Lech Walesa. Under Walesa, Solidarity began openly criticizing the communist government, and helped bring about its downfall. Lech Walesa served as president of Poland from 1990 to 1995. Solidarity is still a political party in Poland today.

Chapter 10 Section 1 **315**

Great Economic Changes L2

Guided Instruction

■ **Vocabulary Builder** Clarify the high-use words **transition** and **invest** before reading.

■ Read Great Economic Changes with students. As they read, check and make sure that individuals can answer the Reading Check question.

■ Ask students **How did Poland change its economy after January 1, 1990?** *(Polish leaders set up a stock market, ended government control over prices, and froze taxes and wages.)*

■ Ask students **Why do you think that Poles decided to make a rapid change to capitalism?** *(Possible answers: Many Poles had been unhappy under communism and wanted to replace it with another economic system as soon as possible; Poles might have felt that a quick transition would be more effective than a slower one.)*

■ Ask students **What led foreigners to begin investing their money in Poland?** *(the collapse of the communist government)* **What other factors might have encouraged foreign investment?** *(Possible answer: Investors might have been encouraged by the economy's rapid transition to capitalism.)*

Differentiated Instruction

For Special Needs Students L1
Before reading the section, show students *Section Reading Support Transparency ER 48*. Tell them that as they read, they should identify the statements on the completed graphic organizer that match the information in the text.

📖 **Europe and Russia Transparencies**
Section Reading Support Transparency ER 48

For Gifted and Talented L3
Tell students to suppose that they work for Poland's largest newspaper in January 1990. Have each student write a newspaper article about new changes in Poland's economy. Use *Rubric for Assessing a Newspaper Article* to evaluate students' articles.

All in One Europe and Russia Teaching Resources, *Rubric for Assessing a Newspaper Article*, p. 348

Links

Read the **Links to Government** on this page. Ask **Why was Solidarity radical?** *(It was the first independent labor union to form in a Soviet-ruled country.)*

Answer

✓ **Reading Check** Most Poles are Catholics.

Chapter 10 Section 1 **315**

Target Reading Skill

Compare and Contrast As a follow up, ask students to do the Target Reading Skill activity in the Student Edition. *(During communist rule, Poland's economy was weak; the government controlled businesses and prices. After the fall of communism, the economy was strengthened due to foreign investment and privatization of businesses.)*

Guided Instruction (continued)

- Have students describe how small businesses in Poland's cities grew after communism ended. *(At first, traders sold goods in street booths. Eventually they earned enough money to take over stores that had once been owned by the government.)*

- Ask students **How did the availability of consumer goods in Poland change after the fall of communism?** *(Poles had more access to consumer goods after the fall of communism.)*

- Ask students **What effect did the transition from communism to capitalism have on farming?** *(Although many farms under communism were privately owned, the government protected farmers by buying their products and ensuring that prices stayed high. After the end of communism, prices dropped and farmers no longer had a guaranteed source of income. As a result, farmers under capitalism have had to be innovative in order to make a living.)*

Independent Practice

Have students continue to fill in their outlines with information from the section.

Monitor Progress

As students fill in their graphic organizers, circulate to make sure they are providing the correct headings and details.

Answers

Chart Skills Compare Slovenia
Infer The standard of living is higher in Germany due to its economic strength and long life expectancy.

316

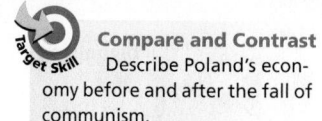 **Compare and Contrast** Describe Poland's economy before and after the fall of communism.

Foreign Investment With the collapse of the communist government, many foreigners began to invest their money in Poland. By 2001, Poland had brought in more foreign investment than had any other Central European country. Foreign investment has greatly strengthened the Polish economy.

Privatization A growth in the number of private businesses has also helped Poland's economy. With the end of communist rule, Poles were free to find new ways of making money. Small businesses soon blossomed in Poland's cities. At first, traders set up booths on the streets. They sold everything they could find, from American blue jeans to old Soviet army uniforms.

Slowly but surely, some traders earned enough money to take over stores that the government had once owned. Now, more than two million businesses are run by entrepreneurs (ahn truh pruh NOORZ). An **entrepreneur** is a person who develops original ideas in order to start new businesses.

Polish industries have also been slowly privatized over the last few years. Poland's most important private industries are food, energy, and mining.

Consumer Goods Poles now have access to more consumer goods than they did under communism. Only half of the homes in Poland had televisions in 1989. Now, almost every home has one. On the streets of cities such as Warsaw, Poland's capital, many people use mobile phones and wear the latest fashions. For these people, the new way of life is good.

Chart Skills

Life expectancy and per capita GDP, or the economic output per person, are two factors used to measure a country's standard of living. **Compare** Which Eastern European country has the highest standard of living?
Infer Why do you think the standard of living is higher in Germany than in the other countries in this chart?

Standard of Living Comparison for Selected European Countries

Country	Per Capita GDP	Life Expectancy	
		Male	Female
Bulgaria	$6,600	68.3	75.6
Czech Republic	$15,300	71.7	78.9
Hungary	$13,300	67.8	76.8
Poland	$9,500	69.8	78.3
Slovenia	$18,000	71.7	79.6
Germany (Western Europe)	$26,600	75.5	81.6

Skills Mini Lesson

Synthesizing Information

1. Tell students that in order to synthesize information, they should analyze each piece of information and then look for connections between them. Finally, they should draw a conclusion based on the connections they found.

2. Have students practice the skill by synthesizing the per capita GDP and life expectancy information in the chart to determine which country has the highest standard of living.

3. Have students apply the skill by synthesizing the information in the chart to compare the standard of living in Hungary and Bulgaria. Tell them to write a few sentences explaining their conclusion.

Changes in Farm Life Unlike many businesses, most farms under communism had remained privately owned. Still, the change to a capitalist economy was harder on farmers than on most other Poles. Under communism, the government always bought produce and meat from farmers, providing them with a reliable income. The government also made sure that prices for farm produce stayed high. After communism, prices dropped, and sales were no longer guaranteed. Farmers learned to be innovative, or creative, to survive.

Some farmers now take on part-time jobs to make extra money. Others invite paying guests from the city to stay on their farms for rural vacations. Some farmers produce organic vegetables, fruits, and meats, which they can sell at higher prices than other farmers' products.

Farmers who cannot find other sources of income often struggle to make a living. Most farms in Poland are small. Many farmers only own about 5 to 12 acres (2 to 5 hectares) of land, which may not produce enough money to live on.

A Polish husband and wife use a draft horse to plow a field in Bialowieza.

✓ **Reading Check** Why did farmers have a steady income under communism?

Future Challenges

Poland has made the change from communism to capitalism with speed and success. It has the strength to compete with other nations as part of the EU. However, the Polish people still face many challenges.

Kraków—A Cultural Treasure
Kraków is Poland's third-largest city. It is also a cultural center with historic architecture, an excellent university, and a marketplace that has existed since the 1200s. **Infer** *How have cities such as Kraków changed since the fall of communism in Poland?*

Guided Instruction

- Read Future Challenges with students.

- Ask students **What effects did coal-mining and steel production during the communist era have on the environment and people of Poland?** (*They created pollution that killed many of the forests in southern Poland and increased rates of diseases among Poles.*) **What steps has the current government taken to help repair the damage to the environment?** (*The government has closed some polluting factories and has invested in equipment to reduce pollution in others; the use of unleaded gasoline has also reduced pollutants coming from cars.*)

- Ask students **Why are rates of unemployment high across Poland?** (*Under the communist government, people were guaranteed jobs, but under the capitalist system jobs are not guaranteed.*) **What is one way that the unemployment problem might be solved?** (*Many Poles hope that as a result of its membership in the EU, more long-term investment will take place in Poland, creating new jobs.*)

Independent Practice

Have students complete the graphic organizer by adding details about pollution and unemployment.

Monitor Progress

- Show *Section Reading Support Transparency ER 48* and ask students to check their graphic organizers individually. Go over key concepts and clarify key vocabulary as needed.

  📖 **Europe and Russia Transparencies,** *Section Reading Support Transparency ER 48*

- Tell students to fill in the last column of their *Reading Readiness Guides.* Probe for what they learned that confirms or invalidates each statement.

  All in One Europe and Russia Teaching Resources, *Reading Readiness Guide,* p. 314

Answers

✓ **Reading Check** The government always bought produce and meat from farmers, which helped keep prices high.

Infer Businesses are now privately owned, and more consumer goods are bought and sold in the marketplaces.

Differentiated Instruction

For Less Proficient Readers L1

As you read this section with students, use simple commands to gain their attention. Try to issue commands that elicit a physical response in which students indicate their readiness to perform various activities. Less-proficient readers often respond well to phrases such as, "find the word 'capitalism' on this page" or "everyone, eyes on me please."

Assess and Reteach

Assess Progress `L2`

Have students complete the Section Assessment. Then administer the *Section Quiz.*

 Europe and Russia Teaching Resources, *Section Quiz,* p. 316

Reteach `L1`

If students need more instruction, have them read this section in the Reading and Vocabulary Study Guide.

Chapter 10, Section 1, **Eastern Hemisphere Reading and Vocabulary Study Guide,** pp. 108–110

Extend `L3`

Divide students into pairs and have them do research in the library and on the Internet to learn more about the events leading to the fall of Poland's communist government in 1989. Then have each pair create a timeline of the major events. Use *Rubric for Assessing a Timeline* to evaluate students' work.

 Europe and Russia Teaching Resources, *Rubric for Assessing a Timeline,* p. 349

Answers

✓ **Reading Check** After the end of communism, some polluting factories were closed, other factories invested in equipment that reduces pollution, and the use of unleaded gasoline reduced pollutants coming from cars.
Conclude Possible answer: transplanting trees into deforested areas will create new jobs for Poles.

Section 1 Assessment

Key Terms
Students' sentences should reflect an understanding of each Key Term.

🔄 **Target Reading Skill**
Under communism, most farmers had reliable income because the government bought meat and produce from farmers and kept prices for farm produce high. After the fall of communism, prices dropped and sales were no longer guaranteed. Some farmers still have a steady income, but they must find more creative ways of making money.

Comprehension and Critical Thinking
1. (a) religion and language **(b)** because it was the main language of the Soviet Union, which ruled Poland

---

Bringing Back the Forests
People on a tree farm plant young trees. Once the trees have grown larger, they will be transplanted to regions that were deforested during the communist years. **Conclude** *How can renewed forests strengthen Poland's economy?*

Pollution During the communist era, coal-mining and steel production in southern Poland caused terrible pollution. This pollution destroyed much of the forests in southern Poland and increased rates of diseases, such as cancer.

After the communists left power, Polish leaders began to repair some of the damage to the environment. Old polluting factories were closed. Other factories invested in equipment to reduce pollution. The use of unleaded gasoline reduced the pollutants coming from cars. By 2003, Poland had reduced many forms of pollution by 50 percent.

Unemployment Poland faces other challenges, such as a high unemployment rate. Under communism, people were guaranteed jobs. In the current capitalist system, there is no such guarantee. Many Poles emigrate to other places in Europe to find work. In fact, about one out three Poles today lives outside of Poland. Other Poles hope that membership in the EU will bring more long-term investment into Poland, creating more jobs.

Poles will have to find ways to deal with such challenges, but they are ready to do whatever is needed. For the first time in many years, their future is in their own hands.

✓ **Reading Check** **How did Poland reduce its air pollution?**

 **Section 1 Assessment**

Key Terms
Review the key terms at the beginning of this section. Use each term in a sentence that explains its meaning.

🔄 **Target Reading Skill**
How is farm life in Poland the same as and different from the way it was under communism?

Comprehension and Critical Thinking
1. (a) Identify What parts of Polish life did not change under communism?

(b) Analyze Information Why did the communist government force Polish schoolchildren to learn Russian?
2. (a) Explain What measures did Poland's leaders take to convert the economy to capitalism?
(b) Identify Point of View How might many Polish farmers view the transition to capitalism?
3. (a) Recall What major challenges does Poland still face?
(b) Predict What further changes might membership in the EU bring to Poland?

Writing Activity
Suppose you are a journalist in Poland today. You interview two Poles—a young entrepreneur in Warsaw and an elderly farmer in the countryside. Write a dialogue that gives their views on how capitalism has changed the country.

> **Writing Tip** Be sure to use appropriate language for each of the two people. Also, consider what is important to people of different ages before you begin writing.

---

2. (a) Polish leaders set up a stock market, ended government control over prices, and froze taxes and wages. **(b)** Possible answers: Some Polish farmers might have been unhappy about the transition to capitalism because they no longer had a reliable income from the government. Others may have welcomed the release from government restraints.

3. (a) environmental pollution and a high unemployment rate **(b)** more long-term investment that will create more jobs

Writing Activity
Use the *Rubric for Assessing a Writing Assignment* to evaluate students' dialogues.

 Europe and Russia Teaching Resources, *Rubric for Assessing a Writing Assignment,* p. 350

New Balkan Nations
A Region Tries to Rebuild

Prepare to Read

Objectives
In this section you will
1. Identify the groups of people who live in the Balkans.
2. Understand how Yugoslavia was created and how it broke up.
3. Identify issues that these Balkan nations face in the future.

Taking Notes
As you read this section, look for important events in the history of these six Balkan nations. Copy the timeline below and record the events in the proper places on it.

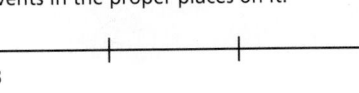

1918

Target Reading Skill

Make Comparisons Comparing two or more situations enables you to see how they are alike. This section is about six countries with similar situations. As you read this section, compare the six nations by considering their histories, economies, cultures, and challenges.

Key Terms
- **civil war** (sih vul wawr) *n.* a war between groups of people within the same nation
- **secede** (sih SEED) *v.* to leave a group, especially a political group or a nation
- **embargo** (em BAHR goh) *n.* a ban on trade
- **economic sanctions** (ek uh NAHM ik SANGK shunz) *n.* actions to limit trade with nations that have violated international laws

---

I n January 1984, the people of the city of Sarajevo (sa ruh YAY voh) were filled with anticipation. They had proudly won the right to host the 1984 Winter Olympics. To prepare for the games, they had built new hotels and restaurants. They had carved ski-racing trails into the mountains and built ski lifts. New bobsled runs and an elegant skating complex awaited the athletes. A shiny new Olympic Village waited to welcome athletes and visitors to the Games.

Ten years later, most of these facilities lay in ruins. So did much of Sarajevo. How could this have happened? The answer is **civil war,** or a war between groups of people within the same nation. Civil war broke up the nation of Yugoslavia and shattered the grand city.

Scenes of Sarajevo's Olympic Village before and after the war

Chapter 10 Section 2 **319**

Target Reading Skill

Make Comparisons Point out the Target Reading Skill. Explain that students can make comparisons to find the similarities between two or more situations.

Model the skill by reading the second paragraph on p. 321 and identifying a similarity between the ethnic groups discussed. (*All of the groups speak the same language—Serbo-Croatian.*)

Give students *Make Comparisons.* Have them complete the activity in groups.

All in One **Europe and Russia Teaching Resources,** *Make Comparisons,* p. 330

Objectives

Social Studies
1. Identify the groups of people who live in the Balkans.
2. Understand how Yugoslavia was created and how it broke up.
3. Identify issues that these Balkan nations face in the future.

Reading/Language Arts
Make comparisons to find out how two or more situations are alike.

Prepare to Read

Build Background Knowledge   L2
Tell students that in this section they will study the history of conflict in the Balkans. Show the video *Rebuilding Kosovo.* Using the Numbered Heads participation strategy (TE, p. T36), ask students how land mines can affect a region after peace has been made. (*Unless land mines are removed, they can continue to injure and kill people years after a war has ended.*)

📼 *Rebuilding Kosovo,* **World Studies Video Program**

Set a Purpose for Reading   L2
- Preview the Objectives.
- Read each statement in the *Reading Readiness Guide* aloud. Ask students to mark the statements true or false.

  All in One **Europe and Russia Teaching Resources,** *Reading Readiness Guide,* p. 318

- Have students discuss the statements in pairs or groups of four, then mark their guides again. Use the Numbered Heads participation strategy (TE, p. T36) to call on students to share their group's perspectives.

Vocabulary Builder
Preview Key Terms   L2
Pronounce each Key Term, and then ask the students to say the word with you. Provide a simple explanation such as, "During the Civil War, many southern states seceded from the United States."

Instruct

COUNTRY PROFILE
Focus on Culture

Guided Instruction L2

Ask students to study the Country Profile on this page. As a class, answer the Map and Chart Skills questions. Allow students to briefly discuss their responses with a partner before sharing answers.

Independent Practice

- Distribute *Using a Map Key.* Have students work in pairs to complete the worksheet.

  All in One **Europe and Russia Teaching Resources,** *Using a Map Key,* p. 341

- Tell students that the map of the Balkan nations in the Student Edition shows the region's ethnic groups. Have them explain what each color in the key stands for. Then ask them to identify what information appears on the map on the worksheet, paying special attention to the map title and key.

Answers

Map and Chart Skills

1. Slovenes

2. Most people in the region practice the Muslim or Christian religions. Most people speak Croation and Serbian.

3. Possible answer: The data shows the religious and ethnic diversity of the region that has led to some of the political unrest—the different groups may have different ideas about politics and government.

Go Online PHSchool.com Students can find more information about this topic on the DK World Desk Reference Online.

COUNTRY PROFILE   Focus on Culture

New Balkan Nations

Ethnic diversity is one of the most enduring characteristics of the Balkans. In ancient times, the region was occupied by different tribes who often fought among themselves. The arrival of Christianity and then Islam brought more diversity and more ethnic and political differences to the region. Political unrest still continues in modern times. The Balkans occupy an area slightly smaller than the state of Texas. As you study the map and the table, think about what challenges great diversity might present to a small region.

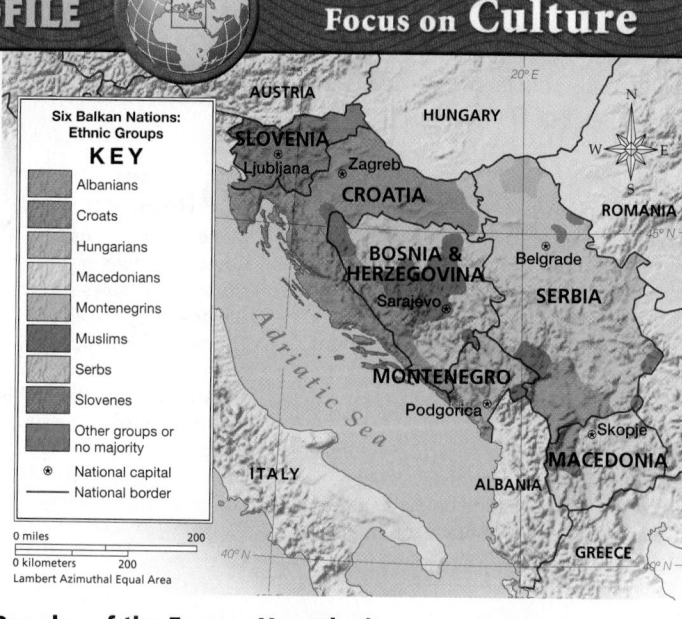

Six Balkan Nations: Ethnic Groups
KEY
- Albanians
- Croats
- Hungarians
- Macedonians
- Montenegrins
- Muslims
- Serbs
- Slovenes
- Other groups or no majority
- ⊛ National capital
- —— National border

0 miles 200
0 kilometers 200
Lambert Azimuthal Equal Area

Peoples of the Former Yugoslavia

Ethnic Group	Population (millions)	Main Homeland(s)	Language	Main Religion
Croats	4.7	Croatia, Bosnia & Herz.	Croatian, Serbian	Roman Catholicism
Serbs	7.5	Bosnia & Herz., Serbia, Montenegro	Serbian, Croatian, Bosnian	Orthodox Christian
Slovenes	1.6	Slovenia	Slovenian	Roman Catholicism
Bosniaks	2.7	Bosnia & Herz.	Bosnian, Croatian, Serbian	Islam
Montenegrins	0.6	Montenegro, Serbia	Serbian	Orthodox Christian
Macedonians	1.3	Macedonia	Macedonian	Macedonian Orthodox
Albanians	2.3	Montenegro, Serbia, Macedonia	Albanian	Islam
Hungarians	0.3	Serbia	Hungarian	Roman Catholicism
Turks	0.8	Serbia, Macedonia	Turkish	Islam
Roma	0.05	Serbia, Macedonia	Roma	Various Beliefs

SOURCE: *CIA World Factbook*

Map and Chart Skills

1. Identify Which ethnic group lives in Slovenia?

2. Analyze Information Which religions do most people in the region practice? What language is spoken by the most people?

3. Apply Information How do the data help explain today's political unrest in the region?

 Use Web Code lde-7502 for DK World Desk Reference Online.

Vocabulary Builder

Use the information below to teach students this section's high-use words.

High-Use Word	Definition and Sample Sentence
principle, p. 323	*n.* a basic truth, law, belief, or doctrine. One of the **principles** of a democratic government is freedom of speech.
prevent, p. 323	*v.* to keep from happening. Using caution can **prevent** forest fires.

Land of Many Peoples

The Balkan Peninsula—also known as the Balkans—is located in southeastern Europe. The Balkans include Serbia, Montenegro, Bosnia and Herzegovina, Macedonia, Croatia, Slovenia, Albania, Romania, Bulgaria, Greece, and European Turkey. This section discusses the first six of these countries, which used to make up the nation of Yugoslavia.

Different ethnic groups in these Balkan countries speak similar languages. The Serbs and Montenegrins (mahnt uh NEE grinz) speak Serbian, Croats (KROH atz) speak Croatian, and Bosniaks speak Bosnian. The Serbian, Croatian, and Bosnian languages are as close as American English and British English. Although these Slavic languages are similar, the Serbian language has a different alphabet than Croatian and Bosnian. Slovenes and Macedonians (mas uh DOH nee unz) speak related Slavic languages.

Although these groups speak related languages, there are important cultural differences among them. Religion may be the most important difference, since it separates groups that speak the same language. Most Serbs, Montenegrins, and Macedonians are Orthodox Christians. Croats and Slovenes are mainly Roman Catholic. Bosniaks are mainly Muslim.

In these six countries, there are also groups that speak non-Slavic languages. These groups include Albanians, Hungarians, Roma, and Turks. The Albanians and Turks are mainly Muslim. The Hungarians are mostly Roman Catholic. The Roma have their own unique customs and religious beliefs.

Faces of the Balkans
Both of the photos above show children of various ethnic groups. The upper photo is from Macedonia, while the lower photo is from Croatia. **Apply Information** *Though these children all live on the Balkan Peninsula, what cultural differences might there be among them?*

✓ Reading Check **What are the largest ethnic groups in the Balkans?**

The Creation of Yugoslavia

For hundreds of years, the Ottoman Empire, based in Turkey, ruled much of the Balkans. Beginning in the late 1800s, several kingdoms within the empire attempted to form their own states. Sometimes they were supported in their efforts by Russia or western nations, who hoped to gain influence in the region. But none of these groups was successful until World War I ended, and the Ottoman Empire broke up.

A New Nation Is Formed Yugoslavia was the first new Balkan nation to emerge from the old Ottoman Empire. Formed in 1918, the new nation joined together many ethnic and religious groups. From the beginning, these groups disagreed about how the government should be structured.

Chapter 10 Section 2 **321**

Land of Many Peoples L2

Guided Instruction

- Use the Paragraph Shrinking strategy (TE, p. T34) to read Land of Many Peoples. As students read, circulate and make sure individuals can answer the Reading Check question.

- Ask students **Which Balkan countries share a Slavic heritage?** (*Serbia, Montenegro, Bosnia and Herzegovina, Macedonia, Croatia, and Slovenia*)

- Discuss with students the differences among the Slavic groups in the Balkans. (*People in the Balkans speak different languages, practice different religions, and have different non-Slavic groups within their populations.*)

Independent Practice

Assign *Guided Reading and Review.*

All in One **Europe and Russia Teaching Resources,** *Guided Reading and Review,* p. 319

Monitor Progress

As students begin the worksheet, circulate to provide assistance as needed.

Answers

Apply Information The children may speak different languages, use different alphabets, and practice different religions.

✓ Reading Check the Serbs and the Croats

Target Reading Skill

Make Comparisons As a follow up, ask students to answer the Target Reading Skill question in the Student Edition. *(In both cases, the people did not always support the government.)*

The Creation of Yugoslavia

L2

Guided Instruction

- **Vocabulary Builder** Clarify the high-use word **principle** before reading.

- Read The Creation of Yugoslavia with students.

- Discuss Yugoslavia's government when it was first formed in 1918. *(Yugoslavia was divided into republics. In each republic, one ethnic group held the majority.)*

- Ask students **How did Yugoslavia change after World War II?** *(Tito became head of the government and changed Yugoslavia into a communist state that allied itself with the Soviet Union. Tito also strengthened the economy and unified Yugoslavia.)*

- Ask students **Why did Yugoslavia begin to break up after Tito's death in 1980?** *(Politicians encouraged their followers to identify with their own ethnic group.)*

Independent Practice

Ask students to create the Taking Notes graphic organizer on a blank piece of paper and fill in important dates and events in Yugoslavia's history. Briefly model how to record dates and events on the timeline.

Monitor Progress

As students begin to fill in the timeline, circulate to help individuals understand which details to include.

Answers

MAP MASTER Skills Activity **Explain** The mountainous terrain may have hindered uniting the nation, but the rivers that cross it may have helped. **Predict** Possible answer: by instituting a strong government and allowing little dissension

Go Online PHSchool.com Students may practice their map skills using the interactive online version of this map.

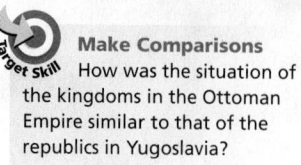
Make Comparisons How was the situation of the kingdoms in the Ottoman Empire similar to that of the republics in Yugoslavia?

Though one nation, Yugoslavia was divided into smaller units called republics. These republics included Serbia, Montenegro, Croatia, Bosnia and Herzegovina, Slovenia, and Macedonia. In each of those republics, one ethnic group held the majority. Yugoslavia's largest republic was Serbia, peopled by Serbs. This republic held the most power, and ran the national government. Other republics, in which Serbs were not the majority, did not always support the government. Resentment against the government grew, along with ethnic conflict among peoples.

The Communist Era During World War II, Germany and Italy occupied Yugoslavia. Josip Broz Tito led the Yugoslav fight against Germany. When the war ended in 1945, Tito became head of the government and changed Yugoslavia into a communist state. Yugoslavia became a firm ally and trade partner of the Soviet Union.

At first, Tito modeled his government after that of the Soviet Union. After a few years, however, he wanted to develop his own government and economic policies. For example, he wanted to maintain trading relations with Western countries in order to strengthen Yugoslavia's economy. This put him in conflict with the Soviet dictator, Joseph Stalin, who broke many ties with Yugoslavia in 1948.

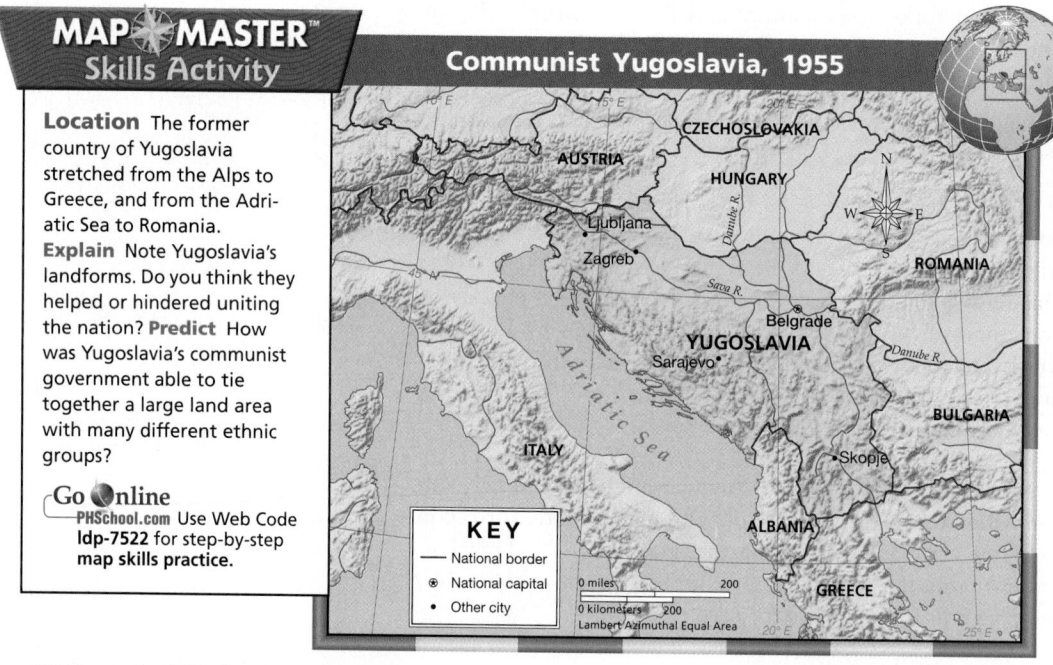

MAP MASTER™ Skills Activity

Communist Yugoslavia, 1955

Location The former country of Yugoslavia stretched from the Alps to Greece, and from the Adriatic Sea to Romania. **Explain** Note Yugoslavia's landforms. Do you think they helped or hindered uniting the nation? **Predict** How was Yugoslavia's communist government able to tie together a large land area with many different ethnic groups?

Go Online PHSchool.com Use Web Code ldp-7522 for step-by-step map skills practice.

KEY
— National border
⊛ National capital
• Other city

0 miles 200
0 kilometers 200
Lambert Azimuthal Equal Area

Differentiated Instruction

For Special Needs Students **L1**
Pair these students with more proficient readers and have them complete the DK Atlas of the World activity *Reading a Political Map*. Then have them use what they learned to help them analyze the map on this page.

All in One **Europe and Russia Teaching Resources,** *DK Compact Atlas of the World Activity: Reading a Political Map,* p. 343

Tito continued to rule Yugoslavia according to communist principles, but he also had good relations with anti-communist nations. For several years, the economy under Tito grew strongly. Tito's strong government also unified Yugoslavia by reducing tensions among ethnic groups. During Tito's time, people began to identify themselves as citizens of a united Yugoslavia.

Yugoslavia Begins to Splinter After Tito's death in 1980, politicians from various ethnic groups struggled for power. They encouraged their followers to once again identify strongly with their own ethnic group. People began to think of themselves less and less as citizens of Yugoslavia.

✓ Reading Check **What event caused Yugoslavia to splinter?**

Yugoslavia Breaks Up

Yugoslavia's problems continued to worsen through the 1980s. In 1989, communism began to crumble in Eastern Europe. Yugoslavia had an unstable government and economy. Many people blamed the Serbs, who still held most of the power in the government. Some republics wanted to govern themselves. In some cases, political change happened almost peacefully. In others, bitter civil wars erupted.

Slovenia and Croatia In 1990, Slovenes and Croats began to pull away from Yugoslavia. That year, the leaders of Slovenia issued a new constitution in which they said they had the right to secede from, or leave, the state of Yugoslavia. Meanwhile, the Yugoslav army threatened to take territory from the republic of Croatia. This alarmed Slovenes and Croats, but also strengthened their desire for independence.

A Croat was elected the new president of Yugoslavia in May 1991. However, Serbia refused to accept the new president. This was the last straw for Slovenia and Croatia. Both republics declared their independence. Serb forces briefly tried to prevent Slovenia from seceding. But soon Serbia recognized the country's independence.

In contrast, war erupted in Croatia. The Serbs attacked Croatian cities. They used terror to drive out the people. This led the United Nations to become involved. In an effort to restore peace, the UN sent peacekeepers to the area and imposed an embargo against Yugoslavia. An **embargo** is a ban on trade. But peace could not be reached until conflict in neighboring Bosnia and Herzegovina was settled.

Links

Read the **Links Across the World** on this page. Ask students **How do the goals of the UN and NATO differ?** *(The UN works to bring about peace, and NATO provides members with defense in case of attack.)*

Yugoslavia Breaks Up L2

Guided Instruction

■ **Vocabulary Builder** Clarify the high-use word **prevent** before reading.

■ Read Yugoslavia Breaks Up with the class.

■ Discuss with students why Slovenia and Croatia seceded from Yugoslavia. *(The Yugoslav army threatened to take territory away from Croatia, and Serbia refused to accept the new Croatian president in 1991, causing resentment in Slovenia and Croatia and leading them to declare independence.)*

■ Ask students **What led to war in Bosnia and Herzegovina?** *(tensions among different ethnic groups)* **Why do you think the United Nations, NATO, and the United States became involved?** *(possible answer: to stop the spread of violence to surrounding areas and to help those who were suffering)*

Differentiated Instruction

For English Language Learners L1
Ask students to create lists of nouns and verbs describing the people, things, and actions in each photograph of this section. Have the students write complete sentences describing the events in each picture. If necessary, pair English Language Learners with native speakers for help with writing their sentences.

Answer

✓ Reading Check Tito's death in 1980

Show students *Rebuilding Kosovo*. Ask **Why did ethnic Albanians leave Kosovo?** *(The ethnic Albanian majority in Kosovo wanted the province to secede from Serbia because of the increasingly brutal rule of the Serbs, but the Serbs would not relinquish control of Kosovo. Years of guerilla war followed, during which many ethnic Albanians were driven from their homes.)*

Guided Instruction (continued)

- Ask **Why did tensions increase between Serbs and Albanians in Kosovo?** *(In 1989, Yugoslavian president Slobodan Milosevic took away many freedoms from Albanians in Kosovo.)* **What did Slobodan Milosevic do to try to end the Albanian uprising in Kosovo?** *(He had Serb forces attack Albanians, destroy their homes and villages, and drive thousands of Albanians from their homes.)*

- Discuss the changes made to Macedonia's constitution. *(The new constitution made Albanian an official language, increased Albanians' access to government jobs, and removed language that had made Albanians second-class citizens.)*

Independent Practice

Have students continue to add dates and events to their timelines.

Monitor Progress

Circulate to make sure students are selecting appropriate dates for their timelines. Provide assistance as needed.

Answer

Infer Possible answer: Tito had helped to unify Yugoslavia and reduced tension among ethnic groups.

Learn about the rebuilding of Kosovo.

Peace Rally in Sarajevo
Before war broke out in 1992, people in Bosnia and Herzegovina held a peace rally. Some of them displayed a picture of Tito. **Infer** *Why might people have used images of Tito to support their drive for peace?*

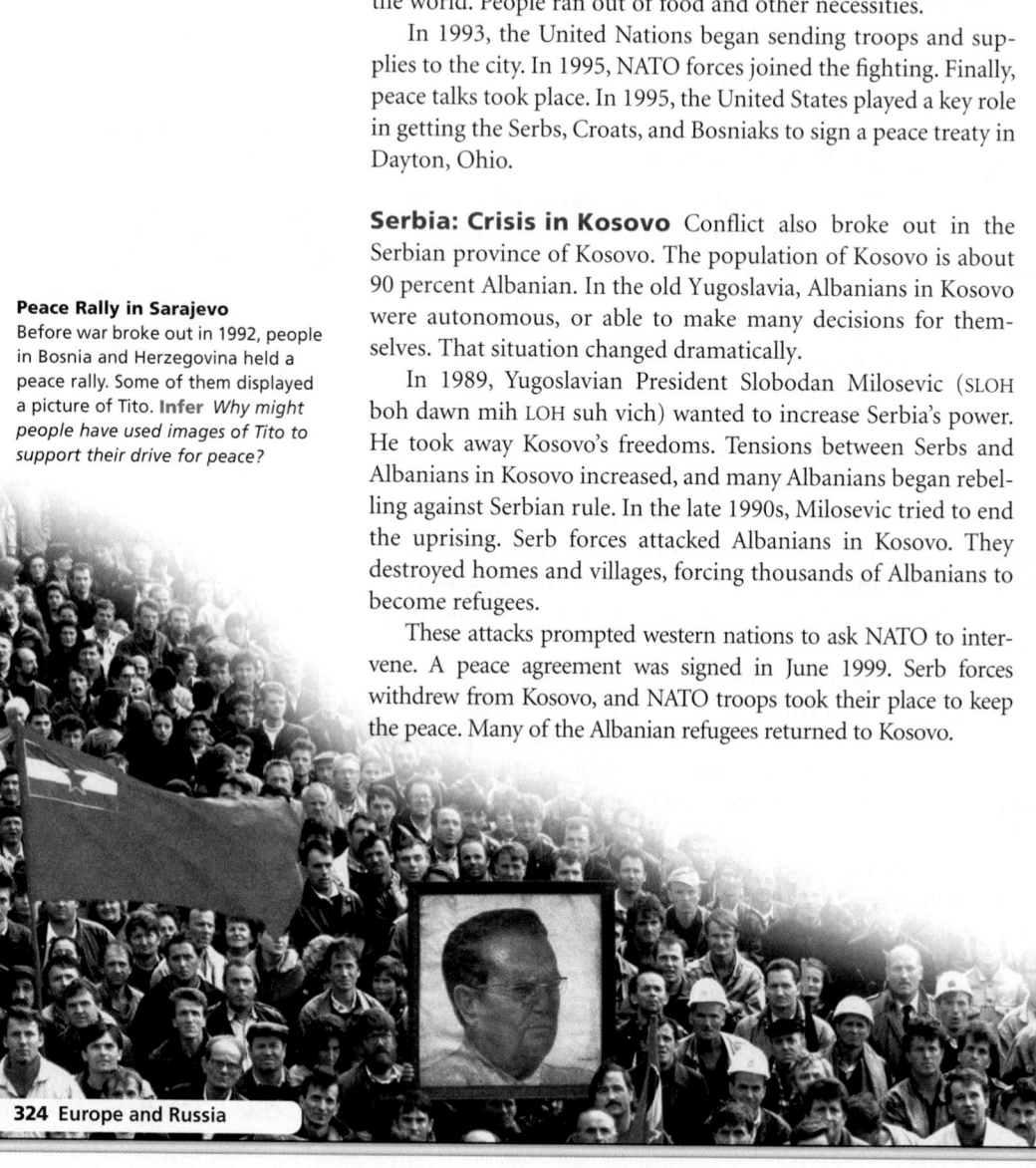

324 Europe and Russia

Bosnia and Herzegovina Tensions among different ethnic groups led to a long and bitter war in Bosnia and Herzegovina, beginning in 1992. People on all sides were mistreated by their enemies. Many people were killed. Some were forced to move away from where they had lived peacefully for years, simply because they were Serbs or Croats.

As you have read, during the war much of Sarajevo, the capital of Bosnia and Herzegovina, was destroyed. Homes and schools were bombed. People were shot as they tried to go about their daily business. Serb armies cut Sarajevo off from the rest of the world. People ran out of food and other necessities.

In 1993, the United Nations began sending troops and supplies to the city. In 1995, NATO forces joined the fighting. Finally, peace talks took place. In 1995, the United States played a key role in getting the Serbs, Croats, and Bosniaks to sign a peace treaty in Dayton, Ohio.

Serbia: Crisis in Kosovo Conflict also broke out in the Serbian province of Kosovo. The population of Kosovo is about 90 percent Albanian. In the old Yugoslavia, Albanians in Kosovo were autonomous, or able to make many decisions for themselves. That situation changed dramatically.

In 1989, Yugoslavian President Slobodan Milosevic (SLOH boh dawn mih LOH suh vich) wanted to increase Serbia's power. He took away Kosovo's freedoms. Tensions between Serbs and Albanians in Kosovo increased, and many Albanians began rebelling against Serbian rule. In the late 1990s, Milosevic tried to end the uprising. Serb forces attacked Albanians in Kosovo. They destroyed homes and villages, forcing thousands of Albanians to become refugees.

These attacks prompted western nations to ask NATO to intervene. A peace agreement was signed in June 1999. Serb forces withdrew from Kosovo, and NATO troops took their place to keep the peace. Many of the Albanian refugees returned to Kosovo.

Background: Biography

Josip Broz Tito (1892–1980) Josip Broz Tito was born in what is now the country of Croatia. While serving in the Austro-Hungarian army during World War I, he was captured by Russians and placed in a prisoner-of-war camp. It was there that Tito was introduced to communism. After he returned to what was then called the Kingdom of the Serbs, Croats, and Slov- enes, he joined the Communist Party of Yugoslavia. As leader of Yugoslavia after World War II, Tito moved the country along an independent path called "non-alignment." He resisted the influence of both the Soviet Union and Western countries during the Cold War.

Macedonia Macedonia declared its independence from Yugoslavia in 1991. From the beginning, ethnic conflict was a problem in the new country. Tensions existed between ethnic Macedonians and ethnic Albanians, who make up a large minority of the population.

Albanians began demanding a number of reforms. The call for reform erupted into violence in 2001. Clashes between ethnic Albanians and the Macedonian military lasted seven months. This prompted fears of another war in the Balkans. A peace agreement was reached after the involvement of NATO.

Soon, Macedonia adopted a new constitution. It made Albanian an official language of the nation. It increased Albanians' access to government jobs. Most important, it removed language in the constitution that had made Albanians second-class citizens.

Ethnic Albanians in Macedonia demand more rights in 2004.

✓ **Reading Check** To which ethnic group do most of the people of Kosovo belong?

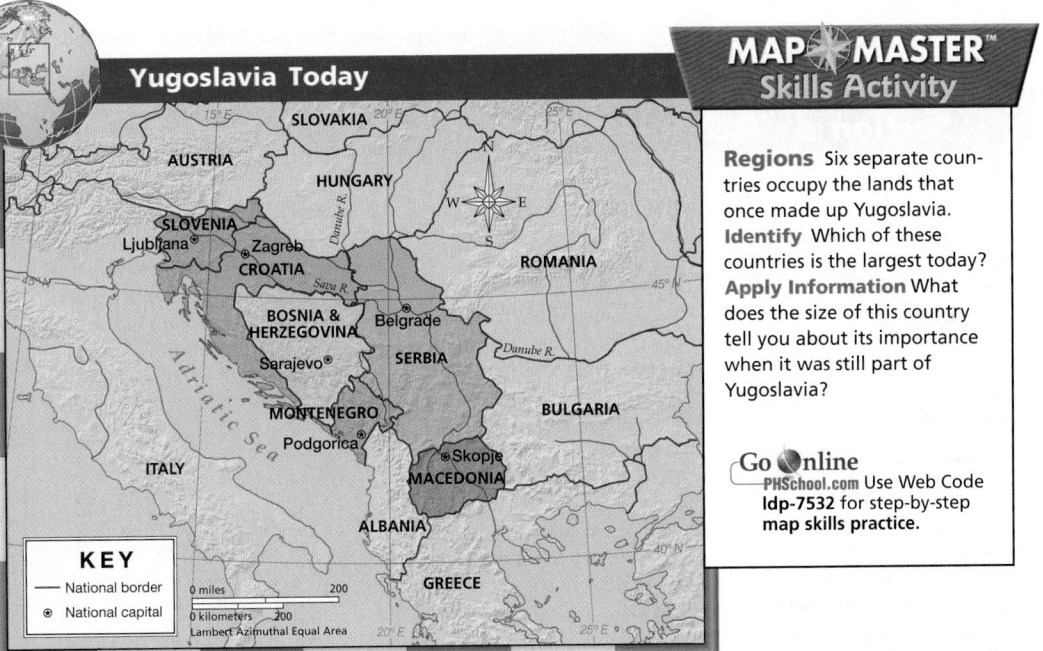

Yugoslavia Today

MAP★MASTER™ Skills Activity

Regions Six separate countries occupy the lands that once made up Yugoslavia. **Identify** Which of these countries is the largest today? **Apply Information** What does the size of this country tell you about its importance when it was still part of Yugoslavia?

Go Online
PHSchool.com Use Web Code ldp-7532 for step-by-step map skills practice.

Chapter 10 Section 2 **325**

The Region's Future L2

Guided Instruction

■ Read The Region's Future with the class.

■ Ask students **How did the United States and Europe show their disapproval of Slobodan Milosevic?** *(They placed economic sanctions on Yugoslavia.)*

■ Discuss with students the problems Balkan nations face in the future. *(They must confront economic problems and overcome a history of ethnic conflict and war.)*

Independent Practice

Have students continue to add dates and events to their timelines.

Monitor Progress

■ Show *Section Reading Support Transparency ER 49* and ask students to check their graphic organizers individually. Go over key concepts and clarify key vocabulary as needed. Provide assistance if necessary.

📖 **Europe and Russia Transparencies,** *Section Reading Support Transparency ER 49*

■ Tell students to fill in the last column of their *Reading Readiness Guides*. Probe for what they learned that confirms or invalidates each statement.

All in One Europe and Russia Teaching Resources, *Reading Readiness Guide*, p. 318

Answers

✓ **Reading Check** Most of the people of Kosovo are Albanians.

MAP★MASTER™ Skills Activity **Identify** Serbia **Apply Information** The people of Serbia probably held significant influence when it was part of Yugoslavia.

Go Online
PHSchool.com Students may practice their map skills using the interactive online version of this map.

Assess and Reteach

Assess Progress L2

Have students complete the Section Assessment. Administer the *Section Quiz*.

All in One **Europe and Russia Teaching Resources,** *Section Quiz,* p. 320

Reteach L1

If students need more instruction, have them read this section in the Reading and Vocabulary Study Guide.

📖 Chapter 10, Section 2, **Eastern Hemisphere Reading and Vocabulary Study Guide,** pp. 111–113

Extend L3

Extend students' understanding of conflict in the Balkans by having them complete the *Enrichment* activity about the destruction of Sarajevo. Ask students to work together in small groups to complete the project.

All in One **Europe and Russia Teaching Resources,** *Enrichment,* p. 333

Answer

✓ **Reading Check** The people of the Balkans are still overcoming ethnic tensions and must resolve economic problems resulting from the conflicts and wars in the region.

Section 2 Assessment

Key Terms

Students' sentences should reflect an understanding of each Key Term.

↻ **Target Reading Skill**

Answers will vary but should be supported with details from the section.

Comprehension and Critical Thinking

1. (a) Serbia, Montenegro, Bosnia and Herzegovina, Macedonia, Croatia, and Slovenia **(b)** People of these nations speak different languages, practice different religions, and include different ethnic groups.

2. (a) the Ottoman Empire **(b)** Yugoslavia was created in 1918 and turned to communism in 1945 when Tito came to power after World War II. **(c)** The collapse of communism led to an unstable government and economy. People of some republics resented the Serbian-controlled government and wanted to rule themselves.

Business has picked up at markets like this one in Slovenia.

The Region's Future

Although several republics in the region gained independence, trouble did not end. The United States and Europe held Slobodan Milosevic responsible for the violence that had occurred in the region. To show their disapproval, they placed economic sanctions on Yugoslavia. **Economic sanctions** are actions to limit trade with nations that have violated international laws.

In 2000, Yugoslavia held new presidential elections. Milosevic was defeated and then arrested by the new government. He was put on trial for war crimes by the court of the United Nations, but he died in 2006, before the trial ended. With Milosevic out of power, the United States and European nations lifted sanctions against Yugoslavia.

In 2003, the two remaining republics of Yugoslavia—Serbia and Montenegro—decided to no longer call themselves Yugoslavia. They became known as the country of Serbia and Montenegro. In 2006, however, the people of Montenegro voted to become independent of Serbia. And many people in Kosovo would like to become independent of Serbia as well.

The destruction that occurred in the 1990s has left the region with deep economic problems. These countries will have to overcome a history of ethnic conflict to move toward peace.

✓ **Reading Check** What problems face people of the Balkans today?

 Section 2 Assessment

Key Terms

Review the key terms at the beginning of this section. Use each term in a sentence that explains its meaning.

↻ **Target Reading Skill**

Compare the histories of these six nations.

Comprehension and Critical Thinking

1. (a) List Which six Balkan nations used to make up the country of Yugoslavia?
(b) Contrast What differences exist among the people of these nations today?

2. (a) Note Which foreign power ruled the Balkans for hundreds of years?
(b) Sequence When was Yugoslavia created? When did its government turn to communism?
(c) Synthesize Information How did the collapse of communism affect Yugoslavia?
3. (a) Identify Who did the United States and European nations hold responsible for the violence in the Balkans?
(b) Identify Effects How did these nations show their disapproval of Yugoslavia's president?

Writing Activity

Choose one of the Balkan nations discussed in this section. What do you think is the most important challenge facing this nation in the future? Write a paragraph that explains why.

For: An activity on the Dayton peace accord
Visit: PHSchool.com
Web Code: ldd-7502

326 Europe and Russia

3. (a) the Yugoslavian president, Slobodan Milosevic **(b)** The nations placed economic sanctions on Yugoslavia. Milosevic was then defeated in the 2000 election and the United Nations tried him for war crimes, but Milosevic died before the trial ended.

Writing Activity

Use the *Rubric for Assessing a Writing Assignment* to evaluate students' paragraphs.

All in One **Europe and Russia Teaching Resources,** *Rubric for Assessing a Writing Assignment,* p. 350

Go Online PHSchool.com Typing in the Web code when prompted will bring students to detailed instructions for this activity.

Ukraine
Independence and Beyond

Prepare to Read

Objectives
In this section you will
1. Understand how Ukraine's history has been shaped by foreign rule.
2. Explain the major issues that Ukrainians have faced since independence.
3. Describe life in Ukraine today.

Taking Notes
As you read this section, look for ways in which the natural resources of Ukraine have shaped its history. Copy the flowchart below and record your findings in it.

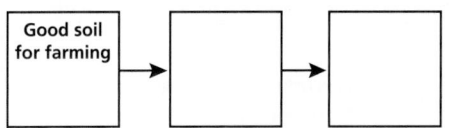

| Good soil for farming | → | | → | |

Target Reading Skill

Compare and Contrast
One way to understand a nation's history is to compare and contrast different times in its history. When you compare, you look at similarities between things. When you contrast, you look at differences. As you read this section, compare and contrast life in Ukraine before and after independence.

Key Terms
- **chernozem** (CHEHR nuh zem) n. rich, black soil
- **collective** (kuh LEK tiv) n. a huge government-controlled farm

H ow many people, linked hand-to-hand, would it take to cover 300 miles (483 kilometers)? The people of Ukraine can tell you, because they did it in 1990. It took about 500,000 Ukrainians to make a human chain that long. It stretched from Kiev, Ukraine's capital, to the city of L'viv (luh VEEF). The chain was a symbol of protest against the Soviet Union's control of Ukraine. It also showed that Ukrainians know how to work together to solve their problems. Today, the people of Ukraine are enjoying their independence and are working hard for a better future.

Ukrainians form a human chain.

Objectives

Social Studies
1. Understand how Ukraine's history has been shaped by foreign rule.
2. Explain the major issues that Ukrainians have faced since independence.
3. Describe life in Ukraine today.

Reading/Language Arts
Compare and contrast different points in history to understand how a nation has changed over time.

Prepare to Read

Build Background Knowledge   L2
Tell students that in this section they will learn about Ukraine, a country that became independent in 1991. Have them preview the section by glancing at headings, Key Terms, and visuals with this question in mind: **How did Ukraine change after gaining independence?** Use the Think-Write-Pair-Share participation strategy (TE, p. T36) to help students brainstorm.

Set a Purpose for Reading   L2
- Preview the Objectives.
- Read each statement in the *Reading Readiness Guide* aloud. Ask students to mark the statements true or false.

  All in One Europe and Russia Teaching Resources, *Reading Readiness Guide,* p. 322

- Have students discuss the statements in pairs or groups of four, then mark their guides again. Use the Numbered Heads participation strategy (TE, p. T36) to call on students to share their group's perspectives.

Target Reading Skill   L2
Compare and Contrast Explain that students can compare and contrast different periods in a country's history to see how it has changed over time.

Model the skill by reading Supplying the Soviets on p. 329 and comparing and contrasting industry before and after the Soviet Union took control of Ukraine. (*Industry grew after the Soviet Union took control of Ukraine.*)

Give students *Compare and Contrast.* Have them complete the activity in groups.

All in One Europe and Russia Teaching Resources, *Compare and Contrast,* p. 329

Vocabulary Builder
Preview Key Terms   L2
Pronounce each Key Term, then ask the students to say the word with you. Provide a simple explanation such as, "Much of Ukraine is covered with chernozem, a rich soil good for growing crops."

Chapter 10 Section 3 **327**

Instruct

COUNTRY PROFILE
Focus on Economics

Guided Instruction
L2

Ask students to study the map and charts on this page. Have students work in pairs to answer the Map and Chart Skills questions and then discuss the answers as a class.

Independent Practice

Have students work with a partner to display the leading import and export partners information in the form of circle graphs. Then have each student write a few sentences explaining which format they think shows the information more clearly and why.

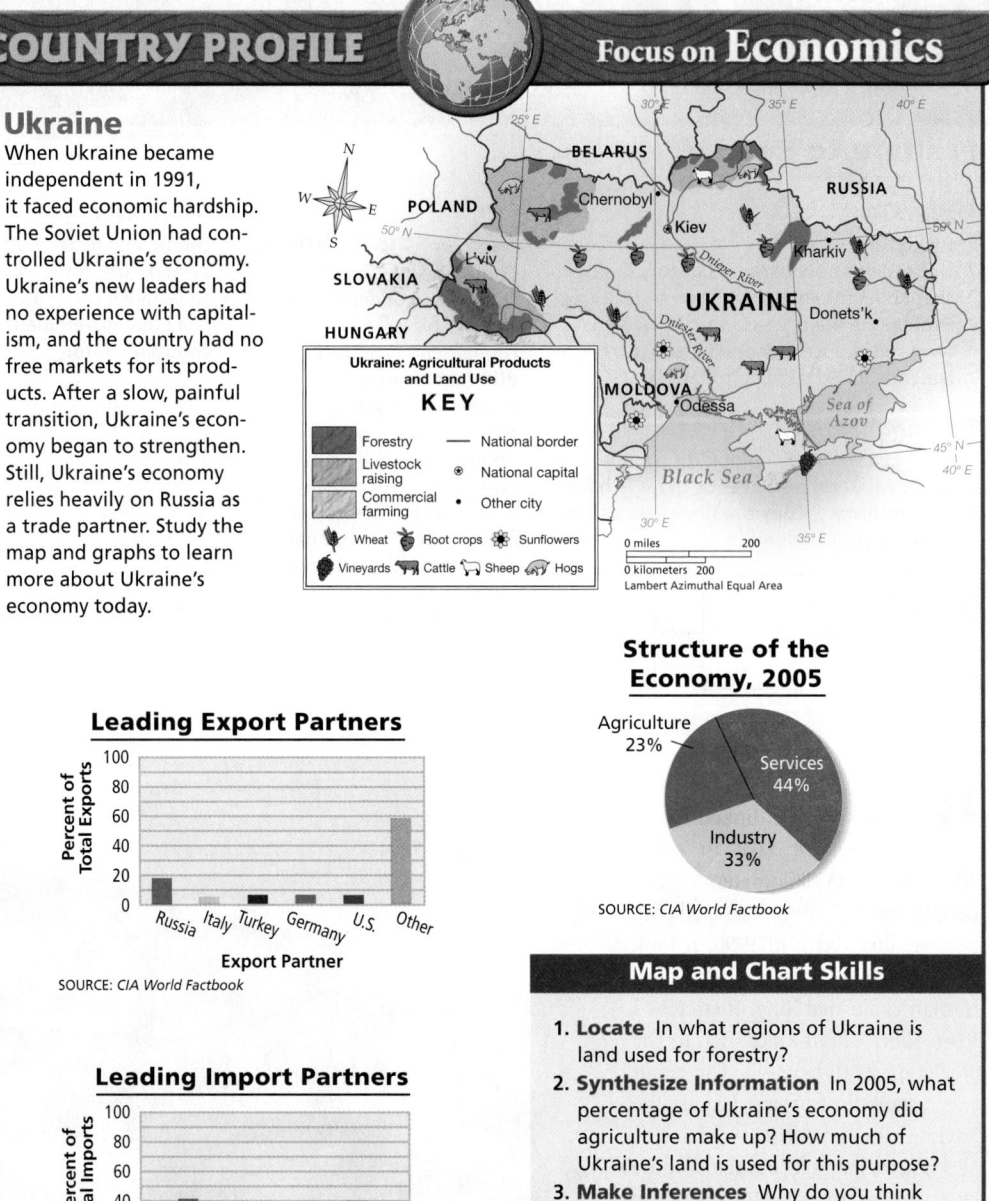

Ukraine

When Ukraine became independent in 1991, it faced economic hardship. The Soviet Union had controlled Ukraine's economy. Ukraine's new leaders had no experience with capitalism, and the country had no free markets for its products. After a slow, painful transition, Ukraine's economy began to strengthen. Still, Ukraine's economy relies heavily on Russia as a trade partner. Study the map and graphs to learn more about Ukraine's economy today.

Ukraine: Agricultural Products and Land Use
KEY

- Forestry
- Livestock raising
- Commercial farming
- ── National border
- ⊛ National capital
- • Other city

🌾 Wheat 🌱 Root crops ❀ Sunflowers
🍇 Vineyards 🐂 Cattle 🐑 Sheep 🐖 Hogs

0 miles 200
0 kilometers 200
Lambert Azimuthal Equal Area

Leading Export Partners

Percent of Total Exports (Russia, Italy, Turkey, Germany, U.S., Other)

Export Partner

SOURCE: *CIA World Factbook*

Leading Import Partners

Percent of Total Imports (Russia, Turkmenistan, Germany, Other)

Import Partners

SOURCE: *CIA World Factbook*

Structure of the Economy, 2005

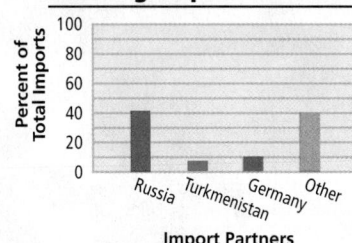

- Agriculture 23%
- Services 44%
- Industry 33%

SOURCE: *CIA World Factbook*

Map and Chart Skills

1. **Locate** In what regions of Ukraine is land used for forestry?
2. **Synthesize Information** In 2005, what percentage of Ukraine's economy did agriculture make up? How much of Ukraine's land is used for this purpose?
3. **Make Inferences** Why do you think Ukraine exchanges more exports and imports with Russia than with its other trade partners?

Use Web Code **lde-7503** for **DK World Desk Reference Online**.

Answers

Map and Chart Skills

1. in the west and the north

2. 23 percent; nearly all of Ukraine's land

3. because Russia controlled Ukraine's economy prior to 1991

Go Online PHSchool.com Students can find more information about this topic on the DK World Desk Reference Online.

Vocabulary Builder

Use the information below to teach students this section's high-use words.

High-Use Word	Definition and Sample Sentence
consume, p. 329	*v.* to eat, drink, or use something up My new car **consumes** less gasoline than my old one.
publish, p. 331	*v.* to print Paul was excited that his first book was about to be **published**.
contaminate, p. 332	*v.* to pollute The oil spill **contaminated** three miles of beach.
produce, p. 333	*n.* something grown on a farm, such as fruits or vegetables The **produce** section has very nice tomatoes today.

A History of Occupation

For hundreds of years, Ukraine was ruled by its more powerful neighbors. You can see how this happened if you look at Ukraine's location on the map on page 303. This huge land lies between Russia and the other nations of Europe. In fact, the name Ukraine means "borderland." Look at the political map of Eastern Europe and Russia at the beginning of this chapter. Notice that to the west of Ukraine are Poland, Slovakia, and Hungary. To the east of Ukraine is Russia. The map makes it easy to see why Ukraine has been open to invasion by its neighbors.

Location has been only part of the problem. The other problem has been Ukraine's vast natural resources. These resources have attracted invaders. At one time or another, Poland, Czechoslovakia, and Romania have occupied areas of Ukraine. During World War II, the German army invaded Ukraine to gain access to its natural resources. Russia has been the most difficult neighbor of all, however. Russia, and later the Soviet Union, ruled Ukraine between the late 1700s and 1991.

Supplying the Soviets Under Soviet rule, Ukrainian industries grew. In time, factories in Ukraine were making nearly 20 percent of the Soviet Union's goods. Ukraine produced much of the equipment for the Soviet armed forces. And Ukrainian mines supplied much of the iron ore, coal, and other minerals for Soviet industries.

The Soviets used other Ukrainian resources as well. Ships used Ukraine's ports on the Black Sea to bring goods into and out of the Soviet Union. Several of Ukraine's rivers reach like highways into other countries. The Soviets made use of these rivers to ship goods.

Because Ukraine was one of Europe's largest grain-producing regions, it became known as the breadbasket of Europe. Why is Ukraine's farmland so productive? More than half of the country is covered by a rich, black soil called **chernozem** (CHEHR nuh zem). When the Soviet Union took control of Ukraine in 1922, Ukrainian farmers were forced to supply the rest of the Soviet Union with food. By the end of the 1980s, they were producing one fourth of the grain and meat consumed by the Soviet Union.

Ukraine Under Foreign Rule

1854 An illustration shows the port of Odessa when Ukraine was part of the Russian Empire.

1941 Ukrainian villagers report to soldiers of the German forces that occupied Ukraine during World War II.

1947 Farmers work on a collective farm during the Soviet rule of Ukraine.

Chapter 10 Section 3 **329**

A History of Occupation L2

Guided Instruction

- **Vocabulary Builder** Clarify the high-use word **consume** before reading.

- Read A History of Occupation, using the Choral Reading strategy (TE, p. T34).

- Ask students **What are two main reasons Ukraine has been invaded frequently?** *(Ukraine's location between Russia and the countries of Eastern Europe leaves it open to invasion by its neighbors; its rich supply of natural resources also has made it attractive to invading countries.)*

- Ask students **How was the Ukrainian economy affected when it was part of the Soviet Union?** *(Ukrainian farms supplied the rest of the Soviet Union with food; Ukrainian industries grew because they supplied about twenty percent of the Soviet Union's goods. However, the Soviet Union collectivized farmland in Ukraine, causing poverty and starvation in the 1930s.)*

- Have students discuss how Ukrainians might have felt about becoming part of the Soviet Union. *(Answers will vary, but students may note that although the Soviet Union presented Ukraine with a large marketplace for its goods and natural resources, many Ukrainians, especially farmers, probably resented Soviet rule.)*

Independent Practice

Ask students to create the Taking Notes graphic organizer on a blank piece of paper. As students read, have them fill in their flowcharts with information about Ukraine's natural resources. Briefly model how to identify which information to record.

Monitor Progress

Circulate to make sure individuals are filling in their graphic organizers correctly. Provide assistance as needed.

Differentiated Instruction

For English Language Learners L2
Pair English language learners with native English speakers to complete *Guided Reading and Review*. Have Spanish speakers complete *Guided Reading and Review (Spanish)*.

All in One **Europe and Russia Teaching Resources**, *Guided Reading and Review*, p. 323

Guided Reading and Review, **Eastern Hemisphere Spanish Support**, p. 102

For Special Needs Students L1
Have students read the section as they listen to the recorded version on the Student Edition on Audio CD. Check for comprehension by pausing the CD and asking students to share their answers to the Reading Checks.

◉ Chapter 10, Section 3, **Student Edition on Audio CD**

Chapter 10 Section 3 **329**

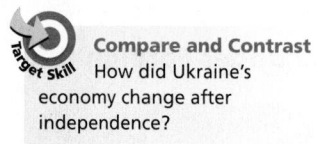

Target Reading Skill L2

Compare and Contrast As a follow up, ask students to answer the Target Reading Skill question in the Student Edition. *(Before independence, Ukraine's industries and resources were controlled by the Soviets. Ukrainian farmers were forced to work on collective farms. After independence, Ukrainian farms and businesses were no longer controlled by the government, so people had to start producing consumer goods and redistribute farmland to improve agricultural production.)*

Independence Brings Challenges L2

Guided Instruction

- **Vocabulary Builder** Clarify the high-use words **publish** and **contaminate** before reading.

- Read Independence Brings Challenges with students. As students read, circulate and make sure individuals can answer the Reading Check question.

- Ask students **What steps has Ukraine taken to strengthen its economy since independence?** *(Ukrainians had to learn how to start new businesses, produce new goods and keep prices under control, and improve their agricultural production by breaking up Soviet-era collectives.)*

Answers

✓ **Reading Check** The Soviets used Ukraine's ports and rivers to ship goods into and out of the Soviet Union.

Compare and Contrast Similarity—Both pictures show a busy port; difference—the photo shows more industry than the illustration.

Compare and Contrast How did Ukraine's economy change after independence?

Odessa—A Thriving Seaport In the 1800s and 1900s, huge quantities of grain were shipped from Odessa to Russia and later the Soviet Union. Today, the city is a major port and a center of Ukrainian industry. **Compare and Contrast** *Compare this photo with the illustration of Odessa on page 329. What similarities and differences do you see?*

330 Europe and Russia

Collectives Bring Starvation To produce all of this grain and meat, Soviet rulers took land away from farmers and created huge government-controlled farms called **collectives.** Most farmers were forced to become workers on these collectives. Other farmers were sent to cities to work in the new factories. All the crops from the collectives went to the government. The people who worked the land were allowed to keep very little of the food they grew. As a result, millions of Ukrainians died of hunger in the 1930s. Over the years, however, life improved on the farms.

✓ **Reading Check** For what purpose did the Soviets use Ukraine's ports and rivers?

Independence Brings Challenges

In 1991, Ukraine won its independence from the Soviet Union. After centuries of foreign rule, the new country now had to decide many important issues for itself.

Building an Independent Economy One of the first issues Ukrainians had to decide was how to build up their economy. Like people in other former Soviet republics, Ukrainians had to learn how to start new businesses. They also needed to learn how to make consumer goods and keep prices under control. Finally, they had to improve their agricultural production by breaking up the inefficient collective farm system put in place by the Soviets.

Differentiated Instruction

For Gifted and Talented L3
Have students work in groups to compose a letter to the local power company asking whether the company obtains power from a nuclear plant and, if so, what measures the power company has taken to ensure that the plant does not have an accident similar to the one at Chernobyl.

Choosing a Language Ukrainians also had to restore their culture. Under Soviet rule, the official language of Ukraine was Russian. Books and newspapers were published only in Russian, and schools used Russian textbooks. As a result, many Ukrainians speak only Russian, especially in the cities and in the eastern part of the nation. Russian is also the language of ethnic Russians, who make up about one fifth of the population. The Ukrainian language is widely spoken only in rural areas and in the western part of the nation.

With independence, Ukrainian was made the official language. Many of the people of Ukraine believe that speaking Ukrainian could tie the country together and free Ukraine from its Soviet past. Elementary and secondary schools have begun using Ukrainian, though Russian is also still used in high schools. Most Ukrainians are pleased about the change. One teacher said, "Language is the anchor of our independence."

A Ukrainian Classroom
Elementary school students sit in class on their first day of school.
Analyze Images *Besides language, what other cultural traditions are important to Ukrainians?*

- Have students explain why Ukrainian became the official language of Ukraine after independence. *(Despite the fact that many Ukrainians spoke only Russian, having Ukrainian as the official language unified the country and distanced it from the Soviet era.)*

- Ask students **How did the disaster at Chernobyl in 1986 affect Ukraine?** *(Many people died or were injured, more than 100,000 people had to move because the area was no longer safe, soil and water were poisoned, and 32,000 acres of farmland were contaminated. Ukraine is still working to repair the damage.)*

- Ask **Which of the three challenges you have just read about—strengthening the economy, establishing a national language, or cleaning up Chernobyl—probably presents the greatest challenge to Ukrainians today? Why?** *(Answers will vary, but opinions should be supported with evidence from the text.)*

Independent Practice
Assign *Guided Reading and Review.*

All in One Europe and Russia Teaching Resources, *Guided Reading and Review,* p. 323

Monitor Progress
Provide students with assistance as they fill in the worksheet.

Differentiated Instruction

For Advanced Readers L3
Have students learn more about the Chernobyl disaster by completing the *Small Group Activity: Chernobyl: Report on a Disaster.*

All in One Europe and Russia Teaching Resources, *Small Group Activity: Chernobyl: Report on a Disaster,* pp. 335–338

Answers

Analyze Images Students may say that education is important to Ukrainians.

Show students *The After-Effects of Chernobyl*. Ask students **How has the Chernobyl accident affected the environment in Ukraine?** *(It has contaminated the soil, making farming difficult.)*

Life in Ukraine

Guided Instruction

- **Vocabulary Builder** Clarify the high-use word **produce** before reading.

- Have students read Life in Ukraine.

- Ask students to compare and contrast economic life in Ukraine before and after the transition to independence. *(Before 1991, certain magazines and newspapers did not exist; farmers were not allowed to own their own farms.)*

- Ask students to make a prediction about the future of Ukraine. *(Students may suggest that life in Ukraine will continue to improve due to new freedoms and many natural resources.)*

Independent Practice

Have students complete their graphic organizers.

Monitor Progress

- Show *Section Reading Support Transparency ER 50* and ask students to check their graphic organizers individually.

  📖 **Europe and Russia Transparencies,** *Section Reading Support Transparency ER 50*

- Tell students to fill in the last column of their *Reading Readiness Guides*.

  All in One Europe and Russia Teaching Resources, *Reading Readiness Guide,* p. 322

Links

Read the **Links to Science** on this page. Ask students to describe in their own words how nuclear energy is produced. *(Answers will vary, but students should accurately explain the process in their own words.)*

Answers

✓ **Reading Check** Traces of dangerous materials from the explosion were found all over the world; much of Ukraine's soil, water, and farmland is still contaminated.

332

Learn about the after-effects of Chernobyl.

Links to Science

Creating Nuclear Power
Nuclear power is produced from a metal called uranium. When uranium is put through a process called nuclear fission, heat is released. The heat can be used to turn water into steam. The steam can be used to power large machines called generators, which produce electricity. When nuclear power is made, radioactive waste is produced. The waste must be carefully stored, because radioactive materials are dangerous to people. If the process of making nuclear power is not tightly controlled, too much heat can destroy the reactor and the entire building that contains it, as happened at Chernobyl. Then radioactive materials can escape into the air. The photo at the right shows a town near Chernobyl after the explosion.

332 Europe and Russia

Recovering From Chernobyl Ukraine is still recovering from a terrible event that occurred during the Soviet period. It became one of the most difficult issues Ukraine has had to face since it gained independence.

Under Soviet rule, Ukrainians built five nuclear power plants. These supply about one third of the country's electricity. The Chernobyl (chehr NOH bul) nuclear plant is located 65 miles (105 kilometers) from the city of Kiev. In 1986, an explosion caused by carelessness rocked the Chernobyl plant. Radioactive materials filled the air. Some people died within days or weeks. Others developed serious health problems that killed them slowly or left them suffering. More than 100,000 people had to be moved out of the area. It was no longer safe to live there. In later years, traces of the dangerous materials released at Chernobyl were found all over the world.

Even today, much of Ukraine's soil and water are still poisoned. More than 32,000 square miles of farmland are contaminated. Some towns and farms remain abandoned. With the help of other nations, the Ukrainians are cleaning up the dangerous materials around Chernobyl, but it may take as long as a hundred years to repair the damage.

✓ **Reading Check** **What are the far-reaching effects of Chernobyl?**

Background: Links Across Place

Three Mile Island The most serious nuclear accident in American history occurred on March 28, 1979 just south of Harrisburg, Pennsylvania. At 4:00 AM, a failure in the cooling system at the Three Mile Island nuclear plant caused a minor leak of radioactive gas. Despite the fact that the health risk was small, thousands living near the plant fled. Though much less serious than the Chernobyl disaster in 1986, the accident at Three Mile Island raised the American public's awareness of the danger of nuclear energy. The Three Mile Island accident caused an increasing number of people to oppose the construction of new nuclear plants.

Life in Ukraine

Independence has brought changes to life in Ukraine. For example, the Kreshchatik (kresh CHAH tik), the main street in Kiev, is often jammed with people. Along this street are many parks, stores, and restaurants. People sell ice cream and pyrohy (pih ROH hee), dumplings filled with vegetables, cheese, or fruit. Newsstands are filled with magazines and newspapers, many of which have been published only since independence. At local markets, farmers sell cheese or produce from their own farms.

Other Ukrainian cities are also alive with the new spirit of freedom. East of Kiev is the city of Kharkiv. Located near huge reserves of iron ore and coal, it is the busiest industrial center in the nation. But Kharkiv is not all work. It is also a vibrant cultural area, where people can attend plays or concerts.

Ukraine is in the early stages of an exciting time in its history. The people have always wanted freedom, and now they have it in their grasp. They know that independence is not easy. But with the land's great resources and the people's ability to work together, the Ukrainians have the ability to make independence succeed.

Vendors sell souvenirs in front of a Roman Catholic church in Kiev.

✓ Reading Check What is Ukraine's busiest industrial center?

Section 3 Assessment

Key Terms
Review the key terms at the beginning of this section. Use each term in a sentence that explains its meaning.

Target Reading Skill
Describe education in Ukraine before and after independence.

Comprehension and Critical Thinking
1. (a) Identify Who controlled Ukraine until 1991?
(b) Find the Main Idea What uses were made of Ukraine's resources?

(c) Predict Now that Ukraine is not supplying another country with its resources, how might that affect its economy?
2. (a) Explain What issues faced Ukraine after independence?
(b) Identify Point of View How might ethnic Russians have reacted when Ukrainian was made the official language?
3. (a) Describe What changes has independence brought to Ukrainian life?
(b) Contrast How was life different in Ukraine before independence?

Writing Activity
Suppose you are a newspaper writer in Ukraine in 1991. Write a short article that describes the views of the people as they start life in an independent country. Be sure to include the views of both Ukrainians and ethnic Russians.

For: An activity on Chernobyl
Visit: PHSchool.com
Web Code: ldd-7503

Chapter 10 Section 3 **333**

Assess and Reteach

Assess Progress L2
Have students complete the Section Assessment. Then administer the *Section Quiz*.

All in One Europe and Russia Teaching Resources, *Section Quiz,* p. 324

Reteach L1
If students need more instruction, have them read this section in the Reading and Vocabulary Study Guide.

Chapter 10, Section 3, **Eastern Hemisphere Reading and Vocabulary Study Guide,** pp. 114–116

Extend L3
Have students learn more about nuclear power by completing the Internet activity *Using Nuclear Power.* After studying the table, students should answer the questions in pairs or small groups.

Go Online PHSchool.com **For:** Environmental and Global Issues: *Using Nuclear Power*
Visit: PHSchool.com
Web Code: ldd-7507

Answer

✓ Reading Check Kharkiv

Writing Activity
Use the *Rubric for Assessing a Newspaper Article* to evaluate students' articles.

All in One Europe and Russia Teaching Resources, *Rubric for Assessing a Newspaper Article,* p. 348

Go Online PHSchool.com Typing in the Web code when prompted will bring students to detailed instructions for this activity.

Section 3 Assessment

Key Terms
Students' sentences should reflect an understanding of each Key Term.

Target Reading Skill
After independence, elementary and secondary schools began teaching in Ukrainian instead of Russian.

Comprehension and Critical Thinking
1. (a) Russia, and later the Soviet Union
(b) The Soviets used Ukraine's natural resources to provide food, goods, minerals, and waterways for transportation.
(c) Answers will vary, but most students will probably suggest that Ukraine's economy will improve because the country now has control over its own resources.

2. (a) After independence, Ukraine needed to build an independent economy and to improve agricultural production. Ukrainians also changed the national language.

(b) Students may suggest that ethnic Russians were fearful that their customs would be forgotten, that they would lose power, or that it would be difficult for them to learn a new language.

3. (a) Ukrainian is now the official language; new magazines and newspapers are being published; farmers at local markets are able to sell produce from their own farms.
(b) Most of Ukraine's resources and farms were controlled by the Soviet Union.

Objective

Learn how to identify frame of reference.

Prepare to Read

Build Background Knowledge L2

Ask students to consider their opinion about the following statement: Students should only have homework two nights a week. Then ask them to consider how teachers would feel about the statement. Explain that the difference in opinion is a matter of frame of reference, or point of view. Tell them that in this lesson they will learn how to identify frame of reference.

Instruct

Identifying Frame of Reference L2

Guided Instruction

■ Read the steps to identifying frame of reference on p. 334 as a class and write them on the board.

■ Complete the Practice the Skill activity on p. 335 together as a class. First identify the main idea of the passage. *(Poland's youth feel it is important for their opinion on the EU to be heard.)* Then discuss the writer's qualifications and experience. *(She is a young woman, so she is part of the Polish youth and may be considered qualified to voice that group's opinion, but we do not know anything about her experience.)*

■ Identify the writer's position *(the opinion of Polish youth on the EU needs to be expressed and heard)*, the tone of the passage *(somewhat forceful and urgent)*, and any emotional language *(words such as demanded)*.

■ Discuss how the writer's age might affect her opinion and why it would be different from the farmer's opinion. *(She is young so her opinion on the EU would probably center around different issues than those of older people who are currently in the workforce. She probably has different concerns than the farmer.)* Finally, put together all

---

> Before Poland joined the European Union, Poles strongly debated the subject. According to 48-year-old Polish farmer Lech Lebedzki, ". . . both of my hands were raised, ready to vote for [it]. . . ." But after hearing that as part of the EU Polish farmers would not receive as much support from the government, he changed his mind. "It's a stab in the back. . . . I will vote against it."

Lebedzki's job as a farmer gave him a certain frame of reference, which influenced his view on EU membership. When you identify a person's frame of reference, you can better understand the influences that shaped his or her position. Writers, for example, may leave information out of an article on purpose to give a stronger argument for their point of view. They may only present one side of the story. Understanding a writer's frame of reference can help you decide whether the writer is a reliable source.

A Polish farmer

Learn the Skill

To identify frame of reference, use the following steps:

1 **Determine the issue.** Read through the passage quickly. What is the main idea?

2 **Look carefully at who the writer is.** What qualifications, if any, does he or she bring to the topic of the passage?

3 **Identify the position taken by the writer.** Look for direct statements of the writer's position. Look also for any emotional language that may give clues to the writer's views. What is the tone, or overall feeling, of the passage? Think about why the writer feels he or she has to write.

4 **Note how the writer's frame of reference may have influenced his or her position on the issue.** Look for connections between who the writer is, the language he or she uses, and the writer's stated position.

5 **Draw a conclusion identifying the writer's position and his or her frame of reference.** Decide whether the writer is giving a reliable picture of the situation.

---

the information that you have learned about Joanna's frame of reference. Write a short paragraph summarizing her frame of reference on the board.

Independent Practice

Assign *Skills for Life* and have students complete it individually.

All in One **Europe and Russia Teaching Resources,** *Skills for Life,* p. 334

Monitor Progress

As students are completing *Skills for Life,* circulate to make sure individuals are applying the skill steps effectively. Provide assistance as needed.

Practice the Skill

Use the steps in Learn the Skill to identify frame of reference in the passage at the right.

① Read through the passage to identify the issue. What main idea does the writer develop in the passage?

② Look at who the writer is. What qualifications does the writer have that enables her to write the article? Does she have any experience that helps her write the article?

③ What is the writer's position? What is the tone of the passage? Can you find any emotional language in the passage?

④ How might the writer's age affect her viewpoint? Why might her opinion be different from the one expressed by the Polish farmer at the beginning of the previous page?

⑤ Write a short paragraph explaining the writer's frame of reference.

Over the months Poland's youth gradually became aware that the issue [of joining the EU] was important to us, because it is we, not our parents, who are going to spend much of our lives in the enlarged EU. Through referenda [votes] and debates in our high schools and universities, we demanded that our voice be heard by those who were longer in the tooth [older]—even though our opinions had no legal value.

—Joanna Margueritte,
a young Polish woman

The University of Warsaw

Agricultural production in Poland is now lower than it's been in any time in the last 50 years. . . . The reason is that the European Union and America and other countries have turned Poland into a dumping ground for overproduction. If we are not treated as equals, if the European Union tries to exploit us . . . we will start a propaganda war and make sure that Poles vote No in the referendum. . . .

—Andrzej Lepper, leader of the
Self Defence Alliance, a Polish
political party

Apply the Skill

Read the passage at the left. Use the steps above to identify the frame of reference of the writer. Then compare this writer's views with those of the writer at the top of this page. How does the tone differ? How would you compare the writers' purposes? Which of these writers do you think is presenting a more reliable picture of the situation?

Assess Progress   L2
Ask students to do the Apply the Skill activity.

Reteach   L1
If students are having trouble applying the skill steps, have them review the skill using the interactive Social Studies Skills Tutor CD-ROM.

⊙ *Identifying Frame of Reference and Point of View,* **Social Studies Skills Tutor CD-ROM**

Extend   L3
Have students read p. 336 and use the steps they have just learned to determine Yura's frame of reference.

Answers
Apply the Skill
Students should recognize that Lepper's membership in a political party gives him the frame of reference of someone who knows he has the power to influence the vote and is warning that if his terms are not met, he will exercise that power. Lepper's tone is more forceful and threatening than Joanna's. Students may suggest that Lepper is presenting a more reliable picture because he presented a fact at the beginning of his statement and has more political experience.

Differentiated Instruction

For Special Needs Students   L1
Partner special needs students with more proficient readers to do Level 1 of the *Identifying Frame of Reference and Point of View* lesson on the Social Studies Skill Tutor CD-ROM together. When students feel more confident, they can move onto Level 2 alone.

⊙ *Identifying Frame of Reference and Point of View,* **Social Studies Skills Tutor CD-ROM**

Section 4
Step-by-Step Instruction

Objectives

Social Studies

1. Investigate the changes that capitalism has brought to Russia.
2. Understand the cultural traditions that have endured throughout Russia.
3. Identify the issues that create challenges for Russians.

Reading/Language Arts

Identify contrasts to find out how two things are different.

Prepare to Read

Build Background Knowledge L2

Tell students that in this section they will learn about Russia and the changes it underwent when it switched from a communist system to a capitalist one. Show students *Life in the "New" Russia*. Ask students to note the effects a capitalist system has had on Russia's capital city of Moscow. Conduct a Give One, Get One activity (TE, p. T37) to allow students to share their answers.

Life in the "New" Russia, **World Studies Video Program**

Set a Purpose for Reading L2

- Preview the Objectives.

- Read each statement in the *Reading Readiness Guide* aloud. Ask students to mark the statements true or false.

  All in One Europe and Russia Teaching Resources, *Reading Readiness Guide,* p. 326

- Have students discuss the statements in pairs or groups of four, then mark their guides again. Use the Numbered Heads participation strategy (TE, p. T36) to call on students to share their group's perspectives.

Vocabulary Builder
Preview Key Terms L2

Pronounce each Key Term, then ask the students to say the word with you. Provide a simple explanation such as, "When inflation occurs, things become more expensive."

Section 4
Russia
A Huge Country Takes a New Path

Prepare to Read

Objectives

In this section you will

1. Investigate the changes that capitalism has brought to Russia.
2. Understand the cultural traditions that have endured throughout Russia.
3. Identify the issues that create challenges for Russians.

Taking Notes

As you read the section, look for details about the changes in Russia since the fall of Soviet communism. Copy the flowchart below and write each detail under the correct heading.

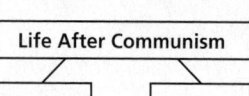

Target Reading Skill

Identify Contrasts When you contrast two regions, you examine how they are different. In this section you will read about two regions in Russia—Moscow and Siberia. As you read, list the differences between these two regions and ways people live in them.

Key Terms

- **investor** (in VES tur) *n.* someone who spends money on improving a business in the hope of making more money
- **inflation** (in FLAY shun) *n.* an increase in the general level of prices when the amount of goods and services remains the same.

Open-air markets like this one in Perm are a more common sight since the fall of communism.

336 Europe and Russia

In 1991, Yura and Tanya Tabak lived in a tiny one-bedroom apartment in Moscow. Soviet communism had ended. Yura had more freedom to pursue his interest in religious studies. Yet life was difficult for the couple. Their wallpaper was peeling off the walls, and their plumbing didn't always work.

In 2002, the Tabaks had a large, bright apartment filled with goods such as a new television. They had even sent their daughter abroad to study. Yura said, "Sometimes I wake up in the morning and want to pinch myself. . . . Are these things really available to us?"

Yet like many Russians, the Tabaks fear what would happen if one of them were to become ill. Medical care used to be free. Now it is expensive and hard to get. Corruption in business and government is widespread, and the economy is unstable. In Russia, many things have changed—but life is still difficult for most Russians.

Target Reading Skill L2

Identify Contrasts Explain that students can contrast two things to find the differences between them.

Model the skill by reading the first two paragraphs on p. 340. Contrast life in Siberia before the fall of the Soviet government with life after the fall. (*Under communist rule, everyone was guaranteed a job, but afterward people had to worry about losing their jobs. Under communist rule people had to live in houses belonging to the state, but afterward people could buy their own homes.*)

Give students *Identify Contrasts*. Have them complete the activity in groups.

All in One Europe and Russia Teaching Resources, *Identify Contrasts,* p. 331

Emerging Capitalism

When the Soviet Union dissolved in 1991, the new Russian Federation—the world's largest country—had to find a new identity for itself. The nation had no experience of democracy, or any laws that supported it. Russian leaders often fought for power within the new government. The new country also struggled to make the transition from communism to a free-market economy.

Moscow, Russia's Capital Moscow is the capital of Russia and the center of its economic activities. It has a population of more than 9 million people. When the Soviet Union first collapsed, business in Moscow boomed. Investors came from many different countries to make money in Moscow. An **investor** is someone who spends money on improving a business in the hope of making more money if the business succeeds.

Some investors became very wealthy. When the first American fast-food chain in Russia opened in Moscow, people lined up in the streets to eat there. The restaurant served 30,000 people on the first day. Ikea, a Swedish furniture store, opened a 250-store mall in Moscow. Russian investors opened 24-hour supermarkets and high-tech companies.

Economic success has not come equally to all Russians. Some Russians have become wealthy because they have influence within the government. For example, a former Soviet official started Russia's largest oil and gas company, Gazprom (GAHS prahm), which is hugely profitable. Other Russians have gained their wealth through corruption.

Explore life in Moscow.

Investment in Moscow
Russia's biggest department store (at the left), built over a hundred years ago in a traditional style, bustles with people and new stores. The modern International Business Center (above) was built in 2001.
Analyze Images *Describe the scene in the department store. Would the scene have been different during Soviet times?*

Emerging Capitalism L2

Guided Instruction
- **Vocabulary Builder** Clarify the high-use words **dissolve** and **enforce** before reading.

- Read Emerging Capitalism using the Paragraph Shrinking strategy (TE, p. T34).

- Discuss with students the problems Russia faced after the Soviet Union was dissolved in 1991. *(Russia had to find a new identity; its leaders often fought for power; it struggled to make the transition from communism to a free-market economy.)*

- Ask students **How many people live in Moscow?** *(more than 9 million)* **How did life change in Moscow after the transition to a free-market economy?** *(Many new businesses opened and investors came from everywhere to make money in Moscow. Some investors and former government leaders became very wealthy.)*

Answer

Analyze Images The department store is bustling with people; during Soviet times, people probably did not shop at such stores since the government controlled businesses and people did not have access to many goods.

Vocabulary Builder

Use the information below to teach students this section's high-use words.

High-Use Word	Definition and Sample Sentence
dissolve, p. 337	*v.* to break up The club **dissolved** after its president quit.
enforce, p. 338	*v.* to cause to be carried out The police help **enforce** our city's laws.
status, p. 341	*n.* the condition of something according to the law His official **status** changed when he became a citizen.
resolve, p. 342	*v.* to find an answer to; to deal with successfully We must **resolve** the disagreement before it leads to a fight.

Guided Instruction (continued)

- Discuss the economic benefits and challenges that ordinary Russians face under capitalism. *(Benefits—Some Russians have been able to start their own businesses, others have opened small factories; some Russians can afford to fix up their apartments and travel abroad. Challenges—Criminal gangs often force money from ordinary business people; in the 1990s bank failures and inflation caused many Russians to lose their life savings.)*

- Have students describe the region of Siberia. *(It is located in eastern Russia and has rich reserves of coal, gold, iron, oil, and natural gas. During the Soviet era the Trans-Siberian Railroad was built to transport materials from Siberia, and factories and mining operations were started. Much of Siberia is rural, but there are also some large cities.)*

- Ask students **How has the fall of the Soviet government and the arrival of free enterprise changed life in Siberia?** *(During the Soviet era, mining and factory jobs were guaranteed; farmers were guaranteed certain prices for their crops; now jobs are not guaranteed and people worry about losing their jobs or farms; Siberians can now buy their own homes and make decisions.)*

Independent Practice

Have students create the Taking Notes graphic organizer on a blank piece of paper. Then have them fill it in with details from the section. Briefly model how to identify which details to record using *Transparency B2: Flow Chart.*

📖 **Europe and Russia Transparencies,** *Transparency B2: Flow Chart*

Monitor Progress

Circulate throughout the classroom to ensure that individuals are filling in their flowcharts with the correct information. Provide assistance as needed.

Links

Read the **Links to Art** on this page. Ask **Why do you think Moscow's subway stations are referred to as "underground palaces?"** *(They contain elaborate artwork and architecture similar to what might be found in a palace.)*

Widespread Corruption Average Russians have been working hard since the collapse of the Soviet government. Many have opened small businesses or factories. Like the Tabaks, more Russians today can afford to fix up their apartments, buy expensive goods, and travel abroad. Yet most Russians still face challenges in their daily lives. Salaries are still low for Russian workers. About 25 percent of all Russians live in poverty.

Corruption is one reason that many Russians have not been able to improve their situations. Criminal gangs often force honest people who own businesses to pay them money. The Russians who own or work in these businesses therefore cannot keep all the money they earn. Laws meant to protect people are often not enforced.

Economic and Health Problems Average Russians also suffer when the economy does not thrive. In the 1990s, large numbers of Russians lost their life savings when banks failed and inflation rose to high levels. **Inflation** is an increase in the general level of prices at a time when the amount of goods and services remains the same. The economy slowly recovered. But some Russians are still working to regain the money they lost years ago.

Finally, as you have read, Russians have major concerns about health care. Life expectancy in Russia is very low for a developed country—just 62 years for men. Hospitals often contain outdated equipment. In some hospitals, patients have to bring their own sheets. Russia's wealthy people can afford better care, but ordinary Russians cannot.

Links to Art

Moscow's "Underground Palaces" When work on Moscow's subway began in the 1930s, its planners wanted to build more than a comfortable, useful mode of transportation. They also wanted to surround the subway riders with beauty. Architects created palace-like subway stations using more than 20 kinds of marble and other different colored stones. The Kievskaya station, shown below, includes domed ceilings hand-painted by famous artists. Others contain stained-glass windows, murals, and statues. Light reflects off of the colored walls of many stations, filling the halls and brightening the day of many passengers.

338 Europe and Russia

Skills Mini Lesson

Recognizing Bias

1. Teach the skill by defining *bias* as a one-sided view. Explain that in determining whether a statement is biased, students should look for false or missing information and for clue words that express emotion instead of fact.

2. Have students practice the skill by determining if the quote by Lech Lebedzki on p. 334 contains bias.

3. Have students apply the skill by analyzing the following statement that could have been made by a former high-ranking Communist party official in the Soviet Union: "We should go back to the way things were before; everything is much worse and nobody is happy."

Russia

As the world's largest country in area, Russia spreads across nearly 180° of latitude. Because of its vast size, the country is divided into eleven separate time zones. While the climate varies from place to place, the summers are generally mild and the winters chilly to bitterly cold. Russia is home to many different landforms, from arctic deserts and tundra to forests, plains, and mountains. Study the map and tables to learn more about Russia's geography.

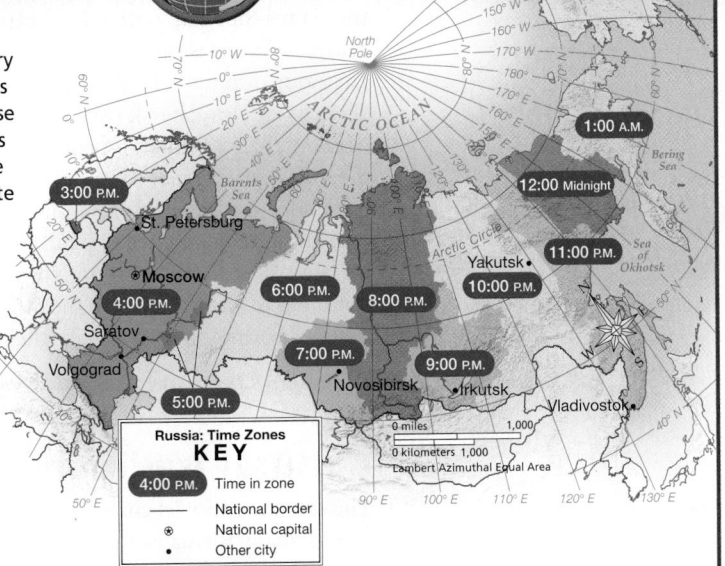

European Railroads by Length

Country	Total Mileage
Russia	
Germany	
France	
Italy	
Spain	
Romania	

This symbol represents 5,000 miles of railroad track.

SOURCE: *DK World Desk Reference*, 2002

World's Largest Countries

Country	Land Area
Russia	6,562,110 sq mi; 16,995,790 sq km
China	3,600,944 sq mi; 9,326,406 sq km
Canada	3,560,234 sq mi; 9,220,968 sq km
United States	3,536,292 sq mi; 9,158,958 sq km
Brazil	3,265,074 sq mi; 8,456,506 sq km

SOURCE: *The World Almanac*, 2004

Map and Chart Skills

1. **Identify** What time is it in Yakutsk when it is noon in Moscow?
2. **Compare** How does Russia's land area compare to that of the United States?
3. **Analyze Information** Why do you think there are so many more miles of railroad track in Russia than in other European countries?

Go Online PHSchool.com Use Web Code lde-7504 for **DK World Desk Reference Online.**

Differentiated Instruction

For Less Proficient Readers   L1

Reinforce students' understanding of Siberia's natural resources by showing them *Color Transparencies ER 13* and *ER 15: Northern Eurasia: Natural Resources*. Have students name the resources and identify their locations.

Europe and Russia Transparencies, *Color Transparency ER 13: Northern Eurasia: Political (Base); Color Transparency ER 15: Northern Eurasia: Natural Resources (overlay)*

For Advanced Readers   L3

Have students explore the creation of the Trans-Siberian Railroad by completing *Activity Shop Interdisciplinary: Plan a New Railroad Line.*

All in One Europe and Russia Teaching Resources, *Activity Shop Interdisciplinary: Plan a New Railroad Line,* pp. 339–340

Guided Instruction   L2

Ask students to study the Country Profile on this page. Have students work in pairs to answer the Map and Chart Skills questions and then discuss the answers as a class.

Independent Practice

Tell students to suppose that they live in Russia. Ask them to write a letter to a friend describing the country's geography. Tell them to include information found in the map and tables on this page.

Answers

Map and Chart Skills

1. 6:00 PM
2. Russia is nearly 2 times larger than the U.S.
3. because Russia is much larger in area than other European countries

Go Online PHSchool.com Students can find more information about this topic on the DK World Desk Reference Online.

Identify Contrasts As a follow up, ask students to answer the Target Reading Skill question in the Student Edition. *(Students may identify two of the following: Siberians worry about losing their jobs or farms; they are able to buy their own homes; they have freedom to make their own decisions.)*

Cultural Traditions Continue [L2]

Guided Instruction

- Have students read Cultural Traditions Continue to learn how Russians have continued to preserve their traditions. As they read, circulate and make sure individuals are able to answer the Reading Check question.

- Ask students to compare life in Moscow in Soviet times to life in Moscow today. *(Moscow is still the cultural center of the nation.)*

- Ask students **How do Siberians prepare for winter?** *(Farmers work overtime to harvest crops before the frost, and collect nuts and honey.)* **Would you call these activities examples of cultural traditions? Why or why not?** *(Possible answers: Yes, they are cultural traditions because Siberians have probably been making the same kinds of preparations for centuries.)*

Independent Practice [L2]

Have students continue to fill in their graphic organizers with information from the section.

Monitor Progress

Circulate among students and provide assistance to individuals as they add details to their flowcharts.

Answers

✓ Reading Check because factory workers and miners are no longer guaranteed jobs, as they were under communism

Generalize Possible answer: Although traditional Russian culture still endures, teenagers may have more freedom and opportunities than they did under Soviet communism.

⤷ **Identify Contrasts** What are two ways that life has changed for Siberians since the fall of Soviet communism?

Changes in Siberia Siberia is a region with rich reserves of coal, gold, iron, oil, and natural gas. During the Soviet years, the government built factories, set up mining operations, and built the Trans-Siberian railroad to carry out materials. Although much of Siberia is rural, large cities developed there over time. In fact, four of the ten largest Russian cities are located in Siberia. The city of Novosibirsk (NOH vuh sih BIHRSK) has a population of more than 1.3 million people. Outside of the cities, much of Siberia is agricultural.

Under the Soviet communist system, factory workers and miners were guaranteed jobs, and farmers were guaranteed certain prices for their crops. Now Siberians worry about losing their jobs or their farms. On the other hand, Siberians are able to buy their own homes and make their own decisions.

✓ Reading Check **Why are Siberians worried about jobs?**

Cultural Traditions Continue

The collapse of Soviet communism brought major changes to the lives of many Russians. But traditional Russian ways endure.

Life in Moscow As it was in Soviet times, Moscow is still the cultural center of the nation. Art, theater, and dance thrive there. The Bolshoi (BOHL shoy) Ballet is based in Moscow. Dancers from this famous Russian school of ballet have performed around the world. And traveling performers, such as folk dancers from northern Russia, come to Moscow.

On Moscow's streets street vendors sell traditional Russian crafts next to vendors selling electronic goods from China. On very cold winter days, some people in Moscow go to the parks to celebrate an old tradition: picnicking in the snow.

Russian Teenagers Teenagers walk across the square in front of St. Basil's Cathedral in Moscow. **Generalize** *How might teenagers' lives have been the same and different before and after the fall of Soviet communism?*

340 Europe and Russia

⌐ Background: Links Across Time ⌐

Russia and the Arts Russians are great readers, and many of the books that are favorites of the Russian people were written before the Russian Revolution of 1917. Favorite authors include Leo Tolstoy, Fyodor Dostoyevsky, and Anton Chekhov. Many of the ballets and operas enjoyed by people in Moscow and St. Petersburg were also created before the revolution, with music by Pyotr Ilyich Tchaikovsky and Nikolay Rimsky-Korsakov. Even with this love for tradition, many Russians enjoy today's rock music from the United States. In addition, American movies are shown regularly.

Life in Rural Siberian Villages Much of Siberia's vast expanse is rural. Few people live in these areas, where change comes slowly. Many homes have no running water. Water has to be hauled from wells. Sometimes the wells freeze in the winter. Then people have to drink and cook with melted snow.

Despite problems like these, Siberians have adapted to life in their frigid climate. Farmers work overtime to harvest crops before the frost. Before winter comes, they start collecting nuts and honey. In winter, some families hang huge pieces of meat from their porches. Temperatures in winter are so cold that the meat freezes solid and does not spoil.

During winter, women wearing many layers of clothing leave their log houses to fetch firewood. Inside the log houses, large stoves are used for both cooking and heating. When the nights become bitterly cold, the family may spread a straw mat on top of the still-warm stove and sleep there to stay warm.

✓ **Reading Check** What are some cultural traditions in Moscow?

Uniting a Vast Nation

Russia is a vast country, covering more than 6 million square miles (17 million square kilometers). Russia has more than 144 million people. The majority of these people are ethnic Russians. However, the nation also includes many different ethnic groups who speak different languages and practice different religions. How can a country with so much land, so many different ethnic groups, and a struggling economy stay united?

War in Chechnya You have read that some Russian republics populated by ethnic minorities have grown tired of Russian rule. One such republic, located in southwestern Russia, is called Chechnya (CHECH nee uh). The people who live in this oil-rich republic are mainly Muslims. In 1991, Chechnya declared its independence from Russia. To prevent the republic from seceding, Russia sent troops into the Chechen capital. For several years during the 1990s, Russian and Chechen troops fought bitterly over the status of the republic. Tens of thousands of people were killed in the struggle. Hundreds of thousands were forced to flee their homes. Although Chechnya remains part of Russia today, conflict still goes on there.

A Nenets mother and child in a reindeer-skin tent in Siberia

Chechen refugees make a temporary home in a train car.

Chapter 10 Section 4 **341**

Uniting a Vast Nation L2

Guided Instruction

- **Vocabulary Builder** Clarify the meaning of the high-use words **status** and **resolve** before reading.

- Have students read Uniting a Vast Nation.

- Have students describe the events that occurred when Chechnya declared independence from Russia. (*To prevent Chechnya from seceding, Russia sent troops to the Chechen capital. Russian and Chechen troops fought for several years, during which tens of thousands of people were killed and hundreds of thousands were forced to leave their homes; Chechnya remains part of Russia today.*)

- Ask students **What are some of Russia's major natural resources?** (*oil, natural gas, and metals*) **How could Russia's dependence on the sale of these resources be a problem?** (*When world prices of the materials are low, the Russian economy suffers.*)

- Ask students **What are some predictions you might make about Russia's future?** (*Possible answers: Russia's economy may improve given its availability of natural resources and a talented workforce. However, economic problems may persist as long as corruption and ethnic tensions remain.*)

Independent Practice
Have students complete their graphic organizers.

Monitor Progress

- Show *Section Reading Support Transparency ER 51* and ask students to check their graphic organizers individually. Go over key concepts and clarify key vocabulary as needed.

    📖 **Europe and Russia Transparencies,** *Section Reading Support Transparency ER 51*

- Tell students to fill in the last column of the *Reading Readiness Guide*. Probe for what they learned that confirms or invalidates each statement.

    All in One Europe and Russia Teaching Resources, *Reading Readiness Guide,* p. 326

Answer

✓ **Reading Check** The Bolshoi Ballet is in Moscow; folk dancers from the north perform there; street vendors sell traditional Russian crafts.

Assess and Reteach

Assess Progress [L2]

Have students complete the Section Assessment. Administer the *Section Quiz*.

All in One **Europe and Russia Teaching Resources,** *Section Quiz,* p. 328

Reteach [L1]

If students need more instruction, have them read this section in the Reading and Vocabulary Study Guide.

Chapter 10, Section 4, **Eastern Hemisphere Reading and Vocabulary Study Guide,** pp. 117–119

Extend [L3]

Have students read the primary source *Housekeeping in Russia Soon After the Revolution* to learn more about another period of change in Russia's history.

All in One **Europe and Russia Teaching Resources,** *Housekeeping in Russia Soon After the Revolution,* p. 345

Answers

Infer Answers may vary, but students will probably say that more average Russians are able to buy dachas today because many work hard at successful jobs.

✓ **Reading Check** When world prices for these materials are low, the Russian economy suffers.

Section 4 Assessment

Key Terms

Students' sentences should reflect an understanding of each Key Term.

↩ Target Reading Skill

After the fall of the Soviet Union, Chechnya tried to secede from Russia and experienced several years of struggle against Russian troops who were sent to prevent the republic from seceding.

Comprehension and Critical Thinking

1. (a) Criminal gangs often force people who own businesses to pay them money. Laws protecting business owners are often not enforced. **(b)** The change to a free-market economy has helped ordinary Russians to start their own businesses or factories and enabled some to fix up their apartments and

---

The Russian Dacha
Country homes called *dachas*, like the one below, were first built by Peter the Great and given to wealthy nobles. In Soviet times, they were usually given to Communist Party officials. **Infer** *Do you think average Russians are able to buy dachas today? Explain why or why not.*

Economic Problems Remain In the early 2000s, Russia's economy shows signs of strengthening. Yet serious economic problems remain. Even one of the country's most important assets—its natural resources—presents problems. For example, Russia has enormous deposits of oil, natural gas, and metals. But Russia depends too heavily on sales of these materials, rather than on creating new jobs. If world prices are low, then Russia's economy suffers.

Corruption is still a problem throughout the country. Laws are still not usually enforced. And banks have never fully recovered from the failures in the 1990s. For these reasons, many Russians distrust the government.

However, Russia is still a powerful nation with many important assets. Besides its natural resources, it has a talented workforce of scientists and engineers. If the country can continue to improve its economy and resolve some of its ethnic tensions, its future should be bright.

✓ **Reading Check** Why is Russia's dependence on its natural resources a problem?

Section 4 Assessment

Key Terms

Review the key terms at the beginning of this section. Use each term in a sentence that explains its meaning.

↩ Target Reading Skill

Contrast the situation in Chechnya before and after the fall of the Soviet Union.

Comprehension and Critical Thinking

1. (a) Explain Why have average Russians had difficulty running their own businesses?

(b) Draw Conclusions How has the change to a free-market economy both helped and harmed ordinary Russians?

2. (a) Describe What cultural traditions have endured throughout Russia?

(b) Contrast How does life in rural Siberia differ from life in Moscow?

3. (a) Recall Which Russian republic declared its independence in 1991?

(b) Infer Why did Russia go to war to prevent that republic from seceding?

Writing Activity

Do you live in a city, a small town, or the countryside? Write a paragraph comparing your life with the lives of Russians in one of the places described in this section.

> **Writing Tip** Before you begin, list details about Russian life in the place you have chosen. For each detail, record a detail about your own life that relates to that topic.

---

travel abroad. Yet many ordinary Russians suffer a lack of job security and have lost money due to bank failures and inflation. There have also been severe food shortages.

2. (a) People from the countryside continue to come to Moscow to buy things; street vendors sell traditional crafts; some people in Moscow still have winter picnics in the snow; traditional art, theater, and dance continue to thrive. **(b)** Life in Siberia is generally rural, and the change to a free-market economy has been slower than in Moscow.

3. (a) Chechnya **(b)** Possible answer: Russia wanted to maintain control of the oil-rich land of Chechnya; it also wanted to discourage other republics from seceding.

Writing Activity

Use the *Rubric for Assessing a Writing Assignment* to evaluate students' comparisons.

All in One **Europe and Russia Teaching Resources,** *Rubric for Assessing a Writing Assignment,* p. 350

Poland

◆ Chapter Summary

Section 1: Poland

- Despite years of foreign rule, cultural traditions and language have endured in Polish life.
- In 1990, Poland's communist-based economy shifted to capitalism.
- Poland must still overcome environmental problems and unemployment.

Section 2: New Balkan Nations

- The Balkans is a diverse region of many ethnic groups, religions, and languages.
- Yugoslavia had a troubled history of ethnic conflict from its beginning.
- The countries created upon the breakup of Yugoslavia hope to overcome a history of ethnic conflict and move towards peace.

Section 3: Ukraine

- Ukraine has a long history of occupation by foreign powers.
- Since independence from the Soviet Union, Ukraine has had to face economic and environmental challenges.
- Life in Ukraine is changing as the country embraces its independence.

Section 4: Russia

- Since the fall of the Soviet government, the transition to capitalism has brought some benefits, but also many economic challenges.
- Many cultural traditions have endured throughout Russia.
- Russia's huge size, ethnic diversity, and economic problems have presented challenges to preserving national unity.

◆ Key Terms

Each of the statements below contains a key term from the chapter. If the statement is true, write *true*. If it is false, replace the term to make it true.

1. In the Eastern Orthodox religion, a shrine is a holy place where visitors often plant crosses.

2. An investor is a person who spends money to make more money.

3. Slovenia and Croatia seceded from Yugoslavia in 1991.

4. Capitalism is an economic system in which the government owns the businesses.

5. More than half of Ukraine is covered with a thick, black soil called collectives.

6. After Yugoslavia broke apart, entrepreneurs erupted in Bosnia and Herzegovina.

Chapter 10 **343**

— Vocabulary Builder —

Revisit this chapter's high-use words.

unique	consume	dissolve
transition	publish	enforce
invest	contaminate	status
principle	produce	resolve
prevent		

Ask students to review the definitions they recorded on their *Word Knowledge* worksheets.

All in One **Europe and Russia Teaching Resources,** *Word Knowledge,* p. 332

Consider allowing students to earn extra credit if they use the words in their answers to the questions in the Chapter Review and Assessment. The words must be used correctly and in a natural context to win the extra points.

Chapter 10
Review and Assessment
Review Chapter Content

- Review and revisit the major themes of this chapter by asking students to classify what Guiding Question each bulleted statement in the Chapter Summary answers. Have students work together in groups to classify the sentences. Refer to p. 139 in the Student Edition for the text of the Guiding Questions.

- Assign *Vocabulary Development* for students to review Key Terms.

    All in One **Europe and Russia Teaching Resources,** *Vocabulary Development,* p. 346

Answers

Key Terms

1. True.
2. True.
3. True.
4. False. Communism is an economic system in which the government owns the businesses.
5. False. More than half of Ukraine is covered with a thick, black soil called chernozem.
6. False. After Yugoslavia broke apart, civil war erupted in Bosnia and Herzegovina.

Comprehension and Critical Thinking

7. (a) Catholicism **(b)** Catholicism in Poland is unique and has been at the center of Polish tradition for centuries; Polish Catholics continued to practice their religion despite discouragement from the communist government; Poles were especially proud when a Pole was selected as pope of the Catholic church.

8. (a) farmers **(b)** It provided them with a reliable income and kept prices high. **(c)** taking on part-time jobs, inviting paying guests to stay with them for vacations, or producing higher-priced organic goods

9. (a) Serbia, Montenegro, Bosnia and Herzegovina, Macedonia, Croatia, Slovenia **(b)** These nations have different languages, practice different religions, and have different non-Slavic ethnic groups. **(c)** After Tito's death and the fall of communism, many people began to support leaders who encouraged them to identify with their own ethnic group, leading many to want to be independent.

10. (a) The nations of this region face economic hardships and must deal with a history of ethnic conflict. **(b)** to help people without food and other supplies, stop conflicts, and create peace treaties

11. (a) The natural resources of Ukraine include rich soil, iron ore, coal, and rivers. **(b)** Ukraine's rich supply of natural resources has made it more likely to be invaded.

12. (a) Some businesses took off and some investors became very wealthy, but ordinary Russians faced challenges in starting new businesses, from bank failures and inflation, and from food shortages. Still, many Russians were able to become successful. **(b)** Capitalism has helped Russians by bringing them new freedoms and opportunities, including the ability to start businesses, fix up their apartments, and travel abroad. However, jobs are no longer guaranteed and corruption and criminal activity affect ordinary Russians' ability to start and maintain profitable businesses.

Skills Practice
Students should identify Havel as a Czech playwright whose tone is persuasive but rational. Students' paragraphs should demonstrate an understanding of the skill.

◆ **Comprehension and Critical Thinking**

7. (a) Identify What religion do most Poles belong to?
(b) Synthesize Information How has religious belief strengthened the pride Poles feel for their country?

8. (a) Name What group of people in Poland has found it hardest to manage the transition to capitalism?
(b) Analyze Information In what ways did communism help Polish farmers?
(c) Identify Effects What are Polish farmers doing to make extra money?

9. (a) List Which six Balkan nations share a Slavic heritage?
(b) Contrast Discuss the differences among the peoples of these nations.
(c) Summarize How did these differences lead to the breakup of Yugoslavia?

10. (a) Recall What problems are faced by all the nations created by Yugoslavia's breakup?
(b) Identify Cause and Effect Why were UN and NATO forces sent to the Balkans several times?

11. (a) Note What are the natural resources of Ukraine?
(b) Identify the Main Idea How have these resources affected Ukraine's history?

12. (a) Describe What changes did the transition to capitalism bring to Russia?
(b) Evaluate Information How has capitalism both helped and hurt average Russians?

◆ **Skills Practice**

Identifying Frame of Reference In the Skills for Life activity in this chapter, you learned how to identify frame of reference. Review the steps you followed to learn this skill. Then reread the quotation by Vaclav Havel on page 233. Identify the writer's tone and qualifications for his position. Then use this information to write a paragraph that explains his frame of reference.

◆ **Writing Activity: Science**

Suppose you are a writer for a science magazine. Your assignment is to write an article about environmental problems in Eastern Europe. Write a short article about the causes and effects of pollution in Poland, or of the Chernobyl accident in Ukraine.

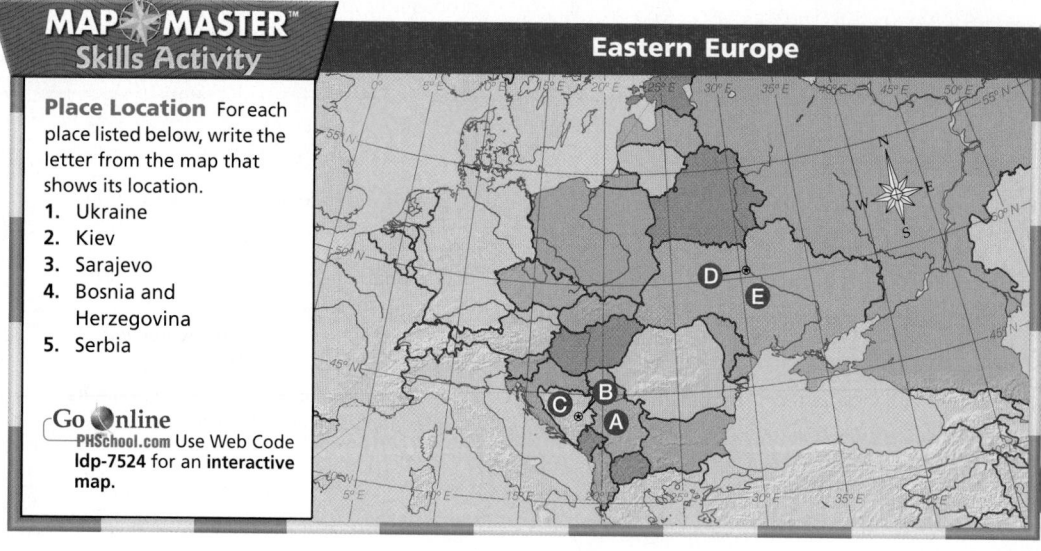

MAP MASTER™ Skills Activity

Place Location For each place listed below, write the letter from the map that shows its location.
1. Ukraine
2. Kiev
3. Sarajevo
4. Bosnia and Herzegovina
5. Serbia

Go Online PHSchool.com Use Web Code ldp-7524 for an interactive map.

Eastern Europe

344 Europe and Russia

Writing Activity: Science
Students' articles will vary, but should make clear the connection between causes and effects. Articles about Poland should note the impact of coal mining, steel production, and the use of unleaded gasoline. Articles about Chernobyl should note the cause of the accident and list several of its effects.

Use *Rubric for Assessing a Newspaper Article* to evaluate students' articles. Tell students how many sources you would like them to use, if any, beyond the textbook.

All in One Europe and Russia Teaching Resources, *Rubric for Assessing a Newspaper Article,* pp. 348

Standardized Test Prep

Test-Taking Tips

Some questions on standardized tests ask you to analyze graphic organizers. Study the table below. Then follow the tips to answer the sample question.

Six Balkan Nations: Ethnic Groups	
Macedonia	Macedonian (64%) Albanian (25%)
Croatia	Croat (90%) Serb (5%)
Bosnia and Herzegovina	Bosniak (48%) Serb (37%)
Serbia	Serb (66%) Albanian (17%)
Montenegro	Montenegrin (43%) Serb (32%)
Slovenia	Slovene (83%) Croat (2%)

TIP Use what you know about history and geography to help you answer the question.

What is the subject of this chart?

A major ethnic groups of countries that make up Eastern Europe

B major ethnic groups of countries that made up the former Soviet Union

C major ethnic groups of countries that were formed after Yugoslavia broke up

D major ethnic groups of countries that were formed at the end of World War II

TIP Try to answer the question before you look at the answer choices.

Think It Through Each of the names in bold print is a country; to the right of each country is its ethnic makeup. You can eliminate A and B. Eastern Europe includes more than these six countries, and the Soviet Union did not include these countries. You may not know which countries were formed after World War II, but you have probably heard most of these six countries mentioned in reference to Yugoslavia. The answer is C.

Practice Questions

Use the tips above and other tips in this book to help you answer the following questions.

1. Which of the following is NOT an important Polish tradition?

A communism   **B** Polish Orthodoxy

C Roman Catholicism   **D** the Polish language

2. In which country is the republic of Kosovo located?

A Macedonia

B Croatia

C Bosnia and Herzegovina

D Serbia

3. What led to the growth of towns and cities in Siberia?

A the collapse of Soviet communism

B the Trans-Siberian Railroad

C the transition to capitalism

D migration from Europe

Use the table below to answer Question 4. Choose the letter of the best answer to the question.

Ukrainian Resources	
Resource	Use by Soviet Union
Farmland	Grain, meat
Minerals	Iron ore, coal for industries
	Shipping of goods to and from Soviet Union

4. Which answer would best fit in the blank space on the table?

A Collectives   **B** Seaports and rivers

C Mines   **D** Factories

Use Web Code lda-7504 for a **Chapter 10 self-test.**

Go Online PHSchool.com Students may practice their map skills using the interactive online version of this map.

Standardized Test Prep
Answers

1. A

2. D

3. B

4. B

Go Online PHSchool.com Students may use the Chapter 10 self-test on PHSchool.com to prepare for the Chapter Test.

Assessment Resources

Teaching Resources
Chapter Tests A and B, pp. 351–356
Final Exams A and B, pp. 363–368

Test Prep Workbook
Europe and Russia Study Sheet, pp. 110–112
Europe and Russia Practice Tests A, B, and C, pp. 37–48

AYP Monitoring Assessments
Europe and Russia Benchmark Test 2, pp. 109–112
Europe and Russia Outcome Tests, pp. 188–193

Technology
◉ *ExamView Test Bank CD-ROM*

- Students can further explore the Guiding Questions by completing hands-on projects.

- Three pages of structured guidance in All-in-One Europe and Russia Teaching Resources support each of the projects described on this page.

  All in One **Europe and Russia Teaching Resources**, *Book Project: Olympic Cities*, pp. 83–85; *Book Project: Folklore Corner*, pp. 86–88

- There are also two additional projects introduced, explained, and supported in the All-in-One Europe and Russia Teaching Resources.

  All in One **Europe and Russia Teaching Resources**, *Book Project: Changing Climates*, pp. 77–79; *Book Project: Tourism in Eastern Europe*, pp. 80–82

- Go over the four project suggestions with students.

- Ask each student to select one of the projects, or design his or her own. Work with students to create a project description and a schedule.

- Post project schedules and monitor student progress by asking for progress reports.

- Assess student projects using rubrics from the All-in-One Europe and Russia Teaching Resources.

  All in One **Europe and Russia Teaching Resources**, *Rubric for Assessing a Student Performance on a Project*, p. 89; *Rubric for Assessing Performance of an Entire Group*, p. 90; *Rubric for Assessing Individual Performance in a Group*, p. 91

 Tell students they can add their completed Book Project as the final item in their portfolios. Assess student portfolios with *Rubric for Assessing a Student Portfolio*.

  All in One **Europe and Russia Teaching Resources**, *Rubric for Assessing a Student Portfolio*, p. 92

Projects

Create your own projects to learn more about Europe and Russia. At the beginning of this book, you were introduced to the **Guiding Questions** for studying the chapters and the special features. You can also find answers to these questions by doing projects on your own or with a group. Use the questions to find topics you want to explore further. Then try the projects described on this page or create your own.

1. **Geography** What are the main physical features of Europe and Russia?

2. **History** How have Europe and Russia been affected by their history?

3. **Culture** How have the people of Europe and Russia been shaped by their cultures?

4. **Government** What types of government have existed in Europe and Russia?

5. **Economics** How have Russian and European economies developed into what they are today?

Project

WRITE A PROPOSAL

Olympic Cities
Plan an Olympic season in a European city. As you read this book, keep track of cities that you find interesting. Research them at the library or on the Internet. After you have gathered your information, choose a city that you think would be a good host of either the summer or winter Olympics. Write a proposal to Olympic officials, explaining what the city has to offer to the Olympics. Include maps or pictures of your city with your proposal.

Project

CREATE A DISPLAY

Folklore Corner
Create a library of folk and fairy tales from countries throughout Europe. As you read about a country in this book, find a traditional tale from that country. Think about how the stories reflect the country's culture. With your classmates, build a Folklore Corner in your classroom. Create a display of books of folk tales. Include objects, drawings, and photographs that represent the culture in these tales. Label each tale with its country of origin.

How to Read Social Studies

Teaching the Target Reading Skills

The Prentice Hall *World Studies* program has interwoven essential reading skills instruction throughout the Student Edition, Teacher's Edition, and ancillary resources. In Africa, students will learn seven reading skills.

Student Edition The *World Studies* Student Edition provides students with reading skills instruction, practice, and application opportunities in each chapter within the program.

Teacher's Edition The *World Studies* Teacher Edition supports your teaching of each skill by providing full modeling in each chapter's interleaf and modeling of the specific sub-skills in each section lesson.

All in One Teaching Resources The *World Studies* All-in-One Teaching Resources provides a worksheet explaining and supporting the elements of each Target Reading Skill. Use these to help struggling students master skills, or as more practice for every student.

Target Reading Skills

The Target Reading Skills introduced on this page will help you understand the words and ideas in this book and in other social studies reading you do. Each chapter in the Africa section focuses on one of these reading skills. Good readers develop a bank of reading strategies, or skills. Then they draw on the particular strategies that will help them understand the text they are reading.

Chapter 11 Target Reading Skill
Clarifying Meaning If you do not understand something you are reading right away, you can use several skills to clarify the meaning of the word or idea. In this chapter you will practice these strategies: rereading, paraphrasing, and summarizing.

Chapter 12 Target Reading Skill
Using the Reading Process Previewing can help you understand and remember what you read. In this chapter you will practice these skills: setting a purpose for reading, predicting, asking questions, and using prior knowledge.

Chapter 13 Target Reading Skill
Comparing and Contrasting You can use comparison and contrast to sort out and analyze information you are reading. In this chapter you will practice these skills: making comparisons, identifying contrasts, and using signal words.

Chapter 14 Target Reading Skill
Using Cause and Effect Recognizing cause and effect will help you understand relationships among the situations and events you are reading about. In this chapter you will practice these skills: recognizing causes and effects and using signal words.

Chapter 15 Target Reading Skill
Identifying the Main Idea Since you cannot remember every detail of what you read, it is important to identify the main ideas. In this chapter you will practice these skills: identifying main ideas, identifying implied main ideas, and identifying supporting details.

Chapter 16 Target Reading Skill
Using Context Using the context of an unfamiliar word can help you understand its meaning. Context includes the words, phrases, and sentences surrounding a word. In this chapter you will practice these skills: using context clues and interpreting non-literal meanings.

Chapter 17 Target Reading Skill
Using Sequence Identifying the sequence, or order, of important events can help you understand and remember the events. In this chapter you will practice these skills: understanding sequence and recognizing words that signal sequence.

Assessment Resources

Use the diagnosing readiness tests from **AYP Monitoring Assessments** to help you identify problems before students begin to study Africa.

Determine students' reading level and identify challenges:
Screening Tests, pp. 1–10

Evaluate students' verbal skills:
Critical Thinking and Reading Tests, pp. 25–34
Vocabulary Tests, pp. 45–52
Writing Tests, pp. 53–60

AFRICA

The name *Africa* may have come from the Latin word *aprica*, which means "sunny." In much of Africa, the sun does shine brightly. Each morning, the African sunrise awakens one eighth of the world's population, in more than fifty different countries. In the chapters that follow, you will spend the day with some of these people.

Guiding Questions

The text, photographs, maps, and charts in this book will help you discover answers to these Guiding Questions.

1. **Geography** What are the main physical features of Africa?

2. **History** How have historical events affected the cultures and nations of Africa?

3. **Culture** What features help define different African cultures?

4. **Government** What factors led to the development of different governments across Africa?

5. **Economics** What factors influence the ways in which Africans make a living?

Project Preview

You can also discover answers to the Guiding Questions by working on projects. Several project possibilities are listed on page 564 of this book.

Africa **349**

Guiding Questions

- This book was developed around five Guiding Questions about Africa. They appear on the reduced Student Edition page to the left. The Guiding Questions are intended as an organizational focus for the book. The Guiding Questions act as a kind of umbrella under which all of the material falls.

- You may wish to add your own Guiding Questions to the list in order to tailor them to your particular course.

- Draw students' attention to the Guiding Questions. Ask them to write the questions in their notebooks for future reference.

- In the Teacher's Edition, each section's themes are linked to a specific Guiding Question at the beginning of each chapter. Then, an activity at the end of the chapter returns to the Guiding Questions to review key concepts.

Project Preview

- The projects for this book are designed to provide students with hands-on involvement in the content area. Students are introduced to some projects on page 564.

- *Book Projects* give students directions on how to complete these projects, and more.

  All in One **Africa Teaching Resources,** *Book Project: Africa on Stage*, pp. 75–77; *Book Project: Africa Conference*, pp. 78–80; *Book Project: Traditional African Masks*, pp. 81–83

- Assign projects as small group activities, whole-class projects, or individual projects. Consider assigning a project at the beginning of the course.

Assess students' social studies skills:

- *Geographic Literacy Tests*, pp. 13–20
- *Visual Analysis Tests*, pp. 21–24
- *Communications Tests*, pp. 35–44

The World Studies program provides instruction and practice for all of these skills. Use students' test results to pinpoint the skills your students have mastered and the skills they need to practice. Then use *Correlation to Program Resources* to prescribe skills practice and reinforcement.

- *Correlation to Program Resources*, pp. 64–77

Objectives

- Describe the size and relative location of Africa.
- Examine how the location of African countries affects their economies.
- Compare the sizes of African countries.
- Identify some key physical features of Africa.
- Investigate vegetation and land use across the continent.

Prepare to Read

Build Background Knowledge **L2**

Conduct an Idea Wave (TE, p. T35) to help students generate a list of words or impressions related to Africa and write them on the board. Tell students that they will either confirm or revise these impressions during their study of the region.

Instruct

Investigate Africa **L2**

Guided Instruction

- Read the introductory, Location, and Regions paragraphs as a class. Tell students to divide the size of Africa by the size of the United States to figure out how many times larger Africa is.
- Hand out the *Regional Overview* worksheets. Direct students to fill in the worksheet as they study the Regional Overview.

All in One **Africa Teaching Resources,**
Regional Overview, pp. 89–91

Investigate Africa

Africa is the second-largest continent in the world after Asia. Africa's climate and physical geography are diverse, ranging from flat, arid deserts to tropical wet rain forests and high mountains. Africa also has a wide range of peoples with their own distinctive languages and cultures. It is a continent potentially rich in natural resources.

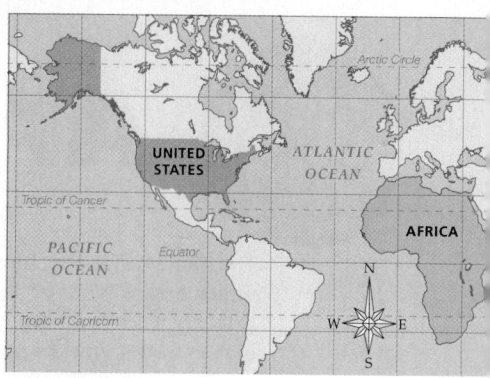

▲ **Tanzania**
The vast, flat grasslands of the savannas support a diverse population of animals.

LOCATION

1 Explore Africa's Location
How would you describe Africa's location? One way would be to compare where it is to where the United States is. What ocean lies between Africa and the United States? Find the Equator. What do you know about the climate of countries near the Equator? How do you think the climates of the United States might differ from the climates of Africa?

REGIONS

2 Estimate the Size of Africa
The United States is 3,500,000 square miles (9,064,958 square kilometers) in land area. How does Africa's size compare to that of the continental United States (all states except Alaska and Hawaii)? Measure mainland Africa at its widest point from east to west. Measure Africa from north to south. Now measure the United States the same way. How do they compare? Estimate Africa's area in square miles.

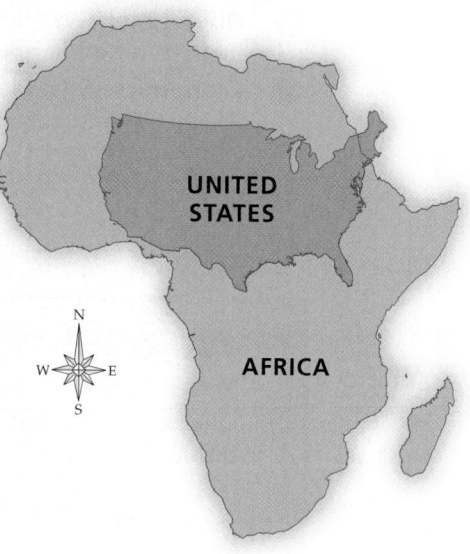

350 Africa

Answers

LOCATION the Atlantic Ocean; countries near the Equator usually have a warm, wet climate; Possible answer: The United States probably has a cooler, drier climate than Africa.

REGIONS Africa is more than three times larger than the United States. Africa is over 10.5 million square miles.

350 *Africa*

Differentiated Instruction

For Special Needs Students **L1**
Display *Color Transparency AF 22: Africa: Political (Base)* and *Color Transparency AF 23: Africa's Size Relative to Several Countries(Overlay)* to reinforce the size of Africa. Have students find each country on the world map in the Student Edition atlas. After they locate each country, refer them back to Africa's location on the map. Tell them to note the size difference. Then partner Special Needs students with Gifted and Talented students to repeat the calculations used to find out how many times larger Africa is than each of the countries.

Africa Transparencies, *Color Transparency AF 22: Africa: Political (Base); Color Transparency AF 23: Africa's Size Relative to Several Countries (Overlay)*

Political Africa

LOCATION

3 Predict How Location Affects Economics

When a country does not border any large body of water, it is described as being landlocked. Make a list of the African countries that are landlocked. Think about how being landlocked might limit the ability of a country to trade with other countries. How might being landlocked affect the economy of a country? How might landlocked countries trade in other ways?

▲ **Farafenni Market, Gambia**
This thriving street market is an important part of the local economy. Farmers sell their produce at such local markets, benefiting themselves and the community.

PLACE

4 Compare the Size of Countries

African countries vary in size. Sudan, Africa's largest country, is about five times the size of France. In contrast, the Seychelles, a group of islands off Africa's eastern coast, has an area of only 175 square miles (453 square kilometers). Find these countries on the map.

Regional Overview **351**

Mental Mapping

Everything in Its Place List the names of some African countries on the chalkboard. Include Egypt, Algeria, Nigeria, Ghana, Mali, Ethiopia, Tanzania, Kenya, Democratic Republic of Congo, and South Africa. Give students a few moments to study the map on this page and then have them close their books.

Distribute *Outline Map 21: Africa: Political*

and ask student to locate as many countries on the map as they can. Tell them to write the names of the countries they can't locate on the water area of the map. Ask them to keep the map so that they may add, correct, or update information as they work though the chapters.

All in One **Africa Teaching Resources,**
Outline Map 21: Africa: Political, p. 92

Independent Practice

Form students into pairs and have them do research to find out the size of one of the other six continents in square miles. Ask them to calculate how much larger or smaller Africa is compared to the continent.

Monitor Progress

Circulate and make sure the pairs are using a reliable source and making the correct calculations.

Political Africa L2

Guided Instruction

■ Read the Location paragraph. Use the Think-Write-Pair-Share strategy (TE, p. T36) to elicit student responses.

■ Have students make a table listing the countries that share a border with a body of water and the name of the body of water. Ask **What types of economic activities might these countries have that landlocked countries do not?** *(Possible answers: Fishing, shipping industries)*

■ Ask students to continue completing the *Regional Overview* worksheet.

All in One **Africa Teaching Resources,**
Regional Overview, pp. 89–91

■ Read the Place paragraph. Have students use the map scale to measure the widths of Algeria and Gabon. How do these countries compare to Sudan? *(Algeria is close to Sudan in size, but Gabon is much smaller.)*

Independent Practice

Have students study the map and predict which African country has the largest area and which has the smallest. Then have them use the Country Databanks (pp. 454–457, 476–483, 508–513, 540–547) to determine if they were correct. *(Sudan is the largest country; Seychelles the smallest.)*

Monitor Progress

Circulate to make sure students can find the appropriate information in the Country Databanks.

Answers

LOCATION Possible answer: Landlocked countries must work with other countries to ship their exports, or find other ways to make money besides exporting goods.

Physical Africa L2

Guided Instruction

- Read the Place paragraph together with students. Ask students to name three deserts on the map besides the Sahara. *(Three of the following: Kalahari Desert, Namib Desert, Libyan Desert, Arabian Desert)*

- Ask **Which country has the highest elevation?** *(Ethiopia)* **How can you tell?** *(Much of the country is colored brown, which is the color that represents the second highest elevation on the map.)*

- Tell students to continue completing the *Regional Overview* worksheet.

  All in One **Africa Teaching Resources,** *Regional Overview,* pp. 89–91

Independent Practice

Have students work individually to complete *Reading a Physical Map* and *Elevation on a Map* to practice using physical maps.

  All in One **Africa Teaching Resources,** *Reading a Physical Map,* p. 93; *Elevation on a Map,* p. 94

Monitor Progress

Circulate while students complete their worksheets. Provide assistance as needed.

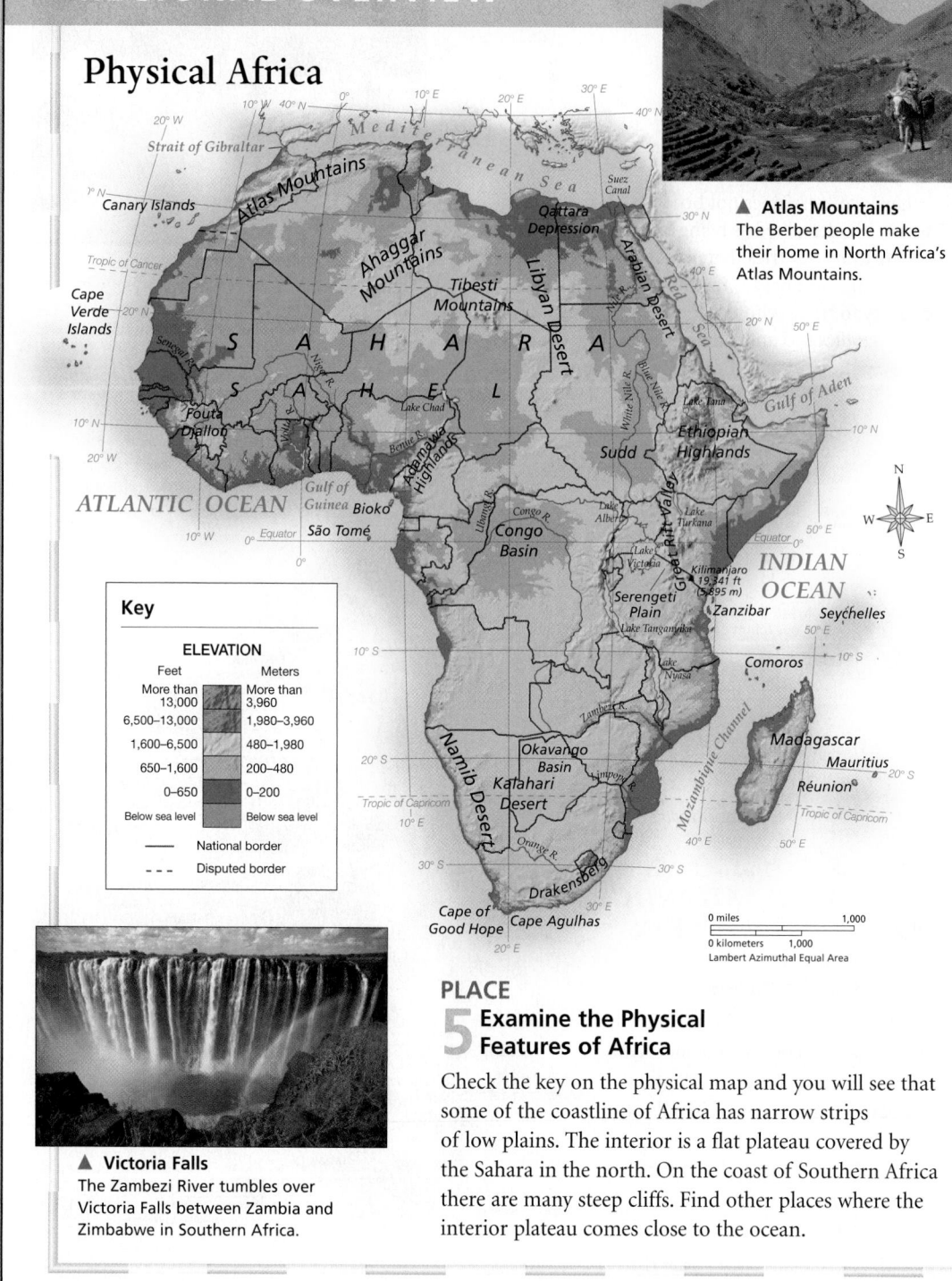

Physical Africa

▲ **Atlas Mountains**
The Berber people make their home in North Africa's Atlas Mountains.

Key

ELEVATION

Feet	Meters
More than 13,000	More than 3,960
6,500–13,000	1,980–3,960
1,600–6,500	480–1,980
650–1,600	200–480
0–650	0–200
Below sea level	Below sea level

—— National border
- - - Disputed border

0 miles 1,000
0 kilometers 1,000
Lambert Azimuthal Equal Area

▲ **Victoria Falls**
The Zambezi River tumbles over Victoria Falls between Zambia and Zimbabwe in Southern Africa.

PLACE

5 Examine the Physical Features of Africa

Check the key on the physical map and you will see that some of the coastline of Africa has narrow strips of low plains. The interior is a flat plateau covered by the Sahara in the north. On the coast of Southern Africa there are many steep cliffs. Find other places where the interior plateau comes close to the ocean.

352 Africa

Differentiated Instruction

For Less Proficient Readers L2

Show students the Africa flyover segment on the Passport to the World CD-ROM. Ask students to list several of the region's major landforms on the board after viewing the segment.

  ◉ *Africa Flyover,* **Passport to the World CD-ROM**

Answer

PLACE along the southwest coast

Africa: Land Use

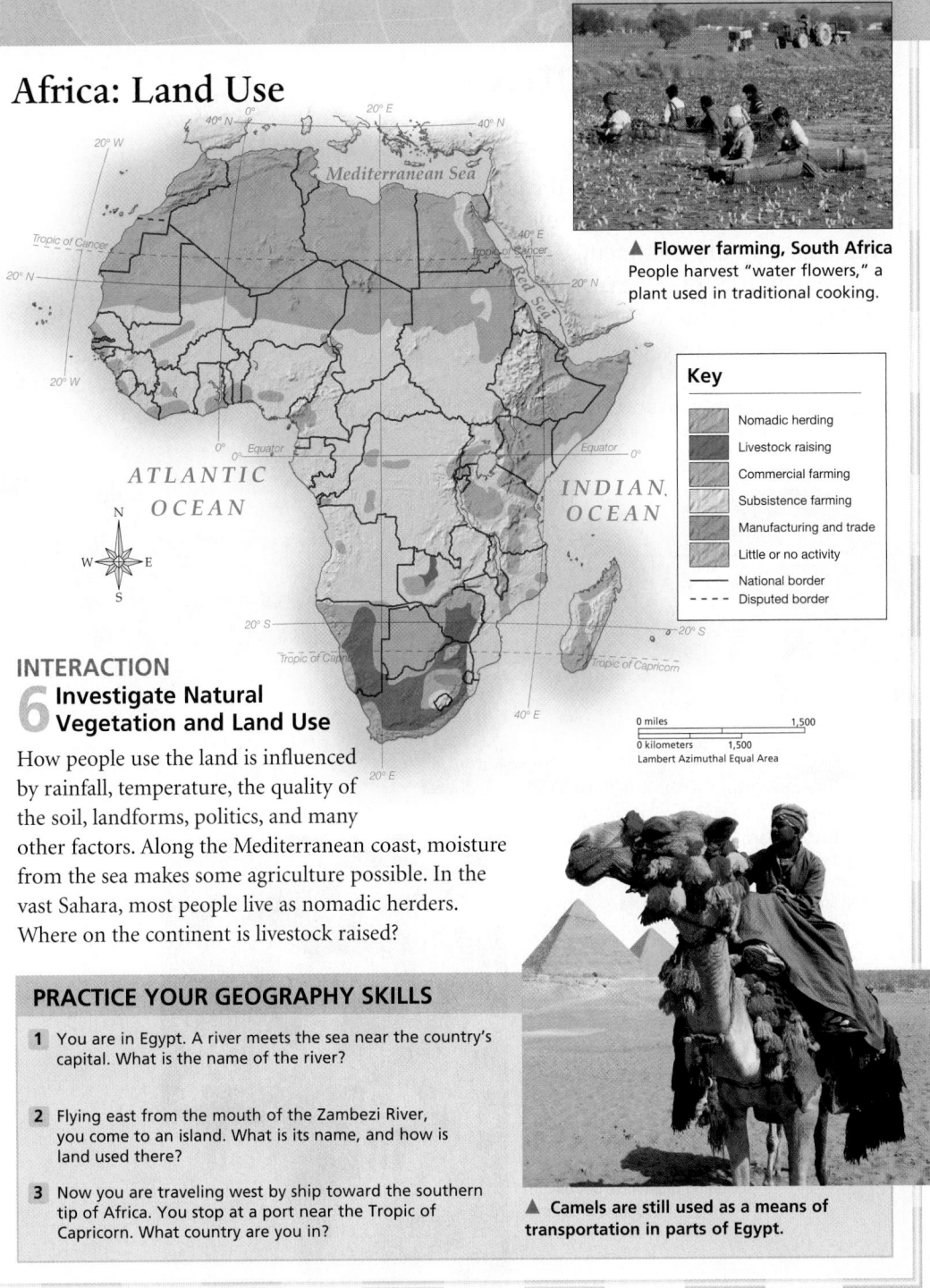

Mediterranean Sea

ATLANTIC OCEAN

INDIAN OCEAN

Key

	Nomadic herding
	Livestock raising
	Commercial farming
	Subsistence farming
	Manufacturing and trade
	Little or no activity
——	National border
- - -	Disputed border

0 miles 1,500
0 kilometers 1,500
Lambert Azimuthal Equal Area

▲ **Flower farming, South Africa**
People harvest "water flowers," a plant used in traditional cooking.

INTERACTION

6 Investigate Natural Vegetation and Land Use

How people use the land is influenced by rainfall, temperature, the quality of the soil, landforms, politics, and many other factors. Along the Mediterranean coast, moisture from the sea makes some agriculture possible. In the vast Sahara, most people live as nomadic herders. Where on the continent is livestock raised?

PRACTICE YOUR GEOGRAPHY SKILLS

1 You are in Egypt. A river meets the sea near the country's capital. What is the name of the river?

2 Flying east from the mouth of the Zambezi River, you come to an island. What is its name, and how is land used there?

3 Now you are traveling west by ship toward the southern tip of Africa. You stop at a port near the Tropic of Capricorn. What country are you in?

▲ **Camels are still used as a means of transportation in parts of Egypt.**

Regional Overview **353**

Africa: Land Use L2

Guided Instruction

- Read the Interaction paragraph and have students study the land use map.
- Have students compare this map to the map on page 352. Ask **How is the land in the Atlas Mountains mainly used?** *(for commercial farming)*
- Direct students to finish the *Regional Overview* worksheet.

  All in One **Africa Teaching Resources,** *Regional Overview*, pp. 89–91

Independent Practice

Have students compare the map on this page to the map of Africa's climate regions on p. 365. Ask them to synthesize the information from the two maps to draw conclusions about the types of land use that occur in the various climate regions. *(Possible answers: Arid regions can only support nomadic herding, but subsistence farming takes place in a number of climate regions.)*

Monitor Progress

Circulate to make sure students are drawing appropriate conclusions. If students need help synthesizing information, have them practice the skill on the Social Studies Skills Tutor CD-ROM.

  ⊙ *Synthesizing Information,* **Social Studies Skills Tutor CD-ROM**

Differentiated Instruction

For English Language Learners L2
Review each type of land use found in the map key with students. Use photographs from the text or from other books and magazines to provide a visual association for each type of land use. For example, have students turn to page 355 in the Regional Overview to see a photo of someone cultivating the land in Kenya.

Answers

INTERACTION in the south

PRACTICE YOUR GEOGRAPHY SKILLS

1. the Nile River

2. Madagascar; nomadic herding, commercial farming

3. Namibia

Focus on Countries in Africa

[L2]

Guided Instruction

- Read the introduction and captions as a class.

- Have students list the ten countries shown in yellow on the map that they will be studying in depth. *(Egypt, Algeria, Nigeria, Ghana, Mali, Ethiopia, Tanzania, Kenya, Democratic Republic of Congo, and South Africa)* Then ask students to use the Country Databanks to determine in which region each country is located. *(Egypt, Algeria—North Africa; Nigeria, Ghana, Mali—West Africa; Ethiopia, Tanzania, Kenya—East Africa; Democratic Republic of Congo, South Africa—Central and Southern Africa.)*

- Ask **What is Africa's third largest country?** *(Democratic Republic of Congo)* **Where do almost all of the people in Egypt live?** *(the fertile valley of the Nile)*

Independent Practice

Form students into five groups. Assign each group one of the countries pictured on pages 354–355. Have groups use the Country Databanks (pp. 454–457, 476–483, 508–513, 540–547), DK Compact Atlas of the World, and the DK World Desk Reference Online (see student pages for Web code) to research the country they have been assigned. Ask groups to focus on the geography, climate, government, and people of the countries. Then, have each group present the information they gathered to the class.

Monitor Progress

Use *Rubric for Assessing an Oral Presentation* to assess students' presentations.

All in One **Africa Teaching Resources,** *Rubric for Assessing an Oral Presentation,* p. 95

Focus on Countries in Africa

Now that you've investigated the geography of Africa, take a closer look at some of the countries that make up this continent. The map shows all of the countries of Africa. The ten countries you will study in depth in the second half of this book are shown in yellow on the map.

Go Online PHSchool.com   Use Web Code lap-5020 for the **interactive maps** on these pages.

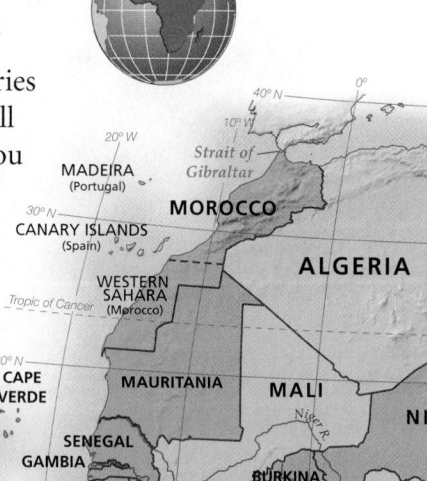

▲ **Nigeria**
The Hausa-Fulani, Igbo, Yoruba, and a number of other, smaller ethnic groups make up Nigeria, where more than 200 languages are spoken. Nigeria is a major oil-producing country.

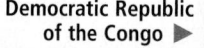

Democratic Republic of the Congo ▶
The Democratic Republic of the Congo is Africa's third-largest country. It is rich in minerals including diamonds, petroleum, cobalt, and copper.

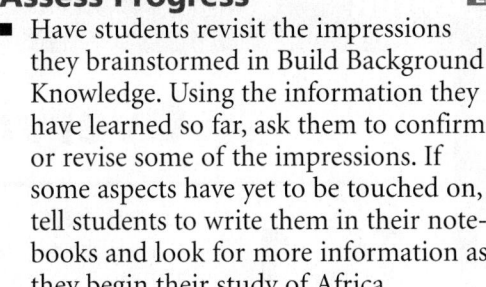

Egypt
Almost all of the people of Egypt live in the fertile valley of the Nile. The vast desert on either side of this river is almost completely unpopulated.

Key

— National border
- - - Disputed border

▨ Countries with in-depth coverage

▨ Non-feature countries

▲ **Kenya**
Two thirds of Kenya's people live in the countryside. Many Kenyan women raise cash crops or work on plantations, while the men work in the cities.

0 miles 1,000
0 kilometers 1,000
Lambert Azimuthal Equal Area

▲ **South Africa**
South Africa, at Africa's southern tip, is bordered by oceans on three sides. It is a resource-rich country with a strong economy.

Assess and Reteach

Assess Progress L2

■ Have students revisit the impressions they brainstormed in Build Background Knowledge. Using the information they have learned so far, ask them to confirm or revise some of the impressions. If some aspects have yet to be touched on, tell students to write them in their notebooks and look for more information as they begin their study of Africa.

■ Ask students to complete the Practice Your Geography Skills questions on page 353.

Reteach L1

For more exploration of the region, have students view the Africa portion of the Passport to the World CD-ROM and complete the Customs Quiz.

◉ *Africa*, **Passport to the World CD-ROM**

Extend L3

Portfolio Activity
One way of assessing students' accomplishments is by having them build a portfolio of their best work. To begin their portfolios for Africa, have students choose a country in Africa that they will not be exploring in depth in this textbook. Have students research their country to create a travel poster that encourages people to visit the country. Tell students to use text, illustrations, and maps in their advertisements.

■ Give students *Using the Library* to teach them how they can gather information for their advertisements.

All in One Africa Teaching Resources, *Using the Library*, p. 96

Background: Global Perspectives

Generating Energy Because Kenya lacks fuel resources, it relies entirely on other countries for oil. Today, Kenya is finding other ways to provide power for factories, homes, and offices. Hydroelectric plants have been built and other, less common, sources of power have been developed, such as geothermal energy, or energy from heat deep within the earth. The sugar industry is even producing alcohol to use as fuel for its factories.

11 Africa: Physical Geography

Overview

Section 1
Land and Water
1. Learn about Africa's four regions and its major landforms.
2. Find out about Africa's major rivers.

Section 2
Climate and Vegetation
1. Discover the factors that influence Africa's climate.
2. Learn the characteristics of each of Africa's vegetation regions.
3. Find out how climate can affect the health of people in Africa.

Section 3
Resources and Land Use
1. Discover the ways in which Africans make use of their agricultural resources.
2. Learn about the mineral and energy resources found in Africa.
3. Find out what African countries are doing to improve their economic health.

The Geography of Africa
Length: 5 minutes, 8 seconds
Use with Section 1
This segment explores the major geographic features of Africa. Students will learn about the Sahara and Kalahari deserts, the savannas, and the rain forests, as well as the Great Rift Valley, Mt. Kilimanjaro, the Nile River, and Lake Victoria.

Technology Resources

Students use embedded Web codes to access Internet activities, chapter self-tests, and additional map practice. They may also access Dorling Kindersley's Online Desk Reference to learn more about each country they study.

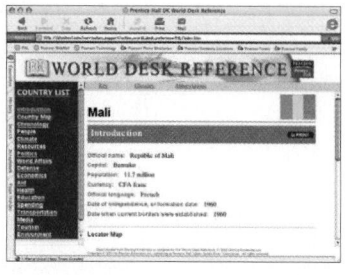

Use the Interactive Textbook to make content and concepts come alive through animations, videos, and activities that accompany the complete basal text—online and on CD-ROM.

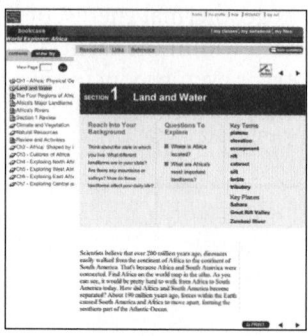

Use this complete suite of powerful teaching tools to make planning lessons and administering tests quicker and easier.

Reading and Assessment

Reading and Vocabulary Instruction

⟳ Model the Target Reading Skill

Clarifying Meaning Explain to students that rereading, paraphrasing, and summarizing can help them understand a text. When they come across a section they do not understand, rereading and then paraphrasing it can help students comprehend and remember the information. Students should finish by summarizing what they have learned to understand key points. Model this skill by thinking about a paragraph from Section 1 aloud:

"The second paragraph on page 359 begins, *The region of North Africa is marked in places by rocky mountains. It is also home to seemingly endless stretches of the world's largest desert, the Sahara.* These sentences are a bit confusing. I'll reread them to get a better understanding of what they say. Now I understand: North Africa contains some mountains and large areas of the Sahara, the world's largest desert.

Now that I have reread and paraphrased part of the paragraph, I will read the rest and summarize it to make sure I remember the important points: The four regions of Africa—North Africa, West Africa, East Africa, and Central and Southern Africa—contain many types of land, including deserts, grasslands, plateaus, rain forests, mountains, and swamps."

Use the following worksheets from All-in-One Africa Teaching Resources (pp. 112–114) to support this chapter's Target Reading Skill.

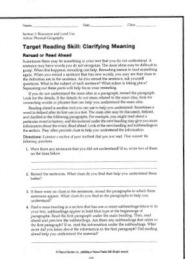  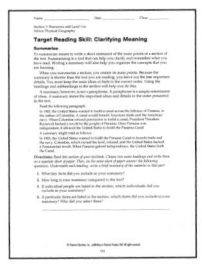

Vocabulary Builder
High-Use Academic Words
Use these steps to teach this chapter's high-use words:

1. Have students rate how well they know each word on their Word Knowledge worksheets (All-in-One Africa Teaching Resources, p. 115).
2. Pronounce each word and ask students to repeat it.
3. Provide a brief definition or sample sentence (provided on TE pp. 359, 365, and 375).
4. Work with students as they fill in the "Definition or Example" column of their Word Knowledge worksheets.

Assessment

Formal Assessment
Test students' understanding of core knowledge and skills.

Chapter Tests A and B, All-in-One Africa Teaching Resources, pp. 132–137

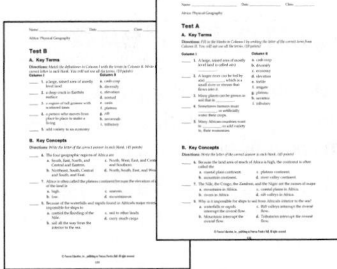

Customize the Chapter Tests to suit your needs.
ExamView® Test Bank CD-ROM

Skills Assessment
Assess geographic literacy.
MapMaster Skills, Student Edition, pp. 357, 360, 365, 369, 377, 380

Assess reading and comprehension.
Target Reading Skills, Student Edition, pp. 361, 371, 376, and in Section Assessments

Chapter 11 Assessment, Eastern Hemisphere Reading and Vocabulary Study Guide, p. 15

Performance Assessment
Assess students' performance on this chapter's Writing Activities using the following rubrics from All-in-One Africa Teaching Resources.

Rubric for Assessing a Writing Assignment, p. 130
Rubric for Assessing a Bar Graph, p. 131

Assess students' work through performance tasks.
Small Group Activity: Simulation: Magazine Article on an African River, All-in-One Africa Teaching Resources, pp. 118–121

Online Assessment
Have students check their own understanding.
Chapter Self-Test

Test Preparation
Screening Tests and Diagnosing Readiness Tests, AYP Monitoring Assessments, pp. 1–11, 13–63

Section 1 Land and Water

 1 period, .5 block

Social Studies Objectives

1. Learn about Africa's four regions and its major landforms.
2. Find out about Africa's major rivers.

Reading/Language Arts Objective

Reread to better understand the meaning of unfamiliar words or ideas in a text.

Prepare to Read	Instructional Resources	Differentiated Instruction
Build Background Knowledge Have students predict which geographic features they will learn about by previewing the section. **Set a Purpose for Reading** Have students evaluate statements on the *Reading Readiness Guide.* **Preview Key Terms** Teach the section's Key Terms. **Target Reading Skill** Introduce the section's Target Reading Skill of **rereading.**	**All in One Africa Teaching Resources** **L2** Reading Readiness Guide, p. 101 **L2** Reread or Read Ahead, p. 112	**Spanish Reading and Vocabulary Study Guide** **L1** Chapter 11, Section 1, pp. 87–88 ELL

Instruct	Instructional Resources	Differentiated Instruction
Africa's Regions and Landforms Ask about the population and landforms of different regions in Africa. **Africa's Rivers** Discuss Africa's four major rivers and their uses. **Target Reading Skill** Review **rereading.**	**All in One Africa Teaching Resources** **L2** Guided Reading and Review, p. 102 **L2** Reading Readiness Guide, p. 101 **Africa Transparencies** **L2** Section Reading Support Transparency AF 33 **World Studies Video Program** **L2** The Geography of Africa	**All in One Africa Teaching Resources** **L3** Enrichment, p. 116 AR, GT **L1** Outline Map 20: Africa: Physical, p. 126 ELL, LPR, SN **Teacher's Edition** **L3** For Gifted and Talented, TE pp. 360, 362 **L3** For Advanced Readers, TE p. 360 **L1** For Special Needs Students, TE p. 362 **Spanish Support** **L2** Guided Reading and Review (Spanish), p. 124 ELL

Assess and Reteach	Instructional Resources	Differentiated Instruction
Assess Progress Evaluate student comprehension with the section assessment and section quiz. **Reteach** Assign the Reading and Vocabulary Study Guide to help struggling students. **Extend** Extend the lesson by assigning a Small Group Activity.	**All in One Africa Teaching Resources** **L2** Section Quiz, p. 103 **L3** Small Group Activity: Simulation: Magazine Article on an African River, pp. 118–121 Rubric for Assessing a Writing Assignment, p. 130 **Reading and Vocabulary Study Guide** **L1** Chapter 11, Section 1, pp. 122–124	**Spanish Support** **L2** Section Quiz (Spanish), p. 125 ELL

Key

L1 Basic to Average   **L3** Average to Advanced

L2 For All Students

LPR Less Proficient Readers
AR Advanced Readers
SN Special Needs Students

GT Gifted and Talented
ELL English Language Learners

Section 2 Climate and Vegetation

 2 periods, 1 block (includes Skills for Life)

Social Studies Objectives
1. Discover the factors that influence Africa's climate.
2. Learn the characteristics of each of Africa's vegetation regions.
3. Find out how climate can affect the health of people in Africa.

Reading/Language Arts Objective
Paraphrase to understand and remember what you have read.

Section Lesson Planner

Prepare to Read	Instructional Resources	Differentiated Instruction
Build Background Knowledge Have students look at a climate map to predict the places in Africa where people are most likely to live. **Set a Purpose for Reading** Have students begin to fill out the *Reading Readiness Guide.* **Preview Key Terms** Teach the section's Key Terms. **Target Reading Skill** Introduce the section's Target Reading Skill of **paraphrasing.**	**All in One Africa Teaching Resources** L2 Reading Readiness Guide, p. 105 L2 Paraphrase, p. 113	**Spanish Reading and Vocabulary Study Guide** L1 Chapter 11, Section 2, pp. 89–90 ELL

Instruct	Instructional Resources	Differentiated Instruction
What Influences Climate? Ask questions about Africa's climate and the factors that affect it. **Vegetation Regions of Africa** Discuss how climate affects vegetation in the different regions of Africa. **Climate and Health** Ask about how the rain forests can breed diseases that pose a danger to humans. **Target Reading Skill** Review **paraphrasing.**	**All in One Africa Teaching Resources** L2 Guided Reading and Review, p. 106 L2 Reading Readiness Guide, p. 105 **Africa Transparencies** L2 Transparency B15: Outline L2 Section Reading Support Transparency AF 34	**All in One Africa Teaching Resources** L3 Reading a Climate Graph, p. 124 AR, GT L3 Activity Shop Interdisciplinary: Desertification, pp. 122–123 AR, GT L2 Skills for Life, p. 117 AR, GT, LPR, SN **Teacher's Edition** L1 For English Language Learners, p. 366 L3 For Advanced Readers, p. 366 L3 For Gifted and Talented, TE p. 369 L1 For Less Proficient Readers, TE p. 370 **Spanish Support** L2 Guided Reading and Review (Spanish), p. 126 ELL

Assess and Reteach	Instructional Resources	Differentiated Instruction
Assess Progress Evaluate student comprehension with the section assessment and section quiz. **Reteach** Assign the Reading and Vocabulary Study Guide to help struggling students. **Extend** Extend the lesson by assigning a research project.	**All in One Africa Teaching Resources** L2 Section Quiz, p. 107 Rubric for Assessing a Writing Assignment, p. 130 **Reading and Vocabulary Study Guide** L1 Chapter 11, Section 2, pp. 125–127	**All in One Africa Teaching Resources** L1 Reading a Diagram, p. 125 ELL, LPR, SN **Teacher's Edition** L1 For Less Proficient Readers, TE p. 373 **Spanish Support** L2 Section Quiz (Spanish), p. 127 ELL

Key

L1 Basic to Average   L3 Average to Advanced   LPR Less Proficient Readers   GT Gifted and Talented

L2 For All Students   AR Advanced Readers   ELL English Language Learners

SN Special Needs Students

Section 3 Resources and Land Use

 2.5 periods, 1.25 blocks (includes Chapter Review and Assessment)

Social Studies Objectives

1. Discover the ways in which Africans make use of their agricultural resources.
2. Learn about the mineral and energy resources found in Africa.
3. Find out what African countries are doing to improve their economic health.

Reading/Language Arts Objective

Summarize to enhance comprehension of a text.

Prepare to Read	Instructional Resources	Differentiated Instruction
Build Background Knowledge Have students preview the section and predict how they think land resources might be used in Africa. **Set a Purpose for Reading** Have students evaluate statements on the *Reading Readiness Guide*. **Preview Key Terms** Teach the section's Key Terms. **Target Reading Skill** Introduce the section's Target Reading Skill of **summarizing**.	**All in One Africa Teaching Resources** L2 Reading Readiness Guide, p. 109 L2 Summarize, p. 114	**Spanish Reading and Vocabulary Study Guide** L1 Chapter 11, Section 3, pp. 91–92 ELL

Instruct	Instructional Resources	Differentiated Instruction
Agricultural Resources Ask questions about African farmers, their crops, and the challenges they face. **Target Reading Skill** Review **summarizing**. **Natural Resources** **Improving Economic Health** Discuss Africa's mineral resources and how they affect the economy.	**All in One Africa Teaching Resources** L2 Guided Reading and Review, p. 110 L2 Reading Readiness Guide, p. 109 **Africa Transparencies** L2 Section Reading Support Transparency AF 35	**All in One Africa Teaching Resources** L3 Mokhtar of the Atlas Mountains, pp. 127–128 AR, GT **Teacher's Edition** L1 For English Language Learners, TE p. 376 L3 For Advanced Readers, TE p. 376 **Africa Transparencies** L1 Color Transparency AF 22: Africa: Political ELL, LPR, SN **Spanish Support** L2 Guided Reading and Review (Spanish), p. 128 ELL

Assess and Reteach	Instructional Resources	Differentiated Instruction
Assess Progress Evaluate student comprehension with the section assessment and section quiz. **Reteach** Assign the Reading and Vocabulary Study Guide to help struggling students. **Extend** Extend the lesson by assigning an oral report.	**All in One Africa Teaching Resources** L2 Section Quiz, p. 111 Rubric for Assessing a Writing Assignment, p. 130 L2 Word Knowledge, p. 115 L2 Vocabulary Development, p. 129 Rubric for Assessing a Bar Graph, p. 131 L2 Chapter Tests A and B, pp. 132–137 **Reading and Vocabulary Study Guide** L1 Chapter 11, Section 3, pp. 128–130	**Spanish Support** L2 Section Quiz (Spanish), p. 129 ELL L2 Chapter Summary (Spanish), p. 130 ELL L2 Vocabulary Development (Spanish), p. 131 ELL

Key

L1 Basic to Average   L3 Average to Advanced
L2 For All Students

LPR Less Proficient Readers   GT Gifted and Talented
AR Advanced Readers   ELL English Language Learners
SN Special Needs Students

Reading Background

Previewing and Prereading

To improve their learning, students should preview each section and set a purpose for reading. Students who do a brief, preliminary reading of complex material are in a strategic position to take control of their learning and comprehension. Previewing helps students consider what they already know about a topic they will be studying and gives some idea of what a text selection is about before they read it. Previewing also helps students identify the text structure and develop a mental framework for ideas they will encounter in the text. This can help students formulate a more realistic reading and study plan. Follow the steps below to teach students how to preview and preread.

1. Tell students that previewing will help them identify the text structure and develop a mental outline of ideas they will encounter in the text.
2. List the various text features you will be previewing in the order in which you would like students to examine them: for example, section title, text headings, list of Key Terms, introduction, questions or tasks in the reading selection, photographs, drawings, maps, charts and other visuals in the text.

Focus students' attention on some of these items, or ask students to look at all of them.

3. Prompt students to reflect after examining various text features. They may ask themselves questions such as: What is this reading selection about? What are some key words I will learn? How should I tackle this reading and divide up the task?

Word Wizard

Encourage students to connect their classroom learning to extracurricular activities and interests. This will not only help to engage students in their academic exercises but will also improve learning outside of the academic setting.

Provide students with a list of Key Terms and high-use words as they are encountered in the text. Invite students to look and listen for the words as they are used in the media (newspapers, radio and television, movies), on the Internet, and in conversation. Have students bring in examples of the words used in these situations. This is an ideal activity for gifted and talented students.

World Studies Background

Lake Victoria

Lake Victoria is Africa's largest lake, covering a total area of 26,828 square miles (69,484 square kilometers). This massive body of water is located mainly in Tanzania and Uganda, but also borders Kenya. The region around the shores of Lake Victoria is one of the most densely populated in Africa. Several million people live within 50 miles of the lake.

The Sahara

The Sahara, the largest desert in the world, covers nearly all of North Africa. As a result of its brutal climate, however, its population density is very low. Though roughly the size of the United States, the

Sahara has an estimated population of only about 2.5 million people—less than one person per square mile—compared with the United States' population of about 280 million people, or about 76 people per square mile.

Africa's Economy

Africa's economy is largely underdeveloped. Many of its countries' economies are dependent on only a few exports, and are therefore sensitive to price fluctuations in those commodities. Other countries' economies have declined due to long periods of internal warfare. Many of Africa's countries are trying to diversify their economies by becoming more industrialized.

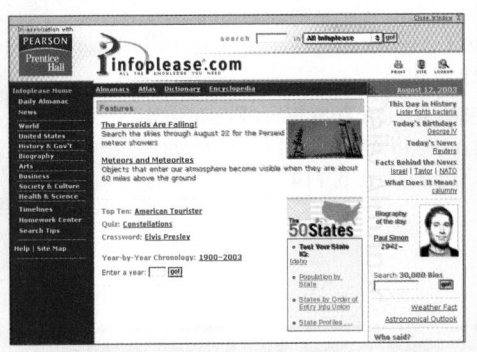

Infoplease® provides a wealth of useful information for the classroom. You can use this resource to strengthen your background on the subjects covered in this chapter. Have students visit this advertising-free site as a starting point for projects requiring research.

Use Web code **lad-5100** for **Infoplease®**.

Chapter 11

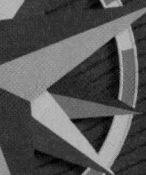

Chapter 11 Africa: Physical Geography

Guiding Questions

Remind students about the Guiding Questions introduced at the beginning of this section.

Section 1 refers to **Guiding Question 1**
What are the main physical features of Africa? (*Africa's main physical features include the Sahara, Namib, and Kalahari deserts; grasslands; Mount Kilimanjaro; coastal plains; the Great Rift Valley; and the Nile, Congo, Zambezi, and Niger rivers.*)

Section 2 refers to **Guiding Question 1**
What are the main physical features of Africa? (*Africa's physical features can affect its climate. For example, temperatures are cooler at higher elevations, such as in the mountains. Climate can also affect physical features. The Sahara and the Sahel make up much of northern Africa. These regions receive very little rainfall.*)

Section 3 refers to **Guiding Question 5**
What factors influence the ways in which Africans make a living? (*Most Africans are farmers. The type of land and amount of rainfall in their region affect what types of crops they grow. Parts of Africa are rich in natural resources. Many people in these regions work in mines.*)

Target Reading Skill

In this chapter, students will learn and apply the reading skill of clarifying meaning. Use the following worksheets to help students practice this skill:

> **All in One** **Africa Teaching Resources,** *Reread or Read Ahead,* p. 112; *Paraphrase,* p. 113; *Summarize,* p. 114

Chapter Preview

This chapter will introduce you to the geography of Africa and show you how geography affects the people of the continent.

Section 1
Land and Water

Section 2
Climate and Vegetation

Section 3
Resources and Land Use

Target Reading Skill

Clarifying Meaning In this chapter you will focus on clarifying, or better understanding, the meaning of what you read. Rereading, paraphrasing, and summarizing can help you better understand sentences and passages.

▶ Elephants walk across the plains below Africa's tallest mountain, Mount Kilimanjaro.

Differentiated Instruction

The following Teacher Edition strategies are suitable for students of varying abilities.

Advanced Readers, pp. 360, 366, 376
English Language Learners, pp. 366, 376
Gifted and Talented, pp. 360, 362, 369
Less Proficient Readers, pp. 370, 373
Special Needs Students, p. 362

Bibliography

For the Teacher
McDade, Barbara E. *Geography of Sub-Saharan Africa,* 2nd ed. Prentice Hall, 2002.
Cutter, Charles H. *Africa 2003 (World Today Series, Africa).* Stryker-Post Publications, 2003.
Reader, John. *Africa.* National Geographic, 2001.

For the Student
L2 Ayo, Yvonne. *Eyewitness: Africa.* Dorling Kindersley, 2000.
L2 Bowden, Rob, and Tony Binns. *The Changing Face of South Africa.* Raintree/Steck-Vaughn, 2002.
L3 Buettner, Dan. *Africatrek: A Journey by Bicycle Through Africa.* Lerner Publications, 1997.

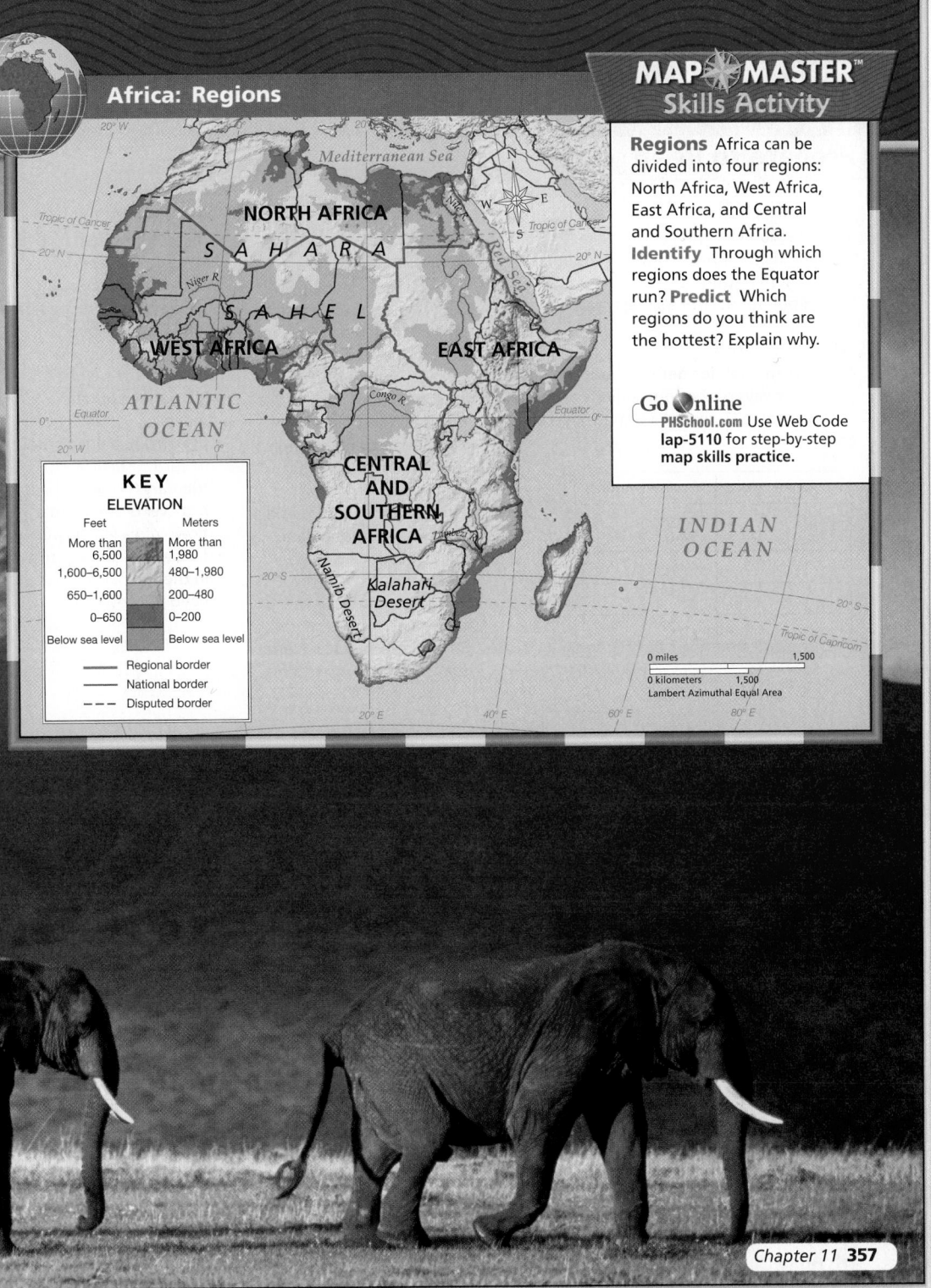

MAP✦MASTER™
Skills Activity

Regions Africa can be divided into four regions: North Africa, West Africa, East Africa, and Central and Southern Africa. **Identify** Through which regions does the Equator run? **Predict** Which regions do you think are the hottest? Explain why.

Go Online
PHSchool.com Use Web Code **lap-5110** for step-by-step map skills practice.

Africa: Regions

NORTH AFRICA
SAHARA
SAHEL
WEST AFRICA
EAST AFRICA
CENTRAL AND SOUTHERN AFRICA
ATLANTIC OCEAN
INDIAN OCEAN
Mediterranean Sea
Niger R.
Congo R.
Namib Desert
Kalahari Desert
Tropic of Cancer
Tropic of Capricorn
Equator

KEY
ELEVATION

Feet	Meters
More than 6,500	More than 1,980
1,600–6,500	480–1,980
650–1,600	200–480
0–650	0–200
Below sea level	Below sea level

—— Regional border
—— National border
- - - Disputed border

0 miles 1,500
0 kilometers 1,500
Lambert Azimuthal Equal Area

MAP✦MASTER™
Skills Activity

- Have students study the map of Africa on this page. Then have them locate the continent on the map of the World on pp. 364–365 of their textbooks. Ask them to note where Africa is in relation to Asia, Europe, and North America.

- Have students name some of the deserts, rivers, and bodies of water located in or bordering Africa.

Go Online PHSchool.com Students may practice their map skills using the interactive online version of this map.

Using the Visual   L2

Reach Into Your Background Tell students to examine the photograph on pp. 356–357 and read the accompanying caption. Ask them to identify the physical features and types of vegetation in the photograph. Do they have similar features and vegetation in their region? If not, how do they differ?

Answers

MAP✦MASTER™ Skills Activity **Identify** Central and Southern Africa and East Africa
Predict Possible answer: The regions nearest the Equator are the hottest because they receive the most direct light from the sun.

Chapter Resources

Teaching Resources
Letter Home, p. 99
L2 Vocabulary Development, p. 129
L2 Skills for Life, p. 117
L2 Chapter Tests A and B, pp. 132–137

Spanish Support
Spanish Letter Home, p. 123
Spanish Chapter Summary, p. 130
Spanish Vocabulary Development, p. 131

Media and Technology
L1 Student Edition on Audio CD
L1 Guided Reading Audiotapes, English and Spanish
L2 Social Studies Skills Tutor CD-ROM
ExamView® Test Bank CD-ROM

PRENTICE HALL
Presentation EXPRESS™
Teach • Connect • Inspire

Teach this chapter's content using the PresentationExpress™ CD-ROM including:
- slide shows
- transparencies
- interactive maps and media
- *ExamView®* QuickTake Presenter

Section 1
Step-by-Step Instruction

Objectives

Social Studies
1. Learn about Africa's four regions and its major landforms.
2. Find out about Africa's major rivers.

Reading/Language Arts
Reread to better understand the meaning of unfamiliar words or ideas in a text.

Prepare to Read

Build Background Knowledge L2
Ask students to preview the headings, photographs, and maps in this lesson. Ask them to compile a list of the geographic features they expect to learn about as they read the lesson. Use the Think-Write-Pair-Share participation strategy (TE, p. T36) to guide the discussion.

Set a Purpose for Reading L2
- Preview the Objectives.
- Read each statement in the *Reading Readiness Guide* aloud. Ask students to mark the statements true or false.
- Have students discuss the statements in pairs or groups of four, then mark their worksheets again. Use the Numbered Heads participation strategy (TE, p. T36) to call on students to share their group's perspectives.

  All in One Africa Teaching Resources, *Reading Readiness Guide,* p. 101

Preview Key Terms L2
Pronounce each Key Term, then ask the students to say the word with you. Provide a simple explanation such as, "After climbing up the steep slope on one edge of the plateau, you'll be tired but you'll have a great view."

Section 1
Land and Water

Prepare to Read

Objectives
In this section you will
1. Learn about Africa's four regions and its major landforms.
2. Find out about Africa's major rivers.

Taking Notes
As you read, look for details about the land and waterways of the four regions of Africa. Copy the table below, and use it to record your findings.

Region of Africa	Physical Features
North	• Land: • Water:

Target Reading Skill
Reread Rereading is a strategy that can help you clarify words and ideas in the text. If you do not understand a certain passage, reread it to look for connections among the words and sentences.

In the following example, you may not know what *level* means. "Much of Africa is made up of raised, mostly level areas of land. Not all of Africa is level, however. Each of Africa's four regions has mountains." If you reread, you will see that level land is land without mountains.

Key Terms
- **plateau** (pla TOH) *n.* a large, level area that rises above the surrounding land; has at least one side with a steep slope
- **elevation** (el uh VAY shun) *n.* the height of land above or below sea level
- **rift** (rift) *n.* a deep crack in Earth's surface
- **tributary** (TRIB yoo tehr ee) *n.* a river or stream that flows into a larger river
- **fertile** (FUR tul) *adj.* rich in the substances plants need to grow well

Dinosaurs like this allosaurus once lived in Africa.

358 Africa

Scientists believe that more than 200 million years ago, dinosaurs were able to walk from Africa to South America. They could do that because Africa and South America were connected then. Turn to page 818 of the Atlas. Find Africa on the map titled The World: Physical. As you can see, it would be impossible to walk from Africa to South America today.

How did Africa and South America become separated? At least 65 million years ago, forces on our planet's surface caused South America and Africa to move apart, forming the southern part of the Atlantic Ocean. In the process, Africa became the second-largest continent on Earth. To learn more about this vast continent, first examine the geography of Africa's regions.

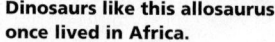

Target Reading Skill L2

Reread Point out the Target Reading Skill. Tell students that rereading a sentence or a paragraph will help them to better understand words and ideas in the text.

Model rereading by reading and rereading the third paragraph on p. 359. Tell students that rereading can help them better understand why Africa is often called the "plateau continent."

Give students *Reread or Read Ahead*. Have them complete the activity in groups.

All in One Africa Teaching Resources, *Reread or Read Ahead,* p. 112

Africa's Regions and Landforms

Africa includes more than 50 countries. This large continent can be divided into four regions: North Africa, West Africa, East Africa, and Central and Southern Africa. Each region contains several different climates and landforms. Turn to the map on page 357 to see the physical features of the four regions.

The Four Regions The region of North Africa is marked in places by rocky mountains. It is also home to seemingly endless stretches of the world's largest desert, the Sahara (suh HA ruh). West Africa, the continent's most populated region, consists mostly of grassland. The soil in the grassland is good for farming. The region of East Africa has many mountains and a few **plateaus,** which are large, raised areas of mostly level land. Grasslands and hills are also found there. Much of Central and Southern Africa is flat or rolling grassland. The region also has thick rain forests, mountains, and swamps. The Namib (NAH mib) Desert and the Kalahari (kah luh HAH ree) Desert are in Southern Africa.

The Plateau Continent Africa is often called the plateau continent because much of the continent is made up of raised, mostly level areas of land that drop off sharply near the sea. Much of this land has a high **elevation,** or height above or below sea level.

Mountains Not all of Africa is level, however. All of Africa's four regions have mountains. The highest are in East Africa. Mount Kilimanjaro in Tanzania is Africa's tallest mountain. It rises to a height of 19,341 feet (5,895 meters).

Learn about the geographic features of Africa.

Rising Up From Flat Land
The Kassala Mountains in the East African country of Sudan rise up from flat land that the people farm. **Analyze Images** *Do these mountains prevent people from farming the land?*

Chapter 11 Section 1 **359**

Vocabulary Builder

Use the information below to teach students this section's high-use words.

High-Use Word	Definition and Sample Sentence
consist, p. 359	*v.* to be made up of The cake **consists** mainly of eggs, flour, and sugar.
trench, p. 360	*n.* a deep furrow in the ground The car had to be towed out of the **trench.**
cycle, p. 362	*n.* a series of events that happen regularly A year is made up of a **cycle** of seasons.
starchy, p. 362	*adj.* of, or containing a food substance found in potatoes and other vegetables My meal of mashed potatoes and yams was very **starchy.**

Show students *The Geography of Africa.* Ask **What are the names of some of Africa's most important geographic features?** *(Students' answers will vary, but may include references to the Sahara and Kalahari deserts, the Great Rift Valley, Mount Kilimanjaro, the Nile, or Lake Victoria.)*

Instruct

Africa's Regions and Landforms L2

Guided Instruction

- **Vocabulary Builder** Clarify the high-use words **consist** and **trench** before reading.

- Read Africa's Regions and Landforms using the Choral Reading strategy (TE, p. T34).

- Have students refer to the map of Africa's regions at the beginning of this chapter and the map of Africa on p. 352 of the Regional Overview as they read the text. Ask students to name the four regions of Africa. *(North Africa, West Africa, East Africa, Central and Southern Africa)*

- Ask students **Which region of Africa is the most populated?** *(West Africa)*

- Ask students **Why do you think West Africa is Africa's most populated region?** *(Students may suggest that the region's fertile grasslands provide an ample source of food, allowing the region to feed and sustain a large population.)*

- Ask students **In which parts of Africa do you suppose the fewest people live? Why?** *(Students may suggest that the deserts of Africa contain the fewest inhabitants because deserts lack sources of water and food.)*

Answer

Analyze Images Possible answer: People probably cannot farm in the mountains, but the photograph shows that it is still possible to farm the flat land around them.

Chapter 11 Section 1 **359**

Guided Instruction (continued)

- Ask students **In which region are the highest mountains of Africa located?** (*East Africa*)

- Ask students to compare and contrast the coastal plain and the Great Rift Valley. (*The coastal plain consists of a strip of land along much of Africa's coast that varies from dry and sandy to marshy and moist; the Great Rift Valley is a deep trench, or rift, that cuts through 4,000 miles of East Africa and includes many of Africa's major lakes.*)

Independent Practice

Have students create the Taking Notes graphic organizer on a separate piece of paper. Then ask them to fill in their graphic organizers by adding details about the landforms in Africa's regions.

Monitor Progress

Circulate to make sure students are adding appropriate details. Provide assistance to individuals as needed.

Answers

MAP MASTER Skills Activity **Locate** northernmost—Egypt; southernmost—Mozambique
Analyze Information Possible answer: The steep walls of the Great Rift Valley make travel and communication difficult.

Go Online PHSchool.com Students may practice their map skills using the interactive online version of this map

✓ **Reading Check** Much of Africa's land area is mostly level with a high elevation.

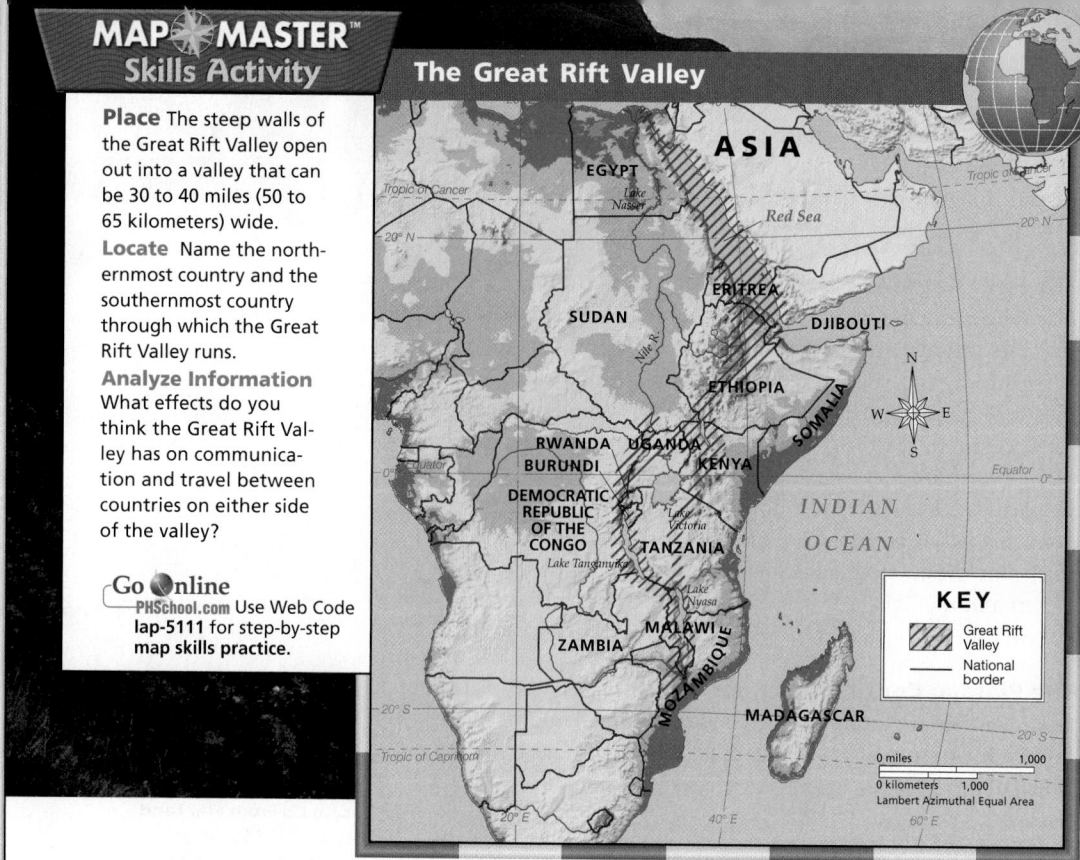

MAP MASTER Skills Activity — The Great Rift Valley

Place The steep walls of the Great Rift Valley open out into a valley that can be 30 to 40 miles (50 to 65 kilometers) wide.

Locate Name the northernmost country and the southernmost country through which the Great Rift Valley runs.

Analyze Information What effects do you think the Great Rift Valley has on communication and travel between countries on either side of the valley?

Go Online PHSchool.com Use Web Code **lap-5111** for step-by-step map skills practice.

KEY
- Great Rift Valley
- National border

0 miles 1,000
0 kilometers 1,000
Lambert Azimuthal Equal Area

Coastal Plains Edge the Continent There is a strip of coastal plain that runs along much of Africa's coast. This land is dry and sandy in some places and marshy and moist in other places. Turn to the political map of Africa on page 351 of the Regional Overview. Find the West African country of Ghana (GAH nuh). The western edge of the coastal strip in Ghana is only about 5 miles (8 kilometers) wide. There, the coastal strip ends in a long, steep slope that rises to a plateau.

The Great Rift Valley Mount Kilimanjaro, Africa's highest peak, is located in East Africa on the edge of the Great Rift Valley. This valley was formed millions of years ago, when the continents pulled apart and left a **rift,** or deep trench. The rift that cuts through East Africa is 4,000 miles (6,400 kilometers) long. Most of Africa's major lakes are located in or near the Great Rift Valley.

✓ **Reading Check** Why is Africa called the plateau continent?

360 Africa

Differentiated Instruction

For Gifted and Talented   L3
Have students complete the *Enrichment* activity on the Great Rift Valley in groups. They may then create a presentation of what they have learned for the rest of the class.

All in One Africa Teaching Resources, *Enrichment,* p. 116

For Advanced Readers   L3
Direct students' attention to the Key Term *plateau.* Point out the suffix *-eau.* Explain that words using this suffix are generally derived from French. Have students list other words that use this suffix (*bureau, beau*). Finally, have them scan the section to identify other words that have foreign word origins.

The Great Rift Valley

Africa's Rivers

Four large rivers carry water from the mountains of Africa's plateaus to the sea. They are the Nile (nyl), the Congo (KAHNG goh), the Zambezi (zam BEE zee), and the Niger (NY jur). Turn to page 352 and find these rivers on the physical map of Africa. Sections of these four rivers may be used for travel. But the rivers are broken in places by large waterfalls or steep rapids. These obstacles make it impossible for ships to sail the whole way between Africa's interior and the sea.

The Nile River   The Nile is the longest river in the world. Its length, more than 4,000 miles (6,400 kilometers), is almost twice the length of the Mississippi River. The White Nile in Sudan and the Blue Nile in the highlands of Ethiopia are tributaries of the Nile. **Tributaries** are rivers and streams that flow into a larger river. After the White Nile and Blue Nile combine to form the Nile, the river flows north into the Mediterranean Sea.

Reread
Reread to clarify what *Africa's interior* means. When you read the paragraph at the left again, look for connections to other words.

Africa's Rivers

Guided Instruction
- **Vocabulary Builder** Clarify the high-use words **cycle** and **starchy** before reading.

- Read about water and its uses in Africa's Rivers.

- Ask students **What are the names of the four major rivers in Africa?** *(the Nile, the Congo, the Zambezi, and the Niger)*

- Ask students to describe the course of the Nile and trace it on the map on the previous page. *(The Nile begins in Uganda at Lake Victoria, proceeds north through the Sudan and Egypt, and empties into the Mediterranean north of Cairo.)*

Target Reading Skill   L2

Reread As a follow up, ask students to perform the Target Reading Skill task in the Student Edition. *(the inland area of the continent that is far away from the coast)*

Background: Global Perspectives

The World's Five Longest Rivers

1. Nile: Africa (about 4,132 miles or 6,650 kilometers)

2. Amazon: South America (about 4,000 miles or 6,400 kilometers)

3. Chang (also called Yangtze): Asia (3,915 miles or 6,300 kilometers)

4. Huang (also called Yellow): Asia (3,395 miles or 5,464 kilometers)

5. Ob-Irtysh: Asia (3,230 miles or 5,200 kilometers)

Guided Instruction (continued)

- Have students list Africa's second, third, and fourth largest rivers in order from longest to shortest. *(the Congo, the Niger, and the Zambezi)*

- Ask **How do people use the Congo, Niger and the Zambezi?** *(People farm near and fish the Congo and Niger rivers. People use the Zambezi for limited transportation and hydroelectricity.)*

- Ask students **On what river is Victoria Falls?** *(the Zambezi)*

Independent Practice

Have students complete the graphic organizer by filling in details about the waterways of Africa.

Monitor Progress

- Show *Section Reading Support Transparency AF 33* and ask students to check their graphic organizers individually. Go over key concepts and clarify key vocabulary as needed.

  Africa Transparencies, *Section Reading Support Transparency AF 33*

- Tell students to fill in the last column of their *Reading Readiness Guides.* Probe for what they learned that confirms or invalidates each statement.

  All in One Africa Teaching Resources, *Reading Readiness Guide,* p. 101

Links

Have students read the **Links To Science** on this page. Ask **Why doesn't the Congo River have a delta?** *(because its current is so strong)* **What does it have instead?** *(a 125-mile canyon beneath the sea)*

Farming on the Banks
Farmers planted the crops shown above near the banks of the Nile River. **Summarize** *What are the benefits of farming near a river?*

Links to
Science

A River Without a Delta
A delta is a plain that forms at the mouth of a river. The Congo River's current is so strong that it does not form a delta. Instead, the river has cut a deep, wide canyon beneath the sea for a distance of about 125 miles (200 kilometers).

362 Africa

Farming Along the Nile People have farmed the land surrounding the Nile for thousands of years. At one time, the Nile flooded its banks regularly. Farmers planted their crops to match the flood cycle of the river. The floods provided water for the crops and left behind a layer of silt, tiny bits of rock and dirt carried downstream by the river. Silt helps make soil **fertile,** or rich in the substances that plants need to grow well.

In the 1960s, Egypt's government built the Aswan High Dam to control the flooding of the Nile. As the water backed up behind the dam, Lake Nasser was created. Waters from the lake are channeled to water crops that grow in the desert. Water rushing through the dam produces electricity. Since the dam was built, the Nile no longer floods the land.

The Congo River The Congo River flows through the rain forests of the Central African countries of the Congo and the Democratic Republic of the Congo. At 2,900 miles (4,677 kilometers), the Congo River is Africa's second-longest river. It is fed by hundreds of tributaries. Many farmers in this region grow yams and cassava (kuh SAH vuh), a starchy plant that is a bit like a potato. They also catch many different types of fish in the Congo River.

Differentiated Instruction

For Special Needs Students L1
Have these students partner with more proficient readers to read about Africa's rivers together. Then have these students label the rivers described in the text on a copy of *Outline Map 20: Africa: Physical.*

All in One Africa Teaching Resources, *Outline Map 20: Africa: Physical,* p. 126

For Gifted and Talented L3
Have students list the various ways that Africans use the water of their rivers and lakes. Then have students write a paragraph to explain the relative importance of each type of water use they list.

Answer

Summarize Farmers could use water from the river to supplement rain or irrigation if necessary.

The Niger River The third-longest river in Africa, the Niger, begins its journey in Guinea (GIH nee). For 2,600 miles (4,180 kilometers), the river flows north and then bends south. It provides water for farms in the river valley. Many people make their living fishing in the river.

The Zambezi River Africa's fourth-longest river, the Zambezi, is in Southern Africa. It runs through or forms the border of six countries: Angola (ang GOH luh), Zambia (ZAM bee uh), Namibia (nuh MIB ee uh), Botswana (baht SWAH nuh), Zimbabwe (zim BAHB way), and Mozambique (moh zum BEEK). The river is 2,200 miles (3,540 kilometers) long, but boats can travel only on about 460 miles (740 kilometers) of it because of its waterfalls and rapids.

People have used the Zambezi's strong current to produce electricity. About halfway to its outlet in the Indian Ocean, the Zambezi plunges into a canyon, creating the spectacular waterfall known as Victoria Falls. Tourists from around the world visit these falls. People can sometimes see the mist and spray of Victoria Falls from as far away as 40 miles (65 kilometers).

✓ **Reading Check** What effect has the Aswan High Dam had on Egypt and on the waters of the Nile?

Victoria Falls is located on the border between Zambia and Zimbabwe.

Section 1 Assessment

Key Terms
Review the key terms at the beginning of this section. Use each term in a sentence that explains its meaning.

Target Reading Skill
Name a word or an idea that you were able to clarify on your own by rereading. Explain it in your own words.

Comprehension and Critical Thinking
1. (a) **Identify** Name the four regions of Africa.

(b) **Compare** What physical features do all of the regions have in common?
(c) **Draw Conclusions** Why might West Africa be the continent's most populated region?
2. (a) **Describe** Describe the course traveled by each of Africa's major rivers.
(b) **Identify Effects** How do Africa's four major rivers affect the lives of its people?
(c) **Draw Inferences** How did farming on the Nile change after the Aswan High Dam was built?

Writing Activity
List several landforms and rivers in Africa that you would like to visit. Explain why you would like to visit them and what you would do on your trip.

> **Writing Tip** Use vivid details to describe your trip. These will help support your explanation of the reasons you chose the landforms you did.

Chapter 11 Section 1 **363**

Assess Progress   L2
Have students complete the Section Assessment. Administer the *Section Quiz.*

📖 **All in One Africa Teaching Resources,**
Section Quiz, p. 103

Reteach   L1
If students need more instruction, have them read this section in the Reading and Vocabulary Study Guide.

📖 Chapter 11, Section 1, **Eastern Hemisphere Reading and Vocabulary Study Guide,** pp. 122–124

Extend   L3
Have students learn more about Africa's physical geography by completing the *Small Group Activity: Simulation: Magazine Article on an African River.* Ask students to work together in small groups to complete the activity.

📖 **All in One Africa Teaching Resources,**
Small Group Activity: Simulation: Magazine Article on an African River, pp. 118–121

Answer

✓ **Reading Check** Water from Lake Nasser, created by the dam, is used for growing crops; water rushing through the dam creates electricity; the Nile no longer produces natural flood cycles.

Writing Activity
Use the *Rubric for Assessing a Writing Assignment* to evaluate students' work.

📖 **All in One Africa Teaching Resources,**
Rubric for Assessing a Writing Assignment, p. 130

Section 1 Assessment

Key Terms
Students' sentences should reflect knowledge of each Key Term.

Target Reading Skill
Students should be able to identify a difficult or unfamiliar word or unclear idea and explain how rereading helped their comprehension.

Comprehension and Critical Thinking
1. (a) North Africa, West Africa, East Africa, and Central and Southern Africa (b) Each of the regions has mountains and coastal plains. (c) Possible answer: The region's fertile grasslands provide an ample source of food, allowing the region to sustain a large population.

2. (a) The Nile flows north to the Mediterranean Sea. The Congo River flows through the Congo and the Democratic Republic of the Congo. The Niger River begins in Guinea and flows north, then turns south. The Zambezi River runs through six countries in southern Africa. (b) Africans use the water from rivers for transportation, growing crops, fishing, producing electricity, and for tourism. (c) Possible answer: Farmers no longer had to worry about the Nile flooding their crops, and waters from Lake Nasser are channeled to water crops that grow in the desert.

Objectives

Social Studies

1. Discover the factors that influence Africa's climate.
2. Learn the characteristics of each of Africa's vegetation regions.
3. Find out how climate can affect the health of people in Africa.

Reading/Language Arts

Paraphrase to understand and remember what you have read.

Prepare to Read

Build Background Knowledge L2

Ask students to scan the climate map on p. 365. Ask students to predict where in Africa they think people would be more or less likely to live. Model the thought process by choosing a climate region and describing what that region might be like to live in. Conduct an Idea Wave (TE, p. T35) in order to generate a list of students' responses.

Set a Purpose for Reading L2

- Preview the Objectives.

- Form students into pairs or groups of four. Distribute the *Reading Readiness Guide*. Ask students to fill in the first two columns of the chart. Use the Numbered Heads participation strategy (TE, p. T36) to call on students to share one piece of information they already know and one piece of information they want to know.

  All in One Africa Teaching Resources, *Reading Readiness Guide,* p. 105

Preview Key Terms L2

Pronounce each Key Term, then ask the students to say the word with you. Provide a simple explanation such as, "A drought occurs when it does not rain for a long period of time."

Prepare to Read

Objectives

In this section you will
1. Discover the factors that influence Africa's climate.
2. Learn the characteristics of each of Africa's vegetation regions.
3. Find out how climate can affect the health of people in Africa.

Taking Notes

Copy the outline below. As you read, find details about Africa's climate and vegetation, and record them in your outline.

> I. Africa's climate factors
>   A. Distance from the Equator
>   1.
>   2.
>   B.
> II. Vegetation regions

Target Reading Skill

Paraphrase Paraphrasing can help you understand what you read. You paraphrase by restating what you have read in your own words.

For example, you could paraphrase the first paragraph on page 368 this way: "Africa has different kinds of vegetation in different parts of the continent. It has rain forests, savannas, and deserts."

As you read this section, paraphrase, or restate, the information following each red or blue heading.

Key Terms

- **irrigate** (IHR uh gayt) *v.* to supply with water through a ditch, pipe, channel, or sprinkler
- **drought** (drowt) *n.* a long period of little or no rain
- **oasis** (oh AY sis) *n.* a fertile place in a desert where there is water and vegetation
- **savanna** (suh VAN uh) *n.* a region of tall grasses with scattered trees
- **nomad** (NOH mad) *n.* a person who has no permanent, settled home and who instead moves from place to place

---

A home in a forest region of Uganda

364 Africa

If you were to travel throughout Africa, you would experience many different climates. Deserts would feel hot and dry. The highlands would feel cool and moist. In some places close to the Equator, hot weather and rainfall would occur throughout the year.

Africa's vegetation is as diverse as its climate. Forest regions are filled with trees and a great variety of plant life. Grasslands are dotted with low trees and scrub bushes. Low mountain areas support plant life, while the highest mountains are covered with snow and ice. A region's climate has a great influence on its vegetation. But what influences climate?

What Influences Climate?

Although people sometimes think of Africa as a hot place, not all parts of it are hot. That is because there are several geographic factors that influence climate. Some key factors are distance from the Equator and elevation. Nearness to large bodies of water and major landforms also affects climate.

Target Reading Skill L2

Paraphrase Point out the Target Reading Skill. Tell students that paraphrasing, or restating what they have read in their own words, can help them understand and remember what they have read.

Model using paraphrasing by restating the information in the second paragraph on p. 366. (*Because Africa is near the Equator, it is warm there. A place's location in relation to the Equator affects its seasons. Seasons in places north of the Equator are the opposite of seasons in places south of the Equator.*)

Give students *Paraphrase.* Have them complete the activity in groups.

All in One Africa Teaching Resources, *Paraphrase,* p. 113

MAP MASTER™
Skills Activity

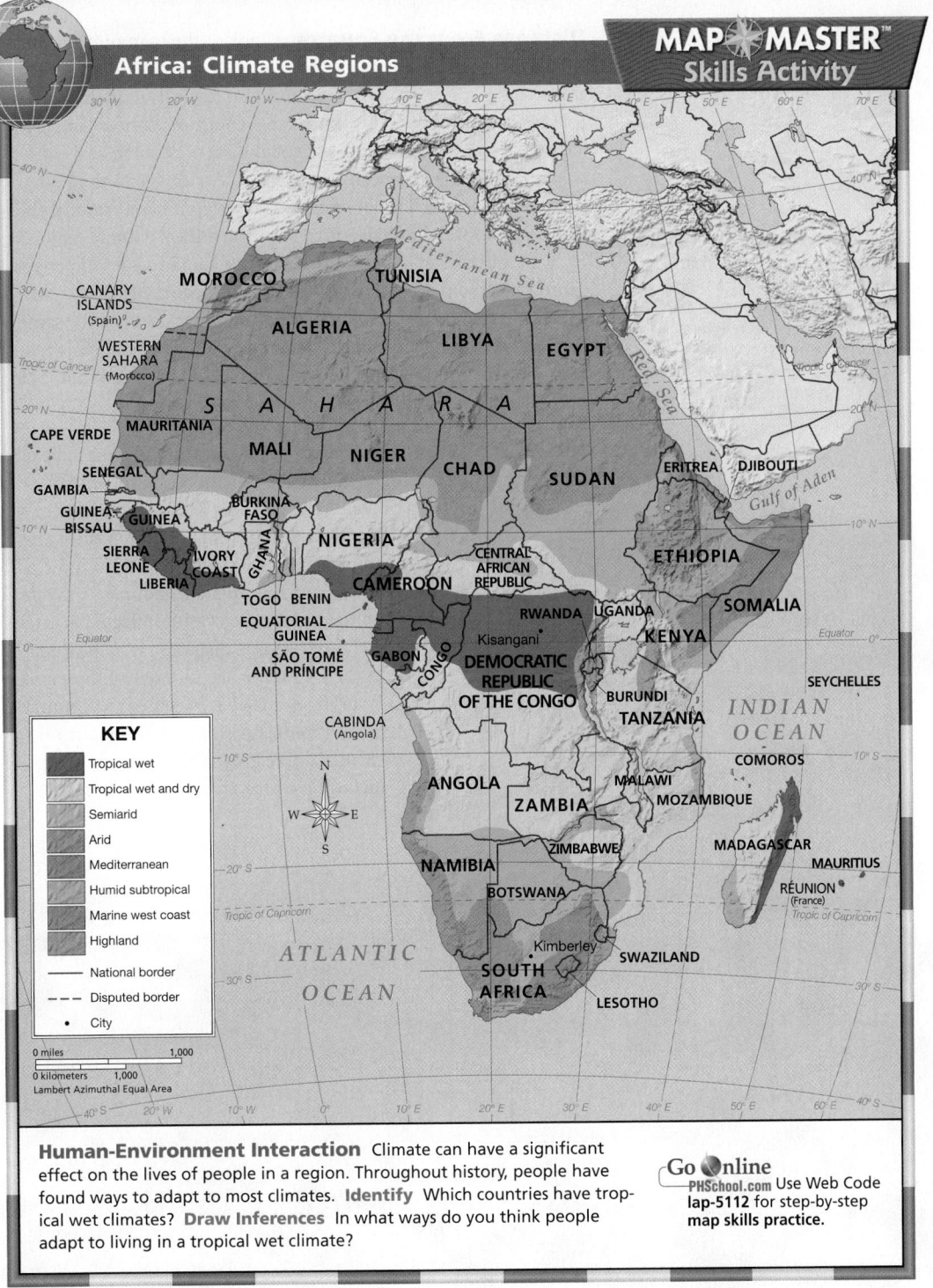

KEY
- Tropical wet
- Tropical wet and dry
- Semiarid
- Arid
- Mediterranean
- Humid subtropical
- Marine west coast
- Highland
— National border
--- Disputed border
• City

0 miles 1,000
0 kilometers 1,000
Lambert Azimuthal Equal Area

Human-Environment Interaction Climate can have a significant effect on the lives of people in a region. Throughout history, people have found ways to adapt to most climates. **Identify** Which countries have tropical wet climates? **Draw Inferences** In what ways do you think people adapt to living in a tropical wet climate?

Go Online
PHSchool.com Use Web Code lap-5112 for step-by-step map skills practice.

Chapter 11 Section 2 **365**

Vocabulary Builder

Use the information below to teach students this section's high-use words.

High-Use Word	Definition and Sample Sentence
factor, p. 364	*n.* something that acts to contribute to the making of a result Your test scores are just one **factor** of your grade in this class.
severe, p. 367	*adj.* serious, extreme The **severe** thunderstorm left the city without electricity.
environment, p. 368	*n.* the conditions that surround people and affect how they live It is difficult to live in the harsh **environment** of the Sahara.
pest, p. 371	*n.* a harmful plant or animal **Pests** destroyed the beautiful tulips in my garden.

Instruct

What Influences Climate?   L2

Guided Instruction
- **Vocabulary Builder** Clarify the high-use words **factor** and **severe** before reading.

- Have students use the ReQuest procedure (TE, p. T35) to read What Influences Climate?

- Draw students' attention to the map on this page. Ask **What climate is common in Africa along the Equator?** *(tropical wet)*

- Ask students **What similarities do you notice about the relative locations of the tropical wet and dry, semiarid, and arid regions of Africa?** *(These three climate regions are usually in the same relative positions as you go north and south from the Equator.)*

Answers
MAP MASTER™ Skills Activity   **Identify** Guinea, Guinea Bissau, Sierra Leone, Liberia, Ivory Coast, Nigeria, Cameroon, Congo, Gabon, Democratic Republic of the Congo, Central African Republic, Equitorial Guinea
Draw Inferences Possible answer: They probably plant crops that grow well in warm, wet climates and wear clothing and construct buildings that keep people as cool and dry as possible.

Go Online
PHSchool.com Students may practice their map skills using the interactive online version of this map.

Chapter 11 Section 2 **365**

Guided Instruction (continued)

- Have students list the factors that influence Africa's climate. *(distance from the Equator; proximity to large bodies of water; major landforms; rainfall; elevation)*

- Ask students **Why is most of Africa warm?** *(A large portion of Africa falls between the Tropic of Cancer and the Tropic of Capricorn, near the Equator.)*

- Ask students **How does elevation affect climate?** *(The higher the elevation, the cooler a place tends to be.)*

Home to Many Animals
The open grasslands of Tanzania's Tarangire National Park are home to many thousands of large animals. Elephants may be seen in herds of 500 or more at a time. **Infer** *Given that animals thrive in this environment, do you think it has a mild or a harsh climate?*

Distance From the Equator Look at the map on page 365 titled Africa: Climate Regions. Notice that the Equator runs through the midsection of the continent. Regions near the Equator are usually hot. Now find the Tropic of Cancer and the Tropic of Capricorn, which are equal distances north and south of the Equator. As you can see, much of Africa lies in the region between these two lines of latitude. This region has a tropical climate. Therefore, much of Africa lies in a tropical climate region.

The location of a place in relation to the Equator influences more than the place's climate—it also influences the place's seasons. North of the Equator, winter and summer occur at the same time as they do in the United States and the rest of the Northern Hemisphere. South of the Equator, the seasons are reversed. For example, July in South Africa is the middle of winter.

The Role of Elevation Recall that elevation is the height of land above sea level. The higher the elevation, the cooler a place tends to be. For example, Mount Kilimanjaro, Africa's highest peak, is located close to the Equator. Yet ice and snow blanket the peak of Kilimanjaro year-round.

The countries of Ethiopia and Somalia provide another example of how elevation affects climate. They are about the same distance from the Equator, yet their climates are different. Ethiopia is on a very high plateau. Much of the country has mild temperatures and abundant rain. Farmers there grow a wide range of crops, including coffee, dates, and cereals.

366 Africa

Differentiated Instruction

For English Language Learners L1
Students may find some of the words in What Influences Climate?, such as *geographic, Equator,* and *irrigate,* hard to pronounce. Have students read silently and note any words they have difficulty pronouncing. Encourage peer-to-peer conferencing so that English learners can learn to pronounce difficult words with the assistance of fellow students.

For Advanced Readers L3
Extend students' abilities to read and interpret climate maps by having them complete *Reading a Climate Graph*. Ask students to work together in pairs to complete the activity.

All in One Africa Teaching Resources, *Reading a Climate Graph,* p. 124

Answer

Infer It probably has a mild climate.

Because Ethiopia usually gets plenty of rain, many farmers there do not irrigate their crops. To **irrigate** is to supply with water through a ditch, pipe, channel, or sprinkler. Even so, the country sometimes goes through a **drought** (drowt), or a long period of little or no rain. With little water, crops and livestock are harder to raise, and food becomes scarce. Ethiopia has suffered severe droughts several times since the 1980s.

Somalia is at a much lower elevation than Ethiopia is. The Somalian climate is hot and dry. Farming is possible only near a river or in or near an oasis, where crops can be irrigated. An **oasis** is a fertile place in a desert, with water and vegetation. Fresh underground water can support life in a region that gets little rain.

Unpredictable Rainfall Rainfall varies greatly from one region of Africa to another. Along parts of the west coast, winds carry moisture from the warm ocean over the land. Rainfall there averages more than 100 inches (250 centimeters) per year. Compare that with your own height. Forty inches (100 centimeters) of rain might fall during June alone. But in parts of the Sahara in the north and the Namib Desert in the south, rain may not fall at all for several years in a row.

Farmers who live in dry regions can never be sure whether there will be enough rain for their crops. Some farmers choose to plant a variety of crops, each needing a different amount of rainfall. These farmers hope they will have at least one successful crop.

✓ **Reading Check** How does elevation affect the climate of regions in Africa?

■ **Graph Skills**

The city of Kimberley is located in a desert region, while the city of Kisangani is located in a tropical region. **Identify** Which city has higher temperatures throughout the year? Which city gets more total rainfall in a year? **Synthesize Information** How does location help explain the differences in temperature and in rainfall?

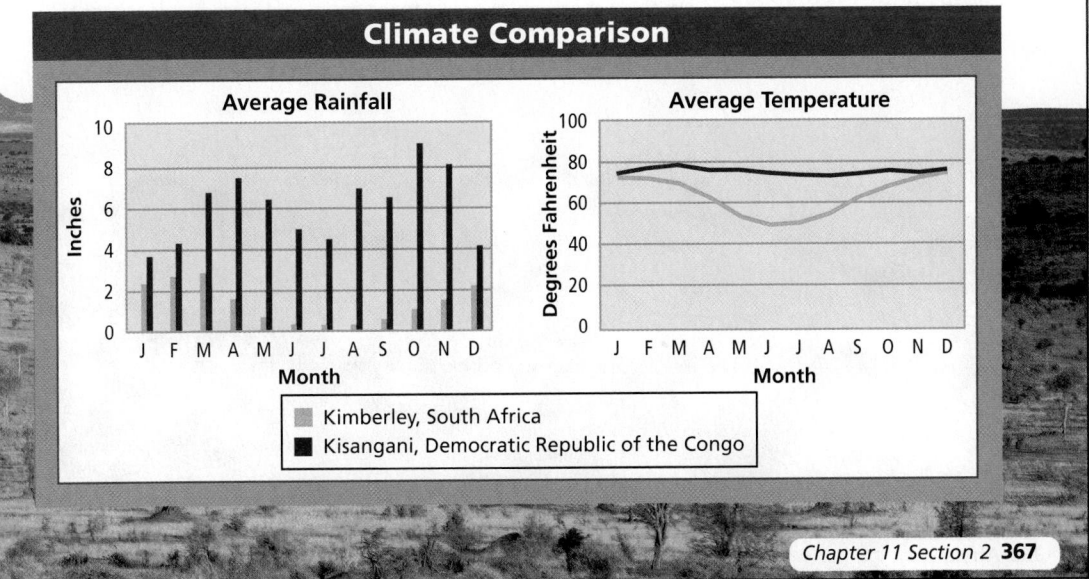

Climate Comparison

Kimberley, South Africa
Kisangani, Democratic Republic of the Congo

■ Ask students **Why is Somalia's climate hotter and dryer than Ethiopia's climate?** (*Somalia is at a much lower elevation than Ethiopia.*)

■ Ask students to make a generalization about the amount of rainfall throughout Africa. (*Students' responses may vary, but should reflect the understanding that rainfall amounts vary greatly throughout the continent. Encourage students to provide details such as the fact that parts of Africa's west coast receive great amounts of rain, whereas deserts such as the Sahara and the Namib often experience no rain for several years in a row.*)

Independent Practice
Ask students to create the Taking Notes graphic organizer on a blank piece of paper. Then have them begin to fill in the outline with information they have just learned. Briefly model how to identify which details to record by providing examples on the *Outline Transparency*.

📖 **Africa Transparencies,** *Transparency B15: Outline*

Monitor Progress
As students fill in the graphic organizer, circulate and help students understand which details about climate to include in their outlines. Provide assistance as needed.

Background Information: Global Perspectives

Earth's Hydrologic Cycle Precipitation, evaporation, and condensation are the three main processes of the world's hydrologic cycle, or water cycle. The hydrologic cycle consists of the continual exchange of water between Earth's surface and the atmosphere. As water evaporates from the ocean, land, and freshwater sources, it forms a vapor that is carried into the atmosphere by air currents.

As the vapor condenses, it forms clouds. Finally, the water returns to Earth's surface in the form of precipitation. On average, the amount of water vapor in the air is equal to about one inch (2.5 centimeters) of water distributed evenly over Earth's surface.

Answers

Graph Skills **Identify** Kisangani; Kisangani **Synthesize Information** Kisangani is very near to the Equator, while Kimberley is farther away.

✓ Reading Check The higher the elevation of a region, the cooler its climate tends to be.

Vegetation Regions of Africa

L2

Guided Instruction

- **Vocabulary Builder** Clarify the high-use word **environment** before reading.

- Read about plant life across Africa in Vegetation Regions of Africa. As students read, circulate and make sure individuals can answer the Reading Check question on p. 370 of the Student Edition.

- Ask students **What kind of vegetation is found near the Equator?** (*rain forests*)

- Ask students **How does the constant rain affect life in the rain forest?** (*The moisture provides a rich environment of trees and plants that supports many types of animals.*)

- Then ask students **How has logging affected life in the rain forests?** (*Logging provides people with timber, yet threatens the forests and the many species that live there.*)

- Ask students to describe the location and climate of Africa's tropical savannas. (*Savannas cover much of Africa north and south of the rain forests. The climate is wet or dry, depending on the season.*)

Answer

Apply Information No; the harsh, dry environment makes it a difficult place for people and animals to live.

Vegetation Regions of Africa

Africa's vegetation varies across the land. Near the Equator, there are rain forests. North and south of the rain forests lie **savanna,** a region of tall grasses with scattered trees. Beyond the savanna, many parts of northern Africa, as well as the southwestern coast of the continent, are covered in desert.

Tropical Rain Forests Tropical rain forests are regions where rain falls often throughout the year. Rain forests exist in parts of West and Central Africa, covering close to 20 percent of the continent. Rain forests are well known for supporting a great number and variety of life forms. Forest moisture provides a rich environment of trees and plants that supports animals such as gorillas and chimpanzees.

People in rain forest regions live in towns, cities, or on farms built on cleared land. Cacao (kuh KAY oh), the plant from which chocolate is made, and cassava grow well in these regions. People also fish, hunt, and harvest timber in the rain forests. However, logging threatens these forests and the many species that live in them.

Tropical Savannas The most common vegetation in Africa is tropical savanna. Tall grasses, thorny bushes, and scattered trees grow in the savanna region. It is also home to large herd animals such as lions, elephants, and zebras. Tropical savannas cover more of Africa than any other type of vegetation.

The savanna has two seasons: dry and wet. During the dry season, farming is impossible. Trees lose their leaves and rivers run dry. Farmers use this time to trade, build houses, and visit friends. In the wet season, the land turns green and farmers plant crops.

World's Largest Desert
The Sahara is famous for sand dunes like the ones shown below. However, most of the Sahara is rock plateau or gravel. Mountains exist there as well.
Apply Information *Do you think the Sahara is an easy place for people and animals to live?*

368 Africa

Skills Mini Lesson

Making Valid Generalizations

1. Teach the skill by telling students that a generalization is a conclusion drawn from specific facts and applied to a broader situation. First identify the generalization, then the facts used to verify it. Then test the generalization for validity.

2. Have students practice the skill by looking at the bar graph on p. 367 and determining the validity of this generalization: "On average, Kisangani receives more yearly rainfall than Kimberley." (*The generalization is valid; the bar graph shows Kisangani receives more rain.*)

3. Have students apply the skill by making their own generalizations based on the line graph on p. 367.

Deserts in Africa Beyond the savanna lie the deserts. The immense Sahara extends across most of North Africa. This desert covers almost as much land as the entire United States. A journalist traveling in the Sahara described what she saw:

> "[H]orizon-to-horizon vistas [views] of sand in a palette of colors, luxurious arches of palm trees swaying in the wind . . . heaving mountains of rough stone unbroken by the slightest sign of vegetation, vast expanses of sand obscured [hidden] by a veil of dust."
> —*Christine Negroni,* The New York Times

The southern edge of the Sahara meets the savanna in a region called the Sahel (sah HEL), which is the Arabic word for "shore" or "border." The Sahel is very hot and dry. Each year it receives only 4 to 8 inches (10 to 20 centimeters) of rain. Small shrubs, grass, and some trees grow there.

The Namib and Kalahari deserts reach across Namibia and Botswana in Southern Africa. Large parts of the Kalahari are covered in scrub and small bushes, while the smaller Namib has more sand dunes.

The fennec fox, the world's smallest fox, lives in the Sahara.

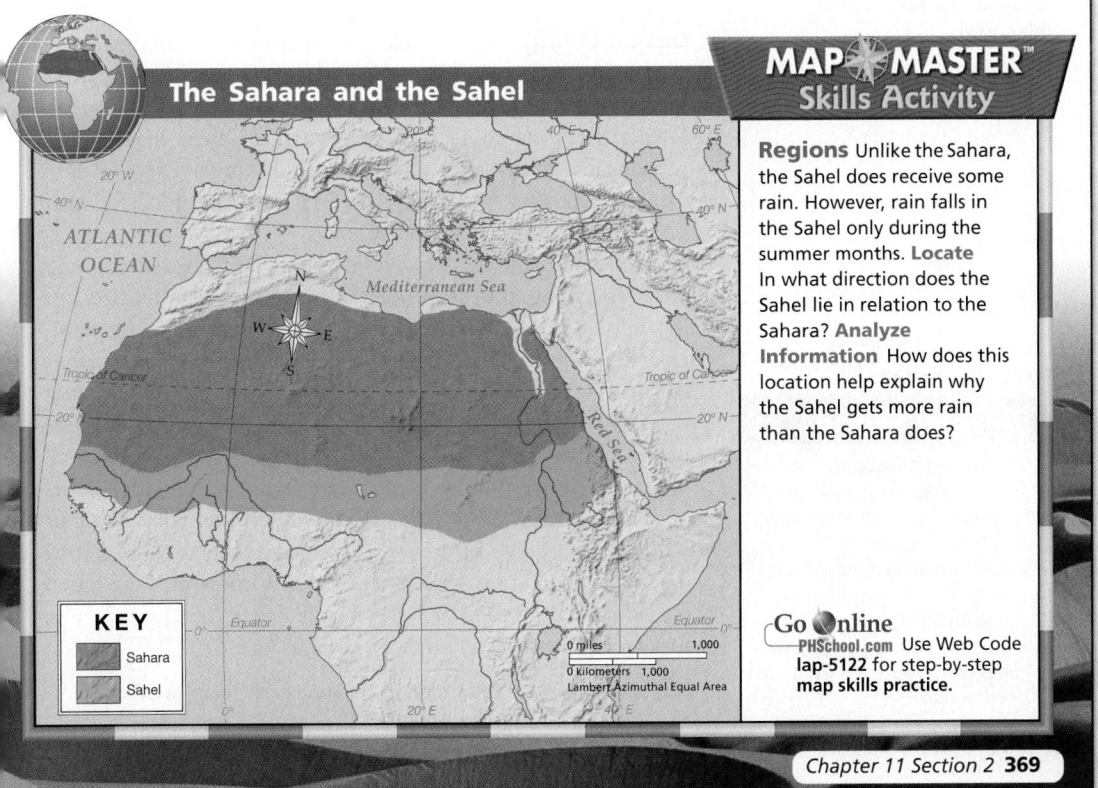

The Sahara and the Sahel

ATLANTIC OCEAN

Mediterranean Sea

Tropic of Cancer

Red Sea

Equator

KEY
- Sahara
- Sahel

0 miles 1,000
0 kilometers 1,000
Lambert Azimuthal Equal Area

MAP MASTER™ Skills Activity

Regions Unlike the Sahara, the Sahel does receive some rain. However, rain falls in the Sahel only during the summer months. **Locate** In what direction does the Sahel lie in relation to the Sahara? **Analyze Information** How does this location help explain why the Sahel gets more rain than the Sahara does?

Go Online
PHSchool.com Use Web Code **lap-5122** for step-by-step map skills practice.

Differentiated Instruction

For Gifted and Talented **L3**
Have students complete *Activity Shop Interdisciplinary: Desertification* to learn more about how deserts are formed. Students should then explain what

they have learned about deserts to the class.

All in One Africa Teaching Resources, *Activity Shop Interdisciplinary: Desertification,* pp. 122–123

Guided Instruction (continued)

- Ask students to describe the Sahara Desert. (*The enormous Sahara lies next to the savanna and extends across most of North Africa. Very little vegetation grows in the Sahara because it is a hot desert.*)

- Ask students **What are nomads?** (*Nomads are people who have no single, settled home.*) Then ask them to describe the movements of nomadic herders. (*They travel to places where they know they can get water and food for their herds.*)

- Ask students to compare the Sahara and the Sahel. (*The Sahara is a vast expanse of sand, covering almost as much land as the United States. The Sahel is the strip of land where the Sahara meets the savanna. It is hot and dry and receives 4 to 8 inches of rain per year. Small trees, shrubs, and grass grow in the Sahel.*)

Independent Practice
Have students continue to fill in their outlines with types of vegetation found in the regions of Africa.

Monitor Progress
As students fill in the outline, circulate and make sure that individuals are choosing appropriate details. Provide assistance as needed.

Answers
MAP MASTER Skills Activity **Locate** south
Analyze Information The Sahel is closer to the Equator where the climate is often wetter.

Climate and Health

Guided Instruction

- **Vocabulary Builder** Clarify the high-use word **pest** before reading.

- Read about the health risks many Africans face in Climate and Health.

- Ask students **How does the environment of the rain forests pose a threat to people?** *(The moist environment is home to many disease-carrying insects.)*

- Ask students **How do Africans fight insects that carry sleeping sickness and malaria?** *(They set traps and sew netting that contains poison into tents to kill tsetse flies. They wear protective clothing and use pesticide to prevent malaria.)*

Independent Practice

Have students complete their outlines with details about how climate and vegetation affect people's health.

Monitor Progress

- Show *Section Reading Support Transparency AF 34* and ask students to check their graphic organizers individually. Go over key concepts and clarify key vocabulary as needed.

    Africa Transparencies, *Section Reading Support Transparency AF 34*

- Tell students to fill in the last column of their *Reading Readiness Guides.* Ask them to evaluate if what they learned was what they had expected to learn.

    All in One Africa Teaching Resources, *Reading Readiness Guide,* p. 105

Links

Read the **Links Across The World** on this page. Ask students **How do desert nomads in the Sahara protect their skin from the sun?** *(by wearing long, loose robes that cover them from head to toe)*

A desert nomad traveling through the Sahara with his camel

Links Across
The World

The Oldest Sunscreen In the United States, people often wear sunscreen to protect their skin from sunburn. But in vast desert regions like the Sahara, sunscreen is unknown. Desert nomads hide their skin from the sun by wearing long, loose robes that cover them from head to toe.

370 Africa

Desert Living Few people live in Africa's deserts. Most of those who do are **nomads,** or people who have no permanent, settled home. Nomads move around to various places, often following the same route each year, to make their living. Most nomads are herders who also take part in trade. They travel to places where they know they can find water and food for their herds of goats, camels, or sheep.

Some nomadic herders live mainly in Africa's mountainous areas. In spring, they leave their winter grazing grounds in the foothills and head up into the mountains. Other nomadic herders live mainly in the flat desert areas. During the dry season, they set up tents near oases (oh AY seez). When the rainy season comes, they move their goats and camels to pastures that are better for grazing.

Desert nomads have herded camels for hundreds of years because the animals are well suited to desert life. They are large, strong animals that can transport goods on their backs over long distances. In addition, when a camel eats, it stores fat in the hump on its back. If no food or water is available, a camel can survive for several days by using the stored fat as food.

✓ **Reading Check** What kinds of vegetation are found in Africa's savanna regions?

Differentiated Instruction

For Less Proficient Readers **L1**
Have students list words they might use to describe nomads. Then encourage students to use the words they list to create sentences. You may wish to model the activity with sentences such as, "*Wander:* Nomads *wander* because they move around to various places.*"*

Answer

✓ **Reading Check** tall grasses, thorny bushes, and scattered trees

Climate and Health

The climate people live in can affect their health. Throughout Africa, there are regions that present health risks to livestock and people. In rain forest regions, the moist environment is home to many disease-carrying insects. Even in the drier grasslands, disease and illness take their toll.

Sleeping Sickness Nearly one fifth of Africa is home to the tsetse (TSET see) fly, a pest that makes raising cattle almost impossible. A tsetse bite can kill cattle and can cause a disease called sleeping sickness in humans. African researchers, together with cattle herders, have worked to find ways to control the spread of the tsetse fly. Cattle herders in Kenya are setting traps for flies. Herders in the country of Uganda catch flies by sewing into tents netting that contains poison.

Malaria Another disease, malaria (muh LEHR ee uh), is spread to humans by the bite of an infected mosquito. Mosquitoes thrive in warm, moist climates and breed in swamps, ponds, and pools of standing water. These conditions make malaria a particular problem in parts of Africa south of the Sahara. Researchers continue to look for ways of fighting the spread of malaria. Protective clothing and insecticide can help prevent infection.

Paraphrase
Use your own words to paraphrase the paragraph at the left. What would be a good way to restate *take their toll*? In your own words, you might say "disease and illness cause serious problems."

✓ **Reading Check** What is being done to control the spread of the tsetse fly?

Section 2 Assessment

Key Terms
Review the key terms at the beginning of this section. Use each term in a sentence that explains its meaning.

Target Reading Skill
Read the paragraphs under Desert Living on page 370. Then, paraphrase the paragraphs in 25 words or fewer.

Comprehension and Critical Thinking
1. (a) **Identify** Name three factors that influence climate.

(b) **Summarize** Give an example of how one of these factors can influence the climate of an area.
2. (a) **Name** Identify the types of vegetation found in each of Africa's four regions.
(b) **Identify Effects** How do climate and vegetation affect the ways Africans make a living?
3. (a) **Recall** What health risks do people and animals in different climate regions of Africa face?
(b) **Draw Conclusions** In which of Africa's climate regions do you think you would be least likely to contract malaria?

Writing Activity
Choose a region of Africa that you would like to live in or visit. Write a short essay about the climate and vegetation. Include several reasons why the region is of interest to you.

For: An activity on vegetation in Africa
Visit: PHSchool.com
Web Code: lad-5102

Paraphrase As a follow up, have students answer the Target Reading Skill question in the Student Edition. (*Possible answer: Africa's climates allow certain diseases to spread easily. These diseases cause serious health problems.*)

Assess and Reteach

Assess Progress [L2]
Have students complete the Section Assessment. Administer the *Section Quiz*.

 Africa Teaching Resources, *Section Quiz,* p. 107

Reteach [L1]
If students need more instruction, have them read this section in the Reading and Vocabulary Study Guide.

 Chapter 11, Section 2, **Eastern Hemisphere Reading and Vocabulary Study Guide,** pp. 125–127

Extend [L3]
Have students do research into how Africans have worked to reduce the threat of the tsetse fly. On the basis of their research, have students suggest additional ways to deal with the challenge of sleeping sickness.

Answers

✓ **Reading Check** Cattle herders in Kenya set traps for the flies; Ugandan herders use netting that contains poison to catch flies.

Writing Activity
Use the *Rubric for Assessing a Writing Assignment* to evaluate students' essays.

 Africa Teaching Resources, *Rubric for Assessing a Writing Assignment,* p. 130

Go Online PHSchool.com Typing in the Web code when prompted will bring students to detailed instructions for this activity.

Section 2 Assessment

Key Terms
Students' sentences should reflect knowledge of each Key Term.

▶ Target Reading Skill [L2]
Answers will vary, but should show that students are paraphrasing the text accurately.

Comprehension and Critical Thinking
1. (a) Possible responses: location relative to the Equator; distance from large bodies of water; influence of major landforms; elevation; rainfall (b) Answers will vary, but should include a concrete example.

2. (a) North Africa: mostly desert scrub or desert; West and Central Africa: tropical savanna and tropical rain forest; East Africa: tropical savanna and grassland; Southern Africa: tropical savanna, with some desert scrub, grassland, and vegetation (b) Students' responses should include that vegetation is dependent on climate and that the amount of vegetation in a place affects how people make a living.

3. (a) Many disease-carrying insects live in the rain forests; malaria thrives in parts of Africa south of the Sahara. (b) dry places such as deserts

Objective
Learn how to interpret diagrams.

Prepare to Read

Build Background Knowledge   L2
Have students study the diagram on p. 372. Point out the diagram's title, labels, and scale. Ask students to brainstorm what information they might learn by studying this diagram. Conduct an Idea Wave (TE, p. T35) to generate a class list on the board.

Instruct

Interpreting Diagrams   L2

Guided Instruction
- Read the steps to interpreting diagrams as a class and write them on the board.

- Practice the skill by following the steps on p. 373 as a class. Read the title to see what the diagram shows. Identify the landforms shown (*basin, mountains, plains, highlands, valley*). Read the labels with students and name the mountain ranges (*Crystal Mts., Mitumba Mts., Virunga Mts.*) and bodies of water (*Atlantic Ocean, Congo River, Lualaba River, Lake Kivu, Lake Victoria, Indian Ocean*). Then list the elevations of three landforms.

- Have students write a few sentences on the board summarizing how the elevation of Africa changes as you travel from the Atlantic Ocean to the Indian Ocean. (*The land starts out close to sea level and then rises slightly through the Crystal Mountains. Then it returns close to sea level in the Congo Basin, rising gradually until you reach the Mitumba Mountains. It dips in the western Great Rift Valley, then plateaus in Lake Victoria and the Serengeti Plain, and then dips again in the eastern Great Rift Valley. The land then rises again in the Kenya Highlands, and gradually decreases elevation toward sea level as you approach the Indian Ocean.*)

 ## Interpreting Diagrams

Africa makes up about one fifth of all the land on Earth. It is a plateau continent with sloping coastal plains, a broad central basin, towering mountains, and a deep rift, or crack, in Earth's surface. If you could drive across the widest stretch of Africa, going 65 miles (105 kilometers) per hour and not stopping for gas or sleep, the trip would take about three full days.

An effective way to learn about Africa's landforms is by looking at a cross-sectional diagram. A cross section is what you would see if you sliced through the continent from its highest point to its lowest point and looked at it from the side.

Learn the Skill
To interpret information in any type of diagram, including a cross-sectional diagram, follow the steps below.

1. **Study the diagram.** Notice the various parts of the diagram. What can you learn from the title? What details are shown?

2. **Read the labels.** Notice the lines that lead from each label to the cross section. Make sure you understand what all the labels refer to.

3. **Summarize the information in the diagram.** Describe what you learned from studying the diagram and its labels.

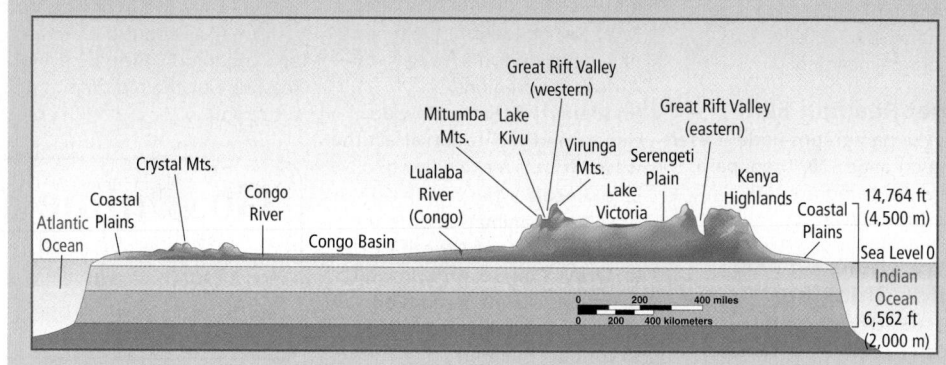

Cross-Sectional Diagram of Africa South of the Sahara

372 Africa

Independent Practice
Assign *Skills for Life* and have students complete it individually.

All in One Africa Teaching Resources, *Skills for Life,* p. 117

Monitor Progress
As students are completing *Skills for Life,* circulate to make sure individuals are applying the skill steps effectively. Provide assistance as needed.

Practice the Skill

Study the cross section of Africa on page 372. Use the steps below to interpret the diagram and learn about Africa's landforms.

1 Look at the diagram. What information can you learn from the title? What kinds of landforms are shown?

2 Examine the labels. Name the mountain ranges and bodies of water shown in the diagram. Identify the elevation of at least three features in the diagram.

3 Write a sentence or two describing the ways in which the elevation of Africa changes as you travel from the Atlantic Ocean to the Indian Ocean.

Apply the Skill

Study the diagram of Earth's movements on pages M2–M3 of the MapMaster Skills Handbook. In a sentence or two, summarize the information given in the diagram.

The Virunga Mountains of East Africa

Assess and Reteach

Assess Progress L2
Ask students to do the Apply the Skill activity.

Reteach L1
Pair struggling students with more able students. Distribute *Reading a Diagram*. Ask the pairs to use the skill steps to complete the worksheet.

All in One **Africa Teaching Resources,** *Reading a Diagram*, p. 125

Extend L3
■ To extend the lesson, ask students to apply the skill steps to the diagrams of Earth on pp. M4–M5 of the MapMaster Skills Handbook in the Student Edition.

■ Have students study the titles and labels of the two large diagrams. Ask students to identify in which hemisphere the latitude 40°N falls. *(the Northern Hemisphere)* Then ask students to identify the name of the line of longitude that divides the globe into the Eastern and Western Hemispheres. *(the Prime Meridian)*

Differentiated Instruction

For Less Proficient Readers L1
Have students create a diagram showing the floor plan of their home, their school, or any other building where they spend a lot of time. Diagrams should include a title and labels for each room. Show students how to create the diagram by sketching a model floor plan on the board.

Answer
Apply the Skill
Possible summary: The diagram shows Earth's orbit around the sun and how it affects the seasons and day and night.

Section 3
Step-by-Step Instruction

Objectives
Social Studies
1. Discover the ways in which Africans make use of their agricultural resources.
2. Learn about the mineral and energy resources found in Africa.
3. Find out what African countries are doing to improve their economic health.

Reading/Language Arts
Summarize to enhance comprehension of a text.

Prepare to Read

Build Background Knowledge L2
In this section, students will learn how resources and land are used in Africa. Have students briefly glance at the headings and visuals of the section. Ask them to list ways they think land and resources might be used in Africa based on their preview of the section. Use the Think-Pair-Write-Share strategy (TE, p. T36) to help students share their ideas.

Set a Purpose for Reading L2
- Preview the Objectives.
- Read each statement in the *Reading Readiness Guide* aloud. Ask students to mark the statements true or false.
- Have students discuss the statements in pairs or groups of four, then mark their worksheets again. Use the Numbered Heads participation strategy (TE, p. T36) to call on students to share their group's perspectives.

  All in One Africa Teaching Resources, *Reading Readiness Guide,* p. 109

Preview Key Terms L2
Pronounce each Key Term, then ask the students to say the word with you. Provide a simple explanation such as, "The economy is the system in which people buy and sell goods and services."

Resources and Land Use

Prepare to Read

Objectives
In this section you will
1. Discover the ways in which Africans make use of their agricultural resources.
2. Learn about the mineral and energy resources found in Africa.
3. Find out what African countries are doing to improve their economic health.

Taking Notes
As you read, look for details about Africa's natural resources. Copy the chart below, and use it to record your findings.

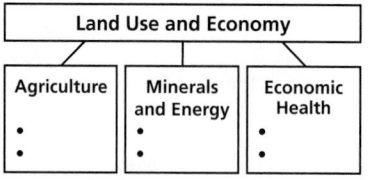

Land Use and Economy
- Agriculture
  - •
  - •
- Minerals and Energy
  - •
  - •
- Economic Health
  - •
  - •

Target Reading Skill
Summarize When you summarize, you review what you have read so far. Then you state the main points in the correct order. Summarizing what you read is a good technique to help you comprehend and study. As you read, pause occasionally to summarize what you have read.

Key Terms
- **subsistence farming** (sub SIS tuns FAHR ming) *n.* raising just enough crops to support one's family
- **cash crop** (kash krahp) *n.* a crop that is raised for sale
- **economy** (ih KAHN uh mee) *n.* a system for producing, distributing, consuming, and owning goods and services
- **diversify** (duh VUR suh fy) *v.* to add variety to; to expand a country's economy by increasing the variety of goods produced

Cacao beans (inset photo) grow on trees as shown below.

374 Africa

> "Here, in this load, I bear the seeds of a wonderful tree which, if cultivated in this land, will bless its sons everlastingly with wealth, and people far and near with health. These are the seeds of the cacao tree which I have brought with me from across the sea. . . . Would you, therefore, be kind enough to grant me a mere acre of land in this neighborhood to try my luck, and yours, and that of this country as a whole?"
>
> —*from the play* Cocoa Comes to Mampong
> *by Michael Francis Dei-Anang*

In the excerpt above, the character Tete Quarshie (TEH tay KWAWR shee) asks for land on which to plant cacao trees in Ghana. These trees, from which cocoa and chocolate are made, originally grew only in Central and South America. As Americans, Europeans, and Africans began to trade with one another, they found that cacao trees could grow in West Africa. In the play, the people grant Tete Quarshie the land, who then raises the first crop of cacao beans in Ghana. Cacao is now one of Africa's many agricultural resources.

Target Reading Skill L2
Summarize Point out the Target Reading Skill. Tell students that when summarizing a passage they should include the main points of the selection in the proper order.

Model the skill by summarizing the second and third paragraphs on p. 376. (*Farmers in all regions of Africa grow cash crops. The amount of land used for cash crops has increased in recent years, sometimes causing food shortages.*)

Give students *Summarize.* Have them complete the activity in groups.

All in One Africa Teaching Resources, *Summarize,* p. 114

MAP MASTER™ Skills Activity

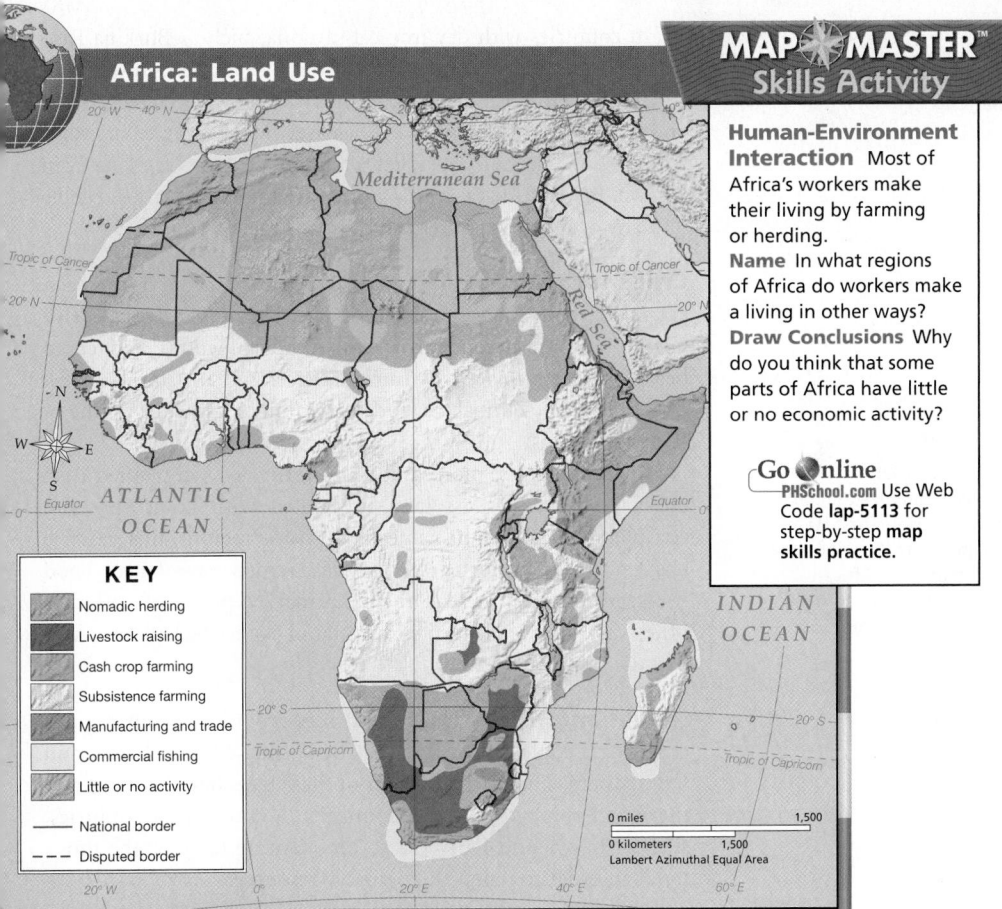

Human-Environment Interaction Most of Africa's workers make their living by farming or herding.
Name In what regions of Africa do workers make a living in other ways?
Draw Conclusions Why do you think that some parts of Africa have little or no economic activity?

Go Online
PHSchool.com Use Web Code **lap-5113** for step-by-step **map skills practice**.

KEY

- Nomadic herding
- Livestock raising
- Cash crop farming
- Subsistence farming
- Manufacturing and trade
- Commercial fishing
- Little or no activity
- ——— National border
- – – – Disputed border

0 miles 1,500
0 kilometers 1,500
Lambert Azimuthal Equal Area

Agricultural Resources

Most Africans are farmers. Some of these farmers live in areas with fertile soil and much rain. But most live on land that is difficult to farm because of poor soil or too little rain. Others lack enough land or tools to make a good living.

Farming to Live On the map above, you can see how much of Africa's land is used for **subsistence farming,** or raising just enough crops to support one's family. Subsistence farmers may sell or trade a few crops for other items they need.

In North African countries such as Morocco, subsistence farmers raise barley and wheat. They also irrigate fields to grow fruits and vegetables. Farms at Saharan oases in Egypt produce dates and small crops of barley and wheat.

Chapter 11 Section 3 **375**

Vocabulary Builder

Use the information below to teach students this section's high-use words.

High-Use Word	Definition and Sample Sentence
grant, p. 374	*v.* to give by legal deed Sandra was **granted** a scholarship for college.
item, p. 375	*n.* a single thing in a group or collection of things The first **item** on her grocery list is bread.
consume, p. 377	*v.* to use up We **consumed** all the food in the house.
conduct, p. 377	*v.* to manage, control, or direct A teacher must be able to **conduct** a classroom effectively.

Instruct

Agricultural Resources [L2]

Guided Instruction

- **Vocabulary Builder** Clarify the high-use words **grant** and **item** before reading.

- Read Agricultural Resources, using the Paragraph Shrinking strategy (TE, p. T34). As students read, circulate and make sure individuals can answer the Reading Check question at the end of the selection.

- Ask students **What difficulties do many African farmers face?** *(Much of the land has poor soil and little rainfall.)*

- Ask students **What is subsistence farming?** *(Subsistence farming is a type of farming in which people raise just enough crops to feed their families.)*

Answers

MAP MASTER Skills Activity **Name** Manufacturing and trade—South Africa and Kenya; commercial fishing—off the northwestern and southern coasts and Madagascar; livestock raising—mainly in the southern region **Draw Conclusions** Possible answer: Few people may live in these parts of Africa.

Go Online
PHSchool.com Students may practice their map skills using the interactive online version of this map.

Guided Instruction (continued)

- Ask students **What types of food do Africans eat besides the crops they grow?** *(They eat fish, goats, or poultry.)*

- Ask students **What are cash crops?** *(Cash crops are crops that are raised for sale.)*

- Ask students to list two causes of food shortages. *(As more land is being used for cash crops, less land is put aside for planting crops to feed families. When cash crops fail, farmers are less able to feed their families. Also, families have less money to buy food when the market prices for cash crops, such as coffee, fall steeply.)*

- Ask students **How do Africans make money from hardwood trees?** *(They cut the trees down and sell them.)*

- Ask students **How are countries such as Kenya and Ivory Coast working to save their forests?** *(They are planting trees by the thousands.)*

Independent Practice

Ask students to create the Taking Notes graphic organizer on a blank piece of paper. Then have them list agricultural resources as they read. Briefly model how to identify which details to record.

Monitor Progress

Circulate to ensure that individuals are filling in their graphic organizers with appropriate details. Provide assistance as needed.

⟳ Target Reading Skill `L2`

Summarize As a follow up, ask students to answer the Target Reading Skill question in the Student Edition. *(Less land is planted with crops to feed families.)*

In countries with dry tropical savanna, such as Burkina Faso (bur KEE nuh FAH soh) and Niger, subsistence farmers grow grains. In regions with more rainfall, farmers also grow vegetables, fruits, and root crops such as yams and cassava. Tapioca (tap ee OH kuh), which is used in the United States to make pudding, is made from cassava. In West Africa, corn and rice are important crops. People in many of Africa's cultures fish or raise goats or poultry.

Crops for Sale In all regions of Africa, farmers grow **cash crops,** or crops that are raised for sale. Farmers in Ivory Coast, Ghana, and Cameroon grow cash crops of coffee and cacao beans. Farmers in Kenya, Tanzania (tan zuh NEE uh), Malawi (MAH lah wee), Zimbabwe, and Mozambique grow tea as one of their cash crops.

In recent years, more and more farmers have planted cash crops. As a result, less land is planted with crops that can completely meet a family's needs. In some regions, this practice has led to food shortages when cash crops have failed. Food shortages can also occur when the market prices of coffee or other cash crops fall steeply. Then families receive less money to buy the things they need.

Harvesting Trees Hardwood trees grow in all four regions of Africa. People can earn money by cutting down the trees and selling them. Thousands of acres of these trees have been cut and the wood shipped to other countries. A number of countries, such as Kenya and Ivory Coast, are planting trees by the thousands in order to renew this valuable resource.

✓ **Reading Check** What are some of the crops grown in Africa, and where are they grown?

⟳ Summarize

Target Skill To summarize the paragraph at the right, first state the main points. An important point is that more African farmers have started to plant cash crops. Which point follows that one?

Replanting the Forest Thousands of Kenyan women have responded to the cutting down of trees in their country. Like the women shown here, they have prepared millions of young trees for local families to plant. **Predict** *How easy do you think it will be for people in Kenya to replace all the cut trees?*

376 Africa

Answers

✓ **Reading Check** Northern African countries such as Morocco: barley, wheat, fruits, vegetables; Saharan oases in Egypt: dates, barley, wheat; dry tropical savanna: grains; regions with more rainfall than savanna: grains, vegetables, fruits, roots such as yams and cassava; West Africa: corn, rice

Predict It will probably be difficult to replace the thousands of acres of cut trees.

Differentiated Instruction

For English Language Learners `L1`

To make the regions of Africa less abstract, show *Color Transparency AF 22: Africa: Political.* Ask individual students to come up and trace North Africa, West Africa, East Africa, and Central and Southern Africa on the transparency's map.

📖 **Africa Transparencies,** *Color Transparency AF 22: Africa: Political*

For Advanced Readers `L3`

To provide an example of subsistence farming, you might refer students to an excerpt from *Mokhtar of the Atlas Mountains,* the true story of a family in Morocco. Ask students to discuss how villagers might use the income from the walnuts.

All in One **Africa Teaching Resources,** *Mokhtar of the Atlas Mountains,* pp. 127–128

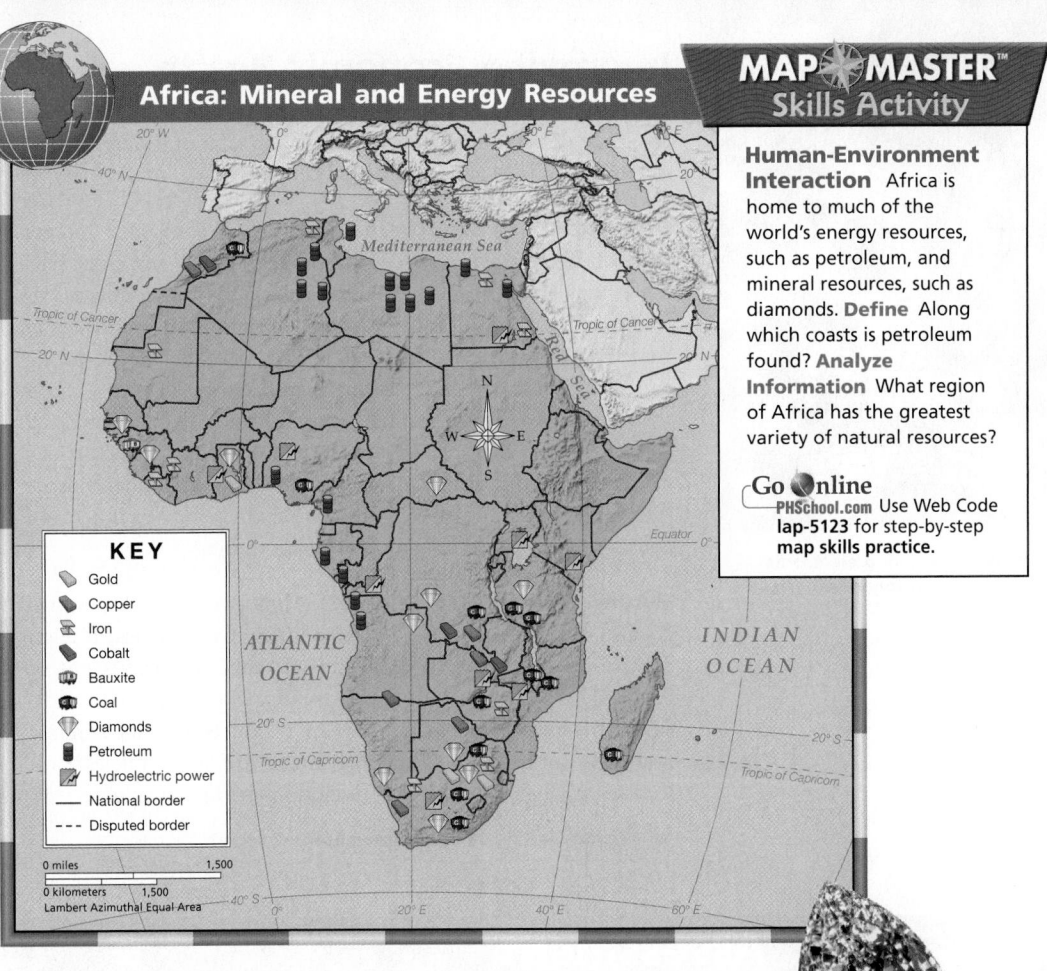

MAP MASTER™
Skills Activity

Human-Environment Interaction Africa is home to much of the world's energy resources, such as petroleum, and mineral resources, such as diamonds. **Define** Along which coasts is petroleum found? **Analyze Information** What region of Africa has the greatest variety of natural resources?

Go Online
PHSchool.com Use Web Code **lap-5123** for step-by-step map skills practice.

KEY

- Gold
- Copper
- Iron
- Cobalt
- Bauxite
- Coal
- Diamonds
- Petroleum
- Hydroelectric power
- National border
- Disputed border

0 miles 1,500
0 kilometers 1,500
Lambert Azimuthal Equal Area

Natural Resources

Each African country has its own economy. An **economy** is a system for producing, distributing, consuming, and owning goods and services. You have read that farming is an important part of many African economies. The same is true of mining. Look at the map above. Notice how many countries conduct mining operations.

Parts of Africa are rich in mineral resources. Some African countries have large amounts of petroleum, which is used to make oil and gasoline. Major oil producers include Libya and Algeria in North Africa, and Nigeria, Cameroon, Gabon, and Angola along the west coast of Africa. Ghana is a leading exporter of gold. Other mineral resources from Africa include copper, silver, uranium, titanium, and diamonds.

✔ **Reading Check** How is petroleum used?

Diamonds that have just been mined (bottom photo) are not nearly as dazzling as ones that have been cut (top photo).

Chapter 11 Section 3 **377**

Natural Resources

Improving Economic Health L2

Guided Instruction
- **Vocabulary Builder** Clarify the high-use words **consume** and **conduct** before reading.

- Read about Africa's mineral resources and its people's efforts to improve their economy in Natural Resources and Improving Economic Health.

- Have students name the mineral resources that can be found in Africa. (*petroleum, gold, copper, silver, uranium, titanium, and diamonds*)

- Ask students **Why is a diverse economy preferable to a specialized economy?** (*A diverse economy is better able to withstand downturns in particular industries without ruining the entire economy.*)

Independent Practice
Have students complete the graphic organizer by filling in details in their outlines about resources found in Africa.

Monitor Progress
- Show *Section Reading Support Transparency AF 35* and ask students to check their graphic organizers individually. Go over key concepts and clarify key vocabulary as needed.

  📖 **Africa Transparencies,** *Section Reading Support Transparency AF 35*

- Tell students to fill in the last column of their *Reading Readiness Guides*. Probe for what they learned that confirms or invalidates each statement.

  All in One Africa Teaching Resources, *Reading Readiness Guide,* p. 109

Skills Mini Lesson

Using Cartographer's Tools L2

1. Teach the skill by pointing out to students that there are certain elements common to most maps. These elements include a scale, compass rose, and map key.

2. Have students practice the skill by looking at the map on this page and using the scale to determine how far the

Equator is from the southern tip of Africa. (*about 2,500 miles or 4,000 kilometers*)

3. Have students apply the skill by answering this question: **In which region of Africa is most of its copper found?** (*in southern Africa*)

Answers

✔ **Reading Check** to make oil and gasoline

MAP MASTER Skills Activity **Define** the northern and western coasts **Analyze Information** Central and Southern Africa

Go Online
PHSchool.com Students may practice their map skills using the interactive online version of this map.

Assess Progress   L2
Have students complete the Section Assessment. Administer the *Section Quiz*.

All in One **Africa Teaching Resources,** *Section Quiz,* p. 111

Reteach   L1
If students need more instruction, have them read this section in the Reading and Vocabulary Study Guide.

📖 Chapter 11, Section 3, **Eastern Hemisphere Reading and Vocabulary Study Guide,** pp. 128–130

Extend   L3
Divide the class into groups of four. Have each group conduct research to compare the resources, land use, and economies of various African countries to those in their own communities. Have students present their findings to the rest of the class as oral reports. Encourage them to supplement their reports with visual aids such as drawings, maps, charts, and graphs.

Answer

✓**Reading Check** A specialized economy is an economy that depends on one kind of farming or industry.

Section 3 Assessment

Key Terms
Students' sentences should reflect knowledge of each Key Term.

🎯 Target Reading Skill   L2
Summaries will vary, but should include main points of the paragraph in the correct order.

Comprehension and Critical Thinking
1. **(a)** poor soil and little rain **(b)** Both kinds of farming depend on climate and the condition of the land. Subsistence farmers grow only enough to support their families. Cash crops are only grown to sell.

2. **(a)** hardwood trees, petroleum, gold, copper, silver, uranium, titanium, and diamonds **(b)** Possible answer: Africans use minerals for their own consumption, as well as to generate income through sales to foreign countries.

3. **(a)** farming **(b)** It would allow countries to weather downturns in specific industries

A man assembling electronic equipment in Johannesburg, South Africa

Improving Economic Health

As you have read, most of Africa's workers are farmers. When an economy of a nation is dependent on one kind of industry, such as farming, it is called a specialized economy.

Strengthening Economies In Africa, economic success relies on farming regions receiving enough rainfall, and crops selling at high enough prices. For that reason, African countries are trying to diversify (duh VUR suh fy) their economies. To **diversify** means to add variety. These countries are working to produce a variety of crops, raw materials, and manufactured goods.

In general, a diverse economy is more flexible than a specialized economy is. For example, suppose a country's major cash crop fails or world prices for one of its major mineral exports suddenly drop. A country with a diverse economy would not be hurt as much as a country that depends only on farming or mining.

Where Does the Money Go? Mining requires many workers and costly equipment. Throughout much of Africa, foreign companies mine African resources and take the profits out of Africa. This system does little to help African economies. In addition, Africa has few factories in which products from its own raw materials can be made. Therefore, many African countries want to diversify their economies by including manufacturing.

✓**Reading Check** What is a specialized economy?

✦ Section 3 Assessment

Key Terms
Review the key terms at the beginning of this section. Use each term in a sentence that explains its meaning.

🎯 Target Reading Skill
Reread the paragraphs under Improving Economic Health. Then write a summary of them. Include at least two main points.

Comprehension and Critical Thinking
1. (a) Recall What makes most land Africans live on hard to farm?

(b) Compare and Contrast Compare subsistence farming with farming to raise cash crops. How are they similar? How are they different?
2. (a) Identify What are some of the important natural resources found in Africa?
(b) Draw Conclusions What do you think happens to most of Africa's mineral resources after they are mined?
3. (a) Recall What kind of work is done by most Africans?
(b) Predict In what ways could African countries benefit from diversifying their economies?

Writing Activity
List some of Africa's natural resources that you and your family use. Which resource would you miss most if you did not have it? Write a paragraph explaining why.

Go Online **PHSchool.com**

For: An activity on natural resources in Africa
Visit: PHSchool.com
Web Code: lad-5103

378 Africa

better than if their economies are structured around only one or two industries.

Writing Activity
Use the *Rubric for Assessing a Writing Assignment* to evaluate students' paragraphs.

All in One **Africa Teaching Resources,** *Rubric for Assessing a Writing Assignment,* p. 130

Go Online **PHSchool.com** Typing in the Web code when prompted will bring students to detailed instructions for this activity.

Review and Assessment

◆ Chapter Summary

Section 1: Land and Water

- Africa can be divided into four regions: North, West, East, and Central and Southern. Africa's major landforms include plateaus, mountains, coastal plains, and a rift valley.
- Africa's four major rivers are the Nile, the Congo, the Zambezi, and the Niger.

Section 2: Climate and Vegetation

- Distance from the Equator and elevation are both factors that influence climate.
- Africa's vegetation regions include tropical rain forests, tropical savannas, and deserts.
- Disease-carrying insects thrive in some of Africa's climate regions, threatening the health of the people who live there.

Section 3: Resources and Land Use

- Africa's agricultural resources are used for subsistence farming and cash crops.
- Natural resources, such as minerals, are an important part of African economies.
- African countries are working to improve their economic health by diversifying their specialized economies.

Taka Mountains, Sudan

Review Chapter Content

- Review and revisit the major themes of this chapter by asking students to classify what Guiding Question each bulleted statement in the Chapter Summary answers. Have students work in groups to classify the statements. Use the Numbered Heads participation strategy (TE, p. T36) to hold a unified group discussion. Refer to p. 349 in the Student Edition for the text of the Guiding Questions.

- Assign *Vocabulary Development* for students to review Key Terms.
  All in One **Africa Teaching Resources,** *Vocabulary Development,* p. 129

◆ Key Terms

Choose the key term from the list that best completes each sentence.

1. _____ is the height of land above or below sea level.
2. A(n) _____ is a deep crack in the surface of Earth.
3. A(n) _____ flows into a river.
4. People who practice _____ raise just enough crops to support their families.
5. A(n) _____ is a region of tall grasses with scattered trees.
6. In areas that receive plenty of rain, many farmers do not need to _____ their crops.
7. A nomad traveling through the Sahara would probably visit a(n) _____ for water.
8. A(n) _____ is a system for producing, distributing, consuming, and owning goods and services.
9. To _____ is to add variety.
10. A period of little or no rainfall is a(n) _____.

Key Terms
plateau
elevation
drought
rift
fertile
tributary
irrigate
oasis
savanna
nomad
subsistence farming
cash crop
economy
diversify

Chapter 11 **379**

Answers

Key Terms

1. elevation
2. rift
3. tributary
4. subsistence farming
5. savanna
6. irrigate
7. oasis
8. economy
9. diversify
10. drought

┌ Vocabulary Builder ─

Revisit this chapter's high-use words:

consist	factor	grant
trench	severe	item
cycle	environment	consume
starchy	pest	conduct

Ask students to review the definitions they recorded on their *Word Knowledge* worksheets.

All in One **Africa Teaching Resources,** *Word Knowledge,* p. 115

Consider allowing students to earn extra credit if they use the words in their answers to the questions in the Chapter Review and Assessment. The words must be used correctly and in a natural context to win the extra points.

Review and Assessment

Comprehension and Critical Thinking

11. **(a)** Nile: longest river in the world, flows north, has fertile banks good for farming; Congo: Africa's second-longest river, has fertile banks good for farming, contains many types of fish people catch for food; Niger: third-longest river in Africa, provides water for farms and fish for food; Zambezi: Africa's fourth-longest river, has strong currents good for generating electricity. **(b)** Yearly flooding provided water and silt for the farmers' crops. The Aswan Dam ended the annual flood cycles. Farmers now use water channeled from Lake Nasser to irrigate their crops.

12. **(a)** The higher the elevation, the cooler a place usually is. Regions near the Equator are usually hot. **(b)** They are at high elevations. **(c)** Ethiopia has mostly mild temperatures and a lot of rain because it lies on a plateau, while Somalia is hot and dry since it is at a lower elevation.

13. **(a)** Tropical savannas: much of Africa north and south of the rain forest; tropical rain forests: West and Central Africa; deserts: the Sahara desert extends across most of North Africa; the Namib and Kalahari extend over much of Namibia and Botswana in Southern Africa. **(b)** Tropical rain forests: year-round rain, a large variety of trees and plants; tropical savannas: two seasons—dry and wet, tall grasses, thorny bushes, scattered trees; deserts: dry and hot, little plant life except for palm trees, and, in places, scrub and small bushes. **(c)** Possible answer: People in the rain forests grow cassava and cacao, which grow well in the warm, wet environment. They use the trees for timber, and they also fish and hunt.

14. **(a)** coffee, cacao, and tea **(b)** The deserts that cover much of North Africa and parts of Southern Africa are hot and dry and not good places to grow crops. **(c)** African countries are strengthening and diversifying their economies by working to produce a variety of crops, raw materials, and manufactured goods.

◆ Comprehension and Critical Thinking

11. **(a) Describe** Describe the physical features of each of the major rivers in Africa.
(b) Identify Cause and Effect How did the regular flooding of the Nile in the past affect farmers in the Nile Valley? How did the building of the Aswan High Dam change life for farmers?

12. **(a) Recall** What do elevation and distance from the Equator have to do with climate?
(b) Explain Why are some parts of Africa cold even though they are near the Equator?
(c) Compare and Contrast Compare the climates of Ethiopia and Somalia. Explain why their climates are similar or different.

13. **(a) Locate** Where in Africa can you find tropical savannas? Tropical rain forests? Deserts?
(b) Describe What characterizes the climate and plant life of each vegetation region?
(c) Apply Information Choose one of these regions and describe how the people who live there adapt to their environment. Give examples.

14. **(a) Name** List three cash crops raised in Africa.
(b) Identify Causes Why is there little or no farming in much of North Africa and parts of Southern Africa?
(c) Summarize Why and in what ways are many African nations trying to strengthen and diversify their economies?

◆ Skills Practice

Interpreting Diagrams You have learned how to interpret diagrams in this chapter's Skills for Life activity. You have also learned how to summarize information found in diagrams.

Review the steps you followed to learn this skill. Then turn to the diagram of Earth's longitude on page M5 of the MapMaster Skills Handbook. Identify and summarize the main ideas in the diagram.

◆ Writing Activity: Math

Make a bar graph that shows the lengths of rivers in Africa. Include the four rivers mentioned in the chapter as well as at least three others that you research on your own. Then write a short paragraph comparing the lengths of the various rivers.

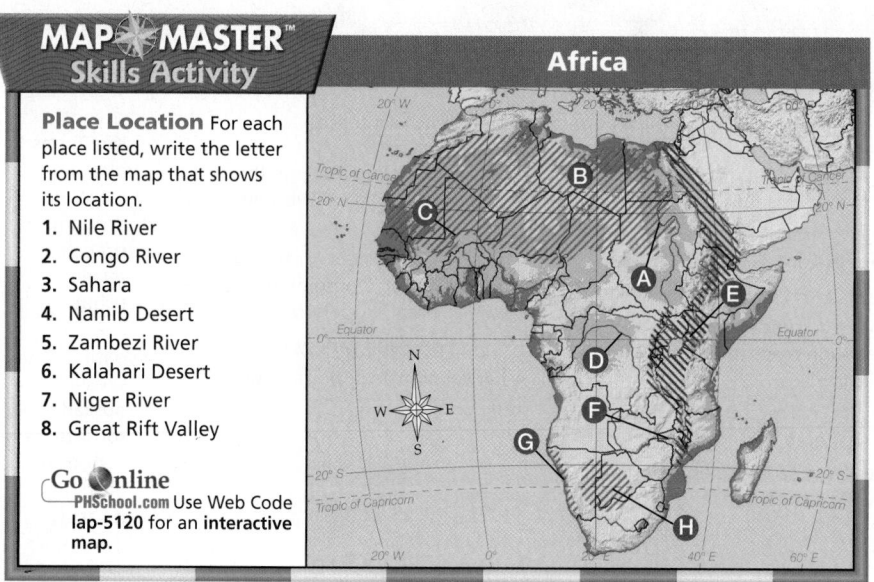

MAP MASTER™ Skills Activity

Place Location For each place listed, write the letter from the map that shows its location.
1. Nile River
2. Congo River
3. Sahara
4. Namib Desert
5. Zambezi River
6. Kalahari Desert
7. Niger River
8. Great Rift Valley

Go Online
PHSchool.com Use Web Code **lap-5120** for an **interactive map.**

Africa

Writing Activity: Math
Students' bar graphs and paragraphs should reflect an understanding of how to construct and interpret a bar graph.

Use *Rubric for Assessing a Bar Graph* and *Rubric for Assessing a Writing Assignment* to evaluate students' graphs and paragraphs.

All in One Africa Teaching Resources,
Rubric for Assessing a Bar Graph p. 131; *Rubric for Assessing a Writing Assignment,* p. 130

Skills Practice
Students summaries should show an understanding of how to interpret diagrams.

Standardized Test Prep

Test-Taking Tips

Some questions on standardized tests ask you to analyze parts of maps. Study the map key below. Then follow the tips to answer the sample question.

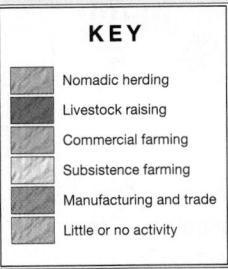

KEY

- Nomadic herding
- Livestock raising
- Commercial farming
- Subsistence farming
- Manufacturing and trade
- Little or no activity

TIP On a map key, the color column lines up with the data in the information column. To find the information you need, move from a given color to the data on the right.

Pick the letter that best answers the question.

On a land-use map, Angola is colored mostly yellow with a small amount of light green. Using the key at the left, you can determine that the people of Angola

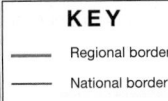

A make a great deal of money.

B use the land mainly to support themselves.

C export many products.

D use their land in many different ways.

TIP Restate the question in your own words to make sure you understand it: *What conclusion can you draw from the map key about the people of Angola and their land?*

Think It Through Yellow on the map stands for subsistence farming. Light green stands for commercial farming. Subsistence farmers grow just enough food to feed and support their families. Since most of Angola is colored yellow, you can rule out A and D. Commercial farmers may raise their crops for export. However, since most of Angola is yellow, you can rule out C also. The correct answer is B.

Practice Questions

Use the tips above and other tips in this book to help you answer the following questions.

1. Most of North Africa is along the border of the

  A Mediterranean Sea.

  B Indian Ocean.

  C Atlantic Ocean.

  D Red Sea.

2. Areas that are higher in elevation

  A tend to be closer to the Equator.

  B tend to be cooler than places lower in elevation.

  C have very mild climates.

  D have little or no rainfall.

3. African economies

  A are based largely on manufacturing.

  B could benefit from increased diversification.

  C rely solely on exports.

  D are usually dependent on a wide variety of industries.

Study the map key below, and then answer the question that follows.

KEY

- Regional border
- National border

4. The boundaries of Egypt are marked by black and red lines. Using the key, you can conclude that

  A Egypt is part of two regions of Africa.

  B Egypt borders other nations of Africa but not other regions.

  C Egypt borders other regions of Africa but not other nations.

  D Egypt borders other regions and nations.

Go Online
PHSchool.com
Use Web Code laa-5100 for **Chapter 11 self-test.**

Chapter 11 **381**

Standardized Test Prep

Answers

1. A

2. B

3. B

4. D

Overview

Section 1 — African Beginnings
1. Examine the ways in which the survival skills of early Africans changed over time.
2. Find out about early civilizations that arose along the Nile River.
3. Learn about the Bantu migrations.

Section 2 — Kingdoms, City-States, and Empires
1. Learn how trade affected the development of early East African civilizations.
2. Examine the forces that shaped the history of the North African trading powers.
3. Find out how West African kingdoms gained wealth and power.

Section 3 — European Conquest of Africa
1. Discover what motivated Europeans to explore the African coast.
2. Find out how the Atlantic slave trade developed in the 1500s.
3. Learn how Europeans colonized regions of Africa.

Section 4 — Independence and Its Challenges
1. Learn about the growth of nationalism in Africa.
2. Find out about the effects of World War II on Africa and on the growing independence movement.
3. Examine the different challenges faced by African nations on their paths to independence.

Section 5 — Issues for Africa Today
1. Learn about the economic issues faced by African nations today.
2. Find out about major social issues and how they affect Africans today.
3. Discover the ways in which Africa is facing current environmental challenges.

Discovery CHANNEL SCHOOL Video

The African Slave Trade
Length: 2 minutes, 52 seconds
Use with Section 3
This segment examines the history of the African slave trade. Students will learn how slave trading began in Africa and what happened when the Europeans began enslaving Africans.

Technology Resources

Go Online PHSchool.com

Students use embedded Web codes to access Internet activities, chapter self-tests, and additional map practice. They may also access Dorling Kindersley's Online Desk Reference to learn more about each country they study.

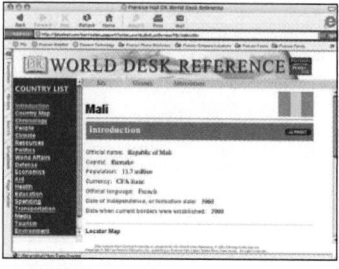

Interactive Textbook

Use the Interactive Textbook to make content and concepts come alive through animations, videos, and activities that accompany the complete basal text—online and on CD-ROM.

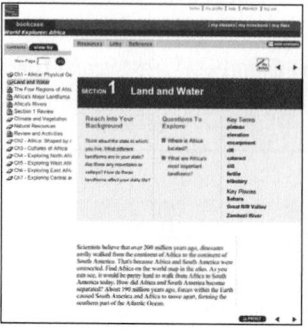

PRENTICE HALL TeacherEXPRESS
Plan • Teach • Assess

Use this complete suite of powerful teaching tools to make planning lessons and administering tests quicker and easier.

Reading and Vocabulary Instruction

🔄 Model the Target Reading Skill

Reading Process Reading actively gives students a chance to engage in the reading process. Setting a purpose gives them something to focus on while reading. Predicting helps them set a purpose and remember what they read. Using prior knowledge calls for students to think about what they already know while scanning a selection. Asking questions allows students to determine what they want to learn from a selection.

Model this process by thinking aloud about Section 1: "Section 1 is called *African Beginnings.* My purpose for reading will be to find out who Africa's first people were and how they lived. Looking at the first heading and subheadings (*Changing Survival Skills, Hunting and Gathering, Farming and Herding, Early Settlements*), I predict that I will be learning about how people in Africa survived. I have learned about people who hunt animals, gather plants, and grow crops for food to survive, but I wonder what herding is and how it relates to survival? Why did the survival skills of early Africans change? I will read the section with my original purpose in mind and see if I can answer these questions."

Use the following worksheets from All-in-One Africa Teaching Resources (pp. 163–166) to support this chapter's Target Reading Skill.

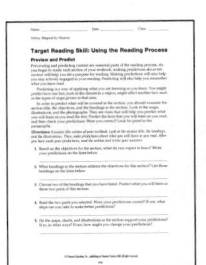 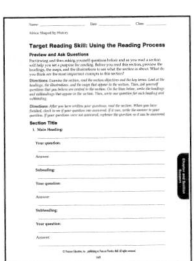

Vocabulary Builder

High-Use Academic Words

Use these steps to teach this chapter's high-use words:

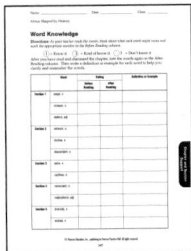

1. Have students rate how well they know each word on their Word Knowledge worksheets (All-in-One Africa Teaching Resources, p. 167).
2. Pronounce each word and ask students to repeat it.
3. Give students a brief definition or sample sentence (provided on TE pp. 385, 391, 399, 406, and 415).
4. Work with students as they fill in the "Definition or Example" column of their Word Knowledge worksheets.

Assessment

Formal Assessment

Test students' understanding of core knowledge and skills.

Chapter Tests A and B, All-in-One Africa Teaching Resources, pp. 191–196

Customize the Chapter Tests to suit your needs.
ExamView Test Bank CD-ROM

Skills Assessment

Assess geographic literacy.

MapMaster Skills, Student Edition, pp. 383, 388, 391, 395, 403, 408, 422

Assess reading and comprehension.

Target Reading Skills, Student Edition, pp. 386, 394, 404, 411, 417, and in Section Assessments

Chapter 11 Assessment, Eastern Hemisphere Reading and Vocabulary Study Guide, p. 147

Performance Assessment

Assess students' performance on this chapter's Writing Activities using the following rubrics from All-in-One Africa Teaching Resources.

Rubric for Assessing a Student Poster, p. 185

Rubric for Assessing a Writing Assignment, p. 186

Rubric for Assessing a Newspaper Article, p. 187

Rubric for Assessing a Journal Entry, p. 188

Rubric for Assessing a Timeline, p. 189

Rubric for Assessing an Oral Presentation, p. 190

Assess students' work through performance tasks.

Small Group Activity: Oral Report on an Ancient African Kingdom, All-in-One Africa Teaching Resources, pp. 170–173

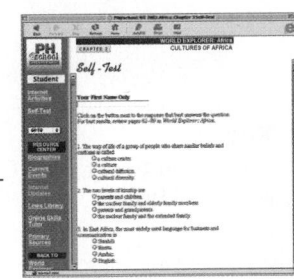

Online Assessment

Have students check their own understanding.

Chapter Self-Test

Section 1 African Beginnings

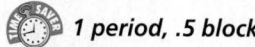 *1 period, .5 block*

Social Studies Objectives
1. Examine the ways in which the survival skills of early Africans changed over time.
2. Find out about early civilizations that arose along the Nile River.
3. Learn about the Bantu migrations.

Reading/Language Arts Objective
Learn how to set a purpose for reading to establish a focus.

Prepare to Read	Instructional Resources	Differentiated Instruction
Build Background Knowledge Have students think about what archaeologists might learn if they studied the students' classroom a thousand years from now. **Set a Purpose for Reading** Have students evaluate statements on the *Reading Readiness Guide*. **Preview Key Terms** Teach the section's Key Terms. **Target Reading Skill** Introduce the section's Target Reading Skill of **setting a purpose for reading**.	**All in One Africa Teaching Resources** L2 Reading Readiness Guide, p. 144 L2 Preview and Set a Purpose, p. 163	**Spanish Reading and Vocabulary Study Guide** L1 Chapter 12, Section 1, pp. 94–95 ELL

Instruct	Instructional Resources	Differentiated Instruction
Changing Survival Skills Discuss how the survival skills of early Africans changed over time. **Target Reading Skill** Review **setting a purpose for reading**. **Civilizations on the Nile** Ask about the elements that characterize a civilization and discuss the ancient Egyptian and Nubian civilizations. **The Bantu Migrations** Ask questions about the causes and effects of the Bantu migrations.	**All in One Africa Teaching Resources** L2 Guided Reading and Review, p. 145 L2 Reading Readiness Guide, p. 144 **Africa Transparencies** L2 Section Reading Support Transparency AF 36 L2 Color Transparency AF 22: Africa: Political	**Teacher's Edition** L1 For Less Proficient Readers, TE p. 386 L1 For Special Needs Students, TE p. 386 L2 For English Language Learners, TE p. 387 **Africa Transparencies** L1 Transparency B5: Flow Chart ELL, LPR, SN **Student Edition on Audio CD** L1 Chapter 12, Section 1 ELL, LPR, SN **Spanish Support** L2 Guided Reading and Review (Spanish), p. 132 ELL

Assess and Reteach	Instructional Resources	Differentiated Instruction
Assess Progress Evaluate student comprehension with the section assessment and section quiz. **Reteach** Assign the Reading and Vocabulary Study Guide to help struggling students. **Extend** Extend the lesson by assigning a Small Group Activity.	**All in One Africa Teaching Resources** L2 Section Quiz, p. 146 L3 Small Group Activity: Oral Report on an Ancient African Kingdom, pp. 170–173 Rubric for Assessing a Student Poster, p. 185 **Reading and Vocabulary Study Guide** L1 Chapter 12, Section 1, pp. 132–134	**Spanish Support** L2 Section Quiz (Spanish), p. 133 ELL

Key
L1 Basic to Average   L3 Average to Advanced

L2 For All Students

LPR Less Proficient Readers
AR Advanced Readers
SN Special Needs Students

GT Gifted and Talented
ELL English Language Learners

Section 2 Kingdoms, City-States, and Empires

 *1 period, .5 block*

Social Studies Objectives
1. Learn how trade affected the development of early East African civilizations.
2. Examine the forces that shaped the history of the North African trading powers.
3. Find out how West African kingdoms gained wealth and power.

Reading/Language Arts Objective
Make predictions to help you set a purpose for reading and remember what you have read.

Prepare to Read

Build Background Knowledge
Have students analyze information from maps.

Set a Purpose for Reading
Have students begin to fill out the *Reading Readiness Guide*.

Preview Key Terms
Teach the section's Key Terms.

Target Reading Skill
Introduce the section's Target Reading Skill of **predicting.**

Instructional Resources

All in One Africa Teaching Resources
- **L2** Reading Readiness Guide, p. 148
- **L2** Preview and Predict, p. 164

Africa Transparencies
- **L2** Color Transparency AF 30: Southwest Asia and North Africa: Physical-Political
- **L2** Color Transparency AF 31: Africa South of the Sahara: Physical-Political

Differentiated Instruction

Spanish Reading and Vocabulary Study Guide
- **L1** Chapter 12, Section 2, pp. 96–97 ELL

Instruct

East African Trading Civilizations
Discuss how trade brought religion, language, and wealth to the societies of East Africa.

Target Reading Skill
Review **predicting.**

North African Trading Powers
Discuss how North Africa's location influenced its history.

West African Kingdoms
Ask questions about West African kingdoms and how they were affected by trade routes.

Instructional Resources

All in One Africa Teaching Resources
- **L2** Guided Reading and Review, p. 149
- **L2** Reading Readiness Guide, p. 148

Africa Transparencies
- **L2** Section Reading Support Transparency AF 37
- **L2** Color Transparency AF Set 2: The Spread of Islam

Differentiated Instruction

All in One Africa Teaching Resources
- **L2** Guided Reading and Review, p. 149 ELL
- **L3** Enrichment, p. 168 AR, GT
- **L1** Al-Bakri Describes the Court of Ghana, p. 177 ELL, LPR, SN
- **L1** Ibn Battuta Praises the Fairness of Mali's People, p. 178 ELL, LPR, SN
- **L1** Leo Africanus Describes Timbuktu and Gao, p. 179 ELL, LPR, SN

Teacher's Edition
- **L3** For Gifted and Talented, TE p. 393
- **L2** For English Language Learners, TE p. 393
- **L3** For Advanced Readers, TE p. 394
- **L1** For Less Proficient Readers, TE p. 395

Spanish Support
- **L2** Guided Reading and Review (Spanish), p. 134 ELL

Assess and Reteach

Assess Progress
Evaluate student comprehension with the section assessment and section quiz.

Reteach
Assign the Reading and Vocabulary Study Guide to help struggling students.

Extend
Extend the lesson by assigning a Book Project.

Instructional Resources

All in One Africa Teaching Resources
- **L2** Section Quiz, p. 150
- **L3** Book Project: Africa on Stage, pp. 75–77 Rubric for Assessing a Writing Assignment, p. 186

Reading and Vocabulary Study Guide
- **L1** Chapter 12, Section 2, pp. 135–137

Differentiated Instruction

Spanish Support
- **L2** Section Quiz (Spanish), p. 135 ELL

Key
- **L1** Basic to Average
- **L2** For All Students
- **L3** Average to Advanced
- LPR Less Proficient Readers
- AR Advanced Readers
- SN Special Needs Students
- GT Gifted and Talented
- ELL English Language Learners

Section 3 European Conquest of Africa

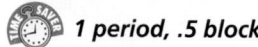 *1 period, .5 block*

Social Studies Objectives

1. Discover what motivated Europeans to explore the African coast.
2. Find out how the Atlantic slave trade developed in the 1500s.
3. Learn how Europeans colonized regions of Africa.

Reading/Language Arts Objective

Preview and ask questions to help you remember what you have read.

Prepare to Read	Instructional Resources	Differentiated Instruction

Build Background Knowledge
Have students preview the section, keeping in mind how the relationship between Europe and Africa changed.

Set a Purpose for Reading
Have students evaluate statements on the *Reading Readiness Guide*.

Preview Key Terms
Teach the section's Key Terms.

Target Reading Skill
Introduce the section's Target Reading Skill of **asking questions**.

All in One Africa Teaching Resources
- L2 Reading Readiness Guide, p. 152
- L2 Preview and Ask Questions, p. 165

Spanish Reading and Vocabulary Study Guide
- L1 Chapter 12, Section 3, pp. 98–99 ELL

Instruct	Instructional Resources	Differentiated Instruction

Europeans on the Coast
Discuss the reasons for European exploration of the African coast and how it affected Africa.

The Atlantic Slave Trade
Discuss the development of the African slave trade.

Europeans Colonize Africa
Discuss how Europeans colonized and ruled territories in Africa.

Target Reading Skill
Review **asking questions**.

All in One Africa Teaching Resources
- L2 Guided Reading and Review, p. 153
- L2 Reading Readiness Guide, p. 152

Africa Transparencies
- L2 Section Reading Support Transparency AF 38
- L2 Color Transparency AF Set 3: Scramble for Africa 1850–1914

Teacher's Edition
- L1 For Special Needs Students, TE p. 401
- L1 For Less Proficient Readers, TE p. 401
- L3 For Gifted and Talented, TE p. 403

Africa Transparencies
- L1 Transparency B16: Venn Diagram ELL, LPR, SN
- L3 Color Transparency AF 27: Africa: Political AR, GT

Reading and Vocabulary Study Guide
- L1 Chapter 12, Section 3, pp. 138–140 ELL, LPR, SN

Spanish Support
- L2 Guided Reading and Review (Spanish), p. 136 ELL

Assess and Reteach	Instructional Resources	Differentiated Instruction

Assess Progress
Evaluate student comprehension with the section assessment and section quiz.

Reteach
Assign the Reading and Vocabulary Study Guide to help struggling students.

Extend
Extend the lesson by showing a video about the African slave trade.

All in One Africa Teaching Resources
- L2 Section Quiz, p. 154
  Rubric for Assessing a Writing Assignment, p. 186

Reading and Vocabulary Study Guide
- L1 Chapter 12, Section 3, pp. 138–140

World Studies Video Program
- L2 The African Slave Trade

Spanish Support
- L2 Section Quiz (Spanish), p. 137 ELL

Key

L1 Basic to Average   L3 Average to Advanced
L2 For All Students

LPR Less Proficient Readers
AR Advanced Readers
SN Special Needs Students

GT Gifted and Talented
ELL English Language Learners

Section 4 Independence and Its Challenges

2 periods, 1 block (includes Skills for Life)

Social Studies Objectives

1. Learn about the growth of nationalism in Africa.
2. Find out about the effects of World War II on Africa and on the growing independence movement.
3. Examine the different challenges faced by African nations on their paths to independence.

Reading/Language Arts Objective

Use prior knowledge to get a head start on learning new information.

Prepare to Read	**Instructional Resources**	**Differentiated Instruction**
Build Background Knowledge Discuss how pride and loyalty led many countries in Africa to work for independence. **Set a Purpose for Reading** Have students begin to fill out the *Reading Readiness Guide*. **Preview Key Terms** Teach the section's Key Terms. **Target Reading Skill** Introduce the section's Target Reading Skill of **using prior knowledge**.	**All in One Africa Teaching Resources** L2 Reading Readiness Guide, p. 156 L2 Preview and Use Prior Knowledge, p. 166	**Spanish Reading and Vocabulary Study Guide** L1 Chapter 12, Section 4, pp. 100–101 ELL **Africa Transparencies** L2 Transparency B6: Flow Chart AR, GT, LPR, SN

Instruct	**Instructional Resources**	**Differentiated Instruction**
The Growth of Nationalism Discuss the development of nationalism in Africa. **Africa and World War II** Discuss Africa's role in World War II. **Different Paths to Independence** Discuss how African countries gained independence and the challenges they faced. **Target Reading Skill** Review **using prior knowledge**.	**All in One Africa Teaching Resources** L2 Guided Reading and Review, p. 157 L2 Reading Readiness Guide, p. 156 **Africa Transparencies** L2 Transparency B8: Cause and Effect Chart L2 Section Reading Support Transparency AF 39	**All in One Africa Teaching Resources** L1 Using the Map Key, p. 174 ELL, LPR, SN L2 Skills for Life, p. 169 AR, GT, LPR, SN **Teacher's Edition** L1 For Less Proficient Readers, TE p. 408 **Spanish Support** L2 Guided Reading and Review (Spanish), p. 138 ELL

Assess and Reteach	**Instructional Resources**	**Differentiated Instruction**
Assess Progress Evaluate student comprehension with the section assessment and section quiz. **Reteach** Assign the Reading and Vocabulary Study Guide to help struggling students. **Extend** Extend the lesson by assigning literature readings.	**All in One Africa Teaching Resources** L2 Section Quiz, p. 158 L3 Interview with Congolese Villagers, 1893, p. 180 L3 Ghanian Leader Speaks Out, p. 181 L3 The Words of Desmond Tutu, pp. 182–183 Rubric for Assessing a Newspaper Article, p. 187 **Reading and Vocabulary Study Guide** L1 Chapter 12, Section 4, pp. 141–143	**All in One Africa Teaching Resources** L1 Reading a Flow Chart, p. 175 ELL, LPR, SN **Teacher's Edition** L1 For Special Needs Students, TE p. 413 **Spanish Support** L2 Section Quiz (Spanish), p. 139 ELL **Social Studies Skills Tutor CD-ROM** L1 Sequencing ELL, LPR, SN

Key

L1 Basic to Average
L2 For All Students
L3 Average to Advanced

LPR Less Proficient Readers
AR Advanced Readers
SN Special Needs Students

GT Gifted and Talented
ELL English Language Learners

Section 5 Issues for Africa Today

 3 periods, 1.5 blocks (includes Chapter Review and Assessment)

Social Studies Objectives

1. Learn about the economic issues faced by African nations today.
2. Find out about major social issues and how they affect Africans today.
3. Discover the ways in which Africa is facing current environmental challenges.

Reading/Language Arts Objective

Make predictions to help you set a purpose for reading and remember what you have read.

Prepare to Read	Instructional Resources	Differentiated Instruction
Build Background Knowledge Discuss the responsibilities that come with independence. **Set a Purpose for Reading** Have students evaluate statements on the *Reading Readiness Guide.* **Preview Key Terms** Teach the section's Key Terms. **Target Reading Skill** Introduce the section's Target Reading Skill of **predicting.**	**All in One Africa Teaching Resources** L2 Reading Readiness Guide, p. 160 L2 Preview and Predict, p. 164	**Spanish Reading and Vocabulary Study Guide** L1 Chapter 12, Section 5, pp. 102–103 ELL

Instruct	Instructional Resources	Differentiated Instruction
Economic Issues Discuss different aspects of the African economy. **Eyewitness Technology** Have students analyze a diagram to learn about South African gold mines. **Target Reading Skill** Review **predicting.** **Social Issues** Discuss education and disease in Africa. **The Environment** Discuss problems facing Africa's environment.	**All in One Africa Teaching Resources** L2 Guided Reading and Review, p. 161 L2 Reading Readiness Guide, p. 160 Rubric for Assessing a Journal Entry, p. 188 **Africa Transparencies** L2 Section Reading Support Transparency AF 40	**All in One Africa Teaching Resources** L1 Reading a Diagram, p. 176 ELL, LPR, SN **Teacher's Edition** L3 For Advanced Readers, TE pp. 416, 418 L1 For Special Needs Students, TE pp. 416, 417 L1 For English Language Learners, TE p. 417 L3 For Gifted and Talented, TE p. 419 **Student Edition on Audio CD** L1 Chapter 12, Section 5 ELL, LPR, SN **PHSchool.com** L3 **For:** Environmental and Global Issues: Life Expectancy; Deforestation AR, GT **Web Codes:** lad-5206, lad-5207

Assess and Reteach	Instructional Resources	Differentiated Instruction
Assess Progress Evaluate student comprehension with the section assessment and section quiz. **Reteach** Assign the Reading and Vocabulary Study Guide to help struggling students. **Extend** Extend the lesson by assigning a Book Project.	**All in One Africa Teaching Resources** L2 Section Quiz, p. 162 L3 Book Project: Africa Conference, pp. 78–80 Rubric for Assessing a Writing Assignment, p. 186 Rubric for Assessing a Timeline, p. 189 Rubric for Assessing an Oral Presentation, p. 190 L2 Vocabulary Development, p. 184 L2 Word Knowledge, p. 167 L2 Chapter Tests A and B, pp. 191–196 **Reading and Vocabulary Study Guide** L1 Chapter 12, Section 5, pp. 144–146	**Spanish Support** L2 Section Quiz (Spanish), p. 141 ELL L2 Chapter Summary (Spanish), p. 142 ELL L2 Vocabulary Development (Spanish), p. 143 ELL

Key

L1 Basic to Average   L3 Average to Advanced
L2 For All Students

LPR Less Proficient Readers
AR Advanced Readers
SN Special Needs Students

GT Gifted and Talented
ELL English Language Learners

Professional Development

Reading Background

Pre-Teaching Vocabulary

Research literature on academic vocabulary instruction indicates that effective strategies require students to go beyond simply looking up dictionary definitions or examining the context. Vocabulary learning must be based on the learner's dynamic engagement in constructing understanding.

If students are not retaining the meaning of the Key Terms or high-use words, use this extended vocabulary sequence to engage them in learning new words.

1. Present the word in writing and point out the part of speech.
2. Pronounce the word and have students pronounce the word.
3. Provide a range of familiar synonyms (or "it's like" words) before offering definitions.
4. Provide an accessible definition and concrete examples, or "showing sentences."
5. Rephrase the simple definition or example sentence, asking students to complete the statement by substituting the word aloud.
6. Check for understanding by providing an application task/ question requiring critical thinking.

Sample instructional sequence:

1. Our first word is *domesticate*. It is a verb, a word that expresses an action.

2. Say the word *domesticate* after me. (Students repeat.)
3. *Domesticating* is similar to *training* or *taming*.
4. The word *domesticate* means *to adapt wild plants or animals for human use.* Pets are *domesticated* animals.
5. Horses that people ride have been _____ by humans. (Students fill in the blank.)
6. Are the plants sold at the florist *domesticated?* Yes-No-Why? (Students answer the question.)

Seed Discussions

Ask students to form small groups, and have them take turns leading their own discussions about what they are reading in the chapter. Tell students that in order to lead a discussion, they will need a strong "seed" to start with.

Model a strong seed versus a weak seed. A strong seed might be a question or opinion about the reading, or something in the chapter that was surprising. An example of a strong seed is: "I wonder why civilizations developed in some places before others." A weak seed might be a restatement of fact, such as: "Settlements were established in Nubia around 6000 B.C."

World Studies Background

Olduvai Gorge

The Olduvai lake basin was sliced into a gorge by millions of years of volcanic activity, fault movements, and erosion. This exposed distinct layers of rock whose age can be determined by their placement and thickness. The basin is rich with artifacts and fossils used by scientists to study early humans.

The *Amistad*

On July 2, 1839, 53 captive Africans aboard the *Amistad,* a Spanish slave ship on its way to Cuba, revolted. The United States navy seized the ship and a trial was held to decide the Africans' fate. A federal court ruled that although slavery in Cuba was legal, importing slaves from Africa

was not. The slaves were considered, therefore, victims of a kidnapping and should be permitted to return home to Africa. The United States Supreme Court upheld the decision.

Léopold Sédar Senghor (1906–2001)

Senghor, born in French West Africa, now Senegal, was a poet and a political leader. He was one of the creators of the idea of Negritude, an artistic and literary movement with an emphasis on African culture. Senghor studied and taught in France, where he became aware of Africa's contributions to modern culture. He became the first president of the independent nation of Senegal in 1960.

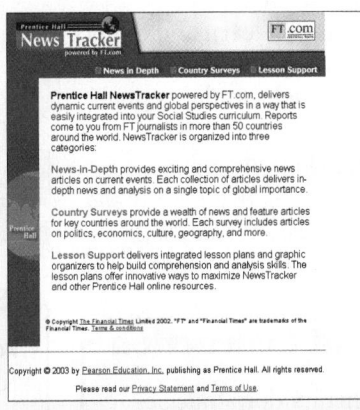

Get in-depth information on topics of global importance with **Prentice Hall Newstracker,** powered by FT.com.

 Use web code **lad-5200** for **Prentice Hall Newstracker.**

Chapter 12

Chapter 12 Africa: Shaped by Its History

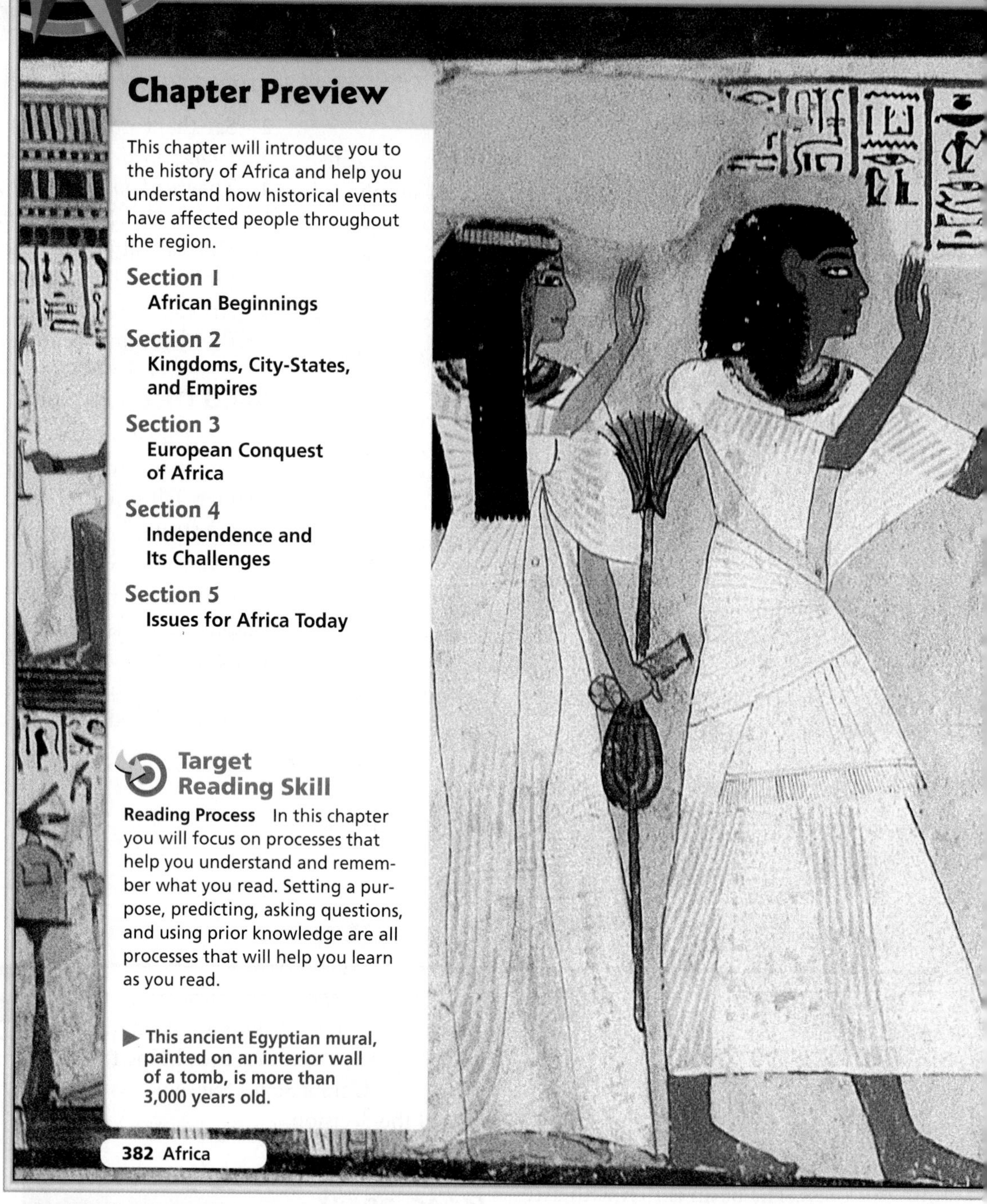

Guiding Questions

Remind students about the Guiding Questions introduced at the beginning of this section.

Section 1 relates to **Guiding Question** ②
How have historical events affected the cultures and nations of Africa? *(The development of farming techniques and the domestication of animals led to the development of ancient civilizations in Africa.)*

Section 2 relates to **Guiding Question** ③
What features help define different African cultures? *(Trade in early African civilizations helped shape the cultures of Africa.)*

Section 3 relates to **Guiding Question** ②
How have historical events affected the cultures and nations of Africa? *(The European colonization of Africa had lasting effects on the continent.)*

Section 4 relates to **Guiding Question** ④
What factors led to the development of different governments across Africa? *(After World War II many African nations won independence from European rule and established different types of governments.)*

Section 5 relates to **Guiding Question** ⑤
What factors influence the ways in which Africans make a living? *(Colonial powers did little to build factories in Africa. Many African countries still have little manufacturing.)*

Target Reading Skill

In this chapter, students will learn and apply the reading skill of reading process. Use the following worksheets to help students practice this skill:

All in One **Africa Teaching Resources,**
Preview and Set a Purpose, p. 163; *Preview and Predict,* p. 164; *Preview and Ask Questions,* p. 165; *Preview and Use Prior Knowledge,* p. 166

Differentiated Instruction

The following Teacher Edition strategies are suitable for students of varying abilities.
Advanced Readers, pp. 394, 416, 418
English Language Learners, pp. 387, 393, 417
Gifted and Talented, pp. 393, 403, 419
Less Proficient Readers, pp. 386, 395, 401, 408
Special Needs Students, pp. 386, 401, 413, 416, 417

Chapter Preview

This chapter will introduce you to the history of Africa and help you understand how historical events have affected people throughout the region.

Section 1
African Beginnings

Section 2
Kingdoms, City-States, and Empires

Section 3
European Conquest of Africa

Section 4
Independence and Its Challenges

Section 5
Issues for Africa Today

Target Reading Skill

Reading Process In this chapter you will focus on processes that help you understand and remember what you read. Setting a purpose, predicting, asking questions, and using prior knowledge are all processes that will help you learn as you read.

▶ This ancient Egyptian mural, painted on an interior wall of a tomb, is more than 3,000 years old.

382 Africa

Bibliography

For the Teacher
Klein, Herbert S. *The Atlantic Slave Trade.* Cambridge University Press, 1999.
Nugent, Paul. *Africa Since Independence: A Comparative History.* Palgrave Macmillan, 2003.
Osborne, Richard E. *World War II in Colonial Africa.* Riebel-Roque Publishing Company, 2001.

For the Student
L1 Thompson, Carol. *Empire of Mali.* Scholastic Library Publishing, 1998.
L2 Newman, Shirlee Petkin. *The African Slave Trade.* Scholastic Library Publishing, 2000.
L3 Oppong, Joseph R., Esther D. Oppong, and Charles F. Gritzner (Editor). *Ghana.* Chelsea House Publishers, 2003.

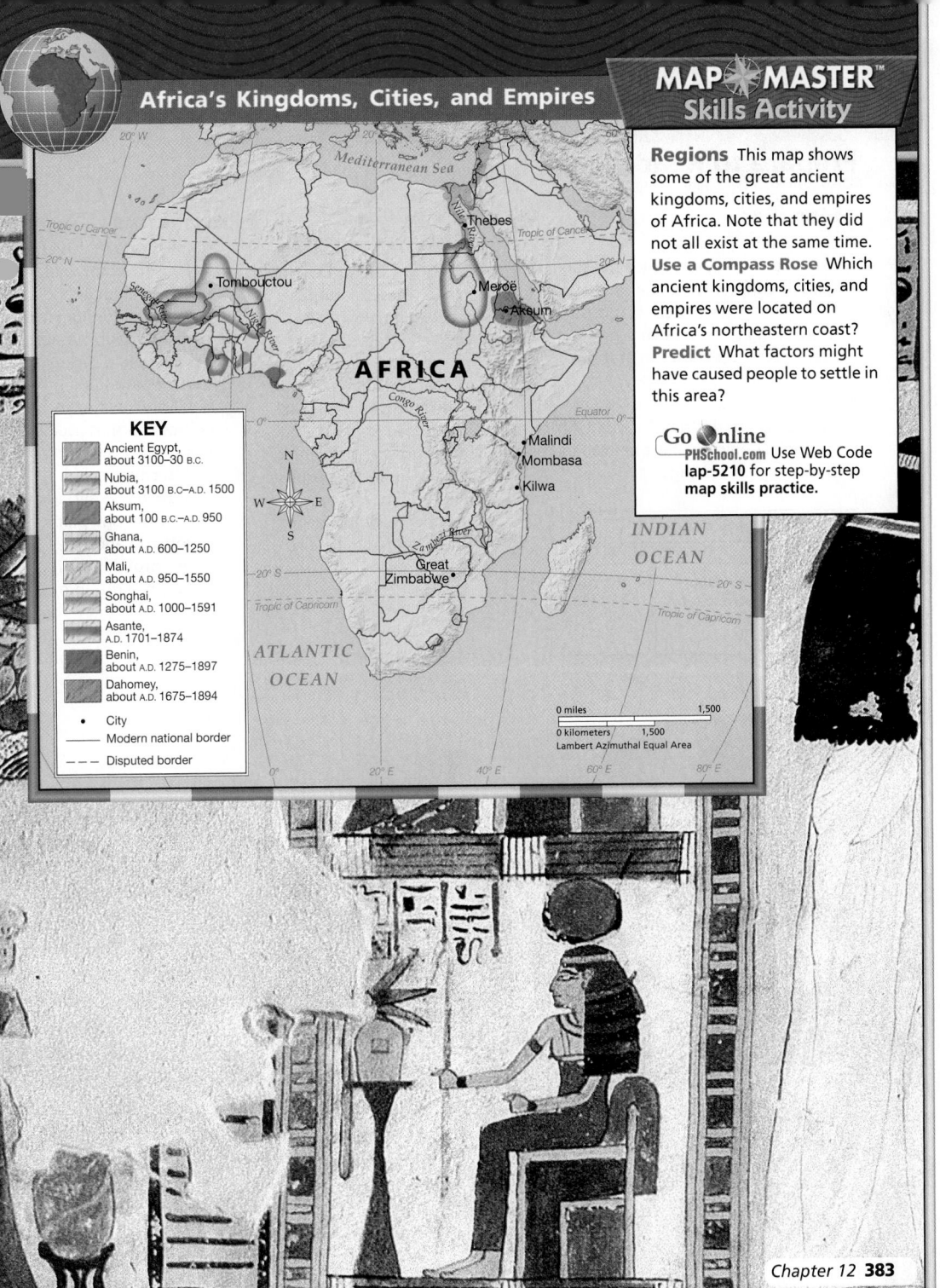

MAP MASTER™
Skills Activity

Regions This map shows some of the great ancient kingdoms, cities, and empires of Africa. Note that they did not all exist at the same time. **Use a Compass Rose** Which ancient kingdoms, cities, and empires were located on Africa's northeastern coast? **Predict** What factors might have caused people to settle in this area?

Go Online
PHSchool.com Use Web Code **lap-5210** for step-by-step **map skills practice.**

KEY

Ancient Egypt, about 3100–30 B.C.
Nubia, about 3100 B.C.–A.D. 1500
Aksum, about 100 B.C.–A.D. 950
Ghana, about A.D. 600–1250
Mali, about A.D. 950–1550
Songhai, about A.D. 1000–1591
Asante, A.D. 1701–1874
Benin, about A.D. 1275–1897
Dahomey, about A.D. 1675–1894

• City
— Modern national border
--- Disputed border

0 miles 1,500
0 kilometers 1,500
Lambert Azimuthal Equal Area

Chapter 12 **383**

MAP MASTER™
Skills Activity

Display *Color Transparency AF 22: Africa: Political*. Have students compare the map on p. 383 with the map of present-day Africa. Tell students to make a table that lists the kingdoms and the names of the present-day countries they stretch across.

📖 **Africa Transparencies,** *Color Transparency AF 22: Africa: Political*

Using the Visual L2

Reach Into Your Background Draw students' attention to the mural on pp. 382–383 and the caption. Discuss what some of the objects in the mural might be and how they might help explain what life was like in ancient Egypt. Ask students to think about what they might paint on a mural to portray their daily lives.

Answers

MAP MASTER™
Skills Activity **Use a Compass Rose**
Ancient Egypt, Aksum, Nubia, Thebes, Meroë **Predict** Possible answers: Access to the Nile River provided water for drinking and farming. Aksum's location on the coast allowed for trade with Southwest Asia and other regions.

Chapter Resources

Teaching Resources
L2 Vocabulary Development, p. 184
L2 Skills for Life, p. 169
L2 Chapter Tests A and B, pp. 191–196

Spanish Support
L2 Spanish Chapter Summary, p. 142
L2 Spanish Vocabulary Development, p. 143

Media and Technology
L1 Student Edition on Audio CD
L1 Guided Reading Audiotapes, English and Spanish
L2 Social Studies Skills Tutor CD-ROM
ExamView Test Bank CD-ROM

PRENTICE HALL
Presentation EXPRESS™
Teach · Connect · Inspire

Teach this chapter's content using the PresentationExpress™ CD-ROM including:
■ slide shows
■ transparencies
■ interactive maps and media
■ *ExamView*® QuickTake Presenter

Objectives

Social Studies

1. Examine the ways in which the survival skills of early Africans changed over time.
2. Find out about early civilizations that arose along the Nile River.
3. Learn about the Bantu migrations.

Reading/Language Arts

Learn how to set a purpose for reading to establish a focus.

Prepare to Read

Build Background Knowledge L2

Tell students that they will learn about Africa's first peoples in this section. Explain that archaeologists study artifacts to learn about ancient people. Ask students to suppose that a thousand years from now, archaeologists are studying your classroom. Challenge students to speculate on what the scientists might learn about them by studying various items such as pencils, a computer, and desks.

Set a Purpose for Reading L2

- Preview the Objectives.

- Read each statement in the *Reading Readiness Guide* aloud. Ask students to mark the statements true or false.

- Have students discuss the statements in pairs or groups of four, then mark their worksheets again. Use the Numbered Heads participation strategy (TE, p. T36) to call on students to share their group's perspectives.

All in One **Africa Teaching Resources,** *Reading Readiness Guide,* p. 144

Vocabulary Builder
Preview Key Terms L2

Pronounce each key term, then ask the students to say the word with you. Provide a simple explanation such as, "Dogs are domesticated animals that were tamed thousands of years ago and today are mainly pets."

Section 1

African Beginnings

Prepare to Read

Objectives

In this section you will

1. Examine the ways in which the survival skills of early Africans changed over time.
2. Find out about early civilizations that arose along the Nile River.
3. Learn about the Bantu migrations.

Taking Notes

As you read, look for details about Africa's first people. Copy the chart below, and use it to record your findings.

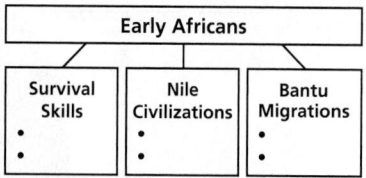

Target Reading Skill

Set a Purpose for Reading
When you set a purpose for reading, you give yourself a focus. Before you read this section, look at the headings and illustrations to see what the section is about. Then set a purpose for reading this section. Your purpose might be to learn about the people who lived in Africa long ago. Finally, read to meet your purpose.

Key Terms

- **domesticate** (duh MES tih kayt) *v.* to adapt wild plants or animals and breed them for human use
- **civilization** (sih vuh luh ZAY shun) *n.* a society that has cities, a central government, and social classes and that usually has writing, art, and architecture
- **migrate** (MY grayt) *v.* to move from one place to settle in another
- **ethnic group** (ETH nik groop) *n.* a group of people who share the same ancestors, culture, language, or religion

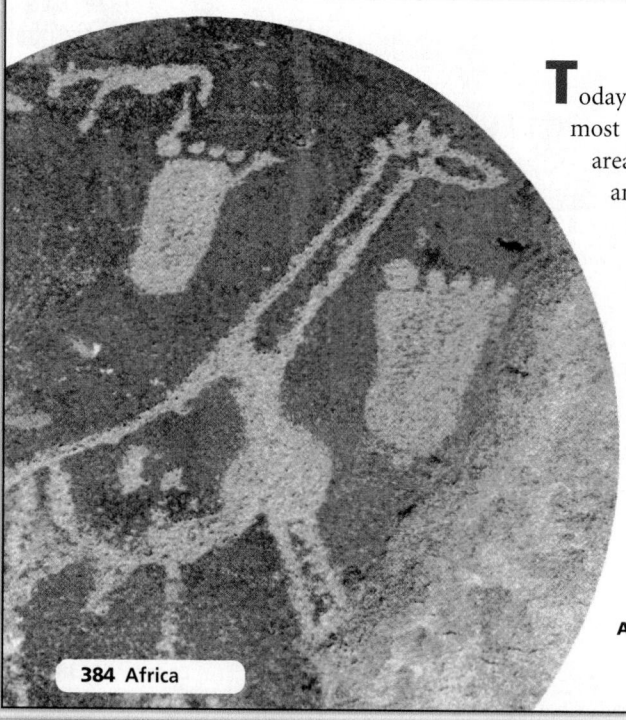

384 Africa

T oday, the dry sands and rocks of the Sahara cover most of North Africa. But 10,000 years ago, this area was wet enough to support many people and animals. Scientists think Africa's first farmers lived in what is now the Sahara. Ancient rock paintings tell their story.

The history of humans in Africa goes back even further in time than the history of those early farmers. Scientists believe that our early human ancestors lived in East Africa at least 2 million years ago. Today, scientists study the stone tools and bones that these ancestors left behind. By doing so, they learn about the ways our early human ancestors found to survive.

Ancient cave painting from Namibia

Target Reading Skill L2

Set a Purpose for Reading Point out the Target Reading Skill. Tell students that setting a purpose for reading will help them to focus on important information as they read.

Model the skill by setting a purpose for reading the Civilizations on the Nile subsection on p. 387. Explain that you will read the subheads and study the photos to help you set your purpose. *(Possible purpose: I will learn about the people who lived in Egypt and Nubia.)*

Give students *Preview and Set a Purpose.* Have them complete the activity in groups.

All in One **Africa Teaching Resources,** *Preview and Set a Purpose,* p. 163

Changing Survival Skills

What skills did our early human ancestors need to survive? Like people today, they needed to find food, water, and shelter to live. Survival skills changed and developed over the course of many thousands of years.

Hunting and Gathering Our early human ancestors were hunter-gatherers. A hunter-gatherer is someone who hunts animals and gathers food in the wild to survive. Hunter-gatherers hunted animals to use the meat for food and the hides and fur for clothing and shelter. They ate foods such as fruits, nuts, and roots. They made tools out of wood, animal bones, and eventually stone. The first use of stone tools marks the beginning of a time period scientists call the Stone Age.

The stone tools made by our early human ancestors worked very well. The scientist Louis Leakey found some of the first evidence of human ancestors in East Africa. He also taught himself how to make and use their tools. Using a two-inch, 25,000-year-old stone knife, Leakey could skin and cut up a gazelle in just 20 minutes.

Studying Early Human Ancestors
This stone tool (above) was made by one of our early human ancestors. For more than 30 years, Louis Leakey studied finds like this one at Olduvai Gorge (left) in Tanzania. His family (below) also studied them. **Analyze Images** *Do you find it easy or hard to tell this stone tool from an ordinary stone?*

Chapter 12 Section 1 **385**

Target Reading Skill

Set a Purpose As a follow up, ask students to answer the Target Reading Skill question in the Student Edition. *(Possible purpose: I will learn about how survival skills changed over time in Africa. If the text did not help students accomplish their purpose, help them set a new one.)*

Guided Instruction (continued)

- Discuss the ways in which the early Africans domesticated plants and animals. *(They threw away the seeds from weak plants and saved seeds from stronger ones. They tamed wild animals and then bred them.)*

- Remind students that food surpluses allowed some early Africans to do other kinds of work. Ask **What other kinds of work might have been needed in a new settlement?** *(Possible answers: builders to create homes, toolmakers to make farming tools)*

Independent Practice

Ask students to create the Taking Notes graphic organizer on a blank piece of paper. Then have them fill in the Survival Skills segment of the chart with the information they have just learned. Briefly model how to identify which details to record.

Monitor Progress

As students fill in their organizers, circulate and make sure individuals are choosing the correct details. Provide assistance as needed.

Answers

Predict domestication of plants and animals, planting and harvesting of crops, and irrigation

✓ Reading Check The Stone Age was the period of time that began with the first use of stone tools.

386 *Africa*

Set a Purpose What purpose did you set for the section? Has the text you have read so far helped you toward achieving this purpose? If not, set a new purpose for the rest of the section.

African Farmers Today In African communities that practice agriculture today, women play a variety of roles. Here, Central African women carry firewood to their homes. **Predict** *What activities are essential to a successful agricultural community?*

386 Africa

Farming and Herding Between 10,000 and 6,000 years ago, some hunter-gatherers began to farm and to herd animals. As you read earlier, farming in Africa probably began in North Africa, when the area that is now the Sahara offered more water than is available there today. The first farmers probably planted wild grains such as barley. At first, gatherers just protected the areas where these grains grew best. Then they began to save some seeds to plant for the next year's crop.

Later, people began to **domesticate** plants, or adapt them for their own use. They threw away seeds from weaker plants and saved seeds from stronger ones. People also domesticated certain wild animals by taming and breeding them.

Early Settlements Domesticating plants and animals meant people could have better control over their food supply. They did not have to travel to places where grains were already growing. Instead, they planted the crops they wanted. As a result, they could settle in one place. Most early farmers settled on fertile land near a water supply. Some communities produced a food surplus, or more than what was needed. Surpluses allowed some people in the community to do work other than farming.

✓ Reading Check What was the Stone Age?

Differentiated Instruction

For Less Proficient Readers · L1

Have students read the section as they listen to the recorded version on the Student Edition on Audio CD. Check for comprehension by pausing the CD and asking students to share their answers to the Reading Checks.

🔘 Chapter 12, Section 1, **Student Edition on Audio CD**

For Special Needs Students · L1

Have students work with more able partners to create a flow chart that shows how early Africans' survival skills changed over time. Display the *Flow Chart Transparency* and model how to fill in the first box.

📖 **Africa Transparencies,** *Transparency B5: Flow Chart*

Civilizations on the Nile

Over a period of hundreds of thousands of years, some Stone Age groups became civilizations. A **civilization** is a society with cities, a government, and social classes. A social class is a group that is made up of people with similar backgrounds, wealth, and ways of living. Social classes form when people do different jobs. The types of jobs people do determine whether they are rich, poor, or in the middle. Civilizations also usually have architecture, writing, and art. A few thousand years ago, two important African civilizations—Egypt and Nubia—arose along the Nile River.

Egypt Each summer, the Nile River used to flood its banks. The flooding waters would cover the ground with a layer of fertile silt that was ideal for farming because it enriched the soil. Around 5000 B.C., people began farming along the river's banks. They settled in scattered villages. Over many years, these villages grew into the civilization of ancient Egypt.

Ancient Egypt was ruled by kings and queens. The kings of Egypt were called pharaohs (FEHR ohz). The people believed that their pharaohs were also gods. When kings and queens died, they were buried in tombs. Some of the tombs were built as large pyramids. People painted murals and picture-writing symbols called hieroglyphs (HY ur oh glifs) on the inner walls of the tombs. The ancient Egyptians became skilled in paper-making, architecture, medicine, and astronomy.

Nubia In about 6000 B.C., settled hunting and fishing communities began to arise along the Nile south of Egypt. About 1,000 years later, these communities began farming. This area was called Nubia. Scientists believe the formation of Nubian kingdoms may have started around 3100 B.C.

One of the greatest Nubian kingdoms was centered in the city of Napata. Around 724 B.C., the Nubians of Napata conquered Egypt. Nubians ruled Egypt for about 60 years. A later Nubian kingdom was based farther south, in the city of Meroë (MEHR oh ee). Meroë began to weaken in the A.D. 200s. It was finally conquered in A.D. 350 by invading forces from the Ethiopian kingdom of Aksum (AHK soom).

Leftover From Ancient Times
The Nubian mural (top) was painted inside a tomb more than 3,000 years ago. The pair of Egyptian leather sandals (above), which are similar to the ones shown in the mural, are more than 5,000 years old. **Infer** *What kind of information can objects like these teach us about ancient civilizations?*

 Reading Check What are social classes, and how are they formed?

Guided Instruction

- **Vocabulary Builder** Clarify the high-use word **conquer** before reading.

- Read Civilizations on the Nile with students. As they read, circulate and make sure individuals can answer the Reading Check question.

- Discuss the elements that characterize a civilization. *(A civilization is a society with cities, a government, and different social classes that form when people do a variety of different jobs. Civilizations also have writing, architecture, and art.)*

- Help students compare and contrast ancient Egypt and Nubia. *(Both arose along the Nile, and farming was important to both. The Nubian civilization started earlier than the Egyptian.)* Then ask **Why do you think the banks of the Nile were a good place to start a civilization?** *(The banks of the Nile were fertile and good for farming. A regular food supply is needed to sustain a civilization.)*

Independent Practice
Ask students to fill in the Nile Civilizations box of the graphic organizer with the information they have just learned.

Monitor Progress
As students fill in the graphic organizer, circulate and make sure individuals are choosing the correct details. Provide assistance as needed.

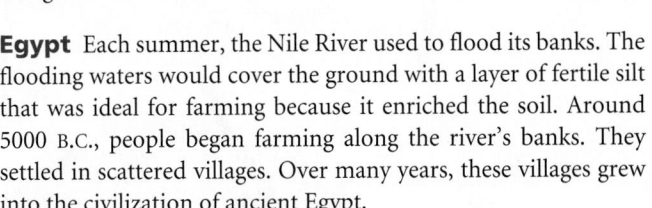

Differentiated Instruction

For English Language Learners   [L2]
Pair students with native speakers to review the use of pronouns throughout this section. Encourage students to discuss the section together, using pronouns to replace some words and phrases, for example, *they* or *them* for *human ancestors, kings and queens; he* or *him* for *Louis Leakey; it* for *the Nile River*. Also ask students to explore the use of *some* and *others* as pronoun references for people.

Answers

Infer Objects like those pictured allow us to learn more about the daily lives of people in ancient civilizations.

Reading Check Social classes are groups made up of people with similar backgrounds, wealth, and ways of living. They are formed when people in a civilization do a variety of jobs.

The Bantu Migrations L2

Guided Instruction

- **Vocabulary Builder** Clarify the high-use academic word **distinct** before reading.

- Read about the spread of Bantu-speaking people in The Bantu Migrations.

- Discuss the chain of events that some people believe led to the Bantu migrations. *(Some experts believe that the ability to grow crops in the tropical rainforest led to an abundance of food, such as yams. The abundance of food may have led to overpopulation. This led the Bantu-speaking people to move to other regions to find new land to farm.)*

- Ask students **Why do you think the Bantu language became dominant in places where Bantu-speaking people were not the native peoples?** *(Possible answer: They had so many skills to teach the native peoples that it became important for native peoples to learn the Bantu language in order to advance their civilizations.)*

Independent Practice

Ask students to complete their charts with the information they have just learned.

Monitor Progress

- Show *Section Reading Support Transparency AF 36* and ask students to check their graphic organizers individually.

  📖 **Africa Transparencies,** *Section Reading Support Transparency AF 36*

- Tell students to fill in the last column of their *Reading Readiness Guides.*

  All in One **Africa Teaching Resources,** *Reading Readiness Guide,* p. 144

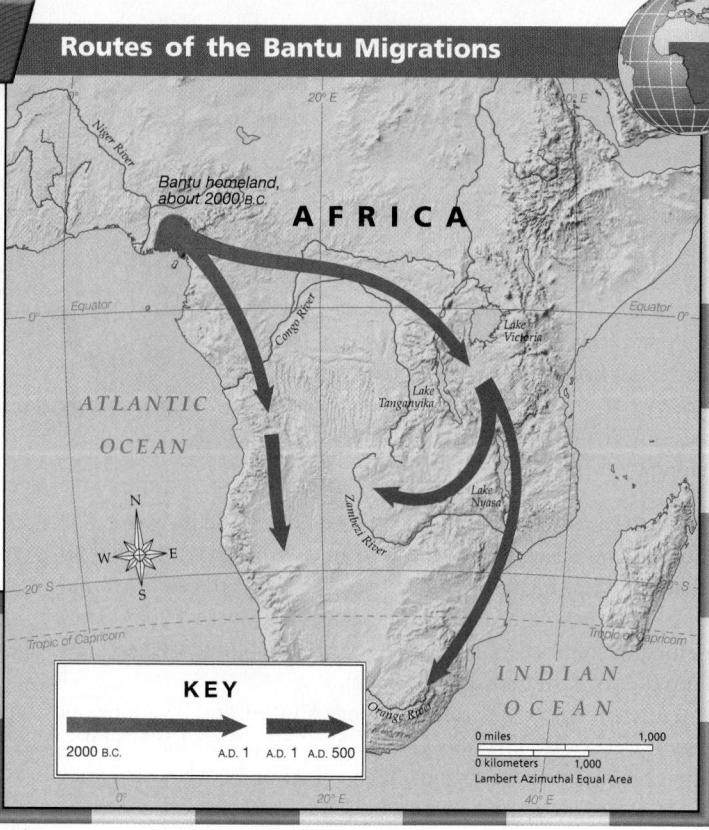

MAP MASTER Skills Activity
Routes of the Bantu Migrations

Movement The Bantu migrations were some of the largest movements of people in history. As a result, millions of Africans today speak Bantu languages. **Identify** Where did the Bantu migrations begin? **Analyze Information** Notice that the arrows on the map change color to show time passing. Which place did the migrations reach first, Lake Tanganyika or the Orange River?

Go Online
PHSchool.com Use Web Code **lap-5211** for step-by-step map skills practice.

KEY

| 2000 B.C. | A.D. 1 | A.D. 1 A.D. 500 |

0 miles 1,000
0 kilometers 1,000
Lambert Azimuthal Equal Area

The Bantu Migrations

About 4,000 years ago, people in Africa began one of the largest migrations that has ever taken place. To **migrate** is to move from one place to resettle in another. Around that time, a group of people who spoke Bantu (BAN too) languages began to migrate out of the region that today forms the border between Nigeria and Cameroon.

Why Migrate? No one knows for certain why the migrations began. Some experts believe that a new ability to grow certain crops in the tropical rain forest made the migrations possible. For example, yams and oil palms became a larger part of people's diet. Then increased food supplies may have led to overpopulation, or overcrowding of people living in one area. As a result, Bantu-speaking farmers migrated, perhaps looking for new land to farm. Over hundreds of years, settlements of Bantu speakers spread across Central and Southern Africa.

Answers

MAP MASTER Skills Activity **Identify** in north central Africa near what is today Nigeria and Cameroon **Analyze Information** Lake Tanganyika

Go Online
PHSchool.com Students may practice their map skills by using the interactive online version of this map.

Skills for Life Skills Mini Lesson

Using Special Purpose Maps

1. Teach the skill by telling students that route maps show a route, or path, from one place to another. They also include other elements common to most maps, such as a compass rose and a scale. Review the purpose of each one.

2. Help students practice the skill by looking at the map on this page to determine in what direction the Bantu traveled.

3. Have students apply the skill by determining how far the Bantu traveled south and southeast from 2000 B.C. to A.D. 1.

Bantus Spread Their Language People had been living in most parts of Africa before the Bantu speakers arrived. As the Bantu-speaking farmers settled, their language became the one that most people spoke. Not everyone agrees on how the Bantu languages spread. People who investigate the migrations have found evidence of various routes Bantu speakers took across Africa. By studying cultural clues and modern African languages, experts may eventually understand how many people followed each route and when.

Language and Ethnic Groups Today, people in Central and Southern Africa belong to hundreds of **ethnic groups**, or groups that share languages, religions, family ties, and customs. People in an ethnic group share an identity separate from others. Most often, this identity is based on a shared history or culture. An ethnic group may also share a distinct language. Most of the ethnic groups living in Central and Southern Africa today are Bantu speakers. In fact, more than 200 million people in the region speak one of the many Bantu languages. The most widely spoken of these languages include Zulu, Xhosa (KOH sah), Shona, and Swahili.

√ **Reading Check** How many people in Central and Southern Africa speak Bantu languages today?

Links Across
The World

Ethnic Groups Ethnic groups can be found around the world. French Canadians are a major ethnic group in Canada. Hispanics, African Americans, and Irish Americans are just a few of the many ethnic groups found in the United States. Below, members of various ethnic groups gather in Paris, France.

Section 1 Assessment

Key Terms
Review the key terms at the beginning of this section. Use each term in a sentence that explains its meaning.

Target Reading Skill
How did having a purpose help you understand the important ideas in this section?

Comprehension and Critical Thinking
1. (a) Locate Where in Africa did farming most likely begin?
(b) Identify Causes Why did people give up hunting and gathering for farming and herding?

(c) Identify Effects What effects did farming have on people?
2. (a) Recall What were some characteristics of the civilizations that arose along the Nile River?
(b) Predict How might the Egyptian and Nubian civilizations have been affected if the Nile River did not regularly flood its banks?
3. (a) Identify What were the Bantu migrations?
(b) Draw Conclusions How do you think the Bantu-speaking farmers adapted to different environments during the hundreds of years of migrations?

Writing Activity
Make a poster that illustrates, step by step, an important idea from this section. For example, your poster could show how scientists learn about early people or how languages spread from one part of Africa to another.

For: An activity on early human ancestors in Africa
Visit: PHSchool.com
Web Code: lad-5201

Links

Read the **Links Across the World** on this page. Ask students **Does the United States have a multicultural population? How do you know?** *(Yes; there are many different ethnic groups.)*

Assess and Reteach

Assess Progress   L2
Have students complete the Section Assessment. Administer the *Section Quiz*.

■ All in One **Africa Teaching Resources,** *Section Quiz,* p. 146

Reteach   L1
If students need more instruction, have them read this section in the Reading and Vocabulary Study Guide.

📖 Chapter 12, Section 1, **Eastern Hemisphere Reading and Vocabulary Study Guide,** pp. 132–134

Extend   L3
Assign the *Small Group Activity,* in which students will research and present an oral report on an ancient African kingdom.

■ All in One **Africa Teaching Resources,** *Small Group Activity: Oral Report on an Ancient African Kingdom,* pp. 170–173

Answers

√ **Reading Check** more than 200 million people

Writing Activity
Use the *Rubric for Assessing a Student Poster* to evaluate students' posters.

■ All in One **Africa Teaching Resources,** *Rubric for Assessing a Student Poster,* p. 185

Go Online PHSchool.com Typing in the Web code when prompted will bring students directly to detailed instructions for this activity.

Section 1 Assessment

Key Terms
Students' sentences should reflect knowledge of each Key Term.

Target Reading Skill
Students should understand that setting a purpose helped them focus their reading.

Comprehension and Critical Thinking
1. (a) North Africa **(b)** to control their food supply and so they no longer had to travel to find food **(c)** People could settle in one place, allowing communities to grow.

2. (a) They were based on farming, and were ruled by kings. **(b)** Students should realize that without the flooding of the Nile, the Egyptian and Nubian civilizations may not have developed.

3. (a) the movement of the Bantu-speaking people from present-day Nigeria and Cameroon to Central and Southern Africa **(b)** Possible answer: The Bantu-speaking farmers probably used their previous farming knowledge to help them come up with new ways to farm in the new environments they encountered.

Section 2
Step-by-Step Instruction

Objectives
Social Studies
1. Learn how trade affected the development of early East African civilizations.
2. Examine the forces that shaped the history of the North African trading powers.
3. Find out how West African kingdoms gained wealth and power.

Reading/Language Arts
Make predictions to help you set a purpose for reading and remember what you have read.

Prepare to Read

Build Background Knowledge **L2**
Display *Color Transparency AF 30: Southwest Asia and North Africa: Physical-Political* and *Color Transparency AF 31: Africa South of the Sahara: Physical-Political.* Ask students to look carefully at the maps and identify places where they think ancient civilizations might have arisen. Encourage them to think about the need for water, fertile land, and trade. Conduct a Give One, Get One activity (TE, p. T37) to generate a list.

📖 **Africa Transparencies,** *Color Transparency AF 30: Southwest Asia and North Africa: Physical-Political; Color Transparency AF 31: Africa South of the Sahara: Physical-Political*

Set a Purpose for Reading **L2**
- Preview the Objectives.

- Form students into pairs or groups of four. Distribute the *Reading Readiness Guide.* Ask the students to fill in the first two columns of the chart. Use the Numbered Heads participation strategy (TE, p. T36) to call on students to share one piece of information they already know and one piece of information they want to know.

All in One Africa Teaching Resources, *Reading Readiness Guide,* p. 148

Vocabulary Builder
Preview Key Terms **L2**
Pronounce each Key Term, then ask the students to say the word with you. Provide a simple explanation such as, "Many Muslims make a pilgrimage to Mecca to worship at this holy place."

Section 2
Kingdoms, City-States, and Empires

Prepare to Read

Objectives
In this section you will
1. Learn how trade affected the development of early East African civilizations.
2. Examine the forces that shaped the history of the North African trading powers.
3. Find out how West African kingdoms gained wealth and power.

Taking Notes
As you read, look for details about important African kingdoms and city-states. Copy the table below, and use it to record your notes.

Early African Civilizations		
Kingdom or City-State	Location	Historical Events

🎯 Target Reading Skill
Predict Making predictions before you read helps you set a purpose for reading and remember what you read. First, preview the section by looking at the headings. Then note illustrations or anything else that stands out. Finally, predict what might be discussed in the text. For example, after previewing this section, you might predict that the text will explain the history of trade in Africa. As you read, compare what you read to your prediction.

Key Terms
- **Swahili** (swah HEE lee) *n.* a Bantu language spoken in much of East Africa; also an ethnic group
- **city-state** (SIH tee stayt) *n.* a city that is also an independent state, with its own traditions, government, and laws
- **pilgrimage** (PIL gruh mij) *n.* a religious journey
- **Tombouctou** (tohm book TOO) *n.* a city in Mali near the Niger River; also spelled *Timbuktu*

Aksum was the first African kingdom to make coins for trade.

390 Africa

In the decades before A.D. 100, a Greek writer made a list of goods for sale in the markets of Adulis, East Africa. The list included the following:

> ❝Cloth made in Egypt . . . many articles of flint glass . . . and brass, which is used for ornament and in cut pieces instead of coin; sheets of soft copper, used for cooking utensils and cut up for bracelets and anklets for the women; iron, which is made into spears used against the elephants and other wild beasts, and in their wars.❞
>
> —*anonymous Greek trader*

Adulis was a bustling trade center along the Red Sea. It was also the main port of the wealthy and powerful kingdom of Aksum.

🎯 Target Reading Skill **L2**

Predict Point out the Target Reading Skill. Explain that making predictions about what you will read helps you to set a purpose for reading and remember what you've read.

Model the skill by making a prediction about what students will learn in the subsection West African Kingdoms, which starts on p. 395. Read the headings aloud and explain what you see in the map and photos. (*I predict that we will learn about how trade affected kingdoms in West Africa.*)

Give students *Preview and Predict.* Have them complete the activity in groups.

All in One Africa Teaching Resources, *Preview and Predict,* p. 164

<footer>

390 *Africa*

</footer>

East African Trading Civilizations

Early East African civilizations grew strong from trade. Turn to the map titled Africa: Regions on page 357. Notice that the boundaries of East Africa include the Red Sea and the Indian Ocean. East Africa's early trading civilizations developed on or near a coastline, providing access to important markets in Arabia, India, and East Asia.

Aksum The kingdom of Aksum was located in East Africa, where the present-day countries of Ethiopia and Eritrea lie. Around 1000 B.C., African and Arab traders began settling along the west coast of the Red Sea. They were the ancestors of the people of Aksum. Over time, Aksum came to control trade in the Red Sea area. By the A.D. 200s, the kingdom controlled a trade network that stretched from the Mediterranean Sea to India.

Ideas, as well as goods, traveled along trade routes. In the A.D. 300s, many people in Aksum became Christian as news about the religion spread. Aksum became a center of the early Ethiopian Christian Church. During the A.D. 600s, Aksum began to decline as Arabs took control of much of the region's trade.

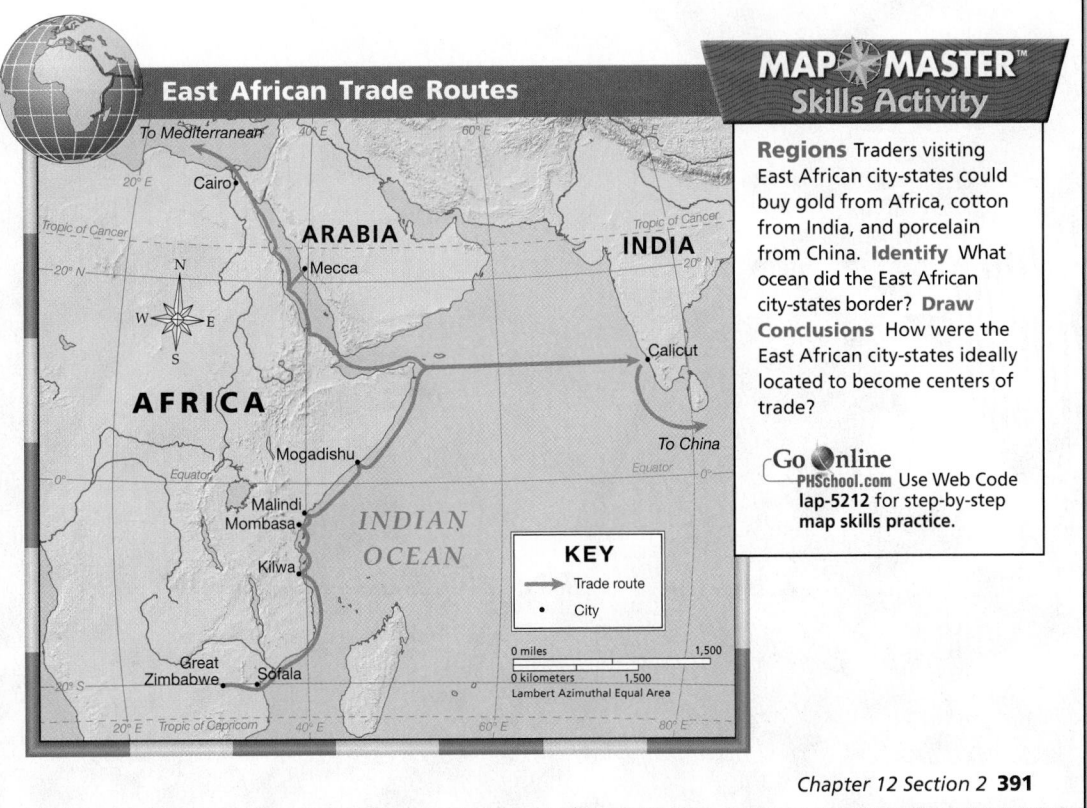

East African Trade Routes

MAP★MASTER™
Skills Activity

Regions Traders visiting East African city-states could buy gold from Africa, cotton from India, and porcelain from China. **Identify** What ocean did the East African city-states border? **Draw Conclusions** How were the East African city-states ideally located to become centers of trade?

Go **Online**
PHSchool.com Use Web Code **lap-5212** for step-by-step map skills practice.

KEY
→ Trade route
• City

0 miles 1,500
0 kilometers 1,500
Lambert Azimuthal Equal Area

Vocabulary Builder

Use the information below to teach students this section's high-use words.

High-Use Word	Definition and Sample Sentence
network, p. 393	*n.* a system, such as roads or routes, that are connected to each other The **network** of roads linked the coast with inland cities.
compete, p. 394	*v.* to be in a state of rivalry The football teams **competed** for the championship trophy.
descendant, p. 397	*n.* from an ancestor Joan is a **descendant** of her great grandmother.

East African Trading Civilizations   L2

Guided Instruction

- **Vocabulary Builder** Clarify the high-use word **network** before reading.

- Read East African Trading Civilizations, using the ReQuest strategy (TE, p. T35).

- Discuss with students how trade influenced the spread of Christianity in East Africa in the A.D. 300s. *(Goods as well as ideas traveled along trade routes. As news about the religion spread, more people in Aksum became Christian.)*

- Ask students **Why do you think Aksum was such a powerful kingdom?** *(It controlled a large trade network that stretched from the Mediterranean Sea to India.)*

Answers

MAP★MASTER **Identify** the Indian Ocean
Skills Activity
Draw Conclusions The East African city-states were on the coast of the Indian Ocean, with routes to India and routes to Arabia and the Mediterranean.

Go **Online**
PHSchool.com **Students may practice their map skills using the interactive online version of this map.**

- Discuss with students how seasonal winds affected East Africa's trade with India and China. *(East African traders followed wind patterns. When winds were blowing in a northeasterly direction, it allowed their boats to travel more quickly and easily toward India and China. When the winds changed direction, traders used the power of the wind to sail back home.)*

- Point out that traders brought both new religions and a new language to East Africa. Then ask **Why do you think these are still practiced and used in East Africa today?** *(Possible answer: East Africans probably passed down their language and their religious beliefs from generation to generation so that today Christianity, Islam, and the Swahili language are still a part of East African society.)*

- Ask **What made both Kilwa and Great Zimbabwe wealthy?** *(trade)*

Origins of Ivory
Ivory comes from elephant tusks such as the one the men below are holding. Although it is no longer legal to trade ivory, a monument (bottom) in Mombasa, Kenya, commemorates the role ivory played in African trade. **Draw Conclusions** *Why do you think it is no longer legal to trade ivory?*

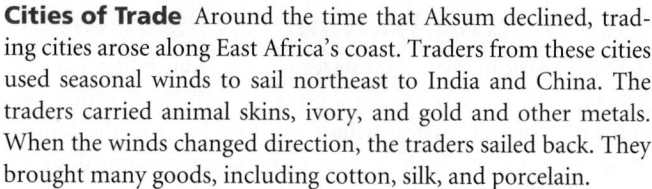

Cities of Trade Around the time that Aksum declined, trading cities arose along East Africa's coast. Traders from these cities used seasonal winds to sail northeast to India and China. The traders carried animal skins, ivory, and gold and other metals. When the winds changed direction, the traders sailed back. They brought many goods, including cotton, silk, and porcelain.

Trade affected the culture of coastal East Africa. Some of the traders who visited the area or settled in it were Muslim. They introduced the religion of Islam to East Africa. As well, a new language, called Swahili (swah HEE lee), developed in the area. **Swahili** is a Bantu language that includes some Arab words. Today, it is the most widely spoken Bantu language in Africa.

Rise of City-States Some East African trading cities grew into powerful city-states. A **city-state** is a city that has its own traditions, government, and laws. It is both a city and an independent state. City-states often control much of the surrounding land. Among the greatest of the East African city-states were Malindi (muh LIN dee), Mombasa (mahm BAH suh), Great Zimbabwe (grayt zim BAHB way), and Kilwa (KEEL wah).

392 Africa

Background: Global Perspectives

City-States The city-state has reappeared again and again throughout history. City-states such as Athens, Corinth, and Thebes were well established by the 500s B.C. These Greek city-states built their wealth through trade and constantly vied with each other for control of the Mediterranean Sea. Uneasy alliances among city-states often disintegrated and sometimes led to wars. About 2,000 years later, the lack of a central authority in Italy allowed the growth of a number of self-governing city-states. One of the most powerful of these was Florence, ruled almost exclusively from 1434 to 1737 by the Medici family. The Medicis were patrons of artists and intellectuals, and their money and patronage helped make Florence one of the most beautiful and important cities of the Renaissance.

Answer

Draw Conclusions Possible answer: Too much trade in ivory may have endangered the African elephant's existence as a species.

Kilwa Ibn Battutah (IB un bat TOO tah) was a Muslim from North Africa who became famous for traveling to and writing about many countries. He visited Kilwa in 1331. He had seen great cities in China, India, and West Africa. Ibn Battutah wrote that Kilwa was "one of the most beautiful and best-constructed towns in the world." In Kilwa, people lived in three- and four-story houses made of stone and sea coral.

Kilwa and other East African city-states grew rich from trade and taxes. Traders had to pay huge taxes on goods they brought into the city. "Any merchant who wished to enter the city paid for every five hundred pieces of cloth, no matter what the quality, one gold [piece] as entrance duty," reported one visitor. "After this, the king took two thirds of all the merchandise, leaving the trader one third."

In the early 1500s, Kilwa and the other East African city-states were conquered and destroyed by the European country of Portugal. The Portuguese wanted to build their own trading empire.

Southern and East African Trade Ties Inland and south from the East African city-states, another great trading civilization developed. Great Zimbabwe was located near the bend of the Limpopo (lim POH poh) River in Southern Africa. It was connected to the trade civilizations of East Africa through a trade network that extended to the coast of the Indian Ocean. Great Zimbabwe reached the peak of its power in about the year 1300. At one time, thousands of people lived in the gigantic stone buildings that covered the area. Today, ruins of Great Zimbabwe remain, including city walls, a fortress, and homes.

Many tall walls of Great Zimbabwe still stand today.

✓ Reading Check What kinds of goods traveled to and from East Africa's trading cities?

Independent Practice
Ask students to create the Taking Notes graphic organizer on a blank piece of paper. Then have them fill in the chart with information on East Africa's city-states and kingdoms. Briefly model how to identify which details to record.

Monitor Progress
As students fill in the graphic organizer, circulate and make sure individuals are choosing the correct details. Provide assistance as needed.

Differentiated Instruction

For Gifted and Talented   L3
Have students conduct further research on one of the kingdoms or city-states of East Africa. Ask them to provide three important facts about the place they choose that are not provided in the text. Encourage them to share their facts with the class.

For English Language Learners   L2
Pair English language learners with native English speakers to complete the *Guided Reading and Review*. If appropriate, distribute the Spanish version as well.

All in One **Africa Teaching Resources,** *Guided Reading and Review,* p. 149

Eastern Hemisphere Spanish Support, *Guided Reading and Review,* p. 134

Answers

✓ Reading Check animal skins, ivory, gold and other metals, cotton, silk, and porcelain

Predict As a follow up, ask students to answer the Target Reading Skill question in the Student Edition. *(Students should assess the accuracy of their predictions and revise them as needed.)*

North African Trading Powers L2

Guided Instruction

- **Vocabulary Builder** Clarify the high-use word **compete** before reading.

- Have students read North African Trading Powers.

- Ask **How did North Africa's location help shape its history?** *(Its location along the Mediterranean Sea attracted traders who established cities there.)*

- Display the *Spread of Islam* transparency set. Ask students to describe the spread of Islam into North Africa using information from the text and the maps. *(From A.D. 600 through A.D. 750, Islam spread into Egypt and through the northern Sahara region.)*

  📖 **Africa Transparencies,** *Color Transparency AF Set 2: The Spread of Islam*

Independent Practice

Ask students to continue filling in their graphic organizers with the information they have just learned about North Africa's history.

Monitor Progress

As students fill in the graphic organizer, circulate and make sure individuals are choosing the correct details.

Answers

Analyze Images Possible answer: Islamic art uses elaborate patterns and curved arches to create a beautiful effect.

✓ **Reading Check** The Phoenicians established Carthage as a trading post in present-day Tunisia.

🔵 **Predict** **Target Skill** Is the text saying what you predicted it would? If not, look over the headings and illustrations again, and then revise your prediction.

Islam and Art
As Islam spread into North Africa, so did Islamic art styles. The gate shown above, which leads into the city of Fès, Morocco, is Islamic in design. **Analyze Images** *How would you describe Islamic art from looking at this gate?*

North African Trading Powers

North Africa's history was shaped in part by its location. The region's major boundaries are the Sahara and the Mediterranean Sea. Its long Mediterranean coastline attracted sea traders. As early as 1000 B.C., ships from Phoenicia (fuh NISH uh) began searching the North African coast for ports that would connect them to Africa's riches. Phoenicia included present-day Lebanon and parts of Syria and Israel.

The Rise and Fall of Carthage By 800 B.C., the Phoenicians had established the city of Carthage (KAHR thij) as a trading post in present-day Tunisia. In time, Carthage became a powerful city-state that controlled the coast of North Africa. Carthage grew rich from the trade of textiles, metals, slaves, and food products. Possibly the wealthiest city in the world at the time, Carthage maintained control over Mediterranean trade from the late 500s B.C. through the 200s B.C. However, wars with the Roman Republic weakened the Carthaginians. In 146 B.C., Carthage fell to the Roman Empire, and the city was destroyed.

Roman and Islamic Influences Under Roman rule, cities grew up in areas that are parts of present-day Morocco, northern Algeria, and Tunisia. Christianity also spread to North African cities. The Romans built thousands of miles of roads throughout the territory, and North Africa's ports flourished.

After the Roman Empire fell in A.D. 476, invading forces competed for control of parts of North Africa. During the A.D. 600s, Arabs took control of Egypt and began to invade areas to the west of it. Thus began a long period of Arab control of North Africa. With Arab rule came the spread of Islam, the major religion of the Arabs. Soon many North Africans became Muslim. Then through trade, North Africa's Muslims helped spread Islam to people in West Africa, many of whom also accepted the religion.

✓ **Reading Check** Why did the Phoenicians establish Carthage?

Differentiated Instruction

For Advanced Readers L3
Have students read the passage in the *Enrichment* activity individually. Then have them discuss the passage with a part-ner before completing the writing assignment at the end of the activity.

📘 **Africa Teaching Resources,** *Enrichment,* p. 168

MAP MASTER™
Skills Activity

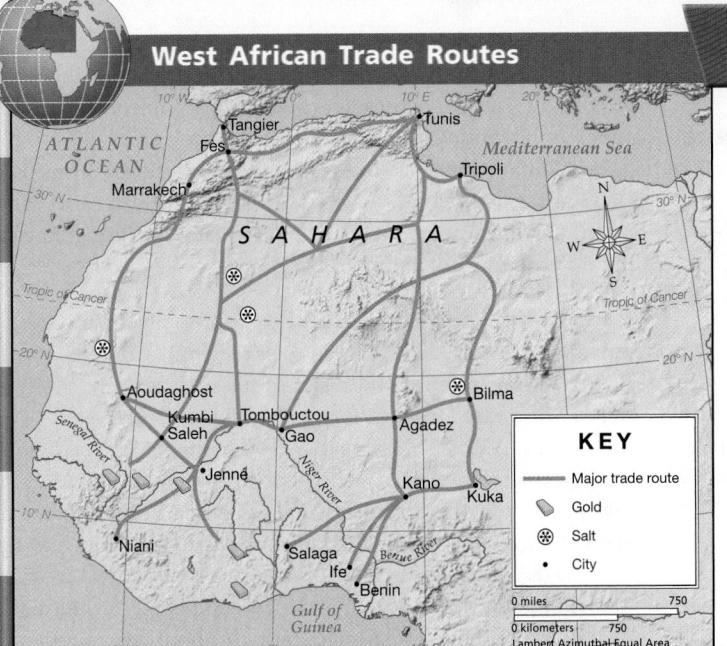

Human-Environment Interaction Temperatures in the Sahara often reach 122°F (50°C). A traveler lost in the Sahara would die of heat and thirst within days. Still, merchants have crossed the desert with trade goods for hundreds of years. **Name** What resources were exchanged along West African trade routes? **Analyze Information** Why was Tombouctou a good location for a trading city?

Go Online
PHSchool.com Use Web Code **lap-5222** for step-by-step **map skills practice.**

KEY
—— Major trade route
◊ Gold
✳ Salt
• City

0 miles 750
0 kilometers 750
Lambert Azimuthal Equal Area

West African Kingdoms

Around the time that East and North African city-states were developing, great trading kingdoms arose on the west side of the continent. The power of the West African kingdoms was based on the trade of salt and gold. People need salt to survive, especially in areas with hot climates such as West Africa. But there were no local sources of salt in the region. However, West Africa had plenty of gold. In North Africa, the opposite was true. There was salt, but no gold.

A brisk trade between North Africa and West Africa quickly grew. Control of this trade brought power and riches to three West African kingdoms: Ghana (GAH nuh), Mali (MAH lee), and Songhai (SAWNG hy). Forest kingdoms such as Benin (beh NEEN) also grew wealthy from trade.

Ghana You can see on the map titled Africa's Kingdoms, Cities, and Empires on page 35 that the kingdom of Ghana was located between the Senegal and Niger rivers. From that location Ghana controlled much of the trade across West Africa. Ghana's kings grew rich from the taxes they charged on the salt, gold, and other goods that flowed through their land. The flow of gold was so great that Arab writers called Ghana "land of gold."

Chapter 12 Section 2 **395**

West African Kingdoms
L2

Guided Instruction

■ **Vocabulary Builder** Clarify the high-use word **descendant** before reading.

■ Have students read West African Kingdoms and trace the trade routes on the map. As students read, circulate and make sure individuals can answer the Reading Check question.

■ Have students explain the importance of the salt and gold trade to some West African kingdoms. *(People living in hot regions of West Africa needed salt to survive. They had no local sources of salt, but they did have a lot of gold. North Africa had salt, but no gold. The regions began trading these goods. Control of this trade brought power and wealth to the West African kingdoms of Ghana, Mali, and Songhai.)*

■ Ask students **How were Ghana and Aksum similar?** *(Both were located near major bodies of water; both grew wealthy and powerful through control of trade routes.)*

■ Discuss with students Mansa Musa's contributions to Mali. *(He brought peace and order to the kingdom. His pilgrimage created new trading ties with other Muslim states.)*

Differentiated Instruction

For Less Proficient Readers
L1
Pair less proficient readers with more advanced readers. Have them read the primary source selections listed below about the Kingdoms of Ghana, Mali, and Songhai, together. Encourage students to answer each others' questions about the passages. Then have them complete the questions at the end of the selections together.

All in One Africa Teaching Resources, *Al-Bakri Describes the Court of Ghana,* p. 177; *Ibn Battuta Praises the Fairness of Mali's People,* p. 178; *Leo Africanus Describes Timbuktu and Gao,* p. 179

Answer

MAP MASTER™ Skills Activity Name gold and salt
Analyze Information Tombouctou was located between the major sources of gold and salt, on the Niger River.

Go Online
PHSchool.com Students may practice their map skills using the Interactive online version of this map.

- Ask students **Why was Tombouctou an important city?** *(It was a caravan stop along the Niger River and a great Muslim learning center.)*

- Ask **Why do you think the people of Benin were willing to trade slaves for guns?** *(Possible answer: They may have wanted guns so that they could conquer other lands and increase their wealth.)*

Independent Practice

Ask students to complete the chart with the information they have just learned.

Monitor Progress

- Show *Section Reading Support Transparency AF 37* and ask students to check their graphic organizers individually. Go over key concepts and clarify key vocabulary as needed.

    Africa Transparencies, *Section Reading Support Transparency AF 37*

- Tell students to fill in the last column of their *Reading Readiness Guides*. Ask them to evaluate if what they learned was what they had expected to learn.

    All in One Africa Teaching Resources, *Reading Readiness Guide,* p. 148

Links

Read the **Links Across the World** on this page. Ask students **How do you think Islam was spread through parts of Africa and Asia?** *(Traders helped to spread the religion.)*

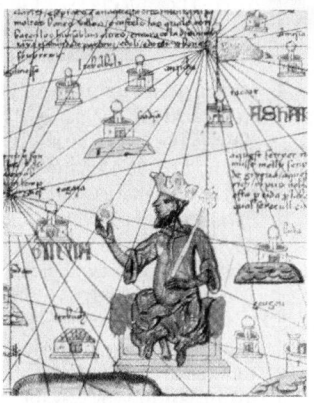

Mansa Musa was so famous that he was portrayed on a Spanish map of the world from the 1300s.

Links Across
The World

The Spread of Islam In the A.D. 600s, Islam began to spread west from Arabia through Southwest Asia and North Africa. Later, it reached West Africa. Islam also spread east—to Central Asia, India, Pakistan, Bangladesh, and Indonesia. About one billion people around the world practice Islam today. On some days, millions of Muslims visit the holy site of Mecca, as shown below.

Mali In time, Ghana lost control of its trade routes to a new power, the kingdom of Mali. This kingdom arose in the mid-1200s in the upper Niger valley. Mali's kings controlled the gold mines of the south and the salt supplies of the north.

In Mali, the king was called *Mansa*, which means "emperor." Mali's most famous king, Mansa Musa (MAHN sah MOO sah), gained the throne in about 1312. His 20-year reign brought peace and order to the kingdom.

Mansa Musa and the Spread of Islam Over hundreds of years, Muslim traders had spread their religion, Islam, into much of Africa. Mansa Musa and many of his subjects were Muslim. Mansa Musa based his laws on the teachings of Islam.

In 1324, Mansa Musa made a **pilgrimage,** or a religious journey, to the Arabian city of Mecca. Muslims consider Mecca a holy place. It is the birthplace of Muhammad, the founder of Islam. Mansa Musa brought 60,000 people with him on his pilgrimage. Each of 80 camels carried 300 pounds (136 kilograms) of gold, which Mansa Musa gave to people as gifts along the way. Mansa Musa's pilgrimage brought about new trading ties with other Muslim states. It also displayed Mali's wealth. Hearing the reports, Europe's rulers eagerly sought Mali's gold.

Songhai After Mansa Musa's death in about 1332, the Songhai empire became West Africa's most powerful kingdom. Songhai's rulers controlled important trade routes and wealthy cities. The wealthiest Songhai trading city was **Tombouctou** (tohm book TOO), an important caravan stop located along the Niger River. People considered Tombouctou a great Muslim learning center.

396 Africa

Background: Links Across Time

The Hajj Today, more than two million people each year make the pilgrimage to Mecca like Mansa Musa did in the 1300s. The pilgrimage is called the hajj. Islam teaches that all Muslims should perform the hajj once in their lifetime if they can afford it and are physically capable of making the trip. The hajj begins on the seventh day of the last month in the Islamic year and ends on the twelfth day. The hajj involves several rituals that must be completed, including kissing and touching the Black Stone. Located in the Great Mosque in Mecca, Islamic legend says that the stone was once white but has turned black by absorbing the sins of those who touch it.

> *"Salt comes from the north, gold from the south, and silver from the city of white men. But the word of God and the treasures of wisdom are only to be found in Tombouctou."*
>
> —*West African proverb*

Invaders from North Africa defeated Songhai in 1591. However, Songhai people still live near the Niger River, and Islam remains important in the region.

Forest Kingdoms Songhai traded with kingdoms located to the south in the forested region of West Africa. One such kingdom, Benin, arose in the late 1200s. Trade in ivory, palm oil, and pepper made the kingdom of Benin wealthy. Benin's artisans worked in ivory, bronze, brass, and wood in a distinctive style. They created some of the finest sculptures and carvings of the time.

Because it was located on the coast, Benin also traded with other African kingdoms as well as with Europeans arriving by sea. In the 1500s, Europeans began to trade guns for slaves from coastal forest kingdoms such as Benin, Asante (uh SAHN tee), and Dahomey (duh HOH mee). Many African Americans are descendants of enslaved people from those kingdoms.

√ **Reading Check** Who was Mansa Musa?

Bronze sculpture from the forest kingdom of Owo

Section 2 Assessment

Key Terms
Review the key terms at the beginning of this section. Use each term in a sentence that explains its meaning.

⟳ Target Reading Skill
What did you predict about this section? Did your prediction help you remember what you read?

Comprehension and Critical Thinking
1. (a) Name Identify two city-states that were important to East African trade.
(b) Identify Effects How did trade affect the coastal culture of East Africa?

(c) Analyze Information Why do you think East African traders had to pay taxes for the right to bring goods into Kilwa?
2. (a) Identify Sequence What forces influenced North Africa throughout its history?
(b) Analyze Information How did Islam become a major religion in North Africa?
3. (a) Describe How did location affect the various kingdoms of West Africa?
(b) Draw Conclusions How did Ghana, Mali, and Songhai become wealthy from gold and salt?

Writing Activity
Suppose you are a traveler visiting one of Africa's ancient kingdoms or city-states during the time that it thrived. Write a short letter home about some of the things that you see and the people that you meet. Explain what your favorite part of the visit has been.

Go Online
PHSchool.com

For: An activity on the empire of Ghana
Visit: PHSchool.com
Web Code: lad-5202

Chapter 12 Section 2 **397**

Assess Progress ▢L2
Have students complete the Section Assessment. Administer the *Section Quiz.*

All in One Africa Teaching Resources, *Section Quiz,* p. 150

Reteach ▢L2
If students need more instruction, have them read this section in the Reading and Vocabulary Study Guide.

📖 Chapter 12, Section 2, **Eastern Hemisphere Reading and Vocabulary Study Guide,** pp. 135–137

Extend ▢L3
Assign *Book Project: Africa on Stage.* Tell students that they may choose a kingdom or city they have already learned about or a different African location that they would like to learn more about.

All in One Africa Teaching Resources, *Book Project: Africa on Stage,* pp. 75–77

Answers

√ **Reading Check** Mansa Musa was Mali's most famous king.

Writing Activity
Use the *Rubric for Assessing a Writing Assignment* to evaluate students' letters.

All in One Africa Teaching Resources, *Rubric for Assessing a Writing Assignment,* p. 186

Go Online
PHSchool.com Typing in the Web code when prompted will bring students directly to detailed instructions for this activity.

Section 2 Assessment

Key Terms
Students' sentences should reflect knowledge of each Key Term.

⟳ Target Reading Skill
Students should state their predictions and explain if they helped students to focus and remember what they read.

Comprehension and Critical Thinking
1. (a) Malindi, Mombasa, Kilwa, and Great Zimbabwe were important city-states.
(b) Trade with other regions exposed the East African people to new ideas, including Christianity. **(c)** Possible answer: The rulers of Kilwa wanted their city-state to profit from being a center of trade.

2. (a) North Africa was controlled first by the Phoenicians, then by the Romans, and later by the Arabs. **(b)** Arabs controlled North Africa for a long period of time and spread Islam throughout the region.

3. (a) The locations of Ghana, Mali, and Songhai allowed them to control trade between North and West Africa. **(b)** The people of West Africa had gold, but needed salt to survive. The people of North Africa had plenty of salt, but needed gold. The regions began trading these items, and control of this trade brought wealth to Ghana, Mali, and Songhai.

Section 3
Step-by-Step Instruction

Objectives

Social Studies

1. Discover what motivated Europeans to explore the African coast.
2. Find out how the Atlantic slave trade developed in the 1500s.
3. Learn how Europeans colonized regions of Africa.

Reading/Language Arts

Preview and ask questions to help you remember what you have read.

Prepare to Read

Build Background Knowledge L2

Tell students that they will learn how Europeans took control of Africa and how it affected the people who lived on the continent. Ask students to preview the headings and visuals of the section with the following question in mind: **What factors contributed to the change in the relationship between Europe and Africa?**

Set a Purpose for Reading L2

- Preview the Objectives.

- Read each statement in the *Reading Readiness Guide* aloud. Ask students to mark the statements true or false.

  All in One **Africa Teaching Resources,** *Reading Readiness Guide,* p. 152

- Have students discuss the statements in pairs or groups of four, then mark their worksheets again. Use the Numbered Heads participation strategy (TE, p. T36) to call on students to share their group's perspectives.

Vocabulary Builder
Preview Key Terms L2

Pronounce each Key Term, then ask the students to say the word with you. Provide a simple explanation such as, "Enslaved Africans worked in the large fields of plantations, picking cotton and harvesting other crops to be sold."

Section 3 European Conquest of Africa

Prepare to Read

Objectives

In this section you will
1. Discover what motivated Europeans to explore the African coast.
2. Find out how the Atlantic slave trade developed in the 1500s.
3. Learn how Europeans colonized regions of Africa.

Taking Notes

As you read, find important details about the European conquest of Africa. Copy the flowchart below, and use it to record your findings.

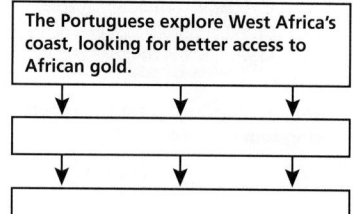

The Portuguese explore West Africa's coast, looking for better access to African gold.

Target Reading Skill

Ask Questions Before you read this section, preview the headings and illustrations to see what the section is about. Write one question that will help you understand or remember something important in the section. For example, you could write this question: "Why did Europeans originally go to Africa?" Then read to answer your question.

Key Terms

- **Cape of Good Hope** (kayp uv good hohp) *n.* a former province of the Republic of South Africa; the point of land at the southern end of Cape Peninsula, South Africa
- **plantation** (plan TAY shun) *n.* a large farm where cash crops are grown
- **Olaudah Equiano** (oh LOW duh ek wee AHN oh) *n.* an antislavery activist who wrote an account of his enslavement
- **colonize** (KAHL uh nyz) *v.* to settle in an area and take control of its government

Many Africans stayed in cells like this one at Gorée.

On the island of Gorée (goh RAY), off the coast of the West African country of Senegal, stands a museum called the House of Slaves. It honors the millions of Africans who were enslaved and then shipped across the Atlantic Ocean. Many Africans passed through the building that now houses the museum. Their last view of Africa was an opening called "The Door of No Return." Beyond it lay the ocean and the slave ships bound for the Americas.

The Atlantic slave trade began in the 1500s and continued through the late 1800s. But contact between Europeans and Africans began long before that. In North Africa, Europeans traded for gold from the empires of Ghana and Mali. Why do you think Europeans' first contacts with Africans took place in North Africa?

398 Africa

Target Reading Skill L2

Ask Questions Draw students' attention to the Target Reading Skill. Tell them that previewing the text and asking questions can help them remember what they have read.

Model the skill by previewing the headings and visuals in Europeans on the Coast on pp. 399–400. Read the headings aloud and then write a possible guiding question on the board, such as "Why did the Portuguese begin exploring Africa?"

Give students *Preview and Ask Questions.* Have them complete the worksheet in groups.

All in One **Africa Teaching Resources,** *Preview and Ask Questions,* p. 165

Europeans on the Coast

After 1500, Europe's relationship with Africa changed. It had begun as trade between equals. But it turned into the enslavement and forced migration of millions of Africans. The African slave trade eventually ended in the 1800s. Afterward, Europeans became more interested in Africa's natural resources. By 1900, European countries had divided Africa among themselves.

Portuguese Exploration In the mid-1400s, the Portuguese began sailing along the West African coast in search of gold. For centuries, gold from West Africa had been transported across the Sahara to North African ports. It was then shipped across the Mediterranean to arrive at European markets. But the Portuguese and other Europeans wanted to trade directly for West African gold and ivory, instead of dealing with North African merchants. They also wanted to trade with Asia.

Many inventions helped the Portuguese explore Africa's coast. The Portuguese used a lateen sail, a triangle-shaped sail designed in North Africa. The lateen sail allowed ships to sail against the wind as well as with it. And better instruments, such as the astrolabe (AS troh layb), helped sailors navigate at sea. With these improvements, Portuguese sailors became the first Europeans to travel south along Africa's coasts.

A Change in Trade Relations At first, Africans and Europeans traded with one another as equals. Africans traded gold, cotton, ivory, skins, metal objects, and pepper. In return, Europeans traded copper, brass, and clothing. Europeans also introduced corn, cassava, and yams from the Americas. These plants became food crops in Africa. Africans in turn introduced Europeans to okra, watermelon, and the best type of rice for growing in the Americas.

Over time, however, the trade relationship changed. In 1498, three Portuguese ships rounded the tip of Southern Africa and sailed north along Africa's east coast. The wealth of the East African city-states amazed the Portuguese. More Portuguese ships followed—not to trade but to seize the riches of the city-states. Portugal controlled the wealth of East Africa's coast until well into the 1600s.

Portuguese Ship, African Sails
This illustration shows a typical Portuguese sailing ship of the 1400s, called a caravel. It used lateen sails.
Synthesize How does this ship show that Europeans adopted elements of African culture?

Instruct

Europeans on the Coast   L2

Guided Instruction

- **Vocabulary Builder** Clarify the high-use word **seize** before reading.

- Read Europeans on the Coast using the Paragraph Shrinking strategy, (TE, p. T34).

- Ask **Why were Europeans interested in exploring the African coast?** (*In the mid-1400s, Portuguese sailors began exploring the West African coast to search for gold. They also wanted to be able to trade directly with West Africans, rather than trade with them through North African merchants.*)

- Ask students **Why do you think Europeans wanted to trade directly with West Africans?** (*Possible answer: They may have thought that they could work out better trade bargains if they dealt with West Africans directly.*)

Vocabulary Builder

Use the information below to teach students this section's high-use words.

High-Use Word	Definition and Sample Sentence
seize, p. 399	*v.* to take possession of The pirates **seized** the trading ship.
captive, p. 402	*n.* person who has been taken prisoner The **captives** were forced to work all day for no pay.

Answer

Synthesize The Portuguese used the lateen sail, designed in North Africa, to help them explore Africa's coast.

Guided Instruction (continued)

- Discuss how Portuguese contact with the East African city-states changed the relationship between Africa and Europe. *(When the Portuguese sailed to the East African coast, they were amazed by the wealth of the East African city-states. Rather than trade with East African merchants, the Portuguese seized the riches of the land and took control of trade along the coast. This prompted other Europeans, like the Dutch, the French, and the British, to begin spreading into Africa, sometimes by force. The relationship between Africans and Europeans worsened.)*

Independent Practice

Ask students to create the Taking Notes graphic organizer on a blank piece of paper. Then have them fill in the chart with the events they have just learned. Briefly model how to identify which details to record.

Monitor Progress

As students fill in the graphic organizer, circulate and make sure individuals are choosing the correct details. Provide assistance as needed.

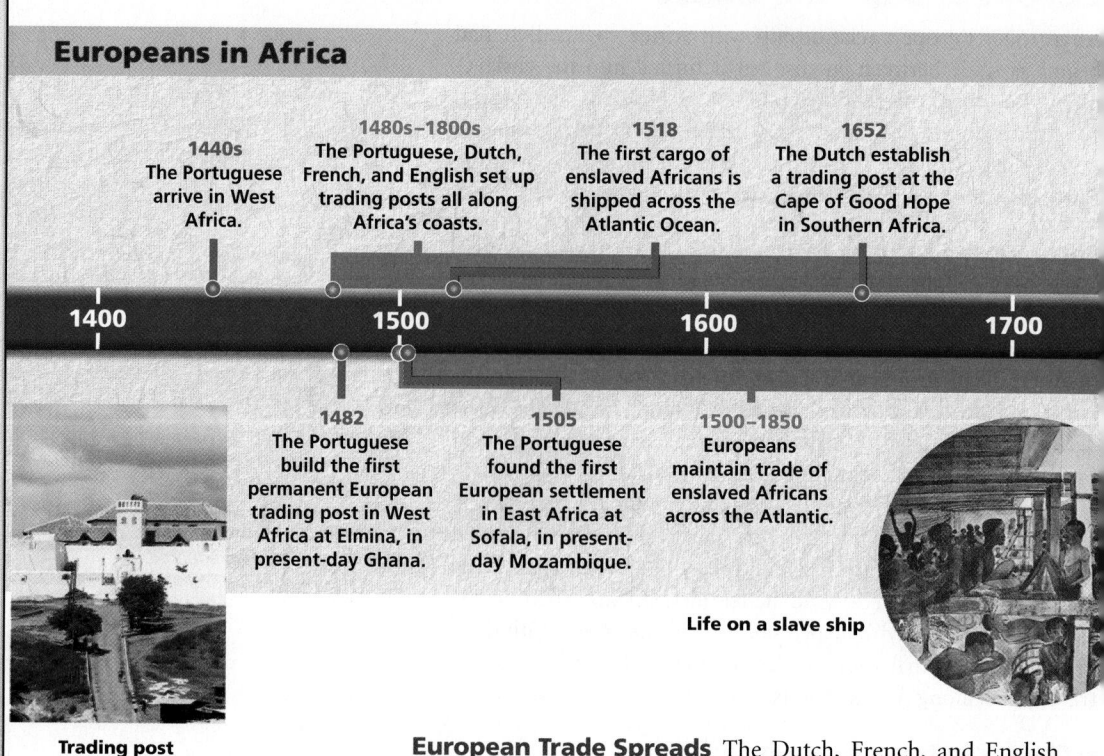

Europeans in Africa

1440s
The Portuguese arrive in West Africa.

1480s–1800s
The Portuguese, Dutch, French, and English set up trading posts all along Africa's coasts.

1518
The first cargo of enslaved Africans is shipped across the Atlantic Ocean.

1652
The Dutch establish a trading post at the Cape of Good Hope in Southern Africa.

1400   1500   1600   1700

1482
The Portuguese build the first permanent European trading post in West Africa at Elmina, in present-day Ghana.

1505
The Portuguese found the first European settlement in East Africa at Sofala, in present-day Mozambique.

1500–1850
Europeans maintain trade of enslaved Africans across the Atlantic.

Life on a slave ship

Trading post at Elmina

European Trade Spreads The Dutch, French, and English soon followed the Portuguese. They set up trading posts along Africa's coasts, where sailors could get supplies. The Dutch built a trading post on the **Cape of Good Hope,** a point of land at Africa's southern tip. Soon, settlers arrived. They moved inland, building homes and farms.

As Europeans spread out, sometimes by force, their relations with Africans worsened. But it was the growing trade in enslaved Africans that poisoned future relations between Africans and Europeans the most.

✓ **Reading Check** What advantages allowed the Portuguese to be the first Europeans to trade directly with West Africans?

The Atlantic Slave Trade

Before the 1500s, slavery was common in some parts of Africa. There, enslaved people became the property of their owners and were forced to work for them. Slaves could win their freedom after a few years. Some became important citizens among the people who had enslaved them. Slaves could even be bought out of slavery by their own people.

400 Africa

Answer

✓ **Reading Check** The lateen sail helped Portuguese vessels sail against the wind as well as with it. Also, the astrolabe helped sailors navigate better at sea.

Skills Mini Lesson

Sequencing

1. Teach the skill by explaining that a timeline is an illustration of events that occur over a given period of time. Events appear in chronological order with a date next to each one. Timelines can help you see the relationship between two events.

2. Help students practice the skill by looking at the timeline in the Student Edition and determining its topic and time span. *(Europeans in Africa, 1400–1914)*

3. Have students apply the skill by writing a sentence summarizing the relationship between two dates on the timeline.

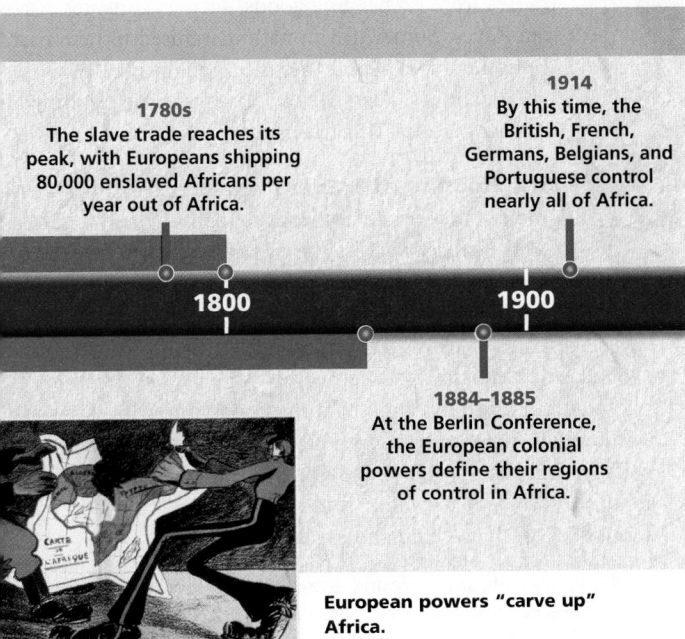

1780s
The slave trade reaches its peak, with Europeans shipping 80,000 enslaved Africans per year out of Africa.

1914
By this time, the British, French, Germans, Belgians, and Portuguese control nearly all of Africa.

1800   1900

1884–1885
At the Berlin Conference, the European colonial powers define their regions of control in Africa.

European powers "carve up" Africa.

■ Timeline Skills

Over the course of 500 years, Europeans had a strong influence on Africa. **Note** When did Europeans establish their first trading post in Africa? **Identify Effects** What were the effects of European trade interests on Africa?

Then the European powers began to establish colonies in North, South, and Central America, as well as the Caribbean. The Europeans practiced a different type of slavery in the Americas. They treated the enslaved Africans as property that they shipped across the Atlantic to the Americas. The Europeans rarely freed their slaves. When the African slave trade ended in the mid-1800s, millions of Africans had been taken from their homelands, most never to return.

The Demand for Slaves European settlers in the Americas needed workers for their mines and plantations. A **plantation** is a large farm where cash crops are grown. Instead of paying plantation workers, the settlers preferred to use enslaved laborers. At first the settlers enslaved Native Americans. But many Native Americans became sick and died from diseases or brutal working conditions. Others ran away.

Therefore the European settlers decided to enslave Africans instead. The settlers knew Africans were skilled farmers, miners, and metal workers. They also thought Africans would easily adapt to the climate of the American tropics, which is similar to that of Africa. And since Africans would be in unfamiliar territory, they would not be able to escape easily.

Learn what the African slave trade was like.

Chapter 12 Section 3 **401**

Guided Instruction

- **Vocabulary Builder** Clarify the high-use word **captive** before reading.

- Read The Atlantic Slave Trade with students. As students read, circulate and make sure individuals can answer the Reading Check question.

- Ask students to describe how the Atlantic slave trade developed. *(European settlers in North and South America needed workers for their mines and plantations. When Native American slaves did not work out, Europeans began to import enslaved Africans.)*

- Ask students **How did the slave trade hurt Africa?** *(The slave trade caused West Africa to lose much of its population. With many skilled workers captured and families destroyed, some African societies broke down.)*

Independent Practice

Ask students to continue to fill in the chart with the information they have just learned.

Monitor Progress

Circulate and make sure individuals are choosing the correct details as they fill in their graphic organizers.

Show students *The African Slave Trade.* Ask **When did the treatment of slaves change?** *(when European traders began buying them from African kings in the 1400s)*

Answers

Timeline Skills Note 1482 **Identify Effects** European trade interests led Europeans to set up trading posts in Africa, begin the Atlantic slave trade, and eventually control much of Africa.

Europeans Colonize Africa

Guided Instruction

- Read about the scramble for Africa and its effect on the continent in Europeans Colonize Africa.

- Discuss with students the purpose of the 1884 meeting of European nations in Berlin. *(European nations set rules for how they could claim African land so that they would not go to war with each other over colonizing Africa.)*

- Ask students **From what you have read, do you think any of the European nations ruled African peoples fairly? Explain.** *(Possible answer: None of the European nations ruled fairly since Africans had limited or no power in government in all of the colonies.)*

The Trials of Slavery
Olaudah Equiano (top right) was a slave who bought his own freedom. He traveled to America in cramped quarters on a slave ship similar to this model (above). **Analyze Images** *Do you think it would have been bearable to live on a ship like this one?*

402 Africa

Answers

✓ **Reading Check** European settlers in the Americas needed workers for their mines and their plantations.

Analyze Images Possible answer: The ship was so crowded that it was probably very difficult to live on it.

The Slave Trade Begins By the 1600s, Portuguese traders were exchanging goods, such as guns, for African slaves. Some African nations refused to take part. But others sold people they captured during battles. By 1780, about 80,000 African slaves were being shipped across the Atlantic each year.

The Horrors of Slavery Captured Africans were often branded with hot irons to identify them as slaves. On the journey across the Atlantic, captives lay side by side on filthy shelves stacked from floor to ceiling. They received little food or water. As many as 20 percent of the slaves died during each crossing. To make up for these losses, ships' captains packed in even more people.

Olaudah Equiano (oh LOW duh ek wee AHN oh) was a slave who bought his own freedom and then fought against slavery. Equiano had been captured and sold at a slave auction in 1756, at about age 11. He felt sure he would die. In a book he later wrote about his experience, Equiano explained,

> **"**[W]hen I looked around the ship and saw a large furnace of copper boiling and a multitude of black people of every description chained together . . . I no longer doubted of my fate.**"**
>
> —*The Interesting Narrative of the Life of Olaudah Equiano, or Gustavus Vassa, the African*, by Olaudah Equiano

Equiano proved luckier than most African slaves. In time, he was able to buy his freedom. For most enslaved people, freedom was little more than a distant dream.

The Effects of Slavery on Africa Some Africans grew wealthy from the slave trade. Overall, however, the slave trade was a disaster for Africa. West Africa lost much of its population. Robbed of skilled workers, and with many families torn apart, many African societies broke down.

✓ **Reading Check** What fueled the European demand for slaves?

Europeans Colonize Africa

In the mid-1800s, the African slave trade ended. Europeans then began to raid Africa's interior for its natural resources. They wanted the resources in order to run factories all across Europe. They also viewed Africa as a place to build empires. Many Africans fiercely resisted European conquest. But their old guns proved no match for modern European weapons.

Background: Links Across Place

Amazing Grace While many sailors earned a living from the slave trade, at least one, John Newton, came to believe that the slave trade was abominable. Newton stopped trading in slaves and began to work to ban slavery in Great Britain. He put his feelings of regret and his hope for forgiveness into words in his hymn *Amazing Grace,* which begins:
"Amazing grace! (how sweet the sound)
That sav'd a wretch like me!
I once was lost, but now I'm found,
Was blind, but now I see."

Africa: European Rule

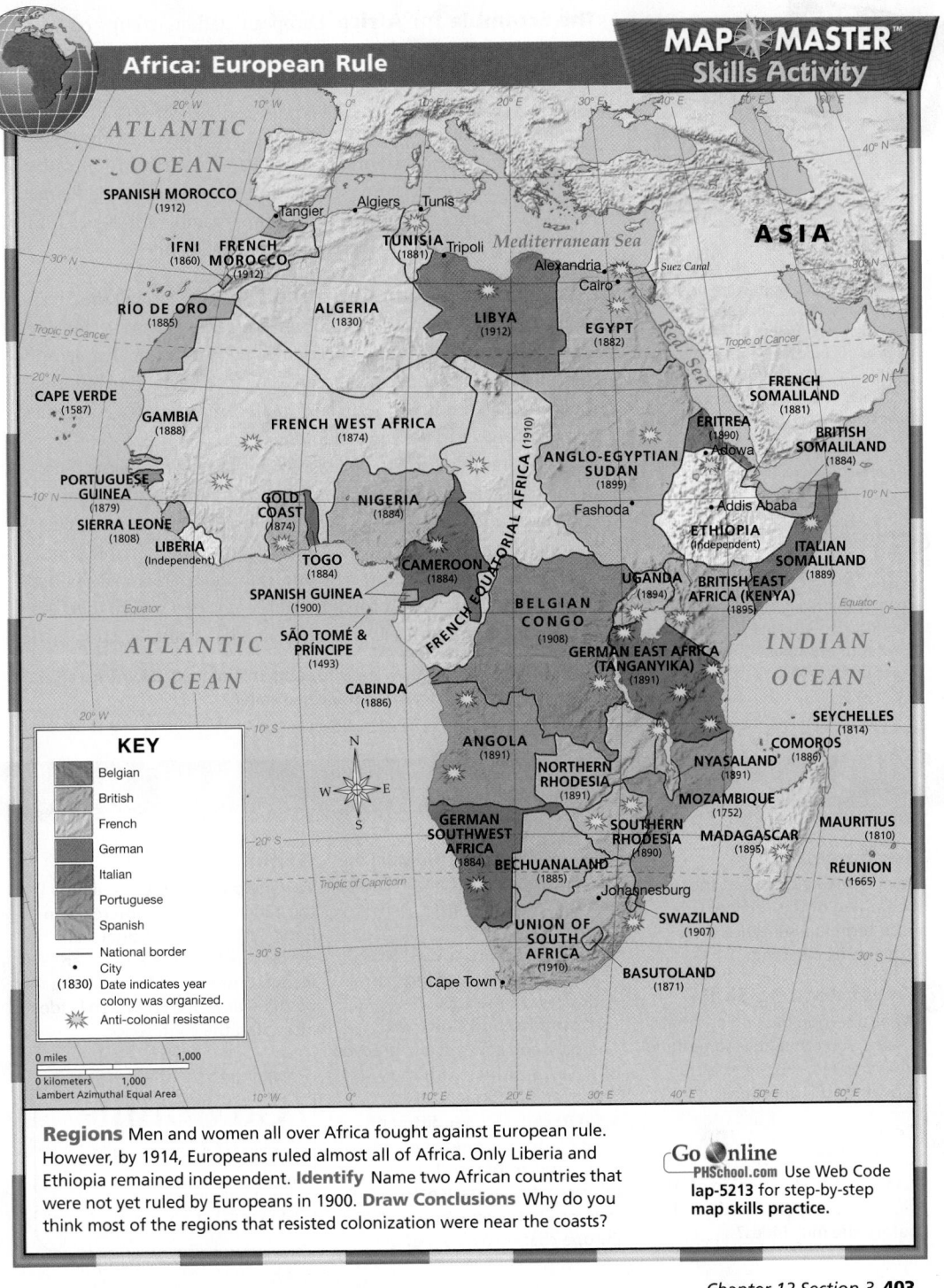

KEY

▨	Belgian
▨	British
▨	French
▨	German
▨	Italian
▨	Portuguese
▨	Spanish
—	National border
•	City
(1830)	Date indicates year colony was organized.
✸	Anti-colonial resistance

0 miles 1,000
0 kilometers 1,000
Lambert Azimuthal Equal Area

Regions Men and women all over Africa fought against European rule. However, by 1914, Europeans ruled almost all of Africa. Only Liberia and Ethiopia remained independent. **Identify** Name two African countries that were not yet ruled by Europeans in 1900. **Draw Conclusions** Why do you think most of the regions that resisted colonization were near the coasts?

Go Online
PHSchool.com Use Web Code **lap-5213** for step-by-step map skills practice.

Chapter 12 Section 3 **403**

Differentiated Instruction

For Gifted and Talented L3

Display the *Africa: Political* transparency. Direct students to examine the similarities and differences between the map on the transparency and the map on this page of the Student Edition. Then have each student write a quiz of five questions about the two maps. Encourage them to write questions that compare the maps, such as *What present-day countries made up French West Africa?* Then have students exchange quizzes and answer the questions.

📖 **Africa Transparencies,** *Color Transparency AF 27: Africa: Political*

Guided Instruction (continued)

- Draw students' attention to the map on this page. Ask **Which country controlled the most territory in Africa?** *(Britain)*

- Display the *Scramble for Africa 1850–1914* transparency set. Show students how Europe claimed more and more of Africa's territory over time. Ask **Which countries were among the first to colonize Africa?** *(Britain, France, Portugal, and Spain)* **Which countries were among the last to colonize Africa?** *(Italy, Germany, and Belgium)*

  📖 **Africa Transparencies,** *Color Transparency AF Set 3, Scramble for Africa 1850–1914*

Independent Practice

Ask students to complete their organizers with the information they have just learned.

Monitor Progress

- Show *Section Reading Support Transparency AF 38* and ask students to check their graphic organizers individually. Go over key concepts and clarify key vocabulary as needed.

  📖 **Africa Transparencies,** *Section Reading Support Transparency AF 38*

- Tell students to fill in the last column of their *Reading Readiness Guides*. Probe for what they learned that confirms or invalidates each statement.

  📘 **Africa Teaching Resources,** *Reading Readiness Guide, p. 152*

Answers

MAP★MASTER Skills Activity **Identify** Ethiopia, Union of South Africa, Belgian Congo, Libya, French Morocco, French Equatorial Africa, Swaziland, and Liberia **Draw Conclusions** Possible answer: The natural resources that Europeans wanted were located in the interior sections of Africa.

Go Online
PHSchool.com Students may practice their map skills by using the interactive online version of this map.

Ask Questions As a follow up, ask students to answer the Target Reading Skill question in the Student Edition. *(European nations rushed to colonize African territory.)*

Assess and Reteach

Assess Progress L2

Have students complete the Section Assessment. Administer the *Section Quiz*.

All in One **Africa Teaching Resources,** *Section Quiz,* p. 154

Reteach L1

If students need more instruction, have them read this section in the Reading and Vocabulary Study Guide.

📖 Chapter 12, Section 3, **Eastern Hemisphere Reading and Vocabulary Study Guide,** pp. 138–140

Extend L3

If you have not already done so, show students *The African Slave Trade.* Tell them to record three facts about the slave trade that they learned from the video that they had not already read in the text.

📼 *The African Slave Trade,* **World Studies Video Program**

Answer

✓ Reading Check They were interested in Africa's natural resources and in colonizing Africa.

Section 3 Assessment

Key Terms
Students' sentences should reflect knowledge of each Key Term.

● **Target Reading Skill**
Students should supply a valid question and a correct answer.

Comprehension and Critical Thinking
1. (a) North Africa **(b)** When the Portuguese saw the riches of East African city-states, they decided to seize them, not trade with them.

2. (a) Slaves were allowed to win their freedom. They also were allowed to be bought by their own people. Once free they could take their place as citizens, side by side with their former owners. **(b)** Both Africans and Europeans considered slaves their property and forced

---

How Stamps Reveal History
These postage stamps were printed in the early 1900s. They are from the German colony in present-day Cameroon and the British colony in present-day Kenya, Uganda, and Tanzania. **Infer** *Did Europeans view their colonies as African or European?*

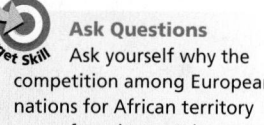

Ask Questions
Ask yourself why the competition among European nations for African territory was referred to as "the scramble for Africa."

The Scramble for Africa European nations competed with one another to gain African territory. But they did not want this competition to lead to war. In 1884, leaders of several European countries met in Berlin, Germany. There, they set rules for which European countries could claim which African land. By 1900, European nations had colonized many parts of Africa. To **colonize** means to settle an area and take control of its government. People began to call this rush for territory "the scramble for Africa." By 1914, only Ethiopia and Liberia remained independent.

Effects of European Control on Africa Not all the European countries ruled their colonies the same way. The Belgian government directly ran the Belgian Congo (now the Democratic Republic of the Congo). Africans governed Nigeria, but they took orders from British officials. In all cases, the African people had little power in their governments.

The scramble for Africa caused long-lasting problems. Europeans had gained power in part by encouraging rivalries among African ethnic groups. Europeans also took the best land to farm. In some areas, they forced Africans to labor under terrible conditions. Europeans also drew new political boundaries that divided some ethnic groups and forced differing groups to live together. Later, these boundaries would cause much conflict in Africa.

✓ Reading Check **Why were Europeans still interested in Africa after the slave trade had ended?**

Section 3 Assessment

Key Terms
Review the key terms at the beginning of this section. Use each term in a sentence that explains its meaning.

● **Target Reading Skill**
What question did you ask that helped you remember something from this section? What is the answer to the question?

Comprehension and Critical Thinking
1. (a) Recall What region of Africa did most Europeans trade with before the mid-1400s?

(b) Identify Causes How did the trade relationship between Europe and Africa change after the late 1400s?
2. (a) Describe How was slavery traditionally practiced in parts of Africa before the 1500s?
(b) Compare and Contrast Compare and contrast the practice of slavery in Africa with the European practice of slavery.
3. (a) Recall In what different ways did the Europeans govern their African colonies?
(b) Identify Sequence How did relations between Africa and Europe change over time?

Writing Activity
Write two brief editorials about the 1884 European conference in Berlin. Write one editorial from the point of view of an African leader. Write the other from the point of view of a European leader attending the conference.

For: An activity on the Boers
Visit: PHSchool.com
Web Code: lad-5203

---

their slaves to work for them. However, in Africa, slaves usually won or bought their freedom, while in the Americas slaves were rarely freed.

3. (a) Some ran their colonies directly, while others had Africans run them with orders coming from the ruling European nation. **(b)** Europeans and Africans began as equal trading partners. However, when Europeans began to take control of trade, establish the slave trade, and colonize the land, relations between the Europeans and Africans worsened.

Writing Activity
Use the *Rubric for Assessing a Writing Assignment* to evaluate students' editorials.

All in One **Africa Teaching Resources,** *Rubric for Assessing a Writing Assignment,* p. 186

Go Online PHSchool.com Typing in the Web code when prompted will bring students directly to detailed instructions for this activity.

Independence and Its Challenges

Prepare to Read

Objectives

In this section you will
1. Learn about the growth of nationalism in Africa.
2. Find out about the effects of World War II on Africa and on the growing independence movement.
3. Examine the different challenges faced by African nations on their paths to independence.

Taking Notes

As you read, find details on the causes and effects of the African movement for independence. Copy the flowchart below, and use it to record your findings.

Causes → Event: African independence movement → Effects

Target Reading Skill

Use Prior Knowledge Prior knowledge is what you already know about a topic before you begin to read. Building on what you already know can give you a head start on learning new information.

Before you begin to read, page through your reading assignment, looking at the headings and illustrations to spark your memory. Write down what you know about a certain topic, such as World War II. As you read, connect what you learn to what you already know.

Key Terms

- **nationalism** (NASH uh nul iz um) *n.* a feeling of pride in one's homeland; a group's identity as members of a nation
- **Pan-Africanism** (pan AF rih kun iz um) *n.* the belief that all Africans should work together for their rights and freedoms
- **boycott** (BOY kaht) *n.* a refusal to buy or use certain products or services
- **democracy** (dih MAHK ruh see) *n.* a government over which citizens exercise power

---

On April 18, 1980, the people of Rhodesia took to the streets. They had recently elected Robert Mugabe (muh GAH bee) prime minister in Rhodesia's first free election. People waited excitedly through the evening. Then, at midnight, the British flag came down for the last time. At that moment, the British colony of Rhodesia became the independent country of Zimbabwe.

The fight for independence had been difficult and sometimes violent. Now, Prime Minister Mugabe asked all the people to work together. They would have to build a new nation. Zimbabwe was one of the last African countries to win independence. But the movement for freedom there had begun many years before.

People in Zimbabwe celebrate the country's independence.

Objectives

Social Studies

1. Learn about the growth of nationalism in Africa.
2. Find out about the effects of World War II on Africa and on the growing independence movement.
3. Examine the different challenges faced by African nations on their paths to independence.

Reading/Language Arts

Use prior knowledge to get a head start on learning new information.

Prepare to Read

Build Background Knowledge   L2

Tell students that in this section they will learn why Africans wanted their countries to be independent, how they gained independence, and what effects independence had on these countries. Ask students to list three to five things about which they feel great pride and loyalty. Encourage them to think about local sports teams, their school, community, state, or country. Conduct an Idea Wave (TE, p. T35) to generate a list of ideas. Then point out that similar feelings of pride and loyalty have motivated people in many countries to seek their independence.

Set a Purpose for Reading   L2

- Preview the Objectives.

- Form students into pairs or groups of four. Distribute the *Reading Readiness Guide*. Ask the students to fill in the first two columns of the chart. Use the Numbered Heads participation strategy (TE, p. T36) to call on students to share one piece of information they already know and one piece of information they want to know.

  All in One Africa Teaching Resources, *Reading Readiness Guide,* p. 156

Vocabulary Builder
Preview Key Terms   L2

Pronounce each Key Term, then ask the students to say the word with you. Provide a simple explanation such as, "In a democracy, all citizens have a say in government."

Target Reading Skill   L2

Use Prior Knowledge Point out the Target Reading Skill. Tell students that they can use what they already know about a subject to help them understand new information on that subject.

Model the skill by directing students' attention to the Building Democracy paragraph on p. 411. Point out that they already know about building a democracy from

their study of United States history. Explain that they can use this prior knowledge to help them understand the challenges of building a democracy in African countries.

Give students *Preview and Use Prior Knowledge.* Have them complete the activity in groups.

All in One Africa Teaching Resources, *Preview and Use Prior Knowledge,* p. 166

The Growth of Nationalism L2

Guided Instruction

- **Vocabulary Builder** Clarify the high-use word **movement** before reading.

- Read The Growth of Nationalism, using the Oral Cloze strategy (TE, p. T33).

- Ask students **What caused nationalism to grow in Africa?** (*European colonial rulers did not consider Africans to be equal and denied them many rights. Nationalism grew out of Africans' desire to gain independence and take back their lands.*)

- Ask students **Why do you think the Pan-Africanism movement developed in the early 1900s?** (*Possible answer: African leaders realized that unity and cooperation would help end colonial rule.*)

Independent Practice

Display the *Cause and Effect Chart Transparency* and ask students to recreate the chart on a blank piece of paper. Ask them to begin filling it in with the information they have just learned. Fill in the first cause with them to get them started.

📖 **Africa Transparencies,** *Transparency B8: Cause and Effect Chart*

Monitor Progress

As students fill in the graphic organizer, circulate and make sure individuals are choosing the correct details. Help students as needed.

Answer

Evaluate In the mid 1990s, when the African National Congress gained power.

406 *Africa*

A Lasting Legacy
Some 80 years after it was founded, the African National Congress, led by Nelson Mandela (below), won an end to South Africa's domination by the descendants of European colonists. People cheer for Mandela during South Africa's 1994 presidential campaign (bottom).
Evaluate *Based on this information, when did South Africa begin to overcome the effects of colonization?*

406 Africa
A better life for all

The Growth of Nationalism

After "the scramble for Africa," many Africans dreamed of independence. In 1897, Mankayi Sontanga (mun KY ee sun TAHN guh) put this dream to music. His song, called "Bless, O Lord, Our Land of Africa," expressed the growing nationalism of Africans. **Nationalism** is a feeling of pride in one's homeland.

Political Parties and Nationalism Most European colonial rulers did not view Africans as their equals. For that reason, many African leaders knew they would have to work hard at developing pride in being African. The colonial powers had drawn political borders that combined many nations and ethnic groups. Some of these groups were old rivals. African leaders saw that to end colonial rule, they would have to build a spirit of unity.

Nationalism grew during the early 1900s. In 1912, Africans in South Africa formed a political party called the South African Native National Congress. (Today this party is the African National Congress, or the ANC.) Party members protested laws that limited the rights of black South Africans. In 1920, African lawyers in British West Africa formed the National Congress of British West Africa. This group also worked to gain rights for Africans, including the right to vote.

Vocabulary Builder

Use the information below to teach students this section's high-use words.

High-Use Word	Definition and Sample Sentence
movement, p. 407	*n.* the actions of a group to achieve a goal. The civil rights **movement** helped African Americans gain equal rights.
sacrifice, p. 407	*n.* the act of giving up one thing for the good of something else Giving up his free afternoon was a **sacrifice,** but he did it because he wanted to help his mother.

Pan-Africanism In the 1920s, Africans formed a movement based on **Pan-Africanism,** the belief that all Africans should work together for their rights and freedoms. This movement stressed unity and cooperation among all Africans, whether they lived in Africa or not. Their slogan was "Africa for Africans." The movement won many supporters.

One of the greatest leaders of the Pan-African movement was Léopold Senghor (lay oh POHLD sahn GAWR) of Senegal. Senghor was a poet and a political leader. He encouraged Africans to study their traditions and be proud of their culture. Senegal became independent in 1960, with Senghor as its first president.

✓ Reading Check **Name two African political parties. What work did these parties do?**

Africa and World War II

A major boost to African independence came unexpectedly in the 1930s and 1940s, when World War II unfolded. The war would inspire many people throughout Africa to seek freedom for their own nations.

The Invasion of North Africa During World War II, Great Britain, France, and the United States formed a group called the Allies. Together, the Allies fought the armies of Germany, Italy, and Japan, which were invading much of the world. German and Italian forces invaded North Africa, much of which was under British or French colonial control. Italian forces also invaded Ethiopia.

These men from Ghana fought in the British Army during World War II.

Some African nations played a major role in supporting the Allies. Countries such as Liberia and the Belgian Congo supplied the Allies with rubber and other needed resources. Allied planes were allowed to use African airfields to move supplies into Asia. Many thousands of African soldiers fought and died to help free Europe from conquest. About 170,000 soldiers from West Africa and 280,000 soldiers from East Africa and Southern Africa served in the British Army.

An Inspirational Victory Africans came home victorious. After the sacrifices they made, however, they wanted their own freedom. One soldier said, "We have been told what we fought for. That is 'freedom.' We want freedom, nothing but freedom."

✓ Reading Check **What parts of Africa were invaded during World War II?**

Background: Global Perspectives

Civil Rights in America World War II proved pivotal in the push for civil rights of African Americans. During the war, African American men joined the military and fought in all-black units. On the home front, African American men and women were able to get high-paying jobs in the war industry—jobs that would have been out of reach before the war. When the war ended, African Americans were not willing to give up the gains they had made. This determination to achieve equality in the United States helped lead to the civil rights movement of the 1950s and 1960s.

Africa and World War II

L2

Guided Instruction

- **Vocabulary Builder** Clarify the high-use word **sacrifice** before reading.

- Read Africa and World War II as a class. As students read, circulate and make sure individuals can answer the Reading Check question.

- Discuss with students how Africa helped the Allied forces in World War II. *(Africa supplied resources, such as rubber, and airfields for Allied planes to move supplies. Many African soldiers fought and died on the side of the Allies.)*

- Ask students to explain the meaning of the soldier's quote in the last paragraph. *(The Allies told Africans that they were helping to fight for Europe's freedom. Africans wanted their freedom as well, and the quote implies that they would be willing to fight for it.)*

Independent Practice

Ask students to continue to fill in their cause and effect charts with the information they have just learned.

Monitor Progress

Circulate and make sure students are correctly filling in the graphic organizer. Provide assistance as needed.

Answers

✓ Reading Check The African National Congress in South Africa protested laws that limited the rights of black South Africans. The National Congress of British West Africa worked to gain rights for Africans, including the right to vote.

✓ Reading Check North Africa and Ethiopia

Different Paths to Independence

L2

Guided Instruction

- Read about the ways some African countries gained independence in Different Paths to Independence.

- Ask students **How did World War II contribute to the end of colonialism?** (*It inspired Africans to win their freedom and weakened the economies of colonial powers like France and Britain, making them unable to afford a colonial empire.*)

- Ask students **What do you think Harold Macmillan meant when he said that the "winds of change were blowing across Africa"?** (*possible answer: that the time for colonialism was ending, and a new era of African independence was beginning*)

ATLANTIC OCEAN

MOROCCO (1956)
TUNISIA (1956)
Mediterranean Sea
WESTERN SAHARA (Morocco)
ALGERIA (1962)
LIBYA (1951)
EGYPT (1922)
CAPE VERDE (1975)
MAURITANIA (1960)
MALI (1960)
NIGER (1960)
CHAD (1960)
SUDAN (1956)
ERITREA (1993)
SENEGAL (1960)
GAMBIA (1965)
GUINEA-BISSAU (1974)
GUINEA (1958)
BURKINA FASO (1960)
NIGERIA (1960)
DJIBOUTI (1977)
GHANA (1957)
SIERRA LEONE (1961)
IVORY COAST (1960)
BENIN (1960)
CENTRAL AFRICA REPUBLIC (1960)
ETHIOPIA
LIBERIA
TOGO (1960)
CAMEROON (1960)
EQUATORIAL GUINEA (1968)
GABON (1960)
CONGO (1960)
RWANDA (1962)
UGANDA (1962)
KENYA (1963)
SOMALIA (1960)
SÃO TOMÉ AND PRÍNCIPE (1975)
DEMOCRATIC REPUBLIC OF THE CONGO (1960)
TANZANIA (1961)
INDIAN OCEAN
BURUNDI (1962)
MALAWI (1964)
SEYCHELLES (1976)
ATLANTIC OCEAN
ANGOLA (1975)
ZAMBIA (1964)
MOZAMBIQUE (1975)
COMOROS (1975)
ZIMBABWE (1980)
MAURITIUS (1968)
NAMIBIA (1990)
BOTSWANA (1966)
MADAGASCAR (1960)
SOUTH AFRICA (1910)
SWAZILAND (1968)
LESOTHO (1966)

KEY

- Independent nations by 1945
- Gained independence 1945–1959
- Gained independence since 1959
- Status in dispute
- Never colonized
- (1960) Date of independence
- ☀ Sites of civil wars and ethnic clashes since 1990
- ——— National border
- – – – Disputed border

0 miles 1,000
0 kilometers 1,000
Lambert Azimuthal Equal Area

Regions Independence was only the first step toward peace in some African countries. Some countries have suffered through major civil wars since independence. **Identify** During what period of time did the most African countries gain independence? **Analyze Information** Why do you think there was an increase in the number of countries that became independent after a certain time?

Go Online
PHSchool.com Use Web Code lap-5214 for step-by-step map skills practice.

408 Africa

Answer

MAP MASTER™
Skills Activity
Identify since 1959
Analyze Information More African countries became independent after World War II ended in 1945 because Africans had been motivated by helping the Allies win the war, and the economies of colonial powers had been weakened.

Go Online
PHSchool.com Students may practice their map skills using the interactive online version of this map.

Differentiated Instruction

For Less Proficient Readers

L1

If students are struggling to read and interpret the map, assign *Using the Map Key* to provide them with further instruction on how to use a map key.

All in One **Africa Teaching Resources,** *Using the Map Key*, p. 174

Different Paths to Independence

World War II did not only inspire Africans to win their freedom. The war also weakened the economies of colonial powers such as France and Great Britain. Colonialism was about to come to an end in Africa.

Winds of Change Public opinion began to turn against the practice of colonialism as well. Many people in Britain felt they could no longer afford a colonial empire. Even the United States and the Soviet Union—Britain's allies during the war—began to speak out against colonialism.

British leader Harold Macmillan realized that Britain would not be able to keep its African colonies. "The winds of change are blowing across Africa," he said. As more and more Africans demanded freedom, European countries began to give up their African colonies. Some colonial powers gave up their colonies peacefully, while others fought to maintain control. Ghana was granted its independence from Britain. But Algeria, a French colony, had to fight for its freedom.

Independence Across Africa
Women in Mauritius in 1965 hold up signs asking for independence from Britain (bottom). Prince Philip of Britain and Prime Minister Jomo Kenyatta of Kenya shake hands at an independence ceremony in 1963 (below). **Predict** Do you think Mauritius and Kenya gained independence peacefully or through fighting?

- Have students contrast the paths to freedom taken by Ghana and Algeria. *(Ghana won its independence peacefully from Britain by means of strikes and boycotts, while Algerians had to fight against France for their independence.)*

- Ask students **What challenges did African countries face after they won independence?** *(The countries were challenged with the task of creating stable governments.)*

- Have students list the pros and cons of the two types of government that emerged in African countries after independence. *(Military government pros: They held together some countries that would have been torn apart by war. Cons: not always fair; people have few rights and may be jailed for protests. Democracy pros: People help make government decisions; people can voice their opinion about government. Cons: takes a long time to establish.)*

Background: Global Perspectives

India From 1858 to 1947, India was a colony of Great Britain. The British had almost complete control over India's government and economy. To facilitate their economic interests in India, the British built railroads; they also established schools, courts, and other institutions modeled after those in England. Until 1920, the call for independence in India was characterized by sporadic violence and the lack of a unified front. In 1920, however, Mohandas K. Gandhi became the leader of the independence movement. He endorsed nonviolent disobedience, such as boycotting British goods. Under Gandhi's charismatic leadership, the independence movement soon involved millions of Indians. Independence was achieved nonviolently.

Answer
Predict Peacefully—the people of Mauritius are using peaceful methods of protest, and Kenya's Prime Minister and England's prince appear to be on good terms.

Independent Practice

Ask students to complete their charts with the information they have just learned.

Monitor Progress

- Show *Section Reading Support Transparency AF 39* and ask students to check their graphic organizers individually. Go over key concepts and clarify key vocabulary as needed.

  📖 **Africa Transparencies,** *Section Reading Support Transparency AF 39*

- Tell students to fill in the last column of their *Reading Readiness Guides.* Ask them to evaluate if what they learned was what they had expected to learn.

  All in One **Africa Teaching Resources,** *Reading Readiness Guide,* p. 156

The Right to Vote
A key part of democracy is allowing all citizens to vote. An elderly woman casts her vote in an election in Mali (below). Voters line up for miles to cast votes in South Africa's first democratic elections in 1994 (bottom).
Apply Information *Why do you think South Africans were willing to walk miles in order to cast a vote?*

From Gold Coast to Ghana In the Gold Coast colony, Kwame Nkrumah (KWAH mee un KROO muh) organized protests against British rule in the early 1950s. The protests were peaceful strikes and boycotts. In a **boycott,** people refuse to buy or use certain products or services. The British jailed Nkrumah several times for his actions, but the protests continued. In 1957, the people achieved their goal: independence. The new country took on the name Ghana, and Nkrumah became its president.

War in Algeria The French people who had settled in Algeria thought of it as more than a colony. To them, it was part of France. Algerians disagreed. They were willing to fight for the right to govern themselves. A bloody war began in Algeria in 1954. The eight-year struggle cost the lives of 100,000 Algerians and 10,000 French. But by 1962, the Algerians had won.

Challenges of Independence The new leaders of Africa had spent many years working for independence. But the colonial powers had rarely allowed Africans to gain experience in government. After agreeing to independence, the colonial powers did little to prepare the new leaders to govern. As a result, many new governments in Africa were unstable.

410 Africa

Answer

Apply Information Possible answer: Many South Africans were denied the right to vote for many years, so they were willing to walk miles to be able to exercise their rights.

In some African countries, African military leaders took control of the government by force. Military governments do not always govern fairly. The people often have few rights. Further, citizens may be jailed if they protest. But military governments have held together some African countries that otherwise might have been torn apart by war.

Building Democracy In many parts of Africa, there is a long history of democracy. A **democracy** is a government over which citizens exercise power. In a democracy, citizens influence governmental decisions. Some countries have made traditional ways a part of governing. For example, in Botswana, lively political debates take place in "freedom squares." These outdoor meetings are like the traditional kgotla (GOHT lah), in which people talk with their leaders.

Most African countries are less than 50 years old. In contrast, the stable, democratic country of the United States is more than 200 years old. Many Africans feel that building stable countries will take time. As one leader said, "Let Africa be given the time to develop its own system of democracy."

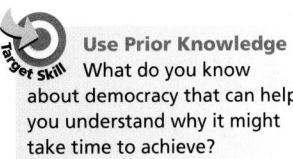
Use Prior Knowledge What do you know about democracy that can help you understand why it might take time to achieve?

✓ **Reading Check** How did Algeria gain independence?

Section 4 Assessment

Key Terms
Review the key terms at the beginning of this section. Use each term in a sentence that explains its meaning.

Target Reading Skill
Look back at what you wrote down about what you already knew. How did what you learned relate to what you already knew?

Comprehension and Critical Thinking
1. (a) Recall How did Africans respond to years of colonial rule?

(b) Infer Why did African leaders encourage people to feel pride about being African?
2. (a) Describe What was Africa's role in World War II?
(b) Identify Effects How did World War II boost the independence movement in Africa?
3. (a) Identify Causes What pressures forced European countries to give up their colonies?
(b) Compare and Contrast How was Ghana's road to independence similar to that of Algeria? How was it different?

Writing Activity
Use a book, an encyclopedia, or the Internet to research an African country that won its independence after 1950. Write a headline and a short newspaper article that might have appeared on the day that country became independent.

Writing Tip Be sure to write a good headline for your newspaper article. The headline should identify the main point of the article. It should also be catchy so that the reader wants to read on.

Chapter 12 Section 4 **411**

Section 4 Assessment

Key Terms
Students' sentences should reflect knowledge of each Key Term.

Target Reading Skill
Answers will vary, but students should be able to explain the link between what they already knew and what they learned.

Comprehension and Critical Thinking
1. (a) They did not like colonial rule and began working toward freedom. **(b)** The political boundaries created by the Europeans brought rival ethnic groups together, and African leaders realized that all Africans needed to have a spirit of togetherness in order to end colonialism.

→ **Target Reading Skill** L2
Use Prior Knowledge As a follow up, ask students to answer the Target Reading Skill question in the Student Edition. (*Encourage students to share what they already know about democracy.*)

Assess and Reteach

Assess Progress L2
Have students complete the Section Assessment. Administer the *Section Quiz*.

All in One **Africa Teaching Resources,** *Section Quiz,* p. 158

Reteach L1
If students need more instruction, have them read this section in the Reading and Vocabulary Study Guide.

📖 Chapter 12, Section 4, **Eastern Hemisphere Reading and Vocabulary Study Guide,** pp. 141–143

Extend L3
Have students read *Interview with Congolese Villagers, 1893; Ghanian Leader Speaks Out;* and *The Words of Desmond Tutu.* Assign students to work in pairs to answer the questions at the end of the selections.

All in One **Africa Teaching Resources,** *Interview with Congolese Villagers, 1893,* p. 180; *Ghanian Leader Speaks Out,* p. 181; *The Words of Desmond Tutu,* pp. 182–183

Writing Activity
Use the *Rubric for Assessing a Newspaper Article* to evaluate students' articles.

All in One **Africa Teaching Resources,** *Rubric for Assessing a Newspaper Article,* p. 187

2. (a) Africa supplied resources and allowed the Allies to use its airfields. African soldiers fought and died to help free Europe.
(b) After helping others to gain their freedom, Africans were inspired to fight for their own freedom.
3. (a) The war weakened the economies of colonial powers, and other Allied nations began speaking out against colonialism.
(b) In both Ghana and Algeria, people had to fight for their freedom. While the people of Ghana fought with peaceful protests, the Algerians had to fight France in a bloody war.

Objective

Learn how to read a diagram for sequence.

Prepare to Read

Build Background Knowledge   L2

Tell students that this skill lesson will teach them how to read a diagram for sequence. Ask students to think about the steps they took to get ready for school this morning. Write the steps you took to get ready on the board (for example, got out of bed, brushed teeth, ate breakfast) in the order that you completed them. Then display the *Flow Chart Transparency* and fill in the steps in order. Explain that flow charts are an effective way to show the sequence of events.

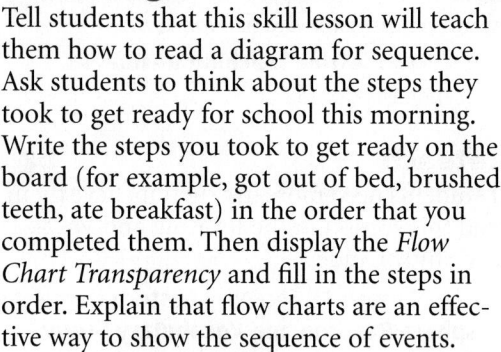 **Africa Transparencies,** *Transparency B6: Flow Chart*

Instruct

Sequencing

Guided Instruction   L2

- Read the steps on p. 412 as a class and then have volunteers write each step on the board.

- Practice the skill by following the steps on p. 413 as a class. First read the title of the flow chart *(Path to Ghana's Independence)*. Then read the flow chart in the order that the arrows indicate. Tell students to think about how one step leads to another. Then use the chart to answer the questions as a class.

Independent Practice

Assign *Skills for Life* and have students complete it individually.

All in One Africa Teaching Resources, *Skills for Life,* p. 169

Monitor Progress

As students complete the Skills for Life activity, circulate to be sure they are applying the skill steps effectively. Provide assistance as needed.

 **Sequencing**

Mr. DeNoto's class had just finished reading about the ways African countries gained independence. Then the class formed groups. Each group was going to build a float to celebrate the independence of an African country.

"Let's make the flag first," said Tamika.

"No, no, we need to build the float frame first," cried Ari.

"Well, I don't see how we can do anything until we buy the materials we need!" complained Sarah.

Mr. DeNoto held up a hand to quiet the class. "Building a float is complicated. The first thing you have to do is make a plan," he said. "Otherwise, you might cover the same ground more than once. You might even forget an important step. Adam, why don't you come up to the board and be our scribe? We're going to make a flowchart to help us plan."

A flowchart shows sequence, or the order in which actions or events happen. Understanding sequence can help you plan an activity or remember what you have read. A flowchart usually uses arrows to show which step or event happens when. A diagram such as a timeline uses dates to show the order of events.

Learn the Skill

Use these steps when you read a diagram for sequence.

1 **Read the title first.** The title will help you understand what the diagram is about. Mr. DeNoto's class titled its flowchart Building a Float. From the title, you know that the flowchart shows how the class plans to build a float.

2 **Find clues that show the order of events.** On a flowchart, the arrows tell you the order in which you should read the chart. Find the beginning and start there. Mr. DeNoto's class decided that their first step would be "Choose a country."

3 **Read the diagram carefully for connections.** Think about how one step leads to the next step. What are the connections? If there are no illustrations, try imagining each step in your head to help you understand the sequence.

Practice the Skill

Follow the steps below to read the flowchart about Ghana.

1 Read the title. What does it tell you the flowchart will be about?

2 Find the beginning of the chart and identify the first step. Start there and follow the arrows through each step.

3 Now reread the flowchart and answer these questions: (a) What is the first step on the flowchart? (b) What step leads to Nkrumah being jailed? (c) What step comes after Nkrumah being jailed? (d) What is the final result of the Gold Coast colony's struggle for independence?

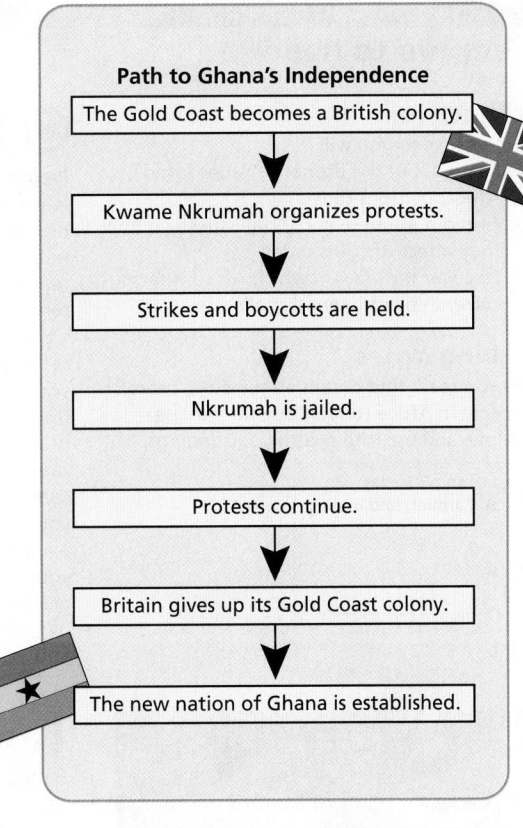

Path to Ghana's Independence

The Gold Coast becomes a British colony.

↓

Kwame Nkrumah organizes protests.

↓

Strikes and boycotts are held.

↓

Nkrumah is jailed.

↓

Protests continue.

↓

Britain gives up its Gold Coast colony.

↓

The new nation of Ghana is established.

After Ghana was established, its government created this coat of arms to represent the nation.

Apply the Skill

Turn to pages 400–401 and study the timeline. Use the steps in this skill to understand what events are shown on the timeline as well as what the sequence of events was.

Differentiated Instruction

For Special Needs Students L1
If students need more instruction on how to read a flow chart, distribute *Reading a Flow Chart*. Pair special needs students with more proficient students and have them complete the activity together.

All in One Africa Teaching Resources, *Reading a Flow Chart,* p. 175

Assess and Reteach

Assess Progress L2
Ask students to do the Apply the Skill activity.

Reteach L2
If students are having trouble applying the skill steps, have them review the skill using the interactive Social Studies Skills Tutor CD-ROM.

 Sequencing, **Social Studies Skills Tutor CD-ROM**

Extend L3
Have students reread Europeans on the Coast on pp. 399–400. Tell them to create a flow chart showing how trade relations between Europe and Africa changed over time. Remind them to give their flow chart a title.

Answer
Apply the Skill
Students should be able to determine that the timeline shows the sequence of events that occurred from the Europeans' arrival in Africa to the point in time when European countries controlled much of Africa.

Section 5
Step-by-Step Instruction

Objectives

Social Studies
1. Learn about the economic issues faced by African nations today.
2. Find out about major social issues and how they affect Africans today.
3. Discover the ways in which Africa is facing current environmental challenges.

Reading/Language Arts
Make predictions to help you set a purpose for reading and remember what you have read.

Prepare to Read

Build Background Knowledge   L2
Ask students to suppose that they have graduated from school and are out on their own for the first time. Have students write a paragraph about some of the decisions they will have to make and some of the responsibilities that come with being independent. Invite students to read their paragraphs aloud. Explain that new nations may face similar challenges when they become independent. Tell students they will learn about these challenges in this section.

Set a Purpose for Reading   L2
■ Preview the Objectives.

■ Read each statement in the *Reading Readiness Guide*. Ask students to mark the statements true or false.

   All in One **Africa Teaching Resources,** *Reading Readiness Guide,* p. 160

■ Have students discuss the statements in pairs or groups of four, then mark their worksheets again. Use the Numbered Heads participation strategy (TE, p. T36) to call on students to share their group's perspectives.

Vocabulary Builder
Preview Key Terms   L2
Pronounce each Key Term, then ask the students to say the word with you. Provide a simple explanation such as, "Growing crops for sale on large farms is called commercial farming."

Section 5
Issues for Africa Today

Prepare to Read

Objectives
In this section you will
1. Learn about the economic issues faced by African nations today.
2. Find out about major social issues and how they affect Africans today.
3. Discover the ways in which Africa is facing current environmental challenges.

Taking Notes
As you read, find details about issues faced by people in Africa today. Copy the outline below, and use it to record your findings.

> I. Economic issues
>   A. Farming and mining
>   1.
>   2.
>   B.
> II.

Target Reading Skill
Predict As you have learned, making predictions before you read helps you set a purpose for reading and helps you remember what you read.

Before you read this section, think about what you know about Africa's history. Then predict some issues the region might face today. As you read, connect what you read to your prediction. If what you learn doesn't support your prediction, revise the prediction.

Key Terms
• **commercial farming** (kuh MUR shul FAHR ming) *n.* the large-scale production of crops for sale
• **hybrid** (HY brid) *n.* a plant that is created by breeding different types of the same plant
• **literate** (LIT ur it) *adj.* able to read and write
• **life expectancy** (lyf ek SPEK tun see) *n.* the average length of time a person can expect to live

A young man digs an irrigation ditch in Niger.

414 Africa

In the past, nothing grew during the dry season in the Sahel. Farmers had to travel to cities to find work. Now, the West African country of Niger has a new irrigation program for its part of the Sahel. Irrigation allows farmers to grow a second crop during the dry season, in addition to their usual crop in the wet season. One farmer says that raising two crops a year means he can stay on village land.

> **Dry-season crops are such a normal practice now that everyone grows them. Before, each year after the harvest, I went to the city to look for work. But today, with the dry-season crops, I have work in the village. Truly it is a good thing.**
>
> —*Adamou Sani, farmer*

Niger's irrigation program is one way Africans are improving their lives. Africans are also finding ways to meet economic, social, and environmental challenges.

Target Reading Skill   L2

Predict Point out the Target Reading Skill. Explain that making predictions about what you will read helps you to set a purpose for reading and remember what you've read.

Model the skill by previewing the headings and photograph on p. 420. Remind students about what they learned about Africa's environment in Chapter 11. Combine this information to predict what types of environmental problems might occur in Africa today. (*I predict that this page will teach me about problems caused by lack of rainfall in parts of Africa.*)

Give students *Preview and Predict*. Have them complete the activity in groups.

All in One **Africa Teaching Resources,** *Preview and Predict,* p. 164

Economic Issues

The colonial powers saw Africa as a source of raw materials and a market for their own manufactured goods. They did little to build factories in Africa. Today, African countries still have little manufacturing. Most economies are based on farming and mining.

Farming Farming is the most important economic activity in Africa. About 60 percent of workers are farmers. And more than half of the goods that African countries sell overseas are farm goods. Africans practice two kinds of farming—subsistence farming and commercial farming. Recall that subsistence farmers work small plots of land. They try to raise as much food as their families need. **Commercial farming** is the large-scale production of cash crops for sale. In Africa, commercial farmers grow cash crops such as coffee, cacao, and bananas.

Mining Many African nations have rich mineral resources. They export minerals to other countries. Nigeria has oil and coal. The Democratic Republic of the Congo and Zambia have copper, while South Africa has gold and diamonds.

Farming for Food or for Profit?
A man bicycles through a banana farm in Ivory Coast (bottom). A woman picks coffee in Zambia (below). **Analyze Information** *Do you think the farms shown are commercial or subsistence farms? Explain why.*

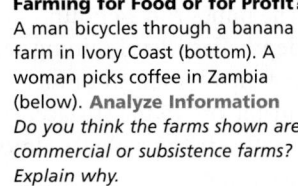

Vocabulary Builder

Use the information below to teach students this section's high-use words.

High-Use Word	Definition and Sample Sentence
diversify, p. 417	*v.* to create variety Juanita **diversified** her garden by planting many kinds of flowers.
expose, p. 420	*v.* to be open to or at risk from Sometimes metal rusts when it is **exposed** to water and air.

South African Gold Mine

Guided Instruction [L2]

Read the introductory paragraph aloud as a class. Then have student volunteers take turns reading each caption aloud. Tell students to answer the Analyze Diagrams question individually. Then allow them to share their answers with a partner.

Independent Practice

Have students write a journal entry as if they worked in this South African mine. Tell them to include details about how the mine works and what it looks like. Use the *Rubric for Assessing a Journal Entry* to evaluate students' entries.

All in One Africa Teaching Resources, *Rubric for Assessing a Journal Entry,* p. 188

South African Gold Mine

In South Africa's deep-level gold mines, miners work as far down as two miles (3.2 kilometers) underground. The mines run 24 hours a day. Because it is so hot at that depth, deep-level mining requires ventilation and cooling. In addition to tunnels, there are shafts, elevators to lift the ore to the surface, and surface processing plants. South Africa produces almost half of the world's gold.

Working in the Mines
Miners like this man train for their jobs by stepping up and down on blocks for hours in a very hot room.

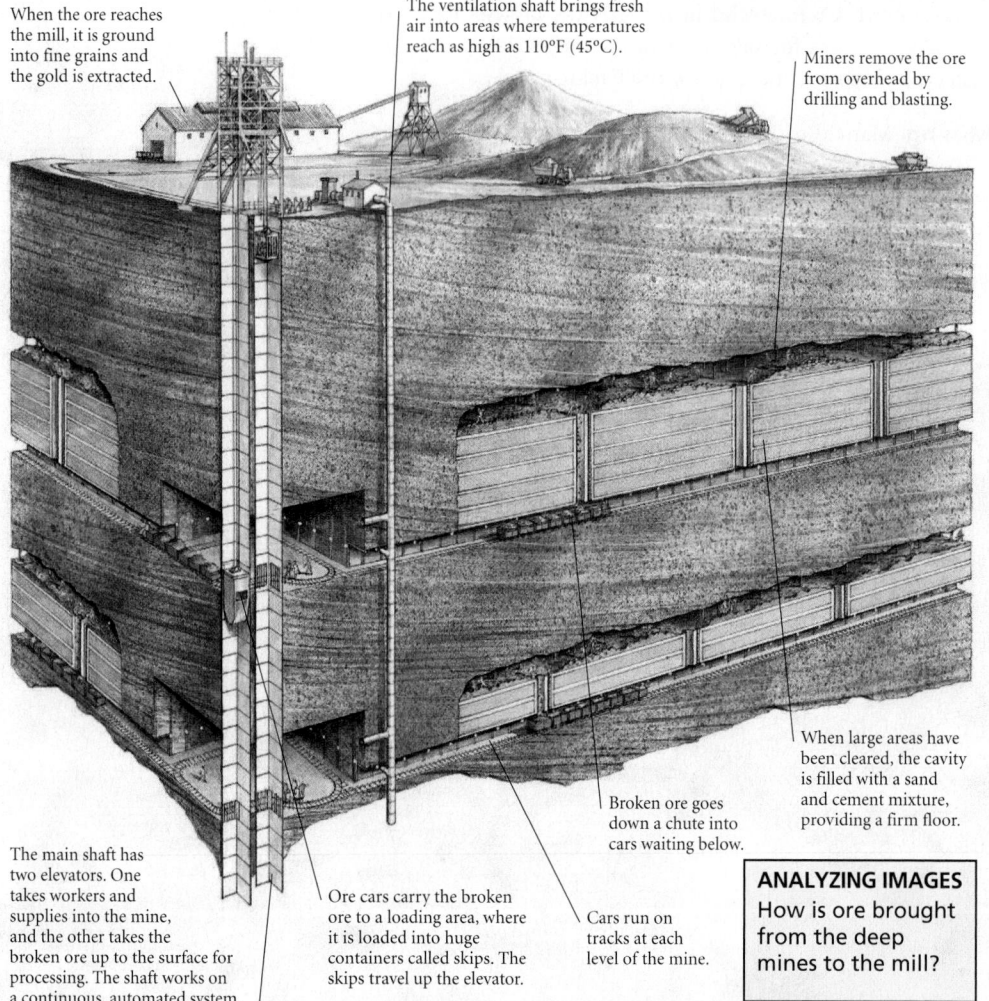

When the ore reaches the mill, it is ground into fine grains and the gold is extracted.

The ventilation shaft brings fresh air into areas where temperatures reach as high as 110°F (45°C).

Miners remove the ore from overhead by drilling and blasting.

When large areas have been cleared, the cavity is filled with a sand and cement mixture, providing a firm floor.

Broken ore goes down a chute into cars waiting below.

The main shaft has two elevators. One takes workers and supplies into the mine, and the other takes the broken ore up to the surface for processing. The shaft works on a continuous, automated system.

Ore cars carry the broken ore to a loading area, where it is loaded into huge containers called skips. The skips travel up the elevator.

Cars run on tracks at each level of the mine.

ANALYZING IMAGES
How is ore brought from the deep mines to the mill?

Differentiated Instruction

For Advanced Readers [L3]

Have students do research to find the top five gold-producing countries in the world. Then ask them to create a bar graph to show how much each country produces. Remind them to label both axes and give the graph a title.

For Special Needs Students [L1]

Distribute *Reading a Diagram* to students who may have trouble analyzing the mine diagram. Circulate to be sure students are correctly answering the questions at the end of the worksheet.

All in One Africa Teaching Resources, *Reading a Diagram,* p. 176

Answer

ANALYZING IMAGES Broken ore goes down a chute and into a car. The cars carry the broken ore to a loading area. The ore is then placed into ships which travel up to the surface by elevator.

Economic Challenges About 75 percent of African countries have specialized economies—they depend on exporting one or two products. Gambia depends on peanuts, while Zambia relies on the export of copper. As a result, African economies are especially sensitive to the rise and fall of world prices. A fall in prices hurts economies that depend on the sale of one crop or mineral.

African countries are now trying to reduce their dependence on one export by diversifying their economies. For example, Senegal became independent in 1960. At that time, more than 70 percent of Senegal's people worked in the peanut industry. Today, Senegal has other major export industries, such as fishing, fish processing, and mining. Peanuts now account for only a small percent of the money Senegal earns from exports.

Farming Improvements African nations face another economic problem—how to feed a growing population. Several governments are trying to help farmers increase the size of their crops. One method they use is to develop hybrid plants. A **hybrid** is a plant created by breeding different types of the same plant. The goal is that the best qualities of each type of plant will show up in the hybrid. Since the late 1990s, West Africans have been planting hybrid rice that combines the best aspects of African and Asian rices. As a result, these farmers have been able to produce more rice.

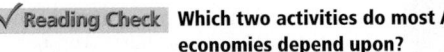 **Reading Check** Which two activities do most African economies depend upon?

Predict Based on what you know about specialized economies, predict whether more African countries are likely to change their economies.

Expanding Economies
Today, fish markets like the ones below are helping Senegal's economy succeed. Fish products have become Senegal's major export. **Generalize** *What advantages do you think the fish industry offers to a country with a specialized economy?*

Chapter 12 Section 5 **417**

Target Reading Skill L2

Predict As a follow up, ask students to perform the Target Reading Skill task in the Student Edition. *(Students should recall that diversifying an economy helps it to flourish. They should predict that some African countries are likely to try to diversify their economies.)*

Guided Instruction (continued)

- Ask students to describe two important economic challenges facing African countries. *(Most African nations make money from only one or two products. This makes them sensitive to the rise and fall of world prices for those goods. Another problem is figuring out how to feed a growing population.)*

- Then ask students to describe how Africans are trying to solve these problems. *(African countries are diversifying their economies with the aim of earning money from more than one product or industry. To feed the growing population, farmers are developing hybrid plants so that plants and crops will be stronger and more plentiful.)*

- Ask students **How might hybrid plants also help the economies of African countries?** *(African countries can increase their profits since hybrid plants can increase the quantity of crops they have to sell.)*

Independent Practice

Ask students to fill in the outline with information they have just learned. Suggest that they use the headings from the section as headings in their outline.

Monitor Progress

As students fill in the graphic organizer, circulate and make sure individuals are choosing the correct headings and details. Provide assistance as needed.

Answers

Generalize Possible answer: Fish are generally plentiful in the ocean and seas so they provide an important resource for both food and trade.

✓ **Reading Check** Most African economies depend upon farming and mining.

Social Issues

L2

Guided Instruction

- Read about social challenges in Africa and how Africans are trying to solve them in Social Issues.

- Ask students **How do parents and children help to make education possible in Africa?** *(Parents help build schools and children help to keep schools clean. Children also take turns going to school so that schools are not overcrowded.)*

- Ask students **Why do you think more African people have learned to read since independence?** *(Possible answer: The colonial powers may have been more concerned with using Africa for its resources than with educating people. They may have wanted to limit education in order to keep control. Once countries became independent, people needed to be educated so that they could fill important roles in society needed to effectively run their countries.)*

- Discuss with students why AIDS is a widespread problem in Southern Africa. *(Many people who are poor cannot afford drugs that might help them and many people do not have access to education that could teach them how to prevent the disease.)*

Independent Practice

Ask students to continue to fill in the outline with information they have just learned.

Monitor Progress

Circulate to check outlines, making sure students are choosing appropriate headings and details. Help students as needed.

A South African girl focuses on her schoolwork.

Social Issues

In addition to making economic improvements, African nations also must provide social services to their growing populations. Many Africans need better access to education and health care.

Education African children must often contribute to their family's income by working on family farms or by selling goods in the market. When girls and boys go to school, families sacrifice. But most Africans are willing to make this sacrifice because they know education can improve their children's lives.

It has long been a tradition in Africa for communities to actively support their schools. If needed, people will construct new schools. For example, parents in South Africa have often helped to build new schools when the government could not do it alone. Even so, many of the schools are overcrowded, so students must take turns attending classes. The headmaster at one such school said that students "who couldn't cram into the desks knelt on the floor or stood on their toes so as not to miss a word the teacher was saying." African students are often expected to help keep their school and its grounds clean. The students might do this by sweeping the floors or disposing of the trash.

Reading and Writing The number of Africans who are literate varies from country to country. Being **literate** means being able to read and write. In all African countries, more people have learned to read and write since independence. When Mozambique gained independence from Portugal in 1975, less than 7 percent of its people were literate. Today, about 48 percent of the people in Mozambique are literate. In Tanzania, progress with literacy has been even more dramatic. When the country gained independence from Britain in 1961, only 15 percent of Tanzania's people were literate. Today, about 78 percent of Tanzanians can read and write.

418 Africa

Differentiated Instruction

For Advanced Readers
L3

Have students work individually to complete *Life Expectancy*. Then have students do research to find the per capita GDP, life expectancy, and literacy rates of five African countries and create a chart similar to the one in the activity. Ask them to write a sentence or two comparing the charts.

Go Online
PHSchool.com **For:** Environmental and Global Issues: *Life Expectancy*
Visit: PHSchool.com
Web Code: lad-5206

Health Another social issue that differs from country to country in Africa is **life expectancy**—the average length of time a person can expect to live. In Morocco, life expectancy is between 67 and 72 years. In Southern Africa, however, the average life expectancy is less than 50 years. In the Southern African country of Botswana, people only live an average of 32 years.

The main reason for low life expectancy in Africa is childhood disease. There are many diseases for which children have low resistance. For example, insects spread diseases such as malaria. Unclean drinking water and living conditions help spread other diseases. The virus called HIV causes AIDS. Millions of African children have been born with HIV, and millions more adults have died of AIDS before age 50.

Preventing Disease Although the problem of AIDS exists around the world, it is worst in Southern Africa. One reason is that many Southern Africans who are poor cannot afford drugs that might help them. Also, many people have not had access to education, so they have not learned how to prevent the disease. African governments are working with groups such as the World Health Organization to prevent and treat health problems. Some progress has been made. For example, individuals and organizations in Uganda have worked hard to reduce the number of HIV infections there. Because of its success, Uganda may serve as a model for preventing and controlling HIV in other countries.

√ Reading Check **What is the main reason for low life expectancy in Africa?**

Health Concerns in Africa
Children surround a health worker at a clinic in Gambia as she writes down information about their health.
Predict *In what ways do you think the health worker can help this community?*

Chapter 12 Section 5 **419**

The Environment L2

Guided Instruction

- **Vocabulary Builder** Clarify the high-use word **expose** before reading.

- Read The Environment with students.

- Ask students to explain why soil erosion has become a problem in Africa. *(Because much of Africa's farmland is of poor quality, people need to use a lot of land to raise enough crops. They sometimes cut down trees to sell or clear land for farming. With no cover from trees, soil is more exposed to wind and rain and it wears away.)*

- Ask students **How might diversifying the economies of African countries contribute to protecting Africa's environment?** *(If countries did not have to rely on farming as much, people would not have to clear as many forests to grow crops.)*

Monitor Progress

- Show *Section Reading Support Transparency AF 40* and ask students to check their graphic organizers individually. Go over key concepts and clarify key vocabulary as needed.

  Africa Transparencies, *Section Reading Support Transparency AF 40*

- Tell students to fill in the last column of their *Reading Readiness Guides*. Probe for what they learned that confirms or invalidates each statement.

  All in One **Africa Teaching Resources,** *Reading Readiness Guide,* p. 160

Differentiated Instruction

For Gifted and Talented L3
Assign *Deforestation* to have students learn more about environmental deforestation as a world problem.

Go Online PHSchool.com **For:** Environmental and Global Issues: *Deforestation*
Visit: PHSchool.com
Web Code: lad-5207

Answers
Predict Possible answer: She can educate people on how to prevent diseases.

√ Reading Check Childhood disease is the main reason for low life expectancy in Africa.

Assess and Reteach

Assess Progress

Have students complete the Section Assessment. Administer the *Section Quiz*.

All in One **Africa Teaching Resources,** *Section Quiz,* p. 162

Reteach

If students need more instruction, have them read this section in the Reading and Vocabulary Study Guide.

Chapter 12, Section 5, **Eastern Hemisphere Reading and Vocabulary Study Guide,** pp. 144–146

Extend

Assign students to work in small groups to complete the *Book Project: Africa Conference.* Suggest that they plan their conference around a topic from this section.

All in One **Africa Teaching Resources,** *Book Project: Africa Conference,* pp. 78–80

Answer

✓ Reading Check Nigerian farmers plant traditional food crops in long rows. They have planted trees that hold the soil in place between the rows.

Section 5 Assessment

Key Terms

Students' sentences should reflect knowledge of each Key Term.

Target Reading Skill

Students' predictions will vary. Students should recognize that their predictions helped them to set a purpose for reading and remember what they read.

Comprehension and Critical Thinking

1. (a) Yes. **(b)** to make their economies more stable and less sensitive to the rise and fall of world prices of one or two goods

2. (a) They need to provide better access to education and health care to a growing population. **(b)** education

3. (a) Africa faces the challenge of reducing soil erosion caused by clearing land for farming. **(b)** In Nigeria, farmers are planting trees in between rows of crops to hold soil in place.

Men plant trees in Madagascar to help prevent erosion.

The Environment

Like other countries around the world, the countries of Africa face a number of environmental challenges. About two thirds of Africa is desert or dry land. High-quality farmland is scarce, and rainfall may vary greatly over the year. These environmental factors make farming especially challenging in parts of Africa.

Soil Problems People in Africa's rural areas often struggle to make a living. Much of the land in Africa is poor for farming. People thus need great areas of land to raise enough crops to support their families. They may cut down trees to use or sell the wood and to clear land for farming. With no cover from trees, soil is exposed to wind and rain. The soil then erodes, or wears away. Soil erosion reduces the amount of land on which food can grow. Without enough farmland, many Africans face starvation.

Solutions From Science Improvements in science can help feed Africans and protect Africa's environment. Irrigation projects, hybrids, and plants that hold water in the ground have all increased crop harvests. To fight soil erosion, Nigerian farmers now plant traditional crops like yams in long rows. Between the rows they plant trees that hold the soil in place. African nations still face many challenges, but they are trying to meet these challenges by using their resources and improving education.

✓ Reading Check **How have Nigerian farmers fought soil erosion?**

Section 5 Assessment

Key Terms
Review the key terms at the beginning of this section. Use each term in a sentence that explains its meaning.

Target Reading Skill
What did you predict about this section? How did your prediction guide your reading?

Comprehension and Critical Thinking
1. (a) Recall Do many African nations today have specialized economies?

(b) Draw Conclusions Why are African nations trying to diversify their economies?
2. (a) Identify What social issues are people facing in Africa today?
(b) Infer Literacy rates in most African countries have increased since independence. Education has also improved. From these facts, what can you infer that people value in Africa?
3. (a) Name Give an example of an environmental challenge African nations face today.
(b) Analyze How is that challenge being addressed?

Writing Activity
Suppose you are the economic advisor to the president of an African country. Write a brief report on some steps the president might take to improve the economy.

Go Online
PHSchool.com
For: An activity on environmental issues in Africa
Visit: PHSchool.com
Web Code: lad-5205

420 Africa

Writing Activity

Use the *Rubric for Assessing a Writing Assignment* to evaluate students' reports.

All in One **Africa Teaching Resources,** *Rubric for Assessing a Writing Assignment,* p. 186

 Typing in the Web code when prompted will bring students directly to detailed instructions for this activity.

◆ Chapter Summary

Section 1: African Beginnings

- Our ancestors were originally hunters and gatherers and became herders and farmers.
- The early African civilizations of Egypt and Nubia arose along the Nile River.
- When Bantu-speaking farmers migrated, Bantu languages spread throughout much of Africa.

Section 2: Kingdoms, City-States, and Empires

- Along East Africa's coast, civilizations grew strong from trade.
- North Africa was shaped by the Carthaginians, the Romans, and the Arabs.
- West African kingdoms grew rich from trade with North Africa.

Bronze head

Section 3: European Conquest of Africa

- Europeans explored Africa's coast to expand their trade ties beyond North Africa.
- Europeans expanded their trade with Africa to include slaves, whom they sent to work on plantations in the Americas.
- European countries claimed African lands for themselves, which had lasting effects on Africa.

Section 4: Independence and Its Challenges

- Fueled by increased feelings of African nationalism, African political parties and leaders worked for the rights of Africans.
- Africans who fought in World War II returned home seeking freedom and independence for their own countries.
- After World War II, African nations gradually gained independence from colonial powers.

Section 5: Issues for Africa Today

- To increase economic stability, African countries are trying to diversify their economies.
- Africans today are working to increase literacy rates and life expectancy.
- Africans are trying to address environmental issues, such as soil erosion, through the help of science, education, and the sensible use of land and other resources.

South Africa

◆ Reviewing Key Terms

Use each key term below in a sentence that shows the meaning of the term.

1. domesticate
2. civilization
3. migrate
4. ethnic group
5. city-state
6. pilgrimage
7. plantation
8. colonize
9. nationalism
10. Pan-Africanism
11. boycott
12. democracy
13. commercial farming
14. hybrid
15. literate
16. life expectancy

Vocabulary Builder

Revisit this chapter's high-use words:

adapt	compete	movement
conquer	descendant	sacrifice
distinct	seize	diversify
network	captive	expose

Ask students to review the definitions they recorded on their *Word Knowledge* worksheets.

All in One Africa Teaching Resources,
Word Knowledge, p. 167
Consider allowing students to earn extra credit if they use the words in their answers to the questions in the Chapter Review and Assessment. The words must be used correctly and in a natural context to earn the extra points.

Review Chapter Content

- Review and revisit the major themes of this chapter by asking students to classify which Guiding Question each bulleted statement in the Chapter Summary answers. Form students into groups and ask them to complete the activity together. Refer to p. 349 in the Student Edition for text of Guiding Questions.

- Assign *Vocabulary Development* for students to review Key Terms.
  All in One Africa Teaching Resources,
  Vocabulary Development, p. 184

Answers

Key Terms
1–16. Students' sentences should reflect knowledge of each Key Term.

Comprehension and Critical Thinking

17. (a) They gathered food and hunted animals to use for food, clothing, and shelter. They also learned how to make tools from wood and bones, and later from stone. **(b)** The onset of farming allowed people to stay in one place since they did not have to travel to find food. This led to the rise of civilizations.

18. (a) East Africa: Aksum, Malindi, Mombasa, Great Zimbabwe, Kilwa; North Africa: Carthage; West Africa: Ghana, Mali, Songhai, Benin **(b)** Ancient African civilizations grew rich and powerful through trade. **(c)** Traders spread the religion of Islam throughout Africa as they traveled to trade their goods.

19. (a) The relationship between Europe and Africa began as an equal trading partnership. **(b)** The relationship became bitter and strained as Europeans began to take African riches and gain control of trade routes. **(c)** The slave trade caused Africa to lose its youngest, healthiest, and most capable people. Robbed of their families and skilled workers, African societies were torn apart.

20. (a) European nations rushed to colonize African territory. **(b)** African nations have faced the challenge of establishing stable governments. **(c)** The colonial powers rarely allowed Africans to share in government, so Africans had little experience governing a country. They also did little to help Africans prepare to govern themselves. In these ways, colonial rule contributed to the problem of maintaining stable governments in the newly independent African countries.

21. (a) Diversifying countries' economies; making schools less crowded; stopping the spread of disease; feeding a growing population; preventing soil erosion **(b)** To improve their economies, African nations are working to reduce their dependency on a single product. They are also building new schools and working with groups like the World Health Organization to improve social conditions.

◆ Comprehension and Critical Thinking

17. (a) List Identify some of the skills early Africans used to survive.
(b) Draw Conclusions How did the onset of farming affect early civilizations in Africa?

18. (a) Name Identify an ancient trading civilization from each of the following areas: East Africa, North Africa, and West Africa.
(b) Explain Why was trade important to ancient African civilizations?
(c) Analyze Information What was the relationship between trade and the spread of Islam in Africa?

19. (a) Recall How did the relationship between Europeans and Africans begin?
(b) Identify Sequence How did the relationship between Europeans and Africans change over time?
(c) Identify Effects Describe the effects of the Atlantic slave trade on Africa.

20. (a) Define What is meant by the phrase "the scramble for Africa"?

(b) Describe What challenges have African nations faced since independence?
(c) Make Inferences In what ways did colonial rule cause problems for African countries after independence?

21. (a) Identify What economic, social, and environmental issues challenge Africans today?
(b) Explain How are Africans working to improve their economies and social conditions?

◆ Skills Practice

Sequencing In the Skills for Life activity in this chapter, you learned how to show sequence. Review the steps you followed to learn this skill. Then make a timeline of key events in this chapter.

◆ Writing Activity: Language Arts

In the 1800s, many people in the United States spoke out against slavery. They were called abolitionists because they wanted to abolish, or put an end to, slavery. Using what you have learned about the slave trade, write a speech that could be used by an abolitionist to help end slavery.

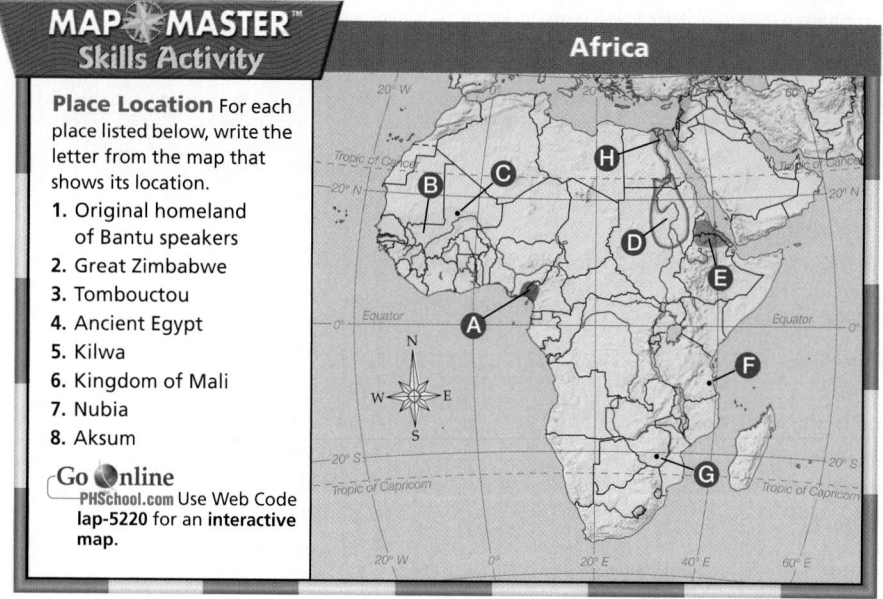

MAP MASTER™ Skills Activity

Africa

Place Location For each place listed below, write the letter from the map that shows its location.
1. Original homeland of Bantu speakers
2. Great Zimbabwe
3. Tombouctou
4. Ancient Egypt
5. Kilwa
6. Kingdom of Mali
7. Nubia
8. Aksum

Go Online
PHSchool.com Use Web Code **lap-5220** for an **interactive map.**

422 Africa

Skills Practice
Answers will vary, but students' timelines should include major events from the chapter listed in order and matched with the appropriate dates.
  Use *Rubric for Assessing a Timeline* to evaluate students' work.
All in One **Africa Teaching Resources,** *Rubric for Assessing a Timeline,* p. 189

Writing Activity: Language and Arts
Students' answers will vary, but should reflect what they have learned about slavery in this section.
  Use *Rubric for Assessing an Oral Presentation* to evaluate students' speeches.
All in One **Africa Teaching Resources,** *Rubric for Assessing an Oral Presentation,* p. 190

Standardized Test Prep

Test-Taking Tips

Some questions on standardized tests ask you to analyze a reading selection. Study the passage below. Then follow the tips to answer the sample question.

> In A.D. 1312, Mansa Musa became emperor of Mali. As emperor, he controlled huge supplies of gold and salt. Mansa Musa brought laws based on Islam to his land. Mali became a safe place to live and travel. The emperor also promoted trade with North Africa. His fame spread to Europe.

TIP Try to identify the main idea, or most important point, in the paragraph. Every sentence in a paragraph helps to support this idea.

Pick the letter that best answers the question.

From this paragraph, it is clear that Mansa Musa

A ~~became too powerful for the good of his people.~~

B ~~was the most powerful ruler in the world at that time.~~

C brought order and prosperity to his land.

D traveled to Europe to promote trade.

TIP Cross out answer choices that don't make sense. Then choose the BEST answer from the remaining choices.

Think It Through You can rule out A and B. Mansa Musa was powerful, but the paragraph doesn't suggest that he was too powerful or that he was the world's most powerful ruler. That leaves C and D. It is true that Mansa Musa's travels promoted trade, but the paragraph doesn't mention a trip to Europe. The correct answer is C.

Practice Questions

Use the tips above and other tips in this book to help you answer the following questions.

1. An early civilization formed in which area along the Nile River?

   A Mali
   B Ghana
   C Nubia
   D Great Zimbabwe

2. During the time of the Atlantic slave trade,

   A Europeans traded weapons for African slaves.
   B slaves in the European colonies usually won their freedom after a few years.
   C almost all slaves survived the voyage across the Atlantic.
   D Africans did not profit from slavery.

3. What was the goal of the Pan-African movement?

   A bringing all Africans together in one nation
   B bringing all Africans living around the world together to work for their rights and freedoms
   C bringing only Africans living in Africa together to work for their rights and freedoms
   D bringing all Africans living outside of Africa back to Africa

Read the passage below, and then answer the question that follows.

> European countries competed with one another to gain African territory. Instead of going to war over territory, they set rules for how they could claim African land. By 1900, European nations had colonized many parts of Africa.

4. What can you conclude from this passage about the colonization of Africa?

   A Africans did not resist colonization.
   B Africa was colonized sometime after 1900.
   C European nations believed they could benefit from controlling Africa's resources.
   D European nations were not good at fighting wars with one another.

Go Online PHSchool.com

Use Web Code laa-5200 for Chapter 12 self-test.

Chapter 12 **423**

Standardized Test Prep

Answers

1. C
2. A
3. B
4. C

Go Online PHSchool.com Students may use the Chapter 12 self-test on PHSchool.com to prepare for the Chapter Test.

Assessment Resources

Use *Chapter Tests A and B* to assess students' mastery of chapter content.

All in One Africa Teaching Resources, *Chapter Tests A and B*, pp. 191–196

Tests are also available on the *ExamView Test Bank CD-ROM.*

⊙ *ExamView Test Bank CD-ROM*

Cultures of Africa

Chapter Overview

Overview

Section 1

The Cultures of North Africa
1. Learn about the elements of culture.
2. Discover how Islam influences life in North Africa.
3. Find out about cultural change in North Africa.

Section 2

The Cultures of West Africa
1. Learn about West Africa's ethnic diversity.
2. Find out about the importance of family ties in West African culture.
3. Examine the West African tradition of storytelling.

Section 3

The Cultures of East Africa
1. Find out how geography has affected the development of East African cultures.
2. Learn how and why ideas about land ownership are changing in East Africa.

Section 4

The Cultures of Southern and Central Africa
1. Learn about the cultural diversity of Southern Africa.
2. Examine different ways of life in Central Africa and learn about the diverse cultures of the region.

African Culture: Textiles and Weaving
Length: 2 minutes, 42 seconds
Use with Section 2
This segment explores weaving as an important element of African culture. Students will learn about different types of cloth and their significance. They will also find out how the importance of textiles has changed throughout Africa's history.

Technology Resources

Students use embedded Web codes to access Internet activities, chapter self-tests, and additional map practice. They may also access Dorling Kindersley's Online Desk Reference to learn more about each country they study.

Use the Interactive Textbook to make content and concepts come alive through animations, videos, and activities that accompany the complete basal text—online and on CD-ROM.

PRENTICE HALL
TeacherEXPRESS
Plan • Teach • Assess

Use this complete suite of powerful teaching tools to make planning lessons and administering tests quicker and easier.

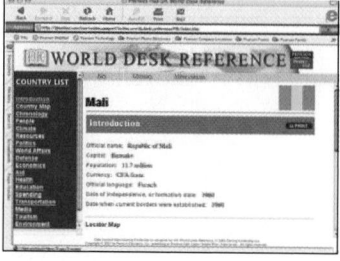
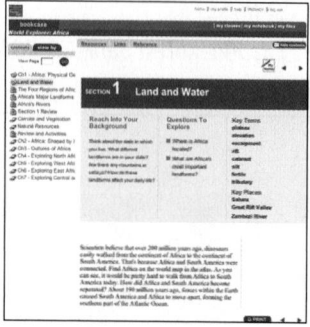

Reading and Assessment

Reading and Vocabulary Instruction

🔊 Model the Target Reading Skill

Comparison and Contrast Explain to students that comparing and contrasting can help them understand relationships between different kinds of information. When students compare two or more ideas or situations, they are looking for similarities between them. Contrasting means looking for differences between two things. Help students understand how to compare and contrast by writing the chart below on the board, leaving the columns empty except for the titles. As you read the chapter with students, fill in the chart with information about each region. The chart might look like this:

North Africa	West Africa	East Africa
Islam is a common bond between people.	Kinship groups are a common bond between people.	Christianity and Islam are a common bond between people.
Arabic is the main language.	There is no common language.	People speak many different languages.

Next, have students use the chart to write sentences comparing and contrasting the information about each region. One example is: *Most people in North Africa are Muslim, whereas most people in East Africa are Muslim or Christian.*

Use the following worksheets from All-in-One Africa Teaching Resources (pp. 221–223) to support the chapter's Target Reading Skill.

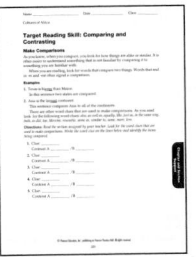 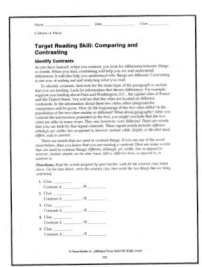 

Vocabulary Builder
High-Use Academic Words

Use these steps to teach this chapter's high-use words:

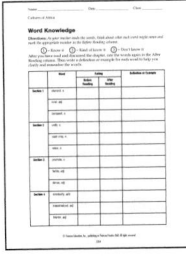

1. Have students rate how well they know each word on their Word Knowledge worksheets (All-in-One Africa Teaching Resources, p. 224).

2. Pronounce each word and ask students to repeat it.

3. Give students a brief definition or sample sentence (provided on TE pp. 427, 433, 441, and 446).

4. Work with students as they fill in the "Definition or Example" column of their Word Knowledge worksheets.

Assessment

Formal Assessment

Test students' understanding of core knowledge and skills.

Chapter Tests A and B, All-in-One Africa Teaching Resources, pp. 239–244

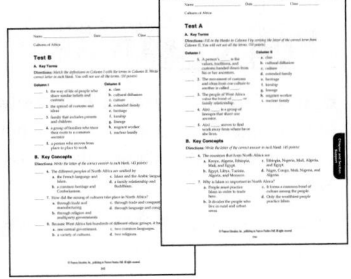

Customize the Chapter Tests to suit your needs.

ExamView Test Bank CD-ROM

Skills Assessment

Assess geographic literacy.

MapMaster Skills, Student Edition pp. 425, 430

Assess reading and comprehension.

Target Reading Skills, Student Edition, pp. 429, 434, 442, 447, and in Section Assessments

Chapter 13 Assessment, Eastern Hemisphere Reading and Vocabulary Study Guide, p. 160

Performance Assessment

Assess students' performance on this chapter's Writing Activities using the following rubrics from All-in-One Africa Teaching Resources.

Rubric for Assessing a Writing Assignment, p. 237

Rubric for Assessing a Report, p. 238

Assess students' work through performance tasks.

Small Group Activity: Telling a Traditional African Story, All-in-One Africa Teaching Resources, pp. 227–230

Online Assessment

Have students check their own understanding.

Chapter Self-Test

Test Preparation

Africa Benchmark Test 1, AYP Monitoring Assessments, pp. 113–116

Section 1 The Cultures of North Africa

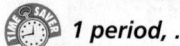 *1 period, .5 block*

Social Studies Objectives

1. Learn about the elements of culture.
2. Discover how Islam influences life in North Africa.
3. Find out about cultural change in North Africa.

Reading/Language Arts Objective

Make comparisons between groups or situations to find similarities.

Prepare to Read

Build Background Knowledge
Ask students to read the introduction to Section 1 and compare and contrast daily life in Marrakech with their own.

Set a Purpose for Reading
Have students begin to fill out the *Reading Readiness Guide*.

Preview Key Terms
Teach the section's Key Terms.

Target Reading Skill
Introduce the section's Target Reading Skill of **making comparisons**.

Instructional Resources

All in One Africa Teaching Resources
- L2 Reading Readiness Guide, p. 206
- L2 Make Comparisons, p. 221

Differentiated Instruction

Spanish Reading and Vocabulary Study Guide
- L1 Chapter 13, Section 1, pp. 105–106 ELL

Instruct

The Elements of Culture
Ask about the elements of culture and discuss how culture can affect the way people behave.

Religion and Culture in North Africa
Discuss the major religions and ethnic groups in North Africa.

Target Reading Skill
Review **making comparisons**.

Cultural Change in North Africa
Discuss how the people of North Africa have been influenced by other cultures.

Instructional Resources

All in One Africa Teaching Resources
- L2 Guided Reading and Review, p. 207
- L2 Reading Readiness Guide, p. 206

Africa Transparencies
- L2 Section Reading Support Transparency AF 41

Differentiated Instruction

All in One Africa Teaching Resources
- L3 A Handful of Dates, pp. 233–234 AR, GT

Teacher's Edition
- L3 For Advanced Readers, TE p. 428
- L1 For Special Needs Students, TE p. 428

Student Edition on Audio CD
- L1 Chapter 13, Section 1 ELL, LPR, SN

Spanish Support
- L2 Guided Reading and Review (Spanish), p. 144 ELL

Assess and Reteach

Assess Progress
Evaluate student comprehension with the section assessment and section quiz.

Reteach
Assign the Reading and Vocabulary Study Guide to help struggling students.

Extend
Extend the lesson by showing students a transparency and having them research the ways in which geography in North Africa influences culture.

Instructional Resources

All in One Africa Teaching Resources
- L2 Section Quiz, p. 208
  Rubric for Assessing a Writing Assignment, p. 237

Reading and Vocabulary Study Guide
- L1 Chapter 13, Section 1, pp. 148–150

Africa Transparencies
- L3 Color Transparency AF 30: Southwest Asia and North Africa: Physical-Political

Differentiated Instruction

Spanish Support
- L2 Section Quiz (Spanish), p. 145 ELL

Key

- L1 Basic to Average
- L2 For All Students
- L3 Average to Advanced

- LPR Less Proficient Readers
- AR Advanced Readers
- SN Special Needs Students

- GT Gifted and Talented
- ELL English Language Learners

Section 2 The Cultures of West Africa

 2 periods, 1 block (includes Skills for Life)

Social Studies Objectives

1. Learn about West Africa's ethnic diversity.
2. Find out about the importance of family ties in West African culture.
3. Examine the West African tradition of storytelling.

Reading/Language Arts Objective

Identify contrasts between groups or situations to find what is unique about each one.

Prepare to Read	Instructional Resources	Differentiated Instruction
Build Background Knowledge Ask students to think about how they would create a newspaper for many groups of people who speak different languages. **Set a Purpose for Reading** Have students evaluate statements on the *Reading Readiness Guide*. **Preview Key Terms** Teach the section's Key Terms. **Target Reading Skill** Introduce the section's Target Reading Skill of **identifying contrasts**.	**All in One Africa Teaching Resources** L2 Reading Readiness Guide, p. 210 L2 Identify Contrasts, p. 222	**Spanish Reading and Vocabulary Study Guide** L1 Chapter 13, Section 2, pp. 107–108 ELL

Instruct	Instructional Resources	Differentiated Instruction
Cultural Diversity of West Africa Discuss the ways in which the cultures of West Africa differ. **Target Reading Skill** Review **identifying contrasts**. **West African Families** Discuss family life and traditions in West Africa. **Keeping Traditions Alive** Discuss how West African culture is preserved and how it influences other cultures.	**All in One Africa Teaching Resources** L2 Guided Reading and Review, p. 211 L2 Reading Readiness Guide, p. 210 **Africa Transparencies** L2 Section Reading Support Transparency AF 42 **World Studies Video Program** L2 African Culture: Textiles and Weaving	**All in One Africa Teaching Resources** L3 Small Group Activity: Telling a Traditional African Story, pp. 227–230 AR, GT L2 Skills for Life, p. 226 AR, GT, LPR, SN **Teacher's Edition** L1 For English Language Learners, TE p. 435 L1 For Less Proficient Readers, TE p. 435 L3 For Gifted and Talented, TE p. 436 **Reading and Vocabulary Study Guide** L1 Chapter 13, Section 2, pp. 151–153 ELL, LPR, SN **Spanish Support** L2 Guided Reading and Review (Spanish), p. 146 ELL

Assess and Reteach	Instructional Resources	Differentiated Instruction
Assess Progress Evaluate student comprehension with the section assessment and section quiz. **Reteach** Assign the Reading and Vocabulary Study Guide to help struggling students. **Extend** Extend the lesson by assigning an Activity Shop activity.	**All in One Africa Teaching Resources** L2 Section Quiz, p. 212 L3 Activity Shop Lab: The Language of Music, pp. 231–232 Rubric for Assessing a Writing Assignment, p. 237 **Reading and Vocabulary Study Guide** L1 Chapter 13, Section 2, pp. 151–153	**Spanish Support** L2 Section Quiz (Spanish), p. 147 ELL **Teacher's Edition** L1 For Less Proficient Readers, TE p. 439 **Africa Transparencies** L1 Transparency B12: Chart/Table ELL, LPR, SN **Social Studies Skills Tutor CD-ROM** L1 Comparing and Contrasting, ELL, LPR, SN

Key

L1 Basic to Average   L3 Average to Advanced   LPR Less Proficient Readers   GT Gifted and Talented

L2 For All Students   AR Advanced Readers   ELL English Language Learners

                                                 SN Special Needs Students

Section 3 The Cultures of East Africa

 1 period, .5 block

Social Studies Objectives
1. Find out how geography has affected the development of East African cultures.
2. Learn how and why ideas about land ownership are changing in East Africa.

Reading/Language Arts Objective
Use signal words to identify comparisons and contrasts in a text.

Prepare to Read	Instructional Resources	Differentiated Instruction
Build Background Knowledge Ask students to brainstorm different kinds of land ownership. **Set a Purpose for Reading** Have students begin to fill out the *Reading Readiness Guide.* **Preview Key Terms** Teach the section's Key Terms. **Target Reading Skill** Introduce the section's Target Reading Skill of **using signal words.**	**All in One Africa Teaching Resources** **L2** Reading Readiness Guide, p. 214 **L2** Compare and Contrast, p. 223	**Spanish Reading and Vocabulary Study Guide** **L1** Chapter 13, Section 3, pp. 109–110 ELL

Instruct	Instructional Resources	Differentiated Instruction
Geography and Cultural Diversity Ask about the different cultures in East Africa and how different religions were introduced to the region. **Target Reading Skill** Review **using signal words.** **Changing Ideas About Land** Ask about and discuss land ownership in Africa.	**All in One Africa Teaching Resources** **L2** Guided Reading and Review, p. 215 **L2** Reading Readiness Guide, p. 214 **Africa Transparencies** **L2** Section Reading Support Transparency AF 43	**Teacher's Edition** **L2** For English Language Learners, TE p. 442 **Spanish Support** **L2** Guided Reading and Review (Spanish), p. 148 ELL

Assess and Reteach	Instructional Resources	Differentiated Instruction
Assess Progress Evaluate student comprehension with the section assessment and section quiz. **Reteach** Assign the Reading and Vocabulary Study Guide to help struggling students. **Extend** Have students write a story that reflects Swahili culture.	**All in One Africa Teaching Resources** **L2** Section Quiz, p. 216 **L3** Writing Stories, p. 235 Rubric for Assessing a Writing Assignment, p. 237 **Reading and Vocabulary Study Guide** **L1** Chapter 13, Section 3, pp. 154–156	**Spanish Support** **L2** Section Quiz (Spanish), p. 149 ELL

Key
L1 Basic to Average   **L3** Average to Advanced
L2 For All Students

LPR Less Proficient Readers   GT Gifted and Talented
AR Advanced Readers   ELL English Language Learners
SN Special Needs Students

Section 4 The Cultures of Southern and Central Africa

⏱ *2.5 periods, 1.25 blocks (includes Chapter Review and Assessment)*

Social Studies Objectives
1. Learn about the cultural diversity of Southern Africa.
2. Examine different ways of life in Central Africa and learn about the diverse cultures of the region.

Reading/Language Arts Objective
Compare and contrast to sort out and analyze information.

Prepare to Read	Instructional Resources	Differentiated Instruction
Build Background Knowledge Ask students to preview the section to identify some characteristics of the cultures of Southern and Central Africa. **Set a Purpose for Reading** Have students evaluate statements on the *Reading Readiness Guide.* **Preview Key Terms** Teach the section's Key Terms. **Target Reading Skill** Introduce the section's Target Reading Skill of **comparing and contrasting.**	**All in One Africa Teaching Resources** L2 Reading Readiness Guide, p. 218 L2 Compare and Contrast, p. 223	**Spanish Reading and Vocabulary Study Guide** L1 Chapter 13, Section 4, pp. 111–112 ELL

Instruct	Instructional Resources	Differentiated Instruction
Diversity in Southern Africa Ask questions about European influence on Southern Africa and how demand for labor affected peoples' lives in nearby countries. **Life in Central Africa** Discuss cultural and economic patterns in Central Africa. **Target Reading Skill** Review **comparing and contrasting.**	**All in One Africa Teaching Resources** L2 Guided Reading and Review, p. 219 L2 Reading Readiness Guide, p. 218 **Africa Transparencies** L2 Section Reading Support Transparency AF 44	**Spanish Support** L2 Guided Reading and Review (Spanish), p. 152 ELL

Assess and Reteach	Instructional Resources	Differentiated Instruction
Assess Progress Evaluate student comprehension with the section assessment and section quiz. **Reteach** Assign the Reading and Vocabulary Study Guide to help struggling students. **Extend** Extend the lesson by assigning an online activity.	**All in One Africa Teaching Resources** L2 Section Quiz, p. 220 Rubric for Assessing a Report, p. 238 L2 Word Knowledge, p. 224 L2 Vocabulary Development, p. 236 L2 Chapter Tests A and B, pp. 239–244 **Reading and Vocabulary Study Guide** L1 Chapter 13, Section 4, pp. 157–159 **PHSchool.com** L3 **For:** Environmental and Global Issues: The Universal Declaration of Human Rights **Web Code:** lad-5305	**Spanish Support** L2 Section Quiz (Spanish), p. 151 ELL L2 Chapter Summary (Spanish), p. 152 ELL L2 Vocabulary Development (Spanish), p. 153 ELL

Key

L1 Basic to Average	L3 Average to Advanced	LPR Less Proficient Readers	GT Gifted and Talented
L2 For All Students		AR Advanced Readers	ELL English Language Learners
		SN Special Needs Students	

Professional Development

Reading Background

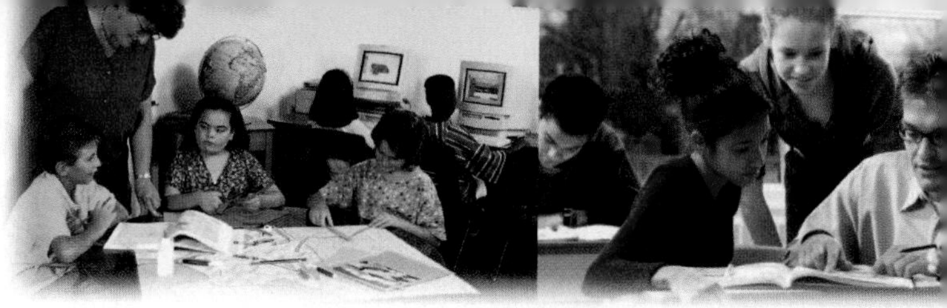

Author's Craft

Tell students that authors plan their writing to present the text clearly and to help the reader learn. Once students learn to determine the author's plan, they will be able to use the text more effectively. To teach students how to identify the author's plan, ask them the following questions about the first two paragraphs on p. 433 of the Student Edition:

1. Does the author let readers know what they are going to learn? *(Yes; the author uses a heading to introduce the selection's theme. The author hints at what will be discussed by asking hypothetical questions for students to think about.)*
2. How does the author introduce the main points? Remind students to reread the paragraph, paying special attention to the sentences at the beginning and end of the paragraph, where the main idea is often found. (*The author explains the main points in the beginning and middle of the paragraph*—The hundreds of ethnic groups in West Africa speak different languages . . . in order to communicate, most West Africans speak more than one language.)
3. Does the author use transition words to present details? *(No; the author lists the details with few transition words. The author uses examples to clarify the details.)*

Create a list of the answers to these questions. Ask students to scan other paragraphs in the section. Is the author's plan consistent for all the paragraphs?

Multiple Meanings

Students may come across a word that has several meanings. For example, the word *compound* can mean *a fenced-in group of homes, consisting of two or more parts,* or *to add to or increase.* Practice identifying the various meanings by creating sentences using the word in various contexts, such as: *The man opened the gate to let us out of the compound; The doctor said the knee was broken in two places, so it was a compound fracture; The wind compounded the difficulty of the tennis match.* Write the sentences on the board, a poster, or a transparency. Have students study the contexts to decide whether the target word has the same meaning in each example. Encourage them to consult a dictionary to help them decide which definition the word has in each sentence.

World Studies Background

North African Influence in Spain

In the eighth century, Muslim Berbers and Arabs from North Africa invaded and conquered Spain, retaining control of the country until 1492. They intermarried with the Spanish and their descendants became known as Moors. The Moors left a strong cultural influence in Spain, especially on its architecture. The Alhambra, a palace overlooking the city of Granada, is one of the most famous Moorish buildings.

Tombouctou and the Sankore Mosque

By the fourteenth century, the city of Tombouctou was a major trading center as well as a center of Islamic culture. The emperor Mansa Musa, inspired by his pilgrimage to Mecca in 1324, built Tombouctou's Great Mosque. An architect who had accompanied Mansa Musa on his pilgrimage was commissioned to build another mosque called the Sankore Mosque. It stands today in Mali.

African Music

Music, integral to African life, is present at social and religious events. Many different instruments are used to create African music. The lamellophone, or "thumb piano," consists of metal strips attached to a piece of wood. To play the instrument, a musician plucks the strips with fingers or thumbs. Other common instruments include xylophones and flutes.

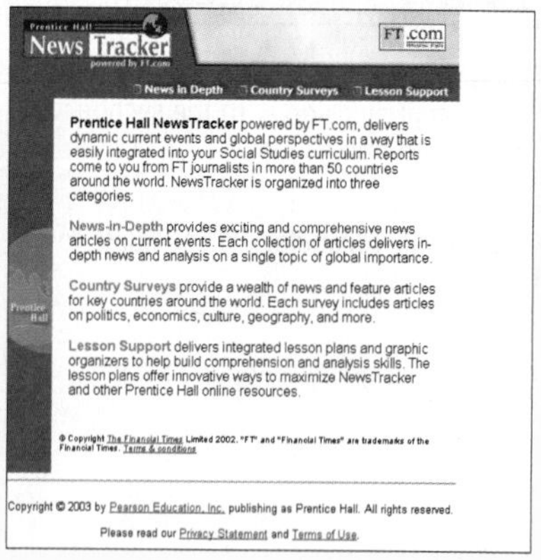

Get in-depth information on topics of global importance with **Prentice Hall Newstracker,** powered by FT.com.

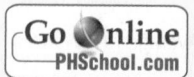

Go Online PHSchool.com Use Web code **lad-5300** for **Prentice Hall Newstracker.**

Reading Background

Reading Strategies for Less Proficient Readers

For many less proficient readers, a lack of confidence is often key to their reading difficulties. You can use a combination of reading strategies, such as Cloze Reading and Choral Reading followed by silent reading, to teach students the skills they need to read confidently.

When using the Cloze Reading strategy, ask students to follow along silently as you read a selection aloud. Leave out every seventh–tenth word, and have students jump in, saying the word aloud together. Students must remain alert during Cloze Reading so that they can be ready to supply the missing word. This can boost students' confidence in their reading abilities because they are able to practice without being singled out.

Following the Cloze Reading with a Choral Reading of the passage further enhances students' reading abilities. Keep the following points in mind as you practice Choral Reading:

1. Encourage students to stay with your voice as you read rather than racing ahead or lagging behind.
2. Use shorter passages of about 300 to 500 words.

3. For students to have a better understanding of the text, follow up with a silent reading of the same passage. Then begin to ask questions about the content of the passage.

Key Terms: Making Choices

The most important part of learning a new word is being able to use it to communicate ideas. Choosing between two descriptions of a vocabulary word can help students internalize its meaning and add the word to their working vocabularies. Ask students to listen as you read two descriptions for each Key Term in the chapter. Explain that one is a description of the term and one is not. Challenge students to identify the correct description.

Example:
Word: *Swahili*
Description 1: *Swahili* people follow only African traditions.
Description 2: *Swahili* culture is a mix of Arab and African ways. *(correct)*

After teaching the Key Terms, challenge students to write their own pairs of descriptions and have a partner choose which is correct.

World Studies Background

Traditional African Societies

Before colonial rule began to change African culture in the nineteenth century, there were six distinct types of societies: hunting and gathering, cattle herding, forest dwelling, fishing, grain raising, and city dwelling.

Most hunting and gathering societies have disappeared, but some of the others were quite successful. The fishing societies, for example, included specialists in boat building and generated large populations because of their nourishing diet of fish. Cattle herding and grain-raising societies were able to trade their surpluses for other necessities. Urban societies were supported by goods from the agricultural societies and became centers of trade.

Contemporary African Societies

Contemporary societies are no longer as distinct because the various groups have intermingled and taken on one another's characteristics. Cattle herders now grow their own vegetables, and grain-raising societies keep cattle. Previously, people living in the same area shared similar jobs and ways of life. Modern African societies, however, are varied in terms of jobs and standards of living.

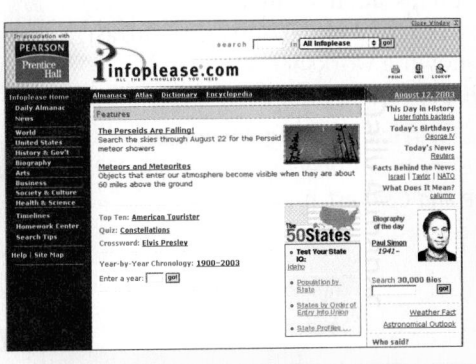

Infoplease® provides a wealth of useful information for the classroom. You can use this resource to strengthen your background on the subjects covered in this chapter. Have students visit this advertising-free site as a starting point for projects requiring research.

 Use Web code **lad-5306** for **Infoplease®**.

Guiding Questions

Remind students about the Guiding Questions introduced at the beginning of this section.

Section 1 relates to **Guiding Question** ③
What features help define different African cultures? *(Culture has many elements, including food, clothing, homes, jobs, language, and people's beliefs. The religion of Islam and the Arabic language help unify the people of North Africa.)*

Section 2 relates to **Guiding Question** ③
What features help define different African cultures? *(West Africa is home to hundreds of ethnic groups that speak different languages and practice different religions.)*

Section 3 relates to **Guiding Question** ③
What features help define different African cultures? *(East Africa's ethnic groups speak different languages, but Swahili is widely used for business and communication.)*

Section 4 relates to **Guiding Question** ③
What features help define different African cultures? *(Southern Africa and Central Africa are both culturally diverse. Southern Africa has been strongly influenced by Europeans. Central Africa has hundreds of ethnic groups and a variety of religions.)*

🕐 Target Reading Skill

In this chapter, students will learn and apply the reading skill of comparison and contrast. Use the following worksheets to help students practice this skill:

> **All in One** **Africa Teaching Resources,** *Make Comparisons,* p. 221; *Identify Contrasts,* p. 222; *Compare and Contrast,* p. 223

Chapter Preview

This chapter will introduce you to the cultures of Africa and help you understand what the lives of the people in the region are like.

Section 1
The Cultures of North Africa

Section 2
The Cultures of West Africa

Section 3
The Cultures of East Africa

Section 4
The Cultures of Southern and Central Africa

 Target Reading Skill

Comparison and Contrast In this chapter you will focus on comparing and contrasting ideas to help you understand the text that you read. Making comparisons, identifying contrasts, and using signal words are all ways for you to learn as you read.

▶ A dancer leaps through the air to the rhythm of the drums at a performance in Burundi.

Differentiated Instruction

The following Teacher Edition strategies are suitable for students of varying abilities.

Advanced Readers, p. 429
English Language Learners, pp. 435, 442
Gifted and Talented, p. 436
Less Proficient Readers, pp. 435, 439
Special Needs Students, p. 429

Bibliography

For the Teacher
Armstrong, Karen. *Islam: A Short History.* Modern Library, 2002.
Brett, Michael, et. al. *South Africa.* DK Publishing, 2003.
Visona, Monica Blakmun. *A History of Art in Africa.* Prentice Hall, 2000.

For the Student
L1 Ayo, Yvonne. *Eyewitness: Africa.* DK Publishing, 2000.
L2 Bennett, Martin. *Tales from West Africa (Oxford Myths and Legends).* Oxford University Press Children's Books, 2001.
L3 Lemasolai-Lekuton, Joseph. *Facing the Lion: Growing Up Maasai on the African Savanna.* National Geographic, 2003.

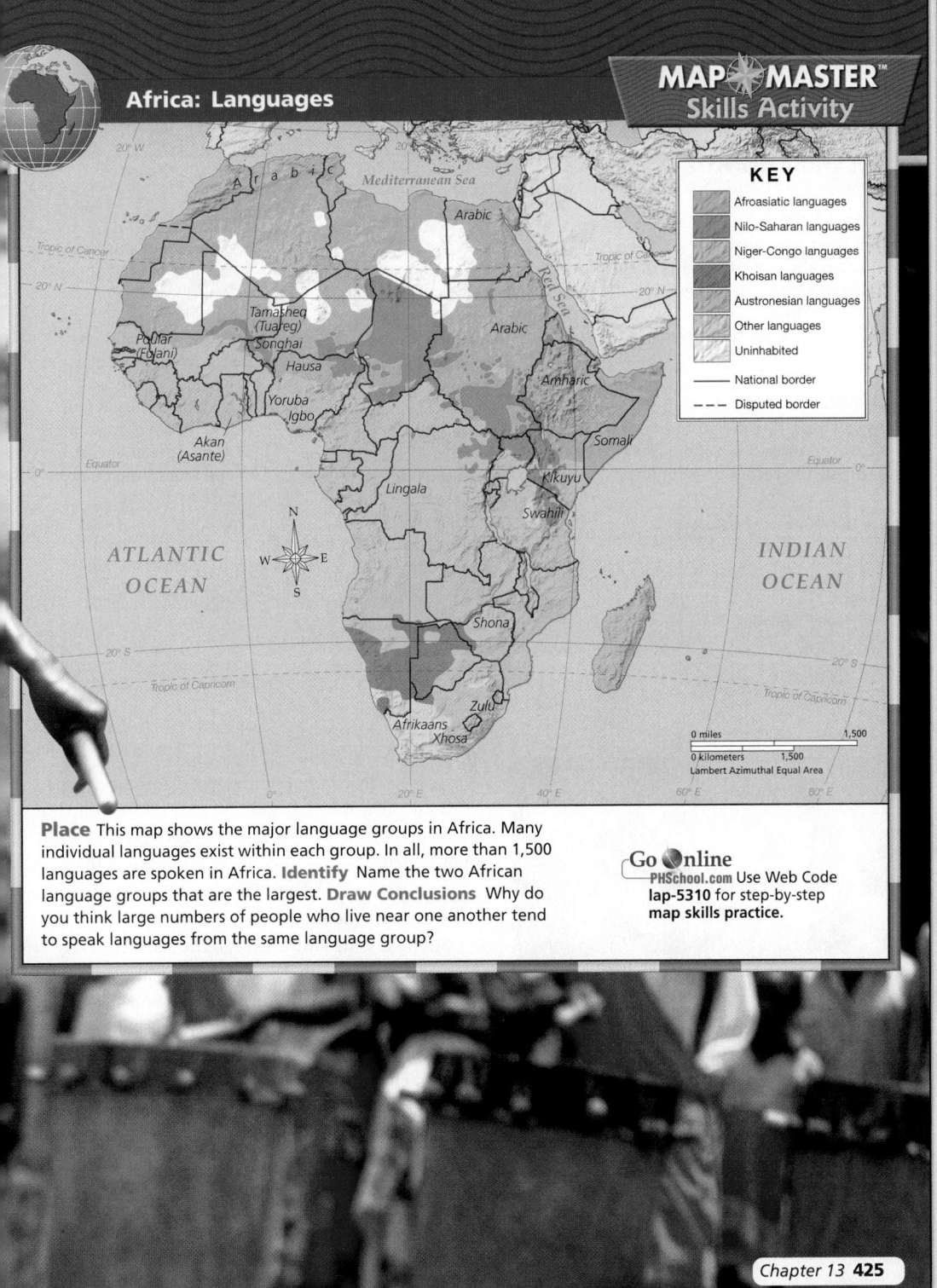

Africa: Languages

KEY

- Afroasiatic languages
- Nilo-Saharan languages
- Niger-Congo languages
- Khoisan languages
- Austronesian languages
- Other languages
- Uninhabited
- ——— National border
- – – – Disputed border

Arabic · Mediterranean Sea · Arabic · Tropic of Cancer · Red Sea · Tamasheq (Tuareg) · Songhai · Poular (Fulani) · Hausa · Arabic · Yoruba · Igbo · Amharic · Akan (Asante) · Somali · Lingala · Kikuyu · Swahili · Shona · Afrikaans · Zulu · Xhosa

ATLANTIC OCEAN · INDIAN OCEAN

0 miles 1,500
0 kilometers 1,500
Lambert Azimuthal Equal Area

Place This map shows the major language groups in Africa. Many individual languages exist within each group. In all, more than 1,500 languages are spoken in Africa. **Identify** Name the two African language groups that are the largest. **Draw Conclusions** Why do you think large numbers of people who live near one another tend to speak languages from the same language group?

Go Online
PHSchool.com Use Web Code lap-5310 for step-by-step **map skills practice.**

Ask students to study the map carefully, paying close attention to the title and map key. Then, have students take turns describing for the class where in Africa each language group is spoken.

Go Online
PHSchool.com Students may practice their map skills using the interactive online version of this map.

Using the Visual L2

Reach Into Your Background Have students study the photograph on pp. 424–425 and read its accompanying caption. Then have students think about dances they have seen or participated in. Ask students to think about how those dances are similar to and different from the one shown in the photo. Use the Think-Write-Pair-Share participation strategy (TE, p. T36) to help students sharpen their ideas.

Answers

Identify Afroasiatic and Niger-Congo languages **Draw Conclusions** Possible answer: The history of the area may influence the languages spoken there. One language spoken in an area hundreds of years ago may have developed into a few related languages over time.

Chapter Resources

Teaching Resources
- **L2** Vocabulary Development, p. 236
- **L2** Skills for Life, p. 226
- **L2** Chapter Tests A and B, pp. 239–244

Spanish Support
- **L2** Spanish Chapter Summary, p. 152
- **L2** Spanish Vocabulary Development, p. 153

Media and Technology
- **L1** Student Edition on Audio CD
- **L1** Guided Reading Audiotapes, English and Spanish
- **L2** Social Studies Skills Tutor CD-ROM
  ExamView Test Bank CD-ROM

PRENTICE HALL
Presentation EXPRESS™
Teach · Connect · Inspire

Teach this chapter's content using the PresentationExpress™ CD-ROM including:
- slide shows
- transparencies
- interactive maps and media
- *ExamView®* QuickTake Presenter

Section 1
Step-by-Step Instruction

Objectives
Social Studies
1. Learn about the elements of culture.
2. Discover how Islam influences life in North Africa.
3. Find out about cultural change in North Africa.

Reading/Language Arts
Make comparisons between groups or situations to find similarities.

Prepare to Read

Build Background Knowledge L2
In this section, students will learn about the cultures of North Africa. As a class, read the paragraph about a typical day in Marrakech, Morocco, on this page of the Student Edition. Then ask students to compare and contrast daily life in Marrakech with their own. Conduct an Idea Wave (TE, p. T35) to generate a list of similarities and differences and write this list on the board.

Set a Purpose for Reading L2
■ Preview the Objectives.

■ Form students into pairs or groups of four. Distribute the *Reading Readiness Guide*. Ask students to fill in the first two columns of the chart. Use the Numbered Heads participation strategy (TE, p.T36) to call on students to share one piece of information they already know and one piece of information they want to know.

All in One **Africa Teaching Resources,** *Reading Readiness Guide,* p. 206

Vocabulary Builder
Preview Key Terms L2
Pronounce each Key Term, and then ask students to say the word with you. Provide a simple explanation such as, "People who share a culture may practice the same religion and celebrate the same holidays."

Prepare to Read

Objectives
In this section you will
1. Learn about the elements of culture.
2. Discover how Islam influences life in North Africa.
3. Find out about cultural change in North Africa.

Taking Notes
As you read, find details about the cultures of North Africa. Copy the outline below, and use it to record your findings.

> I. The elements of culture
>   A.
>   1.
>   2.
>   B.
> II. Islamic influence

Target Reading Skill

Make Comparisons
Making comparisons between groups or situations can help you see what they have in common. As you read this section, compare the ways of life of different peoples in North Africa. Look for similarities among ethnic groups, among people who live in different locations, or among other groups that are logical to compare.

Key Terms
• **culture** (KUL chur) *n.* the way of life of people who share similar customs and beliefs
• **Quran** (koo RAHN) *n.* the sacred book of Islam; also spelled *Koran*
• **cultural diffusion** (KUL chur ul dih FYOO zhun) *n.* the spread of customs and ideas from one culture to another

A carpet salesman in Marrakech

I n the North African country of Morocco, carpets are an export. But they are also part of everyday life. In some Moroccan homes, carpets serve as more than just floor coverings. People may use them as places to sit and to sleep. People also use special carpets as prayer mats.

Suppose your family lives in the Moroccan city of Marrakech (ma ruh KESH). A typical day might unfold in the following way. After breakfast, your mother spends the day weaving carpets. She learned this skill from her mother, who learned it from her mother. Her workday ends at sunset, when she hears the crier who calls out from the nearby mosque (mahsk), the Muslim house of worship. When she hears the call, your mother joins many others in reciting this prayer in Arabic: "There is no god but God, and Muhammad is His messenger."

426 Africa

Target Reading Skill L2

Make Comparisons Point out the Target Reading Skill. Tell students that making comparisons will help them to find things that two groups or situations have in common.

Model making comparisons using the selection on p. 429 under the heading Traditional and Modern Lifestyles. Have students compare urban and rural life in North

Africa, looking for similarities. (*Though they have different ways of life, the majority of urban and rural people in North Africa practice Islam.*)

Give students *Make Comparisons*. Have them complete the activity in groups.

All in One **Africa Teaching Resources,** *Make Comparisons,* p. 221

The Elements of Culture

The way of life you just read about is different in some ways from yours. In other words, Morocco's culture is somewhat different from yours. **Culture** is the way of life of a group of people who share similar customs and beliefs.

What Defines Culture? Culture has many elements. Culture includes food, clothing, homes, jobs, and language. It also includes things that are not so easy to see, such as how people view their world and what their beliefs are. These views and beliefs shape the way people behave. In Morocco, for example, many people take time from their activities to pray several times each day.

Shared Elements Different cultures may have elements in common. People in different places sometimes share the same language, although they may speak different dialects, or versions of that language. Similarly, cultures sometimes share the same religion, although people may practice it in different ways.

Some shared elements of culture are easy to notice. People of different cultures might wear similar clothing or live in similar housing. In many rural villages in Morocco, for example, houses are made of thick adobe (uh DOH bee), a type of brick made from sun-dried clay. Far from Morocco, in Mexico and in the southwestern United States, many people in rural areas also live in adobe houses.

✓ **Reading Check** Name some cultural elements that are easy to see.

Links to Science

Building With Adobe
Adobe bricks are made of clay and plant fibers. The fibers strengthen the bricks and keep them from crumbling. People have built with adobe since ancient times in many parts of the world. Native Americans have built with adobe for hundreds of years in the southwestern United States, where it is still used today.

Adobe is a good building material because it acts as an insulator, a material that helps keep outside heat from traveling inside. This insulating quality is especially important in hot climates, such as Morocco's (below).

Chapter 13 Section 1 **427**

Vocabulary Builder

Use the information below to teach students this section's high-use words.

High-Use Word	Definition and Sample Sentence
element, p. 427	*n.* a basic part of a multipart thing The basic **elements** of the cake mix are flour, sugar, and eggs.
rural, p. 427	*adj.* located in the countryside The **rural** town has only one main road.
conquest, p. 431	*n.* an invasion or take-over The culture of a region can change through **conquest**.

Guided Instruction

- **Vocabulary Builder** Clarify the high-use words **element** and **rural** before reading.

- Read The Elements of Culture, using the Oral Cloze strategy (TE, p. T33).

- Ask students **What are some elements of culture?** (*food, clothing, homes, jobs, language, how people view the world, and what their beliefs are*)

- Ask **How might culture affect the way people behave?** (*Possible answer: People might behave according to religious laws or choose jobs that are popular within their culture.*)

Independent Practice

Ask students to create the Taking Notes graphic organizer on a blank piece of paper. Then have them begin to fill in details about the elements of culture in North Africa.

Monitor Progress

As students fill in the graphic organizer, circulate to make sure individuals are choosing the correct details.

Links

Read the **Links to Science** on this page. Ask students **Why is it convenient for people in North Africa to build with adobe?** (*The materials are readily available, and adobe keeps the heat outside of the building.*)

Answer

✓ **Reading Check** Cultural elements that are easy to see are food, clothing, homes, jobs, and language.

Religion and Culture in North Africa

Guided Instruction

- Read Religion and Culture in North Africa. As students read, circulate to make sure individuals can answer the Reading Check question.

- Ask students **What elements of culture help unify the peoples of North Africa?** *(the Arabic language, Islam)*

- Ask students **What is the Quran?** *(the sacred book of Islam)* **What are some activities that the Quran prohibits?** *(lying, stealing, murder, gambling, eating pork, drinking alcohol)*

Chart Skills

Muslims call Muhammad's most essential teachings the Five Pillars of Islam. These pillars are duties that all Muslims are expected to follow, such as praying daily, as shown above. **Define** What are alms? **Infer** Why do you think Muhammad wanted Muslims to regularly declare their belief in God?

Religion and Culture in North Africa

The peoples of North Africa are spread out over a large area that includes the following countries: Egypt, Libya, Tunisia, Algeria, and Morocco. North Africans have many different backgrounds and ways of life. The Arabic language helps unify the different peoples of North Africa. So does Islam.

Muslim Beliefs Religion is an important part of North African culture. More than 95 percent of North Africans are Muslims. Muslims believe in God, whom they call by the Arabic word *Allah* (AL uh). The founder of Islam was a man named Muhammad. Muslims believe that Muhammad was a prophet, or a religious teacher who speaks for God or a god. In Islam, Jesus and the prophets of the Hebrew Bible, or Christian Old Testament, are also believed to be God's messengers. However, Muhammad is considered God's final messenger.

The sacred book of Islam is called the **Quran** (koo RAHN). Muslims consider the Quran to be the word of God. They believe that God revealed the verses of the Quran to the prophet Muhammad. Like the Hebrew and Christian Bibles, the Quran contains many kinds of writing, including stories, promises, and instructions. The Quran teaches about God, and it also provides a guide to living. The Quran forbids lying, stealing, and murder. It also prohibits gambling, eating pork, and drinking alcohol.

The Five Pillars of Islam

Pillar	Description
Declaration of Faith	Muslims must regularly declare the belief that there is only one God and Muhammad is God's messenger.
Prayer	Muslims must pray five times each day, facing in the direction of the holy city of Mecca.
Almsgiving	Muslims must give alms, or money that goes to the needy.
Fasting	Muslims must fast during daylight hours in the month of Ramadan.
Pilgrimage	Muslims must make a pilgrimage to Mecca at least one time in their lives if they are able.

Differentiated Instruction

For Advanced Readers L3
To learn more about the customs of Islam, have students read the primary source *A Handful of Dates*. Then ask them to discuss the reading and answer the questions in groups.

All in One **Africa Teaching Resources,**
A Handful of Dates, pp. 233–234

For Special Needs Students L1
Have students read the section as they listen to the recorded version of the Student Edition on Audio CD. Check for comprehension by pausing the CD and asking students to share their answers to the Reading Check questions.

⊙ Chapter 13, Section 1, **Student Edition on Audio CD**

Answers

Chart Skills **Define** Alms are donations to the poor. **Infer** possible answer: to remind people of their faith in God

Islam and Law The Islamic system of law is based on the Quran. Islamic law governs many aspects of life, including family life, business practices, banking, and government. Because so many North Africans are Muslims, Islamic law influences the cultures of the region.

Ethnic Groups of North Africa Most North Africans are Arabs. Because the Arab influence is so strong, North Africa is sometimes seen as a part (the western end) of the Arab world. But the region has other ethnic groups besides the Arabs. The largest of these groups is the Berbers, who live mainly in Algeria and Morocco. Most Berbers speak both Berber and Arabic, and almost all are Muslim.

Many Berbers live in cities, while others live in small villages in rugged mountain areas. They make their living by herding and farming. The Tuareg (TWAH reg) are a group of Berbers who live in the Sahara, the enormous desert that stretches across the southern part of North Africa. The Tuareg herd camels, goats, and other livestock and also engage in long-distance trade.

Traditional and Modern Lifestyles In parts of rural North Africa, some people live traditionally, or in ways similar to those of their parents and grandparents. But traditional and modern ways of life mix in towns and large cities such as Cairo (KY roh), in Egypt, and Tunis (TOO nis), in Tunisia.

Some city people work at traditional crafts such as carpet weaving. Others work as architects, scientists, bus drivers, or bankers. Some sell baskets in outdoor markets. Others sell television sets, books, and other items in modern stores. The peoples of North Africa may live vastly different lives, yet Islam helps form a common bond of culture among them.

✓ **Reading Check** What are the two largest ethnic groups of North Africa?

Mixing Old and New
As is traditional for Muslim women, these Moroccan girls are wearing head scarves. At the same time, one is using a cell phone. **Analyze Images** Do you think these girls would say it is easy or difficult to blend old and new ways?

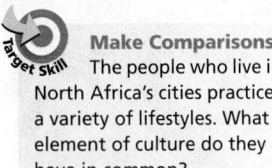
Make Comparisons The people who live in North Africa's cities practice a variety of lifestyles. What element of culture do they have in common?

Chapter 13 Section 1 **429**

Background: Links Across Place

Desert Life Although the Sahara desert in North Africa has one of the harshest climates in the world, people, animals, and plants manage to survive there by adapting to the harsh conditions. For example, some plants are able to store water. Others have roots that can stretch as far as 50 feet underground to find sources of water.

Like plants, animal species here have also adapted to the harsh environment. The camel, for instance, can extract several days' worth of water from the fat stored in its hump. Other animals, like the desert snail, can survive in dormancy for several years before being revived by rainfall.

Cultural Change in North Africa

L2

Guided Instruction

- **Vocabulary Builder** Clarify the high-use word **conquest** before reading.

- Read Cultural Change in North Africa with students. Have students study the map on p. 430.

- Ask **What is cultural diffusion?** *(the movement of customs and ideas from one place to another)* **How does it occur?** *(When people travel, they pick up new ideas and customs and bring them with them.)*

- Ask students **How has North Africa's location affected its cultures?** *(Because of North Africa's location near Europe and Asia, it has been a center of trade and has been influenced by cultures of Europe, Asia, and other parts of Africa.)*

- Have students discuss why some Muslims are concerned about the influence of Western culture on North Africa. *(They are concerned that their countries are becoming too Westernized and fear that this will lead to the loss of Muslim values and traditions.)*

Independent Practice

Have students complete their graphic organizers.

Monitor Progress

- Show *Section Reading Support Transparency AF 41* and ask students to check their graphic organizers individually.

  📖 **Africa Transparencies,** *Section Reading Support Transparency AF 41*

- Tell students to fill in the last column of their *Reading Readiness Guides.*

  All in One **Africa Teaching Resources,** *Reading Readiness Guide,* p. 206

Answer

MAP MASTER Skills Activity **Identify** Spain, France, Italy, and Greece **Analyze Information** Trade goods are probably transported by ship to Europe and Asia and over land routes to other countries in Africa.

Go Online PHSchool.com Students may practice their map skills using the interactive online version of this map.

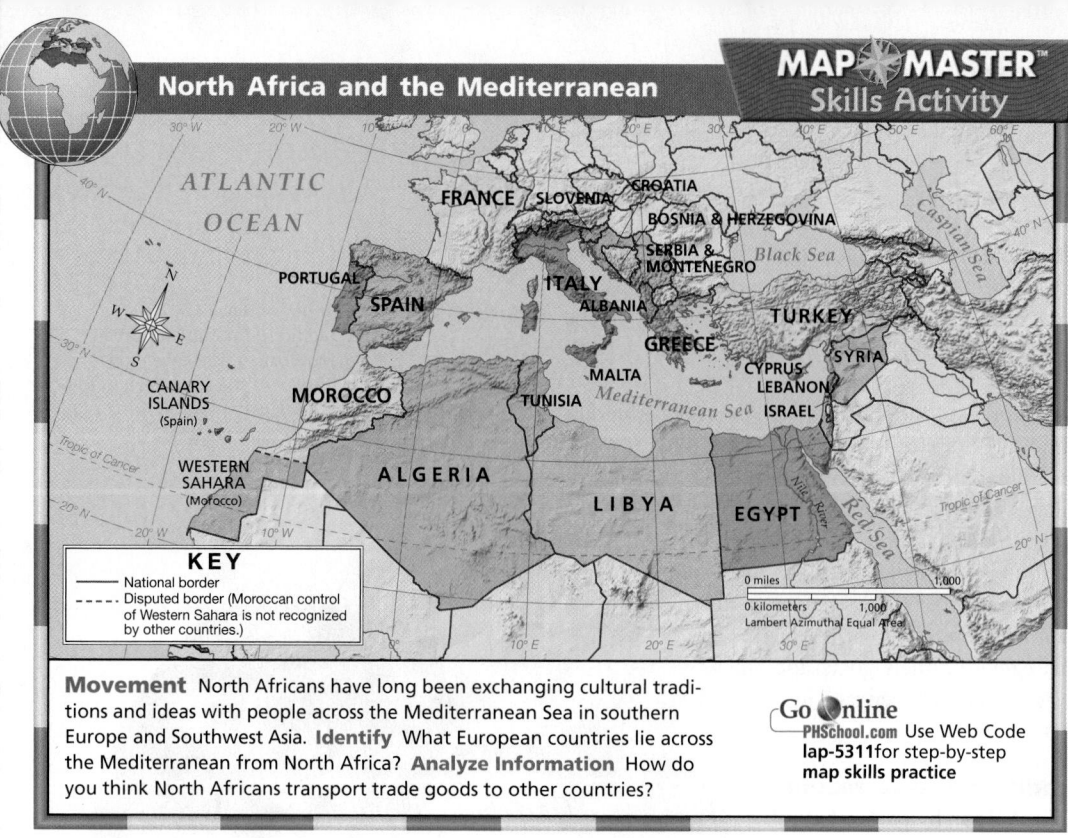

MAP MASTER Skills Activity

North Africa and the Mediterranean

KEY

— National border
- - - Disputed border (Moroccan control of Western Sahara is not recognized by other countries.)

0 miles 1,000
0 kilometers 1,000
Lambert Azimuthal Equal Area

Movement North Africans have long been exchanging cultural traditions and ideas with people across the Mediterranean Sea in southern Europe and Southwest Asia. **Identify** What European countries lie across the Mediterranean from North Africa? **Analyze Information** How do you think North Africans transport trade goods to other countries?

Go Online PHSchool.com Use Web Code lap-5311 for step-by-step map skills practice

Cultural Change in North Africa

North Africa's mix of traditional and modern ways of life shows that culture does not stay the same forever. It changes all the time. Cultural changes often occur when people move from one place to another. As they travel, people share their customs and ideas with others. They also learn about new ideas and customs. The result is **cultural diffusion,** or the spread of customs and ideas to new places. *Diffusion* means "spreading out."

A Hub of Trade Study the map above. An important factor in the diffusion of culture in North Africa is location. Because of its location, North Africa has been a hub, or center, of trade for people from Europe, Asia, North Africa, and other parts of Africa. Thus, the peoples of these regions have come into contact with one another's cultures. Many customs and ideas have spread into and out of North Africa.

Tunisian pottery

430 *Africa*

Background: Links Across Time

Carthage North Africa's cultural interaction with its neighbors has a long history. The city of Carthage, located on the Mediterranean coast in what is now Tunisia, was founded by the ancient Phoenicians in the 800s B.C. The Phoenicians were skilled sailors and made Carthage into a major trading center. They built sturdy ships to bring people and goods from around the Mediterranean in and out of the city. The Phoenicians also manufactured a unique purple dye called Tyrian purple made from the murex, a type of snail. Because it was so expensive, the dye became a signal of rank and prestige.

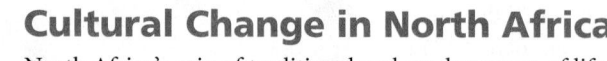

Conquering Empires The mixing of cultures in North Africa did not occur only through trade. It also occurred through conquest. North Africa was home to the ancient Egyptians, one of the world's oldest civilizations. Once the ancient Egyptians had developed trade links with ancient civilizations in both Europe and Southwest Asia, these civilizations competed with one another for power. The ancient Egyptians both conquered and were conquered by other empires. Through these conquests, more cultural diffusion occurred.

Western and Muslim Cultures One of the more recent influences on North Africa is Western culture, meaning the cultures of Europe and North America. Some Muslims are concerned that their countries are becoming too Westernized. More people are wearing Western clothes, buying Western products, seeing films produced by the West, and adopting Western ideas. Some Muslims fear that these influences will lead to the loss of Muslim values and traditions. They want to preserve their way of life. All over Africa, people face the challenge of how to preserve the traditions they value as their countries change.

In Algeria, women in traditional Muslim clothes walk alongside women and men in Western dress.

✓ Reading Check **With what regions have North Africans traditionally traded?**

Section 1 Assessment

Key Terms
Review the key terms at the beginning of this section. Use each term in a sentence that explains its meaning.

Target Reading Skill
Other than religion, what is an element of culture that most North Africans have in common?

Comprehension and Critical Thinking
1. (a) **Name** What are some elements of culture?

(b) **Draw Conclusions** How do you think cultural beliefs shape the way people behave?
2. (a) **Recall** What are the beliefs of the followers of Islam?
(b) **Analyze Information** How has Islam influenced the cultures of North Africa?
3. (a) **Locate** Describe North Africa's location.
(b) **Cause and Effect** How has North Africa's location contributed to cultural diffusion?
(c) **Analyze Information** Do you think that adding new elements to a culture has to lead to the loss of old ones?

Writing Activity
What is your culture? What traditions in your culture do you think are the most important ones to preserve? Write an essay describing these customs and explaining why you value them.

> **Writing Tip** To help you get started, write a list of traditions and customs you practice throughout the year.

Chapter 13 Section 1 **431**

Section 1 Assessment

Key Terms
Students' sentences should reflect knowledge of each Key Term.

Target Reading Skill
Most North Africans are Arabs.

Comprehension and Critical Thinking
1. (a) food, clothing, homes, jobs, language, world views, beliefs (b) Cultural beliefs may influence the foods people eat, the clothes they wear, where they live, what kind of work they do, the language they speak, and how they view the world.
2. (a) Muslims believe that the Quran is the word of God, revealed to the prophet Muhammad. Islam forbids lying, stealing, murder, gambling, eating pork, and drinking alcohol. (b) Islam provides a guide to living. Islamic law influences work and family life, as well as government.
3. (a) North Africa is on the Mediterranean Sea, not far from Europe and Asia and within reach of other parts of Africa. (b) North Africa is a center of trade and travel due to its location on the Mediterranean Sea. It is exposed to many cultures, and its customs have influenced other cultures. (c) Possible answer: No, it is possible to learn new ideas while still keeping older ones alive.

Assess and Reteach

Assess Progress L2
Have students complete the Section Assessment. Administer the *Section Quiz.*

📚 **Africa Teaching Resources,** *Section Quiz,* p. 208

Reteach L1
If students need more instruction, have them read this section in the Reading and Vocabulary Study Guide.

📖 Chapter 13, Section 1, **Eastern Hemisphere Reading and Vocabulary Study Guide,** pp. 32–34

Extend L3
Show students *Color Transparency AF 30: Southwest Asia and North Africa: Physical-Political.* Remind them of what they learned about the climate, vegetation, and natural resources of Africa in Chapter 11. Also remind them that the geography of a country often strongly influences its culture. Students should conduct research on the way the geography of North Africa influences the culture, then create a poster showing the region with the information they have found.

📚 **Africa Transparencies,** *Color Transparency AF 30: Southwest Asia and North Africa: Physical-Political*

Answer

✓ Reading Check North Africa's traditional trading partners include Europe, Asia, and other parts of Africa.

Writing Activity
Use the *Rubric for Assessing a Writing Assignment* to evaluate students' essays.

📚 **Africa Teaching Resources,** *Rubric for Assessing a Writing Assignment,* p. 237

Section 2
Step-by-Step Instruction

Objectives

Social Studies
1. Learn about West Africa's ethnic diversity.
2. Find out about the importance of family ties in West African culture.
3. Examine the West African tradition of storytelling.

Reading/Language Arts
Identify contrasts between groups or situations to find what is unique about each one.

Prepare to Read

Build Background Knowledge L2
Tell students that in this section they will be learning about the cultures of West Africa. Explain that there are many different languages spoken in West Africa. Ask students to suppose they are publishing a newspaper in an area where not every group speaks the same language. Have them think of ways they would use the newspaper to communicate with all the groups. Provide a few simple examples to get students started (*using a language most people are somewhat familiar with, using visuals*). Use the Give One, Get One participation strategy (TE, p. T37) to generate a list.

Set a Purpose for Reading L2
■ Preview the Objectives.

■ Read each statement in the *Reading Readiness Guide* aloud. Ask students to mark the statements true or false.

■ Have students discuss the statements in pairs or groups of four, then mark their worksheets again. Use the Numbered Heads participation strategy (TE, p. T36) to call on students to share their group's perspectives.

All in One **Africa Teaching Resources,** *Reading Readiness Guide,* p. 210

Vocabulary Builder
Preview Key Terms L2
Pronounce each Key Term, then ask students to say the word with you. Provide a simple explanation such as, "When many different ethnic groups live in the same area, it is culturally diverse."

Section 2
The Cultures of West Africa

Prepare to Read

Objectives
In this section you will
1. Learn about West Africa's ethnic diversity.
2. Find out about the importance of family ties in West African culture.
3. Examine the West African tradition of storytelling.

Taking Notes
As you read, look for details about the cultures of West Africa. Copy the flowchart below, and use it to record your findings.

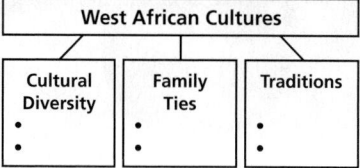

Target Reading Skill

Identify Contrasts Identifying contrasts between two groups or situations can help you see what is unique about each one. As you read this section, contrast the cultures in West Africa with the cultures in the United States. List the differences that relate to language and to family life.

Key Terms
- **cultural diversity** (KUL chur ul duh VUR suh tee) *n.* a wide variety of cultures
- **kinship** (KIN ship) *n.* a family relationship
- **nuclear family** (NOO klee ur FAM uh lee) *n.* the part of a family that includes parents and children
- **extended family** (ek STEN did FAM uh lee) *n.* the part of a family that includes parents, children, and other relatives
- **lineage** (LIN ee ij) *n.* a group of families descended from a common ancestor
- **clan** (klan) *n.* a group of lineages

Mauritanian students in school

432 Africa

In Mauritania (mawr uh TAY nee uh), North Africa meets West Africa. There, the Sahara merges into the tree-dotted grasslands of the savanna. But geography is not the only part of Mauritanian life that reveals major contrasts. Culture does, too. If you were to attend school in one of the small villages in southern Mauritania, you could see this firsthand. You would hear teachers speaking in French, even though they probably also know the country's official language, Arabic. Outside the classroom, students would speak the local language of their ethnic group, which might differ from town to town.

Cultural Diversity of West Africa

Being able to speak more than one language is useful in West Africa, which is home to hundreds of ethnic groups. The region is famous for its **cultural diversity,** or wide variety of cultures. Unlike the ethnic groups of North Africa, those of West Africa are not united by a single religion or a common language.

Target Reading Skill L2

Identify Contrasts Point out the Target Reading Skill. Tell students that identifying contrasts between groups and situations will help them to see what is unique about each one.

Model identifying contrasts using the last paragraph on p. 433 under the heading Rural and Urban Workers. Have students identify contrasts between the lives of West Africans in villages and those living in cities. (*West Africans in villages usually make their living farming, herding animals, or fishing; West Africans in cities often work in hospitals, hotels, or office buildings.*)

Give students *Identify Contrasts.* Have them complete the activity in groups.

All in One **Africa Teaching Resources,** *Identify Contrasts,* p. 222

A Region of Many Languages Think about your community. Imagine that the people who live nearby speak a different language. How could you communicate with them? Suppose you want to shop in a store, eat in a restaurant, or attend a sports event taking place in the next town. It might seem like visiting another country.

This situation is exactly what many West Africans experience. The hundreds of ethnic groups in West Africa speak different languages. Sometimes groups in neighboring villages speak different languages. In order to communicate, most West Africans speak more than one language. Some speak four or five languages. This practice helps unify countries with many ethnic groups. People use these various languages when they travel or conduct business. They often use French, English, Portuguese, or a local language called Hausa to communicate among various ethnic groups.

Rural and Urban Workers The ethnic groups in West Africa differ in more than just the languages they speak. Like North Africans, West Africans make a living in various ways. Many West Africans live in rural areas. A typical village consists of a group of homes surrounded by farmland. The villagers grow food for themselves as well as cash crops to sell. In the Sahara and the dry Sahel just south of it, many people herd cattle, goats, sheep, or camels. Along the coast, most West Africans make a living by fishing. Some West Africans live in large cities where they may work in hospitals, hotels, or office buildings.

✓ **Reading Check** How does cultural diversity affect the people of West Africa?

Many Languages in One Place
If you were shopping at this market in West Africa, you might hear a number of languages being spoken. **Draw Conclusions** *How do you think people communicate in situations like this?*

Vocabulary Builder

Use the information below to teach students this section's high-use words.

High-Use Word	Definition and Sample Sentence
unify, p. 433	*v.* to become one The two small countries **unified** to form one nation.
cash crop, p. 433	*n.* crop grown to be sold rather than consumed on the farm The farm's most profitable **cash crop** is cotton.
value, p. 436	*n.* an admirable principle or quality, something desirable Honesty is an important **value** in life.

Target Reading Skill L2

Identify Contrasts As a follow up, have students perform the Target Reading Skill task on this page of the Student Edition. *(An extended family includes relatives other than parents and their children, such as grandparents and cousins.)*

West African Families L2

Guided Instruction

- As students read the explanation of kinship in West African Families, circulate and make sure that individuals can answer the Reading Check question.

- Ask students to explain the difference between a nuclear family and an extended family. *(nuclear family: parents and children; extended family: parents, children, and other relatives such as grandparents)*

- Ask students **How do extended families work together in West African villages?** *(Neighbors and extended family work together to care for the elderly, the sick, and the children of a village; they also make decisions together.)*

Identify Contrasts A nuclear family and an extended family are similar. Contrast them to understand the important differences between them.

West African Family Ties
Members of an extended family in Nigeria gather in front of their home (bottom). A woman in Ivory Coast cares for her granddaughter (below). **Identify Effects** *What effects do you think the strong kinship ties of West Africa have on communities?*

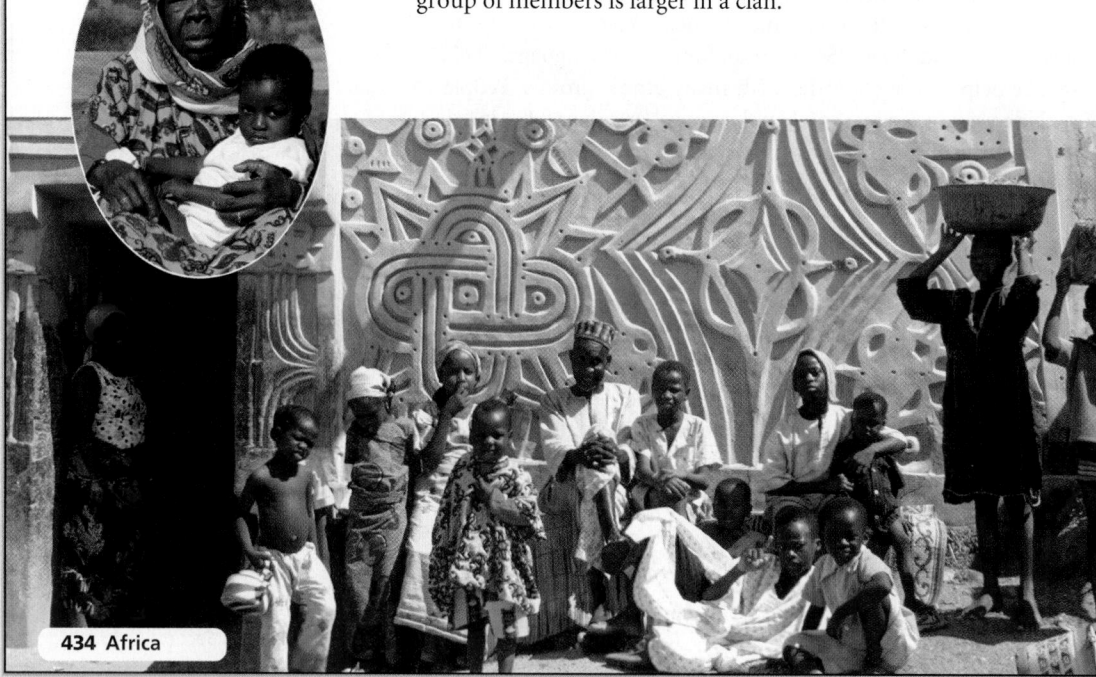

434 Africa

West African Families

Like North Africans, West Africans see themselves as members of a number of groups. Just as you belong to a family, one or more ethnic groups, and a country, so do West Africans.

Kinship and Customs One of the strongest bonds that West Africans have is the bond of **kinship**, or family relationship. The first level of kinship is the **nuclear family**, which consists of parents and their children. The next level is the **extended family**, a group consisting of the nuclear family plus other relatives. It may include grandparents, aunts, uncles, and cousins. Often, members of a West African extended family all live together. They also work together and make decisions together. Family members care for the elderly, the sick, and the less well-off. They also watch over the children of other families in the village and willingly help neighbors.

Larger Kinship Groups In many rural areas, kinship reaches beyond extended families to larger groups. One such group is a **lineage**, or a group of families that can trace their descent back to a common ancestor. Some people also recognize larger kinship groups called clans. A **clan** is a group of lineages. As with a lineage, the people in a clan can all trace their roots back to a common ancestor. Members of a clan may be more distantly related to one another than members of a lineage because the group of members is larger in a clan.

Background: Links Across Place

African Languages There are currently between 800 and 1,000 languages spoken in Africa. Though they have been grouped into four language families, or groups of languages with common origins, there are few shared features among them. However, many African languages are tonal, meaning that they use the voice pitch to show meaning. Some languages of southwestern Africa use unique consonants called "clicks" that can be found nowhere else in the world.

African languages have contributed to other languages around the world. The English words *yam*, *banana*, and *chimpanzee* are all of African origin.

Answer

Identify Effects Possible answers: Strong kinship ties probably make people feel like they are part of a larger group; the ties may help create strong communities.

Kinship

■ Diagram Skills

The diagram shows the extended family of the married couple at the center. The husband's lineage is in purple, and the wife's is in orange. In a matrilineal society, this family would trace descent through the women who are outlined in red. **Identify** How many nuclear families exist in the extended lineage? **Synthesize** What is the relationship of the woman at the top of the purple lineage to the three siblings at the bottom of it?

Tracing Lineage Different traditions govern the ways West African groups trace their ancestry. Some groups are matrilineal (mat ruh LIN ee ul), meaning that they trace their descent through female ancestors. In matrilineal societies, a person's father is not considered part of the person's lineage. Within the lineage, children consider their mother's brother their closest adult male relative. Their father is a member of another lineage. Most groups, however, are patrilineal (pat ruh LIN ee ul)—they trace their descent through the male side of the family.

Changes in Family Life Although traditional family ties are still strong in West Africa, family life is changing. More and more people are moving from rural villages to urban areas. This trend, known as urbanization, is occurring not only in Africa but throughout the world.

Many young men are looking for work to support themselves and their families. They travel long distances to West Africa's cities to find jobs. The women often stay in the rural homes. They raise the children and farm the land. The men come home from time to time to visit their families and to share what they have earned.

Families live close together in West African villages such as this one in Mali.

✓ **Reading Check** What responsibilities do extended family members have toward one another?

Differentiated Instruction

For English Language Learners L1
In pairs, have students read and discuss each paragraph of a section or chapter using the Paragraph Shrinking strategy (TE, p. T34). Students can use their abbreviated paragraphs as an outline to study from later.

For Less Proficient Readers L1
Have students read the section in the Reading and Vocabulary Study Guide. This version provides basic-level instruction in an interactive format with questions and write-on lines.

📖 Chapter 13, Section 2, **Eastern Hemisphere Reading and Vocabulary Study Guide**, pp. 151–153

Guided Instruction (continued)

■ Ask students to describe matrilineal society. *(A matrilineal society traces its descent through female ancestors. A person's father is not considered part of the person's lineage. Children consider their mother's brother to be their closest male relative, so their father is a member of another lineage.)*

■ Ask students **How is family life in West Africa changing?** *(More people are moving from rural villages to cities.)*

■ Ask students **How do you think urbanization will affect the traditions of West Africa?** *(It may offer West Africans new economic opportunities; it may mean that older traditions and ways of doing things will be lost.)*

Independent Practice
Have students add to the graphic organizer by filling in the details under Family Ties.

Monitor Progress
As students continue to fill in the graphic organizer, circulate to make sure individuals are choosing the correct details about family ties.

Answer
Diagram Skills Identify four **Synthesize** grandmother

✓ **Reading Check** Extended family members work together to protect one anothers' children, care for sick or older relatives, and make decisions.

Keeping Traditions Alive

L2

Guided Instruction

- **Vocabulary Builder** Clarify the high-use word **value** before reading.

- Read Keeping Traditions Alive to learn more about how traditions are passed down in West African countries.

- Ask students **How does storytelling preserve West African history, values, and traditions?** *(Griots tell traditional stories and histories that teach cultural values.)*

- Ask students **What other ways can a culture preserve and pass on its values and traditions?** *(Possible answers: through books, museums, education, art, and religion)*

- Discuss with students the influence West African culture has on other cultures. *(West African ideas, stories, dances, music, and customs have spread around the world and influenced other cultures, especially American culture.)*

Independent Practice

Have students complete the graphic organizer by adding details about traditions.

Monitor Progress

- Show *Section Reading Support Transparency AF 42* and ask students to check their graphic organizers individually.

    📖 **Africa Transparencies,** *Section Reading Support Transparency AF 42*

- Tell students to fill in the last column of the *Reading Readiness Guide.*

    All in One **Africa Teaching Resources,** *Reading Readiness Guide,* p. 210

 Show students *African Culture: Textiles and Weaving.* Ask **What is a *haik*?** *(a long, loose garment popular in North Africa)*

Answer

Synthesize Oral storytelling passes traditions, history, and cultural values to the young.

Master of Storytelling
Boys from an Ivory Coast village listen intently as a griot tells them a legend about their ethnic group's history. **Synthesize** *How does oral storytelling help preserve a culture's history?*

Learn about the importance of woven cloth in Africa.

436 Africa

Keeping Traditions Alive

Cultural changes, such as urbanization, affect different families in different ways. As they adapt to these changes, most West Africans try to maintain strong family ties. They pass their history, values, and traditions on to the young.

Storytelling Traditions One important way in which West African traditions are being preserved is through the art of vivid and exciting storytelling. Traditional West African stories are spoken aloud rather than written down. A storyteller called a griot (GREE oh) passes a group's oral traditions on from one generation to another.

Stories of tricksters, animal fables, proverbs, riddles, and songs are all part of West Africa's oral tradition. The details in the stories tell about the histories of ethnic groups and kinships. At the same time, they teach children cultural values. An African proverb reflects the value that West Africans place on handing down traditions from generation to generation: "The young can't teach traditions to the old."

Differentiated Instruction

For Gifted and Talented
L3

Have students complete the *Small Group Activity: Telling a Traditional African Story.* Students can present their traditional African stories to the class, and then discuss them using the suggested questions.

All in One **Africa Teaching Resources,** *Small Group Activity: Telling a Traditional African Story,* pp. 227–230

African musicians perform around the world, from Massachusetts (left) to Ivory Coast (right).

Cultural Influence The traditions of West Africa have greatly influenced other cultures, especially American culture. Many of the enslaved Africans who were brought to the United States came from West Africa. They brought with them the only things they could: their ideas, stories, dances, music, and customs. The trickster tales of Br'er Rabbit, as well as blues and jazz music, have their roots in West Africa.

Today, West African culture—its stories, music, dances, art, cooking, and clothing—is popular in many countries outside of Africa. Griot guitarists and other musicians from West Africa have international followings. In recent years, four Africans have won the Nobel Prize for literature. One of them is West African—the Nigerian writer Wole Soyinka (WOH lay shaw YING kuh).

✓ **Reading Check** What does a griot do?

✦ Section 2 Assessment

Key Terms
Review the key terms at the beginning of this section. Use each term in a sentence that explains its meaning.

➲ Target Reading Skill
Identify one contrast between the way West Africans use language and the way Americans do.

Comprehension and Critical Thinking
1. (a) Recall In what ways is West Africa culturally diverse?

(b) Identify Effects How does cultural diversity create communication challenges for West Africans?

2. (a) Describe What kinds of kinship ties are found in West African societies?

(b) Draw Conclusions How do you think living together with members of one's extended family helps build a sense of community?

3. (a) Explain What purpose does storytelling serve in West African culture?

(b) Analyze What is the meaning of the proverb "The young can't teach traditions to the old"?

Writing Activity
Suppose you live with your extended family in a small village in West Africa. Make a list of the advantages and disadvantages of your way of life. Indicate which are most important to you.

Go Online
PHSchool.com
For: An activity on the cultures of West Africa
Visit: PHSchool.com
Web Code: lad-5302

Chapter 13 Section 2 **437**

Chapter 13 Section 2 **437**

Objective

Learn how to compare and contrast information.

Prepare to Read

Build Background Knowledge `L2`

Ask students to read the paragraphs on the top of p. 438. Have students suppose they are shopping for CDs and have found two that they would like to buy, but have only enough money for one. Then ask how comparing and contrasting the two CDs might help them to make a decision.

Instruct

Comparing and Contrasting `L2`

Guided Instruction

- Read the steps to comparing and contrasting as a class and write them on the board.

- Practice the skill by following the steps on p. 439 as a class. Model each step in the activity by comparing and contrasting the two photographs to determine their similarities and differences. Decide on three categories for comparing and contrasting the photographs. *(animals, plants, land)* Create a chart on the board showing the categories, with space to fill in their similarities and differences. Call on students to identify comparisons and contrasts within the categories and fill them in the chart. *(Possible comparisons/contrasts: Animals— Both photos show wild animals; both show an adult with its young. Plants—The Tanzania photo shows small plants and shrubs; the Kenya photo shows grassland and trees. Land—Forest is depicted in the scene of Tanzania; land in the Kenya scene is more open and includes a lake or pond.)* Make a conclusion about the photographs. *(The photographs are mostly similar because they show an adult animal with its young in a natural setting. A third photograph that would fit the pattern might include an adult tiger and its cub in a grassy plain.)*

Comparing and Contrasting

Nathan and Antonio went to the mall to buy CDs. When Antonio saw the CD Nathan had chosen, he commented, "I like that CD. But I think the band's new CD is better. They use more drums on the new CD."

Nathan argued. "I disagree. I like the way the band sounded on the old CD. They had two singers, and the two voices together sounded better than this one singer's voice alone." The girl working at the register smiled. She couldn't hear any differences in the CDs. She thought they were both great.

When you look for differences between two or more items, you *contrast* them. To *compare*, you do one of two things: you look for similarities between two or more items, or you look for similarities *and* differences between two or more items. If you are asked to compare, ask if you should find similarities only, or similarities and differences.

Learn the Skill

Follow these steps to learn how to compare and contrast.

1 **Identify a topic and purpose.** What do you want to compare or contrast, and why? Some purposes for comparing and contrasting are to make a choice, to understand a topic, or to discover patterns.

2 **Select some categories for comparison and contrast.** For example, if you wanted to choose between two bikes, your categories might be color, cost, and types of tires.

3 **Make notes—or a chart—about the categories you are comparing or contrasting.** Some categories call for a yes or no answer. Other categories, such as color or cost, require that you note specific details.

4 **Notice the similarities and differences.** Are the details the same or different for each item?

5 **Draw conclusions.** Write a few sentences explaining whether the items are more similar or more different.

Independent Practice

Assign *Skills for Life* and have students complete it individually.

All in One **Africa Teaching Resources,** *Skills for Life,* p. 226

Monitor Progress

As students are completing *Skills for Life,* circulate to make sure individuals are applying the skill steps effectively. Provide assistance as needed.

Practice the Skill

Use the steps below, plus your own knowledge, to compare and contrast the two scenes from Africa that are shown in the photographs on this page. Use what you find to determine a pattern in the photographs.

1 What is your topic? What is the purpose?

2 Study the photographs. Then write down at least three categories for comparison and contrast.

3 For each category, take notes on what the photographs show.

4 Now study your notes to see what is similar and what is different about the two photographs.

5 Write a conclusion that explains whether the scenes in the photographs are mostly similar or mostly different. Include a description of one pattern you see in the photographs. Can you describe a third photograph that would fit the pattern?

Chimpanzees in Tanzania

Giraffes in Kenya

Apply the Skill

Reread Sections 1 and 2 of this chapter. Use the steps you learned in this skill to compare and contrast the cultures of North Africa and West Africa.

 **Section 3** **The Cultures of East Africa**

Objectives

Social Studies

1. Find out how geography has affected the development of East African cultures.
2. Learn how and why ideas about land ownership are changing in East Africa.

Reading/Language Arts

Use signal words to identify comparisons and contrasts in a text.

Prepare to Read

Build Background Knowledge [L2]

Tell students that in this section they will learn about the culture of East Africa. Explain to students that before Europeans took control of much of Africa, people did not individually own, buy, and sell land. Ask students to list different kinds of ownership *(homeowners, landowners, national parks)*. Model the thought process by asking them who owns the following: the building they are in, a national park, a neighborhood park, their homes. Then ask who can use these places, using the Think-Write-Pair-Share strategy (TE, p. T36) to elicit responses.

Set a Purpose for Reading [L2]

■ Preview the Objectives.

■ Form students into pairs or groups of four.

■ Distribute the *Reading Readiness Guide*. Ask students to fill in the first two columns of the chart. Use the Numbered Heads participation strategy (TE, p. T36) to call on students to share one piece of information they already know and one piece of information they want to know.

All in One **Africa Teaching Resources,** *Reading Readiness Guide,* p. 214

Vocabulary Builder
Preview Key Terms [L2]

Pronounce each Key Term, then ask students to say the word with you. Provide a simple explanation such as, "Learning about the heritage of different peoples is an important part of social studies."

Prepare to Read

Objectives

In this section you will
1. Find out how geography has affected the development of East African cultures.
2. Learn how and why ideas about land ownership are changing in East Africa.

Taking Notes

As you read, find details about the cultures of East Africa. Copy the concept web below, and use it to record your findings.

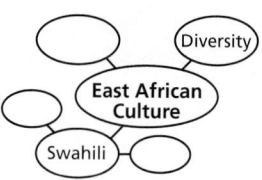

⊙ Target Reading Skill

Use Signal Words
Signal words point out relationships among ideas or events. Certain words or phrases, such as *like* and *as with*, can signal a comparison or a contrast. As you read this section, notice the comparisons between East Africa and other parts of Africa.

Key Terms

• **Swahili** (swah HEE lee) *n.* an ethnic group in East Africa that resulted from the mixing of African and Arab ways more than 1,000 years ago; also a language
• **heritage** (HEHR uh tij) *n.* the values, traditions, and customs handed down from one's ancestors

A woman in Lamu gets her hand decorated with henna.

440 Africa

I n the neighborhood square, old friends often sit together playing dominoes. A man on a donkey may wander past amidst the occasional roar of motorcycles. Down the street, there is a store that sells spices next to a shop that offers fax services and Internet connections. Nearby, behind shuttered windows that filter the hot sun, women take turns making intricate designs on one another's hands using a natural dye called henna. In former East African city-states such as Lamu (LAH moo), in Kenya, and Zanzibar (ZAN zuh bahr), in Tanzania, such traditional and modern ways are interwoven.

Geography and Cultural Diversity

Like West Africa, East Africa is a region of great cultural diversity. In some parts of the region, such as Lamu and Zanzibar, the diversity reveals itself in the contrast between old and new ways. In other parts, it is reflected in the diversity of languages spoken or religions practiced.

⊙ Target Reading Skill [L2]

Use Signal Words Point out the Target Reading Skill. Tell students that identifying signal words can help them to recognize comparisons or contrasts in a text.

Model using signal words using the text on p. 442. Have students skim the page looking for signal words and use them to identify comparisons and contrasts in the text. *(The phrase "As is true of…" at the beginning of the* *second paragraph signals a comparison between East and West Africa. The phrase "As with…" at the beginning of the third paragraph signals a comparison between language and religious beliefs.)*

Give students *Compare and Contrast*. Have them complete the activity in groups.

All in One **Africa Teaching Resources,** *Compare and Contrast,* p. 223

Indian Ocean Connections Much of the cultural diversity of East Africa comes from contact among people from many cultures. Like other Africans, the people of East Africa have often been exposed to other cultures through trade. Turn to the political map of Africa on page 351 of the Regional Overview. Notice how much of East Africa's long coast-line borders the Indian Ocean. This ocean provides a trade and travel route for East Africans as well as for the people living across the ocean to the east. These people include Arabs, Indians, and other Asians, even those from countries as far away from Africa as China and Malaysia.

Swahili Culture The connection across the Indian Ocean dates back to early times. Nearly 2,000 years ago, Arab traders began to settle in the coastal villages of East Africa. Members of various African cultures took on elements of Arab culture from the newcomers. The Arabs took on elements of African culture as well. The **Swahili** are an ethnic group that resulted from this mixing of African and Arab ways.

Most people who live in Lamu or Zanzibar are Swahili. A professor in Zanzibar described the history of the Swahili to a reporter in this way:

> **❝**We have always been middlemen—between the land and the sea, the producers and the buyers, the African and the Arabian. That is not a concern; it is our strength. We will survive. Swahili culture may not be quite the same tomorrow as today, but then nothing living is.**❞**
>
> —Professor Abdul Sheriff

One important strength of the Swahili people is their ability to adapt to other cultures. To adapt is to adjust to new things or circumstances. At the same time, the Swahilis try to preserve their **heritage,** or the values, traditions, and customs handed down from their ancestors.

Swahili Arts and Crafts
Swahili craftsmen are known for carving front doors with detailed decoration on their frames. This one is in Zanzibar, Tanzania. **Analyze Images** *Why do you think people would choose a front door as a place to show their craft?*

Geography and Cultural Diversity ▫L2

Guided Instruction

- **Vocabulary Builder** Clarify the high-use word **promote** before reading.

- Have students read Geography and Cultural Diversity, using the Oral Cloze strategy (TE, p. T33).

- Ask students **How has the location of East Africa affected its cultures?** *(It borders the Indian Ocean and connects East Africans to people in Asia.)*

- Ask students to discuss the factors that produced Swahili culture. *(Arab traders settled in East Africa, and their culture mixed with various East African cultures, resulting in Swahili culture.)*

- Ask students **What is one strength of the Swahili culture?** *(its ability to adapt to new things or circumstances)*

Vocabulary Builder

Use the information below to teach students this section's high-use words.

High-Use Word	Definition and Sample Sentence
promote, p. 442	*v.* to encourage Watering plants will **promote** their growth.
fertile, p. 443	*adj.* good for farming The land is very **fertile,** so the farm produces a lot of crops.
dense, p. 443	*adj.* crowded closely together The house is surrounded by a **dense** group of trees.

Answer

Analyze Images possible answer: probably because it will be seen by many people as they pass by or enter the building

Guided Instruction (continued)

- Ask students what the language map on p. 425 tells them about the cultural diversity of East Africa. *(There are many languages spoken because there are many ethnic groups.)*

- Discuss with students how Islam and Christianity were introduced to East Africa. *(Arab traders introduced Islam; Christianity was introduced to North Africa when it was part of the Roman Empire.)*

Independent Practice

Have students continue filling in the graphic organizer by adding details relating to the cultural diversity of East Africa.

Monitor Progress

As students fill in the graphic organizer, circulate to make sure individuals are choosing the correct details.

Target Reading Skill   L2

Signal Words As a follow up, have students answer the Target Reading Skill question on this page of the Student Edition. *("As is true of")*

Signal Words
What signal words are used to compare the number of languages spoken in East Africa and West Africa?

Widespread Swahili Language Swahilis live along East Africa's coast from Somalia to Tanzania. Recall from Chapter 12 that the Swahili language is a Bantu language that contains many Arabic words. Although the Swahili are just one of hundreds of ethnic groups in East Africa, their language is used among ethnic groups throughout the region for business and communication. In Tanzania, children are educated in Swahili through the primary grades. Later, they learn English as well. By promoting the use of Swahili, East African nations are helping to preserve their African heritage and to establish unity among different peoples.

Other Languages As is true of West Africa, East Africa is home to many ethnic groups who speak different languages. It is not unusual for people in the region to know three languages or more. For example, in Ethiopia more than 80 languages are spoken, and in Kenya about 40 are spoken. About 1,000 languages can be heard in Sudan alone. The variety of languages spoken in the region is largely due to the long history of migrations of ethnic groups from other parts of the continent. For example, the Bantu migration that you read about earlier brought many Bantu-speaking peoples from West Africa to East Africa.

Religion As with languages, religious beliefs in East Africa reflect the cultural diversity of the region. Both Islam and Christianity have large followings there. Islam was introduced to East Africa by Arab traders. Christianity spread into Ethiopia in the A.D. 300s after being introduced to North Africa when the area was a part of the Roman Empire. During the 1800s, Europeans pushed into Africa and spread Christianity even farther. In addition, traditional religions are still practiced in East Africa.

√ **Reading Check** **What religions are practiced by East Africans?**

442 Africa

Differentiated Instruction

For English Language Learners   L2
Students may have difficulty understanding some of the verbs in this section. Read the sentences that contain the words below, then have students paraphrase the sentences in order to determine the meaning of the words. If they have difficulty at first, partner them with a more proficient reader to help them.

extends	*contains*	*change*
produced	*preserve*	*adapt*

Answer

√ **Reading Check** Islam, Christianity, traditional religions

Changing Ideas About Land

In East Africa, as in the rest of Africa, most people live in rural areas, where they farm and tend livestock. The ways in which they work the land and view land ownership are part of the culture of East Africans.

Before Land Was Owned Before Europeans took over parts of Africa in the 1800s, individual Africans did not buy or sell land. The very idea of owning land did not exist. Families had the right to farm plots of land, but the size and location of the plots might change over time.

Traditionally in Africa, extended families farmed the land to produce food for the whole group. Men cleared the land and broke up the soil. Women then planted the seeds, tended the fields, and harvested the crops. Meanwhile, the men herded livestock or traded goods.

The Rise and Fall of Plantations The practice of owning land privately was introduced into much of Africa by European settlers. In parts of East Africa, the British set up plantations. When many African countries became independent, their governments broke up the colonial plantations and sold the land to individual Africans.

Some land in East Africa is still available to buy. But much of it is poor farmland in areas where few people live. In fertile areas such as the Ethiopian Highlands and the Great Rift Valley, most of the land good for farming is already taken. Many people live in these fertile areas. In densely populated countries such as Rwanda (roo AHN duh) and Burundi (boo ROON dee), conflicts have developed over land.

The Legacy of Land
Agriculture is part of life all over East Africa. Farmers work fields of a large plantation (bottom). An Ethiopian farmer tends his fields (inset).
Synthesize Information *Why has farmland caused conflicts in some East African countries?*

Skills Mini Lesson

Identifying Frame of Reference and Point of View

1. Teach the skill by explaining that an opinion or perspective on an issue depends on a person's background, age, and experience, as well as the historical era.

2. Help students practice the skill by reading Julius Nyerere's statement on page 444.

Ask what Nyerere revealed about his background when he expressed how he felt returning to his home village.

3. Have students apply the skill by asking what the quotation from Professor Abdul Sheriff on p. 441 reveals about his frame of reference and point of view on Swahili culture and history.

Changing Ideas About Land

Guided Instruction

- **Vocabulary Builder** Clarify the high-use words **fertile** and **dense** before reading.

- Read about land ownership and farming in East Africa in Changing Ideas About Land. As students read, circulate to make sure individuals can answer the Reading Check question.

- Discuss with students how land was traditionally farmed before Europeans took over parts of Africa in the 1800s. (*Extended families produced food for the whole group. Men cleared land and broke up the soil; women planted seeds, tended the fields, and harvested crops.*)

- Ask students **How have ideas about land ownership changed in Africa?** (*In the 1800s, Europeans introduced the idea of individual land ownership to Africa.*)

- Ask students **Why might densely populated areas have more conflicts over land than other places?** (*Possible answer: More people sharing less land might cause conflict.*)

Independent Practice

Have students complete the graphic organizer by adding details about farming and land ownership in East Africa.

Monitor Progress

- Show *Section Reading Support Transparency AF 43* and ask students to check their graphic organizers individually. Go over key concepts and clarify key vocabulary as needed.

  Africa Transparencies, *Section Reading Support Transparency AF 43*

- Tell students to fill in the last column of the *Reading Readiness Guide*. Ask them to evaluate if what they learned was what they had expected to learn.

  Africa Teaching Resources, *Reading Readiness Guide,* p. 214

Answer

Synthesize Information Most East Africans farm for a living, and the amount of available farmland is limited.

Assess and Reteach

Assess Progress [L2]

Have students complete the Section Assessment. Administer the *Section Quiz*.

 Africa Teaching Resources, *Section Quiz,* p. 216

Reteach [L1]

If students need more instruction, have them read this section in the Reading and Vocabulary Study Guide.

📖 Chapter 13, Section 3, **Eastern Hemisphere Reading and Vocabulary Study Guide,** pp. 154–156

Extend [L3]

Have students write a story that takes place in East Africa. The plot should reflect Swahili culture, and can include information that they find through library or Internet research. Give students *Writing Stories* to focus their ideas before they begin writing.

 Africa Teaching Resources, *Writing Stories,* p. 235

Answer

✔ Reading Check They used land near the village, farming enough to produce food for an entire extended family.

Section 3 Assessment

Key Terms

Students' sentences should reflect knowledge of each Key Term.

🎯 Target Reading Skill

Signal words and comparisons include: pp. 440, 442—"Like" and "as is true" compare West Africa and East Africa; pp. 441, 443, 444—"Like" and "as in" compare East Africa and the rest of Africa; p. 442—"As with" compares languages and religious beliefs.

Comprehension and Critical Thinking

1. (a) along the coast of East Africa from Somalia to Tanzania **(b)** Ethnic groups from other parts of the continent have brought their languages to East Africa. Islam was introduced by Arab traders, and Christianity spread into Ethiopia in the A.D. 300s from North Africa. **(c)** It is used for business and communication among the many ethnic groups in the region.

Julius Nyerere, Tanzania's first president

Where Is Home? Traditionally, Africans feel a strong bond to the land where they grew up. Like the rest of Africa, East Africa is becoming increasingly urban. Yet even people who spend most of their time in a city often do not call it home. If asked where home is, an East African will usually name the village of his or her family or clan. Most people consider their life in the city temporary. They expect to return to their villages at some point.

Tanzania's former president Julius Nyerere (JOOL yus nyuh REHR uh) is one example. After he stepped down as president in 1985, Nyerere moved back to his home village. Although he was far from Dar es Salaam (DAHR es suh LAHM), one of Tanzania's two capital cities, Nyerere continued to be involved in world affairs. Until his death in 1999, he spent his mornings working in the fields, where he grew corn and millet on his farm.

In an interview in 1996, Nyerere said: "In a sense I am a very rural person. I grew up here, and [working in] Dar es Salaam was a duty. I did my duty and after retiring in 1985, I came back here and said, 'Ah, it's good to be back.' " Many other East Africans feel the same. They do their duty by earning money in the city, but they never forget their rural roots.

✔ Reading Check **How did East Africans farm before Europeans arrived?**

✶ Section 3 Assessment

Key Terms

Review the key terms at the beginning of this section. Use each term in a sentence that explains its meaning.

🎯 Target Reading Skill

Make a list of all the signal words you found as you read this section. Describe the comparison that each signal word indicates.

Comprehension and Critical Thinking

1. (a) Locate Where in East Africa do the Swahilis live?

(b) Summarize How did East Africa become a region with great diversity of language and religion?
(c) Make Inferences What is the importance of the Swahili language in East Africa?
2. (a) Recall When was private land ownership introduced to East Africa?
(b) Summarize How have ideas about land ownership changed over time in East Africa?
(c) Identify Point of View How did traditional East African ideas about land differ from those of Europeans who took over parts of Africa?

Writing Activity

Write a description of the place that you consider home. Tell what home means to you and explain why. How does your meaning of home compare to Julius Nyerere's feelings about his homeland?

> **Writing Tip** Before you begin, think of important details about your home that you can use in your description. Use vivid language to make your description come to life.

---

2. (a) when the British took over parts of Africa in the 1800s **(b)** Before colonialism, individual Africans did not own land. Europeans introduced the idea of privately-owned land to Africans and the British introduced plantations. When African countries gained independence, many of the plantations were broken up and sold to individuals. **(c)** Europeans believed in individual ownership of land, whereas the East Africans believed that everyone owned and benefited from the land.

Writing Activity

Use the *Rubric for Assessing a Writing Assignment* to evaluate students' descriptions.

 Africa Teaching Resources, *Rubric for Assessing a Writing Assignment,* p. 237

Section 4 The Cultures of Southern and Central Africa

Prepare to Read

Objectives

In this section you will
1. Learn about the cultural diversity of Southern Africa.
2. Examine different ways of life in Central Africa and learn about the diverse cultures of the region.

Taking Notes

As you read, look for details about the cultures of Southern and Central Africa. Copy the table below, and use it to record your findings.

Southern Africa	Central Africa
•	•
•	•
•	•

Target Reading Skill

Compare and Contrast
Comparing and contrasting can help you sort out and analyze information. When you compare, you examine the similarities between things. When you contrast, you look at the differences.

As you read this section, compare and contrast the cultures of Southern and Central Africa. Look for similarities and differences in ethnic groups and in economic conditions.

Key Terms

- **migrant worker** (MY grunt WUR kur) *n.* a laborer who travels away from where he or she lives to find work
- **compound** (KAHM pownd) *n.* a fenced-in group of homes

A member of South Africa's national soccer team

Soccer is a popular sport all around the world. It is no surprise, then, that it is a favorite sport of people in the country of South Africa. But the fact that the sport is played there reveals more than just that South Africans love fun and recreation. It is proof of the changing political times in South Africa.

Soccer came to South Africa from Europe. As you will read in Chapter 17, Europeans settled in the region from the mid-1600s through the 1800s. After the country gained independence in 1910, the white minority of the population took charge of the government. As part of their rule, the white population denied other members of society certain basic rights. For example, black South Africans were not allowed to play on many of the nation's sports teams.

In 1994, the South African government was restructured, and equal rights were extended to all. Today, when black and white soccer players run onto the field, all South Africans have reason to cheer.

Chapter 13 Section 4 **445**

Objectives

Social Studies

1. Learn about the cultural diversity of Southern Africa.
2. Examine different ways of life in Central Africa and learn about the diverse cultures of the region.

Reading/Language Arts

Compare and contrast to sort out and analyze information.

Prepare to Read

Build Background Knowledge L2

Tell students that in this section they will be learning about the cultures of Southern and Central Africa. Have students preview the section by looking at the headings and visuals with this question in mind: **What are some aspects of the cultures of Southern and Central Africa?** Use the Think-Write-Pair-Share technique (TE, p. T36) to generate a list of possible answers.

Set a Purpose for Reading L2

- Preview the Objectives.

- Read each statement in the *Reading Readiness Guide* aloud. Ask students to mark the statements true or false.

- Have students discuss the statements in pairs or groups of four, then mark their worksheets again. Use the Numbered Heads participation strategy (TE, p. T36) to call on students to share their group's perspectives.

All in One **Africa Teaching Resources,** *Reading Readiness Guide*, p. 218

Vocabulary Builder
Preview Key Terms L2

Pronounce each Key Term, then ask students to say the word or words with you. Provide a simple explanation such as, "A migrant worker does not have a permanent place of employment."

Target Reading Skill L2

Comparison and Contrast Point out the Target Reading Skill. Tell students that comparing and contrasting will help them analyze information.

Model comparing and contrasting using the paragraph on p. 447 under the heading New Roles for Women. Have students compare and contrast the roles of women and men in Africa and list the differences and similarities. (*Differences—Traditionally,*

women raised children and farmed land, while men cared for animals, dealt with local matters, and headed their households. Similarities—After many men migrated to South Africa for work, women were responsible for many of the same tasks as the men had been before they left.)

Give students *Comparison and Contrast.* Have them complete the activity in groups.

All in One **Africa Teaching Resources** *Comparison and Contrast,* p. 223

Diversity in Southern Africa L2

Guided Instruction

- **Vocabulary Builder** Clarify the high-use words **eventually** and **industrialized** before reading.

- Read Diversity in South Africa, using the Structured Silent Reading strategy (TE, p. T34).

- Discuss European influence in Southern Africa. Ask **What groups of European ancestry settled in Southern Africa and why?** *(Portuguese—transported slaves out of Africa in the 1500s; Dutch—farmed, raised cattle, mined; British—farmed and raised cattle.)*

- Ask **How did demand for labor in South Africa affect the lives of people in nearby countries?** *(Migrant workers came from nearby countries to work jobs in South Africa. The working conditions were poor. Families left behind took on new challenges to survive.)*

Independent Practice

Ask students to create the Taking Notes graphic organizer on a blank piece of paper and record details that they just learned about South Africa.

Monitor Progress

As students fill in the graphic organizer, circulate to make sure individuals are choosing the correct details.

Answer

Infer The presence of large cities in a region leads to the growth of urban lifestyles and affects the kinds of jobs people do and the kinds of houses they live in.

Diversity in Southern Africa

Like the rest of Africa, Southern Africa has a great deal of cultural diversity. Most of the people of Southern Africa are black Africans. They belong to a variety of ethnic groups, many of which speak separate languages. In addition, there are certain ethnic groups that have greater numbers of members in Southern Africa than in other parts of Africa—for example, people of European descent.

European Influence Southern Africa attracted Europeans for a variety of reasons. The Portuguese arrived in Mozambique in the 1500s and soon began transporting slaves out of Africa. In the 1600s, Dutch and British settlers moved to the Cape of Good Hope at the southern tip of Africa. They grew wheat and herded cattle. Many of the Dutch eventually spread to the north to places such as Malawi, where they started up a mining industry and enlisted local people as laborers. The British also moved north, to Zimbabwe and Zambia.

European Ethnic Groups Southern Africa is home to three main groups of people with European ancestry. One group is descended from the British settlers. These Africans speak English. Another group is Afrikaners (af rih KAHN urz), who are descendants of the Dutch settlers. They speak Afrikaans (af rih KAHNZ), a language related to Dutch. The third group, descended from the Portuguese settlers, speaks Portuguese.

Urbanization The cultural diversity of Southern Africa extends beyond ethnic differences. It is also represented by the contrast between rural and urban lifestyles. For hundreds of years, people in the region lived in villages or small cities. European settlers started a process of urbanization in Southern Africa. The region now includes a number of cities inhabited by more than 1 million people. The largest are Cape Town and Johannesburg in South Africa and Maputo in Mozambique.

Effects of Urbanization
Even though it sits nestled between ocean and mountains, Cape Town has grown to be one of South Africa's largest cities. Its population is about 3 million people. **Infer** *How do you think the presence of numerous large cities changes the culture of a region?*

446 Africa

Vocabulary Builder

Use the information below to teach students this section's high-use words.

High-Use Word	Definition and Sample Sentence
eventually, p. 446	*adv.* at some time later; in the end **Eventually** I'd like to travel to Europe and Australia.
industrialized, p. 447	*adj.* having many businesses involved in manufacturing and trade The United States is an **industrialized** nation.
interior, p. 448	*adj.* that part of a country that is away from the coast or border Mia, who lives in the **interior** of the country, has never seen the ocean.

Industry in South Africa South Africa is the richest, most urban, and most industrialized country in Africa. During the 1900s, South African industries created a great demand for labor. Hundreds of thousands of people came from nearby countries in Southern Africa to work on South African mines. They formed a large force of **migrant workers,** or laborers who travel away from where they live to find work. These migrant workers had to live together in **compounds,** or fenced-in groups of homes. They were far from their families, clans, and ethnic groups. They worked long hours in dangerous conditions for low wages.

A woman in Zimbabwe spreads fertilizer on corn plants.

New Roles for Women The workers who migrated to South Africa for work were mostly men. While they were gone, the women had to take on the men's responsibilities. Traditionally, women had raised the children and farmed the land. Men had cared for the animals, dealt with local matters, and headed the households. Once the men were gone for a year or two at a time, the women began to make the household and community decisions. For most women, this change was a challenge. For example, many of the women had no training for the new tasks. But the change was also rewarding for many women because they gained new rights, responsibilities, and skills.

 **Reading Check** Name two cities in Southern Africa that have a population of more than one million people.

Life in Central Africa

Like the people of Southern Africa and the rest of Africa, Central Africans went through many cultural changes in the 1900s. But many people in the region still follow old traditions as well.

Economics and Culture In some ways, Central Africa's cultural diversity is a result of sharp economic contrasts that exist in the region. On the Atlantic coast, the countries of Angola, Congo, Gabon, Cameroon, and Equatorial Guinea have large oil reserves. The cities in these coastal areas tend to benefit most from the oil wealth. People living near the coast also gain more exposure to cultures outside of Africa, allowing for the exchange of traditions and customs.

Target Skill **Compare and Contrast** Compare and contrast the ways industry affects culture in Southern and Central Africa. Are there more similarities or more differences?

Chapter 13 Section 4 **447**

Skills for Life **Skills Mini Lesson**

Problem Solving

1. Teach the skill by giving students the four steps to follow when faced with a problem: identify the problem; determine the effect of the problem; identify possible solutions; choose a solution and determine its effectiveness.

2. Students can practice the skill by following the four steps with regard to the problems

of migrant workers. *(Bad living and working conditions affect workers' lives. They could leave the country or try to improve their conditions by forming a union to demand better conditions and pay.)*

3. Have students apply the skill steps to the problem faced by countries with oil-rich coasts and poor interiors.

Life in Central Africa L2

Guided Instruction

- **Vocabulary Builder** Clarify the high-use word **interior** before reading.

- Read Life in Central Africa with students. As students read, circulate to make sure individuals can answer the Reading Check question.

- Ask students **Which areas of Central Africa are most exposed to other cultures? Why?** *(Coastal areas; people there mingle with cultures outside of Africa through work and trade.)*

- Discuss the patterns of economic contrasts in Central Africa. *(People living near the coast tend to have more wealth, while living conditions get poorer as you move into the interior.)*

Independent Practice

Have students complete the graphic organizer by filling in the details they have just learned about Central Africa.

Monitor Progress

- Show *Section Reading Support Transparency AF 44* and ask students to check their graphic organizers individually. Go over key concepts and clarify key vocabulary as needed.

  📖 **Africa Transparencies,** *Section Reading Support Transparency AF 44*

- Tell students to fill in the last column of the *Reading Readiness Guide.* Probe for what they learned that confirms or invalidates each statement.

  All in One Africa Teaching Resources, *Reading Readiness Guide, p. 218*

Target Reading Skill L2

Compare and Contrast As a follow up, ask students to answer the Target Reading Skill question in the Student Edition. *(Southern Africa is rich, urban, and industrialized, while Central Africa's coasts benefit from oil wealth, and its interior areas are poorer. There are more differences than similarities between Southern Africa and Central Africa, though both have significant industrial activity.)*

Answer

✓ **Reading Check** Possible answers: Cape Town, Durban, Johannesburg, Harare

Assess and Reteach

Assess Progress   L2

Have students complete the Section Assessment. Administer the *Section Quiz.*

All in One **Africa Teaching Resources,** *Section Quiz,* p. 220

Reteach   L1

If students need more instruction, have them read this section in the Reading and Vocabulary Study Guide.

Chapter 13, Section 4, **Eastern Hemisphere Reading and Vocabulary Study Guide,** pp. 41–43

Extend   L3

Ask students to complete *The Universal Declaration of Human Rights.* After answering the questions, have them relate the material in the activity to South Africa's history of apartheid.

Go Online PHSchool.com **For:** Environmental and Global Issues: *The Universal Declaration of Human Rights*
Visit: PHSchool.com
Web Code: lad-5305

Answers

✓ **Reading Check** Possible answers: The Congo has about 200 ethnic groups; people practice a mixture of religions.

Section 4 Assessment

Key Terms

Students' sentences should reflect knowledge of each Key Term.

⟳ **Target Reading Skill**   L2

Possible answer: Alike—Both regions have diverse cultures and went through cultural changes in the 1990s. Different—The economy of coastal Central Africa depends heavily on oil reserves, while that of Southern Africa is focused on the industries in South Africa, such as mining. Also, the culture and history of Southern Africa have been more deeply affected by European influence than those of Central Africa have.

448 *Africa*

In contrast, living conditions get poorer as you move in from the coast to the interior areas of Angola, Congo, the Democratic Republic of the Congo, and the Central African Republic. There, village societies are organized by kinship groups, and land is owned by clans. In less-populated rural areas, individual families live and work on their own land.

Diverse Ways of Life Like the rest of the continent, Central Africa contains great cultural diversity. The Democratic Republic of the Congo alone has about 200 ethnic groups.

Millions of people live in crowded shantytowns or cinder-block apartments in Kinshasa, the largest city in the Democratic Republic of the Congo. They walk or take buses or trucks to work in factories, offices, and hotels. Millions of others live in rural areas. Some Central African people are Roman Catholic or Protestant. Others practice religions that blend Christian and traditional African beliefs. Still others are Muslim.

What one writer said about North Africa applies to Central and Southern Africa as well. To define the real North African, he said, "you have to define which one you mean: the rich or the poor, the Berber women of the mountains or the college girls on motorbikes. . . ." Old, new, and mixtures of the two live on in all regions of Africa.

✓ **Reading Check** **What are some examples of cultural diversity in Central Africa?**

Section 4 Assessment

Key Terms
Review the key terms at the beginning of this section. Use each term in a sentence that explains its meaning.

 Target Reading Skill
Name two similarities between Southern Africa and Central Africa. Name two differences.

Comprehension and Critical Thinking
1. (a) Identify When did the process of urbanization in Southern Africa begin?

(b) Explain Why did people from all over Southern Africa migrate to South Africa?
(c) Identify Causes How were the lives of many Southern African women affected by South Africa even though the women never moved there?
2. (a) Recall What industry has brought wealth to some of the countries on Central Africa's Atlantic coast?
(b) Contrast How do the economics and culture of Central Africa's Atlantic coast differ from the economics and culture of its interior areas?

Writing Activity
Write a short report summarizing the ways in which economics have affected culture in Southern Africa and Central Africa. Point out any similarities or differences.

For: An activity on the region of Southern Africa
Visit: PHSchool.com
Web Code: lad-5304

448 Africa

Comprehension and Critical Thinking
1. (a) when European settlers arrived **(b)** South Africa's industry drew workers from other countries. **(c)** Women took on more responsibility at home when the men in their lives went to work in South Africa.

2. (a) the oil industry **(b)** People who live near the coast benefit from the oil wealth and are exposed to more cultures than people who live in the interior.

Writing Activity
Use the *Rubric for Assessing a Report* to evaluate students' reports.

All in One **Africa Teaching Resources,** *Rubric for Assessing a Report,* p. 238

Go Online PHSchool.com Typing in the Web code when prompted will bring students directly to detailed instructions for this activity.

13 Review and Assessment

◆ Chapter Summary

Section 1: The Cultures of North Africa

- Culture has many elements, such as food, language, and beliefs.
- Islam has greatly influenced life in North Africa.
- Because of North Africa's location, the people of the region have been exposed to the cultures of its trading partners, including Europe, Asia, and other parts of Africa.

Morocco

Section 2: The Cultures of West Africa

- West Africa has great ethnic diversity. Most West Africans speak several languages.
- West Africans are bound by strong kinship ties.
- West Africans have kept their cultural values alive by passing them on to younger generations.

Section 3: The Cultures of East Africa

- East Africa's location has contributed to the region's cultural diversity.
- Ideas about land use and ownership have changed over time, but even urban East Africans still feel a bond to their rural villages.

Section 4: The Cultures of Southern and Central Africa

- Southern Africa's diverse culture includes people with three types of European ancestry—Dutch, British, and Portuguese.
- South Africa has had strong economic and cultural influences on Southern Africa.
- Central Africa has great cultural diversity and economic contrasts.

Zimbabwe

Review Chapter Content

- Review and revisit the major themes of this chapter by asking students to classify what Guiding Question each bulleted statement in the Chapter Summary answers. Form students into groups and ask them to complete the activity together. Refer to p. 349 of the Student Edition for the text of the Guiding Questions.

- Assign *Vocabulary Development* for students to review Key Terms.

All in One **Africa Teaching Resources,** *Vocabulary Development*, p. 236

◆ Key Terms

Match the definitions in Column I with the key terms in Column II. There are more terms than definitions.

Column I

1. the spread of customs and ideas from one culture to another
2. a group of families descended from a common ancestor
3. the values, traditions, and customs handed down from one's ancestors
4. the part of a family that includes parents and children only
5. an ethnic group in East Africa
6. a laborer who travels away from where he or she lives to find work

Column II

A Quran
B culture
C cultural diffusion
D cultural diversity
E nuclear family
F extended family
G lineage
H heritage
I Swahili
J migrant worker

── Vocabulary Builder ──

Revisit the chapter's high-use words.

element	cash crop	dense
rural	value	eventually
conquest	promote	industrialized
unify	fertile	interior

Ask students to review the definitions they recorded on their *Word Knowledge* worksheets.

All in One **Africa Teaching Resources,** *Word Knowledge*, p. 224

Consider allowing students to earn extra credit if they use the words in their answers to the questions in the Chapter Review and Assessment. To win the extra points, they must use the words correctly and in a natural context.

Answers

Key Terms

1. C
2. G
3. H
4. E
5. I
6. J

Review and Assessment

Comprehension and Critical Thinking

7. (a) the way of life of people who share similar customs and beliefs **(b)** Most people practice Islam; some people live in houses made of adobe; many people speak the Arabic language.

8. (a) It is a strong bond that encourages working together, making decisions together, taking care of the elderly and sick, and watching over the community's children. **(b)** Families are split up as men go to the city to earn money and women stay in their rural homes.

9. (a) It borders the Indian Ocean. **(b)** The ocean connects East Africa to people living in other countries, such as Arabs and Asians. **(c)** It links many diverse groups, allowing them to communicate and do business together.

10. (a) Individual Africans did not own land; extended families farmed the land to produce food for the entire group. **(b)** After many of the European plantations were broken up into smaller plots, individual Africans began to buy them.

11. (a) The Portuguese exported slaves; the Dutch and British farmed and raised cattle; the Dutch also mined. **(b)** The mining industry created a demand for labor, which drew people from other countries to South Africa. **(c)** Possible answer: the lives of migrant workers are hard—they often live and work under poor conditions and are separated from their families.

12. (a) Central Africa has great cultural diversity. It is organized by kinship groups, with sharp economic divisions between rural and urban inhabitants. **(b)** Like much of Africa, Central Africa is ethnically and economically diverse, and has many religions and languages.

Skills Practice

Students' answers will vary, but should include the major similarities and differences between the two cultural regions, and a conclusion based on their findings.

Review and Assessment (continued)

◆ Comprehension and Critical Thinking

7. (a) Recall What is culture?
(b) Describe What are some elements of North Africa's culture?

8. (a) Identify What is the role of kinship in West African cultures?
(b) Explain How is urbanization changing traditional family life in West Africa?

9. (a) Locate Describe East Africa's location.
(b) Analyze Explain how location has affected East African cultures.
(c) Summarize How does the Swahili language help unite the people of East Africa?

10. (a) Recall What were the traditional African ideas about owning and using land before European rule in the 1800s?
(b) Make Generalizations How do East Africans view land use and land ownership today?

11. (a) Recall In what economic activities did Europeans in Southern Africa take part?
(b) Identify Causes What economic activity in South Africa caused many Southern Africans to migrate to that country?
(c) Make Inferences Is the life of a migrant worker an easy one?

12. (a) Note Describe the cultures of Central Africa.
(b) Compare In what ways are the cultures of Central Africa like those in other parts of Africa?

◆ Skills Practice

Comparing and Contrasting In the Skills for Life activity in this chapter, you learned how to compare and contrast. You learned how to note similarities and differences and then draw a conclusion based on your findings.

Review the steps you followed to learn this skill. Then reread the part of Section 1 called Cultural Change in North Africa and the part of Section 3 called Geography and Cultural Diversity. List the similarities and differences between the cultures of these two regions. Draw a conclusion about these cultures based on your findings.

◆ Writing Activity: Language Arts

Suppose an exchange student from an African country has come to stay at your home for six weeks. You and your family are sharing your first dinner with this visitor. Write a dialogue in which you ask your visitor about African culture and the visitor asks you similar questions about your culture. Use what you have learned in this chapter to write your visitor's answers to questions.

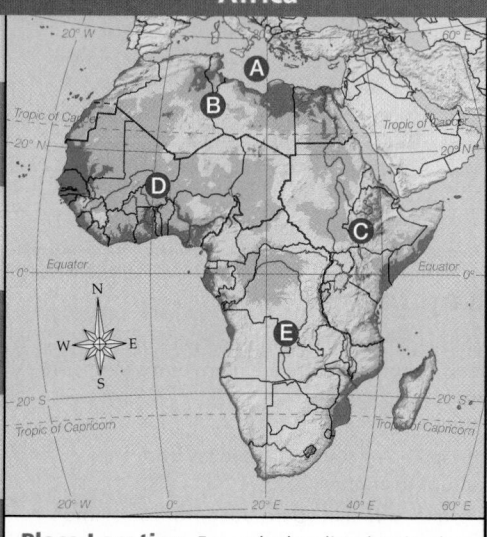

MAP MASTER™
Skills Activity

Africa

Place Location For each place listed, write the letter from the map that shows its location.

1. Mediterranean Sea
2. North Africa
3. West Africa
4. East Africa
5. Southern and Central Africa

Go Online
PHSchool.com Use Web Code **lap-5320** for an **interactive map**.

Writing Activity : Language Arts
Dialogues will vary but should show a clear understanding of the facts and issues presented in the chapter.

Use the *Rubric for Assessing a Writing Assignment* to evaluate students' dialogues.

All in One **Africa Teaching Resources,**
Rubric for Assessing a Writing Assignment, p. 237

Standardized Test Prep

Test-Taking Tips

Some questions on standardized tests ask you to analyze a graphic organizer. Study the concept web below. Then follow the tips to answer the sample question.

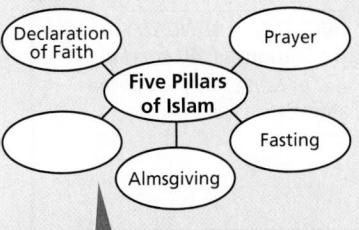

TIP When you study a concept web, notice the kind of information that goes in each oval. The main idea is in the center oval, and the supporting details are in the outer ovals.

Pick the letter that best answers the question.

What is the fifth Pillar of Islam that belongs on this concept web?

A The Quran
B Pilgrimage
C Duties of a Muslim
D The influence of Islam

TIP Use logic, or good reasoning, to be sure you choose an answer that makes sense.

Think It Through The center of the web says "Five Pillars of Islam"—meaning duties required by the religion—and each of the outer ovals shows one duty. What other pillar, or duty, belongs in an outer oval? You can rule out C and D because both are general ideas rather than specific duties. That leaves A and B. Even if you're not sure of the answer, you can see that the other outer ovals involve actions. Because pilgrimage involves an action, you can guess that B is the correct answer.

Practice Questions

Use the tips above and other tips in this book to help you answer the following questions.

1. Which of the following statements is true?
   A Cultural diffusion only occurs on coasts.
   B In general, Africa has little cultural diversity.
   C Cultural changes often occur during travel.
   D Cultural diffusion and cultural diversity are the same thing.

2. Which of the following best explains the meaning of the proverb "The young can't teach traditions to the old"?
   A Traditions do not interest young people.
   B Only adults know customs and traditions.
   C Young people are not the best teachers.
   D Adults must pass traditions on to young people.

3. A cultural group that lives in Southern Africa is the
   A Swahili.   **B** Afrikaners.
   C Berbers.   **D** Tuareg.

Use the Venn diagram below to answer Question 4. Choose the letter of the best answer.

4. Which of the following could be listed in the part of the diagram where *East Africa* and *West Africa* intersect?
   A Cultures affected by coastal trade
   B Indian Ocean location
   C Br'er Rabbit tales
   D Swahili culture

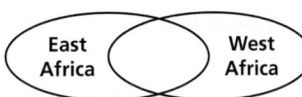

Go Online PHSchool.com

Use Web Code **laa-5300** for **Chapter 13 self-test.**

---

1. A
2. B
3. D
4. C
5. E

Go Online PHSchool.com Students may practice their map skills using the interactive online version of this map.

Standardized Test Prep

Answers

1. C
2. D
3. B
4. A

Go Online PHSchool.com Students may use the Chapter 13 self-test on PHSchool.com to prepare for the Chapter Test.

Assessment Resources

Use *Chapter Tests A and B* to assess students' mastery of chapter content.

All in One *Chapter Tests A and B*, **Africa Teaching Resources,** pp. 239–244

Tests are also available on the *ExamView Test Bank CD-ROM.*

⦿ *ExamView Test Bank CD-ROM*

Use a benchmark test to evaluate students' cumulative understanding of what they have learned in Chapters 1 through 3.

▤ *Africa Benchmark Test 1,* **AYP Monitoring Assessments,** pp. 113–116

Overview

Introducing North Africa
1. Use the map on p. 105 and summary paragraphs to learn about each country.
2. Compare the countries by analyzing the data provided.
3. Name the characteristics shared by most of the countries.
4. Discover the key differences among the countries.

The Geography of North Africa
Length: 5 minutes, 40 seconds
Overview of North Africa, including population density and physical geography.

Section 1

Egypt: A Nation on the Nile
1. Find out how Islam influences Egyptian culture.
2. Learn about daily life in Egypt.

Egypt: The Nile and the Fellaheen
Length: 3 minutes, 3 seconds
Explains the relationship between the Nile and Egyptians' farming techniques.

Section 2

Algeria: Varied Geography, Varied History
1. Learn about the history and people of Algeria.
2. Find out about life in Algeria's different geographic regions.
3. Examine life in Algeria today.

The Sahara: Fruits of the Oasis
Length: 2 minutes, 23 seconds
Shows how people can live and grow food in a Saharan oasis.

Technology Resources

Go Online
PHSchool.com

Students use embedded Web codes to access Internet activities, chapter self-tests, and additional map practice. They may also access Dorling Kindersley's Online Desk Reference to learn more about each country they study.

Interactive Textbook

Use the Interactive Textbook to make content and concepts come alive through animations, videos, and activities that accompany the complete basal text—online and on CD-ROM.

PRENTICE HALL
TeacherEXPRESS™
Plan • Teach • Assess

Use this complete suite of powerful teaching tools to make planning lessons and administering tests quicker and easier.

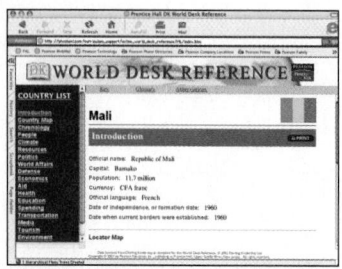

Reading and Assessment

Reading and Vocabulary Instruction

◐ Model the Target Reading Skill

Cause and Effect Explain to students that understanding cause and effect will help them to better understand the events about which they read. By identifying causes and effects and analyzing effects in context, students become more adept at seeing patterns both within and beyond the reading. Model this skill by thinking aloud about the following statements from page 461 of the Student Edition: *Many people move to the cities from rural areas. Cairo is very crowded.*

"One of these sentences states a cause, and the other one states an effect. How will I decide which is which? Let me set up the statements in two ways, using a connection word like *because*, to see which makes more sense. 1) Because many people move to the cities from rural areas, Cairo is very crowded. 2) Because Cairo is very crowded, many people move to the cities from rural areas.

My first statement makes more sense. People moving to the cities happened first, and it caused Cairo to become very crowded, which is the effect."

Use the following worksheets from All-in-One Africa Teaching Resources (pp. 259–260) to support the chapter's Target Reading Skill.

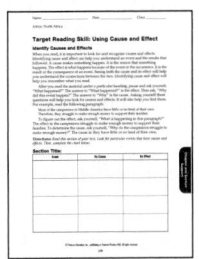 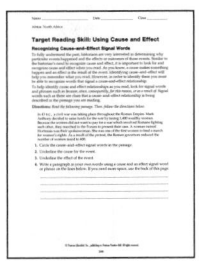

Vocabulary Builder
High-Use Academic Words

Use these steps to teach this chapter's high-use words:

1. Have students rate how well they know each word on their Word Knowledge worksheets (All-in-One Africa Teaching Resources, p. 261).

2. Pronounce each word and ask students to repeat it.

3. Give students a brief definition or sample sentence (provided on TE pp. 459 and 467).

4. Work with students as they fill in the "Definition or Example" column of their Word Knowledge worksheets.

Assessment

Formal Assessment

Test students' understanding of core knowledge and skills.

Chapter Tests A and B, All-in-One Africa Teaching Resources, pp. 279–284

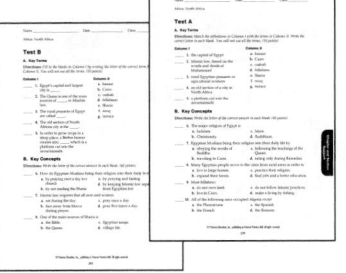

Customize the Chapter Tests to suit your needs.

ExamView Test Bank CD-ROM

Skills Assessment

Assess geographic literacy.

MapMaster Skills, Student Edition, pp. 453, 472

Country Profile Map and Chart Skills, Student Edition, pp. 460, 468

Assess reading and comprehension.

Target Reading Skills, Student Edition, pp. 461, 467, and in Section Assessments

Chapter 14 Assessment, Eastern Hemisphere Reading and Vocabulary Study Guide, p. 167

Performance Assessment

Assess students' performance on this chapter's Writing Activities using the following rubrics from All-in-One Africa Teaching Resources.

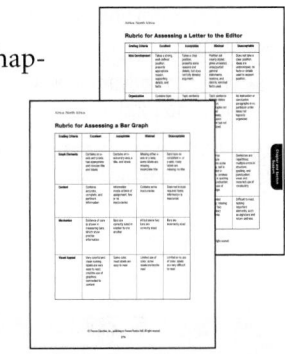

Rubric for Assessing a Bar Graph, p. 276

Rubric for Assessing a Letter to the Editor, p. 277

Rubric for Assessing a Writing Assignment, p. 278

Assess students' work through performance tasks.

Small Group Activity: Writing About the Cities of North Africa, All-in-One Africa Teaching Resources, pp. 264–267

Portfolio Activity, Teacher Edition, p. 457

Online Assessment

Have students check their own understanding.

Chapter Self-Test

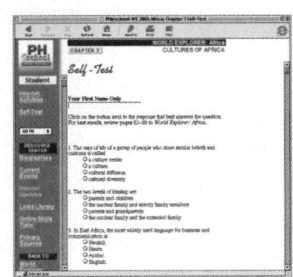

Section 1 Egypt: A Nation on the Nile

 2.5 periods, 1.25 blocks (includes Country Databank and Skills for Life)

Social Studies Objectives
1. Find out how Islam influences Egyptian culture.
2. Learn about daily life in Egypt.

Reading/Language Arts Objective
Determine causes and effects to understand relationships among situations or events.

Prepare to Read

Build Background Knowledge
Ask students to think about how physical geography can affect peoples' lives.

Set a Purpose for Reading
Have students begin to fill out the *Reading Readiness Guide*.

Preview Key Terms
Teach the section's Key Terms.

Target Reading Skill
Introduce the section's Target Reading Skill of **recognizing causes and effects.**

Instructional Resources

All in One Africa Teaching Resources
- L2 Reading Readiness Guide, p. 252
- L2 Identify Causes and Effects, p. 259

Africa Transparencies
- L2 Color Transparency AF 9: The World: Annual Precipitation

Differentiated Instruction

Spanish Reading and Vocabulary Study Guide
- L1 Chapter 14, Section 1, pp. 114–115 ELL

World Studies Video Program
- L2 The Geography of North Africa AR, GT, LPR, SN

Instruct

Islam in Egypt
Discuss the practice of Islam and the role of Sharia in Egyptian culture.

Country Profile
Ask students to derive information from maps, charts, and graphs.

Target Reading Skill
Review **recognizing causes and effects.**

Daily Life in Egypt
Ask about the advantages and disadvantages of living in urban and rural Egypt.

Eyewitness Technology
Read about and discuss the Aswan High Dam.

Instructional Resources

All in One Africa Teaching Resources
- L2 Guided Reading and Review, p. 253
- L2 Reading Readiness Guide, p. 252
- L2 Reading a Population Density Map, p. 268

Africa Transparencies
- L2 Section Reading Support Transparency AF 45

World Studies Video Program
- L2 Egypt: The Nile and the Fellaheen

Differentiated Instruction

All in One Africa Teaching Resources
- L1 Outline Map 22: North Africa, p. 269 ELL, LPR, SN
- L3 A Speech for Peace, pp. 270–273 AR, GT
- L2 Skills for Life, p. 263 AR, GT, LPR, SN

Africa Transparencies
- L3 Transparency AF 27: Africa Political AR, GT

Teacher's Edition
- L3 For Advanced Readers, TE pp. 455, 462
- L1 For Special Needs Students, TE p. 455
- L2 For English Language Learners, TE p. 460
- L3 For Gifted and Talented, TE p. 460

Reading and Vocabulary Study Guide
- L2 Chapter 14, Section 1, pp. 161–163 ELL

Assess and Reteach

Assess Progress
Evaluate student comprehension with the section assessment and section quiz.

Reteach
Assign the Reading and Vocabulary Study Guide to help struggling students.

Extend
Extend the lesson by assigning an Enrichment Activity.

Instructional Resources

All in One Africa Teaching Resources
- L2 Section Quiz, p. 254
- L3 Enrichment, p. 262
- L3 Writing to Describe, p. 274
  Rubric for Assessing a Letter to the Editor, p. 277

Reading and Vocabulary Study Guide
- L1 Chapter 14, Section 1, pp. 161–163

Differentiated Instruction

All in One Africa Teaching Resources
- Rubric for Assessing a Bar Graph, p. 276 AR, GT, LPR, SN

Spanish Support
- L2 Section Quiz (Spanish), p. 155 ELL

Teacher's Edition
- L1 For Special Needs Students, TE p. 465

Social Studies Skills Tutor CD-ROM
- L1 Distinguishing Fact and Opinion ELL, LPR, SN

Key
- **L1** Basic to Average
- **L2** For All Students
- **L3** Average to Advanced

- **LPR** Less Proficient Readers
- **AR** Advanced Readers
- **SN** Special Needs Students

- **GT** Gifted and Talented
- **ELL** English Language Learners

Section 2 Algeria: Varied Geography, Varied History

2.5 periods, 1.25 blocks (includes Chapter Review and Assessment)

Social Studies Objectives
1. Learn about the history and people of Algeria.
2. Find out about life in Algeria's different geographic regions.
3. Examine life in Algeria today.

Reading/Language Arts Objective
Look for signal words that help point out relationships among ideas or events.

Prepare to Read

Build Background Knowledge
Discuss the ways Algeria's weather and landscape differ from students' local weather and landscape.

Set a Purpose for Reading
Have students evaluate statements on the *Reading Readiness Guide*.

Preview Key Terms
Teach the section's Key Terms.

Target Reading Skill
Introduce the section's Target Reading Skill of **using signal words.**

Instructional Resources

All in One Africa Teaching Resources
- L2 Reading Readiness Guide, p. 256
- L2 Recognize Cause-and-Effect Signal Words, p. 260

Differentiated Instruction

Spanish Reading and Vocabulary Study Guide
- L1 Chapter 14, Section 2, pp. 116–117 ELL

Instruct

Algeria's History and People
Discuss how different groups have affected Algeria's culture.

Target Reading Skill
Review **using signal words.**

Country Profile
Ask students to derive and use information from maps, charts, and graphs.

Algeria's Geography

Algeria Today
Discuss life in Algeria and how it compares with students' lives.

Instructional Resources

All in One Africa Teaching Resources
- L2 Guided Reading and Review, p. 257
- L2 Reading Readiness Guide, p. 256

Africa Transparencies
- L2 Transparency B15: Outline
- L2 Section Reading Support Transparency AF 46

World Studies Video Program
- L2 The Sahara: Fruits of the Oasis

Differentiated Instruction

All in One Africa Teaching Resources
- L1 Outline Map 22: North Africa, p. 269 ELL, LPR, SN
- L3 Small Group Activity: Writing About the Cities of North Africa, pp. 264–267 AR, GT

Teacher's Edition
- L1 For Less Proficient Readers, TE p. 468
- L3 For Gifted and Talented, TE p. 469

Spanish Support
- L2 Guided Reading and Review (Spanish), p. 156 ELL

Assess and Reteach

Assess Progress
Evaluate student comprehension with the section assessment and section quiz.

Reteach
Assign the Reading and Vocabulary Study Guide to help struggling students.

Extend
Extend the lesson by having students write letters or postcards about Algeria.

Instructional Resources

All in One Africa Teaching Resources
- L2 Section Quiz, p. 258
- L2 Writing to Describe, p. 274
  Rubric for Assessing a Writing Assignment, p. 278
- L2 Word Knowledge, p. 261
- L2 Vocabulary Development, p. 275
- L2 Chapter Tests A and B, pp. 279–284

Reading and Vocabulary Study Guide
- L1 Chapter 14, Section 2, pp. 164–166

Differentiated Instruction

Spanish Support
- L2 Section Quiz (Spanish), p. 157 ELL
- L2 Chapter Summary (Spanish), p. 158 ELL
- L2 Vocabulary Development (Spanish), p. 159 ELL

Key
- L1 Basic to Average
- L2 For All Students
- L3 Average to Advanced
- LPR Less Proficient Readers
- AR Advanced Readers
- SN Special Needs Students
- GT Gifted and Talented
- ELL English Language Learners

Reading Background

Summarizing

The ability to summarize effectively can help improve students' abilities to comprehend and recall text. Good summarizers take notes from the text and reread as they write. Poor summarizers read the text once and begin writing.

In this chapter students will be asked to summarize their reading using the Paragraph Shrinking strategy. Students may have difficulty summarizing an entire paragraph in a single sentence. Have students read the first paragraph under *City Life* on p. 461 of the Student Edition. Model summarizing by thinking aloud as you follow the steps below.

1. Reread the paragraph aloud as a class.
2. Make notes of the important points on the board. *(Cairo is Egypt's largest city; some parts of Cairo are very old; other areas are very new; most people live in modern apartment buildings; many people shop in traditional bazaars.)*
3. Shrink the paragraph by using the chart on the right.
4. Check back with the text to make sure you have not left anything out or stated anything incorrectly.

What is the topic of the paragraph?	What information does the paragraph begin with?	What information is in the middle of the paragraph?	What information does the paragraph end with?
characteristics of Cairo	*About ten million people live in Cairo, the largest city in Africa.*	*Parts of Cairo are very old while other parts are modern.*	*Most people live in modern apartments, but shop in traditional markets.*

One-sentence summary:
Cairo, the largest city in Africa, is a mixture of the modern and the traditional.

World Studies Background

Alexandria: A Seat of Knowledge

Today, Alexandria is Egypt's leading port and industrial center, but it was once a center for knowledge and learning. It is believed that the Hebrew Bible was translated into Greek in Alexandria around 250 B.C. The city housed a school that was founded and taught by Euclid, the renowned mathematician. For centuries, the Library of Alexandria was the most famous in the ancient world. The library may have held as many as 700,000 volumes before it was partially destroyed when the city was captured by Julius Caesar in 48 B.C. In 2000, the government constructed a new library near the site of the ancient building.

Naguib Mahfouz (1911–)

Egyptian writer Naguib Mahfouz (nuh GEEB mahk FOOS) was born and raised in Cairo and worked in the Egyptian civil service for 37 years. As a result, most of his novels deal with Egyptian values and social issues. He has received international recognition and in 1988 became the first Arab writer to receive the Nobel Prize for Literature.

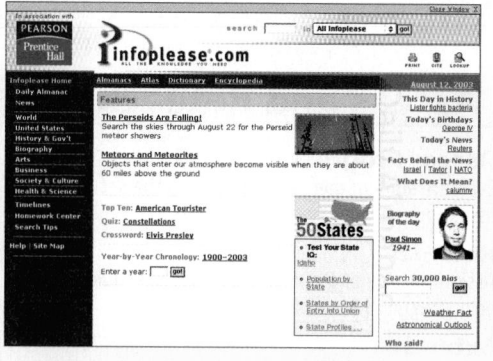

Infoplease® provides a wealth of useful information for the classroom. You can use this resource to strengthen your background on the subjects covered in this chapter. Have students visit this advertising-free site as a starting point for projects requiring research.

Use Web code **lad-5400** for **Infoplease®**.

Reading Background

Using the ReQuest Procedure Effectively

When using the ReQuest Procedure, students and teachers will be asking questions about the text as they read. Facilitate this process by beginning with simple recall questions and progressing to more interpretive questions. For example, when reading the section *Algeria's History and People*, beginning on p. 466 of the Student Edition, ask questions such as:

1. Where is Algeria? *(in North Africa, along the Mediterranean Sea)*
2. What contributes to Algeria's diversity? *(It has been controlled by many different people who left behind elements of culture; the population is made up of Arabs, Berbers, and Europeans; many languages are spoken.)*
3. Why would people want to control Algeria? *(Its port cities on the Mediterranean Sea are valuable to people who want to trade products in Europe and Africa.)*

Read-Cover-Recite-Check

Read-Cover-Recite-Check is a useful strategy for students to retain the information they read. It can be especially effective to help students study for a test. Model the steps for using Read-Cover-Recite-Check to read *Urban Living* on p. 469 of the Student Edition.

1. Read the paragraph quickly to grasp the main ideas. *(Think aloud about the main idea: this paragraph describes characteristics of Algerian cities.)*
2. Reread the paragraph, looking for details and key information. *(Think aloud, noting the details: most Algerians live in cities; there are many mosques and markets in the cities; a souq is an open-air market; old sections, or casbahs, mix with modern sections of the cities.)*
3. Cover the paragraph with your hand or a piece of paper.
4. Recall and repeat the information from the paragraph, including the topic and important details. *(Think aloud: repeat the main idea and details from steps 1 and 2, using different phrasing.)*
5. Rephrase the paragraph in your own words. *(Algerian cities are home to the majority of Algerians, including Arabs and Berbers. Mosques, souqs, and casbahs are common in cities, as is modern architecture.)*
6. Check to make sure you remembered correctly.

World Studies Background

Jehan Sadat (1933–)

Jehan Sadat, wife of former Egyptian president and global peace maker Anwar Sadat, is an ambassador for humanitarian causes. After her husband's assassination in 1981, she pledged to continue his plight for world peace. She devotes her efforts to improving the status of women in Egypt. She established the Talla Society, an organization that helps women become self-sufficient by training them in handicrafts and paying their tuition to secondary schools and universities.

Reforestation in Africa

Algeria and Tunisia are experiencing increased desertification, or the degradation of land, leading to the expansion of the Sahara. This is caused mainly by the disappearance of forests as people cut down trees for fuel and lumber. To correct the resulting ecological imbalance and inhibit erosion, the countries attempted reforestation projects from the 1950s to the 1970s. These efforts were ended due to high costs and failure to reproduce equally diverse forests. In 1996, however, the UN implemented the Convention to Combat Desertification, the first and only program that holds countries legally responsible for taking measures to prevent and end the problem of desertification.

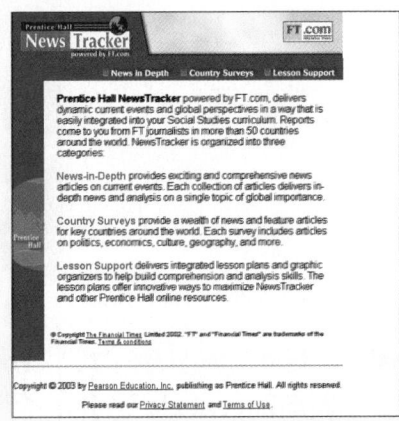

Get in-depth information on topics of global importance with **Prentice Hall Newstracker,** powered by FT.com.

Use Web code **lad-5403** for **Prentice Hall Newstracker.**

Guiding Questions

Remind students about the Guiding Questions introduced at the beginning of this section.

Section 1 relates to **Guiding Question** ③ **What features help define different African cultures?** *(Islam is Egypt's major religion. It affects how Egyptians dress, when they eat and pray, their education, and the nation's laws.)*

Section 2 relates to **Guiding Question** ② **How have historical events affected the cultures and nations of Africa?** *(Algeria is a port city on the Mediterranean Sea, making it an important center for trade. Throughout history it has been occupied by outside groups, including the Phoenicians, Romans, Arabs, Spanish, local pirates, Ottoman Turks and French.)*

⦿ Target Reading Skill

In this chapter, students will learn and apply the reading skill of identifying cause and effect. Use the following worksheets to help students practice this skill:

All in One Africa Teaching Resources, *Identify Causes and Effects,* p. 259; *Recognize Cause-and-Effect Signal Words,* p. 260

Chapter Preview

This chapter will introduce you to some of the countries of North Africa.

Country Databank
The Country Databank provides data and descriptions of each of the countries in the region: Algeria, Egypt, Libya, Morocco, and Tunisia.

Section 1
Egypt
A Nation on the Nile

Section 2
Algeria
Varied Geography, Varied History

 Target Reading Skill

Cause and Effect In this chapter you will focus on understanding causes and effects. Identifying causes and effects and recognizing signal words for causes and effects will help you learn as you read.

▶ Some North Africans live in the Sahara in oasis towns, such as Ghardaia, Algeria, shown here.

452 Africa

Differentiated Instruction

The following Teacher's Edition strategies are suitable for students of varying abilities.

Advanced Readers, pp. 455, 462
English Language Learners, p. 460
Gifted and Talented, pp. 460, 469
Less Proficient Readers, p. 468
Special Needs Students, pp. 455, 465

Bibliography

For the Teacher
History of North Africa. Facts on File, 2003.
McEvedy, Colin. *The Penguin Atlas of African History.* Viking Penguin, 1996.
Nasr, Seyyed Hossein. *The Heart of Islam.* HarperCollins, 2002.

For the Student
L1 Moscovitch, Arlene. *Egypt—the People; Egypt—the Land;* and *Egypt—the Culture.* Crabtree, 2000.
L2 Bramwell, Martyn. *The World in Maps: Africa.* Lerner, 2001.
L3 Kagda, Falaq. *Algeria.* Marshall Cavendish, 1997.

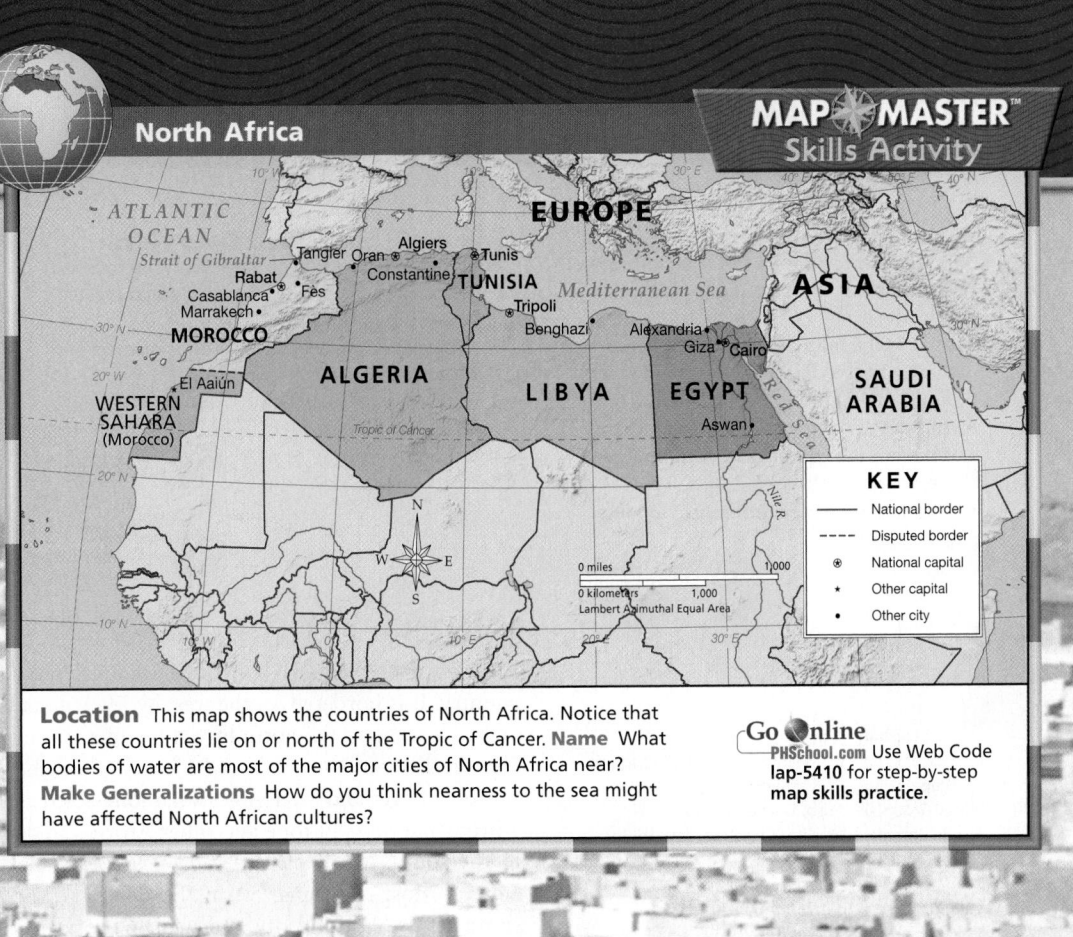

North Africa

ATLANTIC OCEAN

Strait of Gibraltar
Tangier • Oran • Algiers • Tunis
Rabat • Constantine
Casablanca • Fès
Marrakech
MOROCCO

EUROPE

Mediterranean Sea

TUNISIA
• Tripoli
Benghazi • Alexandria
Giza • Cairo

ASIA

El Aaiún
WESTERN SAHARA
(Morocco)

ALGERIA

Tropic of Cancer

LIBYA

EGYPT

Aswan •

SAUDI ARABIA

Red Sea

Nile R.

KEY

— National border
--- Disputed border
⊕ National capital
★ Other capital
• Other city

0 miles   1,000
0 kilometers   1,000
Lambert Azimuthal Equal Area

Location This map shows the countries of North Africa. Notice that all these countries lie on or north of the Tropic of Cancer. **Name** What bodies of water are most of the major cities of North Africa near? **Make Generalizations** How do you think nearness to the sea might have affected North African cultures?

Go Online
PHSchool.com Use Web Code lap-5410 for step-by-step map skills practice.

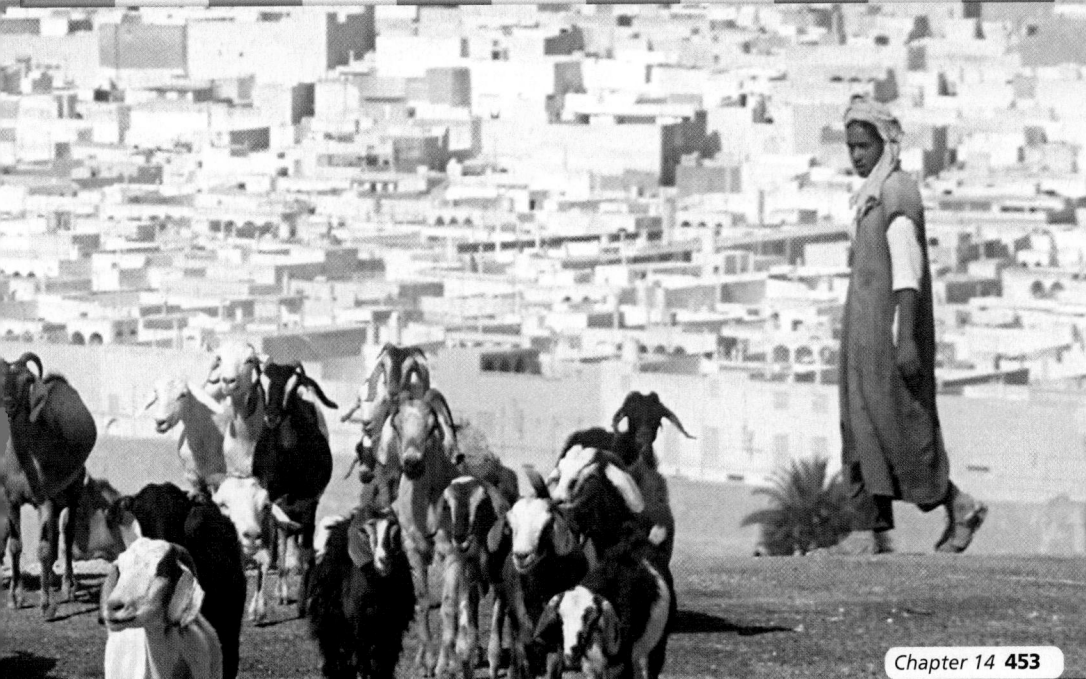

Chapter 14 **453**

■ Show students *Color Transparency AF 9: The World: Annual Precipitation* and ask them to compare the map in the transparency with the map on this page.

📖 **Africa Transparencies,** *Color Transparency AF 9: The World: Annual Precipitation*

■ Have students determine the annual precipitation in the countries of north Africa. (*Most countries have an annual precipitation of under 10 inches; in the northernmost sections, some countries have an annual precipitation of 10–20 inches or 20–40 inches.*) Ask students to think about the challenges people might face in countries with very little rain. How would their lives be different from students' own? Conduct an Idea Wave (TE, p. T35) to elicit student responses.

Go Online
PHSchool.com Students may practice their map skills using the interactive online version of this map.

Using the Visual   L2

Reach Into Your Background Ask students to study the photograph on pp. 452–453, and read the caption on p. 452. Have them describe the scene in their own words. What do they find interesting about this photo? What might the landscape and weather in this region be like? How could location affect the way people live here?

Answers

MAP MASTER Skills Activity **Name** the Atlantic Ocean and the Mediterranean Sea **Make Generalizations** The sea could have been used as a trade route, and allowed the exchange of goods and ideas with other countries.

Chapter Resources

Teaching Resources
L2 Vocabulary Development, p. 275
L2 Skills for Life, p. 263
L2 Chapter Tests A and B, pp. 279–284

Spanish Support
L2 Spanish Chapter Summary, p. 158
L2 Spanish Vocabulary Development, p. 159

Media and Technology
L1 Student Edition on Audio CD
L1 Guided Reading Audiotapes, English and Spanish
L2 Social Studies Skill Tutor CD-ROM
ExamView Test Bank CD-ROM

Discovery World Studies
CHANNEL Video Program
SCHOOL

interactive
Textbook
PRENTICE HALL
TeacherEXPRESS™
Plan • Teach • Assess

Objectives

- Use the map on p. 453 and summary paragraphs to learn about each country.
- Compare the countries by analyzing the data provided.
- Name the characteristics shared by most of the countries.
- Discover the key differences among the countries.

Show students *The Geography of North Africa.* Ask **What are some common features of the region?** *(All countries are on the Mediterranean Sea. The capital cities and greatest population densities in each country are near the Mediterranean or the Nile River because the rest of each country is very arid.)*

Prepare to Read

Build Background Knowledge   **L2**

Conduct an Idea Wave (TE, p. T35) to generate a list of what students think they would need to take on a trip through North Africa. Students should explain why they think each item is necessary, based on what they have learned from the World Studies Video.

The Geography of North Africa, **World Studies Video Program**

Introducing North Africa

Guide for Reading

This section provides an introduction to the five countries that make up the region of North Africa.

- Look at the map on the previous page and then read the paragraphs below to learn about each nation.
- Analyze the data to compare the countries.
- What are the characteristics that most of the countries share?
- What are some key differences among the countries?

Viewing the Video Overview

View the World Studies Video Overview to learn more about each of the countries. As you watch, answer these questions:

- What are some common features of the region?
- How does the availability of water influence where the people of North Africa live?

Explore the geography of North Africa.

Algeria

Capital	Algiers
Land Area	919,590 sq mi; 2,381,740 sq km
Population	32.3 million
Ethnic Group(s)	Arab, Berber, white
Religion(s)	Muslim, Christian, Jewish
Government	republic
Currency	Algerian dinar
Leading Exports	petroleum, natural gas, petroleum products
Language(s)	Arabic (official), Tamazight (official), Kabyle, Shawia, Tamashek, French

Algeria (al JIHR ee uh) is Africa's second-largest country. It is bordered on the west by Mauritania and Morocco, on the north by the Mediterranean Sea, on the east by Tunisia and Libya, and on the south by Niger and Mali. Algeria has long acted as a bridge between Europe and other African lands to the south. Much of Algeria is covered by the Sahara. Most Algerians live in the north, where summers are hot and dry and winters are warm and wet. Following independence from France in 1962, Algeria made improvements in education and literacy. Since the 1990s, Algeria has struggled with economic troubles and civil war.

Algerian girl preparing food

454 Africa

Egypt

Capital	Cairo
Land Area	384,343 sq mi; 995,450 sq km
Population	70.7 million
Ethnic Group(s)	Eastern Hamitic, Nubian, white
Religion(s)	Muslim, Christian
Government	republic
Currency	Egyptian pound
Leading Exports	crude oil and petroleum products, cotton, textiles, metal products, chemicals
Language(s)	Arabic (official), French, English, Berber

Egypt (EE jipt) is bordered on the west by Libya, on the north by the Mediterranean Sea, Israel, and the Gaza Strip, on the east by the Red Sea, and on the south by Sudan. Most of the people live in the fertile valley and delta regions of the Nile River. The rest of Egypt is hot desert. Egypt is famous for the ancient civilization that developed there along the Nile. The ancient Egyptians built pyramids and monuments that today draw tourists and scholars from around the world. Egypt's capital, Cairo, is an important cultural center for the Arabic world.

The Great Pyramids (left) and the Sphinx (below) at Giza, Egypt

Chapter 14 **455**

Introducing North Africa   L2

Guided Instruction

- Have students read the Country Databank using the Structured Silent Reading strategy (TE, p. T34) and study the data tables.

- Ask **What do all the countries of North Africa have in common?** (*All are home to Muslims and have Arabic as an official language.*)

- Ask **Which country was the first to gain its independence: Algeria, Libya, or Morocco?** (*Libya*)

- Draw a Venn diagram on the board with three overlapping circles. Label the circles *Muslim*, *Christian*, and *Jewish*. Ask volunteers to put each country in the appropriate circle(s) in the diagram. Ask **Which countries have the most religious diversity?** (*Algeria, Morocco, Tunisia*)

- Tell students that the acronym OPEC stands for the Organization of Petroleum Exporting Countries. Ask **Which North African countries probably are NOT members of OPEC? Why?** (*Morocco and Tunisia are most likely not OPEC members, because petroleum is not listed among their leading exports.*)

Differentiated Instruction

For Advanced Readers   L3

Have students compare the locations of Rabat, Algiers, Tunis, Tripoli, and Cairo on *Transparency AF 27: Africa: Political* and discuss the possible geographical advantages and disadvantages of each capital's location.

   Africa Transparencies, *Transparency AF 27: Africa: Political*

For Special Needs Students   L1

Have students make a list of countries from greatest land area to least land area. Give students a blank outline map of North Africa. Ask them to label each country with its land area in square miles and square kilometers.

   Africa Teaching Resources, *Outline Map 22: North Africa, p. 269*

Independent Practice

Organize students into five groups. Assign a North African country to each group. Have groups use the information from the data tables and paragraphs to create a travel brochure for their assigned country. Students should include any information of interest to travelers, such as weather, languages, and history.

Monitor Progress

Circulate to make sure students are choosing appropriate information and presenting it accurately.

Introducing North Africa (continued)

Libya

Capital	Tripoli
Land Area	679,358 sq mi; 1,759,540 sq km
Population	5.4 million
Ethnic Group(s)	Arab, Berber, white, Southwest Asian, South Asian
Religion(s)	Muslim
Government	local councils in theory; military dictatorship in practice
Currency	Libyan dinar
Leading Exports	crude oil, refined petroleum products
Language(s)	Arabic (official), Tuareg

Libya (LIB ee uh) is bordered on the west by Algeria and Tunisia, on the north by the Mediterranean Sea, on the east by Egypt and Sudan, and on the south by Chad and Niger. Each year, an average of four inches (10 centimeters) of rain falls in Libya. The country has no rivers that flow year-round. Instead, it relies on groundwater from desert oases and man-made wells. Most Libyans live in urban areas. Large oil and natural gas reserves are important to Libya's economy. Libya gained independence from Italy in 1951. Revolution followed in 1969, leading to the establishment of a military dictatorship.

Morocco

Capital	Rabat
Land Area	172,316 sq mi; 446,300 sq km
Population	31.2 million
Ethnic Group(s)	Arab, Berber
Religion(s)	Muslim, Christian, Jewish
Government	constitutional monarchy
Currency	Moroccan dirham
Leading Exports	phosphates and fertilizers, food and beverages, minerals
Language(s)	Arabic (official), Tamazight, French, Spanish

Morocco (muh RAH koh) is a mountainous country in which earthquakes are common. It is bordered on the west by the Atlantic Ocean, on the north by the Strait of Gibraltar and the Mediterranean Sea, on the east by Algeria, and on the south by Western Sahara. In 1956, Morocco gained independence from France. A year later, Morocco claimed the Spanish colony of Western Sahara as its territory. Today, Morocco occupies Western Sahara, but most countries do not recognize the region as Morocco's possession. Morocco's largest city, Casablanca, lies in the west, along the Atlantic.

Moroccan pottery

Background: Global Perspectives

Eid al-Fitr Eid al-Fitr (id uhl FIT uhr), or The Festival of Breaking the Fast, is one of two major Islamic religious holidays. On the day of the Eid, Muslims celebrate the end of the Ramadan fast. They dress in their best clothes and go to a special morning prayer service. At the end of the service they greet each other with the words "Eid Mubarak," or "Holiday Blessings." Later on, Muslims visit and share holiday meals with family and friends. Homes are decked in lights and decorations, and children may receive gifts.

Tunisia

Capital	Tunis
Land Area	59,984 sq mi; 155,360 sq km
Population	9.8 million
Ethnic Group(s)	Arab, Berber, white
Religion(s)	Muslim, Christian, Jewish
Government	republic
Currency	Tunisian dinar
Leading Exports	textiles, mechanical goods, phosphates and chemicals, agricultural products, hydrocarbons
Language(s)	Arabic (official), French

SOURCES: DK World Desk Reference Online; CIA World Factbook Online, 2002; *The World Almanac*, 2003

The famed ancient port city of Carthage was founded on the Gulf of Tunis, in the land of present-day Tunisia (too NEE zhuh). In A.D. 698, Carthage fell to the Arabs, who then established Tunis. Tunisia is North Africa's smallest country. It is wedged between Algeria on the west and Libya on the east. It is bordered on the north and east by the Mediterranean Sea. Tunisia is one of the Arab world's most liberal countries, where women make up about one third of the workforce. The importance of education is stressed in Tunisia. Since 1995, enrollment in colleges has doubled.

Berber drummers in Tunisia

Assessment

Comprehension and Critical Thinking

1. Compare and Contrast Compare and contrast the physical characteristics of the countries that make up North Africa.

2. Draw Conclusions What are some characteristics that most of the countries share?

3. Analyze Information What are some key differences among the countries?

4. Categorize What kinds of products are the major exports of North Africa?

5. Infer What part of North Africa's history can you infer from reading the list of languages that are spoken in each country?

6. Make a Bar Graph Create a bar graph showing the population of the countries in the region.

Keeping Current

Access the **DK World Desk Reference Online** at **PHSchool.com** for up-to-date information about all five countries in this chapter.

Web Code: lae-5400

Section 1
Egypt
A Nation on the Nile

Objectives

Social Studies

1. Find out how Islam influences Egyptian culture.

2. Learn about daily life in Egypt.

Reading/Language Arts

Determine causes and effects to understand relationships among situations or events.

Prepare to Read

Build Background Knowledge   **L2**

In this section, students will learn about the North African country of Egypt. Ask them to quickly preview the headings and visuals of the section with this question in mind: **How can a physical feature of the land, such as the Nile River, affect where and how people live?** Conduct an Idea Wave (TE, p. T35) to help students generate a list.

Set a Purpose for Reading   **L2**

- Preview the Objectives.

- Form students into pairs or groups of four. Distribute the *Reading Readiness Guide*. Ask the students to fill in the first two columns of the chart. Use the Numbered Heads participation strategy (TE, p. T36) to call on students to share one piece of information they already know and one piece of information they want to know.

  All in One Africa Teaching Resources, *Reading Readiness Guide,* p. 252

Vocabulary Builder
Preview Key Terms   **L2**

Pronounce each Key Term, then ask the students to say the word with you. Provide a simple explanation, such as, "The capital city of Egypt is Cairo."

Prepare to Read

Objectives

In this section you will
1. Find out how Islam influences Egyptian culture.
2. Learn about daily life in Egypt.

Taking Notes

As you read this section, look for details about life in Egypt. Copy the table below, and use it to record your findings.

Islam in Egypt	• •
Everyday Life in Egypt	• •

Target Reading Skill

Identify Causes and Effects Determining causes and effects can help you understand the relationships among situations or events. A cause makes something happen. An effect is what happens. As you read this section, note the effects Islam and the Nile River have had on life in Egypt.

Key Terms

- **Cairo** (KY roh) *n.* the capital of Egypt
- **Sharia** (shah REE ah) *n.* Islamic law, based on the words and deeds of Muhammad and on comments written by Muslim scholars and lawmakers
- **bazaar** (buh ZAHR) *n.* a traditional open-air market with shops or rows of stalls
- **fellaheen** (fel uh HEEN) *n.* peasants or agricultural workers in Egypt and other Arab countries

Egyptian boy at Ramadan evening meal

458 Africa

For one month of the year, the restaurants in **Cairo,** Egypt's capital, stand empty at noon. Egyptian teenagers try not to think about foods such as pita bread or sweet dates. Only certain people, such as the very young or those who are sick, eat regular meals. It is the Muslim holy month of Ramadan (ram uh DAHN). During this month, followers of Islam fast from dawn to dusk. To fast is to go without food for a period of time. During Ramadan, Muslims eat only after the sun has set.

But Muslims do more than fast during the month of Ramadan. They also focus on prayer and obedience to God. They try to avoid thinking unkind thoughts. And they help the poor and other people who are less fortunate than themselves.

Target Reading Skill   **L2**

Identify Causes and Effects Point out the Target Reading Skill. Tell students that recognizing causes and effects can help them understand the relationships between situations and events.

Model recognizing causes and effects by reading the third paragraph on p. 461 with students. Help them see the causes and effects of the increased use of fertilizer by farmers along the Nile River. (*Cause: the Aswan Dam blocks the Nile's rich silt from reaching farmland downstream; Effect: farmers have to use more fertilizer, which threatens Egypt's water supply*)

Give students *Identify Causes and Effects.* Have them complete the activity in groups.

All in One Africa Teaching Resources, *Identify Causes and Effects,* p. 259

Islam in Egypt

Egypt is located in North Africa. It lies across the Red Sea from Saudi Arabia, where Muhammad, the founder of Islam, was born. As you have read, Islam spread from Arabia across North Africa. Today, most North Africans are Muslim. This is true in Egypt, where Islam is the religion that most people practice. However, a minority of Egypt's population is Christian. Most Egyptian Christians are members of the Coptic Church, which is one of the oldest branches of Christianity in the world. Coptic Christianity existed in Egypt for a few hundred years before Islam did.

Islamic Practices Recall from Chapter 13 that the Quran is the sacred book of Islam. One of the Quran's requirements is that Muslims pray five times each day. Many Egyptians pray in mosques. While they pray, they face southeast so that they pray in the direction of the Muslim holy city of Mecca, in Saudi Arabia. Egyptians also often send their children to mosques to receive religious training. There, young students learn to read and memorize the Quran.

Islam and the Law The Quran is one of the main sources of **Sharia** (shah REE ah), or Islamic law. Sharia is based on the words and deeds of Muhammad, as well as on comments written by Muslim scholars and lawmakers. Muslims in North Africa and Southwest Asia try to renew their faith by living each day according to Sharia.

Most Muslims in Egypt agree that, in general, the laws of their country should be based on the laws of Islam. In 1980, the Egyptian government adopted a new constitutional amendment. This amendment identified Sharia as the main source of the laws of Egypt. Still, not all of Egypt's laws are based on Sharia. In recent years, some Egyptians have argued that all of Egypt's laws should match Islamic law exactly. On this issue, however, many Egyptian Muslims disagree.

✓ **Reading Check** Why do Egyptian Muslims face southeast when they pray each day?

Links to Math

Muslim Mathematicians
Beginning around A.D. 800, Muslims throughout the Arab world began developing and using important mathematical concepts. Much of the work done by these Muslim mathematicians has formed the basis of mathematics as it exists today. A number of Muslim mathematicians came from North Africa. For example, Abu Kamil (born A.D. 850) and Ibn Yusun (born A.D. 950) were Egyptian, while Ibn al-Banna (born A.D. 1256) is thought to have been Moroccan.

Muslim men praying in a mosque in Cairo

Instruct

Links

Read the **Links to Math** on this page. Ask **How did the work of Muslim mathematicians influence mathematics today?** *(Their work formed the basis of mathematics as it exists today.)*

Islam in Egypt   L2

Guided Instruction

- **Vocabulary Builder** Clarify the high-use words **minority** and **requirement** before reading.

- Read Islam in Egypt, using the Oral Cloze strategy (TE, p. T33).

- Ask students **What religion do most Egyptians practice?** *(Islam)*

- Ask **What is the role of Sharia in Egyptian culture?** *(It serves as a model for the country's laws, although differing interpretations of Sharia have been a source of conflict.)*

Independent Practice

Ask students to create the Taking Notes graphic organizer on a blank piece of paper. Briefly model how to fill in the organizer with appropriate details from the section.

Monitor Progress

Check students' work as they fill in the graphic organizer. Provide assistance as needed.

Vocabulary Builder

Use the information below to teach students this section's high-use words.

High-Use Word	Definition and Sample Sentence
minority, p. 459	*n.* a smaller group Only a **minority** of the class wanted to have homework over summer vacation.
requirement, p. 459	*n.* a need Being able to run quickly was a **requirement** for joining the soccer team.
densely, p. 461	*adv.* thickly The forest was **densely** overgrown with trees.
shortage, p. 461	*n.* not enough of Because no rain had fallen in months, there was a **shortage** of water in the town.

Answer

✓ **Reading Check** They face southeast so that they pray in the direction of Mecca, the Muslim holy city.

Guided Instruction L2

Ask students to study the Country Profile on this page. As a class, answer the Map and Chart Skills questions. Allow students to briefly discuss their responses with a partner before sharing their answers with the class.

Independent Practice

- Give students *Reading a Population Density Map*. Have students work in pairs to complete the worksheet.

  All in One **Africa Teaching Resources,** *Reading a Population Density Map*, p. 268

- Have students compare the map on this page with the map on the worksheet. Ask students what similarities they notice between the population densities of the two countries. (*In both places, population density is higher near sources of water, such as rivers and oceans.*)

Egypt

The most important body of water in Egypt is the Nile River, which flows from the mountains of East Africa north to the Mediterranean Sea. Nearly all of Egypt's people live on the 4 percent of the land that is closest to the Nile's shores. Irrigation with Nile water allows agriculture to thrive, and one third of Egypt's workforce is employed in agriculture. Each month, however, thousands of Egyptians leave crowded farm communities to begin new lives in the cities. Study the map and charts to learn more about Egypt's changing society.

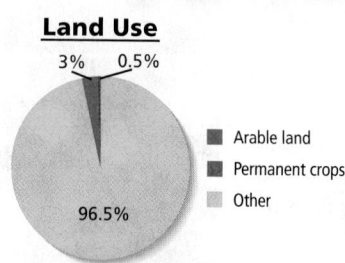

Egypt: Population Density

KEY

Persons per sq. mile	Persons per sq. kilometer
More than 3,119	More than 1,204
520–3,119	200–1,204
260–519	100–199
130–259	50–99
25–129	10–49
1–24	1–9
Less than 1	Less than 1

Urban Areas
- More than 9,999,999
- 5,000,000–9,999,999
- 1,000,000–4,999,999
- 500,000–999,999
- Less than 500,000

— National border

0 miles 300
0 kilometers 300
Lambert Azimuthal Equal Area

Urban and Rural Population

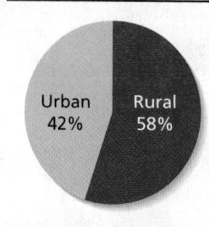

Urban 42%   Rural 58%

SOURCE: *United Nations Population Division*

Land Use

3%   0.5%

96.5%

- Arable land
- Permanent crops
- Other

SOURCE: CIA World Factbook Online, 2003

The Nile River

Map and Chart Skills

1. **Locate** In what part of Egypt are most of the major cities located?
2. **Explain** How does Egypt's geography affect where in the country people live?
3. **Predict** What changes could Egyptians make that would allow them to live in areas where currently few people live?

Go Online PHSchool.com

Use Web Code lae-5401 for **DK World Desk Reference Online.**

Answers

Map and Chart Skills

1. the north
2. Most people live near the Nile River.
3. They could build canals or pipelines to bring water from the Nile to other areas of Egypt or dig more wells.

Go Online PHSchool.com Students can find more information about this topic on the DK World Desk Reference Online.

Differentiated Instruction

For English Language Learners L2
Before students read this section, assign the Reading and Vocabulary Study Guide summary for Chapter 14, Section 1, or read the section aloud to them.

📖 **Eastern Hemisphere Reading and Vocabulary Study Guide,** pp. 161–163

For Gifted and Talented L3
Have students read Egyptian president Anwar el-Sadat's speech before the Israeli Knesset. Ask students to analyze Sadat's references to Islam, Judaism, and Christianity to determine why Sadat included those works in his speech.

All in One **Africa Teaching Resources,** *A Speech for Peace*, pp. 270–273

Daily Life in Egypt

As you can see from the circle graph in the Country Profile on page 460, Egypt's population is fairly evenly divided between people who live in cities and people who live in villages. City dwellers and villagers live very different lives. One thing they have in common, however, is their dependence on the life-giving waters of the Nile River.

Egypt's Water Source Look at the map of Egypt on page 460 in the Country Profile. You can see that Egypt is most densely populated along the Nile River and in the Nile Delta region. Now turn to page 462 and read about the Aswan High Dam. With the help of this dam, the Nile River allows Egypt's crops to be irrigated year-round. The river supplies water to people in the cities and in rural areas.

But farming practices and population pressures threaten Egypt's water supply. The Aswan High Dam blocks the Nile's rich silt from reaching farmland downstream. Without the silt, the Nile Delta has been shrinking. Farmers have to use more fertilizer to grow their crops. The fertilizers they use, along with waste that comes from urban areas, threaten the safety of Egypt's water supply.

City Life Nearly half of all Egyptians live in cities. Cairo is the nation's capital and also its largest city. It is home to more than 10 million Egyptians. Some parts of Cairo are more than 1,000 years old. Other parts are very modern. Most people live in apartment buildings with electric fans or air conditioning. However, they frequently shop in traditional open-air markets called **bazaars.**

Many people move to the cities from rural areas. They hope to find a better education and jobs. As a result, Cairo is very crowded. There are traffic jams and housing shortages. Some people live in tents that they have set up on boats on the Nile. Others live in homes they have built in the huge cemeteries on the outskirts of Cairo. Overcrowding in Egypt's cities has even affected agriculture. Some farmland has been lost because people have built on it instead of farming on it.

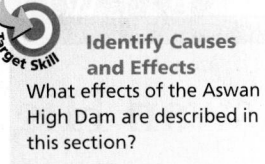

Target Skill Identify Causes and Effects What effects of the Aswan High Dam are described in this section?

Outdoor Markets
At a bazaar in Cairo, people buy goods from vendors who set up stands beneath umbrellas along the streets. **Contrast** How do you think open-air markets are different from indoor shopping centers?

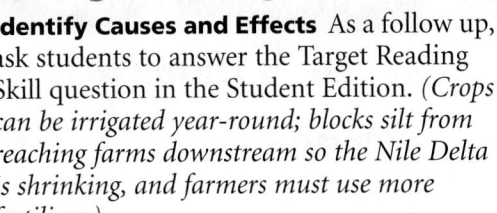

Identify Causes and Effects As a follow up, ask students to answer the Target Reading Skill question in the Student Edition. (*Crops can be irrigated year-round; blocks silt from reaching farms downstream so the Nile Delta is shrinking, and farmers must use more fertilizer.*)

Daily Life in Egypt L2

Guided Instruction

- **Vocabulary Builder** Clarify the meaning of the high-use words **densely** and **shortage** before reading.

- Have students read Daily Life in Egypt. Circulate to make sure students can answer the reading check question.

- Ask **What are the advantages and disadvantages of living in the city and in the countryside in Egypt?** (*City: advantages—more jobs, better education; disadvantages—traffic jams, housing shortages; Countryside: advantages—less crowded, more housing; disadvantages—scarce farmland, fewer jobs, less education*)

Independent Practice
Have students complete the column entitled *Daily Life in Egypt* with information from their reading.

Monitor Progress

- Show *Section Reading Support Transparency AF 45* and ask students to check their graphic organizers individually. Go over key concepts and clarify key vocabulary as needed.

  All in One **Africa Transparencies,** *Section Reading Support Transparency AF 45*

- Tell students to fill in the last column of the *Reading Readiness Guide*. Ask them to evaluate if what they learned was what they had expected to learn.

  All in One **Africa Teaching Resources,** *Reading Readiness Guide*, p. 252

Answer
Contrast Possible answer: In an open-air market, sellers must protect their goods from different kinds of weather and must remove their goods and stalls at night, unlike in a shopping center.

Skills Mini Lesson

Supporting a Position

1. Teach the skill by explaining how to use reasons and evidence to support a position.

2. Help students practice the skill by supporting this position: "The Nile River helps all Egyptians." (*Sample reason: supplies water to cities; evidence: nearly half of Egyptians live in Cairo.*)

3. Have students apply the skill by supporting the position, "Overcrowded cities hurt the entire nation of Egypt." (*Sample reason: Cities take over farmland; evidence: farmland in Egypt is decreasing.*)

Aswan High Dam

Guided Instruction L2

Have students read the text and study the diagrams, labels, photo, and captions on this page. Together with a partner, have students discuss their answer to the Analyzing Images question.

Independent Practice

Working together with a partner, have students use clay or another medium of their choice to construct a model of the Aswan High Dam with identifying labels. Tell students they should use the diagrams in the Student Edition to help them in constructing and labeling their models.

Aswan High Dam

The Aswan High Dam is one of the modern world's greatest engineering projects. A force of 30,000 workers labored for ten years to build the dam out of layers of rock, clay, and cement. The dam serves three major purposes: it controls flooding, it provides electricity, and it supplies water for crops and drinking year-round.

A View From Above
Located on the Nile River near Aswan, Egypt, the dam created the world's third-largest reservoir—Lake Nasser. The lake is 310 miles (500 kilometers) long.

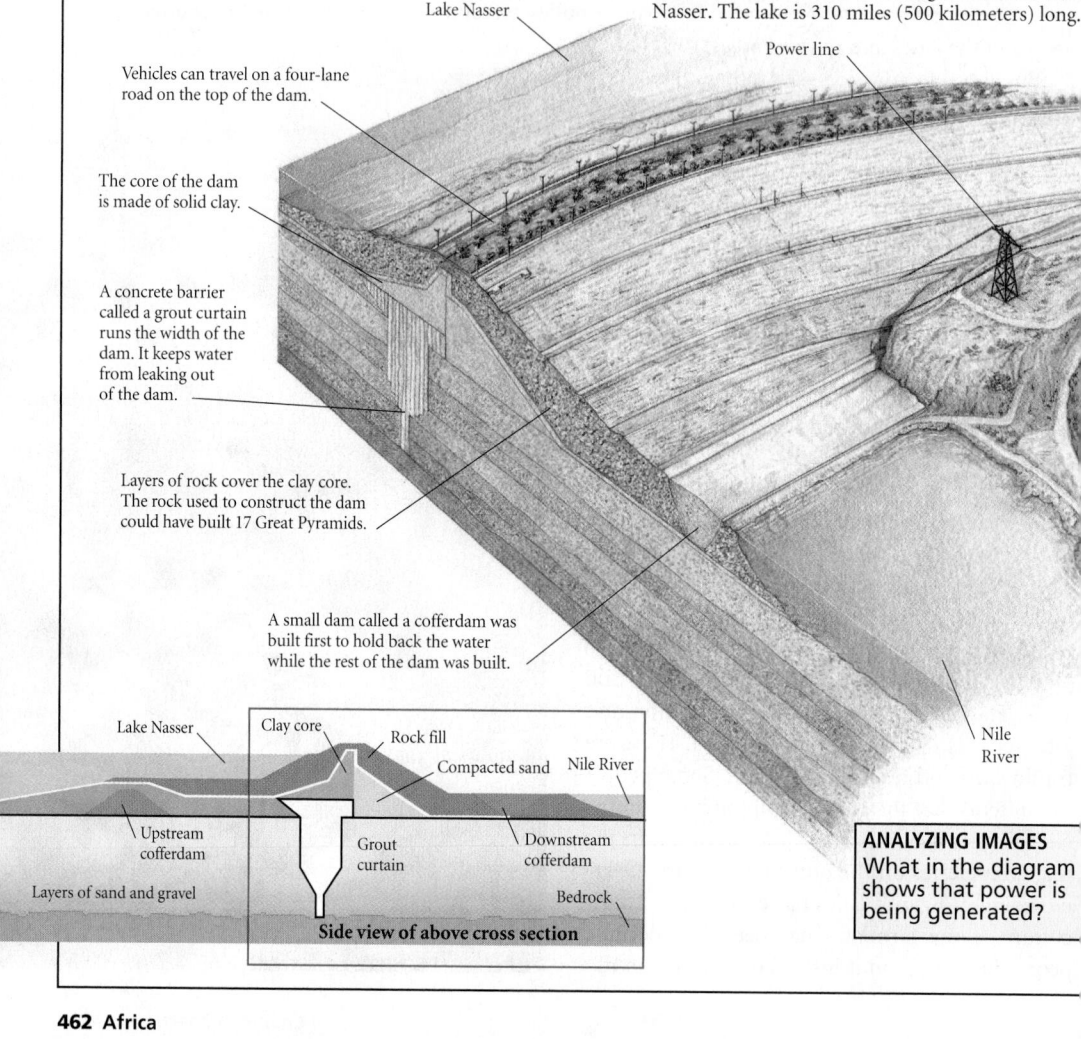

Lake Nasser

Vehicles can travel on a four-lane road on the top of the dam.

The core of the dam is made of solid clay.

A concrete barrier called a grout curtain runs the width of the dam. It keeps water from leaking out of the dam.

Layers of rock cover the clay core. The rock used to construct the dam could have built 17 Great Pyramids.

A small dam called a cofferdam was built first to hold back the water while the rest of the dam was built.

Power line

Nile River

Lake Nasser — Clay core — Rock fill — Compacted sand — Nile River

Upstream cofferdam — Grout curtain — Downstream cofferdam

Layers of sand and gravel — Bedrock

Side view of above cross section

ANALYZING IMAGES
What in the diagram shows that power is being generated?

462 Africa

Differentiated Instruction

For Advanced Readers L3

Have students do research in the library or on the Internet to find the world's five largest dams. Then have them create a table which identifies the name of each dam, where it is located, its size, and when construction on it began and was completed.

Answer

ANALYZING IMAGES power lines

Rural Life Most of the people in Egypt's rural areas live in villages along the banks of the Nile River or in the Nile Delta region. In Egyptian villages, most of the people make their living by farming. Egypt's rural farmers are called **fellaheen** (fel uh HEEN). Most of the fellaheen do not own the land they farm. Good farmland is scarce because the riverbanks are so narrow. Some fellaheen farm small rented plots of land. Others work in the fields of rich landowners.

Many of the fellaheen live in homes built of mud bricks or of stones. Most of these homes are small. They may have from one to three rooms and a courtyard, which the family often shares with its animals. The roofs of the houses are typically flat. Therefore, the fellaheen can use their roofs as places to store food and firewood, to spread dates or other fruits out to dry, and to dry their laundry after washing it.

Learn about farming along the Nile in Egypt.

Fellaheen working near the Great Pyramids at Giza

√ **Reading Check** What land do the fellaheen farm?

Section 1 Assessment

Key Terms
Review the key terms at the beginning of this section. Use each term in a sentence that explains its meaning.

Target Reading Skill
Many Egyptians are Muslim. What are two effects that Islam has had on life in Egypt?

Comprehension and Critical Thinking
1. (a) Recall Describe Egypt's location.

(b) Identify Cause and Effect How did location affect the spread of Islam into North Africa?
(c) Draw Conclusions In what ways does Islam influence Egyptian culture?
2. (a) Identify Where do most people in Egypt live?
(b) Compare How do the lives of city dwellers compare with the lives of villagers in Egypt?
(c) Analyze What is the importance of the Nile River to the people of Egypt?

Writing Activity
Write a letter from the point of view of a rural Egyptian visiting Cairo for the first time. You may want to include observations of things that a rural person would find unfamiliar or familiar.

For: An activity on Egypt
Visit: PHSchool.com
Web Code: lad-5401

Section 1 Assessment

Key Terms
Students' sentences should reflect knowledge of each Key Term.

Target Reading Skill **L2**
Possible answers: how people dress, when they eat, when they pray, their education, the nation's laws.

Comprehension and Critical Thinking
1. (a) Egypt is the easternmost country in North Africa. **(b)** Muhammad, the founder of Islam, was from Saudi Arabia, just across the Red Sea from Egypt. **(c)** Islam affects how people dress, when they eat, when they pray, their education, and the nation's laws.

2. (a) along the Nile River or in the Nile Delta **(b)** City life is very crowded, but more modern than rural life. **(c)** The Nile is Egypt's source of water for people and crops.

Writing Activity
Use the *Rubric for Assessing a Letter to the Editor* to evaluate students' editorials.

All in One **Africa Teaching Resources,**
Rubric for Assessing a Letter to the Editor, p. 277

Go Online PHSchool.com Typing in the Web code when prompted will bring students directly to detailed instructions for this activity.

Assess and Reteach

Assess Progress **L2**
Have students complete the Section Assessment. Administer the *Section Quiz.*

All in One **Africa Teaching Resources,**
Section Quiz, p. 254

Reteach **L1**
If students need more instruction, have them read this section in the Reading and Vocabulary Study Guide.

Chapter 14, Section 1, **Eastern Hemisphere Reading and Vocabulary Study Guide,** pp. 161–163

Extend **L3**
Have students complete the *Enrichment* activity about the architecture of a mosque. Students may use *Writing to Describe* to help them write their paragraphs.

All in One **Africa Teaching Resources,**
Enrichment, p. 262; *Writing to Describe,* p. 274

Answers

√ **Reading Check** They farm either small rented plots or the fields of rich landowners.

Show students *Egypt: The Nile and the Fellaheen.* Ask **How have the fellaheen contributed to Egyptian life over the course of the nation's history?** (*Their methods of farming and harvesting helped build Egypt's wealth and power.*)

Objective

Learn how to distinguish fact and opinion.

Prepare to Read

Build Background Knowledge

L2

Write the following statement on the board: "Geography is the most important subject to learn in school." Ask students **Do you think this statement is true or false? How can it be proved?** Use the Numbered Heads participation strategy (TE p. T36) to elicit student responses.

Instruct

Distinguishing Fact and Opinion

L2

Guided Instruction

- Read the steps to distinguish fact and opinion as a class and write them on the board.

- Practice the skill by following the steps on p. 464 as a class. Model each step in the activity using the following statement: "My name is Ibrahim, and I have lived in Cairo all of my life. Cairo is the capital of Egypt, and about six million people live there. I think that Cairo is the best place to live in all of Egypt."

- Have students identify the facts (*Cairo is the capital of Egypt; about six million people live there.*), tell how they could check whether the facts are true (*by checking in an encyclopedia or other reliable source*), look for opinions (*I think that Cairo is the best place to live.*) Ask whether the opinion is supported by facts or good reasons. (*Possible answer: No; Ibrahim has only lived in Cairo. He has not experienced living in any other places in Egypt.*)

Skills for Life

Distinguishing Fact and Opinion

When Aretha got to class, she looked at the chalkboard. Every day, Mr. Copeland began class by writing a discussion topic on the board. On this day, he had written,

Life in Egyptian cities is better than life in rural Egypt.

Aretha wondered how someone decided this and raised her hand. "That statement doesn't tell the whole story! Whose life is it referring to? Are they wealthy or poor? And when did they live?"

Mr. Copeland smiled. "Exactly, Aretha! The statement cannot be proved. It's somebody's opinion."

Distinguishing between fact and opinion is something you need to do almost every day. Doing it helps you reach your own decisions about what you read, see, or hear.

Learn the Skill

To distinguish fact and opinion, use the following steps.

1 **Look for facts by asking what can be proved true or false.** A fact usually tells who, what, when, where, or how much.

2 **Ask how you could check whether each fact is true.** Could you do your own test, such as measuring or counting, or could you find information in a reliable source, such as an encyclopedia?

3 **Look for opinions by identifying personal beliefs or value judgments.** An opinion cannot be proved true *or* false. Look for words that signal personal feelings, such as *I think*. Look for words that judge, such as *better* and *worse* or *should* and *ought to*.

4 **Ask whether each opinion is supported by facts or good reasons.** A well-supported opinion can help you make up your own mind—as long as you recognize it as an opinion and not a fact.

464 Africa

Independent Practice

- Have students do the Practice the Skill activity on p. 465 in groups of two or three.

- Assign *Skills for Life* and have students complete it individually.

All in One **Africa Teaching Resources,** *Skills for Life*, p. 263

Monitor Progress

As students are completing *Skills for Life*, circulate to make sure individuals are applying the skill steps effectively. Provide assistance as needed.

Practice the Skill

Read the letter below from an American student who is traveling in Egypt with her father. Then use the following steps to analyze the letter for facts and opinions.

1 Identify the facts given about the writer's father.

2 Explain how each fact could be proved true or false.

3 Identify statements within the letter that express opinions. Explain whether each opinion signals a personal feeling or a judgment.

4 Which opinion in the letter do you think has the best factual support?

Dear Brenda,

    I'm sure my dad will help you with your report on ancient Egypt. He has spent years researching the Valley of Kings, where many ancient Egyptian tombs have been found. Scientists like my dad have learned a lot about ancient Egypt because it had a system of writing, called hieroglyphics. Nobody knows more about hieroglyphics than my dad!

    If you could visit while we are here, I know my dad would take you into places that most tourists don't get to see. You would be amazed to see the magnificent tombs. Grave robbers stole many of the mummies and much of the furniture from the tombs. The tomb paintings, which are still there, are unbelievably beautiful. Dad says that the bright colors have faded over time. But I still love looking at them and thinking of how those people lived. You would enjoy it, too, since you like ancient history so much. Please think about coming!

                          Your friend,
                          Dominique

Egyptian hieroglyphs

Apply the Skill

Find the editorial page of a daily newspaper. Read through the editorials and select one that interests you. List several facts and several opinions from the editorial. Can the facts be proved? Are the opinions well supported? Explain what you find.

Differentiated Instruction

For Special Needs Students   **L1**

Partner special needs students with more proficient students to do Level 1 of the Distinguishing Fact and Opinion lesson on the Social Studies Skill Tutor CD-ROM together. When students feel more confident, they can move onto Level 2 alone.

  ⊙ *Distinguishing Fact and Opinion,* **Social Studies Skill Tutor CD-ROM**

Assess and Reteach

Assess Progress   **L2**

Ask students to do the Apply the Skill activity.

Reteach   **L1**

If students are having trouble applying the skill steps, have them review the skill using the interactive Social Studies Skills Tutor CD-ROM.

  ⊙ *Distinguishing Fact and Opinion,* **Social Studies Skills Tutor CD-ROM**

Extend   **L3**

Have students reread pp. 461 and 463 about city and rural life in Egypt. Then divide the class into pairs, and have each student write a journal entry. One student in the pair should write a journal entry as a city resident and the other as a rural resident. Tell students to include both facts and opinions in their journal entries. When they have finished, have each pair trade journal entries with each other, and then underline the facts and circle the opinions in each entry.

Answer
Apply the Skill

Answers will vary, but students should identify facts and opinions in the editorial, and explain how the facts can be proven and whether or not the opinions are well supported.

Objectives

Social Studies
1. Learn about the history and people of Algeria.
2. Find out about life in Algeria's different geographic regions.
3. Examine life in Algeria today.

Reading/Language Arts
Look for signal words that help point out relationships among ideas or events.

Prepare to Read

Build Background Knowledge L2
Discuss with students the ways in which they use water every day *(drinking, cooking, washing)*. Have them think of how their lives would be different if they did not have easy access to water, as is the case in many parts of Algeria. Conduct an Idea Wave (TE, p. T35) to generate a list of ways that Algeria's dry weather and landscape might differ from students' local weather and landscape.

Set a Purpose for Reading L2
■ Preview the Objectives.

■ Read each statement in the *Reading Readiness Guide* aloud. Ask students to mark the statements true or false.

■ Have students discuss the statements in pairs or groups of four, then mark their worksheets again. Use the Numbered Heads participation strategy (TE, p. T36) to call on students to share their group's perspectives.

All in One **Africa Teaching Resources,**
Reading Readiness Guide, p. 256

Vocabulary Builder
Preview Key Terms L2
Pronounce each Key Term, then ask the students to say the word with you. Provide a simple explanation such as, "A souq is an outdoor shopping area."

Prepare to Read

Objectives
In this section you will
1. Learn about the history and people of Algeria.
2. Find out about life in Algeria's different geographic regions.
3. Examine life in Algeria today.

Taking Notes
As you read, find details about Algeria's past and present. Copy the outline below, and use it to record your findings.

> I. Algeria's history and people
>   A. Algeria's past
>   1.
>   2.
>   B.
> II.

 **Target Reading Skill**

Use Signal Words Signal words point out the relationships among ideas or events. To help identify the causes and the effects described in this section, look for words like *because, influence,* or *for that reason* that signal a cause or an effect.

Key Terms
- **souq** (sook) *n.* an open-air marketplace in an Arab city
- **casbah** (KAHZ bah) *n.* an old, crowded section of a North African city
- **terrace** (TEHR us) *n.* a flat platform of earth cut into the side of a slope, used for growing crops in steep places

An Algerian desert home

The Sahara covers all of Algeria south of the Atlas Mountains, which cross the northern portion of Algeria from east to west. Water is in short supply in Algeria's desert lands. For that reason, fewer than 3 percent of Algeria's people live there. Because so much of Algeria is desert, more than 90 percent of Algerians live near the coast, where the weather is milder than in the Sahara.

Algeria's Mediterranean coast, its mountains, and its great desert lands are all part of the country's rich history. Algerians live in modern cities, in rural areas, and in the harsh desert. Geography, history, and culture all influence the way people live in Algeria today.

Algeria's History and People

Algeria has had a long and eventful history. Its Mediterranean location provided easy access to the markets of Europe. Algeria has also participated in trade with other parts of Africa for hundreds of years. Because of its location and resources, Algeria has been a treasure both to its people and to foreign invaders.

 **Target Reading Skill** L2

Use Signal Words Point out the Target Reading Skill. Tell students that when they read, they should look for signal words that point out the cause-and-effect relationships between ideas or events.

Model using signal words by reading the following sentence on this page: "Geography, history, and culture all influence the way people live in Algeria today." Help them identify the signal word (influence) and explain that this word helps them identify the relationship between geography, history, culture, and the way people live in Algeria today.

Give students *Recognize Cause-and-Effect Signal Words*. Have them complete the activity in their groups.

All in One **Africa Teaching Resources,**
Recognize Cause-and-Effect Signal Words, p. 260

Early Foreign Occupations Parts of Algeria have long been occupied by outside groups. The earliest known invaders were the Phoenicians (fuh NISH unz), who were sea traders from the region of present-day Lebanon. The Phoenicians were attracted to Algeria's coast as early as two to three thousand years ago. With help from the Berbers, a North African ethnic group, the Phoenicians set up a trading post on the site of Algiers (al JEERZ). Today, Algiers is the capital of Algeria.

In the A.D. 100s, the Romans invaded Algeria. Berber farmers paid Roman taxes in grain and rented their land from Roman nobles. In the A.D. 600s, Arabs began to spread across North Africa. The Arabs conquered North Africa gradually, over hundreds of years. As a result, the Berber way of life began to change. For example, peace came to the region only after most Berbers accepted the religion of Islam.

Recent Occupations At different times, Algeria's valuable port cities have been commanded by the Spanish, by local pirates, and by the Ottoman Turks. In 1830, the French captured Algiers. The capture resulted in a long period of French colonial rule. Algeria gained independence from France in 1962.

Algeria's People Today, about 75 percent of Algeria's population is Arab, about 24 percent is Berber, and most of the rest is of European descent. Arabs and Berbers alike are Muslim, but many Berbers have combined Islam with their own traditional religious beliefs.

Arabic, several Berber languages, and French are the country's main languages. Many Algerians speak more than one of these languages. Arabic and Tamazight (TAHM uh zyt), a Berber language, are the country's two official languages.

✓ **Reading Check** What foreign influences have been felt in Algeria?

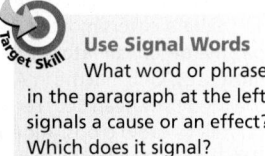
Use Signal Words
What word or phrase in the paragraph at the left signals a cause or an effect? Which does it signal?

City on the Sea
The city of Algiers sits on hills overlooking a bay in the Mediterranean Sea. It has long served as one of Algeria's main ports.
Draw Conclusion Why do you think the Phoenicians chose the site of Algiers for a trading post?

Chapter 14 Section 2 **467**

Vocabulary Builder

Use the information below to teach students this section's high-use words.

High-Use Word	Definition and Sample Sentence
occupy, p. 467	*v.* to take possession of Germany **occupied** France during World War II.
gradually, p. 467	*adv.* developing in small steps The leaves **gradually** changed from green to yellow during the fall.
feature, p. 469	*v.* to have as a characteristic part The new classroom **featured** ten new computers for the students to use.
previous, p. 470	*adj.* occurring earlier This new car is much better than the **previous** one.

Guided Instruction

- **Vocabulary Builder** Clarify the words **occupy** and **gradually** before reading.

- Have students read Algeria's History and People, using the ReQuest strategy (TE, p. T35).

- Ask **Who are the Berbers?** *(an ethnic group that has lived in North Africa since at least 3000 B.C.)*

- Ask **How have outside groups affected the Berbers in Algeria?** *(Phoenicians helped found Algiers, Arabs brought Islam and the Arabic language, and the French brought the French language.)*

- Have students discuss what elements of Algeria's history are reflected in Algerian culture today. *(Seventy-five percent of Algerians are Arab, 24 percent are Berbers, most of the remaining people are of European descent; Berbers have combined the religion of Islam with their own traditional beliefs; Arabic, several Berber languages, and French are the main languages.)*

Independent Practice

Ask students to create the Taking Notes graphic organizer on a blank piece of paper. Briefly model how to fill in the organizer with appropriate details from the section, using the *Outline* transparency.

📖 **Africa Transparencies,** *Transparency B15: Outline*

Monitor Progress

As students fill in their outlines, circulate to make sure individuals are choosing the correct details. Provide assistance as necessary.

🎯 Target Reading Skill L2

Use Signal Words As a follow up, ask students to answer the Target Reading Skill question in the Student Edition. *(word: result; signal: an effect)*

Answers

Draw Conclusions It had easy access to the Mediterranean Sea.

✓ **Reading Check** Phoenicians, Romans, Arabs, Spanish, local pirates, Ottoman Turks, and the French have all influenced Algeria.

Guided Instruction `L2`

Have students study the Country Profile on this page, making sure they pay attention to the map and charts. As a class, answer the Map and Chart Skills questions. Allow students to briefly discuss their responses with a partner before sharing answers.

Independent Practice

- Tell students to review the country profile of Egypt on p. 460. Have them compare the information on both countries.

- Working in pairs, have students write down the answers to the following questions: What similarities do you notice in population density between the two countries? (*It is higher near sources of water, such as the Mediterranean Sea and the Nile River.*) What similarities do you notice in agricultural land use between the two countries? (*Only a small percentage of land in both countries is used for agriculture.*) Why do both countries have only a small percentage of land used for agriculture? (*Possible answer: Both have limited sources of water and are largely covered with deserts that are unsuitable for agriculture.*)

Answers

Map and Chart Skills

1. November, December, and January
2. The Sahara covers most of Algeria, and its climate is unsuitable for agriculture.
3. because the climate near the Mediterranean Sea is milder than in the harsh Sahara to the south

---

COUNTRY PROFILE   Focus on **Geography**

Algeria

Both the climate and the physical geography of Algeria vary from place to place. The climate is very different in the south, where the Sahara lies, and along the Mediterranean coast of the north. The Sahara covers most of Algeria's land, but the desert climate is too harsh for most uses. Only northern Algeria, near the Mediterranean Sea, receives enough rainfall to grow crops. Algeria's population is concentrated in the north, in a narrow band of cities and farmland. Study the map and charts to learn more about Algeria's geography.

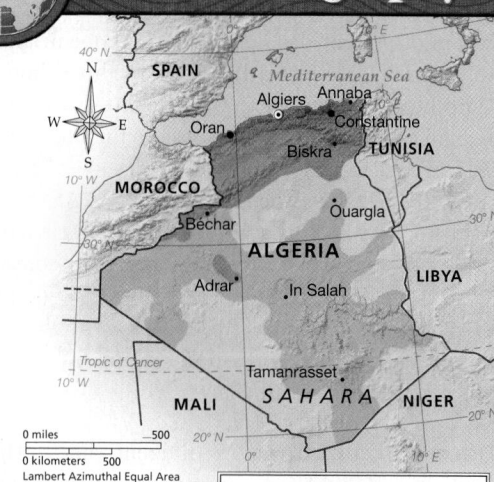

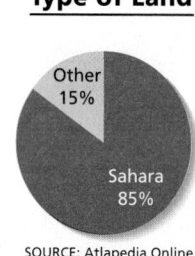

Type of Land

- Other 15%
- Sahara 85%

SOURCE: Atlapedia Online

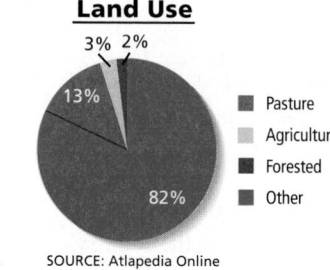

Land Use

- 3% 2%
- 13%
- 82%

Key:
- Pasture
- Agricultural
- Forested
- Other

SOURCE: Atlapedia Online

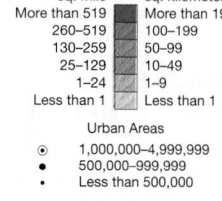

Algeria: Population Density
KEY

Persons per sq. mile	Persons per sq. kilometer
More than 519	More than 199
260–519	100–199
130–259	50–99
25–129	10–49
1–24	1–9
Less than 1	Less than 1

Urban Areas
- ⊙ 1,000,000–4,999,999
- • 500,000–999,999
- · Less than 500,000

— National border
--- Disputed border

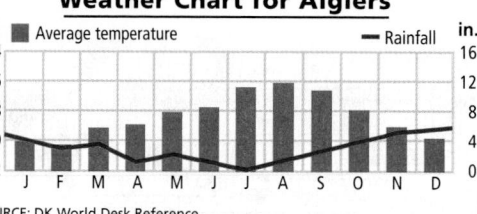

Weather Chart for Algiers

- Average temperature
- Rainfall

SOURCE: DK World Desk Reference

Map and Chart Skills

1. **Identify** In which three months does Algiers receive the greatest amount of rainfall?
2. **Draw Conclusions** Why do you think such a small percent of Algeria's land is used for agriculture?
3. **Synthesize Information** Why do most Algerians live near the Mediterranean Sea?

Use Web Code **lae-5402** for **DK World Desk Reference Online.**

Differentiated Instruction

For Less Proficient Readers `L1`

To help students understand the locations in the chapter, distribute the *North Africa* outline map. As students read, have them label the countries, and shade and label the area of the Sahara.

All in One **Africa Teaching Resources,** *Outline Map 22: North Africa,* p. 269

Algeria's Geography

Most Algerians live in the country's coastal region, called the Tell. Algeria's best farmland is located in this region, as are most of its cities. More than half of Algeria's people live in cities.

Urban Living Many of the Algerians who live in cities are Arab, while some of them are Berber. At the heart of the cities are mosques and open-air marketplaces called **souqs** (sooks). In these souqs, merchants sell food, traditional crafts, and a variety of other goods from their stalls. Older parts of the cities are called **casbahs** (KAHZ bahz). The houses and stores in the casbahs are close together. Children play outside on the narrow, winding streets. Newer parts of the cities are modern, with wide streets and tall buildings made of steel and glass.

Rural Areas Most Berbers and many Arabs live in the countryside. Although the farmland tends to be of poor quality, about one third of Algerians are farmers. Algeria's farmers grow wheat and barley and raise livestock. In the mountains, they build **terraces,** or flat platforms of earth cut into a slope, one above another, for their crops. The terraces increase the amount of farmland and prevent the soil from washing away in the rain.

Traditionally, Algerians live with their extended families. In both urban and rural areas, homes feature several rooms with high walls surrounding an inner courtyard. Family members gather in the courtyard, which might have a garden or fountain.

Desert Dwellers Algeria is more than 80 percent desert. Among the small number of Algerians living in the desert, most settle in oasis towns, where water is available. There, people grow dates or citrus fruits.

Some people who live in the desert work for companies that produce oil and natural gas, Algeria's two main resources. Other desert dwellers are nomads, herding camels and other livestock suited to the climate. Like people in many parts of the world, these nomadic Algerians adapt to their climate by resting during the hottest hours of the day. By being resourceful, Berber and Arab nomads are able to survive the harsh desert conditions.

✓ **Reading Check** How do Algerian desert dwellers make a living?

Finding Land to Farm
Much work goes into building terraces for farming, but the benefits are enormous in areas that are hilly or mountainous. Here, Algerian farmers work the fields below a terraced hillside. **Compare** *How do you think farming on flat land is different from farming on terraced hillsides?*

Learn how people farm in a desert oasis.

Chapter 14 Section 2 **469**

Algeria's Geography L2
Algeria Today L2

Guided Instruction

- **Vocabulary Builder** Clarify the high-use words **feature** and **previous** before reading.

- Have students read Algeria's Geography and Algeria Today. As students read, circulate to make sure they can answer the Reading Check questions.

- Ask **Where do most Algerians live?** *(in a coastal area called the Tell)* **Why do you think so many live there?** *(The country's best farmland and most of its cities are in this region.)*

- Have students compare some of the different ways people make a living in urban, rural, and desert areas of Algeria. *(Urban—merchants sell food, traditional crafts and other goods from stalls; rural—farmers grow crops and raise livestock; desert—people grow dates or citrus fruits, work for companies that produce oil and natural gas, and herd camels and other livestock.)*

- Discuss the modern and traditional aspects of family life in Algeria today. *(Modern—young, urban families having fewer children and living in smaller family groups; Traditional—importance of family, extended families living together, gender roles.)*

- Discuss how the students' educational system compares to Algeria's system. *(Answers will vary but should compare legal requirements, differences between rural and urban areas, ages, languages, and university attendance.)*

Show students *The Sahara: Fruits of the Oasis.* Ask **How has Algeria become one of the largest date producers in Africa?** *(Desert oases provide water to crops through wells, called foggaras, allowing farmers to grow large date crops.)*

Answers

Compare Possible answer: farming on terraced hillsides poses more difficulties, such as reduced access to machinery.

✓ **Reading Check** Algerian desert dwellers farm in oasis towns, work in the oil and gas industry, or herd livestock.

Chapter 14 Section 2 **469**

Independent Practice

Have students complete their graphic organizers with details about Algeria's cities, rural areas, and deserts, and life in Algeria today.

Monitor Progress

- Show the *Section Reading Support Transparency AF 46* and ask students to check their graphic organizers individually. Go over key concepts and clarify key vocabulary as needed.

  Africa Transparencies, *Section Reading Support Transparency AF 46*

- Tell students to fill in the last column of the *Reading Readiness Guide.* Probe for what they learned that confirms or invalidates each statement.

  All in One Africa Teaching Resources, *Reading Readiness Guide,* p. 256

Assess and Reteach

Assess Progress   L2

Have students complete the Section Assessment. Administer the *Section Quiz.*

All in One Africa Teaching Resources, *Section Quiz,* p. 258

Reteach   L1

If students need more instruction, have them read this section in the Reading and Vocabulary Study Guide.

Chapter 14, Section 2, **Eastern Hemisphere Reading and Vocabulary Study Guide,** pp. 164–166

Extend   L3

Ask students to suppose they are traveling through Algeria today. Have them write a letter or postcard to a friend back home, describing the people and places they have seen. You may want to distribute *Writing to Describe* to help students get started.

All in One Africa Teaching Resources, *Writing to Describe,* p. 274

Answer

✓ **Reading Check** Arabic

Section 2 Assessment

Key Terms

Students' sentences should reflect knowledge of each Key Term.

Target Reading Skill

Signal Words: result, resulted

470 *Africa*

An Algerian family

Algeria Today

Throughout the long periods of outside rule, native Algerians preserved many of their traditions. For example, while French was Algeria's official language, many people kept Arabic and Berber languages alive in their homes. Today, Algerians continue to express their customs and traditions.

Modern Home Life In both urban and rural areas, Algerians continue to value family. Many Algerians live with their extended families. However, young couples in urban areas are having fewer children than people did in previous generations. Urban Algerians also tend to live in smaller family groups.

Educating Algeria's Youth While under French rule, few non-European children received a good formal education. Since gaining independence, the Algerian government has worked hard to improve education for its children and young people. Most instruction is in Arabic. Children from ages 6 to 15 are required by law to attend school. Attendance is high in city schools but is lower in rural areas. New universities have been built to educate Algeria's young people. Some students attend colleges in other countries.

 ✓ **Reading Check** Which language is used in most Algerian classrooms today?

Section 2 Assessment

Key Terms
Review the key terms at the beginning of this section. Use each term in a sentence that explains its meaning.

🎯 Target Reading Skill
Review the section Algeria's History and People on pages 466 and 467. Find the words that signal causes or effects related to the foreign occupation of Algeria.

Comprehension and Critical Thinking
1. (a) Name What foreign groups have played a role in the history of Algeria?

(b) Explain What roles did Arabs and Berbers play in the history of Algeria?

2. (a) Identify In which geographic area do most Algerians live?

(b) Compare and Contrast Compare life for Algerians living in urban, rural, and desert areas. How are their lives similar? How are they different?

3. (a) Recall Describe education in Algeria today.

(b) Draw Conclusions What do you think is the importance of the language that is spoken in schools?

Writing Activity
Write an interview that you could conduct with someone living in Algeria today. Think of five questions you would like to ask this person. Try to ask questions that cover a number of different topics.

> **Writing Tip** Try to avoid questions that could be answered with a *yes* or a *no.* Questions that begin with words such as *why* or *how* often lead to more interesting answers.

Comprehension and Critical Thinking
1. (a) Phoenecians, Romans, Spanish, Ottoman, Turks, Arabs and French. **(b)** Berbers have lived in Algeria for thousands of years; they helped found Algiers. Arabs brought Islam and the Arabic language to Algeria beginning around A.D. 600.

2. (a) the Tell **(b)** Similar: family and traditions are important; different: types of housing, ways of earning a living

3. (a) Children ages 6–15 are required to attend school; universities have been built; some students attend college in other countries. **(b)** Possible answer: it provides a common language for all of the students and helps contribute to a sense of community.

Writing Activity
Use the *Rubric for Assessing a Writing Assignment* to evaluate students' interviews.

All in One Africa Teaching Resources, *Rubric for Assessing a Writing Assignment,* p. 278

Review and Assessment

◆ Chapter Summary

Section 1: Egypt
- Islam influences many parts of daily life in Egypt, including daily practices and the country's laws.
- Most of Egypt's population is centered along the Nile River, the country's main source of water in both urban and rural areas.

Cairo, Egypt

Section 2: Algeria
- At times over thousands of years, a variety of foreign groups have occupied Algeria.
- Most Algerians live in modern cities or in rural areas. A small number of Algerians, however, live in the desert.
- Family and education are both valued by Algerians today.

Algerian desert

◆ Key Terms

Each of the statements below contains a key term from the chapter. If the statement is true, write *true*. If it is false, change the highlighted term to make the statement true.

1. A traditional Egyptian open-air market is called a casbah.
2. Egypt's rural farmers are called fellaheen.
3. Souqs are platforms cut into the side of a slope.
4. Islamic law is called Cairo.
5. In Algeria, open-air markets may be called terraces.
6. The old section of Algiers is called the bazaar.
7. Sharia is the capital of Egypt.

Chapter 14 **471**

Vocabulary Builder

Revisit this chapter's high-use words:

minority	shortage	feature
requirement	occupy	previous
densely	gradually	

Ask students to review the definitions they recorded on their *Word Knowledge* worksheets.

All in One Africa Teaching Resources, *Word Knowledge,* p. 261

Consider allowing students to earn extra credit if they use the words in their answers to the questions in the Chapter Review and Assessment. The words must be used correctly and in a natural context to earn the extra points.

Review Chapter Content
- Review and revisit this chapter's themes by asking students to classify what Guiding Question each bulleted statement in the Chapter Summary answers. Form students into groups and ask them to complete the activity together. Refer to p. 349 in the Student Edition for text of the Guiding Questions.

- Assign *Vocabulary Development* for students to review Key Terms.

   All in One Africa Teaching Resources, *Vocabulary Development,* p. 275

Answers

Key Terms
1. False, bazaar
2. True
3. False, terraces
4. False, Sharia
5. False, souqs
6. False, casbah
7. False, Cairo

Comprehension and Critical Thinking

8. (a) fasting during Ramadan, praying five times daily, studying the Quran **(b)** Muslims try to renew their faith by living according to Sharia, or Islamic law.

9. (a) the Nile River **(b)** It helps farms to have a steady supply of water for irrigation; it also blocks silt from reaching farms, leading farmers to use more fertilizers, which pollute the water supply.

10. (a) It is extremely crowded. **(b)** They hope to find jobs and better education. **(c)** traffic jams and housing shortages

11. (a) Algeria's northern coastal area is called the Tell. The Atlas Mountains run east-west across northern Algeria. South of the mountains is part of the Sahara. **(b)** More than 90 percent of Algerians live in the Tell, where the best farmland is located and the weather is milder. This area also has the country's largest cities. People who live in the desert live near oases. **(c)** Its Mediterranean ports facilitated trade, but also made Algeria a tempting target for invaders.

12. (a) Arabic, Berber languages, French **(b)** These languages reflect the original Algerian groups and two outside groups that controlled Algeria in the past.

13. (a) Young urban couples are having fewer children than previous generations had. **(b)** Possible answer: rural Algerians may continue to have a traditional view of family life because their way of life is not changing.

Skills Practice
Answers will vary, but students should list the facts and opinions they found, ways in which the facts can be proven, and whether facts or reasons are given to support each opinion.

◆ Comprehension and Critical Thinking

8. (a) Recall What are some common Islamic religious practices in Egypt?
(b) Analyze Information What is the importance of Sharia to Muslims in Egypt?

9. (a) Identify What is the main source of Egypt's water supply?
(b) Conclude How does the Aswan High Dam affect Egypt's water supply?

10. (a) Describe What is life like in Cairo?
(b) Make Generalizations Why do so many Egyptians move from rural areas to cities such as Cairo?
(c) Identify Effects What are some of the effects of overcrowding in Cairo?

11. (a) Recall Describe the geography of Algeria.
(b) Explain How have people adapted to the geography and climate of Algeria?
(c) Summarize What has been the importance of Algeria's coastal location throughout its history?

12. (a) Identify What languages are spoken in Algeria today?
(b) Apply Information How do these languages reflect the history of Algeria?

13. (a) Explain How has the traditional view of family changed for urban Algerians?
(b) Predict Do you think rural Algerians will change their view of family in a similar way? Explain why or why not.

◆ Skills Practice

Distinguishing Fact and Opinion In the Skills for Life activity in this chapter, you learned how to distinguish fact from opinion.

Review the steps you followed to learn this skill. Next, read a magazine article. List several facts and several opinions that are given in the article. Write down a way that each fact you listed can be proved. Then explain whether facts or reasons are given to support each opinion.

◆ Writing Activity: Science

Do research to learn about how people have used science to help them live in desert climates. Find out about nomadic living as well as life in an oasis town. Write a report describing your findings.

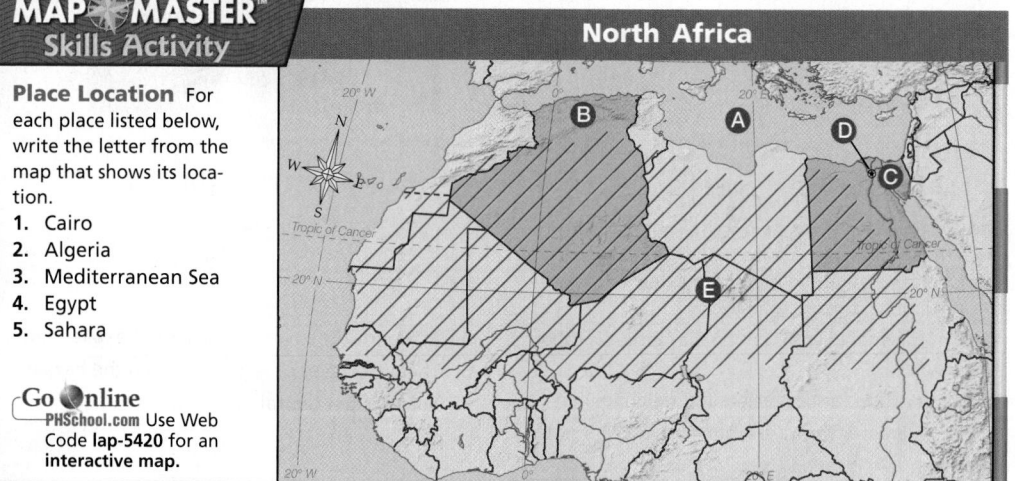

MAP◆MASTER™ Skills Activity

Place Location For each place listed below, write the letter from the map that shows its location.

1. Cairo
2. Algeria
3. Mediterranean Sea
4. Egypt
5. Sahara

Go Online
PHSchool.com Use Web Code **lap-5420** for an interactive map.

North Africa

Writing Activity: Science
Students' reports will vary, but should include information about how people have used science to help them live in desert climates, and what life is like for nomads as well as those who live in oasis towns.

Use the *Rubric for Assessing a Writing Assignment* to evaluate student's reports.

All in One Africa Teaching Resources, *Rubric for Assessing a Writing Assignment,* p. 278

Standardized Test Prep

Test-Taking Tips

Some questions on standardized tests ask you to identify main ideas. Read the paragraph below. Then follow the tips to answer the sample question.

> A Berber household can include grandparents, parents, sons, daughters, and cousins. Family members all share one courtyard. Each married couple within the family has a house that opens onto the courtyard. All the windows of the house face the courtyard. The head of each family is a member of the village assembly that makes village laws.

TIP Some paragraphs have a topic sentence that states the main idea. Every sentence in the paragraph supports this idea.

Pick the letter that best answers the question.

Which topic sentence is missing from this passage?

A The Berbers and the Arabs are Algeria's two main ethnic groups.

B An extended Berber family includes more than just a mother, a father, and children.

C Most Berbers from Algeria live in villages.

D Family is central to every part of Berber village life.

TIP The best way to be sure you have picked the right answer is to read all four answer choices before deciding on one.

Think It Through By reading the paragraph, you will find that every sentence tells about Berber life. You can rule out A because the paragraph is not about Arabs. You can rule out C because the paragraph is not mainly about villages. That leaves B and D. B is about Berber families, but it could be a detail sentence in the paragraph; not all the sentences are about family members. The correct answer is D.

Practice Questions

Use the tips above and other tips in this book to help you answer the following questions. Read the paragraph below to answer Question 1. Choose the letter of the best answer.

> Some desert dwellers work for companies that produce oil and natural gas. Others are nomads who herd camels and other livestock that are suited to the hot, dry climate. Like people in many parts of the world, these Algerians adapt to their climate by resting during the hottest hours of the day.

1. Which topic sentence is missing from the paragraph above?

A Oil and natural gas are Algeria's two most important natural resources.

B Algerians have found ways to work and survive in the desert.

C It is difficult to live in the desert.

D Agriculture and fuel industries thrive in the desert.

2. In Egypt, most people live

A in Cairo.

B in Alexandria.

C in the valley and delta regions of the Nile.

D in the Nile delta region.

3. Which of the following statements is true?

A In Algeria, all Arabs and Berbers are Muslims.

B In Algeria, Arabs and a small percentage of Berbers are Muslims.

C In Egypt, most people are Coptic Christians.

D In Egypt, almost half of the people are Coptic Christians.

Use Web Code laa-5400 for **Chapter 14 self-test.**

Overview

Introducing West Africa
1. Use data to compare countries.
2. Learn what characteristics West African countries share.
3. Identify some key differences among the countries.

The Geography of West Africa
Length: 4 minutes, 31 seconds
Provides an overview of West Africa, including its countries, major cities, and main geographic regions.

Section 1

Nigeria: Land of Diverse Peoples
1. Learn to identify Nigeria's three main ethnic groups.
2. Understand the major events in Nigeria's history.
3. Find out about the conflicts Nigeria faced on its path to democracy.

Nigeria: Can Village Life Survive?
Length: 3 minutes, 33 seconds
Describes how oil drilling and production have affected the environment and people of Nigeria.

Section 2

Ghana: Leading Africa to Independence
1. Learn about the years of British colonial rule in the area that is now called Ghana.
2. Find out about the beliefs that helped move Ghana toward independence.
3. Discover how Ghana changed after achieving independence.

Ghana: Living on the Forest's Edge
Length: 3 minutes, 29 seconds
Explains how local groups are working to save the rain forests in Ghana.

Section 3

Mali: Desert Living
1. Discover how Mali's environment affects its economy.
2. Find out how desert can spread across the land.
3. Learn about the importance of preserving Mali's environment.

Mali: Africa's Grain Basket
Length: 3 minutes, 6 seconds
Explores how life in villages is improving due to new grain-production policies.

Technology Resources

Students use embedded Web codes to access Internet activities, chapter self-tests, and additional map practice. They may also access Dorling Kindersley's Online Desk Reference to learn more about each country they study.

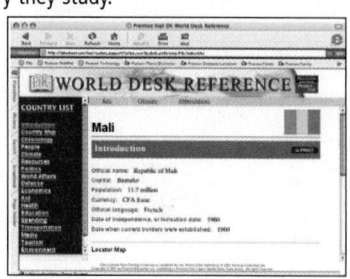

Use the Interactive Textbook to make content and concepts come alive through animations, videos, and activities that accompany the complete basal text—online and on CD-ROM.

Use this complete suite of powerful teaching tools to make planning lessons and administering tests quicker and easier.

Reading and Vocabulary Instruction

🎯 Model the Target Reading Skill

Main Idea Tell students that the main idea is the most important idea in a section. Supporting details are those that give more specific information about the main idea. Write the following paragraph from p. 491 of the Student Edition on the board:

When the British colonized the Gold Coast, their main interest was in controlling the colony's economy. They encouraged farmers to grow cacao, from which cocoa is produced. Once cacao was harvested, the British sent the cocoa to factories in Britain where it was made into chocolate. The British also exported timber and gold.

Help students find the main idea *(the first sentence)*. Have volunteers come to the board and underline the supporting details *(encouraged farmers to grow cocoa; sent the cocoa to factories in Britain; exported timber and gold)*. Ask students how these details support the main idea *(they all describe actions the British took to control the economy of the Gold Coast)*.

Use the following worksheets from All-in-One Africa Teaching Resources (pp. 301–303) to support this chapter's Target Reading Skill.

 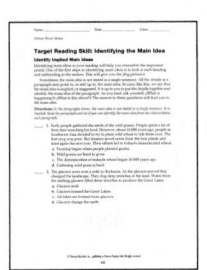 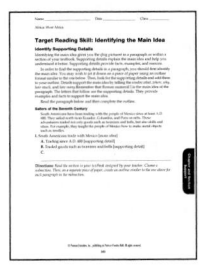

Vocabulary Builder
High-Use Academic Words

Use these steps to teach this chapter's high-use words:

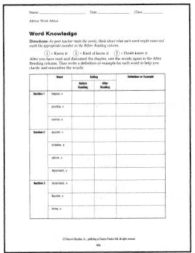

1. Have students rate how well they know each word on their Word Knowledge worksheets (All-in-One Africa Teaching Resources, p. 304).

2. Pronounce each word and ask students to repeat it.

3. Provide a brief definition or sample sentence (provided on TE pp. 485, 491, and 499).

4. Work with students as they fill in the "Definition or Example" column of their Word Knowledge worksheets.

Assessment

Formal Assessment

Test students' understanding of core knowledge and skills.

Chapter Tests A and B, All-in-One Africa Teaching Resources, pp. 323–328

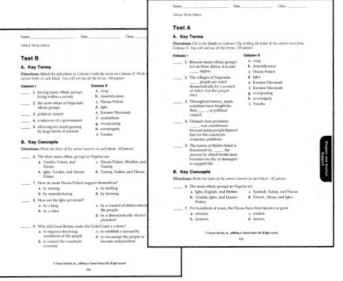

Customize the Chapter Tests to suit your needs.

ExamView Test Bank CD-ROM

Skills Assessment

Assess geographic literacy.

MapMaster Skills, Student Edition, pp. 475, 504

Country Profile Map and Chart Skills, Student Edition, pp. 487, 493, 501

Assess reading and comprehension.

Target Reading Skills, Student Edition, pp. 485, 492, 500, and in Section Assessments

Chapter 15 Assessment, Eastern Hemisphere Reading and Vocabulary Study Guide, p. 177

Performance Assessment

Assess students' performance on this chapter's Writing Activities using the following rubrics from All-in-One Africa Teaching Resources.

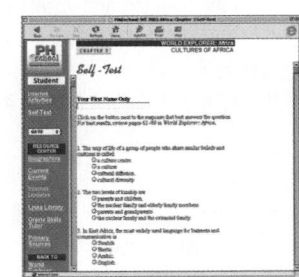

Rubric for Assessing a Newspaper Article, p. 321

Rubric for Assessing a Writing Assignment, p. 322

Assess students' work through performance tasks.

Small Group Activity: Arts and Crafts of West Africa, All-in-One Africa Teaching Resources, pp. 307–310

Portfolio Activity, Teacher Edition, p. 483

Online Assessment

Have students check their own understanding.

Chapter Self-Test

Section 1 Nigeria: Land of Diverse Peoples

 1.5 periods, .75 block (includes Country Databank)

Social Studies Objectives
1. Learn to identify Nigeria's three main ethnic groups.
2. Understand the major events in Nigeria's history.
3. Find out about the conflicts Nigeria faced on its path to democracy.

Reading/Language Arts Objective
Learn how to identify main ideas.

Prepare to Read	**Instructional Resources**	**Differentiated Instruction**
Build Background Knowledge Discuss the challenges of communication between people who speak different languages. **Set a Purpose for Reading** Have students evaluate statements on the *Reading Readiness Guide.* **Preview Key Terms** Teach the section's Key Terms. **Target Reading Skill** Introduce the section's Target Reading Skill of **identifying main ideas.**	**All in One Africa Teaching Resources** L2 Reading Readiness Guide, p. 290 L2 Identify Main Ideas, p. 301	**Spanish Reading and Vocabulary Study Guide** L1 Chapter 15, Section 1, pp. 119–120 ELL **World Studies Video Program** L2 The Geography of West Africa AR, GT, LPR, SN

Instruct	**Instructional Resources**	**Differentiated Instruction**
Target Reading Skill Review **identifying main ideas.** **Ethnic Groups of Nigeria** Discuss different ethnic groups and how they live. **Country Profile** Ask students to derive and use information from maps, charts, and graphs. **Nigeria's History** **The Path to Democracy** Discuss Nigeria's occupation and the challenges that came with independence.	**All in One Africa Teaching Resources** L2 Guided Reading and Review, p. 291 L2 Reading Readiness Guide, p. 290 L2 Reading a Circle Graph, p. 313 **Africa Transparencies** L2 Section Reading Support Transparency AF 47 **World Studies Video Program** L2 Nigeria: Can Village Life Survive?	**All in One Africa Teaching Resources** L3 Outline Map 23: West and Central Africa, p. 316 L3 Enrichment, p. 305 AR, GT L3 Reading a Historical Map, p. 314 AR, GT **Teacher's Edition** L1 For Special Needs Students, TE pp. 477, 488 L1 For Less Proficient Readers, TE pp. 478, 486 L2 For English Language Learners, TE p. 479 L3 For Gifted and Talented, TE pp. 480, 488 L3 For Advanced Readers, TE pp. 481, 486 **Africa Transparencies** L1 Transparency B16: Venn Diagram ELL, LPR, SN **Passport to the World CD-ROM** L1 Nigeria ELL, LPR, SN

Assess and Reteach	**Instructional Resources**	**Differentiated Instruction**
Assess Progress Evaluate student comprehension with the section assessment and section quiz. **Reteach** Assign the Reading and Vocabulary Study Guide to help struggling students. **Extend** Extend the lesson by assigning a Small Group Activity.	**All in One Africa Teaching Resources** L2 Section Quiz, p. 292 L3 Small Group Activity: Arts and Crafts of West Africa, pp. 307–310 Rubric for Assessing a Newspaper Article, p. 321 **Reading and Vocabulary Study Guide** L1 Chapter 15, Section 1, pp. 168–170	**All in One Africa Teaching Resources** Rubric for Assessing a Circle Graph, p. 320 AR, GT, LPR, SN **Spanish Support** L2 Section Quiz (Spanish), p. 161 ELL

Key
L1 Basic to Average   L3 Average to Advanced   LPR Less Proficient Readers   GT Gifted and Talented
L2 For All Students   AR Advanced Readers   ELL English Language Learners
                                              SN Special Needs Students

Section 2 Ghana: Leading Africa to Independence

2 periods, 1 block (includes Skills for Life)

Social Studies Objectives

1. Learn about the years of British colonial rule in the area that is now called Ghana.
2. Find out about the beliefs that helped move Ghana toward independence.
3. Discover how Ghana changed after achieving independence.

Reading/Language Arts Objective

Identify implied main ideas to help you remember the most important ideas that you read.

Prepare to Read

Build Background Knowledge
Show a video and discuss Ghana's most important natural resource.

Set a Purpose for Reading
Have students evaluate statements on the *Reading Readiness Guide.*

Preview Key Terms
Teach the section's Key Terms.

Target Reading Skill
Introduce the section's Target Reading Skill of **identifying implied main ideas.**

Instructional Resources

All in One Africa Teaching Resources
- L2 Reading Readiness Guide, p. 294
- L2 Identify Implied Main Ideas, p. 302

World Studies Video Program
- L2 Ghana: Living on the Forest's Edge

Differentiated Instruction

Spanish Reading and Vocabulary Study Guide
- L1 Chapter 15, Section 2, pp. 121–122 ELL

Instruct

The Colonial Years
Ask questions about British colonization of the Gold Coast.

Target Reading Skill
Review **identifying implied main ideas.**

Moving Toward Independence
Discuss the steps colonies on the Gold Coast took to gain independence.

Country Profile
Ask students to derive and use information from maps, charts, and graphs.

Independence Achieved
Discuss changes in Ghana after independence.

Instructional Resources

All in One Africa Teaching Resources
- L2 Guided Reading and Review, p. 295
- L2 Reading Readiness Guide, p. 294

Africa Transparencies
- L2 Section Reading Support Transparency AF 48

Differentiated Instruction

All in One Africa Teaching Resources
- L3 Reading an Economic Activity Map, p. 315 AR, GT
- L2 Skills for Life, p. 306 AR, GT, LPR, SN

Teacher's Edition
- L3 For Advanced Readers, TE p. 493
- L2 For English Language Learners, TE p. 493

Spanish Support
- L2 Guided Reading and Review (Spanish), p. 162 ELL

Assess and Reteach

Assess Progress
Evaluate student comprehension with the section assessment and section quiz.

Reteach
Assign the Reading and Vocabulary Study Guide to help struggling students.

Extend
Extend the lesson by assigning a research project.

Instructional Resources

All in One Africa Teaching Resources
- L2 Section Quiz, p. 296
  Rubric for Assessing a Writing Assignment, p. 322

Reading and Vocabulary Study Guide
- L1 Chapter 15, Section 2, pp. 171–173

Differentiated Instruction

Spanish Support
- L2 Section Quiz (Spanish), p. 163 ELL

Teacher's Edition
- L1 For Special Needs Students, TE p. 497

Social Studies Skills Tutor CD-ROM
- L1 Decision Making ELL, LPR, SN

Key

- L1 Basic to Average
- L2 For All Students
- L3 Average to Advanced
- LPR Less Proficient Readers
- AR Advanced Readers
- SN Special Needs Students
- GT Gifted and Talented
- ELL English Language Learners

Section 3 Mali: Desert Living

 2.5 periods, 1.25 blocks (includes Chapter Review and Assessment)

Social Studies Objectives

1. Discover how Mali's environment affects its economy.

2. Find out how desert can spread across the land.

3. Learn about the importance of preserving Mali's environment.

Reading/Language Arts Objective

Identify supporting details to get further information about a main idea.

Prepare to Read

Build Background Knowledge
Show a video to introduce students to the importance of farming in Mali.

Set a Purpose for Reading
Have students evaluate statements on the *Reading Readiness Guide.*

Preview Key Terms
Teach the section's Key Terms.

Target Reading Skill
Introduce the section's Target Reading Skill of **identifying supporting details.**

Instructional Resources

All in One Africa Teaching Resources
L2 Reading Readiness Guide, p. 298
L2 Identifying Supporting Details, p. 303

World Studies Video Program
L2 Mali: Africa's Grain Basket

Differentiated Instruction

Spanish Reading and Vocabulary Study Guide
L1 Chapter 15, Section 3, p. 123–124 ELL

Instruct

Mali's Environment
Discuss how the environment influences farming.

Target Reading Skill
Review **identifying supporting details.**

The Desert Spreads
Preserving the Environment
Ask questions about the problem of desertification and possible solutions.

Country Profile
Ask students to derive and use information from maps, charts, and graphs.

Instructional Resources

All in One Africa Teaching Resources
L2 Guided Reading and Review, p. 299
L2 Reading Readiness Guide, p. 298

Africa Transparencies
L2 Section Reading Support Transparency AF 49
L2 Transparency B17: Concept Web

PHSchool.com
L2 **For:** Environmental and Global Issues: Getting Safe Water
Web Code: lad-5505

Differentiated Instruction

All in One Africa Teaching Resources
L3 Activity Shop Lab: Desertification, pp. 311–312 AR, GT
L2 Al-Bakri Describes the Court of Ghana, p. 317 AR, GT, LPR, SN
L2 Ibn Battuta Praises the Fairness of Mali's People, p. 318 AR, GT, LPR, SN

Teacher's Edition
L3 For Gifted and Talented, TE p. 500

Spanish Support
L2 Guided Reading and Review (Spanish), p. 166 ELL

Assess and Reteach

Assess Progress
Evaluate student comprehension with the section assessment and section quiz.

Reteach
Assign the Reading and Vocabulary Study Guide to help struggling students.

Extend
Extend the lesson by assigning an online activity.

Instructional Resources

All in One Africa Teaching Resources
L2 Section Quiz, p. 300
   Rubric for Assessing a Writing Assignment, p. 322
L2 Vocabulary Development, p. 319
   Rubric for Assessing a Newspaper Article, p. 321
L2 Word Knowledge, p. 304
L2 Chapter Tests A and B, pp. 323–328

Reading and Vocabulary Study Guide
L1 Chapter 15, Section 3, pp. 174–176

PHSchool.com
L3 **For:** Long-Term Integrated Projects: Reporting to an Environmental Conference
Web Code: lad-5504

Differentiated Instruction

Spanish Support
L2 Section Quiz (Spanish), p. 165 ELL
L2 Chapter Summary (Spanish), p. 166 ELL
L2 Vocabulary Development (Spanish), p. 167 ELL

Key
L1 Basic to Average   L3 Average to Advanced   LPR Less Proficient Readers   GT Gifted and Talented
L2 For All Students   AR Advanced Readers   ELL English Language Learners
                                                  SN Special Needs Students

Reading Background

Encourage Active Participation

In this chapter, students will use the Think-Write-Pair-Share strategy to develop and share ideas. Explain that it is always acceptable to question a classmate's ideas, but that the approach should be respectful. Below are some sample language strategies students may use to clarify another student's ideas when using Think-Write-Pair-Share:

I don't understand what you mean.
Will you explain that again, please?
I have a question about that.

Questions and Answers

Encourage students to be aware of the fact that there are many different kinds of questions. Questions that require you to:

1. remember a specific fact from the reading
2. synthesize or analyze information from different places in the reading
3. think beyond the reading to make an inference or assumption
4. find the answer somewhere completely outside of the reading

Model this concept by listing the following questions on the board and asking students to state which type of question each is, and where the answer can be found in relation to this chapter.

- What country has the largest population in Africa?
  (Specific fact; Nigeria: page 484)
- What were some advantages and disadvantages of British control of the Gold Coast?
  (Synthesize or analyze; advantages: schools were built, some became wealthy from trade; disadvantages: growing of food crops decreased, dependence on imports: pages 491–492)
- Why might European countries be reluctant to give up their colonies in Africa?
  (Inference or assumption; more colonies meant more land, money, and power: inference from information on pages 491–492)
- How is desertification affecting African countries besides Mali?
  (Outside the reading; could be answered by doing research on the Internet or by reading newspapers or magazines)

After discussing these examples, have students work in teams to develop one question of each type based on the information in each chapter. Challenge students to trade their finished questions with another group and try to identify each type of question and answer it.

World Studies Background

Slave Trade with Africa

The European slave trade began in the fifteenth century when the Portuguese became the first Europeans to reach present-day Nigeria. They purchased captives and agricultural items from Africans along the coast in exchange for European goods. Historians estimate that in the 1700s alone about 5.2 million Africans were sent across the Atlantic Ocean to become slaves in the Americas. In 1807 the British government made the slave trade illegal, but slavery in Africa, and the slave trade, continued for many years.

The Sahel

The Sahel, the semiarid region between the Sahara and the savanna, reaches from the Atlantic Ocean to Sudan. The climate is dry except for the rainy season, which lasts approximately four months. Plants that grow in the Sahel include grass, shrubs, and baobab trees. The Sahel was once forested. Today, the terrain is more open. Cattle, sheep, camels, and oxen are among the livestock raised in the region. Floods by the Niger and Senegal rivers help to water the land, on which crops such as millet and peanuts are raised.

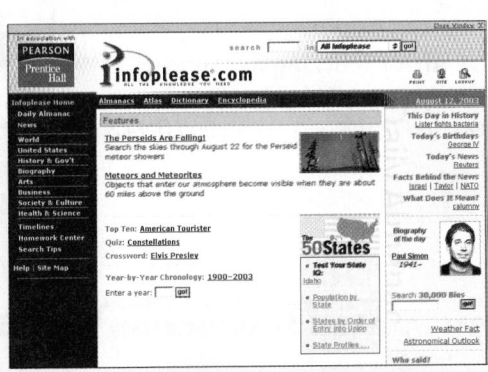

Infoplease® provides a wealth of useful information for the classroom. You can use this resource to strengthen your background on the subjects covered in this chapter. Have students visit this advertising-free site as a starting point for projects requiring research.

Use Web code lad-5500 for **Infoplease®**.

Guiding Questions

Remind students about the Guiding Questions introduced at the beginning of this section.

Section 1 relates to **Guiding Question ②** **How have historical events affected the cultures and nations of Africa?** *(The Fulani conquered the Hausa and the two groups merged, forming the Hausa-Fulani ethnic group; the diversity of Nigeria's ethnic groups made unifying the country under one democratic government a challenge.)*

Section 2 relates to **Guiding Question ③** **What factors led to the development of different governments across Africa?** *(Great Britain colonized the Gold Coast and controlled its economy. Eventually, the people in the Gold Coast demanded their independence and formed a government and the new independent country of Ghana.)*

Section 3 relates to **Guiding Question ⑤** **What factors influence the ways in which Africans make a living?** *(Geography influences the ways Malians make a living—they use the resources of the Sahel to raise crops and animals.)*

⟲ Target Reading Skill

In this chapter, students will learn and apply the reading skill of understanding main ideas. Use the following worksheets to help students practice this skill:

All in One Africa Teaching Resources, *Identify Main Ideas,* p. 301; *Identify Implied Main Ideas,* p. 302; *Identify Supporting Details,* p. 303

West Africa

Chapter Preview

This chapter will introduce you to some of the countries of West Africa.

Country Databank
The Country Databank provides data and descriptions of each of the countries in the region: Benin, Burkina Faso, Cape Verde, Chad, Gambia, Ghana, Guinea, Guinea-Bissau, Ivory Coast, Liberia, Mali, Mauritania, Niger, Nigeria, Senegal, Sierra Leone, and Togo.

Section 1
Nigeria
Land of Diverse Peoples

Section 2
Ghana
Leading Africa to Independence

Section 3
Mali
Desert Living

⟲ Target Reading Skill

Main Idea In this chapter you will focus on understanding main ideas. Identifying main ideas and their supporting details will help you learn as you read.

▶ The large, mud-brick Great Mosque in Djenné, Mali, is a source of pride for many West Africans.

Bibliography

For the Teacher
Fakinlede, Kayode J. *Wealth of the Yoruba People.* Morris Publishing, 2000.
Maier, Karl. *This House Has Fallen: Nigeria in Crisis.* Westview Press, 2003.
Birmingham, David. *Kwame Nkrumah: The Father of African Nationalism.* Ohio University Press, 1998.

For the Student
L1 Vernon-Jackson, Hugh. *African Folk Tales.* Dover, 1999.
L2 McKissack, Pat, Fredrick L. McKissack, and Patricia C. McKissack. *The Royal Kingdoms of Ghana, Mali, and Songhay: Life in Medieval Africa.* Henry Holt & Company, Inc, 1995.
L3 Masoff, Joy. *Mali: Land of Gold and Glory.* Five Ponds Press, 2002.

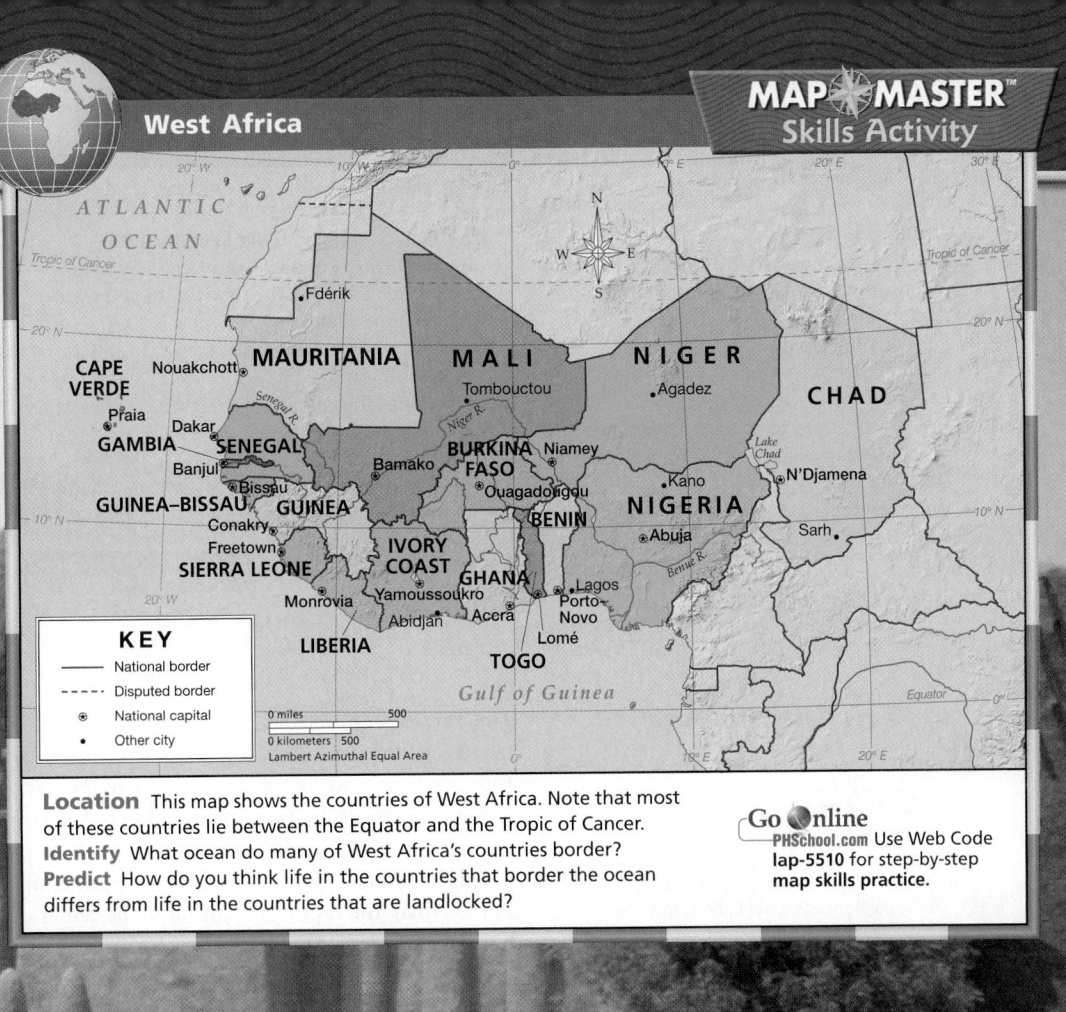

West Africa

MAP MASTER™
Skills Activity

ATLANTIC OCEAN

KEY
— National border
---- Disputed border
⊕ National capital
• Other city

0 miles 500
0 kilometers 500
Lambert Azimuthal Equal Area

Location This map shows the countries of West Africa. Note that most of these countries lie between the Equator and the Tropic of Cancer.
Identify What ocean do many of West Africa's countries border?
Predict How do you think life in the countries that border the ocean differs from life in the countries that are landlocked?

Go Online
PHSchool.com Use Web Code lap-5510 for step-by-step map skills practice.

Chapter 15 **475**

MAP MASTER™
Skills Activity

- Ask students to study the map carefully, paying attention to the names of the countries and their capitals. Working in pairs, have students create a set of flashcards. On one side of the card they should write the name of the country, on the other they should write the name of its capital. Have students take turns quizzing each other with the flashcards.

- For an easier activity, divide students into pairs. Have students take turns asking each other to point to and name the capitals of specific countries. One student should name a country, and the other should locate and name its capital. Then have students switch roles.

Go Online
PHSchool.com **Students may practice their map skills using the interactive online version of this map.**

Using the Visual L2

Reach Into Your Background Ask students to study the photograph on pp. 474–475, and read the caption on p. 474. Ask students to compare the features of this house of worship to others they may have seen. How is it similar? How is it different? Conduct an Idea Wave (TE, p. T35) to elicit student responses.

Answers

MAP MASTER Skills Activity **Identify** the Atlantic Ocean **Predict** Possible answers: People in countries bordering the ocean can take advantage of the resources the ocean provides, such as marine life, and can travel by boat to countries in other parts of the world.

Chapter Resources

Teaching Resources
- L2 Vocabulary Development, p. 319
- L2 Skills for Life, p. 306
- L2 Chapter Tests A and B, pp. 323–328

Spanish Support
- L2 Spanish Chapter Summary, p. 168
- L2 Spanish Vocabulary Development, p. 169

Media and Technology
- L1 Student Edition on Audio CD
- L1 Guided Reading Audiotapes, English and Spanish
- L2 Social Studies Skills Tutor CD-ROM
- *ExamView Test Bank CD-ROM*

PRENTICE HALL
Presentation EXPRESS™
Teach · Connect · Inspire

Teach this chapter's content using the PresentationExpress™ CD-ROM including:
- slide shows
- transparencies
- interactive maps and media
- *ExamView*® QuickTake Presenter

Introducing West Africa

L2

Objectives

- Use data to compare countries.
- Learn what characteristics West African countries share.
- Identify some key differences among the countries.

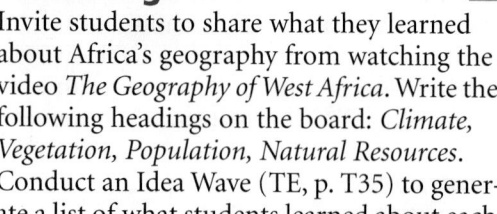

Show students *The Geography of West Africa.* Ask **What are some common features of the region?** (*The Sahara and the Sahel cover much of the region.*) **What natural resources are important to the countries of West Africa?** (*Students may mention fish, oil, gold, peanuts, rubber, cacao, and grasslands for cattle.*)

Prepare to Read

Build Background Knowledge

L2

Invite students to share what they learned about Africa's geography from watching the video *The Geography of West Africa.* Write the following headings on the board: *Climate, Vegetation, Population, Natural Resources.* Conduct an Idea Wave (TE, p. T35) to generate a list of what students learned about each topic. Write their responses under the appropriate heading on the board.

📼 *The Geography of West Africa,* **World Studies Video Program**

Guide for Reading

This section provides an introduction to the 17 countries that make up the region of West Africa.

- Look at the map on the previous page and then read the paragraphs below to learn about each nation.
- Analyze the data to compare the countries.
- What are the characteristics that most of the countries share?
- What are some key differences among the countries?

Viewing the Video Overview

View the World Studies Video Overview to learn more about each of the countries. As you watch, answer these questions:

- What are some common features of the region?
- How does the climate of West Africa affect the people living there?
- What natural resources are important to the countries of West Africa?

Explore the geography of West Africa.

Benin

Capital	Porto-Novo
Land Area	42,710 sq mi; 110,620 sq km
Population	6.9 million
Ethnic Group(s)	42 ethnic groups, including Fon, Adja, Yoruba, Bariba
Religion(s)	traditional beliefs, Muslim, Christian
Government	republic
Currency	CFA franc
Leading Exports	cotton, crude oil, palm products, cocoa
Language(s)	French (official), Fon, Bariba, Yoruba, Adja, Houeda, Somba

The narrow country of Benin (beh NEEN) is bordered on the west by Togo, on the north by Burkina Faso and Niger, on the east by Nigeria, and on the south by the Atlantic Ocean. Seasons are rainy or dry. More than two thirds of Benin's people live in the south. Most live in or near either Porto-Novo, the capital, or Cotonou, the center of business. Present-day Benin was formed by the French in the late 1800s. Since it gained independence in 1960, it has been on a shaky path to democracy and stability. In 1990, Benin successfully opened politics to multiple parties.

Near Porto-Novo, Benin

476 Africa

Burkina Faso

Capital	Ouagadougou
Land Area	105,714 sq mi; 273,800 sq km
Population	12.6 million
Ethnic Group(s)	Mossi, Gurunsi, Senufo, Lobi, Bobo, Mande, Fulani
Religion(s)	traditional beliefs, Muslim, Christian
Government	parliamentary republic
Currency	CFA franc
Leading Exports	cotton, animal products, gold
Language(s)	French (official), Mossi, Fulani, Tuareg, Dyula, Songhai

Burkina Faso (bur KEE nuh FAH soh) is bordered on the west and north by Mali, on the east by Niger and Benin, and on the south by Togo, Ghana, and Ivory Coast. The hot, dry north receives plentiful sunshine. The south is tropical, with more rainfall and a greater range of temperatures. Ninety percent of the population is rural—a higher percentage than in any other West African country. A French colony beginning in the 1890s, it gained independence as Upper Volta in 1960. Its name changed to Burkina Faso in 1984.

Cape Verde

Capital	Praia
Land Area	1,557 sq mi; 4,033 sq km
Population	408,760
Ethnic Group(s)	Creole, black, white
Religion(s)	Roman Catholic, Protestant
Government	republic
Currency	Cape Verde escudo
Leading Exports	fuel, shoes, garments, fish, hides
Language(s)	Portuguese (official), Portuguese Creole

West Africa's smallest nation, Cape Verde (kayp vurd), lies in the Atlantic Ocean, west of Senegal. It consists of ten islands and five islets. One of them, Fogo Island, is home to an active volcano that last erupted in 1995. Throughout its history, periods with little rainfall have brought hardship on the nation. Cape Verde has been inhabited since 1462, when its first settlers arrived from Portugal. They brought enslaved Africans as well. In 1975, Cape Verde gained independence. Today, about half of Cape Verdeans live on the island of São Tiago.

Chad

Capital	N'Djamena
Land Area	486,177 sq mi; 1,259,200 sq km
Population	9 million
Ethnic Group(s)	200 distinct groups, including Arab, Sara
Religion(s)	Muslim, Christian, traditional beliefs
Government	republic
Currency	CFA franc
Leading Exports	cotton, cattle, gum arabic
Language(s)	Arabic (official), French (official), Sara, Maba

Chad (chad) is Africa's fifth-largest country. It is bordered on the west by Cameroon, Nigeria, and Niger; on the north by Libya; on the east by Sudan; and on the south by the Central African Republic. Its northern lands are covered by the Sahara and are spotted with extinct volcanoes. In the south, the Sahel gets slightly more rain. Lake Chad, in the west, was historically a stop for traders crossing the Sahara. The French controlled the region from 1900 to 1960, when it became independent. Chad has since faced civil wars and military takeovers of the government.

Chapter 15 **477**

Guided Instruction (continued)

- Ask **What religious groups are common to all the countries on pp. 478–479?** *(Christian, Muslim, and groups with traditional beliefs)*

- Ask students **Are any languages common to all five of these countries?** *(no)* **How do you think this affects communication among the countries' people and governments?** *(Possible answer: It probably makes communication very challenging.)*

- Discuss the reasons why Ghana is considered to be a leader in African politics. *(Ghana was the first African nation south of the Sahara to achieve independence and was the first African nation to be governed by black leaders.)*

Introducing West Africa

Gambia

Capital	Banjul
Land Area	3,861 sq mi; 10,000 sq km
Population	1.5 million
Ethnic Group(s)	Mandinka, Fulani, Wolof, Jola, Serahuli
Religion(s)	Muslim, Christian, traditional beliefs
Government	republic
Currency	dalasi
Leading Exports	peanuts and peanut products, fish, cotton lint, palm kernels
Language(s)	English (official), Mandinka, Fulani, Wolof, Jola, Sonike

At 295 miles (475 kilometers) in length and 15 to 30 miles (24 to 48 kilometers) in width, Gambia (GAM bee uh) is a narrow country. It is surrounded by Senegal except on the west, where it borders the Atlantic Ocean. The Gambia River flows the entire length of the country. Gambia's economy depends on peanuts as a cash crop. Great Britain ruled Gambia from the early 1600s until 1965. In the early years after independence, Gambia's smooth transition from colonial rule to stable democracy stood as a model for other African nations. Although the government was overthrown in 1994, Gambia has since returned to a stable democracy.

Ghana

Capital	Accra
Land Area	89,166 sq mi; 230,940 sq km
Population	20.2 million
Ethnic Group(s)	Akan, Moshi-Dagomba, Ewe, Ga, Gurma, Yoruba, white
Religion(s)	Christian, traditional beliefs, Muslim
Government	constitutional democracy
Currency	cedi
Leading Exports	gold, cocoa, timber, tuna, bauxite, aluminum, manganese ore, diamonds
Language(s)	English (official), Twi, Fanti, Ewe, Ga, Adangbe, Gurma, Dagomba (Dagbani)

Ghana (GAH nuh) is bordered on the west by Ivory Coast, on the north by Burkina Faso, on the east by Togo, and on the south by the Atlantic Ocean. Ghana is rich in natural resources. It was originally referred to as the Gold Coast because of its abundant supply of gold. In addition, Ghana is viewed as a leader in African politics. The country became independent in 1957, making it the first African nation south of the Sahara to achieve independence as well as the first former European colony to be governed by black leaders.

Gold ornaments from Ghana

478 Africa

Differentiated Instruction

For Less Proficient Readers   L1

Have students create a Venn diagram to show the similarities and differences between Gambia and Ghana. Display the *Venn Diagram* transparency to show students how to sketch the organizer.

Circulate to make sure students are filling in the organizers correctly.

📖 **Africa Transparencies,** *Transparency B16: Venn Diagram*

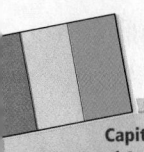

Guinea

Capital	Conakry
Land Area	94,925 sq mi; 245,857 sq km
Population	7.8 million
Ethnic Group(s)	Peuhl, Malinke, Soussou
Religion(s)	Muslim, Christian, traditional beliefs
Government	republic
Currency	Guinea franc
Leading Exports	bauxite, alumina, fish, diamonds, coffee, gold, agricultural products
Language(s)	French (official), Fulani, Malinke, Soussou

Guinea (GIH nee) is neighbored by Guinea-Bissau, Senegal, Mali, Ivory Coast, Sierra Leone, and Liberia. The western border of the country runs along the Atlantic Ocean. Three major rivers—the Gambia, the Senegal, and the Niger—all have their sources in Guinea. The country is rich in natural resources. At least one third of the world's supply of bauxite comes from Guinea, which is the world's second-largest producer of the mineral, after Australia. Farming is also a dominant industry in Guinea, where many people produce cash crops as well as crops to support their families.

Guinea-Bissau

Capital	Bissau
Land Area	10,811 sq mi; 28,000 sq km
Population	1.4 million
Ethnic Group(s)	Balanta, Fula, Manjaca, Mandinga, Papel, white, mixed white and black
Religion(s)	traditional beliefs, Muslim, Christian
Government	republic
Currency	CFA franc
Leading Exports	cashew nuts, shrimp, peanuts, palm kernels, sawn lumber
Language(s)	Portuguese (official), Portuguese Creole, Balante, Fulani, Malinke

The mainland of Guinea-Bissau (GIH nee bih SOW) is bordered by the Atlantic Ocean on the west, Senegal on the north, and Guinea on the east and south. The country also includes a group of islands off its Atlantic coast. Guinea-Bissau's economy revolves mostly around farming. Rice is the main food crop, and cashews are the country's main export. Guinea-Bissau is one of the world's poorest countries. It gained independence from Portugal in 1975 after years of warfare. Since then, it has suffered from civil war and a series of military takeovers. Guinea-Bissau's instability has made it more difficult for the country to escape poverty.

Ivory Coast

Capital	Yamoussoukro
Land Area	122,780 sq mi; 318,000 sq km
Population	16.8 million
Ethnic Group(s)	Akan, Voltaiques (Gur), Northern Mandes, Krous, Southern Mandes
Religion(s)	Muslim, Christian, traditional beliefs
Government	republic
Currency	CFA franc
Leading Exports	cocoa, coffee, timber, petroleum, cotton, bananas, pineapples, palm oil, cotton, fish
Language(s)	French (official), Akan, Kru, Voltaic

Ivory Coast (EYE vur ee kohst) is one of the largest countries on West Africa's coast. It is bordered on the west by Liberia and Guinea, on the north by Mali and Burkina Faso, on the east by Ghana, and on the south by the Gulf of Guinea. Mountains cover most of its western edge. Cocoa and coffee are major agricultural products. Since a 1999 coup, Ivory Coast has faced political instability and violence. A civil war between the government and rebel forces lasted from 2002 to 2003. Despite the presence of African, UN, and French peacekeeping troops, the country remains unstable.

Chapter 15 **479**

Guided Instruction (continued)

- Ask **Which country on p. 479 has the largest population?** (*Ivory Coast*) **Which country's official language is Portuguese?** (*Guinea-Bissau*) **Which country is a leading producer of bauxite?** (*Guinea*) **Which country shares a border with both of the other countries profiled on this page?** (*Guinea*)

- Have students compare and contrast Guinea-Bissau and Ivory Coast. **What do these countries have in common?** (*They both use the CFA franc for currency; have traditional beliefs, Muslim, and Christian religions; export a palm product; and have a republican form of government.*) **What are some differences between the countries?** (*Ivory Coast has a much larger population and more land area. Ivory Coast has a growing urban population while three quarters of Guinea-Bissau's people live in rural areas. They share no common major languages and export many different goods.*)

Differentiated Instruction

For English Language Learners ▨ L2
Before you read about each country with students, have them turn to the map on p. 475 and locate the country. Tell them to trace its border with their fingers. Also, have students locate the countries that border it as they are described in the text.

- Ask **Which country on p. 480 was not colonized by Europeans?** *(Liberia)* **How is Liberia's founding reflected in its official language?** *(Freed slaves from the United States founded Liberia, and they made English the language.)*

- Have students describe Mali's vegetation. *(The northern third of Mali is covered by the Sahara; the partly dry Sahel lies just to the south.)*

- Ask students **What characteristics do Liberia and Mali have in common?** *(They are both republics; both are home to Christians, Muslims, and people who practice traditional beliefs.)*

COUNTRY DATABANK

Introducing West Africa

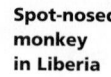
Spot-nosed monkey in Liberia

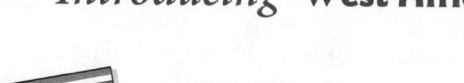

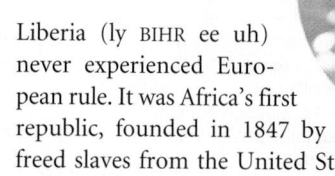
Liberia

Capital	Monrovia
Land Area	37,189 sq mi; 96,320 sq km
Population	3.3 million
Ethnic Group(s)	Kpelle, Bassa, Gio, Kru, Grebo, Mano, Krahn, Gola, Gbandi, Loma, Kissi, Vai, Dei, Bella, Mandingo, Mende, Americo-Liberians, Congo People
Religion(s)	traditional beliefs, Christian, Muslim
Government	republic
Currency	Liberian dollar
Leading Exports	rubber, timber, iron, diamonds, cocoa, coffee
Language(s)	English (official), Kpelle, Vai, Kru Bassa, Grebo, Kissi, Gola, Loma

Liberia (ly BIHR ee uh) never experienced European rule. It was Africa's first republic, founded in 1847 by freed slaves from the United States.

It is bordered on the northwest by Sierra Leone, on the north by Guinea, on the east by Ivory Coast, and on the south and west by the Atlantic Ocean. It has rain forests in which animals such as monkeys and crocodiles live. Beginning in 1990, a chaotic civil war engulfed Liberia. A peace deal was signed in 2003, but about 15,000 UN peacekeeping soldiers remain in the country. Today, 95 percent of Liberians are of African descent. The rest are mostly Americo-Liberians, descendants of the country's American-born founders.

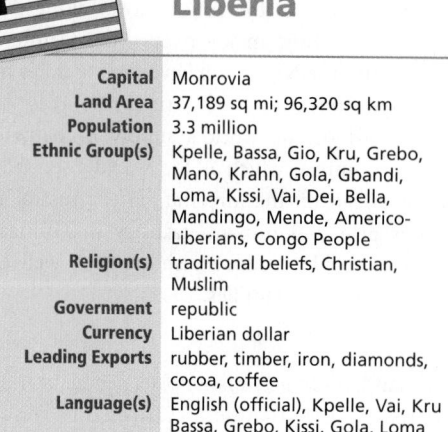
Mali

Capital	Bamako
Land Area	471,042 sq mi; 1,220,000 sq km
Population	11.3 million
Ethnic Group(s)	Mande, Peul, Voltaic, Songhai, Tuareg, Moor
Religion(s)	Muslim, traditional beliefs, Christian
Government	republic
Currency	CFA franc
Leading Exports	cotton, gold, livestock
Language(s)	French (official), Bambara, Fulani, Senufo, Soninke

Mali (MAH lee) is one of West Africa's few landlocked countries. It is bordered on the west by Senegal and Mauritania, on the north by Algeria, on the east by Niger and Burkina Faso, and on the south by Ivory Coast and Guinea. The northern third of Mali is covered by the Sahara. To the south lies the Sahel, where cattle graze widely. The Senegal and Niger rivers flow through Mali. The country is named after an ancient empire that flourished there 700 years ago.

Cattle herders in Mali

Differentiated Instruction

For Gifted and Talented [L3]

Distribute *Outline Map 23: West and Central Africa*. Have students fill in the West African country names using only their memory and the descriptions of the countries' locations found in the Country Databank. When they have finished, have them check their maps against the map on p. 475. Tell them to revise their maps as necessary.

All in One **Africa Teaching Resources,**
Outline Map 23: West and Central Africa, p. 316

Mauritania

Capital	Nouakchott
Land Area	397,837 sq mi; 1,030,400 sq km
Population	2.8 million
Ethnic Group(s)	Maur, black, mixed
Religion(s)	Muslim
Government	republic
Currency	ouguiya
Leading Exports	iron ore, fish, fish products, gold
Language(s)	Arabic (official), Hassaniyah Arabic, Wolof, French

Mauritania (mawr uh TAY nee uh) is bordered on the west by the Atlantic Ocean, on the north by Western Morocco and Algeria, on the east and south by Mali, and on the south by Senegal. About two thirds of the country is covered by the Sahara. Many nomads once lived in the desert, but frequent droughts prevented many of them from staying there. For that reason, the population of the city of Nouakchott (nwahk SHAHT) has grown to around one million people.

Niger

Capital	Niamey
Land Area	489,073 sq mi; 1,226,700 sq km
Population	11.3 million
Ethnic Group(s)	Hausa, Djerma, Songhai, Fula, Tuareg, Beri Beri, Arab, Toubou, Gourmantche
Religion(s)	Muslim, traditional beliefs, Christian
Government	republic
Currency	CFA franc
Leading Exports	uranium ore, livestock products, cowpeas, onions
Language(s)	French (official), Hausa, Djerma, Fulani, Tuareg, Teda

Niger (NY jur) is bordered on the west by Burkina Faso and Mali, on the north by Algeria and Libya, on the east by Chad, and on the south by Nigeria and Benin. Much of the country is arid Sahara or Sahel, although there are savannas in the south. Niger has often faced drought. Also, the country has faced long-term conflict between the northern and southern ethnic groups. Although politically stable after gaining independence in 1960, Niger has struggled to establish democracy. In 1990, seeking fairer treatment, the Tuareg people of the north rebelled against the government. The signing of a peace treaty in 1995 resolved the conflict.

Nigeria

Capital	Abuja
Land Area	351,648 sq mi; 910,768 sq km
Population	129.9 million
Ethnic Group(s)	250 distinct groups, including Hausa, Fulani, Yoruba, Igbo, Ijaw, Kanuri, Ibibio, Tiv
Religion(s)	Muslim, Christian, traditional beliefs
Government	republic
Currency	naira
Leading Exports	petroleum and petroleum products, cocoa, rubber
Language(s)	English (official), Hausa, Yoruba, Igbo

Nigeria (ny JIHR ee uh) has the largest population of any African country. It is bordered on the west by Benin, on the north by Niger, on the east by Chad and Cameroon, and on the south by the Atlantic Ocean. Members of at least 250 ethnic groups live in Nigeria. The country is one of the world's largest oil producers. It is also one of Africa's leaders in education. About 98 percent of Nigerian children attend elementary school, and the country is home to more than 50 colleges and universities. Still, corrupt government, ethnic conflict, and religious conflict have all troubled modern Nigeria.

Chapter 15 **481**

Guided Instruction (continued)

- Discuss some characteristics of Mauritania's population. (*The people are Maur, black, and mixed Maur and black; they are Muslim.*) Ask **How have climate and geography affected Mauritania's population?** (*Many nomads once lived in Mauritania's desert, but frequent droughts prevented them from staying there. This has led to an increase in the population of the city of Nouakchott.*)

- Ask **Which two countries on p. 481 share a border?** (*Niger and Nigeria*) **What are some characteristics that the populations of these two countries have in common?** (*Both have members of the Hausa ethnic group and the Hausa language is spoken in both countries; both practice the same religions; both have republican forms of government.*) **Which common characteristics do you think result from a shared border?** (*the presence of Hausa and the use of the Hausa language*)

Differentiated Instruction

For Advanced Readers L3
Have students conduct Internet or library research to learn more about the Tuareg people. Tell them to write a brief essay describing their way of life and why they rebelled against Niger's government.

Guided Instruction (continued)

- Ask **Which countries on pp. 482–483 share a common form of government?** *(Senegal and Togo)* **What leading exports do Sierra Leone and Togo have in common?** *(cocoa and coffee)* **What leading exports do Senegal and Togo have in common?** *(phosphates and cotton)*

- Tell students to locate Togo, Senegal, and Sierra Leone on the map on p. 475. **What is similar about the locations of these three countries?** *(They are all located on the coast.)* **How do you think this might have affected the development of these countries?** *(Possible answer: It may have helped the economies of these countries by making trade with other nations easier.)*

Independent Practice

- First, have students compare and contrast two West African countries that border each other, using the information in the Country Databank. Tell them to present their findings in either a Venn diagram or a table.

- Then have students compare and contrast any two West African countries that do not border each other.

- Finally, ask them to write a few paragraphs explaining whether the bordering nations they compared had more similar characteristics than the non-bordering nations, and why they think this was or was not so.

Monitor Progress

Circulate to be sure students are making their diagrams and tables correctly and are providing adequate explanations in their paragraphs.

Introducing West Africa

Senegal

Capital	Dakar
Land Area	74,131 sq mi; 192,000 sq km
Population	10.6 million
Ethnic Group(s)	Wolof, Pular, Serer, Jola, Mandinka, Soninke, white, Southwest Asian
Religion(s)	Muslim, Christian, traditional beliefs
Government	republic
Currency	CFA franc
Leading Exports	fish, peanuts, petroleum products, phosphates, cotton
Language(s)	French (official), Wolof, Fulani, Serer, Diola, Malinke, Soninke, Arabic

Senegal (SEN ih gawl) is bordered on the west by the Atlantic Ocean, on the north by Mauritania, on the east by Mali, and on the south by Guinea and Guinea-Bissau. Its capital, Dakar, is located on the westernmost reach of the African continent and is an important port for West Africa. Senegal was colonized by the French, and it became independent in 1960. The first president of the country, Léopold Senghor, is known as one of the great African poets.

Léopold Senghor

Sierra Leone

Capital	Freetown
Land Area	27,652 sq mi; 71,620 sq km
Population	5.6 million
Ethnic Group(s)	20 distinct groups, including Temne, Mende, Creole
Religion(s)	Muslim, traditional beliefs, Christian
Government	constitutional democracy
Currency	leone
Leading Exports	diamonds, rutile, cocoa, coffee, fish
Language(s)	English (official), Mende, Temne, Krio

Sierra Leone (see EHR uh lee OHN) is bordered on the west by the Atlantic Ocean, on the north and east by Guinea, and on the south by Liberia. Its capital city, Freetown, lies beside a huge natural harbor surrounded by low mountains. In 1787, the British established Sierra Leone as a place for freed African slaves to live. It later became a British colony and then gained independence in 1961. Since the 1990s, the country has suffered through intense civil wars. The people of Sierra Leone are known for the carved wooden masks they wear during performances, as well as for their carved ivory figures.

Carved wooden mask from Sierra Leone

482 Africa

Background: Daily Life

Importance of Phosphates Phosphates are important ingredients in many products that we use every day. Phosphate ore is often converted into the more useful phosphoric acid and combined with other elements such as calcium, potassium, and sodium. Different combinations of phosphoric acid and these elements form the main ingredients of products such as antifreeze, dishwasher detergent, paint, and toothpaste.

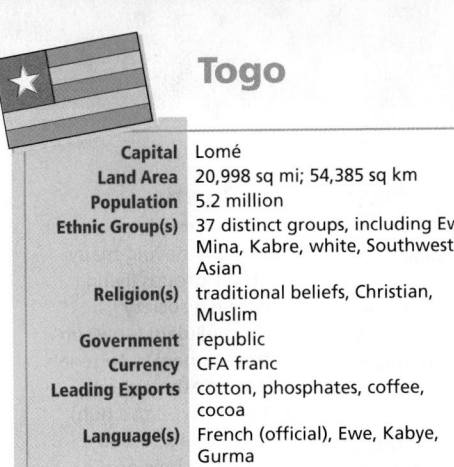

Togo

Capital	Lomé
Land Area	20,998 sq mi; 54,385 sq km
Population	5.2 million
Ethnic Group(s)	37 distinct groups, including Ewe, Mina, Kabre, white, Southwest Asian
Religion(s)	traditional beliefs, Christian, Muslim
Government	republic
Currency	CFA franc
Leading Exports	cotton, phosphates, coffee, cocoa
Language(s)	French (official), Ewe, Kabye, Gurma

Baobab tree

Togo (TOH goh) is bordered on the west by Ghana, on the north by Burkina Faso, on the east by Benin, and on the south by the Atlantic Ocean. The small country includes coastal lands, mountains, rivers, and plateaus. Many trees cover the southern plateaus, including baobab (BAY oh bab) trees, which are famous for their huge trunks. Togo is one of the world's largest producers of the mineral phosphate. Politically, one party has dominated since 1967. In the 1990s, however, the country made the formation of other political parties legal.

SOURCES: DK World Desk Reference Online; CIA World Factbook Online, 2002; *The World Almanac,* 2003

Assessment

Comprehension and Critical Thinking

1. Compare and Contrast Compare and contrast the histories of these countries.

2. Summarize What are some characteristics that most of the countries share?

3. Analyze Information What are some key differences among the countries?

4. Categorize What kinds of products are the major exports of this region?

5. Predict How might the region be affected by the presence of a great number of ethnic groups?

6. Make a Circle Graph Create a circle graph showing the forms of government held by the countries of West Africa and the percentage each form represents.

Keeping Current

Access the **DK World Desk Reference Online** at **PHSchool.com** for up-to-date information about all 17 countries in this chapter.

Go Online
PHSchool.com

Web Code: lae-5500

Assess and Reteach

Assess Progress L2
Direct students' attention back to the lists on the board. Encourage them to suggest more information to fill in under each head based on what they learned from the Country Databank.

Reteach L1
Ask students to create a bar graph showing the populations of the countries of West Africa. Encourage them to display the countries in order from the smallest population to the largest. Remind them to label both axes and give the graph a title.

Extend L3
Have students choose one country in the Country Databank. Ask students to learn more about one or two aspects of the country, using the Internet or other reference sources. Then ask students to suppose that they have visited this country and are writing a letter to a friend about their observations. Students can add their letter to their portfolios.

Assessment

1. Possible answer: Most countries were once under colonial rule and struggled for their independence. While some countries were colonized by the French, others were colonized by the British and Portuguese.

2. Most countries share similar religious groups, history of colonial rule, many different ethnic groups and languages within each country, and a republican form of government.

3. Possible answers: size, population, leading exports, types of ethnic groups, non-official languages.

4. agricultural products and minerals

5. Possible answer: Communication between the groups may be a challenge, and it may have been difficult to unite the groups under one government.

6. Use *Rubric for Assessing a Circle Graph* to evaluate students' work.

All in One **Africa Teaching Resources,** *Rubric for Assessing a Circle Graph,* p. 320

Section 1
Step-by-Step Instruction

Objectives

Social Studies

1. Learn to identify Nigeria's three main ethnic groups.
2. Understand the major events in Nigeria's history.
3. Find out about the conflicts Nigeria faced on its path to democracy.

Reading/Language Arts

Learn how to identify main ideas.

Prepare to Read

Build Background Knowledge   L2

Tell students that they will learn about the different ethnic groups that live in Nigeria. Mention that more than 200 languages are spoken in the country. Have students estimate the number of people they have communicated with so far today. Then have them consider how they would have communicated with these people if they did not share the same language. Use the Think-Write-Pair-Share strategy (TE, p. T36) to generate a list.

Set a Purpose for Reading   L2

- Preview the Objectives.

- Read each statement in the *Reading Readiness Guide* aloud. Ask students to mark the statements true or false.

  All in One **Africa Teaching Resources,** *Reading Readiness Guide,* p. 290

- Have students discuss the statements in pairs or groups of four, then mark their worksheets again. Use the Numbered Heads participation strategy (TE, p. T36) to call on students to share their group's perspectives.

Vocabulary Builder
Preview Key Terms   L2

Pronounce each Key Term, and then ask the students to say the word with you. Provide a simple explanation such as, "A place that is multiethnic has people with different cultures, languages, and backgrounds."

Section 1
Nigeria
Land of Diverse Peoples

Prepare to Read

Objectives

In this section you will
1. Learn to identify Nigeria's three main ethnic groups.
2. Understand the major events in Nigeria's history.
3. Find out about the conflicts Nigeria faced on its path to democracy.

Taking Notes

As you read this section, look for details about Nigeria's three main ethnic groups. Copy the chart below, and use it to record your findings.

Nigeria's Ethnic Groups		
Hausa-Fulani	Yoruba	Igbo
•	•	•
•	•	•

🎯 Target Reading Skill

Identify Main Ideas It is impossible to remember every detail that you read. Therefore, good readers identify the main idea in every paragraph or section. The main idea is the most important point in the section. For example, on page 489, the main idea of the paragraph under the heading Oil is stated here: "Another notable source of tension in Nigeria is the country's wealth of oil resources." All the other information in the paragraph supports this main idea.

Key Terms

- **multiethnic** (mul tee ETH nik) *adj.* having many ethnic groups living within a society
- **Hausa-Fulani** (HOW suh foo LAH nee) *n.* Nigeria's largest ethnic group
- **Yoruba** (YOH roo buh) *n.* Nigeria's second-largest ethnic group
- **Igbo** (IG boh) *n.* Nigeria's third-largest ethnic group

Nigerian youth

484 Africa

If you were planning to travel to Spain, you might learn Spanish. If you were planning to travel to Greece, you might try to learn Greek. But if you were traveling to Nigeria, would you study Nigerian? No, you would not even try to, because there is no such language. In fact, out of the more than 1,000 languages spoken in Africa, at least 200 are spoken in Nigeria alone.

If you find it hard to believe that so many languages can be heard in just one country, picture this: Nigeria is a little larger than the states of California, Oregon, and Washington combined. That means Nigeria could fit inside the United States about 11 times. But Nigeria has nearly half the population of the whole United States. At about 130 million people, Nigeria's population is the largest in Africa.

🎯 Target Reading Skill   L2

Identify Main Ideas Point out the Target Reading Skill. Tell students that the main idea is the most important idea in a section or paragraph.

Model the skill by reading the first paragraph on p. 486 and identifying the sentence that states the paragraph's main idea. (*Historically, the Yoruba have been the most urban of Nigeria's major ethnic groups.*) Point out that you think this sentence expresses the main idea because all of the details in the paragraph support it.

Give students *Identify Main Ideas.* Have them complete the activity in their groups.

All in One **Africa Teaching Resources,** *Identify Main Ideas,* p. 301

Ethnic Groups of Nigeria

Nigeria is **multiethnic,** which means that many ethnic groups live within its borders. In fact, it is home to more than 250 ethnic groups—most of whom speak different languages. English is the official language of Nigeria. However, the languages of Nigeria's major ethnic groups dominate the country.

These ethnic groups have inhabited Nigeria for many centuries. As you can see on the map in the Country Profile on page 487, the people of each group tend to live in certain parts of the country. Most members of Nigeria's largest ethnic group, the **Hausa-Fulani** (HOW suh foo LAH nee), live in the northwest. Nigeria's second-largest ethnic group, the **Yoruba** (YOH roo buh), make their home in the southwest. And the **Igbo** (IG boh), Nigeria's third-largest ethnic group, live mainly in the southeast. In addition, many smaller ethnic groups live in central Nigeria, and others are scattered throughout the country.

The Hausa-Fulani In the early 1800s, the Fulani entered northern Nigeria and conquered the Hausa there. The Fulani then ruled over the Hausa. But instead of imposing their own culture, many of the Fulani adopted the Hausa's language and practices. Over time, many Hausa and Fulani have intermarried, and the two groups have come to be known as the Hausa-Fulani.

The majority of Hausa-Fulani live in the countryside. Some herd cattle, while others farm crops such as peanuts and a grain called sorghum (SAWR gum). Still others produce crafts that are traded in markets. Trade has been an important part of the Hausa economy for hundreds of years—since long before the Fulani arrived. The Hausa built trading cities in northern Nigeria, each of which was enclosed by walls and housed a central market. Today, some of these cities, such as Kano, still thrive as centers of commerce.

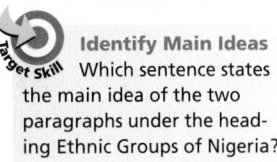

Identify Main Ideas Which sentence states the main idea of the two paragraphs under the heading Ethnic Groups of Nigeria?

Trading City Still Thrives
Kano has been a center of trade for more than 1,000 years. Today, people from around the world visit Kano's Kurmi Market. Vendors sell everything from fabrics (below right) to carved calabash bowls (below left). **Draw Conclusions** *Why do you think trading centers such as Kano have been able to last so long?*

Vocabulary Builder

Use the information below to teach students this section's high-use words.

High-Use Word	Definition and Sample Sentence
impose, p. 485	*v.* to force The citizens feared that the dictator would **impose** unfair laws.
practice, p. 488	*v.* to work at, observe, or carry out an action Her dream was to **practice** medicine one day.
revolve, p. 489	*v.* to be centered His studies will **revolve** around African history.

A Yoruba farming family

Links

Read the **Links to Language Arts** on this page. Ask students **What does Soyinka often write about?** *(He writes about Nigerian society in both serious and humorous ways and Yoruba folklore and traditions.)*

Independent Practice

Ask students to create the Taking Notes graphic organizer on a blank piece of paper. Then have them fill in details about Nigeria's three main ethnic groups. Briefly model how to identify which details to record.

Monitor Progress

As students fill in the graphic organizer, circulate and make sure individuals are choosing the correct details. Provide assistance as needed.

Links to Language Arts

Wole Soyinka Wole Soyinka (WOH lay shaw YING kuh) is a Yoruba man who is known as one of Africa's most talented writers. In 1986, he won the Nobel Prize in Literature—the world's most celebrated prize for writing. Soyinka has written numerous plays, novels, poems, and autobiographical and nonfiction works. In his works, Soyinka often comments on Nigerian society in both serious and humorous ways. He also includes Yoruba folklore and traditions in his writing.

486 Africa

The Yoruba Historically, the Yoruba have been the most urban of Nigeria's major ethnic groups. The Yoruba tradition of building cities began around 1100 and continued for hundreds of years. Each Yoruba city was ruled by a king and was densely populated, including traders and many skilled artisans. Currently, the majority of residents of one of Africa's largest cities, Lagos, are Yoruba. The city was founded in the 1400s and served as the capital of Nigeria from 1960 to 1991.

Today, many Yoruba also live outside cities. Often they are farmers, traders, or craftspeople. The farmers tend to grow cash crops such as cacao. They also grow food for their own families. Yoruba families live in large compounds made up of several houses built around a shared yard. A Yoruba community has many of these compounds.

The Igbo The Igbo have traditionally been rural. They have not built large cities but rather live in small farming villages. The people in a village work closely together. Each village is ruled democratically by a council of elders that the people select. Council members work together to solve problems.

Today, many Igbo also live in cities. Throughout much of the past century, they have served as members of Nigeria's local and federal governments. As you will read, Nigeria became an independent country in 1960, and its first president, Benjamin Nnamdi Azikiwe (NUM dee ah ZEE kway), was Igbo.

✓ **Reading Check** Which of Nigeria's ethnic groups is known as the most urban?

Differentiated Instruction

For Advanced Readers   L3

To better understand another culture's traditions, have students complete the *Enrichment* activity about Yoruba proverbs. Ask students if any of the proverbs are similar to ones they already know.

All in One **Africa Teaching Resources,** *Enrichment,* p. 305

For Less Proficient Readers   L1

Some students may have trouble pronouncing African words in the section. Ask students to make a list of the section's African words. Then ask students to pair up and practice the pronunciations. Students may use other sources, such as the Internet or a geographical dictionary, to find out how to pronounce the words. Assist students with pronunciations if necessary.

Answer

✓ **Reading Check** The Yoruba have been the most urban of Nigeria's ethnic groups.

Nigeria

Nigeria is Africa's most heavily populated country and one of its most diverse. The country is rich in culture, but the differences can result in clashes. With more than 250 ethnic groups, tensions between the different groups have been hard to avoid. In addition, Muslim communities in the north and Christian communities in the south often face conflict today. Many northern states have adopted Islamic law. At the same time, Christian churches have drawn millions of new members. Study the map and charts to learn more about Nigeria's diverse population.

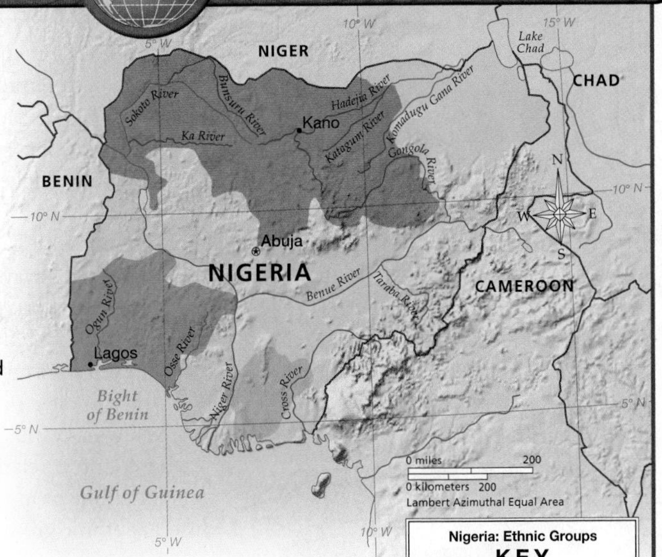

Ethnic Groups

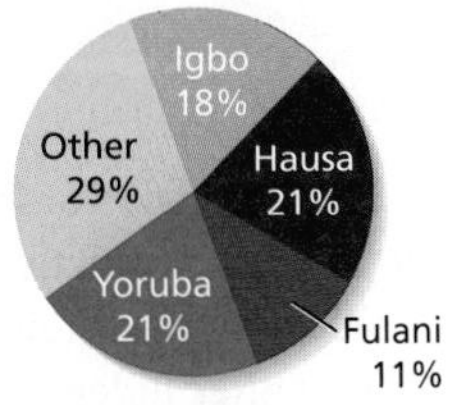

Igbo 18%
Other 29%
Hausa 21%
Yoruba 21%
Fulani 11%

SOURCE: *DK World Desk Reference*

Religions

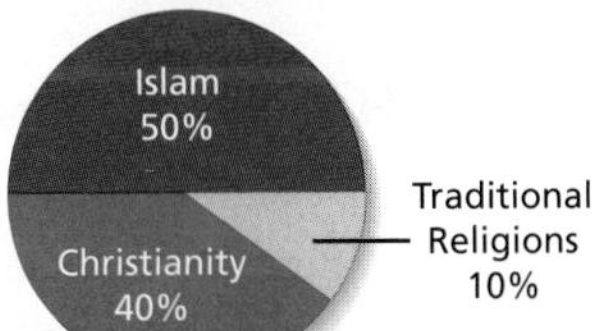

Islam 50%
Christianity 40%
Traditional Religions 10%

SOURCE: *DK World Desk Reference*

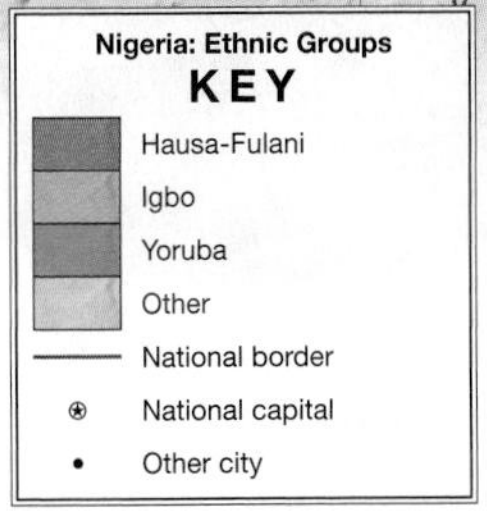

Nigeria: Ethnic Groups
KEY
- Hausa-Fulani
- Igbo
- Yoruba
- Other
- National border
- National capital
- Other city

0 miles 200
0 kilometers 200
Lambert Azimuthal Equal Area

Tall, carved drums like these are made by Igbo people in Nigeria.

Map and Chart Skills

1. **Identify** What are two factors that make Nigeria a diverse country?
2. **Infer** Using the information given in the paragraph and the map above, which of Nigeria's ethnic groups can you infer are Muslim?
3. **Evaluate** Southern Nigeria has large oil reserves. How could this oil wealth play a role in the country's tensions?

Go Online PHSchool.com Use Web Code lae-5501 for **DK World Desk Reference Online.**

Background: Global Perspectives

Diversity in China China is the most populous country in the world and, like Nigeria, its population includes many different ethnic groups. Just as there is no language called Nigerian, there is no one language called Chinese. The language that most non-Chinese call "Chinese" is actually Mandarin, the official language of China. In fact, more than 50 languages are spoken in China in addition to Mandarin, including Mongolian, Tibetan, Uighur, Kazak, Thai, and Korean.

Guided Instruction L2

Ask students to study the Country Profile on this page. As a class, answer the Map and Chart Skills questions. Allow students to briefly discuss their responses with a partner before sharing answers.

Independent Practice

- Distribute *Reading a Circle Graph* and have students work in pairs to complete the worksheet.

  All in One **Africa Teaching Resources,** *Reading a Circle Graph*, p. 313

- Then have students use what they learned to analyze the two circle graphs on p. 487. Tell them to use the information from the two graphs to write a brief paragraph describing the characteristics of Nigeria's population.

Answers

Map and Chart Skills

1. There are more than 250 ethnic groups; people practice different religions, mainly Islam or Christianity.
2. Hausa-Fulani
3. Possible answer: The Igbo and the Yoruba might have control of the oil since they live in the south, which could anger the people of the north—the Hausa-Fulani—who may also want to benefit from oil wealth.

Go Online PHSchool.com Students can find additional useful information about this topic on the DK World Desk Reference Online.

Nigeria's History L2

The Path to Democracy L2

Guided Instruction

- **Vocabulary Builder** Clarify the high-use words **practice** and **revolve** before reading.

- Read Nigeria's History and The Path to Democracy with students.

- Ask **Which European country had taken over Nigeria's government by 1914?** *(Great Britain)*

- Ask students **Why was the Nigerian capital moved?** *(The capital was moved from the south to the middle of the country, making it closer to all major ethnic groups. The aim was to help unite Nigeria.)*

- Ask students **Why was unifying Nigeria's ethnic groups difficult?** *(The groups live in different areas, speak different languages, practice different religions, and have access to different economic resources.)*

- Discuss with students why the oil industry has been a source of tension in Nigeria. *(The government and oil companies profit greatly from the industry, but those who live on the land that oil comes from profit much less.)*

Independent Practice

Have students complete the graphic organizer.

Show students *Nigeria: Can Village Life Survive?* Ask **How has oil production disrupted the soil in the Niger Delta?** *(Oil producers moved fertile topsoil, and oil spills have polluted the soil.)*

Monitor Progress

- Show *Section Reading Support Transparency AF 47* and ask students to check their graphic organizers individually. Go over key concepts and clarify key vocabulary.

  Africa Transparencies, *Section Reading Support Transparency AF 47*

- Tell students to fill in the last column of the *Reading Readiness Guide*. Probe for what they learned that confirms or invalidates each statement.

  All in One Africa Teaching Resources, *Reading Readiness Guide, p. 290*

Answer

✓ Reading Check Abuja

Nigeria's History

For thousands of years, the region of present-day Nigeria was ruled by many different African peoples who formed their own governments. In the late 1400s, however, Portugal began trading for slaves in West Africa. Soon, Great Britain and the Netherlands began trading in the region as well. By 1914, Great Britain had taken over Nigeria's government.

In 1960, Nigeria became an independent nation, with Lagos as its capital. Ethnic groups that had always lived separately had to learn to live and work together as one nation. In 1991, to help unify the country, Nigeria's government moved its capital from Lagos, in the south, to the city of Abuja (uh BOO juh). The new capital has two advantages. It is located in the middle of the country, relatively close to each of the three major ethnic groups. In addition, members of many different ethnic groups live in Abuja.

✓ **Reading Check** What city became Nigeria's new capital in 1991?

Lagos, Nigeria

The Path to Democracy

Unifying Nigeria's many ethnic groups has not been easy. These groups live in different areas, speak different languages, practice different religions, and sometimes have access to different amounts of economic resources. Only a few years after independence, conflicts began to arise. In 1966, a military group took over the government. The next year, civil war broke out as the Igbo tried to separate from Nigeria and form their own country. In 1970, after thousands had been killed or injured, the Igbo surrendered. The fighting ended, and Nigeria remained united. However, tensions remained high, and military control of the country continued for years.

Religion A key source of the tension in Nigeria is the religious diversity among the various ethnic groups. Most of the Hausa-Fulani practice Islam, while some Yoruba practice Islam and others practice Christianity. The Igbo are primarily Christian. Some members of these groups, as well as members of hundreds of others, also practice traditional African religions. Such religious diversity makes Nigeria rich in culture, but it also challenges national unity.

Learn about the impact of oil production on village life.

488 Africa

Differentiated Instruction

For Special Needs Students L1

Students can obtain visual information about Nigeria by taking the *Passport to the World* photo tour of Nigeria and looking at Nigeria's timeline, photo tour, and special purpose map.

⊙ *Nigeria,* **Passport to the World CD-ROM**

For Gifted and Talented L3

Students can learn more about which European nations dominated regions of Africa with the map activity *Reading a Historical Map.*

All in One Africa Teaching Resources, *Reading a Historical Map, p. 314*

Oil Another notable source of tension in Nigeria is the country's wealth of oil resources. Nigeria's economy, which is one of the strongest in Africa, revolves around oil. Ninety-five percent of the income Nigeria earns from its exports to other countries comes from oil. However, while the government and the oil companies earn large profits from oil, the people who live on the oil-rich land do not. That is because most of the oil companies are foreign and use foreign workers. Many Nigerians want to gain a share of the work or income generated by the oil industry.

Democracy for Nigeria Since Nigeria gained its independence in 1960, many Nigerians have struggled to create a democratic government free of military rule. Finally, Nigeria's military leaders gave up their power. On May 29, 1999, an election was held for the first time in more than 15 years. Olusegun Obasanjo (oh loo SEG oon oh bah SAHN joh) was elected president of Nigeria. He was re-elected in 2003.

Oil workers in Port Harcourt, Nigeria

✓ **Reading Check** Which different religions do people in Nigeria practice?

Section 1 Assessment

Key Terms
Review the key terms at the beginning of this section. Use each term in a sentence that explains its meaning.

Target Reading Skill
State three main ideas from Section 1. Tell whether each is the main idea of a paragraph or of a section under a red heading.

Comprehension and Critical Thinking
1. (a) Recall What are the three largest ethnic groups in Nigeria, and in which region does each group live?

(b) Evaluate Information Identify one feature that is unique to each of Nigeria's three major ethnic groups.

2. (a) Locate In what part of Nigeria is the country's capital, Abuja, located?

(b) Identify Causes Why did Nigeria's government think it was necessary to move the country's capital to Abuja?

3. (a) Name Which ethnic group tried to separate itself from Nigeria in 1967?

(b) Synthesize Information How is being a multiethnic country both good and bad for Nigeria?

(c) Predict What can Nigerians do in the future to resolve the conflicts in their country?

Writing Activity
Suppose that you are a Nigerian newspaper editor. Write an editorial supporting a movement for all Nigerians to use one common language. Be sure to say whether you think the common language should be English or another language, and explain why you think so.

Go Online
PHSchool.com

For: An activity on Nigeria
Visit: PHSchool.com
Web Code: lad-5501

Chapter 15 Section 1 **489**

Assess and Reteach

Assess Progress [L2]

Have students complete the Section Assessment. Administer the *Section Quiz.*

All in One **Africa Teaching Resources,** *Section Quiz,* p. 292

Reteach [L1]

If students need more instruction, have them read this section in the Reading and Vocabulary Study Guide.

📖 Chapter 15, Section 1, **Eastern Hemisphere Reading and Vocabulary Study Guide,** pp. 168–170

Extend [L3]

Remind students that the Hausa-Fulani produce and trade crafts in markets. Have students learn more about the crafts of West Africa by completing the *Small Group Activity.*

All in One **Africa Teaching Resources,** *Small Group Activity: Arts and Crafts of West Africa,* pp. 307–310

Answer

✓ **Reading Check** Nigerians practice Islam, Christianity, and traditional religions.

Writing Activity
Use the *Rubric for Assessing a Newspaper Article* to evaluate students' editorials.

All in One **Africa Teaching Resources,** *Rubric for Assessing a Newspaper Article,* p. 321

Go Online PHSchool.com Typing in the Web code when prompted will bring students directly to detailed instructions for this activity.

Section 1 Assessment

Key Terms
Students' sentences should reflect knowledge of each Key Term.

Target Reading Skill
Answers will vary, but students should identify three main points from subsections or paragraphs.

Comprehension and Critical Thinking
1. (a) Hausa-Fulani—northwest, Yoruba—southwest, Igbo—southeast **(b)** Answers may include: Hausa-Fulani—largest Nigerian ethnic group, live in the northwest, composed of the Hausa and Fulani, built trading cities; Yoruba—most urban of Nigeria's ethnic groups, live in the southwest, second largest ethnic group, make up majority of residents of Lagos, live in large compounds of several houses; Igbo—third largest ethnic group, villages ruled democratically by councils of elders, tried to separate from Nigeria, live mostly in the southeast.

2. (a) the middle **(b)** to help unite the country by bringing it close to each of the major ethnic groups

3. (a) the Igbo **(b)** Nigeria is rich in culture, but it is also difficult to unify the people and has led to conflict. **(c)** Possible answer: Nigerians can try to work together and to be more accepting of different ethnic groups.

Chapter 15 Section 1 **489**

Objectives

Social Studies

1. Learn about the years of British colonial rule in the area that is now called Ghana.
2. Find out about the beliefs that helped move Ghana toward independence.
3. Discover how Ghana changed after achieving independence.

Reading/Language Arts

Identify implied main ideas to help you remember the most important ideas that you read.

Prepare to Read

Build Background Knowledge   L2

Tell students that in this section they will be reading about a country whose economy has depended on the export of natural resources throughout history. Show students *Ghana: Living on the Forest's Edge.* Using the Give One, Get One strategy (TE, p. T37), ask students to identify the natural resource discussed in the video, and list some ways in which groups are trying to protect this resource.

📼 *Ghana: Living on the Forest's Edge,* **World Studies Video Program**

Set a Purpose for Reading   L2

■ Preview the Objectives.

■ Read each statement in the *Reading Readiness Guide* aloud. Ask students to mark the statements true or false.

All in One Africa Teaching Resources, *Reading Readiness Guide,* p. 294

■ Have students discuss the statements in pairs or groups of four, then mark their worksheets again. Use the Numbered Heads participation strategy (TE, p. T36) to call on students to share their group's perspectives.

Vocabulary Builder
Preview Key Terms   L2

Pronounce each Key Term, then ask students to say the word with you. Provide a simple explanation such as, "During a coup d'état, an outside group might use force to take over the government."

Prepare to Read

Objectives

In this section you will

1. Learn about the years of British colonial rule in the area that is now called Ghana.
2. Find out about the beliefs that helped move Ghana toward independence.
3. Discover how Ghana changed after achieving independence.

Taking Notes

As you read this section, look for details about events in the history of Ghana's government. Copy the timeline below, and use it to record your findings.

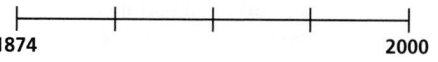
1874   2000

🎯 Target Reading Skill

Identify Implied Main Ideas Identifying main ideas can help you remember the most important ideas in your text. Sometimes the main ideas are not stated directly. In those cases, you must add up all the details in a paragraph or section, and then state the main idea yourself.

Key Terms

• **Kwame Nkrumah** (KWAH mee un KROO muh) *n.* founder of Ghana's independence movement and Ghana's first president
• **sovereignty** (SAHV run tee) *n.* political control
• **coup d'état** (koo day TAH) *n.* the sudden overthrow of a government by force

Kwame Nkrumah

490 Africa

In 1935, a 26-year-old student traveled by ship from Ghana to the United States. At that time, Ghana was called the Gold Coast because of its abundant supply of gold. The region had been ruled by Great Britain for more than 60 years. The student's visit to the United States was a turning point in his life. He was well aware that the people of his country did not have true freedom or equality. When he saw the Statue of Liberty for the first time, he felt determined to bring freedom to both his country and his whole continent. As he looked at the statue, he thought to himself, "I shall never rest until I have carried your message to Africa." The student's name was **Kwame Nkrumah**, and in 1957, he would become the leader who steered Ghana to independence.

🎯 Target Reading Skill   L2

Identify Implied Main Ideas Draw students' attention to the Target Reading Skill. Tell them that sometimes a main idea is not directly stated, but by studying all the details in a paragraph, they can then state a main idea themselves.

Model the skill by reading the second paragraph on p. 494 under Nkrumah Overthrown and state the implied main idea.

(Although Nkrumah was once considered a hero by the people of Nigeria, he was later blamed for the country's economic problems.)

Give students *Identify Implied Main Ideas.* Have them complete the worksheet in groups.

All in One Africa Teaching Resources, *Identify Implied Main Ideas,* p. 302

Links Across
Time

Asante Legacy The Asante did not submit to colonial rule without a struggle. In 1900, Yaa Asantewa (YAH ah uh sahn TEE wah), the Asante king's mother (at the right), led a war against the British. Even with more powerful weapons, the British took four months to defeat the queen mother's troops. After the war, the British began to treat the Asante more respectfully. Asante children still sing a song about "Yaa Asantewa, the warrior woman who carries a gun and a sword of state into battle."

Links
Read **Links Across Time** on this page. Ask students **Why do you think the British treated the Asante more respectfully after Yaa Asantewa's rebellion?** (*Possible answer: because they did not submit to colonial rule and fought against it, even though they did not have modern weapons.*)

The Colonial Years

For hundreds of years, many Africans in the Gold Coast had wanted their people to be free to rule themselves. While the Europeans were trading gold and slaves on the Gold Coast, some members of a large local ethnic group called the Akan (AH kahn) formed the Asante (uh SAHN tee) kingdom. This kingdom became very rich from trade. It controlled parts of the northern savanna and the coastal south. The Asante used their wealth and power to try stopping the European takeover of their kingdom. Despite these efforts, in 1874 Great Britain succeeded in colonizing the Gold Coast. Great Britain then ruled the colony through chiefs it appointed or who already held authority.

Effects of British Control When the British colonized the Gold Coast, their main interest was controlling the colony's economy. They encouraged farmers to grow cacao beans, from which they produced cocoa. The British then sent the cocoa to factories in Britain where it was made into chocolate. The British also exported timber and gold.

The export of raw materials led to problems that became common throughout colonial Africa. For example, people began growing fewer food crops for themselves and more cash crops such as cacao, which brought in more money. Soon, Gold Coast Africans could no longer supply enough food for their own needs, so they had to import it.

A related problem was that processing cacao brought in more money than growing it did. Therefore, most of the profit was gained in Britain, not in the Gold Coast. Yet another concern was that people began spending more time farming and less time making traditional crafts. As a result, Gold Coast people began to depend on buying factory-made goods from the British.

A Symbol of Pride
Colorful kente (KEN tay) cloth was invented in Ghana in the 1100s as a cloth to be worn by royalty. Over time, it became common for all people in Ghana to wear kente. Many West Africans and African Americans wear kente today with great pride. **Analyze Information** *Why would a piece of cloth serve well as a way to show pride in one's heritage?*

Instruct

The Colonial Years L2

Guided Instruction

- **Vocabulary Builder** Clarify the high-use word **appoint** before reading.

- Read The Colonial Years using the Choral Reading strategy (TE, p. T34).

- Ask students **How did the Asante kingdom become rich?** (*through trade*)

- Have students discuss why the British wanted to colonize the Gold Coast. (*to control its economy*) Ask **What effect did the export of cacao have on the Gold Coast?** (*People stopped growing as many food crops and had to import food. Also, because processing cacao was more lucrative than growing it, most of the profits from the crop went to Britain's economy instead of the Gold Coast's economy.*)

- Ask students **How did the old and new mix in the Gold Coast?** (*New schools built by the British introduced Christianity; new ideas and lifestyles brought by the British were introduced to traditional communities, and caused many people to blend old and new ways.*)

Independent Practice

Ask students to create the Taking Notes graphic organizer on a blank piece of paper. Then have them fill it in with dates and information from the section.

Monitor Progress

As students fill in the graphic organizer, circulate and make sure individuals are choosing the correct details. Provide assistance as needed.

Answer

Analyze Information It is an easily seen symbol, and different colors can be used to customize the cloth.

Vocabulary Builder

Use the information below to teach students this section's high-use academic words.

High-Use Words	Definition and Sample Sentence
appoint, p. 491	*v.* to select for a position The principal **appointed** me hall monitor for the entire month.
initiative, p. 492	*n.* taking the first step or move The group leader had **initiative** and began working on the project right away.
reform, p. 495	*v.* make better The candidate promised to **reform** schools across the state.
implement, p. 495	*v.* carry out, or accomplish Teachers should make sure to **implement** classroom rules.

Identify Implied Main Ideas As a follow up, ask students to answer the Target Reading Skill question in the Student Edition. *(The British introduced new ways of life in the Gold Coast and people blended these new ways with the traditional African ways.)*

Moving Toward Independence L2

Guided Instruction

- **Vocabulary Builder** Clarify the high-use word **initiative** before reading.

- Read Moving Toward Independence with students. As students read, circulate and make sure individuals can answer the Reading Check question.

- Ask students **What claim did some Europeans make as a reason for not giving African colonies independence?** *(that the colonies were not ready to rule themselves)* **How did Nkrumah respond to this argument?** *(He pointed out that traditional African governments had ruled Africa for thousands of years.)*

- Have students describe the system of government of the Akan. *(The Akan elders selected rulers from the royal family; if the ruler did not rule fairly, the elders could give power to a new ruler.)*

- Ask students **What actions did Nkrumah take when he returned to the Gold Coast in 1947?** *(He convinced the people to demand independence from Great Britain.)*

Independent Practice

Ask students to continue to fill in the Taking Notes graphic organizer with dates and details from the section.

Monitor Progress

As students fill in the graphic organizer, circulate and make sure individuals are placing the information in chronological order. Provide assistance as needed.

Answers

✓ **Reading Check** The British exported cocoa, timber, and gold.
Draw Conclusions It symbolizes the "seat" of government; the ruler that sits on it would easily be identified as the head of the government.

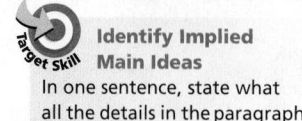 **Identify Implied Main Ideas**
In one sentence, state what all the details in the paragraph at the right express.

Mixing Old and New The British brought changes to some aspects of Gold Coast culture. For example, they built schools in the Gold Coast. Foreign missionaries ran the schools. Christianity began to replace traditional religions in many areas. Over the years, new ideas and ways of doing things came to traditional communities. Many people blended the new ways with the old African ways. For example, Kwame Nkrumah was born a Christian. But he also believed in parts of the traditional African religion. Nkrumah's respect for the old and the new ways helped him govern when Ghana became independent.

✓ **Reading Check** What goods did the British export from the Gold Coast?

Moving Toward Independence

During the 1900s, Africans whose countries were under colonial rule organized to demand independence. The European countries, however, resisted giving up their colonies. Some Europeans claimed that the colonies were not ready to rule themselves. Nkrumah challenged this argument with a reminder that traditional African governments had ruled Africa's lands for thousands of years. The Akan, for example, had long governed much of the Gold Coast.

Traditional Government The Akan are the largest ethnic group in Ghana today. Historically, Akan elders selected their rulers from members of the royal family. If the leader did not rule fairly, the elders had the right to choose another ruler. Each new ruler received this warning about how to behave:

A Symbolic Seat
Stools such as this one carry important symbolism for the Akan. When a new ruler takes office, the people say he has been "enstooled." They believe the stool the ruler sits on contains the soul of the nation.
Draw Conclusions Why do you think people would consider a seat an important symbol?

> ❝ Tell him that
> We do not wish greediness
> We do not wish that he should curse
> We do not wish that his ears should
>   hard of hearing
> We do not wish that he should call
>   people fools
> We do not wish that he should act o
>   his own initiative [act alone] . . .
> We do not wish that it should ever b
>   said 'I have no time. I have no tim
> We do not wish personal abuse
> We do not wish personal violence. ❞
>
> —*Akan statement of political expectati*

Skills Mini Lesson

Identifying Cause and Effect

1. Teach the skill by explaining that cause and effect means that one event happens because of another event. Tell students that identifying causes and effects can help clarify the relationship between events.

2. Help students practice the skill by identifying one effect of exporting cocoa from the Gold Coast to Britain. *(Possible answer: People in the Gold Coast stopped growing so many food crops.)*

3. Have students apply the skill by identifying an effect of foreign missionaries on the Gold Coast. *(Christianity began to replace traditional religions.)*

Nkrumah Takes Action In 1947, after more than a decade of schooling in the United States and England, Nkrumah returned home. He found a region that was poor, despite an abundance of natural resources. Nkrumah believed that people should benefit from the wealth of their land. He traveled throughout the Gold Coast, convincing people to demand independence.

✓ **Reading Check** How did the Akan system of government aim to assure good government?

COUNTRY PROFILE
Focus on Economics

Ghana

Ghana began its period of independence in the late 1950s with a wealth of natural resources. At the time, few people in Ghana had benefited from this wealth. As it has moved from a colony to an independent country with new priorities, Ghana has worked to change its economy. Mining has become much more important than farming. Ghana trades extensively with countries in Europe, North America, and Africa. Study the map and charts to learn more about the economy of Ghana.

Export Destinations

- 15%
- 56%
- 10%
- 7%
- 6%
- 6%

- ■ Netherlands
- ▨ United Kingdom
- ■ United States
- ▨ Germany
- ■ France
- ■ Other

SOURCE: DK World Desk Reference

Income From Mining, 2000

Percent of Income

Diamonds	Maganese	Other Minerals	Gold	Bauxite
2%	2%	24%	71%	1%

SOURCE: United States Geological Survey

Ghana: Natural Resources
KEY
- Gold
- Iron
- Manganese
- Bauxite
- Diamonds
- Natural gas
- Hydroelectric power
- — National border
- ⊛ National capital
- ⊙ Other city

BURKINA FASO

Bolgatanga
Tamale
GHANA
Lake Volta
Kumasi
Volta River
Accra
Sekondi-Takoradi
ATLANTIC OCEAN
Gulf of Guinea
TOGO
BENIN

0 miles 100
0 kilometers 100
Lambert Azimuthal Equal Area

Map and Chart Skills

1. **Locate** Where is most of Ghana's gold located?
2. **Analyze** How much of Ghana's income comes from gold?
3. **Summarize** Explain whether Ghana sells most of its exports to one country or to a variety of countries.

Go Online PHSchool.com
Use Web Code lae-5502 for DK World Desk Reference Online.

Chapter 15 Section 2 **493**

Differentiated Instruction

For Advanced Readers ⬛L3
Students can learn more about economic activity in West Africa by completing *Reading an Economic Activity Map.*

All in One **Africa Teaching Resources,** *Reading An Economic Activity Map,* p. 315

For English Language Learners ⬛L2
Students whose native language is Spanish may benefit by reading the Spanish version of *Guided Reading and Review.*

📄 **Africa Spanish Support,** *Guided Reading and Review (Spanish),* p. 162

COUNTRY PROFILE
Focus on Economics

Guided Instruction ⬛L2
Ask students to study the Country Profile on this page. Remind them to read the map key to understand what the different symbols on the map represent. Also encourage them to study the circle and bar graphs carefully. As a class, answer the Map and Chart Skills questions. Allow students to briefly discuss their responses with a partner before sharing their answers.

Independent Practice
Have students choose one country that buys Ghana's exports and ask them to do research to find out what products that country buys from Ghana. Then ask students to write a few sentences describing the importance of one of those products to the country they chose.

Answers

✓ **Reading Check** Akan elders had the right to replace unfair rulers.

Map and Chart Skills

1. in the south
2. Seventy-one percent of Ghana's mining income comes from gold.
3. Ghana sells its exports to a variety of countries including the United Kingdom, the United States, and the Netherlands.

Go Online PHSchool.com Students can find additional useful information about this topic on the DK World Desk Reference Online.

If you have not already done so, show students *Ghana: Living on the Forest's Edge*. Ask **How are some groups in Ghana trying to help and make use of deforested areas?** *(They offer jobs to people from impoverished villages to collect and process wood that was left to rot, and replant deforested land to grow medicinal plants.)*

Independence Achieved

Guided Instruction
- **Vocabulary Builder** Clarify the high-use words **reform** and **implement** before reading.

- Read Independence Achieved with students.

- Ask students **How did Ghana's independence affect other Africans?** *(It inspired them to push hard for independence.)*

- Have students discuss why Nkrumah was overthrown just nine years after being hailed as a hero. *(He was blamed for Ghana's serious economic problems.)*

- Ask students **What changes did President Jerry Rawlings try to create in Ghana?** *(He tried to reform the government and economy of Ghana.)* **How?** *(He stressed the traditional African values of hard work and sacrifice.)*

Independent Practice
Have students complete the graphic organizer with dates and details from the section.

Monitor Progress
- Show *Section Support Transparency AF 48* and ask students to check their graphic organizers individually. Go over key concepts and clarify key vocabulary as needed.

  Africa Transparencies, *Section Reading Support Transparency AF 48*

- Tell students to fill in the last column of the *Reading Readiness Guide*. Probe for what they learned that confirms or invalidates each statement.

  All in One Africa Teaching Resources, *Reading Readiness Guide*, p. 294

Answer
Draw Inferences Possible answer: that Nkrumah no longer had any power in Ghana

Learn about challenges facing Ghana's environment.

Independence Achieved

In 1957, some 22 years after making his pledge at the Statue of Liberty, Nkrumah gave a moving speech to his people. Great Britain, he said, had finally agreed to grant them **sovereignty** (SAHV run tee), or political control of their own country. Cheering, the people carried Nkrumah through the streets. Crowds sang victory songs to celebrate a dream come true.

Nkrumah became the leader and later the president of the new country. The government named the country Ghana after an African kingdom that flourished hundreds of years ago. Ghana was the first West African colony to gain independence. It was also the second country in all of Africa to become independent of European rule, after South Africa. The achievement of Ghana's independence would soon inspire many other Africans to push hard for—and achieve—freedom.

Nkrumah Overthrown Nine years after he had been carried through the streets a hero, Nkrumah was removed from office by a military **coup d'état** (koo day TAH), or takeover. Most Ghanaian (guh NAY un) citizens did not protest. In fact, many celebrated. Some even pulled down statues of Nkrumah.

How did a hero become an enemy? Nkrumah had formed great plans for Ghana. He borrowed huge amounts of money to make those plans happen quickly. For example, he spent millions of dollars on the construction of a conference center and a superhighway. In addition, he made an agreement with a United States company to build a dam on the Volta River. The dam would provide electricity and irrigation for people in rural areas. But when world prices of Ghana's chief export, cocoa, fell, Ghana could not pay back its loans. Many people blamed Nkrumah for the country's economic problems.

Nkrumah Toppled
Pulled down by angry citizens, the headless statue of Nkrumah lies on the ground in Accra, Ghana. After his overthrow, Nkrumah lived in Guinea and did not return to Ghana before his death. **Draw Inferences** *What do you think Ghanaians thought when they looked at the toppled statue of Nkrumah?*

494 Africa

Background: Global Perspectives

The End of Colonialism Ghana's independence was achieved peacefully, but some African countries had to fight wars to gain their freedom from colonial rule. The Algerians fought for eight years until they finally gained independence from the French in 1962. Angola and Mozambique fought against Portuguese rule before winning independence in 1975. Britain did not formally recognize Zimbabwe's independence until 1980, after a long struggle.

A Hero Again Nkrumah's downfall did not end Ghana's problems. The country alternated between military and democratically elected governments. Few were successful. Over time, people began to think well again of Nkrumah. Many felt that he had done his best to help the country, especially by leading Ghana to independence. When he died in 1972, he was hailed as a national hero. Leaders around the world mourned his death.

Ghana's Government and Economy Today In 1981, Jerry Rawlings seized power, becoming Ghana's second long-term president. Rawlings, an Air Force pilot, had previously overthrown the government and ruled for a few months. As president from 1981 to 2000, Rawlings tried to reform the politics and economy of Ghana. He stressed the importance of Ghana's traditional values of hard work and sacrifice. Ghanaians supported Rawlings, and Ghana's economy began to grow.

Today, Ghana's economy continues to be dependent on the sale of cocoa. Even so, the economy has grown strong enough that Ghana has been able to build better roads and irrigation systems. The government under John Kufuor, who was democratically elected president in 2000, has continued implementing improvements in Ghana.

✓ **Reading Check** How did Nkrumah lose his position as president?

After Nkrumah's death, this mausoleum was built as a national monument in his honor.

Section 2 Assessment

Key Terms
Review the key terms at the beginning of this section. Use each term in a sentence that explains its meaning.

⊙ **Target Reading Skill**
State an implied main idea from Section 2 other than the one you identified on page 492.

Comprehension and Critical Thinking
1. (a) **Explain** How did the Gold Coast's economy change after the British began encouraging farmers to grow cacao beans?
(b) **Summarize** While the British ruled the Gold Coast, did traditional ways stay the same, disappear, or blend with the new?
2. (a) **Recall** When arguing for independence, how did Kwame Nkrumah respond to the European claim that the African colonies were not ready to rule themselves?
(b) **Identify Causes** Why did the economic conditions of the Gold Coast under colonial rule lead Africans there to believe they should rule themselves?
3. (a) **Note** Compared to other African colonies, when did Ghana gain independence?
(b) **Identify Cause and Effect** What caused people's attitudes toward Nkrumah to change before and after his death?

Writing Activity
Work with a partner to write about one or two changes you would like to see happen in your country or community. Consider obstacles to making these changes. Then write a plan that explains each change, how you would make it, and how you would overcome any obstacles.

For: An activity on Ghana
Visit: PHSchool.com
Web Code: lad-5502

Chapter 15 Section 2 **495**

Objective

Learn how to make decisions.

Prepare to Read

Build Background Knowledge L2

Ask students to think about decisions they have made. How did they choose between the alternatives to make a decision? Why might it help to use a grid like the one on p. 149 to make a difficult decision? *(A decision-making grid can help you more easily analyze possible outcomes and see the positives and negatives of each choice.)*

Instruct

Decision Making L2

Guided Instruction

■ Read the skill steps as a class and write them on the board.

■ Practice the skill by following the steps on p. 496 and applying them to the practice decision on p. 497. Draw a decision-making grid on the board. Choose a sample item a student might want to buy and a sample field trip destination.

■ Using an Idea Wave (TE, p. T35), have students offer possible positive and negative outcomes to choosing to spend their money on a field trip or a personal item. Write these on the grid on the board.

■ Have students write down a final decision on a separate piece of paper, along with a reason, and share their response with the class.

Independent Practice

Assign *Skills for Life* and have students complete it individually.

All in One **Africa Teaching Resources,** *Skills for Life,* p. 306

Monitor Progress

As students are completing *Skills for Life*, circulate and make sure individuals are applying the skill steps effectively. Provide assistance as needed.

Decision Making

Julia's neighbor, Mrs. Gonzalez, owns a dog that Julia loves to play with. One day Mrs. Gonzalez offered to pay Julia for walking the dog every morning and afternoon. That sounded to Julia like a fun way to earn some money. But she was already considering joining the swim team. Walking the dog twice a day as well as going to swim practice seemed like too many commitments. Julia realized she would have to decide between the two—but how?

Playing with Buster in the backyard

Some decisions are easy to make because one choice clearly has more to offer than the other. On the other hand, many decisions are difficult to make because all the choices have both positive and negative outcomes. Making good decisions means considering all the options before you decide.

Learn the Skill

Use these steps to make a good decision.

1. **Identify the issue.** Write a question explaining what needs to be decided.

2. **List the alternatives.** When you make a decision, you are choosing between at least two alternatives, or choices.

3. **For each alternative, list the likely outcomes, both positive and negative.** Every decision has outcomes, or effects. Use a decision-making grid like the one on page 497 to list the possible outcomes.

4. **Put a check mark (✓) next to the most important outcomes.** Marking the outcomes that matter most to you can help you reach your decision.

5. **Choose the option that seems best.** Write your decision in a sentence.

My Decision-Making Grid

Decision: Should I take the dog-walking job or join the swim team?

Alternatives	Likely Positive Outcomes	Likely Negative Outcomes
Take the dog-walking job.	Earn money. Get to play with a dog. Help my neighbor.	Don't have time for other activities. Don't get to spend time with friends.
Join the swim team.	Get exercise. Have fun. Meet new people.	Don't have time for other activities. Don't get to spend time with animals.

Practice the Skill

Suppose you win a contest at school and receive money as a prize. There is a certain item you have wanted to buy, and now you can afford it. But in three months your class is taking a field trip, and you know you will need to have some money for the trip. Follow the steps below to decide what to do with your prize money.

1. What is the decision you will make? Write down a question explaining what needs to be decided.

2. List the alternatives that you have to choose from. Are there two alternatives, or more?

3. Create a decision-making grid like the one above. Fill in the likely outcomes.

4. Put a check mark next to the outcomes that are most important to you.

5. Decide which alternative seems best to you. Write down an explanation of your reasoning.

Apply the Skill

Think of an important decision that you might have to make in the near future. It might have to do with school, friends, family, or something else. Create a decision-making grid to analyze the alternatives and outcomes. Then state your decision and your reasons for making it.

Chapter 15 **497**

Assess and Reteach

Assess Progress **L2**
Ask students to do the Apply the Skill activity.

Reteach **L1**
If students are having trouble applying the skill steps, have them review the skill using the interactive Social Studies Skills Tutor CD-ROM.

 Decision Making, **Social Studies Skill Tutor CD-ROM**

Extend **L3**
To extend the lesson, ask students to scan Section 2 again in small groups. Have them focus on details relating to Kwame Nkrumah's life, taking note of times that he may have had to make a decision, such as whether to help liberate Ghana or how to spend money as president of Ghana. Ask students to create a decision-making grid listing one of Nkrumah's decisions and what students believe may have been alternative choices, along with possible negative and positive outcomes. If necessary, students may conduct their own research on Nkrumah's life to learn more about how he made his decisions.

Answer
Apply the Skill
Students' decision-making grids will vary, but should include a decision with two or more alternatives, summaries of the likely positive and negative outcomes of each alternative, and a final decision with a reason.

Section 3
Step-by-Step Instruction

Objectives

Social Studies

1. Discover how Mali's environment affects its economy.
2. Find out how desert can spread across the land.
3. Learn about the importance of preserving Mali's environment.

Reading/Language Arts

Identify supporting details to get further information about a main idea.

Prepare to Read

Build Background Knowledge L2

Show students *Mali: Africa's Grain Basket,* which will introduce students to the importance of farming in Mali. Tell students they will learn more about the role farming plays in Mali's economy and how it is threatened by the spreading of the desert.

📼 *Mali: Africa's Grain Basket,* **World Studies Video Program**

Set a Purpose for Reading L2

- Preview the Objectives.

- Read each statement in the *Reading Readiness Guide* aloud. Ask students to mark the statements true or false.

  All in One **Africa Teaching Resources,** *Reading Readiness Guide,* p. 298

- Have students discuss the statements in pairs or groups of four, then mark their worksheets again. Use the Numbered Heads participation strategy (TE, p. T36) to call on students to share their group's perspectives.

Vocabulary Builder
Preview Key Terms L2

Pronounce each Key Term, then ask students to say the word with you. Provide a simple explanation such as, "Overgrazing occurs when people allow the animals they are raising to eat too many of the plants in an area."

Section 3
Mali
Desert Living

Prepare to Read

Objectives

In this section you will
1. Discover how Mali's environment affects its economy.
2. Find out how desert can spread across the land.
3. Learn about the importance of preserving Mali's environment.

Taking Notes

As you read this section, look for details about the role of the Sahel in the life of the people of Mali. Copy the diagram below, and use it to record your findings.

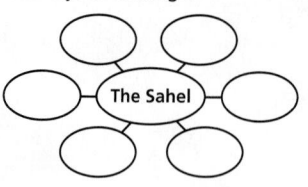

🎯 Target Reading Skill

Identify Supporting Details The main idea of a paragraph or section is supported by details that give further information about it. These details may explain the main idea by giving examples or reasons. As you read, note the details that support each main idea in the text.

Key Terms

- **desertification** (dih zurt uh fih KAY shun) *n.* the process by which fertile land becomes too dry or damaged to support life
- **overgrazing** (oh vur GRAYZ ing) *n.* allowing too much grazing by large herds of animals

Tombouctou, Mali

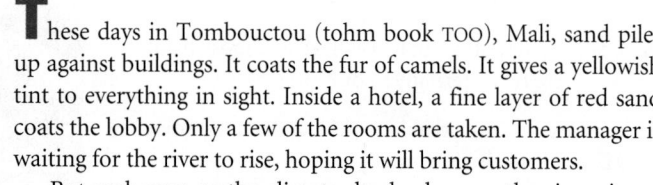

These days in Tombouctou (tohm book TOO), Mali, sand piles up against buildings. It coats the fur of camels. It gives a yellowish tint to everything in sight. Inside a hotel, a fine layer of red sand coats the lobby. Only a few of the rooms are taken. The manager is waiting for the river to rise, hoping it will bring customers.

But each year, as the climate slowly changes, the river rises a little later. "Ten years ago the first boat arrived on July 1," says Tombouctou politician Moulaye Haidara (moo LAH ee HY dah rah). "Five years ago it was July 15. Now, we're lucky if it's here by early August. In another five years, who knows?"

498 Africa

🎯 Target Reading Skill L2

Identify Supporting Details Point out the Target Reading Skill. Tell students that supporting details give examples or more information about a main idea.

Model the skill by identifying the main idea of the first paragraph on p. 151 in A Crossroads Location. (*In the past, the Sahel's location as a crossroads between the Sahara and the savanna has helped its economy flourish.*) Then identify the supporting details found in the paragraph. (*The city of Tombouctou was once a convenient stopping point for many camel caravans traveling between North Africa and the savanna; From the 1300s through the 1500s, Tombouctou thrived as a wealthy center of trade.*)

Give students *Identify Supporting Details.* Have them complete the activity in groups.

All in One **Africa Teaching Resources,** *Identify Supporting Details,* p. 303

Mali's Environment

Tombouctou is located in the partly dry lands of the Sahel. As you can see on the map in the Country Profile on page 501, the Sahel lies between the Sahara and the savanna. The Sahara stretches over much of West Africa, and it is expanding all the time. In Mali, the Sahara covers about one third of the land. Few Malians inhabit the Sahara. Some live in the Sahel, while others live in the savanna, the one area of the country that receives abundant rainfall.

Resources of the Sahel The Sahel extends across Africa from Mauritania in the west to Ethiopia in the east. People have lived in the Sahel for thousands of years. They have long used its resources to earn their living. Malians in the Sahel herd animals and raise food crops to feed their families. Many earn extra money by raising cash crops as well. The rainy season, which lasts from May to October, is an ideal time for farming. During the rest of the year, farming is still possible in the Sahel thanks to water sources that exist year-round, such as the Niger River.

A Crossroads Location In the past, the Sahel's location as a crossroads between the Sahara and the savanna helped its economy flourish. For example, the city of Tombouctou was once a convenient stopping point for many camel caravans traveling between North Africa and the savanna. From the 1300s through the 1500s, Tombouctou thrived as one of Africa's wealthy centers of trade.

Today, people still live in Tombouctou, but they no longer practice trade on a large scale. Once European ships began trading along Africa's coast, trade through the Sahel decreased. Transporting goods by ship was faster and easier than sending them by camel. However, Tombouctou is still a crossroads for people traveling through the area.

✓ **Reading Check** Which months are the best for farming in the Sahel?

Table Skills

The table shows some of the groups of people who pass through Tombouctou and the ways they typically make a living. Below, a trader's camels carry salt to Tombouctou. **Identify** Which groups are traders? **Analyze Information** Based on the way they earn their living, what reasons do you think these groups have for passing through Tombouctou?

Activity in Tombouctou

Ethnic Group	Activities
Bambara	Farmers, traders
Berbers	Nomads
Fulani	Cattle herders
Mandingo	Farmers, traders
Songhai	Traders, gardeners
Tuareg	Nomads

Chapter 15 Section 3 **499**

Vocabulary Builder

Use the information below to teach students this section's high-use words.

High-Use Word	Definition and Sample Sentence
crossroads, p. 499	*n.* a central meeting place The store serves as a **crossroads** for kids going to and from school.
flourish, p. 499	*v.* to gain in wealth Joe hopes his business will **flourish** so he can afford a new house.
thrive, p. 499	*v.* to achieve economic success Jessica's boat rental shop **thrives** in the summer when the weather is warmer.

Target Reading Skill L2

Identify Supporting Details As a follow up, ask students to answer the Target Reading Skill question in the Student Edition. *(The desert is spreading south; fertile land is turning into desert; loose soil is covering the land; drought has turned the land into desert.)*

The Desert Spreads L2

Preserving the Environment L2

Guided Instruction

- Read The Desert Spreads and Preserving the Environment with students. Circulate to make sure individuals can answer the Reading Check questions.

- Ask students to describe the causes of desertification that may be at work in Mali. *(Overgrazing—Soil erodes when animals eat the plants whose roots hold soil in place. Drought—Lack of rain can turn land into desert.)*

- Ask students **What might happen to the Tuareg if desertification continues in Mali?** *(Possible answer: They may no longer be able to raise animals and live as nomads.)*

Independent Practice

Ask students to complete the graphic organizer.

Monitor Progress

- Show *Section Reading Support Transparency AF 49* and ask students to check their graphic organizers individually. Go over key concepts and clarify key vocabulary as needed.

  📖 **Africa Transparencies,** *Section Reading Support Transparency AF 49*

- Tell students to fill in the last column of the *Reading Readiness Guide*. Probe for what they learned that confirms or invalidates each statement.

  All in One **Africa Teaching Resources,** *Reading Readiness Guide,* p. 298

Answers

Diagram Skills Identify Animals pull up the roots of the plants, which loosens the soil. **Predict** Possible answer: They could plant plants with stronger roots or replant regularly.

✓ Reading Check It makes the land dry and infertile.

500 *Africa*

Identify Supporting Details

The main idea under the red heading The Desert Spreads is that desertification is threatening the ways people in Mali make a living. Which details in the paragraphs at the right tell about this problem?

■ **Diagram Skills**

Overgrazing in the Sahara is the result of too much grazing by animals such as sheep, goats, camels, and cattle. **Identify** How does the soil become loosened when animals graze? **Predict** Do you think there are ways in which the people of the Sahara could avoid overgrazing their animals?

The Desert Spreads

Mali has little industry. Most people make their living through trading, farming, or herding. However, these types of work are being threatened by **desertification,** the change of fertile land into land that is too dry or damaged to support life. In Mali and other countries of the Sahel, the desert is spreading south. Even the wetter lands in southwest Mali are at risk of becoming desert. But how does fertile land turn into desert? Scientists have identified two causes of desertification that may be at work in Mali.

Overgrazing One cause of desertification is **overgrazing,** or allowing too much grazing by large herds of animals. When animals graze, they often eat the roots of plants, which hold the soil in place. With the roots gone, the fierce winds of the Sahara erode the soil. The soil then blows into the air, creating yellow dust clouds. This loose soil is one reason that Tombouctou is slowly being covered in sand—the desert is taking over the land.

Drought Another cause of desertification is drought, which you will recall is a long period of little or no rain. Droughts can turn land into desert. Over the last 30 years, the Sahel has received much less rain than it did before. Some scientists argue that a few years of good rainfall could stop desertification.

✓ Reading Check **What does desertification do to fertile land?**

Overgrazing

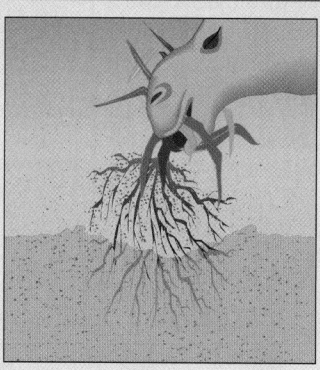

The roots of a plant hold the soil in place.

As a camel eats the plant and pulls up the roots, the soil is loosened.

Wind lifts the loosened soil from the ground and into the air.

500 Africa

Differentiated Instruction

For Gifted and Talented L3
Have students complete *Activity Shop Lab: Desertification* to learn more about how fertile land can change into desert. Tell them to use the worksheet to answer

questions and record results as they do the project.

All in One **Africa Teaching Resources,** *Activity Shop Lab: Desertification,* pp. 311–312

Mali

From north to south, Mali's climate changes from the dry desert of the Sahara to the moderately wet savanna. In between lies the Sahel, a zone where farmers and herders face challenges from year to year due to unpredictable rainfall. The boundaries of the three regions are shifting as the Sahel grows drier and the desert expands southward. Human activity has also endangered farmland and vegetation in the Sahel. Study the map and charts to learn more about the importance of water in shaping the human geography of Mali.

Mali: Physical Regions

KEY

- Sahara
- Sahel
- Savanna
- ———— National border
- ⊛ National capital
- • Other city

ALGERIA
Tropic of Cancer
Sahara
MAURITANIA
MALI
Tombouctou
Niger River
Sahel
SENEGAL
Senegal River
NIGER
Bamako
Bani River
GUINEA
BURKINA FASO
Savanna
IVORY COAST

0 miles 300
0 kilometers 300
Lambert Azimuthal Equal Area

Access to Usable Water

100%	
90%	
80%	
70%	
60%	
50%	
40%	
30%	
20%	
10%	
0%	Urban Residents	Rural Residents

SOURCE: World Health Organization

Average Rainfall

Region	Average Rainfall
Sahara	0–10 in. (0–25 cm)
Sahel	0–40 in. (25–101 cm)
Savanna	30–60 in. (76–152 cm)

SOURCE: Goode's World Atlas

Map and Chart Skills

1. **Identify** Which group has less access to safe drinking water, urban residents or rural residents?

2. **Analyze** A town in Mali received seven inches of rain two years ago. In which region of the country is this town most likely to be found?

Go Online
PHSchool.com
Use Web Code lae-5503 for **DK World Desk Reference Online.**

Preserving the Environment

Many people around the world are concerned about the future of the Sahel. The United Nations has created a committee to help prevent desertification. Before the problem of desertification can be resolved, however, people living in the Sahel must learn how to avoid practices that make the problem worse.

Skills Mini Lesson

Using Reliable Information

1. Teach the skill by explaining how to determine the reliability of information—date published, agreement with other reliable sources, the author's qualifications, and the author's motivation.

2. Help students practice the skill by evaluating the reliability of the information presented in *Al-Bakri Describes the Court of Ghana*.

3. Have students apply the skill by asking them to evaluate the reliability of the information presented in *Ibn Battuta Praises the Fairness of Mali's People.*

All in One **Africa Teaching Resources,** *Al-Bakri Describes the Court of Ghana,* p. 317; *Ibn Battuta Praises the Fairness of Mali's People,* p. 318

Guided Instruction L2

Ask students to study the Country Profile on this page. As a class, answer the Map and Chart Skills questions. Allow students to briefly discuss their responses with a partner before sharing answers.

Independent Practice

- Have students complete the *Getting Safe Water* Internet activity to learn more about how the people of Africa are able to access safe drinking water. Have students work in pairs to complete the activity.

Go Online
PHSchool.com

For: Environmental and Global Issues: *Getting Safe Water*
Visit: PHSchool.com
Web Code: lad-5505

- Then ask students to use the information from the activity and the Country Profile to write a brief news report about how the people of Africa are able to access safe drinking water.

Answers

Map and Chart Skills

1. rural residents

2. the Sahara

Go Online
PHSchool.com Students can find additional useful information about this topic on the DK World Desk Reference Online.

Assess and Reteach

Assess Progress `L2`

Have students complete the Section Assessment. Administer the *Section Quiz*.

 **Africa Teaching Resources,** *Section Quiz,* p. 300

Reteach `L1`

If students need more instruction, have them read this section in the Reading and Vocabulary Study Guide.

📖 Chapter 15, Section 3, **Eastern Hemisphere Reading and Vocabulary Study Guide,** pp. 174–176

 If you have not already done so, show students *Mali: Africa's Grain Basket*. Ask **How do some villages use the money they earn from growing wheat?** (*They build new schools, hire teachers, build infirmaries, and form credit unions.*)

Extend `L3`

Students can learn more about Mali's environmental challenges and possible solutions by completing *Reporting to an Environmental Conference*.

> **Go Online** PHSchool.com
>
> **For:** Long-Term Integrated Projects: *Reporting to an Environmental Conference*
> **Visit:** PHSchool.com
> **Web Code:** lad-5504

Answer

✓ **Reading Check** They faced water and food shortages because of droughts.

Section 3 Assessment

Key Terms

Students' sentences should reflect knowledge of each Key Term.

🎯 Target Reading Skill

Students should list the details that explain how desertification threatens the people of Mali's ways of life and the country's economy, as well as how the government is trying to solve the problem.

Comprehension and Critical Thinking

1. (a) The rainy season and water resources such as the Niger River provide water for

Like this woman, most Tuaregs wear blue from head to toe.

Learn about government changes to farming.

A Way of Life in Danger Many people who live in the Sahel are nomads. The Tuareg (TWAH reg), for example, have lived in the desert and in the Sahel for many hundreds of years. They move their herds of goats, sheep, and camels south in the dry season and north in the wet season. The desertification of countries like Mali is threatening the Tuareg way of life. Moreover, during the 1970s and 1980s, Mali experienced several major droughts. Facing water and food shortages, some of the nomadic Tuareg have settled on farms or moved to cities. Others have built camps outside Tombouctou.

Finding Solutions Desertification has hurt Mali's economy by making it harder for farmers to grow cash crops. To help the economy, Mali's government has encouraged businesses to come to Mali and people to start their own businesses. Also, to help the environment, Mali's government has been studying the problem of desertification and is implementing programs to combat it. With the help of the United Nations, the government is working to educate people about better ways to use land. The government is also sponsoring irrigation and farming projects that will offset the effects of desertification.

✓ **Reading Check** Why did many Tuareg settle on farms, move to cities, or build camps?

 Section 3 Assessment

Key Terms

Review the key terms at the beginning of this section. Use each term in a sentence that explains its meaning.

🎯 Target Reading Skill

State the details that support the main idea of the paragraphs under the red heading Preserving the Environment.

Comprehension and Critical Thinking

1. (a) Identify Name two ways in which the environment of the Sahel makes farming in the region possible.

(b) Compare Compare the effects of the environment on farming and on trade.

2. (a) Recall What are two possible causes of desertification in Mali?

(b) Draw Conclusions How much control do humans have in preventing desertification?

3. (a) Describe How has Mali's government responded to the negative effects of desertification on the economy?

(b) Predict If the government's efforts succeed, do you think some of the Tuareg will be able to return to their nomadic way of life?

Writing Activity

Overgrazing is one possible cause of desertification in the Sahel. In North America, what common activities may present a threat to its environment? Do you think those activities should be discouraged? Write a persuasive essay explaining why or why not.

> **Writing Tip** Be sure to use persuasive language in your essay. Include reasons and examples that clearly support your argument.

502 Africa

---

growing crops. **(b)** Possible answer: Both trade and farming are threatened by desertification. A lack of fertile land makes farming difficult, and the hot, dry conditions of the desert make travel to trade goods difficult.

2. (a) overgrazing and drought **(b)** Possible answer: Humans can prevent some desertification if they stop animals from overgrazing.

3. (a) It encourages people to start their own businesses, encourages existing businesses to come to Mali, and implements educational,

planting, and irrigation projects to help stop desertification. **(b)** Possible answer: Yes, because some are living in camps outside Tombouctou and will probably want to return to their way of life.

Writing Activity

Use the *Rubric for Assessing a Writing Assignment* to evaluate students' essays.

 Africa Teaching Resources, *Rubric for Assessing a Writing Assignment,* p. 322

Chapter 15 Review and Assessment

◆ Chapter Summary

Section 1: Nigeria

- Nigeria is home to more than 250 ethnic groups. The largest are the Hausa-Fulani, the Yoruba, and the Igbo.
- After thousands of years of self-rule, Nigeria became a British colony in 1914. It gained independence from Great Britain in 1960.
- During Nigeria's move toward democracy, Nigerians have faced conflicts over religion and over the wealth gained by the oil industry.

Section 2: Ghana

- In 1874, the British colonized the Gold Coast. They took control of the economy, built schools, and brought Christianity to the region.
- During the 1900s, Africans under colonial rule began organizing for independence. Kwame Nkrumah led the independence movement in the Gold Coast.
- In 1957, Ghana became the first West African country to become independent.

Section 3: Mali

- People in the Sahel have long relied on its resources and its location as a crossroads for trade.
- Desertification is occurring in Mali and other countries of the Sahel. Two possible causes are overgrazing and drought.
- Desertification threatens the ways of life of many people living in the Sahel. Mali's government is working to find solutions to this problem.

Kano, Nigeria

Tuareg woman

◆ Key Terms

Match the definitions in Column I with the key terms in Column II.

Column I

1. Nigeria's second-largest ethnic group
2. having many ethnic groups living within a society
3. the process by which fertile land becomes too dry or damaged to support life
4. Ghana's first president
5. a sudden overthrow of a government by force
6. political control

Column II

A Kwame Nkrumah
B Yoruba
C sovereignty
D coup d'état
E desertification
F multiethnic

Chapter 15 **503**

┌ Vocabulary Builder ┐

Revisit this chapter's high-use words:

impose	initiative	crossroads
practice	reform	flourish
revolve	implement	thrive
appoint		

Ask students to review the definitions they recorded on their *Word Knowledge* worksheets.

All in One Africa Teaching Resources, *Word Knowledge,* p. 304

Consider allowing students to earn extra credit if they use the words in their answers to the questions in the Chapter Review and Assessment. The words must be used correctly and in a natural context to win the extra points.

Chapter 15
Review and Assessment

Review Chapter Content

- Review and revisit the major themes of this chapter by asking students to classify what Guiding Question each bulleted statement in the Chapter Summary answers. Form students into groups and ask them to complete the activity together. Guiding Questions can be found on p. 349 in the Student Edition.

- Assign *Vocabulary Development* for students to review Key Terms.

All in One Africa Teaching Resources, *Vocabulary Development,* p. 319

Answers

Key Terms

1. B
2. F
3. E
4. A
5. D
6. C

Comprehension and Critical Thinking

7. (a) The Hausa-Fulani, Yoruba, and Igbo are the three largest ethnic groups in Nigeria. **(b)** Religious differences and unequal income from the oil industry are sources of conflict in Nigeria. **(c)** Possible answer: Because it is a democracy, people can vote on how to change things that they think are unfair.

8. (a) They grew cash crops such as cocoa instead of food crops and did not have enough food. **(b)** Possible answer: Farmers started to grow cocoa instead of food crops and people had to start importing food. People spent more time farming and less time making traditional crafts so that factory-made goods needed to be imported. **(c)** Yes, because he believed that people should benefit from the wealth of their own land.

9. (a) It was a convenient stopping point for camel caravans traveling between North Africa and the savanna. **(b)** It ended because of both environmental and social change. Once European ships began trading along the coast, trade through the Sahel decreased because it is easier to transport goods by boat than by camel through the hot desert.

Skills Practice

Students' grids should include a statement of the issue, possible alternatives, the outcomes of each alternative, and check marks next to the most important alternatives. Students should write a sentence clearly stating their decision.

Writing Activity: Language Arts

Students' newspaper editorials should clearly state how the problem of overgrazing could be dealt with and include reasons to support their opinion.

Use *Rubric for Assessing a Newspaper Article* to evaluate students' editorials.

All in One **Africa Teaching Resources,**
Rubric for Assessing a Newspaper Article, p. 321

◆ Comprehension and Critical Thinking

7. (a) Name List the three largest ethnic groups that live in Nigeria.
(b) Explain What are two sources of conflict in Nigeria today?
(c) Predict How might Nigeria's government help resolve the country's conflicts?

8. (a) Recall During the colonial years, why did people in the Gold Coast have to start importing their food?
(b) Synthesize Information When the British changed the structure of the Gold Coast's economy, how did the lifestyles of the people living there also change?
(c) Infer According to Kwame Nkrumah's beliefs, did those lifestyle changes matter in the discussion of independence?

9. (a) Explain How did Tombouctou's location in the Sahel allow it to develop as a major trading center in the 1300s?
(b) Summarize Did large-scale trading in Tombouctou end because of environmental change or because of social change? Explain.

◆ Skills Practice

Decision Making In the Skills for Life activity in this chapter, you learned how you can make good decisions.

Review the steps you followed to learn this skill. Then suppose that you have to make a choice between two after-school activities, such as writing for the school newspaper and acting in the school play. Create a decision-making grid. Put check marks next to the most important outcomes. Review the check marks and choose the option that seems best. Write a sentence stating your decision.

◆ Writing Activity: Geography

In the Sahel, overgrazing may be a cause of desertification. It might seem that a simple solution is to stop overgrazing. However, many people of the Sahel make their living from the animals that they graze. To prevent overgrazing, these people would have to change their ways of life. They would have to stop herding animals, herd fewer animals, or move elsewhere to herd their animals. Write a newspaper editorial explaining how you think this problem could be solved.

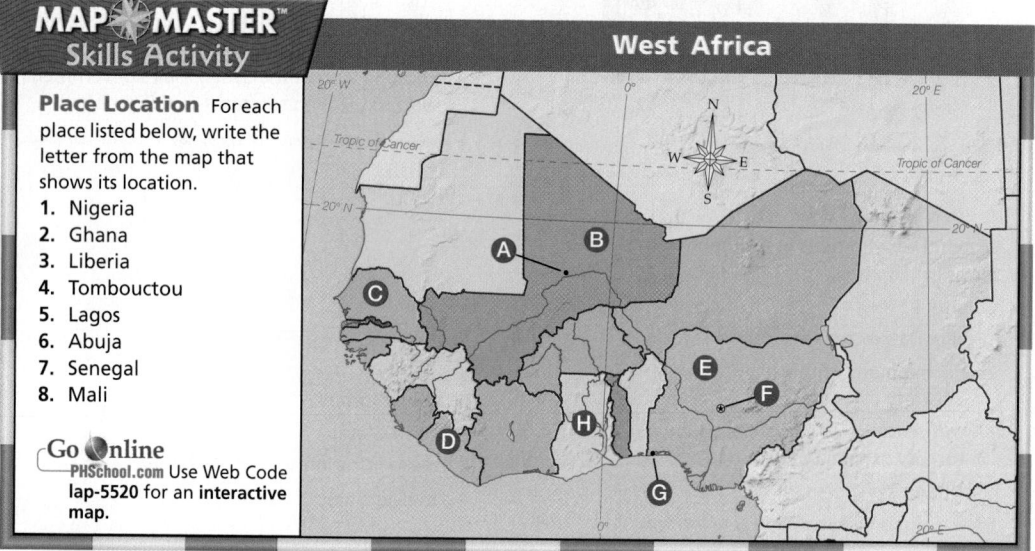

MAP MASTER™ Skills Activity

Place Location For each place listed below, write the letter from the map that shows its location.
1. Nigeria
2. Ghana
3. Liberia
4. Tombouctou
5. Lagos
6. Abuja
7. Senegal
8. Mali

Go Online
PHSchool.com Use Web Code **lap-5520** for an **interactive map**.

West Africa

Standardized Test Prep

Test-Taking Tips

Some questions on standardized tests ask you to analyze an outline. Study the outline below. Then follow the tips to answer the sample question.

> I. The Hausa-Fulani
>   A. Cattle herders, farmers, craftspeople
>   B. Built trading cities
> II. The Yoruba
>   A. Very urban
>   B. Also many farmers, traders, craftspeople
> III. _____
>   A. Rural farmers
>   B. Governed by democratic councils

TIP Pay attention to the organization of the outline. Use that information to help you answer the question.

Pick the letter that best answers the question.

Which of the following major topics belongs next to III?

A The Nigerians
B Ethnic groups of Nigeria
C The Igbo
D Christians

TIP Use what you know about history, geography, or government to find the BEST answer.

Think It Through This outline is organized by major topics and details. The question asks you to find major topic III. Answer B is too general; it could be the subject of an entire outline. Answer D is not an ethnic group. That leaves A and C. You can use your knowledge of geography to help you. Nigerians are a general group—citizens of a country. The Hausa-Fulani and the Yoruba are specific groups—ethnic groups in Nigeria. The Igbo are also a Nigerian ethnic group, so the correct answer is C.

Practice Questions

Use the tips above and other tips in this book to help you answer the following questions. Use the outline below to answer Question 1. Choose the letter of the best answer.

> I. Nkrumah overthrown
>   A. Nkrumah removed from office by a coup d'état
>   B. Nkrumah blamed for economic problems
> II. _____
>   A. Continuing economic problems
>   B. Improvement of public opinion about Nkrumah
> III. Government and economy today

1. According to the outline, which of the following belongs next to II?

A Independence achieved
B A hero again
C Traditional government
D Mixing old and new

2. Which of the following was Nigeria's first capital after independence?

A Kano
B Abuja
C Lagos
D Tombouctou

3. How does Mali's savanna differ from the Sahel and the Sahara?

A It gets less rain.
B It has a more northern location.
C It gets more rain.
D It is inhabited by fewer people.

Use Web Code laa-5500 for Chapter 15 self-test.

Standardized Test Prep

Answers

1. B
2. C
3. C

Go Online PHSchool.com Students may use the Chapter 15 self-test on PHSchool.com to prepare for the Chapter Test.

Assessment Resources

Use *Chapter Tests A and B* to assess students' mastery of chapter content.

All in One **Africa Teaching Resources,** *Chapter Tests A and B*, pp. 323–328

Tests are also available on the *ExamView Test Bank CD-ROM.*

⊙ *ExamView Test Bank CD-ROM*

Chapter Overview

Overview

Introducing East Africa
1. Look at the map and study the data to learn about the nations of East Africa.
2. Analyze data to compare the countries.
3. Identify characteristics that most countries of East Africa share.
4. Find some of the key differences among the countries.

The Geography of East Africa
Length: 4 minutes, 41 seconds
Provides an overview of East Africa's location, including its countries, cities, landforms, and bodies of water. Also shows the people of East Africa.

Section 1 Ethiopia: Religious Roots
1. Learn about the two major religions practiced in Ethiopia.
2. Understand the contrasts in the daily lives of rural and urban Ethiopians.

Ethiopia: Asbeth's Life
Length: 2 minutes, 54 seconds
Portrays the life of an eleven-year-old girl in Ethiopia.

Section 2 Tanzania: Determined to Succeed
1. Find out about early reforms that the government of Tanzania made after independence.
2. Learn about continued social, economic, and political progress and reforms that have been made in Tanzania.

Tanzania: Making a Living on Lake Victoria
Length: 3 minutes, 11 seconds
Discusses the positive and negative effects of the fishing industry on Lake Victoria.

Section 3 Kenya: Ties that Bind
1. Learn about the peoples of Kenya.
2. Discover what life is like in rural Kenya.
3. Find out what life is like in urban Kenya.

Kenya: Once There Was a Bean
Length: 3 minutes, 16 seconds
Describes how growing and producing the "French" bean have positively affected Kenya.

Technology Resources

Students use embedded Web codes to access Internet activities, chapter self-tests, and additional map practice. They may also access Dorling Kindersley's Online Desk Reference to learn more about each country they study.

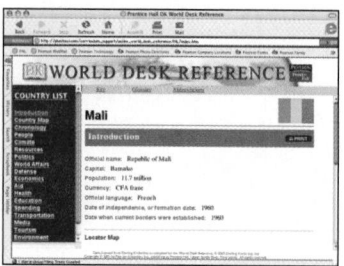

Use the Interactive Textbook to make content and concepts come alive through animations, videos, and activities that accompany the complete basal text—online and on CD-ROM.

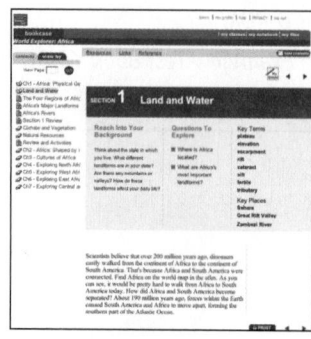

PRENTICE HALL

Use this complete suite of powerful teaching tools to make planning lessons and administering tests quicker and easier.

Reading and Assessment

Reading and Vocabulary Instruction

👁 Model the Target Reading Skill

Context Explain to students that they can decipher the meanings of unfamiliar words or phrases by using clues from the surrounding text. Demonstrate how to use context clues to clarify the meanings of the underlined terms in the following selection from p. 520 of the Student Edition.

He told Tanzanians that independence meant uhuru na kazi— *"freedom and work." By this he meant that only hard work could end poverty. Nyerere said that Tanzania should be self-reliant. He did not want the country to depend on other nations for economic support.*

Explain to students that they can use context clues to determine the meaning of the term *"freedom and work."* The second sentence begins with the phrase *By this he meant.* Ask students what the word *this* refers to. *("freedom and work")* The phrase is a clue that the definition will follow. Have students write down what Nyerere meant by *"freedom and work." (Only hard work could end poverty)*

Next, explain that an author can clarify the meaning of a term by rephrasing it. Ask students to use context clues to read the last two sentences to find the meaning of *self-reliant. (Students should recognize that the second sentence is a restatement of the first; self-reliant means not depending on other nations for economic support.)*

Use the following worksheets from All-in-One Africa Teaching Resources (pp. 347–348) to support the chapter's Target Reading Skill.

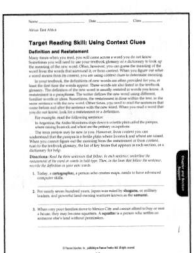
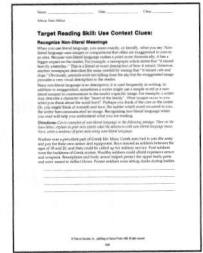

Vocabulary Builder
High-Use Academic Words
Use these steps to teach this chapter's high-use words:

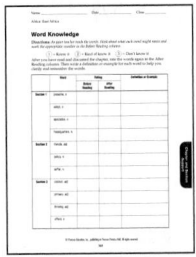

1. Have students rate how well they know each word on their Word Knowledge worksheets (All-in-One Africa Teaching Resources, p. 349).

2. Pronounce each word and ask students to repeat it.

3. Give students a brief definition or sample sentence (provided on TE pp. 515, 520, and 527).

4. Work with students as they fill in the "Definition or Example" column of their Word Knowledge worksheets.

Assessment

Formal Assessment
Test students' understanding of core knowledge and skills.

> **Chapter Tests A and B,** All-in-One Africa Teaching Resources, pp. 376–381

Customize the Chapter Tests to suit your needs.
ExamView Test Bank CD-ROM

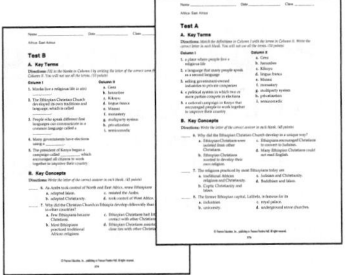

Skills Assessment
Assess geographic literacy.

> **MapMaster Skills,** Student Edition pp. 507, 532
>
> **Country Profile Map and Chart Skills,** Student Edition pp. 517, 522, 528

Assess reading and comprehension.

> **Target Reading Skills,** Student Edition, pp. 516, 520, 529 and in Section Assessments
>
> **Chapter 16 Assessment,** Eastern Hemisphere Reading and Vocabulary Study Guide, p. 187

Performance Assessment
Assess students' performance on this chapter's Writing Activities using the following rubrics from All-in-One Africa Teaching Resources.

> **Rubric for Assessing a Writing Assignment,** p. 373
>
> **Rubric for Assessing an Oral Presentation,** p. 374
>
> **Rubric for Assessing a Newspaper Article,** p. 375

Assess students' work through performance tasks.

> **Small Group Activity: Mural of East African Architecture,** All-in-One Africa Teaching Resources, pp. 352–355
>
> **Portfolio Activity,** Teacher Edition, p. 165

Online Assessment
Have students check their own understanding.

> **Chapter Self-Test**

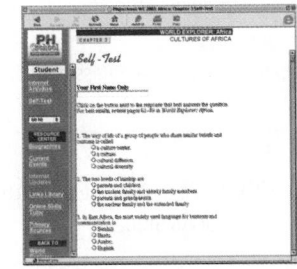

Section 1 Ethiopia: Religious Roots

 1.5 periods, .75 block (includes Country Databank)

Social Studies Objectives
1. Learn about the two major religions practiced in Ethiopia.
2. Understand the contrasts in the daily lives of rural and urban Ethiopians.

Reading/Language Arts Objective
Use context clues to determine the meanings of unfamiliar words.

Prepare to Read	Instructional Resources	Differentiated Instruction
Build Background Knowledge Have students preview the section and discuss what they think might be important to people in Ethiopia. **Set a Purpose for Reading** Have students evaluate statements on the *Reading Readiness Guide.* **Preview Key Terms** Teach the section's Key Terms. **Target Reading Skill** Introduce the section's Target Reading Skill of **using context clues.**	**All in One Africa Teaching Resources** L2 Reading Readiness Guide, p. 336 L2 Use Context Clues: Definition and Description, p. 347	**Spanish Reading and Vocabulary Study Guide** L1 Chapter 16, Section 1, pp. 126–127 ELL **World Studies Video Program** L2 The Geography of East Africa AR, GT, LPR, SN

Instruct	Instructional Resources	Differentiated Instruction
Major Religions of Ethiopia Discuss how Christianity and Islam developed in Ethiopia. **Contrasts in Daily Life** Discuss the people who live in urban and rural areas of Ethiopia and ask about the city of Addis Ababa. **Target Reading Skill** Review **using context clues.** **Country Profile** Ask students to derive information from maps, charts, and graphs.	**All in One Africa Teaching Resources** L2 Guided Reading and Review, p. 337 L2 Reading Readiness Guide, p. 336 L2 Using a Map Key, p. 362 **Africa Transparencies** L2 Section Reading Support Transparency AF 50 **World Studies Video Program** L2 Ethiopia: Asbeth's Life	**All in One Africa Teaching Resources** L2 Outline Map 24, p. 358 AR, GT, LPR, SN L2 Reading a Bar Graph, p. 359 AR, GT, LPR, SN L2 Reading a Circle Graph, p. 360 AR, GT, LPR, SN L2 Reading a Table, p. 361 AR, GT, LPR, SN L3 Small Group Activity, pp. 352–355 AR, GT **Teacher's Edition** L1 For Less Proficient Readers, p. 511 L1 For Special Needs Students, TE pp. 511, 516 L3 For Gifted and Talented, TE p. 516 **Student Edition on Audio CD** L1 Chapter 16, Section 1 ELL, LPR, SN **Passport to the World CD-ROM** L1 Africa ELL, LPR, SN

Assess and Reteach	Instructional Resources	Differentiated Instruction
Assess Progress Evaluate student comprehension with the section assessment and section quiz. **Reteach** Assign the Reading and Vocabulary Study Guide to help struggling students. **Extend** Extend the lesson by assigning an online activity.	**All in One Africa Teaching Resources** L2 Section Quiz, p. 338 **Reading and Vocabulary Study Guide** L1 Chapter 16, Section 1, pp. 178–180 **PHSchool.com** L3 For: Environmental and Global Issues: Urban Population, Past and Projected Web Code: lad-5604	**All in One Africa Teaching Resources** L1 Outline Map 2, p. 356; Outline Map 21, p. 357; Outline Map 24, p. 358 ELL, LPR, SN Rubric for Assessing a Bar Graph, p. 372 AR, GT, LPR, SN **Spanish Support** L2 Section Quiz (Spanish), p. 169 ELL

Key
L1 Basic to Average   L3 Average to Advanced
L2 For All Students

LPR Less Proficient Readers
AR Advanced Readers
SN Special Needs Students

GT Gifted and Talented
ELL English Language Learners

Section 2 Tanzania: Determined to Succeed

 2 periods, 1 block (includes Skills for Life)

Social Studies Objectives

1. Find out about early reforms that the government of Tanzania made after independence.
2. Learn about continued social, economic, and political progress and reforms that have been made in Tanzania.

Reading/Language Arts Objective

Use context clues to clarify the meaning of an unfamiliar word or phrase.

Prepare to Read	Instructional Resources	Differentiated Instruction
Build Background Knowledge Have students brainstorm how a region might change when it becomes independent. **Set a Purpose for Reading** Have students evaluate statements on the *Reading Readiness Guide.* **Preview Key Terms** Teach the section's Key Terms. **Target Reading Skill** Introduce the section's Target Reading Skill of **using context clues.**	**All in One Africa Teaching Resources** L2 Reading Readiness Guide, p. 340 L2 Use Context Clues: Definition and Description, p. 347	**Spanish Reading and Vocabulary Study Guide** L1 Chapter 16, Section 2, pp. 128–129 ELL

Instruct	Instructional Resources	Differentiated Instruction
Early Reforms After Independence Discuss the changes that occurred after Tanzania became independent. **Target Reading Skill** Review **using context clues.** **Progress and Continued Reform** Discuss the progress in Tanzania during and after Nyerere's presidency. **Country Profile** Ask students to derive information from maps, charts, and graphs.	**All in One Africa Teaching Resources** L2 Guided Reading and Review, p. 341 L2 Reading Readiness Guide, p. 340 **Africa Transparencies** L2 Section Reading Support Transparency AF 51 **World Studies Video Program** L2 Tanzania: Making a Living on Lake Victoria	**All in One Africa Teaching Resources** L3 Mukasa, pp. 363–366 AR, GT L2 Skills for Life, p. 351 AR, GT, LPR, SN **Teacher's Edition** L3 For Advanced Readers, TE p. 522 L1 For English Language Learners, TE p. 522 **Spanish Support** L2 Guided Reading and Review (Spanish), p. 170 ELL

Assess and Reteach	Instructional Resources	Differentiated Instruction
Assess Progress Evaluate student comprehension with the section assessment and section quiz. **Reteach** Assign the Reading and Vocabulary Study Guide to help struggling students. **Extend** Extend the lesson by assigning a research project.	**All in One Africa Teaching Resources** L2 Section Quiz, p. 342 Rubric for Assessing an Oral Presentation, p. 374 Rubric for Assessing a Writing Assignment, p. 373 **Reading and Vocabulary Study Guide** L1 Chapter 16, Section 2, pp. 181–183	**Teacher's Edition** L1 For Less Proficient Readers, TE p. 525 **Social Studies Skills Tutor CD-ROM** L1 Identifying Main Ideas ELL, LPR, SN **Spanish Support** L2 Section Quiz (Spanish), p. 171 ELL

Key

L1 Basic to Average	L3 Average to Advanced	LPR Less Proficient Readers	GT Gifted and Talented
L2 For All Students		AR Advanced Readers	ELL English Language Learners
		SN Special Needs Students	

Section 3 Kenya: Ties that Bind

4 periods, 2 blocks (includes Chapter Review and Assessment and Literature)

Social Studies Objectives
1. Learn about the peoples of Kenya.
2. Discover what life is like in rural Kenya.
3. Find out what life is like in urban Kenya.

Reading/Language Arts Objective
Identify and interpret nonliteral language.

Prepare to Read | Instructional Resources | Differentiated Instruction

Build Background Knowledge
Have students preview the section and make predictions about what they will learn.

Set a Purpose for Reading
Have students evaluate statements on the *Reading Readiness Guide*.

Preview Key Terms
Teach the section's Key Terms.

Target Reading Skill
Introduce the section's Target Reading Skill of **interpreting nonliteral meanings.**

All in One Africa Teaching Resources
- L2 Reading Readiness Guide, p. 344
- L2 Recognize Nonliteral Meanings, p. 348

Spanish Reading and Vocabulary Study Guide
- L1 Chapter 16, Section 3, pp. 130–131 ELL

Instruct | Instructional Resources | Differentiated Instruction

Peoples of Kenya
Life in Rural Kenya
Discuss the lives of the people of Kenya.

Country Profile
Ask students to derive information from maps, charts, and graphs.

Target Reading Skill
Review **interpreting nonliteral meanings.**

Life in Urban Kenya
Discuss how the growth of urban populations is affecting people in Kenya.

All in One Africa Teaching Resources
- L2 Guided Reading and Review, p. 345
- L2 Reading Readiness Guide, p. 344
- L2 Reading a Table, p. 361

Africa Transparencies
- L2 Section Reading Support Transparency AF 52

World Studies Video Program
- L2 Kenya: Once There Was a Bean

All in One Africa Teaching Resources
- L2 Determining Tone, Purpose, and Audience, p. 370 AR, GT, LPR, SN

Teacher's Edition
- L3 For Advanced Readers, TE p. 528
- L2 For English Language Learners, TE p. 536

Spanish Support
- L2 Guided Reading and Review (Spanish), p. 172 ELL

Assess and Reteach | Instructional Resources | Differentiated Instruction

Assess Progress
Evaluate student comprehension with the section assessment and section quiz.

Reteach
Assign the Reading and Vocabulary Study Guide to help struggling students.

Extend
Extend the lesson by assigning an Enrichment activity.

All in One Africa Teaching Resources
- L2 Section Quiz, p. 346
- L3 Enrichment, p. 350
  Rubric for Assessing a Writing Assignment, p. 373
- L2 Word Knowledge, p. 349
- L2 Vocabulary Development, p. 371
  Rubric for Assessing a Newspaper Article, p. 375
- L2 Chapter Tests A and B, pp. 376–381

Reading and Vocabulary Study Guide
- L1 Chapter 16, Section 3, pp. 184–186

All in One Africa Teaching Resources
- L3 The Coconut Tree, pp. 367–369 AR, GT

Spanish Support
- L2 Section Quiz (Spanish), p. 173 ELL
- L2 Chapter Summary (Spanish), p. 174 ELL
- L2 Vocabulary Development (Spanish), p. 175 ELL

Key
- L1 Basic to Average
- L2 For All Students
- L3 Average to Advanced

- LPR Less Proficient Readers
- AR Advanced Readers
- SN Special Needs Students

- GT Gifted and Talented
- ELL English Language Learners

Reading Background

Pattern Puzzles

Putting together pattern puzzles can help students understand paragraph structure. This activity calls for students to rearrange sentences in order to construct well-organized paragraphs. It also helps students distinguish between the topic sentence that contains the main ideas and the supporting details. Pattern puzzles also work with any content that requires sequencing of steps and ideas.

To begin, group students into pairs. Write a paragraph on a piece of paper and cut the sentences into separate strips. There should be one sentence on each piece of paper. Place all of the strips in an envelope. Do this with enough envelopes to distribute to each pair. Ask students to arrange the sentences into a logical paragraph.

Extend this strategy by challenging students to recall the plot of a short story, the sequence of events necessary to solve a math problem, or the steps involved in a scientific experiment. Ask students to rearrange the steps or sequence into the correct order. Students should then explain their rationale.

Mapping Word Definitions

In this chapter, students may come across several unfamiliar Key Terms or high-use words. Mapping word definitions can help students develop a way to learn vocabulary independently by charting word meanings. This strategy can expand students' vocabularies and help them build a complete understanding of new words.

After clarifying the meaning of the high-use word *preserve*, ask students to develop a graphic organizer, similar to the one below, including the following information about the word: the definition (in their own words), a synonym, and a sentence using the word.

Preserve	
Definition	to keep or save
Synonym	to continue or protect
Sentence	The leaders signed a peace agreement to preserve harmony between the nations.

World Studies Background

Early Humans in Ethiopia

Many artifacts from our early human ancestors have been found at Hadar, an excavation site in Ethiopia. One groundbreaking discovery occurred in 1974 when an American archaeologist uncovered a partial female skeleton between three and four million years old. Lucy, as the skeleton is popu-larly called, was an important finding for scientists studying early humans.

Pemba Island

Pemba, which means "Green Island" in Arabic, is one of the smaller islands belonging to Tanzania. This fertile island is the world's leading clove producer, and also an exporter of coconuts. Besides coming from Africa and India, some of Pemba's people are descendants of Middle Eastern traders who established settlements on the island in the tenth century.

The Maasai

Many Maasai still live traditional lives as nomadic herders. They raise cattle and move with their herds along the Great Rift Valley in Kenya and Tanzania, gaining most of their food from their cattle. The governments of these nations are encouraging the Maasai to form permanent settlements, however, and to receive a formal education.

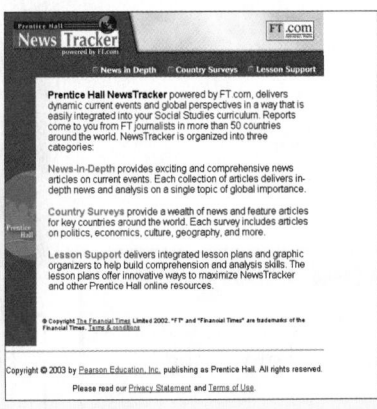

Get in-depth information on topics of global importance with **Prentice Hall Newstracker**, powered by FT.com.

Use Web code **lad-5600** for **Prentice Hall Newstracker**.

Chapter

16 East Africa

Guiding Questions

Remind students about the Guiding Questions introduced at the beginning of this section.

Section 1 relates to **Guiding Question** ❸
What features help define different African cultures? (*Ethiopia's culture is greatly influenced by Christianity, Islam, and the country's combination of urban and rural lifestyles.*)

Section 2 relates to **Guiding Question** ❷
How have historical events affected the cultures and nations of Africa? (*Tanzania's history of colonialism and reforms since independence have greatly affected the culture, economics, language, and politics of the country.*)

Section 3 relates to **Guiding Question** ❸
What features help define different African cultures? (*Kenya's people are ethnically and culturally diverse, and live in both rural and urban areas.*)

Target Reading Skill

In this chapter, students will learn and apply the reading skill of using context clues. Use the following worksheets to help students practice this skill:

 Africa Teaching Resources, *Use Context Clues: Definition and Description,* p. 347; *Recognize Nonliteral Meanings,* p. 348

Chapter Preview

This chapter will introduce you to some of the countries that make up East Africa.

Country Databank
The Country Databank provides data and descriptions of each of the countries in the region: Burundi, Djibouti, Eritrea, Ethiopia, Kenya, Rwanda, Seychelles, Somalia, Sudan, Tanzania, and Uganda.

Section 1
Ethiopia
Religious Roots

Section 2
Tanzania
Determined to Succeed

Section 3
Kenya
Ties That Bind

Target Reading Skill

Context In this chapter you will focus on understanding context. Using context clues and recognizing nonliteral meanings will help you learn as you read.

▶ **Many of the world's fastest runners are Kenyan. This man is training on the plains of Kenya.**

Differentiated Instruction

The following Teacher Edition strategies are suitable for students of varying abilities.

Advanced Readers, pp. 522, 528
English Language Learners,
   pp. 522, 536
Gifted and Talented, p. 516
Less Proficient Readers, pp. 511, 525
Special Needs Students, pp. 511, 516

Bibliography

For the Teacher
Lassieur, Allison and Tadesse Azeb. *Ethiopia.* Bridgestone Books, 2003.
Murphy, Patricia J. *Tanzania.* Bridgestone Books, 2002.
Ngcheong-Lum, Rosline and Victoria Derr. *Welcome to Kenya.* Gareth Stevens, 2000.

For the Student
L1 Fontes, Justine and Ron Fontes. *Kenya (A to Z).* Children's Press, 2003.
L2 Cobb, Vicki. *The Place is Wild: East Africa.* Walker & Co., 2000.
L3 Campbell, Eric. *Papa Tembo.* Harcourt, 1998.

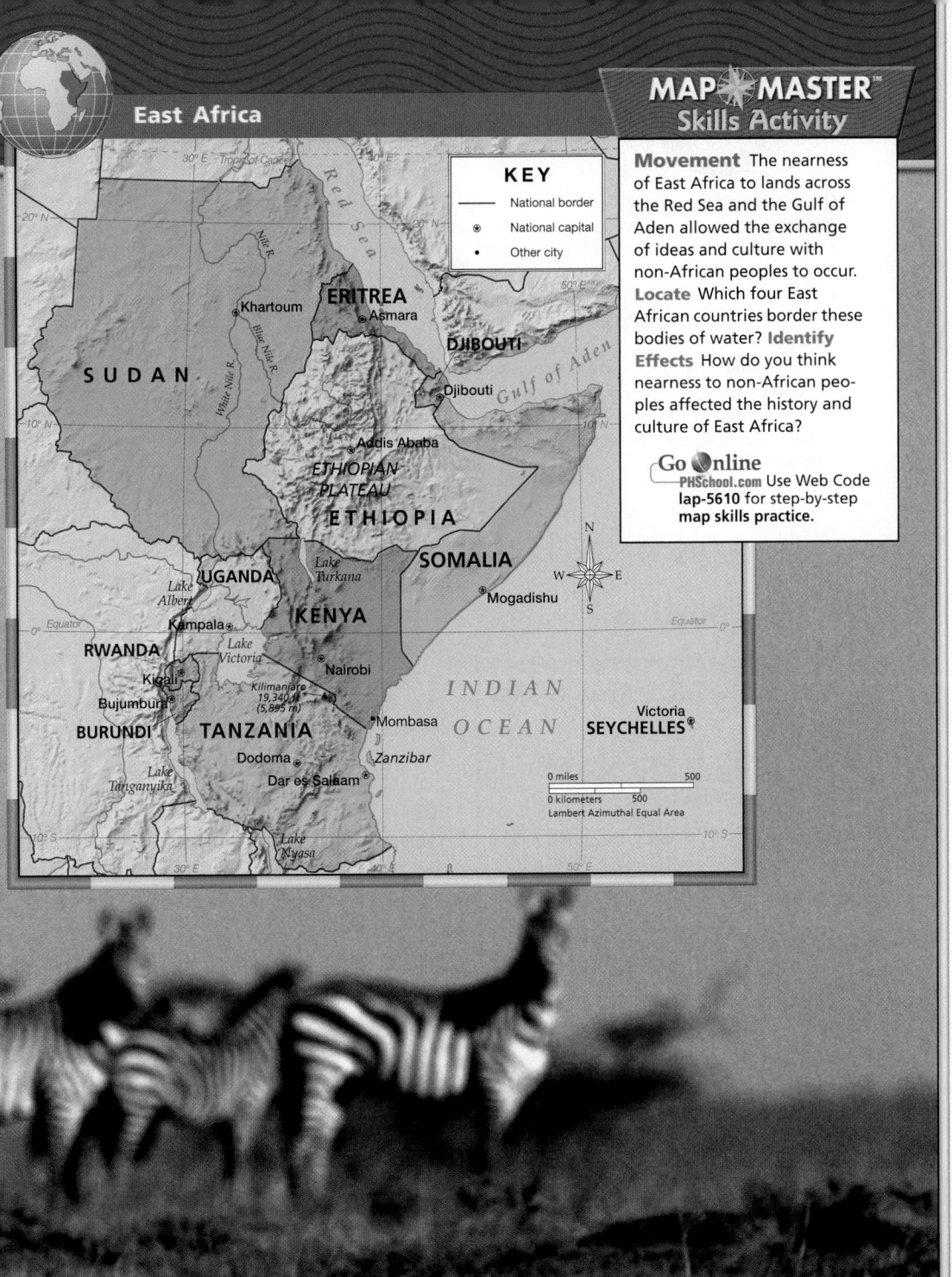

East Africa

KEY

—— National border

⊛ National capital

• Other city

Movement The nearness of East Africa to lands across the Red Sea and the Gulf of Aden allowed the exchange of ideas and culture with non-African peoples to occur. **Locate** Which four East African countries border these bodies of water? **Identify Effects** How do you think nearness to non-African peoples affected the history and culture of East Africa?

Go Online
PHSchool.com Use Web Code **lap-5610** for step-by-step **map skills practice.**

0 miles 500
0 kilometers 500
Lambert Azimuthal Equal Area

Ask students to study the map carefully. Then, on the board, create a table with three columns. Label the first column *Country*, the second *Capital*, and the third *Physical Features.* Have students copy the chart onto a piece of paper, and then use the map to fill in the information.

Go Online
PHSchool.com Students may practice their map skills using the interactive online version of this map.

Using the Visual   L2

Have students study the photograph on pp. 506–507 and read its accompanying caption. Have students think about the kinds of things the man in the photograph might see as he runs on the plains of Kenya. Are they different or similar to the things they might see in their neighborhood? What kinds of challenges might the man face as he trains on this kind of terrain? Conduct an Idea Wave (TE, p. T35) to elicit student responses.

Answers

MAP MASTER™
Skills Activity   **Locate** Eritrea, Djibouti, Somalia, Sudan **Identify Effects** Possible answer: The proximity to non-African countries may have caused non-African influences to play a role in shaping the history and culture of East Africa.

Chapter 16 **507**

Chapter Resources

Teaching Resources
- L2 Vocabulary Development, p. 371
- L2 Skills for Life, p. 351
- L2 Chapter Tests A and B, pp. 376–381

Spanish Support
- L2 Spanish Chapter Summary, p. 174
- L2 Spanish Vocabulary Development, p. 175

Media and Technology
- L1 Student Edition on Audio CD
- L1 Guided Reading Audiotapes, English and Spanish
- L2 Social Studies Skills Tutor CD-ROM
- *ExamView Test Bank CD-ROM*

PRENTICE HALL
Presentation EXPRESS™
Teach · Connect · Inspire

Teach this chapter's content using the PresentationExpress™ CD-ROM including:
- slide shows
- transparencies
- interactive maps and media
- *ExamView*® QuickTake Presenter

Objectives

- Look at the map and study the data to learn about the nations of East Africa.

- Analyze data to compare the countries.

- Identify characteristics that most countries of East Africa share.

- Find some of the key differences among the countries.

Show *The Geography of East Africa.* Ask **What are some common features of the region?** *(East Africa is the most mountainous region of Africa, and the coast is very important to its geography.)*

Prepare to Read

Build Background Knowledge L2

Tell students that the East African countries they saw in the video have many similarities and differences. Have students brainstorm any similarities or differences among East African countries that they can recall from the video. Then have them look over the information in the Country Databank tables, looking for one similarity and one difference between any two countries listed. Create a chart on the board with two columns, one labeled "Similarities" and one labeled "Differences," and conduct an Idea Wave (TE, p. T35) to fill the chart with students' suggestions. *(For example: Similarity—French is an official language of both Burundi and Djibouti. Difference—Burundi's ethnic groups are Hutu, Tutsi, Twa; Djibouti's are Issa, Afar, Somali, white, Arab, and Ethiopian.)*

The Geography of East Africa, **World Studies Video Program**

Introducing
East Africa

Guide for Reading

This section provides an introduction to the eleven countries that make up the region of East Africa.

- Look at the map on the previous page and then read the paragraphs below to learn about each nation.
- Analyze the data to compare the countries.
- What are the characteristics that most of the countries share?
- What are some key differences among the countries?

Viewing the Video Overview

View the World Studies Video Overview to learn more about each of the countries. As you watch, answer these questions:

- What are some common features of the region?
- What are some of the geographic points of interest in East Africa?
- What accounts for the blend of cultures in this region?

Explore the geography of East Africa.

Burundi

Capital	Bujumbura
Land Area	9,903 sq mi; 25,650 sq km
Population	6.4 million
Ethnic Group(s)	Hutu, Tutsi, Twa
Religion(s)	Roman Catholic, Protestant, traditional beliefs, Muslim
Government	republic
Currency	Burundi franc
Leading Exports	coffee, tea, sugar, cotton, hides
Language(s)	French (official), Kirundi (official), Kiswahili

The small country of Burundi (boo ROON dee) is bordered on the west by the Democratic Republic of the Congo, on the north by Rwanda, and on the east and south by Tanzania. Beginning in the 1970s, the country faced fierce fighting between two ethnic groups, the Hutu and the Tutsi. In 2002, a new government signed a peace treaty to help end the conflict. However, the country remains unstable, with small conflicts continuing and the economy weakened from the many years of fighting.

Djibouti

Capital	Djibouti
Land Area	8,873 sq mi; 22,980 sq km
Population	472,810
Ethnic Group(s)	Issa, Afar, Somali, white, Arab, Ethiopian
Religion(s)	Muslim, Christian
Government	republic
Currency	Djibouti franc
Leading Exports	reexports, hides and skins, coffee (in transit)
Language(s)	Arabic (official), French (official), Somali, Afar

Djibouti (jih BOO tee) is bordered on the south by Somalia, on the south and west by Ethiopia, on the north by Eritrea and the Red Sea, and on the east by the Gulf of Aden. It was established in 1977, when it gained independence from France. Its capital, Djibouti, is an important port city for the country's economy. Otherwise, the economy is weak because the country has few natural resources. In the early 1990s, fighting broke out between the nation's two main ethnic groups. In 2000, a peace treaty ended the fighting.

Eritrea

Capital	Asmara
Land Area	46,842 sq mi; 121,320 sq km
Population	4.5 million
Ethnic Group(s)	Tigrinya, Tigre, Kunama, Afar, Saho
Religion(s)	Muslim, Christian
Government	transitional government
Currency	nakfa
Leading Exports	livestock, sorghum, textiles, food, small manufactured goods
Language(s)	Tigrinya (official), English, Tigre, Afar, Arabic, Bilen, Kunama, Nara, Saho, Hadareb

Eritrea (ehr uh TREE uh) is bordered on the west and north by Sudan, on the north and east by the Red Sea, and on the south by Djibouti and Ethiopia. After being ruled by the Italians and then the British during the 1800s and early 1900s, Eritrea was taken over by Ethiopia in 1952. After thirty years of fighting, Eritrea gained its independence in 1993. Then, from 1998 to 2000, Eritrea and Ethiopia fought another destructive war over border disputes. Tensions in the region continue, and Eritrea's economy is weak from many years of war.

An Eritrean girl

Ethiopia

Capital	Addis Ababa
Land Area	432,310 sq mi; 1,119,683 sq km
Population	67.7 million
Ethnic Group(s)	Oromo, Amhara, Tigre, Sidamo, Shankella, Somali, Afar, Gurage
Religion(s)	Muslim, Christian, traditional beliefs
Government	federal republic
Currency	Ethiopian birr
Leading Exports	coffee, qat, gold, leather products, oilseeds
Language(s)	Amharic (official), Tigrinya, Galla, Sidamo, Somali, English, Arabic

Ethiopia (ee thee OH pea uh) is bordered on the west by Sudan, on the north by Eritrea and Djibouti, on the east and south by Somalia, and on the south by Kenya. It is one of the oldest countries in the world. Unlike most African countries, it was never colonized by a European power—at each European attempt, the Ethiopians proved victorious. In the 1990s, Ethiopia became a federal republic with a constitution and free elections. In the past 50 years, the country has experienced war and severe famine, or lack of food. Establishing a stable economy has therefore been difficult.

Chapter 16 **509**

Background: Links Across Place

Coffee Many East African countries export coffee, a crop used to make a beverage brewed from the seeds of the coffee plant. The plant most likely originated in Ethiopia and was first cultivated in Arabia in the 1400s. Coffee is one of the most popular beverages in the world; about one-third of all people drink it.

Coffee beans can be divided into two main groups—Arabica coffee is grown mostly in Latin America, while the Robusta variety is cultivated primarily in Africa. Robusta is especially suited for instant coffee, a product that has grown in popularity since its introduction in 1950.

Guided Instruction   L2

- Read each country paragraph as a class using the Paragraph Shrinking strategy (TE, p. T34). Then ask students to read through each data table.

- Ask students **Which country has the largest population?** *(Ethiopia, with 67.7 million)* **Which has the smallest population?** *(Seychelles, with 80,098)*

- Ask students **Which ethnic groups live in Burundi?** *(Hutu, Tutsi, Twa)* **What is the only other country that shares these same ethnic groups?** *(Rwanda)* Discuss with students how these ethnic groups have influenced recent events in both Burundi and Rwanda. *(Fierce fighting between the Hutu and the Tutsi has troubled both countries in the last 40 years.)*

- Ask students to locate Ethiopia and Eritrea on the map on p. 507, and then describe the relationship between the two countries. *(Eritrea is located north of Ethiopia, and lies between Ethiopia and the Red Sea. In 1952, Ethiopia took Eritrea over after the country had been independent from Britain for ten years. After decades of fighting, Eritrea won independence in 1993. Eritrea and Ethiopia fought a border war from 1998 to 2000, and tensions continue.)*

Guided Instruction (continued)

■ Ask students to compare and contrast the leading exports of Kenya with those of Somalia. *(Both countries export fish, but Kenya's other leading exports include coffee, tea, horticultural and petroleum products, and cement. Somalia's other exports include livestock, bananas, hides, charcoal, and scrap metal.)* **Based on this information, which country would you say has a more developed economy?** *(Kenya, because some of its leading exports, such as petroleum products, are industrial products.)*

■ Have students list the types of governments found in the countries of East Africa. *(republic, transitional government, federal republic, authoritarian regime)* Ask **Which countries are republics?** *(Burundi, Djibouti, Kenya, Rwanda, Seychelles, Tanzania, Uganda; students may also list Ethiopia, which is a federal republic.)*

Introducing East Africa

Cheetahs in a Kenyan national park

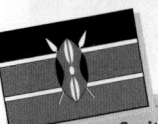

Kenya

Capital	Nairobi
Land Area	219,787 sq mi; 569,250 sq km
Population	31.3 million
Ethnic Group(s)	Kikuyu, Luhya, Luo, Kalenjin, Kamba, Kisii, Meru
Religion(s)	Protestant, Roman Catholic, traditional beliefs, Muslim
Government	republic
Currency	Kenya shilling
Leading Exports	tea, horticultural products, coffee, petroleum products, fish, cement
Language(s)	Kiswahili (official), English (official), Kikuyu, Luo, Kamba

Located along the Equator, Kenya (KEN yuh) is bordered on the west by Lake Victoria and Uganda, on the north by Sudan and Ethiopia, on the east by Somalia and the Indian Ocean, and on the south by Tanzania. The Great Rift Valley runs through the western half of the country. Kenya is home to the Kenyan Highlands, one of the most successful farming regions in Africa. The country is also a major center of business and trade in East Africa. In addition, many rare animals and numerous national parks have made tourism a strong industry in Kenya.

Rwanda

Capital	Kigali
Land Area	9,632 sq mi; 24,948 sq km
Population	7.4 million
Ethnic Group(s)	Hutu, Tutsi, Twa
Religion(s)	Christian, Muslim, traditional beliefs
Government	republic
Currency	Rwanda franc
Leading Exports	coffee, tea, hides, tin ore
Language(s)	French (official), English (official), Kinyarwanda (official), Kiswahili

Rwanda (roo AHN duh) is bordered on the west by the Democratic Republic of the Congo, on the north by Uganda, on the east by Tanzania, and on the south by Burundi. It is the most densely populated country in Africa. Fierce civil war erupted in the early 1990s when nearly 1 million Tutsi were massacred by the majority Hutu. As a result of the war, about 2 million Hutus migrated to neighboring countries. After the war's end, many of them returned to Rwanda. The country's economy is slowly improving.

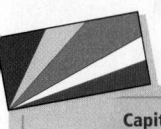

Seychelles

Capital	Victoria
Land Area	176 sq mi; 455 sq km
Population	80,098
Ethnic Group(s)	white, black, South Asian, East Asian, Arab
Religion(s)	Christian
Government	republic
Currency	Seychelles rupee
Leading Exports	canned tuna, cinnamon bark, copra, petroleum products (reexports)
Language(s)	Seselwa (French Creole) (official), English, French

The 115 islands of Seychelles (say SHEL) are located in the Indian Ocean, northwest of Madagascar. The islands are known for their natural beauty and unique plants and animals. They are home to the coco de mer (KOH koh duh mehr), a plant that produces a coconut-like fruit that is one of the largest fruits in the world. In addition, some of the last giant tortoises in the world live there. In 1976, Seychelles gained its independence from the United Kingdom, and in 1993 it became a democracy. Tuna fishing and tourism are the leading economic activities of these islands.

Fishing near Seychelles (left); a giant tortoise (below)

Somalia

Capital	Mogadishu
Land Area	242,215 sq mi; 627,337 sq km
Population	7.8 million
Ethnic Group(s)	Somali, Bantu, Arab
Religion(s)	Muslim
Government	transitional government
Currency	Somali shilling
Leading Exports	livestock, bananas, hides, fish, charcoal, scrap metal
Language(s)	Somali (official), Arabic (official), English, Italian

Somalia (soh MAH lee uh) occupies the Horn of Africa, the easternmost point of the continent. It is bordered on the west by Kenya, Ethiopia, and Djibouti; on the north by the Gulf of Aden; and on the east by the Indian Ocean. Much of Somalia is semiarid desert. There is some fertile land along the coast and in the south near the capital, Mogadishu (moh gah DEE shoo). Most Somalis are farmers or nomadic herders. In recent years, Somalia has faced many severe problems, such as civil war, the collapse of its government, and famine.

Chapter 16 **511**

- Ask students **Which religion is found in nearly all of the countries of East Africa?** *(Islam)* **Which country's population does not include Muslims?** *(Seychelles)* Have students look at the table and paragraph for Seychelles. Then ask **How might the geography of Seychelles affect its lack of religious diversity?** *(Possible answer: Because it is a group of islands located in the Indian Ocean, Seychelles may be culturally isolated from other countries located on Africa's mainland.)*

- Have students look at the languages spoken in each country. Point out that there is no common language shared by all the countries. Discuss with students how having a variety of languages might affect life in East Africa. *(Possible answers: Many people in East Africa may speak more than one language; there are probably newspapers, books, and television and radio programs in many different languages.)*

- Ask students to choose any two countries and compare their currencies, official languages, and religions. *(Answers will vary, but students should accurately compare and contrast the information for the two countries that they choose.)*

Differentiated Instruction

For Less Proficient Readers [L1]

Have students keep a list of any unfamiliar words or terms they come across while reading the Country Databank. Then have them look up the words in a dictionary and record the definition of each word on their lists. Students should then reread the Country Databank text, referring to the lists as necessary.

For Special Needs Students [L1]

Have students become more familiar with the region through the flyover, timeline, and photographs for this region on the Passport to the World CD-ROM.

◉ *Africa,* **Passport to the World CD-ROM**

Independent Practice

- Divide students into groups of three or four and assign each group one category from the country tables, such as Government, Population, or Currency.

- Have groups create a large poster showing the information for their category for each of the countries profiled. Depending on which category the group is working on, groups may choose to organize their information in a chart, a map, or a table.

- Distribute *Outline Map 24: East and Southern Africa, Reading a Bar Graph, Reading a Circle Graph,* and *Reading a Table* to help students decide how to organize their data. When posters are completed, have the groups present their work to the class and explain how they chose to organize their information.

All in One Africa Teaching Resources, *Outline Map 24: East and Southern Africa,* p. 358; *Reading a Bar Graph,* p. 359; *Reading a Circle Graph,* p. 360; *Reading a Table,* p. 361

Monitor Progress

Circulate to make sure students are choosing suitable ways to present their data. Provide assistance as needed.

Introducing East Africa

Sudan

Capital	Khartoum
Land Area	917,374 sq mi; 2,376,000 sq km
Population	37.1 million
Ethnic Group(s)	black, Arab, Beja
Religion(s)	Muslim, traditional beliefs, Christian
Government	authoritarian regime
Currency	Sudanese pound or dinar
Leading Exports	oil and petroleum products, cotton, sesame, livestock, groundnuts, gum arabic, sugar
Language(s)	Arabic (official), Dinka, Nuer, Nubian, Beja, Zande, Bari, Fur, Shilluk, Lotuko

In land area, Sudan (soo DAN) is the largest country in Africa. It is bordered on the west by the Central African Republic, Chad, and Libya; on the north by Egypt; on the east by the Red Sea, Eritrea, and Ethiopia; and on the south by Kenya, Uganda, and the Democratic Republic of the Congo. Both the Blue Nile and White Nile rivers flow through Sudan. Nearly 50 years of civil war have led to millions of deaths, migrations out of the country, and economic problems.

An ancient pyramid at Meroë, in present-day Sudan

Tanzania

Capital	Dar es Salaam and Dodoma
Land Area	342,099 sq mi; 886,037 sq km
Population	37.2 million
Ethnic Group(s)	Bantu, Asian, white, Arab
Religion(s)	Muslim, traditional beliefs, Christian
Government	republic
Currency	Tanzanian shilling
Leading Exports	gold, coffee, cashew nuts, manufactured goods, cotton
Language(s)	English (official), Kiswahili (official), Sukuma, Chagga, Nyamwezi, Hehe, Makonde, Yao, Sandawe

Tanzania (tan zuh NEE uh) is bordered on the west by Zambia, the Democratic Republic of the Congo, Burundi, and Rwanda; on the north by Uganda and Kenya; on the east by the Indian Ocean; and on the south by Mozambique and Malawi. It is home to Mount Kilimanjaro, Africa's tallest mountain. The Great Rift Valley forms the country's southwestern border. In 1964 the newly independent regions of Tanganyika and Zanzibar joined to become Tanzania. It is one of the world's poorest nations, but today Tanzania's manufacturing and mining industries are helping the economy boom.

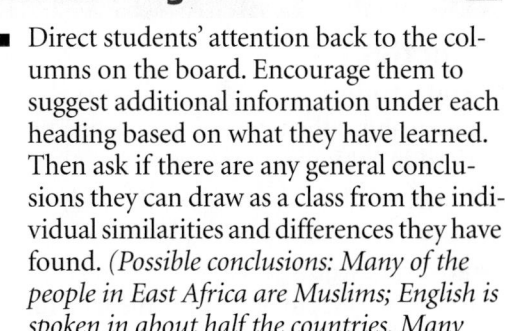

Uganda

Capital	Kampala
Land Area	77,108 sq mi; 199,710 sq km
Population	24.7 million
Ethnic Group(s)	18 distinct groups, including Baganda, Ankole, Basoga, Iteso, Bakiga, Langi, Rwanda, Bagisu
Religion(s)	Roman Catholic, Protestant, traditional beliefs, Hindu, Muslim
Government	republic
Currency	New Uganda shilling
Leading Exports	coffee, fish and fish products, tea, gold, cotton, flowers, horticultural products
Language(s)	English (official), Luganda, Nkole, Chiga, Lango, Acholi, Teso, Lugbara

SOURCES: DK World Desk Reference Online; CIA World Factbook Online; *The World Almanac, 2003*

Uganda (yoo GAN duh) is bordered on the west by the Democratic Republic of the Congo, on the north by Sudan, on the east by Kenya, and on the south by Tanzania, Lake Victoria, and Rwanda. Uganda gained independence from Britain in 1962. It has since faced difficult political challenges. During the 1970s and 1980s, civil war led to hundreds of thousands of deaths as well as the destruction of the country's economy. Since the 1990s, Uganda has been celebrated for its return to economic success. The country has many natural resources, including copper and cobalt, as well as fertile soil and plentiful rain.

Lake Victoria

Assessment

Comprehension and Critical Thinking

1. Draw Conclusions What are some characteristics that most East African countries share?

2. Analyze Information What are some key differences among the countries?

3. Compare Compare the land areas and populations of Burundi and Sudan.

4. Categorize What kinds of products are the major exports of this region?

5. Summarize Which languages are spoken in more than one country in this region?

6. Make a Bar Graph Create a bar graph showing the land area, in square miles, of each of the countries in this region.

Keeping Current

Access the **DK World Desk Reference Online** at PHSchool.com for up-to-date information about all eleven countries in this chapter.

 Go Online
PHSchool.com

Web Code: lae-5600

Chapter 16 **513**

Assess and Reteach

Assess Progress [L2]

- Direct students' attention back to the columns on the board. Encourage them to suggest additional information under each heading based on what they have learned. Then ask if there are any general conclusions they can draw as a class from the individual similarities and differences they have found. *(Possible conclusions: Many of the people in East Africa are Muslims; English is spoken in about half the countries. Many countries have experienced civil unrest.)*

- Ask students to answer the Assessment questions.

Reteach [L1]

If students are having trouble remembering where the countries of East Africa are located, distribute *Outline Map 2: The World: Political, Outline Map 21: Africa: Political,* and *Outline Map 24: East and Southern Africa.* Have students shade in and label the block of countries featured in the Country Databank on each map. Model the process by shading East Africa on the world map as a class.

All in One **Africa Teaching Resources,** *Outline Map 2: The World: Political,* p. 356; *Outline Map 21: Africa: Political,* p. 357; *Outline Map 24: East and Southern Africa,* p. 358

Extend [L3]

Portfolio Activity
Have students choose two countries from the Country Databank. Ask them to conduct library or Internet research about the natural resources of both countries. Have them write a short essay comparing and contrasting the natural resources of the two countries and explaining how the resources affect each country's economy. Have students add their work to their portfolios.

Answers

Assessment

1. There are Muslims in most countries; most of the countries are republics.

2. The countries all have different currencies, capitals, populations, and land areas. For example, Sudan is the largest country in Africa, while the Seychelles is only 176 square miles (455 square kilometers).

3. Burundi's land area is 9,903 sq mi (25,650 sq km); Sudan's land area is 917,374 sq mi (2,376,000 sq km). Burundi's population is 6.4 million; Sudan's is 37.1 million. The land area and population of Sudan are larger than those of Burundi.

4. livestock, agricultural products, natural resources, fish

5. French, Kiswahili, Arabic, Somali, Afar, English

6. Bar graphs should accurately reflect the land area of each country. Use the *Rubric for Assessing a Bar Graph* to evaluate students' work.

All in One **Africa Teaching Resources,** *Rubric for Assessing a Bar Graph,* p. 372

Section 1
Step-by-Step Instruction

Objectives

Social Studies

1. Learn about the two major religions practiced in Ethiopia.
2. Understand the contrasts in the daily lives of rural and urban Ethiopians.

Reading/Language Arts

Use context clues to determine the meanings of unfamiliar words.

Prepare to Read

Build Background Knowledge L2

Tell students that in this section they will learn about the East African country of Ethiopia. Have students preview the headings and visuals in the section, then make a list of what they think might be important to people in Ethiopia. Provide a few simple examples to get students started. *(Possible answer: religion)* Conduct an Idea Wave (TE, p. T35) to generate a list.

Set a Purpose for Reading L2

- Preview the Objectives.

- Read each statement in the *Reading Readiness Guide* aloud. Ask students to mark the statements true or false.

- Have students discuss the statements in pairs or groups of four, then mark their worksheets again. Use the Numbered Heads participation strategy (TE, p. T36) to call on students to share their group's perspectives.

All in One Africa Teaching Resources, *Reading Readiness Guide,* p. 336

Vocabulary Builder
Preview Key Terms L2

Pronounce each Key Term, then ask the students to say the word with you. Provide a simple explanation such as, "The ancient language of Geez is no longer spoken in Ethiopia."

Section 1
Ethiopia
Religious Roots

Prepare to Read

Objectives

In this section you will
1. Learn about the two major religions practiced in Ethiopia.
2. Understand the contrasts in the daily lives of rural and urban Ethiopians.

Taking Notes

As you read this section, look for details about religion and daily life in Ethiopia. Copy the table below, and use it to record your findings.

Culture of Ethiopia	
Religion	**Daily Life**
• •	• •

Target Reading Skill

Use Context Clues When you come across an unfamiliar word, you can sometimes figure out its meaning from clues in the context. The context refers to the surrounding words and sentences. As you read, look at the context for the word *isolated* in the last paragraph on page 515. Use the sentence that follows it as a clue. What do you think *isolated* means?

Key Terms

- **monastery** (MAHN uh stehr ee) *n.* a place where people, especially men known as monks, live a religious life
- **Geez** (gee EZ) *n.* an ancient Ethiopian language that was once used to write literature and religious texts but is no longer spoken

The monastery of Debre Damo, where Iyasus Mo'a became a monk in the 1200s

514 Africa

As a young boy, Iyasus Mo'a (ee YAH soos MOH uh) learned to read and write. Around the year 1241, he traveled from his home in Wag to Tigray (tee GRAY), both in northern Ethiopia. He walked a distance that today would take three days to drive.

Did he plan to enter a university in Tigray? No—at that time there were no universities in Ethiopia. Iyasus entered a Christian monastery. A **monastery** is a place where people, especially men known as monks, live a religious life. As a monk, Iyasus studied hard for many years and eventually also became a famous teacher. His students built monasteries and schools all over the region.

Target Reading Skill L2

Use Context Clues Point out the Target Reading Skill. Tell students that using context clues will help them to define unfamiliar words.

Model using context clues by directing students' attention to the last paragraph on p. 518 under the heading Urban Ethiopia. If students are unfamiliar with the meaning of "conveniences," they can use context clues near the word such as "running water," "electricity," and "modern hospitals" to determine that "conveniences" are technologies that increase comfort or save work.

Give students *Use Context Clues: Definition and Description.* Have them complete the activity in their groups.

All in One Africa Teaching Resources, *Use Context Clues: Definition and Description,* p. 347

Christianity in Ethiopia Today
An Ethiopian man takes part in a Christian celebration, wearing colorful silk clothing and carrying an elaborate gold cross.
Analyze Images What details in the picture provide clues that this man is involved in an important ceremony?

Major Religions of Ethiopia

Iyasus Mo'a learned Ethiopia's ancient traditions. He studied a language called Geez (gee EZ). **Geez** is one of the world's oldest languages. Much of Ethiopia's history was preserved by monks like Iyasus, who copied books in Geez by hand.

The religion Iyasus studied—Christianity—had spread to Ethiopia along trade routes. Ethiopia was a center of trade. It once included present-day Eritrea as well. These lands border the Red Sea. Look at the physical map of Africa on page 352 of the Regional Overview. Find the Red Sea. As people traded goods along the Red Sea, they also learned about one another's religions. The Red Sea connected Ethiopia with Egypt and Palestine, which were early centers of Christianity.

Establishment of Christianity in Ethiopia Alexandria, a city in Egypt, was one of the first centers of Christianity. By the year A.D. 350, missionaries from Alexandria had brought Christianity to Ethiopia. Over time, Christians in Egypt and Ethiopia came to differ with Christians in Rome and Constantinople about certain beliefs. In A.D. 451, Egyptian Christians separated from the rest of the Christian Church. They formed an Egyptian branch of Christianity called the Coptic Christian Church. Ethiopia's Christians also practiced Coptic Christianity.

Over time, Ethiopian Christians became isolated from Christians in other parts of the world. Ethiopia's mountains made it difficult for people who lived in the interior to travel to other areas. Some people did travel overland or along the Red Sea. However, Ethiopian Christians were cut off from these travel routes in the A.D. 600s, when Muslim Arabs arrived in the region.

Links to Language Arts

Written Language Ethiopians began writing in Geez by the A.D. 300s. They used Geez to write literature and religious texts such as the one shown below. Ethiopia and Egypt were the only ancient African countries to develop their own writing systems. Many Islamic kingdoms in Africa did produce written documents for religious and government purposes. However, these texts were written in Arabic, which was developed in Arabia.

Vocabulary Builder

Use the information below to teach students this section's high-use words.

High-Use Word	Definition and Sample Sentence
preserve, p. 515	*v.* to maintain or protect Jane knew it was important to **preserve** her family's holiday traditions.
adopt, p. 516	*v.* to take on as one's own It is often difficult for people to **adopt** new ideas.
specialize, p. 518	*v.* to focus one's efforts in a particular activity The store **specializes** in travel books.
headquarters, p. 518	*n.* the main offices of a business or organization The candidate's **headquarters** were busy the day before the election.

Major Religions of Ethiopia **L2**

Guided Instruction

- **Vocabulary Builder** Clarify the high-use words **preserve** and **adopt** before reading.

- Have students read Major Religions of Ethiopia using the Paragraph Shrinking strategy (TE, p. T34).

- Ask students **Why was Ethiopia a center of trade in ancient times?** *(Because it bordered the Red Sea, which was used for trade.)* **How did this affect Ethiopia?** *(Christianity spread to Ethiopia along trade routes.)*

- Have students discuss how the Coptic Christian Church was formed. *(Christians in Egypt and Ethiopia differed with Christians in Rome and Constantinople, so Egyptian Christians formed the Coptic Christian Church in A.D. 451.)*

- Ask students **How did Islam spread to Ethiopia?** *(It spread over time as Arab traders settled in the region.)*

- Ask students to discuss how Muslims and Christians have interacted in Ethiopia. *(Though they fought in the 1500s, Ethiopian Muslims and Christians have for the most part lived together peacefully.)*

Independent Practice

Ask students to create the Taking Notes graphic organizer on a blank piece of paper. Then have them fill in the "Religion" box with the information they have just learned. Briefly model how to identify which details to record.

Monitor Progress

As students fill in the graphic organizer, circulate and make sure individuals are selecting the correct details. Provide assistance as needed.

Links

Read the **Links To Language Arts** on this page. Ask students **Which were the only two ancient African countries to have developed their own writing systems?** *(Ethiopia and Egypt)*

Answer

Analyze Images He is dressed in elaborate clothing and is carrying a large, gold cross.

Contrasts in Daily Life L2

Guided Instruction

- **Vocabulary Builder** Clarify the high-use words **specialize** and **headquarters** before reading.

- Read Contrasts in Daily Life with students. Circulate to make sure individuals can answer the Reading Check question.

- Ask students **How do people in rural Ethiopia make a living?** (*Some people farm; others herd cattle, fish, or work in trades.*)

- Ask students to describe life in Addis Ababa. (*It is a modern city with running water, electricity, hospitals, businesses, a university, a museum, and palaces. It is also the headquarters of several international organizations working to improve Africa.*)

⏺ Target Reading Skill

Use Context Clues Have students read the Target Reading Skill activity in the Student Edition. As a follow up, ask students to use context clues to figure out the meaning of another word on this page. (*Answers will vary, but students should identify a word and the context clues they used to find its meaning.*)

Independent Practice

Have students complete the graphic organizer by filling in the "Daily Life" box with information from the section.

Monitor Progress

- Show *Section Reading Support Transparency AF 50* and ask students to check their graphic organizers individually. Go over key concepts and clarify key vocabulary as needed.

  📖 **Africa Transparencies,** *Section Reading Support Transparency AF 50*

- Tell students to fill in the last column of the *Reading Readiness Guide*. Probe for what they learned that confirms or invalidates each statement.

  All in One **Africa Teaching Resources,** *Reading Readiness Guide,* p. 336

Answers

Compare From the side, you can see that the church is actually a tall, large building; from above, you can clearly see it was built in the shape of a cross.

✔ Reading Check By A.D. 350 missionaries from Alexandria had spread Christianity to Ethiopia.

Underground Churches
Here you see St. George's Church of Lalibela from a side view (above left) and an overhead view (above right). The church was built in the shape of a cross. **Compare** *Compare the effects of looking at the church from the side and from above.*

 Use Context Clues
If you do not know what *reigned* means, consider the word's context. You know that Lalibela reigned for a few decades. You also know that he was the ruler of Roha. You could conclude that *reigned* means "was the ruler of."

Spread of Islam Into Ethiopia The Muslim Arabs who had begun to settle across North Africa did not attempt to take over Ethiopia. But they did move into nearby areas. Over time, Arab traders built cities along the trade routes of the Red Sea coast. Eventually, Muslim Arabs came to control trade in the entire region. And, in time, some Ethiopians adopted the Muslim faith.

A Unique Form of Christianity As Muslim Arabs took control of Ethiopia's coastal regions, Ethiopian Christians began moving farther inland. Finally, Christian Ethiopia became surrounded by Muslim-controlled areas. As a result, Christians in Ethiopia had very little contact with Christians elsewhere. The Ethiopian Christian Church developed into a unique form of Christianity with its own traditions and language, Geez.

Also unique to Ethiopian Christianity are the churches of a town called Lalibela (lah lee BAY lah). Once called Roha, it was the capital of Christian Ethiopia for about 300 years. It was renamed for its most famous ruler, Lalibela, who reigned during the late 1100s and early 1200s. The ruler Lalibela sponsored the construction of eleven churches unlike any others—they were built below the ground and cut out of solid rock. Many Christians today travel to Lalibela to visit the churches and celebrate their faith.

Christian-Muslim Interaction Throughout most of Ethiopia's history, Christians and Muslims have coexisted peacefully. However, they have sometimes fought over religious issues. For example, they went to war with each other in the 1500s. Today, about 35 percent of Ethiopians are Christians and about 45 percent are Muslims. Most other Ethiopians practice traditional African religions, although a small number practice Judaism.

✔ Reading Check **How did Christianity first come to Ethiopia?**

516 Africa

Differentiated Instruction

For Gifted and Talented L3
Have students complete the *Small Group Activity* for this chapter. After constructing their mural, students should answer the discussion questions together as a group, then explain their artwork to the class.

All in One **Africa Teaching Resources,** *Small Group Activity: Mural of East African Architecture,* pp. 352–355

For Special Needs Students L1
Have students read the section as they listen to the recorded version on the Student Edition on Audio CD. Check for comprehension by pausing the CD and asking students to share their answers to the Reading Check questions.

⏺ Chapter 16, Section 1, **Student Edition on Audio CD**

Ethiopia

People have lived in Ethiopia longer than in most other countries on Earth. And for most of its history, the nation has ruled itself. Except for a short period of time before World War II, Ethiopia was never colonized by a European country.

Today, as for thousands of years, Ethiopian cultures have been centered mainly in the country's highlands. Many ethnic groups exist, but a few are much larger than the rest. Members of each ethnic group tend to live near one another. Study the map and charts to learn more about Ethiopia's people today.

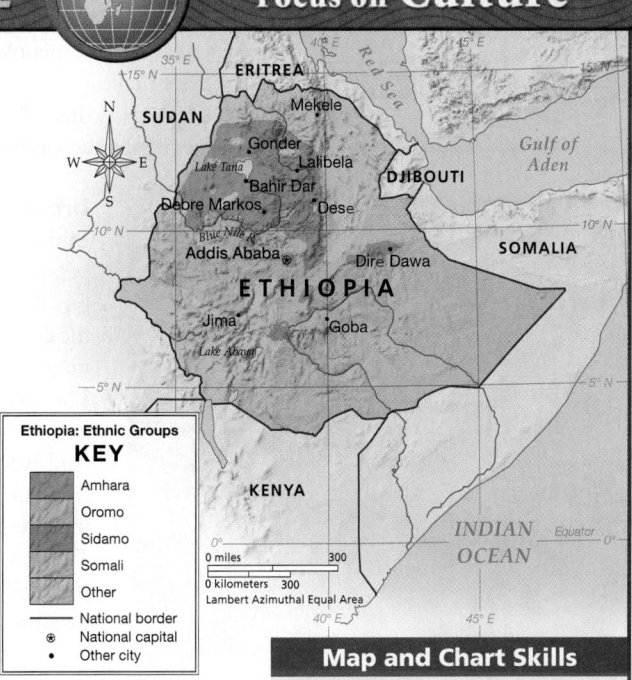

Ethiopia: Ethnic Groups
KEY

- Amhara
- Oromo
- Sidamo
- Somali
- Other

—— National border
⊛ National capital
• Other city

0 miles 300
0 kilometers 300
Lambert Azimuthal Equal Area

Population by Age*

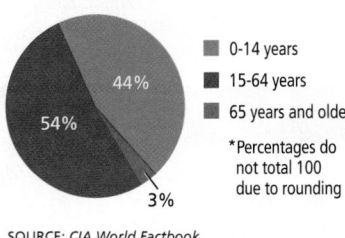

- 0-14 years
- 15-64 years
- 65 years and older

*Percentages do not total 100 due to rounding

44%
54%
3%

SOURCE: *CIA World Factbook*

Ethnic Groups

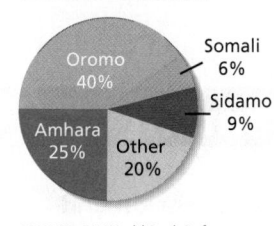

Oromo 40%
Somali 6%
Sidamo 9%
Amhara 25%
Other 20%

SOURCE: *DK World Desk Reference*

Map and Chart Skills

1. **Name** What is the largest ethnic group in Ethiopia?
2. **Identify** What percentage of Ethiopia's population is under 14 years of age?
3. **Analyze** What does this percentage tell you about Ethiopian society?

Go Online
PHSchool.com
Use Web Code lae-5601 for **DK World Desk Reference Online.**

Contrasts in Daily Life

Today, most Ethiopians, regardless of their religious background, live in rural areas. In fact, only about 16 percent of the population lives in cities. How do rural and urban life in Ethiopia differ? A look at the village of Gerba Sefer reveals many clues about rural life in Ethiopia. The capital city of Addis Ababa (ad is AB uh buh), on the other hand, represents the urban life that some Ethiopians know.

Skills Mini Lesson

Transferring Information from One Medium to Another   L2

1. Explain that information can be presented in many forms. Tell students that to transfer information from one medium to another, they should find the main idea, identify key facts, choose a new format, and place each piece of information into the format.

2. Have students practice the skill by reading the text on p. 518 and, as a class, creating a chart comparing life in rural and urban Ethiopia.

3. Have students apply the skill by writing a short paragraph summarizing the information in the circle graph on this page. Students' paragraphs should draw conclusions about the information.

COUNTRY PROFILE
Focus on **Culture**

Guided Instruction

Ask students to study the Country Profile on this page. As a class, answer the Map and Chart Skills questions. Allow students to briefly discuss their responses with a partner before sharing answers.

Independent Practice

- Distribute *Using a Map Key*. Have students work in pairs to complete the worksheet.

  All in One **Africa Teaching Resources,** *Using a Map Key,* p. 362

- Tell students that the map of Ethiopia in the Student Edition shows the country's ethnic groups. Ask them to identify what information appears on the map on the worksheet, paying special attention to the map title and key.

Answers

Map and Chart Skills

1. Oromo
2. 44 percent
3. Possible answer: The country has to devote a large part of its income to education.

Go Online
PHSchool.com Students can find additional useful information about this topic on the DK World Desk Reference Online.

Assess and Reteach

Assess Progress L2

Have students complete the Section Assessment. Administer the *Section Quiz.*

All in One **Africa Teaching Resources,** *Section Quiz,* p. 338

Reteach L1

If students need more instruction, have them read this section in the Reading and Vocabulary Study Guide.

Chapter 16, Section 1, **Eastern Hemisphere Reading and Vocabulary Study Guide,** pp. 178–180

Extend L3

Remind students that only about 16 percent of Ethiopia's population lives in cities. Have them investigate how this percentage compares with the world's urban population by completing *Urban Population, Past and Projected.* They should study the graph independently, then answer the questions in pairs.

Go Online
PHSchool.com **For:** Environmental and Global Issues: *Urban Population, Past and Projected*
Visit: PHSchool.com
Web Code: lad-5604

Answer

✓ Reading Check Most Ethiopians live in rural settings.

Section 1 Assessment

Key Terms

Students' sentences should reflect knowledge of each Key Term.

Target Reading Skill

Answers will vary, but students should state that "coexisted" means "lived together", and should identify clues that helped them arrive at their definitions.

Learn about life in an Ethiopian village.

Rural Ethiopia Public services such as electricity and running water are rare in rural Ethiopia. For example, no one in the village of Gerba Sefer has electricity, and more people own donkeys than cars. The people who live in the areas surrounding Gerba Sefer make a living by farming. In some rural areas, people make a living by herding cattle or by fishing. Some families specialize in jobs such as woodworking and beekeeping.

A street in Addis Ababa

Urban Ethiopia Addis Ababa, the capital of Ethiopia, has a population of almost 3 million people. It is located in the center of the country. People in Addis Ababa have access to all the conveniences of city life—for example, running water, electricity, and modern hospitals. The city also has a university and a museum, as well as palaces built by ancient emperors. And Addis Ababa is a center of business and trade that reflects a diverse population, which includes ethnic groups such as the Amhara, Tigrey, Galla, and Gurage. The city also houses the headquarters of several international organizations that work for the economic, political, and social well-being of Africa.

✓ Reading Check **Do most Ethiopians live in rural or in urban settings?**

Section 1 Assessment

Key Terms

Review the key terms at the beginning of this section. Use each term in a sentence that explains its meaning.

Target Reading Skill

Find the word *coexisted* in the last paragraph on page 516. Use context to figure out its meaning. What do you think it means? What clues helped you arrive at its meaning?

Comprehension and Critical Thinking

1. (a) Recall When did Christianity first come to Ethiopia?
(b) Summarize What led to the unique nature of the Christianity practiced in Ethiopia?
(c) Predict What do you think helps Christians and Muslims exist peacefully in Ethiopia today?
2. (a) Identify In what ways do rural Ethiopians make a living?
(b) Contrast How is life in Ethiopia's rural areas different from life in Addis Ababa?

Writing Activity

Write a paragraph encouraging travelers to visit the historic churches of Lalibela, Ethiopia. In it, explain how the Ethiopian Christian Church has been affected by the country's history.

Go Online
PHSchool.com

For: An activity on Ethiopia
Visit: PHSchool.com
Web Code: lad-5601

518 Africa

Comprehension and Critical Thinking

1. (a) by the year A.D. 350 **(b)** conflict between different groups; geographical and cultural isolation **(c)** Possible answers: The groups live separately; they have a history of fairly peaceful interaction.

2. (a) farming, herding cattle, fishing, trades such as woodworking and beekeeping **(b)** Rural areas lack modern conveniences such as running water, electricity, transportation, and hospitals.

Writing Activity

Use the *Rubric for Assessing a Writing Assignment* to evaluate students' paragraphs.

All in One **Africa Teaching Resources,** *Rubric for Assessing a Writing Assignment,* p. 373

 Typing in the Web code when prompted will bring students directly to detailed instructions for this activity.

Tanzania
Determined to Succeed

Prepare to Read

Objectives
In this section you will
1. Find out about early reforms that the government of Tanzania made after independence.
2. Learn about continued social, economic, and political progress and reforms that have been made in Tanzania.

Taking Notes
As you read this section, look for details about social, economic, and political reforms in Tanzania. Copy the chart below, and use it to record your findings.

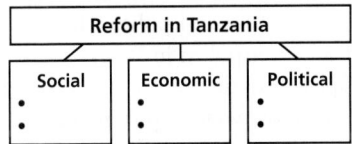

🎯 Target Reading Skill
Use Context Clues You can sometimes clarify the meaning of a word or phrase by using context—the surrounding words, phrases, and sentences. Sometimes the context will give a clear definition or explanation of the word. For example, each word highlighted in blue in this book is followed by a definition. As you read, look for other words that are accompanied by definitions or explanations.

Key Terms
- **lingua franca** (LING gwuh FRANG kuh) *n.* a language used for communication among people who speak different first languages
- **privatization** (pry vuh tih ZAY shun) *n.* the sale of government-owned industries to private companies
- **multiparty system** (MUL tee PAHR tee SIS tum) *n.* a political system in which two or more parties compete in elections

In October 1995, Dar es Salaam (DAHR es suh LAHM), Tanzania, looked ready for a celebration. Flags hung from buildings. People sang in the streets. Was it a holiday? Had a sports team become champions? No—an election was about to start. It would be the first election in more than 30 years to include more than one political party. Finally, voters would have a real choice among candidates with differing views. Tanzanians felt joyful, but they did not know what the future would hold. Other reforms their country had gone through had met with different levels of success.

Early Reforms After Independence

Tanzania lies on the Indian Ocean. This location has made it an important center of trade. Arab traders settled along the coast around 1,200 years ago. In the late 1800s, Germans colonized the entire region. The British took over in the early 1900s. The British named the mainland area Tanganyika (tan guh NYEE kuh). Tanganyika became independent in 1961. In 1964, it joined with the island state of Zanzibar to form Tanzania.

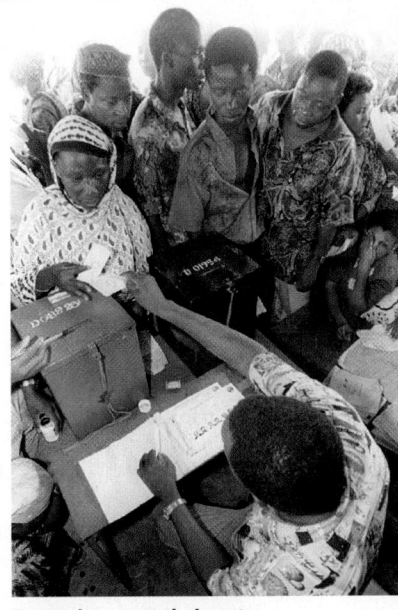

Tanzanians cast their votes.

Objectives
Social Studies
1. Find out about early reforms that the government of Tanzania made after independence.
2. Learn about continued social, economic, and political progress and reforms that have been made in Tanzania.

Reading/Language Arts
Use context clues to clarify the meaning of an unfamiliar word or phrase.

Prepare to Read

Build Background Knowledge L2
Tell students that in this section they will be learning about life in Tanzania. Point out Tanzania on a classroom map, and tell students that the area became independent from Britain in 1961. Ask them to brainstorm how a region might change politically, socially, and economically when it becomes independent. Use the Give One, Get One participation strategy (TE, p. T37) to guide the discussion.

Set a Purpose for Reading L2
- Preview the Objectives.
- Read each statement in the *Reading Readiness Guide* aloud. Ask students to mark the statements true or false.
- Have students discuss the statements in pairs or groups of four, then mark their worksheets again. Use the Numbered Heads participation strategy (TE, p. T36) to call on students to share their group's perspectives.

  All in One Africa Teaching Resources, *Reading Readiness Guide*, p. 340

🎯 Target Reading Skill L2
Use Context Clues Point out the Target Reading Skill. Tell students that an unfamiliar word in the text may be followed by an explanation or definition.

Model using context clues using the term "privatization" in the first sentence on p. 523. Point out that the sentence that follows the term provides a definition:

"Privatization is the sale of government-owned industries to private companies."

Give students *Use Context Clues: Definition and Description*. Have them review the activity in their groups.

All in One Africa Teaching Resources, *Use Context Clues: Definition and Description*, p. 347

Vocabulary Builder
Preview Key Terms
Pronounce each Key Term, then ask the students to say the word with you. Provide a simple explanation such as, "In many countries in East Africa, Swahili is the lingua franca."

Instruct

Early Reforms After Independence L2

Guided Instruction

- **Vocabulary Builder** Clarify the high-use words **literate** and **policy** before reading.

- Read Early Reforms After Independence using the Oral Cloze strategy (TE, p. T33).

- Ask students **When did Tanganyika become independent from British rule?** *(1961)* **What countries joined to form Tanzania?** *(Tanganyika and Zanzibar)*

- Ask students to describe the challenges Tanzania faced after becoming independent. *(poverty, illiteracy, ethnic conflict, lack of medical care and education, many languages, debate over social policies)*

- Ask students **Why did President Nyerere make Swahili the national language of Tanzania?** *(Since Swahili is the* lingua franca, *making it the national language helped all the ethnic groups feel more united.)*

- Ask students **What does** *ujamaa* **mean in Swahili?** *("togetherness" or "being a family")* **How did the** *ujamaa* **villages reflect this meaning?** *(In these villages, farmers worked together and shared resources.)*

Independent Practice

Ask students to create the Taking Notes graphic organizer on a blank piece of paper. Then have them fill in information about reform in Tanzania in the appropriate boxes.

Monitor Progress

As students fill in the graphic organizer, circulate and make sure individuals are selecting the correct details.

🎯 Target Reading Skill L2

Use Context Clues As a follow up, ask students to answer the Target Reading Skill question in the Student Edition. *(Sentences should express that under a one-party system, all candidates are members of the same party.)*

520 *Africa*

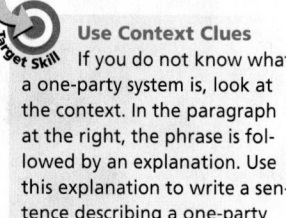

Use Context Clues If you do not know what a one-party system is, look at the context. In the paragraph at the right, the phrase is followed by an explanation. Use this explanation to write a sentence describing a one-party system in your own words.

520 Africa

Challenges for the New Nation When Tanzania became independent, most of its people were poor. Few were literate. According to Tanzania's then president, Julius Nyerere, the new republic had serious problems:

> ❝We had 12 medical doctors in a population of 9 million. About 45 percent of children of schoolgoing age were going to school, and 85 percent of the adult population was illiterate. ❞
>
> —*Julius Nyerere*

A problem Nyerere wanted to avoid was tension among Tanzania's 120 ethnic groups. In many other African nations, ethnic groups fought against one another after independence. To ensure that ethnic conflicts would not occur in Tanzania, Nyerere adopted unusual social policies. Although some of these policies met with approval both at home and abroad, others were sharply criticized. Even today, debate continues over whether or not Nyerere made good choices for Tanzania.

A National Language One of Nyerere's social policies had to do with language. Various languages are spoken in East African homes, but many people also speak Swahili. As you read in Chapter 12, Swahili is one of Africa's most widely spoken languages. In East Africa, Swahili is a lingua franca (LING gwuh FRANG kuh). A **lingua franca** is a language used for communication among people who speak different first languages. To help unite all of Tanzania's ethnic groups, Nyerere made Swahili the national language.

A One-Party System Nyerere also established a new political system. He feared that political parties in Tanzania would be based on ethnic groups. If so, competition among parties could lead to competition or hatred among ethnic groups. This had happened in other newly independent African nations. Therefore, Nyerere established a one-party system. Elections still involved several candidates, but they were all members of the same party. Critics complained that having just one party encouraged corruption in the government.

Economic Changes Next, Nyerere turned to the economy. He told Tanzanians that independence meant *uhuru na kazi* (oo HOO roo nah KAH zee)—"freedom and work." By this he meant that only hard work could end poverty. Nyerere said that Tanzania should be self-reliant. He did not want the country to depend on other nations for economic support.

Vocabulary Builder

Use the information below to teach students this section's high-use words.

High-Use Word	Definition and Sample Sentence
literate, p. 520	*adj.* able to read and write Most people in the United States are **literate**.
policy, p. 520	*n.* a plan or course of action, especially in government The government's new **policy** was very unpopular.
suffer, p. 521	*v.*, to put up with loss or damage I **suffered** only minor injuries from the car accident.

520 *Africa*

To promote self-reliance, Nyerere established a program of *ujamaa* (oo JAH mah), which is Swahili for "togetherness" or "being a family." Tanzania's economy is based on farming. Nyerere called for all farmers to live in ujamaa villages, where they could work together and share resources. He believed this would help boost farm production. It would also make it easier for the government to provide clean water, education, and other services in an organized way.

✓ **Reading Check** What language is the lingua franca of Tanzania?

Progress and Continued Reform

By the time Nyerere stepped down as president in 1985, Tanzania had changed greatly. The country had a national language and very little ethnic conflict. Education and literacy had improved greatly. Proud of his success, Nyerere commented,

> **"When I stepped down, 91 percent of the adult population was literate, 100 percent of the children of school-going age were going to school. . . . We did not have enough engineers, but we had thousands . . . trained by ourselves. We did not have enough doctors, but we had . . . thousands trained by ourselves. That is what we were able to do . . . in a short period of independence."**
>
> —*Julius Nyerere*

However, Tanzania was still one of the poorest countries in the world. The ujamaa program had failed, and the economy was suffering. Many farm families had refused to move to the new villages. Crop production had decreased throughout the nation.

Links Across The World

Kwanzaa In the 1960s, many African Americans began celebrating family, community, and their African heritage with a holiday called Kwanzaa (KWAHN zah). Kwanzaa is based on several traditional African harvest festivals. Its name comes from a Swahili phrase that means "first fruits." The holiday celebrates a set of seven values that also have Swahili names. One of these values is ujamaa. Each night of the week-long holiday, families like the one shown here gather to light a candle and discuss one of the values.

Links
Read the **Links Across the World** on this page. Ask students **What is Kwanzaa?** (*a holiday based on African traditions that is celebrated by many African Americans*)

Progress and Continued Reform   L2

Guided Instruction

- **Vocabulary Builder** Clarify the high-use word **suffer** before reading.

- Read about how new reforms have changed Tanzania in Progress and Continued Reform. As students read, circulate to make sure individuals can answer the Reading Check question.

- Ask students **What progress did Tanzania make under Nyerere?** (*The country established a national language and suffered from little ethnic fighting; education and literacy improved greatly.*) **What problems did Tanzania still face?** (*It was one of the world's poorest countries; the ujamaa program failed and crop production had fallen.*)

- Ask **What changes did the government make to improve the economy after Nyerere retired?** (*The ujamaa program was ended; farmers were encouraged to produce more cash crops and use modern techniques; the government tried privatization and asked foreign countries for loans.*)

Independent Practice
Have students complete the graphic organizer by filling in more details from the section.

Monitor Progress

- Show *Section Reading Support Transparency AF 51* and ask students to check their graphic organizers individually. Go over key concepts and clarify key vocabulary as needed.

  📖 **Africa Transparencies,** *Section Reading Support Transparency AF 51*

- Tell students to fill in the last column of the *Reading Readiness Guide*. Probe for what they learned that confirms or invalidates each statement.

  All in One Africa Teaching Resources, *Reading Readiness Guide*, p. 340

Answer
✓ **Reading Check** Swahili

Background: Links Across Place

Socialism The ideas set forth by Julius Nyerere were partly based on traditional African social systems, but his policies were also a form of socialism—a system in which the community collectively owns land and industry. Socialist ideas began to appear in Europe in the late 1700s and early 1800s as a reaction to the Industrial Revolution. While many became rich during this time of economic growth, many lower class workers struggled. Socialism addressed this split between upper and lower classes by proposing a society based on cooperation and public control of industry. Socialist ideas have had an impact on governments in Europe, Latin America, Asia, and Africa, but several major socialist systems have failed.

COUNTRY PROFILE
Focus on Economics

Guided Instruction

Ask students to study the Country Profile on this page. Point out the map, circle graph, and table. As a class, answer the Map and Chart Skills questions. Allow students to briefly discuss their responses with a partner before sharing answers.

Independent Practice

Have students carefully study the map, and then work with a partner to answer the following: **In what parts of the country are cattle raised?** *(in the north, south, and southeast)* **Where is tea grown?** *(in the north and south)* **Where is coffee grown?** *(in the north)* **What feature do most of the areas of cropland share?** *(Almost all are near bodies of water.)*

 Show students *Tanzania: Making a Living on Lake Victoria.* Ask **How is Lake Victoria important to the Tanzanian economy?** *(About 50,000 fishermen earn their living by fishing in Lake Victoria; the Nile Perch and related products earn Tanzania about 90 million dollars per year.)*

Answers

Map and Chart Skills

1. **(a)** cashews **(b)** sisal
2. Possible answers: advantage—crops such as coffee are used all over the world and so have large markets; disadvantage—a drought or other bad weather can destroy a crop and negatively affect the economy.

Go Online PHSchool.com Students can find additional useful information about this topic on the DK World Desk Reference Online.

COUNTRY PROFILE
Focus on Economics

Tanzania

Like many African nations, Tanzania grows cash crops for export to other countries. The price of these cash crops on the world market greatly influences whether Tanzania's economy improves or declines. When the world price of coffee dropped from about $1.00 per pound in 1996 to less than $.40 per pound in 2003, many Tanzanians suffered. At the same time, the world price of tea rose, helping other Tanzanian farmers. Study the map and charts to learn more about the economy of Tanzania.

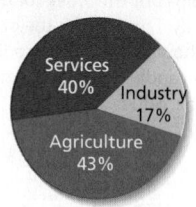

Economic Activity

- Services 40%
- Industry 17%
- Agriculture 43%

SOURCE: *CIA World Factbook*

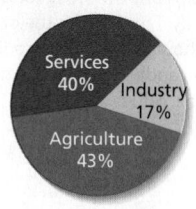

Tanzania: Farming and Land Use
KEY
- Pasture
- Cropland
- Tea
- Coffee
- Cattle
- National border
- ⊛ National capital

Major Cash Crops, 2001

Crop	Exports (billions of Tanzanian shillings*)
Cashews	50.9
Coffee	49.6
Cotton seeds	29.2
Sisal	5.9
Tobacco	32.3

* $1 = approximately 1,000 Tanzanian shillings
SOURCE: Tanzanian Ministry of Agriculture and Food Security

Map and Chart Skills

1. **Identify (a)** Which of Tanzania's cash crops was the most valuable export in 2001? **(b)** Which was least valuable?
2. **Draw Conclusions** You can see that agriculture makes up the largest part of Tanzania's economy. Name one advantage and one disadvantage of basing an economy on selling cash crops to other countries.

 **Go Online** PHSchool.com Use Web Code lae-5602 for **DK World Desk Reference Online.**

Discover how people make a living on Lake Victoria.

522 Africa

A New Era in Economics After Nyerere retired, Ali Hassan Mwinyi (AH lee hah SAHN um WEEN yee) was elected president. His government replaced some of Nyerere's unsuccessful programs. For example, the government ended Nyerere's failing ujamaa program. The government then encouraged farmers to use new farming methods and types of seeds in order to produce more cash crops. It also asked foreign countries for more help, and a number of them have since loaned money to Tanzania.

Differentiated Instruction

For Advanced Readers [L3]

Point out to students that during Julius Nyerere's presidency, some children in Tanzania began going to school for the first time. Have students read *Mukasa*, a story about a young boy in Uganda. Then have students answer the questions.

All in One Africa Teaching Resources, *Mukasa*, pp. 363–366

For English Language Learners [L1]

Students may have difficulty pronouncing some of the longer words in this section, such as *population, criticized, established, independence,* and *experienced.* Show students how to break down these words into smaller parts, and sound out the pronunciations.

The government also decided to try privatization. **Privatization** is the sale of government-owned industries to private companies. Private companies, including some that are foreign-owned, now manage Tanzania's telephone and airline industries. The result of the new economic policies is that Tanzania's economy is improving more quickly and more smoothly than the economies of most other African nations.

Attempts at Political Reform Tanzania's new government also changed the election system. In 1992, the government began to allow new political parties to form. When a country has two or more political parties, it has a **multiparty system.** Tanzania's first elections under the multiparty system were held in October 1995.

But the 1995 and 2000 elections raised some issues that divided people. For example, in both elections, Nyerere's party won the most votes, so power remained with that party. Also, another party suggested that the island of Zanzibar should no longer be part of Tanzania. That would cause exactly the type of social split that Nyerere worried about. Whether Tanzania can achieve the same progress in politics as it has with its economy is still to be seen.

Cashews: A New Cash Crop
Cashew nuts are one of the cash crops that Tanzanian farmers now produce for export to other countries. Coffee and cotton are also major export items. **Summarize** *How can producing cash crops for export help improve a country's economy?*

✓ **Reading Check** What political change occurred in 1992?

Section 2 Assessment

Key Terms
Review the key terms at the beginning of this section. Use each term in a sentence that explains its meaning.

🔁 **Target Reading Skill**
Find the word *self-reliant* on page 520. From its context, what do you think it means?

Comprehension and Critical Thinking
1. (a) Explain Why did Julius Nyerere decide to establish a one-party political system in Tanzania?

(b) Analyze Information In what ways can having a national language help prevent ethnic conflict in a country?
(c) Draw Conclusions If people had not had to move away from their homes, do you think the ujamaa program would have succeeded? Explain.
2. (a) Identify What improvements were made in Tanzania during Nyerere's presidency?
(b) Contrast Contrast the views Nyerere had on foreign involvement in Tanzania with the views that later government leaders had.

Writing Activity
How does Nyerere's slogan *uhuru na kazi,* or "freedom and work," apply to the kind of independence that you develop as you grow up? Write a paragraph explaining your response to this question.

For: An activity on the Ngorongoro Crater
Visit: PHSchool.com
Web Code: lad-5602

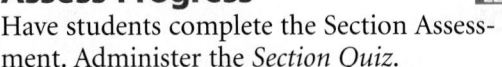

Assess and Reteach

Assess Progress L2
Have students complete the Section Assessment. Administer the *Section Quiz.*

🔲 **Africa Teaching Resources,** *Section Quiz,* p. 342

Reteach L1
If students need more instruction, have them read this section in the Reading and Vocabulary Study Guide.

📖 Chapter 16, Section 2, **Eastern Hemisphere Reading and Vocabulary Study Guide,** pp. 181–183

Extend L3
Divide the class into groups of four and have students find out why some Zanzibaris want Zanzibar to become an independent nation. Suggest that group members look for possible answers by researching Zanzibar's history, economy, and its dominant religion, Islam, in the library or on the Internet. Have group members compile their information and draw conclusions based on what they have learned. Groups should work together to prepare an oral presentation about why some Zanzibaris would like to become independent. Use the *Rubric for Assessing an Oral Presentation* to evaluate students' presentations.

🔲 **Africa Teaching Resources,** *Rubric for Assessing an Oral Presentation,* p. 374

Answers

Summarize It can bring money into the country's economy.

✓ **Reading Check** Tanzania switched to a multi-party system.

Writing Activity
Use the *Rubric for Assessing a Writing Assignment* to evaluate students' paragraph.

🔲 **Africa Teaching Resources,** *Rubric for Assessing a Writing Assignment,* p. 373

Go Online Typing in the Web code when prompted will bring students directly to detailed instructions for this activity.

Section 2 Assessment

Key Terms
Students' sentences should reflect knowledge of each Key Term.

🔁 **Target Reading Skill**
Using the explanation following the term as a clue, students should conclude that it means "depending on oneself rather than on others."

Comprehension and Critical Thinking
1. (a) Nyerere wanted to prevent ethnic strife. **(b)** Possible answer: Ethnic groups would feel like part of one country and be able to communicate more effectively. **(c)** Answers will vary, but should be based on evidence from the text.

2. (a) Nyerere made Swahili the national language and improved education and literacy. **(b)** Nyerere wanted Tanzania to be self-reliant.

Later leaders encouraged privatization and sought foreign aid.

Objective

Learn how to write a summary.

Prepare to Read

Build Background Knowledge   L2

Tell students that in this lesson they will learn how to write a summary. Ask them to turn back to the Chapter 15 Summary on p. 503. Have students count the number of bulleted statements in Section 1. Then ask them to turn to that section and count the number of main headings. Explain that the authors of the text used the main idea under each heading to create each statement in the Chapter Summary.

Instruct

Writing a Summary   L2

Guided Instruction

- Read the steps to summarizing information with the class. Write each step on the board.

- Practice the skill by completing the steps on p. 525 to summarize the Major Religions of Ethiopia on pp. 515–516.

- Read the headings and then identify the main ideas of each paragraph. *(Example: Heading—Spread of Islam Into Ethiopia. Main idea of paragraph—Arab traders spread Islam to Ethiopia.)*

- Identify how the main ideas are related. *(Most of them help to explain how the major religions of Ethiopia developed; the main ideas about Christianity and Islam in Ethiopia also serve as background for understanding the main ideas of A Unique Form of Christianity and Christian-Muslim Interaction.)*

- Write a sample summary paragraph of the reading. *(Summaries will vary, but should include the main ideas of the reading.)*

 # Writing a Summary

Early each morning, the President of the United States listens to a news briefing prepared just for him. His staff members put the briefing together by reading and listening to news from dozens of newspapers, radio stations, and television networks. They then select the most important stories and write a summary of each one.

Writing a summary of any kind of information involves identifying the main ideas and weaving them together based on what they have in common. Knowing how to write a summary will help you take tests, write essays, and understand what you read.

Learn the Skill

Use these steps to summarize information.

1. **Find and state the main idea of each paragraph or section you want to summarize.** You can often find a main idea in the topic sentence of a paragraph.

2. **Identify what the main ideas have in common.** Look for the ways the ideas are presented—for example, in chronological order, as causes and effects, as comparisons, or as a progression of ideas from simple to complex. Doing this will help you identify the overall focus of the information.

3. **Write a summary paragraph that begins with a topic sentence.** The summary should draw together the main ideas into a broad description of the information. The main ideas will be the supporting details of your topic sentence.

U.S. President George W. Bush discusses the day's events with his staff.

524 Africa

Independent Practice

Assign *Skills for Life* and have students complete it individually.

All in One **Africa Teaching Resources,** *Skills for Life,* p. 351

Monitor Progress

As students are completing *Skills for Life*, circulate to make sure students are correctly applying the skill steps. Provide assistance as needed.

Practice the Skill

Read the section titled Major Religions of Ethiopia on pages 515–516. Then follow the steps below to summarize what you read.

1 Read the heading and subheadings in the section. These titles give you a general idea of the content. You can see that both Christianity and Islam are practiced in Ethiopia. Now read each paragraph and list its main idea.

2 The main ideas in this passage are in chronological order. They cover these dates: 350, 451, the 600s, the 1500s, and today. In what other ways are the main ideas related? What overall idea holds these paragraphs together?

3 You might use this topic sentence for your summary: *Ethiopia's location as a crossroads of trade and ideas has shaped its unique religious history.* Use this topic sentence, or write your own, and then complete the summary paragraph by adding explanations and details. The details will come from the main ideas on your list.

Ethiopian places of worship: the Church of St. Mary of Zion (above) and the Nagash mosque (below)

Apply the Skill

Read the section titled Early Reforms After Independence on pages 519–520. Use the steps in this skill to summarize the information.

Chapter 16 **525**

Assess and Reteach

Assess Progress L2
Ask students to do the Apply the Skill activity.

Reteach L1
If students are having trouble remembering the skill steps, have them make flashcards by writing the number and main idea of each step on one side of an index card and the detailed instructions of the step on the other side.

Extend L3
Ask students to choose another short section in the text to read and summarize. Remind them to use the steps on p. 524.

Answer
Apply the Skill
Students should use the topic sentence of each paragraph to help them identify the main ideas and note that the main ideas are presented in chronological order. Summaries should have a topic sentence such as, "President Julius Nyerere adopted many social policies to try to help Tanzania deal with the problems it faced after independence." They should use their main ideas as supporting details for their topic sentence.

Section 3
Step-by-Step Instruction

Objectives

Social Studies

1. Learn about the peoples of Kenya.
2. Discover what life is like in rural Kenya.
3. Find out what life is like in urban Kenya.

Reading/Language Arts

Identify and interpret nonliteral language.

Prepare to Read

Build Background Knowledge   L2

Tell students that in this section they will be learning about the East African country of Kenya. Have students briefly preview the headings, graph, and other visuals in the section. Then ask them to make predictions about what they think they will learn about Kenya. Conduct an Idea Wave (TE, p. T35) to generate a list.

Set a Purpose for Reading   L2

■ Preview the Objectives.

■ Read each statement in the *Reading Readiness Guide* aloud. Ask students to mark the statements true or false.

■ Have students discuss the statements in pairs or groups of four, then mark their worksheets again. Use the Numbered Heads participation strategy (TE, p. T36) to call on students to share their group's perspectives.

All in One Africa Teaching Resources,
Reading Readiness Guide, p. 344

Vocabulary Builder
Preview Key Terms

Pronounce each Key Term, then ask the students to say the word with you. Provide a simple explanation such as, "There are more Kikuyu than Maasai in Kenya."

Section 3
Kenya
Ties That Bind

Prepare to Read

Objectives

In this section you will

1. Learn about the peoples of Kenya.
2. Discover what life is like in rural Kenya.
3. Find out what life is like in urban Kenya.

Taking Notes

As you read this section, look for details about daily life in rural and urban Kenya. Copy the chart below, and use it to record your findings.

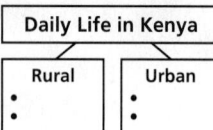

Target Reading Skill

Interpret Nonliteral Meanings Literal language is language that means exactly what it says. Nonliteral language uses images or comparisons to communicate an idea.

In this section you will read about "ties that bind" Kenyans together. When you see these words, ask yourself: Are Kenyans really tied together by something physical, or do the words have another meaning?

Key Terms

- **Kikuyu** (kee KOO yoo) *n.* the largest ethnic group in Kenya
- **Maasai** (mah SY) *n.* a seminomadic ethnic group in Kenya
- **seminomadic** (seh mee noh MAD ik) *adj.* combining nomadic wandering and farming in settlements
- **harambee** (hah RAHM bay) *n.* a social policy started by Jomo Kenyatta and meaning "let's pull together" in Swahili

"Where is your shamba?" is a question that two Kenyans usually ask each other when they first meet. A shamba is a small farm owned and run by a Kenyan family. Even Kenyans who move to the city think of the land where they were born as home. They return to it throughout their lives. Land is very important to Kenyans.

A Maasai family in Kenya standing in front of their land

526 Africa

Target Reading Skill   L2

Interpret Nonliteral Meanings Point out the Target Reading Skill. Tell students that nonliteral language uses images and comparisons to communicate an idea.

Model interpreting nonliteral meanings using the phrase "let's pull together" from the paragraph on p. 528. Ask students to consider what is meant by this phrase. Tell students that people use this phrase when they want to work together to achieve a common goal.

Give students *Recognize Nonliteral Meanings.* Have them complete the activity in their groups.

All in One Africa Teaching Resources,
Recognize Nonliteral Meanings, p. 348

Peoples of Kenya

Kenya's highest mountain, Mount Kenya, lies just south of the Equator. Southwest of Mount Kenya is a region of highlands that receives plenty of rain, so the land is good for farming. Most of Kenya's people are farmers. Many of them live in shambas dotting the countryside of the highlands. Others live along Kenya's coast, a warmer area that also has good farmland.

Kenya's Shared Culture Although some Kenyans are of European, Asian, or Arab descent, most come from families that have always lived in Africa. Kenya has plenty of cultural diversity—including more than 40 ethnic groups. Each ethnic group has distinct cultural features. But many groups have features in common, too. For example, some groups speak the same language as one another, and most Kenyans are either Christian or Muslim. Language and religion are some of the ties that bind the peoples of Kenya together.

Many Kenyans also share common values. Most Kenyans value their families as much as they value the land. Some families have six or more children. Members of extended families can be very close, often considering their cousins to be like brothers and sisters.

Kenya's Ethnic Groups The **Kikuyu** (kee KOO yoo) are Kenya's largest ethnic group. Many Kikuyu live in shambas in the highlands near Mount Kenya. They build round homes with mud walls and thatched roofs. The Kikuyu grow food and cash crops such as coffee and sisal, a fiber used to make rope. The **Maasai** (mah SY) are another ethnic group in Kenya, who traditionally make a living by farming and herding. The Maasai are **seminomadic,** which means they sometimes wander as nomads and sometimes live in settlements where they farm.

✓ **Reading Check** How many ethnic groups live in Kenya?

Life in Rural Kenya

As elsewhere in Africa, the majority of Kenya's farmers are women. They grow fruits and vegetables and herd livestock. Men also farm, but they usually raise cash crops, such as coffee and tea.

The way of life of many Kenyans is changing. As the population increases, many men and some women are moving to the cities to find work. Most women and children, however, stay in rural areas. Women are the primary caretakers of children, and it is expensive for women with children to move to a city. Many find it easier to support their families by farming.

Ethnic Groups of Kenya
These women are Samburu people who, like the Maasai, are seminomadic herders. The women wear traditional Samburu dress—brightly patterned cloths and jewelry made of many colorful beads. **Evaluate** *Why do you think many peoples around the world dress traditionally?*

Learn how growing beans has helped Kenya's economy.

Guided Instruction

- **Vocabulary Builder** Clarify the high-use words **distinct** and **primary** before reading.

- Read Peoples of Kenya and Life in Rural Kenya using the Choral Reading strategy (TE, p. T34).

- Ask **Why is the land southwest of Mount Kenya good for farming?** *(It is a region of highlands that gets plenty of rain.)*

- Discuss Kenya's ethnic makeup with students. *(Some Kenyans are of European, Asian, or Arab descent, but most are African. Kenya has over 40 ethnic groups.)*

- Ask **What do Kenyans have in common with one another?** *(Some groups speak the same language; most are Christian or Muslim; they value land and family.)*

- Ask students to name two of Kenya's ethnic groups. *(Kikuyu and Maasai)* Ask **How are they similar and different?** *(Similar—both groups are farmers; different: the Kikuyu live in shambas, the Maasai live in settlements but are also seminomadic.)*

- Ask **What is harambee?** *(a social policy that encourages people to work together)*

- Ask **How do women's self-help groups help the women of Kenya?** *(Women in the groups contribute money then decide how to use it to help individual women of the community.)*

Show students *Kenya: Once There Was a Bean.* Ask **How is the production of the "French" bean helping Kenya's economy?** *(Money from agriculture is being used for schools and to modernize businesses.)*

Answers

Evaluate Possible answer: It helps remind them of and show others their cultural traditions.

✓ **Reading Check** more than 40

Vocabulary Builder

Use the information below to teach students this section's high-use words.

High-Use Word	Definition and Sample Sentence
distinct, p. 527	*adj.* different, clearly seen I chose three **distinct** flavors—chocolate, vanilla, and strawberry.
primary, p. 527	*adj.* basic; main Ann's **primary** task was to do the dishes.
thriving, p. 529	*adj.,* successful The family's business has been **thriving** for many years.
afford, p. 529	*v.* to have the money to pay for John saved money from his after school job so he could **afford** new CDs.

Independent Practice

Ask students to create the Taking Notes graphic organizer on a blank piece of paper. Then have them fill in information about daily life in rural Kenya.

Monitor Progress

As students fill in the graphic organizer, circulate and make sure individuals are selecting the correct details. Provide assistance as needed.

COUNTRY PROFILE
Focus on Geography

Guided Instruction   L2

Ask students to study the Country Profile on this page. As a class, answer the Map and Chart Skills questions. Allow students to briefly discuss their responses with a partner before sharing answers.

Independent Practice

- Distribute *Reading a Table* to help students practice their chart skills. Have them work in pairs to complete the worksheet.
  All in One **Africa Teaching Resources,** *Reading a Table,* p. 361

- After students have completed the worksheet, ask them to transfer the information in the line graph on this page to a table format.

Answers

Map and Chart Skills

1. corn and coffee

2. in the northeast, which receives the least precipitation

3. Answers will vary; students may suggest that increases in urban population and decreases in rural population will decrease agricultural production as farmers move to the cities.

Go Online PHSchool.com Students can find additional useful information about this topic on the DK World Desk Reference Online.

Kenyans Working Together Kenya gained independence from the British in 1963. The first president, Jomo Kenyatta (JOH moh ken YAH tuh), began a social policy he called **harambee** (hah RAHM bay), which in Swahili means "let's pull together." Kenyatta encouraged harambee in many forms, including politics, farming, and education. For example, he had the government pay for a part of each child's education. In response, many villagers worked together to build and support their schools.

COUNTRY PROFILE   Focus on Geography

Kenya

Most Kenyans live in the countryside. The majority of the country's agricultural products are grown in the highlands region, where rainfall is sufficient for farming. An increasing number of Kenyans have moved to major cities. Nairobi, the largest business center in East Africa, is home both to very wealthy families and to people who live in slums. Study the map and charts to learn more about Kenya's land and people.

Major Agricultural Products, 2005

Production (in metric tons)	
Corn	2,800,000
Cassava	910,000
Plantains	452,000
Sugar cane	489,000
Coffee	1,080,000

SOURCE: USDA Foreign Agricultural Service, 2005

Kenya: Yearly Precipitation

KEY

Inches	Millimeters
More than 59	More than 1,499
40–59	1,000–1,499
20–39	500–999
10–19	250–499

— National border
⊛ National capital
• Other city

0 miles 250
0 kilometers 250
Lambert Azimuthal Equal Area

Urban and Rural Population, 1950–2000

Percent of Population / Year

■ Rural
■ Urban

SOURCE: United Nations Food and Agriculture Organization

Map and Chart Skills

1. **Identify** What products did Kenya produce more than one million metric tons of in 2005?
2. **Infer** In what region do you think Kenyans farm the least?
3. **Synthesize** Study the population graph. How do you think the trend shown has affected Kenya's agriculture?

Use Web Code lae-5603 for **DK World Desk Reference Online.**

528 Africa

Differentiated Instruction

For Advanced Readers   L3

Have students research any products they are not familiar with from the table, such as cassava or plantains. Students should use the library or Internet to find photographs of the products, their uses, and list countries other than Kenya that produce them. They can then present their information to the rest of the class.

Women's Self-Help Groups One of the best examples of how harambee is successful in Kenya is the rise of women's self-help groups in rural areas. Women in rural areas all over Kenya have formed these groups to solve problems in their communities. For example, many women felt it was not easy to farm, chop firewood, haul water, and take care of children all in one day. One woman commented, "My children were educated through the sweat of my brow."

These self-help groups do a great variety of work. Some women's groups grow cash crops in addition to the crops they grow for their families to eat. Then they sell the cash crops and save the money as a group. The women meet to decide what to do with the money they have saved. In the mountain village of Mitero, Kikuyu women's groups have built a nursery school and installed water pipes for the community. They also loan money to women who want to start small businesses. Sometimes they give money to women who need to buy such necessities as a cow or a water tank. They also save money individually and use it to educate their children.

✓ **Reading Check** What is the purpose of women's self-help groups in Kenya?

Life in Urban Kenya

Kenya's capital, Nairobi (ny ROH bee), is an important business center and one of the largest cities in East Africa. It is also East Africa's most important center of industry and manufacturing. Much of East Africa's banking and trade is centered there as well.

Working in the City Because Nairobi is a thriving city, many Kenyans move there looking for jobs. Every day, people arrive in Nairobi by train, bus, or *matatu* (muh TAH too)—minibus. Nairobi's population grew from one million in 1985 to more than two million in 2000. Many of Nairobi's newcomers walk to their jobs from the outskirts of the city. They may walk as far as ten miles each way because they cannot afford the cost of taking the bus to work.

When men move to Nairobi without their families, they often feel homesick for their loved ones in rural villages. Meanwhile, the women who remain in the villages must do much more work. Many people in Kenya have responded to this situation in the spirit of harambee—by working together.

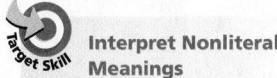

Interpret Nonliteral Meanings What does the woman mean by saying that her children were educated through the sweat of her brow? Did she use the sweat to teach the children or to pay for their schooling? Restate what she means in your own words.

These Kikuyu women have formed a savings and loan club to support local businesses.

Chapter 16 Section 3 **529**

 **Skills Mini Lesson**

Drawing Inferences and Conclusions [L2]

1. Explain that drawing inferences and conclusions means making an educated guess based upon available clues and prior knowledge.

2. Help students practice the skill by drawing inferences and conclusions about life in Nairobi from the text under Life in Urban Kenya. Have students look for clues about the population and distance people travel to work and relate these clues to what they already know about cities.

3. Have students apply the skill by writing a short paragraph about what challenges Nairobi will probably need to address as it continues to grow.

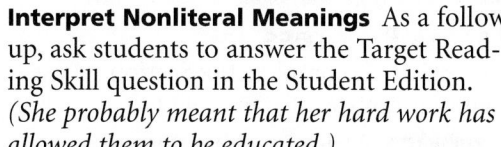 **Target Reading Skill** [L2]

Interpret Nonliteral Meanings As a follow up, ask students to answer the Target Reading Skill question in the Student Edition. *(She probably meant that her hard work has allowed them to be educated.)*

Life in Urban Kenya [L2]

Guided Instruction

- **Vocabulary Builder** Clarify the high-use words **thriving** and **afford** before reading.

- Read how the spirit of harambee helps newcomers to Nairobi in Life in Urban Kenya. Circulate to make sure individuals can answer the Reading Check question.

- Ask students **Why is the population of Nairobi growing?** *(Many Kenyans from rural areas go there to look for jobs.)* **How does this movement from rural areas affect both men and women?** *(Men, who are usually the ones to leave their village for the city, often feel homesick. Women in villages must work harder if the men in their families are working in the city.)*

- Ask students to draw a conclusion about why Kenyans like Moses Mpoke want to keep up their ties to their villages. *(Possible answer: They may want to preserve and continue their traditional way of life.)*

Independent Practice

Have students finish their graphic organizers with details from Life in Urban Kenya. Provide assistance as needed.

Monitor Progress

- Show *Section Reading Support Transparency AF 52* and ask students to check their graphic organizers individually. Go over key concepts and clarify key vocabulary as needed.

  📖 **Africa Transparencies,** *Section Reading Support Transparency AF 52*

- Tell students to fill in the last column of the *Reading Readiness Guide*. Probe for what they learned that confirms or invalidates each statement.

  All in One **Africa Teaching Resources,** *Reading Readiness Guide,* p. 344

Answer

✓ **Reading Check** to deal with community problems

Assess and Reteach

Assess Progress `L2`

Have students complete the Section Assessment. Administer the *Section Quiz*.

All in One **Africa Teaching Resources,** *Section Quiz,* p. 346

Reteach `L1`

If students need more instruction, have them read this section in the Reading and Vocabulary Study Guide.

📖 Chapter 16, Section 3, **Eastern Hemisphere Reading and Vocabulary Study Guide,** pp. 184–186

Extend `L3`

Have students learn more about the Kikuyu of Kenya by completing the *Enrichment* activity. Students can then discuss what they have read as a group before writing their summaries independently.

All in One **Africa Teaching Resources,** *Enrichment,* p. 350

Answer

✓ **Reading Check** Men from the same ethnic group often share rooms and help one another.

Section 3 Assessment

Key Terms

Students' sentences should reflect knowledge of each Key Term.

🔗 Target Reading Skill

It probably means that they are scattered on the landscape randomly, rather than close together like buildings in a city.

Comprehension and Critical Thinking

1. (a) farming **(b)** They value the land and their families; some groups share the same language; most are either Muslim or Christian.

2. (a) Most women are farmers and the primary caretakers of children. **(b)** The government pays for a portion of each child's education; women's self-help groups work together to deal with problems in their communities.

3. (a) Many plan to buy land in the countryside. **(b)** Men often feel homesick; they have to adjust to city life. They may have to walk to work. Women must do more work at home.

Nairobi, Kenya

City Life Men who move to the city also work together. Many are saving money to buy land in the countryside. Men in Nairobi from the same ethnic group often welcome one another, share rooms, and help one another. Take Moses Mpoke (MOH zuz um POH kay) as an example. Mpoke is a Maasai. He owns land that is too dry for farming or grazing, but he could not move his livestock to find better grazing. After finishing high school, Mpoke moved to Nairobi to work.

Living in the city, Mpoke could have forgotten about his Maasai roots. But every weekend, he returns to his village to see his family and friends. When a visitor in his village asked Mpoke which is the real Moses Mpoke, the one in the city or the one in the village, he answered,

> **❝** This is the real Moses Mpoke, but the other is also me. In the week, I can live in the city and be comfortable. At weekends, I can live here [in my village] and be comfortable. The city has not stopped me from being a Maasai. **❞**
>
> —*Moses Mpoke*

✓ **Reading Check** How do Kenyans living in the city support one another?

✳ Section 3 Assessment

Key Terms

Review the key terms at the beginning of this section. Use each term in a sentence that explains its meaning.

🔗 Target Reading Skill

Find the phrase "in shambas dotting the countryside" on page 527. Explain in your own words what this means.

Comprehension and Critical Thinking

1. (a) Recall In what way do most Kenyans make their living?

(b) Compare What other traits do Kenya's different ethnic groups have in common?

2. (a) Explain Why do most Kenyan women stay in rural villages rather than move to the city?

(b) Summarize How have Kenya's government and Kenya's village women used harambee to help benefit village families?

3. (a) Describe What do many Kenyans who live in the city plan to do with the money they earn?

(b) Analyze Information What different hardships do men and women in Kenya face if the men decide to work in Nairobi?

Writing Activity

Consider the concept of harambee. It means that people work together for a common good. Write an account of how you have seen or would like to see harambee in your community or school.

> **Writing Tip** Start your account with an explanation of what harambee is, so that readers can easily understand how your example fits into the concept.

530 Africa

Writing Activity

Use the *Rubric for Assessing a Writing Assignment* to assess students' accounts.

All in One **Africa Teaching Resources,** *Rubric for Assessing a Writing Assignment,* p. 373

16 Review and Assessment

◆ Chapter Summary

Section 1: Ethiopia

- Ethiopia has two major religions—Christianity and Islam. At times Ethiopian Christians and Muslims have fought each other, but today they live together peacefully.
- Most Ethiopians live in rural areas. Their daily lives are very different from those of Ethiopians in urban areas.

Ethiopia

Section 2: Tanzania

- After independence, Tanzania's president Julius Nyerere established Swahili as the country's lingua franca, created a one-party political system, and encouraged farmers to live in ujamaa villages.
- Since Nyerere retired in 1985, Tanzania's government has encouraged privatization and other economic reforms as well as a multiparty political system.

Section 3: Kenya

- Kenyans come from 40 ethnic groups that are distinct but also share some values and characteristics. Many Kenyans are farmers.
- Most Kenyan farmers are women. To help solve community problems, many Kenyan women have formed various self-help groups.
- Many Kenyan men have had to move to the city to find work, but they often return to their villages on weekends or when they retire.

Kenya

◆ Key Terms

Each of the statements below contains a key term from the chapter. If it is true, write *true*. If it is false, change the highlighted term to make the statement true.

1. The Swahili word that means "let's pull together" is harambee.
2. Kikuyu is an ancient Ethiopian language.

3. A place where people live a religious life is a multiparty system.
4. People who speak different languages often communicate by speaking a lingua franca.
5. A country with two or more political parties has a monastery.

Chapter 16 **531**

┌ Vocabulary Builder ─

Revisit this chapter's high-use words:

preserve	literate	primary
adopt	policy	thriving
specialize	suffer	afford
headquarters	distinct	

Ask students to review the definitions they recorded on their *Word Knowledge* worksheets.

All in One Africa Teaching Resources, *Word Knowledge*, p. 349

Consider allowing students to earn extra credit if they use the words in their answers to the questions in the Chapter Review and Assessment. The words must be used correctly and in a natural context to win the extra points.

Chapter 16
Review and Assessment

Review Chapter Content

- Review and revisit the major themes of this chapter by asking students to classify which Guiding Question each bulleted statement in the Chapter Summary answers. Have students do this activity as a class or in groups. Refer to p. 1 in the Student Edition for the text of the Guiding Questions.

- Assign *Vocabulary Development* for students to review Key Terms.

All in One Africa Teaching Resources, *Vocabulary Development*, p. 371

Answers

Key Terms
1. True
2. False. Geez
3. False. monastery
4. True
5. False. multiparty system

Review and Assessment

Comprehension and Critical Thinking

6. (a) Egyptian missionaries brought Christianity to Ethiopia along trade routes; Islam came to Ethiopia when Muslim Arabs began to settle in North Africa. **(b)** Christians in Ethiopia became surrounded by Muslim-controlled areas, isolating them from Christians elsewhere.

7. (a) running water, electricity, and modern transportation **(b)** Answers will vary, but should be supported with information from the chapter. Some students may feel Addis Ababa could be a model for other parts of Ethiopia to become more prosperous, while others may think it would be difficult to change life in rural areas.

8. (a) to help ethnic groups feel more unified **(b)** He established the ujamaa program and instituted a one-party political system. **(c)** A one-party system reduces division between ethnic groups; a multiparty system allows voters to choose among candidates with differing views.

9. (a) Tanzania's economy is improving steadily; the country is working towards the same success in politics. **(b)** Despite the new multiparty system, Nyerere's party remained in power after the 1995 and 2000 elections. One party proposed that the island of Zanzibar be split from the rest of Tanzania.

10. (a) language, religion, and common values such as land and family **(b)** Through the social policy called harambee, people are working together in politics, farming, education, and addressing community problems. **(c)** Men who work in the cities may be able to buy their own land and help their families in their native villages.

Review and Assessment (continued)

◆ Comprehension and Critical Thinking

6. (a) Describe How did Christianity and Islam spread into Ethiopia?
(b) Identify Effects How did the spread of Islam cause Ethiopian Christians to become more isolated?

7. (a) Identify What public services are lacking in Ethiopia's rural areas?
(b) Make Generalizations Do you think the prosperity of Addis Ababa could spread into rural Ethiopia? If it did, how would life change in rural areas?

8. (a) Explain Why did Julius Nyerere establish a lingua franca for Tanzania?
(b) Identify What changes did Julius Nyerere make to Tanzania's economic and political systems?
(c) Contrast What are some advantages of a one-party political system? Of a multiparty system?

9. (a) Recall Has Tanzania had greater success in economics or in politics?
(b) Analyze Information Why has establishing a multiparty political system in Tanzania been a challenge?

10. (a) Recall What are some ties that bind the people of Kenya together?
(b) Summarize How have rural Kenyans worked together to improve their lives?
(c) Identify Effects The movement of men from Kenya's countryside to Nairobi can cause some hardship. How can it also help improve village life?

◆ Skills Practice

Writing a Summary In the Skills for Life activity in this chapter, you learned how to write a summary.

Review the steps you followed to learn this skill. Then reread the part of Section 3 titled Life in Rural Kenya. Find the main idea of each paragraph. Then identify what the main ideas have in common, and write a summary paragraph.

◆ Writing Activity: Language Arts

Think about the community you live in. Is it growing or becoming smaller? Think of reasons why your community may have developed in the way that it has. What are some positive changes that have occurred? What are some negative ones? Use your answers to write a newspaper editorial explaining your opinion on whether your community is developing in a way that benefits its citizens.

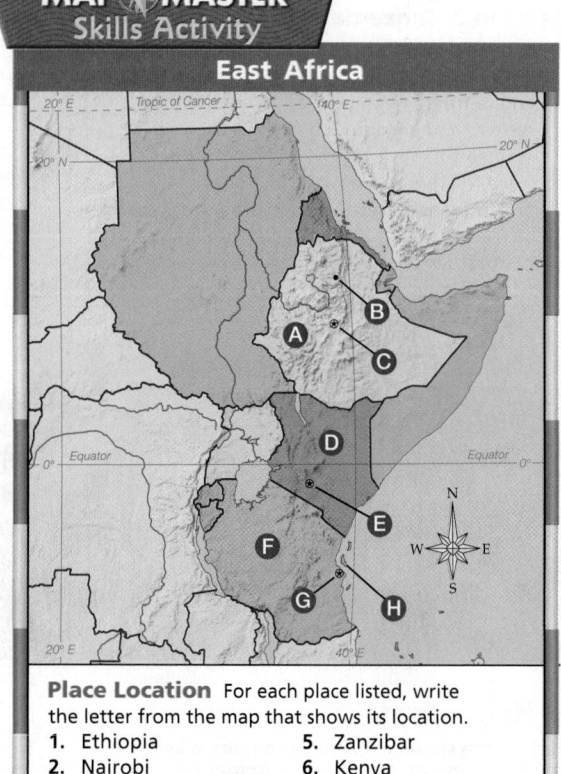

MAP MASTER™ Skills Activity

East Africa

Place Location For each place listed, write the letter from the map that shows its location.
1. Ethiopia
2. Nairobi
3. Tanzania
4. Dar es Salaam
5. Zanzibar
6. Kenya
7. Addis Ababa
8. Lalibela

Go Online
PHSchool.com Use Web Code lap-5620 for an **interactive map**.

Skills Practice
Students' answers will vary, but should summarize the main ideas of each paragraph.

Writing Activity
Students' editorials will vary, but their opinions should be based on changes in their community and how they have affected the people who live there.

All in One Africa Teaching Resources,
Rubric for Assessing a Newspaper Article, p. 375

Standardized Test Prep

Test-Taking Tips

Some questions on standardized tests ask you to analyze a reading selection. Read the passage below. Then follow the tips to answer the sample question.

> Julius Nyerere became the first president of Tanzania in 1964. He made Swahili the national language to help unite his country's many ethnic groups. He encouraged farmers to live together in organized villages and to cooperate. Many more schools were built, and literacy improved dramatically after independence. Many more Tanzanians were trained to be engineers, doctors, and teachers.

TIP Look for topics that are shared by all the sentences in the passage.

Pick the letter that best answers the question.

Which kind of resources in Tanzania does this passage describe?

- A natural resources
- B human resources
- C capital resources
- D entrepreneurial resources

TIP Before you read the paragraph, preview the question. Think about it as you read.

Think It Through The question asks what kind of resources the paragraph describes. Skim over each sentence of the paragraph. Each one mentions something about the people of Tanzania. You can eliminate answer A, natural resources, because those are materials found in the environment. You may not know the words *capital* or *entrepreneurial* in C and D, but you probably know that *human* has to do with people. The correct answer is B.

Practice Questions

Use the tips above and other tips in this book to help you answer the following questions. Use the passage below to answer Question 1. Choose the letter of the best answer.

> Lalibela is a town in Ethiopia. People travel there to visit a group of churches for which Lalibela is famous. Many people who live there, however, do not have electricity. Most of them do not own cars. Most of them earn a living by farming.

1. Which is a detail that is described in this passage?
   - A The people who live in Lalibela love the churches there.
   - B The tourists who visit Lalibela cannot bring cars.
   - C Most of the people who live in Lalibela are farmers.
   - D Most of Lalibela's visitors are farmers.

2. Which of the following was NOT true of Tanzania's ujamaa program?
   - A The program's goal was to boost farm production.
   - B People had to work together to make the program successful.
   - C The government had to help out with the program.
   - D All farm families in Tanzania agreed to take part.

3. Which is the word for a family farm in Kenya?
   - A Maasai
   - B shamba
   - C harambee
   - D Kikuyu

Use Web Code laa-5600 for **Chapter 16 self-test.**

MAP MASTER
Skills Activity

1. A	**2.** E
3. F	**4.** G
5. H	**6.** D
7. C	**8.** B

Go Online PHSchool.com Students may practice their map skills using the interactive online version of this map.

Standardized Test Prep

Answers

1. C
2. D
3. B

Go Online PHSchool.com Students may use the Chapter 16 self-test on PHSchool.com to prepare for the Chapter Test.

Assessment Resources

Use *Chapter Tests A and B* to assess students' mastery of chapter content.

All in One Africa Teaching Resources, *Chapter Tests A and B*, pp. 376–381

Tests are also available on the *ExamView Test Bank CD-ROM.*

⊙ *ExamView Test Bank CD-ROM*

Objectives

1. Explore the natural world from a point of view that may not be familiar to you.

2. Learn how a storyteller can use animals and natural forces as characters to make a story more meaningful.

Prepare to Read

Build Background Knowledge   L2

Tell students that in this story, they will read about a character that makes a promise it is unable to fulfill. Ask students if they have ever made a promise that they did not or could not keep. If students are uncomfortable relating a personal experience, tell them they can create a fictional one. Ask them to think about why they did not keep the promise, and how that made them feel. Conduct an Idea Wave (TE, p. T35) to allow students to share their responses.

Instruct

A Promise to the Sun   L2

Guided Instruction

- Point out that some potentially unfamiliar words are defined for students in the margin. Clarify the meanings of the words before reading.

- Have students read the selection using the Structured Silent Reading strategy (TE, p. T34). Ask them to write the answers to each Reading Check question as they read.

- Ask **What problem do the birds face?** (a severe drought has hit the land of the birds) **What is decided at the meeting they hold?** (that the Bat will go in search of rain)

- Ask students to list the promises made by the characters in the story. (The Sun promises to help the birds by bringing rain; the Bat promises that the birds will build the Sun a nest in return for its help; the birds promise to help the Bat build a nest for the sun.) Then ask **Which promises are broken?** (the Bat's promise to the Sun and the birds' promise to the Bat)

A Promise to the Sun
By Tololwa M. Mollel

Prepare to Read

Background Information

Not all stories were written down when they were first told. Myths like the one you are about to read were originally told aloud. They were part of an oral tradition that people passed down from generation to generation.

These myths are meant to entertain the listener. They are also meant to explain something to the listener. Usually, they explain why aspects of the world are as they are. Myths often provide a moral lesson to the listener as well.

This story was written by Tololwa M. Mollel in the style of Maasai myths heard in his youth in Tanzania. Mollel is a well-known storyteller and author.

Objectives

In this section you will

1. Explore the natural world from a point of view that may not be familiar to you.

2. Learn how a storyteller can use animals and natural forces as characters to make a story more meaningful.

---

savannah alternate spelling of *savanna*

maize (mayz) *n.* corn

shrivel (SHRIH vul) *v.* to wrinkle as moisture is lost

wilt (wilt) *v.* to droop

withered (WITH urd) *adj.* shriveled and shrunken from drying out

---

Long ago, when the world was new, a severe drought hit the land of the birds. The savannah turned brown, and streams dried up. Maize plants died, and banana trees shriveled in the sun, their broad leaves wilting away. Even the nearby forest grew withered and pale.

The birds held a meeting and decided to send someone in search of rain. They drew lots to choose who would go on the journey. And they told the Bat, their distant cousin who was visiting, that she must draw, too. "You might not be a bird," they said, "but for now you're one of us." Everyone took a lot, and as luck would have it, the task fell to the Bat.

Over the trees and the mountains flew the Bat, to the Moon. There she cried, "Earth has no rain, Earth has no food, Earth asks for rain!"

A full moon rises over the Kenyan landscape.

Read Fluently

Form the class into partners. Choose a paragraph from the selection. Have students take turns reading the paragraph aloud. Ask them to underline words that give them trouble as they read. Then, have them decode the problem words with their partner. Provide assistance as needed. Have them reread the paragraph two more times to improve their reading speed. Remind them to stop at the commas and periods and to read with expression.

The Moon smiled. "I can't bring rain. My task is to wash and oil the night's face. But you can try the Stars."

On flew the Bat, until she found the Stars at play. "Away with you!" they snapped, angry at being interrupted. "If you want rain, go to the Clouds!"

The Clouds were asleep but awoke at the sound of the Bat arriving. "We can bring rain," they yawned, "but the Winds must first blow us together, to hang over the Earth in one big lump."

At the approach of the Bat, the Winds howled to a stop. "We'll blow the Clouds together," they said, "but not before the Sun has brought up steam to the sky."

As the Bat flew toward the Sun, a sudden scream shook the sky:

"Stop where you are, foolish Bat, before I burn off your little wings!"

The Bat shrank back in terror, and the Sun smothered its fire in rolls of clouds. Quickly the Bat said, "Earth has no rain, Earth has no food, Earth asks for rain!"

"I'll help you," replied the Sun, "in return for a favor. After the rain falls, choose for me the greenest patch on the forest top, and build me a nest there. Then no longer will I have to journey to the <u>horizon</u> at the end of each day but will rest for the night in the cool and quiet of the forest."

The Bat quickly replied, "I'm only a Bat and don't know how to build nests, but the birds will happily make you one. Nothing will be easier—there are so many of them. They will do it right after the harvest, I promise—all in a day!"

And down the sky's sunlit paths the Bat flew, excited to bring the good news to the birds.

The birds readily promised to build the nest.

"The very day after the harvest," said the Sparrow.

"All in a day," said the Owl.

"A beautiful nest it'll be," said the Canary.

"With all the colors of the rainbow," said the Peacock.

So the Sun burnt down upon the earth, steam rose, Winds blew, and Clouds gathered. Then rain fell. The savannah bloomed, and streams flowed. Green and thick and tall, the forest grew until it touched the sky. Crops flourished and ripened—maize, bananas, cassava, millet, and peanuts—and the birds harvested. The morning after the harvest, the Bat reminded the birds about the nest. Suddenly the birds were in no mood for work. All they cared about was the harvest celebrations, which were to start that night and last several days.

Clouds fill the East African sky.

horizon (huh RY zun) *n.* the place where Earth and sky appear to meet

 **Reading Check**

What promise does the Bat make to the Sun?

Literature **535**

- Ask students **What moral does this story teach about promises?** *(that promises are often easier made than kept)* Then ask **How do the two broken promises teach the moral in different ways?** *(The Bat does everything she can to keep her promise, but is not able to; the birds make no effort to keep their promise because the Sun has already given them the rain they wanted. The two examples show that promises can be broken despite one's best efforts, as well as through carelessness.)*

- Ask **What natural events does the story explain?** *(The story explains why bats are nocturnal and live in caves, why the sun rises and sets, and why the trees sway when it rains.)*

- Discuss with students why they think this myth was created and handed down from generation to generation. *(Possible answers: to explain the behavior of bats; to explain the rising and setting of the sun; to teach that it is important to only make promises that can be kept, and that once a promise is made, it should be kept.)*

Independent Practice

Ask students to work together to determine the tone, purpose, and audience of A Promise to the Sun. Remind students that being aware of these things is important when reading or writing a story. To help them understand this concept, give them *Determining Tone, Purpose, and Audience.* Have them complete the worksheet in pairs, then write a paragraph describing the tone, purpose, and audience of A Promise to the Sun.

All in One **Africa Teaching Resources,** *Determining Tone, Purpose, and Audience,* p. 370

Monitor Progress

As students complete their worksheets and write their paragraphs, circulate to make sure they understand the difference between tone and purpose and have correctly identified the story's tone, purpose, and audience. Provide assistance as necessary.

"I have to adorn myself," said the Peacock.
"I have to practice my flute," said the Canary.
"I have to heat up my drums," said the Owl.
"I have to help prepare the feast," said the Sparrow.
"Wait until after the celebrations," they said. "We'll do it then." But their hearts were not in it, and the Bat knew they would never build the nest.

What was she to do? A promise is a promise, she believed, yet she didn't know anything about making a nest. Even if she did, how could she, all on her own, hope to make one big enough for the sun?

The Sun set, and the Moon rose. The celebrations began. The drums <u>throbbed,</u> the flutes wailed, and the dancers pounded the earth with their feet.

Alone with her thoughts and tired, the Bat fell fast asleep.

She awoke in a panic. The Moon had vanished, the Stars faded. Soon the Sun would rise!

Slowly, the Sun peered out over the horizon in search of the nest.

Certain the Sun was looking for her, the Bat scrambled behind a banana leaf. The Sun moved up in the sky. One of its rays glared over the leaf. With a cry of fear, the Bat fled to the forest.

But even there, she was not long at peace. There was a gust of wind, and the forest opened for a moment overhead. The Bat looked up anxiously. Peeking down at her was the Sun.

She let out a <u>shriek</u> and flew away.

As she flew, a cave came into view below. She dived down and quickly darted in.

There, silent and out of reach, she hid from the glare of the Sun.

She hid from the shame of a broken promise, a shame the birds did not feel.

Outside, the celebrations went on. The Owl's drums roared furiously. The Canary's flute pierced the air. And the Sparrow cheered the Peacock's wild dancing.

The Sun inched down toward the horizon. It lingered over the forest and cast one more glance at the treetops, hoping for a miracle. Then, disappointed, it began to set. The birds carried on unconcerned, the sounds of their festivities reaching into the cave.

throb (thrahb) *v.* to beat

shriek (shreek) *n.* a sharp, shrill sound

Sunrise in Kenya

536 Africa

Differentiated Instruction

For English Language Learners L2
Have students identify any unfamiliar words and write them down. Divide students into pairs, and have each pair look up the unfamiliar words in a dictionary. Then have the students create flashcards with the words on one side and the part of speech and definition on the other. Students may then quiz each other on the words. Students may also make flashcards using the vocabulary words in the margin.

But the Bat did not stir from her hiding place that night. Nor the next day. For many days and nights she huddled in the cave. Then gradually she got up enough courage to venture out—but never in daylight! Only after sunset with Earth in the embrace of night.

Days and months and years went by, but the birds didn't build the nest. The Sun never gave up wishing, though. Every day as it set, it would linger to cast one last, hopeful glance at the forest top. Then, slowly, very slowly, it would sink away below the horizon.

Year after year the Sun continued to drag up steam, so the Winds would blow, the Clouds gather, and rain fall. It continues to do so today, hoping that the birds will one day keep their promise and build a nest among the treetops.

As for the Bat, . . . she made a home in the cave, and there she lives to this day. Whenever it rains, though, she listens eagerly. From the dark silence of her perch, the sound of the down-pour, ripening the crops and renewing the forest, is to her a magical song she wishes she could be out dancing to.

And as she listens, the trees outside sway and bow toward the cave. It is their thank-you salute to the hero who helped turn the forests green and thick and tall as the sky.

venture (VEN chur) *v.* to move forward in the face of danger
embrace (em BRAYS) *n.* hug

About the Selection

A Promise to the Sun is a children's book written by Tololwa M. Mollel and published in 1992.

✓ Reading Check

How does the Bat's life change as a result of what happens in the story?

About the Author

Tololwa M. Mollel (b. 1952) is an Arusha-Maasai born in northern Tanzania. He was educated and has taught writing and theater in Tanzania and Canada. Mollel has written more than 15 children's books. He has based his books on African folklore, including traditional Maasai tales and themes from his childhood.

Review and Assessment

Thinking About the Selection

1. (a) Recall What favor did the Sun ask of the Bat?
(b) Explain Why did the Bat not keep her promise?
(c) Analyze What aspects of how a bat lives are explained by this story? What other natural events are explained by this story?

2. (a) Respond Why do you think that the birds did not feel as ashamed as the Bat did?
(b) Analyze What moral lesson does the story teach about making and keeping promises?

Writing Activity

Write a Myth Using this story as a model, write your own myth. You might want to write a myth in which the Bat makes peace with the Sun, or one in which another animal makes a promise to the Moon.

Literature **537**

Writing Activity
Use *Rubric for Assessing a Writing Assignment* to evaluate students' myths.
All in One Africa Teaching Resources, *Rubric for Assessing a Writing Assignment,* p. 373

Assess and Reteach

Assess Progress L2
Have students answer the assessment questions.

Reteach L1
Help students who are having difficulty analyzing the story by creating a chart with two columns on the board. Label the columns with the following titles: "Storyteller's Purpose" and "Storyteller's Method." Together with students, help them fill in the chart with information from the story.

Extend L3
To extend the lesson, have students read *The Coconut Tree* and answer the questions at the end. Explain to students that although *The Coconut Tree* is from a different part of the world, this story is another example of an attempt to explain a natural occurrence.
All in One Africa Teaching Resources, *The Coconut Tree,* pp. 367–369

Answer

✓ Reading Check As a result of what happens in the story, the Bat makes a home in the cave and only comes out at night.

Answers

Review and Assessment

Thinking About the Selection

1. (a) The Sun asked the Bat to choose the greenest patch on the forest top and build a nest there so that the Sun could rest in the forest at the end of each day instead of journeying to the horizon. **(b)** The birds would not build the nest for the Sun as they said they would. **(c)** The story explains why bats live in caves and only come out at night, how drought affects animals and plants, why the sun rises and sets, why trees sway in the wind, and how rain is created.

2. (a) Possible answer: The birds had not made the promise directly to the Sun, so they did not care about fulfilling it. **(b)** It teaches the importance of only making promises that can be kept, and that once a promise is made, it should be kept.

Chapter Overview

Overview

Introducing Central and Southern Africa
1. Use data to compare countries.
2. Learn what characteristics Central and Southern African countries share.
3. Identify some key differences among the countries.

The Geography of Central and Southern Africa
Length: 4 minutes, 37 seconds
Provides an overview of Central and Southern Africa's geography, vegetation, and resources, with footage of the people of these regions.

Section 1 Democratic Republic of the Congo: A Wealth of Possibilities
1. Discover the physical geography and important natural resources of the Democratic Republic of the Congo.
2. Learn about the country's economic and political challenges since independence.
3. Find out how different groups and leaders have reshaped the nation.

Democratic Republic of Congo: Testing Times
Length: 3 minutes, 26 seconds
Explores the challenges to education in Congo as a result of the civil war, and the steps students are taking to improve their education.

Section 2 South Africa: Struggle for Equality
1. Understand how white rule in South Africa began.
2. Learn about the system of apartheid.
3. Find out how South Africans built a new nation after apartheid.

South Africa: Apartheid's Legacy
Length: 3 minutes, 53 seconds
Describes apartheid's effects on South Africa and how apartheid was finally ended.

Technology Resources

Students use embedded Web codes to access Internet activities, chapter self-tests, and additional map practice. They may also access Dorling Kindersley's Online Desk Reference to learn more about each country they study.

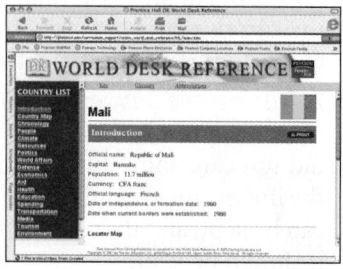

Use the Interactive Textbook to make content and concepts come alive through animations, videos, and activities that accompany the complete basal text—online and on CD-ROM.

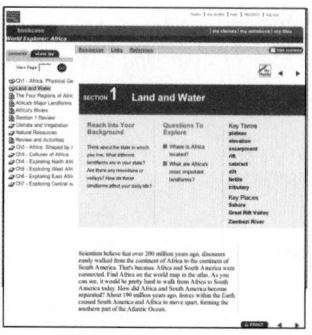

Use this complete suite of powerful teaching tools to make planning lessons and administering tests quicker and easier.

Reading and Assessment

Reading and Vocabulary Instruction

⟳ Model the Target Reading Skill

Sequence Explain to students that sequence is the order in which something occurs. Understanding sequence when reading allows students to recognize the order in which events in history occurred and how one event might influence another. Point out some words that are often used when describing sequence: *first, second, next, then, before, soon.* Use the following selection from p. 548 of the Student Edition to help students understand sequence:

> *In the early 1900s, demand for copper brought Europeans to the area. In 1930, a mining company found copper in an area called Kolwezi. The company built a mine and hired miners and a host of other workers. Soon a small city of workers' houses arose. Meanwhile, miners started to dig down into the earth for the copper.*

Write the selection on the board, and ask students to identify the sequence signal words as you underline them. *(in the early 1900s; in 1930; soon; meanwhile)* Next, create a timeline on the board to show the order in which the events occurred. Point out that the word *meanwhile* indicates that miners started to dig down into the earth at the same time that a city of workers' houses arose, so those events will be placed next to each other on the timeline.

Use the following worksheets from All-in-One Africa Teaching Resources (pp. 395–396) to support the chapter's Target Reading Skill.

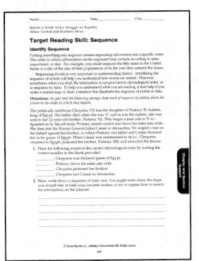 

Vocabulary Builder
High-Use Academic Words

Use these steps to teach this chapter's high-use words:

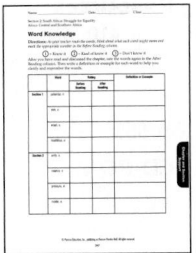

1. Have students rate how well they know each word on their Word Knowledge worksheets (All-in-One Africa Teaching Resources, p. 397).

2. Pronounce each word and ask students to repeat it.

3. Give students a brief definition or sample sentence (provided on TE pp. 549 and 557).

4. Work with students as they fill in the "Definition or Example" column of their Word Knowledge worksheets.

Assessment

Formal Assessment

Test students' understanding of core knowledge and skills.

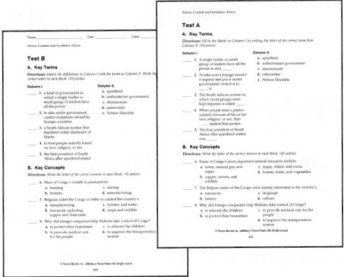

Chapter Tests A and B and Final Exams A and B, All-in-One Africa Teaching Resources, pp. 412–417, pp. 423–428

Customize the Chapter Tests to suit your needs.

ExamView Test Bank CD-ROM

Skills Assessment

Assess geographic literacy.

MapMaster Skills, Student Edition pp. 539, 562

Country Profile Map and Chart Skills, Student Edition pp. 551, 559

Assess reading and comprehension.

Target Reading Skills, Student Edition, pp. 551, 557, and in Section Assessments

Chapter 17 Assessment, Eastern Hemisphere Reading and Vocabulary Study Guide, p. 194

Performance Assessment

Assess students' performance on this chapter's Writing Activities using the following rubrics from All-in-One Africa Teaching Resources.

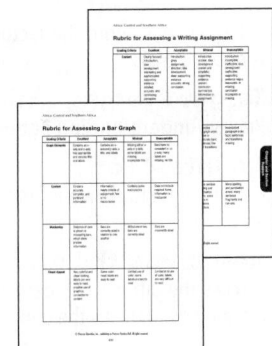

Rubric for Assessing a Bar Graph, p. 410

Rubric for Assessing a Writing Assignment, p. 411

Assess students' work through performance tasks.

Small Group Activity: Musical Instruments of Central and Southern Africa, All-in-One Africa Teaching Resources, pp. 400–403

Portfolio Activity, Teacher Edition, p. 547

Online Assessment

Have students check their own understanding.

Chapter Self-Test

Test Preparation

Africa Practice Tests A, B, and C, Test Prep Workbook, pp. 1–12

Africa Benchmark Test 2 and Outcome Test, AYP Monitoring Assessments, pp. 117–120, 194–199

Section 1 Democratic Republic of the Congo: A Wealth of Possibilities

 2.5 periods, 1.25 blocks (includes Country Databank and Skills for Life)

Social Studies Objectives
1. Discover the physical geography and important natural resources of the Democratic Republic of the Congo.
2. Learn about the country's economic and political challenges since independence.
3. Find out how different groups and leaders have reshaped the nation.

Reading/Language Arts Objective
Sequence events to understand and remember important information.

Prepare to Read

Build Background Knowledge
Have students preview the section to predict what they will learn about the Democratic Republic of the Congo.

Set a Purpose for Reading
Have students evaluate statements on the *Reading Readiness Guide*.

Preview Key Terms
Teach the section's Key Terms.

Target Reading Skill
Introduce the section's Target Reading Skill of **understanding sequence**.

Instructional Resources

All in One Africa Teaching Resources
- L2 Reading Readiness Guide, p. 388
- L2 Identify Sequence, p. 395

Differentiated Instruction

Spanish Reading and Vocabulary Study Guide
- L1 Chapter 17, Section 1, pp. 133–134 ELL

Africa Transparencies
- L2 Transparency B17: Concept Web AR, GT, LPR, SN

World Studies Video Program
- L2 The Geography of Central and Southern Africa ELL, LPR, SN

Instruct

Physical Geography and Resources
Ask questions about and discuss the vegetation and natural resources of the Democratic Republic of the Congo.

Economic and Political Challenges
Ask questions about the factors leading to Congo's economic crisis.

Target Reading Skill
Review **understanding sequence**.

Country Profile
Ask students to derive information from maps, charts, and graphs.

Reshaping the Nation
Discuss the different leaders of Congo and how their regime has affected the country.

Instructional Resources

All in One Africa Teaching Resources
- L2 Guided Reading and Review, p. 389
- L2 Reading Readiness Guide, p. 388

Africa Transparencies
- L2 Transparency B15: Outline
- L1 Transparency B16: Venn Diagram ELL, LPR, SN
- L2 Section Reading Support Transparency AF 53

World Studies Video Program
- L2 Democratic Republic of the Congo: Testing Times

Differentiated Instruction

All in One Africa Teaching Resources
- L3 Reading an Economic Activity Map, p. 404 AR, GT
- L1 Outline Map 21, p. 406 ELL, LPR, SN
- L2 Reading a Bar Graph, p. 405 AR, GT, LPR, SN
- L2 Skills for Life, p. 399 AR, GT, LPR, SN

Teacher's Edition
- L1 For Less Proficient Readers, TE p. 541
- L3 For Gifted and Talented, TE p. 543
- L1 For Special Needs Students, TE p. 544
- L3 For Advanced Readers, TE p. 545
- L1 For English Language Learners, TE pp. 546, 550

Passport to the World CD-ROM
- L1 South Africa ELL

Assess and Reteach

Assess Progress
Evaluate student comprehension with the section assessment and section quiz.

Reteach
Assign the Reading and Vocabulary Study Guide to help struggling students.

Extend
Extend the lesson by assigning a Small Group Activity.

Instructional Resources

All in One Africa Teaching Resources
- L2 Section Quiz, p. 390
- L3 Small Group Activity, pp. 400–403 Rubric for Assessing a Writing Assignment, p. 411

Reading and Vocabulary Study Guide
- L1 Chapter 17, Section 1, pp. 188–190

Differentiated Instruction

All in One Africa Teaching Resources
Rubric for Assessing a Bar Graph, p. 410 AR, GT, LPR, SN

Teacher's Edition
- L1 For Special Needs Students, TE p. 555

Social Studies Skills Tutor CD-ROM
- L1 Analyzing Primary and Secondary Sources ELL, LPR, SN

Key
- L1 Basic to Average
- L3 Average to Advanced
- L2 For All Students
- LPR Less Proficient Readers
- AR Advanced Readers
- SN Special Needs Students
- GT Gifted and Talented
- ELL English Language Learners

Section 2 South Africa: Struggle for Equality

🕐 *2.5 periods, 1.25 blocks (includes Chapter Review and Assessment)*

Social Studies Objectives

1. Understand how white rule in South Africa began.
2. Learn about the system of apartheid.
3. Find out how South Africans built a new nation after apartheid.

Reading/Language Arts Objective

Learn how to recognize words and phrases that signal the order in which events took place.

Prepare to Read	Instructional Resources	Differentiated Instruction
Build Background Knowledge Discuss how the civil rights movement in the United States is similar to the struggle for equality in South Africa. **Set a Purpose for Reading** Have students begin to fill out the *Reading Readiness Guide*. **Preview Key Terms** Teach the section's Key Terms. **Target Reading Skill** Introduce the section's Target Reading Skill of **recognizing words that signal sequence.**	**All in One Africa Teaching Resources** L2 Reading Readiness Guide, p. 392 L2 Recognize Sequence Signal Words, p. 396	**Spanish Reading and Vocabulary Study Guide** L1 Chapter 17, Section 2, pp. 135–136 ELL

Instruct	Instructional Resources	Differentiated Instruction
Target Reading Skill Review **recognizing words that signal sequence.** **Beginning of White Rule** Discuss how apartheid began in South Africa. **System of Apartheid** **Building a New Nation** Discuss the effects of apartheid and how the nation was rebuilt after apartheid was abolished. **Country Profile** Ask students to derive information from maps, charts, and graphs.	**All in One Africa Teaching Resources** L2 Guided Reading and Review, p. 393 L2 Reading Readiness Guide, p. 392 **Africa Transparencies** L2 Section Reading Support Transparency AF 54 **World Studies Video Program** L2 South Africa: Apartheid's Legacy	**All in One Africa Teaching Resources** L3 The Words of Desmond Tutu, pp. 407–408 AR, GT, LPR, SN **Teacher Edition** L3 For Advanced Readers, TE p. 559 L1 For Less Proficient Readers, TE p. 559 **Spanish Support** L2 Guided Reading and Review (Spanish), p. 178 ELL

Assess and Reteach	Instructional Resources	Differentiated Instruction
Assess Progress Evaluate student comprehension with the section assessment and section quiz. **Reteach** Assign the Reading and Vocabulary Study Guide to help struggling students. **Extend** Extend the lesson by assigning an Enrichment activity.	**All in One Africa Teaching Resources** L2 Section Quiz, p. 394 L3 Enrichment, p. 398 Rubric for Assessing a Writing Assignment, p. 411 L2 Word Knowledge, p. 397 L2 Vocabulary Development, p. 409 L2 Chapter Tests A and B, pp. 412–417 **Reading and Vocabulary Study Guide** L1 Chapter 17, Section 2, pp. 191–193	**Spanish Support** L2 Section Quiz (Spanish), p. 179 ELL L2 Chapter Summary (Spanish), p. 180 ELL L2 Vocabulary Development (Spanish), p. 181 ELL

Key

L1 Basic to Average	L3 Average to Advanced	LPR Less Proficient Readers GT Gifted and Talented
L2 For All Students		AR Advanced Readers ELL English Language Learners
		SN Special Needs Students

Professional Development

Reading Background

Organizing Paragraphs

A well-written paragraph clearly identifies a main idea, provides details as factual support, and adds a conclusion. Suggest to students that they follow these guidelines for writing paragraphs:

1. Determine what the main idea of the paragraph will be and then list supporting facts and details. *(main idea: the Congo's richness of natural resources; details: mining is its most profitable industry, has copper and gold deposits, second in diamond production)*

2. Begin the paragraph by writing a topic sentence that states the main idea.

3. Add several examples (3 to 5) in the form of complete sentences. Be sure to use transition words to make the sentences flow smoothly, and vary the length of each sentence. Test each sentence to make sure it supports the main idea.

4. Write a summary sentence.

Provide students with the paragraph below as an example.

The Democratic Republic of the Congo gains most of its wealth from mining. Large copper deposits exist in the south. The country has deposits of gold as well. In addition, Congo is second in the world in diamond production. The nation is rich with natural resources.

Scaffolding Tip

When asking students questions about the text, first ask questions to which the answer can clearly be found in the text. Then ask more difficult questions that require students to make their own interpretations based on the easier questions. For example, in Section 2 you might ask students, "What is apartheid?" and "How did apartheid affect the people of South Africa?" After students have answered these questions, ask, "Why do you think other countries would want to help end apartheid in South Africa?"

World Studies Background

Dian Fossey (1932–1985)

Central Africa is home to many animal species, including the endangered mountain gorilla. Dian Fossey, an American zoologist, devoted her life to studying and saving the mountain gorilla. In 1967 she established a research center in Rwanda to study these animals. Concerned with the poaching that threatened the gorillas she studied, Fossey involved the international media in her crusade to stop it. Fossey's battle ended in 1985 when she was murdered, allegedly by one of the poachers she had struggled against for about a decade.

Gandhi in South Africa

In 1893, Indian lawyer Mohandas Gandhi traveled to South Africa, where he stayed for over 20 years. While in South Africa, he introduced the strategy of passive resistance, or civil disobedience, to try to end discrimination against Asians. After he returned to India in 1915, his use of passive resistance proved instrumental in the movement against British imperialism. Martin Luther King, Jr., and other leaders of the American civil rights movement adopted the concept of civil disobedience in the struggle for equal rights for African Americans.

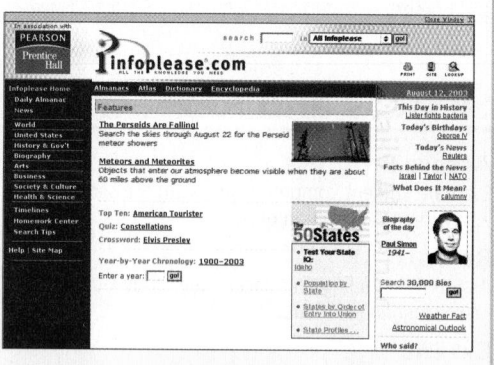

Infoplease® provides a wealth of useful information for the classroom. You can use this resource to strengthen your background on the subjects covered in this chapter. Have students visit this advertising-free site as a starting point for projects requiring research.

Use Web code **lad-5700** for **Infoplease®**.

Professional Development

Reading Background

Power Notes

Power notes can help students distinguish main ideas from details. Creating power notes is easier than outlining, because main ideas are always assigned Level 1. Details are assigned Level 2, 3, or 4. The more specific the detail, the higher the level. Students can use this strategy for organizing their reading, preparing for writing, or studying.

Model creating power notes using information from the chapter. Provide students with a Level 1 idea and have them provide Levels 2 and 3. For example, tell students, "Level 1 is Africa. What will Level 2 be?" *(Congo)* "Great. Now give me another Level 2." *(Namibia)* "Right. Now give me Level 3s that will fit under Congo." *(Congo basin, northern uplands, eastern highlands, southern uplands)*

As students provide you with the levels, write their ideas on the board to show them what a power notes outline looks like. The outline should look like the following:

    Level 1: Africa
        Level 2: Congo
            Level 3: Congo basin
            Level 3: northern uplands
            Level 3: eastern highlands
            Level 3: southern uplands
        Level 2: Namibia

Identifying Author's Craft

Knowing the author's craft, or strategy for writing, can help students understand the text. Explain that authors often present information *chronologically*, using *cause-and-effect*, or by *comparing and contrasting*. Have students choose which of these strategies was used to write each of the following sentences from the chapter:

1. *For example, by the 1400s, the kingdoms of Kongo, Luba, and Lunda ruled much of the area.* (chronology)
2. *Blacks and some whites welcomed the end of apartheid. In some ways, however, South Africa has remained a divided society.* (compare and contrast)
3. *Later, because of an international campaign to end Leopold's abuses, the Belgian government ruled less harshly.* (cause-and-effect)

Challenge students to determine the author's craft in other paragraphs and sections throughout the chapter.

World Studies Background

Television in South Africa

Television, introduced to South Africa in the 1970s, was controlled by the white-ruled government for more than a decade. During that time, the government used the medium to support its policy of apartheid. With the end of apartheid in the 1990s, government control of television broadcasting ended. Television is still, for the most part, publicly owned. The management is now more representative of the population, and the public has a greater influence on the medium.

Flowers in South Africa

South Africa has a diverse agriculture industry due to its large area and variety of climatic conditions. Two of the major agricultural exports are fruit and wine. The exporting of flowers is of growing importance to the economy. About 600 plant producers cultivate the many types of flowers that grow in South Africa. Most of the flowers are shipped to Europe and the United States.

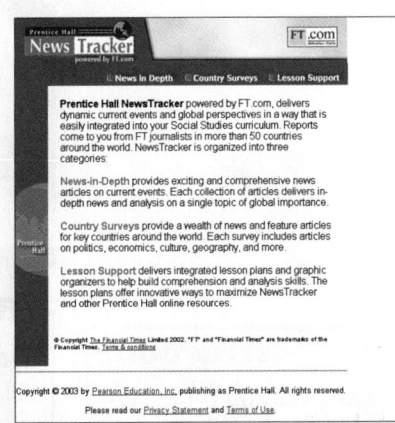

Get in-depth information on topics of global importance with **Prentice Hall Newstracker,** powered by FT.com.

 Use Web code **lad-5703** for **Prentice Hall Newstracker.**

Chapter 17 Central and Southern Africa

Guiding Questions

Remind students about the Guiding Questions introduced at the beginning of this section.

Section 1 relates to **Guiding Question 5** **What factors influence the ways in which Africans make a living?** *(The Democratic Republic of the Congo has large deposits of valuable minerals such as copper, diamonds, and gold. Mining produces most of the country's wealth.)*

Section 2 relates to **Guiding Question 4** **What factors led to the development of different governments across Africa?** *(In 1902, the British took control of Afrikaner states and created the Union of South Africa. They passed laws to keep land and wealth in white hands. In 1948, Afrikaners took control of the country and established the system of apartheid which discriminated against blacks and other ethnic groups. Apartheid separated the races until it was legally ended in 1990.)*

Target Reading Skill

In this chapter, students will learn and apply the reading skill of understanding sequence. Use the following worksheets to help students practice this skill:

All in One **Africa Teaching Resources,** *Identify Sequence*, p. 395; *Recognize Sequence Signal Words*, p. 396

Chapter Preview

This chapter will introduce you to some of the countries of Central and Southern Africa.

Country Databank

The Country Databank provides data and descriptions of each of the countries in the region: Angola, Botswana, Cameroon, Central African Republic, Comoros, Democratic Republic of the Congo, Equatorial Guinea, Gabon, Lesotho, Madagascar, Malawi, Mauritius, Mozambique, Namibia, Republic of the Congo, São Tomé and Príncipe, South Africa, Swaziland, Zambia, and Zimbabwe.

Section 1
Democratic Republic of the Congo
A Wealth of Possibilities

Section 2
South Africa
Struggle for Equality

Target Reading Skill

Sequence In this chapter you will focus on understanding sequence. Identifying sequence and recognizing sequence signal words will help you learn as you read.

▶ Cape Town, South Africa, is an important port and center of industry in Southern Africa.

Differentiated Instruction

The following Teacher Edition Strategies are suitable for students of varying abilities.

Advanced Readers, pp. 545, 559
English Language Learners, pp. 546, 550
Gifted and Talented, p. 543
Less Proficient Readers, pp. 541, 559
Special Needs Students, pp. 544, 555

Bibliography

For the Teacher
Harvey, Robert. *The Fall of Apartheid: The Inside Story From Smuts to Mbeki.* Palgrave MacMillan, 2002.
Edgerton, Robert B. *The Troubled Heart of Africa: A History of the Congo.* St. Martin's Press, 2002.
Sparks, Allister. *Beyond the Miracle: Inside the New South Africa.* University of Chicago Press, 2003.

For the Student
L1 Wynaden, Jo, and Nina Kushner. *Welcome to the Democratic Republic of the Congo.* Gareth Stevens, 2002.
L2 Connolly, Sean. *Apartheid in South Africa.* Raintree Publishers, 2002.
L3 Gogerly, Liz. *Nelson Mandela.* Heinemann Library, 2003.

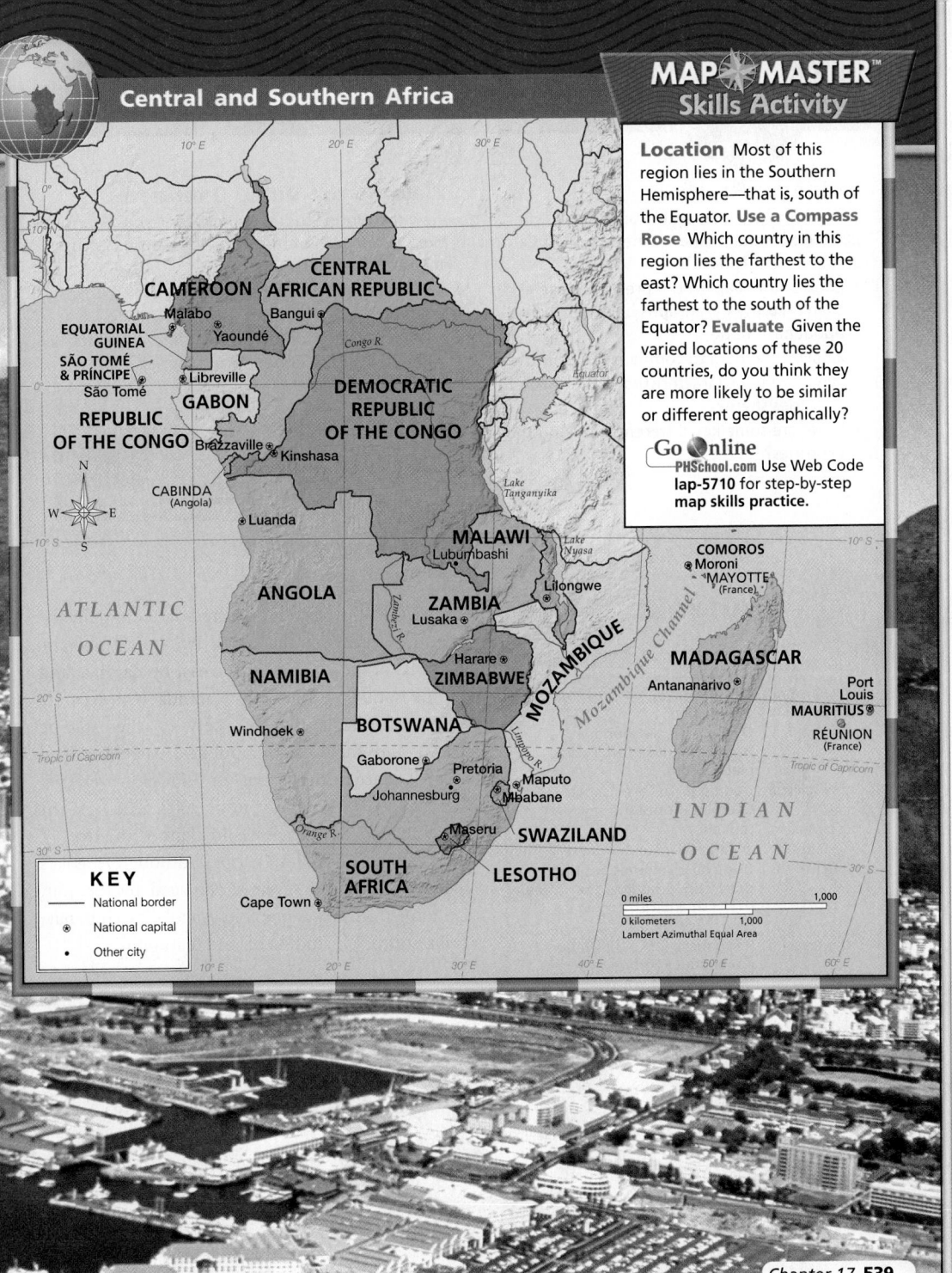

Central and Southern Africa

MAP MASTER™
Skills Activity

Location Most of this region lies in the Southern Hemisphere—that is, south of the Equator. **Use a Compass Rose** Which country in this region lies the farthest to the east? Which country lies the farthest to the south of the Equator? **Evaluate** Given the varied locations of these 20 countries, do you think they are more likely to be similar or different geographically?

Go Online
PHSchool.com Use Web Code **lap-5710** for step-by-step **map skills practice**.

KEY
— National border
⊛ National capital
• Other city

0 miles / 1,000
0 kilometers / 1,000
Lambert Azimuthal Equal Area

Chapter 17 **539**

MAP MASTER™
Skills Activity

Ask students to identify the island countries of Central and Southern Africa. Then have students practice using the map scale by measuring the shortest distance from these countries to mainland Africa. Lead a discussion on how life might be different in the island countries as compared to life in countries on the African continent.

Go Online
PHSchool.com Students may practice their map skills using the interactive online version of this map.

Using the Visual   L2

Reach Into Your Background Draw students' attention to the caption accompanying the picture on pp. 538–539. Ask students to study the image, and have them make a list of what it tells them about Cape Town, South Africa. Then have them compare their observations with what they know about a city in their area.

Answers

MAP MASTER™ Skills Activity **Use a Compass Rose** Mauritius; South Africa **Evaluate** Possible answer: The countries are more likely to be different geographically because the region is spread out across thousands of miles.

Chapter Resources

Teaching Resources
L2 Vocabulary Development, p. 409
L2 Skills for Life, p. 399
L2 Chapter Tests A and B, pp. 412–417

Spanish Support
L2 Spanish Chapter Summary, p. 182
L2 Spanish Vocabulary Development, p. 183

Media and Technology
L1 Student Edition on Audio CD
L1 Guided Reading Audiotapes, English and Spanish
L2 Social Studies Skills Tutor CD-ROM
ExamView Test Bank CD-ROM

PRENTICE HALL
Presentation EXPRESS™
Teach · Connect · Inspire

Teach this chapter's content using the PresentationExpress™ CD-ROM including:
■ slide shows
■ transparencies
■ interactive maps and media
■ *ExamView*® QuickTake Presenter

Objectives

- Look at the map on the previous page to learn more about each nation.

- Use data to compare countries.

- Learn what characteristics Central and Southern African countries share.

- Identify some key differences among the countries.

 Show *The Geography of Central and Southern Africa.* Ask **What are some common features of the region?** *(tropical savanna and abundant mineral resources)*

Prepare to Read

Build Background Knowledge L2

Invite students to share what they learned about Central and Southern Africa's geography from watching the video. Display the *Concept Web* graphic organizer. Write "Natural Resources" in the center circle. Ask students to fill in the outer circles with what they learned about the natural resources of Central and Southern Africa. Then have students create their own concept webs and fill in what they learned about the region's vegetation.

The Geography of Central and Southern Africa, **World Studies Video Program**

Africa Transparencies, *Transparency B17: Concept Web*

Introducing Central and Southern Africa

Guide for Reading

This section provides an introduction to the 20 countries that make up the region of Central and Southern Africa.

- Look at the map on the previous page and then read the paragraphs below to learn about each nation.
- Analyze the data to compare the countries.
- What are the characteristics that most of the countries share?
- What are some key differences among the countries?

Viewing the Video Overview

View the World Studies Video Overview to learn more about each of the countries. As you watch, answer these questions:

- What are some common features of the region?
- What obstacles do children in the Democratic Republic of the Congo face to get an education?

Explore the geography of Central and Southern Africa.

Angola

Capital	Luanda
Land Area	481,551 sq mi; 1,246,700 sq km
Population	10.6 million
Ethnic Group(s)	Ovimbundu, Kimbundu, Bankongo, mixed white and black, white
Religion(s)	traditional beliefs, Roman Catholic, Protestant
Government	republic
Currency	kwanza
Leading Exports	crude oil, diamonds, refined petroleum products, gas, coffee, sisal, fish and fish products, timber, cotton
Language(s)	Portuguese (official), Umbundu, Kimbundu, Kikongo

Angola (ang GOH luh) is bordered on the west by the Atlantic Ocean, on the north by the Democratic Republic of the Congo, on the east by Zambia, and on the south by Namibia. Cabinda is a separate region of Angola that lies between the Atlantic Ocean and the Congo republics. Angola gained independence from Portugal in 1975. However, civil war gripped the country until 2002. The war left many thousands homeless and claimed the lives of an estimated 1.5 million people. Although Angola's economy has been severely damaged by the war, economic recovery is possible. Angola is rich in natural resources, including oil and diamonds.

Thatched-roof houses in Angola

Botswana

Capital	Gaborone
Land Area	226,011 sq mi; 585,370 sq km
Population	1.6 million
Ethnic Group(s)	Tswana, Kalanga, Basarwa, Kgalagadi, white
Religion(s)	traditional beliefs, Christian
Government	parliamentary republic
Currency	pula
Leading Exports	diamonds, copper, nickel, soda ash, meat, textiles
Language(s)	English (official), Tswana, Shona, San, Khoikhoi, Ndebele

Botswana (baht SWAH nuh) is bordered on the west and north by Namibia, on the north and east by Zambia and Zimbabwe, and on the east and south by South Africa. When it was a British colony, Botswana was known as Bechuanaland (bech WAH nah land). After gaining independence in 1966, Botswana's government transformed the economy into one of the fastest-growing in the world. Diamond mining is Botswana's largest industry. AIDS poses a severe health threat to the country. Hundreds of thousands of people have the disease.

Cameroon

Capital	Yaoundé
Land Area	181,251 sq mi; 469,440 sq km
Population	16.1 million
Ethnic Group(s)	Cameroon Highlanders, Bantu, Kirdi, Fulani, Eastern Nigritic
Religion(s)	traditional beliefs, Christian, Muslim
Government	unitary republic
Currency	CFA franc
Leading Exports	crude oil and petroleum products, lumber, cacao beans, aluminum, coffee, cotton
Language(s)	French (official), English (official), Bamileke, Fang, Fulani

Cameroon (kam uh ROON) is bordered on the west by the Atlantic Ocean and Nigeria, on the north by Chad, on the east by the Central African Republic, and on the south by the Republic of the Congo, Gabon, and Equatorial Guinea. It has many forests and rivers and good farmland. Present-day Cameroon was formed in 1961 by merging French Cameroon and a part of British Cameroon. The government has spent the last several decades improving farming conditions and building roads and railways. In terms of oil and agricultural resources, Cameroon is one of Africa's richest countries.

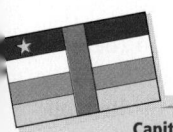

Central African Republic

Capital	Bangui
Land Area	240,534 sq mi; 622,984 sq km
Population	3.6 million
Ethnic Group(s)	Baya, Banda, Mandjia, Sara, Mbouri, M'Baka, Yakoma
Religion(s)	traditional beliefs, Protestant, Roman Catholic, Muslim
Government	republic
Currency	CFA franc
Leading Exports	diamonds, timber, cotton, coffee, tobacco
Language(s)	French (official), Sango, Banda, Gbaya

The Central African Republic (SEN trul AF rih kun rih PUB lik) is bordered on the west by Cameroon, on the north by Chad, on the north and east by Sudan, and on the south by the Democratic Republic of the Congo and the Republic of the Congo. It sits on a low plateau at the southern edge of the Sahel. Once a French colony called Ubangi-Shari (yoo BANG gee SHAH ree), the Central African Republic gained independence in 1960. Since 1993, the government has faced several rebellions. Despite the country's history of instability, the elections of 2005 raised hopes for a more stable future.

Chapter 17 **541**

Instruct

Introducing Central and Southern Africa L2

Guided Instruction

- Read each country paragraph as a class using the Choral Reading strategy (TE, p. T34). Then, ask students to read through each data table.

- Ask students **What event damaged Angola's economy?** *(the civil war that gripped the country from the mid-1970s until 2002)*

- Ask **Which countries on pp. 540–541 use English as an official language?** *(Botswana and Cameroon)* **Why do you think this is so?** *(Botswana and part of Cameroon were once British colonies.)*

- Have students identify the similarities between Cameroon and Central African Republic. Remind them to use both the paragraphs and the data tables. *(Similarities: traditional beliefs and Muslim religions; CFA franc for currency; French as official language; a republican form of government; coffee and cotton as leading exports; France once controlled part of Cameroon and all of the Central African Republic)*

Differentiated Instruction

For Less Proficient Readers L1
Have students create a Venn diagram to show the similarities and differences between Angola and Central African Republic. Display the *Venn Diagram* transparency to show students how to sketch the organizer. Circulate to make sure students are filling in the organizers correctly.

📖 **Africa Transparencies,** *Transparency B16: Venn Diagram*

- Ask students **What religions are practiced in both countries profiled on p. 542?** *(Islam and Roman Catholicism)*

- Point out that both countries on p. 542 have suffered through civil wars. Ask students to think of reasons why many African countries have experienced major rebellions and civil wars. *(Possible answer: After countries gained independence, different groups may have been fighting for control of the country.)*

Introducing Central and Southern Africa

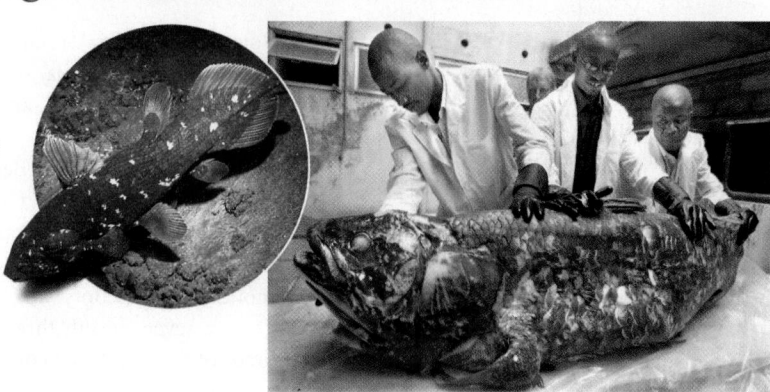

A live coelacanth (left); African scientists studying a dead coelacanth (right)

Comoros

Capital	Moroni
Land Area	838 sq mi; 2,170 sq km
Population	614,382
Ethnic Group(s)	Antalote, Cafre, Makoa, Oimatsaha, Sakalava
Religion(s)	Muslim, Roman Catholic
Government	independent republic
Currency	Comoros franc
Leading Exports	vanilla, ylang-ylang, cloves, perfume oil, copra
Language(s)	Arabic (official), French (official), Comoran (official)

Comoros (KAH muh rohz) is made up of three islands in the Indian Ocean, off the east coast of Mozambique. Numerous species of birds, animals, and fish live on and around the islands. The most famous of these is the coelacanth (SEE luh kanth), an extremely rare fish. Since gaining its independence from France in 1975, Comoros has experienced several major rebellions and civil wars. It is an extremely poor country. The population is growing rapidly, but the country has few natural resources or economic opportunities. Most of the people of Comoros are subsistence farmers.

Congo, Democratic Republic of the

Capital	Kinshasa
Land Area	875,520 sq mi; 2,267,600 sq km
Population	55.2 million
Ethnic Group(s)	more than 200 distinct ethnic groups, including Bantu, Hamitic
Religion(s)	Roman Catholic, Protestant, Muslim, traditional beliefs
Government	dictatorship
Currency	Congolese franc
Leading Exports	diamonds, copper, coffee, cobalt, crude oil
Language(s)	French (official), Kiswahili, Tshiluba, Kikongo, Lingala

The Democratic Republic of the Congo (dem uh KRAT ik rih PUB lik uv thuh KAHNG goh) lies on the Equator. It is bordered on the west by the Republic of the Congo; on the north by the Central African Republic and Sudan; on the east by Uganda, Rwanda, Burundi, and Tanzania; and on the south by Zambia. The rain forests of the Congo River basin cover much of the country. The country has suffered through years of civil war, which led to the deaths of about 3.5 million people. The nation has the potential for a strong economy, with many mineral resources, farmable land, and good soil.

542 Africa

Background: Links Across Place

The Congo and Transportation The Congo River is the second longest river in Africa. The river and its many tributaries flow through several Central and Southern African countries, including Zambia and the Democratic Republic of the Congo. These rivers both help and hinder transportation within the region. Some consider the river system to be the most navigable system on the continent. There are 8,700 miles (14,000 kilometers) of navigable rivers in the Democratic Republic of the Congo alone. The rivers have helped the region develop economically. But, at the same time, the presence of wide waterways hinders transportation over land. Few bridges have been built across the rivers.

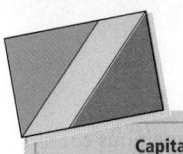

Congo, Republic of the

Capital	Brazzaville
Land Area	131,853 sq mi; 341,500 sq km
Population	3.3 million
Ethnic Group(s)	Kongo, Sangha, M'Bochi, Take
Religion(s)	Christian, traditional beliefs, Muslim
Government	republic
Currency	CFA franc
Leading Exports	petroleum, lumber, plywood, sugar, cocoa, coffee, diamonds
Language(s)	French (official), Kongo, Teke, Lingala

The Republic of the Congo (rih PUB lik uv thuh KAHNG goh) lies on the Equator. It is bordered on the west by Gabon, on the north by Cameroon and the Central African Republic, on the east and south by the Democratic Republic of the Congo, and on the south by Angola. The Congo River forms the border with the Democratic Republic of the Congo. The Republic of the Congo gained independence from France in 1960. Since then, it has faced years of civil war. The nation has large supplies of oil and timber, and sales of oil have brought the country some wealth.

Equatorial Guinea

Capital	Malabo
Land Area	10,830 sq mi; 28,051 sq km
Population	498,144
Ethnic Group(s)	Bioko, Rio Muni
Religion(s)	Christian, traditional beliefs
Government	republic
Currency	CFA franc
Leading Exports	petroleum, timber, cocoa
Language(s)	Spanish (official), French (official), Fang, Bubi

Equatorial Guinea (ee kwuh TAWR ee ul GIH nee) lies just north of the Equator. It consists of five islands and a mainland area. The mainland is bordered on the west by the Atlantic Ocean, on the north by Cameroon, and on the east and south by Gabon. Many species of animals live on the mainland, including gorillas, leopards, antelopes, crocodiles, and snakes. After almost two hundred years as a Spanish colony, Equatorial Guinea gained independence in 1968. The economy is strong due to recently discovered oil reserves. Forestry, farming, and fishing are also important industries.

Gabon

Capital	Libreville
Land Area	99,489 sq mi; 257,667 sq km
Population	1.2 million
Ethnic Group(s)	Bantu, Fang, Bapounou, Nzebi, Obamba
Religion(s)	Christian, traditional beliefs, Muslim
Government	republic
Currency	CFA franc
Leading Exports	crude oil, timber, manganese, uranium
Language(s)	French (official), Fang, Punu, Sira, Nzebi, Mpongwe

Gabon (gah BOHN) is bordered on the west by the Atlantic Ocean, on the north by Equatorial Guinea and Cameroon, and on the east and south by the Republic of the Congo. The country gained its independence from France in 1960, and it became a democracy in 1990. Oil resources have made Gabon's economy very strong in comparison to the economies of other African countries. People live on only a small portion of Gabon's land. More than three quarters of the country is covered by rain forests that are inhabited by many kinds of animals and plants.

Chapter 17 **543**

- Ask **Which of the countries on pp. 544–545 has the largest population?** (*Mozambique*) **Which country has the smallest area?** (*Lesotho*)

- Ask students **What do the governments of Madagascar, Malawi, and Mauritius have in common?** (*They all have representative forms of government.*)

- Have students locate Mauritius on the map on p. 539. **How is Mauritius's location reflected in its economy?** (*Mauritius is made up of islands surrounded by the waters of the Indian Ocean—fish and fish products are some of the country's leading exports.*)

Introducing Central and Southern Africa

Lesotho

Capital	Maseru
Land Area	11,720 sq mi; 30,355 sq km
Population	2.2 million
Ethnic Group(s)	Sotho, white, Asian
Religion(s)	Christian, traditional beliefs
Government	parliamentary constitutional monarchy
Currency	loti
Leading Exports	manufactured goods, wool, mohair, food, live animals
Language(s)	English (off.), Sesotho (off.), Zulu

Lesotho (leh SOO too) is a tiny, mountainous country surrounded on all sides by South Africa. In 1966, the country became independent as a monarchy, or a government led by a king or a queen. Since that time, its government has been unstable. The country has been ruled by a king, by military leaders, and by elected leaders. Lesotho's economy depends heavily on South Africa. Many of Lesotho's men find work in the mines of South Africa. Despite widespread poverty, a large percentage of people in Lesotho are literate.

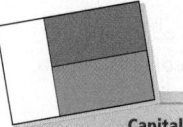

Madagascar

Capital	Antananarivo
Land Area	224,533 sq mi; 581,540 sq km
Population	16.5 million
Ethnic Group(s)	Malayo-Indonesian, Cotier, white, South Asian, Creole, Comoran
Religion(s)	traditional beliefs, Christian, Muslim
Government	republic
Currency	Malagasy franc
Leading Exports	coffee, vanilla, shellfish, sugar, cotton cloth, chromite
Language(s)	French (off.), Malagasy (off.)

Madagascar (mad uh GAS kur) is the world's fourth-largest island. It lies in the Indian Ocean, east of Mozambique. Before the French colonized Madagascar in 1886, it was an independent kingdom. The nation regained its independence in 1960 and became a democracy in the early 1990s. The nation's economy is based mainly on farming, fishing, and forestry. Madagascar is famous for plants and animals that cannot be found anywhere else on Earth. It is also well known for its spices, including vanilla. A larger percentage of people in Madagascar are literate than in most other African countries.

Malawi

Capital	Lilongwe
Land Area	36,324 sq mi; 94,080 sq km
Population	10.7 million
Ethnic Group(s)	Chewa, Nyanja, Tumbuka, Yao, Lomwe, Sena, Tonga, Ngongi, Ngonde, Asian, white
Religion(s)	Protestant, Roman Catholic, Muslim, traditional beliefs
Government	multiparty democracy
Currency	Malawi kwacha
Leading Exports	tobacco, tea, sugar, cotton, coffee, peanuts, wood products, apparel
Language(s)	English (official), Chichewa (official), Lomwe, Yao, Ngoni

Malawi (MAH lah wee) is bordered on the west, east, and south by Mozambique, on the west by Zambia, and on the north by Tanzania. The dominant geographical feature of this tiny country is Lake Nyasa (NYAH sah), Africa's third-largest body of water. In addition, Malawi lies alongside the Great Rift Valley. Malawi was called Nyasaland while under British rule. It became an independent nation in 1964. Malawi then became a democracy in the mid-1990s. The country's economy is mostly agricultural. Almost 90 percent of Malawians live in rural areas.

Differentiated Instruction

For Special Needs Students   **L1**

Distribute *Outline Map 21: Africa: Political.* As you read about each Central and Southern African country as a class, have students fill in the name of the country on their outline map. Refer them to the map on p. 539 if they need guidance. After you have read about and labeled all the countries, have students color them in one color and label the region Central and Southern Africa.

All in One Africa Teaching Resources, *Outline Map 21: Africa: Political,* p. 406

Mauritius

Capital	Port Louis
Land Area	784 sq mi; 2,030 sq km
Population	1.2 million
Ethnic Group(s)	Indo-Mauritian, Creole, Sino-Mauritian, Franco-Mauritian
Religion(s)	Hindu, Roman Catholic, Muslim, Protestant
Government	parliamentary democracy
Currency	Mauritian rupee
Leading Exports	iron ore, fish, fish products, gold
Language(s)	English (official), French Creole, Hindi, Urdu, Tamil, Chinese, French

Mauritius (maw RISH ee us) is made up of islands in the Indian Ocean east of Madagascar. The islands were colonized by Portugal in the 1500s. The country was claimed by the Dutch, the French, and the British before it gained independence in 1968. Since that time, it has turned a weak economy based on agriculture into a healthy economy based on manufacturing, banking, and tourism. Mauritius has a stable, democratic government. A majority of the people of Mauritius are descended from Indians who moved to the islands to work on sugar plantations in the 1800s.

Mozambique

Capital	Maputo
Land Area	302,737 sq mi; 784,090 sq km
Population	19.6 million
Ethnic Group(s)	Shangaan, Chokwe, Manyika, Sena, Makha, white, mixed white and black, South Asian
Religion(s)	traditional beliefs, Christian, Muslim
Government	republic
Currency	metical
Leading Exports	prawns, cashews, cotton, sugar, citrus, timber, electricity
Language(s)	Portuguese (official), Makua, Tsonga, Sena, Lomwe

Mozambique (moh zum BEEK) is bordered on the west by South Africa, Zimbabwe, Zambia, and Malawi; on the north by Tanzania; and on the east and south by the Indian Ocean. The Zambezi River divides the country into dry savanna in the south and fertile lands in the north. When it gained independence from Portugal in 1975, Mozambique was one of the world's poorest countries. It suffered through civil war from 1977 to 1992. Heavy flooding in 1999 and 2000 made the poor economy even worse. The people of Mozambique are relying on economic aid from other countries and new policies to improve their situation.

Namibia

Capital	Windhoek
Land Area	318,694 sq mi; 825,418 sq km
Population	1.8 million
Ethnic Group(s)	Ovambo, Kavango, Herero, Damara, Nama, Caprivian, Bushman, Baster, Tswana
Religion(s)	Christian, traditional beliefs
Government	republic
Currency	Namibian dollar
Leading Exports	diamonds, copper, gold, zinc, lead, uranium, cattle, fish
Language(s)	English (official), Ovambo, Kavango, Bergdama, German, Afrikaans

Namibia (nuh MIB ee uh) is bordered on the west by the Atlantic Ocean, on the north by Angola and Zambia, on the east by Botswana, and on the south by South Africa. Its land includes both the Namib and Kalahari deserts. Its economy is dependent on mining. Once a German colony, Namibia fell under South African rule after World War I. It became an independent country in 1990. Namibia still suffers from the effects of the system of racial inequality that South Africa imposed on it for decades. Its government and people are working to overcome these effects.

Chapter 17 **545**

Guided Instruction (continued)

- Ask students to identify events that contributed to Mozambique's poor economy. *(civil war from 1977 to 1992 and heavy flooding in 1999 and 2000)*

- **Which country was once part of South Africa?** *(Namibia)* **How did being part of South Africa affect Namibia?** *(South Africa imposed a system of racial inequality on Namibia, which the country still suffers effects from.)*

Differentiated Instruction

For Advanced Readers L3

Have students choose two of the six countries found on pp. 544–545. Tell them to use the DK World Desk Reference Online to make information cards similar to the ones in the Country Databank using different statistics, such as the percentage of people living in rural and urban areas and literacy rates. Ask them to use the same types of statistics for both countries. Then have them write a short paragraph explaining the similarities and differences between the countries, based on what they found.

Guided Instruction (continued)

- Ask **How does São Tomé and Príncipe plan on improving its economy in the future?** (*It is working to diversify its crops and make use of the oil reserves located in the Gulf of Guinea.*)

- Ask **Why does Swaziland rely on South Africa to transport its goods?** (*Swaziland is landlocked so it cannot transport goods by sea, while South Africa is located on the coast, giving it access to the sea.*)

- Ask students to identify the similarities among all five countries on pp. 545–546. (*They all have Christianity as a major religion, and they were all once ruled by another country.*)

Independent Practice

- First, have students complete *Reading a Bar Graph*. Then have them create a bar graph showing the populations of all the countries in the Country Databank. Remind students to label both axes and give the graph an appropriate title.

  All in One **Africa Teaching Resources,** *Reading a Bar Graph,* p. 405

Monitor Progress

Circulate to be sure students are labeling the graph appropriately. Provide assistance as needed. Then collect the bar graphs and use the *Rubric for Assessing a Bar Graph* to assess students' work.

  All in One **Africa Teaching Resources,** *Rubric for Assessing a Bar Graph,* p. 410

Introducing Central and Southern Africa

São Tomé and Príncipe

Capital	São Tomé
Land Area	386 sq mi; 1,001 sq km
Population	170,372
Ethnic Group(s)	mixed white and black, angolares, forros, servicais, tongas, white
Religion(s)	Christian
Government	republic
Currency	dobra
Leading Exports	cocoa, copra, coffee, palm oil
Language(s)	Portuguese (official), Portuguese Creole

São Tomé and Príncipe (sow toh MEE and PRIN suh pea) is made up of islands in the Gulf of Guinea, west of Gabon. The Portuguese discovered the uninhabited islands in the 1400s. They immediately built plantations and imported slaves to grow the islands' major resource, sugar cane. The islands began exporting coffee and cocoa in the 1800s. The nation gained independence in 1975. The first free elections were held in 1991. Although a poor country, São Tomé and Príncipe has very fertile land and is working to diversify its crops. It is also hoping to make use of oil reserves located in the Gulf of Guinea.

South Africa

Capital	Pretoria, Cape Town, Bloemfontein
Land Area	471,008 sq mi; 1,219,912 sq km
Population	43.6 million
Ethnic Group(s)	black, white, mixed white and black, South Asian
Religion(s)	Christian, traditional beliefs
Government	republic
Currency	rand
Leading Exports	gold, diamonds, platinum, other metals and minerals, machinery and equipment
Language(s)	Afrikaans, English, Ndebele, Pedi, Sotho, Swazi, Tsonga, Tswana, Venda, Xhosa, Zulu (all official)

South Africa (sowth AF rih kuh) occupies the southern tip of the African continent. With a wealth of natural resources, including gold and diamonds, it has the continent's strongest economy. Ruled by the Dutch after 1652 and by the British after 1806, South Africa became independent in 1931. From that time until 1990, the country was known for apartheid, a harsh political system under which the races were separated from each other and discrimination against nonwhites was the law. After years of struggle, nonwhites won equality in 1994, when apartheid ended. The country then focused on healing the wounds of the past.

Swaziland

Capital	Mbabane
Land Area	6,642 sq mi; 17,203 sq km
Population	1.1 million
Ethnic Group(s)	black, white
Religion(s)	Christian, traditional beliefs, Muslim, Jewish
Government	monarchy
Currency	lilangeni
Leading Exports	soft drink concentrates, sugar, wood pulp, cotton yarn, fruit
Language(s)	English (official), siSwati (official), Zulu, Tsonga

Swaziland (SWAH zee land) is a small country that is surrounded by South Africa and Mozambique. More than 95 percent of the population belongs to the Swazi ethnic group. Swaziland gained independence from Great Britain in 1968. The country has a very diversified economy. Because it is landlocked, Swaziland depends mainly on South Africa to move goods in and out of the country. Swaziland is ruled by a king. However, many Swazis have been pressuring the government for democratic reforms, such as having a multiparty political system.

546 Africa

Differentiated Instruction

For English Language Learners **L1**

Have students study the map, photo tour, and timeline on the *South Africa* portion of the Passport to the World CD-ROM.

⊙ *South Africa,* **Passport to the World CD-ROM**

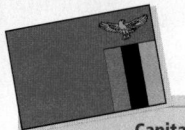

Zambia

Capital	Lusaka
Land Area	285,994 sq mi; 740,724 sq km
Population	10.1 million
Ethnic Group(s)	Bemba, Nyanja, Tonga, Lozi, European, white
Religion(s)	Christian, Muslim, Hindu, traditional beliefs
Government	republic
Currency	Zambian kwacha
Leading Exports	copper, cobalt, electricity, tobacco, flowers, cotton
Language(s)	English (official), Bemba, Nyanja, Tonga, Lunda, Lozi

Zambia (ZAM bee uh) is bordered on the west by Angola, on the north by the Democratic Republic of the Congo and Tanzania, on the east by Malawi and Mozambique, and on the south by Zimbabwe, Botswana, and Namibia. Once a British colony called Northern Rhodesia, Zambia became independent in 1964. For decades, Zambia was under the rule of a single political party. In recent years, it has succeeded in establishing a multiparty democracy. Copper exports have made Zambia prosperous. However, Zambia risks losses if copper prices fall.

Zimbabwe

Capital	Harare
Land Area	149,293 sq mi; 386,670 sq km
Population	11.3 million
Ethnic Group(s)	Shona, Ndebele, Asian, white
Religion(s)	Christian, traditional beliefs, Muslim
Government	parliamentary democracy
Currency	Zimbabwe dollar
Leading Exports	tobacco, gold, ferroalloys, textiles, clothing
Language(s)	English (official), Shona, Ndebele

Zimbabwe (zim BAHB way) is bordered on the west by Botswana and Zambia, on the north by Zambia, on the north and east by Mozambique, and on the south by South Africa. Once the British colony of Southern Rhodesia, Zimbabwe gained independence in 1980. Since then, the country has worked to overcome racial inequality and a troubled economy. Zimbabwe faced additional difficulties under the rule of President Robert Mugabe. These included unfair elections, as well as the destruction of the homes and businesses of about 700,000 people.

SOURCES: DK World Desk Reference Online; CIA World Factbook Online; *The World Almanac*, 2003

Assessment

Comprehension and Critical Thinking

1. Compare and Contrast Compare and contrast the economies of these countries.
2. Summarize What are some characteristics that most of the countries share?
3. Analyze Information What are some key differences among the countries?

4. Infer What can you infer about a country such as South Africa that has eleven official languages?
5. Predict How do you think life in the countries that have no borders on the ocean is different from life in the ones that do?
6. Make a Bar Graph Create a bar graph showing each language that is an official language in this region and how many countries speak that language.

Keeping Current

Access the **DK World Desk Reference Online** at **PHSchool.com** for up-to-date information about all 20 countries in this chapter.

Web Code: lae-5700

Chapter 17 **547**

Assess and Reteach

Assess Progress   L2
Direct students' attention back to the concept webs they made before they began studying the Country Databank. Tell them to make a similar web using some of the information they learned from the Databank, such as a concept web about the economy of São Tomé and Príncipe.

Reteach   L2
Ask students to create a table on a large piece of poster board that shows the religions, governments, leading exports, and languages for all of the countries in the Country Databank. Have them list the categories across the top of the table and the names of the countries along the side. Model filling in the information for one country on the board.

Extend   L2

Have students choose two countries in the Country Databank. Ask them to do library or Internet research to learn more about each country. Then have them write a short essay or create a table to explain the similarities and differences between the two countries. Have students add their work to their portfolios.

4. Possible answer: There are many different ethnic groups living there.

5. Possible answer: People living in land-locked countries may make a living in different ways than people living on the coast; traditions and cultures of coastal countries may be more heavily influenced by those of other countries around the world because they have easier access to them.

6. Students' bar graphs should reflect the correct languages and number of countries in which each language is spoken. Use *Rubric for Assessing a Bar Graph* to evaluate students' graphs.

All in One **Africa Teaching Resources,** *Rubric for Assessing a Bar Graph,* p. 410

Answers

Assessment

1. Most of the countries have struggled to stabilize their economies since independence, but some economies are more stable than others. Some countries have similar leading exports. For example, gold is a leading export for Zimbabwe, South Africa, Namibia, and Mauritius.

2. Most of the countries have some similar major religions, ethnic groups, and languages; all were once ruled by other countries; most have struggled to stabilize their economies and governments since independence.

3. Possible answer: Different products and industries fuel their economies; the sizes of the countries' populations and areas vary greatly.

Section 1
Step-by-Step Instruction

Objectives

Social Studies

1. Discover the physical geography and important natural resources of the Democratic Republic of the Congo.
2. Learn about the country's economic and political challenges since independence.
3. Find out how different groups and leaders have reshaped the nation.

Reading/Language Arts

Sequence events to understand and remember important information.

Prepare to Read

Build Background Knowledge　L2

In this section, students will learn about the resources, people, economy, and government of the Democratic Republic of the Congo. Ask students to preview the headings and visuals and make predictions about what they will learn in this section. Provide a few examples to get them started. Have students engage in a Think-Write-Pair-Share activity (TE, p. T36) to generate a list of predictions. Write their responses on the board.

Set a Purpose for Reading　L2

- Preview the Objectives.

- Read each statement in the *Reading Readiness Guide* aloud. Ask students to mark the statements true or false.

  All in One **Africa Teaching Resources,** *Reading Readiness Guide,* p. 388

- Have students discuss the statements in pairs or groups of four, then mark their worksheets again. Use the Numbered Heads participation strategy (TE, p. T36) to call on students to share their group's perspectives.

Vocabulary Builder
Preview Key Terms　L2

Pronounce each Key Term, then ask students to say the word with you. Provide a simple explanation such as, "In an authoritarian government, one person or a small group of people make all the decisions about how the country will be run."

Section 1

Democratic Republic of the Congo A Wealth of Possibilities

Prepare to Read

Objectives

In this section you will
1. Discover the physical geography and important natural resources of the Democratic Republic of the Congo.
2. Learn about the country's economic and political challenges since independence.
3. Find out how different groups and leaders have reshaped the nation.

Taking Notes

Copy the outline below. As you read this section, look for details about the geography, natural resources, economics, and politics of the Democratic Republic of the Congo. Use the outline to record your findings.

```
I. Physical geography and resources
   A. Geographic regions
      1. _____
      2. _____
   B. Natural resources
```

Target Reading Skill

Understand Sequence A sequence is the order in which a series of events occurs. Noting the sequence of important events can help you understand and remember the events. You can track a sequence of events by simply listing the events in the order in which they happened. As you read this section, list the sequence of events in Congo's political history.

Key Terms

- **authoritarian government** (uh thawr uh TEHR ee un GUV urn munt) *n.* a nondemocratic form of government in which a single leader or a small group of leaders has all the power
- **nationalize** (NASH uh nuh lyz) *v.* to transfer ownership of something to a nation's government

An open-pit copper mine in Congo

Copper has been mined in the present-day Democratic Republic of the Congo since ancient times. In the early 1900s, demand for copper brought Europeans to the area. In 1930, a mining company found copper in an area called Kolwezi (kohl WAY zee). The company built a mine and hired miners and a host of other workers. Soon a small city of workers' houses arose. Meanwhile, miners started to dig down into the earth for the copper. They found it, too—right beneath their houses.

The Kolwezi area proved so rich in copper that, at first, miners found they barely had to scratch the surface to find the mineral. As time went on, however, the miners had to dig deeper. Soon they had dug a huge pit in the ground. They built terraces along the sloping walls of the pit. Then they mined each terrace, in a process called open-pit mining. Miners still dig for copper at the Kolwezi mine today.

Target Reading Skill　L2

Understand Sequence Point out the Target Reading Skill. Tell students that recognizing the sequence of events can help them understand and remember them.

Model the skill by reading Natural Resources in Congo's History on p. 550 and placing the following events in order: (a) King Leopold II takes control of Congo; (b) the Portuguese arrive in the Congo region; (c) Kongo, Luba, and Lunda rule much of the Congo region. *(c, b, a)*

Give students *Identify Sequence*. Have them complete the activity in groups.

All in One **Africa Teaching Resources,** *Identify Sequence,* p. 395

Physical Geography and Resources

Since the 1930s, the Democratic Republic of the Congo has become one of the world's main sources of copper. Congo, as the country is often referred to, also has many other natural resources. These include gold, diamonds, forests, water, and wildlife. Congo's minerals and other resources have played an important role in the nation's history. (The country's neighbor, the Republic of the Congo, is also referred to as Congo. In this section, all references to Congo are to the Democratic Republic of the Congo.)

Geographic Regions The Democratic Republic of the Congo is Africa's third-largest country. It is equal in size to the area of the United States east of the Mississippi River. The country has four major geographic regions: the Congo basin, the northern uplands, the eastern highlands, and the southern uplands.

The Congo basin is covered by dense rain forest. Most Congolese (kahng guh LEEZ) live in the other three regions. The northern uplands, which run along the country's northern border, are covered in savanna. Grasslands and occasional thick forests spread across the eastern highlands. The southern uplands are high plains of grasslands and wooded areas. In each of these three regions, many people make a living as subsistence farmers.

Natural Resources About two thirds of Congo's people are farmers. However, mining produces most of the country's wealth. The Kolwezi and other huge copper deposits exist in the southern province of Katanga (kuh TAHNG guh). Congo is one of the top producers of diamonds in the world. It also has reserves of other valuable minerals such as gold. In addition, Congo has the potential to develop many hydroelectric plants. These are plants that use swiftly flowing river water to generate electricity.

Links to Science

From Water to Electricity
At a hydroelectric plant, electricity is generated by flowing water. For that reason, these plants are usually built at the bottom of a dam. Water that collects behind the dam flows through turbines, which change the energy of the moving water into electricity. The water is not used up in the process—it continues to flow and can be used again for agriculture and other purposes. A large hydroelectric dam (below) sits on Inga Falls, along the Congo River.

Vocabulary Builder

Use the information below to teach students this section's high-use words.

High-Use Word	Definition and Sample Sentence
potential, p. 549	*n.* something that can develop or become actual Rosa has the **potential** to become a great writer.
vow, p. 552	*v.* to promise John **vowed** to clean his room once a week.
erupt, p. 552	*v.* to become active suddenly Applause **erupted** in the auditorium after the class president's speech.
hostilities, p. 553	*n.* acts of war **Hostilities** continued until the countries signed a peace agreement.

Physical Geography and Resources L2

Guided Instruction

- **Vocabulary Builder** Clarify the high-use word **potential** before reading.

- Read Physical Geography and Resources using the Paragraph Shrinking strategy (TE, p. T34).

- Ask students to describe the vegetation that makes up the Democratic Republic of the Congo's four geographic regions. *(Congo basin—dense rain forest; northern uplands—savanna; eastern highlands—grasslands and some thick forests; southern uplands—high flat plains of grasslands and wooded areas)* **In which regions do most people live?** *(the northern uplands, eastern highlands, and southern uplands)*

- Ask students **Why do you think mining produces most of the country's wealth when most people work as farmers?** *(Possible answer: People are subsistence farmers; they farm to feed their families.)*

- Discuss how natural resources helped the kingdoms of Kongo, Luba, and Lunda become powerful. *(because they had fertile soil, plentiful rain, and they used iron to make tools that allowed people to farm more productively)*

Independent Practice

Have students create the Taking Notes graphic organizer on a blank piece of paper. Then have them fill in the details they learned about Congo's geography and natural resources. Display the *Outline* transparency and model how to record the first detail to get them started.

📖 **Africa Transparencies,** *Transparency B15: Outline*

Monitor Progress

As students fill in the outline, circulate and make sure individuals are choosing the correct details. Provide assistance as needed.

Links

Read the **Links to Science** on this page. Ask students to describe an advantage of using water to create electricity. *(Since the water is not used up in the process, it can be used again for other purposes.)*

Economic and Political Challenges

Guided Instruction

- Read about Joseph Mobutu and Congo's economic crisis in Economic and Political Challenges. As students read, circulate and make sure individuals can answer the Reading Check question.

- Ask students **Why did foreign companies in Congo help put Mobutu into power?** (*Various groups in Congo fought each other for power after independence. Foreign companies worried that their businesses would suffer as a result of the unrest. They thought if they put a strong ruler like Mobutu in control, their businesses would thrive.*)

- Ask students to explain why businesses nationalized by Mobutu failed. (*Many government officials who ran the businesses turned out to be poor managers. Some even stole the profits from their companies.*)

- Ask students **What did Mobutu rename Congo?** (*Zaire, a word that has traditional African roots*)

- Discuss the reason why relying on copper for much of its wealth hurt Zaire in the 1970s. (*When world copper prices fell, Zaire earned less money and the economy collapsed. This led Mobutu to cut back government spending, which caused hardship for the poor.*)

Independent Practice

Have students continue to fill in their outlines with details on Congo's economy and government.

Monitor Progress

Circulate to make sure students are structuring their outlines correctly. Help students as needed.

Natural Resources in Congo's History Natural resources have dominated much of the history of the Democratic Republic of the Congo. For example, by the 1400s, the kingdoms of Kongo, Luba, and Lunda ruled much of the area. These kingdoms became powerful largely because they had fertile soil and plentiful rain and their people made iron tools that enabled them to farm more productively. Similarly, when the Portuguese arrived in the area in the 1480s, they came in search of a natural resource—gold.

Some 400 years later, during the scramble for Africa, King Leopold II of Belgium took control of present-day Congo. He ruled brutally, forcing Africans to harvest wild rubber without paying them. Belgium grew wealthy while Africans suffered, starved, and died, probably by the millions. Later, because of an international campaign to end Leopold's abuses, the Belgian government ruled less harshly. But it maintained its interest in Congo's resources, especially its copper and diamonds.

√ **Reading Check** Which industry produces most of Congo's wealth?

Economic and Political Challenges

In spite of its abundant natural resources, the Democratic Republic of the Congo has faced major economic and political challenges. During the 1900s, both the economy and the government of Congo faced a series of crises.

Congo Gains Independence As you have read, calls for independence echoed throughout the African continent during the mid-1900s. In 1960, the Democratic Republic of the Congo won its independence from Belgium. However, Congo's first years as an independent country proved to be difficult.

Celebrating Independence
At a celebration of the country's independence in 1960, boys carry the flag of the newly formed Democratic Republic of the Congo.
Predict *How do you think Congolese people felt when their country gained independence?*

550 Africa

Belgium had done little to prepare Congo for self-rule. In addition, various groups fought one another for power. The foreign companies that controlled Congo's mines feared the unrest would hurt business. In 1965, these foreign companies helped a military leader, Joseph Mobutu (muh BOO too), take power. With a strong ruler in control, they thought their businesses would thrive.

Differentiated Instruction

For English Language Learners L2
Pair students with native English speakers to read the Links to Science on p. 549.

Then have the students work together to draw a rough diagram showing the process of turning water into electricity.

Answers

√ **Reading Check** mining
Predict Possible answer: They probably felt tremendous pride and happiness.

Mobutu Makes Changes Mobutu tried to restore order in the country by setting up an **authoritarian government**—a nondemocratic form of government in which a single leader or small group of leaders has all the power. He also tried to cut ties with the colonial past. First, he renamed the country Zaire (zah IHR), a word that has traditional African roots. And he took on a new name for himself, Mobutu Sese Seko (muh BOO too SAY say SAY koh), which he considered more traditionally African. Then he nationalized foreign-owned industries. To **nationalize** is to transfer ownership to the government.

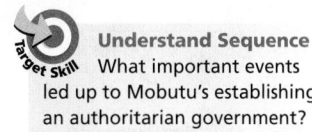

Understand Sequence What important events led up to Mobutu's establishing an authoritarian government?

Target Reading Skill   L2

Understand Sequence As a follow up, ask students to answer the Target Reading Skill question in the Student Edition. (*Congo gained independence and foreign companies helped Mobutu take power.*)

COUNTRY PROFILE
Focus on **Economics**

Guided Instruction
Ask students to study the Country Profile on this page. Remind them to read the map key to help them understand what the map shows. Also encourage them to study the chart and graph carefully and think about the information each provides. As a class, answer the Map and Chart Skills questions. Allow students to briefly discuss their responses with a partner before sharing answers.

Independent Practice
Ask students to synthesize the information in the Country Profile and what they learned from reading the section to write a few sentences answering the following question: **Why do you think Congo exports a majority of its goods to Belgium?** (*Answers will vary, but students should explain that Belgium controlled Congo from the late 1800s to 1960. During that time, it controlled Congo's valuable resources, which include gold and diamonds. Belgium probably remained interested in Congo's resources after the country gained independence.*)

COUNTRY PROFILE
Focus on **Economics**

Democratic Republic of the Congo

Congo's natural resources play a key role in its economy. The country's total earnings from exports in 2002 were around $1.2 billion. Minerals alone made up about 85 percent of those earnings, as they have in most recent years. Most of the economy's diversity comes from the variety of minerals produced. However, Congo does not use all of its natural resources. Thus, the country has potential for greater economic success. Study the map and charts to learn more about Congo's natural resources and economy.

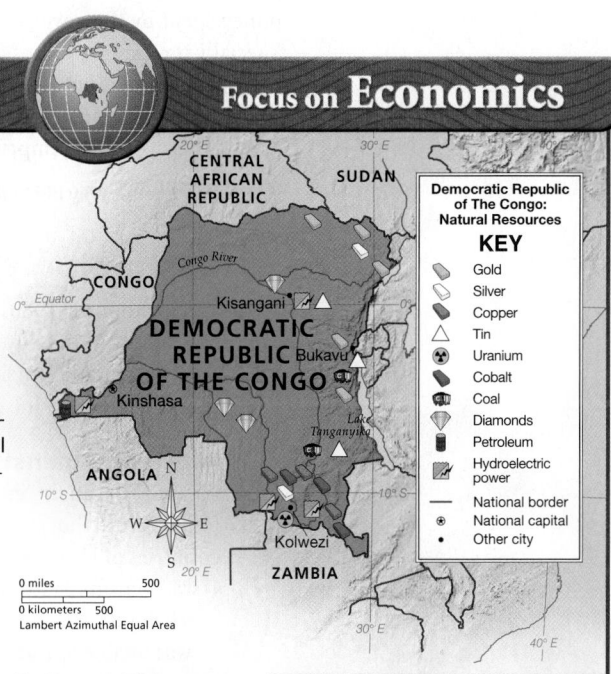

Democratic Republic of The Congo: Natural Resources

KEY
- Gold
- Silver
- Copper
- Tin
- Uranium
- Cobalt
- Coal
- Diamonds
- Petroleum
- Hydroelectric power
- ——— National border
- ⊛ National capital
- • Other city

0 miles 500
0 kilometers 500
Lambert Azimuthal Equal Area

Export Destinations

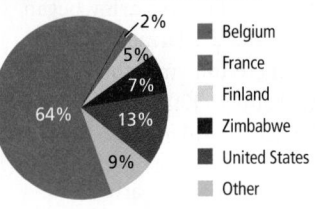

- Belgium 64%
- France 13%
- Finland 9%
- Zimbabwe 7%
- United States 5%
- Other 2%

SOURCE: DK World Desk Reference

Estimated Income From Mining, 2001

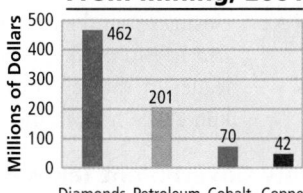

Mineral	Millions of Dollars
Diamonds	462
Petroleum	201
Cobalt	70
Copper	42

SOURCE: The Economist Intelligence Unit's *Country Profile 2003*

Map and Chart Skills

1. **Name** Which two countries buy most of Congo's exports?
2. **Identify** Which mineral earns the most income for Congo?
3. **Infer** How does the map support the idea that Congo has greater potential for using its natural resources?

 Use Web Code **lae-5701** for **DK World Desk Reference Online.**

— Background: Daily Life —

Congolese Cuisine The Congolese diet includes many foods that are grown in the country, such as yams, cassava, peanuts, rice, beans, sweet potatoes, corn, and bananas. People also import a lot of food, including most of their chicken and beef and some grains. The most popular Congolese dish is called *moambé*. It is a stew made of peanuts, palm oil, and chicken. The Congolese usually serve it with yams, rice, or *fufu*, which is mashed cassava.

Answers

Map and Chart Skills
1. Belgium and the United States
2. diamonds
3. The map shows that Congo has a variety of resources that would be valuable if developed for trade.

Go Online PHSchool.com Students can find additional useful information about this topic on the DK World Desk Reference Online.

Mobutu also borrowed money from foreign countries, such as the United States, for projects to improve Zaire's economy. But most of Mobutu's economic moves failed. Many government officials who ran the nationalized companies proved to be poor managers. Others stole their companies' profits. Mobutu and his supporters, too, kept much of Zaire's wealth for themselves.

Crisis In the mid-1970s, the world price of copper fell sharply. Suddenly Zaire was earning less and less from its major export. It could not pay back the money it had borrowed, and the economy quickly collapsed. Mobutu responded by cutting the amount of money spent by the government. The cutbacks caused hardship, especially for Zaire's poorest people. Fewer jobs were available, so many people could not earn a living. When political groups challenged Mobutu's policies, Mobutu crushed their efforts. He had many of his opponents imprisoned or killed.

✓ **Reading Check** Why did Mobutu change the country's name?

Reshaping the Nation

Throughout the 1980s, Mobutu ruled harshly, and Zaire's economy continually declined. Calls for reform came from inside and outside the country. In the early 1990s, Mobutu's grip on the country finally began to weaken.

Rebellion Against Government In 1996, a minor uprising began in eastern Zaire. A small ethnic group fought with the government's troops. The neighboring countries of Uganda, Rwanda, and Burundi supported the small group. With their help, the uprising turned into a rebellion against Mobutu's government. Zaire's army was unable to put down the rebellion.

Within months, the rebels gained control of much of eastern Zaire. By May 1997, the rebel army began closing in on the capital, Kinshasa. Alarmed, Mobutu fled to Morocco. He died there four months later. A leader of the rebel army, Laurent Kabila (law RAHN kuh BEEL uh), became the new president.

Showing Culture in Currency
The upper bill was printed while the name of the country was Zaire. The lower bill was printed after the name became the Democratic Republic of the Congo. **Analyze Images** What aspects of the Congo are represented by the images on these bills?

A New Government Takes Hold The rebel army soon controlled the whole country, which Kabila renamed the Democratic Republic of the Congo. Kabila vowed to establish a new constitution and hold national elections. But months went by without the promised reforms. Criticism quickly erupted. By early 1998, popular support for the new government was fading.

552 Africa

Reshaping the Nation L2

Guided Instruction

- **Vocabulary Builder** Clarify the high-use words **vow, erupt,** and **hostilities** before reading.

- Read Reshaping the Nation with students.

- Discuss how Mobutu was removed from power. *(A rebellion against Mobutu's government began in eastern Zaire with the help of Rwanda, Uganda, and Burundi. The rebel army gained strength and began closing in on the capital. Mobutu fled to Morocco, where he later died.)*

- Ask students to compare and contrast the rule of Laurent Kabila with that of Joseph Kabila. *(Both promised reforms, but Laurent did not follow through while Joseph implemented programs to improve the economy and the government.)*

Independent Practice
Have students complete their outlines with information about Congo's government.

Monitor Progress
- Show *Section Reading Support Transparency AF 53* and ask students to check their graphic organizers individually. Go over key concepts and clarify key vocabulary as needed.

  📖 **Africa Transparencies,** *Section Reading Support Transparency AF 53*

- Tell students to fill in the last column of their *Reading Readiness Guides.* Probe for what they learned that confirms or invalidates each statement.

  All in One Africa Teaching Resources, *Reading Readiness Guide,* p. 388

Answers

✓ **Reading Check** to cut ties with the colonial past

Analyze Images The one on top has a picture of an important figure, probably Mobutu; both bills show wild animals that live in the country.

Skills for Life **Skills Mini Lesson**

Recognizing Bias and Propaganda
1. Explain that bias is a one-sided, or slanted, point of view. Family, culture, or location can influence a person's point of view. Tell students it is important to identify bias to avoid getting an incomplete or incorrect view of a topic.
2. Help students practice the skill by telling them to suppose the following statement was made by a government official appointed by Laurent Kabila: "Laurent Kabila was one of the most effective leaders in Congo's history." Ask students to determine if the statement is biased. *(The statement is biased.)*
3. Apply the skill by asking students to explain how they know the statement above contains bias.

A Second Rebellion In August 1998, another armed rebellion began, this time against Kabila's government. Supported by Uganda and Rwanda, the new rebels threatened to overthrow the government. Angola, Namibia, and Zimbabwe backed Kabila's government. The civil war continued month after month.

Peace and Reform The war in Congo was the first war in post-independence Africa to involve several African nations. In July 1999, the heads of six of these countries met in Zambia to write a peace agreement. However, neither side fulfilled the agreement. Hostilities continued into 2001, when Kabila was killed. His son, Joseph Kabila, became president.

The younger Kabila began making significant reforms. He implemented programs to revive the economy. He replaced many corrupt government officials with well-trained officials. He also allowed the United Nations to send peacekeeping troops to Congo. By the end of 2002, many of the disagreements over the terms of peace had been settled. However, small conflicts did continue in the eastern part of the country. Congo has found that the path to peace is neither smooth nor easy.

Rwandan President Paul Kagame (left) and Joseph Kabila sign peace agreements in 2002.

✓ **Reading Check** How was Congo's civil war unique for Africa?

Section 1 Assessment

Key Terms
Review the key terms at the beginning of this section. Use each term in a sentence that explains its meaning.

⊙ **Target Reading Skill**
Place these events in the correct order: Joseph Kabila becomes president, a rebellion begins, a peace agreement is written.

Comprehension and Critical Thinking
1. (a) List What are some of Congo's natural resources?

(b) Analyze Information What role have these resources played in Congo's history?
2. (a) Describe What changes did Joseph Mobutu make in Congo?
(b) Evaluate What factors prevented Mobutu from bringing stability to Congo?
3. (a) Recall What caused Mobutu to flee the country?
(b) Summarize Once Laurent Kabila became president, how did the civil war in Congo change?
(c) Draw Conclusions In what ways has Joseph Kabila brought positive change to Congo?

Writing Activity
Suppose you are an editor for a newspaper. Write an editorial explaining the challenges Congo has faced and predicting how the country will overcome those challenges once peace returns to the nation.

> **Writing Tip** Be sure to state the opinion you are explaining in your editorial. Then use details to support your opinion.

Assess Progress L2
Have students complete the Section Assessment. Administer the *Section Quiz*.

🔲 **Africa Teaching Resources,** *Section Quiz*, p. 390

Reteach L1
If students need more instruction, have them read this section in the Reading and Vocabulary Study Guide.

📖 Chapter 17, Section 1, **Eastern Hemisphere Reading and Vocabulary Study Guide,** pp. 188–190

Extend L3
Have students work together to complete the *Small Group Activity: Musical Instruments of Central and Southern Africa* to learn more about the culture of the region. Group students of varying abilities together.

🔲 **Africa Teaching Resources,** *Small Group Activity: Musical Instruments of Central and Southern Africa*, pp. 400–403

Answer

✓ **Reading Check** It was the first war in post-independence Africa to involve multiple African countries.

Writing Activity
Use the *Rubric for Assessing a Writing Assignment* to evaluate students' editorials.

🔲 **Africa Teaching Resources,** *Rubric for Assessing a Writing Assignment*, p. 411

Section 1 Assessment

Key Terms
Students' sentences should reflect knowledge of each Key Term.

⊙ **Target Reading Skill**
A rebellion begins; Joseph Kabila becomes president; a peace agreement is written.

Comprehension and Critical Thinking
1. (a) gold, diamonds, copper, water for hydroelectricity **(b)** Those who have ruled Africa have always been interested in the country's natural resources.

2. (a) He changed the name of the country to Zaire, nationalized industries that had been owned by foreign countries, and borrowed money from foreign countries to start projects to improve the economy. **(b)** the ineffectiveness of his economic programs and the fall of world copper prices

3. (a) A rebel army that opposed Mobutu began closing in on the capital. **(b)** Other African countries began to get involved in the civil war. **(c)** He has implemented programs to improve the economy, removed corrupt government officials from office, and worked for peace.

Objective

Learn how to analyze primary sources.

Prepare to Read

Build Background Knowledge   L2

Tell students that in this lesson they will learn what a primary source is and how to analyze it. Ask students to suggest sources they would use to gather information for a report on Joseph Kabila. Guide them to list both primary and secondary sources. Explain that you will refer back to the list after completing this lesson and identify which sources are primary and which are secondary.

Instruct

Analyzing Primary Sources   L2

Guided Instruction

- Read the steps to analyze primary sources. Summarize each step and write it on the board.

- Practice the skill by using the steps on p. 555 to analyze the Nelson Mandela quotation. Identify the speaker and when the quotation was spoken *(Nelson Mandela; 1994)*. Point out that this is a primary source because it is first-hand information.

- Identify the main idea. *(South Africa is now a nation in which all people have a say.)* Determine whether the statement is mostly fact or opinion *(mostly opinion)*. Decide if the statement is biased. *(The statement may be considered biased because Mandela has a definite point of view. The statement may be considered unbiased because his words must have seemed accurate to South Africans.)* Point out that the statement would be useful for writing both a history of South Africa and a biography of Nelson Mandela.

Analyzing Primary Sources

You have probably played the "telephone game." One person makes up a statement and whispers it to the next person. That person whispers it to the next person, and so on. As the statement is passed along, people do not always hear it correctly and it gets confused. By the end, it might not make any sense. If a sentence can get distorted in a matter of minutes, think what can happen to a sentence uttered by someone hundreds of years ago! That is one reason why primary sources are important.

Examples of primary sources

A primary source is information that comes directly from the person who wrote it, said it, or created it. Diaries, photographs, speeches, and recordings are all examples of primary sources. When information does not come directly from the person who created it, it is a secondary source. Newspapers, history books, and Web sites are examples of secondary sources.

Learn the Skill

Use the steps below to analyze a primary source.

1. **Identify who created the information, when it was created, and why.** Before you use any information, determine the source. Is it a primary source?

2. **Identify the main idea.** Make sure you understand what is being communicated, either in words or in visual form.

3. **Separate facts from opinions.** Facts can be proved or disproved. Opinions indicate personal feelings or judgments. A primary source might contain facts and opinions, and both can be valuable.

4. **Look for evidence of bias, or a one-sided view.** If a person's view is biased, it is influenced by certain factors, such as the person's family, culture, or location.

5. **Evaluate whether the source is reliable and whether it suits your purpose.** For factual evidence, you want a primary source that is believable and accurate. For an opinion, you want one that uses good reasoning.

554 Africa

Independent Practice

Assign *Skills for Life* and have students complete it individually.

All in One **Africa Teaching Resources,** *Skills for Life*, p. 399

Monitor Progress

As students are completing *Skills for Life*, circulate to make sure students are correctly applying the skill steps. Provide assistance as needed.

Practice the Skill

Use the steps below to analyze the source in the box.

1 Read the background information and the quotation. Who is the speaker, and when did he speak these words? Is the quotation a primary source?

2 Write a sentence that summarizes Mandela's main point. What situation is he discussing?

3 Using the background information, identify as many facts and opinions as possible. Overall, is this quotation mostly fact or mostly opinion?

4 Do any parts of Mandela's statement show bias?

5 Would this source be of value if you were writing a history of South Africa? A biography of Nelson Mandela? Explain.

> In 1994, democratic elections were held in South Africa for the first time. Never before had all South Africans been allowed to vote. After casting his vote, the man who would be elected president, Nelson Mandela, made this statement:
>
> "This is for all South Africans an unforgettable occasion. It is the realization of hopes and dreams that we have cherished over decades. . . . We are starting a new era of hope, reconciliation [coming together] and nation building. We sincerely hope that by the mere casting of a vote the results will give hope to all South Africans and make all South Africans realize this is our country. We are one nation."
>
> —*Nelson Mandela, April 1994*

Two women in Johannesburg, South Africa, proudly display the identification papers needed for voting in the historic 1994 election.

Apply the Skill

Read the quotation from the South African constitution on page 556.
Follow the steps for analyzing a primary source and answer these questions:
1. What makes the quotation a primary source?
2. What is the main idea?
3. Is the information mostly fact or mostly opinion? Explain.
4. Is the information biased? Explain.
5. For what purpose might you use this source?

Chapter 17 **555**

Assess and Reteach

Assess Progress `L2`
Ask students to do the Apply the Skill activity.

Reteach `L1`
If students are having trouble applying the skill steps, have them review the skill using the Social Studies Skills Tutor CD-ROM.

Analyzing Primary and Secondary Sources, **Social Studies Skills Tutor CD-ROM**

Extend `L3`
- First, have students return to the list of sources they made on the board prior to completing the lesson. Ask them to identify whether each source is primary or secondary.

- Next, tell students to find another primary source in the Student Edition and use the skill steps to analyze it. Allow them to share their work with a partner before turning it in.

Answers
Apply the Skill

1. It is a direct quote from South Africa's constitution.

2. Although some groups have suffered injustices in the past, South Africa now belongs to all the people who live there.

3. Mostly opinion; words such as "believe" indicate an opinion. But, the opinions are based on facts—you can prove that injustices were suffered, people fought for freedom, and many South Africans support the equality of all groups who live there.

4. The information may be considered biased because the people who wrote it had a definite point of view.

5. Possible answer: a report on the changes that took place when apartheid ended in South Africa.

Chapter 17 **555**

Objectives

Social Studies

1. Understand how white rule in South Africa began.
2. Learn about the system of apartheid.
3. Find out how South Africans built a new nation after apartheid.

Reading/Language Arts

Learn how to recognize words and phrases that signal the order in which events took place.

Prepare to Read

Build Background Knowledge L2

Tell students that in this section they will learn how white rule began in South Africa and the struggle for equality among blacks and whites. Lead a discussion on the civil rights movement that took place in the United States. Use the Give One, Get One participation strategy (TE, p. T37) to elicit students' prior knowledge of the movement. List the information they provide on the board.

Set a Purpose for Reading L2

■ Preview the Objectives.

■ Form students into pairs or groups of four. Distribute the *Reading Readiness Guide.* Ask the students to fill in the first two columns of the chart. Use the Numbered Heads participation strategy (TE, p. T36) to call on students to share one piece of information they already know and one piece of information they want to know.

All in One **Africa Teaching Resources,**
Reading Readiness Guide, p. 392

Vocabulary Builder
Preview Key Terms L2

Pronounce each Key Term, then ask students to say the word with you. Provide a simple explanation such as, "During apartheid, the white government of South Africa discriminated against blacks by not allowing them to have certain jobs or live in certain neighborhoods."

Prepare to Read

Objectives

In this section you will
1. Understand how white rule in South Africa began.
2. Learn about the system of apartheid.
3. Find out how South Africans built a new nation after apartheid.

Taking Notes

As you read this section, look for details about South Africa before, during, and after apartheid. Copy the chart below, and use to it to record your findings.

South Africa		
Before Apartheid	**During Apartheid**	**After Apartheid**
• •	• •	• •

 Target Reading Skill

Recognize Words That Signal Sequence

Signal words point out relationships among ideas or events. To help keep the order of events clear as you read, look for words like *after, then,* and *in 1994* that signal the order in which events took place.

Key Terms

• **apartheid** (uh PAHR tayt) *n.* the legal system of South Africa in which the rights of nonwhites were greatly restricted

• **discriminate** (dih SKRIM ih nayt) *v.* to treat people differently, and often unfairly, based on race, religion, or sex

• **Nelson Mandela** (NEL sun man DEL uh) *n.* black leader of the African National Congress and South Africa's first president after apartheid ended

A choir celebrates the new constitution.

"" We, the people of South Africa,
Recognize the injustices of our past;
Honour those who suffered for justice and
    freedom in our land;
Respect those who have worked to build and
    develop our country; and
Believe that South Africa belongs to all who live
    in it, united in our diversity. ""

—*Preamble to the South African Constitution*

So begins the constitution of South Africa. It was written in 1996, soon after nearly a century of harsh and unequal treatment of nonwhite South Africans had officially ended. The constitution's words were shaped by South Africans who came from many backgrounds and political parties. As a result, the 1996 constitution represents all South Africans in a new, democratic South Africa.

556 Africa

Target Reading Skill L2

Recognize Words That Signal Sequence Point out the Target Reading Skill. Tell students that signal words can show them the order in which events took place.

Model the skill by reading the Building a New Nation paragraph on p. 559 and pointing out the sequence signal words and phrases. *(since the 1950s, in 1962, after 28 years, in 1990, in April 1994)*

Give students *Recognize Sequence Signal Words.* Have them complete the activity in groups.

All in One **Africa Teaching Resources,**
Recognize Sequence Signal Words, p. 396

Beginning of White Rule

People have lived in present-day South Africa for thousands of years. In 1652, the first white Europeans arrived in the region and set up a colony. These Dutch settlers called themselves Boers (bohrz), the Dutch word for farmers. As you read in Chapter 13, the descendants of these settlers called themselves Afrikaners. They spoke a language related to Dutch, called Afrikaans.

British and French settlers arrived in South Africa by the late 1700s. For years, black South Africans fought the white settlers, who took their land. But by the late 1800s, the white settlers had forced the Africans off the best land.

Cultures Clash The Afrikaners founded their own states. After diamonds and gold were discovered there, the British wanted control of the land. British prospectors, or people who explore for minerals, pushed Afrikaners off their farms.

The British and Afrikaners fought over the Afrikaner land from 1899 to 1902. The British proved victorious and took control of the Afrikaner states. In 1910, the British created the Union of South Africa by unifying all the land they controlled in the region.

Unequal Treatment The white-led government of the Union of South Africa passed several laws to keep land and wealth in white hands. For example, the government declared that blacks could live and own land in only 8 percent of the country. Blacks could work in white areas, but for very low wages. Other laws passed in the 1920s separated white and black workers. The best jobs and the highest wages were reserved for whites.

√ **Reading Check** When did the first white Europeans arrive in present-day South Africa?

System of Apartheid

The British granted independence to South Africa in 1931. But in 1948, the Afrikaners took political control of the country from the English-speaking whites when the Afrikaner political party, the National Party, won the election.

New Laws Take Hold The new Afrikaner leaders named the system of treating whites and nonwhites by different rules **apartheid** (uh PAHR tayt). In Afrikaans, the word *apartheid* means "apartness." Apartheid laws made it legal to discriminate on the basis of race. To **discriminate** means to treat people differently, and often unfairly, based on race, religion, or sex.

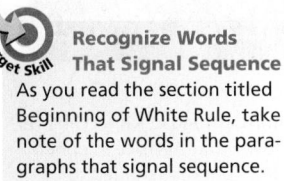

Recognize Words That Signal Sequence
As you read the section titled Beginning of White Rule, take note of the words in the paragraphs that signal sequence.

Keeping People Apart
In this image from the apartheid era, a man sits on a bench designated for Europeans (white South Africans) only. **Analyze Images** *How does this image illustrate discrimination?*

Chapter 17 Section 2 **557**

Target Reading Skill

As a follow up, ask students to perform the Target Reading Skill task in the Student Edition. (*for thousands of years, in 1652, by the late 1700s, for years, by the late 1800s, from 1899 to 1902, in 1910, in the 1920s*)

Instruct

Beginning of White Rule

Guided Instruction

- **Vocabulary Builder** Clarify the high-use words **unify** and **reserve** before reading.

- Read Beginning of White Rule using the Structured Silent Reading strategy (TE, p. T34).

- Ask students **Who are the Afrikaners?** (*descendants of South Africa's Dutch settlers*) Ask students to describe the struggle between the Afrikaners and the British. (*Gold and diamonds were found in Afrikaner states. The British fought the Afrikaners for control of this land. The British won and established the Union of South Africa.*)

- Ask **Why did the government pass laws that discriminated against blacks?** (*The government was run by whites who wanted to keep land and wealth under the control of white people.*)

Independent Practice

Have students create the Taking Notes graphic organizer on a separate piece of paper. Ask them to fill in the Before Apartheid column with the information they just learned. Briefly model how to choose the correct details.

Monitor Progress

Circulate to make sure students are choosing the correct details. Provide assistance as needed.

Answers

Analyze Images The sign on the bench says "For Europeans Only," so blacks were not allowed to sit there.

√ **Reading Check** in 1652

Vocabulary Builder

Use the information below to teach students this section's high-use words.

High-Use Word	Definition and Sample Sentence
unify, p. 557	*v.* to unite or make into one unit The people of the neighborhood **unified** to fight local crime.
reserve, p. 557	*v.* to set aside The school **reserves** a parking space for the school nurse.
pressure, p. 559	*n.* an urgent demand Under **pressure** from his teachers, Billy began to study more.
model, p. 560	*n.* an example for imitation Sandra's good behavior served as a **model** for the rest of the class.

Read the **Citizen Heroes** on this page. Ask **How did Biko help fight against apartheid?** *(He taught that black South Africans had to view themselves as equal to whites in order to gain freedom.)*

System of Apartheid

Building a New Nation [L2]

Guided Instruction

- **Vocabulary Builder** Clarify the high-use words **pressure** and **model** before reading.

- Read System of Apartheid and Building a New Nation as a class. As students read, circulate to make sure that individuals can answer the Reading Check questions.

- Ask students to describe apartheid laws. *(They separated South Africans into groups based on race and denied rights to people who were not white.)*

- Discuss the effects apartheid had on the lives of black South Africans. *(They were forced to live on infertile land and were often poor; they had no citizenship rights; they were forced to work in low-paying jobs and attend poor schools; they were barred from white restaurants and hospitals.)*

- Ask **How did Mandela help to build a more equal nation in South Africa?** *(His government helped create new opportunities for blacks and wrote a constitution that protected the rights of all citizens.)*

Independent Practice

Ask students to complete the graphic organizer by adding details about South Africa during and after apartheid.

Monitor Progress

- Show *Section Reading Support Transparency AF 54* and ask students to check their graphic organizers individually. Go over key concepts and clarify key vocabulary as needed.

  📖 **Africa Transparencies,** *Section Reading Support Transparency AF 54*

- Tell students to fill in the last column of their *Reading Readiness Guides.*

Answers

 Reading Check Some South African protestors were killed and many were imprisoned.

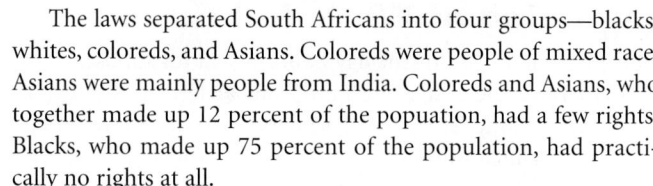

Citizen Heroes

Stephen Biko

Born in 1946 in King William's Town, South Africa, Stephen Biko (BEE koh) studied to become a doctor. Instead, he became a South African hero as a leader of the struggle against apartheid. Biko taught that black South Africans could only become free of white rule if they viewed themselves as equal to whites. His ideas influenced thousands of students and adults throughout South Africa. The white-led government imprisoned Biko for his actions. He died in jail in 1977.

In 1993, Nelson Mandela (left) and F. W. de Klerk (right) together won the Nobel Peace Prize for helping end apartheid.

558 Africa

The laws separated South Africans into four groups—blacks, whites, coloreds, and Asians. Coloreds were people of mixed race. Asians were mainly people from India. Coloreds and Asians, who together made up 12 percent of the popuation, had a few rights. Blacks, who made up 75 percent of the population, had practically no rights at all.

Effects of Apartheid Apartheid affected every aspect of the lives of black South Africans. It forced thousands of them to move to ten poor, rural, all-black areas called homelands. These homelands had the driest and least fertile land in the country. There, blacks lived in poverty. Apartheid also strengthened existing laws that required all blacks to stay in homelands unless they could prove that whites would benefit from hiring them.

In addition, apartheid denied blacks citizenship rights, including the right to vote. The system kept blacks, coloreds, and Asians in low-paying jobs and put them in poor schools. It barred these groups from white restaurants, schools, and hospitals. In short, apartheid kept whites in control of the country.

Struggle to End Apartheid Many South Africans fought apartheid. Starting in the 1950s, blacks and some whites led peaceful protests against it. Over the following decades, South Africa's police met the protesters with deadly force many times. Thousands of men, women, and children were wounded, killed, or imprisoned. Protests, even peaceful ones, were banned. But the demonstrations continued. Many people were willing to risk everything for freedom.

In the 1970s, countries around the world joined the movement against apartheid. Many nations stopped trading with South Africa or lending it money. South Africa's athletes were banned from the Olympic Games. In 1990, these international pressures began to have an effect. F. W. de Klerk, an Afrikaner who was South Africa's president, led the government in abolishing the apartheid laws.

Legally ending apartheid was a major accomplishment. But much work lay ahead to make a reality of legal equality. In 1994, **Nelson Mandela** became South Africa's first black president and the leader who would fight to create a new, more equal system.

✓ **Reading Check** What happened to South Africans who protested against apartheid?

Skills for Life Skills Mini Lesson

Analyzing Images

1. Explain that in order to analyze images, students should identify who and what the image shows, the general feelings they get from it, and who created the image and why.

2. Have students practice the skill by identifying what the image on p. 557 shows,

the general feeling they get from it, and why the photographer may have taken this photograph.

3. Have students apply the skill by analyzing the image on p. 558.

South Africa

South Africa is home to more than 45 million people, and there is a great deal of diversity among them. Numerous black ethnic groups make up almost 90 percent of the population. Of these groups, the Zulu and the Xhosa are the largest. The white population includes people of British, Dutch, German, French, and Portuguese descent. Other South Africans are of Asian descent. Study the map and charts to learn more about the people of South Africa.

Urban and Rural Population

Rural 42%
Urban 58%

SOURCE: The 2003 Revision Population Database

Ethnic Groups*

3%
9%
10%
79%

- Black African
- White
- Other Black
- Indian/Asian

SOURCE: *CIA World Factbook*

*Numbers may not equal 100% due to rounding.

South Africa: Population Density

KEY

Persons per sq. mile	Persons per sq. kilometer
More than 519	More than 199
260–519	100–199
130–259	50–99
25–129	10–49
1–24	1–9
Less than 1	Less than 1

Urban Areas

⊙ 1,000,000–4,999,999
· 250,000–999,999
— National border

(Map labels: BOTSWANA, Tropic of Capricorn, NAMIBIA, MOZAMBIQUE, Pretoria, Tembisa, Johannesburg, Benoni, Soweto, SWAZILAND, Vereeniging, Welkom, Boksburg, Kimberley, Bloemfontein, LESOTHO, Durban, SOUTH AFRICA, INDIAN OCEAN, Mossel Bay, Cape Town, Port Elizabeth, ATLANTIC OCEAN)

0 miles 400
0 kilometers 400
Lambert Azimuthal Equal Area

Map and Chart Skills

1. **Identify** What single ethnic group makes up the largest part of South Africa's population?
2. **Synthesize** Based on the graph, is the population of South Africa mostly rural, mostly urban, or almost evenly divided between rural and urban? How does the information given on the map support this?

Go **Online** PHSchool.com

Use Web Code **lae-5702** for **DK World Desk Reference Online.**

Building a New Nation

Since the 1950s, Mandela had been a leader of the African National Congress (ANC), South Africa's first black-led political party. The ANC had long fought for full voting rights for all South Africans. In 1962, Mandela was sent to prison for life for fighting apartheid. After 28 years of public pressure, de Klerk freed Mandela in 1990. Mandela then became president of the ANC. In April 1994, for the first time, all South Africans were allowed to vote. Mandela and the ANC easily won the presidency.

Learn more about the history of apartheid.

Chapter 17 Section 2 **559**

Guided Instruction

Ask students to study the Country Profile on this page. Encourage them to study the map and graphs carefully to see what information they provide. As a class, answer the Map and Chart Skills questions. Allow students to briefly discuss their responses with a partner before sharing answers.

Independent Practice

Have students use the information from the introduction, circle graphs, and maps to write a paragraph describing the characteristics of South Africa's population.

Show students *South Africa: Apartheid's Legacy.* Ask **How was apartheid harmful to South Africa?** (*Students may say that equal education, health care, and opportunities for a better life were not available to all South Africans under apartheid. Today, many people in South Africa are still unemployed, and a large number of blacks continue to live in poverty.*)

Answers

Map and Chart Skills

1. Black African
2. The population is almost evenly divided between urban and rural. The map shows that the population density of urban and rural areas is roughly equal.

Go **Online** PHSchool.com Students can find additional useful information about this topic on the DK World Desk Reference Online.

Assess and Reteach

Assess Progress
L2

Have students complete the Section Assessment. Administer the *Section Quiz*.

All in One **Africa Teaching Resources,**
Section Quiz, p. 394

Reteach
L1

If students need more instruction, have them read this section in the Reading and Vocabulary Study Guide.

Chapter 17, Section 2, **Eastern Hemisphere Reading and Vocabulary Study Guide,** pp. 191–193

Extend
L3

Have students complete the *Enrichment* activity to learn more about the culture of one of South Africa's ethnic groups—the Zulu.

All in One **Africa Teaching Resources,**
Enrichment, p. 398

Answer

✓ **Reading Check** It was the first time all South Africans were allowed to vote.

Section 2 Assessment

Key Terms
Students' sentences should reflect knowledge of each Key Term.

Target Reading Skill
Starting in the 1950s, over the following decades, in the 1970s, in 1990, began, in 1994.

Comprehension and Critical Thinking
1. (a) The British, the French, and the Dutch **(b)** In both clashes, two groups were fighting each other for control of South Africa.

2. (a) Apartheid separated South Africans into four groups—whites, blacks, coloreds and Asians. The system made it legal for whites to discriminate against the other three groups and gave those groups few rights. **(b)** Possible answer: The groups that were discriminated against had so few rights and were so disadvantaged that it took time for their movement to succeed.

3. (a) Protests by South Africans and pressure from other countries finally led President F.W. de Klerk to pass laws ending apartheid. **(b)** Possible answer: Because the country had been harshly ruled by whites for so long, people may have been fearful that a

Today, South Africans of all races attend school together.

New Challenges Blacks and some whites welcomed the end of apartheid. In some ways, however, South Africa has remained a divided society. For example, blacks and whites usually live in different neighborhoods, and whites control most of the country's biggest businesses. Still, new opportunities have been created for millions of blacks, and tensions have eased. Mandela's government proved it was committed to helping all citizens, regardless of race. In fact, the constitution that Mandela's government wrote in 1996 is considered a world model for human rights.

Democracy Continues In June 1999, South Africa held its second election in which all South Africans were free to vote. Mandela retired, and Thabo Mbeki (TAH boh em BEK ee), also a long-term leader of the ANC, became South Africa's next president. With the equality movement set into motion by Mandela, Mbeki has been able to focus on other important issues as well. He has put great energy into improving the economic situations of all South Africans. In addition, he has continued to strengthen South Africa's new, democratic government. Mbeki was reelected in 2004.

✓ **Reading Check** What was unique about the 1994 election?

Section 2 Assessment

Key Terms
Review the key terms at the beginning of this section. Use each term in a sentence that explains its meaning.

Target Reading Skill
Review the section titled Struggle to End Apartheid on page 558. Find the words that signal the sequence of events that helped end apartheid.

Comprehension and Critical Thinking
1. (a) Name Which groups of white Europeans settled in present-day South Africa?

(b) Compare How was the clash between white settlers and black South Africans similar to the clash between the white groups?
2. (a) Describe Describe the system of apartheid.
(b) Draw Conclusions What do you think it was about the system of apartheid that made the struggle to end it take so long?
3. (a) Explain How did apartheid finally end?
(b) Analyze Information Why do you think South Africans chose someone who was black as their first president after apartheid?

Writing Activity
Suppose you live in South Africa. Write a letter to a friend explaining your view of the changes that have taken place there. Include details about what has changed as well as how you think people have responded to the changes.

For: An activity on South Africa
Visit: PHSchool.com
Web Code: lad-5702

560 Africa

white president would not help blacks overcome the injustices of apartheid.

Writing Activity
Use the *Rubric for Assessing a Writing Assignment* to evaluate students' letters.

All in One **Africa Teaching Resources,**
Rubric for Assessing a Writing Assignment, p. 411

Go Online **PHSchool.com** Typing in the Web code when prompted will bring students directly to detailed instructions for this activity.

Review and Assessment

Review Chapter Content

- Review and revisit the major themes of this chapter by asking students to identify which Guiding Question each bulleted statement in the Chapter Summary answers. Have students write each statement down and work in groups to complete the activity. Refer to p. 349 in the Student Edition for the text of Guiding Questions.

- Assign *Vocabulary Development* for students to review Key Terms.

  All in One **Africa Teaching Resources,** *Vocabulary Development,* p. 409

◆ Chapter Summary

Section 1: Democratic Republic of the Congo

- The Democratic Republic of the Congo is rich in natural resources. These resources have helped shape the country's history.
- From the 1960s to the 1990s, Congo suffered under the authoritarian rule of Joseph Mobutu. It also suffered in the 1970s, when world prices of copper fell.
- During the 1990s, Congo faced civil wars that involved rebels in Congo. A number of neighboring countries also took part in the fighting.

Section 2: South Africa

- The Dutch, the British, and the French settled in South Africa. The British won control of the region and unified its lands as the Union of South Africa in 1910. It became independent in 1931.
- In 1948, the Afrikaners won political control of South Africa and legally established the system of apartheid. Many people who fought against this system were imprisoned, injured, or killed.
- Afrikaner president F. W. de Klerk legally ended apartheid in 1990. Nelson Mandela then became South Africa's first black president. He was followed in office by Thabo Mbeki.

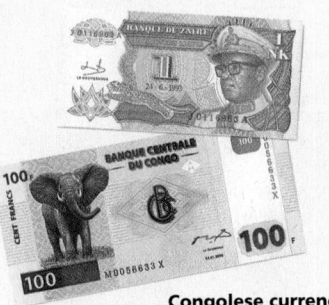

Congolese currency

Nelson Mandela and F. W. de Klerk

◆ Key Terms

Match the definitions in Column I with the key terms in Column II.

Column I

1. the legal system of South Africa in which the rights of nonwhites were greatly restricted
2. black leader of the African National Congress and South Africa's first president after apartheid ended
3. a nondemocratic form of government in which a single leader or a small group of leaders has all the power
4. to treat people differently, and often unfairly, based on race, religion, or sex
5. to transfer ownership of something to a nation's government

Column II

F authoritarian government

G nationalize

H apartheid

I discriminate

J Nelson Mandela

─ Vocabulary Builder ─

Revisit this chapter's high-use words:

potential	hostilities	pressure
vow	unify	model
erupt	reserve	

Ask students to review the definitions they recorded on their *Word Knowledge* worksheets.

All in One **Africa Teaching Resources,** *Word Knowledge,* p. 397

Consider allowing students to earn extra credit if they use the words in their answers to the questions in the Chapter Review and Assessment. The words must be used correctly and in a natural context to win the extra points.

Answers

Key Terms

1. C
2. E
3. A
4. D
5. B

Comprehension and Critical Thinking

6. (a) copper, gold, diamonds, forests, wildlife, and water **(b)** Possible answer: Many people are subsistence farmers—they must grow food to feed their families.

7. (a) authoritarian **(b)** Possible answer: People may have wanted a say in government, leading them to start the rebellion to oust Mobutu from power. **(c)** Laurent Kabila failed to establish a new constitution and hold national elections as he had promised.

8. (a) Zaire; Democratic Republic of the Congo **(b)** Possible answer: Sometimes the name of a country may reflect the type of government it has or is striving for.

9. (a) after the National Party won the 1948 election **(b)** It gave whites power and many rights, Asians and coloreds few rights, and blacks virtually no rights.

10. (a) peaceful protests **(b)** The response was often violent.

11. (a) Protests by South Africans and pressure from other countries led President F.W. de Klerk to pass laws ending apartheid. **(b)** Possible answer: It exemplified the new equality for all groups in South Africa. **(c)** Possible answers: Yes, because laws now call for equality so there is no need to focus on it anymore. No, because it will take many years and much assistance from the government to help blacks achieve full equality after decades of discrimination.

Skills Practice

Possible answer: Nyerere made the statement to express the serious problems Tanzania was facing. The main idea is that medical care and education in Tanzania were problematic. All of the details are statistical facts. There are no opinions in this statement. There is no bias in the statement.

Writing Activity: History

Students' questions and answers will vary. Make sure students are asking relevant and appropriate questions that are answerable by their partners.

◆ Comprehension and Critical Thinking

6. (a) Recall What important natural resources exist in the Democratic Republic of the Congo?
(b) Draw Conclusions If mining produces most of Congo's wealth, why do you think so many Congolese are farmers, not miners?

7. (a) Identify What kind of government did Joseph Mobutu establish in Congo?
(b) Draw Inferences How might this form of government have helped cause rebellion?
(c) Analyze Information What caused the second rebellion in Congo?

8. (a) Name What name did Mobutu give his country? What name did Laurent Kabila give it?
(b) Make Generalizations Why do you think a leader might want to change a country's name?

9. (a) Recall When did the system of apartheid in South Africa begin?
(b) Summarize How did apartheid affect different groups of South Africans?

10. (a) Define What was an important form of protest that black South Africans used against apartheid?
(b) Analyze Information How did the South African government respond to these protests?

11. (a) Explain How did the legal end to apartheid come about?
(b) Draw Conclusions Why was it significant that South Africa's first president after apartheid was not white?
(c) Predict Now that apartheid is over, do you think that South Africans will stop focusing on racial issues in politics? Explain.

◆ Skills Practice

Analyzing Primary Sources In the Skills for Life activity in this chapter, you learned how to analyze primary sources.

Review the steps you followed to learn this skill. Then reread the quotation from Tanzania's former president, Julius Nyerere, on page 521 of Chapter 16. Explain why the statement was made, what its main idea is, and which details are facts and which are opinions. Then explain whether you can identify any bias based on the background of the speaker.

◆ Writing Activity: History

Choose either South Africa or the Democratic Republic of the Congo. Write a list of five interview questions you would ask someone who has been elected president of the country. Be sure to consider what challenges the new president faces. Then exchange questions with a partner. Pretend that you are the president, and write answers to your partner's questions.

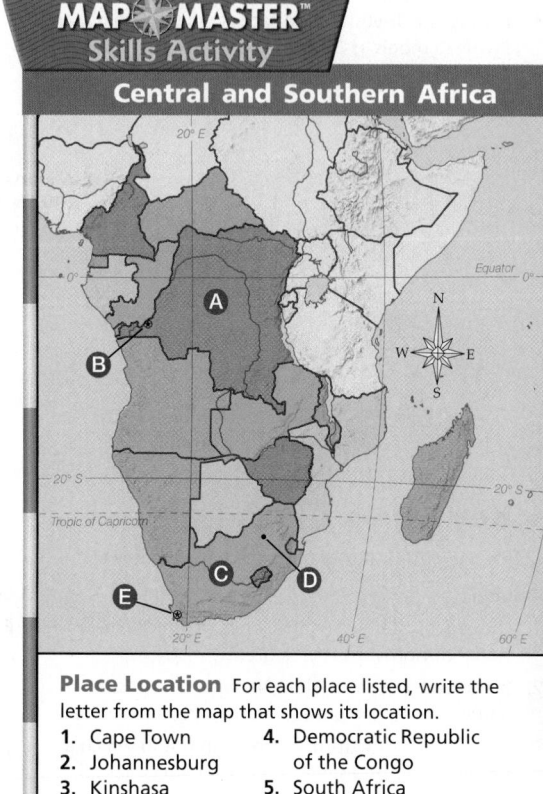

MAP MASTER™
Skills Activity

Central and Southern Africa

Place Location For each place listed, write the letter from the map that shows its location.
1. Cape Town
2. Johannesburg
3. Kinshasa
4. Democratic Republic of the Congo
5. South Africa

Go Online
PHSchool.com Use Web Code lap-5720 for an **interactive map**.

MAP MASTER™
Skills Activity

1. E
2. D
3. B
4. A
5. C

Go Online
PHSchool.com Students may practice their map skills using the interactive online version of this map.

Standardized Test Prep

Test-Taking Tips

Some questions on standardized tests ask you to identify a frame of reference. Read the passage below. Then follow the tips to answer the sample question.

> Apartheid separated South Africa into four groups: blacks, whites, coloreds, and Asians. In 1990, apartheid came to an end. In 1994, South Africa elected Nelson Mandela the nation's first black president. Someone hearing the news shouted, "What a happy day. At last my people will have some opportunities. I never believed this would happen in South Africa."

TIP Think about the author's purpose as you read. Is the author trying to give you information, convince you of something, or teach you how to do something?

Pick the letter that best answers the question.

Which onlooker probably made those comments?

A a white businessman who owned a large diamond mine

B a politician in a pro-Afrikaner party

C a black woman living in a rural homeland

D a white woman who left South Africa to protest apartheid

TIP Watch out for careless errors. Be sure you understand the question and consider each answer choice.

Think It Through Start with the author's purpose: to give you information about the end of apartheid. Then ask yourself: Who would be happy about the end of apartheid? You can rule out A and B because neither was denied opportunities under apartheid. That leaves C and D. A white woman who had left South Africa in protest would probably be happy about the end of apartheid but would not say it meant opportunities for *her* people. The correct answer is C.

Practice Questions

Use the passage below to answer Question 1. Choose the letter of the best answer. Use the tips above and other tips in this book to help you answer the following questions.

> "We need a new government. The one we have now does not rule fairly. It is no better than Mobutu's government. Our neighbors in Rwanda and Uganda agree with us. We must make a change."

1. Who would have been most likely to make this statement?

A Laurent Kabila

B Joseph Kabila

C a member of the first rebellion that occurred in eastern Congo

D a member of the second rebellion that occurred in eastern Congo

2. Which natural resource did NOT play a role in Congo's history?

A diamonds

B silver

C gold

D rubber

3. When did South Africa become independent?

A 1910

B 1931

C 1948

D 1990

Use Web Code laa-5700 for **Chapter 17 self-test.**

Standardized Test Prep

Answers

1. D
2. B
3. B

Go Online PHSchool.com Students may use the Chapter 17 self-test on PHSchool.com to prepare for the Chapter Test.

Assessment Resources

Teaching Resources
Chapter Tests A and B, pp. 412–417
Final Exams A and B, pp. 423–428

Test Prep Workbook
Africa Study Sheet, pp. 97–99
Africa Practice Tests A, B, and C, pp. 1–12

AYP Monitoring Assessments
Africa Benchmark Test 2 and Outcome Test, pp. 117–120; pp. 194–199

Technology
ExamView Test Bank CD-ROM

- Students can further explore the Guiding Questions by completing hands-on projects.

- Three pages of structured guidance in All-in-One Africa Teaching Resources support each of the projects described on this page.

  All in One Africa Teaching Resources, *Book Project: Africa Conference, pp. 78–80; Book Project: Traditional African Masks, pp. 81–83*

- There is an additional project introduced, explained, and supported in the All-in-One Africa Teaching Resources.

  All in One Africa Teaching Resources, *Book Project: Africa on Stage, pp. 75–77*

- Go over the three project suggestions with students.

- Ask each student to select one of the projects, or design his or her own. Work with students to create a project description and a schedule.

- Post project schedules and monitor student progress by asking for progress reports.

- Assess student projects using rubrics from the All-in-One Africa Teaching Resources.

  All in One Africa Teaching Resources, *Rubric for Assessing a Student Performance on a Project, p. 84; Rubric for Assessing Performance of an Entire Group, p. 85; Rubric for Assessing Individual Performance in a Group, p. 86*

 Portfolio Activity Tell students they can add their completed Book Project as the final item in their portfolios. Assess student portfolios with *Rubric for Assessing a Student Portfolio.*

  All in One Africa Teaching Resources, *Rubric for Assessing a Student Portfolio, p. 87*

Projects

Create your own projects to learn more about Africa. At the beginning of this book, you were introduced to the **Guiding Questions** for studying the chapters and special features. But you can also find answers to these questions by doing projects on your own or with a group. Use the questions to find topics you want to explore further. Then try the projects described on this page or create your own.

1. **Geography** What are the main physical features of Africa?
2. **History** How have historical events affected the cultures and nations of Africa?
3. **Culture** What features help define different African cultures?
4. **Government** What factors led to the development of different governments across Africa?
5. **Economics** What factors influence the ways in which Africans make a living?

Project
HOLD AN AFRICA CONFERENCE

Africa in the 2000s
As you read about Africa, organize a conference for the rest of your school about present-day life in Africa. Decide on several major topics for the conference, such as literature, arts, religion, and agriculture. Then form committees to plan the conference. One committee can plan an agenda, or list of events. Another can research the selected topics and give speeches at the conference. A publicity team can make posters to let students in other classes know about the conference. A press committee can write news reports about the speeches given at the conference.

Project
RESEARCH AFRICAN ART

African Masks
As you study Africa, find out about the tradition of mask-making in African countries. Look through books and magazines for information about different African mask-making traditions. Research the kinds of masks people make, the ways of making them, and the meanings that they have. Prepare a mini-museum display with pictures or sketches and detailed explanations of the masks and traditions you research. You may want to try making a mask of your own as well.

The Africa Museum presents The Art of MASK-MAKING

Teaching the Target Reading Skills

The Prentice Hall *World Studies* program has interwoven essential reading skills instruction throughout the Student Edition, Teacher's Edition, and ancillary resources. In Asia and the Pacific, students will learn eight reading skills.

Student Edition The *World Studies* Student Edition provides students with reading skills instruction, practice, and application opportunities in each chapter within the program.

Teacher's Edition The *World Studies* Teacher Edition supports your teaching of each skill by providing full modeling in each chapter's interleaf and modeling of the specific sub-skills in each section lesson.

All in One Teaching Resources The *World Studies* All-in-One Teaching Resources provides a worksheet explaining and supporting the elements of each Target Reading Skill. Use these to help struggling students master skills, or as more practice for every student.

Target Reading Skills

The Target Reading Skills introduced on this page will help you understand the words and ideas in this book and in other social studies reading you do. Each chapter in the Asia and the Pacific section focuses on one of these reading skills. Good readers develop a bank of reading strategies, or skills. Then they draw on the particular strategies that will help them understand the text they are reading.

Chapter 18 Target Reading Skill
Reading Process When you use the reading process, you set a purpose for reading, predict what you are going to read, and ask questions about what you read.

Chapter 19 Target Reading Skill
Clarifying Meaning If you do not understand something right away, you can use several skills to clarify the meaning of words and ideas. In this chapter, you will practice rereading and reading ahead, paraphrasing, and summarizing.

Chapter 20 Target Reading Skill
Main Ideas In this chapter, you will practice these skills: identifying both stated and implied main ideas and identifying supporting details.

Chapter 21 Target Reading Skill
Context Using the context of an unfamiliar word can help you understand its meaning. Context includes the words, phrases, and sentences surrounding a word.

Chapter 22 Target Reading Skill
Word Analysis Word analysis means analyzing a word, or breaking the word into parts to help you recognize and pronounce it. In this chapter, you will analyze words to find roots, prefixes, and suffixes.

Chapter 23 Target Reading Skill
Sequence A sequence is the order in which a series of events occurs. In this chapter, you will practice understanding sequence and recognize words that signal sequence.

Chapter 24 Target Reading Skill
Comparison and Contrast Comparing means examining the similarities between things. Contrasting is looking at differences. In this chapter, you will practice these skills: comparing and contrasting, making comparisons, and identifying contrasts.

Chapter 25 Target Reading Skill
Cause and Effect Identifying cause and effect helps you understand relationships among situations or events. In this chapter, you will practice identifying causes and effects, understanding effects, recognizing multiple causes, and recognizing words that signal cause and effect.

Chapter 26 Target Reading Skill
Main Ideas Focusing on main ideas helps you remember the most important information in what you read. In this chapter, you will have another opportunity to practice identifying main ideas and supporting details.

Assessment Resources

Use the diagnosing readiness tests from **AYP Monitoring Assessments** to help you identify problems before students begin to study Asia and the Pacific.

Determine students' reading level and identify challenges:

📄 *Screening Tests,* pp. 1–10

Evaluate students' verbal skills:

📄 *Critical Thinking and Reading Tests,* pp. 25–34

📄 *Vocabulary Tests,* pp. 45–52

📄 *Writing Tests,* pp. 53–60

ASIA AND THE PACIFIC

Asia and the Pacific is a huge region that covers more than one third of Earth's surface. Asia is the largest continent. It includes some of the world's largest and smallest countries. This region also includes the only continent that is also a country—Australia.

Guiding Questions

The text, photographs, maps, and charts in this book will help you discover answers to these Guiding Questions.

1 **Geography** What are the main physical features of Asia and the Pacific?

2 **History** How have ancient civilizations of Asia and the Pacific influenced the world today?

3 **Culture** What are the main characteristics of the cultures of Asia and the Pacific?

4 **Government** What types of government exist in Asia and the Pacific today?

5 **Economics** How do the people of this region make a living?

Project Preview

You can also discover answers to the Guiding Questions by working on projects. Two projects are listed on page 812 of this book.

Assess students' social studies skills:

- *Geographic Literacy Tests,* pp. 13–20
- *Visual Analysis Tests,* pp. 21–24
- *Communications Tests,* pp. 35–44

The *World Studies* program provides instruction and practice for all of these skills. Use students' test results to pinpoint the skills your students have mastered and the skills they need to practice. Then use *Correlation to Program Resources* to prescribe skills practice and reinforcement.

- *Correlation to Program Resources,* pp. 64–77

Guiding Questions

- This book was developed around five Guiding Questions about Asia and the Pacific. They appear on the reduced Student Edition page to the left. The Guiding Questions are intended as an organizational focus for the book. The Guiding Questions act as a kind of umbrella under which all of the material falls.

- You may wish to add your own Guiding Questions to the list in order to tailor them to your particular course.

- Draw students' attention to the Guiding Questions. Ask them to write the questions in their notebooks for future reference.

- In the Teacher's Edition, each section's themes are linked to a specific Guiding Question at the beginning of each chapter. Then, an activity at the end of the chapter returns to the Guiding Questions to review key concepts.

Project Preview

- The projects for this book are designed to provide students with hands-on involvement in the content area. Students are introduced to some projects on p. 812.

- *Book Projects* give students directions on how to complete these projects, and more.

  All in One **Asia and the Pacific Teaching Resources,** *Book Project: Agricultural Center,* pp. 77–79; *Book Project: Independence Biography,* pp. 80–82; *Book Project: Asian Trade Fair,* pp. 83–85; *Book Project: Travel Log,* pp. 86–88

- Assign projects as small group activities, whole-class projects, or individual projects. Consider assigning a project at the beginning of the course.

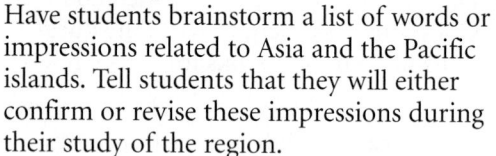
Objectives

- Describe the relative location and size of Asia and the Pacific islands.
- Describe the size of Asia's mainland.
- Examine the physical features of Asia and the Pacific islands.
- Learn about the ring of fire and why it can be a dangerous area.

Prepare to Read

Build Background Knowledge L2

Have students brainstorm a list of words or impressions related to Asia and the Pacific islands. Tell students that they will either confirm or revise these impressions during their study of the region.

Instruct

Investigate Asia and the Pacific Islands L2

Guided Instruction

- Read the introductory, Location, and Regions paragraphs as a class. Have students work in pairs to answer the questions.
- Have students fill in the *Regional Overview* worksheet as they read.
  All in One Asia and the Pacific Teaching Resources, *Regional Overview,* pp. 93–95

Independent Practice

Direct students to the political maps of the United States and Asia in the Student Edition Atlas. Tell them to use the scale to find the length and width of each.

Monitor Progress

If students are having trouble measuring the regions, they can practice using the DK Atlas Activity *Using the Map Scale.*

All in One Asia and the Pacific Teaching Resources, *DK Compact Atlas of the World Activity: Using the Map Scale,* p. 96

Answers

LOCATION the Pacific Ocean; west; east
REGIONS about twice as wide and long

Investigate Asia and the Pacific Islands

Asia is the largest continent in the world. The vast Pacific Ocean contains thousands of scattered islands and another continent—the country of Australia. The continent of Asia includes part of Russia. However, Russian Asia is not covered in these pages. Because most of Russia's people live in Europe, Russia is discussed with Europe.

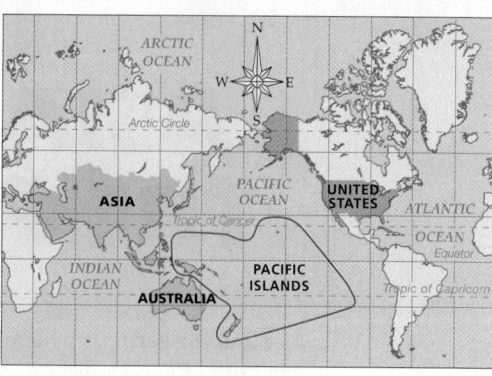

▲ **Myanmar, Asia**
Shwedagon Buddhist Temple, dating from about A.D. 1000.

LOCATION

1 Locate Asia and the Pacific Islands
In this book you will read about Asia, Australia, and the islands of the Pacific Ocean. This region is shaded green on the map above. What ocean lies between Asia and the United States? If you lived on the west coast of the United States, in which direction would you travel to reach Asia? If you lived on the most eastern tip of the Pacific islands, in which direction would you travel to reach the west coast of the United States?

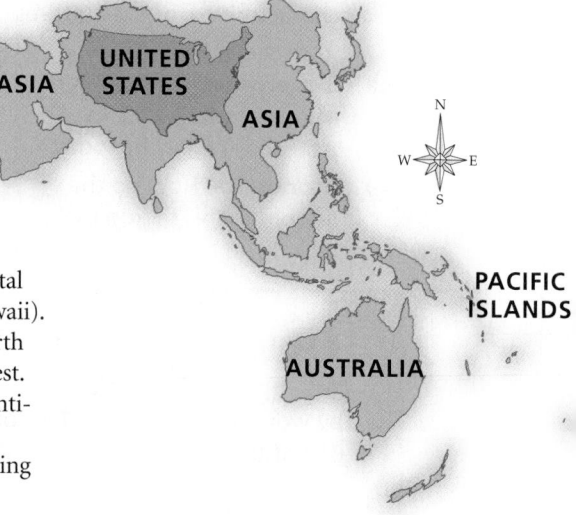

REGIONS

2 Estimate Asia's Size
Compare Asia's mainland to the continental United States (all states except Alaska and Hawaii). With a ruler, measure mainland Asia from north to south. Measure the distance from east to west. Now make the same measurements for the continental United States. About how many times longer and wider is mainland Asia (not including Russia) than the continental United States?

Mental Mapping

Everything in Its Place Divide students into five groups. Give each group one of the outline maps listed below. Write the names of some of the countries from each region on the board. Ask students to locate as many countries on the maps as they can without looking in their textbooks. They can fill in countries they could not locate as they study the region.

All in One Asia and the Pacific Teaching Resources, *Outline Map 26: South Asia: Political,* p. 97; *Outline Map 28: Central and Southwest Asia: Political,* p. 98; *Outline Map 29: East Asia,* p. 99; *Outline Map 30: Southeast Asia,* p. 100; *Outline Map 32: The Pacific Islands,* p. 101

Political Asia

LOCATION

3 Investigate the Countries of Asia

Asia is the largest continent on the Earth. Which Asian country on the map below is the largest? Which country is the second largest? Asia has many countries that are located on islands. Name three of them. Iran is a large country in the western part of Asia. Name three countries that border Iran.

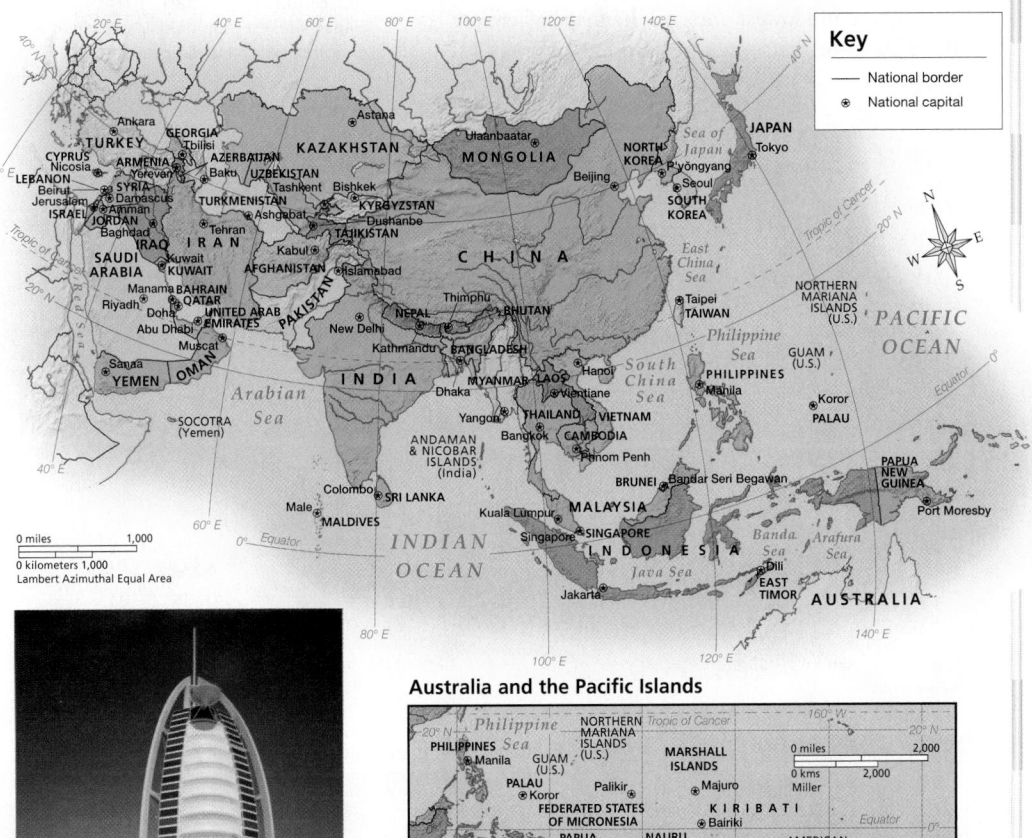

Key

— National border
⊛ National capital

0 miles 1,000
0 kilometers 1,000
Lambert Azimuthal Equal Area

Australia and the Pacific Islands

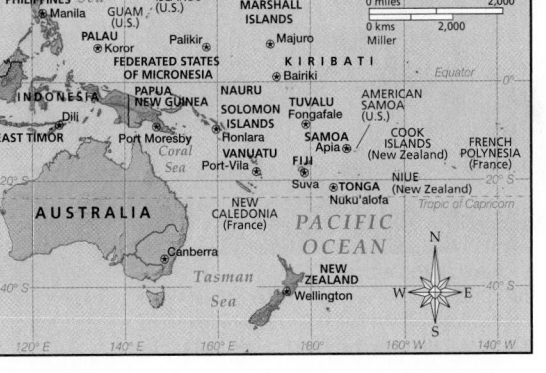

▲ **Dubai, United Arab Emirates**
Wealth from the region's oil resources makes possible such elaborate buildings like this hotel.

Differentiated Instruction

For Special Needs Students **L1**
If possible, show students the Asia flyover segment on the Passport to the World CD-ROM. Ask students to list two facts they

learned about each country visited in the segment.

⊙ *Flyover segment,* **Passport to the World CD-ROM**

Political Asia **L2**

Guided Instruction

- Read the Location paragraph. After students have answered the questions, have them develop a five question quiz about the locations of Asian and Pacific island countries. Give them a sample question such as, "What island country is southeast of India?" (*Sri Lanka*) Tell them to make an answer key on a separate sheet of paper. Then have students exchange quizzes with a partner and take the quiz. When they have finished, have them exchange again to check each other's answers.

- Ask students to continue completing the *Regional Overview* worksheet.

  All in One **Asia and the Pacific Teaching Resources,** *Regional Overview,* pp. 93–95

Independent Practice

Distribute *Reading a Political Map* to give students more practice working with political maps.

All in One **Asia and the Pacific Teaching Resources,** *Reading a Political Map,* p. 53

Monitor Progress

Circulate to ensure that individuals are filling in the correct answers on their worksheets. Provide assistance as needed.

Answer

LOCATION China; India; three of the following: East Timor, Indonesia, Philippines, Palau, Taiwan, Japan, Singapore, Brunei, Sri Lanka, Malaysia; three of the following: Turkmenistan, Afghanistan, Pakistan, Azerbaijan, Armenia, Turkey, Iraq

Physical Asia

Guided Instruction

- Read the Location paragraph. Have students study the physical map of Asia and the Pacific islands. Ask them to write a sentence comparing the elevations of Asia with those of Australia. *(Possible answer: Asia has much higher and lower elevations than Australia.)*

- Ask students to continue completing the *Regional Overview* worksheet.

  All in One Asia and the Pacific Teaching Resources, *Regional Overview*, pp. 93–95

Independent Practice

To give students practice working with physical maps, provide them with the following DK Atlas of the World Activities: *Reading a Physical Map* and *Relief on a Map*. Have students work in pairs to complete the worksheets.

  All in One Asia and the Pacific Teaching Resources, *DK Compact Atlas of the World Activity: Reading a Physical Map*, p. 103; *DK Compact Atlas of the World Activity: Relief on a Map*, p. 104

Monitor Progress

Circulate while students complete their worksheets. Provide assistance as needed.

Answers

LOCATION The highest elevations are located in the Himalayas; the Zagros, Caucasus, and Altei Mountains; Tien Shan and Hindu Kush; and the Plateau of Tibet. The lowest areas are located along the Caspian Sea.

Physical Asia

LOCATION

4 Examine the Physical Features of Asia

Asia is a continent of great physical contrasts, including towering mountains, high plateaus, and low-lying plains. Use the elevation key to identify the highest and lowest areas on the map. Where are they? Describe their physical features.

▲ **Mount Fuji, Japan**
Japan's tallest mountain is actually a volcano, which last erupted in 1707.

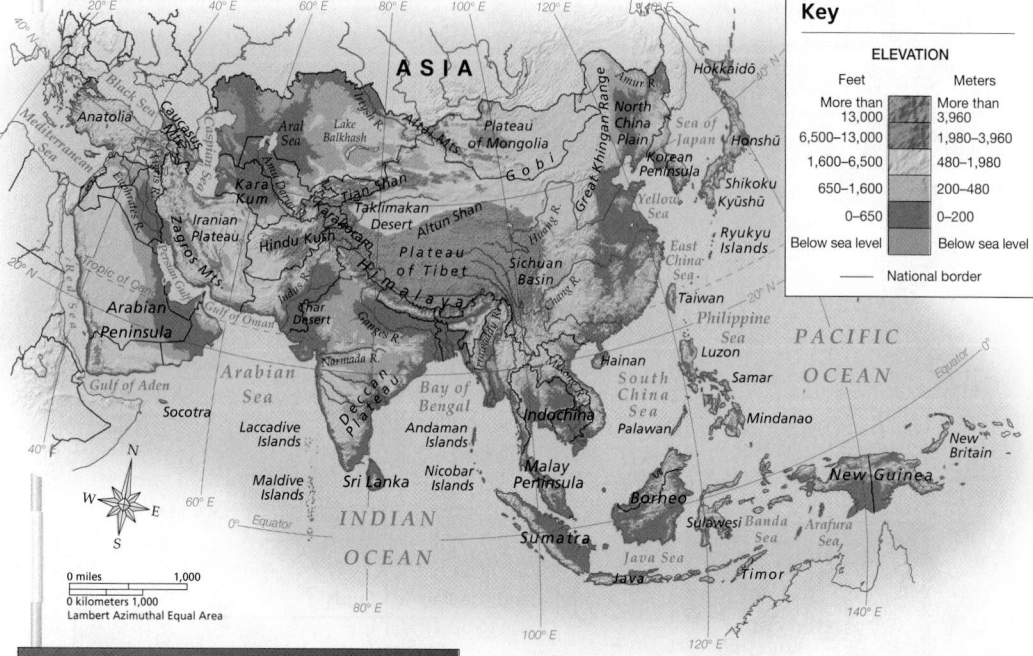

Key

ELEVATION

Feet	Meters
More than 13,000	More than 3,960
6,500–13,000	1,980–3,960
1,600–6,500	480–1,980
650–1,600	200–480
0–650	0–200
Below sea level	Below sea level

—— National border

0 miles 1,000
0 kilometers 1,000
Lambert Azimuthal Equal Area

▲ **Australian Outback**
The outback, in the dry, hot center of the country, is grassland and desert where few people live. Here ranchers raise sheep and cattle.

Australia and the Pacific Islands

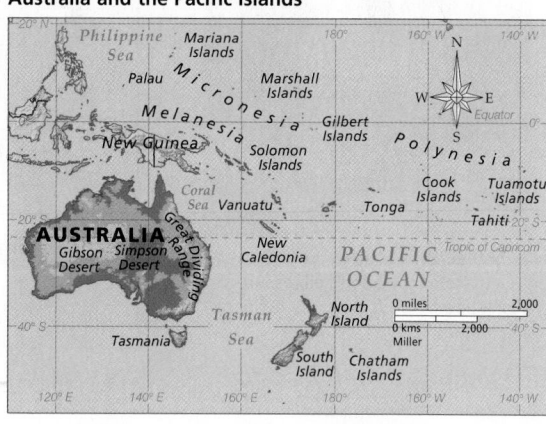

570 Asia and the Pacific

Differentiated Instruction

For English Language Learners L2

To assist students with naming the locations of Asia and the Pacific's important physical features, have students compare the political map of Asia on p. 569 with the map on this page. Have students work in pairs to create a table listing each physical feature on the physical map and the country or countries in which it appears. Have them make a separate table listing the bodies of water and the countries that border them.

The Ring of Fire

Earth's crust is made up of plates that ride on top of molten earth called magma. The magma escapes in the form of lava when volcanoes erupt. Ninety percent of the world's active volcanoes circle the Pacific Ocean. Look at the map below. Why are these volcanoes described as a "Ring of Fire"?

▲ **Puu Oo Volcano, Hawaii**
The Puu Oo volcano spews molten lava as it erupts. The islands that we call Hawaii are the tops of volcanoes that rest on the ocean floor.

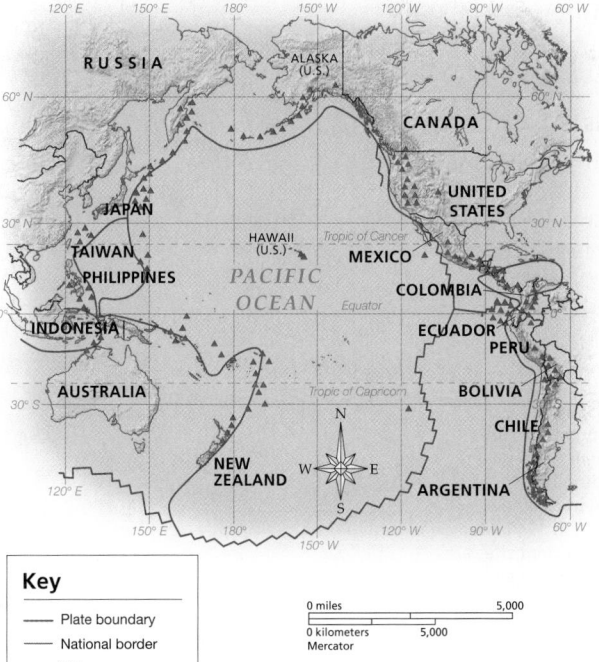

Key
— Plate boundary
— National border
▲ Volcano

0 miles 5,000
0 kilometers 5,000
Mercator

INTERACTION

5 Investigate The Ring of Fire

Where Earth's plates meet, plate boundaries are formed. With your finger, trace the plate boundaries on the map at left. Notice where the volcanoes are located in relation to the plate boundaries. Compare the location of volcanoes to the location of cities on the political map on page 3. Where might volcano eruptions cause the most damage to people?

PRACTICE YOUR GEOGRAPHY SKILLS

1 You begin your boat trip from Australia's north coast and travel west through Indonesia. After you pass Borneo and Java, you cross the Equator and enter a large body of water. What is its name?

2 Today you fly from the Himalayas along the 30z N parallel across the Indus River to the Zagros Mountains. What body of water are you near?

3 There are many volcanoes to the east of this island nation north of the East China Sea. What is the name of this country?

▲ **Boats Moored in Indonesia**

Regional Overview **571**

Background: Links Across Time

Pompeii One of the most famous volcanic eruptions in early history took place far from the Ring of Fire, in what is today Italy. On August 24, A.D. 79, Mount Vesuvius erupted, burying the ancient Roman city of Pompeii in approximately 20 feet of ash, stone and other volcanic debris. The volcanic material actually served to preserve much of the city. Archaeologists were even able to make casts of bodies by pouring plaster into hollows created by the debris. Today, remains of the city provide a unique look at the culture and architecture of the ancient city.

The Ring of Fire L2

Guided Instruction

- Read the introductory paragraph and the Interaction paragraph. Have students refer to the map key to locate the volcanoes along the Ring of Fire.

- Ask students **What continents have volcanoes that are part of the Ring of Fire?** *(North America, South America, Australia, and Asia)*

- Have students list the ways volcanoes can cause damage and death. *(Ash from volcanoes can destroy crops and cause mud flows and tsunamis. Volcanoes also spew hot lava and poisonous gases.)*

- Ask students to look up *tsunami* in a class dictionary. Have students brainstorm reasons why a volcanic eruption might cause a tsunami. *(Possible answer: The violent shaking of the earth caused by volcanoes generates tsunamis.)*

- Direct students to finish the *Regional Overview* worksheet.

   All in One **Asia and the Pacific Teaching Resources**, *Regional Overview*, pp. 93–95

Independent Practice

Have students do research to learn about a volcanic eruption that has occurred in the Ring of Fire. Have them write a newspaper article as if they were reporting on the event at the time it occurred. The article should explain where and when the eruption occurred and how it affected surrounding areas.

Monitor Progress

Distribute *Writing to Describe* to help students with their writing.

   All in One **Asia and the Pacific Teaching Resources**, *Writing to Describe*, p. 105

Answers

Possible answer: The volcanoes are located in a circular formation, and shoot hot lava into the air that resembles fire.
INTERACTION volcanoes near the cities of Tokyo, Japan; Taipei, Taiwan; and Manila, Philippines have the potential to cause a great deal of damage.

PRACTICE YOUR GEOGRAPHY SKILLS

1. Indian Ocean

2. Persian Gulf

3. Japan

Focus on Countries in Asia

L2

Guided Instruction
- Read the introduction and photograph captions as a class.

- Have students list the sixteen yellow countries on the map that they will be studying in depth. (*China, Japan, North Korea, South Korea, India, Afghanistan, Kazakhstan, Kyrgyzstan, Tajikistan, Turkmenistan, Uzbekistan, Pakistan, Israel, Saudi Arabia, Vietnam, and Australia*)

Independent Practice
Have students revisit the outline maps they began filling in during the Mental Mapping activity. Put students back into their groups and have them use the map on pp. 572–573 to fill in the remainder of the countries in their region. Have them color the entire region the same color. Collect all of the maps and affix them to a large piece of poster board to create one map of Asia and the Pacific.

All in One **Asia and the Pacific Teaching Resources,** *Outline Map 26: South Asia: Political,* p. 97; *Outline Map 28: Central and Southwest Asia: Political,* p. 98; *Outline Map 29: East Asia,* p. 99; *Outline Map 30: Southeast Asia,* p. 100; *Outline Map 32: The Pacific Islands,* p. 101

Monitor Progress
Circulate to make sure students are correctly identifying the countries in their region. Provide assistance as needed.

Focus on Countries in Asia

Now that you've investigated the geography of Asia and the Pacific, take a closer look at some of the countries that make up this vast region. The map shows the countries of Asia and the Pacific. The countries that you will study in depth in the second half of this book appear in yellow on the map.

Go Online PHSchool.com Use Web Code lcp-6000 for the **interactive maps** on these pages.

◀ **Israel**
Though it has an ancient history, modern Israel was created as a new nation in 1948. Many of its ancient sites are sacred to Jews, Muslims, and Christians.

Key
- ⎯ National border
- ▨ Countries with in-depth coverage
- ▨ Non-feature countries

India ▶
India is the world's largest democracy and the second-most-populous country in the world. It is home to a number of ethnic groups, and it has 15 official languages.

572 Regional Overview

Background: Links Across Time

Place Names Several Asian countries end with the suffix *-stan*: Afghanistan, Kazakhstan, Kyrgyzstan, Pakistan, Tajikistan, Turkmenistan, and Uzbekistan.

The suffix is generally accepted as the ancient Persian or Farsi word for *land*. Therefore Afghanistan, for example, means *land of the Afghans*.

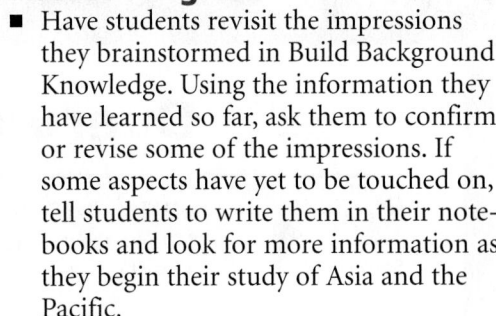

▲ China
The world's most populous country, China is a major economic power today. The products it makes are sold all over the world, and its vast population makes it an important market for international goods.

Australia and the Pacific Islands

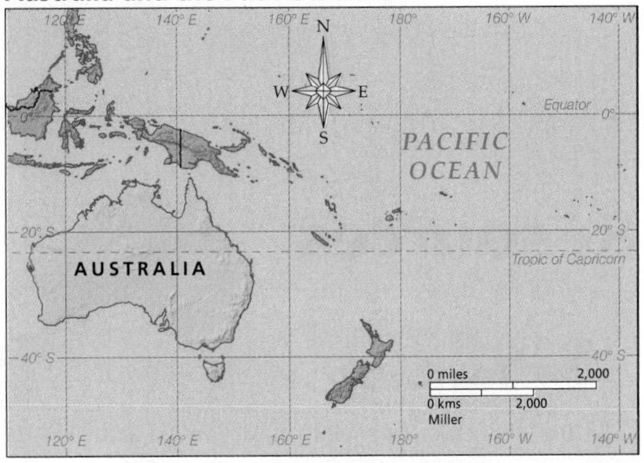

0 miles 2,000
0 kms 2,000
Miller

▲ Seoul, South Korea
The Korean Peninsula is home to one people, but since 1953 they have lived in two separate nations—North Korea and South Korea.

0 miles 1,000
0 kilometers 1,000
Lambert Azimuthal Equal Area

Regional Overview **573**

Assess Progress L2

- Have students revisit the impressions they brainstormed in Build Background Knowledge. Using the information they have learned so far, ask them to confirm or revise some of the impressions. If some aspects have yet to be touched on, tell students to write them in their notebooks and look for more information as they begin their study of Asia and the Pacific.

- Ask students to complete Practice Your Geography Skills on p. 571.

Reteach L1

For more exploration of the region, have students view the Asia and Pacific portion of the Passport to the World CD-ROM and complete the Customs Quiz.

◉ *Asia and the Pacific,* **Passport to the World CD-ROM**

Extend L3

Portfolio Activity
One way of assessing student accomplishments is by having them build a portfolio of their best work. To begin their portfolios for Asia and the Pacific, have students choose one of the countries mentioned on pp. 572–573. Then, have students create a travel brochure for the country. Tell them to include illustrations, historical and geographical sites to visit, and a map.

- Give students *Using the Library* to help them get started on their research.

All in One **Asia and the Pacific Teaching Resources,** *Using the Library,* p. 106

Differentiated Instruction

For Gifted and Talented L3

Assign each student five Asian or Pacific island countries. Have students use the DK World Desk Reference Online to find five facts about each country. Choose the facts you would like each student to find. Possible facts could include area, population size, official language, and urban and rural populations. Have them create an index card for each country. Collect all the cards and create a booklet that students may refer to when they come across new countries as they read the Student Edition.

18 East Asia: Physical Geography

Chapter Overview

Overview

Section 1 Land and Water
1. Learn about the landforms and water bodies found in East Asia.
2. Find out where most of the people in East Asia live.

Section 2 Climate and Vegetation
1. Examine the major climate regions in East Asia.
2. Discover how climate affects people and vegetation in East Asia.

Section 3 Natural Resources and Land Use
1. Learn about East Asia's major natural resources.
2. Find out how the people of East Asia use land to produce food.

Video

The Geography of East Asia
Length: 5 minutes, 54 seconds
Use with Section 1
This segment describes the location of East Asia, with a focus on the nations that make it up. It uses maps and footage to show the major geographical features of the region.

Technology Resources

Students use embedded Web codes to access Internet activities, chapter self-tests, and additional map practice. They may also access Dorling Kindersley's Online Desk Reference to learn more about each country they study.

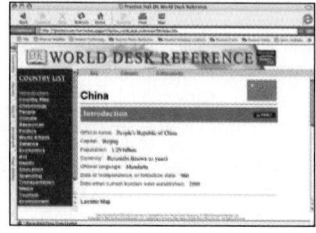

Interactive Textbook

Use the Interactive Textbook to make content and concepts come alive through animations, videos, and activities that accompany the complete basal text—online and on CD-ROM.

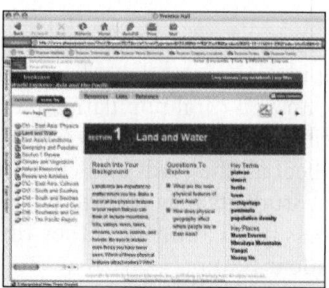

PRENTICE HALL
TeacherEXPRESS
Plan • Teach • Assess

Use this complete suite of powerful teaching tools to make planning lessons and administering tests quicker and easier.

Reading and Assessment

Reading and Vocabulary Instruction

⟳ Model the Target Reading Skill

Reading Process Explain to students that previewing a text and setting a purpose for reading are important steps in reading for comprehension. There are a number of ways to do this, including predicting and asking questions. Previewing and setting a purpose for reading allows the reader to become familiar with the topics discussed in a selection before reading it. Knowing a little about the reading helps the reader to focus his or her attention as he or she reads and recall the main ideas and important details more easily. Using information from Section 1, model the reading process for students:

I see that the first heading is *Landforms and Water Bodies*. I will read this subsection to learn about the landscape, oceans, lakes, and rivers in Asia. Looking at some of the next subheadings—*The Himalayas; Japan: An Island Country;* and *The Koreas: Two Countries, One Peninsula*—I predict that I will learn about the variety of landscapes in East Asia. Why is Japan called *An Island Country?* What exactly is a peninsula? I will read the selection to answer these questions.

Use the following worksheets from All-in-One Asia and the Pacific Teaching Resources (pp. 124–126) to support this chapter's Target Reading Skill.

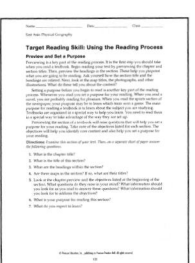 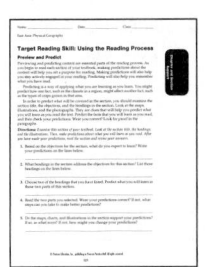 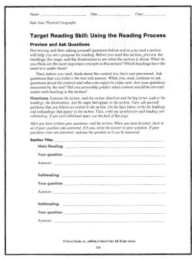

Vocabulary Builder
High-Use Academic Words
Use these steps to teach this chapter's high-use words:

1. Have students rate how well they know each word on their Word Knowledge worksheets (All-in-One Asia and the Pacific Teaching Resources, p. 125).
2. Pronounce each word and ask students to repeat it.
3. Provide a brief definition or sample sentence (see TE pp. 577, 581, and 587).
4. Work with students as they fill in the "Definition or Example" column of their Word Knowledge worksheets.

Assessment

Formal Assessment
Test students' understanding of core knowledge and skills.

Chapter Tests A and B, All-in-One Asia and the Pacific Teaching Resources, pp. 140–145

Customize the Chapter Tests to suit your needs.
ExamView® Test Bank CD-ROM

Skills Assessment
Assess geographic literacy.

MapMaster Skills, Student Edition, pp. 575, 578, 581, 582, 587, 592

Assess reading and comprehension.

Target Reading Skills, Student Edition, pp. 577, 581, 587, and in Section Assessments

Chapter 18 Assessment, Eastern Hemisphere Reading and Vocabulary Study Guide, p. 205

Performance Assessment
Assess students' performance on this chapter's Writing Activities using the following rubrics from All-in-One Asia and the Pacific Teaching Resources.

Rubric for Assessing a Report, p. 138
Rubric for Assessing a Glossary, p. 139

Assess students' work through performance tasks.

Small Group Activity: The Mount Everest Story, All-in-One Asia and the Pacific Teaching Resources, pp. 128–131

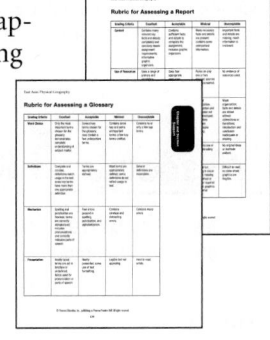

Online Assessment
Have students check their own understanding.

Chapter Self-Test

Test Preparation
Assess students' skills and diagnose problems as students begin their study of this region.

Screening Tests, AYP Monitoring Assessments, pp. 1–11

Diagnosing Readiness Tests, AYP Monitoring Assessments, pp. 13–63

Section 1 Land and Water

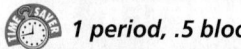 *1 period, .5 block*

Social Studies Objectives

1. Learn about the landforms and water bodies found in East Asia.
2. Find out where most of the people in East Asia live.

Reading/Language Arts Objective

Set a purpose for reading in order to focus on the key information in this section.

Prepare to Read	Instructional Resources	Differentiated Instruction
Build Background Knowledge Have students name well-known landforms in the United States. **Set a Purpose for Reading** Have students evaluate statements on the *Reading Readiness Guide*. **Preview Key Terms** Teach the section's Key Terms. **Target Reading Skill** Introduce the section's Target Reading Skill of **setting a purpose for reading**.	**All in One Asia and the Pacific Teaching Resources** **L2** Reading Readiness Guide, p. 111 **L2** Preview and Set a Purpose, p. 122	**Spanish Reading and Vocabulary Study Guide** **L1** Chapter 18, Section 1, pp. 139–140 ELL

Instruct	Instructional Resources	Differentiated Instruction
Landforms and Water Bodies Discuss the geography of East Asia. **Target Reading Skill** Review **setting a purpose for reading**. **Population in East Asia** Ask about the places most East Asians live and their reasons for living there.	**All in One Asia and the Pacific Teaching Resources** **L2** Guided Reading and Review, p. 112 **L2** Reading Readiness Guide, p. 111 **Asia and the Pacific Transparencies** **L2** Section Reading Support Transparency AP 48 **World Studies Video Program** **L2** The Geography of East Asia and the Pacific	**Teacher's Edition** **L1** For Special Needs Students, TE p. 578 **L1** For English Language Learners, TE p. 578 **Spanish Support** **L2** Guided Reading and Review (Spanish), p. 200 ELL

Assess and Reteach	Instructional Resources	Differentiated Instruction
Assess Progress Evaluate student comprehension with the section assessment and section quiz. **Reteach** Assign the Reading and Vocabulary Study Guide to help struggling students. **Extend** Extend the lesson by having students fill in an outline map.	**All in One Asia and the Pacific Teaching Resources** **L2** Section Quiz, p. 113 **L3** Outline Map 29: East Asia, p. 132 Rubric for Assessing a Writing Assignment, p. 137 **Reading and Vocabulary Study Guide** **L1** Chapter 18, Section 1, pp. 196–198	**Spanish Support** **L2** Section Quiz (Spanish), p. 201 ELL

Key

L1 Basic to Average   **L3** Average to Advanced

L2 For All Students

LPR Less Proficient Readers

AR Advanced Readers

SN Special Needs Students

GT Gifted and Talented

ELL English Language Learners

574c

Section 2 Climate and Vegetation

 1.5 periods, .75 block (includes Skills for Life)

Social Studies Objectives

1. Examine the major climate regions in East Asia.
2. Discover how climate affects people and vegetation in East Asia.

Reading/Language Arts Objective

Preview headings, pictures, and maps to predict what the text might discuss.

Prepare to Read

Build Background Knowledge
Discuss characteristics of East Asia's climate and vegetation.

Set a Purpose for Reading
Have students begin to fill out the *Reading Readiness Guide.*

Preview Key Terms
Teach the section's Key Terms.

Target Reading Skill
Introduce the section's Target Reading Skill of **predicting.**

Instructional Resources

All in One Asia and the Pacific Teaching Resources
- L2 Reading Readiness Guide, p. 115
- L2 Preview and Predict, p. 123

Differentiated Instruction

Spanish Reading and Vocabulary Study Guide
- L1 Chapter 18, Section 2, pp. 141–142 ELL

Instruct

East Asia's Climate Regions
Ask about and discuss the climates of the different regions of East Asia.

Target Reading Skill
Review **predicting.**

The Influences of Climate
Discuss how the Huang River affects farming.

Instructional Resources

All in One Asia and the Pacific Teaching Resources
- L2 Guided Reading and Review, p. 116
- L2 Reading Readiness Guide, p. 115

Asia and the Pacific Transparencies
- L2 Section Reading Support Transparency AP 49

Differentiated Instruction

All in One Asia and the Pacific Teaching Resources
- L2 Skills for Life, p. 127 AR, GT, LPR, SN

Spanish Support
- L2 Guided Reading and Review (Spanish), p. 202 ELL

Assess and Reteach

Assess Progress
Evaluate student comprehension with the section assessment and section quiz.

Reteach
Assign the Reading and Vocabulary Study Guide to help struggling students.

Extend
Extend the lesson by assigning a Book Project.

Instructional Resources

All in One Asia and the Pacific Teaching Resources
- L2 Section Quiz, p. 117
- L3 Book Project: Agriculture Center, pp. 77–79
  Rubric for Assessing a Writing Assignment, p. 137

Reading and Vocabulary Study Guide
- L1 Chapter 18, Section 2, pp. 199–201

Differentiated Instruction

Teacher's Edition
- L1 For Less Proficient Readers, TE p. 585

Social Studies Skills Tutor CD-ROM
- L1 Using Reliable Information, ELL, LPR, SN

Spanish Support
- L2 Section Quiz (Spanish), p. 203 ELL

Key

L1 Basic to Average	LPR Less Proficient Readers	GT Gifted and Talented
L3 Average to Advanced	AR Advanced Readers	ELL English Language Learners
L2 For All Students	SN Special Needs Students	

Section Lesson Planner

Section 3 **Natural Resources and Land Use**

 2 periods, 1 block (includes Chapter Review and Assessment)

Social Studies Objectives
1. Learn about East Asia's major natural resources.
2. Find out how the people of East Asia use land to produce food.

Reading/Language Arts Objective
Turn headings into questions and then read to answer those questions.

Prepare to Read

Build Background Knowledge
Discuss natural resources.

Set a Purpose for Reading
Have students evaluate statements on the *Reading Readiness Guide*.

Preview Key Terms
Teach the section's Key Terms.

Target Reading Skill
Introduce the section's Target Reading Skill of **asking questions**.

Instructional Resources

All in One Asia and the Pacific Teaching Resources
- **L2** Reading Readiness Guide, p. 119
- **L2** Preview and Ask Questions, p. 124

Differentiated Instruction

Spanish Reading and Vocabulary Study Guide
- **L1** Chapter 18, Section 3, pp. 143–144 ELL

Instruct

East Asia's Natural Resources
Ask questions about the relationship between East Asia's natural resources and its economy.

Target Reading Skill
Review **asking questions**.

Using the Land to Produce Food
Discuss how crops are grown in East Asia.

Instructional Resources

All in One Asia and the Pacific Teaching Resources
- **L2** Guided Reading and Review, p. 120
- **L2** Reading Readiness Guide, p. 119

Asia and the Pacific Transparencies
- **L2** Section Reading Support Transparency AP 50

Differentiated Instruction

All in One Asia and the Pacific Teaching Resources
- **L3** Enrichment, p. 126 AR, GT
- **L3** The Year of Impossible Goodbyes, pp. 133–135 AR, GT

Teacher's Edition
- **L3** For Gifted and Talented, TE p. 589
- **L3** For Advanced Readers, TE p. 589

Spanish Support
- **L2** Guided Reading and Review (Spanish), p. 204 ELL

Assess and Reteach

Assess Progress
Evaluate student comprehension with the section assessment and section quiz.

Reteach
Assign the Reading and Vocabulary Study Guide to help struggling students.

Extend
Extend the lesson by assigning a Small Group Activity.

Instructional Resources

All in One Asia and the Pacific Teaching Resources
- **L2** Section Quiz, p. 121
- **L3** Small Group Activity: The Mount Everest Story, pp. 128–131
  Rubric for Assessing a Report, p. 138
- **L2** Vocabulary Development, p. 136
- **L2** Word Knowledge, p. 125
  Rubric for Assessing a Glossary, p. 139
- **L2** Chapter Tests A and B, pp. 140–145

Reading and Vocabulary Study Guide
- **L1** Chapter 18, Section 3, pp. 202–204

Differentiated Instruction

Spanish Support
- **L2** Section Quiz (Spanish), p. 205 ELL
- **L2** Chapter Summary (Spanish), p. 206 ELL
- **L2** Vocabulary Development (Spanish), p. 207 ELL

Key
- **L1** Basic to Average
- **L3** Average to Advanced
- **L2** For All Students
- **LPR** Less Proficient Readers
- **AR** Advanced Readers
- **SN** Special Needs Students
- **GT** Gifted and Talented
- **ELL** English Language Learners

Reading Background

Previewing and Prereading

This chapter's Target Reading Skill asks students to preview each section and set a purpose for reading. Students who do a brief, preliminary reading of complex material are in a strategic position to take control of their learning and comprehension. Previewing helps students consider what they already know about a topic they will be studying and gives some idea of what a text selection is about before they read it. Previewing also helps students identify the text structure and develop a mental framework for ideas to be encountered in the text. This can help them in formulating a more realistic reading and study plan. Follow the steps below to teach students how to preview and preread.

1. Tell students that previewing will help them identify the text structure and develop a mental outline of ideas they will encounter in the text.

2. List the various text features you will be previewing in the order in which you would like students to examine them: section title, text headings, introduction, list of key terms, questions or tasks in the reading selection, photographs, drawings, maps, charts, and other visuals in the text. Focus students' attention on some or all of these items.

3. Prompt students to reflect after examining various text features. They may ask themselves questions such as: What is this reading selection about? What are some key words I will learn? How should I tackle this reading and divide up the task?

Providing Scaffolding

Providing scaffolding for learning gives students the confidence to analyze and comprehend information. In scaffolding the teacher gives the students enough support initially, then provides them with less and less as they become more proficient, ultimately leading to students' being able to do tasks on their own. Below are some tips for using scaffolding.

1. Move from teacher-directed to student-directed instruction.
2. Build on what students already know by organizing questions so that they lead students from easier concepts to more difficult ones.
3. Model skills to illustrate the thinking process students should follow.
4. Have students work in groups.
5. For the more difficult tasks, provide additional structures for students, such as templates that they must complete in order to answer the questions.

World Studies Background

Mountain Formation

Geologically young mountains, such as the Himalayas, are thought to have formed as a result of plate tectonics. According to this theory, continents lie on moving plates and eventually collide with other continents. When they do, the edges of the continents crumple and fold, creating mountains. The Himalayas were probably formed when the continental plate carrying India collided with the Asian plate about 25 million years ago.

Cyclonic Storms

Typhoons are cyclonic storms, or storms composed of winds that swirl around a calm center of low pressure which travels along with the storm. Cyclonic storms begin over oceans, pulling in warm water and warm, moist air to gain power. They lose their source of energy and slow down when they collide with a continent. Cyclonic storms are called hurricanes in the Atlantic Ocean, baquios in the Phillipines, willy-willies in Australia, and cyclones in India.

Hydroelectric Dams

One of the largest dams in East Asia is the Hsin-an River Dam, a hydroelectric dam on a tributary of the Yangtze River. Hydroelectric power dams direct water through turbines, which are wheels with curved blades. The turbines are connected to generators. The higher the water behind the dam, the more pressure it exerts on the turbine blades, and the more power it can produce.

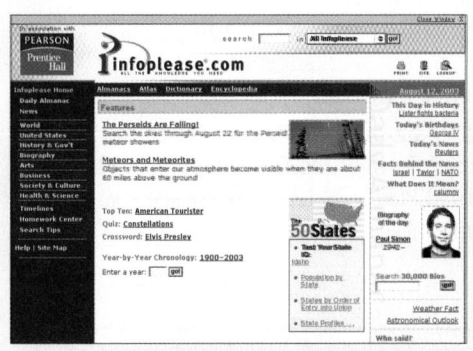

Infoplease® provides a wealth of useful information for the classroom. You can use this resource to strengthen your background on the subjects covered in this chapter. Have students visit this advertising-free site as a starting point for projects requiring research.

Use Web code **lcd-6100** for **Infoplease®**.

Guiding Questions

Remind students about the Guiding Questions introduced at the beginning of this section.

Section 1 relates to **Guiding Question** ❶
What are the main physical features of Asia and the Pacific? *(Many of the countries of East Asia are mountainous; some countries also have plains and plateaus. China is a mix of deserts and mountains, and has two main rivers: the Chang and the Huang. Japan is an archipelago, or group of islands. North and South Korea are located on the Korean Peninsula.)*

Section 2 relates to **Guiding Question** ❶
What are the main physical features of Asia and the Pacific? *(East Asia has five major climate regions: semiarid, arid, humid subtropical, humid continental, and highland. Monsoons have a strong effect on the climates of East Asia.)*

Section 3 relates to **Guiding Question** ❺
How do the people of this region make a living? *(East Asia has natural resources that can be used to produce energy, such as coal, oil, and water for hydroelectric power. In China, people mine copper, tin, and iron. Farming is also a major occupation in East Asia.)*

🎯 Target Reading Skill

In this chapter, students will learn and apply the reading skill of using the reading process. Use the following worksheets to help students practice this skill:

All in One **Asia and the Pacific Teaching Resources,** *Preview and Set a Purpose,* p. 122; *Preview and Predict,* p. 123; *Preview and Ask Questions,* p. 124

Differentiated Instruction

The following Teacher's Edition strategies are suitable for students of varying abilities.

Advanced Readers, p. 589
English Language Learners, p. 578
Gifted and Talented, p. 589
Less Proficient Readers, p. 585
Special Needs Students, p. 578

Chapter Preview

This chapter will introduce you to the region of East Asia. This region includes China, Mongolia, North Korea, South Korea, Japan, and Taiwan.

Section 1
Land and Water

Section 2
Climate and Vegetation

Section 3
Natural Resources and Land Use

 Target Reading Skill

Reading Process In this chapter you will focus on using the reading process to improve your reading skills. When you use the reading process, you set a purpose for reading, predict what you are going to learn, and ask questions about what you read.

▶ The Great Wall of China stretches across the mountains of northern China.

Bibliography

For the Teacher
Japan: Eyewitness Travel Guides. DK Publishing, 2003.
Oberdorfer, Don. *The Two Koreas: A Contemporary History.* Basic Books, 2002.
Haw, Stephen G. et al. *A Traveler's History of China.* Interlink, 2001.

For the Student
L1 Chiarelli, Brunetto et al. *The Atlas of World Cultures.* Peter Bedrick Books, 2001.
L2 National Geographic Society. *National Geographic Student Atlas of the World,* 2001.
L3 Buck, Pearl S. *The Big Wave.* HarperTrophy, 1986 reprint.

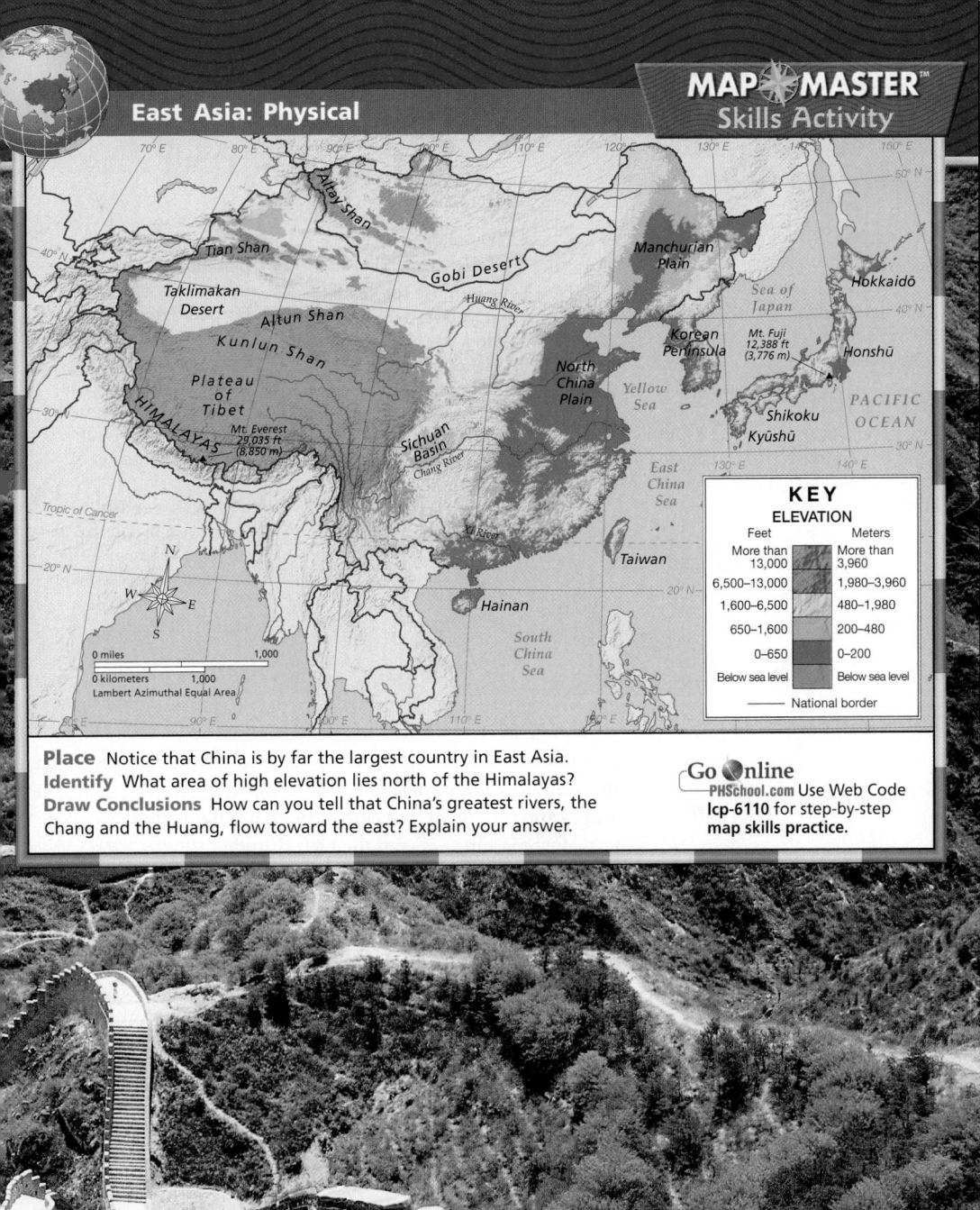

East Asia: Physical

KEY
ELEVATION

Feet	Meters
More than 13,000	More than 3,960
6,500–13,000	1,980–3,960
1,600–6,500	480–1,980
650–1,600	200–480
0–650	0–200
Below sea level	Below sea level

——— National border

Place Notice that China is by far the largest country in East Asia.
Identify What area of high elevation lies north of the Himalayas?
Draw Conclusions How can you tell that China's greatest rivers, the Chang and the Huang, flow toward the east? Explain your answer.

Go Online
PHSchool.com Use Web Code
lcp-6110 for step-by-step
map skills practice.

Chapter 18 **575**

- Tell students that a physical map shows the natural features of a place, while a political map shows boundaries and locations of countries and cities. Ask students to study the physical map on this page, paying special attention to the natural borders. Then ask students to compare the map on this page with a political map of East Asia from an atlas. As a class, locate China, Mongolia, North Korea, South Korea, Japan, and Taiwan on the map on this page.

- Create a table on the board with columns for each of the following features on the map: Manchurian Plain, Korean Peninsula, North China Plain, Taklimakan Desert, and Taiwan. Have students use the map to fill in the table with typical elevations of each place.

Go Online
PHSchool.com Students may practice their map skills using the interactive online version of this map.

Using the Visual L2

Reach Into Your Background Draw students' attention to the photo and caption. Tell students that the Great Wall of China is over 4,000 miles long and thousands of years old. Ask students to think about fences or walls that they see in everyday life and what they are used for. Then have them study the photo of the Great Wall of China and brainstorm what it may have been used for. *(Possible answers: protection from invaders, to show a boundary)*

Answers

MAP MASTER Skills Activity **Identify** the Plateau of Tibet **Draw Conclusions** Because the elevation of East Asia is higher in the west and lower in the east, the rivers flow downhill toward the east.

Chapter Resources

Teaching Resources
Letter Home, p. 109
L2 Vocabulary Development, p. 136
L2 Skills for Life, p. 127
Chapter Tests A and B, pp. 140–145

Spanish Support
Spanish Letter Home, p. 199
L2 Spanish Chapter Summary, p. 206
L2 Spanish Vocabulary Development, p. 207

Media and Technology
L1 Student Edition on Audio CD
L1 Guided Reading Audiotapes, English and Spanish
L2 Social Studies Skills Tutor CD-ROM
ExamView® Test Bank CD-ROM

PRENTICE HALL
Presentation EXPRESS™
Teach · Connect · Inspire

Teach this chapter's content using the PresentationExpress™ CD-ROM including:
- slide shows
- transparencies
- interactive maps and media
- *ExamView®* QuickTake Presenter

Section 1
Step-by-Step Instruction

Objectives

Social Studies

1. Learn about the landforms and water bodies found in East Asia.
2. Find out where most of the people in East Asia live.

Reading/Language Arts

Set a purpose for reading in order to focus on the key information in this section.

Prepare to Read

Build Background Knowledge L2

Tell students that in this section they will be learning about the landforms, water bodies, and population of East Asia. Point out that Mount Fuji, shown on this page of the Student Edition, is often used as a symbol of Japan. When people see this famous mountain, they think of Japan. Ask students to think of some landforms that remind people of the United States. Provide a few simple examples to get students started. (*Grand Canyon, Niagara Falls, Mississippi River*) Conduct an Idea Wave (TE, p. T35) to generate a list.

Set a Purpose for Reading

- Preview the Objectives.

- Read each statement in the *Reading Readiness Guide* aloud. Ask students to mark the statements true or false.

  All in One **Asia and the Pacific Teaching Resources,** *Reading Readiness Guide,* p. 111

- Have students discuss the statements in pairs or groups of four, then mark their worksheets again. Use the Numbered Heads participation strategy (TE, p. T36) to call on students to share their group's perspectives.

Vocabulary Builder
Preview Key Terms L2

Pronounce each Key Term, then ask students to say the word with you. Provide a simple explanation, such as, "A plateau is a high plain with steep slopes around it."

Land and Water

Prepare to Read

Objectives

In this section you will
1. Learn about the landforms and water bodies found in East Asia.
2. Find out where most of the people in East Asia live.

Taking Notes

As you read this section, look for the different types of landforms that dominate East Asia. Copy the web below and record your findings in it.

East Asia's Landforms

Target Reading Skill

Set a Purpose for Reading
When you set a purpose for reading, you give yourself a focus. Before you read this section, look at the headings and pictures. Then set a purpose for reading. In this section, your purpose is to learn about the landforms and water bodies of East Asia.

Key Terms

- **plateau** (pla TOH) *n.* a raised area of level land bordered on one or more sides by steep slopes or cliffs
- **fertile** (FUR tul) *adj.* able to support plant growth
- **archipelago** (ahr kuh PEL uh goh) *n.* a group of islands
- **population density** (pahp yuh LAY shun DEN suh tee) *n.* the average number of people living in a square mile or square kilometer

A view of Mount Fuji, Japan

576 Asia and the Pacific

At 12,388 feet (3,776 meters), Mount Fuji is the highest mountain in Japan. Each year, 150,000 to 200,000 people reach its summit. Visitors heading to the top can stay in mountain lodges and browse in souvenir shops that sell canisters of oxygen to make breathing easier at the high altitude.

Landforms and Water Bodies

Mount Fuji is one of the many spectacular landforms that make up East Asia. A single nation, China, takes up most of East Asia's land. Mountains, highlands, and **plateaus,** or raised areas of level land bordered on one or more sides by steep slopes or cliffs, make up much of China's landscape. The other countries of this region are mountainous, like China. But only China and Mongolia also have wide plains and plateaus. Japan, Taiwan, North Korea, and South Korea have narrow plains that lie mainly along coasts and rivers.

Target Reading Skill L2

Set a Purpose for Reading Point out the Target Reading Skill. Tell students that by setting a purpose for reading, they will be able to focus on the most important information in a section of text.

Model the skill by previewing the headings and pictures on pages 576 and 577 of the Student Edition. Set a purpose based on what you learn from them. For example, "On page 576, I see a picture of a landform. Since the heading mentions landforms and water bodies, I see that I need to focus on the landforms and water bodies of East Asia."

Give students *Preview and Set a Purpose*. Have them complete the activity in their groups.

All in One **Asia and the Pacific Teaching Resources,** *Preview and Set a Purpose,* p. 122

The Himalayas Powerful natural forces created the rugged landscape of East Asia. About 50 million years ago, a huge piece of a continent collided with Asia. The collision caused Earth's surface to fold and buckle, forming the Himalayas and the Plateau of Tibet. The Himalayas are the highest mountains in the world. They include Mount Everest, the highest peak in the world. The Himalayas extend along the border of China and Nepal. The Plateau of Tibet is a huge highland area that lies north of the Himalaya mountains.

Island Landscapes Natural forces also shaped the islands that make up Japan. Earthquakes forced some parts of the country to rise and others to sink. Erupting volcanoes piled up masses of lava and ash, forming new mountains. Japan's Mount Fuji is actually a volcano that has not erupted since 1707. Today, earthquakes and volcanoes are still changing the landscape in many parts of East Asia.

China: More Than One Billion People China is home to one of the oldest civilizations on Earth. With a population of more than one billion people, it also has more people than any other nation in the world.

Mountains and deserts make up more than two thirds of China's land. A desert is a dry region with little vegetation. The area of western and southwestern China has some of the highest mountains in the world. China's Gobi is the northernmost desert on Earth.

China's most important rivers, the Chang and the Huang, begin in Tibet and flow east. The Chang River is deep enough for cargo ships to sail on. More than 100 million people live along the banks of the Huang River. It runs through one of the most fertile regions of China, the North China Plain. **Fertile** soil is capable of supporting abundant plant growth. The North China Plain is covered with deposits of loess (LOH es), a brownish-yellow soil that is very fertile.

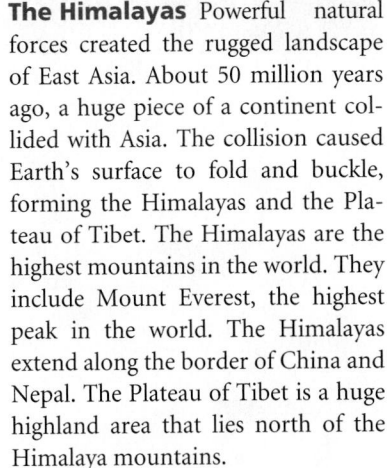

The Plateau of Tibet
The Plateau of Tibet is a vast, high area in China that includes the region of Tibet. These Tibetan women make their living by herding livestock. **Infer** *The Plateau of Tibet is called "the roof of the world." Why do you think this is so?*

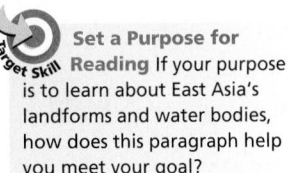
Set a Purpose for Reading If your purpose is to learn about East Asia's landforms and water bodies, how does this paragraph help you meet your goal?

Vocabulary Builder

Use the information below to teach students this section's high-use words.

High-Use Word	Definition and Sample Sentence
spectacular, p. 576	*adj.* amazing; dramatic The view from the top of the mountain is **spectacular**.
rugged, p. 577	*adj.* rough; uneven The **rugged** path was difficult to hike.
previous, p. 579	*adj.* coming before; earlier All of her **previous** jobs had been in clothing stores.

Instruct

Landforms and Water Bodies L2

Guided Instruction

- **Vocabulary Builder** Clarify the high-use words **spectacular** and **rugged** before reading.

- Read Landforms and Water Bodies, using the Oral Cloze reading strategy (TE, p. T33).

- Ask students to name some of the major landforms of East Asia. (*mountains, highlands, plateaus, plains*)

- Have students describe one way in which Japan and the Koreas are similar in geography, and one way in which they are different. (*Both are mountainous; Japan is an archipelago, while North and South Korea are on the Korean Peninsula.*)

Independent Practice

Ask students to create the Taking Notes graphic organizer on a blank piece of paper. Then have them fill in the circles with the types of landforms found in East Asia.

Monitor Progress

- As students fill in the graphic organizer, circulate to make sure individuals are choosing the right details about the dominating landforms in East Asia. Provide assistance as needed.

- Show *Section Reading Support Transparency AP 48* and ask students to check their graphic organizers individually. Go over key concepts and clarify key vocabulary as needed.

    Asia and the Pacific Transparencies, *Section Reading Support Transparency AP 48*

Target Reading Skill L2

Set a Purpose for Reading As a follow up, ask students to answer the Target Reading Skill question on this page of the Student Edition. (*It gives information about East Asia's rivers, and areas of fertile soil.*)

Answer

Infer Possible answer: Its flatness and high elevation make it resemble a roof.

Population in East Asia

Guided Instruction

- **Vocabulary Builder** Clarify the high-use word **previous** before reading.

- Ask students to read Population in East Asia and refer to the maps as directed. As students read, circulate and make sure individuals can answer the Reading Check question.

- Ask students why most people live in the plains and coastal areas of East Asia. (*It is easier to live and grow food there.*)

- Have students consider the positive and negative aspects of having cities, farms, and industries share level ground. (*Positive: Workers are near their workplace, farmers near their markets. Negative: crowding, pollution, disease*)

Independent Practice

Assign *Guided Reading and Review.*

All in One Asia and the Pacific Teaching Resources, *Guided Reading and Review,* p. 112

Monitor Progress

Tell students to fill in the last column of the *Reading Readiness Guide.* Probe for what they learned that confirms or invalidates each statement.

All in One Asia and the Pacific Teaching Resources, *Reading Readiness Guide,* p. 111

 Show students *The Geography of East Asia and the Pacific.* Ask students **What are some of the landforms found in East Asia?** (*Himalayas, Plateau of Tibet, Huang and Chang rivers, archipelago of Japan, the Mongolian steppes, the Gobi Desert*)

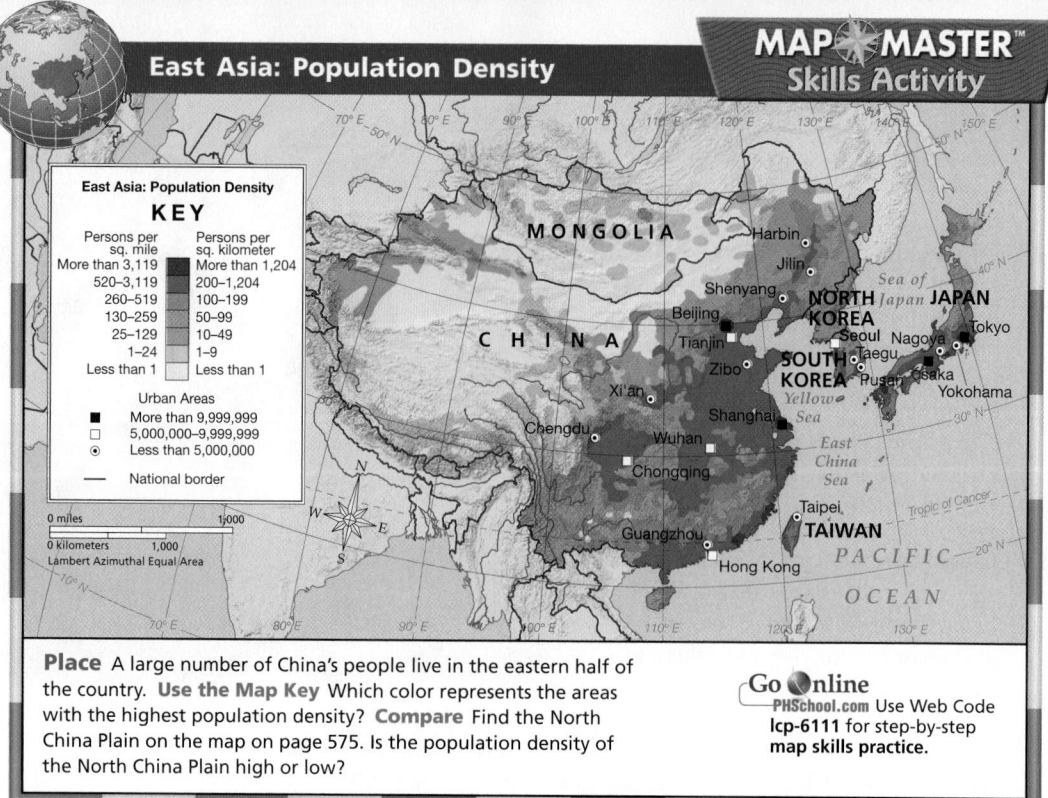

MAP MASTER™ Skills Activity

East Asia: Population Density

East Asia: Population Density

KEY

Persons per sq. mile	Persons per sq. kilometer
More than 3,119	More than 1,204
520–3,119	200–1,204
260–519	100–199
130–259	50–99
25–129	10–49
1–24	1–9
Less than 1	Less than 1

Urban Areas
- ■ More than 9,999,999
- □ 5,000,000–9,999,999
- ⊙ Less than 5,000,000

— National border

0 miles 1,000
0 kilometers 1,000
Lambert Azimuthal Equal Area

Place A large number of China's people live in the eastern half of the country. **Use the Map Key** Which color represents the areas with the highest population density? **Compare** Find the North China Plain on the map on page 575. Is the population density of the North China Plain high or low?

Go Online
PHSchool.com Use Web Code
lcp-6111 for step-by-step map skills practice.

Discovery SCHOOL Video
Learn about the key geographic features in East Asia.

Japan: An Island Country Japan is an **archipelago** (ahr kuh PEL uh goh), or group of islands, in the western Pacific Ocean. Japan has four main islands and more than 3,000 smaller ones. Every major Japanese city is located on the coast. As the map above shows, most of Japan's people live in coastal areas. Nearly 80 percent of the country is mountainous.

Japan's four main islands are Hokkaidō (hoh ky doh), Honshū (hahn shoo), Shikoku (shee koh koo), and Kyūshū (kyoo shoo). The largest and most populated of these is Honshū. Most of Japan's major cities, including its capital city of Tokyo, are located on Honshū.

The Koreas: Two Countries, One Peninsula The Korean Peninsula extends south into the Yellow Sea between China and Japan. A peninsula is a piece of land nearly surrounded by water. Since 1953, Korea has been divided into two separate countries, North Korea and South Korea.

✓ **Reading Check** Which type of landform dominates Japan—mountains or plains?

Answers

✓ **Reading Check** Mountains dominate Japan.

MAP MASTER Skills Activity **Use the Map Key** dark purple **Compare** high

Go Online
PHSchool.com Students may practice their map skills using the interactive version of this map.

Differentiated Instruction

For Special Needs Students L1
Have students locate Japan and Korea on a map as you read aloud the definitions of an archipelago and a peninsula. Have students trace the shoreline of an island, completely surrounded by water; and a peninsula, nearly but not completely surrounded by water. Have students locate an archipelago on the map.

For English Language Learners L1
Have students practice the pronunciations of *island, peninsula,* and *archipelago.* Write the words on the board, then point to examples of each one on a map. At first, point to the correct words so that students can read them. Then have students choose the right ones.

Population in East Asia

As you can see on the map on the previous page, the population of East Asia is spread unevenly across the land. Few people live in the deserts, plateaus, and mountains. Yet almost 1.5 billion people make their homes in East Asia. Most of the people live in the plains and coastal areas, where living and growing food are easier. These parts of East Asia have a very high **population density,** or average number of people living in a square mile (or square kilometer).

Look at the physical map of East Asia on page 575 and find the North China Plain. Now look at the population density map of East Asia on page 578. You can see that this area of China has a very high population density. That is because the land in the North China Plain is better suited for human settlement than the mountains and deserts of China. For example, the North China Plain is level and has fertile soil.

In East Asia, level ground must be shared by cities, farms, and industries. Almost half the population of Japan is crowded onto less than 3 percent of the country's land. In China, most of the population is located in the eastern half of the country, where the plains and coastal areas are located.

A crowded street in Seoul, the capital of South Korea

√ Reading Check **Why does the North China Plain have such a high population density?**

Section 1 Assessment

Key Terms
Review the key terms at the beginning of this section. Use each term in a sentence that explains its meaning.

Target Reading Skill
How did having a purpose help you understand important ideas in this section?

Comprehension and Critical Thinking
1. (a) Recall What are the major landforms in East Asia?

(b) Locate In what part of China is the Plateau of Tibet?
(c) Contrast How are the landforms in eastern China different from the landforms in western China?
2. (a) Identify Name one type of landform in China where there is a high population density. You may refer to the maps in the section to answer.
(b) Draw Conclusions How does the physical geography of East Asia help explain why the eastern part of China is the most densely populated part of the country?

Writing Activity
Suppose that you are a travel agent helping a customer who wants to visit East Asia. Which landforms would you suggest that your customer visit? In which countries are these landforms located? Record your suggestions.

Go Online
PHSchool.com

For: An activity on East Asia
Visit: PHSchool.com
Web Code: lcd-6101

Chapter 18 Section 1 **579**

Writing Activity
Use the *Rubric for Assessing a Writing Assignment* to evaluate students' suggestions.

All in One Asia and the Pacific Teaching Resources, *Rubric for Assessing a Writing Assignment,* p. 137

Go Online
PHSchool.com Typing in the Web code when prompted will bring students directly to detailed instructions for this activity.

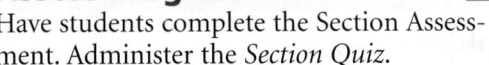
Assess Progress L2
Have students complete the Section Assessment. Administer the *Section Quiz.*

All in One Asia and the Pacific Teaching Resources, *Section Quiz,* p. 113

Reteach L1
If students need more instruction, have them read this section in the Reading and Vocabulary Study Guide.

Chapter 18, Section 1, **Eastern Hemisphere Reading and Vocabulary Study Guide,** pp. 196–198

Extend L3
Give students *Outline Map 29: East Asia.* Using the East Asia physical map in their textbook as a guide, ask students to label all the countries mentioned in Section 1 (China, Mongolia, Taiwan, Japan, North Korea, and South Korea). Have students add several key geographical features to their maps, such as rivers and mountains.

All in One Asia and the Pacific Teaching Resources, *Outline Map 29: East Asia,* p. 132

Answer

√ Reading Check The North China Plain is level and has fertile soil, making it suited for human settlement.

Section 1 Assessment

Key Terms
Students' sentences should reflect knowledge of each Key Term.

Target Reading Skill
Answers will vary, but should include the idea that previewing the section helped students focus on the landforms and water bodies of East Asia.

Comprehension and Critical Thinking
1. (a) mountains, highlands, plateaus, and plains **(b)** Western China, north of the Himalayas **(c)** Eastern China has plains and coasts; mountains and deserts are major features of western China.

2. (a) plains **(b)** Possible answer: The land of eastern China is at a low elevation and is level, making it better for human settlements and farming than the mountains of western China.

Section 2

Climate and Vegetation

Objectives

Social Studies

1. Examine the major climate regions in East Asia.

2. Discover how climate affects people and vegetation in East Asia.

Reading/Language Arts

Preview headings, pictures, and maps to predict what the text might discuss.

Prepare to Read

Build Background Knowledge L2

Tell students that in this section they will be learning about the climate and vegetation of East Asia. Have them preview the visuals in the section and then list some characteristics of East Asia's climate and vegetation . Use the Think-Write-Pair-Share strategy (TE, p. T36) to generate a list. Students can use the list to help them fill out their *Reading Readiness Guides.*

Set a Purpose for Reading

■ Preview the Objectives.

■ Form students into pairs or groups of four. Distribute the *Reading Readiness Guide.* Ask students to fill in the first two columns of the chart. Use the Numbered Heads participation strategy (TE, p. T36) to call on students to share one piece of information they already know and one piece of information they want to know.

All in One Asia and the Pacific Teaching Resources, *Reading Readiness Guide,* p. 115

Vocabulary Builder

Preview Key Terms L2

Pronounce each Key Term, then ask students to say the word with you. Provide a simple explanation, such as, "When monsoon winds change direction, people in East Asia know the weather will also change."

Prepare to Read

Objectives

In this section you will

1. Examine the major climate regions in East Asia.

2. Discover how climate affects people and vegetation in East Asia.

Taking Notes

As you read this section, look for details about how climate affects the people and vegetation in East Asia. Copy the table below and record your findings in it.

East Asia's Climates	
Effect on Vegetation	**Effect on People**
•	• Rice is the main food in southern China.

Target Reading Skill

Predict Making predictions about your text helps you set a purpose for reading and helps you remember what you read. Preview the section by looking at the headings, pictures, and maps. Then predict what the text might discuss about climate and vegetation in East Asia.

Key Terms

• **monsoon** (mahn SOON) *n.* a wind that changes direction with the change of season

• **typhoon** (ty FOON) *n.* a tropical storm that develops over the Pacific Ocean, with winds that reach speeds greater than 74 miles per hour

• **deciduous** (dee SIJ oo us) *adj.* falling off or shedding, as in leaves, seasonally or at a certain stage of development

Y ou and your family are visiting Japan in the middle of February. All of you are trying to decide where to go for a long weekend. Your brother wants to go north to the island of Hokkaidō, where the skiing is perfect. Your parents, though, have had enough of winter. They would like to go to the island of Okinawa (oh kee nah wuh). The water there is warm enough for swimming. Which would you prefer—sun or snow?

East Asia's Climate Regions

Look at the climate map on the next page. It shows that East Asia has seven climate regions. Two of them—the tropical wet region and the subarctic region—cover a comparatively small part of the land. The five major climate regions are semiarid, arid, humid subtropical, humid continental, and highland.

Downhill skiing in Japan

Target Reading Skill L2

Predict Point out the Target Reading Skill. Tell students that predicting will help them set a purpose for reading.

Model the skill by using the headings, pictures, and maps in this section to predict what the text might discuss. "I see that the headings and maps relate to climate and vegetation. I predict that we will learn how climate affects vegetation in East Asia."

Give students *Preview and Predict.* Have them complete the activity in their groups.

All in One Asia and the Pacific Teaching Resources, *Preview and Predict,* p. 123

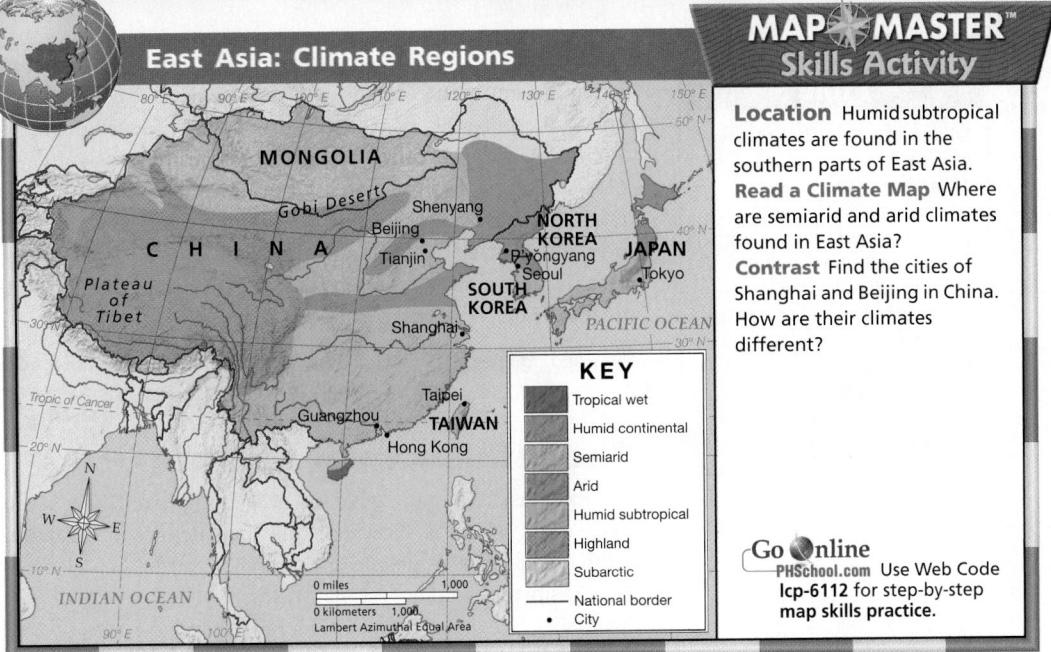

East Asia: Climate Regions

MAP★MASTER™
Skills Activity

MONGOLIA
Gobi Desert
Shenyang
Beijing
Tianjin
CHINA
Plateau of Tibet
NORTH KOREA
P'yongyang
Seoul
SOUTH KOREA
JAPAN
Tokyo
Shanghai
PACIFIC OCEAN
Tropic of Cancer
Guangzhou
Taipei
TAIWAN
Hong Kong
INDIAN OCEAN

KEY
- Tropical wet
- Humid continental
- Semiarid
- Arid
- Humid subtropical
- Highland
- Subarctic
- National border
- City

0 miles 1,000
0 kilometers 1,000
Lambert Azimuthal Equal Area

Location Humid subtropical climates are found in the southern parts of East Asia.
Read a Climate Map Where are semiarid and arid climates found in East Asia?
Contrast Find the cities of Shanghai and Beijing in China. How are their climates different?

Go Online
PHSchool.com Use Web Code
lcp-6112 for step-by-step map skills practice.

A Variety of Climates A large part of eastern China has a humid subtropical climate—cool winters and hot summers with plenty of rain. To the north is a humid continental area of warm summers and cold winters. Because South Korea and Japan are almost completely surrounded by water, summers are a bit cooler and winters are a bit warmer than in other places at the same latitude.

In contrast, the northern interior of China is very dry, with arid and semiarid climate regions. There, temperatures can range from very hot to very cold. To the south, the Plateau of Tibet has a cool, dry, highland climate.

Monsoons Monsoons strongly affect the climates of East Asia. Monsoons are winds that change direction with the change of season. In summer, Pacific Ocean winds blow northwest toward the Asian continent. They bring rainfall that starts in June as a drizzle. The Japanese call this the "plum rain" because it begins just as the plums begin to ripen on the trees. The winds cause hot, humid weather and heavier rain in July.

In winter, the winds blow toward the east. The winds that begin in the interior of northern Asia are icy cold and very dry. In parts of China, the winds produce dust storms that can last for days. Where they cross warm ocean waters, these monsoons pick up moisture. Farther inland, they drop it as rain or snow.

Predict
What did you predict about this section? How did your prediction guide your reading?

Chapter 18 Section 2 **581**

Vocabulary Builder

Use the information below to teach students this section's high-use words.

High-Use Word	Definition and Sample Sentence
comparatively, p. 580	*adv.* relatively; when compared to another thing The theater's dressing room is **comparatively** large.
interior, p. 581	*n.* inside; inner part My office is in the **interior** of the building, so it doesn't have windows.
devastation, p. 582	*n.* major damage; destruction The hurricane caused great **devastation.**

Instruct

East Asia's Climate Regions

L2

Guided Instruction

- **Vocabulary Builder** Clarify the high-use words **comparatively, interior,** and **devastation** before reading.

- Read East Asia's Climate Regions, using the Structured Silent Reading method (TE, p. T34). Refer students to the climate regions maps as they read.

- Ask students to name the five major climate regions in East Asia. (*semiarid, arid, humid subtropical, humid continental, and highlands*) Ask students which region they think gets the least rain. (*arid*)

- Ask students to describe the different types of weather brought by summer and winter monsoons. (*Summer monsoons bring hot, humid weather and rain. Winter monsoons may bring icy weather or dust storms.*)

Independent Practice

Ask students to create the Taking Notes graphic organizer on a blank piece of paper. Then have them begin filling in the chart with details about how each climate affects vegetation and people in East Asia.

Monitor Progress

As students fill in the graphic organizer, circulate to make sure individuals are choosing the correct details. Provide assistance as needed.

Target Reading Skill

L2

Predict As a follow up, ask students to answer the Target Reading Skill questions on this page of the Student Edition. (*Answers will vary, but students should identify elements they referred to when they made their predictions, and explain if and how they had to revise their predictions.*)

Answers

MAP★MASTER Skills Activity **Read a Climate Map** in Mongolia and northern China **Contrast** Shanghai has a humid subtropical climate, while Beijing has a semiarid climate.

Go Online
PHSchool.com Students may practice their map skills using the interactive online version of this map.

The Influences of Climate

 L2

Guided Instruction

■ Ask students to read The Influences of Climate and review the vegetation map for East Asia. Make sure individuals can answer the Reading Check question.

■ Ask students **Why is the Huang River both a blessing and a curse for Chinese farmers?** (*The river makes the North China Plain good for farming. On the other hand, the river also floods.*)

Independent Practice

Have students complete the graphic organizer by filling in the details about how climate affects vegetation and people in East Asia.

Monitor Progress

■ Show *Section Reading Support Transparency AP 49* and ask students to check their graphic organizers individually. Go over key concepts and clarify key vocabulary as needed.

📖 **Asia and the Pacific Transparencies,** *Section Reading Support Transparency AP 49*

■ Tell students to fill in the last column of the *Reading Readiness Guide.* Ask them to evaluate if what they learned was what they had expected to learn.

All in One Asia and the Pacific Teaching Resources, *Reading Readiness Guide,* p. 115

Answers

✔ Reading Check Monsoons are winds that bring rain in summer and cold, dry air in winter; typhoons are violent storms with strong winds and heavy rains.

MAP MASTER Skills Activity **Use a Map Key** Southern China and Taiwan **Compare** fairly dry, because much of the area can support only desert scrub vegetation

582 *Asia and the Pacific*

Divine Winds Typhoons twice saved Japan from invaders. In 1274, Kublai Khan, a great leader of China's Mongol people, sent a fleet of warships to Japan. The Mongols got only as far as the island of Kyūshū. A typhoon frightened them back to China. When Kublai Khan tried again in 1281, a typhoon destroyed his huge fleet. The Japanese called this typhoon *kamikaze*, or "divine wind."

Typhoons East Asia has hurricanes like those that sometime strike the southern coastline of the United States during Augus and September. These violent storms, which develop over th Pacific Ocean, are called **typhoons.** Whirling typhoon wind blow at speeds of 74 miles an hour or more. The winds and heav rains they bring can cause major damage. Killer typhoons hav brought great devastation and death to some countries in Eas Asia. For example, a typhoon that struck China in 1922 resulted in about 60,000 deaths.

✔ Reading Check **Name and describe two types of storms that occur in East Asia.**

The Influences of Climate

In East Asia, climate governs everything from the natura vegetation, which is shown on the map below, to agriculture Climate affects what people grow, how often they can plant, anc how easily they can harvest their fields.

How Climate Affects Vegetation in East Asia Much of the plant life in East Asia is strong enough to stand seasona differences in temperature and rainfall. Bamboo, for example grows remarkably quickly during the wet season in southern China and Japan. Yet it can also survive dry spells by storing food

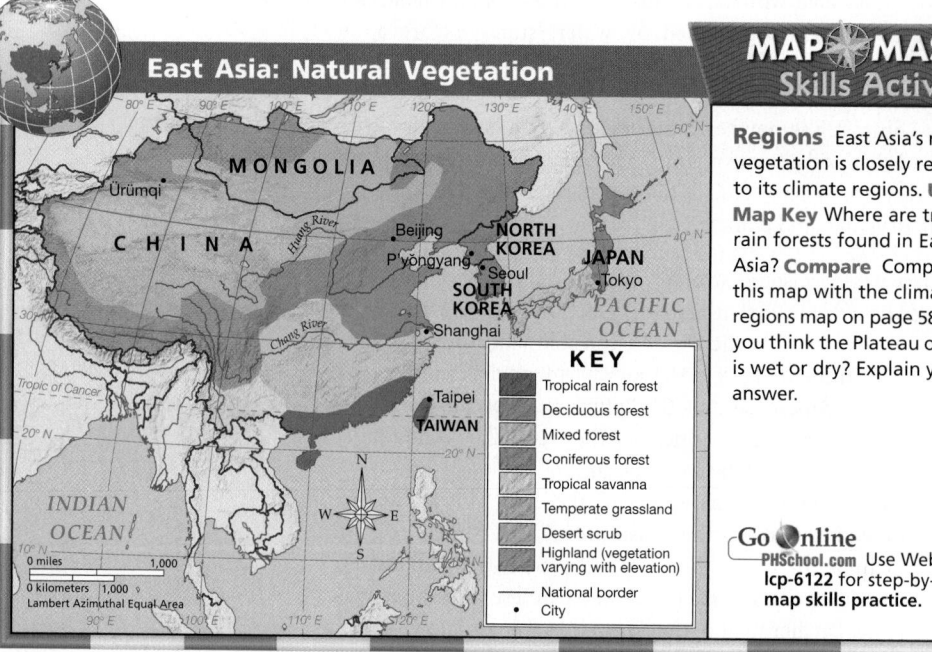

East Asia: Natural Vegetation

KEY
- Tropical rain forest
- Deciduous forest
- Mixed forest
- Coniferous forest
- Tropical savanna
- Temperate grassland
- Desert scrub
- Highland (vegetation varying with elevation)
- —— National border
- • City

0 miles 1,000
0 kilometers 1,000
Lambert Azimuthal Equal Area

MAP MASTER
Skills Activity

Regions East Asia's natural vegetation is closely related to its climate regions. **Use a Map Key** Where are tropical rain forests found in East Asia? **Compare** Compare this map with the climate regions map on page 581. Do you think the Plateau of Tibet is wet or dry? Explain your answer.

Go Online
PHSchool.com Use Web Code lcp-6122 for step-by-step map skills practice.

582 Asia and the Pacific

Skills for Life Skills Mini Lesson

Using the Cartographer's Tools

1. Teach the skill by pointing out to students that most maps have tools that cartographers, or mapmakers, put in to help people use them. These include the compass rose, scale, and map key.

2. Help students practice the skill by looking at the map on this page and determining which tool helps them decide what types of vegetation exist in Mongolia. (*the key*)

3. Have students apply the skill to the map on page 581 by answering this question: How do the climates of Hong Kong and Tokyo differ from areas farther from the ocean? (*The two cities both have humid subtropical climates. Areas farther from the ocean are, for the most part, drier.*)

in its huge root system. Shrubs and many small flowering plants in the deserts of China spring up rapidly after summer rains. **Deciduous** (dih SIJ oo us), or leaf-shedding, trees change with the seasons. Maples, birches, and other trees turn the hillsides of Japan and the Koreas gold, orange, and red, once summer gives way to fall.

How Climate Affects People in East Asia

Climate greatly affects life in East Asia. The region around the Huang River in China is a good example. The Chinese word *Huang* means "yellow." The river gets its name from the brownish-yellow loess that is blown by the desert winds. The river picks up the loess and deposits it to the east on the North China Plain. The loess covers a huge 125,000-square-mile (324,000-square-kilometer) area around the river. This plain is one of the best farming areas in China.

The Huang River also floods. A system of dams helps control the waters. But the river can still overflow during the monsoons. Floods gave the Huang River its nickname, "China's Sorrow."

The diet of East Asians is also affected by climate. Because rice grows best in warm weather, it is the main crop—and food—of people in southern China. In the cooler north, wheat and other grains grow better than rice. This means that people in the north eat more flour products, such as noodles.

√ **Reading Check** How does bamboo survive during dry spells in southern China and Japan?

Brilliant Fall Colors in Japan
Most parts of Japan have spring, summer, fall, and winter. At this teahouse in the city of Nara, it is still warm enough to sit outdoors in October and November. **Analyze Images** *How can you tell the trees in the photo are deciduous trees?*

Section 2 Assessment

Key Terms
Review the key terms at the beginning of this section. Use each term in a sentence that explains its meaning.

Target Reading Skill
What did you predict about this section? How did your prediction guide your reading?

Comprehension and Critical Thinking
1. (a) Recall What are the five major climate regions in East Asia?

(b) Summarize What kind of winters and summers are found in a humid subtropical climate?

2. (a) Identify Name three ways climate affects agriculture in East Asia.
(b) Generalize How does the climate affect what people eat in China?

Writing Activity
Write a letter to a friend who is planning a long trip to East Asia. Explain what climate conditions can occur in different areas. Include suggestions for clothing.

For: An activity on East Asia's climate
Visit: PHSchool.com
Web Code: lcd-6102

Chapter 18 Section 2 **583**

Writing Activity
Use the *Rubric for Assessing a Writing Assignment* to evaluate students' letters.

All in One **Asia and the Pacific Teaching Resources**, *Rubric for Assessing a Writing Assignment*, p. 137

Go Online
PHSchool.com Typing in the Web code when prompted will bring students directly to detailed instructions for this activity.

Assess and Reteach

Assess Progress [L2]
Have students complete the Section Assessment. Then administer the *Section Quiz*.

All in One **Asia and the Pacific Teaching Resources**, *Section Quiz*, p. 117

Reteach [L1]
If students need more instruction, have them read this section in the Reading and Vocabulary Study Guide.

📖 Chapter 18, Section 2, **Eastern Hemisphere Reading and Vocabulary Study Guide,** pp. 199–201

Extend [L3]
Have students learn more about East Asian agriculture by completing the *Book Project: Agriculture Center*. Assign students to groups to work on the project.

All in One **Asia and the Pacific Teaching Resources**, *Book Project: Agriculture Center*, pp. 77–79

Answers

Analyze Images by the color of the leaves

√ **Reading Check** Bamboo survives dry spells by storing food in its huge root system.

Section 2 Assessment

Key Terms
Students' sentences should reflect knowledge of each Key Term.

Target Reading Skill
Answers will vary, but should indicate that students used headings, pictures, and maps to predict what the text might discuss. They should also evaluate the usefulness of their predictions.

Comprehension and Critical Thinking
1. (a) semiarid, arid, humid subtropical, humid continental, highlands **(b)** cool winters; hot summers with lots of rain

2. (a) Climate affects what people plant, how often they plant, and how they harvest.
(b) Rice needs warm weather to grow, so it thrives in warmer southern China, and residents there eat rice products; grains grow better in northern China, which is cooler, so residents eat more flour products.

Objective

Learn to determine the reliability of information on the Internet.

Prepare to Read

Build Background Knowledge **L2**

Tell students that in this lesson they will learn to find reliable Internet sources. Have students think about why it is important to be able to determine how reliable a piece of writing is, especially on the Internet. Conduct an Idea Wave (TE, p. T35) to allow students to share their ideas.

Instruct

Using Reliable Information on the Internet **L2**

Guided Instruction

- Read the steps to using reliable information on the Internet as a class and write them on the board.

- Practice the skill by having students follow the steps on p. 585 as a class. Model each step by having students brainstorm additional search terms *(possible answers: Gobi desert, Gobi climate)*, discuss why an .edu Web site would be helpful to their research *(because .edu addresses are run by schools and universities)*, determine what kinds of topics require recent information *(recent maps and graphs are probably more accurate than information from 50 years ago)*, and identify a reliable source of current information on the Gobi *(a major newspaper Web site, a respected archaeology or science magazine Web site, or an educational Web site run by a university)*.

Using Reliable Information on the Internet

Your teacher has given you an assignment to write a report about the Gobi Desert in Mongolia and China. To research your report, you are asked to find articles, photos, and statistics about the Gobi Desert.

"Use a variety of good sources on the Internet," your teacher urges. "An encyclopedia article is a good start for basic facts. But if you search further, you might find stories from people who live there. You might also find photographs that will help you to describe the land in your own words."

You enter the word *Gobi* on an Internet search engine, and receive 123,000 "hits"—that is, Web sites that contain the word *Gobi*. How can you find reliable, useful information among all these sites?

Learn the Skill

To find information from Web sites you can trust, follow the steps below.

1 **Decide on your search terms.** Make a list of what you are looking for. For example, try *Gobi Desert* or *Gobi climate*.

2 **Notice the Web site's Internet address.** The address, or URL, will include a period followed by a three-letter abbreviation. Among the most common are ".com," ".edu," ".gov," and ".org." Just about anyone can set up a Web site with a .com (commercial) address. Schools and universities use a .edu (education) address. Nonprofit organizations such as museums use .org. Official government sites carry a .gov address.

3 **Try to identify the author and date of information on a Web site.** The author and date often appear on the Web page. But many sites are anonymous—they do not identify the author. Do not use information from anonymous sites. It may be out of date or it may be written by an author who has no particular expertise about the topic.

4 **Choose a reliable source, or use more than one source, if needed.** Encyclopedias are reliable. They are written by people who have knowledge about a wide range of subject areas and they present facts. Sources with .gov and .edu are generally reliable, as are newspapers, magazines, and television network news sites.

584 Asia and the Pacific

Independent Practice

Assign *Skills for Life* and have students complete it individually.

All in One **Asia and the Pacific Teaching Resources**, *Skills for Life*, p. 127

Monitor Progress

As students are completing Skills for Life, circulate to make sure individuals are applying the skill steps effectively. Provide assistance as needed.

Practice the Skill

Use the steps in the skill to do some research on a computer.

1 If a search for *Gobi* gives you thousands of results, what additional search terms could you use to narrow the search?

2 Look for a site with a .gov address from the government of China or Mongolia. Or try a United States government Web site for statistics about the location and size of the Gobi. Why is it a good idea to go to an .edu address to research the Gobi?

3 Would it matter if an online map of the Gobi was created this year or 50 years ago? Would it matter if a graph of average rainfall in the Gobi was from this year or 50 years ago? Explain.

4 Say you read about a recent discovery of dinosaur bones in the Gobi. The news appears on an archaeology Web site, but the author and date are unidentified. Where would you find a reliable source of this news?

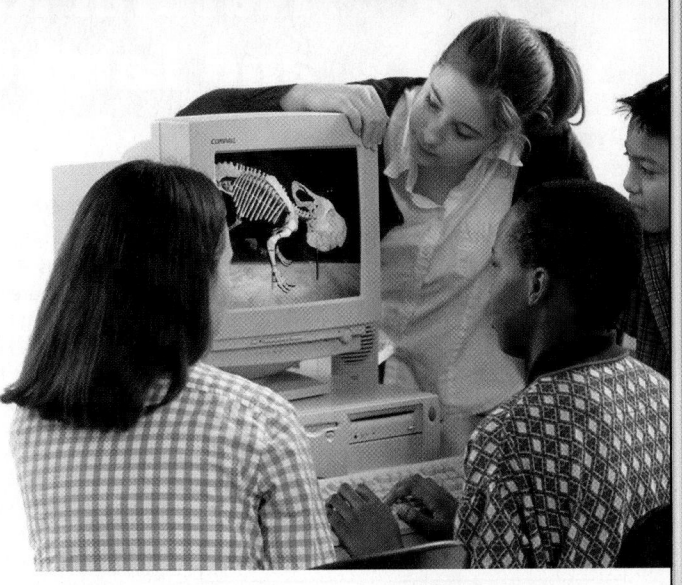

Reliable Web sites can help you research Gobi dinosaurs—or any school assignment.

Apply the Skill

Suppose your neighbor writes a letter to the editor of the Internet edition of your local newspaper. In the letter, she writes, "The population in our community has doubled in the last year." Is this reliable information? Then you go to your local government's Web site and read this: "Town population doubles in just one year, according to government statistics." Is this information reliable? Name two Web sites you could go to in order to find the actual statistics. Explain why each is reliable.

Differentiated Instruction

For Less Proficient Readers L1

To reinforce the lesson, ask each student to find two sources of information, one they deem to be reliable and one they deem to be unreliable. Then form pairs and have students identify which of their partners' sources is reliable and which is unreliable.

Assess and Reteach

Assess Progress L2

Ask students to do the Apply the Skill Activity.

Reteach L1

If students are having trouble applying the skill steps, have them review the skill using the interactive Social Studies Skills Tutor CD-ROM.

> *Using Reliable Information,* **Social Studies Skills Tutor CD-ROM**

Extend L3

Have students choose a topic from the chapter to research on the Internet, such as the Great Wall of China, the Himalayas, the effects of monsoons, or aquaculture. Students should conduct their research on a variety of Web sites and take note of any inconsistencies that they find. Then have students write a paragraph explaining which of their sources they think are the most and least reliable and why.

Answer
Apply the Skill

The neighbor's letter is probably not as reliable as the information from the local government's Web site. The town Web site reporting the population growth probably conducted a census or poll to determine their information, while it is possible the neighbor only guessed or received her information from a source she did not cite. The state government's Web site or the U.S. census bureau's Web site might be able to provide actual statistics.

Objectives

Social Studies

1. Learn about East Asia's major natural resources.
2. Find out how the people of East Asia use land to produce food.

Reading/Language Arts

Turn headings into questions and then read to answer those questions.

Prepare to Read

Build Background Knowledge   **L2**

Tell students that in this section they will be learning about the natural resources of East Asia. Remind students that natural resources are important in every part of the world. They are needed to make everything from food and fuel to buildings and cars. Invite students to share what they know about important natural resources and ways in which these resources are used. Use the Give One, Get One strategy (TE, p. T37) to generate a list of resources and uses.

Set a Purpose for Reading

- Preview the Objectives.

- Read each statement in the *Reading Readiness Guide* aloud. Ask students to mark the statements true or false.

- Have students discuss the statements in pairs or groups of four, then mark their worksheets again. Use the Numbered Heads participation strategy (TE, p. T36) to call on students to share their group's perspectives.

  All in One **Asia and the Pacific Teaching Resources,** *Reading Readiness Guide,* p. 119

Vocabulary Builder
Preview Key Terms   **L2**

Pronounce each Key Term, then ask students to say the word with you. Provide a simple explanation such as, "The United States is a developed country."

Prepare to Read

Objectives

In this section you will
1. Learn about East Asia's major natural resources.
2. Find out how the people of East Asia use land to produce food.

Taking Notes

Copy the table below. As you read, look for the headings that appear in large red type. Turn these headings into questions. Use the table to record your answers to these questions.

Natural Resources and Land Use in East Asia	
Questions	**Answers**

🎯 Target Reading Skill

Ask Questions Preview the headings, pictures, and maps to see what this section is about. Find the main headings in this section. (They appear in large red type.) Turn these headings into questions. Then read to answer your questions. Write your questions and answers in the Taking Notes table.

Key Terms

- **developing country** (dih VEL up ing KUN tree) *n.* a country that has low industrial production and little modern technology
- **developed country** (dih VEL upt KUN tree) *n.* a country with many industries and a well-developed economy
- **terrace** (TEHR us) *n.* a level area in a hillside
- **double-cropping** (DUB ul KRAHP ing) *v.* to grow two or more crops on the same land

Coal miners in China

586 Asia and the Pacific

When planning their economies, all countries ask these three basic questions: What will be produced? How will it be produced? For whom will it be produced? For the countries of East Asia, the answers to these questions depend largely on factors surrounding these two things: natural resources and land use.

Natural resources are materials found in nature. They include fertile land, minerals, water, and forests. Natural resources can be used to produce all sorts of goods, from cars to sweatshirts. Land use is linked to natural resources. To improve their economies, governments have to decide how to use the land and the natural resources they contain.

East Asia's Natural Resources

East Asia's lands and waters are filled with abundant natural resources. As the map on the next page shows, East Asia has natural resources that can be used to produce energy, such as coal, oil, and water for hydroelectric power. Other resources in East Asia are the raw materials for manufactured goods, such as electronic equipment. The water bodies and fertile land of East Asia are also important resources.

🎯 Target Reading Skill   **L2**

Ask Questions Point out the Target Reading Skill. Tell students that being able to turn headings into questions can help them identify the important ideas in what they are reading.

Model turning the first heading on page 586 into a question. For example: "I see that the first heading refers to East Asia's

natural resources, so I ask: What are East Asia's natural resources? I will read to find the answer to that question."

Give students *Preview and Ask Questions.* Have them complete the activity in their groups.

All in One **Asia and the Pacific Teaching Resources,** *Preview and Ask Questions,* p. 124

MAP MASTER™
Skills Activity

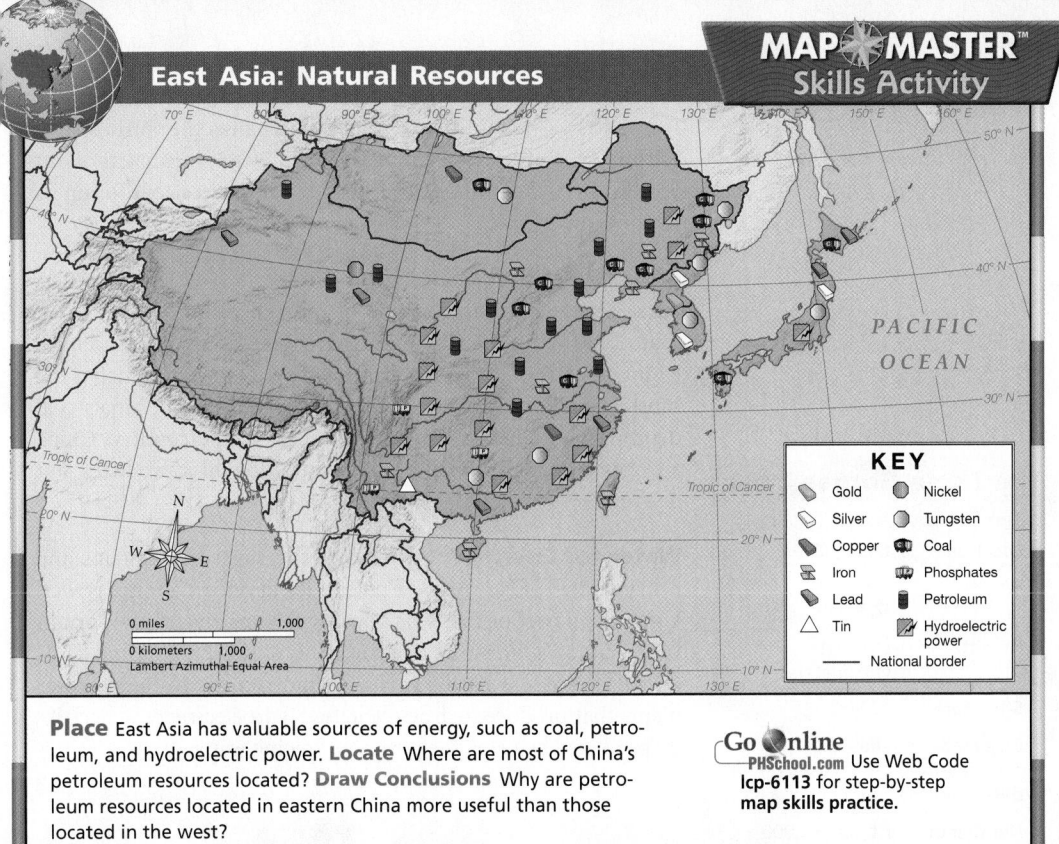

PACIFIC OCEAN

KEY

◇ Gold		◯ Nickel	
◇ Silver		◯ Tungsten	
◇ Copper		🝛 Coal	
⛏ Iron		🝛 Phosphates	
◇ Lead		⬓ Petroleum	
△ Tin		◪ Hydroelectric power	
		— National border	

0 miles 1,000
0 kilometers 1,000
Lambert Azimuthal Equal Area

Place East Asia has valuable sources of energy, such as coal, petroleum, and hydroelectric power. **Locate** Where are most of China's petroleum resources located? **Draw Conclusions** Why are petroleum resources located in eastern China more useful than those located in the west?

Go Online
PHSchool.com Use Web Code
lcp-6113 for step-by-step
map skills practice.

Mineral Resources in the Two Koreas East Asia has plenty of mineral resources, but they are unevenly distributed. Some countries have more and other countries have less. The two Koreas, for example, have limited mineral resources. Coal and iron, which are used in manufacturing, are plentiful in North Korea. But there is little coal or iron in South Korea, where much more manufacturing takes place. The only minerals that are in large supply in the South are tungsten and graphite.

If South Korea could share North Korea's coal and iron, both countries would benefit. But the two do not share resources, since they are hostile toward each other. North Korea is a **developing country**—one that has low industrial production and little modern technology. South Korea is a **developed country**—one with many industries and a well-developed economy. Because of its limited resources, South Korea must import the iron, crude oil, and chemicals it needs for its industries. Nevertheless, it has become one of East Asia's richest economies. It exports, or sells, many manufactured goods to other nations.

Ask Questions
Turn the blue heading into a question. Read the paragraph and then write an answer to your question.

Chapter 18 Section 3 **587**

Vocabulary Builder

Use the information below to teach students this section's high-use words.

High-Use Word	Definition and Sample Sentence
factor, p. 586	*n.* something that helps bring about a result Location is a key **factor** in the success of a new business.
abundant, p. 586	*adj.* plentiful The region has an **abundant** supply of water.
percentage, p. 590	*n.* portion; part of each hundred A large **percentage** of the money will go to charity.
cultivate, p. 590	*v.* to use land to raise crops Machines such as tractors and plows can be used to **cultivate** farmland.

Instruct

East Asia's Natural Resources   **L2**

Guided Instruction

■ **Vocabulary Builder** Clarify the high-use words **factor** and **abundant** before reading.

■ Read East Asia's Natural Resources using the ReQuest Procedure (TE, p. T35).

■ Ask students to give some examples of natural resources. (*fertile land, minerals, water, forests*)

■ Ask students **What important resources are not found in South Korea?** (*coal, iron, crude oil, chemicals*) **How does South Korea make up for this lack of resources?** (*It imports resources from other countries.*)

■ Ask **How are the economies of South Korea and North Korea different?** (*North Korea is a developing country; South Korea is a developed country.*)

⟳ Target Reading Skill

Ask Questions As a follow up, ask students to answer the Target Reading Skill question on this page of the Student Edition. (*What mineral resources do the two Koreas have? North Korea has plentiful coal and iron, while South Korea has tungsten and graphite, but has to import other mineral resources for manufacturing.*)

Answers

MAP MASTER
Skills Activity **Locate** in eastern China
Draw Conclusions Because the resources in eastern China are near the coast, they can be more easily exported to other parts of the world.

Go Online
PHSchool.com Students may practice their map skills, using the interactive online version of this map.

Guided Instruction (continued)
- Have students compare South Korea to China and Japan. In terms of natural resources, is South Korea more like Japan or China? *(South Korea is more like Japan; both have few mineral resources.)*

- Ask students **Why is China building the Three Gorges Dam?** *(to generate hydroelectricity and to control flooding on the Chang River)*

- Ask **Why has aquaculture expanded in East Asia in recent decades?** *(Overfishing and pollution have reduced wild fish supplies. Advances in aquaculture have also helped it to increase.)*

Independent Practice
Ask students to create the Taking Notes graphic organizer on a blank piece of paper. Then have them fill in the chart with answers to the questions they created from the first headings in large red type.

Monitor Progress
As students fill in the graphic organizer, circulate to make sure individuals are creating the right questions and answering them correctly. Provide assistance as needed.

Mineral Resources in Japan Japan is a modern industrial society. Yet Japan—like South Korea—has few mineral resources. It imports vast quantities of minerals. Japan is the world's largest importer of coal, natural gas, and oil. It also imports about 95 percent of the iron ore, tin, and copper that it needs to run its major industries.

Mineral Resources in China Unlike its East Asian neighbors, China has a large supply of mineral resources. For more than 2,000 years, the Chinese have mined copper, tin, and iron. China has one of the world's largest supplies of coal, which is the most important of its mineral resources. Most of China's coal deposits are found in the northern part of the country. China also has oil deposits. China uses most of the oil it produces, but does export some crude oil and oil products.

Water for Energy Production The rugged mountains and heavy rainfall of East Asia are perfect for developing water power. Using the power of East Asia's swiftly flowing rivers is important to the region's industrial development. However, building dams to collect water is costly. It is even more costly to build power plants that produce hydroelectricity. Hydroelectricity is electricity produced by using the power of flowing water.

The Three Gorges Dam

Location	Chang River
Width	1.4 miles (2,309 meters)
Height	607 feet (185 meters)
Start date	1994
Expected completion date	2009
Number of construction workers	About 250,000
Purpose	Flood control, hydroelectricity
Number of people displaced	About 1.5 million

588 Asia and the Pacific

Background: Global Perspectives

Useful Metals Countries such as Japan, China, and South Korea export manufactured goods around the world. East Asian factories rely on many metal resources that are found in the region. Tungsten, for example, is a very strong metal that has an extremely high melting point of about 6,152 °F (3,410 °C). These qualities make tungsten useful for making tools and rocket engine parts. Copper conducts, or carries, electricity very well, so it is a perfect metal for making electrical wires and parts for computers and televisions. Lead is a very heavy and soft metal that is used to make batteries.

In 2004, China produced about 20 percent of its electricity from hydroelectric power. The Chinese government expects this figure to increase when China finishes building the Three Gorges Dam across the Chang River. The Three Gorges Dam will be one and a half miles wide and more than 600 feet high. China is building the dam not only to produce electricity but also to control the frequent floods on the Chang River.

Water for Aquaculture East Asia's ocean and inland waters have been an important source of food for the region's people. Aquaculture, or fish farming, has been practiced in Asia for centuries. During the 1980s and 1990s, however, aquaculture production in Asia greatly expanded. This was due, in part, to the fact that overfishing and pollution had decreased the supply of saltwater and freshwater fish. The increase was also due to advances in the practice of aquaculture. In East Asia, China is the leading aquaculture producer. Japan, South Korea, and Taiwan are also among the top aquaculture producers in the world. Aquaculture includes farm-raised fish, shrimp, oysters, mussels, clams, and seaweed.

✓ Reading Check **Based on what you have read, is Japan a developed country or a developing country?**

The World's Largest Dam
The bottom photo shows the Three Gorges Dam in China under construction. The top photo shows what the Three Gorges area looked like before construction began. The middle photo shows a model of the completed dam. China is building the dam to produce hydroelectricity. **Contrast** *Study the two small photos. How will the dam change the landscape of the Three Gorges area?*

Chapter 18 Section 3 **589**

Using the Land to Produce Food

Guided Instruction

- **Vocabulary Builder** Clarify the high-use words **percentage** and **cultivate** before reading.

- Ask students **What percentage of Japan can be cultivated?** *(12 percent)* **What percentage of Japan cannot be cultivated?** *(88 percent)* **Why is so little land available for agriculture?** *(Mountains and plateaus account for most of the land.)*

- Ask students to describe different ways East Asian farmers try to increase the amount of crops they can raise. *(They use terraces, cutting horizontal ridges into steep hillsides; plant one type of crop between rows of another; use sides of roads and railway lines; practice double-cropping, growing two or more crops on the same land or at the same time; raise crops that ripen fast.)*

Independent Practice

Have students complete the graphic organizer by filling in the answers to their last question.

Monitor Progress

- Show *Section Reading Support Transparency AP 50* and ask students to check their graphic organizers individually. Go over key concepts and clarify key vocabulary as needed.

    📖 **Asia and the Pacific Transparencies,** *Section Reading Support Transparency AP 50*

- Tell students to fill in the last column of the *Reading Readiness Guide*. Probe for what they learned that confirms or invalidates each statement.

    All in One **Asia and the Pacific Teaching Resources,** *Reading Readiness Guide*, p. 119

Answers

Contrast The dam will fill the valley with water.

✓ Reading Check Japan is a developed country.

Assess and Reteach

Assess Progress `L2`

Have students complete the Section Assessment. Then administer the *Section Quiz*.

All in One Asia and the Pacific Teaching Resources, *Section Quiz,* p. 121

Reteach `L1`

If students need more instruction, have them read this section in the Reading and Vocabulary Study Guide.

Chapter 18, Section 3, **Eastern Hemisphere Reading and Vocabulary Study Guide,** pp. 202–204

Extend `L3`

Have students expand their knowledge of East Asia by completing the *Small Group Activity: The Mount Everest Story* in which students will design and create a bulletin board of information on Mount Everest. Have them refer back to the skill on pp. 584–585 to help them with their research.

All in One Asia and the Pacific Teaching Resources, *Small Group Activity: The Mount Everest Story,* pp. 128–131

Answer

✔ **Reading Check** In terrace farming, farmers create more land for crops. In double-cropping, they use existing land to its fullest capacity.

Section 3 Assessment

Key Terms
Students' sentences should reflect knowledge of each Key Term.

Target Reading Skill
Answers will vary, but students' questions should reflect the important information in headings, pictures, and maps in this section.

Comprehension and Critical Thinking
1. (a) coal, oil, water **(b)** China **(c)** The country could import large amounts of mineral resources.

2. (a) terracing, which allows them to cultivate hillside lands; double-cropping, or growing two or more crops on the same land at the same time **(b)** Possible answer: Faster-growing crops would allow farmers to plant more crops during the growing season.

A Japanese farmer displays his harvest of rice.

Using the Land to Produce Food

In order to feed its large population, East Asians need to farm every bit of available land. With so many mountains and plateaus, only a small percentage of the land can be cultivated. Only about 14 percent of China, 12 percent of Japan, and 14 percent of North Korea can be farmed. South Korea's 19 percent is about equal to the percentage of land farmed in the United States.

Terrace Farming In China, Japan, and parts of Korea, farmers cut horizontal steps called **terraces** into steep hillsides to gain a few precious yards of soil for crops. Farmers even use the land at the sides of roads and railway lines for planting.

Double-Cropping Where climate and soil allow, farmers practice **double-cropping,** growing two or more crops on the same land in the same season or at the same time. In China, farmers often plant one type of crop between the rows of another crop in order to grow more food. In some parts of southern China, farmers are even able to grow three crops in a year. In southern Japan, rice seeds are sowed in small fields. When the seedlings are about a foot high, they are replanted in a larger field after wheat has been harvested from it.

✔ **Reading Check** What is the difference between terrace farming and double-cropping?

Section 3 Assessment

Key Terms
Review the key terms at the beginning of this section. Use each term in a sentence that explains its meaning.

Target Reading Skill
What questions did you ask about this section?

Comprehension and Critical Thinking
1. (a) Recall Name three natural resources in East Asia that can be used to produce energy.

(b) Contrast Which country has a larger supply of mineral resources, China or Japan?
(c) Infer How could a country develop its economy without a large supply of mineral resources?
2. (a) Recall What two farming techniques do East Asian farmers use to make up for a shortage of farmland?
(b) Infer Why might East Asian farmers be interested in learning about faster-growing crops?

Writing Activity
Suppose you are a reporter for a television news program. Write a report that tells how the waters of East Asia are an important resource for its people. Include at least two ways water is used in East Asia.

For: An activity on East Asia
Visit: PHSchool.com
Web Code: lcd-6103

Writing Activity
Use the *Rubric for Assessing a Report* to evaluate students' reports.

All in One Asia and the Pacific Teaching Resources, *Rubric for Assessing a Report,* p. 138

Go Online PHSchool.com Typing in the Web code when prompted will bring students directly to detailed instructions for this activity.

◆ Chapter Summary

Section 1: Land and Water

- Mountains, plains, and plateaus are the main landforms in East Asia. The Chang and Huang rivers are major bodies of water.
- Most people in East Asia live in the plains and coastal areas.

China

Section 2: Climate and Vegetation

- East Asia's five major climate regions are semi-arid, arid, humid subtropical, humid continental, and highlands. Monsoons have a strong effect on the climate of East Asia.
- The climate of East Asia supports vegetation, such as bamboo, that is strong enough to stand seasonal differences in temperature and rainfall. Winds blow fertile soil, which is then carried by the Huang River to the North China Plain.

Japan

Section 3: Natural Resources and Land Use

- China has more mineral resources than its neighbors. Water in East Asia is used to produce hydroelectricity and to support aquaculture.
- East Asia's physical landscape leaves a small amount of land available for farming. Terraces and double-cropping are two ways East Asian farmers get the most food out of the land that is used for farming.

◆ Key Terms

Each of the statements below contains a key term from the chapter. If the statement is true, write *true*. If the statement is false, rewrite the statement to make it true.

1. A **plateau** is a dry region with little vegetation.
2. When soil is **fertile,** it is capable of supporting abundant plant growth.
3. **Population density** measures the average number of people living in a square mile or square kilometer.
4. A **monsoon** is a tropical storm that occurs over the Pacific Ocean.
5. **Deciduous** trees shed their leaves in the fall.
6. A **developed country** has a low level of industrial production.
7. A **developing country** has many industries and a well-developed economy.
8. When farmers use **double-cropping,** they build steps into hillsides to increase farmland.

Chapter 18 **591**

┌ Vocabulary Builder ─────────

Revisit the chapter's high-use words:

spectacular	interior	abundant
rugged	devastation	percentage
previous	factor	cultivate
comparatively		

Ask students to review the definitions they recorded on their *Word Knowledge* worksheets.

All in One Asia and the Pacific Teaching Resources, *Word Knowledge*, p. 125

Consider allowing students to earn extra credit if they use the words in their answers to the questions in the Chapter Review and Assessment. They must use the words correctly and in a natural context to win the extra points.

Review Chapter Content

- Review and revisit the major themes of this chapter by asking students to classify what Guiding Question each bulleted statement in the Chapter Summary answers. Form students into groups and ask them to complete the activity together. Guiding Questions can be found on page 567 in the Student Edition.

- Assign *Vocabulary Development* for students to review Key Terms.

  All in One Asia and the Pacific Teaching Resources, *Vocabulary Development*, p. 136

Answers

Key Terms

1. False. A plateau is a raised area of level land bordered by steep slopes or cliffs.
2. True
3. True
4. False. A monsoon is a wind that changes direction with the change of season.
5. True
6. False. A developed country has high industrial production.
7. False. A developing country has low industrial production and little modern technology.
8. False. When farmers use double-cropping, they grow two or more crops on the same land.

Review and Assessment
Comprehension and Critical Thinking

9. (a) China and Mongolia **(b)** along the border of China and Nepal

10. (a) the Chang and Huang **(b)** the Huang **(c)** The river picks up the loess blown by desert winds and deposits it on the plains.

11. (a) Hokkaidō, Honshū, Shikoku, and Kyūshū **(b)** Japan is an archipelago, while Korea is a peninsula.

12. (a) plains and coastal areas **(b)** The land there is level and better suited for living and growing food.

13. (a) Since the countries are almost completely surrounded by water, summers are a bit cooler and winters a bit warmer than other places at the same latitude. **(b)** The summer monsoon blows northwest toward Asia and brings rainfall.

14. (a) What will be produced? How will it be produced? For whom will it be produced? **(b)** They import mineral resources.

15. (a) across the Chang River **(b)** The dam will increase the amount of hydroelectricity available in the country.

16. (a) They use every scrap of available land and techniques that increase the number of crops they can plant at the same time and in the same place. **(b)** Terracing allows farmers to plant on the steep hills of East Asia.

Skills Practice
Students should use the information they learned in the Skills for Life lesson to explain why an Internet encyclopedia is a reliable source.

Writing Activity: Geography
Answers will vary, but should include accurate definitions and real-life examples of each term, all of which are found in East Asia. Tell students what sources you would like them to use beyond the textbook. Use *Rubric for Assessing a Glossary* to assess students' dictionaries.

All in One Asia and the Pacific Teaching Resources, *Rubric for Assessing a Glossary,* p. 139

◆ Comprehension and Critical Thinking

9. (a) Recall Which East Asian countries have mountains, wide plains, and plateaus?
(b) Locate Where are the Himalayas located?

10. (a) Name Name two major rivers in China.
(b) Recall Which of these rivers flows through the North China Plain?
(c) Identify Effect How does this river make the North China Plain a fertile region?

11. (a) List What are Japan's four main islands?
(b) Compare and Contrast How is the physical geography of Japan different from the physical geography of the Koreas?

12. (a) Identify Which parts of East Asia have a very high population density?
(b) Summarize Why does most of the population in China live in the eastern half of the country?

13. (a) Explain How does water affect the climates of the Koreas and Japan?
(b) Summarize What does the summer monsoon do in East Asia and in what direction does it blow?

14. (a) Define What three basic questions do countries ask when planning their economies?

(b) Summarize How do Japan and South Korea make up for their lack of mineral resources?

15. (a) Locate Where is the Three Gorges Dam?
(b) Predict How might the Three Gorges Dam affect energy production in China?

16. (a) Explain How have the farmers of East Asia made the best use of the land for farming?
(b) Apply Information Which farming method is linked to the physical landscape of East Asia?

◆ Skills Practice

Using Reliable Information on the Internet
Review the steps you followed to learn this skill. Then explain why an Internet encyclopedia is a reliable source.

◆ Writing Activity: Geography

Create a geographic dictionary of these items: plateau, plain, volcano, monsoon, mountain, peninsula. Arrange the list in alphabetical order. Write a definition, using your textbook to find a real-life example of each term. The example must be located in East Asia. Include the country where your example is located.

MAP MASTER Skills Activity

Place Location For each place listed below, write the letter from the map that shows its location.
1. Himalayas
2. North China Plain
3. Huang River
4. Plateau of Tibet
5. Chang River
6. Mount Fuji

Go Online
PHSchool.com Use Web Code ldp-6120 for an interactive map.

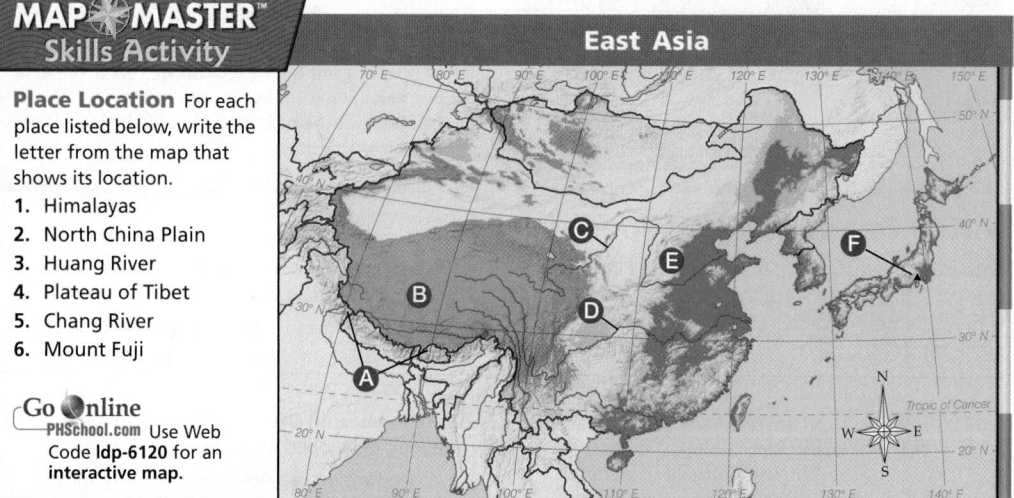

East Asia

Standardized Test Prep

Test-Taking Tips

Some questions on standardized tests ask you to identify the main topic of a reading passage. Study the passage below. Then follow the tips to answer the sample question.

Desert winds blow silt into the Huang River. The Huang, or Yellow, River gets its name from this brownish-yellow loess. The river carries and deposits loess to the east. The loess covers 125,000 square miles (324,000 square kilometers) on the North China Plain. This great plain is one of China's best farming regions.

TIP Some paragraphs contain a topic sentence that states its main idea. All other sentences in the paragraph support this point.

Pick the letter of the statement that best answers the question.
Which is the best topic sentence for this paragraph?

A ~~Climate influences everything from natural vegetation to agriculture.~~

B ~~Loess is rich yellow-brown silt or clay.~~

C Climate affects life in the region around the Huang River.

D The Huang River is known as China's Sorrow because of its damaging floods.

TIP Rule out answer choices that don't make sense. Then pick the best answer from the remaining choices.

Think It Through You can rule out A because the statement is too general. It could be the topic for a paragraph on any region of the world. However, B is too specific; it could be another detail in the paragraph. Similarly, D is another detail, one that might be included in a different paragraph about flooding on the Huang. The correct answer is C.

Practice Questions

Use the passage below to answer Question 1. Use the tips above to help you.

In summer, the monsoon blows northwest from the Pacific Ocean toward the Asian continent. The summer monsoon brings hot, humid weather and rainfall to East Asia. In winter, the monsoon blows toward the east. Where they cross warm ocean waters, such as the South China Sea, these monsoons pick up moisture. Later, they drop it as rain or snow.

1. Which is the best topic sentence for the above paragraph?
   A People need rain to grow crops.
   B Monsoons have a strong effect on climate in East Asia.
   C The South China Sea is located off China's southern coast.
   D The Pacific Ocean is the deepest ocean in the world.

Use the tips above and other tips in this book to help you answer the following questions.

2. Which country takes up most of East Asia's land?
   A Japan   B Mongolia
   C China   D South Korea

3. Most of the people in Japan live
   A in coastal areas.
   B in mountainous areas.
   C on Japan's wide plains.
   D on plateaus.

4. The Huang River runs through a fertile region of East Asia called
   A Mongolia.
   B Taiwan.
   C the North China Plain.
   D Tibet.

Go Online PHSchool.com
Use Web Code lca-6100 for a **Chapter 18 self-test.**

MAP★MASTER Skills Activity

1. A	2. E
3. C	4. B
5. D	6. F

Go Online PHSchool.com Students may practice their map skills using the interactive online version of this map.

Standardized Test Prep

Answers

1. B
2. B
3. A
4. C

Go Online PHSchool.com Students may use the Chapter 18 self-test on PHSchool.com to prepare for the Chapter Test.

Assessment Resources

Use *Chapter Tests A and B* to assess students' mastery of chapter content.

All in One **Asia and the Pacific Teaching Resources,** *Chapter Tests A and B,* pp. 140–145

Tests are also available on the *ExamView®* *Test Bank CD-ROM.*

⊙ *ExamView® Test Bank CD-ROM*

Chapter Overview

Overview

Section 1 — South Asia: Physical Geography
1. Learn about the landforms of South Asia.
2. Discover the most important factor that affects climate in South Asia.
3. Examine how people use the land and resources of South Asia.

Section 2 — Southwest Asia: Physical Geography
1. Learn about the major landforms of Southwest Asia.
2. Find out what the two most important resources in Southwest Asia are.
3. Examine how people use the land in Southwest Asia.

Section 3 — Central Asia: Physical Geography
1. Learn about the main physical features of Central Asia.
2. Discover which natural resources are important in Central Asia.
3. Find out how people use the land in Central Asia.

Discovery CHANNEL SCHOOL Video

The Geography of South, Southwest, and Central Asia
Length: 7 minutes, 12 seconds
Use with Section 1
In this segment, students will learn about the countries that make up South, Southwest, and Central Asia. This segment uses maps to compare and contrast the major landforms of these regions.

Technology Resources

Go Online PHSchool.com

Students use embedded Web codes to access Internet activities, chapter self-tests, and additional map practice. They may also access Dorling Kindersley's Online Desk Reference to learn more about each country they study.

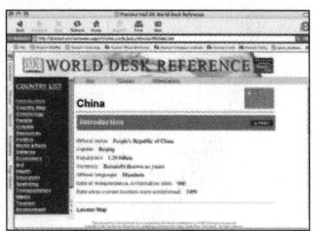

Interactive Textbook

Use the Interactive Textbook to make content and concepts come alive through animations, videos, and activities that accompany the complete basal text—online and on CD-ROM.

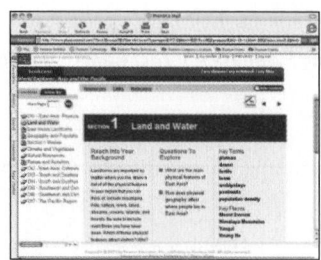

PRENTICE HALL TeacherEXPRESS
Plan • Teach • Assess

Use this complete suite of powerful teaching tools to make planning lessons and administering tests quicker and easier.

Reading and Assessment

Reading and Vocabulary Instruction

⟳ Model the Target Reading Skill

Clarifying Meaning Explain to students that they can use several strategies to understand new words and ideas. They can reread a confusing passage and try to link familiar and unfamiliar words and ideas. They can also read ahead to see if the author provides definitions or examples later in the passage. After reading, students can clarify meaning by summarizing or paraphrasing.

Write the following selection from page 604 of the Student Edition on the board. Model techniques for clarifying meaning by thinking aloud as you read it to the class.

Most of Southwest Asia has an arid or semiarid climate. Think aloud: "I'll reread to make sure I understand. I'm not sure what arid and semiarid are, though. I'll read ahead to find out." *Much of the region receives less than 10 inches (25 centimeters) of rain each year. It is no wonder, then, that nearly two thirds of Southwest Asia is desert!* Think aloud: *"Arid* and *semiarid* must mean that the climate is quite dry. I'll summarize the paragraph in my own words to remember the main ideas: Most of Southwest Asia is desert because it receives very little rainfall."

Use the following worksheets from All-in-One Asia and the Pacific Teaching Resources (pp. 163–165) to support this chapter's Target Reading Skill.

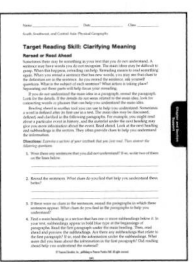 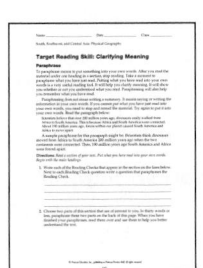 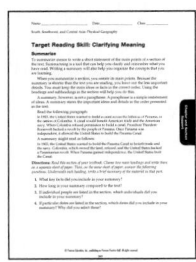

Vocabulary Builder
High-Use Academic Words
Use these steps to teach this chapter's high-use words:

1. Have students rate how well they know each word on their Word Knowledge worksheets (All-in-One Asia and the Pacific Teaching Resources, p. 164).

2. Pronounce each word and ask students to repeat it.

3. Give students a brief definition or sample sentence (provided on TE pp. 597, 602, and 611).

4. Work with students as they fill in the "Definition or Example" column of their Word Knowledge worksheets.

Assessment

Formal Assessment
Test students' understanding of core knowledge and skills.

Chapter Tests A and B,
All-in-One Asia and the Pacific
Teaching Resources, pp. 176–181

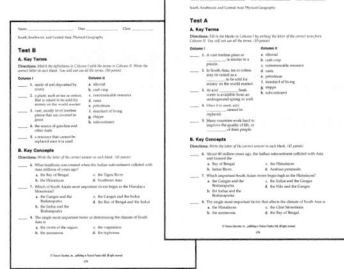

Customize the Chapter
Tests to suit your needs.
*ExamView Test Bank
CD-ROM*

Skills Assessment
Assess geographic literacy.

MapMaster Skills, Student Edition pp. 595, 597, 598, 602, 604, 606, 611, 612, 613, 616

Assess reading and comprehension.

Target Reading Skills, Student Edition, pp. 598, 602, 612 and in Section Assessments

Chapter 19 Assessment, Eastern Hemisphere Reading and Vocabulary Study Guide, p. 215

Performance Assessment
Assess students' performance on this chapter's Writing Activities using the following rubric from All-in-One Asia and the Pacific Teaching Resources.

Rubric for Assessing a Writing Assignment, p. 174

Rubric for Assessing a Newspaper Article, p. 175

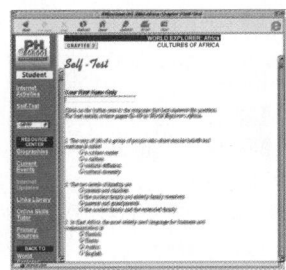

Assess students' work through performance tasks.

Small Group Activity: An Oral Report on Desert Farming,
All-in-One Asia and the Pacific Teaching Resources, pp. 167–170

Online Assessment
Have students check their own understanding.

Chapter Self-Test

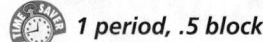
Section 1 South Asia: Physical Geography

1 period, .5 block

Social Studies Objectives

1. Learn about the landforms of South Asia.
2. Discover the most important factor that affects climate in South Asia.
3. Examine how people use the land and resources of South Asia.

Reading/Language Arts Objective

Reread and read ahead to clarify ideas and word meanings.

Prepare to Read	Instructional Resources	Differentiated Instruction
Build Background Knowledge Discuss the Himalayas' effect on the region's history and culture. **Set a Purpose for Reading** Have students evaluate statements on the *Reading Readiness Guide*. **Preview Key Terms** Teach the section's Key Terms. **Target Reading Skill** Introduce the section's Target Reading Skill of **rereading or reading ahead.**	**All in One Asia and the Pacific Teaching Resources** L2 Reading Readiness Guide, p. 150 L2 Reread or Read Ahead, p. 161	**Spanish Reading and Vocabulary Study Guide** L1 Chapter 19, Section 1, pp. 146–147 ELL

Instruct	Instructional Resources	Differentiated Instruction
Major Landforms of South Asia Discuss the landforms of South Asia. **Target Reading Skill** Review **rereading or reading ahead.** **The Climates of South Asia** Discuss monsoons and ask questions about how they affect the people of South Asia. **Land Use in South Asia** Discuss the use of resources in South Asia.	**All in One Asia and the Pacific Teaching Resources** L2 Guided Reading and Review, p. 151 L2 Reading Readiness Guide, p. 150 **Asia and the Pacific Transparencies** L2 Section Reading Support Transparency AP 51 **World Studies Video Program** L2 The Geography of South, Southwest, and Central Asia	**Teacher's Edition** L2 For English Language Learners, TE p. 598 L3 For Advanced Readers, TE p. 599 L1 For Special Needs Students, TE p. 599 **PHSchool.com** L3 For: Environmental and Global Issues: Population Density AR, GT Web Code: lcd-6204 **Spanish Support** L2 Guided Reading and Review (Spanish), p. 208 ELL

Assess and Reteach	Instructional Resources	Differentiated Instruction
Assess Progress Evaluate student comprehension with the section assessment and section quiz. **Reteach** Assign the Reading and Vocabulary Study Guide to help struggling students. **Extend** Extend the lesson by showing students a video.	**All in One Asia and the Pacific Teaching Resources** L2 Section Quiz, p. 152 Rubric for Assessing a Writing Assignment, p. 174 **Reading and Vocabulary Study Guide** L1 Chapter 19, Section 1, pp. 206–208	**Spanish Support** L2 Section Quiz (Spanish), p. 209 ELL

Key

L1 Basic to Average   L3 Average to Advanced
L2 For All Students

LPR Less Proficient Readers
AR Advanced Readers
SN Special Needs Students

GT Gifted and Talented
ELL English Language Learners

Section 2 Southwest Asia: Physical Geography

 1.5 periods, .75 block (includes Skills for Life)

Social Studies Objectives

1. Learn about the major landforms of Southwest Asia.
2. Find out what the two most important resources in Southwest Asia are.
3. Examine how people use the land in Southwest Asia.

Reading/Language Arts Objective

Paraphrase after reading to help you understand what you have read.

Prepare to Read

Build Background Knowledge
Prepare students by having them fill in an outline map of Southwest Asia.

Set a Purpose for Reading
Have students evaluate statements on the *Reading Readiness Guide.*

Preview Key Terms
Teach the section's Key Terms.

Target Reading Skill
Introduce the section's Target Reading Skill of **paraphrasing.**

Instructional Resources

All in One Asia and the Pacific Teaching Resources
- L2 Reading Readiness Guide, p. 154
- L2 Paraphrase, p. 162
- L2 Outline Map 28: Central and Southwest Asia, p. 172

Differentiated Instruction

Spanish Reading and Vocabulary Study Guide
- L1 Chapter 19, Section 2, pp. 148–149 ELL

Instruct

A Dry Region Bordered by Water
Discuss the location and geography of Southwest Asia.

Target Reading Skill
Review **paraphrasing.**

Southwest Asia's Major Natural Resources
Discuss two of the most important resources in Southwest Asia.

Using the Land in Southwest Asia
Discuss land use in Southwest Asia.

Instructional Resources

All in One Asia and the Pacific Teaching Resources
- L2 Guided Reading and Review, p. 155
- L2 Reading Readiness Guide, p. 154

Asia and the Pacific Transparencies
- L2 Section Reading Support Transparency AP 52

PHschool.com
- L2 For: Environmental and Global Issues: Alternative Sources of Energy
  Web Code: lcd-6205

Differentiated Instruction

All in One Asia and the Pacific Teaching Resources
- L1 Reading a Climate Map, p. 171 ELL, LPR, SN
- L2 Skills for Life, p. 166 AR, GT, LPR, SN

Teacher's Edition
- L1 For Special Needs Students, TE p. 604
- L1 For Less Proficient Readers, TE p. 605

Student Edition on Audio CD
- L1 Chapter 19, Section 2 ELL, LPR, SN

Spanish Support
- L2 Guided Reading and Review (Spanish), p. 210 ELL

Assess and Reteach

Assess Progress
Evaluate student comprehension with the section assessment and section quiz.

Reteach
Assign the Reading and Vocabulary Study Guide to help struggling students.

Extend
Extend the lesson by assigning a Small Group Activity.

Instructional Resources

All in One Asia and the Pacific Teaching Resources
- L2 Section Quiz, p. 156
- L3 Small Group Activity: An Oral Report on Desert Farming, pp. 167–170
  Rubric for Assessing a Writing Assignment, p. 174

Reading and Vocabulary Study Guide
- L1 Chapter 19, Section 2, pp. 209–211

Differentiated Instruction

Spanish Support
- L2 Section Quiz (Spanish), p. 211 ELL

Teacher's Edition
- L3 For Gifted and Talented, TE p. 609

Social Studies Skills Tutor CD-ROM
- L1 L3 Identifying Main Ideas AR, GT, ELL, LPR, SN

Key

- L1 Basic to Average
- L2 For All Students
- L3 Average to Advanced

- LPR Less Proficient Readers
- AR Advanced Readers
- SN Special Needs Students

- GT Gifted and Talented
- ELL English Language Learners

Section 3 Central Asia: Physical Geography

 2 periods, 1 block (includes Chapter Review and Assessment)

Social Studies Objectives
1. Learn about the main physical features of Central Asia.
2. Discover which natural resources are important in Central Asia.
3. Find out how people use the land in Central Asia.

Reading/Language Arts Objective
Summarize to review main ideas and better understand a text.

Prepare to Read	Instructional Resources	Differentiated Instruction
Build Background Knowledge Discuss natural resources and land use in the students' region or community. **Set a Purpose for Reading** Have students evaluate statements on the *Reading Readiness Guide*. **Preview Key Terms** Teach the section's Key Terms. **Target Reading Skill** Introduce the section's Target Reading Skill of **summarizing**.	**All in One Asia and the Pacific Teaching Resources** **L2** Reading Readiness Guide, p. 158 **L2** Summarize, p. 163	**Spanish Reading and Vocabulary Study Guide** **L1** Chapter 19, Section 3, pp. 150–151 ELL

Instruct	Instructional Resources	Differentiated Instruction
Central Asia's Main Physical Features Discuss the countries and physical features of Central Asia. **Target Reading Skill** Review **summarizing**. **Natural Resources in Central Asia** **Land Use in Central Asia** Discuss natural resources and how people use the land in Central Asia.	**All in One Asia and the Pacific Teaching Resources** **L2** Guided Reading and Review, p. 159 **L2** Reading Readiness Guide, p. 158 **Asia and the Pacific Transparencies** **L2** Section Reading Support Transparency AP 53 **L2** Transparency B3: Tree Map/Flow Chart	**All in One Asia and the Pacific Teaching Resources** **L3** Enrichment, p. 165 AR, GT **Teacher's Edition** **L3** For Gifted and Talented, TE p. 612 **L1** For Less Proficient Readers, TE p. 612 **Reading and Vocabulary Study Guide** **L1** Chapter 19, Section 3, pp. 212–214 ELL, LPR, SN

Assess and Reteach	Instructional Resources	Differentiated Instruction
Assess Progress Evaluate student comprehension with the section assessment and section quiz. **Reteach** Assign the Reading and Vocabulary Study Guide to help struggling students. **Extend** Extend the lesson by assigning an Internet activity.	**All in One Asia and the Pacific Teaching Resources** **L2** Section Quiz, p. 160 Rubric for Assessing a Writing Assignment, p. 174 **L2** Word Knowledge, p. 164 **L2** Vocabulary Development, p. 173 Rubric for Assessing a Newspaper Article, p. 175 **L2** Chapter Tests A and B, pp. 176–181 **Reading and Vocabulary Study Guide** **L1** Chapter 19, Section 3, pp. 212–214 **PHSchool.com** **L3** **For:** Long-Term Integrated Projects: Reporting to an Environmental Conference **Web Code:** lcd-6206	**Spanish Support** **L2** Section Quiz (Spanish), p. 213 ELL **L2** Chapter Summary (Spanish), p. 214 ELL **L2** Vocabulary Development (Spanish), p. 215 ELL

Key
L1 Basic to Average   **L3** Average to Advanced   LPR Less Proficient Readers   GT Gifted and Talented
L2 For All Students   AR Advanced Readers   ELL English Language Learners
                                           SN Special Needs Students

Professional Development

Reading Background

Pre-Teaching Vocabulary

Research literature on academic vocabulary instruction indicates that effective strategies require students to go beyond simply looking up dictionary definitions or examining the context. Vocabulary learning must be based on the learner's dynamic engagement in constructing understanding.

If students are not retaining the meaning of the Key Terms or high-use words, use this extended vocabulary sequence to engage them in learning new words.

1. Present the word in writing and point out the part of speech.
2. Pronounce the word and have students pronounce the word.
3. Provide an accessible definition and concrete examples, or "showing sentences."
4. Rephrase the simple definition or example sentence, asking students to complete the statement by substituting the word aloud.
5. Check for understanding by providing an application task/question requiring critical thinking.

Sample instructional sequence:

1. Our first key term is *cash crop*. It is a noun, a word that names a person, place, or thing.
2. Say the words *cash crop* after me. (Students repeat.)
3. The word *cash crop* means *a crop that is raised for sale in a market*; The farm did not sell enough of its *cash crop* to make a profit.
4. Oranges are a _____ grown in Florida. (Students substitute the word.)
5. Are the flowers grown in your garden a *cash crop*? Yes-No-Why? (Students answer the question.)

Word Wizard

It is important for students to learn vocabulary both inside and outside the classroom. One way to spark students' interest in learning new words is to allow them to earn points for every Key Term from the chapter that they recognize on television or in the news. For example, they might hear a newscaster refer to the Indian *subcontinent* or see a poster advertising a benefit concert to protect a *rainforest*. Give students points for bringing in evidence of having heard or seen a Key Term or high-use word outside the classroom. Have students earn extra points for bringing in evidence of hearing a new word that relates to the chapter, along with its definition.

World Studies Background

Adam's Bridge

Sri Lanka and India are separated by Adam's Bridge, a chain of limestone shoals and sandbars. Some of these are never covered by water, and at high tide, only about four feet of water cover the rest. Evidence suggests that Adam's Bridge represents a former land connection between Sri Lanka and India. A Muslim legend has it that Adam crossed the shoals to reach Adam's Peak in Ceylon where he stood on one foot for 1,000 years to apologize for his sins.

The Dead Sea

The Dead Sea is a 390 square mile (1,010 square kilometer) salt lake that lies between Israel and Jordan. The aptly named Dead Sea is so salty that it supports little life. The salt and minerals found there, however, are an important natural resource. Factories on the shore extract minerals for commercial use, and health spas in the area are taking advantage of the medical benefits of the Dead Sea.

The Roof of the World

Pamir, a mountainous region of central Asia, is located mostly in Tajikistan. The area is also known as the "roof of the world" because many of its peaks are more than 20,000 feet high, and it is the meeting point of four great mountain ranges.

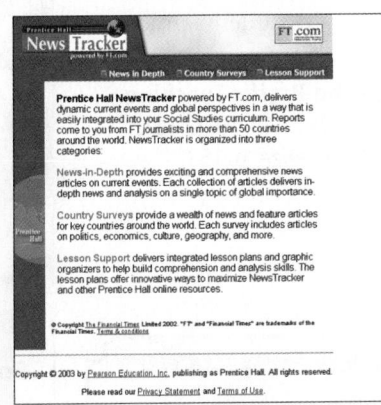

Get in-depth information on topics of global importance with **Prentice Hall Newstracker,** powered by FT.com.

 Use Web code **lcd-6200** for **Prentice Hall Newstracker.**

594f

Chapter 19

Guiding Questions

Remind students about the Guiding Questions introduced at the beginning of the book.

Section 1 relates to **Guiding Question 1**
What are the main physical features of Asia and the Pacific? *(The main physical features of South Asia include the Himalayas, the Ganges and Indus rivers, large alluvial plains in the north, the Deccan Plateau, the Western Ghats, and the Eastern Ghats.)*

Section 2 relates to **Guiding Question 1**
What are the main physical features of Asia and the Pacific? *(The main physical features of Southwest Asia include the Rub' al-Khali desert; the Tigris, Euphrates, and Shatt-al-Arab rivers; the Zagros and Elburz mountains; the Red, Mediterranean, Black, and Caspian seas; and the Persian Gulf.)*

Section 3 relates to **Guiding Question 1**
What are the main physical features of Asia and the Pacific? *(The main physical features of Central Asia include highlands, the Tien Shan and Pamir mountains, the Hindu Kush, the Kara Kum and Kyzyl Kum deserts, the Kirghiz Steppe, and the Caspian and Aral seas.)*

Target Reading Skill

In this chapter, students will learn the reading skill of clarifying meaning. Use the following worksheets to help students practice this skill:

All in One Asia and the Pacific Teaching Resources, *Reread or Read Ahead,* p. 161; *Paraphrase,* p. 162; *Summarize,* p. 163

Differentiated Instruction

The following Teacher's Edition strategies are suitable for students of varying abilities.

Advanced Readers, p. 599
English Language Learners, p. 598
Gifted and Talented, pp. 609, 612
Less Proficient Readers, pp. 605, 612
Special Needs Students, pp. 599, 604

Chapter 19
South, Southwest, and Central Asia: Physical Geography

Chapter Preview

In this chapter, you will examine the physical geography of South, Southwest, and Central Asia. This huge region includes many countries and a range of landforms.

Section 1
South Asia
Physical Geography

Section 2
Southwest Asia
Physical Geography

Section 3
Central Asia
Physical Geography

Target Reading Skill

Clarifying Meaning In this chapter, you will focus on understanding what you read by rereading and reading ahead, paraphrasing, and summarizing.

▶ An American climbing team below the summit of Mount Everest, the world's tallest peak

594 Asia and the Pacific

Bibliography

For the Teacher
Shrestha, Nanda R. *Nepal and Bangladesh: A Global Studies Handbook.* ABC-CLIO, Inc., 2002.
Amery, Hussein A., and Aaron T. Wolf. *Water in the Middle East: A Geography of Peace.* University of Texas Press, 2000.
Kort, Michael. *Central Asian Republics.* Facts on File, 2003.

For the Student
L1 Weintraub, Aileen. *The Dead Sea: The Saltiest Sea.* Powerkids Press, 2003.
L2 Barter, James. *The Ganges.* Lucent Books, 2002.
L3 Cartlidge, Cherese, and Charles Clark. *The Central Asian States.* Lucent Books, 2001.

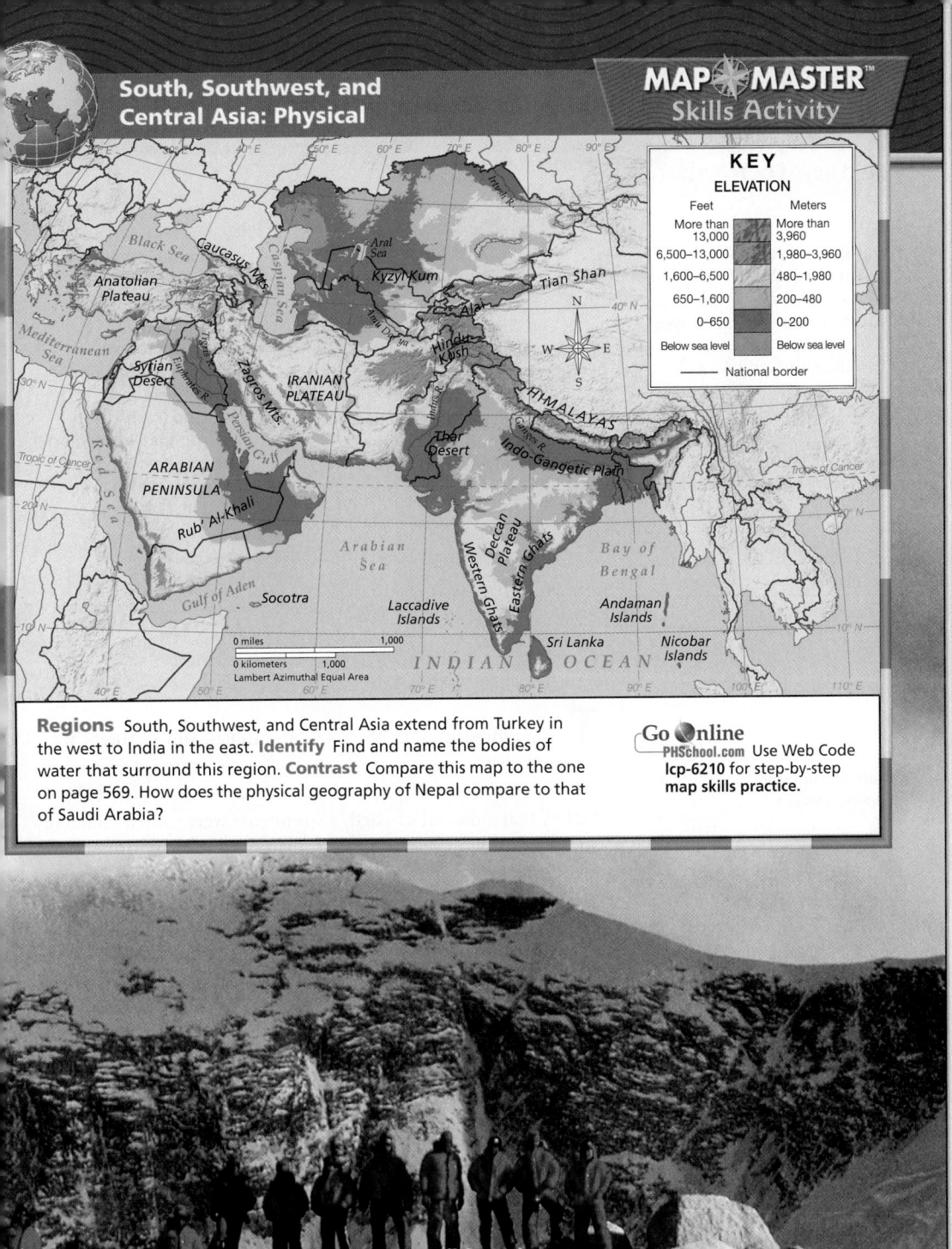

South, Southwest, and Central Asia: Physical

MAP★MASTER™ Skills Activity

KEY
ELEVATION

Feet	Meters
More than 13,000	More than 3,960
6,500–13,000	1,980–3,960
1,600–6,500	480–1,980
650–1,600	200–480
0–650	0–200
Below sea level	Below sea level

— National border

0 miles 1,000
0 kilometers 1,000
Lambert Azimuthal Equal Area

Regions South, Southwest, and Central Asia extend from Turkey in the west to India in the east. **Identify** Find and name the bodies of water that surround this region. **Contrast** Compare this map to the one on page 569. How does the physical geography of Nepal compare to that of Saudi Arabia?

Go Online PHSchool.com Use Web Code lcp-6210 for step-by-step map skills practice.

Chapter 19 **595**

MAP★MASTER™ Skills Activity

Point out the map of South, Southwest, and Central Asia on this page. The map shows the region's physical geography, including its elevation. Help students to understand that the map uses colors to represent different elevation ranges. Explain that when an area of land has an elevation of 0 feet, it is level with the ocean, or sea. This is called "sea level." Ask students to find areas on the map with elevations above 13,000 feet (3,960 meters).

Go Online PHSchool.com Students may practice their map skills using the interactive online version of this map.

Using the Visual   L2

Reach Into Your Background Draw students' attention to the photo and caption on pp. 594–595. Lead a discussion on the challenges the climbers might have faced as they climbed Mt. Everest. Encourage them to think about physical geography and climate using the photograph and their own prior knowledge.

Answers

MAP★MASTER™ Skills Activity **Identify** Mediterranean Sea, Black Sea, Red Sea, Gulf of Aden, Arabian Sea, Indian Ocean, Bay of Bengal, Persian Gulf **Contrast** Saudi Arabia, Iran, and India are much larger than Israel and Nepal.

Chapter Resources

Teaching Resources
- L2 Vocabulary Development, p. 173
- L2 Skills for Life, p. 166
- L2 Chapter Tests A and B, pp. 176–181

Spanish Support
- L2 Spanish Chapter Summary, p. 214
- L2 Spanish Vocabulary Development, p. 215

Media and Technology
- L2 Student Edition on Audio CD
- L2 Guided Reading Audiotapes, English and Spanish
- L2 Social Studies Skills Tutor CD-ROM
- *ExamView Test Bank CD-ROM*

PRENTICE HALL
Presentation EXPRESS™
Teach · Connect · Inspire

Teach this chapter's content using the PresentationExpress™ CD-ROM including:
- slide shows
- transparencies
- interactive maps and media
- *ExamView®* QuickTake Presenter

Section 1
Step-by-Step Instruction

Objectives

Social Studies

1. Learn about the landforms of South Asia.
2. Discover the most important factor that affects climate in South Asia.
3. Examine how people use the land and resources of South Asia.

Reading/Language Arts

Reread and read ahead to clarify ideas and word meanings.

Prepare to Read

Build Background Knowledge **L2**

Have students preview p. 597 by reading the headings and studying the map. Ask them which geographic feature they think is being referred to as a "natural barrier." *(the Himalayas)* Using the Give One, Get One participation strategy (TE, p. T37), lead a discussion on the effect this natural barrier may have had on the region's history and culture.

Set a Purpose for Reading **L2**

■ Preview the Objectives

■ Read each statement in the *Reading Readiness Guide* aloud. Ask students to mark the statements true or false.

All in One Asia and the Pacific Teaching Resources, *Reading Readiness Guide*, p. 150

■ Have students discuss the statements in pairs or groups of four, then mark their worksheets again. Use the Numbered Heads participation strategy (TE, p. T36) to call on students to share their group's perspectives.

Vocabulary Builder
Preview Key Terms **L2**

Pronounce each key term, then ask students to say the word with you. Provide a simple explanation such as, "Crops can easily be grown on alluvial plains because they have rich soil that comes from rivers."

Section 1
South Asia
Physical Geography

Prepare to Read

Objectives

In this section, you will
1. Learn about the landforms of South Asia.
2. Discover the most important factor that affects climate in South Asia.
3. Examine how people use the land and resources of South Asia.

Taking Notes

As you read this section, look for details about the physical features of South Asia. Copy the table below and record your findings in it.

Physical Features	Details
Himalayas	
Indus River	

Target Reading Skill

Rereading or Reading Ahead   If you do not understand a certain passage, reread it to look for connections among the words and sentences. It might also help to read ahead, because a word or an idea may be explained further on.

Key Terms

- **subcontinent** (SUB kahn tih nunt) *n.* a large landmass that is a major part of a continent
- **alluvial** (uh LOO vee ul) *adj.* made of soil deposited by rivers
- **cash crop** (kash krahp) *n.* a crop that is raised or gathered to be sold for money on the local or world market

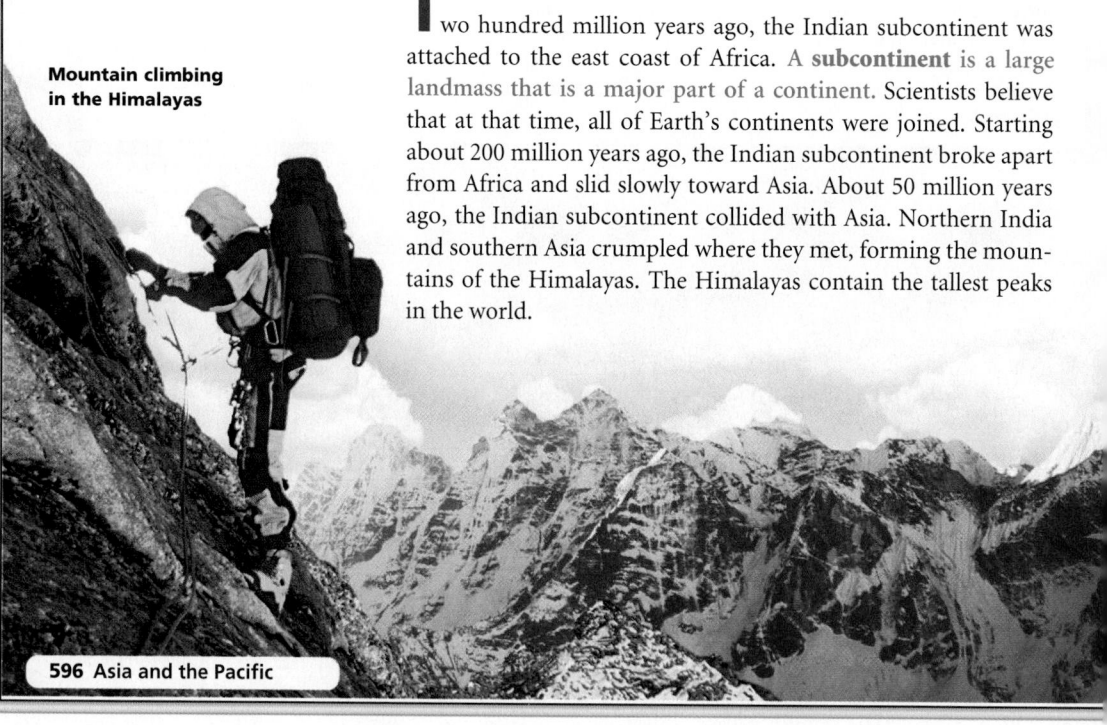

Mountain climbing in the Himalayas

Two hundred million years ago, the Indian subcontinent was attached to the east coast of Africa. A **subcontinent** is a large landmass that is a major part of a continent. Scientists believe that at that time, all of Earth's continents were joined. Starting about 200 million years ago, the Indian subcontinent broke apart from Africa and slid slowly toward Asia. About 50 million years ago, the Indian subcontinent collided with Asia. Northern India and southern Asia crumpled where they met, forming the mountains of the Himalayas. The Himalayas contain the tallest peaks in the world.

596 Asia and the Pacific

Target Reading Skill **L2**

Rereading or Reading Ahead Point out the Target Reading Skill. Tell students that rereading or reading ahead can help them understand unfamiliar words and ideas.

Use the Plains and Plateaus paragraph on p. 598 to model rereading. Explain that students can reread to look for connections between the words *river, soil, deposited*, and the Key Term *alluvial* to help them understand the content.

To model reading ahead, use the sentence on p. 599, "Monsoons are the single most important factor that affects the climate of South Asia." Show students that the effects are provided later on the page.

Give students *Reread or Read Ahead*. Have them complete the activity in groups.

All in One Asia and the Pacific Teaching Resources, *Reread or Read Ahead*, p. 161

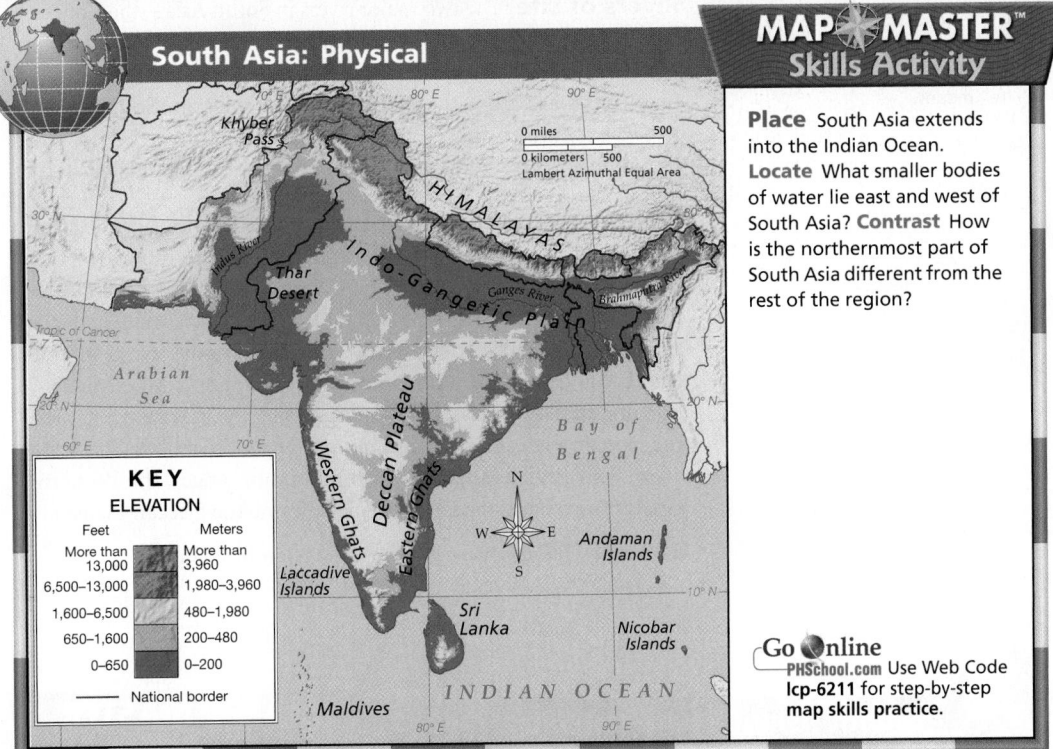

South Asia: Physical

Khyber Pass

HIMALAYAS

Indus River

Thar Desert

Indo-Gangetic Plain

Ganges River

Brahmaputra River

Arabian Sea

Tropic of Cancer

Western Ghats

Deccan Plateau

Eastern Ghats

Bay of Bengal

Andaman Islands

Laccadive Islands

Sri Lanka

Nicobar Islands

Maldives

INDIAN OCEAN

0 miles 500
0 kilometers 500
Lambert Azimuthal Equal Area

KEY
ELEVATION

Feet		Meters
More than 13,000		More than 3,960
6,500–13,000		1,980–3,960
1,600–6,500		480–1,980
650–1,600		200–480
0–650		0–200

—— National border

MAP MASTER Skills Activity

Place South Asia extends into the Indian Ocean.
Locate What smaller bodies of water lie east and west of South Asia? **Contrast** How is the northernmost part of South Asia different from the rest of the region?

Go Online
PHSchool.com Use Web Code lcp-6211 for step-by-step map skills practice.

Major Landforms of South Asia

The largest nation in South Asia is India. It extends from the Himalayas down to the narrow tip of the Indian subcontinent in the south. Pakistan (PAK ih stan) and Afghanistan (af GAN ih stan) lie to the west of India. Along India's northern border, the kingdoms of Nepal (nuh PAWL) and Bhutan (BOO tahn) lie along the slopes of the Himalayas. To the east is Bangladesh (BAHNG luh DESH). The island nations of Sri Lanka (sree LAHNG kuh) and the Maldives (MAL dyvz) lie off the southern tip of India.

A Natural Barrier Find the Himalayas on the map above. Notice that they form a barrier between South Asia and the rest of Asia. This huge mountain range stretches some 1,550 miles (2,500 kilometers) from east to west. Mount Everest, the world's tallest mountain, is located in the Himalayas. Mount Everest rises to 29,035 feet (8,850 meters). That's about five and a half miles high! More than 100 mountains in the Himalayas soar above 24,000 feet (7,300 meters). The Himalayas present the greatest challenge in the world to mountain climbers.

Discovery SCHOOL Video
Explore the land of South, Southwest, and Central Asia.

Chapter 19 Section 1 **597**

Vocabulary Builder

Use the information below to teach students this section's high-use words.

High-Use Word	Definition and Sample Sentence
collide, p. 596	*v.* to come together with direct impact The cars **collided** during the accident.
wedge, p. 598	*n.* something that is roughly triangular-shaped and comes to a point at the tip She put the small end of the **wedge** under the door to prop it open.
moist, p. 599	*adj.* damp; slightly wet My shoes were **moist** after I left them in the rain.
economy, p. 600	*n.* the system of managing the production, distribution, and use of money, goods, natural resources, and services Trade helped the nation's **economy** to grow.

Instruct

Major Landforms of South Asia   L2

Guided Instruction

- **Vocabulary Builder** Clarify the high-use words **collide** and **wedge** before reading.

- Read Major Landforms of South Asia, using the Choral Reading strategy (TE, p. T34).

- Ask **What are the major landforms of South Asia?** *(the Himalayas, Indus and Ganges rivers, alluvial plains, Deccan Plateau, Eastern Ghats, Western Ghats)*

- Discuss how South Asia might be different if the Himalayas did not exist. *(South Asia's two major rivers, the Ganges and the Indus, begin in the Himalayas. If the Himalayas did not exist, the region might not have the fertile alluvial plains created by the Indus and Ganges rivers. Without the two rivers, the plains probably could not support a large population.)*

Independent Practice

Have students create the Taking Notes graphic organizer on a blank piece of paper. Students should begin filling in details they have learned about the physical features of South Asia.

Monitor Progress

As students fill in the chart, circulate and help students as needed.

Show *The Geography of South, Southwest, and Central Asia.* Ask **What nations make up the region of South Asia?** *(Pakistan, India, Nepal, Bhutan, Bangladesh, and Sri Lanka)*

Answer

MAP MASTER Skills Activity **Locate** the Arabian Sea and the Bay of Bengal **Contrast** The northernmost part has higher elevations.

Go Online
PHSchool.com Students may practice their map skills using the interactive online version of this map.

Target Reading Skill

Reading Ahead As a follow up, ask students to answer the Target Reading Skill question in the Student Edition. (*The phrase "Rivers of Life" refers to the Ganges and Indus rivers, which carry the water and minerals necessary to grow crops that feed people.*)

The Climates of South Asia

Guided Instruction

- **Vocabulary Builder** Clarify the high-use word **moist** before reading.

- Have students read about the effect of monsoons on South Asia's climate in The Climates of South Asia.

- Ask **What has the greatest influence on the South Asian climate?** (*monsoons*)

- Discuss with students how the inland areas of South Asia are able to get rain from the summer monsoons. (*The rains that fall along the coastline cool the coastline and the next air mass travels farther inland before losing moisture.*)

- Ask students **Why does South Asia remain warm during the winter monsoon?** (*The Himalayas block the cold air blowing from the northeast.*)

Independent Practice

Have students complete the chart by filling in the remaining details about the Himalayas.

Monitor Progress

Show *Section Reading Support Transparency AP 51* and ask students to check their graphic organizers individually. Go over key concepts and clarify key vocabulary as needed.

📖 **Asia and the Pacific Transparencies,** *Section Reading Support Transparency AP 51*

Answers

✓ Reading Check the Ganges and the Indus rivers

MAP MASTER *Skills Activity* **Read a Map Key** arid **Infer** Colombo, because it has a tropical wet climate

Go Online PHSchool.com Students may practice their map skills using the interactive online version of this map.

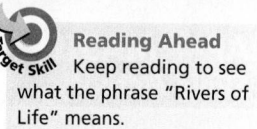

Reading Ahead Keep reading to see what the phrase "Rivers of Life" means.

Rivers of Life The two major rivers in South Asia—the Ganges and the Indus—begin in the Himalayas. The Ganges flows across northern India and empties into the Bay of Bengal. The Indus flows westward from the Himalayas into Pakistan. South Asia's rivers carry water and minerals to support farming. The plains around the rivers, therefore, are fertile and heavily populated.

Plains and Plateaus Huge plains cover the northern part of the Indian subcontinent. They stretch from the mouth of the Indus River to the mouth of the Ganges River. These plains are **alluvial,** which means they are made of soil deposited by rivers. Alluvial plains have rich, fertile soil. As a result, parts of the Indus, Ganges, and Brahmaputra (brah muh POO truh) river valleys are excellent areas for farming. South of India's plains lies the Deccan Plateau. The word *deccan* means "south" in Sanskrit, an ancient Indian language. Two mountain ranges, the Western Ghats (gawts) and the Eastern Ghats, frame the Deccan Plateau.

✓ **Reading Check** Name the two major rivers in South Asia.

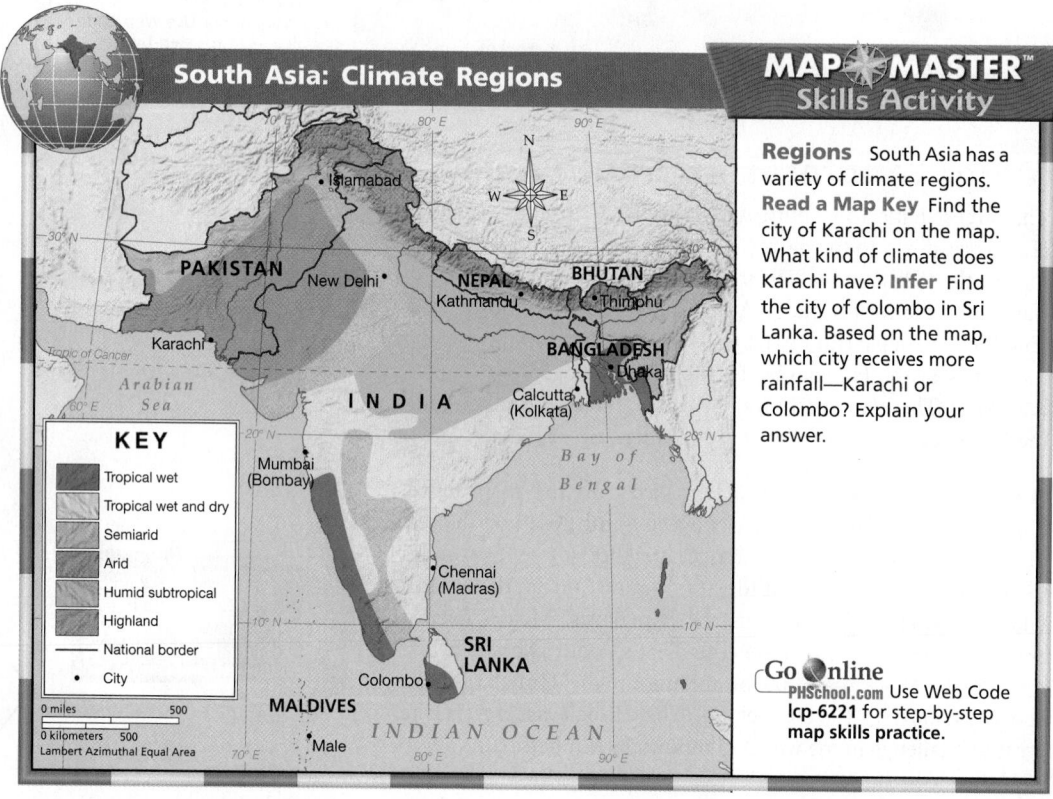

South Asia: Climate Regions

KEY
- Tropical wet
- Tropical wet and dry
- Semiarid
- Arid
- Humid subtropical
- Highland
- National border
- City

0 miles 500
0 kilometers 500
Lambert Azimuthal Equal Area

MAP MASTER *Skills Activity*

Regions South Asia has a variety of climate regions. **Read a Map Key** Find the city of Karachi on the map. What kind of climate does Karachi have? **Infer** Find the city of Colombo in Sri Lanka. Based on the map, which city receives more rainfall—Karachi or Colombo? Explain your answer.

Go Online PHSchool.com Use Web Code lcp-6221 for step-by-step map skills practice.

598 Asia and the Pacific

Differentiated Instruction

For English Language Learners L2
As you read the section with students, pause after each sentence that contains a new landform or river in South Asia. Have students point to each landform or river on the map on page 597.

Background: Biography

Tenzing Norgay (1914–1986) Tenzing Norgay of Nepal, a member of the Sherpa ethnic group, and Edmund Hillary of New Zealand became the first people to set foot on the summit of Mount Everest on May 29, 1953. During their brief celebration Tenzing ate a piece of cake, took some photographs and, as a devout Buddhist, left an offering of food.

The Climates of South Asia

Monsoons are the single most important factor that affects the climate of South Asia. Monsoons are winds that change direction with the change of seasons. The summer monsoons blow across South Asia from the southwest. During the winter, the winds change direction and blow from the northeast.

The Summer Monsoons From June to early October, steady winds blow over the surface of the Arabian Sea and the Indian Ocean. The air picks up a great deal of moisture. Then, the air passes over the hot land along the western tip of India. As the moist air passes over the hot land, it rises and loses its moisture in the form of rain. The rains that fall along the coastline cool the land somewhat. When the next air mass blows in, it travels farther inland before losing its supply of moisture. In this way, the monsoon rains work their way inland until they finally reach the Himalayas.

The Winter Monsoons During the winter months, the monsoons change direction, and the winds blow from the frigid northeast. These winds move dry, cold air toward South Asia. The Himalayas block the cold air. The countries of South Asia enjoy dry winter weather, with temperatures averaging 70°F (21°C).

✓ **Reading Check** What are monsoons?

Land Use in South Asia

About 70 percent of the population in South Asia live in rural areas. Most of these people are crowded into fertile river valleys. Here, they grow whatever crops the soil and climate of their particular region will allow.

Tea Harvest in India
Tea is a major crop in India. Workers harvest fresh tea leaves by hand. The leaves are then processed and dried. Dried tea is sometimes packed in tea bags. **Infer** *How can you tell harvesting leaves is labor-intensive?*

Chapter 19 Section 1 **599**

Chapter 19 Section 1 **599**

Assess and Reteach

Assess Progress
L2

Have students complete the Section Assessment. Administer the *Section Quiz*.

All in One **Asia and the Pacific Teaching Resources**, *Section Quiz*, p. 152

Reteach
L1

If students need more instruction, have them read this section in the Reading and Vocabulary Study Guide.

Chapter 19 Section 1, **Eastern Hemisphere Reading and Vocabulary Study Guide,** pp. 206–208

Extend
L3

If you have not already done so, show students *The Geography of South, Southwest, and Central Asia* to learn more about the regions' landforms. Have students make a table comparing and contrasting the landforms of each region.

The Geography of the South, Southwest, and Central Asia, **World Studies Video Program**

Answers

✓ Reading Check Most people in South Asia live in rural areas.

Section 1 Assessment

Key Terms
Students' sentences should reflect knowledge of each Key Term.

⟳ Target Reading Skill
Students' word choices will vary, but should include high-use words and other challenging words.

Comprehension and Critical Thinking
1. (a) the Himalayas **(b)** The Ganges and Indus rivers both begin in the Himalayas.
2. (a) the southwest **(b)** The summer monsoon brings rain to much of South Asia, while the winter monsoon brings dry air; they come from opposite directions.

The densely populated city of Dhaka is Bangladesh's capital.

Cash Crops Some countries of South Asia produce cash crops such as tea, cotton, coffee, and sugar cane. A **cash crop** is one that is raised or gathered to be sold for money on the local or world market. Growing cash crops often brings in a great deal of money, but it can also cause problems. The economy of a region can become dependent on world prices for the crops. When prices fall, the cash crops do not bring in enough money. When cash crops fail, farmers may not earn enough money.

Mineral Resources The earth beneath India holds a vast supply of mineral wealth. Iron ore and coal are plentiful. Other important minerals include copper, limestone, and bauxite—an ore that contains aluminum. India has only a small amount of oil. Because of this, India relies heavily on hydroelectricity and nuclear power plants.

Population and Land Use South Asia is one of the most densely populated regions in the world. Most of the people live in areas that have plenty of rainfall. These include coastal areas, as well as northeastern India and the country of Bangladesh. The population is lower in areas where it is more difficult for people to live.

✓ Reading Check Where do most of the people in South Asia live?

Section 1 Assessment

Key Terms
Review the key terms at the beginning of this section. Use each term in a sentence that explains its meaning.

⟳ Target Reading Skill
What words were you able to clarify by rereading?

Comprehension and Critical Thinking
1. (a) Recall Which landform forms a natural barrier between South Asia and the rest of Asia?

(b) Connect How do the Ganges and the Indus rivers relate to this landform?
2. (a) Identify From which direction does the summer monsoon blow across South Asia?
(b) Contrast How is the winter monsoon different from the summer monsoon in South Asia?
3. (a) List Give some examples of the cash crops raised in South Asia.
(b) Summarize Why may cash crops cause problems for the economies of South Asian countries?

Writing Activity
Write a two-paragraph description of a television show about the geography and resources of South Asia. In your description, include at least three locations in South Asia. Tell what your camera crew will film in each location.

For: An activity on South Asia
Visit: PHSchool.com
Web Code: lcd-6201

600 Asia and the Pacific

3. (a) tea, cotton, coffee, and sugar cane
(b) They make a country's entire economy dependent on the fluctuating world prices for these crops.

Writing Activity
Use the *Rubric for Assessing a Writing Assignment* to evaluate students' descriptions.

All in One **Asia and the Pacific Teaching Resources,** *Rubric for Assessing a Writing Assignment,* p. 174

Go Online **PHSchool.com** Typing in the Web code when prompted will bring students directly to detailed instruction for this activity.

Southwest Asia
Physical Geography

Prepare to Read

Objectives

In this section, you will

1. Learn about the major landforms of Southwest Asia.
2. Find out what the two most important resources in Southwest Asia are.
3. Examine how people use the land in Southwest Asia.

Taking Notes

As you read this section, look for details about Southwest Asia's major physical features, including climate. Copy the table below and record your findings in it.

Physical Features of Southwest Asia	Details
Desert	
Persian Gulf	
Arabian Peninsula	
Dry climate	

🎯 Target Reading Skill

Paraphrasing When you paraphrase, you state what you have read in your own words. Here is a paraphrase of the first paragraph under the red heading on page 607: "Land in Southwest Asia is used mainly for agriculture, nomadic herding, and producing oil. The region has a small percentage of arable land. Most farming takes place in the northern part of the region."

As you read this section, paraphrase the first paragraph after each red heading.

Key Terms

- **oasis** (oh AY sis) *n.* an area in a desert region where fresh water is usually available from an underground spring or well
- **petroleum** (puh TROH lee um) *n.* an oily liquid formed from the remains of ancient plants and animals; a fuel
- **nonrenewable resource** (nahn rih NOO uh bul REE sawrs) *n.* a natural resource that cannot be quickly replaced once it is used
- **standard of living** (STAN durd uv LIV ing) *n.* a measurement of a person's or a group's education, housing, health, and nutrition

A parachutist lands in the Rub' al-Khali desert in Saudi Arabia.

The Rub' al-Khali (roob ahl KHAH lee), or "Empty Quarter," of the Arabian Peninsula is the largest all-sand desert in the world. Almost nothing lives in this flat, hot territory. Ten years may pass between rainfalls. The sand dunes do not stay in one place—they gradually move as they are blown by the wind.

🎯 Target Reading Skill L2

Paraphrasing Point out the Target Reading Skill. Tell students that one way to clarify meaning is to paraphrase what they have read. Define paraphrasing as writing a passage in their own words.

Model the skill by paraphrasing the second paragraph on p. 604. *(Southwest Asia is very hot during the day because there are no clouds in the sky to block the sun. But temperatures at night can get very cool.)*

Give students *Paraphrase*. Have them complete the activity in groups.

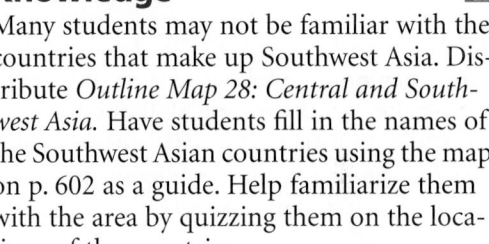 **Asia and the Pacific Teaching Resources,** *Paraphrase*, p. 162

Objectives
Social Studies

1. Learn about the major landforms of Southwest Asia.
2. Find out what the two most important resources in Southwest Asia are.
3. Examine how people use the land in Southwest Asia.

Reading/Language Arts

Paraphrase after reading to help you understand what you have read.

Prepare to Read

Build Background Knowledge L2

Many students may not be familiar with the countries that make up Southwest Asia. Distribute *Outline Map 28: Central and Southwest Asia.* Have students fill in the names of the Southwest Asian countries using the map on p. 602 as a guide. Help familiarize them with the area by quizzing them on the locations of the countries.

All in One **Asia and the Pacific Teaching Resources,** *Outline Map 28: Central and Southwest Asia*, p. 172

Set a Purpose for Reading L2

- Preview the Objectives.

- Read each statement in the *Reading Readiness Guide* aloud. Ask students to mark the statements true or false.

  All in One **Asia and the Pacific Teaching Resources,** *Reading Readiness Guide*, p. 154

- Have students discuss the statements in pairs or groups of four, then mark their worksheets again. Use the Numbered Heads participation strategy (TE, p. T36) to call on students to share their group's perspectives.

Vocabulary Builder
Preview Key Terms L2

Pronounce each Key Term, then ask the students to say the word with you. Provide a simple explanation such as, "A desert traveler will find water and shade at an oasis."

Instruct

A Dry Region Bordered by Water

L2

Guided Instruction

■ Have students use the Paragraph Shrinking strategy (TE, p. T34) to read A Dry Region Bordered by Water. Remind students to refer to the maps on pp. 602 and 604 as they read.

■ Ask **What bodies of water surround the Arabian Peninsula?** (*The Arabian Peninsula is surrounded by the Mediterranean Sea, the Red Sea, the Gulf of Aden, the Indian Ocean, the Arabian Sea, and the Persian Gulf. Students may also identify the Strait of Hormu and the Bab el Mandeb.*)

■ Ask **What is the largest country on the Arabian Peninsula?** (*Saudi Arabia*)

⟳ Target Reading Skill

L2

Paraphrasing As a follow up, ask students to answer the Target Reading Skill question in the Student Edition. (*Students' answers will vary but should contain a synonym for* relieved, *such as* comforted.)

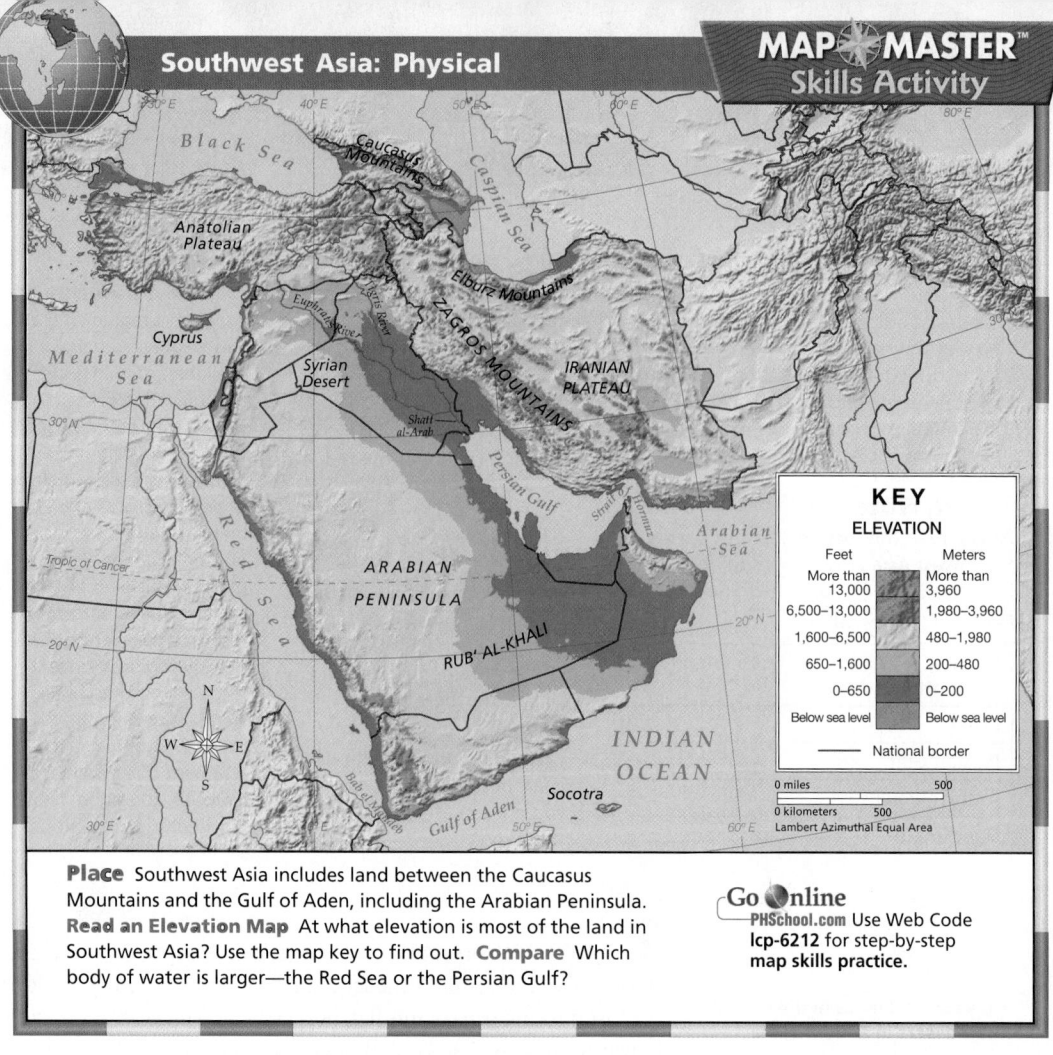

Southwest Asia: Physical

MAP MASTER
Skills Activity

KEY
ELEVATION

Feet		Meters
More than 13,000		More than 3,960
6,500–13,000		1,980–3,960
1,600–6,500		480–1,980
650–1,600		200–480
0–650		0–200
Below sea level		Below sea level

—— National border

0 miles 500
0 kilometers 500
Lambert Azimuthal Equal Area

Place Southwest Asia includes land between the Caucasus Mountains and the Gulf of Aden, including the Arabian Peninsula. **Read an Elevation Map** At what elevation is most of the land in Southwest Asia? Use the map key to find out. **Compare** Which body of water is larger—the Red Sea or the Persian Gulf?

Go Online
PHSchool.com Use Web Code **lcp-6212** for step-by-step **map skills practice.**

A Dry Region Bordered by Water

Southwest Asia contains some of Earth's largest deserts. The Rub'al-Khali is almost as big as the state of Texas. Deserts also cover much of the country of Iran, Syria, and Iraq. Many parts of Southwest Asia receive little rain. Water is very valuable here.

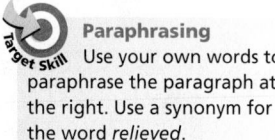

Paraphrasing
Use your own words to paraphrase the paragraph at the right. Use a synonym for the word *relieved*.

Some of the region's deserts are covered with sand. In others, the land is strewn with pebbles, gravel, and boulders. Travelers passing through these dry areas are relieved when they find an oasis (oh AY sis). An **oasis** is a small area in a desert region where fresh water is usually available from an underground spring or well. Sometimes, an oasis can support a community of people. Farmers can grow crops. Nomadic shepherds can raise livestock.

602 Asia and the Pacific

Answer

MAP MASTER
Skills Activity **Read an Elevation Map** 1,600–6,500 feet (480–1,980 meters) **Compare** the Red Sea

Go Online
PHSchool.com Students may practice their map skills using the interactive online version of this map.

Vocabulary Builder

Use the information below to teach students this section's high-use words.

High-Use Word	Definition and Sample Sentence
flammable, p. 605	*adj.* capable of catching fire easily and burning quickly Be careful to keep the **flammable** cloth away from the stove.
reserve, p. 605	*n.* something available for future use We keep a food **reserve** in the basement just in case we need it.
permanent, p. 606	*adj.* continuing without real change The car has a **permanent** parking spot in the garage.
arable, p. 607	*adj.* usable for growing crops They built houses on the land that was not **arable**.

Two Historic Rivers Few plants grow in most Southwest Asian deserts. Some of the most fertile soil in the world, however, lies along the Tigris (TY gris) and Euphrates (yoo FRAY teez) rivers. When these rivers flood, they deposit rich soil along their banks. The Tigris and the Euphrates rivers begin in Turkey and flow south through Iraq. They join to form the Shatt-al-Arab, which flows into the Persian Gulf. In ancient times, the land between these two rivers supported one of the world's first civilizations. The region was known as Mesopotamia. Here, people learned to raise plants and animals for food, relying on the rich soil provided by the rivers.

Mountains and Plateaus As you can see on the physical map of Southwest Asia, the Tigris and Euphrates rivers begin in the mountains of Turkey. Iran also has mountains. The Zagros Mountains extend along the western part of Iran. The Elburz Mountains extend along the northern coast of Iran. The mountains give way to large plateaus in both Turkey and Iran.

Seas and Gulfs Much of the land of Southwest Asia borders bodies of water that separate countries within the region. These bodies of water also separate Southwest Asia from other regions. The Red Sea separates Southwest Asia and Africa. The Mediterranean Sea forms Southwest Asia's western border. The Black Sea forms Turkey's northern border. The Caspian Sea forms part of the boundary between Southwest Asia and Central Asia. The Persian Gulf separates Iran from the Arabian Peninsula.

Iraq's capital, Baghdad, lies on both banks of the Tigris River. The small photo shows a mosque, or Islamic place of worship, in Istanbul, Turkey.

Chapter 19 Section 2 **603**

Guided Instruction (continued)

■ Ask students to scan the text and physical map and make a list of the major land-forms and bodies of water of Southwest Asia. (*Arabian Peninsula, Rub' al-Khali, Syrian Desert, Tigris and Euphrates rivers, Shatt-al-Arab, Zagros and Elburz mountains, Anatolian Plateau, Iranian Plateau, Red Sea, Mediterranean Sea, Black Sea, Caspian Sea, Arabian Sea, Persian Gulf, Gulf of Aden, Strait of Hormuz*)

■ Have students take out the outline maps they began filling in at the beginning of the section. Ask them to fill in the bodies of water listed on p. 603. Encourage them to use only the information from the Seas and Gulfs paragraph as a guide.

All in One **Asia and the Pacific Teaching Resources,** *Outline Map 28: Central and Southwest Asia,* p. 172

■ Ask **What is the climate like on the coast of Syria, Lebanon, and Israel?** (*Mediterranean—hot, dry summers and mild, rainy winters*)

■ Ask **Why do you think one of the world's first civilizations grew up between the Tigris and Euphrates rivers?** (*Possible answer: Its fertile valleys allowed people to grow enough food to sustain a large civilization.*)

Background: Daily Life

Dates Dates are the small, brownish fruit of the date palm, a tree that has been grown for some 4,000 years along the Tigris and Euphrates rivers. Date palms can grow up to 100 feet tall. A mature tree produces about 100 to 200 pounds of dates per year. The date palm has many uses in addition to providing dates for food. The sap can be made into sugar or a fermented drink. Roasted date seeds can serve as a substitute for coffee beans. Date seeds are pressed for oil and the leftovers used to feed livestock. Woven mats and baskets are made from date palm leaves, and the tree's wood is used for construction.

Independent Practice

Have students create the Taking Notes graphic organizer on a blank piece of paper. Students should complete the organizer by filling in details they have learned about the physical features of Southwest Asia.

Monitor Progress

Show *Section Reading Support Transparency AP 52* and ask students to check their graphic organizers individually. Go over key concepts and clarify key vocabulary as needed.

📖 **Asia and the Pacific Transparencies,** *Section Reading Support Transparency AP 52*

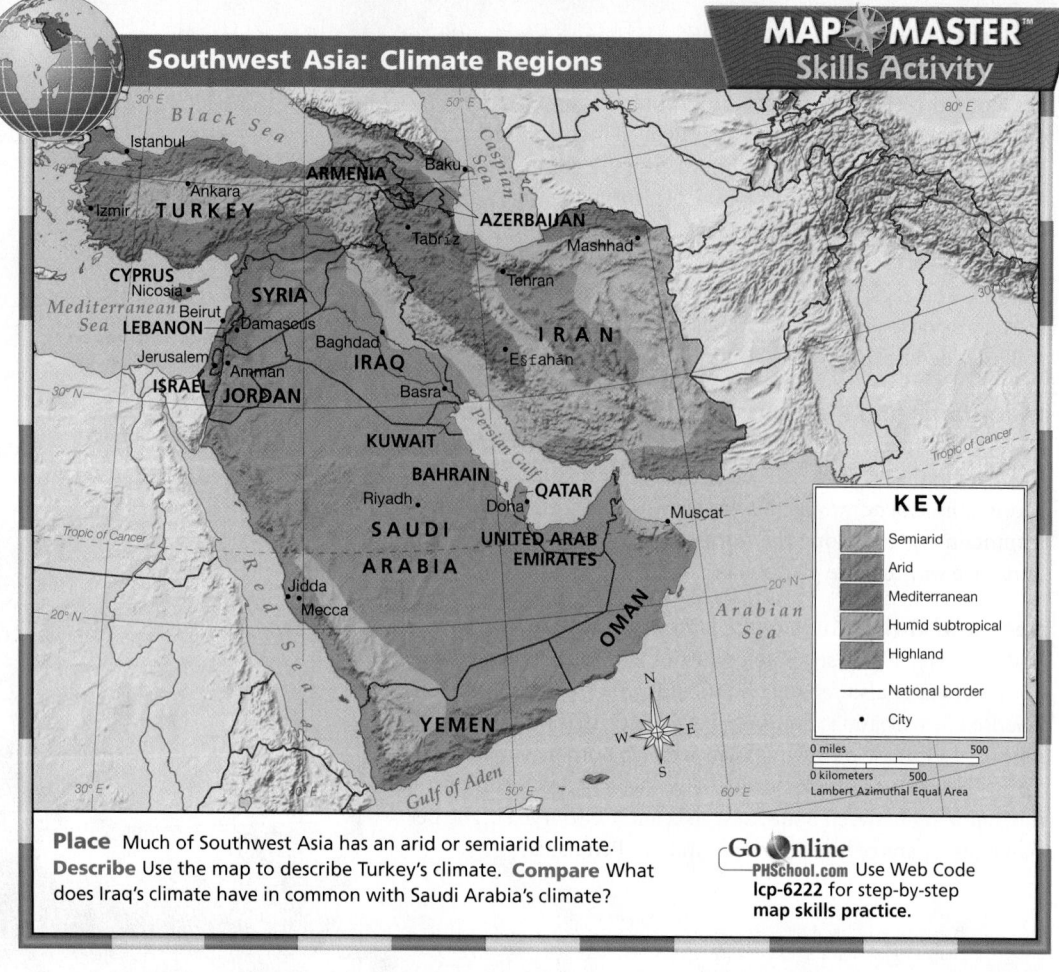

MAP MASTER™
Skills Activity

Southwest Asia: Climate Regions

KEY

- Semiarid
- Arid
- Mediterranean
- Humid subtropical
- Highland
- National border
- City

0 miles 500
0 kilometers 500
Lambert Azimuthal Equal Area

Place Much of Southwest Asia has an arid or semiarid climate. **Describe** Use the map to describe Turkey's climate. **Compare** What does Iraq's climate have in common with Saudi Arabia's climate?

Go Online
PHSchool.com Use Web Code **lcp-6222** for step-by-step map skills practice.

A Hot, Dry Climate Most of Southwest Asia has an arid or a semiarid climate. Much of the region receives less than 10 inches (25 centimeters) of rain each year. It is no wonder, then, that nearly two thirds of Southwest Asia is desert!

Because the desert air contains little moisture, few clouds form over the dry land. As a result, temperatures may reach as high as 125°F (52°C) during the day. At night, they may drop to as low as 40°F (4°C).

Some parts of Southwest Asia have a Mediterranean climate, with hot, dry summers and mild, rainy winters. The coasts of the Mediterranean, Black, and Caspian seas as well as the mountainous areas of the region have a Mediterranean climate.

✓ **Reading Check** Which two countries in Southwest Asia have mountains?

604 Asia and the Pacific

Answers

✓ **Reading Check** Turkey and Iran

MAP MASTER™ **Describe** Turkey has a Mediterranean climate on the coast and a semiarid climate inland. **Compare** Both climates are mostly arid with a small area that is semiarid.

Go Online PHSchool.com Students may practice their map skills using the interactive online version of this map.

Differentiated Instruction

For Special Needs Students 🔲 **L1**
Pair special needs students with more able students and have them complete *Reading a Climate Map* so that they may better understand the map of Southwest Asian

climate regions. Then have students answer the MapMaster Skills Activity questions on p. 604 together.

All in One **Asia and the Pacific Teaching Resources,** *Reading a Climate Map,* p. 171

Southwest Asia's Major Natural Resources

The two most important natural resources in Southwest Asia are petroleum and water. **Petroleum** (puh TROH lee um) is an oily, flammable liquid formed from the remains of ancient plants and animals. It is found under Earth's surface. Petroleum deposits take millions of years to form. Petroleum is a **nonrenewable resource**—a natural resource that cannot be quickly replaced once it is used.

Petroleum is the source of gasoline and other fuels. People all over the world depend on petroleum to fuel cars and trucks, provide energy for industry, and heat homes. Petroleum is the natural resource that brings the most money into Southwest Asia. Water, however, is the resource that people there need most. Since much of Southwest Asia has a dry climate, the water in the region must be used carefully.

Petroleum Large deposits of petroleum, also called oil, can be found in only a few places on Earth. As a result, petroleum-rich countries play a key role in the world's economy. Southwest Asia is the largest oil-producing region in the world. Petroleum is Southwest Asia's greatest export.

Oil wealth allows many Southwest Asian countries to increase the standard of living of their people. **Standard of living** is a measurement of a person's or a group's education, housing, health, and nutrition. These countries have enough money to build schools and hospitals and to import goods from other countries. They can also import workers. Most of the people living in oil-rich Kuwait are citizens of other countries, including Pakistan, India, and Bangladesh.

Southwest Asia has more than half of the world's oil reserves. But some countries in the region have little or no oil. These countries tend to have a lower standard of living than their oil-rich neighbors. They do not have the income that petroleum brings.

Oil pipelines in Saudi Arabia

Southwest Asia's Major Natural Resources L2

Guided Instruction

- **Vocabulary Builder** Clarify the high-use words **flammable, reserve,** and **permanent** before reading.

- Have students read Southwest Asia's Major Natural Resources and study the map on p. 606.

- Ask **What are the two most important resources in Southwest Asia?** (*petroleum and water*) Discuss the uses of these resources. (*petroleum—used to make gasoline and other fuels to power vehicles and industry, and to heat homes; water—to irrigate crops*)

- Ask **Why is petroleum so valuable?** (*It is found in only a few places on Earth, but is in high demand.*)

- Ask **Why must countries be careful about irrigation use?** (*Possible answer: Too much irrigation can use up water, and when a river runs through more than one country, each nation can be affected by the others' irrigation systems.*)

Independent Practice

To learn more about other sources of energy besides oil, have students work in groups or pairs on the *Alternative Sources of Energy* Internet activity. Then have them complete the questions at the end of the activity.

Go Online
PHSchool.com **For:** Environmental and Global Issues: *Alternative Sources of Energy*
Visit: PHSchool.com
Web Code: lcd-6205

Monitor Progress

Circulate and check student's progress. Provide assistance as needed.

Differentiated Instruction

For Less Proficient Readers L1
Have students read the section as they listen to the recorded version on the Student Edition on Audio CD. Check for comprehension by pausing the CD after each paragraph and asking students to summarize what they have just read.

- Chapter 19, Section 2, **Student Edition on Audio CD**

Read the **Links to Science** on p. 607. Ask students **How does the Dead Sea help support Israel's economy?** (*Israelis harvest potash and other minerals for export.*)

Using the Land in Southwest Asia

Guided Instruction

- **Vocabulary Builder** Clarify the high-use word **arable** before reading.

- Read Using the Land in Southwest Asia.

- Have students list the three major ways land is used in Southwest Asia. (*agriculture, nomadic herding, producing oil*)

- Ask **What type of farming takes place along the coasts?** (*commercial farming*) **Why can a wide variety of crops be grown there?** (*because of the Mediterranean climate*)

- Discuss with students how Bedouins from Southwest Asia have lived in the past. (*They have herded camels, goats, and sheep, and have moved from place to place searching for grass and water for their animals.*)

Independent Practice

Assign *Guided Reading and Review.*

All in One **Asia and the Pacific Teaching Resources,** *Guided Reading and Review,* p. 155

Monitor Progress

Tell students to fill in the last column of the *Reading Readiness Guide.*

All in One **Asia and the Pacific Teaching Resources,** *Reading Readiness Guide,* p. 154

Answers

✓ **Reading Check** Income from oil exports has raised the standard of living in some Southwest Asian countries.

MAP MASTER Skills Activity **Read a Natural Resource Map** along the Persian Gulf **Predict** the Persian Gulf

Go Online PHSchool.com Students may practice their map skills using the interactive online version of this map.

606 *Asia and the Pacific*

Water from the Sea of Galilee is carried to southern Israel by the National Water Carrier.

Water To grow crops in this dry region, people usually must irrigate their land. Saudi Arabia, for example, has no permanent rivers. It has wadis (WAH deez), or stream beds that may hold water when seasonal rains fall but are dry much of the year. People there irrigate their crops by pumping water from deep underground wells. In other parts of Southwest Asia, wells are not as necessary. People use water from rivers and streams to irrigate the dry areas of the country.

The nations of Southwest Asia have continued to build irrigation systems. But irrigation cannot solve the problem of water scarcity. Too much irrigation can use up the water that is available. In an area with little rainfall, water that is taken from a river is not soon replaced. When a river runs through more than one nation, each nation is affected by the others' irrigation systems.

✓ **Reading Check** **What benefits has petroleum brought to the countries of Southwest Asia?**

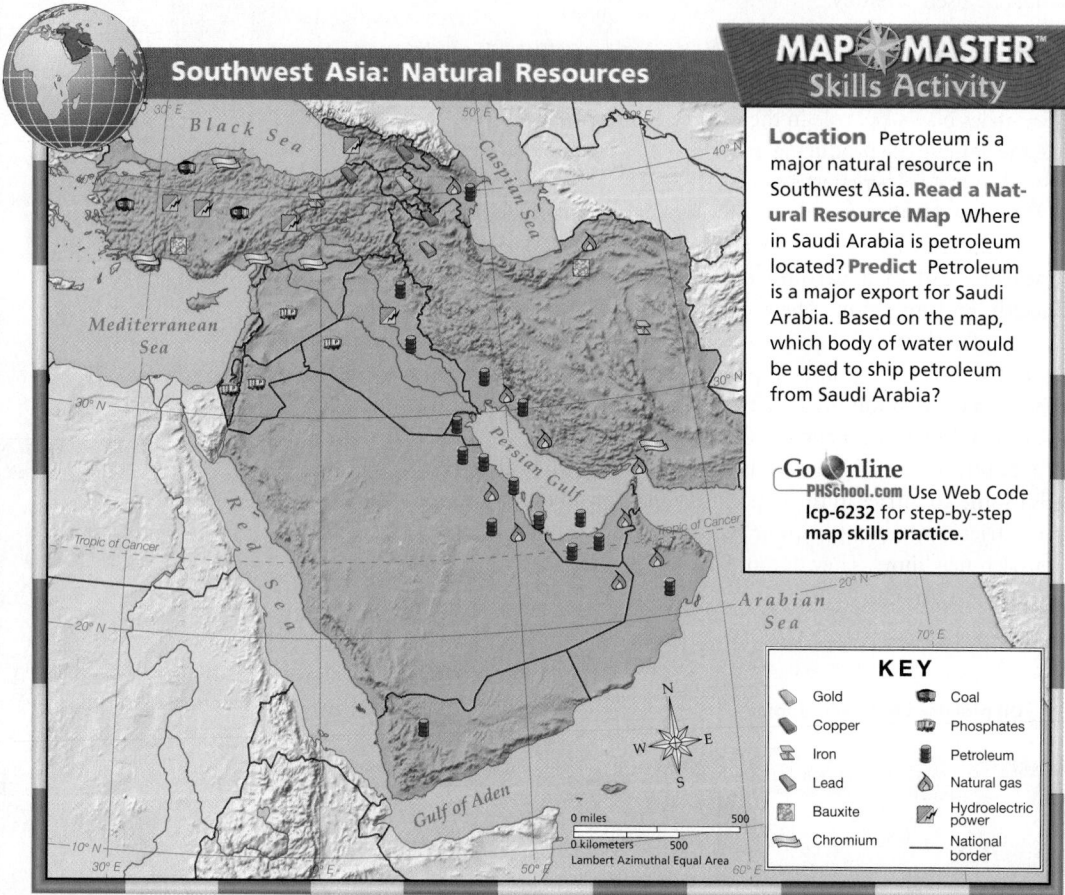

Southwest Asia: Natural Resources

MAP MASTER Skills Activity

Location Petroleum is a major natural resource in Southwest Asia. **Read a Natural Resource Map** Where in Saudi Arabia is petroleum located? **Predict** Petroleum is a major export for Saudi Arabia. Based on the map, which body of water would be used to ship petroleum from Saudi Arabia?

Go Online PHSchool.com Use Web Code lcp-6232 for step-by-step map skills practice.

KEY

Gold	Coal
Copper	Phosphates
Iron	Petroleum
Lead	Natural gas
Bauxite	Hydroelectric power
Chromium	National border

0 miles 500
0 kilometers 500
Lambert Azimuthal Equal Area

606 Asia and the Pacific

Skills for Life: Skills Mini Lesson

Problem Solving

1. Teach students the four steps of problem solving: (1) identify the problem, (2) determine the effects, (3) identify possible solutions, and (4) choose a solution and evaluate its effectiveness.

2. Help students practice the skill by identifying the problem with water in Southwest Asia and its possible effects.

(*problem—water is scarce; effect—people have little water for farming.*)

3. Have students apply the skill by identifying a solution and evaluating its effectiveness. (*Possible answer: Water could be pumped from the surrounding seas and scientists could try to chemically treat the water to make it usable for farming. This could be an effective solution but may prove to be too costly.*)

Using the Land in Southwest Asia

People use the land in Southwest Asia in three major ways: for agriculture, for nomadic herding, and for producing oil. Because of the region's climate, only a small percentage of the region is made up of arable land. Most of this farmland is located in the northern part of the region, with commercial farming taking place along the coasts. There, the Mediterranean climate makes it possible for people to grow a wide variety of crops.

Various commercial farm products are raised in Israel and Turkey. In Israel, these include citrus fruits, cotton, peanuts, and sugar cane. Turkey's commercial farms produce such crops as wheat, barley, cotton, sugar beets, fruits, olives, and corn.

For centuries, Arabic-speaking nomadic herders known as Bedouins (BED oo inz) have lived in Southwest Asia's deserts herding camels, goats, and sheep. Instead of settling in one place, Bedouins moved over a large area of land, seeking grass and water for their animals. Today the Bedouin make up about 10 percent of the population of Southwest Asia. In recent times, settlement policies of countries in Southwest Asia have forced many Bedouins to settle in one place.

✓ **Reading Check** What are some of Turkey's commercial farming crops?

Links to Science

Dead Sea Alive With Minerals The Dead Sea, a lake between Israel and Jordan, is too salty to support fish or plant life. But it does help support Israel's economy. The sea is full of minerals. The Israelis take out potash—a mineral used for explosives and fertilizer—as well as table salt and a variety of other minerals for export.

Section 2 Assessment

Key Terms
Review the key terms at the beginning of this section. Use each term in a sentence that explains its meaning.

Target Reading Skill
Reread the first paragraph after the heading Two Historic Rivers on page 603. Then, using your own words, paraphrase the paragraph. Begin your paraphrase with the sentence, "Rich soil lies along the banks of the Tigris and Euphrates rivers."

Comprehension and Critical Thinking
1. (a) Recall What kind of land covers much of Southwest Asia?
(b) Identify Name one major desert, two seas, and one mountain range in Southwest Asia.
(c) Explain Give a location for the desert, the seas, and the mountain range in the previous question.
2. (a) Identify What are the two most important natural resources in Southwest Asia?
(b) Explain Why are irrigation systems important in Southwest Asia?
3. (a) Recall What are three major ways that people use the land in Southwest Asia?
(b) Summarize What are some commercial farm products of Southwest Asia?

Writing Activity
Write a paragraph that describes water from the point of view of a person living in the United States on the coast of the Atlantic Ocean. Then write another paragraph from the point of view of a person living in a desert region in Southwest Asia. Exchange your paragraphs with a partner. How are your paragraphs similar to or different from those of your partner?

Go Online PHSchool.com
For: An activity on Southwest Asia
Visit: PHSchool.com
Web Code: lcd-6202

Section 2 Assessment

Key Terms
Students' sentences should reflect knowledge of each Key Term.

Target Reading Skill
Possible answer: Rich soil lies along the banks of the Tigris and Euphrates rivers. The rivers begin in Turkey and flow through Iraq. The land between the rivers, known as Mesopotamia, supported the world's first civilizations.

Comprehension and Critical Thinking
1. (a) desert **(b)** Rub' al-Khali; any two of the following: Red Sea, Black Sea, Caspian Sea, Arabian Sea, and Mediterranean Sea; Zagros or Elburz mountains **(c)** Rub' al-Khali—Arabian peninsula; Red Sea—between Southwest Asia and Africa; Black Sea—on Turkey's northern border; Caspian Sea—between Southwest Asia and Central Asia; Arabian Sea—southeast of Arabian Peninsula; Mediterranean Sea—northwestern border of Southwest Asia; Zagros or Elburz mountains—western Iran or Iran's northern coast

2. (a) petroleum and water **(b)** Irrigation is important because much of Southwest Asia receives less than 10 inches of rain annually.
3. (a) agriculture, nomadic herding, and producing oil **(b)** citrus fruits, cotton, peanuts, sugar cane, wheat, barley, sugar beets, olives, corn

---

Assess and Reteach

Assess Progress [L2]
Have students complete the Section Assessment. Administer the *Section Quiz*.

All in One **Asia and the Pacific Teaching Resources,** *Section Quiz,* p. 156

Reteach [L1]
If students need more instruction, have them read this section in the Reading and Vocabulary Study Guide.

📖 Chapter 19, Section 2, **Eastern Hemisphere Reading and Vocabulary Study Guide,** pp. 209–211

Extend [L3]
Organize students into groups. Have them learn more about agriculture in the deserts of Southwest Asia by completing the *Small Group Activity*.

All in One **Asia and the Pacific Teaching Resources,** *Small Group Activity: Simulation: An Oral Report on Desert Farming,* pp. 167–170

Answers

✓ **Reading Check** wheat, barley, cotton, sugar beets, fruits, olives, and corn

Writing Activity
Use the *Rubric for Assessing a Writing Assignment* to evaluate students' paragraphs.

All in One **Asia and the Pacific Teaching Resources,** *Rubric for Assessing a Writing Assignment,* p. 174

Go Online PHSchool.com Typing in the Web code when prompted will bring students directly to detailed instruction for this activity.

Objective

Learn how to identify main ideas.

Prepare to Read

Build Background Knowledge L2

Reread Using the Land in Southwest Asia on p. 607 with students. Ask students to list what they learned from the passage on the board. Discuss what all the ideas they recorded have in common. Then write one sentence on the board that tells what they learned. Explain that this is the main idea of the passage.

Instruct

Identifying Main Ideas L2

Guided Instruction

- Read the steps to identifying main ideas as a class and write them on the board.

- Model the skill with students by completing the Practice the Skill activity on the next page. First, identify the topic of the paragraph. *(petroleum and water in Southwest Asia)* Then write down what each sentence is about. For example, the first sentence is about petroleum and water, and the second sentence explains what petroleum is. Identify the common ideas among the sentences in the paragraph. *(The sentences all provide information about petroleum.)*

- Discuss why the first statement given in Step 3 is too broad. *(The paragraph only focuses on petroleum. It does not focus on all of Southwest Asia's natural resources.)* Then discuss why the second statement is too specific. *(It only explains the information given in one sentence of the paragraph.)* Finally, help students write a sentence that states the main idea. *(Petroleum is an important, nonrenewable resource found in Southwest Asia.)*

Skills for Life — Identifying Main Ideas

Keith was just starting his homework when his mother popped her head into the room.

"What assignment are you working on?" she asked.

"I'm reading an article on petroleum mining in Southwest Asia," Keith replied. "Did you know that more than half of Saudi Arabia's oil reserves are found in just eight oil fields, including the largest onshore oil field in the world?"

"That's a fascinating detail," Keith's mother said. "What's the main idea of the article?"

"That's the assignment," Keith answered. "We have to read the article and identify the main idea."

Identifying main ideas is an essential study skill.

608 Asia and the Pacific

A main idea is the most important information in a paragraph or reading passage. A main idea is not the same as a topic. Knowing how to identify main ideas will make you a better reader and a better student.

Learn the Skill

To identify the main idea in a paragraph, follow these steps:

1. **Identify the topic of the paragraph.** The topic of a paragraph tells what the paragraph is about. Look for a sentence that identifies the topic. It is called a "topic sentence," and it is often the first sentence of a paragraph. Also, it sometimes—but not always—states the main idea.

2. **Look for an idea that all the sentences in the paragraph have in common.** In a well-written paragraph, most of the sentences provide details that support or explain the main idea.

3. **State the main idea in your own words.** Write what you think is the main idea in your own words. Write a complete sentence. Avoid writing a sentence that is too broad or too specific. Remember that a main idea focuses on the most important information about the topic. Even if a detail is interesting, it may not be the most important information. A main idea should always be a complete sentence.

Independent Practice

Assign *Skills for Life* and have students complete it individually.

All in One Asia and the Pacific Teaching Resources, *Skills for Life,* p. 166

Monitor Progress

As students are completing *Skills for Life,* circulate and make sure individuals are applying the skills steps effectively. Provide assistance as needed.

Practice the Skill

Now turn to page 605 and study the first paragraph under the heading Southwest Asia's Major Natural Resources. Use the steps on the previous page to find the main idea of the paragraph.

1. What is the topic of the paragraph? Remember that the topic of a paragraph is not necessarily the same as a main idea. For example, the topic of a paragraph is usually a subject, such as petroleum mining in Southwest Asia.

2. In a word or phrase, write down what you think each sentence is about. Then look at the words you've listed and find a common idea among them.

3. Look for the most important information about the topic. Write a complete sentence that states the most important information. Be sure your sentence focuses on the most important information. Why is the following statement too broad? *Southwest Asia has many natural resources.* Why is the following statement too specific? *Petroleum is found under Earth's surface.*

Apply the Skill

Read the following paragraph. Use the steps you learned to write a statement giving the main idea of this paragraph.

With about one fourth of the world's oil, Saudi Arabia is the leading country in the Organization of Petroleum Exporting Countries (OPEC). OPEC is an organization of countries with economies that rely on money from oil exports. As a group, OPEC decides how much oil its members will produce and at what price to sell it. Besides Saudi Arabia, members consist of Algeria, Indonesia, Iran, Iraq, Kuwait, Libya, Nigeria, Qatar, the United Arab Emirates, and Venezuela. OPEC produces about 40 percent of the world's crude oil.

Chapter 19 **609**

Differentiated Instruction

For Gifted and Talented   L3
Have students complete Level 2 of the *Identifying the Main Idea* activity on the Social Studies Skills Tutor CD-ROM individually.

⊙ *Identifying Main Ideas,* **Social Studies Skills Tutor CD-ROM**

Assess Progress   L2
Ask students to do the Apply the Skill activity.

Reteach   L1
If students are having trouble applying the skills steps, have them review the skill using the interactive Social Studies Skills Tutor CD-ROM.

⊙ *Identifying Main Ideas,* **Social Studies Skills Tutor CD-ROM**

Extend   L3
To extend the lesson, have students follow the skill steps to identify the main idea of the second paragraph on p. 606.

Answer
Apply the Skill
Main idea: Saudi Arabia is the leading country in OPEC, an organization of countries with economies that rely heavily on oil exports.

Section 3
Step-by-Step Instruction

Objectives
Social Studies
1. Learn about the main physical features of Central Asia.
2. Discover which natural resources are important in Central Asia.
3. Find out how people use the land in Central Asia.

Reading/Language Arts
Summarize to review main ideas and better understand a text.

Prepare to Read

Build Background Knowledge L2
Tell students that in this section they will learn about natural resources and land use in Central Asia. Ask students if they know of any important natural resources in their region, state, or community. Then ask how people use the land in their area. Begin the discussion by providing an example of a local resource and one way the land is used. Use the Idea Wave participation strategy (TE, p. T35) to generate a list.

Set a Purpose for Reading
- Preview the Objectives.

- Read each statement in the *Reading Readiness Guide* aloud. Ask students to mark the statements true or false.
  All in One Asia and the Pacific Teaching Resources, *Reading Readiness Guide,* p. 158

- Have students discuss the statements in pairs or groups of four, then mark their worksheets again. Use the Numbered Heads participation strategy (TE, p. T36) to call on students to share their group's perspectives.

Vocabulary Builder
Preview Key Terms L2
Pronounce the Key Term, then ask the students to say the word with you. Provide a simple explanation such as, "If you were traveling through the steppe of Central Asia, the land would be mostly flat and you would not see any trees."

Section 3 Central Asia
Physical Geography

Prepare to Read

Objectives
In this section, you will
1. Learn about the main physical features of Central Asia.
2. Discover which natural resources are important in Central Asia.
3. Find out how people use the land in Central Asia.

Taking Notes
As you read this section, look for details about the physical geography of Central Asia. Copy the diagram below and record your findings in it.

Land	Climate	Natural Resources
•	•	•
•	•	•

🎯 Target Reading Skill
Summarizing When you summarize, you review and state the main points you have read. Summarizing is a good technique to help you better understand a text. A good summary identifies the main ideas, states them in the order in which they appear, and notes when one event causes another to happen. As you read, pause occasionally to summarize what you have read.

Key Term
- **steppe** (step) *n.* vast, mostly level, treeless plains that are covered in grasses

610 Asia and the Pacific

On the treeless plains of Central Asia sprawls the Baikonur (by kuh NOOR) Cosmodrome, the largest space-launch center in the world. Baikonur is the site of several historic spaceflights. In 1957, the first artificial satellite was launched from Baikonur. The first mission to put a human in space blasted off from Baikonur in 1961. In 2003, the *Mars Express,* a European mission to send a spacecraft to Mars, was launched from Baikonur.

Baikonur is located in Kazakhstan (kah zahk STAHN), the largest and northernmost country in Central Asia. To its south are Uzbekistan (ooz BEK ih stan), Kyrgyzstan (kihr gih STAN), Turkmenistan (turk MEN ih stan), and Tajikistan (tah jik ih STAN). Afghanistan forms the southern border of Central Asia. Except for Afghanistan, the countries of Central Asia were once part of the Soviet Union.

This rocket, carrying the *Mars Express,* was launched from Baikonur in 2003.

🎯 Target Reading Skill L2

Summarizing Point out the Target Reading Skill. Explain that summarizing will help students review main ideas. Tell students that a summary lists the main points of a reading selection in order and notes any cause-and-effect relationships.

Model summarizing, using the first paragraph on this page. Explain that you can create a summary by stating the main ideas of the paragraph in the order that they

appear. *(Baikonur Cosmodrome, located on the plains of Central Asia, is the largest space-launch center in the world. A number of important space missions have been launched from there.)*

Give students *Summarize.* Have them complete the activity in groups.

All in One Asia and the Pacific Teaching Resources, *Summarize,* p. 163

Central Asia's Main Physical Features

Central Asia's main physical features are highlands, deserts, and steppes. **Steppes** are vast, mostly level, treeless plains covered with grassland vegetation. Central Asia's mountains are in the southeastern part of the region. The Tian Shan and Pamir mountain ranges cover much of Kyrgyzstan and Tajikistan. The Tian Shan range also extends into China. The Pamir extend into Afghanistan, where they meet the Hindu Kush mountains.

To the west of these mountain ranges, the elevation drops and the land flattens. The Kara Kum desert covers much of the land in Turkmenistan. The Kyzyl Kum desert covers much of neighboring Uzbekistan. The Kirghiz Steppe is located in Kazakhstan.

Steppes in Central Asia

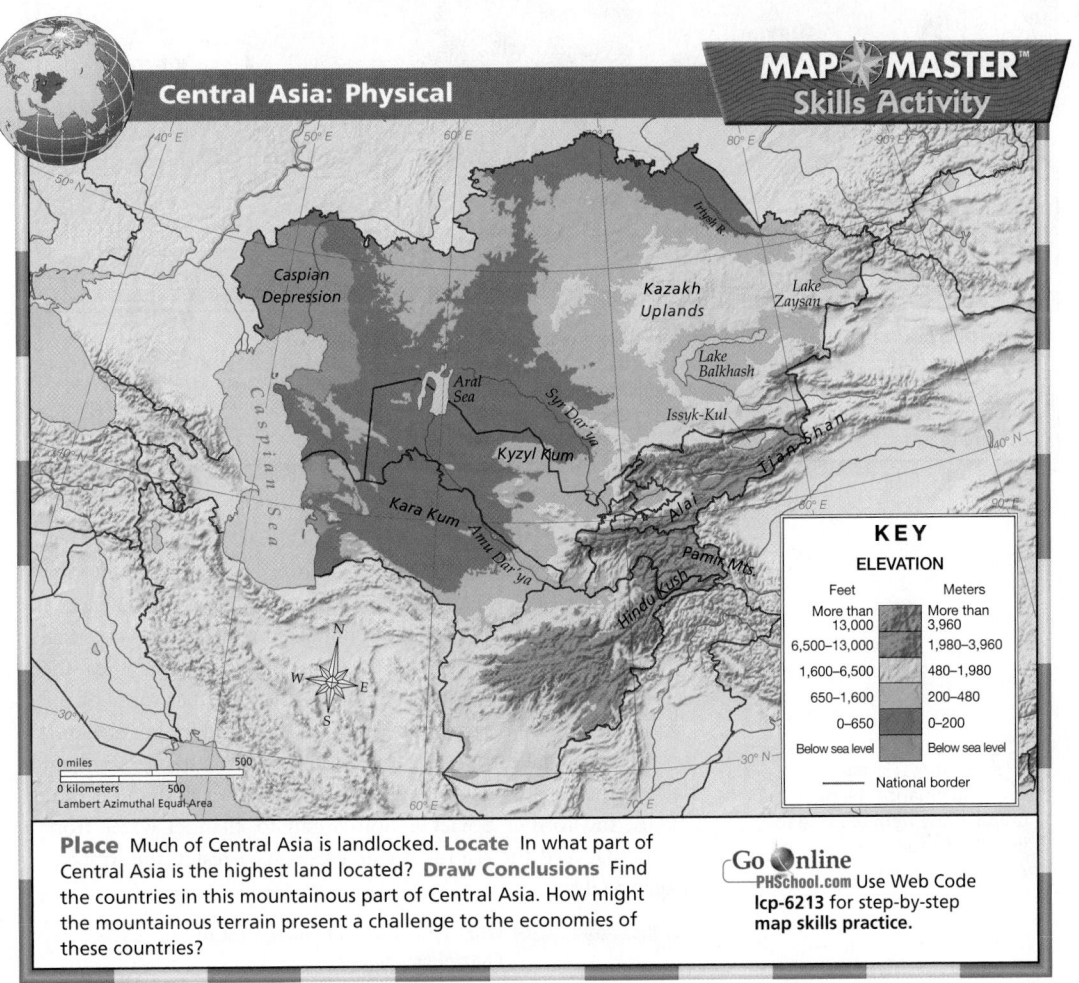

Central Asia: Physical

MAP★MASTER™ Skills Activity

KEY
ELEVATION

Feet	Meters
More than 13,000	More than 3,960
6,500–13,000	1,980–3,960
1,600–6,500	480–1,980
650–1,600	200–480
0–650	0–200
Below sea level	Below sea level

—— National border

Place Much of Central Asia is landlocked. **Locate** In what part of Central Asia is the highest land located? **Draw Conclusions** Find the countries in this mountainous part of Central Asia. How might the mountainous terrain present a challenge to the economies of these countries?

Go Online
PHSchool.com Use Web Code
lcp-6213 for step-by-step
map skills practice.

Vocabulary Builder

Use the information below to teach students this section's high-use words.

High-Use Word	Definition and Sample Sentence
channel, p. 612	*v.* to direct into or through a waterway The farmer **channeled** water from the river to his crops.
export, p. 613	*v.* to send goods to other countries for sale or trade The United States **exports** many goods to Canada.
production, p. 614	*n.* the amount created The factory's **production** went up this year.
disaster, p. 614	*n.* an event causing much suffering or loss The hurricane was a **disaster** for the small town.

Instruct

Central Asia's Main Physical Features   L2

Guided Instruction

- **Vocabulary Builder** Clarify the high-use word **channel** before reading.

- Have students read Central Asia's Main Physical Features, using the Structured Silent Reading strategy (TE, p. T34). Remind students to refer to the maps on pp. 611 and 612 as they read.

- Write the names of the countries of Central Asia on the board. As you write each name, say it aloud and have students repeat it with you. Then have students locate each country on the map on p. 612. (*Kazakhstan, Uzbekistan, Kyrgyzstan, Turkmenistan, Tajikistan, Afghanistan*)

- Ask **What are the main physical features of Central Asia?** (*highlands, deserts, and steppes*). Have students name the features and state the country in which each is located. (*Kyrgyzstan and Tajikistan—Tien Shan and Pamir mountains; Afghanistan—Pamir and Hindu Kush mountains; Turkmenistan—Kara Kum desert; Uzbekistan—Kyzyl Kum desert; Kazakhstan—Kirghiz Steppe*)

- Have students find Kazakhstan on the maps on pp. 611 and 612. Ask **Why might the plains of Central Asia be a good place to build a space-launch center?** (*Possible answer: The land is flat and there is little chance of rain delaying a launch.*)

Answers

MAP★MASTER™ Skills Activity **Locate** in the mountains of eastern Tajikistan **Draw Conclusions** The mountainous terrain might make transportation between these countries difficult.

Go Online
PHSchool.com Students may practice their map skills using the interactive online version of this map.

Guided Instruction (continued)

- Tell students to create a table listing the two major bodies of water in Central Asia and facts about each. *(Possible details about the Caspian and Aral seas: Caspian Sea is largest lake in the world; is a salt lake; has some of the world's largest oil reserves. Aral Sea was once the fourth largest inland lake in the world; it has begun to dry up and become saltier as it is used for irrigation of crops.)*

Independent Practice

Have students create the Taking Notes graphic organizer on a blank piece of paper. Students should complete the bulleted lists under *Land* and *Climate* with the information they have just learned. Display the *Transparency B3: Tree Map/Flow* and fill in the *Land* box with students to get them started.

📖 **Asia and the Pacific Transparencies,** *Transparency B3: Tree Map/Flow Chart*

Monitor Progress

Check students' work as they fill in the graphic organizer. Provide assistance as needed.

🎯 Target Reading Skill   L2

Summarize As a follow up, ask students to answer the Target Reading Skill question in the Student Edition. *(Answers will vary, but students should mention irrigation as the cause.)*

Answers

✓ **Reading Check** a dry climate

MAP MASTER Skills Activity **Locate** in central and northern Kazakhstan and in the northern portions of Uzbekistan and Turkmenistan **Analyze Information** in a thin sliver of land in Turkmenistan, extending east from the Caspian Sea

Go Online PHSchool.com Students may practice their map skills using the interactive online version of this map.

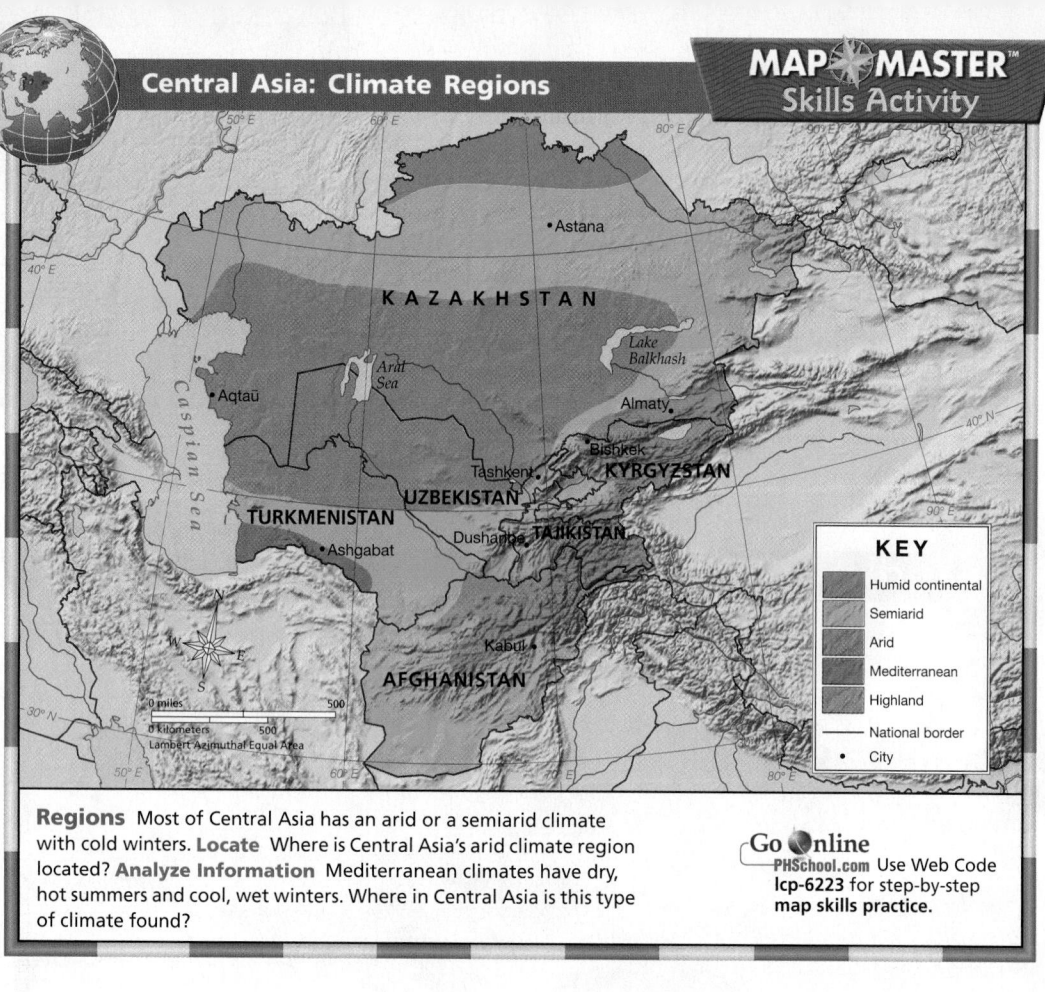

Central Asia: Climate Regions

MAP MASTER Skills Activity

KEY
- Humid continental
- Semiarid
- Arid
- Mediterranean
- Highland
— National border
• City

Regions Most of Central Asia has an arid or a semiarid climate with cold winters. **Locate** Where is Central Asia's arid climate region located? **Analyze Information** Mediterranean climates have dry, hot summers and cool, wet winters. Where in Central Asia is this type of climate found?

Go Online PHSchool.com Use Web Code lcp-6223 for step-by-step map skills practice.

Most of Central Asia has a dry climate. A wide band of semiarid land surrounds the arid region that covers much of the interior. The arid areas receive less precipitation than the semiarid areas.

Two bodies of water stand out in the dry region of Central Asia. They are the Caspian Sea and the Aral Sea. The Caspian Sea, the largest lake in the world, is actually a salt lake. It has some of the world's largest oil reserves. The Aral Sea is located in the interior.

Also a salt lake, the Aral Sea was once the fourth-largest inland lake in the world. Now many boats there rest on dry land. In the 1960s, the former Soviet Union began to channel water from rivers that feed the sea to irrigate crops. As a result, the Aral Sea began to dry up.

🎯 **Target Skill** **Summarizing** Summarize the paragraph at the right. Be sure to include the reason why the Aral Sea is drying up.

✓ **Reading Check** What type of climate does most of Central Asia have?

Differentiated Instruction

For Gifted and Talented L3

Have students complete the *Enrichment* activity to learn about the Khyber Pass that runs through the Hindu Kush.

All in One **Asia and the Pacific Teaching Resources,** *Enrichment,* p. 165

For Less Proficient Readers L2

Have students read the section in the Reading and Vocabulary Study Guide to help them better understand section content. This version provides basic-level instruction in an interactive format with questions and write-on lines.

📖 Chapter 19, Section 3, **Eastern Hemisphere Reading and Vocabulary Study Guide,** pp. 212–214

Natural Resources in Central Asia

As in Southwest Asia, petroleum is a major natural resource in Central Asia. Another major natural resource in the region is natural gas. Kazakhstan is one of three Central Asian countries that have large oil and gas reserves. The other two are Uzbekistan and Turkmenistan. Turkmenistan has the fifth-largest reserve of natural gas in the world. These countries are working to develop the oil and gas industry.

Central Asia has other valuable minerals in addition to petroleum and natural gas. Kazakhstan has rich deposits of coal, much of which it exports to Russia, Ukraine, and Kyrgyzstan. Kazakhstan is the largest exporter of coal to other former Soviet republics as well. Kyrgyzstan, Tajikistan, and Uzbekistan are important gold producers. Other major mineral resources in the region are copper, iron ore, lead, and uranium.

Drilling for oil in Kazakhstan

✓ **Reading Check** What are two major natural resources in Central Asia?

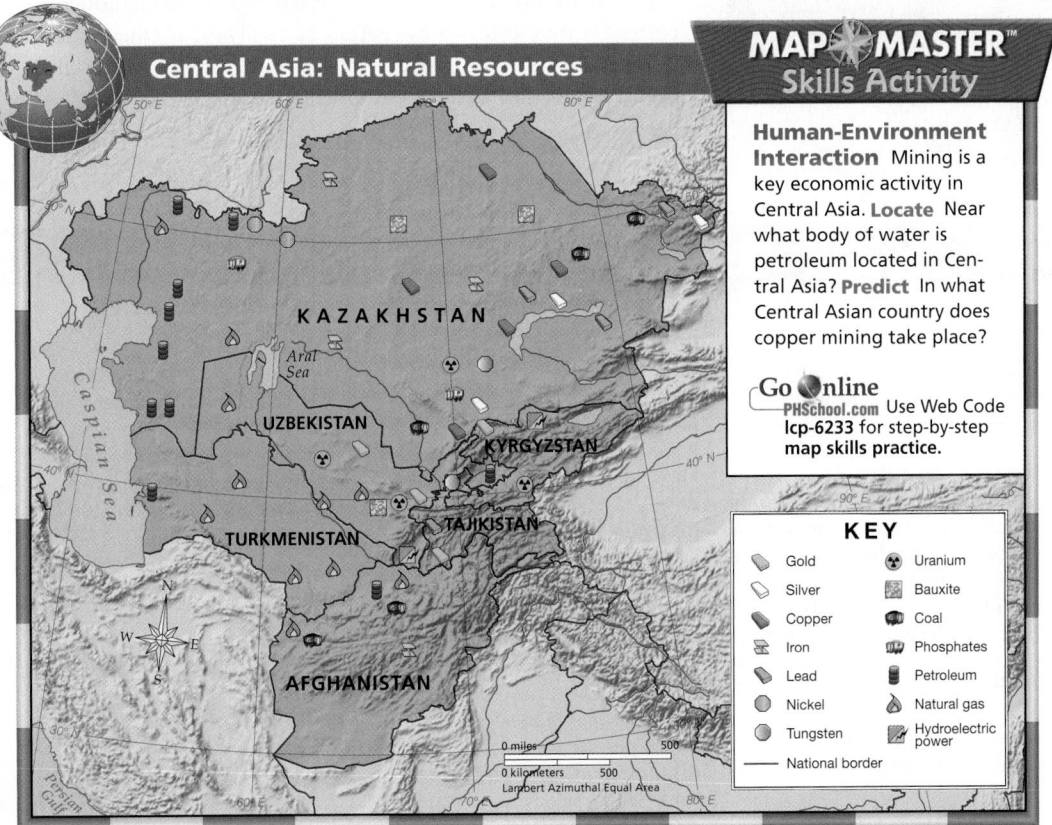

Central Asia: Natural Resources

MAP MASTER™ Skills Activity

Human-Environment Interaction Mining is a key economic activity in Central Asia. **Locate** Near what body of water is petroleum located in Central Asia? **Predict** In what Central Asian country does copper mining take place?

Go Online
PHSchool.com Use Web Code lcp-6233 for step-by-step map skills practice.

KEY

Gold	Uranium
Silver	Bauxite
Copper	Coal
Iron	Phosphates
Lead	Petroleum
Nickel	Natural gas
Tungsten	Hydroelectric power
	National border

Chapter 19 Section 3 **613**

Skills for Life — Skills Mini Lesson

Analyzing Images L2

1. Teach the skill by pointing out to students that visuals can help them learn more about a topic. While studying images, students should ask themselves the following questions: Who or what is the image showing? Where and when does the scene take place? What feeling do I get from it? Why do I think this image was created?

2. Help students practice the skill by asking What does the photo on p. 613 show? Why is the man wearing gloves and a hard hat?

3. Have students apply the skill by looking at the photo on p. 614. Ask: Why might this photo have been taken? Why do you think the ships were abandoned?

Guided Instruction

■ **Vocabulary Builder** Clarify the high-use words **export, production,** and **disaster** before reading.

■ Have students read Natural Resources of Central Asia and Land Use in Central Asia. Have students answer the Reading Checks.

■ Ask **Which Central Asian countries have large oil and gas reserves?** *(Kazakhstan, Uzbekistan, and Turkmenistan)* Have students locate these resources on the map.

■ Ask **Why might foreign banks and companies want to help Central Asia develop a larger oil and gas industry?** *(Possible answer: This industry can be very profitable. If they help develop the industry, they could make a lot of money.)*

■ Have students list the ways people use most of the land in Central Asia. *(Most of the land is used for agriculture, especially livestock raising and commercial farming.)*

Independent Practice

Have students complete the Taking Notes graphic organizer.

Monitor Progress

■ Show *Section Reading Support Transparency AP 53* and ask students to check their graphic organizers individually.

All in One **Asia and the Pacific Teaching Resources,** *Section Reading Support Transparency AP 53*

■ Tell students to fill in the last column of the *Reading Readiness Guide.*

All in One **Asia and the Pacific Teaching Resources,** *Reading Readiness Guide,* p. 158

Answers

MAP MASTER Skills Activity **Locate** Caspian Sea
Predict Kazakhstan

Go Online
PHSchool.com Students may practice their map skills using the interactive online version of this map.

✓ **Reading Check** petroleum and natural gas

Assess and Reteach

Assess Progress `L2`

Have students complete the Section Assessment. Administer the *Section Quiz.*

> **All in One Asia and the Pacific Teaching Resources,** *Section Quiz,* p. 160

Reteach `L1`

If students need more instruction, have them read this section in the Reading and Vocabulary Study Guide.

> Chapter 19 Section 3, **Eastern Hemisphere Reading and Vocabulary Study Guide,** pp. 212–214

Extend `L3`

Have students learn more about environmental damage in Central Asia and the rest of the world, as well as possible solutions by working on *Reporting to an Environmental Conference.*

> **Go Online** PHSchool.com **For:** Long-Term Integrated Projects: *Reporting to an Environmental Conference*
> **Visit:** PHSchool.com
> **Web Code:** lcd-6206

Answers

> ✓ **Reading Check** Irrigation supports commercial cotton farming. It has also led to the drying up of the Aral Sea.

Section 3 Assessment

Key Terms
Students' sentences should reflect knowledge of the Key Term.

⟳ **Target Reading Skill**
Students' summaries will vary, but should include the main points of the paragraph in order and should be written in their own words.

Comprehension and Critical Thinking
1. (a) highlands, deserts, and steppes
(b) mountains—in Kyrgyzstan, Tajikistan, and Afghanistan; deserts—in Turkmenistan and Uzbekistan; steppes—in Kazakhstan
2. (a) petroleum and natural gas **(b)** Possible answer: Turkmenistan; It has the world's fifth-largest natural gas reserve.

Abandoned boats lie rusting on land that was once the bottom of the Aral Sea.

Land Use in Central Asia

Most of the land in Central Asia is used for agriculture, especially livestock raising and commercial farming. People in Central Asia have raised sheep, horses, goats, and camels for thousands of years. Cotton is a major crop in Uzbekistan, Turkmenistan, and Tajikistan.

Agriculture in Central Asia depends on irrigation. In the 1960s, the Soviet Union started a huge irrigation project to bring water to Central Asia. The Soviet Union wanted to increase cotton production. Canals were built to carry fresh water from two rivers to irrigate the cotton fields. Between 1960 and 1980, cotton production in the Soviet Union more than tripled.

The irrigation projects turned Central Asia into a leading cotton producer. But they also caused major damage to the Aral Sea. The Amu Darya and Sry Darya rivers flow into the Aral Sea. Over the decades, heavy irrigation has taken great amounts of water from these two rivers. As a result, the Aral Sea is drying up. The land around the Aral Sea is affected, too. Huge quantities of pesticides were used on the cotton crops. These chemicals have polluted the soil. The destruction of the Aral Sea has been called one of the world's worst environmental disasters.

> ✓ **Reading Check** How has irrigation affected the land in Central Asia?

Section 3 Assessment

Key Terms
Review the key terms at the beginning of the section. Use each term in a sentence that explains its meaning.

⟳ **Target Reading Skill**
Write a summary of the first paragraph under the heading Natural Resources in Central Asia. Be sure to use your own words and include the main idea and details in the order in which they appeared.

Comprehension and Critical Thinking
1. (a) Recall What are Central Asia's three main physical features?

(b) Transfer Information If you were to draw a map of Central Asia, where would these main physical features be located?
2. (a) Identify What are two important natural resources in Central Asia?
(b) Draw Inferences With which Central Asian country might an American energy company want to work to develop natural gas resources? Explain why.
3. (a) Explain What major crop raised in Uzbekistan, Turkmenistan, and Tajikistan depends on irrigation?
(b) Identify Cause and Effect What were the effects of irrigation on the Aral Sea?

Writing Activity
As in many regions around the world, the economies of Central Asian countries depend on the availability of water. Write a paragraph suggesting ways in which your community can wisely conserve water.

> **Go Online PHSchool.com**
> **For:** An activity on Central Asia
> **Visit:** PHSchool.com
> **Web Code:** lcd-6203

3. (a) cotton **(b)** Irrigation has increased cotton production, but it also lowered the water level of the Aral Sea dramatically. The remaining water is much saltier. Pesticides used on the cotton pollute the surrounding area.

Writing Activity
Use the *Rubric for Assessing a Writing Assignment* to evaluate students' paragraphs.

All in One Asia and the Pacific Teaching Resources, *Rubric for Assessing a Writing Assignment,* p. 174

>  Typing in the Web code when prompted will bring students directly to detailed instruction for this activity.

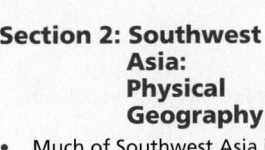
♦ **Chapter Summary**

Section 1: South Asia: Physical Geography

- The Himalayas are a major landform in South Asia. The region also includes the Ganges and Indus rivers, fertile plains, and a plateau framed by the Western Ghats and the Eastern Ghats.
- The climate of South Asia is greatly affected by the monsoons.
- South Asia is a densely populated and generally rural region. Most of the people work in agriculture, and most of the land is used for farming.

Israel

Section 2: Southwest Asia: Physical Geography

- Much of Southwest Asia is a peninsula. The region has a dry climate and contains some of Earth's largest deserts.
- Petroleum and water are Southwest Asia's most important and valuable natural resources.
- Land in Southwest Asia is used mainly for agriculture, for nomadic herding, and for producing oil.

Section 3: Central Asia: Physical Geography

- Highlands, deserts, steppes, and a generally dry climate are Central Asia's main physical features. Much of the region is located inland.
- Central Asia's most valuable natural resources are oil and natural gas.
- Most of the land in Central Asia is used for agriculture, especially livestock raising and commercial farming. Because the region is dry, agriculture in Central Asia depends on irrigation.

India

- Review and revisit the major themes of this chapter by asking students to classify what Guiding Question each bulleted statement in the Chapter Summary answers. Have students work in groups to classify the statements. Refer to page 567 in the Student Edition for the text of the Guiding Questions.

- Assign *Vocabulary Development* for students to review Key Terms.

  All in One **Asia and the Pacific Teaching Resources,** *Vocabulary Development*, p. 173

♦ **Key Terms**

Match the definitions in Column I with the key terms in Column II.

Column I

1. a large landmass that is a major part of a continent
2. a crop that is raised to be sold for money on the local or world market
3. an oily liquid used as a fuel
4. an area in a desert region where fresh water is usually found
5. a natural resource that cannot be quickly replaced once it is used up
6. a measurement of a person's or group's education, housing, health, and nutrition
7. a vast, mostly level, treeless plain

Column II

A standard of living
B oasis
C steppe
D petroleum
E subcontinent
F nonrenewable resource
G cash crop

Chapter 19 **615**

Vocabulary Builder

High-Use Academic Words

Revisit this chapter's high-use words:

collide	flammable	channel
wedge	reserve	export
moist	permanent	production
economy	arable	disaster

Ask students to review the definitions they recorded on their *Word Knowledge* worksheets.

All in One **Asia and the Pacific Teaching Resources,** *Word Knowledge*, p. 164

Consider allowing students to earn extra credit if they use the words in their answers to the questions in the Chapter Review and Assessment. The words must be used correctly and in a natural context to earn the extra points.

Answers

Key Terms

1. E
2. G
3. D
4. B
5. F
6. A
7. C

Comprehension and Critical Thinking

8. (a) the Indus and the Ganges rivers
(b) They deposit fertile soil in which crops can be grown.

9. (a) about 70 percent **(b)** Population is concentrated in the areas with the most rainfall.

10. (a) They begin in Turkey and flow south through Iraq. **(b)** The Arabian Peninsula is mainly desert, while Mesopotamia has some of the most fertile farmland on Earth.

11. (a) petroleum **(b)** Possible answer: The United States uses a lot of oil.

12. (a) One of the following: agriculture, nomadic herding, or producing oil
(b) Turkey—most of Southwest Asia's arable land is in the northern part of the region, where Turkey is located, and Saudi Arabia has no permanent rivers to serve as sources of irrigation water.

13. (a) Possible answer: Central Asia's main physical features are highlands, deserts, and steppes. Most of Central Asia has a dry climate. The Caspian and Aral seas are major bodies of water in this region. **(b)** Large amounts of water have been diverted from the rivers that feed the Aral Sea to irrigate cotton farms.

Skills Practice

Possible answer Oil and natural gas are major natural resources in Central Asia.

Writing Activity: Science

Students' articles will vary, but should include the causes of the current environmental problems and proposed solutions.

Use *Rubric for Assessing a Newspaper Article* to evaluate students' reports.

All in One Asia and the Pacific Teaching Resources, *Rubric for Assessing a Newspaper Article,* p. 175

MAP MASTER
Skills Activity

1. C   **2.** A
3. B   **4.** E
5. F   **6.** D

Go Online Students may practice their map skills using the interactive online version of this map.

◆ Comprehension and Critical Thinking

8. (a) Define What are the two most important rivers in South Asia?
(b) Identify Effects How do the rivers of South Asia affect farmland?

9. (a) Recall What percentage of the population in South Asia lives in rural areas?
(b) Apply Information How does rainfall relate to population patterns in South Asia?

10. (a) Locate Where are the Tigris and Euphrates rivers located?
(b) Analyze Information What are some of the factors that explain why one of the world's first civilizations grew in Mesopotamia rather than on the Arabian Peninsula?

11. (a) Identify What is Southwest Asia's greatest export?
(b) Infer Southwest Asia has more than half of the world's oil reserves. Why might the United States have an interest in this region?

12. (a) Name Name one way that people use the land in Southwest Asia.

(b) Predict Where would you expect to find a commercial farm in Southwest Asia—in Saudi Arabia or in Turkey? Give at least two reasons to support your answer.

13. (a) List What are three facts about the geography of Central Asia?
(b) Summarize Why is the Aral Sea shrinking?

◆ Skills Practice

Identifying Main Ideas Review the steps you followed on page 608 to learn how to identify main ideas. Then re-read the first paragraph on page 613. Write a sentence that states the main idea.

◆ Writing Activity: Science

Suppose that you are a science reporter assigned to write about the Aral Sea. Do research to learn more about how the area around the Aral Sea has been affected by heavy irrigation. Write a brief article about the current situation.

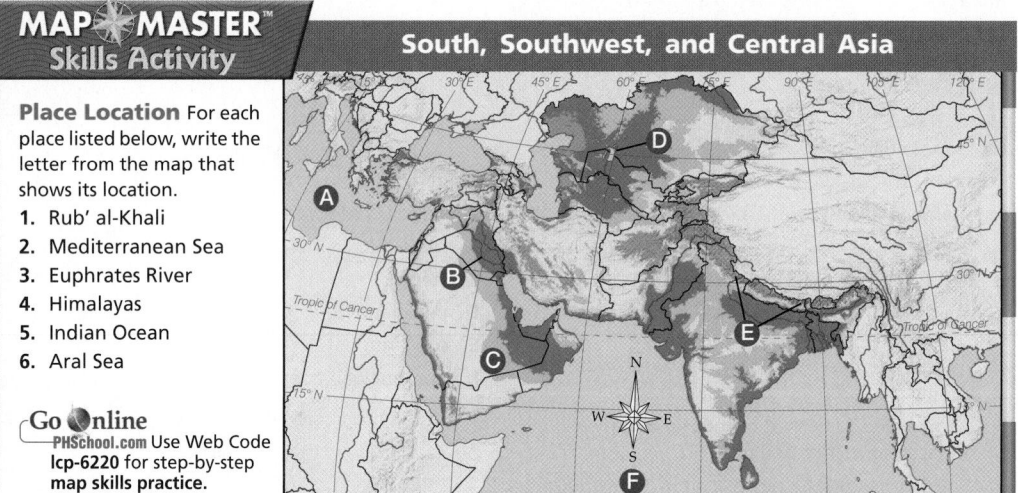

MAP MASTER™
Skills Activity

South, Southwest, and Central Asia

Place Location For each place listed below, write the letter from the map that shows its location.
1. Rub' al-Khali
2. Mediterranean Sea
3. Euphrates River
4. Himalayas
5. Indian Ocean
6. Aral Sea

Go Online
PHSchool.com Use Web Code **lcp-6220** for step-by-step map skills practice.

Standardized Test Prep

Test-Taking Tips

Some questions on standardized tests ask you to analyze parts of a map. Study the map key below. Then follow the tips to answer the sample question.

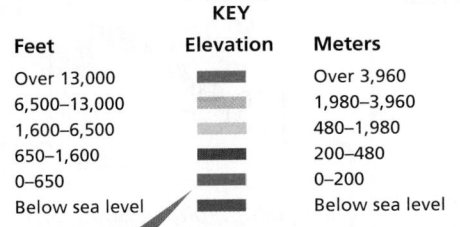

KEY

Feet	Elevation	Meters
Over 13,000		Over 3,960
6,500–13,000		1,980–3,960
1,600–6,500		480–1,980
650–1,600		200–480
0–650		0–200
Below sea level		Below sea level

TIP On a map key, the color column lines up with the data on the information column or columns. To find the required information, move from a given color to the data on the left or right.

Pick the letter that best answers the question.

On an elevation map, most of the area around the Ganges River is colored green. According to the key at the left, how many meters is the elevation in that area?

A below sea level
B 0–200
C 0–650
D 650–1,600

TIP Preview the question. Keep it in mind as you study the information on the map key.

Practice Questions

Use the tips above and other tips in this book to help you answer the following questions.

1. Scientists think that about 50 million years ago, the Indian subcontinent slowly collided with Asia to form
  A the island nation of Sri Lanka.
  B the Western Ghats.
  C the Himalayas.
  D Mesopotamia.

2. The alluvial plains in northern India make the area ideal for
  A mining.
  B farming.
  C aquaculture.
  D hydroelectricity.

3. South Asian countries have climates with warm, dry winters because
  A they are located along the Equator.
  B they are located in a desert region.
  C the Himalayas block cold air blown by the winter monsoon.
  D the Eastern Ghats block cold air blown by the winter monsoon.

Use the passage below to answer Question 4.

> In the winter, the people of eastern Kazakhstan wrap themselves in fur to brave the freezing temperatures. Snow covers the ground as far as the eye can see. Livestock must dig through the ice to feed on the tough grass underneath. But the straight roads of the countryside never need to be plowed. Engineers built the roads slightly higher than the surrounding land. The strong winds keep the roads free of snow.

4. This paragraph is missing a topic sentence. What is the best topic sentence for this paragraph?
  A Winters in eastern Kazakhstan are extremely cold and snowy.
  B Engineers in Kazakhstan are among the best in the world.
  C Some people in eastern Kazakhstan raise livestock for a living.
  D Summers in Kazakhstan are extremely hot.

Use Web Code lca-6200
for **Chapter 19 self-test.**

Standardized Test Prep

Answers

1. C
2. B
3. C
4. A

Go Online PHSchool.com Students may use the Chapter 19 self-test on PHSchool.com to prepare for the Chapter Test.

Assessment Resources

Use *Chapter Tests A and B* to assess students' mastery of chapter content.

All in One **Asia and the Pacific Teaching Resources,** *Chapter Tests A and B,* pp. 176–181

Tests are also available on the *ExamView Test Bank CD-ROM.*

◉ *ExamView Test Bank CD-ROM*

20 Southeast Asia and the Pacific Region: Physical Geography

Overview

Section 1

Southeast Asia: Physical Geography
1. Learn about the major landforms of Southeast Asia.
2. Find out about the kinds of climate and vegetation in Southeast Asia.
3. Examine how people use the land and resources of Southeast Asia.

Section 2

Australia and New Zealand: Physical Geography
1. Find out why Australia and New Zealand have unique physical environments.
2. Learn about Australia's physical geography.
3. Explore New Zealand's physical geography.

Section 3

The Pacific Islands: Physical Geography
1. Examine features of high islands and low islands.
2. Learn about the three main island groups.
3. Find out what kind of climate and vegetation the islands have.
4. Discover how land is used in the Pacific islands.

DISCOVERY CHANNEL SCHOOL Video

The Geography of Southeast Asia and the Pacific
Length: 6 minutes, 23 seconds
Use with Sections 2 and 3

Using a political map, students will learn about the mainland and island countries of Southeast Asia, as well as the countries of the Pacific region. The focus will be on the physical geography, vegetation, and climates of these regions.

Technology Resources

Go Online
PHSchool.com

Students use embedded Web codes to access Internet activities, chapter self-tests, and additional map practice. They may also access Dorling Kindersley's Online Desk Reference to learn more about each country they study.

Interactive Textbook

Use the Interactive Textbook to make content and concepts come alive through animations, videos, and activities that accompany the complete basal text—online and on CD-ROM.

PRENTICE HALL
TeacherEXPRESS
Plan • Teach • Assess

Use this complete suite of powerful teaching tools to make planning lessons and administering tests quicker and easier.

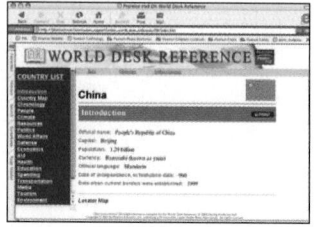

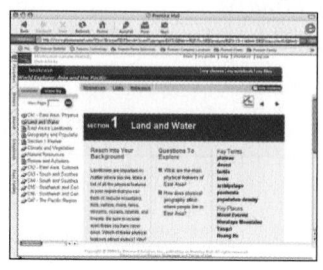

Reading and Vocabulary Instruction

⟳ Model the Target Reading Skill

Identifying Main Ideas Explain to students that the main idea is the most important point in a paragraph or section. All of the details in a well-written paragraph should add to the main idea. Write the paragraph below, from page 627 of the Student Edition, on the board. Point out the supporting details by underlining each one.

What bird is <u>strange looking, has a long bill, does not fly, and only comes out at night to hunt?</u> If you said a kiwi, you are right. <u>The people of New Zealand are so proud of this unusual bird that they have made it their national symbol.</u> <u>The people even call themselves "Kiwis."</u> The bird is one of many unique animals found in New Zealand and its neighbor to the west, Australia.

Model identifying the main idea by analyzing the supporting details: What do these details have in common? *(They all have to do with the kiwi bird, found in Australia and New Zealand.)* Ask yourself: What main idea do these details add up to? *(The kiwi bird is unique to Australia and New Zealand.)*

Use the following worksheets from All-in-One Asia and the Pacific Teaching Resources (pp. 197–199) to support the chapter's Target Reading Skill.

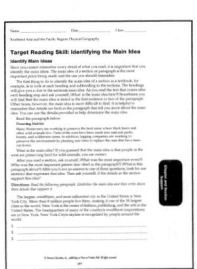 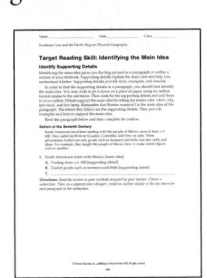 

Vocabulary Builder
High-Use Academic Words
Use these steps to teach this chapter's high-use words:

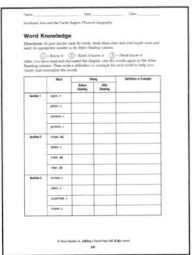

1. Have students rate how well they know each word on their Word Knowledge worksheets (All-in-One Asia and the Pacific Teaching Resources, p. 200).
2. Pronounce each word and ask students to repeat it.
3. Give students a brief definition or sample sentence (provided on TE pp. 621, 628, and 635).
4. Work with students as they fill in the "Definition or Example" column of their Word Knowledge worksheets.

Assessment

Formal Assessment
Test students' understanding of core knowledge and skills.

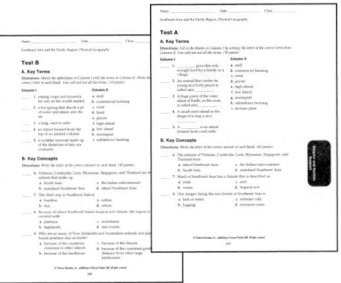

Chapter Tests A and B, All-in-One Asia and the Pacific Teaching Resources, pp. 215–220

Customize the Chapter Tests to suit your needs.
ExamView Test Bank CD-ROM

Skills Assessment
Assess geographic literacy.
MapMaster Skills, Student Edition pp. 619, 621, 622, 625, 629, 640

Assess reading and comprehension.
Target Reading Skills, Student Edition, pp. 625, 628, 637, and in Section Assessments

Chapter 20 Assessment, Eastern Hemisphere Reading and Vocabulary Study Guide, p. 225

Performance Assessment
Assess students' performance on this chapter's Writing Activities using the following rubric from All-in-One Asia and the Pacific Teaching Resources.

Rubric for Assessing a Writing Assignment, p. 214

Assess students' work through performance tasks.

Small Group Activity: Making a Geography Trivia Game, All-in-One Asia and the Pacific Teaching Resources, pp. 203–206

Online Assessment
Have students check their own understanding.
Chapter Self-Test

Test Preparation
Asia and the Pacific Benchmark Test 1, AYP Monitoring Assessments, pp. 121–124

Section 1 Southeast Asia: Physical Geography

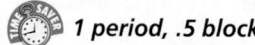 *1 period, .5 block*

Social Studies Objectives

1. Learn about the major landforms of Southeast Asia.
2. Find out about the kinds of climate and vegetation in Southeast Asia.
3. Examine how people use the land and resources of Southeast Asia.

Reading/Language Arts Objective

Determine the main idea to remember the main points.

Prepare to Read	Instructional Resources	Differentiated Instruction
Build Background Knowledge Have students think about the effects of floods. **Set a Purpose for Reading** Have students evaluate statements on the *Reading Readiness Guide*. **Preview Key Terms** Teach the section's Key Terms. **Target Reading Skill** Introduce the section's Target Reading Skill of **identifying main ideas.**	**All in One Asia and the Pacific Teaching Resources** **L2** Reading Readiness Guide, p. 186 **L2** Identify Main Ideas, p. 197	**Spanish Reading and Vocabulary Study Guide** **L1** Chapter 20, Section 1, pp. 153–154 ELL

Instruct	Instructional Resources	Differentiated Instruction
The Land of Southeast Asia Ask questions about the location of Southeast Asia and the "Ring of Fire." **Climate and Vegetation** Discuss the climate of Southeast Asia. **Using the Land and Resources of Southeast Asia** Ask about crops and resources that are important to the region. **Target Reading Skill** Review **identifying main ideas.**	**All in One Asia and the Pacific Teaching Resources** **L2** Guided Reading and Review, p. 187 **L2** Reading Readiness Guide, p. 186 **Asia and the Pacific Transparencies** **L2** Section Reading Support Transparency AP 54	**All in One Asia and the Pacific Teaching Resources** **L1** Using the Compass Rose, p. 207 ELL, LPR, SN **L3** Outline Map 30: Southeast Asia, p. 208 AR, GT **Teacher's Edition** **L1** For Special Needs Students, TE p. 623 **L3** For Advanced Readers, TE p. 623 **Spanish Support** **L2** Guided Reading and Review (Spanish), p. 216 ELL

Assess and Reteach	Instructional Resources	Differentiated Instruction
Assess Progress Evaluate student comprehension with the section assessment and section quiz. **Reteach** Assign the Reading and Vocabulary Study Guide to help struggling students. **Extend** Extend the lesson by assigning a Small Group Activity.	**All in One Asia and the Pacific Teaching Resources** **L2** Section Quiz, p. 188 **L3** Small Group Activity: Making a Geography Trivia Game, pp. 203–206 Rubric for Assessing a Writing Assignment, p. 214 **Reading and Vocabulary Study Guide** **L1** Chapter 20, Section 1, pp. 216–218	**Spanish Support** **L2** Section Quiz (Spanish), p. 217 ELL

Key

L1 Basic to Average	**L3** Average to Advanced	LPR Less Proficient Readers
L2 For All Students		AR Advanced Readers
		SN Special Needs Students

GT Gifted and Talented
ELL English Language Learners

Section 2 Australia and New Zealand: Physical Geography

 1.5 periods, .75 block (includes Skills for Life)

Social Studies Objectives
1. Find out why Australia and New Zealand have unique physical environments.
2. Learn about Australia's physical geography.
3. Explore New Zealand's physical geography.

Reading/Language Arts Objective
Look for supporting details that further explain the main idea of a paragraph.

Prepare to Read	Instructional Resources	Differentiated Instruction
Build Background Knowledge Ask students to look at a map of Australia and New Zealand and note the elevations and major landforms. **Set a Purpose for Reading** Have students evaluate statements on the *Reading Readiness Guide.* **Preview Key Terms** Teach the section's Key Terms Using a "See It—Remember It" chart. **Target Reading Skill** Introduce the section's Target Reading Skill of **identifying supporting details.**	**All in One Asia and the Pacific Teaching Resources** L2 Reading Readiness Guide, p. 190 L2 Identify Supporting Details, p. 198	**Spanish Reading and Vocabulary Study Guide** L1 Chapter 20, Section 2, pp. 155–156 ELL

Instruct	Instructional Resources	Differentiated Instruction
Unique Physical Environments Discuss why Australia's and New Zealand's plants and animals are unique. **Target Reading Skill** Review **identifying** supporting details. **Australia's Physical Geography** Discuss Australia's size and geographical regions. **New Zealand's Physical Geography** Discuss the physical geography of New Zealand and compare its natural resources with those of Australia.	**All in One Asia and the Pacific Teaching Resources** L2 Guided Reading and Review, p. 191 L2 Reading Readiness Guide, p. 190 **Asia and the Pacific Transparencies** L2 Section Reading Support Transparency AP 55 **World Studies Video program** L2 The Geography of Southeast Asia and the Pacific	**All in One Asia and the Pacific Teaching Resources** L2 Skills for Life, p. 202 AR, GT, LPR, SN **Teacher's Edition** L2 For English Language Learners, TE p. 630 L1 For Less Proficient Readers, TE p. 630 **Spanish Support** L2 Guided Reading and Review (Spanish), p. 218 ELL **Passport to the World CD-ROM** L1 Australia: Photo Tour ELL, LPR, SN

Assess and Reteach	Instructional Resources	Differentiated Instruction
Assess Progress Evaluate student comprehension with the section assessment and section quiz. **Reteach** Assign the Reading and Vocabulary Study Guide to help struggling students. **Extend** Have students complete an Enrichment activity.	**All in One Asia and the Pacific Teaching Resources** L2 Section Quiz, p. 192 L3 Enrichment, p. 201 Rubric for Assessing a Writing Assignment, p. 214 **Reading and Vocabulary Study Guide** L1 Chapter 20, Section 2, pp. 219–221	**Spanish Support** L2 Section Quiz (Spanish), p. 219 ELL **Teacher's Edition** L1 For Less Proficient Readers, TE p. 633 **Social Studies Skills Tutor CD-ROM** L1 Identifying Cause and Effect, ELL, LPR, SN

Key
L1 Basic to Average   L3 Average to Advanced   LPR Less Proficient Readers   GT Gifted and Talented

L2 For All Students   AR Advanced Readers   ELL English Language Learners

SN Special Needs Students

Section Lesson Planner

Section 3 The Pacific Islands: Physical Geography

 2 periods, 1 block (includes Chapter Review and Assessment)

Social Studies Objectives

1. Examine features of high islands and low islands.
2. Learn about the three main island groups.
3. Find out what kind of climate and vegetation the islands have.
4. Discover how land is used in the Pacific islands.

Reading/Language Arts Objective

Use details in a paragraph to figure out an unstated main idea.

Prepare to Read	**Instructional Resources**	**Differentiated Instruction**
Build Background Knowledge Show a video and discuss living in the Pacific Island region. **Set a Purpose for Reading** Have students evaluate statements on the *Reading Readiness Guide*. **Preview Key Terms** Teach the section's Key Terms using a "See It—Remember It" chart. **Target Reading Skill** Introduce the section's Target Reading Skill of **identifying implied main ideas.**	**All in One Asia and the Pacific Teaching Resources** L2 Reading Readiness Guide, p. 194 L2 Identify Implied Main Ideas, p. 199 **World Studies Video Program** L2 The Geography of Southeast Asia and the Pacific	**Spanish Reading and Vocabulary Study Guide** L1 Chapter 20, Section 3, pp. 157–158 ELL

Instruct	**Instructional Resources**	**Differentiated Instruction**
High Islands and Low Islands Discuss the features of high islands and low islands. **Melanesia, Micronesia, and Polynesia** Discuss the features of these three island groups. **Climate and Vegetation of the Pacific Islands** **Natural Resources and Land Use** Discuss the climate and land use in the Pacific Islands. **Target Reading Skill** Review **identifying implied main ideas.**	**All in One Asia and the Pacific Teaching Resources** L2 Guided Reading and Review, p. 195 L2 Reading Readiness Guide, p. 194 **Asia and the Pacific Transparencies** L2 Section Reading Support Transparency AP 56	**All in One Asia and the Pacific Teaching Resources** L1 Outline Map 32: The Pacific Islands, p. 209 ELL, LPR, SN **Teacher's Edition** L1 For Special Needs Students, TE p. 637 L3 For Gifted and Talented, TE p. 637 **Spanish Support** L2 Guided Reading and Review (Spanish), p. 220 ELL

Assess and Reteach	**Instructional Resources**	**Differentiated Instruction**
Assess Progress Evaluate student comprehension with the section assessment and section quiz. **Reteach** Assign the Reading and Vocabulary Study Guide to help struggling students. **Extend** Extend the lesson by having students read a primary source.	**All in One Asia and the Pacific Teaching Resources** L2 Section Quiz, p. 196 L3 The Coconut Tree, pp. 210–212 Rubric for Assessing a Writing Assignment, p. 214 L2 Word Knowledge, p. 200 L2 Vocabulary Development, p. 213 L2 Chapter Tests A and B, pp. 215–220 **Reading and Vocabulary Study Guide** L1 Chapter 20, Section 3, pp. 222–224	**Spanish Support** L2 Section Quiz (Spanish), p. 221 ELL L2 Chapter Summary (Spanish), p. 222 ELL L2 Vocabulary Development (Spanish), p. 223 ELL

Key

L1 Basic to Average   L3 Average to Advanced
L2 For All Students

LPR Less Proficient Readers
AR Advanced Readers
SN Special Needs Students

GT Gifted and Talented
ELL English Language Learners

Reading Background

Author's Craft

Knowing the author's organizational plan can help students grasp the information in a text, especially in a difficult selection. Read the following selection from page 620 of the Student Edition aloud:

In 1991, the Mount Pinatubo volcano erupted in the Philippines, a Southeast Asian country. It was the second-largest volcanic eruption of the twentieth century. About 58,000 people moved to safety, but about 800 people died.

Knowing that the text is organized using cause-and-effect helps clarify that the eruption was the cause, and its effects were the displacement of 58,000 people and the death of 800.

Ask students to determine the organizational plan used in Section 2. For example, is the text organized chronologically or does it compare and contrast information? Ask students to write down what clues they used to determine the organizational plan. *(The content is organized in a compare and contrast structure. First Australia's geography is examined, then New Zealand's, and finally both are compared.)*

Writing Tips

Knowing the components that make up a paragraph is essential for writing successful paragraphs. Model the following steps using a sample paragraph before students write their own paragraph:

1. Begin with a topic sentence. *(Living on a low Pacific island would be a challenge.)*
2. Provide examples that expound upon the topic sentence with transition words. *(First of all, it is difficult to grow food on low islands due to the lack of nutrients in the soil. Secondly, fresh water is not readily available, making it difficult for humans as well as crops to survive.)*
3. End with a summary sentence. *(Few people live on low islands in the Pacific.)*

Remind students to vary the length and structure of their sentences.

World Studies Background

Growing Rice in Southeast Asia

In many Asian countries, farmers still cultivate and harvest rice without the use of machines. The fields are often tilled using plows pulled by water buffalo. The fields are then fertilized naturally, smoothed with a rolling log, and flooded with water. Seedlings are hand-transplanted into the flooded fields. Before selling the rice, farmers must pound it to remove its brown hull.

Plants and Animals of Australia and New Zealand

As isolated landmasses, Australia and New Zealand have many plants and animals found nowhere else in the world. The giant eucalyptus, the flying opossum, the kangaroo, the koala, and the platypus are all unique to Australia. New Zealand also has many unusual animals including the kiwi, a flightless bird, and the tuatara, a relative of a prehistoric reptile.

Easter Island

Easter Island in the South Pacific is famous for the more than 600 mysterious statues found there by Europeans in 1722. Experiments conducted in the 1900s helped solve the puzzle of how these statues—many weighing over 50 tons—were scattered throughout the island without the use of modern machinery. Reenactments proved that the statues could be maneuvered with logs used as levers, and it took only 12 people 18 days to lift a 25-ton statue.

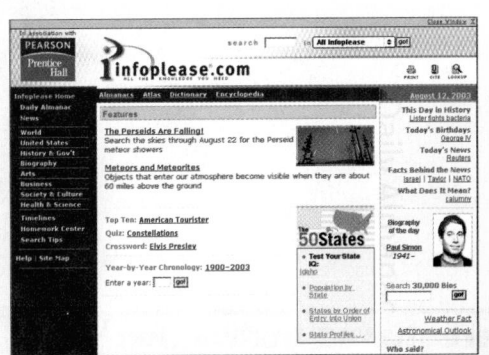

Infoplease® provides a wealth of useful information for the classroom. You can use this resource to strengthen your background on the subjects covered in this chapter. Have students visit this advertising-free site as a starting point for projects requiring research.

Use Web code **lcd-6300** for **Infoplease**.

Chapter 20

Guiding Questions

Remind students about the Guiding Questions introduced at the beginning of this section.

Section 1 relates to **Guiding Question** **5**
How do people of this region make a living?
(Many people in Southeast Asia work on either small subsistence farms or large commercial farms.)

Section 2 relates to **Guiding Question** **1**
What are the main physical features of Asia and the Pacific? *(Australia's east coast has a vast plain with fertile farmland, while New Zealand's North and South islands have volcanoes, hot springs, mountains, fiords, glaciers, and fertile plains.)*

Section 3 relates to **Guiding Question** **5**
How do people of this region make a living? *(Some people of the Pacific islands fish, work in the tourism industry, or grow crops such as sugar, coconuts, taro, yams, and sweet potatoes.)*

⟳ Target Reading Skill

In this chapter, students will learn and apply the reading skill of identifying the main idea. Use the following worksheets to help students practice this skill:

> **All in One Asia and the Pacific Teaching Resources,** *Identify Main Ideas,* p. 197; *Identify Supporting Details,* p. 198; *Identify Implied Main Ideas,* p. 199

Chapter 20

Southeast Asia and the Pacific Region: Physical Geography

Chapter Preview

In this chapter, you will learn about Southeast Asia and the Pacific Region—a region of the world that includes islands, peninsulas, and the world's smallest continent.

Section 1
Southeast Asia
Physical Geography

Section 2
Australia and New Zealand
Physical Geography

Section 3
The Pacific Islands
Physical Geography

 Target Reading Skill

Main Idea In this chapter, you will focus on identifying the main ideas in the sections and paragraphs you read. You will also focus on identifying the details that support each main idea.

▶ A lush rain forest in the Philippines

618 Asia and the Pacific

⌐ Differentiated Instruction ¬

The following Teacher Edition strategies are suitable for students of varying abilities.
Advanced Readers, p. 623
English Language Learners, p. 630
Gifted and Talented, p. 637
Less Proficient Readers, pp. 630, 633
Special Needs Students, pp. 623, 637

⌐ Bibliography

For the Teacher
Bachman, Bill and Tim Winton. *Australian Colors: Images of the Outback.* Amphoto, 2001.
National Wildlife Federation and Sandra Stotsky. *Rainforests: Tropical Treasures (Ranger Rick's Naturescope).* Chelsea House Publishing, 1998.

For the Student
L1 Berger, Melvin and Gilda Berger. *Does it Always Rain in the Rain Forest? Questions and Answers About Tropical Rain Forest.* Scholastic, 2002.
L2 Vierow, Wendy. *Australia (Atlas of the Seven Continents).* Rosen Publishing Group, 2004.

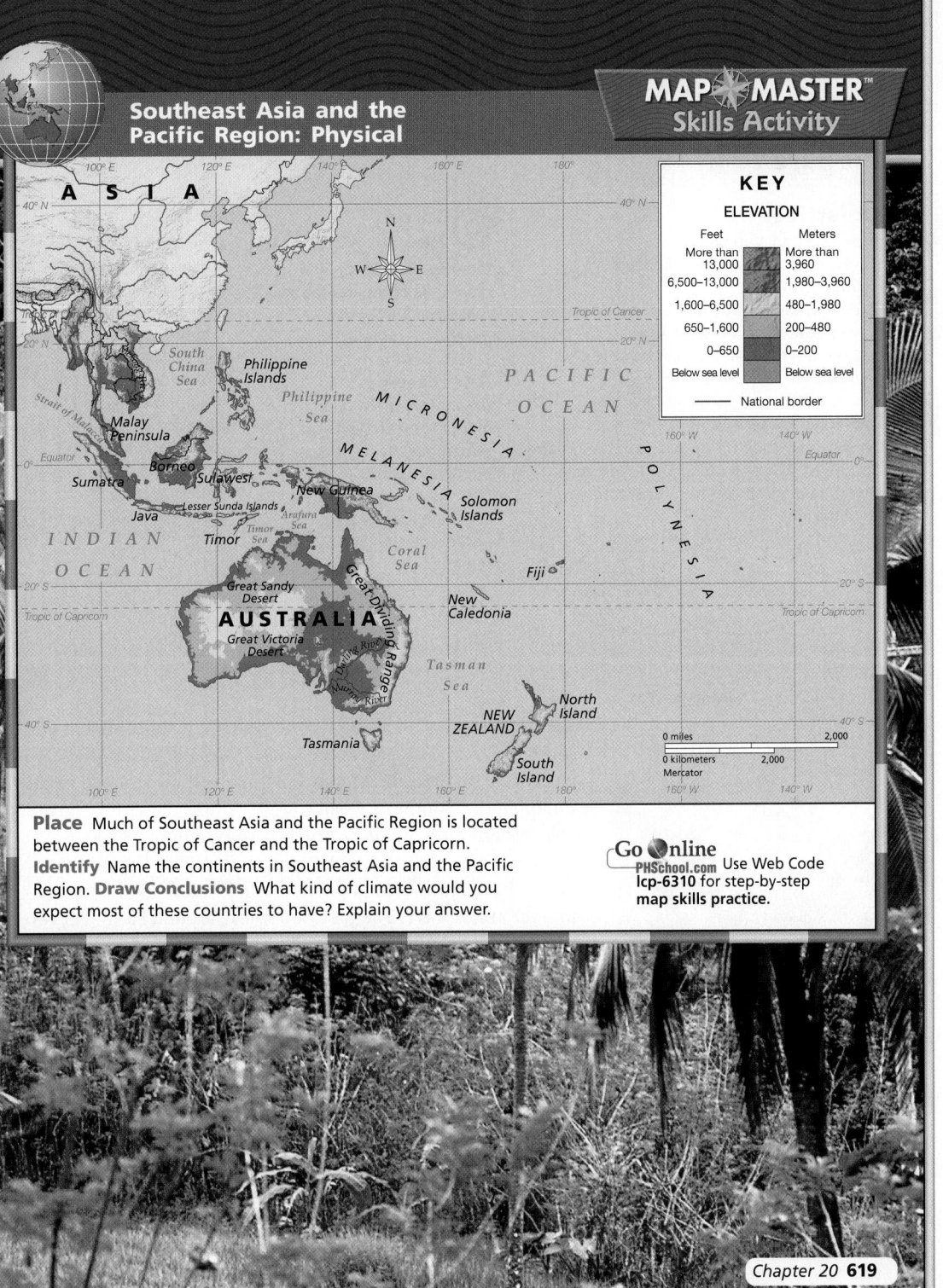

Southeast Asia and the Pacific Region: Physical

KEY

ELEVATION

Feet	Meters	
More than 13,000	More than 3,960	
6,500–13,000	1,980–3,960	
1,600–6,500	480–1,980	
650–1,600	200–480	
0–650	0–200	
Below sea level	Below sea level	

— National border

Place Much of Southeast Asia and the Pacific Region is located between the Tropic of Cancer and the Tropic of Capricorn. **Identify** Name the continents in Southeast Asia and the Pacific Region. **Draw Conclusions** What kind of climate would you expect most of these countries to have? Explain your answer.

Go Online
PHSchool.com Use Web Code
lcp-6310 for step-by-step
map skills practice.

Chapter 20 **619**

Have students look at the map of Southeast Asia and the Pacific region on page 619. Point out that Australia is the smallest of Earth's seven continents, and that it is the only continent that is also a country. Ask students why they think Australia is categorized as a continent and not an island. (*It is much larger than most islands.*)

Go Online
PHSchool.com Students may practice their map skills using the interactive online version of this map.

Using the Visual L2

Reach Into Your Background Draw students' attention to the photograph on pp. 618–619. Ask them to compare and contrast the vegetation shown to the vegetation in their area.

Answers

MAP MASTER™
Skills Activity **Identify** Asia and Australia; **Draw Conclusions** Possible response: The region probably has a warm climate because much of it is located near the Equator.

Chapter Resources

Teaching Resources
- L2 Vocabulary Development, p. 213
- L2 Skills for Life, p. 202
- L2 Chapter Tests A and B, pp. 215–220

Spanish Support
- L2 Spanish Chapter Summary, p. 222
- L2 Spanish Vocabulary Development, p. 223

Media and Technology
- L1 Student Edition on Audio CD
- L1 Guided Reading Audiotapes, English and Spanish
- L2 Social Studies Skills Tutor CD-ROM
- *ExamView Test Bank CD-ROM*

PRENTICE HALL
Presentation EXPRESS™
Teach · Connect · Inspire

Teach this chapter's content using the PresentationExpress™ CD-ROM including:
- slide shows
- transparencies
- interactive maps and media
- *ExamView®* QuickTake Presenter

Section 1
Step-by-Step Instruction

Objectives

Social Studies

1. Learn about the major landforms of Southeast Asia.
2. Find out about the kinds of climate and vegetation in Southeast Asia.
3. Examine how people use the land and resources of Southeast Asia.

Reading/Language Arts

Determine the main idea to remember main points.

Prepare to Read

Build Background Knowledge ▣L2

Have students look at the photographs on page 623. Ask students if they know if floods have ever affected their community, state, or region. What effects might floods have on the land and how people live and travel? Use an Idea Wave (TE, p. T35) to generate responses. *(Possible answers: Floods may bring much-needed water for crops. They may also destroy bridges, dams, homes, or buildings, and make it almost impossible to travel.)*

Set a Purpose for Reading ▣L2

■ Preview the Objectives.

■ Read each statement in the *Reading Readiness Guide* aloud. Ask students to mark the statements true or false.

   All in One **Asia and the Pacific Teaching Resources,** *Reading Readiness Guide,* p. 186

■ Have students discuss the statements in pairs or groups of four, then mark their guides again. Use the Numbered Heads participation strategy (TE, p. T36) to call on students to share their groups' perspectives.

Vocabulary Builder
Preview Key Terms ▣L2

Pronounce each Key Term, and then ask the students to say the word with you. Provide a simple explanation such as, "In subsistence farming, families grow only enough food to provide for their needs."

Section 1
Southeast Asia
Physical Geography

Prepare to Read

Objectives

In this section, you will

1. Learn about the major landforms of Southeast Asia.
2. Find out about the kinds of climate and vegetation in Southeast Asia.
3. Examine how people use the land and resources of Southeast Asia.

Taking Notes

As you read, look for details about mainland Southeast Asia and island Southeast Asia. Copy the diagram below, and record your findings in it.

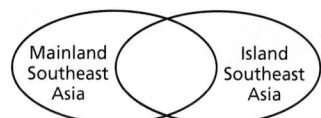

🎯 Target Reading Skill

Identify Main Ideas The main idea of a paragraph tells what the whole paragraph is about. Sometimes the main idea is stated directly in the paragraph. Identifying main ideas can help you remember the most important points in the text. As you read, identify the main idea of each paragraph that follows a red heading.

Key Terms

• **subsistence farming** (sub SIS tuns FAHR ming) *n.* farming that provides only enough food for a family or for a village
• **commercial farming** (kuh MUR shul FAHR ming) *n.* raising crops and livestock for sale on the local or world market
• **paddy** (PAD ee) *n.* a level field that is flooded to grow rice, especially in Asia

Mount Pinatubo erupting in 1991

620 Asia and the Pacific

Southeast Asia is located east of the Indian subcontinent and south of China. This part of the world has many earthquakes and volcanoes. In 1991, the Mount Pinatubo volcano erupted in the Philippines, a Southeast Asian country. It was the second-largest volcanic eruption of the twentieth century. About 58,000 people moved to safety, but about 800 people died. The eruption threw nearly 20 millions tons of gas and ash 21 miles (34 kilometers) into the atmosphere. The gas cloud spread around Earth. For two years, this gas cloud caused global temperatures to drop by about 1°F (0.5°C). Volcanoes are one physical feature of Southeast Asia. What are other major physical features of Southeast Asia? How do they affect land use in the region?

The Land of Southeast Asia

Southeast Asia is divided into mainland and island areas. The mainland is a peninsula that juts south from the main area of Asia. The islands extend east and west between the Indian and the Pacific oceans. Locate the mainland and the islands on the map on the next page.

🎯 Target Reading Skill ▣L2

Identify Main Ideas Point out the Target Reading Skill. Tell students that being able to identify the main idea of a paragraph can help them to remember the most important part of what they have read.

Model identifying main ideas by reading the paragraph following The Land of Southeast Asia on p. 620. Think aloud as you

choose the sentence that is the main idea. *(Southeast Asia is divided into mainland and island areas.)*

Give students *Identify Main Ideas.* Have them complete the activity in their groups.

   All in One **Asia and the Pacific Teaching Resources,** *Identify Main Ideas,* p. 197

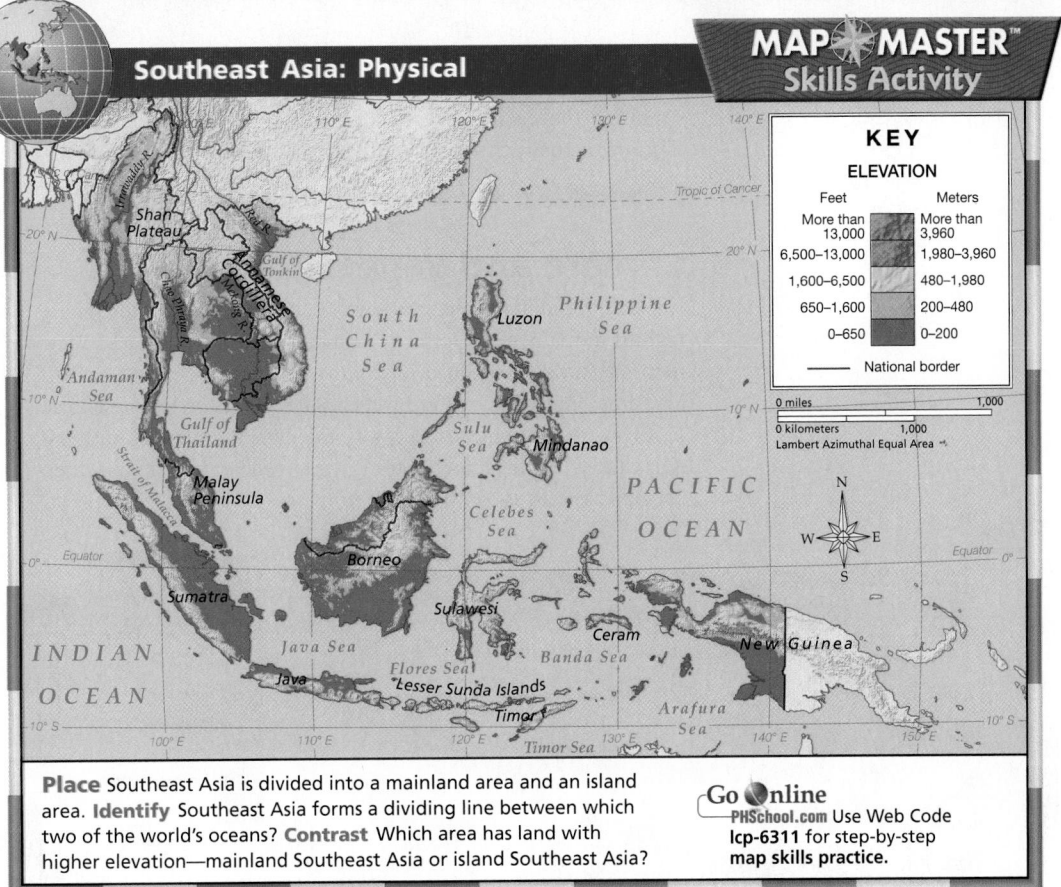

Southeast Asia: Physical

MAP MASTER™
Skills Activity

KEY
ELEVATION

Feet		Meters
More than 13,000		More than 3,960
6,500–13,000		1,980–3,960
1,600–6,500		480–1,980
650–1,600		200–480
0–650		0–200

—— National border

0 miles 1,000
0 kilometers 1,000
Lambert Azimuthal Equal Area

Place Southeast Asia is divided into a mainland area and an island area. **Identify** Southeast Asia forms a dividing line between which two of the world's oceans? **Contrast** Which area has land with higher elevation—mainland Southeast Asia or island Southeast Asia?

Go Online
PHSchool.com Use Web Code lcp-6311 for step-by-step map skills practice.

Mainland Southeast Asia The nations of mainland Southeast Asia are Cambodia, Laos (LAH ohs), Malaysia (muh LAY zhuh), Myanmar (MYUN mahr), Thailand (TY land), and Vietnam. Note that Malaysia is part of mainland Southeast Asia as well as of island Southeast Asia. Much of this area is covered by forested mountains. Most people live in the narrow river valleys between mountain ranges.

Island Southeast Asia Five major nations make up island Southeast Asia: Singapore, Malaysia, Brunei (broo NY), Indonesia, and the Philippines. The largest of the island nations is Indonesia. Indonesia's biggest island is Sumatra. Singapore is a tiny nation, located at the tip of the Malay Peninsula. The country of Malaysia lies partly on the mainland and partly on the island of Borneo. The Philippines is a country made up of some 7,000 islands.

Tourists riding elephants through the forests of Thailand

Vocabulary Builder

Use the information below to teach students this section's high-use words.

High-Use Word	Definition and Sample Sentence
region, p. 622	*n.* geographic area with characteristics that set it apart from other areas They lived in the Northeast **region** of the United States.
pattern, p. 623	*n.* set of actions or characteristics that does not change The scientists studied the **pattern** of the dogs' behavior.
conserve, p. 625	*v.* to protect from loss, harm, or waste She wanted to **conserve** her energy for the game.
generate, p. 626	*v.* to produce or bring into existence The concert **generated** much excitement among the audience members.

Instruct

The Land of Southeast Asia L2

Guided Instruction

- **Vocabulary Builder** Clarify the high-use word **region** before reading.

- Read The Land of Southeast Asia, using the Oral Cloze strategy (TE, p. T33).

- Ask students to name the nations of island Southeast Asia. (*Singapore, Malaysia, Brunei, Indonesia, and the Philippines*)

- Ask students **Which nation is part of both mainland and island Southeast Asia?** (*Malaysia*)

- Ask students **Why do you think the term "Ring of Fire" is used to refer to the region of volcanoes and earthquakes of which Southeast Asia is a part?** (*Possible answer: The word "ring" might refer to the region of volcanoes and earthquakes that surrounds the Pacific Ocean, and the word "fire" might refer to the extremely hot lava that flows from volcanoes.*)

Independent Practice

Ask students to create the Taking Notes graphic organizer on a blank piece of paper. Then have them fill in details about Southeast Asia's mainland and island regions in the two circles. Briefly model how to identify which details to record.

Monitor Progress

As students fill in the graphic organizer, circulate and make sure individuals are choosing the correct details. Provide assistance as needed.

Answers

MAP MASTER Skills Activity **Identify** the Pacific Ocean and Indian Ocean; **Contrast** island Southeast Asia

Go Online
PHSchool.com Students may practice their map skills using the interactive online version of this map.

Climate and Vegetation

L2

Guided Instruction

- **Vocabulary Builder** Clarify the high-use word **pattern** before reading.

- Read Climate and Vegetation with students. As students read, circulate and make sure individuals can answer the Reading Check question.

- Ask students **Which regions of Southeast Asia have a tropical wet climate?** (*west coast of Myanmar, southeastern coast of Vietnam, and most of island Southeast Asia*)

- Discuss with students the differences between the two summer monsoons of Southeast Asia. (*The Indian Ocean summer monsoon blows from the southwest and most of the rain falls on Myanmar. The Pacific Ocean summer monsoon blows from the southeast and brings heavy rains to the southeastern coast of Vietnam.*)

- Discuss how climate affects living conditions. **Why might someone avoid living in a region where typhoons are common?** (*because of property damage and loss of life*)

Answers

✓ **Reading Check** Indonesia is the largest nation in island Southeast Asia.

MAP MASTER Skills Activity **Read a Climate Map** island Southeast Asia; **Contrast** The Philippines has a tropical wet climate, while Thailand has a mix of tropical wet, tropical wet and dry, and humid subtropical climates.

Go Online PHSchool.com Students may practice their map skills using the interactive version of this map.

The Ring of Fire The islands of Southeast Asia are part of the Ring of Fire. That is a region of volcanoes and earthquakes surrounding the Pacific Ocean. Most of the mountainous islands there are actually the peaks of underwater volcanoes.

✓ **Reading Check** Name the largest nation in island Southeast Asia.

Climate and Vegetation

Look at the climate map of Southeast Asia below. The climate regions in mainland Southeast Asia between Myanmar and Vietnam are similar to those in South Asia. On the west coast of Myanmar, there is a tropical wet climate, just as on the west coast of India. As you move eastward through mainland Southeast Asia, the climate changes to tropical wet and dry and then becomes humid subtropical.

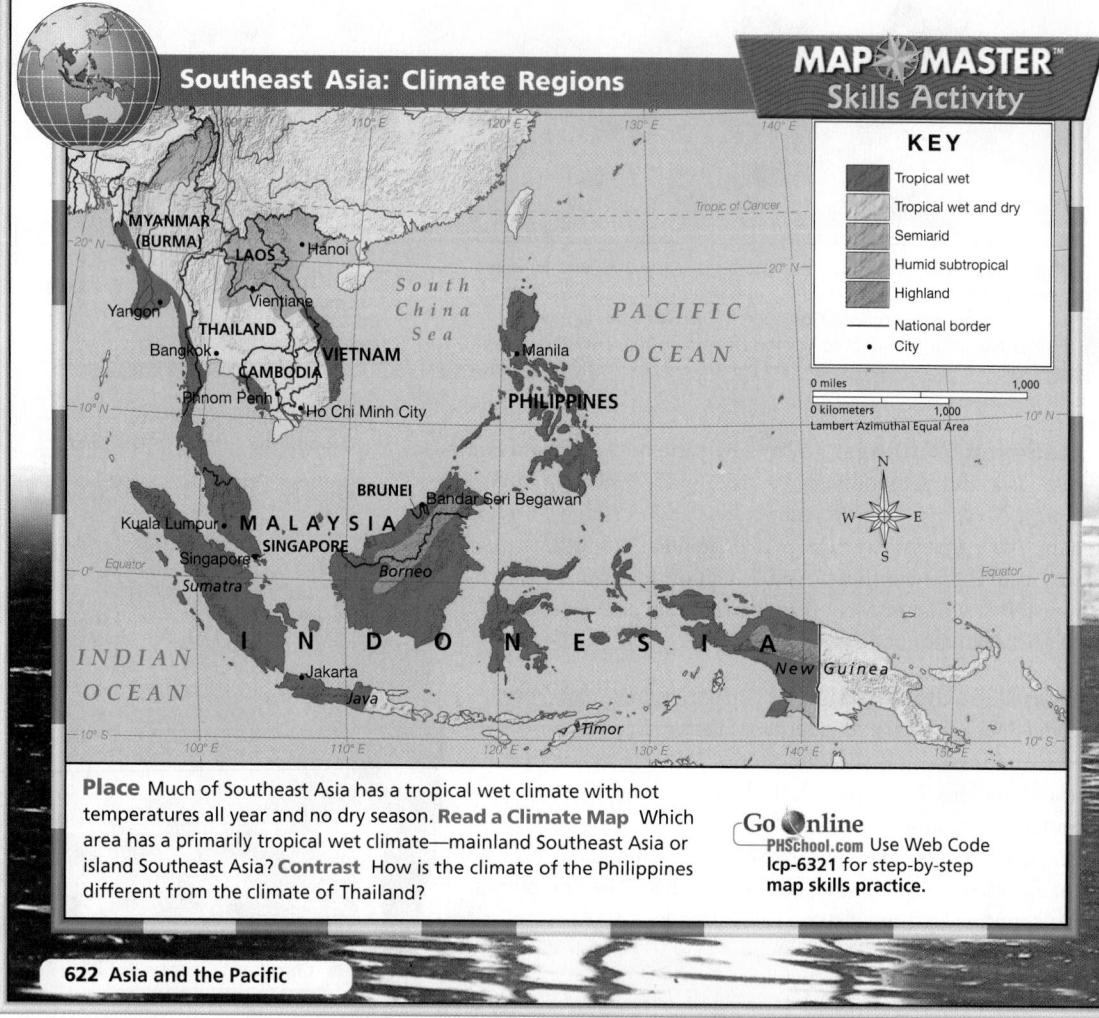

MAP MASTER Skills Activity

Southeast Asia: Climate Regions

KEY
- Tropical wet
- Tropical wet and dry
- Semiarid
- Humid subtropical
- Highland
- National border
- • City

0 miles 1,000
0 kilometers 1,000
Lambert Azimuthal Equal Area

Place Much of Southeast Asia has a tropical wet climate with hot temperatures all year and no dry season. **Read a Climate Map** Which area has a primarily tropical wet climate—mainland Southeast Asia or island Southeast Asia? **Contrast** How is the climate of the Philippines different from the climate of Thailand?

Go Online PHSchool.com Use Web Code lcp-6321 for step-by-step map skills practice.

622 Asia and the Pacific

Background: Links Across Place

Typhoons A typhoon is a tropical cyclone, a storm that has winds of over 74 miles (119 kilometers) per hour, and often involves heavy rains. Typhoons can last one to thirty days. The winds of a tropical cyclone spin counterclockwise in the Northern Hemisphere and clockwise in the Southern Hemisphere.

Meteorologists use the Saffir-Simpson scale to rate the severity of a tropical cyclone. The scale, ranging from category 1 (minimal) to 5 (catastrophic), measures the potential damage and flooding that the storm may cause along the coast. A category 5 cyclone has winds greater than 155 miles per hour and causes major flooding and complete destruction of some buildings. Towns near the shoreline are usually evacuated before a category 5 storm reaches the coast.

Multiple Monsoons However, when you get to the southeastern coast of Vietnam, the pattern changes. The climate is again tropical wet. It supports tropical rain forests—thick forests that receive at least 60 inches (152 centimeters) of rain a year. Why is this area so wet? The answer is that summer monsoons bring rains to this coast just as they do to the western coast.

In fact, there are two separate summer monsoons. An Indian Ocean monsoon blows from the southwest, and a Pacific Ocean monsoon blows from the southeast. Each brings heavy summer rain to the Southeast Asian coast that it hits. Also, during the Northern Hemisphere's winter, winds off the central Pacific Ocean blow from the northeast. This winter monsoon brings heavy rains to the southern Philippines and Indonesia. Because most of Indonesia is in the Southern Hemisphere, the heavy rain from December to March is a summer monsoon there.

Effects of a Tropical Wet Climate Most of island Southeast Asia has a tropical wet climate that supports tropical rain forests. Southeast Asia contains the second-largest tropical rain forest region in the world.

The rain forests of Southeast Asia are lush and thick with vegetation. However, there are disadvantages to living in the tropical climate of Southeast Asia—typhoons. When typhoons hit land, the high winds and heavy rain often lead to widespread property damage and loss of life.

√ **Reading Check** How does the northeast monsoon affect the southern Philippines and Indonesia?

Monsoons in Southeast Asia
The photos below show the effect of monsoons in Cambodia. Monsoons bring rains that can sometimes flood streets. **Analyze Images** *How do people get around when monsoon flooding is severe?*

Differentiated Instruction

For Special Needs Students **L1**
Have students review directions using the *DK Atlas Activity: Using the Compass Rose* in order to better understand the path of monsoons as described in Climate and Vegetation.

All in One **Asia and the Pacific Teaching Resources,** *DK Atlas Activity: Using the Compass Rose,* p. 207

For Advanced Readers **L3**
Ask students to draw the path of the monsoons described in Climate and Vegetation using the outline map of Southeast Asia. Students may wish to consult other maps in atlases or on the Internet.

All in One **Asia and the Pacific Teaching Resources,** *Outline Map 30: Southeast Asia,* p. 208

Independent Practice
Have students continue to fill in the graphic organizer with details about Southeast Asia's climate and vegetation.

Monitor Progress
As students fill in the graphic organizer, circulate and make sure individuals are choosing the correct details. Provide assistance as necessary.

Answers

√ Reading Check The northeast monsoon brings heavy rains to the southern Philippines and Indonesia.

Analyze Images People may walk or ride on rafts to travel during floods.

- **Vocabulary Builder** Clarify the high-use words **conserve** and **generate** before reading.

- Ask students to read Using the Land and Resources of Southeast Asia, and review the map on page 625 with students.

- Ask **What crops do people grow in Southeast Asia?** (*coffee, tea, rubber, soybeans, sugar cane, fruit, and rice*)

- Discuss how certain crops need special conditions to grow. **What conditions in Southeast Asia make it ideal for growing rice?** (*It has a hot climate and plenty of water.*)

Growing Rice in Indonesia
In most of Southeast Asia, people grow rice by hand. Farmers use water buffalo to plow the fields. Rice seedlings are transplanted by hand to the fields, which have been flooded with water. **Analyze Images** *Which photo shows people transplanting rice seedlings to the fields?*

Using the Land and Resources of Southeast Asia

Many of the people in Southeast Asia make their living from the land. Some live in villages, where they build their own houses and grow their own food. Farming that provides only enough for a family or for a village is called **subsistence farming**. Many use the same building and farming methods that their ancestors relied upon thousands of years ago. Other people in Southeast Asia work on plantations—large farming operations designed to raise crops for profit, or cash crops. Plantation agriculture is a type of commercial farming. **Commercial farming** is the raising of crops and livestock for sale on the local or world market.

Farming Farming is a major economic activity in Southeast Asia, even though the region's cities and industries have been growing rapidly. In most Southeast Asian countries, more than 40 percent of the population work in agriculture. People farm—and live—in the river valleys of mountainous mainland Southeast Asia and on the lowland plains of island Southeast Asia. Crops include cash crops such as coffee, tea, and rubber. In Indonesia and Malaysia, rubber is grown on plantations and is a major export crop. Other major crops are soybeans, sugar cane, fruit, and, most important, rice.

The Importance of Rice Rice has been the chief crop in Southeast Asia for centuries. Rice needs a hot climate and plenty of water to grow. In fact, rice grows best when it is planted in the water. In Southeast Asia, farmers use the paddy system to grow rice. A **paddy** is a level field that is flooded to grow rice. Indonesia and Thailand are among the top rice-producing countries in the world. In Southeast Asia, rice is also an important part of the people's diet. It is a food crop as well as a cash crop.

624 Asia and the Pacific

Comparing and Contrasting

1. Teach the skill by outlining the steps for students: Identify things to be compared and contrasted. Look for clue words that compare, such as *like* or *as*, and words that contrast, such as *but* or *different*. Finally, identify similarities and differences.

2. Help students practice the skill by comparing and contrasting subsistence and commercial farming.

3. Have students apply the skill by answering the question: **How are the places of work in subsistence and commercial farming similar and different?**

Answer

Analyze Images The bottom photograph shows people transplanting rice seedlings to the fields.

Southeast Asia: Rain Forest Destruction

MAP MASTER™ Skills Activity

KEY

Extent of rain forest, 3000 B.C.

Present-day extent of rain forest

— National border
• City

0 miles 600
0 kilometers 600
Lambert Azimuthal Equal Area

Human-Environment Interaction Rain forests have a thin layer of topsoil. When people clear rain forests for farms, heavy rains often wash the topsoil away. Then people must clear more land for crops. **Locate** Where are rain forests located in Southeast Asia today? **Compare** On which island has rain forest destruction been greater—Sumatra or Java?

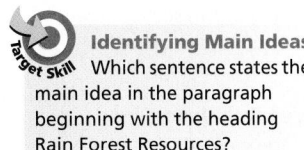

Go Online
PHSchool.com Use Web Code **lcp-6331** for step-by-step map skills practice.

Rain Forest Resources Southeast Asia's tropical rain forests cover large areas in the region. Rain forests contain a great variety of plant and animal life. In Southeast Asia, rain forests are a source of lumber, medicines, and chemicals used in industry. Tropical rain forests once covered nearly all of Southeast Asia. Over the years, huge sections have been cut down to provide lumber and to create farmland. On the island of Java in Indonesia, more than 90 percent of the rain forest has been cleared.

One challenge for the nations of Southeast Asia is balancing the need for economic growth with the need for rain forests. Thailand has made some progress toward conserving its rain forests. In 1988, hundreds of people in Thailand were killed by huge mudslides. The mudslides occurred because trees that had held the soil on the hillsides had been cut down. In 1989, Thailand banned logging in natural forests.

Target Skill — **Identifying Main Ideas** Which sentence states the main idea in the paragraph beginning with the heading Rain Forest Resources?

Background: Global Perspectives

Rain Forests Tropical rain forests, which are warm year-round with plenty of rainfall, are located near the Equator in Southeast Asia, Africa, South America, and Central America. Trees in rain forests can grow as tall as 200 feet (61 meters). These tall trees form a canopy with their leaves that allow very little sunlight to reach the ground. Because of the lack of sunlight at ground level, very few shorter plants such as bushes grow in rain forests. For this reason, people can walk easily through some areas of a rain forest. However, areas of dense plant growth can occur where much sunlight reaches the ground, such as near a river.

Guided Instruction (continued)

- Ask students **What products have people made from resources found in rain forests?** *(lumber, medicines, and chemicals)*

- Have students look at the map on this page. Ask **Which nations that once had rain forests no longer have any?** *(Myanmar, Laos, Thailand, Cambodia, Vietnam, and the Philippines)*

- Ask students **Why might Indonesia, Malaysia, and Thailand want to use their own reserves of natural gas to generate electricity instead of importing oil?** *(Students might conclude that it may be easier and cheaper to use a source of energy already in the country rather than to import it.)*

Independent Practice

Have students complete the graphic organizer with details about Southeast Asia's land and resources.

Monitor Progress

- Show *Section Reading Support Transparency AP 54* and ask students to check their graphic organizers individually. Go over key concepts and clarify key vocabulary as needed.

  Asia and the Pacific Transparencies, *Section Reading Support Transparency AP 54*

- Tell students to fill in the last column of their *Reading Readiness Guides*. Probe for what they learned that confirms or invalidates each statement.

  All in One Asia and the Pacific Teaching Resources, *Reading Readiness Guide,* p. 186

Target Reading Skill — L2

Identifying Main Ideas As a follow up, ask students to answer the Target Reading Skill question in the Student Edition. *(the first sentence)*

Answers

MAP MASTER Skills Activity Locate They are located in Malaysia and Indonesia. **Compare** Java

Go Online
PHSchool.com Students may practice their map skills using the interactive online version of this map.

Assess and Reteach

Assess Progress `L2`

Have students complete the Section Assessment. Administer the *Section Quiz*.

All in One **Asia and the Pacific Teaching Resources,** *Section Quiz,* p. 188

Reteach `L1`

If students need more instruction, have them read this section in the Reading and Vocabulary Study Guide.

📖 Chapter 20, Section 1, **Eastern Hemisphere Reading and Vocabulary Study Guide,** pp. 216–218.

Extend `L3`

To extend the lesson, ask students to complete the *Small Group Activity.* Have each group create trivia cards, game pieces, and a game board using the information from this section.

All in One **Asia and the Pacific Teaching Resources,** *Small Group Activity: Making a Geography Trivia Game,* pp. 203–206

Answer

✓ **Reading Check** Huge sections of rain forest have been cut down for lumber and to create farmland.

Section 1 Assessment

Key Terms
Students' sentences should reflect knowledge of each Key Term.

🔁 Target Reading Skill
Southeast Asia is divided into mainland and island areas. The climate regions in mainland Southeast Asia are similar to those in South Asia. Many of the people in Southeast Asia make their living from the land.

Comprehension and Critical Thinking
1. (a) a peninsula **(b)** Possible answer: Similar—Both get typhoons and monsoons, both have many people who work in agriculture, both have many forest and mineral resources, both have rainforests with tropical wet climate, the nation of Malaysia is part of both regions, and mountains cover much of both regions. Different—The mainland is a peninsula while the islands are not, and the islands are part of the "Ring of Fire."

Bamboo stems being used as scaffolding in Laos

Bamboo as a Resource One forest resource that Southeast Asian people have long used for shelter is bamboo. Bamboo is a type of fast-growing grass that produces a woody stem. Giant bamboo can grow to about 100 feet (30 meters) tall. Millions of people in Southeast Asia live in houses made of bamboo. It is also used to make irrigation pipes, ropes, and bridges. Bamboo is important to the economies of several Southeast Asian countries. The Philippines is one of the world's largest suppliers of bamboo to the world market.

Mineral Resources The countries of Southeast Asia are rich in minerals. Indonesia, Myanmar, and Brunei have large deposits of oil. Even more plentiful, however, are the region's reserves of natural gas. Among the Southeast Asian countries, Indonesia and Malaysia have the largest reserves of natural gas. Thailand has large natural gas reserves in the Gulf of Thailand. These countries are using their own supplies of natural gas to generate electricity instead of importing oil.

✓ **Reading Check** Why does Southeast Asia now have fewer areas of tropical rain forests than in the past?

Section 1 Assessment

Key Terms
Review the key terms at the beginning of this section. Use each term in a sentence that explains its meaning.

🔁 Target Reading Skill
Write the main idea of each paragraph that follows a red heading in this section.

Comprehension and Critical Thinking
1. (a) Recall What kind of landform makes up mainland Southeast Asia?
(b) Compare and Contrast How is mainland Southeast Asia similar to and different from island Southeast Asia?
2. (a) Recall What kind of climate does most of island Southeast Asia have?
(b) Synthesize Information Why does the southeastern coast of Vietnam have the same climate as most of island Southeast Asia?
3. (a) List Give some examples of cash crops raised in Southeast Asia.
(b) Contrast What is the difference between subsistence farming and commercial farming?
(c) Draw Conclusions How can rice be a product of both commercial and subsistence farming?

Writing Activity
Write a paragraph that explains why commercial logging and commercial farming have a destructive effect on tropical rain forests.

For: An activity about Southeast Asia's geography
Visit: PHSchool.com
Web Code: lcd-6301

626 Asia and the Pacific

2. (a) tropical wet climate **(b)** The Pacific Ocean summer monsoon blows from the southeast, bringing heavy rains and a tropical wet climate.

3. (a) coffee, tea, rubber, soybeans, sugar cane, fruit, and rice **(b)** Subsistence farming provides for a family or village, while commercial farming involves sale on the world market. **(c)** Possible answer: Enough rice could be grown to provide food for a family and also to be sold on the world market.

Writing Activity
Use the *Rubric for Assessing a Writing Assignment* to evaluate students' paragraphs.

All in One **Asia and the Pacific Teaching Resources,** *Rubric for Assessing a Writing Assignment,* p. 214

Go Online **PHSchool.com** Typing in the Web code when prompted will bring students to detailed instructions for this activity.

626 *Asia and the Pacific*

Australia and New Zealand:
Physical Geography

Prepare to Read

Objectives

In this section, you will
1. Find out why Australia and New Zealand have unique physical environments.
2. Learn about Australia's physical geography.
3. Explore New Zealand's physical geography.

Taking Notes

As you read, look for details about the physical geography of Australia and New Zealand. Copy the table below, and record your findings in it.

Physical Geography	
Australia	New Zealand

Target Reading Skill

Identify Supporting Details The main idea of a paragraph is supported by details that give further information about it. These details may explain the main idea or give examples or reasons. Look at the first paragraph on page 628. The first sentence is the main idea. The rest of the sentences support this main idea. How do the details about marsupials support the main idea?

Key Terms

- **marsupial** (mahr SOO pea ul) *n.* an animal, such as a kangaroo, that carries its young in a body pouch
- **tectonic plate** (tek TAHN ik playt) *n.* a huge slab of rock that moves very slowly over a softer layer beneath the surface of Earth's crust
- **geyser** (GY zur) *n.* a hot spring that shoots a jet of water and steam into the air
- **fiord** (fyawrd) *n.* a long, narrow inlet or arm of the sea bordered by steep slopes created by glaciers

Objectives

Social Studies
1. Find out why Australia and New Zealand have unique physical environments.
2. Learn about Australia's physical geography.
3. Explore New Zealand's physical geography.

Reading/Language Arts
Look for supporting details that further explain the main idea of a paragraph.

Prepare to Read

Build Background Knowledge L2

In this section, students will learn about the geography of Australia and New Zealand. Have students look at the map on p. 629, taking note of the elevations and the names of major landforms. Using the Give One, Get One strategy (TE, p. T37), have students note similarities and differences between Australia and New Zealand based only on information from the map. (*Answers may include: both have mountains and plains, only Australia has land below sea level, only New Zealand has land above 6,500 feet in elevation, only Australia has deserts.*)

Set a Purpose for Reading L2

- Preview the Objectives.

- Read each statement in the *Reading Readiness Guide* aloud. Ask students to mark the statements true or false.

  All in One Asia and the Pacific Teaching Resources, *Reading Readiness Guide,* p. 190

- Have students discuss the statements in pairs or groups of four, then mark their worksheets again. Use the Numbered Heads participation strategy (TE, p. T36) to call on students to share their group's perspectives.

W hat bird is strange looking, has a long bill, does not fly, and only comes out at night to hunt? If you said a kiwi, you are right. The people of New Zealand are so proud of this unusual bird that they have made it their national symbol. The people even call themselves "Kiwis." The bird is one of many unique animals found in New Zealand and its neighbor to the west, Australia.

The kiwi has appeared on New Zealand stamps since 1898.

Unique Physical Environments

Australia lies between the Pacific Ocean and the Indian Ocean. New Zealand lies in the Pacific Ocean to the east of Australia. Both countries are in the Southern Hemisphere, south of the Equator. This means that their seasons are the opposite of those in the United States. They are far from other continents, which has made them unique.

Target Reading Skill L2

Identify Supporting Details Point out the Target Reading Skill. Tell students that supporting details give more information about the main idea, including examples and reasons.

Model the skill by reading the first paragraph on page 628. Identify the main idea and details that support it. (*The first sentence tells the main idea and the other sentences provide details about the main idea, including which animals are found only in New Zealand and Australia, and how most of Australia's mammals are marsupials.*)

Give students *Identify Supporting Details.* Have them complete the activity in groups.

All in One Asia and the Pacific Teaching Resources, *Identify Supporting Details,* p. 198

Vocabulary Builder
Preview Key Terms L2

Create a three-column "See It—Remember It" chart of Key Terms on the board. Write a term in the first column, a short definition in the second column, and a sketch in the third column. Guide students as they complete the chart.

Instruct

Unique Physical Environments L2

Guided Instruction

- **Vocabulary Builder** Clarify the high-use words **unique** and **isolated** before reading.

- Read A Unique Physical Environment, using the Choral Reading strategy (TE, p. T34).

- Ask students **How do mammals of Australia compare with mammals elsewhere on Earth?** (*In Australia almost all native mammals are marsupials. This is not the case anywhere else on Earth.*)

- Discuss with students **Why are many of New Zealand's and Australia's animals and plants found nowhere else on Earth?** (*New Zealand and Australia are far from other landmasses, and changes in its plants and animals did not spread to other regions.*)

Independent Practice

Assign *Guided Reading and Review*.

All in One **Asia and the Pacific Teaching Resources,** *Guided Reading and Review,* p. 191

Monitor Progress

As students complete *Guided Reading and Review*, circulate and make sure that individuals are completing the worksheet correctly.

Target Reading Skill

Identifying Supporting Details As a follow up, ask students to answer the Target Reading Skill question on this page of the Student Edition. (*The second and third sentences tell that small changes occurred in plants and animals over the centuries, such as birds losing the ability to fly.*)

Answer

√ **Reading Check** Australia and New Zealand are located in the Southern Hemisphere.

Ayers Rock, known in the Aboriginal language as Uluru, is located in central Australia. Kangaroos are common in Australia.

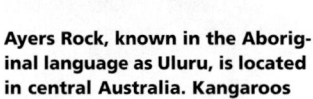

Identifying Supporting Details
Which details in the paragraph at the right tell about change over time?

Unique Plants and Animals New Zealand and Australia are so far from other continents that many of their animals and plants are found nowhere else on Earth. Only in New Zealand can you find kiwis and yellow-eyed penguins. Eighty-four percent of the plants in New Zealand's forests grow nowhere else. Australia has many unique creatures, such as the kangaroo and the koala. They are **marsupials** (mahr SOO pea ulz), or animals that carry their young in a body pouch. Marsupials *are* found elsewhere in the world. The opossum of North America, for instance, is a marsupial. But in Australia, almost all mammals are marsupials. This is not true anywhere else on Earth.

Moving Plates of Rock The uniqueness of New Zealand and Australia is the result of forces beneath Earth's surface. According to the theory of plate tectonics, the outer "skin," or crust of Earth, is broken into huge, moving slabs of rock called **tectonic plates.** These plates move independently, sometimes colliding and sometimes sliding against one another. Australia, New Zealand, and the Pacific islands are all part of the Indo-Australian plate. Once, it was part of a landmass that included Africa. Then, several hundred million years ago, the Indo-Australian plate broke away. Slowly—at a rate of an inch or two each year—it moved northeast toward Asia.

Movement and Change Over Time As the plates moved, Australia and the Pacific islands moved farther from Africa. Over the centuries, small changes have occurred naturally in the animals and plants of Australia and the islands. For instance, many birds have lost the ability to fly, even though they still have small wings. Because Australia and the islands are so isolated, these animals have not spread to other regions.

√ **Reading Check** In which hemisphere are Australia and New Zealand located?

628 Asia and the Pacific

Vocabulary Builder

Use the information below to teach students this section's high-use words.

High-Use Word	Definition and Sample Sentence
unique, p. 627	*adj.* one of a kind She had a **unique** experience during her trip to Europe.
isolate, p. 628	*v.* to keep separate He was **isolated** from other children until he got over the flu.
ample, p. 629	*adj.* more than enough; abundant The new car had **ample** trunk space.
major, p. 630	*adj.* greater in size or importance Silver and gold are the country's **major** exports.

Australia's Physical Geography

Australia is Earth's smallest continent. It is about as large as the continental United States (the part of the United States located between Canada and Mexico, not including Alaska and Hawaii). Most Australians live along Australia's eastern and southeastern coasts. Australia's physical geography explains why.

Find the region along Australia's east coast on the map below. This region receives ample rain. Winds blowing westward across the Pacific Ocean pick up moisture. As the winds rise to cross the Great Dividing Range, the moisture falls as rain. These winds also help make the climate mild and pleasant. Most Australians live here, in cities. Australia's most important rivers, the Murray and the Darling, flow through the region. They flow across a vast plain that contains Australia's most fertile farmland.

✓ **Reading Check** How does the physical geography of Australia explain where the people live?

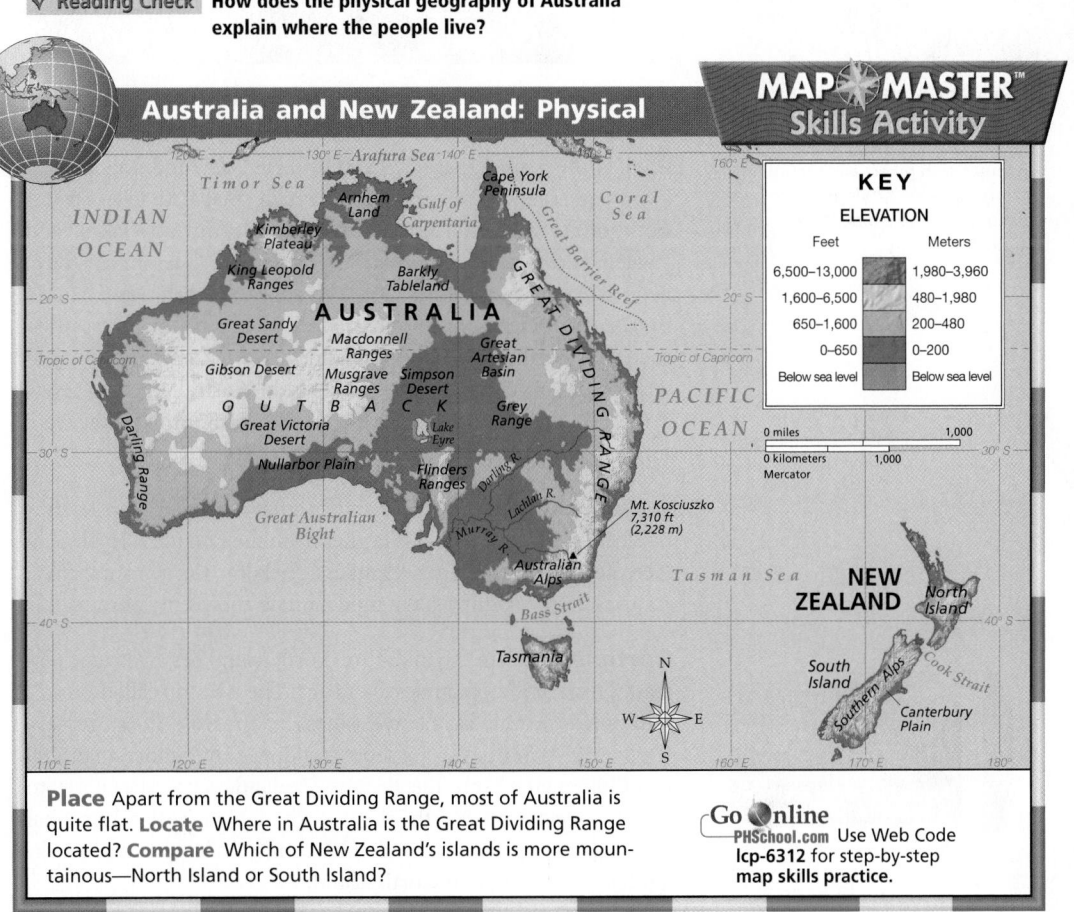

Australia and New Zealand: Physical

MAP MASTER™ Skills Activity

KEY
ELEVATION

Feet	Meters
6,500–13,000	1,980–3,960
1,600–6,500	480–1,980
650–1,600	200–480
0–650	0–200
Below sea level	Below sea level

Place Apart from the Great Dividing Range, most of Australia is quite flat. **Locate** Where in Australia is the Great Dividing Range located? **Compare** Which of New Zealand's islands is more mountainous—North Island or South Island?

Go Online PHSchool.com Use Web Code lcp-6312 for step-by-step map skills practice.

Background: Links Across Time

Formation of the Continents Many geologists believe that the continents were once part of one huge continent, which they call Pangaea. This "supercontinent" is thought to have existed about 175 to 275 million years ago. Eventually, Pangaea split into the continents of Laurasia and Gondwanaland. Laurasia included the present-day continents of North America, Europe, and most of Asia. Gondwanaland included Africa, Antarctica, Australia, South America, and India. By about 50 million years ago, the continents had neared their present locations.

Australia's Physical Geography

Guided Instruction

- **Vocabulary Builder** Clarify the high-use word **ample** before reading.

- Read Australia's Physical Geography with students. As students read, circulate and make sure individuals can answer the Reading Check question.

- Ask students **What is Earth's smallest continent?** (*Australia*)

- Ask students **What are Australia's most important rivers?** (*the Murray and Darling rivers*) **Where are they located?** (*They are located on Australia's eastern coast.*)

- Have students look at the map on this page. Ask **Where in Australia is the elevation below sea level?** (*in southern Australia, north of Flinders Ranges*)

Independent Practice

Ask students to create the Taking Notes graphic organizer on a blank piece of paper. Then have them fill in details about Australia's physical geography in the column labeled "Australia." Briefly model how to identify which details to record.

Monitor Progress

As students fill in the graphic organizer, circulate and make sure individuals are choosing the correct details. Provide assistance as needed.

Answers

✓ **Reading Check** Most people live along Australia's eastern and southeastern coasts because that is where there is ample rain, a pleasant climate, and fertile farmland.

MAP MASTER Skills Activity **Locate** along the eastern coast; **Compare** South Island

Go Online PHSchool.com Students may practice their map skills, using the interactive online version of this map.

New Zealand's Physical Geography

Guided Instruction

- **Vocabulary Builder** Clarify the high-use word **major** before reading.

- Read New Zealand's Physical Geography with students. Review the physical map of Australia and New Zealand on p. 629 with students.

- Ask students to contrast the geography of North Island and South Island of New Zealand. (*North Island has volcanoes and hot springs, while South Island has mountains, glaciers, fiords, and a plain suitable for farmland.*)

- Ask students to compare the natural resources of Australia and New Zealand. (*Both have coal, iron ore, and natural gas. Both also have sheep and cattle and grow similar crops.*)

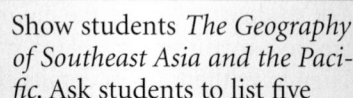

Show students *The Geography of Southeast Asia and the Pacific*. Ask students to list five facts they have learned about Australia and New Zealand from the video. (*Students' answers will vary.*)

Independent Practice

Have students complete the graphic organizer by filling in the "New Zealand" column and finishing the "Australia" column.

Monitor Progress

- Show *Section Reading Support Transparency AP 55* and ask students to check their graphic organizers individually. Go over key concepts and clarify key vocabulary as needed.

    Asia and the Pacific Transparencies, *Section Reading Support Transparency AP 55*

- Tell students to fill in the last column of their *Reading Readiness Guides*. Probe for what they learned that confirms or invalidates each statement.

    All in One Asia and the Pacific Teaching Resources, *Reading Readiness Guide,* p. 190

Answer

Infer a day hike; they do not have any mountain-climbing equipment with them

Mount Cook National Park
New Zealand's Mount Cook National Park, located in the Southern Alps, is popular with hikers and mountain climbers. **Infer** *Is this group of people out to climb a mountain or enjoy a day hike?*

Explore the land of Southeast Asia and the Pacific Region.

New Zealand's Physical Geography

Look at the map on page 629 and find New Zealand. Made up of two major islands, New Zealand is much smaller than Australia. Both of its major islands have highlands, forests, lakes, and rugged, snowcapped mountains. New Zealand's landforms have been shaped by volcanoes. The volcanoes, in turn, were caused by the movement of tectonic plates. Where plates meet, often there are earthquakes and volcanoes. New Zealand is located where the Pacific plate meets the Indo-Australian plate. New Zealand's major islands, North Island and South Island, were formed by volcanoes when these plates collided.

A Mild Climate New Zealand's climate is cooler than Australia's because New Zealand is farther from the Equator. No place in New Zealand is more than 80 miles (129 kilometers) from the sea. As a result, the country has a mild climate and plenty of rainfall.

North Island In the middle of North Island lies a volcanic plateau. Three of the volcanoes are active. The volcano called Mount Egmont, however, is inactive. North of the volcanoes, **geysers** (GY zurz), or hot springs, shoot scalding water more than 100 feet (30.5 meters) into the air. New Zealanders use this energy to produce electricity. North Island is where New Zealand's capital city of Wellington is located. The country's largest city, Auckland, is also located on North Island.

630 Asia and the Pacific

Differentiated Instruction

For English Language Learners L2

Ask English learners to take out their "See It—Remember It" chart of Key Terms that they created early in the lesson. Have them work with English-speaking students to use dictionaries to write definitions and draw pictures that illustrate the following words: *Equator, volcano, earthquake, glacier, cattle,* and *coal.*

For Less Proficient Readers L1

Help students obtain a visual image of Australia's geographic features by taking the Passport to the World photo tour of Australia.

Australia: Photo Tour, **Passport to the World CD-ROM**

South Island South Island has a high mountain range called the Southern Alps. Mount Cook, the highest peak in the range, rises to 12,349 feet (3,764 meters). Glaciers cover the mountainsides. Below, crystal-clear lakes dot the landscape. **Fiords** (fyawrds), or narrow inlets bordered by steep slopes, slice the southwest coastline. Here, the mountains reach the sea. To the southeast lies a flat, fertile land called the Canterbury Plain. This is where farmers produce most of New Zealand's crops. Ranchers also raise sheep and cattle here.

Comparing Australia and New Zealand New Zealand is like Australia in several ways. In both countries, most of the population lives in cities along the coast. More than four out of five New Zealanders live in towns and cities. Both Australia and New Zealand have important natural resources such as coal, iron ore, and natural gas. The two countries also raise sheep and cattle and grow similar crops.

New Zealand is different from Australia in a number of ways, too. New Zealand is much smaller but has higher mountains than those in Australia. New Zealand has glaciers, while Australia does not. The two countries also have different climates.

✓ **Reading Check** Where do most people in New Zealand live— in urban areas or in rural areas?

Links Across
The World

Steam Heat Geysers are found in three places in the world: the northwestern United States, Iceland, and New Zealand. In these places, movements of tectonic plates have created deep cracks in Earth's crust. Water seeps down into the cracks until it reaches very hot rocks. The heat raises the temperature of the water until it is so hot that it bursts upward in a shower of water and steam.

Links
Read the **Links Across the World** on this page. Ask students **Where are geysers found?** (*northwestern United States, Iceland, and New Zealand*)

Assess and Reteach

Assess Progress
Have students complete the Section Assessment. Administer the *Section Quiz.*

All in One **Asia and the Pacific Teaching Resources,** *Section Quiz,* p. 192

Reteach
If students need more instruction, have them read this section in the Reading and Vocabulary Study Guide.

Chapter 20, Section 2, **Eastern Hemisphere Reading and Vocabulary Study Guide,** pp. 219–221

Extend
Have students learn more about Australia's geography by completing the *Enrichment* activity on Australia's Great Barrier Reef.

All in One **Asia and the Pacific Teaching Resources,** *Enrichment,* p. 201

Answer

✓ **Reading Check** Most people in New Zealand live in urban areas.

Writing Activity
Use the *Rubric for Assessing a Writing Assignment* to evaluate students' lists.

All in One **Asia and the Pacific Teaching Resources,** *Rubric for Assessing a Writing Assignment,* p. 214

Go Online PHSchool.com Typing in the Web code when prompted will bring students directly to detailed instructions for this activity.

Section 2 Assessment

Key Terms
Review the key terms at the beginning of this section. Use each term in a sentence that explains its meaning.

Target Reading Skill
The main idea of the last paragraph in this section is that Australia and New Zealand are different in many ways. State the details that support this main idea.

Comprehension and Critical Thinking
1. (a) Recall Where do most of the people in Australia live?

(b) Identify Cause and Effect How have Australia's geography and climate affected where Australians live?
2. (a) Recall How were New Zealand's North Island and South Island formed?
(b) Compare and Contrast How is the physical geography of New Zealand different from that of Australia? How is it similar?
3. (a) Explain How are the population patterns similar in Australia and New Zealand?
(b) Draw Conclusions Why do most of the people in New Zealand live near the coasts?

Writing Activity
Write a list of adjectives that describe Australia. Then write a list of adjectives that describe New Zealand. Include at least three adjectives for each country. Using the information in this section, write a fact related to each adjective on your list.

Go Online PHSchool.com
For: An activity about Australia
Visit: PHSchool.com
Web Code: lcd-6302

Chapter 20 Section 2 **631**

Section 2 Assessment

Key Terms
Students' sentences should reflect knowledge of each Key Term.

Target Reading Skill
New Zealand is smaller, and has glaciers, higher mountains, and a different climate than Australia.

Comprehension and Critical Thinking
1. (a) the eastern and southeastern coasts **(b)** Most people live along Australia's eastern and southeastern coasts because that is where there is ample rain, a pleasant climate, and fertile farmland.

2. (a) Both islands were formed by volcanoes when the Pacific and Indo-Australian plates collided. **(b)** Possible answers: Different— New Zealand consists of two islands while Australia is a continent; New Zealand is

smaller than Australia and has higher mountains. New Zealand has glaciers while Australia does not. Similar—Both have fertile plains and mountains.

3. (a) In both countries most of the population lives in cities along the coast. **(b)** Possible answer: No place in New Zealand is more than 80 miles from the sea, and several active volcanoes are located in the middle of North Island.

Objective

Learn how to identify cause and effect.

Prepare to Read

Build Background Knowledge `L2`

Tell students that they can see cause and effect relationships everyday. Ask them about activities with possible effects that they have done or will do today, such as riding the school bus, completing homework on time, or eating lunch. Use the Numbered Heads participation strategy (TE, p. T36) to create a list of causes and effects.

Instruct

Identifying Cause and Effect `L2`

Guided Instruction

- Read the steps to identifying cause and effect as a class and write them on the board.

- Draw two columns on the board, one labeled *cause* and the other labeled *effect*. Practice the skill by following the steps on p. 632 and applying them to the practice paragraph on p. 633. Using an Idea Wave (TE, p. T35), go through each of the four steps with students.

- If necessary, repeat the process in Practice the Skill, but find effects instead of causes. Change the question in step 2 to read: "What are the effects of tsunamis on land?"

Independent Practice

Assign *Skills for Life* and have students complete it individually.

All in One Asia and the Pacific Teaching Resources, *Skills for Life,* p. 202

Monitor Progress

Monitor the students while they are doing the *Skills for Life* worksheet, checking to make sure individuals understand the skill steps.

Identifying Cause and Effect

Have you ever tossed a stone into a pond and watched what happens? As soon as that stone hits the surface and sinks, circles of ripples, or waves, begin to move away from that spot in ever-widening circles. This is one case of cause and effect. Tossing the stone started the waves moving away from the spot where the stone landed. Understanding this relationship between cause and effect is useful in school and in daily life.

Learn the Skill

Being able to identify causes and effects helps you to understand what you read. To learn this skill, follow the steps below.

1 **Look for a cause-and-effect relationship.** Remember the pebble in the pond. As you read, ask yourself, "Why did this happen?" or "How did this happen?" Look for words such as *because, so,* and *as a result.* These words sometimes signal a cause-and-effect relationship.

2 **Identify the effect or effects.** Like the ripples that appear in a pond, an effect is what happens. A cause may have more than one effect. List the effect(s) you have identified.

3 **Identify the cause or causes.** A cause makes something happen. An effect may have more than one cause. List the cause(s) of the effect(s) you identified in Step 2.

4 **State the cause and effect.** A simple cause-and-effect statement might read, "A caused B." A is the cause, and B is the effect. A cause that produced three effects might be stated as, "A caused B, C, and D." A is the cause; its effects are B, C, and D.

A stone tossed into this pond caused the ripples to form. The stone is the cause, and the ripples are the effect.

Practice the Skill

To practice identifying a cause-and-effect relationship, read the paragraph below, using the steps on the previous page.

1 What words signal a possible cause-and-effect situation?

2 Identify the effect by filling in the blank in the following sentence: "Why do _____ happen?" The word you use to fill in the blank is the effect.

3 The effect you identified is triggered by two causes. What are the two causes?

4 State the cause-and-effect relationship in a sentence. Your sentence should give an answer to this question: What causes tsunamis?

A Japanese woodblock print of a tsunami

Tsunamis (soo NAH mees) are powerful waves caused by earthquakes or volcanic eruptions that take place underwater. When an earthquake happens under the ocean floor or when an underwater volcano erupts, both of these actions cause circles of waves like the ones that form when you throw a stone into a pond. The result is a wave that is extremely forceful and fast. In deep water, tsunamis can move as fast as 500 to 600 miles (800 to 960 kilometers) per hour. As a tsunami approaches land, the speed slows down and the wave grows in height, sometimes as high as a ten-story building. The wave pushes inland, carrying boulders, boats, and buildings along until its energy is gone. In 2004, a huge tsunami struck at least 12 countries along the Indian Ocean. Entire villages were destroyed, and at least 225,000 people were killed.

Apply the Skill

Read the passages titled Moving Plates of Rock and Movement and Change Over Time on page 628. Use the steps in the skill to identify one cause that explains why New Zealand and Australia are unique.

Chapter 20 **633**

Section 3
Step-by-Step Instruction

Objectives

Social Studies

1. Examine features of high islands and low islands.
2. Learn about the three main island groups.
3. Find out what kind of climate and vegetation the islands have.
4. Discover how land is used in the Pacific islands.

Reading/Language Arts

Use details in a paragraph to figure out an unstated main idea.

Prepare to Read

Build Background Knowledge L2

Tell students that in this section they will learn about the geography of the Pacific islands. Show the Discovery Channel School Video, and then ask students what advantages and disadvantages they think there are to living in this region compared to their community. Use the Think-Write-Pair-Share strategy (TE, p. T36) to solicit answers.

The Geography of Southeast Asia and the Pacific, **World Studies Video Program**

Set a Purpose for Reading L2

■ Preview the Objectives.

■ Read each statement in the *Reading Readiness Guide* aloud. Ask students to mark the statements true or false.

All in One Asia and the Pacific Teaching Resources, *Reading Readiness Guide,* p. 194

■ Have students discuss the statements in pairs or groups of four, then mark their guides again. Use the Numbered Heads participation strategy (TE, p. T36) to call on students to share their group perspectives.

Vocabulary Builder
Preview Key Terms L2

Create a three column "See It—Remember It" chart of the Key Terms on the board. Write a term in the first column, a short definition in the second column, and a sketch in the third column. Guide students as they copy and complete the chart.

Section 3
The Pacific Islands
Physical Geography

Prepare to Read

Objectives

In this section, you will

1. Examine features of high islands and low islands.
2. Learn about the three main island groups.
3. Find out what kind of climate and vegetation the islands have.
4. Discover how land is used in the Pacific islands.

Taking Notes

As you read this section, look for details about the three major Pacific island groups. Copy the diagram below, and record your findings in it.

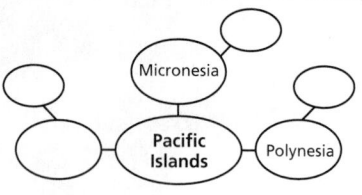

Target Reading Skill

Identify Main Ideas
Sometimes the main idea in a paragraph or reading passage is not stated directly. All the details add up to a main idea, but you must state the main idea yourself. As you read, look for main ideas that are not stated directly.

Key Terms

- **high island** (hy EYE lund) *n.* an island formed from the mountainous top of an ancient volcano
- **low island** (loh EYE lund) *n.* an island formed from coral reefs or atolls
- **atoll** (A tawl) *n.* a small coral island in the shape of a ring
- **coral** (KAWR ul) *n.* a rock-like material made up of the skeletons of tiny sea creatures, most plentiful in warm ocean water

Scuba diving in the Pacific islands

634 Asia and the Pacific

The Pacific Ocean, which covers nearly one third of Earth's surface, is dotted with thousands of islands. Some are barely large enough for a person to stand on. Others cover thousands of square miles. The Pacific islands include the second-largest island in the world. This is New Guinea. Half of this island is actually part of Indonesia. The other half is the independent country of Papua New Guinea (PAP yoo uh noo GIH nee). The Pacific islands also include the world's smallest independent island nation. This is the country of Nauru (NAH oo roo), which has a total land area of just 8 square miles (21 square kilometers).

Geographers divide these thousands of islands into three main groups. Melanesia (mel uh NEE zhuh) means "black islands." Micronesia (my kruh NEE zhuh) means "small islands." Polynesia (pahl uh NEE zhuh) means "many islands." Each of these groups covers a particular area, and any island that falls inside the boundaries of one of these areas belongs to that group.

Target Reading Skill L2

Identify Implied Main Ideas Point out the Target Reading Skill. Tell students that when a main idea is not stated directly, readers can combine important details to express the main idea.

Model the skill using the last paragraph on p. 635. Explain your thought process as you identify the implied main idea. (*Low islands have very few conditions that allow for a large population.*)

Give students *Identify Implied Main Ideas.* Have them complete the activity in groups.

All in One Asia and the Pacific Teaching Resources, *Identify Implied Main Ideas,* p. 199

634 *Asia and the Pacific*

High Islands and Low Islands

Geographers also divide the Pacific islands into high islands and low islands. **High islands** are mountainous and have been formed by volcanoes. The soil, which consists of volcanic ash, is very fertile. Because of their size and because people can grow crops there, high islands can support more people than low islands.

Low islands are made up of coral reefs or atolls. An **atoll** (A tawl) is a small coral island in the shape of a ring. The ring encloses a shallow pool of ocean water called a lagoon. Often, the lagoon has one or more openings to the sea. An atoll may rise only a few feet above the water. Low islands have this shape and low elevation because they are coral reefs. **Coral** is a rocklike material made up of the skeletons of tiny sea creatures. A reef develops until it nears the surface. Then sand and other debris accumulate on the reef's surface, raising the island above the level of the water.

Far fewer people live on low islands than on high islands. In part, this is because low islands are quite small. Also, low islands have poor, sandy soil and little fresh water, so it is difficult to raise crops. Most low islanders survive by fishing. They may also grow coconuts, yams, and a starchy root called taro.

A traditional house on a high island in Polynesia

✓ **Reading Check** On which type of island do most Pacific island people live?

A Coral Atoll

A South Pacific Atoll
The diagram below shows how a coral atoll is formed. **1** It begins as a fringe of coral around a volcanic island. **2** The coral continues to build as the island is worn away. **3** Eventually, only a ring of coral remains. The aerial view of an atoll at the left shows the ring structure of the coral.

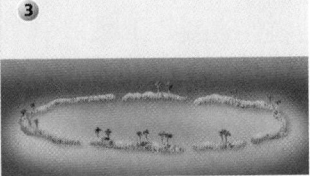

Chapter 20 Section 3 **635**

Vocabulary Builder

Use the information below to teach students this section's high-use words.

High-Use Word	Definition and Sample Sentence
enclose, p. 635	*v.* to close in on all sides; surround A fence **enclosed** the field.
debris, p. 635	*n.* remains of something destroyed The **debris** from the collapsed building was collected for study.
accumulate, p. 635	*v.* to gather or pile up The top of the table **accumulated** dust.
income, p. 638	*n.* money earned by working The **income** from her new job allowed her to support her family.

Instruct

High Islands and Low Islands   L2

Guided Instruction

■ **Vocabulary Builder** Clarify the high-use words **enclose, debris** and **accumulate** before reading.

■ Read High Islands and Low Islands, using the Structured Silent Reading strategy (TE, p. T34).

■ Ask students to compare the soil of high islands and low islands. *(High islands have fertile soil consisting of volcanic ash, while low islands have poor, sandy soil that is not ideal for raising crops.)*

■ Discuss the sequence of events in the creation of a low island by asking students **How does a low island develop?** *(Coral reef develops until it nears the surface. Then sand and debris accumulate on the reef's surface, creating an island above the surface of the water.)*

Independent Practice

Assign *Guided Reading and Review.*

All in One **Asia and the Pacific Teaching Resources,** *Guided Reading and Review,* p. 195

Monitor Progress

As students complete *Guided Reading and Review,* circulate and make sure that individuals are completing the worksheet correctly.

Answer

✓ **Reading Check** Most people of the Pacific islands live on high islands.

Melanesia, Micronesia, and Polynesia L2

Guided Instruction

- Read Melanesia, Micronesia, and Polynesia with students. As students read, circulate and make sure individuals can answer the Reading Check question.

- Ask students **Which island group has the most people?** (*Melanesia*)

- Compare the types of islands in the different island groups by asking students these questions: **Which two island groups contain many high islands?** (*Melanesia and Polynesia*) **Which island group contains mostly low islands?** (*Micronesia*)

Independent Practice

Ask students to create the Taking Notes graphic organizer on a blank piece of paper and complete it by filling in details about each of the island groups of the Pacific. Briefly model how to identify which details to record.

Monitor Progress

Show *Section Reading Support Transparency AP 56* and ask students to check their graphic organizers individually. Go over key concepts and clarify key vocabulary as needed.

Asia and the Pacific Transparencies, *Section Reading Support Transparency AP 56*

Answer

 Reading Check Hawaii is part of Polynesia.

636 *Asia and the Pacific*

Melanesia, Micronesia, and Polynesia

The island group with the most people is Melanesia, which is north and east of Australia. Most of Melanesia's large islands are high islands. New Guinea, for example, has two ranges of high mountains. The western half of New Guinea is called Irian Jaya (IHR ee ahn JAH yuh). It is part of the country of Indonesia. The eastern half is Papua New Guinea, the largest and most populated Melanesian country. Some smaller Melanesian islands are Fiji, the Solomon Islands, and New Caledonia.

Made up largely of low islands, Micronesia covers an area of the Pacific as large as the continental United States. Most of the islands of Micronesia lie north of the Equator. Some of Micronesia's 2,000 islands are less than 1 square mile (2.6 square kilometers) in area. The largest is Guam, which is 209 square miles (541 square kilometers). Most of Micronesia's islands are divided into groups. The largest are the Caroline, Gilbert, Marshall, and Mariana islands. Guam is part of the Marianas.

Polynesia is the largest island group in the Pacific. It includes the fiftieth state of the United States, Hawaii. Polynesia consists of a great many high islands, such as Tahiti and Samoa. Dense rain forests cover their high volcanic mountains. Along the shores are palm-fringed, sandy beaches. The Tuamotus and Tonga are examples of Polynesia's few low islands and atolls.

✓ Reading Check **Which island group contains Hawaii?**

Living in the Pacific Islands
The bottom photo on the opposite page shows a traditional canoe in Fiji. Below left, fishers haul nets in the waters of Fiji. Below right, some people in Papua New Guinea farm for a living. The inset photo on the opposite page shows children playing volleyball in Vanuatu.

636 Asia and the Pacific

Skills for Life — Skills Mini Lesson

Transferring Information from One Medium to Another

1. Teach the skill by outlining the steps to transfer information from a visual to a written format: state the main idea of the visual, identify the details, and write complete sentences describing each section of the visual aid.

2. Help students practice the skill by choosing one of the pictures in the chart on p. 635 and writing one sentence that describes the main idea.

3. Have students apply the skill by writing one sentence that summarizes the entire chart. (*Possible answer: Atolls do not begin as coral islands, but develop over time.*)

Climate and Vegetation of the Pacific Islands

The Pacific islands lie in the tropics. Temperatures are hot year-round. Daytime temperatures can reach as high as the 80s and mid-90s in degrees Fahrenheit (around 30°C). Nighttime temperatures average about 75°F (24°C). The ocean winds keep the temperatures from getting too high.

Some Pacific islands have wet and dry seasons. Most islands, however, receive heavy rainfall all year long. In Hawaii, for example, volcanic peaks such as Mauna Kea (MOW nuh KAY uh) receive 100 inches (250 centimeters) of rain each year. Usually the rain falls in brief, heavy downpours. Some low islands, however, receive only scattered rainfall.

Because of high temperatures, plentiful rainfall, and fertile soil, high islands such as Papua New Guinea and the Hawaiian Islands have rich vegetation. Tropical rain forests cover the hills. Savanna grasses grow in the lowlands. Low islands, on the other hand, have little vegetation. The poor soil supports only palm trees, grasses, and small shrubs.

Identify Main Ideas In one sentence, state what the paragraph at the left is about.

✓ **Reading Check** Why do low islands have little vegetation?

Differentiated Instruction

For Special Needs Students `L1`
Help students visualize the information they read about on p. 636 by labeling the island groups and some of their nations on the outline map of the Pacific islands. Students may wish to consult other maps in atlases or on the Internet to label their maps.

 **Asia and the Pacific Teaching Resources,** *Outline Map 32: The Pacific Islands,* p. 209

For Gifted and Talented `L3`
Have students read the section Climate and Vegetation of the Pacific Islands and pick out some of the adjectives in the passage, such as *heavy, fertile, rich,* and *poor.* Ask them to think of words with similar meanings that could be used as replacements. Remind students that some words have several meanings, and that they should study each word's context carefully.

Climate and Vegetation of the Pacific Islands `L2`

Natural Resources and Land Use `L2`

Guided Instruction

■ **Vocabulary Builder** Clarify the high-use word **income** before reading.

■ Read Climate and Vegetation of the Pacific Islands and Natural Resources and Land Use with students. Review the photos and captions on pp. 636–638 with students.

■ Ask students **What is the climate of the Pacific islands like?** *(The temperature is hot year-round with rainfall ranging from heavy on the high islands to scattered on the low islands.)*

■ Ask students **How is the land of the Pacific islands used by people to support themselves?** *(People support themselves by fishing, harvesting coconuts, working in tourism, or growing sugarcane, taro, yams, and sweet potatoes.)*

Independent Practice
Have students create a list of activities they would like to do if they were tourists in Fiji or French Polynesia. Allow them to conduct library or Internet research to find possible activities.

Monitor Progress
Tell students to fill in the last column of their *Reading Readiness Guides.* Probe for what they learned that confirms or invalidates each statement.

Asia and the Pacific Teaching Resources, *Reading Readiness Guide,* p. 194

Target Reading Skill `L2`

Identify Main Ideas As a follow up, ask students to complete the Target Reading Skill activity in the Student Edition. *(Some Pacific islands have a wet and dry season, but most have rainfall all year, whether heavy or scattered.)*

Answer

✓ **Reading Check** The poor soil does not support much vegetation.

Assess and Reteach

Assess Progress `L2`

Have students complete the Section Assessment. Administer the *Section Quiz*.

All in One **Asia and the Pacific Teaching Resources,** *Section Quiz,* p. 196

Reteach `L1`

If students need more instruction, have them read this section in the Reading and Vocabulary Study Guide.

📖 Chapter 20, Section 3, **Eastern Hemisphere Reading and Vocabulary Study Guide,** pp. 222–224

Extend `L3`

Have students learn more about the Pacific islands by reading *The Coconut Tree* in pairs or groups and discussing the Think It Over questions at the end.

All in One **Asia and the Pacific Teaching Resources,** *The Coconut Tree,* pp. 210–212

Answer

✓ **Reading Check** Sugar cane and copra, or dried coconut, are cash crops in the Pacific islands.

Section 3 Assessment

Key Terms
Students' sentences should reflect knowledge of each Key Term.

🎯 **Target Reading Skill**
Students' sentences will vary, but should include the idea that tourism is important to the economies of the Pacific islands.

Comprehension and Critical Thinking
1. (a) High islands are mountainous and formed by volcanoes. They have fertile soil of volcanic ash on which people can grow crops. Low islands are made up of coral reefs or atolls and have poor, sandy soil with little fresh water, making growing crops difficult. **(b)** Because high islands are larger and have fertile soil, people there can grow more crops than people living on low islands.

2. (a) Melanesia, Micronesia, Polynesia **(b)** Possible answer: Most of Melanesia's large islands are high islands that support more people than low islands. **(c)** Possible answer: It might be difficult for these islands to make money by exporting goods; they would need to import many goods from other nations.

A worker harvests ripe coconuts in Fiji.

Natural Resources and Land Use

The Pacific island region has few natural resources. The coconut palm is its most important resource. It provides food, clothing, and shelter. Another important resource is fish.

Cash Crops Some Pacific island countries, such as the nation of Fiji, grow cash crops. Fiji is a nation of some 300 islands in Melanesia. The Fiji islands' fertile, volcanic soil and hot, wet climate are good for growing sugar cane. Sugar is a major export for Fiji. Another important cash crop for many Pacific island countries is copra. Copra, or dried coconut, is used in margarine, cooking oils, soaps, and cosmetics. The people in Fiji also work as subsistence farmers, growing their own food crops such as taro, yams, and sweet potatoes.

Tourism The Pacific islands' most valuable resource may be their natural beauty. Tourism provides a key source of income in the region. Many Pacific island nations are working to develop their tourist industries. The greatest number of visitors to the Pacific islands come from Australia. Nearly as many come from the United States.

✓ **Reading Check** Give two examples of cash crops grown in the Pacific islands.

Section 3 Assessment

Key Terms
Review the key terms at the beginning of this section. Use each key term in a sentence that explains its meaning.

🎯 **Target Reading Skill**
Read the paragraph titled Tourism, above. Write a sentence that states the main idea.

Comprehension and Critical Thinking
1. (a) Explain Tell the difference between high islands and low islands in the Pacific.

(b) Make Generalizations The people on high islands often have a better standard of living than people on low islands. Explain why this might be so.
2. (a) Recall Name the three Pacific island groups.
(b) Apply Information Why do most of the people in the Pacific islands live in Melanesia?
(c) Draw Conclusions Most Pacific islands have few natural resources. How might this affect trade between these islands and industrial nations around the world?

Writing Activity
Suppose that you have decided to live on one of the Pacific islands. Write a paragraph explaining why you have decided to move. How will you handle the challenges of island life? Will you live on a high island or a low island?

For: An activity on the Pacific islands
Visit: PHSchool.com
Web Code: lcd-6303

638 Asia and the Pacific

Writing Activity
Use the *Rubric for Assessing a Writing Assignment* to evaluate students' paragraphs.

All in One **Asia and the Pacific Teaching Resources,** *Rubric for Assessing a Writing Assignment,* p. 214

Go Online PHSchool.com Typing in the Web code when prompted will bring students directly to detailed instructions for this activity.

◆ Chapter Summary

Section 1: Southeast Asia Physical Geography

- Southeast Asia is divided into mainland and island areas. Mainland Southeast Asia is a peninsula. Island Southeast Asia is part of the Ring of Fire, a region of volcanoes and earthquakes.
- Most of Southeast Asia has a tropical wet climate.
- Farming is a major economic activity in Southeast Asia, although the region's cities and industries have been growing rapidly.
- Southeast Asian rain forests are a source of lumber, medicines, and materials used in industry. The region's remaining rain forests are in danger of destruction from commercial logging and farming.

Section 2: Australia and New Zealand Physical Geography

- Because Australia and New Zealand are far from other landmasses, many of their plants and animals are found nowhere else on Earth.
- Australia is the smallest continent. Most people live along its eastern and southern coasts.
- New Zealand is made up of two mountainous islands.

Cambodia

Australia

Section 3: The Pacific Islands Physical Geography

- The Pacific islands are divided into three main groups: Melanesia, Micronesia, and Polynesia.
- Within these groups, there are high islands and low islands.
- Because the Pacific islands lie in the tropics, temperatures are hot all year.
- The Pacific islands have few natural resources, but some island countries are able to grow cash crops such as sugar and copra, or dried coconut. Tourism is growing in importance in the region.

◆ Key Terms

Use each key term in a sentence that explains its meaning.

1. fiord
2. paddy
3. subsistence farming
4. commercial farming
5. marsupial
6. tectonic plate
7. geyser
8. high island
9. low island
10. coral

Chapter 20 **639**

─ Vocabulary Builder ─

High-Use Academic Words

Revisit this chapter's high-use words:

region   unique   enclose
pattern   isolate   debris
conserve   ample   accumulate
generate   major   income

Ask students to review the definitions they recorded on their *Word Knowledge* worksheets.

All in One Asia and the Pacific Teaching Resources, *Word Knowledge*, p. 200

Consider allowing students to earn extra credit if they use the words in their answers to the questions in the Chapter Review and Assessment. The words must be used correctly and in a natural context to win the extra points.

Review Chapter Content

- Review and revisit the major themes of this chapter by asking students to classify what Guiding Question each bulleted statement in the Chapter Summary answers. Form students into groups and ask them to complete the activity together. Refer to page 567 in the Student Edition for the text of Guiding Questions.

- Assign *Vocabulary Development* for students to review Key Terms.

  All in One Asia and the Pacific Teaching Resources, *Vocabulary Development*, p. 213

Answers

Key Terms

1–10. Answers will vary. Students' sentences should reflect knowledge of each Key Term.

Comprehension and Critical Thinking

11. (a) Cambodia, Laos, Malaysia, Myanmar, Thailand, Vietnam **(b)** It lies on the mainland, but also includes part of the island of Borneo.

12. (a) The Indian Ocean monsoon blows from the southwest and a Pacific Ocean monsoon blows from the southeast. **(b)** The monsoons bring heavy rain which support rain forests.

13. (a) Indonesia and Thailand **(b)** Possible answer: A subsistence farmer grows enough food for a family or village, not for the world market. Rubber is not a food product and is usually grown on plantations.

14. (a) Great Dividing Range **(b)** It is located west of the coastal plain on the eastern coast.

15. (a) Possible answer: New Zealand is made up of two major islands shaped by volcanoes; both islands have highlands, forests, lakes, and mountains; no place is more than 80 miles from the sea; the North Island has geysers and three active volcanoes; the South Island has glaciers, fiords, and a fertile plain. **(b)** Similar—most of the population lives in cities along the coast; both have natural resources of coal, iron ore, and natural gas; people raise sheep and cattle and grow similar crops; both have plants and animals found nowhere else on Earth; Different—New Zealand is smaller than Australia; both have different climates. New Zealand has glaciers, while Australia does not; New Zealand's mountains are higher than those in Australia.

16. (a) high islands **(b)** More people live on high islands because they have better conditions to support a large population, including larger area, better soil for crops, and more fresh water.

Skills Practice

Effects of the eruption of Mount Pinatubo include: 58,000 people had to move to safety, 800 people died, 20 million tons of gas and ash were thrown 21 miles into the atmosphere, and this gas cloud caused global temperatures to drop by about 1°F for two years.

◆ Comprehension and Critical Thinking

11. (a) List Which countries make up mainland Southeast Asia?
(b) Explain Why is Malaysia part of both mainland Southeast Asia and island Southeast Asia?

12. (a) Explain Why does Southeast Asia have more than one summer monsoon?
(b) Summarize Describe the effects of summer monsoons in Southeast Asia.

13. (a) Name Which two Southeast Asian countries are among the world's leading rice producers?
(b) Analyze Information Why would a subsistence farmer in Southeast Asia raise rice instead of rubber?

14. (a) Name What is one mountain range in Australia?
(b) Locate Where is this mountain range located relative to Australia's east coast?

15. (a) Recall Describe the major features of New Zealand's geography.
(b) Compare and Contrast How are Australia and New Zealand different from and similar to each other?

16. (a) Identify Where do most people in the Pacific islands live—on high islands or on low islands?
(b) Draw Conclusions You have read about high islands and low islands. What conclusion can you reach about why more people live on one kind than another?

◆ Skills Practice

Identifying Cause and Effect Review the steps you followed to learn this skill. Then reread the first paragraph on page 620. Identify three effects of the eruption of Mount Pinatubo.

◆ Writing Activity: Math

Suppose that it is Monday at 12 noon where you live. Calculate what day and time it is in Bangkok, Thailand; in Jakarta, Indonesia; and in Sydney, Australia. You will need to use a world time zones map, which you can find in an atlas. Do research to learn more about time zones and the International Date Line. Then write a paragraph about the International Date Line.

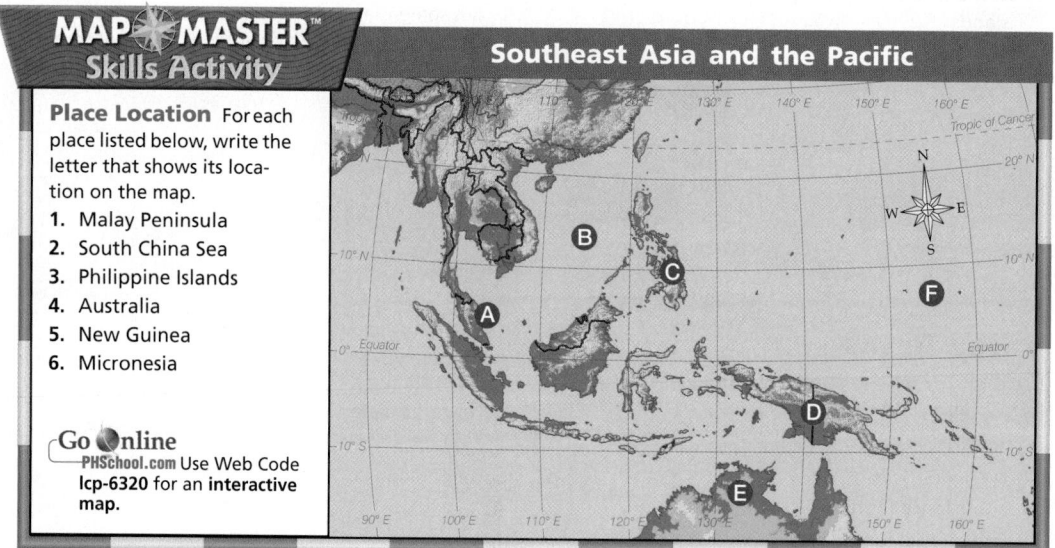

MAP✦MASTER™ Skills Activity

Southeast Asia and the Pacific

Place Location For each place listed below, write the letter that shows its location on the map.

1. Malay Peninsula
2. South China Sea
3. Philippine Islands
4. Australia
5. New Guinea
6. Micronesia

Go Online
PHSchool.com Use Web Code lcp-6320 for an **interactive map.**

640 Asia and the Pacific

Writing Activity: Math

Answers will vary depending on where students live. Students' paragraphs should include an explanation that the International Date Line is an imaginary line running from the North Pole to the South Pole that distinguishes one day from the next.

Use *Rubric for Assessing a Writing Assignment* to evaluate students' paragraphs.

All in One Asia and the Pacific Teaching Resources, *Rubric for Assessing a Writing Assignment,* p. 214

Standardized Test Prep

MAP*MASTER
Skills Activity

1. A   2. B
3. C   4. E
5. D   6. F

Test-Taking Tips

Some questions on standardized tests ask you to analyze graphic organizers. Study the Venn diagram below. Then follow the tips to answer the sample question.

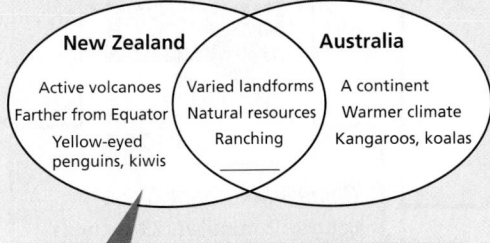

New Zealand   **Australia**

Active volcanoes | Varied landforms | A continent
Farther from Equator | Natural resources | Warmer climate
Yellow-eyed penguins, kiwis | Ranching | Kangaroos, koalas

TIP A Venn diagram lists ways that two things are the same and different. This kind of chart is good for writing or note-taking.

Pick the letter that best answers the question.

Which of the following belongs in the blank in the overlapping space?

- **A** compare and contrast
- **B** population mostly in cities
- **C** Great Dividing Range
- **D** geysers

Think It Through The question asks you to choose another example for the overlapping space—in other words, ways that both countries are the same. You can rule out C and D because the Great Dividing Range is in Australia and geysers are only in New Zealand. You can eliminate A, because it describes the chart—not an example in the chart. The correct answer is B, because the population of both countries is mostly in cities.

Practice Questions

Use the tips above and other tips in this book to help you answer the following questions.

1. Thailand, Cambodia, and Vietnam are part of
   - **A** island Southeast Asia.
   - **B** Polynesia.
   - **C** Micronesia.
   - **D** mainland Southeast Asia.

2. Most Australians live along Australia's eastern and southeastern coasts. Based on this information, what conclusion can be drawn about the location of Australia's cities?
   - **A** Most of Australia's cities are located in the interior of the continent.
   - **B** Most of Australia's cities are located along Australia's eastern and southeastern coasts.
   - **C** Most of Australia's cities are located along Australia's northern coast.
   - **D** Most of Australia's cities are located along Australia's western coast.

3. New Zealand's North Island and South Island were formed by
   - **A** volcanoes.   **B** coral.
   - **C** earthquakes.   **D** geysers.

Use the Venn diagram below to answer Question 4.

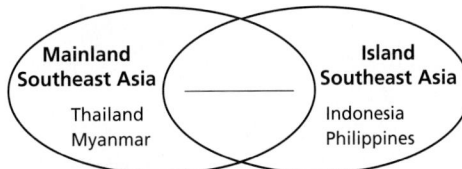

Mainland Southeast Asia   **Island Southeast Asia**

Thailand   Indonesia
Myanmar   Philippines

4. Which of the following belongs in the blank in the overlapping space?
   - **A** Vietnam   **B** Australia
   - **C** Malaysia   **D** Cambodia

Go Online
PHSchool.com

Use Web Code lca-6300 for
Chapter 20 self-test.

Go Online
PHSchool.com Students may practice their map skills using the interactive online version of this map.

Standardized Test Prep

Answers

1. D
2. B
3. A
4. C

Go Online
PHSchool.com Students may use the Chapter 20 self-test on PHSchool.com to prepare for the Chapter Test.

Assessment Resources

Use *Chapter Tests A and B* to assess students' mastery of chapter content.

All in One **Asia and the Pacific Teaching Resources**, *Chapter Tests A and B*, pp. 215–220

Tests are also available on the *ExamView Test Bank CD-Rom.*

◉ *ExamView Test Bank CD-ROM*

Overview

Section 1

Historic Traditions
1. Learn about civilizations of East Asia.
2. Learn how Chinese culture influenced the rest of East Asia.
3. Find out how East Asia was affected by Western nations.

Section 2

People and Cultures
1. Examine some ways in which East Asia's past affects its modern-day culture.
2. Find out how the people of China are different from the people of the Koreas and Japan.

DISCOVERY CHANNEL SCHOOL Video

China's Merchant Class
Length: 2 minutes, 23 seconds
Use with Section 2
Students will explore the development of China's merchant class, from ancient times to the present. This segment explains the importance of the merchant culture to China and to the history of Asia.

Technology Resources

Go Online
PHSchool.com

Students use embedded Web codes to access Internet activities, chapter self-tests, and additional map practice. They may also access Dorling Kindersley's Online Desk Reference to learn more about each country they study.

Interactive Textbook

Use the Interactive Textbook to make content and concepts come alive through animations, videos, and activities that accompany the complete basal text—online and on CD-ROM.

PRENTICE HALL
TeacherEXPRESS
Plan • Teach • Assess

Use this complete suite of powerful teaching tools to make planning lessons and administering tests quicker and easier.

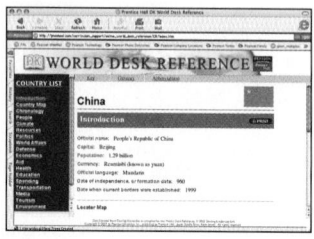

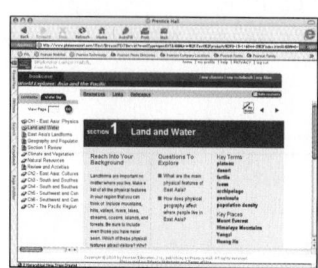

Reading and Assessment

Reading and Vocabulary Instruction

⟳ Model the Target Reading Skill

Use Context Clues Explain to students that they can decipher the meanings of unfamiliar words or phrases using clues from the surrounding text. Sometimes a word will be defined in the same sentence in which it appears. Other times it may be necessary to read ahead to find a context clue. Demonstrate how to use context to find the meanings of the italicized words below.

1. To *irrigate* means to supply water by using ditches and canals.

2. Japanese leaders came to believe that *isolation*, or separation, was the best way to keep the country united.

3. Although they have a common written language, they speak different *dialects* from region to region. Each dialect varies in vocabulary and pronunciation.

Model this skill by thinking aloud: *What context clues help me to understand the italicized word in each sentence? (1)* Irrigate *is defined in the same sentence. The word* means is a clue that the definition follows. (2) Another word for* isolation *helps to define the term; the word* or *is a clue. (3) Reading ahead provides the context clue to the meaning of* dialect. *The next sentence explains that a dialect of a language can vary in vocabulary and pronunciation.)*

Use the following worksheet from All-in-One Asia and the Pacific Teaching Resources (p. 231) to support this chapter's Target Reading Skill.

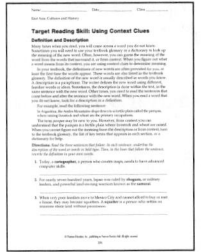

Vocabulary Builder
High-Use Academic Words

Use these steps to teach this chapter's high-use words:

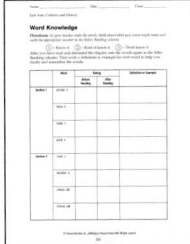

1. Have students rate how well they know each word on their Word Knowledge worksheets (All-in-One Asia and the Pacific Teaching Resources, p. 232).

2. Pronounce each word and ask students to repeat it.

3. Give students a brief definition or sample sentence (provided on TE pp. 645 and 653).

4. Work with students as they fill in the "Definition or Example" column of their Word Knowledge worksheets.

Assessment

Formal Assessment

Test students' understanding of core knowledge and skills.

Chapter Tests A and B,
All-in-One Asia and the Pacific
Teaching Resources, pp. 247–252

Customize the Chapter
Tests to suit your needs.
*ExamView Test Bank
CD-ROM*

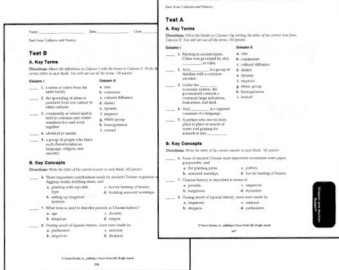

Skills Assessment

Assess geographic literacy.

MapMaster Skills, Student Edition, pp. 643, 651, 655, 658

Assess reading and comprehension.

Target Reading Skills, Student Edition, pp. 646, 654, and in Section Assessments

Chapter 21 Assessment, Eastern Hemisphere Reading and Vocabulary Study Guide, p. 232

Performance Assessment

Assess students' performance on this chapter's Writing Activities using the following rubrics from All-in-One Asia and the Pacific Teaching Resources.

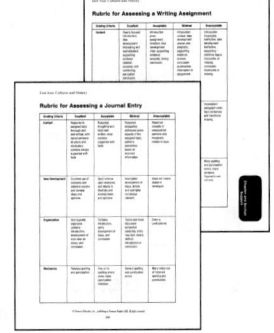

Rubric for Assessing a Writing Assignment, p. 245

Rubric for Assessing a Journal Entry, p. 246

Assess students' work through performance tasks.

Small Group Activity: Organizing a Japan Fair, All-in-One Asia and the Pacific Teaching Resources, pp. 235–238

Online Assessment

Have students check their own understanding.

Chapter Self-Test

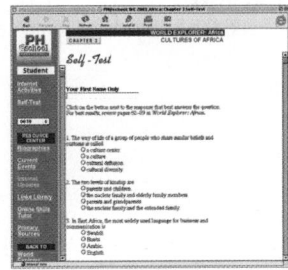

Section 1 Historic Traditions

 1.5 periods, .75 block (includes Skills for Life)

Social Studies Objectives

1. Learn about civilizations of East Asia.
2. Learn how Chinese culture influenced the rest of East Asia.
3. Find out how East Asia was affected by Western nations.

Reading/Language Arts Objective

Use context clues to determine the meaning of unfamiliar words.

Prepare to Read	**Instructional Resources**	**Differentiated Instruction**
Build Background Knowledge Discuss how students' lives have been affected by other cultures. **Set a Purpose for Reading** Have students begin to fill out the *Reading Readiness Guide.* **Preview Key Terms** Teach the section's Key Terms. **Target Reading Skill** Introduce the section's Target Reading Skill of **using context clues.**	**All in One Asia and the Pacific Teaching Resources** L2 Reading Readiness Guide, p. 224 L2 Use Context Clues: Definition and Description, p. 231	**Spanish Reading and Vocabulary Study Guide** L1 Chapter 21, Section 1, pp.160–161 ELL

Instruct	**Instructional Resources**	**Differentiated Instruction**
Civilizations of East Asia Discuss achievements and traditions in East Asian countries. **Target Reading Skill** Review **using context clues.** **Eyewitness Technology** Have students read about and discuss paper making. **The Spread of Cultures in East Asia Westerners in East Asia** Discuss how the countries of East Asia changed over time and were influenced by Westerners.	**All in One Asia and the Pacific Teaching Resources** L2 Guided Reading and Review, p. 225 L2 Reading Readiness Guide, p. 224 **Asia and the Pacific Transparencies** L2 Section Reading Support Transparency AP 57	**All in One Asia and the Pacific Teaching Resources** L3 Book Project: Travel Log, pp. 86–88 AR, GT L2 Skills for Life, p. 234 AR, GT, LPR, SN **Asia and the Pacific Transparencies** L1 Color Transparency AP 42: Terra Cotta Soldiers ELL, LPR, SN **Teacher's Edition** L3 For Gifted and Talented, TE p. 647 L1 For Less Proficient Readers, TE p. 647

Assess and Reteach	**Instructional Resources**	**Differentiated Instruction**
Assess Progress Evaluate student comprehension with the section assessment and section quiz. **Reteach** Assign the Reading and Vocabulary Study Guide to help struggling students. **Extend** Extend the lesson by assigning a literature selection.	**All in One Asia and the Pacific Teaching Resources** L2 Section Quiz, p. 226 L3 Tankas, p. 243 Rubric for Assessing a Journal Entry, p. 246 **Reading and Vocabulary Study Guide** L1 Chapter 21, Section 1, pp. 226–228	**All in One Asia and the Pacific Teaching Resources** L1 Using the Map Key, Using the Compass Rose, pp. 241, 242 ELL, LPR, SN L3 Understanding Road Maps, Reading Road Maps, pp. 239, 240 AR, GT **Spanish Support** L2 Section Quiz (Spanish), p. 225 ELL **Teacher's Edition** L1 For Special Needs Students, TE p. 651 L1 For English Language Learners, TE p. 651 **Social Studies Skills Tutor CD-ROM** L1 Analyzing and Interpreting Special Purpose Maps ELL, LPR, SN

Key

L1 Basic to Average   L3 Average to Advanced

L2 For All Students

LPR Less Proficient Readers
AR Advanced Readers
SN Special Needs Students

GT Gifted and Talented
ELL English Language Learners

Section 2 People and Cultures

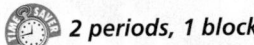 *2 periods, 1 block*

Social Studies Objectives
1. Examine some ways in which East Asia's past affects its modern-day culture.
2. Find out how the people of China are different from the people of the Koreas and Japan.

Reading/Language Arts Objective
Read ahead to find context clues to determine the meaning of unfamiliar words.

Prepare to Read	Instructional Resources	Differentiated Instruction
Build Background Knowledge Have students predict what the section will be about by looking at the title, Key Terms, photographs, and the map. **Set a Purpose for Reading** Have students evaluate statements on the *Reading Readiness Guide*. **Preview Key Terms** Teach the section's Key Terms. **Target Reading Skill** Introduce the section's Target Reading Skill of **using context clues.**	**All in One Asia and the Pacific Teaching Resources** L2 Reading Readiness Guide, p. 228 L2 Use Context Clues: Definition and Description, p. 231	**Spanish Reading and Vocabulary Study Guide** L1 Chapter 21, Section 2, pp. 162–163 ELL

Instruct	Instructional Resources	Differentiated Instruction
Tradition and Change Discuss the changes that occurred in China after 1949. **Target Reading Skill** Review **using context clues.** **East Asia's People** Discuss ethnic groups in East Asia.	**All in One Asia and the Pacific Teaching Resources** L2 Guided Reading and Review, p. 229 L2 Reading Readiness Guide, p. 228 **Asia and the Pacific Transparencies** L2 Section Reading Support Transparency AP 58 **World Studies Video Program** L2 China's Merchant Class	**All in One Asia and the Pacific Teaching Resources** L3 Enrichment, p. 233 AR, GT **Asia and the Pacific Transparencies** L2 Section Reading Support Transparency AP 58 ELL, LPR, SN **Teacher's Edition** L3 For Advanced Readers, TE p. 654 L1 For Less Proficient Readers, TE p. 654 **Spanish Support** L1 Guided Reading and Review (Spanish), p. 226 ELL

Assess and Reteach	Instructional Resources	Differentiated Instruction
Assess Progress Evaluate student comprehension with the section assessment and section quiz. **Reteach** Assign the Reading and Vocabulary Study Guide to help struggling students. **Extend** Extend the lesson by assigning a Small Group Activity.	**All in One Asia and the Pacific Teaching Resources** L2 Section Quiz, p. 230 L3 Small Group Activity: Organizing a Japan Fair, pp. 235–238 Rubric for Assessing a Writing Assignment, p. 245 L2 Word Knowledge, p. 232 L2 Vocabulary Development, p. 244 L2 Chapter Tests A and B, pp. 247–252 **Reading and Vocabulary Study Guide** L1 Chapter 21, Section 2, pp. 229–231	**Spanish Support** L2 Section Quiz (Spanish), p. 227 ELL L2 Chapter Summary (Spanish), p. 228 ELL L2 Vocabulary Development (Spanish), p. 229 ELL

Key
L1 Basic to Average
L2 For All Students
L3 Average to Advanced
LPR Less Proficient Readers
AR Advanced Readers
SN Special Needs Students
GT Gifted and Talented
ELL English Language Learners

Reading Background

Discussion Ideas

One way to enrich a lesson is to encourage students to discuss the material from the chapter. Ideas for discussion must be complex enough to spark an interesting dialogue. They can relate to something students do not understand, something that seems interesting, or something that relates to information students already know.

Read aloud the sayings of Confucius on page 644 in the Student Edition and model the difference between strong and weak discussion ideas.

For example, a strong discussion idea for what you have just read might be:

I am not sure what Confucius meant when he said, "When you have faults, do not fear to abandon them." Maybe he meant that one should not be afraid to change bad habits.

A weak discussion idea might be:

Socrates was a teacher.

As students read, ask them to write down one idea that could be used to conduct an interesting discussion. Begin the class discussion by having one student present his or her idea. Monitor the discussion to ensure that an adequate number of students have had a chance to respond before you introduce another idea.

Read-Cover-Recite-Check

Read-Cover-Recite-Check is a useful strategy for students to retain the information they read. It can be especially effective to help students study for a test. Model the steps for using Read-Cover-Recite-Check to read the paragraph under Civilizations of East Asia on page 645 of the Student Edition.

1. Read the paragraph quickly to grasp the main ideas. (*Think aloud about the main idea: Many regions of East Asia produced important civilizations.*)
2. Reread the paragraph, looking for details and key information. (*Think aloud, noting the details: China's ancient civilization has survived; The civilizations of Korea and Japan have long histories.*)
3. Cover the paragraph with your hand or a piece of paper.
4. Recall and repeat the information from the paragraph, including the topic and important details. (*Think aloud: Repeat the information from steps 1 and 2.*)
5. Rephrase the paragraph in your own words. (*Although East Asia's civilizations are not the oldest, they are important. China's is the only ancient civilization that still exists, and Japan's and Korea's civilizations also have valuable histories.*)
6. Check to make sure you remembered correctly.

World Studies Background

China

China is the world's third largest country in land area, after Russia and Canada. With an estimated 1.27 billion people in 2000, China has the largest population on Earth, and it is growing by about 15 million people each year. Because it is difficult to provide increasing amounts of necessities like food and shelter to match this kind of growth, population control is a constant challenge for China.

The Shinto Religion in Japan

The Shinto religion originated in Japan. Shinto is the worship of spirits, or *kami*, that are believed to be inherent in every object in the universe. In 1868, Shinto became the state religion and the

foundation for many political affairs. After World War II it was abolished as such by the Allied Powers. It remains an important belief system and way of life for many Japanese.

Korean Surnames

Although Korea has a population of about 65 million, only about 270 surnames exist. In the past, many Korean families belonged to one clan with a common name, which led to a smaller variety of surnames today. More than half of the population shares only five surnames—Kim, Li, Pak, Choe, and Chong—with about 10 million people possessing the most common, Kim.

Infoplease® provides a wealth of useful information for the classroom. You can use this resource to strengthen your background on the subjects covered in this chapter. Have students visit this advertising-free site as a starting point for projects requiring research.

 Use Web code **lcd-6400** for **Infoplease®**.

Power Notes

Power Notes are simplified outlines that can help students clarify the difference between main ideas and details. When creating Power Notes outlines, main ideas and details are assigned different numbers. Main ideas are power 1 ideas. Details are either power 2s or 3s. Students can use this technique as a method of organization for reading, writing, and studying.

Write the following on the board to show students what a Power Notes outline looks like:

Power 1: Main Idea
    Power 2: Detail or support for power 1
        Power 3: Detail or support for power 2

Model this approach by using information from the chapter:

Power 1: China's government
    Power 2: Empires
        Power 3: Regions controlled by one government
    Power 2: Dynasties
        Power 3: Emperors from one family

Another way to practice this skill is to write power 1s from the chapter on the board and have students take turns filling in the supporting details.

Question-Answer Relationships

Explain to students that there are many different types of questions. Understanding what a question is asking for will help students write better answers. Explain that they can identify different types of questions. Give students an example of these different types, referring to Tradition and Change on pages 652 and 653 of the Student Edition.

Questions with:

1. Answers that are found explicitly in one or two sentences in the book. (example: *When did communism in China begin?*)
2. Answers that are found in several different paragraphs in the book. (example: *How did communism change the Chinese way of life?*)
3. Answers that are not found directly in the book, but instead require you to think about what you've read. (example: *What might be the advantages and disadvantages of living on a commune?*)
4. Answers that are not found directly in the book and which you can answer without having read the book. (example: *What are some traditions in your family?*)

Have students practice recognizing question-answer relationships by writing their own questions. Ask them to explain which type of question it is and to provide the answer.

The Tokaido Megalopolis

Japan has the eighth largest population in the world and a high population density, with about three quarters of its residents living in cities. The highest concentration of people exists in the Tokaido Megalopolis, a 350-mile area along the Pacific coast. The Tokaido Megalopolis includes six of the seven largest cities in Japan—including Tokyo, Japan's capital—and is a hub for business, finance and education.

Mongols

Under the leadership of Genghis Khan, the Mongols invaded China from the north during the early 1200s. They were disciplined fighters who conquered most of China and much of Asia. The conquest of China was completed by Genghis Khan's grandson Kublai Khan, who established the Yuan dynasty that ruled China for more than a century. Mongol rule ended in 1368, when the Chinese restored rule under the Ming emperors.

The Tale of Genji

In the early eleventh century, Lady Shikibu Murasaki penned what is considered to be the world's first full-length novel, *The Tale of Genji*. The 54-chapter novel, set in Japan's court society, follows the life of Prince Genji through many romances. Besides its significance for world literature, *The Tale of Genji* is also thought to be one of the greatest works of Japanese literature.

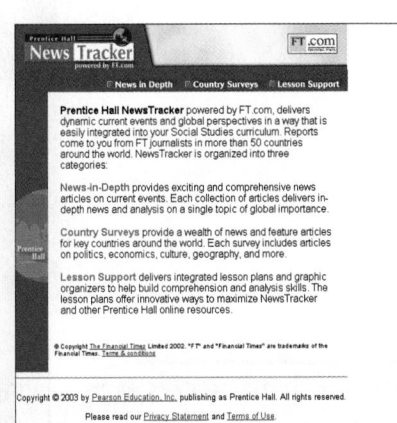

Get in-depth information on topics of global importance with **Prentice Hall Newstracker,** powered by FT.com.

Use Web code **lcd-6404** for **Prentice Hall Newstracker.**

Guiding Questions

Remind students about the Guiding Questions introduced at the beginning of this section.

Section 1 relates to **Guiding Question ❷**
How have ancient civilizations of Asia and the Pacific influenced the world today? *(Buddhism spread from ancient civilizations in India to China and then to other East Asian nations and countries around the world. China invented many products we still use today such as paper, gunpowder, silk weaving, the magnetic compass, the printing press, and clockworks.)*

Section 2 relates to **Guiding Question ❸**
What are the main characteristics of the cultures of Asia and the Pacific? *(In China, Japan, and Korea, old tr;aditions still influence culture, but more modern ways are visible as well.)*

⦿ Target Reading Skill

In this chapter, students will learn and apply the reading skill of using context clues. Use the following worksheet to help students practice this skill:

All in One Asia and the Pacific Teaching Resources, *Use Context Clues: Definition and Description,* p. 231

Chapter Preview

East Asian cultures are among the oldest in the world. In this chapter, you will learn about East Asian cultures and their long histories.

Section 1
Historic Traditions

Section 2
People and Cultures

⦿ **Target Reading Skill**

Context In this chapter, you will focus on using context to help you understand the meanings of unfamiliar words. Context includes the words, phrases, and sentences surrounding a particular word.

▶ The Great Buddha of Kamakura is the second-largest statue of Buddha in Japan.

642 Asia and the Pacific

Differentiated Instruction

The following Teacher's Edition strategies are suitable for students of varying abilities.

Advanced Readers, p. 654
English Language Learners, p. 651
Gifted and Talented, p. 647
Less Proficient Readers, pp. 647, 654
Special Needs Students, p. 651

Bibliography

For the Teacher
Oberdorfer, Don. *The Two Koreas: A Contemporary History* (rev. ed.). Basic Books, 2002.
McClain, James L. *Japan: A Modern History.* Norton, 2001.
Shaughnessy, Edward. *China: Empire and Civilization.* Oxford University Press, 2000.

For the Student
L1 Harvey, Miles. *Look What Came From China!* Orchard Books, 1999.
L2 Landau, Elaine. *Korea.* Children's Book Press, 2000.
Teague, Ken. *Growing Up In Ancient China.* Troll Associates, 1997.
L3 O'Connor, Jane. *The Emperor's Silent Army: Terracotta Warriors of Ancient China.* Viking Children's Books, 2002.

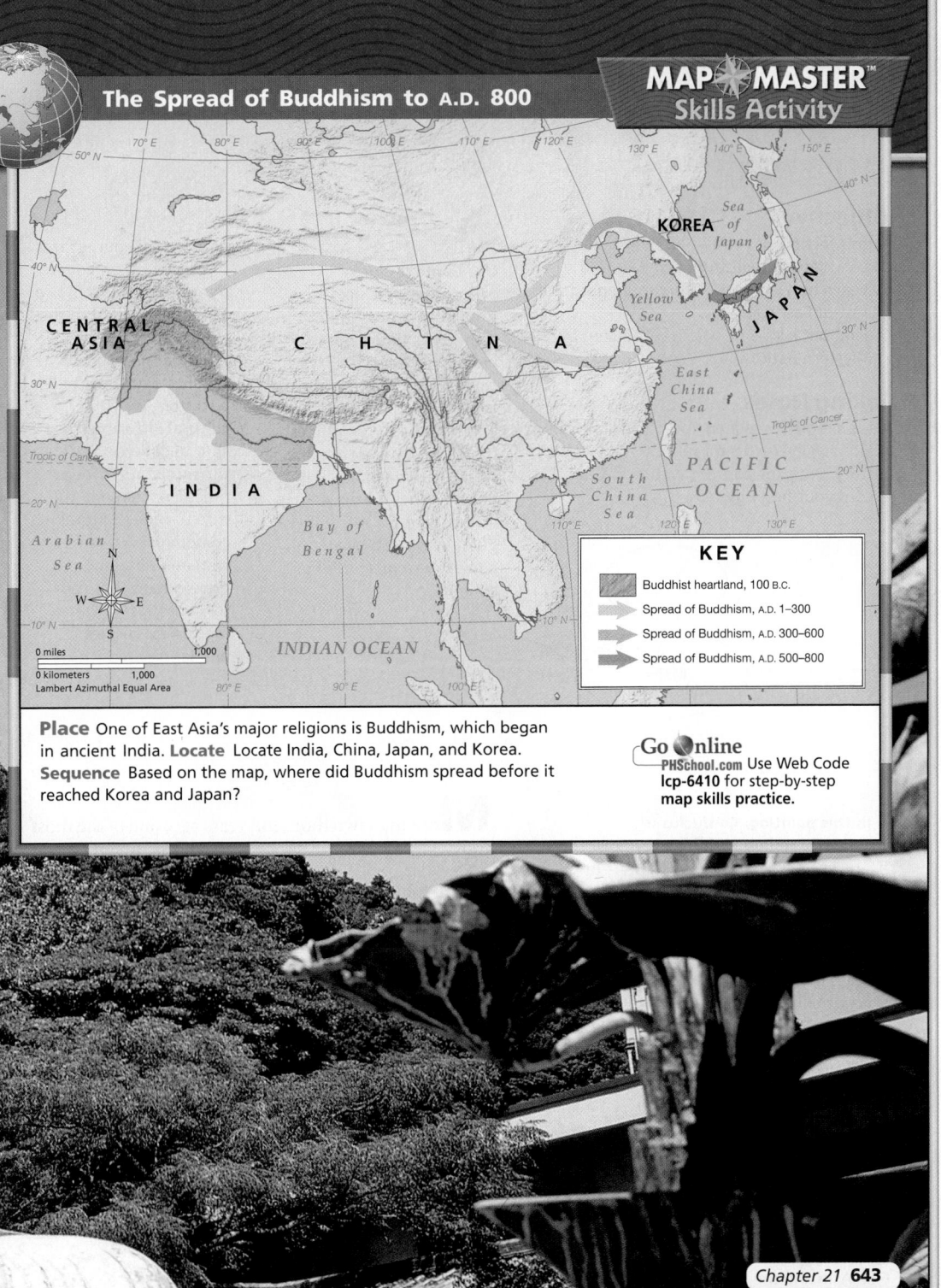

The Spread of Buddhism to A.D. 800

MAP MASTER™
Skills Activity

KOREA

Sea of Japan

CENTRAL ASIA

C H I N A

JAPAN

Yellow Sea

East China Sea

Tropic of Cancer

PACIFIC OCEAN

South China Sea

I N D I A

Arabian Sea

Bay of Bengal

INDIAN OCEAN

0 miles 1,000
0 kilometers 1,000
Lambert Azimuthal Equal Area

KEY
Buddhist heartland, 100 B.C.
Spread of Buddhism, A.D. 1–300
Spread of Buddhism, A.D. 300–600
Spread of Buddhism, A.D. 500–800

Place One of East Asia's major religions is Buddhism, which began in ancient India. **Locate** Locate India, China, Japan, and Korea. **Sequence** Based on the map, where did Buddhism spread before it reached Korea and Japan?

Go Online
PHSchool.com Use Web Code lcp-6410 for step-by-step map skills practice.

Chapter 21 **643**

Ask students to summarize what the map shows by writing a paragraph describing the spread of Buddhism to A.D. 800.

Go Online
PHSchool.com Students may practice their map skills using the interactive online version of this map.

Using the Visual

Reach Into Your Background Draw students' attention to the photograph on pp. 642–643 and its caption. Have students discuss statues or any other landmarks or symbols in their community that represent parts of their history or culture.

Answers

MAP MASTER™ *Skills Activity* **Locate** India is in South Asia; Korea is a peninsula in East Asia; Japan is an archipelago off the coast of East Asia. **Sequence** It spread across China before reaching Japan and Korea.

Chapter Resources

Teaching Resources
- L2 Vocabulary Development, p. 244
- L2 Skills for Life, p. 234
- L2 Chapter Tests A and B, pp. 247–252

Spanish Support
- L2 Spanish Chapter Summary, p. 228
- L2 Spanish Vocabulary Development, p. 229

Media and Technology
- L1 Student Edition on Audio CD
- L1 Guided Reading Audiotapes, English and Spanish
- L2 Social Studies Skills Tutor CD-ROM
- *ExamView Test Bank CD-ROM*

PRENTICE HALL
Presentation EXPRESS™
Teach · Connect · Inspire

Teach this chapter's content using the PresentationExpress™ CD-ROM including:
- slide shows
- transparencies
- interactive maps and media
- *ExamView®* QuickTake Presenter

Objectives

Social Studies

1. Learn about civilizations of East Asia.
2. Learn how Chinese culture influenced the rest of East Asia.
3. Find out how East Asia was affected by Western nations.

Reading/Language Arts

Use context clues from surrounding phrases to determine the meaning of unfamiliar words.

Prepare to Read

Build Background Knowledge L2

Tell students that in this section they will learn about the history of East Asia and how the region was affected by other cultures. Ask students to list the ways in which their lives might have been affected by other cultures. Provide a few examples to get students started, such as types of food or styles of clothing. Conduct an Idea Wave (TE p. T35) to generate a list.

Set a Purpose for Reading L2

- Preview the Objectives.

- Form students into pairs or groups of four. Distribute the *Reading Readiness Guide*. Ask students to fill in the first two columns of the chart. Use the Numbered Heads participation strategy (TE, p. T36) to call on students to share one piece of information they already know and one piece of information they want to know.

  All in One Asia and the Pacific Teaching Resources, *Reading Readiness Guide*, p. 224

Vocabulary Builder
Preview Key Terms L2

Pronounce each Key Term, then ask the students to say the word with you. Provide a simple explanation such as, "Every year the families of the clan have a reunion to celebrate their common ancestor."

Prepare to Read

Objectives

In this section you will

1. Learn about civilizations of East Asia.
2. Learn how Chinese culture influenced the rest of East Asia.
3. Find out how East Asia was affected by Western nations.

Taking Notes

As you read this section, look for details about major achievements throughout East Asia's history. Copy the concept web below, and record your findings in it.

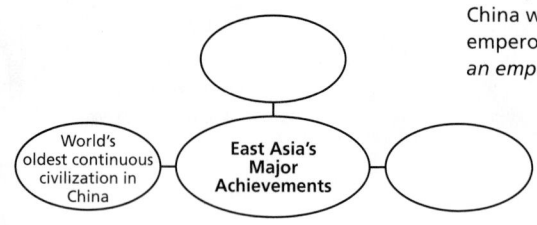

Target Reading Skill

Use Context Clues
When you come across an unfamiliar word, you can sometimes figure out its meaning from clues in the context. The context refers to the surrounding words and sentences. Sometimes the context will define the word. In this example, the phrase in italics tells what an emperor is: "Ancient China was ruled by an emperor—*a male ruler of an empire.*"

Key Terms

- **emperor** (EM pur ur) *n.* a male ruler of an empire
- **dynasty** (DY nus tee) *n.* a series of rulers from the same family
- **clan** (klan) *n.* a group of families with a common ancestor
- **cultural diffusion** (KUL chur ul dih FYOO zhun) *n.* the spreading of ideas or practices from one culture to other cultures
- **communist** (KAHM yoo nist) *adj.* relating to a government that controls a country's large industries, businesses, and land

---

In this painting, Confucius is shown standing with his students.

More than two thousand years ago, one of the most important thinkers of ancient times gave this advice:

> **❝Let the ruler be a ruler and the subject a subject.**
>
> **A youth, when at home, should act with respect to his parents, and, abroad, be respectful to his elders. He should be earnest and truthful. He should overflow in love to all, and cultivate the friendship of the good.**
>
> **When you have faults, do not fear to abandon them.❞**

These words are from the teachings of Confucius (kun FYOO shus), who lived in China about 500 B.C. He taught that all individuals have duties and responsibilities. If a person acts correctly, the result will be peace and harmony. Confucius's ideas helped to guide Chinese life for hundreds of years.

Target Reading Skill L2

Use Context Clues Point out the Target Reading Skill. Tell students that information surrounding an unknown word can provide clues to the word's meaning.

Model context clues to find the meaning of *shoguns* in this sentence from page 646: "Instead, shoguns, or 'emperor's generals,' made the laws." (*The phrase in quotations tells what a shogun is: an "emperor's general."*)

Give students *Use Context Clues: Definition/Description*. Have them complete the activity in their groups.

All in One Asia and the Pacific Teaching Resources, *Use Context Clues: Definition and Description*, p. 231

Civilizations of East Asia

Regions of Asia and Africa produced civilizations earlier than China's. A civilization has cities, a central government, workers who do specialized jobs, and social classes. Of the world's early civilizations, however, only China's has survived. This makes it the oldest continuous civilization in the world. Korea and Japan are not as old, but they, too, have long histories.

China's Middle Kingdom For much of its history, China had little to do with the rest of the world. The Great Wall of China first started in the 600s B.C. as many small unconnected walls between warring states. Over time, it became a symbol of China's desire to keep the world at a distance. In fact, Chinese leaders had such pride that they named their country the Middle Kingdom. To them, it was the center of the universe.

Ancient Achievements The Chinese had reason to believe that their civilization was the greatest in the world. They invented paper, gunpowder, silk weaving, the magnetic compass, the printing press, and clockworks. Chinese engineers were experts at digging canals, building dams and bridges, and setting up irrigation systems. Chinese scientists made major discoveries in mathematics and medicine.

Dynasties in China Starting in ancient times, China was governed by an **emperor**—a male ruler of an empire. An empire is an area of many territories and people that are controlled by one government. A series of emperors from the same family is a **dynasty.** Chinese history is described in terms of dynasties. The chart below lists major dynasties of China.

The Great Wall of China

■ **Chart Skills**

The chart below shows major dynasties of China. They ruled China from ancient times to A.D. 1911. **Identify** Which dynasty was the first to develop the Chinese calendar? **Sequence** Which was developed in China first—paper money or iron tools?

Major Dynasties of China

Major Dynasty	Major Achievements
Shang (c. 1766–c. 1122 B.C.)	Well-developed writing, first Chinese calendar, bronze casting.
Zhou (c. 1122–c. 256 B.C.)	Writing laws, iron tools and plows in use.
Qin (221 B.C.–206 B.C.)	First great Chinese Empire. Much of the Great Wall built.
Han (206 B.C.–A.D. 220)	Government based on Confucianism. Buddhism introduced.
Tang (A.D. 618–A.D. 907)	Sculpture and poetry flourish.
Song (A.D. 906–A.D. 1279)	Block printing and paper money developed. Gunpowder first used.
Ming (A.D. 1318–A.D. 1644)	Porcelain, the novel, and drama flourish.
Qing (A.D. 1644–A.D. 1911)	Increased trade with Europe. Last Chinese dynasty.

Chapter 21 Section 1 **645**

Instruct

Civilizations of East Asia L2

Guided Instruction

- **Vocabulary Builder** Clarify the high-use words **symbol** and **noble** before reading.

- Read about the accomplishments of China in Civilizations of East Asia using the Oral Cloze strategy (TE, p. T33).

- Ask students **Why is China considered to be the world's oldest civilization?** *(It is the only early civilization that has survived.)*

- Have students discuss the Great Wall of China and what it became a symbol for. *(It became a symbol of China's desire to keep the world at a distance.)*

- Have students list some of the achievements of ancient Chinese people. *(The Chinese were responsible for major inventions such as paper, gunpowder, silk weaving, the magnetic compass, the printing press, and clockworks, and engineering feats such as irrigation systems and building dams and bridges. Their scientists made major discoveries in mathematics and medicine.)*

- Discuss why and how China's inventions and discoveries may have spread to Korea. *(Possible answer: As people from China migrated to Korea to escape troubles at home, they brought their knowledge and customs to Korea.)*

- Ask students why for many centuries Japan's emperors did not have as much power as China's emperors. *(For much of Japan's history, laws were made by shoguns and enforced by samurai.)*

Vocabulary Builder

Use the information below to teach students this section's high-use words.

High-Use Word	Definition and Sample Sentence
symbol, p. 645	*n.* something that stands for something else, usually an idea or concept The Statue of Liberty is a **symbol** of freedom.
noble, p. 646	*n.* a person born to a high rank A **noble** had a higher standing in society than a peasant.
adopt, p. 648	*v.* to take and use as one's own Billy **adopted** his friend's taste in music.
grant, p. 648	*v.* to allow or permit The teacher **granted** the class permission to go outside for recess.

Answers

Chart Skills Identify the Shang Dynasty **Sequence** iron tools

Target Reading Skill ⓛ②

Use Context Clues As a follow up, ask students to perform the Target Reading Skill task in the Student Edition. *(Unified means brought together as one country.)*

Independent Practice

Ask students to create the Taking Notes graphic organizer on a blank piece of paper. Then have them record details about major achievements throughout East Asia's history. Briefly model how to identify which details to record.

Monitor Progress

Show *Section Reading Support Transparency AP 57* and ask students to check their graphic organizers individually. Go over key concepts and clarify key vocabulary as needed.

📖 **Asia and the Pacific Transparencies,** *Section Reading Support Transparency AP 57*

Use Context Clues If you do not know what *unified* means, look in the surrounding words for a context clue. Here, the phrase following *unified* explains what the term means.

■ **Timeline Skills**

Japan has interacted with other countries and regions except for one period in its history. **Note** When did Japan close its borders to the rest of the world? **Analyze Information** Which European country introduced Christianity to Japan?

Korea and China Although Korea's original settlers came from north-central Asia, Korea's history is closely tied to China. Around 1200 B.C., during a time of troubles in China, some Chinese moved to the Korean Peninsula. Later, other Chinese settled in the southern part of the peninsula. In this way, Chinese people brought Chinese knowledge and customs to the Koreans.

As in China, dynasties ruled Korea. While China had many dynasties, Korea had only three. The first was the Shilla. The Shilla dynasty unified Korea as one country in A.D. 668.

Years of Isolation in Japan For much of Japan's history, **clans,** or groups of families who claim a common ancestor, fought each other for land and power. Around A.D. 500, one clan, the Yamato (yah MAH toh), became powerful. Claiming descent from the sun goddess, Yamato leaders took the title of emperor. Many emperors sat on Japan's throne. For a long time they had little power. Instead, shoguns (SHOH gunz), or "emperor's generals," made the laws. Warrior nobles, the samurai (SAM uh ry), enforced these laws. Together, the shoguns and samurai ruled Japan for more than 700 years.

Japan was isolated from the outside world from about 1640 to 1853. Japanese leaders believed that isolation, or separation, was the best way to keep the country united. Japan finally was forced to trade with the West in the 1800s.

✔ **Reading Check** **Name at least four major achievements of the Chinese civilization.**

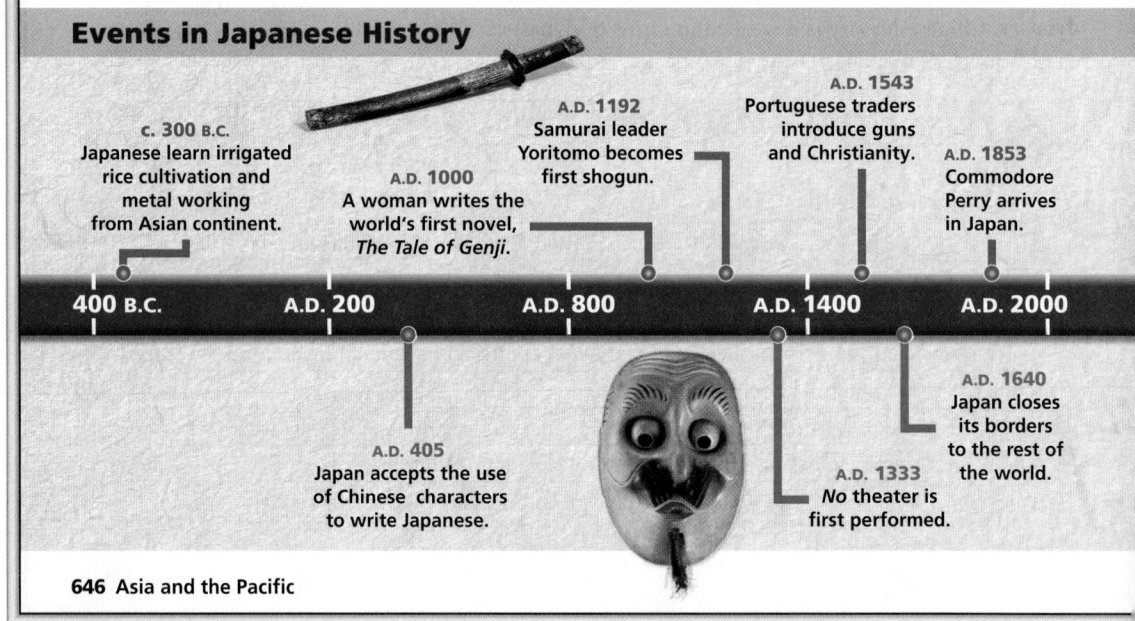

Events in Japanese History

c. 300 B.C. Japanese learn irrigated rice cultivation and metal working from Asian continent.

A.D. 1000 A woman writes the world's first novel, *The Tale of Genji.*

A.D. 1192 Samurai leader Yoritomo becomes first shogun.

A.D. 1543 Portuguese traders introduce guns and Christianity.

A.D. 1853 Commodore Perry arrives in Japan.

400 B.C. — A.D. 200 — A.D. 800 — A.D. 1400 — A.D. 2000

A.D. 405 Japan accepts the use of Chinese characters to write Japanese.

A.D. 1333 *No* theater is first performed.

A.D. 1640 Japan closes its borders to the rest of the world.

646 Asia and the Pacific

Answers

✔ **Reading Check** Achievements include inventions such as paper, gunpowder, silk weaving, the magnetic compass, the printing press, clockworks, and engineering feats such as irrigation and transportation systems, and scientific discoveries in mathematics and medicine.

Timeline Skills
Note in about 1640
Analyze Information Portugal

Skills for Life **Skills Mini Lesson**

Sequencing

1. Teach the skill by telling students that a timeline shows events in chronological, or time, order. A timeline can help them see the "big picture" of key events during a time period and make it easier to see possible relationships between events.

2. Help students practice the skill by looking at the timeline on this page. Ask:

What came first, Commodore Perry's arrival or Japan closing its borders? *(Japan closing its borders)*

3. Have students apply the skill by answering this question: **What event on the timeline might have been influenced by the acceptance of Chinese characters for writing?** *(the writing of the world's first novel)*

Paper Making

Civilization developed as people learned first to speak and to draw, and then to write. By the time of the Han dynasty in China, civilization included government, trade, record-keeping, and poetry. Paper was needed for all of these activities. Cai Lun, an official of the Han dynasty, is said to have invented this useful material.

Making paper pulp
People in Xishuangbanna, China, split open bamboo stems to extract pulp.

3 A paper mold—a box with wooden sides and a fine wire screen—is dipped into a vat of pulp and slowly raised.

4 Workers then shake the mold until the water drains off and the wet fibers cover the screen with a thin web of pulp.

2 Workers pound the water-soaked fibers to a pulp.

1 Fibers are gathered from bamboo, mulberry bark, cotton or linen cloth, grass, straw, or wood—and then chopped up, beaten, and soaked in water.

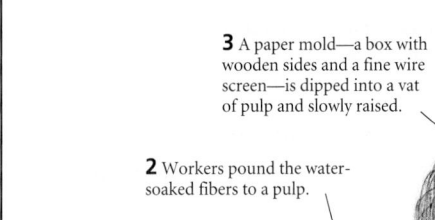

5 While still damp, the sheet of paper is peeled off the mold.

6 The paper sheets are pasted on a wall to dry. A fire might be lit to help the drying process.

ANALYZING IMAGES
Why did it make sense to make paper near a source of water?

Paper dyeing
Women lay out freshly dyed paper to dry in Bhaktapur, Nepal.

Differentiated Instruction

For Gifted and Talented [L3]
Now that these students have read about the geographical, cultural, and historic aspects of several Asian countries, assign the *Travel Log* book project.

All in One Asia and the Pacific Teaching Resources, *Book Project: Travel Log,* pp. 86–88

For Less Proficient Readers [L1]
Show students the *Terra Cotta Soldiers Transparency.* Explain that over 7,000 of these figures were part of the tomb of the first emperor of the Qin dynasty. Have students describe these figures in their own words.

Asia and the Pacific Transparencies, *Color Transparency AP 42: Terra Cotta Soldiers*

Paper Making [L2]

Guided Instruction
Ask students to study Paper Making by reading the text and captions, and examining the diagram and photos. As a class, answer the Analyzing Images question. Allow students to briefly discuss their responses with a partner before sharing answers.

Independent Practice
Have students do research in the library or on the Internet on the history of paper making and how it spread after its origins in China. Ask students to write a report summarizing their findings.

The Spread of Cultures in East Asia [L2]

Westerners in East Asia [L2]

Guided Instruction
■ **Vocabulary Builder** Clarify the high-use words **adopt** and **grant** before reading.

■ Have students read The Spread of Cultures in East Asia and Westerners in East Asia. As students read, survey the class to make sure individuals can answer the Reading Check questions.

■ Ask **What were among the first ideas passed along from China to Korea and Japan?** *(the teachings of Confucius)* **What religion later spread to Korea and Japan?** *(Buddhism)*

■ Have students discuss why Western nations wanted to trade with East Asian nations. *(Western nations wanted markets for their increasingly large amounts of manufactured goods.)*

■ Ask **How did Commodore Perry's actions affect Japan?** *(Perry forced Japan to grant trading rights to the United States.)*

Answer
ANALYZING IMAGES It was necessary to soak the fibers used to make paper in water.

Guided Instruction (continued)

- Discuss the events leading up to the Korean War. *(After World War II, Korea was divided into two parts—North Korea and South Korea. Communists ruled North Korea and South Korea turned to Western nations for support. North Korea invaded South Korea in 1950.)* Ask **What was the role of the United States in the Korean War?** *(The United States supported South Korea and sent 480,000 troops to help them. Many United States soldiers lost their lives in the war.)*

Independent Practice

Assign *Guided Reading and Review.*

All in One **Asia and the Pacific Teaching Resources,** *Guided Reading and Review,* p. 225

Monitor Progress

Tell students to fill in the last column of their *Reading Readiness Guides.* Ask them to evaluate if what they learned was what they expected to learn.

All in One **Asia and the Pacific Teaching Resources,** *Reading Readiness Guide,* p. 224

Answers

✓ Reading Check the spread from China to Korea of the teachings of Confucius and the religion of Buddhism

Analyze Images Koizumi is the man standing up and bowing to the other members of the Diet who are applauding him.

Government in Japan
Japan's legislative branch is called the Diet. The Diet elects a prime minister, who heads the executive branch. Members of the Diet are shown in 2001 applauding the election of Junichiro Koizumi as prime minister. **Analyze Images** *Which man in the photo is Koizumi? Explain your answer.*

648 Asia and the Pacific

The Spread of Cultures in East Asia

In ancient times, China was far ahead of the rest of the world in inventions and discoveries. Thus, it is not surprising that many Chinese discoveries spread to Korea and Japan. This process of **cultural diffusion,** or spreading of ideas from one culture to other cultures, happened early. The teachings of Confucius were among the first ideas to be passed along. The religion of Buddhism (BOOD iz um), which China had adopted from India, later spread to Korea and Japan. East Asian culture owes much to the early exchanges among China, Japan, and Korea. In each case, the countries changed what they borrowed until the element of culture became their own.

✓ Reading Check **Give an example of cultural diffusion between China and Korea.**

Westerners in East Asia

In the 1800s, Europeans and Americans began to produce great amounts of manufactured goods. East Asia seemed to be a good place to sell these products. Western trading ships began to sail to Asian ports.

The Opening of East Asia In 1853, U.S. Commodore Matthew Perry sailed with four warships to Japan. He forced Japan to grant trading rights to the United States. The opening up of China to Europe was different. The British, French, Germans, Portuguese, Russians, and Japanese gained control over parts of China. Other countries then feared losing the opportunity to share in China's riches. In 1899, the United States announced the policy that China should be open for trade with all nations equally. For a while, nations halted their efforts to divide up China.

New Forces in the 1900s Many Chinese blamed the emperor for the foreign powers in their country. In 1911, revolution broke out in China. The rule of emperors ended, and a republic was set up.

Meanwhile, Japan was becoming more powerful. Its leaders sought to control other Asian countries. One of their reasons was to make sure that Japan would have resources to fuel its growing industries. Japanese attacks on other Asian and Pacific lands led to the start of World War II in East Asia in 1941. In 1945, the United States and its allies defeated Japan.

Background: Biography

Confucius (551 B.C.–479 B.C.) Confucius is known for devoting his entire life to education. He believed in the importance of education for all men. Before Confucius, only wealthy families hired tutors to educate their sons.

Teaching became a way of life for Confucius. He believed that educating people would improve society. Therefore, Confucius began a humanities program for future leaders and provided access to education for all. As a teacher, Confucius believed that self-improvement was just as important as acquiring knowledge.

After World War II ended, civil war broke out in China between two groups, the Nationalists and the Communists. The Communists won the war in 1949 and made China a **communist** nation, one in which the government owns large industries, businesses, and most of the country's land.

After World War II, Korea was divided into two parts. Communists ruled North Korea. South Korea turned to Western nations for support. In 1950, North Korea invaded South Korea. The United States sent 480,000 troops to help South Korea. The Korean War lasted for three years, killing about 37,000 U.S. soldiers and more than 2 million Koreans. Neither side won. The battle line at the end of the war, in 1953, remains the border between the two Koreas today.

✓ **Reading Check** How did Japan's actions lead to the start of World War II in East Asia?

American veterans visiting a memorial in South Korea marking the 50th anniversary of the Korean War

Section 1 Assessment

Key Terms
Review the key terms at the beginning of this section. Use each term in a sentence that explains its meaning.

⊙ **Target Reading Skill**
Find the phrase *foreign powers* on page 648. Use context clues to figure out its meaning. What clues helped you figure out its meaning?

Comprehension and Critical Thinking
1. **(a) List** Name at least four achievements of the Chinese civilization.
(b) Find Main Ideas How was the Chinese civilization ruled from ancient times to 1911?

2. **(a) Identify** Give one example of cultural diffusion in East Asia.
(b) Make Generalizations Cultural diffusion can take place when people move from one place to another. When they do, they take their culture with them. Based on what you have read in this section, what are some other ways in which cultural diffusion can happen?
3. **(a) Recall** Why did U.S. Commodore Matthew Perry sail to Japan in 1853?
(b) Compare and Contrast How was the opening up of China to Europe different from the opening up of Japan?

Writing Activity
Suppose that you are a European merchant traveling through China in the 1300s. Use the chart on page 645 to write three short diary entries about the inventions and achievements you find there.

For: An activity on East Asia's history
Visit: PHSchool.com
Web Code: lcd-6401

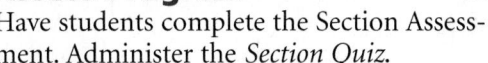

Assess and Reteach

Assess Progress L2
Have students complete the Section Assessment. Administer the *Section Quiz.*

All in One **Asia and the Pacific Teaching Resources,** *Section Quiz,* p. 226

Reteach L1
If students need more instruction, have them read this section in the Reading and Vocabulary Study Guide.

📖 Chapter 21, Section 1, **Eastern Hemisphere Reading and Vocabulary Study Guide,** pp. 226–228

Extend L3
To give the class an appreciation of one of Japan's cultural contributions, have students read the literature selection *Tankas* and answer the questions. You may encourage students who are inspired by these examples to write their own tankas. Make sure students' poems have 31 syllables and 5 lines.

All in One **Asia and the Pacific Teaching Resources,** *Tankas,* p. 243

Answers

✓ **Reading Check** To fuel its growing industries, Japan attacked other Asian and Pacific lands to gain access to their resources.

Writing Activity
Use the *Rubric for Assessing a Journal Entry* to evaluate students' diary entries.

All in One **Asia and the Pacific Teaching Resources,** *Rubric for Assessing a Journal Entry,* p. 246

Go Online PHSchool.com Typing in the Web code when prompted will bring students directly to detailed instructions for this activity.

Section 1 Assessment

Key Terms
Students' sentences should reflect knowledge of each Key Term.

⊙ **Target Reading Skill**
The term *foreign powers* means "other countries." Clues are in the sentence before and the sentence after.

Comprehension and Critical Thinking
1. **(a)** Any four of the following: paper, silk weaving, gunpowder, magnetic compass, printing press, clockworks. **(b)** by emperors
2. **(a)** Possible answers: Buddhism's spread from India to China and then to Korea and Japan; the spread of the teachings of Confucius from China to Korea and Japan. **(b)** Possible answer: Cultural diffusion can happen through trade between countries.

3. **(a)** Commodore Perry wanted to force Japan to grant trading rights to the United States. **(b)** Western nations traded goods with Japan, whereas European countries gained control of parts of China.

Objective

Learn how to read a route map.

Prepare to Read

Build Background Knowledge L2

Tell students to suppose they wanted to walk to a friend's house but were not sure where their friend's street was located. What would they do? Lead students to respond that they would probably look for their friend's street on a road map of their town. Explain that they will learn how to read such a map in this lesson.

Instruct

Reading Route Maps L2

Guided Instruction

- Read the steps to reading a route map on p. 650 as a class. Then write the steps on the board.

- Complete the Practice the Skill activity on p. 651 with students. Read the title of the map *(The Silk Road)* and determine what region is shown *(Asia)*. Point out that this is a historical route map and explain that its purpose is to show the Silk Road trade routes.

- Direct students' attention to the map key. Explain that it shows the symbols that represent the Silk Road, cities, and the Great Wall of China. Tell students to trace the Silk Road with their finger starting at Chang'an. Describe some of the landforms it traveled over *(mountains and rivers)*. Identify landforms it avoided *(the Taklimakan Desert)*. Name the city where it ends *(Antioch)*. Explain that students can use all the information they just learned about the route to draw conclusions about the route and why it took the particular path shown on the map.

Independent Practice

Assign *Skills for Life* and have students complete it individually.

All in One Asia and the Pacific Teaching Resources, *Skills for Life,* p. 234

Think of three inventions that had an important effect on human progress. What comes to mind: Farming? Books? Cars?

Did you think of *roads?*

The development of road networks has helped human civilization to grow and spread. Roads have been the lifelines of trade, communication, and human migration for thousands of years. Some of the world's oldest roads are in East Asia.

650 Asia and the Pacific

Learn the Skill

A map that shows roads is called a route map. Follow these steps to learn how to read a route map.

1. **Read the title of the map and become familiar with its features.** First, get a general idea of what region the map shows. Use the compass rose to figure out direction on the map.

2. **Study the key to understand its symbols.** Most modern road maps use colored lines to indicate various types of roads, from country roads to interstate highways. Other maps use colors to show land, sea, and air routes. The colors and what they represent are shown in the key. Notice what other symbols in the key represent, including cities.

3. **Trace routes on the map.** Gather information about the route by studying the features on the map. Use the scale of miles to calculate distances. Notice physical features and landmarks along the journey. Make note of any geographic barriers that would affect speed or comfort on the trip.

4. **Interpret the map.** Use information you gather from the map to draw conclusions about the route. On historical maps you can draw conclusions about why travelers and traders took certain routes and traveled at certain times of the year.

Monitor Progress

As students are completing the worksheet, circulate to make sure students are applying the skill steps effectively. Help students as needed.

The Silk Road

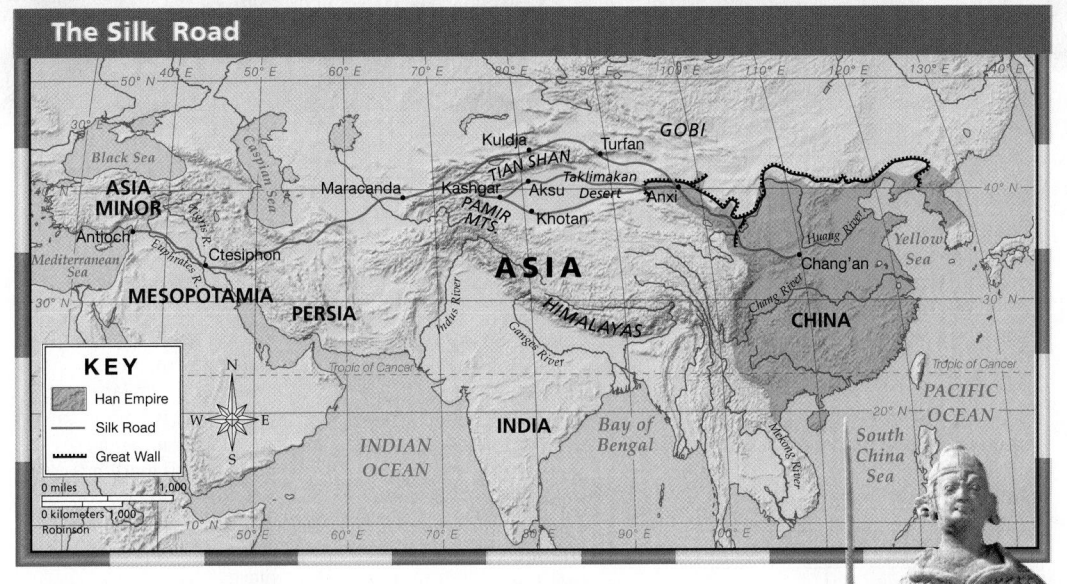

KEY

- Han Empire
- Silk Road
- Great Wall

0 miles 1,000
0 kilometers 1,000
Robinson

Practice the Skill

Study the map and follow the steps on the previous page to practice reading a route map.

1 Read the title of the map and study the map to observe its main features. What region does it show? What type of map is it—modern or historical, a standard road map, or some other kind? What is its purpose?

2 Look at the key on this map. What features does it identify?

3 With your finger, start at the city of Chang'an, in China, and trace the general paths of the Silk Road. Using the compass rose, determine the direction of the route. What continents or regions did the Silk Road cross? Where did it end? Did it include travel over mountains?

4 The Silk Road was created over time, as local and regional routes became connected to form one long route. Write a paragraph that describes the route and draws conclusions about how and why it took the particular path shown on the map.

Apply the Skill

Find a street map of your community. Use the steps in the Learn the Skill section to trace the route from your house to your school or to some other location you know, such as a park. Write a paragraph that draws conclusions about the route you found.

Differentiated Instruction

For Special Needs Students L1

Some students may need to review basic map skills to help them interpret route maps. Distribute *Using the Map Key* and *Using the Compass Rose* to these students and have them work with more proficient students to complete the worksheets.

All in One **Asia and the Pacific Teaching Resources,** *Using the Map Key,* p. 241; *Using the Compass Rose,* p. 242

For English Language Learners L1

Pair native English-speaking students with English learners and have them do the Apply the Skill activity. Encourage students to help each other in writing their paragraphs, and answer each other's questions about the skill. Circulate and ask students questions about the skill to be sure they understand what they have read.

Assess and Reteach

Assess Progress L2

Ask students to do the Apply the Skill activity.

Reteach L1

If students are having trouble applying the skill steps, have them review the skill using the Social Studies Skills Tutor CD-ROM. Route maps are reviewed in Level 2 of *Analyzing and Interpreting Special Purpose Maps.*

◉ *Analyzing and Interpreting Special Purpose Maps,* **Social Studies Skills Tutor CD-ROM**

Extend L3

Have students complete *Understanding Road Maps* and *Reading Road Maps* to further practice the skill.

All in One **Asia and the Pacific Teaching Resources,** *Understanding Road Maps,* p. 239; *Reading Road Maps,* p. 240

Answer
Apply the Skill

Students' routes will vary but check to make sure the routes they trace are appropriate. Students' conclusions should explain why they chose their particular route.

Section 2
Step-by-Step Instruction

Objectives

Social Studies

1. Examine some ways in which East Asia's past affects its modern-day culture.
2. Find out how the people of China are different from the people of the Koreas and Japan.

Reading/Language Arts

Read ahead to find context clues to determine the meaning of unfamiliar words.

Prepare to Read

Build Background Knowledge   L2

Before students read, lead them on a quick "section tour" focusing their attention on the title, Key Terms, photographs, and the map. Ask students to predict what this section is about. Write their predictions on the board. After they have read the section, revisit the predictions and revise them as necessary.

Set a Purpose for Reading   L2

- Preview the Objectives.

- Read each statement in the *Reading Readiness Guide* aloud. Ask students to mark the statements true or false.

- Have students discuss the statements in pairs or groups of four, then mark their worksheets again. Use the Numbered Heads participation strategy (TE, p. T36) to call on students to share their group's perspectives.

  All in One Asia and the Pacific Teaching Resources, *Reading Readiness Guide,* p. 228

Vocabulary Builder
Preview Key Terms   L2

Pronounce each Key Term, then ask the students to say the word with you. Provide a simple explanation such as, "The nomad lives on the hillside in summer and moves to the valley in the fall."

Section

2 People and Cultures

Prepare to Read

Objectives

In this section you will

1. Examine some ways in which East Asia's past affects its modern-day culture.
2. Find out how the people of China are different from the people of the Koreas and Japan.

Taking Notes

As you read, look for details about the people and culture of East Asia. Copy the chart below, and record your findings in it.

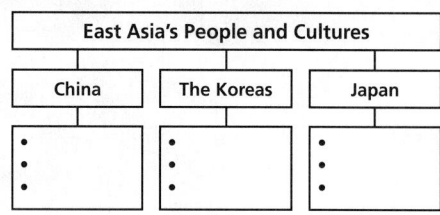

Target Reading Skill

Use Context Clues
Context, the words and phrases surrounding a word, can help you understand a word or phrase you do not know. Sometimes you may need to keep reading to find a context clue. On page 653, find the phrase *many marriages are still arranged.* The sentence that follows this phrase explains what an arranged marriage is.

Key Terms

- **commune** (KAHM yoon) *n.* a community in which people own land as a group and where they live and work together
- **dialect** (DY uh lekt) *n.* a variation of a language that is unique to a region or an area
- **nomad** (NOH mad) *n.* a person who has no settled home but who moves from place to place
- **homogeneous** (hoh moh JEE nee us) *adj.* identical or similar
- **ethnic group** (ETH nik groop) *n.* a group of people who share such characteristics as language, religion, and ancestry

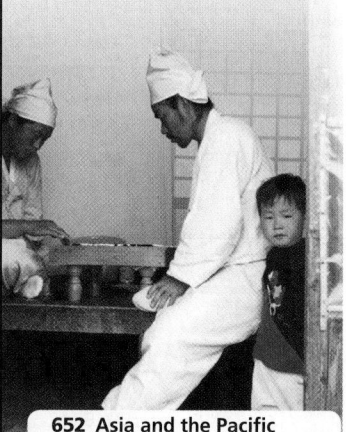

Two men play a game of Go in a small South Korean village.

652 Asia and the Pacific

The Chinese game weiqi (WAY chee) has ancient cultural roots. One player has 181 black stones standing for night. The other has 180 white stones standing for day. The goal is to surround and capture the opponent's stones. But to the Chinese, weiqi is more than a game. For centuries, Buddhists have used it to discipline the mind. Today, you can see people playing this ancient game throughout East Asia. Another name for this traditional Chinese game is Go.

Tradition and Change

In East Asia, tradition mixes with change in a thousand ways. Businesspeople in Western suits greet each other in the traditional way—with a bow. Ancient palaces stand among skyscrapers. Everywhere in Japan, China, and the Koreas, reminders of the past mingle with activities of the present.

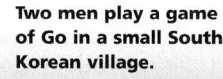

Target Reading Skill   L2

Use Context Clues Point out the Target Reading Skill. Tell students that in order to understand an unfamiliar word, they must sometimes read ahead to find a clue to its meaning.

Model context clues to find the meaning of "privileges" in this sentence in the third paragraph on p. 653: "Chinese families with only one child could receive special privileges."

(Reading ahead to the next two sentences, I learn that privileges are rewards.)

Give students *Use Context Clues: Definition and Description.* Have them complete the activity in their groups.

All in One Asia and the Pacific Teaching Resources, *Use Context Clues: Definition and Description,* p. 231

Communism Changes Chinese Farming When the Communists took power in 1949, they began to make major changes. The government ended the old system of land ownership. It created **communes**, communities in which land is held in common and where members live and work together.

Many Chinese farmers were bitter at losing their land. They were accustomed to living in family groups that worked together in small fields. The farmers resisted the communes. Food production fell, and China suffered terrible food shortages. Only when the government allowed some private ownership did food production grow.

Changes in Chinese Life Beginning in the 1970s, the Communists also tried to slow China's population growth by attacking the idea of large families. Chinese couples were supposed to wait until their late twenties to marry. They were not supposed to have more than one child per family. Chinese families with only one child could receive special privileges. For example, couples in urban areas could receive a payment of money. In rural areas, the reward could be more land.

Under communism, the position of women improved. One of the first laws the Communists passed allowed a woman to own property, choose her husband, and get a divorce. Today, however, men still hold most of the power, and many marriages are still arranged. That is, parents or other family members decide who will marry whom.

Shanghai at Night
Shanghai, China, is a bustling city with skyscrapers and superhighways. The small photo shows Nanjing Road, one of the principal streets in Shanghai. **Analyze Images** *Do you think Shanghai is a large or a small city? Explain your answer.*

Vocabulary Builder

Use the information below to teach students this section's high-use words.

High-Use Word	Definition and Sample Sentence
resist, p. 653	*v.* to stand firm against Susan **resisted** changes to her plan for a new playground.
variation, p. 655	*n.* difference, alternative There are many **variations** of the Chinese language.
unique, p. 655	*adj.* the only one of its kind Ann bought a **unique** painting to hang in her bedroom.
diverse, p. 655	*adj.* not all the same; varied The class has a **diverse** group of students.

Guided Instruction

- **Vocabulary Builder** Clarify the high-use word **resist** before reading.

- Read Tradition and Change, using the Structured Silent Reading strategy (TE, p. T34).

- Ask students **What happened in China in 1949?** (*The Communists came into power.*)

- Ask students to compare and contrast the life of a Chinese farmer before and after 1949. (*Before—farmers owned land and lived in family groups that worked together; after—farmers lost their land and had to join communes.*)

- Ask students **What were the results of Chinese farmers having to live on communes?** (*The farmers resisted the communes and food production fell, resulting in serious food shortages.*)

- Discuss some ways in which Chinese traditions have mixed with modern ways. (*Possible responses: women have the right to own property, choose their husbands, and get divorced, but many marriages are still arranged; pedicabs share the roads with more modern means of transportation, such as cars and buses; tiny shops exist side by side with modern buildings.*)

Answer

Analyze Images Possible answer: Shanghai looks like a large city because it has many skyscrapers, highways, and lights.

- Ask students **How is daily life in Korea still influenced by traditions?** *(The family is still important and takes care of all its members.)*

- Ask students **What evidence supports the main idea that Japan is the most modern of the East Asian countries?** *(Nearly 80 percent of its population lives in cities.)*

- Ask students **How does Japan's past still influence its present?** *(At home, many Japanese still wear traditional dress and may sit on mats at a low table to eat dinner.)*

Independent Practice

Ask students to create the Taking Notes graphic organizer on a blank piece of paper. Then have them record details about the peoples and cultures of China, the Koreas, and Japan, using the information they have just read. Briefly model how to identify which details to record.

Monitor Progress

As students fill in the graphic organizer, survey the class to determine if individuals are selecting the correct details. Provide assistance as needed.

Target Reading Skill   L2

Use Context Clues As a follow up, ask students to answer the Target Reading Skill question in the Student Edition. *(The last two sentences describe habits that Japanese people have had for many years, so students may deduce that traditional customs are long-held habits.)*

Japan's Capsule Hotels
In densely populated Japan, people have developed unique ways to use space. Capsule hotels are one such example. They are used mainly by businessmen who have missed the last train home. Each capsule usually has a bed, a television, a radio, and an alarm clock.
Analyze Images *What are most of the people in the photo doing?*

Use Context Clues
Use the last two sentences in this paragraph to help you define *traditional customs.* Check your definition by looking up *traditional* and *custom* in a dictionary.

Old and New in China Old traditions in China are strongest in rural areas. Yet even in the cities, a visitor sees examples of the old China. In cities like Beijing, the capital of China, the streets are filled with three-wheeled cabs pedaled like tricycles. These pedicabs share the roads with buses, cars, and taxis. Tiny shops exist side by side with modern buildings.

Changes in the Koreas In both Koreas, daily life is influenced by long-standing traditions. The family is still important, although the average family is smaller today than before. In rural areas, grandparents, parents, aunts, and uncles may live in one household. In the cities, usually just parents and children live as one household.

As in China, modern ways are much more visible in Korean urban areas. Also, as is true all over the world, the role of women has changed. In the past, Korean women had few opportunities. Today, women can work and vote.

A Blend of Old and New in Japan Japan is the most modern of the East Asian countries. The Japanese use more modern technology than the rest of East Asia. Nearly 80 percent of the population lives in urban areas. Once Japanese workers reach home, however, many still follow traditional customs. For example, they may change into kimonos, or robes. They may sit on mats at a low table to have dinner.

✓ **Reading Check** **Which is the most modern country in East Asia?**

Differentiated Instruction

For Advanced Readers   L3
Have students look at the *Enrichment* worksheet to learn about the Korean martial art Tae Kwon Do. Ask them to choose one of the questions to research and write a brief report.

All in One Asia and the Pacific Teaching Resources, *Enrichment,* p. 233

For Less Proficient Readers   L1
Show students the *Section Reading Support Transparency* before reading to provide them with an overview of key ideas and concepts in this section.

Asia and the Pacific Transparencies, *Section Reading Support Transparency AP 58*

Answers

Analyze Images Most of the people in the photo seem to be lying down reading, or getting ready to lie down.

✓ **Reading Check** Japan

East Asia's People

East Asia is a mix of cultures both old and new. Within each of the area's countries, however, the people tend to share a single culture.

China: The Han and Other Chinese Ethnic Groups

About 19 of every 20 Chinese people trace their ancestry to the Han ethnic group. As you can see on the map below, the Han live mostly in the eastern half of China. Although they have a common written language, they speak different dialects from region to region. A **dialect** is a variation of a language that is unique to a region or area. The other Chinese come from 55 different minority groups. These groups live mainly in western and southern China. With so many different ethnic groups, China is one of the most ethnically diverse nations in the world.

Learn about the history of China's merchant class.

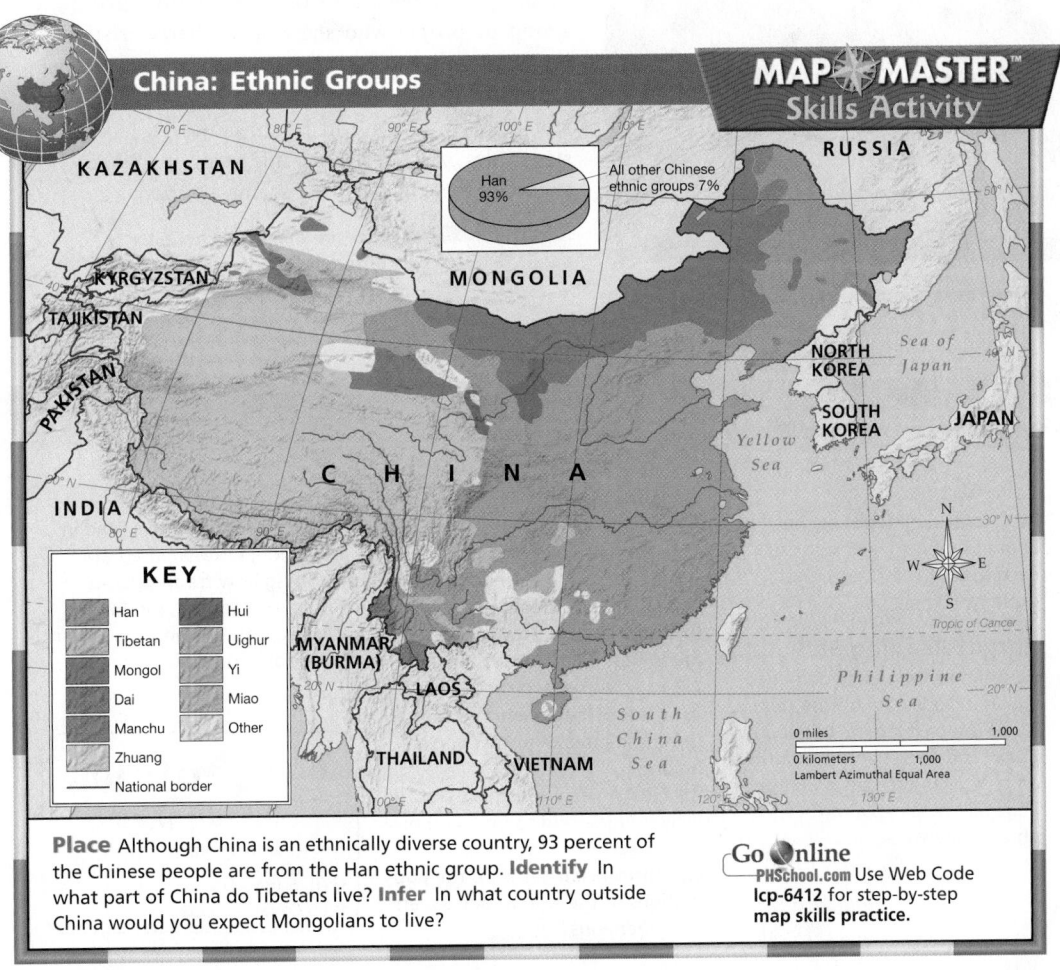

China: Ethnic Groups

MAP MASTER™ Skills Activity

KAZAKHSTAN

KYRGYZSTAN

TAJIKISTAN

PAKISTAN

INDIA

Han 93%

All other Chinese ethnic groups 7%

RUSSIA

MONGOLIA

NORTH KOREA

SOUTH KOREA

JAPAN

Sea of Japan

Yellow Sea

C H I N A

MYANMAR (BURMA)

LAOS

THAILAND

VIETNAM

South China Sea

Philippine Sea

Tropic of Cancer

KEY

Han	Hui
Tibetan	Uighur
Mongol	Yi
Dai	Miao
Manchu	Other
Zhuang	

— National border

0 miles 1,000
0 kilometers 1,000
Lambert Azimuthal Equal Area

N E S W

Place Although China is an ethnically diverse country, 93 percent of the Chinese people are from the Han ethnic group. **Identify** In what part of China do Tibetans live? **Infer** In what country outside China would you expect Mongolians to live?

Go Online
PHSchool.com Use Web Code lcp-6412 for step-by-step map skills practice.

Chapter 21 Section 2 **655**

Skills Mini Lesson

Identifying Point of View

1. Teach the skill by defining point of view as an opinion or perspective on an issue or topic. Explain that recognizing point of view can help students identify and interpret peoples' beliefs and opinions.

2. Help students practice the skill by having them identify whether this statement is

the point of view of a teacher or student: "I believe that homework should be given every night and turned in on time."

3. Have students apply the skill by answering these questions: What was the point of view of many Chinese farmers about communism? What information helps to support their point of view?

Assess and Reteach

Assess Progress L2

Have students complete the Section Assessment. Administer the *Section Quiz*.

 **Asia and the Pacific Teaching Resources,** *Section Quiz,* p. 230

Reteach L1

If students need more instruction, have them read this section in the Reading and Vocabulary Study Guide.

📖 Chapter 21, Section 2, **Eastern Hemisphere Reading and Vocabulary Study Guide,** pp. 229–231

Extend L3

To extend the lesson distribute the *Small Group Activity: Organizing a Japan Fair.* Have students work in groups to complete the activity.

 **Asia and the Pacific Teaching Resources,** *Small Group Activity: Organizing a Japan Fair,* pp. 235–238

Answer

✓ **Reading Check** There are more minority groups in China while the people of the Koreas and Japan belong to homogenous ethnic groups.

Section 2 Assessment

Key Terms

Students' sentences should reflect knowledge of each Key Term.

🕑 Target Reading Skill L2

The phrase "tradition mixes with change" helps you to understand what the last sentence of the paragraph means.

Comprehension and Critical Thinking

1. (a) They started communes and improved the position of women. **(b)** Modern ways are more visible in cities. People in urban areas wear modern clothes. Modern transportation such as buses, cars, and taxis fill city streets. Traditions are stronger in rural areas and in homes.

2. (a) the Han **(b)** China has 55 different minority groups. **(c)** Korea: nomad groups lost their separate traditions and formed one homogeneous group. Japan: it is an island country that isolated itself for a long time, and nearly all the people belong to the same ethnic group.

Shoppers in Seoul, South Korea

Korea and Japan: Few Minorities Historians believe that the ancient Korean language was brought to Korea by nomads from the north. **Nomads** are people who have no settled home but who move from place to place, usually on a seasonal basis. Over centuries, these groups lost their separate traditions. They formed one **homogeneous** (hoh moh JEE nee us) group, which means identical or similar. Today, even with the division of Korea into two countries, the population is quite homogeneous. There are few minority groups.

Because it is an island nation that isolated itself from the world for a long time, Japan has one of the most homogeneous populations on Earth. Nearly all of the people belong to the same **ethnic group,** a group of people who share such characteristics as language, religion, ancestry, and cultural traditions. Minority groups are few. Small numbers of Koreans and Chinese also live in Japan. However, Japan has strict rules on immigration. It is hard for anyone who is not Japanese by birth to become a citizen.

✓ **Reading Check** How are the people of China different from the people of the Koreas and Japan?

 Section 2 Assessment

Key Terms

Review the key terms at the beginning of this section. Use each term in a sentence that explains its meaning.

🕑 Target Reading Skill

Find the last sentence on page 652. It includes the phrase *reminders of the past mingle with activities of the present.* Which phrases and words in the paragraph on page 652 help explain what the phrase means?

Comprehension and Critical Thinking

1. (a) Recall In what two major ways did the Communists make changes in the Chinese way of life?
(b) Summarize How is modern life in East Asia more visible in urban areas than in rural areas?
2. (a) Identify To which ethnic group do most Chinese people belong?
(b) Find Main Ideas and Details Why is China said to be an ethnically diverse country?
(c) Summarize Why are the populations of the Koreas and Japan homogeneous?

Writing Activity

Based on what you have read in this section, write a paragraph describing how tradition and change exist together in East Asia. Include at least three supporting details for your topic sentence.

For: An activity on East Asia's culture
Visit: PHSchool.com
Web Code: lcd-6402

656 Asia and the Pacific

Writing Activity

Use the *Rubric for Assessing a Writing Assignment* to evaluate students' paragraphs.

 **Asia and the Pacific Teaching Resources,** *Rubric for Assessing a Writing Assignment,* p. 245

Go Online PHSchool.com Typing in the Web code when prompted will bring students directly to detailed instructions for this activity.

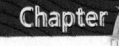

Review and Assessment

◆ Chapter Summary

Section 1: Historic Traditions

- China has the oldest continuous civilization in the world. Starting in ancient times, a series of dynasties ruled China.
- Paper, gunpowder, silk weaving, and the magnetic compass are among China's many cultural and technical achievements.
- The Shilla people unified Korea as one country. A series of shoguns ruled Japan for more than 700 years.
- In the 1800s, western nations became interested in East Asia as a market to sell goods.

Japanese *No* mask

Section 2: People and Cultures

- China has been governed under a Communist system since 1949. The Communist party has made major changes in the Chinese way of life.
- Although China is becoming more modern, old traditions are still followed, especially in rural areas of the country.
- As in China, modern ways of life in the Koreas are more visible in urban areas. Japan is the most modern of the East Asian countries but also lives by its historic traditions.
- Most people in China belong to the Han ethnic group. Korea's history resulted in a homogeneous population. As in the Koreas, nearly all Japanese people belong to the same ethnic group.

Shanghai, China

◆ Key Terms

Each of the statements below contains a key term from the chapter. If the statement is true, write *true*. If it is false, rewrite the statement to make it true.

1. An emperor is the male ruler of an empire.
2. A clan is a series of rulers from the same family.
3. A dynasty is a group of families with a common ancestor.
4. Cultural diffusion is the spreading of ideas or practices from one culture to other cultures.
5. People with the same dialect use a variation of a language that is unique to their region or area.
6. A nomad is a community in which people own land as a group and where they live together and work together.
7. A homogeneous group includes people who are identical or similar.
8. An ethnic group shares such characteristics as language, religion, ancestry, and cultural traditions.

Chapter 21 **657**

┌ Vocabulary Builder ─

Revisit this chapter's high-use words:

symbol	grant	unique
noble	resist	diverse
adopt	variation	

Ask students to review the definitions they recorded on their *Word Knowledge* worksheets.

All in One **Asia and the Pacific Teaching Resources**, *Word Knowledge*, p. 232

Consider allowing students to earn extra credit if they use the words in their answers to the questions in the Chapter Review and Assessment. The words must be used correctly and in a natural context to win the extra points.

Review and Assessment
Review Chapter Content

- Review and revisit the major themes of this chapter by asking students to classify what Guiding Question each bulleted statement in the Chapter Summary answers. Form students into groups and ask them to complete the activity together. Refer to page 567 in the Student Edition for text of the Guiding Questions.

- Assign *Vocabulary Development* for students to review Key Terms.

  All in One **Asia and the Pacific Teaching Resources**, *Vocabulary Development*, p. 244

Answers

Key Terms

1. True
2. False; A clan is a group of families with a common ancestor.
3. False; A dynasty is a series of rulers from the same family.
4. True
5. True
6. A nomad is a person who has no settled home but who moves from place to place.
7. True
8. True

Comprehension and Critical Thinking

9. (a) a complex, highly organized social order, with cities, a central government, workers who do specialized jobs, and social classes **(b)** achievements include inventing paper, gunpowder, silk weaving, magnetic compass, printing press, and clockworks; engineering achievements include canals, dams, bridges, and irrigation systems; scientific discoveries were made in medicine and mathematics. **(c)** Possible answers: Clothes are made from silk, fireworks are made from gunpowder, books are made from paper, and compasses are used to guide ships and planes.

10. (a) the Han **(b)** China is more diverse, with 55 ethnic groups. Korea and Japan are more homogenous.

11. (a) a series of rulers from the same family **(b)** In ancient times emperors ruled China. Today Communist leaders rule China.

12. (a) nearly 80 percent **(b)** People may wear modern clothing to work but traditional dress at home or during festivals; women have more rights today, but many marriages are still arranged; families look after the welfare of all their members. **(c)** Possible answer: People in rural areas are more isolated and less likely to be influenced by cultural diffusion, so their traditions have changed less than in urban areas.

13. (a) 1949 **(b)** The Communists took over most of the land, industries, and businesses.

Skills Practice

Tigris and Euphrates rivers; Euphrates

Writing Activity: History

Students' paragraphs will vary, but should include information about the invention's development and use, as well as how it spread to and affected other parts of the world.

Use the *Rubric for Assessing a Writing Assignment* to evaluate students' paragraphs.

All in One **Asia and the Pacific Teaching Resources,** *Rubric for Assessing a Writing Assignment,* p. 245

◆ Comprehension and Critical Thinking

9. (a) Explain What is a civilization?
(b) Describe What are some achievements of the ancient Chinese civilization?
(c) Make Generalizations Give some examples of how ancient Chinese achievements still affect the world today.

10. (a) Recall To which ethnic group do most of the people in China belong?
(b) Summarize How does China's population differ from the populations of Japan and the Koreas in terms of ethnic diversity?

11. (a) Define What is a dynasty?
(b) Contrast How is China governed today, and how is that government different from China's government in ancient times?

12. (a) Recall About what percentage of people in Japan live in urban areas?
(b) Synthesize Information Give examples of how life in East Asia reflects past traditions and present traditions.
(c) Predict Why might past traditions be followed more in rural areas of East Asia than in urban areas?

13. (a) Recall When did the Communists come into power in China?
(b) Summarize What changes did the Communists make to the Chinese way of life?

◆ Skills Practice

Reading Route Maps In the Skills for Life activity in this chapter, you learned how to read route maps. Review the steps you followed to learn this skill. Then use the map on page 651 to name two rivers in Mesopotamia that the Silk Road crossed. If a traveler was heading west on the Silk Road, which river would he cross first?

◆ Writing Activity: History

As you have read in this chapter, paper was invented in ancient China, as were many other things. Choose one of the inventions named in this chapter, and do research in the library or on the Internet to learn more about it. Find out how it was made and used in ancient China. Also, find out how the invention spread to other parts of the world. Write a paragraph about what you have learned.

MAP MASTER™ Skills Activity

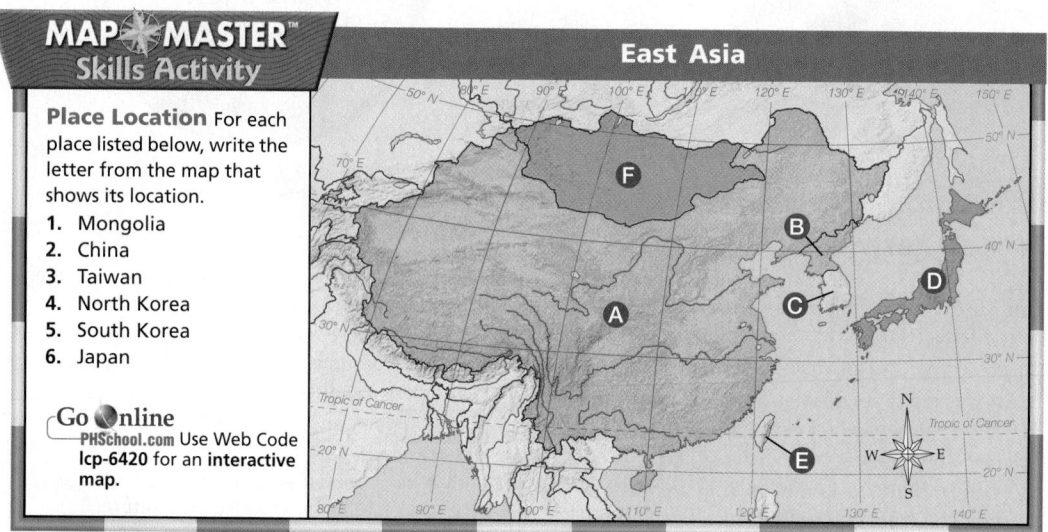

East Asia

Place Location For each place listed below, write the letter from the map that shows its location.
1. Mongolia
2. China
3. Taiwan
4. North Korea
5. South Korea
6. Japan

Go Online PHSchool.com Use Web Code lcp-6420 for an **interactive map.**

658 Asia and the Pacific

MAP MASTER™ Skills Activity

1. F
2. A
3. E
4. B
5. C
6. D

Go Online PHSchool.com Students may practice their map skills using the interactive online version of this map.

Standardized Test Prep

Test-Taking Tips

Some questions on standardized tests ask you to analyze timelines. Study the timeline below. Then follow the tips to answer the sample question.

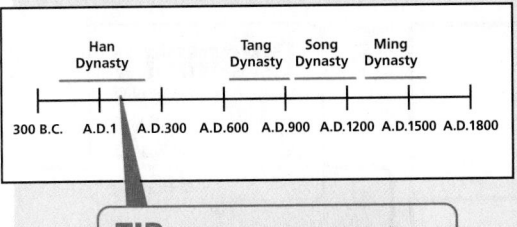

Han Dynasty   Tang Dynasty   Song Dynasty   Ming Dynasty

300 B.C.   A.D.1   A.D.300   A.D.600   A.D.900   A.D.1200   A.D.1500   A.D.1800

TIP To read a timeline, first figure out the timespan between dates (in this case it is 300 years). Then line up each event or dynasty with the nearest date or dates and estimate.

Pick the letter that best answers the question.

The world's oldest printed book was found in China. It was made around A.D. 868, during the

- A Han dynasty.
- B Tang dynasty.
- C Song dynasty.
- D Ming dynasty.

Think It Through The oldest book was made around A.D. 868. You can eliminate Han and Ming (A and D) because they are not near that date. Now look closely at the timeline: A.D. 868 is between A.D. 600 and A.D. 900. The Song Dynasty started *after* A.D. 900. So the correct answer is B, the Tang Dynasty.

TIP Rewrite the sentence in your own words to make sure you understand what it is asking: *During which dynasty was the oldest book made?*

Practice Questions

Use the tips above and other tips in this book to help you answer the following questions.

1. Based on the timeline above, the Tang dynasty lasted about
   - A 100 years.
   - B 200 years.
   - C 300 years.
   - D 400 years.

2. The religion of Buddhism, which China adopted from India, is an example of
   - A cultural migration.
   - B irrigation.
   - C cultural diffusion.
   - D Communist rule.

3. Which statement correctly describes Chinese culture?
   - A Everyone in China belongs to the same ethnic group.
   - B Chinese people speak different dialects from region to region.
   - C Old traditions and ways of life are illegal in China.
   - D There are two ethnic groups in China.

Go **Online**
PHSchool.com

Use Web Code lca-6400
for **Chapter 21 self-test.**

Go **Online**
PHSchool.com Students may use the Chapter 21 self-test on PHSchool.com to prepare for the Chapter Test.

Assessment Resources

Use Chapter Tests A and B to assess students' mastery of chapter content.

All in One **Asia and the Pacific Teaching Resources,** *Chapter Tests A and B,* pp. 247–252

Test are also available on the *ExamView Test Bank CD-ROM.*

⦿ *ExamView Test Bank CD-ROM*

Chapter Overview

Overview

Section 1

South Asia: Cultures and History
1. Find out which religions became part of South Asian cultures.
2. Understand which empires shaped the history of South Asia.
3. Learn about the present-day religions and languages of South Asian cultures.

Section 2

Southwest Asia: Cultures and History
1. Find out that one of the world's earliest civilizations grew in Southwest Asia.
2. Understand that three of the world's great religions began in Southwest Asia.
3. Examine the different ethnic groups and religions of Southwest Asia.
4. Learn about the conflict between Arabs and Israelis in Southwest Asia.

Section 3

Central Asia: Cultures and History
1. Learn that many cultures and peoples influenced Central Asia in ancient times.
2. Discover how Central Asian nations became independent and why they are a focus of world interest.

Istanbul, Aleppo, and Jerusalem: Crossroads of Trade
Length: 3 minutes, 6 seconds
Use with Section 2
This segment introduces three of the major cities in Southwest Asia. Students will learn why these cities are important centers for trade.

Technology Resources

Students use embedded Web codes to access Internet activities, chapter self-tests, and additional map practice. They may also access Dorling Kindersley's Online Desk Reference to learn more about each country they study.

Use the Interactive Textbook to make content and concepts come alive through animations, videos, and activities that accompany the complete basal text—online and on CD-ROM.

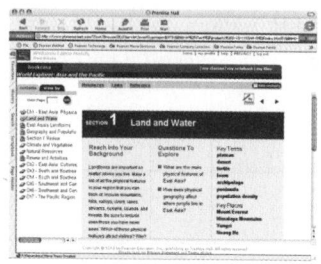

PRENTICE HALL

Use this complete suite of powerful teaching tools to make planning lessons and administering tests quicker and easier.

Reading and Assessment

Reading and Vocabulary Instruction

🔊 Model the Target Reading Skill

Word Analysis Explain to students that as they read, they may encounter difficult or unfamiliar words. Analyzing unfamiliar words can help students determine their meaning. Model this skill by analyzing the word *independence*, found on page 667 of the Student Edition.

Think aloud: *If I did not know the meaning of this word, I could look at its parts to help figure it out. For example, this word has a prefix, -in, and a suffix, -ence. That leaves the root word,* depend. *I know that* depend *means "to hang on to, rely on, or be a part of." The prefix* -in *means "not." The suffix* -ence *means "a state of being." So, by analyzing the parts of this word, I can tell that* independence *means something like "not being a part of" or "not hanging on to others."*

Use the following worksheets from All-in-One Asia and the Pacific Teaching Resources, (pp. 267–269) to support the chapter's Target Reading Skill.

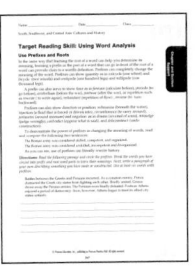 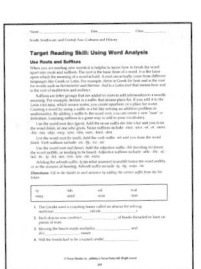 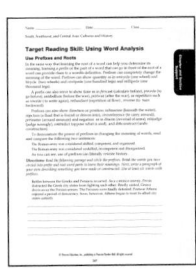

Vocabulary Builder
High-Use Academic Words

Use these steps to teach this chapter's high-use words:

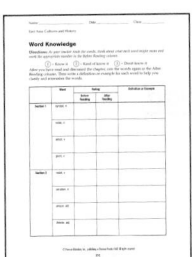

1. Have students rate how well they know each word on their Word Knowledge worksheets (All-in-One Asia and the Pacific Teaching Resources, p. 270).

2. Pronounce each word and ask students to repeat it.

3. Give students a brief definition or sample sentence (provided on TE pp. 663, 670, and 679).

4. Work with students as they fill in the "Definition or Example" column of their Word Knowledge worksheets.

Assessment

Formal Assessment

Test students' understanding of core knowledge and skills.

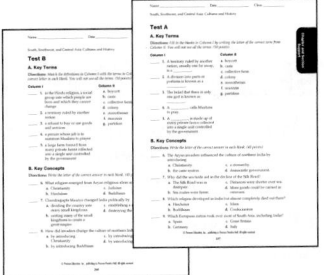

Chapter Tests A and B, All-in-One Asia and the Pacific Teaching Resources, pp. 287–292

Customize the Chapter Tests to suit your needs.

ExamView Test Bank CD-ROM

Skills Assessment

Assess geographic literacy.

MapMaster Skills, Student Edition pp. 661, 663, 670, 684

Assess reading and comprehension.

Target Reading Skills, Student Edition, pp. 666, 674, 682 and in Section Assessments

Chapter 22 Assessment, Eastern Hemisphere Reading and Vocabulary Study Guide, p. 242

Performance Assessment

Assess students' performance on this chapter's Writing Activities using the following rubric from All-in-One Asia and the Pacific Teaching Resources.

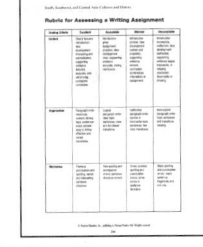

Rubric for Assessing a Writing Assignment, p. 286

Assess students' work through performance tasks.

Small Group Activity: Reporting on Hinduism and Buddhism, All-in-One Asia and the Pacific Teaching Resources, pp. 273–276

Online Assessment

Have students check their own understanding.

Chapter Self-Test

Section 1 South Asia: Cultures and History

 *1 period, .5 block*

Social Studies Objectives

1. Find out which religions became part of South Asian cultures.
2. Understand which empires shaped the history of South Asia.
3. Learn about the present-day religions and languages of South Asian cultures.

Reading/Language Arts Objective

Analyze word parts to determine the meanings and pronunciations of unfamiliar words.

Prepare to Read	**Instructional Resources**	**Differentiated Instruction**

Build Background Knowledge
Ask students to preview the section and think about things that might be important to the people of South Asia.

Set a Purpose for Reading
Have students begin to fill out the *Reading Readiness Guide*.

Preview Key Terms
Teach the section's Key Terms.

Target Reading Skill
Introduce the section's Target Reading Skill of **analyzing word parts**.

All in One Asia and the Pacific Teaching Resources
L2 Reading Readiness Guide, p. 256
L2 Use Prefixes and Roots, p. 267

Spanish Reading and Vocabulary Study Guide
L1 Chapter 22, Section 1, pp. 165–166 ELL

Instruct	**Instructional Resources**	**Differentiated Instruction**

New Religions
Discuss the Indus Valley civilization, Aryan culture, and religions of South Asia.

From Empires to Nations
Ask questions about the empires and rulers of South Asia before the independence of India.

Target Reading Skill
Review **analyzing word parts**.

South Asian Cultures Today
Discuss language and religion in South Asia today.

All in One Asia and the Pacific Teaching Resources
L2 Guided Reading and Review, p. 257
L2 Reading Readiness Guide, p. 256

Asia and the Pacific Transparencies
L2 Section Reading Support Transparency AP 59

All in One Asia and the Pacific Teaching Resources
L3 A Great Asian Thinker, p. 279 AR, GT
L3 Writing Stories, p. 282 AR, GT

Asia and the Pacific Transparencies
L1 Transparency B20: Timeline ELL, LPR, SN

Teacher's Edition
L3 For Gifted and Talented, TE pp. 665, 666, 667
L1 For Less Proficient Readers, TE p. 665
L1 For English Language Learners, TE pp. 666, 667

Student Edition on Audio CD
L1 Chapter 22, Section 1 ELL, LPR, SN

Assess and Reteach	**Instructional Resources**	**Differentiated Instruction**

Assess Progress
Evaluate student comprehension with the section assessment and section quiz.

Reteach
Assign the Reading and Vocabulary Study Guide to help struggling students.

Extend
Extend the lesson by assigning a Small Group Activity.

All in One Asia and the Pacific Teaching Resources
L2 Section Quiz, p. 258
L3 Small Group Activity: Reporting on Hinduism and Buddhism, pp. 273–276
Rubric for Assessing a Writing Assignment, p. 286

Reading and Vocabulary Study Guide
L1 Chapter 22, Section 1, pp. 233–235

Spanish Support
L2 Section Quiz (Spanish), p. 233 ELL

Key

L1 Basic to Average   L3 Average to Advanced
L2 For All Students

LPR Less Proficient Readers
AR Advanced Readers
SN Special Needs Students

GT Gifted and Talented
ELL English Language Learners

Section 2 Southwest Asia: Cultures and History

 1.5 periods, .75 block (includes Skills for Life)

Social Studies Objectives
1. Find out that one of the world's earliest civilizations grew in Southwest Asia.
2. Understand that three of the world's great religions began in Southwest Asia.
3. Examine the different ethnic groups and religions of Southwest Asia.
4. Learn about the conflict between Arabs and Israelis in Southwest Asia.

Reading/Language Arts Objective
Learn to use suffixes and roots to help figure out the meanings of unfamiliar words.

Prepare to Read

Build Background Knowledge
Discuss what students know about the Middle East, or Southwest Asia.

Set a Purpose for Reading
Have students evaluate statements on the *Reading Readiness Guide*.

Preview Key Terms
Teach the section's Key Terms.

Target Reading Skill
Introduce the section's Target Reading Skill of **analyzing word parts**.

Instructional Resources

All in One Asia and the Pacific Teaching Resources
- L2 Reading Readiness Guide, p. 260
- L2 Use Roots and Suffixes, p. 268

Differentiated Instruction

Spanish Reading and Vocabulary Study Guide
- L1 Chapter 22, Section 2, pp. 167–168 ELL

Instruct

Mesopotamia
Discuss the location and achievements of Mesopotamia.

Birthplace of Three Religions
Discuss the three major religions of Southwest Asia.

Diverse Cultures in Southwest Asia
Discuss the major ethnic groups of Southwest Asia.

Southwest Asia: Recent History
Discuss the conflicts between the peoples of Southwest Asia.

Target Reading Skill
Review **analyzing word parts**.

Instructional Resources

All in One Asia and the Pacific Teaching Resources
- L2 Guided Reading and Review, p. 261
- L2 Reading Readiness Guide, p. 260
- L2 Preparing for Presentations, p. 283
- L2 Doing Searches on the Internet, p. 284

Asia and the Pacific Transparencies
- L2 Section Reading Support Transparency AP 60

World Studies Video Program
- L2 Istanbul, Aleppo, and Jerusalem: Crossroads of Trade

Differentiated Instruction

All in One Asia and the Pacific Teaching Resources
- L3 Reading a Circle Graph, p. 277 AR, GT
- L3 Moses and the Ten Commandments, p. 280 AR, GT
- L3 Enrichment, p. 271 AR, GT
- L2 Skills for Life, p. 272 AR, GT, LPR, SN

Asia and the Pacific Transparencies
- L1 Section Reading Support Transparency AP 60 ELL, LPR, SN
- L1 Transparency B15: Outline ELL, LPR, SN

Teacher's Edition
- L3 For Advanced Readers, TE pp. 671, 673, 674
- L1 For Special Needs Students, TE pp. 671, 673
- L1 For Less Proficient Readers, TE p. 674

Assess and Reteach

Assess Progress
Evaluate student comprehension with the section assessment and section quiz.

Reteach
Assign the Reading and Vocabulary Study Guide to help struggling students.

Extend
Extend the lesson by assigning a research project.

Instructional Resources

All in One Asia and the Pacific Teaching Resources
- L2 Section Quiz, p. 262
- L3 Writing a Cause-and-Effect Essay, p. 285
  Rubric for Assessing a Writing Assignment, p. 286

Reading and Vocabulary Study Guide
- L1 Chapter 22, Section 2, pp. 236–238

Differentiated Instruction

Spanish Support
- L2 Section Quiz (Spanish), p. 233 ELL

Teacher's Edition
- L3 For Gifted and Talented, TE p. 677

Social Studies Skills Tutor CD-ROM
- L1 Recognizing Bias ELL, LPR, SN

Key
- L1 Basic to Average
- L3 Average to Advanced
- L2 For All Students
- LPR Less Proficient Readers
- AR Advanced Readers
- SN Special Needs Students
- GT Gifted and Talented
- ELL English Language Learners

Section 3 Central Asia: Cultures and History

2 periods, 1 block (includes Chapter Review and Assessment)

Social Studies Objectives

1. Learn that many cultures and peoples influenced Central Asia in ancient times.
2. Discover how Central Asian nations became independent and why they are a focus of world interest.

Reading/Language Arts Objective

Recognize word origins to better understand the meanings of words.

Prepare to Read	Instructional Resources	Differentiated Instruction
Build Background Knowledge Discuss how location and geography influence culture. **Set a Purpose for Reading** Have students evaluate statements on the *Reading Readiness Guide*. **Preview Key Terms** Teach the section's Key Terms. **Target Reading Skill** Introduce the section's Target Reading Skill of **recognizing word origins**.	**All in One Asia and the Pacific Teaching Resources** L2 Reading Readiness Guide, p. 264 L2 Recognize Word Origins, p. 269	**Spanish Reading and Vocabulary Study Guide** L1 Chapter 22, Section 3, pp. 169–170 ELL

Instruct	Instructional Resources	Differentiated Instruction
Meeting Place of Empires Discuss trade, the Silk Road, and the effects of Soviet rule in Central Asia. **After Independence** Discuss the results of independence in Central Asia.	**All in One Asia and the Pacific Teaching Resources** L2 Guided Reading and Review, p. 265 L2 Reading Readiness Guide, p. 264 **Asia and the Pacific Transparencies** L2 Section Reading Support Transparency AP 61	**All in One Asia and the Pacific Teaching Resources** L1 Outline Map 27: Central and Southwest Asia: Physical, p. 278 ELL, LPR, SN **Teacher's Edition** L1 For Less Proficient Readers, TE p. 681

Assess and Reteach	Instructional Resources	Differentiated Instruction
Assess Progress Evaluate student comprehension with the section assessment and section quiz. **Reteach** Assign the Reading and Vocabulary Study Guide to help struggling students. **Extend** Extend the lesson by assigning an online activity. **Target Reading Skill** Review **recognizing word origins**.	**All in One Asia and the Pacific Teaching Resources** L2 Section Quiz, p. 266 Rubric for Assessing a Writing Assignment, p. 286 L2 Word Knowledge, p. 270 L2 Vocabulary Development, p. 281 L2 Chapter Tests A and B, pp. 287–292 **Reading and Vocabulary Study Guide** L1 Chapter 22, Section 3, pp. 239–241 **PHSchool.com** L3 **For:** Long-Term Integrated Projects: Mapping World Trade **Web Code:** lcd-6504	**Spanish Support** L2 Section Quiz (Spanish), p. 235 ELL L2 Chapter Summary (Spanish), p. 236 ELL L2 Vocabulary Development (Spanish), p. 237 ELL

Key

L1 Basic to Average   L3 Average to Advanced   LPR Less Proficient Readers   GT Gifted and Talented
L2 For All Students   AR Advanced Readers   ELL English Language Learners
                                                     SN Special Needs Students

Professional Development

Reading Background

Oral Cloze Reading

In this chapter, students will use the Oral Cloze Reading strategy. To make this strategy effective, preview the selection to determine which words you will be leaving out as you read. Do not drop very difficult words that most students do not know or cannot read. Prepositions and conjunctions may be avoided. Here is an example of words that might be dropped, using a sentence from page 669 of the Student Edition. Words to be dropped have been underlined:

Hammurabi's Code was <u>written</u> about 3,800 years ago in <u>Southwest Asia.</u> People have described its <u>laws</u> as demanding "an eye for an <u>eye</u>."

You may want to use this strategy with the text on the section opener page to engage students' interest. After you have read the first few paragraphs together using the Oral Cloze, have students go back and read the material silently.

Word Mapping

Mapping words is a way for students to create their own definitions for unfamiliar words. Word mapping provides students with a more well-rounded idea of a word rather than a one-sentence definition. Model word mapping using the high-use word *flourish* and a graphic organizer similar to the one below:

definition	*to grow; to thrive*
synonym/ antonym	*do well/wither*
example	*crops that flourish in rich soil*
sentence	*The city flourished due to its prosperity.*

Ask students to create word maps for other key terms or high-use words. Have students work in pairs to review each other's work and make any necessary corrections.

World Studies Background

The Civil Rights Movement

American civil rights leader Martin Luther King, Jr., was influenced by Mohandas Gandhi's methods of nonviolent resistance. Like Gandhi, King led a boycott to gain recognition of injustice and to force change. African Americans boycotted the Montgomery, Alabama, public bus service in 1955 and 1956 to protest laws that restricted them to certain seats on buses. The boycott was successful and led to new laws that eventually ended racial segregation in the South.

Jerusalem

A focal point in the ongoing struggle between Arabs and Israelis is the city of Jerusalem, holy to both Jews and Muslims. Jerusalem was the capital of an ancient Israeli kingdom and contains the Western Wall, the remains of the Second Temple of Jerusalem. For Muslims, the city is the site of the Dome of the Rock from which Muhammad is believed to have ascended to heaven. Because the Western Wall surrounds the Dome of the Rock, the two peoples have long fought over its control.

Silk

The process of silk-making, or sericulture, was developed in China around 3000 B.C., but long remained a carefully kept secret. By A.D. 200, however, silk had reached Persia, which became a major center of silk trade. The secrets of sericulture itself, however, did not make it to Europe until the A.D. 500s, when the Byzantine emperor Justinian I had two monks smuggle silkworms out of China.

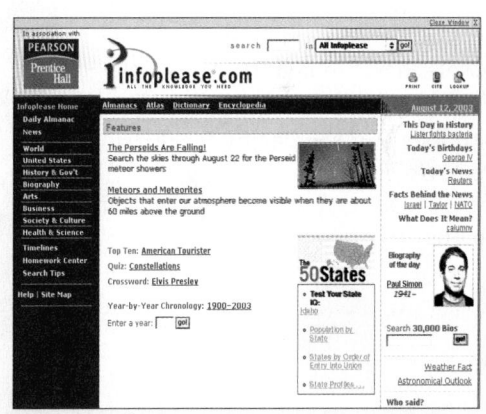

Infoplease® provides a wealth of useful information for the classroom. You can use this resource to strengthen your background on the subjects covered in this chapter. Have students visit this advertising-free site as a starting point for projects requiring research.

Use Web code lcd-6500 for **Infoplease®**.

Chapter 22

Guiding Questions

Remind students about the Guiding Questions introduced at the beginning of this section.

Section 1 relates to **Guiding Question ❷** **How have ancient civilizations of Asia and the Pacific influenced the world today?** *(The Indus Valley civilization, the Maurya empire, the Gupta empire, and the Mughal empire contributed to the mix of cultures in Central and South Asia today.)*

Section 2 relates to **Guiding Question ❸** **What are the main characteristics of the cultures of Asia and the Pacific today?** *(The various ethnic groups and religions of Southwest Asia combine to make a unique culture, though differences among groups have led to conflict between Arabs and Israelis.)*

Section 3 relates to **Guiding Question ❸** **What are the main characteristics of the cultures of Asia and the Pacific today?** *(Many newly independent nations of Central Asia are working to preserve their culture while learning to govern themselves.)*

⟳ Target Reading Skill

In this chapter, students will learn and apply the reading skill of word analysis. Use the following worksheets to help students practice this skill:

All in One Asia and the Pacific Teaching Resources, *Use Prefixes and Roots,* p. 267, *Use Roots and Suffixes,* p. 268, *Recognize Word Origins,* p. 269

Differentiated Instruction

The following Teacher Edition strategies are suitable for students of varying abilities.

Advanced Readers, pp. 671, 673, 674
English Language Learners, pp. 666, 667
Gifted and Talented, pp. 665, 666, 667, 677
Less Proficient Readers, pp. 665, 674, 681
Special Needs Students, pp. 671, 673

Chapter 22 — South, Southwest, and Central Asia: Cultures and History

Chapter Preview

In this chapter, you will learn about the cultures and history of three regions in Asia: South Asia, Southwest Asia, and Central Asia.

Section 1
South Asia
Cultures and History

Section 2
Southwest Asia
Cultures and History

Section 3
Central Asia
Cultures and History

⟳ Target Reading Skill

Word Analysis In this chapter, you will focus on analyzing words. For example, you will learn to break unfamiliar words into parts to understand the words.

▶ Amber Fort is one of the many forts and palaces of South Asia. It is located in India.

Bibliography

For the Teacher

Arnett, Robert. *India Unveiled.* Atman Press, 2002.
Harding, Paul and Simon Richmond. *Lonely Planet Istanbul to Katmandu: A Classic Overland Route.* Lonely Planet, 2001.
Nemet-Nejat, Karen Rhea. *Daily Life in Ancient Mesopotamia.* Hendrickson Publishers, Inc., 2002.

For the Student

L1 Chatterjee, Manini and Anita Roy. *Eyewitness: India.* DK Publishing, 2002.
L2 Ali, Daud et al. *Great Civilizations of the East.* Southwater Publishing, 2001.
L3 Nye, Naomi Shihab, ed. *The Space Between Our Footsteps: Poems and Paintings from the Middle East.* Simon & Schuster, 1998.

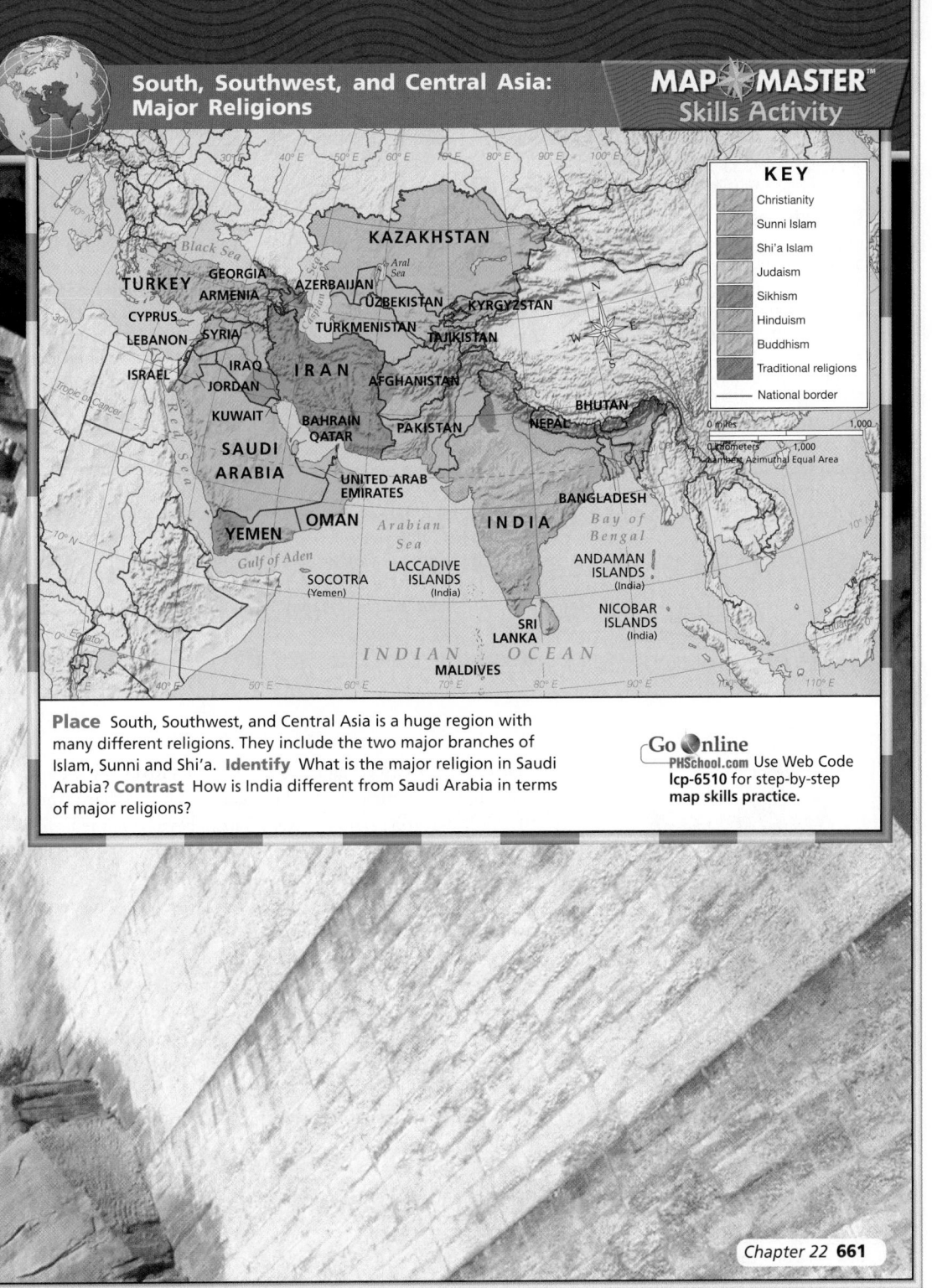

South, Southwest, and Central Asia: Major Religions

MAP☀MASTER™
Skills Activity

KEY
- Christianity
- Sunni Islam
- Shi'a Islam
- Judaism
- Sikhism
- Hinduism
- Buddhism
- Traditional religions
- ——— National border

Place South, Southwest, and Central Asia is a huge region with many different religions. They include the two major branches of Islam, Sunni and Shi'a. **Identify** What is the major religion in Saudi Arabia? **Contrast** How is India different from Saudi Arabia in terms of major religions?

Go Online PHSchool.com Use Web Code **lcp-6510** for step-by-step map skills practice.

Have students transfer the information on the map into another medium, such as a table. Suggest that they list each country in one column and the religions practiced there in another column.

Go Online PHSchool.com Students may practice their map skills using the interactive online version of this map.

Using the Visual   L2

Have students read the caption and study the photograph on pp. 660–661. Ask them why palaces and forts such as Amber Fort might be important in South Asia. Have students share their ideas.

Answers

MAP☀MASTER™ Skills Activity **Identify** Sunni Islam **Contrast** Hinduism is the major religion in India; Sunni Islam is the major religion in Saudi Arabia.

Chapter Resources

Teaching Resources
- L2 Vocabulary Development, p. 281
- L2 Skills for Life, p. 272
- L2 Chapter Tests A and B, pp. 287–292

Spanish Support
- L2 Spanish Chapter Summary, p. 236
- L2 Spanish Vocabulary Development, p. 237

Media and Technology
- L1 Student Edition on Audio CD
- L1 Guided Reading Audiotapes, English and Spanish
- L2 Social Studies Skills Tutor CD-ROM
- *ExamView Test Bank CD-ROM*

PRENTICE HALL Presentation EXPRESS™
Teach · Connect · Inspire

Teach this chapter's content using the PresentationExpress™ CD-ROM including:
- slide shows
- transparencies
- interactive maps and media
- *ExamView*® QuickTake Presenter

Section 1
Step-by-Step Instruction

Objectives

Social Studies
1. Find out which religions became part of South Asian cultures.
2. Understand which empires shaped the history of South Asia.
3. Learn about the present-day religions and languages of South Asian cultures.

Reading/Language Arts
Analyze word parts to determine the meanings and pronunciations of unfamiliar words.

Prepare to Read

Build Background Knowledge   L2
Tell students that in this section they will learn about the cultures and history of South Asia. Ask students to quickly preview the headings and visuals in the section, then ask them to predict a few things that they think might be important to the people of South Asia. Conduct an Idea Wave (TE, p. T35) to elicit students' responses.

Set a Purpose for Reading   L2
■ Preview the Objectives.

■ Form students into pairs or groups of four. Distribute the *Reading Readiness Guide*. Ask students to fill in the first two columns of the chart. Use the Numbered Heads participation strategy (TE, p. T36) to call on students to share one piece of information they already know and one piece of information they want to know.

All in One Asia and the Pacific Teaching Resources, *Reading Readiness Guide,* p. 256

Vocabulary Builder
Preview Key Terms   L2
Pronounce each Key Term, and then ask students to say the word with you. Provide a simple explanation such as, "The thirteen American colonies were originally ruled by Great Britain."

Section 1

South Asia
Cultures and History

Prepare to Read

Objectives
In this section, you will
1. Find out which religions became part of South Asian cultures.
2. Understand which empires shaped the history of South Asia.
3. Learn about the present-day religions and languages of South Asian cultures.

Taking Notes
As you read this section, look for main ideas about the history and cultures of South Asia. Copy the web below, and record your findings in it.

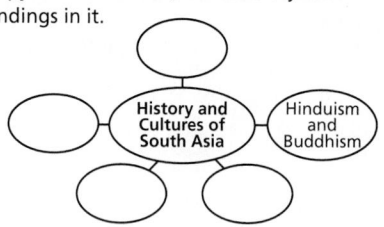

Target Reading Skill
Analyze Word Parts When you come across a word you do not know, break the word into parts to help you recognize it and pronounce it. This may help you find its root and prefix. A root is the part of the word that has meaning by itself. A prefix goes in front of the root and changes its meaning. In this section you will find the word *nonviolent*. Break it into a root and a prefix to learn its meaning.

Key Terms
- **caste** (kast) *n.* in the Hindu religion, a social group into which people are born and which they cannot change; each group with assigned jobs
- **colony** (KAHL uh nee) *n.* a territory ruled by another nation
- **boycott** (BOY kaht) *n.* a refusal to buy or use goods and services to show disapproval or bring about change
- **partition** (pahr TISH un) *n.* a division into parts or portions

In 1921, scientists digging near the Indus River came upon the ruins of an ancient city they called Mohenjo-Daro (moh HEN joh DAH roh). The city was amazingly well planned, with wide, straight streets and large buildings. It had a sewer system and a large walled fortress. Mohenjo-Daro was part of a civilization that developed about 4,500 years ago. The people who lived there were part of the Indus Valley civilization, one of the world's oldest civilizations.

Over the centuries, many other people moved into South Asia. All of them contributed to South Asian culture. South Asian culture, in turn, influenced cultures of other regions. Hinduism (HIN doo iz um) and Buddhism (BOO diz um), two religions that developed in South Asia, are practiced by hundreds of millions of people all over the world.

This ancient statue of a priest-king was unearthed at Mohenjo-Daro.

662 Asia and the Pacific

Target Reading Skill   L2

Analyze Word Parts Point out the Target Reading Skill. Tell students that studying the prefixes and roots of a word will help them better understand a word they already know or define an unfamiliar word.

Model analyzing word parts using the passage containing the word *nonviolent* on p. 667: "However, Gandhi stressed that they use nonviolent means." (*The prefix non-means "not" or "the opposite of," so nonviolent must mean not violent or peaceful.*)

Give students *Use Prefixes and Roots.* Have them complete the activity in groups.

All in One Asia and the Pacific Teaching Resources, *Use Prefixes and Roots,* p. 267

New Religions

The Indus Valley civilization flourished from about 2500 B.C. to about 1600 B.C. By 1500 B.C., however, the civilization was coming to an end. Scholars are uncertain why this happened.

About the same time that the Indus Valley civilization was weakening, newcomers came to the region, probably from Central Asia. They brought different languages and beliefs to the region. The newcomers merged with the people of the Indus Valley. A new culture combined the ancient languages and beliefs of the region with the language and religion of the newcomers. This mixed culture is known as Aryan culture. The people who practiced this culture are known as Aryans (AYR ee unz).

The Aryans ruled northern India for more than 1,000 years. They divided people into four classes—priests and the educated; rulers and warriors; farmers, artisans, and merchants; and laborers. Europeans later called the division the caste (kast) system. A **caste** is a social group into which people are born and which they cannot change.

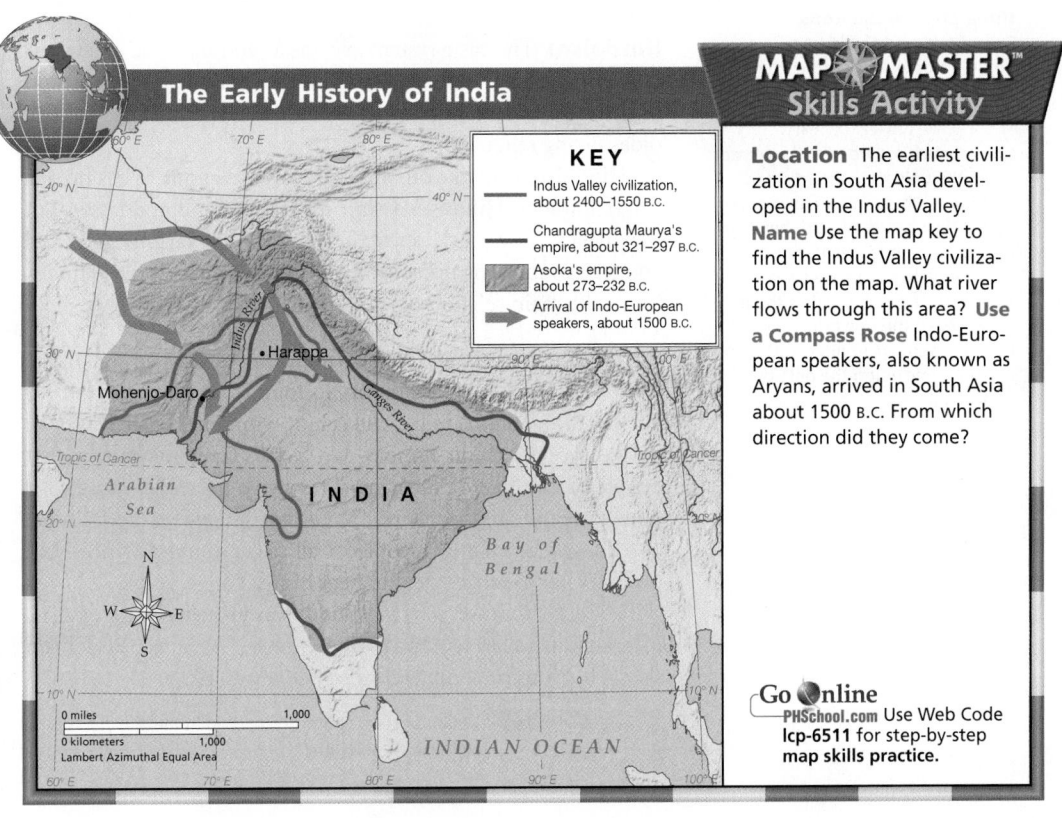

The Early History of India

MAP MASTER™
Skills Activity

KEY

—— Indus Valley civilization, about 2400–1550 B.C.

—— Chandragupta Maurya's empire, about 321–297 B.C.

▨ Asoka's empire, about 273–232 B.C.

➡ Arrival of Indo-European speakers, about 1500 B.C.

Location The earliest civilization in South Asia developed in the Indus Valley. **Name** Use the map key to find the Indus Valley civilization on the map. What river flows through this area? **Use a Compass Rose** Indo-European speakers, also known as Aryans, arrived in South Asia about 1500 B.C. From which direction did they come?

Go Online
PHSchool.com Use Web Code **lcp-6511** for step-by-step map skills practice.

Vocabulary Builder

Use the information below to teach students this section's high-use words.

High-Use Word	Definition and Sample Sentence
flourish, p. 663	*v.* to grow; to thrive Most plants cannot **flourish** without water and sunlight.
merge, p. 663	*v.* to combine or unite The two companies **merged** last June.
emerge, p. 664	*v.* to slowly grow out of or appear The stars **emerged** in the night sky.

New Religions L2

Guided Instruction

- **Vocabulary Builder** Clarify the high-use words **flourish, merge,** and **emerge** before reading.

- Read New Religions, using the Structured Silent Reading technique (TE, p. T34).

- Ask **When did the Indus Valley civilization flourish?** *(about 2500 B.C. to about 1600 B.C.)* **When did it decline?** *(1500 B.C.)*

- Ask **How did Aryan culture develop?** *(Aryan culture combined ancient languages and beliefs of the Indus Valley civilization with those of newcomers to the area from Central Asia.)*

Answers

MAP MASTER *Skills Activity* **Name** the Indus River **Use a Compass Rose** from the northwest

Go Online PHSchool.com Students may practice their map skills using the interactive online version of this map.

- Ask students **What two major religions developed in South Asia?** *(Hinduism and Buddhism)*

- Ask students to explain the significance of the caste system in Hinduism. *(A caste is a social group into which people are born and which cannot change. The caste system is a central idea in Hinduism.)*

- Ask students **Who was Siddhartha Gautama?** *(He was a prince born around 560 B.C. in what is now Nepal. He became known as the Buddha, or "Enlightened One," and founded the religion of Buddhism.)*

- Discuss the ideas of Buddhism with students. Ask them to brainstorm how wealth, power, and pleasure might cause suffering. *(Possible answer: Wealth, power, and pleasure may bring happiness, but can also cause anxiety about the possibility of losing these things.)*

Independent Practice

Have students create the Taking Notes graphic organizer on a blank piece of paper and label the ovals accordingly. Briefly model how to add more ovals to record information about Hinduism and Buddhism.

Monitor Progress

As students fill in the graphic organizer, circulate and make sure that individuals are choosing the correct details. Provide assistance as needed.

Answer

✓ **Reading Check** Hinduism is widely practiced in India today.

Three Main Hindu Gods
One of the world's oldest religions, Hinduism dates back more than 3,000 years. Shown here are the three main gods in the Hindu trinity

1. Brahma is regarded as the creator of the universe. According to Hindu writings, Brahma originally had five heads. His fifth head was destroyed by Shiva because Brahma had offended him.
2. Vishnu is worshipped as the preserver of the universe.
3. Shiva appears in many different forms, including the destroyer of the universe.

Hinduism The caste system became a central part of a new system of belief that also emerged from Aryan religious ideas and practices. This system of beliefs, Hinduism, is one of the world's oldest living religions.

Hinduism is unlike other major world religions. It has no one single founder. Hindus worship many gods and goddesses, but they believe in a single spirit. To Hindus, the various gods and goddesses represent different parts of this spirit. Today, Hinduism is the main religion of India.

Buddhism Buddhism, like Hinduism, developed in India. According to Buddhist tradition, its founder was a prince named Siddhartha Gautama (sih DAHR tuh GOW tuh muh). He was born in about 560 B.C., in present-day Nepal. Gautama taught that people can be free of suffering if they give up selfish desires for power, wealth, and pleasure. He became known as the Buddha, or "Enlightened One." People of all backgrounds, princes and ordinary people alike, went to hear his teachings.

Buddha's followers spread Buddhism to many parts of Asia. Although it spread to China, Tibet, Korea, and Japan, Buddhism slowly but almost completely died out in India.

✓ **Reading Check** Which ancient religion founded in India is a main religion there today?

664 Asia and the Pacific

Background: Global Perspectives

Buddhism The Buddhist religion is based on the Buddha's Four Noble Truths: that existence is suffering; that suffering is caused by a desire for pleasure; that the need for pleasure can be controlled; and that suffering can be eliminated by following a certain series of steps, known as the Eightfold Path. Buddhists believe that following this path leads to *nirvana*, or a blissful state of no desires, which brings an end to the cycle of *samsara*, or rebirth. The two main branches of Buddhism are Theravada and Mahayana. Another type, Vajrayana, or Tibetan Buddhism, has become popular in the West in recent years. Zen Buddhism is another important tradition, practiced in Japan; it is also popular in the West. Today there are over 350 million Buddhists worldwide.

From Empires to Nations

Today, South Asia is a region of independent countries. Starting in ancient times, however, a series of empires rose and fell in the region. Before South Asian countries became independent in the 1900s, the region was under European control.

The Maurya Empire Around 321 B.C., a leader named Chandragupta Maurya (chun druh GOOP tuh MOWR yuh) conquered many kingdoms. By the time of his death in 298 B.C., the Maurya Empire covered much of the Indian subcontinent.

Chandragupta's grandson, Asoka (uh SOH kuh), became emperor in 268 B.C. After one bloody battle, Asoka gave up war and violence. He changed his beliefs to Buddhism and vowed to rule peacefully. Asoka had stone pillars set up across India. Carved into the pillars were his laws and beliefs in fair and just government.

The Maurya Empire lost power not long after Asoka's death. By about 185 B.C. the empire collapsed as rival leaders fought for power.

The Gupta Empire About 500 years after the Mauryas, the Gupta Empire again united much of the Indian subcontinent. The Guptas ruled from A.D. 320 to about A.D. 550. Gupta emperors set up a strong central government that was supported by trade and farming.

Under Gupta rule, India enjoyed a period of great cultural achievement. Gupta mathematicians developed the system of writing numerals that we use today. These numerals are called "Arabic" numerals. Arabs carried them from India to Southwest Asia and Europe. People built splendid temples of stone decorated with carvings. Artists created wall paintings of Buddhist stories in temples built inside caves at Ajanta (uh JUN tuh) in western India.

Weak rulers and foreign invaders led to the fall of the Gupta Empire. The empire lasted until about A.D. 550.

The Mughal Empire In the A.D. 700s, people from the north began moving into northern India. They introduced the religion of Islam to the area. According to its followers, Islam is the set of beliefs revealed to the prophet Muhammad. He began teaching these beliefs around A.D. 610 in Southwest Asia. Islam eventually spread westward into North Africa and eastward into Central and South Asia.

This lion sculpture originally stood at the top of one of Asoka's pillars.

Links to Math

Decimal Numbers By about A.D. 600, Indian astronomers were using the decimal system—a numbering system based on tens. Their system also had place values and a zero. This made it easy to add, subtract, multiply, and divide. Europeans were using Roman numerals at this time. They later switched to this decimal, or Hindu-Arabic, system, which is used worldwide today.

From Empires to Nations

Guided Instruction

- Read about the groups who ruled the subcontinent and the eventual independence of the region in From Empires to Nations.

- Have students list the groups who ruled South Asia before the independence of India. (*Aryan; Maurya; Gupta; Mughal; British*)

- Ask students **How did the Maurya Empire change over time?** (*Both Chandragupta Maurya and his grandson Asoka conquered other kingdoms, but Asoka eventually became Buddhist and vowed to rule more peacefully.*)

- Ask **When did the Guptas rule?** (*from about A.D. 320 to about A.D. 550*) **How did the Gupta Empire contribute to the culture of South Asia?** (*The Guptas set up a strong empire and developed a system of numbers still used today; art and architecture flourished.*)

Links

Read the **Links to Math** on this page. Ask students to name one advantage of using the decimal system rather than Roman numerals. (*The decimal system makes it easier to add, subtract, multiply, and divide.*)

Differentiated Instruction

For Gifted and Talented [L3]
Select a quotation from the primary source *A Great Asian Thinker* and write it on the board. Tell students that the quotation is by Siddhartha Gautama. Discuss the meaning of the quotation with students.

All in One Asia and the Pacific Teaching Resources, *A Great Asian Thinker,* p. 279

For Less Proficient Readers [L1]
Have students create a simple timeline showing the order of groups who ruled South Asia—from the arrival of the Aryans, about 1500 B.C., to Indian independence in 1947. Show students the *Timeline Graphic Organizer* to help them.

Asia and the Pacific Transparencies, *Transparency B20: Timeline*

Guided Instruction (continued)

- Ask students **How did Mughal leaders contribute to the culture of South Asia?** *(Akbar allowed freedom of religion and supported the arts, and Shah Jahan built many striking buildings.)*

- Ask students **How did the British influence begin in South Asia?** *(Great Britain gained control through a trading company called the British East India Company.)*

- Discuss the role of Mohandas Gandhi in the Indian independence movement. Ask **How did Gandhi work to gain India's independence from Great Britain?** *(He urged people to use nonviolent methods in resisting the British, such as boycotts. His efforts played a large part in greatly influencing the British to give up their rule of India.)*

- Have students describe the history of the relationship between India and Pakistan. *(In 1947, the subcontinent was divided into Pakistan, a Muslim nation, and India, a Hindu nation. Fighting continued over Kashmir, and the area is still unstable today.)*

Independent Practice

Have students continue to work on their graphic organizers by labeling additional ovals and recording details on the history and cultures of South Asia.

Monitor Progress

As students fill in the graphic organizer, circulate to make sure individuals are choosing appropriate labels and details. Provide assistance as needed.

Target Reading Skill L2

Analyze Word Parts As a follow up, ask students to perform the Target Reading Skill task in the Student Edition. *(The prefix sub- in this instance mean "lesser than" or "a piece of." A continent is a very large landmass—there are seven continents on Earth. So a subcontinent is a landmass that is smaller than a continent, but still very large.)*

Answer

Analyze Images The left side of the building is exactly the same as the right side; each side has the same number and style of towers and windows.

Asia and the Pacific

The Taj Mahal, India
The Taj Mahal is considered to be one of the world's most beautiful buildings. Emperor Shah Jahan had it built as a tomb for his wife. The small photo shows the actual tomb inside the marble structure. **Analyze Images** *How does the large photo show symmetry in the design of the Taj Mahal?*

Analyze Word Parts Look for the word *subcontinent* in this paragraph. The prefix *sub-* means "under." Now define the word *subcontinent.*

Asia and the Pacific

Among these Muslims, or followers of Islam, who settled in India were the Mughals (MOO gulz). They arrived in the 1500s and established an empire. Akbar (AK bahr), who ruled the Mughal Empire from 1556 to 1605, allowed all people to worship freely, regardless of their religion. He also generously supported the arts and literature.

Akbar's grandson, Shah Jahan (shah juh HAHN), built many grand buildings. Perhaps the greatest is the Taj Mahal (tahzh muh HAHL), which still stands today. He had it built as a magnificent tomb for Mumtaz Mahal (mum TAHZ muh HAHL), his wife. The cost of this and other of Jahan's building projects was enormous. It drained the empire of money and, eventually, helped to cause the empire's collapse in the 1700s.

The British in India By the late 1700s, much of the Indian subcontinent had come under British rule. Until 1858, a trading company known as the British East India Company controlled most of India. The British government ended the rule of the British East India Company in 1858. From that time until 1947, India was controlled by Britain as a colony of Britain's empire. A **colony** is a territory ruled by another nation.

Differentiated Instruction

For Gifted and Talented L3
Tell students that the Mauryan leader Asoka erected huge pillars with inscriptions urging people to treat one another justly and humanely. His guiding principles were honesty, mercifulness, consideration, and respect. Have students write their own inscriptions based on Asoka's principles.

For English Language Learners L1
Have students read the section as they listen to the recorded version on the Student Edition on Audio CD. Check for comprehension by pausing the CD and asking students to share their answers to the Reading Checks.

Chapter 22, Section 1, **Student Edition on Audio CD**

Asia and the Pacific

Independence and Division In the early 1900s, a strong independence movement emerged in India. Its leader was Mohandas K. Gandhi (GAHN dee). Gandhi called for people to resist British rule. However, Gandhi stressed that they use nonviolent means. For example, he urged a boycott of British goods. A **boycott** means a refusal to buy or use goods and services to show disapproval or bring about change. Gandhi played a major part in forcing Britain to grant India its independence in 1947.

As independence approached, Muslims feared that their rights would not be protected in a land where Hindus were the majority. Fighting erupted as demands arose for a state where Muslims would be the majority. In 1947 this led to the **partition**, or division, of the subcontinent into two nations, Pakistan and India. Muslims would be the majority in Pakistan. Hindus would be the majority in India.

This partition did not stop the fighting. About one million people were killed. Gandhi himself was murdered by a Hindu who was angered at Gandhi's concern for Muslims.

Conflict in South Asia Conflict between India and Pakistan continued throughout the 1900s. In 1971, Indian troops helped East Pakistan break away from Pakistan to form the nation of Bangladesh (BAHNG luh desh). Pakistan and India have fought over the question of which country controls Kashmir (KASH mihr), an area on the border of India and Pakistan. In 1998, both nations tested nuclear weapons. The continuing threat of conflict that might involve nuclear weapons in the region concerns the United States and other countries.

✓ Reading Check **What are some contributions from the Maurya, Gupta, and Mughal empires?**

Indian Independence leader Mohandas Gandhi

Republic Day in India
Every January 26, Indians celebrate Republic Day to mark the adoption of the Indian constitution on January 26, 1950.
Infer *Which national flag do you think is shown in the photo?*

Chapter 22 Section 1 **667**

South Asian Cultures Today L2

Guided Instruction

- With students, read about some aspects of modern cultures in South Asia in South Asian Cultures Today.

- Ask students **What religions are practiced in South Asia?** *(Hinduism, Islam, Christianity, Sikhism, Jainism)*

- Ask students **Where are Dravidian languages spoken?** *(in southern India)* **Where are Indo-European languages spoken?** *(in northern India and the rest of South Asia)* **What is an example of an Indo-European language in India?** *(Hindi)*

- Ask students **Why do you think English is widely used in India?** *(Students may suggest the fact that the British colonized India and brought the English language to all parts of the country.)*

Independent Practice
Have students complete their graphic organizers by adding details about culture in South Asia today.

Monitor Progress

- Show *Section Reading Support Transparency AP 59* and ask students to check their graphic organizers individually. Go over key concepts and clarify key vocabulary as needed.

  Asia and the Pacific Transparencies, *Section Reading Support Transparency AP 59*

- Tell students to fill in the last column of the *Reading Readiness Guide*. Ask them to evaluate if what they learned was what they had expected to learn.

  All in One Asia and the Pacific Teaching Resources, *Reading Readiness Guide,* p. 256

Answers

✓ Reading Check Maurya: conquered territory and spread Buddhist ideas; Gupta: set up a strong central government, brought about advances in mathematics and architecture; Mughal: introduced Islam and allowed religious freedom.

Infer India's national flag

Assess and Reteach

Assess Progress `L2`

Have students complete the Section Assessment. Administer the *Section Quiz.*

All in One **Asia and the Pacific Teaching Resources,** *Section Quiz,* p. 258

Reteach `L1`

If students need more instruction, have them read this section in the Reading and Vocabulary Study Guide.

📖 Chapter 22, Section 1, **Eastern Hemisphere Reading and Vocabulary Study Guide,** pp. 233–235

Extend `L3`

To extend the lesson, assign students *Small Group Activity: Reporting on Hinduism and Buddhism.* Give groups time to discuss each other's finished reports.

All in One **Asia and the Pacific Teaching Resources,** *Small Group Activity: Reporting on Hinduism and Buddhism,* pp. 273–276

Answer

✓ **Reading Check** India and Nepal

Section 1 Assessment

Key Terms

Students' sentences should reflect an understanding of each Key Term.

 Target Reading Skill
Uncertain means "not sure."

Comprehension and Critical Thinking

1. **(a)** Aryans **(b)** Hinduism

2. **(a)** the Mughal Empire **(b)** Muslims were a minority in the newly independent India and were afraid that their rights would not be protected.

3. **(a)** Islam **(b)** People bring their language with them to a new land. Their words mingle with the native language, or their language may take over and become the primary language.

668 *Asia and the Pacific*

Selling spices at an open-air market in India

South Asian Cultures Today

South Asia's long history continues to shape its cultures. Two major examples are religion and languages.

Many Religions Hinduism and Islam are the major religions of South Asia today. About 80 percent of the people in India are Hindus. Hinduism is also the major religion in Nepal. Islam is the main religion in Pakistan and Bangladesh. Other religions in South Asia include Christianity, Sikhism (SEEK iz um), and Jainism (JY niz um). Sikhism began as a religion that combined Hindu and Muslim beliefs. Followers of Jainism believe that violence toward or injury of any living thing is wrong.

Many Languages Many different languages are spoken in South Asia. The languages of South Asia generally belong to two families. Dravidian (druh VID ee un) languages are spoken in southern India. Indo-European languages are spoken in northern India and most of the rest of South Asia. The Aryans who came into South Asia in ancient times spoke Indo-European languages. One of the languages in this group is Hindi (HIN dee). About 30 percent of the people in India speak Hindi. Hindi is one of 15 languages recognized by the Indian government. English is also widely used as an official language in India.

✓ **Reading Check** **In which two South Asian countries is Hinduism the major religion?**

 **Section 1 Assessment**

Key Terms
Review the key terms at the beginning of this section. Use each term in a sentence that explains its meaning.

🔄 **Target Reading Skill**
Find the word *uncertain* on page 663 in the first paragraph under the heading New Religions. The prefix *un-* means "not." What is the meaning of *uncertain*?

Comprehension and Critical Thinking
1. **(a) Recall** Which group of people developed the caste system?
(b) Sequence Which developed first, Hinduism or Buddhism?
2. **(a) Name** Which empire introduced Islam to South Asia?
(b) Identify Effect What major issues led to the partition of India in 1947?
3. **(a) Identify** What is the main religion in Pakistan?
(b) Make Generalizations How can the movement of people from one place to another affect language in a region?

Writing Activity
Suppose you are traveling throughout South Asia. Write a letter to your family in which you describe ways in which the history of the region is shown in its present-day culture.

Writing Tip Your letter should begin with a greeting and end with a closing and a signature. The body of the letter contains the information you want to communicate to your reader.

668 Asia and the Pacific

Writing Activity

Use the *Rubric for Assessing a Writing Assignment* to evaluate students' letters.

All in One **Asia and the Pacific Teaching Resources,** *Rubric for Assessing a Writing Assignment,* p. 286

Section 2
Southwest Asia
Cultures and History

Prepare to Read

Objectives
In this section, you will
1. Find out that one of the world's earliest civilizations grew in Southwest Asia.
2. Understand that three of the world's great religions began in Southwest Asia.
3. Examine the different ethnic groups and religions of Southwest Asia.
4. Learn about the conflict between Arabs and Israelis in Southwest Asia.

Taking Notes
As you read this section, look for details about the three main religions that developed in Southwest Asia. Copy the chart below, and record your findings in it.

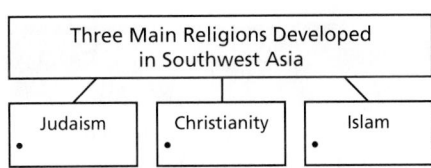

Three Main Religions Developed in Southwest Asia
- Judaism
- Christianity
- Islam

Target Reading Skill

Analyze Word Parts
Breaking an unfamiliar word into parts can help you understand the word. Word parts include roots and suffixes. A root is the base of a word that has meaning by itself. A suffix comes at the end of a root word. Suffixes change the meanings of root words. In this section you will read the word *creation*. The suffix *-ion* makes the word a noun. If you know what *create* means, you can figure out the meaning of *creation*.

Key Terms
- **monotheism** (MAHN oh thee iz um) *n.* a belief that there is only one god
- **muezzin** (myoo EZ in) *n.* a person whose job is to call Muslims to pray
- **Holocaust** (HAHL uh kawst) *n.* the systematic killing of more than six million European Jews and others by Nazi Germany before and during World War II

Hammurabi's Code was written about 3,800 years ago in Southwest Asia. People have described its laws as demanding "an eye for an eye." But there was more to the code than that.

> **If the robber is not caught, the man who has been robbed shall formally declare whatever he has lost . . . and the city and the mayor . . . shall replace whatever he has lost for him. . . . If a person is too lazy to make the dike of his field strong and there is a break in the dike and water destroys his own farmland, that person will make good the grain [tax] that is destroyed.**
> —from Hammurabi's Code

The law punished people severely for wrongdoings. But it also offered justice to people who had been hurt through no fault of their own.

In this ancient carving, Hammurabi receives his code of laws from the sun god.

Chapter 22 Section 2 **669**

Objectives

Social Studies
1. Find out that one of the world's earliest civilizations grew in Southwest Asia.
2. Understand that three of the world's great religions began in Southwest Asia.
3. Examine the different ethnic groups and religions of Southwest Asia.
4. Learn about the conflict between Arabs and Israelis in Southwest Asia.

Reading/Language Arts
Learn to use suffixes and roots to help figure out the meanings of unfamiliar words.

Prepare to Read

Build Background Knowledge L2
Tell students that in this section they will learn about the cultures and history of Southwest Asia. Draw a concept web on the board. In the center oval write "Southwest Asia." Explain to students that this area is often referred to as part of the Middle East. Ask students what they know or have heard on the news about the area. Use the Give One, Get One participation strategy (TE, p. T37) to elicit ideas to add to the web.

Set a Purpose for Reading L2
- Preview the Objectives.
- Distribute the worksheet and read each statement in the *Reading Readiness Guide* aloud. Ask students to mark the statements true or false.

  All in One Asia and the Pacific Teaching Resources, *Reading Readiness Guide*, p. 260

- Have students discuss the statements in pairs or groups of four, then mark their worksheets again. Use the Numbered Heads strategy (TE, p. 36) to call on students to share their group's perspectives.

Vocabulary Builder
Preview Key Terms L2
Pronounce each Key Term, and then ask students to say the word with you. Provide a simple explanation such as, "Judaism is a monotheistic religion."

Target Reading Skill L2

Analyze Word Parts Point out the Target Reading Skill. Tell students that being able to break up a word and study its parts—for example, its root and suffix—will help them to figure out the meaning of an unfamiliar word or better understand a word they already know.

Model analyzing word parts using the word *percentage* in the last paragraph on p. 673. The prefix *per-* means "for every" or

"apiece," and the root word *cent* comes from the Latin *centum*, meaning "one hundred." The suffix *-age* means "result of." So a *percentage* is the result of taking a part of one hundred, or a part of a whole.

Give students *Use Roots and Suffixes*. Have them complete the activity in groups.

All in One Asia and the Pacific Teaching Resources, *Use Roots and Suffixes*, p. 268

Instruct

Mesopotamia L2

Guided Instruction

- **Vocabulary Builder** Clarify the high-use word **surplus** before reading.

- Read Mesopotamia using the Oral Cloze reading strategy (TE, p.T33).

Show students *Istanbul, Aleppo, and Jerusalem: Crossroads of Trade.* Then have them write a summary explaining how the locations of the cities covered in the video have made them important centers of trade over time.

- Ask students **Where was Mesopotamia located?** *(in present-day Iraq, between the Tigris and Euphrates rivers)* **What were some of its achievements?** *(People in Mesopotamia developed writing and laws.)*

- Ask students **How did people of this region produce a surplus of crops?** *(They dug irrigation ditches to bring water to fields far from rivers.)*

Independent Practice

Assign *Guided Reading and Review.*

All in One Asia and the Pacific Teaching Resources, *Guided Reading and Review,* p. 261

Monitoring Progress

Circulate to make sure individuals are filling in the worksheet correctly. Provide assistance as needed.

Answers

✓ Reading Check Iraq

MAP MASTER Skills Activity **Locate** They both run through Mesopotamia to the Persian Gulf. **Draw Conclusions** the Syrian Desert, because there is little water there for farming or drinking

Go Online PHSchool.com Students may practice their map skills using the interactive online version of this map.

Mesopotamia

Hammurabi ruled the city of Babylon from about 1800 B.C. to 1750 B.C. He united the region along the Tigris and Euphrates rivers. Located in present-day Iraq, this region was called Mesopotamia, which is derived from Greek words meaning "between the rivers." Mesopotamia was one of the world's earliest civilizations.

The people of Mesopotamia developed a system of writing. They also produced ideas about law that still affect people today. For example, they believed that all citizens must obey the same set of laws.

People had lived in Mesopotamia for thousands of years before Hammurabi united it. By 3500 B.C., the area became a center of farming and trade. The Tigris and Euphrates rivers flooded every year, leaving fertile soil along their banks. People dug irrigation ditches to bring water to fields that lay far from the river. Irrigation helped them to produce crop surpluses, or more than they needed for their own use.

Explore the history of trade in Southwest Asia.

✓ Reading Check In what present-day country did Mesopotamia develop?

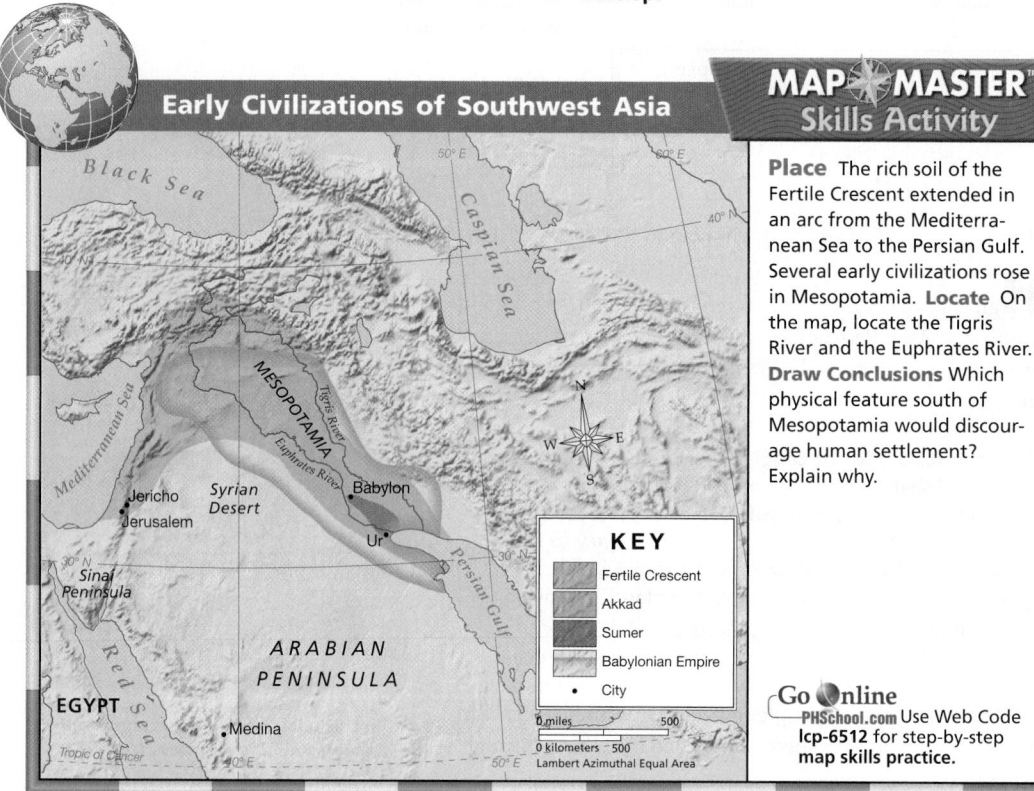

Early Civilizations of Southwest Asia

MAP MASTER Skills Activity

Place The rich soil of the Fertile Crescent extended in an arc from the Mediterranean Sea to the Persian Gulf. Several early civilizations rose in Mesopotamia. **Locate** On the map, locate the Tigris River and the Euphrates River. **Draw Conclusions** Which physical feature south of Mesopotamia would discourage human settlement? Explain why.

KEY
- Fertile Crescent
- Akkad
- Sumer
- Babylonian Empire
- • City

Go Online PHSchool.com Use Web Code lcp-6512 for step-by-step map skills practice.

670 Asia and the Pacific

Vocabulary Builder

Use the information below to teach stuents this section's high-use words.

High-Use Word	Definition and Sample Sentence
surplus, p. 670	*n.* an extra amount All the party guests took home some of the **surplus** food.
sacred, p. 672	*adj.* holy; highly valued Most religions include **sacred** festivals or holidays.
majority, p. 673	*n.* the larger number or part of something; more than half The **majority** of the class voted for Elaine for treasurer.
refugee, p. 674	*n.* person forced to flee to another country The organization raises money to help **refugees.**

Guided Instruction

- **Vocabulary Builder** Clarify the high-use word **sacred** before reading.

- With students, read about the development of three major world religions in Birthplace of Three Religions.

- Ask students to list the three major religions that originated in Southwest Asia and their founders. *(Judaism—Abraham, Christianity—Jesus, Islam—Muhammad)*

- Discuss with students the similarities among Judaism, Christianity, and Islam. Encourage students to share information that they may know from their own lives or other sources. *(Possible answers: All were founded in Southwest Asia; all practice monotheism.)*

Birthplace of Three Religions

Three of the world's greatest religions—Judaism, Christianity, and Islam—have their roots in Southwest Asia. About 2000 B.C., according to Hebrew religious writings, a man later known as Abraham founded the religion that would become known as Judaism. He lived in present-day Israel. Almost 2,000 years later, Jesus, the founder of Christianity, began preaching in present-day Israel. In about A.D. 600, Islam's founder and prophet, Muhammad, began teaching in present-day Saudi Arabia.

People who practice these three religions share a belief in monotheism. **Monotheism** is a belief in only one god. The followers of these religions also worship the same God—known as Allah in Islam.

Islam Of the three religions, Islam has by far the most followers in Southwest Asia today. They are called Muslims. The sights and sounds of Islam are everywhere in Southwest Asia. One sound is the call of the **muezzin** (myoo EZ in), a person whose job is to call Muslims to pray. Five times a day, Muslims stop what they are doing and pray. In large cities, the call to prayer is broadcast over loudspeakers. Throughout Southwest Asia, as well as other regions in the world, Muslims gather to worship in buildings called mosques. One of the most famous is the Dome of the Rock, shown in the photo on this page.

Jerusalem, A Holy City
Jerusalem is holy to Jews, Christians, and Muslims because events important to their religions took place there. The golden-domed building is the Dome of the Rock. It stands over the rock from which Muslims believe the prophet Muhammad rose into heaven. **Infer** *Why might Muslims from around the world want to visit Jerusalem?*

Differentiated Instruction

For Advanced Readers L3
Have students research and create a circle graph showing the number of followers of the world religions they have learned about in this chapter. Have them complete *Reading a Circle Graph* to familiarize themselves with the format.

  All in One **Asia and the Pacific Teaching Resources,** *Reading a Circle Graph*, p. 277

For Special Needs Students L1
Show students *Section Reading Support Transparency AP 60* before they read the section. Then have them identify and check off each item in the flow chart as they read.

  Asia and the Pacific Transparencies, *Section Reading Support Transparency AP 60*

Independent Practice

Have students create the Taking Notes graphic organizer on a blank piece of paper. Then have students fill in the chart with information they have just learned. Briefly model labeling the chart and recording details.

Monitor Progress

As students fill in the graphic organizer, circulate and make sure that individuals are choosing the correct details. Provide assistance as needed. When students are finished with their flow charts, show *Section Reading Support Transparency AP 60* and ask students to check their work. Go over key concepts and clarify key vocabulary as needed.

Asia and the Pacific Transparencies, *Section Reading Support Transparency AP 60*

Diverse Cultures in Southwest Asia L2

Guided Instruction

- **Vocabulary Builder** Clarify the high-use word **majority** before reading.

- With students, learn about the mixture of peoples in the region in Diverse Cultures in Southwest Asia.

- Ask students **How has the location of Southwest Asia affected its culture?** *(Southwest Asia was at the center of trading routes that stretched across Europe, Africa, and Asia over 3,000 years ago. Because of these routes and various conquering groups, people of many different ethnic groups and religions settled there. This has resulted in the unique mix of people in Southwest Asia today.)*

- Ask students **What is the main ethnic group in Southwest Asia today?** *(Arab)* **Where do most non-Arab people live?** *(Israel, Turkey, and Iran)* **What are the largest ethnic groups in each of these countries?** *(Israel—Jewish, Turkey—Turkish, Iran—Persian)*

Answer

✓ Reading Check All three religions were founded in that region.

These women are praying at the Western Wall, held sacred by Jews as the remains of the Second Temple.

The New Testament of the Christian Bible describes Jesus as a good shepherd who lays down his life for his sheep.

Judaism At the heart of Judaism is the Torah (TOH ruh), five books that make up the Jews' most sacred text. According to the Torah, about 2000 B.C. Abraham, a Mesopotamian man, became convinced that there was one god, not many. He migrated to Canaan, where he became the ancestor of the Jewish people. Canaan was an area of land located along the eastern shore of the Mediterranean Sea. Hundreds of years later, it became known as Palestine. From ancient times, Jews saw Palestine as their homeland. The Torah also contains the Ten Commandments. They established religious duties toward God as well as rules for moral and ethical behavior.

Christianity Christianity first developed around A.D. 30. The religion is based on the teachings of Jesus, a Jew who traveled throughout Palestine. Christians later adopted the Torah as the first five books of the Old Testament of the Christian Bible. The first four books of the New Testament of the Christian Bible are the Gospels. They tell about the life and teachings of Jesus. According to the Gospels, Jesus taught that his followers would have eternal life. Like Islam and Judaism, Christianity began in Southwest Asia and spread throughout the world.

✓ Reading Check Why is Southwest Asia considered the birthplace of Judaism, Christianity, and Islam?

672 Asia and the Pacific

Background: Links Across Time

The Hanging Gardens of Babylon The famous Hanging Gardens of Babylon were considered one of the seven wonders of the ancient world. Built in what today is Iraq, the gardens are usually attributed to King Nebuchadnezzar II, who ruled Babylon in the sixth century B.C. No certain physical evidence of the garden has survived, but writers of the time described the gardens in detail. Laid out on a series of large terraces built one on top of the other, the gardens stood on the roof of Babylon's royal palace. They included tropical flowers and paths lined with palm trees, and were irrigated by pumps from the Euphrates River. The king is said to have built them for his wife Amytis, who missed the mountains and trees found in her homeland. From the shaded rooftop, the king and queen could look out over their city.

Diverse Cultures in Southwest Asia

More than 3,000 years ago, the land of Southwest Asia was at the center of trading routes that extended across Europe, Africa, and Asia. Time after time, groups from within and outside the region conquered it. The movement of people across Southwest Asia gave the region a unique character. People of many different ethnic groups and religious beliefs settled there.

Arabic-speaking Arabs are the largest ethnic group in the region, and Islam is their main religion. But not all Southwest Asians are Arabs. Many Southwest Asians do not speak Arabic and many people, including Arabic-speaking Arabs, practice religions other than Islam.

A Mix of Ethnic Groups The people in Southwest Asia belong to a mix of ethnic groups. Today, Arabs are the main ethnic group in Saudi Arabia, Jordan, Syria, Iraq, Lebanon, and other countries on the Arabian Peninsula. Arabs also live in territories occupied by Israel. Non-Arab people live mainly in Israel, Turkey, and Iran. In Israel, about 80 percent of the population is Jewish. The remaining 20 percent is mostly Arab. In Turkey, about 80 percent of the population is Turkish. The rest of Turkey's population is Kurdish. Kurdish people also live in communities in Syria, Iraq, and Iran. In Iran, about 50 percent of the people are Persian. The rest belong to a number of different ethnic groups.

A Variety of Religions Except for Israel, the majority of the people in each country in Southwest Asia are Muslim. Even within the Islamic religion, however, there are differences. Muslims are divided into two main groups—Sunnis (SOO neez) and Shi'as (SHEE uz). Today, about 90 percent of Muslims are Sunni. Most of the Muslims in both Iran and Iraq, however, are Shi'as.

In Israel, about 80 percent of the people are Jewish. Muslims make up about 20 percent of the population. A small percentage of people in Israel are Christian. Christians also live in Syria, Turkey, Lebanon, and Iraq.

✔ **Reading Check** To which branch of Islam do most Muslims belong?

About half of Iran's population is Persian.

Differentiated Instruction

For Special Needs Students L1
Suggest that students use a ruler to help them keep their place as they read, line to line, down a page. Have students mark unfamiliar words or ideas with a sticky note, and periodically help them understand what they have marked.

For Advanced Readers L3
Tell students that Moses is a figure who is important to several different religions practiced in Southwest Asia. Assign students *Moses and the Ten Commandments*.

All in One Asia and the Pacific Teaching Resources, *Moses and the Ten Commandments,* p. 280

Guided Instruction (continued)

■ Ask students **What is the main religion practiced in Southwest Asia today?** *(Islam)* **What are the two main groups of Muslims?** *(Sunni and Shi'a)*

■ **What percentage of people in Israel are Jewish?** *(about 80 percent)* **What percentage are Muslims?** *(about 20 percent)*

■ Ask students to discuss the possible benefits and challenges of having a mix of ethnic groups and religions in Southwest Asia. *(Benefits—the people of Southwest Asia are exposed to languages, cultures, and religions other than their own. Challenges—groups who speak different languages have trouble communicating with each other; differences among groups can cause serious conflicts.)*

Independent Practice
Divide the class into groups and assign each an ethnic group mentioned in Diverse Cultures in Southwest Asia. Have them do library or Internet research on the ethnic group's history and traditions, then present the information to the rest of the class. Have them use *Preparing for Presentations* to help them organize their information.

All in One Asia and the Pacific Teaching Resources, *Preparing for Presentations,* p. 283

Monitor Progress
Circulate while students are preparing for their presentations, making sure individuals are contributing and are using reliable sources for their information. Provide assistance as needed.

Answer
✔ **Reading Check** Sunni

Southwest Asia: Recent History

L2

Guided Instruction

- **Vocabulary Builder** Clarify the high-use word **refugee** before reading.

- Read Southwest Asia: Recent History.

- Ask students **Why do Israelis and Arabs both claim land in Palestine?** (*Palestine is important in Jewish and Arab history.*)

- Ask students **Why do you think many Jews migrated to Palestine after World War II?** (*Possible answer: After the killing of millions of Jews in Europe during World War II, Jews may have felt that migrating to Palestine would protect them from further persecution.*)

- Ask students **What efforts were made toward peace in the 1990s and in 2003?** (*In 1993, the Israeli and Palestinian governments formally recognized each other; in 2003, Israeli and PLO leaders agreed to a new peace plan.*)

- Have students draw a conclusion about why the United States wanted to set up a democratic government in Iraq after the fall of Saddam. (*Possible answer: Americans believed that a democratic government in Iraq would be more peaceful and less likely to build dangerous weapons.*)

Independent Practice

Have each student summarize two current articles on the conflict over Palestine in newspapers or on the Internet. Give students *Doing Searches on the Internet* to help them with their research.

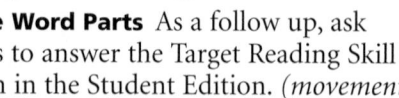 **Asia and the Pacific Teaching Resources**, *Doing Searches on the Internet*, p. 284

Monitor Progress

Tell students to fill in the last column of their *Reading Readiness Guides*.

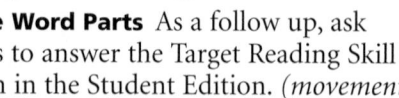 **Asia and the Pacific Teaching Resources**, *Reading Readiness Guide*, p. 260

Target Reading Skill

L2

Analyze Word Parts As a follow up, ask students to answer the Target Reading Skill question in the Student Edition. (*movement from one place to another*)

Answer

Infer People who have friends from other cultures may be more likely to be willing to compromise and try to avoid conflicts.

Scenes of Hope
A Jewish boy and a Palestinian boy walk together in Israel (left). Israeli troops supervise the evacuation of Jewish residents from the Gaza Strip in 2005 (right). **Infer** *Why might friendship and compromise help solve conflict?*

 **Analyze Word Parts**
If *migrate* means "move from one country or place to another," what is a *migration*?

Southwest Asia: Recent History

Differences among various groups of people have led to conflict in Southwest Asia. As you have read, Judaism has ancient roots in Palestine. Over many years, a few Jews continued to live in Palestine. But most had been forced in ancient times to migrate to other parts of the world. In the late 1800s, Jews from around the world began to return to their homeland. This alarmed the Arabs who lived there. For hundreds of years, they had claimed Palestine as their homeland, too.

The Formation of Israel Before and during World War II, Nazi Germany killed more than six million Jews in Europe solely because they were Jewish. This became known as the **Holocaust**. After the war, many of those who had survived decided to migrate to Palestine. On May 14, 1948, Jews declared the formation of their own state, Israel. Their state was recognized by the United Nations.

Arab-Israeli Conflict The day after the state of Israel was declared, the Arab nations of Egypt, Iraq, Jordan, Lebanon, and Syria invaded Israel. These nations supported the Palestinians. Israel drove away the Arab forces. Hundreds of thousands of Palestinians fled from Jewish territory. They lived as refugees in other Arab nations or in territories under Israeli rule. Even larger numbers of Jews were forced to leave Arab countries, and most resettled in Israel. Since 1948, Israel and the Arab nations that border it have fought a number of bloody wars.

674 Asia and the Pacific

Differentiated Instruction

For Advanced Readers
L3

Have students complete the *Enrichment* activity about the Dead Sea. Encourage students to illustrate their stories. When the stories are complete, bind them together into a classroom book of Dead Sea Tales. If possible, display the book at the library for other classes to see.

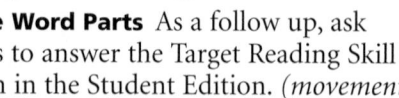 **Asia and the Pacific Teaching Resources**, *Enrichment*, p. 271

For Less Proficient Readers
L1

Have students create an outline of the chapter as they read using the headings as a guide. To help them organize their outlines, show students the *Outline Transparency*.

📖 **Asia and the Pacific Transparencies**, *Transparency B15: Outline*

Efforts Toward Peace In 1993, Israel and the Palestinian government—known as the Palestine Liberation Organization (PLO)—formally recognized each other. In 2000, fighting broke out between Israel and the Palestinians once again. In 2003, Israeli leaders and the PLO agreed on a new peace plan, which called for the co-existence of Israel and a democratic Palestine. In 2005, Israel withdrew its settlements from the Gaza Strip. Due to renewed fighting in the area, however, future progress is uncertain.

War With Iraq After Iraq's defeat in the 1991 Persian Gulf War, Iraqi leader Saddam Hussein (suh DAHM hoo SAYN) refused to cooperate with United Nations inspectors sent to ensure that Iraq destroyed its most dangerous weapons. In March 2003, U.S. forces attacked Iraq in an invasion supported by Great Britain and several other nations. Three weeks after the start of the war, Saddam fell from power. He was captured by U.S. troops in December 2003. Although Iraq remains unstable, it successfully held democratic national elections and approved a constitution in 2005.

Iraqis line up to vote for new leaders in the city of Suleimaniya in 2005.

✓ **Reading Check** Give one example of conflict in Southwest Asia.

Section 2 Assessment

Key Terms
Review the key terms at the beginning of this section. Use each term in a sentence that explains its meaning.

Target Reading Skill
Define *irrigation*. The root word means "to supply with water by artificial methods." The suffix *–ion* means "act or process."

Comprehension and Critical Thinking
1. (a) Identify Tell where Mesopotamia is located.
(b) Summarize What are two achievements of the civilizations of Mesopotamia?

2. (a) List What three major religions grew in Southwest Asia?
(b) Contrast What do all three religions have in common?
3. (a) Name What is Southwest Asia's main ethnic group today?
(b) Analyze Information Give one example of ethnic or religious diversity in the region of Southwest Asia.
4. (a) Name What area do both Palestinians and Israelis claim as a homeland?
(b) Summarize How has Iraq moved toward establishing a democratic form of government?

Writing Activity
Write a paragraph that begins with this topic sentence: *Southwest Asia is a region with different ethnic groups and religious beliefs.* Include supporting details about at least three countries in the region.

> **Writing Tip** Include at least two sentences about ethnic groups and at least two sentences about religions. Be sure to include supporting details.

Assess Progress L2
Have students complete the Section Assessment. Administer the *Section Quiz*.

📘 **Asia and the Pacific Teaching Resources,** *Section Quiz,* p. 262

Reteach L1
If students need more instruction, have them read this section in the Reading and Vocabulary Study Guide.

📖 Chapter 22, Section 2, **Eastern Hemisphere Reading and Vocabulary Study Guide,** pp. 236–238

Extend L3
To extend the lesson, have students do research and write a report on the events leading to the creation of the state of Israel in the period after World War II. Distribute *Writing a Cause-and-Effect Essay* to help students with their reports.

📘 **Asia and the Pacific Teaching Resources,** *Writing a Cause-and-Effect Essay,* p. 285

Answers

✓ **Reading Check** Possible response: Hundreds of thousands of Palestinians were forced to live as refugees in other nations. Even larger numbers of Jews were forced to leave Arab countries. The United States attacked Iraq because of the actions of its leader Saddam Hussein.

Writing Activity
Use the *Rubric for Assessing a Writing Assignment* to evaluate students' paragraphs.

📘 **Asia and the Pacific Teaching Resources,** *Rubric for Assessing a Writing Assignment,* p. 286

Section 2 Assessment

Key Terms
Students' sentences should reflect an understanding of each Key Term.

Target Reading Skill
the act of supplying water

Comprehension and Critical Thinking
1. (a) in present-day Iraq between the Tigris and Euphrates rivers **(b)** Possible answers: a system of writing, ideas about law, and an irrigation system
2. (a) Judaism, Christianity, Islam **(b)** They are monotheistic.
3. (a) Arab **(b)** Possible answers: In Iran, 50 percent of the people are Persian, and the other 50 percent belong to other ethnic groups. Kurdish people live in Turkey, Syria, Iraq, and Iran. In Israel, about 80 percent of the population are Jewish, while about 20 percent are Muslims.
4. (a) Palestine **(b)** After the U.S. capture of Saddam Hussein in December 2003, Iraq has successfully held democratic national elections and also approved a constitution in 2005.

Objective
Learn how to recognize bias.

Prepare to Read

Build Background Knowledge L2
Have students read the examples of bias in the introduction. Using these examples, have students discuss how bias can cause problems. Conduct an Idea Wave (TE, p. T35) to share individuals' ideas with the class.

Instruct

Recognizing Bias L2

Guided Instruction
- Read the steps to recognize bias as a class and write them on the board.

- Practice the skill by following the steps on p. 676 as a class. Model each step using the activity on p. 677. Students should refer to the report on the left as, "Report 1" and the one on the right as "Report 2." Have students identify which report contains opinion words. (*Report 2 uses the word "should."*) Next have students analyze loaded phrases. (*"Greedy American tourists" in Report 2 is a loaded phrase because it describes all American travelers as having one trait and cannot be proved with evidence; Report 2 also uses the phrase "buying everything in sight," which is probably an exaggeration.*) Then have students look for facts. (*Report 1 includes the facts that there were "150 American tourists," that "the group arrived at 7 a.m. just as the sellers opened for business," and that "four tourists bumped into a display and knocked it over.)* Identify positive or negative point of view. (*Report 2 presents a negative point of view about American tourists*), and finally ask students to decide which report shows bias (*Report 2 is biased against American tourists because it describes them as greedy, lazy, impatient, and rude.*)

 **Recognizing Bias**

A baseball coach chooses his own son over other, better players, to play in a tournament game. The mayor hires her friends to fill important city jobs instead of seeking the most qualified people. The politician who wants to give business to family members says his son-in-law is the best builder to build a new school.

All these situations are examples of bias. Bias is an attitude that favors one way of feeling or acting over any other. Bias prevents someone from making a fair judgment based on facts and reason. Biased speech or writing often contains opinions stated as facts.

Learn the Skill
Knowing how to recognize bias is an important skill you will need in school and in life. To identify bias in what you read, follow the steps below.

1. **Look for opinions.** Opinions are beliefs that cannot be proved. Biased statements often appear to be facts but are actually opinions.

2. **Look for loaded words and phrases and exaggerations.** Loaded words and phrases cannot be proved. They are intended to produce a strong emotional response. To exaggerate means to enlarge a fact or statement beyond what is actual or true.

3. **Look for missing facts.** Biased speech often leaves out facts that do not support the author's bias.

4. **Determine whether the text presents only one point of view.** Writing that is biased presents only one point of view about an issue or a topic. The point of view may be positive or negative.

5. **Determine whether the text contains bias.** Review the text and draw a conclusion about it.

676 Asia and the Pacific

Independent Practice
Assign *Skills for Life* and have students complete it individually.

All in One **Asia and the Pacific Teaching Resources,** *Skills for Life,* p. 272

Monitor Progress
As students are completing *Skills for Life,* circulate to make sure individuals are applying the skill steps effectively. Provide assistance as needed.

Traveling Through Turkey by Bus

A group of 150 American tourists spent a busy morning at a market in Istanbul, Turkey, arriving at 7 AM just as sellers opened for business.

The Americans were visiting Istanbul on a tour to study the cultures of Turkey. The tourists spent about an hour shopping at the market.

"We usually don't get such a large group so early in the morning," one shop owner commented.

The tourists arrived so early that some shop owners had not yet opened for business. In a narrow section of the market, four tourists bumped into a display and knocked it over. The visitors stopped to help the shop owner fix the display.

The next stop for the Americans' cultural tour will be Turkey's capital, Ankara. The group is traveling through Turkey by bus.

Greedy Tourists Mob Market

A crowd of greedy American tourists invaded a market in the city of Istanbul, Turkey, buying everything in sight.

In a burst of energy rarely seen from Americans who prefer to drive everywhere instead of walk, the bargain-hunters swarmed out of tour buses to examine the products on display. Shop owners were overwhelmed as the impatient Americans roamed through the market.

One group of tourists overturned tables in their quest for bargains.

Americans should use better manners when they shop in other countries instead of barging into stores and being rude.

The next stop for the mob of American tourists is Turkey's capital city, Ankara.

A market in Istanbul, Turkey

Practice the Skill

Read the two reports above. Then use the steps on the previous page to determine which report shows bias.

1 Opinions often contain words such as *I believe* and *should*. Which report contains an opinion?

2 Look for loaded words or phrases and exaggerations in the reports. How is the phrase "greedy American tourists" an example of a loaded phrase? Which report contains the phrase "buying everything in sight"? Is this a factual statement or an exaggeration?

3 Which report includes facts, such as the number of tourists and the time of day?

4 Which report presents a point of view about American tourists? Is the point of view negative or positive?

5 Based on your review, which report shows bias? State the bias in a complete sentence.

Apply the Skill
Find an article about Turkey in the news, either in a newspaper or a magazine. Use the steps shown here to decide whether the article contains bias. Explain your reasoning.

Assess and Reteach

Assess Progress   L2
Ask students to do the Apply the Skill Activity.

Reteach   L1
If students are having trouble applying the skill steps, have them review the skill using the interactive Social Studies Skills Tutor CD-ROM.

◉ *Recognizing Bias,* **Social Studies Skills Tutor CD-ROM**

Extend   L3
Provide students with a copy of the "Letters to the Editor" section of a newspaper or magazine. Have students choose one letter and apply the skill steps to it, making sure to look for loaded words and phrases and for missing facts. Then ask students to write a paragraph summarizing the letter, explaining if the letter is biased or not, and if so, recommending what steps could be taken to make the letter more fair.

Answer
Apply the Skill
Answers will vary, but should show that students understand and are able to apply the skill steps. Students should first look for opinions, loaded words and phrases, and exaggerations. They should then check for any missing facts, determine whether the text presents only one point of view, and review the text and their observations to decide whether or not the article is biased.

Objectives

Social Studies

1. Learn that many cultures and peoples influenced Central Asia in ancient times.
2. Discover how Central Asian nations became independent and why they are a focus of world interest.

Reading/Language Arts

Recognize word origins to better understand the meanings of words.

Prepare to Read

Build Background Knowledge L2

Tell students that in this section they will learn about the cultures and history of Central Asia. Tell students the location and geography of Central Asia made it an important area for trade and influenced the culture found there today. Ask students to think how location and geography influence the culture where they live. Use the Think-Write-Pair-Share participation strategy (TE, p. T36) to elicit responses.

Set a Purpose for Reading L2

- Preview the Objectives.

- Distribute the worksheet and read each statement aloud in the *Reading Readiness Guide*. Ask students to mark the statements true or false.

   All in One **Asia and the Pacific Teaching Resources,** *Reading Readiness Guide,* p. 264

- Have students discuss the statements in pairs or groups of four, then mark their worksheets again. Use the Numbered Heads participation strategy (TE, p. T36) to call on students to share their group's perspectives.

Vocabulary Builder
Preview Key Terms L2

Pronounce the Key Term, and then ask students to say the word with you. Provide a simple explanation such as, "A collective farm is controlled by the government."

Prepare to Read

Objectives

In this section, you will

1. Learn that many cultures and peoples influenced Central Asia in ancient times.
2. Discover how Central Asian nations became independent and why they are a focus of world interest.

Taking Notes

As you read this section, look for details about the topics listed in the outline below. Copy and continue the outline and record your details in it.

> I. Meeting Place of Empires
>   A. Early history
>   1. _____
>   2. _____
>   B. The Silk Road
>   1. _____
>   2. _____

🎯 Target Reading Skill

Recognize Word Origins A word's origin is where the word comes from. The word *government* contains the root word *govern*, which comes from the Latin word *gubernare*, meaning "to steer." The suffix *-ment* means "act or process." Knowing a word's origin can better help you understand the word's meaning. How is government related to the process of "steering" a country?

Key Term

- **collective farm**
  (kuh LEK tiv farhm) *n.*
  in a Communist country, a large farm formed from many private farms collected into a single unit controlled by the government

678 Asia and the Pacific

American fighter planes prepare for takeoff at an airbase in Central Asia. They are part of a new U.S. military force in the region. American soldiers came to fight a war in Afghanistan in 2001. Now they are based in several Central Asian countries.

American troops are not the only foreign visitors in Central Asia these days. Russian soldiers are also there. Political leaders from various countries are making official visits. Investors and business leaders are arriving too. They are coming from the United States, Russia, China, France, Turkey, and other countries. All these foreign visitors reflect Central Asia's growing international importance. The new countries of Central Asia are becoming the focus of world attention.

A growing film industry is one example of change in Central Asia.

🎯 Target Reading Skill L2

Recognize Word Origins Point out the Target Reading Skill. Tell students that knowing where a word comes from can help them to better understand its meaning and the meanings of related words.

Model recognizing word origins using the word *inventions* on p. 679. Tell students that the root of the word, *invent*, comes from the Latin word *invenire*, which means "to come

upon or to find." The suffix *-ion* means "an act or a process" or "the result of an act or process." So an *invention* is the result of a discovery.

Give students *Recognize Word Origins*. Have them complete the activity in groups.

   All in One **Asia and the Pacific Teaching Resources,** *Recognize Word Origins,* p. 269

Samarkand, Uzbekistan
A Silk Road caravan is the subject of a sculpture near the Registan, an ancient square in Samarkand. Samarkand was a major city along the Silk Road, an ancient trade route crossing Central Asia that linked China and Europe.
Apply Information *Based on what you know about Central Asia's location, how can you be certain the Silk Road was a land route?*

Meeting Place of Empires

Long ago, Central Asia was a meeting place for ancient cultures and peoples. Located between East Asia and Europe, Central Asia was a crossroads for trade caravans and conquering armies. Over time, dozens of ethnic groups settled there. Each group brought new ideas and ways of living.

The Silk Road More than 2,000 years ago, a trade route called the Silk Road linked China and Europe. The Silk Road brought Central Asia into contact with East Asia, Southwest Asia, and Europe. For hundreds of years, caravans brought Chinese silk and Asian spices to the West. They carried items such as glass, wool, gold, and silver to the East. Along with goods, the traders exchanged ideas and inventions. Cities like Samarkand (sam ur KAND), in present-day Uzbekistan (ooz BEK ih stan), grew up at oases along the route and became wealthy centers of trade and learning.

Invasion and Conquest The Silk Road generated wealth, but it also attracted invaders. Waves of conquerors fought to control Central Asia. Although some ruled for hundreds of years, each group was eventually replaced by new invaders.

Each conqueror left a mark on the region. For example, about A.D. 700, a Muslim empire spread across large stretches of Central Asia. The Muslims had the greatest impact on the culture of the region. Many of the people of Central Asia adopted Islam. Today, most people in this region are Muslims.

Links Across The World

Lands for Empires In the 1200s, much of Central Asia was part of the largest land empire the world has ever known. Genghis Khan (GEN gis kahn), a leader of the Mongols, united his nomadic people into a strong fighting force. He conquered much of China and then swept west over Central Asia. At his death in 1227, his empire extended from the Sea of Japan to the Caspian Sea.

Chapter 22 Section 3 **679**

Vocabulary Builder

Use the information below to teach students this section's high-use words.

High-Use Word	Definition and Sample Sentence
decline, p. 680	*n.* period when something is coming to an end The club's membership is in **decline.**
nomadic, p. 680	*adj.* having no fixed home; wandering **Nomadic** groups often move according to the seasons.
refer, p. 681	*v.* to call or direct attention Are you **referring** to the new restaurant on Main Street?
native, p. 681	*n.* a person who was born in a particular place or country He is a **native** of Italy.

Guided Instruction (continued)

- Ask **Why did the Silk Road decline?** (*Sea routes developed that were faster and easier than the land route.*)

- Ask students **How did Russia affect Central Asia between 1865 and the early 1920s?** (*Russia captured the city of Tashkent, Uzbekistan, in 1865 and built railroads, factories, and farms in the area. Some Russians moved to the region, bringing their way of life with them.*)

- Ask students **What were some effects of Soviet rule in Central Asia?** (*Communist rule forced many people to give up their traditional ways of life and work on collective farms. The farms did not always produce enough food, and a large number of people starved. The Soviets made religion illegal and destroyed mosques.*)

- Have students summarize the Soviet conflict with Afghanistan. (*In 1979, the Soviet Union invaded Afghanistan and clashed with Afghan forces for the next ten years. The Soviets withdrew in 1989, but warfare continued as Afghans struggled against each other for power.*)

Independent Practice

Have students create the Taking Notes graphic organizer on a blank sheet of paper. Students should then fill in the outline with details they learn as they read. Briefly model the activity by filling in the first item under "A. Early history" with details such as, "Heavy trading area; Silk Road."

Monitor Progress

As students fill in the outline, circulate to make sure that individuals are choosing appropriate details.

Answer

Compare and Contrast Similar—at an outdoor market, there are probably a variety of vendors and products, much like an American shopping mall; some Americans may shop at outdoor flea markets or tag sales; Different—most Americans shop at indoor stores.

Ashgabat's Sunday Market
Ashgabat is the capital and largest city of Turkmenistan. Its Sunday market attracts thousands of people. Here, a family displays the traditional dark red carpets of Turkmenistan.
Compare and Contrast *How is shopping at an outdoor market similar to and different from the way most Americans shop?*

By the late 1200s, the rise of sea trade led to the decline of the Silk Road. Ships began carrying goods between China and the seaports of Europe. These sea routes were faster and easier than the overland routes across Asia. As a result, trade declined in Central Asia. This, however, did not stop foreign powers from trying to control the region.

Under Russian Rule In the 1800s, both Russia and Britain tried to expand their empires into Central Asia. Russia was more successful. One of the most important cities Russia captured was the city of Tashkent, Uzbekistan, in 1865.

Russia built railroads, factories, and large farms in Central Asia. Some Russians moved into the region, bringing new ways of life. But most people continued to live as they always had. They practiced Islam and lived as nomadic herders.

The Soviet Union In 1922, Russian Communists formed the Soviet Union. The Soviets extended Communist control over a vast area of Central Asia. They divided the region into five separate states, which they called republics. They also forced people to stop living as nomads and give up their traditional way of life. People had to work on **collective farms**, large farms controlled by the government. The Communist government formed collectives by taking over smaller private farms and livestock herds and combining them into larger units. Soviet collectives did not always produce enough food for people to eat. At least one million Central Asians starved to death during the 1930s.

680 Asia and the Pacific

 **Skills Mini Lesson**

Supporting a Position   L2

1. Point out to students that to persuade people to agree with your opinion on an issue, you must state your position and the reasons why you hold that position, provide evidence to support each reason, and anticipate opposing arguments.

2. Help students practice the skill by supporting the following position: Soviet rule in Central Asia had negative effects on the region. Write students' responses on the board. (*Have students reference the text on Student Edition pp. 680–682.*)

3. Have students work in pairs to support opposing positions on this statement: Central Asia benefited from the breakup of the Soviet Union in 1991.

While the Soviets built new industries, schools, and hospitals in Central Asia, they allowed people few freedoms. The Soviets outlawed the practice of religion and tried to stamp out Muslim culture. Many mosques—places of Islamic worship—were torn down in the mid-1900s.

War in Afghanistan In 1979, the Soviets tried to extend their control over Central Asia by invading Afghanistan. Afghan forces fought the Soviets, and the Afghan fighters called themselves mujahedin (moo jah heh DEEN), or Islamic holy warriors. In ten years of warfare, the Soviet army never defeated the Afghan forces. In 1989, the Soviets finally gave up and withdrew their troops.

War continued, however, as the Afghans fought each other for power. Eventually, in the mid 1990s, a group known as the Taliban took control of most of the country. The brutal regime collapsed in 2001 after a U.S.-led military invasion. Hamid Karzai was elected president of Afghanistan in a 2004 democratic election. Members of the National Assembly were elected the following year.

✓ Reading Check **What impact did Soviet rule have on Central Asia?**

After Independence

The Soviet defeat in Afghanistan helped bring an end to Soviet power. In 1991, the Soviet Union broke up. The five Soviet republics of Central Asia became independent nations.

The New States After independence, each of these countries adopted a name that reflected its main ethnic group. The suffix *-stan* is a Persian term that means "place of, or land." So, for example, Kazakhstan means "place of the Kazakhs," or "Kazakh land." Together with Afghanistan, these countries are sometimes referred to as "the Stans."

The new countries are different in many ways. The largest country, Kazakhstan, is mostly flat and has important natural resources, such as oil and natural gas. The smallest country, Tajikistan, is mountainous and very poor. Nevertheless, the countries have many things in common, including Islamic culture. They also face many of the same challenges as they work to develop their economies.

A woman in Kyrgyzstan plays a traditional stringed instrument.

Chapter 22 Section 3 **681**

After Independence L2

Guided Instruction

- **Vocabulary Builder** Clarify the high-use word **refer** before reading.

- With students, read about the changes that occurred after the break-up of the Soviet Union in After Independence.

- Ask students **How did the former Soviet territories in Central Asia change after the Soviet Union broke up?** *(After independence, these countries had to learn how to govern themselves, and many adopted new names that reflected their main ethnic group. They began to develop natural resources, restore their religious practices, and use their native languages.)*

- Ask students **What do the new countries have in common?** *(They share Islamic culture, and many are struggling to establish new governments and stable economies.)*

Independent Practice

Have students continue their outlines by adding "II. After Independence," and adding details using the first part of the outline as a model.

Monitor Progress

- Show *Section Reading Support Transparency AP 61* and ask students to check their work individually. Go over key concepts and clarify key vocabulary as needed. Discuss students' answers for the additional section of their outlines.

  Asia and the Pacific Transparencies, Section Reading Support Transparency AP 61

- Tell students to fill in the last column of their *Reading Readiness Guides*. Probe for what they learned that confirms or invalidates each statement.

  All in One *Asia and the Pacific Teaching Resources, Reading Readiness Guide, p. 264*

Differentiated Instruction

For Less Proficient Readers L1
Have students use *Outline Map 27* to make a map showing which areas of Central Asia were a part of the Soviet Union before it broke up. Have students outline the borders of the Soviet Union in one color and the borders of the newly independent nations in another color, then create a key explaining what the colors represent.

All in One **Asia and the Pacific Teaching Resources,** *Outline Map 27: Central and Southwest Asia: Physical, p. 278*

Answer

✓ Reading Check Under Soviet rule many people starved. Religion was outlawed and mosques were destroyed. The Soviets built new industries, schools, and hospitals.

Assess and Reteach

Assess Progress
L2

Have students complete the Section Assessment. Administer the *Section Quiz.*

All in One **Asia and the Pacific Teaching Resources,** *Section Quiz,* p. 266

Reteach
L1

If students need more instruction, have them read this section in the Reading and Vocabulary Study Guide.

📖 Chapter 22, Section 3, **Eastern Hemisphere Reading and Vocabulary Study Guide,** pp. 239–241

Extend
L3

Assign students the *Long-Term Integrated Project: Mapping World Trade.* Have students focus the project on countries in South, Southwest, and Central Asia.

Go Online
PHSchool.com **For:** Long-Term Integrated Projects: *Mapping World Trade*
Visit: PHSchool.com
Web Code: lcd-6504

🎯 Target Reading Skill
L2

Recognize Word Origins As a follow up, have students answer the Target Reading Skill question on this page of the Student Edition. *(The words have different suffixes, but have related meanings. A* government *is the group of people in charge of managing a country, and* governing *means ruling a country.)*

Answer

✓ Reading Check "place of" or "land"

Section 3 Assessment

Key Terms

Each student's sentence should reflect an understanding of the Key Term.

🎯 Target Reading Skill

A *benefit* is "something good that comes from or out of something."

Comprehension and Critical Thinking

1. (a) between East Asia and Europe
(b) Possible answer: People were forced to give up their nomadic way of life and live and work on collective farms.

Children at their desks at a school in Kyrgyzstan

 **Recognize Word Origins**
Find the word *governing* in the first sentence of this paragraph. Compare this word to the word *government.* What is the same? What is different?

Challenges and Opportunities Since independence, the new countries of Central Asia have learned to start governing themselves. Most are weighed down by weak economies. Many people do not have jobs. Health care and education are poor and hard to get.

However, all the countries of Central Asia now proudly celebrate their culture and Islam. Mosques that had fallen into ruin are being rebuilt. The people of Central Asia are teaching their children about their religion. Other benefits of independence include the right to use native languages in schools, literature, and the daily news media.

✓ Reading Check **What does the suffix** *-stan* **mean in the names of the Central Asian countries?**

🧭 Section 3 Assessment

Key Terms
Review the key terms at the beginning of this section. Use each term in a sentence that explains its meaning.

🎯 Target Reading Skill
You read about the benefits of independence in Central Asia in this section. The Latin root word *bene* means "good or well." What do you think *benefit* means?

Comprehension and Critical Thinking
1. (a) Recall Where is Central Asia located?

(b) Identify Effects Describe one way that Soviet rule affected Central Asia.
2. (a) Explain How did the Central Asian republics under Soviet control gain their independence?
(b) Identify Central Issues How has Central Asia changed since becoming independent from the former Soviet Union?
(c) Make Generalizations Central Asian countries are now in charge of their own governments. You read that the root word of *governing* means "to steer." How is governing a country related to the idea of steering?

Writing Activity
The countries of Central Asia have many tasks to accomplish as they organize their nations. Using the information in this section, write a list of the challenges facing Central Asian countries. Write a brief explanation of why you think each challenge is an important one to tackle.

For: An activity about Central Asia
Visit: PHSchool.com
Web Code: lcd-6503

---

2. (a) The Soviet Union broke up, releasing them from Soviet rule. **(b)** The new countries renamed themselves, learned to govern themselves, and are rebuilding and modernizing their societies and economies. **(c)** People who govern a country direct it, or steer it in a certain direction.

Writing Activity

Use the *Rubric for Assessing a Writing Assignment* to evaluate students' work.

All in One **Asia and the Pacific Teaching Resources,** *Rubric for Assessing a Writing Assignment,* p. 286

Go Online
PHSchool.com Typing in the Web code when prompted will bring students directly to detailed instructions for this activity.

22 Review and Assessment

Chapter 22

Review and Assessment

Review Chapter Content

- Review and revisit the major themes of this chapter by asking students to identify what Guiding Question each bulleted statement in the Chapter Summary answers. Form students into groups and ask them to complete the activity together. Refer to p. 567 in the Student Edition for text of Guiding Questions.

- Assign *Vocabulary Development* for students to review Key Terms.

All in One Asia and the Pacific Teaching **Resources,** *Vocabulary Development,* p. 281

◆ Chapter Summary

Section 1: South Asia Cultures and History

- Two ancient religions, Hinduism and Buddhism, developed in India. Hinduism is a major religion in South Asia today.
- During its long history, South Asia has been shaped by Indian empires and British rule.
- South Asia's religions and languages have been affected by the region's history.

Ancient Indian sculpture

Section 3: Central Asia Cultures and History

- A crossroads between East Asia and Europe, Central Asia was influenced by many cultures and peoples in ancient times.
- After decades of Soviet rule, independent nations emerged in Central Asia and are working to govern themselves.

Samarkand, Uzbekistan

Section 2: Southwest Asia Cultures and History

- One of the world's earliest civilizations grew in Southwest Asia.
- Three of the world's greatest religions have their roots in Southwest Asia.
- People of many different ethnic groups and religious beliefs settled in Southwest Asia.
- Differences among various people, especially over land claims, have led to conflict and struggle in Southwest Asia.

◆ Key Terms

Each of the statements below contains a key term from the chapter. If the statement is true, write *true*. If the statement is false, rewrite the statement to make it true.

1. According to Hinduism, a caste is a social group into which people are born and which they cannot change.

2. A boycott is a refusal to buy or use goods and services to show disapproval or bring about social or political change.

3. A colony is an independent nation that has its own government.

4. Monotheism is the belief that there is only one god.

5. A muezzin is a person whose job is to call Muslims to prayer.

6. More than six million Jews and others died in the Holocaust.

7. A collective farm is owned and operated by one farmer.

Chapter 22 **683**

┌ Vocabulary Builder ─────

Revisit this chapter's high-use words.

flourish	sacred	nomadic
merge	majority	refer
emerge	refugee	native
surplus	decline	

Ask students to review the definitions they recorded on the *Word Knowledge* worksheets.

All in One Asia and the Pacific Teaching **Resources,** *Word Knowledge,* p. 270

Consider allowing students to earn extra credit if they use the words in their answers to the questions in the Chapter Review and Assessment. The words must be used correctly and in a natural context to win extra points.

Answers

Key Terms

1. True

2. True

3. False. A colony is an area that is ruled by another country.

4. True

5. True

6. True

7. False. A collective farm is controlled by a government.

Review and Assessment

Comprehension and Critical Thinking

8. (a) an ancient city of the Indus Valley civilization **(b)** around 1500 B.C. **(c)** Hinduism

9. (a) Siddhartha Gautama, the Buddha **(b)** Buddhism had a huge following in India for a time after the Buddha's death, and his followers also spread the religion to China, Tibet, Korea, and Japan. However, Buddhism slowly died out in India.

10. (a) Asoka was a Mauryan who became emperor around 268 B.C. **(b)** He changed from being a violent conqueror to a peaceful ruler.

11. (a) Gupta Empire **(b)** Mughal Empire **(c)** The Guptas were Buddhists, and the Mughals were Muslims.

12. (a) Mohandas Gandhi **(b)** India was a mostly Hindu country and the Muslim minority was afraid that their rights would not be respected after independence.

13. (a) Hinduism and Islam **(b)** Christianity, Jainism, and Sikhism

14. (a) Islam **(b)** Judaism

15. (a) Arab **(b)** Possible answer: In Israel, the majority of the people are Jews, but 20 percent are Muslims, and a small number of people are Christians.

Skills Practice

Answers will vary, but students' sentences should accurately explain what bias is.

Writing Activity: Language Arts

Students' paragraphs should indicate that they researched each word in the activity and should give the Arabic roots. The paragraphs should also offer some conclusion about the contributions of the Arabic language to English. Use the *Rubric for Assessing a Writing Assignment* to evaluate students' paragraphs.

All in One Asia and the Pacific Teaching Resources, *Rubric for Assessing a Writing Assignment,* p. 286

Review and Assessment (continued)

◆ Comprehension and Critical Thinking

8. (a) Identify Identify Mohenjo-Daro. **(b) Sequence** When did Aryans first come to South Asia? **(c) Identify Effects** What new religion grew out of Aryan beliefs and practices?

9. (a) Recall Who is considered the founder of the religion Buddhism? **(b) Summarize** Describe the spread of Buddhism after its founder's death.

10. (a) Identify Who was Asoka? **(b) Identify Effects** How did Buddhist beliefs affect Asoka?

11. (a) Name Under which empire did India experience a period of great cultural achievement? **(b) Sequence** Which empire followed that one? **(c) Contrast** How were these two empires different in terms of religious beliefs?

12. (a) Recall Who played a major part in forcing Britain to grant independence to India? **(b) Analyze** Why was India's independence followed by heavy fighting between Hindu and Muslim groups?

13. (a) Recall What are the two main religions in South Asia today?

(b) Apply Information What are other religions in South Asia?

14. (a) Identify Of the three religions founded in Southwest Asia, which has the most followers there today? **(b) Sequence** Of the three religions founded in Southwest Asia, which is the oldest?

15. (a) Name What is the largest ethnic group in Southwest Asia today? **(b) Synthesize Information** Give an example showing that Southwest Asia is a region of many different ethnic groups and religious beliefs.

◆ Skills Practice

Recognizing Bias Review the steps you followed on page 676 to learn this skill. Then write a sentence that explains what bias is.

◆ Writing Activity: Language Arts

The English language includes contributions from the Arabic language. Use a dictionary to research and learn about the history of these words: *admiral, algebra, cipher, cotton, sherbet,* and *zenith.* Write a paragraph on what you learned about the Arabic and English languages.

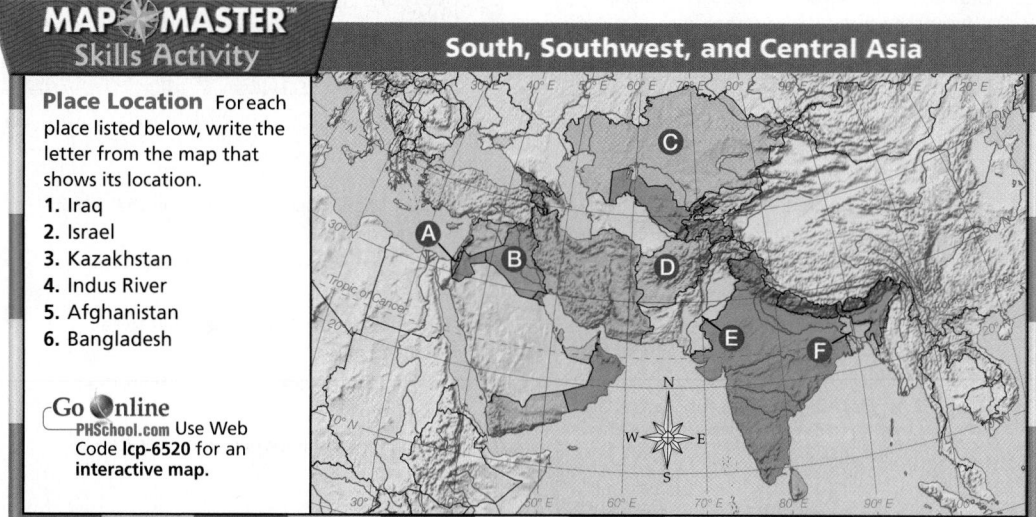

MAP MASTER™ Skills Activity

South, Southwest, and Central Asia

Place Location For each place listed below, write the letter from the map that shows its location.
1. Iraq
2. Israel
3. Kazakhstan
4. Indus River
5. Afghanistan
6. Bangladesh

Go Online PHSchool.com Use Web Code lcp-6520 for an interactive map.

MAP MASTER™ Skills Activity

1. B	**2.** A
3. C	**4.** E
5. D	**6.** F

Go Online PHSchool.com Students may practice their map skills using the interactive online version of this map.

Standardized Test Prep

Test-Taking Tips

Some questions on standardized tests ask you to analyze a reading selection. Read the passage below. Then follow the tips to answer the sample question.

> The Silk Road was an important trade route across Central Asia that linked China and Europe more than 2,000 years ago. Caravans carried Chinese silk to the west. They also brought glass, wool, gold, and silver eastward. Merchants traded more than just goods. They also exchanged ideas and inventions. Many ancient cities along the Silk Road, including Samarkand, became wealthy centers of trade and learning.

Pick the letter that best answers the question.

One city that sprang up in Central Asia along the Silk Road was

- **A** China.
- **B** Europe.
- **C** Mohenjo-Daro.
- **D** Samarkand.

TIP Use what you know about geography and history to find the BEST answer choice.

Think It Through Reread the question: The answer must be a city in Central Asia. You can rule out A and B as they are not cities. That leaves C and D. In Section 1, you read that Mohenjo-Daro is an ancient city in South Asia. In Section 2, you read that Samarkand is in Central Asia. The correct answer is D.

Practice Questions

Use the reading selection below to answer Question 1.

> The discovery and production of oil in the Arabian Peninsula brought dramatic changes to Riyadh, Saudi Arabia's capital. Once a small country town, Riyadh is now a modern city with wide highways and skyscrapers of steel and glass. It boasts luxury hotels, large hospitals, and one of the biggest airports in the world. By 2003, Riyadh was one of the world's fastest-growing cities.

1. What conclusion can be made from this reading selection?

- **A** Riyadh benefited from a worldwide increase in air travel.
- **B** Riyadh is a fast-growing city because it has luxury hotels.
- **C** Wealth from Arabian oil production has transformed Riyadh.
- **D** Riyadh was the smallest town in Saudi Arabia.

Use the tips above and other tips in this book to help you answer the following questions.

2. Which of the following events in South Asia happened last?

- **A** Asoka ruled the Maurya Empire in India.
- **B** Aryans came to South Asia probably from Central Asia.
- **C** India became a colony in the British Empire.
- **D** During the Gupta Empire, mathematicians developed Arabic numerals.

3. People who practice Judaism, Christianity, and Islam share a belief in

- **A** the caste system.
- **B** monotheism.
- **C** many gods.
- **D** Buddha.

Use Web Code lca-6500 for a **Chapter 22 self-test.**

Standardized Test Prep
Answers

1. C
2. C
3. B

Go Online PHSchool.com Students may use the Chapter 22 self-test on PHSchool.com to prepare for the Chapter Test.

Assessment Resources

Use Chapter Tests A and B to assess students' mastery of chapter content.

All in One Asia and the Pacific Teaching Resources, *Chapter Tests A and B,* pp. 287–292

Tests are also available on the *ExamView Test Bank CD-ROM.*

⊙ *ExamView Test Bank CD-ROM*

CHAPTER 23 — Southeast Asia and the Pacific Region: Cultures and History

Chapter Overview

Overview

1 Southeast Asia: Cultures and History
1. Find out why Southeast Asia is a culturally diverse region.
2. Learn how colonial powers affected Southeast Asia.
3. Understand how years of conflict affected Vietnam, Cambodia, and Laos.

2 The Pacific Region: Cultures and History
1. Find out how people settled Australia and New Zealand.
2. Learn which groups shaped the cultures of Australia and New Zealand.
3. Understand how Pacific island nations have been affected by other cultures.

Thai Festivals of Water and Light
Length: 3 minutes, 21 seconds
Use with Section 2
In this segment, students will learn about Thailand's many festivals. The festivals combine the beliefs of the different religions found in the country and serve to unite Thailand's people.

Technology Resources

Students use embedded Web codes to access Internet activities, chapter self-tests, and additional map practice. They may also access Dorling Kindersley's Online Desk Reference to learn more about each country they study.

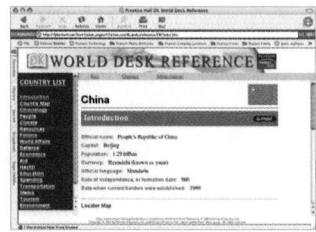

Use the Interactive Textbook to make content and concepts come alive through animations, videos, and activities that accompany the complete basal text—online and on CD-ROM.

PRENTICE HALL
TeacherEXPRESS — Plan • Teach • Assess

Use this complete suite of powerful teaching tools to make planning lessons and administering tests quicker and easier.

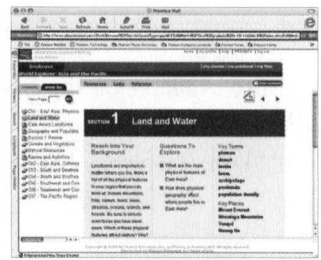

686a

Reading and Assessment

Reading and Vocabulary Instruction

🎯 Model the Target Reading Skill

Sequence Recognizing the sequence, or order, of events in written material can help students to organize ideas and analyze patterns. Becoming familiar with words that signal sequence is one way for students to strengthen and apply this skill.

Model this skill using the paragraph *Colonial Rule in Southeast Asia* from page 690 of the Student Edition:

Europeans brought more than Christianity to Southeast Asia. Traders from Europe arrived in the region in the 1500s. They hoped to gain control of the rich trade in silks, iron, silver, pearls, and spices. At first, Portugal, the Netherlands, and other European nations built trading posts there. From these small posts, Europeans expanded their power. By the 1800s, European nations had gained control of most of Southeast Asia.

Think aloud: "I'll begin by underlining words that seem like they are clues to the order of events." (*Underline 1500s; 1800s; At first; From these.*) "Now that I have my clue words, I will try to list the events in sequence." (*Write the following sequence on the board.*)

1. *1500s: European traders arrive in Southeast Asia.*
2. *Europeans build small trading posts in Southeast Asia.*
3. *European nations expand their powers in Southeast Asia.*
4. *1800s: European nations control most of Southeast Asia.*

Use the following worksheets from All-in-One Asia and the Pacific Teaching Resources (pp. 305–306) to support the chapter's Target Reading Skill.

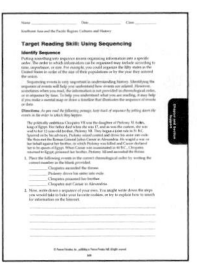 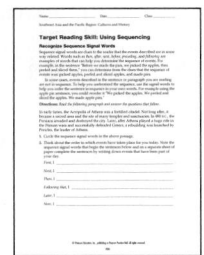

Vocabulary Builder
High-Use Academic Words

Use these steps to teach this chapter's high-use words:

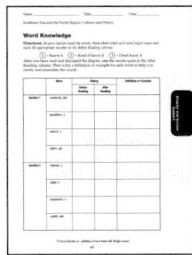

1. Have students rate how well they know each word on their Word Knowledge worksheets (All-in-One Asia and the Pacific Teaching Resources, p. 307).
2. Pronounce each word and ask students to repeat it.
3. Give students a brief definition or sample sentence (provided on TE pp. 689 and 697).
4. Work with students as they fill in the "Definition or Example" column of their Word Knowledge worksheets.

Assessment

Formal Assessment

Test students' understanding of core knowledge and skills.

Chapter Tests A and B, All-in-One Asia and the Pacific Teaching Resources, pp. 322–327

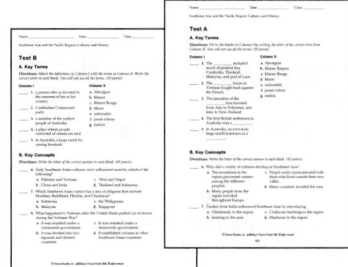

Customize the Chapter Tests to suit your needs.

ExamView Test Bank CD-ROM

Skills Assessment

Assess geographic literacy.

MapMaster Skills, Student Edition pp. 687, 690, 702

Assess reading and comprehension.

Target Reading Skills, Student Edition, pp. 690, 697, and in Section Assessments

Chapter 23 Assessment, Eastern Hemisphere Reading and Vocabulary Study Guide, p. 249

Performance Assessment

Assess students' performance on this chapter's Writing Activities using the following rubrics from All-in-One Asia and the Pacific Teaching Resources.

Rubric for Assessing a Writing Assignment, p. 320

Rubric for Assessing a Timeline, p. 321

Assess students' work through performance tasks.

Small Group Activity: Create a Legend About Pacific Explorers, All-in-One Asia and the Pacific Teaching Resources, pp. 310–313

Online Assessment

Have students check their own understanding.

Chapter Self-Test

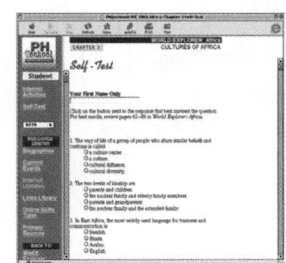

Test Preparation

Benchmark Test 2, AYP Monitoring Assessments, pp. 125–128

Section 1 Southeast Asia: Cultures and History

 1.5 periods, .75 block (includes Skills for Life)

Social Studies Objectives
1. Find out why Southeast Asia is a culturally diverse region.
2. Learn how colonial powers affected Southeast Asia.
3. Understand how years of conflict affected Vietnam, Cambodia, and Laos.

Reading/Language Arts Objective
Notice sequence while reading to help you understand and remember events.

Prepare to Read

Build Background Knowledge
Discuss how festivals might help to unite people of different religions.

Set a Purpose for Reading
Have students begin to fill out the *Reading Readiness Guide.*

Preview Key Terms
Teach the section's Key Terms.

Target Reading Skill
Introduce the section's Target Reading Skill of **understanding sequence.**

Instructional Resources

All in One Asia and the Pacific Teaching Resources
- **L2** Reading Readiness Guide, p. 298
- **L2** Identify Sequence, p. 305

Asia and the Pacific Transparencies
- **L2** Transparency B12: Chart/Table

World Studies Video Program
- **L2** Thai Festivals of Water and Light

Differentiated Instruction

Spanish Reading and Vocabulary Study Guide
- **L1** Chapter 23, Section 1, pp. 172–173 ELL

Instruct

A Region of Diversity
Discuss how the geography of Southeast Asia has influenced its culture.

Colonial Rule in Southeast Asia
Discuss how colonial rule affected Southeast Asia and how its countries gained independence.

Target Reading Skill
Review **understanding sequence**.

Vietnam, Cambodia, and Laos
Discuss the Vietnam War and the Khmer Rouge.

Instructional Resources

All in One Asia and the Pacific Teaching Resources
- **L2** Guided Reading and Review, p. 299
- **L2** Reading Readiness Guide, p. 298

Asia and the Pacific Transparencies
- **L2** Section Reading Support Transparency AP 62
- **L2** Transparency B20: Timeline

Differentiated Instruction

All in One Asia and the Pacific Teaching Resources
- **L3** Enrichment, p. 308 AR, GT
- **L2** Skills for Life, p. 309 AR, GT, LPR, SN

Asia and the Pacific Transparencies
- **L1** Section Reading Support Transparency AP 62 ELL, LPR, SN

Teacher's Edition
- **L3** For Advanced Readers, TE p. 691
- **L1** For Special Needs Students, TE p. 691
- **L3** For Gifted and Talented, TE p. 692

PHSchool.com
- **L3** For: Environmental and Global Issues: Why Do Wars Begin? AR, GT
  Web Code: lcd-6604

Assess and Reteach

Assess Progress
Evaluate student comprehension with the section assessment and section quiz.

Reteach
Assign the Reading and Vocabulary Study Guide to help struggling students.

Extend
Extend the lesson by assigning a Book Project.

Instructional Resources

All in One Asia and the Pacific Teaching Resources
- **L2** Section Quiz, p. 300
- **L3** Book Project: Independence Biography, pp. 80–82
- **L3** Gathering Details, p. 318
  Rubric for Assessing a Writing Assignment, p. 320

Reading and Vocabulary Study Guide
- **L1** Chapter 23, Section 1, pp. 243–245

Differentiated Instruction

Spanish Support
- **L2** Section Quiz (Spanish), p. 239 ELL

Asia and the Pacific Transparencies
- **L3** Color Transparency AP 39: Southeast Asia: Physical-Political AR, GT

Teacher's Edition
- **L3** For Gifted and Talented, TE p. 695

Social Studies Skills Tutor CD-ROM
- **L1** Drawing Inferences and Conclusions ELL, LPR, SN

Key
- **L1** Basic to Average
- **L3** Average to Advanced
- **L2** For All Students
- LPR Less Proficient Readers
- AR Advanced Readers
- SN Special Needs Students
- GT Gifted and Talented
- ELL English Language Learners

Section 2 The Pacific Region: Cultures and History

 2.5 periods, 1.25 blocks (includes Chapter Review and Assessment and Literature)

Social Studies Objectives
1. Find out how people settled Australia and New Zealand.
2. Learn which groups shaped the cultures of Australia and New Zealand.
3. Understand how Pacific island nations have been affected by other cultures.

Reading/Language Arts Objective
Learn to recognize signal words that indicate sequence.

Prepare to Read	Instructional Resources	Differentiated Instruction
Build Background Knowledge Have students think about things they associate with Australia, New Zealand, and the Pacific Islands. **Set a Purpose for Reading** Have students begin to fill out the *Reading Readiness Guide.* **Preview Key Terms** Teach the section's Key Terms. **Target Reading Skill** Introduce the section's Target Reading Skill of **recognizing signal words.**	**All in One Asia and the Pacific Teaching Resources** L2 Reading Readiness Guide, p. 302 L2 Recognize Sequence Signal Words, p. 306	**Spanish Reading and Vocabulary Study Guide** L1 Chapter 23, Section 2, pp. 174–175 ELL

Instruct	Instructional Resources	Differentiated Instruction
Settlement Discuss the Aborigine and Maori cultures. **Target Reading Skill** Review **recognizing signal words.** **The Cultures of Australia and New Zealand** Discuss the various ethnic groups of Australia and New Zealand. **The Cultures of the Pacific Islands** Discuss the lives of the Pacific islanders and how they were affected by settlers from other places.	**All in One Asia and the Pacific Teaching Resources** L2 Guided Reading and Review, p. 303 L2 Reading Readiness Guide, p. 302 **Asia and the Pacific Transparencies** L2 Section Reading Support Transparency AP 63	**All in One Asia and the Pacific Teaching Resources** L3 The Coconut Tree, pp. 314–316 AR, GT **Teacher's Edition** L3 For Advanced Readers, TE p. 699 L1 For Less Proficient Readers, TE p. 699 L1 For English Language Learners, TE p. 700 **Spanish Support** L2 Guided Reading and Review (Spanish), p. 240 ELL

Assess and Reteach	Instructional Resources	Differentiated Instruction

Assess Progress
Evaluate student comprehension with the section assessment and section quiz.
 	
Reteach
Assign the Reading and Vocabulary Study Guide to help struggling students.
 	
Extend
Extend the lesson by assigning a Small Group Activity.
	All in One Asia and the Pacific Teaching Resources
	L2 Section Quiz, p. 304
	L3 Small Group Activity: Create a Legend About Pacific Explorers, pp. 310–313
	    Rubric for Assessing a Timeline, p. 321
	L2 Word Knowledge, p. 307
	L2 Vocabulary Development, p. 319
	    Rubric for Assessing a Writing Assignment, p. 320
	L2 Chapter Tests A and B, pp. 322–327
	Reading and Vocabulary Study Guide
	L1 Chapter 23, Section 2, pp. 246–248
		All in One Asia and the Pacific Teaching Resources
		L3 The Tale of the Frog, p. 317 AR, GT
		    Rubric for Assessing a Writing Assignment, p. 320
		Spanish Support
		L2 Section Quiz (Spanish), p. 241 ELL
		L2 Chapter Summary (Spanish), p. 242 ELL
		L2 Vocabulary Development (Spanish), p. 243 ELL

Key
L1 Basic to Average   L3 Average to Advanced
L2 For All Students

LPR Less Proficient Readers
AR Advanced Readers
SN Special Needs Students

GT Gifted and Talented
ELL English Language Learners

Reading Background

Making Choices

To assist students in learning and remembering key terms and high-use words, have them choose between correct and incorrect descriptions of the words.

Word: *eventually*
Description 1: The family finally reaches its destination after much traveling. *(correct)*
Description 2: The family quickly reaches its destination after little traveling.

Word: *Maori*
Description 1: The native people of Australia have lived there for over 1,000 years.
Description 2: The native people of New Zealand have lived there for over 1,000 years. *(correct)*

Word: *impress*
Description 1: The books by the new science fiction author amaze Alan. *(correct)*
Description 2: The books by the new science fiction author bore Alan.

Word: *station*
Description 1: We'll need extra help at the dock to close down for the winter.
Description 2: We'll need extra help at the ranch to shear the sheep. *(correct)*

Word Wizard

Students often remember new words more easily when they see them used in everyday contexts. Bring in news magazines and newspapers and ask students to work in small groups to find instances in which the chapter's Key Terms and high-use words are used in those sources. Ask students to record each sentence in which a Key Term or high-use word is used. When the time for the activity has elapsed, ask students to share the sentences they have found, and initiate a class discussion in which students analyze how the word is used in each example.

World Studies Background

Vietnam War Memorial

The Vietnam War lasted from 1959 until 1975, and U.S. forces were present in large numbers starting in 1965. During the conflict, about 58,000 Americans died, as well as over 3 million Vietnamese and nearly 2 million Cambodians and Laotians. The names of the U.S. soldiers who were killed in the war are permanently etched into a memorial constructed in 1982. Located in Washington, D.C., the memorial was designed by Maya Lin, an architecture student who was only 21 years old at the time.

The Capitals of Cambodia

The first capital of what we now know as Cambodia was called Angkor and served as the capital of the Khmer Empire for about 600 years. In 1434, Phnom Penh replaced Angkor as the Khmer capital, and became Cambodia's capital in 1867. In the 1970s, the Khmer Rouge forced 2 million residents out of the city to rural areas, and shut down many of the city's institutions. Since 1980, Phnom Penh has been resettled and some of its many museums and universities have been reopened. Approximately 1 million people currently live there.

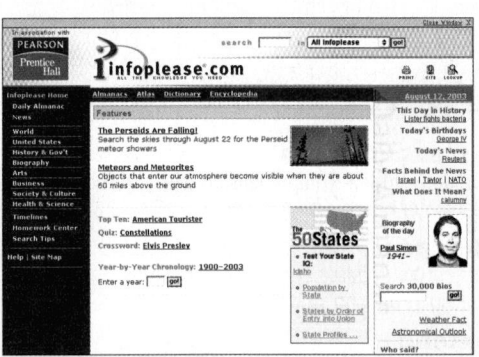

Infoplease® provides a wealth of useful information for the classroom. You can use this resource to strengthen your background on the subjects covered in this chapter. Have students visit this advertising-free site as a starting point for projects requiring research.

Use Web code **lcd-6600** for **Infoplease®**.

Using the Reciprocal Questioning Strategy

In Section 1, students will be asked to use the Reciprocal Questioning (ReQuest) strategy. To use this strategy, the teacher begins by modeling questions and answers to encourage students to ask themselves questions as they read. Questions should progress from those that require factual recall to those that require more interpretation. Model Reciprocal Questioning using the text on pages 688–689 of the Student Edition. Teacher-modeled questions and answers might include:

- What was the Khmer Empire? (*a civilization that included much of present day Cambodia, Thailand, Malaysia, and part of Laos*)

- What effects did the arrival of Indian traders have on the Khmer Empire? (*Indians brought the religions of Hinduism and Buddhism, along with Indian arts and culture, with them, and these things were incorporated into the culture of the Khmer Empire.*)

- Why is this section called *A Region of Diversity? (The people of Southeast Asia practice a variety of religions and incorporate many cultural influences into their society.*)

Summarizing

Help students take effective notes on the reading by encouraging them to organize their notes into summaries. Ask students to read and take notes on *The Cultures of the Pacific Islands* on page 700 of the Student Edition. Students might write down a variety of details. However, to organize their notes into a summary, ask students to eliminate any idea or detail that is not essential to the passage. A final summary might read: *Native peoples of the Pacific islands developed a variety of cultures, all of which were greatly impacted by European colonization in the 1800s.* Students' summaries will vary, but should express the main idea of the passage without extraneous details. Pair students and ask them to exchange summaries and help each other with revisions.

Australia's Reconciliation Movement

Reconciliation is the name given to the Australian government's attempts to right the wrongs done to the Aboriginal people in the past. In 1991, Australia formed the Council for Aboriginal Reconciliation to work on a plan to increase unity in the country and improve the standard of living for Aboriginal Australians. Today, an organization called Reconciliation Australia continues to work toward raising awareness of the need for reconciliation and how it can be achieved.

The Treaty of Waitangi

New Zealand became a British colony in the nineteenth century through the sign-ing of a controversial treaty. In 1840, Captain William Hobson was sent from Britain to negotiate with the Maori. He received enough signatures from the Maori leaders to make the treaty official, but not all the leaders were present to sign his proposal. Historians now believe that the translation of the treaty from English to Maori may have also been misleading. Some believed that the treaty gave the British power only over the British subjects in New Zealand—not the Maori people or their lands. The British understood the treaty to mean that all of New Zealand—its land and its people—became a British colony.

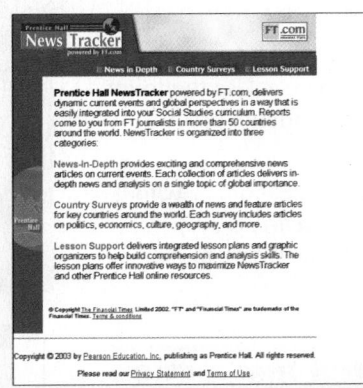

Get in-depth information on topics of global importance with **Prentice Hall Newstracker,** powered by FT.com.

Use Web code **lcd-6605** for Prentice Hall Newstracker.

Guiding Questions

Remind students about the Guiding Questions introduced at the beginning of this section.

Section 1 relates to **Guiding Question** ❸ **What are the main characteristics of the cultures of Asia and the Pacific?** *(The culture of Southeast Asia developed independently because the region's mountains kept groups of people apart from one another. But later, China and India influenced the region's culture. People from India brought Islam to Southeast Asia. People in Vietnam used Chinese farming techniques, and the ideas of Confucius influenced their government. Hinduism, Buddhism, and Islam are the major religions in Southeast Asia.)*

Section 2 relates to **Guiding Question** ❸ **What are the main characteristics of the cultures of Asia and the Pacific?** *(Australia, once a British colony, is heavily influenced by British culture. Australian Aborigines were forced to adopt European ways during the colonial period. Australia also has a large Chinese population. The Maoris of New Zealand were also forced to adopt British ways. Recently though the Maori have gained more power, and new laws allow them to practice their own customs. Pacific island nations have varied cultures due to the large distances between them.)*

↻ Target Reading Skill

In this chapter, students will learn and apply the reading skill of sequence. Use the following worksheets to help students practice this skill:

AllinOne Asia and the Pacific Teaching Resources, *Identify Sequence,* p. 305; *Recognize Sequence Signal Words,* p. 306

┌ Differentiated Instruction ┐

The following Teacher Edition strategies are suitable for students of varying abilities.

Advanced Readers, pp. 691, 699
English Language Learners, p. 706
Gifted and Talented, pp. 692, 695
Less Proficient Readers, p. 699
Special Needs Students, p. 691

Chapter Preview

In this chapter, you will learn about the cultures and history of Southeast Asia and Australia, New Zealand, and the Pacific islands.

Section 1
Southeast Asia
Cultures and History

Section 2
The Pacific Region
Cultures and History

 Target Reading Skill

Sequence In this chapter, you will focus on understanding the order in which a series of events occurs. This is called sequence.

▶ Women sell prepared food and fruits and vegetables at a floating market in Thailand.

686 Asia and the Pacific

⌐ Bibliography

For the Teacher
Einfeld, Jann. *Life in the Australian Outback (Way People Live).* Lucent Books, 2003.
Mack, Stevie, and Lori Philips. *Island Worlds: Art and Culture in the Pacific.* Crizmac, 1998.
Maraniss, David. *They Marched Into Sunlight.* Simon and Schuster, 2003.

For the Student
L1 Taus-Bolstad, Stacy. *Thailand in Pictures (Visual Geography Series).* Lerner Publications Company, 2003.
L2 Arnold, Caroline. *Uluru : Australia's Aboriginal Heart.* Clarion Books, 2003.
L2 Gifford, Clive. *The Water Puppets: A Story from the War in Vietnam.* Barrons Educational Series, 2002.
L3 Ihimaera, Witi. *The Whale Rider.* Harcourt Paperbacks, 2003.

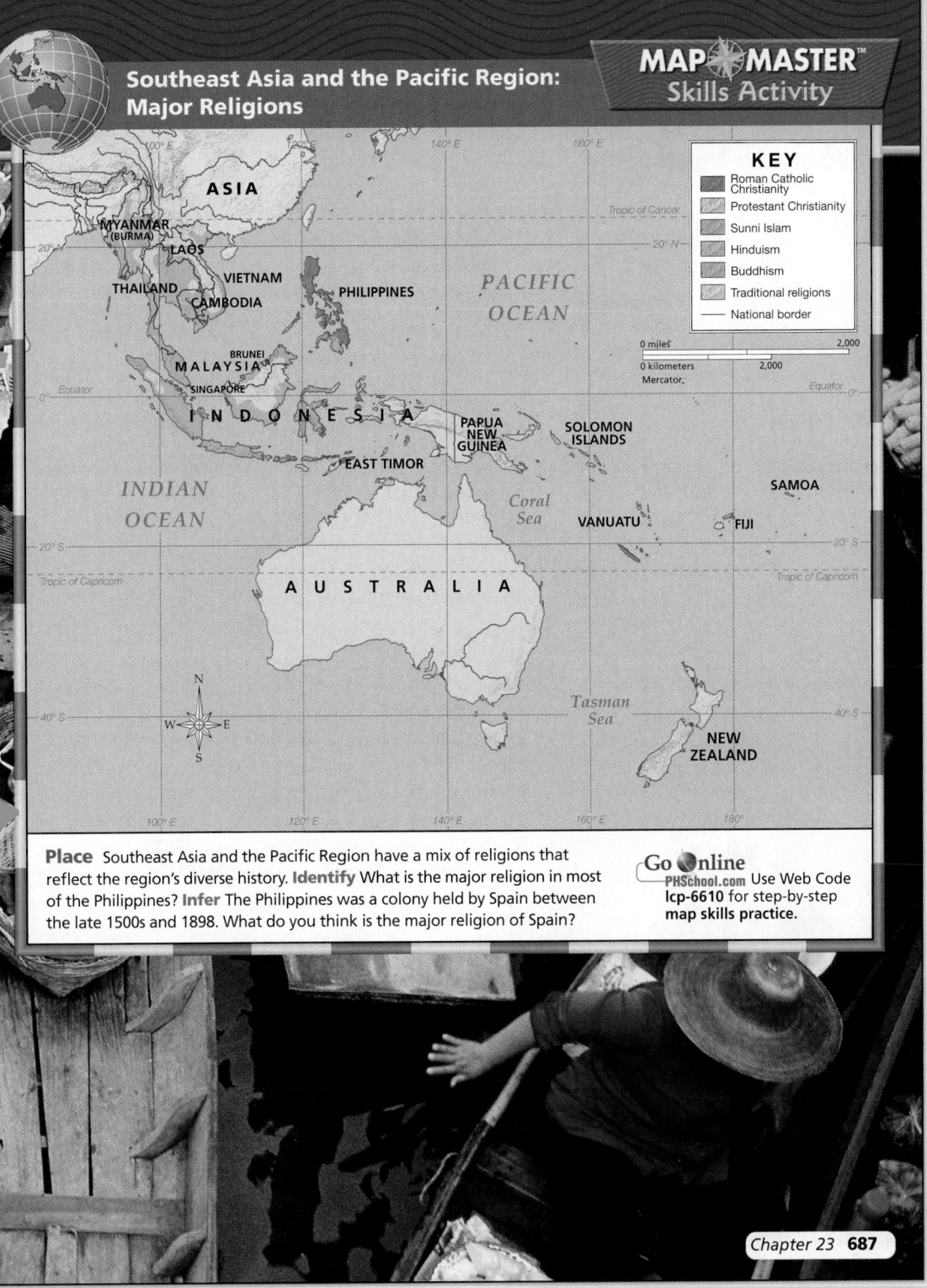

Southeast Asia and the Pacific Region: Major Religions

KEY

Roman Catholic Christianity
Protestant Christianity
Sunni Islam
Hinduism
Buddhism
Traditional religions
— National border

ASIA

MYANMAR (BURMA)
LAOS
THAILAND
VIETNAM
CAMBODIA
PHILIPPINES
BRUNEI
MALAYSIA
SINGAPORE
INDONESIA
PAPUA NEW GUINEA
EAST TIMOR
SOLOMON ISLANDS
SAMOA
VANUATU
FIJI
AUSTRALIA
NEW ZEALAND

PACIFIC OCEAN
INDIAN OCEAN
Coral Sea
Tasman Sea

Tropic of Cancer
Equator
Tropic of Capricorn

0 miles   2,000
0 kilometers   2,000
Mercator

Place Southeast Asia and the Pacific Region have a mix of religions that reflect the region's diverse history. **Identify** What is the major religion in most of the Philippines? **Infer** The Philippines was a colony held by Spain between the late 1500s and 1898. What do you think is the major religion of Spain?

Go Online
PHSchool.com Use Web Code
lcp-6610 for step-by-step
map skills practice.

Have students create a chart showing the religions practiced in each country shown on the map. Display the *Chart/Table Transparency* to show students how to create their charts.

Asia and the Pacific Transparencies, *Transparency B12: Chart/Table*

Go Online
PHSchool.com Students may practice their map skills using the interactive online version of this map.

Using the Visual
L2

Reach Into Your Background Draw students' attention to the photograph and caption. Ask them to think about the geography of their town or city. Would a floating market be possible? Why or why not? If it were, how might it benefit the people living in the area?

Answers
MAP MASTER™
Skills Activity **Identify** Roman Catholic Christianity **Infer** probably Roman Catholic Christianity

---

Chapter Resources

Teaching Resources
L2 Vocabulary Development, p. 319
L2 Skills for Life, p. 309
L2 Chapter Tests A and B, pp. 322–327

Spanish Support
L2 Spanish Chapter Summary, p. 242
L2 Spanish Vocabulary Development, p. 243

Media and Technology
L1 Student Edition on Audio CD
L1 Guided Reading Audiotapes, English and Spanish
L2 Social Studies Skills Tutor CD-ROM
ExamView Test Bank CD-ROM

PRENTICE HALL
Presentation **EXPRESS**™
Teach · Connect · Inspire

Teach this chapter's content using the PresentationExpress™ CD-ROM including:
■ slide shows
■ transparencies
■ interactive maps and media
■ *ExamView*® QuickTake Presenter

Objectives

Social Studies

1. Find out why Southeast Asia is a culturally diverse region.
2. Learn how colonial powers affected Southeast Asia.
3. Understand how years of conflict affected Vietnam, Cambodia, and Laos.

Reading/Language Arts

Notice sequence while reading to help you understand and remember events.

Prepare to Read

Build Background Knowledge   L2

Tell students that they will be reading about the cultures of Southeast Asia in this section, and that religion is one aspect of culture. Show the video *Thai Festivals of Water and Light*, and then ask students why they think festivals might help to unite people of different religions. Use the Idea Wave participation strategy (TE, p. T35) to solicit answers.

📼 *Thai Festivals of Water and Light,* **World Studies Video Program**

Set a Purpose for Reading   L2

- Preview the Objectives.

- Form students into pairs or groups of four. Distribute the *Reading Readiness Guide*. Ask the students to fill in the first two columns of the chart. Use the Numbered Heads participation strategy (TE, p. T36) to call on students to share one piece of information they already know and one piece of information they want to know.

All in One **Asia and the Pacific Teaching Resources,** *Reading Readiness Guide,* p. 298

Preview Key Terms   L2

Pronounce the Key Terms, and then ask the students to say the words with you. Provide a simple explanation such as, "A nationalist is very dedicated to his or her country."

Prepare to Read

Objectives

In this section you will
1. Find out why Southeast Asia is a culturally diverse region.
2. Learn how colonial powers affected Southeast Asia.
3. Understand how years of conflict affected Vietnam, Cambodia, and Laos.

Taking Notes

As you read this section, look for details about events in Southeast Asia. Copy the timeline below, and record your findings on it.

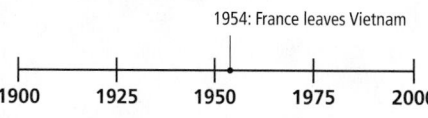

1954: France leaves Vietnam

| 1900 | 1925 | 1950 | 1975 | 2000 |

🎯 Target Reading Skill

Understand Sequence
A sequence is the order in which a series of events occurs. Noting the sequence of events can help you understand and remember the events. You can track events by making a timeline, like the one shown at the left. As you read this section, add events to the timeline in the order in which they happened.

Key Terms

- **Khmer Empire** (kuh MEHR EM pyr) *n.* an empire that included much of present-day Cambodia, Thailand, Malaysia, and part of Laos
- **nationalist** (NASH uh nul ist) *n.* a person who is devoted to the interests of his or her country
- **Khmer Rouge** (kuh MEHR roozh) *n.* the Cambodian Communist party

One of the majestic stone buildings at Angkor Wat

688 Asia and the Pacific

Deep in the rain forests of Cambodia lies Angkor Wat—the largest temple in the world. Angkor Wat is a Hindu temple built of stone. It was built in the A.D. 1100s by the Khmer (kuh MEHR) civilization. At its greatest extent, the **Khmer Empire** included much of present-day Cambodia, Thailand, Malaysia, and part of Laos. The empire was at its height from about A.D. 800 to 1434. The Khmer Empire was one of many kingdoms in Southeast Asia.

A Region of Diversity

The peoples of Southeast Asia developed their own cultures before outside influences shaped the region. Southeast Asia's mountains kept groups of people apart from one another. As a result, each group developed its own way of life.

When outside influences came to Southeast Asia, many of them came from India and China. Southeast Asia is located between India and China. Because of this location, the cultures of Southeast Asia were strongly affected by India and China.

🎯 Target Reading Skill   L2

Understand Sequence Tell students that understanding sequence will help them to understand and remember events in history.

Model understanding sequence using the text under the heading The Impact of India and China on p. 689. Write the following statements on the board: **(a)** *Indians bring Buddhism to Southeast Asia.* **(b)** *Indian trad-* ers sail to the lands of Southeast Asia. **(c)** *Indians introduce Hinduism to Southeast Asia.* Explain that the correct order is *b, c, a.* Tell students they can find the sequence by using clue words, such as "later."

Give students *Identify Sequence.* Have them complete the activity in groups.

All in One **Asia and the Pacific Teaching Resources,** *Identify Sequence,* p. 305

The Impact of India and China India affected Southeast Asian cultures mainly through trade. Nearly 2,000 years ago, Indian traders sailed across the Indian Ocean to Southeast Asia. Indians introduced the religion of Hinduism to the region. Later, around A.D. 200, Indians brought Buddhism to Southeast Asia.

Long after Hinduism and Buddhism spread throughout the region, Indians brought Islam to Southeast Asia. Muslim traders from northern India, then under Muslim rule, carried Islam to Indonesia and the Philippines.

China's effect on Southeast Asia was felt primarily in Vietnam. In 111 B.C., the Chinese conquered Vietnam. They ruled the country for more than 1,000 years. During that time, the Vietnamese began using Chinese ways of farming. They also began using the ideas of Confucius, the ancient Chinese philosopher, to run their government.

Major Religions of Southeast Asia Today, there are Hindus in Indonesia and Malaysia. Buddhists and Muslims, however, eventually outnumbered Hindus in the region. Buddhism is the main religion in Myanmar, Thailand, Laos, Vietnam, and Cambodia today. Islam is the religion of the majority of the people in Malaysia and Indonesia. In fact, Indonesia has the largest Muslim population in the world. Singapore has a mix of religions that include Muslims, Buddhists, Hindus, and Christians.

European missionaries brought Christianity to Southeast Asia in the 1500s. Today, most of the people in the Philippines are Christian. There are small groups of Christians in Malaysia and Indonesia, too.

Learn about festivals in Thailand.

Buddhism in Southeast Asia
According to Buddhist tradition, Buddhism was founded in India in the 500s B.C. by Siddhartha Gautama, known as the Buddha. This gigantic sculpture of the Buddha is in Laos. **Apply Information** *Name another Southeast Asian country where Buddhism is the main religion.*

✓ **Reading Check** What are the major religions of Southeast Asia?

Chapter 23 Section 1 **689**

Vocabulary Builder

Use the information below to teach students this section's high-use words.

High-Use Word	Definition and Sample Sentence
eventually, p. 689	*adv.* at a later time The winter season seems long, but spring will **eventually** arrive.
population, p. 689	*n.* total number of people in a group or living in an area The **population** of our town doubled in the last five years.
expand, p. 690	*v.* to make larger or spread out She hoped to **expand** her computer business within the next year.
stable, p. 693	*adj.* secure, steady The platform is **stable** enough to hold several hundred people.

Colonial Rule in Southeast Asia

L2

Guided Instruction

- **Vocabulary Builder** Clarify the high-use word **expand** before reading.

- Have students read Colonial Rule in Southeast Asia and examine the map on this page. Circulate to make sure individuals can answer the Reading Check question.

- Ask students **Why did Europeans arrive in Southeast Asia in the 1500s?** (*They hoped to gain control of the trade in silks, iron, silver, pearls, and spices.*)

- Have students look at the map on this page. Ask **Which country did the United States control?** (*Philippines*)

Target Reading Skill

L2

Understand Sequence As a follow up, ask students to answer the Target Reading Skill question in the Student Edition. (*after the Spanish-American War*)

Colonial Rule in Southeast Asia

Europeans brought more than Christianity to Southeast Asia. Traders from Europe arrived in the region in the 1500s. They hoped to gain control of the rich trade in silks, iron, silver, pearls, and spices. At first, Portugal, the Netherlands, and other European nations built trading posts there. From these small posts, Europeans expanded their power. By the 1800s, European nations had gained control of most of Southeast Asia.

As the map below shows, by 1914 Thailand was the only country in Southeast Asia that was not under colonial rule. Thailand was known as Siam until 1939. Spain ruled the Philippines for about 350 years. In 1898, however, the United States defeated Spain in the Spanish-American War. Control of the Philippines passed to the United States.

Target Skill **Understand Sequence** When did control of the Philippines pass to the United States, before or after the Spanish-American War?

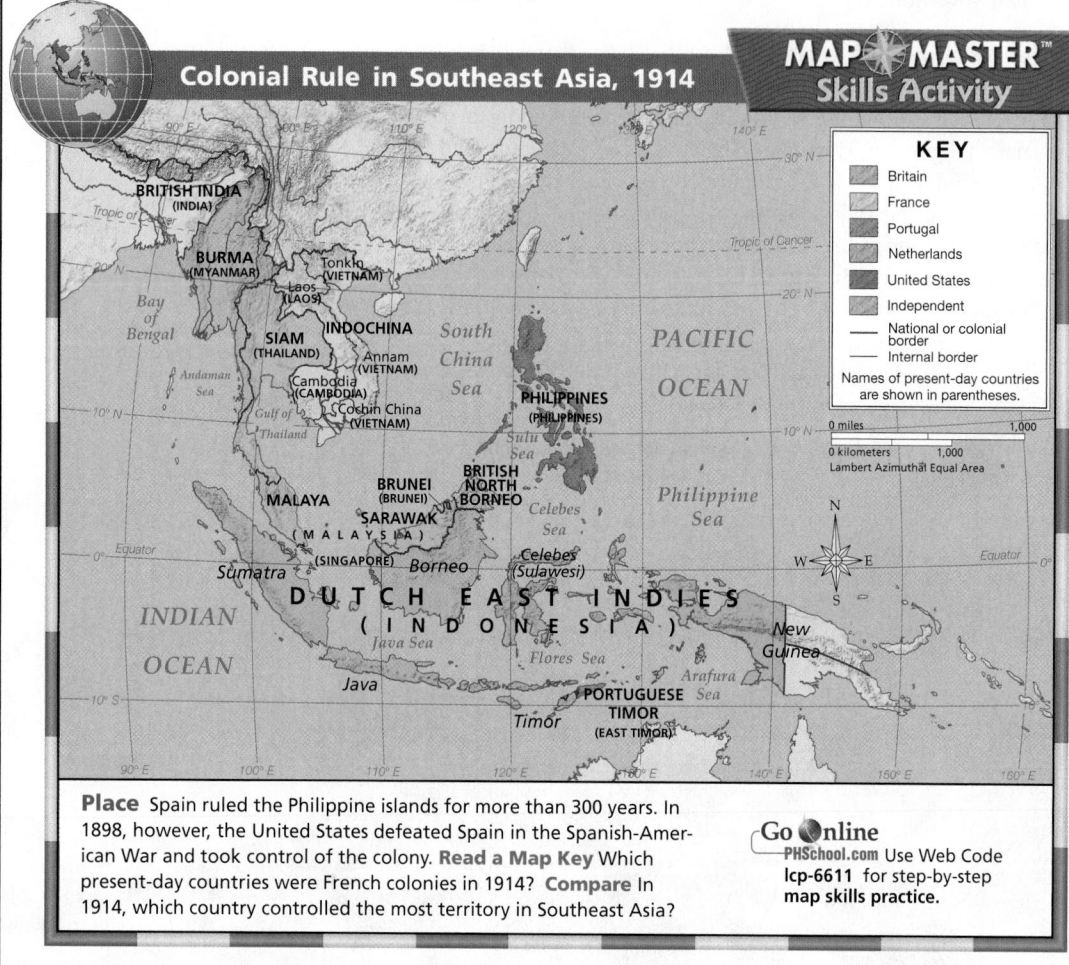

Place Spain ruled the Philippine islands for more than 300 years. In 1898, however, the United States defeated Spain in the Spanish-American War and took control of the colony. **Read a Map Key** Which present-day countries were French colonies in 1914? **Compare** In 1914, which country controlled the most territory in Southeast Asia?

Go Online PHSchool.com Use Web Code lcp-6611 for step-by-step map skills practice.

690 Asia and the Pacific

Answers

MAP MASTER Skills Activity **Read a Map Key** Laos, Vietnam, and Cambodia
Compare Netherlands

Go Online PHSchool.com Students may practice their map skills using the interactive online version of this map.

Background: Daily Life

Singapore's Colonial Legacy In the 1820s the British gained control of the island nation of Singapore. The location of Singapore, between the Indian Ocean and South China Sea, and the fact that ships did not have to pay taxes there, helped to turn Singapore into a busy and prosperous port. Following World War II, the British gradually relinquished control of Singapore, and it officially became self-governing in 1959.

However, more than 100 years of colonial rule had left its mark. Singapore based its government upon the British parliamentary model. In addition, English is one of Singapore's four official languages. Most governmental, commercial, and industrial business is conducted in English, and it is the language in which classes in school are taught.

Effects of Colonial Rule Colonial rulers built a network of roads, bridges, ports, and railroads in Southeast Asia. Good transportation was essential for the economic success of the colonies. This new network made moving people and goods across the region much easier. The colonial powers also built schools, which helped to produce skilled workers for colonial industries. Education gave some Southeast Asians the skills to become teachers, doctors, government workers, and more.

The Road to Independence By the early 1900s, nationalists were organizing independence movements throughout the countries of Southeast Asia. A **nationalist** is someone who is devoted to the interests of his or her country. But, by the time World War II broke out in 1939, the Japanese had begun to move into Southeast Asia. During the war, the Japanese invaded mainland Southeast Asia and drove out the European colonial powers.

After the Japanese were defeated in World War II, Western nations hoped to regain power in Southeast Asia. But Southeast Asians had other hopes. They wanted independence.

Southeast Asian countries did gain independence. Some, like the Philippines and Burma (now called Myanmar), won their freedom peacefully. Others, including Laos, Cambodia, Vietnam, Malaysia, and Indonesia, had to fight for it.

✓ **Reading Check** How did the United States gain control of the Philippines?

Citizen Heroes

Aung San Suu Kyi

The country of Myanmar has had a military government since 1962. The key leader in Myanmar's fight for democracy was a woman named Aung San Suu Kyi (awn san soo chee). The government tried to stop her efforts. Suu Kyi was placed under house arrest from 1989 to 1995. In 1991, Suu Kyi won the Nobel Peace Prize for her work to bring democracy and human rights to Myanmar through peaceful means. In spite of the government's efforts to stop her, she stayed in Myanmar and continued to work for freedom and democracy.

Chapter 23 Section 1 **691**

Guided Instruction (continued)

- Ask **Why did colonial rulers think it was important to build roads, bridges, ports, and railroads?** *(Good transportation made it easier to move people and goods across the region.)*

- Ask students why they think Japanese forces moved into Southeast Asia during World War II and fought against the colonial powers there. *(Possible answer: Japan wanted the resources of Southeast Asia for itself.)*

- Ask **Which countries gained independence peacefully?** *(Burma, now known as Myanmar, and the Philippines)* **Which countries fought for independence?** *(Laos, Cambodia, Vietnam, Malaysia, and Indonesia)*

Independent Practice

Have students continue to fill in their timelines with events in Southeast Asia's history.

Monitor Progress

As students work on the timeline, circulate to ensure that they are choosing relevant events and placing them in the correct order.

Citizen Heroes

Read the **Citizen Heroes** on this page. Ask students **Why do you think Suu Kyi stayed in Myanmar despite government efforts to stop her work?** *(Possible answer: She cared about the people of Myanmar and wanted to bring democracy and freedom to them.)*

Differentiated Instruction

For Advanced Readers L3
Point out that students have been reading about the importance of transportation networks in Southeast Asia. Explain that waterways also serve as important transportation routes. Have them complete the *Enrichment* activity to learn more about boats in Southeast Asia.

All in One **Asia and the Pacific Teaching Resources,** *Enrichment, p. 308*

For Special Needs Students L1
Show special needs students *Section Reading Support Transparency AP 62* before they read in order to help them focus on the organization and facts of the section.

📖 **Asia and the Pacific Transparencies,** *Section Reading Support Transparency AP 62*

Answer

✓ Reading Check The United States took control of the Philippines from Spain when it defeated Spain in the Spanish-American War.

Vietnam, Cambodia, and Laos

L2

Guided Instruction

- **Vocabulary Builder** Clarify the high-use word **stable** before reading.

- Read Vietnam, Cambodia, and Laos with students.

- Ask students to discuss the cause of the Vietnam War, and which countries around the world had an interest in the war's outcome. *(North Vietnam had a Communist government while South Vietnam had a non-Communist government. North Vietnam wanted to unite both parts of Vietnam under Communist rule. The United States supported the non-Communist South Vietnamese. The Soviet Union hoped to see the Communist North Vietnamese win.)*

- Ask **What was the Khmer Rouge and what were some effects of its rule?** *(Communist Cambodians called the Khmer Rouge took over the Cambodian government in 1975 and opposed technology and Western ways of life. The Khmer Rouge government forced urban dwellers to move to rural areas to work on farms. In its four-year rule, the Khmer Rouge killed more than one million Cambodians. Even after it was overthrown, fighting continued among different groups.)*

Independent Practice

Have students complete the timeline by adding important events that took place in Vietnam, Cambodia, and Laos after 1945.

Monitor Progress

- Show *Section Reading Support Transparency AP 62* and ask students to check their graphic organizers individually. Go over key concepts and clarify key vocabulary as needed.

    📖 **Asia and the Pacific Transparencies,** *Section Reading Support Transparency AP 62*

- Tell students to fill in the last column of the *Reading Readiness Guide*. Ask them to evaluate if what they learned was what they had expected to learn.

    All in One Asia and the Pacific Teaching Resources, *Reading Readiness Guide,* p. 298

Vendors display their fruit on bicycles in Hanoi, Vietnam.

Vietnam, Cambodia, and Laos

The road to independence was especially violent in Laos, Cambodia, and Vietnam. These countries were formerly controlled by France. Together, they were known as French Indochina. After World War II ended in 1945, France tried to take back Indochina from Japan. Nationalist forces in Vietnam fought back against the French. In 1954, they forced France to give up power and leave.

The Vietnam War The Vietnamese forces that defeated France declared Vietnam's independence. They wanted Vietnam to be a Communist country. This concerned leaders in the United States. Since the end of World War II, the United States had worked to prevent communism from spreading. Its main rival, the Soviet Union, had worked to expand communism by bringing other countries under its control.

In 1954, Vietnam was divided into two parts. The government of North Vietnam was Communist. The government of South Vietnam was non-Communist. Communist leaders in North Vietnam used force in an effort to unite the country under Communist rule. Helped by the United States, South Vietnam fought back.

At first, the United States sent military advisers and supplies to South Vietnam. Later, it sent hundreds of thousands of American soldiers to Vietnam. After years of fighting, the United States began to withdraw its forces. In 1975, North Vietnam took over South Vietnam and reunited the country under a Communist government.

692 Asia and the Pacific

Differentiated Instruction

For Gifted and Talented
L3

Have students further explore the fundamental issues behind wars by completing the Internet activity entitled *Why Do Wars Begin?* As students learn about the basic causes of war, ask them to identify which cause best applies to the conflict in Vietnam.

Go Online
PHSchool.com

For: Environmental and Global Issues: *Why Do Wars Begin?*
Visit: PHSchool.com
Web Code: lcd-6604

Cambodia and Laos Cambodia and Laos had gained independence from France in 1953. Pulled into the conflict over Vietnam, both countries went through years of violence as Communists and non-Communists struggled for power. During the war, the United States bombed Cambodia and Laos to destroy Communist North Vietnamese forces there.

In 1975, the Cambodian Communist party called the **Khmer Rouge** (kuh MEHR roozh) took over the government of Cambodia. Opposed to Western ways of life, the Khmer Rouge moved the entire urban population to rural areas and forced them to work in the fields. Over the next four years, the Khmer Rouge killed more than a million Cambodians. Even after the Khmer Rouge leader, Pol Pot, was driven out in 1979, fighting continued. After Pol Pot died in 1998, the Khmer Rouge surrendered, and the country became more stable. A new coalition government formed in 2004. Local elections are scheduled for 2007 and national elections for 2008.

Cambodian children reading in school

✓ **Reading Check** Which country did the United States support with troops during the Vietnam War?

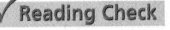 **Section 1 Assessment**

Key Terms
Review the key terms at the beginning of this section. Use each term in a sentence that explains its meaning.

Target Reading Skill
List these events in the order in which they occurred: Vietnam comes under Communist rule; Nationalists organize independence movements throughout Southeast Asia; elections are held in Cambodia.

Comprehension and Critical Thinking
1. (a) Recall Between which two large Asian countries is Southeast Asia located?

(b) Summarize How did this location affect the development of Southeast Asia's cultures?
(c) Apply Information Give one example showing that Southeast Asia has diverse religions.
2. (a) Explain Why did Europeans begin traveling to Southeast Asia in the 1500s?
(b) Identify Effects What were some positive and negative effects of colonial rule in Southeast Asia?
3. (a) Identify What present-day countries made up French Indochina?
(b) Sequence What happened in Vietnam in 1954?
(c) Identify Point of View Why was the United States concerned about Vietnam in 1954?

Writing Activity
Complete this sentence: *Southeast Asian cultures have been shaped by____.* Use your completed sentence as a topic sentence for a paragraph about Southeast Asian cultures. Use the information in this section to write your paragraph.

> **Writing Tip** To complete the topic sentence, review this section. Choose two or three features that have shaped Southeast Asian cultures. Be sure to include supporting details for your topic sentence.

Assess Progress [L2]
Have students complete the Section Assessment. Administer the *Section Quiz*.

📕 **All in One** **Asia and the Pacific Teaching Resources,** *Section Quiz*, p. 300

Reteach [L1]
If students need more instruction, have them read this section in the Reading and Vocabulary Study Guide.

📙 Chapter 23, Section 1, **Eastern Hemisphere Reading and Vocabulary Study Guide,** pp. 243–245

Extend [L3]
Have students complete the *Book Project: Independence Biography* in small groups to learn more about those who helped the colonies of Southeast Asia gain independence. To help students prepare for this project, have them complete the *Gathering Details* worksheet in advance of their research.

📕 **All in One** **Asia and the Pacific Teaching Resources,** *Book Project: Independence Biography*, pp. 80–82; *Gathering Details*, p. 318

Answer

✓ **Reading Check** South Vietnam

Writing Activity
Use the *Rubric for Assessing a Writing Assignment* to evaluate students' paragraphs.

📕 **All in One** **Asia and the Pacific Teaching Resources,** *Rubric for Assessing a Writing Assignment*, p. 320

Section 1 Assessment

Key Terms
Students' sentences should reflect knowledge of each Key Term.

Target Reading Skill
Nationalists organized independence movements throughout Southeast Asia; Vietnam comes under Communist rule; Elections are held in Cambodia.

Comprehension and Critical Thinking
1. (a) India and China **(b)** People from India brought Hinduism, Buddhism, and Islam to Southeast Asia. People in Vietnam adopted Chinese farming techniques and used the ideas of Confucius to run their government. **(c)** The diverse religions of Southeast Asia can be shown by the presence of Hinduism, Buddhism, Islam, and Christianity in the region.

2. (a) to gain control of the trade in silks, iron, silver, pearls, and spices **(b)** Positive: Transportation networks and schools were built. Negative: Colonial rulers controlled trade and the economy.

3. (a) French Indochina was composed of Laos, Cambodia, and Vietnam. **(b)** Vietnamese nationalists forced France out of the country. Vietnam was divided into North and South Vietnam. **(c)** The United States did not want to see Vietnam become a Communist country.

Objective

Learn how to draw conclusions.

Prepare to Read

Build Background Knowledge L2

Ask students to give examples of times they have drawn conclusions or might do so. You may need to offer a model conclusion, such as, "Based on the items he packed in his suitcase, I concluded that he was going away to a warm place for his vacation." Write the sample conclusions on the board, and then ask students for facts that support their conclusions. Write these on the board as well.

Instruct

Drawing Conclusions L2

Guided Instruction

■ Read the steps to drawing conclusions as a class and write them on the board. Practice the skill by following the steps on p. 694 and applying them to Practice the Skill on p. 695.

■ Divide students into small groups to work on writing the answers to the Practice the Skill questions. (*Step 1—Vietnamese forces defeated the French and declared independence. The Soviet Union was the main rival of the United States after World War II. The United States sent soldiers to help the South Vietnamese fight the Communist North Vietnamese. Step 3 possible conclusion— The people of the United States wanted troops to come home after years of fighting and no progress against an experienced enemy.*)

■ Write each group's conclusion on the board and go over any differences with the class. Have each group give facts that support their conclusion.

Independent Practice

Assign *Skills for Life* and have students complete it individually.

All in One **Asia and the Pacific Teaching Resources,** *Skills for Life,* p. 309

 # Drawing Conclusions

Ena walked into class wearing a bright red silk dress. Her anklet of tiny bells chimed each time she moved. Smiling, she took some objects out of a large box.

Maria watched as Ena put up a beautiful picture of the full moon. Next, Ena placed a small, handmade boat on the table. Then she put a small dish of rice next to it.

Maria looked at the calendar. The date was April 13. Tonight there would be a full moon.

Maria smiled. "Ena is going to tell us about the Cambodian New Year." "How do you know?" Paul asked. Maria laughed. "Yesterday we read about how Cambodians celebrate the New Year," she reminded Paul. "In April when the moon is full, they send boats down the river and make offerings to relatives. Look at what Ena has in her display." Maria had noticed some important details and drew the correct conclusion.

Drawing conclusions means adding clues, or evidence, that you read or see, to what you already know. A conclusion is a judgment.

Learn the Skill

Follow the steps below to learn how to draw a reliable conclusion.

1 **Identify what you know is true.** Use these facts as clues. Maria identified the following facts as clues:

a. Ena was dressed up and wore an anklet of tiny bells.

b. Ena displayed a picture of a full moon along with a boat and a bowl of rice.

2 **Add these facts to what you already know.** Maria had heard about the Cambodian New Year. She knew how Cambodians celebrated this special holiday.

3 **Add two or more clues to what you already know to draw a reasoned conclusion.** Maria put together the two clues she saw with what she already knew to reach the conclusion that Ena was going to tell about the Cambodian New Year.

Monitor Progress

As students are completing *Skills for Life,* circulate and make sure individuals are applying the skill steps effectively. Provide assistance as needed.

Practice the Skill

Read the passage titled The Vietnam War, on page 692. Then use the steps on the previous page to draw conclusions about why the United States withdrew its troops from Vietnam in 1973.

1 Answer these questions in order to find facts: How did Vietnam become independent after World War II? What country was the main rival of the United States after the end of World War II? Why did the United States send soldiers to Vietnam?

2 Use the facts to build on what you already know. For example, you know that the Vietnamese were successful in driving the French out of their country. If Vietnam had that kind of military success with the French, maybe they could defeat the United States forces, too.

3 Add the clues you have discovered to what you already know. What conclusion can you draw about why the United States withdrew its troops from Vietnam in 1973?

Women dressed in silk clothing attend a New Year's celebration in Hanoi, Vietnam.

Apply the Skill

Turn to page 691 and reread the passage titled Effects of Colonial Rule. Then use the steps in this skill to draw a conclusion about why Southeast Asians fought for independence from their colonial rulers.

Assess and Reteach

Assess Progress   L2
Ask students to do the Apply the Skill activity.

Reteach   L1
If students are having trouble applying the skill steps, have them review the skill using the interactive Social Studies Skills Tutor CD-ROM.

 Drawing Inferences and Conclusions, **Social Studies Skills Tutor CD-ROM**

Extend   L3
To extend the lesson, have student groups repeat the skill steps using information from Section 1. Have them draw a conclusion about why present-day Southeast Asian countries have such a diverse mix of religions. (*Possible conclusion: The influence of other countries over thousands of years led to Southeast Asia's religious diversity today. Supporting facts: Indian traders came to Southeast Asia almost 2,000 years ago and brought Hinduism. Indians also brought Buddhism to the region around A.D. 200, and later, the religion of Islam. European missionaries brought Christianity to Southeast Asia in the 1500s.*)

Differentiated Instruction

For Gifted and Talented   L3
Tell students that they may also use maps to help them draw conclusions. Have students look at the transparency *Southeast Asia: Physical-Political.* Using the information they learned from p. 689 as well, ask students to draw a conclusion about why China's effect on Southeast Asia was felt primarily in Vietnam instead of other regions of Southeast Asia.

📖 **Asia and the Pacific Transparencies,** *Color Transparency AP 39: Southeast Asia: Physical-Political*

Answer
Apply the Skill
Possible conclusion: As Southeast Asians gained greater economic success, they wanted to be ruled by people from their own country, not people from foreign countries who had little interest in their welfare.

Objectives

Social Studies

1. Find out how people settled Australia and New Zealand.
2. Learn which groups shaped the cultures of Australia and New Zealand.
3. Understand how Pacific island nations have been affected by other cultures.

Reading/Language Arts

Learn to recognize signal words that indicate sequence.

Prepare to Read

Build Background Knowledge [L2]

Tell students that in this section they will learn about the cultures and history of Australia, New Zealand, and the Pacific islands. Ask students to brainstorm words and images they associate with these three regions. Use the Give One, Get One strategy (TE, p. T37) to generate a list. Then preview the photographs and captions in this section to see if students' responses match any of the images.

Set a Purpose for Reading [L2]

■ Preview the Objectives.

■ Form students into pairs or groups of four. Distribute the *Reading Readiness Guide*. Ask the students to fill in the first two columns of the chart. Use the Numbered Heads participation strategy (TE, p. T36) to call on students to share one piece of information they already know and one piece of information they want to know.

All in One **Asia and the Pacific Teaching Resources,** *Reading Readiness Guide,* p. 302

Preview Key Terms [L2]

Pronounce each Key Term, and then ask the students to say the words with you. Provide a simple explanation such as, "The Maori people have lived in New Zealand longer than any other group."

Prepare to Read

Objectives

In this section you will

1. Find out how people settled Australia and New Zealand.
2. Learn which groups shaped the cultures of Australia and New Zealand.
3. Understand how Pacific island nations have been affected by other cultures.

Taking Notes

As you read this section, look for details about the cultures and history of Australia, New Zealand, and the Pacific islands. Copy and complete the outline below.

> I. Settlement
>   A. The Maori of New Zealand
>   B. Aborigines in Australia
>   C. The Arrival of the British
> II. The Cultures of Australia and New Zealand

 **Target Reading Skill**

Recognize Signal Words
Signal words point out relationships among ideas or events. To help keep the order of events clear, look for words like *first, before, later, next,* and *recently.* These words help show the order in which events took place. Signal words sometimes, but not always, come at the beginning of a sentence.

Key Terms

• **Maori** (MAH oh ree) *n.* a native of New Zealand whose ancestors first traveled from Asia to Polynesia, and later to New Zealand

• **Aborigine** (ab uh RIJ uh nee) *n.* a member of the earliest people of Australia, who probably came from Asia

• **penal colony** (PEEN ul KAHL uh nee) *n.* a place where people convicted of crimes are sent

• **station** (STAY shun) *n.* in Australia, a large ranch for raising livestock

Stone statues on Easter Island

696 Asia and the Pacific

Hundreds of giant stone statues dot the landscape of Easter Island, a tiny island in the South Pacific. Made of volcanic rock, the statues are from 10 to 40 feet (3 to 12 meters) high. Some weigh more than 50 tons (45 metric tons). A European who saw them in 1722 was amazed:

> ❝ The stone images . . . caused us to be struck with astonishment because we could not comprehend how it was possible that these people, who are devoid of heavy thick timber for making any machines . . . had been able to erect such images. ❞
>
> —*Dutch explorer Jacob Roggeveen, 1722*

Settlement

Easter Island's statues still impress people. Easter Island is part of the island group of Polynesia. The island belongs to Chile, a country in South America. Scientists have wondered how people first came to this faraway island, as well as to the other parts of the Pacific region.

🎯 Target Reading Skill [L2]

Recognize Signal Words Direct students to the Target Reading Skill. Explain that by identifying signal words that show time order, readers can more easily understand sequence.

Model recognizing signal words using the second paragraph on p. 698. On the board, list words and terms that signal sequence. (*since, in the colonial period, starting in the 1800s, continuing into the 1960s, today*)

Give students *Recognize Sequence Signal Words.* Have them complete the activity in groups.

All in One **Asia and the Pacific Teaching Resources,** *Recognize Sequence Signal Words,* p. 306

The Maori of New Zealand The earliest people in New Zealand were the Maori (MAH oh ree). **Maori** are natives of New Zealand. Their ancestors first traveled from Asia to Polynesia. Then, about 1,000 years ago, the Maori traveled across the ocean to New Zealand. According to Maori legend, seven groups set out in long canoes to find a new homeland. A storm tossed their boats ashore on New Zealand. The Maori quickly adapted to their new home. They settled in villages, making a living as hunters and farmers. But the Maori also prized fighting and conquering their enemies. They often fought other groups of Maori over the possession of land. The Maori used storytelling to pass on their beliefs and tales of their adventures.

Aborigines in Australia Many scientists think that the earliest settlers in Australia, the **Aborigines** (ab uh RIJ uh neez), came from Asia more than 40,000 years ago. For thousands of years, they hunted and gathered food along the coasts and river valleys.

During this time, the Aboriginal population in Australia flourished. People lived in small family groups that moved from place to place in search of food and water. All had strong religious beliefs about nature and the land.

The Arrival of the British In 1788, the British founded the first colony in Australia as a penal colony. A **penal colony** is a remote place where people convicted of crimes are sent. Soon, other colonists settled in Australia. Some worked for the prison facilities. Others went to find new land. Then, in 1851, gold was discovered. The population soared. Not long after, Britain stopped sending convicts to Australia. In 1901, Australia gained its independence.

The British settled New Zealand at about the same time as Australia. In 1840, the British took control of New Zealand. The colony, with its fine harbors and fertile soil, attracted many British settlers. New Zealand gained independence in 1947.

✔ **Reading Check** How did people settle Australia and New Zealand?

Recognize Signal Words
In the paragraph at the left, which words signal, or tell you, when and how the Maori came to New Zealand?

Links to Art

Maori Canoes The Maori showed their standing in society by the works of art they owned. For instance, a person might own elaborately carved and painted war canoes. Some were as long as 100 feet (30 meters). Human figures were carved along the hull and into the prow, which is the front part of the boat. The figures often had eyes made of mother-of-pearl. Canoes were painted red and decorated with feather streamers. Today these canoes are important artifacts preserved in museums.

Chapter 23 Section 2 **697**

Vocabulary Builder

Use the information below to teach students this section's high-use words.

High-Use Word	Definition and Sample Sentence
impress, p. 130	*v.* to have a strong effect He was **impressed** with his little brother's tennis skills.
adapt, p. 131	*v.* to adjust It took a while for the immigrant family to **adapt** to life in the United States.
possession, p. 131	*n.* ownership They took **possession** of a new house.
rapidly, p. 133	*adv.* marked by a fast rate of activity The flowers grew **rapidly** once spring began.

Instruct

Settlement   L2

Guided Instruction

- **Vocabulary Builder** Clarify the high-use words **impress, adapt,** and **possession** before reading.

- Read Settlement using the Paragraph Shrinking technique (TE, p. T34).

- Ask students **How long ago did Maoris arrive in New Zealand?** *(about 1,000 years ago)* **How long ago did Aborigines arrive in Australia?** *(more than 40,000 years ago)* **Which happened first?** *(The Aborigines arrived in Australia first.)*

- Have students describe early Aboriginal settlements. *(small family groups that moved around to find food and water)*

- Discuss with students the different reasons that the British settled Australia. *(Some people were convicts sent to the penal colony, some people worked for the prison facilities, and others wanted new land or gold.)*

Target Reading Skill   L2

Recognize Signal Words As a follow up, ask students to answer the Target Reading Skill question in the Student Edition. *(when: "earliest," "first" and "about 1,000 years ago" how: "set out in long canoes")*

Links
Read the **Links to Art** on this page. Ask students **Why do you think that Maori canoes are preserved in museums today?** *(Possible answer: Canoes are an important part of Maori history.)*

Independent Practice

Ask students to create the Taking Notes graphic organizer on a blank piece of paper. Help students fill in details under the first heading to get them started.

Monitor Progress

Circulate to make sure students are properly filling in the outline.

Answer

✔ **Reading Check** Aborigines lived in small nomadic groups, as hunters and gatherers. Maoris settled in villages and hunted and farmed.

The Cultures of Australia and New Zealand L2

Guided Instruction

■ **Vocabulary Builder** Clarify the high-use word **rapidly** before reading.

■ Read The Cultures of Australia and New Zealand to learn more about Aborigines, Maoris, and other groups in Australia and New Zealand.

■ Ask students **In addition to the British, what groups have settled in Australia?** (*Chinese, Irish, Italians, Yugoslavs, Greeks, Germans, and Vietnamese*)

■ Ask students **How are the Maori working to preserve their traditional way of life in modern times?** (*The Maori have worked to gain power and to be allowed to practice their own customs. Many continue to speak Maori.*)

■ Ask students to name the other ethnic groups that make up New Zealand's population. (*Europeans, Polynesians, and Asians*)

Independent Practice

Have students continue working with the Taking Notes graphic organizer by asking them to expand and complete the sections of the outline under The Cultures of Australia and New Zealand.

Monitor Progress

Circulate to make sure students are choosing the correct supporting details for their outlines. Provide assistance as needed.

The Cultures of Australia and New Zealand

Today, most Australians and New Zealanders are descendants of British settlers. They share British culture, holidays, and customs. Most Australians and New Zealanders enjoy a high standard of living. Employment in farming, mining, manufacturing, and service industries have made the nations prosperous.

Aborigines Since the arrival of Europeans, the Aborigines have suffered great hardships. In the colonial period, settlers forced these native peoples off their lands. Tens of thousands died of European diseases. Others were forced to work on sheep and cattle **stations,** which in Australia are extremely large ranches. The settlers forced Aborigines to adopt European ways. As a result, the Aborigines began to lose their own customs and traditions. More tragically, starting in the 1800s and continuing into the 1960s, Aboriginal children were taken from their families, often by force, to live with non-Aborigines. Today, Aborigines make up less than 1 percent of the country's population.

European and Asian Immigrants People other than the British also settled in Australia. During the gold rush of the 1850s, many people came, including Chinese. Chinese people continue to settle in Australia today. About 2.6 percent of Australia's population is Chinese.

Australians All
About 92 percent of Australians are Caucasian, 7 percent are Asian, and less than 1 percent are Aborigine. Australia's Aborigine heritage was honored at the 2000 Olympic Games when track athlete Kathy Freeman, an Aborigine, lit the Olympic torch.
Summarize *How were Aborigines affected by the arrival of Europeans?*

698 Asia and the Pacific

Answer

Summarize Europeans forced Aborigines off their land, unknowingly brought diseases that killed Aborigines who lacked immunity to them, and made Aborigines adopt European ways. Aborigines began to lose their customs and traditions. From the 1800s to the 1960s, Aborigine children were taken from their families and forced to live with non-Aborigines.

Skills for Life — Skills Mini Lesson

Analyzing Primary Sources

1. Teach the skill by explaining that primary sources are information from someone who experienced or witnessed what is being described. Analyzing a primary source includes identifying the author, thinking about why the source was written, finding the main idea, looking for evidence of bias, and evaluating the reliability of the source.

2. Have students practice the skill by looking at the quoted text on p. 696. Ask them to paraphrase the main idea of the text, identify when the source was written, and identify who wrote the passage.

3. Have students apply the skill by recognizing any biases and evaluating the reliability of the source.

Farmers planting vegetables in Tasmania, an island south of Australia

After World War II, many Europeans migrated to Australia. They came from Ireland, Italy, Yugoslavia, Greece, and Germany. In the 1970s, people fleeing the war in Vietnam settled in Australia. Today, people from all over the world continue to arrive.

The Maori Way of Life When New Zealand became a British colony, Britain promised to protect Maori land. Settlers, however, broke that promise. For many years, the settlers and the Maori clashed violently. The settlers defeated the Maori in 1872. After their defeat, the Maori were forced to adopt English ways. Maori culture seemed in danger of being destroyed. Slowly, however, Maori leaders gained more power. Laws now allow the Maori to practice their customs and ceremonies.

Today about 15 percent of New Zealand's population is Maori. Most Maori now live in urban areas. Many speak both Maori and English. Thanks to their artists, writers, and singers, Maori culture is an important part of New Zealand life.

Other Peoples of New Zealand After World War II, many Europeans migrated to New Zealand. People from Polynesia have settled there as well. Today, more Polynesians live in New Zealand's largest city, Auckland, than in any other city in the world. Although most New Zealanders are of European background, the Asian population has grown rapidly.

✓ Reading Check **What is the main ethnic group in Australia and New Zealand today?**

The Cultures of the Pacific Islands [L2]

Guided Instruction

- Read The Cultures of the Pacific Islands together with students. Make sure students are able to answer the Reading Check question.

- Discuss why groups living in the Pacific islands developed separate languages, customs, and beliefs. *(The distances between islands prevented groups from communicating with each other or influencing each other.)*

- Ask **How might the arrival of British, French, German, and American settlers have affected the lives of the Pacific island peoples?** *(Possible answers: The island people may have adopted some of the ways of life of the new settlers. Once their lands were colonized, Pacific islanders may have struggled to maintain their traditions and ways of life, and may have lost control of their economies.)*

Independent Practice

Have students complete the outline with the information they have learned about Pacific island cultures.

Monitor Progress

- Show *Section Reading Support Transparency AP 63* and ask students to check their graphic organizers individually. Go over key concepts and clarify key vocabulary as needed.

  📖 **Asia and the Pacific Transparencies,** *Section Reading Support Transparency AP 63*

- Tell students to fill in the last column of the *Reading Readiness Guide*. Ask them to evaluate if what they learned was what they had expected to learn.

  All in One **Asia and the Pacific Teaching Resources,** *Reading Readiness Guide,* p. 302

Differentiated Instruction

For Advanced Readers [L3]
Have students read *The Coconut Tree,* a story from the Cook Islands in the South Pacific. Then have them answer the questions at the end of the selection.

All in One **Asia and the Pacific Teaching Resources,** *The Coconut Tree,* pp. 314–316

For Less Proficient Readers [L1]
Pre-teach important words in the section. Make large flash cards with the words *cultures, variety, colonies,* and *independence.* On the flip side of each card, write a simple definition of the word. Have students work with the cards before reading, partnering students to check each other's understanding of each word.

Answer

✓ Reading Check European

Assess and Reteach

Assess Progress
L2
Have students complete the Section Assessment. Administer the *Section Quiz*.

 Asia and the Pacific Teaching Resources, *Section Quiz,* p. 304

Reteach
L1
If students need more instruction, have them read this section in the Reading and Vocabulary Study Guide.

📖 Chapter 23, Section 2, **Eastern Hemisphere Reading and Vocabulary Study Guide,** pp. 246–248

Extend
L3
Direct students to complete the *Small Group Activity.* Remind students that they will be thinking about not only who these explorers were, but also how they traveled and why they decided to make the journey.

 Asia and the Pacific Teaching Resources, *Small Group Activity: Create a Legend About Pacific Explorers,* pp. 310–313

Answer

✓ Reading Check   Since World War II, most Pacific islands have cultures that blend traditional island cultures with those from Europe, America, and other countries. Many Pacific islanders read and speak English.

Section 2 Assessment

Key Terms
Students' sentences should reflect knowledge of each Key Term.

🎯 Target Reading Skill
Words that signal time include *In 1788; Soon; Then, in 1851; Not long after;* and *In 1901.*

Comprehension and Critical Thinking
1. (a) Asia **(b)** Both are thought to have originally come from Asia; both are native peoples in their homelands; and the native lands of both groups were settled by the British.

2. (a) Great Britain **(b)** It caused hardship and suffering for the native peoples, as they were often forced to leave their lands and adopt European ways of life.

3. (a) Southeast Asia **(b)** Possible answer: The water surrounding the island might keep travelers from bringing the influences of other cultures.

Girls from the Cook Islands, in Polynesia, wearing flower garlands, or *leis*.

The Cultures of the Pacific Islands

Scientists believe that the first people to inhabit the Pacific islands came from Southeast Asia more than 30,000 years ago.

A Variety of Cultures Because of the distances between islands, groups could not easily communicate with one another. Therefore, each group developed its own language, customs, and religious beliefs. However, the island people did have many things in common. Their ocean environment shaped their lives. It fed them and was their main means of transportation and trade. Most built their lives around their small villages.

From Colonies to Independence In the 1800s, Western nations began to take an interest in the Pacific islands. Britain, France, and Germany set up trading posts and naval bases on many islands. By 1900, the United States, Britain, France, and Germany had claimed nearly every island in the region.

After World War II, most Pacific islands gained independence, and life began to improve. By then, traditional island cultures had blended with cultures from Europe, America, and other countries. Most governments were democratic. Most churches were Christian. Many Pacific islanders read and spoke English.

✓ Reading Check   **What were Pacific island cultures like after World War II?**

Section 2 Assessment

Key Terms
Review the key terms at the beginning of this section. Use each term in a sentence that explains its meaning.

🎯 Target Reading Skill
Reread the paragraph on page 697 with the heading The Arrival of the British. Find the words that signal time related to the settlement of Australia.

Comprehension and Critical Thinking
1. (a) Apply Information From where do scientists believe the native peoples of Australia came?

(b) Compare In what ways are the histories of the Aborigines and the Maori similar?

2. (a) Recall From which country are most of the people in Australia and New Zealand descended?

(b) Identify Effects How did the settlement of Australia and New Zealand affect native peoples there?

3. (a) Recall From where do scientists believe the first people to live in the Pacific islands came?

(b) Draw Conclusions Why might people who live on an island be able to preserve their culture for a long period without change?

Writing Activity
Write 10 brief entries for a timeline that shows events in the history and cultures of Australia, New Zealand, and the nearby Pacific islands.

Writing Tip Use complete sentences for your timeline entries. This will help make the sequencing of events easier to follow.

Writing Activity
Use the *Rubric for Assessing a Timeline* to evaluate students' work.

 Asia and the Pacific Teaching Resources, *Rubric for Assessing a Timeline,* p. 321

23 Review and Assessment

◆ Chapter Summary

Section 1: Southeast Asia Cultures and History

- The people of Southeast Asia developed cultures that later blended with influences from India, China, and Europe.
- By the 1800s, European nations had gained control of most of Southeast Asia.
- After World War II ended in 1945, Southeast Asian countries gained independence.
- After Vietnam became independent, it was divided into Communist North Vietnam and non-Communist South Vietnam. In the Vietnam War, the two sides fought for control of the country for nearly 30 years.
- The United States supported South Vietnam during the Vietnam War. Hundreds of thousands of American soldiers fought in Vietnam. Fighting spread to Cambodia and Laos.
- The Vietnam War ended in 1975 when North Vietnam took over South Vietnam and united the country under a Communist government.

The Cook Islands, Polynesia

Section 2: The Pacific Region Cultures and History

- Aborigines first settled Australia, and the Maori first settled New Zealand.
- In 1788, the British set up their first colony in Australia. Australia was a British colony until it became independent in 1901.
- Britain took control of New Zealand in 1840. New Zealand became independent in 1947.
- Most Australians and New Zealanders are descended from the British and share British culture, holidays, and customs.
- Australia's population now includes Aborigines, Asians, and people with European backgrounds. New Zealand's population includes Maori, Asians, and Polynesians.

Buddha sculpture, Laos

◆ Key Terms

Match the definitions in Column I with the key terms in Column II.

Column I

1. a remote place where people convicted of crimes are sent
2. a member of the earliest people of Australia
3. a person who is devoted to the interests of his or her country
4. in Australia, a large ranch for raising livestock
5. a member of the native people of New Zealand

Column II

A nationalist
B Aborigine
C Maori
D penal colony
E station

Review Chapter Content

- Review and revisit the major themes of this chapter by asking students to classify what Guiding Question each bulleted statement in the Chapter Summary answers. Form students into groups and ask them to complete the activity together. Refer to page 567 of the Student Edition for the text of the Guiding Questions.

- Assign *Vocabulary Development* for students to review Key Terms.

  All in One Asia and the Pacific Teaching Resources, *Vocabulary Development*, p. 319

— Vocabulary Builder —

Revisit this chapter's high-use words:

eventually	stable	possession
population	impress	rapidly
expand	adapt	

Ask students to review the definitions they recorded on their *Word Knowledge* worksheets.

All in One Asia and the Pacific Teaching Resources, *Word Knowledge*, p. 307

Consider allowing students to earn extra credit if they use the words in their answers to the questions in the Chapter Review and Assessment. The words must be used correctly and in a natural context to win the extra points.

Answers

Key Terms

1. D
2. B
3. A
4. E
5. C

Review and Assessment

Comprehension and Critical Thinking

6. (a) The Khmer Empire included much of what is now Cambodia, Thailand, Malaysia, and part of Laos, and reached its height from about A.D. 800 to 1434. **(b)** Traders from India brought the religions to Southeast Asia.

7. (a) three of the following: Buddhism, Islam, Christianity, and Hinduism **(b)** three of the following: Myanmar, Thailand, Laos, Vietnam, and Cambodia

8. (a) French Indochina was an area controlled by France, made up of present-day Laos, Cambodia, and Vietnam. **(b)** Vietnamese Nationalists forced the French to give up power and leave. **(c)** The conflict in Vietnam took place between the Communist North Vietnamese, who wanted all of Vietnam to become a Communist country, and the South Vietnamese, who tried to prevent communism from spreading into non-Communist South Vietnam and were backed by the United States. The war involved hundreds of thousands of United States soldiers, and lasted until 1975, when the United States withdrew, and North Vietnam took over South Vietnam and established a Communist government.

9. (a) Aborigines lived in small family groups that moved from place to place in search of food and water. **(b)** Today, Maori make up 15 percent of New Zealand's population. Most Maori live in cities. Many are working to preserve the Maori culture.

10. (a) The British founded the first colony in Australia in 1788. **(b)** Both Australia and New Zealand were once British colonies.

11. (a) The Maori first settled on Polynesia. **(b)** Since World War II, Pacific island culture has reflected a blend of traditional island culture and the cultures from Europe, America, and other countries. Most people read and speak English and are Christian.

Skills Practice

Possible conclusion: Creating a Maori canoe requires a high level of skill.

◆ Comprehension and Critical Thinking

6. (a) Identify Identify the Khmer Empire.
(b) Identify Cause How did Hinduism and Buddhism come to Southeast Asia?

7. (a) List What are three religions in Southeast Asia today?
(b) Apply Information Name three countries in Southeast Asia in which Buddhism is the main religion today.

8. (a) Identify Identify French Indochina.
(b) Identify Causes Why did the French leave Vietnam in 1954?
(c) Summarize Describe the conflict in Vietnam, including U.S. involvement.

9. (a) Explain How did Aborigines live before the British came to Australia?
(b) Summarize Describe life for the Maori today.

10. (a) Recall What happened in Australia in 1788?
(b) Draw Conclusions How does the history of Australia and New Zealand help explain why their cultures reflect a British heritage?

11. (a) Name On what island group do historians believe the people of the Pacific islands first settled?
(b) Make Generalizations Describe Pacific island cultures after World War II.

◆ Skills Practice

Drawing Conclusions Review the steps you followed on page 694 to learn this skill. Then reread Links to Art on page 697 and draw a conclusion about the level of skill needed to make a Maori canoe.

◆ Writing Activity: Math

Population density is the average number of people living in a square mile or square kilometer. To calculate a country's population density, divide the total population by the total land area. Use an almanac or encyclopedia to find the land areas in square miles and populations for Australia, Thailand, and Vietnam. Be sure to find whole numbers. Calculate the population density of each country to the nearest whole number. Create a table that shows your data. Then write a short paragraph about your findings.

MAP MASTER™ Skills Activity

Southeast Asia and the Pacific Region

Place Location For each place listed below, write the letter from the map that shows its location.
1. Thailand
2. Vietnam
3. Indonesia
4. Australia
5. New Zealand
6. The Philippines

Go Online
PHSchool.com Use Web Code lcp-6620 for an interactive map.

Writing Activity: Math
Answers will vary slightly, depending on the source used. Be sure the table includes columns for country names, area, population, and population density. Check students' calculations.

Students' paragraphs should compare and contrast the information in their tables. Possible paragraph: Although Australia is the largest country in land area, it has the lowest population density. Vietnam is the smallest country in land area, but has the highest population density. Thailand also seems to have a high population density for its small size.

Use the *Rubric for Assessing a Writing Assignment* to assess students' paragraphs.

All in One Asia and the Pacific Teaching Resources, *Rubric for Assessing a Writing Assignment,* p. 320

Standardized Test Prep

Test-Taking Tips

Some questions on standardized tests ask you to find cause and effect. Read the passage below. Then follow the tips to answer the sample question at the right.

> In the 1100s, the Khmer Empire extended across much territory. It included lands that are now Cambodia and much of Laos, Thailand, and Vietnam. There were many other kingdoms in Southeast Asia at that time. Because of geography, however, the others were small. The mountains of Southeast Asia isolated people, who had little contact with anybody outside their own valley. Each group developed its unique way of life. The region became rich in cultures.

TIP In a cause-and-effect relationship, the effect is what happens and the cause is what makes it happen.

Pick the letter that best answers the question.

Southeast Asia was rich in cultures because—

A the Khmer Empire extended across much territory.

B mountains isolated groups of people in their own valleys.

C there were many other kingdoms in Southeast Asia in the 1100s.

D the Khmer Empire forced different groups to pull together.

TIP Look for words, such as *because, so,* and *as a result* that point to a cause-and-effect relationship.

Think It Through The fourth sentence in the passage says that "because of geography" many Southeast Asian kingdoms were small. You can eliminate A and D because the Khmer Empire did not produce these small kingdoms. C simply restates the idea that the area is rich in cultures. The correct answer is B.

Practice Questions

Use the passage below to answer Question 1.

> Beginning in the early 1900s, Australia's population grew steadily. Until the end of World War II in 1945, most of Australia's immigrants came from Great Britain. After the war ended, large numbers of immigrants came from other countries in Europe. In recent years, many immigrants have come from East Asia and Southeast Asia because of Australia's nearby location, and because of Australia's high standard of living.

1. Many immigrants recently have come to Australia from Asian countries because

   A they were not welcome in other countries.

   B Australia has a high standard of living.

   C they could afford to travel to Australia.

   D many immigrants from Great Britain were making Asian countries too crowded.

2. During the Vietnam War, fighting spread to

   A Malaysia.

   B Australia.

   C the Philippines.

   D Cambodia.

3. The first colony in Australia was set up by

   A Great Britain.

   B the United States.

   C China.

   D France.

Use Web Code lca-6600 for a **Chapter 23 self-test.**

Assessment Resources

Use *Chapter Tests A and B* to assess students' mastery of chapter content.

All in One Asia and the Pacific Teaching Resources, *Chapter Tests A and B,* pp. 322–327

Tests are also available on the *ExamView Test Bank CD-ROM.*

⊙ *ExamView Test Bank CD-ROM*

Use a benchmark test to evaluate students' cumulative understanding of what they have learned in Chapters 4 through 6.

📄 *Asia and the Pacific Benchmark Test 2,* **AYP Monitoring Assessments,** pp. 125–128

Objectives

- Discover how Jantu deals with the challenge of living in a refugee camp.

- Find out how the author uses point of view to tell a story.

- Identify devices of persuasion and determine their effectiveness.

Prepare to Read

Build Background Knowledge **L2**

Tell students that they will be reading a story about a girl who makes toys using everyday materials around her, such as twigs and leaves. Ask students to think of some objects that may be reused for something other than their original purpose. Write a list of students' responses on the board. You may need to provide an example, such as a tin can that can be used to hold pencils.

Instruct

The Clay Marble **L2**

Guided Instruction

- Point out that some words are defined for students in the margin. Clarify **sarong, mortar, recruit, resistance army, saunter,** and **retrieve** before reading.

- Read the first two paragraphs of the story with students using the Oral Cloze strategy (TE, p. T33). Then have students read the entire story by themselves. As students read, circulate and make sure individuals can answer the Reading Check questions.

- Ask students **What words are used in the story to describe Jantu's hands?** (*"quick fingers," "ordinary," "fingernails grimy," and "palms slightly calloused"*) Ask **Why do you think the author uses these words to describe Jantu?** (*Possible answer: The author is trying to show the reader that Jantu is very skilled, loves her craft, and works tirelessly.*)

The Clay Marble
By Minfong Ho

Prepare to Read

Background Information

Think of someone you admire. What special gift or quality does that person have? Some people have the ability to show us a new way of looking at things.

In 1980, civil war in Cambodia forced thousands of Cambodians to leave their homes and move to refugee camps near the border of Thailand and Cambodia. Among these refugees were many children. There was very little food, and living conditions were poor. *The Clay Marble* tells the story of twelve-year-old Dara, who lives in one such camp. Dara's friend Jantu, another girl in the camp, makes toys out of little scraps and trinkets she finds at the camp.

Objectives

In this selection, you will
1. Discover how Jantu deals with the challenge of living in a refugee camp.
2. Find out how the author uses point of view to tell a story.

I t amazed me, the way she shaped things out of nothing. A knobby branch, in her deft hands, would be whittled into a whirling top. She would weave strips of a banana leaf into plump goldfish or angular frogs. A torn plastic bag and a scrap from some newspaper would be cut and fashioned into a graceful kite with a long tail. A couple of old tin cans and a stick would be transformed into a toy truck.

One of the many refugee camps along the Thai-Cambodian border. The last refugee camp closed in 1999.

704 Asia and the Pacific

Read Fluently

Form the class into partners. Choose a paragraph from the selection. Have students take turns reading the paragraph aloud. Ask them to underline words that give them trouble as they read. Then, have them decode the problem words with their partner. Provide assistance as needed. Have them reread the paragraph two more times to improve their reading speed. Remind them to stop at the commas and periods and to read with expression.

Whenever Jantu started making something, she would withdraw into her own private world and ignore everything around her. Leaving me to mind her baby brother, she would hunch over her project, her fierce scowl keeping at bay anybody who might come too close or become too noisy. But if I was quiet and kept my distance, she didn't seem to mind my watching her.

And so I would stand a little to one side, holding the baby on my hip, as Jantu's quick fingers shaped, twisted, smoothed, rolled whatever material she happened to be working with into new toys.

"How do you do it?" I asked her one day, after she had casually woven me a delicate bracelet of wild vines.

"Well, you take five vines of about the same length—elephant creeper vines like this work well—and you start braiding them, see. Like this . . ."

"No, I don't mean just this bracelet," I said. "I mean the goldfish, too, and the kites and toy trucks and . . ."

"But they're all different," Jantu said. "You make them different ways."

"But how do you know what to make? Is there some . . . some kind of magic in your hands, maybe?"

Jantu looked puzzled. "I don't know," she said, turning her hands over and examining them with vague interest. They looked like ordinary hands, the fingernails grimy, the palms slightly calloused. "I don't see anything there," she said. "Nothing that looks like magic." She shrugged and dismissed the subject.

Yet the more I watched her, the more convinced I became that Jantu's hands were gifted with some special powers, some magic. How else could anyone explain how she made that wonderful mobile, of two delicate dolls husking rice?

Even from the start, I knew it was going to be something special. For three days Jantu had kept me busy scrounging up a collection of old cloth and string. Then, as I sat cross-legged watching her, she fashioned two straw dolls in <u>sarongs</u> and straw hats and, with dabs of sticky rice, glued their feet onto a smooth branch. Carefully she tied strings connecting the dolls' wrists and waists, so that when one doll bent down, the other one straightened up. Each doll held a long thin club, with which, in turn, one would pound at a tiny <u>mortar</u> as the other doll lifted up its club in readiness. Jantu held up the mobile and showed me how a mere breath of wind would set the two dolls in motion.

About the Selection

This reading selection is from a chapter in *The Clay Marble*, a novel for young readers written by Minfong Ho and published in 1991.

sarong (suh RAWNG) *n.* a loose garment made of a long strip of cloth wrapped around the body

mortar (MAWRT ur) *n.* a dish in which seed or grain is pounded or ground

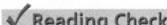

✓ Reading Check

What materials does Jantu use to make the dolls?

Chapter 23 **705**

Guided Instruction (continued)

■ Ask students **In what ways did Dara help Jantu as she made toys?** (*Dara sometimes took care of Jantu's baby brother, and at other times helped collect materials for the toys.*)

■ Discuss with students how Chnay's behavior made Dara feel. (*Dara was angry and sad that Chnay broke a toy that Jantu worked so long on, and blamed herself for not protecting it better.*) Ask **What language does the author use to show Dara's emotions?** (*Possible answer: The author uses strong words like "exclaim" and "bitterly" to convey Dara's anger.*)

■ Ask **How does the author show that Jantu and Dara have different points of view towards the mud?** (*The author explains that Dara just sees a lump of mud and a mud ball. On the other hand, Jantu notices that the mud is like clay and can easily be molded with her hands into a marble.*) Ask **How does Jantu persuade Dara that the mud ball is special?** (*She blows on it and tells Dara that it is a magic marble.*)

■ Ask **Why do you think Dara felt better by the end of the story?** (*Possible answer: Dara was happy because Jantu made another toy for her and helped her realize that there is potential fun in many of the everyday objects around her.*)

■ Ask students **How do you think Jantu decides what to make materials into?** (*Possible answer: Jantu may be inspired by objects or people around her, or things she has heard of.*)

Answer

✓ Reading Check cloth, string, straw, rice, and branches

Independent Practice

Have students create a chart about the three main characters in the story—Dara, Jantu, and Chnay. In one column, have students make a list of words that they think describe the characters' personalities. In another column, have students list passages from the story that support their descriptions.

Monitor Progress

Make sure that students are using appropriate passages from the story to support their descriptions.

A Cambodian family leaving their refugee camp to return home

recruit (rih KROOT) v. to persuade someone to join
resistance army (rih ZIS tuns AHR mee) n. an army of people resisting, or opposing, the group holding political power in a country
saunter (SAWN tur) v. to walk in an idle or a casual manner

retrieve (rih TREEV) v. to get something back again

Pound and lift, up and down, the two dolls took turns crushing the rice with exactly the same jerky rhythm that real village women pounded it to get the brown husks off. There were even some real grains in the miniature mortar set between the two dolls. It was the cleverest thing I had ever seen.

Children crowded around Jantu, pressing in from all sides to watch her work it. "Let me hold it," I begged, standing next to Jantu. "I helped you find the stuff for the dolls."

Jantu nodded. Breathlessly I held it carefully and blew on it. It worked! One of the dolls bent down and pounded the mortar with its club. The other doll straightened up and waited its turn. I was still engrossed with it when someone shouted a warning: "Watch out, Chnay's coming!"

Even in my short stay at the camp, I'd heard of Chnay. He liked to break things, and he was a bully. An orphan, Chnay made his way to the Border alone. Too young to be <u>recruited</u> into the <u>resistance army</u>, Chnay roamed the fields by himself, scrounging for food and sleeping wherever he liked.

Chnay <u>sauntered</u> up and shoved his way through to us. "What've you got there?" he demanded.

"Nothing," I said, trying to hide the toy behind me.

Laughing, Chnay snatched it away from me. One of the dolls was ripped loose and dropped to the ground.

As I bent over to <u>retrieve</u> it, Chnay pushed me aside. "Leave it," he said. "That's for kids. Look what I have." He thrust his arm out. It was crawling with big red ants, the fierce kind that really sting when they bite. "I'm letting them bite me. See?" he bragged. Already small fierce welts were swelling up on his arm, as some ants kept biting him.

"That's dumb!" I exclaimed. Dodging behind him, I tried to snatch the mobile back from him.

Chnay flung the toy to the ground, scattering straw and red ants into the air.

I grabbed on to his hand, but he was taller than I, and much stronger. He shoved me aside and stomped on the dolls until they were nothing but a pile of crushed sticks and rags. Then, kicking aside a boy who stood in his way, Chnay strode off, angrily brushing red ants off his arm.

I squatted down beside the bits of dolls and tried to fit them together, but it was no use. The delicate mobile was beyond repair. I could feel my eyes smarting with angry tears. "I should've held on to it more tightly," I said bitterly. "I shouldn't have let him grab it away from me."

706 Asia and the Pacific

Differentiated Instruction

For English Language Learners L1
English language learners might find some of the words in the story difficult to pronounce or define. Pair English language learners with more advanced students and have them make a chart with three columns. One column will contain verbs from the story that describe Jantu's actions as she makes her toys, such as *whittled, weave,* and *transformed.* Have partners look up the words in a dictionary and enter the definition and pronunciation in the other two columns of the chart.

Jantu knelt next to me and took the fragments of the dolls out of my hands. "Never mind," she said quietly, putting them aside. "We can always start something new."

"But it took you so long to make it," I said.

Idly Jantu scooped up a lump of mud from a puddle by her feet and began to knead it in her hands. "Sure, but the fun is in the making," she said.

She looked down at the lump of mud in her hands with sudden interest. "Have you ever noticed how nice the soil around here is?" she asked. "Almost like clay." She smoothed the ball with quick fingers, then rolled it between her palms.

When she opened her palm and held it out to me, there was a small brown ball of mud cupped in it. "For you," she announced.

I looked at it. Compared to the delicate rice-pounding mobile, this was not very interesting at all. "I don't want it," I said. "It's just a mud ball."

"No, it's not. It's a marble," Jantu said. Her eyes sparkling, she blew on it. "There! Now it's a magic marble."

I took it and held it. Round and cool, it had a nice solid feel to it. I glanced at Jantu. She was smiling. Slowly I smiled back at her.

Maybe, I thought, maybe she did put some magic in the marble. After all, why else would I feel better, just holding it?

✓ **Reading Check**

What happens to Jantu's dolls?

About the Author

Minfong Ho (b. 1951) was born in Rangoon, Myanmar (Burma). She grew up in Singapore and Thailand and studied at Cornell University in New York. In 1980, Ho worked as a volunteer in a refugee camp on the Cambodian-Thai border. Her experiences helped her write *The Clay Marble*. She is the author of numerous children's fiction books about life in Southeast Asia.

Review and Assessment

Thinking About the Selection

1. (a) Respond How did you feel about Chnay while reading this selection?
(b) Infer How do you think Jantu felt about what Chnay did to the dolls?

2. (a) Recall How would Jantu act when she started to make something?
(b) Analyze For Jantu, what is important, making toys or the toys themselves? Give evidence for your answer.

3. (a) Recall What does Jantu do with the lump of mud she scoops up?

(b) Contrast How is Dara's opinion of the lump of mud different from Jantu's opinion?
(c) Conclude What symbolic meaning might the clay marble have?

Writing Activity

Write an Essay Choose a person who has been important in your life. Write an essay that tells who the person is and what special qualities he or she has. Tell why these qualities are important to you. Include an introduction and a conclusion in your essay.

Chapter 23 **707**

Assess and Reteach

Assess Progress L2
Have students answer the assessment questions.

Reteach L1
If students need more instruction, have them think about from which character's point of view the story is being told *(Dara)*, and write down why they think the author chose to write the story this way. *(Possible answer: The reader may be more familiar with the point of view of Dara, who admires Jantu's skills and wonders how she is able to make toys.)*

Extend L3
To learn more about the effects of nature and people on each other, have students read the poem *The Tale of the Frog* and discuss the questions in groups.

All in One **Asia and the Pacific Teaching Resources,** *The Tale of the Frog,* p. 317

Answers

✓ Reading Check They break when Chnay throws them to the ground and stomps on them.

Review and Assessment

Thinking About the Selection

1. (a) Answers will vary. Students may say Chnay makes them sad or angry that he broke something Jantu worked so hard on.
(b) Possible answer: While Jantu may have been disappointed at first, she was able to focus on starting a new project.

2. (a) Jantu withdrew into her own private world and ignored everything around her.
(b) Possible answer: Making toys is more important, because Jantu is not as upset as Dara when Chnay breaks the dolls, and Jantu tells Dara that the fun is in the making of the toy, not the toy itself.

3. (a) She makes a marble. **(b)** Dara is not interested in what she sees as just mud, but Jantu imagines what could be made out of the mud. **(c)** The clay marble could teach us to look at the potential special quality of everyday objects.

Writing Activity
Use the *Rubric for Assessing a Writing Assignment* to evaluate students' stories.

All in One **Asia and the Pacific Teaching Resources,** *Rubric for Assessing a Writing Assignment,* p. 320

CHAPTER 24 **East Asia**

Chapter Overview

Overview

Introducing East Asia
1. Look at a map and study the data to learn about the nations of East Asia.
2. Analyze data to compare the countries.
3. Identify characteristics East Asian countries share.
4. Find some of the key differences among the countries.

The Geography of East Asia
Length: 5 minutes, 54 seconds
Provides overview of Asia and the Pacific. Illustrates the geography of the region with maps and footage.

 Section **1**

China: Transforming Itself
1. Find out how China controlled its economy from 1949 to 1980.
2. Learn about the growth of Taiwan since 1949.
3. Discover how China's government operated after the death of Mao Zedong.
4. Examine aspects of life in China today.

China's Great Green Wall
Length: 3 minutes, 9 seconds
Explains how the Chinese are combating desertification.

 Section **2**

Japan: Tradition and Change
1. Learn about the growth of Japan's economy.
2. Find out about successes and challenges in Japan's economy.
3. Examine aspects of life in Japan.

The Samurai of Japan
Length: 5 minutes, 26 seconds
Explores the tools and techniques of the samurai.

 Section **3**

The Koreas: A Divided Land
1. Understand why North Korea has been slow to develop.
2. Find out how South Korea became an economic success.

The Koreas: Rich and Poor
Length: 2 minutes, 57 seconds
Overview of North and South Korea and how their policies have affected their economies.

Technology Resources

Students use embedded Web codes to access Internet activities, chapter self-tests, and additional map practice. They may also access Dorling Kindersley's Online Desk Reference to learn more about each country they study.

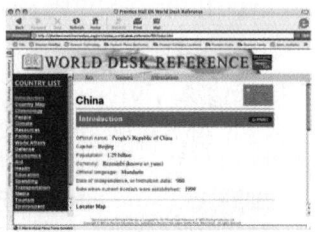

Use the Interactive Textbook to make content and concepts come alive through animations, videos, and activities that accompany the complete basal text—online and on CD-ROM.

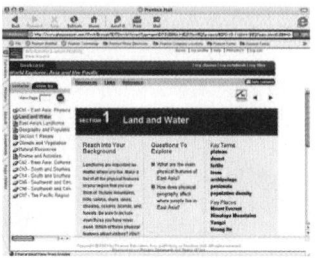

Use this complete suite of powerful teaching tools to make planning lessons and administering tests quicker and easier.

Reading and Assessment

Reading and Vocabulary Instruction

🎯 Model the Target Reading Skill

Comparison and Contrast Explain to students that comparing and contrasting can help them analyze information by noting similarities and differences between things. Using Venn diagrams can help students organize information for comparing and contrasting. Draw a Venn diagram on the board and ask students to name two different sports. *(example: basketball and running)* Draw the Venn diagram below to show similarities and differences between the two.

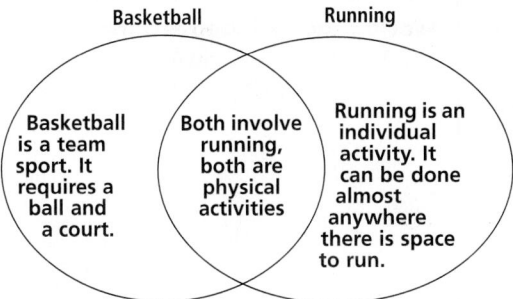

Basketball — Running

- **Basketball is a team sport. It requires a ball and a court.**
- **Both involve running, both are physical activities**
- **Running is an individual activity. It can be done almost anywhere there is space to run.**

Continue to use a Venn diagram to compare and contrast information from the chapter.

Use the following worksheets from All-in-One Asia and the Pacific Teaching Resources (pp. 343–345) to support the chapter's Target Reading Skill.

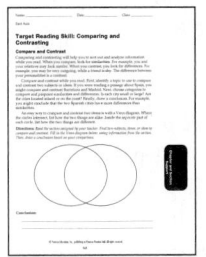 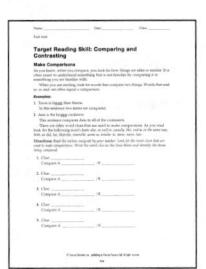 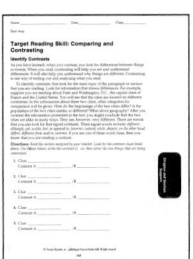

Vocabulary Builder
High-Use Academic Words
Use these steps to teach this chapter's high-use words:

1. Have students rate how well they know each word on their Word Knowledge worksheets (All-in-One Asia and the Pacific Teaching Resources, p. 346).

2. Pronounce each word and ask students to repeat it.

3. Give students a brief definition or sample sentence (provided on TE pp. 715, 721, and 729).

4. Work with students as they fill in the "Definition or Example" column of their Word Knowledge worksheets.

Assessment

Formal Assessment
Test students' understanding of core knowledge and skills.

Chapter Tests A and B, All-in-One Asia and the Pacific Teaching Resources, pp. 360–365

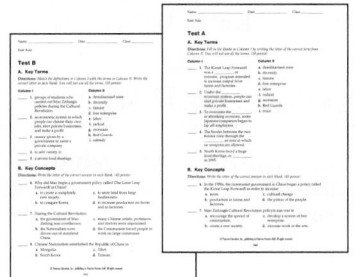

Customize the Chapter Tests to suit your needs.

ExamView Test Bank CD-ROM

Skills Assessment
Assess geographic literacy.

MapMaster Skills, Student Edition pp. 709, 734

Country Profile Map and Chart Skills, Student Edition pp. 717, 723, 731

Assess reading and comprehension.

Target Reading Skills, Student Edition, pp. 719, 722, 730, and in Section Assessments

Chapter 24 Assessment, Eastern Hemisphere Reading and Vocabulary Study Guide, p. 259

Performance Assessment

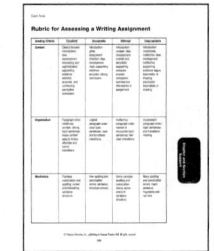

Assess students' performance on this chapter's Writing Activities using the following rubrics from All-in-One Asia and the Pacific Teaching Resources.

Rubric for Assessing a Writing Assignment, p. 359

Assess students' work through performance tasks.

Small Group Activity: The Divided Koreas, All-in-One Asia and the Pacific Teaching Resources, pp. 349–352

Portfolio Activity, Teacher Edition, p. 713

Online Assessment
Have students check their own understanding.

Chapter Self-Test

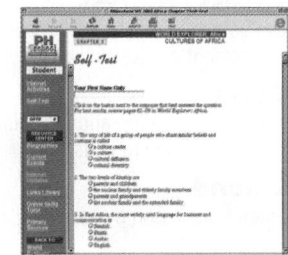

Section 1 China: Transforming Itself

 1.5 periods, .75 block (includes Country Databank)

Social Studies Objectives

1. Find out how China controlled its economy from 1949 to 1980.
2. Learn about the growth of Taiwan since 1949.
3. Discover how China's government operated after the death of Mao Zedong.
4. Examine aspects of life in China today.

Reading/Language Arts Objective

Learn how to compare and contrast to help analyze information.

Prepare to Read	Instructional Resources	Differentiated Instruction
Build Background Knowledge Have students think about how their communities have changed over time. **Set a Purpose for Reading** Have students evaluate statements on the *Reading Readiness Guide*. **Preview Key Terms** Teach the section's Key Terms. **Target Reading Skill** Introduce the section's Target Reading Skill of **comparing and contrasting**.	**All in One Asia and the Pacific Teaching Resources** L2 Reading Readiness Guide, p. 332 L2 Compare and Contrast, p. 343	**Spanish Reading and Vocabulary Study Guide** L1 Chapter 24, Section 1, pp. 177–178 ELL **World Studies Video Program** L2 The Geography of East Asia AR, GT, LPR, SN

Instruct	Instructional Resources	Differentiated Instruction
China's Economy, 1949–1980 Discuss the Great Leap Forward, the Cultural Revolution, and the leadership of Mao Zedong. **Taiwan Since 1949** Discuss Taiwan's economic and cultural growth. **Country Profile** Ask students to derive information from maps, charts, and graphs. **Changes in China** Discuss the benefits of Deng Xiaoping's leadership. **China Today** Discuss some of the issues that modern China faces. **Target Reading Skill** Review **comparing and contrasting**.	**All in One Asia and the Pacific Teaching Resources** L2 Guided Reading and Review, p. 333 L2 Reading Readiness Guide, p. 332 **Asia and the Pacific Transparencies** L2 Section Reading Support Transparency AP 64	**All in One Asia and the Pacific Teaching Resources** L2 Using the Map Key, p. 353 AR, GT, LPR, SN L2 Outline Map 29: East Asia, p. 354 AR, GT, LPR, SN L3 City Kids in China, pp. 355–356 AR, GT **Asia and the Pacific Transparencies** L1 Transparency B16: Venn Diagram ELL, LPR, SN **Teacher's Edition** L1 For Special Needs Students, TE p. 712 L2 For English Language Learners, TE p. 712 L1 For Less Proficient Readers, TE p. 716 L3 For Advanced Readers, TE p. 716 **Passport to the World CD-ROM** L1 China ELL, LPR, SN

Assess and Reteach	Instructional Resources	Differentiated Instruction
Assess Progress Evaluate student comprehension with the section assessment and section quiz. **Reteach** Assign the Reading and Vocabulary Study Guide to help struggling students. **Extend** Extend the lesson by assigning a Book Project.	**All in One Asia and the Pacific Teaching Resources** L2 Section Quiz, p. 334 L3 Book Project: Asia Trade Fair, pp. 83–85 **Reading and Vocabulary Study Guide** L1 Chapter 24, Section 1, pp. 250–252 **World Studies Video Program** L2 China's Great Green Wall	**All in One Asia and the Pacific Teaching Resources** Rubric for Assessing a Bar Graph, p. 408 AR, GT, LPR, SN **Spanish Support** L2 Section Quiz (Spanish), p. 245 ELL **Asia and the Pacific Transparencies** L1 Color Transparency AP 32: East Asia: Political ELL, LPR, SN

Key
L1 Basic to Average   L3 Average to Advanced   LPR Less Proficient Readers   GT Gifted and Talented
L2 For All Students   AR Advanced Readers   ELL English Language Learners
SN Special Needs Students

Section 2 Japan: Tradition and Change

1.5 periods, .75 block (includes Skills for Life)

Social Studies Objectives

1. Learn about the growth of Japan's economy.
2. Find out about successes and challenges in Japan's economy.
3. Examine aspects of life in Japan.

Reading/Language Arts Objective

Compare information to identify similarities.

Prepare to Read	Instructional Resources	Differentiated Instruction
Build Background Knowledge Discuss the qualities of a good employee. **Set a Purpose for Reading** Have students begin to fill out the *Reading Readiness Guide.* **Preview Key Terms** Teach the section's Key Terms. **Target Reading Skill** Introduce the section's Target Reading Skill of **making comparisons.**	**All in One Asia and the Pacific Teaching Resources** **L2** Reading Readiness Guide, p. 336 **L2** Make Comparisons, p. 344	**Spanish Reading and Vocabulary Study Guide** **L1** Chapter 24, Section 2, pp. 179–180 ELL

Instruct	Instructional Resources	Differentiated Instruction
Building a Developed Economy Discuss the economy and industry of Japan. **Target Reading Skill** Review **making comparisons.** **Successes and Challenges** Discuss Japan's economy in the 1980s and ask about Japanese spending habits. **Country Profile** Ask students to derive information from maps, charts, and graphs. **Life in Japan** Discuss Japan's culture.	**All in One Asia and the Pacific Teaching Resources** **L2** Guided Reading and Review, p. 337 **L2** Reading Readiness Guide, p. 336 **Asia and the Pacific Transparencies** **L2** Section Reading Support Transparency AP 65 **World Studies Video Program** **L2** The Samurai of Japan	**All in One Asia and the Pacific Teaching Resources** **L2** Skills for Life, p. 348 AR, GT, LPR, SN **Teacher's Edition** **L1** For Less Proficient Readers, TE p. 722 **L3** For Gifted and Talented, TE p. 723 **L1** For Special Needs Students, TE p. 724 **L1** For English Language Learners, TE p. 724 **Spanish Support** **L2** Guided Reading and Review (Spanish), p. 246 ELL

Assess and Reteach	Instructional Resources	Differentiated Instruction
Assess Progress Evaluate student comprehension with the section assessment and section quiz. **Reteach** Assign the Reading and Vocabulary Study Guide to help struggling students. **Extend** Extend the lesson by assigning an Enrichment activity.	**All in One Asia and the Pacific Teaching Resources** **L2** Section Quiz, p. 338 **L3** Enrichment, p. 347 Rubric for Assessing a Writing Assignment, p. 359 **Reading and Vocabulary Study Guide** **L1** Chapter 24, Section 2, pp. 253–255	**Spanish Support** **L2** Section Quiz (Spanish), p. 247 ELL **Teacher's Edition** **L1** For Special Needs Students, TE p. 727 **Social Studies Skills Tutor CD-ROM** **L1** Synthesizing Information ELL, LPR, SN

Key

L1 Basic to Average	**L3** Average to Advanced	**LPR** Less Proficient Readers	**GT** Gifted and Talented
L2 For All Students		**AR** Advanced Readers	**ELL** English Language Learners
		SN Special Needs Students	

Section 3 The Koreas: A Divided Land

 2 periods, 1 block (includes Chapter Review and Assessment)

Social Studies Objectives
1. Understand why North Korea has been slow to develop.
2. Find out how South Korea became an economic success.

Reading/Language Arts Objective
Learn how to identify contrasts to examine differences in information.

Prepare to Read

Build Background Knowledge
Discuss the separation of North and South Korea using a hypothetical situation.

Set a Purpose for Reading
Have students evaluate statements on the *Reading Readiness Guide*.

Preview Key Terms
Teach the section's Key Terms.

Target Reading Skill
Introduce the section's Target Reading Skill of **identifying contrasts.**

Instructional Resources

All in One Asia and the Pacific Teaching Resources
- L2 Reading Readiness Guide, p. 340
- L2 Identify Contrasts, p. 345

Differentiated Instruction

Spanish Reading and Vocabulary Study Guide
- L1 Chapter 24, Section 3, pp. 181–182 ELL

Instruct

North Korea: Economic Challenges
Discuss North Korea's economy.

South Korea: Economic Growth
Discuss South Korea's economy.

Target Reading Skill
Review **identifying contrasts.**

Country Profile
Ask students to derive information from maps, charts, and graphs.

Years of Tension
Discuss tensions between North and South Korea.

Instructional Resources

All in One Asia and the Pacific Teaching Resources
- L2 Guided Reading and Review, p. 341
- L2 Reading Readiness Guide, p. 340

Asia and the Pacific Transparencies
- L2 Section Reading Support Transparency AP 66

World Studies Video Program
- L2 The Koreas: Rich and Poor

Differentiated Instruction

All in One Asia and the Pacific Teaching Resources
- L3 Doing Searches on the Internet, p. 357 AR, GT

Teacher's Edition
- L1 For Special Needs Students, TE p. 730
- L3 For Advanced Readers, TE p. 731
- L3 For Gifted and Talented, TE p. 731

Spanish Support
- L2 Guided Reading and Review (Spanish), p. 248 ELL

Assess and Reteach

Assess Progress
Evaluate student comprehension with the section assessment and section quiz.

Reteach
Assign the Reading and Vocabulary Study Guide to help struggling students.

Extend
Extend the lesson by assigning a Small Group Activity.

Instructional Resources

All in One Asia and the Pacific Teaching Resources
- L2 Section Quiz, p. 342
- L3 Small Group Activity: The Divided Koreas, pp. 349–352
  Rubric for Assessing a Writing Assignment, p. 359
- L2 Word Knowledge, p. 346
- L2 Vocabulary Development, p. 358
- L2 Chapter Tests A and B, pp. 360–365

Reading and Vocabulary Study Guide
- L1 Chapter 24, Section 3, pp. 256–258

Differentiated Instruction

Spanish Support
- L2 Section Quiz (Spanish), p. 249 ELL
- L2 Chapter Summary (Spanish), p. 250 ELL
- L2 Vocabulary Development (Spanish), p. 251 ELL

Key
- L1 Basic to Average
- L3 Average to Advanced
- L2 For All Students

- LPR Less Proficient Readers
- AR Advanced Readers
- SN Special Needs Students

- GT Gifted and Talented
- ELL English Language Learners

Reading Background

Using Summary Sentence Frames to Compare and Contrast

Students can utilize the skill of summarizing to help them compare and contrast information. Writing one-sentence summaries can help students learn information because it requires them to highlight the main points in the briefest way possible. Using sentence frames can help students with this process. A common sentence frame for comparing and contrasting is:

> (X) and (Y) are similar in that they both_____, but (X)_____, while (Y)_____.

Use the following steps to model how to write a one-sentence summary:

1. Read the section aloud.
2. List four or five details from the section.
3. Show how to combine these details into one sentence, using a sentence frame.

Provide students with the following sentence frames to use with the chapter:

Section 1

Mao Zedong and Deng Xiaoping were similar in that they both were *(Chinese leaders)*, but Mao *(was more radical)*, while Deng *(was more pragmatic)*.

Section 2

The role of women in Japan today is similar to what it was many years ago in that *(marriage is important)*, but Japanese women today *(are delaying marriage)*, while women in the past *(married earlier)*.

Section 3

North Korea and South Korea are similar in that they both *(share the Korean peninsula, culture, and language)*, but North Korea is a *(communist country)*, while South Korea is a *(democracy)*.

Choral Reading Strategy

In this chapter, students will use the Choral Reading strategy to engage them in actively reading the chapter. Remember that the following tips can help improve the effectiveness of the Choral Reading strategy:

1. Make sure that students say the words with you, without lagging behind or racing ahead in their speech.
2. Use only short passages of less than 500 words.
3. Follow the choral reading with a silent reading of the same passage to allow students to review the materials now that they are familiar with the content.

World Studies Background

Communist China and the Soviet Union

Although they were both communist countries for many years, China and the Soviet Union had a tumultuous relationship during the mid 1900s. In the 1940s, when the Chinese Communist Party (CCP) was struggling for power against the Nationalists, the Soviet Union backed the Nationalists because Stalin believed the Nationalists were more loyal to Soviet principles. When the CCP finally gained control over China, the CCP and the Communist Party of the Soviet Union often disagreed over foreign policy and ideology. Tensions caused the Communist parties of China and the Soviet Union to break all ties with each other in the 1960s.

Japan's Postwar Government

Japan underwent great political changes after World War II. During the Allied occupation from 1945 to 1952, Japan was required to implement a new constitution. This document marked a radical departure from Japanese tradition. It declared that power lay with the people, not with the emperor, who previously had been considered divine. The emperor is still the head of state, but he is no longer worshipped as a deity.

Infoplease® provides a wealth of useful information for the classroom. You can use this resource to strengthen your background on the subjects covered in this chapter. Have students visit this advertising-free site as a starting point for projects requiring research.

 Use Web code **lcd-6700** for **Infoplease®**.

Chapter 24

Guiding Questions

Remind students about the Guiding Questions introduced at the beginning of this section.

Section 1 relates to **Guiding Question ⑤** **How do the people of this region make a living?** *(China's economy has been transformed from an economy controlled by the government to an increasingly free enterprise one.)*

Section 2 relates to **Guiding Question ⑤** **How do the people of this region make a living?** *(Japan has one of the largest economies in the world, based on manufacturing and service industries. However, it does not have a growing labor force.)*

Section 3 relates to **Guiding Question ④** **What types of government exist in Asia and the Pacific today?** *(After World War II, the Korean Peninsula was divided into two countries: North Korea and South Korea. North Korea is a communist country ruled by a dictatorship, while South Korea is a democracy with an economy based on free enterprise.)*

Target Reading Skill

In this chapter, students will learn and apply the reading skill of comparing and contrasting. Use the following worksheets to help students practice this skill:

All in One Asia and the Pacific Teaching Resources, *Compare and Contrast,* p. 343; *Make Comparisons,* p. 344; *Identify Contrasts,* p. 345

Chapter Preview

This chapter focuses on key countries in East Asia: China, Japan, North Korea, and South Korea.

Country Databank
The Country Databank provides data and descriptions of each of the countries of East Asia: China, Japan, North Korea, South Korea, Taiwan, and Mongolia.

Section 1
China
Transforming Itself

Section 2
Japan
Tradition and Change

Section 3
The Koreas
A Divided Land

Target Reading Skill

Comparison and Contrast In this chapter, you will focus on using comparison and contrast to help you analyze information.

▶ Dressed in traditional clothing, a Korean man plays a stringed instrument called a komungo.

Differentiated Instruction

The following Teacher Edition strategies are suitable for students of varying abilities.

Advanced Readers, pp. 671, 716, 731
English Language Learners, pp. 712, 724
Gifted and Talented, pp. 723, 731
Less Proficient Readers, pp. 716, 722
Special Needs Students, pp. 712, 724, 727, 730

Bibliography

For the Teacher
Cornell, Eric. *North Korea Under Communism.* Routledge Curzon, 2002.
Jansen, Marius B. *The Making of Modern Japan.* Belknap Press, 2002.
Spence, Jonathan D. *The Search for Modern China.* W.W. Norton and Company, 2001.

For the Student
L1 Wells, Ruth. *A to Zen: A Book of Japanese Culture.* Simon and Schuster Children's Publishing, 1992.
L2 Allan, Tony. *The Rise of Modern China (20th Century Perspectives).* Heinemann Library, 2002.
L3 Dudley, William. *North and South Korea (Opposing Viewpoints).* Greenhaven Press, 2002.

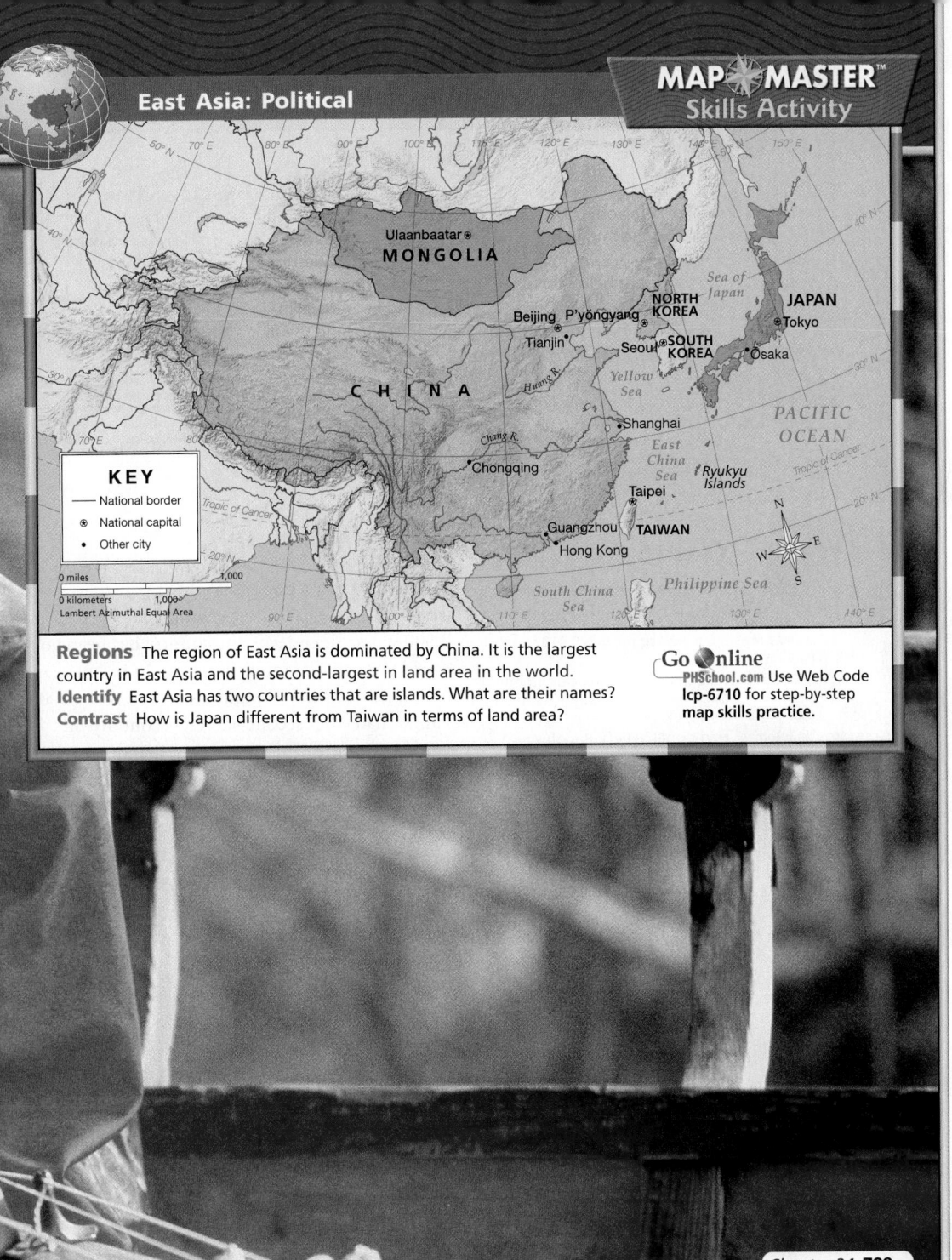

East Asia: Political

KEY
— National border
⊙ National capital
• Other city

0 miles   1,000
0 kilometers   1,000
Lambert Azimuthal Equal Area

Regions The region of East Asia is dominated by China. It is the largest country in East Asia and the second-largest in land area in the world.
Identify East Asia has two countries that are islands. What are their names?
Contrast How is Japan different from Taiwan in terms of land area?

Go Online
PHSchool.com Use Web Code lcp-6710 for step-by-step map skills practice.

Divide students into pairs and have each pair carefully study the map on this page. Draw a table on the board with four columns. Label the first column *Name of country,* the second *National capital,* the third *Other cities,* and the fourth *Country or countries that border it.* Have students copy the table and fill it in with the correct details about the countries shown on the map. Circulate among students to make sure that they are putting the information in the correct columns.

Go Online
PHSchool.com Students may practice their map skills using the interactive online version of this map.

Using the Visual   L2

Reach Into Your Background Ask students to study the photograph on pp. 708 and 709, and read the caption on p. 708. Have students discuss the musical instrument in the photograph. Can they think of other musical instruments in their own cultures that are similar? Conduct an Idea Wave (TE, p. T35) to elicit student responses, and then record them on the board.

Answers

Identify Japan, Taiwan **Contrast** Japan's land area is larger, although it is made up of many islands, while Taiwan's land area is smaller and made up of only one island.

Chapter Resources

Teaching Resources
L2 Vocabulary Development, p. 358
L2 Skills for Life, p. 348
L2 Chapter Tests A and B, pp. 360–365

Spanish Support
L2 Spanish Chapter Summary, p. 250
L2 Spanish Vocabulary Development, p. 251

Media and Technology
L1 Student Edition on Audio CD
L1 Guided Reading Audiotapes, English and Spanish
L2 Social Studies Skill Tutor CD-ROM
ExamView Test Bank CD-ROM

PRENTICE HALL
Presentation EXPRESS™
Teach · Connect · Inspire

Teach this chapter's content using the PresentationExpress™ CD-ROM including:
■ slide shows
■ transparencies
■ interactive maps and media
■ *ExamView*® QuickTake Presenter

Objectives

- Look at a map and study the data to learn about the nations of East Asia.

- Analyze data to compare the countries.

- Identify characteristics East Asian countries share.

- Find some of the key differences among the countries.

Show *The Geography of East Asia.* Ask **How does the land use in China compare to the land use in Japan?** *(Students may say that in China, proximity to the sea and fertile soil continue to make agriculture and fishing important to a majority of Chinese — despite pockets of industrialization and modern city life. In Japan, farmers are much scarcer than business people. Most people live in urban areas, and technology thrives.)*

Prepare to Read

Build Background Knowledge   L2

Remind students of the distinctive physical features of East Asia that they saw in *The Geography of East Asia.* *(The Himalayas, the Plateau of Tibet, the archipelago of Japan, the Korean Peninsula, the Mongolian steppes, and the Gobi Desert)* Then have them quickly preview the information in the tables of the Country Databank. Discuss with students how the physical geography of a country can affect its economy, such as how people make a living and what kind of goods a country might export. Use the Numbered Heads participation strategy (TE, p. T36) to encourage class discussion.

The Geography of East Asia, **World Studies Video Program**

Introducing
East Asia

Guide for Reading

This section provides an introduction to the countries that make up the region of East Asia.

- Look at the map on the previous page and then read the paragraphs below to learn about each nation.

- Analyze the data to compare the countries.

- What are the characteristics that most of the countries share?

- What are some key differences among the countries?

Viewing the Video Overview

View the World Studies Video Overview to learn more about each of the countries. As you watch, answer this question:

- How does the land use in China compare to land use in Japan?

Learn about the key geographic features in East Asia.

China

Capital	Beijing
Land Area	3,600,927 sq mi; 9,326,410 sq km
Population	1.31 billion
Ethnic Group(s)	Han, Zhuang, Uygur, Hui, Tibetan, Miao, Manchu, Mongol, Buyi, Korean
Religion(s)	traditional beliefs, Buddhist, Muslim, Christian
Government	Communist state
Currency	yuan
Leading Exports	machinery and equipment, textiles and clothing, footwear, toys and sporting goods, mineral fuels
Language(s)	Mandarin (official), Wu, Cantonese, Hsiang, Min, Hakka, Kan

With more than one billion people, China (CHY nuh) is the most populous country in the world. The history and culture of China date back about 3,500 years. Since 1949, the country has been governed under a Communist system. In recent years, China has worked to build its economy. In 2005, China had the second-largest economy in the world, after the United States. Expanding private businesses and trade with countries around the world have helped China's economy grow rapidly.

Beijing, China

710 Asia and the Pacific

A priest outside a temple in Japan

Japan

Capital	Tokyo
Land Area	144,689 sq mi; 374,744 sq km
Population	127 million
Ethnic Group(s)	Japanese, Korean, Chinese, Brazilian, Southwest Asian
Religion(s)	traditional beliefs, Buddhist, Christian
Government	constitutional monarchy
Currency	yen
Leading Exports	motor vehicles, semiconductors, office machinery, chemicals
Language(s)	Japanese (official), Korean, Chinese

Japan (juh PAN) is an island country located east of North Korea and South Korea. Japan's four main islands and thousands of small islands lie between the Sea of Japan and the Pacific Ocean. Most of Japan's land is rugged and mountainous. Japan succeeded in building a strong economy in the decades after World War II. Although its economy has declined in recent years, Japan still has one of the largest economies in the world. Japan is among the world's leading producers of motor vehicles and electronic equipment.

Mongolia

Capital	Ulaanbaatar
Land Area	600,540 sq mi; 1,555,400 sq km
Population	2.6 million
Ethnic Group(s)	Mongol, Turkic, Tungusic, Chinese, Russian
Religion(s)	Buddhist, Muslim, traditional beliefs, Christian
Government	parliamentary
Currency	tugrik
Leading Exports	copper, livestock, animal products, cashmere, wool, hides, fluorspar, other nonferrous metals
Language(s)	Khalka Mongolian, Kazakh, Chinese, Russian

Mongolia (mahn GOH lee uh) is a landlocked country bordered by Russia to the north and China to the south. Mongolia has very little land suitable for growing crops. Most of the labor force works in raising and herding livestock. Industry in Mongolia takes place chiefly in the capital city of Ulaanbaatar and consists primarily of livestock products, such as dairy products, meats, and woolen textiles. Mongolia is rich in mineral resources as well. The mining of copper, gold, coal, and other minerals contributes to Mongolia's economy.

Chapter 24 **711**

Instruct

Introducing East Asia L2

Guided Instruction

- Read each country paragraph as a class using the Oral Cloze strategy (TE, p. T33). Then, ask students to read through each data table.

- Ask **Which country has the largest land area?** *(China, with 3,600,927 sq mi; 9,326,410 sq km)* **Which has the smallest land area?** *(Taiwan, with 12,456 sq mi; 32,260 sq km)*

- Discuss the religions listed for each country. **What religions do all of the countries share?** *(Buddhism, Christianity, and traditional beliefs)* **In which countries do Muslims live?** *(China and Mongolia)*

- Discuss with students how they think the different physical geographies of Japan and Mongolia affect their exports. *(Answers will vary, but may include the following: Japan is an island country that has a rugged and mountainous landscape, which might make it difficult to raise crops or livestock; it has built a strong industrial economy and exports goods such as motor vehicles and semiconductors; Mongolia has little land suitable for growing crops, but most of its labor force raises livestock, and the country is rich in mineral deposits, therefore livestock, animal products, and minerals are leading exports.)*

Background: Links Across Place

Japan's Technology Giant One of the most successful post-World War II Japanese companies was the Sony Corporation, which was founded in 1946 as the Tokyo Telecommunications Engineering Corporation. The company was founded by some of those who had helped to create new technology for use during World War II. The purpose of their new company was to find ways to apply this technology to consumer products. One of its first popular products was the audio tape recorder, which it introduced in 1950. In 1957, it introduced the first pocket-sized transistor radio. Sony was also a pioneer in early television technology, introducing a transistor television set in 1960 and color televisions in 1968.

Guided Instruction (continued)

- Ask students **What are some of the major differences between North and South Korea?** *(population size, kinds of ethnic groups, types of government, leading exports)* **Based on Korea's history, why do you think these countries have so many differences?** *(When Korea was divided after World War II, North Korea was occupied by the Soviet Union, and South Korea was occupied by the United States; these countries influenced North and South Korea in different ways.)*

- Ask **What is one type of leading export that both North and South Korea have in common?** *(fish and fishery products)* **What about the location of the Koreas do you think makes this possible?** *(Both countries have ocean coasts.)*

Independent Practice

- Have students complete *Using the Map Key*, and then divide the class into pairs or groups and give them *Outline Map 29: East Asia*. Ask them to choose one type of data in the Country Databank (such as Government or Official Language) and show it for each country on their maps. Guide them to avoid Ethnic Groups and Leading Exports. Refer them to p. 709 for a map of the region.

  All in One **Asia and the Pacific Teaching Resources,** *Using the Map Key*, p. 353; *Outline Map 29: East Asia*, p. 354

- Remind them to create a map key that clearly explains the meanings of any colors or symbols on their maps.

- Students should also include the capital of each country on their maps.

Monitor Progress

Circulate to make sure students have chosen appropriate data and are expressing it correctly.

Introducing East Asia

North Korea

Capital	Pyongyang
Land Area	46,490 sq mi; 120,410 sq km
Population	22.3 million
Ethnic Group(s)	Korean, Chinese, Japanese
Religion(s)	Buddhist, traditional beliefs, Christian
Government	authoritarian socialist
Currency	North Korean won
Leading Exports	minerals, metallurgical products, manufactured goods (including armaments), agricultural and fishery products
Language(s)	Korean (official), Chinese

South Korea

Capital	Seoul
Land Area	37,911 sq mi; 98,190 sq km
Population	48.3 million
Ethnic Group(s)	Korean, Chinese
Religion(s)	Christian, Buddhist, traditional beliefs
Government	republic
Currency	South Korean won
Leading Exports	electronic products, machinery and equipment, motor vehicles, steel, ships, textiles, clothing, footwear, fish
Language(s)	Korean (official), Chinese

Children eating dinner in South Korea

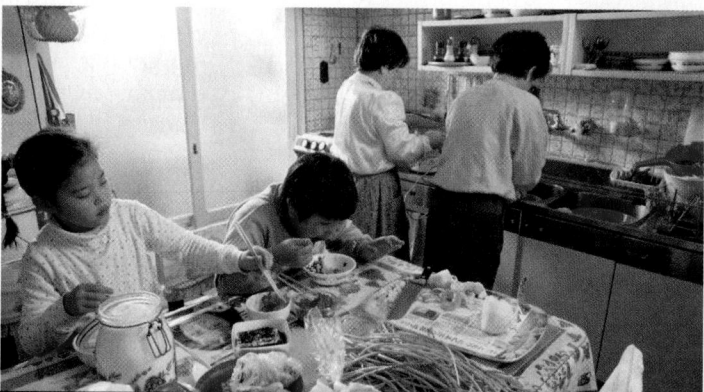

North Korea (nawrth kuh REE uh) is located on the northern part of the Korean Peninsula. Before World War II ended in 1945, Korea was one country. From 1910 to 1945, Korea was controlled by Japan. When Japan was defeated in World War II, Korea was divided into two parts. The northern part was occupied by the Soviet Union and the southern part was occupied by the United States. In 1948, North Korea and South Korea were established as separate nations. Since then, North Korea has been governed under a communist system. The government supports a huge military and an extensive weapons program, including weapons of mass destruction.

The nation of South Korea (sowth kuh REE uh) was established in 1948. South Korea is located on the southern half of the Korean Peninsula. South Korea went through many years of political unrest under a number of different rulers. The country's first democratic elections were held in 1987. Since the 1960s, South Korea has achieved remarkable economic growth. Despite an economic slowdown in the late 1990s, South Korea's economy continued to grow in 2002. Its major industries include car production, electronics, shipbuilding, steel, textiles, and footwear. Political relations between South Korea and North Korea have been strained since the Korean War in the 1950s.

712 Asia and the Pacific

Differentiated Instruction

For Special Needs Students **L1**

Have students become more familiar with China, the largest country in East Asia, through the special purpose map, photo tour, and timeline for this country on the Passport to the World CD ROM.

⊙ *China,* **Passport to the World CD-ROM**

For English Language Learners **L2**

If students are having trouble comparing the data, have them create a table on a large piece of poster board that shows the data for all of the countries in the Country Databank. They should list the categories across the top of the table and the names of the countries along the side. Model filling in the information for one country on the board.

Taiwan

Capital	Taipei
Land Area	12,456 sq mi; 32,260 sq km
Population	22.5 million
Ethnic Group(s)	Taiwanese, Chinese, aborigine
Religion(s)	Buddhist, traditional beliefs, Christian
Government	multiparty democracy
Currency	Taiwan dollar
Leading Exports	machinery and electrical equipment, metals, textiles, plastics, chemicals
Language(s)	Mandarin Chinese (official), Amoy Chinese, Hakka Chinese

SOURCES: DK World Desk Reference Online; CIA World Factbook Online; *World Almanac*, 2003

Taiwan (ty wahn) is an island country located off the southeastern coast of China. The formation of Taiwan as a nation was the result of a power struggle between two political parties in China. One party, the Chinese Communists, gained control of China in 1949. The other party, the Nationalists, fled to Taiwan and set up a government there. During the 1950s and 1960s, Taiwan built a strong economy based on manufacturing industries. Manufacturing is still important in Taiwan today, but growing service industries, such as banking, bring in more money to the nation's economy.

An aerial view of Taipei, Taiwan

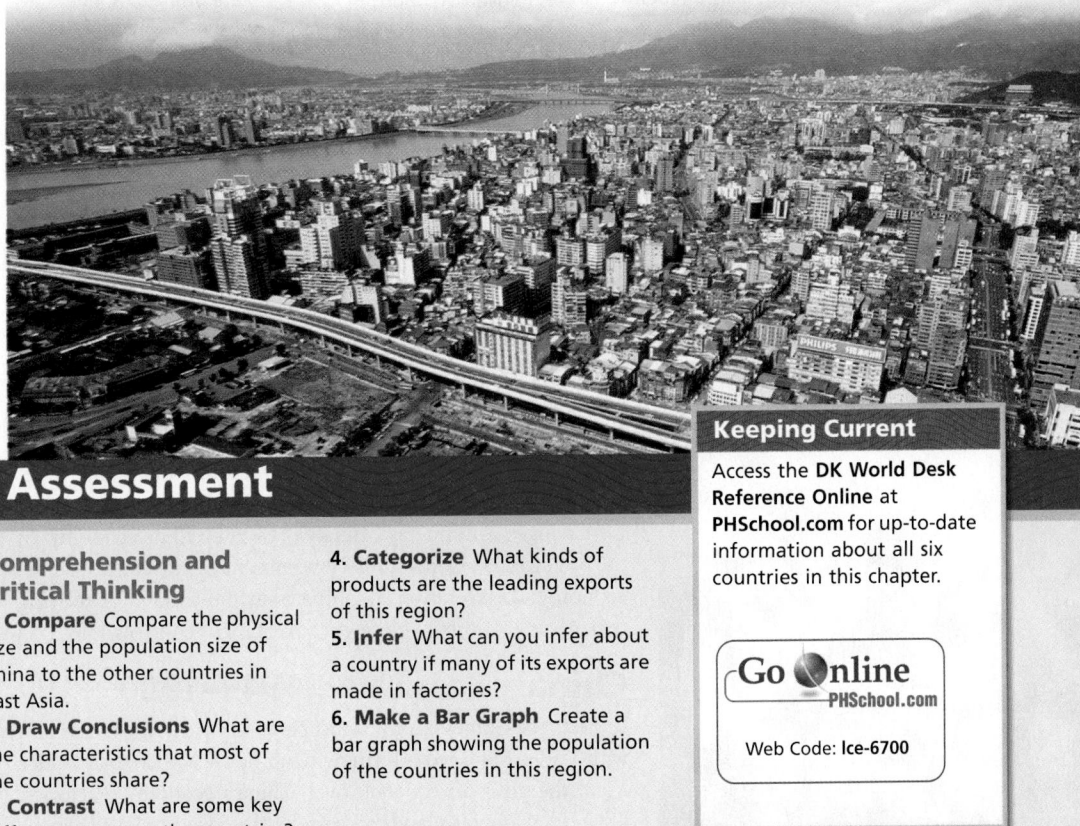

Assessment

Comprehension and Critical Thinking

1. Compare Compare the physical size and the population size of China to the other countries in East Asia.

2. Draw Conclusions What are the characteristics that most of the countries share?

3. Contrast What are some key differences among the countries?

4. Categorize What kinds of products are the leading exports of this region?

5. Infer What can you infer about a country if many of its exports are made in factories?

6. Make a Bar Graph Create a bar graph showing the population of the countries in this region.

Keeping Current

Access the **DK World Desk Reference Online** at **PHSchool.com** for up-to-date information about all six countries in this chapter.

Go Online
PHSchool.com

Web Code: lce-6700

Assess Progress L2

- Ask students to think back to the connections they made between the physical geography of a country and ways in which it might influence that country's economic activity. What connections did they notice?

- Ask students to answer the Assessment questions.

Reteach L1

Help reinforce the location of each country in the Country Databank by showing *Color Transparency AP 32: East Asia: Political.* As you read about each country with students, have one student come up and locate the country on the transparency. Have them trace its border with their fingers and locate the countries that border it.

Asia and the Pacific Transparencies, *Color Transparency AP 32: East Asia Political*

Extend L3

Portfolio Activity
Have students choose one country in the Country Databank. Ask them to research the country, using the DK World Desk Reference Online as a starting point. Then, have them create a paragraph, short story, chart, graph, map, or illustration about the country to add to their portfolios.

Answers

Assessment

1. China has the largest land area and largest population.

2. Most countries have the same religions.

3. Key differences include land area, population, ethnic groups, government, currency, leading exports, and languages.

4. Leading exports include manufactured goods, such as electronics, machinery and equipment, motor vehicles, and electrical products.

5. Possible answer: It has an industrial economy.

6. Students' bar graphs should reflect the countries' populations accurately. Use *Rubric for Assessing a Bar Graph* to evaluate students' work.

   All in One Asia and the Pacific Teaching Resources, *Rubric for Assessing a Bar Graph,* p. 408

Objectives

Social Studies

1. Find out how China controlled its economy from 1949 to 1980.
2. Learn about the growth of Taiwan since 1949.
3. Discover how China's government operated after the death of Mao Zedong.
4. Examine aspects of life in China today.

Reading/Language Arts

Learn how to compare and contrast to help analyze information.

Prepare to Read

Build Background Knowledge L2

Tell students that in this section they will read about China, a country that has experienced and continues to experience tremendous changes. Ask students to think about the ways in which their community has changed during their lifetime. Have new buildings been constructed? Have some been demolished? Have new businesses opened or old ones closed? What have been the effects of these changes? Are there more changes they would like to see? Conduct a Think-Write-Pair-Share (TE, p. T36) to generate ideas.

Set a Purpose for Reading L2

- Preview the Objectives.

- Read each statement in the *Reading Readiness Guide* aloud. Ask students to mark each statement true or false.

  All in One **Asia and the Pacific Teaching Resources,** *Reading Readiness Guide,* p. 332

- Have students discuss the statements in pairs or groups of four, then mark their worksheets again. Use the Numbered Heads participation strategy (TE, p. T36) to call on students to share their group's perspective.

Vocabulary Builder
Preview Key Terms

Pronounce each Key Term, then ask the students to say the word with you. Provide a simple explanation such as, "Someone who dramatically alters their appearance makes a radical change."

Prepare to Read

Objectives

In this section, you will

1. Find out how China controlled its economy from 1949 to 1980.
2. Learn about the growth of Taiwan since 1949.
3. Discover how China's government operated after the death of Mao Zedong.
4. Examine aspects of life in China today.

Taking Notes

As you read this section, look for details about how China was governed under the Communist party. Copy the diagram below, and record your findings in it. Write the similarities in the space where the ovals overlap. Write the differences in the space where the ovals do not overlap.

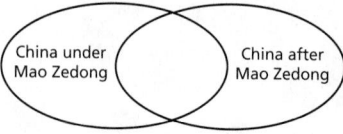

China under Mao Zedong | China after Mao Zedong

🎯 Target Reading Skill

Compare and Contrast
Comparing and contrasting can help you analyze information. When you compare, you look at the similarities between things. When you contrast, you look at the differences. As you read this section, look for similarities and differences in how China was governed under the Communist party. Write the information in your Taking Notes table.

Key Terms

- **radical** (RAD ih kul) *adj.* extreme
- **Red Guards** (red gahrdz) *n.* groups of students who carried out Mao Zedong's policies during the Cultural Revolution
- **free enterprise system** (free ENT ur pryz SIS tum) *n.* an economic system in which people can choose their own jobs, start private businesses, own property, and make a profit
- **gross domestic product** (grohs duh MES tik PRAHD ukt) *n.* the total value of all goods and services produced in an economy

Bicycles remain a major form of transportation in China.

714 Asia and the Pacific

In 1985, the total number of cars, buses, and trucks in all of China was about 320,000. Most people in cities rode bicycles or walked to get around. In 2005, the number of cars, buses, and trucks had grown to about 25 million. During that time, China had experienced tremendous economic growth.

Changes continue as China works to build its economy. In the past, China's Communist government tightly controlled the economy. Today, however, China is in the process of moving toward an economy with fewer government controls.

China's Economy, 1949–1980

In 1949, the Chinese Communist party set up a new government with leader Mao Zedong (mow dzuh doong) in charge. Under Mao, the government took over China's economy. Factories, businesses, and farmland came under the government's control.

🎯 Target Reading Skill L2

Compare and Contrast Point out the Target Reading Skill. Tell students that being able to compare and contrast information will help them identify the similarities and differences between things.

Model comparing and contrasting by reading the text on this page. Point out the similarities and differences the text reveals between China in the early 1980s and China today. *(Similarities: still a lot of bicycles; differences: more cars, buses, and trucks, better roads, less government control over the economy)*

Give students *Compare and Contrast.* Have them complete the activity in groups.

All in One **Asia and the Pacific Teaching Resources,** *Compare and Contrast,* p. 343

The Great Leap Forward In 1958, Mao began a **radical,** or extreme, program called the "Great Leap Forward." Its goal was to increase output from farms and factories. The program turned out to be a giant step backward. The Communists rushed to increase production by forcing people to work on large communes. But they ignored the need for experience and planning. For example, they ordered a huge increase in steel production. Thousands of untrained workers built backyard furnaces for making steel and other products. Much of the steel they produced was of poor quality and useless.

The focus on industry took farmers away from farming. At the same time, poor weather destroyed crops, resulting in a severe food shortage. Between 1959 and 1961, an estimated 30 million people died from starvation.

The Cultural Revolution In 1966, Mao introduced another radical policy called the Cultural Revolution. His aim was to create a completely new society with no ties to the past. He began by closing schools and urging students to rebel against their teachers and their families. The students formed bands of radicals called Red Guards. These bands destroyed some of China's most beautiful ancient buildings. They beat and imprisoned many Chinese artists, professors, and doctors. Anyone they considered to be against Mao's policies was attacked.

When the Red Guards raged out of control and began to threaten Mao's government, they were imprisoned, too. The Cultural Revolution kept China in turmoil until its conclusion in 1976. Years of chaos left China in disorder, with hundreds of thousands of its citizens dead. The focus on political revolution disrupted China's economic growth.

✔ **Reading Check** What was the purpose of China's Great Leap Forward?

China Under Mao
Mao launched the Great Leap Forward in order to improve China's economy. The small photo above shows a poster promoting the program. Mao declared the Cultural Revolution in 1966. In the large photo, Red Guards read a book of Mao's writings. **Summarize** *How did the Great Leap Forward affect China's economy?*

Instruct

China's Economy, 1949–1980 L2

Guided Instruction

- **Vocabulary Builder** Clarify the high-use words **output** and **turmoil** before reading.

- Read China's Economy, 1949–1980, using the Structured Silent Reading strategy (TE, p. T34).

- Describe the Great Leap Forward and the Cultural Revolution. (*The Great Leap Forward was an economic program whose goal was to increase output from farms and factories. The Cultural Revolution was aimed at creating a new society with no ties to the past.*)

- Ask students **How did the Great Leap Forward and the Cultural Revolution reflect the failure of Mao's leadership?** (*The Great Leap Forward failed to achieve its goals, causing about 30 million people to die from starvation. The Cultural Revolution led to destructive acts by bands of radicals called Red Guards.*)

- Ask **How do you think Mao could have avoided China's economic problems?** (*Answers will vary. Possible answers: Mao could have left land and businesses in the hands of private citizens instead of controlling them through the government; encouraged more job training for workers; allowed more farmers to raise crops.*)

Independent Practice
Ask students to create the Taking Notes graphic organizer on a blank piece of paper. Have them fill in the "China under Mao Zedong" circle with information they have just learned.

Monitor Progress
As students fill in the graphic organizer, circulate and make sure individuals are choosing the correct details. Provide assistance as needed.

Answers

Summarize It weakened the economy.

✔ **Reading Check** Its goal was to increase output from farms and factories.

Vocabulary Builder

Use the information below to teach students this section's high-use words.

High-Use Word	Definition and Sample Sentence
output, p. 715	*n.* work done or amount produced over a certain period of time The workers in the shoe factory increased their **output** to 1,000 pairs per day.
turmoil, p. 715	*n.* condition of extreme confusion The meeting was in **turmoil** when the president of the club resigned.
moderate, p. 718	*adj.* within reasonable limits The teacher gave us a **moderate** amount of homework over the weekend.
record, p. 719	*n.* collection of known facts The candidate's civil rights **record** helped her win the election.

Taiwan Since 1949 L2

Guided Instruction

- Read Taiwan Since 1949. As students read, circulate and make sure individuals can answer the Reading Check question.

- Ask students **What is a free enterprise system?** *(an economic system where people can choose their own jobs, start private businesses, own property, and make profits)*

- Discuss some of the effects of Taiwan's free enterprise economy. *(The Chinese on Taiwan started programs that increased farm output and brought in more money that was used to build ports and railroads.)*

- Ask students **Why do you think both the Nationalists and the Communists claimed the right to rule the other group's country?** *(Answers will vary, but may include that both the Nationalists and the Communists were groups from the mainland country of China; the Nationalists felt they were still Chinese even though they no longer lived on the mainland.)*

Independent Practice

Assign *Guided Reading and Review.*

All in One Asia and the Pacific Teaching Resources, *Guided Reading and Review,* p. 333

Monitor Progress

As students fill in *Guided Reading and Review,* circulate and make sure individuals are completing the assignment correctly. Provide assistance as needed.

Answer

✓ **Reading Check** Taiwan has a free enterprise system.

Links Across Time

China's Government
China's government is a dictatorship. In a dictatorship, the power to govern is held by one person. By contrast, a democracy is a form of government in which the power to govern rests with the people. A dictatorship has complete power over the people. It may also have control of nearly everything people do. Examples of dictatorships in the past include those in the former Soviet Union and Germany. Shown below is Mao Zedong, leader of China's government from 1949 to 1976.

China launched the world's first magnetic levitation, or maglev, passenger train system. Powerful magnets work to lift and propel the train.

Taiwan Since 1949

After their defeat by the Communists in 1949, the Nationalists fled to Taiwan, an island 100 miles (161 kilometers) off mainland China's southeast coast. They formed a new government and called their country the Republic of China. The Communists on mainland China, however, still claimed the right to rule Taiwan. The Nationalists on Taiwan also claimed the right to rule the rest of China.

In Taiwan, the Nationalists followed the free enterprise system. Under the **free enterprise system,** people can choose their own jobs, start private businesses, own property, and make profits. Taiwan's free enterprise economy quickly became one of Asia's strongest. New programs increased farm output and brought in money to help build new ports and railroads.

Businesses in Taiwan export many goods, such as computer products and electronics, to other countries. These exports, along with new service jobs, have helped the economy grow dramatically. Taiwan has also developed a democratic government. Following the 2000 elections, a new ruling party peacefully took power for the first time in Taiwan's modern history.

✓ **Reading Check** What kind of economic system does Taiwan have?

Changes in China

Meanwhile, many Western countries refused to trade with China. At the same time, some of Mao's policies hurt the country. During the 1970s, the Communists realized that they needed new policies in order to improve China's economy and its relations with the rest of the world.

First, China began repairing relations with the West. In 1971, China was allowed to join the United Nations. In 1972, Richard Nixon became the first American president to visit China. This historic trip opened up trade between the two nations.

Differentiated Instruction

For Less Proficient Readers L1
Have students practice the Target Reading Skill by creating a Venn diagram that compares and contrasts life in China and life in Taiwan since 1949. Briefly model how to record details using the *Venn Diagram Transparency.*

📖 **Asia and the Pacific Transparencies,** *Transparency B16: Venn Diagram*

For Advanced Readers L3
Have students read the primary source *City Kids in China.* Then have them write a short essay explaining what the passage tells them about modern life in China.

All in One Asia and the Pacific Teaching Resources, *City Kids in China,* pp. 355–356

China

China has a large and complex economy. Much of China's land is devoted to farming to feed its large population. Most of this land is used for subsistence farming, or growing food mainly for the farm family rather than for sale. Now look at the graphs below. China's exports, or sales to other countries, are greater than its imports, or purchases from other countries. These exports have helped China's economy to grow. Many young workers have moved from rural areas to cities to find higher-paying jobs. However, agriculture remains the main source of jobs in China.

CHINA

Huang He
Yellow Sea
Chang R.
East China Sea
Tropic of Cancer
Xi R.
South China Sea
PACIFIC OCEAN
Amur R.
Brahmaputra

0 miles 1,000
0 kilometers 1,000
Lambert Azimuthal Equal Area

China: Land Use
KEY

- Commercial farming (without rice)
- Commercial farming (with rice)
- Subsistence farming (without rice)
- Subsistence farming (with rice)
- Nomadic herding
- Forestry
- Manufacturing and trade
- Little or no activity
- National border

Foreign Trade

$752 billion
$632 billion
Billions of Dollars
800 700 600 500 400 300 200 100 0
Exports   Imports

SOURCE: CIA World Factbook

Labor Force by Sector

Agriculture 49%
Services 29%
Industry 22%

SOURCE: CIA World Factbook

Exports by Sector

Services 19%
Agriculture 4%
Industry 77%

SOURCE: World Trade Organization

Map and Chart Skills

1. **Identify** Which economic sector in China uses the most land and employs the most people?
2. **Contrast** Which economic sector accounts for most of China's exports?
3. **Infer** How might large population movements from rural to urban areas affect farming?

Go Online PHSchool.com Use Web Code Ice-6711 for **DK World Desk Reference Online.**

Chapter 24 Section 1 **717**

Skills Mini Lesson

Distinguishing Fact and Opinion

1. Teach the skill by explaining that facts are statements that can be proved or disproved, while opinions are statements that cannot be proved or disproved.
2. Help students practice the skill by writing the following sentences on the board, and then determining if the statements are fact or opinion and why as a class. "China had more cars in 2005 than it did in 1980." "I think it's good that there are more cars now in China."
3. Have students apply the skill by finding facts and opinions in the following sentences: "In 1972, Richard Nixon became the first American President to visit China. I think that it was a good decision for him to visit China."

Guided Instruction [L2]

Ask students to study the Country Profile on this page. As a class, answer the Map and Chart Skills questions. Allow students to briefly discuss their responses with a partner before sharing their answers.

Independent Practice

Pair students and ask them to analyze the land use map on this page. Ask them to work together to write a one-sentence description of the difference between commercial farming and subsistence farming.

Changes in China [L2]

Guided Instruction

- **Vocabulary Builder** Clarify the high-use word **moderate** before reading.

- Read Changes in China. As students read, circulate and make sure individuals can answer the Reading Check question.

- Ask students **What was the "Four Modernizations"?** (*a program carried out by Deng Xiaoping to improve China's farming, industry, science, and defense*)

- Ask students **What changes did Deng Xiaoping make to China's economic system and what were the results?** (*Areas were set up where foreign companies could own and operate businesses, helping China's economy grow and bringing money into the economy; some Chinese citizens were allowed to run private businesses, which eventually produced about 75 percent of China's gross domestic product; China took control of Hong Kong but allowed its economy to operate without changes for the next 50 years and to govern itself.*)

Answers

Map and Chart Skills

1. agriculture
2. industry
3. There will be fewer workers on farms as a result and production may suffer.

Go Online PHSchool.com Students can find more information about this topic on the DK World Desk Reference Online.

Independent Practice

Ask students to continue filling in their graphic organizers with information they have just learned.

Monitor Progress

As students fill in the graphic organizer, circulate and make sure individuals are choosing the correct details. Provide assistance as needed.

China Today ▪ L2

Guided Instruction

- **Vocabulary Builder** Clarify the high-use word **record** before reading.

- Read China Today with students.

- Describe the events that occurred in China in 1989. (*The Chinese government killed or wounded thousands of people who gathered in Tiananmen Square in Beijing to demand greater political freedoms.*)

- Ask students **Why do you think some countries struggle with the issue of whether they should trade with China?** (*Answers will vary, but may include that although China has a huge market for goods and manufactures many items, its government has a poor human rights record.*)

Independent Practice

Ask students to complete the graphic organizer with the information they have just read.

Monitor Progress

- Show *Section Reading Support Transparency AP 64* and ask students to check their graphic organizers individually.

  📖 **Asia and the Pacific Transparencies,** *Section Reading Support Transparency AP 64*

- Tell students to fill in the last column of their *Reading Readiness Guides.*

  All in One **Asia and the Pacific Teaching Resources,** *Reading Readiness Guide,* p. 332

Answers

Compare and Contrast Similar: It has stores, a food court, a movie complex, and some car parking. Different: It has many more parking spaces for bicycles than for cars.

✓ Reading Check China regained control over Hong Kong.

The New China
Sun Dong An Plaza in Beijing, China, includes seven floors of stores, a food court, a multiscreen movie complex, and parking for about 500 cars and about 3,500 bicycles. **Compare and Contrast** *How is Sun Dong An Plaza similar to and different from an American shopping mall?*

New Leaders After Mao died in 1976, moderate leaders gained power in China. By 1981, Deng Xiaoping (dung show ping) was leader of China. Deng carried out a program called the Four Modernizations. This program focused on improvements in farming, industry, science, and defense. During the next 20 years, China gradually allowed some free enterprise. Privately owned Chinese factories began to make electronic equipment, clothes, computer parts, toys, and many other products.

New Economic Plans Under Deng, China set up areas where foreign companies could own and operate businesses. These areas included five "special economic zones" and 14 cities along China's coast. They helped bring in money to China's economy. The Chinese Communist party also allowed some Chinese citizens to run private businesses. By the end of the 1990s, private businesses were producing about 75 percent of China's gross domestic product. **Gross domestic product** is the total value of all goods and services produced in an economy.

Hong Kong Returns to China In 1997, China took back control of Hong Kong, which had been a British colony since the late 1800s. Hong Kong had long been a major center for trade, banking, and shipping. China agreed to allow the economy of Hong Kong to operate without changes for the next 50 years. China also agreed that during this period Hong Kong could largely govern itself.

✓ Reading Check **What happened to Hong Kong in 1997?**

718 Asia and the Pacific

Background: Biography

Deng Xiaoping Deng Xiaoping had a career of many highs and lows. The son of a landowner, Deng became a follower of communism while studying in France. Although he held many key positions in government, Deng's desire to push the country forward economically often conflicted with Mao's strong Communist ideology. During the Cultural Revolution Mao supporters forced Deng from political power for several years. However, he was later appointed deputy premier under premier Zhou Enlai. After Zhou's death, Deng was again forced from power. After Mao's death and the imprisonment of the Gang of Four, Deng regained power and eventually became the leader of China.

China Today

Today, China is a major economic power. It has formed good relations with many nations. Yet the government has often been criticized for the way it treats its people. China has one political party, which is the Chinese Communist party. Under China's government, its citizens do not have political freedom.

The Chinese government has used violence against people who have called for a democratic government. In 1989, tens of thousands of people gathered in Tiananmen Square in Beijing, China's capital, to demand greater political freedoms. When the people refused to leave, the government sent in tanks and troops. Thousands of people were killed or wounded.

Many nations question how they should relate to a country with such a poor human rights record. Still, most of them continue to remain trade partners with China. China's population makes it a huge market for goods, and China manufactures many items for other countries. In 2003, Hu Jintao became China's president and leader of the Chinese Communist party. Experts on China expected Hu to keep developing an economy with fewer government controls. With the Chinese Communist party firmly in control, however, the country's political system was not expected to change.

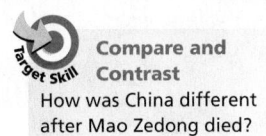
Compare and Contrast
How was China different after Mao Zedong died?

✓ **Reading Check** How did China's government respond to the democracy movement in 1989?

Learn about desertification in China.

Section 1 Assessment

Key Terms
Review the key terms at the beginning of this section. Use each term in a sentence that explains its meaning.

Target Reading Skill
Explain one way China's government was the same and one way it was different after Mao's death?

Comprehension and Critical Thinking
1. (a) Identify Who took control of China in 1949?

(b) Summarize Why did the Chinese government launch the Great Leap Forward?
2. (a) Define What is the Republic of China?
(b) Contrast How is Taiwan different from China?
3. (a) Identify Identify Deng Xiaoping.
(b) Find the Main Idea What economic changes took place under Deng's leadership?
(c) Explain Why has the Chinese government been criticized for the way it treats its people?

Writing Activity
Write a paragraph comparing and contrasting China before and after Mao Zedong's death. Include a description of how China's economy has changed during this time.

> **Writing Tip** Compare and contrast the Great Leap Forward with the Four Modernizations program. How were these programs alike? How were they different?

Chapter 24 Section 1 **719**

Target Reading Skill L2

Compare and Contrast As a follow up, ask students to answer the Target Reading Skill in the Student Edition. *(The government allowed more free enterprise and the economy became more developed.)*

Assess and Reteach

Assess Progress L2
Have students complete the Section Assessment. Administer the *Section Quiz*.

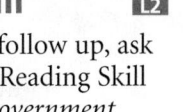 **Asia and the Pacific Teaching Resources,** *Section Quiz,* p. 334

 Show students *China's Great Green Wall.* Ask **How are people in China combating desertification?** *(They are planting trees to prevent topsoil from being blown away, turning dry desert back into fertile land.)*

Reteach L1
If students need more instruction, have them read this section in the Reading and Vocabulary Study Guide.

 Chapter 24, Section 1, **Eastern Hemisphere, Reading and Vocabulary Study Guide,** pp. 250–252

Extend L3
Have students learn more about products made in China and other Asian countries by beginning the *Book Project: Asia Trade Fair.*

Asia and the Pacific Teaching Resources, *Book Project: Asia Trade Fair* pp. 83–85

Answers

✓ **Reading Check** The government tried to end it, killing or wounding thousands of people in the process.

Writing Activity
Use the *Rubric for Assessing a Writing Assignment* to evaluate students' answers.

Asia and the Pacific Teaching Resources, *Rubric for Assessing a Writing Assignment,* p. 359

Section 1 Assessment

Key Terms
Students' sentences should reflect knowledge of each Key Term.

Target Reading Skill
Same: People had few political rights.
Different: There was more free enterprise and industry was stronger.

Comprehension and Critical Thinking
1. (a) Mao Zedong and the Communist Party **(b)** to increase output from farms and factories

2. (a) Taiwan **(b)** Unlike China, it has had a free enterprise system and a strong economy since the 1950s.

3. (a) leader of China after Mao Zedong, who made changes in order to develop China's economy **(b)** Some free enterprise, private businesses, and foreign businesses were

allowed. The economy grew stronger. **(c)** Citizens do not have political freedom and the government has a poor human rights record.

Section 2
Step-by-Step Instruction

Objectives

Social Studies

1. Learn about the growth of Japan's economy.
2. Find out about successes and challenges in Japan's economy.
3. Examine aspects of life in Japan.

Reading/Language Arts
Compare information to identify similarities.

Prepare to Read

Build Background Knowledge `L2`

Tell students that in this section they will read how hard work and teamwork have helped Japan develop a successful economy. Discuss with students what qualities they think makes a person a good worker or employee. *(Examples: works hard, is always on time, takes pride in work)* Conduct an Idea Wave (TE, p. T35) to generate a list and record student responses on the board.

Set a Purpose for Reading `L2`

- Preview the Objectives.

- Form students into pairs or groups. Distribute the *Reading Readiness Guide*. Ask the students to fill in the first two columns of the chart. Use the Numbered Heads participation strategy (TE, p. T36) to call on students to share one piece of information they already know and one piece of information they want to know.

  All in One Asia and the Pacific Teaching Resources, *Reading Readiness Guide,* p. 336

Vocabulary Builder
Preview Key Terms

Pronounce each Key Term, then ask the students to say the word with you. Provide a simple explanation such as, "During a recession, businesses make less money, affecting the overall economy."

Section 2
Japan
Tradition and Change

Prepare to Read

Objectives
In this section, you will
1. Learn about the growth of Japan's economy.
2. Find out about successes and challenges in Japan's economy.
3. Examine aspects of life in Japan.

Taking Notes
As you read this section, look for ways in which tradition and change have helped Japan develop its economy. Copy the web diagram below, and record your findings in it.

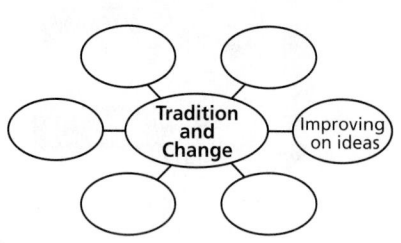

Target Reading Skill
Make Comparisons When you make comparisons, you note how things are alike. As you read this section, compare tradition and change in terms of how they have helped Japan build its economy. Write your information in the Taking Notes web diagram.

Key Terms
- **subsidy** (SUB suh dee) *n.* money given by a government to assist a private company
- **recession** (rih SESH un) *n.* a period during which an economy and the businesses that support it shrink, or make less money
- **birthrate** (BURTH rayt) *n.* the number of live births each year per 1,000 people
- **labor** (LAY bur) *n.* the work people do for which they are paid

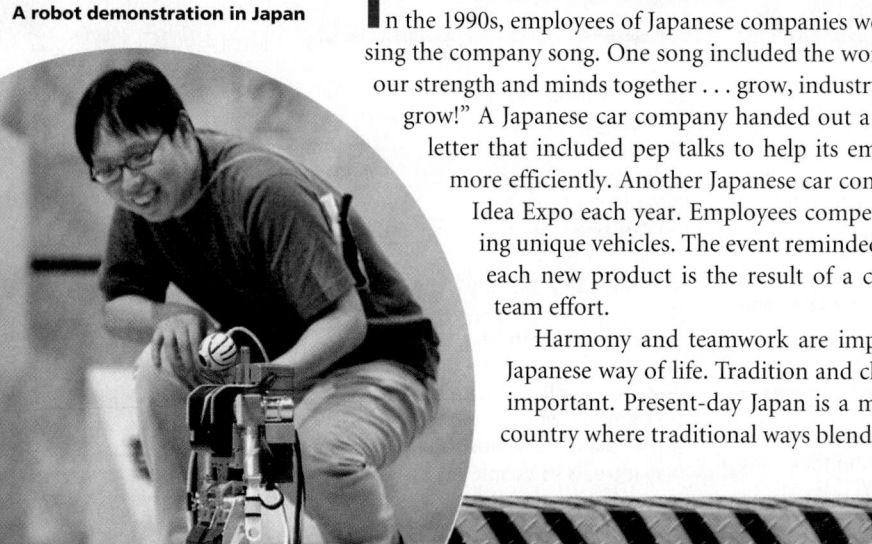

A robot demonstration in Japan

720 Asia and the Pacific

In the 1990s, employees of Japanese companies would gather to sing the company song. One song included the words, "Let's put our strength and minds together . . . grow, industry, grow, grow, grow!" A Japanese car company handed out a weekly newsletter that included pep talks to help its employees work more efficiently. Another Japanese car company held an Idea Expo each year. Employees competed in designing unique vehicles. The event reminded workers that each new product is the result of a company-wide team effort.

Harmony and teamwork are important in the Japanese way of life. Tradition and change are also important. Present-day Japan is a modern, urban country where traditional ways blend with the new.

Target Reading Skill `L2`

Make Comparisons Point out the Target Reading Skill. Tell students that comparing information helps them identify how things are alike.

Model comparing by reading the first paragraph on p. 721. Compare Japan's economy in the 1800s and the 1920s. *(In the 1800s, Japan opened its ports and welcomed new ideas and inventions from the West, and*

used them to help build its industries. By the 1920s it had become an important manufacturing country.)

Give students *Make Comparisons.* Have them complete the activity in groups.

All in One Asia and the Pacific Teaching Resources, *Make Comparisons,* p. 344

Building a Developed Economy

Once Japan finally opened its ports to other countries in the 1800s, it welcomed new ideas and inventions from the West. For years, the Japanese worked to build major industries. By the 1920s, Japan had become an important manufacturing country.

Japan's Economy After World War II After World War II ended in 1945, however, Japan was in ruins. The United States helped to rebuild Japan's industries. In addition, the Japanese government helped industries by giving them subsidies. A **subsidy** is money given by a government to assist a private company. This allowed companies to build large factories and sell more goods, which boosted the country's economy.

High-Technology Industries Since the 1960s, Japan has produced some of the world's most modern industrial robots. By the 1970s, the Japanese were making more watches and cameras than the Swiss and the Germans. By the 1980s, Japan made and sold a large share of the world's cars, electronic goods, skiing gear, and bicycles. Japan also produced huge amounts of steel, ships, televisions, and CDs.

In addition, Japanese companies improved existing products. For example, the videocassette recorder (VCR) was invented in the United States. But production costs for making VCRs in the United States were thought to be too high. A Japanese company bought the invention. Japan today is a leading maker of VCRs.

Japanese companies also had new ideas of their own. You are probably familiar with portable stereos and small, hand-held electronic games. These products were invented by the Japanese. In 1983, a European company and a Japanese company introduced the first compact disc. Working with European and American companies, Japanese companies also developed the digital video disc (DVD).

✓ **Reading Check** What are some high-technology products made in Japan?

Japan's Robotics Industry
Below, a Japanese robotics designer watches as a humanoid robot steps over a barrier. Increased robot use may be one solution for Japan's labor shortage. **Analyze** *What characteristics does this robot have that would make it suitable as a replacement for a human worker?*

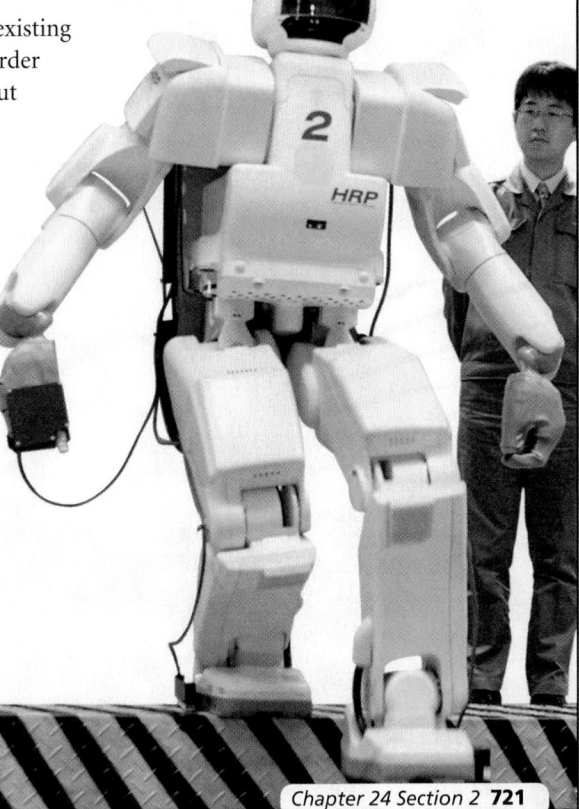

Vocabulary Builder

Use the information below to teach students this section's high-use words.

High-Use Word	Definition and Sample Sentence
assist, p. 721	*v.* to help I **assisted** my teacher in creating the bulletin board.
position, p. 724	*n.* rank or standing The president has a higher **position** than the vice-president.
maintain, p. 725	*v.* to keep He must **maintain** his good grades if he wants to graduate.

Instruct

Building a Developed Economy ⬛ L2

Guided Instruction
- **Vocabulary Builder** Clarify the high-use word **assist** before reading.

- Read about the growth of Japan's economy in Building a Developed Economy, using the Oral Cloze strategy (TE, p. T33).

- Describe how Japan's economy recovered after World War II. (*The United States helped rebuild Japan's industries, and the Japanese government helped industries by giving them subsidies.*)

Independent Practice
Ask students to create the Taking Notes graphic organizer on a blank piece of paper. Then have them fill in some of the outer circles with information they have just learned.

Monitor Progress
As students fill in the graphic organizer, circulate and make sure individuals are choosing the correct details. Provide assistance as needed.

Answers

Analyze It is built to look and perform tasks like a human worker would.

✓ Reading Check Answers will vary, but might include televisions, CDs, VCRs, portable stereos, small hand-held electronic games, and DVDs.

Make Comparisons As a follow up, ask students to answer the Target Reading Skill question in the Student Edition. (*Unemployment in Japan rose.*)

Successes and Challenges L2

Guided Instruction

- Read more about Japan's economy in Successes and Challenges. As students read, circulate and make sure individuals can answer the Reading Check question.

- Discuss the state of Japan's economy in the 1980s. (*Japan had one of the largest and strongest economies in the world; it depended on exporting products to the rest of the world.*)

- Ask students **How did Japanese spending habits contribute to poor trade relations between Japan and other countries?** (*The Japanese people did not buy many imported goods. This led some countries to grow angry because although they bought Japanese products, Japan did not buy their products.*)

Independent Practice

Have students fill in more of the outer circles on the graphic organizer with information they have just learned.

Monitor Progress

As students fill in the graphic organizer, circulate and make sure individuals are choosing the correct details. Provide assistance as needed.

Answer

✓ Reading Check Businesses made less money and unemployment rose.

⊙ **Make Comparisons** In what ways have tradition and change affected Japan's economy?

Inspecting a turbine in Yokohama, Japan (large photo); a Japanese-made electronic book reader (small photo)

722 Asia and the Pacific

Successes and Challenges

By the 1980s, Japan had one of the world's largest and strongest economies. Japan's economy depended on exporting its products to the rest of the world. Americans and Europeans eagerly bought Japanese products—particularly cars, television sets, and electronics. Yet Japanese people did not buy many goods from America and Europe.

Other countries grew angry because even though they bought many Japanese products, the Japanese did not buy theirs. This led to poor trade relations between Japan and other countries. On top of that, in the early 1990s, the Japanese economy suffered a severe recession. A **recession** is a period of time when an economy and the businesses that support it shrink, or make less money. To overcome the recession, some companies began laying off their employees. Unemployment in Japan rose.

Since 2004, Japan has experienced improved economic growth, and it still has one of the largest economies in the world. Manufacturing remains an important part of Japan's economy. Today, however, more people work in Japan's service industries than in manufacturing. Service industries include jobs in banking, communications, sales, hotels, and restaurants. More of the country's wealth comes from service industries as well.

✓ Reading Check **How was Japan affected by the recession in the 1990s?**

Differentiated Instruction

For Less Proficient Readers L1

Have students create the Taking Notes graphic organizer on p. 720 on a blank piece of paper, leaving out the word already filled in. Have them fill in the blank organizer with details from the text under the heading "High-Technology Indus-tries" on p. 721. Ask them to write "High-Technology Industries" in the center circle, and fill in the outer circles with examples of Japanese industries from the text, such as robots and televisions. Encourage them to modify the graphic organizer if necessary, by adding or taking away outer circles.

Japan

Japan is one of the world's most densely populated countries. Japan is about the same size as the states of California or Montana. But it has almost half as many people as the entire United States. The bar graph below the map shows that Japan has about the same population density as Massachusetts. Massachusetts is one of the most densely populated U.S. states. Yet, as you can see on the map, forests and farmland cover most of Japan. How is this possible? Japan preserves large areas of forest and farmland because most of its people are crowded into the small part of the country that is urban. Compare the circle graphs below showing land use in Massachusetts and Japan. Even though Japan has nearly the same overall population density as Massachusetts, it devotes much less of its space to urban development. This is mainly because its cities are compact, with little of the sprawling suburban development that we know in the United States.

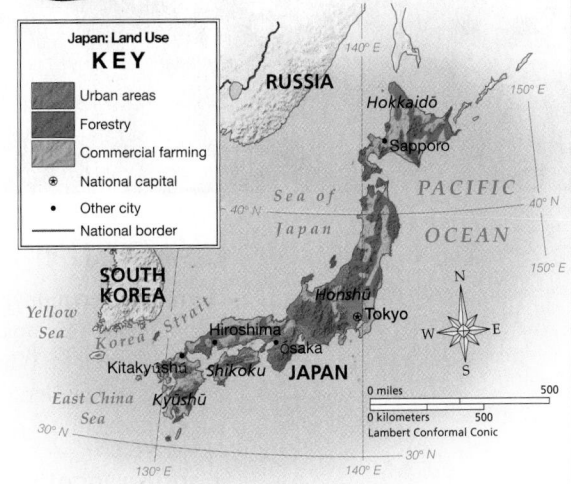

Japan: Land Use
KEY
- Urban areas
- Forestry
- Commercial farming
- ⊛ National capital
- • Other city
- — National border

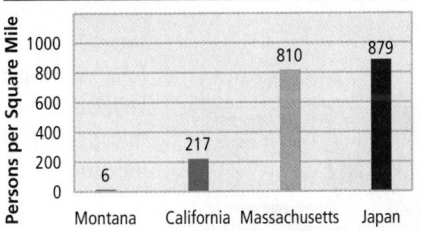

Population Density Comparison

Persons per Square Mile

Montana	California	Massachusetts	Japan
6	217	810	879

SOURCE: U.S. Census Bureau, Prentice Hall DK World Desk Reference

Land Use

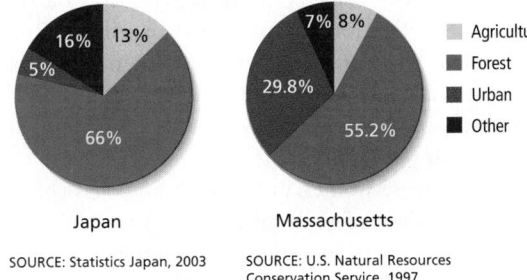

Japan
- 13%
- 16%
- 5%
- 66%

Massachusetts
- 8%
- 7%
- 29.8%
- 55.2%

KEY
- Agriculture
- Forest
- Urban
- Other

Japan

Massachusetts

SOURCE: Statistics Japan, 2003

SOURCE: U.S. Natural Resources Conservation Service, 1997

Map and Chart Skills

1. **Identify** What percentages of Japan's land are devoted to agriculture and forest?
2. **Compare** Does Japan devote more or less land to agriculture and forest than Massachusetts?
3. **Synthesize** What explains this difference?

 Go Online PHSchool.com

Use Web Code **Ice-6712** for **DK World Desk Reference Online.**

COUNTRY PROFILE
Focus on Geography

Guided Instruction   L2

Ask students to study the Country Profile on this page. Point out the map, bar graph, and circle graphs. As a class, answer the Map and Chart Skills questions.

Independent Practice

Ask students to research the population of their own state. Ask them to recreate the bar graph on this page on a separate piece of paper, adding a bar to show their state's density. Ask them to write a statement comparing the population density of their state with that of Japan and the other states on the bar graph.

Answers

Map and Chart Skills

1. agriculture: 13 percent; forest: 66 percent
2. more
3. Japan preserves large areas of forest and farmland because most of its population is crowded into smaller urban areas.

Go Online PHSchool.com Students can find more information about this topic on the DK World Desk Reference Online.

Differentiated Instruction

For Gifted and Talented   L3

Have students do research to find out what countries are major importers of Japanese goods, and what those goods are. Then have them present the information in a table. Encourage students to be creative when making their tables, such as by adding drawings or photos of the products.

Life in Japan L2

Guided Instruction

- **Vocabulary Builder** Clarify the high use words **position** and **maintain** before reading.

- Read more about Japanese culture and about future issues for the country in Life in Japan.

- Ask students **What is *keiretsu*?** (*a Japanese term for a group of companies that join together to work toward one another's success*) **How does it reflect the traditions of Japan?** (*Working together as a group is a Japanese tradition.*)

 Show students *The Samurai of Japan.* Ask **When were shoguns powerful in Japan?** (*from about 1200 to 1700*)

- Ask students **How has the role of women in the Japanese work force changed since World War II?** (*Before the war, few women in Japan worked outside the home; today more women work full or part time than those who stay at home full time, and half of Japan's work force is made up of women.*)

- Ask students **What are some challenges facing Japan's labor force?** (*Japan has an aging population, a low birth rate, and has had limited immigration in the past. These factors contribute to a current shortage of younger workers.*)

Independent Practice

Have students complete the graphic organizer by filling in any remaining outer circles with information they have just learned.

Monitor Progress

- Show *Section Reading Support Transparency AP 65* and ask students to check their graphic organizers individually. Go over the key concepts and clarify vocabulary as needed.

  📖 **Asia and the Pacific Transparencies,** *Section Reading Support Transparency AP 65*

- Tell students to fill in the last column of the *Reading Readiness Guide.* Ask them to evaluate if what they learned was what they had expected to learn.

  All in One Asia and the Pacific Teaching Resources, *Reading Readiness Guide,* p. 336

Life in Japan

Harmony, ceremony, and order have long been important in Japanese culture. Japanese people have generally followed these traditional values. While the past is honored, however, new ways of living and working have been introduced in Japan. The result is a modern culture with features that are unique to the country.

Working Together Working together as a group has long been a tradition in Japan. One way Japanese manufacturing companies have worked together is by forming *keiretsu* (kay ret soo). This is a Japanese term that describes a group of companies that join together to work toward one another's success. Some *keiretsu* included the companies that make goods, the companies that provide the raw materials for those goods, and the companies that sell the goods. The Japanese car industry has followed this model. Although still part of the country's economy, *keiretsu* have been joined by a growing number of small businesses.

Learn about the ways of the samurai in Japan.

Changing Roles The role of marriage is another example of tradition and change in Japan. Marriage has been the most acceptable social position for a Japanese man or woman. Today, however, more and more Japanese men and women are choosing not to marry or to delay marriage. One result is that Japan's birthrate is low. A country's **birthrate** measures the number of live births each year per 1,000 people.

The role of Japanese women in the work force has changed, too. Before World War II, few women in Japan worked outside the home. Today, there are more Japanese women working full time or part time than women who stay at home full time.

Although about half of Japan's work force is made up of women, men hold most of the management positions. In 2005, women headed about 6 percent of the companies in Japan. This compared with some 40 percent of U.S. companies being headed by women.

724 Asia and the Pacific

Differentiated Instruction

For Special Needs Students L1

After students read through each section, have them go back and make flash cards of the Key Terms and their definitions. Then, working in pairs, have students use the flash cards to test each other's knowledge of Key Terms.

For English Language Learners L1

As students read through the section, have them write down any new or unfamiliar words they encounter. After they have completed the section, have them look up any unfamiliar words not defined in the text and then write sentences using the new words.

Japanese Students
Like American schoolchildren, these Japanese students enjoy clowning for the camera. Most public school students in Japan wear uniforms. **Analyze** *What purpose do you think school uniforms serve?*

Facing the Future As Japan heads into the future, its challenge is to find a way of maintaining its wealth. One of the resources a country needs to produce goods and services is labor. **Labor** is the work people do for which they are paid. Japan does not have a growing labor force of young workers. In the United States and Europe, a steady supply of immigrants helps keep the labor force growing. In the past, Japan has limited immigration.

Japan's low birthrate affects the labor force. Fewer and fewer workers have to support an aging population no longer working. This makes the cost of producing goods and services higher in Japan than in countries with growing populations.

✓ **Reading Check** Why is the cost of producing goods and services higher in Japan than in other Asian countries?

Section 2 Assessment

Key Terms
Review the key terms at the beginning of this section. Use each term in a sentence that explains its meaning.

Target Reading Skill
What are two ways in which tradition and change have helped Japan build its economy?

Comprehension and Critical Thinking
1. (a) **Recall** Describe what Japan's economy was like by the 1920s.

(b) **Summarize** Tell how Japan's economy grew from the 1960s to the 1980s.
2. (a) **Identify** What happened that disturbed Japan's economy in the early 1990s?
(b) **Identify Effects** How did this affect Japan?
3. (a) **Explain** What tradition helps explain why Japanese companies formed *keiretsu?*
(b) **Identify** What is one resource a country needs to produce goods and services?
(c) **Draw Conclusions** How would a low birthrate affect a country's labor force?

Writing Activity
Japan has an aging population. Based on the information in this section, brainstorm a list of what Japan can do to increase its labor force. Write your list and add a short description of each idea.

Go Online
PHSchool.com

For: An activity on Japan
Visit: PHSchool.com
Web Code: lcd-6702

Chapter 24 Section 2 **725**

Assess and Reteach

Assess Progress L2
Have students complete the Section Assessment. Administer the *Section Quiz*.

All in One **Asia and the Pacific Teaching Resources,** *Section Quiz,* p. 338

Reteach L1
If students need more instruction, have them read this section in the Reading and Vocabulary Study Guide.

Chapter 24, Section 2, **Eastern Hemisphere Reading and Vocabulary Study Guide,** pp. 253–255

Extend L3
Have students learn more about the Japanese language and the characters of its alphabet by completing the *Enrichment* activity.

All in One **Asia and the Pacific Teaching Resources,** *Enrichment,* p. 347

Answers

Analyze Possible answers: They ensure that everyone is dressed appropriately for school; they prevent competition between students.

✓ **Reading Check** Fewer workers have to support an increasing number of older people.

Writing Activity
Use the *Rubric for Assessing a Writing Assignment* to evaluate students' lists.

All in One **Asia and the Pacific Teaching Resources,** *Rubric for Assessing a Writing Assignment,* p. 359

Go Online
PHSchool.com Typing in the Web code when prompted will bring students directly to detailed instructions for this activity.

Objective

Learn how to synthesize information.

Prepare to Read

Build Background Knowledge L2

Ask students to identify the information sources they might use when writing a report or preparing a presentation. *(library, encyclopedia, the Internet)* Then have them think about the ways they combine the information to use it in a report or presentation. Conduct an Idea Wave (TE, p. T35) to elicit student responses. Explain to students that when they gather information, they have to be able to synthesize, or combine the information that comes from different sources, in order to find the main ideas and draw a conclusion.

Instruct

Synthesizing Information L2

Guided Instruction

- Read the steps to synthesizing information as a class and write them on the board.

- Practice the skill by following the steps on p. 726 as a class. Model each step in the activity using the information under the heading Facing the Future on p. 725. Identify the main idea *(Japan needs to find ways to maintain its wealth)*, identify several details *(Japan does not have a growing labor force, it has limited immigration and a low birthrate; the cost of producing goods and services is higher in Japan than in other countries)*, look for connections and draw a conclusion *(because the country does not have a growing labor force, the cost of producing goods and services is higher, which makes it a challenge for Japan to maintain its wealth)*.

Independent Practice

Assign *Skills for Life* and have students complete it individually.

All in One **Asia and the Pacific Teaching Resources,** *Skills for Life*, p. 348

Skills for Life # Synthesizing Information

James and his family were going to host a Japanese exchange student for the summer. The student, Hiro, would be arriving in three weeks.

James decided to send information about his town to Hiro. First, he got a map that showed the mountains and lakes in the area. Then, James took photos of his favorite places in town. James added photos of his friends at school and playing soccer. His mother gave him a brochure that told about the area. Finally, James made a video showing his family, his apartment, and even his cat.

Soon, James had a mountain of information. He showed it to his dad.

"You've done a great job," his dad said. "But maybe you should synthesize some of this information. After all, Hiro may not have time to digest all of these things."

When you synthesize information, you combine information from several different sources. You find the main ideas and weave them into a conclusion. Synthesizing information is a very important skill in school and in life.

Learn the Skill

Follow these steps to synthesize information.

1. **Identify the main idea in each piece of information.** Main ideas are big, important ideas that are supported by details. You may want to write the main ideas down. The main idea for James is to tell about his town.

2. **Find details that support your main ideas.** Details will give you more information about your main ideas. One detail that James chose to share was that some children in his town like to play soccer.

3. **Look for connections between the pieces of information.** These connections might be similarities, differences, causes, effects, or examples. Jot down these connections.

4. **Draw conclusions based on the connections you found.** What broad, general statements can you make that tie your main ideas together?

726 Asia and the Pacific

Monitor Progress

As students are completing *Skills for Life*, circulate to make sure individuals are applying the skill steps effectively. Provide assistance as needed.

Japan's Modern Economy

Main Ideas	Supporting Details	Connections
1. By the 1980s Japan had one of the world's largest and strongest economies.	• Japan loaned large amounts of money to other countries. • Japan exported its products to the rest of the world.	• Japan imported few goods.
2. In the early 1990s Japan suffered a severe recession.		

Practice the Skill

Use the steps on the previous page to synthesize information about Japan's modern economy. Reread the text on page 722 under the heading Successes and Challenges. Then make a table like the partially completed one above.

1. Study the information about Japan's economy from the 1980s to the present. Add one or two main ideas to the two ideas on the table above.

2. Now find details that support each main idea and add them to the chart. The details already listed add more information about Japan's strong economy in the 1980s.

3. Are the pieces of information connected in some way? Consider cause and effect. The connection already included is a possible cause for the decline in Japan's economy. Add other connections to the chart.

4. Draw some conclusions from the connections you find. See whether you can use these conclusions to answer the question, "Why did Japan's economy decline in the early 1990s?"

The Tokyo Stock Exchange is part of Japan's economy. This stock trader is using a hand signal to show he wants to sell stocks.

Apply the Skill

Use the steps on the previous page to synthesize information about how life has changed in modern Japan. Select information from the text and photos in the section Life in Japan on page 724. Focus on a single aspect of Japanese life, such as family life or work life.

Differentiated Instruction

For Special Needs Students [L1]

Partner special needs students with more proficient students to do Level 1 of the *Synthesizing Information* lesson on the Social Studies Skill Tutor CD-ROM

together. When students feel more confident, they can move onto Level 2 alone.

 Synthesizing Information, **Social Studies Skills Tutor CD-ROM**

Assess and Reteach

Assess Progress [L2]

Ask students to do the Apply the Skill activity.

Reteach [L1]

If students are having trouble applying the skill steps, have them review the skill using the interactive Social Studies Skills Tutor CD-ROM.

 Synthesizing Information, **Social Studies Skills Tutor CD-ROM**

Extend [L3]

Ask students to suppose they are going on a trip to a place they have never been to before. Have them identify the kinds of information that they might want to have with them. *(maps, brochures with pictures, information from books or the Internet)* Working in groups or pairs, have students choose a location they would like to travel to, and do research at the library or on the Internet to gather information about that place. Then have them synthesize and create a table with the information, and present it to the class.

Answer
Apply the Skill

Answers will vary, but students should focus on a single aspect of Japanese life from the section, and choose and synthesize the information from the text and photos.

Section 3
Step-by-Step Instruction

Objectives

Social Studies

1. Understand why North Korea has been slow to develop.
2. Find out how South Korea became an economic success.

Reading/Language Arts

Learn how to identify contrasts to examine differences in information.

Prepare to Read

Build Background Knowledge L2

Tell students that in this section they will learn about North and South Korea, two countries on the Korean Peninsula that have been separated from each other for a half century. Ask students to suppose that the classroom was divided into two parts, and that students on one side of the classroom would not be allowed to cross from one side of the room to the other, and forbidden to talk to the students there. What kind of challenges would this create? How would they feel? Use the Give One, Get One activity (TE, p. T37) to generate ideas.

Set a Purpose for Reading L2

■ Preview the Objectives.

■ Read each statement in the *Reading Readiness Guide* aloud. Ask students to mark each statement true or false.

All in One Asia and the Pacific Teaching Resources, *Reading Readiness Guide,* p. 340

■ Have students discuss the statements in pairs or groups of four, then mark their worksheets again. Use the Numbered Heads participation strategy (TE, p. T36) to call on students to share their group's perspectives.

Vocabulary Builder
Preview Key Terms

Pronounce each Key Term, then ask the students to say the word with you. Provide a simple explanation such as, "During a famine, many people do not have enough to eat."

Section 3
The Koreas
A Divided Land

Prepare to Read

Objectives

In this section, you will
1. Understand why North Korea has been slow to develop.
2. Find out how South Korea became an economic success.

Taking Notes

As you read this section, look for differences between North Korea and South Korea. Copy the table below, and record your findings in it.

North Korea	South Korea
•	• High economic growth

🎯 Target Reading Skill

Identify Contrasts When you identify contrasts, you examine differences. North Korea and South Korea are very different. As you read, look for differences between these two countries. Write them down in the Taking Notes table.

Key Terms

- **demilitarized zone** (dee MIL uh tuh ryzd zohn) *n.* an area in which no weapons are allowed
- **truce** (troos) *n.* a cease-fire agreement
- **diversify** (duh VUR suh fy) *v.* to add variety to
- **famine** (FAM in) *n.* a huge food shortage

North Korea and South Korea have a border unlike any other in the world. On a map, the border looks like a simple line. In reality, the border runs through the middle of what former President Bill Clinton called "the scariest place on Earth."

The border runs through the DMZ or **demilitarized zone** (dee MIL uh tuh ryzd zohn), an area in which no weapons are allowed. The DMZ is about 2.5 miles (4 kilometers) wide and about 151 miles (248 kilometers) long. Barbed wire, land mines, watchtowers, and thousands of weapons line both sides.

Children in South Korea

728 Asia and the Pacific

🎯 Target Reading Skill L2

Identify Contrasts Point out the Target Reading Skill. Tell students that identifying contrasts in information can help them understand differences between people, places, and things in their reading.

Model identifying contrasts by reading the first two paragraphs under the heading North Korea: Economic Challenges on p. 729. Note that the first paragraph says that until the end of World War II, North Korea was the industrial center of the Korean Peninsula. Ask students to contrast that with the description of North Korea in the second paragraph. (*North Korea's economy today is in poor shape and cannot compete with South Korea.*)

Give students *Identify Contrasts.* Have them complete the activity in groups.

All in One Asia and the Pacific Teaching Resources, *Identify Contrasts,* p. 345

On North Korea's side, an estimated one million troops patrol the border. South Korea has about 600,000 troops. Why does the DMZ exist? In 1953, a **truce**, or cease-fire agreement, ended the Korean War. But no peace treaty was signed. Since then, the world's most heavily armed border has divided the two countries.

More than the DMZ divides the Koreas. The two countries have very different economies and governments as well.

A section of the DMZ that divides North Korea and South Korea

North Korea: Economic Challenges

North Korea (the Democratic People's Republic of Korea) is a communist country under a dictatorship. The government runs the economy. The country has kept itself closed to much of the world. This has kept out new technology and fresh ideas. Yet North Korea is rich in mineral resources. Until the end of World War II, it was the industrial center of the Korean Peninsula.

Today, North Korea manufactures poor-quality goods in government-owned factories. Little has been done to **diversify**, or add variety to, the economy. Although the government briefly opened some private markets in 2004, it still controls the economy. Overall, North Korea's economy is in poor shape.

Farming methods, too, are outdated in North Korea. In 1995, North Koreans faced **famine**, or a huge food shortage, and starvation. About 220,000 people died from famine between 1995 and 1998. Without farming reforms, food shortages have continued. To help combat starvation, many countries and international organizations provided humanitarian food aid to North Korea. However, in 2005, the government said that it would stop accepting humanitarian aid.

✓ **Reading Check** How has North Korea's isolation affected its economy?

A North Korean man saw his South Korean grandmother for the first time in more than 50 years when North Korea allowed separated families to reunite in 2005.

Vocabulary Builder

Use the information below to teach students this section's high-use words.

High-Use Word	Definition and Sample Sentence
manufacture, p. 729	*v.* to make a product by hand or machinery The toy company **manufactured** many items, including board games.
outdated, p. 729	*adj.* no longer current or popular The typewriter has become **outdated** since the invention of the computer.
focus, p. 730	*v.* to concentrate on one thing Over the weekend, I **focused** on studying for Monday's test.
material, p. 730	*n.* what a thing is made from or used for The blanket was made from a very soft **material**.

North Korea: Economic Challenges L2

Guided Instruction

■ **Vocabulary Builder** Clarify the high-use words **manufacture** and **outdated** before reading.

■ Read about the state of North Korea's economy in North Korea: Economic Challenges. As students read, circulate and make sure individuals can answer the Reading Check question.

■ Discuss the state of North Korea's economy. *(It is in poor shape because its factories produce poor-quality goods and little has been done to diversify.)*

■ Ask students **How have the lack of farming reforms affected North Koreans?** *(Without farming reforms, North Koreans have had to deal with continued food shortages, which have led to starvation.)*

Independent Practice

Ask students to create the Taking Notes graphic organizer on a blank piece of paper. Then have them fill it in with information about North Korea's economy.

Monitor Progress

As students fill in the graphic organizer, circulate and make sure individuals are choosing the correct details. Provide assistance as needed.

Answer

✓ **Reading Check** The government-run economy has meant little economic diversification and an overall poor economic performance.

South Korea: Economic Growth

Guided Instruction

- **Vocabulary Builder** Clarify the meaning of the high-use words **focus** and **material** before reading.

- Read South Korea: Economic Growth, using the Paragraph Shrinking strategy (TE, p. T34).

- Discuss South Korea's economic development from after World War II to the present. (*After World War II, the country focused on making cloth and processed foods; later it developed heavy industry; today it is a leader in shipbuilding and has a growing electronics industry. It also has large oil refineries.*)

- Ask students **How do you think South Korea's government and economic structure have contributed to its economic success?** (*Answers will vary, but should include that having a democratic government and a free enterprise system enables people to sell and buy more goods, thereby contributing to a successful economy.*)

Independent Practice

Have students complete their graphic organizers by filling in information about South Korea's economy in the appropriate column.

Monitor Progress

Show *Section Reading Support Transparency AP 66* and ask students to check their graphic organizers individually. Go over key concepts and clarify key vocabulary as needed.

📖 **Asia and the Pacific Transparencies,** *Section Reading Support Transparency AP 66*

🔄 **Target Reading Skill** L2

As a follow up, ask students to answer the Target Reading Skill question in the Student Edition. (*North Korea's government is a Communist dictatorship, while South Korea's government is a democracy.*)

Answer

✓ Reading Check Answers may include ships, electronics, silicon chips, plastics, and rubber.

Soccer is a popular sport in South Korea.

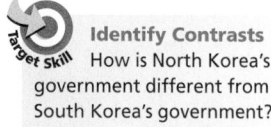
Identify Contrasts How is North Korea's government different from South Korea's government?

South Korea: Economic Growth

In the mid-1950s, South Korea (the Republic of Korea) had agricultural resources but few industries. Fifty years later, South Korea has become a leading economic power.

South Korea is a democracy with an economy based on free enterprise. After World War II, South Korea's factories focused on making cloth and processed foods. Later, South Korea developed heavy industry. Today, South Korea is among the world's leading shipbuilders. It has a growing electronics industry that exports radios, televisions, and computers. South Korea is a leading producer of the silicon chips used in computers. South Korea also has large refineries, or factories that process oil. The oil products are used to make plastics, rubber, and other goods.

The government of South Korea has focused on the growth of industry. But it has also helped farmers. Some programs helped increase crop production. Other programs improved housing, roads, and water supplies and brought electricity to rural areas.

Despite its successes, South Korea faces a number of challenges. Like Japan, it lacks many natural resources. It must import large amounts of raw materials to keep industry running. Major imports are oil, iron, steel, and chemicals.

✓ Reading Check **What are some products made in South Korea?**

Differentiated Instruction

For Special Needs Students L1

Before students read the section, show them *Section Reading Support Transparency AP 66* to give them a preview of the material. You may wish to leave the transparency up so that students can refer to it as they read.

📖 **Asia and the Pacific Transparencies,** *Section Reading Support Transparency AP 66*

Background

The Korean War The Korean War was the first war in which the United Nations played a major role. The war began on June 25, 1950, when Communist North Korea invaded South Korea. The United Nations asked member nations to aid South Korea. Sixteen members sent troops. The war ended on July 27, 1953, when the United Nations and North Korea signed a truce.

Years of Tension

Many Koreans hope that one day North Korea and South Korea will once again be one country. But relations between the two Koreas have remained tense since the end of the Korean War. North Korean and South Korean troops have had numerous violent clashes. Better relations seemed possible in 2000. The leaders of the two countries met in Pyongyang, the capital of North Korea, and agreed to work toward peace and cooperation.

Compare and contrast North and South Korea.

Show students *The Koreas: Rich and Poor.* Ask students to write a brief summary of what they learned.

COUNTRY PROFILE
Focus on Economics

The Koreas

The Koreas have very different economies. The map at right shows that North Korea is rich in natural resources. However, its communist system has hurt its economy. The graph below shows that South Korea's gross domestic product, or economic output, has soared, while North Korea's has failed to grow.

Manufacturing electronics in South Korea

The Koreas: Natural Resources
KEY

- Gold
- Silver
- Copper
- Iron
- Lead
- Tungsten
- Coal
- Graphite
- Hydroelectric power
- Manufacturing
- ⊛ National capital
- National border

CHINA

NORTH KOREA

P'yŏngyang

Sea of Japan

Seoul

SOUTH KOREA

Yellow Sea

Korea Strait

Cheju-Do

0 miles 250
0 kilometers 250
Lambert Conformal Conic

Gross Domestic Product, 1985–2005

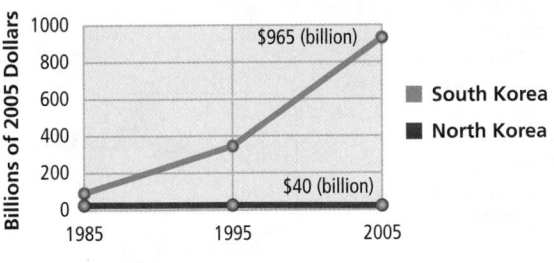

$965 (billion)

$40 (billion)

■ South Korea
■ North Korea

SOURCE: *CIA World Factbook*

Map and Chart Skills

1. **List** Using the map, name at least three natural resources that are found in North Korea but not South Korea.
2. **Contrast** Based on your reading and the graph at the left, discuss the differences between the economies of North and South Korea.

 **Go Online** PHSchool.com

Use Web Code **Ice-6713** for **DK World Desk Reference Online.**

Chapter 24 Section 3 **731**

COUNTRY PROFILE
Focus on Economics

Guided Instruction L2

Ask students to study the Country Profile on this page. As a class, answer the Map and Chart Skills questions.

Independent Practice

Have students work in pairs to create a Venn diagram comparing the natural resources of North Korea and South Korea.

Years of Tension L2

Guided Instruction

- Read Years of Tension with students.

- Ask students **How did North's Korea's announcement in 2002 affect South Korea and the world?** (*North Korea's leaders announced that the country had been developing nuclear weapons, which damaged hopes for peace with South Korea and caused concern worldwide.*)

Independent Practice

Assign *Guided Reading and Review.*

All in One Asia and the Pacific Teaching Resources, *Guided Reading and Review,* p. 341

Monitor Progress

Tell students to fill in the last column of their *Reading Readiness Guides.*

All in One Asia and the Pacific Teaching Resources, *Reading Readiness Guide,* p. 340

Answers

Map and Chart Skills

1. gold, silver, iron, lead
2. North Korea is rich in natural resources, yet its communist system has hindered its economic growth; South Korea does not have a communist system, and its economy has grown rapidly.

Go Online PHSchool.com Students can find more information about this topic on the DK World Desk Reference Online.

Links

Read the **Links to Science** on this page. Ask students **Why has the DMZ become a haven for wildlife?** *(The land inside the DMZ has been untouched by human settlement for more than 50 years.)*

Assess and Reteach

Assess Progress   L2

Have students complete the Section Assessment. Adminster the *Section Quiz.*

> All in One **Asia and the Pacific Teaching Resources,** *Section Quiz,* p. 342

Reteach   L1

If students need more instruction, have them read this section in the Reading and Vocabulary Study Guide.

> Chapter 24, Section 3, **Eastern Hemisphere Reading and Vocabulary Study Guide**, pp. 256–258

Extend   L3

Have students learn more about how the division of North and South Korea affects the lives of families who live in both countries, by completing the *Small Group Activity.*

> All in One **Asia and the Pacific Teaching Resources,** *Small Group Activity: The Divided Koreas,* pp. 349–352

Answer

> ✓ Reading Check "Six Party Talks" led to a new agreement with North Korea.

Section 3 Assessment

Key Terms
Students' sentences should reflect knowledge of each Key Term.

🔁 **Target Reading Skill**
South Korea is a democracy with a strong free-enterprise economy, while North Korea is a communist dictatorship with a weak economy.

Comprehension and Critical Thinking
1. (a) It has a democratic government with a free-enterprise economy. **(b)** It is a democracy based on free enterprise, and the government has focused on improving both industry and agriculture.

2. (a) It has a communist government run by a dictator and a government-run economy. **(b)** It has kept out new technology and ideas.

3. (a) Leaders from the two sides met in 2000 and agreed to work toward peace and cooperation. **(b)** "Six Party Talks" led to a new agreement with North Korea. **(c)** He meant that one day the North Koreans will live in a free society.

Writing Activity
Use the *Rubric for Assessing a Writing Assignment* to evaluate students' paragraphs.

> All in One **Asia and the Pacific Teaching Resources,** *Rubric for Assessing a Writing Assignment,* p. 359

Go Online
PHSchool.com   Typing in the Web code when prompted will bring students directly to detailed instructions for this activity.

Links to Science

Nature in the DMZ The land inside the DMZ has been untouched by human settlement for more than 50 years. As a result, the DMZ has become a peaceful haven for wildlife. Living in the DMZ are several rare and endangered species. They include eagles, cranes, and bears. Some people believe there are tigers in the DMZ. If North Korea and South Korea ever sign a peace agreement, some people want to preserve the DMZ as a peace park. Other people want to use the land to develop Korea's economy.

In 2002, North Korea's government made a shocking announcement. Even though it had previously agreed not to, North Korea said it had been developing nuclear weapons. The news damaged hopes for peace between the two countries and caused worldwide concern. In 2005, North Korea announced that it had made nuclear weapons. Later that year, "Six-Party Talks" among North Korea, the United States, Russia, China, Japan, and South Korea led to a new agreement. In exchange for giving up its nuclear weapons, North Korea would receive increased aid and diplomatic relations. However, the agreement has not yet been carried out.

In 2005, U.S. President George W. Bush visited several countries in Asia. On that trip, he said,

> ❝We will not forget the people of North Korea. The 21st century will be freedom's century for all Koreans—and one day every citizen of that peninsula will live in dignity and freedom and prosperity at home, and in peace with their neighbors abroad. ❞
>
> — *President George W. Bush*

✓ Reading Check   **What happened when North Korea announced it had made nuclear weapons?**

Section **3** Assessment

Key Terms
Review the key terms at the beginning of this section. Use each term in a sentence that explains its meaning.

🔁 **Target Reading Skill**
Using your Taking Notes chart, explain ways in which North Korea and South Korea are different.

Comprehension and Critical Thinking
1. (a) Identify What kind of government and economy does South Korea have?
(b) Identify Causes What are some reasons for South Korea's economic success?

2. (a) Identify What kind of government does North Korea have?
(b) Analyze Why has North Korea's economy lagged behind South Korea's?

3. (a) Explain What event seemed to point to better relations between North Korea and South Korea?
(b) Identify Effects What was the effect of North Korea's development of nuclear weapons?
(c) Draw Inferences What did President Bush mean when he said, "We will not forget the people of North Korea"?

Writing Activity
When North Korea and South Korea were divided, families were divided, too. Based on what you have read about the Koreas, write a paragraph that states your viewpoint on the issue of reunifying the two countries.

Go Online
PHSchool.com
For: An activity on the Koreas
Visit: PHSchool.com
Web Code: lcd-6703

◆ Chapter Summary

Section 1: China
- China tried two economic programs from 1949 to 1980, including the Great Leap Forward and the Cultural Revolution.
- Under a free enterprise system, Taiwan developed a successful economy.
- After the death of Chinese leader Mao Zedong, China followed a different path that included many changes to develop the economy.
- China today is a major economic power with a government that has fewer controls over the economy, but that does not allow political freedom for its citizens.

Section 2: Japan
- Japan worked hard to build a successful, highly developed economy.
- After an economic decline in the 1990s, Japan continues its recovery with one of the largest economies in the world.
- Japan has a modern culture that combines traditional Japanese values with new ways of working and living.
- One of Japan's challenges for the future is finding a way of maintaining its wealth, despite an aging population and a low birthrate.

China

Section 3: The Koreas
- South Korea has a democratic government with an economy based on free enterprise.
- North Korea has a communist government that controls the economy.

Japan

◆ Key Terms

Match the definitions in Column I with the key terms in Column II.

Column I

1. an economic system in which people can choose their own jobs, start private businesses, own property, and make a profit
2. extreme
3. a huge food shortage
4. to add variety to
5. the number of live births in a nation each year per 1,000 people

Column II

A   radical
B   free enterprise system
C   birthrate
D   diversify
E   famine

─ Vocabulary Builder ─

Revisit this chapter's high-use words:

output	assist	outdated
turmoil	position	focus
moderate	maintain	material
record	manufacture	

Ask students to review the definitions they recorded on their *Word Knowledge* worksheets.

All in One **Asia and the Pacific Teaching Resources,** *Word Knowledge,* p. 346

Consider allowing students to earn extra credit if they use the words in their answers to the questions in the Chapter Review and Assessment. The words must be used correctly and in a natural context to win the extra points.

Review Chapter Content
- Review and revisit the major themes of this chapter by asking students to classify what Guiding Question each bulleted statement in the Chapter Summary answers. Form students into groups and ask them to complete the activity together. Refer to p. 567 in the Student Edition for the text of the Guiding Questions.

- Assign *Vocabulary Development* for students to review Key Terms.

All in One **Asia and the Pacific Teaching Resources,** *Vocabulary Development,* p. 358

Answers

Key Terms

1. B
2. A
3. E
4. D
5. C

Comprehension and Critical Thinking

6. (a) to create a completely new society with no ties to the past **(b)** The Cultural Revolution focused on social changes, while the Great Leap Forward focused on the economy. Both were harmful to China.

7. (a) an island 100 miles off mainland China's southeast coast, and the location of a country known as the Republic of China **(b)** It believes it should be ruling all of mainland China.

8. (a) a program aimed at improving farming, industry, science, and defense in China **(b)** Answers may include any of the following: more free enterprise was allowed; farmers could sell crops for a profit; foreign-owned factories were allowed.

9. (a) robots, watches, cameras, electronic goods, televisions, CDs, VCRs, personal stereos, small handheld games, DVDs

10. Groups of companies joined together to work towards each other's success.

11. (a) work people do for which they are paid **(b)** Its birthrate has been shrinking, and it has little immigration.

12. (a) It was the industrial center of the Korean Peninsula. **(b)** North Korea is a communist dictatorship with a weak economy, while South Korea is a democracy with a strong free-enterprise economy.

13. (a) Possible answers: cloth, processed foods, ships, radios, televisions, computers, silicon chips, plastics, rubber **(b)** Like Japan, South Korea lacks many natural resources and must import large amounts of raw materials to keep its industry running.

Skills Practice

Answers will vary, but students should synthesize the information in the text and captions in Section 1, and draw a conclusion about how China has changed since 1949.

Writing Activity: Language Arts

Use the *Rubric for Assessing a Writing Assignment* to evaluate students' reports.

All in One **Asia and the Pacific Teaching Resources,** *Rubric for Assessing a Writing Assignment,* p. 359

◆ Comprehension and Critical Thinking

6. (a) Identify What was the purpose of the Cultural Revolution?
(b) Compare and Contrast How was the Cultural Revolution similar to and different from the Great Leap Forward?

7. (a) Define Where and what is Taiwan?
(b) Identify Point of View How does the government of Taiwan view China?

8. (a) Explain What was the Four Modernizations program of the 1990s?
(b) Identify Effects Describe one change in China's economy under this program.

9. (a) Note Give examples of some of the high-technology products made in Japan.

10. (a) Summarize How was the formation of *keiretsu* an example of the Japanese tradition of working together?

11. (a) Define What is labor?
(b) Summarize What is one reason that Japan has a declining labor force?

12. (a) Describe What was North Korea like before the end of World War II?

(b) Contrast How is North Korea's government and economy different from South Korea's?

13. (a) List Name four products that are made in South Korea.
(b) Compare Why is South Korea similar to Japan in terms of what the country must do to keep industry running?

◆ Skills Practice

Synthesizing Information Review the steps you learned in the Skills for Life lesson in this chapter. Then review the text and pictures in Section 1. Synthesize the information and draw a conclusion about how China has changed since 1949.

◆ Writing Activity: Language Arts

Written Chinese is based on characters, rather than on an alphabet. Each Chinese character represents a word or an idea. The complete Chinese writing system has more than 40,000 characters. Use an encyclopedia to look up information about the Chinese language and the Chinese writing system. Write a brief report that describes Chinese writing.

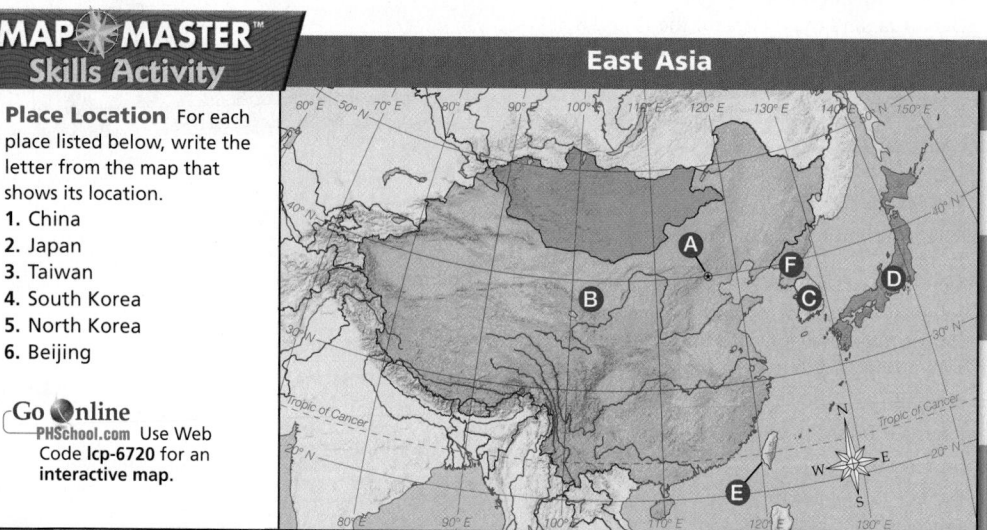

MAP MASTER™
Skills Activity

East Asia

Place Location For each place listed below, write the letter from the map that shows its location.
1. China
2. Japan
3. Taiwan
4. South Korea
5. North Korea
6. Beijing

Go Online
PHSchool.com Use Web Code **lcp-6720** for an interactive map.

734 Asia and the Pacific

Standardized Test Prep

Test-Taking Tips

Some questions on standardized tests ask you to analyze graphic organizers. Study the concept web below. Then follow the tips to answer the sample question at the right.

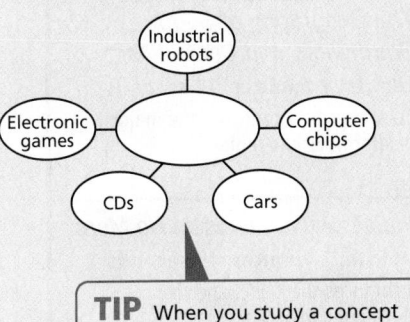

TIP When you study a concept web, think about what kind of information belongs in each part.

Pick the letter that best answers the question.

Which title should go in the center of the web?

A Skiing Gear
B Exports
C Japanese Exports
D Japanese Imports

TIP Read all four answer choices. Then choose the BEST answer from the remaining choices.

Think It Through The question asks you to choose a title for the center of the web—in other words, an idea that covers the information in all of the outer circles. You can rule out A because it is too specific: skiing gear belongs in an outer circle. However, B is too general. Although it is correct, there is probably a better answer. That leaves C or D. Look over the items in the outer circles. Are they goods that Japan sells to the rest of the world (exports) or buys from other countries (imports)? Look for at least one product on the web that you are sure is an export or import. (For instance, do you know any Americans who own a Japanese car?) The correct answer is C.

Practice Questions

Use the tips above and other tips in this book to help you answer the following questions.

1. How are the governments of China and North Korea similar?
   A They are both ruled by kings.
   B They both have communist governments.
   C They both follow the free enterprise system.
   D They both have democratic governments.

2. In Japan, you could expect to find
   A special economic zones.
   B a high birthrate.
   C a growing labor force.
   D an economy based on manufacturing goods for export.

3. In 1997, Hong Kong was returned to
   A Taiwan.
   B China.
   C Japan.
   D South Korea.

Use the concept web below to answer Question 4.

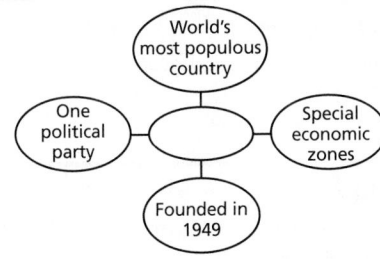

4. Which title should go in the center of the web?
   A Japan
   B North Korea
   C China
   D Taiwan

Use Web Code lca-6700 for **Chapter 24 self-test.**

Chapter 24 **735**

Standardized Test Prep
Answer
1. B
2. D
3. B
4. C

Assessment Resources

Use *Chapter Tests A and B* to assess students' mastery of chapter content.

All in One **Asia and the Pacific Teaching Resources,** *Chapter Tests A and B,* pp. 360–365

Tests are also available on the *ExamView Test Bank CD-ROM.*

💿 *ExamView Test Bank CD-ROM*

Overview

Introducing South, Southwest, and Central Asia
1. Use a map and data to learn about the nations of South, Southwest, and Central Asia.
2. Analyze data to compare the countries.
3. Identify characteristics they share.
4. Find some of the key differences among the countries.

The Geography of South, Southwest, and Central Asia
Length: 7 minutes, 12 seconds
Compares and contrasts the major landforms of the region.

Section 1 India: In the Midst of Change
1. Learn about key features of India's population.
2. Examine the state of India's economy.
3. Understand major challenges facing India.

India's Dalits: Outcasts No More
Length: 2 minutes, 49 seconds
Introduces the Dalits and the challenges they face.

Section 2 Pakistan: An Economy Based on Agriculture
1. Find out that Pakistan's economy is based on agriculture.
2. Learn about Pakistan's industries.

Pakistan: Improving Education
Length: 3 minutes, 24 seconds
Explains Pakistani efforts to improve education in rural areas.

Section 3 Israel: Economics and Cultures
1. Discover how Israel's economy has grown and changed over the years.
2. Learn about the different peoples living in Israel.

Jerusalem: Whose Holy City?
Length: 4 minutes, 25 seconds
Depicts Jerusalem and the religious mix found there.

Section 4 Saudi Arabia: Oil and Islam
1. Learn how oil has affected Saudi Arabia's development and economy.
2. Discover how Islam affects everyday life in Saudi Arabia.
3. Understand the main features of Saudi Arabia's government.

The Call to Mecca
Length: 3 minutes, 19 seconds
Explores the traditional pilgrimage to Mecca.

Section 5 The Stans: A Diverse Region
1. Examine the factors that have caused war and conflicts in the Stans.
2. Learn about the economies of the Stans.
3. Discover how environmental issues affect life in the Stans.

The Disappearing Aral Sea
Length: 3 minutes, 9 seconds
Explains the shrinkage of the Aral Sea and its effects on people of the region.

Technology Resources

Students use embedded Web codes to access Internet activities, chapter self-tests, and additional map practice. They may also access Dorling Kindersley's Online Desk Reference to learn more about each country they study.

Use the Interactive Textbook to make content and concepts come alive through animations, videos, and activities that accompany the complete basal text—online and on CD-ROM.

Use this complete suite of powerful teaching tools to make planning lessons and administering tests quicker and easier.

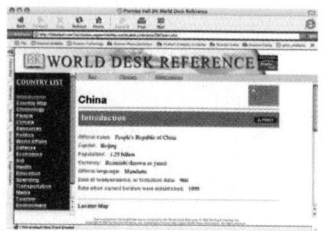
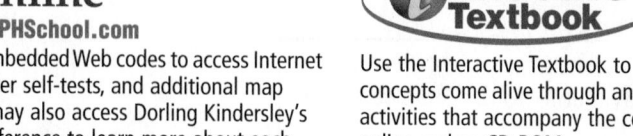
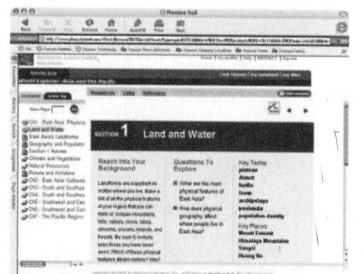

Reading and Assessment

CHAPTER 25

Reading and Vocabulary Instruction

⟳ Model the Target Reading Skill

Identify Causes and Effects Explain to students that identifying causes and effects helps to clarify the relationship between events or situations. To identify causes and effects, follow these steps: (1) Pick one event or condition as a starting point. (2) Look at earlier events or conditions for possible causes—look for clue words such as *reason*, *because*, *produced*, and *purpose*. (3) Look at later events or conditions for possible effects—look for clue words such as *brought about*, *effect*, *led to*, *outcome*, *produced*, *reaction*, *result*, *so*, *then*, *therefore*, and *this*. (4) Summarize the cause-effect relationships; a diagram can show them at a glance.

Model identifying causes and effects using the following sentences from the *Link to Science* feature on page 771.

In Saudi Arabia, some parts of the desert have what is called "sweet" sand. This sand is not too salty, so plants can grow on it.

Think aloud: "When I look at these sentences, I see the word *so*. This signals to me that there is a cause and effect relationship. The word *so* signals an effect. The effect is that plants can grow. The cause of plants growing is that the sand is not too salty."

Use the following worksheets from All-in-One Asia and the Pacific Teaching Resources (pp. 389–392) to support the chapter's Target Reading Skill.

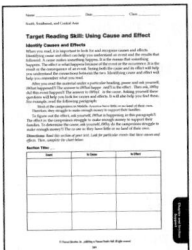 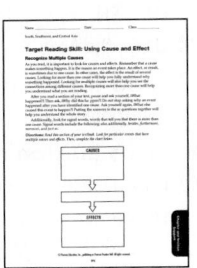 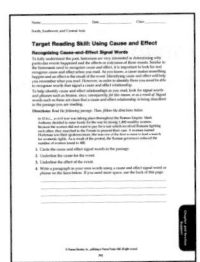

Vocabulary Builder
High-Use Academic Words

Use these steps to teach this chapter's high-use words:

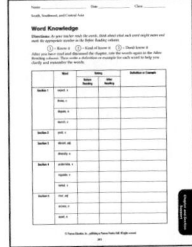

1. Have students rate how well they know each word on their Word Knowledge worksheets (All-in-One Asia and the Pacific Teaching Resources, p. 393).
2. Pronounce each word and ask students to repeat it.
3. Give students a brief definition or sample sentence (provided on pp. 751, 757, 762, 767, 775).
4. Work with students as they fill in the "Definition or Example" column of their Word Knowledge worksheets.

Assessment

Formal Assessment

Test students' understanding of core knowledge and skills.

Chapter Tests A and B, All-in-One Asia and the Pacific Teaching Resources, pp. 412–417

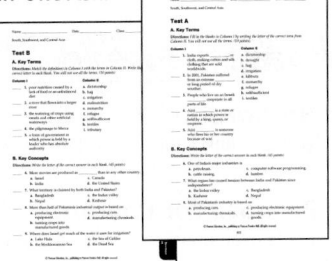

Customize the Chapter Tests to suit your needs.

ExamView Test Bank CD-ROM

Skills Assessment

Assess geographic literacy.

MapMaster Skills, Student Edition pp. 737, 782

Country Profile Map and Chart Skills, Student Edition pp. 753, 759, 763, 768, 777

Assess reading and comprehension.

Target Reading Skills, Student Edition pp. 754, 758, 767, 775, and in Section Assessments

Chapter 25 Assessment, Eastern Hemisphere Reading and Vocabulary Study Guide, p. 275

Performance Assessment

Assess students' performance on this chapter's Writing Activities using the following rubrics from All-in-One Asia and the Pacific Teaching Resources.

Rubric for Assessing a Bar Graph, p. 408

Rubric for Assessing a Journal Entry, p. 409

Rubric for Assessing a Writing Assignment, p. 410

Rubric for Assessing a Newspaper Article, p. 411

Assess students' work through performance tasks.

Small Group Activity: Creating a Brochure on Buildings of Southwest and Central Asia, All-in-One Asia and the Pacific Teaching Resources, pp. 396–399

Portfolio Suggestions, Teacher Edition, p. 749

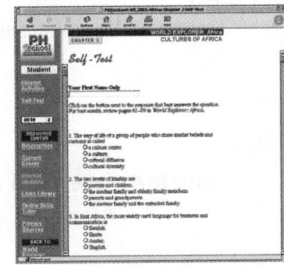

Online Assessment

Have students check their own understanding.

Chapter Self-Test

Section 1 India: In the Midst of Change

 1.5 periods, .75 block (includes Country Databank)

Social Studies Objectives
1. Learn about key features of India's population.
2. Examine the state of India's economy.
3. Understand major challenges facing India.

Reading/Language Arts Objective
Determine causes and effects to understand how events and situations are related.

Prepare to Read

Build Background Knowledge
Ask students to think about what they know about India.

Set a Purpose for Reading
Have students evaluate statements on the *Reading Readiness Guide*.

Preview Key Terms
Teach the section's Key Terms.

Target Reading Skill
Introduce the section's Target Reading Skill of **identifying causes and effects.**

Instructional Resources

All in One Asia and the Pacific Teaching Resources
- **L2** Reading Readiness Guide, p. 370
- **L2** Identify Causes and Effects, p. 389

Passport to the World CD ROM
- **L2** India: Photo Tour

Differentiated Instruction

Spanish Reading and Vocabulary Study Guide
- **L1** Chapter 25, Section 1, pp. 184–185 ELL

World Studies Video Program
- **L2** The Geography of South, Southwest, and Central Asia AR, GT, LPR, SN

Instruct

Key Features of India's Population A Growing Economy
Discuss the population and economy of India.

Country Profile
Ask students to derive information from maps, charts, and graphs.

Progress and Challenges
Discuss the major challenges facing India.

Target Reading Skill
Review **identifying causes and effects.**

Instructional Resources

All in One Asia and the Pacific Teaching Resources
- **L2** Guided Reading and Review, p. 371
- **L2** Reading Readiness Guide, p. 370

Asia and the Pacific Transparencies
- **L2** Section Reading Support Transparency AP 67

World Studies Video Program
- **L2** India's Dalits: Outcasts No More

Differentiated Instruction

All in One Asia and the Pacific Teaching Resources
- **L2** Outline Maps 26 and 28, pp. 401, 402 AR, GT, LPR, SN
- **L2** Using the Map Key, p. 400 AR, GT, LPR, SN

Asia and the Pacific Transparencies
- **L1** Transparency B16: Venn Diagram ELL, LPR, SN

Teacher's Edition
- **L3** For Advanced Readers, TE p. 739
- **L3** For Gifted and Talented, TE p. 742
- **L1** For Less Proficient Readers, TE pp. 743, 754
- **L1** For Special Needs Students, TE p. 746
- **L2** For English Language Learners, TE p. 747

Assess and Reteach

Assess Progress
Evaluate student comprehension with the section assessment and section quiz.

Reteach
Assign the Reading and Vocabulary Study Guide to help struggling students.

Extend
Extend the lesson by having students read an ancient Indian tale.

Instructional Resources

All in One Asia and the Pacific Teaching Resources
- **L2** Section Quiz, p. 372
- **L3** Savitri: A Tale of Ancient India, pp. 403–406
  Rubric for Assessing a Journal Entry, p. 409

Reading and Vocabulary Study Guide
- **L1** Chapter 25, Section 1, pp. 260–262

Differentiated Instruction

All in One Asia and the Pacific Teaching Resources
  Rubric for Assessing a Bar Graph, p. 408 AR, GT, LPR, SN

Spanish Support
- **L2** Section Quiz (Spanish), p. 253 ELL

Key
- **L1** Basic to Average
- **L3** Average to Advanced
- **L2** For All Students

LPR Less Proficient Readers
AR Advanced Readers
SN Special Needs Students

GT Gifted and Talented
ELL English Language Learners

Section 2 Pakistan: An Economy Based on Agriculture

 *1.5 periods, .75 block*

Social Studies Objectives
1. Find out that Pakistan's economy is based on agriculture.
2. Learn about Pakistan's industries.

Reading/Language Arts Objective
Find multiple effects produced by one cause to establish relationships between different pieces of information.

Prepare to Read	Instructional Resources	Differentiated Instruction
Build Background Knowledge Discuss water conservation. **Set a Purpose for Reading** Have students evaluate statements on the *Reading Readiness Guide*. **Preview Key Terms** Teach the section's Key Terms. **Target Reading Skill** Introduce the section's Target Reading Skill of **understanding effects**.	**All in One Asia and the Pacific Teaching Resources** L2 Reading Readiness Guide, p. 374 L2 Understand Effects, p. 390	**Spanish Reading and Vocabulary Study Guide** L1 Chapter 25, Section 2, pp. 186–187 ELL

Instruct	Instructional Resources	Differentiated Instruction
An Agricultural Nation Discuss the dependency of Pakistan's economy on agriculture. **Target Reading Skill** Review **understanding effects**. **Industry in Pakistan** Discuss three major industries in Pakistan. **Country Profile** Ask students to derive information from maps, charts, and graphs.	**All in One Asia and the Pacific Teaching Resources** L2 Guided Reading and Review, p. 375 L2 Reading Readiness Guide, p. 374 **Asia and the Pacific Transparencies** L2 Section Reading Support Transparency AP 68 **World Studies Video Program** L2 Pakistan: Improving Education	**Teacher's Edition** L3 For Advanced Readers, TE p. 759 **PHSchool.com** L3 **For:** Environmental and Global Issues: Water Use Around the World AR, GT **Web Code:** lcd-6806 **Spanish Support** L2 Guided Reading and Review (Spanish), p. 254 ELL

Assess and Reteach	Instructional Resources	Differentiated Instruction
Assess Progress Evaluate student comprehension with the section assessment and section quiz. **Reteach** Assign the Reading and Vocabulary Study Guide to help struggling students. **Extend** Extend the lesson by assigning an Internet activity.	**All in One Asia and the Pacific Teaching Resources** L2 Section Quiz, p. 376 Rubric for Assessing a Writing Assignment, p. 410 **Reading and Vocabulary Study Guide** L1 Chapter 25, Section 2, pp. 263–265 **PHSchool.com** L3 **For:** Environmental and Global Issues: Local Water Use **Web Code:** lcd-6810	**Spanish Support** L2 Section Quiz (Spanish), p. 255 ELL

Key
L1 Basic to Average L3 Average to Advanced
L2 For All Students

LPR Less Proficient Readers
AR Advanced Readers
SN Special Needs Students

GT Gifted and Talented
ELL English Language Learners

Section 3 Israel: Economics and Cultures

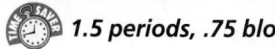 *1.5 periods, .75 block*

Social Studies Objectives

1. Discover how Israel's economy has grown and changed over the years.

2. Learn about the different peoples who live in Israel.

Reading/Language Arts Objective

Find multiple causes that lead to one effect.

Prepare to Read	Instructional Resources	Differentiated Instruction
Build Background Knowledge Discuss water management with students. **Set a Purpose for Reading** Have students evaluate statements on the *Reading Readiness Guide*. **Preview Key Terms** Teach the section's Key Terms. **Target Reading Skill** Introduce the section's Target Reading Skill of **recognizing multiple causes**.	**All in One Asia and the Pacific Teaching Resources** L2 Reading Readiness Guide, p. 378 L2 Recognize Multiple Causes, p. 391	**Spanish Reading and Vocabulary Study Guide** L1 Chapter 25, Section 3, pp. 188–189 ELL

Instruct	Instructional Resources	Differentiated Instruction
Israel's Economy Discuss the economy and industry of Israel. **Country Profile** Ask students to derive information from maps, charts, and graphs. **The People of Israel** Discuss the different cultures found in Israel and the tensions between Israelis and Arabs. **Target Reading Skill** Review **recognizing multiple causes**.	**All in One Asia and the Pacific Teaching Resources** L2 Guided Reading and Review, p. 379 L2 Reading Readiness Guide, p. 378 **Asia and the Pacific Transparencies** L2 Section Reading Support Transparency AP 69 **World Studies Video Program** L2 Jerusalem: Whose Holy City?	**Teacher's Edition** L1 For English Language Learners, TE p. 763 **Spanish Support** L2 Guided Reading and Review (Spanish), p. 256 ELL

Assess and Reteach	Instructional Resources	Differentiated Instruction
Assess Progress Evaluate student comprehension with the section assessment and section quiz. **Reteach** Assign the Reading and Vocabulary Study Guide to help struggling students. **Extend** Extend the lesson by assigning a research project.	**All in One Asia and the Pacific Teaching Resources** L2 Section Quiz, p. 380 Rubric for Assessing a Writing Assignment, p. 410 **Reading and Vocabulary Study Guide** L1 Chapter 25, Section 3, pp. 266–268	**Spanish Support** L2 Section Quiz (Spanish), p. 257 ELL

Key

L1 Basic to Average	L3 Average to Advanced	LPR Less Proficient Readers	GT Gifted and Talented
L2 For All Students		AR Advanced Readers	ELL English Language Learners
		SN Special Needs Students	

Section 4 Saudi Arabia: Oil and Islam

 2 periods, 1 block (includes Skills for Life)

Social Studies Objectives
1. Learn how oil has affected Saudi Arabia's development and economy.
2. Discover how Islam affects everyday life in Saudi Arabia.
3. Understand the main features of Saudi Arabia's government.

Reading/Language Arts Objective
Find multiple effects produced by one cause.

Prepare to Read

Build Background Knowledge
Discuss the uses for oil.

Set a Purpose for Reading
Have students evaluate statements on the *Reading Readiness Guide*.

Preview Key Terms
Teach the section's Key Terms.

Target Reading Skill
Introduce the section's Target Reading Skill of **understanding effects**.

Instructional Resources

All in One Asia and the Pacific Teaching Resources
- L2 Reading Readiness Guide, p. 382
- L2 Understand Effects, p. 390

Differentiated Instruction

Spanish Reading and Vocabulary Study Guide
- L1 Chapter 25, Section 4, pp. 190–191 ELL

Instruct

Target Reading Skill
Review **understanding effects**.

Oil Wealth and Saudi Arabia
Discuss Saudi Arabia's dependence on oil for wealth.

Country Profile
Ask students to derive information from maps, charts, and graphs.

Everyday Life in Saudi Arabia

The Government of Saudi Arabia
Discuss how Islam influences the life and politics of people in Saudi Arabia.

Eyewitness Technology
Have students read about drilling for oil.

Instructional Resources

All in One Asia and the Pacific Teaching Resources
- L2 Guided Reading and Review, p. 383
- L2 Reading Readiness Guide, p. 382

Asia and the Pacific Transparencies
- L2 Section Reading Support Transparency AP 70
- L2 Transparency B6: Flow Chart

World Studies Video Program
- L2 The Call to Mecca

Differentiated Instruction

All in One Asia and the Pacific Teaching Resources
- L3 Enrichment, p. 394 AR, GT
- L3 Small Group Activity, pp. 396–399 AR, GT
- L2 Skills for Life, p. 395 AR, GT, LPR, SN

Asia and the Pacific Transparencies
- L1 Transparency B17: Concept Web ELL, LPR, SN

Teacher's Edition
- L3 For Gifted and Talented, TE p. 768
- L3 For Advanced Readers, TE p. 768
- L1 For Special Needs Students, TE p. 769
- L1 For Less Proficient Readers, TE p. 770

PHSchool.com
- L1 For: Environmental and Global Issues: The Imbalance of Energy Consumption
  Web Code: lcd-6811 ELL, LPR, SN

Assess and Reteach

Assess Progress
Evaluate student comprehension with the section assessment and section quiz.

Reteach
Assign the Reading and Vocabulary Study Guide to help struggling students.

Extend
Extend the lesson by assigning an Internet activity.

Instructional Resources

All in One Asia and the Pacific Teaching Resources
- L2 Section Quiz, p. 384
  Rubric for Assessing a Writing Assignment, p. 410

Reading and Vocabulary Study Guide
- L1 Chapter 25, Section 4, pp. 269–271

PHSchool.com
- L3 For: Environmental and Global Issues: World Oil Reserves
  Web Code: lcd-6807

Differentiated Instruction

Spanish Support
- L2 Section Quiz (Spanish), p. 259 ELL

Teacher's Edition
- L1 For Special Needs Students, TE p. 773

Social Studies Skills Tutor CD-ROM
- L1 Analyzing Graphic Data ELL, LPR, SN

Key
- L1 Basic to Average
- L3 Average to Advanced
- L2 For All Students
- LPR Less Proficient Readers
- AR Advanced Readers
- SN Special Needs Students
- GT Gifted and Talented
- ELL English Language Learners

Section 5 The Stans: A Diverse Region

 2 periods, 1 block (includes Chapter Review and Assessment)

Social Studies Objectives

1. Examine the factors that have caused war and conflicts in the Stans.
2. Learn about the economies of the Stans.
3. Discover how environmental issues affect life in the Stans.

Reading/Language Arts Objective

Use signal words to recognize cause-and-effect relationships.

Prepare to Read	**Instructional Resources**	**Differentiated Instruction**
Build Background Knowledge Discuss the suffix *-stan*. **Set a Purpose for Reading** Have students evaluate statements on the *Reading Readiness Guide*. **Preview Key Terms** Teach the section's Key Terms. **Target Reading Skill** Introduce the section's Target Reading Skill of **recognizing cause-and-effect signal words**.	**All in One Asia and the Pacific Teaching Resources** L2 Reading Readiness Guide, p. 386 L2 Recognize Cause-and-Effect Signal Words, p. 392	**Spanish Reading and Vocabulary Study Guide** L1 Chapter 25, Section 5, pp. 192–193 ELL

Instruct	**Instructional Resources**	**Differentiated Instruction**
Warfare and Unrest in Afghanistan Discuss political unrest in Afghanistan. **Target Reading Skill** Review **recognizing cause-and-effect signal words**. **Conflicts in Other Central Asian Countries** Discuss the conflicts in other Central Asian countries. **Country Profile** Ask students to derive information from maps, charts, and graphs. **Economic Conditions in Central Asia** Discuss why most Central Asian countries are poor. **Environmental Issues** Discuss environmental challenges in Central Asia.	**All in One Asia and the Pacific Teaching Resources** L2 Guided Reading and Review, p. 387 L2 Reading Readiness Guide, p. 386 **Asia and the Pacific Transparencies** L2 Section Reading Support Transparency AP 71 L2 Transparency B1: Flow Chart **World Studies Video Program** L2 The Disappearing Aral Sea	**Teacher's Edition** L3 For Gifted and Talented, TE p. 776 L1 For Less Proficient Readers, TE p. 777, 779 L1 For English Language Learners, TE p. 779 **PHSchool.com** L3 **For:** Environmental and Global Issues: Conflict and Quality of Life AR, GT Web Code: lcd-6809 **Student Edition on Audio CD** L1 Chapter 25, Section 5 ELL, LPR, SN **Spanish Support** L2 Guided Reading and Review (Spanish), p. 260 ELL

Assess and Reteach	**Instructional Resources**	**Differentiated Instruction**
Assess Progress Evaluate student comprehension with the section assessment and section quiz. **Reteach** Assign the Reading and Vocabulary Study Guide to help struggling students. **Extend** Extend the lesson by assigning an online activity.	**All in One Asia and the Pacific Teaching Resources** L2 Section Quiz, p. 388 Rubric for Assessing a Newspaper Article, p. 411 L2 Word Knowledge, p. 393 L2 Vocabulary Development, p. 407 Rubric for Assessing a Bar Graph, p. 408 L2 Chapter Tests A and B, pp. 412–417 **Reading and Vocabulary Study Guide** L1 Chapter 25, Section 5, pp. 272–274 **PHSchool.com** L3 **For:** Long-Term Integrated Projects: Reporting to an Environmental Conference Web Code: lcd-6808	**Spanish Support** L2 Section Quiz (Spanish), p. 261 ELL L2 Chapter Summary (Spanish), p. 262 ELL L2 Vocabulary Development (Spanish), p. 263 ELL

Key

L1 Basic to Average	L3 Average to Advanced	LPR Less Proficient Readers	GT Gifted and Talented
L2 For All Students		AR Advanced Readers	ELL English Language Learners
		SN Special Needs Students	

Reading Background

Paragraph Puzzles

Explain to students that creating paragraphs using puzzles can help them become more adept at writing paragraphs. Paragraph puzzles involve rearranging the sentences in a paragraph and having students put them back together in the correct order. This activity teaches students to distinguish a topic sentence that contains the main idea from the supporting details. Paragraph puzzles also work with any content that requires sequencing of steps and ideas.

Begin by writing the following paragraph from page 751 of the Student Edition on a piece of paper with each sentence on its own line.

India has a population of more than one billion people. This large population is growing. India has one of the world's highest population growth rates. By 2050, India is expected to be the world's most-populated country.

Cut the sentences into narrow strips, and place the strips in an envelope. Divide students into pairs and distribute one envelope to each pair. Ask students to arrange the sentences into a logical paragraph. Remind students to look for a main idea, supporting details, and transition words. The first time students do this, model the reasoning:

Think aloud: "The main idea seems to be that India has one of the highest population growth rates. The main idea usually comes at the end or the beginning of a paragraph. The other sentences are details. The word *This* in the second sentence signals that it follows the first paragraph, about India's population. The final sentence is the conclusion because it discusses what is expected to happen as a result of India's high population growth rate."

Processing Information: Discussion Ideas

As students read, ask them to write down an idea that would be a good topic for a discussion. Tell students that the ideas could relate to something that interests them, something that they don't understand, or something that relates to something that is in the text. Model the process by providing examples of both good and poor ideas for discussion. After reading, have students share their ideas with the class, using an Idea Wave (TE, p. T35).

World Studies Background

India, Pakistan, and Kashmir

Kashmir has been a source of conflict between India and Pakistan since 1947. During that year, British rule in South Asia came to an end, and the Indian subcontinent was divided into the countries of India and Pakistan. The allocation of the region of Kashmir was not finalized. India and Pakistan continue to struggle over claims to the area, which is administered by India in the south and southeast, by Pakistan in the north and west, and by China in the northeast.

Saudi Arabian Oil

Saudi Arabia has the world's largest oil reserve. Its oil can be found in the Arabian-Iranian basin region. Earth's largest oil field, discovered in Saudi Arabia in 1948, contains 82 billion barrels of oil. Saudi Arabia also controls the largest offshore oil field, which is located in the Persian Gulf.

Ethnic Groups of Central Asia

The people of Central Asia are divided into five main ethnic groups. The largest group is the Uzbeks. The other four groups, from largest to smallest, are the Kazaks, Tajiks, Turkmens, and Kyrgyz. Many other groups immigrated to the area after Russia's expansion into Central Asia. These groups included Jews, Germans, Koreans, Russians, and Ukrainians. However, many left the region after the collapse of the Soviet Union.

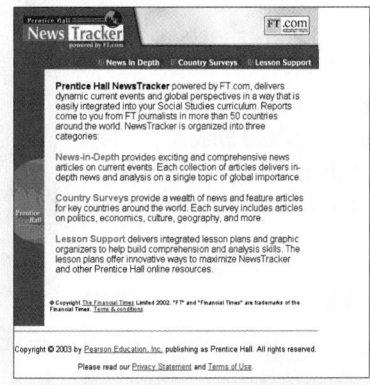

Get in-depth information on topics of global importance with **Prentice Hall Newstracker,** powered by FT.com.

Use Web code **lcd-6800** for **Prentice Hall Newstracker.**

Chapter 25 South, Southwest, and Central Asia

Guiding Questions

Remind students about the Guiding Questions at the beginning of the book.

Section 1 relates to **Guiding Question** ❺ **How do the people of this region make a living?** *(People in India work in computer programming, manufacturing, film, and agriculture.)*

Section 2 relates to **Guiding Question** ❺ **How do the people of this region make a living?** *(Many people in Pakistan work in agriculture. Others work in manufacturing.)*

Section 3 relates to **Guiding Question** ❺ **How do the people of this region make a living?** *(People in Israel work in agriculture and industries such as high technology, textiles, processed foods, fertilizer, and plastics.)*

Section 4 relates to **Guiding Question** ❹ **What types of government exist in Asia and the Pacific today?** *(Saudi Arabia is an absolute monarchy ruled under Islamic law.)*

Section 5 relates to **Guiding Question** ❺ **How do the people of this region make a living?** *(People in the poor countries of Central Asia work in agriculture and industries such as mining, oil, farm equipment, and textiles.)*

🎯 Target Reading Skill   L2

In this chapter, students will learn and apply the reading skill of identifying causes and effects. Use the following worksheets to help students practice this skill:

All in One Asia and the Pacific Teaching Resources, *Identify Causes and Effects,* p. 389; *Understand Effects;* p. 390; *Recognize Multiple Causes,* p. 391; *Recognize Cause-and-Effect Signal Words,* p. 392

Differentiated Instruction

The following Teacher Edition strategies are suitable for students of varying abilities.

Advanced Readers, pp. 739, 759, 768
English Language Learners, pp. 747, 763, 779
Gifted and Talented, pp. 742, 768, 776
Less Proficient Readers, pp. 743, 754, 770, 777, 779
Special Needs Students, pp. 746, 769, 773

Chapter Preview

This chapter focuses on four key countries in South Asia and Southwest Asia: India, Pakistan, Israel, and Saudi Arabia. The chapter also focuses on the countries of the Stans, in Central Asia.

Country Databank
The Country Databank provides data and descriptions of each of the countries of South Asia, Southwest Asia, and Central Asia.

Section 1
  India
  In the Midst of Change

Section 2
  Pakistan
  An Economy Based on Agriculture

Section 3
  Israel
  Economics and Cultures

Section 4
  Saudi Arabia
  Oil and Islam

Section 5
  The Stans
  A Diverse Region

🎯 Target Reading Skill

Cause and Effect In this chapter, you will practice understanding causes and effects.

▶ A man docking a small boat in Jordan

Bibliography

For the Teacher
al-Rasheed, Madawi. *A History of Saudi Arabia.* Cambridge University Press, 2002.

Everett-Health, Tom, ed. *Central Asia: Ethnicity, Modernity.* Curzon Press, 2003.

Wolpert, Stanley A. *A New History of India.* Oxford University Press, 1999.

For the Student
L2 Boraas, Tracey. *Israel (Countries and Cultures).* Bridgestone Books, 2002.

L3 Cartlidge, Cherese et al. *The Central Asian States (Former Soviet Republics).* Lucent Books, 2001.

L3 Goodwin, William. *India (Modern Nations of the World).* Lucent Books, 2000.

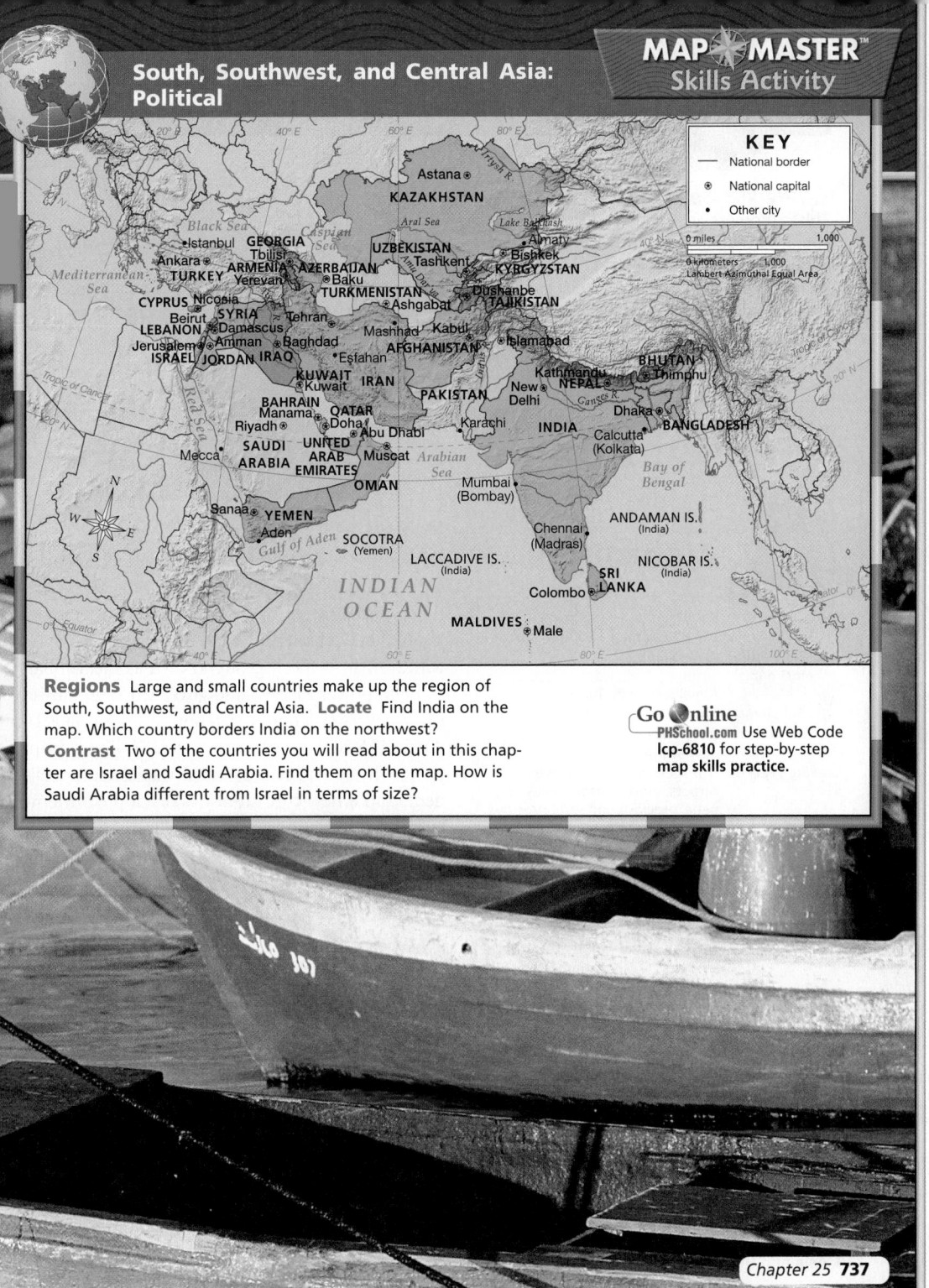

MAP MASTER™ Skills Activity

South, Southwest, and Central Asia: Political

KEY
— National border
⊛ National capital
• Other city

0 miles 1,000
0 kilometers 1,000
Lambert Azimuthal Equal Area

Regions Large and small countries make up the region of South, Southwest, and Central Asia. **Locate** Find India on the map. Which country borders India on the northwest? **Contrast** Two of the countries you will read about in this chapter are Israel and Saudi Arabia. Find them on the map. How is Saudi Arabia different from Israel in terms of size?

Go Online
PHSchool.com Use Web Code lcp-6810 for step-by-step map skills practice.

Chapter 25 **737**

MAP MASTER™ Skills Activity

Ask students to create a table listing each country on the map and its capital. Encourage students to list the countries in alphabetical order. Then have them categorize the countries in different ways, such as by size (large to small) or location (landlocked, coastal).

Go Online
PHSchool.com Students may practice their map skills using the interactive online version of this map.

Using the Visual   L2

Reach Into Your Background Draw students' attention to the caption accompanying the picture on pp. 736–737. Ask them to think about possible uses for small boats like the ones in the photograph. *(transporting goods or people, fishing)* Then have them study the image for clues as to what the man pictured might be using his boat for.

Answers

MAP MASTER™ Skills Activity **Locate** Pakistan
Contrast Saudi Arabia is much larger than Israel.

Chapter Resources

Teaching Resources
- L2 Vocabulary Development, p. 407
- L2 Skills for Life, p. 395
- L2 Chapter Tests A and B, pp. 412–417

Spanish Support
- L2 Spanish Chapter Summary, p. 262
- L2 Spanish Vocabulary Development, p. 263

Media and Technology
- L1 Student Edition on Audio CD
- L1 Guided Reading Audiotapes, English and Spanish
- L2 Social Studies Skills Tutor CD-ROM
- *ExamView Test Bank CD-ROM*

PRENTICE HALL
Presentation EXPRESS™
Teach · Connect · Inspire

Teach this chapter's content using the PresentationExpress™ CD-ROM including:
- slide shows
- transparencies
- interactive maps and media
- *ExamView®* QuickTake Presenter

Objectives

- Use a map and data to learn about the nations of South, Southwest, and Central Asia.

- Analyze data to compare the countries.

- Identify characteristics they share.

- Find some of the key differences among the countries.

Show *The Geography of South, Southwest, and Central Asia.* Ask **What are some of the geographic extremes of South, Southwest, and Central Asia?** *(There are extreme differences in elevation, climate, and vegetation.)*

Prepare to Read

Build Background Knowledge L2

Have students quickly preview the information in the tables of the Country Databank. Discuss with students how the physical characteristics of a country can affect its economy. For example, have them identify countries that have crude oil or petroleum-related products among their exports. Would students expect these countries to have large oil reserves? Use the Numbered Heads participation strategy (TE, p. T36) to encourage class discussion.

Introducing South, Southwest, and Central Asia

Guide for Reading

This section provides an introduction to the countries that make up the region of South, Southwest, and Central Asia.

- Look at the map on the previous page and then read the paragraphs below to learn about each nation.

- Analyze the data to compare the countries.

- What are the characteristics that most of the countries share?

- What are some key differences among the countries?

Viewing the Video Overview

View the World Studies Video Overview to learn more about each of the countries. As you watch, answer this question:

- South, Southwest, and Central Asia encompass many geographic extremes. What are some of them?

Explore the land of South, Southwest, and Central Asia.

Afghanistan

Capital	Kabul
Land Area	250,000 sq mi; 647,500 sq km
Population	27.8 million
Ethnic Group(s)	Pashtun, Tajik, Hazara, Uzbek, Aimaks, Baloch, Turkmen
Religion(s)	Muslim
Government	transitional
Currency	new afghani
Leading Exports	fruits and nuts, handwoven carpets, wool, cotton, hides and pelts, precious and semi-precious gems
Language(s)	Pashtu (official), Dari (official), Tajik, Farsi, Uzbek, Turkmen

A girl reading out loud in an Afghanistan classroom

Afghanistan (af GAN ih stan) is a landlocked country in Central Asia. Conflict and war have troubled this poor country. A ten-year war with the Soviet Union left Afghanistan in ruins when Soviet forces withdrew in 1989. A group known as the Taliban came to power in 1996 and governed Afghanistan under a very strict interpretation of Islamic law. In 2001, U.S.-led forces drove the Taliban from power. In 2004, Hamid Karzai was elected president, and a new constitution was adopted. Members of the National Assembly were elected in 2005. The new government is working to bring peace to the country.

738 Asia and the Pacific

Armenia

Capital	Yerevan
Land Area	10,965 sq mi; 29,400 sq km
Population	3.3 million
Ethnic Group(s)	Armenian, Azeri, Russian, Kurd
Religion(s)	Christian, traditional beliefs
Government	republic
Currency	dram
Leading Exports	diamonds, scrap metal, machinery and equipment, copper ore
Language(s)	Armenian (official), Russian

Located in Southwest Asia east of Turkey, Armenia (ahr MEE nee uh) is a small, landlocked country with an ancient history. Ancient Armenia was the first country in the world to officially adopt Christianity as its religion. The Ottoman Empire conquered Armenia in the 1500s. During World War I, Armenians suffered greatly under Ottoman rule. An estimated 600,000 to 1.5 million Armenians died in what historians called the first genocide in the 1900s. Between 1920 and 1991, Armenia was part of the Soviet Union. Armenia declared its independence from the Soviet Union in 1991.

Azerbaijan

Capital	Baku
Land Area	33,243 sq mi; 86,100 sq km
Population	7.8 million
Ethnic Group(s)	Azeri, Dagestani, Russian, Armenian
Religion(s)	Muslim, Christian
Government	republic
Currency	manat
Leading Exports	oil and gas, machinery, cotton, foodstuffs
Language(s)	Azerbaijani (official), Russian

Azerbaijan (ahz ur by JAHN) is a small country in Southwest Asia located on the west coast of the Caspian Sea. Once part of the Soviet Union, Azerbaijan was the first Soviet republic to declare its independence. Within Azerbaijan is a region called Nagorno-Karabakh (nah GAWR noh kahr ah BAHK). Armenians living in this region wish to become part of Armenia. Between 1988 and 1994, Azerbaijan and Armenia fought a war over which country would control Nagorno-Karabakh. The issue remains a concern today. Azerbaijan has plentiful petroleum and natural gas resources.

Bahrain

Capital	Manama
Land Area	257 sq mi; 665 sq km
Population	656,397
Ethnic Group(s)	Bahraini, Arab, Asian
Religion(s)	Muslim
Government	constitutional hereditary monarchy
Currency	Bahraini dinar
Leading Exports	petroleum and petroleum products, aluminum, textiles
Language(s)	Arabic (official)

Bahrain (bah RAYN) is a tiny island country located in the Persian Gulf east of Saudi Arabia. Bahrain has used its petroleum resources to develop its economy. Aware that it is running out of oil, Bahrain has turned to petroleum processing and refining and has established itself as an international banking center. Unemployment and shrinking oil reserves are major economic problems in Bahrain.

Chapter 25 **739**

Instruct

Introducing South, Southwest, and Central Asia L2

Guided Instruction

- Have students read each country paragraph and its accompanying data table using the Paragraph Shrinking strategy (TE, p. T34).

- Ask **Which country has the largest land area?** *(India, with 1,147,949 sq mi; 2,973,190 sq km)* **Which has the smallest land area?** *(Maldives, with 116 sq mi; 300 sq km)*

- Ask **What major religion do almost all of the countries share?** *(Islam)* **What other religious groups are there?** *(Christian, traditional beliefs, Hindu, Buddhist, Jewish)*

- Ask **What resource do Azerbaijan and Bahrain share?** *(oil)* **What problem does Bahrain face concerning its major resource, and what has happened as a result?** *(Bahrain's oil reserves are shrinking, and it is running out of oil; as a result, it has turned to petroleum processing and refining and international banking to help its economy.)*

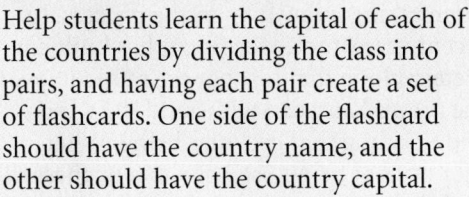

Differentiated Instruction

For Advanced Readers L3

Help students learn the capital of each of the countries by dividing the class into pairs, and having each pair create a set of flashcards. One side of the flashcard should have the country name, and the other should have the country capital.

Have students take turns quizzing each other. Once students have learned the country capitals, you may choose to have students repeat the exercise using different information, such as population or government.

Guided Instruction (continued)

- Ask **How does the location of Bangladesh affect the lives of its people?** (*Most of Bangladesh lies on a plain near the Bay of Bengal and is close to sea level. This feature, combined with heavy rainfall, makes Bangladesh prone to heavy flooding that can cause major damage and ruin the country's crops.*)

- Ask **Why does the government limit the number of people who visit Bhutan?** (*to protect its environment and preserve its mostly Buddhist culture*) **How do you think this policy might affect Bhutan's economy?** (*It might cause problems for Bhutan's economy, since tourism is an important economic activity.*)

- Ask **What is unique about the population of Cyprus?** (*Greek Cypriots live in the southern two-thirds of the island, and Turkish Cypriots live in the northern third.*) **What historical event lead to this situation?** (*In 1974, Turkey invaded Cyprus and won control over a northern region of the island.*)

Introducing South, Southwest, and Central Asia

Bangladesh

Capital	Dhaka
Land Area	51,705 sq mi; 133,910 sq km
Population	133.4 million
Ethnic Group(s)	Bengali
Religion(s)	Muslim, Hindu
Government	parliamentary democracy
Currency	taka
Leading Exports	clothing, jute and jute goods, leather, frozen fish and seafood
Language(s)	Bengali (official), Urdu, Chakma, Marma (Magh), Garo, Khasi, Santhali, Tripuri, Mro

Bangladesh (BAHNG luh desh) is located in South Asia. Most of Bangladesh lies on a plain formed by the soil deposited by three powerful rivers that empty into the Bay of Bengal. Most of the country is close to sea level and has a tropical wet climate with heavy rainfall. Low elevation and heavy rainfall contribute to floods that sometimes cause major damage. In 1998, the worst flooding in Bangladesh's history left nearly two thirds of the country underwater. Agriculture is an important part of Bangladesh's economy, and serious flooding can ruin the crops.

Bhutan

Capital	Thimphu
Land Area	18,147 sq mi; 47,000 sq km
Population	2.1 million
Ethnic Group(s)	Bhote, Nepalese, indigenous tribes
Religion(s)	Buddhist, Hindu
Government	monarchy
Currency	ngultrum
Leading Exports	electricity, cardamom, gypsum, timber, handicrafts, cement, fruit, precious stones, spices
Language(s)	Dzongkha (official), Nepali, Assamese

Bhutan (BOO tahn) is a small, landlocked country in South Asia located between India and China. Mountains cover most of Bhutan. These are the Himalayas, the highest mountains in the world. Bhutan's economy is based on agriculture and forestry. Although about 3 percent of Bhutan's land is suitable for growing crops, about 90 percent of the labor force works in farming. Most of the people live in small rural villages. Tourism is an important economic activity in Bhutan. To protect the environment and preserve Bhutan's mostly Buddhist culture, the government limits the number of people who visit Bhutan each year.

Cyprus

Capital	Nicosia
Land Area	3,568 sq mi; 9,240 sq km
Population	767,314
Ethnic Group(s)	Greek, Turkish
Religion(s)	Christian, Muslim
Government	republic
Currency	Cypriot pound and Turkish lira
Leading Exports	citrus, potatoes, grapes, cement, clothing and shoes, textiles
Language(s)	Greek (official), Turkish (official)

Cyprus (SY prus) is an island country located south of Turkey in the Mediterranean Sea. The majority of the people in Cyprus are Greek. About 12 percent of the population is Turkish. In 1974, Turkey invaded Cyprus and won control over a northern region of the island. Today, Greek Cypriots live in the southern two thirds of the island while the Turkish Cypriots occupy the northern third. In 1983, the Turkish region declared independence as a separate nation, which was recognized only by Turkey. The Greek Cypriot region has a prosperous economy.

740 Asia and the Pacific

Background: Daily Life

Cyclones Bangladesh, which lies close to sea level on the Bay of Bengal, often experiences devastating storms called cyclones. Cyclones, which form over warm areas in tropical oceans, bring damaging winds, heavy rains, and storm surges, or giant waves, that sweep over the land, destroying everything in their path. Because of the land's low elevation and the fact that many homes are poorly constructed, cyclones can cause widespread damage and destruction, often taking many lives in the process. In recent years, the government has built concrete cyclone shelters that are raised above the ground and can withstand the winds and flooding that cyclones bring. When they are not being used as shelters, these buildings often serve as schools.

Georgia

Capital	Tbilisi
Land Area	26,911 sq mi; 69,700 sq km
Population	5 million
Ethnic Group(s)	Georgian, Armenian, Russian, Azeri, Ossetian, Greek, Abkhaz
Religion(s)	Christian, Muslim
Government	republic
Currency	lari
Leading Exports	scrap metal, machinery, tea, chemicals, citrus fruits, other agricultural products
Language(s)	Georgian (official), Abkhazian (official), Russian

Georgia (JAWR juh) emerged as an independent nation in 1991 during the collapse of the Soviet Union. Georgia is located in Southwest Asia between Turkey and Russia. Mountains cover much of the country. Since independence, differences among Georgia's many ethnic groups have led to violence and civil war. Farming is a major economic activity. Georgia is rich in minerals, including copper. An oil pipeline extending from Azerbaijan across Georgia to Turkey is expected to strengthen the economy.

India

Capital	New Delhi
Land Area	1,147,949 sq mi; 2,973,190 sq km
Population	1.05 billion
Ethnic Group(s)	Indo-Aryan, Dravidian, Mongoloid
Religion(s)	Hindu, Muslim, Christian, Buddhist, traditional beliefs
Government	federal republic
Currency	Indian rupee
Leading Exports	textile goods, gems and jewelry, engineering goods, chemicals
Language(s)	Hindi (official), English (official), Urdu, Bengali, Marathi, Telugu, Tamil, Bihari, Gujarati, Kanarese

India (IN dee uh) is the largest country in South Asia and the second-most-populated country in the world. Only China has a larger population than India. India's history dates back to ancient times, with one of the world's earliest civilizations developing in the Indus Valley. A former British colony, India today consists of 28 states governed under a democratic system. A wide range of activities support India's economy. These include farming and modern industries such as textiles, steel, and computer software.

Iran

Capital	Tehran
Land Area	631,660 sq mi; 1,636,000 sq km
Population	66.6 million
Ethnic Group(s)	Persian, Azari, Gilaki and Mazandariani, Kurd, Arab, Lur, Baloch, Turkmen
Religion(s)	Muslim, Jewish, Christian
Government	theocratic republic
Currency	Iranian rial
Leading Exports	petroleum, carpets, fruits and nuts, iron and steel, chemicals
Language(s)	Farsi (official), Azerbaijani, Gilak, Mazanderani, Kurdish, Baluchi, Arabic, Turkmen

Known as Persia until 1935, Iran (ih RAN) became a republic governed under Islamic law in 1979. Islam is the official religion and nearly 100 percent of Iranians are Muslim. Iran's economy depends on the oil industry. Despite recent high oil prices, inflation and unemployment remain high. In 1980, Iraq invaded Iran, beginning an indecisive eight-year war fought over territory claimed by both countries. Iran's commitment to developing nuclear weapons and its support of terrorism have led to tense relations with many countries, including the United States.

Chapter 25 **741**

Guided Instruction (continued)

- Have students review the map on p. 737, and ask them to draw a conclusion about Georgia's geographic location and its different ethnic groups. *(Georgia is located near Russia, Armenia, Azerbaijan, and has easy access to Greece. A number of its ethnic groups come from these places.)*

- Ask students to identify India's official languages. *(Hindi, English)* Ask **Based on India's history, why do you think that English is one of its official languages?** *(India was a British colony, and English became a common language for a linguistically diverse nation.)*

- Have students compare the governments of India and Iran. *(India is a federal republic, made up of 28 states that are governed under a democratic system, while Iran is a theocratic republic governed under Islamic law.)*

Guided Instruction (continued)

- Ask students **What is Iraq's leading export?** *(crude oil)* **What challenges might a country face with an economy based on only one product?** *(Possible answer: The economy might suffer if the product suddenly runs out or is no longer available, or if the price for the product drops drastically.)*

- Discuss with students the similarities and differences between the population and land area of Israel and Jordan. *(Israel and Jordan have about the same populations, but Jordan has a much larger land area.)*

Introducing South, Southwest, and Central Asia

Iraq

Capital	Baghdad
Land Area	166,858 sq mi; 432,162 sq km
Population	24.7 million
Ethnic Group(s)	Arab, Kurd, Turkoman, Assyrian
Religion(s)	Muslim, Christian
Government	republic
Currency	Iraqi dinar
Leading Exports	crude oil
Language(s)	Arabic (official), Kurdish, Turkic languages, Armenian, Assyrian

Iraq (ih RAHK) became the focus of world attention when it invaded neighboring Kuwait in 1990. The United States led a group of 32 countries in the Persian Gulf War, defeating Iraq. After the war, the United Nations required Iraq to give up its chemical and nuclear weapons programs. Iraq's refusal to do so led to a second U.S.-led invasion in 2003. Dictator Saddam Hussein and his government were quickly removed, and a new government was elected in 2005. Violence remains a problem.

Israel

Capital	Jerusalem
Land Area	7,849 sq mi; 20,330 sq km
Population	6 million
Ethnic Group(s)	Jewish, Arab
Religion(s)	Jewish, Muslim, Christian
Government	parliamentary democracy
Currency	shekel
Leading Exports	machinery and equipment, cut diamonds, software, agricultural products, chemicals, textiles and clothing
Language(s)	Hebrew (official), Arabic (official), Yiddish, German, Russian, Polish, Romanian, Persian

Israel (IZ ree ul) lies between Egypt and Lebanon and borders the Mediterranean Sea. After World War II, the United Nations allowed Israel to form as a Jewish state, but Arab nations in Southwest Asia opposed its formation. They fought a series of wars in which the Israelis were victorious and gained new territories. However, violence beween Israel and Palestinian residents of these areas continued. Peace talks over the last several decades have been hampered by Palestinian terrorist attacks, aggressive Israeli military counter-terrorism operations, and mistrust on both sides. In 2005, Israel began pulling out of the Gaza Strip and parts of the West Bank.

Jordan

Capital	Amman
Land Area	35,510 sq mi; 91,971 sq km
Population	5.3 million
Ethnic Group(s)	Arab, Circassian, Armenian
Religion(s)	Muslim, Christian
Government	constitutional monarchy
Currency	Jordanian dinar
Leading Exports	phosphate, fertilizers, potash, agricultural products, manufactured goods, pharmaceuticals
Language(s)	Arabic (official)

Jordan (JAWRD un) is a Southwest Asian country located northwest of Saudi Arabia. After gaining its independence from the British in 1946, the country was ruled for more than forty years by King Hussein. King Hussein established parliamentary elections and a peace treaty with Israel. After King Hussein's death in 1999, his son, Abdullah, took the throne and worked to bring economic reforms. Recent trade agreements with other countries and increased foreign investment have improved Jordan's economy. The economy is based on tourism, shipping, and the export of phosphate.

742 Asia and the Pacific

Differentiated Instruction

For Gifted and Talented L3

Using information in the Country Databank, have students make a resource map of South, Southwest, and Central Asia. Break students into two groups and give one group *Outline Map 28: Central and Southwest Asia: Political* and the other group *Outline Map 26: South Asia: Political.* Then ask them to fill in the industries shown in the Country Databank, using a small symbol to represent each industry. The map should include a key, giving the meaning of each symbol.

All in One **Asia and the Pacific Teaching Resources,** *Outline Map 26: South Asia: Political,* p. 401; *Outline Map 28: Central and Southwest Asia: Political,* p. 402

Kazakhstan

Capital	Astana
Land Area	1,030,810 sq mi; 2,669,800 sq km
Population	16.7 million
Ethnic Group(s)	Kazakh, Russian, Ukrainian, Uzbek, Uighur
Religion(s)	Muslim, Christian
Government	republic
Currency	tenge
Leading Exports	oil and oil products, ferrous metals, machinery, chemicals, grain, wool, meat, coal
Language(s)	Kazakh (official), Russian, Uighur, Korean, German

Kazakhstan (kah zahk STAHN) is a former Soviet republic, located northwest of China, that struggles to find its national identity. The native people of the area are descendants of Turkic and Mongol tribes who for years did not think of themselves as a nation. Russia conquered these peoples in the 1700s. During the mid-1900s, many Soviet citizens came to cultivate the country's northern pastures as part of a governmental agricultural project. After the country gained independence in 1991, some of these native Russians left. Today, the country is moving quickly to establish a market economy as well as a national identity.

Kuwait

Capital	Kuwait City
Land Area	6,880 sq mi; 17,820 sq km
Population	2.1 million
Ethnic Group(s)	Arab, South Asian
Religion(s)	Muslim, Christian, Hindu, traditional beliefs
Government	nominal constitutional monarchy
Currency	Kuwaiti dinar
Leading Exports	oil and refined products, fertilizers
Language(s)	Arabic (official), English

Kuwait (koo WAYT) is a small country on the Persian Gulf. Its neighbors are Iran, Iraq, and Saudi Arabia. Mainly desert, the country has large oil and gas reserves. Ninety-five percent of its export earnings are from oil. In 1990, Kuwait was invaded by neighboring Iraq. The United States and other countries came to Kuwait's defense in a conflict known as the Persian Gulf War. After the war ended in 1991, Kuwait spent billions on repairs to its oil infrastructure and built a wall on its Iraqi border.

Kuwaitis celebrating the end of the Persian Gulf War

Chapter 25 **743**

Guided Instruction (continued)

- Point out to students the different ethnic groups of Kazakhstan. Ask **Based on Kazakhstan's history, why do you think the country continues to struggle for a national identity?** *(Possible answer: The native people of Kazakhstan never thought of themselves as a nation. In the 1700s, Russia conquered them, and many Soviet citizens came to the country in the mid-1900s. All of these different ethnic groups living in one area, combined with Soviet rule of the country until 1991, might make it difficult for Kazakhstan to establish its own national identity.)*

- Ask students **What happened in Kuwait in 1991?** *(It was invaded by Iraq, and the United States and other countries came to the country's defense in the Persian Gulf War.)* **What steps did Kuwait take after the war ended?** *(It made billions of dollars worth of repairs to its oil infrastructure and built a wall on its Iraqi border.)*

- Have students identify the similarities between Kazakhstan and Kyrgyzstan. *(Both were under Soviet rule until gaining independence; have Russian, Ukrainian, and white ethnic groups; have Muslims and Christians; have leading exports of wool and meat; have people who speak Russian; are republics; and are working to improve their economy.)*

Differentiated Instruction

For Less Proficient Readers L1

Working in pairs, have students create a Venn diagram showing the similarities and differences between Kazakhstan and Kyrgyzstan. Display the *Venn Diagram* transparency to show students how to sketch the organizer. Circulate to make sure students are filling in the organizers correctly.

📖 **Asia and the Pacific Transparencies,** *Transparency B16: Venn Diagram*

Guided Instruction (continued)

- Ask students **What are the two main religions in Lebanon?** *(Islam, Christianity)* **What portion of the population is part of these groups?** *(Muslims are the majority of the population, and Christians make up a large minority of the population.)*

- Have students identify the leading exports of the Maldives. *(fish, clothing)* Ask **Why do you think fish is a leading export?** *(The Maldives are islands and have easy access to fishing in the surrounding Indian Ocean.)*

Introducing South, Southwest, and Central Asia

Kyrgyzstan

Capital	Bishkek
Land Area	73,861 sq mi; 191,300 sq km
Population	4.8 million
Ethnic Group(s)	Kyrgyz, Russian, Uzbek, Tatar, Ukrainian
Religion(s)	Muslim, Christian
Government	republic
Currency	som
Leading Exports	cotton, wool, meat, tobacco, gold, mercury, uranium, hydropower, machinery, shoes
Language(s)	Kyrgyz (official), Russian (official)

Kyrgyzstan (kihr gih STAN) is a mountainous Central Asian country located west of China. In the late 1800s, Kyrgyzstan was annexed by Russia. It gained its independence from the Soviet Union more than one hundred years later. Currently, Kyrgyzstan's rural population is growing faster than its urban population. The country is agriculturally self-sufficient, which gives it an economic advantage. Kyrgyzstan is focused on many of the same issues that face other nations in the region. These include improving its economy and making democratic reforms.

Lebanon

Capital	Beirut
Land Area	3,950 sq mi; 10,230 sq km
Population	3.7 million
Ethnic Group(s)	Arab, Armenian
Religion(s)	Muslim, Christian
Government	republic
Currency	Lebanese pound
Leading Exports	foodstuffs, textiles, chemicals, metal products, electrical products, jewelry, paper products
Language(s)	Arabic (official), French, Armenian, Assyrian

Lebanon (LEB uh nahn) is a Southwest Asian nation on the Mediterranean Sea, bordered by Israel and Syria. Although it only became a nation in modern times, it has some of the world's most ancient human settlements. The country has a Muslim majority and a large minority of Christians. Lebanon has suffered from a 16-year civil war, an invasion by Israel in 1981, and fighting between Hezbollah terrorists based in southern Lebanon and Israel in 2006. It faces many challenges as it tries to rebuild. Lebanon has one of the highest literacy rates in the region and is a vibrant economic and cultural center.

Maldives

Capital	Malé
Land Area	116 sq mi; 300 sq km
Population	320,165
Ethnic Group(s)	South Indian, Sinhalese, Arab
Religion(s)	Muslim
Government	republic
Currency	rufiyaa
Leading Exports	fish, clothing
Language(s)	Dhivehi (Maldivian)

Maldives (MAL dyvz) is a group of about 1,300 islands in the Indian Ocean southwest of India. Today, only about 200 of these small coral islands are inhabited. Located at the center of Arab trade routes, the islands were a stopping place for Arab traders who brought Islam with them. For much of their history, the Maldives were ruled by Muslim sultans, but the islands became a British protectorate in 1887. The country gained independence from the British in 1965. A major economic goal for the Maldives is the growth of a tourist trade.

Nepal

Capital	Kathmandu
Land Area	52,818 sq mi; 136,800 sq km
Population	25.9 million
Ethnic Group(s)	Brahman, Chetri, Newar, Gurung, Magar, Tamang, Rai, Limpu, Sherpa, Tharu
Religion(s)	Hindu, Buddhist, Muslim
Government	parliamentary democracy and constitutional monarchy
Currency	Nepalese rupee
Leading Exports	carpets, clothing, leather goods, jute goods, grain
Language(s)	Nepali (official), Maithilli, Bhojpuri

Nepal (nuh PAWL) is a country with a recent history of troubled leadership. Though a kingdom traditionally ruled by a series of royal families, in 1990 Nepal formed a multiparty government with a modern constitution. This began a period of political turmoil, including the killing of most of the royal family, a dissolved parliament, and the postponement of elections. The current king is working to resolve differences and hold elections once again. One of the poorest nations in the world, Nepal's economy depends on agriculture and the tourists who come to see the Himalayas that dominate the country's physical geography.

Oman

Capital	Muscat
Land Area	82,030 sq mi; 212,460 sq km
Population	2.7 million
Ethnic Group(s)	Arab, Baluchi, South Asian, African
Religion(s)	Muslim, Hindu
Government	monarchy
Currency	Omani rial
Leading Exports	petroleum, reexports, fish, metals, textiles
Language(s)	Arabic (official), Baluchi

Oman (oh MAHN) shares a western border with Yemen, the United Arab Emirates, and Saudi Arabia. To the east, it is bordered by the Arabian Sea, the Gulf of Oman, and the Persian Gulf. The nation is ruled by a monarch. Although the country is the least developed of the Persian Gulf nations, the current sultan's efforts to modernize have increased Oman's standing in the international community. Oil exports have brought some prosperity to Oman. The country also has a large fishing industry.

Pakistan

Capital	Islamabad
Land Area	300,664 sq mi; 778,720 sq km
Population	147.7 million
Ethnic Group(s)	Punjabi, Sindhi, Pashtun (Pathan), Baloch, Muhajir
Religion(s)	Muslim, Christian, Hindu
Government	federal republic
Currency	Pakistani rupee
Leading Exports	textiles (clothing, cotton cloth, and yarn), rice, other agricultural products
Language(s)	Urdu (official), Punjabi, Sindhi, Pashtu, Baluchi, Brahui

Pakistan (PAK ih stan) is a nation with a history of conflict among its many religious and ethnic groups. Pakistan is located on the shores of the Arabian Sea with India to the east, Iran and Afghanistan to the west, and China to the north. Pakistan was created in 1947, when tensions between Muslims and Hindus caused the British to divide British India into Muslim Pakistan and mostly-Hindu India. In 1971, East Pakistan became the separate country of Bangladesh. Tensions with India have continued since Pakistan was created. At the end of the 1900s, Pakistan began testing nuclear weapons.

Chapter 25 **745**

Guided Instruction (continued)

- Ask students **What physical feature dominates Nepal's geography?** (*the Himalayas*) **What role does this physical feature play in the country's economy?** (*Tourism to the Himalayas brings money into the economy.*) **What other country in this region depends on the Himalayas in the same way?** (*Bhutan*)

- Have students identify the bodies of water that border Oman. (*the Arabian Sea, the Gulf of Oman, and the Persian Gulf*) Ask **How do you think these bodies of water influence the country's economy?** (*They can be used for fishing and to ship oil to other countries.*)

- Have students describe the creation of Pakistan. (*In 1947, after tensions arose between Muslims and Hindus, the British divided British India into Muslim Pakistan and mostly-Hindu India.*) Ask **Did the creation of Pakistan help relieve tensions between Muslims and Hindus?** (*No, not entirely, because tensions continue today between Pakistan and India.*)

Background: Daily Life

Sherpas Originally from Tibet, Sherpas migrated into the Himalayan region over 500 years ago. Over time, the Sherpas' bodies have adapted to life in the thin air and cold climate of the Himalayas. The ability to survive in this extreme climate is one of the reasons that some Sherpas have become world-famous mountain-climbers. For over 50 years, people seeking to climb to the top of Mount Everest and other high mountains in the Himalayas have relied on the mountain-climbing expertise of Sherpa guides. Today, about 70,000 Sherpas live in northeast Nepal.

Guided Instruction (continued)

- Have students identify the similarities and differences between Qatar and Saudi Arabia. (*Similarities: ethnic groups, religion, government, some exports, language; Differences: capital, land area, population, currency, some exports*)

- Ask students **Why is Qatar one of the wealthiest nations in Southwest Asia?** (*It has plentiful oil and natural gas resources.*) **How does the country's wealth benefit its citizens?** (*They receive free health care and education.*)

- Ask students **What effect did Iraq's invasion of Kuwait have on Saudi Arabia?** (*Saudi Arabia received 400,000 Kuwaiti refugees and served as a launching point for the United States military effort to free Kuwait from Iraqi occupation.*)

Introducing South, Southwest, and Central Asia

Qatar

Capital	Doha
Land Area	4,416 sq mi; 11,437 sq km
Population	793,341
Ethnic Group(s)	Arab, South Asian
Religion(s)	Muslim
Government	traditional monarchy
Currency	Qatari riyal
Leading Exports	petroleum products, fertilizers, steel
Language(s)	Arabic (official)

Qatar (kah TAHR) is an oil-rich monarchy on the northeastern tip of the Arabian Peninsula. The country is a small peninsula in the Persian Gulf. A single family has ruled Qatar since the mid-1800s. With plentiful oil and natural gas resources, Qatar is one of the wealthiest nations in Southwest Asia and provides free health care and education to its citizens. It has a large immigrant population, made up of people from northern Africa, the Indian subcontinent, and Iran, who come to Qatar to work in the oil industry.

Saudi Arabia

Capital	Riyadh and Jiddah
Land Area	756,981 sq mi; 1,960,582 sq km
Population	23.5 million
Ethnic Group(s)	Arab, mixed black and Asian
Religion(s)	Muslim
Government	monarchy
Currency	Saudi riyal
Leading Exports	petroleum and petroleum products
Language(s)	Arabic (official)

Saudi Arabia (SAW dee uh RAY bee uh) is an oil-rich nation bordering the Red Sea and the Persian Gulf north of Yemen. Medina and Mecca, two of Islam's holiest cities, are located in Saudi Arabia. This large country is more than 95 percent desert, but oil discovered there in the 1930s quickly brought it into a position of economic power. In 1990, Saudi Arabia received 400,000 Kuwaiti refugees following Iraq's invasion of Kuwait. It played a key role as a launching point for the United States-led military effort to free Kuwait from Iraqi occupation. Today, the royal family of Saudi Arabia faces the issues of a growing population and a petroleum-dominated economy.

Sri Lanka

Capital	Colombo
Land Area	24,996 sq mi; 64,740 sq km
Population	19.6 million
Ethnic Group(s)	Sinhalese, Tamil, Moor, Burgher, Malay, Vedda
Religion(s)	Buddhist, Hindu, Christian, Muslim
Government	republic
Currency	Sri Lankan rupee
Leading Exports	textiles and clothing, tea, diamonds, coconut products, petroleum products
Language(s)	Sinhala (official), Tamil (official), English (official), Sinhalese-Tamil

Sri Lanka (sree LAHNG kuh) is made up of a large island and several small coral islands in the Indian Ocean off the coast of India. This small nation was controlled by other countries until 1948, when it finally gained its independence. Independence did not, however, bring stability to the country. Civil war between the majority Sinhalese group, made up of Buddhists, and the minority Tamil group, made up mainly of Hindus and Muslims, has raged for more than 20 years. A land of great physical and cultural diversity, Sri Lanka is the world's largest exporter of tea.

746 Asia and the Pacific

Differentiated Instruction

For Special Needs Students `L1`

Help students understand the location of the countries in the Country Databank by continuously referring to the map on p. 737. As you read the name of each country, have students turn to the map and place their finger on the country and locate its capital.

A lace shop at an outdoor market in Syria

■ Have students describe the physical geography and location of Sri Lanka. (*It is made up of a large island and several small coral islands, and is located in the Indian Ocean off the coast of India.*) Ask **What other country in this region shares a similar physical geography and location?** (*Maldives, which is made up of 1,300 small coral islands in the Indian Ocean, southwest of India*)

■ Ask students **How does Syria's use of its income from oil supplies differ from the way in which Qatar uses its income from oil?** (*Syria uses much of its oil income for its military, while Qatar uses its income to provide free health care and education to its citizens.*)

■ Ask students **What happened to Tajikistan after gaining independence from the Soviet Union?** (*The nation went through a five-year civil war and three changes in government.*) **What challenges does Tajikistan continue to face?** (*an unstable economy, poor health care, continuing conflict between ethnic groups*)

Syria

Capital	Damascus
Land Area	71,062 sq mi; 184,050 sq km
Population	17.2 million
Ethnic Group(s)	Arab, Kurd, Armenian
Religion(s)	Muslim, Christian
Government	republic under military regime
Currency	Syrian pound
Leading Exports	crude oil, textiles, fruits and vegetables, raw cotton
Language(s)	Arabic (official), French, Kurdish, Armenian, Circassian, Turkic languages, Assyrian, Aramaic

Syria (SIHR ee uh) is a Southwest Asian country on the shores of the Mediterranean Sea, between Lebanon and Turkey. After World War I, the French controlled Syria until its independence in 1946. Since that time, Syria has been governed by a series of military leaders. The country opposes its neighbor, Israel, to whom it lost an area known as the Golan Heights in 1967 during the Arab-Israeli War. Though Syria has large oil supplies, much of its income from oil is spent on military defense.

Tajikistan

Capital	Dushanbe
Land Area	55,096 sq mi; 142,700 sq km
Population	6.7 million
Ethnic Group(s)	Tajik, Uzbek, Russian
Religion(s)	Muslim
Government	republic
Currency	somoni
Leading Exports	aluminum, electricity, cotton, fruits, vegetable oil, textiles
Language(s)	Tajiki (official), Russian

Tajikistan (tah jik ih STAN) is a struggling former Soviet republic located in Central Asia. After gaining independence from the Soviet Union in 1991, the nation went through a five-year civil war and three changes in government. The country has 14 percent of the world's uranium reserves, but has not successfully developed this resource. Tajikistan faces many challenges, including an unstable economy, poor health care, and continuing conflict among ethnic groups.

Chapter 25 **747**

Differentiated Instruction

For English Language Learners L2
Encourage students to read through the Country Databank and make a list of any unfamiliar words. Have them look up the words in a dictionary, and then note the spelling, definition, and part of speech of each word. Then have them choose five of the words on their lists and write a sentence for each of the words.

Guided Instruction (continued)

- Ask students **What is unique about the United Arab Emirates?** *(It was created when seven Southwest Asian states united as a single nation.)* **How do you think forming one nation could benefit these small states that are located in an area that is mostly desert?** *(Possible answer: They can work together on irrigation systems to benefit all areas, and can also benefit from the oil and natural gas resources in each state.)*

- Have students compare the resources of the former Soviet republics of Turkmenistan and Uzbekistan. *(Turkmenistan has almost no land suitable for agriculture, but has abundant natural gas reserves, Uzbekistan's economy depends on agriculture, and it is the fourth largest exporter of cotton, but it also has extensive mineral and oil resources; both countries are working to improve and develop their ability to take advantage of their resources.)*

Independent Practice

- Have students complete *Using the Map Key,* and then divide the class into pairs or groups. Give half of the groups *Outline Map 26: South Asia: Political* and the other half *Outline Map 28: Central and Southwest Asia: Political.* Then ask them to use the Country Databank to help them create a map that shows the official language for each country in their region. Tell students to use different colors for each official language, and shade the countries with the color that corresponds to the official language. If a country has more than one official language, have them alternate bands of two or three colors to show that information. They should explain what each color represents in their map keys.

  All in One **Asia and the Pacific Teaching Resources,** *Using the Map Key,* p. 400; *Outline Map 26: South Asia: Political,* p. 401; *Outline Map 28: Central and Southwest Asia: Political,* p. 402

Monitor Progress

Circulate to make sure students are filling in their maps correctly. Provide assistance as needed.

Introducing South, Southwest, and Central Asia

Turkey

Capital	Ankara
Land Area	297,590 sq mi; 770,760 sq km
Population	67.3 million
Ethnic Group(s)	Turkish, Kurd
Religion(s)	Muslim
Government	republican parliamentary democracy
Currency	Turkish lira
Leading Exports	clothing, foodstuffs, textiles, metal manufactured goods, trasport equipment
Language(s)	Turkish (official), Kurdish, Arabic, Circassian, Armenian, Greek, Georgian, Ladino

Turkey (TUR kee) is a primarily Muslim country that straddles two continents—Asia and Europe. Its location on the Black Sea and Mediterranean Sea has always made it a crossroads of trade and culture. Turkey has a strong economy and has great influence in the region. However, a major fault line leaves many Turkish cities vulnerable to earthquakes. The country's two main ethnic groups, Turks and Kurds, are in conflict. Many Kurds seek to form their own state.

Turkmenistan

Capital	Ashgabat
Land Area	188,455 sq mi; 488,100 sq km
Population	4.7 million
Ethnic Group(s)	Turkmen, Uzbek, Russian, Kazakh
Religion(s)	Muslim, Christian
Government	republic
Currency	manat
Leading Exports	gas, oil, cotton fiber, textiles
Language(s)	Turkmen (official), Uzbek, Russian

Turkmenistan (turk MEN ih stan) is a former Soviet republic which borders the Caspian Sea between Kazakhstan and Iran. Turkmenistan is mostly desert. Only 2 percent of the total land area is suitable for agriculture. The country gained its independence in 1991 and formed a democracy, but the president exercises complete control over the government. Culturally, Turkmenistan is dominated by Sunni Muslims. It has abundant natural gas reserves and is currently working to improve its ability to extract and transport this valuable resource.

United Arab Emirates

Capital	Abu Dhabi
Land Area	32,000 sq mi; 82,880 sq km
Population	2.4 million
Ethnic Group(s)	Arab, South Asian
Religion(s)	Muslim
Government	federation
Currency	UAE dirham
Leading Exports	crude oil, natural gas, reexports, dried fish, dates
Language(s)	Arabic (official), Farsi, Indian and Pakistani languages, English

The United Arab Emirates (yoo NYT id AR ub EM ur uts) was created when seven Southwest Asian states united as a single nation. The United Arab Emirates (UAE) is bordered by the Gulf of Oman and the Persian Gulf between Saudi Arabia and Oman. The UAE is mostly desert. With few water resources, the country relies on an extensive irrigation system. The UAE is rich in oil and natural gas resources. It has a strong economy and good health care and education. It has taken on an important role in the affairs of the region.

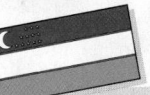

Uzbekistan

Capital	Tashkent
Land Area	164,247 sq mi; 425,400 sq km
Population	25.5 million
Ethnic Group(s)	Uzbek, Russian, Tajik, Kazakh, Karakalpak, Tatar
Religion(s)	Muslim, Christian
Government	republic
Currency	som
Leading Exports	cotton, gold, energy products, mineral fertilizers, ferrous metals, textiles, food products, automobiles
Language(s)	Arabic (official)

Uzbekistan (ooz bek ih STAN) is a former Soviet republic in Central Asia north of Afghanistan. Conquered by Russia in the late 1800s, it came under Communist control in 1924. Heavy growing of cotton and grain by the Soviet Union depleted its water supplies and polluted the land in many areas. Since it gained its independence in 1991, Uzbekistan has looked to develop its extensive mineral and oil resources. However, the country's economy still depends on agriculture. Uzbekistan is one of the largest exporters of cotton in the world.

Yemen

Capital	Sana
Land Area	203,849 sq mi; 527,970 sq km
Population	18.7 million
Ethnic Group(s)	Arab, mixed black and Arab, South Asian
Religion(s)	Muslim
Government	republic
Currency	Yemeni rial
Leading Exports	crude oil, coffee, dried and salted fish
Language(s)	Arabic

Yemen (YEM un) is located at the southern tip of the Arabian Peninsula. Bordered by Saudi Arabia and Oman, it occupies a fertile strip along the Red Sea. Yemen's recent history is one of conflict, including years of civil war that led to the country being divided in half. In 1990, the country was reunited, but still remains politically unstable. Yemen has large oil, gas, and mineral reserves. Agriculture continues to support most of the population.

SOURCES: DK World Desk Reference Online; CIA World Factbook Online; *World Almanac*, 2003

Assessment

Comprehension and Critical Thinking

1. Identify What is the most common ethnic group in the region?

2. Apply Information What is the language in countries that include this ethnic group?

3. Draw Conclusions What are the characteristics that most of the countries share?

4. Contrast What are some key differences among the countries?

5. Summarize In which region is petroleum a leading export, South Asia or Southwest Asia?

6. Make a Bar Graph Create a bar graph showing the population of the four most populous countries in this region.

Keeping Current

Access the **DK World Desk Reference Online** at **PHSchool.com** for up-to-date information about the countries in this chapter.

Go Online
PHSchool.com

Web Code: Ice-6800

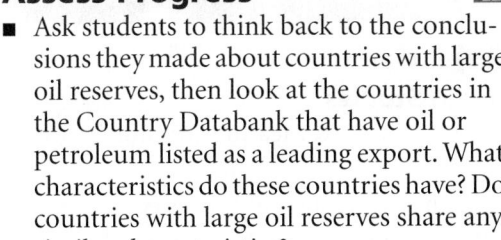

Assess Progress   L2

■ Ask students to think back to the conclusions they made about countries with large oil reserves, then look at the countries in the Country Databank that have oil or petroleum listed as a leading export. What characteristics do these countries have? Do countries with large oil reserves share any similar characteristics?

■ Ask students to answer the Assessment questions.

Reteach   L1

Help reinforce the location of each country in the Databank for students by distributing *Outline Map 26: South Asia: Political* and *Outline Map 28: Central and Southwest Asia: Political*. As you read about each country with students, have them look on p. 737 for the location of the country, and fill it in on the appropriate outline map.

📖 **Asia and the Pacific Teaching Resources,** *Outline Map 26: South Asia: Political*, p. 401; *Outline Map 28: Central and Southwest Asia Political*, p. 402

Extend   L3

Portfolio Activity

Have students choose one country in the Country Databank. Ask them to research the country, using the DK World Desk Reference Online as a starting point. Then, have them create a paragraph, short story, chart, graph, map, or illustration about the country to add to their portfolios.

Answers

Assessment

1. Arab
2. Arabic
3. religions, such as Muslim, Hindu, Buddhist and Christian, and some leading exports such as petroleum products

4. Key differences include land area, size of population, ethnic groups, types of government, currency used, leading exports, and languages spoken.
5. Southwest Asia
6. Students' bar graphs should reflect the country populations for India, Pakistan, Bangladesh, and Iran accurately. Use *Rubric for Assessing a Bar Graph* to evaluate students' work.

Asia and the Pacific Teaching Resources, *Rubric for Assessing a Bar Graph*, p. 408

Section 1
Step-by-Step Instruction

Objectives

Social Studies
1. Learn about key features of India's population.
2. Examine the state of India's economy.
3. Understand major challenges facing India.

Reading/Language Arts
Determine causes and effects to understand how events and situations are related.

Prepare to Read

Build Background Knowledge L2
Ask students to think about what they have heard and seen about India. Conduct an Idea Wave (TE, p. T35) to generate a list of impressions and list some on the board. Then have students take the *India: Photo Tour* on the Passport to the World CD-ROM. Ask students if the tour confirmed or disproved their impressions.

⊙ *India: Photo Tour,* **Passport to the World CD-ROM**

Set a Purpose for Reading L2
■ Preview the Objectives.

■ Read each statement in the *Reading Readiness Guide* aloud. Ask students to mark the statements true or false.

All in One Asia and the Pacific Teaching Resources, *Reading Readiness Guide,* p. 370

■ Have students discuss the statements in pairs or groups of four, then mark their worksheets again. Use the Numbered Heads participation strategy (TE, p. T36) to call on students to share their group's perspectives.

Vocabulary Builder
Preview Key Terms L2
Pronounce each Key Term, then ask students to say the word with you. Provide a simple explanation such as, "In parts of the world where people do not have enough to eat, malnutrition is a major problem."

Section 1
India
In the Midst of Change

Prepare to Read

Objectives
In this section you will
1. Learn about key features of India's population.
2. Examine the state of India's economy.
3. Understand major challenges facing India.

Taking Notes
As you read this section, look for ways in which India's growing population has an effect on its development. Copy the chart below, and record your findings in it.

CAUSE		EFFECTS
• India's population is growing.	⇨	•

🎯 Target Reading Skill

Identify Causes and Effects Identifying causes and effects helps you understand how events and situations are related. A cause makes something happen. An effect is what happens as a result. As you read this section, think of India's growing population as a cause. What are the effects of this cause on India's development?

Key Terms
• **textiles** (TEKS tylz) *n.* cloth made by weaving or by knitting
• **malnutrition** (mal noo TRISH un) *n.* poor nutrition caused by a lack of food or an unbalanced diet
• **life expectancy** (lyf ek SPEK tun see) *n.* the average number of years a person is expected to live
• **literacy rate** (LIT ur uh see rayt) *n.* the percentage of a population age 15 and over that can read and write

Students at a private school for boys in Rajasthan, India

In Chapter 24, you read that the gross domestic product (GDP) is the total value of all the goods and services produced in an economy. India's gross domestic product is $3.6 trillion. This makes India's GDP the fourth highest in the world. Yet the standard of living in India is very low compared with many other countries, even though India's GDP is higher. This is because India's $3.6 trillion is shared by more than one billion people. If you divided that $3.6 trillion by India's population, each person would have about $3,300. By comparison, Germany's GDP is about $2.5 trillion. But Germany has a much lower population than India has. If you divided Germany's $2.5 trillion by its population, each person would have about $30,400.

India's large population presents many challenges to the country. At the same time, India's people are an important resource in the drive to develop the country.

🎯 Target Reading Skill L2

Identify Causes and Effects Point out the Target Reading Skill. Tell students that identifying causes and effects in a selection can help them understand the relationship between situations.

Model the skill by identifying the cause and effect in these sentences from p. 750: "Yet the standard of living in India is very low compared with many other countries, even though India's GDP is higher. This is because

India's $3.6 trillion is shared by more than one billion people." (*Cause: India's GDP is shared by more than one billion people; Effect: a low standard of living.*)

Give students *Identify Causes and Effects.* Have them complete the activity in their groups.

All in One Asia and the Pacific Teaching Resources, *Identify Causes and Effects,* p. 389

Key Features of India's Population

India is the second-most-populated country in the world. Only China's population is bigger. India's population is changing in ways that affect the country's development.

A Growing Population India has a population of more than one billion people. This large population is growing. India has one of the world's highest population growth rates. By 2050, India is expected to be the world's most populated country.

Growing Urban Areas About 72 percent of India's population lives in rural areas. But with such a large population, that means nearly 300 million people were living in urban areas in 2000. By 2030, the urban population of India is expected to reach more than 600 million. Using 2006 population figures, that equals the combined total populations of the United States, Russia, Mexico, and South Korea.

An Expanding Middle Class About one fourth of India's people lives in poverty. They earn just enough money to buy the food they need to survive. In recent years, however, India's middle class has been growing. People in the middle class are neither very rich nor very poor. They earn enough money to buy goods and services that improve their lives. By some estimates, India's middle class is one of the largest in the world.

√ **Reading Check** What are some key features of India's population?

India's Middle Class
Although about one fourth of India's population is poor, India has a growing middle class that earns enough money to spend on consumer goods from pizza to cars. The growth of India's middle class is one result of its growing economy. **Analyze Images** *Do you think this photo shows an urban area or a rural area? Explain your answer.*

Learn about the effects of India's caste system.

Instruct

Key Features of India's Population

A Growing Economy   [L2]

Guided Instruction

■ **Vocabulary Builder** Clarify the high-use words **expect** and **thrive** before reading.

■ Read Key Features of India's Population and A Growing Economy using the Oral Cloze strategy (TE, p. T33).

■ Ask students **How does India's population rank among the world's countries?** *(India is the second-most-populated country in the world.)*

■ Ask **How does India's population growth affect the country's economic progress?** *(The growing middle class provides a huge market for goods and services, which boosts the economy.)*

■ Have students name the factors that are helping India's economy grow faster. *(The government has made it easier for foreign companies to do business in India, the middle class provides a large market for goods, and industries such as computer software programming are expanding.)*

Show students *India's Dalits: Outcasts No More.* Ask **How are the Dalits empowering themselves?** *(by bringing medical education to their communities)*

Answers

Analyze Images Possible answer: It probably shows an urban area because there appears to be more than one store or restaurant on the street, which would be more likely to occur in an urban area.

√ **Reading Check** second-most-populated country in the world; a growing population; 72 percent live in rural areas; large, growing urban population; one-fourth live in poverty; has what may be the world's largest middle class

Vocabulary Builder

Use the information below to teach students this section's high-use words.

High-Use Word	Definition and Sample Sentence
expect, p. 751	*v.* to look forward to the occurrence of Susan **expected** her dinner guests to arrive at 8 p.m.
thrive, p. 752	*v.* to grow vigorously; flourish Jim's ski shop **thrives** in the winter.
tension, p. 754	*n.* any strained state or relationship There is **tension** between the two nations.
launch, p. 754	*v.* to set in motion The teacher **launched** an after-school program for interested students.

Independent Practice

Ask students to create the Taking Notes graphic organizer on a blank piece of paper. Then have them fill in the effects of India's growing population. Briefly model how to identify which details to record.

Monitor Progress

Circulate as students complete the chart to make sure they are choosing the correct details. Help students as needed.

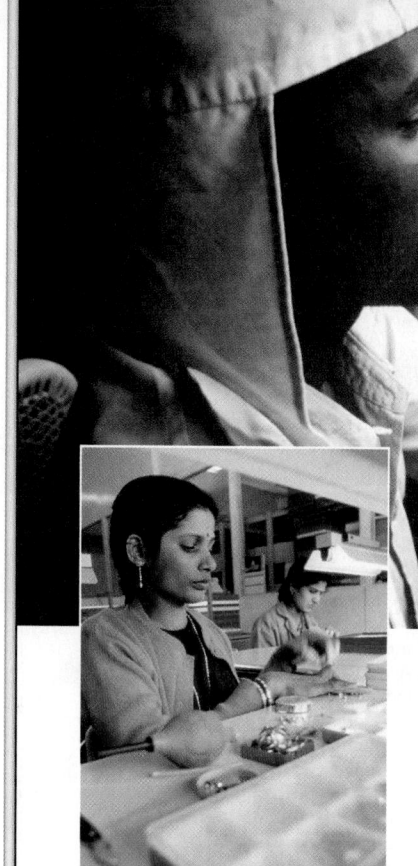

A worker checks electronic circuit boards in Bangalore (large photo); other workers assemble watches (small photo).

A Growing Economy

India has the second-fastest-growing economy in Asia. Only China's economy is growing faster. A democratic government supports India's economy. In the early 1990s, the government made changes to speed economic progress. For example, the government made it easier for foreign companies to do business in India. India's middle class helps the economy, too. The middle class provides a huge market for goods and services produced and sold in India. As the middle class grows, the number of poor people in India is expected to decrease.

Expanding industries in India are also helping the country's economy. One of India's major industries is computer software programming. India has large numbers of highly educated and skilled workers in the computer software industry. India's computer software has become a major export. Products such as electrical appliances are being manufactured in greater numbers. India also has a thriving film industry. More movies are produced in India than in any other country.

India imports more than it exports, but the country can produce all its own food. India exports **textiles,** or cloth, making cotton and silk clothing that are sold worldwide. Gemstones and jewelry are another major export. The United States buys the largest share of India's exports.

✓ Reading Check What are some major industries in India?

752 Asia and the Pacific

Answer

✓ Reading Check computer software programming, film industry, electrical appliance manufacturing, textiles, gemstone and jewelry exporting

Skills for Life Skills Mini Lesson

Making Valid Generalizations

1. Teach the skill by outlining the steps for making a generalization: 1) identify the subject; 2) identify facts and look for patterns among them; 3) make a generalization and then revise it if necessary.

2. Help students to practice the skill by identifying a valid generalization and its supporting facts under the heading A Growing Economy. (*Generalization: One of India's major industries is computer software programming; Supporting facts: large number of workers in the industry, software is a major export.*)

3. Have students apply the skill by reading the paragraph under Health Care on p. 188 and making a generalization. (*Possible generalization: Disease and malnutrition are still problems in India, but some progress has been made.*)

India

India has great cultural diversity, or variety. Most Indians are Hindus. As you can see on the map, however, Muslims, followers of Islam, are a majority in one of India's states. But there are Muslims in every other state in India. Millions of Indians practice Christianity, Sikhism, and other religions. Indians also speak hundreds of different languages. Hindi has more speakers than any other language in India. However, many other languages have millions of speakers, and most Indians speak a language other than Hindi.

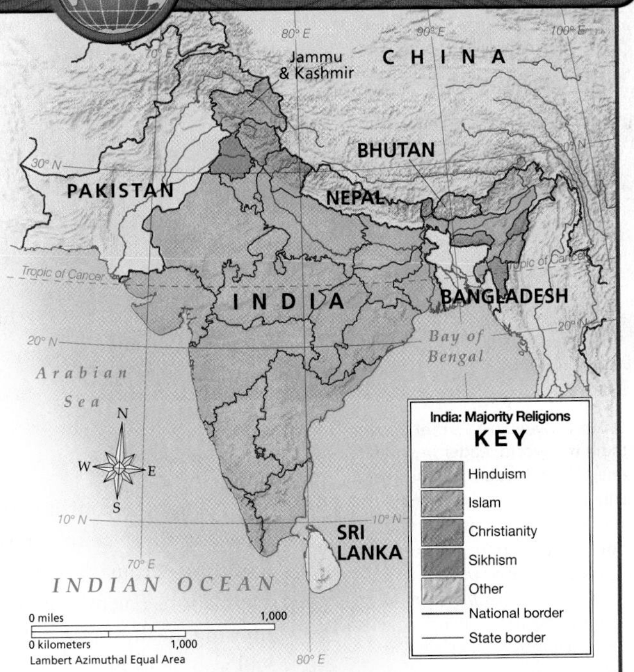

India: Majority Religions
KEY
- Hinduism
- Islam
- Christianity
- Sikhism
- Other
- —— National border
- —— State border

0 miles 1,000
0 kilometers 1,000
Lambert Azimuthal Equal Area

Religions

2% 2% 2%
13%
81%

- Hinduism
- Islam
- Christianity
- Sikhism
- Other

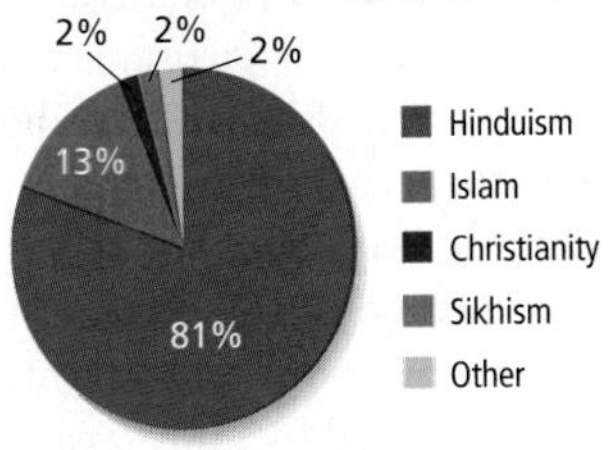

SOURCE: *CIA World Factbook*

Where Muslims Live

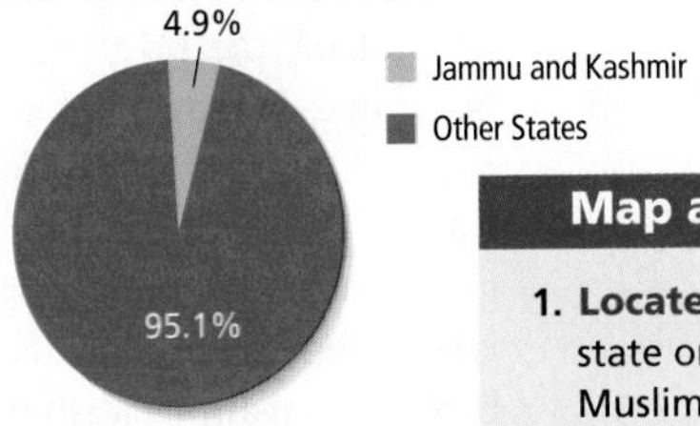

4.9%
95.1%

- Jammu and Kashmir
- Other States

SOURCE: Census of India

Languages

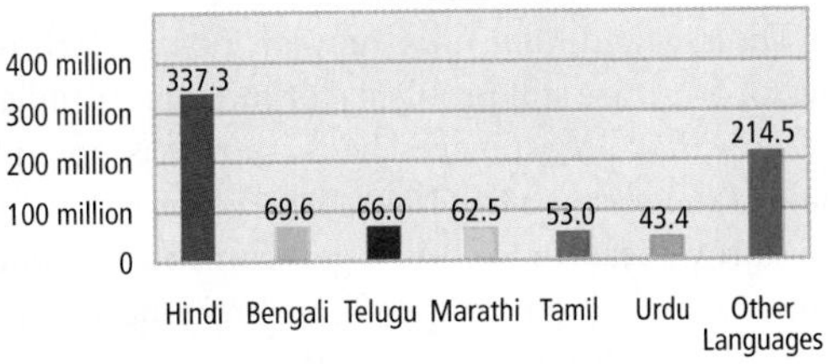

Hindi	337.3
Bengali	69.6
Telugu	66.0
Marathi	62.5
Tamil	53.0
Urdu	43.4
Other Languages	214.5

(400 million, 300 million, 200 million, 100 million, 0)

SOURCE: Census of India, 1991

Map and Chart Skills

1. **Locate** Which is the only state on the map with a Muslim majority?
2. **Note** Based on the graphs, what percentage of India's Muslims live in that state?
3. **Infer** Would you expect states with a Hindu majority to have many people belonging to other religions?

Go Online
PHSchool.com
Use Web Code Ice-6801 for DK World Desk Reference Online.

Guided Instruction   L2

Ask students to study the Country Profile on p. 753. As a class, answer the Map and Chart Skills questions. Allow students to briefly discuss their responses with a partner before sharing their answers.

Independent Practice

Have students practice transferring information from one medium to another. Ask them to convert the Languages bar graph into a table. Then have them write a brief statement explaining which medium is better for displaying the information, and why.

Answers

Map and Chart Skills

1. Jammu and Kashmir
2. about 4.9 percent
3. Possible answer: Yes, because India's population is so large, that even though a majority of people in a state are Hindu, there are probably many other people living in the state who practice other religions.

Go Online
PHSchool.com Students can find additional useful information about this topic on the DK World Desk Reference Online.

Progress and Challenges

L2

Guided Instruction

- **Vocabulary Builder** Clarify the high-use words **tension** and **launch** before reading.

- Read Progress and Challenges with students. As students read, circulate and make sure individuals can answer the Reading Check question.

- Discuss the major challenges facing India. (*Challenges include easing tensions with Pakistan, and providing jobs, housing, health care, and education for the growing population.*)

Independent Practice

Have students complete the graphic organizer with information from this section.

Monitor Progress

- Show *Section Reading Support Transparency AP 67* and ask students to check their graphic organizers individually. Go over key concepts and clarify key vocabulary as needed.

   📖 **Asia and the Pacific Transparencies,** *Section Reading Support Transparency AP 67*

- Tell students to fill in the last column of their *Reading Readiness Guides*. Probe for what they learned that confirms or invalidates each statement.

   All in One Asia and the Pacific Teaching Resources, *Reading Readiness Guide*, p. 370

🎯 Target Reading Skill

L2

Identify Causes and Effects As a follow up, ask students to answer the Target Reading Skill question in the Student Edition. (*It can increase the need for jobs, educators, schools, and housing.*)

Wind Power and Camel Power
India is a world leader in wind energy production. In many rural villages, however, people still use traditional methods to obtain power. At the right, a camel turns a wheel that pumps water.
Identify Effects *India's monsoons bring strong winds to much of the country. How does this affect the potential to create electricity from wind power?*

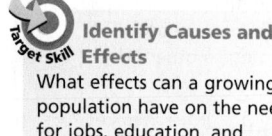

🎯 **Identify Causes and Effects**
What effects can a growing population have on the need for jobs, education, and housing?

Progress and Challenges

With about one fourth of its people living in poverty, India has a long way to go before all of its people enjoy higher living standards. India must meet the challenge of taking care of its growing population. The millions of people born each year will need jobs, housing, health care, and education. Food, water, and electricity will also be in higher demand. Another challenge facing India is its relations with its neighbor Pakistan.

Tensions Between India and Pakistan Kashmir is an area of land on the northern borders of India and Pakistan. Since becoming independent in 1947, India and Pakistan have both claimed Kashmir as part of their territory. The disagreement over Kashmir has led to fighting between the two countries. Tensions grew worse after India tested nuclear weapons in 1998. Pakistan responded by holding its own nuclear weapons tests. Fighting broke out again in Kashmir in 2003, followed by more weapons tests by both countries. However, a 2004 cease fire and continuing peace talks have brought new hope to the troubled region.

Health Care Disease and **malnutrition,** or poor nutrition caused by a lack of food, are still problems for millions of Indian people. Yet progress has been made. The country has not suffered from major famine since the 1940s. The government has taken steps to improve health care. More government-paid doctors work in rural areas. The government has also launched programs that protect people from certain diseases.

754 Asia and the Pacific

Differentiated Instruction

For Less Proficient Readers   L1
Have these students work with more proficient readers to make a table in which they list India's challenges in one column and signs of the country's progress in another.

Answer

Identify Effects The strong winds make it easier to create electricity from wind power.

As a result of these efforts, people in India are living longer. The average life expectancy in India has increased from 53 years in 1981 to 63 years in 2003. **Life expectancy** is the average number of years a person is expected to live. It is an important measure of how well a country is caring for its citizens.

Education Another way that is used to measure how well a country is taking care of its people is the literacy rate. A country's **literacy rate** shows the percentage of the population age 15 and over that can read and write. India's literacy rate is far lower than the literacy rate in the United States, but it is rapidly rising. In 1991, just over 50 percent of India's population were literate. In 2001, the literacy rate had risen to about 65 percent. Thanks to ongoing efforts to improve education, India's literacy rate is continuing to rise.

✓ **Reading Check** How has India improved health care and education for its people?

People in India, like these young students, benefit from being educated.

Section 1 Assessment

Key Terms
Review the key terms at the beginning of this section. Use each term in a sentence that explains its meaning.

Target Reading Skill
Using your Taking Notes chart, identify three effects of India's growing population.

Comprehension and Critical Thinking
1. (a) Recall What is the population of India?
(b) Find Main Ideas Why is India expected to be the world's most populated country by 2050?

(c) Identify Effects One effect of rapid urban growth is increased pollution. What might be some other effects of India's rapid urban growth?
2. (a) Note How does India's middle class help the country's economy?
(b) Identify Causes What are some other factors that are helping India's economy?
3. (a) Explain How have changes in health care increased life expectancy in India?
(b) Predict Give some reasons that a nation would want its citizens to read and write.

Writing Activity
Write an entry in your journal describing some of the challenges India must meet to take care of its growing population. Be sure to consider such factors as food and health care. Which of these challenges do you think is most important? Give one or two reasons for your answer.

For: An activity on India
Visit: PHSchool.com
Web Code: lcd-6801

Chapter 25 Section 1 **755**

Section 1 Assessment

Key Terms
Students' sentences should reflect knowledge of each Key Term.

Target Reading Skill
Three of the following: The standard of living is low; India is expected to be the world's most-populated country by 2050; the urban population is growing; the population will need jobs, housing, health care, education, food, water, and electricity.

Comprehension and Critical Thinking
1. (a) more than one billion people **(b)** It has one of the world's highest population growth and birth rates. **(c)** Possible answers: a greater demand for goods, services, jobs, housing, health care, education, food, water, and electricity

Assess Progress [L2]
Have students complete the Section Assessment. Administer the *Section Quiz*.

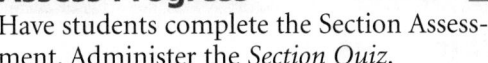 **Asia and the Pacific Teaching Resources,** *Section Quiz*, p. 372

Reteach [L1]
If students need more instruction, have them read this section in the Reading and Vocabulary Study Guide.

📖 Chapter 25, Section 1, **Eastern Hemisphere Reading Vocabulary Study Guide,** pp. 260–262

Extend [L3]
Have students expand their knowledge of India by reading an ancient tale that is popular among the country's Hindus.

All in One **Asia and the Pacific Teaching Resources,** *Savitri: A Tale of Ancient India,* pp. 403–406

Answer
✓ **Reading Check** There are more government-paid doctors working in rural areas and the government has launched programs to protect people from getting certain diseases. India's literacy rate is rising, thanks to ongoing efforts to improve education.

Writing Activity
Use the *Rubric for Assessing a Journal Entry* to evaluate students' journal entries.

All in One **Asia and the Pacific Teaching Resources,** *Rubric for Assessing a Journal Entry,* p. 409

Go Online PHSchool.com Typing in the Web code when prompted will bring students to detailed instructions for this activity.

2. (a) They provide a huge market for goods and services. **(b)** The government has made it easier for foreign companies to do business; expanding industries help the economy.

3. (a) People are living longer because more government-paid doctors are working in rural areas, and the government has launched programs that protect people from certain diseases. **(b)** Possible answer: Educated people and skilled workers can help the economy to grow.

Section 2
Step-by-Step Instruction

Objectives

Social Studies
1. Find out that Pakistan's economy is based on agriculture.
2. Learn about Pakistan's industries.

Reading/Language Arts
Find multiple effects produced by one cause to establish relationships between different pieces of information.

Prepare to Read

Build Background Knowledge L2
Tell students that in this section they will be reading about a country that has little water. Ask students to write down different ways of conserving water. Ask students to list reasons why they think conserving water might be important. Have students share their ideas using the Think-Write-Pair-Share strategy (TE, p. T36).

Set a Purpose for Reading L2
■ Preview the Objectives.

■ Read each statement in *Reading Readiness Guide* aloud. Ask students to mark the statements true or false.

> **All in One Asia and the Pacific Teaching Resources**, *Reading Readiness Guide*, p. 374

■ Have students discuss the statements in pairs or groups of four, then mark their worksheets again. Use the Numbered heads participation strategy (TE, p. T36) to call on students to share their group's perspectives.

Vocabulary Builder
Preview Key Terms L2
Pronounce each Key Term, then ask students to say the word with you. Provide a simple explanation such as, "During a drought, there is a shortage of water for drinking or crops."

Section 2 Pakistan
An Economy Based on Agriculture

Prepare to Read

Objectives
In this section you will
1. Find out that Pakistan's economy is based on agriculture.
2. Learn about Pakistan's industries.

Taking Notes
As you read this section, look for ways in which Pakistan's water supply has affected its economy. Copy the chart below, and record your findings in it.

CAUSE	EFFECTS
• Water is in short supply in Pakistan.	•

Target Reading Skill
Understand Effects A cause makes something happen. An effect is what happens as the result of a specific cause. Sometimes one cause may produce several effects. As you read this section, note the effects of Pakistan's water supply on its economy. Write the effects in the Taking Notes chart.

Key Terms
• **drought** (drowt) *n.* a long period of dry weather
• **Green Revolution** (green rev uh LOO shun) *n.* a worldwide effort to increase food production in developing countries
• **self-sufficient** (self suh FISH unt) *adj.* able to supply one's own needs without any outside assistance
• **tributary** (TRIB yoo tehr ee) *n.* a river that flows into a larger river

Rainfall is scarce throughout much of Pakistan. What water the country gets is a precious resource. Pakistan's water supply includes three main sources: the Indus River, monsoon rains, and slow-melting glaciers. To make the most of its water supply, Pakistan built the world's largest irrigation system. Without rainfall, however, the gigantic system of dams, canals, ditches, and reservoirs cannot deliver the water needed for Pakistan's farms.

In 2001, Pakistan was in the middle of an extreme **drought**—a long period of dry weather. The government was so concerned over the lack of water that it considered melting part of the glaciers in northern Pakistan. One idea was to spray on charcoal, which would raise the temperature of the ice. Later that year, however, the government decided to give up the plan due to environmental concerns.

Tarbela Dam on the Indus River provides water for irrigation.

756 Asia and the Pacific

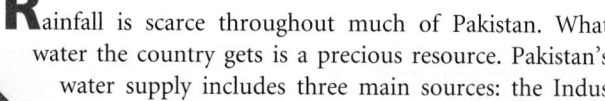

Target Reading Skill L2

Understand Effects Point out the Target Reading Skill. Tell students that sometimes one cause results in many effects.

Model how to understand effects using the last three sentences under Managing the Water Supply and the first three under Industry in Pakistan on p. 758. (*The cause,* *releasing water from the dam, has two effects: it provides water for irrigation canals and produces hydroelectricity.*)

Give students *Understand Effects*. Have them complete the activity in groups.

> **All in One Asia and the Pacific Teaching Resources**, *Understand Effects*, p. 390

An Agricultural Nation

Pakistan's economy is based mostly on agriculture. That is why water is so important there. About half of Pakistan's labor force works in agriculture.

Farming Most of Pakistan's farming takes place in the Indus River basin, where the irrigation system is located. Cotton, wheat, sugar cane, and rice are grown there. Pakistan is among the world's top ten cotton producers. Farmers in Pakistan grow so much rice that the country exports it to other countries.

Wheat is the major food crop in Pakistan. The green revolution has helped Pakistan's farmers grow more wheat. Starting in the 1940s, **the Green Revolution** was a worldwide effort to increase food production in developing countries, including Pakistan and India. The program introduced modern farming methods and special varieties of wheat, rice, and corn that yielded more grain. The year 2000 was the first year in recent history that Pakistan did not have to import wheat. Instead, the country had enough wheat to export its extra to Afghanistan. Becoming self-sufficient in wheat production and having enough to export are major goals in Pakistan. Being **self-sufficient** means Pakistan can supply its own goods without outside assistance.

Wheat Harvest in Pakistan
Although most of Pakistan's wheat is used for food within the country, Pakistan succeeded in exporting wheat for the first time in 2000. **Analyze Images** *How does the lack of modern farm machinery indicate that this wheat was raised by a subsistence farmer?*

Learn about Pakistan's efforts to improve education.

Chapter 25 Section 2 **757**

Vocabulary Builder

Use the information below to teach students this section's high-use word.

High-Use Word	Definition and Sample Sentence
yield, p. 757	*v.* to produce as a result of cultivation The tomato plant **yielded** more tomatoes than John had expected.

Guided Instruction

- **Vocabulary Builder** Clarify the high-use word **yield** before reading.

- Read An Agricultural Nation, using the Choral Reading strategy (TE, p. T34).

- Ask **What is Pakistan's economy based on?** *(agriculture)* **What percentage of the labor force works in agriculture?** *(about 50 percent)*

- Have students list the effects the green revolution had on Pakistan. *(It introduced modern farming methods and special varieties of wheat, rice, and corn that yielded more grain; it allowed Pakistan to export wheat for the first time.)*

- Ask students to describe the problems Pakistan has with its water supply and their solutions. *(Pakistan often does not have enough water for crops, so it has created an irrigation system. Sometimes, Pakistan has too much water because of the monsoons. The government has built large dams to combat the problem.)*

Show students *Pakistan: Improving Education.* Ask **In what areas has Pakistan spent most of its education money?** *(in building schools and hiring new teachers in cities)*

Independent Practice

Ask students to create the Taking Notes graphic organizer on a blank piece of paper. Then have them fill in the effects Pakistan's water supply has on its economy. Model how to identify which details to record.

Monitor Progress

As students fill in the graphic organizer, circulate and make sure individuals are choosing the correct details. Provide assistance as needed.

Answer

Analyze Images Because the farmer is harvesting the wheat by hand.

Understand Effects As a follow up, ask students to answer the Target Reading Skill question in the Student Edition. *(drought; the building of extensive irrigation systems; salt build-up in the soil)*

Links

Read the **Links Across the World** on this page. Ask **How did cricket become popular in Pakistan?** *(Cricket is popular in Great Britain, and Pakistan was once a British territory.)*

Industry in Pakistan   L2

Guided Instruction

- Read Industry in Pakistan with students. Circulate and make sure individuals can answer the Reading Check question.

- Tell students to list three industries in Pakistan. *(Students should name three of the following: agriculture, textile, chemical, cement, steel.)*

- Ask students to explain why a lack of water could affect Pakistan's textile industry. *(Textile mills need moving water to produce hydroelectric power.)*

Monitor Progress

- Show *Section Support Transparency AP 68* and ask students to check their graphic organizers individually. Go over key concepts and clarify key vocabulary as needed.

  Asia and the Pacific Transparencies, *Section Reading Support Transparency AP 68*

- Tell students to fill in the last column of the *Reading Readiness Guide*. Probe for what they learned that confirms or invalidates each statement.

  All in One Asia and the Pacific Teaching Resources, *Reading Readiness Guide*, p. 374

Independent Practice

Have students complete the graphic organizer by filling in the remaining effects Pakistan's water supply has on its economy.

Answer

✓ **Reading Check** Irrigation allows farmers to maintain a steady flow of water to raise crops.

 Understand Effects In this section, look for details about what happens in Pakistan because of the limited water supply. What are the effects of Pakistan's limited water supply?

Links Across
The World

Cricket One of the most popular sports in Pakistan is cricket. Played with a bat and a ball, cricket is a team sport widely played in Great Britain and in former colonies of the British Empire. Cricket is also popular in India, Bangladesh, Sri Lanka, Australia, and New Zealand. Like Pakistan, these countries were once British territories. In 1992, Pakistan's international cricket team won the Cricket World Cup.

Managing the Water Supply Pakistan's farmers use thousands of canals and ditches to move water from the Indus River and its tributaries to their fields. A **tributary** is a river that flows into a larger river. In this way, farmers maintain a steady flow of water, even during droughts. As more land is irrigated, more acres are farmed. This increases the amount of crops.

Irrigation solves many farming problems, but it creates others. For example, river water contains small amounts of salts. When water evaporates, the salts are left behind. Over time, salts build up in the soil, causing plant growth to slow. Pakistani scientists are trying to find a way to treat the salt-damaged soil. They are also working to develop a type of wheat that can grow in salty soil.

Pakistanis have another water problem, one that is the opposite of drought. During the monsoon season, damaging floods can occur. One solution is the large dams built by the government. The dams catch and hold monsoon rains. The waters are then released, as needed, into irrigation canals.

✓ **Reading Check** How has irrigation helped Pakistan develop an economy based on agriculture?

Industry in Pakistan

In addition to helping farmers, dams such as the Tarbela—on the Indus River in northern Pakistan—speed industrial growth. Dams capture the energy of rushing water to create hydroelectricity. In Pakistan, hydroelectric power plants produce electricity to run textile mills and other factories. Most industry is located near the sources of hydroelectric power, on the plains of the Indus River.

Making steel at a small factory near Lahore, Pakistan

Background: Links Across Time

Water Power Flowing water has been used throughout time to generate power. In order for water to generate power, it must flow from a higher place to a lower place. In the past, a water wheel was one way to utilize the power of flowing water. The oldest type of water wheel probably originated in the Middle East more than 2,000 years ago. Before the invention of the steam engine in the nineteenth century, large water wheels were used to drive machinery in factories and flour mills. Today, water flowing from a dam or waterfall is used to power a turbine, which then drives electric generators. This is called hydroelectric power, which is a principal source of energy today. Unlike one of the main sources of energy—fossil fuels—hydroelectric power is renewable.

Pakistan

As the map and graphs show, Pakistan has several different ethnic groups, whose members speak several different languages. However, Islam is very much the dominant religion. Islam is the majority religion for every major ethnic group in Pakistan. Only very small minorities practice religions other than Islam.

A Pashtun woman in Pakistan

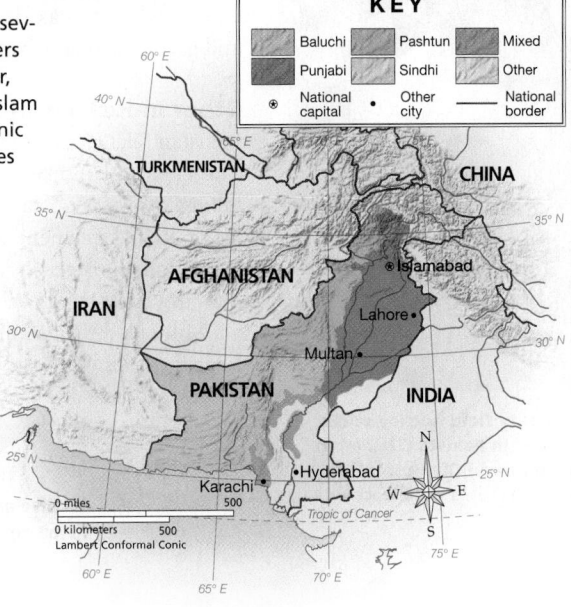

Pakistan: Ethnic Groups
KEY

Baluchi	Pashtun	Mixed
Punjabi	Sindhi	Other
⊛ National capital	• Other city	National border

Religions*

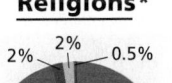
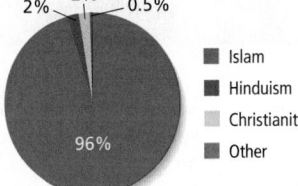

2% | 2% | 0.5%
96%

- Islam
- Hinduism
- Christianity
- Other

SOURCE: Pakistan Statistics Division
*Numbers may not equal 100% due to rounding.

Languages

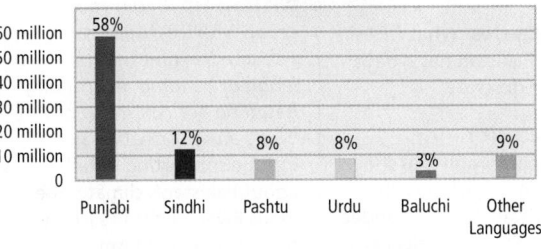

60 million	58%
50 million	
40 million	
30 million	
20 million	
10 million	12% 8% 8% 3% 9%
0	

Punjabi Sindhi Pashtu Urdu Baluchi Other Languages

SOURCE: CIA World Factbook

Map and Chart Skills

1. **Locate** Based on the map, which two languages are spoken across the largest areas of Pakistan?
2. **Identify** Based on the graph, which of these languages has the most speakers?
3. **Synthesize** What might explain why one language has so many more speakers, even though both are spoken across areas of similar size?

 **Go Online** PHSchool.com
Use Web Code **Ice-6802** for **DK World Desk Reference Online.**

Chapter 25 Section 2 **759**

Differentiated Instruction

For Advanced Readers L3

Have students complete *Water Use Around the World*. Challenge them to find the statistics on Pakistan's water use on the Internet or in the library and add them to the graph.

 Go Online PHSchool.com

For: Environmental and Global Issues: Water Use Around the World
Visit: PHSchool.com
Web Code: lcd-6806

COUNTRY PROFILE
Focus on **Culture**

Guided Instruction L2

Ask students to study the Country Profile on this page. As a class, answer the Map and Chart Skills questions. Allow students to briefly discuss their responses with a partner before sharing their answers.

Independent Practice

Ask students to write a paragraph summarizing the characteristics of Pakistan's population. Remind them to use the information in the map, graphs, and the introductory paragraph.

Answers

Map and Chart Skills

1. Punjabi and Baluchi
2. Punjabi
3. Possible answer: The area over which Baluchi is spoken might have a smaller population than that over which Punjabi is spoken.

Go Online PHSchool.com Students can find additional useful information about this topic on the DK World Desk Reference Online.

Assess and Reteach

Assess Progress L2
Have students complete the Section Assessment. Administer the *Section Quiz*.

 **Asia and the Pacific Teaching Resources,** *Section Quiz,* p. 376

Reteach L1
If students need more instruction, have them read this section in the Reading and Vocabulary Study Guide.

📖 Chapter 25, Section 2, **Eastern Hemisphere Reading and Vocabulary Study Guide**, pp. 263–265

Extend L3
Have students discover how much water they use in an average day and arrive at possible solutions to deal with a water shortage by completing *Water: Local Water Use.*

Go Online PHSchool.com

For: Environmental and Global Issues: *Local Water Use*
Visit: PHSchool.com
Web Code: lcd-6810

Answer

✓ Reading Check the textile industry

Section 2 Assessment

Key Terms
Students' sentences should reflect knowledge of each Key Term.

🎯 Target Reading Skill
Possible answer: Water allows farmers to raise crops, which is important since Pakistan's economy is based on agriculture. Water also speeds industrial growth by providing hydroelectric power.

Comprehension and Critical Thinking
1. (a) in the Indus River basin **(b)** It introduced modern farming methods and special varieties of crops that yielded more grain. **(c)** Salt builds up in the soil and slows plant growth.

2. (a) Textiles account for more than 60 percent of the country's exports. **(b)** The textile industry is based on agriculture, Pakistan's main industry.

760 *Asia and the Pacific*

Industry Based on Agriculture Pakistan began its growth in industry by building on what its people knew best: agriculture. Today, Pakistan's economy depends largely on its textile industry. More than 60 percent of the country's exports come from the textile industry. Pakistan's textile products include yarn, cloth, and garments made from cotton grown by the country's farmers.

Other Industries in Pakistan Although most industries in Pakistan relate to farming, the nation has other industries as well. The chemical industry produces paint, soap, dye, and insect-killing sprays. Pakistan uses one of its natural resources, limestone, to make cement. Several steel mills allow Pakistan to make almost all the steel it needs. Producing steel can be less costly than buying it from other countries.

Millions of Pakistanis work in small workshops instead of in large factories. Workshops produce field hockey sticks, furniture, knives, saddles, and carpets. Pakistan is famous for its beautiful carpets. Some sell for as much as $25,000 in Pakistan—and $50,000 in New York or London.

Top-quality field hockey sticks are made in Pakistan. Pakistan has won three Olympic gold medals in men's field hockey.

 **Give an example of an industry in Pakistan based on agriculture.**

⭐ Section 2 Assessment

Key Terms
Review the key terms at the beginning of this section. Use each term in a sentence that explains its meaning.

🎯 Target Reading Skill
Describe two or more effects of Pakistan's water supply on the economy. Use the information in your Taking Notes chart.

Comprehension and Critical Thinking
1. (a) Recall Where does most of the farming in Pakistan take place?

(b) Summarize How did the green revolution help Pakistan's farmers grow more wheat?
(c) Identify Effects What is one negative effect of heavy irrigation in Pakistan?

2. (a) Explain How does Pakistan's textile industry help the country's economy?
(b) Identify Causes What factor explains why Pakistan has a developed textile industry?

Writing Activity
Write a brief paragraph that shows your understanding of how the people of Pakistan have responded to conditions in their physical envi- ronment. Be sure to include ways Pakistan has developed an economy based mainly on agriculture even though it has a dry climate.

Writing Tip Begin your paragraph with this topic sentence: *Pakistan has met the challenge of building an economy based on agriculture by developing a vast irrigation system.* Include supporting details about Pakistan's climate, the Indus River, Pakistan's irrigation system, and farming.

760 Eastern Hemisphere

Writing Activity
Use the *Rubric for Assessing a Writing Assignment* to evaluate students' paragraphs.

 Asia and the Pacific Teaching Resources, *Rubric for Assessing a Writing Assignment,* p. 410

Israel
Economics and Cultures

Prepare to Read

Objectives
In this section you will
1. Discover how Israel's economy has grown and changed over the years.
2. Learn about the different peoples living in Israel.

Taking Notes
As you read this section, look for the major ideas about the economy and cultures of Israel. Copy the diagram below, and record your findings in it.

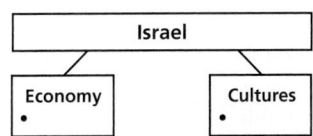

Target Reading Skill
Recognize Multiple Causes Sometimes multiple causes make one effect happen. As you read, look for three causes that have contributed to Israel's success in agriculture.

Key Terms
- **irrigation** (ihr uh GAY shun) *n.* the watering of crops using canals and other artificial waterways
- **kibbutz** (kih BOOTS) *n.* a cooperative settlement
- **West Bank** (west bank) *n.* a disputed region on the western bank of the Jordan River
- **Gaza Strip** (GAHZ uh strip) *n.* a disputed region on the Mediterranean coast

It is spring in the country of Israel. The khamsin (kam SEEN) has come. The khamsin is a wind—a hot wind—that blows into the country from the south. *Khamsin* means "wind of 50 days."

For many days, the hot khamsin will blow over a harsh landscape. The southern half of Israel is the unforgiving Negev Desert, an arid land of plains and mountains. As the wind continues north, it raises waves on a huge saltwater lake with little life. The lake is called the Dead Sea. The shore of the Dead Sea is the lowest spot on Earth. Rocky highlands lie north of the lake.

Israel is a rugged land, as harsh as the khamsin is hot. Yet the peoples of Israel have turned this dry and rocky place into a country with a modern economy and vibrant cultures.

Harvesting hay on a kibbutz in Galilee, Israel

Target Reading Skill

Recognize Multiple Causes Point out the Target Reading Skill. Explain that sometimes more than one cause can lead to one effect.

Model the skill by reading Jews on p. 764 and identifying the causes for the diversity of Israel's Jewish population. *(When Israel was founded, most of the Jewish people came from Europe and North America. Later Jews came from other Middle Eastern countries, Ethiopia, and Russia.)*

Give students *Recognize Multiple Causes.* Have them complete the activity in groups.

All in One Asia and the Pacific Teaching Resources, *Recognize Multiple Causes*, p. 391

Objectives

Social Studies
1. Discover how Israel's economy has grown and changed over the years.
2. Learn about the different peoples living in Israel.

Reading/Language Arts
Find multiple causes that lead to one effect.

Prepare to Read

Build Background Knowledge L2
Tell students that they will learn more about water management as they read about Israel. Have them share what they learned about ways to manage water in Section 2. Write students' responses on the board. Ask students to compare the methods Israel uses to manage water with Pakistan's methods as they read.

Set a Purpose for Reading L2
- Preview the Objectives.
- Read each statement in the *Reading Readiness Guide* aloud. Ask students to mark the statements true or false.

  All in One Asia and the Pacific Teaching Resources, *Reading Readiness Guide*, p. 378

- Have students discuss the statements in pairs or groups of four, then mark their worksheets again. Use the Numbered Heads participation strategy (TE, p. T36) to call on students to share their group's perspectives.

Vocabulary Builder
Preview Key Terms L2
Pronounce each Key Term, then ask students to say the word with you. Provide a simple explanation such as, "A kibbutz is a type of community in which people share work and the profits from it."

Instruct

Israel's Economy   L2

Guided Instruction

- **Vocabulary Builder** Clarify the high-use word **vibrant** before reading.

- Read Israel's Economy, using the Structured Silent Reading strategy (TE, p. T34).

- Lead a discussion on Israel's changing economy by asking the following questions: **Why is farming difficult in Israel?** *(Israel does not have a lot of arable land, so irrigation is needed.)* **Other than agriculture, what types of industries are important in Israel?** *(manufacturing and service)* Then have students list Israel's manufacturing and service industries. *(Manufacturing: textiles, processed foods, fertilizer, plastics, cut diamonds, high technology; service: banking, communication, transportation, food services and trade)*

- Ask students to compare and contrast kibbutzim and moshavim. *(Both involve cooperation among workers. Moshavim and some kibbutzim are based on farming, but many kibbutzim today are based on manufacturing. Kibbutz members share profits equally, while moshavims share farming equipment.)*

Independent Practice

Ask students to create the Taking Notes graphic organizer on a blank piece of paper and fill in the main ideas about Israel's economy. Help them identify the first main idea to get them started.

Monitor Progress

As students fill in the graphic organizer, circulate and make sure individuals are choosing appropriate main ideas. Provide assistance as needed.

Israel's Economy

Fresh water and land suitable for farming are in especially short supply in Israel. Historically, people in the region made their living by herding animals across the desert, not by farming.

Agriculture The people of Israel have managed to make farms in their desert. They grow fruits, vegetables, cotton, and other crops. How can they farm in a land with little water?

As in Pakistan, the answer is irrigation. **Irrigation** is the watering of crops using canals and other artificial waterways. Water from the Sea of Galilee, a freshwater lake in northern Israel, is pumped through a vast network of canals and pipelines. Other technological achievements have contributed to Israel's success in agriculture. During the 1950s, the Israelis drained Lake Hula, in northern Israel, and nearby swamps. This created an additional 12,000 acres of farmland.

Another factor in the success of Israeli agriculture has been cooperation among farm workers. Most of them live in small farming villages called *moshavim* (moh shah VEEM). The workers cooperate by combining their money to buy equipment and sharing information about new methods of farming. They also pool their crops to get a better price.

Manufacturing Today, about one in four Israelis work in manufacturing. Major Israeli industries include textiles, processed foods, fertilizers, and plastics. Many companies manufacture goods for the Israeli military. But most Israeli industry is in high technology. Israeli electronic and scientific equipment is respected around the world.

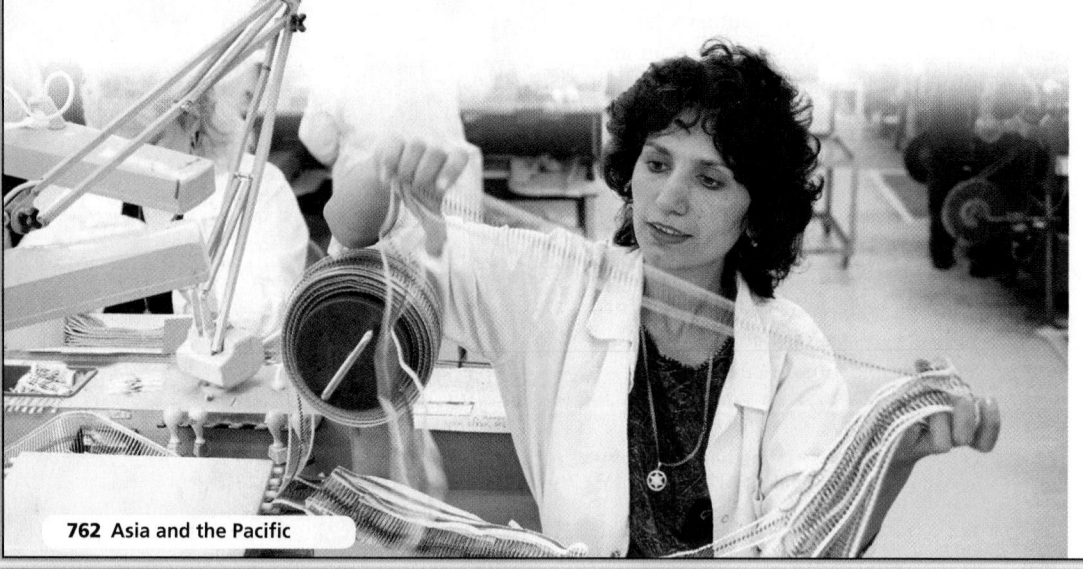

This woman is making electronic cash registers at a factory in Dimona, a town in the Negev Desert.

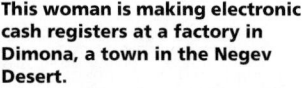

Vocabulary Builder

Use the information below to teach students this section's high-use words.

High-Use Word	Definition and Sample Sentence
vibrant, p. 761	*adj.* pulsating with life or vigor Jill captured the **vibrant** colors of the flowers in her painting.
diversity, p. 764	*n.* variety The **diversity** of items on the menu made Mary's choice difficult.

Kibbutzim Some manufacturing is done on cooperative settlements called kibbutzim. People who live on a **kibbutz** (kih BOOTS) cooperate in all parts of life. They eat together, work together, and share profits equally. Originally, most kibbutzim were farming communities. Today, modern farming machinery has replaced the need for many farm workers. As a result, many kibbutzim have turned to manufacturing.

COUNTRY PROFILE   Focus on Government

Israel

Israel controls two types of land. The orange area on the map is Israel within its pre-1967 borders, which the United States and other countries consider part of Israel. Its people are mostly Israeli Jews. Since 1967, Israel has controlled the lands known by the Palestinians as the "occupied territories." The people who live there are mostly non-Israeli Arabs. However, in 2005 Israel withdrew from the Gaza Strip. Including the occupied territories, Israel controls an area slightly larger than New Jersey. Yet the population under Israeli control is larger than New Jersey's. Partly because there is so little land, there are sharp conflicts between Israelis and Arabs over control of this land.

Israel, 2006: Political

KEY

- Israel
- Occupied by Israel after 1967 (Final status to be resolved in negotiations)
- — National border
- ---- Disputed border
- ⊛ National capital
- • City

*Limited areas of Palestinian autonomy not shown.

0 miles 100
0 kilometers 100
Lambert Conformal Conic

Israel: Population, 2000

- 22% Jewish
- 78% Arab and other

SOURCE: *Encyclopedia Britannica*

Land Area Comparison

	Square Miles
Israel, 2006	8,100
Golan Heights, West Bank, Gaza Strip	2,930
New Jersey	8,721

SOURCE: *CIA World Factbook*

Map and Chart Skills

1. **Identify** Of the two areas currently under Israeli control, which is larger?
2. **Locate** Which of these areas borders the Sea of Galilee?
3. **Synthesize** What percentage of the population of Israel is not Jewish?

Go Online PHSchool.com Use Web Code Ice-6803 for **DK World Desk Reference Online.**

Differentiated Instruction

For English Language Learners   L1

English language learners whose native language is Spanish can increase their comprehension of section content by completing the Spanish version of *Guided Reading and Review.*

📄 *Guided Reading and Review (Spanish),* **Eastern Hemisphere Spanish Support,** p. 258

COUNTRY PROFILE
Focus on Government

Guided Instruction   L2

Ask students to study the Country Profile on this page. As a class, answer the Map and Chart Skills questions. Allow students to briefly discuss their responses with a partner before sharing their answers.

Independent Practice

Ask students to use the DK World Desk Reference Online to find the population of Israel. Then have them calculate the country's population density using the land area figure provided in this profile. Ask students to list some challenges Israel might face as a result of its dense population.

Answers

Map and Chart Skills

1. the West Bank
2. Golan Heights
3. 22 percent

Go Online PHSchool.com Students can find additional useful information about this topic on the DK World Desk Reference Online.

Show students *Jerusalem: Whose Holy City?* Ask **For which religions does Jerusalem serve as a holy city?** (*Christianity, Judaism, and Islam*)

The People of Israel L2

Guided Instruction

- **Vocabulary Builder** Clarify the high-use word **diversity** before reading.

- Read The People of Israel with students. As students read, circulate and make sure individuals can answer the Reading Check question.

- Lead a discussion on the diversity among Jewish peoples in Israel. Ask **From what parts of the world have Jews come to live in Israel?** (*Europe, North America, Middle Eastern countries, Russia, Ethiopia*)

- Ask students **Why is there tension between Israelis and Arabs?** (*Israelis and Arabs disagree over who should control the West Bank and the Gaza Strip.*)

Independent Practice

Have students complete the flow chart by filling in the Cultures box.

Monitor Progress

- Show *Section Reading Support Transparency AP 69* and ask students to check their graphic organizers individually. Go over key concepts and clarify key vocabulary as needed.

  📖 **Asia and the Pacific Transparencies,** *Section Reading Support Transparency AP 69*

- Tell students to fill in the last column of the *Reading Readiness Guide*. Probe for what they learned that confirms or invalidates each statement.

  All in One Asia and the Pacific Teaching Resources, *Reading Readiness Guide*, p. 378

Answer

✔ **Reading Check** the service industry

Explore the city of Jerusalem in Israel.

Service Industries Today, service industries are the most important part of the Israeli economy. Service industries are industries that provide services instead of manufactured goods.

One type of service industry is trade. Israel borders the Mediterranean Sea. Its chief port city is Haifa, which has a deep-water harbor, excellent for docking ships. Many Israeli exports leave through Haifa. Many imports arrive there as well. Israel must import much of what it needs, since it has few natural resources. Imports include oil for energy and grain for food.

✔ **Reading Check** What industry is the most important part of the Israeli economy?

The People of Israel

Israel is home to about 6.5 million people. More than 90 percent of them live in cities. Israel's largest cities are Jerusalem, the manufacturing center of Tel Aviv, and the coastal city of Haifa.

Jews Today, about 80 percent of the people of Israel consider themselves to be Jews. Yet there is great diversity among Israeli Jews. When Israel was founded in 1948, most of the Jewish people who moved to Israel came from Europe and North America. They helped shape the culture and government of their new country. Because these people came from modern, developed countries, Israel became a modern, developed country, too.

Later, groups of Jews came from Middle Eastern countries. Beginning in the mid-1970s, tens of thousands of Ethiopian Jews from Africa have emigrated to Israel. More recently, many Jewish immigrants have come from Russia—nearly a million in the 1990s. Overall, nearly 3 million people have settled in Israel since the country was founded.

Children and teachers create crafts at a kibbutz daycare school in Israel.

764 Asia and the Pacific

Background: Links Across Place

Jewish Ethnic Groups Within Israel's Jewish population, there are two main ethnic groups. Ashkenazic are Jews who originally came from eastern and central Europe, while the Sephardic Jews came from North Africa and the Mediterranean area. Each group follows its own traditions. Cultural differences between the groups have led to tensions. Another factor contributing to tensions is the fact that throughout most of Israel's history, many of the Sephardic Jews were poorer and held fewer high political positions.

Religious Diversity Most people in Israel practice Judaism. A small percentage of the country's population is Christian or follows other religions. The single largest religion after Judaism, however, is Islam. About 16 percent of Israel's population is Muslim.

Palestinian Arabs Most Muslims living under Israeli control are Palestinian Arabs. Israel was founded in 1948 on land that was known as Palestine. Both Jews and Palestinian Arabs have long claimed Palestine as their homeland. In a series of wars with its Arab neighbors, Israel won portions of Egypt, Jordan, and Syria. Arabs called these areas the "occupied territories." Today, the occupied territories include the West Bank and the Golan Heights. The **West Bank** is an area on the west bank, or edge, of the Jordan River. Israel gave up control of the Gaza Strip to the Palestinians in 2005. The **Gaza Strip** is a small area of land along the Mediterranean Sea.

For decades, relations between the Palestinians and the Israelis have been marked by violence despite efforts on both sides to achieve peace. Several issues have divided the two groups. For example, many Palestinians fled after the Arab-Israeli wars, and Israelis have opposed the return of large numbers of Palestinians. Many Israelis insisted that a peace agreement protect Israeli settlements in the occupied territories. Palestinians, however, have opposed this idea.

√ Reading Check **What is the single largest religion in Israel after Judaism?**

A Palestinian open-air market in Jerusalem, Israel

Section 3 Assessment

Key Terms
Review the key terms at the beginning of this section. Use each term in a sentence that explains its meaning.

Target Reading Skill
What are three causes of Israel's success in agriculture?

Comprehension and Critical Thinking
1. (a) Explain How can Israeli farmers grow crops in a desert?

(b) Main Idea What type of industry is most important to the Israeli economy?
(c) Synthesize Information Why do you think high technology has become an important part of the Israeli economy?
2. (a) Recall About what percentage of Israel's population is Muslim?
(b) Identify the Main Idea Give an example of the diversity among Israeli Jews.

Writing Activity
Would you enjoy living on a kibbutz? Write a paragraph that explains why or why not.

> **Writing Tip** Give specific reasons for your explanation. Your first sentence should answer the basic question—whether or not you would like to live on a kibbutz. The following sentences should give specific reasons for your answer.

Chapter 25 Section 3 **765**

Assess and Reteach

Assess Progress
Have students complete the Section Assessment. Administer the *Section Quiz*.

All in One **Asia and the Pacific Teaching Resources,** *Section Quiz,* p. 380

Reteach
If students need more instruction, have them read this section in the Reading and Vocabulary Study Guide.

Chapter 25, Section 3, **Eastern Hemisphere Reading and Vocabulary Study Guide,** pp. 266–268

Extend
Have students do more research on what life is like on a kibbutz or moshav. Have them write journal entries as if they lived on one. Tell them to include what they do for work and aspects of daily life.

Answer

√ Reading Check Islam

Writing Activity
Use the *Rubric for Assessing a Writing Assignment* to evaluate students' paragraphs.

All in One **Asia and the Pacific Teaching Resources,** *Rubric for Assessing a Writing Assignment,* p. 410

Section 3 Assessment

Key Terms
Students' sentences should reflect knowledge of each Key Term.

Target Reading Skill
successful irrigation; other technological advances such as the draining of lakes and swamps; cooperation among farm workers

Comprehension and Critical Thinking
1. (a) by using irrigation and draining swamps and lakes to create more arable land **(b)** service industries **(c)** Possible answer: The demand for high technology, such as electronic equipment, has increased worldwide and those products produced in Israel are respected around the world.

2. (a) 16 percent **(b)** Possible answer: Groups of Jews from places all over the world, such as North America, Europe, Russia, and Ethiopia, have moved to Israel.

Section 4
Step-by-Step Instruction

Objectives

Social Studies

1. Learn how oil has affected Saudi Arabia's development and economy.
2. Discover how Islam affects everyday life in Saudi Arabia.
3. Understand the main features of Saudi Arabia's government.

Reading/Language Arts

Find multiple effects produced by one cause.

Prepare to Read

Build Background Knowledge [L2]

Tell students that in this section they will learn about a country that has more oil than any other country in the world. Ask students to think of ways that oil is used. Use the Give One, Get One participation strategy (TE, p. T37) to generate a list. *(Possible answers: fuel for transportation, heat, electricity, chemicals, lubricants)* Then explain that because it has so many uses, oil is in great demand around the world. Tell students to think about how this affects the economy of a major oil producer like Saudi Arabia *(Saudi Arabia probably exports a lot of oil, which helps to boost its economy.)*

Set a Purpose for Reading [L2]

- Preview the Objectives.

- Read each statement in the *Reading Readiness Guide* aloud. Ask students to mark the statements true or false.

  All in One **Asia and the Pacific Teaching Resources,** *Reading Readiness Guide,* p. 382

- Have students discuss the statements in pairs or groups of four, then mark their worksheets again. Use the Numbered Heads participation strategy (TE, p. T36) to call on students to share their group's perspectives.

Vocabulary Builder
Preview Key Terms [L2]

Pronounce each Key Term, then ask students to say the word with you. Provide a simple explanation such as, "In a monarchy, the head of the government is a king, a queen, or an emperor, who usually inherits this position of power."

Prepare to Read

Objectives

In this section you will
1. Learn how oil has affected Saudi Arabia's development and economy.
2. Discover how Islam affects everyday life in Saudi Arabia.
3. Understand the main features of Saudi Arabia's government.

Taking Notes

As you read this section, look for ways in which oil and Islam have shaped Saudi Arabia. Copy the table below, and record your findings in it.

Oil	Islam
•	•
•	•

Target Reading Skill

Understand Effects

Sometimes one cause may produce several effects. As you read, note two effects of oil wealth on the development of Saudi Arabia. Write them in your Taking Notes chart.

Key Terms

- **hajj** (haj) *n.* a pilgrimage or journey to Mecca undertaken by Muslims during the month of the hajj
- **Quran** (koo RAHN) *n.* the holy book of Islam
- **monarchy** (MAHN ur kee) *n.* a state or a nation in which power is held by a monarch—a king, a queen, or an emperor

Kingdom Tower in Riyadh

For more than a thousand years, Muslims from all over the world have been making pilgrimages to Mecca, Saudi Arabia. By going to Mecca, they honor the memory of Abraham, who is said to have built the first house of worship there. The pilgrimage to Mecca is called the **hajj** (haj). Muslims must make the hajj at least once in their lifetime. The hajj used to be long, hard, and dangerous. Muslims traveled across mountains and deserts by foot, horse, or camel to reach Mecca. Today, many pilgrims travel there by airplane. Roads link Mecca with other Saudi Arabian cities. Modern hotels line the streets of Mecca. Mecca is the birthplace of Islam's founder, Muhammad, and considered the holiest city in Islam.

Oil Wealth and Saudi Arabia

In 1900, Mecca was a very poor town. Saudi Arabia was one of the poorest countries in the world. Many of its people made a living by herding livestock. Like most of the countries of Southwest Asia, Saudi Arabia is mostly desert.

Target Reading Skill [L2]

Understand Effects Point out the Target Reading Skill. Tell students that sometimes one cause results in many effects.

Model how to find the effects of a cause using the following sentences found under An Economy Based on Oil on p. 767: "When oil prices are high, buildings go up at a rapid pace. Money pours in, allowing communities like Riyadh to modernize." *(Cause: high oil prices; effects: buildings go up rapidly, money allows communities to modernize)*

Give students *Understand Effects*. Have them complete the activity in groups.

All in One **Asia and the Pacific Teaching Resources,** *Understand Effects,* p. 390

An Economy Based on Oil But in the 1930s, everything changed. People discovered oil in Southwest Asia. Oil reserves changed the fortunes of Saudi Arabia and several other countries in the region. It made them rich. When night falls in Riyadh (ree YAHD), Saudi Arabia's capital, the skyline begins to glow. The lights of the many apartment and office buildings flicker on. Large buildings line the city streets. When oil prices are high, buildings go up at a rapid pace. Money pours in, allowing communities like Riyadh to modernize. But when oil prices are down, the economy of the entire country is affected. Many large building projects grind to a stop.

Saudi Arabia has the most important oil economy in the world. Under its deserts lie more than 260 billion barrels of oil. Saudi Arabia has about one fourth of the world's oil. No other country on Earth exports more petroleum.

Changes From Oil Wealth Projects paid for with oil money have changed the lives of all Saudi Arabians. Beginning in the late 1960s, the Saudi Arabian government spent billions of dollars from oil sales to modernize the country. The Saudis built modern highways, airports, seaports, and a telephone system. Villages that had always depended on oil lamps were hooked up to electric power grids.

The nation's oil wealth made it possible to build a large school system. Saudi Arabia built thousands of schools. The country has eight major universities. In 1900, many Saudi Arabians could not read or write. But today, Saudi students are becoming doctors, scientists, and teachers.

✓ **Reading Check** About how much of the world's oil is in Saudi Arabia?

Understand Effects How does the blue heading signal information on the effects of oil on Saudi Arabia's economy?

Saudi and American men working at the Saudi American Bank in Riyadh

Vocabulary Builder

Use the information below to teach students this section's high-use words.

High-Use Word	Definition and Sample Sentence
undermine, p. 769	*v.* to weaken Cheating **undermines** the rules of a game.
regulate, p. 769	*v.* to direct according to rules The commissioner **regulates** all aspects of the football league.
reveal, p. 771	*v.* to make known Jen **revealed** her desire to learn new dance steps to her instructor.

⤷ **Target Reading Skill** L2

Understand Effects As a follow up, ask students to answer the Target Reading Skill question in the Student Edition. *(The heading indicates that Saudi Arabia's economy is affected by oil in numerous ways.)*

Instruct

Oil Wealth and Saudi Arabia L2

Guided Instruction

- Read Oil Wealth and Saudi Arabia using the Choral Reading strategy (TE, p. T34).

- Discuss how Saudi Arabia has changed with oil wealth. *(Before discovering oil, Saudi Arabia was one of the poorest countries in the world. After the discovery of oil, the country became rich and could afford to modernize.)*

- Ask students **Why might it be a problem that Saudi Arabia relies so heavily on oil for wealth?** *(The economy of the entire country is shaken when world oil prices drop.)*

Independent Practice

Ask students to create the Taking Notes graphic organizer on a blank piece of paper. Then have them fill in the table with details about how oil has shaped Saudi Arabia's economy and development. Briefly model how to identify which details to record.

Monitor Progress

As students fill in the graphic organizer, circulate and make sure individuals are choosing the correct details. Help students as needed.

Answer

✓ Reading Check one fourth of the world's oil

Guided Instruction L2

Ask students to study the Country Profile on this page. As a class, answer the Map and Chart Skills questions. Allow students to briefly discuss their responses with a partner before sharing their answers.

Independent Practice

Have students use the information on this page to create a flow chart showing why Saudi Arabia's gross domestic product per capita has not changed in recent years. Display the *Flow Chart Transparency* to show students how to draw their charts.

📖 **Asia and the Pacific Transparencies,** *Transparency B6: Flow Chart*

COUNTRY PROFILE
Focus on **Economics**

Saudi Arabia

Saudi Arabia has the world's largest known oil reserves. Its economy is heavily dependent on oil. As you can see on the map, much of Saudi Arabia's land area has little or no activity other than oil production. The rest of the land supports a thin population of nomadic herders. One result of Saudi Arabia's heavy dependence on oil is that its gross domestic product per capita, or the average value of goods and services per person, has not increased much over the years. This is because oil prices have been fairly steady in recent years. Although Saudi Arabia has increased oil production, its population has increased, too, so production per person has not changed much.

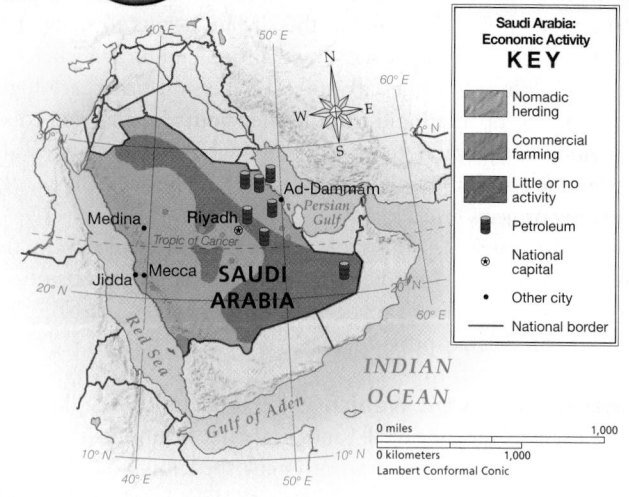

Saudi Arabia: Economic Activity KEY
- Nomadic herding
- Commercial farming
- Little or no activity
- Petroleum
- ⊛ National capital
- • Other city
- —— National border

0 miles 1,000
0 kilometers 1,000
Lambert Conformal Conic

Exports

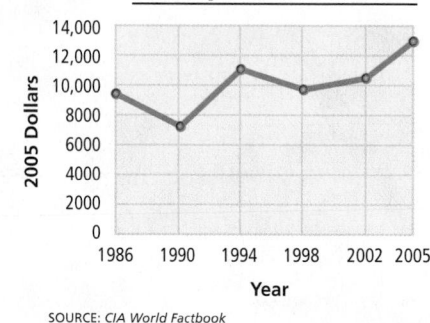

- Oil and oil products
- All other products and services

90%
10%

SOURCE: *CIA World Factbook*

Gross Domestic Product Per Capita, 1986–2005

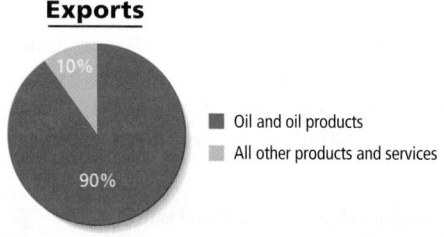

2005 Dollars: 0, 2000, 4000, 6000, 8000, 10,000, 12,000, 14,000

Year: 1986, 1990, 1994, 1998, 2002, 2005

SOURCE: *CIA World Factbook*

Map and Chart Skills

1. **Identify** What percentage of Saudi Arabia's exports is made up of oil and oil products?
2. **Infer** How does the map help to explain Saudi Arabia's dependence on oil?
3. **Predict** How would Saudi Arabia's economy be affected if oil prices dropped sharply? If oil prices jumped?

Go Online PHSchool.com
Use Web Code **Ice-6804** for **DK World Desk Reference Online.**

768 Asia and the Pacific

Answers

Map and Chart Skills

1. 90 percent
2. The map shows that oil production is the only economic activity taking place over much of Saudi Arabia's land area.
3. If oil prices dropped sharply, Saudi Arabia's economy would begin to collapse. If prices jumped quickly, the economy would flourish.

Differentiated Instruction

For Gifted and Talented L3

Have students learn about how Kuwait, another Southwest Asian nation, has been affected by its development of oil resources by completing the *Enrichment* activity.

All in One Asia and the Pacific Teaching Resources, *Enrichment*, p. 394

For Advanced Readers L3

Remind students that Saudi Arabian building projects boom when oil prices are high. Have students complete the *Small Group Activity* below.

All in One Asia and the Pacific Teaching Resources, *Small Group Activity: Creating a Brochure on Buildings of the Southwest and Central Asia*, pp. 396–399

Everyday Life in Saudi Arabia

Using their oil wealth, Saudis have imported computers, cellular phones, and televisions. But before a new product is used, the nation's religious leaders study it. They decide whether each import may be used by Muslims. Only imports that they believe do not undermine Muslim values may be used in daily life. In Saudi Arabia, Islam regulates most people's lives.

Islamic Traditions For example, cities like Riyadh have department stores, hotels, and universities. But they have no movie theaters or night clubs. The Wahhabi (wah HAH bee) branch of Islam, which most Saudi Arabians follow, forbids such entertainment.

Alcohol and pork are illegal in Saudi Arabia. All shops close five times a day when Muslims pray. Saudi Arabians use Western inventions to improve their lives, but they make sure these inventions do not interfere with Islamic traditions.

The Role of Women Many laws and traditions in Saudi Arabia deal with the role of women. Women are forbidden to do certain things. For example, Saudi women are not allowed to vote or drive cars.

However, women in Saudi Arabia today have more opportunities than in the past. Women can work as doctors, as journalists, and in other professions. They can own businesses and sit on the boards of local chambers of commerce. Today, more women than men are studying in Saudi Arabian universities.

Despite the changes, women and men usually remain separate. Boys and girls go to different schools. At the university level, women study separately from men. Female students watch male teachers over a video system.

Saudi Arabian Women
According to Islamic law, Saudi Arabian women appearing in public must wear a long, black cloak, a scarf, and a veil covering the face, (bottom photo). The small photo shows a female Saudi doctor examining a male patient.

The Government of Saudi Arabia L2

Guided Instruction

- **Vocabulary Builder** Clarify the high-use words **undermine, regulate,** and **reveal** before reading.

- Read Everyday Life in Saudi Arabia and The Government of Saudi Arabia with students. As students read, circulate and make sure individuals can answer the Reading Check questions.

- Have students provide examples of how Islam affects daily life in Saudi Arabia. (*Possible answers: The nation's religious leaders control what products are available to people. Some cities like Riyadh do not allow certain forms of entertainment, such as movie theaters. Women are not allowed to vote or drive a car. Girls and boys attend separate schools.*)

- Ask students **Under what type of law is Saudi Arabia's government ruled?** (*Islamic law*)

Independent Practice

Have students complete their graphic organizers by filling in details about how Islam shapes daily life and government in Saudi Arabia.

Monitor Progress

- Show *Section Support Transparency AP 70* and ask students to check their graphic organizers individually. Go over key concepts and clarify key vocabulary as needed.

  📖 **Asia and the Pacific Transparencies,** *Section Reading Support Transparency AP 70*

- Tell students to fill in the last column of the *Reading Readiness Guide*. Probe for what they learned that confirms or invalidates each statement.

  All in One **Asia and the Pacific Teaching Resources,** *Reading Readiness Guide,* p. 382

Differentiated Instruction

For Special Needs Students L1
Have students who learn better visually create a graphic organizer of Saudi Arabia's government. Students may use a concept web to organize the main parts of the government. Display the *Concept Web Transparency* and fill in the first circle with them to get them started. Ask students to include a brief description of the function of each branch on their organizers.

📖 **Asia and the Pacific Transparencies,** *Transparency B17: Concept Web*

Drilling for Oil

Guided Instruction

Ask students to study the Eyewitness Technology on this page. As a class, answer the questions. Allow students to briefly discuss their responses with a partner before sharing their answers.

Independent Practice

Have students do research to find the top ten oil-producing countries in the world. Then have them make a bar graph showing how much oil these countries produce in a year.

Drilling for Oil

The modern world depends on oil. Oil affects people every day, in almost every way. It fuels cars, heats homes, and is used to create electricity. Oil is located deep within Earth's surface, on land and under the oceans. The rotary drill, shown here, is often used to extract oil from land. It works like a giant screwdriver. As the drill turns round and round, it forces itself deeper through the ground.

Working the Drill
Workers operate machinery in the new oil fields of western China's Xinjiang-Uygur region.

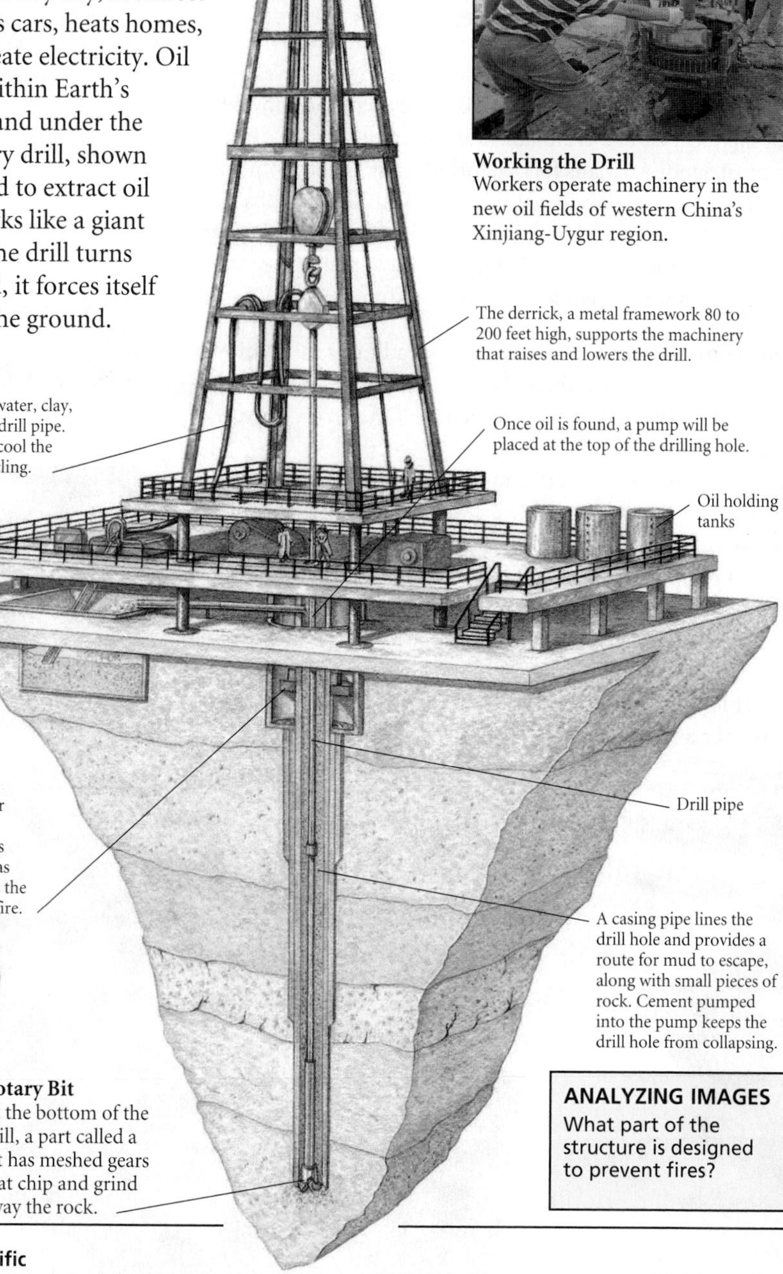

The derrick, a metal framework 80 to 200 feet high, supports the machinery that raises and lowers the drill.

Drilling "mud," made of water, clay, and chemicals, enters the drill pipe. It flows down the pipe to cool the drill, and returns for recycling.

Once oil is found, a pump will be placed at the top of the drilling hole.

Oil holding tanks

The drill may come across gas or oil under high pressure. The blowout preventer has valves that keep the gas or oil from rushing to the surface and catching fire.

Drill pipe

A casing pipe lines the drill hole and provides a route for mud to escape, along with small pieces of rock. Cement pumped into the pump keeps the drill hole from collapsing.

Rotary Bit
At the bottom of the drill, a part called a bit has meshed gears that chip and grind away the rock.

ANALYZING IMAGES
What part of the structure is designed to prevent fires?

770 Asia and the Pacific

Differentiated Instruction

For Less Proficient Readers
Pair these students with more proficient students and have them work on *The Imbalance of Energy Consumption* to learn more about world oil consumption.

For: Environmental and Global Issues: *The Imbalance of Energy Consumption*
Visit: PHSchool.com
Web Code: lcd-6811

Answer

ANALYZING IMAGES the blowout preventer

Go Online PHSchool.com Students can find additional useful information about this topic on the DK World Desk Reference Online.

The Influence of the Quran Most of the rules governing daily life in Saudi Arabia come from the **Quran,** the holy book of Islam. The word *Quran* means "the recitation" or "the reading." It consists of 114 chapters said to have been revealed by God to Muhammad. Muslims view the Quran as a guide for living. It provides guidelines on all aspects of life and religion.

✓ Reading Check How is Islam a part of daily life in Saudi Arabia?

The Government of Saudi Arabia

Islam guides more than daily life in Saudi Arabia. Saudi Arabia's government is based on the Quran and Islamic law. The country is an absolute monarchy ruled under Islamic law. A **monarchy** is a state or a nation in which power is held by a monarch. A monarch is a king, a queen, or an emperor.

The king serves as head of the Council of Ministers, which acts as the executive and legislative branches of the government. The king decides who will serve on the Council of Ministers. Traditionally, the Council includes the Crown Prince and members of the royal family. Political parties and elections are not allowed in Saudi Arabia.

✓ Reading Check What kind of government does Saudi Arabia have?

Links to
Science

Circles of Wheat In Saudi Arabia, some parts of the desert have what is called "sweet" sand. This sand is not too salty, so plants can grow in it. In a place with sweet sand, wells are dug and fields are planted. Often, the fields are circular, with the well at the center. A long pipe with sprinklers swings around the well, irrigating the field. Wheat, alfalfa, and even pumpkins are grown in such areas.

Learn what brings millions of Muslims to Mecca each year.

⭐ **Section 4 Assessment**

Key Terms
Review the key terms at the beginning of this section. Use each term in a sentence that explains its meaning.

🎯 **Target Reading Skill**
What are two ways that oil wealth has affected the development of Saudi Arabia?

Comprehension and Critical Thinking
1. (a) Recall On what natural resource is Saudi Arabia's economy based?

(b) Apply Information How did wealth from oil change Saudi Arabia?
(c) Generalize How has the Saudi Arabian government used oil wealth to improve the lives of its citizens?
2. (a) Explain Give two examples of the ways Islam affects daily life in Saudi Arabia.
(b) Identify Point of View How do Muslims view the Quran?
3. (a) Describe Describe Saudi Arabia's system of government.
(b) Evaluate Information Why do you think political parties are not permitted in Saudi Arabia?

Writing Activity
Economists estimate that Saudi Arabia has enough oil to last for about 90 years of production at its present rate. In recent years, the Saudi Arabian government has used oil wealth to develop industries outside of petroleum. These include the iron and steel industries, construction, and chemicals. Write a paragraph that explains why Saudi Arabia might want to diversify its economy.

Writing Tip As you work on your paragraph, keep in mind that petroleum is a nonrenewable resource.

Links
Read the **Links to Science** on this page. Ask **What is sweet sand?** (*sand that plants can grow in because it is not too salty*)

Assess and Reteach

Assess Progress L2
Have students complete the Section Assessment. Administer the *Section Quiz.*

All in One **Asia and the Pacific Teaching Resources,** *Section Quiz,* p. 384

Show students *The Call to Mecca.* Ask **Why do millions of Muslims travel to Mecca?** (*to complete the hajj*)

Reteach L1
If students need more instruction, have them read this section in the Reading and Vocabulary Study Guide.

📖 Chapter 25, Section 4, **Eastern Hemisphere Reading and Vocabulary Study Guide,** pp. 269–271

Extend L3
Have students complete the *World Oil Reserves* activity.

Go Online
PHSchool.com

For: Environmental and Global Issues: *World Oil Reserves*
Visit: PHSchool.com
Web Code: lcd-6807

Answers

✓ Reading Check It regulates the daily lives of Saudi Arabians.

✓ Reading Check an absolute monarchy ruled under Islamic law.

Writing Activity
Use the *Rubric for Assessing a Writing Assignment* to evaluate students' paragraphs.

All in One **Asia and the Pacific Teaching Resources,** *Rubric for Assessing a Writing Assignment,* p. 410

Section 4 Assessment

Key Terms
Students' sentences should reflect knowledge of each Key Term.

🎯 **Target Reading Skill**
Possible answers: It allowed for the modernization of the country and the construction of many public works.

Comprehension and Critical Thinking
1. (a) oil **(b)** Oil has made it wealthy. **(c)** It built highways, airports, seaports, telephone systems, electrical hookups, and schools.

2. (a) Possible answers: clothes and education **(b)** as a guide for living

3. (a) It is an absolute monarchy ruled under Islamic law. **(b)** Possible answer: Since the king is an absolute monarch, there would be no function for political parties to fill.

Objective
Learn how to interpret bar graphs.

Prepare to Read

Build Background Knowledge   L2
Tell students that this lesson will teach them how to interpret a bar graph. Refer them back to the Country Profile on p. 759 to show them an example of a bar graph that they have already seen. Familiarize them with the features of a bar graph by having them read the title and labels and then trace their finger along each bar.

Instruct

Interpreting Bar Graphs   L2

Guided Instruction
- Read the steps to interpreting a bar graph. Summarize each step and write it on the board.

- Practice the skill by using the steps to interpret the bar graph titled Saudi Arabia Crude Oil Production, 1998–2003 on p. 773. Discuss what the graph shows. (*the amount of crude oil Saudi Arabia produced each year from 1998 to 2003*)

- Help students identify the *x*- and *y*-axes. Read their labels. (*x-axis—each year from 1998 to 2003; y-axis—number of barrels of oil in billions*)

- Work with students to answer the questions in Step 3. (*Saudi Arabia produced about 8.5 billion barrels of oil in 1998; about 10 billion in 2003; in 2002, Saudi Arabia produced 9.5 billion barrels of oil.*)

- Make a prediction about how much oil Saudi Arabia produced in 2004. (*Possible answer: Because Saudi Arabia's oil production seems to steadily increase, Saudi Arabia probably produced more than 10 billion barrels in 2004.*)

 **Skills for Life   Interpreting Bar Graphs**

Look at the picture below. The man is pushing a standard-size oil barrel that holds 42 gallons. The barrel is about the size of a large trash can.

Imagine 20 of these barrels standing together in a corner of your classroom. Would they fill up your classroom? If you stacked them, how many could fit into the room? You could probably squeeze in a few hundred.

If just a few hundred barrels of oil would fill your classroom, imagine how much space 8 million barrels would fill! You probably can't even picture that many barrels. Yet it is important for people to visualize huge numbers like these because they often represent facts we need to understand.

772 Asia and the Pacific

A bar graph is a useful tool for thinking about and comparing large numbers. It is a simple, easy-to-read way of showing a large amount of information.

Learn the Skill
Review the following steps to help you understand how to read bar graphs.

1. **Read the title to see what the bar graph is about.** The title identifies the topic of the bar graph.

2. **Read the labels to find out what each axis represents.** An axis is a line at the side or bottom of a graph. The horizontal axis is called the *x*-axis. Here you will find the categories of your data. The vertical axis is called the *y*-axis. The *y*-axis shows value or quantity.

3. **Look at the data to see if you can find similarities, differences, increases, or decreases.** What information does the horizontal axis show? What information does the vertical axis show?

4. **Make one or more general statements about what the graph shows.** You will have to compare and analyze the data in the bar graph in order to draw a conclusion or make a prediction about the topic of the bar graph.

Independent Practice
Assign *Skills for Life* and have students complete it individually.

All in One **Asia and the Pacific Teaching Resources,** *Skills for Life*, p. 395

Monitor Progress
As students are completing *Skills for Life*, circulate to make sure students are correctly applying the skill steps. Provide assistance as needed.

Practice the Skill

Use the steps you have just learned to read the bar graph on the right.

1 Jot down the subject of the bar graph. What does the bar graph show?

2 Look at the labels. What does the *x*-axis represent? What does the *y*-axis represent?

3 Now compare the data. What information can you read from the *x*-axis and the *y*-axis? Use it to answer the following questions: About how much oil did Saudi Arabia produce in 1998? In 2003? In what year did Saudi Arabia produce 9.5 billion barrels of oil?

4 Analyze the data to make a prediction. From 2002 to 2003, Saudi Arabia increased its crude oil production by about half a billion barrels per year. Based on this rate of increase, how much crude oil would you expect Saudi Arabia to have produced in 2004?

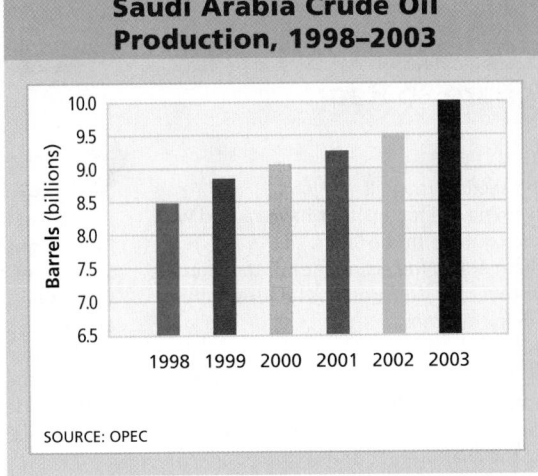

Saudi Arabia Crude Oil Production, 1998–2003

SOURCE: OPEC

Apply the Skill

Follow the steps in this skill lesson to read the bar graph below. What is the bar graph about? What does the *x*-axis represent? The *y*-axis? Which country has the greatest reserves?

Oil Reserves in selected Southwest Asian Countries

SOURCE: *The NY Times Almanac*

Chapter 25 **773**

Assess and Reteach

Assess Progress L2
Ask students to do the Apply the Skill activity.

Reteach L1
If students are having trouble applying the skill steps, have them review the skill using the Social Studies Skills Tutor CD-ROM.

⊙ *Analyzing Graphic Data*, **Social Studies Skills Tutor CD-ROM**

Extend L3
Ask students to poll the class to determine what their favorite food is. Then have them make a bar graph showing the data they collected. Remind them to label each axis and give the graph a title.

Answer
Apply the Skill

The graph shows oil reserves in selected Southwest Asian countries. The *x*-axis shows each country, and the *y*-axis shows how many barrels of oil each country produced in billions. Saudi Arabia has the greatest oil reserves of all of the countries shown on the graph.

Chapter 25 **773**

Objectives

Social Studies

1. Examine the factors that have caused war and conflicts in the Stans.
2. Learn about the economies of the Stans.
3. Discover how environmental issues affect life in the Stans.

Reading/Language Arts

Use signal words to recognize cause-and-effect relationships.

Prepare to Read

Build Background Knowledge **L2**

Write the names of the following countries on the board: *Kazakhstan, Uzbekistan, Kyrgyzstan, Tajikistan, Afghanistan, Pakistan,* and *Turkmenistan.* Ask students to identify what these country names have in common. *(They all end in the suffix -stan.)* Explain that *stan* is generally accepted as the ancient Persian or Farsi word for *land.* Tell students they will learn about life in these lands in this section.

Set a Purpose for Reading **L2**

- Preview the Objectives.

- Read each statement in the *Reading Readiness Guide* aloud. Ask students to mark the statements true or false.

  All in One **Asia and the Pacific Teaching Resources,** *Reading Readiness Guide,* p. 386

- Have students discuss the statements in pairs or groups of four, then mark their worksheets again. Use the Numbered Heads participation strategy (TE, p. T36) to call on students to share their group's perspectives.

Vocabulary Builder
Preview Key Terms **L2**

Pronounce each Key Term, then ask students to say the word with you. Provide a simple explanation such as, "A country that is landlocked is completely surrounded by land."

Prepare to Read

Objectives

In this section you will
1. Examine the factors that have caused war and conflicts in the Stans.
2. Learn about the economies of the Stans.
3. Discover how environmental issues affect life in the Stans.

Taking Notes

As you read, look for details about the challenges facing Central Asian countries. Copy the chart below, and record your findings in it.

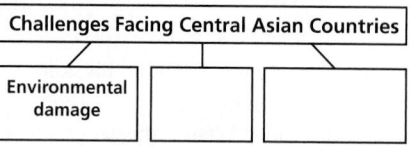

Challenges Facing Central Asian Countries

- Environmental damage

Target Reading Skill

Recognize Cause-and-Effect Signal Words Sometimes certain words, such as *because, affect,* or *as a result,* signal a cause or an effect. In this section, look for these words to better understand conditions in Central Asia.

Key Terms

- **refugee** (ref yoo JEE) *n.* a person who flees war or other disasters
- **dictatorship** (DIK tay tur ship) *n.* a form of government in which power is held by a leader who has absolute authority
- **landlocked** (LAND lahkt) *adj.* having no direct access to the sea

774 Asia and the Pacific

Sharbat Gula was a child when she first experienced the hardships of war. The Soviet Union invaded Afghanistan in 1979. Her village was destroyed in the fighting. Her parents were killed. She fled to neighboring Pakistan, where she lived in a camp for **refugees,** people who flee war or other disasters.

In 1985, a photographer named Steve McCurry took a picture of Sharbat at a refugee camp in Pakistan. The picture became famous. People around the world became more aware of the war and suffering in Afghanistan.

Seventeen years later, McCurry went back to the region to find Sharbat. He managed to trace her to a small village in Afghanistan. She was married and had children. She said she hoped that her children would have more opportunities than she had. She hoped they would get an education. Many people in Central Asia share Sharbat's hope for a better life. In addition to Afghanistan, this region includes Kazakhstan, Uzbekistan, Tajikistan, Turkmenistan, and Kyrgyzstan.

Sharbat Gula holds the magazine that made her picture famous.

Target Reading Skill **L2**

Recognize Cause-and-Effect Signal Words Point out the Target Reading Skill. Tell students that some words, such as *because, affect,* and *as a result,* help to point out cause-and-effect relationships.

Model the skill by identifying the signal words in this sentence from the Links to Art feature on p. 779: "Many works of art have been destroyed, however, as a result of war

and other conflicts." *(The phrase* as a result *signals that war and conflict have caused the destruction of artwork.)*

Give students *Recognize Cause-and-Effect Signal Words.* Have them complete the activity in groups.

All in One **Asia and the Pacific Teaching Resources,** *Recognize Cause-and-Effect Signal Words,* p. 392

Warfare and Unrest in Afghanistan

The war that caused Sharbat to flee Afghanistan lasted for ten years, until the Soviet troops withdrew in 1989. But that wasn't the end of the fighting in Afghanistan.

Conflict in Afghanistan A group of militant Islamic people called the Taliban gained power in Afghanistan in 1996. The Taliban established very strict Islamic rule. It limited freedoms and executed or severely punished those who violated their laws. Under the Taliban, girls were not allowed to attend school, and women were barred from working outside the home. Television, music, and the Internet were banned.

The Taliban had the support of radical Muslims from other countries. One of these supporters was Osama bin Laden, a wealthy Saudi Arabian who moved to Afghanistan. In 1996, the Taliban placed bin Laden under its protection.

A Campaign Against Terrorism Bin Laden was the leader of al-Qaeda, a terrorist group. He was the leading suspect in the terrorist attacks of September 11, 2001 that destroyed the World Trade Center in New York City, damaged the Pentagon in Washington, D.C., and killed nearly 3,000 people. Because the Taliban refused to hand bin Laden over to the United States, American troops invaded Afghanistan in October 2001. Aided by Afghan rebels opposed to the Taliban, the United States quickly overthrew the Taliban government. Since 2001, Afghanistan has had a democratic government and, in 2004, Hamid Karzai became the country's first democratically elected president.

✓ **Reading Check** What happened in Afghanistan after the terrorist attacks on September 11, 2001?

An Afghan Classroom
This picture of a girl's school in Kabul was taken when schools reopened after the fall of the Taliban government. The Taliban shut down most schools when it took over in 1996. **Analyze** *Why was the reopening of schools in Afghanistan seen as a return to a stable life?*

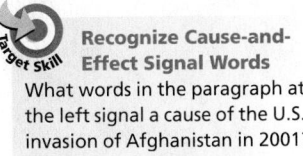

Recognize Cause-and-Effect Signal Words
What words in the paragraph at the left signal a cause of the U.S. invasion of Afghanistan in 2001?

Vocabulary Builder

Use the information below to teach students this section's high-use words.

High-Use Word	Definition and Sample Sentence
radical, p. 775	*adj.* advocating extreme change Jamel had **radical** ideas about how to use new kinds of energy.
rival, p. 776	*adj.* competing The two football teams came from **rival** cities.
access, p. 779	*n.* ability to enter The key only provided **access** to the back door, not the front door.
asset, p. 780	*n.* an item of value The rare stamp was Kate's most expensive **asset.**

Conflicts in Other Central Asian Countries

Guided Instruction

- **Vocabulary Builder** Clarify the high-use word **rival** before reading.

- Read Conflicts in Other Central Asian Countries with students. As students read, circulate and make sure individuals can answer the Reading Check question.

- Ask students **When did tensions in Central Asia increase?** *(when Soviet rule ended)*

- Ask students to describe the conflict in Kazakhstan. *(Kazaks and Russians disputed issues of political and economic power under the new government.)*

- Ask students **Why do you think the situation in Tajikistan was considered to be worse than the situation in Kazakhstan?** *(In Tajikistan, conflicts between rival groups erupted into violence, followed by a civil war that left the country in ruins.)*

Independent Practice

Have students continue to fill in the graphic organizer with details about challenges faced by Central Asian countries.

Monitor Progress

Circulate to check students' organizers and provide assistance as needed.

Children in Kyrgyzstan outside a yurt, a portable dwelling used by nomads in Central Asia

Conflicts in Other Central Asian Countries

Afghanistan was not the only Central Asian country to experience conflict. Tensions among rival leaders, clans, and ethnic groups also affected other countries in the region.

Ethnic Disputes Central Asia is a mixture of various ethnic groups and cultures. For many years, strong Soviet rule kept ethnic and clan tensions under control. As Soviet rule came to an end, however, these tensions increased. In some countries, competing groups came into conflict. In Kazakhstan, for example, disputes arose between Kazakhs and Russians over issues of political and economic power under the new government.

Political Conflicts The situation in Tajikistan was worse. There, conflicts between rival groups erupted in violence. A bloody civil war raged through much of the 1990s and left the country in ruins. In Uzbekistan, conflict broke out in the Ferghana Valley. This fertile region, which borders Tajikistan and Kyrgyzstan, came under attack from radical Muslim groups. They wanted to overthrow the government of Uzbekistan and found an Islamic state.

Uzbekistan's government fought back against its opponents. It jailed critics of the government and outlawed radical groups. Other governments in the region also cracked down on opponents. They curbed political freedoms and violated human rights. Since independence, several countries of Central Asia have turned toward **dictatorship**—a form of government in which authority is held by an all-powerful ruler.

776 Asia and the Pacific

Help for Central Asia The United States and other Western countries expressed concern about the rise of dictators in the region. They called on the Stans to create democratic governments. The United States also took steps to help the region. It provided training, equipment, and money—$594 million in 2002—to build democracy and to improve economies. One program, for example, trained judges in Kyrgyzstan and Tajikistan.

✓ Reading Check **What conflicts have disrupted life in the Stans?**

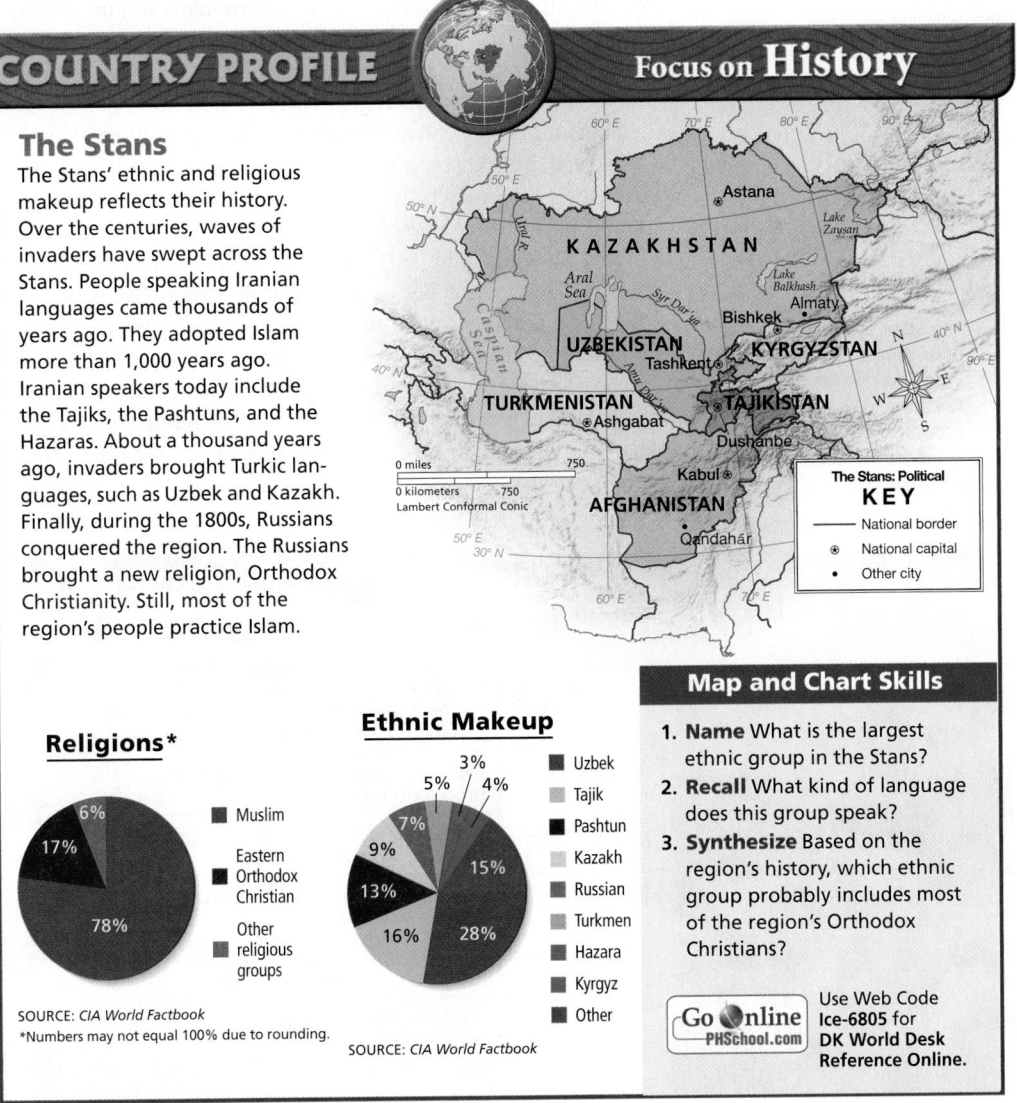

COUNTRY PROFILE   Focus on **History**

The Stans

The Stans' ethnic and religious makeup reflects their history. Over the centuries, waves of invaders have swept across the Stans. People speaking Iranian languages came thousands of years ago. They adopted Islam more than 1,000 years ago. Iranian speakers today include the Tajiks, the Pashtuns, and the Hazaras. About a thousand years ago, invaders brought Turkic languages, such as Uzbek and Kazakh. Finally, during the 1800s, Russians conquered the region. The Russians brought a new religion, Orthodox Christianity. Still, most of the region's people practice Islam.

Religions*

- Muslim
- Eastern Orthodox Christian
- Other religious groups

6%
17%
78%

SOURCE: *CIA World Factbook*
*Numbers may not equal 100% due to rounding.

Ethnic Makeup

3%
5% 4%
7%
9%
13%
16%
28%
15%

- Uzbek
- Tajik
- Pashtun
- Kazakh
- Russian
- Turkmen
- Hazara
- Kyrgyz
- Other

SOURCE: *CIA World Factbook*

Map and Chart Skills

1. **Name** What is the largest ethnic group in the Stans?
2. **Recall** What kind of language does this group speak?
3. **Synthesize** Based on the region's history, which ethnic group probably includes most of the region's Orthodox Christians?

Go Online
PHSchool.com
Use Web Code **Ice-6805** for **DK World Desk Reference Online.**

Differentiated Instruction

For Less Proficient Readers L1
Have students read the section as they listen to the recorded version on the Student Edition on Audio CD. Circulate and check students' comprehension by pausing the CD and asking students the Reading Check question.

◉ Chapter 25, Section 5, **Student Edition on Audio CD**

COUNTRY PROFILE
Focus on **History**

Guided Instruction   L2
Ask students to study the Country Profile on this page. As a class, answer the Map and Chart Skills questions. Allow students to briefly discuss their responses with a partner before sharing their answers.

Independent Practice
Ask students to consider the Religions circle graph on this page. Explain that it shows how the region's population is divided among different religions. Ask students to write a paragraph comparing the percentages of people in the region who are Sunni Muslim, Shi'a Muslim, and Eastern Orthodox Christian. Encourage students to include information on how this breakdown relates to the region's history.

Answers

✓ Reading Check conflict between Kazaks and Russians over political and economic issues in Kazakhstan, bloody conflicts between rival groups in Tajikistan, and conflict in Uzbekistan when radical Muslim groups attacked the country

Map and Chart Skills

1. Uzbek
2. Uzbek
3. Russian

Economic Conditions in Central Asia

Guided Instruction

- **Vocabulary Builder** Clarify the high-use word **access** before reading.

- Read Economic Conditions in Central Asia with students.

- Ask students **Are the countries of Central Asia generally rich or poor?** (*generally poor*)

- Ask students **What are most farms like in Central Asia?** (*They are small, and it is difficult to grow enough food on them to provide a living.*)

- Ask students **Why do you think that being landlocked is a problem for exporting oil and gas?** (*Possible answer: There is no way to get the oil or gas to ships that would transport it to places around the world.*)

Independent Practice

Have students continue to fill in the graphic organizer with details about challenges faced by Central Asian countries.

Monitor Progress

Continue to check students' organizers to be sure they are identifying the challenges Central Asia faces. Help students as needed.

Economic Conditions in Central Asia

The Stans are generally poor countries. Agriculture is the main economic activity, although manufacturing, mining, and energy production are increasingly important. The growth of industry may offer better economic prospects in the future.

Agriculture Farming is the mainstay of Central Asian economies. During the Soviet era, large cotton farms produced huge amounts of cotton for export. Cotton farming is still important in the region—especially around the Ferghana Valley—but other types of farming have also increased. Production of grains, fruits, vegetables, and livestock has grown in recent years.

Some farms in Central Asia are large, like the cotton farms of Uzbekistan, but most are small. For most small farmers, life is a struggle. It is difficult to grow enough food or earn enough money to provide a decent living.

Sharbat Gula's life is typical for people who live in the country. Her village lies in the hills of eastern Afghanistan. Villagers plant small plots of corn, wheat, and rice on terraces built into the hillsides. They may also have a few walnut trees and maybe a sheep or two. To make money, Sharbat's husband works at a bakery in a nearby city. He makes less than one dollar a day. That's barely enough for Sharbat's family to buy the things they need to survive.

■ Chart Skills

The Stans are generally poor countries with developing economies. **Compare** What is one economic activity all the countries in the Stans have in common?

Economies of Central Asian Countries

Country	Economic Activities
Afghanistan	Farming and livestock raising. Small-scale production of textiles, furniture, cement.
Kazakhstan	Farming, oil and coal mining, steel production, textiles.
Kyrgyzstan	Farming and livestock raising. Cotton, tobacco, wool and meat.
Tajikistan	Mainly farming, mostly cotton. One large aluminum plant.
Turkmenistan	Major cotton-producing country. Production of natural gas, oil, and textiles.
Uzbekistan	Major cotton exporter. Large producer of gold and oil.

778 Asia and the Pacific

┌ Background: Links Across Time ─────────

Pipelines Pipelines have been used for thousands of years. At first, pipelines were mainly used to transport water for irrigation. The Romans and Persians built aqueducts, which were above-ground pipelines that carried water for hundreds of miles. The Chinese made pipelines out of bamboo, and around 400 B.C. transported natural gas in these pipes. This natural gas was used to light the capital city of Peking. In the 1800s, steel pipes came into use. The strongest pipes created to date, these pipes allowed for the transport of oil and natural gas over long distances.

Answer
Chart Skills Compare farming

Industry Not all Central Asians live in rural areas, however. Many live in growing cities, like Almaty, Kazakhstan, and Tashkent, Uzbekistan. Many residents live in apartments and work in offices or factories. Many of the industries in the Stans date back to the Soviet era. They are generally old and unproductive. Gradually, however, some factories and mines are being modernized. Much of the focus is on the development of Central Asia's energy and mineral resources.

Several of the Stans are rich in oil, natural gas, and minerals such as coal, gold, iron ore, and uranium. Kazakhstan has major oil reserves, while Turkmenistan is rich in natural gas. Foreign oil and gas companies are exploring ways to develop and export these resources. One problem is that these countries are **landlocked,** with no direct access to the sea. Plans are underway to build pipelines to carry oil and gas out of the region.

√ Reading Check **What are the main features of Central Asian economies?**

Environmental Issues

The new countries of Central Asia face the challenging task of restoring and protecting the environment. In the past, the Soviet Union caused great environmental damage in the region.

One major environmental challenge involves nuclear fallout. For years, the Soviet Union conducted nuclear tests in northern Kazakhstan. Nuclear explosions left the region with severe radiation pollution. Radiation has caused serious health problems, including cancer and birth defects. This pollution will take years, even decades, to clean up.

Chapter 25 Section 5 **779**

Links to Art

Saving Art Central Asia has a rich artistic tradition. Many works of art have been destroyed, however, as a result of war and other conflicts. In Kabul, Afghanistan, for example, the Taliban destroyed priceless art in the National Museum. They also destroyed two giant Buddha statues at Bamiyan. Efforts are now underway to restore or save the remaining art treasures. Foreign countries and international agencies, such as the United Nations, are working with the Afghan government to preserve the country's artistic heritage. An ancient bronze sculpture from the National Museum in Kabul is shown below.

Environmental Issues

Guided Instruction

■ **Vocabulary Builder** Clarify the high-use word **asset** before reading.

■ Read about environmental challenges in Central Asia in Environmental Issues.

■ Ask students to describe two major environmental challenges facing Central Asia. *(The region must clean up the nuclear fallout produced by Soviet Union weapon testing and try to stop the drying up of the Aral Sea.)*

■ Ask students **How might the undamaged and undeveloped lands of Central Asia serve as an important asset?** *(Possible answers: The lands would offer safe places to grow food, raise families, and conduct business; they might encourage tourism.)*

Independent Practice

Have students complete the graphic organizer by filling in the environmental challenges facing Central Asian countries.

Monitor Progress

■ Show *Section Reading Support Transparency AP 71* and ask students to check their graphic organizers individually. Go over key concepts and clarify key vocabulary as needed.

📖 **Asia and the Pacific Transparencies,** *Section Reading Support Transparency AP 71*

■ Tell students to fill in the last column of the *Reading Readiness Guide.* Probe for what they learned that confirms or invalidates each statement.

All in One **Asia and the Pacific Teaching Resources,** *Reading Readiness Guide,* p. 386

Answer

√ Reading Check agriculture, manufacturing, mining, and energy production

Differentiated Instruction

For English Language Learners L1
To help students better understand the minerals mentioned on p. 779, ask them to work in small groups to find pictures on the Internet or in magazines of coal, gold, iron ore, and uranium. Have students make a poster including a labeled drawing of each mineral. Then have them list some products that are made from each mineral on the poster.

For Less Proficient Readers L1
Remind students that each paragraph has a main idea, and that main ideas are often stated in the first sentence of a paragraph. Ask students to find the main idea in the second and third paragraphs of Environmental Issues that tell about two challenges facing Central Asia. *(The main ideas are located in the first sentences of these two paragraphs.)*

Assess and Reteach

Assess Progress L2

Have students complete the Section Assessment. Administer the *Section Quiz*.

 **Asia and the Pacific Teaching Resources,** *Section Quiz,* p. 388

 Show students *The Disappearing Aral Sea.* Ask **By how much has the Aral Sea shrunk over the past forty years?** *(by half)*

Reteach L1

If students need more instruction, have them read this section in the Reading and Vocabulary Study Guide.

 Chapter 25, Section 5, **Eastern Hemisphere Reading and Vocabulary Study Guide,** pp. 272–274

Extend L3

Have students complete the *Reporting to an Environmental Conference* Internet activity.

For: Long-Term Integrated Projects: *Reporting to an Environmental Conference*
Visit: PHSchool.com
Web Code: lcd-6808

Answer

✓ Reading Check Nuclear fallout in Kazakhstan left the region with radiation damage.

Section 5 Assessment

Key Terms
Students' sentences should reflect knowledge of each Key Term.

Target Reading Skill
Possible answers: the effects; caused; as a result

Comprehension and Critical Thinking
1. (a) After Soviet troops pulled out of the country, the Taliban defeated other rebel groups in a fight for power. **(b)** The Taliban refused to hand over Osama bin Laden.

2. (a) Possible answers: Kazakhstan, Tajikistan, Uzbekistan **(b)** It has tried to build democracies and improve economies.

3. (a) agriculture **(b)** They could sell their minerals to other countries.

4. (a) It has caused radiation pollution. **(b)** the diversion of rivers for irrigation

Writing Activity
Use the *Rubric for Assessing a Newspaper Article* to evaluate students' news reports.

As you read in Chapter 19, another major challenge is the drying of the Aral Sea. For years, the Soviets diverted water from rivers feeding the sea to irrigate cotton fields. As a result, the sea is now drying up.

Still, vast areas of Central Asia remain undeveloped and undamaged. These environmentally healthy lands are a key resource for Central Asia. If the Stans can preserve their environment, it will be an important asset for their future.

Learn why the Aral Sea is shrinking.

✓ **Reading Check** How have environmental problems affected the Stans?

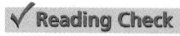

Section 5 Assessment

Key Terms
Review the key terms at the beginning of this section. Use each term in a sentence that explains its meaning.

 Target Reading Skill
Review the text about environmental issues. Find the words that signal effects on Central Asia's environment.

Comprehension and Critical Thinking
1. (a) Explain How did the Taliban come to power in Afghanistan?
(b) Summarize Why did the United States invade Afghanistan in 2001?

2. (a) Recall Name a Central Asian country other than Afghanistan that has experienced recent conflicts.
(b) Make Generalizations In general, how has the United States helped Central Asian countries?
3. (a) Identify What is the main economic activity in Central Asian countries?
(b) Apply Information How might mineral resources help Central Asian countries develop their economies?
4. (a) Recall How has nuclear testing affected Kazakhstan?
(b) Identify Causes What caused the Aral Sea to shrink?

Writing Activity
Suppose that you are a news reporter covering Central Asia. Write a brief news report about economic conditions and challenges in Central Asia.

For: An activity on the Stans
Visit: PHSchool.com
Web Code: lcd-6805

 **Asia and the Pacific Teaching Resources,** *Rubric for Assessing a Newspaper Article,* p. 411

Go Online PHSchool.com Typing in the Web code when prompted will bring students directly to detailed instructions for this activity.

Review and Assessment

◆ Chapter Summary

Section 1: India
- India is the second-most-populated country in the world. India also has a rapidly growing population.
- India has a large middle class that provides a huge market for goods and services.
- Despite India's fast-growing economy, about one fourth of the population lives in poverty.

India

Section 2: Pakistan
- Pakistan has been working hard to improve its economy.
- Pakistan's economy is based largely on agriculture.
- Pakistan's textile industry is an important part of the economy. Other industries include making chemicals and steel.

Israel

Section 3: Israel
- Service industries are the most important part of Israel's well-developed economy.
- About 80 percent of the people of Israel are Jewish. About 16 percent are Muslims.
- In 2005, Israel gave control of parts of the occupied territories to the Palestinians.

Section 4: Saudi Arabia
- Oil production is the main economic activity in Saudi Arabia. No other country in the world exports more petroleum.
- Saudi Arabia has used its wealth from oil to make the country more modern.
- Islam guides daily life in Saudi Arabia and is the basis for Saudi Arabia's laws.

Section 5: The Stans
- The countries of Central Asia face many challenges in creating prosperous, stable nations.
- Agriculture is the main economic activity in Central Asia. Manufacturing, mining, and energy production are becoming important.

◆ Key Terms

Each of the statements below contains a key term from the chapter. If the statement is true, write *true*. If it is false, rewrite the statement to make it true.

1. Life expectancy measures the percentage of the population age 15 or over that can read and write.

2. Poor nutrition caused by a lack of food or an unbalanced diet is called malnutrition.

3. Drought, a long period of dry weather, is a major problem in Pakistan.

4. Irrigation is a worldwide effort to increase food production in developing countries.

5. Today, many Muslims make the hajj by airplane.

6. A refugee is a person who flees war or other disasters.

┌ Vocabulary Builder ─────────

Revisit this chapter's high-use words:

expect	vibrant	radical
thrive	diversity	rival
tension	undermine	access
launch	regulate	asset
yield	reveal	

Ask students to review the definitions they recorded on their *Word Knowledge* worksheets.

AllᵢnOne Asia and the Pacific Teaching Resources, *Word Knowledge,* p. 393

Consider allowing students to earn extra credit if they use the words in their answers to the questions in the Chapter Review and Assessment. The words must be used correctly and in a natural context to win the extra points.

Review and Assessment

Review Chapter Content

- Review and revisit the major themes of this chapter by asking students to classify what Guiding Question each bulleted statement in the Chapter Summary answers. Form students into groups and ask them to complete the activity together. Refer to p. 567 in the Student Edition for the text of the Guiding Questions.

- Assign *Vocabulary Development* for students to review Key Terms.

  AllᵢnOne Asia and the Pacific Teaching Resources, *Vocabulary Development,* p. 407

Answers

Key Terms

1. False. Life expectancy is the average number of years a person is expected to live.

2. True

3. True

4. False. Irrigation is the artificial watering of crops.

5. True

6. True

Comprehension and Critical Thinking

7. (a) more than 1 billion **(b)** It has one of the world's highest population growth rates and birth rates.

8. (a) The people of the middle class provide a huge market for goods and services. **(b)** People are living longer.

9. (a) Rainfall is scarce and the economy is highly dependent on agriculture. **(b)** A dam creates hydroelectric power, which can be used to run mills and factories. **(c)** Educated people can become skilled in many professions that would help a nation's economy thrive.

10. (a) Possible answers: it helped them create advanced irrigation systems; it helped them create new arable land. **(b)** They provide jobs and help bring revenue from trade.

11. (a) oil **(b)** Oil wealth has enabled the country to build new highways, airports, seaports, telephone systems, electricity, and schools.

12. (a) The government is an absolute monarchy. **(b)** Saudi Arabia's government is ruled under Islamic law.

13. (a) Afghanistan **(b)** Possible answers: tensions between rival leaders, clans, and ethnic groups; the breakup of the Soviet Union

Skills Practice
Possible answers: Armenia, Azerbaijan, Georgia, Israel, Jordan, Lebanon, Syria; through library or Internet research

Writing Activity: Math
Students' bar graphs should include a title, labels for the *x*- and *y*-axes, and the population of each country listed in the Country Databank.

Use the *Rubric for Assessing a Bar Graph* to evaluate students' graphs.

All in One Asia and the Pacific Teaching Resources, *Rubric for Assessing a Bar Graph,* p. 408

◆ Comprehension and Critical Thinking

7. (a) Recall What is the population of India?
(b) Summarize Why is India expected to have the world's largest population by 2050?

8. (a) Explain How does India's middle class help the nation's economy?
(b) Identify Effects What is one effect of India's efforts to improve health care?

9. (a) Explain Why is water shortage a major problem for Pakistan?
(b) Draw Inferences Why might a manufacturing company in Pakistan be located on the plains of the Indus River?
(c) Make Generalizations Why would education be considered important in making a nation more prosperous?

10. (a) Identify Give one example of how technology has helped Israel succeed in agriculture.
(b) Summarize How do the manufacturing and service industries improve Israel's economy?

11. (a) Identify What natural resource has helped Saudi Arabia build its economy and modernize the country?

(b) Identify Effects How has oil wealth affected the lives of Saudi Arabians?

12. (a) Describe What kind of government does Saudi Arabia have?
(b) Analyze What is the connection between Islam and the government of Saudi Arabia?

13. (a) Name Which Central Asian country was controlled by the Taliban?
(b) Summarize What factors have caused wars and conflicts in the Stans?

◆ Skills Practice

Interpreting Bar Graphs Name one Southwest Asian country that is not shown on the graph on the bottom of page 773. How would you find out whether it had any oil reserves?

◆ Writing Activity: Math

Use the Country Databank on pages 738–749 to look up the population of five countries discussed in this chapter. Make a bar graph that shows each country's population. Be sure to label the horizontal axis and the vertical axis of the graph. Include a title for your graph.

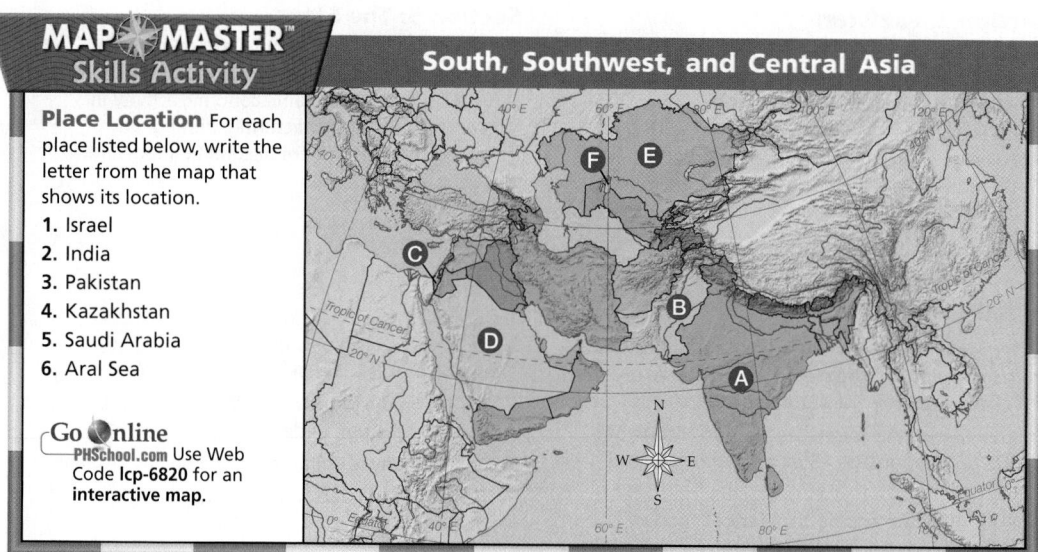

MAP MASTER™
Skills Activity

South, Southwest, and Central Asia

Place Location For each place listed below, write the letter from the map that shows its location.
1. Israel
2. India
3. Pakistan
4. Kazakhstan
5. Saudi Arabia
6. Aral Sea

Go Online
PHSchool.com Use Web Code lcp-6820 for an interactive map.

782 Asia and the Pacific

Standardized Test Prep

Test-Taking Tips

Some questions on standardized tests ask you to analyze a reading selection. Read the passage below. Then follow the tips to answer the sample question at the right.

> The Negev Desert takes up two thirds of Israel's land. Only three or four inches of rain fall there each year. Yet Israeli farmers grow fruits and vegetables on the desert. They also plant trees there to prevent erosion. For water, Israeli farmers use an irrigation system that is controlled by computer. Plastic tubes carry underground water straight to the crops. This water is salty, so Israelis developed plants that can soak up the water but not the salt.

> **TIP** Think about the author's purpose as you read. Is the author trying to give information, convince you about something, or explain how something works?

Pick the letter that best answers the question.

This paragraph answers which question?

A What is the Negev Desert in Israel like?

B What are Israeli farms like?

C How has Israel reclaimed the Negev Desert for farmland?

D How can an irrigation system bring water to desert land?

Think It Through Start with the author's purpose: to give you information about Israeli farms in the Negev Desert. What question is the passage answering about Israeli farms on the Negev Desert? You can eliminate D because it is not related specifically to Israeli farms. You can rule out A because it does not address the question of farms at all. That leaves B and C. Both ask questions about Israeli farms, but B does not include the Negev Desert. The correct answer is C.

Practice Questions

Use the tips above and other tips in this book to help you answer the following questions.

Use the passage below to answer Question 1.

> Landlocked Kazakhstan is the largest of the five former Soviet republics in Central Asia. It is about four times the size of Texas. Kazakhstan's most important natural resource is oil. In 2003, the country's oil reserves were estimated to be between 9 and 17.6 million barrels.

1. What information best supports the prediction that Kazakhstan could be a major oil exporter?

A Kazakhstan is the largest of the former Soviet republics in Central Asia.

B Kazakhstan is larger than Texas.

C Kazakhstan's oil reserves are estimated to be as great as 17.6 million barrels.

D Kazakhstan is landlocked.

2. What is one effect of India's efforts to improve health care?

A India's literacy rate is increasing.

B India's life expectancy is increasing.

C Malnutrition is increasing.

D India's film industry is growing.

Use Web Code **lca-6800** for **Chapter 25 self-test.**

MAP MASTER Skills Activity

1. C   2. A
3. B   4. E
5. D   6. F

Go Online PHSchool.com Students may practice their map skills using the interactive online version of this map.

Standardized Test Prep

Answers

1. C

2. B

Go Online PHSchool.com Students may use the Chapter 25 self-test on PHSchool.com to prepare for the Chapter Test.

Assessment Resources

Use *Chapter Tests A and B* to assess students' mastery of chapter content.

All in One Asia and the Pacific Teaching Resources, *Chapter Tests A and B,* pp. 412–417

Tests are also available on the *ExamView Test Bank CD-ROM.*

⊙ *ExamView Test Bank CD-ROM.*

Overview

Introducing Southeast Asia and the Pacific Region
1. Analyze data to compare countries.
2. Learn what characteristics countries in Southeast Asia and the Pacific region share.
3. Identify some key differences among the countries.

The Geography of Southeast Asia and the Pacific
Length: 6 minutes, 23 seconds
Uses a political map to show the physical geography, vegetation, and climates of the countries of Southeast Asia and the Pacific region.

Section 1 Vietnam: A Nation Rebuilds
1. Find out how Vietnam was divided by conflicts and war.
2. Learn how Vietnam has rebuilt its economy.

The Extended Family in Vietnam
Length: 3 minutes, 10 seconds
Explores family life in rural and urban Vietnam.

Section 2 Australia: A Pacific Rim Country
1. Learn about the major economic activities in Australia.
2. Find out how Aboriginal people in Australia are working to improve their lives.

Australia: A World of Its Own
Length: 3 minutes, 21 seconds
Provides a geographic overview of the diverse continent of Australia.

Technology Resources

Go Online
PHSchool.com

Students use embedded Web codes to access Internet activities, chapter self-tests, and additional map practice. They may also access Dorling Kindersley's Online Desk Reference to learn more about each country they study.

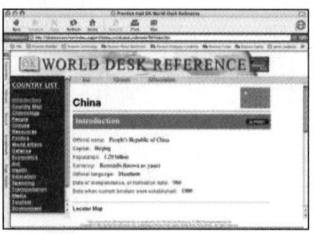

Interactive Textbook

Use the Interactive Textbook to make content and concepts come alive through animations, videos, and activities that accompany the complete basal text—online and on CD-ROM.

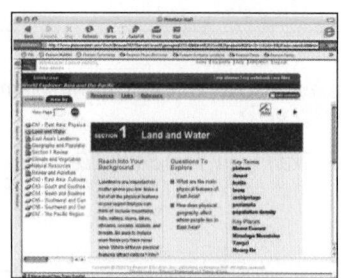

PRENTICE HALL
TeacherEXPRESS
Plan • Teach • Assess

Use this complete suite of powerful teaching tools to make planning lessons and administering tests quicker and easier.

Reading and Assessment

Reading and Vocabulary Instruction

🎯 Model the Target Reading Skill

Identify Main Ideas Explain to students that the main idea is the most significant or key point in a paragraph. The supporting details in a well thought-out paragraph should add up to the main idea. Write the paragraph below, from page 800 of the Student Edition, on the board. Point out the supporting details by underlining them.

> *Most Vietnamese <u>live in rural areas.</u> In spite of some progress, these <u>areas remain poor.</u> Whole families live on a few hundred dollars a year. Most houses have <u>no indoor toilets or running water.</u> <u>Children suffer</u> from a lack of healthy food. Vietnam is still among the poorest nations in Asia.*

Ask yourself aloud: "What do all the underlined details have in common?" *(They all have to do with what life is like in rural Vietnam.)* Then ask yourself: "What main idea do these details add up to?" *(Vietnam is still among the poorest nations in Asia.)*

Use the following worksheets from All-in-One Asia and the Pacific Teaching Resources (pp. 431–432) to support the chapter's Target Reading Skill.

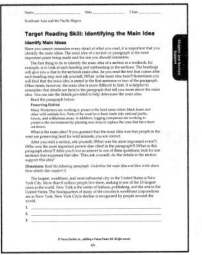 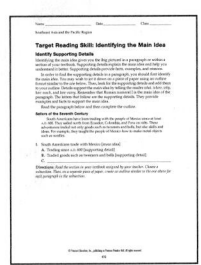

Vocabulary Builder
High-Use Academic Words

Use these steps to teach this chapter's high-use words:

1. Have students rate how well they know each word on their Word Knowledge worksheets (All-in-One Asia and the Pacific Teaching Resources, p. 433).

2. Pronounce each word and ask students to repeat it.

3. Give students a brief definition or sample sentence (provided on TE pp. 797 and 805).

4. Work with students as they fill in the "Definition or Example" column of their Word Knowledge worksheets.

Assessment

Formal Assessment

Test students' understanding of core knowledge and skills.

Chapter Tests A and B,

Final Exams A and B, All-in-One Asia and the Pacific Teaching Resources, pp. 452–457, 461–466

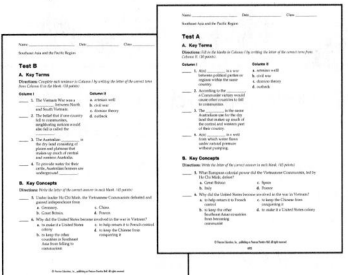

Customize the Chapter Tests to suit your needs.

ExamView Test Bank CD-ROM

Skills Assessment

Assess geographic literacy.

MapMaster Skills, Student Edition pp. 785, 810

Country Profile Map and Chart Skills, Student Edition pp. 799, 806

Assess reading and comprehension.

Target Reading Skills, Student Edition, pp. 801, 805, and in Section Assessments

Chapter 26 Assessment, Eastern Hemisphere Reading and Vocabulary Study Guide, p. 282

Performance Assessment

Assess students' performance on this chapter's Writing Activities using the following rubric from All-in-One Asia and the Pacific Teaching Resources.

Rubric for Assessing a Newspaper Article, p. 451

Assess students' work through performance tasks.

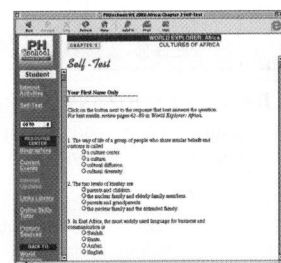

Small Group Activity: Touring Vietnam, All-in-One Asia and the Pacific Teaching Resources, pp. 436–439

Portfolio Suggestions, Teacher Edition, p. 795

Online Assessment

Have students check their own understanding.

Chapter Self-Test

Test Preparation

Practice Tests A, B, and C, Test Prep Workbook, pp. 25–36

Benchmark Test 3 and Outcome Test, AYP Monitoring Assessments, pp. 129–132, 200–205

Section 1 Vietnam: A Nation Rebuilds

 2 periods, 1 block (includes Country Databank and Skills for Life)

Social Studies Objectives

1. Find out how Vietnam was divided by conflicts and war.
2. Learn how Vietnam has rebuilt its economy.

Reading/Language Arts Objective

Find the main idea to identify what a paragraph is about.

Prepare to Read

Build Background Knowledge
Discuss the conflicts that divided Vietnam.

Set a Purpose for Reading
Have students begin to fill out the *Reading Readiness Guide.*

Preview Key Terms
Teach the section's Key Terms.

Target Reading Skill
Introduce the section's Target Reading Skill of **identifying main ideas.**

Instructional Resources

All in One Asia and the Pacific Teaching Resources
- L2 Reading Readiness Guide, p. 424
- L2 Identify Main Ideas, p. 431

Differentiated Instruction

Spanish Reading and Vocabulary Study Guide
- L1 Chapter 26, Section 1, pp. 195–196 ELL

World Studies Video Program
- L2 The Geography of Southeast Asia and the Pacific AR, GT, LPR, SN

Asia and the Pacific Transparencies
- L2 Transparency B17: Concept Web

Instruct

Decades of Conflict and War
Discuss the conflicts that arose in Vietnam after World War II.

Country Profile
Ask students to derive information from maps, charts, and graphs.

After the Vietnam War
Discuss Vietnam's economy after the war.

Target Reading Skill
Review **identifying main ideas.**

Instructional Resources

All in One Asia and the Pacific Teaching Resources
- L2 Guided Reading and Review, p. 425
- L2 Reading Readiness Guide, p. 424

Asia and the Pacific Transparencies
- L2 Section Reading Support Transparency AP 72
- L2 Transparency B17: Concept Web

World Studies Video Program
- L2 The Extended Family in Vietnam

Differentiated Instruction

All in One Asia and the Pacific Teaching Resources
- L3 Reading a Cartogram, p. 440 AR, GT
- L1 Outline Maps 30 and 32, pp. 442, 443 ELL, LPR, SN
- L2 Skills for Life, p. 435 AR, GT, LPR, SN

Asia and the Pacific Transparencies
- L1 Transparency B16: Venn Diagram ELL, LPR, SN
- L2 Transparency B20: Timeline AR, GT, LPR, SN

Teacher's Edition
- L3 For Gifted and Talented, TE pp. 788, 793
- L3 For Advanced Readers, TE p. 789
- L1 For Special Needs Students, TE pp. 790, 800
- L1 For Less Proficient Readers, TE pp. 792, 800

Assess and Reteach

Assess Progress
Evaluate student comprehension with the section assessment and section quiz.

Reteach
Assign the Reading and Vocabulary Study Guide to help struggling students.

Extend
Extend the lesson by assigning a Small Group Activity.

Instructional Resources

All in One Asia and the Pacific Teaching Resources
- L2 Section Quiz, p. 426
- L3 Small Group Activity: Touring Vietnam, pp. 436–439
- Rubric for Assessing a Writing Assignment, p. 450

Reading and Vocabulary Study Guide
- L1 Chapter 26, Section 1, pp. 276–278

Differentiated Instruction

All in One Asia and the Pacific Teaching Resources
- Rubric for Assessing a Bar Graph, p. 449 AR, GT, LPR, SN
- L1 Reading a Flow Chart, p. 441 ELL, LPR, SN

Spanish Support
- L2 Section Quiz (Spanish), p. 265 ELL

Teacher's Edition
- L1 For Special Needs Students, TE p. 803

Key
- L1 Basic to Average
- L2 For All Students
- L3 Average to Advanced
- LPR Less Proficient Readers
- AR Advanced Readers
- SN Special Needs Students
- GT Gifted and Talented
- ELL English Language Learners

Section 2 Australia: A Pacific Rim Country

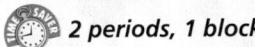 *2 periods, 1 block*

Social Studies Objectives
1. Learn about the major economic activities in Australia.
2. Find out how Aboriginal people in Australia are working to improve their lives.

Reading/Language Arts Objective
Learn to identify which details support the main idea of a paragraph.

Prepare to Read	**Instructional Resources**	**Differentiated Instruction**
Build Background Knowledge Discuss how new settlers have affected local peoples in the United States and Australia. **Set a Purpose for Reading** Have students begin to fill out the *Reading Readiness Guide*. **Preview Key Terms** Teach the section's Key Terms. **Target Reading Skill** Introduce the section's Target Reading Skill of **identifying supporting details**.	**All in One Asia and the Pacific Teaching Resources** **L2** Reading Readiness Guide, p. 428 **L2** Identify Supporting Details, p. 432	**Spanish Reading and Vocabulary Study Guide** **L1** Chapter 26, Section 2, pp. 197–198 ELL

Instruct	**Instructional Resources**	**Differentiated Instruction**
Target Reading Skill Review **identifying supporting details**. **Economic Activities** Discuss Australia's economy. **Country Profile** Ask students to derive information from maps, charts, and graphs. **Aborigines: Improving Lives** Discuss how Aborigines are working to protect their culture.	**All in One Asia and the Pacific Teaching Resources** **L2** Guided Reading and Review, p. 429 **L2** Reading Readiness Guide, p. 428 **Asia and the Pacific Transparencies** **L2** Section Reading Support Transparency AP 73 **World Studies Video Program** **L2** Australia: A World of Its Own	**All in One Asia and the Pacific Teaching Resources** **L3** Writing a Letter, p. 447 AR, GT **L3** Family Council, pp. 444–446 AR, GT **Teacher's Edition** **L1** For English Language Learners, TE p. 806 **L3** For Gifted and Talented, TE p. 807 **L3** For Advanced Readers, TE p. 807 **Passport to the World CD-ROM** **L1** Australia ELL, LPR, SN

Assess and Reteach	**Instructional Resources**	**Differentiated Instruction**
Assess Progress Evaluate student comprehension with the section assessment and section quiz. **Reteach** Assign the Reading and Vocabulary Study Guide to help struggling students. **Extend** Extend the lesson by assigning an Enrichment activity.	**All in One Asia and the Pacific Teaching Resources** **L2** Section Quiz, p. 430 **L3** Enrichment, p. 434 Rubric for Assessing a Newspaper Article, p. 451 **L2** Word Knowledge, p. 433 **L2** Vocabulary Development, p. 448 Rubric for Assessing a Writing Assignment, p. 450 **L2** Chapter Tests A and B, pp. 452–457 **L2** Final Exams A and B, pp. 461–466 **Reading and Vocabulary Study Guide** **L1** Chapter 26, Section 2, pp. 279–281	**Spanish Support** **L2** Section Quiz (Spanish), p. 267 ELL **L2** Chapter Summary (Spanish), p. 268 ELL **L2** Vocabulary Development (Spanish), p. 269 ELL

Key

L1 Basic to Average	**L3** Average to Advanced	**LPR** Less Proficient Readers	**GT** Gifted and Talented
L2 For All Students		**AR** Advanced Readers	**ELL** English Language Learners
		SN Special Needs Students	

Reading Background

Mapping Word Definitions

In this chapter, students may come across unfamiliar words. Graphic organizers can help students develop a way to learn vocabulary independently by charting word meanings. This strategy can expand students' vocabularies and help them to master unfamiliar ideas. As students read the chapter, suggest that they create their own glossaries. Below is a sample vocabulary strategy for independent learning.

Ask students to study the word *opponent*. Ask them to develop a complete definition of the word by answering these three questions: What is it? *(someone who takes the opposite position in a conflict)* What is it like? *(an enemy)* What are some examples? *(two players of a tennis match; two people running for president)*

Simplified Outlining

Simplified outlining helps students clarify the difference between main ideas and details. Simplified outlining is similar to creating an outline, but less complicated because main ideas and details are assigned numbers. Main ideas are level 1 ideas. Details are either level 2 or level 3. Students can use this technique as a method of organization for reading, writing, or studying.

Write the following model for a simplified outline on the board:

> **Level 1:** Main Idea
>> **Level 2:** Detail or support for Level 1
>>> **Level 3:** Detail or support for Level 2

Model this approach by outlining the information in *Economic Activities* from page 239 of the Student Edition:

> **Level 1:** Australia's economy
>> **Level 2:** supported by Pacific Rim countries
>>> **Level 3:** trade with Australia
>> **Level 2:** farming
>>> **Level 3:** wheat
>> **Level 2:** ranching
>>> **Level 3:** sheep
>>> **Level 3:** cattle

Give students more practice by having them read a selection from the chapter. Provide students with the level 1s and ask them to fill in the level 2s and 3s, or write down the level 2s and 3s and have students provide you with the level 1s.

World Studies Background

The Geneva Conference of 1954

The Geneva Conference was convened to end the fighting in Vietnam between France and the Vietnamese independence fighters. The Geneva treaty divided Vietnam into two parts to separate the opposing forces, with a provision to hold elections to reunite the country. However, the elections were not held. Fighting continued, eventually leading to the involvement of the United States military.

Australian Outback

The term *outback* has been used since the 1800s to refer to the remote interior of Australia. Other phrases to describe the outback include "back of beyond," "back country," and "the bush." Enormous ranching stations are isolated in the outback and can range in size from 30 to 5,800 square miles (80 to 15,000 square kilometers), with anywhere from 15 to 50 residents. These self-sufficient stations usually contain an airstrip, garage and machine shops, a butchery, a shearing shed, a main house for the owners, and separate buildings for the manager, overseer, and workers. The Royal Flying Doctor Service provides medical services to these isolated ranches. Children are educated through correspondence schools that instruct students using two-way radio equipment and television.

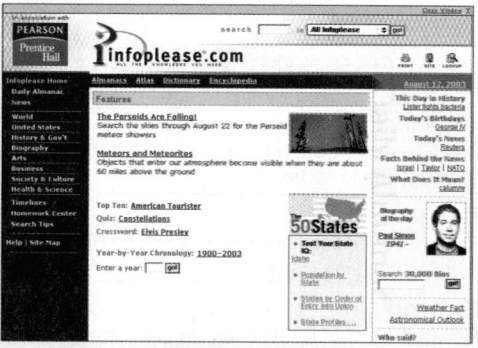

Infoplease® provides a wealth of useful information for the classroom. You can use this resource to strengthen your background on the subjects covered in this chapter. Have students visit this advertising-free site as a starting point for projects requiring research.

 Use Web code **lcd-6900** for **Infoplease®**.

Using Paragraph Shrinking Effectively

Students can use the Paragraph Shrinking strategy to help them learn important ideas in the text. The first part of this strategy involves reading and rereading the paragraph independently. To minimize students' anxiety when reading, tell students that they can take as much time as they need to read the selection. You will let them know when it is time to move on to the next step. If they finish the paragraph before the time is up, they can read it again more slowly. Then monitor the class for signs that all students have finished their silent reading.

Repeated Use

Explain to students that one word can have several slightly different definitions. Showing students the different ways in which a word can be used can often help reinforce its meanings. One way to do this is to write a word on the board, explain its multiple meanings, and give sentences using the word as examples of its various uses.

For example, point out to students that the high-use word *reflect* in Section 2 of this chapter is used to mean *to show* or *to make apparent*. A sentence using *reflect* in this sense might be, *The expression on your face can reflect your mood.* Explain that *reflect* can also mean *to mirror.* An example might be, *The deer saw its own face reflected on the pond's surface.* Other high-use words with multiple meanings from this chapter are *launch* and *conduct.*

Have students become more proficient at recognizing the different meanings one word may have by finding appropriate Key Terms or high-use words used in everyday life. Ask them to bring in newspaper or magazine clippings, or to write down sentences they hear on the news that involve the word. Emphasize the importance of listening for multiple meanings of the same word.

Language in Vietnam

Vietnam has great variety in spoken languages. The Vietnamese make up more than 85 percent of the country, and their language is largely influenced by Chinese. About 50 minority groups live in the Vietnamese highlands, however, many speaking a unique dialect. Some of these dialects are similar to Indonesian languages, others reflective of Cambodian languages. Groups in northern Vietnam share aspects of their languages with people in Thailand and Laos.

Australian Aborigines

By the late 1700s, it is estimated that there were from 300,000 to 1,000,000 Aborigines and Torres Islanders living in different communities throughout Australia. Each group had its own culture and traditions. European settlement had a profound effect on these communities, however. Removal from their traditional lands has led to poverty, loss of culture, and disease in the Aboriginal people. Today, Aboriginal people live throughout Australia and many groups are trying to reclaim their culture. Although a mere fraction of the total population, the Aboriginal population has nearly quadrupled from 115,000 in 1971 to 410,000 in 2001. However, this is still less than two percent of Australia's population.

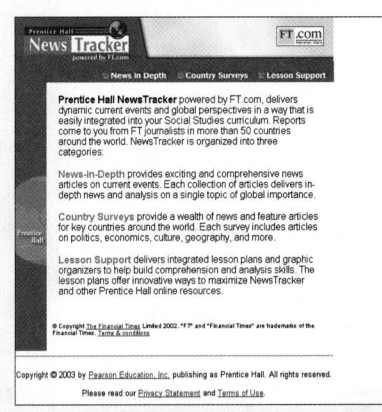

Get in-depth information on topics of global importance with **Prentice Hall Newstracker,** powered by FT.com.

Use Web code **lcd-6903** for **Prentice Hall Newstracker.**

Chapter 26

Guiding Questions

Remind students about the Guiding Questions introduced at the beginning of this section.

Section 1 relates to **Guiding Question 4**
What types of government exist in Asia and the Pacific today? *(Vietnam has a Communist government.)*

Section 2 relates to **Guiding Question 5**
How do the people of this region make a living? *(The people of Australia work in trade, agriculture, and ranching.)*

⟳ Target Reading Skill

In this chapter, students will learn and apply the reading skill of identifying main ideas and supporting details. Use the following worksheets to help students practice this skill:

All in One Asia and the Pacific Teaching Resources, *Identify Main Ideas*, p. 431; *Identify Supporting Details*, p. 432

Chapter

26 Southeast Asia and the Pacific Region

Chapter Preview

This chapter focuses on Vietnam, a country in mainland Southeast Asia, and on Australia, the only country that is also a continent.

Country Databank
The Country Databank provides data and descriptions of each of the countries of Southeast Asia and the Pacific Region.

Section 1
Vietnam
A Nation Rebuilds

Section 2
Australia
A Pacific Rim Country

⟳ Target Reading Skill

Main Idea In this chapter you will focus on identifying main ideas and supporting details.

▶ Hiking in the mountains of New Zealand

Differentiated Instruction

The following Teacher's Edition strategies are suitable for students of varying abilities.

Advanced Readers, pp. 789, 807
English Language Learners, p. 806
Gifted and Talented, pp. 788, 793, 807
Less Proficient Readers, pp. 792, 800
Special Needs Students, pp. 790, 800, 803

Bibliography

For the Teacher
Bachman, Bill and Tim Winton. *Australian Colors: Images of the Outback.* Amphoto, 2001.
Bell, Ken. *100 Missions North: A Fighter Pilot's Story of the Vietnam War.* Brasseys, Inc., 2003.
Herring, George. *America's Longest War: The United States and Vietnam, 1950–1975.* McGraw-Hill, 2001.

For the Student
L1 Landau, Elaine. *Australia and New Zealand.* Children's Book Press, 1999.
L2 Garland, Sherry. *Children of the Dragon: Selected Tales from Vietnam.* Harcourt, 2001.
L3 Myers, Walter Dean. *Patrol: An American Soldier in Vietnam.* HarperCollins, 2002.

MAP MASTER™
Skills Activity

Map: Southeast Asia and the Pacific

PACIFIC OCEAN

Tropic of Cancer

MYANMAR (BURMA)
Hanoi
Yangon
LAOS
Vientiane
THAILAND
VIETNAM
Bangkok
CAMBODIA
Phnom Penh
Ho Chi Minh City
South China Sea
Philippine Sea
Manila
PHILIPPINES
NORTHERN MARIANA ISLANDS (U.S.)
GUAM (U.S.)
20° N
MARSHALL ISLANDS
Strait of Malacca
Andaman Sea
BRUNEI
MALAYSIA
Bandar Seri Begawan
Koror
PALAU
Palikir
Majuro
Kuala Lumpur
SINGAPORE
Singapore
FEDERATED STATES OF MICRONESIA
Equator
0°
Sumatra
Borneo
INDONESIA
NAURU
Tarawa
K I R I B A T I
Jakarta
Java Sea
Surabaya
Java
Dili
EAST TIMOR
New Guinea
PAPUA NEW GUINEA
SOLOMON ISLANDS
Honiara
Port Moresby
TUVALU
Fongafale
TOKELAU (New Zealand)
Arafura Sea
Coral Sea
VANUATU
Port-Vila
SAMOA
Apia
AMERICAN SAMOA (U.S.)
COOK ISLANDS (New Zealand)
FIJI
Suva
20° S
NEW CALEDONIA (France)
Nuku'alofa
TONGA
FRENCH POLYNESIA (France)
20° S
Tropic of Capricorn
AUSTRALIA
Tropic of Capricorn
INDIAN OCEAN
Perth
Sydney
Canberra
Melbourne
Auckland
North Island
40° S
Tasmania
Tasman Sea
South Island
Wellington
NEW ZEALAND
40° S

KEY
— National border
⊛ National capital
• Other city

0 miles 2,000
0 kilometers 2,000
Mercator

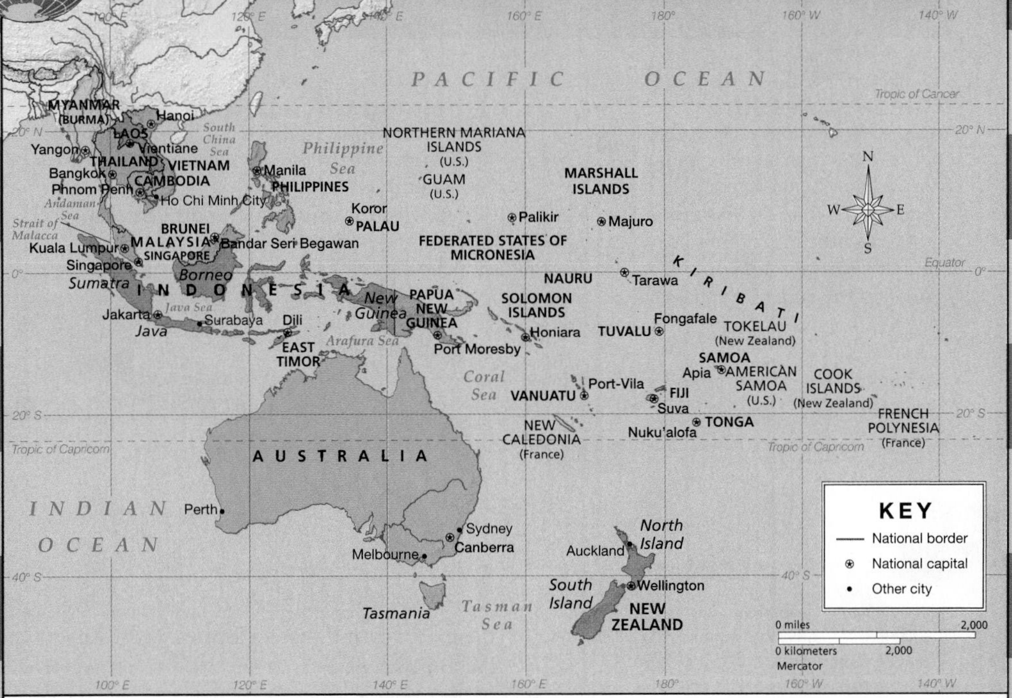

Regions Much of Southeast Asia and the Pacific Region is located between the Tropic of Cancer and the Tropic of Capricorn.
Identify Which countries have land south of the Tropic of Capricorn?
Contrast What climate would you expect most of these countries to have? Explain your answer.

Go Online
PHSchool.com Use Web Code
lcp-6910 for step-by-step
map skills practice.

Point out that many of the countries in Southeast Asia and the Pacific are islands. Ask students to identify the countries that are located entirely on mainland Asia. (*Myanmar, Laos, Vietnam, Thailand, Cambodia*)

Go Online
PHSchool.com Students may practice their map skills using the interactive online version of this map.

Using the Visual L2

Reach Into Your Background Draw students' attention to the photo on pp. 784–785 and its accompanying caption. Discuss the photograph with students. Have them describe the physical features of the landscape. Ask them to think about how the physical features of a place might effect how people live and work there. What kinds of challenges would people in this area face? Conduct an Idea Wave (TE, p. T35) to elicit student responses.

Answers

MAP MASTER™
Skills Activity
Identify Australia and New Zealand **Contrast** Most countries probably have a warm climate because areas around the Equator generally have warm climates.

Chapter 26 **785**

Chapter Resources

Teaching Resources
L2 Vocabulary Development, p. 448
L2 Skills for Life, p. 435
L2 Chapter Tests A and B, pp. 452–457
L2 Final Exams A and B, pp. 461–466

Spanish Support
L2 Spanish Chapter Summary, p. 268
L2 Spanish Vocabulary Development, p. 269

Media and Technology
L1 Student Edition on Audio CD
L1 Guided Reading Audiotapes, English and Spanish
L2 Social Studies Skills Tutor CD-ROM
ExamView Test Bank CD-ROM

PRENTICE HALL
Presentation EXPRESS™
Teach · Connect · Inspire

Teach this chapter's content using the PresentationExpress™ CD-ROM including:
- slide shows
- transparencies
- interactive maps and media
- *ExamView*® QuickTake Presenter

Objectives

- Analyze data to compare countries.

- Learn what characteristics countries in Southeast Asia and the Pacific region share.

- Identify some key differences among the countries.

Show *The Geography of Southeast Asia and the Pacific*. Ask **How do the countries in Southeast Asia and the Pacific depend on their diverse natural resources to support people?** *(Possible answer: Volcanic ash on the islands and river systems on the mainland have made the soil especially fertile for crops such as rubber, rice, and tea. Most of the world's teak wood comes from the dense forests here, and the surrounding oceans yield great quantities of fish.)*

Prepare to Read

Build Background Knowledge L2

Invite students to share what they learned about Southeast Asia and the Pacific's geography from watching the World Studies Video. Display the *Concept Web* graphic organizer. Write "Geographic Features" in the center circle. Ask students to fill in the outer circles with information they learned about the physical geography of Southeast Asia and the Pacific.

📼 *The Geography of Southeast Asia and the Pacific*, **World Studies Video Program**

📖 **Asia and the Pacific Transparencies,** *Transparency B17: Concept Web*

Introducing Southeast Asia and the Pacific Region

Guide for Reading

This section provides an introduction to the countries that make up the region of Southeast Asia and the Pacific Region.

- Look at the map on the previous page and then read the paragraphs below to learn about each nation.

- Analyze the data to compare the countries.

- What are the characteristics that most of the countries share?

- What are some key differences among the countries?

Viewing the Video Overview

View the World Studies Video Overview to learn more about each of the countries. As you watch, answer this question:

- How do the countries in Southeast Asia and the Pacific depend on their diverse natural resources to support their people?

Explore the land of Southeast Asia and the Pacific Region.

Australia

Capital	Canberra
Land Area	2,941,283 sq mi; 7,617,930 sq km
Population	19.6 million
Ethnic Group(s)	white, Asian, Aboriginal
Religion(s)	Protestant, Roman Catholic, traditional beliefs
Government	democratic, federal-state system recognizing the British monarch as sovereign
Currency	Australian dollar
Leading Exports	coal, gold, meat, wool, aluminum, iron ore, wheat, machinery and transport equipment
Language(s)	English (official), Italian, Cantonese, Greek, Arabic, Vietnamese, Aboriginal languages

Australia (aw STRAYL yuh) is both a continent and a country. The country is divided into five continental states and two territories. Most Australians live on the coast, as the interior is extremely dry. All the state capitals, including Sydney, are on the coast. The national capital, Canberra, is located inland. Australia is a country of great physical diversity, from deserts to snow-capped mountains. It also has the Great Barrier Reef, the largest coral reef in the world. Tourism is Australia's main industry, although it also has important farming and mining industries.

Wool is a leading Australian export.

786 Asia and the Pacific

Brunei

Capital	Bandar Seri Begawan
Land Area	2,035 sq mi; 5,270 sq km
Population	366,000
Ethnic Group(s)	Malay, Chinese, indigenous tribes
Religion(s)	Muslim, Buddhist, Christian, traditional beliefs
Government	constitutional sultanate
Currency	Brunei dollar
Leading Exports	crude oil, natural gas, refined products
Language(s)	Malay (official), English, Chinese

Brunei (broo NY) is a largely Muslim country in Southeast Asia. The same family, the Sultanate of Brunei, has been in power for more than six hundred years. At one point between the 1400s and 1600s, the nation controlled parts of Borneo and the Philippines. Later, the country experienced problems related to royal succession, colonization, and piracy. In the late 1800s, Brunei came under British rule for almost one hundred years, until it gained its independence in 1984. The nation is rich in oil and natural gas and has a relatively strong economy.

Cambodia

Capital	Phnom Penh
Land Area	68,154 sq mi; 176,520 sq km
Population	14.5 million
Ethnic Group(s)	Khmer, Vietnamese
Religion(s)	Buddhist
Government	multiparty democracy under a constitutional monarchy
Currency	riel
Leading Exports	clothing, timber, rubber, rice, fish
Language(s)	Khmer (official), French, English

Cambodia (kam BOH dee uh) is located on the Gulf of Thailand in Southeast Asia. It is bordered by Thailand, Vietnam, and Laos. Communist Khmer Rouge forces took over Cambodia in 1975. More than a million people died or were executed when the Khmer Rouge ordered the evacuation of all cities and towns. After decades of violent political conflict, the surrender of the Khmer Rouge in 1998 brought renewed political stability to Cambodia. Today, with massive international donations, Cambodia struggles to maintain a stable government and establish a working economy.

East Timor

Capital	Dili
Land Area	5,794 sq mi; 15,007 sq km
Population	820,000
Ethnic Group(s)	Austronesian (Malayo-Polynesian), Papuan, Chinese
Religion(s)	Roman Catholic, Muslim, Protestant, Hindu, Buddhist, traditional beliefs
Government	republic
Currency	U.S. dollar
Leading Exports	coffee, sandalwood, marble
Language(s)	Tetum (Portuguese-Austronesian) (official), Portuguese (official), Indonesian, English

East Timor (eest TEE mawr) is located in Southeast Asia, northwest of Australia. East Timor includes the eastern half and the Oecussi region of the island of Timor as well as two smaller islands. Once a Portuguese colony, East Timor declared its independence in 1975. Nine days after declaring independence, however, it was invaded and occupied by Indonesia. In 1999, the United Nations supervised an election in which the people of East Timor voted for independence from Indonesia. Though Indonesian militias protested with violence, East Timor was internationally recognized as an independent democratic nation in May 2002.

Chapter 26 **787**

Instruct

Introducing Southeast Asia and the Pacific Region L2

Guided Instruction

■ Read each country paragraph as a class using the Choral Reading strategy (TE, p. T34). Then, ask students to read through each data table.

■ Ask **Which country on pp. 786–787 is also a continent?** *(Australia)* Tell students to turn to the map on p. 785 and locate Australia and Brunei. Then have them study the data on these countries. Ask **Why do you think these two countries have little in common?** *(They are located far from one another. Brunei is much closer to mainland Asia, and much smaller than Australia. These factors may have influenced the countries' development.)*

■ Ask students to locate Cambodia and East Timor on the map on p. 785. Ask **Do you think these countries have similar climates? Why or why not?** *(Possible answer: They probably have similar climates because they are located about the same distance from the Equator.)*

Background: Daily Life

Aborigine Storytelling For Aborigines in Australia, raising children is the responsibility of everyone in the community. Teaching children about their Aboriginal culture and history through storytelling is part of everyday life. Elders tell stories while preparing food, getting water, or at night while the campfire is burning.

Through storytelling, children learn about the creation of the land, plants, animals, and humans according to Aboriginal beliefs. They also learn about their ancestors. When children grow up it is their responsibility to pass the stories on to younger generations.

- Ask **Which country on pp. 788–789 has the smallest area?** (*Federated States of Micronesia*) **Which country has the largest population?** (*Indonesia*) **Which country is located entirely on the Asian continent?** (*Laos*)

- Ask **What is the official language of the Federated States of Micronesia?** (*English*) **Why do you think this is so?** (*The country was once controlled by the United States.*)

- Have students compare and contrast the characteristics of Fiji and Indonesia. (*Similarities: Both countries have Muslims, Protestants, Roman Catholics, and Hindus; both have republican forms of government; both were once controlled by other countries. Differences: Fiji is much smaller in area and population; the countries have different ethnic groups, currency, leading exports, and official language.*)

Introducing Southeast Asia and the Pacific Region

Federated States of Micronesia

Capital	Palikir
Land Area	271 sq mi; 702 sq km
Population	135,869
Ethnic Group(s)	Micronesian, Polynesian
Religion(s)	Roman Catholic, Protestant
Government	constitutional government
Currency	U.S. dollar
Leading Exports	fish, clothing, bananas, black pepper
Language(s)	English (official), Trukese, Pohnpeian, Mortlockese, Losrean

The Federated States of Micronesia (FED ur ayt id stayts uv my kruh NEE zhuh) is an island group in the North Pacific Ocean. It consists of all the Caroline Islands except Palau. Once under United States control, the Federated States of Micronesia (FSM) became independent in 1986. The United States still provides the country with financial aid and military protection. The FSM is working to overcome long-term concerns such as high unemployment, overfishing, and dependence on United States aid. Most Micronesians live without running water or electricity.

Fiji

Capital	Suva
Land Area	7,054 sq mi; 18,270 sq km
Population	856,346
Ethnic Group(s)	Fijian, South Asian, white, other Pacific Islander, East Asian
Religion(s)	Hindu, Protestant, Roman Catholic, Muslim
Government	republic
Currency	Fiji dollar
Leading Exports	sugar, clothing, gold, timber, fish, molasses, coconut oil
Language(s)	English (official), Fijian, Hindi, Urdu, Tamil, Telugu

Fiji (FEE jee) is an island group in the South Pacific Ocean. Fiji consists of two main islands and hundreds of smaller islands. After nearly one hundred years as a British colony, Fiji became an independent democracy in 1970. Fiji has a history of ethnic conflict between native Fijians and those of Indian ancestry. This conflict has caused great political instability over the past few decades and has weakened Fiji's economy.

Indonesia

Capital	Jakarta
Land Area	705,188 sq mi; 1,826,440 sq km
Population	231.3 million
Ethnic Group(s)	Javanese, Sundanese, Madurese, coastal Malay
Religion(s)	Muslim, Protestant, Roman Catholic, Hindu, Buddhist
Government	republic
Currency	rupiah
Leading Exports	oil and gas, electrical appliances
Language(s)	Bahasa Indonesia (official), Javanese, Sundanese, Madurese, Dutch

Indonesia (in duh NEE zhuh) is an island nation located between the Indian and Pacific Oceans. It is Southeast Asia's largest and most populous country, and the world's largest archipelago. It is also the world's most populous Muslim nation. Once known as the Dutch East Indies, Indonesia achieved independence from the Netherlands in 1949. When a giant tsunami struck in 2004, parts of Indonesia faced destruction, and about 129,000 people were killed. Although poverty and terrorism remain problems, the nation's government and economy have grown more stable.

788 Asia and the Pacific

Differentiated Instruction

For Gifted and Talented   L3

Have students complete *Reading a Cartogram* to learn about the gross national product (GNP) of Indonesia and how it compares to other Asian countries.

 Asia and the Pacific Teaching Resources, *Reading a Cartogram*, p. 440

Kiribati

Capital	Bairiki (Tarawa Atoll)
Land Area	313 sq mi; 811 sq km
Population	96,335
Ethnic Group(s)	Micronesian, Polynesian
Religion(s)	Roman Catholic, Protestant, Muslim, traditional beliefs
Government	republic
Currency	Australian dollar
Leading Exports	copra, coconuts, seaweed, fish
Language(s)	English (official), Micronesian dialect

Kiribati (kihr uh BAS) is a group of 33 coral atolls in the Pacific Ocean. It lies on the Equator about halfway between Hawaii and Australia. Once called the Gilbert Islands, part of a British colony, Kiribati became independent in 1979. Great Britain had mined the islands for their phosphate deposits for decades. Although the phosphate ran out in 1980, Kiribati succeeded in winning some payment from Britain for what it had taken. With very few natural resources, Kiribati has a limited economy. However, it grows enough food to support its citizens without imports.

Laos

Capital	Vientiane
Land Area	89,112 sq mi; 230,800 sq km
Population	5.8 million
Ethnic Group(s)	Lao Loum, Lao Theung, Lao Soung, Vietnamese, East Asian
Religion(s)	Buddhist, traditional beliefs
Government	communist state
Currency	new kip
Leading Exports	wood products, clothing, electricity, coffee, tin
Language(s)	Lao (official), Mon-Khmer, Yao, Vietnamese, Chinese, French

Laos (LAH ohs) is a landlocked Communist country in Southeast Asia bordered by Vietnam, Cambodia, Thailand, Myanmar, and China. After six hundred years as a monarchy, Laos became a communist nation in 1975. The country has many mineral resources and produces large amounts of coffee and timber. Still, it is one of the world's least developed countries and depends on foreign aid. Laotians are mostly Buddhists. The majority of the population lives in rural areas and works in farming.

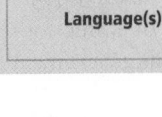

Malaysia

Capital	Kuala Lumpur and Putrajaya
Land Area	126,853 sq mi; 328,550 sq km
Population	22.7 million
Ethnic Group(s)	Malay, East Asian, indigenous tribes, South Asian
Religion(s)	Muslim, Buddhist, traditional beliefs, Hindu, Christian
Government	constitutional monarchy
Currency	ringgit
Leading Exports	electronic equipment, petroleum and liquefied natural gas, wood
Language(s)	Bahasa Malaysia (official), Malay, Chinese, Tamil, English

Malaysia (muh LAY zhuh) consists of a peninsula and the northern third of the island of Borneo in the South China Sea. It shares borders with Thailand, Indonesia, Singapore, and Brunei. The country, made up of parts of former British colonies, was formed in 1963. Although Malaysia is considered a developing country, its economy was one of the fastest growing in the world from 1987 to 1997. The Asian financial crash of 1997 slowed but did not stop this growth. Malaysia exports large amounts of oil, natural gas, and palm oil.

Chapter 26 **789**

- Ask **Which country on pp. 788–789 is ruled by a Communist government?** *(Laos)* **What type of government did this country have previously?** *(a monarchy)*

- Discuss the relationship between Great Britain and Kiribati. *(Kiribati was once a British colony called the Gilbert Islands. Great Britain mined Kiribati's phosphates, which eventually ran out. Kiribati has been able to win some payment from Great Britain for what it has taken. Great Britain's influence on Kiribati is also reflected in Kiribati's official language—English.)*

- Have students identify the similarities between Malaysia and Kiribati, using both the data and the paragraphs beside them. *(Both were British colonies; both have people who are Muslim and people who practice traditional beliefs.)*

Differentiated Instruction

For Advanced Readers L3

Have students choose two of the countries found on pp. 788–789. Tell them to use the DK World Desk Reference Online to make information cards similar to the ones in the Country Databank using different statistics, such as the percentage of people living in rural and urban areas and literacy rates. Ask them to use the same types of statistics for both countries. Then have them write a short paragraph explaining the similarities and differences between the countries based on what they found.

Guided Instruction (continued)

- Ask students **What do the Marshall Islands, Nauru, and Palau have in common?** *(Possible answer: They are all tiny island nations with under 100,000 citizens.)* **How is Nauru different from the other two nations?** *(Possible answer: Nauru, made up of one small island, is the smallest independent republic in the world. Unlike the Marshall Islands and Palau, its economy is not supported by financial aid from the United Nations or the United States.)*

- Point out that Nauru has only one leading export—phosphates. Discuss the potential problems Nauru could face by relying heavily on this one export. *(Possible answers: The country's economy is sensitive to world phosphate prices—when prices are down, the country's economy will suffer. When phosphates run out, Nauru will need another major industry to keep the economy strong.)*

Introducing Southeast Asia and the Pacific Region

Marshall Islands

Capital	Majuro
Land Area	70 sq mi; 181.3 sq km
Population	73,360
Ethnic Group(s)	Micronesian
Religion(s)	Christian
Government	constitutional government in free association with the United States
Currency	U.S. dollar
Leading Exports	copra (dried coconut), coconut oil, handicrafts
Language(s)	English (official), Marshallese (official), Japanese, German

The Marshall Islands (MAHR shul EYE lundz) is a group of 34 islands in the North Pacific Ocean. Once under United States control, the Marshall Islands became independent in 1986. The island nation maintains ties to the United States and heavily depends on it for economic support. The money the United States provides the islands makes up almost two thirds of its total income. The Marshall Islands faces ongoing problems of few natural resources, high unemployment, and poverty.

Myanmar

Capital	Rangoon
Land Area	253,953 sq mi; 657,740 sq km
Population	42.2 million
Ethnic Group(s)	Burman, Shan, Karen, Rakhine, East Asian, South Asian, Mon
Religion(s)	Buddhist, Christian, Muslim, traditional beliefs
Government	military regime
Currency	kyat
Leading Exports	clothing, food, wood products, precious stones
Language(s)	Burmese (Myanmar) (official), Karen, Shan, Chin, Kachin, Mon, Palaung, Wa

Myanmar (MYUN mahr), also known as Burma, is a Southeast Asian nation bordered by Thailand, China, India, the Andaman Sea, and the Bay of Bengal. There are mountains in the north, but the fertile Irrawaddy basin dominates the rest of the country. Myanmar is rich in natural resources, and its economy is mainly agricultural. Once a British colony, Myanmar gained its independence in 1948. Since that time, it has had a history of ethnic conflict and political instability. Today, its government is run by the military.

Nauru

Capital	Yaren District
Land Area	8 sq mi; 21 sq km
Population	12,329
Ethnic Group(s)	Nauruan, Pacific Islanders, East Asian, white
Religion(s)	Protestant, Roman Catholic
Government	republic
Currency	Australian dollar
Leading Exports	phosphate
Language(s)	Nauruan (official), Kiribati, Chinese, Tuvaluan, English

Nauru (nah OO roo) is an island in the South Pacific Ocean. The world's smallest independent republic, Nauru was once a German and then a British colony. It gained its independence in 1968. For decades, the United Kingdom, New Zealand, and Australia mined Nauru for its phosphate. The income from phosphate, Nauru's only export, has made its people very wealthy. However, mining activities caused great environmental damage. With phosphate mining expected to run out, Nauru faces the great challenge of keeping its economy from collapsing.

790 Asia and the Pacific

Differentiated Instruction

For Special Needs Students L1

Distribute *Outline Map 30: Southeast Asia* and *Outline Map 32: The Pacific Islands*. As you read about each country in Southeast Asia and the Pacific Region as a class, have students fill in the name of the country on their outline map. Refer them to the map on p. 785 if they need guidance.

All in One **Asia and the Pacific Teaching Resources**, *Outline Map 30: Southeast Asia*, p. 442; *Outline Map 32: The Pacific Islands*, p. 443

Sea kayaks in Milford Sound in Fiordland National Park, New Zealand

New Zealand

Capital	Wellington
Land Area	103,737 sq mi; 268,680 sq km
Population	3.8 million
Ethnic Group(s)	white, Maori, Pacific Islander, Asian
Religion(s)	Protestant, Roman Catholic
Government	parliamentary democracy
Currency	New Zealand dollar
Leading Exports	dairy products, meat, wood and wood products, fish, machinery
Language(s)	English (official), Maori (official)

New Zealand (noo ZEE lund) is made up of two large islands and a number of smaller islands in the South Pacific Ocean. It lies about 1,000 miles southeast of Australia. Settled by the Polynesian Maori in about A.D. 800, New Zealand became a British colony during the 1800s and an independent nation in 1907. New Zealand's economy is based on agricultural exports—particularly butter and wool—as well as manufacturing. New Zealand has some of the world's most varied scenery, and tourism is an important industry.

Palau

Capital	Koror
Land Area	177 sq mi; 458 sq km
Population	19,409
Ethnic Group(s)	Palauan, Asian, white
Religion(s)	Christian, traditional beliefs
Government	constitutional government in free association with the United States
Currency	U.S. dollar
Leading Exports	shellfish, tuna, copra, clothing
Language(s)	Palauan (official), English (official), Japanese, Angaur, Tobi, Sonsorolese

Palau (pah LOW) is an archipelago made up of several hundred islands in the North Pacific Ocean southeast of the Philippines. Palau, once governed by the United States and the United Nations, became independent in 1994. It is now a constitutional democracy but maintains close ties to the United States and relies on it for financial aid. Its economy is developing and is primarily agricultural, with a growing tourism industry.

Chapter 26 **791**

- Ask **Which country on this page gained independence first?** *(New Zealand)* **Which country uses the United States dollar as its currency?** *(Palau)* Ask students to think of possible reasons why Palau uses the United States dollar as its currency. *(Palau only became independent from the United Nations and the United States in 1994, and still receives a great deal of financial aid from the United States.)*

- Have students study the leading exports of New Zealand and Palau. Then tell students to locate the countries on the map on p. 785. Ask **How are the locations of these countries reflected in their economies?** *(Both countries are made up of islands, and the export of ocean animals is a key part of each country's economy—fish is a leading export for New Zealand, and shellfish and tuna are leading exports for Palau.)*

Guided Instruction (continued)

- Ask **Which countries on pp. 792–793 have English as an official language?** *(Papua New Guinea, the Philippines, Samoa, Singapore, and the Solomon Islands—every country but Thailand)* **Why might Thailand not have a European language as an official language?** *(Possible answer: Thailand was never taken over by a European power.)*

- **Which country is an important Asian trading port?** *(Singapore)* **How do you think this affects its economy?** *(Possible answer: It probably helps Singapore's economy thrive.)*

- Ask students to compare and contrast the religions of the Philippines and Samoa. *(Protestantism and Roman Catholicism are practiced in both countries but Buddhists and Muslims are listed only for the Philippines.)* Tell students to identify additional similarities between the two countries. *(English is an official language for both; both are island nations.)* Ask students to look at the locations of the Philippines and Samoa on the map on p. 785. Then ask students if they are surprised by the number of similarities the two countries share. *(Answers will vary. Students may say they are surprised because the two island nations are quite far apart, or that they are not surprised because being in the same region may have caused the two countries to have similar climates and histories.)*

Introducing Southeast Asia and the Pacific Region

Papua New Guinea

Capital	Port Moresby
Land Area	174,849 sq mi; 452,860 sq km
Population	5.2 million
Ethnic Group(s)	Melanesian, Papuan, Negrito, Micronesian, Polynesian
Religion(s)	Protestant, Roman Catholic, traditional beliefs
Government	constitutional monarchy with parliamentary democracy
Currency	kina
Leading Exports	oil, gold, copper ore, logs, palm oil, coffee, cocoa, crayfish, prawns
Language(s)	English (official), Pidgin English, Papuan, Motu, around 750 native languages

Papua New Guinea (pap YOO uh noo GIH nee) is a group of islands—including the eastern half of the island of New Guinea—located between the Coral Sea and the South Pacific Ocean. Papua New Guinea became independent from Australia in 1975. Since then, its political situation has been somewhat unstable due to conflicts between many political parties. Papua New Guinea's people are extraordinarily diverse, with around 750 different languages spoken there. Its economy is mainly agricultural, though it has significant mineral and oil resources as well. A gas pipeline between Papua New Guinea and Australia is expected to bring in almost $220 million per year.

Philippines

Capital	Manila
Land Area	115,123 sq mi; 298,170 sq km
Population	84.5 million
Ethnic Group(s)	Malay, East Asian
Religion(s)	Roman Catholic, Protestant, Muslim, Buddhist
Government	republic
Currency	Philippine peso
Leading Exports	electronic equipment, machinery and transport equipment
Language(s)	English (official), Filipino (official), Tagalog, Cebuano, Hiligaynon, Samaran, Ilocano, Bikol

The Philippines (FIL uh peenz) is an island nation in the western Pacific Ocean, between the Philippine Sea and the South China Sea. It consists of more than 7,000 islands, about 1,000 of which are inhabited. The Philippines became independent from the United States in 1946. Since that time, it has suffered a troubled political history, including dictatorships. The Philippines has more than 100 ethnic groups and is the only Christian nation in Southeast Asia. It has large mineral deposits that have not been fully developed.

Samoa

Capital	Apia
Land Area	1,133 sq mi; 2,934 sq km
Population	178,631
Ethnic Group(s)	Samoan, mixed white and Polynesian, white
Religion(s)	Protestant, Roman Catholic
Government	constitutional monarchy
Currency	tala
Leading Exports	fish, coconut oil and cream, copra
Language(s)	Samoan (official), English (official)

Samoa (suh MOH uh) is a group of nine volcanic islands located in the South Pacific Ocean. Only four of the nine islands are inhabited, and more than 70 percent of the population lives on one island. Samoa became independent from New Zealand in 1962, when it established a democratic government. Samoa is one of the world's least developed countries and is dependent on foreign aid. However, its expanding manufacturing and tourism industries and increasing agricultural exports are helping its economy to grow.

792 Asia and the Pacific

Differentiated Instruction

For Less Proficient Readers   L1

Have students create a Venn diagram to show the similarities and differences between Papua New Guinea and New Zealand. Display the *Venn Diagram* transparency to show students how to sketch the graphic organizer. Circulate to make sure students are filling in the organizers correctly.

📖 **Asia and the Pacific Transparencies,** *Transparency B16: Venn Diagram*

Singapore

Capital	Singapore
Land Area	264 sq mi; 683 sq km
Population	4.5 million
Ethnic Group(s)	East Asian, Malay, South Asian
Religion(s)	Buddhist, Muslim, Christian, Hindu, traditional beliefs
Government	parliamentary republic
Currency	Singapore dollar
Leading Exports	machinery and equipment (including electronics), consumer goods, chemicals, mineral fuels
Language(s)	Malay (official), English (official), Mandarin (official), Tamil (official)

Singapore (SING uh pawr) is a group of islands located in Southeast Asia between Malaysia and Indonesia. Singapore was established as a British trading colony in 1819. It became independent in 1965. Singapore is currently one of the most important trading ports in Asia and one of the world's most prosperous countries. Ethnic Chinese make up about 80 percent of its population.

Solomon Islands

Capital	Honiara
Land Area	10,633 sq mi; 27,540 sq km
Population	494,786
Ethnic Group(s)	Melanesian, Polynesian, Micronesian, white, East Asian
Religion(s)	Protestant, Roman Catholic, traditional beliefs
Government	parliamentary democracy
Currency	Solomon Islands dollar
Leading Exports	timber, fish, copra, palm oil, cocoa
Language(s)	English (official), Pidgin English, Melanesian Pidgin

The Solomon Islands (SAHL uh mun EYE lundz) is a group of islands in the South Pacific Ocean east of Papua New Guinea. The Solomons are an archipelago of several hundred islands spread over 250,000 square miles. Most are coral reefs, and the majority of the population lives on the six largest islands. The Solomon Islands have been settled for thousands of years. In 1978, the island nation achieved independence from the United Kingdom. However, ethnic conflict and a high crime rate have caused instability and weakened the economy in recent years.

Thailand

Capital	Bangkok
Land Area	197,594 sq mi; 511,770 sq km
Population	62.5 million
Ethnic Group(s)	Thai, East Asian
Religion(s)	Buddhist, Muslim, Christian, Hindu
Government	constitutional monarchy
Currency	baht
Leading Exports	computers, transistors, seafood, clothing, rice
Language(s)	Thai (official), Chinese, Malay, Khmer, Karen, Miao

Thailand (TY land) is located in Southeast Asia, between the Andaman Sea and the Gulf of Thailand. It is bordered by Laos, Cambodia, Myanmar, and Malaysia. Thailand's central plain is fertile and densely populated. The country has enjoyed rapid economic growth in recent decades. However, this growth has used up many of its natural resources and strained its water supplies. Thailand, once called Siam, is the only Southeast Asian country that has never been taken over by a European power. It is now a constitutional monarchy.

Chapter 26 **793**

Guided Instruction (continued)

- Ask students to list the countries on pp. 792–793 in order from largest to smallest population. *(Philippines, Thailand, Papua New Guinea, Singapore, Solomon Islands, Samoa)*

- Have students compare and contrast Singapore and Thailand. *(Similarities: East Asians live in both countries; Buddhists, Christians, Hindus, and Muslims live in both countries; both have growing economies. Differences: land area, population, other ethnic groups, government, currency, leading exports, official language, and Singapore was once a colony while Thailand was not)*

Differentiated Instruction

For Gifted and Talented [L3]

Direct students' attention to the populations and land areas of the Philippines, Singapore, and Thailand. Then have them note the relative size of these countries by locating them on the map on p. 785. Point out that in these countries, a large number of people live on a small amount of land. Ask students to find the population density of each country by dividing the number of people by the area of the land. Ask them to make a table listing the countries and their population densities in order from highest to lowest.

Guided Instruction (continued)

- Ask students to identify the similarities among the countries on p. 794. *(All have English as an official language; all are island nations located in the South Pacific Ocean; agriculture is important to all three countries.)* Ask students **From what unusual source does Tuvalu gain about $50 million a year?** *(from leasing out its Internet domain name ".tv")*

- Ask students to create a timeline illustrating the brief history of Vietnam described on p. 795. Display the *Timeline Transparency* to help students set up their timelines.

  Asia and the Pacific Transparencies, *Transparency B20: Timeline*

Independent Practice

Have students use the information in the Country Databank to create a chart showing the year each island country in this region gained its independence, and what country the island nation broke away from. Tell them to do research on the Internet if they need more information to fill in their charts.

Monitor Progress

Circulate to be sure students are creating charts with one column for each country's name, one for its date of independence, and a third for the parent country. Provide assistance as needed.

Introducing Southeast Asia and the Pacific Region

Tonga

Capital	Nuku'alofa
Land Area	277 sq mi; 718 sq km
Population	106,137
Ethnic Group(s)	Polynesian, white
Religion(s)	Christian
Government	hereditary constitutional monarchy
Currency	pa'anga (Tongan dollar)
Leading Exports	squash, fish, vanilla beans, root crops
Language(s)	Tongan (official), English (official)

Tonga (TAHNG guh) is an archipelago of 170 islands located in the South Pacific Ocean northeast of New Zealand. Tonga's economy is based on agriculture and tourism but depends heavily on foreign aid. The country also imports much of its food. Tonga remains the only monarchy in the Pacific region and its king controls the nation's politics, despite calls in recent years for greater democracy.

Tuvalu

Capital	Fongafale
Land Area	10 sq mi; 26 sq km
Population	10,800
Ethnic Group(s)	Polynesian, Micronesian
Religion(s)	Protestant, traditional beliefs
Government	constitutional monarchy with a parliamentary democracy
Currency	Australian dollar and Tuvaluan dollar
Leading Exports	copra, fish
Language(s)	English (official), Tuvaluan, Kiribati

Tuvalu (too vuh LOO) is a tiny island group located in the South Pacific Ocean. It lies about halfway between Hawaii and Australia, or about 650 miles north of Fiji. Tuvalu has a total land area of about 10 square miles (26 square kilometers). Tuvalu was part of a British colony until its independence in 1978. Tuvalu's economy is based mainly on subsistence farming and fishing. However, the tiny nation also gets about $50 million per year from leasing out its Internet domain name ".tv."

Vanuatu

Capital	Port-Vila
Land Area	4,710 sq mi; 12,200 sq km
Population	196,178
Ethnic Group(s)	Melanesian, white, Southeast Asian, East Asian, Pacific Islander
Religion(s)	Protestant, Roman Catholic, traditional beliefs
Government	parliamentary republic
Currency	vatu
Leading Exports	copra, kava, beef, cocoa, timber, coffee
Language(s)	Bislama (official), English (official), French (official)

Vanuatu (van wah TOO) is a small island nation located in the South Pacific Ocean. It lies about three quarters of the way from Hawaii to Australia, or about 500 miles west of Fiji. Vanuatu is an archipelago of 80 volcanic islands spread over about 450 miles. However, only about 12 of the islands are of any size. Vanuatu was once called the New Hebrides. The islands were settled in the 1800s and ruled jointly by Great Britain and France from 1906. In 1980, Vanuatu became an independent republic. The economy is based primarily on agriculture and fishing.

794 Asia and the Pacific

⌐ Background: Links Across Time ¬

The Trung Sisters Just as Ho Chi Minh City is named after a famous leader, so too is one of the city's streets. Prior to France's rule, China ruled Vietnam for some 1,000 years. The Vietnamese were discontent under Chinese rule, however. In the years 39 and 40, two Vietnamese sisters, Trung Trac and Trung Nhi, led a Vietnamese army in freeing 65 towns from Chinese rule. They established an independent state, declared themselves queens, and ruled for over three years. Although the Chinese eventually crushed the independent nation, the Vietnamese continue to honor the Trung sisters with the street in Ho Chi Minh City named for them.

Vietnam

Capital	Hanoi
Land Area	125,621 sq mi; 325,360 sq km
Population	81.1 million
Ethnic Group(s)	Vietnamese, East Asian, Hmong, Thai, Khmer, Cham
Religion(s)	Buddhist, Christian, traditional beliefs, Muslim
Government	communist state
Currency	dông
Leading Exports	crude oil, marine products, rice, coffee, rubber, tea, clothing, shoes
Language(s)	Vietnamese (official), Chinese, Thai, Khmer, Muong, Nung, Miao, Yao, Jarai

SOURCES: DK World Desk Reference Online; CIA World Factbook Online; *World Almanac*, 2003

Vietnam (vee et NAHM) is located along the eastern coast of the Indochinese peninsula in the South China Sea. France occupied Vietnam during the late 1800s. France continued to rule until 1954, when Communist forces under leader Ho Chi Minh defeated the French and took over the northern part of the country. The United States then helped South Vietnam resist Communist rule by fighting the North Vietnamese in the Vietnam War. The United States withdrew its military forces in 1973, and all of Vietnam was united under Communist rule. Still recovering from years of war, the government has allowed some private enterprise to strengthen its weak economy.

A woman weaves in a village in Vietnam. Most people in Vietnam live in rural areas.

Assessment

Comprehension and Critical Thinking

1. Name Name two Southeast Asian countries that are island nations.

2. Draw Conclusions What are the characteristics that most of the countries share?

3. Contrast What are some key differences among the countries?

4. Categorize Which countries in the region have monarchies?

5. Contrast How are the governments of Laos and Vietnam different from those of the other countries in the region?

6. Make a Bar Graph Create a bar graph showing the land area of the five most populous countries in this region.

Keeping Current

Access the **DK World Desk Reference Online** at **PHSchool.com** for up-to-date information about all the countries in this chapter.

Go Online
PHSchool.com

Web Code: lce-6900

Assess and Reteach

Assess Progress [L2]

Direct students' attention back to the concept webs they made before they began studying the Country Databank. Tell them to make a similar web using some of the information they learned from the Country Databank, such as a concept web about the economy of New Zealand.

Reteach [L1]

To review information from the Country Databank, have each student write ten questions and answers about Southeast Asia and the Pacific Region. Collect students' questions and form the class into two teams. Use the students' questions to quiz each team alternately. Give one point for each question the teams answer correctly. If neither team can answer a certain question, allow them to use their textbooks to find the answer.

Extend [L3]

Portfolio Activity

Have students choose two countries in the Country Databank. Ask them to do library or Internet research to learn more about each country. Then have them write a short essay or create a table to explain the similarities and differences between the two countries. Have students add their work to their portfolios.

Assessment

1. Two of the following: Brunei, East Timor, Indonesia, Palau, Philippines, and Singapore

2. Most are island nations that were once colonized by another country.

3. land area, population size, ethnic groups, religions, governments, leading exports, official languages

4. Cambodia, Malaysia, Papua New Guinea, Samoa, Thailand, Tonga, Tuvalu

5. Laos and Vietnam are the only Communist states in the region.

6. Students' bar graphs should include the land areas of the following countries: Indonesia, Myanmar, Philippines, Thailand, and Vietnam. Use *Rubric for Assessing a Bar Graph* to evaluate students' graphs.

All in One Asia and the Pacific Teaching Resources, *Rubric for Assessing a Bar Graph,* p. 449

Section 1
Step-by-Step Instruction

Objectives

Social Studies

1. Find out how Vietnam was divided by conflicts and war.
2. Learn how Vietnam has rebuilt its economy.

Reading/Language Arts

Find the main idea to identify what a paragraph is about.

Prepare to Read

Build Background Knowledge L2

Tell students that in this section they will learn about the conflicts that divided Vietnam. Ask them to recall what they learned about the governments of the Koreas in Chapter 24. Explain that, like the Koreas, Vietnam also had different types of governments in the north and south and this was one cause of conflicts between the two regions.

Set a Purpose for Reading L2

- Preview the Objectives.

- Form students into pairs or groups of four. Distribute the *Reading Readiness Guide*. Ask the students to fill in the first two columns of the chart. Use the Numbered Heads participation strategy (TE, p. T36) to call on students to share one piece of information they already know and one piece of information they want to know.

  All in One **Asia and the Pacific Teaching Resources,** *Reading Readiness Guide,* p. 424

Vocabulary Builder
Preview Key Terms

Pronounce the Key Term, then ask the students to say the word with you. Provide a simple explanation such as, "The civil war between the northern and southern states of the United States took place between 1861 and 1865."

Vietnam
A Nation Rebuilds

Prepare to Read

Objectives

In this section you will
1. Find out how Vietnam was divided by conflicts and war.
2. Learn how Vietnam has rebuilt its economy.

Taking Notes

As you read this section, look for details about how Vietnam has developed since the Vietnam War. Copy the diagram below and record your findings in it.

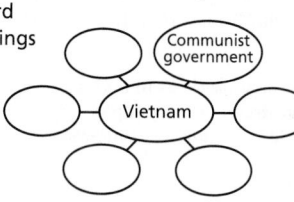

Target Reading Skill

Identify Main Idea The main idea of a paragraph tells what the whole paragraph is about. On page 800, the main idea of the paragraph with the heading Rebirth in Ho Chi Minh City is "Vietnam's greatest successes have been in rebuilding its cities." As you read this section, identify the main idea of each paragraph that follows a blue heading.

Key Terms

- **civil war** (SIV ul wawr) *n.* a war between political parties or regions within the same country
- **domino theory** (DAHM uh noh THEE uh ree) *n.* a belief that if one country fell to communism, neighboring nations would also fall, like a row of dominoes

New industries in Vietnam

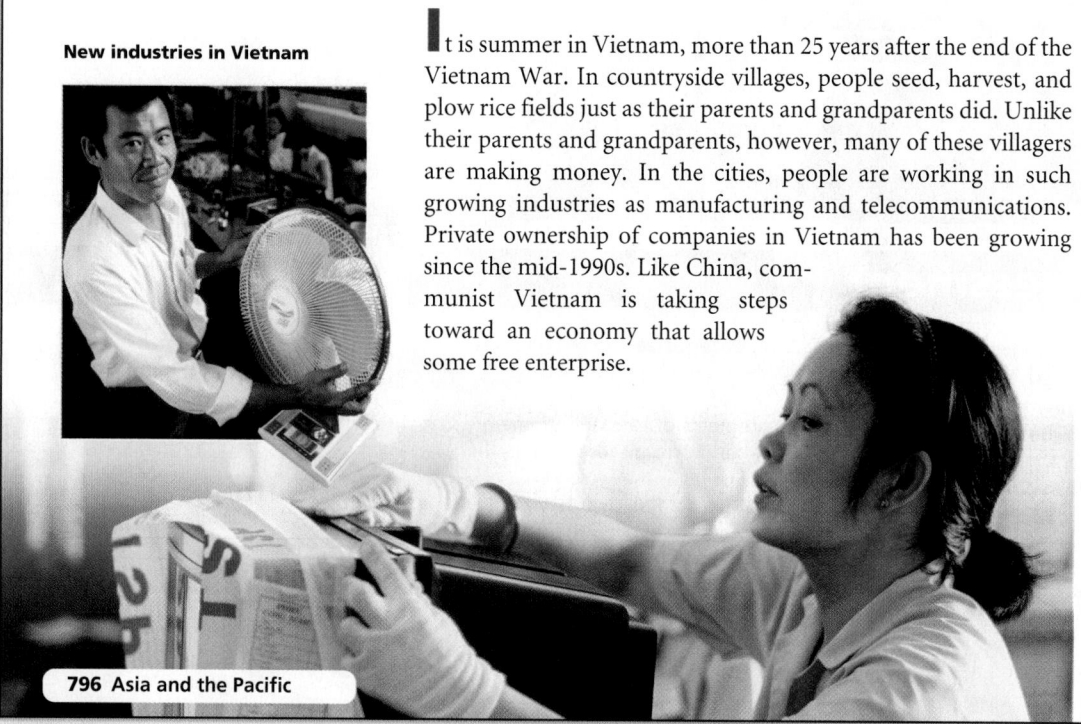

It is summer in Vietnam, more than 25 years after the end of the Vietnam War. In countryside villages, people seed, harvest, and plow rice fields just as their parents and grandparents did. Unlike their parents and grandparents, however, many of these villagers are making money. In the cities, people are working in such growing industries as manufacturing and telecommunications. Private ownership of companies in Vietnam has been growing since the mid-1990s. Like China, communist Vietnam is taking steps toward an economy that allows some free enterprise.

796 Asia and the Pacific

Target Reading Skill L2

Identify Main Idea Point out the Target Reading Skill. Tell students that the main idea of a paragraph is the central point of the whole paragraph.

Model the skill by reading the first paragraph on p. 797 aloud and stating the main idea. *(The people of Vietnam have survived a long period of conflict.)*

Give students *Identify Main Ideas*. Have them complete the activity in groups.

All in One **Asia and the Pacific Teaching Resources,** *Identify Main Ideas,* p. 431

Decades of Conflict and War L2

Guided Instruction

- **Vocabulary Builder** Clarify the high-use words **reunite** and **achieve** before reading.

- Read about the struggle between the people of North and South Vietnam in Decades of Conflict and War, using the Paragraph Shrinking reading strategy (TE p. T34).

- Have students briefly describe the two conflicts that took place in Vietnam following World War II. (*First, the Vietnamese fought the French for independence. Then, North and South Vietnam fought because the Communist north was trying to unite the two regions under communism.*)

- Ask students **How was Vietnam divided after the French were defeated?** (*A treaty divided Vietnam into northern and southern parts.*)

- Ask students to infer why the United States sent troops to South Vietnam. (*Possible answers: It wanted to prevent North Vietnam from reuniting the country under a Communist government; it wanted South Vietnam to become a democratic nation.*)

- Ask students **How did the conflict in Vietnam spread to Cambodia and Laos?** (*The conflict spread to Cambodia and Laos because the United States and South Vietnam wanted to stop the Viet Cong from getting supplies to its troops in South Vietnam. In 1970, the United States bombed the Ho Chi Minh trail, which went through Cambodia and Laos. In 1971, South Vietnamese troops attacked North Vietnamese bases in Laos.*)

Decades of Conflict and War

The people of Vietnam have survived a long period of conflict. First, an alliance of Communists and Nationalists in Vietnam fought against France from 1946 to 1954. Second, a civil war followed. A **civil war** is a war between political parties or regions within the same country. During the Vietnam War, North Vietnam fought South Vietnam and its ally, the United States.

Vietnam Divided After the French defeat in 1954, a treaty divided Vietnam into northern and southern parts. Communists controlled the northern half. A non-communist government supported by the United States ruled South Vietnam. The treaty said that, eventually, an election would be held to reunite the country under one government.

These elections were never held, largely because the United States and Ngo Dinh Diem (en GOH din dee EM), the leader of South Vietnam, feared that the Communists might win. At that time, U.S. leaders believed in the **domino theory**. They thought that a Communist victory would cause other countries in Southeast Asia to fall to communism, like a row of dominoes.

Meanwhile, the Communists were trying to take over the south by force. In 1959, they launched a war to achieve this goal. They were led by Communist leader Ho Chi Minh (hoh chee min). Ho Chi Minh's forces were called the Viet Cong.

Presidential Palace in Hanoi
The Presidential Palace is used as offices for Vietnam's government. The palace was built by the French and used as headquarters for the French government until 1954. Note the flag of Vietnam is displayed. **Analyze Images** *How are change and continuity shown in this photo?*

Vocabulary Builder

Use the information below to teach students this section's high-use words.

High-Use Word	Definition and Sample Sentence
reunite, p. 797	*v.* to bring together again The family members were **reunited** after not seeing each other for a year.
achieve, p. 797	*v.* to do or carry out successfully Dan **achieved** his goal of hitting five home runs this season.
devastate, p. 800	*v.* to destroy or ruin by violent action The town was **devastated** by the tornado's damaging winds.
strictly, p. 800	*adv.* inflexibly maintained Rules in the jail were **strictly** enforced.

Answer

Analyze Images The display of the Vietnam flag represents change while the French-style palace represents continuity.

Read the **Links to Art** on this page. Ask students to describe a water puppet show. *(A pond is used for the stage. The audience sits at the water's edge and watches as the puppeteer guides wooden puppets so that they look like they are wading in water.)*

Independent Practice

Assign *Guided Reading and Review.*

All in One **Asia and the Pacific Teaching Resources,** *Guided Reading and Review,* p. 425

Monitor Progress

As students work on *Guided Reading and Review,* circulate to make sure they are answering the questions correctly and provide assistance as needed.

U.S. troops taking part in a mission in South Vietnam in 1967

Links to Art

Water Puppets In Vietnam, a type of puppet theater uses a pond for a stage. Water puppet shows started centuries ago. In these shows, a puppeteer guides wooden figures so that they appear to wade through the water. The puppets are attached to rods and strings hidden underwater. Audiences sit at the water's edge. Stage settings of trees and clouds are also placed on the pond.

798 Asia and the Pacific

American Involvement in the Vietnam War Communist leader Ho Chi Minh wanted to unite Vietnam under northern rule. Operating from the north, he aided Communist forces in the south. As the Communists threatened South Vietnam, the United States took an active role. At first, the United States sent thousands of military advisors to help the South Vietnamese. Later, hundreds of thousands of American troops arrived. Through the 1960s, the United States sent more troops to Vietnam. By 1968, there were more than 500,000 U.S. troops in Vietnam.

By the early 1970s, Vietnam had been at war for more than 30 years. The fighting spread to neighboring Laos and Cambodia as well. North Vietnam sent supplies along the Ho Chi Minh Trail through Laos and Cambodia to its troops in South Vietnam. In 1970, the United States bombed the Ho Chi Minh Trail and then invaded Cambodia. In 1971, South Vietnamese troops attacked North Vietnamese bases in Laos.

As the fighting continued, American casualties increased. Millions of people in the United States were calling for an end to the war. In 1973, the United States finally ended its part in the war when the last American combat soldiers left South Vietnam. More than 3 million Americans had served in the Vietnam War. More than 58,000 American troops died in the war, and another 150,000 were seriously wounded.

✓ **Reading Check** **Why did North Vietnam launch a war against South Vietnam?**

 **Skills Mini Lesson**

Decision Making

1. Teach the skill by explaining the decision making steps: identify the problem, evaluate the options, choose the best option.

2. Help students practice the skill as a class by analyzing the following scenario:

Mae has been saving for six months to buy a new scooter. Before she buys the scooter, Mae's friends invite her to a concert. The concert tickets cost the same as the scooter.

3. Have students apply the skill by analyzing the decision the United States made to end its part in the Vietnam War.

Answer

✓ **Reading Check** North Vietnam wanted to create a unified Communist country.

Vietnam

Most people in Vietnam are ethnic Vietnamese, but Vietnam has more than 90 ethnic minorities. Ethnic Vietnamese live mainly in the lowlands of the north, the south, and a thin coastal strip. Fertile soils in the lowlands support a dense population, as you can see on the map. The largest minority, the ethnic Chinese, live mainly in lowland cities. Other minorities inhabit the rugged highlands, where farming is difficult and population densities are low.

Vietnam: Population Density

KEY

Persons per sq. mile	Persons per sq. kilometer
More than 3,119	More than 1,204
520–3,119	200–1,204
260–519	100–199
130–259	50–99
25–129	10–49
1–24	1–9

Urban Areas
⊙ 1,000,000–4,999,999
• 500,000–999,999
— National border

0 miles 300
0 kilometers 300
Lambert Conformal Conic

Ethnic Groups

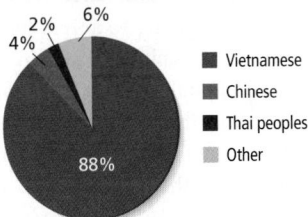

- 88% Vietnamese
- 4% Chinese
- 2% Thai peoples
- 6% Other

SOURCE: DK World Desk Reference

Peoples of Vietnam

Ethnic Group	Where They Live
Vietnamese	Coastal strip, lowlands, major cities
Chinese	Major cities, northern lowlands
Tai peoples	Northern highlands
Hmong peoples	Northern highlands
Other minorities	Northern and central highlands, border regions

SOURCE: Ethnologue

Map and Chart Skills

1. **Identify** What percentage of Vietnam's people are ethnically Vietnamese or Chinese?
2. **Describe** These groups live in the fertile lowlands, with more than 259 persons per square mile. Do these lowlands cover more than 50 percent of Vietnam's area?
3. **Analyze** How can you explain the difference between these percentages?

Use Web Code **Ice-6901** for **DK World Desk Reference Online.**

Chapter 26 Section 1 **799**

COUNTRY PROFILE
Focus on Culture

Guided Instruction   L2

Ask students to study the Country Profile on p. 799. As a class, answer the Map and Chart Skills questions. Allow students to briefly discuss their responses with a partner before sharing their answers.

Independent Practice

Have students create a map of Vietnam's ethnic groups. First, ask them to sketch a map of Vietnam on a separate piece of paper. Then, using the information on this page, have them fill in the names of Vietnam's ethnic groups in the appropriate areas on the map.

Answers

Map and Chart Skills

1. 92 percent
2. No, the lowlands do not cover more than 50 percent of Vietnam's area.
3. Possible answer: Vietnam probably contains a low percentage of non-Vietnamese ethnic groups because the country has undergone many years of conflict, causing few people to immigrate there.

Go Online PHSchool.com Students can find more information about this topic on the DK World Desk Reference Online.

Show students *The Extended Family in Vietnam.* Discuss how life is similar in the rural village and in the city of Hanoi. *(People in both places maintain their traditions and value their extended families.)*

After the Vietnam War L2

Guided Instruction

- **Vocabulary Builder** Clarify the high-use words **devastate** and **strictly** before reading.

- Read After the Vietnam War with students. Circulate to make sure that students can answer the Reading Check question.

- Ask students **What are some ways in which Vietnam is rebuilding its economy?** *(possible answers: by rebuilding cities, allowing some free enterprise, and attracting foreign investors)*

- Ask students to draw a conclusion about why Ho Chi Minh City is the most prosperous city in Vietnam. *(Possible answers: It is the center of trade; the many businesses there help stimulate the economy.)*

Independent Practice

Ask students to create the Taking Notes graphic organizer on a blank piece of paper. Then have them record details about changes in Vietnam since the Vietnam War. Use the *Concept Web Transparency* to demonstrate how to fill in the details.

📖 **Asia and the Pacific Transparencies,** *Transparency B17: Concept Web*

Monitor Progress

- Show *Section Reading Support Transparency AP 72* and ask students to check their graphic organizers individually. Go over key concepts as needed.

All in One **Asia and the Pacific Transparencies,** *Section Reading Support Transparency AP 72*

- Tell students to fill in the last column of the *Reading Readiness Guide.* Ask them to evaluate if what they learned was what they expected to learn.

All in One **Asia and the Pacific Teaching Resources,** *Reading Readiness Guide, p. 424*

Learn about family life in urban and rural Vietnam.

Contruction projects reflect the spirit of change in Vietnam. Here, workers lay a foundation for a new building in Ho Chi Minh City.

800 Asia and the Pacific

After the Vietnam War

After the United States pulled out its troops, North Vietnam conquered South Vietnam in 1975. In 1976, the country was reunited under a communist government. Vietnam had been devastated by the war. More than a million Vietnamese had been killed or wounded. Homes, farms, factories, and forests had been destroyed. Bombs had torn cities apart. Fields were covered with land mines, or hidden explosives. The Vietnamese people were worn out. Still ahead was the huge effort of rebuilding.

The Vietnamese Rebuild In the years after the war, the communist government in Vietnam strictly controlled the lives of its citizens. As time passed, however, it was clear that the economy was not growing. Like the Chinese, the Vietnamese had to adapt their approach to economic growth. Although it is still a communist country, Vietnam now allows some free enterprise. This has helped many Vietnamese improve their lives.

Most Vietnamese live in rural areas. In spite of some progress, these areas remain poor. Whole families live on a few hundred dollars a year. Most houses have no indoor toilets or running water. Children suffer from a lack of healthy food. Vietnam is still among the poorest nations in Asia.

Rebirth in Ho Chi Minh City Vietnam's greatest success has been in rebuilding its cities. Hanoi in the north is the capital. The city of Saigon (sy GAHN), in the south, was renamed Ho Chi Minh City after the Communist leader. It is the most prosperous city in Vietnam and is the center of trade. Americans who visit Ho Chi Minh City today find some of the same things they would find at home, such as American-style ice cream and cable news networks on television.

Some Vietnamese who live in the city enjoy greater prosperity. They buy designer clothing and watches, stereo systems, video recorders, and jewelry. Many of these people run restaurants or hotels, buy and sell land or buildings, or own factories, all of which help stimulate Vietnam's economy.

Differentiated Instruction

For Special Needs Students L1
Before reading, give students a paper copy of *Section Reading Support Transparency AP 72.* Tell them to check off each piece of information as they read the section.

📖 **Asia and the Pacific Transparencies,** *Section Reading Support Transparency AP 72*

For Less Proficient Readers L1
Pair less proficient readers with more able readers and have them create a timeline of the events in the section. Display the *Timeline Transparency* and fill in the first event with students to get them started.

📖 **Asia and the Pacific Transparencies,** *Transparency B20: Timeline*

A girl from the Hmong ethnic group (left) and a city shopper (inset) show rural and urban life in Vietnam.

Economic Recovery In 1986, Vietnam's government began an economic recovery program aimed chiefly at attracting foreign investors. As a result, Vietnam became one of the fastest-growing economies in the world. From 1990 to 1997, the economy grew each year by an average of about 8 percent. Agricultural output doubled, turning Vietnam from a country once dependent on food imports to the world's second-largest exporter of rice. Government-led reforms have helped modernize the economy and promote economic growth in the 2000s. After committing to trade agreements with other countries, including the United States, Vietnam's exports have greatly increased.

Identify Main Ideas Which sentence states the main idea in the paragraph on this page?

✓ **Reading Check** Which city in Vietnam is the most prosperous and the nation's center of trade?

Section 1 Assessment

Key Terms
Review the key terms at the beginning of this section. Use each term in a sentence that explains its meaning.

Target Reading Skill
Write the main idea of each paragraph that follows a blue heading in this section.

Comprehension and Critical Thinking
1. (a) **Recall** When did the United States withdraw from the Vietnam War?

(b) **Summarize** What conflicts have divided Vietnam since the end of World War II?
2. (a) **Describe** Describe conditions in Vietnam when the Vietnam War ended.
(b) **Make Generalizations** What successes has Vietnam had in rebuilding its economy?
(c) **Identify Point of View** Why do you think Saigon was renamed Ho Chi Minh City after the Vietnam War?

Writing Activity
Write a summary that describes Vietnam since the Vietnam War. Use this title for your summary: Vietnam: A Country, Not a War. Focus on the country's economic development.

> **Writing Tip** Be sure to look closely at the pictures and the Country Profile in this section to help you as you write your description.

Chapter 26 Section 1 **801**

Section 1 Assessment

Key Terms
Students' sentences should reflect knowledge of the Key Term.

Target Reading Skill
Vietnam Divided—After the French defeat in 1954, a treaty divided Vietnam into a northern part, run by a Communist government, and a southern part, run by a non-communist government. American Involvement in the Vietnam War—As Communists threatened

South Vietnam to unite the country under northern rule, the United States sent troops to help the South Vietnamese.

The Vietnamese Rebuild—In the years after the war, the Communist government strictly controlled the lives of its citizens but later loosened control to help the economy grow. Rebirth in Ho Chi Minh City—Vietnam's greatest successes have been in rebuilding its cities, such as Hanoi and Ho Chi Minh City. Economic Recovery—Vietnam's economy became one of the fastest-growing economies in the world.

Identify Main Idea As a follow up, ask students to answer the Target Reading Skill question in the Student Edition. (*As a result, Vietnam's economy became one of the fastest-growing economies in the world.*)

Assess and Reteach

Assess Progress L2
Have students complete the Section Assessment. Administer the *Section Quiz*.

All in One **Asia and the Pacific Teaching Resources,** *Section Quiz,* p. 426

Reteach L2
If students need more instruction, have them read this section in the Reading and Vocabulary Study Guide.

Chapter 26, Section 1, **Eastern Hemisphere Reading and Vocabulary Study Guide,** pp. 276–278

Extend L3
Assign the *Small Group Activity* in which students will organize a tour of Vietnam.

All in One **Asia and the Pacific Teaching Resources,** *Small Group Activity: Touring Vietnam,* pp. 436–439

Answer

✓ **Reading Check** Ho Chi Minh City

Writing Activity
Use the *Rubric for Assessing a Writing Assignment* to evaluate students' summaries.

All in One **Asia and the Pacific Teaching Resources,** *Rubric for Assessing a Writing Assignment,* p. 450

Comprehension and Critical Thinking
1. (a) in 1973 (b) The Vietnamese first fought for independence from France. After the country was divided into North and South Vietnam, the two regions fought a long civil war.

2. (a) More than a million people had been killed or wounded; homes, farms, and factories were destroyed; cities were torn apart by bombs; land mines filled fields. (b) Ho Chi Minh City has become a prosperous center of trade; government-led reforms have helped modernize the economy and promote economic growth in the 2000s. (c) Possible answer: After the Communist North conquered South Vietnam, it probably wanted to change the name of the city to reflect the victory of the leader of the Communist forces.

Objective

Learn how to use a flowchart.

Prepare to Read

Build Background Knowledge L2

Tell students that in this lesson they will learn how to read a flowchart. Explain that flowcharts can show the order of events or steps in a clear way. Ask students to write down five steps explaining what they do when they get up in the morning. Tell them they will use this information to create a flowchart after they have completed the lesson.

Instruct

Using a Flowchart L2

Guided Instruction

■ Read the steps to using a flowchart. Summarize each step and write it on the board.

■ Practice the skill by using the steps on p. 803 to answer the questions about the flowchart on p. 802. Read the title of the flowchart (*Traditional Rice Farming*) and discuss what the flowchart shows (*the sequence of traditional rice farming*).

■ Direct students' attention to the first step in the chart and read it aloud. Then have students follow the arrows to each step with their finger as you read each step aloud.

■ Help students answer the questions in Step 3. (*Farmers build a rice paddy; farmers use water buffalo to plow and smooth out the paddy; four to six inches tall; when the rice turns from green to gold*)

Using a Flowchart

Rice is one of the most important crops in Vietnam. It is grown on almost 75 percent of all cultivated land. Most Vietnamese farmers live in the lowland and delta area. This area's wetlands and heavy rains make it perfect for growing rice.

Most Southeast Asian farmers grow rice the same way that their ancestors did thousands of years ago. They build shallow fields called paddies. They flood the paddies with water. They plant rice in seedling beds. Farmers transplant the rice seedlings in the paddies by hand. They also harvest the rice by hand.

You've just read a description of how rice is grown. But sometimes it is easier to figure out how something works by following the steps in a flowchart.

Traditional Rice Farming

Farmers build a rice paddy.

↓

The paddy is flooded with water.

↓

Farmers use water buffalo to plow and smooth out the paddy.

↓

Farmers prepare seedling beds alongside the paddy and plant rice seed in seedling beds.

↓

After seedlings are 4 to 6 inches tall, farmers transplant them into the paddy.

↓

Farmers weed, fertilize, and add water regularly to the paddy.

↓

When the rice turns from green to gold, it is harvested.

802 Asia and the Pacific

A flowchart shows the sequence of steps used to complete an activity. It shows the steps in the order they happen. Sometimes the steps are illustrated. A flowchart usually uses arrows to show how steps follow one another.

Learn the Skill

Here are the steps you will need to follow when you read a flowchart.

1 **Read the title.** Read the title first to find out what the flowchart is about. The title of the flowchart at the left is Traditional Rice Farming.

2 **Find the arrows.** The arrows will tell you the order in which you should read the chart. Find the beginning and start there.

3 **Read the flowchart carefully.** If there are illustrations, study them, but be sure to read the text next to them. Think about how one step leads to the next step. What are the connections? If there are no illustrations, try imagining each step to help you understand the sequence.

Independent Practice

Assign *Skills for Life* and have students complete it individually.

> **All in One** **Asia and the Pacific Teaching Resources,** *Skills for Life,* p. 435

Monitor Progress

As students are completing *Skills for Life,* circulate to make sure students are correctly applying the skill steps. Provide assistance as needed.

Practice the Skill

Use the steps and the flowchart on the previous page to practice reading a flowchart.

1. Read the title of the flowchart first. Explain what the flowchart will tell you.

2. Find the beginning of the chart. Identify the first step of the chart. Start there and follow the arrows through each step.

3. Now read the flowchart carefully. Your reading of the flowchart should help you understand the steps in traditional rice farming. Now answer these questions: What is the first step in traditional rice farming? What happens after the paddy is flooded with water? Where do the farmers prepare seedling beds? How tall are the rice seedlings when the farmers transplant them into the paddy? How do the farmers know when it is time to harvest the rice?

Traditional Rice Processing

Thresh, or beat, the rice plants to separate the rice husks from the plant.

↓

Dry the rice husks.

↓

Thresh the rice husks to remove the rice grains from the husks.

↓

Thresh the rice again to separate the husks from rice grains.

↓

Store the rice in a dry place.

Apply the Skill

Use the steps in this skill to read the flowchart above. What is the chart about? How are the rice husks separated from the plant? Why is the rice threshed three times?

Assess and Reteach

Assess Progress　L2

Ask students to do the Apply the Skill activity.

Reteach　L1

If students are having trouble applying the skill steps, have students reread Learn the Skill with a partner. Circulate to answer any questions they may have.

Extend　L3

Ask students to return to the list of steps they wrote in the Build Background Knowledge activity. Tell them to create a flowchart displaying these steps.

Differentiated Instruction

For Special Needs Students　L1
If students need further instruction, have them complete *Reading a Flowchart* with a partner.

All in One Asia and the Pacific Teaching Resources, *Reading a Flowchart*, p. 441

Answers
Apply the Skill

The flowchart shows the sequence of how traditional rice processing is performed; the rice husks are threshed or beaten; the first time to separate the rice husks from the plant, the second time to remove the rice grains from the husks, and the third time to separate the husks from the rice grains.

Section 2
Step-by-Step Instruction

Objectives

Social Studies

1. Learn about the major economic activities in Australia.
2. Find out how Aboriginal people in Australia are working to improve their lives.

Reading/Language Arts

Learn to identify which details support the main idea of a paragraph.

Prepare to Read

Build Background Knowledge `L2`

Ask students to think about what happened to Native American lands and ways of life when European settlers moved west across the United States. Tell them that in this section they will learn what happened when European settlers in Australia moved into Aboriginal lands in the 1800s. Ask them to make a list of predictions about what they think happened to the Aborigines based on what they know about Native Americans.

Set a Purpose for Reading `L2`

■ Preview the Objectives.

■ Form students into pairs or groups of four. Distribute the *Reading Readiness Guide*. Ask the students to fill in the first two columns of the chart. Use the Numbered Heads participation strategy (TE, p. T36) to call on students to share one piece of information they already know and one piece of information they want to know.

All in One Asia and the Pacific Teaching Resources, *Reading Readiness Guide,* p. 428

Vocabulary Builder
Preview Key Terms

Pronounce each Key Term, then ask the students to say the word with you. Provide a simple explanation such as, "Artesian wells are drilled in some deserts in order to bring water to the surface."

Section 2 Australia
A Pacific Rim Country

Prepare to Read

Objectives

In this section you will

1. Learn about the major economic activities in Australia.
2. Find out how Aboriginal people in Australia are working to improve their lives.

Taking Notes

Copy the diagram. As you read, record details about Australia's economy.

Target Reading Skill

Identify Supporting Details On page 806, look at the paragraph with the heading Ranching. The first sentence is the main idea. The rest of the sentences support the main idea. What details in this paragraph explain the part ranching plays in Australia's economy?

Key Terms

• **outback** (OWT bak) *n.* the dry land consisting of plains and plateaus that makes up much of central and western Australia
• **artesian well** (ahr TEE zhun wel) *n.* a well from which water flows under natural pressure without pumping

Michael Chang owns a successful trading company in Sydney, Australia's largest city. From his office in a modern glass skyscraper, he sometimes watches Sydney's busy harbor. What interests him most are the large cargo ships.

John Koeyers and his family own a huge cattle ranch in northwest Australia. He uses helicopters and trucks to round up the herds on his ranch. The Koeyers sell most of their cattle to companies in Asian nations.

Charlie Walkabout is director of Anangu Tours. Anangu Tours is owned and run by Aboriginal people. The company has won awards for its tours of Uluru, also known as Ayers Rock.

Sydney, Australia, has a beautiful and busy harbor.

804 Asia and the Pacific

Target Reading Skill `L2`

Identify Supporting Details Point out the Target Reading Skill. Tell students that the supporting details in a paragraph are the sentences that support the main idea.

Model the skill by identifying the details in the second paragraph under Aborigines: Improving Lives on p. 807 that support the main idea stated in the first sentence of the paragraph. *(Their schools now teach Aborigi-*

nal languages. Aborigines celebrate important events with ancestral songs and dances. Artists have strengthened culture by creating traditional Aboriginal paintings.)

Give students *Identify Supporting Details.* Have them complete the activity in groups.

All in One Asia and the Pacific Teaching Resources, *Identify Supporting Details,* p. 432

Economic Activities

Michael Chang, the Koeyers, and Charlie Walkabout are all Australians. The meaning of *Australian* has changed since Australia achieved independence. It is no longer "British." It now reflects the diversity of Australia's people. Today, Australia has close ties with other nations of the Pacific Rim. These nations border the Pacific Ocean. They include Japan, South Korea, China, and Taiwan. The United States is another major Pacific Rim nation. It is one of Australia's key trading partners. Australia's economy depends on trade with Pacific Rim countries.

Trade Michael Chang's trading company is just one of hundreds of companies that do business with Pacific Rim countries. He sends various products to many countries in Asia. Rancher John Koeyers is involved in trade, too. Large cargo ships transport his cattle to South Korea and Taiwan. Other cargo ships carry products such as Australian wool and meat to foreign markets. Cargo ships also carry Australia's minerals to Japan.

Farming It seems strange that farm products are an important export for Australia, because only about 7 percent of Australia's land is good for farming. Most of this land is in southeastern Australia and along the east coast. The country's few rivers are in those areas. Farmers use the river water to irrigate their crops. Australian farmers raise barley, oats, and sugar cane. However, their most valuable crop is wheat. Australia is one of the world's leading wheat growers and exporters.

Target Skill Identify Supporting Details
What details in this paragraph explain the meaning of the "Pacific Rim"?

Chapter 26 Section 2 **805**

Vocabulary Builder

Use the information below to teach students this section's high-use words.

High-Use Word	Definition and Sample Sentence
reflect p. 805	*v.* to show; make apparent Mr. Kim's large mansion **reflects** the extent of his wealth.
scarce, p. 807	*adj.* not plentiful Water is **scarce** in the desert.
conduct, p. 807	*v.* to lead Lee did a great job of **conducting** the orchestra in playing the song.
resolve, p. 808	*v.* to deal with successfully The plumber **resolved** the problem with our kitchen sink.

Target Reading Skill   L2

Identify Supporting Details As a follow up, ask students to answer the Target Reading Skill question in the Student Edition. *(These nations border the Pacific Ocean. They include Japan, South Korea, China, and Taiwan. The United States is another major Pacific Rim nation.)*

Instruct

Economic Activities   L2

Guided Instruction

- **Vocabulary Builder** Clarify the high-use words **reflect** and **scarce** before reading.

- Read Economic Activities using the Choral Reading strategy (TE, p. T34).

- Tell students to name five countries discussed in this section that are part of the Pacific Rim. *(Five of the following: Australia, Japan, South Korea, China, Taiwan, United States)* Ask **Why are Pacific Rim countries important to Australia's economy?** *(Australia's economy depends on trade with Pacific Rim countries.)*

- Ask students **What are two other important economic activities in Australia?** *(farming and ranching)*

- Ask **Why do you think grass is scarce on many cattle stations?** *(Possible answer: Many cattle stations are located in Australia's interior which is very hot and receives little rainfall, making it difficult for grass to grow.)*

Independent Practice

Ask students to create the Taking Notes graphic organizer on a blank piece of paper. Then have them fill in what they have learned about Australia's economic activities.

Monitor Progress

Show *Section Reading Support Transparency AP 73* and ask students to check their graphic organizers individually. Go over key concepts and clarify key vocabulary as needed.

📖 **Asia and the Pacific Transparencies**
Section Reading Support Transparency AP 73

Guided Instruction   L2

Ask students to study the Country Profile on this page. As a class, answer the Map and Chart Skills questions. Allow students to briefly discuss their responses with a partner before sharing answers.

Independent Practice

Ask students to use the information in the map and graph to write a brief paragraph summarizing the types of jobs people in urban areas of Australia have and those that people in rural areas have.

Ranching Ranching is another major part of Australia's economy. Australian sheep and cattle provide lamb, mutton, and beef for export. Australia is the world's leading wool producer. Most cattle and sheep are raised on large ranches called stations. Some of the largest stations are in the outback. The **outback** is the name Australians use for the dry land that makes up much of the central and western part of the country. Few people live on its plains and plateaus.

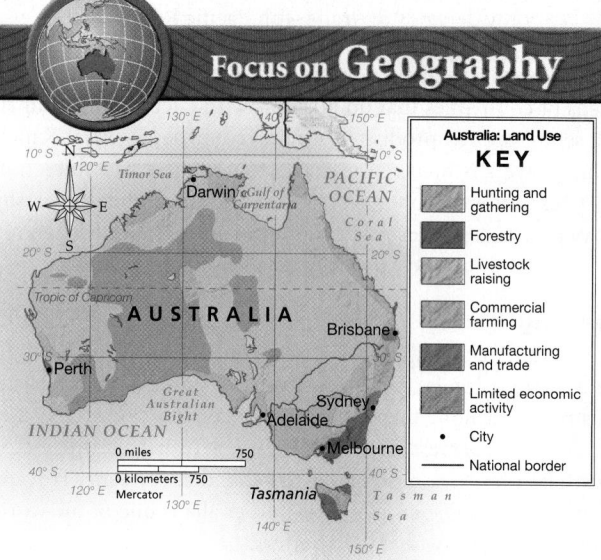

COUNTRY PROFILE   Focus on Geography

Australia

Australia is a large but thinly populated country. It covers about the same area as the United States, not including Alaska and Hawaii. But it has only about 20 million people, a smaller population than Texas. As the graph shows, most of its people live in urban areas. Australia's largest urban areas lie along its southeast coast. On the map, they are the areas labeled "manufacturing and trade." They cover only a very small part of the country. Much of the country consists of huge ranches and farms—labeled "livestock raising" and "commercial farming" on the map—and large deserts—labeled "limited economic activity." There are also forests in the southeast and aboriginal land, used for hunting and gathering, mainly in the north.

Australia: Land Use
KEY
- Hunting and gathering
- Forestry
- Livestock raising
- Commercial farming
- Manufacturing and trade
- Limited economic activity
- • City
- — National border

Urban and Rural Population

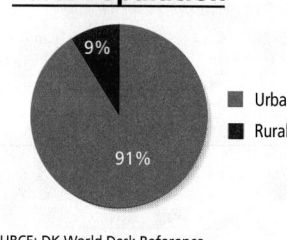

- Urban
- Rural

9%
91%

SOURCE: DK World Desk Reference

Map and Chart Skills

1. **Recall** Where do most Australians live?
2. **Infer** About how many people live in Australia's rural areas?
3. **Compare** How does Australia's population density compare with that of the United States?

Use Web Code **Ice-6902** for **DK World Desk Reference Online.**

Answers

Map and Chart Skills

1. in urban areas

2. almost 2 million

3. Australia has a lower population density than the United States.

Go Online PHSchool.com Students can find more information about this topic on the DK World Desk Reference Online.

Differentiated Instruction

For English Language Learners   L1

To reinforce section content and provide visual associations, have students study the maps, photos, and timeline in the Australia section of the *Passport to the World CD-ROM*.

🔘 *Australia,* **Passport to the World CD-ROM**

For example, the Koeyers' ranch is in a hot, dry area in northwest Australia. It covers 1 million acres (404,686 hectares) and has about 7,000 head of cattle. Another outback station, near Alice Springs in the center of Australia, is even larger. It covers nearly 12,000 square miles (31,080 square kilometers)—larger than the state of Maryland. Even with this much land, sometimes the cattle can barely find enough grass for grazing. Fresh water also is scarce. Rain falls rarely, and the region has only a few small streams. To supply water for their cattle, ranchers use underground **artesian wells**. These are wells from which water flows under natural pressure without pumping.

✓ Reading Check   **How does ranching help Australia's economy?**

Aborigines: Improving Lives

The people of Anangu Tours are proud of the awards they have won for their tours of Uluru. Aboriginal guides conduct the tours in their own language and an interpreter translates the words into English. Aboriginal people in Australia are working hard to preserve their culture. They are having a growing role in the economic life of the country.

Aboriginal leaders have worked to improve the lives of their people. Their schools now teach Aboriginal languages. Aborigines again celebrate important events with ancestral songs and dances. Artists have strengthened Aboriginal culture by creating traditional rock paintings and tree bark paintings.

British Heritage in Australia
The majority of Australians have a British ancestry. Australia's British heritage is shown in Australia's national flag, which includes the flag of the United Kingdom. Australia's flag also includes the Southern Cross, a constellation visible in the Southern Hemisphere. **Conclude** *Why is the Southern Cross an appropriate symbol for Australia?*

Aborigines: Improving Lives   L2

Guided Instruction

- **Vocabulary Builder** Clarify the high-use words **conduct** and **resolve** before reading.

- Have students read about how life is changing for Aboriginal people in Aborigines: Improving Lives. Circulate to make sure students can answer the Reading Check question.

- Discuss the ways in which Aborigines are working to improve the lives of their people. *(Aborigines teach their languages in schools; they celebrate important events with ancestral songs and dances; artists are strengthening Aboriginal culture by creating traditional paintings; Aboriginal leaders have influenced the government, which has begun building schools and hospitals and protects some sacred Aboriginal places.)*

- Ask students to make a generalization about why Aborigines believe it is important to regain ancestral lands. *(Possible answers: Some of the land is sacred; they want to preserve their way of life; they want to build strong Aboriginal communities.)*

Independent Practice
Assign *Guided Reading Review.*

All in One Asia and the Pacific Teaching Resources, *Guided Reading and Review*, p. 429

Monitor Progress
Tell students to fill in the last column of the *Reading Readiness Guide.* Probe for what they learned that confirms or invalidates each statement.

All in One Asia and the Pacific Teaching Resources, *Reading Readiness Guide*, p. 428

Differentiated Instruction

For Gifted and Talented   L3
Tell students to suppose that they are Aborigines living in Australia. Ask them to write a letter to a government official listing changes they believe are still needed. Give students *Writing a Letter* to get them started.

All in One Asia and the Pacific Teaching Resources, *Writing a Letter*, p. 447

For Advanced Readers   L3
Have students read *Family Council*, a memoir in which an Aborigine reflects on how family decisions were made within her family unit. Then have them answer the questions at the end of the selection.

All in One Asia and the Pacific Teaching Resources, *Family Council*, pp. 444–446

Answers

Conclude because Australia is located in the Southern Hemisphere

✓ Reading Check Australia exports products that come from ranches, such as wool, mutton, lamb, and beef.

Show students *Australia: A World of Its Own*. Ask **In what regions do Australians raise sheep?** (*in the grassy plains*)

Assess and Reteach

Assess Progress `L2`

Have students complete the Section Assessment. Administer the *Section Quiz*.

 Asia and the Pacific Teaching Resources, *Section Quiz,* p. 430

Reteach `L1`

If students need more instruction, have them read this section in the Reading and Vocabulary Study Guide.

📖 Chapter 26, Section 2, **Eastern Hemisphere Reading and Vocabulary Study Guide,** pp. 279–281

Extend `L3`

Have students complete *Enrichment* to learn more about Aborigine culture.

 Asia and the Pacific Teaching Resources, *Enrichment,* p. 434

Answers

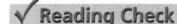 to regain ancestral land

Section 2 Assessment

Key Terms
Students' sentences should reflect knowledge of each Key Term.

⟳ **Target Reading Skill**
Australia exports lamb, mutton, and beef; Australia is the world's leading wool producer.

Comprehension and Critical Thinking
1. (a) the countries that border the Pacific Ocean, including Australia, South Korea, Japan, China, Taiwan, and the United States **(b)** These countries make up some of Australia's most accessible trading partners, since Australia is located far south in the Pacific Ocean.

2. (a) Two of the following: Aborigines teach their languages in schools; they celebrate important events with ancestral songs and dances; artists are strengthening Aboriginal culture by creating traditional paintings; Aborigine leaders have influenced the

---

Learn about the different regions of Australia.

Aboriginal leaders have helped their people in another important way, too. They have influenced the government of Australia. The government has begun to return Aboriginal land to them. The government has also built schools and hospitals on their land. It has begun to protect some of their sacred places as well.

Aborigines have gained more rights. But their main goal is to regain their ancestral lands. Though Australia's courts have helped, many ranchers and farmers now live on those lands. These people strongly oppose giving the land back. This issue may take many years to resolve.

✓ **Reading Check** What is a main goal for Aboriginal people in Australia?

Australian Aboriginal cave paintings date back thousands of years and are among the world's earliest art.

 **Section 2 Assessment**

Key Terms
Review the key terms at the beginning of this section. Use each term in a sentence that explains its meaning.

 Target Reading Skill
Find the text on ranching on page 806. What details support the information about ranching in Australia?

Comprehension and Critical Thinking
1. (a) Explain What is the Pacific Rim?

(b) Apply Information Based on what you know about Australia's location, explain why Australia's economy depends on trade with Pacific Rim countries.
2. (a) Recall Give two examples showing how Aboriginal people are working to improve their lives.
(b) Compare As the United States grew, Native Americans were forced from their homelands and moved to reservations. For years, Native Americans have been fighting to regain their original homelands. How does this compare with the history and struggle of the Aborigines?

Writing Activity
Use the information in this section and in the Country Profile on page 786 to write an article about Australia for a news magazine. The article should describe the main types of work people do in Australia.

Go Online
PHSchool.com

For: An activity about Australia
Visit: PHSchool.com
Web Code: lcd-6902

---

government, which has begun building schools and hospitals and has set aside some sacred Aboriginal places. **(b)** Native Americans and Aborigines have a similar history. They are both struggling to regain their homelands and maintain their cultures.

Writing Activity
Use the *Rubric for Assessing a Newspaper Article* to evaluate students' articles.

 **Asia and the Pacific Teaching Resources,** *Rubric for Assessing a Newspaper Article,* p. 451

Go Online
PHSchool.com Typing in the Web code when prompted will bring students directly to detailed instructions for this activity.

Review and Assessment

Review Chapter Content

- Review and revisit the major themes of this chapter by asking students to classify what Guiding Question each bulleted statement in the Chapter Summary answers. Form students into groups and ask them to complete the activity together. Refer to page 567 in the Student Edition for the text of the Guiding Questions.

- Assign *Vocabulary Development* for students to review Key Terms.

  All in One **Asia and the Pacific Teaching Resources,** *Vocabulary Development*, p. 448

◆ Chapter Summary

Section 1: Vietnam

- After decades of conflict and war, Vietnam is now a communist country that allows some free enterprise.
- In recent years, Vietnam has made great strides toward modernizing and strengthening its economy.
- Vietnam has become a leading exporter of rice.

Section 2: Australia

- Australia is a Pacific Rim country with an economy based on trade.
- Farming and ranching are key parts of Australia's economy.
- Aboriginal people in Australia are working to preserve their culture and have a role in the economic life of the country.

Vietnamese water puppets

Sydney, Australia

◆ Key Terms

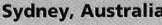

Match the definitions in Column I with the key terms in Column II.

Column I

1. a well from which water flows under natural pressure without pumping
2. a war between political parties or regions within the same country
3. a belief that if one country fell to communism, neighboring nations would also fall, like a row of dominoes
4. the dry land that makes up much of central and western Australia

Column II

A civil war

B outback

C artesian well

D domino theory

─ Vocabulary Builder ─

Revisit this chapter's high-use words:

reunite	strictly	conduct
achieve	reflect	resolve
devastate	scarce	

Ask students to review the definitions they recorded on their *Word Knowledge* worksheets.

All in One **Asia and the Pacific Teaching Resources,** *Word Knowledge*, p. 433

Consider allowing students to earn extra credit if they use the words in their answers to the questions in the Chapter Review and Assessment. The words must be used correctly and in a natural context to win the extra points.

Answers

Key Terms

1. C
2. A
3. D
4. B

Review and Assessment

Comprehension and Critical Thinking

5. (a) France **(b)** They were Ho Chi Minh's Communist forces that set out to conquer South Vietnam. **(c)** The United States sent more than 500,000 troops to try to stop Communist North Vietnam from taking control of South Vietnam.

6. (a) Many people in the U.S. objected to the war. **(b)** Possible answer: Homes, farms, factories, and forests were destroyed; many lives were lost.

7. (a) in rural areas **(b)** Most rural areas are poor, while Ho Chi Minh City is the most prosperous city in Vietnam.

8. (a) Hanoi **(b)** in northern Vietnam **(c)** Possible answer: After the Communist North conquered South Vietnam, they probably wanted to change the name of the city to reflect the victory of Communist leaders.

9. (a) farm products, especially wheat, and wool, lamb, mutton, and beef **(b)** The outback is hot and dry and fresh water is scarce.

10. (a) to preserve their culture, gain more rights, and regain their ancestral lands **(b)** They conduct their tours in their own Aboriginal language.

Skills Practice

Farmers then weed, fertilize, and water the paddy regularly. Then, when the rice turns from green to gold, it is harvested.

Writing Activity: Language Arts

Students' reports will vary but should include an accurate summary of the folk tale.

Use *Rubric for Assessing a Writing Assignment* to assess students' reports.

All in One Asia and the Pacific Teaching Resources, *Rubric for Assessing a Writing Assignment,* p. 450

◆ Comprehension and Critical Thinking

5. (a) Recall Who was Vietnam in conflict with from 1946 to 1954?
(b) Explain What were the Viet Cong?
(c) Summarize Describe the involvement of the United States in the Vietnam War.

6. (a) Recall Why did the United States end its involvement in the Vietnam War?
(b) Identify Effects What was one result of the Vietnam War?

7. (a) Note Where do most people in Vietnam live?
(b) Contrast How are rural areas in Vietnam different from Ho Chi Minh City?

8. (a) Name What is the capital of Vietnam?
(b) Locate In what part of Vietnam is Hanoi located?
(c) Apply Information Why was Saigon renamed Ho Chi Minh City?

9. (a) Recall On what kinds of products does Australia depend for a prosperous foreign trade?
(b) Infer Why do few people make their home in Australia's outback?

10. (a) Note What are important goals for Australia's Aboriginal people?
(b) Conclude How is Anangu Tours helping to preserve Aboriginal culture?

◆ Skills Practice

Using a Flowchart In the Skills for Life activity in this chapter, you learned how to read a flowchart. Review the steps you learned to use this skill. Then use the flowchart on page 802 to tell what happens after farmers transplant rice seedlings into the rice paddy.

◆ Writing Activity: Language Arts

Storytelling is an important part of Aboriginal culture. Do library research to find and read an Aboriginal folk tale from Australia. Write a report that summarizes the folk tale.

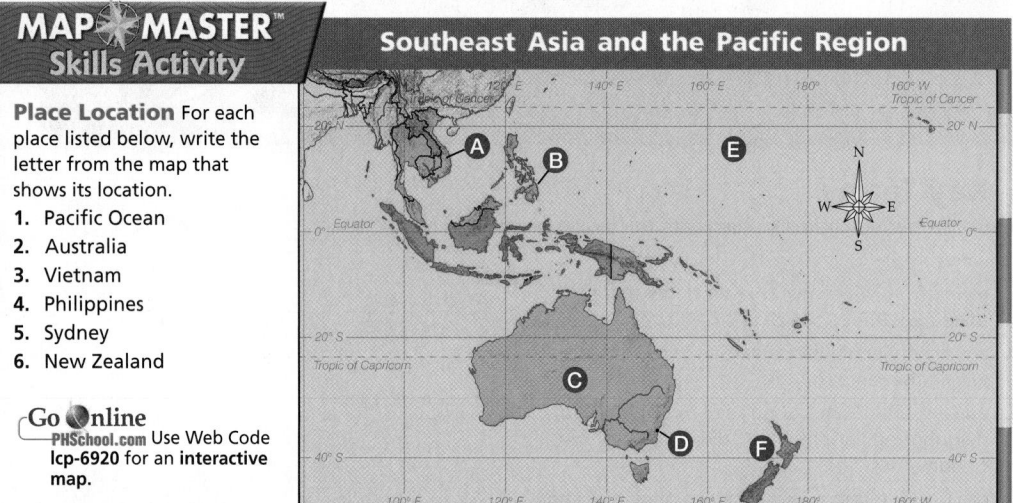

MAP MASTER™ Skills Activity

Southeast Asia and the Pacific Region

Place Location For each place listed below, write the letter from the map that shows its location.
1. Pacific Ocean
2. Australia
3. Vietnam
4. Philippines
5. Sydney
6. New Zealand

Go Online
PHSchool.com Use Web Code **lcp-6920** for an **interactive map.**

Standardized Test Prep

Test-Taking Tips

Some questions on standardized tests ask you to analyze point of view. Read the passage below. Then, follow the tips to answer the sample question.

> In 1973, the United States ended its part in the Vietnam War. American military advisers and troops were sent home. As American helicopters flew off from the capital, someone watching them said, "I had better hurry to the American embassy. Maybe one of my American friends there can help me escape from Vietnam and go to America."

Pick the letter that best answers the question.

Which onlooker might have made that statement?

TIP Be sure you understand the question. Who said the words that begin, "I had better hurry to the American embassy . . ."?

A a North Vietnamese soldier who had been fighting for years

B an American soldier who got separated from his company

C a South Vietnamese woman who had worked for the Americans

D a protestor who had been supporting North Vietnam during the war

Think It Through You can eliminate A and D because neither person would have friends at the American embassy. You can eliminate B because an American soldier would not have a reason to escape from Vietnam. The correct answer is C.

Practice Questions

Use the tips above and other tips in this book to help you answer the following questions.

1. What did the United States fear would happen if it did NOT help South Vietnam fight against North Vietnam?

   A The French would take control.

   B North Vietnam would invade China.

   C Communists would take over South Vietnam.

   D The United States would lose control of North Vietnam.

2. The Vietnam War finally ended in 1975 when

   A North Vietnam surrendered.

   B U.S. forces invaded Cambodia.

   C North Vietnam gained control over all of South Vietnam.

   D the United States signed a peace treaty with North Vietnam.

3. Some of Australia's trading partners in the Pacific Rim include the United States, China, Taiwan, and

   A India.

   B Italy.

   C Egypt.

   D Japan.

Go Online
PHSchool.com

Use Web Code **lca-6900** for **Chapter 26 self-test.**

MAP MASTER™ Skills Activity

1. E	**2.** C
3. A	**4.** B
5. D	**6.** F

Go Online
PHSchool.com Students may practice their map skills using the interactive online version of this map.

Standardized Test Prep

Answers

1. C
2. C
3. D

Go Online
PHSchool.com Students may use the Chapter 26 self-test on PHSchool.com to prepare for the Chapter Test.

Assessment Resources

Teaching Resources

Chapter Tests A and B, pp. 452–457
Final Exams A and B, pp. 461–466

Test Prep Workbook

Asia and the Pacific Study Sheet, pp. 103–109
Asia and the Pacific Practice Tests A, B, and C, pp. 25–36

AYP Monitoring Assessments

Asia and the Pacific Benchmark Test 3, pp. 129–132
Asia and the Pacific Outcome Test, pp. 200–205

Technology

⊙ ExamView Test Bank CD-ROM

Projects

- Students can further explore the Guiding Questions by completing hands-on projects.

- Three pages of structured guidance in All-in-One Asia and the Pacific Teaching Resources support each of the projects described on this page.

  All in One Asia and the Pacific Teaching Resources, *Book Project: Agricultural Center, pp. 77–79; Book Project: Asian Trade Fair, pp. 83–85*

- There are also two additional projects introduced, explained, and supported in the All-in-One Asia and the Pacific Teaching Resources.

  All in One Asia and the Pacific Teaching Resources, *Book Project: Independence Biography, pp. 80–82; Book Project: Travel Log, pp. 86–88*

- Go over the four project suggestions with students.

- Ask each student to select one of the projects, or design his or her own. Work with students to create a project description and a schedule.

- Post project schedules and monitor student progress by asking for progress reports.

- Assess student projects using rubrics from the All-in-One Asia and the Pacific Teaching Resources.

  All in One Asia and the Pacific Teaching Resources, *Rubric for Assessing a Student Performance on a Project, p. 89; Rubric for Assessing Performance of an Entire Group, p. 90; Rubric for Assessing Individual Performance in a Group, p. 91*

 Tell students they can add their completed Book Project as the final item in their portfolios. Assess student portfolios with *Rubric for Assessing a Student Portfolio.*

All in One Asia and the Pacific Teaching Resources, *Rubric for Assessing a Student Portfolio, p. 92*

Projects

Create your own projects to learn more about Asia and the Pacific. At the beginning of this book, you were introduced to the **Guiding Questions** for studying the chapters and special features. But you can also find answers to these questions by doing projects on your own or with a group. Use the questions to find topics you want to explore further. Then try the projects described on this page or create your own.

1. **Geography** What are the main physical features of Asia and the Pacific?

2. **History** How have ancient civilizations of Asia and the Pacific influenced the world today?

3. **Culture** What are the main characteristics of the cultures of Asia and the Pacific?

4. **Government** What types of government exist in Asia and the Pacific today?

5. **Economics** How do the people of this region make a living?

Project
RESEARCH EXPORTS AND TRADE

Asia and the Pacific Trade Fair
With your class, plan a trade fair for the countries of Asia and the Pacific. As you read this book, choose a country to research. Find out about its major products, factories, and trading partners. Set up a booth to show and tell visitors about trade in your country. Bring books about the country and make posters, pamphlets, and charts for your booth.

Project
CREATE A MAP AND POSTER DISPLAY

Agriculture in Asia and the Pacific
Draw a large map of Asia and the Pacific and hang it in your classroom. As you read about different kinds of farm products, mark them on the appropriate location on your map. Choose ten farm products and design a small poster for each one. On each poster, write the farm product and a country in Asia and the Pacific where this product comes from. Find or draw a picture for each poster.

812 Asia and the Pacific

Reference

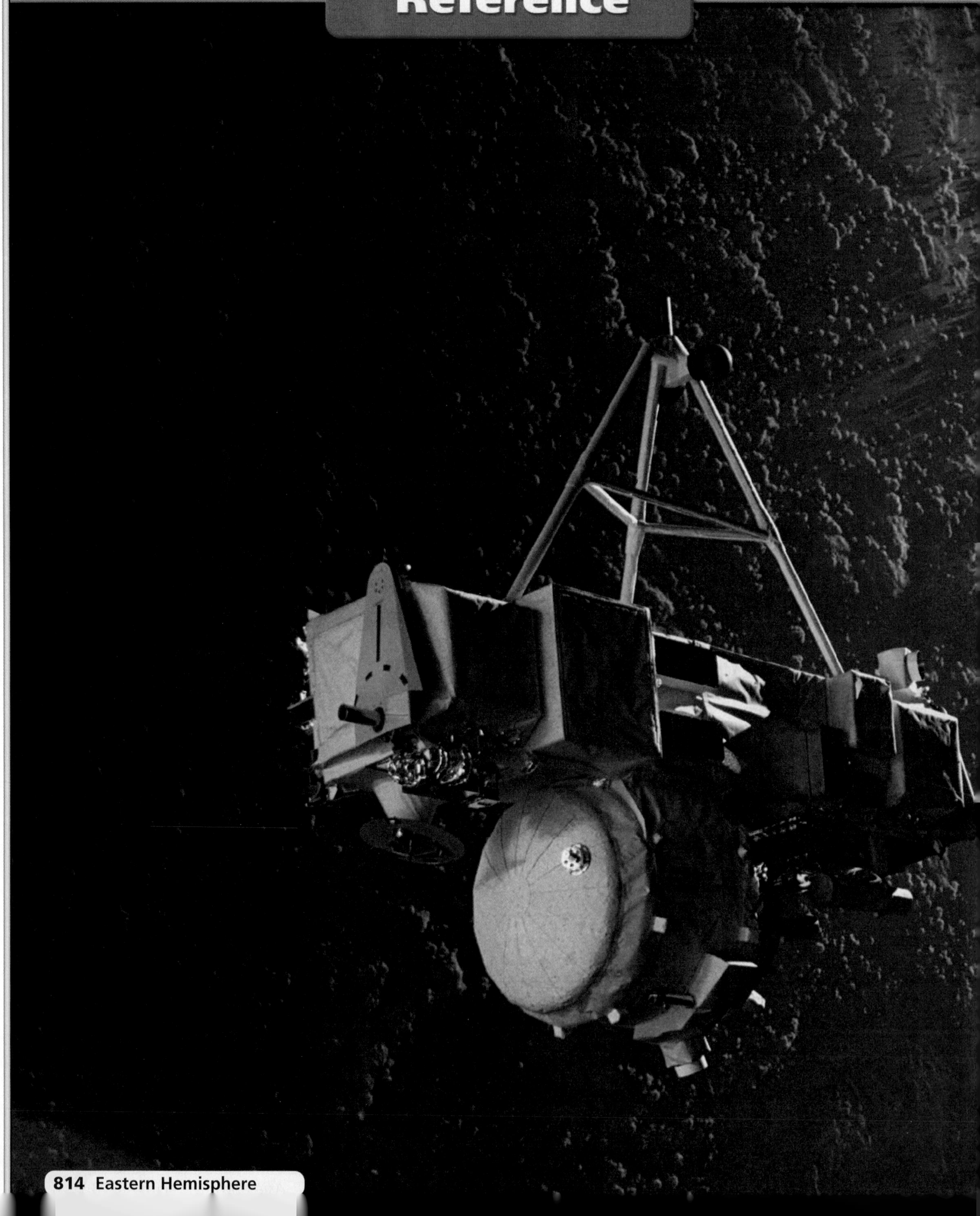

Table of Contents

The World: Political

ARCTIC OCEAN

RUSSIA

GREENLAND
(Denmark)

Arctic Circle

ALASKA
(U.S.)

Reykjavík

C A N A D A

NORTH
AMERICA

Ottawa

80° N

UNITED STATES

Washington, D.C.

A T L A N T I C
O C E A N

40° N

M
E
X
I
C
O

CENTRAL AMERICA
AND THE CARIBBEAN
For detail, see map
North and South
America: Political.

CAPE
VERDE

Tropic of Cancer

HAWAII (U.S)

20° N

Mexico City

Praia

MARSHALL
ISLANDS

Caracas

Majuro

VENEZUELA Georgetown

K I R I B A T I

Equator

PALMYRA ATOLL (U.S.)

GALÁPAGOS ISLANDS
(Ecuador)

Quito

Bogotá

Paramaribo

FRENCH GUIANA
(France)

NAURU

0°

Tarawa

COLOMBIA

GUYANA
SURINAME

ECUADOR

SOUTH
AMERICA

TUVALU

N

BRAZIL

SOLOMON
ISLANDS

Funafuti

Lima

PERU

Honiara

W   E

COOK
ISLANDS
(New Zealand)

P A C I F I C
O C E A N

La Paz

Brasília

VANUATU

SAMOA

S

BOLIVIA

Port-Vila

FIJI

Apia

AMERICAN
SAMOA
(U.S.)

FRENCH POLYNESIA
(France)

Sucre

Suva

PARAGUAY

NIUE (New Zealand)

20° S

Nuku'alofa TONGA

PITCAIRN
ISLANDS
(U.K.)

Asunción

CHILE

NEW
CALEDONIA
(France)

Tropic of Capricorn

A
R
G
E
N
T
I
N
A

URUGUAY

Santiago

Montevideo

Buenos Aires

NEW
ZEALAND

40° S

Wellington

FALKLAND ISLANDS
(U.K.)

SOUTH GEORGIA &
SOUTH SANDWICH ISLANDS
(U.K.)

60° S

S O U T H E R N   O C E A N

Antarctic Circle

80° S

ANTARCTICA

180° 160° W 140° W 120° W 100° W 80° W 60° W 40° W 20° W

0 miles   2,000

0 kilometers   2,000

Robinson

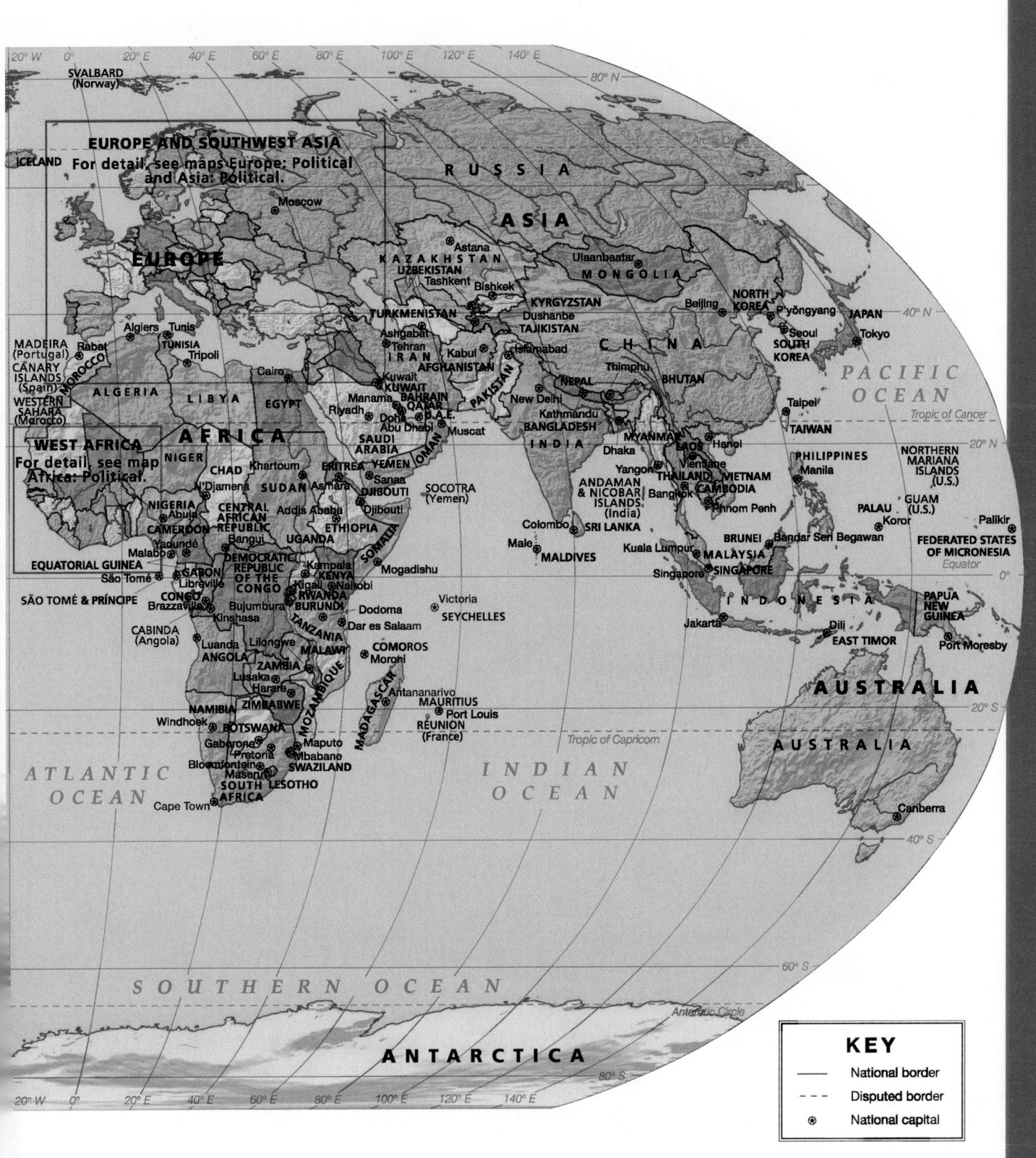

SVALBARD
(Norway)

EUROPE AND SOUTHWEST ASIA
For detail, see maps Europe: Political
and Asia: Political.

ICELAND

RUSSIA

ASIA

EUROPE

Moscow

Astana
KAZAKHSTAN
UZBEKISTAN
Tashkent Bishkek
KYRGYZSTAN
Dushanbe
TAJIKISTAN

Ulaanbaatar

MONGOLIA

Beijing

NORTH
KOREA P'yŏngyang

JAPAN

Tokyo

PACIFIC
OCEAN

MADEIRA
(Portugal)
CANARY
ISLANDS
(Spain)
WESTERN
SAHARA
(Morocco)

Rabat
MOROCCO

Algiers Tunis
TUNISIA
Tripoli

TURKMENISTAN
Ashgabat
Tehran
IRAN Kabul
AFGHANISTAN

PAKISTAN

Islamabad

Kathmandu

CHINA

Thimphu

BHUTAN

SOUTH
KOREA

Seoul

Taipei

Tropic of Cancer

Cairo

ALGERIA LIBYA EGYPT

AFRICA

WEST AFRICA
For detail, see map
Africa: Political.

NIGER

CHAD

Khartoum

SUDAN

SAUDI
ARABIA YEMEN

Kuwait
KUWAIT
Manama BAHRAIN
Riyadh QATAR
Doha U.A.E.
Abu Dhabi

ERITREA
Asmara DJIBOUTI

Muscat

OMAN

SOCOTRA
(Yemen)

New Delhi

INDIA

Dhaka

BANGLADESH

Kathmandu

NEPAL

MYANMAR Hanoi
LAOS
Yangon Vientiane
THAILAND VIETNAM
Bangkok CAMBODIA
Phnom Penh

TAIWAN

20° N

PHILIPPINES

Manila

NORTHERN
MARIANA
ISLANDS
(U.S.)

N'Djamena

NIGERIA
Abuja
CAMEROON
Yaoundé

CENTRAL
AFRICAN
REPUBLIC
Bangui

Addis Ababa

ETHIOPIA

UGANDA

Colombo
Male SRI LANKA
MALDIVES

ANDAMAN
& NICOBAR
ISLANDS
(India)

PALAU
Koror

GUAM
(U.S.)

Palikir

EQUATORIAL GUINEA
Malabo

SÃO TOMÉ & PRÍNCIPE

São Tomé

GABON
Libreville

CONGO
Brazzaville

DEMOCRATIC
REPUBLIC
OF THE
CONGO
Kinshasa

Kampala
KENYA
Kigali Nairobi
RWANDA
Bujumbura
BURUNDI
TANZANIA
Dodoma
Dar es Salaam

SOMALIA

Mogadishu

Victoria
SEYCHELLES

BRUNEI Bandar Seri Begawan

Kuala Lumpur
MALAYSIA
Singapore SINGAPORE

FEDERATED STATES
OF MICRONESIA

Equator

INDONESIA

PAPUA
NEW
GUINEA

CABINDA
(Angola)

Luanda Lilongwe
ANGOLA MALAWI
Lusaka
ZAMBIA

Harare

COMOROS
Moroni

Jakarta

Dili
EAST TIMOR

Port Moresby

NAMIBIA ZIMBABWE

Windhoek

BOTSWANA
Gaborone
Pretoria
Bloemfontein
Maseru
SOUTH
Cape Town AFRICA

Maputo
Mbabane
SWAZILAND
LESOTHO

MOZAMBIQUE

MADAGASCAR

Antananarivo
MAURITIUS
Port Louis
RÉUNION
(France)

AUSTRALIA

AUSTRALIA

20° S

ATLANTIC
OCEAN

INDIAN
OCEAN

Tropic of Capricorn

Canberra

40° S

SOUTHERN OCEAN

Antarctic Circle

ANTARCTICA

80° S

KEY

————— National border

- - - - - Disputed border

⊛ National capital

The World: Physical

ARCTIC OCEAN

80° N

Beaufort Sea

Greenland

Baffin Island

Yukon R.

Mackenzie R.

Hudson Bay

Labrador Sea

Bering Sea

ROCKY MOUNTAINS

NORTH AMERICA

CANADIAN SHIELD

Aleutian Islands

GREAT PLAINS

Great Lakes

St. Lawrence R.

40° N

Missouri R.

APPALACHIAN MTS.

ATLANTIC OCEAN

Colorado R.

Mississippi R.

Tropic of Cancer

Rio Grande

Gulf of Mexico

West Indies

20° N

Hawaiian Islands

Caribbean Sea

N

MICRONESIA

Galápagos Islands

Orinoco R.

GUIANA HIGHLANDS

Equator

0°

W   E

AMAZON BASIN

Amazon R.

SOUTH AMERICA

ANDES

MELANESIA

S

POLYNESIA

PACIFIC OCEAN

BRAZILIAN HIGHLANDS

20° S

Tropic of Capricorn

Tasman Sea

North Island

PAMPAS

Rio de la Plata

40° S

PATAGONIA

South Island

Cape Horn

60° S

Drake Passage

SOUTHERN OCEAN

ANTARCTIC PENINSULA

Antarctic Circle

Weddell Sea

Ross Sea

80° S

ANTARCTICA

180°   160° W   140° W   120° W   100° W   80° W   60° W   40° W   20° W

0 miles   2,000

0 kilometers   2,000

Robinson

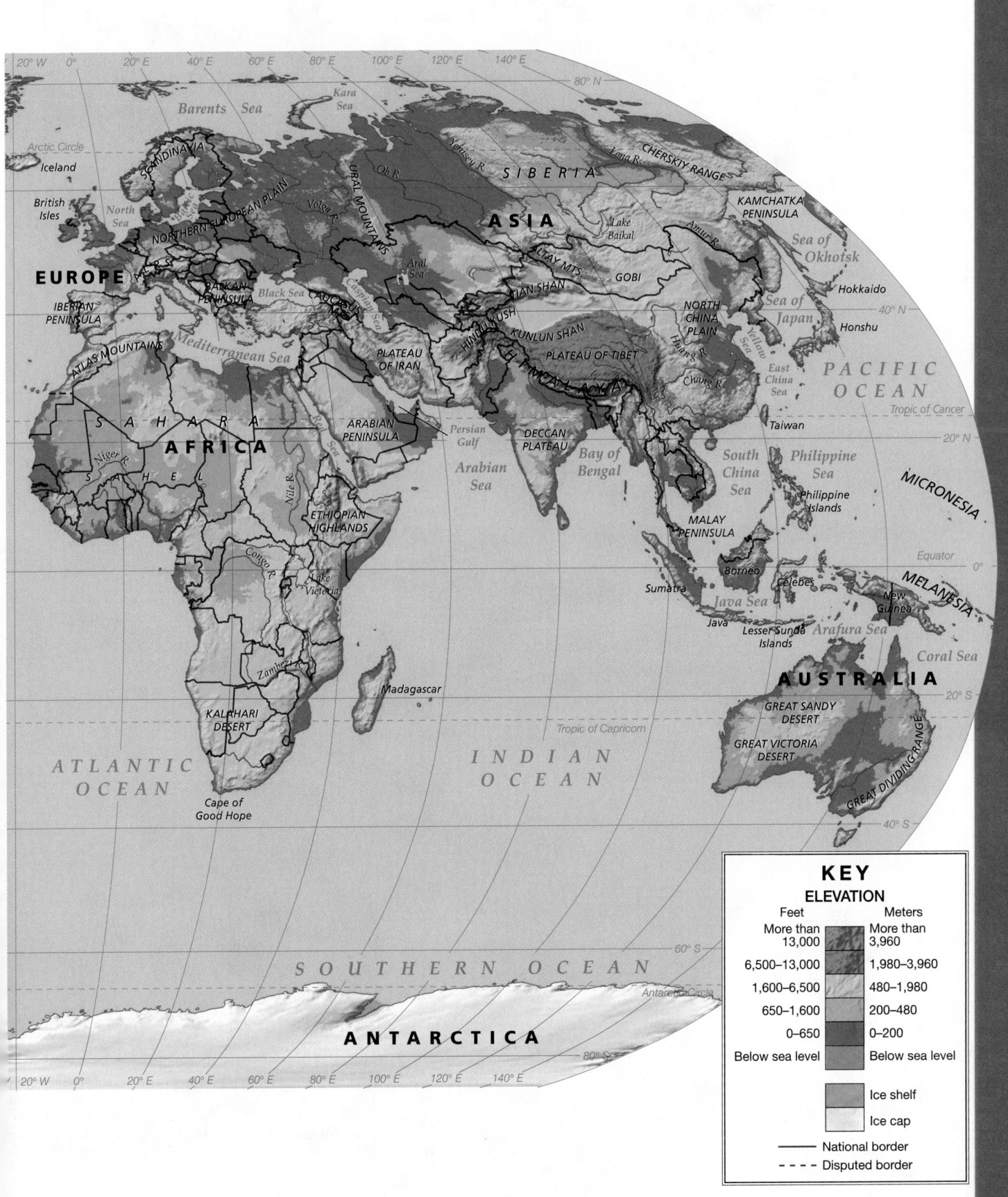

20° W 0° 20° E 40° E 60° E 80° E 100° E 120° E 140° E 80° N

Barents Sea
Kara Sea

Arctic Circle
Iceland

SCANDINAVIA

British Isles
North Sea
NORTHERN EUROPEAN PLAIN

URAL MOUNTAINS

Ob R.
Volga R.
Yenisey R.

SIBERIA

Lena R.

CHERSKIY RANGE

KAMCHATKA PENINSULA

ASIA

Lake Baikal

Amur R.

Sea of Okhotsk

EUROPE
ALPS
BALKAN PENINSULA
Aral Sea
Caspian Sea
ALTAY MTS.

GOBI

Hokkaido
40° N
Sea of Japan

IBERIAN PENINSULA
Black Sea
CAUCASUS
TIAN SHAN
NORTH CHINA PLAIN
Honshu

ATLAS MOUNTAINS
Mediterranean Sea
PLATEAU OF IRAN
HINDU KUSH
KUNLUN SHAN
PLATEAU OF TIBET
Huang R.
Yellow Sea
East China Sea
PACIFIC OCEAN

S A H A R A
ARABIAN PENINSULA
Persian Gulf
DECCAN PLATEAU
HIMALAYA
Chang R.
Tropic of Cancer

AFRICA
Niger R.
S A H E L
Red Sea
Nile R.
Arabian Sea
Bay of Bengal
Taiwan
20° N

South China Sea
Philippine Sea

ETHIOPIAN HIGHLANDS
Philippine Islands

MICRONESIA

MALAY PENINSULA
Equator 0°

Congo R.
Lake Victoria
Borneo
Celebes
MELANESIA

Sumatra
Java Sea
New Guinea

Zambezi R.
Madagascar
Java
Lesser Sunda Islands
Arafura Sea
Coral Sea

AUSTRALIA

KALAHARI DESERT
GREAT SANDY DESERT
20° S

Tropic of Capricorn
GREAT VICTORIA DESERT

ATLANTIC OCEAN
INDIAN OCEAN
GREAT DIVIDING RANGE

Cape of Good Hope
40° S

60° S

S O U T H E R N   O C E A N

Antarctica Circle

ANTARCTICA
80° S

20° W 0° 20° E 40° E 60° E 80° E 100° E 120° E 140° E

KEY

ELEVATION

Feet		Meters
More than 13,000		More than 3,960
6,500–13,000		1,980–3,960
1,600–6,500		480–1,980
650–1,600		200–480
0–650		0–200
Below sea level		Below sea level

Ice shelf

Ice cap

—— National border

- - - - Disputed border

North and South America: Political

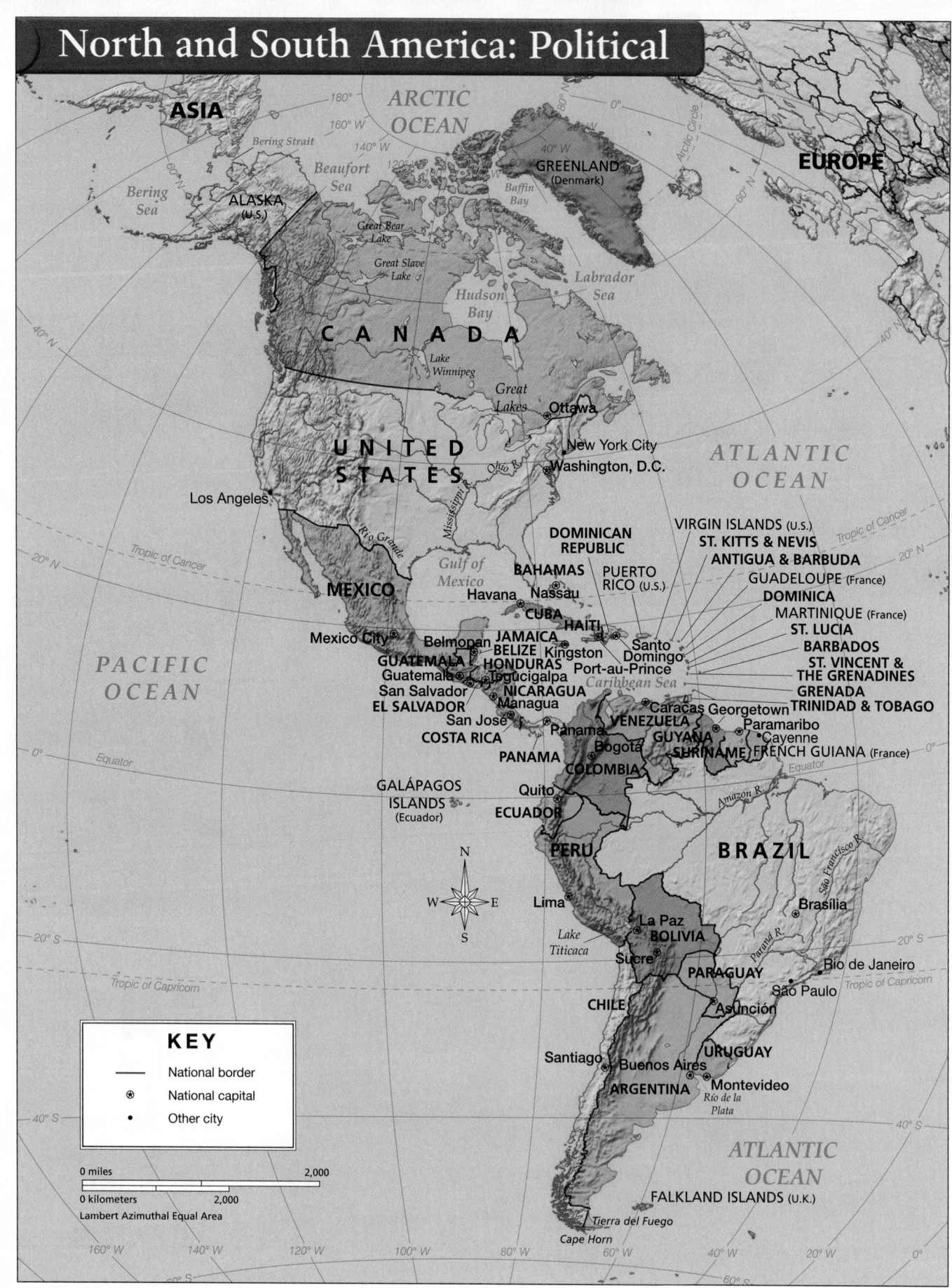

ASIA

Bering Strait

ARCTIC OCEAN

180°

160° W

140° W

Bering Sea

Beaufort Sea

40° W

GREENLAND
(Denmark)

EUROPE

0°

Arctic Circle

ALASKA
(U.S.)

Great Bear Lake

Baffin Bay

Great Slave Lake

Labrador Sea

C A N A D A

Lake Winnipeg

60° N

Great Lakes

Ottawa

Hudson Bay

U N I T E D
S T A T E S

New York City

Washington, D.C.

ATLANTIC OCEAN

40° N

Ohio R.

Los Angeles

Rio Grande

Mississippi

DOMINICAN
REPUBLIC

VIRGIN ISLANDS (U.S.)

ST. KITTS & NEVIS

Tropic of Cancer

20° N

Tropic of Cancer

Gulf of Mexico

BAHAMAS

PUERTO
RICO (U.S.)

ANTIGUA & BARBUDA

GUADELOUPE (France)

MEXICO

Havana

Nassau

DOMINICA

MARTINIQUE (France)

Mexico City

CUBA

HAITI

Santo
Domingo

ST. LUCIA

Belmopan

JAMAICA

Kingston

BARBADOS

GUATEMALA

BELIZE

HONDURAS

Port-au-Prince

ST. VINCENT &
THE GRENADINES

Guatemala

Tegucigalpa

Caribbean Sea

GRENADA

San Salvador

NICARAGUA

EL SALVADOR

Managua

Caracas Georgetown

TRINIDAD & TOBAGO

San José

VENEZUELA

Paramaribo

COSTA RICA

Panama

GUYANA

Cayenne

*PACIFIC
OCEAN*

PANAMA

Bogotá

SURINAME

FRENCH GUIANA (France)

COLOMBIA

Equator

0°

Equator

GALÁPAGOS
ISLANDS
(Ecuador)

Quito

Amazon R.

ECUADOR

PERU

B R A Z I L

São Francisco R.

N

W   E

Lima

Brasília

S

La Paz

20° S

Lake Titicaca

BOLIVIA

20° S

Sucre

Paraná R.

Rio de Janeiro

Tropic of Capricorn

PARAGUAY

Tropic of Capricorn

São Paulo

CHILE

Asunción

KEY

— National border

⊛ National capital

• Other city

Santiago

URUGUAY

Buenos Aires

Montevideo

ARGENTINA

Río de la Plata

40° S

0 miles   2,000

40° S

0 kilometers   2,000

Lambert Azimuthal Equal Area

*ATLANTIC
OCEAN*

FALKLAND ISLANDS (U.K.)

Tierra del Fuego

Cape Horn

160° W

140° W

120° W

100° W

80° W

60° W

40° W

20° W

0°

60° S

North and South America: Physical

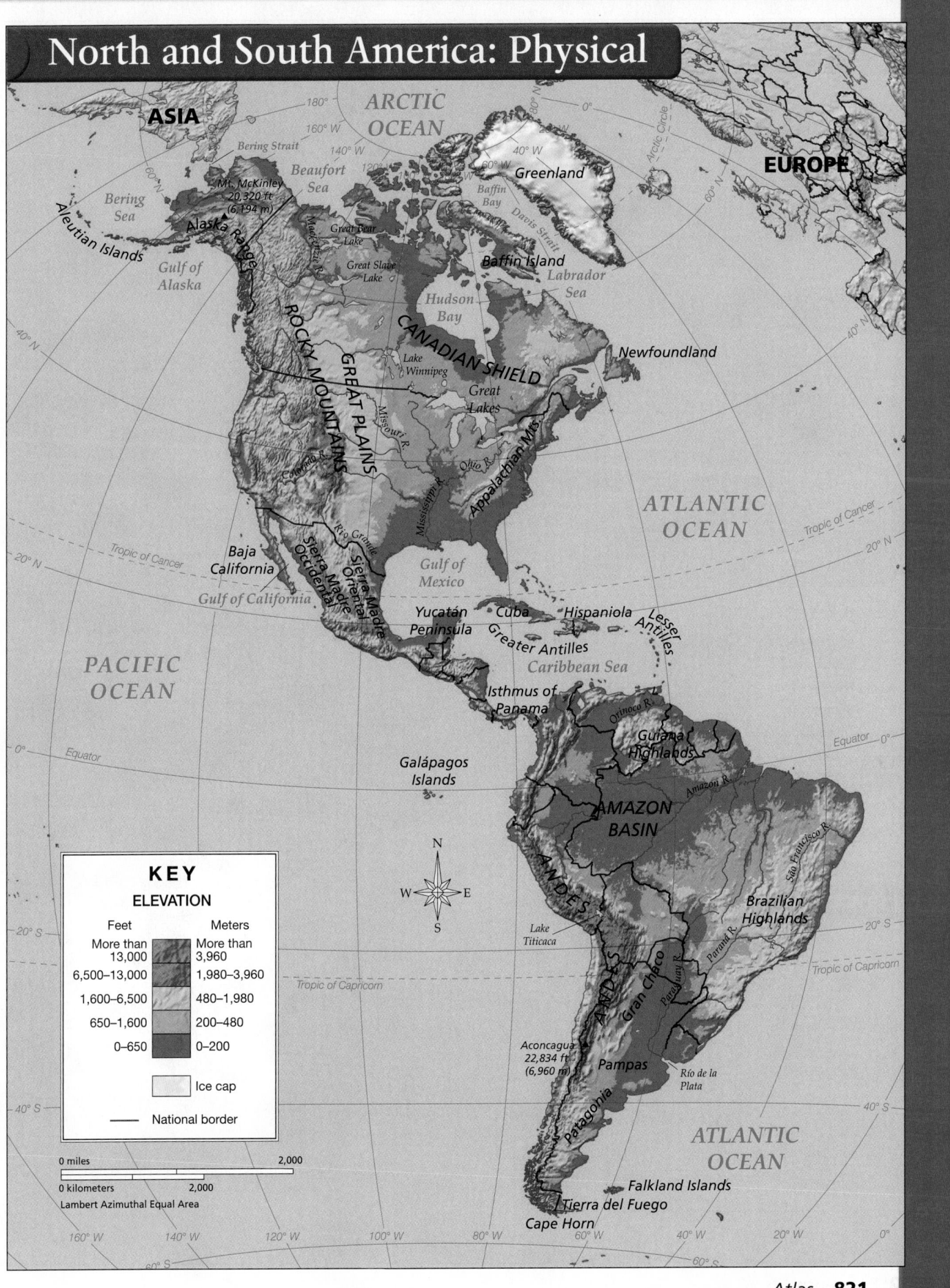

ASIA

ARCTIC OCEAN

180°
160° W
140° W
120°
100° W
80° N
0°
40° W
60° W

Bering Strait

Beaufort Sea

Greenland

EUROPE

Mt. McKinley
20,320 ft
(6,194 m)

Bering Sea

Aleutian Islands

Alaska Range

Gulf of Alaska

Baffin Bay

Davis Strait

Mackenzie R.

Great Bear Lake

Baffin Island

Great Slave Lake

Labrador Sea

Arctic Circle

60° N

ROCKY MOUNTAINS

GREAT PLAINS

Hudson Bay

CANADIAN SHIELD

Newfoundland

40° N

Lake Winnipeg

Missouri R.

Great Lakes

40° N

Colorado R.

Ohio R.

Appalachian Mts.

ATLANTIC OCEAN

Tropic of Cancer

Mississippi R.

Tropic of Cancer

20° N

Baja California

Rio Grande

Sierra Madre Oriental

Gulf of Mexico

20° N

Gulf of California

Sierra Madre Occidental

Yucatán Peninsula

Cuba

Hispaniola

Lesser Antilles

PACIFIC OCEAN

Greater Antilles

Caribbean Sea

Isthmus of Panama

Orinoco R.

Guiana Highlands

Equator

0°

Equator

0°

Galápagos Islands

Amazon R.

AMAZON BASIN

ANDES

Brazilian Highlands

20° S

Lake Titicaca

São Francisco R.

Paraná R.

KEY

ELEVATION

Feet	Meters
More than 13,000	More than 3,960
6,500–13,000	1,980–3,960
1,600–6,500	480–1,980
650–1,600	200–480
0–650	0–200

Ice cap

National border

N
W E
S

Gran Chaco

Paraguay R.

Tropic of Capricorn

20° S

Tropic of Capricorn

Aconcagua
22,834 ft
(6,960 m)

Pampas

Río de la Plata

Patagonia

40° S

ATLANTIC OCEAN

40° S

0 miles 2,000

0 kilometers 2,000

Lambert Azimuthal Equal Area

Falkland Islands

Tierra del Fuego

Cape Horn

160° W
140° W
120° W
100° W
80° W
60° W
40° W
20° W
0°
60° S

United States: Political

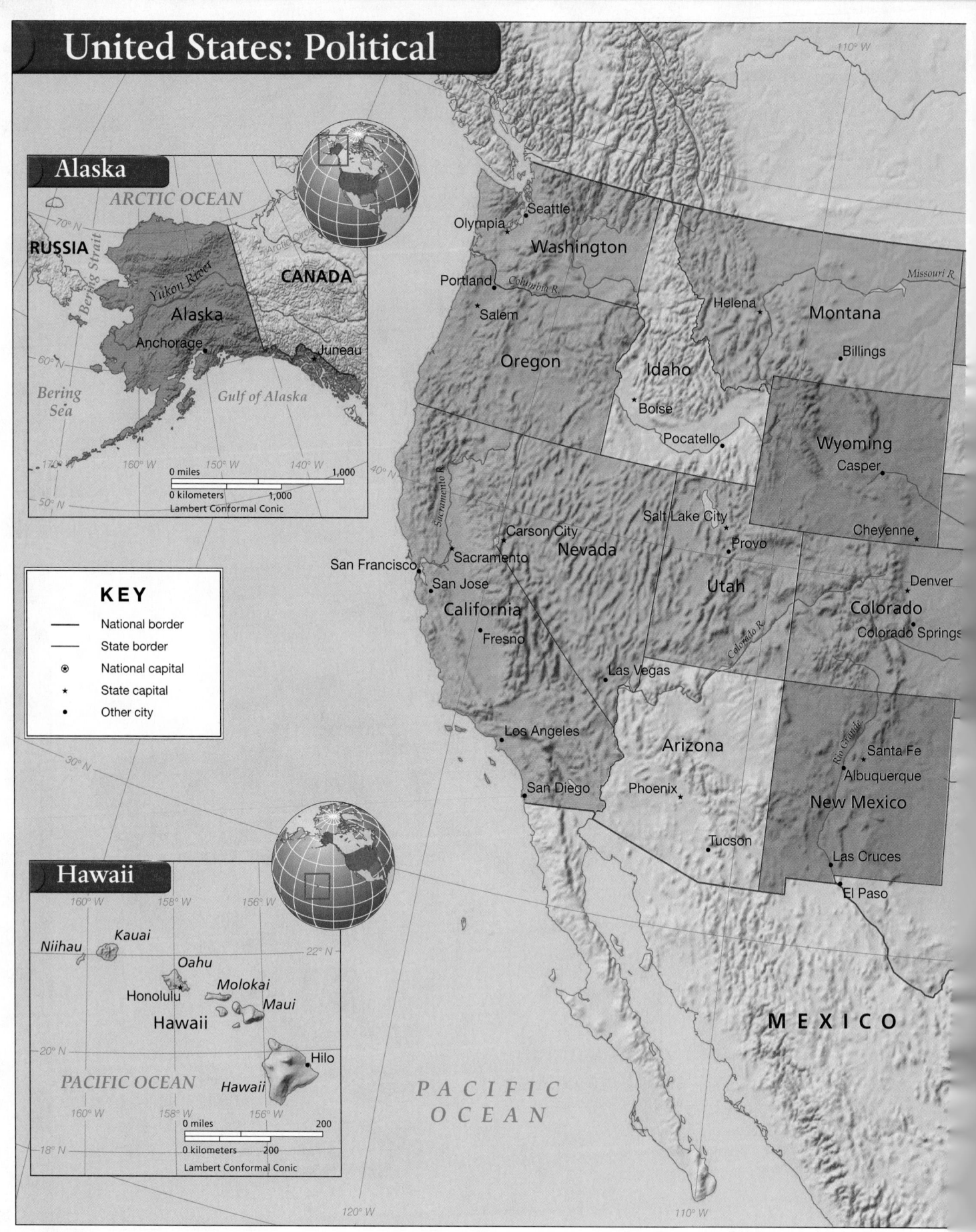

Alaska

ARCTIC OCEAN

RUSSIA

CANADA

Yukon River

Alaska

Anchorage

Juneau

Bering Strait

Arctic Circle

70° N

60° N

Bering
Sea

Gulf of Alaska

170°   160° W   150° W   140° W

50° N

40° N

0 miles   1,000

0 kilometers   1,000

Lambert Conformal Conic

KEY

—— National border

—— State border

⊛ National capital

★ State capital

• Other city

Hawaii

160° W   158° W   156° W

Niihau   Kauai

Oahu

Molokai

Honolulu   Maui

Hawaii

22° N

20° N

Hilo

PACIFIC OCEAN   Hawaii

160° W   158° W   156° W

18° N

0 miles   200

0 kilometers   200

Lambert Conformal Conic

110° W

Seattle

Olympia

Washington

Portland   Columbia R.

Salem

Helena

Montana

Missouri R.

Oregon   Idaho

Boise

Pocatello

Billings

Wyoming

Casper

Carson City

Salt Lake City

Provo

Cheyenne

San Francisco   Sacramento   Nevada

San Jose

California

Fresno

Utah

Colorado R.

Denver

Colorado

Colorado Springs

Sacramento R.

30° N

Los Angeles

Las Vegas

Arizona

Rio Grande

Santa Fe

Albuquerque

San Diego   Phoenix

New Mexico

Tucson

Las Cruces

El Paso

PACIFIC
OCEAN

M E X I C O

120° W   110° W

Europe: Political

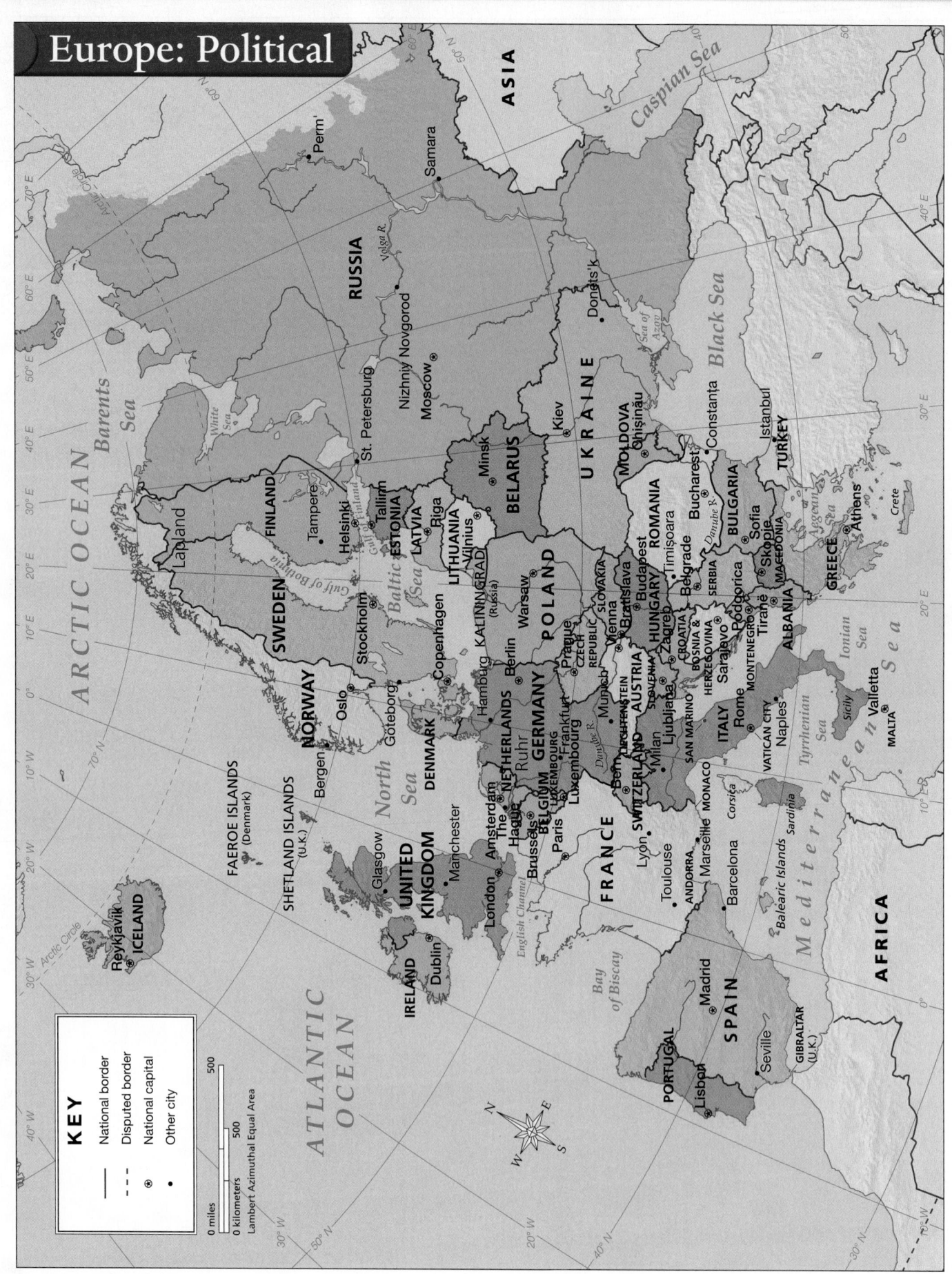

KEY

— National border
- - - Disputed border
⊛ National capital
• Other city

0 miles 500
0 kilometers 500
Lambert Azimuthal Equal Area

824 Reference

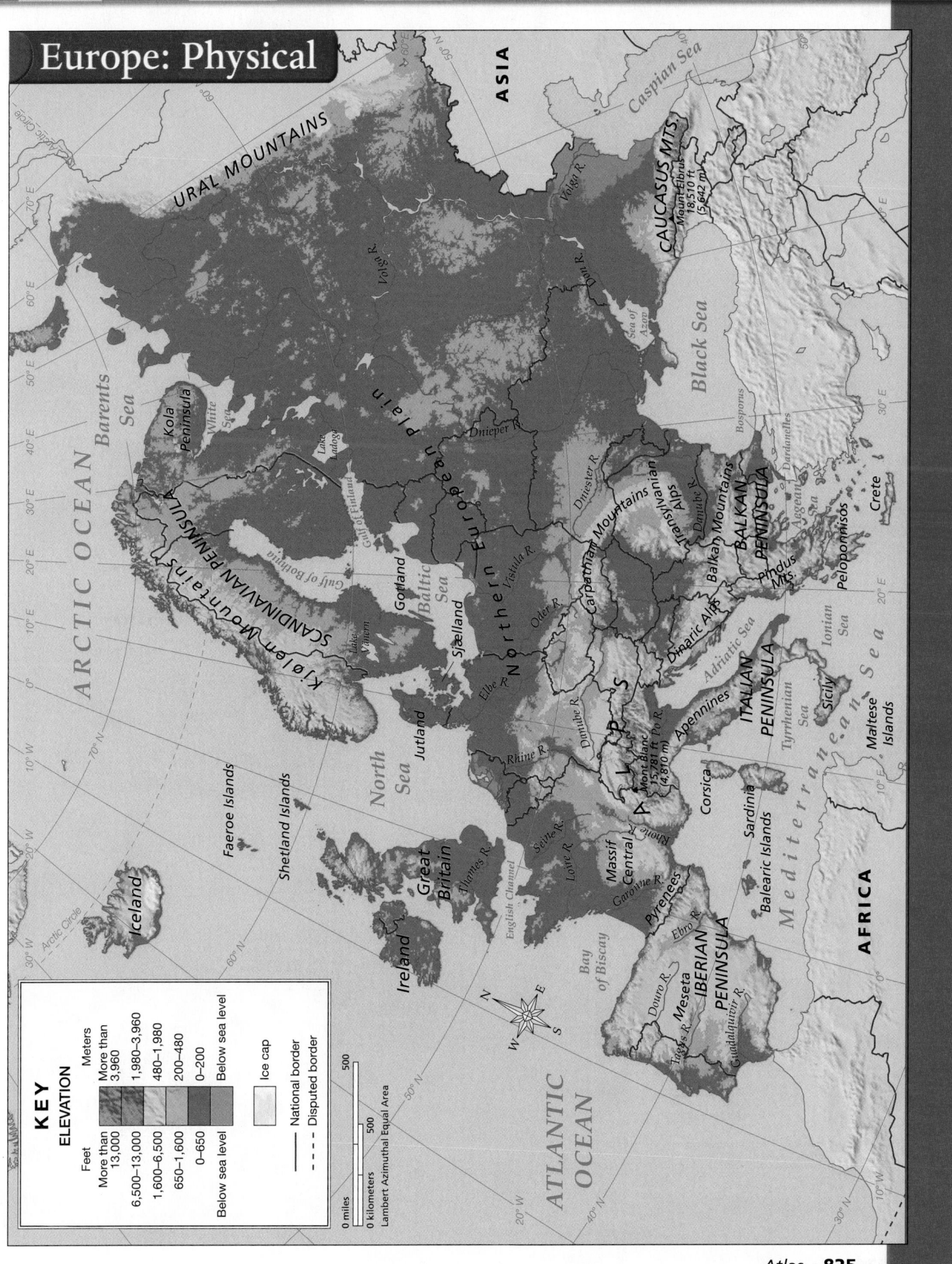

Europe: Physical

ASIA

URAL MOUNTAINS

Caspian Sea

CAUCASUS MTS.
Mount Elbrus
18,510 ft
(5,642 m)

Volga R.

Volga R.

Don R.

Sea of Azov

Black Sea

Barents Sea

ARCTIC OCEAN

Kola Peninsula

White Sea

Lake Ladoga

Gulf of Finland

Dnieper R.

Northern European Plain

Dniester R.

Carpathian Mountains

Transylvanian Alps

Danube R.

Balkan Mountains

BALKAN PENINSULA

Pindus Mts.

Bosporus

Dardanelles

KJØLEN MOUNTAINS

SCANDINAVIAN PENINSULA

Gulf of Bothnia

Lake Vänern

Gotland

Baltic Sea

Sjælland

Vistula R.

Oder R.

Elbe R.

Dinaric Alps

Adriatic Sea

Aegean Sea

Crete

Peloponnisos

Ionian Sea

ITALIAN PENINSULA

Apennines

Tyrrhenian Sea

Sicily

Maltese Islands

Mediterranean Sea

Faeroe Islands

Shetland Islands

North Sea

Jutland

Great Britain

Thames R.

Rhine R.

Seine R.

Loire R.

Danube R.

A L P S

Mont Blanc
15,781 ft
(4,810 m)

Rhone R.

Po R.

Corsica

Sardinia

Balearic Islands

Iceland

Arctic Circle

Ireland

English Channel

Bay of Biscay

Massif Central

Garonne R.

Pyrenees

Ebro R.

IBERIAN PENINSULA

Meseta

Douro R.

Tagus R.

Guadalquivir R.

AFRICA

ATLANTIC OCEAN

N
E
S
W

KEY

ELEVATION

Feet	Meters
More than 13,000	More than 3,960
6,500–13,000	1,980–3,960
1,600–6,500	480–1,980
650–1,600	200–480
0–650	0–200
Below sea level	Below sea level

Ice cap

—— National border

‑ ‑ ‑ Disputed border

0 miles 500

0 kilometers 500

Lambert Azimuthal Equal Area

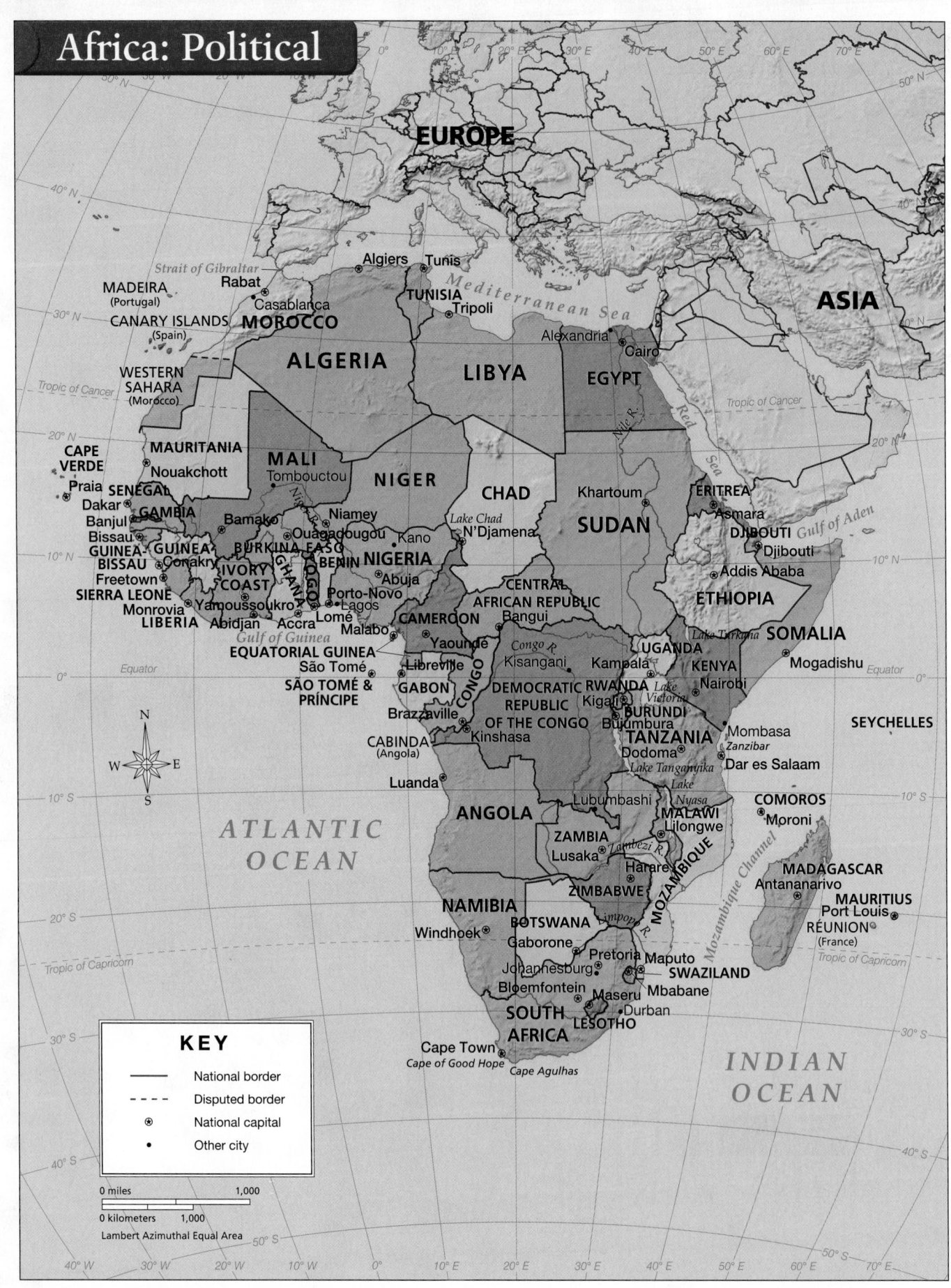

Africa: Political

EUROPE

ASIA

Strait of Gibraltar

Mediterranean Sea

MADEIRA
(Portugal)

Algiers   Tunis
Rabat
TUNISIA
Casablanca   •Tripoli
CANARY ISLANDS
(Spain)   MOROCCO

Alexandria•   •Cairo

Tropic of Cancer

ALGERIA   LIBYA   EGYPT

WESTERN
SAHARA
(Morocco)

Red Sea

Tropic of Cancer

CAPE
VERDE   MAURITANIA   MALI   NIGER   CHAD
•Nouakchott   Khartoum•   ERITREA
•Praia   SENEGAL   Tombouctou   •Asmara
Dakar⊛   Niamey   Lake Chad   DJIBOUTI   *Gulf of Aden*
GAMBIA   Bamako• •Ouagadougou   •N'Djamena   SUDAN   •Djibouti
Banjul⊛   •Kano
Bissau•   BURKINA FASO   •Addis Ababa
GUINEA-   GUINEA   •Conakry BENIN   NIGERIA
BISSAU   IVORY GHANA TOGO •Abuja   CENTRAL   ETHIOPIA
Freetown⊛   COAST   AFRICAN REPUBLIC
SIERRA LEONE   Yamoussoukro Porto-Novo •Bangui
Monrovia⊛   •Lagos
LIBERIA   Abidjan Accra Lomé Malabo CAMEROON   SOMALIA
Gulf of Guinea   Yaoundé•   UGANDA   Lake Turkana
EQUATORIAL GUINEA   Kisangani• Kampala⊛ KENYA   •Mogadishu   *Equator*
Equator   São Tomé   •Libreville   *Congo R.*   RWANDA Lake •Nairobi
                SÃO TOMÉ &   GABON   CONGO DEMOCRATIC Kigali⊛ Victoria
                PRÍNCIPE   REPUBLIC BURUNDI   SEYCHELLES
                          Brazzaville•   OF THE CONGO Bujumbura• •Mombasa
                                    Kinshasa   TANZANIA   Zanzibar
              CABINDA   Dodoma⊛
              (Angola)   Lake Tanganyika •Dar es Salaam
                                                      Lake
                Luanda•   Lubumbashi• Nyasa   COMOROS
                                                          MALAWI   •Moroni
ATLANTIC   ANGOLA   ZAMBIA Lilongwe⊛
OCEAN   •Lusaka   MADAGASCAR
                                                  Zambezi R.   Antananarivo⊛
                                          ZIMBABWE •Harare MOZAMBIQUE   MAURITIUS
                      NAMIBIA   Port Louis⊛
                              BOTSWANA *Limpopo R.*   RÉUNION
                Windhoek⊛   •Gaborone   (France)
                                              Pretoria⊛ •Maputo   *Tropic of Capricorn*
Tropic of Capricorn   Johannesburg•   SWAZILAND
                        Bloemfontein⊛ •Mbabane
                          SOUTH   Maseru⊛ •Durban
                          AFRICA LESOTHO
                Cape Town⊛
                Cape of Good Hope Cape Agulhas   INDIAN
                                                      OCEAN

KEY

—————— National border

- - - - - Disputed border

⊛ National capital

• Other city

0 miles ————————— 1,000

0 kilometers ————————— 1,000

Lambert Azimuthal Equal Area

Africa: Physical

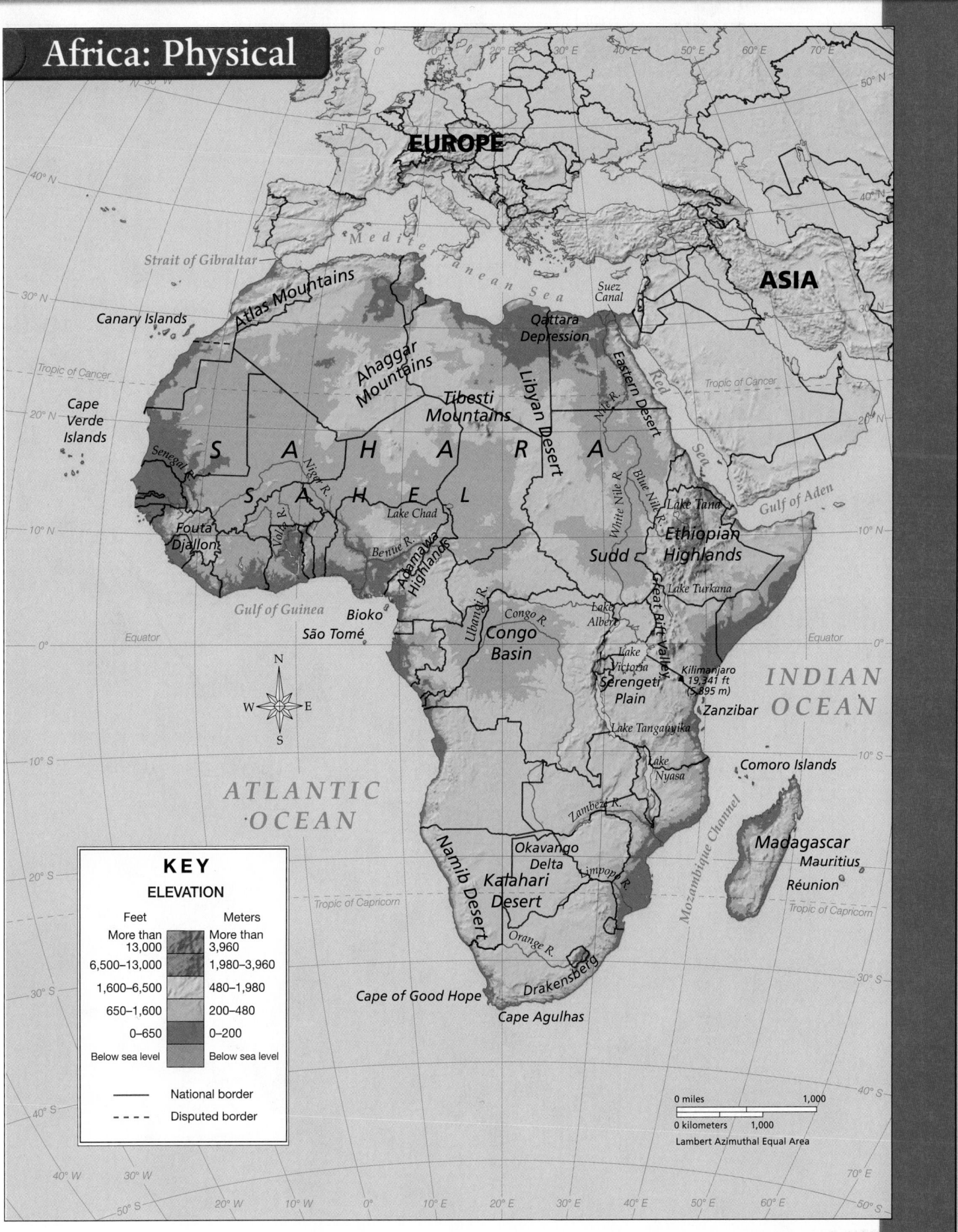

EUROPE

ASIA

Strait of Gibraltar

Canary Islands

Cape Verde Islands

Atlas Mountains

Ahaggar Mountains

Tibesti Mountains

Qattara Depression

Suez Canal

Libyan Desert

Eastern Desert

Red Sea

S A H A R A

S A H E L

Senegal R.

Niger R.

Volta R.

Fouta Djallon

Lake Chad

Benue R.

Adamawa Highlands

Gulf of Guinea

Bioko

São Tomé

Ubangi R.

Congo R.

Congo Basin

White Nile R.

Blue Nile R.

Lake Tana

Niger R.

Ethiopian Highlands

Sudd

Lake Turkana

Gulf of Aden

Lake Albert

Great Rift Valley

Lake Victoria

Kilimanjaro 19,341 ft (5,895 m)

Serengeti Plain

Zanzibar

Lake Tanganyika

INDIAN OCEAN

Equator

ATLANTIC OCEAN

N
W E
S

Lake Nyasa

Comoro Islands

Zambezi R.

Okavango Delta

Limpopo R.

Mozambique Channel

Madagascar

Mauritius

Réunion

Namib Desert

Kalahari Desert

Orange R.

Cape of Good Hope

Drakensberg

Cape Agulhas

Tropic of Cancer

Equator

Tropic of Capricorn

KEY

ELEVATION

Feet	Meters
More than 13,000	More than 3,960
6,500–13,000	1,980–3,960
1,600–6,500	480–1,980
650–1,600	200–480
0–650	0–200
Below sea level	Below sea level

——— National border

- - - - Disputed border

0 miles 1,000

0 kilometers 1,000

Lambert Azimuthal Equal Area

Asia: Political

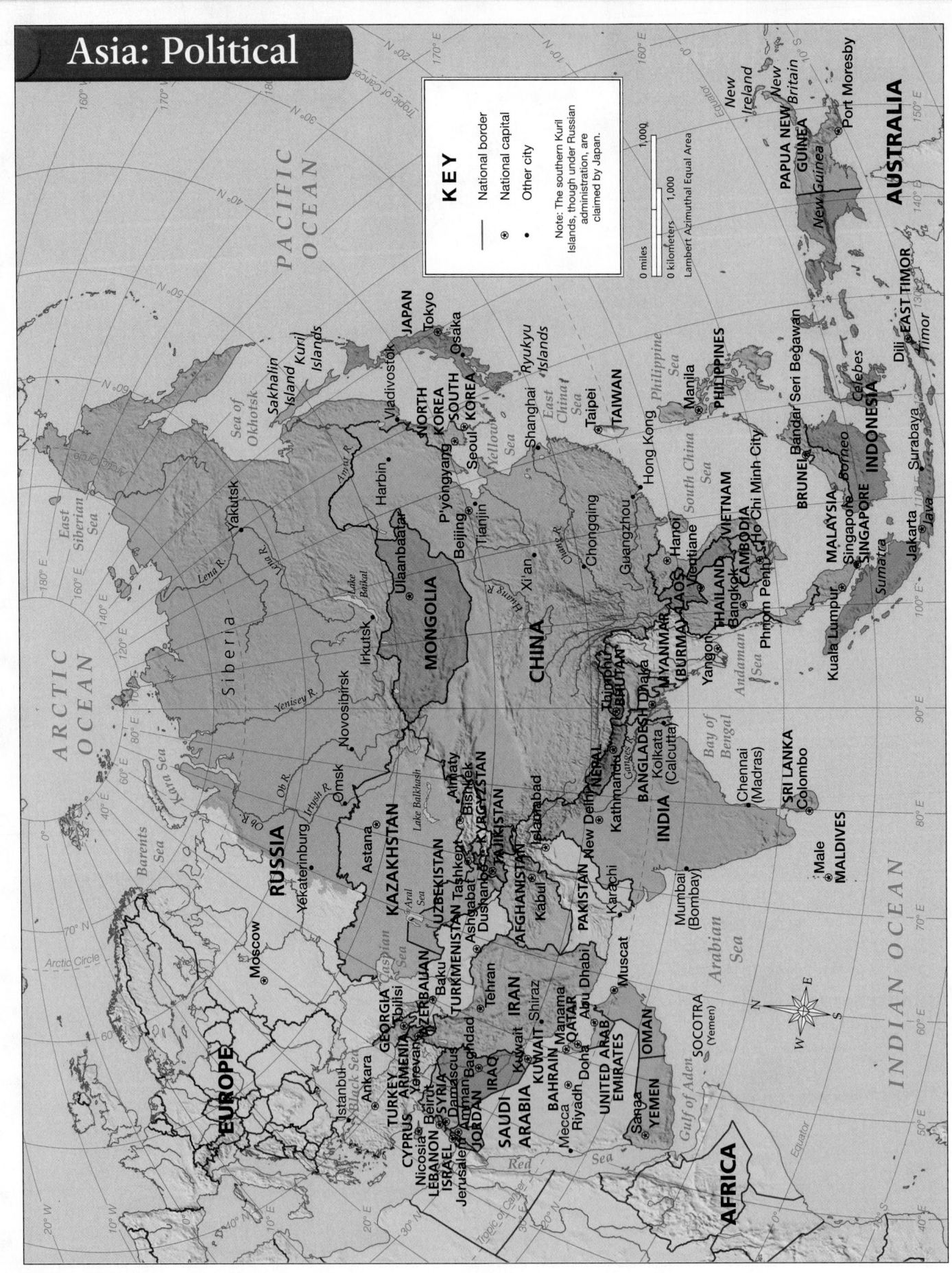

KEY

— National border
⊛ National capital
• Other city

Note: The southern Kuril Islands, though under Russian administration, are claimed by Japan.

Lambert Azimuthal Equal Area

ARCTIC OCEAN

PACIFIC OCEAN

INDIAN OCEAN

EUROPE

AFRICA

AUSTRALIA

RUSSIA

Siberia

Moscow

Yekaterinburg

Omsk

Novosibirsk

Irkutsk

Yakutsk

Lake Baikal

Lena R.

Yenisey R.

Ob R.

Irtysh R.

Amur R.

Sea of Okhotsk

Sakhalin Island

Kuril Islands

East Siberian Sea

Kara Sea

Barents Sea

Arctic Circle

Black Sea

Caspian Sea

Aral Sea

Lake Balkhash

KAZAKHSTAN

Astana

Almaty

Bishkek

KYRGYZSTAN

Tashkent

UZBEKISTAN

TURKMENISTAN

Ashgabat

Dushanbe

TAJIKISTAN

MONGOLIA

Ulaanbaatar

CHINA

Beijing

Tianjin

Harbin

Xi'an

Chongqing

Guangzhou

Shanghai

Hong Kong

Chang R.

Huang R.

NORTH KOREA

P'yŏngyang

SOUTH KOREA

Seoul

JAPAN

Tokyo

Osaka

Vladivostok

Yellow Sea

East China Sea

Ryukyu Islands

TAIWAN

Taipei

Philippine Sea

PHILIPPINES

Manila

South China Sea

VIETNAM

Hanoi

Ho Chi Minh City

LAOS

Vientiane

THAILAND

Bangkok

CAMBODIA

Phnom Penh

MYANMAR (BURMA)

Yangon

Andaman Sea

Bay of Bengal

BANGLADESH

Dhaka

BHUTAN

Thimphu

NEPAL

Kathmandu

INDIA

New Delhi

Kolkata (Calcutta)

Chennai (Madras)

Mumbai (Bombay)

SRI LANKA

Colombo

MALDIVES

Male

PAKISTAN

Islamabad

Karachi

AFGHANISTAN

Kabul

IRAN

Tehran

Shiraz

Ganges R.

GEORGIA

Tbilisi

ARMENIA

Yerevan

AZERBAIJAN

Baku

TURKEY

Ankara

CYPRUS

Nicosia

LEBANON

Beirut

ISRAEL

Jerusalem

SYRIA

Damascus

JORDAN

Amman

IRAQ

Baghdad

KUWAIT

Kuwait

SAUDI ARABIA

Riyadh

Mecca

BAHRAIN

Manama

QATAR

Doha

UNITED ARAB EMIRATES

Abu Dhabi

OMAN

Muscat

YEMEN

Sanaa

SOCOTRA (Yemen)

Arabian Sea

Gulf of Aden

Red Sea

Istanbul

Tropic of Cancer

Equator

MALAYSIA

Kuala Lumpur

SINGAPORE

Singapore

BRUNEI

Bandar Seri Begawan

INDONESIA

Jakarta

Surabaya

Sumatra

Borneo

Java

Celebes

EAST TIMOR

Dili

Timor

PAPUA NEW GUINEA

Port Moresby

New Guinea

New Britain

New Ireland

0 miles 1,000

0 kilometers 1,000

Asia: Physical

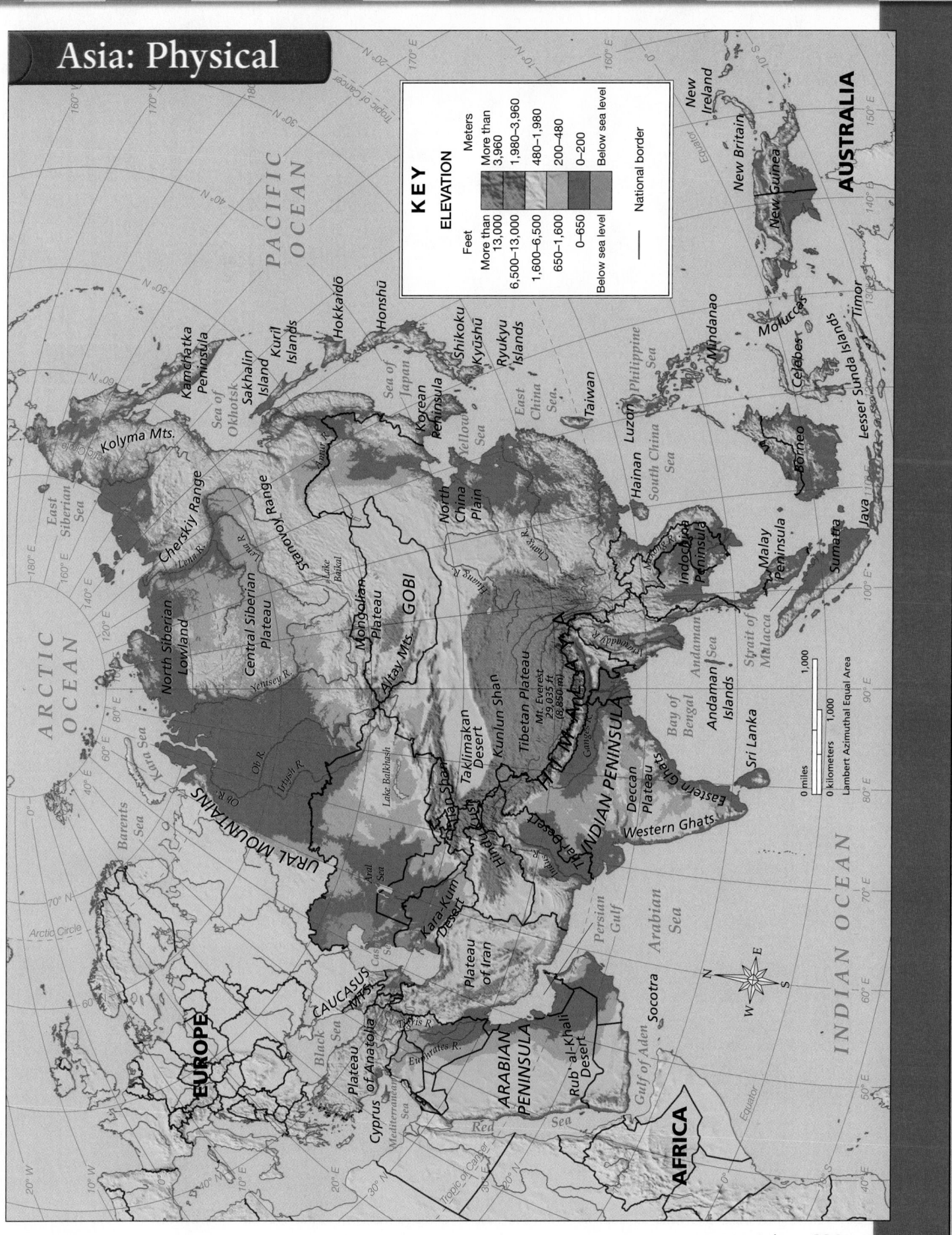

KEY

ELEVATION

Feet	Meters
More than 13,000	More than 3,960
6,500–13,000	1,980–3,960
1,600–6,500	480–1,980
650–1,600	200–480
0–650	0–200
Below sea level	Below sea level

—— National border

PACIFIC OCEAN

ARCTIC OCEAN

INDIAN OCEAN

EUROPE

AFRICA

AUSTRALIA

New Ireland

New Britain

New Guinea

Kamchatka Peninsula

Kolyma Mts.

East Siberian Sea

Cherskiy Range

Lena R.

Central Siberian Plateau

North Siberian Lowland

Yenisey R.

Sea of Okhotsk

Sakhalin Island

Kuril Islands

Hokkaidō

Honshū

Sea of Japan

Korean Peninsula

Amur R.

Stanovoy Range

Lake Baikal

Mongolian Plateau

GOBI

Altay Mts.

Tien Shan

Ob R.

Irtysh R.

Lake Balkhash

URAL MOUNTAINS

Ob R.

Kara Sea

Barents Sea

Aral Sea

Kara Kum Desert

Caspian Sea

Plateau of Iran

CAUCASUS MTS.

Black Sea

Plateau of Anatolia

Cyprus

Mediterranean Sea

Tigris R.

Euphrates R.

ARABIAN PENINSULA

Rub' al-Khali Desert

Red Sea

Gulf of Aden

Socotra

Persian Gulf

Arabian Sea

Hindu Kush

Taklimakan Desert

Kunlun Shan

Tibetan Plateau

Mt. Everest 29,035 ft (8,850 m)

HIMALAYAS

Indus R.

Thar Desert

Ganges R.

INDIAN PENINSULA

Deccan Plateau

Western Ghats

Eastern Ghats

Sri Lanka

Bay of Bengal

Andaman Islands

Andaman Sea

Irrawaddy R.

Indochina Peninsula

Mekong R.

Malay Peninsula

Strait of Malacca

Sumatra

Java

Borneo

Celebes

Lesser Sunda Islands

Timor

Moluccas

Mindanao

Philippine Sea

Luzon

South China Sea

Hainan

Taiwan

East China Sea

Yellow Sea

North China Plain

Huang R.

Chang R.

Shikoku

Kyūshū

Ryukyu Islands

Tropic of Cancer

Arctic Circle

Equator

0 miles 1,000

0 kilometers 1,000

Lambert Azimuthal Equal Area

Oceania

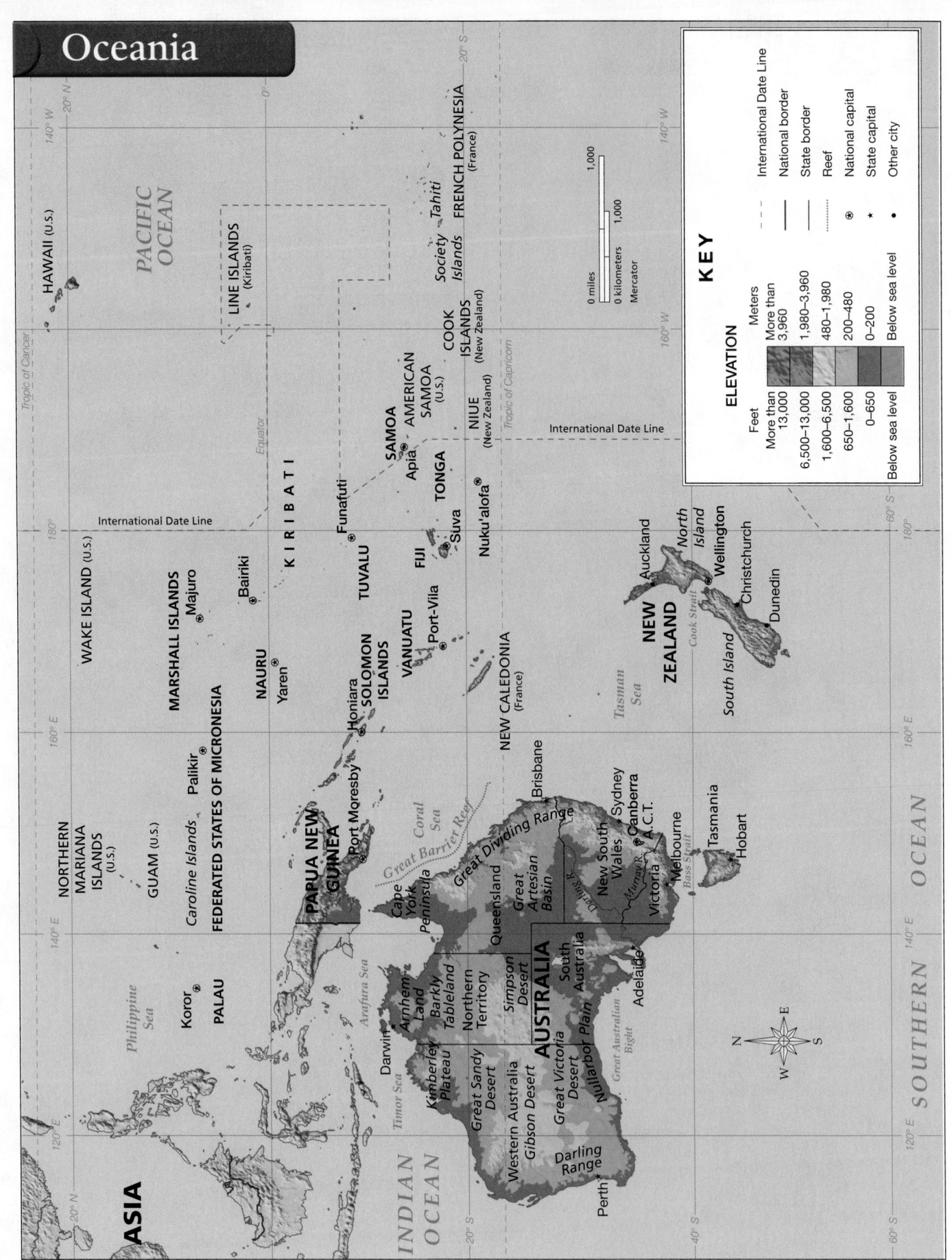

ASIA

INDIAN OCEAN

Philippine Sea

Koror ✪
PALAU

Caroline Islands   Palikir ✪
FEDERATED STATES OF MICRONESIA

NORTHERN MARIANA ISLANDS (U.S.)

GUAM (U.S.)

WAKE ISLAND (U.S.)

MARSHALL ISLANDS
Majuro ✪

Bairiki ✪

NAURU
Yaren ✪

KIRIBATI

HAWAII (U.S.)

PACIFIC OCEAN

Tropic of Cancer

Equator

LINE ISLANDS
(Kiribati)

International Date Line

International Date Line

Funafuti ✪
TUVALU

SOLOMON ISLANDS
Honiara ✪

Port Moresby ✪
PAPUA NEW GUINEA

Arafura Sea

Timor Sea

Darwin

Arnhem Land

Kimberley Plateau

Great Sandy Desert

Western Australia

Gibson Desert

Darling Range

Perth

Great Victoria Desert

Nullarbor Plain

Great Australian Bight

Barkly Tableland

Northern Territory

Simpson Desert

South Australia

AUSTRALIA

Adelaide

Cape York Peninsula

Coral Sea

Great Barrier Reef

Queensland

Great Artesian Basin

Great Dividing Range

Brisbane

New South Wales

Sydney
Canberra ✪ A.C.T.

Murray R.

Darling R.

Victoria

Melbourne

Bass Strait

Tasmania

Hobart

VANUATU
Port-Vila ✪

FIJI
Suva ✪

NEW CALEDONIA (France)

Tasman Sea

Nuku'alofa ✪
TONGA

Apia ✪
SAMOA

AMERICAN SAMOA (U.S.)

NIUE (New Zealand)

Tropic of Capricorn

COOK ISLANDS (New Zealand)

Society Islands   Tahiti
FRENCH POLYNESIA (France)

Auckland
North Island

Wellington ✪
Christchurch

Cook Strait

South Island

NEW ZEALAND

Dunedin

SOUTHERN OCEAN

N
E
W
S

KEY

ELEVATION

Feet	Meters
More than 13,000	More than 3,960
6,500–13,000	1,980–3,960
1,600–6,500	480–1,980
650–1,600	200–480
0–650	0–200
Below sea level	Below sea level

- - - - International Date Line
———— National border
———— State border
·········· Reef
✪ National capital
★ State capital
• Other city

0 miles   1,000
0 kilometers   1,000
Mercator

20° N

20° N

20° S

40° S

120° E   140° E   160° E   180°   160° W   140° W   20° S

60° S

60° S

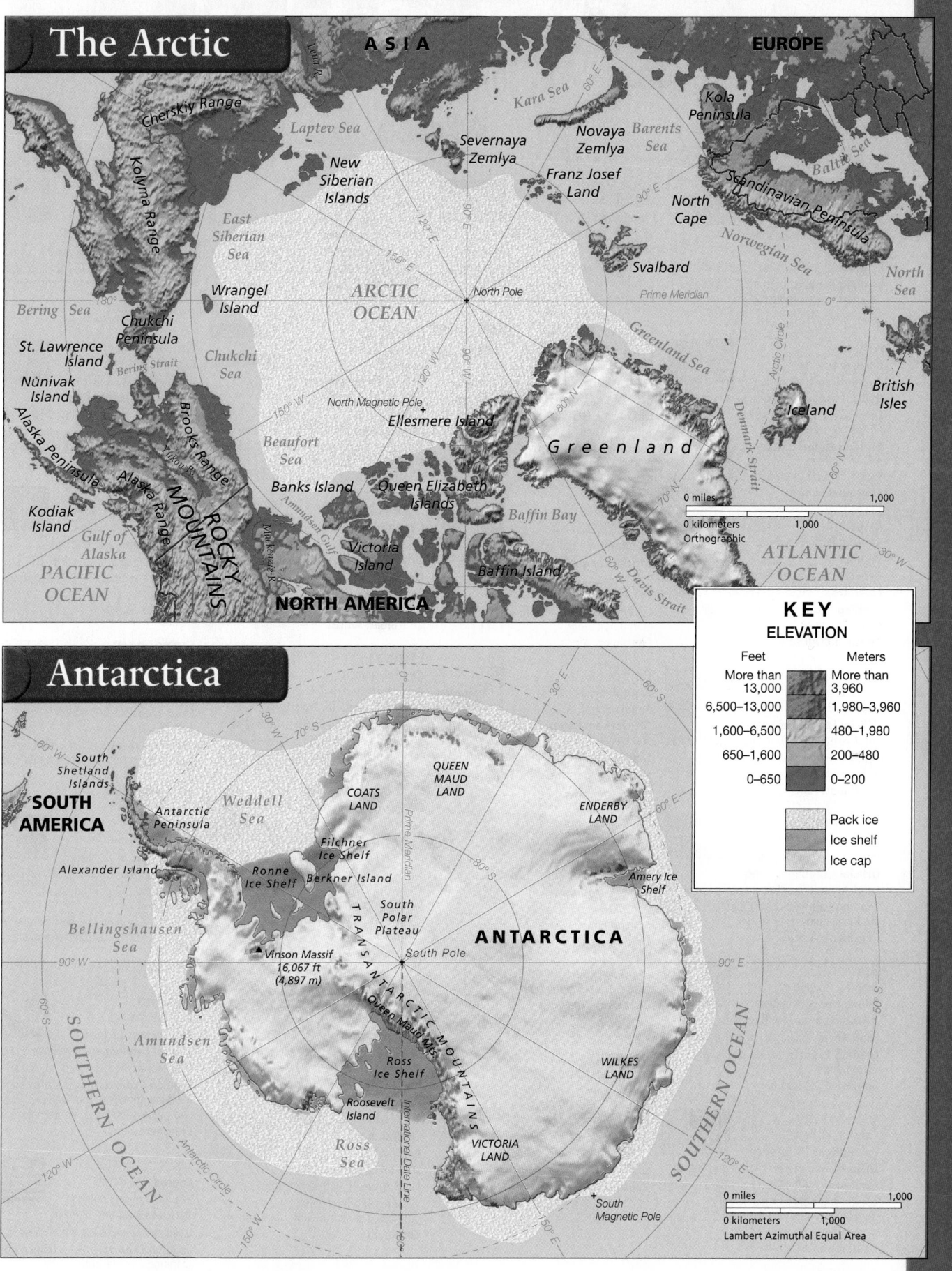

The Arctic

ASIA

EUROPE

Cherskiy Range

Lena R.

Kara Sea

60° E

Kola Peninsula

British Sea

Baltic Sea

Laptev Sea

Severnaya Zemlya

Novaya Zemlya

Barents Sea

Kolyma Range

New Siberian Islands

Franz Josef Land

North Cape

Scandinavian Peninsula

East Siberian Sea

30° E

Norwegian Sea

North Sea

Wrangel Island

ARCTIC OCEAN

Svalbard

Prime Meridian

0°

Bering Sea

80° N

North Pole

Greenland Sea

Chukchi Peninsula

Chukchi Sea

Arctic Circle

St. Lawrence Island

Bering Strait

150° W

Iceland

British Isles

Nunivak Island

North Magnetic Pole

Denmark Strait

Beaufort Sea

Ellesmere Island

Greenland

60° N

Brooks Range

ROCKY MOUNTAINS

Yukon R.

Banks Island

Queen Elizabeth Islands

70° N

Alaska Peninsula

Alaska Range

Amundsen Gulf

Baffin Bay

0 miles 1,000

Kodiak Island

Mackenzie R.

Victoria Island

Baffin Island

0 kilometers 1,000

Gulf of Alaska

Orthographic

PACIFIC OCEAN

Davis Strait

60° W

ATLANTIC OCEAN

30° W

NORTH AMERICA

Antarctica

KEY
ELEVATION

Feet	Meters
More than 13,000	More than 3,960
6,500–13,000	1,980–3,960
1,600–6,500	480–1,980
650–1,600	200–480
0–650	0–200

Pack ice

Ice shelf

Ice cap

SOUTH AMERICA

South Shetland Islands

30° W

0°

70° S

QUEEN MAUD LAND

30° E

60° S

Antarctic Peninsula

Weddell Sea

COATS LAND

ENDERBY LAND

60° E

Filchner Ice Shelf

Prime Meridian

Alexander Island

Ronne Ice Shelf

Berkner Island

Amery Ice Shelf

Bellingshausen Sea

80° S

South Polar Plateau

ANTARCTICA

90° E

90° W

▲ Vinson Massif 16,067 ft (4,897 m)

TRANSANTARCTIC MOUNTAINS

South Pole

Queen Maud Mts.

WILKES LAND

Amundsen Sea

Ross Ice Shelf

50° S

60° S

Roosevelt Island

International Date Line

VICTORIA LAND

120° E

SOUTHERN OCEAN

Ross Sea

120° W

Antarctic Circle

South Magnetic Pole

0 miles 1,000

150° W

0 kilometers 1,000

Lambert Azimuthal Equal Area

Country Databank

Africa

Algeria
Capital: Algiers
Population: 32.3 million
Official Languages: Arabic and Tamazight
Land Area: 2,381,740 sq km; 919,590 sq mi
Leading Exports: petroleum, natural gas, petroleum products
Continent: Africa

Angola
Capital: Luanda
Population: 10.6 million
Official Language: Portuguese
Land Area: 1,246,700 sq km; 481,551 sq mi
Leading Exports: crude oil, diamonds, refined petroleum products, gas, coffee, sisal, fish and fish products, timber, cotton
Continent: Africa

Benin
Capital: Porto-Novo
Population: 6.9 million
Official Language: French
Land Area: 110,620 sq km; 42,710 sq mi
Leading Exports: cotton, crude oil, palm products, cocoa
Continent: Africa

Botswana
Capital: Gaborone
Population: 1.6 million
Official Language: English
Land Area: 585,370 sq km; 226,011 sq mi
Leading Exports: diamonds, copper, nickel, soda ash, meat, textiles
Continent: Africa

Burkina Faso
Capital: Ouagadougou
Population: 12.6 million
Official Language: French
Land Area: 273,800 sq km; 105,714 sq mi
Leading Exports: cotton, animal products, gold
Continent: Africa

Burundi
Capital: Bujumbura
Population: 6.4 million
Official Languages: Kirundi and French
Land Area: 25,650 sq km; 9,903 sq mi
Leading Exports: coffee, tea, sugar, cotton, hides
Continent: Africa

Cameroon
Capital: Yaoundé
Population: 16.1 million
Official Languages: English and French
Land Area: 469,440 sq km; 181,251 sqmi
Leading Exports: crude oil and petroleum products, lumber, cocoa, aluminum, coffee, cotton
Continent: Africa

Cape Verde
Capital: Praia
Population: 408,760
Official Language: Portuguese
Land Area: 4,033 sq km; 1,557 sq mi
Leading Exports: fuel, shoes, garments, fish, hides
Location: Atlantic Ocean

Central African Republic
Capital: Bangui
Population: 3.6 million
Official Language: French
Land Area: 622,984 sq km; 240,534 sq mi
Leading Exports: diamonds, timber, cotton, coffee, tobacco
Continent: Africa

Chad
Capital: N'Djamena
Population: 9 million
Official Languages: Arabic and French
Land Area: 1,259,200 sq km; 486,177 sq mi
Leading Exports: cotton, cattle, gum arabic
Continent: Africa

Comoros
Capital: Moroni
Population: 614,382
Official Languages: Arabic, Comoran, and French
Land Area: 2,170 sq km; 838 sq mi
Leading Exports: vanilla, ylang-ylang, cloves, perfume oil, copra
Location: Indian Ocean

Congo, Democratic Republic of the
Capital: Kinshasa
Population: 55.2 million
Official Language: French
Land Area: 2,267,600 sq km; 875,520 sq mi
Leading Exports: diamonds, copper, coffee, cobalt, crude oil
Continent: Africa

Congo, Republic of the
Capital: Brazzaville
Population: 3.3 million
Official Language: French
Land Area: 341,500 sq km; 131,853 sq mi
Leading Exports: petroleum, lumber, sugar, cocoa, coffee, diamonds
Continent: Africa

Djibouti
Capital: Djibouti
Population: 472,810
Official Languages: Arabic and French
Land Area: 22,980 sq km; 8,873 sq mi
Leading Exports: reexports, hides and skins, coffee (in transit)
Continent: Africa

Egypt
Capital: Cairo
Population: 70.7 million
Official Language: Arabic
Land Area: 995,450 sq km; 384,343 sq mi
Leading Exports: crude oil and petroleum products, cotton, textiles, metal products, chemicals
Continent: Africa

Equatorial Guinea
Capital: Malabo
Population: 498,144
Official Languages: Spanish and French
Land Area: 28,050 sq km; 10,830 sq mi
Leading Exports: petroleum, timber, cocoa
Continent: Africa

Eritrea
Capital: Asmara
Population: 4.5 million
Official Language: Tigrinya
Land Area: 121,320 sq km; 46,842 sq mi
Leading Exports: livestock, sorghum, textiles, food, small manufactured goods
Continent: Africa

Ethiopia
Capital: Addis Ababa
Population: 67.7 million
Official Language: Amharic
Land Area: 1,119,683 sq km; 432,310 sq mi
Leading Exports: coffee, qat, gold, leather products, oilseeds
Continent: Africa

Gabon
Capital: Libreville
Population: 1.2 million
Official Language: French
Land Area: 257,667 sq km; 99,489 sq mi
Leading Exports: crude oil, timber, manganese, uranium
Continent: Africa

Gambia
Capital: Banjul
Population: 1.5 million
Official Language: English
Land Area: 10,000 sq km; 3,861 sq mi
Leading Exports: peanuts and peanut products, fish, cotton lint, palm kernels
Continent: Africa

Ghana
Capital: Accra
Population: 20.2 million
Official Language: English
Land Area: 230,940 sq km; 89,166 sq mi
Leading Exports: gold, cocoa, timber, tuna, bauxite, aluminum, manganese ore, diamonds
Continent: Africa

Guinea
Capital: Conakry
Population: 7.8 million
Official Language: French
Land Area: 245,857 sq km; 94,925 sq mi
Leading Exports: bauxite, alumina, gold, diamonds, coffee, fish, agricultural products
Continent: Africa

Guinea-Bissau
Capital: Bissau
Population: 1.4 million
Official Language: Portuguese
Land Area: 28,000 sq km; 10,811 sq mi
Leading Exports: cashew nuts, shrimp, peanuts, palm kernels, lumber
Continent: Africa

Ivory Coast
Capital: Yamoussoukro
Population: 16.8 million
Official Language: French
Land Area: 318,000 sq km; 122,780 sq mi
Leading Exports: cocoa, coffee, timber, petroleum, cotton, bananas, pineapples, palm oil, cotton, fish
Continent: Africa

Kenya
Capital: Nairobi
Population: 31.3 million
Official Languages: Swahili and English
Land Area: 569,250 sq km; 219,787 sq mi
Leading Exports: tea, horticultural products, coffee, petroleum products, fish, cement
Continent: Africa

Lesotho
Capital: Maseru
Population: 2.2 million
Official Languages: Sesotho and English
Land Area: 30,355 sq km; 11,720 sq mi
Leading Exports: manufactured goods (clothing, footwear, road vehicles), wool and mohair, food and live animals
Continent: Africa

Liberia
Capital: Monrovia
Population: 3.3 million
Official Language: English
Land Area: 96,320 sq km; 37,189 sq mi
Leading Exports: rubber, timber, iron, diamonds, cocoa, coffee
Continent: Africa

Libya
Capital: Tripoli
Population: 5.4 million
Official Language: Arabic
Land Area: 1,759,540 sq km;
679,358 sq mi
Leading Exports: crude oil, refined
petroleum products
Continent: Africa

Madagascar
Capital: Antananarivo
Population: 16.5 million
Official Languages: French and
Malagasy
Land Area: 581,540 sq km;
224,533 sq mi
Leading Exports: coffee, vanilla,
shellfish, sugar, cotton cloth, chromite,
petroleum products
Location: Indian Ocean

Malawi
Capital: Lilongwe
Population: 10.7 million
Official Languages: English and
Chichewa
Land Area: 94,080 sq km; 36,324 sq mi
Leading Exports: tobacco, tea, sugar,
cotton, coffee, peanuts, wood products,
apparel
Continent: Africa

Mali
Capital: Bamako
Population: 11.3 million
Official Language: French
Land Area: 1,220,000 sq km;
471,042 sq mi
Leading Exports: cotton, gold, livestock
Continent: Africa

Mauritania
Capital: Nouakchott
Population: 2.8 million
Official Language: Arabic
Land Area: 1,030,400 sq km;
397,837 sq mi
Leading Exports: iron ore, fish and fish
products, gold
Continent: Africa

Mauritius
Capital: Port Louis
Population: 1.2 million
Official Language: English
Land Area: 2,030 sq km;
784 sq mi
Leading Exports: clothing and textiles,
sugar, cut flowers, molasses
Location: Indian Ocean

Morocco
Capital: Rabat
Population: 31.2 million
Official Language: Arabic
Land Area: 446,300 sq km;
172,316 sq mi
Leading Exports: phosphates and
fertilizers, food and beverages, minerals
Continent: Africa

Mozambique
Capital: Maputo
Population: 19.6 million
Official Language: Portuguese
Land Area: 784,090 sq km;
302,737 sq mi
Leading Exports: prawns, cashews,
cotton, sugar, citrus, timber, bulk
electricity
Continent: Africa

Namibia
Capital: Windhoek
Population: 1.8 million
Official Language: English
Land Area: 825,418 sq km;
318,694 sq mi
Leading Exports: diamonds, copper,
gold, zinc, lead, uranium, cattle,
processed fish, karakul skins
Continent: Africa

Niger
Capital: Niamey
Population: 11.3 million
Official Language: French
Land Area: 1,226,700 sq km;
489,073 sq mi
Leading Exports: uranium ore,
livestock products, cowpeas, onions
Continent: Africa

Nigeria
Capital: Abuja
Population: 129.9 million
Official Language: English
Land Area: 910,768 sq km;
351,648 sq mi
Leading Exports: petroleum and
petroleum products, cocoa, rubber
Continent: Africa

Rwanda
Capital: Kigali
Population: 7.4 million
Official Languages: Kinyarwanda,
French, and English
Land Area: 24,948 sq km; 9,632 sq mi
Leading Exports: coffee, tea, hides,
tin ore
Continent: Africa

São Tomé and Príncipe
Capital: São Tomé
Population: 170,372
Official Language: Portuguese
Land Area: 1,001 sq km; 386 sq mi
Leading Exports: cocoa, copra, coffee,
palm oil
Location: Atlantic Ocean

Senegal
Capital: Dakar
Population: 10.6 million
Official Language: French
Land Area: 192,000 sq km;
74,131 sq mi
Leading Exports: fish, groundnuts
(peanuts), petroleum products,
phosphates, cotton
Continent: Africa

Seychelles
Capital: Victoria
Population: 80,098
Official Languages: English and French
Land Area: 455 sq km; 176 sq mi
Leading Exports: canned tuna,
cinnamon bark, copra, petroleum
products (reexports)
Location: Indian Ocean

Sierra Leone
Capital: Freetown
Population: 5.6 million
Official Language: English
Land Area: 71,620 sq km; 27,652 sq mi
Leading Exports: diamonds, rutile,
cocoa, coffee, fish
Continent: Africa

Somalia
Capital: Mogadishu
Population: 7.8 million
Official Languages: Somali and Arabic
Land Area: 627,337 sq km;
242,215 sq mi
Leading Exports: livestock, bananas,
hides, fish, charcoal, scrap metal
Continent: Africa

South Africa
Capital: Cape Town,
Pretoria, and Bloemfontein
Population: 43.6 million
Official Languages: Eleven official
languages: Afrikaans, English, Ndebele,
Pedi, Sotho, Swazi, Tsonga, Tswana,
Venda, Xhosa, and Zulu
Land Area: 1,219,912 sq km;
471,008 sq mi
Leading Exports: gold, diamonds,
platinum, other metals and minerals,
machinery and equipment
Continent: Africa

Sudan
Capital: Khartoum
Population: 37.1 million
Official Language: Arabic
Land Area: 2,376,000 sq km;
917,374 sq mi
Leading Exports: oil and petroleum
products, cotton, sesame, livestock,
groundnuts, gum arabic, sugar
Continent: Africa

Swaziland
Capital: Mbabane
Population: 1.1 million
Official Languages: English and siSwati
Land Area: 17,20 sq km; 6,642 sq mi
Leading Exports: soft drink concen-
trates, sugar, wood pulp, cotton yarn,
refrigerators, citrus and canned fruit
Continent: Africa

Tanzania
Capital: Dar es Salaam
and Dodoma
Population: 37.2 million
Official Languages: Swahili and
English
Land Area: 886,037 sq km;
342,099 sq mi
Leading Exports: gold, coffee, cashew
nuts, manufactured goods, cotton
Continent: Africa

Togo
Capital: Lomé
Population: 5.2 million
Official Language: French
Land Area: 54,385 sq km; 20,998 sq mi
Leading Exports: cotton, phosphates,
coffee, cocoa
Continent: Africa

Tunisia
Capital: Tunis
Population: 9.8 million
Official Language: Arabic
Land Area: 155,360 sq km;
59,984 sq mi
Leading Exports: textiles, mechanical
goods, phosphates and chemicals, agri-
cultural products, hydrocarbons
Continent: Africa

Uganda
Capital: Kampala
Population: 24.7 million
Official Language: English
Land Area: 199,710 sq km;
77,108 sq mi
Leading Exports: coffee, fish and fish
products, tea, gold, cotton, flowers, hor-
ticultural products
Continent: Africa

Zambia
Capital: Lusaka
Population: 10.1 million
Official Language: English
Land Area: 740,724 sq km;
285,994 sq mi
Leading Exports: copper, cobalt,
electricity, tobacco, flowers, cotton
Continent: Africa

Zimbabwe
Capital: Harare
Population: 11.3 million
Official Language: English
Land Area: 386,670 sq km;
149,293 sq mi
Leading Exports: tobacco, gold, iron
alloys, textiles and clothing
Continent: Africa

Asia and the Pacific

Afghanistan
Capital: Kabul
Population: 27.8 million
Official Languages: Pashtu and Dari
Land Area: 647,500 sq km; 250,000 sq mi
Leading Exports: agricultural products, hand-woven carpets, wool, cotton, hides and pelts, precious and semiprecious gems
Continent: Asia

Armenia
Capital: Yerevan
Population: 3.3 million
Official Language: Armenian
Land Area: 29,400 sq km; 10,965 sq mi
Leading Exports: diamonds, scrap metal, machinery and equipment, brandy, copper ore
Continent: Asia

Australia
Capital: Canberra
Population: 19.6 million
Official Language: English
Land Area: 7,617,930 sq km; 2,941,283 sq mi
Leading Exports: coal, gold, meat, wool, alumina, iron ore, wheat, machinery and transport equipment
Continent: Australia

Azerbaijan
Capital: Baku
Population: 7.8 million
Official Language: Azerbaijani
Land Area: 86,100 sq km; 33,243 sq mi
Leading Exports: oil and gas, machinery, cotton, foodstuffs
Continent: Asia

Bahrain
Capital: Manama
Population: 656,397
Official Language: Arabic
Land Area: 665 sq km; 257 sq mi
Leading Exports: petroleum and petroleum products, aluminum, textiles
Continent: Asia

Bangladesh
Capital: Dhaka
Population: 133.4 million
Official Language: Bengali
Land Area: 133,910 sq km; 51,705 sq mi
Leading Exports: garments, jute and jute goods, leather, frozen fish and seafood
Continent: Asia

Bhutan
Capital: Thimphu
Population: 2.1 million
Official Language: Dzongkha
Land Area: 47,000 sq km; 18,147 sq mi
Leading Exports: electricity, cardamom, gypsum, timber, handicrafts, cement, fruit, precious stones, spices
Continent: Asia

Brunei
Capital: Bandar Seri Begawan
Population: 350,898
Official Language: Malay
Land Area: 5,270 sq km; 2,035 sq mi
Leading Exports: crude oil, natural gas, refined products
Continent: Asia

Cambodia
Capital: Phnom Penh
Population: 12.8 million
Official Language: Khmer
Land Area: 176,520 sq km; 68,154 sq mi
Leading Exports: timber, garments, rubber, rice, fish
Continent: Asia

China
Capital: Beijing
Population: 1.29 billion
Official Languages: Mandarin and Chinese
Land Area: 9,326,410 sq km; 3,600,927 sq mi
Leading Exports: machinery and equipment, textiles and clothing, footwear, toys and sports goods, mineral fuels
Continent: Asia

Cyprus
Capital: Nicosia
Population: 767,314
Official Languages: Greek and Turkish
Land Area: 9,240 sq km; 3,568 sq mi
Leading Exports: citrus, potatoes, grapes, wine, cement, clothing and shoes
Location: Mediterranean Sea

East Timor
Capital: Dili
Population: 952,618
Official Languages: Tetum and Portuguese
Land Area: 15,007 sq km; 5,794 sq mi
Leading Exports: coffee, sandalwood, marble
Continent: Asia

Fiji
Capital: Suva
Population: 856,346
Official Language: English
Land Area: 18,270 sq km; 7,054 sq mi
Leading Exports: sugar, garments, gold, timber, fish, molasses, coconut oil
Location: Pacific Ocean

Georgia
Capital: Tbilisi
Population: 5 million
Official Languages: Georgian and Abkhazian
Land Area: 69,700 sq km; 26,911 sq mi
Leading Exports: scrap metal, machinery, chemicals, fuel reexports, citrus fruits, tea, wine, other agricultural products
Continent: Asia

India
Capital: New Delhi
Population: 1.05 billion
Official Languages: Hindi and English
Land Area: 2,973,190 sq km; 1,147,949 sq mi
Leading Exports: textile goods, gems and jewelry, engineering goods, chemicals, leather manufactured goods
Continent: Asia

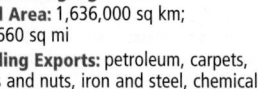

Indonesia
Capital: Jakarta
Population: 231.3 million
Official Language: Bahasa Indonesia
Land Area: 1,826,440 sq km; 705,188 sq mi
Leading Exports: oil and gas, electrical appliances, plywood, textiles, rubber
Continent: Asia

Iran
Capital: Tehran
Population: 66.6 million
Official Language: Farsi
Land Area: 1,636,000 sq km; 631,660 sq mi
Leading Exports: petroleum, carpets, fruits and nuts, iron and steel, chemicals
Continent: Asia

Iraq
Capital: Baghdad
Population: 24.7 million
Official Language: Arabic
Land Area: 432,162 sq km; 166,858 sq mi
Leading Exports: crude oil
Continent: Asia

Israel
Capital: Jerusalem
Population: 6.0 million
Official Languages: Hebrew, Arabic
Land Area: 20,330 sq km; 7,849 sq mi
Leading Exports: machinery and equipment, software, cut diamonds, agricultural products, chemicals, textiles and apparel
Continent: Asia

Japan
Capital: Tokyo
Population: 127 million
Official Language: Japanese
Land Area: 374,744 sq km; 144,689 sq mi
Leading Exports: motor vehicles, semiconductors, office machinery, chemicals
Continent: Asia

Jordan
Capital: Amman
Population: 5.3 million
Official Language: Arabic
Land Area: 91,971 sq km; 35,510 sq mi
Leading Exports: phosphates, fertilizers, potash, agricultural products, manufactured goods, pharmaceuticals
Continent: Asia

Kazakhstan
Capital: Astana
Population: 16.7 million
Official Language: Kazakh
Land Area: 2,669,800 sq km; 1,030,810 sq mi
Leading Exports: oil and oil products, ferrous metals, machinery, chemicals, grain, wool, meat, coal
Continent: Asia

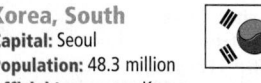

Kiribati
Capital: Bairiki (Tarawa Atoll)
Population: 96,335
Official Language: English
Land Area: 811 sq km; 313 sq mi
Leading Exports: copra, coconuts, seaweed, fish
Location: Pacific Ocean

Korea, North
Capital: Pyongyang
Population: 22.3 million
Official Language: Korean
Land Area: 120,410 sq km; 46,490 sq mi
Leading Exports: minerals, metallurgical products, manufactured goods (including armaments), agricultural and fishery products
Continent: Asia

Korea, South
Capital: Seoul
Population: 48.3 million
Official Language: Korean
Land Area: 98,190 sq km; 37,911 sq mi
Leading Exports: electronic products, machinery and equipment, motor vehicles, steel, ships, textiles, clothing, footwear, fish
Continent: Asia

Kuwait
Capital: Kuwait City
Population: 2.1 million
Official Language: Arabic
Land Area: 17,820 sq km; 6,880 sq mi
Leading Exports: oil and refined products, fertilizers
Continent: Asia

Kyrgyzstan
Capital: Bishkek
Population: 4.8 million
Official Languages: Kyrgyz and Russian
Land Area: 191,300 sq km; 73,861 sq mi
Leading Exports: cotton, wool, meat, tobacco, gold, mercury, uranium, hydropower, machinery, shoes
Continent: Asia

Laos
Capital: Vientiane
Population: 5.8 million
Official Language: Lao
Land Area: 230,800 sq km; 89,112 sq mi
Leading Exports: wood products, garments, electricity, coffee, tin
Continent: Asia

Lebanon

Capital: Beirut
Population: 3.7 million
Official Language: Arabic
Land Area: 10,230 sq km; 3,950 sq mi
Leading Exports: foodstuffs and tobacco, textile, chemicals, precious stones, metal and metal products, electrical equipment and products, jewelry, paper and paper products
Continent: Asia

Malaysia

Capital: Kuala Lumpur and Putrajaya
Population: 22.7 million
Official Language: Bahasa Malaysia
Land Area: 328,550 sq km; 126,853 sq mi
Leading Exports: electronic equipment, petroleum and liquefied natural gas, wood and wood products, palm oil, rubber, textiles, chemicals
Continent: Asia

Maldives

Capital: Malé
Population: 320,165
Official Language: Dhivehi (Maldivian)
Land Area: 300 sq km; 116 sq mi
Leading Exports: fish, clothing
Location: Indian Ocean

Marshall Islands

Capital: Majuro
Population: 73,360
Official Languages: Marshallese and English
Land Area: 181.3 sq km; 70 sq mi
Leading Exports: copra cake, coconut oil, handicrafts
Location: Pacific Ocean

Micronesia, Federated States of

Capital: Palikir (Pohnpei Island)
Population: 135,869
Official Language: English
Land Area: 702 sq km; 271 sq mi
Leading Exports: fish, garments, bananas, black pepper
Location: Pacific Ocean

Mongolia

Capital: Ulaanbaatar
Population: 2.6 million
Official Language: Khalkha Mongolian
Land Area: 1,555,400 sq km; 600,540 sq mi
Leading Exports: copper, livestock, animal products, cashmere, wool, hides, fluorspar, other nonferrous metals
Continent: Asia

Myanmar (Burma)

Capital: Rangoon (Yangon)
Population: 42.2 million
Official Language: Burmese (Myanmar)
Land Area: 657,740 sq km; 253,953 sq mi
Leading Exports: apparel, foodstuffs, wood products, precious stones
Continent: Asia

Nauru

Capital: Yaren District
Population: 12,329
Official Language: Nauruan
Land Area: 21 sq km; 8 sq mi
Leading Exports: phosphates
Location: Pacific Ocean

Nepal

Capital: Kathmandu
Population: 25.9 million
Official Language: Nepali
Land Area: 136,800 sq km; 52,818 sq mi
Leading Exports: carpets, clothing, leather goods, jute goods, grain
Continent: Asia

New Zealand

Capital: Wellington
Population: 3.8 million
Official Languages: English and Maori
Land Area: 268,680 sq km; 103,737 sq mi
Leading Exports: dairy products, meat, wood and wood products, fish, machinery
Location: Pacific Ocean

Oman

Capital: Muscat
Population: 2.7 million
Official Language: Arabic
Land Area: 212,460 sq km; 82,030 sq mi
Leading Exports: petroleum, reexports, fish, metals, textiles
Continent: Asia

Pakistan

Capital: Islamabad
Population: 147.7 million
Official Languages: Urdu and English
Land Area: 778,720 sq km; 300,664 sq mi
Leading Exports: textiles (garments, cotton cloth, and yarn), rice, other agricultural products
Continent: Asia

Palau

Capital: Koror
Population: 19,409
Official Languages: English and Palauan
Land Area: 458 sq km; 177 sq mi
Leading Exports: shellfish, tuna, copra, garments
Location: Pacific Ocean

Papua New Guinea

Capital: Port Moresby
Population: 5.2 million
Official Language: English
Land Area: 452,860 sq km; 174,849 sq mi
Leading Exports: oil, gold, copper ore, logs, palm oil, coffee, cocoa, crayfish, prawns
Location: Pacific Ocean

Philippines

Capital: Manila
Population: 84.5 million
Official Languages: Filipino and English
Land Area: 298,170 sq km; 115,123 sq mi
Leading Exports: electronic equipment, machinery and transport equipment, garments, coconut products
Continent: Asia

Qatar

Capital: Doha
Population: 793,341
Official Language: Arabic
Land Area: 11,437 sq km; 4,416 sq mi
Leading Exports: petroleum products, fertilizers, steel
Continent: Asia

Samoa

Capital: Apia
Population: 178,631
Official Languages: Samoan and English
Land Area: 2,934 sq km; 1,133 sq mi
Leading Exports: fish, coconut oil cream, copra, taro, garments, beer
Location: Pacific Ocean

Saudi Arabia

Capital: Riyadh and Jiddah
Population: 23.5 million
Official Language: Arabic
Land Area: 1,960,582 sq km; 756,981 sq mi
Leading Exports: petroleum and petroleum products
Continent: Asia

Singapore

Capital: Singapore
Population: 4.5 million
Official Languages: Malay, English, Mandarin, Chinese, and Tamil
Land Area: 683 sq km; 264 sq mi
Leading Exports: machinery and equipment (including electronics), consumer goods, chemicals, mineral fuels
Continent: Asia

Solomon Islands

Capital: Honiara
Population: 494,786
Official Language: English
Land Area: 27,540 sq km; 10,633 sq mi
Leading Exports: timber, fish, copra, palm oil, cocoa
Location: Pacific Ocean

Sri Lanka

Capital: Colombo
Population: 19.6 million
Official Language: Sinhala, Tamil, and English
Land Area: 64,740 sq km; 24,996 sq mi
Leading Exports: textiles and apparel, tea, diamonds, coconut products, petroleum products
Continent: Asia

Syria

Capital: Damascus
Population: 17.2 million
Official Language: Arabic
Land Area: 184,050 sq km; 71,062 sq mi
Leading Exports: crude oil, textiles, fruits and vegetables, raw cotton
Continent: Asia

Taiwan

Capital: Taipei
Population: 22.5 million
Official Language: Mandarin Chinese
Land Area: 32,260 sq km; 12,456 sq mi
Leading Exports: machinery and electrical equipment, metals, textiles, plastics, chemicals
Continent: Asia

Tajikistan

Capital: Dushanbe
Population: 6.7 million
Official Language: Tajik
Land Area: 142,700 sq km; 55,096 sq mi
Leading Exports: aluminum, electricity, cotton, fruits, vegetables, oil, textiles
Continent: Asia

Thailand

Capital: Bangkok
Population: 62.5 million
Official Language: Thai
Land Area: 511,770 sq km; 197,564 sq mi
Leading Exports: computers, transistors, seafood, clothing, rice
Continent: Asia

Tonga

Capital: Nuku'alofa
Population: 106,137
Official Languages: Tongan and English
Land Area: 718 sq km; 277 sq mi
Leading Exports: squash, fish, vanilla beans, root crops
Location: Pacific Ocean

Turkey

Capital: Ankara
Population: 67.3 million
Official Language: Turkish
Land Area: 770,760 sq km; 297,590 sq mi
Leading Exports: apparel, foodstuffs, textiles, metal manufactured goods, transport equipment
Continent: Asia

Turkmenistan

Capital: Ashgabat
Population: 4.7 million
Official Language: Turkmen
Land Area: 488,100 sq km; 188,455 sq mi
Leading Exports: gas, oil, cotton fiber, textiles
Continent: Asia

Asia and the Pacific (continued)

Tuvalu

Capital: Fongafale
Population: 10,800
Official Language: English
Land Area: 26 sq km; 10 sq mi
Leading Exports: copra, fish
Location: Pacific Ocean

United Arab Emirates
Capital: Abu Dhabi
Population: 2.4 million
Official Language: Arabic
Land Area: 82,880 sq km; 32,000 sq mi
Leading Exports: crude oil, natural gas, reexports, dried fish, dates
Continent: Asia

Uzbekistan
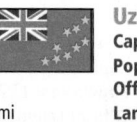
Capital: Tashkent
Population: 25.5 million
Official Language: Uzbek
Land Area: 425,400 sq km; 164,247 sq mi
Leading Exports: cotton, gold, energy products, mineral fertilizers, ferrous metals, textiles, food products, automobiles
Continent: Asia

Vanuatu
Capital: Port-Vila
Population: 196,178
Official Languages: English, French, and Bislama
Land Area: 12,200 sq km; 4,710 sq mi
Leading Exports: copra, kava, beef, cocoa, timber, coffee
Location: Pacific Ocean

Vietnam
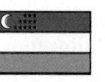
Capital: Hanoi
Population: 81.1 million
Official Language: Vietnamese
Land Area: 325,320 sq km; 125,621 sq mi
Leading Exports: crude oil, marine products, rice, coffee, rubber, tea, garments, shoes
Continent: Asia

Yemen

Capital: Sanaa
Population: 18.7 million
Official Language: Arabic
Land Area: 527,970 sq km; 203,849 sq mi
Leading Exports: crude oil, coffee, dried and salted fish
Continent: Asia

Europe and Russia

Albania
Capital: Tiranë
Population: 3.5 million
Official Language: Albanian
Land Area: 27,398 sq km; 10,578 sq mi
Leading Exports: textiles and footwear, asphalt, metals and metallic ores, crude oil, vegetables, fruits, tobacco
Continent: Europe

Andorra
Capital: Andorra la Vella
Population: 68,403
Official Language: Catalan
Land Area: 468 sq km; 181 sq mi
Leading Exports: tobacco products, furniture
Continent: Europe

Austria
Capital: Vienna
Population: 8.2 million
Official Language: German
Land Area: 82,738 sq km; 31,945 sq mi
Leading Exports: machinery and equipment, motor vehicles and parts, paper and paperboard, metal goods, chemicals, iron and steel, textiles, foodstuffs
Continent: Europe

Belarus
Capital: Minsk
Population: 10.3 million
Official Languages: Belarussian and Russian
Land Area: 207,600 sq km; 80,154 sq mi
Leading Exports: machinery and equipment, mineral products, chemicals, textiles, food stuffs, metals
Continent: Europe

Belgium
Capital: Brussels
Population: 10.3 million
Official Languages: Dutch and French
Land Area: 30,230 sq km; 11,172 sq mi
Leading Exports: machinery and equipment, chemicals, metals and metal products
Continent: Europe

Bosnia and Herzegovina
Capital: Sarajevo
Population: 4.0 million
Official Language: Serbo-Croat
Land Area: 51,129 sq km; 19,741 sq mi
Leading Exports: miscellaneous manufactured goods, crude materials
Continent: Europe

Bulgaria
Capital: Sofia
Population: 7.6 million
Official Language: Bulgarian
Land Area: 110,550 sq km; 42,683 sq mi
Leading Exports: clothing, footwear, iron and steel, machinery and equipment, fuels
Continent: Europe

Croatia
Capital: Zagreb
Population: 4.4 million
Official Language: Croatian
Land Area: 56,414 km; 21,781 sq mi
Leading Exports: transport equipment, textiles, chemicals, foodstuffs, fuels
Continent: Europe

Czech Republic
Capital: Prague
Population: 10.3 million
Official Language: Czech
Land Area: 78,276 sq km; 29,836 sq mi
Leading Exports: machinery and transport equipment, intermediate manufactured goods, chemicals, raw materials and fuel
Continent: Europe

Denmark
Capital: Copenhagen
Population: 5.4 million
Official Language: Danish
Land Area: 42,394 sq km; 16,368 sq mi
Leading Exports: machinery and instruments, meat and meat products, dairy products, fish, chemicals, furniture, ships, windmills
Continent: Europe

Estonia
Capital: Tallinn
Population: 1.4 million
Official Language: Estonian
Land Area: 43,211 sq km; 16,684 sq mi
Leading Exports: machinery and equipment, wood products, textiles, food products, metals, chemical products
Continent: Europe

Finland
Capital: Helsinki
Population: 5.2 million
Official Languages: Finnish and Swedish
Land Area: 305,470 sq km; 117,942 sq mi
Leading Exports: machinery and equipment, chemicals, metals, timber, paper, pulp
Continent: Europe

France

Capital: Paris
Population: 59.8 million
Official Language: French
Land Area: 545,630 sq km; 310,668 sq mi
Leading Exports: machinery and transportation equipment, aircraft, plastics, chemicals, pharmaceutical products, iron and steel, beverages
Continent: Europe

Germany
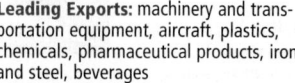
Capital: Berlin
Population: 83 million
Official Language: German
Land Area: 349,223 sq km; 134,835 sq mi
Leading Exports: machinery, vehicles, chemicals, metals and manufactured goods, foodstuffs, textiles
Continent: Europe

Greece
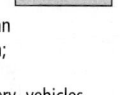
Capital: Athens
Population: 10.6 million
Official Language: Greek
Land Area: 130,800 sq km; 50,502 sq mi
Leading Exports: food and beverages, manufactured goods, petroleum products, chemicals, textiles
Continent: Europe

Holy See (Vatican City)

Capital: Vatican City
Population: 900
Official Languages: Latin and Italian
Land Area: 0.44 sq km; 0.17 sq mi
Leading Exports: no information available
Continent: Europe

Hungary

Capital: Budapest
Population: 10.1 million
Official Language: Hungarian
Land Area: 92,340 sq km; 35,652 sq mi
Leading Exports: machinery and equipment, other manufactured goods, food products, raw materials, fuels and electricity
Continent: Europe

Iceland

Capital: Reykjavík
Population: 279,384
Official Language: Icelandic
Land Area: 100,250 sq km; 38,707 sq mi
Leading Exports: fish and fish products, animal products, aluminum, diatomite, ferrosilicon
Location: Atlantic Ocean

Ireland

Capital: Dublin
Population: 3.9 million
Official Languages: Irish Gaelic and English
Land Area: 68,890 sq km; 26,598 sq mi
Leading Exports: machinery and equipment, computers, chemicals, pharmaceuticals, live animals, animal products
Continent: Europe

Italy

Capital: Rome
Population: 57.7 million
Official Language: Italian
Land Area: 294,020 sq km; 113,521 sq mi
Leading Exports: fruits, vegetables, grapes, potatoes, sugar beets, soybeans, grain, olives, beef, diary products, fish
Continent: Europe

Latvia

Capital: Riga
Population: 2.4 million
Official Language: Latvian
Land Area: 63,589 sq km; 24,552 sq mi
Leading Exports: wood and wood products, machinery and equipment, metals, textiles, foodstuffs
Continent: Europe

Liechtenstein

Capital: Vaduz
Population: 32,842
Official Language: German
Land Area: 160 sq km; 62 sq mi
Leading Exports: small specialty machinery, dental products, stamps, hardware, pottery
Continent: Europe

Lithuania

Capital: Vilnius
Population: 3.6 million
Official Language: Lithuanian
Land Area: 65,200 sq km; 25,174 sq mi
Leading Exports: mineral products, textiles and clothing, machinery and equipment, chemicals, wood and wood products, foodstuffs
Continent: Europe

Luxembourg

Capital: Luxembourg
Population: 448,569
Official Languages: Luxembourgish, French, and German
Land Area: 2,586 sq km; 998 sq mi
Leading Exports: machinery and equipment, steel products, chemicals, rubber products, glass
Continent: Europe

Macedonia, The Former Yugoslav Republic of

Capital: Skopje
Population: 2.1 million
Official Languages: Macedonian and Albanian
Land Area: 24,856 sq km; 9,597 sq mi
Leading Exports: food, beverages, tobacco, miscellaneous manufactured goods, iron and steel
Continent: Europe

Malta

Capital: Valletta
Population: 397,499
Official Languages: Maltese and English
Land Area: 316 sq km; 122 sq mi
Leading Exports: machinery and transport equipment, manufactured goods
Location: Mediterranean Sea

Moldova

Capital: Chişinău
Population: 4.4 million
Official Language: Moldovan
Land Area: 33,371 sq km; 12,885 sq mi
Leading Exports: foodstuffs, textiles and footwear, machinery
Continent: Europe

Monaco

Capital: Monaco
Population: 31,987
Official Language: French
Land Area: 1.95 sq km; 0.75 sq mi
Leading Exports: no information available
Continent: Europe

Montenegro

Capital: Podgorica
Population: 620,145
Official Language: Serbian
Land Area: 13,812 sq km; 5,333 sq mi
Leading Exports: food products
Continent: Europe

Netherlands

Capital: Amsterdam and The Hague
Population: 16.1 million
Official Language: Dutch
Land Area: 33,883 sq km; 13,082 sq mi
Leading Exports: machinery and equipment, chemicals, fuels, foodstuffs
Continent: Europe

Norway

Capital: Oslo
Population: 4.5 million
Official Language: Norwegian
Land Area: 307,860 sq km; 118,865 sq mi
Leading Exports: petroleum and petroleum products, machinery and equipment, metals, chemicals, ships, fish
Continent: Europe

Poland

Capital: Warsaw
Population: 38.6 million
Official Language: Polish
Land Area: 304,465 sq km; 117,554 sq mi
Leading Exports: machinery and transport equipment, intermediate manufactured goods, miscellaneous manufactured goods, food and live animals
Continent: Europe

Portugal

Capital: Lisbon
Population: 10.1 million
Official Language: Portuguese
Land Area: 91,951 sq km; 35,502 sq mi
Leading Exports: clothing and footwear, machinery, chemicals, cork and paper products, hides
Continent: Europe

Romania

Capital: Bucharest
Population: 22.3 million
Official Language: Romanian
Land Area: 230,340 sq km; 88,934 sq mi
Leading Exports: textiles and footwear, metals and metal products, machinery and equipment, minerals and fuels
Continent: Europe

Russia

Capital: Moscow
Population: 145 million
Official Language: Russian
Land Area: 16,995,800 sq km; 6,592,100 sq mi
Leading Exports: petroleum and petroleum products, natural gas, wood and wood products, metals, chemicals, and a wide variety of civilian and military manufactured goods
Continents: Europe and Asia

San Marino

Capital: San Marino
Population: 27,730
Official Language: Italian
Land Area: 61 sq km; 24 sq mi
Leading Exports: building stone, lime, wood, chestnuts, wheat, wine, baked goods, hides, ceramics
Continent: Europe

Serbia

Capital: Belgrade
Population: 9.4 million
Official Language: Serbian
Land Area: 88,361 sq km; 34,116 sq mi
Leading Exports: food and live animals, manufactured goods, raw materials
Continent: Europe

Slovakia

Capital: Bratislava
Population: 5.4 million
Official Language: Slovak
Land Area: 48,800 sq km; 18,842 sq mi
Leading Exports: machinery and transport equipment, intermediate manufactured goods, miscellaneous manufactured goods, chemicals
Continent: Europe

Slovenia

Capital: Ljubljana
Population: 1.9 million
Official Language: Slovene
Land Area: 20,151 sq km; 7,780 sq mi
Leading Exports: manufactured goods, machinery and transport equipment, chemicals, food
Continent: Europe

Spain

Capital: Madrid
Population: 40.1 million
Official Languages: Spanish, Galician, Basque, and Catalan
Land Area: 499,542 sq km; 192,873 sq mi
Leading Exports: machinery, motor vehicles, foodstuffs, other consumer goods
Continent: Europe

Europe and Russia (continued)

Switzerland
Capital: Bern
Population: 7.3 million
Official Languages: German, French, and Italian
Land Area: 39,770 sq km; 15,355 sq mi
Leading Exports: machinery, chemicals, metals, watches, agricultural products
Continent: Europe

Ukraine
Capital: Kiev
Population: 48.4 million
Official Language: Ukrainian
Land Area: 603,700 sq km; 233,090 sq mi
Leading Exports: ferrous and nonferrous metals, fuel and petroleum products, machinery and transport equipment, food products
Continent: Europe

United Kingdom
Capital: London
Population: 59.8 million
Official Languages: English and Welsh
Land Area: 241,590 sq km; 93,278 sq mi
Leading Exports: manufactured goods, fuels, chemicals, food, beverages, tobacco
Continent: Europe

Vatican City
(Holy See)
Capital: Vatican City
Population: 900
Official Languages: Latin and Italian
Land Area: 0.44 sq km; 0.17 sq mi
Leading Exports: no information available
Continent: Europe

Latin America

Antigua and Barbuda
Capital: Saint John's
Population: 67,448
Official Language: English
Land Area: 442 sq km; 171 sq mi
Leading Exports: petroleum products, manufactured goods, machinery and transport equipment, food and live animals
Location: Caribbean Sea

Argentina
Capital: Buenos Aires
Population: 37.8 million
Official Language: Spanish
Land Area: 2,736,690 sq km; 1,056,636 sq mi
Leading Exports: edible oils, fuels and energy, cereals, feed, motor vehicles
Continent: South America

Bahamas
Capital: Nassau
Population: 300,529
Official Language: English
Land Area: 10,070 sq km; 3,888 sq mi
Leading Exports: fish and crawfish, rum, salt, chemicals, fruit and vegetables
Location: Caribbean Sea

Barbados
Capital: Bridgetown
Population: 276,607
Official Language: English
Land Area: 431 sq km; 166 sq mi
Leading Exports: sugar and molasses, rum, other foods and beverages, chemicals, electrical components, clothing
Location: Caribbean Sea

Belize
Capital: Belmopan
Population: 262,999
Official Language: English
Land Area: 22,806 sq km; 8,805 sq mi
Leading Exports: sugar, bananas, citrus, clothing, fish products, molasses, wood
Continent: North America

Bolivia
Capital: La Paz and Sucre
Population: 8.5 million
Official Languages: Spanish, Quechua, and Aymara
Land Area: 1,084,390 sq km; 418,683 sq mi
Leading Exports: soybeans, natural gas, zinc, gold, wood
Continent: South America

Brazil
Capital: Brasília
Population: 176 million
Official Language: Portuguese
Land Area: 8,456,510 sq km; 3,265,059 sq mi
Leading Exports: manufactured goods, iron ore, soybeans, footwear, coffee, autos
Continent: South America

Chile
Capital: Santiago
Population: 15.5 million
Official Language: Spanish
Land Area: 748,800 sq km; 289,112 sq mi
Leading Exports: copper, fish, fruits, paper and pulp, chemicals
Continent: South America

Colombia
Capital: Bogotá
Population: 41 million
Official Language: Spanish
Land Area: 1,038,700 sq km; 401,042 sq mi
Leading Exports: petroleum, coffee, coal, apparel, bananas, cut flowers
Continent: South America

Costa Rica
Capital: San José
Population: 3.8 million
Official Language: Spanish
Land Area: 51,660 sq km; 19,560 sq mi
Leading Exports: coffee, bananas, sugar, pineapples, textiles, electronic components, medical equipment
Continent: North America

Cuba
Capital: Havana
Population: 11.2 million
Official Language: Spanish
Land Area: 110,860 sq km; 42,803 sq mi
Leading Exports: sugar, nickel, tobacco, fish, medical products, citrus, coffee
Location: Caribbean Sea

Dominica
Capital: Roseau
Population: 73,000
Official Language: English
Land Area: 754 sq km; 291 sq mi
Leading Exports: bananas, soap, bay oil, vegetables, grapefruit, oranges
Location: Caribbean Sea

Dominican Republic
Capital: Santo Domingo
Population: 8.7 million
Official Language: Spanish
Land Area: 48,380 sq km; 18,679 sq mi
Leading Exports: ferronickel, sugar, gold, silver, coffee, cocoa, tobacco, meats, consumer goods
Location: Caribbean Sea

Ecuador
Capital: Quito
Population: 13.5 million
Official Language: Spanish
Land Area: 276,840 sq km; 106,888 sq mi
Leading Exports: petroleum, bananas, shrimp, coffee, cocoa, cut flowers, fish
Continent: South America

El Salvador
Capital: San Salvador
Population: 6.4 million
Official Language: Spanish
Land Area: 20,720 sq km; 8,000 sq mi
Leading Exports: offshore assembly exports, coffee, sugar, shrimp, textiles, chemicals, electricity
Continent: North America

Grenada
Capital: Saint George's
Population: 89,211
Official Language: English
Land Area: 344 sq km; 133 sq mi
Leading Exports: bananas, cocoa, nutmeg, fruit and vegetables, clothing, mace
Location: Caribbean Sea

Guatemala
Capital: Guatemala City
Population: 13.3 million
Official Language: Spanish
Land Area: 108,430 sq km; 41,865 sq mi
Leading Exports: coffee, sugar, bananas, fruits and vegetables, cardamom, meat, apparel, petroleum, electricity
Continent: North America

Guyana
Capital: Georgetown
Population: 698,209
Official Language: English
Land Area: 196,850 sq km; 76,004 sq mi
Leading Exports: sugar, gold, bauxite/alumina, rice, shrimp, molasses, rum, timber
Continent: South America

Haiti
Capital: Port-au-Prince
Population: 7.1 million
Official Languages: French and French Creole
Land Area: 27,560 sq km; 10,641 sq mi
Leading Exports: manufactured goods, coffee, oils, cocoa
Location: Caribbean Sea

Honduras
Capital: Tegucigalpa
Population: 6.6 million
Official Language: Spanish
Land Area: 111,890 sq km; 43,201 sq mi
Leading Exports: coffee, bananas, shrimp, lobster, meat, zinc, lumber
Continent: North America

Jamaica

Capital: Kingston
Population: 2.7 million
Official Language: English
Land Area: 10,831 sq km; 4,182 sq mi
Leading Exports: alumina, bauxite, sugar, bananas, rum
Location: Caribbean Sea

Mexico

Capital: Mexico City
Population: 103.4 million
Official Language: Spanish
Land Area: 1,923,040 sq km; 742,486 sq mi
Leading Exports: manufactured goods, oil and oil products, silver, fruits, vegetables, coffee, cotton
Continent: North America

Nicaragua

Capital: Managua
Population: 5 million
Official Language: Spanish
Land Area: 120,254 sq km; 46,430 sq mi
Leading Exports: coffee, shrimp and lobster, cotton, tobacco, beef, sugar, bananas, gold
Continent: North America

Panama

Capital: Panama City
Population: 2.9 million
Official Language: Spanish
Land Area: 75,990 sq km; 29,340 sq mi
Leading Exports: bananas, shrimp, sugar, coffee, clothing
Continent: North America

Paraguay

Capital: Asunción
Population: 5.9 million
Official Language: Spanish
Land Area: 397,300 sq km; 153,398 sq mi
Leading Exports: electricity, soybeans, feed, cotton, meat, edible oils
Continent: South America

Peru

Capital: Lima
Population: 28 million
Official Languages: Spanish and Quechua
Land Area: 1,280,000 sq km; 494,208 sq mi
Leading Exports: fish and fish products, gold, copper, zinc, crude petroleum and byproducts, lead, coffee, sugar, cotton
Continent: South America

Saint Kitts and Nevis

Capital: Basseterre
Population: 38,736
Official Language: English
Land Area: 261 sq km; 101 sq mi
Leading Exports: machinery, food, electronics, beverages, tobacco
Location: Caribbean Sea

Saint Lucia

Capital: Castries
Population: 160,145
Official Language: English
Land Area: 606 sq km; 234 sq mi
Leading Exports: bananas, clothing, cocoa, vegetables, fruits, coconut oil
Location: Caribbean Sea

Saint Vincent and the Grenadines

Capital: Kingstown
Population: 116,394
Official Language: English
Land Area: 389 sq km; 150 sq mi
Leading Exports: bananas, eddoes and dasheen, arrowroot starch, tennis racquets
Location: Caribbean Sea

Suriname

Capital: Paramaribo
Population: 436,494
Official Language: Dutch
Land Area: 161,470 sq km; 62,344 sq mi
Leading Exports: alumina, crude oil, lumber, shrimp and fish, rice, bananas
Continent: South America

Trinidad and Tobago

Capital: Port-of-Spain
Population: 1.2 million
Official Language: English
Land Area: 5,128 sq km; 1,980 sq mi
Leading Exports: petroleum and petroleum products, chemicals, steel products, fertilizer, sugar, cocoa, coffee, citrus, flowers
Location: Caribbean Sea

Uruguay

Capital: Montevideo
Population: 3.4 million
Official Language: Spanish
Land Area: 173,620 sq km; 67,100 sq mi
Leading Exports: meat, rice, leather products, wool, vehicles, dairy products
Continent: South America

Venezuela

Capital: Caracas
Population: 24.3 million
Official Language: Spanish
Land Area: 882,050 sq km; 340,560 sq mi
Leading Exports: petroleum, bauxite and aluminum, steel, chemicals, agricultural products, basic manufactured goods
Continent: South America

United States and Canada

Canada

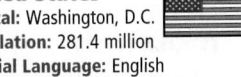

Capital: Ottawa
Population: 31.9 million
Official Languages: English and French
Land Area: 9,220,970 sq km; 3,560,217 sq mi
Leading Exports: motor vehicles and parts, industrial machinery, aircraft, telecommunications equipment, chemicals, plastics, fertilizers, wood pulp, timber, crude petroleum, natural gas, electricity, aluminum
Continent: North America

United States

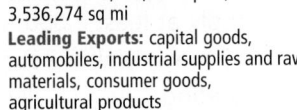

Capital: Washington, D.C.
Population: 281.4 million
Official Language: English
Land Area: 9,158,960 sq km; 3,536,274 sq mi
Leading Exports: capital goods, automobiles, industrial supplies and raw materials, consumer goods, agricultural products
Continent: North America

SOURCE: CIA World Factbook Online, 2002

Glossary of Geographic Terms

basin
an area that is lower than surrounding land areas; some basins are filled with water

bay
a body of water that is partly surrounded by land and that is connected to a larger body of water

butte
a small, high, flat-topped landform with cliff-like sides

▲ **butte**

canyon
a deep, narrow valley with steep sides; often with a stream flowing through it

cataract
a large waterfall or steep rapids

◀ **cataract**

delta
a plain at the mouth of a river, often triangular in shape, formed where sediment is deposited by flowing water

flood plain
a broad plain on either side of a river, formed where sediment settles during floods

glacier
a huge, slow-moving mass of snow and ice

hill
an area that rises above surrounding land and has a rounded top; lower and usually less steep than a mountain

island
an area of land completely surrounded by water

isthmus
a narrow strip of land that connects two larger areas of land

mesa
a high, flat-topped landform with cliff-like sides; larger than a butte

mountain
a landform that rises steeply at least 2,000 feet (610 meters) above surrounding land; usually wide at the bottom and rising to a narrow peak or ridge

▶ **glacier**

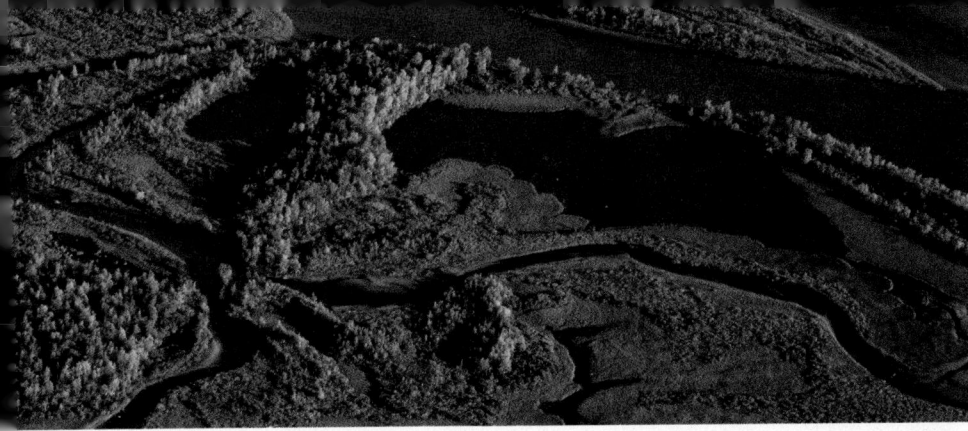

◀ delta

mountain pass
a gap between mountains

peninsula
an area of land almost completely surrounded by water but connected to the mainland

plain
a large area of flat or gently rolling land

plateau
a large, flat area that rises above the surrounding land; at least one side has a steep slope

river mouth
the point where a river enters a lake or sea

strait
a narrow stretch of water that connects two larger bodies of water

tributary
a river or stream that flows into a larger river

valley
a low stretch of land between mountains or hills; land that is drained by a river

volcano
an opening in Earth's surface through which molten rock, ashes, and gases escape from the interior

▶ **volcano**

Glossary of Geographic Terms **841**

Gazetteer

A

Abuja (9°12′ N, 7°11′ E) the capital of Nigeria, p. 488

Addis Ababa (9°2′ N, 38° 42′ E) the capital of Ethiopia, p. 518

Africa (10° N, 22° E) the world's second-largest continent, surrounded by the Mediterranean Sea, the Atlantic Ocean, the Indian Ocean, and the Red Sea, p. 15

Aksum an ancient city in northern Ethiopia that was a powerful kingdom and trade center from about A.D. 200 to A.D. 600, p. 391

Algeria (28° N, 3° E) a country in North Africa, officially the Democratic and Popular Republic of Algeria, p. 466

Algiers (36°47′ N, 3°3′ E) the capital of Algeria, p. 467

Alice Springs (23°42′ S, 133°53′ E) a town in Northern Territory, Australia, p. 807

Almaty (43°15′ N, 76°57′ E) the largest city of Kazakhstan, a country in Central Asia, p. 779

Alpine Mountain System (46° N, 10° E) a range of mountains that extends through south-central Europe; Europe's highest mountain system, p. 151

Angkor Wat (13°26′ N, 103°52′ E) an archaeological site in present-day Angkor, in northwest Cambodia; the world's largest religious temple complex, p. 688

Antarctic Circle (66°30′ S) a line of latitude around Earth near the South Pole, p. 32

Antarctica (87° S, 60° E) the continent that contains the South Pole; almost completely covered by an ice sheet, p. 35

Antofagasta (23°39′ S, 70°24′ W) a coastal city in Chile, p. 43

Appalachian Mountains (41° N, 77° W) a mountain system in eastern North America, p. 39

Aral Sea (45° N, 60° E) an inland saltwater sea in Kazakhstan and Uzbekistan, p. 612

Arctic a region located around the North Pole, p. 31

Arctic Circle (66°30′ N) a line of latitude around Earth near the North Pole, p. 30

Asia (50° N, 100° E) the world's largest continent, the main part of the Eurasian landmass, surrounded by the Arctic Ocean, the Pacific Ocean, the Indian Ocean, the Mediterranean Sea, and Europe, p. 54

Athens (37°58′ N, 23°43′ E) the capital city of modern Greece; the world's most powerful cultural center in the 400s B.C., p. 177

Auckland (36°52′ S, 174°46′ E) the largest city in New Zealand, located on North Island, p. 630

Australia (25° S, 135° E) a continent in the Southern Hemisphere, the world's smallest continent; also a country including the continent and Tasmania, p. 68

B

Balkan Peninsula (44° N, 23° E) a region in southeastern Europe, also known as the Balkans, p. 321

Bangladesh (24° N, 90° E) a coastal country in South Asia, officially the People's Republic of Bangladesh, p. 66

Benin an ancient African kingdom in the forest region of West Africa, p. 397

Berlin (52°31′ N, 13°24′ E) the capital city of Germany; once divided into East Berlin and West Berlin, p. 292

Bosnia and Herzegovina (44° N, 18° E) a country in Eastern Europe, p. 324

Brazil (10° S, 55° W) the largest country in South Amercia, p. 71

C

Cairo (30°3′ N, 31°15′ E) the capital and most populous city of Egypt, p. 458

Canada (60° N, 95° W) a large country in North America, p. 63

Canterbury Plain (44° S, 172° E) the lowland area of east-central South Island, New Zealand, p. 631

Cape of Good Hope (34°18′ S, 18°26′ E) the cape at the southern end of the Cape Peninsula in South Africa, p. 400

Cape Town (33°48′ S, 18°28′ E) one of the capitals and largest cities in South Africa, p. 446

Carthage an ancient city-state established in present-day Tunisia by the Phoenicians, which maintained control over Mediterranean trade from the late 500s B.C. through the 200s B.C., p. 394

Central America (11° N, 80° W) the part of Latin America south of Mexico and north of South America. It includes the seven republics of Guatemala, Honduras, El Salvador, Nicaragua, Costa Rica, Panama, and Belize, p. 103

Central Africa countries in the central and southern regions of Africa, p. 359

Central Asia a region in Asia including Kazakhstan, Kyrgystan, Tajikistan, Turkmenistan, Uzbekistan, and other countries, p. 610

Central Uplands a region of mountains and plateaus in the center of Southern Europe, p. 151

Chang River (32° N, 121° E) the longest river in Asia, flowing through China to the East China Sea, p. 577

Chernobyl (51°16' N, 30°14' E) the city in northern Ukraine where a nuclear power station accident occurred in 1986, p. 332

China (35° N, 105° E) a large country in East Asia, officially the People's Republic of China, p. 20

Congo, Democratic Republic of the (4° S, 25° E) a country in Central Africa, formerly called Zaire, p. 548

Congo River (6°4' S, 12°24' E) a river in Central Africa that flows into the Atlantic Ocean, p. 361

Cuba (22° N, 80° W) the largest island country in the Caribbean Sea, p. 68

Czechoslovakia a former Central European country that contained the present-day countries of the Czech Republic and Slovakia, p. 233

D

Danube River (45° N, 30° E) a river that flows 1,770 miles (2,850 kilometers) from Germany to the Black Sea, p. 153

Dar es Salaam (6°48' S, 39°17' E) one of two capitals of Tanzania, p. 444

Denmark (56° N, 10° E) a country in Northern Europe, p. 118

E

East Africa countries in the eastern region of Africa, p. 359

East Asia a region of Asia including China, Japan, Mongolia, North Korea, South Korea, and Taiwan, p. 575

Eastern Ghats (14° N, 79° E) a mountain range forming the eastern edge of the Deccan Plateau in India, p. 598

Egypt (27° N, 30° E) a country in North Africa, officially the Arab Republic of Egypt, p. 60

Equator (0°) a line of latitude that circles Earth at the center of the tropics, midway between the North and South poles, along which days and nights are always equal in length, p. 11

Ethiopia (9° N, 39° E) a country in East Africa, p. 514

Euphrates River (31° N, 46° E) a river that flows south from Turkey through Syria and Iraq. The ancient civilizations of Babylon and Ur were situated near its banks. p. 603

Eurasia the world's largest landmass; contains the continents of Europe and Asia, p. 149

Europe (50° N, 28° E) the world's second-smallest continent; a peninsula of the Eurasian landmass bordered by the Arctic Ocean, the Atlantic Ocean, the Mediterranean Sea, and Asia, p. 43

F

Florida (28° N, 8° W) a state in the southeastern United States that is largely a peninsula, p. 12

France (46° N, 2° E) a country in Western Europe, p. 268

G

Ganges River (23° N, 90° E) a river in India and Bangladesh flowing from the Himalaya Mountains to the Bay of Bengal; considered by Hindus to be the most holy river in India, p. 598

Genoa (44°25' N, 8°57' E) a seaport city of Italy, p. 104

Georgia (33° N, 83° W) a state in the southeastern United States, p. 12

Germany (51° N, 10° E) a country in Western Europe, p. 97

Ghana (8° N, 1° W) a country in West Africa, officially the Republic of Ghana, p. 490; an early African empire located in parts of present-day Mauritania and Mali, p. 395

Great Dividing Range (25° S, 147° E) a series of plateaus and mountain ranges in eastern Australia, p. 629

Great Plains (42° N, 100° W) a semiarid plain located in North America, stretching from the Rio Grande at the U.S.-Mexico border in the south to the Mackenzie River Delta in the north, and from the Canadian Shield in the east to the Rocky Mountains in the west, p. 128

Great Rift Valley the major branch of the East African Rift System, p. 360

Great Wall of China (41° N, 117° E) a fortification wall which, with all its extensions, stretches 4,000 miles (6,400 kilometers) through China; constructed from about 600 B.C. to A.D. 1600, p. 645

Great Zimbabwe an ancient city-state in southeastern Zimbabwe that was a powerful trade center from about A.D. 1100 to 1500, p. 393

Greece (39° N, 22° E) a country in southeastern Europe, p. 93

Greenland (70° N, 40° W) a self-governing island in the northern Atlantic Ocean; a possession of Denmark; Earth's largest island, p. 18

Greenwich (51°28' N, 0°) a borough of London, England, and location of the Royal Greenwich Observatory, whose site serves as the basis for longitude and for setting standard time, p. 12

Gulf Stream a warm ocean current in the North Atlantic; flowing northeastward off the North American coast, p. 43

H

Himalayas (28° N, 84° E) the Central Asian mountain range extending along the India-Tibet border, through Pakistan, Nepal, and Bhutan, and containing the world's highest peaks, p. 577

Hindu Kush (36° N, 72° E) a mountain range in Central Asia, p. 611

Ho Chi Minh City (10°45' N, 106°40' E) the largest city in Vietnam, named for a former President of North Vietnam; formerly Saigon, p. 797

Huang River (38° N, 118° E) the second-longest river in China, flowing across northern China to the Yellow Sea; also known as the Yellow River, p. 577

I

India (20° N, 77° E) a large country occupying most of the Indian subcontinent in South Asia, p. 40

Indonesia (5° S, 120° E) a country in Southeast Asia consisting of many islands, p. 93

Indus River (24° N, 68° E) a river rising in Tibet and flowing through India and Pakistan into the Arabian Sea, p. 598

Iran (32° N, 53° W) a country in Southwest Asia, p. 82

Iraq (33° N, 44° E) a country in Southwest Asia, officially the Republic of Iraq, p. 602

Italy (43° N, 13° E) a boot-shaped country in Southern Europe, p. 104

J

Jakarta (6°10' S, 106°48' E) the capital and largest city of Indonesia, p. 71

Japan (36° N, 138° E) an island country in the Pacific Ocean off the east coast of Asia, consisting of four main islands, p. 63

Java (7° S, 110° E) the fourth-largest island in the Republic of Indonesia, an archipelago in the Indian and Pacific oceans, p. 625

K

Kalahari Desert a desert in Southern Africa, p. 359

Kashmir (34° N, 76° E) a disputed territory in northwest India, parts of which have been claimed by India, Pakistan, and China since 1947, p. 667

Kazakhstan (48° N, 68° E) the largest country in Central Asia, officially the Republic of Kazakhstan, p. 610

Kenya (1° N, 38° E) a country in East Africa, officially the Republic of Kenya, p. 526

Kilwa an Islamic city-state, located on an island off the coast of present-day Tanzania, that was powerful during the A.D. 1300s, p. 393

Kuwait (29° N, 48° E) a country in Southwest Asia, officially the Republic of Kuwait, p. 743

L

Lagos (6°27′ N, 3°24′ E) a city and main port of Nigeria, p. 488

Lalibela (12°2′ N, 39°02′ E) a town in Ethiopia that is famous for its stone churches carved in the 1100s, p. 516

Libya (27° N, 17° E) a country in North Africa, p. 82

London (51°30′ N, 0°10′ W) the capital and largest city of the United Kingdom, p. 22

M

Macedonia (42° N, 22° E) a country in Eastern Europe, p. 325

Malaysia (3° N, 113° E) a country in Southeast Asia, p. 103

Mali (17° N, 4° E) a country in West Africa, officially the Republic of Mali, p. 498; an ancient African empire located in present-day Mali, p. 396

Mecca (21°27′ N, 39°49′ E) a city in western Saudi Arabia; bithplace of the prophet Muhammad and most holy city for Islamic people, p. 766

Mediterranean Sea (35° N, 20° E) the large sea that separates Europe and Africa, p. 603

Melanesia (13° S, 164° E) the most populous of the three groups of Pacific islands; includes Fiji, Papua New Guinea, and others, p. 634

Mesopotamia a historic region in western Asia between the Tigris and Euphrates rivers; one of the cradles of civilization, p. 603

Mexico (23° N, 102° W) a country in North America, south of the United States, p. 67

Miami (25°46′ N, 80°11 W) a city on the southeast coast of Florida, p. 12

Micronesia (11° N, 159° E) one of the three groups of Pacific islands; includes Guam, the Marshall Islands, and others, p. 634

Middle Kingdom the name given to China by its Chinese leaders, p. 645

Milky Way a galaxy consisting of several billions of stars, including the sun, p. 28

Montenegro (43° N, 19° E) a country in Eastern Europe, p. 326

Moscow (55°45′ N, 37°35′ E) the capital city of modern Russia; the home of the tsars, p. 201

Mount Everest (27°59′ N, 86°56′ E) the highest point on Earth, located in the Himalayas on the border between Nepal and China, p. 54

Mount Fuji (35°22′ N, 138°44′ E) the highest mountain in Japan; a dormant volcano and sacred symbol of Japan, p. 576

Mount Kenya (0°9′ S, 37°19′ E) a volcanic mountain in central Kenya, p. 527

Mount Kilimanjaro (3°04′ S, 37°22′ E) the tallest mountain in Africa, located in Tanzania, p. 359

Myanmar (22° N, 98° E) a country in Southeast Asia, also known as Burma, p. 82

N

Nairobi (1°17′ S, 36°49′ E) the capital of Kenya, p. 529

Namib Desert a desert extending along the Atlantic Coast of Southern Africa, p. 359

Negev Desert (30° N, 35° E) a triangular, arid region in southwest Israel, touching the Gulf of Aqaba, p. 761

Nepal (28° N, 83° E) a country in South Asia, p. 54

Netherlands, the (52° N, 6° E) a country in Northern Europe, p. 148

New York (43° N, 75° W) a state in the northeastern United States, p. 132

New York City (40°43′ N, 74°1′ W) a large city and port at the mouth of the Hudson River in the state of New York; the largest city in the United States, p. 84

New Zealand (41° S, 174° E) an island country in the Pacific Ocean, p. 122

Niger River (5°33′ N, 6°33′ E) a river in West Africa that flows from Guinea into the Gulf of Guinea, p. 361

Nigeria (10° N, 8° E) a country in West Africa, officially the Federal Republic of Nigeria, p. 484

Nile River (30°10′ N, 31°6′ E) the longest river in the world, flowing through northeastern Africa into the Mediterranean Sea, p. 361

Nile Valley the fertile land located on both sides of the Nile River in northeastern Africa; site of one of the earliest civilizations, p. 63

North Africa the countries of northern Africa, p. 359

North America (45° N, 100° W) the world's third-largest continent, consisting of Canada, the United States, Mexico, Central America, and many islands, p. 17

North Atlantic Current a warm ocean current in the North Atlantic, flowing northeastward toward Europe, p. 43

North China Plain a large, fertile plain in northeastern China, p. 577

North European Plain a plain extending from Russia to France; contains Europe and Russia's most productive farmland and largest cities, p. 151

North Island (39° S, 176° E) the smaller and more northern of the two islands that make up New Zealand, p. 630

North Korea (40° N, 127° E) a country in East Asia, officially the Democratic People's Republic of Korea, p. 82

North Pole (90° N) the northernmost end of Earth's axis, located in the Arctic Ocean, p. 11

North Sea (56° N, 3° E) an arm of the Atlantic Ocean located between Great Britain and the European mainland, p. 164

Northwestern Highlands a mountainous, forested region in Northern Europe, p. 151

Norway (62° N, 10° E) a country in Northern Europe, p. 118

Nubia an ancient region in North Africa, p. 387

P

Palestine (32° N, 35° E) a historical region at the east end of the Mediterranean Sea, now divided between Israel and Jordan, p. 672

Pamir (38° N, 73° E) a mountain range in Central Asia, p. 611

Pangaea according to scientific theory, a single landmass that broke apart to form today's separate continents; thought to have existed about 180 million years ago, p. 38

Papua New Guinea (6° S, 150° E) an island country in the southwest Pacific; the eastern half of New Guinea, officially the Independent State of Papua New Guinea, p. 634

Paris (48°52′ N, 2°20′ E) the capital city of France, p. 268

Peru Current a cold-water current of the southeast Pacific Ocean; flows northward between 40° S and 4° S, p. 43

Philippines (13° N, 122° E) an island country in Southeast Asia, officially the Republic of the Philippines, p. 67

Poland (52° N, 19° E) a country in Eastern Europe, p. 312

Polynesia (4° S, 156° W) largest of the three groups of Pacific islands; includes New Zealand, Hawaii, Easter, and Tahiti islands, p. 634

R

Rhine River (52° N, 6° E) a river that flows about 865 miles (1,391 kilometers) from Switzerland to the Netherlands, p. 153

Ring of Fire a circle of volcanic mountains that surrounds the Pacific Ocean, including those on the islands of Japan and Indonesia, in the Cascades of North America, and in the Andes of South America, p. 33

Riyadh (24°38′ N, 46°43′ E) the capital of Saudi Arabia, p. 767

Rocky Mountains (48° N, 116° W) the major mountain range in western North America, extending from central New Mexico to northeastern British Columbia, p. 12

Rome (41°54′ N, 12°29′ E) the capital of modern Italy; one of the world's greatest ancient civilizations and empires, p. 81

Rotterdam (51°55′ N, 4°28′ E) a seaport city in the Netherlands, p. 131

Rub' al-Khali (20° N, 51° E) the largest all-sand desert in the world, located on the Arabian peninsula; the "Empty Quarter," p. 601

Ruhr (51° N, 7° E) an industrial region in Germany; also a river there, p. 166

Russia (60° N, 80° E) a country stretching across eastern Europe and northern Asia, the largest country in the world, p. 3

S

Sahara the largest tropical desert in the world, covering almost all of North Africa, p. 53

Sahel the region in West and Central Africa that forms an intermediate climate zone between the dry Sahara to the north and the humid savannas to the south, p. 369

St. Louis (38°37′ N, 90°11′ W) a major city in Missouri, on the Mississippi River, p. 45

St. Petersburg (59°55′ N, 30°15′ E) a city and important cultural center in Russia, p. 243

Samarkand (39°40′ N, 67°15′ E) a city in Uzbekistan, p. 679

San Francisco (37°46′ N, 122°25′ W) a coastal city in California, p. 45

São Paulo (23°32′ S, 46°37′ W) the largest city in Brazil, p. 48

Sarajevo (43°52′ N, 18°25′ E) the capital city of Bosnia and Herzegovina, p. 319

Saudi Arabia (25° N, 45° E) a country in Southwest Asia, p. 101

Scandinavia a historical region of Northern Europe that included Norway, Finland, Sweden, Denmark, and Iceland, p. 161

Seoul (37°33′ N, 125°58′ E) the capital of South Korea, p. 579

Serbia (44° N, 21° E) a country in Eastern Europe, p. 326

Siberia (65° N, 110° E) a resource-rich region of northeastern Russia; contains the West Siberian Plain, the Central Siberian Plateau, and the East Siberian Uplands, p. 151

Silesia (51° N, 17° E) a coal-rich region where Poland, the Czech Republic, and Germany meet, p. 167

Silk Road a 4,000-mile-long ancient trade route linking China to the Mediterranean area in the west, p. 651

Slovenia (46° N, 15° E) a country in Eastern Europe, p. 323

Songhai an ancient African empire located in present-day Mali, Niger, and Nigeria, p. 396

South Africa (30° S, 26° E) a country in Southern Africa, officially the Republic of South Africa, p. 70

South America (15° S, 60° W) the world's fourth-largest continent, bounded by the Caribbean Sea, the Atlantic Ocean, and the Pacific Ocean, and linked to North America by the Isthmus of Panama, p. 17

South Asia a region of Asia that includes Afghanistan, Bangladesh, Bhutan, India, Maldives, Nepal, Pakistan, and Sri Lanka, p. 597

South Island (43° S, 171° E) the larger and more southern of the two islands composing New Zealand, p. 630

South Korea (37° N, 128° E) a country in East Asia, p. 67

South Pole (90° S) the southernmost end of Earth's axis, located in Antarctica, p. 12

Southeast Asia a region of Asia including Brunei, Cambodia, Indonesia, Laos, Malaysia, Myanmar (Burma), Philippines, Singapore, Thailand, Timor, and Vietnam, p. 620

Southern Africa countries in the southern regions of Africa, p. 359

Southwest Asia a region of Asia including Iran, Iraq, Israel, Jordan, Kuwait, Lebanon, Saudi Arabia, Syria, Turkey, and others, p. 602

Soviet Union a former communist country that included present-day Russia and several other Eastern European countries, p. 209

Sweden (62° N, 15° E) a country in Northern Europe, p. 276

Switzerland (47° N, 121° E) a country in central Europe, p. 78

Sydney (33°52′ S, 151°13′ E) the capital of New South Wales, on the southeastern coast of Australia, and the largest city in Australia, p. 804

T

Taiwan (23° N, 121° E) a large island country off the southeast coast of mainland China, formerly Formosa; since 1949, the Nationalist Republic of China, p. 713

Tanzania (6° S, 35° E) a country in East Africa, officially the United Republic of Tanzania, p. 519

Thailand (15° N, 100° E) a country in Southeast Asia, officially the Kingdom of Thailand, p. 793

Tigris River (31° N, 47° E) a river that flows through Turkey, Iraq, and Iran to the Persian Gulf. The ancient civilizations of Nineveh and Ur were situated near its banks. p. 603

Tokyo (35°42′ N, 139°46′ E) the capital and largest city of Japan, also the largest city in the world, p. 63

Tombouctou (16°46′ N, 3°1′ E) a city in Mali near the Niger River; in the past an important center of Islamic education and a stop along trans-Saharan trade routes (also spelled *Timbuktu*), p. 498

Tropic of Cancer (23°30′ N) the northern boundary of the tropics, or the band of Earth that receives the most direct light and heat energy from the sun. Such a region lies on both sides of the Equator, p. 30

Tropic of Capricorn (23°30′ S) the southern boundary of the tropics. *See Tropic of Cancer,* p. 31

U

Ukraine (49° N, 32° E) a country in Eastern Europe, p. 327

United Kingdom (54° N, 2° E) a nation in Northern Europe that includes Great Britain and Northern Ireland, p. 260

United States (38° N, 97° W) a large country in North America, p. 12

Ural Mountains (60° N, 60° E) a mountain range in northern Eurasia that forms the border between Europe and Asia, p. 149

V

Vatican City (41°54′ N, 12°27′ E) a city-state completely surrounded by Rome, Italy; the seat of the Roman Catholic Church, p. 81

Vietnam (16° N, 108° E) a country in Southeast Asia, officially the Socialist Republic of Vietnam, p. 67

Volga River (46° N, 48° E) Europe's longest river, flowing 2,291 miles (3,687 kilometers) through western Russia to the Caspian Sea, p. 153

W

West Africa countries in the western region of Africa, p. 359

Western Ghats (14° N, 75° E) a mountain range forming the western edge of the Deccan Plateau in India, p. 598

Y

Yugoslavia a former Eastern European country that contained the present-day countries of Serbia, Montenegro, Bosnia and Herzegovina, Croatia, Slovenia, and Macedonia, p. 219

Z

Zambezi River a river in Central and Southern Africa that flows into the Indian Ocean, p. 361

Glossary

A

Aborigine (ab uh RIJ uh nee) *n.* a member of the earliest people of Australia, who probably came from Asia, p. 697

absolute location (AB suh loot loh KAY shun) *n.* the exact position of a place on Earth, p. 12

absolute monarchy (AB suh loot MAHN ur kee) *n.* a system of complete control by a king or a queen who inherits the throne by birth, p. 82

acculturation (uh kul chur AY shun) *n.* the process of accepting new ideas from one culture and fitting them into another culture, p. 106

aerial photograph (EHR ee ul FOHT uh graf) *n.* a photographic image of Earth's surface taken from the air, p. 17

agriculture (AG rih kul chur) *n.* farming, including growing crops and raising livestock, p. 94

alliance (uh LY uns) *n.* a formal agreement to pursue common interests, formed between governments, often for military purposes, p. 196

alluvial soil (uh LOO vee ul soyl) *n.* soil deposited by water; fertile topsoil left by rivers after a flood, p. 598

apartheid (uh PAHR tayt) *n.* the former legal system of South Africa in which the rights of nonwhites were greatly restricted, p. 557

archipelago (ahr kuh PEL uh goh) *n.* a group of islands, p. 578

arid (A rid) *adj.* dry, p. 44

artesian well (ahr TEE zhun wel) *n.* a well from which water flows under natural pressure without pumping, p. 807

atmosphere (AT muh sfeer) *n.* a layer of gases surrounding a planet, p. 35

atoll (A tawl) *n.* a small coral island in the shape of a ring, p. 635

B

authoritarian government (uh thawr uh TEHR ee un GUV urn munt) *n.* a nondemocratic form of government in which a single leader or small group of leaders has all the power, p. 551

axis (AK sis) *n.* an imaginary line around which a planet turns. Earth's axis runs through its center from the North Pole to the South Pole. p. 29

barometer (buh RAHM uh tur) *n.* an instrument for forecasting changes in the weather; anything that indicates a change, p. 89

basilica (buh SIL ih kuh) *n.* a Roman Catholic church that has a special, high status because of its age or history, p. 284

bazaar (buh ZAHR) *n.* a traditional open-air market with shops or rows of stalls, p. 461

biodiversity (by oh duh VUR suh tee) *n.* a large variety of living things in a region, p. 129

birthrate (BURTH rayt) *n.* the number of live births each year per 1,000 people, p. 64

blizzard (BLIZ urd) *n.* a heavy snowstorm with strong winds, p. 47

boycott (BOY kaht) *n.* a refusal to buy or use certain products or services, p. 410

C

Cairo (KY roh) *n.* the capital of Egypt and the most populous city in Africa, p. 458

canopy (KAN uh pea) *n.* the dense mass of leaves and branches forming the top layer of a forest, p. 52

Cape of Good Hope (kayp uv good hohp) *n.* a former province of the Republic of South Africa; the point of land at the southern end of the Cape Peninsula, South Africa, p. 400

capitalism (KAP ut ul iz um) *n.* an economic system in which private individuals or private groups of people own most businesses, p. 75

cardinal directions (KAHR duh nul duh REK shunz) *n.* north, east, south, and west, p. 11

casbah (KAHZ bah) *n.* an old, crowded section of a North African city, p. 469

cash crop (kash krahp) *n.* a crop grown mostly for sale rather than for the needs of a farmer's family, p. 376

caste (kast) *n.* in the Hindu religion, a social group into which people are born and which they cannot change. Each group has assigned jobs. p. 663

chernozem (CHEHR nuh zem) *n.* rich, black soil, productive for farming, p. 329

city-state (SIH tee stayt) *n.* a city with its own government that was both a city and an independent state, p. 81

civil engineering (SIV ul en juh NIHR ing) *n.* the technology for building structures that alter the landscape, such as dams, roads, and bridges, p. 131

civil war (SIV ul wawr) *n.* a war between political parties or regions within the same country, p. 797

civilization (sih vuh luh ZAY shun) *n.* a society that has cities, a central government, and social classes and that usually has writing, art, and architecture, p. 94

clan (klan) *n.* a group of families with a common ancestor, p. 434

climate (KLY mut) *n.* the average weather of a place over many years, p. 40

collective farm (kuh LEK tiv fahrm) *n.* in a Communist country, a large farm formed from many private farms collected into a single unit and controlled by the government, p. 330

colonization (kahl uh nih ZAY shun) *n.* the movement of settlers and their culture to a new country, p. 125

colonize (KAHL uh nyz) *v.* to settle in an area and take control of its government, p. 404

colony (KAHL uh nee) *n.* a territory ruled by another nation, p. 188

commercial farmer (kuh MUR shul FAHR mur) *n.* a farmer who grows most of his or her food for sale rather than for the needs of his or her family, p. 76

commercial farming (kuh MUR shul FAHR ming) *n.* the raising of crops and livestock for sale on the local or world market, p. 415

commune (KAHM yoon) *n.* a community in which people own land as a group and in which they live and work together, p. 653

communism (KAHM yoo niz um) *n.* an economic system in which the central government owns farms, factories, and offices, p. 75

communist (KAHM yoo nist) *adj.* relating to a government that controls a country's large industries, businesses, and land, p. 649

compass rose (KUM pus rohz) *n.* a diagram of a compass showing direction on a map, p. 21

compound (KAHM pownd) *n.* a fenced-in group of homes, p. 447

conformal map (kun FAWR mul map) *n.* a flat map of the entire planet Earth, which shows correct shapes but not true distances or sizes; also known as a Mercator projection after geographer Gerardus Mercator, p. 18

coniferous tree (koh NIF ur us tree) *n.* a tree that produces cones that carry seeds, p. 52

constitution (kahn stuh TOO shun) *n.* a set of laws that defines and limits a government's power, p. 83

constitutional monarchy (kahn stuh TOO shun ul MAHN ur kee) *n.* a government in which the power of the king or the queen is limited by law, p. 83

consumer (kun SOOM ur) *n.* a person who buys and uses goods and services, p. 74

copse (kahps) *n.* a thicket of small trees or shrubs, p. 89

coral (KAWR ul) *n.* a rocklike material made up of the skeletons of tiny sea creatures, most plentiful in warm ocean water, p. 635

core (kawr) *n.* the ball of hot metal at the center of Earth, p. 34

crust (krust) *n.* the thin layer of rocks and minerals that surrounds Earth's mantle, p. 34

cultural diffusion (KUL chur ul dih FYOO zhun) *n.* the movement of customs and ideas from one culture to other cultures, p. 106

cultural diversity (KUL chur ul duh VUR suh tee) *n.* a wide variety of cultures, p. 432

cultural landscape (KUL chur ul LAND skayp) *n.* the parts of a people's environment that they have shaped and that reflect their culture, p. 93

cultural trait (KUL chur ul trayt) *n.* a skill, custom, idea, or way of doing things that forms part of a culture, p. 92

culture (KUL chur) *n.* the way of life of a people, including their language, beliefs, customs, and practices, p. 92

D

death rate (deth rayt) *n.* the number of deaths each year per 1,000 people, p. 64

deciduous tree (dee SIJ oo us tree) *n.* a tree that loses its leaves in the fall, p. 52

deforestation (dee fawr uh STAY shun) *n.* a loss of forest cover in a region, p. 129

degrees (dih GREEZ) *n.* units that measure angles or temperature, p. 11

demilitarized zone (dee MIL uh tuh ryzd zohn) *n.* an area in which no weapons are allowed, p. 728

democracy (dih MAHK ruh see) *n.* a government over which citizens exercise power, p. 177

demography (dih MAH gruh fee) *n.* the scientific study of population change and population distribution, p. 60

dependency (dee PEN dun see) *n.* a region that belongs to another state, p. 81

desert (DEZ urt) *n.* a dry region with little vegetation, p. 52

desert scrub (DEZ urt skrub) *n.* desert vegetation that needs little water, p. 52

desertification (dih zurt uh fih KAY shun) *n.* the process by which fertile land becomes too dry or damaged to support life, p. 500

developed nation (dih VEL upt NAY shun) *n.* a nation with many industries and advanced technology, p. 76

developing nation (dih VEL up ing NAY shun) *n.* a nation with few industries and simple technology, p. 76

dialect (DY uh lekt) *n.* a variation of a language that is unique to a region or area, p. 231

dictator (DIK tay tur) *n.* a ruler with complete power over a country, p. 82

dictatorship (DIK tay tur ship) *n.* a form of government in which the power is held by a leader who has absolute authority, p. 776

direct democracy (duh REKT dih MAHK ruh see) *n.* a form of government in which all adults take part in decisions, p. 82

discriminate (dih SKRIM ih nayt) *v.* to treat people differently, and often unfairly, based on race, religion, or sex, p. 557

distortion (dih STAWR shun) *n.* loss of accuracy. Every map projection causes some distortion of shape or size, p. 17

diversify (duh VUR suh fy) *v.* to add variety; to expand a country's economy by increasing the variety of goods produced, p. 378

domesticate (duh MES tih kayt) *v.* to adapt wild plants or animals and breed them for human use, p. 386

domino theory (DAHM uh noh THEE uh ree) *n.* a belief that if one country fell to communism, neighboring nations would also fall, like a row of dominoes, p. 797

double-cropping (DUB ul KRAHP ing) *v.* to grow two or more crops on the same land in the same season or at the same time, p. 590

drought (drowt) *n.* a long period of dry weather, p. 367

dynasty (DY nus tee) *n.* a series of rulers from the same family, p. 645

E

economic sanctions (ek uh NAHM ik SANGK shunz) *n.* actions to limit trade with nations that have violated international laws, p. 326

economy (ih KAHN uh mee) *n.* a system for producing, distributing, consuming, and owning goods, services, and wealth, p. 74

elevation (el uh VAY shun) *n.* the height of land above or below sea level, p. 359

embargo (em BAHR goh) *n.* a ban on trade, p. 323

emperor (EM pur ur) *n.* a male ruler of an empire, p. 645

empire (EM pyr) *n.* a state containing several countries, p. 81

energy (EN ur jee) *n.* usable heat or power; capacity for doing work, p. 115

entrepreneur (ahn truh pruh NOOR) *n.* a person who develops original ideas in order to start new businesses, p. 316

environment (en VY run munt) *n.* natural surroundings, p. 120

equal-area map (EEK wul EHR ee uh map) *n.* a map showing landmasses with the correct sizes, but with altered shapes, p. 19

Equator (ee KWAYT ur) *n.* the line of latitude around the middle of the globe, p. 11

Equiano, Olaudah (ek wee AHN oh, oh LOW duh) *n.* an antislavery activist who wrote an account of his enslavement, p. 402

equinox (EE kwih nahks) *n.* one of two days in the year when the sun is directly over the Equator and the day is almost exactly as long as the night; known as spring and fall equinoxes, p. 30

erosion (ee ROH zhun) *n.* a process in which water, ice, or wind removes pieces of rock, p. 39

ethics (ETH iks) *n.* the standards or code of moral behavior distinguishing between right and wrong, p. 101

ethnic group (ETH nik groop) *n.* a group of people who share the same ancestors, culture, language, or religion, p. 231

euro (YUR oh) *n.* the official currency of the European Union, p. 209

extended family (ek STEN did FAM uh lee) *n.* a family that includes several generations, p. 97

F

famine (FAM in) *n.* a huge food shortage, p. 729

fault (fawlt) *n.* a crack in Earth's crust, p. 37

fellaheen (fel uh HEEN) *n.* peasants or agricultural workers in Egypt and other countries of the Arab world, p. 463

fertile (FUR tul) *adj.* able to support plant growth, p. 577

feudalism (FYOOD ul iz um) *n.* a system in which land was owned by kings or lords but held by vassals in return for their loyalty, p. 181

fiord (fyawrd) *n.* a long, narrow inlet or arm of the sea bordered by steep cliffs created by glaciers, p. 631

foreign minister (FAWR in MIN is tur) *n.* a government official who is in charge of a nation's foreign affairs, p. 211

fossil fuel (FAHS ul FYOO ul) *n.* a fuel formed over millions of years from animal and plant remains, including coal, petroleum, and natural gas, p. 117

free enterprise system (free ENT ur pryz SIS tum) *n.* an economic system in which people can choose their own jobs, start private businesses, own property, and make a profit, p. 716

G

Gaza Strip (GAHZ uh strip) *n.* a disputed region on the Mediterranean coast, p. 765

Geez (gee EZ) *n.* an ancient Ethiopian language that was once used to write literature and religious texts but is no longer spoken, p. 515

geographic information systems (jee uh GRAF ik in fur MAY shun SIS tumz) *n.* computer-based systems that store and use information linked to geographic locations, p. 17

geography (jee AHG ruh fee) *n.* the study of Earth, p. 10

geyser (GY zur) *n.* a hot spring that shoots a jet of water and steam into the air, p. 630

globe (glohb) *n.* a model of Earth with the same round shape as Earth itself, p. 16

goods (gudz) *n.* physical products, p. 75

government (GUV urn munt) *n.* a system that sets up and enforces laws and institutions in a region, p. 80

Green Revolution (green rev uh LOO shun) *n.* the increased use of chemicals and machinery in agriculture since the 1950s that has greatly increased the world's food supply. It has also created environmental challenges. p. 65

gross domestic product (grohs duh MES tik PRAHD ukt) *n.* the total value of all goods and services produced in an economy, p. 718

H

hajj (haj) *n.* a pilgrimage or journey to Mecca undertaken by Muslims during the month of the hajj, p. 766

harambee (hah RAHM bay) *n.* a social policy started by Jomo Kenyatta and meaning "let's pull together" in Swahili, p. 528

Hausa-Fulani (HOW suh foo LAH nee) *n.* Nigeria's largest ethnic group, p. 485

hemisphere (HEM ih sfeer) *n.* one half of Earth, p. 11

hemlock (HEM lahk) *n.* an evergreen tree with drooping branches and short, flat needles, p. 89

heritage (HEHR uh tij) *n.* the customs and practices passed from one generation to the next, p. 239

high island (hy EYE lund) *n.* an island formed from the mountainous tops of ancient volcanoes, p. 635

high latitudes (hy LAT uh toodz) *n.* the areas north of the Arctic Circle and south of the Antarctic Circle, p. 32

hill (hil) *n.* a landform with a rounded top that rises above the surrounding land but that is lower and less steep than a mountain, p. 35

Holocaust (HAHL uh kawst) *n.* the killing of millions of Jews and others by the Nazis in World War II, p. 295

homogeneous (hoh moh JEE nee us) *adj.* to be the same or similar, p. 656

human-environment interaction (HYOO mun en VY run munt in tur AK shun) *n.* how people affect the environment and the physical characteristics of their surroundings and how the environment affects them, p. 13

humid continental climate (HYOO mid kahn tuh NENT ul KLY mut) *n.* a climate with moderate to hot summers but very cold winters, supporting grasslands and forests, p. 51

hurricane (HUR ih kayn) *n.* a violent tropical storm, or cyclone, that forms over the Atlantic Ocean, p. 47

hybrid (HY brid) *n.* a plant that is created by cross breeding different types of the same plant, p. 417

hydroelectric power (hy droh ee LEK trik POW ur) *n.* the power produced by water-driven turbines, p. 166

I

Igbo (IG boh) *n.* Nigeria's third-largest ethnic group, p. 485

I

Igbo (IG boh) *n.* Nigeria's third-largest ethnic group, p. 485

immigrant (IM uh grunt) *n.* a person who moves to a new country in order to settle there, p. 67

imperialism (im PIHR ee ul iz um) *n.* the pursuit of economic and political control over foreign territories, p. 195

Industrial Revolution (in DUS tree ul rev uh LOO shun) *n.* the life-changing period in the 1800s when the production of goods shifted from hand work to machines in factories, p. 191

industrialization (in dus tree ul ih ZAY shun) *n.* the development of manufacturing in an economy, p. 125

inflation (in FLAY shun) *n.* an increase in the general level of prices, p. 338

institution (in stuh TOO shun) *n.* a custom or organization with social, educational, or religious purposes, p. 95

interdependent (in tur dee PEN dunt) *adj.* dependent on one another, p. 79

international (in tur NASH uh nul) *adj.* involving more than one nation, p. 84

investor (in VES tur) *n.* someone who spends money on improving a business in the hope of making more money if the business succeeds, p. 337

irrigation (ihr uh GAY shun) *n.* the watering of crops using canals and other artificial waterways, p. 94

K

key (kee) *n.* the section of a map that explains the symbols and shading on the map, p. 21

Khmer Empire (kuh MEHR EM pyr) *n.* an empire that included much of present-day Cambodia, Thailand, and Malaysia, and part of Laos, p. 688

Khmer Rouge (kuh MEHR roozh) *n.* a Communist party that took over the government of Cambodia in 1975, p. 693

kibbutz (kih BOOTS) *n.* a cooperative settlement in Israel, p. 763

Kikuyu (kee KOO yoo) *n.* the largest ethnic group in Kenya, p. 527

kinship (KIN ship) *n.* a family relationship, p. 434

L

labor (LAY bur) *n.* the work people do, for which they are paid, p. 725

land reform (land ree FAWRM) *n.* the process of dividing large properties into smaller ones, p. 288

landform (LAND fawrm) *n.* a shape or type of land, p. 35

landlocked (LAND lahkt) *adj.* having no direct access to the sea, p. 779

landmass (LAND mas) *n.* a large area of land, p. 19

latitude (LAT uh tood) *n.* the distance north or south of the Equator, measured in units called degrees, p. 11

lichen (LY kun) *n.* a plant that is a combination of a fungus and an algae and that grows and spreads over rocks and tree trunks, p. 39

life expectancy (lyf ek SPEK tun see) *n.* the average number of years a person is expected to live, p. 65

lineage (LIN ee ij) *n.* a group of families descended from a common ancestor, p. 434

lingua franca (LING gwuh FRANG kuh) *n.* a language used for communication among people who speak different first languages, p. 520

literacy rate (LIT ur uh see rayt) *n.* the percentage of a population age 15 and older that can read and write, p. 755

literate (LIT ur it) *adj.* able to read and write, p. 418

loess (LOH es) *n.* a type of rich, dustlike soil, p. 165

low latitudes (loh LAT uh toodz) *n.* the area between the Tropic of Cancer and the Tropic of Capricorn, p. 32

M

Maasai (mah SY) *n.* a seminomadic ethnic group in Kenya, p. 527

magma (MAG muh) *n.* soft, hot, molten rock, p. 36

malnutrition (mal noo TRISH un) *n.* poor nutrition caused by a lack of food or an unbalanced diet, p. 754

Mandela, Nelson (man DEL uh, NEL sun) *n.* black leader of the African National Congress and South Africa's first president after apartheid ended, p. 558

mantle (MAN tul) *n.* the thick, rocky layer around Earth's core, p. 34

manufacturing (man yoo FAK chur ing) *n.* the process of turning raw materials into finished products, p. 123

Maori (MAH oh ree) *n.* a native of New Zealand whose ancestors first traveled from Asia to Polynesia, and later to New Zealand, p. 697

marine west coast climate (muh REEN west kohst KLY mut) *n.* moderate climate occurring in areas cooled by ocean currents, supporting forests more often than grasses, p. 51

marsupial (mahr SOO pea ul) *n.* an animal that carries its young in a body pouch, such as a kangaroo, p. 628

Mediterranean climate (med uh tuh RAY nee un KLY mut) *n.* moderate climate that receives most of its rain in winter and has hot and dry summers, supporting plants with leathery leaves that hold water, p. 51

meridian (muh RID ee un) *n.* a line of longitude, p. 12

Middle Ages (MID ul AY juz) *n.* the time between ancient and modern times, about A.D. 500–1500, p. 176

middle latitudes (MID ul LAT uh toodz) *n.* the areas between the high and low latitudes, p. 32

migrant worker (MY grunt WUR kur) *n.* a laborer who travels away from where he or she lives to find work, p. 447

migration (my GRAY shun) *n.* the movement of people from one country or region to another in order to make a new home, p. 67

mineral (MIN ur ul) *n.* a natural resource that is obtained by mining, such as gold, iron, or copper, p. 114

monarch (MAHN urk) *n.* the ruler of a kingdom or an empire, such as a king or a queen, p. 186

monarchy (MAHN ur kee) *n.* a state or a nation in which power is held by a monarch—a king, a queen, or an emperor, p. 771

monastery (MAHN uh stehr ee) *n.* a place where people, especially men known as monks, live a religious life, p. 514

monotheism (MAHN oh thee iz um) *n.* a belief that there is only one god, p. 671

monsoon (mahn SOON) *n.* a wind that changes direction with the change of season, occurring especially in southern Asia and Africa, p. 581

mountain (MOWN tun) *n.* a steep landform that usually rises more than 2,000 feet (610 meters) above sea level or the surrounding flatlands, p. 35

muezzin (myoo EZ in) *n.* a person whose job is to call Muslims to pray, p. 671

multiethnic (mul tee ETH nik) *adj.* having many ethnic groups living within a society, p. 485

multiparty system (MUL tee pahr tee SIS tum) *n.* a political system in which two or more parties compete in elections, p. 523

N

national debt (NASH uh nul det) *n.* the amount of money a government owes, p. 280

nationalism (NASH uh nul iz um) *n.* pride in one's country, p. 406

nationalist (NASH uh nul ist) *n.* a person who is devoted to the interests of his or her country, p. 691

nationalize (NASH uh nuh lyz) *v.* to transfer ownership of something to a nation's government, p. 551

nation-state (NAY shun stayt) *n.* a state that is independent of other states, p. 81

natural resource (NACH ur ul REE sawrs) *n.* a material found in nature, such as minerals, soil, and vegetation, p. 114

navigable (NAV ih guh bul) *adj.* wide and deep enough for ships to travel through, p. 154

Nkrumah, Kwame (un KROO muh, KWAH mee) *n.* founder of Ghana's independence movement and Ghana's first president, p. 490

nomad (NOH mad) *n.* a person who has no settled home but moves from place to place, p. 370

nonrenewable resource (nahn rih NOO uh bul REE sawrs) *n.* a natural resource that cannot be replaced once it is used, p. 116

nuclear family (NOO klee ur FAM uh lee) *n.* a mother, a father, and their children, p. 97

O

oasis (oh AY sis) *n.* an area in a desert where fresh water is usually available from a spring or well, p. 367

ocean current (OH shun KUR unt) *n.* a moving stream of water in the ocean created by uneven heating of Earth's surface, p. 42

oligarchy (AHL ih gahr kee) *n.* a government controlled by a small group of people, p. 82

orbit (AWR bit) *n.* the path one body makes as it circles around another, p. 28

outback (OWT bak) *n.* the dry land consisting of plains and plateaus that makes up much of central and western Australia, p. 806

overgrazing (oh vur GRAYZ ing) *n.* allowing too much grazing by large herds of animals, p. 500

P

paddy (PAD ee) *n.* a level field that is flooded to grow rice, especially in Asia, p. 624

Pan-Africanism (pan AF rih kun iz um) *n.* the belief that all Africans should work together for their rights and freedoms, p. 407

parallel (PA ruh lel) *n.* in geography, a line of latitude, p. 12

Parliament (PAHR luh munt) *n.* the lawmaking body of the United Kingdom, p. 264

partition (pahr TISH un) *n.* a division into parts or portions, p. 667

penal colony (PEEN ul KAHL uh nee) *n.* a place where people convicted of crimes are sent, p. 697

permafrost (PUR muh frawst) *n.* a permanently frozen layer of ground below the top layer of soil, p. 161

petroleum (puh TROH lee um) *n.* an oily liquid formed from the remains of ancient plants and animals; used as a fuel, p. 116

philosophy (fih LAHS uh fee) *n.* a system of ideas and beliefs, p. 269

pilgrimage (PIL gruh mij) *n.* a religious journey, p. 396

plain (playn) *n.* a large area of flat or gently rolling land, p. 35

plantation (plan TAY shun) *n.* a large farm where cash crops are grown, p. 401

plate (playt) *n.* in geography, a huge section of Earth's crust, p. 36

plateau (pla TOH) *n.* a large, raised area of mostly level land bordered on one or more sides by steep slopes or cliffs, p. 35

polar climate (POH lur KLY mut) *n.* a climate of the high latitudes that is cold all year and has short summers, p. 50

pollution (puh LOO shun) *n.* waste, usually made by people, which makes a place's air, water, or soil less clean, p. 132

population (pahp yuh LAY shun) *n.* total number of people in an area, p. 60

population density (pahp yuh LAY shun DEN suh tee) *n.* the average number of people living in a square mile or square kilometer, p. 62

population distribution (pahp yuh LAY shun dis trih BYOO shun) *n.* the way the population is spread out over an area, p. 60

precipitation (pree sip uh TAY shun) *n.* water that falls to the ground as rain, sleet, hail, or snow, p. 40

Prime Meridian (prym muh RID ee un) *n.* the meridian that runs through Greenwich, England; 0° longitude, p. 11

privatization (pry vuh tih ZAY shun) *n.* selling government-owned industries to private companies, p. 523

producer (pruh DOOS ur) *n.* a person who makes products that are used by other people, p. 74

projection (proh JEK shun) *n.* the method of mapping Earth on a flat surface, p. 18

propaganda (prahp uh GAN duh) *n.* the spread of ideas designed to support a cause, p. 242

push-pull theory (push pul THEE uh ree) *n.* a theory of migration claiming that difficulties "push" people to leave their old homes, while a hope for better living conditions "pulls" them to a new country or region, p. 68

Q

Quran (koo RAHN) *n.* the holy book of Islam; also spelled Koran, p. 428

R

radical (RAD ih kul) *adj.* extreme, p. 715

rain shadow (rayn SHAD oh) *n.* the area on the dry, sheltered side of a mountain, which receives little rainfall, p. 157

raw materials (raw muh TIHR ee ulz) *n.* natural resources that must be processed to be useful, p. 114

recession (rih SESH un) *n.* a period during which an economy and the businesses that support it shrink, or make less money, p. 722

Red Guards (red gahrdz) *n.* groups of students who carried out Mao Zedong's policies during the Cultural Revolution, p. 715

refugee (ref yoo JEE) *n.* a person who leaves his or her homeland for personal safety or to escape persecution, p. 774

region (REE jun) *n.* an area with a unifying characteristic such as climate, land, population, or history, p. 12

relative location (REL uh tiv loh KAY shun) *n.* the location of a place described in relation to places near it, p. 12

Renaissance (REN uh sahns) *n.* a period of European history that was characterized by the rebirth of interest in learning and art, p. 184

renewable resource (rih NOO uh bul REE sawrs) *n.* a natural resource that can be replaced, p. 115

representative (rep ruh ZEN tuh tiv) *n.* a person who represents, or stands for, a group of people, p. 264

representative democracy (rep ruh ZEN tuh tiv dih MAHK ruh see) *n.* a government run by representatives that the people choose, p. 83

reunification (ree yoo nih fih KAY shun) *n.* the process of becoming unified again, p. 297

revolutionary (rev uh LOO shuh neh ree) *adj.* relating to or causing the overthrow of a government or other great change, p. 204

rift (rift) *n.* a deep crack in Earth's surface, p. 360

rotation (roh TAY shun) *n.* a complete turn, p. 29

rural (ROOR ul) *adj.* having to do with the countryside, p. 71

S

sanitation (san uh TAY shun) *n.* disposal of sewage and waste, p. 65

satellite image (SAT uh lyt IM ij) *n.* an image of Earth's surface taken from a satellite in orbit, p. 17

savanna (suh VAN uh) *n.* a region of tall grasses with scattered trees, p. 52

scale (skayl) *n.* relative size, p. 16

secede (sih SEED) *v.* to leave a group, especially a political group or a nation, p. 323

self-sufficient (self suh FISH unt) *n.* able to supply one's own needs without outside assistance, p. 757

semiarid climate (sem ee A rid KLY mut) *n.* a hot, dry climate with little rain, supporting only shrubs and grasses, p. 51

seminomadic (seh mee noh MAD ik) *adj.* combining nomadic wandering and farming in settlements, p. 527

services (SUR vih siz) *n.* work done for other people that does not produce goods, p. 123

Sharia (shah REE ah) *n.* Islamic law, based on the words and deeds of Muhammad and on comments written by Muslim scholars and lawmakers, p. 459

shrine (shryn) *n.* a holy place, p. 313

single market (SIN gul MAHR ket) *n.* system in which goods, services, and capital move freely with no barrier; used to describe the European Union, p. 210

social class (SOH shul klas) *n.* a grouping of people based on rank or status, p. 97

social structure (SOH shul STRUK chur) *n.* a pattern of organized relationships among groups of people within a society, p. 96

society (suh SY uh tee) *n.* a group of people sharing a culture and social structure, p. 96

solstice (SAHL stis) *n.* one of two days in the year when the sun is directly overhead at its farthest point from the Equator. Summer solstice, in the hemisphere where the sun is overhead, is the longest day and the shortest night of the year. Winter solstice, on the same day in the opposite hemisphere, is the shortest day and the longest night of the year, p. 30

souq (sook) *n.* an open-air marketplace in an Arab city, p. 469

sovereignty (SAHV run tee) *n.* political control, p. 494

standard of living (STAN durd uv LIV ing) *n.* the level at which a person or nation lives, as measured by the availability of food, clothing, shelter, and so forth, p. 605

state (stayt) *n.* a region that shares a government, p. 80

station (STAY shun) *n.* in Australia, a large ranch for raising livestock, p. 698

steppe (step) *n.* vast, mostly level treeless plains that are covered in grass, p. 611

subarctic climate (sub AHRK tik KLY mut) *n.* a continental dry climate with cool summers and cold winters, p. 51

subcontinent (SUB kahn tih nunt) *n.* a large landmass that is a major part of a continent, p. 596

subsidy (SUB suh dee) *n.* money given by a government to assist a private company, p. 721

subsistence farming (sub SIS tuns FAHR ming) *n.* farming that provides only enough food for a family or a village, p. 77

subsidy (SUB suh dee) *n.* money given by a government to assist a private company, p. 721

subsistence farming (sub SIS tuns FAHR ming) *n.* farming that provides only enough food for a family or a village, p. 77

Swahili (swah HEE lee) *n.* an ethnic group of Africans who have mixed African and Arab ancestry and who live along the coast of East Africa; also a Bantu language, p. 441

T

technology (tek NAHL uh jee) *n.* any way of putting knowledge to practical use, p. 76

tectonic plate (tek TAHN ik playt) *n.* a huge slab of rock that moves very slowly over a softer layer beneath the surface of Earth, p. 628

temperature (TEM pur uh chur) *n.* the hotness or coldness of air or some other substance, p. 40

terrace (TEHR us) *n.* a horizontal ridge made in a hillside to create farmland, save water, or lessen erosion, p. 469

textile (TEKS tyl) *n.* a cloth product, p. 192

Tombouctou (tohm book TOO) *n.* city in Mali near the Niger River; also spelled *Timbuktu*, p. 396

tornado (tawr NAY doh) *n.* a storm in the form of a swirling funnel of wind, moving as fast as 200 miles (320 kilometers) per hour, p. 47

treaty (TREE tee) *n.* an agreement in writing made between two or more countries, p. 84

tributary (TRIB yoo tehr ee) *n.* a river or stream that flows into a larger river, p. 153

tropical cyclone (TRAWP ih kul SY klohn) *n.* an intense wind and rain storm that forms over oceans in the tropics, p. 47

truce (troos) *n.* a cease-fire agreement, p. 729

tsar (zahr) *n.* emperor of Russia, p. 202

tundra (TUN druh) *n.* a cold, dry region covered with snow for more than half the year, p. 51

typhoon (ty FOON) *n.* a tropical storm in which winds reach speeds greater than 74 miles (118 kilometers) an hour and that occurs over the Pacific Ocean, p. 582

U

urban (UR bun) *adj.* located in cities and nearby towns, p. 71

urbanization (ur bun ih ZAY shun) *n.* the movement of people to cities, p. 70

V

vegetation (vej uh TAY shun) *n.* plants that grow in a region, p. 50

vertical climate (VUR tih kul KLY mut) *n.* the overall weather patterns of a region, as influenced by elevation; the higher the elevation, the colder the climate, p. 54

W

weather (WETH ur) *n.* the condition of the air and sky from day to day, p. 40

weathering (WETH ur ing) *n.* a process that breaks rocks down into tiny pieces, p. 39

welfare state (WEL fair stayt) *n.* a country in which many services and benefits are paid for by the government, p. 277

West Bank (west bank) *n.* a disputed region on the western bank of the Jordan River, p. 765

westernization (wes tur nuh ZAY shun) *n.* the adoption of Western culture, p. 200

Y

Yoruba (YOH roo buh) *n.* Nigeria's second-largest ethnic group, p. 485

Index

radio, 106, 107
radioactivity, 118, 332, 779
railroads, 105p, 222, 222p, 339g
rain, 40, 41, 42m, 157, 157g, 367, 501g
  climate graphs, 48–49, 48g, 56
  dry climates, 51
  storms, 47
  temperate marine climates, 51
  tropical climates, 50
  tropical cyclones, 47
  water cycle, 35, 41g, 115
rain forests, 4p, 50, 52, 52p, 129p, 368, 480,
  543, 549, 625
rain shadow, 157, 857
Ramadan, 458, 458p
ranching, 806–807, 806g, 806m
Rangoon, Myanmar, 790
raw materials, 112f, 114, 128, 857
Rawlings, Jerry, 495
reading skills
  analyze author's purpose, RW1
  analyze word parts, 662, 668, 669, 675
  ask questions, 164, 398, 586
  clarifying meaning, 8, 174, 356, 594
  compare and contrast, 54, 58, 60, 302, 312,
    327, 424, 426, 445, 708, 714
  context, 26, 28, 33, 40, 50, 642
  context clues, 28, 30, 32, 33, 35, 39, 40, 50,
    52, 644, 649, 652, 656
  distinguish between facts and opinions,
    RW1
  evaluate credibility, RW1
  identify cause and effect, 452, 458, 736, 750
  identify contrasts, 67, 336, 432
  identify evidence, RW1
  identify implied main ideas, 128, 490
  identify main ideas, 87, 112, 114, 135, 211,
    222, 238, 474, 484, 618, 620, 634, 784, 796
  identify supporting details, 120, 229, 498,
    627, 804
  informational texts, RW1
  interpret nonliteral meanings, 526
  make comparisons, 74, 319, 720
  paraphrase, 16, 22, 183, 364, 601
  predict, 155, 390, 414, 580
  preview, 164
  read ahead, 10, 200, 208, 596
  reading process, 146, 382, 574
  recognize cause and effect signal words,
    774
  recognize contrast signal words, 80
  recognize multiple causes, 761
  recognize root words, 682
  recognize signal words, 104, 696, 700
  reread, 10, 176, 208, 358, 596
  sequence, 90, 92, 96, 538, 548, 556, 686,
    688, 693
  set a purpose, 148, 384, 576
  summarizing, 191, 374, 610
  understand effects, 756, 766
  understanding context, 506
  use context clues, 28, 30, 32, 33, 35, 39, 40,
    50, 52, 248, 260, 268, 276, 283, 292, 514,
    519
  use contrast signal words, 80

  use prereading strategies, 42
  use prior knowledge, 405
  use signal words, 440, 466, 556
  word analysis, 660
  word origins, 678
  See also writing skills
recession, 722, 857
recycling, 116, 132, 132p
Red Guards, 715, 857
Red Sea, 507m, 602m, 603
refugees, 774, 857
regions, M1, 12, 350, 350m, 568, 568m, 857
Reichstag, 225p
relative location, M1, 12, 857
relief, M11
religion, 95, 98, 100m, 101, 110m
  in Afghanistan, 738
  in Aksum, 391
  in Algeria, 454, 467
  in ancient Rome, 180, 180p
  in Angola, 540
  in Australia, 786
  in Balkan Peninsula, 320, 320g, 320m, 321
  in Bangladesh, 740
  in Benin, 476
  in Botswana, 541
  in Burkina Faso, 477
  in Burundi, 508
  in Cambodia, 787
  in Cameroon, 541
  in Cape Verde, 477
  in Central Africa, 448
  in Central African Republic, 541
  in Central Asia, 661m, 679
  in Chad, 477
  in China, 710
  in Comoros, 542
  in daily life, 98
  in Democratic Republic of the Congo, 542
  in Djibouti, 508
  in East Africa, 391, 392, 442
  in Egypt, 455, 458, 458p, 459, 459p
  in Equatorial Guinea, 543
  in Eritrea, 509
  in Ethiopia, 509, 514–516, 514p, 515p,
    516p, 525
  ethnic groups and, 231, 231p
  in Gabon, 543
  in Gambia, 478
  in Ghana, 478, 492
  in Guinea, 479
  in Guinea-Bissau, 479
  in India, 665, 668, 741
  in Indonesia, 788
  in Iran, 741
  in Iraq, 742
  in Israel, 742, 764–765
  in Italy, 288
  in Ivory Coast, 479
  in Japan, 711, 711p
  in Jordan, 742
  in Kazakhstan, 743
  in Kenya, 510, 527
  in Kuwait, 743
  in Kyrgyzstan, 744

  in Laos, 789
  in Lebanon, 744
  in Lesotho, 544
  in Liberia, 480
  in Libya, 456
  in Madagascar, 544
  in Malawi, 544
  in Malaysia, 789
  in Mali, 480
  in Mauritania, 481
  in Mauritius, 545
  in Middle Ages, 182, 182p
  in Morocco, 456
  in Mozambique, 545
  in Myanmar, 790
  in Namibia, 545
  in Nepal, 745
  in New Zealand, 791
  in Niger, 481
  in Nigeria, 481, 487, 487g, 488
  in North Africa, 396, 428–429, 428g, 428p
  in North Korea, 712
  in Pacific Region, 687m, 700
  in Pakistan, 745
  in Philippines, 792
  in Poland, 232, 313, 313p
  in Republic of the Congo, 543
  in Russia, 238, 238p, 239, 240, 341
  in Rwanda, 510
  in São Tomé and Príncipe, 546
  in Saudi Arabia, 746, 769
  in Senegal, 482
  in Seychelles, 511
  in Sierra Leone, 482
  in Singapore, 793
  in Somalia, 511
  in South Africa, 546
  in South Asia, 661m, 663–664, 664p, 668
  in South Korea, 712
  in Southeast Asia, 687m
  in Southwest Asia, 661m, 671–672, 671p,
    672p, 673
  in Soviet Union, 238
  in Sri Lanka, 746
  in Sudan, 512
  in Swaziland, 546
  in Syria, 747
  in Tajikistan, 747
  in Tanzania, 512
  in Thailand, 793
  in Togo, 483
  in Tunisia, 457
  in Turkey, 748
  in Turkmenistan, 748
  in Uganda, 513
  in Vietnam, 795
  in West Africa, 396
  in Zambia, 547
  in Zimbabwe, 547
  See also specific religions
religious diversity
  in Western Europe, 227
Renaissance, 857
  art, 184–185, 184p, 185p
  in Europe, 184–187, 184p, 185p, 186p, 187p

Acknowledgments

Cover Design

Pronk&Associates

Staff Credits

The people who made up *World Studies* team—representing design services, editorial, editorial services, educational technology, marketing, market research, photo research and art development, production services, project office, publishing processes, and rights & permissions—are listed below. Bold type denotes core team members.

Greg Abrom, Ernie Albanese, Rob Aleman, Susan Andariese, **Rachel Avenia-Prol,** Leann Davis Alspaugh, Penny Baker, Barbara Bertell, **Peter Brooks,** Rui Camarinha, John Carle, **Lisa Del Gatto,** Paul Delsignore, Kathy Dempsey, Anne Drowns, Deborah Dukeshire, Marlies Dwyer, **Frederick Fellows,** Paula C. Foye, Lara Fox, Julia Gecha, **Mary Hanisco,** Salena Hastings, Lance Hatch, Kerri Hoar, **Beth Hyslip,** Katharine Ingram, Nancy Jones, John Kingston, Deborah Levheim, Constance J. McCarty, **Kathleen Mercandetti,** Art Mkrtchyan, Ken Myett, **Mark O'Malley,** Jen Paley, Ray Parenteau, **Gabriela Pérez Fiato,** Linda Punskovsky, Kirsten Richert, **Lynn Robbins,** Nancy Rogier, Bruce Rolff, Robin Samper, Mildred Schulte, Siri Schwartzman, **Malti Sharma,** Lisa Smith-Ruvalcaba, Roberta Warshaw, Sarah Yezzi

Additional Credits

Jonathan Ambar, Tom Benfatti, Lisa D. Ferrari, Paul Foster, Florrie Gadson, Phil Gagler, Ella Hanna, Jeffrey LaFountain, Karen Mancinelli, Michael McLaughlin, Lesley Pierson, Debi Taffet

The DK Designs team who contributed to *World Studies* were as follows: Hilary Bird, Samantha Borland, Marian Broderick, Richard Czapnik, Nigel Duffield, Heather Dunleavy, Cynthia Frazer, James A. Hall, Lucy Heaver, Rose Horridge, Paul Jackson, Heather Jones, Ian Midson, Marie Ortu, Marie Osborn, Leyla Ostovar, Ralph Pitchford, Ilana Sallick, Pamela Shiels, Andrew Szudek, Amber Tokeley.

Maps

Maps and globes were created by **DK Cartography.** The team consisted of Tony Chambers, Damien Demaj, Julia Lunn, Ed Merritt, David Roberts, Ann Stephenson, Gail Townsley, Iorwerth Watkins.

Illustrations

Kenneth Batelman: **177, 223, 372, 438;** Richard Bonson/DK Images: **416, 647;** Richard Draper/DK Images: **462;** Chris Orr/DK Images: **241, 769;** DK Images: **31, 34, 36, 41, 43, 194, 769 bl;** DK Images/Still Pictures: **769 t;** Trevor Johnston: **189;** Kevin Jones Associates: **140;** Jen Paley: **148, 155, 157, 162, 164, 169, 176, 183, 186, 191, 193, 200, 208, 222, 229, 237, 238, 247, 260, 262, 268, 269, 272, 276, 278, 280, 283, 285, 291, 292, 294, 312, 314, 316, 319, 320, 327, 328, 336, 339, 345, 358, 364, 367, 374, 384, 390, 398, 400, 401, 405, 413, 414, 426, 428, 432, 435, 439, 440, 451, 458, 460, 465, 466, 468;** Jun Park: **500, 635;** Pronk&Associates: **484, 485, 490, 493, 497, 498, 499, 501, 517, 519, 522, 526, 528, 548, 551, 556, 559**

Photos

Cover Photos

tl, Romana Huq/First Light Associated Photographers; **tm,** Mary Louise MacDonald/Masterfile Corporation; **tr,** Charles Cecil/Cecil Images; **b,** Elinor Donohoe/Getty Images Inc.

Title Page

Elinor Donohoe/Getty Images Inc.

Table of Contents

iv–v b, K Yamashita/Mon Tresor/Panoramic Images; **v t,** Galen Rowell/Corbis; **vi t,** Demetrio Carrasco/Dorling Kindersley; **vi b,** Bob Krist/Corbis; **vii t,** Wolfgang Kaehler/Corbis; **vii b,** AP Photo/Boris Grdanoski; **viii t,** The British Library/Topham-HIP/Image Works; **viii b,** Hicks/Premium/Panoramic Images;

ix t, SuperStock, Inc.; **ix b,** Robert Frerck/Odyssey Productions, Inc.; **x t,** Robert Everts/Getty Images Inc.; **x–xi b,** Dave Starrlet/Artbase, Inc.; **xi t,** Dave Bartruff/Danita Delimont; **xii t,** Karen Su/Getty Images, Inc.; **xii–xiii b,** Macduff Everton/Getty Images, Inc.; **xiii t,** Camermann International; **xiv t,** Reuters/Corbis; **xiv b,** Alison Wright/Corbis; **xv t,** AP/Wide World Photos; **xv b,** Dallas & John Heaton/Corbis; **xvi,** Staffan Widstrand/Corbis; **xviii,** Christie's Images; **xix,** Bettmann/Corbis; **xx both,** Discovery Channel School; **xxii all,** The British Museum; **xxiv–xxv,** Wolfgang Kaehler/Corbis

Learning With Technology

xxvi, Discovery Channel School

Reading and Writing Handbook

RW, Michael Newman/PhotoEdit; **RW1,** Walter Hodges/Getty Images, Inc.; **RW2,** Digital Vision/Getty Images, Inc.; **RW3,** Will Hart/PhotoEdit; **RW5,** Jose Luis Pelaez, Inc./Corbis

MapMaster Skills Handbook

M, James Hall/DK Images; **M1,** Mertin Harvey/Gallo Images/Corbis; **M2–3 m,** NASA; **M2–3,** (globes) Planetary Visions: **M5 br,** Barnabas Kindersley/DK Images; **M6 tr,** Mike Dunning/DK Images; **M10 b,** Bernard and Catherine Desjeux/Corbis; **M11,** Hutchinson Library; **M12 b,** Pa Photos; **M13 r,** Panos Pictures; **M14 l,** Macduff Everton/Corbis; **M14 t,** MSCF/NASA; **M15 b,** Ariadne Van Zandbergen/Lonely Planet Images; **M16 l,** Bill Stormont/Corbis; **M16 b,** Pablo Corral/Corbis; **M17 t,** Stone Les/Sygma/Corbis; **M17 b,** W. Perry Conway/Corbis

Guiding Questions

1, Christine Osborne/World Religions Photo Library

World Overview

2 l, 2 t, DK Images; **3 l,** Daniel Laine/Corbis; **3 tr,** DK Images; **3 br,** Sipa/Rex Features; **4 bl,** Layne Kennedy/Corbis; **4 tr,** DK Images; **5 t,** Royalty Free Images/Corbis; **6 t,** Roger Ressmeyer/Corbis; **7 br,** Amet Jean Pierre/Sygma/Corbis; **7 tr,** DK Images

Chapter One

8–9, Johnson Space Center/NASA; **10,** Steve Gorton/DK Images; **13,** M. Balan/DK Images; **14,** Will & Deni McIntyre/Corbis; **15 b,** Richard Powers/Corbis; **15 t,** DK Images; **16,** Peter Wilson/DK Images; **17,** MSFC/NASA; **23,** Johnson Space Center/NASA

Chapter Two

26–27, George H. Huey/Corbis; **28,** Daniel Pyne/DK Images; **30 bl,** Alan Briere/DK Images; **30–31,** sun, DK Images; globes, Planetary Visions; **31 tr,** Barnabas Kindersley/DK Images; **33,** Brenda Tharp/Corbis; **35,** C. M. Leask/Eye Ubiquitous; **36 bl,** James Balog/Getty Images; **37 tr,** James A. Sugar/Corbis; **39,** Alan Hills/DK Images; **40,** Galen Rowell/Corbis; **41 tr,** Hutchison Library; **43 tr,** Royalty Free Images/Corbis; **44 b,** Demetrio Carrasco/DK Images; **45 bl,** Chris Stowers/DK Images; **46 m,** DK Images; **46 bl,** NASA; **46 tr,** N.H.P.A.; **46 mr,** Lelan Statom, meteorologist; Mark Martin, photojournalist/network operations manager, WTVF-Newschannel 5 Network, Nashville, Tenn.; **47,** Chris Graythen/Getty Images; **48 t,** Michael S. Yamashita/Corbis; **50,** Liu Liqun/Corbis; **51 br,** Terry W. Eggers/Corbis; **51 tr,** Denver Museum of Nature and Science; **52,** Alan Watson/DK Images; **53 t,** Photowood Inc./Corbis; **53 bl,** Neil Lukas; **53 br,** Stephen Hayward/DK Images; **54,** Galen Rowell/Corbis; **55,** George H. Huey/Corbis

Chapter Three

58–59, Keren Su/Corbis; **60,** James Strachan/Getty Images; **61 t,** Royalty Free Images/Corbis; **62 bl,** Wolfgang Kaehler/Corbis; **63 br,** Peter Wilson/DK Images; **64 t,** Howard Davies/Corbis; **65 b,** Patricia Aithie/Ffotograff; **66,** Dirk R. Frans/Hutchison Library; **67,** Bettmann Corbis; **68,** Dave King/DK Images; **69 bl,** Bettmann/Corbis; **70 bl,** Hulton-Deutsch Collection/Corbis; **70 br,** Paul Almasy/Corbis; **71,** Stephanie Maze/Corbis; **72,** Bill Ross/Corbis; **74,** Rob

Macduff Everton/Corbis; **283,** John Miller/Robert Harding World Imagery; **284,** Owen Franken/Corbis; **286 t,** Discovery Channel School; **286 b,** Hulton Archive Photos/Getty Images Inc.; **287 t,** Allsport UK/Getty Images, Inc.; **287 b,** Mimmo Jodice/Corbis; **288,** Shaun Egan/Getty Images, Inc.; **289,** Burstein Collection/Corbis; **290,** Stephen Studd/Getty Images, Inc.; **292,** AP/Wide World Photos; **293,** Hulton-Deutsch Collection/Corbis; **294,** Collection of Stuart S. Corning, Jr. Photo © Rob Huntley/Lightstream; **295 t,** Sovfoto/Eastfoto; **295 b,** Bettmann/Corbis; **296,** David Brauchli/Corbis; **297 t,** Bettmann/Corbis; **297 b,** Discovery Channel School; **298,** Ken Straiton/Corbis; **299,** Burstein Collection/Corbis

Chapter Ten

302–303, Jonathan Blair/Corbis; **304,** Discovery Channel School; **306,** Niall Benvie/Corbis; **309 t,** Topham Picturepoint/Image Works; **309 b,** Dave King/Dorling Kindersley; **310,** Tim Thompson/Corbis; **312,** Hideo Haga/The Image Works; **313 t,** AP/Wide World Photos/Rudi Blaha; **313 b,** Raymond Gehman/Corbis; **315 t,** Discovery Channel School; **315 b,** Peter Turnley/Corbis; **317 t,** Raymond Gehman/Corbis; **317 b,** Hicks/Premium/Panoramic Images; **318,** Raymond Gehman/Corbis; **319 t,** David Cannon/Allsport/Getty Images, Inc.; **319 b,** AP/Wide World Photos/Rikard Larma; **321 t,** Jonathan Blair/Corbis; **321 b,** Jim McDonald/Corbis; **323,** Jules Frazier/Getty Images, Inc.; **324 t,** Discovery Channel School; **324 b,** Ron Haviv/VII Photo; **325,** AP/Wide World Photos/EPA/Georgi Licovski; **326,** Janez Skok/Corbis; **327,** Novosti/Sovfoto; **329 t,** Mary Evans Picture Library; **329 m,** TASS/Sovfoto; **329 b,** Robert Capa/Magnum Photo Library; **330–331 b,** TASS/Sovfoto; **331 t,** Ed Kashi/Corbis; **332 t,** Discovery Channel School; **332 b,** Yann Arthus-Bertrand/Corbis; **333,** Sean Sprague/Peter Arnold, Inc.; **334,** Raymond Gehman/Corbis; **335,** Paul Almasy/Corbis; **336,** Peter Turnley/Corbis; **337 t,** Discovery Channel School; **337 m,** TASS/Sovfoto; **337 b,** Demetrio Carrasco/Getty Images, Inc.; **338,** TASS/Sovfoto; **340,** Alain Le Garsmeur/Getty Images, Inc.; **341 t,** B&C Alexander/AgPix; **341 b,** Reuters NewMedia Inc./Corbis; **342,** Marc Garanger/Corbis; **343,** Hideo Haga/The Image Works

Projects

346 t, Andy Crawford/Dorling Kindersley; **346 b,** Wally McNamee/Corbis

Guiding Questions

349 t, Christie's Images/SuperStock, Inc.; **349 b,** Heini Schneebeli/Bridgeman Art Library

Regional Overview

350 l, G. Hind/Still Pictures; **351 t,** Liba Taylor/Corbis; **352 t,** Chris Lisle/Corbis; **352 b,** Patrick Ward/Corbis; **353 t,** Sharna Balfour/Gallo Images; **353 b,** David Ball/Corbis; **354 ml,** Liba Taylor/Corbis; **354 b,** Leanne Logan/Lonely Planet Images; **355 t,** Geert Cole/Lonely Planet Images; **355 mr,** Harlmut Schwarzbach/Still Pictures; **355 br,** Gallo Images/Corbis

Chapter Eleven

356–357, Tim Davis/Corbis; **358,** Richard Cummins/Corbis; **359 t,** Discovery Channel School; **359 b,** Martin Rogers/Getty Images, Inc.; **360–361,** Jason Lauré/Lauré Communications; **362,** Roger Wood/Corbis; **363,** SuperStock, Inc.; **364,** Jason Edwards/Lonely Planet Images; **366 t,** Hal Beral/Corbis; **366–367 b,** Panoramic Images; **368–369 b,** SuperStock, Inc.; **369 t,** F. Lemmens/Masterfile Corporation; **370,** Lorne Resnick/Getty Images, Inc.; **371,** Robert Patrick/Corbis Sygma; **373,** Ariadne Van Zandbergen/Lonely Planet Images; **374,** Victor Englebert/Victor Englebert Photography; **374 inset,** Dave King/Dorling Kindersley; **376,** Jason Lauré/Lauré Communications; **377 t,** AFP/Corbis; **377 b,** Tim Boyle/Getty Images, Inc.; **378,** Eric Miller/iAfrika Photos; **379,** Martin Rogers/Getty Images, Inc.

Chapter Twelve

382–383, J. D. Dallet/AGE Fotostock; **384,** Juan Carlos Munoz/AGE Fotostock; **385 t,** Lauros/Giraudon/The Bridgeman Art Library; **385 m,** John Reader/Photo Researchers, Inc.; **385 b,** Robert Sisson/National Geographic Image Collection;

386, Martin Harvey/Gallo Images/Corbis; **387 t,** Erich Lessing/Art Resource, NY; **387 b,** The Art Archive/Egyptian Museum Turin/Dagli Orti; **389,** David Turnley/Corbis; **390 all,** The British Museum; **392 t,** Anthony Bannister/Gallo Images/Corbis; **392 b,** Corbis; **393,** David Reed/Corbis; **394 both,** Pictor International/Agency ImageState/Alamy; **396 t,** The Granger Collection, New York; **396 b,** Saudi Arabia-Ramadan/AFP/Corbis; **397,** Christie's Images/SuperStock, Inc.; **398,** Yann Arthus-Bertrand/Corbis; **399,** Dorling Kindersley/The Science Museum London; **400 l,** Ingrid Roddis/Lonely Planet Images; **400 r,** The Granger Collection, New York; **401 t,** The Granger Collection, New York; **401 b,** Discovery Channel School; **402 t,** The Granger Collection, New York; **402 b,** Wilberforce Museum, Hull/Dorling Kindersley; **404 t,** The Art Archive/Private Collection; **404 b,** The British Library, London, UK/Topham-HIP/The Image Works; **405,** Chris Steele-Perkins/Magnum Photos; **406 both,** Peter Turnley/Corbis; **407,** Corbis; **409 l,** Hulton-Deutsch Collection/Corbis; **409 r,** M. & E. Bernheim/Woodfin Camp & Associates; **410 t,** Joao Silva/New York Times Pictures; **410–411 b,** Peter Turnley/Corbis; **413,** One Mile Up, Inc./Fotosearch Stock Photography; **414,** Michael S. Lewis/Corbis; **415 t,** A. Ramey/Woodfin Camp & Associates; **415 b,** Charles O. Cecil/Words & Pictures/PictureQuest; **416 t,** Michael S. Lewis/Corbis; **417 t,** Yann Arthus-Bertrand/Corbis; **417 b,** Sandro Vannini/Corbis; **418,** Willem de Lange/PictureNET Africa; **419,** Liba Taylor/Corbis; **420,** Wolfgang Kaehler Photography; **421 l,** Christie's Images/SuperStock, Inc.; **421 r,** Peter Turnley/Corbis

Chapter Thirteen

424–425, Kennan Ward/Corbis; **426,** Getty Images, Inc.; **427,** Glen Allison/Getty Images, Inc.; **428,** Francois Perri/Cosmos/Woodfin Camp & Associates; **429,** Jim Erickson/Corbis; **430,** Jon Arnold Images/Alamy; **431,** Francois Perri/Cosmos/Woodfin Camp & Associates; **432,** Jason Lauré/Lauré Communications; **433,** M. & E. Bernheim/Woodfin Camp & Associates; **434 t,** Craig Pershouse/Lonely Planet Images; **434 b,** Robert Frerck/Odyssey Productions, Inc.; **435,** Yann Arthus-Bertrand/Corbis; **436 t,** M. & E. Bernheim/Woodfin Camp & Associates; **436 b,** Discovery Channel School; **437 l,** Courtesy of Balla Tounkara; **437 r,** Bob Burch/ Index Stock Imagery/PictureQuest; **439 l,** Gunter Ziesler/Peter Arnold, Inc.; **439 r,** Rich Kirchner/NHPA; **440,** Ariadne Van Zandbergen/Lonely Planet Images; **441,** Yadid Levy/AGE Fotostock; **442–443 b,** Wolfgang Kaehler Photography; **443 t,** Peter Marlow/Magnum Photos; **444,** Sipa Press; **445,** Popperfoto/Alamy Images; **446,** Chris Harvey/Stone Allstock/Getty Images Inc.; **447,** Ian Murphy/Getty Images, Inc.; **448,** Christie's Images, Inc.; **449 l,** Jim Erickson/Corbis; **449 r,** Ian Murphy/Getty Images

Chapter Fourteen

452–453, Photolibrary.com; **454 t,** Discovery Channel School; **454 b,** Claudia Wiens/Peter Arnold, Inc.; **455 t,** F. J. Jackson/Alamy Images; **455 b,** Paul Hardy/Corbis; **456,** Damien Simonis/Lonely Planet Images; **457,** Patrick Ward/Corbis; **458,** Harry Gruyaert/Magnum Photos; **459,** Stock Image/SuperStock, Inc.; **460,** Nik Wheeler/Corbis; **461,** Nik Wheeler; **462,** Lloyd Cluff/Corbis; **463 t,** Discovery Channel School; **463 b,** Mark Henley/Panos Pictures; **464,** David Young-Wolff/PhotoEdit; **465,** Carmen Redondo/Corbis; **466,** Robert Everts/Getty Images Inc.; **467,** Francoise Perri/Woodfin Camp & Associates; **469 t,** Abbas/Magnum Photos; **469 b,** Discovery Channel School; **470,** Tiziana and Gianni Baldizzone/Corbis; **471 l,** Harry Gruyaert/Magnum Photos; **471 r,** Robert Everts/Getty Images Inc.

Chapter Fifteen

474–475, Yann Arthus-Bertrand/Corbis; **476 b,** Art Directors/Jane Sweeney; **478 bl,** Ancient Art&Architecture/DanitaDelimont.com; **478 br,** Robert Burch/Bruce Coleman Inc.; **480 tr,** Robert Burch; **480 b,** AP/Wide-World Photos; **482 mr,** AFP/Corbis; **482 b,** Beryl Goldberg; **483 tr,** Luis Marden/National Geographic/Getty Images, Inc.; **484 bl,** Sally Mayman/Getty Images, Inc.; **485 br,** Paul Almasy/Corbis; **485 bl,** Werner Forman/Art Resource NY; **486 bl,** McPherson Colin/Corbis/Sygma; **486 tr,** Betty Press/Panos Pictures; **487 b,** Hamill Gallery of African Art, Boston MA; **488 tl,** Bruno Barbey/Magnum Photos; **489 tr,** Campbell William/Corbis/Sygma; **490–491,** Dave

Starrett/Artbase Inc.; **490 bl**, Bettman/Corbis; **491 tr**, Hulton-Deutsch Collection/Corbis; **492 bl**, Hamill Gallery of African Art, Boston MA; **494 b**, AP/Wide World Photos; **495 tr**, Robert Burch; **496 ml**, Imagestate/firstlight.ca; **497 mr**, Jonathan Nourok/PhotoEdit Inc.; **497 br**, Dave Starrett/Artbase Inc.; **498–499**, Ali Atay/Atlas; **498 bl**, Wolfgang Kaehler/Corbis; **502 tl**, Art Directors/ Mary Jelliffe; **503 ml**, Paul Almasy/Corbis; **503 mr**, Art Directors/Mary Jelliffe

Chapter Sixteen

506–507, Robert Bourgoing; **509 tr**, Sheila McKinnon/Mira.com; **510 t**, Edwards Roderick, Edward/MaXx Images; **511 m**, © 2003 Norbert Wu/www.nobertwu.com; **511 mr**, Wolfgang Kaehler Photography; **512 tr**, AFP/Corbis; **513 m**, Art Directors/Fiona Good; **514 b**, Robert Patrick/Corbis/Sygma; **515 br**, M. & E. Bernheim/Woodfin Camp & Associates; **515 tl**, Dave Bartruff/Danita Delimont; **516 tr**, Dave Bartruff/Danita Delimont; **516 tl**, Kal Muller/Woodfin Camp & Associates; **518 ml**, Robert Caputo/Aurora Photos; **519 br**, Reuters; **521 t**, Kwame Zikomo/SuperStock; **523 tr**, Howard Davies/Corbis; **524 bl**, Eric Draper/White House/Getty Images, Inc.; **525 tr**, Art Directors/Andrew Gasson; **525 br**, David Pluth/Fotografx; **526 b**, Robert Burch; **527 tr**, Michele Burgess/MaXx Images; **529 mr**, Betty Press/Woodfin Camp & Associates; **530 tl**, DigtalVision/Artbase Inc.; **531 tr**, Dave Bartruff/Danita Delimont; **531 m**, Robert Burch; **534 br**, Paul Souders/Getty Images, Inc.; **535 tr**, PhotodiscRed/Artbase Inc.; **536 bl**, Jeremy Woodhouse/Masterfile Corporation; **537**, Tololwa M. Mollel

Chapter Seventeen

538–539, Eric Nathan/Alamy Images; **540 b**, Volkmar Wentzel/Getty Images, Inc.; **542 tr**, AFP/Corbis; **542 tl**, Max-Planck-Institut Seewiesen; **548**, Jason Lauré/Lauré Communications; **549 b**, Patrick Roberts/Corbis/Sygma; **550 bl**, Bettmann/Corbis; **552 bl**, Artbase Inc.; **553 tr**, Reuters/Corbis; **554 tl**, Photodisc/Artbase Inc.; **554 ml**, Photodisc/Artbase Inc.; **554 bl**, Photodisc/Artbase Inc.; **555 m**, Paula Bronstein/Impact Visuals; **556 bl**, Charles O'Rear/Corbis; **557 br**, TimeLifePictures/Getty Images, Inc.; **558 br**, AP/WideWorld Photos; **560 tl**, Owen Franken/Corbis; **561 ml**, Artbase Inc.; **561 mr**, AP/WideWorld Photos

Projects

564, Heini Schneebeli/Bridgeman Art Library

Guiding Questions

567, AFP/Corbis

Regional Overview

568 l, David Ball/Corbis; **569 bl**, Massimo Listri/Corbis; **570 t**, José Fuste Raga/Corbis; **570 bl**, Paul A. Souders/Corbis; **571 t**, James A. Sugar/Corbis; **571 b**, David Samuel Robbins/Corbis; **572 l**, Richard T. Nowitz/Corbis; **572 br**, Jeremy Horner/Corbis; **573 tr**, Damien Simonis/Lonely Planet Images; **573 bl**, Bohemian Nomad Picturemakers/Corbis

Chapter Eighteen

574–575, Boden-Ledingham/Masterfile; **576 bl**, Dallas&John Heaton/Corbis; **577 tr**, Keren Su/Getty Images; **578 bl**, Michael S. Yamashita/Corbis; **579 tr**, Catherine Karnow/Corbis; **580 b**, Scott Markewitz/Getty Images; **582 ml**, Private Collection/Ancient Art and Architecture Collection Ltd/Bridgeman Art Library; **583 tr**, Heatons/Firstlight.ca; **585 tr**, Mug Shots/Corbis; **585 tr(inset)**, Kevin Schafer/Corbis; **586 bl**, AFP/Corbis; **588–589 b**, Liu Liqun/ Corbis; **589 tr**, Keren Su/Corbis; **589 br**, Keren Su/Corbis; **590 tl**, B.S.P.I./Corbis; **591 ml**, Keren Su/Getty Images; **591 mr**, Scott Markewitz/Getty Images

Chapter Nineteen

594–595, Galen Rowell/Corbis; **596 b**, Alan Kearney/Getty Images; **599 b**, Will Curtis/Getty Images; **599 lr**, Eisenhut&Mayer/Foodpix; **599 mr**, Artbase Inc.; **600 tl**, R. Ian Lloyd/Masterfile; **601 b**, George Steinmetz; **603 b**, George Gerster/Photo Researchers Inc.; **603 mr**, H. Spichtinger/zefa; **605 r**, George Steinmetz; **606 tl**, Israel Talby; **607 tr**, Hugh Sitton/Getty Images; **608 bl**, Myrleen Ferguson/Photoedit Inc.; **609 tr**, Business Essentials/Artbase Inc.; **609 br**, Donovan Resse/Getty Images; **609 tr (inset)**, George Steinmetz; **610 bl**, TASS/Sovfoto/

Sergei Kazak; **611 tr**, James Strachan/Getty Images; **613 tr**, Reuters/Corbis; **614 tl**, TASS-S-54679/Sovfoto/Eastfoto; **615 ml**, James Strachan/Getty Images; **615 tr**, Israel Talby

Chapter Twenty

618–619, Paul A. Souders/Corbis; **620 bl**, Photodisc/ArtBase Inc.; **621 br**, Dorling Kindersley/DK Images; **622–623 bg**, ACE; **623 (inset)**, AFP/Corbis; **624 ml**, Martin Puddy/Getty Images; **624 b**, R. Ian Lloyd/Masterfile; **626 tl**, Frank Siteman/Maxximages.com; **627 br**, Tui De Roy/Auscape; **627 mr**, Artbase Inc.; **628 ml**, Jeremy Woodhouse/Masterfile; **628 t**, Tim Flach/Getty Images; **630 t**, Mike Langford/Auscape; **631 tr**, John Lamb/Getty Images; **632 b**, William Gottlieb/Corbis; **633 bg**, The Bridgeman Art Library/Getty Images; **634 bl**, G.Bell/Zefa/Masterfile; **635 bm**, Yann Arthurs-Bertrand/Corbis; **635 tr**, Trip/Ask Images; **636 br**, Photography.com.au; **636 bl**, Photography.com.au; **636–637 bg**, Macduff Everton/Getty Images; **637 mr**, James Strachan/Getty Images; **638 tl**, Trip/M.Jelliffe; **639 tr**, AFP/Corbis; **639 bm**, Jeremy Woodhouse/Masterfile; **639 bm**, Tim Flach/Getty Images

Chapter Twenty-One

642–643, John Dakers-Eye Ubiquitous/Corbis; **644 bl**, Bridgeman Art Library; **645 tr**, Carl & Ann Purcell/Corbis; **646 b**, © Lee Boltin/Boltin Picture Library; **647 t**, DK Images/Wolfgang Kaehler/Corbis; **647 b**, Macduff Everton/Corbis; **648 bl**, Haruyoshi Yamaguchi/Corbis/Sygma; **649 tr**, AFP/Getty Images; **650 l**, Michael S. Yamashita/Corbis; **651 mr**, Werner Forman/Art Resource, NY; **652 bl**, SETBOUN/Corbis; **653 t**, Daryl Benson/Masterfile; **653 mr**, Dale Wilson/ Masterfile; **654 t**, Paul Chesley/Getty Images; **656 tl**, James A. Sugar/Corbis; © Lee Boltin/Boltin Picture Library; **657 mr**, Dale Wilson/Masterfile

Chapter Twenty-Two

660–661, Bob Krist/Corbis; **662 bl**, Archivo Iconografico S.A./Corbis; **664 tl**, Michael Freeman/Corbis; **664 tm**, Burstein collection/Corbis; **664 tr**, Burstein collection/Corbis; **665 tr**, Camermann International; **666 t**, Miles Ertman/Masterfile; **666 inset**, Archivo Iconografico S.A./Corbis; **667 tl**, Hulton Deutsch Collection/Corbis; **667 b**, Kapoor Baldev/Corbis; **668 tl**, Frans Lemmens/ZEFA/Masterfile; **669 br**, Gianni Dagli Orti/Corbis; **671 t**, Shai Ginott/Corbis; **672 tr**, Paul Chesley/Getty Images; **672 l**, Scala/Art Resource; **673 r**, Peter Turnley/Corbis; **674 tl**, Ricki Rosen/Corbis; **674 tr**, Eddie Gerald/Alamy Images; **675 tr**, Pool/Reuters; **676 l**, Ed Brock/Corbis; **677 r**, David W. Hamilton/Getty Images; **678 bl**, Dean Conger/Corbis; **679 t**, Daniel Sheehan/The Image Works; **679 br**, The Bridgeman Art Library/Getty Images; **680 t**, David Samuel Robbins/Corbis; **681 br**, David Samuel Robbins/Corbis; **682 tr**, Nevada Weir/Corbis; **683 tl**, Camermann International; **683 mr**, Daniel Sheehan/The Image Works

Chapter Twenty-Three

686–687, David Noton/Masterfile; **688 bl**, DK Images; **689 b**, Manfred Gottschalk/agefotostock/firstlight.ca; **691 tl**, Miles Ertman/Masterfile; **692 t**, Paul Chesley/Getty Images; **693 tr**, Howard Davies/Corbis; **694 bl**, Chad Elhers/Getty Images; **694 inset**, Foodphotography/MaXximages.com; **695 b**, Leonard de Selva/Corbis; **696 bl**, Kevin Schafer/Getty Images; **697 b**, Graeme Matthews/PhotoNewZealand.com; **698 br**, Reuters/Corbis; **698 bl**, Rob Walls; **699 t**, R. Ian Lloyd/Masterfile; **700 tl**, Nicolas DaVore/Getty Images; **701 bl**, Manfred Gottschalk/agefotostock/firstlight.ca; **701 tr**, Nicolas DaVore/Getty Images; **704 b**, Time-Life Pictures/Getty Images; **706 tl**, Jason Bleibtreu/ Corbis/Sygma

Chapter Twenty-Four

708–709, John Elk/Getty Images; **710 b**, Grant Faint/Getty Images; **711 t**, Don Stevenson/MaxXImages.com; **712 b**, Nathan Benn/Corbis; **713 m**, Bill Lai/IndexStock/MaXX Images; **714 bl**, Chris Shinn/Getty Images; **715 t**, Bettmann/Corbis; **715 mr**, Collection: Stefan Landsberger; **716 ml**, Bettmann/ Corbis; **716 br**, Reuters/Corbis; **718 t**, Walter Bibikow/Getty Images; **718 inset**, Walter Bibikow/Getty Images; **720 bl**, APWideWorld; **721 br**, Reuters/Corbis; **722 ml**, AFP/Corbis; **722 b**, Alan Levinson/Getty Images; **724–725 t**, Ettagale

Blauer/Laure Communications; **726 ml,** Bob Daemmrich/StockBoston; **727 mr,** The Cover Story/Corbis; **728 b,** Janet Wishnetsky/Corbis; **729 b,** AP Wide World Photos; **730 t,** APWideWorld; **731 ml,** DigitalVision/Artbase Inc.; **732 ml,** Corbis/Artbase Inc.; **733 tr,** Chris Shinn/Getty Images; **734 mr,** Reuters/Corbis

Chapter Twenty-Five

736–737, Annie Griffiths Belt/Corbis; **738 r,** AFP/Corbis; **743 b,** Peter Turnley/Corbis; **747 t,** Alison Wright/Corbis; **750 bl,** Anna Clopet/Corbis; **751 t,** Kapoor Baldev/Corbis; **752 t,** Derimais Lionel/Corbis/Sygma; **752 (inset),** David H. Wells/Corbis; **754 tl,** Michael S. Yamashita/Corbis; **754 tr,** Sheldon Collins/Corbis; **755 tr,** David Katzenstein/Corbis; **756 bl,** Christine Osborne/Corbis; **757 t,** Jonathan Blair/Corbis; **757 (inset),** Jonathan Blair/Corbis; **758 br,** AFP/Corbis; **759 ml,** Antoine Serra/Corbis; **760 tl,** AFP/Corbis; **761 br,** Richard T. Nowitz/Corbis; **762 b,** Ricki Rosen/Saba/Corbis; **764 b,** Zev Radovan/PhotoEdit Inc.; **765 tr,** Izzet Keribar/Coral Planet; **766 bl,** James Sparshatt/Corbis; **767 b,** John Moore/The Image Works; **769 (inset),** Jacques Langeuin/Corbis/Sygma; **769 b,** David Turnley/Corbis; **770 t,** DK Images/Still Pictures; **770 bl,** DK Images; **772 l,** Caroline Penn/Corbis; **773 b,** R. Ian Lloyd; **774 bl,** Steve McCurry/Magnum Photos Inc.; **775 t,** AFP/Corbis; **776 b,** Janet Wishnetsky/Corbis; **778 bl,** Zylberman Lauren/Corbis/Sygma; **779 br,** Volker Thewalt; **779 tl,** Zylberman Lauren/Corbis/Sygma; **780 tr,** James Strachan/Getty Images

Chapter Twenty-Six

784–785, Philip&Karen Smith/Getty Images; **786 b,** J. Raga/Zefa/Masterfile; **791 t,** Paul A. Souders/Corbis; **795 m,** Alyx Kellington/MaxXimages.com; **796 ml,** Owen Franken/Corbis; **796 b,** Steve Raymer/Corbis; **797 t,** R. Ian Lloyd/Masterfile; **798 bl,** Dallas&John Heaton/Corbis; **798 tr,** Bettman/Corbis; **800 bl,** Tim Page/Corbis; **801 tl,** Charles Coates/Impact Photos; **801 tr,** AP WideWorld; **803 b,** BohemianNomadPicturemakers/Corbis; **804–805 b,** Ray Juno/Corbis; **807 t,** Corbis/Artbase Inc.; **808 mr,** John Van Hasselt/Corbis; **809 mc,** Ray Juno/Corbis; **809 tr,** Dallas&John Heaton/Corbis

Projects

812 b, Robert Essel NYC/Corbis; **812 mr,** AFP/Corbis

Reference

814–815, Johnson Space Center/NASA

Glossary of Geographic Terms

840 t, A & L Sinibaldi/Getty Images, Inc; **840 b,** John Beatty/Getty Images, Inc; **840–841 b,** Spencer Swanger/Tom Stack & Associates; **841 t,** Hans Strand/Getty Images, Inc.; **841 m,** Paul Chelsey/Getty Images, Inc.

Text

Chapter Three

88–89, Excerpt from *My Side of the Mountain* by Jean Craighead George. Copyright © 1959 by Jean Craighead George.

Chapter Seven

216, Excerpt from *Pearl in the Egg: A Tale of the Thirteenth Century* by Dorothy van Woerkom. Copyright © 1980 by Dorothy van Woerkom.

Chapter Eleven

369, Excerpt from "Where Hospitality Is an Oasis," by Christine Negroni, *The New York Times,* January 19, 2003. **374,** From *Cocoa Comes to Mampong,* by Dei Anang. Copyright © 1949. Reprinted with the permission of Methodist Book Depot.

Chapter Thirteen

441, Excerpt from "Swahili Coast: East Africa's Ancient Crossroads," by Robert Caputo, *National Geographic,* October 2001. **444,** From "African Statesman Still Sowing Seeds for Future," by James C. McKinley, Jr., *The New York Times.*

Chapter Fifteen

492, From *Ghana in Transition,* by David E. Apter. Copyright © 1955, 1963, and 1972 by Princeton University Press.

Chapter Sixteen

520–521, From "Three Leaders," by Andrew Meldrum, *Africa Report,* September–October 1994. Copyright © 1994 by *Africa Report.* **530,** From "Back to No Man's Land," by George Monbiot, *Geographical Magazine,* July 1994. Copyright © 1994 by *Geographical Magazine.* **534,** From *A Promise to the Sun* by Tololwa M. Mollel. Text Copyright © 1991 by Tololwa M. Mollel. By permission of Little, Brown, and Company.

Chapter Seventeen

555, Excerpt from "Nelson Mandela's Statement After Voting in South Africa's First Democratic Election, Inanda, Kwazulu Natal, 27 April 1994," by Nelson Mandela, the African National Congress. **556,** Excerpt from "Preamble: Constitution of the Republic of South Africa by the Constitutional Assembly," Policy and Law Online News.

Chapter Twenty-Three

704, Excerpt from *The Clay Marble,* by Minfong Ho. Copyright © 1991, by Minfong Ho.

Note: Every effort has been made to locate the copyright owner of material used in this textbook. Omissions brought to our attention will be corrected in subsequent editions.